Politics in America 2014

113th Congress

By CQ Roll Call Staff • Chris White and Amanda H. Allen, Editors

Keith White, Executive Vice President and Managing Director, CQ/Capitol Advantage

Susan Benkelman, Editorial Director and Senior Vice President

Dennis Arndt, Senior Vice President and Publisher, Politics in America

Beth Bronder, Senior Vice President, Advertising

Published by CQ-Roll Call, Inc.
77 K Street NE
8th Floor
Washington, DC 20002
202-650-6500; toll-free, 1-800-432-2250
www.cqrollcall.com

The paper used in this publication exceeds the requirements of the American National Standard for Information Sciences — Permanence of Paper for Printed Library Materials, ANSI Z39.48-1992.

Printed and bound in the United States of America

13 12 11 10 09 08 07 5 4 3 2 1

ISBN 978-1-4522-7782-0 (cloth) ISBN 978-1-4522-7783-7 (paper)
ISSN 1064-6809

The Library of Congress catalogued an earlier edition of this title as follows:

Congressional Quarterly's Politics in America: 1994, the 103rd Congress / by CQ's political staff: Phil Duncan, Editor

p. cm.

Includes index.

1. United States. Congress — Biography. 2. United States. Congress — Committees. 3. United States. Congress — Election districts — Handbooks, manuals, etc. I. Duncan, Phil. II. Congressional Quarterly Inc. III. Title: Politics in America.

JK1010.C67 1993 328.73'073'45'0202

Politics in America 2014

113th Congress

EDITORS
Amanda H. Allen, Chris White

DEPUTY EDITOR
Stacey Goers

MANAGING EDITORS
Angela Kim, Sara Smith

CONTRIBUTING EDITORS
Nell Benton, George Cahlink, David Meyers

SENIOR WRITER
Shawn Zeller

POLITICAL ANALYSIS
John Cranford, Ryan Kelly (vote studies)

CONTRIBUTING WRITERS
Kate Ackley, Rebecca Adams, Ambreen Ali, Joanna Anderson, Melissa Attias, Rachael Bade, Jasmine Baker, Amanda Becker, John Bicknell, Chad Brand, Kristin Broughton, Emily Cadei, Emily Cahn, Scott Campbell, Eliza Newlin Carney, Charlene Carter, Richard Cohen, Kristin Coyner, Steven T. Dennis, Michael DeFilippis, John M. Donnelly, Emma Dumain, Emily Ethridge, Ellyn Ferguson, Matt Fuller, Karin Fuog, Lauren Gardner, Emil Georgi, Sam Goldfarb, Aaron Guerrero, Clayton Hanson, David Harrison, Hannah Hess, David Higgins, Emily Holden, Jay Hunter, Nathan Hurst, Paul Jenks, Ryan Kelly, Elham Khatami, Anne L. Kim, Ashley Kongs, Geof Koss, Kaitlin Kovach, Paul M. Krawzak, Niels Lesniewski, Adam Levin, Jacqueline Linnane, Abby Livingston, Janie Lorber, Rob Margetta, Anna McGeehan, Caitlin McGlade, Tait Militana, Joshua Miller, Manuel Moya, Eugene Mulero, Eric Naing, Chris Nehls, Daniel Newhauser, Connor O'Brien, Frank Oliveri, Sandra Opanga, Alan K. Ota, Daniel Peake, Carolyn Phenicie, Emily Poe, Peter Rocco, Warren Rojas, Humberto Sanchez, Adam Schank, Joseph J. Schatz, Jennifer Scholtes, Megan Scully, Neda Semnani, Rebecca Shabad, Mary Shaffrey, Meredith Shiner, Annie Shuppy, Lauren Smith, Tim Starks, Jonathan Strong, Gail Sullivan, Michael Teitelbaum, Shira Toeplitz, Robert Tomkin, Kyle Trygstad, Kate Tummarello, Ben Weyl, Sean Winkler, Chris Wright, Kerry Young

SENIOR RESEARCHERS
Jay Hunter, Ryan Kelly

RESEARCHERS
Jasmine Baker, Nell Benton, Tait Jany, Kaitlin Kovach, Sarah Lawrence, Chris Nehls, Emily Poe, Peter Rocco, Sean Winkler, Tim Yoder

SENIOR COPY EDITOR
Arwen Bicknell

COPY EDITORS
Kevin Barnard, Sara Bondioli, Colin Degen, Jamisha Ford, David Higgins, Julie Klavens, Kaitlin Kovach, Alex Muller, Melinda W. Nahmias, Mary Ann Nyamweya, Aleksandra Robinson, Debra Rubin, Jennifer Rubio, Joe Warminsky, Khari Williams

PHOTOGRAPHY
Bill Clark, Douglas Graham, Tom Williams

LAYOUT AND DESIGN / DISTRICT MAPS
John Irons, Michael Stanaland / © Map Resources

INDEX
Nell Benton

PUBLISHING SOFTWARE
Erin Miller, Mark Logic – San Carlos, Calif.

DATA SUPPORT
George Codrea, Jessica Cuellar, Amanda Hicks

IT SUPPORT
Ron Brodmann, John Hanna, Jason Pritchard

PIA ONLINE EDITION
Andrew Boney, Jerry Orvedahl, CQ Press, an imprint of SAGE Publications Inc. – Thousand Oaks, Calif.

PRODUCTION MANAGER
Paul Pressau, CQ Press, an imprint of SAGE Publications Inc. – Thousand Oaks, Calif.

BUSINESS MANAGER
Dennis Arndt

MARKETING MANAGER
Dionne Williams

Politics in America

17th Edition

ON NOVEMBER 6, 2012, Barack Obama was re-elected president, Democrats kept control of the Senate and Republicans held on to the House. A status quo election? It was anything but.

Democrats were buoyed by the reality of a second term for Obama, who took almost all the battleground states despite a still-lagging economy. While Republicans held the House, they lost eight seats as the tea party lost some of its luster. They were left to wrestle with their identity: Did they need to better motivate their base or broaden it to include younger people and Latinos? That tension continued to play out in the early months of the 113th Congress.

And then there were the Senate surprises. The incumbent seen as most vulnerable when the campaign began ended up winning by 16 points. After Republican Rep. Todd Akin talked about a woman's ability to get pregnant from "legitimate rape," Missouri voters sent Democrat Claire McCaskill back to Washington. The addition of five new female senators brought the number of women in the chamber to 20, the most ever.

These women would band together early in 2013 on issues including the Violence Against Women Act and sexual assault in the military. They also took control of the Senate's fiscal agenda, with Maryland's Barbara A. Mikulski in the Appropriations chair and Patty Murray of Washington heading the Budget Committee. "For the first time, there was a traffic jam in the Senate women's bathroom," said Amy Klobuchar of Minnesota.

This book paints the rich portrait of the 113th Congress — the most the diverse in history, with more openly gay members than ever and plenty of new faces. Thanks in part to reapportionment and redistricting, 164 current House members and 30 current senators have arrived since the decade began, disrupting longstanding alliances and further shaking up the old guard.

Freshman or veteran, though, most lawmakers arrived in January with the economy on their minds — specifically the needs to curb the deficit, update the tax code and create jobs. But hot-button issues kept drawing them in. Immigration came to the forefront. And by spring, there was already talk of a second-term curse on Obama, as Republicans went on the offensive on a number of domestic and foreign issues where they saw him as vulnerable.

Whether you're looking at this book as a field guide as these issues unfold, or as a reference work years later, you'll find what you need in this 17th edition of Politics in America. Unlike the first edition of 1981, of course, this is the print output of a living version of our members database on CQ.com.

In this era of noise and distraction, I like looking at this book the way some people study maps — to absorb the detail and to have a chance encounter with a random fact that helps me understand this community on a hill. But if you're using it for research purposes, we know you'll find its information rock-solid.

For that, we thank the people who put it together: co-editors Chris White and Amanda H. Allen, and deputy editor Stacey Goers. They collected these profiles from the CQ Roll Call writers who know the members best, compiled the data and edited it all into the 541-chapter narrative that follows.

Chris, Amanda and Stacey occupy a corner of our newsroom owned by our members information team. They are fun and full of trivia about members of Congress, their personalities, their districts and their vital statistics. But these professionals are dead serious when it comes to their data and their book, which they have lived and breathed for the past two years. We think their work is the most objective and authoritative source of information on Congress available anywhere, and we hope you'll agree.

Susan Benkelman
Editorial Director and Senior Vice President, CQ Roll Call

MANY PEOPLE ENJOY SCREAMING ABOUT GOVERNMENT, and a lucky few of us are paid to do so. As you may have heard, the environment in Washington has never been more toxic, and ulcerative colitis has slightly higher approval ratings than Congress. The institution, by many accounts, is broken.

What's lacking in that analysis is historical perspective. Things have been worse. The 12th and 13th Congresses argued bitterly about defense spending while the British were actually invading America, with guns and everything. Personal attacks leveled by 19th-century politicians make modern-day blog commenters look like the Algonquin Round Table. The "corrupting influence" of money in politics was direct bribes, not this namby-pamby business with super PACs. Huge swaths of the population were not even fully empowered (at least under the law) until 1920 and 1965. There also might have been a civil war somewhere in there.

In terms of congressional politics, we are nowhere near the low point. Quite the opposite, in fact. As polarized as they seemed, the debates of the 112th Congress were a celebration of our sprawling society. Ethnic, racial, gender, generational, religious, ideological, social and economic groups have been energized by the ease of both communication and organization in the Information Age; they also have become remarkably efficient at formulating and promoting their agendas.

One of the quieter members of Congress, Nebraska Republican Adrian Smith, summarized the situation nicely: "The beauty of Congress, even amidst our low approval ratings, is the House is reflective of America and the diversity of America — the variability. It's amazing that we can boil anything down to a yes-or-no vote."

The point of "Politics in America," to my mind, is to outline that diversity and provide meaningful context for the actions of the legislative branch — something deeper than superficial complaints of a broken system. This book offers 1,200 pages of empathy, so when people call for bipartisanship or compromise, it's clear exactly what they're asking.

There are cynics on Capitol Hill (they're part of our diversity), but there are also sincere advocates. If a Republican truly believes that federal deficits and an overreaching government will end the greatest experiment in democracy, how can he give ground? If a Democrat truly believes that the shrinking of government will unfairly inflict untold misery on vulnerable constituents, what could make her budge?

Those are difficult questions, and they might not have answers. But the personal, professional and political stories crammed into this book are usually the starting point for understanding progress, or the lack thereof — no matter how you choose to define progress. The district descriptions broaden that understanding by providing snapshots of the economic and cultural realities that lawmakers face back home.

It's all worth studying. No matter what happens in the 113th Congress, there's probably going to be a 114th, and it will represent a nation that has become even more diverse, in just about every way imaginable. If there isn't a 114th, then the aliens have attacked, and I, for one, welcome our new insect overlords.

And now some personal advice: If you decide to produce a textbook on every member of Congress, you're going to want an excellent group of diligent co-workers. The process will also go much more smoothly if you have the greatest spouse in the known universe. The latter is impossible, as Allyson Jaffe is already married, but I'm sure you can find someone who is a distant but respectable second. Best of luck.

Chris White
May 2013

About the Editors

Amanda H. Allen joined the staff of "Politics in America" in 2006 to work on congressional and territorial district descriptions. The intensely nerdy project was right in her wheelhouse, and she has spent seven years focusing on the fine points of congressional membership, elections and districts. She is currently a deputy members editor, and this is the fourth edition of PIA she has worked on. After being licensed by the Maryland bar, Amanda got into news because that's what you do when you're an Allen. Her father was a longtime reporter for UPI, her brother is a well-known reporter in D.C., and her sister-in-law moved from news to a Hill job to speech writing. Amanda's mother, an academic-turned-public-servant, is the smartest one in the family.

Chris White started his career as a reporter and editor with the Bureau of National Affairs. He soon joined the Washington Post Writers Group, where he served as a copy editor and fact-checker for some of the most prominent opinion writers in the business. After five years, he abandoned the stable and high-paying world of journalism for the even-more-secure world of entertainment, traveling the country as a stand-up comedian. Chris returned to full-time journalism in 2010 with CQ Roll Call, and in 2011 he became a deputy members editor. This is the third edition of "Politics in America" that he has worked on. He is also a presidential history enthusiast, to the unending joy of his wife, Allyson Jaffe. They live in Washington.

Capitol Hill's Great Divides

Political polarization overhangs most every debate and decision on Capitol Hill, despite the lamentations of pundits and ordinary people alike that the difficult issues of the day require lawmakers to work cooperatively. Yet it's no secret that America is a closely divided country on most matters of political significance — and Congress is, if anything, a representative body.

Paradoxically, Americans don't seem to want Congress to reflect the deep divisions within the electorate. Surveys routinely show a preference for lawmakers to stop fighting and resolve the tough issues. Moreover, Americans frequently say they want their elected representatives to choose compromise positions that navigate between the extremes.

Frankly, that wish may be naïve, given the country's long history of political discord. Perhaps the public should get over its fascination with moderation and embrace the conflict within the body politic — and the resulting gridlock and tension. There are few signs that polarization will lessen, and it might even be getting more pronounced.

Congressional Quarterly (now CQ Roll Call) has been studying partisanship since the end of World War II by analyzing "party unity" votes, where majorities of Republicans and Democrats line up on opposite sides. The data for the two years of the 112th Congress reveal the House — back under GOP control after four years under the Democrats — to have been a place where party unity was stronger than at any time since 1953.

One measure of partisanship is how frequently roll call votes split the parties. A half-century ago, that happened less than half the time in either chamber. But in 2012, almost 75 percent of House votes and 60 percent of Senate votes met that standard. That pattern seems to have continued in the early months of the 113th Congress, although it's the Senate where three-fourths of votes have broken along party lines.

The tendency of Congress to split along partisan lines is hardly surprising. Every poll, every election and almost every issue reveals fissures — and at the same time reveals a relatively thin margin separating the two sides.

The Pew Research Center's annual "Trends in American Values" survey found that partisanship is now the dominant source of disagreement on issues, far surpassing differences that can be attributed to race, wealth or educational attainment. "Since 1987 — and particularly over just the past decade — the country has experienced a stark increase in partisan polarization," Pew reported in June 2012. "In most cases, this represents a widening of already existing partisan differences — particularly when it comes to the role of government."

Partisanship has increased even while fewer people associate with a party. In 2012, 38 percent of those surveyed by Pew called themselves political independents — the highest in more than 70 years. But they are still a polarized bunch. "Political polarization is not limited to the narrowed partisan bases," Pew wrote. "Even independents who say they only lean toward one or the other party have grown further apart in their values and beliefs. On most of the core attitudes about the role and effectiveness of government, the values of these partisan leaners track very closely with those of partisans."

Some of this fracturing is tied to conflicts that date to the founding of the republic and involve such broad issues as the size and role of government. At their center, these disagreements often are founded on interpretations of constitutional intent and on the willingness, or lack thereof, of 21st-century Americans to adapt long-held principles to modern circumstances.

No issue on which the public is closely divided better illustrates this point than gun control. But it's far from the only fight where both sides believe they hold the key to the truth. Spending limits, the structure of the tax code, access to health care and the crisis in immigration policy all stir polarized debates. Each of those issues has been front and center in the first months of the 113th Congress, and each is likely to be pivotal for some segment of the electorate when voters go to the polls in 2014.

Lest this trend toward ideological division seem transitory, history suggests that polarization has long been the norm in the United States. Research by Keith T. Poole of the University of Georgia, Howard L. Rosenthal of New York University and Nolan McCarty of Princeton University shows that Congress was highly partisan throughout the 19th century. Polarization declined in the early part of the 20th century and reached a low point in the years just before and after World War II.

Poole, who with his colleagues has done extensive analysis of roll call voting patterns back to the beginning of the republic, writes that the past two decades "mark an acceleration of the trend (especially in the House)." Notably, he observes that "polarization in the House and Senate is now at the highest level since the end of Reconstruction." CQ noticed this trend, and in its first years did annual studies of "bipartisanship," until it became evident that the opposite dynamic was the controlling force.

For students of Congress, the central question is how lawmakers can function in such an environment. Especially at a time of divided government, partisanship blocks action on Capitol Hill more often than it drives action.

The House can still — at least much of the time — be force-marched into following the lead of the majority. But that doesn't mean that the House position can prevail at the end of the day. In the Senate, where majority rule is no longer the order of the day and 60 votes are needed to conduct any business, polarization has to be overcome if lawmakers are to do their fundamental job, which is to legislate.

The previous two Congresses (2009-12) amply illustrated the limitations of a polarized and divided government. When the Democrats had the White House, both chambers of Congress and — fleetingly — a 60-vote majority in the Senate, they were barely able to work their will. President Barack Obama's biggest achievement, the 2010 health care overhaul, was a result of partisan force. It won him no friends on the other side of the aisle and perhaps cost him his House majority in 2010. The inability of Republicans and Democrats to agree on much of anything since then isn't burnishing Washington's image.

Among the difficult issues facing the 113th Congress, immigration may provide the best opportunity for compromise, while a gridlocked fiscal policy will require accommodation, if not agreement, across party lines to avert serious consequences.

How these and other front-burner issues play out before the 2014 election may affect who grabs the reins of power in the 114th Congress. One thing is clear, however: America has to choose whether it is comfortable living in a starkly polarized world, or whether it wants to reverse course. The voters will decide.

John Cranford
Editor, CQ Weekly

2010 Census and Congressional Apportionment

STATE	2010 POPULATION	2000 POPULATION	PERCENT CHANGE	SEATS IN HOUSE 2013-2023	GAIN/ LOSS
California	37,253,956	33,871,648	10.0	53	0
Texas	25,145,561	20,851,820	20.6	36	4
Florida	18,801,310	15,982,378	17.6	27	2
New York	19,378,102	18,976,457	2.1	27	-2
Illinois	12,830,632	12,419,293	3.3	18	-1
Pennsylvania	12,702,379	12,281,054	3.4	18	-1
Ohio	11,536,504	11,353,140	1.6	16	-2
Georgia	9,687,653	8,186,453	18.3	14	1
Michigan	9,883,640	9,938,444	-0.6	14	-1
North Carolina	9,535,483	8,049,313	18.5	13	0
New Jersey	8,791,894	8,414,350	4.5	12	-1
Virginia	8,001,024	7,078,515	13.0	11	0
Washington	6,724,540	5,894,121	14.1	10	1
Arizona	6,392,017	5,130,632	24.6	9	1
Indiana	6,483,802	6,080,485	6.6	9	0
Massachusetts	6,547,629	6,349,097	3.1	9	-1
Tennessee	6,346,105	5,689,283	11.5	9	0
Maryland	5,773,552	5,296,486	9.0	8	0
Minnesota	5,303,925	4,919,479	7.8	8	0
Missouri	5,988,927	5,595,211	7.0	8	-1
Wisconsin	5,686,986	5,363,675	6.0	8	0
Alabama	4,779,736	4,447,100	7.5	7	0
Colorado	5,029,196	4,301,261	16.9	7	0
South Carolina	4,625,364	4,012,012	15.3	7	1
Kentucky	4,339,367	4,041,769	7.4	6	0
Louisiana	4,533,372	4,468,976	1.4	6	-1
Connecticut	3,574,097	3,405,565	4.9	5	0
Oklahoma	3,751,351	3,450,654	8.7	5	0
Oregon	3,831,074	3,421,399	12.0	5	0
Arkansas	2,915,918	2,673,400	9.1	4	0
Iowa	3,046,355	2,926,324	4.1	4	-1
Kansas	2,853,118	2,688,418	6.1	4	0
Mississippi	2,967,297	2,844,658	4.3	4	0
Nevada	2,700,551	1,998,257	35.1	4	1
Utah	2,763,885	2,233,169	23.8	4	1
Nebraska	1,826,341	1,711,263	6.7	3	0
New Mexico	2,059,179	1,819,046	13.2	3	0
West Virginia	1,852,994	1,808,344	2.5	3	0
Hawaii	1,360,301	1,211,537	12.3	2	0
Idaho	1,567,582	1,293,953	21.1	2	0
Maine	1,328,361	1,274,923	4.2	2	0
New Hampshire	1,316,470	1,235,786	6.5	2	0
Rhode Island	1,052,567	1,048,319	0.4	2	0
Alaska	710,231	626,932	13.3	1	0
Delaware	897,934	783,600	14.6	1	0
Montana	989,415	902,195	9.7	1	0
North Dakota	672,591	642,200	4.7	1	0
South Dakota	814,180	754,844	7.9	1	0
Vermont	625,741	608,827	2.8	1	0
Wyoming	563,626	493,782	14.1	1	0
TOTAL	**308,143,815**	**280,849,847**	**9.7**	**435**	

TABLE OF CONTENTS

Florida

Georgia

Hawaii

Idaho

Illinois

Indiana

Iowa

Kansas

Kentucky

New Hampshire

New Jersey

New Mexico

New York

North Carolina

North Dakota

Ohio

Oklahoma

Oregon

Pennsylvania

Explanation of Statistics

State Profiles

State profile pages contain information on governors, compositions of state legislatures, statewide statistics and information about major cities. Details about the makeup of the state legislatures, elected officials' salaries, the legislative schedule, registered voters and state term limits were obtained from state officials and reflect their status as of June 2013.

POPULATION AND URBAN STATISTICS

Statistical information was obtained from the U.S. Census Bureau, the Defense Department and the FBI. Place of origin statistics, violent crime rates, poverty rates, and federal worker and military personnel statistics are from 2009.

STATISTICS BY DISTRICT

Demographic information relates to current congressional district lines. The figures for racial composition, Hispanic origin, median household income, age, education, urban versus rural residences and size of each congressional district are from the Census Bureau.

The college education table shows the percentage of people age 25 and older who have earned at least a bachelor's degree. The district's area is presented in square miles of land area.

The tables include percentages for the Democratic and Republican candidates for president in 2008 and 2012. The Associated Press calculated the presidential vote in every House district to reflect the results within the district boundaries in effect for the 2012 elections (for the 113th Congress). Seven states — Alaska, Delaware, Montana, North Dakota, South Dakota, Vermont and Wyoming — have only one House district.

District Descriptions

In most states, congressional district lines were redrawn in 2011 to reflect reapportionment and changes in population patterns revealed in the 2010 census.

The district description briefly sets forth the economic, sociological, demographic and political forces that are the keys to elections and that influence the legislative agenda of the district's member of Congress.

Military base figures are compiled by CQ Roll Call from information provided by each base. The military base listings do not include Coast Guard, National Guard or reserve bases, and do not include all depots and arsenals due to space limitations.

Party Abbreviations	
ABA	Abundant America
AC	American Constitution
AEL	Americans Elect
BFC	Bednarski for Congress
BFJ	Bob's for Jobs
C	Conservative
CHA	Change Change Change
CNSTP	Constitution
CONSTL	Constitutional
D	Democratic
GR	Grassroots
GREEN	Green
I	Independent
IA	Independent American
IDP	Independent Progressive
IGREEN	Independent Green
INDC	Independence
IRFM	Independent Reform
LIBERT	Libertarian
LU	Liberty Union
MOUNT	Mountain
NJC	New Jersey Conservative
NOP	Non Party
NPA	No Party Affiliation
OCG	Opposing Congressional Gridlock
PAC	Politicians Are Crooks
PACGRN	Pacific Green
PNP	New Progressive (Puerto Rico)
POPDEM	Popular Democratic (Puerto Rico)
PRI	Puerto Rican Independence
PRO	Progressive
R	Republican
RAP	Restoring America's Promise
REF	Reform

(continued on p. xvi)

(continued from p. xv)

S	Socialist
SGREEN	Statehood Green
SW	Socialist Workers
UIS	Unity is Strength
UMJ	United States Marijuana
UNA	Unaffiliated
USTAX	U.S. Taxpayers
WCP	Wyoming Country Party
WFM	Working Families
WTP	We The People

Note: In the New York election results, last names only were used for lawmakers to accommodate multiple party designations.

Member Profiles

COMMITTEES

Committee assignments are as of June 4, 2013, and a complete roster for each panel begins on page 1151.

CAREER AND POLITICAL HIGHLIGHTS

The member's principal occupations before becoming a full-time public official are given, with the most recent occupation listed first. Often, lawmakers' prior political offices were part-time jobs, and the member continued working at his or her "career" job. Political highlights listed include elected positions in government, high party posts, posts requiring legislative confirmation and unsuccessful candidacies for public office. Dates given cover years of service, not election dates.

ELECTIONS

Results for 2010 and 2012 are listed for House members, with primary results for 2012. For senators and governors, the most recent election results are listed. Because candidates who received less than 1 percent of the vote are not listed and percentages have been rounded, election results do not always add up to 100 percent.

Earlier election victories are noted for members of the House and Senate, with the member's percentage of the vote given. If no percentage is given for a year, the member either did not run or lost the election.

For special elections and primaries where a candidate would have won outright if he or she had received a majority of the votes, two election tallies are given, one for the initial election and one for the subsequent runoff.

PRIMARY ELECTIONS

California and Washington conduct elections under a "top two" primary system in which voters are able to vote for one candidate from among all candidates running for each office without having to declare a party affiliation or select a party ballot. The two candidates in each race who receive the most votes qualify for the general election, provided the candidate received at least 1 percent of the total votes cast for that office. In Washington, candidates for partisan office have the opportunity to state a political party preference on the primary ballot, but that preference is not an indication of approval, support, nomination, endorsement or association by the party that is listed.

Key Votes

Profiles of members who served in the 112th Congress (2011-12) are accompanied by key votes chosen by CQ Roll Call editors from that Congress. Following is a description of those votes, including President Barack Obama's position on that particular vote, if he unambiguously took one beforehand.

KEY SENATE VOTES

2012

Surface Transportation Authorization/Religious Exemptions for Health Care (Senate Vote 24): Murray, D-Wash., motion to table (kill) the Blunt, R-Mo., amendment to the Reid, D-Nev., amendment to the bill (S 1813). The Blunt amendment would allow health insurance plans to deny coverage for medical services that run counter to the plan sponsor's or employer's religious beliefs. It also would establish a private right of legal action for enforcement of the coverage exemptions. Motion agreed to 51-48: D 48-3; R 1-45; I 2-0. A "yea" was a vote in support of the president's position. March 1, 2012.

Surface Transportation Authorization/Keystone XL Pipeline (Senate Vote 34): Hoeven, R-N.D., amendment that would provide for approval of the Keystone XL pipeline between Canada and the United States. The amendment to the bill (S 1813) would require that the route for the pipeline in Nebraska be submitted by the state of Nebraska. It also would provide for certain environmental protections. Rejected 56-42: D 11-40; R 45-0; I 0-2. (By unanimous consent, the Senate agreed to raise the majority requirement for adoption of the Hoeven amendment to 60 votes.) A "nay" was a vote in support of the president's position. March 8, 2012.

Small-Business Startups/Passage (Senate Vote 55): Passage of the bill (HR 3606) that would define "emerging growth companies" and exempt them from certain independent auditing requirements. It would increase from $5 million to $50 million the annual public offering threshold for companies to be exempt from full Securities and Exchange Commission (SEC) filing requirements and raise the number of shareholders that would trigger mandatory SEC registration from 750 to 2,000. It also would raise to 2,000 the number of shareholders that would trigger a requirement for SEC registration for a bank. The bill would lift an SEC ban that prevents small, privately held companies from using advertisements to solicit investors and allow companies to sell up to $1 million worth of securities. As amended, it also would require anyone acting as a "crowdfunding" intermediary to register with securities regulators. Passed 73-26: D 26-25; R 46-0; I 1-1. A "yea" was a vote in support of the president's position. March 22, 2012.

Farm Programs/Passage (Senate Vote 164): Passage of the bill (S 3240) that would reauthorize federal farm and nutrition programs for five years, including crop subsidies, conservation, rural development and foreign food aid programs, for a total projected cost of roughly $969 billion over the next decade. It would reauthorize the Supplemental Nutrition Assistance Program for five years. The bill would eliminate direct payments and counter-cyclical payments and replace them with a new supplemental coverage option, which would allow producers to purchase additional crop insurance coverage on an area yield and loss basis. Those with losses of between 11 percent and 21 percent could receive payment from the supplemental coverage, while losses in excess of 21 percent would be covered by crop insurance. The bill would authorize $175 million annually for the

KEY VOTE SYMBOLS

CQ Roll Call editors selected key votes from roll call votes taken during the 112th Congress. The following symbols are used to indicate how votes were cast:

YES	VOTED FOR
No	VOTED AGAINST
#	PAIRED FOR
+	ANNOUNCED FOR
X	PAIRED AGAINST
-	ANNOUNCED AGAINST
P	VOTED "PRESENT"
C	VOTED "PRESENT" TO AVOID POSSIBLE CONFLICT OF INTEREST
?	DID NOT VOTE OR OTHERWISE MAKE A POSITION KNOWN
I	INELIGIBLE
S	SPEAKER EXERCISED HIS DISCRETION TO NOT VOTE

KEY VOTE SYMBOLS

CQ Roll Call editors selected key votes from roll call votes taken during the 112th Congress. The following symbols are used to indicate how votes were cast:

Yes	**VOTED FOR**
No	**VOTED AGAINST**
#	**PAIRED FOR**
+	**ANNOUNCED FOR**
X	**PAIRED AGAINST**
-	**ANNOUNCED AGAINST**
P	**VOTED "PRESENT"**
C	**VOTED "PRESENT" TO AVOID POSSIBLE CONFLICT OF INTEREST**
?	**DID NOT VOTE OR OTHERWISE MAKE A POSITION KNOWN**
I	**INELIGIBLE**
S	**SPEAKER EXERCISED HIS DISCRETION TO NOT VOTE**

Key Senate Votes cont.

Emergency Food Assistance Program, which provides assistance to food banks. It also would reauthorize the Export Credit Guarantee Program, which helps finance the export of U.S. agricultural products to countries where financing might not be available, but it would reduce export credit guarantees from $5.5 billion to $4.5 billion annually. The bill would lower the acreage cap of the Conservation Reserve Program, which pays farmers and ranchers to remove erodible land from their production, from 33 million acres to 25 million acres. It also would make any person or entity with a non-farm adjusted gross income of more than $750,000 ineligible for payments from commodity programs, capped at $50,000 per entity under the bill. Passed 64-35: D 46-5; R 16-30; I 2-0. (By unanimous consent, the Senate agreed to raise the majority requirement for passage of the bill to 60 votes.) A "yea" was a vote in support of the president's position. June 21, 2012.

Cybersecurity Standards/Cloture (Senate Vote 187): Motion to invoke cloture (thus limiting debate) on the bill (S 3414) that would create voluntary security standards for vital digital infrastructure. Motion rejected 52-46: D 45-6; R 5-40; I 2-0. Three-fifths of the total Senate (60) is required to invoke cloture. A "yea" was a vote in support of the president's position. Aug. 2, 2012.

Convention on the Rights of Persons with Disabilities/Adoption (Senate Vote 219): Adoption of the resolution of ratification of the Convention on the Rights of Persons with Disabilities (Treaty Doc 112-7), which would establish global standards for the treatment of people with disabilities. The resolution would state that current U.S. law fulfills or exceeds the obligations of the treaty. Rejected 61-38: D 51-0; R 8-38; I 2-0. A two-thirds majority of those present and voting (66 in this case) is required for adoption of resolutions of ratification. A "yea" was a vote in support of the president's position. Dec. 4, 2012.

Disaster Supplemental/Passage (Senate Vote 248): Passage of the bill (HR 1) that would provide $60.4 billion in emergency spending for communities hit by Superstorm Sandy, including an additional $9.7 billion in borrowing authority for the National Flood Insurance Program, $13 billion for mitigation projects, $11.5 billion for the Federal Emergency Management Agency's Disaster Relief Fund and $10.8 billion for the Federal Transit Administration to rebuild public transit systems. As amended, the bill would provide $17 billion for the Community Development Fund, with $500 million designated for regions that suffered major disasters or for "small, economically distressed areas" with less severe calamities in 2011 and 2012. The bill would allow the transfer of previously appropriated foreign operations funds to pay for increased security at U.S. embassies and other overseas posts. Passed 62-32: D 48-0; R 12-32; I 2-0. A "yea" was a vote in support of the president's position. Dec. 28, 2012.

Tax Rates Extensions/Passage (Senate Vote 251): Passage of the bill (HR 8) that would permanently extend the 2001 and 2003 tax rates for individual income below $400,000 and joint-filer income below $450,000. Rates for income above those thresholds would rise to 39.6 percent from 35 percent. It also would permanently extend the tax rates on dividends and capital gains for individual income below $400,000 and joint-filer income below $450,000. Rates for the dividends and capital gains taxes would rise to 20 percent for income above those thresholds. The measure would delay the automatic, across-the-board cuts known as the "sequester" for two months. Half of the sequester delay would be offset by discretionary cuts, split between defense and non-defense accounts, and the other half

Key Senate Votes cont.

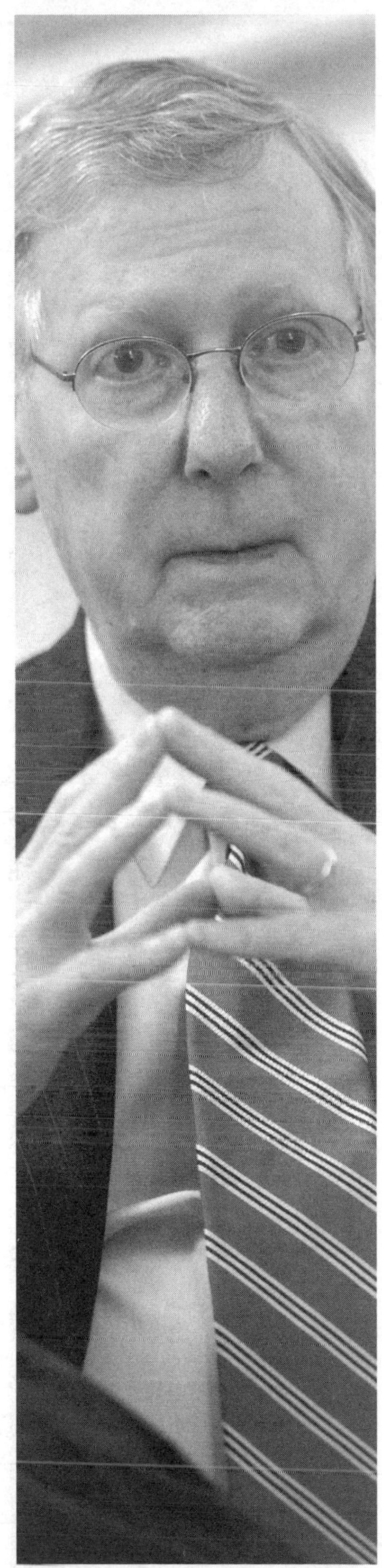

would be offset by revenue raised through the voluntary transfer of traditional IRAs to Roth IRAs, which would tax retirement savings when transferred. It also would tax individual estates valued over $5 million and joint estates valued over $10 million at 40 percent. It would extend the Milk Income Loss Contract (MILC) program at current rates, and it would permanently "patch" the alternative minimum tax to account for inflation. Unemployment insurance would be extended through 2013. The bill would block scheduled cuts to Medicare physician payment rates and extend for five years tax credits included in the 2009 stimulus law, including the child tax credit and the earned-income tax credit. It would permanently institute the Personal Exemption Phase-out tax, which would reduce the value of exemptions for individual income over $250,000. It would allow the 2 percent payroll tax holiday to expire. Passed 89-8: D 47-3; R 40-5; I 2-0. (By unanimous consent, the Senate agreed to raise the majority requirement for passage of the bill to 60 votes.) A "yea" was a vote in support of the president's position. Jan. 1, 2013 (in the session that began on and the Congressional Record dated Dec. 31, 2012).

2011

Small-Business Research/Prohibition on EPA Regulations (Senate Vote 54): McConnell, R-Ky., amendment to a small-business research bill (S 493). The amendment would block the EPA from regulating carbon dioxide and other greenhouse gases under the Clean Air Act. Rejected 50-50: D 4-47; R 46 1; I 0-2. (By unanimous consent, the Senate agreed to raise the majority requirement for adoption of the McConnell amendment to 60 votes.) A "nay" was a vote in support of the president's position. April 6, 2011 (on the legislative day April 5, 2011).

Patriot Act Extensions/Motion to Concur (Senate Vote 84): Reid, D-Nev., motion to concur in the House amendment with a Reid substitute amendment to the bill (S 990) that would extend through June 1, 2015, three provisions of the anti-terrorism law known as the Patriot Act. The provisions allow the government to seek court orders for roving wiretaps on suspects who use multiple devices or modes of communication, to request access to "any tangible thing" deemed related to a terrorism investigation and to seek warrants to conduct surveillance of "lone wolf" foreign terrorist suspects who may not be connected to a larger terrorist group. Motion agreed to 72-23: D 30-18; R 41-4; I 1-1. A "yea" was a vote in support of the president's position. May 26, 2011.

Debt Limit/Motion to Concur (Senate Vote 123): Reid, D-Nev., motion to concur in the House amendment to the bill (S 365) that would provide a process to reduce the deficit by up to $2.4 trillion. The measure would allow the president to raise the debt limit immediately by $400 billion, with an additional $500 billion subject to a resolution of disapproval. It would set discretionary spending caps that would reduce the deficit by $917 billion in fiscal 2012 through 2021 and establish a firewall between security and non-security spending for fiscal 2012 and 2013. It would establish a bipartisan, bicameral committee tasked with making recommendations to reduce the deficit by $1.5 trillion. It would require across-the-board cuts to non-exempt discretionary and mandatory accounts by up to $1.2 trillion over fiscal 2013 through 2021 if committee reductions totaling $1.2 trillion were not enacted. The measure would require Congress to vote on a balanced-budget constitutional amendment by the end of 2011. It also would provide for an additional debt limit increase of $1.2 trillion

Key Senate Votes cont.

to $1.5 trillion, subject to a resolution of disapproval. Motion agreed to (thus clearing the bill for the president) 74-26: D 45-6; R 28-19; I 1-1. (By unanimous consent, the Senate agreed to raise the majority requirement for the motion to concur to 60 votes.) A "yea" was a vote in support of the president's position. Aug. 2, 2011.

Patent Overhaul/Passage (Senate Vote 129): Passage of the bill (HR 1249) that would overhaul the U.S. patent system, changing how patents are awarded, reviewed and challenged. It would change the basis for awarding patents from a "first to invent" to a "first inventor to file" standard. It also would alter the process for challenging the validity of issued patents through the U.S. Patent and Trademark Office review proceedings, as well as authorize a re-examination of certain previously issued business method patents. It would require excess revenue from fees collected by the patent office to be set aside in an account for use pending further appropriations and would broaden the scope of the prior-user rights defense in infringement cases to include prior commercial use of a process. Passed (thus cleared for the president) 89-9: D 47-3; R 40-6; I 2-0. A "yea" was a vote in support of the president's position. Sept. 8, 2011.

Colombia Trade Agreement/Passage (Senate Vote 163): Passage of the bill (HR 3078) that would implement a trade agreement between the United States and Colombia. The agreement would reduce most tariffs and duties on goods traded between the two countries, reduce barriers to trade in services, increase protections for intellectual property and require Colombia to take steps to strengthen its labor and environmental enforcement standards. Passed (thus cleared for the president) 66-33: D 21-30; R 44-2; I 1-1. A "yea" was a vote in support of the president's position. Oct. 12, 2011.

Halligan Nomination/Cloture (Senate Vote 222): Motion to invoke cloture (thus limiting debate) on President Barack Obama's nomination of Caitlin Joan Halligan of New York to be a judge for the U.S. Court of Appeals for the District of Columbia Circuit. Motion rejected 54-45: D 51-0; R 1-45; I 2-0. Three-fifths of the total Senate (60) is required to invoke cloture. A "yea" was a vote in support of the president's position. Dec. 6, 2011.

Year-End Extensions/Substitute (Senate Vote 232): Reid, D-Nev., substitute amendment that would extend the 4.2 percent employee payroll tax rate through February 2012. The amendment to the bill (HR 3630) also would provide for an extension of Medicare payment rates to doctors through February 2012, delaying a reduction scheduled to occur in 2012. The amendment also would extend workers' eligibility for certain expanded unemployment benefits through February 2012. It would be offset through an increase in loan fees levied by government-backed mortgage lenders Fannie Mae and Freddie Mac for guaranteeing loans purchased in the secondary mortgage market. Adopted 89-10: D 49-2; R 39-7; I 1-1. (By unanimous consent, the Senate agreed to raise the majority requirement for adoption of the Reid-McConnell amendment to 60 votes. Subsequently the bill was passed by unanimous consent). A "yea" was a vote in support of the president's position. Dec. 17, 2011.

KEY HOUSE VOTES

2012

Payroll Tax Relief Extension/Conference Report (House Vote 72): Adoption of the conference report on the bill (HR 3630) that would extend the 4.2 percent employee payroll tax rate through 2012. It also would renew long-term unemployment benefits into January 2013, with three stages of reductions. The current Medicare reimbursement rate for physicians would be preserved through 2012, preventing a scheduled 27.4 percent payment cut. The cost of the legislation would be partially offset by requiring larger pension payments from newly hired federal employees and from lawmakers, by auctioning blocks of electromagnetic spectrum used by television broadcasters and by reducing funds for certain programs tied to the 2010 health care overhaul. Adopted (thus sent to the Senate) 293-132: R 146-91; D 147-41. A "yea" was a vote in support of the president's position. Feb. 17, 2012.

Small-Business Startups/Motion to Concur (House Vote 132): Bachus, R-Ala., motion to suspend the rules and concur in the Senate amendment to the bill (HR 3606) that would define "emerging growth companies" and exempt them from certain independent auditing requirements. It would increase from $5 million to $50 million the annual public offering threshold for companies to be exempt from full Securities and Exchange Commission (SEC) filing requirements and raise the number of shareholders that would trigger mandatory SEC registration from 750 to 2,000. It also would raise to 2,000 the number of shareholders that would trigger a requirement for SEC registration for a bank. The bill would lift an SEC ban that prevents small, privately held companies from using advertisements to solicit investors and allow companies to sell up to $1 million worth of securities without registering with the SEC. It also would require anyone acting as a "crowdfunding" intermediary to register with securities regulators. Motion agreed to (thus clearing the bill for the president) 380-41: R 235-0; D 145-41. A two thirds majority of those present and voting (263 in this case) is required for passage under suspension of the rules. A "yea" was a vote in support of the president's position. March 27, 2012.

Student Loan Interest Rates/Passage (House Vote 195): Passage of the bill (HR 4628) that would extend for one year, through June 30, 2013, the 3.4 percent interest rate for federally subsidized, undergraduate student loans. It would be offset by repealing the Prevention and Public Health Fund established by the health care overhaul law and rescinding unobligated amounts in the fund. Passed 215-195: R 202-30; D 13-165. A "nay" was a vote in support of the president's position. April 27, 2012.

Holder Contempt Resolution/Adoption (House Vote 441): Adoption of the resolution (H Res 711) that would cite Attorney General Eric H. Holder Jr. for contempt of Congress for refusing to comply with the subpoena issued by the House Oversight and Government Reform Committee to provide documents to the committee regarding the Operation Fast and Furious gun-tracking program. Adopted 255-67: R 238-2; D 17-65. A "nay" was a vote in support of the president's position. June 28, 2012.

STEM Visa Program/Passage (House Vote 613): Passage of the bill (HR 6429) that would create a new visa program under which foreign students earning advanced degrees in science, technology, engineering or mathematics (STEM) at eligible U.S. colleges and universities could remain in the United States to work in those fields.

KEY VOTE SYMBOLS

CQ Roll Call editors selected key votes from roll call votes taken during the 112th Congress. The following symbols are used to indicate how votes were cast:

YES	VOTED FOR
No	VOTED AGAINST
#	PAIRED FOR
+	ANNOUNCED FOR
X	PAIRED AGAINST
-	ANNOUNCED AGAINST
P	VOTED "PRESENT"
C	VOTED "PRESENT" TO AVOID POSSIBLE CONFLICT OF INTEREST
?	DID NOT VOTE OR OTHERWISE MAKE A POSITION KNOWN
I	INELIGIBLE
S	SPEAKER EXERCISED HIS DISCRETION TO NOT VOTE

KEY VOTE SYMBOLS

CQ Roll Call editors selected key votes from roll call votes taken during the 112th Congress. The following symbols are used to indicate how votes were cast:

YES	**VOTED FOR**
No	**VOTED AGAINST**
#	**PAIRED FOR**
+	**ANNOUNCED FOR**
X	**PAIRED AGAINST**
-	**ANNOUNCED AGAINST**
P	**VOTED "PRESENT"**
C	**VOTED "PRESENT" TO AVOID POSSIBLE CONFLICT OF INTEREST**
?	**DID NOT VOTE OR OTHERWISE MAKE A POSITION KNOWN**
I	**INELIGIBLE**
S	**SPEAKER EXERCISED HIS DISCRETION TO NOT VOTE**

Key House Votes cont.

The bill would eliminate the Diversity Visa Program and would reallocate 55,000 visas to the new STEM visa program. It would allow spouses and children of a STEM graduate to reside in the United States without work authorization after a one-year waiting period. Passed 245-139: R 218-5; D 27-134. A "nay" was a vote in support of the president's position. Nov. 30, 2012.

Tax Rates Extensions/Motion to Concur (House Vote 659): Camp, R-Mich., motion to concur in the Senate amendments to the bill (HR 8) that would permanently extend the 2001 and 2003 tax rates for individual income below $400,000 and joint-filer income below $450,000. Rates for income above those thresholds would rise to 39.6 percent from 35 percent. It also would permanently extend the tax rates on dividends and capital gains for individual income below $400,000 and joint-filer income below $450,000. Rates for the dividends and capital gains taxes would rise to 20 percent for income above those thresholds. The measure would delay the automatic, across-the-board cuts known as the "sequester" for two months. Half of the sequester delay would be offset by discretionary cuts, split between defense and non-defense accounts, and the other half would be offset by revenue raised through the voluntary transfer of traditional IRAs to Roth IRAs, which would tax retirement savings when transferred. It also would tax individual estates valued over $5 million and joint estates valued over $10 million at 40 percent. It would extend the Milk Income Loss Contract (MILC) program at current rates, and it would permanently "patch" the alternative minimum tax to account for inflation. Unemployment insurance would be extended through 2013. The bill would block scheduled cuts to Medicare physician payment rates and extend for five years tax credits included in the 2009 stimulus law, including the child tax credit and the earned-income tax credit. It would permanently institute the Personal Exemption Phase-out tax, which would reduce the value of exemptions for individual income over $250,000. It would allow the 2 percent payroll tax holiday to expire. Motion agreed to (thus clearing the bill for the president) 257-167: R 85-151; D 172-16. A "yea" was a vote in support of the president's position. Jan. 1, 2013.

2011

Fiscal 2011 Continuing Appropriations/F-35 Alternative Engine (House Vote 46): Rooney, R-Fla., amendment to the bill (HR 1) that would reduce funding for Army and Air Force research, development, testing and evaluation by $450 million, with the aim of reducing funding by that amount for the F-35 Joint Strike Fighter alternative engine. Adopted in Committee of the Whole 233-198: R 110-130; D 123-68. A "yea" was a vote in support of the president's position. Feb. 16, 2011.

EPA Greenhouse Gas Regulation/Passage (House Vote 249): Passage of the bill (HR 910) that would prohibit the EPA from regulating greenhouse gases in any effort to address climate change. It would amend the Clean Air Act to strike specific elements from the definition of "air pollutant," unless regulation of those chemicals is not used in an attempt to address climate change. It also would clarify that the bill does not limit the authority of a state to regulate the emission of a greenhouse gas, unless the regulation attempts to address climate change. Passed 255-172: R 236-0; D 19-172. A "nay" was a vote in support of the president's position. April 7, 2011.

Key House Votes cont.

Patriot Act Extensions/Motion to Concur (House Vote 376): Smith, R-Texas, motion to concur in the Senate amendment to the House amendment to the bill (S 990) that would extend through June 1, 2015, three provisions of the anti-terrorism law known as the Patriot Act. The provisions allow the government to seek court orders for roving wiretaps on suspects who use multiple devices or modes of communication, to request access to "any tangible thing" deemed related to a terrorism investigation and to seek warrants to conduct surveillance of "lone wolf" foreign terrorist suspects who may not be connected to a larger terrorist group. Motion agreed to (thus clearing the bill for the president) 250-153: R 196-31; D 54-122. A "yea" was a vote in support of the president's position. May 26, 2011.

Use of Ground Forces in Libya/Adoption (House Vote 411): Adoption of the resolution (H Res 292) that would direct the administration to transmit certain documents to the House and direct the president to transmit a report within 14 days containing certain information about the military activity in Libya. It would state that the armed forces should be used exclusively to defend and advance U.S. national security interests, that the president did not provide "compelling rationale" to Congress regarding the action in Libya, and that the president should not deploy ground forces in Libya unless it is to rescue a member of the armed forces in imminent danger. Adopted 268-145: R 223-10; D 45-135. June 3, 2011.

Patent Overhaul/Passage (House Vote 491): Passage of the bill (HR 1249) that would overhaul the U.S. patent system, changing how patents are awarded, reviewed and challenged. It would change the basis for awarding patents from a "first to invent" to a "first inventor to file" standard. It also would alter the process for challenging the validity of issued patents through the U.S. Patent and Trademark Office review proceedings, as well as authorize a re-examination of certain previously issued business method patents. It would require excess revenue from fees collected by the patent office to be set aside in an account for use pending further appropriations and would broaden the scope of the prior-user rights defense in infringement cases to include prior commercial use of a process. Passed 304-117: R 168-67; D 136-50. A "yea" was a vote in support of the president's position. June 23, 2011.

Debt Limit/Passage (House Vote 690): Passage of the bill (S 365) that would provide a process to reduce the deficit by up to $2.4 trillion. The measure would allow the president to raise the debt limit immediately by $400 billion, with an additional $500 billion subject to a resolution of disapproval. It would set discretionary spending caps that would reduce the deficit by $917 billion in fiscal 2012 through 2021 and establish a firewall between security and non-security spending for fiscal 2012 and 2013. It would establish a bipartisan, bicameral committee tasked with making recommendations to reduce the deficit by $1.5 trillion. It would require across-the-board cuts to non-exempt discretionary and mandatory accounts by up to $1.2 trillion over fiscal 2013 through 2021 if committee reductions totaling $1.2 trillion were not enacted. The measure would require Congress to vote on a balanced-budget constitutional amendment by the end of 2011. It also would provide for an additional debt limit increase of $1.2 trillion to $1.5 trillion, subject to a resolution of disapproval. Passed 269-161: R 174-66; D 95-95. A "yea" was a vote in support of the president's position. Aug. 1, 2011.

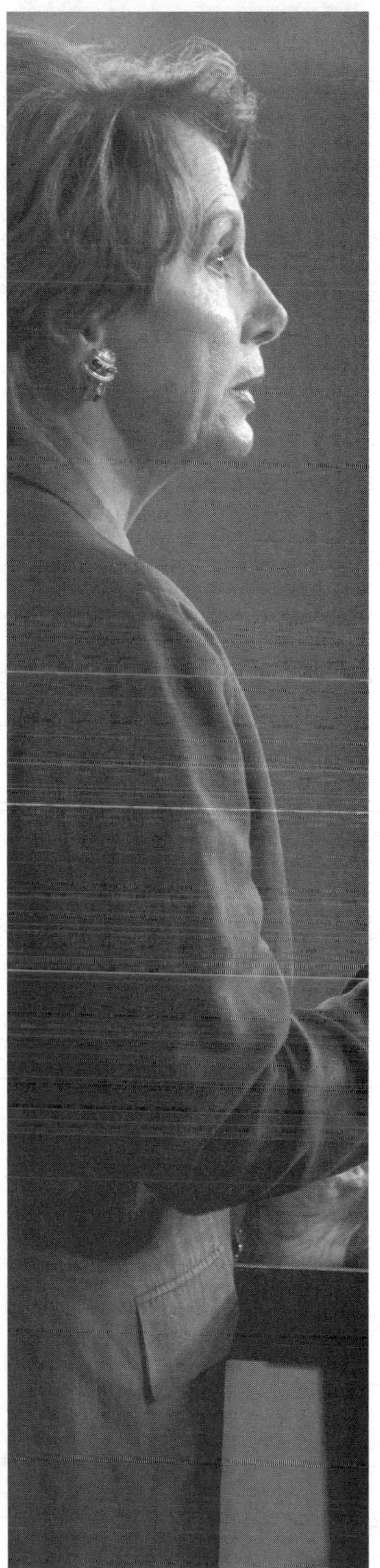

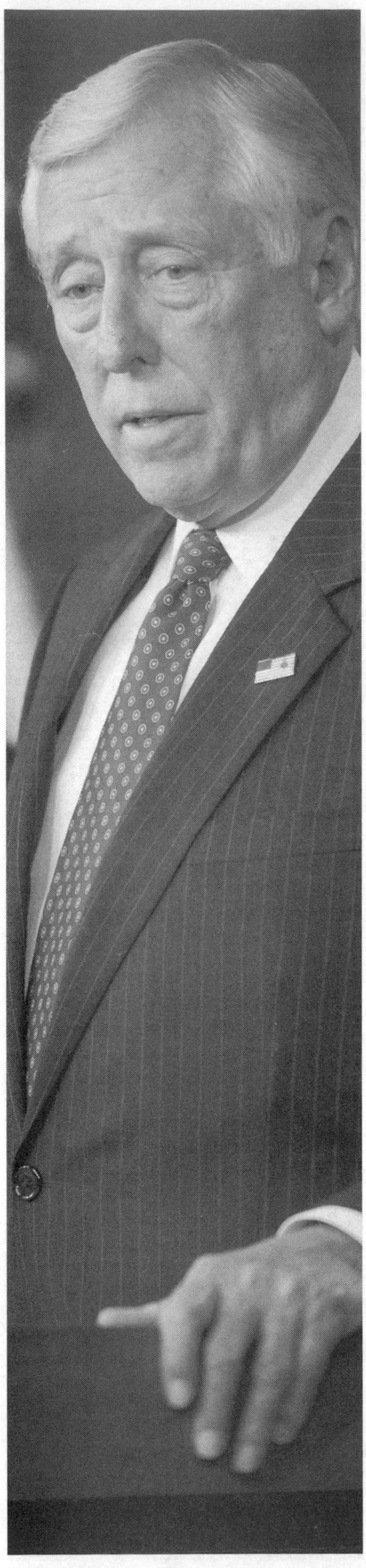

Key House Votes cont.

South Korea, Colombia and Panama Trade Agreements/Rule (House Vote 771): Adoption of the rule (H Res 425) that would provide for House floor consideration of bills that would implement trade agreements with Colombia (HR 3078), Panama (HR 3079) and South Korea (HR 3080). It also would provide for consideration of the Senate amendment to a bill (HR 2832) that would extend Trade Adjustment Assistance programs and the Generalized System of Preferences. Adopted 281-128: R 232-1; D 49-127. Oct. 11, 2011.

Vote Studies

Each year, CQ studies the frequency with which each member of Congress supports or opposes the position of their own party's majority and the position of the president. Scores are based only on votes cast; not voting does not alter a member's score. All votes have equal statistical weight in the analysis. Scores are rounded to the nearest whole percentage point, although rounding is not used to increase any score to 100 percent or to reduce any score to zero.

PARTY UNITY

Party unity votes are defined as all votes in the Senate and House that split the two parties — a majority of voting Democrats opposing a majority of voting Republicans. Votes on which the parties agree, or on which one party divides evenly, are excluded. In recent years, more than half of all votes in the Senate and the House have been designated as party unity votes. In 2012, nearly three-fourths of votes in the House were party unity votes — the third-highest proportion on record.

Support scores represent the percentage of party unity votes on which a member voted yes or no in agreement with a majority of the member's party. Opposition scores represent the percentage of party unity votes on which a member voted yes or no in disagreement with a majority of the member's party.

PRESIDENTIAL SUPPORT

CQ tries to determine what the president personally, as distinct from other administration officials, wants or does not want in the way of legislative action. This is done by reviewing messages to Congress, news conference remarks and other public statements and documents. Every roll call vote in the House and Senate is reviewed in that context, and those votes where the editors of CQ decide that the president had a clear stake in the outcome carry presidential positions. Occasionally, important bills are so extensively amended that it is impossible to characterize votes on final passage as a victory or a defeat for the president. At the same time, procedural votes on motions to recommit, to reconsider or to table (kill) sometimes govern the outcome and these are included in the presidential support tabulations. In the House in recent years, fewer than 10 percent of all votes have been judged to carry presidential positions. In the Senate, 30 percent or more of all votes typically meet the definition.

Support scores represent the percentage of votes on which a member voted yes or no in agreement with the president's position. Opposition scores represent the percentage of votes on which a member voted yes or no in disagreement with president's position.

CONGRESS BY ITS NUMBERS

A new Congress is elected in each even-numbered year and convenes at the beginning of each odd-numbered year. As a shorthand, this book frequently refers to the actions of a particular Congress by its number. The sequence began with the 1st Congress, which was elected in 1788.

Congress	Year elected	Years in session
113th	2012	2013 and 2014
112th	2010	2011 and 2012
111th	2008	2009 and 2010
110th	2006	2007 and 2008
109th	2004	2005 and 2006
108th	2002	2003 and 2004
107th	2000	2001 and 2002
106th	1998	1999 and 2000
105th	1996	1997 and 1998
104th	1994	1995 and 1996
103rd	1992	1993 and 1994
102nd	1990	1991 and 1992
101st	1988	1989 and 1990
100th	1986	1987 and 1988

Interest Group Ratings

Ratings for members by four advocacy groups are chosen to reflect labor, liberal, business and conservative viewpoints.

AFL-CIO

The AFL-CIO was formed when the American Federation of Labor and the Congress of Industrial Organizations merged in 1955. For senators, ratings are based on 11 votes in 2008, 18 in 2009, 16 in 2010, 19 in 2011 and 11 in 2012. For House members, ratings are based on 18 votes in 2008, 21 in 2009, 14 in 2010, 29 in 2011 and 21 in 2012. (www.aflcio.org)

ADA

Americans for Democratic Action was founded in 1947 by a group of liberal Democrats that included Minnesota Sen. Hubert H. Humphrey and Eleanor Roosevelt. The ADA ratings are based on 20 votes each year in each chamber of Congress. (www.adaction.org)

CCUS

The Chamber of Commerce of the United States represents local, regional and state chambers as well as trade and professional groups. It was founded in 1912 to be "a voice for organized business." For senators, ratings are based on eight votes in 2008, seven in 2009, 11 in 2010, 11 in 2011 and eight in 2012. For House members, ratings are based on 18 votes in 2008, 15 in 2009, nine in 2010, 16 in 2011 and 12 in 2012. (www.uschamber.com)

ACU

The American Conservative Union was founded in 1964 "to mobilize resources of responsible conservative thought across the country and further the general cause of conservatism." The organization intends to provide education in: political activity; "prejudice in the press"; foreign and military policy; domestic economic policy; the arts; professions and sciences. For senators, ratings are based on 25 votes in 2008, 25 in 2009, 25 in 2010, 20 in 2011 and 25 in 2012. For House members, the ratings are based on 25 votes in 2008, 25 in 2009, 24 in 2010, 25 in 2011 and 25 in 2012. (www.conservative.org)

ALABAMA

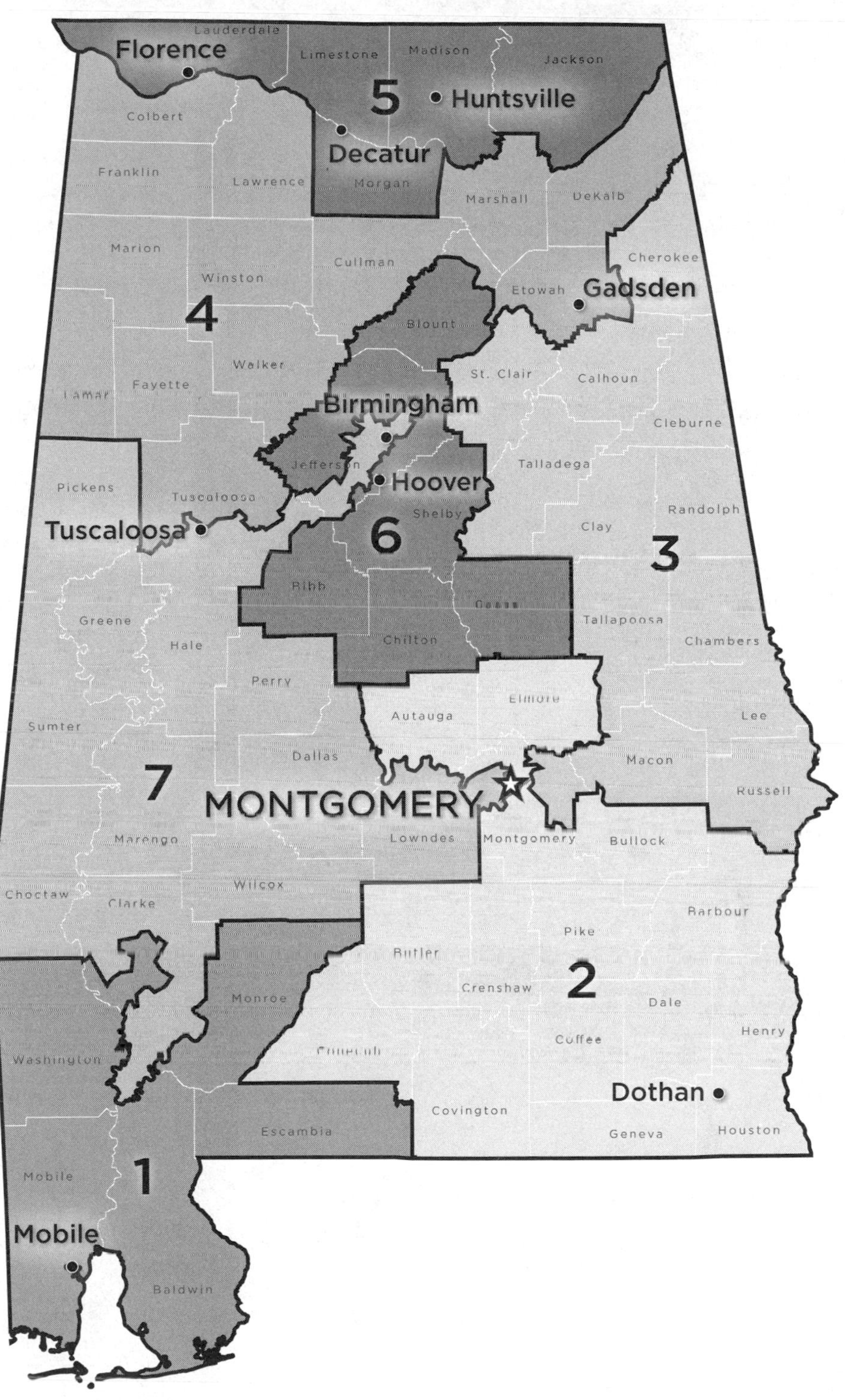
Lauderdale
Florence
Limestone
Madison
Jackson
5
Huntsville
Colbert
Decatur
Franklin
Lawrence
Morgan
Marshall
DeKalb
Marion
Winston
Cullman
Cherokee
Etowah
Gadsden
4
Blount
Walker
St. Clair
Calhoun
Lamar
Fayette
Birmingham
Cleburne
Jefferson
Hoover
Talladega
Pickens
Tuscaloosa
Shelby
Randolph
Tuscaloosa
6
Clay
3
Bibb
Greene
Tallapoosa
Chambers
Hale
Chilton
Perry
Elmore
Autauga
Lee
Sumter
Dallas
Macon
7
MONTGOMERY
Russell
Marengo
Lowndes
Montgomery
Bullock
Choctaw
Wilcox
Clarke
Barbour
Pike
Butler
Crenshaw
2
Monroe
Dale
Henry
Coffee
Washington
Dothan
Covington
Escambia
Geneva
Houston
Mobile
1
Mobile
Baldwin

Gov. Robert Bentley (R)

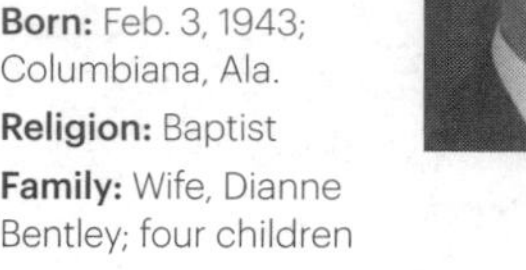

First elected: 2010
Length of term: 4 years
Term expires: 1/15
Salary: $120,936
Phone: (334) 242-7100
Residence: Tuscaloosa
Born: Feb. 3, 1943; Columbiana, Ala.
Religion: Baptist
Family: Wife, Dianne Bentley; four children
Education: U. of Alabama, B.S. 1964 (chemistry), M.D. 1968
Career: Physician
Political highlights: Ala. House, 2002-10

ELECTION RESULTS

2010 GENERAL

Robert Bentley (R)	860,052	57.9%
Ron Sparks (D)	625,052	42.1%

Lt. Gov. Kay Ivey (R)

First elected: 2010
Length of term: 4 years
Term expires: 1/15
Salary: $74,036
Phone: (334) 242-7900

LEGISLATURE

Legislature: Annually, limit of 30 legislative days within 105 calendar days
Senate: 35 members, 4-year terms
2013 ratios: 23 R, 11 D, 1 independent; 30 men, 5 women.
Salary: $10/day; $50/day per diem; $4,398/month expenses.
Phone: (334) 242-7800
House: 105 members, 4-year terms
2013 ratios: 66 R, 38 D, 1 I; 91 men, 14 women, 1 vacancy
Salary: $10/day; $50/day per diem; $4,398/month expenses.
Phone: (334) 242-7600

TERM LIMITS

Governor: 2 consecutive terms
Senate: No
House: No

URBAN STATISTICS

CITY	POPULATION
Birmingham	212,237
Montgomery	205,764
Mobile	195,111
Huntsville	180,105
Tuscaloosa	90,468

REGISTERED VOTERS

Voters do not register by party.

POPULATION

2010 population	4,779,736
2000 population	4,447,100
1990 population	4,040,587
Percent change (2000-2010)	+7.5%
Rank among states (2010)	23
Median age	37.2
Born in state	70.9%
Foreign born	2.8%
Violent crime rate	450/100,000
Poverty level	17.5%
Federal workers	64,817
Military	11,896

ELECTIONS

STATE ELECTION OFFICIAL
(334) 242-7210
DEMOCRATIC PARTY
(334) 262-2221
REPUBLICAN PARTY
(205) 212-5900

MISCELLANEOUS

Web: www.alabama.gov
Capital: Montgomery

U.S. CONGRESS

Senate: 2 Republicans
House: 6 Republicans, 1 Democrat

STATISTICS BY DISTRICT

	2012 Vote for President		2008 Vote for President										
District	Obama	Romney	Obama	McCain	Black	Asian	Hispanic	Median Income	Over 64	Under 20	College Education	Rural	Sq. Miles
1	37%	62%	38%	61%	28%	1%	3%	$43,258	14%	27%	22%	33%	6,067
2	36	63	35	64	30	1	3	41,360	14	27	21	47	10,142
3	37	62	37	63	26	1	3	39,261	14	26	20	51	7,544
4	24	75	26	73	7	<1	6	36,336	16	26	15	66	8,889
5	35	64	36	63	17	1	5	46,886	14	26	28	34	3,677
6	25	74	26	74	14	2	5	55,897	13	26	33	31	4,171
7	72	28	71	29	64	1	2	30,327	13	28	18	29	10,156
STATE	**38**	**61**	**39**	**60**	**26**	**1**	**4**	**41,415**	**14**	**26**	**22**	**42**	**50,645**
U.S.	**51**	**47**	**53**	**46**	**12**	**5**	**17**	**50,052**	**13**	**27**	**29**	**21**	**3,531,905**

Sen. Richard C. Shelby (R)

Capitol Office
224-5744
shelby.senate.gov
304 Russell Bldg. 20510-0103; fax 224-3416

Committees
Appropriations - Ranking Member
Banking, Housing & Urban Affairs
Rules & Administration

Residence
Tuscaloosa

Born
May 6, 1934; Birmingham, Ala.

Religion
Presbyterian

Family
Wife, Annette Nevin Shelby; two children

Education
U. of Alabama, A.B. 1957, LL.B. 1963

Career
Lawyer; city prosecutor

Political Highlights
Ala. Senate, 1971-79 (served as a Democrat); U.S. House, 1979-87 (served as a Democrat)

ELECTION RESULTS

2010 GENERAL		
Richard C. Shelby (R)	968,181	65.2%
William Barnes (D)	515,619	34.7%
2010 PRIMARY		
Richard C. Shelby (R)	405,398	84.4%
N.C. "Clint" Moser (R)	75,190	15.6%

Previous Winning Percentages
2004 (68%); 1998 (63%); 1992 (65%); 1986 (50%); 1984 House Election (97%); 1982 House Election (97%); 1980 House Election (73%); 1978 House Election (94%)

Elected 1986; 5th term

Shelby is a shrewd and courteous operator, known to approach tasks cautiously but deliver on his commitments when it's time for legislation to move. As the top Republican on the Appropriations Committee, he has indicated his resolve to fortify his party's economic platform. "We don't have a revenue problem," he said in early 2013. "We've got a hell of a spending problem."

Fiscal restraint isn't a new theme for Shelby, who became the ranking member on Appropriations at the start of the 113th Congress (2013-14). Since 1981 — when he was a House member, and a Democrat — he has promoted his version of a balanced-budget amendment to the Constitution, which also would cap spending at 20 percent of the gross domestic product.

During the 104th Congress (1995-96), his first as a Republican, he started advocating a "flat tax" as a means to shrink government and increase economic growth.

Shelby was one of only five Senate Republicans to reject the January 2013 "fiscal cliff" deal, which averted scheduled income tax increases only on earnings under $400,000. On Fox News the day after the vote, Shelby said a grand bargain is needed to restructure costly entitlement programs and reduce spending. "We've got to get real about this," he said. "We're heading down the road that Europe's already on."

But Shelby also has acted in the mold of a more traditional appropriator at times. He has a record of voting for compromise spending packages struck with Democrats. He has been effective at directing money to projects in Alabama, and he has been frustrated by the ban on earmarks that started in 2011. "I had a big plan for the universities" in Birmingham, he told the Birmingham News when the ban was put in place. "But it's gone now. It's gone."

Shelby still looks out for his state as much as possible, and in the 113th he's also the top Republican on the Commerce-Justice-Science Appropriations Subcommittee. He has helped support the space and defense economy in Huntsville, home to NASA's Marshall Space Flight Center and the Army's Redstone Arsenal.

A Shelby provision included in the fiscal 2010 budget helped protect NASA spending on the Ares rocket, part of which is built in Alabama, even after the program was effectively canceled. In the Senate's draft of the fiscal 2013 Defense spending bill, Shelby championed funds for the Medium Extended Air Defense System even after congressional authorizers found it wasteful. Some development work on the system takes place at a Lockheed Martin facility in Huntsville. The final fiscal 2013 spending law included $381 million for completion of the project.

And he was one of nine Senate Republicans to vote in 2013 for a $50 billion package of relief related to Superstorm Sandy — much of it "emergency" spending outside of the federal budget. His own state has been hit hard by hurricanes and tornados over the years.

Shelby's authority on fiscal matters is further cemented by his post on the Banking, Housing and Urban Affairs Committee. He was its chairman from 2003 through 2006 and its ranking member from 2007 through 2012. He now occupies the No. 2 Republican spot on the panel.

He opposed the 2010 overhaul of financial regulation known as Dodd-Frank. Speaking to the U.S. Chamber of Commerce in 2012, he said it "does not simplify or modernize our overly complex and arcane financial regulatory system. It is now more complex and arcane than it ever was."

Shelby sees far too much power in the hands of regulators, and he's particularly offended by the Consumer Financial Protection Bureau created by the law. Republicans frequently complain that Congress has little authority over the CFPB. He would also like a law directing financial regulators to undertake cost-benefit analyses before making rules. "No regulation should see the light of day if its costs outweigh its benefits," he told the Chamber.

Shelby opposed the $700 billion bailout of the financial services industry in 2008, and he's not thrilled with Fannie Mae and Freddie Mac, the housing mortgage giants currently held in conservatorship by the government. He says he wants an overhaul of those government-sponsored enterprises that would likely reduce their role in the housing market. But true to his deliberative style, he didn't outline a specific plan in the 112th Congress (2011-12) and called for more-intensive study of the matter.

Sometimes, Shelby's slow pace and aversion to "crisis" legislation can delay action that other people describe as necessary. It took Congress more than two years to crack down on financial services and insurance companies that prey on members of the military, in large part because Shelby insisted on waiting for a series of reports on the abuses from government agencies. The bill was enacted in 2006.

In an effort to advance priorities important to his home state, Shelby has used procedural tools available to senators to gum up the works in the chamber. He placed what amounted to a blanket hold on President Barack Obama's nominations in an effort to get the administration to release funds appropriated for an FBI center in Huntsville, and to protest how the Air Force was proceeding on a tanker contract that could have benefited contractors in Alabama. (Boeing won that contract in 2011, with most of the work slated for Washington.)

One of Congress' first party-switchers of the 1990s, Shelby says he became a Republican because the Democratic Party moved to the left. "Philosophically, I was not tuned in to the Democratic Party; I had not been. The party had become more liberal," he told CNN in 2001. "I always had espoused the idea of a smaller, efficient government, people keeping more taxes — that's the opposite of the Democratic Party. And I thought, after reflecting on it many, many months, that it was time to leave." He also cited the demise of the pro-defense, conservative wing of the party.

He made the switch to the GOP immediately after learning Republicans had won control of Congress in the 1994 election. As a reward, he ended up with a coveted Appropriations seat. The switch also followed an attempt by the Clinton administration to move some space programs out of Alabama after Shelby had criticized President Bill Clinton's budget while standing next to Vice President Al Gore in front of TV cameras.

Prior to his party switch, Shelby never voted with a majority of Democrats against a majority of Republicans more than 63 percent of the time in a given year — that percentage was often below 50. Since his switch, he has stuck with Republican majorities at least 80 percent of the time each year.

Shelby spent most of the 1960s as a prosecutor in Tuscaloosa. He served eight years in the state Senate, where he was often at odds with Gov. George C. Wallace. Although he initially was interested in running for lieutenant governor in 1978, more than a dozen other Democrats had the same idea. When one of his former law partners, Democrat Walter Flowers, gave up his House seat that year to run for the Senate, Shelby was easily persuaded to change course and run for Congress.

Shelby operated largely behind the scenes in the House for eight years, working on federal projects for his district and often siding with Republicans. His election to the Senate as a Democrat in 1986 was a slim victory over one-term incumbent Jeremiah Denton, a celebrated Vietnam veteran who had been a prisoner of war.

All of his re-elections have been by comfortable margins. In 2010, he won 65 percent of the vote against Democrat William Barnes.

Key Votes

2012	
Prohibit health insurance plans from denying coverage based on the sponsor's religious beliefs	NO
Require approval of the Keystone XL oil pipeline	YES
Ease securities rules to expand small-business access to capital	YES
Reauthorize farm and nutrition programs for five years	NO
Limit debate on a bill that would create private-sector cybersecurity standards	NO
Consent to ratification of a treaty setting global standard for the treatment of people with disabilities	NO
Provide $60.4 billion in disaster relief following Superstorm Sandy	YES
Extend most Bush-era income tax rates while allowing rates for top-bracket earners to rise (Jan. 1, 2013)	NO
2011	
Prevent EPA from regulating greenhouse gas emissions to address climate change	YES
Extend certain provisions of Patriot Act for four years	YES
Clear compromise debt limit increase plan and establish future spending limits	NO
Overhaul patent law	YES
Implement Colombia free trade agreement	YES
Limit debate on confirmation of Caitlin J. Halligan to D.C. Circuit Court of Appeals	NO
Extend payroll tax cut and unemployment benefits for two months	NO

CQ Vote Studies

	PARTY UNITY		PRESIDENTIAL SUPPORT	
	SUPPORT	OPPOSE	SUPPORT	OPPOSE
2012	90%	10%	47%	53%
2011	91%	9%	52%	48%
2010	96%	4%	41%	59%
2009	83%	17%	58%	42%
2008	95%	5%	74%	26%
2007	88%	12%	80%	20%
2006	88%	12%	86%	14%
2005	94%	6%	89%	11%
2004	94%	6%	86%	14%
2003	96%	4%	95%	5%

Interest Groups

	AFL-CIO	ADA	CCUS	ACU
2012	18%	0%	100%	76%
2011	11%	5%	91%	90%
2010	13%	0%	100%	96%
2009	22%	10%	86%	88%
2008	20%	15%	75%	84%
2007	21%	20%	73%	88%
2006	7%	10%	83%	74%
2005	23%	10%	89%	88%
2004	25%	20%	88%	84%
2003	15%	10%	82%	90%

Sen. Jeff Sessions (R)

Capitol Office
224-4124
sessions.senate.gov
326 Russell Bldg. 20510-0104; fax 224-3149

Committees
Armed Services
Budget - Ranking Member
Environment & Public Works
Judiciary

Residence
Mobile

Born
Dec. 24, 1946, Hybart, Ala.

Religion
Methodist

Family
Wife, Mary Sessions; three children

Education
Huntingdon College, B.A. 1969 (history); U. of Alabama, J.D. 1973

Military Service
Army Reserve, 1973-86

Career
Lawyer; teacher

Political Highlights
Assistant U.S. attorney, 1975-77; U.S. attorney, 1981-93; Ala. attorney general, 1995-97

ELECTION RESULTS

2008 GENERAL		
Jeff Sessions (R)	1,305,383	63.4%
Vivian Davis Figures (D)	752,391	36.5%
2008 PRIMARY		
Jeff Sessions (R)	199,690	92.3%
Earl Mack Gavin (R)	16,718	7.7%

Previous Winning Percentages
2002 (59%); 1996 (52%)

Elected 1996; 3rd term

Sessions won't back down from a fight, and as the top Republican on the Budget Committee he is in the middle of some of the biggest rhetorical battles in Congress. He assails Democrats' numbers while selling the Republican vision for welfare programs. It's a similar story on the Judiciary Committee, where he argues against Democrats' judicial picks and immigration plans.

Trim, courtly and unpretentious, Sessions does not cut an intimidating figure. But John Cornyn of Texas, the GOP whip, has described him as a "scrapper." Rhode Island Democrat Sheldon Whitehouse, who serves with Sessions on both the Judiciary and Budget committees, called him a "good advocate for his side." Whitehouse also noted that he has been able to work with Sessions: "He has stuck once he's given his word."

Sessions had an extensive career as a prosecutor, and he leaned on that experience upon becoming the ranking member of the Budget Committee at the start of the 112th Congress (2011-12). He uses hearings to draw sharp distinctions with Democratic views and hammers at discrete points. "When somebody comes in and we have this sort of public debate — not too much unlike a trial — and one side's got an untenable position, it reminds me of asking a jury to convict," he said.

In the first Budget hearing of the 113th Congress (2013-14), Sessions maneuvered the head of the Congressional Budget Office into agreeing that the projected growth of federal debt — and debt service payments — will cripple government activity.

Sessions wants a balanced budget within 10 years. When President Barack Obama released a budget proposal in 2012 that the administration said would achieve "primary balance" by 2017, Sessions pounced. "This was one of the most stunning financial misrepresentations in the history of the world," he said. His displeasure carried over to the next year: Sessions loudly opposed the nomination of Jacob J. Lew, Obama's budget director and then chief of staff, to become Treasury secretary.

He sees hazards in long term reliance on safety net programs and in the argument that they pump money into the economy. "Compassionate help for the poor and struggling amounts to more than just borrowing money and sending out more money in the form of checks," he said in 2013.

Sessions led Republicans on the Judiciary Committee from May 2009 through the end of the 111th Congress (2009-10), then relinquished that spot to Charles E. Grassley of Iowa (who had reached a term limit for holding the top spot on the Finance Committee).

In 2010, Sessions spearheaded resistance to a House-passed bill that would have provided a path to legalization for hundreds of thousands of young adults brought illegally to the United States as children. When the Senate passed a bill in 2006 offering guest-worker permits and a path to citizenship for those in the country illegally, he called it "the worst piece of legislation to come before the Senate since I've been here." He was pessimistic about a comprehensive overhaul introduced in spring 2013.

In recent years, most immigrants, illegal and legal, have been poor. Sessions describes their entry as a threat to government budgets. "One of the bedrock legal principles of immigration is that those coming to America should not be reliant on federal assistance," he said in 2012. "That principle has been steadily eroded."

During the 111th, Sessions garnered the most attention for his role in the confirmation battles over Obama's nominees to the Supreme Court. He conceded that Sonia Sotomayor had a "well-rounded résumé" and "a wonderful personal story," but he voiced concerns that she had exhibited a pattern of activism in her speeches and writings.

He then led opposition to Elena Kagan, questioning her qualifications and what he called an activist judicial philosophy. "I believe she does not have the gifts and the qualities of mind or temperament that one must have to be a justice," he said. "And, worse still, she possesses a judicial philosophy that does not properly value discipline, restraint and rigorous intellectual honesty." He didn't try to block a vote on either nominee, however.

From the Armed Services Committee, Sessions is an advocate for a missile defense system and seeks more development of space-based devices, which could help his state's aerospace industry. He frowned on a strategic arms reduction treaty with Russia that the Senate approved in late 2010.

Sessions criticized Obama for setting a withdrawal date for U.S. forces in Afghanistan, arguing that victory should determine the timing. He was displeased that Congress wasn't consulted about a strategic partnership with Afghanistan that was finalized in May 2012 — the fiscal 2013 defense policy law includes his provision that slashes the funds available for the Executive Office of the President if a bilateral security agreement with Afghanistan transpires in a similar fashion.

He generally dislikes deviations from established procedural norms. He called it a "tragedy" that the Democratic Senate didn't adopt a budget in 2010, 2011 or 2012. Sessions voted against an August 2011 deficit reduction deal because it created a special congressional panel charged with negotiating further deficit reduction behind closed doors.

Although he has supported trade pacts, Sessions is sensitive to practices that he views as unfair. He has gone to bat for Exxel Outdoors, an Alabama-based sleeping bag manufacturer that was threatened by duty-free treatment of sleeping bags imported from Bangladesh. Arguing that it was a violation of the Generalized System of Preferences to waive duties on foreign-made bags if the waiver would adversely affect a domestic manufacturer, he forced a temporary expiration of the program in 2010. The next year, Obama removed "certain non-down sleeping bags" from eligibility for duty-free treatment.

Sessions grew up in the towns of Hybart and Camden, southwest of Montgomery. His father owned a general store and then a farm equipment dealership, and Sessions worked in both. He was also active in the Boy Scouts, eventually earning the rank of Eagle Scout. "I grew up with people who didn't get to go to college, had less money than we did," he said at a 2013 hearing. "I think I understand something about human beings who work hard and try to do the right thing and how to help them improve."

At Huntingdon College in Alabama, Sessions joined the Young Republicans and served as student body president. After earning a law degree, he joined a law firm in Russellville, becoming assistant U.S. attorney in 1975 and U.S. attorney for the Southern District of Alabama in 1981.

President Ronald Reagan nominated Sessions for a judgeship in 1986, but Sessions was effectively rejected by the Judiciary Committee. Critics accused him of "gross insensitivity" on racial issues. Justice Department lawyers said he called the National Association for the Advancement of Colored People and the American Civil Liberties Union "communist-inspired" and claimed they tried to "force civil rights down the throats of people." Sessions said his words were misrepresented.

In 1994, he ran for state attorney general. With a corruption scandal raging in Montgomery, he rode to victory on a vow to clean up the mess. Two years later, Sessions entered the Senate race to succeed retiring Democrat Howell Heflin. He won a seven-way primary and a runoff, then defeated Democrat Roger Bedford, giving Alabama two Republican senators for the first time since Reconstruction. Sessions easily won his next two Senate contests.

Key Votes

2012	
Prohibit health insurance plans from denying coverage based on the sponsor's religious beliefs	NO
Require approval of the Keystone XL oil pipeline	YES
Ease securities rules to expand small-business access to capital	YES
Reauthorize farm and nutrition programs for five years	NO
Limit debate on a bill that would create private-sector cybersecurity standards	NO
Consent to ratification of a treaty setting global standard for the treatment of people with disabilities	NO
Provide $60.4 billion in disaster relief following Superstorm Sandy	NO
Extend most Bush-era income tax rates while allowing rates for top-bracket earners to rise (Jan. 1, 2013)	YES
2011	
Prevent EPA from regulating greenhouse gas emissions to address climate change	YES
Extend certain provisions of Patriot Act for four years	YES
Clear compromise debt limit increase plan and establish future spending limits	NO
Overhaul patent law	YES
Implement Colombia free trade agreement	YES
Limit debate on confirmation of Caitlin J. Halligan to D.C. Circuit Court of Appeals	NO
Extend payroll tax cut and unemployment benefits for two months	NO

CQ Vote Studies

	PARTY UNITY		PRESIDENTIAL SUPPORT	
	SUPPORT	OPPOSE	SUPPORT	OPPOSE
2012	93%	7%	48%	52%
2011	95%	5%	54%	46%
2010	98%	2%	40%	60%
2009	96%	4%	41%	59%
2008	98%	2%	74%	26%
2007	92%	8%	85%	15%
2006	96%	4%	91%	9%
2005	97%	3%	90%	10%
2004	97%	3%	96%	4%
2003	98%	2%	99%	1%

Interest Groups

	AFL-CIO	ADA	CCUS	ACU
2012	9%	0%	100%	88%
2011	11%	5%	90%	90%
2010	7%	5%	82%	100%
2009	13%	5%	60%	96%
2008	10%	20%	50%	84%
2007	16%	10%	40%	83%
2006	20%	0%	92%	92%
2005	14%	0%	78%	100%
2004	8%	10%	88%	96%
2003	0%	0%	100%	75%

Rep. Jo Bonner (R)

Capitol Office
225-4931
bonner.house.gov
2236 Rayburn Bldg. 20515-0101; fax 225-0562

Committees
Appropriations

Residence
Mobile

Born
Nov. 19, 1959; Selma, Ala.

Religion
Episcopalian

Family
Wife, Janee Bonner; two children

Education
U. of Alabama, B.A. 1982 (journalism), attended 1998 (law)

Career
Congressional and campaign aide

Political Highlights
No previous office

ELECTION RESULTS

2012 GENERAL		
Jo Bonner (R)	196,374	97.9%
Write-in (WRI)	4,302	2.1%
2012 PRIMARY		
Jo Bonner (R)	48,481	55.6%
Dean Young (R)	21,216	24.3%
Pete Riehm (R)	13,744	15.7%
Peter Gounares (R)	3,828	4.4%
2010 GENERAL		
Jo Bonner (R)	129,063	82.6%
David Walter (CNSTP)	26,357	16.9%

Previous Winning Percentages
2008 (98%); 2006 (68%); 2004 (63%); 2002 (61%)

Elected 2002; 6th term

Bonner has announced his intention to resign from the House in August 2013 to become the vice chancellor of government relations and economic development for the University of Alabama. The school is his alma mater, and Judy Bonner, his sister, became its president in November 2012.

His departure will create an opening on the Appropriations Committee, a panel he has been associated with for decades. He served as an aide to the panel during nearly 18 years working for appropriator Sonny Callahan, his immediate predecessor. He also interned for Jack Edwards, the appropriator who preceded Callahan.

Bonner didn't break the mold of his political forebears: He is easygoing, he steadily supports Republican priorities, and he does what he can to help out the diverse industrial and shipping concerns back home. "Some of my constituents want me to be on Fox News every night, questioning the president. ... That's not who I am," he said.

After years of going to bat for the defense and aeronautics company EADS, Bonner was added to the Defense Appropriations Subcommittee in 2011. The company sought a contract to build Air Force refueling tankers, and EADS North America initially won the competition (with plans to do much of the work in the Gulf Coast). But it lost out to the Boeing Co. in 2011 when bidding was reopened following an appeal. "I still believe [Boeing] bought the contract," Bonner said in 2012, and he vowed to ensure "that they are going to deliver the plane at the price that they promised."

That battle may have had some spoils for his district. EADS announced in 2012 that its Airbus division would open its first U.S. factory in Mobile, and construction began in April 2013. Bonner called the decision "the product of seven-and-a-half years of building relationships."

Bonner also was among the Gulf Coast lawmakers working to secure more funds for recovery from the 2010 Gulf of Mexico oil spill. A reauthorization of surface transportation programs enacted in 2012 included a provision steering most Clean Water Act fines resulting from the spill to the affected states. The same year, Bonner introduced a bill to prohibit any company from writing off as business expenses the compensation paid for damage caused by the spill.

Bonner joined GOP calls for fiscal restraint in the 112th Congress (2011-12), though his votes weren't as aggressive as those of some conservatives. He made the case for a return of earmarking — allowing lawmakers to request spending for specific projects back home — if proper oversight can be devised. Even local projects can have national benefits, Bonner said; for example, improvements to Mobile's ports could boost international trade once the Panama Canal expansion is completed. The ban on earmarks, meant to cut wasteful spending and reduce the potential for ethics violations, leaves too many spending decisions to the executive branch, he said.

Bonner served as the ranking member on the Ethics Committee in the 111th Congress (2009-10), then took the gavel for the 112th Congress. "Nobody lobbies to be on the Ethics Committee," he said, but Bonner took the assignment as a compliment. "It's a committee where you can do your best to try to bring some credibility back [to Congress], even if it can't always be in the light of day that some of us would like."

Lawmakers and outside groups accused the panel of botching the probe of California Democrat Maxine Waters, who was alleged to have improperly intervened with regulators on behalf of a bank in which her husband had a financial stake. Just before a public hearing was to begin in November 2011, the committee postponed proceedings and hired an independent counsel to investigate whether committee members and staff had improperly released information regarding the case.

That investigation found that the Waters case wasn't compromised, but Bonner and five other panel members recused themselves from further involvement in February 2012. Waters was cleared several months later.

Another high-profile inquiry that the committee took up during his tenure was the 2010 ethics trial of Charles B. Rangel, which culminated in censuring the New York Democrat for multiple financial misdeeds. "Mr. Rangel should only look into the mirror if he wants to know who to blame," Bonner said before the House voted on censure.

Bonner comes from a prominent Alabama family. His grandfather was a banker in Wilcox County, and his great-uncles were a doctor, a lawyer and a newspaper publisher. Bonner, whose given name is Josiah Robins Bonner Jr., is named for his father, a county judge.

At one time he thought he'd be a journalist. As a kid in Camden, he launched a community newspaper with a press loaned by the local newspaper editor. He earned a degree in journalism, but his interest in politics led him to work on the 1982 gubernatorial campaign of George McMillan, who was challenging incumbent George C. Wallace Jr. in the Democratic primary.

McMillan lost, but during the campaign Bonner met Callahan, who was a Republican candidate for lieutenant governor. Callahan also lost, but two years later he was elected to the House and hired Bonner to be his press secretary. Bonner eventually rose to chief of staff.

Callahan quietly encouraged his aide to prepare himself to run for the seat. In 1997, Bonner moved from Washington to the 1st District. He paid close attention to constituent service, joining the local Rotary Club and the board of the local Junior League. When Callahan announced his retirement in 2002, Bonner was ready.

His toughest competition came from Tom Young, a Mobile native who was chief of staff for another Alabama Republican, Sen. Richard C. Shelby. It was one of the most expensive and hotly contested races of the season.

Bonner finished first in a seven-way primary but fell short of the majority needed to win outright. That forced him into a runoff election, which he won with 62 percent of the vote. In November, Bonner easily defeated Democratic businesswoman Judy McCain Belk.

Bonner had few electoral difficulties after that. He faced three challengers in the 2012 GOP primary, several of them in the tea party mold. An outside group spent $121,000 running advertisements criticizing Bonner for a few of his less conservative votes. He still took more than 55 percent of the vote in the primary, and he had no Democratic opponent in November.

Key Votes

2012	
Extend a Social Security payroll tax cut and unemployment benefits	NO
Ease securities rules to expand small-business access to capital	YES
Extend for one year subsidized student loan interest rates financed by a cut in health care spending	YES
Cite Attorney General Eric H. Holder Jr. for contempt of Congress	YES
Create a visa program for foreign graduates in high-tech fields	?
Extend most Bush-era income tax rates while allowing rates for top-bracket earners to rise (Jan. 1, 2013)	NO
2011	
Strike funding for F-35 alternative engine	NO
Prevent EPA from regulating greenhouse gas emissions to address climate change	YES
Extend certain provisions of Patriot Act for four years	YES
Declare opposition to use of ground troops in Libya	YES
Overhaul patent law	YES
Pass compromise debt limit increase plan and establish future spending limits	YES
Allow consideration of measures to implement three trade agreements	YES

CQ Vote Studies

	PARTY UNITY		PRESIDENTIAL SUPPORT	
	SUPPORT	OPPOSE	SUPPORT	OPPOSE
2012	92%	8%	10%	90%
2011	93%	7%	26%	74%
2010	94%	6%	29%	71%
2009	87%	13%	22%	78%
2008	97%	3%	76%	24%

Interest Groups

	AFL-CIO	ADA	CCUS	ACU
2012	16%	0%	100%	78%
2011	0%	10%	100%	72%
2010	7%	0%	88%	95%
2009	5%	0%	87%	92%
2008	13%	15%	94%	83%

Alabama 1

Southwest — Mobile

The 1st District sits in Alabama's southwestern corner around Mobile Bay, and Mobile anchors the state's only Gulf Coast district. Almost 60 percent of the district's population lives in Mobile County west of the bay and another 27 percent in Baldwin County to the east. Gulf Coast beaches give way to pine forests and soybean and cotton fields to the north.

The 1st depends heavily on its economic ties to the Gulf of Mexico. The white sand beaches and local resorts draw tourists. Visitor rates in both counties have rebounded following the Deepwater Horizon oil spill in 2010 even as sport fishing in Mobile Bay has lagged. Carnival Cruise Lines stopped running cruises out of Mobile in late 2011.

Shipbuilding and manufacturing in Mobile remain strong. Austal USA builds naval combat ships at its Mobile shipyard and expects to have 4,500 employees in the district by 2016. International Shipholding runs cargo operations out of the port, where officials hope to lure traffic following expansion of the Panama Canal. The first Airbus plane manufacturing site in the U.S. is under construction in Mobile, adding to an already significant aerospace industry centered on the Brookley Aeroplex just south of the port.

Farming dominates the inland areas of the district, and timber production in rural Monroe County rounds out the natural-resources-based economy. Manufacturing in Washington County, west of the Tombigbee River, took a hit with layoffs at a ThyssenKrupp steel factory and at chemical plants.

The shift to the GOP seen in much of the South took root early in Alabama's 1st. Republicans have held the U.S. House seat since 1965, and the district has overwhelmingly favored Republican presidential candidates for decades. Mobile County, which is more than one-third black, provides some votes for Democrats.

Major Industry
Shipbuilding, aerospace, tourism, distribution

Cities
Mobile, Pritchard, Daphne

Notable
Author Harper Lee based the fictional setting of "To Kill a Mockingbird" on her hometown of Monroeville; Mobile has retained a few remnants of a Louisiana-centered tradition: The city has celebrated Mardi Gras for 150 years and Dauphin Street emulates the New Orleans French Quarter vibe.

Rep. Martha Roby (R)

Capitol Office
225-2901
roby.house.gov
428 Cannon Bldg. 20515-0102; fax 225-8913

Committees
Agriculture
Armed Services
(Oversight & Investigations - Chairwoman)
Education & the Workforce

Residence
Montgomery

Born
July 26, 1976; Montgomery, Ala.

Religion
Presbyterian

Family
Husband, Riley Roby; two children

Education
New York U., B.M. 1998 (music, business and technology); Samford U., J.D. 2001

Career
Lawyer

Political Highlights
Montgomery City Council, 2004-11

ELECTION RESULTS

2012 GENERAL		
Martha Roby (R)	180,591	63.6%
Therese Ford (D)	103,092	36.3%
2012 PRIMARY		
Martha Roby (R)		unopposed
2010 GENERAL		
Martha Roby (R)	111,645	51.0%
Bobby Bright (D)	106,865	48.8%

Elected 2010; 2nd term

The youthful and smiling Roby has ambitions for a greater role in the Republican Party. Early in her career, she has backed up GOP positions on education, national security and agriculture. Her loudest overtures, however, are on the party's most common theme: fiscal restraint.

A former Montgomery City Council member, Roby is amiable, polite and still in her 30s. She has thus far avoided allegiances that might pin her down ideologically, joining none of the major Republican caucuses in the House.

But her rhetoric on budgets is right out of the GOP playbook. In early 2012, she teamed with Alabama Republican Sen. Jeff Sessions, adapting for the House his bill to overhaul the federal budgeting process. Their measure would make it harder to designate "emergency" spending outside of normal budget rules, set up stricter spending limits for federal programs and change the way loan guarantees are counted in the budget, among other things.

And in both 2012 and 2013, she proposed a balanced-budget amendment to the Constitution that tracks with the version long favored by her state's senior senator, Richard C. Shelby. It would also cap spending at 20 percent of gross domestic product.

She has supported the budgets put forth by Wisconsin Republican Paul D. Ryan, who proposes structural changes to entitlement programs as a means to long-term fiscal stability. The more austere budgets of the conservative Republican Study Committee haven't won her approval, but she has said that curtailing federal spending should be the top priority of the Republican Party. She voted against the January 2013 "fiscal cliff" agreement, which extended lower income tax rates for most people but included no spending cuts.

Roby argued on the House floor in September 2012 that uncertainty caused by the national debt was stifling job creation. "I've traveled around and looked into the eyes of folks, and they can't take any more," she said. "Their businesses are on the line, and that then, in turn, is a reflection of what's going to happen in their households."

Roby draws the line at substantial cuts to defense accounts. She sits on the Armed Services Committee, where she chairs the Subcommittee on Oversight and Investigations. She has fought to maintain and expand the missions of Maxwell-Gunter Air Force Base — headquarters of the Air University and the 42nd Air Base Wing — and Fort Rucker, the Army's primary air training base. In August 2011, Roby voted against a deal to raise the federal debt limit and cut spending, citing the hundreds of billions of dollars in potential defense cuts in the agreement.

Roby also attends to a few parochial concerns as a member of the Agriculture Committee. She and Georgia Democrat Sanford D. Bishop Jr. established the Peanut Caucus in March 2012. Her 2nd District is one of the nation's top peanut-producing districts, with many family farms that grow the crop, in addition to soybeans and cotton. When the Agriculture Committee approved its version of a reauthorization of federal farm programs in 2012, it was more favorable to Southern rice and peanut producers than the Senate's bill.

That bill included Roby's plan for systems to check the eligibility of those seeking federal nutrition benefits — similar to the E-Verify system to check employment eligibility.

Roby is a mother of two, and she said party leaders asked her to serve on the Education and the Workforce Committee. A rewrite of the federal education law known as No Child Left Behind is on tap for the 113th Congress (2013-14).

On education, "I'm a huge proponent of local and parental control," Roby said. "It's very important to me that I am doing everything I can as a member of Congress to put more control into the hands of those closest to our children: the local school boards, the state school board, and, of course, the parents of the children in the school system."

She said she was pursuing greater flexibility for families when she wrote a 2013 bill that would allow more private employers to give workers "comp time" instead of overtime pay. (Under the bill, comp hours would accumulate at the same time-and-a-half rate as overtime wages.) Democrats said it was a threat to workers' rights — it passed that May along mostly partisan lines.

Roby is socially conservative. She calls herself "unapologetically pro-life" and worked for a pro-life ministry while in Montgomery. She was an original co-sponsor to a 2011 resolution by Republican Diane Black of Tennessee that would have blocked funding for Planned Parenthood in the 2010 health care overhaul.

Roby was born in Montgomery and received her bachelor's degree in music, specializing in music business and technology, from New York University. She played the trumpet briefly in the fourth grade and sang through high school; she wanted to be involved in the music industry, though not necessarily as a performer.

She got a degree in 2001 from Samford University's Cumberland School of Law, where she met her husband. After going to Nashville following her second year in law school, Roby decided the music industry's "appeal had worn off." Returning to Alabama, she practiced law for two years, a choice that pleased her father, a U.S. appeals court judge. Roby then won, at age 27, a seat on the Montgomery City Council, where she served for seven years.

She was the GOP establishment's candidate for the U.S. House in 2010 but fell just short of a majority in the primary and was forced into a second round against businessman and retired U.S. Marine Rick Barber. He had the support of local tea party activists, but Roby coasted to an easy 20-point victory in the runoff election. In the general election she faced first-term lawmaker Bobby Bright, the first Democrat to hold the 2nd District seat since 1965. She won with 51 percent of the vote. Roby and Democrat Terri A. Sewell that year became the first women elected to Congress from Alabama.

Redistricting for the 2012 election gave the district more of a Republican lean. Roby had no challengers in the primary and took more than 63 percent of the vote against Democrat Therese Ford, a former deputy attorney general.

Near the end of her freshman term, Roby tried to join the House Republican leadership, but she lost to Lynn Jenkins of Kansas in the race for the No. 5 position of conference vice chairwoman.

She was, however, named the Southern regional chairwoman of the National Republican Congressional Committee for the 2014 election cycle.

Key Votes

2012	
Extend a Social Security payroll tax cut and unemployment benefits	NO
Ease securities rules to expand small-business access to capital	YES
Extend for one year subsidized student loan interest rates financed by a cut in health care spending	YES
Cite Attorney General Eric H. Holder Jr. for contempt of Congress	YES
Create a visa program for foreign graduates in high-tech fields	YES
Extend most Bush-era income tax rates while allowing rates for top-bracket earners to rise (Jan. 1, 2013)	NO
2011	
Strike funding for F-35 alternative engine	YES
Prevent EPA from regulating greenhouse gas emissions to address climate change	YES
Extend certain provisions of Patriot Act for four years	YES
Declare opposition to use of ground troops in Libya	YES
Overhaul patent law	YES
Pass compromise debt limit increase plan and establish future spending limits	NO
Allow consideration of measures to implement three trade agreements	YES

CQ Vote Studies

	PARTY UNITY		PRESIDENTIAL SUPPORT	
	SUPPORT	OPPOSE	SUPPORT	OPPOSE
2012	92%	8%	11%	89%
2011	94%	6%	26%	74%

Interest Groups

	AFL-CIO	ADA	CCUS	ACU
2012	14%	0%	100%	76%
2011	0%	5%	94%	84%

Alabama 2

Southeast — part of Montgomery, Dothan

Changes to the 2nd after decennial remapping solidified the GOP's hold on the district. Black-majority Lowndes County and western parts of Montgomery were moved into the 7th District, and the 2nd now grabs most of Montgomery County, pushing past downtown in a narrow strip of white-majority neighborhoods. A large military retiree population underscores a conservative bent overall. Dothan, the small towns that dot Alabama's coastal plain, farmland and military bases fill out the rest of the district.

Montgomery's major military and state government employers form the district's population and economic hub. Maxwell Air Force Base and its Gunter Annex contribute more than $1 billion annually to the Alabama River Region's economy and sustain aerospace industry facilities in neighboring Elmore County. Some blue-collar residents of the 2nd also work at a Hyundai assembly plant south of downtown Montgomery, in the 7th District.

Dothan sits amid the piney grasslands that cover portions of southwestern Georgia, southeastern Alabama and the Florida Panhandle. The city supports manufacturing and trucking industries, and Fort Rucker, 20 miles to the northwest, is an Army aviation training center. Agriculture is still vital to the economy in the district's rural areas. The 2nd grows enough peanuts to make Alabama one of the nation's leading producers of the legume. A nuclear plant east of the city on the Georgia border also provides jobs.

Among the district's many historical sites, its section of Montgomery hosts the State Capitol Complex, the first White House of the Confederacy and the Dexter Avenue Baptist Church, where the 1955 bus boycott was launched. Officials have pushed redevelopment plans to aid blighted areas.

Major Industry
Defense, manufacturing, government, agriculture

Military Bases
Maxwell-Gunter Air Force Base, 3,600 military, 3,900 civlian (2010); Fort Rucker (Army), 5,850 military, 2,800 civilian

Cities
Montgomery (pt.), Dothan, Enterprise, Troy

Notable
The Boll Weevil Monument in Enterprise honors the insect, whose taste for cotton compelled local farmers to grow peanuts.

Rep. Mike D. Rogers (R)

Capitol Office
225-3261
mike-rogers.house.gov
324 Cannon Bldg. 20515-0103; fax 226-8485

Committees
Agriculture
Armed Services
(Strategic Forces - Chairman)
Homeland Security

Residence
Anniston

Born
July 16, 1958; Hammond, Ind.

Religion
Baptist

Family
Wife, Donna Elizabeth "Beth" Rogers; three children

Education
Jacksonville State U., B.A. 1981 (political science & psychology), M.P.A. 1985; Birmingham School of Law, J.D. 1991

Career
Lawyer, laid-off worker assistance program director; psychiatric counselor

Political Highlights
Calhoun County Commission, 1987-91; candidate for Ala. House, 1990; Ala. House, 1995-2002 (minority leader, 1998-2000)

ELECTION RESULTS

2012 GENERAL		
Mike D. Rogers (R)	175,306	64.0%
John Andrew Harris (D)	98,141	35.8%
2012 PRIMARY		
Mike D. Rogers (R)		unopposed
2010 GENERAL		
Mike D. Rogers (R)	117,736	59.4%
Steve Segrest (D)	80,204	40.5%

Previous Winning Percentages
2008 (53%); 2006 (59%); 2004 (61%); 2002 (50%)

Elected 2002; 6th term

Rogers is an in-your-face Republican who vigorously pushes his ideas on national security and dings members of either party who get in the way. He's tasked with a new policy focus in the 113th Congress as the chairman of the Armed Services Subcommittee on Strategic Forces.

Prior to the 113th (2013-14), a lot of Rogers' publicized work on Armed Services dealt with the military bases in and near his district: Anniston Army Depot, Maxwell-Gunter Air Force Base and Fort Benning. He frequently backs bills to provide a litany of employment and housing benefits for veterans.

The end of the Iraq War and the drawdown in Afghanistan are affecting depot employment. Rogers, whose father was a firefighter at the depot, wrote in March 2012 to warn constituents of "the president's unwillingness to fully fund a national defense strategy I believe we need." He promised to work with unions and local business leaders to preserve as many jobs as possible.

The Strategic Forces panel handles space- and missile-related programs, and Alabama has facilities dealing with each. Rogers has been disappointed with the Obama administration regarding nuclear arms policies. He interpreted a February 2013 underground nuclear test conducted by North Korea as a very bad sign.

"North Korea continues to provoke the world, and its supporters in Beijing and Tehran appear unconcerned with potential reactions from the United States," Rogers wrote. "President Obama has been the world leader on reduction of nuclear weapons, but he's only succeeded in reducing the deterrent that protects the American people and its allies."

His meatiest work in recent years was on the Homeland Security Committee, where in the 112th Congress (2011-12) he chaired the Transportation Security Committee. Anyone who saw a Rogers-run hearing — of which there were many — knows his watchwords for the homeland security apparatus: leaner and smarter.

"I don't think that any reasonable person would argue that we can't do with less," he said in 2012. "One of the things I'm fully cognizant of is we've spent $400 billion on homeland security over the last 11 years, and now the nation is broke. We're not going to have $400 billion going forward."

Rogers sees lots of slack in the Transportation Security Administration, the labor-intensive agency that has been cursed, fairly or unfairly, by millions of travelers. Rogers in the 112th suggested to TSA Director John S. Pistole that the agency could cut its workforce by as much as 40 percent, in part by allowing the private sector to take over screening operations at more airports.

He describes new screening technologies developed by or purchased for the TSA as intrusive and ineffective, advocating instead lower-tech resources such as trained dogs. He says financial resources (and many hours standing in airport lines) can be saved by switching to "risk-based" screening, where various techniques are used to identify people more likely to pose threats. But Rogers hasn't called for the outright elimination of the TSA, as some conservatives have demanded.

Border security is one area where Rogers might be OK with more spending. He called George W. Bush an "open borders president" and said Barack Obama is "even worse." Rogers has set tighter border control as a precondition for his acceptance of an overhaul of immigration laws.

He came agonizingly close to chairing the Homeland Security Committee in the 113th Congress. The GOP Steering Committee, which recommends chairmen, reached several three-way ties between Rogers, Michael McCaul of Texas and Candice S. Miller of Michigan, then more ties between McCaul and Rogers. McCaul eventually won in a squeaker.

The blow was likely softened for Rogers by his return to the Agriculture Committee. He was off that panel in the 112th, but he's looking out for Southern farmers again as work continues on a long-term rewrite of farm programs.

Rogers is a conservative, though not a hard-core one. He is a member of the Republican Study Committee but didn't back its fiscal 2013 budget, which was more austere than the blueprint produced by the Budget Committee. He bristled when GOP leaders began their campaign against earmarked spending, which is now banned. Rogers has said that the relatively small percentage of federal spending going to local projects isn't a threat to his fiscal conservatism.

His mother was a textile worker, and Rogers defends that diminished industry in his state. He opposes free trade with China and is wary of any pacts that might hurt the domestic textile industry in Alabama. He voted for 2011 agreements with South Korea, Colombia and Panama, but he also supported an expansion of federal assistance for workers who lose their jobs because of international trade.

Rogers is generally gregarious, but his propensity for chirping at opponents sometimes earns him some criticism. In a 2009 speech at Auburn University-Montgomery, he described Speaker Nancy Pelosi of California as "mean as a snake," "crazy" and "Tom DeLay in a skirt" — a reference to the former GOP majority leader known as "The Hammer." Rogers later refused to apologize. "She can't do anything to me," he said.

Neither of Rogers' parents graduated from high school, but he and his wife — whom he met while working at the United Way as a career counselor — attended law school at night. After graduating, she continued working at the local power company and he started his own law practice in Anniston.

His interest in politics started early. Rogers told the Opelika-Auburn News how he was entertained by watching the 1968, 1972, and 1976 conventions and started considering politics as a career. "I admired a lot of different politicians," he said. "Ronald Reagan had personal appeal. I looked up to Lyndon Johnson for being able to get things done."

At 28, Rogers became the first Republican elected to the Calhoun County Commission. In 1994, Rogers, who traces his ancestry back five generations in eastern Alabama, was elected to the state House, where he eventually became minority leader.

When Republican Rep. Bob Riley ran successfully for governor in 2002, Rogers jumped into the race for his House seat. Rogers won by 2 points, and his subsequent victories have been by wider margins. He won with 64 percent of the vote in 2012 against Democratic challenger John Andrew Harris, a retired food preparer for Auburn city schools and Lee County commissioner.

Key Votes

2012	
Extend a Social Security payroll tax cut and unemployment benefits	NO
Ease securities rules to expand small-business access to capital	YES
Extend for one year subsidized student loan interest rates financed by a cut in health care spending	YES
Cite Attorney General Eric H. Holder Jr. for contempt of Congress	YES
Create a visa program for foreign graduates in high-tech fields	YES
Extend most Bush-era income tax rates while allowing rates for top-bracket earners to rise (Jan. 1, 2013)	NO
2011	
Strike funding for F-35 alternative engine	NO
Prevent EPA from regulating greenhouse gas emissions to address climate change	YES
Extend certain provisions of Patriot Act for four years	YES
Declare opposition to use of ground troops in Libya	YES
Overhaul patent law	YES
Pass compromise debt limit increase plan and establish future spending limits	YES
Allow consideration of measures to implement three trade agreements	YES

CQ Vote Studies

	PARTY UNITY		PRESIDENTIAL SUPPORT	
	SUPPORT	OPPOSE	SUPPORT	OPPOSE
2012	91%	9%	11%	89%
2011	93%	7%	27%	73%
2010	95%	5%	26%	74%
2009	80%	20%	42%	58%
2008	88%	12%	53%	47%

Interest Groups

	AFL-CIO	ADA	CCUS	ACU
2012	19%	0%	100%	72%
2011	3%	10%	100%	72%
2010	7%	5%	75%	96%
2009	29%	15%	93%	80%
2008	40%	50%	89%	50%

Alabama 3

East — Auburn, Anniston

Comprising much of eastern Alabama from Montgomery County to rural Appalachia, the 3rd is a mix of rural piedmont counties, old mill towns and bedroom communities in the Birmingham orbit and outside of Montgomery. Despite losing most of Montgomery County, including almost all of the city of Montgomery, to the 2nd and 7th districts during decennial remapping, the solidly Republican 3rd District retained fast-growing areas in the northeastern part of the county. Talladega National Forest spans the northern tier of the district from Sylacauga past Anniston.

The district has a diverse economy that includes technology firms, regional medical centers, manufacturing and higher education. Auburn University is one of the state's largest employers and a national leader in agricultural research. A university program also has aided efforts to redevelop a former textile mill in Valley along Interstate 85 — mill towns in the cotton-producing counties along the Georgia border boomed a century ago, but the last mills have been shuttered or demolished in recent decades. Industrial growth cushioned the blow to the textile sector. Honda is expanding its 4,000-employee SUV and minivan plant in Lincoln, and many Alabamians near Valley work at a Kia plant over the border in West Point, Ga.

Defense and government jobs also sustain the district's workforce. Anniston Army Depot hosts combat vehicle maintenance facilities. The base, a former conventional and chemical weapons storage facility, is also an EPA superfund site, and a nearby FEMA center trains first-responders for chemical, biological and nuclear terrorist attacks. Fort Benning, the massive Army base almost entirely across the Chattahoochee River in Georgia from Russell County, continues personnel and construction expansion.

Major Industry
Manufacturing, defense, higher education

Military Bases
Anniston Army Depot, 2 military, 2,873 civilian; Fort Benning (Army), 27,436 military, 3,250 civilian (shared with Georgia's 2nd District)

Cities
Montgomery (pt.), Auburn, Phenix City, Opelika

Notable
Tuskegee University, founded in 1881, was the first historically black college to be recognized as a National Historic Landmark.

Rep. Robert B. Aderholt (R)

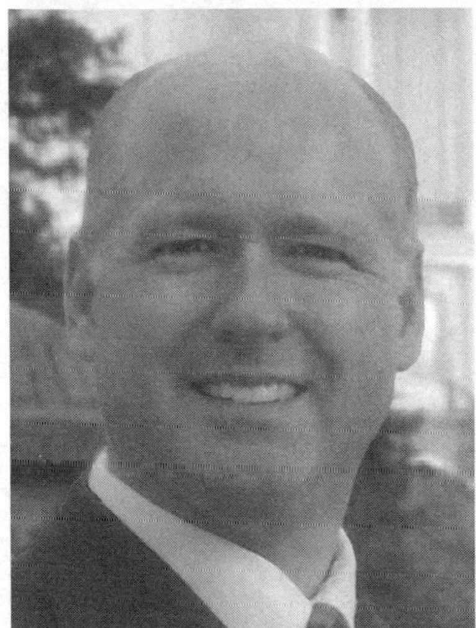

Capitol Office
225-4876
aderholt.house.gov
2369 Rayburn Bldg. 20515-0104; fax 225-5587

Committees
Appropriations
(Agriculture - Chairman)

Residence
Haleyville

Born
July 22, 1965; Haleyville, Ala.

Religion
Congregationalist Baptist

Family
Wife, Caroline Aderholt; two children

Education
Birmingham-Southern College, B.A. 1987 (history & political science); Samford U., J.D. 1990

Career
Lawyer; gubernatorial aide

Political Highlights
Republican nominee for Ala. House, 1990; Haleyville municipal judge, 1992-96

ELECTION RESULTS

2012 GENERAL		
Robert B. Aderholt (R)	199,071	74.0%
Daniel H. Boman (D)	69,706	25.9%
2012 PRIMARY		
Robert B. Aderholt (R)		unopposed
2010 GENERAL		
Robert B. Aderholt (R)	167,714	98.8%
write-ins (WRI)	2,007	1.2%

Previous Winning Percentages
2008 (75%); 2006 (70%); 2004 (75%); 2002 (87%); 2000 (61%); 1998 (56%); 1996 (50%)

Elected 1996; 9th term

Aderholt commits himself to reining in government spending, and that commitment is regularly tested by his service on the Appropriations Committee. He spent the 112th Congress mulling the best ways to pay for disaster relief, even as storms and tornadoes punished his district. Now he's in charge of the Agriculture Subcommittee, giving him a say in the funding of federal programs that affect the biggest industry in his state.

He joined Appropriations as a freshman, and he inherited the Agriculture gavel from Jack Kingston of Georgia at the start of the 113th Congress (2013-14). It was a fortuitous exchange for Southern farmers, as agriculture interests often break along regional lines. Aderholt (ADD-er-holt) also inherited the challenges Kingston faced — he's looking to find savings and eliminate inefficiencies in safety net programs for both farmers and those in need of food assistance. Passions run hot among advocates of both groups.

But Aderholt is a congenial lawmaker, and he has experience with tricky political situations. He had served only a few months as the chairman of the Homeland Security Subcommittee in the 112th Congress (2011-12) when storms and tornadoes hit the southeastern United States, including his district.

Aderholt stuck with fellow conservatives in demanding that any proposed injections of cash into the nation's Disaster Relief Fund be offset by cuts elsewhere. In May 2011, he proposed providing an extra $1 billion for the fund in fiscal 2011 while taking $1 billion from an advanced-care program favored by Democrats. Senate Democrats refused, but Aderholt stuck to his demand for an offset. "Shoring up the Disaster Relief Fund by insisting on 'truth in budgeting' has been a key priority for me this year, but some in Washington struggle with ensuring the DRF has adequate resources," Aderholt said.

In the end, no extra money was provided for the fund in fiscal 2011. Though Aderholt acceded to emergency spending outside of approved limits for fiscal 2012, he voted against a $50 billion relief package related to Superstorm Sandy in January 2013, most of which had the emergency designation.

Aderholt's subcommittee in the 112th worked steadily to reduce overall spending, and a fiscal 2013 bill it produced would have trimmed homeland accounts by about a half-billion dollars from the previous year. (No regular fiscal 2013 spending bills were enacted, however.)

While Aderholt supports lower taxes and smaller government, he and other longtime GOP appropriators are less zealous about budget cuts than the more conservative wing of their party. He belongs to the Republican Study Committee, but he didn't support its fiscal 2013 budget, which was more austere than the blueprint produced by the Budget Committee.

Aderholt has defended earmarking, the practice of requesting federal funds for specific projects back home, such as the $350,000 earmark he secured in fiscal 2010 for the Alabama Technology Network in Birmingham. Earmarks are currently banned by the House.

But he still seeks ways to bring money and jobs to his swath of Alabama. Aderholt fought to end U.S. tariff reductions for certain sleeping bags, a move that would aid Exxel Outdoors, a company based in Aderholt's hometown of Haleyville. Aderholt and Republican Sen. Jeff Sessions introduced identical bills in 2011, seeking to remove an advantage intended for products made in certain poor nations. The Obama administration made the change in late 2011.

The president also signed Aderholt's 2012 bill to add some flexibility to rules on the energy efficiency of manufactured products — essentially allowing manufacturers to hit regulatory targets by using new technologies that old standards can't account for. Aderholt cited the case of HH Technologies, an

Alabama-based manufacturer of walk-in freezers; he said regulations were hindering its use of superior designs.

In 2005 he voted for the Central America Free Trade Agreement, but only after receiving written assurances from top administration officials — and a personal phone call from President George W. Bush — that they would help protect domestic sock makers from import surges. The trade pact passed the House by two votes. When a local sock manufacturer closed its doors in 2008, Aderholt blamed what he said was the Bush administration's failure to live up to the deal. Aderholt voted against a South Korea pact in 2011 that the textile industry opposed.

Aderholt was raised in a deeply conservative community. His father was a judge and a Baptist pastor, and he believes in bringing religious values into the public sphere. During his first term in Congress, Aderholt got the House to go on record promoting the Ten Commandments. In 2003, when a federal judge ordered the removal of a stone display of the Ten Commandments from the state judicial complex in Montgomery, Aderholt said it was a "scene one would expect to see in the former Soviet Union, not the United States of America."

He is a member of the Commission on Security and Cooperation in Europe (also known as the Helsinki Commission), which monitors human rights in Europe and the countries of the former Soviet Union. Aderholt has pursued a campaign for freedom of religious expression overseas, particularly in Georgia and Turkmenistan.

Aderholt's religious faith has influenced his government work. In 2010, the D. James Kennedy Center for Christian Statesmanship named him its distinguished statesman of the year. In 2007, he had a chance to travel in Alabama with Bush — but he chose to remain in Washington to vote for what is known as the Mexico City policy, a restriction on foreign aid to groups that provide abortions.

Aderholt grew up with politics. When he was 5, he wrote a campaign letter touting his father in a local election, and he recalls meeting Republican Sen. Bob Dole of Kansas when he was about 11. A month after his graduation from law school, he was nominated for a state House seat, but he lost the general election. He was appointed a municipal judge in 1992 and went to work as an aide to Republican Gov. Fob James Jr. in 1995.

When Democrat Tom Bevill retired in 1996 after 15 terms, Aderholt made a run for the seat. Democrats nominated former state Sen. Robert T. "Bob" Wilson, who was nearly as conservative as Aderholt on social issues. Aderholt prevailed by less than 2 points but has won handily since. With no serious opposition in 2012, he was able to contribute more than $350,000 of his campaign funds to the National Republican Congressional Committee.

Key Votes

2012	
Extend a Social Security payroll tax cut and unemployment benefits	NO
Ease securities rules to expand small-business access to capital	YES
Extend for one year subsidized student loan interest rates financed by a cut in health care spending	YES
Cite Attorney General Eric H. Holder Jr. for contempt of Congress	YES
Create a visa program for foreign graduates in high-tech fields	YES
Extend most Bush-era income tax rates while allowing rates for top-bracket earners to rise (Jan. 1, 2013)	NO
2011	
Strike funding for F-35 alternative engine	NO
Prevent EPA from regulating greenhouse gas emissions to address climate change	YES
Extend certain provisions of Patriot Act for four years	YES
Declare opposition to use of ground troops in Libya	YES
Overhaul patent law	NO
Pass compromise debt limit increase plan and establish future spending limits	YES
Allow consideration of measures to implement three trade agreements	YES

CQ Vote Studies

	PARTY UNITY		PRESIDENTIAL SUPPORT	
	SUPPORT	OPPOSE	SUPPORT	OPPOSE
2012	89%	11%	13%	87%
2011	94%	6%	23%	77%
2010	95%	5%	29%	71%
2009	84%	16%	28%	72%
2008	96%	4%	67%	33%

Interest Groups

	AFL-CIO	ADA	CCUS	ACU
2012	20%	0%	100%	76%
2011	3%	15%	88%	76%
2010	7%	0%	88%	92%
2009	10%	5%	92%	92%
2008	21%	25%	82%	92%

Alabama 4

North central — Gadsden, Cullman, Jasper

The Republican 4th spans the width of Alabama, rising from the Tennessee Valley across large waterways and through cave-pocked foothills to the Appalachian Mountains. A small black population and the absence of a major city distinguish the relatively poor district from the rest of Alabama.

The western portion of the district stretches from Muscle Shoals south to the outskirts of Tuscaloosa. The central part of the 3rd bottlenecks north of Birmingham and south of Huntsville; its eastern edge follows Interstate 59 from Gadsden into the Appalachians at the Georgia border.

Gadsden, which has relied on factory jobs for decades, is the district's only sizable city. Manufacturing plants across the district are still important to the economy, although the once-dominant textile industry has collapsed. Volatility in the coal market and environmental concerns have created uncertainty for mining interests. Local officials and the Appalachian Regional Commission expect the 2014 completion of "Corridor X," an interstate route following U.S. 78 from Memphis to Birmingham, to draw new midsize businesses to the western part of the district.

The industrial sector has diversified beyond steel and textiles to include food processing and wood products. The 4th also is one of the nation's largest poultry producers, although tornadoes in 2011 hurt the industry. At opposite ends of the district, chicken-processing plants in DeKalb and Franklin counties have drawn thousands of Hispanic immigrants during the past decade, making Latinos the largest minority group by far in each.

Guntersville Reservoir, shared with the 5th, supports a shipping- and tourism-based economy in Guntersville. The district's mountainous landscape provides opportunities for outdoor recreation, including at Smith Lake.

Major Industry
Manufacturing, food processing, agriculture, tourism

Cities
Gadsden, Albertville, Cullman

Notable
Fame Recording Studios in Muscle Shoals — source of the "Muscle Shoals Sound" that blended rhythm and blues, country and gospel — recorded hit records for Percy Sledge, Wilson Pickett, Aretha Franklin, the Staple Singers, Paul Simon and the Rolling Stones.

Rep. Mo Brooks (R)

Capitol Office
225-4801
brooks.house.gov
1230 Longworth Bldg. 20515-0105; fax 225-4392

Committees
Armed Services
Foreign Affairs
Science, Space & Technology

Residence
Huntsville

Born
April 29, 1954; Charleston, S.C.

Religion
Christian

Family
Wife, Martha Brooks; four children

Education
Duke U., B.A. 1975 (economics & political science); U. of Alabama, J.D. 1978

Career
Special assistant state attorney general; lawyer; county prosecutor

Political Highlights
Ala. House, 1983-91; Madison County district attorney, 1991-93; defeated for election as Madison County district attorney, 1992; Madison County Commission, 1996-2011; sought Republican nomination for lieutenant governor, 2006

ELECTION RESULTS

2012 GENERAL		
Mo Brooks (R)	189,185	64.9%
Charlie L. Holley (D)	101,772	34.9%
2012 PRIMARY		
Mo Brooks (R)	65,163	70.9%
Parker Griffith (R)	26,694	29.1%
2010 GENERAL		
Mo Brooks (R)	131,109	57.9%
Steve Raby (D)	95,192	42.1%

Elected 2010; 2nd term

Frank, conservative and having an affinity for details, Brooks takes a prosecutorial approach to legislating. It's his natural role after a long legal career in Alabama.

Brooks was a county prosecutor, as well as a special assistant attorney general under Jeff Sessions, who now represents Alabama in the Senate. His policy work touches on a mix of local and national interests. Brooks pushes for a balanced-budget amendment to the Constitution, looks out for the military and research interests in his home state and wants substantive changes to federal immigration law. "I want to do anything I can to remove illegal aliens from America. It's really quite simple," he said.

Brooks sees his agenda as a means to making the United States fiscally solvent and competitive on the international stage. He is, in general, a competitive guy. He says he plays "a pretty mean game of table tennis."

"Pingpong is when you're in a garage with beer in your hand," according to Brooks. "Table tennis is when you're running all over the place. Each point is life or death."

Brooks might be competing with Sessions for the title of most conservative member of the Alabama delegation. He took a very fiscally conservative tack in his first term. Brooks co-sponsored a bill to eliminate federal taxes and the IRS and replace them with a national sales tax.

As the parties battled over raising the federal debt limit in 2011, Brooks introduced a bill to increase the debt limit in $750 billion increments — once upon congressional adoption of a balanced-budget amendment to the Constitution, and once on its ratification. He calls such an amendment "necessary for America's financial security." His first bill of the 113th Congress (2013-14) was an updated version with $1 trillion increases.

"I think the only way Democrats will ever agree to being financially responsible is if we force them to do that while they are kicking and screaming the whole way," he said. He was one of 33 Republicans who refused to support a short-term elimination of the debt limit in January 2013. That vote came just a few weeks after he rejected a "fiscal cliff" deal that extended lower income tax rates for most people, but didn't cut spending.

His budget views affect his work on the Armed Services Committee, as well as the Foreign Affairs Committee, which he joined in the 113th.

Brooks is hesitant to support some funding for the Afghanistan War while there are continuing federal budget concerns. He's also not convinced Afghanistan can sustain its own police or national defense force. "I, like a lot of Americans, am ready to leave a country where our financial sacrifices and sacrifices of young lives are not fully appreciated by who we fight for," he told an Alabama newspaper.

Brooks' district is home to the Army's Redstone Arsenal for rocket and missile programs, and he has a seat on the Strategic Forces Subcommittee (which is chaired by fellow Alabaman Mike D. Rogers). He is wary of allowing missile defense technology to be used as a "bargaining chip" in future treaty negotiations with Russia, and the fiscal 2012 defense authorization law contained his provision to prohibit sharing that technology with Russia. Brooks also added it to a fiscal 2013 defense spending bill that wasn't enacted.

He wants to reduce foreign aid to all countries but has voted against doing so for Pakistan, citing the use of that nation for ground troop movement to Afghanistan. "Once we get out of Afghanistan, I'd give Pakistan zippo," he said. In early 2013, the Rules Committee rejected a proposed Brooks amendment that would have cut $21 billion from foreign aid — except for Israel,

Afghanistan and Pakistan — to offset spending on Superstorm Sandy relief.

Brooks also sits on the Science, Space and Technology Committee. He chaired the Research and Science Education Subcommittee as a freshman, and in the 113th he's the vice chairman of the subcommittee overseeing NASA. The Marshall Space Flight Center, a NASA facility that develops rocket propulsion technology and spaceflight vehicles, is in his district. Brooks supports NASA and space exploration programs, in particular the heavy-lift space launch system.

As a freshman, Brooks served on the Homeland Security panel but gave his seat to Bob Turner of New York, who was sworn into the House in September 2011. He didn't give up his interest in border and immigration policy. He introduced a bill allowing states and local governments to further strengthen illegal immigration laws. Brooks believes illegal immigrants "adversely affect" the lives of citizens by driving up the costs of health care and other public services and competing with citizens for employment opportunities. "Don't get me wrong, removing illegal aliens from America is not a cure-all, but it helps with almost every issue we face," he said.

Born in South Carolina, Brooks moved when he was a boy to Huntsville, where he now resides. His father was an electrical engineer and his mother was a high school teacher. In addition to playing basketball and baseball, Brooks was an active member of his high school debate team, winning a scholarship to the University of Alabama.

But he attended Duke University — a good move, considering it's where he met his wife, Martha. He graduated in three years with a double major in economics and political science. He received a law degree from the University of Alabama in 1978, then worked a few years as a Tuscaloosa County assistant district attorney. He served in the Alabama House from 1983 to 1991, then became the Madison County district attorney.

Brooks briefly served under Sessions in the mid-1990s, when the now-senator was Alabama's attorney general. "I've been urging Sen. Sessions to run for president," Brooks said in July 2011. "He won't do that. But I think he would make a great president."

In 2010, he ran for the House, handily beating incumbent Parker Griffith in the primary and then topping Democrat Steve Raby in the general election with almost 58 percent of the vote. Brooks is the first Republican elected from Alabama's 5th District since Reconstruction — Griffith was elected as a Democrat before switching to the GOP in December 2009.

Two years later, the district was made more Republican-friendly by decennial redistricting. Brooks faced Griffith again and bested him by more than 40 points. He then won the general election with about 65 percent of the vote.

Key Votes

2012	
Extend a Social Security payroll tax cut and unemployment benefits	NO
Ease securities rules to expand small-business access to capital	YES
Extend for one year subsidized student loan interest rates financed by a cut in health care spending	YES
Cite Attorney General Eric H. Holder Jr. for contempt of Congress	YES
Create a visa program for foreign graduates in high-tech fields	YES
Extend most Bush-era income tax rates while allowing rates for top-bracket earners to rise (Jan. 1, 2013)	NO
2011	
Strike funding for F-35 alternative engine	NO
Prevent EPA from regulating greenhouse gas emissions to address climate change	YES
Extend certain provisions of Patriot Act for four years	YES
Declare opposition to use of ground troops in Libya	YES
Overhaul patent law	NO
Pass compromise debt limit increase plan and establish future spending limits	NO
Allow consideration of measures to implement three trade agreements	YES

CQ Vote Studies

	PARTY UNITY		PRESIDENTIAL SUPPORT	
	SUPPORT	OPPOSE	SUPPORT	OPPOSE
2012	96%	4%	20%	80%
2011	96%	4%	19%	81%

Interest Groups

	AFL-CIO	ADA	CCUS	ACU
2012	14%	10%	83%	92%
2011	3%	10%	88%	88%

Alabama 5

North — Huntsville

The 5th sits in the northern tier of the state. The Tennessee River forms the western half of the district's southern border, and Huntsville and its Morgan County suburbs fill in the central portion of the 5th. Small towns and parts of the Guntersville Reservoir and Appalachians make up the district's east.

Federal investment in both the Shoals and Huntsville is the foundation of the 5th's economy. The Shoals was undeveloped rural land until Tennessee Valley Authority dams spurred industrial growth beginning in the 1930s, and manufacturing sites along the river's shores remain vital to the district.

Huntsville relies on federal government, defense and contracting jobs. The nation's ballistic missile program at Huntsville's Redstone Arsenal transformed the one-time farming and railroad town into "Rocket City U.S.A." by the 1950s. Tens of thousands of area residents are employed in technology, manufacturing and research industries, working on projects including missile defense, space telescopes and heavy-lift rocket engines. NASA's Marshall Space Flight Center, adjacent to Redstone Arsenal, develops rocket propulsion technology and spaceflight vehicles. Madison County's Cummings Research Park has 25,000 employees. High-tech jobs near Huntsville has given the area the state's highest percentage of college graduates. Agriculture — soybeans, corn and cotton — is a healthy sector of the 5th's economy outside of Huntsville, particularly in Limestone County.

After a century and a half of backing Democrats, 2009 marked the beginning of a now-complete shift to the GOP at the federal level. The addition of Morgan County south of Huntsville and the loss of some Muscle Shoals-area communities south of the Tennessee River during decennial redistricting have swung the 5th. Lawrence County, the only county where Rep. Mo Brooks lost in 2010, was shifted to the already firmly Republican 4th District.

Major Industry
Defense, technology, manufacturing, agriculture

Military Bases
Redstone Arsenal (Army), 1,000 military, 17,000 civilian (2012)

Cities
Huntsville, Decatur, Madison, Florence

Notable
Florence's Rosenbaum House is the state's only Frank Lloyd Wright building.

Rep. Spencer Bachus (R)

Capitol Office
225-4921
bachus.house.gov
2246 Rayburn Bldg. 20515-0106; fax 225-2082

Committees
Financial Services
Judiciary
(Regulatory Reform, Commercial & Antitrust Law - Chairman)

Residence
Vestavia Hills

Born
Dec. 28, 1947; Birmingham, Ala.

Religion
Baptist

Family
Wife, Linda Bachus; five children

Education
Auburn U., B.A. 1969; U. of Alabama, J.D. 1972

Military
Ala. National Guard, 1969-71

Career
Lawyer; sawmill owner

Political Highlights
Ala. Senate, 1983; Ala. House, 1983-87; Ala. Board of Education, 1987-91; candidate for Ala. attorney general, 1990; Ala. Republican Party chairman, 1991-92

ELECTION RESULTS

2012 GENERAL		
Spencer Bachus (R)	219,262	71.2%
Penny H. Bailey (D)	88,267	28.6%
2012 PRIMARY		
Spencer Bachus (R)	63,360	61.4%
Scott Beason (R)	28,673	27.8%
David Standridge (R)	8,120	7.9%
Al Mickle (R)	2,930	2.8%
2010 GENERAL		
Spencer Bachus (R)	205,288	98.0%

Previous Winning Percentages
2008 (98%); 2006 (98%); 2004 (99%); 2002 (90%); 2000 (88%); 1998 (72%); 1996 (71%); 1994 (79%); 1992 (52%)

Elected 1992; 11th term

In a six-year run as the top Republican on the Financial Services Committee, Bachus saw his political stock fluctuate like the markets he closely observed. He's not currently in charge of a full committee, but his party reserved him a panel overseeing the business and financial communities: Bachus now has the gavel of the Judiciary subcommittee handling commercial law and regulations.

Bachus (BACK-us) had two years as Financial Services chairman before Republican term limits on committee leaders closed out his reign. As chairman in the 112th Congress (2011-12) he stuck with the anti-regulatory, smaller-government message that underpins most of the GOP agenda. He attacked rules written by the Obama administration and the 2010 overhaul of financial regulations that Democrats enacted.

"Our economy is hobbled not only by our deficits and debt, but also by the cumulative weight of Washington over-regulation," he said. Bachus warned that regulations stemming from the 2010 law would ultimately slow loans to, and investments in, businesses. He had one significant victory in that regard — enactment of a 2012 bill to help startup businesses get access to capital.

Other efforts weren't so successful. Most prominently, Bachus proposed placing the Consumer Financial Protection Bureau created by the 2010 law under the governance of a bipartisan board appointed by the president and approved by the Senate. Republicans had complained that the CFPB would be largely unaccountable to Congress and far too powerful. The House passed legislation to make the change, but it was ignored by the Democratic Senate.

It was a common problem for Bachus. Democrats shot down his efforts to restrict regulation of the complex financial instruments known as derivatives, to bar the CFPB from giving trial lawyers information collected from banks and to overhaul the Securities and Exchange Commission to give some of its power to an industry self-regulatory body.

Bachus was also undermined by a kerfuffle over his personal finances. A November 2011 report on the news program "60 Minutes" alleged that he used "insider" information in 2008 to make stock trades. Bachus had received a briefing from top George W. Bush administration officials and soon thereafter put a stock market bet on a market collapse. Bachus' frequent stock trading has long been a point of interest in Washington.

Bachus denied the allegation, and the Office of Congressional Ethics dropped its inquiry into the matter in May 2012. But a cloud hung over his head for a few months. Bachus pressed for legislation to require congressmen to place their assets in a blind trust (which went nowhere), as well as a bill to tighten restrictions on lawmakers or congressional staffers using "privileged information" to make stock trades (which was enacted). He was challenged in the March GOP primary by conservative state Sen. Scott Beason, who wrote tough immigration legislation and was assisted by a conservative political action committee. When the votes were counted, Bachus won in a landslide, trouncing Beason by nearly 35,000 votes.

The episode wasn't the first time Bachus irked conservatives, despite being fairly right-of-center himself. Bachus was the ranking member on Financial Services from 2007 through 2010. As markets tumbled and the GOP divided on solutions during the 2008 financial crisis, Bachus found himself alone among party leaders in negotiating a financial services industry rescue plan. In fall 2008, his decision to work with Democratic leaders on the $700 billion proposal to stabilize the economy led conservatives to accuse him of "drinking the Kool-Aid." Minority Leader John A. Boehner of Ohio eventually blocked him from speaking for the GOP at the deliberations.

And Bachus had worked with Democrats before that. He was one of the early critics of subprime lending and supported a 2007 plan by Barney Frank of Massachusetts — who was then the Financial Services chairman — to keep more bad mortgages from being issued.

Californian Ed Royce challenged Bachus for the committee gavel after Republicans gained control of the House in the 2010 elections. Bachus' status as a prolific fundraiser for the party and support from incoming Majority Leader Eric Cantor of Virginia helped him secure the chairmanship.

Bachus retains a seat on Financial Services as chairman emeritus. He also rejoined the Judiciary Committee for the 113th Congress (2013-14). He has a new angle to approach some of his recent work, as the chairman of the Regulatory Reform, Commercial and Antitrust Law Subcommittee.

As the full Judiciary Committee began discussing possible changes to immigration law early in the 113th Congress, Bachus supported some common Republican positions. He said he prefers smaller bills to a "comprehensive" overhaul, and that expanding the visa program for highly skilled workers is a good place to start.

Bachus is a devout Baptist. His religious beliefs have led to his support of Third World debt relief — he has had unusual alliances on the issue with the likes of U2 front man Bono and liberal California Democrat Maxine Waters, the current ranking member on Financial Services. Bachus says canceling the debt of poorer countries can help stabilize their governments, fight poverty and prevent terrorism.

He's also a strong backer of autism research and treatment. Mitchell's Place, an autism treatment center in Birmingham, has received federal funding to those ends.

Bachus was born in Birmingham. His father, Spencer T. Bachus Jr., was a World War II veteran who went on to become a partner in a construction company. Like his father, Bachus graduated from Auburn University.

Early in his career, Bachus owned a sawmill, but for the most part he earned a living as a trial lawyer. He began his career in elective office in 1983, serving first in the state legislature. He went on to serve on the state board of education and then as chairman of the Alabama Republican Party.

In his first House bid, Bachus benefited from the remapping of Alabama's congressional districts done after the 1990 census — it transformed the district held for five terms by Democrat Ben Erdreich into a Republican bastion. Bachus took 52 percent of the vote in 1992 and has been re-elected with at least 70 percent of the vote in each subsequent general election. In the 2012 cycle he continued to be a prolific fundraiser, contributing hundreds of thousands of dollars to fellow Republicans.

Key Votes

2012	
Extend a Social Security payroll tax cut and unemployment benefits	NO
Ease securities rules to expand small-business access to capital	YES
Extend for one year subsidized student loan interest rates financed by a cut in health care spending	YES
Cite Attorney General Eric H. Holder Jr. for contempt of Congress	YES
Create a visa program for foreign graduates in high-tech fields	YES
Extend most Bush-era income tax rates while allowing rates for top-bracket earners to rise (Jan. 1, 2013)	NO
2011	
Strike funding for F-35 alternative engine	NO
Prevent EPA from regulating greenhouse gas emissions to address climate change	YES
Extend certain provisions of Patriot Act for four years	YES
Declare opposition to use of ground troops in Libya	YES
Overhaul patent law	YES
Pass compromise debt limit increase plan and establish future spending limits	YES
Allow consideration of measures to implement three trade agreements	YES

CQ Vote Studies

	PARTY UNITY		PRESIDENTIAL SUPPORT	
	SUPPORT	OPPOSE	SUPPORT	OPPOSE
2012	91%	9%	12%	88%
2011	94%	6%	27%	73%
2010	95%	5%	32%	68%
2009	86%	14%	29%	71%
2008	94%	6%	68%	32%

Interest Groups

	AFL-CIO	ADA	CCUS	ACU
2012	19%	0%	100%	83%
2011	0%	5%	100%	80%
2010	7%	0%	88%	96%
2009	11%	5%	80%	92%
2008	20%	20%	94%	84%

Alabama 6

Central — suburban Birmingham

The 6th unites rural counties of central Alabama with the white-majority suburbs around Birmingham into a solidly Republican seat. Although the district takes in most of Jefferson County, it excludes almost all of Birmingham itself — the 7th narrowly cuts out much of the city from the 6th.

Jefferson County and fast-growing suburban Shelby County to its south are home to the vast majority of the district's voters. Reflective of the city's painful racial history, many of the tony hilltop communities southeast of downtown Birmingham are nearly all white, while the inner-city neighborhoods that fall in the 7th District are overwhelmingly black. Racial divisions are beginning to soften elsewhere in the district, particularly as middle-class blacks move into suburbs near Interstate 65 both north and south of Birmingham.

In the late 20th century, Birmingham transitioned from a struggling steel town into a major health care and banking hub. Some district residents work at the Mercedes-Benz auto plant in Vance (in the strip of the 7th slicing between the 6th and 4th in Tuscaloosa County), but the 6th District has a mostly white-collar workforce that floods daily into the city's downtown.

Towns settled along the district's highways have some of the worst suburban commute times in the nation. A boom in the late 1990s, when six Fortune 500 companies had headquarters in Birmingham, was on the wane before nationwide economic slowdowns led to high unemployment rates and municipal budget shortfalls. The area has been slow to recover.

Birmingham's suburbs are encroaching on the district's rural areas — as far as parts of Bibb County southwest of Shelby and Blount County (shared with the 4th) northeast of Jefferson — but agriculture remains important to the district's economic health and peaches are a point of pride in Chilton County. Rural and poor Coosa County continues to lose population.

Major Industry
Health care, financial services, manufacturing, agriculture

Cities
Birmingham (pt.), Hoover, Vestavia Hills, Alabaster

Notable
The district's portion of Birmingham includes the city's botanical garden and zoo.

Rep. Terri A. Sewell (D)

Capitol Office
225-2665
sewell.house.gov
1133 Longworth Bldg. 20515-0107; fax 226-9567

Committees
Financial Services
Select Intelligence

Residence
Birmingham

Born
Jan. 1, 1965; Huntsville, Ala.

Religion
African Methodist Episcopal

Family
Single

Education
Princeton U., A.B. 1986 (public and international affairs); Oxford U., M.A. 1988 (Marshall scholar), Harvard U., J.D. 1992

Career
Lawyer

Political Highlights
No previous office

ELECTION RESULTS

2012 GENERAL		
Terri A. Sewell (D)	232,520	75.8%
Don Chamberlain (R)	73,835	24.1%
2012 PRIMARY		
Terri A. Sewell (D)		unopposed
2010 GENERAL		
Terri A. Sewell (D)	136,696	72.4%
Don Chamberlain (R)	51,890	27.5%

Elected 2010; 2nd term

Sewell is a bright star in the Alabama Democratic Party. For now, she's also its only star. Her isolation isn't slowing her progress on the national political scene — she has made inroads into the House leadership team, prominent committees and campaign operations.

She started her House career by making history: Sewell (SUE-ell) is the first African-American woman from Alabama to serve in Congress, and she and Republican Martha Roby are the first Alabama women to be elected rather than appointed to a congressional term.

She was also the first black valedictorian at her Selma high school, and her mother was the first black woman on the Selma City Council. She and Roby "stand on the shoulders of so many pioneering women from Alabama who paved the way for us to be where we are," Sewell said in 2011. "It's a tremendous honor."

Gregarious and a loud laugher, the self-described "daughter of the Black Belt" was president of the nine-member Democratic freshman class of 2010. She was named a chief deputy whip in the 113th Congress (2013-14), and she serves as a vice chairwoman of the fundraising effort at the Democratic Congressional Campaign Committee. Party leaders also picked her to serve on the Intelligence Committee.

All this, while being the only readily recognizable Democratic politician from her state. At the start of 2013, all statewide offices and the other six House seats in Alabama were held by Republicans, and the GOP had huge majorities in the state legislature. Alabaman Jimmy Buffett might have raised more money headlining a single Barack Obama fundraiser in 2012 than any of the state's Democratic candidates did in the entire campaign cycle.

Sewell operates with those electoral realities in mind, and she sometimes tries to work within the constraints of the cost-cutting plans of House Republicans. She backed fiscal 2011 and 2012 bills that cut overall discretionary spending, as well as a deficit reduction package in August 2011.

But her district is the poorest in the state. That makes job creation a top priority for Sewell, and she has tried to secure infrastructure funding for the region. Four months into her freshman term, her district was hit by a series of tornadoes, killing more than 200. Sewell tried to make the best of the tragedy: "If we're going to rebuild, we're going to rebuild better," she said. The storms were also an early test of her constituent services operation, which Sewell says is essential to her philosophy of being a lawmaker: "As my mother would say, bloom where you are planted."

Sewell joined the Financial Services Committee for the 113th Congress. Birmingham, in her district, isn't the banking center it once was, but it still has large financial institutions for her to look after. Sewell once worked as a securities lawyer in New York, and on moving back to Alabama she was a public finance attorney.

As the committee considered its oversight plan in February 2013, Sewell asked that it pay close attention to the way international banking conventions, particularly regarding capitalization requirements, are affecting community banks. Mandatory cash reserves are "a key component of any efficient and solvent financial system that can adequately withstand financial shock," she said, but they might lock up so much money that small banks don't have the flexibility to perform basic lending functions.

Sewell looked out for small farmers and West Alabama's burgeoning catfish industry as a member of the Agriculture Committee in her freshman term. She voted in committee against a long-term reauthorization of farm programs that included $16 billion in cuts to the Supplemental Nutrition Assistance Program. Citing the need to open markets to Alabama farmers, Sewell voted in 2011 for free-trade agreements with Panama and South Korea. She's a member of the business-friendly New Democrat Coalition.

She also sat on the Science, Space and Technology Committee as a freshman and promoted STEM (science, technology, engineering and mathematics) education. Those fields are important for children in her district who rely on schooling to boost them beyond tough economic starting points, Sewell said: "For me, growing up in rural America, it was education that gave me the opportunity to be where I am." She has degrees from Princeton, Oxford and Harvard.

Sewell, whose father had multiple strokes and uses a wheelchair, defends the health care law enacted in 2010. "Health care should be a right and not a fight," she said. "Look, was it a perfect bill? No. But was it a really great start? Yes. Is it a premise from which to build upon? Absolutely."

She held no elected office before winning her House seat, but during her college summers, "I was working as a college intern for my congressman from this district." The lawmaker was Democrat Richard C. Shelby—who later won a Senate seat and switched to the Republican Party in 1994. Entering the House, she said, was a "full-circle moment."

Sewell graduated from Princeton in 1986 and received her master's degree in politics from Oxford in 1988. She then received her law degree from Harvard in 1992. Sewell knew Obama in law school, and she knew his wife even earlier. When studying at Princeton, Sewell was mentored by Michelle Obama, before the future first lady met the future president.

She clerked for a federal judge, then worked in New York for more than a decade before becoming a partner in a Birmingham firm—giving her a "business acumen" she believes is important to her as a legislator.

In 2010, Democratic Rep. Artur Davis made an unsuccessful gubernatorial bid, giving up the 7th District seat he held for four terms. A well-funded but relatively unknown Sewell faced a crowded Democratic field in the 2010 primary. Candidates included state Rep. Earl Hilliard Jr., whose father held the seat for a decade, and Jefferson County Commissioner Sheila Smoot. Sewell finished first in the primary, taking 37 percent of the vote, then bested Smoot six weeks later in the runoff, 55 percent to 45 percent.

That was tantamount to election in the heavily Democratic district. In November, she took 72 percent of the vote against Republican Don Chamberlain, a retired Marine.

In the 2012 election, she faced Chamberlain again, this time netting 75 percent of the vote.

Key Votes

2012	
Extend a Social Security payroll tax cut and unemployment benefits	YES
Ease securities rules to expand small-business access to capital	YES
Extend for one year subsidized student loan interest rates financed by a cut in health care spending	NO
Cite Attorney General Eric H. Holder Jr. for contempt of Congress	?
Create a visa program for foreign graduates in high-tech fields	NO
Extend most Bush-era income tax rates while allowing rates for top-bracket earners to rise (Jan. 1, 2013)	YES
2011	
Strike funding for F-35 alternative engine	NO
Prevent EPA from regulating greenhouse gas emissions to address climate change	YES
Extend certain provisions of Patriot Act for four years	YES
Declare opposition to use of ground troops in Libya	NO
Overhaul patent law	YES
Pass compromise debt limit increase plan and establish future spending limits	YES
Allow consideration of measures to implement three trade agreements	YES

CQ Vote Studies

	PARTY UNITY		PRESIDENTIAL SUPPORT	
	SUPPORT	OPPOSE	SUPPORT	OPPOSE
2012	92%	8%	79%	21%
2011	88%	12%	85%	15%

Interest Groups

	AFL-CIO	ADA	CCUS	ACU
2012	90%	70%	33%	8%
2011	90%	75%	56%	0%

Alabama 7

West central — parts of Birmingham and Tuscaloosa

Western rural counties, predominately black portions of southwestern Montgomery, and most of Tuscaloosa and Birmingham come together in the 7th to form the state's only black-majority district. Consolidating urban and industrial areas with struggling rural counties, the district is among the poorest in the nation. Tuscaloosa's population is growing modestly, but middle-class residents have left Birmingham for nearby suburban communities and rural areas are hemorrhaging population.

The 7th's part of Birmingham includes downtown's Civil Rights District as well as the University of Alabama-Birmingham. The university's medical center anchors the health care industry in the city, which also still relies on a dwindling steel and heavy industry sector. Downtown Birmingham also hosts financial services firms, although many members of the white-collar workforce live in the surrounding 6th District. The Birmingham airport and cargo rail lines drive regional transportation interests.

Tuscaloosa boasts the University of Alabama flagship campus. Mercedes-Benz operates a plant northeast of Tuscaloosa in Vance and the automaker is adding more than $2 billion of investment and expansion there. A Hyundai Motors plant south of downtown Montgomery and Alabama State University in the city provide jobs.

Beyond Birmingham and Tuscaloosa, almost all of the rest of the district — including Lowndes County and the slice of Montgomery added during redistricting — falls into the western half of the state's Black Belt, a historically poverty-filled region of rich soil that stretches from Texas to Virginia. The district has been held by three African-American representatives, including Rep. Terri A. Sewell, Alabama's first black female U.S. House member.

Major Industry
Health care, higher education, manufacturing

Cities
Birmingham (pt.), Tuscaloosa (pt.), Bessemer, Selma

Notable
Edmund Pettus Bridge in Selma was the site of "Bloody Sunday," when Alabama state troopers assaulted peaceful civil rights marchers — who were led by current Georgia Democratic Rep. John Lewis — on their way to Montgomery in 1965.

ALASKA

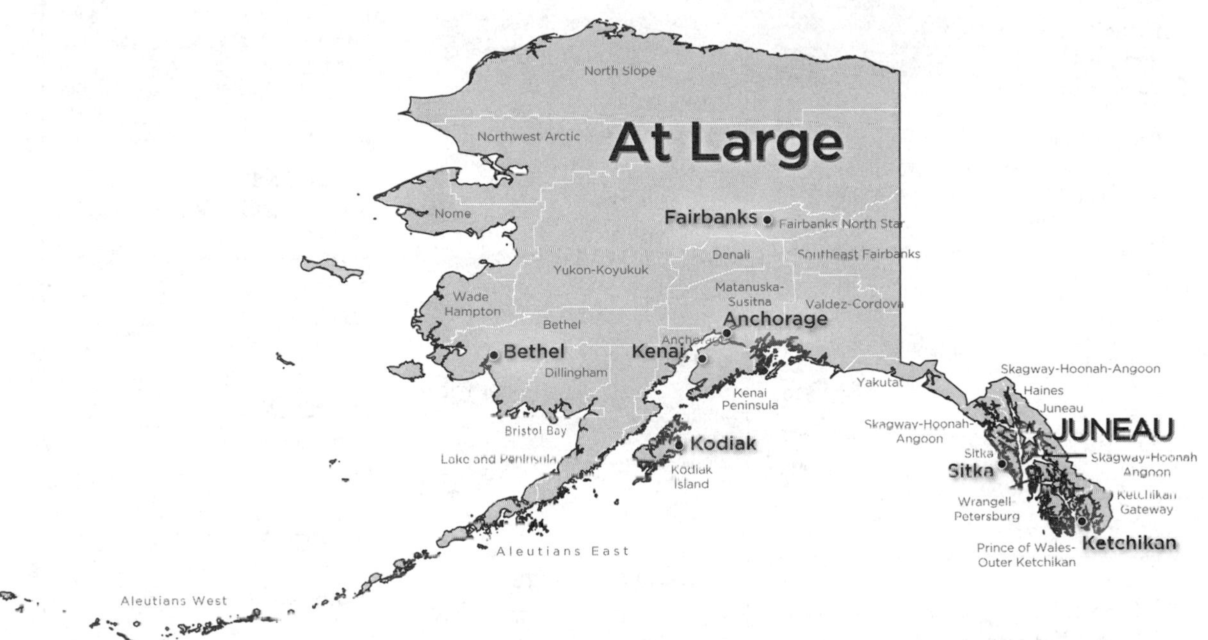
North Slope
Northwest Arctic
At Large
Nome
Fairbanks
Fairbanks North Star
Denali
Southeast Fairbanks
Yukon-Koyukuk
Matanuska-Susitna
Wade Hampton
Valdez-Cordova
Anchorage
Bethel
Bethel
Kenai
Dillingham
Yakutat
Kenai Peninsula
Skagway-Hoonah-Angoon
Haines
Juneau
JUNEAU
Bristol Bay
Skagway-Hoonah-Angoon
Kodiak
Lake and Peninsula
Kodiak Island
Sitka
Sitka
Skagway-Hoonah Angoon
Ketchikan Gateway
Wrangell-Petersburg
Prince of Wales-Outer Ketchikan
Ketchikan
Aleutians East
Aleutians West

Gov. Sean Parnell (R)

First elected: 2010
Took office July 26, 2009, due to the resignation of Sarah Palin, R.

Length of term: 4 years

Term expires: 12/14

Salary: $145,000

Phone: (907) 465-3500

Residence: Juneau

Born: Nov. 19, 1962; Hanford, Calif.

Religion: Christian

Family: Wife, Sandy Parnell; two children

Education: Pacific Lutheran U., B.B.A. 1984; U. of Puget Sound, J.D. 1987

Career: Lawyer; state natural resources official; lobbyist

Political highlights: Alaska House, 1993-97; Alaska Senate, 1997-2001; lieutenant governor, 2006-09; sought Republican nomination for U.S. House 2008

ELECTION RESULTS

2010 GENERAL

Sean Parnell (R)	151,318	59.1%
Ethan Berkowitz (D)	96,519	37.7%
Don R. Wright (AKI)	4,775	1.9%
William Toien (LIBERT)	2,682	1.0%

Lt. Gov. Mead Treadwell (R)

First elected: 2010

Length of term: 4 years

Term expires: 12/10

Salary: $115,000

Phone: (907) 465-3520

LEGISLATURE

Legislature: January to April

Senate: 20 members, 4-year terms

2013 ratios: 13 R, 7 D; 16 men, 4 women

Salary: $50,400

Phone: (907) 465-3701

House: 40 members, 2-year terms

2013 ratios: 26 R, 14 D; 27 men, 13 women

Salary: $50,400

Phone: (907) 465-3725

TERM LIMITS

Governor: 2 consecutive terms

Senate: No

House: No

URBAN STATISTICS

CITY	POPULATION
Anchorage	291,826
Fairbanks	31,535
Juneau	31,275
Sitka	8,881
Ketchikan	8,050

REGISTERED VOTERS

Others	58%
Republican	27%
Democrat	14%

POPULATION

2010 population	710,231
2000 population	626,932
1990 population	550,043
Percent change (2000-2010)	+13.3%
Rank among states (2010)	47
Median age	32.7
Born in state	39.5%
Foreign born	6.3%
Violent crime rate	633/100,000
Poverty level	9.0%
Federal workers	22,244
Military	23,178

ELECTIONS

STATE DIVISION OF ELECTIONS
(907) 465-4611

DEMOCRATIC PARTY
(907) 258-3050

REPUBLICAN PARTY
(907) 276-4467

MISCELLANEOUS

Web: www.alaska.gov

Capital: Juneau

U.S. CONGRESS

Senate: 1 Democrat, 1 Republican

House: 1 Republican

STATISTICS BY DISTRICT

	2012 Vote for President		2008 Vote for President										
District	Obama	Romney	Obama	McCain	Black	Asian	Hispanic	Median Income	Over 64	Under 20	College Education	Rural	Sq. Miles
AL	41%	55%	38%	59%	3%	5%	6%	$67,825	8%	29%	26%	40%	570,641
STATE	41	55	38	59	3	5	6	67,825	8	29	26	40	570,641
U.S.	51	47	53	46	12	5	17	50,052	13	27	29	21	3,531,905

Sen. Lisa Murkowski (R)

Capitol Office
224-6665
murkowski.senate.gov
709 Hart Bldg. 20510-0202; fax 224-5301

Committees
Appropriations
Energy & Natural Resources - Ranking Member
Health, Education, Labor & Pensions
Indian Affairs

Residence
Girdwood

Born
May 22, 1957; Ketchikan, Alaska

Religion
Roman Catholic

Family
Husband, Verne Martell; two children

Education
Willamette U., attended 1975-77; Georgetown U., B.A. 1980 (economics); Willamette U., J.D. 1985

Career
Lawyer; state legislative aide

Political Highlights
Anchorage district attorney, 1987-89; Alaska House, 1999-2002

ELECTION RESULTS

2010 GENERAL		
Lisa Murkowski (WRI)	101,091	39.2%
Joe Miller (R)	90,839	35.3%
Scott T. McAdams (D)	60,045	23.3%
write-ins (WRI)	2,719	1.1%

Previous Winning Percentages
2004 (49%)

Elected 2004; 2nd full term

Appointed 2002

Murkowski charts a course for herself that isn't always on the same map used by a majority of Republicans. Putting Alaska firmly at the center of energy policy debates, she's a leading Senate moderate who invests a lot of time pitching her state as a proving ground for new development.

Whether considering geothermal power, ocean energy or biomass, "allow us to be that demonstration project and figure out how you can then take this from a small, rural, remote village in Alaska to somewhere else," she urged during a 2012 speech at the progressive think tank Center for American Progress. "I think we can really prove the difference."

As the ranking member of the Energy and Natural Resources Committee, Murkowski will have a role in efforts to legislate an "all of the above" energy strategy, addressing everything from renewable sources to delivery infrastructure. She has shown disdain for Republicans who focus solely on fossil fuel production, and for Democrats hell-bent on conservation.

At the start of the 113th Congress (2013-14), she released a more than 100-page outline of policy suggestions, some new, some old. Among the newer ideas: a trust fund for "advanced energy" research, fed by a portion of the revenue from new energy leasing by the government; making sure that the tax code and energy programs don't favor any one category of energy production; and defining clean energy, for the purpose of production targets and future policy, as a source that has fewer environmental drawbacks than its "likeliest alternative" (meaning fossil fuels could be clean in some cases).

She's still not in favor of a cap-and-trade system for greenhouse gas emissions, and she told Fox Business Network in early 2013 that the idea of a carbon tax "is going absolutely nowhere."

Murkowski has cultivated relationships that could make her agenda succeed. In the 112th Congress (2011-12) she strengthened her ties to Oregon Democrat Ron Wyden, who became the Energy chairman in 2013. She studied wind farms and oil shale deposits with West Virginia Democrat Joe Manchin III and founded the Oceans Caucus with Rhode Island Democrat Sheldon Whitehouse.

And drilling did factor into her efforts. As top Republican on the Interior-Environment Appropriations Subcommittee, Murkowski successfully inserted into a fiscal 2012 spending law a provision to speed up oil projects off the coasts of Alaska. The language transferred the clean-air permit authority for those seas from the EPA to the Interior Department, which Murkowski said has shown a much better turnaround time on applications; she has described permitting as the biggest obstacle to energy development in her state.

Time and again, Murkowski has proved to be a moderate with little taste for political standoffs when Alaska's direct interests aren't at stake. She and Wyden have teamed up to propose new disclosure requirements for political donations to super PACs.

In January 2013 she told the Fairbanks News-Miner that she didn't want to use the statutory limit on government borrowing (and the threat of a federal default) as a tool to force concessions from Democrats on fiscal matters. She is one of the five or so Republicans that Democrats regularly court as they try to reach the 60 votes needed to overcome procedural hurdles.

In fact, the biggest obstacle to Murkowski in recent years has been the conservative wing of her own party.

First welcomed to Washington in 2002 — her father, Frank H. Murkowski, appointed her to his old seat after he was elected governor — Lisa won her first full term in 2004 with 49 percent of the vote.

As she neared the end of that term, she had amassed some clout. Murkowski got the top GOP spot on the energy panel in 2009 and was named a counsel to Minority Leader Mitch McConnell of Kentucky. A few months later she was elected Republican Conference vice chairwoman.

But her 2010 campaign was a dramatic affair involving a battle with tea party conservatives. Murkowski lost the Republican primary to challenger Joe Miller by 2,006 votes, then re-entered the race as a write-in candidate. Because she was challenging the nominated Republican, she resigned from her leadership post.

Murkowski claimed victory two weeks after Election Day but had to wait until the final day of the year before Miller threw in the towel on his legal challenges. With 39 percent of the vote, she became the first write-in candidate to win a Senate race since Strom Thurmond of South Carolina in 1954.

She still sticks with her party on some of its key agenda items. She joined a losing effort on a bill to limit EPA authority to regulate greenhouse gases, and she supported a procedural effort to force a vote on repeal of the 2010 health care law. (It was rejected.) Murkowski has tried to stave off cuts to defense spending in her state, particularly at Eielson Air Force Base; the fiscal 2013 defense policy law contained her provision delaying the relocation of equipment or aircraft by the Air Force until at least 2014.

Cultural clashes, however, make her a little wary. An Obama administration policy to require health care plans to cover women's contraceptives riled many Republicans, and Missouri's Roy Blunt in 2012 offered a "conscience clause" amendment to exempt employers with religious objections from complying. Democrats blasted the attempt as a GOP "war on women," putting Murkowski and other moderates on the spot. She voted against a Democratic motion that killed the amendment, but said that "we kind of lost the discussion there. We sure missed what the public was seeing."

A member of the Health, Education, Labor and Pensions Committee, she has joined with Democrats to push proposals to improve prevention and treatment of cardiovascular diseases in women, and to get junk food out of schools.

On the Indian Affairs panel, where she was the top Republican in the 110th Congress (2007-08), she worked with then-Chairman Byron L. Dorgan of North Dakota on efforts to improve American Indian housing and health care. She also worked with Sen. Barack Obama on a bill to ban exports of mercury, which can result in fish — a staple among Alaska's native peoples — being unsafe to eat. That bill was signed into law in 2008.

One of Murkowski's bipartisan team-ups for 2012 had a distinct tie to her state. A Justice Department investigation found that prosecutors had withheld evidence detrimental to their case in the 2008 corruption trial of Alaska Sen. Ted Stevens — who was convicted and lost his re-election bid that year. Judiciary Chairman Patrick J. Leahy, a Democrat from Vermont, cheered Murkowski as she introduced a measure to require uniform disclosure standards for exculpatory evidence. "This is truly one of the Justice Department's darkest moments," Murkowski testified before Leahy's panel.

The second of six children, Murkowski was born in Ketchikan and raised in the Alaskan Panhandle. She interned for Stevens after attending high school in Fairbanks, then went to Willamette University in Oregon. She later transferred to Georgetown University.

Her father launched his first Senate campaign in 1980, the year she graduated, and she and her siblings joined the effort. Later, with a law degree from Willamette, she spent two years as court attorney for the Anchorage District Court. She practiced with a commercial law firm for eight years before opening a solo law practice.

She ran successfully for the state House in 1998, was re-elected twice, and was chosen by her peers late in 2002 as majority leader, a post that she never filled because of her appointment to the U.S. Senate.

Key Votes

2012	
Prohibit health insurance plans from denying coverage based on the sponsor's religious beliefs	NO
Require approval of the Keystone XL oil pipeline	YES
Ease securities rules to expand small-business access to capital	YES
Reauthorize farm and nutrition programs for five years	NO
Limit debate on a bill that would create private-sector cybersecurity standards	NO
Consent to ratification of a treaty setting global standard for the treatment of people with disabilities	YES
Provide $60.4 billion in disaster relief following Superstorm Sandy	YES
Extend most Bush-era income tax rates while allowing rates for top-bracket earners to rise (Jan. 1, 2013)	YES
2011	
Prevent EPA from regulating greenhouse gas emissions to address climate change	YES
Extend certain provisions of Patriot Act for four years	NO
Clear compromise debt limit increase plan and establish future spending limits	YES
Overhaul patent law	YES
Implement Colombia free trade agreement	YES
Limit debate on confirmation of Caitlin J. Halligan to D.C. Circuit Court of Appeals	YES
Extend payroll tax cut and unemployment benefits for two months	YES

CQ Vote Studies

	PARTY UNITY		PRESIDENTIAL SUPPORT	
	SUPPORT	OPPOSE	SUPPORT	OPPOSE
2012	51%	49%	69%	31%
2011	71%	29%	65%	35%
2010	83%	17%	60%	40%
2009	70%	30%	66%	34%
2008	72%	28%	72%	28%
2007	71%	29%	77%	23%
2006	82%	18%	89%	11%
2005	93%	7%	87%	13%
2004	92%	8%	87%	13%
2003	94%	6%	93%	7%

Interest Groups

	AFL-CIO	ADA	CCUS	ACU
2012	45%	35%	100%	36%
2011	21%	40%	91%	50%
2010	21%	20%	100%	73%
2009	56%	35%	71%	68%
2008	40%	25%	86%	58%
2007	32%	30%	91%	67%
2006	13%	5%	100%	71%
2005	14%	20%	100%	83%
2004	50%	35%	94%	74%
2003	15%	20%	86%	70%

Sen. Mark Begich (D)

Capitol Office
224-3004
begich.senate.gov
111 Russell Bldg. 20510; fax 224-2354

Committees
Appropriations
Commerce, Science & Transportation
(Oceans, Atmosphere, Fisheries & Coast Guard - Chairman)
Homeland Security & Governmental Affairs
(Emergency Management & District of Columbia - Chairman)
Indian Affairs
Veterans' Affairs

Residence
Anchorage

Born
March 30, 1962; Anchorage, Alaska

Religion
Roman Catholic

Family
Wife, Deborah Bonito; one child

Education
U. of Alaska, Anchorage, attended 1981-88

Career
Property development company owner; city government employee

Political Highlights
Anchorage Assembly, 1988-98 (chairman, 1993, 1996-98); candidate for mayor of Anchorage, 1994, 2000; mayor of Anchorage, 2003-09

ELECTION RESULTS

2008 GENERAL		
Mark Begich (D)	151,767	47.8%
Ted Stevens (R)	147,814	46.5%
Bob Bird (AKI)	13,197	4.2%
2008 PRIMARY		
Mark Begich (D)	63,747	90.8%
Ray Metcalfe (D)	5,480	7.8%
Frank Vondersaar (D)	965	1.4%

Elected 2008; 1st term

Begich sometimes strains against both the slow pace of the Senate and the Democratic agenda. Party leaders consider him an effective messenger for the moderate segment of their caucus, and he hopes his centrist approach will prolong his congressional career in a Republican state.

A former mayor of Anchorage, Begich is in tune with many aspects of Alaska's political culture — he supports all kinds of energy development, defends gun rights and has no qualms about steering federal funds to Alaska (a practice perfected by Republican Ted Stevens, whom Begich defeated in 2008). An entrepreneurial history stretching back to his teen years helps him identify with small-business concerns. There are Democrats in the Senate "who worked in business and had great titles and fancy corporate stuff," he said, "but I actually had to build a business from scratch."

In the 112th Congress (2011-12), Begich accepted an invitation to take charge of the Democratic Steering and Outreach Committee, making him a part of the Senate leadership team. His stated intention was to improve party relations with business groups, veterans and other constituencies that are conventionally aligned with Republicans. "I think it's important [the leadership] have a moderate voice — Democrats who are pro-development, pro-oil and-gas, NRA supporters — in that mix," he said. "I'm very blunt. ... If I think there's something wrong, I'm gonna say it, I'm not gonna hesitate, and if they kick me out of leadership, so be it."

They didn't. He still has the job in the 113th Congress (2013-14).

Begich says conversations between business groups and his party have been uncomfortable at times, but also productive. As an example, he cites the regulatory streamlining provisions in a two-year surface transportation law enacted in 2012. Some liberal senators had environmental concerns, but an outreach call to contractors may have loosened up resistance.

Centrism probably offers Begich his best chance of victory in the 2014 election. Alaska favored GOP presidential candidate Mitt Romney over President Barack Obama by 14 points in 2012, and Begich will have to shuttle back from Washington to campaign against the eventual GOP nominee. In 2008, he barely outran the 85-year-old Stevens, who days before the election was found guilty on seven corruption charges of making false statements on financial disclosure forms. (The charges were later vacated after the judge criticized prosecutors for failing to turn over documents to defense lawyers.)

Begich picked up some Alaska-friendly committee assignments in the 113th Congress that might boost his support among voters. He joined the Appropriations and Indian Affairs panels, giving up seats on the Budget and Armed Services committees to do so.

His most notable work in the 112th Congress was done on the Commerce, Science and Transportation Committee. Dating back to his mayoral days, Begich professes to "love building stuff," and he waxes enthusiastic when discussions turn to bonds and infrastructure financing. While a big fan of the regulatory streamlining in the 2012 highway law, he favors a bigger federal investment in infrastructure and a longer-term law to provide "the certainty that the contractors need, the communities need on planning." Begich also calls for greater federal investments in ports.

As chairman of the Oceans, Atmosphere, Fisheries and Coast Guard Subcommittee, Begich pursues a major parochial goal: a comprehensive approach to development in the Arctic as climate changes make it more accessible. "People still are wondering, 'Are we going to develop it?' That's not the question anymore," he said. "It's not if, it's how we're going to manage and develop it in the most environmentally safe way, but yet recognize the commerce that's up there. Commerce in multiple areas: transportation, fisheries, science, oil and gas, tourism."

To set the ground rules for international disputes in the Arctic, Begich wants the United States to ratify the United Nations' Convention of the Law of the Sea. To keep sea lanes clear and support economic development, he wants an increase in Coast Guard funding and the commissioning of new icebreakers — in 2012, Obama signed a Coast Guard reauthorization bill that included a Begich provision requiring a feasibility study for a deep-water port in the Arctic. To protect Alaska's fisheries, he has introduced bills to require tighter federal controls over genetically modified salmon.

And to get energy development humming, he has proposed the creation of new offices to process lease applications for drilling on the outer continental shelf. "When the president calls me at times, I'm usually in his face about oil and gas issues," Begich said in 2013. He wants Alaska's share of revenue from offshore energy production bumped up to 37.5 percent, the same rate enjoyed by Gulf Coast states.

Begich promotes the development of renewable energy as much as fossil fuels; he is among those senators who call for a national requirement for electricity production from renewable sources (Alaska has such a mandate). He partners with Alaska Republican Lisa Murkowski on energy. They argue that the state can be a "test bed" for renewable-energy technologies, and Begich supports an active federal role in promoting energy through tax incentives, research and regulatory streamlining.

He also serves on the Veterans' Affairs Committee and the Homeland Security and Governmental Affairs Committee. Begich figures to be active on Alaska's behalf as the U.S. military shifts more resources to the Asia-Pacific theater.

In the 112th Congress, he worked to keep a number of military assets in the state, particularly at Joint Base Elmendorf-Richardson, which hosts the Air Force's extensive Red Flag-Alaska training exercises. When the Pentagon moved to lay off workers at the base in 2011, Begich criticized overall deployments. "We've got two brigades in Germany that shouldn't be there," he said. "Bring them home."

Begich supports abortion rights, and he favors allowing same-sex couples to receive benefits through their partners.

Begich is the third of six children born to schoolteachers who moved from Minnesota to Alaska in the late 1950s. His father, Nick Begich, was elected to the House as a Democrat in 1970. The senior Begich disappeared in 1972 with House Democratic leader Hale Boggs of Louisiana aboard a plane that was never found.

Mark Begich never graduated from college, instead making use of a business license he got at the age of 16. He and a brother had several ventures, including a nightclub for teens and a vending-machine operation. He later managed apartment buildings that catered to low-income renters and became a real estate agent in the 1990s.

His political career started in the 1980s, when he worked for Anchorage Mayor Tony Knowles, a Democrat who went on to serve two terms as governor. At 26, Begich was elected to the Anchorage Assembly. He served 10 years there, including three years as chairman and two as vice chairman. He lost 1994 and 2000 mayoral races before being elected in 2003. He was the first Alaska-born citizen to serve as Anchorage's top elected official.

The race against Stevens in 2008 was too close to call weeks after Election Day. During the campaign, Begich highlighted his respect for Stevens but said the state would benefit from a changing of the guard. Stevens led by more than 3,000 votes in the initial tally, but absentee ballots allowed Begich to defeat the incumbent by fewer than 4,000 votes.

Key Votes

2012	
Prohibit health insurance plans from denying coverage based on the sponsor's religious beliefs	YES
Require approval of the Keystone XL oil pipeline	YES
Ease securities rules to expand small-business access to capital	NO
Reauthorize farm and nutrition programs for five years	YES
Limit debate on a bill that would create private-sector cybersecurity standards	YES
Consent to ratification of a treaty setting global standard for the treatment of people with disabilities	YES
Provide $60.4 billion in disaster relief following Superstorm Sandy	YES
Extend most Bush-era income tax rates while allowing rates for top-bracket earners to rise (Jan. 1, 2013)	YES
2011	
Prevent EPA from regulating greenhouse gas emissions to address climate change	NO
Extend certain provisions of Patriot Act for four years	NO
Clear compromise debt limit increase plan and establish future spending limits	YES
Overhaul patent law	YES
Implement Colombia free trade agreement	NO
Limit debate on confirmation of Caitlin J. Halligan to D.C. Circuit Court of Appeals	YES
Extend payroll tax cut and unemployment benefits for two months	YES

CQ Vote Studies

	PARTY UNITY		PRESIDENTIAL SUPPORT	
	SUPPORT	OPPOSE	SUPPORT	OPPOSE
2012	93%	7%	93%	7%
2011	91%	9%	93%	7%
2010	93%	7%	97%	3%
2009	93%	7%	93%	7%

Interest Groups

	AFL-CIO	ADA	CCUS	ACU
2012	100%	85%	63%	4%
2011	89%	85%	55%	0%
2010	100%	85%	27%	4%
2009	100%	100%	57%	12%

Rep. Don Young (R)

Capitol Office
225-5765
donyoung.house.gov
2314 Rayburn Bldg. 20515-0201; fax 225-0425

Committees
Natural Resources
(Indian & Alaska Native Affairs - Chairman)
Transportation & Infrastructure

Residence
Fort Yukon

Born
June 9, 1933; Meridian, Calif.

Religion
Episcopalian

Family
Widowed; two children

Education
Yuba Junior College, A.A. 1952; Chico State College, B.A. 1958

Military
Army, 1955-57

Career
Elementary school teacher; riverboat captain

Political Highlights
Fort Yukon City Council, 1960-64; mayor of Fort Yukon, 1964-68; Alaska House, 1967-70; Alaska Senate, 1971-73; Republican nominee for U.S. House, 1972

ELECTION RESULTS

2012 GENERAL

Don Young (R)	185,296	63.9%
Sharon M. Cissna (D)	82,927	28.6%
Jim C. McDermott (LIBERT)	15,028	5.2%
Ted Gianoutsos (WRI)	5,589	1.9%

Previous Winning Percentages
2010 (69%); 2008 (50%); 2006 (57%); 2004 (71%); 2002 (75%); 2000 (70%); 1998 (63%); 1996 (59%); 1994 (57%); 1992 (47%); 1990 (52%); 1988 (63%); 1986 (56%); 1984 (55%); 1982 (71%); 1980 (74%); 1978 (55%); 1976 (71%); 1974 (54%); 1973 Special Election (51%)

Elected 1973; 20th full term

The self-described "alpha wolf" of Alaska politics no longer runs at the front of the pack as a committee chairman, despite sitting at No. 2 on the House Republican seniority chart. But Young has kept his focus on Alaska, pressing for energy development and keeping an eye on public lands issues.

He sits on two panels where he once held the gavel: Natural Resources (1995-2000) and Transportation and Infrastructure (2001-06). He served as the ranking member on Natural Resources as recently as the 110th Congress (2007-08), before stepping aside to address possible ethics charges which ultimately were not brought up by the Ethics Committee.

A return to the top of either committee is unlikely, considering Young's age and his acerbic personality. He did himself no favors in spring 2013, when he used the term "wetback" in a radio interview to refer to Hispanic workers on the California farm where he grew up. He apologized — while also defending the remark as innocuous by the standards of his childhood. He was excoriated by Republicans and Democrats alike.

Plus, Young's voting record reflects little concern for the party line. Alaska has traditionally looked to the federal government for a wide variety of needs, and Young votes against many attempts to increase cuts to grant and assistance programs. When Heritage Action for America finalized its House voting scorecard for the 112th Congress (2011-12), it ranked only Ohio's Steven C. LaTourette as less conservative that young — and he has retired.

Republicans have found Young a niche, however, handing him the gavel of the revived Natural Resources Subcommittee on Indian and Alaska Native Affairs. "I asked the chairman to resurrect the subcommittee, because I'm actively involved in the whole Native American area," Young said in 2011. "I need the ability to be heard to a greater extent on issues that affect Alaska." Young's wife Lu, who died in 2009, was an Alaska Native.

A longtime proponent of increased energy exploration, including in the Arctic National Wildlife Refuge, Young sponsored a bill to ease federal regulation of such development on American Indian-owned land; it would establish at least five Indian Energy Development Offices to provide tribes with more information. In 2012, the House passed a bill containing Young's provision finalizing the land claims of Sealaska Corp., one of 12 regional corporations Congress created through the Alaska Native Claims Settlement Act; timber harvesting on that land would be an economic boon, Young said. A slightly modified version was introduced in 2013.

Young sometimes joins with Democrats in promoting routine measures such as public land swaps and funding to fight forest fires, but he typically takes the opposing side on broad land management and environmental issues. He continues to introduce a slew of Alaska-centered measures, whether regarding Alaska Natives, fisheries or Coast Guard management.

He was on the conference committee for a 27-month reauthorization of surface transportation programs that was enacted in 2012; Young boasted of restoring funding in the final version for Alaska ferry and rail programs.

Young's style has made him susceptible to criticism over the years. During the 2008 campaign, news reports indicated that he was the subject of a Justice Department probe for his ties to VECO Corp., an oil services company at the center of the public corruption probe of a fellow Alaska Republican, Sen. Ted Stevens. Young denied accepting personal gifts and doing favors for the company. His campaign spent more than $1 million on his legal expenses and tried to reimburse a VECO executive for $37,626 in expenses for annual pig roasts the executive had sponsored for Young over 10 years. The Public Integrity

Section of the Justice Department cleared him of wrongdoing in 2010.

And as the chief House steward of a six-year surface transportation law in 2005, Young promoted a $10 million design study for the "Coconut Road" highway interchange off Interstate 75 in Florida. In 2008 the Senate included a provision in a technical corrections law that directed the Justice Department to examine the earmark's origin. Young denied that the funding set-aside, which was revised after the bill had cleared both chambers, was intended to aid a developer and other interests that donated to his campaign.

Young and Stevens in 2005 were also the chief proponents of a more than $200 million earmark for a bridge to the sparsely populated Gravina Island. Dubbed the "Bridge to Nowhere" by critics, it became a rallying point in the campaign against earmarks and pork barrel spending.

Young has been unapologetic for his pursuit of funding for his state, and he dislikes the current ban on earmarks. As Republicans considered House rules for the 113th Congress, he prepared an amendment to change the definition of the term, so that it wouldn't include any measure that funds a federal, state or local governmental entity without increasing the appropriations amount allocated by the Budget Committee. He eventually withdrew it.

Young was introduced to Alaska through his favorite book, Jack London's "The Call of the Wild." After completing college and military service, he headed for Alaska in 1959 and settled in as a fifth-grade teacher for Alaska Native students at a school in Fort Yukon, seven miles above the Arctic Circle. He taught school in the winter and captained his own tug and barge operation in the summer, ferrying supplies to villages along the Yukon River.

He served as mayor of Fort Yukon and as a state House member before moving to a state Senate seat in 1971. The only election he ever lost was his first U.S. House race, in 1972. His opponent, freshman Democrat Nick Begich, disappeared without a trace, along with House Majority Leader Hale Boggs, during an October flight from Anchorage to Juneau. But Begich still beat Young by almost 12,000 votes in November. After Begich's seat was declared vacant, Young edged out Emil Notti, the former state Democratic Party chairman, in a 1973 special election. (Begich's son Mark defeated Stevens in 2008.)

On the campaign trail in 2008, Young made the case that Alaskans needed him to take care of the state's interests with Democrats gaining clout in Washington. He survived a primary challenge by Lt. Gov. Sean Parnell by just 304 votes, then edged Democrat Ethan Berkowitz, a former state legislator, with 50 percent of the vote. He scored big victories in 2010 and 2012.

The House Ethics Committee announced in March 2013 that it is investigating reports, stemming from the Coconut Road case, that Young has misused campaign funds for hunting trips, charter flights and other personal expenses.

Key Votes

2012	
Extend a Social Security payroll tax cut and unemployment benefits	YES
Ease securities rules to expand small-business access to capital	YES
Extend for one year subsidized student loan interest rates financed by a cut in health care spending	YES
Cite Attorney General Eric H. Holder Jr. for contempt of Congress	YES
Create a visa program for foreign graduates in high-tech fields	?
Extend most Bush-era income tax rates while allowing rates for top-bracket earners to rise (Jan. 1, 2013)	YES
2011	
Strike funding for F-35 alternative engine	NO
Prevent EPA from regulating greenhouse gas emissions to address climate change	?
Extend certain provisions of Patriot Act for four years	NO
Declare opposition to use of ground troops in Libya	YES
Overhaul patent law	YES
Pass compromise debt limit increase plan and establish future spending limits	YES
Allow consideration of measures to implement three trade agreements	YES

CQ Vote Studies

	PARTY UNITY		PRESIDENTIAL SUPPORT	
	SUPPORT	OPPOSE	SUPPORT	OPPOSE
2012	88%	12%	14%	86%
2011	90%	10%	18%	82%
2010	81%	19%	38%	62%
2009	71%	29%	42%	58%
2008	88%	12%	54%	46%

Interest Groups

	AFL-CIO	ADA	CCUS	ACU
2012	38%	0%	100%	71%
2011	46%	30%	85%	63%
2010	30%	10%	100%	75%
2009	40%	10%	90%	75%
2008	77%	55%	73%	71%

Alaska

At Large

Alaska's remoteness belies its dependence on Washington, D.C., from which it receives billions of dollars in annual federal spending. Nevertheless, state and local governments — which together provide the largest number of jobs in the state — are waging a never-ending battle against federal control of the local economy that has made voters hostile to Washington.

The state's proximity to Russia and the Far East makes it a military stronghold, and its vulnerable economic boosters — oil and gas, minerals and timber — lie mostly on federally owned land. Most Alaskans and local lawmakers view opening land to oil and gas exploration as the best way to independence and heavily favor drilling in the Arctic National Wildlife Refuge. But economic turmoil has delayed construction of a natural gas pipeline from Prudhoe Bay through Canada to the lower 48 states.

Alaska has not had state sales and income taxes since black gold was discovered near Prudhoe Bay in the 1970s. The private-sector economy includes retail and health care jobs. Tourism, especially cruise-line-based travel, is big business.

Alaska tends to support Republicans at the federal level — voters in the state overwhelmingly backed the 2008 GOP presidential ticket, which included then-Gov. Sarah Palin, and gave Republican Mitt Romney a 14-point victory over Barack Obama in 2012. But some cities, the panhandle and the isolated tundra trend more Democratic, and moderates dominate the Alaska Legislature.

Most residents in this cold, conservative frontier state pay more attention to personality than to party affiliation and register as either third-party or unaffiliated voters.

Major Industry
Oil and gas, defense, government, tourism, fishing, timber, mining

Military Bases
Joint Base Elmendorf-Richardson, 13,314 military, 2,113 civilian; Fort Wainwright (Army), 6,400 military, 870 civilian (2012); Eielson Air Force Base, 1,895 military, 439 civilian; Fort Greely (Army), 1 military, 271 civilian (2009)

Cities
Anchorage, Fairbanks, Juneau

Notable
Mt. McKinley is the highest point in North America, at 20,320 feet.

ARIZONA

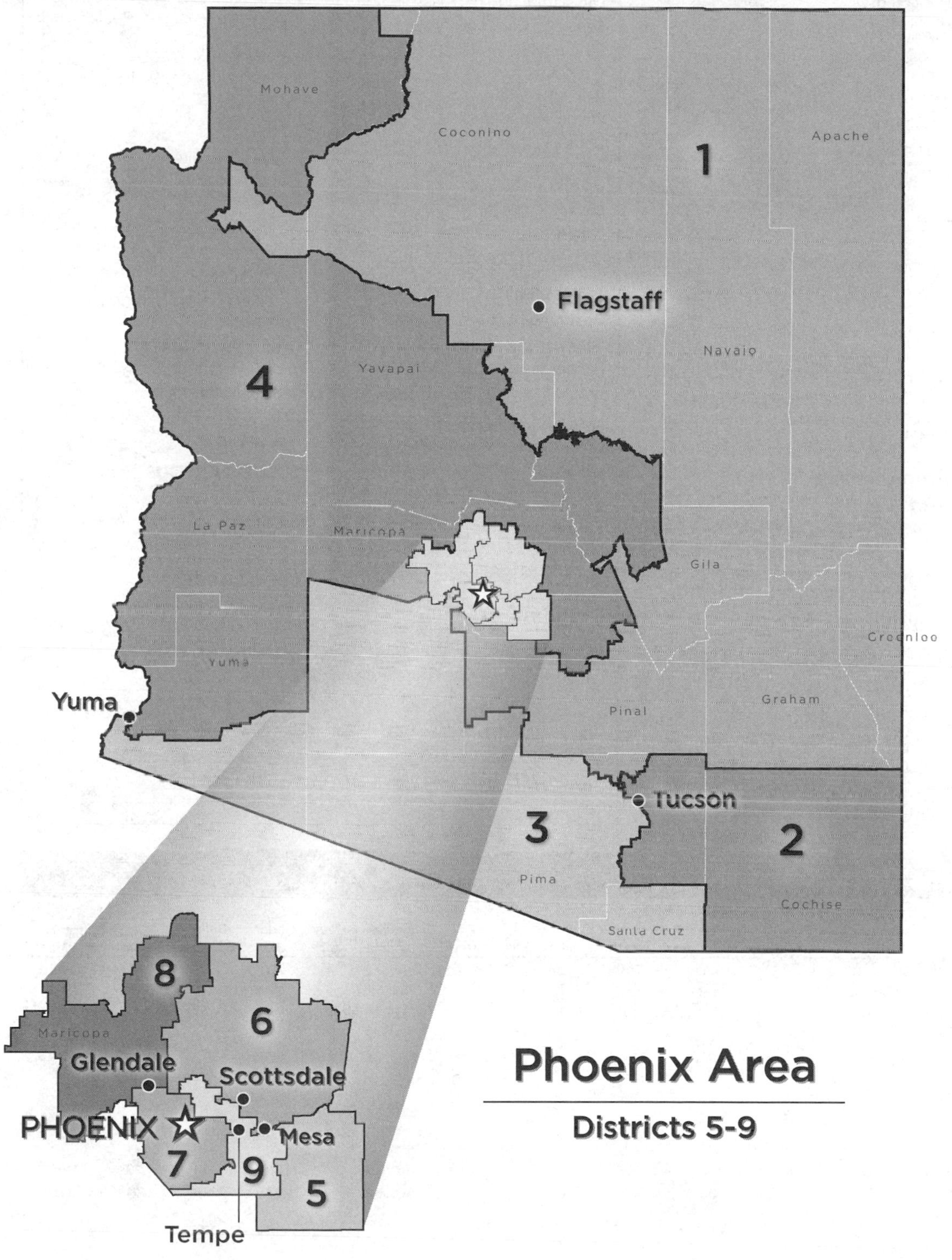

Phoenix Area

Districts 5-9

Gov. Jan Brewer (R)

First elected: 2010
Took office Jan. 21, 2009, due to the resignation of Janet Napolitano, D.

Length of term: 4 years

Term expires: 1/15

Salary: $95,000

Phone: (602) 542-4331

Residence: Glendale

Born: Sept. 26, 1944; Los Angeles, Calif.

Religion: Lutheran — Missouri Synod

Family: Husband, John Brewer; three children (one deceased)

Education: Verdugo Hills H.S., graduated 1962

Career: Homemaker, office manager

Political highlights: Ariz. House, 1983-87; Ariz. Senate, 1987-96 (minority whip, 1993-96); Maricopa County Board of Supervisors, 1997-2002; Ariz. Secretary of State, 2003-09

ELECTION RESULTS

2010 GENERAL

Jan Brewer (R)	938, 934	54.3%
Terry Goddard (D)	733,935	42.5%
Barry Hess (LIBERT)	38,722	2.2%

Secretary of State Ken Bennet (R)

(no lieutenant governor)

Assumed office: 2009

Length of term: 4 years

Term expires: 1/15

Salary: $70, 000

Phone: (602) 542-4285

LEGISLATURE

Legislature: 100 days January-April

Senate: 30 members, 2-year terms

2013 ratios: 17 R, 13 D; 17 men, 13 women

Salary: $24,000

Phone: (602) 926-3559

House: 60 members, 2-year terms

2013 ratios: 36 R, 24 D; 41 men, 19 women

Salary: $24,000

Phone: (602) 926-3032

TERM LIMITS

Governor: 2 consecutive terms

Senate: 4 consecutive terms

House: 4 consecutive terms

URBAN STATISTICS

CITY	POPULATION
Phoenix	1,445,632
Tucson	520,116
Mesa	439,041
Chandler	236,123
Glendale	226,721

REGISTERED VOTERS

Republican	35%
Democrat	30%
Other	35%

POPULATION

2010 population (est.)	6,392,017
2000 population	5,130,632
1990 population	3,665,228
Percent change (2000-2010)	+24.6%
Rank among states (2010)	16
Median age	34.8
Born in state	36.2%
Foreign born	14.6%
Violent crime rate	408/100,000
Poverty level	16.5%
Federal workers	69,533
Military	21,343

ELECTIONS

STATE ELECTION OFFICIAL
(602) 542-4285

DEMOCRATIC PARTY
(602) 298-4200

REPUBLICAN PARTY
(602) 957-7770

MISCELLANEOUS

Web: www.az.gov

Capital: Phoenix

U.S. CONGRESS

Senate: 2 Republicans

House: 5 Democrats, 4 Republicans

STATISTICS BY DISTRICT

	2012 Vote for President		2008 Vote for President										
District	Obama	Romney	Obama	McCain	Black	Asian	Hispanic	Median Income	Over 64	Under 20	College Education	Rural	Sq. Miles
1	48%	50%	47%	51%	2%	2%	20%	$43,377	14%	29%	24%	40%	55,040
2	48	50	49	50	4	3	26	44,921	18	23	30	11	7,838
3	61	37	58	41	4	1	61	37,771	10	33	16	12	15,689
4	31	67	35	64	2	1	19	40,802	22	24	18	29	33,199
5	35	64	36	63	3	4	18	60,624	15	30	33	<1	293
6	39	60	41	58	2	4	15	58,582	15	25	39	3	625
7	72	27	64	35	9	2	66	31,611	7	34	13	<1	205
8	37	62	38	61	3	3	18	55,454	19	25	28	2	540
9	51	47	51	47	6	4	26	48,033	9	26	34	<1	165
STATE	**45**	**54**	**45**	**54**	**4**	**3**	**30**	**46,709**	**14**	**28**	**26**	**12**	**113,594**
U.S.	**51**	**47**	**53**	**46**	**12**	**5**	**17**	**50,052**	**13**	**27**	**29**	**21**	**3,531,905**

Sen. John McCain (R)

Capitol Office
224-2235
mccain.senate.gov
241 Russell Bldg. 20510-0303; fax 228-2862

Committees
Armed Services
Foreign Relations
Homeland Security & Governmental Affairs
Indian Affairs

Residence
Phoenix

Born
Aug. 29, 1936; Panama Canal Zone, Panama

Religion
Episcopalian

Family
Wife, Cindy McCain; seven children

Education
U.S. Naval Academy, B.S. 1958; National War College, attended 1973-74

Military Service
Navy, 1958-81

Career
Navy officer; Navy Senate liaison; beer distributor

Political Highlights
U.S. House, 1983-87; sought Republican nomination for president, 2000; Republican nominee for president, 2008

ELECTION RESULTS

2010 GENERAL		
John McCain (R)	1,005,615	58.9%
Rodney Glassman (D)	592,011	34.6%
David F. Nolan (LIBERT)	80,097	4.7%
Jerry Joslyn (GREEN)	24,603	1.4%
2010 PRIMARY		
John McCain (R)	333,744	56.2%
J.D. Hayworth (R)	190,229	32.1%
Jimmie Lee Deakin (R)	69,328	11.7%

Previous Winning Percentages
2004 (77%); 1998 (69%); 1992 (56%); 1986 (61%); 1984 House Election (78%); 1982 House Election (66%)

Elected 1986; 5th term

McCain billed himself as a maverick conservative during his 2008 presidential campaign. After his loss, he resumed life as a senator as if nothing had happened — he was feisty, funny and focused on his policy agenda. To critics, though, he was not substantively the same on the issues.

Many commentators said McCain moved further to the right heading into a 2010 re-election campaign, then stayed there during the 112th Congress (2011-12). Conservatives complained about his bipartisanship — especially on campaign finance issues — to the point where former Rep. J.D. Hayworth opposed him in the 2010 GOP primary. Whether McCain was inoculating himself against such criticism or simply opposing the policies of the Obama administration, he was closer to the GOP fold for several years. Although he still saw himself as a maverick conservative, his actions seemed to emphasize the second part of that construction.

But he has been constant in the areas that largely define his career: defense and foreign policy. McCain is the son and grandson of famous admirals, and as a naval aviator he spent five and a half brutal years in solitary confinement in a North Vietnamese prison. McCain has been one of the most senior Republicans on the Armed Services Committee for years. He isn't its top Republican for the 113th Congress (2013-14) — party-imposed term limits forced him from that spot — but his policy clout is undiminished. He has also joined the Foreign Relations Committee.

McCain is an advocate of high levels of defense spending, and he tried hard in 2012 to block some $500 billion in cuts to the coming decade's defense budgets. (The automatic cuts were put in place by the August 2011 law raising the debt limit.) But he criticizes military spending when he thinks it's out of control. From 2002 through 2005, he almost single-handedly took down a scandal-plagued Air Force program to acquire midair refueling planes. He is a relentless critic of earmarked spending, and he never spared Republicans in his critiques.

McCain is not shy about recommending military action or the threat of its use. He was one of the most ardent backers of the Iraq War, and he was arguably the leading congressional proponent of the 2007 "surge" of troops that is perceived as having helped drive down violence in Iraq. He consistently supported high troop levels in Afghanistan and opposed setting a timetable for troop withdrawals.

He backed the use of force in Libya in 2011. Late in 2012, after militants there attacked a consulate and killed the U.S. ambassador and three other Americans, McCain and others argued that the Obama administration had misled the public about the terrorist nature of the attack. Appearing on "Meet the Press" in February 2013, he accused the administration of a "massive cover-up" of its response to the attacks.

McCain has said that he takes an "internationalist" approach to foreign relations. Speaking at a Human Rights First summit in 2012, he described America's "unique responsibilities of world leadership, especially our support for the values of human rights, rule of law, and democracy." As a civil war erupted in Syria in 2011, McCain waged a sometimes lonely but insistent campaign in favor of arming Syrian rebels seeking to overthrow Bashar al-Assad's government. He never lets up in defending Israel's actions and in depicting Iran's nuclear ambitions as a threat to world peace.

McCain, a member of the Homeland Security and Governmental Affairs Committee, played a central role in debates on cybersecurity legislation in 2012. He opposed efforts to set mandatory standards for private computer networks and wants Defense Department agencies, not the Department of Homeland Security, to have primary responsibility for cybersecurity.

His history as a prisoner of war gave him virtually unquestioned credibility when he stood against harsh interrogation of terrorist detainees during President George W. Bush's administration. He pushed Congress to bar such tactics in the U.S. military, and Bush eventually signed a ban into law.

On domestic issues, McCain is perhaps best known for his co-sponsorship of the McCain-Feingold law that regulated campaign contributions, although the Supreme Court overturned parts of the law. McCain depicts electoral cash as a corrupting influence in American democracy.

McCain is also somewhere near the political middle on immigration. In 2005, he and Massachusetts Democrat Edward M. Kennedy wrote a comprehensive overhaul bill. When that effort sputtered out, he spent the next few years emphasizing the need for border security before any overhaul could happen. But after the November 2012 elections, he said changes were needed to keep Republicans viable with Hispanic voters. "There is no doubt whatsoever that the demographics are not on our side," he said on Fox News. He is part of the bipartisan group of eight senators that produced an overhaul bill in the opening months of 2013. Their plan includes creating a path to citizenship for illegal immigrants already in the country.

In a chamber where members are expected to treat one another with deference, McCain sometimes discards courtesies and comes across as self-righteous. He is also volatile, sometimes going from amusing and charming to blunt and testy in the same sitting — several colleagues have endured his obscenity-laced tirades. Yet he is also famously self-deprecating. A favorite campaign line of his was, "I am older than dirt and have more scars than Frankenstein."

McCain was born in the Panama Canal Zone. His mother, in her mid-90s, campaigned with him for president in 2007 and 2008.

He attended the Naval Academy in Annapolis to follow in the footsteps of his father and grandfather. Although McCain never achieved the rank of admiral, he is widely admired for his bravery as a prisoner. During the Vietnam War, McCain's fighter plane was shot down, and he was captured by the North Vietnamese.

McCain ran for Congress in 1982, transitioning from his position as the Navy's Senate liaison. After two terms in the House, he pursued the Senate seat that opened when conservative icon Barry Goldwater retired. McCain won with 61 percent of the vote.

Shortly thereafter, he was accused of interceding with federal regulators on behalf of a wealthy savings and loan operator and was given a mild rebuke in 1991, after a protracted Ethics Committee investigation. He has pointed to that incident as his inspiration for becoming a crusader for changes in the campaign finance system. Following the scandal, he was held to 56 percent of the vote in 1992.

In 2000 he sought the GOP presidential nomination, but lost to Bush. He was easily re-elected to the Senate in 2004, then made another run for the White House in 2008. He trailed in early polls and lost in the Iowa caucuses, but recovered to win the nomination.

His choice of Alaska Gov. Sarah Palin as his vice presidential candidate was a typically maverick move for McCain, although results were mixed. She sparked interest in his campaign among conservative voters, who were generally unenthusiastic about his nomination, but she was not popular among the independent voters McCain himself tended to attract. Unable to compete with Barack Obama's fundraising and mantra of change, McCain lost the election.

After dispatching Hayworth in the GOP primary in 2010, he cruised to a 24-point victory over Democrat Rodney Glassman in November.

Key Votes

2012	
Prohibit health insurance plans from denying coverage based on the sponsor's religious beliefs	NO
Require approval of the Keystone XL oil pipeline	YES
Ease securities rules to expand small-business access to capital	YES
Reauthorize farm and nutrition programs for five years	NO
Limit debate on a bill that would create private-sector cybersecurity standards	NO
Consent to ratification of a treaty setting global standard for the treatment of people with disabilities	YES
Provide $60.4 billion in disaster relief following Superstorm Sandy	NO
Extend most Bush-era income tax rates while allowing rates for top-bracket earners to rise (Jan. 1, 2013)	YES
2011	
Prevent EPA from regulating greenhouse gas emissions to address climate change	YES
Extend certain provisions of Patriot Act for four years	YES
Clear compromise debt limit increase plan and establish future spending limits	YES
Overhaul patent law	NO
Implement Colombia free trade agreement	YES
Limit debate on confirmation of Caitlin J. Halligan to D.C. Circuit Court of Appeals	NO
Extend payroll tax cut and unemployment benefits for two months	YES

CQ Vote Studies

	PARTY UNITY		PRESIDENTIAL SUPPORT	
	SUPPORT	OPPOSE	SUPPORT	OPPOSE
2012	88%	12%	57%	43%
2011	93%	7%	59%	41%
2010	98%	2%	39%	61%
2009	96%	4%	43%	57%
2008	93%	7%	89%	11%
2007	90%	10%	95%	5%
2006	76%	24%	89%	11%
2005	84%	16%	77%	23%
2004	79%	21%	92%	8%
2003	86%	14%	91%	9%

Interest Groups

	AFL-CIO	ADA	CCUS	ACU
2012	0%	10%	75%	92%
2011	11%	15%	80%	80%
2010	6%	0%	100%	100%
2009	17%	15%	71%	96%
2008	0%	5%	100%	63%
2007	0%	10%	100%	80%
2006	7%	15%	100%	65%
2005	7%	10%	72%	80%
2004	33%	35%	67%	72%
2003	15%	35%	61%	75%

Sen. Jeff Flake (R)

Capitol Office
224-4521
flake.senate.gov
368 Russell Bldg. 20510; fax 228-0515

Committees
Energy & Natural Resources
Foreign Relations
Judiciary
Special Aging

Residence
Mesa

Born
Dec. 31, 1962; Snowflake, Ariz.

Religion
Mormon

Family
Wife, Cheryl Flake; five children

Education
Brigham Young U., B.A. 1986 (international relations), M.A. 1987 (political science)

Career
Public policy think tank director; lobbyist; international democratic advocacy organization director

Political Highlights
U.S. House, 2001-13

ELECTION RESULTS

2012 GENERAL		
Jeff Flake (R)	1,104,457	49.2%
Richard Carmona (D)	1,036,542	46.2%
Marc Victor (LIBERT)	102,109	4.6%
2012 PRIMARY		
Jeff Flake (R)	357,360	69.2%
Wil Cardon (R)	110,150	21.3%
Clair Van Steenwyk (R)	29,159	5.6%
Bryan Hackbarth (R)	19,174	3.7%

Previous Winning Percentages
2010 House Election (66%); 2008 House Election (62%); 2006 House Election (75%); 2004 House Election (79%); 2002 House Election (66%); 2000 House Election (54%)

Elected 2012; 1st term

Unyielding stands against federal spending made Flake a fringe figure in the Republican Party and a conservative folk hero throughout his 12-year House career. He's now in the Senate, where his philosophical independence from party leaders makes him a lawmaker to watch — for select policy areas, particularly on the Judiciary Committee, he is a potential swing vote.

Flake has good looks, a friendly demeanor and an affinity for Barry Goldwater. He once ran a think tank named for that Arizona senator, who was a conservative icon and the 1964 Republican presidential nominee. Goldwater espoused the virtues of small government, free enterprise and a strong national defense, and Flake essentially does the same.

His signature issue in the House was eradicating earmarks — provisions in laws that direct federal spending to specific projects in lawmakers' states or districts. In his third term, Flake started introducing a spate of amendments to strip earmarks from bills; he invited people to explain their requests on the House floor. Colleagues were publicly irritated by Flake's crusade. Many argued that their knowledge of local affairs made earmarks an efficient vehicle for spending, and that his challenges implied some ethical lapse on their part. Meanwhile, some Arizonans complained that Flake wasn't an effective advocate for bringing federal funds to their state.

After losing just about every battle, Flake won the war. Burgeoning concern about budget deficits and a few high-profile ethics cases solidified public opinion against earmarking, and House Republicans banned the practice in the 112th Congress (2011-12). House GOP leaders granted Flake's request to join the Appropriations Committee.

Flake continued to push for smaller government. He voted against the final spending deals for fiscal 2011 and 2012, as well as a deficit reduction package in August 2011; none of them did enough to control government spending, he said. Budget Chairman Paul D. Ryan endorsed him, calling him a "lonely leader" ahead of his time: "Jeff Flake was an economic fiscal conservative against all the pork before it was cool."

While Flake can frustrate colleagues, it's hard to find people who admit to a personal distaste for the man. In an interview with Esquire, Flake's mother called him her "peaceable boy." He has a goofy sense of humor and was a regular on the basketball courts in the House gym. At the 2012 State of the Union address, Flake sat with Democratic Rep. Gabrielle Giffords, who was recovering from a gunshot wound to the head; whenever she wanted to stand to applaud President Barack Obama, Flake also stood to help her get up.

For his first years in the Senate, Flake sits on the Energy and Natural Resources Committee, the Foreign Relations Committee, and the Judiciary Committee — he served on similar panels at various times in the House.

Some of Flake's libertarian leanings make him an intriguing figure on the Judiciary Committee. He often says that Republicans and Democrats alike trample on the principle of federalism, overriding states on everything from regulatory affairs to social policy — a lot of which runs through Judiciary. He opposes abortion and supported a proposed constitutional amendment to ban recognition of gay marriage, but more recently he has said that marriage should be decided by the states.

Flake is willing to negotiate an overhaul of immigration law. In the closing years of the George W. Bush administration, he helped prepare a proposal that included a pathway to citizenship for illegal immigrants already in the country. He later walked back from that position and emphasized the need to focus on border security first. But when Republicans were drubbed in the competition for the Hispanic vote in the 2012 election, talk of a comprehensive bill was revived, and Flake joined a bipartisan working group on the issue at the start of the 113th Congress (2013-14).

On Foreign Relations, Flake has an interest in promoting free trade. He opposes the embargo on Cuba. "The only solid path toward long-term, sustainable development in the global market is through free trade," he said in 2011. Flake stood with Republicans in support of the Iraq War, despite some reservations about the military's progress along the way. After visiting Afghanistan in January 2013, he posted on his Facebook page that he thought a withdrawal of troops by the end of 2014 was reasonable.

On the Energy and Natural Resources Committee, he is more of a classic Western Republican. He wants expansion of domestic energy production and less regulation of the energy sector. Flake did join in a 2009 proposal to tax fossil fuel energy production while reducing payroll taxes — but he does not like cap-and-trade systems favored by Democrats. He's an advocate for his state's mining industry and the Navajo Generating Station, a huge coal-fired plant in his state. Flake was disappointed by the government's early 2013 proposal to require major environmental upgrades at the plant.

The fifth of 11 children, Flake grew up near Snowflake, about 100 miles northeast of Phoenix. Established in 1878, it is named after its Mormon founders, Erastus Snow and William Flake, the lawmaker's great-great-grandfather. Flake's father is a former mayor of the town, and his uncle was speaker of the Arizona House. Flake spent his childhood working on the family ranch. The size of the family made a modest upbringing a necessity.

At 19, Flake began a two-year church mission to Zimbabwe and South Africa; on his return he got a bachelor's degree in international relations and a master's degree in political science from Brigham Young University. He married his college sweetheart, Cheryl. They have five children, and Flake became a grandfather about two weeks before Election Day 2012. His wife worked to help pay for Flake's studies.

After a stint as a Washington lobbyist, Flake moved to Namibia in 1989 as director of the Foundation for Democracy, a group helping the country develop a constitution after its break from South Africa. He returned to Arizona in 1992 to lead the Goldwater Institute.

Flake's first bid for public office was the 2000 race to succeed GOP Rep. Matt Salmon, who was retiring to satisfy a term limit pledge. Flake — who also made a term limit pledge — won a five-way primary with Salmon's endorsement, then beat Democratic labor lobbyist David Mendoza by 11 points. Flake broke his pledge when he ran in 2006, telling USA Today that such a promise was a "mistake."

Sen. Jon Kyl announced his retirement early in the 112th Congress. Soon after Flake announced his campaign to succeed Kyl, several prominent Republicans ended theirs. But real estate investor Wil Cardon ran against Flake in the primary and spent millions on negative television advertisements, mainly focusing on Flake's positions on climate change and immigration. Flake won easily, but the battle prepared the field for the Democratic candidate, former Surgeon General Richard Carmona.

Carmona used a common attack against Flake: that his ideological stands aren't helpful for Arizona. Flake unleashed attack ads of his own; one showed Carmona's former boss saying that he has "issues with anger, with ethics, and with women." He had the support of the anti-tax Club for Growth, which gave Flake a perfect rating throughout his House career.

Flake won by 3 points, taking only 49 percent of the vote. Libertarian candidate Marc Victor may have made the race considerably tighter, by taking nearly 5 percent of the vote. At the same time, Salmon recaptured the House seat Flake had vacated — though Flake endorsed Salmon's opponent in the GOP primary.

Key Votes (while House member)

2012	
Extend a Social Security payroll tax cut and unemployment benefits	NO
Ease securities rules to expand small-business access to capital	YES
Extend for one year subsidized student loan interest rates financed by a cut in health care spending	NO
Cite Attorney General Eric H. Holder Jr. for contempt of Congress	YES
Create a visa program for foreign graduates in high-tech fields	YES
Extend most Bush-era income tax rates while allowing rates for top-bracket earners to rise (Jan. 1, 2013)	NO
2011	
Strike funding for F-35 alternative engine	YES
Prevent EPA from regulating greenhouse gas emissions to address climate change	YES
Extend certain provisions of Patriot Act for four years	?
Declare opposition to use of ground troops in Libya	NO
Overhaul patent law	NO
Pass compromise debt limit increase plan and establish future spending limits	NO
Allow consideration of measures to implement three trade agreements	YES

CQ Vote Studies (while House member)

	PARTY UNITY		PRESIDENTIAL SUPPORT	
	SUPPORT	OPPOSE	SUPPORT	OPPOSE
2012	96%	4%	24%	76%
2011	95%	5%	19%	81%
2010	97%	3%	20%	80%
2009	97%	3%	8%	92%
2008	99%	1%	85%	15%
2007	95%	5%	89%	11%
2006	86%	14%	72%	28%
2005	91%	9%	74%	26%
2004	93%	7%	74%	26%
2003	90%	10%	70%	30%

Interest Groups (while House member)

	AFL-CIO	ADA	CCUS	ACU
2012	5%	20%	83%	100%
2011	7%	5%	75%	100%
2010	0%	10%	75%	96%
2009	0%	0%	71%	100%
2008	0%	0%	61%	100%
2007	4%	5%	68%	100%
2006	0%	20%	79%	100%
2005	7%	0%	70%	96%
2004	13%	15%	81%	96%
2003	13%	25%	67%	92%

Rep. Ann Kirkpatrick (D)

Capitol Office
225-3361
kirkpatrick.house.gov
330 Cannon Bldg. 20515-0301; fax 225-3462

Committees
Transportation & Infrastructure
Veterans' Affairs

Residence
Flagstaff

Born
March 24, 1950; McNary, Ariz.

Religion
Roman Catholic

Family
Husband, Roger Curley; two children

Education
U. of Arizona, B.A. 1972 (social studies), J.D. 1979

Career
Lawyer; county prosecutor; teacher

Political Highlights
Ariz. House, 2005-07; U.S. House, 2009-11; defeated for re-election to U.S. House, 2010

ELECTION RESULTS

2012 GENERAL		
Ann Kirkpatrick (D)	122,774	48.8%
Jonathan Paton (R)	113,594	45.2%
Kim Allen (LIBERT)	15,227	6.0%
2012 PRIMARY		
Ann Kirkpatrick (D)	33,831	63.7%
Wenona Benally Baldenegro (D)	19,247	36.3%

Previous Winning Percentages
2008 (56%)

Elected 2008; 2nd term

Did not serve 2011-13

The independent-minded Kirkpatrick in 2012 won back the 1st District seat that she lost two years earlier. Changes to the district's borders have made it friendlier to a Democrat, but Kirkpatrick still has incentives to seek ideological balance. The huge swath of territory she represents includes well-to-do Sedona environmentalists, conservative rural dwellers and a large, desperately poor Native American population.

Kirkpatrick, who had a moderate and relatively robust legislative record in her first term, enjoyed no honeymoon when she returned to Washington. In January 2013, the EPA proposed air pollution limits for the Navajo Generating Station, a coal-fired power plant located on the Navajo reservation in far northern Arizona, fewer than 20 miles from the Grand Canyon. The EPA said the plant is one of the largest sources of nitrogen oxide emissions in the country and is the cause of a perpetual haze that hangs over the canyon, as well as a spate of serious respiratory problems.

But the plant is a major employer of American Indians and a source of revenue for area tribes. It powers the disbursement of water throughout the state. Kirkpatrick was in a fix: Part of her 2012 campaign platform was encouraging the development of newer, cleaner power sources, which sometimes have trouble competing with less-expensive electricity from coal.

She declined to endorse or oppose the EPA's move and said she hoped the Obama administration would consider the views of all stakeholders. "It's about finding the right balance," she said. "We want clean air, but the Navajo Generating Station is unique in that it's on tribal land in an area that's got no other jobs. We don't want to do anything to set back the fragile economy. And we don't want to make water more expensive for farmers in the district. It's a complicated issue."

She faced lots of complicated issues in the 111th Congress (2009-10), especially regarding government regulation. Kirkpatrick was one of 44 House Democrats to oppose a 2009 bill to establish a cap-and-trade system to regulate greenhouse gases, and one of seven opposing new regulation of cigarettes.

In 2010 she was one of 19 House Democrats to vote against the financial regulatory overhaul known as Dodd-Frank. "It didn't make sense to me that we should be adding a new layer of regulation," she said. "I'm really concerned about a new level of bureaucracy. As a former prosecutor, I want to enforce the laws we already have on the books."

Still, Kirkpatrick was unusually successful for a freshman member in getting her colleagues to enact laws to advance the interests of her district. In collaboration with Republican Sen. John McCain, she led the effort to repeal a law known as the "Bennett Freeze," which was an impediment to economic growth on Native American reservations that prevented even simple expansion of the use of electricity and running water.

As member of the Veterans' Affairs Committee in her first term, she also shepherded legislation to increase cost-of-living adjustments for disabled veterans and to boost federal-housing assistance for disabled veterans who are also Native Americans. Kirkpatrick is back on that panel and is the top Democrat on its oversight subcommittee.

At the start of the 113th Congress (2013-14) she was the only Arizonan on the Transportation and Infrastructure Committee. A lot of Arizona's surface water is found in her district, and Kirkpatrick is on the Water Resources and Environment Subcommittee. She's also on the highways subcommittee and plans to work on the proposed Interstate 11 between Phoenix and Las Vegas.

Kirkpatrick was born on the Fort Apache Indian Reservation — her father ran a general store in Whiteriver and her mother taught school. Kirkpatrick says the first words she uttered as a child were in Apache.

After graduating from the University of Arizona, she became a substitute teacher to supplement the income of her family, which was struggling after the death of her father during her junior year. She later obtained a law degree and worked as a county prosecutor and as the city attorney for Sedona. Kirkpatrick eventually opened her own firm.

She bested a Native American candidate to win a seat in the Arizona House in 2004, and she was re-elected in 2006. Before resigning to seek a seat in the U.S. House, she proved an effective advocate for increased government support for infrastructure development on the reservations.

When Kirkpatrick ran for the House in 2008, she was seeking an open seat. Republican Rep. Rick Renzi, who was indicted in 2008 for his role in a land deal that allegedly enriched a former business partner, wasn't seeking re-election. (Renzi's case was not resolved as of early 2013.) She took 47 percent of the vote in a four-way primary, then easily defeated Republican mining lobbyist Sydney Hay in November.

Her legislative successes during the 111th didn't insulate Kirkpatrick from the surge in Republicans' popularity in 2010. Kirkpatrick annoyed some constituents with her support for the 2009 stimulus law and the 2010 health care overhaul. Dentist Paul Gosar, a political novice backed by the tea party movement, was her Republican opponent in 2010. Kirkpatrick had trouble explaining some of her positions, especially as they contrasted with her statements on the campaign trail. Her vote against the cap-and-trade bill was a prime example, since she had mentioned her concern about global warming during her 2008 run. Gosar won by 6 points, and Kirkpatrick almost immediately began raising funds for a rematch.

The new district lines announced for the 2012 race played to her advantage, as they cut out the heavily Republican Yavapai County. Kirkpatrick caught another break when Gosar decided to run for re-election in the 4th District, which had become more friendly to a Republican candidate.

Jonathan Paton, a former state senator from the district's far southern reaches, won the GOP nomination. Kirkpatrick criticized Paton for his work earlier in his career as a lobbyist for the payday lending industry. Paton tried to tar Kirkpatrick with her votes on the stimulus and health care laws. Kirkpatrick reclaimed her seat, but she won less than 49 percent of the vote — and a Libertarian candidate may have siphoned off votes that would have propelled her Republican opponent to victory.

Gosar also won, and Kirkpatrick said they have "put politics aside" to work together for their state.

CQ Vote Studies

	PARTY UNITY		PRESIDENTIAL SUPPORT	
	SUPPORT	OPPOSE	SUPPORT	OPPOSE
2010	67%	33%	80%	20%
2009	74%	26%	67%	33%

Interest Groups

	AFL-CIO	ADA	CCUS	ACU
2010	83%	60%	57%	36%
2009	76%	60%	67%	36%

Arizona 1

North and east — Flagstaff; southern Phoenix suburbs

With a footprint the size of Pennsylvania, the 1st District covers nearly two-thirds of Arizona from the Utah border to just north of Tucson. Encompassing Navajo, Hopi Mesas and Zuni Pueblo tribes, among others, the 1st hosts the nation's largest American Indian population. Twenty-three percent of the population is Native American and another 20 percent is Hispanic.

Flagstaff, the largest city in the district, is a center for scientific research, including the U.S. Geological Survey's Flagstaff Science Campus, Lowell Observatory's Discovery Channel Telescope and federal observatories, all of which benefit from the city's commitment to maintaining the dark skies needed for astronomy. It also draws more than 5 million visitors annually thanks to its proximity to Grand Canyon National Park. Northern Arizona University, Flagstaff's largest employer, allows Olympic hopefuls and professional sports teams to use its facilities for altitude training.

Scenic Sedona hosts luxury resorts, art galleries and retirement communities. An hour east of Phoenix, retirees have joined environmentalists to fight proposed copper mining near the border with the 4th in the southeastern corner of Tonto National Forest.

The district takes in most of the Navajo Nation, including the Canyon de Chelly National Monument, which brings tourism revenue to the tribe. On the heavily forested San Carlos Apache Reservation, logging and gaming are significant economic drivers. Still, tribal rates of unemployment and poverty sit significantly higher than national averages, and the population is plagued by alcoholism and crime.

Democrats have an edge in voter registration, and many residents focus on environmental issues. In the 1st, though, nearly one-third of voters do not register with either major party and Republican Mitt Romney took a 2-percentage-point win in the 2012 presidential election. The U.S. House seat changed party hands in each of the last four races.

Major Industry

Tourism, government, mining, agriculture

Cities

Flagstaff, Casa Grande, Maricopa

Notable

The Petrified Forest National Park contains dinosaur fossils and the nation's largest deposits of petrified wood.

Rep. Ron Barber (D)

Capitol Office
225-2542
barber.house.gov
1029 Longworth Bldg. 20515-0308; fax 225-0378

Committees
Armed Services
Homeland Security
Small Business

Residence
Tucson

Born
Aug. 25, 1945; Wakefield, United Kingdom

Religion
Roman Catholic

Family
Wife, Nancy Barber; two children

Education
U. of Arizona, B.A. 1967 (government)

Career
Congressional district aide; toy store owner; state disability program official; county Head Start director

Political Highlights
No previous office

ELECTION RESULTS

2012 GENERAL		
Ron Barber (D)	147,336	50.4%
Martha E. McSally (R)	144,884	49.6%
2012 PRIMARY		
Ron Barber (D)	51,206	82.0%
Matt Heinz (D)	11,213	18.0%
2012 SPECIAL		
Ron Barber (D)	111,204	52.2%
Jesse Kelly (R)	96,465	45.3%
Charlie Manolakis (GREEN)	4,869	2.3%

Elected 2012; 1st full term

A tragic event was the catalyst for Barber's ascent from congressional aide to congressman.

Barber was the district director for Democratic Rep. Gabrielle Giffords, and he was at a January 2011 constituent event in suburban Tucson when a mentally unstable gunman opened fire. Giffords suffered the head injury that was the impetus for her January 2012 resignation. Barber was shot several times and spent months recovering from his injuries, which included loss of movement in his left leg.

With Giffords' blessing, he was elected as her replacement for the last quarter of the 112th Congress (2011-12). Stepping into turbulent debates on federal spending, Barber sought to offer peace. "I want to go to Congress to be as bipartisan as I can possibly be," he said — a sentiment suited to both his district, which is closely divided between Republicans and Democrats, and the moderate style of his former boss.

His career has long had an element of public service. Barber held jobs with Head Start and then the Arizona Division of Developmental Disabilities. He also spent years operating a toy store with his wife, who acts as a postpartum doula. "If you're fortunate enough to have an education, even if you don't, just to be alive, and to live a life, one of the most important responsibilities that you can carry out is to serve your community," he said.

Barber became a full-time district director for Giffords after the 2006 election; he had volunteered for her campaign before that. After the 2011 shooting, Barber started a nonprofit organization that seeks to advance civility and respect by tackling issues such as bullying in schools.

Barber has committee assignments that, in many instances, do not lend themselves to drastically partisan debates. He joined the Armed Services and Homeland Security panels when he first came to the House, and he picked up a seat on the Small Business Committee in the 113th Congress (2013-14).

Born in Wakefield in the United Kingdom, Barber was raised on the Davis-Monthan Air Force Base by his stepfather. That base is in now in his district, and, together with the Army's Fort Huachuca, it accounts for a significant portion of the region's economy. Barber works to protect both installations on the Armed Services Committee. He worries that across-the-board cuts to defense budgets could indiscriminately harm their operations.

On the Homeland Security Committee, he's the top Democrat on the Oversight and Management Efficiency panel. Barber's district borders Mexico, and he wants to strengthen border security through greater manpower and the use of more high-tech devices, including unmanned aerial vehicles. A Government Accountability Office study pinpointing Border Patrol weaknesses will drive his committee work, he says.

He also supports the deployment of National Guard troops at the border: "The guard's presence allows the Border Patrol to focus on its mission of apprehending those who enter the United States illegally and keep those who live and work near the border safe," he said.

A second tragic event sketched out another of his legislative priorities. In December 2012, the shooting at Sandy Hook Elementary School in Connecticut prompted debate on gun-related violence. Barber says he supports Second Amendment rights but also restrictions on the availability of certain weapons and related hardware. He has been more outspoken, however, on the treatment of mental illness.

Barber is a vice chairman of a congressional task force on gun violence prevention. In a January 2013 letter to Vice President Joseph R. Biden Jr., Barber laid out his case: "I approach the issue of gun violence prevention in several ways: as a supporter of the Second Amendment, as a survivor of a mass shooting and as a grandfather," he said. "I have worked for 32 years with individuals living with mental illness and know the struggles they face, along with their families, to fight stigma and get the treatment they need."

He introduced a bill to further authorize state grants for mental health training. During the sentencing for the Tucson shooter, Jared Lee Loughner, in November 2012, Barber called for more awareness of mental illness: "We know for a fact that 90 percent of people with a mental illness never commit a violent act," he said. "In your case, Mr. Loughner, I believe that your behaviors preceding the shooting should have alerted others that you needed mental health treatment."

Given his district's makeup, Barber is unlikely to be a lock-step Democratic vote. He does trend liberal on social issues — he doesn't want to block federal funding for Planned Parenthood, for example, even though he is Roman Catholic. On fiscal issues, he opposed the fiscal 2013 budget put forth by House Republicans, and during his special-election campaign he said he would "responsibly adjust" Medicare and Medicaid. He supported the January 2013 measure extending lower tax rates only for income under $400,000.

After Giffords announced that she would resign from the House, she directly asked Barber to run in the June 2012 special election to replace her in the 8th District. Media and money were drawn to the campaign: There was the emotional story of filling "Gabby's seat." Both Republicans and Democrats tried to use the campaign as a barometer for the general elections in November.

Iraq War veteran Jesse Kelly, who opposed Giffords in 2010, won the Republican nomination. More than $2 million was spent on the race, much in the form of television ads, by House campaign committees and outside political groups. Giffords came out toward the end of campaigning to support Barber, who won by 7 points.

He immediately turned his attention to winning again in November, only this time in the new 2nd District. Created for the 2012 congressional map, it contains most of the old 8th District but no longer includes any of Santa Cruz County.

Kelly announced that he wouldn't challenge Barber again, but Martha E. McSally emerged as a top-notch GOP candidate. An Air Force combat pilot with a master's degree from Harvard, she proved a tough campaigner.

The results were too close to declare a winner on Election Day, and McSally attended orientation for incoming members on Capitol Hill as provisional ballots were counted. The race was finally called for Barber after a week and a half. He won by about 2,400 votes.

Key Votes

2012	
Cite Attorney General Eric H. Holder Jr. for contempt of Congress	NO
Create a visa program for foreign graduates in high-tech fields	+
Extend most Bush-era income tax rates while allowing rates for top-bracket earners to rise (Jan. 1, 2013)	YES

CQ Vote Studies

	PARTY UNITY		PRESIDENTIAL SUPPORT	
	SUPPORT	OPPOSE	SUPPORT	OPPOSE
2012	88%	12%	70%	30%

Interest Groups

	AFL-CIO	ADA	CCUS	ACU
2012	100%		40%	

Arizona 2

Southeast — part of Tucson

Nestled in the state's southeastern corner, the 2nd is home to independent-minded swing voters. Formerly designated the 8th District, it begins in the eastern half of Tucson, Arizona's second-largest city, then stretches through the giant cacti of Saguaro National Park and sparsely populated desert grasslands and mountain ranges of Cochise County to the New Mexico border. The population, concentrated in Pima County near Tucson, is one-fourth Hispanic and majority white.

Most of Tucson's economic engines — the University of Arizona, the airport and Raytheon Missile Systems — are in the adjacent 3rd. The 2nd hosts Davis-Monthan Air Force Base, powered in part by a solar array, and its active-duty and civilian workforces. Health care facilities support the city's military retirees. The 2nd also captures part of the city's high-tech sector.

The 2nd follows suburban Tucson's growth north toward Casas Adobes and Catalina Foothills. The district also includes Sahuarita to the south of Tucson down Interstate 19, where population increased six-fold between 2000 and 2010. Large subdivisions have drawn families seeking more space, but planners and environmentalists criticize the sprawl as a strain on resources.

Tourism is important for much of the district, including Sierra Vista, which attracts nature lovers with its large hummingbird population. Bisbee, a former mining town, is now a liberal artists' mecca and hub for the state's gay and lesbian community.

Concerns about the federal government's handling of illegal immigration helped the GOP edge out Democrats in Cochise County's voter rolls within the past decade. Law enforcement officials here work to secure more than 80 miles of the Mexico border from drug trafficking and human smuggling.

Major Industry
Military, tourism, health care, mining, ranching

Military Bases
Davis-Monthan Air Force Base, 6,624 military, 2,400 civilian (2012), Fort Huachuca (Army), 3,197 military, 3,113 civilian (2010)

Cities
Tucson (pt.), Casas Adobes (unincorporated), Catalina Foothills

Notable
Tucson's annual Gem and Mineral Show is the largest in the world.

Rep. Raúl M. Grijalva (D)

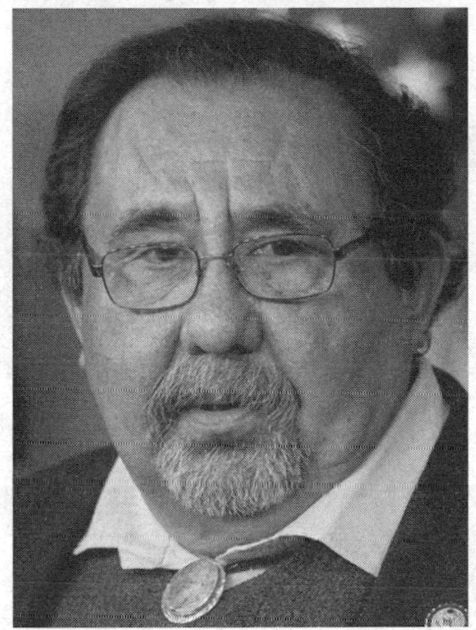

Capitol Office
225-2435
grijalva.house.gov
1511 Longworth Bldg. 20515-0307; fax 225-1541

Committees
Education & the Workforce
Natural Resources

Residence
Tucson

Born
Feb. 19, 1948; Tucson, Ariz.

Religion
Roman Catholic

Family
Wife, Mona Grijalva; three children

Education
U. of Arizona, B.A. 1987 (sociology)

Career
University dean; community center director

Political Highlights
Candidate for Tucson Unified School District Governing Board, 1972; Tucson Unified School District Governing Board, 1974-86; Pima County Board of Supervisors, 1989-2002 (chairman, 1997, 2001-02)

ELECTION RESULTS

2012 GENERAL		
Raúl M. Grijalva (D)	98,468	58.4%
Gabriela Saucedo Mercer (R)	62,663	37.1%
Blanca Guerra (LIBERT)	7,567	4.5%
2012 PRIMARY		
Raúl M. Grijalva (D)	24,044	65.6%
Amanda Aguirre (D)	9,484	25.9%
Manny Arreguin (D)	3,105	8.5%
2010 GENERAL		
Raúl M. Grijalva (D)	79,935	50.2%
Ruth McClung (R)	70,385	44.2%
Harley Meyer (I)	4,506	2.8%
George Keane (LIBERT)	4,318	2.7%

Previous Winning Percentages
2008 (63%); 2006 (61%); 2004 (62%); 2002 (59%)

Elected 2002; 6th term

Grijalva's experiences in local politics, activism and social work have shaped his starkly liberal thinking on education, health care and the environment. His efforts on those topics can be overshadowed, however, by his impassioned demands on immigration.

The son of a Mexican immigrant, Grijalva (gree-HAHL-va) spent a dozen years on a school board and another dozen in county government. He also has worked as the director of a community center. He sees those jobs as especially relevant to his current work in Congress. "I think the mantra now is, 'I'm a businessman, so therefore I know how to run something,'" he said in 2012. "Government is not a business."

The 113th Congress (2013-14) marks his third term as co-chairman of the Congressional Progressive Caucus, the group of the most-liberal members of the House. Grijalva embraces "the added responsibility" of representing the Latino population as a Hispanic lawmaker, but he resents what he thinks is "an initial effort to pigeonhole" minority members as being concerned only with civil rights issues. For example, the environmental community used to question his interest in their causes, he says.

They're probably past their doubts. Grijalva, who sits on the Natural Resources Committee, has fought GOP attempts to roll back environmental restrictions and whittle public lands in the West. He first got involved with environmental issues in the Tucson area after solvent waste was dumped in the sewer system and leaked into an aquifer. The neighborhood where the contamination occurred — and where he has lived his whole life — was predominately Latino. "Suddenly the link became real obvious to me, about clean air, water, and how it's so important to preserve areas with historical, cultural and air quality issues," he said. "I started out that this is an issue of justice and civil rights — and it was — but it was much more than that."

As the top Democrat on the Public Lands and Environmental Regulations Subcommittee, Grijalva rejects the notion that the government owns and underutilizes too much land: "The idea that by privatizing our federal lands and our public lands, that that's going to be the magic panacea that's going to turn the environment around, stop unemployment, make us energy independent and raise the living standard for all Americans ... it's a false premise."

He wants a rewrite of a 19th-century mining law that allows companies to extract resources from federal lands without having to pay royalties. He also has fought a GOP push to preserve uranium mining on land near the Grand Canyon. "Cities all across the Southwest ... rely on the Colorado River watershed for their water supply," Grijalva said in 2012. "What would it mean for our national security if 25 million people did not have access to clean water?"

If the opportunity arises, Grijalva wants to become the top Democrat on the full committee. He and Peter A. DeFazio of Oregon are the top contenders to succeed Edward J. Markey of Massachusetts, should Markey win a special election for a Senate seat in June 2013.

Grijalva also sits on the Education and the Workforce Committee. He urges robust federal involvement in education, from preschool through Pell grants for college students. The cause that introduced him to education policy, he says, was making sure poor kids and Latinos had equal access to quality public education. During a 2007 reauthorization of the Head Start program, he worked to ensure funding to help children with limited English proficiency and children from American Indian and migrant worker families.

Grijalva frequently engages in passionate debate with Republicans, which he says he enjoys. "It's not so much about persuading each other — because here it's numbers that count more than persuasion, unfortunately — it's about coexisting," he said. "I'm fine with coexisting."

He'll sometimes get passionate with Democrats as well, when they aren't as liberal as he would like. Grijalva was disappointed that his party's 2010 health care law did not create a government-run "public option" insurance plan. He resigned himself to the realities of legislative sausage-making and supported the bill: "It became an issue of getting something done."

But he can be most passionate about immigration. In April 2010, Grijalva called for an economic boycott of his own state after Republican Gov. Jan Brewer signed into law a measure empowering law enforcement officers to check the immigration status of those they have detained for other suspected offenses — such as a traffic violation.

Constituent anger at Grijalva was palpable; that November, he had his worst showing in a House race. But he says the anger subsided — not because of any contrition on his part, but as people appreciated "the reality of what that law meant." The Supreme Court struck down much of the law in 2012, but upheld the portion on checking immigration status. Grijalva still took a victory lap, writing in the Yuma Sun that Brewer and other people who criticized him should "apologize to the state and the country for the damage they've done."

Grijalva wants a codified path to citizenship for those who come to the United States either illegally or on a guest worker program. Anything less risks creating a "permanent, hidden subclass of people in our country without any chance for hope," he said.

His father came to the United States with the infamous "bracero" labor program, under which migrant Mexican workers flocked to low-wage farm jobs created by World War II labor shortages. He then married a U.S. citizen.

Grijalva attended the University of Arizona, but quit to get married. He became a social worker and community activist, then ran for the Tucson school board in 1972 and was "embarrassingly" defeated. In his second attempt in 1974, he followed through with voter ID work and door-to-door campaigning. His time on the Pima County Board of Supervisors began in 1989. While in local government, he frequently advised young people to stay in school. To set an example, he earned the nine credit hours he needed to complete his sociology degree, graduating from college at 39.

When redistricting created a new seat in southern Arizona in 2002, Grijalva jumped into a crowded primary race. In the general election, the district's Hispanic-majority makeup ensured Grijalva's victory. He enjoyed easy re-elections until Republican Ruth McClung, a physicist, held him to 50 percent of the vote in 2010. Remapping for 2012 shrank and renumbered his district, and he scored an easy 21-point victory.

Key Votes

2012	
Extend a Social Security payroll tax cut and unemployment benefits	YES
Ease securities rules to expand small-business access to capital	NO
Extend for one year subsidized student loan interest rates financed by a cut in health care spending	NO
Cite Attorney General Eric H. Holder Jr. for contempt of Congress	?
Create a visa program for foreign graduates in high-tech fields	NO
Extend most Bush-era income tax rates while allowing rates for top-bracket earners to rise (Jan. 1, 2013)	YES
2011	
Strike funding for F-35 alternative engine	YES
Prevent EPA from regulating greenhouse gas emissions to address climate change	NO
Extend certain provisions of Patriot Act for four years	NO
Declare opposition to use of ground troops in Libya	NO
Overhaul patent law	NO
Pass compromise debt limit increase plan and establish future spending limits	NO
Allow consideration of measures to implement three trade agreements	?

CQ Vote Studies

	PARTY UNITY		PRESIDENTIAL SUPPORT	
	SUPPORT	OPPOSE	SUPPORT	OPPOSE
2012	98%	2%	88%	12%
2011	97%	3%	78%	22%
2010	96%	4%	80%	20%
2009	99%	1%	93%	7%
2008	99%	1%	10%	90%

Interest Groups

	AFL-CIO	ADA	CCUS	ACU
2012	95%	100%	17%	0%
2011	100%	95%	13%	8%
2010	92%	90%	13%	0%
2009	100%	100%	33%	0%
2008	100%	100%	44%	8%

Arizona 3

South; western Phoenix suburbs

Stretching from Yuma County's San Luis in the state's southwestern corner into the desert beyond Nogales, the 3rd tracks more than 300 miles of the Mexico border. The district only crosses north of Interstate 8 in Maricopa County, where it reaches some western Phoenix suburbs.

North of Nogales, Tucson is the district's population hub and economic engine, fueled by the University of Arizona and Raytheon Missile Systems. Air Force Reserve F-16s and planes full of tourists land at Tucson International Airport. Copper and gold mining operations have their headquarters here, and open-pit mines carve into the land south of the city.

Water from the Colorado River irrigates desert-like soil in Yuma County. Lettuce, wheat and dates are top crops. Many of the tens of thousands of seasonal farmworkers who work the harvest cross the border daily. Nogales is another major crossing, where trains and trucks account for nearly $20 billion in annual two-way trade between Mexico and the U.S. It also serves as an entry point for illegal traffic of drugs and humans.

The Barry M. Goldwater Range offers air-to-ground combat training. Operations are occasionally interrupted by illegal immigrants and drug smugglers attempting to cross the Sonoran Desert. Decennial redistricting moved another large desert training center, the Army's Yuma Proving Ground, as well as Marine Corps Air Station Yuma, to the 4th District.

The district leans Democratic, with Pima and Santa Cruz counties' liberal populations countering conservative sentiments in Yuma and Maricopa counties. In the 2012 Senate race, Republican Jeff Flake eked out a win in Yuma County, while Democrat Richard Carmona bested him in Pima.

More than 37,000 American Indians reside in the 3rd, the second-largest population among Arizona districts. Many are members of the Tohono O'odham Nation. One quarter of the voters in this Hispanic-majority district live in southern and western Tucson (shared with the 2nd).

Major Industry

Agriculture, higher education, mining, aviation

Cities

Phoenix (pt.), Tucson (pt.), Avondale (pt.), Goodyear (pt.), Buckeye (pt.)

Notable

Somerton hosts Arizona's largest tamale festival.

Rep. Paul Gosar (R)

Capitol Office
225 2315
gosar.house.gov
504 Cannon Bldg. 20515-0301; fax 226-9739

Committees
Natural Resources
Oversight & Government Reform

Residence
Prescott

Born
Nov. 27, 1958, Rock Springs, Wyo.

Religion
Roman Catholic

Family
Wife, Maude Gosar; three children

Education
Creighton U., B.S. 1981 (biology), D.D.S. 1985

Career
Dentist

Political Highlights
No previous office

ELECTION RESULTS

2012 GENERAL		
Paul Gosar (R)	162,907	66.8%
Johnnie Robinson (D)	69,154	28.4%
Joe Pamelia (LIBERT)	9,306	3.8%
2012 PRIMARY		
Paul Gosar (R)	40,033	51.3%
Ron Gould (R)	24,617	31.6%
Rick Murphy (R)	13,315	17.1%
2010 GENERAL		
Paul Gosar (R)	112,816	49.7%
Ann Kirkpatrick (D)	99,233	43.7%
Nicole Patti (LIBERT)	14,869	6.6%

Elected 2010; 2nd term

Gosar entered Congress under the auspices of the tea party, then planted his flag in the border and land-use issues important to Arizona. He thinks of himself as a constitutionalist, but he tries to find ways to make that philosophy palatable to the public. "We may have the right message, but we're very poor at our marketing," he says.

The stereotypical description of a tea party politician is actually well-suited to Gosar (go-SAR). He was a successful professional who never held public office. Concern for the direction of the nation, fueled in part by the perceived overreach of a Democrat-controlled Congress, propelled him into a campaign for a House seat in 2010. He says his political style is rooted in his career as a dentist, which required him to listen carefully before solving a problem.

In geographic terms, Gosar already has represented most of Arizona. He was first elected in the rural 1st District, which covered most of northeast Arizona, including both sides of the Grand Canyon and several national forests. He switched to the new 4th District in the 113th Congress (2013-14), which includes almost the entire western border of the state.

Mining, forestry and the use of federal land are hot topics in those regions, and Gosar sits on the Natural Resources Committee. He has a personal affinity for the land. His father was a geologist, and Gosar, the first of 10 children, likes to "play in the dirt" in his spare time, messing around with tractors and in the garden. "As a dentist, I would trade services for dirt and rocks. I built Mt. Gosar at my house," he said.

He won a legislative victory when President Barack Obama signed his 2011 bill to settle jurisdictional disputes over federal management of the C.C. Cragin Dam in central Arizona.

Like most Republicans, Gosar argues that government bureaucracy is choking economic activity on public lands, with little benefit to the public. "What's happening right now in our forests is insanity," he said in 2011. Gosar suggests that a more-permissive approach to tree thinning will both prevent forest fires and create private sector lumber jobs.

The House passed Gosar's 2011 bill to allow the Resolution Copper Co. to swap some of its land holdings for federal property near Superior, which could become the largest copper mine in the country. GOP lawmakers first proposed the land swap in 2005, and John McCain has been the standard-bearer in the Senate. Environmentalists have said mining operations could deplete or contaminate area water supplies, and some Apache leaders have called the area sacred. Gosar says it's a "stimulus" plan without the need for federal funds. He teamed with Democratic Rep. Ann Kirkpatrick to reintroduce the bill in 2013.

Gosar supports an "all of the above" energy strategy. He voted for several measures to expand offshore drilling and is the lead sponsor of a bipartisan measure to speed up the permitting process for renewable-energy projects on federal land — Arizona's deserts are considered good spots for solar arrays. Gosar has frowned on the EPA's regulatory agenda. A 2012 package of coal-related measures included his provisions to limit EPA regulation of power facilities on tribal lands (including the Navajo Generating Station in his state). The Senate didn't take up the bill.

Gosar has used the Oversight and Government Reform Committee as his gateway to border issues. He supported Arizona's efforts to enforce federal immigration law, though portions of the state law that set that effort in motion were struck down by the Supreme Court in 2012. When President Barack Obama issued a policy directive in June 2012 to stop the deportation of some immigrants brought to the country illegally as children, Gosar called it an "unconstitutional, de facto amnesty program."

He was heavily involved in the Oversight investigation of Fast and Furious, a Justice Department gun-walking operation on the Mexican border that was embroiled in controversy — weapons meant to be tracked by the government were used to kill a Border Patrol agent in December 2010. In a mostly partisan vote, the House found Attorney General Eric H. Holder Jr. in contempt of Congress for declining to turn over some documents requested by investigators. Gosar kept pressing his own resolution to express no confidence in Holder, and in January 2013 he again introduced a resolution requesting Holder's resignation.

Gosar's constitutionalist beliefs make him sympathetic to limited government and, in turn, cost-cutting. He did support some compromise deficit reduction measures, such as a fiscal 2011 spending deal and an August 2011 package that cut spending and raised the federal debt limit. He did not back a January 2013 measure to permanently extend lower tax rates on income under $400,000. Most House Republicans couldn't swallow the package's lack of spending cuts.

Gosar had been active in the professional dental community, holding various chairmanships and association posts. He said patients and his family encouraged him to run for the House in 2010, and he was also motivated by the 2010 health care law.

The health care system is "in the process of disintegrating," he said, and he wants a system that incorporates more patient responsibility. Gosar has celiac disease, and "if I don't take care of myself, you shouldn't have to share that," he said. "It's my burden."

In 2010, Gosar won a crowded GOP primary, with help from an endorsement by former Alaska Gov. Sarah Palin. He then bested Kirkpatrick, a one-term Democrat, taking just under 50 percent of the vote.

Redistricting for the 2012 election made the 1st District more Democrat-friendly, and Kirkpatrick was hoping for a rematch. Gosar instead switched to the more conservative 4th District (which has about 200,000 of his old constituents), where the primary election would be his biggest challenge.

Some tea party groups had soured on Gosar since 2010, feeling that he was too willing to accept compromises regarding fiscal restraint. Activists were incensed by Gosar's comments on political strategy at a Washington event: "If all you do is stand for the Constitution, you will lose," he said. The Club for Growth backed state Sen. Ron Gould. But Gosar ran a solid campaign and won by almost 20 points. He then easily won the general election.

Meanwhile, Kirkpatrick returned to the House with a narrow victory.

Key Votes

2012	
Extend a Social Security payroll tax cut and unemployment benefits	?
Ease securities rules to expand small-business access to capital	YES
Extend for one year subsidized student loan interest rates financed by a cut in health care spending	NO
Cite Attorney General Eric H. Holder Jr. for contempt of Congress	YES
Create a visa program for foreign graduates in high-tech fields	YES
Extend most Bush-era income tax rates while allowing rates for top-bracket earners to rise (Jan. 1, 2013)	NO
2011	
Strike funding for F-35 alternative engine	YES
Prevent EPA from regulating greenhouse gas emissions to address climate change	YES
Extend certain provisions of Patriot Act for four years	YES
Declare opposition to use of ground troops in Libya	YES
Overhaul patent law	NO
Pass compromise debt limit increase plan and establish future spending limits	YES
Allow consideration of measures to implement three trade agreements	YES

CQ Vote Studies

	PARTY UNITY		PRESIDENTIAL SUPPORT	
	SUPPORT	OPPOSE	SUPPORT	OPPOSE
2012	97%	3%	20%	80%
2011	95%	5%	22%	78%

Interest Groups

	AFL-CIO	ADA	CCUS	ACU
2012	17%	20%	75%	96%
2011	0%	5%	94%	84%

Arizona 4

West and central — Lake Havasu City, Prescott

Sliding down nearly the state's entire western border, the sprawling and newly redrawn 4th covers massive tracts of desert and veers east into Arizona's forests. The population is mostly white, rural conservatives but includes pockets of Hispanics on the outskirts of Yuma (most of which is in the 3rd) and American Indians living in some of the state's smaller reservations. Republicans hold a significant advantage in party registration.

Colorado River towns Bullhead City and Lake Havasu City are the largest cities in the district's western expanses. Casinos across the river in Nevada boost Bullhead City's economy. Farther south, irrigation along the Gila River gives the 4th a piece of Yuma County's vibrant agricultural economy. Illegal immigration is a hot issue for the suburbs of Yuma and the Mohawk Valley. The Army tests weapon systems at the Yuma Proving Ground.

Most of the district's land is in Mohave County, where mining is contentious. In 2012, the county sued the federal government over a ban on new uranium mining claims near the Grand Canyon, arguing the ban unfairly suppressed economic development in the region. High copper prices have led to renewed efforts to capture deposits around Kingman.

With an abundance of sunlight and strategic location between Las Vegas and Phoenix, there are plans for solar energy developments in the district. The dry, flat land has also attracted automotive testing facilities; Chrysler and Toyota have invested in proving grounds. At the district's eastern end near Gilbert and Chandler (in the 5th), the collapsing real estate market decimated the construction industry. Retail and health services now make up a large portion of the economy in Apache Junction and San Tan Valley.

Major Industry
Retail, agriculture, gaming

Military Bases
Marine Corps Air Station Yuma, 4,462 military, 220 civilian; Yuma Proving Ground (Army), 30 military, 450 civilian

Cities
San Tan Valley, Lake Havasu City, Apache Junction

Notable
Yuma Territorial Prison — a late-19th-century penitentiary — was once a high school, and then a shelter for railroad vagrants, and now is a state historic park.

Rep. Matt Salmon (R)

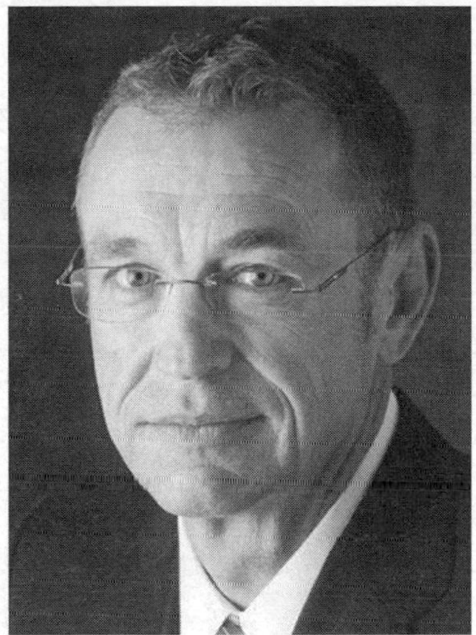

Capitol Office
225-2635
salmon.house.gov
2349 Rayburn Bldg. 20515-0601; fax 226-4386

Committees
Education & the Workforce
Foreign Affairs
(Western Hemisphere - Chairman)

Residence
Mesa

Born
Jan. 21, 1958; Salt Lake City, Utah

Religion
Mormon

Family
Wife, Nancy; four children

Education
Arizona State U., B.A. 1981 (English literature); Brigham Young U., M.P.A. 1986

Career
Lobbyist; campaign aide; education nonprofit director; telecommunications company executive

Political Highlights
Ariz. Senate, 1991-95; U.S. House, 1995-2001; Republican nominee for governor, 2002; Ariz. Republican Party chairman, 2005-07

ELECTION RESULTS

2012 GENERAL		
Matt Salmon (R)	183,470	67.2%
Spencer Morgan (D)	89,589	32.8%
2012 PRIMARY		
Matt Salmon (R)	41,078	51.8%
Kirk Adams (R)	38,152	48.2%

Previous Winning Percentages
1998 (65%); 1996 (60%); 1994 (56%)

Elected 2012; 4th term

Also served 1995-2001

As one of the most conservative members of the 1994 Republican Revolution, Salmon keyed on balancing budgets, rethinking entitlement programs and shaping foreign policy. He then quit the House to satisfy a term limit pledge. Disputes over his favorite subjects intensified during his 12-year absence, and his plan for his second tour is to stick to his principles while taking a respectful approach to the opposition: "I think this place has gotten way too acrimonious," he says.

There are several lessons that Salmon says he gleaned from his first run in the House, when a Republican Congress clashed with the Clinton administration. "It's so easy to get sucked up into the process that you forget that lives hang in the balance," he said. "I think more than anything, I realize that we are here to do the bidding of people — it's not a game."

Many people decried the maneuvering of both parties in the 112th Congress (2011-12), and Salmon tried to artfully register his displeasure. During the initial roll call vote to choose the speaker of the 113th Congress (2013-14), he abstained — then changed to support a second term for John A. Boehner just before the vote was closed. Salmon said he was sending a message to the GOP Conference: "That we were sent here for a specific reason, and our duration will be very finite — two years — if we don't show the American people that we are going to rise above where past Congresses have been."

It wasn't the first time Salmon had ruffled a Republican speaker. He was one of the hard-core conservatives who led a coup in July 1997 against Newt Gingrich. After that failed, he sustained his public criticisms of Gingrich — who resigned in early 1999.

When Salmon is politely hostile, it's likely in relation to government spending; he plans to "fight with everything I got to try to balance the budget as quickly as we possibly can." Salmon likes plans by the conservative Republican Study Committee to balance the budget within five years. He wants a revamp of Social Security and Medicare that includes changes to eligibility ages.

For the 113th, Salmon has return engagements on two committees: Foreign Affairs and Education and the Workforce. On the former, he's the chairman of the Western Hemisphere Subcommittee.

Arizona's biggest trading partners are Canada and Mexico, so Salmon is particularly invested in those economic relationships. He has been impressed by Brazil's economic development efforts and wonders if the United States might want to emulate any parts of them. Similarly, he has spoken admiringly of pension privatization in Chile and a need to study it further — Salmon proposed a partial privatization of Social Security in the 1990s, inspired by Chile.

The stability of Mexico has a direct effect on immigration, security and a host of other things, so Salmon seeks ways to improve government transparency and the rule of law in the neighboring country. He worries that current Mexican leadership may be fumbling counternarcotics operations. "I am really concerned that the new administration is going to take at least a step, if not a few steps, backward, in how it deals with cartels," he said in 2013.

Salmon also has a keen interest in the Eastern Hemisphere. "From a global standpoint, I don't think there is a more important relationship that exists in the world today than that that exists between us and China," he said. Salmon was once a Mormon missionary in Taiwan, and he's fluent in Mandarin.

"I am a strong believer that increased trade with China is going to ultimately move them toward a more Western-friendly government, and also a government that moves more toward democratization," Salmon said. He doubts that

China will attack Taiwan, because Taiwan invests so heavily in China: "They aren't that stupid." After North Korea conducted an underground nuclear test in February 2013, Salmon called on China to pressure its neighbor to abandon that initiative.

Education and the Workforce has some jurisdiction over health care, which is another area of interest for Salmon. He wants greater coordination among cancer researchers, believing that the current grants process encourages recipients to hide their work from competitors. Salmon has also tried in the past to strengthen hospice programs, introducing a bill to give physicians wider authority in determining whether a Medicare beneficiary is eligible for hospice care.

Born in Salt Lake City, Salmon studied English literature at Arizona State University and got a master's in public administration from Brigham Young University. Many of his jobs outside politics have involved lobbying or government relations.

He won election to the state Senate in 1990 and eventually became assistant majority leader and chairman of the Rules Committee. In 1994, one-term Democrat Sam Coppersmith decided to give up his 1st District House seat and gamble on a Senate race, which he ultimately lost. Salmon entered the race to succeed him and bested four other Republicans in the primary. He won the general election by 17 points.

Salmon pledged to serve no more than three terms, and he says in hindsight that it hampered some of his work: "I was a lame duck from the first term." But he kept his word, and his departure cleared a path for Republican Jeff Flake to succeed him.

He stayed involved in politics. Salmon was the unsuccessful GOP candidate for governor in 2002 (losing to Janet Napolitano, who is now Homeland Security secretary). He chaired the state Republican Party for several years and worked as a lobbyist.

Flake announced early in the 2012 cycle that he was running for Arizona's open Senate seat. Salmon said he was encouraged by many people to run again, and that his wife's support tipped the balance. The new congressional map for 2012 made the district, now numbered the 5th, the most Republican one in Arizona, so the primary election was the one to watch.

Salmon faced former state House Speaker Kirk Adams, who had some stunning endorsements: Sarah Palin, Sen. John McCain, retiring Sen. Jon Kyl, Flake and Gingrich. Salmon had in his corner Gov. Jan Brewer and Maricopa County Sheriff Joe Arpaio, a well-known advocate for tough enforcement of immigration laws.

Salmon played up his experience and bested Adams by nearly 4 points, then took more than two-thirds of the vote in November.

Arizona 5

Southeast Phoenix suburbs — Gilbert

Shifted into the southeastern corner of Maricopa County, the renumbered 5th has large concentrations of Mormons, wealthy retirees and GOP voters. Many residents were drawn to the area east of Phoenix for the dry air and ample sunshine of its desert climate. Referred to by locals as the East Valley, the district includes part of Mesa and Chandler and all of Gilbert.

Close to 70 percent of Mesa's voting-age population lives in the 5th, many in master-planned luxury retirement communities such as Sunland Village, Leisure World and Fountain of the Sun. Mesa drew national attention in 2009 during the real estate crisis and foreclosure rates remain high, a trend that has sparked an unprecedented boom in rental demand. In an effort to revitalize blighted areas, Mesa's mayor launched iMesa, an online suggestion box oriented toward community improvements.

One of the district's largest employers is Boeing, which builds Apache helicopters at its Mesa plant. The Phoenix-Mesa Gateway Airport, formerly Williams Air Force Base, hosts more than 40 companies and accommodates foreign trade. Chandler is a major semiconductor and computing technology manufacturing hub.

Incorporated in 1920 as a hay-shipping community, Gilbert has maintained a small-town feel while evolving from its agricultural roots. Attracting a young, highly educated population, the town grew from around 5,000 in 1980 to more than 200,000 by 2010. Gilbert recently welcomed cancer treatment and research centers, making it a regional leader in the biomedical and life science industries, and leaders have implemented a five-year plan aimed at attracting more high-tech companies.

The conservative 5th is the most Republican-heavy district in the state, with a pro-business constituency that tends to be more moderate, and even libertarian, on social issues.

Major Industry

Manufacturing, health care, biomedicine

Cities

Mesa (pt.), Chandler (pt.), Gilbert, Queen Creek

Notable

Chandler's annual Ostrich Festival features ostrich races and ostrich burgers.

Rep. David Schweikert (R)

Capitol Office
225-2190
schweikert.house.gov
1205 Longworth Bldg. 20515-0305; fax 225-0096

Committees
Science, Space & Technology
Small Business
(Investigations, Oversight & Regulations - Chairman)

Residence
Fountain Hills

Born
March 3, 1962; Los Angeles, Calif.

Religion
Roman Catholic

Family
Wife, Joyce Schweikert

Education
Scottsdale Community College, A.A. 1985; Arizona State U., B.S. 1987 (real estate), M.B.A. 2005

Career
Real estate company owner; county deputy treasurer; financial consultant; Realtor

Political Highlights
Sought Republican nomination for Ariz. House, 1988; Ariz. House, 1991-95 (majority whip, 1993-94); sought Republican nomination for U.S. House, 1994; Ariz. State Board of Equalization chairman, 1995-2003; Maricopa County treasurer, 2004-06; Republican nominee for U.S. House, 2008

ELECTION RESULTS

2012 GENERAL		
David Schweikert (R)	179,706	61.3%
Matt Jette (D)	97,666	33.3%
Jack Anderson (LIBERT)	10,167	3.5%
Mark Salazar (GREEN)	5,637	1.9%
2012 PRIMARY		
David Schweikert (R)	41,821	51.5%
Ben Quayle (R)	39,414	48.5%
2010 GENERAL		
David Schweikert (R)	110,374	52.0%
Harry E. Mitchell (D)	91,749	43.2%
Nick Coons (LIBERT)	10,127	4.8%

Elected 2010; 2nd term

Schweikert is a fierce campaigner, a caffeine addict and a number-cruncher. His ardent fiscal conservatism puts him further to the right than most Republicans, and his unwillingness to vote against his principles has gotten him into trouble with party leaders.

Although he started his congressional career as a member of the GOP whip operation, he left the leadership team after breaking with his party on multiple near-party-line votes. And after the 2012 elections, leaders removed him from the Financial Services Committee for the 113th Congress (2013-14), reportedly as a punishment for too often dissenting from a majority of the GOP.

Schweikert and a few other conservative colleagues who were similarly punished did not take it in stride; they issued indignant press releases and demanded public explanations. It was the leading edge of intraparty strife that exploded during deficit reduction negotiations at the end of the 112th Congress (2011-12).

Bloody but unbowed, Schweikert intends to stay the course. A former deputy county treasurer, he often references his old standby calculator. He explains his views to constituents via multiple charts and slide shows on his website; he says he feels like a "one-man truth squad," translating data to the public and his colleagues. The Washington staff supporting this crusade is fueled by lattes and cappuccinos made by Schweikert.

"I have a personal fixation that you can't have honest discussions about numbers if people are going to make them up," he said. "I understand this is a clash of math and politics, and math often doesn't facilitate the political agenda. But at some point it's the truth."

He supported the budgets prepared by Wisconsin Republican Paul D. Ryan in the 112th and voted for a balanced-budget amendment to the Constitution. He wants the government to switch the dollar bill to a coin, believing it will save funds over the long term.

But he voted against all the major spending and deficit reduction bills of the 112th, saying they did not do enough to constrain federal debt.

During his one term on Financial Services, Schweikert looked at improving businesses' access to capital. By April 2012, two of Schweikert's bills were part of a larger package signed into law. The legislation aimed to scale down Securities and Exchange Commission regulations in an effort to make it easier for small businesses to go public and raise capital in the private market.

One of his measures increases from $5 million to $50 million the size of a public offering that triggers many SEC regulations. "The number of companies going public has just crashed," he said. "Some of that is because of the regulatory environment, and some of it is alternative accesses to capital, so we're just trying to provide an alternative out there." His other measure raises from 500 to 1,000 the number of shareholders for securities issuers that would trigger mandatory registration with the SEC.

He now studies small-business policy as member of the Small Business Committee. Schweikert chairs the Subcommittee on Investigations, Oversight and Regulations.

Schweikert introduced another bill as part of the effort to dismantle Fannie Mae and Freddie Mac. He and some fellow House Republicans oppose government involvement in the mortgage industry and blame those government-sponsored enterprises for causing the 2008 financial crisis. Schweikert proposed codifying current practices prohibiting the entities from engaging in new activities or businesses while in conservatorship or receivership.

But the very first measure Schweikert introduced on entering the House evinced his desire to improve clarity: He wants to prohibit the House from considering any bill that carries more than one subject. He also introduced legislation that would require agency hearings for any rule issued under the 2010 health care overhaul law to be open to broadcast on radio and television.

Immigration is a big topic in Arizona. Schweikert backs cracking down on companies that hire illegal immigrants, continuing construction of border fencing and beefing up other aspects of border security — including additional use of the unmanned Predator-B aircraft to patrol the border. The Science, Space and Technology Committee, on which Schweikert also sits, has some sway over the use of unmanned aircraft in U.S. airspace.

Born in California, Schweikert was adopted as an infant — a circumstance he says inspired his anti-abortion views. In Arizona, Schweikert's parents ran in the same social circles as Republican icon Sen. Barry Goldwater, whose family lived down the street.

Schweikert received a bachelor's from Arizona State University in real estate and an MBA in 2005. He has worked in real estate and ran a consulting business with his wife. When he was homesick during his first few months in Congress, his wife flew his dog, a wheaten terrier named Charlie, to Washington to keep him company.

Schweikert was a frequent candidate for public office before winning election to the House in 2010. He ran for the Arizona House in 1988, lost, then ran again in 1990 and won. He made his first congressional run in 1994, but lost in the primary. He tried again in 2008 and won the party's nomination, but lost to incumbent Democrat Harry E. Mitchell. In 2010, he beat out five other Republicans in the primary, and then rode the GOP wave that year to a 9-point win over Mitchell.

He spent a lot of his freshman term campaigning in his home state. Because of decennial redistricting, Schweikert was forced into a bitter primary against fellow freshman Rep. Ben Quayle.

The new district takes in of parts of Scottsdale and northeast Phoenix and Paradise Valley. Schweikert emphasized his "everyman" roots and Quayle's political family ties. (He is the son of Dan Quayle, a former vice president.) It was an expensive and personal race, and it was highly publicized. Schweikert won by 3 points.

Matt Jette, an adjunct business professor, won the Democratic primary, then changed his voter registration in September and announced that he was running as an independent. (He previously had run in the 2010 gubernatorial primary as a Republican.)

Schweikert had far superior campaign finances, and he swamped Jette in the Republican-leaning district.

Key Votes

2012	
Extend a Social Security payroll tax cut and unemployment benefits	YES
Ease securities rules to expand small-business access to capital	YES
Extend for one year subsidized student loan interest rates financed by a cut in health care spending	NO
Cite Attorney General Eric H. Holder Jr. for contempt of Congress	YES
Create a visa program for foreign graduates in high-tech fields	?
Extend most Bush-era income tax rates while allowing rates for top-bracket earners to rise (Jan. 1, 2013)	NO
2011	
Strike funding for F-35 alternative engine	YES
Prevent EPA from regulating greenhouse gas emissions to address climate change	YES
Extend certain provisions of Patriot Act for four years	YES
Declare opposition to use of ground troops in Libya	NO
Overhaul patent law	YES
Pass compromise debt limit increase plan and establish future spending limits	NO
Allow consideration of measures to implement three trade agreements	YES

CQ Vote Studies

	PARTY UNITY		PRESIDENTIAL SUPPORT	
	SUPPORT	OPPOSE	SUPPORT	OPPOSE
2012	97%	3%	25%	75%
2011	96%	4%	15%	85%

Interest Groups

	AFL-CIO	ADA	CCUS	ACU
2012	5%	20%	73%	100%
2011	0%	5%	94%	96%

Arizona 6

Northeast Phoenix suburbs — Scottsdale

Once known for cattle ranches and citrus farms, the 6th has evolved into a mecca for art dealers, young families and retirees. A plurality of the population lives in northeastern Phoenix suburbs. The arid district also includes mountain preserves, most of Scottsdale, Paradise Valley and Fountain Hills.

Hikers frequent the North Mountain Preserve in northern Phoenix for its trails, abundant wildflowers and cacti, especially on "Silent Sundays" when the park's roadways are closed to motorized vehicles. Large, master-planned communities have made the area surrounding the mountain a popular option for home buyers. Multi-family apartment complexes also are springing up in the area, which continues to rebound from the housing market crisis.

To the east, posh Paradise Valley is the home of affluent seniors. Many receive health care treatment at the nearby Mayo Clinic, a top employer for the district. The community is lushly landscaped and exclusively zoned for single-family residences.

Scottsdale (shared with the 9th) was settled by health-seekers in the early 1900s, who hoped desert air would cure their respiratory ailments, and later evolved into a destination for travelers seeking warm winter recreation. The popular WestWorld Equestrian Center offers year-round horseback riding. Downtown's weekly ArtWalk features displays from more than 100 galleries. Several Major League Baseball teams hold spring training in Scottsdale.

Land conservation is a priority in the northern tip of the district, where endangered plants and species live in the foothills of the Sonoran Desert. In Cave Creek, tourists are invited to learn about the archaeology of the desert, and explore via trail rides and biking.

The district — which was renumbered and made more compact during decennial remapping — is more than 75 percent white; Hispanics make up the largest minority population. The GOP has a nearly 20-point advantage over Democrats in voter registration; one-third sign up as independents.

Major Industry

Health care, tourism

Cities

Phoenix (pt.), Scottsdale, Fountain Hills

Notable

A memorial to Barry Goldwater is in Paradise Valley, where he retired after three decades of serving Arizona in the U.S. Senate.

Rep. Ed Pastor (D)

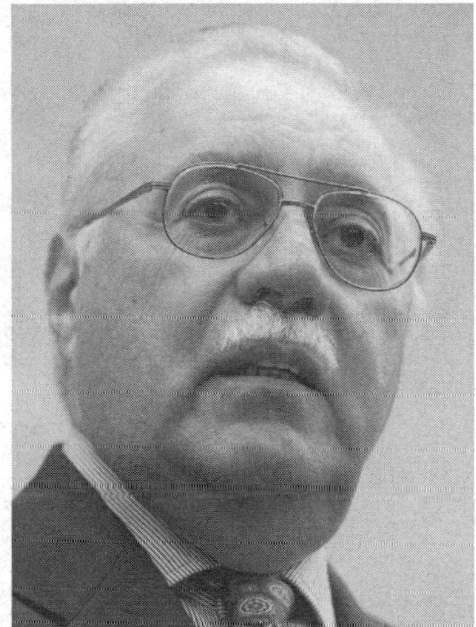

Capitol Office
225-4065
pastor.house.gov
2465 Rayburn Bldg. 20515-0304; fax 225-1655

Committees
Appropriations
Select Intelligence

Residence
Phoenix

Born
June 28, 1943; Claypool, Ariz.

Religion
Roman Catholic

Family
Wife, Verma Mendez Pastor; two children

Education
Arizona State U., B.A. 1966 (chemistry), J.D. 1974

Career
Teacher; gubernatorial aide; public policy consultant

Political Highlights
Maricopa County Board of Supervisors, 1977-91

ELECTION RESULTS

2012 GENERAL		
Ed Pastor (D)	104,489	81.7%
Joe Cobb (LIBERT)	23,338	18.3%
2012 PRIMARY		
Ed Pastor (D)	22,664	79.0%
Rebecca DeWitt (D)	6,013	21.0%
2010 GENERAL		
Ed Pastor (D)	61,524	66.9%
Janet Contreras (R)	25,300	27.5%
Joe Cobb (LIBERT)	2,718	3.0%
Rebecca DeWitt (GREEN)	2,365	2.6%

Previous Winning Percentages
2008 (72%); 2006 (73%); 2004 (70%); 2002 (67%); 2000 (69%); 1998 (68%); 1996 (65%); 1994 (62%); 1992 (66%); 1991 Special Election (56%)

Elected 1991; 11th full term

Pastor rarely pops up in the national news, seldom speaks on the House floor, doesn't send out many press releases and introduces few bills. He's an insider trusted by the Democratic leadership, and he values the leverage provided by his seat on the Appropriations Committee. "Where the money is is how policy is implemented," he says.

Pastor (pas-TORE) has been one of his party's chief deputy whips since 1999 and advises the leadership team on policy. He belongs to the Congressional Progressive Caucus, the bloc of the most-liberal House members, and he voted for all of President Barack Obama's major initiatives during the 111th Congress (2009-10), including the health care and financial regulatory overhauls. As a member of the minority party, he sees the whip job as "trying to see where your caucus members are, and hopefully being the loyal opposition."

He also has clout as an appropriator. In the 113th Congress (2013-14), Pastor gained a little more leverage as the ranking member of the Transportation-HUD Appropriations Subcommittee. It's his second run as the top Democrat on a spending panel — he had a taste of control in the 111th Congress when Indiana Democrat Peter J. Visclosky, caught up in an ethics investigation, temporarily handed over his Energy-Water gavel to Pastor. Managing a spending bill for the first time "was very satisfying," he said.

Pastor also sits on the Financial Services Appropriations Subcommittee, and Democratic leaders added him to the Intelligence Committee in 2013.

He has proved adept at directing federal money not just to his district, but to all of Arizona. Hundreds of millions of dollars have gone to his Phoenix-based district and the state over the years, especially for transportation and water projects.

Phoenix's rapid population growth is creating serious strains, Pastor said. "When I was a county supervisor, the biggest scare was that Phoenix was going to one day wake up and be like L.A.," he said. "We looked like L.A. in size, but we didn't in freeways." He helped get a federal commitment of $587 million for a light-rail project for the city that began operating in late 2008.

Pastor drew some unflattering attention in 2007. The Arizona Republic reported that he had directed $1 million in earmarks to a local community college scholarship program just months after his daughter was hired to direct it. But he said he had nothing to do with her hire: "Sometimes perception is worse than the actual conduct."

House Republicans imposed a ban on earmarked spending at the start of the 112th Congress (2011-12), so Pastor has sought other ways to aid the state. He helped beat back an attempt to allow uranium mining near the Grand Canyon, and he worked to secure grants for hospitals affected by cuts to the state's Medicaid program.

Pastor was the first the first Hispanic elected to Congress from Arizona, and he takes an interest in immigration law. He pushed unsuccessfully for comprehensive changes in the immigration system during the 110th (2007-08) and 111th Congresses.

Nowhere are tensions higher over illegal immigration than in Arizona, especially after the state enacted a tough anti-illegal-immigration measure in April 2010. Pastor harshly criticized the law, which empowers police to check the immigration status of people detained for some other reason. Several parts of the law were struck down by the Supreme Court in 2012, but the provision allowing the status checks was left standing.

Pastor has endorsed plans to combine increased border security with a guest-worker program and a path to citizenship for most illegal immigrants.

He has long held naturalization workshops in his district and staffed them with volunteers, including local lawyers who help legal immigrants apply for citizenship.

Pastor chaired the Congressional Hispanic Caucus in 1995 and 1996, and he opposed GOP efforts to roll back bilingual education and to make English the official language of the federal government. His wife, Verma, was a longtime director of bilingual programs for the Arizona Department of Education.

The oldest son of a copper miner, Pastor grew up in a working-class household about 85 miles east of Phoenix. Many of his peers were destined for jobs in the mines, but "both my parents were very determined that they were going to see their kids educated and get out of a mining town," he said. "My dad was a sucker for every encyclopedia salesman because he wanted his kids to have everything to read."

His father pushed him to deliver newspapers so that he could qualify for a college scholarship sponsored by the The Arizona Republic. Through high school, he delivered papers, while also lettering in football and baseball and being elected senior class president. He went to Arizona State University on a scholarship — he was the first member of his family to attend college — and worked in the mines during the summers to help pay expenses.

After graduating with a degree in chemistry and a teaching certificate, Pastor taught high school and worked nights helping adults learn to read and write. He got involved with a nonprofit group, The Guadalupe Organization Inc., and eventually became its deputy director.

During that time, Pastor got interested in the Chicano movement and its charismatic leader, Cesar Chavez. Believing that Mexican-Americans needed more decisive political leadership, he started volunteering for the campaigns of Mexican-American candidates in south Phoenix. He also went to law school.

After working for the successful gubernatorial campaign of Democrat Raul Castro in 1974, he became one of the governor's aides. Pastor was elected to the Maricopa County Board of Supervisors in 1976.

Democrat Morris K. Udall, who suffered from Parkinson's disease, resigned his House seat in May 1991. Two days later, Pastor quit his post on the board to campaign for the seat. "I said, the hell with it, let's go," he remembers.

In the five-person special primary, he prevailed by 5 points over the mayor of Tucson. His 11-point victory in the special election over a Yuma County supervisor remains his closest House election.

Pastor thought about running for the Senate in 2012 but ultimately opted for a re-election campaign in the 7th District — after congressional maps were redrawn following the 2010 census, it covered most of the same territory as his old 4th District. He had no Republican opponent.

Key Votes

2012	
Extend a Social Security payroll tax cut and unemployment benefits	YES
Ease securities rules to expand small-business access to capital	NO
Extend for one year subsidized student loan interest rates financed by a cut in health care spending	NO
Cite Attorney General Eric H. Holder Jr. for contempt of Congress	NO
Create a visa program for foreign graduates in high-tech fields	NO
Extend most Bush-era income tax rates while allowing rates for top-bracket earners to rise (Jan. 1, 2013)	YES
2011	
Strike funding for F-35 alternative engine	YES
Prevent EPA from regulating greenhouse gas emissions to address climate change	NO
Extend certain provisions of Patriot Act for four years	NO
Declare opposition to use of ground troops in Libya	NO
Overhaul patent law	NO
Pass compromise debt limit increase plan and establish future spending limits	NO
Allow consideration of measures to implement three trade agreements	NO

CQ Vote Studies

	PARTY UNITY		PRESIDENTIAL SUPPORT	
	SUPPORT	OPPOSE	SUPPORT	OPPOSE
2012	91%	9%	82%	18%
2011	92%	8%	73%	27%
2010	98%	2%	90%	10%
2009	99%	1%	96%	4%
2008	99%	1%	13%	87%

Interest Groups

	AFL-CIO	ADA	CCUS	ACU
2012	90%	90%	25%	0%
2011	100%	95%	25%	8%
2010	93%	85%	14%	0%
2009	100%	100%	33%	0%
2008	100%	100%	50%	4%

Arizona 7

Downtown Phoenix; part of Glendale

Situated in central and southern Phoenix, the 7th District captures the government mall of the most populous state capital in the nation. It also grabs a portion of Glendale to the north and the tiny towns of Guadalupe and Tolleson to the east and west. The Democratic-leaning district is nearly 66 percent Hispanic, a higher proportion than in any other Arizona district, and about 9 percent black.

A bright spot for downtown development is the newest and rapidly expanding campus of Arizona State University, including construction of a $25 million student recreation facility. But municipal budgets are strained and neighborhood park projects have been put on hold. Community leaders teamed up for a makeover of the grounds surrounding Arizona's state legislative complex, and private fundraisers are working on a long-term plan to renovate the capitol building.

State government is the top employer in the Greater Phoenix area. The long-awaited light-rail line has also aided the city's economy, carrying weekend travelers to restaurants and recreation venues. Downtown also includes US Airways Center, the home court of basketball's Suns and Mercury, and Chase Field, where baseball's Diamondbacks play.

South Phoenix includes the headquarters for the Apollo Group, the education behemoth behind the online University of Phoenix. Nearby, the joint civilian-military Phoenix Sky Harbor International Airport is one of the busiest in the nation, carrying passengers to domestic destinations and travel spots in Mexico.

During the recession, Phoenix was hit hard by the housing crisis and suffered one of the worst declines in employment among major metro areas. The housing market is recovering and there are rising home prices, but families still struggle to afford housing. Many of the region's job gains have been in low-wage service industries.

Major Industry
State government, transportation, higher education

Cities
Phoenix (pt.), Glendale, Tolleson, Guadalupe

Notable
Guadalupe imposes fines on visitors who try to photograph the Yaqui Indians' holy Easter dance ceremonies.

Rep. Trent Franks (R)

Capitol Office
225-4576
franks.house.gov
2435 Rayburn Bldg. 20515-0302; fax 225-6328

Committees
Armed Services
Judiciary
(Constitution & Civil Justice - Chairman)

Residence
Peoria

Born
June 19, 1957; Uravan, Colo.

Religion
Baptist

Family
Wife, Josephine Franks; two children

Education
Ottawa U. (Ariz.), attended 1989-90

Career
Oil company executive; conservative think tank president; state children's programs director

Political Highlights
Ariz. House, 1985-87; defeated for re-election to Ariz. House, 1986; sought Republican nomination for U.S. House, 1994

ELECTION RESULTS

2012 GENERAL		
Trent Franks (R)	172,809	63.3%
Gene Scharer (D)	95,635	35.1%
Stephen Dolgos (AEL)	4,347	1.6%
2012 PRIMARY		
Trent Franks (R)	57,257	83.2%
Tony Passalacqua (R)	11,572	16.8%
2010 GENERAL		
Trent Franks (R)	173,173	64.9%
John Thrasher (D)	82,891	31.1%
Powell Gammill (LIBERT)	10,820	4.0%

Previous Winning Percentages
2008 (59%); 2006 (59%); 2004 (59%); 2002 (60%)

Elected 2002; 6th term

The Republican Party has shifted toward Franks in recent years, but it would have to move a lot further to the right to meet him. His staunch fiscal and social conservatism is accompanied by hawkish stands on military issues.

Franks is a self-made millionaire from his work in the oil business, and he founded an Arizona think tank to promote socially conservative policy. Unsurprisingly, he's confident and assertive when expressing his political views. "We fight on fronts that are moving," he has said. "I've just gotten louder, is all."

He sits on the Armed Services and Judiciary committees, two panels that give him plenty of opportunities to challenge the Obama administration and congressional Democrats on high-profile issues.

Fighting abortion has long been one of his signature causes. In the 112th Congress (2011-12), Franks used his chairmanship of the Judiciary Constitution Subcommittee to hold hearings on socially conservative legislation, including two abortion-related bills he sponsored — hallmark measures for a lawmaker who was known around the Arizona statehouse for wearing a tie tack in the shape of a fetus' feet. Franks has called the Supreme Court decision legalizing abortion "the greatest holocaust in the history of mankind."

One of his bills was to outlaw late-term abortions in Washington, D.C., while the other was to ban abortions based on the sex of the fetus. The Judiciary Committee approved both measures in 2012, but they were brought up on the House floor under suspension of the rules. That status requires a two-thirds majority for passage, and both bills fell short. After the vote on the D.C. bill, Franks likened aborted fetuses to a "hidden class of victims" and said America is on the cusp of realizing "the humanity of the victim and the inhumanity of what was being done to them."

Franks fiercely defends gun rights. "I don't trust the left to back away from their lifelong commitment to destroy the Second Amendment," he said in early 2013.

He's also passionate about national security threats and military assets, such as missile defense systems and strategic nuclear weapons. He has been particularly critical of the Obama administration's approach to the Iranian threat. He wrote in December 2012 that Iran and North Korea "have successfully duped this president into sitting on the sidelines" as they develop nuclear capabilities.

A co-founder of the Israel Allies Caucus, Franks has pushed the administration to make it "unequivocally clear to Iran and to the entire world that we will do everything necessary, including direct military intervention, to prevent this rogue nation from gaining nuclear weapons with which to threaten either the United States or our allies."

He uses his seat on Armed Services to look out for Luke Air Force base in his district. The base was selected in 2012 to be a pilot training center for the F-35 Joint Strike Fighter.

Franks is one of the most pro-growth fiscal conservatives in the House, with stellar ratings from activist groups such as Heritage Action for America and the Club for Growth. Along with fellow Arizona Republican Jeff Flake — who was elected to the Senate in November 2012 — Franks stridently opposed earmarks in spending bills before the practice was banned by House Republicans at the start of the 112th Congress.

He traditionally votes against all legislative efforts aimed at boosting federal spending to stimulate the economy. Upset over federal spending levels, Franks was one of 48 House Republicans opposing a stopgap spending bill to keep the government running at the start of fiscal 2012.

The defeat of the bill was a major embarrassment for GOP leaders, but when a second version was brought to the floor, Franks was one of 24 Republicans who still voted against it.

He also refused to support the August 2011 deal to raise the federal debt limit. "The question before our nation now is whether our budget will balance due to proactive work by those of us sent to fix the broken system in Washington, or by financial calamity due to the unwillingness of so many to stop a looming disaster when we had the opportunity to do so," he said at the time.

Franks is the oldest of five children of a geologist and a nurse. He grew up in the uranium- and vanadium-mining town of Uravan, Colo., which is now a ghost town. He was born with severe lip and palate deformities that took nine surgeries to correct. He is an active booster of Operation Smile, which provides free surgeries in 60 countries to babies with birth defects.

When he was just out of high school, he and a brother went looking for oil in Texas. Starting with a truck-mounted rig, the two were so young they had to hire an 18-year-old friend to get a drilling permit. They drilled a lot of dry holes and lived out of a trailer, but they eventually sank a modest well that produced a few barrels and earnings of $100 a day.

Busy with the growing oil-drilling business, Franks never finished college. He settled in the Phoenix suburbs after getting married to his wife, Josephine, in 1980. Franks is the wealthiest member of the Arizona delegation, according to congressional disclosure forms.

In 1984, he made a successful bid for a state House seat but was defeated for re-election. He then founded a think tank, the Arizona Family Research Institute (now the Center for Arizona Policy). In 1987, he was appointed director of the Arizona Governor's Office for Children by Republican Evan Mecham.

He lost the 1994 GOP primary for the open 4th District seat to John Shadegg. Franks tried another congressional run in 2002, this time in the 2nd District, and edged past Lisa Atkins, former chief of staff for retiring GOP Rep. Bob Stump of the 3rd District, by just 797 votes. He handily won the November election. He has won relatively easily since.

His district was significantly altered by reapportionment-based remapping after the 2010 census. Mapmakers lopped off the sparsely populated northwest corner of the state and the Hopi reservation in the northeast, leaving just a suburban area west of Phoenix.

Franks' Democratic opponent was Gene Scharer, who had made unsuccessful bids for Congress in 2000, 2004 and 2006. Scharer raised almost no money for the race, and Franks took more than 63 percent of the vote in what is now the 8th District.

Key Votes

2012	
Extend a Social Security payroll tax cut and unemployment benefits	NO
Ease securities rules to expand small-business access to capital	YES
Extend for one year subsidized student loan interest rates financed by a cut in health care spending	NO
Cite Attorney General Eric H. Holder Jr. for contempt of Congress	YES
Create a visa program for foreign graduates in high-tech fields	YES
Extend most Bush-era income tax rates while allowing rates for top-bracket earners to rise (Jan. 1, 2013)	NO
2011	
Strike funding for F-35 alternative engine	NO
Prevent EPA from regulating greenhouse gas emissions to address climate change	YES
Extend certain provisions of Patriot Act for four years	YES
Declare opposition to use of ground troops in Libya	YES
Overhaul patent law	NO
Pass compromise debt limit increase plan and establish future spending limits	NO
Allow consideration of measures to implement three trade agreements	YES

CQ Vote Studies

	PARTY UNITY		PRESIDENTIAL SUPPORT	
	SUPPORT	OPPOSE	SUPPORT	OPPOSE
2012	97%	3%	16%	84%
2011	95%	5%	22%	78%
2010	99%	1%	21%	79%
2009	99%	1%	10%	90%
2008	99%	1%	87%	13%

Interest Groups

	AFL-CIO	ADA	CCUS	ACU
2012	5%	15%	83%	100%
2011	0%	5%	88%	100%
2010	0%	5%	75%	100%
2009	0%	0%	73%	100%
2008	0%	0%	76%	100%

Arizona 8

Northwest Phoenix suburbs — most of Peoria, Surprise

Comprising much of the former 3rd District, the redrawn 8th takes in towns northwest of Phoenix, including fast-growing Peoria, a portion of Glendale and the retirement community of Sun City. Remapping carved out growing Hispanic areas in Glendale and shifted the 8th west to Sun City West and Surprise, retaining the district's mainly conservative and white identity.

Retail, education, health care, manufacturing and aerospace drive the diverse economy here. Aviation- and defense-based Honeywell Aerospace has several locations in the district and nearby towns. Redistricted into the 8th in 2011, Luke Air Force Base is Glendale's largest public employer, providing $2 billion to the economy each year. It will serve as a training center for new F-35 fighter jet pilots; some 1,000 new jobs are expected.

Gambling is a divisive issue in the area. In 2012, a federal court upheld a plan by the Tohono O'odham Nation to create a reservation and casino near the border of Peoria and Glendale on an unincorporated piece of land. Opponents in Glendale had hoped to annex the property.

The district's construction industry crumbled when the Phoenix area housing bubble burst, and while Peoria has maintained some the higher median home values in the West Valley, they are well below their peak. Construction of the Northern Parkway, a new east-west artery that speeds commuters to Phoenix, and an entertainment and hotel project proposed for the 2015 Super Bowl, could bring more jobs. The football's Cardinals and hockey's Coyotes play across the street from each other in Glendale. Arizona State University has a branch campus in Glendale with nearly 9,000 students.

Major Industry
Aerospace, retail, manufacturing

Military Bases
Luke Air Force Base, 3,649 military, 900 civilian

Cities
Peoria, Glendale (pt.), Surprise, Sun City

Notable
Peoria is home to the Challenger Space Center of Arizona, a Smithsonian Institution affiliate museum dedicated to science education and honoring the lives of the astronauts lost in the Space Shuttle Challenger disaster.

Rep. Kyrsten Sinema (D)

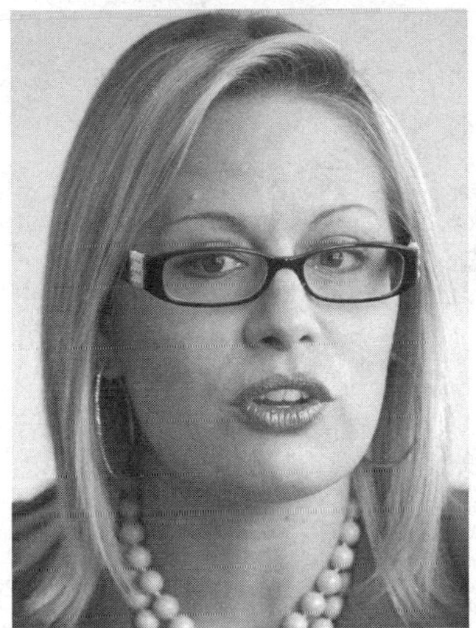

Capitol Office
225-9888
sinema.house.gov
1237 Longworth Bldg. 20515-0302; fax 225-9731

Committees
Financial Services

Residence
Phoenix

Born
July 12, 1976; Tucson, Ariz.

Religion
None

Family
Single

Education
Brigham Young U., B.S.W. 1995; Arizona State U., M.A. 1999 (social work), J.D. 2004, Ph.D. 2012 (justice studies)

Career
Lawyer; college instructor; social worker

Political Highlights
Candidate for Phoenix City Council, 2001; independent nominee for Ariz. House, 2002; Ariz. House, 2005-11; Ariz. Senate, 2011-12

ELECTION RESULTS

2012 GENERAL		
Kyrsten Sinema (D)	121,881	48.7%
Vernon B. Parker (R)	111,630	44.6%
Powell Gammill (LIBERT)	16,620	6.6%
2012 PRIMARY		
Kyrsten Sinema (D)	15,536	40.8%
David Schapira (D)	11,419	30.0%
Andrei Cherny (D)	11,146	29.2%

Elected 2012; 1st term

Sinema is effervescent, confident and accomplished for her age. She's a liberal Democrat but says she wants to adopt a bipartisan approach — which isn't a bad strategy for her competitive district.

Sinema (full name: KEER-sten SIN-eh-ma) cites her personal story when explaining her political philosophy. She grew up with very limited means — her family was homeless for a time — but she turned to schooling to improve her fortunes. She became a social worker and later a criminal defense attorney. "I will always be on the side of ordinary families who have been kicked around and held down by powerful forces that have damaged our country's prosperity," she said in 2012. She was a bit further to the left in her early 20s, when she was active in the Green Party and espoused anti-war and anti-capitalist views.

Starting at age 28, she spent six years in the state House and one year in the state Senate. The Arizona Republic described her as "eager for the spotlight." She was a noted critic of Arizona's 2010 immigration enforcement law (which was partially struck down in 2012), and she served as a White House liaison for Arizona during the developmental stages of the 2010 health care overhaul.

She said she ran for the U.S. House to battle Republicans' priorities: "They seem more intent on legislating birth control than they do solving Arizona's mortgage crisis or high unemployment," according to Sinema. She now sits on the Financial Services Committee and its housing subcommittee.

Sinema was raised Mormon, but some people now describe her as agnostic. She is the first openly bisexual member of Congress.

The campaign for the 9th District was very competitive. In the Democratic primary, Sinema defeated the minority leader of the Arizona Senate and a former chairman of the Arizona Democratic Party. She then faced Republican Vernon B. Parker, a former mayor of Paradise Valley and civil rights official in the George W. Bush administration. Sinema won with less than 49 percent of the vote, aided in part by a Libertarian candidate drawing off GOP support.

Arizona 9

Tempe; parts of Phoenix, Chandler and Mesa

Wealth abounds in the 9th, which captures country clubs, luxury golf courses and high-end shopping centers. Contained within metro Phoenix, the 9th takes in Tempe, much of Mesa and Chandler from the west, southern Scottsdale, and parts of southeastern Phoenix and Paradise Valley. The district hosts the state's largest undergraduate population at Tempe's Arizona State University campus. A new district following reapportionment, the 9th was drawn to be politically competitive: there are more independent or minor-party-affiliated voters than either registered Republicans or Democrats. Barack Obama managed a 4-percentage-point win here in the 2012 presidential race; Libertarian candidate Gary Johnson pulled in 2 percent.

Phoenix's upscale neighborhoods account for the largest concentration of the district's voters. Gated mansions with private golf courses in Biltmore serve as havens for the city's richest, with some home values surpassing $10 million. Orange, lemon and grapefruit trees dot the lawns of large properties in Arcadia, a former citrus grove. Fancy homes overlook immigrant housing developments in eccentric Sunnyslope.

The technology sector provides many jobs for residents of the East Valley, who focus their energy on production of semiconductors and engineering innovations at Scottsdale's SkySong center. Intel is the largest employer in Chandler, and the company is expanding its presence with a new research and development facility. The headquarters for US Airways is expected to move to Texas after a merger with American Airlines, but the airline will still keep a presence in Tempe. Baseball's spring training season draws sports fans from around the nation to watch games in the Cactus League. The Phoenix Zoo is another major tourist attraction.

More than one-fourth of the 9th's population is Hispanic, although whites remain a majority. Mesa is home to much of the district's growing Latino population, many of whom have converted from Catholicism to Mormonism, which retains its historical significance in the city.

Major Industry
Technology, higher education, tourism

Cities
Phoenix (pt.), Mesa (pt.), Chandler (pt.), Scottsdale, Tempe

Notable
Piestewa Peak is named after the first Native American woman in the U.S. military to be killed in combat

ARKANSAS

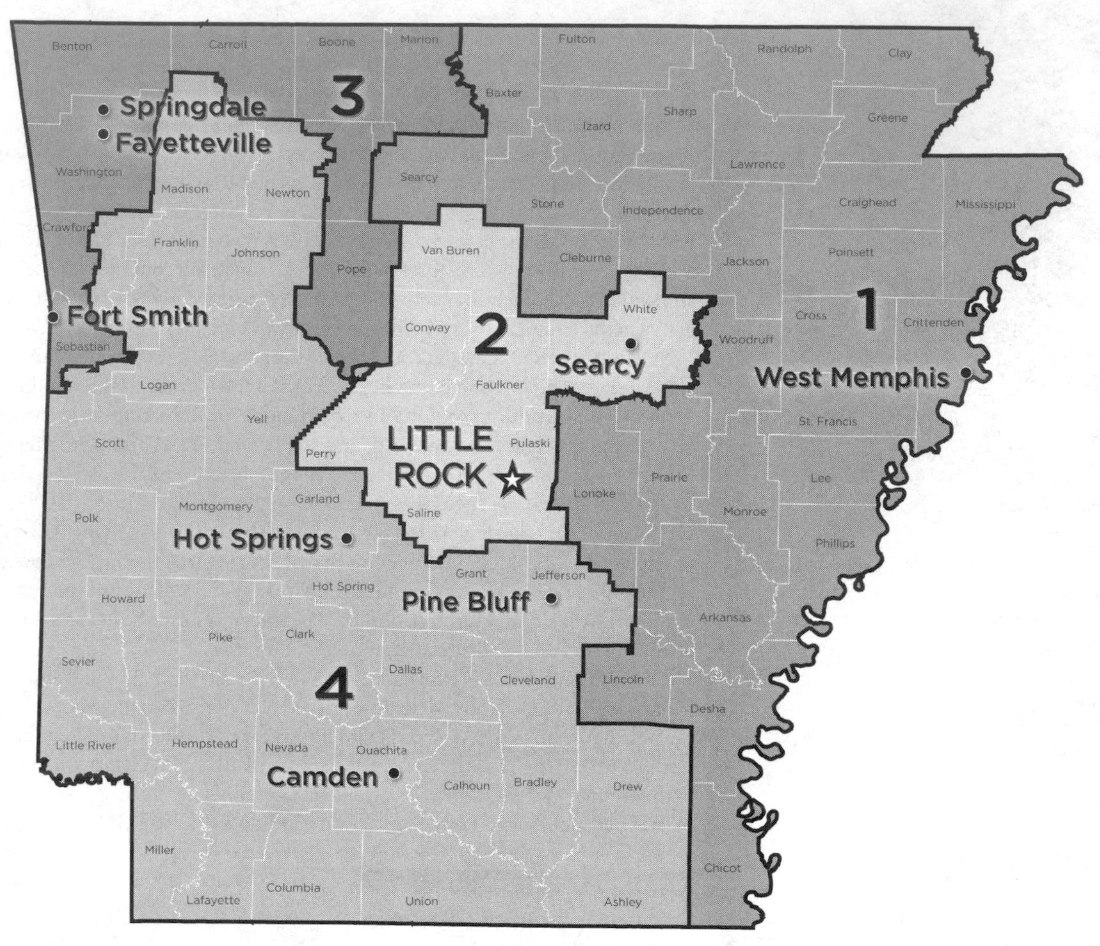

Benton
Carroll
Boone
Marion
Fulton
Randolph
Clay
Baxter
3
Springdale
Fayetteville
Sharp
Izard
Greene
Washington
Madison
Newton
Searcy
Lawrence
Stone
Independence
Craighead
Mississippi
Crawford
Franklin
Johnson
Van Buren
Cleburne
Poinsett
Pope
Jackson
Fort Smith
White
1
Conway
2
Cross
Crittenden
Sebastian
Woodruff
Searcy
West Memphis
Logan
Faulkner
St. Francis
Yell
Scott
LITTLE ROCK
Pulaski
Perry
Lee
Prairie
Lonoke
Polk
Montgomery
Garland
Saline
Monroe
Hot Springs
Phillips
Grant
Jefferson
Howard
Hot Spring
Pine Bluff
Arkansas
Pike
Clark
Sevier
Dallas
Cleveland
Lincoln
4
Desha
Little River
Hempstead
Nevada
Ouachita
Camden
Calhoun
Bradley
Drew
Miller
Chicot
Columbia
Lafayette
Union
Ashley

Gov. Mike Beebe (D)

Pronounced: BEE-bee
First elected: 2006
Length of term: 4 years
Term expires: 1/15
Salary: $86,890
Phone: (501) 682-2345
Residence: Searcy
Born: Dec. 28, 1946; Amagon, Ark.
Religion: Episcopalian
Family: Wife, Ginger Beebe; three children
Education: Arkansas State U., B.A. 1968 (political science); U. of Arkansas, J.D. 1972
Military service: Army Reserve, 1968-74
Career: Lawyer
Political highlights: Ark. Senate, 1983-2003 (president pro tempore, 2001-03); Ark. attorney general, 2003-07

ELECTION RESULTS
2010 GENERAL

Mike Beebe (D)	503,336	64.4%
Jim Keet (R)	262,784	33.6%
Jim Lendall (Green)	14,513	1.9%

Lt. Gov. Mark A. Darr (R)

First elected: 2010
Length of term: 4 years
Term expires: 1/15
Salary: $41,896
Phone: (501) 682-2144

LEGISLATURE

General Assembly: At least 60 days, even-numbered years beginning in February
Senate: 35 members, 4-year terms
2013 ratios: 21 R, 14 D; 29 men, 6 women
Salary: $15,869
Phone: (501) 682-6107
House: 100 members, 2-year terms
2013 ratios: 51 R, 48 D, 1 Green; 83 men, 17 women
Salary: $15,869
Phone: (501) 682-7771

TERM LIMITS

Governor: 2 terms
Senate: 2 terms
House: 3 terms

URBAN STATISTICS

CITY	POPULATION
Little Rock	193,524
Fort Smith	86,209
Fayetteville	73,580
Springdale	69,797
Jonesboro	67,263

REGISTERED VOTERS

Voters do not register by party.

POPULATION

2010 population (est.)	2,915,918
2000 population	2,673,400
1990 population	2,350,725
Percent change (2000-2010)	+9.1%
Rank among states (2010)	32
Median age	36.9
Born in state	61.1%
Foreign born	3.8%
Violent crime rate	518/100,000
Poverty level	18.8%
Federal workers	28,860
Military	6,717

ELECTIONS

STATE ELECTION OFFICIAL
(501) 682-5070
DEMOCRATIC PARTY
(501) 374-2361
REPUBLICAN PARTY
(501) 372-7301

MISCELLANEOUS

Web: www.arkansas.gov
Capital: Little Rock

U.S. CONGRESS

Senate: 1 Democrat, 1 Republican
House: 4 Republicans

STATISTICS BY DISTRICT

	2012 Vote for President		2008 Vote for President										
District	Obama	Romney	Obama	McCain	Black	Asian	Hispanic	Median Income	Over 64	Under 20	College Education	Rural	Sq. Miles
1	36%	61%	39%	58%	18%	<1%	3%	$34,704	16%	27%	15%	57%	19,318
2	43	55	44	54	22	1	5	45,415	13	26	28	29	4,978
3	32	65	34	64	3	2	13	41,109	13	28	24	34	5,401
4	36	62	37	60	20	<1	5	34,630	17	26	15	60	22,338
STATE	**37**	**61**	**39**	**59**	**15**	**1**	**6**	**38,758**	**15**	**27**	**20**	**45**	**52,035**
U.S.	**51**	**47**	**53**	**46**	**12**	**5**	**17**	**50,052**	**13**	**27**	**29**	**21**	**3,531,905**

Sen. Mark Pryor (D)

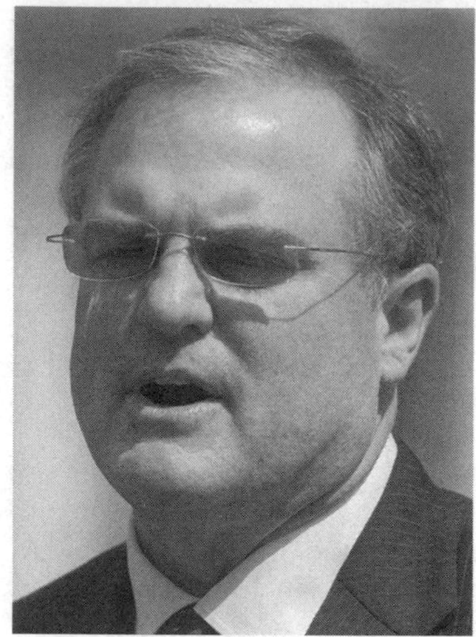

Capitol Office
224-2353
pryor.senate.gov
255 Dirksen Bldg. 20510; fax 228-0908

Committees
Appropriations
(Agriculture - Chairman)
Commerce, Science & Transportation
(Communications, Technology & the Internet - Chairman)
Homeland Security & Governmental Affairs
Rules & Administration
Small Business & Entrepreneurship
Select Ethics

Residence
Little Rock

Born
Jan. 10, 1963; Fayetteville, Ark.

Religion
Christian

Family
Separated; two children

Education
U. of Arkansas, B.A. 1985 (history), J.D. 1988

Career
Lawyer

Political Highlights
Ark. House, 1991-95; sought Democratic nomination for Ark. attorney general, 1994; Ark. attorney general, 1999-2003

ELECTION RESULTS

2008 GENERAL		
Mark Pryor (D)	804,678	79.5%
Rebekah Kennedy (GREEN)	207,076	20.5%
2008 PRIMARY		
Mark Pryor (D)		unopposed

Previous Winning Percentages
2002 (54%)

Elected 2002; 2nd term

Pryor says the political center is the place where things get done. He has stuck with that view as Congress has become more polarized and his home state has become more Republican. "My modus operandi is to work across the aisle," he says.

He's counting on his record of bipartisanship to sustain him in 2014, as he seeks a third term — two-term Democrat Blanche Lincoln, herself a noted centrist, was easily defeated by Republican John Boozman in a 2010 Senate race. Pryor explained his decision to run in a 2012 campaign letter. "Unfortunately, conditions have worsened in the nation's capital over the last few years, but we need consensus now more than ever," he wrote.

Pryor, the son of former Arkansas governor and three-term senator David Pryor, can point to some successes in recent years. Republicans often seek him as a partner when they need a Democratic vote, giving him leverage to encourage Arkansas-friendly changes in legislation. He has committee assignments that lend themselves to bipartisan efforts: Pryor sits on the Appropriations Committee; he tackles consumer protection measures from the Commerce, Science and Transportation Committee; and he uses his seat on the Homeland Security and Governmental Affairs Committee to address preparedness and disaster recovery.

Democrats have tried to give Pryor a boost heading into his re-election campaign. He was named the chairman of the Agriculture Appropriations Subcommittee in the 113th Congress (2013-14), giving him the opportunity to shape spending for his state's biggest industry.

A two-year reauthorization of surface transportation programs enacted in 2012 contained several examples of Pryor's handiwork. The bill was packaged with a reauthorization of federal flood insurance, and it originally required insurance for many homes and businesses near levees and dams. Boozman credited Pryor with leading the bipartisan group that "successfully stripped this arbitrary, unfair and overreaching language from the bill. ... The burden this mandate would have placed on Arkansans who live behind sound flood control infrastructure was completely unnecessary given the investments these communities have already made in flood protection."

The highway part of the law contains a provision by Pryor and Tennessee Republican Lamar Alexander intended to reduce accidents caused by fatigue. It directs the Transportation Department to issue regulations requiring commercial trucks to carry electronic "black boxes" to track a driver's hours of service. Safety advocates were thrilled; the trucking industry less so.

Safety and consumer initiatives are not new to Pryor, who often did similar work as Arkansas' attorney general. He was one of Parents magazine's three "movers and shakers" in Washington for efforts to keep toxic toys out of stores. In the 110th Congress (2007-08), he steered to enactment a law to ban lead in children's products, protect whistle-blowers and outlaw the use of certain plastic softeners, called phthalates, in toys.

In the 111th Congress (2009-10), he helped produce a law requiring software makers, smartphone manufacturers and Internet service companies to provide user-friendly features for blind and deaf consumers. During the 110th Pryor won permanent extension of the Do Not Call Registry that limits telemarketing calls to consumers. He's now the chairman of the Commerce subcommittee covering communications and the Internet.

The 112th Congress (2011-12) found Pryor open to some GOP positions on taxes, spending and regulation. In July 2012, he was the lone Democrat to vote in favor of a failed GOP measure that would have extended the George

W. Bush-era tax cuts entirely, preserving lower rates even on the highest levels of income. Pryor and Ohio Republican Rob Portman were the Senate sponsors of a bill to overhaul the rule-writing process for federal entities and require more cost-benefit analyses of new rules. (The House passed its version in 2011, but the Senate version stalled.) He has supported efforts to block the EPA from regulating greenhouse gas emissions and urged approval of the Keystone XL pipeline connecting Canada's tar sands to U.S. refineries.

He's not completely in step with Republicans, however. Pryor would not endorse a plan by Arkansas Rep. Tim Griffin to block many regulations until the national unemployment rate reaches 6 percent or lower. "Some regulation is good. For example, we just passed the highway bill, and there is going to be a lot of safety regulation that is part of this highway bill — that's a good thing," Pryor told a Little Rock radio station in July 2012. Griffin's bill "might stop that, and that's not smart."

Over the years, Pryor has been a leader of his party's centrist faction, often serving as a catalyst for the formation of coalitions to resolve stalemates. He made his first big mark in 2005 as part of the "Gang of 14" — seven Democrats and seven Republicans — that was formed to end Democratic filibusters of George W. Bush's judicial nominees, while blocking GOP leaders from using a parliamentary procedure to abolish such filibusters.

Pryor took heat from both liberals and conservatives in Arkansas over the health care overhaul in 2009 and 2010. He voted for the Senate version of the bill in December 2009; it became law in March 2010. That month, he objected to a follow-up bill designed to adjust the overhaul. Pryor opposed the $65 billion price tag, a payroll tax on unearned income and fines on employers who do not offer employee health insurance. He was one of three Democrats to vote against the bill, which passed 56-43.

His positions on abortion and gun rights are tied more to his state than his party. In 2006, he was among six Democrats to support a bill making it a crime to take a minor across state lines to obtain an abortion, a practice that could be used to circumvent state parental consent laws. In another vote, Pryor, who says neither the "pro-choice" nor "pro-life" label fits him, declined to affirm the principles of Roe v. Wade.

Pryor was 15 when his family moved to the Washington area after his father's 1978 election to the Senate. He got an early start in politics as class president at Walt Whitman High School in Bethesda, Md., and he was a congressional page, as his father had been.

Hoping for a political career, Pryor returned to his hometown of Fayetteville and earned undergraduate and law degrees from the University of Arkansas. He was elected to the state House in 1990 at age 27, but four years later he lost the Democratic primary for attorney general.

Shortly thereafter, he was diagnosed with sarcoma, a rare cancer. For a year following surgery, he was unable to walk unassisted. After the cancer went into remission, Pryor restarted his political career in 1998. He was elected attorney general in his second bid for the job.

Pryor defeated conservative Republican Sen. Tim Hutchinson by 8 points in 2002. Hutchinson, a Baptist minister who had campaigned as a "traditional values" Republican, had divorced his wife of 29 years and married a former Senate aide. Pryor never spoke directly about the divorce but touted his own commitment to his religion and his family. However, Pryor in 2012 quietly announced that he and his wife were in the process of divorcing.

Presidential politics seemed to work to Pryor's advantage in 2008. Former Arkansas Gov. Mike Huckabee ran unsuccessfully for the GOP presidential nomination, and on ending that campaign he decided he wasn't interested in a Senate race. There wasn't anyone behind him on the Republican bench. Pryor found himself to be the only incumbent senator without major-party opposition in that election cycle.

Key Votes

2012	
Prohibit health insurance plans from denying coverage based on the sponsor's religious beliefs	YES
Require approval of the Keystone XL oil pipeline	YES
Ease securities rules to expand small-business access to capital	YES
Reauthorize farm and nutrition programs for five years	NO
Limit debate on a bill that would create private-sector cybersecurity standards	NO
Consent to ratification of a treaty setting global standard for the treatment of people with disabilities	YES
Provide $60.4 billion in disaster relief following Superstorm Sandy	YES
Extend most Bush-era income tax rates while allowing rates for top-bracket earners to rise (Jan. 1, 2013)	YES
2011	
Prevent EPA from regulating greenhouse gas emissions to address climate change	YES
Extend certain provisions of Patriot Act for four years	YES
Clear compromise debt limit increase plan and establish future spending limits	YES
Overhaul patent law	YES
Implement Colombia free trade agreement	YES
Limit debate on confirmation of Caitlin J. Halligan to D.C. Circuit Court of Appeals	YES
Extend payroll tax cut and unemployment benefits for two months	YES

CQ Vote Studies

	PARTY UNITY		PRESIDENTIAL SUPPORT	
	SUPPORT	OPPOSE	SUPPORT	OPPOSE
2012	85%	15%	91%	9%
2011	85%	15%	95%	5%
2010	85%	15%	92%	8%
2009	91%	9%	95%	5%
2008	79%	21%	46%	54%
2007	81%	19%	46%	54%
2006	76%	24%	64%	36%
2005	80%	20%	58%	42%
2004	81%	19%	68%	32%
2003	84%	16%	60%	40%

Interest Groups

	AFL-CIO	ADA	CCUS	ACU
2012	73%	70%	75%	16%
2011	72%	75%	73%	20%
2010	80%	65%	60%	29%
2009	94%	90%	57%	8%
2008	100%	85%	75%	4%
2007	84%	70%	45%	12%
2006	73%	75%	75%	20%
2005	79%	90%	78%	24%
2004	92%	85%	71%	20%
2003	85%	70%	61%	30%

Sen. John Boozman (R)

Capitol Office
224-4843
boozman.senate.gov
320 Hart Bldg. 20510-0404; fax 228-1371

Committees
Agriculture, Nutrition & Forestry
Appropriations
Environment & Public Works
Veterans' Affairs

Residence
Rogers

Born
Dec. 10, 1950; Shreveport, La.

Religion
Baptist

Family
Wife, Cathy Boozman; three children

Education
U. of Arkansas, attended 1969-72; Southern College of Optometry, O.D. 1977

Career
Optometrist; cattle farm owner

Political Highlights
Rogers Public Schools Board of Education, 1994-2001; U.S. House, 2001-11

ELECTION RESULTS

2010 GENERAL		
John Boozman (R)	451,618	57.9%
Blanche Lincoln (D)	288,156	36.9%
Trevor Drown (I)	25,234	3.2%
John Laney Gray III (GREEN)	14,430	1.8%
2010 PRIMARY		
John Boozman (R)	75,010	52.7%
Jim Holt (R)	24,826	17.4%
Gilbert Baker (R)	16,540	11.6%
Conrad Reynolds (R)	7,128	5.0%
Curtis Coleman (R)	6,928	4.9%
Kim Hendren (R)	5,551	3.9%
Randy Alexander (R)	4,389	3.1%
Fred Ramey (R)	1,888	1.3%

Previous Winning Percentages
2008 House Election (78.5%); 2006 House Election (62%); 2004 House Election (59%); 2002 House Election (99%); 2001 Special House Election (56%)

Elected 2010; 1st term

Boozman was once an offensive tackle for the University of Arkansas Razorbacks, performing one of the most team-oriented and anonymous jobs on the football field. He now takes to the role of rank-and-file senator, supporting the Republican Party platform while taking care of his home state.

Mild-mannered and courteous, Boozman (BOZE-man) professes to "really enjoy the committee work and really enjoy getting things done." He works on panels suited to helping Arkansas' infrastructure and agriculture, and he promotes humanitarian causes he pursued during his 10 years in the House.

On the fiscal issues that have dominated headlines as of late, Boozman sticks with the GOP message. During the 112th Congress (2011-12), he described America as being at a pivotal moment in its financial history. "If somebody writes a book about this, we'll be the people that they talked about who acted appropriately and who did the best they could for their country," he said.

Boozman supports Republican plans for a tax code overhaul, reducing regulatory burdens, increasing free trade and expanding all kinds of energy production. He signed off on the big fiscal deals of the 112th: an August 2011 agreement to cut spending and raise the debt limit; and a January 2013 package that prevented higher income tax rates for earnings under $400,000.

He even went along with the GOP earmark moratorium in the Senate, days after saying he was worried about what such a restriction would mean for some projects under way in Arkansas. "While not all earmarks are bad, it is clear that the system is broken and in need of reform," he said. Boozman has a more direct hand in spending in the 113th Congress (2013-14), having joined the Appropriations Committee.

Boozman does most of his heavy lifting on his committees, and he's willing to work with Democrats when it benefits his state.

He joined the Agriculture, Nutrition and Forestry Committee after defeating its chairwoman, Democrat Blanche Lincoln, in 2010. Congress didn't clear a long-term reauthorization of farm and nutrition programs in the 112th, meaning Boozman gets to refight some battles in the 113th Congress. He and 29 other Republicans opposed the farm bill passed by the Senate in 2012, as did Arkansas Democrat Mark Pryor. Both Boozman and Pryor wanted greater support for Southern rice and peanut farmers and hoped to make adjustments in a conference committee that never came.

Boozman and many other farm-state lawmakers panned a proposed Labor Department rule on agriculture-related child labor, which was eventually withdrawn in 2012. "There was no common sense, science or reason behind this proposal, and it seemed to be written by bureaucrats who lack a full understanding of farm operations," said Boozman, a cattle farm owner.

In a stance at odds with many other conservative Republicans, Boozman advocates ending the U.S. trade embargo against Cuba — the rice and poultry farmers in his state see that country as a potentially lucrative market. (Arkansas is the nation's top producer of rice.) He backed the 2011 ratification of trade agreements with Colombia, Panama and South Korea, touting their benefit to Arkansas farmers.

The Environment and Public Works Committee is his platform to fight environmental regulations that he sees as burdening farmers. It's also where he promotes the extension of Interstate 49. While in the House, Boozman secured politically popular funding for the interstate, which is planned to cut through western Arkansas as it connects Kansas City, Mo., to port cities in Louisiana.

Boozman is the second of three children of an Air Force master sergeant. The family moved around with his father's service assignments, and Boozman spent his early childhood in London, attending an all-boys British school. Eventually, the family returned to Fort Smith, where it had roots dating to the late 19th century.

Boozman served on the House Veterans' Affairs Committee and now sits on its Senate counterpart. He wants the federal government to help recent veterans apply the professional training they have picked up in the military — working as medics, truck drivers, office managers and the like — to the private sector. He and Alaska Democrat Mark Begich introduced a bill to expand the Transition Assistance Program, which helps veterans and spouses shifting to non-military employment, to operate at off-base locations. He also introduced a bill to improve rehabilitative services for veterans with traumatic brain injuries. Boozman cites the benefit claims backlog at the Veterans Affairs Department as a major problem.

A former member of the House Foreign Affairs Committee, Boozman pursues his interests in international affairs through the Senate's Hunger and Malaria caucuses. He sees no conflict between his desire to reduce national spending and calls for international aid. "We have to use the resources in a really wise way to make sure that those moneys are going to the individuals we want to be affected," he said. "Malaria is something that, if the Western world would get together on, it is something that can be defeated, accomplished, relatively easily."

He gave up his seat on the Commerce, Science and Transportation Committee to become an appropriator, but he still looks out for Arkansas-based Wal-Mart Stores Inc. and Tyson Foods Inc.

The 6-foot-3-inch Boozman was a standout football player at Northside High School in Fort Smith before going to the University of Arkansas.

He was going to be a dentist until his brother, Fay, who was studying ophthalmology, persuaded him to go to optometry school so they could practice together. They co-founded the Boozman-Hof Regional Eye Clinic in 1977 in their hometown of Rogers. Early in his House career, Boozman pushed to enactment a bill that categorized all contact lenses, even decorative ones, as medical devices subject to regulation.

Fay Boozman, who died in March 2005 in an accident while working on his farm, was always the higher-profile politician. He had served in the state Senate and eventually ran, unsuccessfully, against Lincoln in the 1998 open-seat U.S. Senate race.

John Boozman grew up among Southern Democrats, but was drawn to the GOP by President Ronald Reagan in the 1980s. He began his political career on the Rogers school board, where he served for six years.

When President George W. Bush appointed GOP Rep. Asa Hutchinson to head the Drug Enforcement Administration, Fay Boozman passed on a chance to seek the seat. John, who had never been to Washington, jumped in. He finished first in the four-candidate GOP primary but was forced into a runoff by state Sen. Gunner DeLay, a distant cousin of House Majority Whip Tom DeLay, a Texas Republican.

Endorsed by GOP Gov. Mike Huckabee, Boozman won both the primary runoff and the 2001 special election. He had little trouble getting re-elected in the following years. As his state's lone Republican House member, Boozman modeled himself after John Paul Hammerschmidt, a member of the GOP who represented the 3rd District from 1967 until 1993.

As the 2010 elections neared, Boozman emerged as the early favorite to take on Lincoln, who faced a challenge from the left in her own party and barely fended off Lt. Gov. Bill Halter. During the general-election campaign, Boozman showed sizable leads in virtually every poll, then coasted to a 21-point victory.

Key Votes

2012	
Prohibit health insurance plans from denying coverage based on the sponsor's religious beliefs	NO
Require approval of the Keystone XL oil pipeline	YES
Ease securities rules to expand small-business access to capital	YES
Reauthorize farm and nutrition programs for five years	NO
Limit debate on a bill that would create private-sector cybersecurity standards	NO
Consent to ratification of a treaty setting global standard for the treatment of people with disabilities	NO
Provide $60.4 billion in disaster relief following Superstorm Sandy	NO
Extend most Bush-era income tax rates while allowing rates for top-bracket earners to rise (Jan. 1, 2013)	YES
2011	
Prevent EPA from regulating greenhouse gas emissions to address climate change	YES
Extend certain provisions of Patriot Act for four years	YES
Clear compromise debt limit increase plan and establish future spending limits	YES
Overhaul patent law	YES
Implement Colombia free trade agreement	YES
Limit debate on confirmation of Caitlin J. Halligan to D.C. Circuit Court of Appeals	NO
Extend payroll tax cut and unemployment benefits for two months	YES

CQ Vote Studies

	PARTY UNITY		PRESIDENTIAL SUPPORT	
	SUPPORT	OPPOSE	SUPPORT	OPPOSE
2012	86%	14%	46%	54%
2011	93%	7%	55%	45%
2010	96%	4%	30%	70%
2009	96%	4%	22%	78%
2008	95%	5%	71%	29%
2007	91%	9%	74%	26%
2006	97%	3%	92%	8%
2005	96%	4%	77%	23%
2004	96%	4%	82%	18%
2003	97%	3%	93%	7%

Interest Groups

	AFL-CIO	ADA	CCUS	ACU
2012	9%	10%	100%	76%
2011	16%	15%	100%	90%
2010	7%	0%	88%	100%
2009	10%	0%	80%	96%
2008	13%	25%	94%	84%
2007	13%	15%	90%	92%
2006	21%	5%	100%	92%
2005	15%	0%	93%	96%
2004	13%	10%	100%	96%
2003	7%	10%	97%	84%

Rep. Rick Crawford (R)

Capitol Office
225-4076
crawford.house.gov
1711 Longworth Bldg. 20515-0401; fax 225-5602

Committees
Agriculture
(Livestock, Rural Development & Credit - Chairman)
Transportation & Infrastructure

Residence
Jonesboro

Born
Jan. 22, 1966; Homestead Air Force Base, Fla.

Religion
Southern Baptist

Family
Wife, Stacy Crawford; two children

Education
Southwest Missouri State U., attended 1991-93; Arkansas State U., B.S. 1996 (agriculture business economics)

Military
Army, 1985-89

Career
Agricultural news service owner; radio and television broadcaster; rodeo announcer; automotive decal and sign shop employee

Political Highlights
No previous office

ELECTION RESULTS

2012 GENERAL		
Rick Crawford (R)	138,800	56.2%
Scott Ellington (D)	96,601	39.1%
Jessica Paxton (LIBERT)	6,427	2.6%
Jacob Holloway (GREEN)	5,015	2.0%
2012 PRIMARY		
Rick Crawford (R)		unopposed
2010 GENERAL		
Rick Crawford (R)	93,224	51.8%
Chad Causey (D)	78,267	43.5%
Ken Adler (GREEN)	8,320	4.6%

Elected 2010; 2nd term

By Crawford's estimation, the urban-rural divide is bigger than any gap between Republicans and Democrats, and he thinks of himself as a protector of the rural way of life. He's the first Republican to represent his poor, farming-dependent district since the 1870s and believes it was conservative values — not a party label — that won him the job.

Crawford, whose 2010 House campaign was his first run for office, spent most of his working life in agriculture-related news services. He had stints as an agriculture reporter for TV and radio stations and owned AgWatch, a farm news radio and TV network broadcast in several Southern states. In 2006, former Republican Rep. Asa Hutchinson enlisted Crawford as an agriculture adviser to his (ultimately unsuccessful) gubernatorial campaign.

He sits on the Agriculture Committee, and in the 113th Congress (2013-14) he's chairing the Subcommittee on Livestock, Rural Development and Credit. "Fundamentally, what we need to do is make sure that we continue to maintain the cheapest, safest, most abundant food supply in the world," he said.

Crawford was sorely disappointed that Congress didn't clear a long-term reauthorization of farm programs in the 112th Congress (2011-12) — the House never voted on the bill approved by the Agriculture Committee. Crawford skipped the Republican National Convention in August 2012 and emphasized to constituents that he was spending the time working on farm problems.

He co-founded the Rice Caucus and the Chicken Caucus as a freshman to promote some of his state's biggest products, and in farm bill negotiations he has tried to preserve the federal programs that are he says are optimal for Southern growers. Crawford supports trade agreements that expand market access for Arkansas farmers. He called a 2012 law normalizing trade relations with Russia a "tremendous opportunity" for poultry producers.

Unlike many fiscal conservatives, Crawford supports subsidies for farmers, which he says are misunderstood by taxpayers. He sees them as "pass-through subsidies" that essentially keep food prices down, although he adds that "it's a tough argument to make."

He voted for a fiscal 2012 Agriculture spending bill but lamented its lack of funding for the Farm Service Agency's Biomass Crop Assistance Program, which gives incentive payments to farmers for collection and storage of biomass — organic material used to create energy.

Crawford also joins in the GOP's anti-regulatory efforts, paying particular attention to EPA actions that he thinks are unfair to farmers. The House in 2012 passed his bill to allow more exemptions to the EPA's spill prevention guidelines for fuel containers — such as the large ones found on many farms. The Senate did not act on the measure, and Crawford quickly reintroduced it in January 2013.

Mostly, he says he wants to see more understanding from urban colleagues: "I know it's probably not as exciting as going to Afghanistan or Israel, but I would love for people to come down to my district and see cotton farms and rice farms and get an up-close view of where the food and fiber comes from," he said in 2011.

Crawford has also found ways to address rural concerns from his seat on the Transportation and Infrastructure Committee. His district experienced flooding in both 2011 and 2012, and while dealing with recovery Crawford also worried that constituents might be forced to purchase costly flood insurance that they didn't need.

He was a conferee on a two-year reauthorization of surface transportation programs in 2012 that also included a reauthorization of the National Flood

Insurance Program. Crawford applauded when the final measure did not include Senate provisions that would have forced many people living near dams or levees to buy insurance. He said a few of the law's provisions also would allow for more-accurate flood zone mapping.

Crawford in 2011 introduced legislation to require the Transportation Department to keep a clearinghouse of records pertaining to alcohol and other substance testing for commercial motor vehicle drivers, expanding on a model already used in some states.

Crawford hasn't hacked at the federal budget quite as vigorously as some conservative colleagues; he endorsed several compromise spending and deficit reduction packages that hard-liners rejected as insufficiently austere. In January 2013, Crawford was one of 49 House Republicans to vote for $50 billion in disaster relief tied to Superstorm Sandy, even though most of it was "emergency" funding that was not within federal spending caps.

But a few weeks earlier, he had voted against the "fiscal cliff" deal. Although it permanently extended the George W. Bush-era tax cuts for income under $400,000, the package needed spending reductions to address the growing federal debt, Crawford said. He wants "permanent spending controls," and he introduced a bill at the start of the 113th to make an increase in the federal debt limit contingent on the president submitting to the states a constitutional amendment requiring either a balanced budget or spending caps.

Crawford grew up in a military family. Before he was 20 he had joined the Army, where he worked as a bomb-disposal technician. (He still has the look, thanks to a close-cropped haircut.) Crawford earned a bachelor's degree in agriculture business economics from Arkansas State University in 1996 before going into broadcasting. Included on his résumé is time behind a microphone as a rodeo announcer. He also used to participate in the events, though less so over the years.

Crawford told an Arkansas paper that he "saw such a fundamental change" in the way the country was run that he decided to enter the race for retiring Democratic Rep. Marion Berry's seat in the 2010 cycle. Crawford plays guitar, and when he first announced his candidacy for the 1st District seat, he played with a local band and sang a few country songs. He won the GOP nomination with almost 72 percent of the vote, then faced Berry's former chief of staff, Chad Causey, in the general election. Crawford won with almost 52 percent of the vote.

For the 2012 cycle, he was unopposed in the Republican primary. Democrat Scott Ellington, a prosecutor, tried to associate Crawford with congressional inaction on the farm bill, but he couldn't sway enough voters. Crawford won 56 percent of the vote.

Key Votes

2012	
Extend a Social Security payroll tax cut and unemployment benefits	YES
Ease securities rules to expand small-business access to capital	YES
Extend for one year subsidized student loan interest rates financed by a cut in health care spending	YES
Cite Attorney General Eric H. Holder Jr. for contempt of Congress	YES
Create a visa program for foreign graduates in high-tech fields	YES
Extend most Bush-era income tax rates while allowing rates for top-bracket earners to rise (Jan. 1, 2013)	NO
2011	
Strike funding for F-35 alternative engine	YES
Prevent EPA from regulating greenhouse gas emissions to address climate change	YES
Extend certain provisions of Patriot Act for four years	YES
Declare opposition to use of ground troops in Libya	YES
Overhaul patent law	YES
Pass compromise debt limit increase plan and establish future spending limits	YES
Allow consideration of measures to implement three trade agreements	YES

CQ Vote Studies

	PARTY UNITY		PRESIDENTIAL SUPPORT	
	SUPPORT	OPPOSE	SUPPORT	OPPOSE
2012	91%	9%	17%	83%
2011	95%	5%	26%	74%

Interest Groups

	AFL-CIO	ADA	CCUS	ACU
2012	14%	0%	100%	76%
2011	3%	5%	100%	76%

Arkansas 1

East — Jonesboro, Mississippi Delta

The 1st District traces the state's entire Mississippi riverfront. Crops dominate in the east amid the Mississippi Delta and fertile plains, while the Ozark Mountains rise up to the northwest.

Agriculture, including a history of plantation cotton farming, has defined this region for centuries. Cotton remains vital to the district's economy, but the 1st also is one of the nation's largest rice-producing districts.

Manufacturing near Jonesboro, the district's largest city, boosts Craighead County, and steel production still props up Mississippi County. In Marion and West Memphis, near the Tennessee border, shipping and distribution are key. Baxter County in the northwest corner of the 1st has established retirement communities that boast golfing and fishing. Visitors from across the Mid-South flock to the White River National Wildlife Refuge and to the flooded rice fields and Delta bayous for duck hunting.

Remapping after the 2010 census added Lincoln County and a part of Jefferson County east of Pine Bluff and shed a corner of Searcy County in the northwest, while tacking on three southern Delta counties from the adjacent 4th District. The southern Delta counties, already very rural, have experienced significant population loss over the last decade, but areas around Jonesboro and in western counties have steadily gained residents.

District politics typically split the heavily Democratic and predominately poor, black southern Delta from the Republican-leaning and white majority counties to the north and west. Desha and Chicot counties in the southeastern corner — added to the 1st after decennial redistricting — supported Democrat Barack Obama for president in 2012, as did most counties along the Mississippi. Obama had some of his strongest support in Phillips. But Republican Rep. Rick Crawford benefited from the population density in the district's north, and won re-election to the U.S. House. Before 2010, the GOP had not carried the 1st since Reconstruction.

Major Industry
Agriculture, steel production

Cities
Jonesboro, West Memphis, Paragould

Notable
Stuttgart hosts the World's Championship Duck Calling Contest annually during Thanksgiving week.

Rep. Tim Griffin (R)

Capitol Office
225-2506
griffin.house.gov
1232 Longworth Bldg. 20515-0402; fax 225-5903

Committees
Ways & Means

Residence
Little Rock

Born
Aug. 21, 1968; Charlotte, N.C.

Religion
Baptist

Family
Wife, Elizabeth Griffin; two children

Education
Hendrix College, B.A. 1990 (economics and business); Oxford U., attended 1991 (history); Tulane U., J.D. 1994

Military
Army Reserve, 1996-present

Career
Lawyer; political consultant; White House aide; federal prosecutor; party official; congressional aide; associate investigative counsel

Political Highlights
Assistant U.S. attorney, 2006-07

ELECTION RESULTS

2012 GENERAL		
Tim Griffin (R)	158,175	55.2%
Herb Rule (D)	113,156	39.5%
Barbara Ward (GREEN)	8,566	3.0%
Chris Hayes (LIBERT)	6,701	2.3%
2012 PRIMARY		
Tim Griffin (R)		unopposed
2010 GENERAL		
Tim Griffin (R)	122,091	57.9%
Joyce Elliott (D)	80,687	38.3%
Lance Levi (I)	4,421	2.1%
Lewis Kennedy (GREEN)	3,599	1.7%

Elected 2010; 2nd term

Griffin had the luster of a Republican Party insider before coming to Congress and has shown some political skill since getting there. For now, he says, he's forgetting about bids for the Senate or the governorship to focus on the Ways and Means Committee, which he joined for his second term.

For two years in the late 1990s, Griffin worked on Capitol Hill as the senior investigative counsel for the House Committee on Government Reform. He moved to the Republican National Committee and was often described as a protégé of Karl Rove, President George W. Bush's adviser. Griffin worked for the RNC during both the 2000 and 2004 presidential campaigns — one of his specialties was opposition research — then moved over to the White House in 2005 as an aide.

His job representing the 2nd District is his first elected office, but as he rounded out his freshman term in 2012 he offered new lawmakers advice that jibes with his analytical and precise approach: "Learn all you can before you draw your conclusions."

Griffin stayed close to the GOP line in the 112th Congress (2011-12) and worked as an assistant whip; in the 113th Congress (2013-14) he's serving as the vice chairman for communications and strategy at the National Republican Congressional Committee.

He favors broad plans to simplify the tax code and lower many rates. Griffin voted for a 2012 bill to extend the George W. Bush-era tax cuts for all income levels, but he couldn't bring himself to support the "fiscal cliff" deal at the start of 2013 that made those cuts permanent only for earnings below $400,000. According to Griffin, Congress needed to include more spending cuts as part of the deal.

"I have supported every single major bipartisan agreement proposed by the president, the Senate majority leader and House speaker since I was elected, but this one is a bridge too far," he wrote.

In both of his terms, Griffin has introduced bills to eliminate federal estate and gift taxes — a major goal of farmers in his state.

The Ways and Means Committee handles health care issues, and that industry is a big employer in Griffin's district. When Republican efforts to repeal the 2010 health care overhaul law died in the Democratic Senate, Griffin introduced a bill to amend the law by providing greater disclosure in the federal process for waiving annual limitation requirements for essential health benefits. He called the 2012 Supreme Court decision upholding the law a "monumental error."

His aversion to the health care law fits with his general distaste for bigger government. The House in 2012 passed his bill to prohibit federal agencies from issuing new rules that have an annual economic cost of more than $50 million until the unemployment rate drops to or below 6 percent.

Griffin has extensive military and legal experience, which he put to use as a freshman on the Armed Services, Foreign Affairs and Judiciary committees.

Since 1996 he has been an active member of the Army Reserve. Griffin was deployed to Iraq in 2006 and counts the 2007 troop surge there as a military and political success. He says the United States has an obligation to leave Afghanistan stable.

Griffin supports continued aid and security assistance to Israel, and in 2013 he said military aid to Egypt should be held up until that country's fledgling government demonstrates "respect for Israel and its people."

On Foreign Affairs, Griffin wanted a clarification of U.S. intent toward Libya when NATO intervened in that country's 2011 civil war. "My concerns over the legality of our actions in Libya should not be equated with objecting to the substance of what's going on in Libya," he said. "I can't get to that discussion until we start complying with the law." He voted against a resolution in June 2011 to withdraw forces from the country.

His service on the Judiciary Committee was colored by his professional past. In 2006 the Bush administration did some midterm housecleaning and dismissed several U.S. attorneys; Griffin was then appointed to fill the vacancy in the Eastern District of Arkansas. Democrats complained that the firings were politically motivated, and as criticism intensified, Attorney General Alberto R. Gonzales resigned (citing no reason) the next year. Griffin resigned after serving only six months on the job.

Griffin was born in Charlotte, N.C., and grew up in Magnolia, Ark. He graduated from Hendrix College, received a law degree from Tulane University and spent some time at Oxford in a graduate program.

He studied C.S. Lewis during college and, while at Oxford, worked at the pub, the Eagle and Child, where Lewis had spent time with J.R.R. Tolkien. Books have remained an important part of his life. "I've got probably 1,000 books," he said. "In my new house I built a room where every wall is shelves."

Griffin practiced law after quitting as U.S. attorney, and he considered running for the Senate. He eventually decided to challenge Democratic Rep. Vic Snyder, announcing his intention in 2009.

But Snyder announced in January 2010 that he was retiring, making the seat a prime target for a Republican takeover. Griffin won the GOP nomination with 62 percent of the vote. Democrat Joyce Elliott tried to make hay with Griffin's ties to Rove and the U.S. attorney firings, but voters sided with Griffin, giving him 58 percent of the vote.

During the campaign, Griffin — who is a social conservative and opposes both abortion and new restrictions on gun rights — continued to emphasize his Arkansas roots.

"You've heard my accent. You know I'm not from D.C.," Politico reported Griffin saying in February 2010. "I'm a fifth-generation Arkansan. I'm from Arkansas, my wife's from Arkansas, my daughter's from Arkansas. Went to college in Arkansas. So good luck with that one. It's pretty clear where I'm from, and my values are certainly conservative Arkansas values."

In 2012, he was unopposed in the primary. Herb Rule, a lawyer who worked at the Rose Law Firm (the former employer of Hillary Rodham Clinton), won the Democratic nomination.

Griffin campaigned largely on the Republican Party platform, and Rule was hindered by an August arrest — he was charged with driving while intoxicated. Griffin won 55 percent of the vote.

Key Votes

2012	
Extend a Social Security payroll tax cut and unemployment benefits	YES
Ease securities rules to expand small-business access to capital	YES
Extend for one year subsidized student loan interest rates financed by a cut in health care spending	YES
Cite Attorney General Eric H. Holder Jr. for contempt of Congress	YES
Create a visa program for foreign graduates in high-tech fields	YES
Extend most Bush-era income tax rates while allowing rates for top-bracket earners to rise (Jan. 1, 2013)	NO
2011	
Strike funding for F-35 alternative engine	YES
Prevent EPA from regulating greenhouse gas emissions to address climate change	YES
Extend certain provisions of Patriot Act for four years	YES
Declare opposition to use of ground troops in Libya	YES
Overhaul patent law	YES
Pass compromise debt limit increase plan and establish future spending limits	YES
Allow consideration of measures to implement three trade agreements	YES

CQ Vote Studies

	Party Unity		Presidential Support	
	Support	Oppose	Support	Oppose
2012	95%	5%	15%	85%
2011	96%	4%	22%	78%

Interest Groups

	AFL-CIO	ADA	CCUS	ACU
2012	14%	0%	92%	80%
2011	0%	5%	100%	76%

Arkansas 2

Central — Little Rock

An urban hub in a rural state, the 2nd takes in most of the Little Rock metro area. The Natural State's wealthiest and best-educated district, the 2nd has a well-established white-collar workforce anchored by state government and health care industries. More than a decade of downtown redevelopment in Little Rock also has brought entertainment and tourist revenue.

In Little Rock, a University of Arkansas campus and the system's medical school lead regional higher education and health care research efforts, employing thousands of district residents. Professionals also work in financial services and information technology sectors. Little Rock's River Market District hosts club and bar venues, and the Quapaw Quarter's Victorian buildings draw history buffs to downtown. The nearby Clinton Presidential Center also sits along the Arkansas River, and the entertainment district spills across the Big Dam Bridge to North Little Rock.

Little Rock-area suburbs along Interstates 30 and 40 have experienced a decade of population growth driven by economic stability, but the local tide has not lifted all boats. In addition to pockets of higher poverty rates, this boom also has created significant sprawl and traffic congestion.

Little Rock, by far the state's most populous city, remains strongly Democratic, but decades of white flight from inner Pulaski County shows no signs of letting up and has contributed to growing Republican electoral strength in the surrounding counties and in suburban Pulaski. Wide margins for the GOP in White and Saline counties push Republican candidates to victory. Small but rapidly growing Hispanic populations in all counties of the 2nd may further complicate the region's racial politics — more than 50 years after federal troops were required to integrate Little Rock's Central High School, equal opportunity in education remains a problem here.

Major Industry
State government, health care, higher education

Military Bases
Little Rock Air Force Base, 5,500 military, 1,200 civilian (2010)

Cities
Little Rock, North Little Rock, Conway, Benton

Notable
Little Rock Air Force Base boasts the largest C-130 training and airlift facility in the world.

Rep. Steve Womack (R)

Capitol Office
225-4301
womack.house.gov
1119 Longworth Bldg. 20515-0403; fax 225-5713

Committees
Appropriations

Residence
Rogers

Born
Feb. 18, 1957; Russellville, Ark.

Religion
Baptist

Family
Wife, Terri Womack; three children

Education
Arkansas Tech, B.A. 1979 (speech)

Military
Ark. National Guard, 1979-2009

Career
Securities broker; college ROTC program director; radio station manager

Political Highlights
Rogers City Council, 1983-84, 1997-98; mayor of Rogers, 1999-2010

ELECTION RESULTS

2012 GENERAL		
Steve Womack (R)	186,467	75.9%
Rebekah Kennedy (GREEN)	39,318	16.0%
David Pangrac (LIBERT)	19,875	8.1%
2012 PRIMARY		
Steve Womack (R)		unopposed
2010 GENERAL		
Steve Womack (R)	148,581	72.4%
David Whitaker (D)	56,542	27.6%

Elected 2010; 2nd term

Womack says there are two people he doesn't want to disappoint while serving in the House: his father and Kentucky GOP Rep. Harold Rogers, chairman of the Appropriations Committee. Rogers "gave me a chance to serve on the Appropriations Committee, and without his endorsement, I probably wouldn't be there," Womack said.

Before coming to the House he was mayor of, appropriately enough, the city of Rogers. Womack had a reputation for being straightforward and strong-willed; he was in the National Guard for three decades and retired as a colonel. Republican leaders put him to work as a member of the whip team, and he didn't miss a vote in his first term.

In the 113th Congress (2013-14), Womack was added to the Appropriations subcommittees handling the biggest pieces of the federal budget — Defense and Labor-HHS-Education — and kept his slot on the Financial Services subcommittee. But service on the spending panel comes with the chance to chime in on a wide range of issues. Womack thus far has gone with a classic appropriator's formula: broad support for his party's agenda plus attention to home-state needs.

Womack wants to see the proposed Interstate 49 corridor come to fruition, and he supports public-private partnerships for transportation projects and funding of local airport expansions and rehabilitations.

His district has many farms, and in 2011 he introduced a bill with Democrat Dan Boren of Oklahoma to repeal tax credits for ethanol production. Womack says that the diversion of corn supplies to that pursuit has driven up feed costs for farmers in his district.

Womack was among the Arkansas lawmakers trying to block changes to the 188th Fighter Wing at Fort Smith, but a fiscal 2013 defense policy bill allowing the removal of several fighters was enacted.

Arkansas is the home of Wal-Mart, and Womack pushes legislation to overturn a 1992 Supreme Court decision and allow states to tax online retailers outside their borders, while including exemptions for small businesses. "In short, this bill levels the playing field in the world of retails sales," he said at a 2012 hearing. "This is not a new tax. This is an existing, lawfully due tax imposed on consumers." Wyoming Republican Michael B. Enzi has worked on a similar bill in the Senate. Womack maintains that the current rules for online taxation hurt all brick-and-mortar retailers, from Wal-Mart to mom-and-pop stores.

As mayor, he was among the first to sign up his city's police officers for "287(g) training," allowing them to serve as U.S. immigration agents in the field or at jails. He wants to strengthen current laws against illegal immigration and pass new ones to "increase our ability to monitor who is in our country."

He backed a bill in the 112th Congress (2011-12) to make the E-Verify employment verification system mandatory for employers; he also successfully amended the House version of a fiscal 2012 Financial Services spending bill to prohibit the use of its funds for federal hires if the employees were not first checked through E-Verify. Womack says the poultry industry — Tyson Foods is in his district — and the draw of inexpensive labor have led to a large number of illegal immigrants in Arkansas.

Womack also looks beyond the parochial at the broader fiscal situation of the nation. His first legislative victory was a contentious one. In March 2011, he introduced a measure stipulating that if by April 6 the Senate did not pass an appropriations bill for the remainder of fiscal 2011, a House-passed, Republican-sponsored spending bill would be enacted.

The bill would have suspended lawmakers' pay during a government shutdown lasting more than 24 hours. The House passed it on April Fool's Day, much to the delight of Democrats. "It didn't come without ridicule," Womack said. "But that's OK. At least people know that we're trying to get something accomplished."

Hard-line conservatives are more assertive than Womack regarding spending cuts, but he broadly supports budget reductions. He voted in the 112th for the budgets of Wisconsin Republican Paul D. Ryan and the final version of a deficit reduction package in August 2011.

Womack placed blame for the fiscal situation on previous Congresses for "not swallowing hard and doing the right thing." Even so, he was in the minority of House Republicans voting for the January 2013 "fiscal cliff" deal, which prevented an increase in income tax rates on earnings under $400,000 — but without accompanying spending reductions.

"The notion that because we didn't get the spending cuts we wanted and should therefore raise taxes is absurd, and the discussion on spending is far from over," Womack wrote after the vote.

Born in Russellville, Womack graduated from Arkansas Tech in 1979. He started his National Guard service that year. Womack was deployed to Egypt after the Sept. 11 attacks; he was inducted in 2011 into the Officer Candidate School Hall of Fame. His favorite movie is "An Officer and a Gentleman."

Womack worked as a radio station manager until 1990, then became executive officer of the Army ROTC program at the University of Arkansas. He briefly worked as a broadcaster and as a broker for Merrill Lynch. After his second pass through the Rogers City Council, Womack ran for mayor in 1998. He won and served three terms.

Republican John Boozman decided to vacate the 3rd District House seat for a Senate run in 2010, and Womack ran to succeed him. He finished first in the June primary, beating his nearest competitor by 18 points. He won the runoff by nearly 4 points. That all but assured him a seat in Congress in a very Republican district. Womack took 72 percent of the vote against Democrat David Whitaker, a Fayetteville attorney.

In 2012, his Democratic opponent dropped out before the general election, and Womack took more than 75 percent of the vote.

His placement on Appropriations as a freshman and his selection as a deputy whip were likely aided by his campaign contributions during the 2010 cycle. Womack turned $50,000 of his campaign funds over to the National Republican Congressional Committee and made donations directly to 14 GOP House candidates, eight of whom were elected. He continued the practice during the 2012 cycle.

Key Votes

2012	
Extend a Social Security payroll tax cut and unemployment benefits	YES
Ease securities rules to expand small-business access to capital	YES
Extend for one year subsidized student loan interest rates financed by a cut in health care spending	YES
Cite Attorney General Eric H. Holder Jr. for contempt of Congress	YES
Create a visa program for foreign graduates in high-tech fields	YES
Extend most Bush-era income tax rates while allowing rates for top-bracket earners to rise (Jan. 1, 2013)	YES
2011	
Strike funding for F-35 alternative engine	YES
Prevent EPA from regulating greenhouse gas emissions to address climate change	YES
Extend certain provisions of Patriot Act for four years	YES
Declare opposition to use of ground troops in Libya	YES
Overhaul patent law	YES
Pass compromise debt limit increase plan and establish future spending limits	YES
Allow consideration of measures to implement three trade agreements	YES

CQ Vote Studies

	PARTY UNITY		PRESIDENTIAL SUPPORT	
	SUPPORT	OPPOSE	SUPPORT	OPPOSE
2012	89%	11%	15%	85%
2011	95%	5%	26%	74%

Interest Groups

	AFL-CIO	ADA	CCUS	ACU
2012	14%	0%	100%	76%
2011	0%	5%	100%	76%

Arkansas 3

Northwest — Fort Smith, Fayetteville

Previously encompassing the entire northwestern corner of the state, the 3rd District now forms an arc from Fort Smith north to Eureka Springs and back south to Russellville in Pope County. Retail outlets, interstates and suburbia in the district's western arm give way to forests and sparsely populated counties in the east.

Explosive growth in Benton and Washington counties forced Arkansas legislators to shift out three whole counties and parts of three others during decennial redistricting following the 2010 census, hollowing out the 3rd. Although Fayetteville, a Democratic stronghold and home of the University of Arkansas, remains in the district, remapping solidified the overall Republican dominance here, a U.S. House seat the GOP has held since 1966.

The corridor of cities from Bentonville to Fayetteville along Interstate 540 forms the commercial hub of the district. Hometown giants Wal-Mart Stores in Bentonville, Tyson Foods in Springdale and J.B. Hunt trucking in Lowell all provide jobs. The district's diversified economy is a bright spot for Arkansas. Unemployment rates are lower than statewide and national averages, and trends in the construction sector anticipate further growth.

The district is majority white but does have the highest percentage of Hispanic residents statewide, at almost 13 percent. Between 2000 and 2010, Benton County's Hispanic population more than doubled.

The loss of much of the Ozark National Forest to the 4th District will lessen the 3rd's reliance on outdoors-related tourism, but Beaver Lake remains a draw. History buffs visit Civil War sites such as Pea Ridge National Military Park, as well as the museums and landmarks in Fort Smith, which cover everything from the founding of the namesake fort to the Belle Grove Historic District. The new Crystal Bridges art museum, opened in 2011 by Wal-Mart heiress Alice Walton, is in Bentonville. Religion-oriented tourism in Carroll County illustrates the district's conservative, Bible Belt character.

Major Industries
Retail, tourism, health care

Cities
Fort Smith, Fayetteville, Springdale, Rogers, Bentonville

Notable
The Daisy Company has its Airgun Museum in Rogers.

Rep. Tom Cotton (R)

Capitol Office
225-3772
cotton.house.gov
415 Cannon Bldg. 20515-0404; fax 225-1314

Committees
Financial Services
Foreign Affairs

Residence
Dardanelle

Born
May 13, 1977; Dardanelle, Ark.

Religion
Methodist

Family
Single

Education
Harvard U., A.B. 1998 (government); Claremont Graduate University, attended 1998-99; Harvard U., J.D. 2002

Military
Army, 2004-09

Career
Management consultant; lawyer

Political Highlights
No previous office

ELECTION RESULTS

2012 GENERAL		
Tom Cotton (R)	154,149	59.5%
Gene Jeffress (D)	95,013	36.7%
Bobby Tullis (LIBERT)	4,984	1.9%
Josh Drake (GREEN)	4,807	1.9%
2012 PRIMARY		
Tom Cotton (R)	20,899	57.6%
Beth Anne Rankin (R)	13,460	37.1%
John Cowart (R)	1,953	5.4%

Elected 2012; 1st term

Republican strategists salivate over Cotton's potential — he's a Harvard-educated lawyer, an Army veteran with combat experience, and a young conservative who's comfortable in front of a TV camera.

He says the Sept. 11 terrorist attacks motivated him to join the military. Cotton was in law school at the time — he earned his degree, worked for several years to pay down student loans, then enlisted. He deployed to Baghdad in 2006 with the 101st Airborne, and he also served in Afghanistan in 2008.

Cotton was given a seat on the Foreign Affairs Committee and its nonproliferation subcommittee. He quickly criticized Obama administration policy toward Iran and North Korea. After a nuclear test by North Korea in February 2013, Cotton said the United States should be "crippling the Kim regime through strict sanctions."

After his military service, Cotton worked as a management consultant, advising companies across a range of industries. He's a member of the Financial Services Committee, and Cotton has expressed his displeasure with both the 2010 financial regulatory overhaul law and the Federal Reserve's "quantitative easing" strategy. "Hardworking families and small-business owners bear the ultimate burden" of those policies, he said in 2013.

Cotton is a sixth-generation Arkansan. He grew up on his family's cattle farm, pitching in as needed. He came of age during Bill Clinton's presidential campaign and credits Clinton for sparking his interest in current affairs.

He announced his candidacy in the fall of 2011, a few months after Rep. Mike Ross, a six-term conservative Democrat, announced his retirement. He put on a bravura fundraising performance for the GOP primary and bested Beth Anne Rankin, who lost to Ross in 2010. He was confident enough of victory in the general election that he donated hundreds of thousand of dollars to other Republican candidates around the country.

Cotton has been mentioned as a possible Senate candidate in 2014.

Arkansas 4

South and west — Pine Bluff, Hot Springs

Planted across most of Arkansas' south and west, the 4th District is the state's geographically largest district. An abundant timber industry, small farming communities and one of the state's most lucrative tourist areas drive the district's economy.

Tourism revolves around Hot Springs and its historic mineral baths and the nearby Ouachita Mountains; the Ozark National Forest (shared with the 3rd) also stretches across Johnson and Newton counties. The pine woodlands of the Ouachita Mountains also sustain a significant forestry industry. Southern Arkansas is one of the nation's largest poultry and farmed-fish producing regions. Local farmers provide chickens to processing plants run by Tyson Foods and other companies across Arkansas.

The district has the lowest median income in the state. In Texarkana, in the district's southwestern corner, the poverty rate is more than 20 percent and in Hope, it stretches to more than 30 percent. The drive for cheap labor at chicken plants has attracted a booming Hispanic immigrant population, legal and illegal. Yell County adds thousands more Hispanic residents to the 4th; Tyson's is the largest employer in that county.

The addition of Republican-friendly areas north of the Arkansas River and the loss of several Mississippi Delta counties in the east during the decennial remapping process made the 4th less likely to support Democrats. African-American communities in the Delta have been moved into the neighboring 1st District, although black-majority Pine Bluff was kept in the 4th. Despite more than a decade of representation in the U.S. House by a Democrat, statewide and federal elections have swung in favor of the GOP. In Polk County, along the Oklahoma border, Republican Mitt Romney took more than 77 percent of the 2012 presidential vote, his highest percentage statewide.

Major Industry
Timber, livestock, agriculture, tourism

Military Bases
Pine Bluff Arsenal (Army), 1 military, 960 civilian

Cities
Pine Bluff, Hot Springs, Texarkana, El Dorado

Notable
Visitors can pan for diamonds at Crater of Diamonds State Park in Murfreesboro, the only public diamond mine in the world.

CALIFORNIA

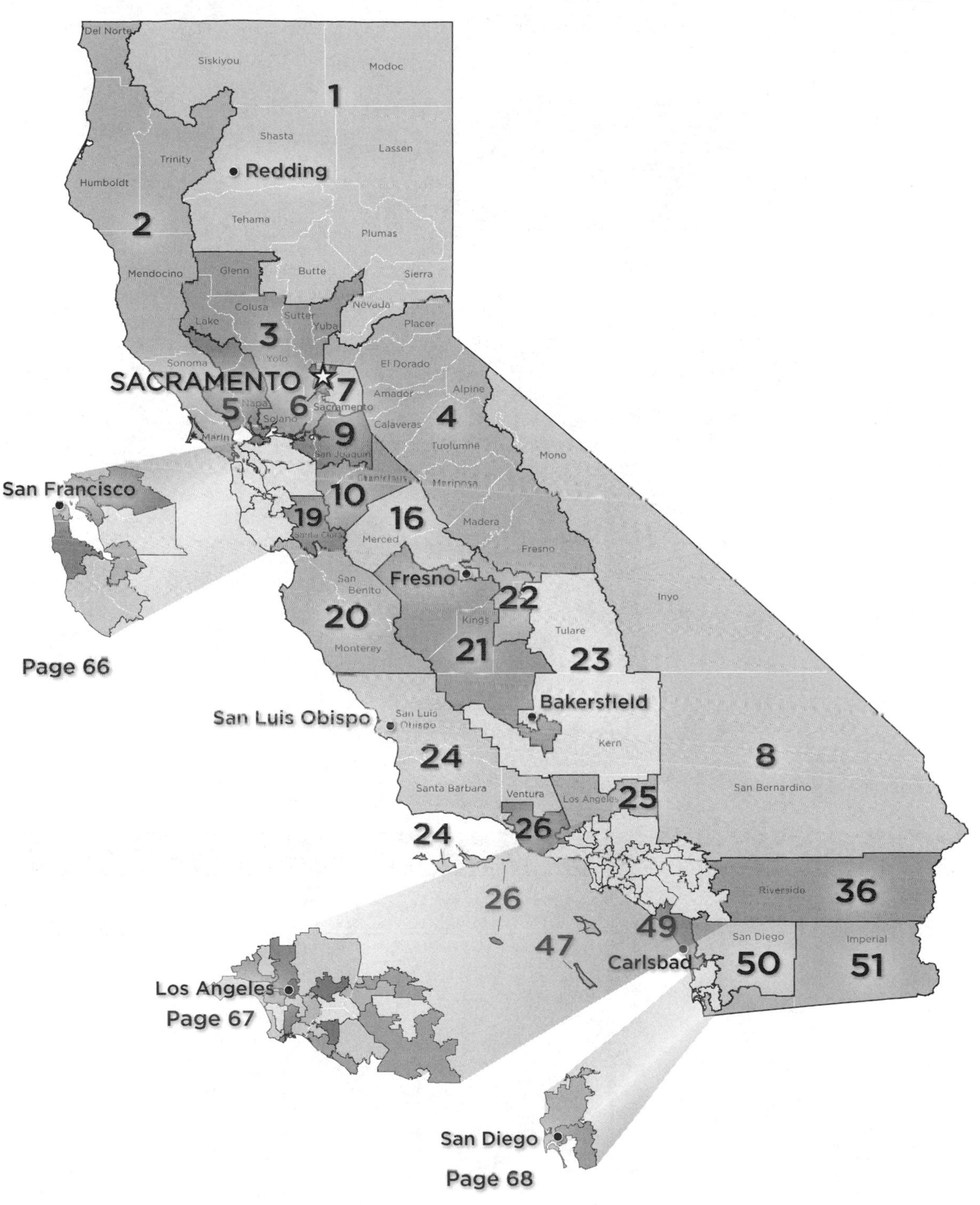

Page 66
Page 67
Page 68

San Francisco Area

Districts 11-15, 17-18

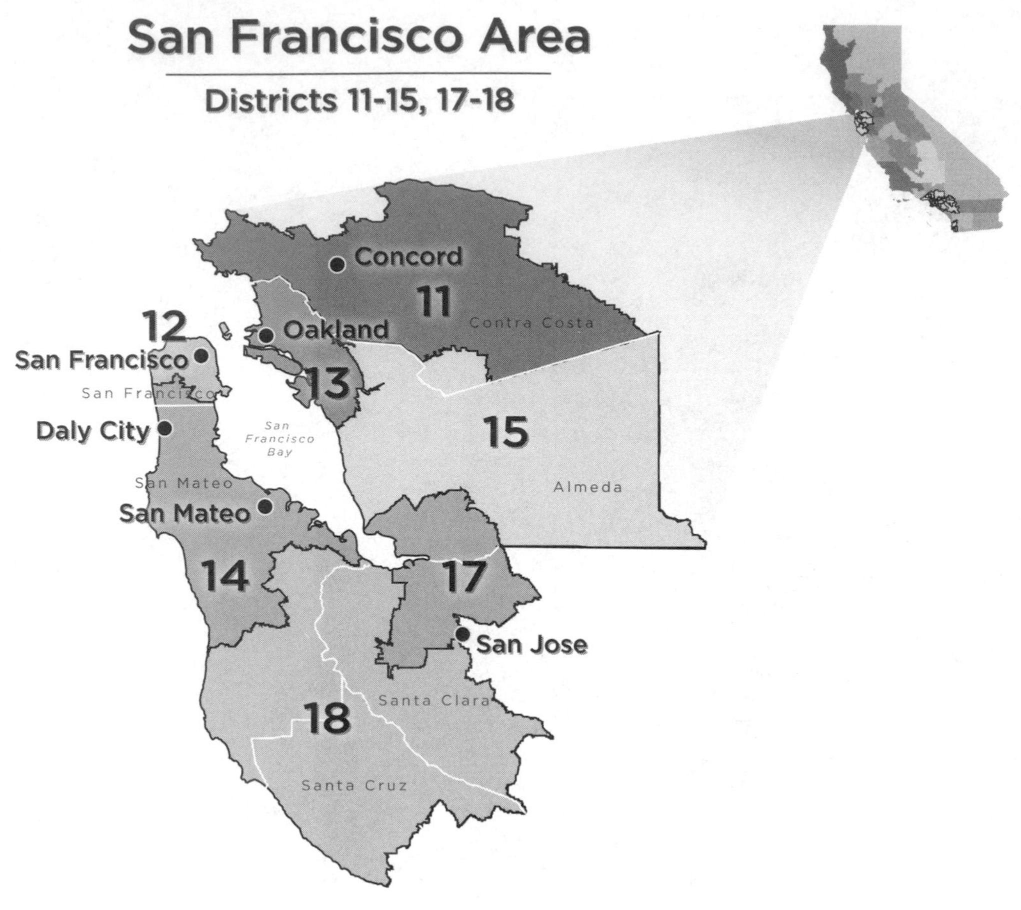

STATISTICS BY DISTRICT

District	2012 Vote for President Obama	Romney	2008 Vote for President Obama	McCain	Black	Asian	Hispanic	Median Income	Over 64	Under 20	College Education	Rural	Sq. Miles
1	40%	57%	44%	56%	1%	3%	12%	$41,709	18%	23%	22%	40%	28,089
2	69	27	74	26	2	4	17	56,576	16	23	38	27	12,952
3	54	43	56	44	6	11	29	53,602	12	28	23	15	6,184
4	40	58	44	56	1	4	13	61,303	16	24	31	43	12,836
5	70	27	72	28	7	11	26	58,942	14	25	30	10	1,731
6	69	28	70	30	12	17	26	44,523	10	29	25	<1	175
7	51	47	53	47	8	12	17	60,537	12	27	31	3	549
8	42	56	44	56	8	3	36	45,879	11	31	16	20	32,867
9	58	40	58	42	8	13	39	52,209	11	32	19	8	1,245
10	51	47	51	49	4	6	40	49,660	10	32	18	8	1,819
11	68	30	71	29	9	13	25	69,586	14	26	41	1	494
12	84	12	87	13	6	31	15	69,046	13	15	54	0	39
13	88	9	90	10	20	21	21	56,906	12	23	45	0	97
14	74	24	75	25	4	31	25	79,287	14	23	40	1	260
15	68	30	69	31	6	28	24	82,179	10	27	39	1	599

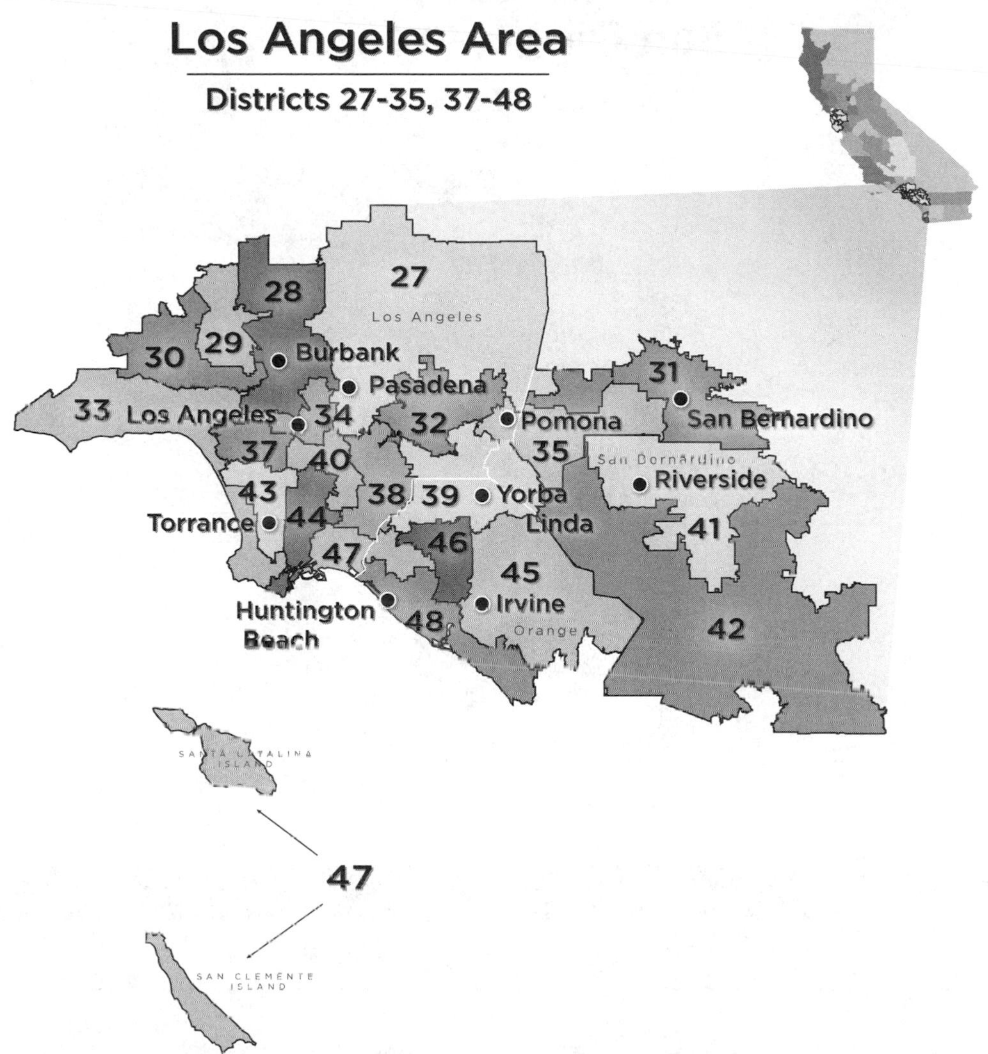

STATISTICS BY DISTRICT

District	2012 Vote for President Obama	2012 Vote for President Romney	2008 Vote for President Obama	2008 Vote for President McCain	Black	Asian	Hispanic	Median Income	Over 64	Under 20	College Education	Rural	Sq. Miles
16	59%	39%	59%	41%	6%	9%	58%	$36,372	9%	35%	11%	9%	2,840
17	72	26	71	29	3	49	19	92,030	10	26	50	<1	185
18	68	29	72	28	2	20	17	97,001	13	25	57	5	696
19	71	27	70	30	3	26	41	71,479	11	27	31	2	915
20	71	26	73	27	2	5	52	55,752	11	29	26	12	4,874
21	55	44	54	46	4	3	72	37,228	7	35	9	16	6,730
22	42	57	44	56	3	7	46	49,844	11	32	22	8	1,165
23	36	62	37	63	7	5	35	51,232	11	31	18	16	9,898
24	54	43	58	42	2	5	35	56,943	14	26	32	11	6,883
25	48	50	51	49	8	8	38	68,551	9	32	26	7	1,691
26	54	44	58	42	2	7	43	72,804	13	28	32	3	939
27	63	35	63	37	4	36	26	63,561	15	23	40	<1	700
28	70	27	72	28	2	14	25	51,500	14	18	42	<1	218
29	77	21	76	24	4	8	68	43,780	9	29	18	<1	92
30	65	32	67	33	4	13	29	67,079	14	23	40	<1	136

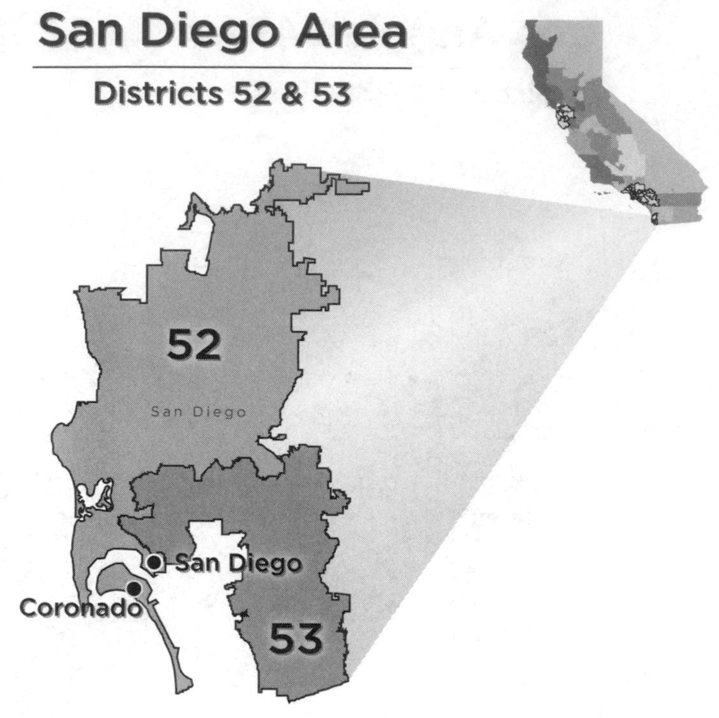

Statistics by District

District	2012 Vote for President Obama	2012 Vote for President Romney	2008 Vote for President Obama	2008 Vote for President McCain	Black	Asian	Hispanic	Median Income	Over 64	Under 20	College Education	Rural	Sq. Miles
31	57%	41%	58%	42%	10%	7%	49%	$50,882	9%	32%	22%	<1%	218
32	65	32	64	36	3	16	62	57,062	11	28	20	<1	124
33	61	37	66	34	3	14	12	89,354	15	22	62	2	289
34	83	14	80	20	4	19	66	32,667	10	26	20	0	48
35	67	31	66	34	7	6	70	51,699	8	33	13	<1	169
36	51	48	52	48	4	4	48	42,922	19	27	19	8	5,913
37	85	13	86	14	24	10	39	46,081	11	24	36	0	55
38	65	33	64	36	4	14	61	59,781	11	29	21	0	101
39	47	51	49	51	2	28	35	76,748	12	27	39	1	204
40	81	17	80	20	6	2	87	37,876	7	35	8	0	58
41	62	36	61	39	10	5	59	49,887	8	35	15	1	317
42	41	57	45	55	6	9	33	71,073	10	30	25	6	936
43	78	20	77	23	24	13	46	44,230	11	29	23	0	72
44	85	14	83	17	15	5	70	43,956	9	34	11	0	79
45	43	55	48	52	1	21	19	89,383	12	26	50	<1	330

Gov. Jerry Brown (D)

First elected: 2010
Length of term: 4 years
Term expires: 1/15
Salary: $173,000
Phone: (916) 445-2841
Residence: Oakland
Born: April 7, 1938; San Francisco, Calif.
Religion: Roman Catholic
Family: Wife, Anne Gust
Education: Santa Clara U., attended 1955-56; U. of California, B.A. 1961 (classics); Yale U., J.D. 1964
Career: Lawyer; international relations think tank chairman
Political highlights: Los Angeles Community College Board of Trustees, 1969-71; Calif. secretary of state, 1971-75; governor, 1975-83; sought Democratic nomination for president, 1976, 1980; Democratic nominee for U.S. Senate, 1982; Calif. Democratic Party chairman, 1989-91; sought Democratic nomination for president, 1992; mayor of Oakland, 1999-2007; Calif. attorney general, 2007-11

ELECTION RESULTS

2010 GENERAL

Jerry Brown (D)	5,428,149	53.8%
Meg Whitman (R)	4,127,391	40.9%
Chelene Nightingale (AMI)	166,312	1.7%
Laura Wells (GREEN)	129,224	1.2%
Dale F. Ogden (LIBERT)	150,895	1.5%

Lt. Gov. Gavin Newsom (D)

First elected: 2010
Length of term: 4 years
Term expires: 1/15
Salary: $130,490
Phone: (916) 445-8994

LEGISLATURE

Legislature: Year-round with recess; 2-year session
Senate: 40 members, 4-year terms
2013 ratios: 28 D, 11 R, 1 vacancy; 28 men, 11 women
Salary: $90,526
Phone: (916) 651-4181
Assembly: 80 members, 2-year terms
2013 ratios: 54 D, 25 R, 1 vacancy; 58 men, 21 women
Salary: $90,526
Phone: (916) 319-2856

TERM LIMITS

Governor: 2 terms
Senate: 2 terms
Assembly: 3 terms

URBAN STATISTICS

CITY	POPULATION
Los Angeles	3,792,621
San Diego	1,307,402
San Jose	945,942
San Francisco	805,235
Fresno	494,665

REGISTERED VOTERS

Democrat	44%
Republican	29%
Other	27%

POPULATION

2010 population	37,253,956
2000 population	33,871,648
1990 population	29,760,021
Percent change (2000-2010)	+10.0%
Rank among states (2010)	1
Median age	34.6
Born in state	52.9%
Foreign born	26.1%
Violent crime rate	472/100,000
Poverty level	14.2%
Federal workers	335,024
Military	117,806

ELECTIONS

STATE ELECTION OFFICIAL
(916) 657-2166
DEMOCRATIC PARTY
(916) 442-5707
REPUBLICAN PARTY
(818) 841-5210

MISCELLANEOUS

Web: www.ca.gov
Capital: Sacramento

U.S. CONGRESS

Senate: 2 Democrats
House: 38 Democrats, 15 Republicans

Statistics by District

District	2012 Vote for President		2008 Vote for President										
	Obama	Romney	Obama	McCain	Black	Asian	Hispanic	Median Income	Over 64	Under 20	College Education	Rural	Sq. Miles
46	61%	36%	60%	40%	2%	11%	67%	$51,899	8%	31%	16%	0%	72
47	60	37	59	41	8	20	35	55,590	11	28	29	<1	216
48	43	55	48	52	1	18	20	76,077	15	23	42	<1	145
49	46	52	51	49	2	7	26	68,129	13	27	39	1	553
50	38	60	40	60	2	5	30	54,971	12	28	24	13	2,787
51	69	29	67	33	8	7	69	38,528	10	32	13	7	4,792
52	52	46	56	44	3	19	14	77,409	12	23	55	<1	267
53	61	36	62	38	7	13	32	59,959	11	24	34	<1	135
STATE	**60**	**37**	**61**	**37**	**6**	**13**	**38**	**57,287**	**12**	**28**	**30**	**6**	**155,779**
U.S.	**51**	**47**	**53**	**46**	**12**	**5**	**17**	**50,052**	**13**	**27**	**29**	**21**	**3,531,905**

Sen. Dianne Feinstein (D)

Capitol Office
224-3841
feinstein.senate.gov
331 Hart Bldg. 20510-0504; fax 228-3954

Committees
Appropriations
(Energy-Water - Chairwoman)
Judiciary
Rules & Administration
Select Intelligence - Chairwoman

Residence
San Francisco

Born
June 22, 1933; San Francisco, Calif.

Religion
Jewish

Family
Husband, Richard Blum; one child, three stepchildren

Education
Stanford U., A.B. 1955 (history)

Career
Homemaker

Political Highlights
San Francisco Board of Supervisors, 1970-78 (president, 1970-71, 1974-75, 1978); candidate for mayor of San Francisco, 1971, 1975; mayor of San Francisco, 1978-89; Democratic nominee for governor, 1990

ELECTION RESULTS

2012 GENERAL		
Dianne Feinstein (D)	7,864,624	62.5%
Elizabeth Emken (R)	4,713,887	37.5%
2012 PRIMARY (Open)		
Dianne Feinstein (D)	2,392,822	49.3%
Diane Stewart (D)	97,782	2.0%
Michael Strimling (D)	97,024	2.0%
David Alex Levitt (D)	76,482	1.6%
Colleen Fernald (D)	51,623	1.1%

Previous Winning Percentages
2006 (59%); 2000 (56%); 1994 (47%); 1992 Special Election (54%)

Elected 1992; 4th full term

Feinstein is deliberative and level-headed. She's comfortable working with Republicans on thorny political problems, and she's equally at ease when staking out liberal positions that have little hope of picking up GOP support.

"I'm probably less an ideologue than I am one for solving the problem of the day, whatever it might be," she said. "Most problems around here require bipartisan solutions; therefore, I think working across partisan lines is very important where one can."

Despite holding many positions that put her in the left wing of her party, Feinstein (FINE-stine) has never been a "San Francisco liberal," even as a former mayor of that city. She is known for often-protracted consideration before making up her mind — a trait that makes her seem less overtly partisan than many of her colleagues.

That style has helped Feinstein become one of the most popular politicians in her state. She passed on the governor's race in 2010 and instead won re-election in 2012 with more than 60 percent of the vote.

Her philosophical duality is on display when she works on national security. In the Senate, her top concern is chairing the Intelligence Committee, which makes her highly visible during debates on defense and foreign policy.

In the 112th Congress (2011-12) she worked to smooth over Senate opposition to a reauthorization of a 2008 electronic surveillance law, as requested by the White House; President Barack Obama signed that bill late in 2012. Yet she initiated an investigation into the deadly attack on a U.S. consulate in Libya — at a time when Republicans were making the attack into an election issue for 2012. She criticized the Obama administration over a spate of leaks of classified national security information — but when Republican presidential candidate Mitt Romney seized on her remarks about how much the White House knew about the disclosures, she issued a statement rebuffing Romney.

During debate on the fiscal 2013 defense authorization bill, she brokered a compromise amendment prohibiting detention without charge or trial of a U.S. citizen or a permanent resident apprehended in the United States. It prompted Kentucky Republican Rand Paul, a stringent civil libertarian, to lift his hold on the legislation.

Together with Intelligence Vice Chairman Saxby Chambliss of Georgia and their House counterparts, she has restored regular enactment of annual intelligence authorization bills. Those measures were once a magnet for controversial policy riders, but lately their passage has been a more innocuous ritual. Feinstein describes the bills as one of the few vehicles by which Congress can put its stamp on spy operations.

Feinstein in the 113th Congress (2013-14) is escalating cybersecurity oversight. She wrote in 2013 that legislation is needed to "remove legal barriers to full sharing of information" between the public and private sectors and "to provide liability protections to encourage the best cyber measures possible." A report of increased hacking by China in February 2013 prompted Feinstein to call for a "binding international agreement among nations to prohibit cybercrimes and attacks."

She also might be looking at offensive operations — the U.S. intelligence community's role in developing the Stuxnet worm with Israel has made headlines and raised questions about the legal justifications for contributing to attacks.

As the No. 2 Democrat on the Judiciary Committee, she often has helped shape national security legislation that comes through that panel as well, such as a 2011 extension of several expiring surveillance provisions in the anti-terrorism law known as the Patriot Act.

When it comes to gun control, a topic dear to party liberals, Feinstein is a fierce proponent. She was the author of a federal ban on certain semi-automatic weapons, which expired in 2004. Feinstein has sought its renewal, and her quest became more urgent after a gunman killed 26 people, most of them children, at a Connecticut school in late 2012.

A few weeks into the 113th Congress she introduced an expanded version of her earlier law. It would ban the future sale, transfer, manufacture and importation of 157 specific kinds of semi-automatic guns, as well as some kinds of ammunition magazines. It beefs up background checks for the sale or transfer of existing weapons. Feinstein admitted in March 2013 that her plan had virtually no chance of passage — it was resoundingly defeated in an April vote — but she added that "I don't give up."

She came to support stricter gun control in part through tragic firsthand experience. In November 1978, while president of San Francisco's Board of Supervisors, Feinstein discovered the body of Mayor George Moscone in his office after he and Harvey Milk, the city's first openly gay supervisor, were gunned down by Dan White, a former supervisor. Feinstein, as board president, replaced Moscone as mayor.

Feinstein holds the gavel of the Energy-Water Appropriations Subcommittee, which is a platform to discuss nuclear weapons, research laboratories and water projects — all critical components of California's economy.

Most notably, her fiscal 2013 appropriations bill included a provision to fund temporary nuclear-waste storage facilities, an attempt to move past the political impasse surrounding the disposal of such waste, which for three decades has focused on burying spent fuel under Nevada's Yucca Mountain. The bill wasn't enacted — no regular spending bills were in 2012 — but the Energy Department in early 2013 announced a pilot program for interim nuclear-waste storage.

"Regardless of whether the United States proceeds with Yucca Mountain or another geologic repository, this country will need interim storage for more than 20 years," Feinstein wrote in approving of the decision.

Feinstein in 2011 helped take down what had been one of the most resilient federal energy policies, leading the charge to end tax subsidies for ethanol production. A resounding vote of approval for Feinstein's proposal to end the subsidy was seen as its death knell, and it expired in 2012. Critics note that the existing federal mandate for renewable-fuel production still can be considered a market-distorting subsidy to corn growers and ethanol producers, however.

Feinstein's mother was a former model; her father was a surgeon. Her marriage to investment banker Richard Blum has made her one of the wealthiest members of Congress, but also has resulted in her being a frequent target of criticism that his government contracts and other business dealings present a conflict of interest. Feinstein has uniformly denied any connection between her legislative positions and her husband's interests.

Her affinity for politics began in college as she built on her volunteer work to become Stanford's student body vice president. In 1960, Gov. Pat Brown named her to the women's parole board. She started her service on the board of supervisors in 1970 and made several unsuccessful runs for mayor. She held the mayoral post for a decade, leaving City Hall in 1989 to prepare for a 1990 gubernatorial campaign against GOP Sen. Pete Wilson.

She lost that battle, but two years later she ran for the Senate and defeated Republican incumbent John Seymour, whom Wilson had appointed as his successor. Two years later, Feinstein got a scare from Rep. Michael Huffington, an oil family scion who spent millions of his own money on the race. But she prevailed, as she did in 2000 against moderate Republican Rep. Tom Campbell. Feinstein coasted to victory in both 2006 and 2012.

Key Votes

2012	
Prohibit health insurance plans from denying coverage based on the sponsor's religious beliefs	YES
Require approval of the Keystone XL oil pipeline	NO
Ease securities rules to expand small-business access to capital	NO
Reauthorize farm and nutrition programs for five years	YES
Limit debate on a bill that would create private-sector cybersecurity standards	YES
Consent to ratification of a treaty setting global standard for the treatment of people with disabilities	YES
Provide $60.4 billion in disaster relief following Superstorm Sandy	YES
Extend most Bush-era income tax rates while allowing rates for top-bracket earners to rise (Jan. 1, 2013)	YES
2011	
Prevent EPA from regulating greenhouse gas emissions to address climate change	NO
Extend certain provisions of Patriot Act for four years	YES
Clear compromise debt limit increase plan and establish future spending limits	YES
Overhaul patent law	YES
Implement Colombia free trade agreement	YES
Limit debate on confirmation of Caitlin J. Halligan to D.C. Circuit Court of Appeals	YES
Extend payroll tax cut and unemployment benefits for two months	YES

CQ Vote Studies

	PARTY UNITY		PRESIDENTIAL SUPPORT	
	SUPPORT	OPPOSE	SUPPORT	OPPOSE
2012	93%	7%	97%	3%
2011	98%	2%	99%	1%
2010	97%	3%	98%	2%
2009	96%	4%	96%	4%
2008	91%	9%	38%	62%
2007	93%	7%	39%	61%
2006	90%	10%	54%	46%
2005	92%	8%	40%	60%
2004	95%	5%	62%	38%
2003	91%	9%	49%	51%

Interest Groups

	AFL-CIO	ADA	CCUS	ACU
2012	100%	95%	38%	4%
2011	79%	90%	64%	5%
2010	94%	90%	27%	8%
2009	100%	100%	43%	0%
2008	100%	100%	63%	4%
2007	89%	90%	45%	0%
2006	100%	90%	50%	0%
2005	62%	95%	50%	12%
2004	100%	100%	65%	4%
2003	92%	90%	39%	5%

Sen. Barbara Boxer (D)

Capitol Office
224-3553
boxer.senate.gov
112 Hart Bldg. 20510-0505; fax 224-0454

Committees
Commerce, Science & Transportation
Environment & Public Works - Chairwoman
Foreign Relations
(International Operations & Organizations - Chairwoman)
Select Ethics - Chairwoman

Residence
Rancho Mirage

Born
Nov. 11, 1940; Brooklyn, N.Y.

Religion
Jewish

Family
Husband, Stewart Boxer; two children

Education
Brooklyn College, B.A. 1962 (economics)

Career
Congressional aide; journalist; stockbroker

Political Highlights
Candidate for Marin County Board of Supervisors, 1972; Marin County Board of Supervisors, 1977-83 (president, 1980); U.S. House, 1983-93

ELECTION RESULTS

2010 GENERAL

Barbara Boxer (D)	5,218,441	52.2%
Carly Fiorina (R)	4,217,366	42.2%
Gail K. Lightfoot (LIBERT)	175,242	1.8%
Marsha Feinland (PFP)	135,093	1.4%
Duane Roberts (GREEN)	128,510	1.3%
Edward C. Noonan (AMI)	125,441	1.2%

2010 PRIMARY

Barbara Boxer (D)	1,957,920	80.9%
Brian Quintana (D)	338,442	14.0%
Robert M. "Mickey" Kaus (D)	123,573	5.1%

Previous Winning Percentages
2004 (58%); 1998 (53%); 1992 (48%); 1990 House Election (68%); 1988 House Election (73%); 1986 House Election (74%); 1984 House Election (68%); 1982 House Election (52%)

Elected 1992; 4th term

Boxer is often the mental stand-in when conservatives visualize and grouse about California liberals. She's anti-war, favors strong environmental protections, seethes at possible gender discrimination and can be uncomfortably blunt to both friends and foes when expressing herself. But after years of limited legislative success, in recent Congresses she has demonstrated increasing pragmatism and steered more major bills to passage.

The daughter of Jewish immigrants, Boxer grew up in New York City. She was married by her early 20s and worked as a stockbroker while her husband finished law school; they moved to California in 1965 and settled near San Francisco a few years later. They were involved in the anti-war and environmental movements while raising a family, and Boxer was elected to the Marin County Board of Supervisors in 1976.

Six years later she won a House seat and took over for her longtime friend and mentor, Rep. John L. Burton, when he retired. A decade later she was elected to the Senate. Along the way, critics accused her of self-promotion and excessively partisan behavior; they also noted that virtually none of her bills made it through the Senate.

"My political style is to be extremely candid and straight from the shoulders, and not to be mealy-mouthed or waffle," she once said. "When I believe in something, I believe in it strongly."

Memories of that intractability may be overshadowing some of her recent work. There aren't many lawmakers associated more closely with environmental causes than Boxer, and since 2007 she has chaired the Environment and Public Works Committee. In 2012, she and her very conservative ranking Republican, James M. Inhofe of Oklahoma, in tandem found the votes to pass a two-year reauthorization of surface transportation programs. Boxer worked with House Transportation and Infrastructure Chairman John L. Mica, a Florida Republican, to build support for the Boxer-Inhofe bill in that chamber. Throughout the process she publicly praised GOP colleagues for their cooperation.

The final version had provisions that satisfied both parties. Republicans liked regulatory streamlining that gave states more flexibility in selecting and executing transportation projects. Democrats were able to block the inclusion of one provision to expedite construction of an oil pipeline from Canada and another to block EPA regulation of coal ash.

"I have to find a sweet spot," Boxer told MSNBC in March 2012. "We must reach across the aisle, and we did it."

In May 2013, Boxer won overwhelming Senate passage of an authorization of water infrastructure projects — it includes a streamlined project review process similar to the highway law. In 2007, when President George W. Bush vetoed a $23.2 billion water infrastructure bill, Inhofe and Boxer worked together to override the veto in the Senate.

But Boxer still has her combative side. Not long after the 2012 elections, she vowed to move legislation to mitigate man-made climate change. She and Vermont independent Bernard Sanders have proposed a "carbon tax" to be paid by polluters; most of the revenue raised would go to taxpayers to help them cope with the higher energy costs that would result. Her new ranking member for the 113th Congress (2013-14), Louisiana's David Vitter, panned the idea, but Boxer said in February 2013 that she was ready for a fight. "It is going to make making sausage look pretty," she warned.

As a chief deputy whip, Boxer has been called upon to build consensus among her Democratic colleagues. During the health care debate of the 111th

Congress (2009-10), she engineered a compromise on abortion provisions that was suitable to anti-abortion Democrats led by Sen. Ben Nelson of Nebraska, facilitating enactment of the 2010 health care law. In the lame-duck session of 2010, Boxer agreed to back a two-year extension of the Bush-era tax cuts for all income levels after being a vociferous critic of the tax cuts when they were enacted — the inclusion of extended unemployment insurance won her over.

Boxer is the No. 2 Democrat on the Foreign Relations Committee, where she has paid close attention to anything involving human rights or Israel. She was the Senate sponsor of a 2012 law to enhance U.S.-Israeli cooperation on security issues; it expanded loan guarantees available to Israel and provided assistance for the development of defenses to rocket and missile attacks. When Israeli Prime Minister Benjamin Netanyahu questioned U.S. commitment to his country just months after President Barack Obama signed the bill, Boxer dashed off a terse letter to Netanyahu. "I know that President Obama's support for Israel is unshakable," she wrote.

Boxer chairs the subcommittee on international operations and organizations, which includes jurisdiction over global women's issues. When she took that gavel in 2009, she expressed her hope to "stamp out violence against women in the world."

She is vigilant — and closer to her reputation for scathing partisanship — when she perceives threats to women's rights at home. When the Susan G. Komen foundation in 2012 reversed its decision to stop its funding of Planned Parenthood, Boxer told MSNBC that "women's health triumphed over right-wing politics."

She was an enthusiastic participant as Democrats in 2012 rallied to accuse Republicans of promoting an anti-woman agenda. "They say there's no war on women," she said on MSNBC in April 2012, but "there are no less than 500 bills in the various states of the union, they're completely outrageous. Ninety percent of them ... are written by Republicans." A few months later, she said that Republican vice presidential candidate Paul D. Ryan of Wisconsin "stood hand in hand with Todd Akin in trying to redefine rape, trying to criminalize abortion" — a reference to controversial comments that Akin, a Senate candidate in Missouri, had made about "legitimate rape."

Boxer also chairs the Ethics Committee. She oversaw appointment of a special counsel in early 2011 to lead the ethics investigation of Nevada Republican John Ensign, who faced allegations that he tried to cover up an affair with the spouse of his former top aide. Though Ensign resigned, the committee elected to release a report of the counsel's findings. She said on the floor at the time that they were "so disturbing" that, had he not voluntarily left the Senate, it was "substantial enough to warrant the consideration of expulsion."

Boxer counts Democrat Nancy Pelosi, the House minority leader, as a friend — their relationship goes back to the 1980s, when they represented adjoining House districts. Since 2000, Boxer and her husband have lived in Southern California. Their home is in the Republican-leaning Riverside County community of Rancho Mirage, which is adjacent to Palm Springs.

Boxer has used her time flying back and forth between Washington and the Golden State to write books. She co-wrote the novel "A Time to Run" with Mary-Rose Hayes. The book is about a female senator whose former lover attempts to sabotage her career. A second novel is titled "Blind Trust."

A nonfiction book about women and politics called "Strangers in the Senate" was completed shortly after Boxer won her first Senate race, in 1992, by 5 points over TV commentator Bruce Herschensohn.

Boxer doubled that margin in 1998, then doubled it again in 2004. Republicans targeted her in 2010, and they had a strong recruit in former Hewlett Packard CEO Carly Fiorina. Boxer still won by 10 points.

Key Votes

2012	
Prohibit health insurance plans from denying coverage based on the sponsor's religious beliefs	YES
Require approval of the Keystone XL oil pipeline	NO
Ease securities rules to expand small-business access to capital	NO
Reauthorize farm and nutrition programs for five years	YES
Limit debate on a bill that would create private-sector cybersecurity standards	YES
Consent to ratification of a treaty setting global standard for the treatment of people with disabilities	YES
Provide $60.4 billion in disaster relief following Superstorm Sandy	?
Extend most Bush-era income tax rates while allowing rates for top-bracket earners to rise (Jan. 1, 2013)	YES
2011	
Prevent EPA from regulating greenhouse gas emissions to address climate change	NO
Extend certain provisions of Patriot Act for four years	YES
Clear compromise debt limit increase plan and establish future spending limits	YES
Overhaul patent law	NO
Implement Colombia free trade agreement	NO
Limit debate on confirmation of Caitlin J. Halligan to D.C. Circuit Court of Appeals	YES
Extend payroll tax cut and unemployment benefits for two months	YES

CQ Vote Studies

	Party Unity		Presidential Support	
	Support	Oppose	Support	Oppose
2012	97%	3%	96%	4%
2011	98%	2%	95%	5%
2010	97%	3%	98%	2%
2009	97%	3%	96%	4%
2008	99%	1%	30%	70%
2007	97%	3%	34%	66%
2006	97%	3%	47%	53%
2005	99%	1%	30%	70%
2004	96%	4%	65%	35%
2003	99%	1%	44%	56%

Interest Groups

	AFL-CIO	ADA	CCUS	ACU
2012	100%	90%	38%	4%
2011	95%	95%	45%	0%
2010	100%	95%	18%	0%
2009	100%	100%	43%	0%
2008	100%	95%	57%	4%
2007	100%	80%	30%	4%
2006	100%	95%	25%	8%
2005	92%	100%	24%	12%
2004	100%	95%	56%	4%
2003	100%	95%	22%	10%

Rep. Doug LaMalfa (R)

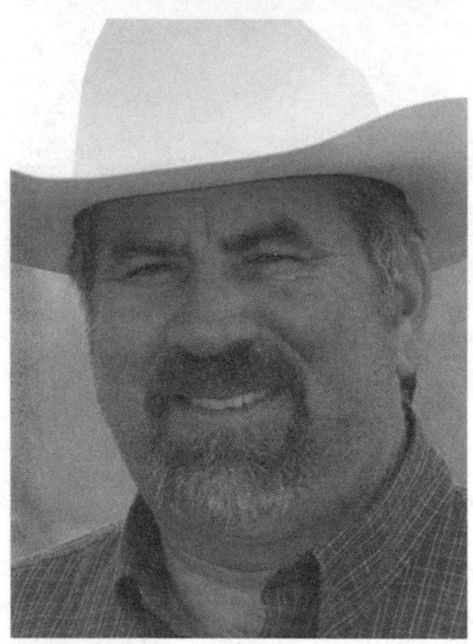

Capitol Office
225-3076
lamalfa.house.gov
506 Cannon Bldg. 20515-0912; fax 226-0852

Committees
Agriculture
Natural Resources

Residence
Richvale

Born
July 2, 1960; Oroville, Calif.

Religion
Christian

Family
Wife, Jill LaMalfa; four children

Education
Butte College, A.A. 1980 (agricultural business); California Polytechnic State U., B.S. 1982 (agricultural management)

Career
Farmer

Political Highlights
Calif. Assembly, 2002-08; Calif. Senate, 2010-12

ELECTION RESULTS

2012 GENERAL		
Doug LaMalfa (R)	168,827	57.4%
Jim Reed (D)	125,386	42.6%
2012 PRIMARY (Open)		
Doug LaMalfa (R)	66,527	37.9%
Sam Aanestad (R)	25,224	14.4%
Michael Dacquisto (R)	10,530	6.0%
Pete Stiglich (R)	10,258	5.8%
Gregory Cheadle (R)	4,939	2.8%

Elected 2012; 1st term

In LaMalfa, California Republicans have another soldier in the water wars that have swamped state politics. He's an experienced legislator with a preference for smaller government and hands-on experience with agriculture.

He spent three terms in the California Assembly and a few more years in the state Senate, but LaMalfa identifies most strongly as a rice farmer. His great-grandfather founded his family farming business in the 1930s, and LaMalfa's college degrees are in agriculture business and management. He is frequently seen wearing a cowboy hat.

LaMalfa has a seat on the Agriculture Committee and wants a long-term reauthorization of farm programs. He told the Capital Press website in 2013 that specialty crop funding favored by farmers in his state could be reduced. "I think what they're looking for is help with marketing and research, and that's something that we can probably help on, but they're going to see a haircut, too," he said. LaMalfa has received federal subsidies for his farm.

He also sits on the Natural Resources Committee and its panels on water, public land and the environment. LaMalfa as a state legislator promoted an expansion of water storage infrastructure, and he dislikes regulations that steer water supplies to the habitats of threatened species rather than to farms.

LaMalfa wants to see devolution of federal land ownership to states and private entities. He maintains that the government's purview should be limited to core constitutional duties such as border defense and public safety.

As a social conservative, he defends gun rights. He also supported California ballot initiatives to ban same-sex marriage and limit affirmative action.

LaMalfa isn't the clear successor to any prior lawmaker — the 1st District created for the 2012 election has large pieces of two old districts. But 13-term Republican Rep. Wally Herger, who retired, gave LaMalfa his endorsement. He finished well ahead of the field in the "open" primary, then easily dispatched Democrat Jim Reed in the general election.

California 1

Northeast — Redding, Chico

Cobbled together from parts of two GOP-heavy districts during decennial remapping, the 1st District sits in northeastern and north-central California. This enormous district stretches from the Interstate 80 crossing of the mountainous Nevada border north of Lake Tahoe, across the northern Sierra Nevada Mountains, and takes in areas west of Interstate 5 in Shasta and Siskiyou counties.

Butte County, in the northern Sacramento Valley, is the 1st's population center. California State University, Chico, a large commuter school, is a major employer and lone Democratic rampart. Butte farms and orchards produce large rice, walnut and almond crops.

Counties on the district's northern and eastern edges are isolated and sparsely populated. Federal agencies manage 60 percent of the land both in sylvan Siskiyou County and in the alkaline Modoc Plateau region of California's northeast. As the site of two state penitentiaries, Lassen County has nearly one prisoner for every four residents.

Outdoor attractions and abundant scenic vistas draw tourists to the district. Shasta Lake, the state's largest reservoir, is popular with houseboat renters and water skiers. Auburn hosts a number of annual long-endurance running and mountain biking events. Skiing in the Sierra Nevada range is big business, but the cluster of resorts in the Lake Tahoe area is just to the south in the 4th District.

The GOP enjoys a 13-point advantage in voter registration and leads Democrats in each of the 11 counties wholly or partly in the district. Republican nominee Elizabeth Emken won all but one county in the 1st in her unsuccessful bid to unseat U.S. Sen. Dianne Feinstein in 2012 — Nevada County narrowly backed Feinstein even though Republicans outnumber Democrats and GOP presidential nominee Mitt Romney won by less than 1 percentage point. Romney won his highest percentage statewide (70 percent) in Modoc County.

Major Industry
Agriculture, timber, tourism, higher education

Military Bases
Sierra Army Depot, 3 military, 1,350 civilian

Cities
Redding, Chico, Paradise

Notable
Sierra Nevada Brewing Company, one of the pioneers of the American craft beer industry, was founded in Chico in 1980.

Rep. Jared Huffman (D)

Capitol Office
225-5161
huffman.house.gov
1630 Longworth Bldg. 20515-2002; fax 225-5163

Committees
Budget
Natural Resources

Residence
San Rafael

Born
Feb. 18, 1964; Independence, Mo.

Religion
Unspecified

Family
Wife, Susan Huffman; two children

Education
U. of California, Santa Barbara, B.A. 1986 (political science); Boston College, J.D. 1990

Career
Lawyer; national team volleyball player

Political Highlights
Marin Municipal Water District Board of Directors, 1995-2006; Calif. Assembly, 2006-12

ELECTION RESULTS

2012 GENERAL		
Jared Huffman (D)	226,216	71.2%
Daniel W. Roberts (R)	91,310	28.8%
2012 PRIMARY (Open)		
Jared Huffman (D)	63,922	37.5%
Norman Solomon (D)	25,462	14.9%
Stacey Lawson (D)	16,946	9.9%
Susan L. Adams (D)	14,041	8.2%
Tiffany Renee (D)	3,033	1.8%
William L. Courtney (D)	2,385	1.4%
Andy Caffrey (D)	1,737	1.0%

Elected 2012; 1st term

Environmental causes brought Huffman into politics and are still a major part of his work. He has a reputation as a non-flashy and liberal lawmaker.

As a child in Independence, Mo., Huffman was a neighbor of a Democratic icon — Harry S. Truman, whom he sometimes saw walking around the town square. Huffman headed west to attend the University of California at Santa Barbara, where he was a volleyball star. He was a member of the 1987 world-champion U.S. volleyball team.

He ended up back in California after getting his law degree. The book "Cadillac Desert," about development-driven water policies in the West, inspired him to run for the Marin County Municipal Water District Board, where he served for 12 years. Huffman also worked for a time as an attorney for the Natural Resources Defense Council, participating in the legal effort to restore water flows in the San Joaquin River to protect salmon.

Elected to the state Assembly in 2006, he advanced a lot of legislation related to water use and the promotion of renewable energy. He continues those efforts as a member of the Natural Resources Committee. "The intersection between job creation and economic growth and environmental sustainability is where I like to focus," he says.

Huffman joined the Congressional Progressive Caucus, and on the Budget Committee he promotes liberal priorities — including collecting more federal revenue from the wealthiest Americans and reducing military spending.

Huffman was in his final term in the Assembly (thanks to a term limit law) when Democrat Lynn Woolsey announced her retirement from Congress. That opened up the 2nd District, where she would have run. Huffman had stiff Democratic competition in activist Norman Solomon and Stacey Lawson, a businesswoman who raised more than $1 million for her campaign. Solomon finished third in the "jungle" primary, 173 votes behind a Republican candidate. That guaranteed Huffman's November victory in the very liberal district.

California 2

Northern Coast — Eureka; Marin County

A motorist would not leave the 2nd while taking Highway 101 from the northern terminus of the Golden Gate Bridge to the Oregon border, a trip of more than 400 miles. Taking in northern coastal counties, affluent Marin County and most of vineyard-covered Sonoma County (shared with the 5th), the district also pulls in land-locked Trinity County. Defined by its geographical breadth, the 2nd even has diverse weather patterns — rainy forests in the north give way to arid farmland in the south.

In the south, wine grapes dominate in warm, dry Mendocino and Sonoma counties. The vineyards of Sonoma are split with the 5th; the Russian River Valley, Green Valley and Dry Creek Valley areas fall in the 2nd. Dairy-rich Marin County boasts gourmet cheese makers. The housing market continues to be an albatross in the southern portion of the 2nd. Home values have plummeted in Mendocino and Sonoma counties since 2007, but the overall cost of living remains high.

Marin's suburban population — many residents are self-employed or commute into San Francisco for high-tech or other white-collar jobs — is mainly divided between foothill towns such as Mt. Tamalpais and waterfront locales like tony Sausalito and Tiburon. Tourists take getaways to Point Reyes National Seashore and Muir Woods.

Farther north, the environmental politics that gripped Humboldt County during the 1990s, driven by opposition to clear-cut logging, are subdued. Humboldt redwood forests account for roughly one-third of California timber industry revenue, but harvests are only two-fifths of what they were two decades ago. The 2nd also relies on commercial fishing in Crescent City, Eureka and Fort Bragg.

Democrats have a more than 2-to-1 lead in voter registration, and independent and unaffiliated voters outnumber Republicans. The GOP has a slight edge in sparsely populated Del Norte and Trinity: In the 2012 presidential election, GOP nominee Mitt Romney won easily in Del Norte County and with a slim plurality in Trinity as Barack Obama dominated in the district's other counties.

Major Industry
Agriculture, tourism, timber

Cities
Petaluma, San Rafael, Novato, Eureka

Notable
San Quentin State Prison in Marin County is the state's oldest correctional facility.

Rep. John Garamendi (D)

Capitol Office
225-1880
garamendi.house.gov
2438 Rayburn Bldg. 20515-0510; fax 225-5914

Committees
Agriculture
Armed Services
Transportation & Infrastructure

Residence
Walnut Grove

Born
Jan. 24, 1945; Camp Blanding, Fla.

Religion
Christian

Family
Wife, Patricia Wilkinson Garamendi; six children

Education
U. of California, Berkeley, B.S. 1966 (business administration); Harvard U., M.B.A. 1970

Career
Rancher; Peace Corps volunteer

Political Highlights
Calif. Assembly, 1974-76; Calif. Senate, 1976-90 (majority leader, 1982-84); sought Democratic nomination for governor, 1982; sought Democratic nomination for Calif. controller, 1986; Calif. insurance commissioner, 1991-95; sought Democratic nomination for governor, 1994; deputy Interior secretary, 1995-98; Calif. insurance commissioner, 2003-07; lieutenant governor, 2007-09

ELECTION RESULTS

2012 GENERAL		
John Garamendi (D)	126,882	54.2%
Kim Dolbow Vann (R)	107,086	45.8%
2012 PRIMARY (Open)		
John Garamendi (D)	59,546	51.5%
2010 GENERAL		
John Garamendi (D)	137,578	58.8%
Gary Clift (R)	88,512	37.9%
Jeremy Cloward (GREEN)	7,716	3.3%

Previous Winning Percentages
2009 Special Election (53%)

Elected 2009; 2nd full term

Backed by an extensive résumé in California politics, Garamendi punches above his relative weight on issues such as health care, industrial policy and offshore oil drilling. He is willing to draw attention his way as a promoter of liberal positions.

Garamendi's support of gay and lesbian rights, a government-run health care program, gun control and climate change legislation have made him a darling in many Democratic circles. But some find his self-confidence off-putting, and he's had his share of setbacks.

He was rebuffed in two attempts at the Democratic nomination for governor and a bid for state controller. Colleagues in the state Senate dumped him from the majority leader's job after two years, saying he was too focused on his own political ambitions, according to the Los Angeles Times. As lieutenant governor in 2009, he had most of his office's budget stripped after he called Republican Arnold Schwarzenegger the "worst governor in California history."

Even so, Garamendi racked up lots of experience: his state legislative career lasted 16 years; he was California's first elected insurance commissioner and succeeded in forcing rate rollbacks; and he got his feet wet in Washington as a deputy Interior secretary during the Clinton administration. Garamendi views himself as "a problem solver" and places the blame for Capitol Hill's dysfunction on Republicans — they too often believe that "if the facts don't fit, the facts are wrong," he said.

He has stood by Democratic priorities. One of his first votes upon joining Congress in 2009 was for the House version of a Democratic health care overhaul bill. He proceeded to chip in on the insurance provisions for the version of the overhaul that was enacted in 2010.

In the 112th Congress (2011-12) Garamendi became a leading proponent of the Democrats' "Make It in America" agenda, introducing two bills to require more domestic purchasing in federally funded transportation programs and put similar restrictions on the use of renewable-energy tax credits. "Don't tell me the Founding Fathers wanted the government to play no role" in the economy, he said. "Washington and Hamilton advocated an industrial policy that included the government playing an active role in developing the nation's infrastructure."

He's back on the Transportation and Infrastructure Committee in the 113th Congress (2013-14) and serves as the ranking member of the Coast Guard and Maritime Transportation panel. He also has a seat on the water resources panel — an important post for the huge farming industry in the 3rd District. Democrats seem to be helping Garamendi for a possible tough re-election campaign, as he was also granted a seat on the Agriculture Committee.

Garamendi is a strong environmentalist — he volunteered in a 2011 interview with comedian Stephen Colbert that "you could call me a tree-hugger." During the 111th Congress (2009-10) he introduced a bill to permanently ban offshore drilling in federal waters off California, Oregon and Washington, and while he was at Interior, he felt the agency overseeing offshore drilling safety was "the handmaiden of the industry."

He nevertheless advocates development of natural gas and next-generation nuclear reactors, along with waste-processing capabilities. Garamendi finds the objections of some environmentalists to nuclear power to be impractical: "The world is going to use nuclear. China and India are moving ahead. What are you going to do about the problem of waste? If they have a better solution, I'd like to know what it is."

From his seat on the Armed Services Committee he takes a common approach for Democrats: attempting to shrink defense spending while still championing local installations. Garamendi in the 112th Congress sponsored a number of unsuccessful amendments to limit funding for the Afghanistan War and missile defense programs. Regardless, he remains a supporter of Travis Air Force Base and Beale Air Force Base.

Garamendi has deep California roots. His mother's side of the family arrived there from Ireland via Massachusetts during the gold rush of the 1860s. They started out as miners, then settled down as ranchers. His father's family is from the Basque region of Spain. Garamendi grew up on a ranch.

He and his wife, Patricia, now have their own cattle ranch in Mokelumne Hill, in the Sierra foothills, where they also grow pears. Their six children and 10 grandchildren continue to live nearby. The two married when Garamendi was a senior at Berkeley. A second-team All-American offensive guard on the Cal football team, Garamendi decided not to apply for the NFL draft, instead following his wife to Ethiopia for two years in the Peace Corps. He says President John F. Kennedy is his political hero.

He entered the state Assembly at age 29, soon after completing Harvard Business School, and two years later jumped to the state Senate. In the middle of his Senate tenure, in 1982, he unsuccessfully sought the Democratic nomination for governor. Four years later, he made his failed bid for controller.

The race for insurance commissioner in 1990 was his first statewide success, but state Treasurer Kathleen Brown beat him in his second try for a gubernatorial nomination in 1994. Shortly after, he headed to Washington to work at Interior.

Garamendi had a second stint as insurance commissioner before winning the race for lieutenant governor in 2006. He had planned to run for governor in 2010, but he abandoned that effort when he was down in the polls and Democratic Rep. Ellen O. Tauscher stepped down in 2009 to take a post at the State Department.

During the special-election campaign to succeed Tauscher, Garamendi topped the 15-candidate primary field with 26 percent of the vote, then beat GOP businessman David Harmer by 10 points in a runoff. He easily won the 2010 race for a full term.

The state's congressional map was dramatically altered for the 2012 elections. Garamendi ran in the new 3rd District, which contains parts of his old district but is overall farther from San Francisco — it centers more on Sacramento and counties to the north. Republicans thought they had a good shot at winning, and their candidate was Colusa County Supervisor Kim Dolbow Vann. Garamendi won by more than 8 points, but Republicans quickly identified him as a target for 2014.

Key Votes

2012

Extend a Social Security payroll tax cut and unemployment benefits	YES
Ease securities rules to expand small-business access to capital	YES
Extend for one year subsidized student loan interest rates financed by a cut in health care spending	NO
Cite Attorney General Eric H. Holder Jr. for contempt of Congress	?
Create a visa program for foreign graduates in high-tech fields	YES
Extend most Bush-era income tax rates while allowing rates for top-bracket earners to rise (Jan. 1, 2013)	YES

2011

Strike funding for F-35 alternative engine	YES
Prevent EPA from regulating greenhouse gas emissions to address climate change	NO
Extend certain provisions of Patriot Act for four years	NO
Declare opposition to use of ground troops in Libya	YES
Overhaul patent law	NO
Pass compromise debt limit increase plan and establish future spending limits	YES
Allow consideration of measures to implement three trade agreements	NO

CQ Vote Studies

	PARTY UNITY		PRESIDENTIAL SUPPORT	
	SUPPORT	OPPOSE	SUPPORT	OPPOSE
2012	90%	10%	77%	23%
2011	97%	3%	85%	15%
2010	99%	1%	83%	17%
2009	100%	0%	100%	0%

Interest Groups

	AFL-CIO	ADA	CCUS	ACU
2012	95%	65%	42%	20%
2011	100%	85%	19%	0%
2010	100%	100%	0%	0%
2009	100%		14%	0%

California 3

Sacramento Valley — Fairfield, Davis, Yuba City

The 3rd follows the Sacramento River from the wetlands of Glenn County south into Grizzly Bay. It unites rural Sacramento Valley counties north of the state capital (in the neighboring 6th) with Sacramento suburbs and East Bay bedroom communities. In the northeastern reaches of Yuba County, the district creeps into the rural Tahoe National Forest.

Remapping following the 2010 census kept Colusa, Sutter, Yolo and Yuba counties together, and added Lake County north of Clear Lake and most of Glenn and Solano counties. The 3rd grabs the southwestern arm of Sacramento County. West of Sacramento in Yolo County, Davis hosts a University of California campus that is a major employer.

Water is a perennial issue here. Vast swathes of farmland — amid which are small towns — produce hundreds of millions of dollars worth of rice annually, as well as large tomato, almond, walnut and livestock feed crops. Growers ship plums to Sunsweet's Yuba City prune processing plant. Farmers are wary of state government plans to expand existing floodways for the Sacramento River, which could potentially put more fields underwater.

Environmentalists and residents in downstream communities, meanwhile, worry about inadequate flood protection from existing levies, potential harm to salmon stock and the impact of farm runoff on water reserves.

These divisions are evident in the political geography of the district. Its portions of Glenn, Colusa, Sacramento, Sutter and Yuba counties supported GOP U.S. Senate candidate Elizabeth Emken in 2012 and host more registered Republicans than Democrats. Democrats dominate in Yolo and Solano counties, where most of the district's electorate live. The 3rd is mainly white, although nearly 30 percent of its residents are Hispanic.

Major Industry
Agriculture, food processing

Military Bases
Travis Air Force Base, 7,900 military, 3,500 civilian; Beale Air Force Base, 4,587 military, 1,436 civilian

Cities
Fairfield, Vacaville, Davis

Notable
Much of the Pacific Coast migratory waterfowl, including 3 million ducks, spend the winter in the Sacramento National Wildlife Refuge.

Rep. Tom McClintock (R)

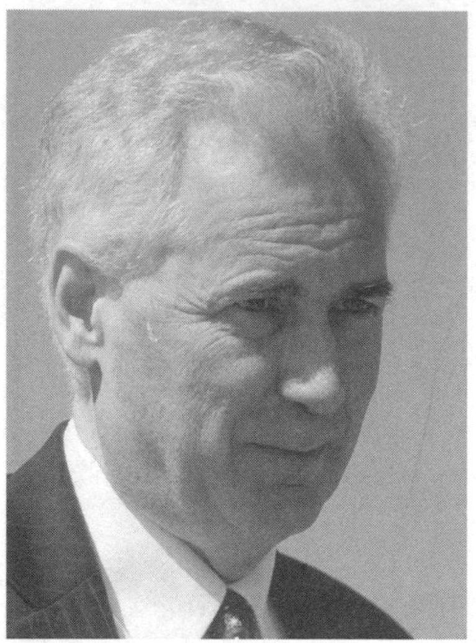

Capitol Office
225-2511
mcclintock.house.gov
434 Cannon Bldg. 20515-0504; fax 225-5444

Committees
Budget
Natural Resources
(Water & Power - Chairman)

Residence
Elk Grove

Born
July 10, 1956; Bronxville, N.Y.

Religion
Baptist

Family
Wife, Lori McClintock; two children

Education
U. of California, Los Angeles, B.A. 1978 (political science)

Career
Conservative public policy group director; state legislative aide; newspaper columnist

Political Highlights
Ventura County Republican Central Committee chairman, 1979-81; Calif. Assembly, 1982-92; Republican nominee for U.S. House, 1992; Republican nominee for Calif. controller, 1994; Calif. Assembly, 1996-00; Calif. Senate, 2000-08; Republican nominee for Calif. controller, 2002; candidate for governor (recall election), 2003; Republican nominee for lieutenant governor, 2006

ELECTION RESULTS

2012 GENERAL		
Tom McClintock (R)	197,803	61.1%
Jack Uppal (D)	125,885	38.9%
2012 PRIMARY (Open)		
Tom McClintock (R)	114,311	64.8%
2010 GENERAL		
Tom McClintock (R)	186,397	61.3%
Clint Curtis (D)	95,653	31.4%
Benjamin "Ben" Emery (GREEN)	22,179	7.3%

Previous Winning Percentages
2008 (50%)

Elected 2008; 3rd term

McClintock's conservatism has a theological flair. He has an abiding faith in the "elegant simplicity" of markets, he looks at the writings of the founders as essential texts, and he has followers who admire his tenacity navigating 30 years of Democratic control of California politics.

In fact, the 112th Congress (2011-12) marked the first time in McClintock's long political career that he was part of majority party. But he still places his small-government beliefs ahead of the wishes of Republican leaders.

One of his earliest memories of politics is his attendance as a third-grader at a Barry Goldwater rally in 1964. Hiking, camping, scuba diving and other activities fell by the wayside as "politics just kind of gradually crowded everything else out," and McClintock hasn't eased up over the years.

"I believe in the principles of the American founding: individual liberty, constitutionally limited government and personal responsibility," he said. "My objective has always been to restore those principles as the foundation of our public policy."

McClintock often quotes George Washington, Patrick Henry and other revolutionaries (relative latecomer Abraham Lincoln is his favorite), and his speeches feature both vivid metaphors and blunt statements. During the first week of the 112th, he laid down a marker on the House floor: "Government exists to ensure that the currency is stable and reliable and that property rights are secure."

Beyond that mission, McClintock can do without government. A member of the Budget Committee, he said the fiscal 2011 and 2012 appropriations laws provided too much spending, and he faulted GOP leaders for placating a Democratic Senate.

"It is not the responsibility of the House Republican majority to pass legislation that [Senate Majority Leader] Harry Reid likes," he said. "It is our responsibility to pass legislation that comports with the promises that we made to the people who elected us as a majority. It is Harry Reid's responsibility to pass really crappy legislation, because that's what he promised to do."

McClintock applauds presidents who oversaw a cut in spending relative to gross domestic product, including Calvin Coolidge, Harry S. Truman and Bill Clinton. He scorns George W. Bush and Barack Obama, who did the opposite.

He gathered 40 signatures on a letter urging the continuation of "open rules" on the fiscal 2013 spending bills to allow numerous cost-cutting amendments; McClintock then tried to zero out spending on energy development and research, whether for fossil fuels or renewable sources. "When government makes those investments, it's not making them based upon economic considerations, it's making them based upon political considerations," he said. "And that is guaranteed not to end well." He also tried to wipe out Community Development Block Grants.

The Natural Resources Committee approved his 2011 bill to repeal $3.25 billion in borrowing authority for the Energy Department's Western Area Power Administration. It was seen as a response to the collapse of Solyndra Inc., a solar panel maker that had received substantial loan guarantees from the Energy Department. "It astonishes me that it is the policy of the government and has been for many years to encourage the most expensive possible forms of electricity generation while discouraging — actively discouraging — the cheapest forms of electricity generation," McClintock said.

Hydropower is one such source, and McClintock chairs the Natural Resources Subcommittee on Water and Power. Water management is a hot topic in the West, and McClintock states a simple goal for his panel: "restoring abundance." That would require significant new infrastructure for water storage, which should "be paid for by the beneficiaries of those projects in proportion to their use," he said. "I don't believe in subsidies."

The biggest obstacle to abundance is, according to McClinktock, "this radical and retrograde ideology that somehow if we stop providing for the needs of a growing population, those needs will go away." He has pinned dam removal in the Northwest on "the most extreme elements of the environmental left," and McClintock blames efforts to protect endangered fish for the diversion of water that could go to the farms of California's Central Valley.

McClintock's philosophy of government leads him to civil libertarian stances. He voted against 2011 extensions of surveillance provisions in the anti-terrorism law known as the Patriot Act, and he opposed defense policy bills in the 112th that would allow indefinite detention of suspected terrorists or terrorist associates.

McClintock was born in Bronxville, N.Y. His father was an accountant and his mother worked in real estate. Inspired by an enthusiastic teacher and his parents' involvement in local politics, he talked his way into a trip to the Goldwater rally.

The family moved to Southern California. McClintock wrote letters to the editor as a teenager, which led to a column in the Thousand Oaks Chronicle, then to a 10-paper syndicated column after he graduated from UCLA.

McClintock worked as a chief of staff in the state Senate before winning an Assembly seat in 1982, representing a suburban Los Angeles district. He served 14 years in two stints, followed by eight years in the state Senate, where he led the charge to roll back a motor vehicle registration fee and voted against nearly every state budget. Along the way, he lost one U.S. House race, two races for state controller, one for lieutenant governor and one for governor.

He had a tough battle in his 2008 bid to succeed Republican Rep. John T. Doolittle, who was retiring from the district covering the northeast corner of the state. His primary- and general-election opponents accused McClintock of being a carpetbagger, as he had moved his family to the Sacramento area in the mid-1990s so they could be together during the legislative session — and on top of that, he lived outside the district he was running in. McClintock raised nearly $3.7 million to Democrat Charlie Brown's $2.6 million and eked out a nearly 2,000-vote victory. His first re-election campaign, however, was a 30-point cakewalk.

The 4th District as drawn for the 2012 election had starkly different borders, taking in the Sierra Nevada foothills and running southeast from Sacramento. But it is solidly Republican territory, and McClintock defeated token Democratic opposition to secure a third term.

Key Votes

2012	
Extend a Social Security payroll tax cut and unemployment benefits	NO
Ease securities rules to expand small-business access to capital	YES
Extend for one year subsidized student loan interest rates financed by a cut in health care spending	NO
Cite Attorney General Eric H. Holder Jr. for contempt of Congress	YES
Create a visa program for foreign graduates in high-tech fields	?
Extend most Bush-era income tax rates while allowing rates for top-bracket earners to rise (Jan. 1, 2013)	NO
2011	
Strike funding for F-35 alternative engine	YES
Prevent EPA from regulating greenhouse gas emissions to address climate change	YES
Extend certain provisions of Patriot Act for four years	NO
Declare opposition to use of ground troops in Libya	YES
Overhaul patent law	NO
Pass compromise debt limit increase plan and establish future spending limits	NO
Allow consideration of measures to implement three trade agreements	YES

CQ Vote Studies

	PARTY UNITY		PRESIDENTIAL SUPPORT	
	SUPPORT	OPPOSE	SUPPORT	OPPOSE
2012	92%	8%	33%	67%
2011	93%	7%	18%	82%
2010	95%	5%	29%	71%
2009	97%	3%	13%	87%

Interest Groups

	AFL-CIO	ADA	CCUS	ACU
2012	14%	45%	73%	92%
2011	3%	10%	88%	100%
2010	0%	0%	88%	100%
2009	0%	0%	73%	100%

California 4

Sierra Nevada foothills

The newly redrawn 4th includes California's elbow-shaped corner of the Nevada border, following the Sierra Nevada foothills south from Lake Tahoe to take in Yosemite National Park and areas near Sacramento.

The 4th includes a majority of Placer County, containing the district's three largest cities — Roseville, Rocklin and Lincoln — which are bedroom communities at the edge of the Sacramento area. The housing boom expanded populations in Roseville and Rocklin before the housing bust squeezed local economies. Roseville, known for affluence and an upscale shopping mall, hosts a longtime campus of Hewlett-Packard as well as small computer plants. "Green"-tech companies have been a recent focus for growth.

A shift from timber to small technology companies to tourism-based economies has occurred throughout the district's mountain region, where the federal government owns most of the forests; land-use policy and environmental regulation can be particularly divisive. The sliver of Nevada County in the district relies on revenue from ski resorts. In El Dorado County, which splits Lake Tahoe with Placer, more than a quarter of the workforce works in recreation service or retail. Calaveras County, which includes Yosemite National Park, relies heavily on tourism and its retiree communities. Vineyards have been growing in the area for decades, capturing more tourist dollars.

With a population that's 86 percent white, the 4th is one of the less ethnically diverse districts in the state. The only outlier is Madera County, an agricultural area with a majority Hispanic population and nearly 19 percent of residents below the poverty line. Madera is also the state's top fig producer, and No. 2 for raisin grapes and pistachios.

Registered Republicans outnumber Democrats here. Only the district's portions of Alpine and Nevada backed Barack Obama in the 2012 presidential race — overall, Republican Mitt Romney won with 58 percent of the district's vote. The three most populous counties — Placer, El Dorado and Tuolumne — have maintained Republican majorities for the past decade.

Major Industry
Tourism, agriculture, technology

Cities
Roseville, Rocklin, Lincoln, South Lake Tahoe

Notable
Union Pacific's J.R. Davis Yard (Roseville) is the largest West Coast rail facility.

Rep. Mike Thompson (D)

Capitol Office
225-3311
mikethompson.house.gov
231 Cannon Bldg. 20515-0501; fax 225-4335

Committees
Ways & Means
Select Intelligence

Residence
St. Helena

Born
Jan. 24, 1951; St. Helena, Calif.

Religion
Roman Catholic

Family
Wife, Janet Thompson; two children

Education
California State U., Chico, B.A. 1982 (political science), M.A. 1996 (public administration)

Military
Army, 1969-73

Career
Grape farmer; winery maintenance supervisor; state legislative aide; college instructor

Political Highlights
Calif. Senate, 1990-98

ELECTION RESULTS

2012 GENERAL		
Mike Thompson (D)	202,872	74.5%
Randy Loftin (R)	69,545	25.5%
2012 PRIMARY (Open)		
Mike Thompson (D)	95,748	72.2%
2010 GENERAL		
Mike Thompson (D)	147,307	62.8%
Loren Hanks (R)	72,803	31.0%
Carol Wolman (GREEN)	8,486	3.6%
Mike Rodrigues (LIBERT)	5,996	2.6%

Previous Winning Percentages
2008 (68%); 2006 (66%); 2004 (67%); 2002 (64%); 2000 (65%); 1998 (62%)

Elected 1998; 8th term

Thompson holds fiscally conservative views that often set him apart from his fellow House Democrats. But his fundraising prowess and solid support on other issues have kept him in the party fold, and Democrats have chosen him as a leader of their campaign to curb gun violence.

He's a long-standing member of both the Blue Dog Coalition and the Ways and Means Committee, and he unobtrusively uses those platforms to express disagreement with Democrats' fiscal plans. In early 2012 he was one of 41 House Democrats to oppose a bill, favored by the Obama administration, to extend a one-year reduction in Social Security payroll taxes. "They borrowed $100 billion to do that," he told The Press Democrat of Santa Rosa. "Tax cuts ought to be paid for."

Still, he has backed some major stimulus and "bailout" measures meant to stabilize the economy, justifying his support in Keynesian terms. "I'm willing to borrow and spend a little money now to get the things we need," he said. The time to cut spending is "when we have the money."

With the economy struggling, Thompson favors maintaining tax relief for small businesses, as well as preventing steep cuts to reimbursements for doctors under Medicare. Thompson has long called for exempting more inherited wealth from estate taxes, as well as exempting functioning family farms from that levy as they are handed to the next generation.

Thompson once led the California Senate's Budget Committee and stays involved in California-focused issues such as renewable energy, agriculture, conservation and rural health care.

He seeks out GOP partners to promote renewable energy. In February 2013, Thompson was on a bipartisan team introducing a measure to accelerate the permitting process for renewable-energy projects on public lands. Working with Texas Republican Ted Poe in 2012, he proposed a bill to allow renewable-energy projects to operate under "master limited partnerships" — a tax structure appealing to private investors that many fossil fuel projects utilize.

Thompson comes from a family of grape growers, and he owns a vineyard where he grows sauvignon blanc grapes, hay and olives. He is a founder and co-chairman of the Congressional Wine Caucus, one of the more popular groups on Capitol Hill. He works to expand trade markets for California's wine and produce — he supported free-trade pacts with South Korea and Panama in 2011 — and presses for federal dollars to fight insect-borne crop diseases.

Thompson is the No. 2 Democrat on the Intelligence Committee, where he has served since 2007. He opposed both the Iraq War's authorization in 2002 and increases to troop levels in 2007. He was similarly wary of troop increases made in Afghanistan. "Counterinsurgency plans don't work unless you have a strong partner government, which we do not have," he said. After a trip to Israel and Palestine in February 2013, he was optimistic about the Palestinian government, saying it had shown "a genuine commitment to a counterterrorism strategy."

He has military experience. Thompson dropped out of high school and joined the Army, serving as a staff sergeant and platoon leader with the 173rd Airborne Brigade in Vietnam, where he was wounded and received a Purple Heart. He belongs to the Congressional Sportsmen's Caucus and several times has won "Top Gun" honors at an annual congressional shooting competition. "I grew up a poor kid," he said. "If we shot a shotgun shell, it better put dinner on the table."

Late in 2012, Democrats chose Thompson as the chairman of a task force on gun violence prevention — its creation was spurred by a horrific shooting at a Connecticut elementary school. Thompson jumped into a series of meetings to gather public input, and a month later he said a "comprehensive" approach was required, including more mandatory criminal background checks, improved mental health services and restrictions on high-capacity ammunition magazines.

"I'm not interested in giving up my guns, and I wouldn't ask anyone else to give up their guns," he said in February 2013, but he did endorse a ban on so-called assault weapons: "I carried an assault weapon in Vietnam. I've seen them in action. I know what they're used for. I know what they're designed for. ... And they don't have any place in our streets or in our communities."

Beyond his policy efforts, Thompson has been very effective at raising funds for the Democratic Party year after year. During the 2012 cycle, between his political action committee and his personal campaign funds he gave more than $500,000 to Democratic candidates and organizations. At one time he was considered for the chairmanship of the Democratic Congressional Campaign Committee.

Thompson grew up in his district before the wine boom, picking walnuts and prunes to make extra money and spending a lot of time outdoors. As a young man, he worked as a maintenance supervisor at the Beringer Vineyards in Napa Valley.

"I was the guy the Hispanic field laborers would come to with their problems," he said. When he once sought to intervene on behalf of a Hispanic worker who had been cheated by a mechanic, Thompson recalled, "The guy in the repair shop said: 'What do you care? The guy's just a Mexican.'"

Outraged by the incident, Thompson said, he realized that to be able to help people effectively, he would have to complete his education. In his late 20s and early 30s, he earned his high school diploma and a college degree.

Thompson won a fellowship working with the state legislature and later served as chief of staff for Assemblyman Lou Papan. When Papan left the chamber, Thompson packed up his office and prepared to leave the legislature, agreeing only to help Papan's successor, Jackie Speier, find a replacement. Speier persuaded him to stay. (Thompson supported Speier's successful bid for Congress in a special election in 2008.)

Thompson first ran for elective office in 1990, winning a seat in the state Senate. Term limited, he set his sights on Congress in 1998. He easily defeated Napa County Supervisor Mark Luce, a Republican. Since then, his re-elections have not been remotely difficult.

His district as redrawn after the 2010 census still contains Napa County, but it shed a huge chunk of coastal real estate to the northwest and a segment near Sacramento.

Key Votes

2012	
Extend a Social Security payroll tax cut and unemployment benefits	NO
Ease securities rules to expand small-business access to capital	YES
Extend for one year subsidized student loan interest rates financed by a cut in health care spending	NO
Cite Attorney General Eric H. Holder Jr. for contempt of Congress	NO
Create a visa program for foreign graduates in high-tech fields	NO
Extend most Bush-era income tax rates while allowing rates for top-bracket earners to rise (Jan. 1, 2013)	YES
2011	
Strike funding for F-35 alternative engine	YES
Prevent EPA from regulating greenhouse gas emissions to address climate change	NO
Extend certain provisions of Patriot Act for four years	NO
Declare opposition to use of ground troops in Libya	NO
Overhaul patent law	YES
Pass compromise debt limit increase plan and establish future spending limits	YES
Allow consideration of measures to implement three trade agreements	YES

CQ Vote Studies

	Party Unity		Presidential Support	
	Support	Oppose	Support	Oppose
2012	96%	4%	90%	10%
2011	93%	7%	87%	13%
2010	97%	3%	88%	12%
2009	98%	2%	96%	4%
2008	95%	5%	15%	85%

Interest Groups

	AFL-CIO	ADA	CCUS	ACU
2012	90%	85%	33%	4%
2011	93%	85%	31%	4%
2010	100%	100%	13%	0%
2009	100%	100%	40%	0%
2008	100%	90%	56%	8%

California 5

Napa County; Santa Rosa; northeast Bay Area

California's 5th District is a liberal bastion of vineyard towns and a high-tech workforce in the northeastern Bay Area. It includes Lake County southwest of Clear Lake and all of Napa County, as well as portions of southeastern Sonoma County and corners of Solano and industrial Contra Costa counties situated along the San Pablo Bay.

The wineries of Napa and eastern Sonoma generate billions in wine sales and tourism revenue annually, and together, are the second-most visited destination in the state after Disneyland, with plush resorts and restaurants catering to oenophiles. The famed Culinary Institute of America operates a branch campus in an old winery at Greystone.

With sizable Hispanic, black and Filipino communities, Vallejo, the district's second-largest city, is its most diverse. The affluent and suburban Benicia and Hercules sit on the bay to the south. Nearby, in Rodeo, Phillips 66 operates a crude oil refinery.

The health care industry is a major component of the economy of the district's largest towns. Hospitals employ thousands in Napa and Vallejo. Santa Rosa is home to several medical device manufacturers. Medical diagnostics firms operate in Benicia, drawing the community into the emerging Solano County life sciences cluster. The 5th has not been immune to recent economic downturns: Housing markets plummeted after 2007, and recovery has been slow, especially in Vallejo.

Solidly Democratic, the district's affluent residents tend to have progressive views. Democrats dominate voter registration and the GOP has only the smallest of toeholds in the district. Lake County, the least populous jurisdiction in the district, has the narrowest voter registration margin and gave Democratic Rep. Mike Thompson his lowest percentage in 2012.

Major Industry
Agriculture, tourism, health care

Cities
Santa Rosa, Vallejo, Napa, Rohnert Park

Notable
The Charles M. Schulz Museum in Santa Rosa displays the famous cartoonist's studio as well as the bedroom wall on which he drew several Peanuts characters for his young daughter in 1951.

Rep. Doris Matsui (D)

Capitol Office
225-7163
matsui.house.gov
2434 Rayburn Bldg. 20515-0505; fax 225-0566

Committees
Energy & Commerce

Residence
Sacramento

Born
Sept. 25, 1944; Poston, Ariz.

Religion
Methodist

Family
Widowed; one child

Education
U. of California, Berkeley, B.A. 1966 (psychology)

Career
Lobbyist; White House aide; homemaker; state computer systems analyst

Political Highlights
No previous office

ELECTION RESULTS

2012 GENERAL		
Doris Matsui (D)	160,667	75.0%
Joseph McCray Sr. (R)	53,406	24.9%
2012 PRIMARY (Open)		
Doris Matsui (D)	67,174	71.4%
2010 GENERAL		
Doris Matsui (D)	124,220	72.0%
Paul A. Smith (R)	43,577	25.3%
Gerald Allen Frink (PFP)	4,594	2.7%

Previous Winning Percentages
2008 (74%); 2006 (71%); 2005 Special Election (68%)

Elected 2005; 4th full term

Matsui was a party insider long before she was elected to Congress. She has ties to the current Democratic House leadership and an advantageous spot on the Energy and Commerce Committee for working on high-profile issues.

She served as a White House aide for six years during the Bill Clinton administration and was a lobbyist after that. Matsui also was connected to Congress through her husband, Rep. Robert T. Matsui, who died days before the start of his 14th term in 2005. She won a special election that year to replace him, with Minority Leader Nancy Pelosi of California drumming up support for Matsui's campaign.

Matsui started out on the Rules Committee, which shapes the debate on major bills. In 2008, she was also awarded a seat on the Energy and Commerce Committee. When Democratic losses in the 2010 election shrank committee rosters, Matsui had to choose between the two panels — and she opted for policy over process.

She is a constant promoter of clean-energy technology, which is a prominent industry in her Sacramento district. The House in 2010 passed her bill to help develop an export strategy for U.S.-made clean-energy technology and assist producers in finding foreign markets; Matsui brought the measure back in 2011 and 2013. Another Matsui bill would establish a loan guarantee program to assist small businesses that manufacture clean-energy technologies.

Matsui usually shares the positions of Democratic leaders, but she sometimes breaks from the caucus regarding exports. She helped push through the North American Free Trade Agreement as a Clinton aide, and in 2011 she voted for free-trade deals with South Korea and Panama. When she opposes trade deals — the 2011 Colombia pact is an example — it is usually over what she sees as inadequate environmental or labor protections.

Along with Texas Republican Michael McCaul, Matsui co-chairs the High Tech Caucus, and she says she is "committed to providing greater access to technology for all Americans." She has urged the collection of fees from telecom providers to subsidize the cost of broadband Internet service in lower-income households, saying a lack of access is too disadvantageous in the modern economy — especially as things like health care services migrate online.

Matsui supported the Federal Communications Commission's 2011 "net neutrality" rules, which are designed to prevent telecom providers from restricting access to parts of the Internet, and she was happy that the United States in 2012 didn't ratify a U.N. telecommunications treaty — Mastsui said it "would open the door for government to control the Internet."

She also keeps tabs on health care. During the 111th Congress (2009-10), Matsui used her seats on the Rules Committee and the Energy and Commerce Committee to help usher the Democratic health care overhaul to enactment. One of her bills became a basis for the Prevention and Public Health Fund, which provides funding to programs aimed at preventing tobacco use, obesity, heart disease, stroke and cancer.

House Republicans in 2012 passed a bill to eliminate the prevention fund, as a budgetary offset to keep student loan interest rates from doubling. Matsui called Republican efforts to repeal the health care law unfortunate. "Health care is a right and not a privilege," she said. "Why not try to help everyone?"

Flood protection is her district's key concern, Matsui says. She pursues continued federal funding for flood control infrastructure in her district. "Public safety must not be compromised just to meet a bottom line," she wrote in 2012.

In 2008, despite opposition from local developers and the mayor, she refused to challenge the Federal Emergency Management Agency's designation of parts of northern Sacramento as a floodplain. Since then, she has tried to limit the increases in premiums paid by homeowners now living in mandatory coverage areas — she fought for a five-year phase-in of higher premiums in a reauthorization of flood insurance programs enacted in 2012.

As part of her husband's legacy, Matsui promotes legislation to preserve as historic sites the World War II Japanese-American internment camps, in which both of them spent part of their childhoods. She was born in the Poston camp in Arizona, but was too young to remember the experience; her family moved out when she was 3 months old. Her parents tried to shield her from their painful memories.

Growing up on a small farm in the Central Valley of California, Matsui never felt drawn to politics. But her father, who raised and sold flowers for a living, had a strong interest in government, which encouraged her to explore the field. "If the composition of Congress were different [at the time of internment] and there were people who understood, he didn't believe the internment would've happened," she said.

Matsui met her husband at a college dance, and they married in 1966. While her husband pursued a political career, Matsui raised their son and worked with Sacramento-area nonprofit organizations in the years before they moved to Washington.

During their early years in D.C., "we got to know a lot of people, and it didn't matter what side of the aisle because families were here," she said. "Even if there were policy differences between members, the humanizing aspect of family helped out a great deal."

Matsui volunteered to work on Clinton's campaign for president, and her early support was rewarded when Clinton gave her a spot on his eight-member presidential transition committee in 1992. She became a deputy assistant to the president and the highest-ranking Asian-American official in the White House. After leaving the Clinton administration in 1998, she went to work as a lobbyist and as government relations director at the Washington law firm Collier Shannon Scott, a job she held until running for Congress.

Her private sector experience, she said, taught her the importance of weighing private sector concerns in order to produce good legislation.

Though he had been diagnosed with a rare bone disease, Robert Matsui was re-elected in November 2004. But he was admitted to the hospital shortly afterward and died on New Year's Day 2005.

As he lay dying in the hospital, he encouraged his wife to run for the seat. She won 68 percent of the vote in the special election to replace him and took more than 70 percent in each of the following four elections. "I just felt that I needed to at least continue what he was doing," Matsui said.

Key Votes

2012	
Extend a Social Security payroll tax cut and unemployment benefits	YES
Ease securities rules to expand small-business access to capital	YES
Extend for one year subsidized student loan interest rates financed by a cut in health care spending	NO
Cite Attorney General Eric H. Holder Jr. for contempt of Congress	?
Create a visa program for foreign graduates in high-tech fields	NO
Extend most Bush-era income tax rates while allowing rates for top-bracket earners to rise (Jan. 1, 2013)	YES
2011	
Strike funding for F-35 alternative engine	YES
Prevent EPA from regulating greenhouse gas emissions to address climate change	NO
Extend certain provisions of Patriot Act for four years	NO
Declare opposition to use of ground troops in Libya	NO
Overhaul patent law	NO
Pass compromise debt limit increase plan and establish future spending limits	NO
Allow consideration of measures to implement three trade agreements	YES

CQ Vote Studies

	PARTY UNITY		PRESIDENTIAL SUPPORT	
	SUPPORT	OPPOSE	SUPPORT	OPPOSE
2012	90%	2%	90%	10%
2011	96%	4%	86%	14%
2010	100%	0%	90%	10%
2009	100%	0%	96%	4%
2008	99%	1%	13%	87%

Interest Groups

	AFL-CIO	ADA	CCUS	ACU
2012	95%	95%	25%	0%
2011	93%	85%	19%	4%
2010	100%	100%	13%	0%
2009	100%	100%	40%	0%
2008	100%	100%	56%	0%

California 6

Sacramento

While it may have a new number after decennial redistricting, the 6th District still closely resembles the old 5th and remains Sacramento-based. Key changes to its boundaries include the addition of West Sacramento and two political plums — Sacramento International Airport and the city's major cargo port. Rosemont, Rancho Cordova and Florin were shifted into the redrawn 7th District, and now the 6th much more closely resembles Sacramento's municipal borders, especially to the south and east.

State politics and triple-digit temperatures dominate the northern Central Valley district. With one out of every eight workers in Sacramento employed by the state government, the district's economy has suffered acutely from California's budget crisis. Unemployment has remained above 10 percent since early 2009, and state budget deals will close several government agencies and cut some employee pay. A California State University campus in Sacramento draws young residents.

The port, now named the Port of West Sacramento, exports nearly $150 million worth of cargo each year, including much of the agricultural output from the fertile farmlands surrounding the capital region. It is linked to the San Francisco Bay and Pacific Ocean via the Sacramento River.

Health care and technology drive private-sector employment here. Tens of thousands of area residents work for hospitals within the district and at the University of California, Davis, medical campus. Siemens and Intel facilities in the area are also top employers.

Sacramento boasts more than a decade of recognition as a highly racially and ethnically diverse city, and most of the residential neighborhoods to the north and south of downtown have blended communities. The geographic revisions to the district's boundaries should increase an already-solidly Democratic lean here: Democrats outnumber registered Republicans by 2-to-1.

Major Industry
State government, health care, shipping, technology

Cities
Sacramento, West Sacramento

Notable
Sacramento lured fortune hunters after gold was found on the banks of the river in 1848, and the Old Sacramento Historic District preserves more than 50 buildings from the Gold Rush.

Rep. Ami Bera (D)

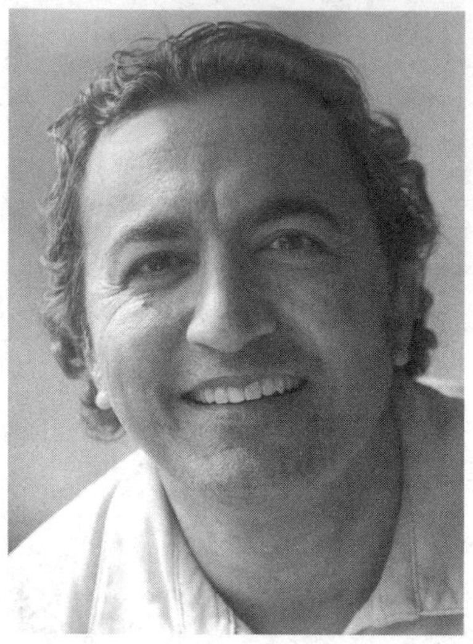

Capitol Office
225-5716
bera.house.gov
1408 Longworth Bldg. 20515-6601; fax 226-1298

Committees
Foreign Affairs
Science, Space & Technology

Residence
Elk Grove

Born
March 2, 1965; Los Angeles, Calif.

Religion
Unitarian

Family
Wife, Janine Bera; one child

Education
U. of California, Irvine, B.S. 1987 (biological sciences), M.D. 1991

Career
Professor; county health official; physician

Political Highlights
Democratic nominee for U.S. House, 2010

ELECTION RESULTS

2012 GENERAL		
Ami Bera (D)	141,241	51.7%
Dan Lungren (R)	132,050	48.3%
2012 PRIMARY (Open)		
Ami Bera (D)	49,433	41.0%

Elected 2012; 1st term

Bera positions himself as a business-friendly lawmaker who wants to improve to the nation's long-term fiscal outlook.

He's also the third Indian-American lawmaker in the history of Congress. His parents arrived from Gujarat in the 1950s and went into the hotel business. Their son went into medicine. Bera (full name: AH-mi BEAR-uh), one of the few Democratic doctors currently serving in the House, spent two decades as an internist, tried out public life as the chief medical officer for Sacramento County, then taught medicine at the University of California at Davis.

Bera joined the New Democrat Coalition and received an assignment to the Science, Space and Technology Committee; his experience at a research university comes into play on the Research Subcommittee. The Sacramento area has a large number of technology companies.

He wants to boost exports to Asia as a member of the Foreign Affairs Committee. And his medical experience will come in handy on the subcommittee handling global health. For domestic health care, he emphasizes letting the private sector find efficiencies, with government overseeing quality of care.

In his campaign, Bera harped on the budget calamities of the 112th Congress (2011-12). Early in the 113th Congress (2013-14), he was in the minority of House Democrats voting for a bill to block lawmakers' salaries if a budget isn't adopted on time. He also split from most Democrats to back a pay freeze for federal workers through 2013.

Bera was the Democratic nominee in the 3rd District in 2010, but he lost a fairly close contest to Republican Rep. Dan Lungren. He challenged Lungren again in 2012 in the new 7th District, capitalizing on his old campaign organization and a huge swell of outside support — independent groups spent almost $5 million attacking Lungren.

Groups opposing Bera spent $3 million, but it didn't save Lungren. Bera won by less than 10,000 votes.

California 7

Sacramento suburbs — Elk Grove, Citrus Heights

Uniting eastern Sacramento suburbs, the 7th District represents the heart of the former, much larger 3rd District. Already hotly contested political turf prior to redistricting following the 2010 census, this slimmed-down district promises to remain an electoral battleground.

This new district retains about 80 percent of the votes cast in the old 3rd, which delivered a split-ticket result in the congressional and gubernatorial contests in 2010. The new 7th has a nearly identical number of registered Republicans and Democrats; independent voters do lean Democratic and Barack Obama took 51 percent of the district's vote in the 2012 presidential election.

The 7th's boundaries largely adhere to the Sacramento city and county borders — the district takes in none of the capital city and is contained entirely within the county. State Highway 99 forms most of the district's southwestern limit. The district does not extend west of Elk Grove and Florin.

Technology and health care jobs have attracted well-educated and highly paid professionals to the 7th. Elk Grove, the district's largest city, tripled in size between 2000 and 2010. More than one-third of its households earn more than $100,000 annually. In Folsom, the district's most affluent town, microchip maker Intel employs more than one-fourth of the workforce; the city's second-largest employer is the state prison. The towns between these two suburbs — including Rancho Cordova, Arden-Arcade, Carmichael and Citrus Heights — have median household incomes below the state average.

During hot summer months, Folsom Lake State Recreation Area (shared with the 4th District) offers an attractive recreational option for the region's residents and visitors. The lake is created by Folsom Dam, which protects farmland and residential communities in the region from seasonal floods. The recreation area includes the powerhouse of one of the largest early hydroelectric power plants in the world, opened in 1895.

Major Industry
Health care, technology, state government

Cities
Elk Grove, Citrus Heights, Folsom, Rancho Cordova

Notable
Johnny Cash's "At Folsom Prison," a live album recorded over two shows in the maximum security prison in 1968, has sold more than 3 million copies.

Rep. Paul Cook (R)

Capitol Office
225-5861
cook.house.gov
1222 Longworth Bldg. 20515-6601; fax 225-6498

Committees
Armed Services
Foreign Affairs
Veterans' Affairs

Residence
Yucca Valley

Born
March 3, 1943; Meriden, Conn.

Religion
Roman Catholic

Family
Wife, Jeanne Cook; two children

Education
Southern Connecticut State U., B.S. 1966 (education); California State U., San Bernardino, M.P.A. 1996; U. of California, Riverside, M.A. 2000 (political science)

Military
Marine Corps, 1966-92

Career
College instructor; chamber of commerce director; Marine Corps officer

Political Highlights
Yucca Valley Town Council, 1998-2006; Calif. Assembly, 2006-12

ELECTION RESULTS

2012 GENERAL		
Paul Cook (R)	103,093	57.4%
Gregg Imus (R)	76,551	42.6%
2012 PRIMARY (Open)		
Gregg Imus (R)	12,754	15.6%
Paul Cook (R)	12,517	15.3%
Phil Liberatore (R)	12,277	15.0%
Brad Mitzelfelt (R)	8,801	10.8%
Angela Valles (R)	4,924	6.0%
Ryan McEachron (R)	3,181	3.9%
Bill Jensen (R)	1,850	2.3%
George Craig (R)	1,376	1.7%
Joseph D. Napolitano (R)	1,050	1.3%

Elected 2012; 1st term

Cook thinks Republican policies can spur job creation in the sparsely populated and enormous swath of California that he represents. Part of his plan is promoting investments in the military, one of the region's biggest employers.

The new 8th District was created largely from pieces of Republican districts represented by Rep. Jerry Lewis — who retired — and Armed Services Chairman Howard "Buck" McKeon. Cook inherited several military installations from McKeon's old district, and he sits on the Armed Services and Veterans' Affairs committees.

Cook, the oldest GOP freshman, is a retired Marine Corps colonel — during 26 years of service he earned two Purple Hearts and a Bronze Star. He served in the California Assembly, and despite being in the minority party he was appointed to chair its Veterans Affairs Committee. "I won't let Washington replicate the past, where they forgot about veterans returning from Vietnam," he said while campaigning. He also sits on the Foreign Affairs Committee.

He joined the moderate Main Street Partnership, but he has signaled his support for the regulatory rollbacks favored by House GOP leaders. Looser federal regulation might help tourism and energy development back home — a lot of the land in his district is owned by the government.

Cook grew up in Connecticut. When he retired from the military, he settled permanently in California, resumed his education, taught history and political science at a few colleges and got involved in politics as a member of the Yucca Valley Town Council. He was first elected to the Assembly in 2006.

Republicans took the top three spots in the 8th District's "open" primary in 2012. Cook finished second to tea party favorite Gregg Imus and just 240 votes ahead of accountant and businessman Phil Liberatore, who spent more than $1 million of his own money on the campaign.

Cook had a far superior campaign organization to Imus and easily defeated him in the general election.

California 8

Most of San Bernardino County; Mono and Inyo counties

The 8th tracks nearly the state's entire eastern border from the Sierra Nevada Mountains into vast deserts. The only population center is to the far southwest in San Bernardino County.

New to the redistricted 8th is San Bernardino County's populous Victor Valley, which has struggled with high unemployment rates. Like much of the Inland Empire, the valley is heavily Latino and growing as a manufacturing and distribution hub. Southern California Logistics Airport aids the Valley's economy. Solar power is an emerging industry in the desert. Overall, many residents live below the poverty line; in Victorville, the district's largest city, incomes are roughly half the statewide average.

Alfalfa farms, cattle ranches and outdoor tourism are crucial to the 8th. Tourists visit Inyo's Death Valley National Park and Mount Whitney. Lakes attract visitors in the summer, and ski resorts carry the winter, leaving local businesses to scrape for revenue during off-seasons.

The federal government owns almost all of the land in Inyo and Mono, and several large military sites are scattered in the district's southern half. Regulation of lakes and deserts can clash with locals' focus on tourism; water resources are another perennial issue, especially in the more populated sections of western San Bernardino County closer to Los Angeles.

Sparsely populated Mono and Inyo counties have large elderly populations; moderate population growth in both is due in part to an influx of Latino residents. The district is majority white and generally backs Republicans.

Major Industry
Military, tourism, distribution, agriculture

Military Bases
Fort Irwin, 4,997 military, 5,637 civilian; Edwards Air Force Base (shared with the 23rd), 2,142 military, 5,369 civilian; Naval Air Warfare Center Weapons Division, China Lake (shared with the 23rd), 646 military, 4,216 civilian; Marine Corps Air Ground Combat Center, Twentynine Palms, 3,500 military, 3,000 civilian; Marine Corps Logistics Base Barstow, 500 military, 2,500 civilian

Cities
Victorville, Hesperia, Apple Valley, Highland

Notable
Death Valley is home to the lowest point in the western hemisphere: 282 feet below sea level.

Rep. Jerry McNerney (D)

Capitol Office
225-1947
mcnerney.house.gov
1210 Longworth Bldg. 20515-0511; fax 225-4060

Committees
Energy & Commerce

Residence
Stockton

Born
June 18, 1951; Albuquerque, N.M.

Religion
Roman Catholic

Family
Wife, Mary McNerney; three children

Education
U.S. Military Academy, attended 1969-71; U. of New Mexico, B.S. 1973 (mathematics), M.S. 1975 (mathematics), Ph.D. 1981 (mathematics)

Career
Wind engineering company owner; wind engineer; renewable energy consultant and researcher

Political Highlights
Democratic nominee for U.S. House, 2004

ELECTION RESULTS

2012 GENERAL		
Jerry McNerney (D)	118,373	55.6%
Ricky Gill (R)	94,704	44.4%
2012 PRIMARY (Open)		
Jerry McNerney (D)	45,696	47.8%
2010 GENERAL		
Jerry McNerney (D)	115,361	48.0%
David Harmer (R)	112,703	46.9%
David Christensen (AMI)	12,439	5.2%

Previous Winning Percentages
2008 (55%); 2006 (53%)

Elected 2006; 4th term

McNerney is an expert on renewable energy. Political breakthroughs in that area have been hard to come by in a divided Congress, but there's no shortage of other issues for McNerney to tackle in the meantime. His district is a battlefield in California's current water wars, and its biggest city has been crippled by the state's fiscal crises.

He worked several years as a contractor to Sandia National Laboratories in New Mexico, and he eventually ended up in California with a senior engineering position with U.S. Windpower. Prior to his election in 2006 — he defeated Richard W. Pombo, the Republican chairman of the Resources Committee — McNerney was an energy consultant and CEO of a startup company that manufactured wind turbines. (A daughter of McNerney's goes by her middle name, Windy.)

He's still an avid publicist for renewable energy. McNerney in 2011 published "Clean Energy Nation," a book describing the "tyranny of fossil fuels" and the economic and environmental consequences of relying on them. McNerney opposes offshore drilling and the proposed Keystone XL pipeline from Canada's tar sands to the refineries of the Gulf Coast. He did not sympathize as Republicans in the 112th Congress (2011-12) tried to ease regulation of the coal industry.

McNerney would like government to actively build up alternatives to fossil fuels. "It's really a matter of putting the right resources and incentives in place to get people to make investments in clean energy, and to make sure that those investments pay dividends," he told The Browser website in 2011.

The political environment hasn't cooperated, however. As a member of the Energy and Commerce Committee in the 111th Congress (2009-10), he backed the 2009 Democratic bill to create a cap-and-trade system to regulate greenhouse gas emissions, but it died in the Senate. McNerney's bills to promote the creation of "smart grid" systems have thus far stalled. In 2011 he defended an Energy Department loan guarantee program after one participant, solar panel manufacturer Solyndra Inc., went bankrupt. But the next year, in a possible nod to election year politics, he voted for a bill to severely limit the activities of that program.

He did have a victory in 2012, when President Barack Obama signed a bill with his provision to allow a 200-acre solar energy project near the city of Tracy. California Republican Jeff Denham helped him promote that measure, as Tracy is now in Denham's district for the 113th Congress (2013-14).

McNerney's new district is the heart of the Sacramento-San Joaquin River Delta, which provides water for California's farms and southern cities. He aligns with other regional Democrats against plans to divert the delta's water. California Gov. Jerry Brown and the U.S. Interior Department have developed a huge infrastructure plan to use either underground tunnels or canals to carry more water south, to make delivery to farms and cities there more consistent. Opponents such as McNerney warn of an environmental and economic disaster should the plan go through; McNerney maintains that people in the delta have been ignored in the planning process.

He opposed a 2012 House-passed bill by California Republican Devin Nunes that would transfer water allocated to fish and wildlife conservation in the region to a San Joaquin Valley irrigation project. The bill would "ship even more water out of the delta, turning this precious estuary into a salty, stagnant marsh, crushing the local economy, and costing the delta region thousands of jobs," McNerney said on the House floor. He proposes bolstering federal programs to help develop alternative water sources, such as recycling.

McNerney also represents the entire city of Stockton, which is in dire straits. The city declared bankruptcy in 2012 and has had one of the highest home foreclosure rates in the country. Much of McNerney's constituent outreach has been trying to help residents facing foreclosure, and he introduced a bill to accelerate the approval of "short sales," when the sale price of a home is less than the debts of the seller.

His first bill of the 113th Congress was to increase the federal resources available to communities fighting high rates of methamphetamine addiction — California's Central Valley is a hub for meth distribution.

On most fiscal and social issues, McNerney takes conventional Democratic positions. "I will work for the middle class and not the wealthy in this country," he said in a 2012 campaign debate.

McNerney was born in Albuquerque, N.M., the youngest of five children. His father was a civil engineer, and his mother was a secretary at a local high school. His political inclinations stem from his father, who was a San Francisco union organizer before serving in the Philippines during World War II and earning his engineering degree.

Along with his twin brother, John, McNerney attended St. Joseph's Military Academy in Hays, Kan. He won appointment to the U.S. Military Academy in 1969 but left West Point two years later because he opposed the Vietnam War. He registered for the draft but was not called. Subsequently, he enrolled at the University of New Mexico, eventually earning a Ph.D. in mathematics.

McNerney's son, Michael, is a reserve officer in the Air Force. When Michael received an absentee ballot in 2004 he was furious to see Pombo — a blunt conservative who clashed with environmentalists — running unopposed. He persuaded his dad to run, but McNerney lost by 23 points.

In 2006, with strong backing from environmental groups, he defeated Pombo by 7 points. He had an easier race in 2008, but in 2010, with Republicans surging nationally, he ran one of the closest House races in the country, defeating Republican lawyer David Harmer by just 2,658 votes.

An independent redistricting commission made dramatic changes to California's congressional map for the 2012 elections. McNerney moved to San Joaquin County to run in the new 9th District, which had parts of his old 11th District and an overall Democratic lean.

His Republican opponent was 25-year-old Ricky Gill, a former member of the state board of education. Gill raised almost $3 million to campaign for the seat, and he also had some outside support — the National Republican Congressional Committee and the U.S. Chamber of Commerce combined to spend almost $3 million to oppose McNerney.

McNerney still won by 11 points.

Key Votes

2012	
Extend a Social Security payroll tax cut and unemployment benefits	YES
Ease securities rules to expand small-business access to capital	YES
Extend for one year subsidized student loan interest rates financed by a cut in health care spending	NO
Cite Attorney General Eric H. Holder Jr. for contempt of Congress	NO
Create a visa program for foreign graduates in high-tech fields	YES
Extend most Bush-era income tax rates while allowing rates for top-bracket earners to rise (Jan. 1, 2013)	YES
2011	
Strike funding for F-35 alternative engine	NO
Prevent EPA from regulating greenhouse gas emissions to address climate change	NO
Extend certain provisions of Patriot Act for four years	NO
Declare opposition to use of ground troops in Libya	YES
Overhaul patent law	NO
Pass compromise debt limit increase plan and establish future spending limits	NO
Allow consideration of measures to implement three trade agreements	NO

CQ Vote Studies

	PARTY UNITY		PRESIDENTIAL SUPPORT	
	SUPPORT	OPPOSE	SUPPORT	OPPOSE
2012	90%	10%	79%	21%
2011	94%	6%	87%	13%
2010	91%	9%	86%	14%
2009	90%	10%	93%	7%
2008	93%	7%	17%	83%

Interest Groups

	AFL-CIO	ADA	CCUS	ACU
2012	81%	75%	50%	8%
2011	100%	90%	19%	4%
2010	93%	85%	25%	8%
2009	100%	100%	40%	12%
2008	100%	85%	61%	13%

California 9

Stockton and parts of Contra Costa and Sacramento counties

The 9th draws together an area previously represented by three different U.S. House members, encompassing most of the Sacramento-San Joaquin Delta, including most of San Joaquin County, and wedges of Contra Costa and Sacramento counties. The 9th also splits Antioch with the 11th District.

The new 9th reunites San Joaquin County's Delta region with the city of Stockton. Unlike liberal-leaning Stockton, Delta residents have swung between Republican and Democratic candidates in recent presidential and gubernatorial elections. The new boundaries give Democrats a 9-point advantage in registered voters.

This district sits atop the largest estuary on the Pacific Coast and is crisscrossed by more than 1,100 miles of levees that protect the fertile farmland. State and federal agencies oversee water pumping systems that provide drinking water to more than 20 million Californians and irrigate farms. Dairy products and wine grapes, particularly grapes grown in Lodi, are primary goods. Lodi and Tracy (in the 10th District) are major trucking centers and the port on the San Joaquin River is a bulk cargo center for the export of agricultural products. Canning, food-processing and distribution companies provide blue-collar jobs.

Forty percent of the state's surface water flows through here; the 9th is the epicenter of California's stormy water-related politics. Urban centers in Southern California and valley farmers tussle over water diversion, while environmentalists and private-sector interests battle over wildlife protection and land use — some farmland has given ground to development.

Stockton also illustrates the housing crisis. The city grew rapidly after 2000 as East Bay-oriented commuters sought cheaper housing and now has one of the nation's highest foreclosure rates and underfunded city services.

Major Industry
Agriculture, distribution, health care

Military Bases
Defense Distribution Depot San Joaquin, 34 military, 2,510 civilian

Cities
Stockton, Antioch, Lodi

Notable
More than 40,000 pounds of asparagus is eaten at Stockton's annual festival.

Rep. Jeff Denham (R)

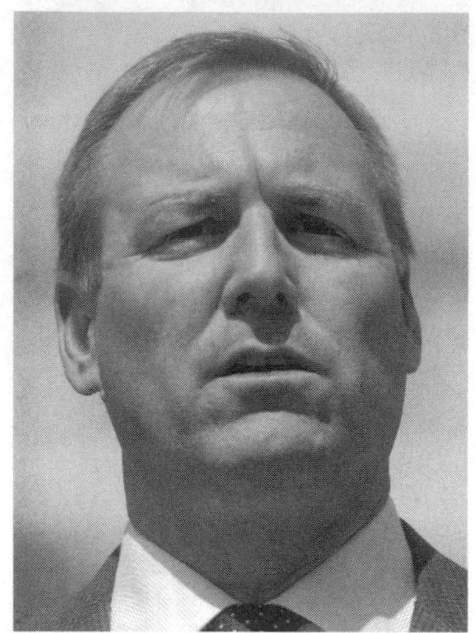

Capitol Office
225-4540
denham.house.gov
1730 Longworth Bldg. 20515-0519; fax 225-3402

Committees
Agriculture
Transportation & Infrastructure
(Railroads, Pipelines & Hazardous Materials - Chairman)
Veterans' Affairs

Residence
Turlock

Born
July 29, 1967; Hawthorne, Calif.

Religion
Presbyterian

Family
Wife, Sonia Denham; two children

Education
Victor Valley Junior College, A.A. 1989 (liberal arts); California Polytechnic State U., B.A. 1992 (political science)

Military
Air Force, 1984-88; Air Force Reserve, 1988-2000

Career
Agricultural packaging company owner; packaged food company shipping manager; almond orchard owner

Political Highlights
Republican nominee for Calif. Assembly, 2000; Calif. Senate, 2002-10

ELECTION RESULTS

2012 GENERAL		
Jeff Denham (R)	110,265	52.7%
Jose M. Hernandez (D)	98,934	47.3%
2012 PRIMARY (Open)		
Jeff Denham (R)	45,779	49.2%
2010 GENERAL		
Jeff Denham (R)	128,394	64.6%
Loraine Goodwin (D)	69,912	35.1%

Elected 2010; 2nd term

Redistricting changed Denham's home turf from safe Republican ground to a closely divided swing district. If tough campaigns are in his future, he has assets to draw on: ties to House GOP leaders, and committee assignments perfect for the farming and water needs of the San Joaquin Valley.

Denham knows a bit about holding a competitive seat. He overcame a significant Democratic voter-registration advantage to win a 2002 race for the state Senate. In his second term there, he voted against a state budget that had too much deficit spending for his tastes, and Democratic foes engineered a recall election against him; Denham held his seat with 75 percent of the vote. He has a flashy smile, speaks fluent Spanish (in a region with many Hispanics) and emphasizes the importance of "customer service" when handling constituent requests.

He also knows the agriculture industry, which is the biggest economic concern in his district. Denham grew up on a cattle ranch, and early in his career he worked for Fresh Express, which makes bagged salads. He eventually founded his own company making plastic containers used by farmers. He also shares a particular farming interest with Democrat Jim Costa of the neighboring 16th District — they both operate almond orchards.

Republicans added Denham to the Agriculture Committee for the 113th Congress (2013-14), giving him the opportunity to work on a reauthorization of farm programs. Denham says he can live with an end to direct subsidies for farmers, and he backs bolstering crop insurance programs, "as long as it's fair for the West Coast as well." He would like to see the bill sharpen the focus on agriculture research, notably for pest control.

The Transportation and Infrastructure Committee is where he addresses California's serious water management disputes. Water is "by far the most difficult thing that I am working on," Denham said. "There are no easy solutions to water."

Denham wants localities to have more flexibility in deciding how to store or manage excess water in wet years. He introduced a bill in his first term to allow the Federal Energy Regulatory Commission to consider a proposal to expand the size of Lake McClure during wet seasons; conservationists voiced concerns that the plan would damage portions of the Merced River. Ultimately he wants a 50-year plan for water storage across the nation.

Denham has cultivated cross-party appeal while often voting with House leaders. As a member of the California Senate, he roomed in Sacramento with fellow state legislator Kevin McCarthy, who is now the House GOP whip. Denham is a member of McCarthy's whip team, and for part of the 112th Congress (2011-12) he withdrew from the Republican Study Committee, which was reportedly organizing opposition to the plans of Speaker John A. Boehner.

He voted with Boehner — but against McCarthy — to support a January 2013 measure averting an increase in income tax rates, but only for earnings under $400,000. Denham fell short in his bid for an official spot on the leadership team in November 2012, losing the race for GOP Conference secretary to Virginia Foxx of North Carolina.

For the 113th Congress, Denham chairs the Transportation and Infrastructure subcommittee on railroads as Congress looks at reauthorizations of both Amtrak and rail safety laws. Denham and the Obama administration are not on the same page regarding high-speed rail. The House passed his amendment to a fiscal 2013 transportation spending bill to prevent federal funding of such a project in his state. "It would be fun to have, but the question you have to ask yourself is, 'Can we afford to have something fun, can we afford to have a luxury right now, and can we afford to do it with no viable plan and no private investment?'" Denham said.

In the 112th he chaired the subcommittee on public buildings and emergency management. Denham introduced a 2011 bill to create a commission to evaluate federal properties, decide if they are being used efficiently and sell off the dead wood. The plan received bipartisan praise, and Denham reintroduced it in February 2013.

A month earlier, the $50 billion spending law tied to Superstorm Sandy contained Denham's provision to streamline the environmental reviews process tied to the dispersal of disaster aid. His language also provides more options for how that aid is spent.

Denham joined the Air Force as a teenager and was a member of the Air Force Reserve until 2000. He served in both Iraq and Somalia, and he now sits on the Veterans' Affairs Committee.

President Barack Obama in 2012 signed a bill by Denham and Minnesota Democrat Tim Walz; it directs the heads of federal licensing authorities to consider and apply any relevant training received by members of the armed forces toward certification requirements for federal licenses.

After his full-time military service ended, Denham went to college. He played football at California Polytechnic State University and ended up with a degree in political science. His jobs in the agriculture business were followed by the December 2000 founding of Denham Plastics. He started almond ranching in 2004.

Denham has two kids, and he has said that frustrations with California's education bureaucracy got him into politics. He lost a 2000 bid to join the state Assembly, then won a Senate seat two years later. In 2010, term limits were forcing him from that job, and retiring eight-term Rep. George P. Radanovich asked if he would run in the reliably Republican 19th District. Denham won a GOP primary that included former Rep. Richard W. Pombo, then cruised to victory in November.

Redistricting for 2012 dismantled the old 19th, so Denham ran in the new 10th District, which has an even balance of Republicans and Democrats. He handily won the state's new "jungle" primary, which sent him to a matchup with the second-place finisher, Democrat Jose M. Hernandez, a former NASA astronaut. Denham won by more than 5 points, even as Obama carried the district in the presidential race.

Denham learned Spanish to speak with the grandmother of his then-fiancée and now wife. "Now my wife and I primarily speak in Spanish when we don't want the kids to know what we're talking about," he said in 2011. "They are learning it now. We need to find a new language."

Key Votes

2012	
Extend a Social Security payroll tax cut and unemployment benefits	YES
Ease securities rules to expand small-business access to capital	YES
Extend for one year subsidized student loan interest rates financed by a cut in health care spending	YES
Cite Attorney General Eric H. Holder Jr. for contempt of Congress	YES
Create a visa program for foreign graduates in high-tech fields	NO
Extend most Bush-era income tax rates while allowing rates for top-bracket earners to rise (Jan. 1, 2013)	YES
2011	
Strike funding for F-35 alternative engine	YES
Prevent EPA from regulating greenhouse gas emissions to address climate change	YES
Extend certain provisions of Patriot Act for four years	YES
Declare opposition to use of ground troops in Libya	YES
Overhaul patent law	NO
Pass compromise debt limit increase plan and establish future spending limits	YES
Allow consideration of measures to implement three trade agreements	YES

CQ Vote Studies

	PARTY UNITY		PRESIDENTIAL SUPPORT	
	SUPPORT	OPPOSE	SUPPORT	OPPOSE
2012	93%	7%	21%	79%
2011	97%	3%	21%	79%

Interest Groups

	AFL-CIO	ADA	CCUS	ACU
2012	19%	5%	92%	88%
2011	0%	5%	94%	84%

California 10

Central Valley — Modesto, Tracy

Representing the heart of the San Joaquin Valley, the 10th District combines some of the nation's richest farmland with rapidly growing suburbs along the Interstate 5 corridor. The district covers all of Stanislaus County and the southern third of San Joaquin County, an area that was split among three different districts before the latest decennial remapping process.

Much of the district west of the interstate is farmland. With unemployment in Modesto — the population center of the district — above 12 percent, the agricultural sector is pivotal to the local economy. The value of products produced by Stanislaus County farms grew over the last decade and the overall agricultural economic impact is around $9 billion. The county is one of the nation's largest producers of milk, almonds and walnuts.

This agricultural impact ripples through the rest of the district's economy. Stanislaus County is home to large fruit, vegetable and poultry processing plants, including several Del Monte facilities. Foster Farms Dairy headquarters are in Modesto; Gallo Winery operates a bottling plant there as well. Tracy, in San Joaquin County, is an important grocery distribution hub.

The 10th is 40 percent Hispanic, a ratio similar to the state as a whole, but many Hispanic residents in the district live in heavily segregated neighborhoods within primary population hubs. Public services do not always extend into these communities, causing tension between residents and local governments. Areas like Modesto also battle gang-related violence.

With nearly the same number of registered Democrats as Republicans, federal races are tight in the 10th. Democrats have a slight edge in Stanislaus County, and the portion of the county in the 10th backed Barack Obama by 3 percentage points over GOP nominee Mitt Romney in the 2012 presidential election. Rep. Jeff Denham held off a Democratic challenger by a similar margin in the U.S. House race — there are more registered Republicans in the district's portion of San Joaquin, but Denham managed a larger win in Stanislaus.

Major Industry
Agriculture, food processing, distribution

Cities
Modesto, Tracy, Turlock

Notable
Modesto annually honors native son George Lucas with Graffiti Summer, a classic car and oldies rock festival that celebrates his movie "American Graffiti," which was filmed in the city.

Rep. George Miller (D)

Capitol Office
225-2095
georgemiller.house.gov
2205 Rayburn Bldg. 20515-0507; fax 225-5609

Committees
Education & the Workforce - Ranking Member

Residence
Martinez

Born
May 17, 1945; Richmond, Calif.

Religion
Roman Catholic

Family
Wife, Cynthia Miller; two children

Education
San Francisco State U., B.A. 1968; U. of California, Davis, J.D. 1972

Career
Lawyer; state legislative aide

Political Highlights
Democratic nominee for Calif. Senate, 1969

ELECTION RESULTS

2012 GENERAL		
George Miller (D)	200,743	69.7%
Virginia Fuller (R)	87,136	30.3%
2012 PRIMARY (Open)		
George Miller (D)	76,163	58.5%
John Fitzgerald (D)	9,092	7.0%
Cheryl Sudduth (D)	4,635	3.6%
2010 GENERAL		
George Miller (D)	122,435	68.3%
Rick Tubbs (R)	56,764	31.7%

Previous Winning Percentages
2008 (73%); 2006 (84%); 2004 (76%); 2002 (71%); 2000 (76%); 1998 (77%); 1996 (72%); 1994 (70%); 1992 (70%); 1990 (61%); 1988 (68%); 1986 (67%); 1984 (66%); 1982 (67%); 1980 (63%); 1978 (63%); 1976 (75%); 1974 (56%)

Elected 1974; 20th term

Miller has a feisty persona and clear ideological leanings as a founder of the liberal Congressional Progressive Caucus. He reliably advocates more public education funding, stronger workers' rights and tougher consumer safety and environmental laws.

He's an avuncular figure in the Democratic Party. His Capitol Hill home, which he bought in the late 1970s, also is the address of Richard J. Durbin of Illinois and Charles E. Schumer of New York — the No. 2 and No. 3 Democrats in the Senate leadership. The list of past renters includes Leon E. Panetta of California, who went on to become a CIA director and Defense secretary in the Obama administration.

Those kinds of personal connections and his seniority — Miller came to the House in the post-Watergate election and only three Democrats have been in the chamber longer — have been instrumental to his success. He has served on the committee overseeing education since his first term and chaired it during the most recent Democratic majority. His early support for fellow California Democrat Nancy Pelosi as she climbed the Democrats' leadership ladder yielded him the co-chairmanship of the Democratic Steering and Policy Committee in 2003.

He stepped down from the post at the end of 2012, saying he wanted to focus on the heavy workload of the Education and the Workforce Committee.

As ranking member of that panel, Miller is still a respected negotiator. Some of his legislative successes have come from letting prominent Republicans or subcommittee leaders share the spotlight on high-profile deals. He also knows how to exact revenge — he has warned opponents that if they want to go head-to-head with him, "they better bring lunch."

Miller and Minnesota Republican John Kline, the panel's current chairman, have a personal camaraderie. But good will didn't bridge political divides in the 112th Congress (2011-12).

Miller, Kline and their staffs met early on to survey common ground for a reauthorization of the 2002 federal education law known as No Child Left Behind. That bipartisan spirit soon dissipated. Republicans turned to narrower, partisan measures: one to eliminate the unpopular school accountability system in the law and another to require states to implement teacher evaluation systems based partly on student test scores.

The bills stalled after the committee approved them on party-line votes in 2012, and the reauthorization is right back at the top of the agenda for the 113th Congress (2013-14) — along with a reauthorization of higher education programs, which expire in 2013, and an overhaul of student aid. Miller wants stronger consumer protections for borrowers with private student loans (such as discharging the debt via bankruptcy) and more money for Pell grants.

As chairman, Miller helped secure more than $100 billion for education in the $787 billion economic stimulus law in 2009. In final negotiations, he helped restore funds for some education programs that had been stripped from the bill in the Senate. In the end, the legislation included money to shore up local school budgets and Pell grants, as well as money for school modernization and construction. The No Child Left Behind program also received its full authorized funding for the first time.

Miller is on the front lines as Democrats defend their 2010 health care law. His committee was the first to approve the overhaul in 2009. The overall measure, which included his proposal to make the government the sole provider of student loans backed by a federal guarantee, changed considerably before reaching President Barack Obama's desk, but Miller was a constant presence among the Democratic supporters who negotiated and pushed for the law.

He is a major supporter of organized labor and stronger worker protections. In early 2009, he orchestrated passage of a bill to extend the period when people are able to file a claim of gender-based wage discrimination; it was the second measure signed by Obama.

He was unsuccessful, however, in promoting a bill to allow unions to organize a workplace without a secret ballot.

When Democrats took control of the House in 2007, Miller helped the party achieve one of its big promises from the 2006 campaign: an increase in the minimum wage. Miller and Iowa Democratic Sen. Tom Harkin applauded when Obama, in his 2013 State of the Union address, asked for another increase, to $9 an hour—their own plan is to set the wage at $10.10.

Democratic losses in 2010 pushed Miller off the Natural Resources Committee, where he had battled GOP attempts to revise environmental laws. He opposes drilling for oil off California's coast and in Alaska's Arctic National Wildlife Refuge. Miller's views are informed by a personal interest in the outdoors. Every year, he and a group of buddies take a major camping trip; in 2012, they hiked in Yosemite National Park.

Even without a spot on Natural Resources, he keeps an eye on the water issues that are important to all California politicians. Miller and several other Democrats were furious with the Interior Department and California Gov. Jerry Brown upon the 2012 unveiling of the Bay Delta Conservation Plan—its proposed tunnel system under the Sacramento-San Joaquin Delta to ship water south from Northern California would end up "economically and environmentally devastating the region," they wrote.

Miller developed his interest in politics as a youngster, watching his father, George Jr., broker deals on water issues and education during a 20-year career in the state Senate. The Bay Area has a physical testament to the father and son's complementary work: A bridge named for the younger Miller that opened in 2007 sits alongside an older bridge named for his father.

His grandfather, George Miller Sr., was the assistant civil engineer in Richmond, Calif. Miller's son, George Miller IV, became a lobbyist working on issues before the California state legislature.

Miller was a law student in 1969 when his father died. He went to work as a legislative aide to state Sen. George Moscone, the Democratic floor leader and later San Francisco mayor.

He was 29 in 1974 when he was elected to succeed Democratic Rep. Jerome Waldie, who ran unsuccessfully for governor. Miller won his seat in part by capitalizing on the Watergate scandal, which was fresh in voters' minds. He took 56 percent of the vote and has won re-election easily ever since.

Key Votes

2012	
Extend a Social Security payroll tax cut and unemployment benefits	YES
Ease securities rules to expand small-business access to capital	NO
Extend for one year subsidized student loan interest rates financed by a cut in health care spending	NO
Cite Attorney General Eric H. Holder Jr. for contempt of Congress	NO
Create a visa program for foreign graduates in high-tech fields	NO
Extend most Bush-era income tax rates while allowing rates for top-bracket earners to rise (Jan. 1, 2013)	YES
2011	
Strike funding for F-35 alternative engine	YES
Prevent EPA from regulating greenhouse gas emissions to address climate change	NO
Extend certain provisions of Patriot Act for four years	-
Declare opposition to use of ground troops in Libya	+
Overhaul patent law	NO
Pass compromise debt limit increase plan and establish future spending limits	NO
Allow consideration of measures to implement three trade agreements	NO

CQ Vote Studies

	PARTY UNITY		PRESIDENTIAL SUPPORT	
	SUPPORT	OPPOSE	SUPPORT	OPPOSE
2012	96%	4%	91%	9%
2011	97%	3%	84%	16%
2010	99%	1%	88%	12%
2009	99%	1%	97%	3%
2008	99%	1%	13%	87%

Interest Groups

	AFL-CIO	ADA	CCUS	ACU
2012	95%	85%	18%	4%
2011	100%	95%	13%	4%
2010	100%	100%	13%	0%
2009	100%	95%	33%	0%
2008	100%	95%	50%	0%

California 11

Most of Contra Costa County

Situated on the southeastern shore of San Pablo Bay and along the marshes and deltas where the Sacramento and San Joaquin rivers merge, the 11th District combines industrial and suburban areas of Contra Costa County. Geography dominates — waterways, Mount Diablo, state parks and reserves, and transportation access to the rest of the Bay Area — in this East Bay district. Like much of the Bay Area, the new 11th is heavily Democratic. The party enjoys a 2-to-1 advantage in registered voters here.

Representing two-thirds of Contra Costa County's population, the 11th is a microcosm of post-World War II American suburbanization. The port city of Richmond was a major shipbuilding boomtown during the war, but lost population over succeeding decades, particularly as "white flight" led many blue-collar workers east into the county's interior. During the 1960s, '70s, and '80s, towns such as Concord and Walnut Creek grew rapidly. In recent decades, once-sleepy towns even farther east and south such as Pittsburg have experienced rapid development and some of the attendant foreclosure issues of the modern housing market.

Transportation, accordingly, is a major issue. Much of the workforce commutes out of Contra Costa County daily and traffic bottlenecks on the major highways create some of the worst traffic congestion in the nation. Expansion projects for state Route 4 and BART commuter rail are ongoing.

The area's military footprint, stamped down during World War II, is almost gone. A cargo transport facility is the only active military installation in the district, and much of Richmond's former Kaiser Shipyards has been redeveloped. Steel for shipbuilding came out of nearby Pittsburg, which is no longer a regional industrial giant. Chevron's oil refinery in Richmond is one of the state's primary refining sites.

Major Industry
Petrochemicals, health care, steel

Military Bases
Military Ocean Terminal, Concord, 15 military, 100 civilian

Cities
Concord, Richmond, Walnut Creek, Pittsburg

Notable
The Rosie the Riveter World War II Home Front National Historical Park in Richmond honors the contributions of women who held industrial jobs.

Rep. Nancy Pelosi (D)

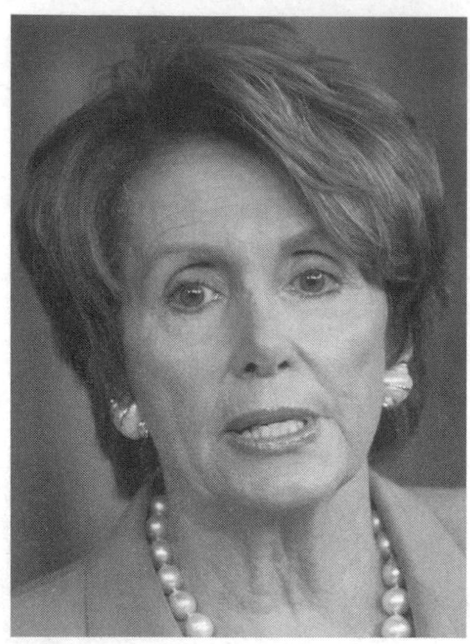

Capitol Office
225-4965
pelosi.house.gov
235 Cannon Bldg. 20515-0508; fax 225-8259

Committees
No committee assignments

Residence
San Francisco

Born
March 26, 1940; Baltimore, Md.

Religion
Roman Catholic

Family
Husband, Paul Pelosi; five children

Education
Trinity College (D.C.), A.B. 1962

Career
Public relations consultant; senatorial campaign committee finance chairwoman; homemaker

Political Highlights
Calif. Democratic Party chairwoman, 1981-83

ELECTION RESULTS

2012 GENERAL		
Nancy Pelosi (D)	253,709	85.1%
John Dennis (R)	44,478	14.9%
2012 PRIMARY (Open)		
Nancy Pelosi (D)	89,446	74.9%
David Peterson (D)	3,756	3.1%
Summer Justice Shields (D)	2,146	1.8%
Americo Arturo Diaz (D)	1,499	1.3%
2010 GENERAL		
Nancy Pelosi (D)	167,957	80.1%
John Dennis (R)	31,711	15.1%
Gloria E. La Riva (PFP)	5,161	2.5%
Philip Berg (LIBERT)	4,843	2.3%

Previous Winning Percentages
2008 (72%); 2006 (80%); 2004 (83%); 2002 (80%); 2000 (84%); 1998 (86%); 1996 (84%); 1994 (82%); 1992 (82%); 1990 (77%); 1988 (76%); 1987 Special Runoff (63%)

Elected 1987; 13th full term

Pelosi established herself as a historic figure by breaking through what she calls the "marble ceiling" — in 2002 she became the first woman to lead a party caucus, and in 2007 she became the first female speaker of the House.

She has an iron grip on the Democratic Caucus, but voters swept her party from control of the House in 2010. It's a tough climb back to the majority, in part because of significant GOP redistricting victories after the 2010 census. There have been grumblings that Pelosi herself is a ceiling, preventing the rise of a younger generation of Democratic leaders.

Still, she continues as minority leader. Her influence is diminished — major negotiations are mostly between Republican Speaker John A. Boehner and President Barack Obama, and Pelosi hasn't been known as an across-the-aisle deal-maker. But she remains relentlessly on-message and optimistic about her party's future.

Pelosi said in late 2012 that she'd rather be minority leader under a Democratic president than speaker under a Republican one: "There's a certain enthusiasm when you have your president in the White House, newly elected ... and all of us picking up seats in the Senate and House of Representatives." She also said that a major 2012 campaign theme is what holds her caucus together: "Our unifying principle is that we are here for working families."

A key question facing the liberal Pelosi is whether she'll build up a successor or let the more moderate minority whip, Steny H. Hoyer of Maryland, become the top House Democrat. Had Pelosi stepped down in 2010 or 2012, Hoyer would have been a lock to replace her — he has long aspired to hold the top job. Although he has been fairly effective working with Pelosi, their rivalry goes back at least to 2002, when Pelosi defeated him in a head-to-head contest for the job of minority whip.

Democratic aides and lawmakers list three younger Pelosi allies as possible successors: Democratic Caucus Chairman Xavier Becerra of California, Democratic Congressional Campaign Committee Chairman Steve Israel of New York, and Chris Van Hollen of Maryland, the ranking member on the Budget Committee. Pelosi's preferences are known only to her, as she is ruthlessly efficient at controlling information.

Whatever comes to pass, Pelosi already cemented a legislative legacy in the 111th Congress (2009-10). She shepherded a $787 billion economic stimulus bill to enactment in 2009, and in 2010 she engineered major overhauls of the health care system and financial sector regulations. The House even passed a 2009 bill to create a cap-and-trade system regulating greenhouse gas emissions. That plan died in the Senate, however.

Pelosi was involved in the intimate details of all those measures. When it came time to finalize the make-or-break deals to push bills forward, it was Pelosi — not the relevant committee chairmen — who made the decisions. On health care, for example, she negotiated with Michigan's Bart Stupak, a leader of anti-abortion Democrats, on language that his allies could accept. That bloc provided the winning margin for the House version of the bill.

The concentration of such power in a speaker hadn't been seen in decades. It won Pelosi wide admiration among Democrats, and it allowed Republicans to use her as a bogeyman in their electoral and fundraising campaigns.

Pelosi admits that her biggest disappointment as speaker was the failure to end the Iraq War, a conflict she had opposed from its outset. After Obama was elected, she said, she was forced to make the toughest appeal of her career — asking anti-war Democrats to vote for the funding of continued operations as a way of giving Obama time to implement a withdrawal.

Even without the same legislative stroke she had as speaker, Pelosi tries to set a liberal tone for her party. During deficit reduction negotiations late in the 112th Congress (2011-12), Pelosi indicated that spending cuts shouldn't be part of any deal — the exact opposite demand of most Republicans.

"In the course of this Congress, we have voted for the Budget Control Act and we have voted for a few hundred billion dollars more in cuts," she said, referring to fiscal 2011 and 2012 appropriations and an August 2011 deficit reduction law. "That's over the next 10 years: $1.6 trillion in cuts. That's enough."

Wheeling and dealing come naturally to Pelosi. Her father was Thomas D'Alesandro Jr., a New Deal Democratic congressman from Baltimore who also served three terms as that city's mayor. Politics was a family affair for Pelosi and her five brothers, who grew up in a corner row house in crowded Little Italy.

They took turns staffing a desk in the D'Alesandro home, where constituents stopped in to ask for help finding a job, finding a doctor, getting food or making the rent. It was a constant lesson in retail politics, where favors and constituent services could translate into votes and loyalty. Pelosi notes that her mother, Anunciata (for whom she is named), played a big behind-the-scenes role in D'Alesandro's long political success.

Pelosi attended Catholic schools in Baltimore, then went to Trinity College in Washington. While in college, she met San Franciscan Paul Pelosi, who was a student at Georgetown University. They married in 1963, and Pelosi gave birth to her five children over the next six years while the couple lived in New York City.

The Pelosis moved to Paul's hometown, and she became increasingly active in Democratic Party politics as that city was fashioning itself into a bastion of liberalism. She rose to become state party chairwoman and played a role in hosting the 1984 Democratic National Convention.

She became a close ally of Rep. Phillip Burton, the firebrand Democratic liberal from San Francisco who narrowly lost a race for majority leader and whose brother, former Rep. John Burton, remains a close Pelosi friend.

When Burton died in 1983, he was succeeded by his widow, Sala Burton, another Pelosi friend who had a reputation as a tough, focused politician. Pelosi's career in elective politics began in 1987, when Sala Burton was diagnosed with cancer and personally summoned Pelosi to her hospital room to ask her to run for the seat.

With her youngest child already in high school, Pelosi took the plunge, winning a wild Democratic primary and runoff to score a victory in her first run for public office. Pelosi has since been re-elected overwhelmingly.

Key Votes

2012	
Extend a Social Security payroll tax cut and unemployment benefits	YES
Ease securities rules to expand small-business access to capital	YES
Extend for one year subsidized student loan interest rates financed by a cut in health care spending	NO
Cite Attorney General Eric H. Holder Jr. for contempt of Congress	?
Create a visa program for foreign graduates in high-tech fields	NO
Extend most Bush-era income tax rates while allowing rates for top-bracket earners to rise (Jan. 1, 2013)	YES
2011	
Strike funding for F-35 alternative engine	YES
Prevent EPA from regulating greenhouse gas emissions to address climate change	NO
Extend certain provisions of Patriot Act for four years	NO
Declare opposition to use of ground troops in Libya	NO
Overhaul patent law	NO
Pass compromise debt limit increase plan and establish future spending limits	YES
Allow consideration of measures to implement three trade agreements	NO

CQ Vote Studies

	PARTY UNITY		PRESIDENTIAL SUPPORT	
	SUPPORT	OPPOSE	SUPPORT	OPPOSE
2012	98%	2%	95%	5%
2011	98%	2%	90%	10%
2010	100%	0%	95%	5%
2009	100%	0%	100%	0%
2008	98%	2%	25%	75%

Interest Groups

	AFL-CIO	ADA	CCUS	ACU
2012	95%	80%	25%	4%
2011	93%	70%	27%	0%
2010	100%		0%	0%
2009	100%		17%	0%
2008	100%	50%	38%	0%

California 12

San Francisco

The slightly redrawn 12th represents almost all of San Francisco — nearly 90 percent of the city's residents live in the district, and decennial redistricting swung the western portion of the 12th to the south to include the misleadingly named Sunset District, a notoriously foggy area and popular home for middle-class families. Only the southwestern corner of the city, including San Francisco State University and the zoo, falls outside the 12th.

Although San Francisco's financial district keeps money moving in the 12th, most non-locals focus on the scenic vistas and iconic neighborhoods. Tourism is a multibillion-dollar industry. Visitors concentrate on bayfront attractions like Fisherman's Wharf, Golden Gate National Recreation Area and Alcatraz prison. The city's bustling Chinatown, one of the largest in North America, draws more visitors than does the Golden Gate Bridge (its northern terminus is in the 2nd). Southeast of Chinatown is the Bay Bridge, which crosses the neck of the bay over Treasure Island to Oakland (in the 13th). More ambitious sightseers can take a tour of the murals of Balmy Alley in the Mission District, a Hispanic neighborhood that became trendy during the dot-com boom.

Montgomery Street, the "Wall Street of the West," is the heart of the city's financial district. Banking titans such as Wells Fargo and Transamerica — in its pyramid-shaped skyscraper — have their world headquarters here. Along with financial services, the 12th boasts strong computing, biotech and technology sectors, and city residents tend to be highly educated. The University of California, San Francisco, campus includes a medical center and is a major biomedical hub.

The famously liberal San Francisco routinely gives Democrats more than 80 percent of the vote in elections — 85 percent of registered voters are either Democrats or unaffiliated and skewing far to the left. A longtime mecca for gays and lesbians, the city has a high proportion of same-sex couples, and the nation's first GLBT history museum opened in the Castro district in 2011.

Major Industry

Tourism, financial services, biotechnology

Cities

San Francisco (pt.)

Notable

The Letterman Digital Arts Center at the Presidio is the headquarters of Lucasfilm — a fountain at the entrance shows a life-size statue of the Jedi Master Yoda.

Rep. Barbara Lee (D)

Capitol Office
225-2661
lee.house.gov
2267 Rayburn Bldg. 20515-2661; fax 225-9817

Committees
Appropriations
Budget

Residence
Oakland

Born
July 16, 1946; El Paso, Texas

Religion
Baptist

Family
Divorced; two children

Education
Mills College, B.A. 1973 (psychology); U. of California, Berkeley, M.S.W. 1975

Career
Congressional aide

Political Highlights
Calif. Assembly, 1990-96; Calif. Senate, 1996-98

ELECTION RESULTS

2012 GENERAL		
Barbara Lee (D)	250,436	86.8%
Marilyn M. Singleton (NPA)	38,146	13.2%
2012 PRIMARY (Open)		
Barbara Lee (D)	94,709	83.1%
Justin Jelincic (D)	5,741	5.0%
2010 GENERAL		
Barbara Lee (D)	180,400	84.3%
Gerald Hashimoto (R)	23,054	10.8%
Dave Heller (GREEN)	4,848	2.3%
James Eyer (LIBERT)	4,113	1.9%

Previous Winning Percentages
2008 (86%); 2006 (86%); 2004 (85%); 2002 (81%); 2000 (85%); 1998 (83%); 1998 Special Election (67%)

Elected 1998; 8th full term

Lee is a boundary stone. If you get to her left, you're no longer in the Democratic Party. Her anti-war and hyper-progressive stances play well with her very liberal constituents in Oakland and Berkeley, and in a few instances her House colleagues have moved a lot closer to positions she has held for years.

She says her own life started with an incident of inequality and discrimination. In 1946 in El Paso, Texas, her mother, in labor with Lee, was initially refused treatment at the hospital because she was black.

Even after she was admitted, she was left unattended for so long that she became delirious with pain. Lee was delivered at the last minute with forceps, which left a mark on her forehead for years to come.

"My birth put me on the path" of progressive politics, Lee said. "You look at the fact that I almost didn't get into this world, almost died — almost was not born — because of racism. My whole life has been about trying to make life better for people who were discriminated against, shut out and disenfranchised."

Her preferences for government intervention in the economy can be close to radical. She wants the government to codify the goal of reducing poverty rates by half over 10 years. "That should be a national strategy that cuts across party lines," she said in 2012. "Every ethnic group and region should be putting forward resolutions and policies." She'd like "to push the party to be what I think the true Democratic Party should be."

Her goal for the Republican Party is obstructing its plans. Lee sits on the Appropriations and Budget committees, and her ambition for the 113th Congress (2013-14) is to stop funding reductions for Medicaid, Medicare and the Supplemental Nutrition Assistance Program. She said decisions in the 112th Congress (2011-12) were bad enough, and that the GOP promises "terrible cuts that would hurt the most vulnerable: our seniors, low-income people, middle-class people, the poor."

Lee isn't afraid to act alone — she famously was the only House member to vote against authorizing military force in response to the Sept. 11 attacks — but she's not a loner. Lee is a former chairwoman of both the Congressional Black Caucus and the Congressional Progressive Caucus. And she finds more allies as Democrats try to counter an aggressive GOP majority in the House. Lee fervently backs abortion rights, and she was livid at Republican attempts in the 112th to stop federal funding of Planned Parenthood and to allow insurance providers with religious objections to drop contraception coverage. She takes credit for coining the phrase "war on women," which Democrats used relentlessly against GOP candidates in 2012.

Exhaustion over the conflicts in Iraq and Afghanistan has brought more colleagues closer to her anti-war positions as well. Talking about defense budgets on an MSNBC appearance late in 2012, she said "we could cut at least $100 billion dollars and not even tamper with our national security."

She wasn't pleased with NATO's involvement in Libya in 2011 but accepted the humanitarian goals of its intervention; Lee has introduced a resolution to express that the United States should annually spend an amount equal to at least 1 percent of its gross domestic product on nonmilitary foreign aid. "It's really good to see that people are beginning to focus on global peace and security, smart security, not a military solution," she said in 2012.

Lee in the 113th is the new champion for a measure once pushed by Ohio Democrat Dennis J. Kucinich, who was defeated for re-election. It would create a Department of Peacebuilding to address "the root causes of violence."

Her undeniable legislative successes involve HIV/AIDS. Lee founded and co-chairs the Congressional HIV/AIDS Caucus. In 2008, President George W. Bush signed an AIDS bill that included her provision to eliminate the administrative ban on HIV-positive visitors to the United States. That allowed San Francisco to host the International AIDS Conference in July 2012. She continues to introduce sweeping measures to combat AIDS and ban discrimination against those with AIDS.

Before joining the Appropriations Committee for the 110th Congress (2007-08), Lee approached her AIDS work and other international issues as a member of the Foreign Affairs Committee.

Lee spent her early years in El Paso, where the public school system was segregated. She and her sister attended a Catholic school where, Lee said, they were the only black students.

Her family moved to Southern California in 1960. Her public high school had never chosen a black cheerleader, so she set about to become the first. With the help of the NAACP, she put pressure on the selection committee to make the audition process more transparent and inclusive, and ultimately won a spot on the team.

Lee first registered to vote in 1972, when a course at Mills College in Oakland required her to work for a political campaign. She was, at first, prepared to flunk the class: "I didn't feel the two-party system, or politics, was a way to make change," she said.

But her outlook shifted when Democratic Rep. Shirley Chisholm of New York came to Mills to speak before the Black Student Union, which Lee headed. Chisholm, the first African-American woman to elected to Congress, was readying herself to become the first black female candidate for president.

"I went up to her and talked to her about this class I was getting ready to flunk," Lee said, "and she took me to task and said, she's running for president, so why didn't I help her?"

Lee was inspired by Chisholm's progressive agenda and social consciousness. She registered to vote and went on to run the Chisholm for President Northern California campaign. Lee ended up with an "A" in the course, a passion for politics and a new belief in the potential for enacting change within the two party system. It was reinforced by her experiences with another liberal Democrat, Rep. Ronald V. Dellums of California.

In 1975, after earning a master's degree in social work, Lee went to work for Dellums in California and Washington. She then ran for the state legislature and served for six years in the Assembly and 17 months in the Senate.

When Dellums decided to leave Congress in 1998, he endorsed Lee to succeed him. She easily won the special election and has never gotten less than 80 percent of the vote in a re-election campaign.

Key Votes

2012	
Extend a Social Security payroll tax cut and unemployment benefits	NO
Ease securities rules to expand small-business access to capital	NO
Extend for one year subsidized student loan interest rates financed by a cut in health care spending	NO
Cite Attorney General Eric H. Holder Jr. for contempt of Congress	?
Create a visa program for foreign graduates in high-tech fields	NO
Extend most Bush-era income tax rates while allowing rates for top-bracket earners to rise (Jan. 1, 2013)	YES
2011	
Strike funding for F-35 alternative engine	YES
Prevent EPA from regulating greenhouse gas emissions to address climate change	NO
Extend certain provisions of Patriot Act for four years	NO
Declare opposition to use of ground troops in Libya	NO
Overhaul patent law	NO
Pass compromise debt limit increase plan and establish future spending limits	NO
Allow consideration of measures to implement three trade agreements	NO

CQ Vote Studies

	PARTY UNITY		PRESIDENTIAL SUPPORT	
	SUPPORT	OPPOSE	SUPPORT	OPPOSE
2012	98%	2%	84%	16%
2011	97%	3%	78%	22%
2010	98%	2%	85%	15%
2009	99%	1%	93%	7%
2008	99%	1%	14%	86%

Interest Groups

	AFL-CIO	ADA	CCUS	ACU
2012	100%	95%	17%	0%
2011	100%	95%	6%	8%
2010	93%	95%	0%	0%
2009	100%	100%	33%	0%
2008	100%	100%	41%	4%

California 13

Northwest Alameda County — Oakland, Berkeley

Taking in Alameda County's progressive bastion Berkeley as well as multicultural and urban Oakland, the 13th District is rock-solid for the Democratic Party — unaffiliated voters outnumber registered Republicans by greater than a 2-to-1 margin, and the district gave Barack Obama his highest percentage statewide in the 2012 presidential election (88 percent). Redistricting following the 2010 census reassigned the rural hills east of Lake Chabot to the adjacent 15th.

More than half of the racially diverse 13th — white residents make up a plurality; Hispanic, black and Asian communities each account for about one-fifth of the population — lives in Oakland. Downtown Oakland is coming to the end of a residential redevelopment effort initiated by then-mayor Jerry Brown more than a decade ago. The city has added thousands of new housing units in an often-controversial process that detractors have opposed because of the displacement of impoverished Oaklanders. Although budget shortfalls kept the initiative from meeting full expectations, music venues, art galleries and brewpubs dot the city center.

Oakland has been a major commercial port since 1962, when it became the first West Coast facility to cater to containerships. The Port of Oakland also operates the city's international airport, which includes a major FedEx air freight sorting center. A 5,000-acre industrial area abuts the port.

Just north of Oakland in the Berkeley Hills, Berkeley is home to the world-renowned flagship of the University of California system. Lawrence Berkeley National Laboratory scientists research atomic physics, medical science and cosmology — 13 of its scholars have won Nobel Prizes. Tucked between Oakland and Berkeley, Emeryville is a major high-tech and pharmaceutical hub. The small town is home to the studios of film studio Pixar and video game maker Maxis. South of Oakland, San Leandro is home to Ghirardelli Chocolate, Otis Spunkmeyer's cookie empire and the North Face, which produces outdoor gear.

Major Industry

Higher education, research, technology, shipping

Cities

Oakland, Berkeley, San Leandro

Notable

Emeryville's Wham-O Toys has marketed many famous toys, including the Frisbee, Hula Hoop, Hacky Sack and Slip 'n Slide.

Rep. Jackie Speier (D)

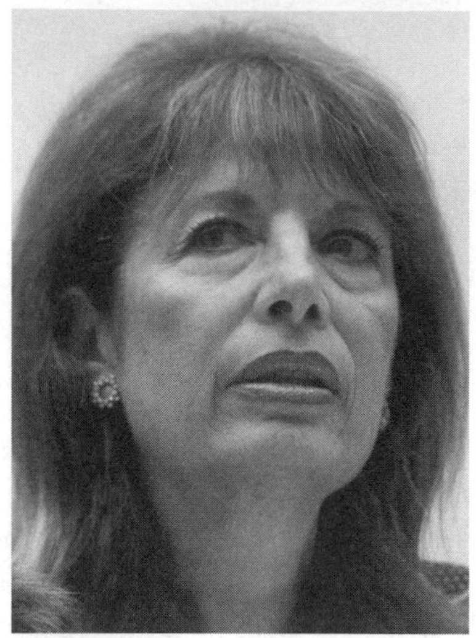

Capitol Office
225-3531
speier.house.gov
211 Cannon Bldg. 20515-0512; fax 226-4183

Committees
Armed Services
Oversight & Government Reform

Residence
Hillsborough

Born
May 14, 1950; San Francisco, Calif.

Religion
Roman Catholic

Family
Husband, Barry Dennis; two children

Education
U. of California, Davis, B.A. 1972 (political science); U. of California, Hastings, J.D. 1976

Career
Lawyer; game software company executive; disability services nonprofit officer; congressional aide

Political Highlights
Candidate for U.S. House (special election), 1979; San Mateo County Board of Supervisors, 1981-86; Calif. Assembly, 1986-96; Calif. Senate, 1998-2006; sought Democratic nomination for lieutenant governor, 2006

ELECTION RESULTS

2012 GENERAL		
Jackie Speier (D)	203,828	78.9%
Deborah "Debbie" Bacigalupi (R)	54,455	21.1%
2012 PRIMARY (Open)		
Jackie Speier (D)	80,850	74.3%
Michael J. Moloney (D)	4,607	4.2%
2010 GENERAL		
Jackie Speier (D)	152,044	75.6%
Mike Moloney (R)	44,475	22.1%
Mark Paul Williams (LIBERT)	4,611	2.3%

Previous Winning Percentages
2008 (75%); 2008 Special Election (78%)

Elected 2008; 3rd full term

Speier has asserted herself in national security policy debates, building on a liberal voting record and a commitment to consumer protection as a state legislator.

The events that motivated her to become a politician are famous. Speier (SPEAR) was working as an aide to California Democratic Rep. Leo J. Ryan in 1978 during his investigation of Jonestown, a Guyana compound of the Peoples Temple cult. When cult members opened fire on their party, Ryan and five others were killed. Speier was shot five times and underwent 10 surgeries; she still has two bullets in her body.

As she recovered, "I realized that I had a decision to make," she said. "Did I want to be a victim, or did I want to be a survivor?" In 1979, she ran in a crowded special election to succeed Ryan, finishing fourth. She won a county government election the next year and went on to serve 18 years in the California Legislature.

In the 112th Congress (2011-12), some of Speier's most public work was on behalf of other survivors: servicemembers who have been raped or sexually assaulted. Speier started on the issue as a member of the Oversight and Government Reform Committee and continued her efforts upon joining the Armed Services Committee in 2012, filling the vacancy created by the resignation of Arizona Democrat Gabrielle Giffords.

Few incidents are reported, even fewer perpetrators are court-martialed, and victims might be drummed out of the service to silence them, she said. The fiscal 2013 defense policy law contains provisions by Speier to further the study of the problem and review how the military justice system handles related cases.

Her other stated goal for Armed Services is fiscal oversight. "There is a blank-check mentality in that committee that is shocking to me," she said. "The committee shouldn't be a subsidiary of the defense contractors." Too many procurement programs have little practical value, Speier said. She has openly criticized the military's spending on F-22 jets: "I mean, the F-22 is about fighter-to-fighter combat, which we're not going to ever see again."

Speier urged a quicker end to U.S. involvement in Afghanistan and voted for a 2011 resolution to end U.S. involvement in Libya's civil war. She also opposed the U.S.-led invasion of Iraq, using one of her first speeches on the House floor after winning a 2008 special election to criticize President George W. Bush's war strategy. Republicans booed her.

Much of Speier's earlier work involved protecting consumers, including consumers of government services. She led numerous oversight investigations of state spending during her time in the state legislature.

In Washington, she has sought ways to revamp earmarking, the process lawmakers use for directing funding to projects in their districts. Speier in 2009 had requests for her district vetted by a board of local officials, community leaders and businesses; such a system eliminates the appearance of a quid pro quo arrangement, she said.

A former member of the Financial Services Committee, Speier was an early supporter of the creation of a Consumer Financial Protection Bureau in the 2010 overhaul of financial sector regulations. She has also introduced a series of bills to help consumers prevent the collection and redistribution of data on their finances and online activities.

Online consumers might be less enthusiastic about one Speier initiative, however. Working with Arkansas Republican Steve Womack, she has called for the collection of state sales taxes by online retailers, saying their exemption from doing so provides an unfair advantage over brick-and-mortar stores.

Speier's consistent support for her party landed her a senior whip posting in 2011, and she also sits on the Democratic Steering and Policy Committee. In the 113th Congress (2013-14) she has a good spot to defend a huge swath of the Democratic agenda. Speier is the ranking member of the Oversight and Government Reform Subcommittee on Energy Policy, Health Care and Entitlements. The chairman, James Lankford of Oklahoma, heads up policy development for House Republicans.

Spurred by a horrific shooting at a Connecticut elementary school late in 2012, Speier committed herself anew to seeking both a ban on so-called assault weapons and stricter requirements for background checks linked to gun purchases. In 2013, she was named a vice chairwoman of a task force on gun violence that includes colleagues who also experienced injury or loss from incidents involving firearms.

And she wrote a powerful opinion piece incorporating her own experiences as a shooting victim and the remorse she felt for not championing the cause more fervently. "I regret that I haven't done more to stop the unspeakable," she wrote. "I've learned my lesson, and now I am in all the way."

Her life story sometimes reads like a melodrama screenplay. Years after the trauma of Jonestown, Speier and her first husband, physician Steve Sierra, adopted a baby — but a short while later, the birth mother changed her mind. When Speier was pregnant with her second child, Sierra was killed by a drunken driver.

With two co-authors, she drew on her life experiences to write a book in 2007, "This Is Not the Life I Ordered: 50 Ways to Keep Your Head Above Water When Life Keeps Dragging You Down."

Speier thinks of herself as a mentor for women, in part because of her personal struggles. Early in 2011, she caused a stir when she announced during a House floor debate on funding for Planned Parenthood that she had undergone an abortion procedure nearly two decades earlier. She is a former co-chairwoman of Women LEAD, a Democratic Party program aimed at growing the number of women in Congress.

Speier is a San Francisco native who became infatuated with politics at age 16 while working on Ryan's 1966 re-election campaign for the state Assembly. During college she interned for him, which eventually led to a full-time job. She followed Ryan to Washington when he won a House seat in 1972.

She lost a hotly contested primary for lieutenant governor in 2006. But in 2008, she easily won a special congressional election to succeed Democratic Rep. Tom Lantos, who had died of esophageal cancer. Speier flirted with a run for state attorney general in 2010.

Key Votes

2012	
Extend a Social Security payroll tax cut and unemployment benefits	YES
Ease securities rules to expand small-business access to capital	YES
Extend for one year subsidized student loan interest rates financed by a cut in health care spending	NO
Cite Attorney General Eric H. Holder Jr. for contempt of Congress	NO
Create a visa program for foreign graduates in high-tech fields	?
Extend most Bush-era income tax rates while allowing rates for top-bracket earners to rise (Jan. 1, 2013)	YES
2011	
Strike funding for F-35 alternative engine	YES
Prevent EPA from regulating greenhouse gas emissions to address climate change	NO
Extend certain provisions of Patriot Act for four years	NO
Declare opposition to use of ground troops in Libya	NO
Overhaul patent law	YES
Pass compromise debt limit increase plan and establish future spending limits	YES
Allow consideration of measures to implement three trade agreements	NO

CQ Vote Studies

	PARTY UNITY		PRESIDENTIAL SUPPORT	
	SUPPORT	OPPOSE	SUPPORT	OPPOSE
2012	96%	4%	87%	13%
2011	95%	5%	83%	17%
2010	99%	1%	87%	13%
2009	95%	5%	92%	8%
2008	99%	1%	10%	90%

Interest Groups

	AFL-CIO	ADA	CCUS	ACU
2012	94%	85%	40%	0%
2011	100%	85%	38%	0%
2010	100%	95%	13%	0%
2009	95%	95%	33%	4%
2008	100%	60%	43%	0%

California 14

Most of San Mateo County; part of San Francisco

Wedged between San Francisco and Silicon Valley, the overwhelmingly Democratic 14th blends scenic coastal mountains and densely packed suburbs clustered along U.S. Route 101 and the Junipero Serra Freeway.

Decennial remapping expanded this district — formerly numbered the 12th — south and reduced its footprint in San Francisco County. It now takes in almost of all of San Mateo County's residents, most of whom live on the San Francisco Bay side of the Santa Cruz Mountains. Along the Bay, the 14th represents Redwood City, North Fair Oaks and East Palo Alto. The district's Pacific Coast includes a number of state parks and redwood forest preserves. Half Moon Bay on Highway 1 has a number of beaches and hosts an annual big-wave surfing competition.

Although not as dominant a feature of the local economy as in districts to the north and south, the 14th boasts a vital computer software sector. Video game publisher Electronic Arts and software giant Oracle have headquarters in the planned community of Redwood City. In the north, drugmaker Genentech and United Airlines are major employers.

Transportation provides jobs and revenue and allows district residents to contribute to the daily congestion on the way to San Francisco and cities in the Silicon Valley. The San Francisco International Airport is in the central part of the district; the BART and Caltrain commuter rail systems serve several cities in the 14th. District commuters should also benefit from an agreement between the California High-Speed Rail Authority and Caltrain to operate service between San Jose and San Francisco.

Asians comprise about 31 percent of the 14th's residents, giving the district the third-highest proportion statewide. Daly City and South San Francisco have large Filipino communities. There are also Hispanic-majority communities near the airport in South San Francisco and San Bruno. Mexican immigrants make up large communities in Redwood City and East Palo Alto.

Major Industry
Software, pharmaceuticals, transportation

Cities
San Francisco (pt.), Daly City, San Mateo, South San Francisco

Notable
The Farallon Islands are a national wildlife sanctuary for marine mammals and seabirds, and brave visitors can dive with great white sharks.

Rep. Eric Swalwell (D)

Capitol Office
225-5065
swalwell.house.gov
501 Cannon Bldg. 20515-3604; fax 226-3805

Committees
Homeland Security
Science, Space & Technology

Residence
Dublin

Born
Nov. 16, 1980; Sac City, Iowa

Religion
Christian

Family
Single

Education
Campbell U., attended 1999-2001; U. of Maryland, B.A. 2003 (government and politics), J.D. 2006

Career
County prosecutor

Political Highlights
Dublin Heritage and Cultural Arts Commission, 2006-08; Dublin Planning Commission, 2008-10; Dublin City Council, 2010-13

ELECTION RESULTS

2012 GENERAL		
Eric Swalwell (D)	120,388	52.1%
Pete Stark (D)	110,646	47.9%
2012 PRIMARY (Open)		
Pete Stark (D)	39,943	42.1%
Eric Swalwell (D)	34,347	36.2%

Elected 2012; 1st term

Swalwell became one of youngest members of the House by beating one of the oldest: 20-term Democrat Pete Stark. He vows to be less partisan than his famously prickly predecessor.

Swalwell has blue-collar roots; his dad is a retired police officer and his mother was a secretary (they are Republicans, however). His family moved to California when he was in elementary school. Swalwell had an athletic scholarship to a North Carolina school, but he transferred to the University of Maryland after injuries ended his dreams of playing professional soccer.

He eventually got a law degree, and he interned on Capitol Hill while in the region. Swalwell worked as a county prosecutor and got involved in government on his return to California, winning election as a Dublin city councilman.

His district has lots of technology companies and the Lawrence Livermore National Laboratory, which works on nuclear weapons programs, anti-terrorism and energy research. Swalwell has seats on the Homeland Security and Science, Space and Technology Committees.

On the latter, he's the top Democrat on the Energy Subcommittee. Swalwell says he'll be a "champion for renewable energy" and try to direct more federal spending toward private sector development on that front.

Swalwell supports rewriting the tax code to reward domestic manufacturers for keeping jobs in the United States, and he wants to provide tax credits to cover the moving expenses of plants that close overseas production to move back to U.S. soil.

Stark did not take Swalwell's challenge graciously — he accused Swalwell of taking bribes as a councilman and implied that Swalwell was a secret Republican. But the new 15th District was less liberal than Stark, and many voters were turned off by the 80-year-old's animosity. Swalwell finished second in the all-party "open" primary, then beat Stark by 4 points on Election Day.

Several Democrats are mulling a challenge to Swalwell in 2014.

California 15

East Bay — Hayward, part of Fremont; Livermore

Traversed by three major interstate highways and serving as one terminus of the San Mateo Bridge, the 15th is the crossroads of the East Bay. It represents wealthy and rapidly growing towns filling the spaces between Oakland, Silicon Valley and the fertile Central Valley.

The 15th unifies areas previously spread across four U.S. House districts. Its redrawn boundaries include about 40 percent of Alameda, including the entire eastern half of the county as well as Hayward, Union City and about one-third of Fremont near the San Francisco Bay. It also represents the Contra Costa County city of San Ramon, which grew by more than 60 percent between 2000 and 2010.

As in other San Francisco Bay area districts, Democrats enjoy comfortable voter registration advantages and past electoral successes in the 15th. Democratic strength wanes, however, in communities farthest from the Bay. In 2010, Democratic gubernatorial candidate Jerry Brown bested Republican Meg Whitman only by roughly 1,100 votes in San Ramon, 900 in Pleasanton and 500 in Livermore.

High-tech and heavy-industry sectors buoy the economy here. The Lawrence Livermore and Sandia National Laboratories employ more than 10,000 regional residents in cutting-edge energy, life sciences and nuclear research. San Ramon is home to Chevron's global headquarters and a regional AT&T office, while towns closer to Silicon Valley enjoy a spillover of electronics manufacturing and biotechnology jobs.

The 15th is racially diverse, and although whites comprise the majority of residents, Asian and Hispanic populations are significant. Large Mexican communities straddle Interstate 880 in Hayward; Union City and Hayward both have significant Chinese, Indian and Filipino populations. Asian-majority communities also have developed outside of Dublin and San Ramon.

Major Industry
Technology, manufacturing, telecommunications

Cities
Hayward, Livermore, Fremont (pt.), San Ramon

Notable
A breakthrough at Lawrence Livermore National Laboratory in the 1950s was the development of a nuclear warhead small enough to be launched by missile from submarines.

Rep. Jim Costa (D)

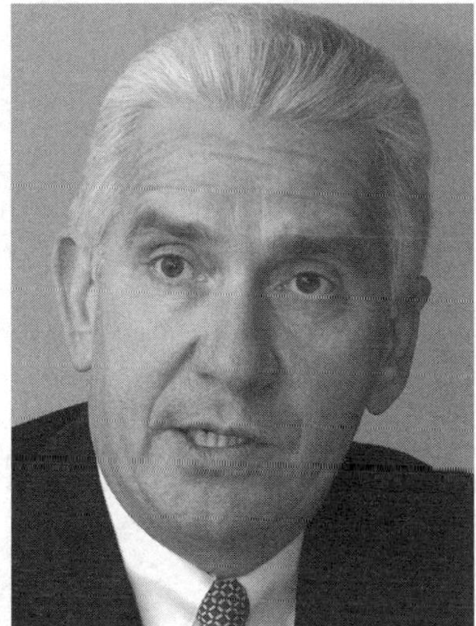

Capitol Office
225-3341
costa.house.gov
1314 Longworth Bldg. 20515-0520; fax 225-9308

Committees
Agriculture
Natural Resources

Residence
Fresno

Born
April 13, 1952; Fresno, Calif.

Religion
Roman Catholic

Family
Single

Education
California State U., Fresno, B.A. 1974 (political science)

Career
Government relations firm owner; state legislative aide; congressional district aide; almond orchard owner

Political Highlights
Calif. Assembly, 1978-94; Democratic nominee for Calif. Senate, 1993; Calif. Senate, 1994-2002

ELECTION RESULTS

2012 GENERAL		
Jim Costa (D)	84,649	57.4%
Brian Daniel Whelan (R)	62,801	42.6%
2012 PRIMARY (Open)		
Jim Costa (D)	25,355	42.7%
Loraine Goodwin (D)	5,703	9.6%
2010 GENERAL		
Jim Costa (D)	46,247	51.7%
Andy Vidak (R)	43,197	48.3%

Previous Winning Percentages
2008 (74%); 2006 (100%); 2004 (53%)

Elected 2004; 5th term

The San Joaquin Valley anchors Costa's personal and political lives. He was raised on a family-run dairy farm in Fresno, and he was a player on water policy, agriculture and infrastructure long before entering the House in 2005.

Costa, the grandson of Portuguese immigrants, is a 24-year veteran of state government. He seeks aid for the farmers and laborers in his district, and he belongs to the Blue Dog Coalition of fiscally conservative Democrats.

On votes in the 112th Congress (2011-12) where majorities of the two parties were opposed, few Democrats broke ranks more than Costa. He has sided with Republicans on expanding offshore energy development; he opposed the Democrats' 2009 cap-and-trade plan to limit greenhouse gas emissions; and he supported a balanced-budget constitutional amendment in 2011.

With seats on both the Agriculture and Natural Resources committees, Costa is immersed in the water politics of his state.

He wants to improve California's "plumbing" so that the heavily farmed San Joaquin Valley is ensured a stable water supply — Costa is one of the handful of House Democrats pushing for the Bay Delta Conservation Plan, which proposes large tunnels or canals to move water south to the San Joaquin Valley.

Costa proposes giving California additional regulatory flexibility to allot more water to the valley. He and other California lawmakers have complained that resources sometimes are directed toward the protection of endangered fish species. He wrote in early 2013 that it was "absurd to put a few fish before millions of Californians."

Costa backed a 2011 bill by Republican Devin Nunes to limit environmental regulation as a means to improve central California's access to water — even though he was frustrated that Democrats were not consulted on its development. Most members of his party believed it would override the state's right to manage its resources.

In the 113th Congress (2013-14), Costa is the top Democrat on the Agriculture Subcommittee on Livestock, Rural Development and Credit.

He has many ties to farming. Costa's grandfather was milking cows from the day he arrived in the Central Valley from the island of Terceira in the Azores. Costa's father and uncle later ran a farm, and Costa started helping out at age 7. The family sold its dairy herd in the 1970s, and the farm was divided after his father and uncle died. Costa still runs his acreage as an almond orchard. "Eat a handful a day," he says. "They are good for you."

Dairy prices have been volatile, and Costa feels that federal regulations on the prices for dairy products purchased by distributors have "outgrown their usefulness." He has proposed preventing the overproduction of milk by taxing dairies when their production reaches a defined threshold.

As the Agriculture Committee worked on a long-term reauthorization of farm programs in the 112th, Costa kept an eye on block grants and research funding tied to specialty crops, which are a large part of central California's output. He was pleased at funding increases for those programs in the panel-approved version of the bill, but he opposed large cuts to nutrition assistance programs that Republicans wrote into the measure. (It never got a floor vote.)

Costa supports free-trade deals, in part as a means to expand the market for farm goods. He voted in 2011 for pacts with Colombia, Panama and South Korea, and Costa is chairman of the U.S. steering committee of the Trans-atlantic Policy Network, a nongovernmental group working on trade relations with the European Union.

He's in line with most Democrats in supporting some major federal infrastructure projects. Costa has wanted high-speed rail in his region for a number of years. "With unemployment in my area as high as 20 percent, this is an opportunity to create hundreds of thousands of jobs — good-paying jobs, real jobs," he said at a Transportation and Infrastructure Committee hearing in December 2011.

Costa comes from a politically active family. His father served as treasurer for a friend running for the county board of supervisors. His mother served on a county social services board and as a school trustee. She belonged to Democratic clubs and thought President Harry S. Truman was "a heck of a guy," Costa told the Fresno Bee.

Despite his parents' civic involvement, it wasn't until he interned in the office of California Democratic Rep. B.F. Sisk in the summer of 1973 and attended the Senate Watergate hearings that Costa caught the political bug.

He worked on the winning 1974 House campaign of California Democrat John Krebs, then was an aide in his Washington office. He returned home to help on a state legislative race. After 18 months as the legislator's administrative assistant, Costa in 1978 successfully ran for an open Assembly seat.

When term limits forced him out of the state Senate in 2002, Costa opened his own lobbying firm. Having flirted with a House run three previous times, Costa quickly declared his candidacy when six-term Democrat Cal Dooley announced his retirement. The state Senate district Costa represented for eight years included the entire congressional district he was seeking.

Costa trounced Dooley's former chief of staff in the 2004 primary. The campaign featured a TV ad citing Costa's 1986 arrest in a prostitution sting, for which he had earlier apologized, and a 1994 incident in which police found marijuana in his apartment. (The drug was never linked to him and no charges were filed.) He beat a well-funded GOP state senator by 7 points in the general election.

Costa had several easy re-election campaigns, and voter turnout in the district was anemic. In 2010, however, he won one of the closest House races, nipping Republican Andy Vidak by barely 3,000 votes while receiving fewer than 50,000.

When new district lines for the 2012 election were revealed, Costa found that his home was in the 16th District — along with the home of his close friend, Democratic Rep. Dennis Cardoza. Rather than duke it out with Costa, Cardoza opted to retire.

Costa hadn't represented most of the 16th — it has no portion of Kings or Kern counties, which he had represented, and a lot less of Fresno County. Instead, it takes in more of the city of Fresno, as well as Merced and Madera counties to the northwest. But it is still a solidly Democratic area. Costa defeated Republican attorney Brian Daniel Whelan by almost 15 points.

Key Votes

2012	
Extend a Social Security payroll tax cut and unemployment benefits	YES
Ease securities rules to expand small-business access to capital	YES
Extend for one year subsidized student loan interest rates financed by a cut in health care spending	+
Cite Attorney General Eric H. Holder Jr. for contempt of Congress	?
Create a visa program for foreign graduates in high-tech fields	NO
Extend most Bush-era income tax rates while allowing rates for top-bracket earners to rise (Jan. 1, 2013)	YES
2011	
Strike funding for F-35 alternative engine	YES
Prevent EPA from regulating greenhouse gas emissions to address climate change	YES
Extend certain provisions of Patriot Act for four years	YES
Declare opposition to use of ground troops in Libya	NO
Overhaul patent law	YES
Pass compromise debt limit increase plan and establish future spending limits	YES
Allow consideration of measures to implement three trade agreements	YES

CQ Vote Studies

	PARTY UNITY		PRESIDENTIAL SUPPORT	
	SUPPORT	OPPOSE	SUPPORT	OPPOSE
2012	64%	36%	58%	42%
2011	55%	45%	68%	32%
2010	86%	14%	93%	7%
2009	91%	9%	93%	7%
2008	94%	6%	26%	74%

Interest Groups

	AFL-CIO	ADA	CCUS	ACU
2012	71%	40%	75%	29%
2011	79%	65%	73%	20%
2010	86%	70%	50%	8%
2009	90%	85%	67%	12%
2008	100%	80%	67%	9%

California 16

Central Valley — Merced County, Madera, most of Fresno

Remapping following the 2010 census drastically altered the Central Valley's representation. The land in the new 16th had previously fallen into three districts. It follows the Golden State Highway to take in most of Fresno and all of Merced and Madera. Grids of farmland separate its population hubs.

The 16th's portion of Fresno County accounts for about 45 percent of the district's population. About 60 percent of the residents of the city of Fresno live in the district — the rest are in the 22nd. There is a mix of ethnicities with Hispanic, Hmong and Armenian groups, and many residents of the district are foreign-born. Significant black and Asian populations live in the city's southwest, an area historically prone to gang violence. Overall, Hispanics (58 percent) outnumber any other group in the 16th.

Government and professional services are top employers in downtown Fresno, which includes city hall as well as county and federal courthouses. The 16th also takes in the Tower District, centered on the art deco Tower Theater, a landmark anchoring a clutch of arts and entertainment venues.

Northwest of Fresno, Merced, which already struggled with poverty, was hit hard by the economic downturn; unemployment and foreclosure rates remain high. The University of California campus in Merced has been competing for funds to support its fledgling medical program, designed to address a physician shortage in the Central Valley. Locals hope the state's approval of a high-speed rail line to connect Los Angeles with San Francisco will revitalize the region with a station in the valley. Across Interstate 5 in western Merced County are reservoirs and mountains of the Diablo Range. The district's farms produce fruits, vegetables and nuts. Dairy and food processing are also key.

Democrats have a voter registration edge, but residents tend to be more socially conservative than Democrats elsewhere in the state. Barack Obama won here by 20 percentage points in the 2012 presidential race.

Major Industry
Manufacturing, telecommunications, technology

Cities
Fresno (pt.), Merced, Madera, Los Banos

Notable
The Hmong Memorial Statue in Fresno's Courthouse Park honors Hmong and Laotian soldiers who aided U.S. troops in the Vietnam War.

Rep. Michael M. Honda (D)

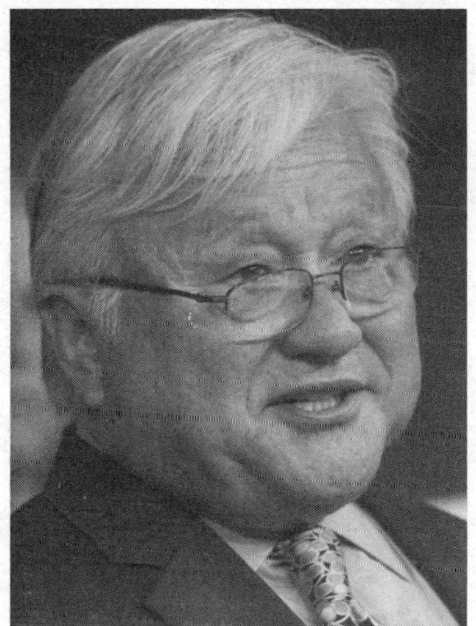

Capitol Office
225-2631
honda.house.gov
1713 Longworth Bldg. 20515-0515; fax 225-2699

Committees
Appropriations

Residence
San Jose

Born
June 27, 1941; Stockton, Calif.

Religion
Protestant

Family
Widowed; two children

Education
San Jose State U., B.S. 1969 (biological sciences), B.A. 1970 (Spanish), M.A. 1973 (education)

Career
Teacher; principal; Peace Corps volunteer

Political Highlights
San Jose School Board, 1981-90; Santa Clara County Board of Supervisors, 1990-96; Calif. Assembly, 1996-2000

ELECTION RESULTS

2012 GENERAL		
Michael M. Honda (D)	159,392	73.5%
Evelyn Li (R)	57,336	26.5%
2012 PRIMARY (Open)		
Michael M. Honda (D)	60,252	66.7%
2010 GENERAL		
Michael M. Honda (D)	126,147	67.6%
Scott Kirkland (R)	60,468	32.4%

Previous Winning Percentages
2008 (72%); 2006 (72%); 2004 (72%); 2002 (66%); 2000 (54%)

Elected 2000; 7th term

Honda sometimes seems like a mellow guy, and that image doesn't do justice to his passion for liberal causes. He outlines legislative plans as a leader in the Congressional Progressive Caucus and works on expanding the Democratic Party's base.

A former science teacher and school principal, Honda is used to public speaking. But he admits that campaign debates aren't his venue, and his speeches don't have much emotional zing. Honda's version of high dudgeon sounds like a light scolding. He's not a cable news staple.

Honda has found other ways to contribute, however. He specializes in minority outreach. Honda, a Japanese-American, spent seven years leading the Congressional Asian Pacific American Caucus, and in the 2012 election he claimed to use 20 different languages in get-out-the-vote efforts for his own House campaign. He's fluent in Spanish — Honda spent two years in El Salvador with the Peace Corps in the 1960s.

From 2005 through early 2013, he was a vice chairman of the Democratic National Committee. Honda's district includes part of Silicon Valley and is packed with tech companies, so he paid extra attention to his party's new-media strategies. He might have been forced from the job, however — the political team of President Barack Obama reportedly tried to consolidate its grip on the DNC by replacing several longtime officeholders. The Bay Area News Group reported that Honda reluctantly stepped aside.

His politics are across-the-board liberal, and he sits on the Appropriations Committee, which lets him touch on just about any matter before Congress. He criticized Republicans' priorities in the 112th Congress (2011-12) as described in the blueprints of Budget Chairman Paul D. Ryan of Wisconsin. "It is simply unfathomable that Paul Ryan's budget — which he claims is inspired by his Judeo-Christian faith — asks the most sacrifice from those with the least," Honda said, calling GOP plans "social Darwinism."

Honda prepared alternatives in the 112th as the chairman of the CPC Budget Task Force. The "People's Budget" and the "Budget for All" concentrate spending reductions in defense accounts (Honda opposes many foreign interventions, including the Afghanistan War) while calling for a liberal wish list of policies: higher taxes on the rich and fossil fuel companies; tax breaks for clean-energy producers and manufacturers; huge federal investments in infrastructure and new jobs programs; and leaving entitlement programs alone.

For the 113th Congress (2013-14), Honda returned to the Labor-HHS-Education Appropriations Subcommittee, which handles one of the largest pieces of the federal budget. He also serves on the subcommittee that provides funding for science and space programs, which is advantageous for Silicon Valley and the NASA Ames Research Center near his district.

Beyond fiscal matters, Honda publicizes a number of other issues. As California's cap-and-trade system for regulating greenhouse gas emissions took effect in November 2012, Honda's office dashed off opinion pieces urging more attempts at creating a federal version.

Immigration is a hot topic in the 113th, and Honda wants to create a path to citizenship for those currently in the country illegally. He focuses on expediting "reunification" cases, where family members of an immigrant are allowed to enter the country; Honda made his bill on the subject as liberal as possible by expanding the definition of eligible family to include gay partners.

Honda doesn't advocate government solutions for every problem. Citing his experiences as a teacher, he has commented that parental interest is usually the determining factor in the success of a child's education. But he often sees ways the government might pitch in. Amid many news reports of school bullying incidents, Honda in 2012 founded the Congressional Anti-Bullying Caucus and called for more federal funding to train school employees to deal with bullying.

He says his political outlook is rooted in his family history. After the bombing attack on Pearl Harbor, Honda, then an infant, was held along with his family for two and a half years in an internment camp for Japanese-Americans in Colorado. Honda's late wife, Jeanne, whom he married in 1967 and who died in 2004, survived the atomic bombing of Hiroshima.

After being released from the camp, Honda's family moved to Chicago, where his father worked for Navy intelligence, before they returned to California in 1953. Honda's parents became strawberry sharecroppers. He worked janitorial and delivery jobs to pay his way through San Jose State University, but he described himself as an aimless student. He was one credit shy of graduation when he joined the Peace Corps in 1965, looking for direction in life. After two years in El Salvador, where he helped build schools and medical clinics, he returned to California to finish college.

"I saw the niche that I needed to fill. ... I had to teach myself to learn from others, then try to figure out through the political process or educational process to seek change, reconciliation," he said. He went into teaching.

Honda remembers little of his internment. But he was a key participant in the Japanese-American lobbying campaign that culminated in a 1988 law providing a formal apology and compensation to interned Japanese-Americans. Congress in 2011 awarded a Gold Medal to Japanese-American veterans of World War II, a group that included his late father.

Honda got his start in public service volunteering for San Jose city councilman Norman Y. Mineta — another Japanese-American who spent time in an internment camp as a child. After being elected mayor, Mineta named Honda to the city planning commission in 1971.

In 1981, Honda won election to the local school board, and later to the county board of supervisors and the California Assembly. (Mineta went on to become a House member, a co-founder of CAPAC and George W. Bush's secretary of Transportation.)

When moderate Republican Rep. Tom Campbell left the 15th District seat open in 2000 to pursue a second run for the Senate, Honda entered the race. A phone call from President Bill Clinton convinced him the national party would back his bid, and Honda won by 12 points.

Honda has easily won re-election, bolstered by his ties to the large minority communities in his district. Redistricting for the 113th Congress made his home turf, the new 17th District, approximately half Asian.

Key Votes

2012	
Extend a Social Security payroll tax cut and unemployment benefits	YES
Ease securities rules to expand small-business access to capital	YES
Extend for one year subsidized student loan interest rates financed by a cut in health care spending	NO
Cite Attorney General Eric H. Holder Jr. for contempt of Congress	?
Create a visa program for foreign graduates in high-tech fields	NO
Extend most Bush-era income tax rates while allowing rates for top-bracket earners to rise (Jan. 1, 2013)	YES
2011	
Strike funding for F-35 alternative engine	YES
Prevent EPA from regulating greenhouse gas emissions to address climate change	NO
Extend certain provisions of Patriot Act for four years	NO
Declare opposition to use of ground troops in Libya	NO
Overhaul patent law	NO
Pass compromise debt limit increase plan and establish future spending limits	NO
Allow consideration of measures to implement three trade agreements	NO

CQ Vote Studies

	PARTY UNITY		PRESIDENTIAL SUPPORT	
	SUPPORT	OPPOSE	SUPPORT	OPPOSE
2012	98%	2%	93%	7%
2011	98%	2%	79%	21%
2010	97%	3%	90%	10%
2009	99%	1%	94%	6%
2008	100%	0%	15%	85%

Interest Groups

	AFL-CIO	ADA	CCUS	ACU
2012	90%	100%	25%	0%
2011	100%	90%	13%	4%
2010	100%	95%	0%	0%
2009	100%	100%	33%	0%
2008	100%	95%	50%	0%

California 17

South Bay and most of Fremont

The industrially diverse 17th is the birthplace of the microprocessor and the iPod as well as a longtime blue-collar center of salt refining and auto manufacturing. The Silicon Valley cities are home to a largely affluent populace, and the district as a whole is ethnically diverse and overwhelmingly Democratic.

The geographically smallest of the three districts representing Silicon Valley, the 17th now takes in towns in Santa Clara and Alameda counties that arc around the lower San Francisco Bay. It includes the cities of Cupertino, Sunnyvale and Santa Clara to the southeast, a portion of San Jose and the city of Milpitas at its elbow, and the cities of Fremont and Newark in Alameda County in the East Bay area.

The cities of this district are home to technology giants and ambitious start-ups. Cupertino-based Apple has driven a local commercial development surge — groundbreaking in Cupertino on a new, futuristic headquarters is expected in 2013 or 2014, and the company has added office space in Sunnyvale. Sunnyvale already is home to microchip maker AMD, data storage giant NetApp and Internet mainstay Yahoo. Intel, in Santa Clara, and Cisco, in San Jose, also have their corporate headquarters in the 17th. A focus on innovative technology here extends to civic endeavors — in 2010, Santa Clara was ranked the No. 1 Green Power Community in the nation by the EPA because its city-owned utility generates 30 percent of its power through renewable sources.

Roughly half of the district's residents are Asian; the 17th has the largest percentage of Asian residents (49) among districts in the contiguous United States. Many groups are represented within that broad category: Cupertino, parts of San Jose, and Fremont all have attracted large Chinese and Indian populations; roughly 17 percent of Milpitas residents are Filipino; and several tracts of San Jose have large Vietnamese communities.

Major Industry
Computing hardware, software, biotechnology

Cities
Sunnyvale, San Jose, Fremont

Notable
Don Edwards San Francisco Bay National Wildlife Refuge, the nation's first urban wildlife preserve, occupies 30,000 acres of salt marsh, mudflat and upland.

Rep. Anna G. Eshoo (D)

Capitol Office
225-8104
eshoo.house.gov
241 Cannon Bldg 20515-0514; fax 225-8890

Committees
Energy & Commerce

Residence
Menlo Park

Born
Dec. 13, 1942; New Britain, Conn.

Religion
Roman Catholic

Family
Divorced, two children

Education
Canada College, A.A. 1975 (English literature)

Career
State legislative aide; homemaker

Political Highlights
Candidate for San Mateo County Community College Board of Trustees, 1977; Democratic National Committee, 1980-92; San Mateo County Board of Supervisors, 1982-92 (president, 1986); Democratic nominee for U.S. House, 1988

ELECTION RESULTS

2012 GENERAL		
Anna G. Eshoo (D)	212,831	70.5%
Dave Chapman (R)	89,103	29.5%
2012 PRIMARY (Open)		
Anna G. Eshoo (D)	86,851	61.5%
William Parks (D)	6,504	4.6%
2010 GENERAL		
Anna G. Eshoo (D)	151,217	69.1%
Dave Chapman (R)	60,917	27.8%
Paul Lazaga (LIBERT)	6,735	3.1%

Previous Winning Percentages
2008 (70%); 2006 (71%); 2004 (70%); 2002 (68%); 2000 (70%); 1998 (69%); 1996 (65%); 1994 (61%); 1992 (57%)

Elected 1992; 11th term

Even though Eshoo is immersed in the rapidly evolving world of technology, her approach as a legislator has been consistent over two decades. Her solidly liberal beliefs are seasoned with a desire to promote the interests of tech companies that call her district home.

Silicon Valley "is a place that constantly reinvents itself," Eshoo said. "If there's anything that motivates me and is a source of inspiration to me, it's my constituents and what they do. I pack up their ideas and put them in my suitcase, and bring them here to my work."

In the 112th Congress (2011-12) she became the top Democrat on the Energy and Commerce Subcommittee on Communications and Technology, where even as a member of the minority she had opportunities to push government involvement in shaping technology infrastructure and accessibility.

She and Chairman Greg Walden of Oregon share the mission of shuffling the federally regulated allocations of the broadcast spectrum "to help satiate the enormous appetite for spectrum that's needed in order to support all that's going on with wireless," she said. Eshoo was pleased with the 2012 law authorizing the Federal Communications Commission to implement a voluntary auction to allow current license holders to sell back their spectrum for reuse. As spectrum allocations are shuffled, Eshoo wants to maintain some unlicensed segments — which could be used for citywide wireless Internet networks, among other things.

The 2012 law also achieved a longtime goal of hers: authorizing the FCC to create an interoperable, nationwide broadband public safety network. Eshoo and Illinois Republican John Shimkus helped found the E911 Caucus in 2003, inspired in large part by the difficulties first-responders had communicating with each other during the Sept. 11 terrorist attacks. "People in our communities across the country will benefit from that for years to come," she said.

Eshoo wants to make "high-speed, affordable broadband" available to all, and she doesn't mind using the federal government to do it. A 2012 White House executive order was similar to her 2011 "dig once" bill to require the installation of broadband fiber-optic conduits when federal highway projects are undertaken. She has pushed for a permanent ban on Internet access taxes.

She's also a defender of network neutrality — the idea that broadband providers should be barred from blocking or slowing access to certain Internet content. Republicans were livid at 2011 net neutrality rules put in place by the FCC, calling them an unprecedented expansion of government regulation of the Internet. It is one area where Eshoo and some constituents part ways. She opposed a 2010 proposal by Google, which is based in Mountain View, that wireless broadband providers be excluded from such rules.

Google was more on board with Eshoo's battle against a 2011 anti-piracy measure to allow law enforcement agencies to shut down offending websites by obtaining a court order. Opponents said the bill would create a system ripe for abuse, where those operating the sites would have few opportunities to defend themselves. The measure was scuttled after tech companies ignited a populist campaign against it.

Eshoo can be intense and hard-driving. She has described herself as a lawmaker who "will work with anyone and everyone who really wants to push the edges of the envelope out and create new opportunities." But she also has some very powerful Democratic friends. Eshoo and Minority Leader Nancy Pelosi have known each other for more than 30 years; Eshoo performed the rites for the wedding of one of Pelosi's daughters in 2008.

In her 2008 autobiography, Pelosi described Eshoo as "one of my dearest friends in the world," and Eshoo would often preside over the House during tough floor fights when Pelosi was speaker.

Eshoo stepped up on a big Democratic priority in the 112th: campaign finance. She was aghast at a 2010 Supreme Court ruling that allowed the creation of super PACs, advocacy groups independent of official campaigns that can accept unrestricted donations from individuals or organizations.

"I think that our democracy is being hijacked, but we can't identify the hijackers," Eshoo said. "This is secret money, secret donors, secret everything. This is not who and what we are."

Eshoo championed new FCC rules requiring broadcasters to make data about political advertisements available online. She wants shareholders to have more access to information about corporate political spending. And she was disappointed that the White House did not go through with a 2011 plan to require all federal contractors to disclose their political contributions. (Republicans said it would be used to deny contracts to entities that opposed White House positions.)

She has promoted high-speed rail in California and worked to bring a regional U.S. Patent and Trademark Office to Silicon Valley. A former member of the Intelligence Committee, Eshoo has also promoted cybersecurity and pushed for more integration and oversight of intelligence agencies.

And Eshoo will always have a place in the heart of many a TV viewer. She wrote the 2011 law requiring television commercials to be played at the same volume level as the shows during which they appear. After the rules to implement the law went into effect in late 2012, Eshoo said that her efforts got the most positive feedback of anything she has done in Congress.

The daughter of immigrants of Armenian and Assyrian descent, Eshoo was drawn to politics in her native New Britain, Conn. Her father was a New Deal Democrat who named his daughter after Franklin D. Roosevelt's wife, whose full name was Anna Eleanor Roosevelt.

The family eventually moved west to California. Eshoo married (she has been divorced since the 1980s) and devoted herself to motherhood while earning an associate's degree in English literature from a local college. Yet she continued her political activity, taking an internship with California Assembly Speaker Leo T. McCarthy, who was also a close Pelosi friend, and later serving as his chief of staff.

In 1982, McCarthy urged her to run for the San Mateo County Board of Supervisors, where she served for a decade. In 1988, she lost a House race to Republican Tom Campbell. Four years later, Campbell ran for the Senate, so Eshoo tried again. She won an eight-candidate primary and hasn't been in a close election since then.

Key Votes

2012	
Extend a Social Security payroll tax cut and unemployment benefits	YES
Ease securities rules to expand small-business access to capital	YES
Extend for one year subsidized student loan interest rates financed by a cut in health care spending	NO
Cite Attorney General Eric H. Holder Jr. for contempt of Congress	NO
Create a visa program for foreign graduates in high-tech fields	NO
Extend most Bush-era income tax rates while allowing rates for top-bracket earners to rise (Jan. 1, 2013)	YES
2011	
Strike funding for F-35 alternative engine	YES
Prevent EPA from regulating greenhouse gas emissions to address climate change	NO
Extend certain provisions of Patriot Act for four years	NO
Declare opposition to use of ground troops in Libya	NO
Overhaul patent law	NO
Pass compromise debt limit increase plan and establish future spending limits	YES
Allow consideration of measures to implement three trade agreements	YES

CQ Vote Studies

	PARTY UNITY		PRESIDENTIAL SUPPORT	
	SUPPORT	OPPOSE	SUPPORT	OPPOSE
2012	95%	5%	90%	10%
2011	95%	5%	85%	15%
2010	99%	1%	93%	7%
2009	99%	1%	97%	3%
2008	99%	1%	14%	86%

Interest Groups

	AFL-CIO	ADA	CCUS	ACU
2012	95%	95%	25%	0%
2011	93%	85%	25%	0%
2010	100%	95%	13%	0%
2009	100%	100%	33%	0%
2008	100%	90%	61%	0%

California 18

Western Santa Clara County; southern San Mateo and northern Santa Cruz counties

Characterized by scenic landscapes and well-funded bank accounts, the 18th District is made up of Pacific Coast beaches and Silicon Valley cities nestled in the foothills of the Santa Cruz Mountains. Decennial remapping made the district more compact than the former 14th. About 20 percent of the population lives in a corner of San Jose, but the real activity of the district is centered in Menlo Park, Palo Alto, Los Altos and Mountain View.

Home to the headquarters of Internet and software heavyweights Google, Facebook, Netflix, Mozilla, Symantec and LinkedIn, as well as Stanford University, the 18th hosts educated and high-earning residents. Although the recent economic downturn took some of the shine off its economy, the 18th has the third-highest median household income nationwide and highest in the state; finding affordable housing is a concern for segments of the workforce. Researchers at a NASA facility near Mountain View collaborate with firms and colleges on high-tech and space-related projects — the Kepler Mission telescope has discovered thousands of planet-like bodies in our galaxy. Venture capital is another outlet for economic growth here.

Southwest of Silicon Valley, the 18th contains a number of state parks and open-space preserves in the Santa Cruz Mountains. Big Basin Redwoods State Park is California's oldest. The district's coastal stretch runs south from San Gregorio State Beach to a state park just north of Santa Cruz.

Unlike neighboring districts, the Democratic 18th has a majority-white population, while Asians — mainly ethnic Chinese, Indian, Korean and Japanese — comprise the district's largest minority group, at 20 percent.

Voters in the 18th are liberal on social and environmental issues, especially in Santa Cruz County. Many residents are more conservative regarding economic policy, and small Republican voting blocs exist in wealthy areas in Santa Clara County.

Major Industry
Computing hardware, software, biotechnology

Cities
San Jose (pt.), Mountain View, Palo Alto

Notable
Stanford University's Cantor Arts Center has the nation's largest concentration of bronze sculptures by Auguste Rodin.

Rep. Zoe Lofgren (D)

Capitol Office
225-3072
zoelofgren.house.gov
1401 Longworth Bldg. 20515-0516; fax 225-3336

Committees
House Administration
Judiciary
Science, Space & Technology

Residence
San Jose

Born
Dec. 21, 1947; San Mateo, Calif.

Religion
Lutheran

Family
Husband, John Marshall Collins; two children

Education
Stanford U., A.B. 1970 (political science), U. of Santa Clara, J.D. 1975

Career
Lawyer; nonprofit housing development director; law professor; congressional aide

Political Highlights
San Jose-Evergreen Community College District Board of Trustees, 1979-81; Santa Clara County Board of Supervisors, 1981-95

ELECTION RESULTS

2012 GENERAL		
Zoe Lofgren (D)	162,300	73.2%
Robert Murray (R)	59,313	26.8%
2012 PRIMARY (Open)		
Zoe Lofgren (D)	60,726	65.2%
2010 GENERAL		
Zoe Lofgren (D)	105,841	67.8%
Daniel Sahagun (R)	37,913	24.3%
Edward Gonzalez (LIBERT)	12,304	7.9%

Previous Winning Percentages
2008 (71%); 2006 (73%); 2004 (71%); 2002 (67%); 2000 (72%); 1998 (73%); 1996 (66%); 1994 (65%)

Elected 1994; 10th term

Democrats trust Lofgren to get out front on some contentious subjects — which is a recognition of both her support for party causes and her willingness to fight for incremental victories when big deals are out of reach. She's an expert on immigration and technology policy, a portfolio that suits the needs of her Silicon Valley district.

The 2012 elections raised Lofgren's profile. Republicans did so poorly with Hispanic voters that an immigration overhaul seemed viable for the first time in years. Lofgren (full name: ZO LOFF-gren) was an immigration attorney and law professor, and she's now the top Democrat on the Judiciary Subcommittee on Immigration and Border Security. She took the initiative as part of an eight-person bipartisan House working group drafting a comprehensive overhaul.

She pans the current immigration system. "Americans don't realize how bulky and inefficient and counterintuitive it is until someone they know gets involved," she said. Her notion of a comprehensive overhaul is shared by many Democrats. Lofgren wants increases in enforcement paired with the creation of a path to citizenship for illegal immigrants already in the United States. She rejects the term "amnesty" for the latter.

"What we're saying is, over some period of time that's arduous, you might gain legal permanent residence in the United States, and then if you pay thousands of dollars, learn everything there is to know about the American government, learn English so well you can pass the test and then swear you can defend the Constitution and be willing to fight for your country, only in that case could you become an American citizen," she said at an early 2013 hearing.

Lofgren strongly supported a 2012 policy directive by President Barack Obama to stop or slow enforcement against certain immigrants who were brought to the country illegally as children.

She attempted smaller bites in the 112th Congress (2011-12). Lofgren negotiated with Judiciary Chairman Lamar Smith of Texas on a plan to expand the visa program for workers in high-tech fields — the employers in her district approve heartily of such efforts. But she couldn't countenance Smith's plan to offset the expansion with reductions to other kinds of visas.

She'd also like to eliminate per country limits on employment-based green cards. Lofgren has spoken in support of Republican bills that have similar provisions, which would allow greater numbers of skilled immigrants from countries such as India and China, which have a higher demand for visas.

When Lofgren chaired the immigration subcommittee in the 111th Congress (2009-10), she famously invited comedian Stephen Colbert to testify, based on a segment for "The Colbert Report" in which he spent a day with migrant farm workers in upstate New York. Republicans derided it as a publicity stunt — and it did lead to a crush of media attention.

Lofgren tackles tech issues as a member of the Judiciary subcommittee on the Internet, and as the No. 2 Democrat on the Science, Space and Technology Committee. She is wary of plans, public or private, that might limit the flow of information. "Technology, and specifically communications technology ... is the biggest opportunity for ideas to be widely disseminated and freedom to flourish that society has ever seen," she said. "That's pretty exciting, isn't it?"

She supports "network neutrality" rules set by the Federal Communications Commission in 2011 that are meant to prevent service providers from slowing or preventing access to certain Internet content. Republicans have called the rules a Trojan horse to allow future regulation of the Internet; Lofgren has called them a consumer protection. She opposes cybersecurity measures if she thinks they would give government too much power to pry into people's

Internet-usage habits and overall privacy.

Lofgren frequently takes the side of Internet activists and Web companies against content creators and government agencies that enforce copyright laws. In another bit of showmanship, Lofgren in 2013 used the website Reddit to "crowdsource" ideas for a bill to slow down the government's seizure of website domains accused of copyright infringement.

Her workload was particularly formidable when Democrats were in the majority. In the 111th Congress, Lofgren chaired a subcommittee on election law, the immigration subcommittee and one of Capitol Hill's most labor-intensive panels — what is now known as the Ethics Committee. Her time on Ethics required her to oversee cases against Democrats Charles B. Rangel of New York and Maxine Waters of California. As both cases dragged on, accusations of improper conduct by committee members and staff flew back and forth between the parties; Lofgren and the panel's top Republican, Jo Bonner of Alabama, were feuding publicly. She left the panel early in 2011.

Lofgren grew up in a blue-collar neighborhood in south Palo Alto. Her father was a truck driver and her mother was a secretary and a school cafeteria cook. While other mothers went door to door collecting for the March of Dimes, Lofgren's mother went after "dollars for Democrats."

After completing her undergraduate studies at Stanford University on a scholarship, she headed to Washington, landing an internship with Democratic Rep. Don Edwards of California. She stayed on as a staffer through the 1970s and was inspired to go to law school when a draft bill she developed was "ripped to shreds" by the House legislative counsel. She practiced immigration law as a partner in the firm Webber & Lofgren and taught the subject at the University of Santa Clara. Lofgren's husband, John Marshall Collins, is a lawyer in San Jose whom she met one election night while working for Edwards.

She was the first executive director of the San Jose nonprofit Community Housing Developers. In 1979, a colleague urged her to run for the local community college board of trustees; she won.

In 1980, she was elected to the Santa Clara County Board of Supervisors, where she stayed for 14 years and was often in conflict with San Jose Mayor Tom McEnery, a Democrat, who pushed downtown redevelopment while Lofgren argued for more money for education and human services.

When Edwards retired from the House after 32 years, the 1994 Democratic primary featured a face-off between Lofgren and McEnery. She benefited from an uproar that ensued when state election officials barred her from describing herself as "county supervisor/mother" on the ballot. She went on to win the primary and has enjoyed easy general-election victories. Since 2003, Lofgren has chaired California's Democratic congressional delegation.

Key Votes

2012	
Extend a Social Security payroll tax cut and unemployment benefits	YES
Ease securities rules to expand small-business access to capital	YES
Extend for one year subsidized student loan interest rates financed by a cut in health care spending	NO
Cite Attorney General Eric H. Holder Jr. for contempt of Congress	NO
Create a visa program for foreign graduates in high-tech fields	NO
Extend most Bush-era income tax rates while allowing rates for top-bracket earners to rise (Jan. 1, 2013)	YES
2011	
Strike funding for F-35 alternative engine	YES
Prevent EPA from regulating greenhouse gas emissions to address climate change	NO
Extend certain provisions of Patriot Act for four years	NO
Declare opposition to use of ground troops in Libya	?
Overhaul patent law	NO
Pass compromise debt limit increase plan and establish future spending limits	NO
Allow consideration of measures to implement three trade agreements	YES

CQ Vote Studies

	PARTY UNITY		PRESIDENTIAL SUPPORT	
	SUPPORT	OPPOSE	SUPPORT	OPPOSE
2012	93%	7%	85%	15%
2011	95%	5%	82%	18%
2010	98%	2%	90%	10%
2009	99%	1%	93%	7%
2008	99%	1%	14%	86%

Interest Groups

	AFL-CIO	ADA	CCUS	ACU
2012	95%	100%	17%	4%
2011	100%	80%	7%	8%
2010	93%	95%	0%	4%
2009	100%	95%	40%	0%
2008	100%	100%	56%	0%

California 19

Santa Clara County — most of San Jose

The Democratic 19th, renumbered and redrawn entirely within Santa Clara County, boasts both the urban, technology-centric hub of Silicon Valley and the more-remote farmland surrounding Gilroy, the self-proclaimed "Garlic Capital of the World." Most constituents live in San Jose, of which the 19th takes a majority from a three-way split with the 17th and 18th. The third-largest city in California, San Jose's footprint has spread over four decades of aggressive annexation of Santa Clara County territory.

The 19th follows the path of the Highway 101 from San Jose Airport and the Rosemary Gardens neighborhood through downtown and southeast into Coyote Valley. It includes the small town of Morgan Hill and the western half of Gilroy. The limits of Santa Clara County form its eastern and much of the district's southern border.

Downtown San Jose offers white-collar jobs at leading computing, technology and financial services firms. New high-rise condominium buildings tower over what was the city's poorest area a decade ago. City residents can walk to the state-of-the-art HP Pavilion, home of hockey's San Jose Sharks.

The education-intensive nature of Silicon Valley's labor market creates a complicated demographic picture for the 19th. The district's Asian population, which is one-fourth of its populace, includes South and East Asians working in tech sector-related fields; San Jose's 95,000 Vietnamese residents have a much higher incidence of poverty. Neighborhoods east of downtown San Jose and in the western half of Gilroy are predominately Mexican, and income levels in San Jose vary between white and Hispanic communities.

Gilroy, in the southern reaches of the district and shared with the 20th, is a major agricultural center for Santa Clara County. Family-owned Christopher Ranch is the largest garlic processor in the U.S. and a major sponsor of the city's annual Garlic Festival. Gilroy is also home to flower seed production.

Major Industry
Computing hardware, software, biotechnology, agriculture

Cities
San Jose (pt.), Morgan Hill, Gilroy

Notable
San Jose's Japantown is one of three such Japanese cultural districts remaining in the country.

Rep. Sam Farr (D)

Capitol Office
225-2861
farr.house.gov
1126 Longworth Bldg. 20515-0517; fax 225-6791

Committees
Appropriations

Residence
Carmel

Born
July 4, 1941; San Francisco, Calif.

Religion
Episcopalian

Family
Wife, Shary Baldwin Farr; one child

Education
Willamette U., B.S. 1963 (biology)

Career
State legislative aide; Peace Corps volunteer

Political Highlights
Monterey County Board of Supervisors, 1975-80; Calif. Assembly, 1980-93

ELECTION RESULTS

2012 GENERAL		
Sam Farr (D)	172,996	74.1%
Jeff Taylor (R)	60,566	25.9%
2012 PRIMARY (Open)		
Sam Farr (D)	68,895	64.4%
Art Dunn (D)	4,095	3.8%
2010 GENERAL		
Sam Farr (D)	118,734	66.6%
Jeff Taylor (R)	53,176	29.8%
Eric Petersen (GREEN)	3,397	1.9%
Mary V. Larkin (LIBERT)	2,742	1.5%

Previous Winning Percentages
2008 (74%); 2006 (76%); 2004 (67%); 2002 (68%); 2000 (69%); 1998 (65%); 1996 (59%); 1994 (52%); 1993 Special Runoff (54%)

Elected 1993; 10th full term

California's "salad bowl" region is home to thriving agriculture, stunning Pacific Coast scenery and Farr — a cagey progressive who operates from the Appropriations Committee.

Government's role, according to Farr, is "to take care of the people who fall through the cracks." He sees his personal obligations extending further. "I try to tell people that when you're elected to office, you're not just the voice of voting people," he said. "You're the voice for all living things."

Farr's Central Coast district supports scores of different crops and is responsible for billions of dollars in sales of small-acreage produce. "This isn't the Midwest, where they get commodity support like the corn, wheat, soybeans," Farr says. "This is just free-market agriculture. You go out there and take risks. If it rains too much or it's too dry or bugs get in your crop, too bad. No government's going to come in and help you out, which they do with those other crops." Thanks to California's more-rigorous labor and environmental standards, production costs in the state can run relatively high.

Farr sees successful agriculture as both good business for his district and essential to fending off the urban sprawl that has claimed a significant amount of land elsewhere in California. As the ranking Democrat on the Agriculture Appropriations Subcommittee, Farr advocates land-conservation programs and other federal supports. And he relishes the opportunity to fund nutrition and housing programs. "The Department of Agriculture is essentially the department of the poor and needy in America," he said.

He's also a supporter of helping the needy overseas. He said the fiscal 2013 Agriculture spending bill, which wasn't enacted, would have cut too much from foreign assistance. "We all know that in tough budget times everyone has to tighten their belts," he said, but the reductions to international food aid were "beyond lean."

On the Military Construction-VA Subcommittee he looks out for numerous military installations in his district. The closing of Fort Ord during Farr's freshman term was one of the largest single-base closures in U.S. history. He has since worked for the conversion of the base to civilian use. It's now home to the campus of California State University, Monterey Bay, as well as to commercial property and low-income housing.

Farr has been critical of the earmark ban imposed by Republicans, saying it shirks Congress' responsibility of determining how taxpayer money should be spent. He said that federal funding formulas shortchange rural districts like his in favor of urban areas, and he sees the earmarking process as a vehicle for getting a fair shake.

Environmental protection has always been a key interest for Farr, who is a founder and co-chairman of the House Oceans Caucus. He fought GOP efforts to block funding for implementation of the recommendations of the U.S. Commission on Ocean Policy that were enacted by executive order in 2010. A 2012 law contains Farr's provision to remove the "sunset" clause for funding of the Marine Debris Program. He says he is "leading the sustainable oceans concept" in the House, and he has backed a measure, with California Democrat John Garamendi, to ban new offshore oil drilling along the Pacific Coast.

Looking inland, Farr was partly responsible for the country's newest national park. President Barack Obama in January 2013 signed his bill to upgrade the designation of the Pinnacles National Monument.

Farr, whose district relies upon migrant agricultural labor and is home to a large Latino population, wants a comprehensive immigration law overhaul. He praised Obama's 2012 policy directive to halt the deportation of some undocumented youths who were born in the Unites States.

Farr is noted for his photography, both at the Capitol and at home in California. He credits his early interest in the field to his exposure to famed landscape photographer Ansel Adams — a family friend — as well as his family's penchant for taking pictures. Referring to himself as photojournalist, Farr says, "I think that I've always loved the visual arts, and photography just struck me as a way of being able to communicate, but knowing how to do it well." Adams served as an honorary campaign chairman during Farr's first run for the state Assembly. (He died four years later at age 82.)

Farr is a fifth-generation Californian whose father was a longtime state senator and, under President Lyndon Johnson, the first national director of highway beautification programming. A 1963 graduate of Willamette University in Salem, Ore., Farr joined the Peace Corps, serving as a community organizer in Medellin, Colombia.

His approach to that vocation is reflected in his approach in the House; Farr says that teaching people to represent themselves is the best course to take in public service. "It may be a lifetime of work, but when you leave, you should've empowered your constituency to be able to do a lot of problem-solving, to petition government without having to depend on" a particular lawmaker, he said.

His mother died of cancer during his service. His family visited him in Colombia and, while on an outing, his younger sister was thrown from a horse and injured her head. She died on the operating table.

Farr in 2011 co-sponsored a bill to implement a free-trade agreement with Colombia and was one of only 31 Democrats to vote for it. "My party wasn't keen on that," Farr said. "But it was good for Colombia, and it was good for my district. It was the right thing to do."

Farr credits his time in the Peace Corps with leading him to a career in public service. "If I wasn't in the Peace Corps I'd probably be a high school biology teacher," he said. "But I would've been a pretty radical teacher. I would want kids to question authority and petition government to right wrongs. I've always been an advocate of that."

After leaving the Peace Corps, Farr got a staff job in the California Assembly. He won election to the Monterey County Board of Supervisors in 1975, and was elected to the Assembly in 1980, serving for more than a dozen years.

In 1993, he won a special election to replace Democratic Rep. Leon E. Panetta, who became the budget director for President Bill Clinton. Farr took 54 percent of the vote in a runoff against the GOP nominee, Pebble Beach lawyer Bill McCampbell. He won their 1994 rematch, and has been re-elected easily each time since then.

Key Votes

2012	
Extend a Social Security payroll tax cut and unemployment benefits	NO
Ease securities rules to expand small-business access to capital	YES
Extend for one year subsidized student loan interest rates financed by a cut in health care spending	?
Cite Attorney General Eric H. Holder Jr. for contempt of Congress	NO
Create a visa program for foreign graduates in high-tech fields	NO
Extend most Bush-era income tax rates while allowing rates for top-bracket earners to rise (Jan. 1, 2013)	YES
2011	
Strike funding for F-35 alternative engine	YES
Prevent EPA from regulating greenhouse gas emissions to address climate change	NO
Extend certain provisions of Patriot Act for four years	NO
Declare opposition to use of ground troops in Libya	NO
Overhaul patent law	NO
Pass compromise debt limit increase plan and establish future spending limits	NO
Allow consideration of measures to implement three trade agreements	YES

CQ Vote Studies

	PARTY UNITY		PRESIDENTIAL SUPPORT	
	SUPPORT	OPPOSE	SUPPORT	OPPOSE
2012	97%	3%	90%	10%
2011	96%	4%	83%	17%
2010	99%	1%	86%	14%
2009	99%	1%	94%	6%
2008	99%	1%	13%	87%

Interest Groups

	AFL-CIO	ADA	CCUS	ACU
2012	90%	95%	25%	0%
2011	93%	95%	19%	4%
2010	100%	90%	13%	0%
2009	100%	100%	33%	0%
2008	100%	100%	61%	0%

California 20

Monterey and San Benito counties — Salinas; Santa Cruz

The 20th District is located on California's central coast and takes in most of Santa Cruz County and all of its namesake city as well as affluent Monterey Bay communities in Santa Cruz and Monterey counties. Southeast of the bay is the agrarian Salinas Valley and San Benito County.

The Monterey Bay region has several marine research and higher education sites, including the Monterey Bay Aquarium Research Institute and the University of California, Santa Cruz. Exclusive Pebble Beach is home to movie stars and Silicon Valley executives.

Salinas Valley, in the center of Monterey County, is home to the area's nearly $6 billion agricultural industry as well as large Hispanic communities. The "salad bowl" is a top producer of strawberries, artichokes, lettuce and other vegetables. Environmental issues are not simply a matter of farm production here: Santa Cruz supports several conservation and "green" programs, and the district's southwestern coast contains Los Padres National Forest.

Registered Democrats have a commanding lead in voter registration and make up a majority of district voters, with less than one-fourth of voters registered as Republicans. Unaffiliated voters in the area tend to lean Democratic. Farming areas south of Salinas are only slightly more conservative than reliably liberal Santa Cruz. The military has a major presence here, with research centers in Monterey and Fort Hunter Liggett to the south. The National Guard's Camp Roberts also straddles the district's southern border.

Major Industry

Agriculture, tourism, higher education

Military bases

Fort Hunter Liggett (Army), 7,632 military, 241 civilian; Defense Language Institute Foreign Language Center/Presidio of Monterey (Army), 3,500 military, 3,300 civilian; Naval Postgraduate School, 1,647 military, 737 civilian; Fleet Numerical Meteorology and Oceanography Center, 40 military, 133 civilian (2011)

Cities

Salinas, Santa Cruz, Watsonville, Hollister

Notable

Monterey Canyon is the deepest submarine canyon off the Pacific Ocean's North American coast.

Rep. David Valadao (R)

Capitol Office
225-4695
valadao.house.gov
1004 Longworth Bldg. 20515-1703; fax 225-3196

Committees
Appropriations

Residence
Hanford

Born
April 14, 1977; Hanford, Calif.

Religion
Roman Catholic

Family
Wife, Terra Valadao; three children

Education
College of the Sequoias, attended 1996-98

Career
Dairy farmer

Political Highlights
Calif. Assembly, 2010-12

ELECTION RESULTS

2012 GENERAL		
David Valadao (R)	67,164	57.8%
John Hernandez (D)	49,119	42.2%
2012 PRIMARY (Open)		
David Valadao (R)	27,251	57.0%

Elected 2012; 1st term

Dairy farmers don't get to take vacations, so Valadao should be mentally prepared for a nonstop effort to secure his grip on a competitive district.

Valadao (val-a-DAY-oh) grew up working on the farm his parents established in Hanford after they emigrated from Portugal's Azores islands in 1969. He and his brothers went on to run what has grown into two separate dairies and farmland used to grow feedstock. Valadao served on dairy and agriculture trade groups, and in 2010 he won a seat in the California Assembly.

In the House, Valadao belongs to the moderate Main Street Partnership, and he's one of two Republican freshmen on the Appropriations Committee. He sits on subcommittees overseeing spending for agricultural and environmental programs. Like many Republicans, he says overregulation is hurting farms and other businesses.

He joins GOP calls for tighter budgets — he'd be happy to axe funds for high-speed rail in his state — but in January 2013 he was one of 49 in his party to vote for a $50 billion spending package tied to Superstorm Sandy.

Valadao has endorsed some changes to immigration law, namely an improvement of guest worker programs and "ensuring a realistic and responsible path to earned legal status." His district is overwhelmingly Hispanic.

In 2010 another Hanford farmer, Republican Andy Vidak, finished around 3,000 votes shy of beating Democratic Rep. Jim Costa in the 20th District. When district lines were redrawn for 2012, the new 21st had a lot of the same turf as the old 20th. But Costa ran elsewhere, creating an open seat.

Valadao, whose Assembly district was entirely in the new 21st, ran against two Democrats from Fresno, which is outside the district: City Councilman Blong Xiong and John Hernandez, the CEO of the Central California Hispanic Chamber of Commerce. Valadao and Hernandez made it through the all-party "open" primary, and in November Valadao won by more than 15 points, even as Barack Obama won the district's presidential vote.

California 21

Southern Central Valley

Much of the population of the largely rural and Hispanic majority 21st District is scattered amid the farmland of Kings County in the San Joaquin Valley. The district extends north to the Fresno city limits and snakes around Kern County's Bakersfield in the south to take in that city's southeast side and smaller communities nearby. Interstate 5, a major route for transporting goods and agricultural products between northern and southern California, traverses the western, desert upland tier of the district.

Agriculture fuels the region's economy. Farms produce fruits, vegetables, nuts, cotton and dairy, while food-processing plants and canneries are grouped in the cities and towns. Selma, south of Fresno, claims to be the raisin capital of the world, and Sun-Maid Growers has its headquarters in nearby Kingsburg. Mexican and Asian immigrants shore up the blue-collar labor force, but farm-based employment is particularly vulnerable to economic uncertainty caused by drought or other weather conditions.

The valley region was already struggling with among the highest poverty rates and lowest education levels in the state before the financial and housing crises hit. Hanford has rebounded faster than some other San Joaquin Valley towns. Surrounded by mountains, the region also tends to collect air pollution from as far away as San Francisco, leading to unusually smoggy conditions for a rural area. A state prison in Coalinga, along Interstate 5, provides more jobs.

The 21st has the second-highest percentage of Hispanics (72 percent) statewide, and other ethnic groups include a significant population of Hmong. Registered Democrats outnumber Republicans in the district by about a 15-point margin, but Kings County trends reliably Republican and the loss of urban parts of Fresno during decennial redistricting has made the new 21st District more competitive.

Major Industry
Agriculture, dairy, food processing, prisons

Military Bases
Naval Air Station Lemoore, 6,123 military, 1,077 civilian

Cities
Bakersfield (pt.), Hanford, Delano, Wasco

Notable
Naval Air Station Lemoore is home to the Pacific Strike Fighter Wing, the Navy's West Coast air-attack force.

Rep. Devin Nunes (R)

Capitol Office
225-2523
nunes.house.gov
1013 Longworth Bldg. 20515-0521; fax 225-3404

Committees
Ways & Means
(Trade - Chairman)
Select Intelligence

Residence
Tulare

Born
Oct. 1, 1973; Tulare, Calif.

Religion
Roman Catholic

Family
Wife, Elizabeth Nunes; three children

Education
College of the Sequoias, A.A. 1993 (agriculture); California Polytechnic State U., B.S. 1995 (agricultural business), M.S. 1996 (agriculture)

Career
Farmer; U.S. Agriculture Department program administrator

Political Highlights
College of the Sequoias Board of Trustees, 1996-2002; sought Republican nomination for U.S. House, 1998

ELECTION RESULTS

2012 GENERAL		
Devin Nunes (R)	132,386	61.9%
Otto Lee (D)	81,555	38.1%
2012 PRIMARY (Open)		
Devin Nunes (R)	67,386	70.6%
2010 GENERAL		
Devin Nunes (R)		unopposed

Previous Winning Percentages
2008 (68%); 2006 (67%); 2004 (73%); 2002 (70%)

Elected 2002; 6th term

Nunes is in the core group of younger, fiscally conservative Republicans with broad plans to reshape the relationship between citizens and government. He says his motivation is his Democrat-dominated and fiscally unstable home state: "Every day I wake up and try to put forth ideas that can be implemented that will fix the problems at hand, so that the United States doesn't end up like the state of California."

He grew up in a farming family in one of the most productive agricultural regions in the country and moved into politics in his early 20s. Nunes (NEW-ness) was not yet 40 at the start of the 113th Congress (2013-14), but he's already fifth in GOP seniority on the Ways and Means Committee, which has jurisdiction over taxes, entitlement programs and trade.

Nunes lacks the name recognition of Paul D. Ryan of Wisconsin, the Budget Committee chairman, Ways and Means member and former vice presidential nominee whose ideas have been adopted as the GOP standard in fiscal debates. But he's a close ally of Ryan, and since Republicans regained the House majority in the 2010 elections, Nunes has been promoting bold legislation within the Ryan framework. "It's taking some of these ideas that we've been working on for many years and adding meat to the bones," he said.

In 2012 Nunes put forth an alternative to the Democrats' 2010 health care law. His bill would create a voluntary 10-year pilot program where Medicare and Medicaid recipients are provided the equivalent of their benefits in debit card form to purchase health insurance and pay out-of-pocket expenses. "It will encourage widespread entrepreneurship, innovation and competition as providers seek to meet the needs of empowered consumers," Nunes wrote in The Wall Street Journal. "It will harness the free market to drive reforms that will benefit all Americans, particularly the poorest."

A few months later, Nunes promoted plans to restructure business taxes to what he described as a pro-growth system. He would allow one deduction — for 100 percent of business expenses (including payroll) paid in the United States in a year — and tax any eligible income at a 25 percent rate. The same rules would apply to businesses of all sizes.

In 2013, Nunes became the chairman of the Ways and Means Subcommittee on Trade. He has been so bold as to suggest a realignment of U.S. foreign policy so that free trade, rather than military intervention or multilateral diplomacy, becomes the operative principle for international relations. Nunes said he will be encouraging expansion of the Trans-Pacific Partnership and a pact with the European Union. He has an able partner in Texas Republican Kevin Brady, the former Trade chairman who still sits on the panel.

Nunes' family hails from the Azores, the island chain off the coast of Portugal, and Nunes speaks "just enough Portuguese to be dangerous." (His district has a large concentration of Portuguese-Americans.) He is co-chairman of the Congressional Brazil Caucus and has long urged stronger relationships with both Brazil and Mexico. In 2003, Nunes married Elizabeth Tamariz, a Portuguese-American who teaches elementary school. He has known her since they were children.

Since the 112th Congress (2011-12) Nunes has served on the Intelligence Committee. He criticized the Obama administration for leaks of sensitive national security materials and its response to a 2012 attack on a U.S. consulate in Libya. Still, he called his work on the panel "the most rewarding experience I've had since I've been in public office. ... Republicans or Democrats, doesn't matter — we're working together to try and make the country safe."

Nunes' immigrant grandfather established a 640-acre family farm in the

San Joaquin Valley. His grandmother later ran a dairy operation with the help of two of Nunes' uncles. He and his brother, Anthony, once ran an alfalfa hay harvesting business. His current involvement in agriculture is an ownership stake in the Alpha Omega winery in Rutherford and some attempts at wine-making for personal use. "It's more like vinegar, but I'm still trying," he said.

Nunes says the woes of the agriculture-heavy region were a major motivator for his entry into politics. He blames persistently high unemployment in the agricultural sector on a regulatory and tax regime imposed by an overwhelmingly Democratic state government in the thrall of environmentalists and congressional Democrats. "California is run by extremists, from the senators to Nancy Pelosi to [George] Miller," Nunes said. "These are people who are dangerous individuals."

He is engaged in a running battle over water allocations from the San Joaquin River. The issue stems from a court settlement reached by environmentalists and some local officials to restore water to a 60-mile dry stretch of the river in the hope of returning Chinook salmon to the area. Initially a supporter, Nunes has since opposed the 2006 agreement, arguing that a disproportionate amount of his district's water would be allocated for the plan.

In February 2012, Nunes won House passage of a bill to transfer water resources allocated to fish and wildlife conservation in the region to the Central Valley Project, a federal bureau designed to irrigate farmland in the San Joaquin Valley. Democrats were not pleased with the measure, which went nowhere in the Senate.

After graduating from California Polytechnic State University with a master's degree in agriculture in 1996, Nunes volunteered to help a candidate for the board of the two-year College of the Sequoias, which he had attended. The candidate unexpectedly quit, and Nunes, then 22, decided to run. He ousted a seasoned incumbent.

While on the school board, he met Bill Thomas, the local congressman. In 1998, he agreed to an all-but-hopeless challenge to Democratic incumbent Cal Dooley in the 20th District and lost in the primary. In 2000, Nunes campaigned for GOP presidential candidate George W. Bush. He was rewarded when Thomas helped him get appointed as state director for the Agriculture Department's rural development program when Bush became president.

Reapportionment gave California an additional House seat for the 2002 elections. Nunes beat two better-known Republicans, Fresno Mayor Jim Patterson and state Rep. Mike Briggs, in the primary for the 21st District. He cruised to victory in the general election and has easily won re-election since.

Nunes is serving as one of five regional chairmen of the National Republican Congressional Committee for the 2014 cycle.

Key Votes

2012	
Extend a Social Security payroll tax cut and unemployment benefits	YES
Ease securities rules to expand small-business access to capital	YES
Extend for one year subsidized student loan interest rates financed by a cut in health care spending	?
Cite Attorney General Eric H. Holder Jr. for contempt of Congress	YES
Create a visa program for foreign graduates in high-tech fields	YES
Extend most Bush-era income tax rates while allowing rates for top-bracket earners to rise (Jan. 1, 2013)	NO
2011	
Strike funding for F-35 alternative engine	NO
Prevent EPA from regulating greenhouse gas emissions to address climate change	YES
Extend certain provisions of Patriot Act for four years	YES
Declare opposition to use of ground troops in Libya	YES
Overhaul patent law	YES
Pass compromise debt limit increase plan and establish future spending limits	NO
Allow consideration of measures to implement three trade agreements	YES

CQ Vote Studies

	PARTY UNITY		PRESIDENTIAL SUPPORT	
	SUPPORT	OPPOSE	SUPPORT	OPPOSE
2012	94%	6%	15%	85%
2011	97%	3%	26%	74%
2010	99%	1%	27%	73%
2009	97%	3%	18%	82%
2008	97%	3%	83%	17%

Interest Groups

	AFL-CIO	ADA	CCUS	ACU
2012	15%	0%	100%	88%
2011	0%	5%	94%	84%
2010	0%	0%	100%	100%
2009	0%	0%	73%	96%
2008	7%	0%	94%	100%

California 22

Central Valley — part of Fresno, Visalia

In the heart of the Central Valley, the 22nd District includes wealthier neighborhoods of northern Fresno and all of the nearby city of Clovis, as well as the farmland of northwest Tulare County.

Following decennial remapping, the newly drawn 22nd contains most of the same population centers as the former 21st District while being confined to a much smaller geographic footprint. The majestic national parks of the Sierra Nevada mountain range and the Sequoia National Forest were shifted into the vast, rural 8th District to the east.

While 46 percent of the new district's residents say they have Hispanic roots, the 22nd has a large white population as well as the most registered Republicans among the Fresno-area districts — they outnumber Democrats by more than 10 percentage points in this socially conservative district.

One of the nation's top-producing regions for fruit, vegetables, nuts and dairy, Fresno and Tulare counties rely heavily on agriculture and food packaging and processing plants, vying each year for the title of top farm-goods-producing county in the nation. Export and trade issues are important for the valley's wholesalers, while competition for scarce resources — especially water — can cause tension in a state with a strong environmentalist streak and dense population centers.

In the more affluent neighborhoods of northern Fresno, median home values are well above state averages. Clovis has several higher education institutions; the 22nd includes a California State University's campus in Fresno. To the south, the district includes Visalia, one of the state's fastest-growing cities. Fourteen percent of the city's population is foreign born and there is a significant Lao influence there. Overall, some areas in the 22nd struggle with high poverty and unemployment rates and declining home values.

Major Industry
Agriculture, dairy, food processing

Cities
Fresno (pt.), Visalia, Clovis, Tulare

Notable
The city of Tulare hosts the annual World Ag Expo, the world's largest agricultural exposition, which draws an attendance of more than 100,000 people from more than 70 countries.

Rep. Kevin McCarthy (R)

Capitol Office
225-2915
kevinmccarthy.house.gov
2421 Rayburn Bldg. 20515-0522; fax 225-2908

Committees
Financial Services

Residence
Bakersfield

Born
Jan. 26, 1965; Bakersfield, Calif.

Religion
Baptist

Family
Wife, Judy McCarthy; two children

Education
Bakersfield College, attended 1984-85; California State U., Bakersfield, B.S. 1989 (business administration), M.B.A. 1994

Career
Congressional district director; sandwich store owner

Political Highlights
Kern County Republican Central Committee, 1992-2002; Kern County Community College District Board of Trustees, 2000-02; Calif. Assembly, 2002-06 (minority leader, 2004-06)

ELECTION RESULTS

2012 GENERAL		
Kevin McCarthy (R)	158,161	73.2%
Terry Phillips (NPA)	57,842	26.8%
2012 PRIMARY (Open)		
Kevin McCarthy (R)	71,109	72.2%
Eric Parker (R)	10,414	10.6%
2010 GENERAL		
Kevin McCarthy (R)	173,490	98.8%
John Uebersax (WRI)	2,173	1.2%

Previous Winning Percentages
2008 (100%); 2006 (71%)

Elected 2006; 4th term

McCarthy helped Republicans take control of the House with his consummate skill as a political strategist, and his reward for doing so was the post of majority whip. Keeping the caucus united has proved challenging. McCarthy's laid-back style sometimes appears ill-suited to managing headstrong and anti-establishment GOP factions.

He ascended to the No. 3 post in the House GOP leadership at the start of the 112th Congress (2011-12), which was just his third term. From the start, he had few carrots or sticks to encourage votes favored by leaders. Speaker John A. Boehner has tried to keep the legislative process fairly open, and the GOP banned earmarks — appropriations for specific projects that affect members' districts, which have often been attached to bills to entice reluctant supporters.

"There's no earmarks; the speaker doesn't punish people. It's a different philosophy," he said in March 2012. "So it's harder where you have to grab something ahead of time and work it through the process."

Rhetorical persuasion and a winning personality have been his best tools. He cultivated relationships with the large Class of 2010, opening his Capitol office as a hangout between votes. Instead of being an enforcer, McCarthy sometimes acted as the rank and file's voice in leadership meetings, telling Boehner when his goals weren't feasible.

His charm and camaraderie have kept the party together on many votes, but the nice-guy approach has its limits. In the 112th, there were several episodes in which the leadership team lost on the House floor or retreated: Hard-line conservative lawmakers who were particularly worried about federal spending levels blocked the progress of long-term reauthorizations of farm and surface transportation programs. Senior Republicans groused about the difficulty of operating without earmarks, but McCarthy was an enthusiastic supporter of the ban.

The leadership team had made a small show of its authority after the 2012 elections, removing four prominent dissidents from their preferred committee assignments. It didn't help. Conservatives openly revolted against Boehner during deficit reduction negotiations in December 2012, which led to his embarrassing withdrawal from the talks.

McCarthy is still popular, however. He returned as whip, and early in the 113th Congress (2013-14) he got a standing ovation at a GOP Conference meeting as he rallied the party for the next confrontation over federal spending.

His rapid rise is a testament to McCarthy's political savvy and his devotion to behind-the-scenes work. It's also a byproduct of his ability to raise money — and his willingness to share it.

As Republicans worked to regain their footing after the 2008 elections, McCarthy emerged as a secret weapon of sorts. Young, telegenic and devoted to the cause, he impressed the right people. After only one term in the House, McCarthy was appointed chief deputy whip for the 111th Congress (2009-10), charged with helping Minority Whip Eric Cantor of Virginia count votes. He also served on the executive committee of the National Republican Congressional Committee, where he had spectacular success recruiting House candidates for 2010.

His efforts to get Republicans elected are not restricted to his own recruits. He contributed millions of dollars to GOP campaigns in the 2012 election cycle.

Known for his detailed political knowledge, McCarthy uses his plane rides from Washington to Bakersfield to study the economic and political characteristics of colleagues' districts, looking for ways to market his policy ideas. "Hopefully, I can get to where I understand their districts better than them,"

McCarthy has said. "They may be able to be part of some legislation and not know it."

McCarthy has spent nearly his entire adult life in politics. He served as an aide to his predecessor, Republican Bill Thomas, and as a state legislator before easily winning the seat after Thomas' retirement in 2006. Like Thomas, McCarthy is a fiscal conservative who tends to be only marginally engaged on the issues that preoccupy social conservatives. His lack of forcefully voiced ideological convictions have led even close friends to wonder aloud about where his views lie within the Republican spectrum.

But McCarthy's personality is the polar opposite of that of the abrasive Thomas, who was often condescending to his colleagues and hostile to the press. McCarthy is congenial and approachable; whether it is a staff member or a stranger, he greets a visitor with a pat on the back, and it is not unusual for him to conduct a meeting with his feet propped on a desk.

McCarthy's mother was a dental assistant who then stayed home to raise her three children. His father was a full-time firefighter who also worked as a furniture mover. After turning 18, the younger McCarthy earned a certification and worked three summers as a firefighter.

In high school, McCarthy was class president. He supported President Ronald Reagan's re-election in 1984, which meant going against the strong pro-union sentiment in his family. His father belonged to the firefighters union, and his grandfather was a railroad worker.

To help pay for college, McCarthy bought cars at auctions in Los Angeles and resold them in Bakersfield. On the second day of the California lottery, McCarthy, then 19, won $5,000 from a scratch-off ticket. He invested part of his winnings in the stock market and part to open Kevin O's Deli. Before finishing college, he sold the deli at a profit, after which he worked as an unpaid intern in Thomas' district office. The internship turned into a full-time position; he eventually filled almost every role in that office, from clipping newspapers to handling casework to serving as district director.

In 2000, McCarthy won election to the Kern County Community College board of trustees. Two years later, voters sent him to the state Assembly, where he was the first freshman to be elected Republican leader. As leader, he was included in California's "Big 5," an informal decision-making group that also counted as members GOP Gov. Arnold Schwarzenegger, the Senate president pro tempore, the GOP Senate leader and the Speaker of the Assembly.

In the race to succeed Thomas, McCarthy defeated two lesser-known candidates in the GOP primary, then breezed past Democrat Sharon M. Beery in the general election with 71 percent of the vote. He hasn't had a Democratic opponent since then.

Key Votes

2012	
Extend a Social Security payroll tax cut and unemployment benefits	YES
Ease securities rules to expand small-business access to capital	YES
Extend for one year subsidized student loan interest rates financed by a cut in health care spending	YES
Cite Attorney General Eric H. Holder Jr. for contempt of Congress	YES
Create a visa program for foreign graduates in high-tech fields	YES
Extend most Bush-era income tax rates while allowing rates for top-bracket earners to rise (Jan. 1, 2013)	NO
2011	
Strike funding for F-35 alternative engine	NO
Prevent EPA from regulating greenhouse gas emissions to address climate change	YES
Extend certain provisions of Patriot Act for four years	YES
Declare opposition to use of ground troops in Libya	YES
Overhaul patent law	YES
Pass compromise debt limit increase plan and establish future spending limits	YES
Allow consideration of measures to implement three trade agreements	YES

CQ Vote Studies

	PARTY UNITY		PRESIDENTIAL SUPPORT	
	SUPPORT	OPPOSE	SUPPORT	OPPOSE
2012	97%	3%	15%	85%
2011	97%	3%	26%	74%
2010	97%	3%	30%	70%
2009	96%	4%	24%	76%
2008	97%	3%	73%	27%

Interest Groups

	AFL-CIO	ADA	CCUS	ACU
2012	16%	0%	100%	86%
2011	0%	5%	100%	80%
2010	0%	0%	100%	95%
2009	5%	0%	80%	100%
2008	13%	10%	94%	100%

California 23

Most of Bakersfield; parts of Tulare and Los Angeles counties

Energy and the military loom large in the 23rd District, which takes in nearly all of Bakersfield, mineral-rich deserts of southeast Kern County, the citrus-farming areas of eastern Tulare County and a slice of Lancaster on the outer edge of Los Angeles County.

The district's largest employers are military bases — Edwards Air Force Base and China Lake Naval Weapons Center — located in the Mojave Desert. The 23rd's southeastern border bisects Lancaster, the Antelope Valley's largest city and an aerospace hub: NASA maintains research centers nearby.

Energy is big in the district's arid areas. Kern County is responsible for about 75 percent of California's oil production and nearly 60 percent of its total natural gas. Tehachapi produces nearly half of the state's wind energy. Alternative-energy projects with biomass and solar power are in development. Energy regulation is a hot-button issue with the locally powerful oil industry, and the extraction technique known as hydraulic fracturing, or fracking, remains contentious. The rich borate mines in Boron supply jobs; gold mines are re-opening in Rosamond's Soledad Mountain.

The district's northern panhandle is a stretch of the Sequoia National Forest. Towns such as Porterville in the Sierra Nevada western foothills rely on the citrus farms of the Orange Belt, where water access and drought are concerns. Kernville, surrounding Lake Isabella and the Kern River, depends on tourism.

The 23rd is one of the state's most conservative districts and remapping carved out heavily Latino cities of Lamont and Alvin near Bakersfield. It includes nearly one-fourth of agrarian Tulare County, which has backed GOP candidates for years; the slice of Los Angeles County is competitive.

Major Industry
Energy, aerospace, military

Military Bases
Edwards Air Force Base (shared with 8th), 2,142 military, 5,637 civilian; Naval Weapons Station China Lake (shared with 8th), 646 military, 4,216 civilian

Cities
Bakersfield (pt.), Lancaster (pt.), Porterville, Ridgecrest

Notable
Pilot Chuck Yeager broke the sound barrier in 1947 at Edwards Air Force Base.

Rep. Lois Capps (D)

Capitol Office
225-3601
capps.house.gov
2231 Rayburn Bldg. 20515-5023; fax 225-5632

Committees
Energy & Commerce

Residence
Santa Barbara

Born
Jan. 10, 1938; Ladysmith, Wis.

Religion
Lutheran

Family
Widowed; three children (one deceased)

Education
Pacific Lutheran U., B.S. 1959 (nursing); Yale U., M.A. 1964 (religion); U. of California, Santa Barbara, M.A. 1990 (education)

Career
Elementary school nurse; college instructor

Political Highlights
No previous office

ELECTION RESULTS

2012 GENERAL		
Lois Capps (D)	156,749	55.1%
Abel Maldonado (R)	127,746	44.9%
2012 PRIMARY (Open)		
Lois Capps (D)	72,356	46.4%
2010 GENERAL		
Lois Capps (D)	111,768	57.8%
Tom Watson (R)	72,744	37.6%
John V. Hager (I)	5,625	2.9%
Darrell M. Stafford (LIBERT)	3,326	1.7%

Previous Winning Percentages
2008 (68%); 2006 (65%); 2004 (63%); 2002 (59%); 2000 (53%); 1998 (55%); 1998 Special Runoff Election (53%)

Elected 1998; 8th full term

Surveys by Washingtonian magazine have several times identified Capps as the nicest person in the House, but she shows steely resolve on issues close to her heart. After decades as a registered nurse, she won't give ground in discussions about health care. And she's a passionate environmentalist, a position inspired in part by the picturesque coastlines of her district.

Her committee assignment clashes with her personality: She sits on Energy and Commerce, a panel that lends itself to cantankerous debates. As a member of the Health Subcommittee, Capps defends the 2010 health care law, while also promoting a number of measures addressing narrower health issues.

Republicans in the 112th Congress (2011-12) intensified their efforts to stop taxpayer funds from being spent on abortion — proposals included blocking health-care-related tax credits for entities that might use them to provide insurance plans that cover abortion. Capps was resolute in her opposition, calling GOP plans "extreme, extreme manipulation of the tax code." She also defended an Obama administration rule requiring most employers to provide health insurance plans that cover contraceptive services.

Capps — who increased her promotion of preventive medicine after the loss of her daughter, Lisa, to lung cancer in 2000 — drew conservative jeers during an April 2012 House floor debate. A Republican bill to extend lower interest rates on student loans was offset by cutting a prevention fund created by the 2010 law. Capps introduced a procedural motion to prohibit cuts in health benefits for women and children. Speaker John A. Boehner of Ohio rebuked her characterization that the cut was part of a "war on women," protesting on the floor, "Give me a break!" A compromise extension with a different offset was enacted the following July.

She founded the Congressional Nursing Caucus and keeps her nurse's license current, studying and taking an exam every two years, even though it's no longer her primary occupation. The House in 2013 quickly passed her bill to allow the National Institutes of Health to facilitate the creation of research consortia focusing on pediatric diseases. It also passed a bill by Capps and Illinois Republican Adam Kinzinger to make it easier for veterans with military medical training to become civilian EMTs.

Capps has become more outspoken on environmental issues over the years. Her district is considered one of the birthplaces of the modern environmental movement. A 1969 oil well rupture that fouled beaches there made her a determined foe of offshore drilling.

She would like states to have the authority to impose air pollution standards for offshore energy exploration that are more stringent than the EPA's. She also wants to maintain state authority over offshore permit issuance. Capps fought efforts to allow the sale of gas and oil leases in the Santa Maria and Santa Barbara/Ventura basins as part of an oil shale development bill that the House considered in February 2012.

"I find it ironic that some of the same people in this body who decry an overarching federal government seem to have no qualms about forcing new drilling upon a local population which is directly against its wishes," she said during floor debate.

In 2009, she was a supporter of the Democrats' cap-and-trade bill to reduce greenhouse gas emissions, which the House passed but the Senate never considered. In February 2013, she vowed that the Democratic Caucus would keep pushing for ways to reduce greenhouse gas emissions: "Climate change is not going away, and neither are we."

In 2005, she nearly outmaneuvered Republicans on the potential liability for costs of cleaning up water contaminated by the fuel additive methyl tertiary butyl ether. As the House considered a GOP energy policy bill, Capps challenged a provision exempting U.S. producers of MTBE from lawsuits over water contamination. Though her challenge failed on a close vote, it brought national attention to new allegations of MTBE contamination. Capps in the 112th Congress offered a number of amendments, typically defeated along party lines, to require policymakers to consider the public health impact of environmental deregulation.

Capps belongs to the business-friendly New Democrat Coalition. She has introduced legislation meant to increase the availability, through local Workforce Investment Boards, of self-employment training programs for local entrepreneurs and small-business startups. She promotes federal support, such as tax credits, for the renewable-energy industry.

But since 2003, Capps has rarely voted against a majority of Democrats when they oppose a majority of Republicans. And she is socially liberal. Capps has drawn attention to the rights of lesbian, gay, bisexual and transgender individuals by introducing anti-bullying legislation and advocating employee non-discrimination policies among federal contractors. In the 112th Congress she opposed a Republican-written reauthorization of federal programs to combat domestic violence — Capps said it lacked protections for abused immigrant women and LGBT individuals.

The daughter and granddaughter of Lutheran ministers, Capps grew up in small towns in Wisconsin and Montana. She earned a master's degree in religion from Yale, worked as a nurse for many years in Santa Barbara schools and ran the county's teen pregnancy counseling project.

When her husband, Walter Capps, ran for the House in 1996, she stood in for him at campaign events while he recovered from injuries suffered in a car accident caused by a drunken driver. When he had a fatal heart attack less than a year into his first term, she ran for his seat in a special election to represent what was then the 22nd District. Staying focused on local issues, Capps bested conservative state Rep. Tom Bordonaro by 9 points in a runoff.

Capps had a fairly easy time holding the seat, but the new congressional map for 2012 significantly changed her district. Previously a narrow strip of land along the coast, it lost the city of Oxnard and was extended inland to take in all of Santa Barbara and San Luis Obispo counties. A huge Democratic voter registration advantage became a small one.

Republican Abel Maldonado, who served eight and a half months as an appointed lieutenant governor, was her biggest competition, but he didn't get enough traction to overcome Capps' solid campaign effort.

She won by 10 points.

Key Votes

2012	
Extend a Social Security payroll tax cut and unemployment benefits	YES
Ease securities rules to expand small-business access to capital	YES
Extend for one year subsidized student loan interest rates financed by a cut in health care spending	NO
Cite Attorney General Eric H. Holder Jr. for contempt of Congress	NO
Create a visa program for foreign graduates in high-tech fields	NO
Extend most Bush-era income tax rates while allowing rates for top-bracket earners to rise (Jan. 1, 2013)	YES
2011	
Strike funding for F-35 alternative engine	YES
Prevent EPA from regulating greenhouse gas emissions to address climate change	NO
Extend certain provisions of Patriot Act for four years	NO
Declare opposition to use of ground troops in Libya	NO
Overhaul patent law	YES
Pass compromise debt limit increase plan and establish future spending limits	YES
Allow consideration of measures to implement three trade agreements	NO

CQ Vote Studies

	Party Unity		Presidential Support	
	Support	Oppose	Support	Oppose
2012	97%	3%	90%	10%
2011	98%	2%	90%	10%
2010	100%	0%	98%	2%
2009	99%	1%	97%	3%
2008	99%	1%	14%	86%

Interest Groups

	AFL-CIO	ADA	CCUS	ACU
2012	95%	95%	25%	0%
2011	100%	85%	25%	0%
2010	100%	95%	25%	0%
2009	100%	100%	29%	0%
2008	100%	100%	61%	0%

California 24

Central Coast — Santa Maria, Santa Barbara, San Luis Obispo

Taking in all of Santa Barbara and San Luis Obispo counties as well as a sliver of Ventura County, the 24th combines areas split between three other districts before decennial redistricting. Sixty percent of the district's population lives in Santa Barbara County, where in the past decade the heavily Hispanic Santa Maria eclipsed Santa Barbara as the most populous city.

Cultural and economic differences divide along geographical lines here. Agricultural and blue-collar interests are represented in the more conservative San Luis Obispo County, Santa Maria and inland areas of Santa Barbara, while research, higher education and tourism drive liberal coastal cities.

San Luis Obispo and northern Santa Barbara counties are agriculturally focused; strawberries, wine grapes, broccoli and other vegetables thrive in the moderate coastal weather. Southern Santa Barbara's beaches and sunshine support a robust tourism and resort industry, supplemented by nearby wineries. Aerospace and defense manufacturing are big employers; computer firms such as Citrix's online division have a presence in Goleta. The southern branch of Los Padres National Forest winds through the center of the 24th, which also includes several of the largely uninhabited Channel Islands off the coast of Santa Barbara.

Overall, the district's population is majority white and 35 percent Hispanic. Democrats hold a slight edge in party registration. San Luis Obispo County tends to be more conservative than Santa Barbara County, but the University of California, Santa Barbara, and California Polytechnic State University in San Luis Obispo add liberal votes. Barack Obama won San Luis Obispo in the 2012 presidential race with a slim 1-point margin and less than 50 percent of the vote; he did better in Santa Barbara County (58 percent).

Major Industry
Agriculture, tourism, aerospace

Military Bases
Vandenberg Air Force Base, 2,924 military, 1,143 civilian

Cities
Santa Maria, Santa Barbara, San Luis Obispo, Lompoc

Notable
Santa Maria's namesake barbecue is sliced sirloin, salsa and pinquito beans.

Rep. Howard 'Buck' McKeon (R)

Capitol Office
225-1956
mckeon.house.gov
2310 Rayburn Bldg. 20515-0525; fax 226-0683

Committees
Armed Services - Chairman
Education & the Workforce

Residence
Santa Clarita

Born
Sept. 9, 1938; Los Angeles, Calif.

Religion
Mormon

Family
Wife, Patricia McKeon; six children

Education
Brigham Young U., B.S. 1985

Career
Clothing store owner

Political Highlights
William S. Hart School Board, 1978-87; Santa Clarita City Council, 1987-92 (mayor, 1987-88)

ELECTION RESULTS

2012 GENERAL		
Howard "Buck" McKeon (R)	129,593	54.8%
Lee C. Rogers (D)	106,982	45.2%
2012 PRIMARY (Open)		
Howard "Buck" McKeon (R)	39,997	50.5%
Dante Acosta (R)	10,387	13.1%
Cathie Wright (R)	5,215	6.6%
2010 GENERAL		
Howard "Buck" McKeon (R)	118,308	61.8%
Jackie Conaway (D)	73,028	38.2%

Previous Winning Percentages
2008 (58%); 2006 (60%); 2004 (64%); 2002 (65%); 2000 (62%); 1998 (75%); 1996 (62%); 1994 (65%); 1992 (52%)

Elected 1992; 11th term

The amiable McKeon has a sharp edge when it comes to defense policy, his overriding legislative concern. "I cannot say it strongly enough," he said in 2011 during his first hearing as chairman of the Armed Services Committee. "I will not support any measures that stress our forces and jeopardize the safety of our men and women in uniform."

His focus shifted markedly in 2009, when he gave up the top Republican seat on the Education and the Workforce Committee to become the ranking member on Armed Services. McKeon became chairman at the start of the 112th Congress (2011-12), and in that role he has been a leading advocate for maintaining a large defense budget.

In the cost-cutting atmosphere that pervaded the 112th, however, he oversaw reductions. McKeon voted for an August 2011 deficit reduction law setting defense spending caps for the next decade that would knock hundreds of billions of dollars out of Pentagon accounts.

But he couldn't stomach the law's "sequestration" cuts of around $500 billion, which were written to take effect in 2013 if Congress didn't find other ways to reduce the deficit. Weeks before those cuts were set to take place, McKeon was forthright: "That was a bad bet," he said. He resolved to let the cuts happen, hoping that the alarms sounded by stakeholders would inspire a political breakthrough.

McKeon hasn't found much to like in the Obama administration's military strategy. He panned the early 2012 announcement of reduced troop levels and a move away from the two-war strategy, whereby readiness is defined by the ability to fight two wars in different theaters simultaneously. In an interview with the American Enterprise Institute, McKeon called it an "unrealistic posture" that would be insufficient to handle threats to the United States.

He also took issue with the plan to "pivot" resources to the Pacific. "It's baffling that, in this fiscal environment, the president would be talking about a pivot to Asia before our work is done in the Middle East," he told AEI.

McKeon blamed the president's foreign policy for the September 2012 embassy attack in Libya that killed four Americans, including the U.S. ambassador to that country. In the 110th Congress (2007-08) he opposed Democratic efforts to set a timeline for the withdrawal of U.S. troops from Iraq, and he similarly opposed President Barack Obama's deadlines for Afghanistan. The House-passed fiscal 2012 defense policy bill contained his provision to authorize the use of force against a broader array of militant groups around the world, but it didn't make it into the final law.

Preparing for possible conflicts with nations such as China will require more spending, particularly in naval and aerospace power, McKeon says. Missile defense has been a major concern, and McKeon has assailed the Pentagon for revising President George W. Bush's plans for an antimissile shield in Europe.

Prior to a GOP ban on earmarked spending, McKeon was known for ensuring that funds were steered to California aerospace manufacturers and military bases in his district. In the fiscal 2012 defense authorization bill, he created a $1 billion fund largely for members' parochial projects, although the awards would have been competitive. The provision, which never became law, was called out by taxpayer groups as an end-run around the earmark ban. He did not repeat it the following year.

He opposed repealing the 1993 "don't ask, don't tell" law, which barred openly gay people from serving in the military. But the repeal became law and was implemented with no apparent adverse result, and McKeon hasn't made any symbolic attempts to undo the new policy.

McKeon has saved his seat on the Education and the Workforce panel. He chaired that committee in 2006, succeeding John A. Boehner of Ohio, who became majority leader. McKeon switched to ranking member in the 110th Congress, and in the minority he complained about "pretty much just playing defense."

With a Democratic White House, his frustrations grew. McKeon raised questions about the inclusion of $100 billion in education spending in the $787 billion economic stimulus law in early 2009. During the 110th, he had to watch as California colleague George Miller guided bills to boost mine safety and raise the minimum wage over his objections. He could do little as Democrats made the government the sole provider of federal student loans in 2010.

The top GOP spot on Armed Services opened up when Obama picked Republican Rep. John M. McHugh of New York to become Army secretary. As a close ally of Boehner and a solid fundraiser for GOP candidates, McKeon had the inside track as Republicans considered McHugh's replacement.

Before he became immersed in politics, McKeon worked in his family business, a chain of Western-style clothing stores based in Santa Clarita that was founded by his parents in 1962. The business closed in 1999, but McKeon still has a soft spot for ostrich-skin cowboy boots.

Fears that his oldest daughter would be bused from their Santa Clarita home into a neighboring school district prompted his first foray into elected office in 1978. He won a 14-person race for the local school board.

Years later, after McKeon had served as a city council member, the first mayor of Santa Clarita and chairman of a start-up bank, naïveté drove his bid for a newly created congressional district in suburban Los Angeles. A mayor of a neighboring town called and asked for his support for the seat. Instead, McKeon decided in 1991 to launch his own campaign. "I thought, 'If he could do it, I could do it,'" McKeon said. "I didn't know what a congressman did. I'd only met two."

After a fierce campaign, McKeon narrowly defeated a 14-year state assembly veteran in the primary. In November, McKeon defeated his Democratic opponent by 19 points.

His district picked up a huge swath of GOP-friendly territory along California's eastern border (and lots of military bases) in redistricting after the 2000 census. But it shrank back to a suburban district on the map drawn for the 2012 election. McKeon was challenged by 34-year-old Democrat Lee C. Rogers, a podiatric surgeon.

Rogers tried to pin several allegations of unethical behavior on McKeon, but superior fundraising and experience won the day. McKeon prevailed by more than 9 points.

Key Votes

2012	
Extend a Social Security payroll tax cut and unemployment benefits	YES
Ease securities rules to expand small-business access to capital	YES
Extend for one year subsidized student loan interest rates financed by a cut in health care spending	YES
Cite Attorney General Eric H. Holder Jr. for contempt of Congress	YES
Create a visa program for foreign graduates in high-tech fields	YES
Extend most Bush-era income tax rates while allowing rates for top-bracket earners to rise (Jan. 1, 2013)	YES
2011	
Strike funding for F-35 alternative engine	NO
Prevent EPA from regulating greenhouse gas emissions to address climate change	YES
Extend certain provisions of Patriot Act for four years	?
Declare opposition to use of ground troops in Libya	YES
Overhaul patent law	YES
Pass compromise debt limit increase plan and establish future spending limits	YES
Allow consideration of measures to implement three trade agreements	YES

CQ Vote Studies

	PARTY UNITY		PRESIDENTIAL SUPPORT	
	SUPPORT	OPPOSE	SUPPORT	OPPOSE
2012	92%	8%	15%	85%
2011	94%	6%	26%	74%
2010	96%	4%	26%	74%
2009	88%	12%	28%	72%
2008	97%	3%	78%	22%

Interest Groups

	AFL-CIO	ADA	CCUS	ACU
2012	15%	0%	100%	83%
2011	0%	5%	100%	80%
2010	7%	0%	86%	96%
2009	14%	15%	87%	96%
2008	7%	5%	100%	88%

California 25

Northern Los Angeles County — Santa Clarita, Palmdale, most of Simi Valley

North of Los Angeles, the 25th District is a conservative-leaning collection of upper-middle class cities and bedroom communities among the foothills of the San Gabriel Mountains. It includes most of Simi Valley and the Angeles National Forest to its west, stretching east across northern Los Angeles County to grab part of Antelope Valley and edges of the Mojave Desert.

Decades of population growth in the Antelope Valley, particularly in Hispanic-majority Palmdale and neighboring Lancaster (shared with the 23rd), resulted in the loss of much of the former district's footprint during decennial redistricting. The sparsely populated stretch of rural mountains and deserts to the east and north was redrawn into the new 8th District, and the 25th now is contained in the Los Angeles suburbs. The San Andreas Fault runs through Palmdale; the entire region is surrounded by faults and prone to earthquakes. The hot and dry climate makes wildfires a constant threat to hillside homes.

Specialized manufacturing is a major economic driver, including tools, machine parts and aerospace technology. Lockheed Martin, Northrop Grumman and Boeing all have operations here, supporting Edwards Air Force Base in the 8th and 23rd districts just northeast of the district's border.

Santa Clarita's economy is boosted by entertainment and tourism venues, including the Six Flags Magic Mountain amusement park and filming locations. Valencia is home to the California Institute of the Arts, established in 1961 by Walt and Roy Disney and now one of the nation's top arts schools.

Unlike the liberal Los Angeles districts to the south, the 25th leans conservative. Republicans hold the advantage in voter registration and GOP candidates Mitt Romney and Elizabeth Emken each won the district by roughly 2 percentage points in the 2012 presidential and U.S. Senate races. While the district's overall population is more than one-third Hispanic, white residents maintain a plurality.

Major Industry

Manufacturing, aerospace, entertainment, tourism

Cities

Santa Clarita, Palmdale, Simi Valley (pt.), Lancaster (pt.), Los Angeles (pt.)

Notable

The Ronald Reagan Presidential Library is located in Simi Valley and regularly hosts debates for Republican presidential candidates.

Rep. Julia Brownley (D)

Capitol Office
225-5811
juliabrownley.house.gov
1019 Longworth Bldg. 20515-6601; fax 225-1100

Committees
Science, Space & Technology
Veterans' Affairs

Residence
Oak Park

Born
Aug. 28, 1952; Aiken, S.C.

Religion
Episcopalian

Family
Divorced; two children

Education
Mount Vernon College, B.A. 1975 (political science); American U., M.B.A. 1979

Career
Homemaker; office furniture company product manager; shipping equipment company sales manager

Political Highlights
Candidate for Santa Monica-Malibu Unified School District Board of Education, 1992; Santa Monica-Malibu Unified School District Board of Education, 1994-2006 (president, 1997, 2002, 2006); Calif. Assembly, 2006-12

ELECTION RESULTS

2012 GENERAL		
Julia Brownley (D)	139,072	52.7%
Tony Strickland (R)	124,863	47.3%
2012 PRIMARY (Open)		
Julia Brownley (D)	29,892	26.9%
Jess Herrera (D)	7,244	6.5%
David Cruz Thayne (D)	2,809	2.5%
Albert Goldberg (D)	1,880	1.7%

Elected 2012; 1st term

Brownley quit a business career to be with her children. Being with her children led to involvement on school boards. Her education work led to three terms in the California Assembly. And that, in turn, propelled her to the House.

She isn't a stranger to Washington; Brownley grew up in Virginia and went to college in the District. She moved to California at the start of the 1980s and worked in sales and marketing before stepping away from the business world.

First elected to the Assembly in 2006, she chaired the Education Committee and worked on setting curriculum standards; Brownley wants new federal involvement to enhance after-school education programs. She has some input on education as a member of the Science, Space and Technology Committee, which addresses science, technology, engineering and math programs.

She can also continue her environmental work from the Environment Subcommittee. Among other California efforts, Brownley led a public campaign to do away with plastic bags at supermarkets, enlisting Hollywood stars such as Rosario Dawson for the cause.

Brownley has a parochial interest in promoting research programs: Biotech giant Amgen Inc. is based in her district.

Her other committee is Veterans' Affairs, where she is the ranking member on the Health panel. Brownley has said she favors expanding benefits for veterans, especially women who served in Iraq and Afghanistan.

Republican Rep. Elton Gallegly decided to retire rather than run in the newly drawn 26th District, where Democrats have a slight registration edge.

Brownley was the leading Democratic vote-getter in the all-party "open" primary, finishing second overall to Republican state Sen. Tony Strickland. The general-election campaign was expensive and closely watched. Brownley played up her support for Democratic policies and got an endorsement from President Bill Clinton, while Strickland tried to appeal to independents. Her 5-point win was close enough that Republicans are targeting the seat in 2014.

California 26

Most of Ventura County — Oxnard, Thousand Oaks

The newly redrawn 26th District takes in most of Ventura County on California's central coast, including the major cities of Oxnard and the more affluent Thousand Oaks, as well as a sliver of conservative Simi Valley in Los Angeles County to the south. A section of Los Padres National Forest makes up the district's northern border, and the district also includes San Nicolas Island, the Anacapa Islands and part of the Santa Monica National Recreation Area in Ventura County.

Ventura County's traditional strength is in agriculture, especially strawberries, celery, lemons, raspberries and avocados, although the county's farm industry has been shrinking. Technology and aerospace are major pillars of the economy, and biotechnology giant Amgen has its headquarters in Thousand Oaks.

International trade issues affect Oxnard's Port Hueneme, the only deep-water port in central California and a major thoroughfare for farm produce and auto exports. The district's largest single employer is Naval Base Ventura County near the port.

The city of San Buenaventura (Ventura) hosts the headquarters of outdoors outfitter Patagonia. While municipal budgets here are strained, home prices are improving and the median household income remains above the state average.

An ethnically split district — the 26th is nearly equally white and Hispanic — many Latino residents in the district live in Oxnard and the farmland to the east. Overall, Democrats hold a slight voter registration edge but conservative-leaning independents can swing races. Overall, Barack Obama took 54 percent of the district's vote in the 2012 presidential election.

Major Industry
Agriculture, military, manufacturing, biotechnology

Military bases
Naval Base Ventura County, 5,200 military, 5,300 civilian

Cities
Oxnard, Thousand Oaks, Ventura

Notable
Established in 1932, the Anacapa Island Light Station off the coast of the Port of Hueneme in the Channel Islands was the last lighthouse constructed by the federal Bureau of Lighthouses in the continental United States.

Rep. Judy Chu (D)

Capitol Office
225-5464
chu.house.gov
1520 Longworth Bldg. 20515-0532; fax 225-5467

Committees
Judiciary
Small Business

Residence
Monterey Park

Born
July 7, 1953; Los Angeles, Calif

Religion
Unspecified

Family
Husband, Mike Eng

Education
U. of California, Santa Barbara, attended 1970-73; U. of California, Los Angeles, B.A. 1974 (mathematics); California School of Professional Psychology, Los Angeles, Ph.D. 1979 (clinical psychology)

Career
Professor

Political Highlights
Garvey School District Board of Education, 1985-88; Monterey Park City Council, 1988-2001 (mayor, 1994-95, 1999); sought Democratic nomination for Calif. Assembly, 1994, 1998; Calif. Assembly, 2001-06; Calif. Board of Equalization, 2007-09 (chairwoman, 2008-09)

ELECTION RESULTS

2012 GENERAL		
Judy Chu (D)	154,191	64.0%
Jack Orswell (R)	86,817	36.0%
2012 PRIMARY (Open)		
Judy Chu (D)	50,203	57.8%
2010 GENERAL		
Judy Chu (D)	77,759	71.0%
Edward "Ed" Schmerling (R)	31,697	29.0%

Previous Winning Percentages
2009 Special Election (62%)

Elected 2009; 2nd full term

Chu is friendly, direct and almost completely in step with her fellow liberals. She's the first Chinese-American woman to serve in Congress and has taken a leadership role among Asian-American lawmakers.

She has held a number of government jobs in a political career stretching back to the mid-1980s. Chu started out on local school boards and eventually became a city council member and mayor of Monterey Park. After a few attempts she secured a seat in the California Assembly, where she was an appropriations chairwoman. Her last political gig before coming to the House was on the state tax commission.

Before completing a second full year of service in Washington, Chu was chosen by colleagues as the chairwoman of the Congressional Asian Pacific American Caucus. She continues that role in the 113th Congress (2013-14), and thanks to a redrawn congressional map she now represents the district with the second-highest population of Asian-Americans in California. (Democrat Michael M. Honda's 17th District is first.)

When her Hispanic constituents are also factored in, a significant number of people from her district are foreign-born. That makes immigration an important issue in the region, and Chu is one of the non-lawyers with a seat on the Judiciary Committee. She quips that the panel "benefits from a consumer's perspective."

Chu has long urged a comprehensive overhaul of the federal immigration system. She supports legal protections for guest workers, to keep them in the country during investigations of misconduct by their employers. In the 112th Congress (2011-12) Chu applauded the Obama administration's directives to stop or limit deportation actions against some illegal immigrants who were brought into the country as children.

She also backed a Democratic proposal to increase by 50,000 the visas available to foreign students who come to America and obtain degrees in science, technology, engineering and math (STEM) fields. Republicans had a similar bill, but Chu didn't like how their plan offset the increase by shrinking other visa programs.

Chu represents employers that might benefit from more STEM workers. The California Institute of Technology and NASA's Jet Propulsion Laboratory, which employ more than 5,000 scientists and engineers, are in her district. In 2012 she said the White House's proposed budget cuts for NASA "would devastate this industry and force many to seek employment elsewhere."

She also represents a lot of people tied to the motion picture industry. As a member of the Judiciary panel overseeing intellectual property law and the Internet, she calls for maintaining strong IP protections both domestically and internationally.

Chu seldom goes against a majority of her party when it opposes a majority of Republicans, and she belongs to the liberal Congressional Progressive Caucus. But some of her more bipartisan work has happened on the Small Business Committee, where for the 113th Congress she is the top Democrat on the Subcommittee on Economic Growth, Tax and Capital Access.

In the 112th she worked on bills to increase access to Small Business Administration startup and mentoring programs. One measure by Chu and Illinois Republican Bobby Schilling would have expanded the SBA's mentor-protégé program, which pairs current or recent recipients of SBA assistance with other small businesses to help them obtain federal contracts through joint ventures.

Chu has a natural interest in education policy, thanks to her professional background: She taught psychology at community colleges for 20 years. Chu was a member of the American Federation of Teachers and has been strongly supported by unions in her political career.

She emphasizes the importance of flexibility and collaboration between teachers, principals, parents, administrators, community leaders and local businesses. Chu has introduced a number of bills designed to better link the curriculums of high schools and colleges, an approach that "connects strong academics with real-world experience in a wide range of fields, like engineering, arts and media and biomedical science," she said.

In 2011, she also adopted the personal cause of fighting military hazing. Her 21-year-old nephew, a Marine, committed suicide after a hazing incident. Chu called for an Armed Services Committee hearing on the subject. After sitting in on the 2012 testimony of military leaders, she said that better records of hazing incidents should be kept and that stricter penalties should be imposed. The fiscal 2013 defense policy law includes a provision requiring reports from each military service on its evaluation of and response to hazing incidents.

Chu grew up in south Los Angeles as a third-generation Chinese-American. Her grandfather ran a Chinese restaurant in the Watts neighborhood of Los Angeles. Her father was an electrician for the Pacific Telephone Company, while her mother shifted between being a stay-at-home parent and a cannery worker with a Teamsters card.

She entered college during the Vietnam War and initially planned to be a computer scientist. While walking on campus, she was handed a flier for an Asian-American studies course. "I went to college going to be this quiet little math major, and I took ethnic and women's studies classes and was appalled at the disparities I discovered," she once recalled. "I was soon involved in the anti-war movement." Chu received her undergraduate degree in mathematics and later obtained a doctorate in clinical psychology.

She won an Assembly seat in 2000 on her third try. Rep. Hilda L. Solis, another California Democrat, endorsed Chu's successful Assembly campaign in a legislative district that was heavily Hispanic.

In 2009, Solis was named secretary of Labor. She endorsed Chu as her successor. Other Hispanic leaders, including California Democratic Rep. Loretta Sanchez, also backed her. That insulated Chu from obstacles she otherwise might have faced in the May 2009 special election, which included several Hispanic contenders. Chu comfortably defeated her closest Democratic rival, state Sen. Gil Cedillo, in the primary. She then crushed Republican Betty Chu in the general election by almost 30 points. She was re-elected easily in 2010.

Redistricting cut her old 32nd District in half, so Chu opted to run in the new 27th District in 2012—it contained her Monterey Park home and had a definite Democratic lean. She cruised to a second full term.

Key Votes

2012	
Extend a Social Security payroll tax cut and unemployment benefits	YES
Ease securities rules to expand small-business access to capital	YES
Extend for one year subsidized student loan interest rates financed by a cut in health care spending	NO
Cite Attorney General Eric H. Holder Jr. for contempt of Congress	?
Create a visa program for foreign graduates in high-tech fields	YES
Extend most Bush-era income tax rates while allowing rates for top-bracket earners to rise (Jan. 1, 2013)	YES
2011	
Strike funding for F-35 alternative engine	NO
Prevent EPA from regulating greenhouse gas emissions to address climate change	NO
Extend certain provisions of Patriot Act for four years	NO
Declare opposition to use of ground troops in Libya	NO
Overhaul patent law	YES
Pass compromise debt limit increase plan and establish future spending limits	NO
Allow consideration of measures to implement three trade agreements	NO

CQ Vote Studies

	PARTY UNITY		PRESIDENTIAL SUPPORT	
	SUPPORT	OPPOSE	SUPPORT	OPPOSE
2012	98%	2%	86%	14%
2011	98%	2%	84%	16%
2010	99%	1%	88%	12%
2009	100%	0%	100%	0%

Interest Groups

	AFL-CIO	ADA	CCUS	ACU
2012	95%	95%	25%	0%
2011	100%	95%	19%	4%
2010	100%	100%	0%	0%
2009	100%		40%	0%

California 27

Part of the San Gabriel Valley — most of Pasadena, Alhambra

Covering the western edge of the San Gabriel Valley, on the eastern edge of the city of Los Angeles, and most of the Angeles National Forest, the 27th is a liberal stronghold and one of only two districts in the state where Asian residents (36 percent) comprise the largest segment of the population.

Pasadena, a small part of which is in the 28th District, is the district's largest city. The local economy is firmly wrapped up in higher education and research institutions, primarily Pasadena's California Institute of Technology, which also sustains the city's engineering and biotechnology businesses. Cal Tech is also a large driver behind NASA's Jet Propulsion Laboratory on the district's western border, shared with the 28th. In Claremont, on the eastern edge of the district, the Claremont Colleges are the largest employer. The 27th is home to Los Angeles County Public Works as well as Southern California Edison utilities, both of which provide jobs.

With a large number of suburban commuters who work in Los Angeles, traffic and transit remain constant issues for the 27th. Congestion has long dogged Pasadena and Alhambra, in particular, and a proposed freeway extension that would bisect South Pasadena has sparked local opposition and ongoing legal battles. Similarly, California's on-again, off-again high-speed rail project has mapped a route straight through the San Gabriel Valley.

The 27th's second- through seventh-largest cities — Alhambra, Monterey Park, Arcadia, Rosemead, San Gabriel, Temple City — all have majority or plurality Asian populations, but incomes vary widely across these communities. Registered Democrats outnumber Republicans in the new district, and tend to win elections, but there are areas where conservatives can compete. The district's portion of Los Angeles County trends Democratic, whereas its section of San Bernardino County is more GOP-friendly.

Major Industry
Research, higher education

Cities
Pasadena (pt.), Alhambra, Monterey Park, Arcadia, Rosemead

Notable
California State Assembly District 49, centered on Alhambra, was California's first Asian-majority state or federal legislative district.

Rep. Adam B. Schiff (D)

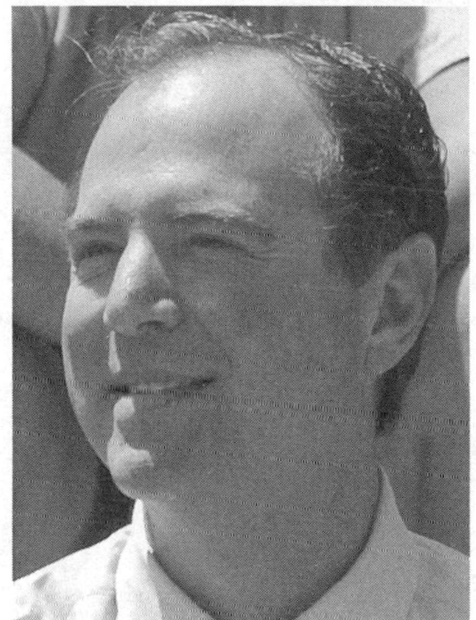

Capitol Office
225-4176
schiff.house.gov
2411 Rayburn Bldg. 20515-0529; fax 225-5828

Committees
Appropriations
Select Intelligence

Residence
Burbank

Born
June 22, 1960; Framingham, Mass.

Religion
Jewish

Family
Wife, Eve Schiff; two children

Education
Stanford U., A.B. 1982 (political science & pre-med); Harvard U., J.D. 1985

Career
Federal prosecutor; lawyer

Political Highlights
Assistant U.S. attorney, 1987-93; Democratic nominee for Calif. Assembly (special election), 1994; Democratic nominee for Calif. Assembly, 1994; Calif. Senate, 1996-2000

ELECTION RESULTS

2012 GENERAL		
Adam B. Schiff (D)	188,703	76.5%
Phil Jennerjahn (R)	58,008	23.5%
2012 PRIMARY (Open)		
Adam B. Schiff (D)	42,797	59.0%
Sal Genovese (D)	2,829	3.9%
Massie Munroe (D)	2,437	3.4%
Jonathan Ryan Kalbfeld (D)	2,119	2.9%
2010 GENERAL		
Adam B. Schiff (D)	104,374	64.8%
John P. Colbert (R)	51,534	32.0%
William P. Cushing (LIBERT)	5,218	3.2%

Previous Winning Percentages
2008 (69%); 2006 (63%); 2004 (65%); 2002 (63%); 2000 (53%)

Elected 2000; 7th term

Schiff has interests tailored to the post-Sept. 11 world. He promotes soft power as a means to stabilize hotbeds of anti-Americanism, keeps close tabs on the spy community and brings experience as a lawyer to discussions of the war on terrorism. He wants his Democratic Party "to speak more knowledgeably, more forcefully" on those issues.

Los Angeles' iconic entertainment studios are in and around Schiff's district, and he professes to be a movie buff. Put in cinematic terms, his preferred policies come from character-driven independent films and Tom Clancy-inspired thrillers. He sits on the Appropriations panel handling foreign aid and the State Department, and he serves on the Intelligence Committee.

Schiff has some fiscally conservative tendencies, and he describes foreign aid as "important, cost-effective investments in our own security." He says that it's a "much better and cheaper investment to spend proactively than wait till you are attacked from another country."

Schiff wants the United States to enable economic growth, freedom of the press and minority and women's rights in developing or unstable countries. In 2012, he called himself an "optimist about the Arab Spring," the revolutionary wave that swept aside several regimes starting in 2011. It is the "greatest threat to the al-Qaida narrative since the beginning of al-Qaida," he said, noting that the terrorist network uses disaffection with governments in its recruiting.

He has proposed the use of public-private partnerships to spur investments in Egypt and Tunisia, and he applauded the State Department's 2011 decision to shift some funds toward similar goals. "To the degree that we can help countries avoid falling into chaos and division, we can potentially avoid another Afghanistan in the making," he said.

Schiff serves as co-chairman of the Congressional Caucus for the Freedom of the Press; he wrote legislation, enacted in 2010, that requires the State Department to identify countries where press freedoms are violated and report whether the governments are taking action.

The spying issues before the Intelligence Committee find Schiff with a foot in both Republican and Democratic camps.

Schiff backed a broad use of the state secrets privilege to keep intelligence information out of open court; he favored a lower standard of cause for certain types of electronic surveillance of terrorist suspects; and in 2011 he was one of 54 House Democrats to vote for a four-year extension of expiring surveillance provisions in the anti-terrorism law known as the Patriot Act.

But he also has civil-liberties concerns. Schiff and Arizona Republican Jeff Flake fought for a provision, included in a 2008 update of the Foreign Intelligence Surveillance Act, to require a special court to sign off on spying on anyone in the United States when they are communicating with terrorism suspects who are overseas.

Schiff, a former federal prosecutor, has said the president needs the option to try military detainees in either civilian or military courts. In the 113th Congress (2013-14), he's looking at possible legal reviews of targeted killings via unmanned aerial vehicles when the target is a U.S. citizen.

Whether the threat comes from rogue states or terrorists, Schiff is acutely concerned about the possibility of a nuclear strike. Schiff and Nebraska Republican Jeff Fortenberry founded the Congressional Caucus on Nuclear Security, and he was the sponsor of legislation enacted in 2010 to make the Domestic Nuclear Detection Office responsible for developing a method for "fingerprinting" nuclear materials in order to trace them to their points of origin.

The Commerce-Justice-Science Appropriations Subcommittee is a useful platform from which Schiff can address several other concerns. Many of Schiff's constituents work at the famed Jet Propulsion Laboratory, and he is critical of efforts to cut spending on planetary sciences; he says money spent on the Mars program will be easily recouped through the technological advances achieved. With the tech and entertainment industries in mind, he has been open to giving law enforcement new tools to fight online piracy.

Schiff also supports any means possible to promote the use of DNA testing in criminal cases, saying that "we've only sort of seen the tip of the iceberg in terms of its power" to convict or exonerate people. He wrote the 2012 law allowing Justice Department grants to states trying to establish DNA collection programs for those arrested for various felonies.

His district is home to one of the largest Armenian communities in the world, and winning U.S. recognition of the Armenian genocide has been central to Schiff's political life. He has sponsored related legislation, such as a resolution to require the president to characterize as genocide the deaths of 1.5 million Armenians between 1915 and 1923 at the hands of the Ottoman Empire, now modern-day Turkey.

Schiff was born in Massachusetts. When he was 11, his family moved to northern California, where his father bought a lumber yard. He and his brother helped out in the business.

Schiff majored in both pre-med and political science at Stanford University and was accepted to medical school and law school. Although his parents urged him to become a doctor, Schiff chose law. "All my doctor friends say I made the right decision, and all my lawyer friends say I messed up," Schiff said. "Now that I'm in politics, everyone says I messed up."

After getting his law degree from Harvard, he returned to California and clerked for a federal judge, then worked in the U.S. attorney's office.

He was unsuccessful in his first attempt at electoral politics, losing to Republican James E. Rogan in a 1994 contest for an Assembly seat. He rebounded in 1996, winning a state Senate seat. In 2000, he again faced Rogan, by then a U.S. House member who had played a high-profile role in the GOP attempt to impeach President Bill Clinton. The race was viewed nationally as a referendum on the impeachment proceedings, though Schiff said it turned on local concerns.

He defeated Rogan by 9 points and has been re-elected easily since. Significant alterations to his district before the 2012 election — the redrawn version had parts of six districts from 2010 — didn't slow him down.

Schiff stays physically active, and in recent years he has started competing in triathlons. "It clears my head," he says, since it requires focusing on "things like not drowning."

Key Votes

2012	
Extend a Social Security payroll tax cut and unemployment benefits	YES
Ease securities rules to expand small-business access to capital	YES
Extend for one year subsidized student loan interest rates financed by a cut in health care spending	NO
Cite Attorney General Eric H. Holder Jr. for contempt of Congress	?
Create a visa program for foreign graduates in high-tech fields	NO
Extend most Bush-era income tax rates while allowing rates for top-bracket earners to rise (Jan. 1, 2013)	YES
2011	
Strike funding for F-35 alternative engine	YES
Prevent EPA from regulating greenhouse gas emissions to address climate change	NO
Extend certain provisions of Patriot Act for four years	YES
Declare opposition to use of ground troops in Libya	NO
Overhaul patent law	NO
Pass compromise debt limit increase plan and establish future spending limits	YES
Allow consideration of measures to implement three trade agreements	YES

CQ Vote Studies

	PARTY UNITY		PRESIDENTIAL SUPPORT	
	SUPPORT	OPPOSE	SUPPORT	OPPOSE
2012	95%	5%	90%	10%
2011	95%	5%	93%	7%
2010	99%	1%	98%	2%
2009	99%	1%	97%	3%
2008	98%	2%	14%	86%

Interest Groups

	AFL-CIO	ADA	CCUS	ACU
2012	90%	85%	25%	4%
2011	93%	80%	31%	0%
2010	100%	90%	25%	0%
2009	100%	100%	33%	0%
2008	100%	90%	61%	4%

California 28

Northern Los Angeles suburbs — Glendale, part of Burbank; West Hollywood

Taking in the historic home of the film industry, the 28th is a destination for studio bigwigs, aspiring actors and tourists. Hollywood and West Hollywood are along the district's southern border, while the production studios and residential areas of Burbank and Glendale make up the center. To the north are upscale mansions of La Cañada Flintridge and La Crescenta-Montrose, and a portion of Angeles National Forest.

Iconic landmarks such as the world-famous Hollywood sign, the Hollywood Walk of Fame and Sunset Boulevard can all be found in the district's southern tier. More than 40 percent of the businesses in West Hollywood specialize in the creative fields that feed the performing arts industry. Across the district, well-developed service and hospitality sectors cater to upscale clientele and international tourism.

Much of the actual film and television production, however, takes place in Burbank, which is split with the 30th. The 28th's share of major production headquarters includes Walt Disney Studios, Cartoon Network and Nickelodeon. Copyright and digital distribution are big issues here.

Entertainment has a smaller presence in neighboring Glendale, which has higher unemployment and lower incomes than other communities in the district. The city's modest manufacturing and financial sectors have declined, but like the rest of the region, Glendale is increasingly hitching itself to the Hollywood film industry. With a Disney creative campus and DreamWorks studios, the city touts itself as a destination for animation.

While the wealthier enclaves in the district's north are more conservative, the 28th as a whole is a liberal bastion. Registered Democrats far outnumber Republicans. The district, which is majority white, has an active gay community in West Hollywood.

Major Industry
Film and entertainment, hospitality, tourism

Cities
Los Angeles (pt.), Glendale, Burbank (pt.), West Hollywood, La Cañada Flintridge, Pasadena (pt.)

Notable
During World War II, the military camouflaged Lockheed's Burbank aircraft plant, now Bob Hope Airport, to look like a residential subdivision from the air.

Rep. Tony Cárdenas (D)

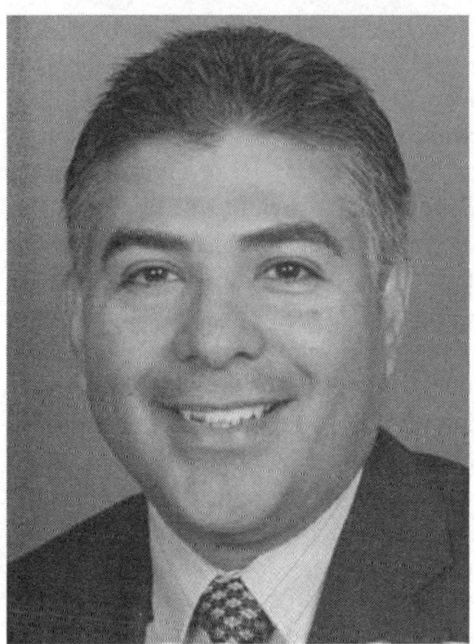

Capitol Office
225-6131
cardenas.house.gov
1508 Longworth Bldg. 20515-6601; fax 225-0819

Committees
Budget
Natural Resources
Oversight & Government Reform

Residence
Los Angeles

Born
March 31, 1963; San Fernando, Calif.

Religion
Christian

Family
Wife, Norma Cárdenas; four children

Education
U. of California, Santa Barbara, B.S. 1986 (electrical engineering)

Career
Real estate company owner; Realtor; insurance agent; computer support technician

Political Highlights
Calif. Assembly, 1996-2002; candidate for Los Angeles City Council (special election), 2002; Los Angeles City Council, 2003-13

ELECTION RESULTS

2012 GENERAL		
Tony Cárdenas (D)	111,287	74.0%
David R. Hernandez Jr. (NPA)	38,994	25.9%
2012 PRIMARY (Open)		
Tony Cárdenas (D)	24,882	64.4%
Richard A. Valdez (D)	5,379	13.9%

Elected 2012; 1st term

Cárdenas comes to Congress from the Los Angeles City Council, and before that the state Assembly. He's an assertive, business-friendly Democrat who is positioned to contribute in budget and energy discussions.

His parents emigrated from Mexico so his father could work on California farms. Cárdenas, the youngest of 11 children, grew up helping out at his father's gardening business, then went to college to study electrical engineering. He eventually settled into a career in real estate — Cárdenas is one of the few House Democrats with that kind of business background.

Elected to the Assembly in 1996, he fell short in a bid to become its speaker, but he did chair the Budget Committee. As a councilman, he headed up a panel on business taxes. He now sits on the House Budget Committee and calls himself a fiscal moderate.

Term limits forced him out of the Assembly, but before long he was on the City Council. He chaired its Energy and Natural Resources Committee and backed plans to boost Los Angeles' use of "clean" energy. Cárdenas sits on the Natural Resources Committee and its panels on energy and water.

He's also on the subcommittee for Indian and Alaska Native Affairs. Cárdenas has gotten a lot of campaign donations from Indian tribes over the years and was a defender of Indian gaming in the Assembly. His political opponents have criticized his ties to tribal interests as possibly unethical.

He wants a comprehensive overhaul of immigration policy and would "absolutely" support creating a path to citizenship for the children of illegal immigrants who were brought to the United States as youngsters.

Cárdenas had no problem winning in the 29th, which was drawn by an independent redistricting commission for the 2012 elections as a Hispanic-majority seat. Democrat Adam B. Schiff, who previously represented parts of the district — and who worked with Cárdenas on anti-gang measures in the state legislature — ran elsewhere. Cárdenas faced no significant opposition.

California 29

Eastern San Fernando Valley

The Hispanic-majority 29th District is centered on a portion of the San Fernando Valley communities of northern Los Angeles, including Van Nuys, Panorama City, Sylmar, North Hollywood and the city of San Fernando. Largely made up of areas from the former 27th and 28th districts before decennial remapping following the 2010 census, the new 29th has Van Nuys Airport to the west, abuts Bob Hope Airport in the 28th to the east and heads into the San Gabriel Mountains to the north. Burbank Boulevard forms most of its southern border.

Historically possessing its own water supply, San Fernando is an independent city that has resisted annexation even as Los Angeles expanded to completely encircle it. It is also the oldest settlement in the valley — an 18th century Spanish mission there is still active. It has a long history of Mexican settlements; the city's population is 90 percent Hispanic.

The once-booming community of Van Nuys used to be home to major auto and aerospace plants, but the manufacturing sector has been in decline since General Motors closed its doors there in the 1990s. Still, small manufacturers continue to operate, and Pepsi has a large bottling center in San Fernando.

Like much of California, the region was badly bruised by declining property values and increasing foreclosures after the 2008 financial crisis. North Hollywood, on the district's southeastern corner, has undergone some revitalization, with new housing developments and the trendy NoHo Arts District developing an arts and entertainment hub.

Despite losing the more affluent Sherman Oaks neighborhood and the film-and-TV-driven Studio City in redistricting, entertainment still looms large in the district: North Hollywood is home to the Academy of Television Arts & Sciences. This arts culture, along with large Latino and immigrant populations, helps make the 29th a Democratic stronghold. Registered Democrats have a greater than 3-to-1 voter registration margin in the district, and there are more unaffiliated voters than Republicans.

Major Industry
Service, retail, manufacturing

Cities
Los Angeles (pt.), San Fernando

Notable
The César E. Chávez Memorial in San Fernando is the nation's largest honoring the labor and civil rights leader.

Rep. Brad Sherman (D)

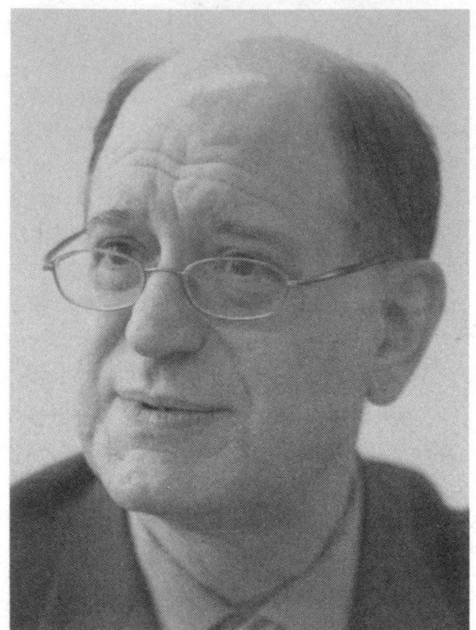

Capitol Office
225-5911
bradsherman.house.gov
2242 Rayburn Bldg. 20515-0527; fax 225-5879

Committees
Financial Services
Foreign Affairs

Residence
Sherman Oaks

Born
Oct. 24, 1954; Los Angeles, Calif.

Religion
Jewish

Family
Wife, Lisa N. K. Sherman; three children

Education
U. of California, Los Angeles, B.A. 1974 (political communication); Harvard U., J.D. 1979

Career
Accountant; lawyer

Political Highlights
Calif. State Board of Equalization, 1991-97 (chairman, 1991-95)

ELECTION RESULTS

2012 GENERAL		
Brad Sherman (D)	149,456	60.3%
Howard L. Berman (D)	98,395	39.7%
2012 PRIMARY (Open)		
Brad Sherman (D)	40,589	42.4%
Howard L. Berman (D)	31,086	32.4%
2010 GENERAL		
Brad Sherman (D)	102,927	65.2%
Mark Reed (R)	55,056	34.8%

Previous Winning Percentages
2008 (69%); 2006 (69%); 2004 (62%); 2002 (62%); 2000 (66%); 1998 (57%); 1996 (50%)

Elected 1996; 9th term

Sherman is both a fiscal populist and a foreign policy hawk — he's a critic of free trade, which he says hurts workers, and an advocate for international institutions such as the nuclear nonproliferation treaty. He sometimes defies party labels, and he likes it that way. "The more I sound like the talking points of the Republican Party, the Democratic Party, the New Democrats, the Purple Democrats, the Green Democrats, the more useless I am," he says.

Sherman therefore reserves many of his comments for dissent, and his one-liners are just as likely to sting the Obama administration as they are GOP lawmakers. His gadfly persona is a selling point for his San Fernando Valley constituents, but it hasn't always endeared him to Capitol Hill colleagues.

That fact played out vividly in his 2012 re-election campaign, a testy contest against Rep. Howard L. Berman in the new 30th District. Berman, the 15-term Democrat who was the ranking member on the Foreign Affairs Committee, won the endorsement of 24 Democrats and 10 Republicans in California's House delegation. Only two House Democrats endorsed Sherman.

But the redrawn district included more than half of Sherman's old constituents and just a quarter of Berman's. Sherman beat Berman handily in both California's "jungle" primary — which candidates of all parties enter — and the general election, in which the top two primary finishers compete. The campaign's drawn-out nature and the huge sums of money spent by both sides increased the bitterness. At one debate in October, the candidates almost came to blows, an episode caught on video and circulated in the media. Sherman criticized Berman for spending too much time traveling abroad — a move that rankled other members of Foreign Affairs, where Sherman also has a seat.

After the election, Sherman made a bid to succeed Berman as the top Democrat on Foreign Affairs. Eliot L. Engel of New York had more years of service on the committee, but Sherman had a higher rank because Engel had left the panel for a brief period. Democrats weren't persuaded by Sherman's pitch, and he withdrew after it became clear he didn't have enough support to win the ranking-member position.

Hard feelings from the 2012 election might have been lingering a few weeks later, when Sherman did not get the top Democratic spot on the subcommittee on the Middle East, as he was anticipating. Instead, in the 113th Congress (2013-14) he again is the ranking member of the Subcommittee on Terrorism, Nonproliferation and Trade.

Two of Sherman's biggest concerns throughout his House career have been Israel's security and Iran's nuclear program. Sherman is one of the lawmakers calling loudest for sanctions to crush Iran's economy. A number of provisions included in stand-alone bills he introduced in the 111th and 112th Congresses (2009-12) were incorporated into laws that were enacted in 2010 and 2012; they have effectively cut Iran's energy and financial sectors out of the global economy. However, the current sanctions program is more than a decade late, according to Sherman.

"I feel like I've been in a car for 15 years, 14 years screaming, 'Go faster!' as the car went about 5 miles an hour," he said. "Now we're up to 30 miles an hour, but having given up 14 years, we'd have to floor it."

Sherman challenged the White House over its decision to get involved, along with NATO, in Libya's 2011 civil war. Convinced that President Barack Obama had violated a law requiring congressional consent for prolonged military involvement, he introduced several successful amendments to House-passed spending bills that would block funding for Libya operations.

As chairman of the non-proliferation panel in 2009, he called the spread of nuclear weapons "perhaps the only thing that poses a national security threat to ordinary Americans and a threat to their safety and to our way of life."

Sherman has similarly stark thoughts about international commerce. "Our trade policies are terrible," he said in 2012. "We have a huge trade deficit and a huge dearth of jobs. If we had balanced trade right now, we'd be talking about a labor shortage." Sherman maintains that current policies have been good only for "the elites."

A former certified public accountant and lawyer, Sherman is a co-founder and co-chairman of the Congressional CPA caucus. He brings his experience to bear on the Financial Services Committee. He says his preoccupation there is preventing a "second precipitous decline in home values" and making sure "that middle-class families can get mortgages to buy what in Los Angeles is a middle-class house, but has a price tag of the biggest mansion of Omaha." To that end, he has proposed to set permanently high thresholds for the limits on loans offered by government-backed mortgage providers Fannie Mae and Freddie Mac in high-cost areas.

His populist instincts manifest as a general aversion to government bailouts. Sherman opposed the $700 billion rescue package for the financial-services sector in 2008, and he says his most important work in Congress was successfully removing the executive branch's permanent unlimited bailout authority included in early drafts of a 2010 financial regulatory overhaul. He said it would have allowed Wall Street to take more risks while shifting the entire downside to taxpayers. "If the devil made a pact with me — you will never have a name on a bill, but you will often be able to stop bad bills, or take bad provisions out of bills — I'm ready to sign up," he says.

Sherman was one of the authors of a 2009 bill to create an agency to supervise banks and punish abusive financial practices; the idea was baked into the 2010 overhaul as the Consumer Financial Protection Bureau. He was also involved in drafting a 2009 law providing a "bill of rights" for credit card users.

Sherman got his start in politics as a child, stuffing envelopes for Democratic Rep. George E. Brown Jr., a family friend. Sherman was elected to the California State Board of Equalization, which administers the state's tax regime, in 1990 and 1994.

In 1996, he ran for the seat of retiring 10-term Democratic Rep. Anthony C. Beilenson. Prior to the primary Sherman sewed up the backing of most area Democrats, including Beilenson.

His willingness to finance his own campaign (he eventually spent nearly $400,000) helped him easily outpace six foes in the primary. He then won the general election by 8 points. After that, he was in no truly competitive races until his 2012 contest with Berman.

Key Votes

2012	
Extend a Social Security payroll tax cut and unemployment benefits	YES
Ease securities rules to expand small-business access to capital	YES
Extend for one year subsidized student loan interest rates financed by a cut in health care spending	NO
Cite Attorney General Eric H. Holder Jr. for contempt of Congress	NO
Create a visa program for foreign graduates in high-tech fields	NO
Extend most Bush-era income tax rates while allowing rates for top-bracket earners to rise (Jan. 1, 2013)	YES
2011	
Strike funding for F-35 alternative engine	YES
Prevent EPA from regulating greenhouse gas emissions to address climate change	NO
Extend certain provisions of Patriot Act for four years	NO
Declare opposition to use of ground troops in Libya	NO
Overhaul patent law	NO
Pass compromise debt limit increase plan and establish future spending limits	YES
Allow consideration of measures to implement three trade agreements	NO

CQ Vote Studies

	Party Unity		Presidential Support	
	Support	Oppose	Support	Oppose
2012	95%	5%	93%	7%
2011	95%	5%	83%	17%
2010	97%	3%	98%	2%
2009	99%	1%	96%	4%
2008	98%	2%	14%	86%

Interest Groups

	AFL-CIO	ADA	CCUS	ACU
2012	95%	80%	25%	4%
2011	100%	85%	19%	0%
2010	100%	90%	25%	0%
2009	100%	100%	33%	0%
2008	100%	85%	61%	9%

California 30

Part of the San Fernando Valley; part of Burbank

While most of the 30th District is within Los Angeles, people who live here do not generally think of themselves as residents of the city, instead identifying as part of communities in the San Fernando Valley. Bounded by mountains and hills on three sides, the 30th takes in the western half of the valley. The southern border follows in part the iconic routes of Ventura Boulevard and Mulholland Drive, taking in Encino, Sherman Oaks and Studio City. The film and entertainment industry dominates the region's economy, supported by hospitality and health care industries.

Ventura Boulevard runs into the southern tier of the district east to Burbank. Several of the world's largest film and television production studios are clustered there, including Warner Bros., NBC and Universal Studios. The valley is also home to much of the nation's adult entertainment industry. The 30th has a stable hospitality industry, particularly hotels and small conference sites, because of the proximity to Hollywood and airports.

Northrop Grumman and Pratt & Whitney both operate plants in the 30th. Biomedical firms provide jobs and health company Quest Diagnostics has a clinical trials site in Northridge. The area is served by California State University, Northridge, as well as the University of West Los Angeles law school.

At the district's western edge are the wealthy gated communities of Bell Canyon and the aptly named Hidden Hills, where the median household income is more than $200,000 — home to music and movie stars and media moguls, and the only sliver of the district that reliably leans Republican. The 30th is overwhelmingly Democratic, with Republicans facing a more than 20-point disadvantage in party registration. Hispanics are the largest minority here at 29 percent of the population; the valley also has large populations of Asian, Iranian and Russian immigrants.

Major Industry

Entertainment, service, tourism, retail

Cities

Los Angeles (pt.), Burbank (pt.), Hidden Hills

Notable

The Universal Studios Hollywood theme park and surrounding hotels are located on an unincorporated plot of land known as Universal City.

Rep. Gary G. Miller (R)

Capitol Office
225-3201
garymiller.house.gov
2467 Rayburn Bldg. 20515-0542; fax 226-6962

Committees
Financial Services
Transportation & Infrastructure

Residence
Rancho Cucamonga

Born
Oct. 16, 1948; Huntsville, Ark.

Religion
Protestant

Family
Wife, Cathy Miller; four children

Education
Mt. San Antonio Community College, attended 1968-70

Military
Army, 1967

Career
Real estate developer

Political Highlights
Diamond Bar Municipal Advisory Council, 1988-89; Diamond Bar City Council, 1989-90; sought Republican nomination for Calif. Senate, 1990; Diamond Bar City Council, 1991-95 (mayor, 1993-94); sought Republican nomination for Calif. Senate (special election), 1994; Calif. Assembly, 1995-98

ELECTION RESULTS

2012 GENERAL		
Gary G. Miller (R)	88,964	55.2%
Robert Dutton (R)	72,255	44.8%
2012 PRIMARY (Open)		
Gary G. Miller (R)	16,708	26.7%
Robert Dutton (R)	15,557	24.8%
2010 GENERAL		
Gary G. Miller (R)	127,161	62.2%
Michael Williamson (D)	65,122	31.9%
Mark Lambert (LIBERT)	12,115	5.9%

Previous Winning Percentages
2008 (60%); 2006 (100%); 2004 (68%); 2002 (68%); 2000 (59%); 1998 (53%)

Elected 1998; 8th term

Miller is a business-minded conservative and a team player in the Republican Party. On one subject where the GOP is still working out its game plan — housing — he cites his professional expertise and the realities of Southern California as he presses for continued federal involvement.

He made a fortune in real estate. After attending community college but leaving without a degree, Miller formed a partnership with a building contractor. They bid on Department of Housing and Urban Development home improvement contracts. He says he learned construction skills on the job and moved on to build single-family homes and, eventually, planned communities. His prowess as a developer has made him one of the wealthiest members of Congress, and in the 113th Congress (2013-14) he is the vice chairman of the Financial Services Committee.

Miller frequently states that some government backing of the mortgage market is necessary to keep homeownership affordable — even for his well-off constituents. That backing has come from Fannie Mae and Freddie Mac, government-sponsored enterprises that buy up mortgages and sell securities based on their value. By taking mortgages (and their inherent risks) off the balance sheets of lenders, the GSEs allow lenders to make more loans. The GSEs were placed under federal conservatorship in 2008, when they could not absorb losses from a cascade of defaults on high-risk mortgages.

Several Republicans on Financial Services, led by New Jersey's Scott Garrett and Chairman Jeb Hensarling of Texas, call for dissolution of the GSEs and a switch to a totally privatized mortgage market. Miller argues that private companies can't match the performance of the GSEs. "Have they made mistakes?" he asked at a 2011 hearing. "Absolutely, without a doubt. But they're still outperforming everybody else, so that's got to be part of the debate. You can't say they're awful, let's get rid of them."

In 2011, Miller and New York Democrat Carolyn McCarthy introduced a bill to replace Fannie and Freddie with a single entity that would issue mortgage-backed securities guaranteed by the federal government; unlike Fannie and Freddie, it wouldn't have shareholders, and profits would go to the Treasury.

A 2008 mortgage rescue law included Miller's provision to increase the size of home loans that Fannie and Freddie could purchase, while increasing the size of loans that the Federal Housing Administration could insure. He pushed to continue the higher loan limits in 2011; Congress ultimately chose to let the higher limits lapse for Fannie and Freddie, but not for the FHA.

Not all federal housing investments have Miller's support. As part of a Republican salvo against President Barack Obama's housing policies, the House passed Miller's 2011 bill to eliminate the Neighborhood Stabilization Program, which helps governments purchase abandoned and foreclosed properties. Miller called the program "ineffective and unaccountable."

In the 112th Congress (2011-12), Miller chaired the Subcommittee on International Monetary Policy and Trade. He sponsored the 2012 reauthorization of the Export-Import Bank, which helps U.S. companies selling products overseas. Some conservatives opposed the bank as a distorter of free markets, but Miller said it was still necessary "to ensure there's a level playing field for American companies when they compete with foreign competitors who are supported by aggressive credit agencies."

Miller's strong opinions on the Financial Services Committee haven't kept him from working with party leaders. He sharply criticizes Obama's plans, and he stood with Speaker John A. Boehner to vote for the January 2013 "fiscal cliff" bill that allowed higher income tax rates on earnings over $400,000 in exchange for permanently lower rates below that threshold. Most rank-and-file Republicans opposed it. He also vows to protect the tax deduction for mortgage interest.

Miller has a seat on the Transportation and Infrastructure Committee. A 2012 reauthorization of surface transportation programs included provisions he helped write to accelerate the regulatory review of infrastructure projects. That committee assignment is also an important one for the water issues of great consequence to Southern California — Miller has blasted restrictions on pumping water in the Sacramento-San Joaquin Delta intended to protect the delta smelt.

A vocal opponent of illegal immigration, Miller supports legislation that would deny "birthright citizenship" to children born in the United States whose parents are illegal immigrants. He has co-sponsored measures requiring that ballots for federal elections be printed only in English.

Miller is a Civil War buff and owns a large collection of history books, which he reads on flights between California and D.C. His study of history has translated into legislative action. In 2002, he won enactment of a law to provide federal grants to states and localities to preserve battle sites. He secured $4 million in 2004 for the Richard Nixon Library (which was in his district at the time) to house Nixon's presidential papers and tapes.

Miller was raised by his mother and grandparents. When he was young, his family moved from Arkansas to Whittier, Calif., where other poor families from Oklahoma and Arkansas had settled. His mother worked as a checker at a grocery store, and his grandfather was a school custodian.

Miller began his political career on the Diamond Bar Municipal Advisory Council. He was a member of Diamond Bar's first council after the city was incorporated in 1989 and became mayor in 1993. Two years later, he won a seat in the California Assembly.

In 1998, three-term Republican Rep. Jay C. Kim was convicted of violating campaign finance laws, and Miller challenged him for the seat. He was the winner of an "open" primary, in which the top two finishers advance to the general election regardless of party. Kim was third, behind the only Democrat on the ballot. Miller easily won the general election.

Redistricting for 2012 left Miller with no great options. He chose to run in the Democratic-leaning 31st District rather than face a fellow GOP incumbent elsewhere. In another open primary, Miller took almost 27 percent of the vote. Four Democrats on the ballot canceled each other out, allowing Republican state Sen. Bob Dutton to finish second. In the general election, Miller bested Dutton by about 10 points, but Obama easily won the district's presidential vote. Democrats quickly named Miller as one of their top targets for 2014.

Key Votes

2012	
Extend a Social Security payroll tax cut and unemployment benefits	YES
Ease securities rules to expand small-business access to capital	YES
Extend for one year subsidized student loan interest rates financed by a cut in health care spending	YES
Cite Attorney General Eric H. Holder Jr. for contempt of Congress	YES
Create a visa program for foreign graduates in high-tech fields	YES
Extend most Bush-era income tax rates while allowing rates for top-bracket earners to rise (Jan. 1, 2013)	YES
2011	
Strike funding for F-35 alternative engine	NO
Prevent EPA from regulating greenhouse gas emissions to address climate change	YES
Extend certain provisions of Patriot Act for four years	YES
Declare opposition to use of ground troops in Libya	YES
Overhaul patent law	YES
Pass compromise debt limit increase plan and establish future spending limits	YES
Allow consideration of measures to implement three trade agreements	YES

CQ Vote Studies

	PARTY UNITY		PRESIDENTIAL SUPPORT	
	SUPPORT	OPPOSE	SUPPORT	OPPOSE
2012	95%	5%	15%	85%
2011	97%	3%	23%	77%
2010	98%	2%	29%	71%
2009	87%	13%	27%	73%
2008	97%	3%	79%	21%

Interest Groups

	AFL-CIO	ADA	CCUS	ACU
2012	16%	0%	100%	95%
2011	0%	5%	100%	96%
2010	0%	0%	100%	96%
2009	13%	5%	77%	90%
2008	27%	5%	100%	81%

California 31

San Bernardino; Rancho Cucamonga

Taking up an arc of the densely populated southwestern corner of San Bernardino County's Inland Empire south of the San Gabriel Mountains, the 31st stretches from Rancho Cucamonga to Redlands. The city of San Bernardino occupies much of the central part of the district. Small, more isolated towns, such as Devore Heights and Small Canyon, edge the mountains to the north. Population growth in the region has made the district's transportation corridors — the Foothills Freeway and parts of three major interstates — prime features of the landscape.

San Bernardino County is the nation's largest by land area, but most of it falls into the sprawling, rural 8th District to the east. The 31st's small slice of the county grabs one-third of its population, including its and the district's largest city. The city of San Bernardino, the county seat, relies on state and county government jobs, a California State University campus and the service industry. The city's budgets are strained, however, and high crime rates worry residents. Rancho Cucamonga, in the district's west, is a major hub for logistics companies and is home to a generic pharmaceutical manufacturing company, Amphastar.

Residents here are low- to middle-income, unlike many wealthy Southern California communities. Inland Empire unemployment and housing market stability remain issues, although the lower home prices in some established suburbs may continue to lure a diverse workforce.

Nearly 50 percent Hispanic overall, the district also has Southern California's largest proportion of black residents outside of Los Angeles (10 percent). Although there are slightly more registered Democrats than Republicans in the district, 20 percent of voters are unaffiliated and Republicans can win federal elections here.

Major industry
Government, higher education, manufacturing

Cities
San Bernardino, Rancho Cucamonga, Redlands

Notable
Minor League baseball's Inland Empire 66er's take their name from the famous Route 66 that ran through San Bernardino, and the city hosts an annual car festival focused on the highway.

Rep. Grace F. Napolitano (D)

Capitol Office
225-5256
napolitano.house.gov
1610 Longworth Bldg. 20515-0538; fax 225-0027

Committees
Natural Resources
Transportation & Infrastructure

Residence
Norwalk

Born
Dec. 4, 1936; Brownsville, Texas

Religion
Roman Catholic

Family
Husband, Frank Napolitano; five children

Education
Brownsville H.S., graduated 1954

Career
Regional transportation claims agent

Political Highlights
Norwalk City Council, 1986-92 (mayor, 1989-90); Calif. Assembly, 1992-98

ELECTION RESULTS

2012 GENERAL		
Grace F. Napolitano (D)	124,903	65.7%
David L. Miller (R)	65,208	34.3%
2012 PRIMARY (Open)		
Grace F. Napolitano (D)	24,094	46.1%
G. Bill Gonzalez (D)	6,322	12.1%
2010 GENERAL		
Grace F. Napolitano (D)	85,459	73.4%
Robert Vaughn (R)	30,883	26.5%

Previous Winning Percentages
2008 (82%); 2006 (75%); 2004 (100%); 2002 (71%); 2000 (71%); 1998 (68%)

Elected 1998; 8th term

Napolitano has a reputation as a caretaker. She prides herself on being highly responsive to the needs of her constituents and fiercely protective of federal resources used by those under her watch. "I'm focused on rendering service to the people who elected me to be here," she said. "I'm their voice."

She is best known for her grandmotherly image. Recognizable by her bright white hair — usually cropped short and teased high — she's quick to talk about her grandchildren and prepares food for her staff. "I treat my friends and my relations the same as I do my family. And what I cook for them, I cook for my family," she said.

Napolitano touts her work with local officials and has fought throughout her career for funding for her district. She believes earmarks are appropriate when the projects are "based on need"; in 2012, California State Polytechnic University named an aerospace lab in her honor after she helped secure more than $5 million in federal funding for wind tunnels and lab equipment.

With earmarks banned in the 112th Congress (2011-12), she explored other avenues of assistance. In 2011, she helped persuade the White House to eliminate duty-free importation of sleeping bags made in Bangladesh. The move brought jobs for Exxel Outdoors, a sleeping bag manufacturer, back to her district. Exxel had lobbied for the change for several years.

Water is always a pressing concern for California, and Napolitano is the top Democrat on the Natural Resources Subcommittee on Water and Power. She chaired the panel during the 111th Congress (2009-10).

"The days of building large regional water projects are behind us," she wrote in a 2010 issue of Irrigation Leader magazine. A more sustainable strategy, she said, would focus on conservation, water recycling, desalination and improved water treatment.

She has had some success moving water legislation through the Republican-controlled House. Her bill to fund water desalination research passed as part of a fiscal 2012 appropriations package, and Napolitano introduced another bill to extend such funding in the 113th Congress (2013-14). She worked with Nevada Republican Joe Heck on a Hoover Dam power allocation bill, which was signed into law in late 2011.

Napolitano enjoys favorable ratings from environmental groups and backs strong state and federal water quality standards. In that vein, she opposes hydraulic fracturing, the injection of high-pressure fluids into rock layers to allow access to new deposits of gas and oil — there hasn't been enough research into its effect on local water supplies, she said. It's a key issue in her region. The city of Whittier, which was in Napolitano's old 38th District, voted in 2011 to re-open local oil wells.

From her seat on the Transportation and Infrastructure Committee, Napolitano pays a lot of attention to railroad safety, spurred by a series of derailments in or near her district. A 2008 railroad safety law included her provision barring safety inspections performed in Mexico from satisfying U.S. standards without certification from the Transportation Department. She has fought to maintain the funding and schedule for the implementation of positive train control systems included in that law.

But she has been less committed to a proposed $68 billion high-speed rail line running from San Diego to San Francisco that received about $1.8 billion from the 2009 economic stimulus legislation. "I don't oppose high-speed rail," she said. "I just don't propose that they take away from current transportation projects that affect my community or my area." Her priority is expanding transit systems in her district. "We need to be able to take people to work and get cars off the streets," she said. "The high-speed rail's not going to do it."

She has a passion for mental-health issues that stems from her work on the Norwalk City Council in the 1980s and '90s, when hospitals in her area began closing and sending mentally ill patients onto the streets. She co-chairs the Congressional Mental Health Caucus and has proposed creating a competitive grant program for schools that partner with community groups to increase student access to mental-health resources.

As Democrats began a push in the 113th Congress for measures to curb gun violence, Napolitano was named a vice chairwoman of a task force on the subject. Her initial policy suggestions were all tied to strengthening federal support for mental health services — including cementing guidelines to ensure that insurance companies treat mental illnesses the same as physical ones, as required by law.

Napolitano, a former chairwoman of the Congressional Hispanic Caucus, is the daughter of a divorced Mexican immigrant who raised her two children on a shoestring budget. In 2007, Napolitano played a key role in writing a Democratic immigration overhaul proposal that would have created a guest-worker program and provided a path for illegal immigrants to gain legal status.

She married at 18 and had five children by 23; she worked for the California government and then spent two decades with Ford Motor Co., starting as a secretary and working her way into the transportation division.

Napolitano caught the political bug as a volunteer in Norwalk's efforts to cultivate a sister-city relationship with Hermosillo, Mexico. Though she "hated politics" and had a fear of public speaking, she says she got involved to show her children and "other youngsters on this side how lucky they were."

She launched her first political campaign, for city council, with $35,000 she borrowed against her home, and won by just 28 votes. She served six years, two as mayor, before moving over to the California Assembly for six years.

In 1998, she ran for the House seat of retiring Democrat Esteban E. Torres and defeated his son-in-law by 618 votes in the primary. Napolitano sailed to victory in the general election and has easily won her re-election bids.

Napolitano drew some scrutiny in 2009 when Bloomberg News revealed that she had earned more than $200,000 in interest over the years on a $150,000 loan she had made to her initial 1998 campaign.

The new congressional map for 2012 dismantled her old district and created a new 38th District where both she and Democratic Rep. Linda T. Sánchez were residents. After some consideration, she opted to run in the 32nd District, most of which was new to her. Napolitano said it was better to have "two strong Latina congresswomen representing the people of this area instead of just one." She easily defeated Republican David L. Miller.

Key Votes

2012	
Extend a Social Security payroll tax cut and unemployment benefits	YES
Ease securities rules to expand small-business access to capital	NO
Extend for one year subsidized student loan interest rates financed by a cut in health care spending	NO
Cite Attorney General Eric H. Holder Jr. for contempt of Congress	?
Create a visa program for foreign graduates in high-tech fields	NO
Extend most Bush-era income tax rates while allowing rates for top bracket earners to rise (Jan. 1, 2013)	YES
2011	
Strike funding for F-35 alternative engine	YES
Prevent EPA from regulating greenhouse gas emissions to address climate change	NO
Extend certain provisions of Patriot Act for four years	NO
Declare opposition to use of ground troops in Libya	NO
Overhaul patent law	+
Pass compromise debt limit increase plan and establish future spending limits	NO
Allow consideration of measures to implement three trade agreements	-

CQ Vote Studies

	PARTY UNITY		PRESIDENTIAL SUPPORT	
	SUPPORT	OPPOSE	SUPPORT	OPPOSE
2012	98%	2%	85%	15%
2011	98%	2%	78%	22%
2010	98%	2%	83%	17%
2009	99%	1%	93%	7%
2008	99%	1%	10%	90%

Interest Groups

	AFL-CIO	ADA	CCUS	ACU
2012	100%	90%	17%	0%
2011	100%	90%	13%	8%
2010	100%	100%	13%	0%
2009	100%	100%	33%	0%
2008	100%	95%	44%	8%

California 32

Central San Gabriel Valley — El Monte, West Covina

California's 32nd District is a collection of primarily residential cities in the San Gabriel Valley, east of the Los Angeles city limits and west of the Inland Empire. The district's population is anchored in the west by working- and middle-class cities like El Monte and West Covina, with Hispanic-majority populations and sizable Asian communities. It centers itself geographically on Covina and West Covina, and is crisscrossed by four major freeways.

Manufacturers and distributors of construction components and consumer goods in the foreign trade-oriented city of Industry are a big source of jobs. Covina hosts small-scale technology manufacturing firms, and nearby Irwindale relies on sand and gravel industries, as well as bottling plants for Miller Brewing and Pepsi. The district is home to distribution warehouses for food companies as well as corporate offices for Wells Fargo Bank and fast-food company Jack in the Box.

Industrial dumping years ago created groundwater contamination issues that the region still battles, now with EPA assistance. West Covina is negotiating ways to repurpose the land from the toxic BKK Landfill site it shut down years ago. The city of Industry is an almost entirely industrial area (its population is just more than 200) along the district's southern edge, but the once-thriving employment hub has diminished.

Ramona is an affluent alcove with a dominant Asian population, while San Dimas is a mostly white, conservative-voting suburb with higher income levels than other communities in Los Angeles County. While such conservative enclaves in the valley had previously been included in safe Republican districts before redistricting following the 2010 census, the newly drawn 32nd is now considered a safe Democratic seat, with registered Democrats outnumbering Republicans by a 20-point margin overall.

Major Industry

Manufacturing, distribution

Cities

El Monte, West Covina, Baldwin Park, Covina, Azusa, La Puente, San Dimas

Notable

San Dimas Canyon Park hosts a nature reserve and animal sanctuary.

Rep. Henry A. Waxman (D)

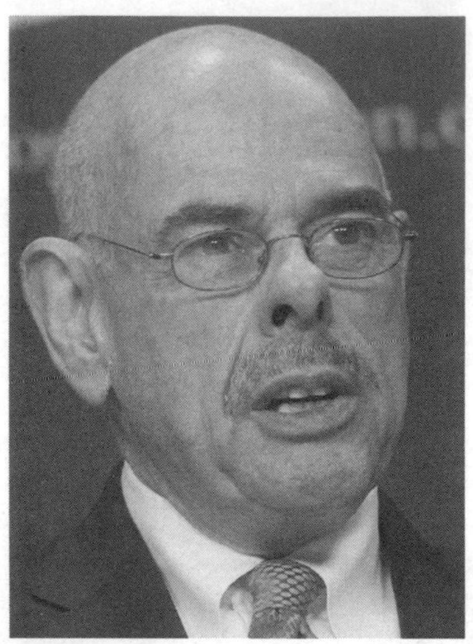

Capitol Office
225-3976
waxman.house.gov
2204 Rayburn Bldg. 20515-0530; fax 225-4099

Committees
Energy & Commerce - Ranking Member

Residence
Beverly Hills

Born
Sept. 12, 1939; Los Angeles, Calif.

Religion
Jewish

Family
Wife, Janet Waxman; two children

Education
U. of California, Los Angeles, B.A. 1961 (political science), J.D. 1964

Career
Lawyer

Political Highlights
Calif. Assembly, 1968-74

ELECTION RESULTS

2012 GENERAL		
Henry A. Waxman (D)	171,860	54.0%
Bill Bloomfield (NPA)	146,660	46.0%
2012 PRIMARY (Open)		
Henry A. Waxman (D)	51,235	45.3%
Bruce Martin Margolin (D)	5,020	4.4%
Zein E. Obagi (D)	1,988	1.8%
2010 GENERAL		
Henry A. Waxman (D)	153,663	64.6%
Charles E. Wilkerson (R)	75,948	31.9%
Erich D. Miller (LIBERT)	5,021	2.1%
Richard R. Castaldo (PFP)	3,115	1.3%

Previous Winning Percentages
2008 (100%); 2006 (71%); 2004 (71%); 2002 (70%); 2000 (76%); 1998 (74%); 1996 (68%); 1994 (68%); 1992 (61%); 1990 (69%); 1988 (72%); 1986 (88%); 1984 (63%); 1982 (65%); 1980 (64%); 1978 (63%); 1976 (68%); 1974 (64%)

Elected 1974; 20th term

Waxman was a relentless leader on health care and energy when Democrats controlled the House. He's often in a defensive posture now that Republicans are in charge, but he's no less vigorous. The Energy and Commerce Committee, where Waxman is the top Democrat, remains a partisan battleground.

In the 112th Congress (2011-12), "most of what Republicans wanted, they have not achieved. ... Democrats have taken them on, and I have been part of that," he said. "We have been very successful in defending current law. ... The public is with us, even though we don't always prevail."

He rejects the suggestion that he's a reflexive critic of GOP alternatives to his policy preferences, but he takes credit for highlighting and stymieing what he views as egregious proposals. Waxman is a close ally of Minority Leader Nancy Pelosi and has a reputation for single-minded focus on his job.

As the chairman of Energy and Commerce in the 111th Congress (2009-10), he was a major player on several of President Barack Obama's chief priorities, most notably a health care overhaul, which became law in 2010, and legislation designed to curb greenhouse gas emissions, which died in the Senate.

House Republicans sought to reverse Democratic gains and pare federal regulations when they took control in the 112th, and Waxman met those efforts with rhetorical bombardments. A repeal of the health care law would "take essential health benefits from millions of struggling Americans and give new powers and profits to insurance companies," he said.

Waxman vigorously attacked Republican oversight of the law, which he called "fishing expeditions ... designed to prevent agencies from carrying out their responsibilities." (He was accused of such tactics when serving as chairman of the Oversight and Government Reform Committee during the last two years of the George W. Bush administration.)

He pounced on Republican budget proposals as eliminating "basic Medicare and Medicaid guarantees." His criticism occasionally extended to the Obama administration, as when the Health and Human Services Department said it would not implement a costly long-term care program that was part of the health care law. The program, he said, had not been canceled but "simply stands in recess."

Waxman also responded to moves to restrict the EPA's regulatory authority and weaken the Clean Air Act. A House-passed bill to halt the EPA's greenhouse gas regulations was a "distraction from the imperative of developing new sources of energy," he said. Waxman began cataloging online votes that he felt demonstrated Republicans' "anti-environment" record. "Their approach is: Deny the science, stop regulating and roll back the law," he said. He started the 113th Congress (2013-14) with a public relations campaign urging government action to mitigate the effects of climate change. "The biggest energy challenge we face as a country is carbon pollution," he said at a February 2013 hearing.

Illinois Republican John Shimkus accused Waxman of sabotaging a 2011 investigation of whether the head of the Nuclear Regulatory Commission had acted illegally in closing Nevada's Yucca Mountain facility for nuclear waste storage. In a hearing, Waxman read aloud accusatory emails gathered as part of the probe; Shimkus said he had requested secrecy from Waxman.

Politics aside, it's hard to deny Waxman's expertise on energy and health issues. For 16 years before the 1995 GOP takeover, he chaired the Energy and Commerce Health and Environment Subcommittee.

In that post, Waxman, a former smoker who had a tough time quitting, became a crusader against tobacco. At a 1994 hearing, he grilled the chief executives of the seven largest tobacco companies, all of whom testified under oath that they did not believe nicotine was addictive. The hearing helped lay the groundwork for multibillion-dollar lawsuits against the industry and for Waxman's successful fight a decade and a half later to expand the Food and Drug Administration's power to regulate tobacco advertising and marketing.

His work foreshadowed his efforts in 2010 to hold oil industry executives' feet to the fire after the oil rig explosion that spurred a massive oil spill in the Gulf of Mexico.

Waxman's political chops were on display in 2008 as he took the Energy and Commerce gavel from Michigan's John D. Dingell, the House's longest-serving member and the panel's top Democrat since 1981. His rivalry with Dingell dates to the 1980s, when the two clashed on environmental issues. An uneasy truce collapsed in 2008 when Dingell, a defender of Michigan's auto industry, revived a proposal to bar Waxman's home state and others from setting tougher vehicle emissions standards than the federal government.

A handful of issues found Waxman working with the opposition in the 112th. He cooperated on a measure, enacted in 2012, to set aside part of the broadcast spectrum for an interoperable public safety network for first-responders. He also worked across the aisle on a 2012 reauthorization of the FDA user fees that fund the agency's approval process for prescription drugs and medical devices. "Patients will have access to new and innovative therapies in a timely way," he said.

Waxman grew up in an apartment above a Los Angeles grocery store run by his father. The elder Waxman, a New Deal Democrat, was the son of Russian Jewish immigrants. Waxman's political career began at UCLA in the 1960s, when he became active in California's Federation of Young Democrats. In 1968, after a term as chairman of the federation, Waxman challenged Democratic state Assemblyman Lester McMillan in a primary and beat him handily.

He entered Congress in the huge Democratic wave of 1974 and is one of three "Watergate babies" in the House. (The others are fellow Californian George Miller and Minnesota's Rick Nolan, who returned in 2013 after a 32-year absence.)

Waxman had never been seriously challenged for re-election, but Bill Bloomfield, a real estate entrepreneur and former Republican running with no party affiliation, stepped up in 2012. Bloomfield spent more than $7 million of his own money on the campaign, and, on top of that, the new congressional map had added several wealthy Republican enclaves to Waxman's district.

Waxman took 54 percent of the vote in the general election — his worst performance in 20 campaigns.

Key Votes

2012	
Extend a Social Security payroll tax cut and unemployment benefits	YES
Ease securities rules to expand small-business access to capital	NO
Extend for one year subsidized student loan interest rates financed by a cut in health care spending	NO
Cite Attorney General Eric H. Holder Jr. for contempt of Congress	NO
Create a visa program for foreign graduates in high-tech fields	NO
Extend most Bush-era income tax rates while allowing rates for top-bracket earners to rise (Jan. 1, 2013)	YES
2011	
Strike funding for F-35 alternative engine	YES
Prevent EPA from regulating greenhouse gas emissions to address climate change	NO
Extend certain provisions of Patriot Act for four years	NO
Declare opposition to use of ground troops in Libya	NO
Overhaul patent law	NO
Pass compromise debt limit increase plan and establish future spending limits	NO
Allow consideration of measures to implement three trade agreements	NO

CQ Vote Studies

	PARTY UNITY		PRESIDENTIAL SUPPORT	
	SUPPORT	OPPOSE	SUPPORT	OPPOSE
2012	98%	2%	87%	13%
2011	97%	3%	84%	16%
2010	99%	1%	95%	5%
2009	99%	1%	99%	1%
2008	99%	1%	16%	84%

Interest Groups

	AFL-CIO	ADA	CCUS	ACU
2012	100%	100%	25%	0%
2011	96%	90%	13%	8%
2010	100%	90%	25%	0%
2009	100%	100%	33%	0%
2008	100%	95%	61%	4%

California 33

Coastal Los Angeles County — Santa Monica, Redondo Beach; Beverly Hills

The 33rd now slides down the Southern California coast from west of Malibu to near Los Angeles Harbor. Tourists and locals flock to the Santa Monica and Venice beaches and Santa Monica Mountain trails. Tony mansions and condos host wealthy residents in such famous locales as Beverly Hills, Bel Air, Brentwood and Pacific Palisades, as well as Agoura Hills in the north. Few places in the district's northern tier have not been immortalized by movies or television. Oil refineries, aerospace jobs and ritzy enclaves from El Segundo to Rancho Palos Verdes define the slice of coast to the south.

A varied economy based on tourism and hospitality, entertainment, and research and higher education supports the glamorous hotels of Beverly Hills, biomedical firms and institutions such as UCLA, Pepperdine University and the Cedars-Sinai Medical Center. Major entertainment firms are strewn throughout the district. New Line Cinema and MGM have headquarters in Beverly Hills, while Santa Monica includes corporate offices of MTV Networks, Activision video game developers and Universal Music Group.

Several of Los Angeles' major museums can be found on "Museum Row" near Beverly Hills, including the Page Museum at La Brea Tar Pits with its 3 million Ice Age fossils, and Los Angeles County Museum of Art, which is the largest art museum in the western U.S. The Getty Museum overlooks Interstate 405 between the San Fernando Valley and downtown Los Angeles.

In contrast with large Hispanic populations in surrounding areas, the 33rd is primarily white. Income and education levels are high overall, but some areas match national and regional averages. Nearly half of the district's voters are registered Democrats, and the 33rd backs Democrats at all levels.

Major Industry
Tourism and hospitality, entertainment, research, higher education

Military Bases
Los Angeles Air Force Base, 1,497 military, 869 civilian (2010)

Cities
Los Angeles (pt.), Santa Monica, Redondo Beach, Torrance

Notable
Santa Monica Airport, formerly Clover Field, was the takeoff and landing point in 1924 for the first circumnavigation of the Earth by air.

Rep. Xavier Becerra (D)

Capitol Office
225-6235
becerra.house.gov
1226 Longworth Bldg. 20515-0531; fax 225-2202

Committees
Ways & Means

Residence
Los Angeles

Born
Jan. 26, 1958; Sacramento, Calif.

Religion
Roman Catholic

Family
Wife, Carolina Reyes; three children

Education
Stanford U., A.B. 1980 (economics), J.D. 1984

Career
State prosecutor; state legislative aide; lawyer

Political Highlights
Calif. Assembly, 1990-92; candidate for mayor of Los Angeles, 2001

ELECTION RESULTS

2012 GENERAL		
Xavier Becerra (D)	120,367	85.6%
Stephen C. Smith (R)	20,223	14.4%
2012 PRIMARY (Open)		
Xavier Becerra (D)	27,939	77.3%
2010 GENERAL		
Xavier Becerra (D)	76,363	83.8%
Stephen C. Smith (R)	14,740	16.2%

Previous Winning Percentages
2008 (100%); 2006 (100%); 2004 (80%); 2002 (81%); 2000 (83%); 1998 (81%); 1996 (72%); 1994 (66%); 1992 (58%)

Elected 1992; 11th term

Becerra runs with some of the most powerful House Democrats, but it remains to be seen if he overcomes his weaknesses to reach the highest rungs on the party's leadership ladder.

He is renowned as a policy expert and has been a close ally of fellow California Democrat Nancy Pelosi, the former speaker and current minority leader. She has trusted Becerra to protect the party's interests in fiscal debates. Becerra was appointed to both President Barack Obama's 2010 special fiscal commission (widely known as Simpson-Bowles) and the Joint Committee on Deficit Reduction, or "supercommittee," created by the August 2011 deal to raise the debt limit.

But Becerra didn't play a particularly visible role on either panel. He voted against the deficit reduction plan drafted by the commission, saying it did not do enough to address the "drivers of our economic crisis" — according to Becerra, the wars in Iraq and Afghanistan, the Medicare prescription drug benefit enacted in 2003 and the George W. Bush-era tax cuts. The supercommittee never even considered a plan before disbanding.

Still, Becerra secured a promotion from vice chairman of the Democratic Caucus to chairman in the 113th Congress (2013-14). (Former Chairman John B. Larson of Connecticut reached a term-limit restriction.) In Democratic leadership meetings he represents the views of the party's liberal Congressional Progressive Caucus and the Hispanic Caucus, which he once led.

Becerra's policy chops, closeness to Pelosi and Hispanic background have helped his rise into leadership. But colleagues have faulted him for arrogance, and he can be somewhat stiff when delivering the party's message in public. "I understand the politics," Becerra once told the Los Angeles Times. "I'm not the best at playing the game."

He keeps trying, however. In opening months of the 113th, Becerra was revealed as a member of a bipartisan working group trying to generate legislation to overhaul immigration law.

Becerra favors plans that emphasize keeping families together and providing a route to permanent U.S. residency for illegal immigrants already in the country. He applauded Obama's policy directive to halt deportations on some immigrants who entered the country illegally as children.

Taxes and entitlement programs will also occupy the 113th Congress, and Becerra has a voice on such matters as a member of the Ways and Means Committee. The first Hispanic to serve on the panel, Becerra sees himself as a guardian of lower-income taxpayers. Several times he has introduced a "taxpayer's bill of rights" measure that would expand filing assistance to lower-income taxpayers and boost oversight of private tax preparation services.

Becerra is the top Democrat on the Social Security Committee. He put distance between himself and Pelosi in early 2013 by telling C-SPAN that he would oppose fiscal measures that include cuts to Social Security benefits — both Pelosi and Obama had indicated that they might be OK with indexing benefits to a "chained consumer price index," which would mean smaller growth in payouts over the long term than under the current system.

Democrats also chatter about whether he harmed his relationship with Pelosi by tacking to her left in the health care battles of 2010. That year, he was an enthusiastic supporter of the Democrats' health care overhaul, saying the measure would "lay the groundwork for a more just and prosperous America." But he supported a government-run "public option" insurance plan, which was not included in the final version of the bill. He subsequently became a co-sponsor of legislation to create one.

Becerra sometimes goes along with Republicans on free trade — one of the nation's largest seaports sits near his downtown Los Angeles district. He opposes trade agreements that Democrats criticize as having inadequate protections for workers, such as the 2005 Central America Free Trade Agreement and a 2011 pact with Colombia.

But Becerra did break with the majority of his party in 2011 to vote for pacts with South Korea and Panama. In December 2008, he turned down an offer to become Obama's U.S. trade representative.

Beyond trade, he's almost always a soundly liberal vote. An opponent of the Iraq War, he voted repeatedly against supplemental funding for the wars in Iraq and Afghanistan; in 2011 he expressed reservations about the cost of U.S. intervention in Libya. In 2008 he joined other liberals in opposing two $700 billion measures — the second of which became law — to assist the ailing financial services sector. He said the legislation didn't do enough for taxpayers or businesses.

Becerra sought the caucus vice chairmanship in 2006 but backed out when Larson, also a Pelosi ally, decided to keep the post. Pelosi responded by creating an "assistant to the speaker" slot that gave Becerra a seat in leadership meetings. When Larson became the caucus chairman in late 2008, Becerra beat the more centrist Marcy Kaptur of Ohio for the vice chairmanship.

Becerra was born in Sacramento. But his mother was born in Mexico, and his American-born father spent much of his early life moving back and forth across the border to earn money by shining shoes, canning tomatoes and working on highway construction crews. Becerra still wears his father's wedding ring as a reminder of his humble origins.

He earned a bachelor's in economics and a law degree from Stanford, paying his way in part by working summers on road construction crews in Sacramento and tutoring students in the community during the school year. A state Senate fellowship cemented his interest in advocacy and policy work. He then worked with a legal services firm in Worcester, Mass., that specialized in helping mentally ill clients. After returning to California, Becerra was an aide for a state senator and worked for the state attorney general.

In 1990, he ran a successful race for a state Assembly seat. Two years later, his interest in the "bigger-picture issues" of national and foreign policy led him to run for Congress.

He easily outdistanced nine other candidates in the 1992 primary, then bested a Republican and three minor-party candidates in November with 58 percent of the vote. He has been re-elected handily since.

In 2001, Becerra ran for mayor of Los Angeles, finishing fifth in a field of 14 candidates.

Key Votes

2012	
Extend a Social Security payroll tax cut and unemployment benefits	YES
Ease securities rules to expand small-business access to capital	NO
Extend for one year subsidized student loan interest rates financed by a cut in health care spending	NO
Cite Attorney General Eric H. Holder Jr. for contempt of Congress	?
Create a visa program for foreign graduates in high-tech fields	NO
Extend most Bush-era income tax rates while allowing rates for top-bracket earners to rise (Jan. 1, 2013)	NO
2011	
Strike funding for F-35 alternative engine	YES
Prevent EPA from regulating greenhouse gas emissions to address climate change	NO
Extend certain provisions of Patriot Act for four years	-
Declare opposition to use of ground troops in Libya	NO
Overhaul patent law	YES
Pass compromise debt limit increase plan and establish future spending limits	NO
Allow consideration of measures to implement three trade agreements	NO

CQ Vote Studies

	PARTY UNITY		PRESIDENTIAL SUPPORT	
	SUPPORT	OPPOSE	SUPPORT	OPPOSE
2012	99%	1%	88%	12%
2011	97%	3%	88%	12%
2010	98%	2%	90%	10%
2009	99%	1%	100%	0%
2008	99%	1%	10%	90%

Interest Groups

	AFL-CIO	ADA	CCUS	ACU
2012	100%	100%	25%	0%
2011	93%	85%	25%	4%
2010	100%	95%	13%	0%
2009	100%	100%	33%	4%
2008	100%	100%	50%	8%

California 34

Downtown Los Angeles

An urban center of thriving business and entertainment as well as some persistent poverty, the Hispanic-majority 34th District takes in the heart of Los Angeles. Centered on a portion of downtown skyscrapers and City Hall, the crescent-shaped district's western wing takes in Koreatown, while its northern edge stretches to residential communities farther from the city center and Occidental College in the Eagle Rock neighborhood.

The district is home to city government and white-collar financial services firms. Farmers Insurance Group, one of Los Angeles' largest employers, has its headquarters just beyond the district's west side. The east-west artery of Wilshire Boulevard, on the southern edge of Koreatown, includes a cluster of professional schools and colleges amid corporate high rises.

Sports and entertainment are also key to the local economy and culture. To the north is baseball's Dodger Stadium, and to the south is the Staples Center, home to basketball's Lakers, Clippers and Sparks and hockey's Kings. Developers hope to build a stadium at the convention center to bring an NFL team back to the city. Other destinations include Walt Disney Concert Hall, home of the Los Angeles Philharmonic; and the Dorothy Chandler Pavilion, home of the Los Angeles Opera.

Transportation hub Union Station and the terminus of the 20-mile Alameda Corridor rail link connecting the city to the ports of Los Angeles and Long Beach are also here. To the southeast are warehouses and wholesalers, as well as poverty- and crime-ravaged areas. Upscale residential communities make up the district's northern half, bordering Glendale and Pasadena.

The relatively compact and downtown-oriented 34th is more than 65 percent Hispanic. Asians — mostly Koreans — account for about 20 percent of the population. The district is one of the most liberal in the state, and less than 13 percent of voters register as Republicans.

Major Industry
Government, entertainment, financial services

Cities
Los Angeles (pt.)

Notable
Dodger Stadium has largest seating capacity of any baseball park in the world, accommodating 56,000 fans.

Rep. Gloria Negrete McLeod (D)

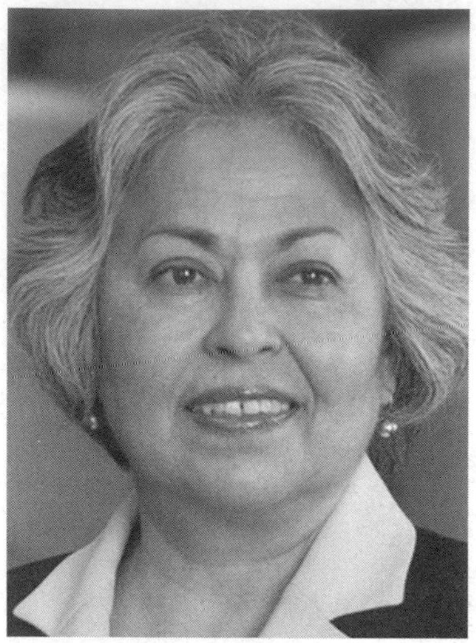

Capitol Office
225-6161
negretemcleod.house.gov
1641 Longworth Bldg. 20515-3005; fax 225-8671

Committees
Agriculture
Veterans' Affairs

Residence
Chino

Born
Sept. 6, 1941; Los Angeles, Calif.

Religion
Roman Catholic

Family
Husband, Gilbert L. McLeod; 10 children

Education
Chaffey Community College, A.A. 1979 (general education)

Career
College instructional aide; homemaker

Political Highlights
Sought Democratic nomination for Calif. Assembly, 1998; Chaffey Community College Board, 1995-2000 (president, 1999-2000); Calif. Assembly, 2000-06; Calif. Senate, 2006-12

ELECTION RESULTS

2012 GENERAL		
Gloria Negrete McLeod (D)	79,698	55.9%
Joe Baca (D)	62,982	44.1%
2012 PRIMARY (Open)		
Joe Baca (D)	15,388	45.0%
Gloria Negrete McLeod (D)	12,425	36.3%

Elected 2012; 1st term

Negrete McLeod focuses on Democratic policies suited to her middle-class constituents, but it's hard to ignore the soap opera that led to her election.

She was a homemaker married to a policeman — Negrete McLeod is a mother of 10, a grandmother of 27 and a great-grandmother many times over. In her 30s she got a community college degree, then worked as an instructional aide. She eventually served on the board of her alma mater. Regarding education, Negrete McLeod pitches spending on early-childhood programs as an investment that results in economic growth and lower crime rates.

In 1999, Negrete McLeod did some field work for state Sen. Joe Baca, who that year won a seat in the U.S. House in a special election. The next year, she won a seat in the state Assembly. In 2006, she was elected to the state Senate — beating Baca's son for the job. As a state legislator, she worked intensively on shoring up California's public employees retirement system.

In 2012, she ran in a new Hispanic-majority 35th District that was similar to her state legislative district. But she was challenged by Baca, who lived outside the district. He raised far more money for the campaign, but a super PAC upset with his ambivalent record on gun control spent more than $3 million in support of Negrete McLeod. Baca planned on a rematch, then changed his mind. He is now targeting the 31st District, a Democratic-leaning area represented by Republican Gary G. Miller.

With that drama behind her, Negrete McLeod is plugging away on behalf of her district. It has a lot of transportation infrastructure that needs tending. Negrete McLeod, who sits on the Agriculture Committee, has also been active in efforts to improve California's water supply.

She also sits on the Veterans' Affairs Committee, having served on its equivalent in the state Senate. Negrete McLeod has a clear agenda on the panel: "I will simply not stand for any attempt to strip military families of their benefits," she wrote on her campaign website.

California 35

Southwestern San Bernardino County — Ontario, most of Fontana; Pomona

Almost all of the 35th District's population lives in the dense cities strung from Pomona in Los Angeles County east into the San Bernardino County suburbs of the Inland Empire, all the way to Fontana. The mainly middle-income cities that make up this district, which is home to the state's fourth-largest Hispanic population, have relatively young populations. The district lost land north of Interstate 210 and west to San Bernardino after decennial redistricting following the 2010 census, but gained tracts to the west and south stretched along the San Bernardino Freeway.

A traditional agricultural heritage has waned over decades as dairy interests have given way to residential development and retail growth. Despite some volatility during recent national economic slowdowns, construction in the region continues. Some residents commute along the Pomona and San Bernardino freeways to jobs outside the district in Los Angeles. Fontana, to the east, is mainly industrially oriented, although a Kaiser Permanente facility provides health care jobs.

Major employers in the 35th include the Pomona campus of the California State Polytechnic University, which falls mainly in the 39th District. The school has a huge impact on the local economy, accounting for more than 3,000 jobs and generating millions of dollars in tax revenue.

The L.A./Ontario International Airport was once considered a top alternative to Los Angeles International, but drops in passenger volume have hurt the city. Freight traffic remains key, however, and residents rely on the airport and affiliated employers, including UPS and FedEx.

The district is 70 percent Hispanic and safely Democratic, with a 20-point voter registration lead for Democrats. All electoral competition here is intraparty.

Major industry
Transportation, health care, higher education

Cities
Fontana (pt.), Ontario, Pomona, Chino (pt.)

Notable
Fontana is birthplace of the Hells Angels motorcycle club.

Rep. Raul Ruiz (D)

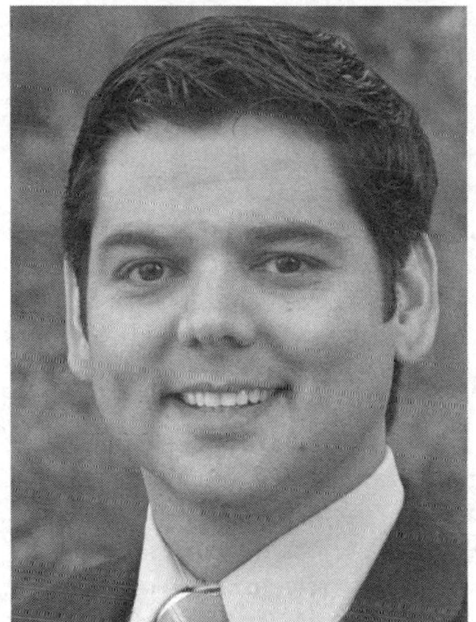

Capitol Office
225-5330
ruiz.house.gov
1319 Longworth Bldg. 20515-1305; fax 225-1238

Committees
Natural Resources
Veterans' Affairs

Residence
Palm Desert

Born
Aug. 25, 1972; Zacatecas, Mexico

Religion
Seventh-day Adventist

Family
Single

Education
U. of California, Los Angeles, B.S. 1994 (physiological science); Harvard U., M.D. 2001, M.P.P. 2001, M.P.H. 2007

Career
Physician

Political Highlights
No previous office

ELECTION RESULTS

2012 GENERAL		
Raul Ruiz (D)	110,189	52.9%
Mary Bono Mack (R)	97,953	47.1%
2012 PRIMARY (Open)		
Raul Ruiz (D)	37,847	41.9%

Elected 2012; 1st term

Ruiz defeated a prominent Republican moderate to win his seat, and it's a good bet that he'll be taking a few moderate stands of his own as he learns the ropes in Congress. His district's expanding energy sector can benefit from his placement on the Natural Resources Committee.

Ruiz was adopted by migrant farmworker relatives as a baby. He was a high-achieving student who decided at an early age to become a doctor, and he eventually got a medical degree from Harvard. He came home to work as an emergency physician.

His campaign against Rep. Mary Bono Mack was his first run for public office. Ruiz said he was not a politician, but a "public servant and physician, dedicated to serving the community." He came close to matching Bono Mack in fundraising, did very well with Latino voters and won by more than 5 points.

He cast some centrist votes early in 2013, especially on fiscal matters. He was in the minority of Democrats supporting measures to compel the adoption of a budget and freeze the pay of federal workers.

Ruiz says he wants to diversify the economy of the Coachella Valley, a vast expanse of fruit and vegetable fields between Los Angeles and Arizona. In part, that means more federal support for wind and solar power — he sits on the Natural Resources subcommittees covering energy and water.

He's also on the Veterans' Affairs Committee, and he can apply some of his medical experience from its Health Subcommittee.

Like many Democrats, Ruiz says his main prescription for slowing the growth of Medicare is to allow the government to negotiate with pharmaceutical companies for lower prices. Like many physicians (but not very many Democrats), he says the other big step toward controlling health care costs should be curbing medical malpractice litigation and damage awards.

In addition to his Harvard medical degree, Ruiz also has master's degrees in public policy and public health from the university.

California 36

Riverside County — Hemet, Palm Springs

The 36th encompasses almost all of Riverside County but accounts for less than one-third of its population. Rural and sparsely populated, this wide swath of southeastern California stretches over the San Jacinto Mountains and the fertile farms of Coachella Valley through the resorts of Palm Springs. It traverses east along Interstate 10 through Joshua Tree National Park to the wind farms near the Arizona border. Agriculture, tourism and alternative energy are economic drivers.

The Coachella Valley is a farming center that relies on irrigation from the waters of the Colorado River and legions of seasonal migrant workers. Cities in the valley have dense Latino communities and high rates of poverty. San Jacinto's citrus-heavy farming and health care prop up the city. The high desert microclimate it shares with nearby Hemet allows for grapefruit harvests in the summer, when major producers elsewhere are spent.

Populations here have boomed. A byproduct of the housing expansion are unsanctioned garbage dumps and recycling plants, leading to conflicts with sovereign Native American lands and EPA regulations. Several American Indian reservations are in the district with tribal casinos in the Palm Springs resort area.

About one third of all jobs in the Palm Springs, Cathedral City and Palm Desert area are provided by the hospitality and retail sectors. With the construction industry dragging, Palm Springs has focused on expanding tourism, tapping the Los Angeles market and the growing industry of gay vacation resorts. The Coachella Valley is also popular with retirees.

The alternative-energy industry is growing. The western edge of Palm Springs is dotted with windmills, and huge solar projects are under way in the vast desert region to the east.

Hispanic residents (48 percent) barely edge out whites for a plurality here. The district is a toss-up — Republicans hold a slim edge in voter registration but even GOP voters are not overwhelmingly conservative. Barack Obama took 51 percent of the district's vote in the 2012 presidential election.

Major Industry
Agriculture, tourism, energy

Cities
Hemet, Indio, Cathedral City, Palm Desert, Palm Springs, San Jacinto

Notable
The "Cactus to Clouds" trail to the San Jacinto Peak has a more than 10,000-foot elevation gain.

Rep. Karen Bass (D)

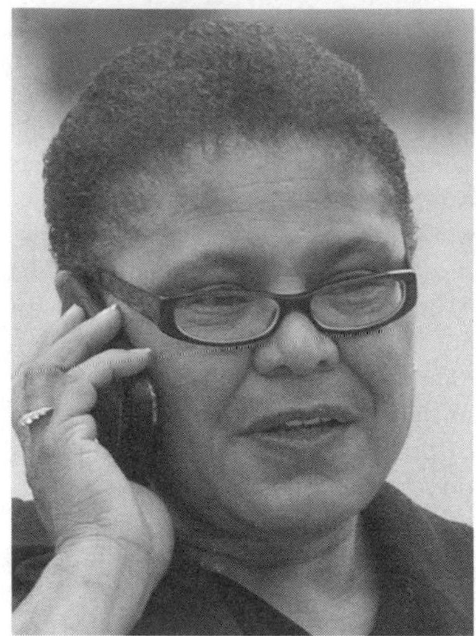

Capitol Office
225-7084
karenbass.house.gov
408 Cannon Bldg. 20515-0533; fax 225-2422

Committees
Foreign Affairs
Judiciary

Residence
Los Angeles

Born
Oct. 3, 1953; Los Angeles, Calif.

Religion
Baptist

Family
Divorced; one child (deceased) and four stepchildren

Education
San Diego State U., attended 1971-73 (philosophy); California State U., Dominguez Hills, B.S. 1990 (health sciences)

Career
Nonprofit community activism organization founder; college instructor; physician's assistant; nurse

Political Highlights
Calif. Assembly, 2004-10 (majority floor leader, 2006-08; speaker, 2008-10)

ELECTION RESULTS

2012 GENERAL		
Karen Bass (D)	207,039	86.4%
Morgan Osborne (R)	32,541	13.6%
2012 PRIMARY (Open)		
Karen Bass (D)	54,345	99.9%
2010 GENERAL		
Karen Bass (D)	131,990	86.1%
James L. Andion (R)	21,342	13.9%

Elected 2010; 2nd term

Bass was a quick study in the California Assembly, rising from novice politician to speaker in four years and winning praise for her work ethic. As she absorbs the patterns of the House and learns about life in the legislative minority, she keeps her focus on social welfare and human rights.

Bass practiced as a nurse and a physician's assistant before establishing the Community Coalition in 1990. That nonprofit started out trying to address the conditions that contributed to the Los Angeles crack cocaine epidemic and related social ills. She served as executive director for 14 years, then won a seat in the Assembly in her first bid for public office.

A combination of high turnover (members were limited to three terms at the time) and natural talent let Bass sprint up the ladder. She became majority whip, majority floor leader, and then the first black woman speaker of a state house in U.S. history.

During her tenure, California's economy was crashing. She worked to rally Democrats, appease Republicans and move job creation bills. Bass and other Assembly leaders won the John F. Kennedy Profile in Courage Award for their efforts. Republican Gov. Arnold Schwarzenegger praised her for earning her post "the old-fashioned way — she worked."

Bass has brown belts in tae kwon do and hapkido, and she says those disciplines teach a respect for opponents that she has found useful in politics. "I can have political differences, but I do not have to personalize," she said. "I can be opposed to you, and I don't have to yell and scream."

That attitude makes her a spiritual successor to New Jersey Democrat Donald M. Payne, who quietly went about his business on the Foreign Affairs Committee. When Payne died in March 2012, Bass took his place as the top Democrat on the subcommittee covering Africa, global health and human rights. She has kept that job for the 113th Congress (2013-14).

Bass introduces legislation to help those she sees as the most vulnerable in society, and so she takes a particular interest in the victims of human trafficking. She wants a State Department task force to prevent and combat Internet-facilitated human trafficking. Bass has also proposed improving training so that employees of state welfare agencies can better identify, document, educate and counsel children who are susceptible to or victims of trafficking. The fiscal 2013 defense policy law included her provision meant to stop any Pentagon contractors from contributing to human trafficking.

Bass generally supports a multilateral approach to international affairs and would like a greater focus on humanitarian problems, such as the famine in Africa or abuses in Libya. She agreed with President Barack Obama's rationale for intervening in Libya's 2011 civil war as part of NATO, saying the action could prevent a humanitarian crisis. Bass supported a 2012 extension of preferential import treatment for Africa-produced garments made from third-country fabrics.

Early in 2013, she laid down a marker for involvement in central Africa. Bass wrote in Roll Call that U.S. leadership was needed to address the seemingly endless humanitarian crisis in the Democratic Republic of the Congo. "The great depths of this conflict and its implications for American foreign policy demand nothing less than an actionable commitment to finally develop a comprehensive response," she said.

For the 113th, Bass has joined the Judiciary Committee, where she continues her pre-politics work with the criminal justice and family court systems.

Bass is a leading congressional advocate for improving the lives of foster children. "I grew up in a very loving, two-parent household and had great parents," she said. "I just can't imagine kids who don't have any parents. I happen to really, fundamentally believe that it is the role of society to take care of its children."

A reauthorization of child welfare programs signed by Obama in 2011 included a Bass provision requiring a study on recruitment and retention of foster parents. Bass and Democratic Sen. Mary L. Landrieu of Louisiana introduced bills in the 112th Congress (2011-12) to award grants for both public and private foster care mentoring programs.

Bass also has something to say about intellectual property laws. Her district and its economy have many links to television and movie production. She co-sponsored a controversial 2011 measure that would have allowed law enforcement agencies to get court orders to shut down websites posting pirated material. That bill was withdrawn after a huge netroots protest.

As a freshman, Bass served on the Budget Committee, where she said most of 2011 felt like a "Groundhog Day" rehash of her state battles. Bass has largely stayed with her party on fiscal matters. She panned GOP budgets but voted for a compromise package to cut spending and raise the federal debt limit in August 2011. Bass almost always voted with a majority of House Democrats when they diverged from a majority of Republicans.

Bass grew up in Los Angeles. She briefly studied philosophy at San Diego State University and protested the war in Vietnam. She got a health science degree from California State University, Dominguez Hills, in 1990, the same year she founded Community Coalition. When she ran for the state Assembly in 2004, she was carried to victory with the support of African-Americans, Hispanics and organized labor.

While Bass was in the Assembly in 2006, she faced personal tragedy when her daughter, Emilia, and son-in-law were killed in a car accident.

Democratic Rep. Diane Watson announced her retirement in February 2010, and Bass used contacts from her years of community service to emerge as the overwhelming favorite. She took the primary with 85 percent of the vote and the general election with 86 percent.

She had Watson's blessing throughout, and Watson even gave her a place to rent for her first few months in Washington. "She left me her apartment, with everything in it," said Bass. She quickly developed close relationships with the other eight Democrats in the class of 2010, meeting for regular dinner parties. "We all really get along and all genuinely like each other and like spending time together," she said.

In 2012, she did not face a formidable candidate in the state's new "open" primary system and ran in a district similar to her old 33rd. For the general election, she again took more than 86 percent of the vote.

Key Votes

2012	
Extend a Social Security payroll tax cut and unemployment benefits	YES
Ease securities rules to expand small-business access to capital	YES
Extend for one year subsidized student loan interest rates financed by a cut in health care spending	NO
Cite Attorney General Eric H. Holder Jr. for contempt of Congress	?
Create a visa program for foreign graduates in high-tech fields	NO
Extend most Bush-era income tax rates while allowing rates for top-bracket earners to rise (Jan. 1, 2013)	YES
2011	
Strike funding for F-35 alternative engine	YES
Prevent EPA from regulating greenhouse gas emissions to address climate change	NO
Extend certain provisions of Patriot Act for four years	NO
Declare opposition to use of ground troops in Libya	NO
Overhaul patent law	YES
Pass compromise debt limit increase plan and establish future spending limits	YES
Allow consideration of measures to implement three trade agreements	YES

CQ Vote Studies

	PARTY UNITY		PRESIDENTIAL SUPPORT	
	SUPPORT	OPPOSE	SUPPORT	OPPOSE
2012	97%	3%	93%	7%
2011	98%	2%	87%	13%

Interest Groups

	AFL-CIO	ADA	CCUS	ACU
2012	95%	100%	30%	0%
2011	100%	85%	25%	0%

California 37

West Los Angeles; Culver City

The 37th District is a highly diverse collection of Los Angeles communities, stretching from the junction of Interstates 405 and 10 east through Culver City, Baldwin Hills and Exposition Park to the University of Southern California. Several of the economically distressed neighborhoods of South Los Angeles fall into this racially diverse district: Hispanics comprise nearly 40 percent of the population and the 24 percent black population here is the highest percentage of any district statewide.

Culver City is the former hub of golden-age Hollywood film production and the city retains some of the industry despite other parts of the region hosting more studios. Although the economy relies on health care and service industry jobs, Sony Pictures is the city's largest employer and NPR West's office is also in the city.

The district's southeastern corner includes some of Los Angeles' most violent neighborhoods, and city blocks are marked by varying degrees of blight and crime. Gentrification has crept in to some historically low-income black and Hispanic communities, such as Mid-City near Wilshire Boulevard.

The 37th is home to the large and private University of Southern California, a major research institution with about 40,000 students. The surrounding University Park neighborhood is predominately Hispanic and largely poor, and less than half of residents there have a high school diploma. The university has recently undertaken an expansion of 350,000 square feet of mixed-use development in the neighborhood. Nearby Exposition Park contains a monumental museum campus which includes the Natural History Museum with its new Dinosaur Hall, as well as the African American Museum.

The entirely urban district is a Democratic stronghold, with Democrats making up nearly two-thirds of registered voters — more than six times as many as are affiliated with the GOP.

Major Industry
Service, higher education, retail

Cities
Los Angeles (pt.), Culver City, Inglewood (pt.)

Notable
Aviator and film producer Howard Hughes built his infamous wooden cargo plane, the "Spruce Goose," in Culver City.

Rep. Linda T. Sánchez (D)

Capitol Office
225-6676
lindasanchez.house.gov
2423 Rayburn Bldg. 20515-0539; fax 226-1012

Committees
Ethics - Ranking Member
Ways & Means

Residence
Whittier

Born
Jan. 28, 1969; Orange, Calif.

Religion
Roman Catholic

Family
Husband, Jim Sullivan; one child, three stepchildren

Education
U. of California, Berkeley, B.A. 1991 (Spanish literature); U. of California, Los Angeles, J.D. 1995

Career
Union official; campaign aide; lawyer; secretary

Political Highlights
No previous office

ELECTION RESULTS

2012 GENERAL		
Linda T. Sánchez (D)	145,280	67.5%
Benjamin Campos (R)	69,807	32.5%
2012 PRIMARY (Open)		
Linda T. Sánchez (D)	33,223	56.0%
2010 GENERAL		
Linda T. Sánchez (D)	81,590	63.3%
Larry S. Andre (R)	42,037	32.6%
John Smith (AMI)	5,334	4.1%

Previous Winning Percentages
2008 (70%); 2006 (66%); 2004 (61%); 2002 (55%)

Elected 2002; 6th term

Sánchez has spun through a range of committee assignments over a decade in the House, with a few constants emerging: sharply liberal positions; an interest in immigration and women's issues; and her irrepressible personality.

She is the younger sister of California Democratic Rep. Loretta Sanchez (who uses no accent in her name). The siblings have highlighted their upbringing when meditating on their public careers.

Sánchez has said that she often questioned why her traditional Latino family gave males special status. "There was a very clear distinction between what boys could do and what girls could do," she said. She is stridently liberal regarding women's health, combating gender discrimination and protecting Title IX funding for women's sports programs in schools. Several times, she has been the only woman in the annual CQ Roll Call Congressional Baseball Game for charity, sporting "IX" as her jersey number. She quit the Congressional Hispanic Caucus in 2007, charging that its chairman, Democrat Joe Baca of California, had been demeaning to women; she returned in 2009 when Democrat Nydia M. Velázquez of New York became chairwoman.

She often gets a laugh in hearings, a skill she attributes to being teased "unmercifully" by her brothers: "I learned to be quick with a comeback." Like Loretta, she is not afraid to inject a little personality into her work; whereas her sister has been known for cat-themed Christmas cards, Linda has a kid-friendly section of her congressional website that stars her beagle, Chavo. Having a dog in the office helps her to "stop and smell the roses," she said.

Sánchez has served on many House panels, including incarnations of the Small Business, Education and the Workforce, Oversight and Government Reform, Foreign Affairs and Veterans' Affairs committees. In 2013, she began a second stint on the Ways and Means Committee, where she previously served in the 111th Congress (2009-10).

She has a seat on the Select Revenue Measures Subcommittee, which puts her in the vanguard as Democrats critique GOP plans for the tax code. Sánchez has developed some nonpartisan tax plans as well. She argues for lifting the ban on taxation of some aspects of Internet-based commerce, suggesting that it could be giving an unfair advantage to online retailers and shortchanging states that would love to have that extra revenue in their budgets.

Sánchez also serves as the top Democrat on the Ethics Committee, which has the labor-intensive task of vetting hundreds of interactions and transactions by lawmakers and staffers. She took the assignment, which is viewed as a great way to curry favor with party leaders, in 2011. (Sánchez also serves as a senior whip.)

Despite Sánchez's outgoing nature, the business of the Ethics Committee has been quieter since she took the ranking member position. In the 111th Congress, panel leaders — Alabama Republican Jo Bonner and California Democrat Zoe Lofgren — exchanged accusations of misconduct in the investigation of Maxine Waters, another California Democrat. Waters was alleged to have used her office to intervene on behalf of a bank in which her husband had a financial stake. Bonner and Sánchez oversaw the conclusion of the probe in 2012, with Waters cleared of wrongdoing.

The committee was unanimous in finding that California Democrat Laura Richardson had required her congressional staffers to perform campaign work. In 2012, the House adopted a public reprimand, and Richardson was defeated in her bid for re-election.

In her first five terms, Sánchez served on the Judiciary Committee, where she addressed both women's issues and the concerns of her mostly Hispanic constituency. She is a proponent of a comprehensive overhaul of immigration law and favors the creation of opportunities for illegal immigrants in the country to become citizens.

She hailed the Obama administration's June 2012 policy directive halting enforcement actions against some illegal immigrants brought to the country as children. "These changes will make a world of difference to the hundreds of young people in my district who want to give back to the country they call home," she wrote.

Sánchez made stabbing criticisms of efforts by some states to toughen enforcement of federal immigration law. She said a 2010 Arizona law condoned racial profiling "to win a few more votes from the hate-monger wing of the Republican Party." The Supreme Court struck down much of the law in 2012, but upheld the provision allowing law enforcement officials to check the immigration status of anyone they detain in the course of their regular duties.

When states arrest illegal immigrants for violations of state and local law, however, Sánchez wants the federal government to help with the tab. She often pushes for greater funding of the State Criminal Alien Assistance Program, which reimburses states and localities for incarceration costs.

Her father, Ignacio, worked as a mechanic at a tire shop, where he met her mother, Maria Macias, an accountant and union organizer. Sánchez started her political activism in high school in Anaheim. Upset by her congressman, conservative Republican Robert K. Dornan, Sánchez in 1986 knocked on doors for Democratic challenger Dave Carter, who lost.

Sánchez worked her way through college as a nanny, a security guard, a bilingual teacher's aide and an ESL instructor. She says a speech by farm labor organizer Cesar Chavez inspired her to go back to school for a law degree and get involved in organizing labor. She eventually became executive secretary treasurer of the AFL-CIO in Orange County. She also practiced civil rights and labor law.

In 1996, Sánchez was the field organizer for sister Loretta's winning race against Dornan. She had no experience of her own in local or state government before her 2002 run for Congress, but vigorous campaigning and assistance from Loretta's fundraising network helped her secure a victory.

Redistricting after the 2010 census put Sánchez and Democratic Rep. Grace F. Napolitano into the new 38th District together. Napolitano opted to run in the nearby 32nd District in 2012 rather than face Sánchez — who easily beat Republican Benjamin Campos to secure a sixth term.

Sánchez has been open about her personal life. In November 2008 she announced that she was pregnant, and after that announcement she married the father, Jim Sullivan.

Key Votes

2012	
Extend a Social Security payroll tax cut and unemployment benefits	YES
Ease securities rules to expand small-business access to capital	YES
Extend for one year subsidized student loan interest rates financed by a cut in health care spending	NO
Cite Attorney General Eric H. Holder Jr. for contempt of Congress	?
Create a visa program for foreign graduates in high-tech fields	NO
Extend most Bush-era income tax rates while allowing rates for top-bracket earners to rise (Jan. 1, 2013)	YES
2011	
Strike funding for F-35 alternative engine	YES
Prevent EPA from regulating greenhouse gas emissions to address climate change	NO
Extend certain provisions of Patriot Act for four years	NO
Declare opposition to use of ground troops in Libya	NO
Overhaul patent law	YES
Pass compromise debt limit increase plan and establish future spending limits	NO
Allow consideration of measures to implement three trade agreements	?

CQ Vote Studies

	Party Unity		Presidential Support	
	SUPPORT	OPPOSE	SUPPORT	OPPOSE
2012	98%	2%	91%	9%
2011	98%	2%	83%	17%
2010	99%	1%	85%	15%
2009	99%	1%	95%	5%
2008	99%	1%	10%	90%

Interest Groups

	AFL-CIO	ADA	CCUS	ACU
2012	95%	90%	25%	0%
2011	100%	95%	20%	4%
2010	100%	100%	13%	0%
2009	100%	85%	36%	5%
2008	100%	100%	50%	8%

California 38

Eastern Los Angeles County — Norwalk, Whittier

The 38th District, made up of cities and towns in Los Angeles County and a tiny corner of Orange County (La Palma), lies southeast of Los Angeles itself. The district curves south from the southern San Gabriel Valley city of South El Monte through Whittier and Norwalk to Cerritos and Hawaiian Gardens on the Orange County line. It includes portions of the cities of Lakewood and Bellflower, and the major transportation corridors of Interstates 605 and 5 slice across the district.

Norwalk, which is mainly a bedroom community, is the largest city in the district. Like Whittier, it has more-affluent residents than much of Los Angeles County. The district overall is more than 60 percent Hispanic, and both Norwalk and Whittier have sizable Hispanic communities. Local industrial and retail centers in Whittier keep much of the blue-collar workforce in the 38th instead of commuting to jobs in Los Angeles.

Norwalk also is home to the Joint Regional Intelligence Center, a collaborative law enforcement center covering the greater Los Angeles area. Whittier's demographic makeup has led to a particular focus for Whittier College — educational attainment rates of Hispanic students. Gang violence still plagues parts of Whittier, and residents in South El Monte have a lower than average education rate at both the high school and college levels.

Democrats are a plurality of registered voters in the 38th, some areas of which share more in common ideologically with their more conservative Orange County neighbors than other Los Angeles area cities, but Republicans make up less than 30 percent of the electorate overall. Cerritos — which has a well-educated, wealthy and largely Asian population living in residential areas that quickly sprang up out of former farmland when the dairy industry dried up in the mid-20th century — is more friendly to the GOP, though Democrats still lead in voter registration statistics.

Major Industry
Manufacturing, health care, aerospace

Cities
Norwalk, Whittier, Pico Rivera, Cerritos

Notable
Until 1967, Cerritos was incorporated as the City of Dairy Valley, reflecting its connection to the region's primary agricultural output.

Rep. Ed Royce (R)

Capitol Office
225-4111
royce.house.gov
2185 Rayburn Bldg. 20515-0540; fax 226-0335

Committees
Financial Services
Foreign Affairs - Chairman

Residence
Fullerton

Born
Oct. 12, 1951; Los Angeles, Calif.

Religion
Roman Catholic

Family
Wife, Marie Royce

Education
California State U., Fullerton, B.A. 1977 (accounting & finance)

Career
Tax manager

Political Highlights
Calif. Senate, 1982-92

ELECTION RESULTS

2012 GENERAL		
Ed Royce (R)	145,607	57.8%
Jay Chen (D)	106,360	42.2%
2012 PRIMARY (Open)		
Ed Royce (R)	62,874	66.3%
2010 GENERAL		
Ed Royce (R)	119,455	66.8%
Christina Avalos (D)	59,400	33.2%

Previous Winning Percentages
2008 (63%); 2006 (67%); 2004 (68%); 2002 (68%); 2000 (63%); 1998 (63%); 1996 (63%); 1994 (66%); 1992 (57%)

Elected 1992; 11th term

Ronald Reagan's well-articulated themes struck a chord with Royce, helping inspire his first political run in 1982. More than 30 years later, he still adheres to the principles of small government, free trade and national defense, and he is in position to apply them on a global scale as the chairman of the Foreign Affairs Committee.

Royce is an understated and serious lawmaker — he won the top spot on Foreign Affairs despite having a very low national profile. (At 5 feet, 5 inches tall, he also has a low physical profile.) A member of the panel since his freshman term, he beat out New Jersey's Christopher H. Smith to claim the gavel for the 113th Congress (2013-14). Royce had been chairman of the Subcommittee on Terrorism, Nonproliferation and Trade, and he has plans to emphasize each of those specialties in directing the full committee.

Free-market principles gird many of Royce's foreign policy positions.

He likes to use trade as a tool in international relations. He has fought for economic liberalization and free trade as a means to improve conditions in Africa. In 2006, Royce successfully backed a bill allowing negotiations on the sale of civilian nuclear materials to India; that deal was approved in 2008. He supported free-trade pacts with Colombia, Panama and South Korea in 2011.

He's also willing to use economics as a weapon. After North Korea conducted an underground nuclear test early in 2013, Royce announced his plans for sanctions that would essentially cut off that country from the international banking system. "It's disappointing that we do not have a proactive policy to change the regime in North Korea," he said at a 2012 hearing.

Royce has advocated aggressive military and diplomatic options to combat terrorist groups. He has suggested making aid to Pakistan conditional on steps taken by the Pakistani government to crack down on terrorism, and he was one of 69 House Republicans to back an amendment to the fiscal 2013 defense policy bill to bar the use of its funds to assist Pakistan. It was rejected.

When the French military started fighting Islamic militants in the northern part of Mali in early 2013, Royce was disappointed that the Obama administration seemed to hesitate before providing operational support. "There should be no doubt that this militancy in northern Mali and the region threatens us all," he said at a hearing. "This is a NATO ally fighting al Qaida-linked terrorists. It shouldn't be that hard."

And he also has an interest in human rights issues. A 2012 law written by Royce removes barriers to adopting North Korean refugees abandoned or orphaned in the Chinese countryside.

At the start of the 112th Congress (2011-12), Royce introduced legislation to bar Vietnamese officials complicit in human rights abuses from traveling to the United States and doing business with U.S. companies. "With the communist government in Vietnam increasing its crackdown on human rights, Congress needs to respond. Those squashing freedom must pay a price," Royce said.

The selection of Royce as chairman might have been aided by his "team player" approach to the party — Royce has served as a vice chairman of the National Republican Congressional Committee, the campaign arm for House Republicans. He had also been mentioned as a potential chairman of the Financial Services Committee, and Royce, a former tax manager, is still a senior member of that panel.

Writing in 2012, he criticized the effect of sweeping 2002 and 2010 financial regulatory overhauls: "Legislation such as Sarbanes-Oxley and Dodd-Frank have driven up the cost of raising capital in our markets, impairing the ability of U.S. businesses (especially start-ups) to expand and hire."

The 2010 overhaul (Dodd-Frank) was intended in part to end the concept of "too big to fail" — institutions that the government would have to rescue to prevent national or global economic calamity. Royce is a fan of requiring banks to have large financial reserves to protect themselves, as required by some international banking conventions. "Capital, capital and more capital," he said at a 2012 hearing. "This is the only way to ensure that banks are going to be able to absorb unforeseen losses."

He generally rejects government-centric solutions. Royce described as "state socialism" the $700 billion rescue of the financial services sector the George W. Bush administration pushed in 2008.

He also aims at smaller targets; in 2011 he proposed eliminating a trust fund created in 2008 to build and support affordable rental housing. Royce said the program is susceptible to waste and abuse and that the money could be funneled to support a political agenda.

Despite growing up in a blue-collar Democratic household, Royce developed a conservative viewpoint early on. In high school, he was intrigued by the free-market message in Henry Hazlitt's book "Economics in One Lesson." He found himself defending those viewpoints to fellow students and teachers, honing his debating skills as a result.

At California State University in Fullerton, he came to the aid of a young woman staffing a College Republicans recruiting table after three men overturned it and caused a disturbance.

"I stepped in and was explaining the concept of free speech and nonviolence on campus," he recalls. He wound up joining the College Republicans and became a leader of the Young Americans for Freedom in Southern California.

Reagan's 1980 victory spurred Royce to give politics a try himself, and in 1982 he won election to the California Senate at the age of 31.

After 10 years there, Royce decided to run for the House when Republican William E. Dannemeyer gave up his seat to run for the Senate. Royce had represented a sizable portion of the congressional district in the state Senate, and he drew no primary opposition. His Democratic opponent proved too liberal for Orange County and Royce prevailed by almost 20 points.

Due to redistricting following the 2010 census, Royce ran in the new 39th District in 2012. He escaped a costly primary race against Republican Rep. Gary G. Miller, a fellow member of Financial Services, when Miller opted to run in the new 31st District, which has a Democratic lean. Miller won, but Democrats are targeting him for 2014.

Royce, meanwhile, took almost 58 percent of the vote to defeat Democrat Jay Chen, a 34-year-old school board president.

Key Votes

2012	
Extend a Social Security payroll tax cut and unemployment benefits	NO
Ease securities rules to expand small-business access to capital	YES
Extend for one year subsidized student loan interest rates financed by a cut in health care spending	YES
Cite Attorney General Eric H. Holder Jr. for contempt of Congress	YES
Create a visa program for foreign graduates in high-tech fields	YES
Extend most Bush-era income tax rates while allowing rates for top-bracket earners to rise (Jan. 1, 2013)	YES
2011	
Strike funding for F-35 alternative engine	YES
Prevent EPA from regulating greenhouse gas emissions to address climate change	YES
Extend certain provisions of Patriot Act for four years	YES
Declare opposition to use of ground troops in Libya	YES
Overhaul patent law	NO
Pass compromise debt limit increase plan and establish future spending limits	YES
Allow consideration of measures to implement three trade agreements	YES

CQ Vote Studies

	PARTY UNITY		PRESIDENTIAL SUPPORT	
	SUPPORT	OPPOSE	SUPPORT	OPPOSE
2012	94%	6%	25%	75%
2011	96%	4%	19%	81%
2010	99%	1%	26%	74%
2009	98%	2%	11%	89%
2008	99%	1%	82%	18%

Interest Groups

	AFL-CIO	ADA	CCUS	ACU
2012	10%	10%	92%	100%
2011	0%	5%	94%	96%
2010	7%	0%	88%	100%
2009	5%	0%	80%	100%
2008	0%	0%	83%	100%

California 39

Northern Orange County; parts of Los Angeles and San Bernardino counties

Split geographically among Orange, Los Angeles and San Bernardino counties east of Los Angeles proper, the 39th District is home to several medium-size cities and an ethnically diverse and conservative-leaning populace. Most of the district's residents live in largely upper-middle-class Orange County communities, including affluent Yorba Linda.

Fullerton is the district's largest city. Aerospace firms provide skilled manufacturing and high-paying white-collar jobs. The city's California State University campus is one of the area's major employers despite ongoing budget cuts. Traffic remains a hot issue, and a long-awaited bridge project aimed at alleviating congestion from the growing community into other parts of Southern California is expected to be completed 2014. Yorba Linda, home to highly educated white-collar workers, continues to thrive, and median household incomes exceed $110,000. Further north, Hacienda Heights, in Los Angeles County, has experienced a bump in home prices, after dramatic drops in residential values from 2008 through 2011.

Chino Hills in San Bernardino County used to be a predominately rural community, but has grown significantly during the last two decades. It is mainly residential, blanketed with subdivisions encircling elementary and high schools and retail clusters. Most residents in Chino Hills commute and work outside the district. Chino Hills State Park sits along the district's eastern edge.

In Los Angeles County, Diamond Bar and Rowland Heights have large Asian populations, and Orange County's Brea, La Habra and Placentia have Hispanic and Asian communities. Voter registration in the 39th favors Republicans and in the 2012 presidential race, GOP candidate Mitt Romney took 51 percent of the district's vote.

Major industry

Aerospace, higher education

Cities

Fullerton, Chino Hills, Yorba Linda

Notable

Yorba Linda, the birthplace and burial site of President Richard Nixon, is the home of the Nixon Library; Buena Park hosts the Knott's Berry Farm amusement park.

Rep. Lucille Roybal-Allard (D)

Capitol Office
225-1766
roybal-allard.house.gov
2330 Rayburn Bldg. 20515-0534; fax 226-0350

Committees
Appropriations

Residence
Downey

Born
June 12, 1941; Boyle Heights, Calif.

Religion
Roman Catholic

Family
Husband, Edward Allard; four children

Education
California State U., Los Angeles, B.A. 1965 (speech)

Career
Nonprofit worker

Political Highlights
Calif. Assembly, 1987-92

ELECTION RESULTS

2012 GENERAL		
Lucille Roybal-Allard (D)	73,940	58.9%
David Sanchez (D)	51,613	41.1%
2012 PRIMARY (Open)		
Lucille Roybal-Allard (D)	16,596	65.4%
David Sanchez (D)	8,777	34.6%
2010 GENERAL		
Lucille Roybal-Allard (D)	69,382	77.2%
Wayne Miller (R)	20,457	22.8%

Previous Winning Percentages
2008 (77%); 2006 (77%); 2004 (74%); 2002 (74%); 2000 (85%); 1998 (87%); 1996 (82%); 1994 (81%); 1992 (63%)

Elected 1992; 11th term

Roybal-Allard primarily works on behalf of those in uncertain legal, educational and economic positions. Among her Angeleno constituents, that often means women, Hispanics and other minorities.

Her family has a long history of engaging those populations. She is the daughter and successor of Edward R. Roybal, a 15-term House member who founded the Congressional Hispanic Caucus. Prior to serving in elected office, Roybal-Allard worked for United Way and was the assistant director on the Alcoholism Council of East Los Angeles. Much like her father — who began his political career on the Los Angeles City Council — Roybal-Allard started in local politics, serving in the California Assembly for nearly six years before running for Congress in 1992.

In Washington, Roybal-Allard has taken legislative steps and rhetorical stands meant to provide women with increased protection from domestic violence and expand their health care. She's the first Mexican-American woman elected to Congress and has pressed for stronger legal protections for immigrants and their children. But no endeavor has been without challenges.

Her plans for an overhaul of U.S. immigration policy were stymied in the 111th Congress (2009-10), so in the 112th Congress (2011-12) she pushed hard for President Barack Obama to issue a policy directive granting clemency to illegal immigrants brought to the United States at a young age by their parents. She became so frustrated at an April 2012 meeting between members of the CHC and a White House adviser that she walked out. Obama issued the directive that June.

Roybal-Allard co-wrote the 2011 version of legislation known as the Dream Act, which would provide a path to legal standing for that class of immigrant. "The immigrant youth this bill would benefit aren't criminals," she said during a June 2011 YouTube town hall. "Brought over our borders as children by their parents, they had no say in the decision to enter the United States. We have a responsibility to remove impediments so they can accomplish their personal goals and our society can reap the benefits of their strengths and skills."

She was encouraged by the renewed efforts toward an overhaul at the start of the 113th Congress (2013-14).

Roybal-Allard is measured and well spoken when she takes to the House floor — the Sunlight Foundation in 2012 ranked her as having some of the best oratory skills in Congress. She has occupied a seat on the Appropriations Committee since 1999, often using her post to further her favored causes. Before bans on earmarks began to take hold in 2009, she had considerable success steering millions of dollars to Los Angeles for targeted programs.

She argued against the fiscal 2013 Homeland Security appropriations bill after Republicans introduced a series of amendments that she saw as targeting immigrants, and she argued against a proposed $1.1 billion worth of cuts in the 2012 version of the bill, specifically noting reductions for first-responders.

Roybal-Allard also took issue with fiscal 2013 bills to reduce housing assistance funds. "By systematically underfunding ... three major rental assistance programs, this bill increases the chances of greater homelessness in our country, especially for those already living in unstable housing conditions," she said in a 2012 floor speech.

She sits on the Labor-HHS-Education Appropriations Subcommittee and in the 112th chaired the CHC's task force on health care. Roybal-Allard voted against the August 2011 agreement to raise the federal debt ceiling and cut spending, in part because of potential cuts to health care services in the deal.

"Some of the most damaging proposals being discussed in these budget debates are those that involve the Medicaid program," she wrote at the time. "While I agree that we must look for savings and inefficiencies in all of our social programs, it is imperative that we do not decimate what has been the essential primary health coverage for millions."

Roybal-Allard belongs to the Congressional Progressive Caucus, the group of the most liberal House members. She opposed a 2012 Republican bill to reauthorize federal programs to investigate and prosecute violent crimes against women, as it did not contain provisions for equal protection of gay and lesbian abuse victims and took away the right of immigrant victims of domestic abuse to confidentially apply for permanent residency.

She was part of a successful effort to expand the definition of rape in the FBI's Uniform Crime Report, writing in an October 2011 letter to FBI director Robert S. Mueller that the definition unfairly excluded victims who had been drugged or impaired by alcohol and "explicitly excludes men." The definition was officially changed in 2012 to include victims of any gender and instances where drugs or alcohol are involved. She has made numerous legislative efforts to keep minors from drinking.

Roybal-Allard has worked across the aisle when California is involved. She won praise in the late 1990s as the first elected chairwoman of the California Democratic delegation, coordinating with the state's Republicans on a number of parochial issues.

Still, she's a very reliable Democratic vote, notably taking a protectionist tack when she feels manufacturing or labor interests in her district are threatened. She joined many in her party in voting against Obama's wishes and opposing free-trade deals with South Korea, Colombia and Panama in 2011.

Roybal-Allard has spoken of discrimination experienced as a child. She recalls being punished for speaking Spanish in school and the disdain shown her family when her father entered politics. "The racial slurs and not-so-quiet whispers directed at him and our family when we attended events and dinners remain vivid in our minds even today," she said in 2008.

Some relatives were skeptical when her father sent his daughters to college, and her own siblings discouraged her from entering politics, thinking of the difficulties her father faced. But she has enjoyed a relatively smooth ride at the polls. California's new "open primary" system for 2012 led to her poorest showing in a House election. Community college instructor David Sanchez, a Democrat, finished second in the primary, which guaranteed him a spot on the November ballot. Sanchez raised hardly any money for the general election but still won 41 percent of the vote.

Roybal-Allard's current district has the highest percentage of Hispanic residents of any district in the nation.

Key Votes

2012	
Extend a Social Security payroll tax cut and unemployment benefits	YES
Ease securities rules to expand small-business access to capital	YES
Extend for one year subsidized student loan interest rates financed by a cut in health care spending	NO
Cite Attorney General Eric H. Holder Jr. for contempt of Congress	?
Create a visa program for foreign graduates in high-tech fields	-
Extend most Bush-era income tax rates while allowing rates for top-bracket earners to rise (Jan. 1, 2013)	YES
2011	
Strike funding for F-35 alternative engine	NO
Prevent EPA from regulating greenhouse gas emissions to address climate change	NO
Extend certain provisions of Patriot Act for four years	NO
Declare opposition to use of ground troops in Libya	NO
Overhaul patent law	YES
Pass compromise debt limit increase plan and establish future spending limits	NO
Allow consideration of measures to implement three trade agreements	NO

CQ Vote Studies

	PARTY UNITY		PRESIDENTIAL SUPPORT	
	SUPPORT	OPPOSE	SUPPORT	OPPOSE
2012	98%	2%	91%	9%
2011	98%	2%	85%	15%
2010	98%	2%	93%	7%
2009	99%	1%	97%	3%
2008	99%	1%	11%	89%

Interest Groups

	AFL-CIO	ADA	CCUS	ACU
2012	90%	90%	30%	4%
2011	100%	90%	19%	4%
2010	100%	100%	13%	0%
2009	100%	100%	33%	0%
2008	100%	95%	44%	8%

California 40

East Los Angeles; Downey

With the highest percentage of Hispanic residents (87 percent) of any district in the nation, the 40th incorporates parts of East Los Angeles and the more industrial and suburban communities southeast of Los Angeles.

A chunk of the city of Los Angeles takes up the northwestern corner of the 40th, east of Interstate 110 and south of Interstate 10. To the east are Vernon and predominately Mexican-American areas of East Los Angeles. Heading south is a string of cities from Commerce to Paramount.

Light industry is the district's economic driver. The industrial region of Vernon, south of downtown Los Angeles, which is in the 34th, is chockablock with food-processing plants and industrial warehouses that employ thousands from the neighboring communities.

The city's population explodes during the workday as people head to its plants — business-friendly zoning and utilities laws have long kept Vernon a haven for industry, and a potential disincorporation could see it annexed by a neighbor.

Downey is the district's main population center outside the Los Angeles city limits. It once thrived as an aerospace hub, with sites that supported the Apollo program for NASA, but cuts in the 1990s left the job base depleted. A film production company operated on part of the former Boeing site, but has since closed, and the city grapples with how to best preserve its aerospace roots. The area now relies on health care jobs at a Kaiser Permanente site and the Rancho Los Amigos Rehabilitation Center.

Overall the district is overwhelmingly Democratic. Democrats account for 61 percent of all registered voters, and more voters register without a party affiliation than with the GOP.

Major Industry

Light industry, food processing and wholesale, health care

Cities

Los Angeles (pt.), Downey, Huntington Park, Paramount, Bell Gardens, Bellflower (pt.)

Notable

The Iceland ice skating rink in the city of Paramount opened in 1940 by Frank Zamboni, who developed the iconic ice-resurfacing machine that now bears his name.

Rep. Mark Takano (D)

Capitol Office
225-2305
takano.house.gov
1507 Longworth Bldg. 20515-4328; fax 225-7018

Committees
Science, Space & Technology
Veterans' Affairs

Residence
Riverside

Born
Dec. 10, 1960; Riverside, Calif.

Religion
Methodist

Family
Single

Education
Harvard U., A.B. 1983 (government); U. of California, Riverside, M.F.A. 2010 (creative writing)

Career
Teacher

Political Highlights
Riverside Community College District Board of Trustees, 1990-2012 (president 1992, 1997, 1998, 2005, 2006); Democratic nominee for U.S. House, 1992, 1994

ELECTION RESULTS

2012 GENERAL		
Mark Takano (D)	103,578	59.0%
John F. Tavaglione (R)	72,074	41.0%
2012 PRIMARY (Open)		
Mark Takano (D)	20,860	36.7%
Anna Nevenic (D)	4,991	8.8%

Elected 2012; 1st term

In Takano's quest for a House seat, the third time was the charm — but it came 18 years after the second time. He ran in the 43rd District in 1992 and lost by 519 votes to Republican Ken Calvert. In the 1994 rematch, Takano got stomped. When an open, Democratic-leaning 41st District was drawn for the 2012 election, he didn't hesitate. Takano beat GOP Riverside County Supervisor John F. Tavaglione by 18 points.

A Riverside native, Takano crossed the country to attend Harvard. When he returned home, he became a high school teacher. He also served more than two decades on the board of trustees for the local community college.

Takano, a gay Japanese-American, joined the Congressional Progressive Caucus, the group of the most-liberal House members.

When Republicans advanced a bill in February 2013 that said the president had "allowed" the federal deficit to grow, Takano proposed an amendment to put the blame on Congress. "The budgets passed by the House Republicans are less valuable than the paper they are written on," he said on the House floor. "They do nothing to bring both sides of the aisle together and are a complete waste of time and taxpayers' money."

He says attaining the "American dream" is increasingly difficult due to rising education costs and fewer job-training opportunities. He proposes creating a National Critical Skills Development Fund to offer job-training loans to people entering fields such as health care that are experiencing workforce shortages. And he has floated the idea of getting the government involved in microlending to young people, to "give young graduates the tools to start their own businesses."

His didn't get a seat on the Education and the Workforce Committee, but Takano is the top Democrat on the Veterans' Affairs Economic Opportunity Subcommittee. His first bill was to extend the eligibility window for a program that helps veterans with service-connected disabilities find employment.

California 41

Northwestern Riverside County — Riverside, Moreno Valley

Wedged into northwestern Riverside County, the Inland Empire-based 41st District includes densely populated cities to the north and rural, unincorporated stretches along Interstate 215.

The cities of Riverside and Moreno Valley contrast with the vast landscape of the south, especially outside of Perris, where skydiving is advertised. Productive farmland in Riverside County has been driven farther east; decades of population growth has suburbanized this corner of the county, and one-third of Riverside's population falls into the 41st. Predominately residential, the district is home to retail and service employers that support the local population.

The high density, growing residential sprawl and a population dependent on interstates and freeways to reach other parts of Southern California make the district part of the greater Los Angeles "smog belt."

A University of California campus in Riverside employs thousands of residents of the region. March Air Reserve Base is Moreno Valley's largest employer. The base is home to the 452nd Air Mobility Wing and hosts units of the Army, Navy and Marine Corps reserves, as well as the National Guard. Long-term uncertainty in the area's traditional manufacturing sector continues.

Unemployment is in double digits across the district, and new home construction rates have fallen in Moreno Valley. A medical school campus at UC, Riverside, was scheduled to open in 2012 but will not open until the fall of 2013 because of state budget cuts.

While the Inland Empire has historically been Republican turf, changing demographics have places in the 41st shifting to the middle. The majority-Hispanic district gives an edge to Democrats in voter registration and elections, although many voters still hold onto conservative sentiments.

Major Industry
Manufacturing, higher education, retail

Cities
Riverside, Moreno Valley, Perris

Notable
The California Citrus State Historic Park in Riverside preserves the culture and landscape of the area's longtime agricultural touchstone.

Rep. Ken Calvert (R)

Capitol Office
225-1986
calvert.house.gov
2269 Rayburn Bldg. 20515-0544; fax 225-2004

Committees
Appropriations
Budget

Residence
Corona

Born
June 8, 1953; Corona, Calif.

Religion
Protestant

Family
Divorced

Education
Chaffey College, A.A. 1973 (business); San Diego State U., B.A. 1975 (economics)

Career
Real estate executive, restaurant executive

Political Highlights
Sought Republican nomination for U.S. House, 1982; Riverside County Republican Party chairman, 1984-88

ELECTION RESULTS

2012 GENERAL		
Ken Calvert (R)	130,245	60.6%
Michael Williamson (D)	84,702	39.4%
2012 PRIMARY (Open)		
Ken Calvert (R)	35,392	51.3%
Clayton Thibodeau (R)	6,374	9.2%
Eva Johnson (R)	5,678	8.2%
2010 GENERAL		
Ken Calvert (R)	107,482	55.6%
Bill Hedrick (D)	85,784	44.4%

Previous Winning Percentages
2008 (51%); 2006 (60%); 2004 (62%); 2002 (64%); 2000 (74%); 1998 (56%); 1996 (55%); 1994 (55%); 1992 (47%)

Elected 1992; 11th term

Calvert sticks to his principles on spending and immigration, but he is more than willing to work across the aisle — and across the Capitol — to support his Southern California district. That inclination has been particularly notable regarding water issues and highway funding to help resolve traffic problems in the Inland Empire.

A member of the Appropriations Committee since 2007, Calvert has in recent years kept a low profile in Washington. He backs reductions in government spending but still stands closer to the center than most of his GOP colleagues on fiscal issues — he was one of 85 House Republicans who acceded to the January 2013 "fiscal cliff" deal, which allowed higher income tax rates on earnings over $400,000. Calvert is a member of the Main Street Partnership, a more moderate group of lawmakers.

On other issues he is further to the right. Calvert supports limited federal regulation of private property and stricter controls on immigration. He wrote the legislation that created the E-Verify program, which allows businesses to confirm the employment eligibility of new hires, and he has encouraged making its use mandatory. "If we cut off the job magnet, that will end the incentive for people to cross the border illegally in the first place," he told The San Diego Union-Tribune in 2013.

Calvert disapproved of the California law enacted in 2011 that prohibited cities and counties from requiring businesses to use E-Verify. He also panned President Barack Obama's 2012 policy directive that would allow illegal immigrants brought to the country as children to avoid deportation. Calvert pointed to immigration concerns when voting against a bill, signed into law in early 2009, to expand the Children's Health Insurance Program — the expansion was an effort to provide benefits to illegal immigrants, he said.

The Appropriations Interior-Environment Subcommittee gives him a venue to focus on water. When he chaired the Natural Resources Subcommittee on Water and Power in 2004, he worked with California Democratic Sen. Dianne Feinstein to win enactment of a bill to reauthorize and restructure the California Federal Bay-Delta Program, or Calfed, which provides irrigation and drinking water for two-thirds of the state's population.

Calvert and Feinstein also worked together in the 112th Congress (2011-12). They introduced companion legislation that would shift 14 air tankers from the U.S. Air Force to the Forest Service to help fight wildfires. They also helped persuade Transportation Secretary Ray LaHood to provide a $445 million loan to help subsidize the widening of Highway 91 through Corona, and they introduced a bill to provide loan guarantees for public entities seeking to acquire land for wildlife habitat conservation.

Calvert occasionally sides with Democrats, but regarding the Obama administration's major economic initiatives he has solidly stuck with his party. He supported a deal to cut spending and raise the debt limit in 2011 but later said it was a mistake to cut Pentagon spending as part of that deal. "We are still a nation at war," he told the Marine Corps Times after supporting a House Republican budget in 2012 that would significantly increase defense spending. Calvert has seats on both the Defense Appropriations Subcommittee and the Budget Committee.

He was born in Corona, just west of Riverside County. His father, who changed parties to become a Republican in the 1960s, won election to the city council and then served as Corona's mayor. The younger Calvert worked on Richard Nixon's 1968 presidential campaign and interned in the Capitol Hill office of Rep. Victor Veysey, a California Republican.

Calvert's political career has included close races and serious challenges from both the left and right. His electoral prospects have been boosted by the regular redrawing of the congressional map.

In 1982, Calvert entered an open-seat House race in a district that contained most of Riverside County, losing the GOP primary by just 868 votes on his 29th birthday. But he stayed active in party affairs, helping run the gubernatorial campaigns of Republicans George Deukmejian and Pete Wilson.

When reapportionment changed the borders of the 43rd District in western Riverside County in 1992, Calvert ran again; Election Day tallies showed him behind, but when write-in ballots were counted he was the victor. Tragedy marred his triumph: That September, Calvert's father had committed suicide.

Calvert had a rough start in Congress. A tryst with a prostitute drew widespread notice. He said his "inappropriate" behavior stemmed from depression over his recent divorce and his father's suicide. Calvert won the 1994 GOP primary by just 2 points, and the national surge that delivered the House to the GOP carried him to victory. (His victories in 1992 and 1994 were over Democrat Mark Takano, who was elected in 2012 to represent the 41st District.)

Redistricting that took effect in 2002 put Calvert in a slightly more Republican-leaning district, and he scored solid wins until the 2008 campaign. Calvert had been under increasing criticism from bloggers, and watchdog groups questioned whether he used his seat on the Appropriations Committee to increase the value of some of his personal real estate deals. They pointed to a 2006 Los Angeles Times report that Calvert and a partner held numerous properties near transportation projects that Calvert had supported with federal earmarks — member-directed funding set-asides for specific projects. Calvert denied wrongdoing, and an FBI review of public documents never led to any action.

But the Democratic tidal wave of 2008, combined with the questions raised about his financial activities, held him to a 2-point victory over Democrat Bill Hedrick. In the 2010 cycle he had to deal with a primary challenge from the right but prevailed with 66 percent of the vote. He went on to once again defeat Hedrick, that time by 11 points.

An independent redistricting commission redrew the congressional lines for 2012, and Calvert was one of the benefactors. He ran in the now GOP-friendly 42nd District — it contains Corona, but the city of Riverside from his previous district is now in the 41st. Calvert was wiped off the Democratic target list for the foreseeable future.

He easily won a six-way primary under California's new all-party format, taking 51 percent of the vote. He had a huge fundraising advantage over Democrat Michael Williamson and won by 21 points in November.

Key Votes

2012	
Extend a Social Security payroll tax cut and unemployment benefits	YES
Ease securities rules to expand small-business access to capital	YES
Extend for one year subsidized student loan interest rates financed by a cut in health care spending	YES
Cite Attorney General Eric H. Holder Jr. for contempt of Congress	YES
Create a visa program for foreign graduates in high-tech fields	YES
Extend most Bush-era income tax rates while allowing rates for top-bracket earners to rise (Jan. 1, 2013)	YES
2011	
Strike funding for F-35 alternative engine	NO
Prevent EPA from regulating greenhouse gas emissions to address climate change	YES
Extend certain provisions of Patriot Act for four years	YES
Declare opposition to use of ground troops in Libya	YES
Overhaul patent law	YES
Pass compromise debt limit increase plan and establish future spending limits	YES
Allow consideration of measures to implement three trade agreements	YES

CQ Vote Studies

	PARTY UNITY		PRESIDENTIAL SUPPORT	
	SUPPORT	OPPOSE	SUPPORT	OPPOSE
2012	91%	9%	15%	85%
2011	94%	6%	27%	73%
2010	96%	4%	27%	73%
2009	86%	14%	24%	76%
2008	96%	4%	76%	24%

Interest Groups

	AFL-CIO	ADA	CCUS	ACU
2012	14%	0%	100%	79%
2011	0%	5%	100%	84%
2010	7%	0%	100%	96%
2009	14%	10%	87%	92%
2008	13%	15%	100%	83%

California 42

Western Riverside County — Corona, Murrieta

East of Los Angeles and north of San Diego, the 42nd District contains almost one-third of Riverside County's residents in the county's western tip. Once rural farmland, decades of population growth and a shift of much of the region's agricultural production east has transformed some of these suburbs into satellites of the greater Los Angeles area. The 42nd stretches up past Corona in the northwest and curls in a "U" to pull in Lake Perris in its northeast. The Santa Ana Mountains rise to the district's west; Diamond Valley Lake reservoir is to the east. The rugged eastern reaches of the district remain sparsely populated.

Corona is a diverse bedroom community for white-collar Orange County. Traffic congestion in the northwestern arm of the district puts transportation and infrastructure funding at the top of local agendas. Residents pushed farther from jobs in Los Angeles and Orange counties have settled in towns in the southwestern part of the district, and the expansion of Interstate 15 — which runs from Corona to Murrieta just east of the Santa Ana Mountains — over the last 20 years aided development of areas such as Menifee and Wildomar. Some residents of these cities and the district's portion of Temecula (mostly in the 50th) will commute to Marine Corps Base Camp Pendleton along the Pacific Coast in the 49th. A Navy analysis and assessment station is in Norco. The district also hosts some vineyards in part of the popular Temecula Valley.

The minority-majority district is more than one-third Hispanic, although white residents constitute a plurality of almost 47 percent. The 42nd District supports Republicans and the GOP has a roughly 16-point voter registration margin over Democrats here. But nearly 20 percent of the voters here do not list a party affiliation.

Major Industry
Manufacturing, health care, retail

Cities
Corona, Murrieta, Menifee, Lake Elsinore

Notable
Norco is known as "Horsetown USA" because it has 81 miles of horse trails throughout the city to promote the rural lifestyle — ties for horses can be seen next to parking lots.

Rep. Maxine Waters (D)

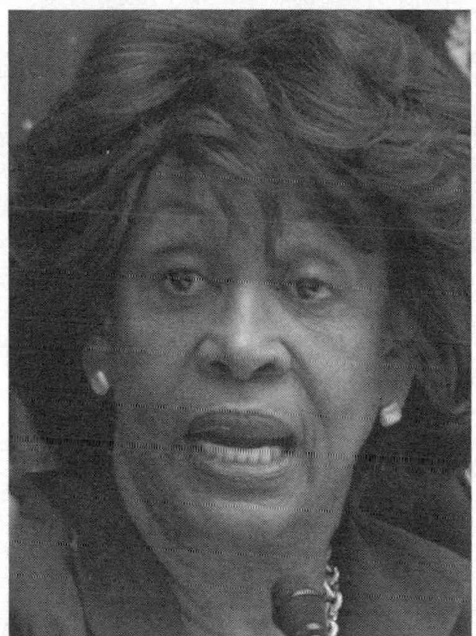

Capitol Office
225-2201
waters.house.gov
2221 Rayburn Bldg. 20515-0535; fax 225-7854

Committees
Financial Services - Ranking Member

Residence
Los Angeles

Born
Aug. 15, 1938; St. Louis, Mo.

Religion
Christian

Family
Husband, Sidney Williams; two children

Education
California State U., Los Angeles, B.A. 1970

Career
City council aide; public relations firm owner; Head Start program coordinator; telephone company service representative; clothing factory worker

Political Highlights
Calif. Assembly, 1976-90

ELECTION RESULTS

2012 GENERAL		
Maxine Waters (D)	143,123	71.2%
Bob Flores (D)	57,771	28.8%
2012 PRIMARY (Open)		
Maxine Waters (D)	36,062	65.4%
Bob Flores (D)	19,061	34.6%
2010 GENERAL		
Maxine Waters (D)	98,131	79.3%
K. Bruce Brown (R)	25,561	20.7%

Previous Winning Percentages
2008 (83%); 2006 (84%); 2004 (81%); 2002 (78%); 2000 (87%); 1998 (89%); 1996 (86%); 1994 (78%); 1992 (83%); 1990 (79%)

Elected 1990; 12th term

Many politicians present a genteel exterior regardless of their feelings. When stoked by Republicans or her perceptions of injustice, Waters does not. "Anger is not a permanent state of mind," she says, "but anger has a place in an honest display of emotions."

As memories of past barbs fade, Waters creates new ones. Speaking at an August 2011 event in Los Angeles, she said the tea party "can go straight to hell." That was a few days after a Congressional Black Caucus event in Detroit where she accused President Barack Obama of neglecting black communities: "Our people are hurting," she said. "The unemployment is unconscionable."

At California's Democratic convention in 2012 she called House Republican leaders "demons" who would "rather do whatever they can to destroy this president rather than for the good of the country."

It is fair to say that Waters runs through conflicts rather than around them. But she has forced both Republican and Democratic administrations to address her concerns, and she also has attained positions of authority. A drawn-out ethics investigation of Waters ended in 2012, in time for her to become the top Democrat on the Financial Services Committee for the 113th Congress (2013-14).

Waters supports many government interventions in the marketplace, which puts her in opposition to Chairman Jeb Hensarling of Texas, another solid partisan. She wants full implementation of the regime created by Dodd-Frank — the 2010 financial regulatory overhaul law which Republicans say is paralyzing the private sector. She supports the Federal Reserve's "quantitative easing" monetary policy. "I sincerely believe our central bank's actions have provided critical support for our nation's economic recovery," she said at a 2013 hearing. And she's not about to concede the withdrawal of the federal government from the housing sector.

She calls extra attention to policies affecting her poor and mostly minority constituents. Waters was the chairwoman of the subcommittee on housing when the residential housing sector collapsed in 2008. Working with full-committee Chairman Barney Frank of Massachusetts, she secured reauthorizations of several low-income housing programs.

As the committee assembled a momentous bill overhauling the Federal Housing Administration and authorizing the effective takeover of mortgage giants Fannie Mae and Freddie Mac, Waters fought for inclusion of an affordable-housing trust fund and $3.9 billion in grants to buy and rehabilitate foreclosed homes. President George W. Bush threatened to veto any measure that included either provision, but Waters and Frank stared down the threat. "The president is attempting to get a lot in this bill," Waters said. "You don't give him all this and not get something else."

Waters introduced a bill to revamp the FHA's shaky finances in 2010, and a provision allowing FHA to increase mortgage insurance premiums was peeled off and enacted.

In the 111th Congress (2009-10) she stalled the regulatory overhaul bill to force the inclusion of $4 billion to help prevent home mortgage foreclosures. Waters led the 10 Black Caucus members on the committee to boycott the panel vote. She had no regrets about holding it up — even though she agrees with its goals and considers the Consumer Financial Protection Bureau created by the law to be a triumph.

Waters' posturing can obscure the fact that she does listen to the complaints of the business community — and sometimes sympathizes. "I look forward to working with financial institutions so that they can make a profit and do good," she said in late 2012. In the 112th Congress (2011-12) she went along with bills to aid the flow of capital to small businesses and startup companies.

Waters also uses her financial services connections for international causes, such as debt forgiveness. She wrote the 2010 bill, signed by Obama, to encourage lending institutions to cancel Haiti's foreign debt to help in that nation's recovery from a January earthquake.

For most of 2012, Waters' ascension to the ranking member post was no sure thing. In the summer of 2010, the House ethics committee charged that Waters violated House rules in seeking federal help for OneUnited Bank, a Los Angeles institution where her husband had been a board member and owned a minimum of $500,000 in stock in 2007. Waters said she was acting on behalf of small, minority- and women-owned banks, not just OneUnited. She was vehement in proclaiming her innocence. Chaos on the ethics committee resulted in delays of the investigation, but Waters was cleared of wrongdoing in September 2012. That also cleared her to take the ranking member position from Frank, who retired.

Waters is undoubtedly a liberal. "The government must keep people safe and secure; it must give the opportunity to have a voice; it must provide decent quality of life," she said in 2012. "The government has responsibility for providing opportunity."

She is a former member of the Judiciary Committee, and she often introduces bills to cover testing and treatment of HIV/AIDS in prisons and to ensure that health care plans cover routine testing. She sponsored a bill to focus federal prosecution on major drug offenses, rather than all drug offenses.

Born in St. Louis as one of 13 children in a family on welfare, Waters bused tables in a segregated restaurant as a teenager. Her high school class voted her as "most likely to become speaker of the House." She married after graduating.

In 1961 she moved with her first husband and two children to Los Angeles, where she worked at a clothing factory and a telephone company. Waters' public career began in 1965 when she took a job as a program coordinator for Head Start while in college. She got involved in community organizing, which led her to politics. After working as a volunteer and a consultant in several races, she won an upset victory in 1976 for a seat in the California Assembly.

In 1990, Waters ran to succeed Democratic Rep. Augustus F. Hawkins, who was retiring after 14 terms. She had been preparing for the move. During redistricting debates in the Assembly in 1982, Waters maneuvered to remove from Hawkins' district a blue-collar, mainly white suburb she saw as unfriendly territory.

She won the 1990 race with 79 percent of the vote, and has won every election since with at least 70 percent of the vote.

Key Votes

2012	
Extend a Social Security payroll tax cut and unemployment benefits	YES
Ease securities rules to expand small-business access to capital	YES
Extend for one year subsidized student loan interest rates financed by a cut in health care spending	NO
Cite Attorney General Eric H. Holder Jr. for contempt of Congress	?
Create a visa program for foreign graduates in high-tech fields	NO
Extend most Bush-era income tax rates while allowing rates for top-bracket earners to rise (Jan. 1, 2013)	YES
2011	
Strike funding for F-35 alternative engine	YES
Prevent EPA from regulating greenhouse gas emissions to address climate change	NO
Extend certain provisions of Patriot Act for four years	NO
Declare opposition to use of ground troops in Libya	P
Overhaul patent law	NO
Pass compromise debt limit increase plan and establish future spending limits	NO
Allow consideration of measures to implement three trade agreements	NO

CQ Vote Studies

	PARTY UNITY		PRESIDENTIAL SUPPORT	
	SUPPORT	OPPOSE	SUPPORT	OPPOSE
2012	97%	3%	91%	9%
2011	95%	5%	77%	23%
2010	97%	3%	78%	22%
2009	98%	2%	93%	7%
2008	98%	2%	18%	82%

Interest Groups

	AFL-CIO	ADA	CCUS	ACU
2012	95%	100%	17%	0%
2011	100%	90%	7%	8%
2010	93%	90%	25%	4%
2009	100%	90%	36%	0%
2008	100%	95%	47%	0%

California 43

Southwestern Los Angeles County — most of Inglewood, parts of Torrance and Los Angeles

The 43rd District takes in some of the state's poorest communities. The northern bar of the "T"-shaped district stretches from Los Angeles International Airport through Inglewood to the junction of Interstates 105 and 110. Extending south through Hawthorne, the 43rd crosses Interstate 405 into Torrance (shared with the far wealthier 33th). The Hispanic-plurality district is also nearly one-quarter black, the state's second-highest proportion.

The communities of Inglewood, Westmont, Hawthorne and Lennox are all characterized as low-income with low educational attainment. Many residents here are young and communities struggle with high unemployment rates. Torrance and Gardena are home to residents with more wealth and education, as well as significant Asian communities.

Despite the economic struggles of many district residents, there are several major employers based within the boundaries of the 43rd, pivotal not just to the district, but to the state overall. Los Angeles International Airport is one of the top 10 busiest in the world and the third-busiest in the nation. It is currently undergoing a major renovation project that will cost more than $4 billion and is expected to generate thousands of jobs. Just north of the airport sits Loyola Marymount University. Toyota and Honda also have major American corporate headquarters here. Aviation interests are not limited to LAX: Two general aviation airports, Hawthorne Municipal Airport and Zamperini Field, are in the 43rd and the aerospace industry south of Los Angeles includes firms based in Torrance.

The district is solid Democratic territory at the statewide and federal levels. Nearly 60 percent of voters in the 43rd are registered Democrats and more residents are unaffiliated than register as Republicans.

Major Industry
Airports, service, aerospace

Cities
Los Angeles (pt.), Inglewood (pt.), Hawthorne, Torrance (pt.)

Notable
The Armed Forces parade held annually in Torrance since 1960 is the longest running annual municipal military parade in the country.

Rep. Janice Hahn (D)

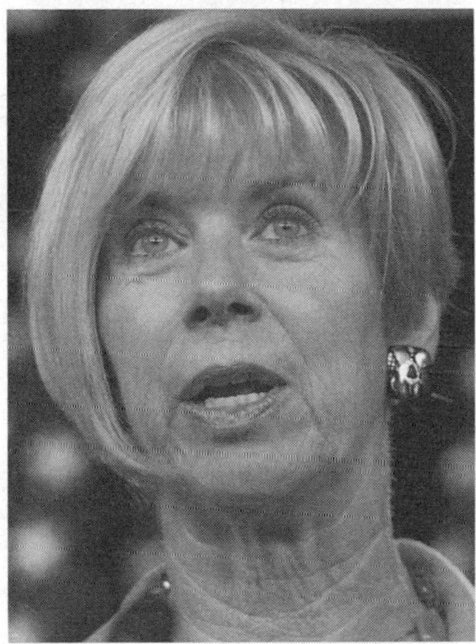

Capitol Office
225-8220
hahn.house.gov
404 Cannon Bldg. 20515-0536; fax 226-7290

Committees
Small Business
Transportation & Infrastructure

Residence
Los Angeles

Born
March 30, 1952; Los Angeles, Calif.

Religion
Church of Christ

Family
Divorced; three children

Education
Pepperdine U., attended 1972-73; Abilene Christian College, B.S. 1974 (education)

Career
Utility company public affairs director; investment banker; commercial real estate development company marketing director; homemaker; teacher

Political Highlights
Candidate for Los Angeles City Council, 1993; Los Angeles Charter Reform Commission, 1997-99; Democratic nominee for U.S. House, 1998; Los Angeles City Council, 2001-11; sought Democratic nomination for lieutenant governor, 2010

ELECTION RESULTS

2012 GENERAL		
Janice Hahn (D)	99,909	60.2%
Laura Richardson (D)	65,989	39.8%
2012 PRIMARY (Open)		
Janice Hahn (D)	24,843	60.1%
Laura Richardson (D)	16,523	39.9%
2011 SPECIAL		
Janice Hahn (D)	47,000	54.9%
Craig Huey (R)	38,624	45.1%

Elected July 2011; 1st full term

Hahn's young congressional career has been an extension of her work in Los Angeles city government — she's an energetic booster of liberal causes and her hometown's infrastructure. As she scales her positions up to national level, Hahn says she is guided by the principles of her father, a longtime Los Angeles County supervisor: "He really believed government was there to make people's lives better."

Politics is her family's business. Hahn's father, Kenneth, was a county supervisor for 40 years; her uncle, Gordon, served on the Los Angeles City Council for a decade; and her brother, James, was elected to a number of city jobs, the last being mayor.

Hahn was a relative latecomer — her first electoral victory put her on the city council only in 2001 — but admirers noted her natural skill as well as her enthusiasm (she was a college cheerleader and mascot). A fellow council member told the Los Angeles Times in 2005 that "Janice has great instincts as a street politician."

Her home turf on the city council included Los Angeles' port, and Hahn also chaired the council committee overseeing the port and the airport. When she came to the House in July 2011 after a special-election victory, she identified those hubs as a top priority. "No one before me, or after me, will ever have the knowledge of the Port of Los Angeles or the [Los Angeles] International Airport like I do," she said.

Hahn got a seat on the Transportation and Infrastructure Committee in the 113th Congress (2013-14), but she started advancing her agenda well before then. She and Texas Republican Ted Poe launched the Ports Caucus in 2011 to promote the economic importance and security needs of U.S. ports.

The House in 2012 passed her bill to require the Department of Homeland Security to report on its plans to address gaps in port security. She supports a "risk-based" method for awarding homeland security funding, which favors high-density and high-traffic areas such as Los Angeles.

Hahn and Poe have said that the Harbor Maintenance Trust Fund is one of their top concerns; they want to make sure that all the fees collected for the fund are used for dredging and port maintenance and not diverted to other accounts. She sits on the subcommittees covering maritime transportation and water infrastructure.

Hahn urges development of a national freight policy to speed the movement of goods from ports to consumers. In 2012, she asked conferees on a two-year reauthorization of surface transportation programs to consider such a provision, and she applauded when the Transportation Department created a Freight Policy Council to formulate one in accordance with the law. (She also professes to be an "unabashed supporter" of high-speed passenger rail.)

As a member of the Small Business Committee, Hahn has spoken of the need to help employers find export markets.

All of those causes are nonpartisan, but Hahn is unmistakably a liberal. She belongs to the Congressional Progressive Caucus; her involvement in transportation and infrastructure includes very strong support for the unions that operate in those industries; and she wants to cut troop and contractor levels in Iraq and Afghanistan.

She also defends the 2010 health care law. Hahn is the top Democrat on the Small Business Health and Technology Subcommittee, which gives her a front row seat as employers attempt to navigate the law's new demands.

Hahn takes common Democratic stances on the nation's fiscal health. "Hardworking Americans, seniors, students did not cause this financial crisis that we now find ourselves in," she said at a 2012 event. "The financial crisis was caused by the Wall Street bankers who carelessly gambled with our economy. It was caused by policymakers who thought we could build an economy on a foundation of financial sand. And that is why we must create another New Deal, a deal in which work is rewarded. ... This deal for all builds upon our values by asking the richest Americans to recognize that they didn't get to where they are on their own."

And she pushes for changes to immigration law in order to provide illegal immigrants paths to citizenship. She briefly gained national attention in 2010 for helping write a city council resolution to boycott businesses in the state of Arizona in response to its passage of a contentious law cracking down on illegal immigrants.

Hahn was born the same year her father joined the county board. Her mother, Ramona, was the daughter of missionaries and a lifelong member of the Church of Christ. Hahn herself is religious. She attended Pepperdine University in California and graduated from Abilene Christian University in Texas, both schools affiliated with the church. (Poe also attended Abilene.)

Hahn's aspiration in college was to teach physical education. She worked as a teacher for a time but also had stints in finance and marketing while raising three children.

She has said that her parents groomed her brother for public service while trying to keep her out of politics. The call was too strong, however. She lost a 1993 bid for the city council and was the unsuccessful Democratic nominee in a 1998 House race before winning election to the city council.

A decade later, Democratic Rep. Jane Harman resigned from the 36th District to lead the Woodrow Wilson Center, a foreign-policy think tank. Hahn, who had tried to secure the Democratic nomination for lieutenant governor in 2010, entered the House race. After a short and nasty campaign, she beat Republican Craig Huey by almost 10 points.

The campaigning didn't stop there. Redistricting for the 2012 election forced a matchup between Hahn and Democratic Rep. Laura Richardson in a contest for the redrawn 44th District. Hahn quickly raised campaign cash and locked up endorsements from labor unions and various Democratic interest groups; in an open primary, she bested Richardson by 20 points as they both advanced to the general election.

Richardson ran a lackluster campaign and was plagued by ethics investigations, one of which resulted in an August 2012 House reprimand for her use of congressional staff in campaign activities.

Several House colleagues endorsed Hahn, and she defeated Richardson by 20 points on Election Day.

Key Votes

2012	
Extend a Social Security payroll tax cut and unemployment benefits	YES
Ease securities rules to expand small-business access to capital	YES
Extend for one year subsidized student loan interest rates financed by a cut in health care spending	NO
Cite Attorney General Eric H. Holder Jr. for contempt of Congress	?
Create a visa program for foreign graduates in high-tech fields	NO
Extend most Bush-era income tax rates while allowing rates for top-bracket earners to rise (Jan. 1, 2013)	YES
2011	
Pass compromise debt limit increase plan and establish future spending limits	NO
Allow consideration of measures to implement three trade agreements	NO

CQ Vote Studies

	PARTY UNITY		PRESIDENTIAL SUPPORT	
	SUPPORT	OPPOSE	SUPPORT	OPPOSE
2012	97%	3%	84%	16%
2011	99%	1%	82%	18%

Interest Groups

	AFL-CIO	ADA	CCUS	ACU
2012	89%	95%	17%	0%
2011		25%	11%	

California 44

Southern Los Angeles County — Compton, Carson, parts of Los Angeles

The 44th runs along the industrial Alameda Corridor to San Pedro and the Port of Los Angeles, also taking in a small portion of the city of Los Angeles. The district is primarily lower- and middle-class suburbs of Los Angeles that struggle economically. Minorities make up more than 90 percent of the district and Hispanics (70 percent) account for the largest racial group here.

The Alameda Corridor runs through Compton, linking both the ports of Long Beach (in the 47th) and Los Angeles with distribution hubs in the city of Los Angeles to the north. A critical path for trade, 25 percent of all American waterborne international cargo travels this route.

Another large blue-collar employer in the region, BP, announced in early 2012 it was selling its facility in Carson to Tesoro, eliminating or transferring some 1,200 jobs. Though lacking entertainment venues, historical sites or scenic vistas common to other Los Angeles-area districts, tourism is a key economic driver here — most major cruise lines that depart from Los Angeles set sail from San Pedro. The largely commuter-based California State University, Dominguez Hills, is located in Carson.

The cities of South Gate, Compton and Lynwood all share socio-economic characteristics. They are very densely populated, with median household incomes under $45,000 and around 20 percent of their populations living below the poverty line. The district overall has a high percentage of young residents, many of whom lack a high school diploma. South Gate is 95 percent Hispanic and has a high unemployment rate. Compton has a history of gang-related violence.

In addition to its predominant Hispanic population, the 44th also has a significant percentage of black residents (15 percent). Barack Obama took 85 percent of the district's vote in the 2012 presidential election.

Major Industry

Trade, shipping, tourism, service

Cities

Los Angeles (pt.), Compton, South Gate, Carson, Long Beach

Notable

The StubHub Center's multiuse sports complex in Carson is home to soccer's Chivas USA and LA Galaxy.

Rep. John Campbell (R)

Capitol Office
225-5611
campbell.house.gov
2331 Rayburn Bldg. 20515-0548; fax 225-9177

Committees
Budget
Financial Services
(Monetary Policy & Trade - Chairman)
Joint Economic

Residence
Irvine

Born
July 19, 1955; Los Angeles, Calif.

Religion
Presbyterian

Family
Wife, Catherine Campbell; two children

Education
U. of California, Los Angeles, B.A. 1976 (economics); U. of Southern California, M.S. 1977 (business taxation)

Career
Car dealership president; accountant

Political Highlights
Calif. Assembly, 2000-04; Calif. Senate, 2004-05

ELECTION RESULTS

2012 GENERAL		
John Campbell (R)	171,417	58.5%
Sukhee Kang (D)	121,814	41.5%
2012 PRIMARY (Open)		
John Campbell (R)	54,346	51.0%
John Webb (R)	17,014	16.0%
2010 GENERAL		
John Campbell (R)	145,481	59.9%
Beth Krom (D)	88,465	36.4%
Mike Binkley (LIBERT)	8,773	3.6%

Previous Winning Percentages
2008 (56%); 2006 (60%); 2005 Special Election (44%)

Elected December 2005; 4th full term

Campbell is crisp and engaging when he outlines his conservative vision of free markets and reduced federal spending. But he can also be a provacateur among Republicans as the party formulates its legislative plans, particularly regarding the financial sector. His proposed alternatives have been met with both wonkish curiosity and occasional GOP grumbling.

You can pin down Campbell's beliefs on just about any issue by skimming the blogs on his House website. Campbell updates often, writes engagingly and mixes in a fair share of humor; he ends many posts with the salutation "drive fast and live free," a nod to his car obsession. Campbell made a fortune operating dealerships and collects classic automobiles; he seems to have geek-level enthusiasm and energy for all his professional and personal interests.

"I believe in the Austrian School of Economics and think John Maynard Keynes was messed up," he wrote in a 2011 post. "I am a devotee of Ayn Rand and don't have much time for Upton Sinclair."

With those bright lines painted, he still calls for practicality, remembering the frustrations of other businessmen-turned-politicians from his time in the California Legislature. "This is democracy," he said. "It's not supposed to work like a business. It is designed so that no one gets their own way."

Campbell road-tests that philosophy on the Financial Services Committee. Scott Garrett of New Jersey and Chairman Jeb Hensarling of Texas are leading the charge toward a conservative dream: the dissolution of Fannie Mae and Freddie Mac and the transition to a housing market free of the federal guarantees backing home loans.

Campbell—whose Orange County district has pricey real estate—protests, predicting that a withdrawal of guarantees will collapse the housing market. He and Michigan Democrat Gary Peters in the 112th Congress (2011-12) introduced a bill to replace Fannie and Freddie with several private companies to issue mortgage-backed securities; for a fee, the government would explicitly guarantee those securities. The companies would have higher capitalization requirements than Fannie and Freddie. Many in the banking industry applauded the plan, while Garrett panned it as keeping taxpayers on the hook to pay for a rescue in the event of a future market collapse.

Intraparty disagreements dissipate when it comes to the 2010 financial regulatory overhaul law. Campbell believes it did not eliminate the need for government bailouts if large companies collapse. "To go overboard on regulation and not fix the fundamental problem of the 2008 crisis ... is not good," he said. Campbell favors requirements for much bigger capital reserves when companies reach a certain size: "I understand that's going to squeeze your profitability, and if you don't like it, break yourself up."

For the 113th Congress (2013-14), Campbell chairs the subcommittee on monetary policy. At a February 2013 hearing he laid out his objections to the Federal Reserve's "quantitative easing," in which the government prints money, then uses it to buy financial assets to keep long-term interest rates down. According to Campbell, it might be creating a bubble in the bond markets, disrupting the ability of businesses to "price risk" and undermining retirement savings, among other things. In 2011 he wrote that it looks "a bit like a Ponzi scheme that will soon unravel."

Campbell, who sits on the Budget and Joint Economic committees, calls for shrinking government. The National Taxpayers Union Foundation credited him as the House member who proposed the greatest number of spending cuts ($308 billion) during the 111th Congress (2009-10), and when Republicans early in 2011 passed their version of a catchall spending bill with substantial reductions, Campbell was one of three in his party to oppose it—it did not go far enough, he said. He rejects as "intellectually dishonest" the idea that defense spending should not be reduced.

He's not a reflexive hatchet man, though. While chairing the Republican Study Committee's budget task force in 2008, Campbell backed the George W. Bush administration's $700 billion proposal to shore up the ailing financial services industry. In 2012, he helped round up GOP support for a multi-year reauthorization of the Export-Import Bank, which conservatives targeted as a boondoggle.

Campbell also offers creative ideas for financing traditional federal duties. Diving into his "tax geekiness," he has proposed "master limited partnerships" for infrastructure, whereby private entities build things such as roads, get accelerated depreciation or other favorable tax treatment, then hand over the infrastructure to the public once the project is paid off by tolls or other fees.

One of three children, Campbell grew up in the Hancock Park area of Los Angeles in a very conservative household. "My mother told me many times, we were Taft Republicans," he said. "Eisenhower was too liberal for them." The family's GOP ties go back many years. His great-grandfather Alexander was elected to the California Assembly in 1860 on the same GOP ticket as Abraham Lincoln. (Campbell used to participate in Civil War re-enactments.)

Writing is another "family trait," Campbell says. His grandfather edited the Los Angeles Herald Examiner for William Randolph Hearst, and his father for a time was the paper's financial editor. Campbell's middle name is Bayard Taylor, after the 19th-century poet and journalist.

Campbell's father was heavily involved in the California GOP until 1966, when he lost a state Senate race. Campbell remembers stuffing envelopes for Barry Goldwater in 1964 and volunteered in every election up to the 1980s, when he stayed involved as a campaign donor.

After earning degrees in economics and business taxation, Campbell in 1978 moved to Orange County to be a corporate comptroller for car dealerships. He spent almost 25 years in the industry as an executive and an owner of franchises that sold Nissan, Mazda, Ford, Saturn, Porsche and Saab models.

In 2000, he was recruited to run for the Assembly and won. He moved to the state Senate in 2004. The retirement of Republican Rep. Christopher Cox to become chairman of the Securities and Exchange Commission opened a path to Washington. Campbell easily bested a diverse field of candidates to win the 2005 special election.

Democrat Sukhee Kang, the mayor of Irvine, challenged Campbell in 2012, but the new boundaries of the 45th District where the race was contested are very Republican. Campbell won by 17 points.

Key Votes

2012	
Extend a Social Security payroll tax cut and unemployment benefits	?
Ease securities rules to expand small-business access to capital	YES
Extend for one year subsidized student loan interest rates financed by a cut in health care spending	YES
Cite Attorney General Eric H. Holder Jr. for contempt of Congress	YES
Create a visa program for foreign graduates in high-tech fields	NO
Extend most Bush-era income tax rates while allowing rates for top-bracket earners to rise (Jan. 1, 2013)	NO
2011	
Strike funding for F-35 alternative engine	YES
Prevent EPA from regulating greenhouse gas emissions to address climate change	YES
Extend certain provisions of Patriot Act for four years	NO
Declare opposition to use of ground troops in Libya	NO
Overhaul patent law	YES
Pass compromise debt limit increase plan and establish future spending limits	YES
Allow consideration of measures to implement three trade agreements	YES

CQ Vote Studies

	PARTY UNITY		PRESIDENTIAL SUPPORT	
	SUPPORT	OPPOSE	SUPPORT	OPPOSE
2012	92%	8%	39%	61%
2011	93%	7%	15%	85%
2010	95%	5%	18%	82%
2009	97%	3%	14%	86%
2008	97%	3%	89%	11%

Interest Groups

	AFL-CIO	ADA	CCUS	ACU
2012	5%	25%	82%	96%
2011	8%	15%	94%	91%
2010	0%	10%	83%	95%
2009	15%	10%	86%	92%
2008	0%	5%	76%	86%

California 45

Central Orange County — Irvine, most of Mission Viejo

An inland chunk of Orange County, the 45th District grabs planned suburbs filled with wealthy, well-educated white-collar workers and the wilderness of the Santa Ana Mountains. Some very affluent enclaves to the south include Laguna Hills and Laguna Woods.

Sprawling Irvine accounts for about 30 percent of the district's population and a significant portion of its geography. It is sliced by congested traffic routes — Interstates 5 and 405, as well as several state routes — and occupies a central location in Southern California's landscape.

The sheer number of people who commute into the 45th from the north and east makes transportation among the toughest problems here, as traffic backs up and increases the threat of pollution. Toll roads in the area have helped, and regional mass transit and bus systems have expanded.

Smog, crime and other problems endemic to Los Angeles generally do not affect these areas: Irvine consistently rates as the nation's safest city with more than 100,000 people, based on the FBI's crime reporting statistics.

Irvine's University of California campus, whose student body is mainly commuter-based, is the largest employer in the district and is well-known for its scientific and engineering research. The district also hosts engineering, telecommunications, health care and pharmaceutical companies, including Edwards Lifesciences, the developer of the world's first heart valve replacement.

The majority-white district has sizable Asian (21 percent) and Hispanic (19 percent) populations, and voters here are conservative. The GOP has a nearly 20-point lead in voter registration, and Republican candidate Mitt Romney took 55 percent of the district's vote in the 2012 presidential election. Lake Forest is home to the mega-church Saddleback Community Church, one of the largest congregations in the nation.

Major Industry
Higher education, technology, health care

Cities
Irvine, Mission Viejo (pt.), Lake Forest, Tustin, Orange (pt.)

Notable
The Ayn Rand Institute is located in Irvine.

Rep. Loretta Sanchez (D)

Capitol Office
225-2965
lorettasanchez.house.gov
1114 Longworth Bldg. 20515-0547; fax 225-5859

Committees
Armed Services
Homeland Security
Joint Economic

Residence
Santa Ana

Born
Jan. 7, 1960; Lynwood, Calif.

Religion
Roman Catholic

Family
Husband, Jack Einwechter

Education
Chapman College, B.S. 1982 (economics); American U., M.B.A. 1984 (finance)

Career
Financial adviser; strategic management associate

Political Highlights
Candidate for Anaheim City Council, 1994

ELECTION RESULTS

2012 GENERAL		
Loretta Sanchez (D)	95,694	63.9%
Jerry Hayden (R)	54,121	36.1%
2012 PRIMARY (Open)		
Loretta Sanchez (D)	25,706	52.1%
2010 GENERAL		
Loretta Sanchez (D)	50,832	53.0%
Van Tran (R)	37,679	39.3%
Cecilia "Ceci" Iglesias (I)	7,443	7.8%

Previous Winning Percentages
2008 (69%); 2006 (62%); 2004 (60%); 2002 (61%); 2000 (60%); 1998 (56%); 1996 (47%)

Elected 1996; 9th term

Sanchez is one of the most prominent national security Democrats in the House. Gregarious and opinionated, she isn't reluctant to lay out her thoughts on topics under that umbrella — or most other issues.

The second of seven children, Sanchez says she grew up a "shy, quiet girl" who did not speak English. (A younger sister, Linda T. Sánchez — who uses the accent — represents California's 38th District.) Her Mexican immigrant parents worked at a manufacturing plant, where her father was a machinist and her mother was a secretary.

She seems to have gotten over her shyness. Sanchez's ascent over the past decade and a half was facilitated by her prodigious fundraising abilities and a close relationship with Minority Leader Nancy Pelosi of California. Sanchez is a regular guest on news shows and a frequent speaker on the House floor.

And she can be outgoing in quirky ways — many political observers await her annual Christmas card, which for years featured Sanchez in poses with her cat, Gretzky. After the death of Gretzky in 2010, Sanchez's husband started appearing; in a nod to fiscal debates, the 2012 edition showed them dancing near the edge of a cliff.

Sanchez is the No. 2 Democrat on both the Armed Services and Homeland Security committees. But as a member of the minority party, she has limits on her reach.

In the 112th Congress (2011-12) she was the ranking member of the Armed Services Strategic Forces Subcommittee. Sanchez resisted with little success House GOP initiatives to increase spending on nuclear weapons infrastructure and missile defense — particularly a proposal favored by Chairman Michael R. Turner of Ohio to build a missile defense site on the East Coast. Sanchez opposes investing in new missile defense sites on U.S. soil until it is clear that sites in California and Alaska are effective. "If I'm living in L.A., I'm not feeling too comfortable" with their current success rate in tests, she said.

Sanchez in the 113th Congress (2013-14) became the ranking member of the Tactical Air and Land Forces Subcommittee, which oversees the purchase, research and development of jet fighters, tanks and a host of other weapons. The switch kept her paired up with Turner, who is that subcommittee's new chairman.

She continues to pursue women's issues relating to the military. In 2011 she created the Congressional Caucus on Women in the Military to elevate awareness of the roles women play in the modern military, while also highlighting the danger of sexual assault in the service; she calls for victims to have access to legal and counseling services. The fiscal 2013 defense policy law includes provisions, also pushed by California Democrat Jackie Speier, to require further study of the problem.

In a non-military context, Sanchez in 2013 again introduced a bill — working with North Carolina Republican Virginia Foxx — to update federal stalking laws to account for the use of the Internet and other technologies.

Sanchez thinks about cybersecurity quite a bit. Her seat on Armed Services lets her tackle it from the defense and intelligence realm, and as the chairwoman of the Terrorism, Unconventional Threats and Capabilities Subcommittee in the 111th Congress (2009-10) she served as an unofficial coordinator for Democrats' cybersecurity discussions. Her seat on the Homeland Security Committee comes with jurisdiction over cybersecurity for the rest of government and the private sector. "I don't know that there is another member that has the vantage point that I have," she said.

Sanchez calls for a significant expansion of cybersecurity personnel and resources at the Homeland Security Department; she wants more direct federal research into cybersecurity and a mandate to quickly share breakthroughs with the private sector.

The homeland panel also takes her into the realm of border security and immigration law, and Sanchez considers herself a spokeswoman for America's growing Latino population. She believes the United States should offer a path to citizenship for illegal immigrants who have otherwise abided by the law. Sanchez in 2012 teamed with New York Republican Michael G. Grimm to introduce a bill to make targeted visa program changes in the high-skilled sector, so that students and entrepreneurial immigrants would have an easier time staying in America and starting new companies.

She belongs to both the New Democrat Coalition, a business-friendly caucus, and the fiscally conservative Blue Dog Coalition. She doesn't belong to the Congressional Hispanic Caucus. Sanchez had a public dispute in 2007 with California Democrat Joe Baca, the CHC chairman at the time, charging that Baca had demeaned women, abused the group's political action committee and held improper elections. Baca denied the accusations, but Sanchez and her sister quit. Linda returned two years later, but Loretta never did.

Sanchez credits government with her success. "I am a Head Start child, a public school kid, a Pell grant recipient," she said. She opposed the GOP's unsuccessful effort, in the 108th Congress (2003-04), to restructure Head Start, an early-childhood development program for low-income preschoolers. She invoked her own experience growing up poor with a speech impediment.

She worked her way through college and earned a master's degree in business administration. Sanchez worked as a finance adviser but felt isolated as a Hispanic woman in the financial world. Her first foray into politics was in 1994, when she lost a race for an Anaheim City Council seat.

In 1996, she took on conservative GOP Rep. Robert K. Dornan. After winning a four-way primary with 35 percent of the vote, she drew attention from liberal groups. Voter turnout linked to a backlash against a ballot initiative to end state affirmative action programs helped Sanchez score a 984-vote upset. Pelosi, already on her way up in the House, backed Sanchez's campaign.

In a 1998 rematch, Sanchez defeated Dornan by 17 points. Her subsequent re-elections were by larger margins until 2010. That year, matched up against Republican Van Tran in a district with a large Vietnamese community, Sanchez caused a stir in September when she said in a Spanish-language interview that "the Vietnamese" were trying to take her seat.

Sanchez has been a vocal advocate for human rights in Vietnam over her House career, but that controversy and a strong Republican year squeezed her margin of victory to less than 14 points.

Key Votes

2012	
Extend a Social Security payroll tax cut and unemployment benefits	YES
Ease securities rules to expand small-business access to capital	YES
Extend for one year subsidized student loan interest rates financed by a cut in health care spending	NO
Cite Attorney General Eric H. Holder Jr. for contempt of Congress	NO
Create a visa program for foreign graduates in high-tech fields	NO
Extend most Bush-era income tax rates while allowing rates for top-bracket earners to rise (Jan. 1, 2013)	YES
2011	
Strike funding for F-35 alternative engine	NO
Prevent EPA from regulating greenhouse gas emissions to address climate change	NO
Extend certain provisions of Patriot Act for four years	?
Declare opposition to use of ground troops in Libya	NO
Overhaul patent law	NO
Pass compromise debt limit increase plan and establish future spending limits	YES
Allow consideration of measures to implement three trade agreements	NO

CQ Vote Studies

	PARTY UNITY		PRESIDENTIAL SUPPORT	
	SUPPORT	OPPOSE	SUPPORT	OPPOSE
2012	96%	4%	85%	15%
2011	94%	6%	76%	24%
2010	99%	1%	86%	14%
2009	97%	3%	94%	6%
2008	96%	4%	9%	91%

Interest Groups

	AFL-CIO	ADA	CCUS	ACU
2012	89%	90%	27%	0%
2011	96%	80%	36%	4%
2010	100%	95%	0%	0%
2009	100%	90%	36%	0%
2008	93%	80%	41%	8%

California 46

West central Orange County — most of Santa Ana and Anaheim

Centered on Anaheim and entirely within Orange County, the 46th is a mainly suburban district bisected by one of the state's main north-south thoroughfares, Interstate 5. Unlike most of the rest of the county — which is affluent, white and Republican — the 46th is Hispanic-majority with a strong Democratic base. Residents here tend to have lower levels of English proficiency, education and income than much of the rest of Orange County.

Anaheim is the most populous city in Orange County, and more than 80 percent of its residents live in the 46th. The largest employer in the district is family vacation mecca Disneyland. On what was once a rural enclave on the outskirts of Los Angeles, Anaheim's Disney campus is Orange County's economic mainstay, adding billions of dollars annually to the local economy. Corporate, commercial and residential development in the southern part of the city has boosted activity near the homes of hockey's Ducks and baseball's Angels.

But apart from Disneyland, no single employer dominates the economy. Small businesses are scattered throughout the district, and in Santa Ana, the Orange County seat, local government and support industries provide jobs. In the private sector, Fortune 100 technology distributor Ingram Micro has its headquarters here. Santa Ana's blue-collar workforce is more vulnerable to job cuts than other areas of the county. The district's portion of the city of Orange includes the University of California, Irvine, medical campus (the main campus is 15 miles away in the 45th) at a major freeway junction.

Santa Ana is one of only a few Orange County cities that trends Democratic, and the 46th also takes in some Democratic areas of Anaheim. Rep. Loretta Sanchez was the only Democratic candidate for a U.S. House seat to have won his or her portion of Orange County in 2012.

Major Industry
Tourism, government

Cities
Santa Ana (pt.), Anaheim (pt.), Orange (pt.)

Notable
The musical instrument manufacturer Rickenbacker is based in Santa Ana and produced the first modern electric guitars.

Rep. Alan Lowenthal (D)

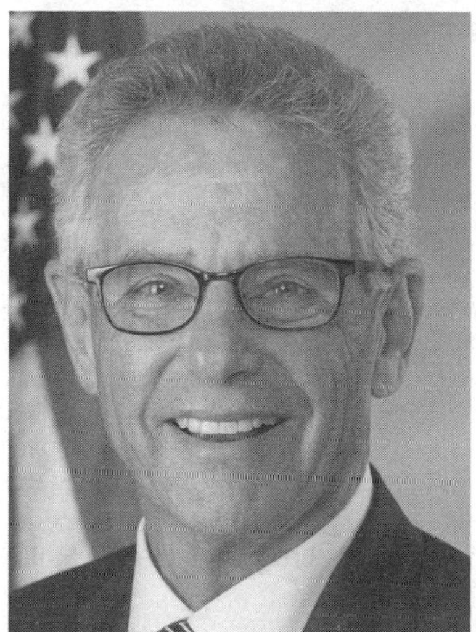

Capitol Office
225-7924
lowenthal.house.gov
515 Cannon Bldg. 20515-1390; fax 225-7926

Committees
Foreign Affairs
Natural Resources

Residence
Long Beach

Born
March 8, 1941; Manhattan, N.Y.

Religion
Jewish

Family
Wife, Deborah Malumed; two children

Education
Hobart College, B.A. 1962 (psychology); Ohio State U., M.A. 1965 (psychology), Ph.D. 1967 (psychology)

Career
Professor; psychologist

Political Highlights
Long Beach City Council, 1992-98; Calif. Assembly, 1998-2004; Calif. Senate, 2004-12

ELECTION RESULTS

2012 GENERAL		
Alan Lowenthal (D)	130,093	56.6%
Gary DeLong (R)	99,919	43.4%
2012 PRIMARY (Open)		
Alan Lowenthal (D)	27,356	33.8%
Peter Mathews (D)	7,951	9.8%
Usha Shah (D)	2,350	2.9%
Jay Shah (D)	2,273	2.8%

Elected 2012; 1st term

Liberal activism drives Lowenthal's politics. He's a student (and teacher) of community psychology, which "tries to look at the person in relationship to their environment and prevent problems," he told the Long Beach Post.

Lowenthal, the oldest member of the freshman class, grew up in and around New York City. After a getting a Ph.D. in psychology, he was an intern in San Francisco in the late 1960s—he was enthralled by the political consciousness of that time and place. He started teaching psychology in Long Beach in 1969.

He agitated for years on behalf of environmental and community causes. Six years on the Long Beach City Council were followed by six in the state Assembly and eight in the state Senate. In a Press-Telegram story from 2006, he was described as "extremely progressive on social issues, but always in favor of localized control."

Lowenthal looks after the ports in Los Angeles and Long Beach, and he is eager to refocus the national job-creation debate by highlighting the need to transport goods through the nation's urban areas using the latest technologies. Lowenthal speaks passionately about "green-collar jobs" and touts his efforts to improve environmental conditions at the port complexes.

He works on energy and environmental policy from the Natural Resources Committee, and he can try to shape trade policy (which affects ports) from his seat on the Foreign Affairs Committee. Lowenthal also supports strong government investments in education, calling it "the best job developer."

Lowenthal had a hand in creating the electoral madness in California in 2012. As a state senator, he was an early proponent of creating an independent redistricting commission. Such a panel redrew California's congressional map after the 2010 census, creating the 47th District where he ran.

The "open" primary featured four Republicans and four Democrats, but Lowenthal had the most star power of any candidate. He finished first, then beat Long Beach GOP Councilman Gary DeLong by 13 points in November.

California 47

Most of Long Beach; part of northeastern Orange County

Most of the residents in the 47th live in Los Angeles County inland of the high-traffic Port of Long Beach. The city itself is split with the 44th District (which also is home to the adjacent Port of Los Angeles), but the 47th includes the stretch of Long Beach Harbor from the port south to the Alamitos Bay marina at the Orange County line. In Orange County, the district grabs only inland cities, such as Cypress, Stanton and Los Alamitos.

Revenue losses at the port following global financial downturns were mitigated by a 2012 deal to bring more container-ship and cargo jobs, and Long Beach is expected to surpass the Port of Los Angeles in volume of traffic in a decade. The port directly employs 30,000 people in the city of Long Beach, and is responsible for tens of thousands more in Southern California overall. Labor disputes are not uncommon and can rattle the economy. Pollution and other environmental concerns remain issues for the industrial area; most of Long Beach is middle-class, suburban and a mix of ethnicities and languages.

A once-dominant aerospace industry has diminished, but Boeing still has a manufacturing plant in the district and Air Industries in Garden Grove is a small-parts aerospace manufacturer. Other economic drivers in the district include Los Alamitos' California National Guard-operated Joint Forces Training Base.

Westminster's Little Saigon is in the 48th, but many other Vietnamese retail shops and residential areas fall in the 47th. Areas near Washington and Wilmore have heavy concentrations of Hispanic residents. And with nearly equal proportions of white and Hispanic residents overall, the district is one of the more diverse in the state. Although the Orange County portions of the district support conservative candidates, the larger population in more blue-collar Los Angeles County puts the district in Democratic hands.

Major Industry
Shipping, trade, service

Cities
Long Beach (pt.), Garden Grove (pt.), Westminster (pt.), Cypress

Notable
The district includes two channel islands: Santa Catalina and San Clemente.

Rep. Dana Rohrabacher (R)

Capitol Office
225-2415
rohrabacher.house.gov
2300 Rayburn Bldg. 20515-0546; fax 225-0145

Committees
Foreign Affairs
(Europe, Eurasia & Emerging Threats - Chairman)
Science, Space & Technology

Residence
Costa Mesa

Born
June 21, 1947; Coronado, Calif.

Religion
Christian

Family
Wife, Rhonda Rohrabacher; three children

Education
Los Angeles Harbor College, attended 1965-67; California State U., Long Beach, B.A. 1969 (history); U. of Southern California, M.A. 1971 (American studies)

Career
White House speechwriter; newspaper reporter

Political Highlights
No previous office

ELECTION RESULTS

2012 GENERAL		
Dana Rohrabacher (R)	177,144	61.0%
Ron Varasteh (D)	113,358	39.0%
2012 PRIMARY (Open)		
Dana Rohrabacher (R)	73,302	66.3%
2010 GENERAL		
Dana Rohrabacher (R)	139,822	62.2%
Ken Arnold (D)	84,940	37.8%

Previous Winning Percentages
2008 (53%); 2006 (60%); 2004 (62%); 2002 (62%); 2000 (62%); 1998 (59%); 1996 (61%); 1994 (69%); 1992 (55%); 1990 (59%); 1988 (64%)

Elected 1988; 13th term

Rohrabacher says he's "somewhere between a libertarian conservative and a conservative libertarian. ... I always think of myself just as a patriot for the people and the United States and liberty and justice." His governing philosophy is embodied in a motto that hangs on his wall and decorates coffee cups: "Fighting for Freedom ... and Having Fun."

Rohrabacher (ROAR-ah-BAH-ker) credits his father — who grew up "dirt poor" in North Dakota and then flew spy missions for the Marines during the Cold War — with helping shape his politics. "My dad was very opinionated," someone who "didn't put up with nonsense," he said. That mentality co-exists with another side of Rohrabacher: the Southern California surfer who supports things like medical marijuana.

It makes for an interesting blend. Rohrabacher spars with Democrats, but he also splits with Republicans on some key issues. In the 113th Congress (2013-14), he's indulging both habits as chairman of the Foreign Affairs Subcommittee on Europe, Eurasia and Emerging Threats.

Rohrabacher butts heads with his own party over the war in Afghanistan. He was an early voice calling for troop withdrawals. He opposed the surge of troops that President Barack Obama announced in 2010 and was one of seven GOP co-sponsors of a bill to require a Pentagon report outlining the U.S. exit strategy from Afghanistan.

"I think once you've decided to withdraw and once you have eliminated Osama bin Laden and driven the Taliban out of the country, it's time to come home ASAP," he said in 2012. "I think we have overstayed our stay."

Rohrabacher's ties to Afghanistan run deep. In 1988, after he was first elected to Congress but before he took his seat, he traveled with a mujahedeen unit fighting the Soviet army. He has an ongoing relationship with some Afghan warlords and minority group leaders who are political rivals of President Hamid Karzai, and his trenchant criticism of Karzai caused a minor diplomatic row in 2012. The State Department asked Rohrabacher to abandon a trip to Afghanistan with other Republican colleagues after Karzai threatened to block his entry.

He is good at causing a stir overseas. In February 2012, Rohrabacher introduced a resolution stating that the Baloch people, currently split between Iran, Pakistan and Afghanistan, have a right to self-determination. As chairman of the Subcommittee on Oversight and Investigations, he held a hearing on Pakistan's Balochistan province. The agitation led to Pakistani rioting and condemnations from Islamabad.

He has courted controversy by backing an Iranian exile group known as the Mujahedeen-e-Kalq, which was removed from the State Department's list of terrorist organizations in 2012. Experts consider the group, regarded as a fringe movement within Iran, as cult-like, though no longer violent. Rohrabacher met with its leader in February 2013 and said the United States should be encouraging the MEK to become an alternative to Iran's current government.

Rohrabacher frames these incidents as occupational hazards that come with fighting for human rights. "I have a history of helping people and supporting people who are struggling for freedom," he said.

And he says his constituents understand and appreciate that focus. "When I was elected, people elected me for my work in the Reagan White House," where he served as a speech writer. "I was not elected as a hometown boy. They elected me as a champion of American values."

Rohrabacher's style has hampered his ability to climb the political ladder. He made a bid to chair the Science, Space and Technology Committee in the

113th, but lost to Lamar Smith of Texas. Ed Royce of California has less seniority than Rohrabacher on Foreign Affairs, but nonetheless leapfrogged him to take the gavel of that committee.

He was named vice chairman of the Science committee, however. Rohrabacher wants Congress take a more aggressive approach to science and technology, complaining that the Science committee has "been a backwater for many years." He pushes legislation to promote the commercial space industry and collaboration between the public and private sectors on space exploration (Boeing Co.'s space division is one of his district's largest employers).

As chairman of the subcommittee on space and aeronautics from 1997 to 2005, he introduced several bills to foster private space flight, including one to offer a prize of up to $100 million for the first private spacecraft to make three orbits of the Earth.

That one went nowhere, but he did push through a law supporting the development of commercial space projects and allowing the Federal Aviation Administration to regulate private spacecraft. "We can be the leading power in space even though we have declining budgets," he said.

Rohrabacher supports aggressive steps to combat illegal immigration, but on other social and civil liberties issues he has found himself allied with liberals. He voted in 2006 to override a veto of a bill expanding federal funding of embryonic stem cell research. In 2011 he and 30 other House Republicans opposed an extension of surveillance provisions in the anti-terrorism law known as the Patriot Act.

Rohrabacher is an avid surfer and scuba diver. Among his friends are writers, artists and musicians, including heavy metal vocalist Sammy Hagar and folk singer Joan Baez. During his younger days, he was a hard-drinking, banjo-playing wanderer who worked as a house painter. He says actor John Wayne showed him how to drink tequila — in a small glass with one ice cube and a squeeze of lime. The father of triplets born in 2004, he says he now drinks less tequila than he used to.

He was a reporter for City News Service and an editorial writer for the Orange County Register. Before his gig at the White House, he was an assistant press secretary for Ronald Reagan's 1976 and 1980 presidential campaigns.

His 1988 campaign was his first bid for elective office. He ran for the House seat being vacated by Republican Rep. Dan Lungren, who later returned to Congress, and beat out GOP competitors who had name recognition and Lungren's support. Rohrabacher had fairly easy re-elections until 2008, when Huntington Beach Democratic Mayor Debbie Cook held him to less than 53 percent of the vote.

He won 61 percent of the vote in the newly drawn 48th district in 2012.

Key Votes

2012	
Extend a Social Security payroll tax cut and unemployment benefits	NO
Ease securities rules to expand small-business access to capital	YES
Extend for one year subsidized student loan interest rates financed by a cut in health care spending	YES
Cite Attorney General Eric H. Holder Jr. for contempt of Congress	YES
Create a visa program for foreign graduates in high-tech fields	YES
Extend most Bush-era income tax rates while allowing rates for top-bracket earners to rise (Jan. 1, 2013)	NO
2011	
Strike funding for F-35 alternative engine	YES
Prevent EPA from regulating greenhouse gas emissions to address climate change	YES
Extend certain provisions of Patriot Act for four years	NO
Declare opposition to use of ground troops in Libya	YES
Overhaul patent law	NO
Pass compromise debt limit increase plan and establish future spending limits	YES
Allow consideration of measures to implement three trade agreements	YES

CQ Vote Studies

	PARTY UNITY		PRESIDENTIAL SUPPORT	
	SUPPORT	OPPOSE	SUPPORT	OPPOSE
2012	95%	5%	21%	79%
2011	93%	7%	11%	89%
2010	97%	3%	24%	76%
2009	91%	9%	23%	77%
2008	95%	5%	74%	26%

Interest Groups

	AFL-CIO	ADA	CCUS	ACU
2012	14%	20%	83%	96%
2011	7%	20%	88%	88%
2011	7%	20%	88%	88%
2010	7%	5%	88%	96%
2009	10%	5%	73%	100%

California 48

Coastal Orange County — Huntington Beach, Costa Mesa

The 48th District hugs the Orange County coast from Seal Beach to Laguna Niguel, taking in beautiful beaches and expensive homes. Aerospace workers, surfers and wealthy families mix in the largely affluent district, which is also is roughly 60 percent white.

Newport Beach regularly ranks as one of the wealthiest cities in America. The median income is more than $100,000 and the average home price is $1 million. While other areas of the district do not reach those levels, local wealth supports high-end retail shopping.

The district has not been immune to housing slumps, and some areas of the district await full recovery from the national market decline. White-collar workers who live and work in the district have watched the aerospace industry slim down as Boeing has cut jobs. Hyundai announced in early 2012 that it would build its new U.S. headquarters in Fountain Valley, a bedroom community experiencing a boost of local construction projects.

Beaches are crucial to the district's stability, from tourism to housing prices. Smaller beaches, such as Laguna Beach to the south, may struggle with the effects of erosion and environmental changes, while Huntington Beach and Newport Beach attract more visitors.

During decennial remapping after the 2010 census, the 48th dropped farther along the coast while losing land inland. The area's growing Hispanic population accounts for 20 percent of this solidly GOP district — nearly 45 percent of registered voters are Republican, and Democrats are at 28 percent. Little Saigon, considered to be the largest concentration of Vietnamese people outside of Vietnam, is in the 48th and adds to its diversity.

Major Industry
Aerospace, technology

Military Bases
Naval Weapons Station Seal Beach, 150 military, 650 civilian

Cities
Huntington Beach, Costa Mesa, Newport Beach, Laguna Niguel

Notable
Huntington Beach is home to the International Surfing Museum.

Rep. Darrell Issa (R)

Capitol Office
225-3906
issa.house.gov
2437 Rayburn Bldg. 20515-0549; fax 225-3303

Committees
Judiciary
Oversight & Government Reform - Chairman

Residence
Vista

Born
Nov. 1, 1953; Cleveland, Ohio

Religion
Antioch Orthodox Christian Church

Family
Wife, Kathy Issa; one child

Education
Kent State U., A.A. 1976 (general studies); Siena Heights College, B.A. 1976 (business administration and management)

Military
Army, 1970-72; Army, 1976-80; Army Reserve, 1980-88

Career
Car alarm company owner; electronics manufacturing company executive

Political Highlights
Sought Republican nomination for U.S. Senate, 1998

ELECTION RESULTS

2012 GENERAL		
Darrell Issa (R)	159,725	58.2%
Jerry Tetalman (D)	114,893	41.8%
2012 PRIMARY (Open)		
Darrell Issa (D)	71,329	61.1%
Jerry Tetalman (D)	35,816	30.7%
2010 GENERAL		
Darrell Issa (R)	119,088	62.8%
Howard Katz (D)	59,714	31.5%
Dion Clark (AMI)	6,585	3.5%
Mike Paster (LIBERT)	4,290	2.3%

Previous Winning Percentages
2008 (58%); 2006 (63%); 2004 (63%); 2002 (77%); 2000 (61%)

Elected 2000; 7th term

Showcasing a bold personality and armed with subpoena power, Issa embraces the theatrical side of politics as chairman of the Oversight and Government Reform Committee. Along with high-profile investigations, he takes a hands-on approach to his panel's less glamorous jurisdictions.

Critics have called him ambitious to the point of arrogance, but few question that Issa (EYE-sah) worked hard to win the Oversight job. He leapfrogged more-senior members by throwing himself into his work and mastering mundane subjects such as government procurement. Issa became the top Republican in 2009 and replaced much of the panel's GOP staff with seasoned investigators; he became chairman when his party regained the House majority in 2011. Barring a waiver of his party's term limits on committee leaders, the 113th Congress (2013-14) will be his last atop the panel.

Several Issa investigations of the executive branch have met the meticulous, thorn-in-the-side standard that Democrats were expecting when he took over.

He conducted an extensive probe of Operation Fast and Furious, a botched gun-tracking operation in which Justice Department officials allowed weapons to be sold into Mexico, where they might have been used by drug cartels in attacks on federal agents and others.

Attorney General Eric H. Holder Jr. claimed to be unaware of the operation's controversial tactics; Issa eventually acknowledged that no definitive evidence of his prior knowledge had been uncovered. But he conducted a slew of hearings — Democrats called it overkill — and panel Republicans made scores of television appearances to discuss the case and call for Holder's resignation.

President Barack Obama invoked executive privilege to allow Holder to withhold some documents subpoenaed by the committee. Issa retaliated by introducing a resolution to find Holder in criminal contempt of Congress. His panel adopted it along party lines, and the full House adopted it in June 2012 with the backing of 17 Democrats. An adopted civil contempt resolution allowed further legal action to obtain more documents.

Issa produced more fodder for Republicans to use on the campaign trail with a protracted look at the bankruptcy of Solyndra Inc., a solar panel manufacturer that had received a $529 million loan guarantee from the Energy Department. The case was used to deride "clean energy" policies of the Obama administration.

Other Issa-led investigations developed along less partisan lines. In the 112th Congress (2011-12) he issued reports on a three-year investigation of a VIP loan program at Countrywide Financial, which allegedly gave lawmakers and staff deals on mortgages and rental agreements. Issa forwarded to the Ethics Committee the names of four House members, three of them Republicans, believed to have received preferential treatment. No action was taken by the Ethics Committee.

Beyond investigations, Issa used the Oversight panel to promote Republicans' attempts to scale down federal regulations. And when federal spending is in the spotlight, Issa often looks at the government workforce. Issa has called federal salaries and pension plans "overly generous," and he put forward a plan to make federal workers pay an additional $82 billion in pension contributions over 10 years. He has also suggested extending an existing federal pay freeze, started in 2011, through 2015.

The Postal Service has a huge chunk of federal workers, and Issa led House Republicans in preparing a contentious overhaul of the cash-strapped agency. Issa introduced tough-love legislation to establish an independent commission to shutter postal facilities and create a new body to seize control if the

Postal Service defaults on its financial obligations for an extended period of time — which happened for the first time in August 2012. Substantial distance between Issa's bill and a Senate version pushed the debate to the 113th.

Like his investigations, Issa's legislative efforts also find occasional bipartisan support. In 2011 he surprised District of Columbia Del. Eleanor Holmes Norton by collaborating on an effort to give the District autonomy over its own budget. Work stalled over Republican attempts to add controversial policy provisions, such as restrictions on funding of abortion providers, but Norton praised Issa's outreach. He increased his involvement with the city by adding District affairs to the jurisdiction of the full committee in 2013.

Issa's personal story is distinctive. A Lebanese-American, he was born in Cleveland, where his father was a salesman and an X-ray technician. Issa quit high school at 17 and joined the Army. After he served for two years, the Army paid for his college education, requiring him to return to duty upon graduation.

In 1972, he and his older brother, William, were arrested for allegedly stealing a Maserati from a car dealership. The charges were dropped. In 1980, the two were charged with faking the theft of Issa's Mercedes-Benz; again, the charges were dropped. In both cases, Issa blamed his brother.

After fulfilling his Army obligation, Issa returned to Cleveland and used his $7,000 in savings to purchase assets from a struggling electronics business. He and his wife turned those into a highly profitable operation that gained renown as the maker of the popular Viper automobile anti-theft device.

In 1985, they moved the business to Vista. Before selling the company in 2000, Issa was chairman of the board of the Consumer Electronics Association for two years; he sits on the Judiciary Committee, and in the 110th Congress (2007-08) he worked on an ill-fated bid to revamp the country's patent approval process to protect high-tech companies from infringement litigation. Issa backed a patent overhaul enacted in 2011.

He is easily one of the richest members of Congress, and he has at times thrown his money around for political purposes. In 1998, Issa spent $11 million on a failed bid for the GOP Senate nomination. He hit the campaign trail again in 2000, when Republican Ron Packard announced his retirement from the reliably Republican 48th District. Weathering a packed primary and sinking $2 million into the race, he won the general election with 61 percent of the vote.

In 2003, Issa bankrolled the recall effort that ousted California Democratic Gov. Gray Davis and led to Republican Arnold Schwarzenegger's election. Although Issa wanted to replace Davis himself, several GOP House colleagues persuaded him to step aside for Schwarzenegger.

Changes to his district's borders before the 2012 election didn't affect his political fortunes. Issa won 58 percent of the vote.

Key Votes

2012	
Extend a Social Security payroll tax cut and unemployment benefits	YES
Ease securities rules to expand small-business access to capital	YES
Extend for one year subsidized student loan interest rates financed by a cut in health care spending	YES
Cite Attorney General Eric H. Holder Jr. for contempt of Congress	YES
Create a visa program for foreign graduates in high-tech fields	YES
Extend most Bush-era income tax rates while allowing rates for top-bracket earners to rise (Jan. 1, 2013)	NO
2011	
Strike funding for F-35 alternative engine	NO
Prevent EPA from regulating greenhouse gas emissions to address climate change	YES
Extend certain provisions of Patriot Act for four years	YES
Declare opposition to use of ground troops in Libya	YES
Overhaul patent law	YES
Pass compromise debt limit increase plan and establish future spending limits	YES
Allow consideration of measures to implement three trade agreements	YES

CQ Vote Studies

	PARTY UNITY		PRESIDENTIAL SUPPORT	
	SUPPORT	OPPOSE	SUPPORT	OPPOSE
2012	98%	2%	15%	85%
2011	97%	3%	23%	77%
2010	95%	5%	29%	71%
2009	98%	2%	19%	81%
2008	99%	1%	79%	21%

Interest Groups

	AFL-CIO	ADA	CCUS	ACU
2012	10%	0%	100%	92%
2011	0%	5%	100%	84%
2010	0%	0%	88%	100%
2009	14%	5%	73%	100%
2008	7%	10%	94%	100%

California 49

Coastal San Diego and southern Orange counties

The 49th District tracks Interstate 5 along the Pacific Coast from southern Orange County to the Torrey Pines Golf Course and the University of California, San Diego, at the very northern tip of that city. Before decennial remapping following the 2010 census, the district stretched miles inland and included beachfront only from San Clemente to Oceanside. The newly drawn 49th is shore-based and extends past Dana Point in the north and through Del Mar in the south. It hosts the massive Camp Pendleton Marine Corps Base as well as several affluent San Diego bedroom communities.

The largest single employer in the district is Camp Pendleton. The Marine Corps base, which is powered in part by a large solar energy field, sits on the largest undeveloped portion of coast in Southern California. But the 49th depends less on government contracts than its San Diego or Orange County neighbors. A new hospital on base, funded in large part by the 2009 economic stimulus law, is scheduled to open by 2014.

In addition to the military, the district also has a strong manufacturing sector, including biotechnology and communications. And tourism plays a key role, especially for Oceanside. Health care networks provide more jobs, and Carlsbad is home to the international weight-loss program Jenny Craig.

The 49th is mostly white, although there are sizable Hispanic populations and illegal immigration is an issue here. Coastal Del Mar, Carlsbad and Encinitas, where beach pollution and the environment are concerns, add some liberals, but the GOP has a double-digit voter registration edge overall.

Major Industry

Manufacturing, defense, health care

Military Bases

Camp Pendleton Marine Corps Base, Air Station and Naval Hospital, 42,572 military, 3,681 civilian; Naval Weapons Station Seal Beach, Detachment Fallbrook, 0 military, 260 civilian

Cities

Oceanside, Carlsbad, Vista, San Clemente

Notable

The Casa Romantica mansion in San Clemente, built in 1927 as a family home, is now a cultural center, hosting special events.

Rep. Duncan Hunter (R)

Capitol Office
225-5672
hunter.house.gov
223 Cannon Bldg. 20515-0552; fax 225-0235

Committees
Armed Services
Education & the Workforce
Transportation & Infrastructure
(Coast Guard & Maritime Transportation - Chairman)

Residence
Alpine

Born
Dec. 7, 1976; San Diego, Calif.

Religion
Baptist

Family
Wife, Margaret Hunter; three children

Education
San Diego State U., B.S. 2001 (business administration)

Military
Marine Corps, 2002-05; Marine Corps Reserve, 2005-08

Career
Residential real estate developer; business strategies analyst

Political Highlights
No previous office

ELECTION RESULTS

2012 GENERAL		
Duncan Hunter (R)	174,838	67.7%
David B. Secor (D)	83,455	32.3%
2012 PRIMARY (Open)		
Duncan Hunter (R)	76,818	67.4%
Terri R. Linnell (R)	3,275	2.9%
2010 GENERAL		
Duncan Hunter (R)	139,460	63.1%
Ray Lutz (D)	70,870	32.1%
Michael Benoit (LIBERT)	10,732	4.8%

Previous Winning Percentages
2008 (56%)

Elected 2008; 3rd term

The hawkish and conservative Hunter has made security overseas and along America's borders his political mission. He's also in the mix on education and transportation policy.

Hunter is among the younger members of Congress and the handful who can claim military service in Iraq and Afghanistan. He sits on the Armed Services Committee — a panel once chaired by his father, whom he succeeded in the House — and questions reductions to military spending.

Defense accounts took a $450 billion hit in an August 2011 law that also raised the federal debt limit. Hunter, who was one of 66 House Republicans to oppose that deal, called that amount "the most the national security budget can absorb without doing irreparable harm to military readiness and core capability."

Coming from the San Diego area, Hunter has a deep interest in the Navy. He sits on the Seapower and Projection Forces Subcommittee and loudly protests the shrinking of the U.S. fleet. Hunter was incensed when President Barack Obama seemed to condone a smaller fleet during a 2012 campaign debate. Writing in Roll Call, Hunter said Obama's own plan to shift military focus to the Pacific makes a larger fleet necessary: "The Navy will be the tip of the spear, establishing a presence in the Asia-Pacific region while still executing missions elsewhere in the world."

Hunter picked up responsibility for another fleet in the 113th Congress (2013-14) when he became the chairman of the Transportation and Infrastructure subcommittee overseeing the Coast Guard. At the first hearing he called in 2013, he highlighted a report that many Coast Guard vessels and aircraft have "surpassed their service lives and become increasingly prone to failures."

The day after the Sept. 11 terrorist attacks, Hunter quit his job as an information technology analyst and joined the Marine Corps. He deployed to Iraq twice — he was ambushed just five hours into his first tour, and later fought in the first battle of Fallujah — and served one tour in Afghanistan as a reservist before retiring.

Hunter has joined with Virginia Republican Frank R. Wolf to request the creation of an Afghanistan-Pakistan Study Group that would assess the U.S. mission in that region. Hunter wrote that objectives have been "clouded by uncertainty and mixed messages" as the focus shifts to a military withdrawal from Afghanistan, and he said that "we have seen little in the way of presidential leadership in this regard." He was one of 69 Republicans voting for a 2012 amendment to a defense policy measure that would bar the use of any funds in that bill for aid to Pakistan.

He also co-chairs, along with Minnesota Democrat Tim Walz, the House caucus looking out for the National Guard and Reserve. Hunter supports the use of the National Guard to secure the Mexican border, and he says that military spending cuts were the reason for a reduction in such deployments at the end of 2011.

The border is a major concern in San Diego. Hunter takes a hard line on illegal immigration, and he has been strongly supportive of states that attempt to use their resources to enforce federal immigration law. He wrote in the San Diego Union Tribune in December 2012 that "there is no such thing as immigration reform if the border is not secured," and his interest in the Coast Guard is partly tied to its border security mission.

Hunter's third committee is Education and the Workforce, where in the 112th Congress (2011-12) he chaired the Subcommittee on Early Childhood, Elementary and Secondary Education. In that role, he convened hearings promoting alternative teacher certification programs, which would get aspiring teachers into those jobs faster than traditional teacher education programs.

He also used his post to advocate charter schools. The House showed significant bipartisanship in passing his 2011 bill to authorize $300 million over five years for charter school programs; it consolidates facility financing assistance programs, uses competitive grants to encourage states to develop and expand charter schools, and installs accountability standards. That bill and other education measures were held up as the House and Senate struggled throughout the 112th with a reauthorization of the 2002 education law known as No Child Left Behind.

Hunter is a member of the conservative Republican Study Committee, and he has served as part of the GOP whip team. But in an unusual turn for a conservative, he has some protectionist instincts.

Hunter was one of 21 Republicans to oppose a free-trade pact with South Korea in 2011, citing its effect on manufacturing. "The enticements of free trade and imbalanced trade practices, essentially putting foreign interests above our own, have been a major contributing factor to the outsourcing of American jobs and lagging economic recovery," he wrote in the Washington Times in 2011.

Hunter was 4 years old when his father arrived in Washington for the first of 14 terms; he attended schools in the District of Columbia and later earned a business administration degree from San Diego State University.

As a college sophomore, Hunter and a friend started Jones Hunter Web Design. After graduation, they sold the company and Hunter accepted a position as an information technology analyst. Aides say he remains tech-savvy, often acting as the IT guy in his Capitol Hill office.

His father made it known in early 2007 that he planned to leave the House, paving the way for his son's bid. The younger Hunter was absent for nearly eight months of the primary and general-election campaign while he completed his final tour with the reserves. Election laws prohibit active-duty military personnel from taking partisan positions, making campaign speeches or fundraising, so Hunter turned his campaign over to his wife, Margaret, before heading to training for his deployment.

When Hunter returned from combat, he campaigned vigorously and cruised past three other primary candidates with more than 72 percent of the vote. He then faced Democrat Mike Lumpkin, a retired Navy SEAL commander, who sought to make an issue of the Hunters trying to keep the seat in the family. Hunter outraised Lumpkin by 3-to-1, and the district's GOP tilt enabled Hunter to win with 56 percent of the vote.

His re-election campaigns haven't been close.

Key Votes

2012	
Extend a Social Security payroll tax cut and unemployment benefits	YES
Ease securities rules to expand small-business access to capital	YES
Extend for one year subsidized student loan interest rates financed by a cut in health care spending	YES
Cite Attorney General Eric H. Holder Jr. for contempt of Congress	YES
Create a visa program for foreign graduates in high-tech fields	YES
Extend most Bush-era income tax rates while allowing rates for top-bracket earners to rise (Jan. 1, 2013)	NO
2011	
Strike funding for F-35 alternative engine	NO
Prevent EPA from regulating greenhouse gas emissions to address climate change	YES
Extend certain provisions of Patriot Act for four years	YES
Declare opposition to use of ground troops in Libya	YES
Overhaul patent law	NO
Pass compromise debt limit increase plan and establish future spending limits	NO
Allow consideration of measures to implement three trade agreements	YES

CQ Vote Studies

	PARTY UNITY		PRESIDENTIAL SUPPORT	
	SUPPORT	OPPOSE	SUPPORT	OPPOSE
2012	97%	3%	12%	88%
2011	97%	3%	20%	80%
2010	98%	2%	26%	74%
2009	95%	5%	21%	79%

Interest Groups

	AFL-CIO	ADA	CCUS	ACU
2012	20%	0%	92%	100%
2011	4%	15%	81%	92%
2010	7%	0%	88%	100%
2009	10%	5%	80%	100%

California 50

Northeastern San Diego County — Escondido, San Marcos; most of Temecula

Decennial redistricting renumbered and changed the boundaries of the district. The 50th gained mountainous areas of northern San Diego County, including Escondido, and most of Temecula in Riverside County. It is the only district in San Diego County that does not include residents of the city of San Diego itself.

Nearly all of the district's population is clustered near its western edge; several state and national parks and forests, including the Anza-Borrego Desert State Park and the Cuyamaca Rancho State Park, cover much of the district east of Interstate 15 all the way to the Imperial County border. Valleys in the rural areas that take up most of the district to the east grow fruit and flowers, and the Temecula Valley has vineyards. Unincorporated Ramona is known for its thoroughbred horse farms.

The densely packed residential areas near San Diego drive the economy. About one-third of the district's population lives in Escondido and San Marcos. Technology companies and defense contractors in the region provide jobs, and the California State University campus in San Marcos has a technology focus. Despite proximity to white-collar industries in San Diego, most residents in the district have incomes lower than the regional average.

Between the population hubs of the Escondido and San Marcos area and Temecula, the northwestern corner of the district abuts the massive Camp Pendleton Marine Corps Base (in the 49th). A conservative and majority-white population gives the 50th the state's largest proportion of registered Republicans; Mitt Romney took a 22-percentage-point win in the 2012 presidential race. Hispanics account for the largest minority group here at about 30 percent of the population.

Major Industry

Technology, agriculture

Cities

Escondido, San Marcos, Temecula (pt.), Santee, El Cajon

Notable

The Anza-Borrego Desert State Park is the largest state park in California and is a stopover on the Swainson's Hawks' 6,000-mile migration from Argentina to their breeding grounds far to the north.

Rep. Juan C. Vargas (D)

Capitol Office
225-8045
vargas.house.gov
1605 Longworth Bldg. 20515-1406; fax 225-9073

Committees
Agriculture
Foreign Affairs
House Administration

Residence
San Diego

Born
March 7, 1961; National City, Calif.

Religion
Roman Catholic

Family
Wife, Adrienne Vargas; two children

Education
U. of San Diego, B.A. 1983 (political science); Fordham U., M.A. 1987 (philosophy); Harvard U., J.D. 1991

Career
Insurance company government affairs executive; lawyer; Jesuit novice

Political Highlights
Sought Democratic nomination for U.S. House, 1992; San Diego City Council, 1993-2000; sought Democratic nomination for U.S. House, 1996; Calif. Assembly, 2000-06; sought Democratic nomination for U.S. House, 2006; Calif. Senate, 2010-13

ELECTION RESULTS

2012 GENERAL		
Juan C. Vargas (D)	113,934	71.5%
Michael Crimmins (R)	45,464	28.5%
2012 PRIMARY (Open)		
Juan C. Vargas (D)	30,143	46.0%
Denise Moreno Ducheny (D)	10,107	15.4%
John Brooks (D)	3,290	5.0%
Daniel C. "Danny" Ramirez (D)	2,794	4.3%

Elected 2012; 1st term

A Los Angeles Times story from 1997 said Vargas was "arguably the most successful Latino politician in San Diego history," and he has built up his résumé a great deal since then. The former Jesuit missionary champions social welfare programs and community-based initiatives, and he also has some expertise in business and finance.

His parents came to the country from Mexico as part of a guest worker program. Vargas, one of 10 children, was raised on a chicken ranch. After college he traveled as a missionary, then left the order to go back to school. He lost a 1992 congressional campaign shortly after getting a Harvard law degree, but ended up replacing the city councilman — Democrat Bob Filner — who won.

Vargas went on to serve three terms in the state Assembly, where he chaired the insurance committee. He then worked in the insurance industry for a few years before winning a state Senate seat. There, he chaired the banking committee. Vargas is a member of the business-friendly New Democrat Coalition.

The businesses of his district are often tied to trade and agriculture. International commerce is a local concern for Vargas — the southern edge of his district is the California-Mexico border — and he holds a seat on the Foreign Affairs subcommittee on trade.

Vargas also belongs to the Agriculture subcommittee on horticulture, which covers policies regarding the fruits and vegetables grown in his district. He wants to "ensure labor shortages are solved" for farmers — which could mean a push for more agricultural guest workers.

Vargas tried to unseat Filner in 1996 and 2006, and he expressed frustration that local Hispanic leaders didn't back him up. But Filner stepped aside in 2012 to run for mayor. To keep his toughest Democratic opponent from advancing out of the all-party "open" primary, Vargas spent campaign cash on behalf of Republican Michael Crimmins to boost him to a second-place finish. He then easily beat Crimmins in November in the very Democratic district.

California 51

Southern San Diego; Imperial County

The part-urban, part-rural 51st District runs the state's entire length of its border with Mexico, taking in all of Imperial County as well as the southernmost tier of San Diego County and its coastline at Imperial Beach. More than 40 percent of the district's population is packed into the city of San Diego, and National City and Chula Vista (shared with the 53rd) just south add another 25 percent. The district also takes in part of the below-sea-level Salton Sea to the east.

The dry and hot Imperial County is rural and agricultural. High unemployment and poverty rates in the predominately Hispanic county illustrate the area's overall economic stagnation. Energy development opportunities, such as geothermal, are being explored here.

While Imperial accounts for most of the district's footprint, the majority of the population in the 51st comes from San Diego County. Retail shopping in Chula Vista and National City lures shoppers from Mexico, but crime rates remain high in the working-class and heavily Hispanic areas of San Diego east and south of downtown. South of Chula Vista and across the border from Tijuana, Otay Mesa is a busy port of entry that is known for manufacturing plants that have twin sites in Mexico. Blue-collar jobs at the Port of San Diego (in the 52nd) draw from the regional workforce.

The district is overwhelmingly Democratic. Illegal immigration fills many agricultural jobs in the district, and ranchers and growers see it as a necessary source of labor while other residents say it threatens the district's quality of life. Border issues go beyond immigration to include border-crossing efficiency and volume. Water resources and the environmental impact of alternative water sources are concerns here, as both Imperial and San Diego counties are under pressure to reduce their dependency on the Colorado River.

Major Industry
Agriculture, trade

Military Bases
Naval Base San Diego, 26,037 military, 3,786 civilian (2011); El Centro Naval Air Facility, 294 military, 303 civilian (2010)

Cities
San Diego (pt), Chula Vista (pt), National City, El Centro, Calexico

Notables
El Centro is the winter training home of the Navy's Blue Angels.

Rep. Scott Peters (D)

Capitol Office
225-0508
scottpeters.house.gov
2410 Rayburn Bldg. 20515-0504; fax 225-2558

Committees
Armed Services
Science, Space & Technology

Residence
San Diego

Born
June 17, 1958; Springfield, Ohio

Religion
Lutheran

Family
Wife, Lynn Gorguze; two children

Education
Duke U., B.A. 1980 (economics & political science); New York U., J.D. 1984

Career
Lawyer; deputy county attorney; EPA economist

Political Highlights
San Diego City Council, 2000-08 (president, 2006-08); candidate for San Diego city attorney, 2008; San Diego Unified Port District Board of Port Commissioners, 2009-12

ELECTION RESULTS

2012 GENERAL		
Scott Peters (D)	151,451	51.2%
Brian P. Bilbray (R)	144,459	48.8%
2012 PRIMARY (Open)		
Scott Peters (D)	34,106	22.6%
Lori Saldana (D)	33,387	22.1%
Shirley Decourt-Park (D)	2,368	1.6%

Elected 2012; 1st term

Peters dealt with the ugly realities of government budgeting as a leader in San Diego politics and lists fiscal responsibility as a big concern. He also has lots of experience navigating environmental disputes. "I'm not a real fiery speech maker," he says. "I'm a pretty good listener."

As an attorney, he was specializing in tax and environment law when he moved to San Diego in the late 1980s. He spent two terms on the City Council starting in 2000 and helped guide the transition to a "strong mayor" system in his second term; he also endured a budget crisis that the council helped create by fully funding the city's pension system after years of underfunding.

He was involved in environment and infrastructure discussions as a member of commissions overseeing California's coasts and San Diego's port.

Peters, a member of the New Democrat Coalition, has spoken of the need to shrink federal deficits, in part through changes to the tax code. But he opposed $85 billion in spending cuts that took effect in March 2013, saying they were "drastic." He's involved in military spending talks as a member of the Armed Services Committee, and his spot on the seapower subcommittee is particularly relevant to San Diego's huge Navy presence.

Peters says he's very interested in reducing energy consumption as a means to mitigate the effects of climate change. He has a seat on the Science, Space and Technology Committee.

In 2012, Peters finished second in the all-party "open" primary, just ahead of former state Rep. Lori Saldaña. The general election pitted him against GOP Rep. Brian P. Bilbray. The 52nd District now is closely divided between the parties; Bilbray stayed away from his signature issue (illegal immigration) and criticized Peters' city government work. Peters campaigned against inaction in Washington, and he loaned himself $2.75 million over the course of the cycle. National committees from both parties also sank millions of dollars into TV ads. It took 11 days before Bilbray conceded a 4-point loss.

California 52

Downtown San Diego; Poway

Military bases, wide beaches, technology companies and medical research labs are the pillars of the renumbered 52nd District. Nearly half of the population of San Diego resides in the 52nd, which slides up the coast west of downtown before turning inland through Miramar and Poway. Parks dot the landscape among residential communities filled with white-collar workers, and tourist attractions include SeaWorld and PETCO Park, where baseball's Padres play.

San Diego is the heart of the 52nd, and its portion of the city includes the Gaslamp Quarter shopping and nightlife district, the airport and part of the massive port along the Pacific Ocean, as well as nearly all of the sprawling areas to the north. It takes in the seaside La Jolla and the neighborhood's multimillion-dollar homes and stretches to the east to include the San Diego Zoo Safari Park.

The district's own bases — including Marine Corps Air Station Miramar — fuel the economy and are linked to the region's other military installations. Major defense contractors provide stability in the military-oriented district, and technology, energy and computer firms draw on the well-educated workforce. The University of San Diego downtown and the University of California, San Diego, in La Jolla and shared with the 49th, add research jobs, especially at UCSD science research park and Scripps Memorial Hospital.

The 52nd has many conservative voters and registration does slightly favor the GOP, but Barack Obama took 52 percent of the district's vote in the 2012 presidential election. Sizable minority populations — Asians make up 19 percent and Hispanics 13 percent — make the district competitive.

Major Industry
Technology, agriculture

Military Bases
Naval Air Station North Island/Naval Amphibious Base Coronado, 21,237 military, 4,765 civilian; Naval Base Point Loma, 4,633 military, 8,303 civilian (2011), Marine Corps Air Station Miramar, 7,785 military, 664 civilian (2010); Marine Corps Recruit Depot San Diego, 5,717 military, 394 civilian (2011)

Cities
San Diego (pt.), Poway, Coronado

Notable
The Cabrillo National Monument on Point Loma identifies the spot where, in 1542, the first European landed on what is now the West Coast of the United States.

Rep. Susan A. Davis (D)

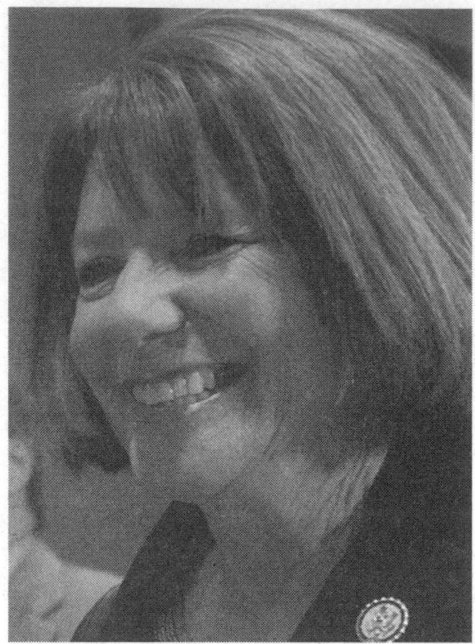

Capitol Office
225-2040
house.gov/susandavis
1526 Longworth Bldg. 20515-0553; fax 225-2948

Committees
Armed Services
Education & the Workforce

Residence
San Diego

Born
April 13, 1944; Cambridge, Mass.

Religion
Jewish

Family
Husband, Steve Davis; two children

Education
U. of California, Berkeley, B.A. 1965 (sociology); U. of North Carolina, M.A. 1968 (social work)

Career
High school leadership program director; public television producer; social worker

Political Highlights
San Diego Unified School District Board of Education, 1983-92 (president, 1989-92); Calif. Assembly, 1994-2000

ELECTION RESULTS

2012 GENERAL		
Susan A. Davis (D)	164,825	61.4%
Nick Popaditch (R)	103,482	38.6%
2012 PRIMARY (Open)		
Susan A. Davis (D)	70,462	57.8%
2010 GENERAL		
Susan A. Davis (D)	104,800	62.3%
Michael Crimmins (R)	57,230	34.0%
Paul Dekker (LIBERT)	6,298	3.7%

Previous Winning Percentages
2008 (68%); 2006 (68%); 2004 (66%); 2002 (62%); 2000 (50%)

Elected 2000; 7th term

Davis calls herself a "social worker at heart" and says she is more interested in listening than talking. She's happy to remain in the background if it helps move her legislative priorities on defense and education.

A longtime member of the Armed Services Committee, Davis often addresses the social side of defense issues as the top Democrat on the Military Personnel Subcommittee. She chaired that panel in the 111th Congress (2009-10) and became the ranking member to South Carolina Republican Joe Wilson starting in 2011.

Her knowledge of military families includes firsthand experience. She was studying social work in graduate school in North Carolina when she met Steve Davis, who was studying to be a psychiatrist; they married and spent two years in Japan while he served in the Air Force. Her San Diego district is also home to thousands of servicemembers.

Davis was a leading voice opposing the ban on openly gay servicemembers. When the "don't ask, don't tell" policy officially ended following 2010 legislative action and the military's certification of the repeal in 2011, Davis said it closed "a chapter of discrimination against gays and lesbians."

She brought attention to sexual assaults in the ranks, making them the topic of her first hearing as chairwoman. For several years, Davis has inserted into annual defense policy bills provisions to increase the reporting and study of such incidents, as well as expand legal protections for victims.

Working with California Republican Duncan Hunter, in the 112th Congress (2011-12) she introduced a bill to allow military personnel to refinance homes even if they aren't living in them. She also has pushed legislation to maintain military families' eligibility for such government programs as free or reduced-cost school lunches and Supplemental Security Income, which provides payments to the poor, elderly and disabled.

Davis also brings firsthand experience to the Education and the Workforce Committee, as she served on the San Diego school board for a decade. To keep America competitive, she said, we need to start by "valuing our teachers and believing that they can be very much a part of improving education in their schools."

Davis would like to improve teacher evaluations and give teachers more constructive feedback on their work. She has said the 2002 education law known as No Child Left Behind should be altered so that there is more support and less punishment for schools falling short of national standards. Davis has proposed the creation of an "online hub" for education professionals to share best practices, as well as a corps of experts to assist struggling schools.

A few other issues have found their way into her portfolio over the years. In the 110th Congress (2007-08) she began her efforts to overhaul and standardize absentee balloting rules. Davis said it is a civil rights issue; if long lines at the polls or other obstacles keep people from voting, they "should be able to vote when it's convenient for them."

The House in 2009 passed a bill by Davis and California Republican Kevin McCarthy to help states set up a system for voters to track their absentee ballots. She has also repeatedly introduced a bill to prohibit states from requiring voters to declare an excuse in order to vote absentee.

Davis quietly scored some victories during the health care debates of the 111th Congress. Three of her provisions made it into the Democrats' 2010 health care law: a diabetes prevention provision; a provision requiring insurance plans to allow women direct access to their OB/GYN without needing a referral from a primary care physician; and a provision that would permit matching funds for state Medicaid payments for freestanding birth center facility fees.

Davis' military ties make her a little more open to some security measures. She was one of 54 House Democrats to back a 2011 extension of surveillance provisions in the anti-terrorism law known as the Patriot Act.

As a member of the pro-business New Democrat Coalition, she also will break with her party on trade. In 2001, she was among 21 Democrats who voted in favor of giving the president authority to negotiate trade agreements that cannot be amended by Congress. She voted for 2003 trade agreements with Chile and Singapore, then did the same in 2011 for pacts with Colombia, South Korea and Panama.

And she does bend toward the middle on matters of fiscal restraint. Davis supported a fiscal 2011 spending package that was full of cuts that a majority of Democrats opposed.

Davis was raised in Richmond, Calif., the daughter of a pediatrician. She said a desire to help people led her to the mental health field, which in turn led her to her to graduate school in North Carolina.

When she and her husband returned from Japan and settled in San Diego, Davis became active in community affairs. She joined the League of Women Voters, serving as president of the San Diego chapter, and worked at the local public TV station.

In 1983, when Democrat Bob Filner left the San Diego school board to run for the city council, Davis won the election to replace him. (Filner went on to become a congressman, and in 2012 he was elected as mayor of San Diego.) While on the school board, she helped start a local fellowship program for preteens and teenagers to learn how business and government work. She did not seek re-election to the board in 1992 and became the fellowship program's first executive director.

Two years later, Davis won the first of three terms in the California Assembly. Term limits barred her from running for the Assembly in 2000, but the political vulnerability of the 49th District's GOP incumbent, Brian P. Bilbray, handed Davis an opportunity.

She had support from California Democratic Rep. Nancy Pelosi, and President Bill Clinton flew to San Diego to campaign on her behalf—though Davis refused to skip a vote in Sacramento to attend the event. She captured the seat by 3 points.

In her first re-election bid in the new 53rd District, her 2001 vote in favor of President George W. Bush's trade legislation cost her the support of the AFL-CIO. But she benefited from the political makeup of the newly drawn district, won with 62 percent, and hasn't been seriously threatened since.

Key Votes

2012

Extend a Social Security payroll tax cut and unemployment benefits	YES
Ease securities rules to expand small-business access to capital	YES
Extend for one year subsidized student loan interest rates financed by a cut in health care spending	NO
Cite Attorney General Eric H. Holder Jr. for contempt of Congress	?
Create a visa program for foreign graduates in high-tech fields	NO
Extend most Bush-era income tax rates while allowing rates for top-bracket earners to rise (Jan. 1, 2013)	YES

2011

Strike funding for F-35 alternative engine	YES
Prevent EPA from regulating greenhouse gas emissions to address climate change	NO
Extend certain provisions of Patriot Act for four years	YES
Declare opposition to use of ground troops in Libya	NO
Overhaul patent law	YES
Pass compromise debt limit increase plan and establish future spending limits	YES
Allow consideration of measures to implement three trade agreements	YES

CQ Vote Studies

	PARTY UNITY		PRESIDENTIAL SUPPORT	
	SUPPORT	OPPOSE	SUPPORT	OPPOSE
2012	94%	6%	83%	17%
2011	95%	5%	96%	4%
2010	98%	2%	95%	5%
2009	99%	1%	97%	3%
2008	99%	1%	15%	85%

Interest Groups

	AFL-CIO	ADA	CCUS	ACU
2012	95%	85%	33%	4%
2011	90%	80%	44%	0%
2010	100%	90%	25%	0%
2009	100%	100%	40%	0%
2008	100%	95%	56%	0%

California 53

Eastern San Diego; inland San Diego County

Urban, diverse and liberal, the 53rd now stretches east from the intersection of Interstate 8 and Interstate 5, through areas such as University Heights and College West to El Cajon. South of La Mesa, it takes in Latino-majority communities reaching roughly two-and-a-half miles north of the Mexico border.

The military plays a major role throughout the San Diego region, and many residents of the 53rd work at the district-based naval medical center or commute to the other installations nearby. Defense contractors, research firms and high-tech telecommunications companies with operations in the county provide white-collar jobs. San Diego State University is home to several research facilities and accounts for hundreds of millions of dollars annually in the local economy. The mild climate and attractions — such as Balboa Park (including the San Diego Zoo) and Qualcomm Stadium, where football's Chargers play — draw tourists.

Some economic uncertainty, especially concerning the housing market, has troubled areas in the 53rd. The portion of Chula Vista in the district has had the highest number of foreclosures of any area in San Diego County, and unemployment rates in El Cajon, Lemon Grove and Spring Valley all have been in the double digits.

The 53rd includes Hispanic Democratic sections of the city in places such as Lemon Grove. It also contains central city areas such as North Park and Hillcrest, which is one of the area's most liberal and Democratic neighborhoods and the center of San Diego's gay community. Overall, Democrats have a double-digit lead in voter registration.

Major Industry
Defense, tourism, technology, higher education

Military Bases
Naval Medical Center San Diego, 3,200 military, 2,100 civilian

Cities
Oceanside, Carlsbad, Vista, San Clemente

Notables
The United States Olympic Training center for rowing sports is in the southern portion of the district along the Lower Otay Reservoir.

COLORADO

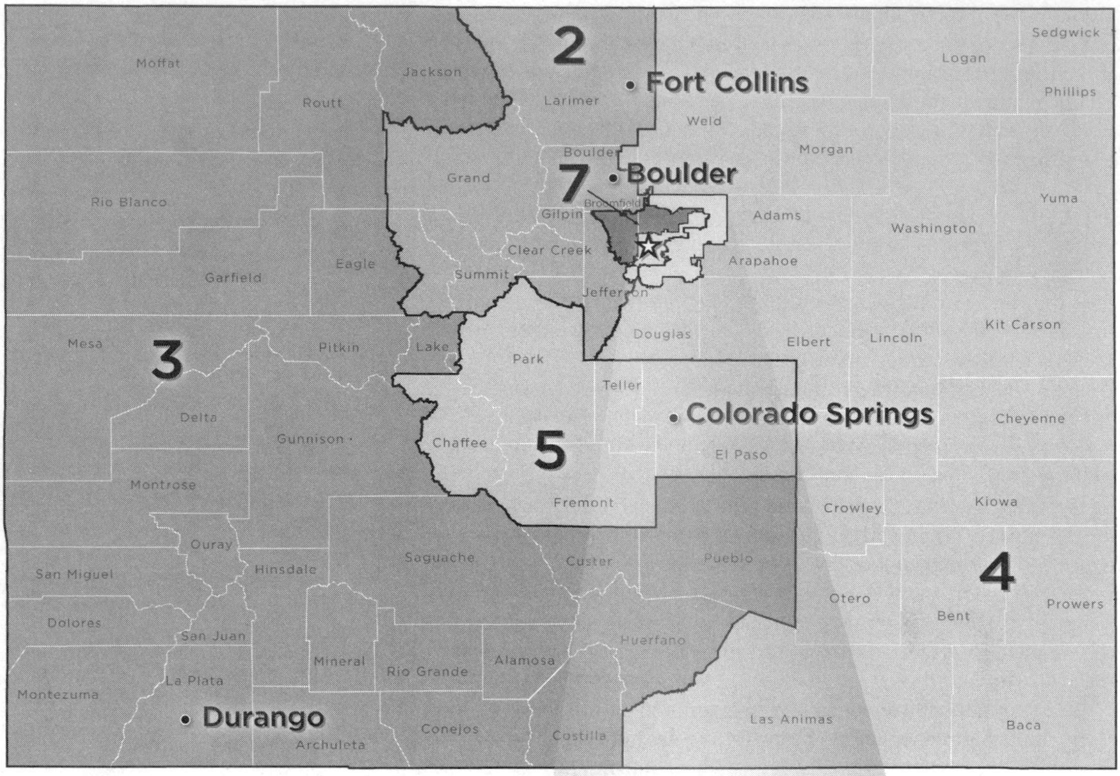

2
Fort Collins
Boulder
7
3
5
Colorado Springs
4
Durango
Moffat
Jackson
Routt
Larimer
Weld
Logan
Sedgwick
Phillips
Morgan
Boulder
Grand
Rio Blanco
Broomfield
Gilpin
Adams
Yuma
Washington
Clear Creek
Eagle
Garfield
Summit
Arapahoe
Jefferson
Douglas
Elbert
Lincoln
Kit Carson
Mesa
Pitkin
Lake
Park
Teller
Delta
Gunnison
Chaffee
El Paso
Cheyenne
Montrose
Fremont
Crowley
Kiowa
Ouray
San Miguel
Hinsdale
Saguache
Custer
Pueblo
Dolores
San Juan
Otero
Bent
Prowers
Mineral
Rio Grande
Alamosa
Huerfano
La Plata
Montezuma
Conejos
Archuleta
Costilla
Las Animas
Baca

Denver Area
Districts 1 & 6
Adams
1
DENVER
Denver
6
Arapahoe

Gov. John W. Hickenlooper (D)

First elected: 2010
Length of term: 4 years
Term expires: 1/15
Salary: $90,000
Phone: (303) 866-2471
Residence: Denver
Born: Feb. 7, 1952; Narberth, Pa.
Religion: Episcopalian
Family: Separated; one child
Education: Wesleyan U., B.A. 1974 (English), M.S. 1980 (earth and environmental science)
Career: Brewery owner and restaurateur; real estate developer; geologist
Political highlights: Mayor of Denver, 2003-11

ELECTION RESULTS

2010 GENERAL

John W. Hickenlooper (D)	912,005	51.0%
Tom Tancredo (AC)	651,232	36.4%
Dan Maes (R)	199,034	11.1%

Lt. Gov. Joseph Garcia (D)

First elected: 2010
Length of term: 4 years
Term expires: 1/15
Salary: $68,500
Phone: (303) 866-2087

LEGISLATURE

General Assembly: 120 days, January-May
Senate: 35 members, 4-year terms
2013 ratios: 20 D, 15 R; 21 men, 14 women
Salary: $30,000
Phone: (303) 866-2316
House: 65 members, 2-year terms
2013 ratios: 37 D, 28 R; 37 men, 28 women
Salary: $30,000
Phone: (303) 866-2904

TERM LIMITS

Governor: 2 terms
Senate: 2 consecutive terms
House: 4 consecutive terms

URBAN STATISTICS

CITY	POPULATION
Denver	600,158
Colorado Springs	416,427
Aurora	325,078
Fort Collins	143,986
Lakewood	142,980

REGISTERED VOTERS

Other	34%
Democrat	33%
Republican	33%

POPULATION

2010 population	5,029,196
2000 population	4,301,261
1990 population	3,294,394
Percent change (2000-2010)	+16.9%
Rank among states (2010)	22
Median age	35.5
Born in state	42.2%
Foreign born	9.5%
Violent crime rate	338/100,000
Povery level	12.9%
Federal workers	66,435
Military	35,404

ELECTIONS

STATE ELECTION OFFICIAL
(303) 894-2200
DEMOCRATIC PARTY
(303) 623-4762
REPUBLICAN PARTY
(303) 758-3333

MISCELLANEOUS

Web: www.colorado.gov
Capital: Denver

U.S. CONGRESS

Senate: 2 Democrats
House: 4 Republicans, 3 Democrats

STATISTICS BY DISTRICT

District	2012 Vote for President		2008 Vote for President					Median	Over	Under	College		
	Obama	Romney	Obama	McCain	Black	Asian	Hispanic	Income	64	20	Education	Rural	Sq. Miles
1	69%	29%	71%	28%	9%	3%	29%	$50,168	11%	24%	43%	<1%	190
2	58	40	61	37	1	3	10	63,571	11	25	52	24	7,535
3	46	52	48	50	1	1	24	47,012	14	26	30	41	49,732
4	39	58	42	56	1	2	22	57,836	11	29	30	29	38,103
5	38	59	40	59	6	2	15	53,691	11	27	34	17	7,266
6	52	46	54	45	9	5	20	63,513	9	30	39	1	475
7	56	41	57	41	2	3	27	55,341	12	26	29	1	342
STATE	**51**	**46**	**54**	**45**	**4**	**3**	**21**	**55,387**	**11**	**27**	**36**	**17**	**103,642**
U.S.	**51**	**47**	**53**	**46**	**12**	**5**	**17**	**50,052**	**13**	**27**	**29**	**21**	**3,531,905**

Sen. Mark Udall (D)

Capitol Office
224-5941
markudall.senate.gov
730 Hart Bldg. 20510; fax 224-6471

Committees
Armed Services
(Strategic Forces - Chairman)
Energy & Natural Resources
(National Parks - Chairman)
Select Intelligence

Residence
Eldorado Springs

Born
July 18, 1950; Tucson, Ariz.

Religion
Christian

Family
Wife, Maggie Fox; two children

Education
Williams College, B.A. 1972 (American civilization)

Career
Colo. Outward Bound School executive director; mountain guide

Political Highlights
Colo. House, 1997-99; U.S. House, 1999-2009

ELECTION RESULTS

2008 GENERAL

Mark Udall (D)	1,230,994	52.8%
Bob Schaffer (R)	990,755	42.5%
Douglas Campbell (AC)	59,733	2.6%
Bob Kinsey (GREEN)	50,004	2.2%

2008 PRIMARY

Mark Udall (D)	unopposed

Previous Winning Percentages
2006 House Election (68%); 2004 House Election (67%); 2002 House Election (60%); 2000 House Election (55%); 1998 House Election (50%)

Elected 2008; 1st term

Udall has a reputation as a deal-maker, but it hasn't been tested much in the polarized Senate. The avid outdoorsman finds the lack of cooperation vexing. Congress is climbing "political mountains," he said, and "when you're on a serious mountain, you don't ever think about cutting the rope."

America's debt and deficit problems were the highest peak in the 112th Congress (2011-12), and Udall is one of the more fiscally hawkish Democrats; 19 of his caucus colleagues (and one Republican) voted for his 2011 resolution proposing a balanced-budget amendment to the Constitution.

He openly criticizes President Barack Obama's economic agenda. Udall favors plans based on the work of a 2010 special fiscal commission, known as Simpson-Bowles, which would cut deficits by $4 trillion over 10 years through a mix of spending reduction and revenue increases.

"So much would ripple out from creating certainty about the federal government's financial situation," including more faith in Congress, he said. "The president missed an opportunity to fully embrace Simpson-Bowles. That's probably my biggest disappointment with this administration."

In pursuit of productivity, Udall has been party to some procedural accomplishments. He joined a charge to abolish a single senator's ability to block legislation and nominations — a practice known as a secret hold. The effort succeeded early in 2011 as part of a package of changes intended to speed up the pace of floor action. The Senate rejected his proposed ban on earmarks late in the 111th Congress (2009-10), but the Appropriations Committee instituted one the following year.

In 2011, he spearheaded a movement toward bipartisan seating in the House chamber during the annual State of the Union address. "I think we've permanently changed the tradition," he said.

And he has scored some parochial victories. Obama signed his 2011 bill to allow ski areas on U.S. Forest Service land to repurpose their grounds for summer recreational activities such as mountain biking and concerts — a move aimed at stimulating tourism and creating jobs in mountainous states.

Tall and telegenic, Udall has benefited from being part of what can be considered the West's first family of politics. His father, Morris K. Udall, represented Arizona in the House and also ran for president in 1976. His uncle, Stewart L. Udall, was Interior secretary under presidents John F. Kennedy and Lyndon B. Johnson and also served in the House.

Mark was elected to the House — and later the Senate — at the same time as his cousin Tom Udall, a Democrat from neighboring New Mexico. (Their House service overlapped with the tenure of another cousin, Republican Sen. Gordon H. Smith of Oregon.)

Udall's political moderation has served him well in his state, which includes conservative bastions such as Colorado Springs and liberal havens such as Boulder — which Udall represented during his decade in the House.

His work on energy and environmental issues has spanned both chambers. In the closing weeks of the 111th Congress, Udall, a member of the Energy and Natural Resources Committee, helped marshal support among Senate Democrats for legislation that would require 15 percent of electricity to be generated from renewable sources such as wind or solar by 2021. During the 110th Congress (2007-08), he and cousin Tom played a key role in seeing similar legislation pass the House.

Udall has supported efforts to enact cap-and-trade legislation to reduce greenhouse gas emissions — but he has drawn criticism for trying to ease the expected impact on coal-dependent states. He acknowledges the dilemma of attempting to protect the environment and the economy simultaneously, noting that his last name creates an expectation that he "bleeds green."

His energy interests carry over to the Armed Services Committee. He successfully tweaked the fiscal 2013 defense authorization law to make sure the Pentagon could continue to develop and use renewable energy, even when it is more expensive than fossil fuels.

His clout regarding national security is growing. In the 113th Congress (2013-14), he is the chairman of the Strategic Forces Subcommittee, which oversees cybersecurity, missile defense and space-based assets, all of which are important to military facilities in his state. As the Senate discussed cybersecurity plans in the 112th, he proposed permanently establishing cyberdefense training programs at the U.S. Air Force Academy in Colorado.

Udall also sits on the Intelligence Committee. He has repeatedly raised concerns about the government's interpretation of the anti-terrorism law known as the Patriot Act. Udall and Oregon Democrat Ron Wyden have said that the FBI is conducting unspecified domestic surveillance that does not reflect a plain reading of the statute. When Udall opposed an extension of the Foreign Intelligence Surveillance Act in 2012, he said it didn't require the government to disclose whether Americans' calls and emails are being searched without a judge's approval.

Udall was 10 when his father, "Mo," a legendary wit and energetic liberal, first won election to the House in 1961. He remembers being roused from sleep to join his five pajama-clad siblings to celebrate. He didn't see his father much after age 13 (his parents divorced when he was 15), but one of his proudest moments was witnessing his dad become the first prominent House Democrat to come out against Johnson's troop buildup in Vietnam in 1967.

He cited his father's 1964 vote in favor of the Gulf of Tonkin resolution when he announced in October 2002 that he would not support the resolution that gave President George W. Bush the authority to use military force against Iraq. The elder Udall, the son said, regretted that Tonkin vote.

Udall maintains that his mother "was actually the really cool person in my family." She was a National Rifle Association member who spent five years in Nepal with the Peace Corps in her late 50s, and he calls her his best example of "connective public service."

After graduating from Williams College in 1972, Udall didn't go home to Arizona, but rather moved to Colorado's Western Slope and launched a career as a mountain guide with the Colorado Outward Bound School. He was a course director for 10 years and served as executive director from 1985 to 1995. "There were years where I spent more nights under the stars than I did under a roof," he said.

Udall has scaled Kanchenjunga in the Himalayas, the third-highest peak in the world; Aconcagua, the highest point in South America; and Alaska's Mount McKinley, the highest peak in North America. In 1994, he reached 26,000 feet on Mount Everest via a route that has been climbed only once.

Thinking of his two young children, Udall has given up high-altitude climbing, but that has not kept him away from tamer mountains. He scheduled seven Colorado ascents for the summer of 2012 to round out his quest to summit the 100 highest peaks in his state.

His first House race was one of the most costly contests of 1998. Udall campaigned door to door to prove he was a "legitimate Coloradan" and was not trying to capitalize on a famous name. He prevailed by 5,500 votes. A month after the election, his father died of Parkinson's disease.

With each re-election bid, he took an increasing share of the vote. Udall announced early in 2005 that he would try in 2008 for the Senate seat then occupied by Republican Wayne Allard, who announced in 2007 that he would retire. Udall faced Republican Bob Schaffer in a good year for Democrats, and he was the superior fundraiser. He won by 10 points.

Key Votes

2012	
Prohibit health insurance plans from denying coverage based on the sponsor's religious beliefs	YES
Require approval of the Keystone XL oil pipeline	NO
Ease securities rules to expand small-business access to capital	YES
Reauthorize farm and nutrition programs for five years	YES
Limit debate on a bill that would create private-sector cybersecurity standards	YES
Consent to ratification of a treaty setting global standard for the treatment of people with disabilities	YES
Provide $60.4 billion in disaster relief following Superstorm Sandy	YES
Extend most Bush-era income tax rates while allowing rates for top-bracket earners to rise (Jan. 1, 2013)	YES
2011	
Prevent EPA from regulating greenhouse gas emissions to address climate change	NO
Extend certain provisions of Patriot Act for four years	NO
Clear compromise debt limit increase plan and establish future spending limits	YES
Overhaul patent law	YES
Implement Columbia free trade agreement	YES
Limit debate on confirmation of Caitlin J. Halligan to D.C. Circuit Court of Appeals	YES
Extend payroll tax cut and unemployment benefits for two months	YES

CQ Vote Studies

	PARTY UNITY		PRESIDENTIAL SUPPORT	
	SUPPORT	OPPOSE	SUPPORT	OPPOSE
2012	93%	7%	97%	3%
2011	90%	10%	95%	5%
2010	90%	10%	95%	5%
2009	93%	7%	97%	3%
2008	94%	6%	21%	79%
2007	94%	6%	8%	92%
2006	92%	8%	30%	70%
2005	91%	9%	20%	80%
2004	94%	6%	32%	68%
2003	95%	5%	24%	76%

Interest Groups

	AFL-CIO	ADA	CCUS	ACU
2012	91%	95%	29%	4%
2011	79%	90%	64%	5%
2010	94%	90%	18%	8%
2009	94%	95%	43%	16%
2008	93%	80%	61%	13%
2007	96%	90%	60%	4%
2006	93%	85%	53%	16%
2005	87%	90%	37%	8%
2004	93%	100%	53%	8%
2003	83%	80%	32%	18%

Sen. Michael Bennet (D)

Capitol Office
224-5852
bennet.senate.gov
458 Russell Bldg. 20510-0605; fax 228-5036

Committees
Agriculture, Nutrition & Forestry
(Conservation, Forestry & Natural Resources - Chairman)
Finance
(Taxation & IRS Oversight - Chairman)
Health, Education, Labor & Pensions

Residence
Denver

Born
Nov. 28, 1964; New Delhi, India

Religion
Unspecified

Family
Wife, Susan Daggett; three children

Education
Wesleyan U., B.A. 1987 (history); Yale U., J.D. 1993

Career
School superintendent; mayoral and gubernatorial aide; investment company executive; lawyer

Political Highlights
No previous office

ELECTION RESULTS

2010 GENERAL		
Michael Bennet (D)	851,590	48.0%
Ken Buck (R)	822,731	46.4%
Bob Kinsey (GREEN)	38,768	2.2%
Maclyn "Mac" Stringer (LIBERT)	22,589	1.3%
Jason Napolitano (IRFM)	19,415	1.1%
2010 PRIMARY		
Michael Bennet (D)	184,714	54.1%
Andrew Romanoff (D)	156,419	45.8%

Elected 2010; 1st full term

Appointed 2009

Competing missions complicate Bennet's young political career. He continues sincere attempts to shape bipartisan legislative breakthroughs, while also tackling the nakedly partisan job of managing campaign operations for Senate Democrats in the 2014 election cycle.

Appointed to his seat in 2009, Bennet had never run for public office until a narrow victory in 2010. In line with the divided politics of Colorado, he frequently bucks Democratic leaders, particularly as he seeks to impose fiscal discipline on the federal government.

"The longer that I'm here, the less I think that this conversation — this left-right conversation — is of any use, and the more I think the conversation that we should be having is one about future versus the past," Bennet said in 2012. "And how we create an economic environment in this country where we're generating wage growth and job growth again."

Bennet called for bipartisan action during the budget battles of the 112th Congress (2011-12). Early in 2011, he and Nebraska Republican Mike Johanns circulated a letter among senators asking President Barack Obama to support a comprehensive deficit reduction package. Signed by 32 Republicans and 32 Democrats, the letter said discretionary spending cuts, changes to entitlement programs and a tax code overhaul should all be on the table.

He and Johanns eventually became the seventh and eighth members of an informal group of senators who attempted to produce deficit reduction legislation based on the work of the 2010 special fiscal commission known as Simpson-Bowles. He was one of three Democratic senators to oppose the January 2013 "fiscal cliff" deal, which averted income tax increases on earnings under $400,000 but didn't cut spending. He said he couldn't support a bill that did nothing to seriously address federal deficits.

At the start of the 113th Congress (2013-14), Bennet emerged as part of another bipartisan eight-man working group — this time trying to create a framework for changes to immigration law. The bill they produced in spring 2013 includes tougher enforcement and border security provisions, as well as a path for illegal immigrants to eventually become citizens.

Bennet, a former superintendent of Denver public schools, plays a leading role in education from his post on the Health, Education, Labor and Pensions Committee. In 2011, that panel incorporated several of his provisions into its rewrite of the 2002 education law known as No Child Left Behind. One would allow states to create and expand academies for preparing teachers and principals to serve in high-need schools. Another would establish a commission to examine school regulations in an effort to cut red tape and improve testing practices — it drew on legislation Bennet introduced with Tennessee Republican Lamar Alexander, a former secretary of Education.

"There is a lot of distance between our schools and our classrooms and this place, and I tried to bring the perspective of our kids and of our teachers, and what is really going on on a day-to-day basis," Bennet said. No reauthorization was enacted in the 112th, so the work continues.

Bennet also used his HELP seat to push for several provisions included in the successful 2012 reauthorization of Food and Drug Administration user fee programs. He contributed language to improve the safety of the drug supply chain and expedite approval of breakthrough drugs. He won praise from the panel's top Republican and Democrat for his work.

There are a few areas where Bennet sides with liberals. He pushed hard for the creation of a government-run health insurance plan, a feature that was ultimately left out of the 2010 health care overhaul law. He railed against "backroom deals" that had been cut to secure support for the measure, but he joined Democrats in voting for it. He also wants to use tax incentives to encourage behavior that he says will mitigate the effects of climate change.

In addition to his other assignments, Bennet chairs the Agriculture Subcommittee on Conservation, Forestry and Natural Resources. He has focused on the conservation title of a rewrite of farm programs. A farm bill approved by the full committee in May 2013 included Bennet provisions to promote the use of conservation easement agreements.

Democrats hope Bennet's battle-hardened moderation is an asset in 2014, when a large number of the party's senators are up for re-election. He agreed to chair the Democratic Senatorial Campaign Committee, which puts him at the helm of campaign fundraising and support operations. It's a partisan job that might cramp Bennet's style, but for his trouble he was awarded a seat on the Finance Committee. Not only that, he's the chairman of the Finance subcommittee on taxation — a lofty spot for publicizing his fiscal ideals.

Despite his lack of political experience, Bennet was no stranger to Washington. His father, Douglas Bennet, was a State Department official who went on to become president of National Public Radio and Wesleyan University. The younger Bennet attended one of the city's boys schools before attending Wesleyan and earning a law degree from Yale.

He later left a prestigious law firm to become a counsel in the Clinton administration's Justice Department, where one of his responsibilities was writing speeches for Attorney General Janet Reno. But Bennet grew weary of the law and followed his future wife, Susan Daggett, to Montana, where he spent his time repairing furniture for their cabin.

They moved to Denver when Daggett was offered a position with the Earthjustice Legal Defense Fund in 1997. Looking for a job, Bennet was referred by a fellow Wesleyan alumnus to Phil Anschutz, the billionaire entrepreneur and donor to conservative causes. Bennet had no business experience, but Anschutz eventually gave him the task of refurbishing a movie theater chain. His success earned him a multimillion-dollar payday.

During his time on Anschutz's staff, he befriended John Hickenlooper, another Wesleyan alumnus. Bennet advised Hickenlooper in a 2003 run for mayor; once elected, Hickenlooper hired Bennet to be his chief of staff.

Two years later, Hickenlooper asked him to run Denver's public school system, even though he had no experience in education. As superintendent, Bennet promoted a merit pay system for teachers that increased starting salaries and linked bonuses to student achievement. He also closed underperforming schools. His work caught the eye of Obama, who reportedly considered making Bennet his secretary of Education.

Instead he was appointed to the Senate in 2009 as the replacement for Ken Salazar, who became Obama's secretary of Interior. Bennet's legislative inexperience spurred skepticism back home. Almost from the moment he arrived in Washington for the 111th Congress (2009-10), he found himself campaigning, first to prove himself worthy of the appointment, then to fend off a vigorous primary challenge by former Colorado House Speaker Andrew Romanoff — an old friend of Bill Clinton's who had the former president's endorsement. Obama campaigned on Bennet's behalf.

In the August 2010 Democratic primary, Bennet beat Romanoff by 8 points. He went on to face Republican Ken Buck, a tea-party-backed district attorney from Weld County.

Bennet raised more than $11 million, and outside groups spent millions more on his behalf. Buck received generous aid from ideological groups who tied Bennet to the Democratic agenda. The race ended up costing more than $45 million. Bennet edged Buck, 48 percent to 46 percent.

His campaign manager for that race, Guy Cecil, is the current executive director of the DSCC.

Key Votes

2012	
Prohibit health insurance plans from denying coverage based on the sponsor's religious beliefs	YES
Require approval of the Keystone XL oil pipeline	NO
Ease securities rules to expand small-business access to capital	YES
Reauthorize farm and nutrition programs for five years	YES
Limit debate on a bill that would create private-sector cybersecurity standards	YES
Consent to ratification of a treaty setting global standard for the treatment of people with disabilities	YES
Provide $60.4 billion in disaster relief following Superstorm Sandy	YES
Extend most Bush-era income tax rates while allowing rates for top-bracket earners to rise (Jan. 1, 2013)	NO
2011	
Prevent EPA from regulating greenhouse gas emissions to address climate change	NO
Extend certain provisions of Patriot Act for four years	YES
Clear compromise debt limit increase plan and establish future spending limits	YES
Overhaul patent law	YES
Implement Colombia free trade agreement	YES
Limit debate on confirmation of Caitlin J. Halligan to D.C. Circuit Court of Appeals	YES
Extend payroll tax cut and unemployment benefits for two months	YES

CQ Vote Studies

	PARTY UNITY		PRESIDENTIAL SUPPORT	
	SUPPORT	OPPOSE	SUPPORT	OPPOSE
2012	92%	8%	97%	3%
2011	91%	9%	95%	5%
2010	87%	13%	98%	2%
2009	92%	8%	96%	4%

Interest Groups

	AFL-CIO	ADA	CCUS	ACU
2012	91%	90%	29%	4%
2011	79%	90%	64%	5%
2010	88%	85%	36%	8%
2009	94%	95%	57%	8%

Rep. Diana DeGette (D)

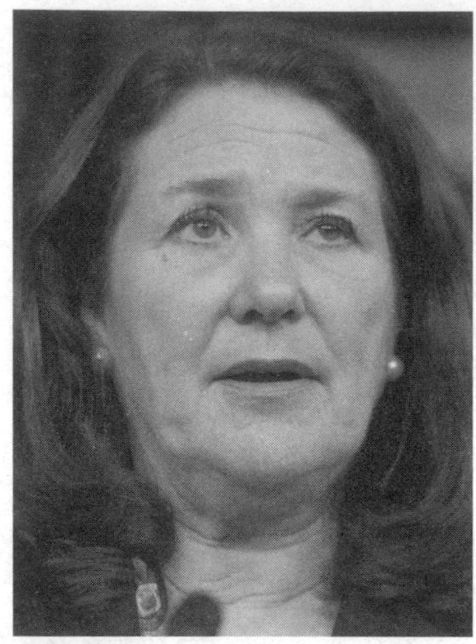

Capitol Office
225-4431
degette.house.gov
2368 Rayburn Bldg. 20515-0601; fax 225-5657

Committees
Energy & Commerce

Residence
Denver

Born
July 29, 1957; Tachikawa, Japan

Religion
Presbyterian

Family
Husband, Lino Lipinsky; two children

Education
Colorado College, B.A. 1979 (political science); New York U., J.D. 1982

Career
Lawyer; state public defender

Political Highlights
Colo. House, 1993-96 (assistant minority leader, 1995-96)

ELECTION RESULTS

2012 GENERAL		
Diana DeGette (D)	237,579	68.2%
Danny Stroud (R)	93,217	26.8%
Frank Atwood (LIBERT)	12,585	3.6%
Gary Swing (GREEN)	4,829	1.4%
2012 PRIMARY		
Diana DeGette (D)		unopposed
2010 GENERAL		
Diana DeGette (D)	140,073	67.4%
Mike Fallon (R)	59,747	28.8%
Gary Swing (GREEN)	2,923	1.4%
Clint Jones (LIBERT)	2,867	1.4%
Chris Styskal (AC)	2,141	1.0%

Previous Winning Percentages
2008 (72%); 2006 (80%); 2004 (74%); 2002 (66%); 2000 (69%); 1998 (67%); 1996 (57%)

Elected 1996; 9th term

There are many approaches to serving in the minority, and DeGette excels at several of them. She's a public critic of the Republican agenda who also accumulates bipartisan support for yearslong legislative campaigns. "If you find a key issue and you stick with it long enough, it becomes sort of en vogue," she says.

Her persistence earned her a spot on the Democratic leadership team — DeGette (de-GET) has served as a chief deputy whip since 2005. It also laid the groundwork for victories on stem cell research and children's health care when her party was ascendant in the 111th Congress (2009-10).

DeGette was assigned to the Energy and Commerce Committee as a freshman and still sits on the panel today. It's the arena for some of the most heated battles between Republicans and Democrats, and DeGette participates as the ranking member of the Oversight and Investigations Subcommittee. "I love investigations," says DeGette, a former litigator.

In the 112th Congress (2011-12) she complained that oversight was too partisan. The subcommittee "seems to have devolved into ... sort of a party organ of the Republican Party," she said, with the GOP giving short shrift to consumer and public health issues. DeGette wasn't timid as she accused Republicans of being nakedly political. "It seems to me, having sat on this committee for a number of years, that Republicans only woke up to their vehement opposition to a government role in green energy when President Obama was elected," she said at a 2012 hearing.

But even as she challenged Republicans, she continued building coalitions to advance her priorities. DeGette worked with Florida Republican Tom Rooney to address prescription drug shortages in hospitals. The two collaborated on a measure to require drug manufacturers to notify the Food and Drug Administration of a potential interruption in supply, so providers could make contingency plans. Their language was included in a 2012 law reauthorizing FDA user fee programs.

One of DeGette's daughters has diabetes, and she hopes stem cell research can provide an improved treatment or a cure. After George W. Bush in 2006 vetoed her bill to expand funding, DeGette campaigned for candidates who shared her position, picking up 14 votes when she pushed her bill through the House a second time in 2007. The final count was still short of the two-thirds majority required to override a veto, however.

Her book on the saga, "Sex, Science and Stem Cells: Inside the Right Wing Assault on Reason," was released in 2008, and President Barack Obama in 2009 issued an executive order lifting restrictions on federally funded embryonic stem cell research. Pennsylvania Republican Charlie Dent co-sponsored her 2011 bill to codify that order.

"I do think that the Republicans trust me," she said. "I can fight just as hard for something as anybody else, but they know that I won't be unfair, they know that I won't undercut them and that I will be respectful."

A strong defender of abortion rights, DeGette is outspoken when she thinks Republicans are trying to limit women's access to health care. GOP lawmakers in 2012 protested an Obama administration rule that would require most private insurance plans to offer contraceptives without co-payments — Republicans said organizations with religious objections should have exemptions. DeGette said the GOP wanted to take women back "to the Dark Ages." A chairwoman of the Pro-Choice Caucus, DeGette led teams of Democratic women in emphasizing the benefits of access to birth control and started a series of "Women's Health Wednesdays" speeches on the House floor.

DeGette has also been in the thick of debates on energy policy. She introduced legislation that would require disclosure of the chemicals used in hydraulic fracturing, which involves fracturing rocks by injecting water and chemicals under high pressure to release oil and gas.

In 2012 and 2013, the House passed a bill by DeGette and Washington Republican Cathy McMorris Rodgers meant to speed up federal permitting of smaller hydropower projects.

In her capacity as a whip, DeGette counts as one of her biggest successes a 2007 bipartisan effort on legislation to set national standards for renewable-energy production — although the bill fell one vote short in the Senate.

In the 113th Congress (2013-14), DeGette got involved with legislative efforts to curb gun violence — there were several high-profile mass shootings in 2012, including one in the Denver suburb of Aurora. She was ridiculed in April 2013 when, during a Denver Post forum, she didn't seem to know that ammunition magazines can be refilled and re-used — even though she has introduced several bills to regulate the size of magazines.

Born in Japan, where her father was stationed with the Air Force, DeGette spent most of her childhood in the Denver area. She was deeply affected by news coverage of the assassination of the Rev. Martin Luther King Jr. "It hit me, the whole idea of social justice and fighting for equality. I decided I was going to become a lawyer." She remembers being a fan — possibly the only one — of the 1970 television show "The Storefront Lawyers."

After earning a law degree at New York University, DeGette became a public defender in Denver and then went into private practice, specializing in cases about discrimination based on disability, sex and age. She volunteered in Federico Peña's mayoral campaign, which spurred her interest in public service. "I can do these cases one at a time," she recalls thinking, "or I can get elected to office and I can affect many people by changing the laws."

She won a Colorado House seat in 1992. As a freshman member of the minority party, DeGette won enactment of a law — upheld by the Supreme Court in 2000 — requiring protesters to stay eight feet from anyone within 100 feet of entrances to clinics where abortions are performed. DeGette moved up to the party leadership in the chamber but resigned in early 1996 to concentrate on her bid to succeed Democrat Patricia Schroeder in the U.S. House.

DeGette defeated Republican Joe Rogers, a lawyer and former congressional aide, by nearly 17 points. Each of her re-elections has been with at least two-thirds of the vote. When Obama named Colorado's Sen. Ken Salazar as Interior secretary in 2009, DeGette figured in speculation about his successor. But she took herself out of the running, saying she could be more effective as Colorado's senior House member.

Key Votes

2012	
Extend a Social Security payroll tax cut and unemployment benefits	YES
Ease securities rules to expand small-business access to capital	YES
Extend for one year subsidized student loan interest rates financed by a cut in health care spending	NO
Cite Attorney General Eric H. Holder Jr. for contempt of Congress	?
Create a visa program for foreign graduates in high-tech fields	?
Extend most Bush-era income tax rates while allowing rates for top-bracket earners to rise (Jan. 1, 2013)	YES
2011	
Strike funding for F-35 alternative engine	YES
Prevent EPA from regulating greenhouse gas emissions to address climate change	NO
Extend certain provisions of Patriot Act for four years	NO
Declare opposition to use of ground troops in Libya	NO
Overhaul patent law	NO
Pass compromise debt limit increase plan and establish future spending limits	NO
Allow consideration of measures to implement three trade agreements	NO

CQ Vote Studies

	PARTY UNITY		PRESIDENTIAL SUPPORT	
	SUPPORT	OPPOSE	SUPPORT	OPPOSE
2012	98%	2%	93%	7%
2011	97%	3%	86%	14%
2010	99%	1%	92%	8%
2009	99%	1%	97%	3%
2008	99%	1%	13%	87%

Interest Groups

	AFL-CIO	ADA	CCUS	ACU
2012	95%	90%	27%	0%
2011	93%	85%	19%	4%
2010	100%	95%	13%	0%
2009	100%	100%	33%	0%
2008	100%	80%	59%	0%

Colorado 1

Denver

The Denver-based 1st encompasses the capital city and the airport in Denver County as well as several towns to the southwest. As a result of decennial remapping, areas around Columbine and Ken Caryl in Jefferson County were moved into the 1st from the former 6th District. The population of Denver County increased by more than 8 percent from 2000 to 2010, and most of that growth was among white and Hispanic communities.

Equidistant between Chicago and Los Angeles, Denver is an economic and transportation hub. State and federal government offices provide public sector jobs in the metropolitan area, and varied financial services, technology, aerospace and other white-collar industries drive the local economy. Merrill Lynch Wealth Management relocated its regional headquarters to the city; development at the Fitzsimons Life Science District in neighboring Aurora (in the 6th) and major research hospitals downtown support the region's buoyant health care sector.

Denver International Airport has become one of the nation's busiest. Ongoing redevelopment of the lively "LoDo" district, what locals call the lower downtown neighborhood, has attracted visitors to historic buildings, galleries, restaurants and breweries. The Uptown district boasts dining and nightlife. Other tourism spots — such as Sports Authority Field at Mile High, home to football's Broncos — are in the 1st.

Denver has been the center of the 1st District since the state first joined the union in 1876, and the 1st remains the geographically smallest of Colorado's seven districts. The district has been represented by a Democrat for all but five years since 1933 and is a bastion of liberalism. Diana DeGette has easily held on to her U.S. House seat since she was first elected in 1996. In the 2012 presidential contest, Democrat Barack Obama took his highest percentage statewide in the 1st (69 percent).

Major Industry
Government, health care, tourism

Major Cities
Denver

Notable
Colfax Avenue in Denver is the longest continuous running street in the United States; the annual Great American Beer Festival offers more than 2,000 beers for tasting.

Rep. Jared Polis (D)

Capitol Office
225-2161
polis.house.gov
1433 Longworth Bldg. 20515-0602; fax 226-7840

Committees
Education & the Workforce
Rules

Residence
Boulder

Born
May 12, 1975; Boulder, Colo.

Religion
Jewish

Family
Partner, Marlon Reis; one child

Education
Princeton U., A.B. 1996 (politics)

Career
Internet entrepreneur and venture capitalist; at-risk charter schools founder

Political Highlights
Colo. Board of Education, 2001-07 (chairman, 2004-05)

ELECTION RESULTS

2012 GENERAL		
Jared Polis (D)	234,758	55.7%
Kevin Lundberg (R)	162,639	38.6%
Randy Luallin (LIBERT)	13,770	3.3%
Susan P. Hall (GREEN)	10,413	2.5%
2012 PRIMARY		
Jared Polis (D)		unopposed
2010 GENERAL		
Jared Polis (D)	148,720	57.4%
Stephen Bailey (R)	98,171	37.9%
Jenna Goss (AC)	7,080	2.7%
Curtis Harris (LIBERT)	5,056	2.0%

Previous Winning Percentages
2008 (63%)

Elected 2008; 3rd term

Polis is enterprising, aggressive and heavily involved in the operations of the Democratic Party. He has liberal instincts and approaches a lot of his work with the mind-set of an Information Age businessman.

His business career started early. Polis (POE-liss) graduated from high school in three years and enrolled at Princeton University at 17. As a college student he founded American Information Systems, a web-hosting company. He went on to co-found BlueMountain.com and ProFlowers.com and open a chain of movie theaters catering to Spanish-speaking audiences.

Polis' political activism also started at a young age. His journalist-turned-poet mother and physicist-turned-artist father were anti-war activists during the 1960s. They took their young son with them to demonstrations against nuclear proliferation. As a teenager Polis volunteered for Michael Dukakis' 1988 presidential campaign and founded a Democratic Club in San Diego, where he attended high school.

The marriage of activism and business has been productive for Polis. Prior to his election to Congress, he was a member of a group of wealthy donors who poured money into Colorado state races and helped elect several Democrats in districts long held by Republicans. The proceeds from the sale of his companies allowed Polis to self-fund significant portions of his campaign races. He is one of the richest members of Congress.

Polis' commitment to the Democratic Party and the logistics of political campaigns has won him the ear of party leaders. He is the national chairman for candidate services at the Democratic Congressional Campaign Committee in the 113th Congress (2013-14) — he was given the job shortly after wrapping up his tenure as co-chairman of the DCCC's Red to Blue program, which supports candidates in districts that are open or held by Republicans.

Polis is currently serving his third term on the Rules Committee, which sets rules for floor debate, and he is the parliamentarian of the Democratic whip team. His attention seems to have spread across the party's full ideological spectrum. He belongs to both the Congressional Progressive Caucus of the most-liberal House Democrats and the business-oriented New Democrat Coalition. He also serves as an honorary co-chairman for the public policy think tank Third Way.

When turning to policy, Polis dedicates much of his time to increasing access to education. He returned to the Education and the Workforce Committee in 2013. Prior to coming to Congress, he served for several years on the Colorado Board of Education and founded a public charter school that provides a high school education to new immigrants.

He has proposed grant funding as a means to several ends: improving the education of pregnant students and those who are parents; turning around low-performing schools; strengthening elementary and secondary computer science education; and encouraging charter schools to increase childhood nutrition and wellness education. Polis has called for an expanded system of continuing education for teachers, and he considers increasing the number of high-performing charter schools to be a priority.

In the 113th he has introduced a bill to encourage states to revise guidelines and teacher training for early-childhood learning. Polis took over as the lead House Democratic sponsor of the measure when Hawaii's Mazie K. Hirono moved over to the Senate in 2013. He has also collaborated with Wisconsin Republican Tom Petri on a bill to greatly simplify the federal student loan program for higher education.

Polis is liberal — for example, he favors strong environmental protections and opposes hydraulic fracturing, a method of extracting fossil fuels that critics say can contaminate groundwater. He has introduced a bill with Oregon Democrat Earl Blumenauer to de-criminalize marijuana at the federal level.

But he occasionally stakes out middle ground on fiscal issues. He was one of only 22 House Democrats to vote for a fiscal 2013 budget — widely viewed as a compromise plan — that would cut deficits by $4 trillion over 10 years through spending reduction and revenue increases. (More in line with liberals, he wants a lot of spending reductions to come from the military.)

Polis was the first openly gay man elected to Congress as a non-incumbent. He and his partner, Marlon Reis, welcomed a son in 2011, making Polis the first openly gay parent in Congress. He regularly co-sponsors measures to address what he sees as discriminatory practices against gay, lesbian, bisexual or transgender people. In 2012, Polis continued calling for repeal of the law that bans the federal government from recognizing same-sex unions. "States are where the definition of marriage resides," he said during a CNN interview.

Drawing on his Internet background, Polis was a strong opponent of 2011 bills meant to curb online piracy. The measures would have allowed the attorney general to seek a court order against websites involved in online piracy. Opponents said the bills' standards were too loose, allowing the potential for censorship if abused by the government; Polis told the technology website CNET that the measures were too much like a "wish list for rights holders rather than a balanced approach." Speaking on the House floor, he said that "these bills threaten free discourse, free speech and the very infrastructure of the Internet, itself." The measures stalled.

Polis uses social media to maintain close contact with his constituents. A regular Twitter user, he has more than 20,000 followers. He considers himself to be one of the more tech-savvy members of Congress and frequently supports technology initiatives.

Polis was born in Boulder. He attended school in San Diego, returning to Colorado with his family during the summers. His interest in business started as a child. He started a scrap metal business, sold tomatoes and even spent a summer in Russia trading privatization vouchers.

At Princeton he was active in Jewish community activities, student government, the College Democrats and the ROTC.

When Democratic Rep. Mark Udall decided to run for the Senate in 2008, Polis spent more than $5 million of his own money in the primary to succeed him — he rejected donations from political action committees associated with industries while pointing out that his opponents accepted money from oil and mining interests. He won that primary with almost 42 percent of the vote, and the general elections in his district haven't been close contests.

Key Votes

2012	
Extend a Social Security payroll tax cut and unemployment benefits	YES
Ease securities rules to expand small-business access to capital	YES
Extend for one year subsidized student loan interest rates financed by a cut in health care spending	NO
Cite Attorney General Eric H. Holder Jr. for contempt of Congress	?
Create a visa program for foreign graduates in high-tech fields	NO
Extend most Bush-era income tax rates while allowing rates for top-bracket earners to rise (Jan. 1, 2013)	YES
2011	
Strike funding for F-35 alternative engine	YES
Prevent EPA from regulating greenhouse gas emissions to address climate change	NO
Extend certain provisions of Patriot Act for four years	NO
Declare opposition to use of ground troops in Libya	-
Overhaul patent law	-
Pass compromise debt limit increase plan and establish future spending limits	YES
Allow consideration of measures to implement three trade agreements	?

CQ Vote Studies

	PARTY UNITY		PRESIDENTIAL SUPPORT	
	SUPPORT	OPPOSE	SUPPORT	OPPOSE
2012	89%	11%	91%	9%
2011	92%	8%	89%	11%
2010	97%	3%	81%	19%
2009	97%	3%	88%	12%

Interest Groups

	AFL-CIO	ADA	CCUS	ACU
2012	80%	85%	25%	4%
2011	89%	80%	23%	8%
2010	71%	90%	25%	4%
2009	90%	95%	47%	4%

Colorado 2

North central — Boulder, Fort Collins

The 2nd drops down from the border with Wyoming past Fort Collins to Boulder. It picks up Interstate 70 west of the Denver metro area to reach the slopes of Breckenridge and Vail. Forests, parks, lakes and the majestic peaks of the Rockies dominate much of the district's geographical expanse.

Boulder, at the foothills of the Rocky Mountains, is at the heart of the 2nd. It's here where students and faculty at the University of Colorado's flagship campus, scientists at high-tech federal facilities and a committed corps of environmentalists and outdoors enthusiasts mingle. The National Institute of Standards and Technology, just south of the school, is a federal research site for physics, optics, statistics and computer science and is the nation's official timekeeper. Google also has a facility in Boulder.

Education and technology are also key to Larimer County. Colorado State University in Fort Collins has environmental, business and biotechnology programs; Hewlett-Packard has a large campus in the city near Interstate 25 that anchors a semiconductor sector. Outside of Fort Collins, Larimer County is home to bioscience research and renewable energy firms.

Both Boulder and Fort Collins are cycling-oriented, and outdoor sports remain the most popular pastimes in the region. Skiing is king in the mountain counties of Eagle (shared with the 3rd), Summit and Grand. The 2nd's portion of Eagle is home to the resort city of Vail, and Breckenridge is in Summit. Sprawling national forests and the scenic Rocky Mountain National Park draw tourists year round.

A generally liberal culture in Boulder pulls the district to the left, and environmental issues play heavily here. Despite adding conservative Larimer County in the north and parts of GOP-leaning Jefferson and Park counties after decennial redistricting, the 2nd remains friendly to Democrats and voter registration overall is split among Democrats, Republicans and independents.

Major Industry
Technology, research, higher education, tourism

Cities
Boulder, Fort Collins

Notable
The Eisenhower-Johnson Memorial Tunnel, one of the world's highest vehicular tunnels, takes Interstate 70 across the Continental Divide about 60 miles west of Denver.

Rep. Scott Tipton (R)

Capitol Office
225-4761
tipton.house.gov
218 Cannon Bldg. 20515-0603; fax 226-9669

Committees
Agriculture
Natural Resources
Small Business
(Agriculture, Energy & Trade - Chairman)

Residence
Cortez

Born
Nov. 9, 1956; Espanola, N.M.

Religion
Anglican

Family
Wife, Jean Tipton; two children

Education
Fort Lewis College, B.A. 1978 (political science)

Career
Pottery company owner

Political Highlights
Montezuma County Republican Party chairman, 1980-84; Republican nominee for U.S. House, 2006; Colo. House, 2009-10

ELECTION RESULTS

2012 GENERAL		
Scott Tipton (R)	185,291	53.4%
Sal Pace (D)	142,619	41.1%
Tisha T. Casida (UNA)	11,125	3.2%
Gregory Gilman (LIBERT)	8,212	2.4%
2012 PRIMARY		
Scott Tipton (R)		unopposed
2010 GENERAL		
Scott Tipton (R)	129,257	50.1%
John Salazar (D)	118,048	45.8%
Gregory Gilman (LIBERT)	5,678	2.2%
Jake Segrest (UNA)	4,982	1.9%

Elected 2010; 2nd term

Tipton keeps a low profile while steadily promoting small-business and land management policies pertinent to his huge district. He's a fiscal conservative with a civil-libertarian streak, describing himself as "more of your typical citizen legislator."

Tipton made his money running a pottery business. He is as comfortable describing the Native American carvings on a vase as he is talking about his plans to boost Colorado's economy. "I'm a small-town, small-business guy," he says. He wants lower corporate income taxes, greater flexibility for states to manage natural resources, and enactment of a farm bill that protects the growers of specialty crops.

His seats on the Agriculture and Natural Resources committees are useful when Tipton wants to shape forest policies. His district contains lots of National Forest land. (A 73-foot Engelmann spruce from the White River National Forest was decorated as the U.S. Capitol Christmas Tree in 2012.) He favors less federal regulation of forest conditions: "I believe that local communities know their forests best and know what needs to be done to restore them to healthy conditions," he said at a Colorado forest summit in 2012.

Tipton and several Colorado colleagues introduced a 2012 bill to give states more management authority (for activities like forest thinning) in forests deemed "high risk" by governors or the Agriculture secretary; an updated version was rolled out early in 2013. He argued it would help prevent the spread of wildfires and bark beetles. He was pleased when the Bureau of Land Management dropped its "wild lands" policy in June 2011; many Republicans feared the Obama administration would use that designation to close federal land to economic development without the usual congressional approval.

Like most Republicans, Tipton wants greater U.S. energy development, particularly of oil shale reserves. But he is also open to expanding renewable energy sources. In April 2013, the House passed his bill to expedite development of small hydropower stations on existing federal canals and pipelines. He stumped for extension of the tax credit for wind energy — Vestas Wind Systems has a plant in Pueblo. That credit was extended in the "fiscal cliff" package enacted early in 2013, along with lower income tax rates for earnings under $400,000. Tipton voted against it, however. He wanted the overall agreement to include substantial spending cuts.

On the Small Business Committee, Tipton is the chairman of the Agriculture, Energy and Trade panel — a job he has held since the start of his freshman term. Tipton contends that the export programs helping small businesses are often duplicating the work of state programs and can be needlessly confusing. He has worked with Small Business Chairman Sam Graves of Missouri on bills to simplify the programs for business owners.

He sides with many farmers and small-business owners who dislike the estate tax. "It's my belief that families intending to maintain the family business following the passing of the former owner shouldn't be routed by the crippling effects of the estate tax," he said:

Tipton is the son of sharecroppers, and he calls agriculture the "backbone" of the 3rd District. In July 2012, he voted in the Agriculture Committee for a long-term farm bill, and he wants any final measure to continue specialty crop research and pest management programs. Overall, he supports new agricultural research initiatives, mainly aimed at increasing yields. He also supports free trade as a way to increase market access for farmers. Tipton voted for pacts with South Korea, Panama and Colombia in 2011.

"A very critical point for our national security and our national well-being is our ability to be able to feed ourselves," Tipton said. "If we get to the point where we are relying on other nations to supply us with our foodstuffs, we're in bad shape."

Tipton has some vintage Republican views. He supports gun owners' rights, opposes a path to citizenship for illegal immigrants and says abortion should be limited to cases of rape, incest or threat to the life of the woman. He says the definition of marriage should be left to states, "not co-opted by judges and the federal government." He advertised his fiscal conservatism by voting against the final spending packages for fiscal 2011 and fiscal 2012, as well as an August 2011 deficit reduction package. In each case he said he wanted more spending cuts than the bills provided.

He also has some libertarian instincts. Tipton opposed a 2011 extension of surveillance provisions in the 2001 anti-terrorism law known as the Patriot Act. He later voted against a fiscal 2012 defense policy bill that he felt would allow indefinite detention of U.S. citizens.

In September 2012, President Barack Obama declared Chimney Rock in the San Juan National Forest a national monument under control of the Forest Service. A few months earlier, the House had passed Tipton's bill that would have made that designation. The "natural observatory," where every 18.6 years the moon rises precisely between two rock spires, has religious significance to Indian tribes. Tipton says the designation will boost tourism. "You gotta come out and take a look," he says.

Tipton graduated from Fort Lewis College in Durango with a degree in political science in 1978. He co-founded Mesa Verde Pottery with his brother, selling handmade Navajo and Ute items.

He unsuccessfully sought the 3rd District seat in 2006, taking just 37 percent of the vote in losing to incumbent Democrat John Salazar. Two years later Tipton won election to the Colorado House. His victory over tea party favorite Bob McConnell in the 2010 GOP primary set up a rematch with Salazar. Tipton improved on his previous performance, taking 50 percent of the vote for a 4-point win. That sent him to D.C. to work with his opponent's brother, Ken, who was serving as the Interior secretary for Obama.

In 2012, he faced Democrat Sal Pace, a former state House minority leader and district director for John Salazar. Pace was considered a strong opponent, and he emphasized Tipton's support for GOP budgets that would cut spending and revamp entitlement programs. Tipton still won by 12 points.

Tipton briefly battled ethics questions in May 2011 when reports surfaced that his daughter, who works for a company that organizes telephone-based town hall meetings, sent emails soliciting business using his name. Politico reported that Tipton sent a letter of apology to the House Ethics Committee.

Key Votes

2012	
Extend a Social Security payroll tax cut and unemployment benefits	YES
Ease securities rules to expand small-business access to capital	YES
Extend for one year subsidized student loan interest rates financed by a cut in health care spending	YES
Cite Attorney General Eric H. Holder Jr. for contempt of Congress	YES
Create a visa program for foreign graduates in high-tech fields	YES
Extend most Bush-era income tax rates while allowing rates for top-bracket earners to rise (Jan. 1, 2013)	NO
2011	
Strike funding for F-35 alternative engine	YES
Prevent EPA from regulating greenhouse gas emissions to address climate change	YES
Extend certain provisions of Patriot Act for four years	NO
Declare opposition to use of ground troops in Libya	YES
Overhaul patent law	YES
Pass compromise debt limit increase plan and establish future spending limits	NO
Allow consideration of measures to implement three trade agreements	YES

CQ Vote Studies

	PARTY UNITY		PRESIDENTIAL SUPPORT	
	SUPPORT	OPPOSE	SUPPORT	OPPOSE
2012	90%	10%	16%	84%
2011	95%	5%	21%	79%

Interest Groups

	AFL-CIO	ADA	CCUS	ACU
2012	14%	5%	92%	84%
2011	0%	5%	94%	92%

Colorado 3

Western Slope; Pueblo

Spanning all of or part of 29 counties, the 3rd stretches down the Utah border from Wyoming to the Four Corners area in the southwest before heading east across half of Colorado's border with New Mexico. The state's geographically largest district, it takes in almost all of Colorado's Western Slope, rural communities in sparsely populated counties and two population centers — Grand Junction in the west and Pueblo in the east.

The 3rd displays some of the variety found outside the state's urban centers: rural poor, resort rich, old steel-mill towns and isolated Hispanic counties. Significant rural swathes of the district struggle with high poverty rates, in stark contrast to the wealth in resort destinations Aspen and Steamboat Springs.

Pueblo, the district's largest city, used to rely on steel and has seen its fair share of both boom and bust. Manufacturing interests remain, and Colorado State University props up the economy. Outside of Pueblo and Grand Junction, the large district is filled with more trees than people, and vast wilderness and majestic scenery dominate the landscape. Potential development of what is largely privately owned land and water usage for the rivers flowing down the Western Slope are perennial political issues.

Natural resources-based tourism in the north and west is around national parks and ski resorts. Although once-robust mining areas have dwindled, many areas rely on the remaining coal jobs. Local vintners have made inroads in rural areas near Grand Junction, but extended drought conditions have hurt agricultural production overall.

Pueblo is a Democratic stronghold, but many areas in the district tend to back conservative candidates. Overall, voter registration gives a narrow edge to Republicans, and unaffiliated voters slightly outnumber Democrats. In the 2012 presidential contest, Mitt Romney took 52 percent of the district's vote.

Major Industry
Tourism, mining

Cities
Pueblo, Grand Junction

Notable
The Federal Citizen Information Center — a clearinghouse of federal information for consumers — has its own zip code in Pueblo.

Rep. Cory Gardner (R)

Capitol Office
225-4676
gardner.house.gov
213 Cannon Bldg. 20515-0604; fax 225-5870

Committees
Energy & Commerce

Residence
Yuma

Born
Aug. 22, 1974; Yuma, Colo.

Religion
Lutheran - Missouri Synod

Family
Wife, Jaime Gardner; two children

Education
Colorado State U., B.A. 1997 (political science); U. of Colorado, J.D. 2001

Career
Lawyer; congressional aide; agricultural advocacy organization spokesman; farm equipment parts dealer

Political Highlights
Colo. House, 2005-10

ELECTION RESULTS

2012 GENERAL		
Cory Gardner (R)	200,006	58.4%
Brandon Shaffer (D)	125,800	36.7%
Josh Gilliland (LIBERT)	10,682	3.1%
Doug Aden (AC)	5,848	1.7%
2012 PRIMARY		
Cory Gardner (R)		unopposed
2010 GENERAL		
Cory Gardner (R)	138,634	52.5%
Betsy Markey (D)	109,249	41.4%
Doug Aden (AC)	12,312	4.7%
Ken "Wasko" Waszkiewicz (UNA)	3,986	1.5%

Elected 2010; 2nd term

GOP leaders trusted Gardner enough to put him on the Energy and Commerce Committee when he was a freshman. He repaid that kindness by sticking with the party's sales pitch for energy policy and expressing his conservative views in a non-disruptive manner. Youthful and tactful, he is likely to be involved as House Republicans tweak their branding.

Gardner managed to be both amicable and partisan in the 112th Congress (2011-12). He had prior experience with the political process, including stints as spokesman for a trade association in Washington, an aide to Republican Sen. Wayne Allard and a member of the Colorado House. Gardner says he hopes to be seen as "approachable" by members of any party.

Late in 2012, he supported a wave of kinder, gentler candidates seeking leadership roles. When Steve Scalise of Louisiana ran for chairman of the conservative Republican Study Committee, promising a less combative direction for the RSC, Gardner helped him round up votes. He also whipped up support for Cathy McMorris Rodgers of Washington in her successful bid for the chairmanship of the Republican Conference.

"As we sort of break down the silos that we couldn't penetrate this past election, she's somebody that can communicate our message to voters we need to be reaching," Gardner told The Hill. In the 113th Congress (2013-14), Gardner is helping to run the Patriot Program, the House GOP campaign operation that focuses on assisting incumbents.

On the Energy and Commerce Committee, Gardner offers unqualified support for an "all of the above" energy strategy and the loosening of federal regulations. Republican bills to realize those goals mostly bounced off the Democratic Senate in the 112th, but Gardner plugged away.

He introduced a plan to link the release of oil from the nation's Strategic Petroleum Reserve with increases in the amount of public land available for oil and gas development. Republicans liked the bill enough to make it the vessel for six other measures to expand energy production. The package passed in June 2012. The year before, the House passed his bill to set a six-month deadline for the EPA to take action on pollution permit applications for energy development on the outer continental shelf. "It's frightening that an agency with as much regulatory authority as the EPA doesn't appear to care about jobs," Gardner said.

Gardner joined the chorus of Republicans fretting about possible federal regulation of hydraulic fracturing, the injection of high-pressure fluids into rock layers to allow access to new deposits of gas and oil. The Bureau of Land Management proposed rules in 2012, and Gardner wrote the Interior Department to say they violate state water laws. "The rules give BLM veto authority over water use related to oil and natural gas development on federal lands, which is entirely inappropriate and an affront to Colorado's system of prior appropriation," he said.

It's not all oil and gas with Gardner. As a state House member, he counted his work on the creation of the Colorado Clean Energy Development Authority as a top accomplishment. He supported extension of the tax credit for wind energy (though he voted against the early 2013 "fiscal cliff" package that ultimately contained the extension, because he wanted it to include more spending reductions). Gardner and Democrat Peter Welch of Vermont in December 2012 formed a caucus to promote energy-efficiency measures.

He wants to develop what he terms "American energy zones." Gardner says the concept came from the Healthy Forests Initiative, a George W. Bush-era initiative that expedited the cutting of timber in areas prone to wildfires. The zones would be areas pre-approved at the local, state and federal levels for the development of certain energy sources, such as gas, oil and wind. "It's all based on local support and getting the work done up front," he said.

Like many of his Western colleagues, Gardner keeps close tabs on water policy. He references a poem by Thomas Hornsby Ferril, found in a mural within the Colorado capitol, that describes the state: "Here is a land where life is written in water." Gardner says federal regulations are slowing the development of water storage projects in his state.

Gardner is a fiscal conservative, and some of his notable (and few) departures from the preferences of party leaders came on fiscal votes. He did not support the spending bills for fiscal 2011 or 2012, or a plan to defer spending decisions for fiscal 2013 to the 113th Congress.

Gardner grew up in Colorado, working various jobs in his family's farm implement dealership. (He has introduced bills to allow the creation of tax-deductible savings accounts to start or expand small businesses.) "My dad was a Democrat, my granddad was a Democrat," he said. "So when I turned 18 in high school, I went down and registered as a Democrat. I quickly realized going through college that that's not who I was or what I believed in." When he was at the University of Colorado's law school, he was president of the conservative Federalist Society.

After receiving his law degree, Gardner became the communications director at the National Corn Growers Association in Washington. In 2002, he moved to Allard's office and then was appointed to the Colorado House in 2005 after a few dominoes fell his way.

The state treasurer, Republican Mike Coffman, left for a tour in Iraq with the Marine Corps Reserve; a state senator filled the position; and a state representative took the senator's seat. Gardner was appointed to that vacancy and later won election to the post. (Coffman was elected to the House from Colorado's 6th District in 2008.)

Gardner made his first bid for Congress in 2010. His opponent, one-term Rep. Betsy Markey, had become the first Democrat elected to the seat in decades when she defeated incumbent Republican Marilyn Musgrave by 13 points. Gardner won an often feisty campaign with nearly 53 percent of the vote to Markey's 41 percent.

For the 2012 election, he was aided by decennial redistricting with the addition of more conservative regions to his largely rural, agriculture-focused district. After running unopposed in his primary, he beat the state Senate president, Democrat Brandon Shaffer, by almost 22 points.

Gardner, an antiques buff, lives in the home his great-grandparents owned and is trying to restore it to its likely state in the early 1900s.

Key Votes

2012	
Extend a Social Security payroll tax cut and unemployment benefits	NO
Ease securities rules to expand small-business access to capital	YES
Extend for one year subsidized student loan interest rates financed by a cut in health care spending	YES
Cite Attorney General Eric H. Holder Jr. for contempt of Congress	YES
Create a visa program for foreign graduates in high-tech fields	YES
Extend most Bush-era income tax rates while allowing rates for top-bracket earners to rise (Jan. 1, 2013)	NO
2011	
Strike funding for F-35 alternative engine	YES
Prevent EPA from regulating greenhouse gas emissions to address climate change	YES
Extend certain provisions of Patriot Act for four years	YES
Declare opposition to use of ground troops in Libya	YES
Overhaul patent law	YES
Pass compromise debt limit increase plan and establish future spending limits	YES
Allow consideration of measures to implement three trade agreements	YES

CQ Vote Studies

	PARTY UNITY		PRESIDENTIAL SUPPORT	
	SUPPORT	OPPOSE	SUPPORT	OPPOSE
2012	97%	3%	13%	87%
2011	96%	4%	21%	79%

Interest Groups

	AFL-CIO	ADA	CCUS	ACU
2012	10%	5%	92%	92%
2011	0%	5%	100%	84%

Colorado 4

Eastern plains; Greeley

High, snowy peaks tend to dominate images of Colorado, but the 4th District looks more like the Kansas prairies than the rugged Rockies. The district touches five states — Wyoming, Nebraska, Kansas, Oklahoma and New Mexico — and includes many rural areas and some of the state's poorest counties. The eastern landscape appears flat, but the sparsely populated farmland slopes gradually for more than 150 miles west to the foothills of the Rockies and the fast-growing cities between Denver (in the 1st) and Colorado Springs (in the 5th).

Most of the district's population lives to the northwest in the outer ring of burgeoning Denver-area communities, particularly in Weld County between Longmont and Greeley and in Douglas County along Interstate 25 south of the E-470 tollway. The population in the 4th's portion of Douglas County, which is shared with the 6th, is more than several of the southeastern counties combined. The towns of Parker and Castle Rock, about a half hour outside of Denver, boast median incomes well above the state average. To the east, poverty is more prevalent; in Lamar and Trinidad, more than 20 percent of the residents live below the poverty line.

Thanks to intensive irrigation, the district has productive wheat and corn fields; Yuma County grows about one-fourth of the state's corn. Volatility in the climate — with summer hailstorms and occasionally dry winters or unseasonable snow in the spring — and in market prices can hurt the agricultural economy. Greeley focuses on agribusiness, meatpacking and poultry processing — JBS has its headquarters in the city.

The addition of most of conservative Douglas County during decennial redistricting solidified the 4th's Republican lean. In the 2012 presidential contest, both Adams and Arapahoe counties supported Barack Obama, but their portions in the 4th gave GOP candidate Mitt Romney more than 60 percent. In Cheyenne and Kiowa counties, Romney had his highest percentages statewide, at more than 80 percent.

Major Industry

Agriculture, food processing

Cities

Greeley, Longmont, Castle Rock

Notable

Greeley hosts the Greeley Stampede rodeo and music festival each year leading up to July Fourth.

Rep. Doug Lamborn (R)

Capitol Office
225-4422
lamborn.house.gov
2402 Rayburn Bldg. 20515-0605; fax 226-2638

Committees
Armed Services
Natural Resources
(Energy & Mineral Resources - Chairman)
Veterans' Affairs

Residence
Colorado Springs

Born
May 24, 1954; Leavenworth, Kan.

Religion
Christian

Family
Wife, Jeanie Lamborn; five children

Education
U. of Kansas, B.S. 1978 (journalism), J.D. 1985

Career
Lawyer

Political Highlights
Republican nominee for Kan. House, 1982; Colo. House, 1995-98; Colo. Senate, 1998-2007 (president pro tempore, 1999-2000)

ELECTION RESULTS

2012 GENERAL		
Doug Lamborn (R)	199,639	65.0%
Dave Anderson (NPA)	53,318	17.4%
Jim Pirtle (LIBERT)	22,778	7.4%
Misha Luzov (GREEN)	18,284	6.0%
Kenneth R. Harvell (AC)	13,212	4.3%
2012 PRIMARY		
Doug Lamborn (R)	43,929	61.7%
Robert Blaha (R)	27,245	38.3%
2010 GENERAL		
Doug Lamborn (R)	152,829	65.8%
Kevin Bradley (D)	68,039	29.3%
Brian "Barron X" Scott (AC)	5,886	2.5%
Jerell Klaver (LIBERT)	5,680	2.4%

Previous Winning Percentages
2008 (60%); 2006 (60%)

Elected 2006; 4th term

Lamborn is a custodian of the GOP's "all of the above" energy agenda. He's also among the most conservative members of the House.

"I'm going back to the values our country was founded upon: limited government, personal responsibility, living within one's means," he says. "And then I have a strong faith as well, and I think that that also connects me to traditional values."

His beliefs are generally well-received in the über-conservative Colorado Springs region, a magnet for outdoorsmen and military families. Lamborn sits on the Natural Resources, Armed Services and Veterans' Affairs committees — he also is an avid hiker, and one of his hobbies is climbing the dozens of 14,000-foot peaks in the state.

In 2011 he began serving as the chairman of the Natural Resources Subcommittee on Energy and Mineral Resources, with hopes of decreasing regulations on and increasing study of oil shale reserves. Oil shale, a rock that contains petroleum when processed properly, is found in many areas of Colorado.

Voting mostly along partisan lines, the House in 2012 passed Lamborn's bill to expand the number of exploration leases issued by the government for oil shale deposits, as well as lock in George W. Bush-era regulations for such energy development. It was also used as a vehicle for several Republican-favored energy provisions: expanding offshore energy development, opening parts of Alaska's Arctic National Wildlife Refuge to development and attempting to expedite approval of a pipeline to carry oil from Canada's tar sands to U.S. refineries. It wasn't considered in the Democratic Senate.

Another Lamborn bill to speed up permitting for energy projects on federal lands passed the House as part of a separate legislative package. Speaking to a mining group in early 2013, Lamborn vowed to continue those kinds of efforts — for both energy and mineral extraction.

The Obama administration's "anti-energy policies continuously hinder rather than help job creation," Lamborn said at a 2012 field hearing in Colorado. Oil shale development relies in part on hydraulic fracturing, the injection of high-pressure fluids into rock layers to allow access to new deposits of gas and oil; environmentalists and others have said the practice can contaminate groundwater. Lamborn says regulation of "fracking" should be left to states, and at that hearing he accused the Obama administration of seeking to "hijack those efforts and impose their own blanket set of regulations with little or no consultation with the states or tribes that would be affected."

His work on Armed Services and Veterans' Affairs often has a parochial bent, almost by necessity: His district is home to large Air Force facilities (including the Air Force Academy), part of the Army's Fort Carson, and a huge veteran population. Critics accused Lamborn early in his House career of tepid efforts as an advocate for local bases, but since joining Armed Services in 2007 he has touted his attempts to steer military funding to the 5th District.

As part of that process, he has become a leading congressional supporter of missile defense programs. Lamborn co-chairs the House Missile Defense Caucus and has been highly critical of any attempts to reduce spending on those programs. Threats from rogue nations justify the investment, according to Lamborn.

Some of his most notable stands, however, have been to reduce federal spending. Lamborn rejected all the final fiscal 2011 and fiscal 2012 spending bills, believing they did not do enough to cut spending. He vehemently opposed raising the debt ceiling in August 2011 and was among the Republicans who were dubious that the government could not service its debts without an increase in its borrowing limits.

Lamborn has introduced bills to prevent an increase in the federal debt limit unless a budget is in place. Another of his measures would include disaster relief funding, often appropriated as "emergency" funding outside of regular budget constrains, as part of discretionary spending. "If we were living within our means in our country, we would be much more prosperous," he said.

House Republicans in the 112th did sustain Lamborn's continuing crusade against federal funding of public broadcasting entities. His bill to block funding for NPR passed the House in early 2011. "What I oppose is subsidizing an organization that no longer provides, if it ever did, an essential government service," he wrote in The Hill newspaper. He also strongly opposes abortion and limitations to gun rights.

Lamborn's energetic conservatism isn't always reflected in floor speeches or committees. But he has on occasion run afoul of public opinion.

In July 2011 he called President Obama a "tar baby" while discussing the debt ceiling on a Denver talk radio program. "I don't even want to have to be associated with him," Lamborn said. "It's like touching a tar baby and you get it, you're stuck, and you're a part of the problem now and you can't get away." Lamborn later sent Obama an apology letter for using "a term some find insensitive." In a 2007 telephone message, he threatened a Colorado Springs couple with "consequences" for criticizing a campaign donation Lamborn had accepted; he later apologized.

Lamborn grew up on a family farm near Leavenworth, Kan. His mother was a homemaker, his father was a farmer who supplemented the family income by working at a federal penitentiary. He and his three brothers attended a three-room school near Fairmount before graduating from Lansing High School. Lamborn was class valedictorian and went on to obtain journalism and law degrees from the University of Kansas.

He was inspired to enter politics when Ronald Reagan was elected president. In 1982, Lamborn ran unsuccessfully for a seat in the Kansas Legislature. He moved to Colorado Springs with his wife in 1986 and won a seat in the Colorado House in 1994. Three years later he joined the state Senate.

Republican Rep. Joel Hefley's retirement in 2006 sparked a free-for-all in the August GOP primary. With the backing of the conservative Club for Growth, Lamborn edged ex-Hefley aide Jeff Crank in a chippy primary, which was tantamount to a November victory in the conservative district. He easily dispatched Crank in the 2008 primary rematch.

Banker Robert Blaha challenged Lamborn in the 2012 primary, loaning his campaign more than $750,000 of his own money. It was a negative campaign on both sides, but Lamborn won almost 62 percent of the vote.

Key Votes

2012	
Extend a Social Security payroll tax cut and unemployment benefits	NO
Ease securities rules to expand small-business access to capital	YES
Extend for one year subsidized student loan interest rates financed by a cut in health care spending	NO
Cite Attorney General Eric H. Holder Jr. for contempt of Congress	YES
Create a visa program for foreign graduates in high-tech fields	YES
Extend most Bush-era income tax rates while allowing rates for top-bracket earners to rise (Jan. 1, 2013)	NO

2011	
Strike funding for F-35 alternative engine	NO
Prevent EPA from regulating greenhouse gas emissions to address climate change	YES
Extend certain provisions of Patriot Act for four years	YES
Declare opposition to use of ground troops in Libya	YES
Overhaul patent law	NO
Pass compromise debt limit increase plan and establish future spending limits	NO
Allow consideration of measures to implement three trade agreements	YES

CQ Vote Studies

	PARTY UNITY		PRESIDENTIAL SUPPORT	
	SUPPORT	OPPOSE	SUPPORT	OPPOSE
2012	99%	1%	13%	87%
2011	98%	2%	20%	80%
2010	99%	1%	21%	79%
2009	99%	1%	13%	87%
2008	99%	1%	83%	17%

Interest Groups

	AFL CIO	ADA	CCUS	ACU
2012	5%	5%	91%	96%
2011	0%	5%	88%	100%
2010	0%	5%	75%	100%
2009	5%	0%	73%	100%
2008	0%	0%	83%	100%

Colorado 5

South central — Colorado Springs

God and country rule the 5th, an overwhelmingly conservative district in the shadows of the Rocky Mountains in central Colorado. Military bases employ tens of thousands in the Colorado Springs area, and James Dobson's Focus on the Family and other evangelical groups are based in the 5th.

The district has made itself an indispensable arm of the military. Colorado Springs in El Paso County houses the Air Force Space Command, the North American Aerospace Defense Command (NORAD) and the U.S. Northern Command at Peterson Air Force Base. The city has broadened its economic base beyond the military and satellite research, but much of the 5th's industry — including superconductor and computer development — still depends on the defense sector. Uncertainty regarding military spending has officials worried about job losses. The city also hosts Progressive Insurance's second largest information hub, and health care systems provide numerous jobs.

The Colorado Springs area is a prime destination for tourists who stop at spots such as Pikes Peak — the most visited mountain in North America — and the nearby Garden of the Gods sandstone formation. Colorado Springs consistently ranks among the nation's safest big cities to live in

Teller, Chaffee and Fremont counties are also wholly within the district, as is a portion of Park. Republican voters outnumber Democrats and independents in every jurisdiction in the district, and the main political contests for U.S. House races are typically at the primary level. But in the 2012 presidential election, Democrat Barack Obama squeaked out a win in Chaffee County by less than 1 percentage point even though the county has more registered GOP voters than Democrats.

Major Industry

Military, defense, tourism

Military Bases

Fort Carson (Army), 26,000 military, 5,800 civilian (2012) (shared with the 3rd); Peterson Air Force Base, 3,685 military, 4,459 civilian (2012); U.S. Air Force Academy, 1,965 military, 2,045 civilian; Schriever Air Force Base, 2,055 military, 607 civilian

Cities

Colorado Springs

Notable

The U.S. Olympic Committee headquarters is in Colorado Springs.

Rep. Mike Coffman (R)

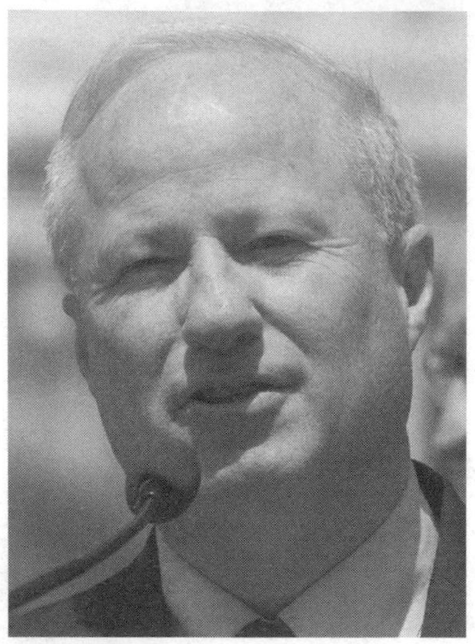

Capitol Office
225-7882
coffman.house.gov
2443 Rayburn Bldg. 20515-0606; fax 226-4623

Committees
Armed Services
Small Business
Veterans' Affairs
(Oversight & Investigations - Chairman)

Residence
Aurora

Born
March 19, 1955; Fort Leonard Wood, Mo.

Religion
United Methodist

Family
Wife, Cynthia Coffman

Education
U. of Colorado, B.A. 1979 (political science)

Military
Army, 1972-74; Army Reserve, 1975-79; Marine Corps, 1979-83; Marine Corps Reserve, 1983-94; Marine Corps Reserve, 2005-06

Career
Property management company owner

Political Highlights
Candidate for Aurora City Council, 1985; Colo. House, 1989-94; Colo. Senate, 1994-98; Colo. treasurer, 1999-2007; Colo. secretary of state, 2007-08

ELECTION RESULTS

2012 GENERAL

Mike Coffman (R)	163,938	47.8%
Joe Miklosi (D)	156,937	45.8%
Kathy Polhemus (UNA)	13,442	3.9%
Patrick E. Provost (LIBERT)	8,597	2.5%

2012 PRIMARY

Mike Coffman (R)	unopposed

Previous Winning Percentages
2010 (66%); 2008 (61%)

Elected 2008; 3rd term

Conservatism has always been a big part of Coffman's political identity. He now has to see if it's a liability in his district, which has been transformed into the most competitive political turf in Colorado.

When Coffman was first elected to the House in 2008, he represented a solidly Republican 6th District in suburban Denver — its prior representative was Tom Tancredo, an archconservative nationally known for hard-line stances on illegal immigration. But Coffman was on the short end of redistricting heading into the 2012 election. The 6th no longer has a strong Republican lean; it has a much higher proportion of Hispanic residents and takes in the entire city of Aurora, which tends to favor Democrats.

The saving grace for Coffman is that Aurora is his hometown. He was born at Fort Leonard Wood, Mo., where his father was stationed for Army service. The family lived there for about a year before bouncing between Alaska, Arkansas and Europe. They settled in Aurora when Coffman was 9. His father later set up a heating and air-conditioning business there.

As a teenager, Coffman volunteered at Fitzsimons Army Medical Center (now closed), where he saw wounded soldiers returning from Vietnam. He dropped out of high school at 17 to enlist. After several years of service, he switched over to the Army Reserve while getting a degree at the University of Colorado. When he graduated, he joined the Marine Corps.

In 1983, Coffman moved over to the Marine Corps Reserve and started a property management firm in the Denver area. He lost a race for the Aurora City Council in 1985 but three years later won a seat in the state House.

He was a member of that chamber when he was summoned to lead combat troops during the first Gulf War. It turned him from a somewhat obscure lawmaker into "a celebrity in House chambers just by not being there," the Rocky Mountain News reported in 2008. He parlayed that fame into a Colorado Senate seat and statewide offices.

Coffman's work in state government had a decidedly fiscal bent. He chaired the Finance Committee in the state Senate and spent eight years as Colorado's treasurer, battling with the governor while earning praise from conservatives and the Colorado Union of Taxpayers. He was narrowly elected Colorado secretary of state in 2006, then had little difficulty winning the race to succeed Tancredo, who retired from the House.

It was a different story in 2012. The new district lines encouraged a strong Democratic challenger, state Rep. Joe Miklosi, who painted Coffman as far too extreme for the district. Coffman raised more than twice the money that Miklosi did, but campaign organizations for House Democrats far outspent their GOP counterparts in trying to win the race.

Coffman won by only 2 points, taking less than 48 percent of the vote. Democrats early in 2013 announced plans to target Coffman, and former Colorado House Speaker Andrew Romanoff declared his candidacy in February.

For his part, Coffman started out the 113th Congress (2013-14) with some politically moderate displays. He introduced a bill to allow noncitizens to serve in the military and gain a path to citizenship. He's no longer listed on the roster of the conservative Republican Study Committee. And he left the Natural Resources Committee, home to energy and environmental debates. Instead, he's on the Veterans' Affairs Committee and chairs its oversight panel, giving him opportunities to tackle far less partisan problems.

But Coffman still has a record more conservative than the average Republican's, particularly on fiscal matters. He enthusiastically supported the moratorium on earmarks in 2010, and that same year he co-founded the Balanced-

Budget Amendment Caucus. Coffman looks to extend his brand of spending discipline across the government, including the military services where he spent large stretches of his life.

At the start of the 113th, Coffman didn't join many Republicans in trying to stop impending cuts to defense budgets that had been put in place by an August 2011 deficit reduction law — instead, he promoted his bill to allow the Pentagon to be more discriminating in where those cuts are made. He sits on the Armed Services Committee, and as the House debated the fiscal 2013 defense policy bill, Coffman ruffled feathers with an amendment to authorize the end of permanent combat brigades in Europe.

Some Republicans blanched in 2011 when Coffman proposed half a billion dollars in spending cuts affecting education reimbursements and military health care accounts, among other things. Coffman has suggested that active-duty military personnel are too expensive to maintain over long periods, and he has been skeptical of long-term interventions around the world.

"I think this nation made a terrible mistake in relying on nation-building as a principal tool for achieving our national security interests," he said of Afghanistan during a 2010 CNN appearance. Coffman himself helped organize local elections in Iraq in 2005 and 2006. Though he was the state treasurer at the time, he signed up again with the Marine Corps Reserve. Despite his reservations about nation-building, he had heard that the Marines needed people with both government and military experience: "There wasn't the right troop numbers and the right strategy to provide enough security that would allow the political process to move forward where the Iraqis would have the capacity to take care of the situation themselves," he said.

Tapping Coffman's reputation for frugality, House leaders named him to a special Panel on Defense Acquisition Reform, which led to legislation enacted in May 2009 to boost oversight of the Defense Department's procurement process to limit cost growth and improve delivery times.

Coffman also sits on the Small Business Committee, where in the 112th Congress (2011-12) he chaired its Subcommittee on Investigations, Oversight and Regulations. He used hearings to highlight cases of fraud when small businesses contract with the federal government and to advance the GOP claim that the regulatory and lending environment created by the Democratic administration has been detrimental to businesses.

Coffman's frustrations with the administration boiled over in the spring of 2012. Speaking at a campaign event in his home state, Coffman said of President Barack Obama, "in his heart, he's not an American." He later apologized, calling his comment "boneheaded" in an op-ed in the Denver Post. "I should never have questioned the president's devotion to our country," he wrote.

Key Votes

2012

Extend a Social Security payroll tax cut and unemployment benefits	YES
Ease securities rules to expand small-business access to capital	YES
Extend for one year subsidized student loan interest rates financed by a cut in health care spending	YES
Cite Attorney General Eric H. Holder Jr. for contempt of Congress	YES
Create a visa program for foreign graduates in high-tech fields	YES
Extend most Bush-era income tax rates while allowing rates for top-bracket earners to rise (Jan. 1, 2013)	NO

2011

Strike funding for F-35 alternative engine	YES
Prevent EPA from regulating greenhouse gas emissions to address climate change	YES
Extend certain provisions of Patriot Act for four years	YES
Declare opposition to use of ground troops in Libya	YES
Overhaul patent law	NO
Pass compromise debt limit increase plan and establish future spending limits	YES
Allow consideration of measures to implement three trade agreements	YES

CQ Vote Studies

	PARTY UNITY		PRESIDENTIAL SUPPORT	
	SUPPORT	OPPOSE	SUPPORT	OPPOSE
2012	93%	7%	15%	85%
2011	94%	6%	23%	77%
2010	95%	5%	29%	71%
2009	98%	2%	24%	76%

Interest Groups

	AFL-CIO	ADA	CCUS	ACU
2012	15%	0%	91%	92%
2011	0%	10%	94%	96%
2010	7%	0%	88%	100%
2009	15%	5%	73%	92%

Colorado 6

Eastern Denver suburbs — Aurora

Anchored by Aurora, the state's third-largest city, the 6th arcs through outer suburbs north, east and south of Denver. Most of the district's population lives in the white-collar suburbs of Arapahoe County, but the southern edge of the 6th dips into fast-growing Douglas County, and it wraps around to the north in Adams County. A slice of Denver falls into the district as well.

Aurora has long lived in the shadow of Denver, but technology manufacturing, major medical facilities and a military base support an independent economy. Raytheon employs more than 2,000 area residents at its Aurora satellite and intelligence systems facility. The renovation of the Fitzsimons Army Medical Center into the University of Colorado Anschutz Medical Campus has brought millions of dollars to the regional health care and research hub.

Buckley Air Force Base, a link in the Air Force Space Command satellite tracking system, is another major employer in the district. Intelligence and global missile defense work at the base, as well as classified federal contracts at the district's aerospace and technology firms, draw a highly skilled and highly educated workforce to the 6th.

Middle- to upper-class Littleton and Centennial are both in the district's southwest, and unincorporated Highlands Ranch is a growing bedroom community for Denver.

Explosive population growth across the district since 2000 forced a change in shape for the 6th during remapping following the 2010 census. A once strongly Republican district with the state's lowest minority population now offers the GOP only a single-digit percentage point edge in voter registration, supported Barack Obama in the 2012 presidential election with 52 percent of its vote, and is 20 percent Hispanic.

Major Industry
Technology, health care, aerospace

Military Bases
Buckley Air Force Base, 3,100 military, 2,400 civilian

Cities
Aurora, Centennial, Littleton

Notable
General aviation Front Range Airport has applied for designation by the FAA as Colorado's official commercial spaceport.

Rep. Ed Perlmutter (D)

Capitol Office
225-2645
perlmutter.house.gov
1410 Longworth Bldg. 20515-0607; fax 225-5278

Committees
Financial Services

Residence
Golden

Born
May 1, 1953; Denver, Colo.

Religion
Protestant

Family
Wife, Nancy Perlmutter; three children

Education
U. of Colorado, B.A. 1975 (political science), J.D. 1978

Career
Lawyer

Political Highlights
Colo. Senate, 1995-2003 (president pro tempore, 2001-03)

ELECTION RESULTS

2012 GENERAL		
Ed Perlmutter (D)	182,460	53.5%
Joe Coors (R)	139,066	40.8%
Douglas Campbell (AC)	10,296	3.0%
Buck Bailey (LIBERT)	9,148	2.7%
2012 PRIMARY		
Ed Perlmutter (D)		unopposed
2010 GENERAL		
Ed Perlmutter (D)	112,667	53.4%
Ryan Frazier (R)	88,026	41.8%
Buck Bailey (LIBERT)	10,117	4.8%

Previous Winning Percentages
2008 (63%); 2006 (55%)

Elected 2006; 4th term

Perlmutter has slid into the background as a member of the minority, pressing his priorities on renewable energy and financial services regulation from behind the scenes. With Republicans running the House floor, he's also had more chances to break from his party on business-minded measures.

A former bankruptcy attorney, Perlmutter developed a reputation for crossing party lines when he served in the Colorado Senate. He took opportunities to be personable with the opposition when he joined the U.S. House as a member of the new Democratic majority in 2007, but tactically he was a team player. Perlmutter raises impressive amounts of campaign cash for his colleagues, and in the 111th Congress (2009-10) party leaders put him on the Rules Committee, which dictates the terms of floor debate.

The landscape changed when Republicans took control of the chamber in 2011. Perlmutter continues to back his party in most things but no longer sits on Rules. A member of the business-friendly New Democrat Coalition, he lines up closer to the middle on fiscal matters.

Perlmutter accepted the spending reductions in the fiscal 2011 and 2012 appropriations laws, and he was one of 22 House Democrats to vote for a fiscal 2013 budget based on the work of a 2010 special fiscal commission created by President Barack Obama. The blueprint, widely viewed as middle ground between Republicans and Democrats, proposed to cut deficits by $4 trillion over 10 years through a mix of spending reduction and revenue increases.

In recent years, Perlmutter has also rolled out fewer bills on one of his biggest priorities going back to his state Senate days: renewable energy.

He was active on the issue, though. Perlmutter often champions energy independence as a way to boost economic growth. He says he believes in the "all of the above" approach to energy production. Perlmutter in 2012 campaigned for an extension of the tax credit for production related to wind energy — it was extended as part of the January 2013 "fiscal cliff" law — and in 2012 he made pleas to House leaders to retain funding for the Energy Department program that in turn feeds the National Renewable Energy Laboratory in Colorado. Perlmutter had contributed to a $300 million boost to the program's funding in 2007.

Perlmutter also pays more than lip service to fossil fuels. He split with environmentalists in his party to call for the granting of a permit for the Keystone XL pipeline, which would connect Canada's oil sands to U.S. refineries. He was one of 41 House Democrats to vote for a bill to stop tougher EPA regulation of industrial boilers — rules seen by many as detrimental to coal use.

Perlmutter sometimes pursues his energy goals on the Financial Services Committee, the one panel he has sat on throughout his House career. In his freshman term, he tried unsuccessfully to require public-housing authorities and government-backed mortgage companies to support energy-efficiency standards for low- and moderate-income housing.

He supports the 2010 financial regulatory overhaul known as Dodd-Frank, and has dismissed many GOP complaints that it is too burdensome for businesses. When the law was enacted, Perlmutter said it would end "the Wild West era on Wall Street."

He also praised Obama's $787 billion economic stimulus law, enacted in February 2009, for its investments in mass transit and energy efficiency upgrades to public housing. He said it would help his state's burgeoning renewable-energy sector.

Perlmutter has been less thrilled over the years with Obama's plans for the space program. He joined other Colorado officials in a lobbying effort to save the Orion space vehicle, which was built in their state, from administration plans to cancel the Constellation, a manned space flight program. Perlmutter and Texas Republican Lamar Smith wrote a scolding letter to NASA leaders in September 2012, warning them to keep the program on track for a 2014 test flight. "America needs to lead on the frontiers of space," they wrote.

On social issues, Perlmutter generally aligns with Democrats. He historically skirted discussions of gun control, but a deadly mass shooting in an Aurora movie theater in 2012 put his district on the front page. (All of Aurora is now in the 6th District, however.) Perlmutter and fellow Colorado Democrats called for regulation over certain types of firearms, and he has continued that push in the 113th Congress (2013-14). More Democrats joined in after a Connecticut elementary school shooting in late 2012.

Perlmutter drew unwelcome headlines in 2009 when he and other Colorado lawmakers were a subject of news reports focused on a potential connection between campaign contributions from the now-defunct lobbying firm The PMA Group and earmarks it secured for clients. He denied wrongdoing in obtaining an earmark for IHS Inc., a defense consulting firm and PMA client. His spokeswoman said he did not receive money from IHS, but from PMA's political action committee. He gave the money to charity.

For decades, Perlmutter's grandfather and father ran a cement business in the Denver area, where Perlmutter was born and raised. His father was active in the Democratic Party, and Perlmutter's first taste of politics came by walking precincts with his family and handing out fliers.

He worked his way through law school as a laborer on the family business' construction projects, then spent nearly 30 years at one law firm, mostly focusing on bankruptcy cases.

Perlmutter was elected to the Colorado Senate in 1994 in a district traditionally held by Republicans. He considered a run for Congress in 2002 but demurred; in 2004, he co-chaired John Kerry's presidential campaign operation in Colorado. He saw an opportunity to run for the House in 2006 when incumbent Republican Bob Beauprez launched an unsuccessful bid for governor. Perlmutter's GOP opponent was Rick O'Donnell, a former state education commissioner. What was originally viewed as a toss-up race turned into a resounding victory for Perlmutter, who also won easily the next two cycles.

His district once surrounded Denver on three sides, but the new congressional map for 2012 took away most of the territory to the east of the city. Republican Joe Coors — of the famous brewing company family — spent $3.5 million of his own money trying to unseat Perlmutter. Raising more than enough money to stage a solid defense in the Democratic-leaning district, Perlmutter won by almost 13 points.

Key Votes

2012	
Extend a Social Security payroll tax cut and unemployment benefits	YES
Ease securities rules to expand small-business access to capital	YES
Extend for one year subsidized student loan interest rates financed by a cut in health care spending	NO
Cite Attorney General Eric H. Holder Jr. for contempt of Congress	NO
Create a visa program for foreign graduates in high-tech fields	NO
Extend most Bush-era income tax rates while allowing rates for top-bracket earners to rise (Jan. 1, 2013)	YES
2011	
Strike funding for F-35 alternative engine	YES
Prevent EPA from regulating greenhouse gas emissions to address climate change	NO
Extend certain provisions of Patriot Act for four years	NO
Declare opposition to use of ground troops in Libya	NO
Overhaul patent law	YES
Pass compromise debt limit increase plan and establish future spending limits	YES
Allow consideration of measures to implement three trade agreements	?

CQ Vote Studies

	PARTY UNITY		PRESIDENTIAL SUPPORT	
	SUPPORT	OPPOSE	SUPPORT	OPPOSE
2012	85%	15%	85%	15%
2011	84%	16%	84%	16%
2010	98%	2%	95%	5%
2009	97%	3%	97%	3%
2008	97%	3%	16%	84%

Interest Groups

	AFL-CIO	ADA	CCUS	ACU
2012	89%	70%	33%	4%
2011	100%	85%	38%	4%
2010	93%	95%	29%	4%
2009	100%	95%	40%	0%
2008	93%	95%	59%	0%

Colorado 7

Western and northern Denver suburbs — Lakewood, Arvada

The 7th District is made up mostly of Denver's northern and western suburbs, curving from Lakewood and Golden through Arvada, Westminster and Commerce City, past the Rocky Mountain Arsenal National Wildlife Refuge.

The district's portion of Jefferson County relies on federal government jobs. Lakewood is home to the Denver Federal Center, which hosts 55 federal buildings and more than 6,000 government employees on its 600-acre campus. The Social Security Administration and the FBI are two of the agencies at the center of the complex. The National Renewable Energy Laboratory and the National Earthquake Information Center are both located in Golden, which is also home to the engineering- and natural-resources-focused Colorado School of the Mines and several Coors Brewing Company facilities, including the brewery where some 11 million barrels of beer are produced each year.

Westminster and Arvada are split between Jefferson and Adams counties, taking in densely packed suburbs as well as open spaces, parks and nature refuges. East of Commerce City in Adams, the former Rocky Mountain Arsenal is now a national wildlife refuge and the largest contiguous open space in the Denver metropolitan area. The district's cities are overwhelmingly white. Some areas in the otherwise well-educated suburbs have problems with poverty.

Colorado gained a seventh district following the 2000 census, and it was drawn to be competitive, although it shifted to the left in the latter part of the decade. Remapping after the 2010 census shed sparsely populated portions of Adams County in favor of closer-in suburbs and re-established a competitive environment for federal races. Registered Democrats slightly outnumber GOP voters; there are as many unaffiliated voters as Republicans in the district. In the 2012 presidential race, Barack Obama took a comfortable 56 percent of the district's vote.

Major Industry
Government, technology

Cities
Lakewood, Westminster, Arvada, Golden

Notable
Commerce City is home to the Colorado Rapids' soccer stadium.

CONNECTICUT

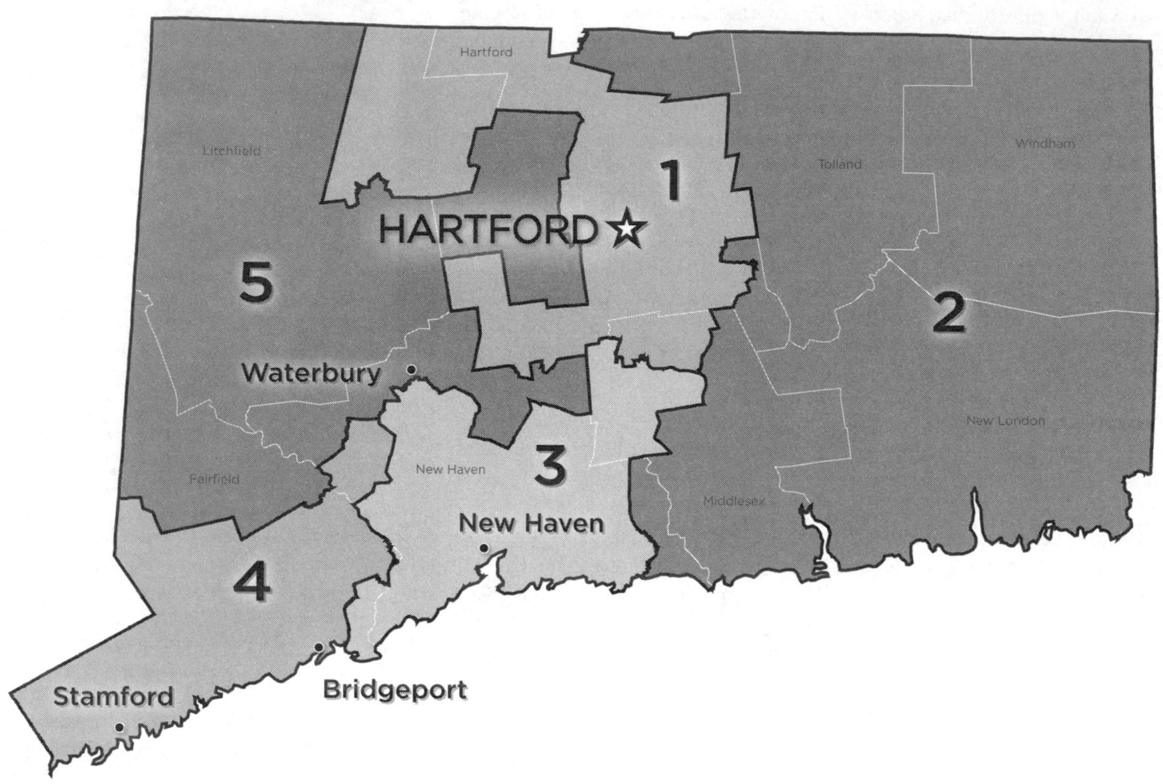

Gov. Dannel P. Malloy (D)

First elected: 2010
Length of term: 4 years
Term expires: 1/15
Salary: $150,000
Phone: (860) 566-4840
Residence: Stamford
Born: July 21, 1955; Stamford, Conn.
Religion: Roman Catholic
Family: Wife, Cathy Malloy; two children
Education: Boston College, B.A. 1977, J.D. 1980
Career: Lawyer; city prosecutor
Political highlights: Stamford Board of Finance, 1983-94; mayor of Stamford, 1995-2009; sought Democratic nomination for governor, 2006

ELECTION RESULTS

2010 GENERAL

Dannel P. Malloy (D)	567,278	49.5%
Tom Foley (R)	560,874	48.9%
Thomas Marsh (I)	17,629	1.5%

Lt. Gov. Nancy Wyman (D)

First elected: 2010
Length of term: 4 years
Term expires: 1/15
Salary: $110,000
Phone: (860) 524-7384

LEGISLATURE

General Assembly: January-June in odd-numbered years; February-May in even-numbered years
Senate: 36 members, 2-year terms
2013 ratios: 22 D, 14 R; 27 men, 9 women
Salary: $28,000
Phone: (860) 240-0500
House: 151 members, 2-year terms
2013 ratios: 98 D, 52 R, 1 vacancy; 104 men, 46 women
Salary: $28,000
Phone: (860) 240-0400

TERM LIMITS

Governor: No
Senate: No
House: No

URBAN STATISTICS

CITY	POPULATION
Bridgeport	144,229
New Haven	129,779
Hartford	124,775
Stamford	122,643
Waterbury	110,366

REGISTERED VOTERS

Other	40%
Democrat	37%
Republican	20%

POPULATION

2010 population (est.)	3,574,097
2000 population	3,405,565
1990 population	3,287,116
Percent change (2000-2010)	+4.9%
Rank among states (2010)	29
Median age	39
Born in state	55.9%
Foreign born	12.5%
Violent crime rate	299/100,000
Poverty level	9.4%
Federal workers	24,973
Military	1,914

ELECTIONS

STATE ELECTION OFFICIAL
(860) 509-6200
DEMOCRATIC PARTY
(860) 560-1775
REPUBLICAN PARTY
(860) 422-8211

MISCELLANEOUS

Web: www.ct.gov
Capital: Hartford

U.S. CONGRESS

Senate: 2 Democrats
House: 5 Democrats

STATISTICS BY DISTRICT

District	2012 Vote for President: Obama	Romney	2008 Vote for President: Obama	McCain	Black	Asian	Hispanic	Median Income	Over 64	Under 20	College Education	Rural	Sq. Miles
1	63%	36%	66%	33%	14%	5%	15%	$60,572	15%	25%	34%	6%	675
2	56	43	59	40	4	3	7	68,925	14	24	33	31	1,988
3	63	36	63	36	13	4	13	61,277	15	25	34	3	470
4	55	44	60	40	12	5	17	79,097	14	28	47	4	461
5	54	45	56	43	7	3	16	63,275	14	26	34	15	1,248
STATE	**58**	**41**	**61**	**38**	**10**	**4**	**13**	**65,753**	**15**	**25**	**36**	**12**	**4,842**
U.S.	**51**	**47**	**53**	**46**	**12**	**5**	**17**	**50,052**	**13**	**27**	**29**	**21**	**3,531,905**

Sen. Richard Blumenthal (D)

Capitol Office
224-2823
blumenthal.senate.gov
724 Hart Bldg. 20510; fax 224-9673

Committees
Armed Services
Commerce, Science & Transportation
Judiciary
(Oversight, Federal Rights & Agency Action - Chairman)
Veterans' Affairs
Special Aging

Residence
Greenwich

Born
Feb. 13, 1946; Brooklyn, N.Y.

Religion
Jewish

Family
Wife, Cynthia Blumenthal; four children

Education
Harvard U., A.B. 1967 (political science); Cambridge U., attended 1967-68; Yale U., J.D. 1973

Military Service
Marine Corps Reserve, 1970-76

Career
Lawyer; congressional aide; White House aide

Political Highlights
U.S. attorney, 1977-81; Conn. House, 1984-87; Conn. Senate, 1987-91; Conn. attorney general, 1991-2011

ELECTION RESULTS

2010 GENERAL

Richard Blumenthal (D, WFM)	636,040	55.2%
Linda McMahon (R)	498,341	43.2%

2010 PRIMARY

Richard Blumenthal (D)	unopposed

Elected 2010; 1st term

Blumenthal is a private person in a public profession — a popular politician who is not a natural back-slapper. A 2004 Hartford Courant profile described him, not unkindly, as "the ultimate carnival performer, hiding behind a public mask, trick mirrors and spotlights."

A traditional Northeastern Democrat, he has voted in much the same tradition as his predecessor, Democrat Christopher J. Dodd. A lot of Blumenthal's work has a parochial bent, but he has been loyal to his party. In each of his first two years in the Senate, Blumenthal stuck with a majority of Democrats on at least 95 percent of the votes where they opposed a majority of Republicans.

Blumenthal took a civic-minded tack early in his career. During the Richard Nixon administration, he worked in the White House for Democrat Daniel Patrick Moynihan, who was counseling the president on urban affairs (and went on to become a New York senator). When Blumenthal was 31, President Jimmy Carter appointed him as a U.S. attorney — at the recommendation of Connecticut Sen. Abraham Ribicoff, whom Blumenthal had served as an administrative aide.

Blumenthal later became a state legislator and state attorney general, earning the appellation "the perennial golden boy of New England politics." He always seemed ready to move up, but he held the attorney general post for two decades. Dodd's retirement finally gave him the opening he wanted.

He works to protect his state's defense interests as a member of the Armed Services Committee. "We in Connecticut produce weaponry that fits that new kind of warfare," Blumenthal told the Norwich Bulletin. "I will fight relentlessly and resourcefully for those defense products made in Connecticut."

Blumenthal, like Dodd, opposed President Barack Obama's decision to cancel the F-22 fighter program — the plane's engine is made in Connecticut — and said he would fight to restart production. He cheered when Congress eliminated funding for an alternative engine for the F-35, leaving East Hartford-based Pratt & Whitney as the sole provider of engines for the project.

He has emphasized humanitarian goals when looking at broader security policy. Working with Ohio Republican Rob Portman, he helped secure language in the fiscal 2013 defense authorization law that seeks to stop Pentagon contractors from engaging in human trafficking. Blumenthal traveled to the Middle East in early 2013 and called for a large increase in humanitarian assistance to those affected by Syria's civil war. He described aid for children as an investment in future security: "They are the prey for extremists and jihadists who will eventually attack United States interests," he said.

He also engages in humanitarian work as a member of the Commission on Security and Cooperation in Europe — aka the Helsinki Commission.

At the start of the 113th Congress (2013-14), Blumenthal joined the Veterans' Affairs Committee. It's an assignment he sought despite a sticky situation tied to his own military service. Blumenthal received multiple draft deferments during the Vietnam War. When they were exhausted, he enlisted in the Marine Corps Reserve, but he never served in Vietnam.

During his 2010 Senate campaign, The New York Times reported that Blumenthal had, as he put it, "misspoken" about his service. "We have learned something important since the days that I served in Vietnam," the Times quoted Blumenthal as saying to a group in Norwalk in March 2008. He had made similar allusions to being in the theater of war on other occasions.

As a freshman Blumenthal was placed on the Judiciary Committee, and for the 113th he was added to the Commerce, Science and Transportation Committee. Both of those panels are forums for the consumer watchdog efforts he championed as an attorney general.

He was named the chairman of a new Judiciary subcommittee at the start of the 113th, overseeing the federal rulemaking process. Blumenthal has been disappointed at the pace of some regulatory efforts — he signed a June 2012 letter complaining that the government was too slow in implementing the 2010 financial regulatory overhaul law and its consumer protections. He has called for investigations into banks' handling of foreclosures.

Consumer privacy is very important to Blumenthal. In September 2011, the Judiciary Committee approved his bill to set notification requirements for companies that suffer a data breach of consumers' personal information, as well as establish legal measures to recover damages from companies that allow preventable breaches. He emphasizes privacy protections when discussing public-private data sharing meant to help cybersecurity efforts.

As attorney general, Blumenthal was a lead negotiator for the 1998 Master Settlement Agreement with large cigarette manufacturers. He was one of three senators in September 2012 who called on the surgeon general to look into the effect that sugary drinks have on U.S. obesity rates.

The horrifying shooting of more than 20 people at a Connecticut elementary school in late 2012 increased Blumenthal's involvement in gun control efforts. Early in the 113th he introduced a bill to require background checks for ammunition purchases.

The Commerce committee is also a good spot for Blumenthal to promote manufacturing in his state. Connecticut has sought to position itself as a leader in fuel cell technology, and Blumenthal wants to extend the federal "48c" tax credit, enacted as part of the 2009 stimulus, for "clean" energy manufacturers. (It was capped at $2.3 billion when written.)

Blumenthal was born in Brooklyn in the first wave of the baby boom. He is the son of a German Jewish immigrant who came to the United States in the 1930s to escape Nazi persecution and built a successful import-export business. Blumenthal attended the private Riverdale Country School in the Bronx and graduated Phi Beta Kappa from Harvard, where he served as chairman of the Harvard Crimson newspaper. He followed that with a year as an intern at The Washington Post and had plans to become a journalist.

But he left journalism to take a job at the White House, where he worked under Moynihan and met future Defense Secretary Donald H. Rumsfeld. He and Rumsfeld, then head of the Office of Economic Opportunity, became tennis partners. After his stint at the White House, Blumenthal attended Yale Law School, where he edited the law journal and won a clerkship with Supreme Court Justice Harry A. Blackmun.

Blumenthal was elected state attorney general in 1990 — making him a successor to Joseph I. Lieberman, who had run successfully for the Senate in 1988. A rapid rise was expected after that, but he remained attorney general. He might have been elected to the Senate in 2000 if Lieberman, running for vice president on the Democratic ticket with Al Gore, had not chosen to simultaneously seek re-election to the Senate. Instead, he turned the attorney general's office into a consumer protection division.

When Dodd announced he would retire in 2010, Blumenthal was the automatic choice of Connecticut Democrats to succeed him. Often accused of being too cautious to take on a tough electoral challenge, he certainly faced one in the 2010 Senate race, overcoming a self-financed opponent, his own missteps and a banner year for Republicans nationwide.

Professional wresting magnate Linda McMahon secured the GOP nomination and outspent Blumenthal about 6-to-1, but he still garnered 55 percent of the vote.

Blumenthal was the wealthiest member of the congressional Class of 2010, and one of the richest members overall. Blumenthal's wealth stems in part from his wife, Cynthia, daughter of New York real estate mogul Peter Malkin.

Key Votes

2012

Prohibit health insurance plans from denying coverage based on the sponsor's religious beliefs	**YES**
Require approval of the Keystone XL oil pipeline	**NO**
Ease securities rules to expand small-business access to capital	**NO**
Reauthorize farm and nutrition programs for five years	**YES**
Limit debate on a bill that would create private-sector cybersecurity standards	**YES**
Consent to ratification of a treaty setting global standard for the treatment of people with disabilities	**YES**
Provide $60.4 billion in disaster relief following Superstorm Sandy	**YES**
Extend most Bush-era income tax rates while allowing rates for top-bracket earners to rise (Jan. 1, 2013)	**YES**

2011

Prevent EPA from regulating greenhouse gas emissions to address climate change	**NO**
Extend certain provisions of Patriot Act for four years	**?**
Clear compromise debt limit increase plan and establish future spending limits	**YES**
Overhaul patent law	**YES**
Implement Colombia free trade agreement	**NO**
Limit debate on confirmation of Caitlin J. Halligan to D.C. Circuit Court of Appeals	**YES**
Extend payroll tax cut and unemployment benefits for two months	**YES**

CQ Vote Studies

	PARTY UNITY		PRESIDENTIAL SUPPORT	
	SUPPORT	OPPOSE	SUPPORT	OPPOSE
2012	90%	2%	97%	3%
2011	95%	5%	94%	6%

Interest Groups

	AFL-CIO	ADA	CCUS	ACU
2012	100%	90%	38%	0%
2011	95%	95%	45%	5%

Sen. Christopher S. Murphy (D)

Capitol Office
224-4041
murphy.senate.gov
303 Hart Bldg. 20510; fax 228-9604

Committees
Foreign Relations
(European Affairs - Chairman)
Health, Education, Labor & Pensions
Joint Economic

Residence
Cheshire

Born
Aug. 3, 1973; White Plains, N.Y.

Religion
Protestant

Family
Wife, Cathy Holahan; two children

Education
Williams College, B.A. 1996 (history & political science); U. of Connecticut, J.D. 2002

Career
Lawyer; state legislative and campaign aide

Political Highlights
Southington Planning & Zoning Commission, 1997-99; Conn. House, 1999-2003; Conn. Senate, 2003-07; U.S. House, 2007-13

ELECTION RESULTS

2012 GENERAL		
Christopher S. Murphy (D)	828,761	54.8%
Linda McMahon (R)	651,089	43.1%
Paul Passarelli (LIBERT)	25,045	1.7%
2012 PRIMARY		
Christopher S. Murphy (D)	94,424	66.7%
Susan Bysiewicz (D)	47,109	33.3%

Previous Winning Percentages
2010 House Election (54%); 2008 House Election (59%); 2006 House Election (56%)

Elected 2012; 1st term

Murphy is something of a political wunderkind. Starting at the age of 25, he quickly worked his way up the ladder in local and state politics, never staying in any one office longer than four years. He moved to a national stage when he was elected to the House in his 30s, and he showed a knack for making friends among fellow Democrats in his state's delegation. He's now the youngest member of the Senate.

Part of Murphy's appeal as a politician is his lack of ideological rigidity. His views on the environment and social issues align with those of most liberals, but as a House member he belonged to the business-friendly New Democrat Coalition. The mold that most reliably shapes his interests is Connecticut — when Murphy takes up causes, they tend to resonate with his state.

The most prominent example is also a tragic one. Murphy supported the idea of stronger gun control laws, but it was not a priority for him during his three terms in the House. A tragic shooting in his district in December 2012, just weeks after he was elected to the Senate, changed all that. Twenty first-graders and six teachers were killed at an elementary school in Newtown.

"Sometimes you find issues and sometimes issues find you," says Murphy, who has become one of Capitol Hill's loudest proponents of restrictions on access to guns. He is also one of the fiercest critics of the National Rifle Association, the powerful lobby that opposes most restrictions.

"I have been personally changed by what happened in Newtown," Murphy said. Even in a country largely inured to stories about gun violence, the school shooting captured national attention and prompted a new push by the White House on gun control. Murphy is fully on board with that effort. Specifically, he supports proposals to strengthen background check requirements for gun purchases, prevent gun trafficking and bar high-capacity magazines.

He would also like to see a new version of the "assault weapons" ban that expired in 2004, but Murphy doesn't see such legislation making it through the Senate. Democratic leaders conceded as much in March 2013.

Murphy's newfound passion on gun control influenced his early work on the Foreign Relations Committee. He wants to be "a strong voice for an international arms trade agreement" — negotiations on such a treaty began in 2012 and continued in March 2013 at the United Nations.

Murphy served on the Foreign Affairs Committee during his last term in the House but was not active on the panel. He is likely to be a much bigger player on foreign policy in the Senate, as the new chairman of the Subcommittee on European Affairs. From there, he will be able to exert influence on the negotiation of a new free-trade agreement with the European Union, something President Barack Obama announced he intended to pursue during his 2013 State of the Union address.

The contours of that pact will be significant for the U.S. economy and Connecticut in particular, according to Murphy. "Connecticut is a state that has a lot at stake when it comes to the world economy and export policy," he said. Murphy points to a manufacturing sector that, as a proportion of the state economy, is bigger than the national average. Connecticut is home to multinational corporations such as United Technologies and General Electric.

As a House member, Murphy never voted for a free-trade agreement — he said he had concerns about labor and environmental standards in the pacts that came before Congress. But he maintains that he's not "philosophically opposed to free trade."

"I'm looking forward to being part of the drafting of this agreement so I can make it one that some of us who have traditionally been opposed to free-trade agreements can support," he said.

Murphy is known as a supporter of U.S. manufacturing interests and an opponent of outsourcing. He founded the Buy American Caucus in 2010 with North Carolina Republican Walter B. Jones to draw attention to government purchases from foreign vendors, most notably in defense contracts. He intends to promote a similar agenda in the Senate. "The government can't preach about not off-shoring jobs when it's off-shoring jobs," he said.

Murphy first ran for the House in 2006, and he says his primary motivation was to vote for a national health care law. That goal was achieved with passage of the health care overhaul in the 111th Congress (2009-10). The law doesn't include the government-run "public option" insurance plan that he favored, but he still defends it — now as a member of the Health, Education, Labor and Pensions Committee.

He wants the law implemented "in the strongest way possible," and he is preparing for two battles that could be pivotal in determining the law's reach. The first is over the creation of health insurance exchanges, which need to attract a large number of patients and insurers to be effective, Murphy says.

The second is over changes to the delivery systems by which Americans obtain health care. "We can largely solve the entitlement problem within Medicare by running a more efficient delivery system," he argues. His worry is that the Obama administration might not be aggressive enough in pushing the sort of overhaul that could make Medicare solvent. "Every day that we waste time not implementing delivery system reforms, it becomes more likely that we're going to balance the Medicare books on the backs of beneficiaries," he said.

The HELP Committee handles workforce issues, and Murphy is a supporter of organized labor. He attributes his allegiance to his grandfather and great-grandfather, who worked at a New Britain ball bearing factory. "My family is tied to the industrial past," he said.

Murphy's parents weren't politically active, but they raised him and his two siblings "to live our lives in a way that gave back and tried to lift other people up who weren't in our circumstances." His brother went to work for a humanitarian organization, his sister was a social worker and he went into politics.

He was initially drawn in by an interest in local environmental issues. "I remember helping to clean up the Connecticut River and thinking to myself, I could come down here with my little clean-up group and help clean up the river every two weeks, or I could start paying attention to why the thing is polluted in the first place," he said.

Murphy is still interested in the environment, and, as a Foreign Relations member, he supports the idea of global climate talks.

Murphy went to Williams College, where he earned a dual degree in history and political science. In his first job out of college, he managed the congressional campaign of activist Charlotte Koskoff, who came within 1,600 votes of upsetting veteran Republican Rep. Nancy L. Johnson. Ten years later, Murphy finished the job, ousting Johnson by a solid margin in an election season that heavily favored his party.

Connecticut had an open Senate seat in the 2012 election, thanks to the retirement of independent Joseph I. Lieberman. Murphy easily won the Democratic primary to claim his party's nomination.

In the general election he faced big-spending former World Wrestling Entertainment CEO Linda McMahon. It was her second attempt at securing an open Senate seat — in the 2010 race to succeed retiring Democrat Christopher J. Dodd, McMahon lost to Democrat Richard Blumenthal.

It was a testy and competitive race, and McMahon spent almost $50 million of her own money on the campaign. Murphy was able to pull away and win by more than 10 points, buoyed by strong Democratic turnout in the state and President Barack Obama's re-election win.

Key Votes (while in the House)

2012	
Extend a Social Security payroll tax cut and unemployment benefits	YES
Ease securities rules to expand small-business access to capital	YES
Extend for one year subsidized student loan interest rates financed by a cut in health care spending	NO
Cite Attorney General Eric H. Holder Jr. for contempt of Congress	NO
Create a visa program for foreign graduates in high-tech fields	?
Extend most Bush-era income tax rates while allowing rates for top-bracket earners to rise (Jan. 1, 2013)	YES
2011	
Strike funding for F-35 alternative engine	YES
Prevent EPA from regulating greenhouse gas emissions to address climate change	NO
Extend certain provisions of Patriot Act for four years	NO
Declare opposition to use of ground troops in Libya	NO
Overhaul patent law	YES
Pass compromise debt limit increase plan and establish future spending limits	NO
Allow consideration of measures to implement three trade agreements	NO

CQ Vote Studies (while in the House)

	PARTY UNITY		PRESIDENTIAL SUPPORT	
	SUPPORT	OPPOSE	SUPPORT	OPPOSE
2012	93%	7%	88%	12%
2011	92%	8%	89%	11%
2010	97%	3%	90%	10%
2009	97%	3%	97%	3%
2008	98%	2%	17%	83%
2007	96%	4%	5%	95%

Interest Groups (while in the House)

	AFL-CIO	ADA	CCUS	ACU
2012	95%	90%	44%	0%
2011	100%	85%	19%	4%
2010	93%	95%	13%	4%
2009	100%	100%	40%	4%
2008	100%	95%	61%	0%
2007	96%	100%	50%	0%

Rep. John B. Larson (D)

Capitol Office
225-2265
larson.house.gov
1501 Longworth Bldg. 20515-0701; fax 225-1031

Committees
Ways & Means

Residence
East Hartford

Born
July 22, 1948; Hartford, Conn.

Religion
Roman Catholic

Family
Wife, Leslie Larson; three children

Education
Central Connecticut State U., B.S. 1971 (history)

Career
Insurance company owner; high school teacher

Political Highlights
East Hartford Board of Education, 1978-79; East Hartford Town Council, 1979-83; Conn. Senate, 1983-95 (president pro tempore, 1987-95); sought Democratic nomination for governor, 1994

ELECTION RESULTS

2012 GENERAL		
John B. Larson (D)	206,973	69.7%
John Henry Decker (R)	82,321	27.7%
Michael DeRosa (GREEN)	5,477	1.8%
2012 PRIMARY		
John B. Larson (D)		unopposed
2010 GENERAL		
John B. Larson (D)	138,440	61.2%
Ann Brickley (R)	84,076	37.2%
Kenneth J. Krayeske (GREEN)	2,564	1.1%

Previous Winning Percentages
2008 (72%); 2006 (74%); 2004 (73%); 2002 (67%); 2000 (72%); 1998 (58%)

Elected 1998; 8th term

Larson was the chairman of the House Democratic Caucus, a position that reflected his excellent standing with both the party rank and file and Minority Leader Nancy Pelosi. A term limit forced him from that job at the end of 2012, however, and he now fulfills more amorphous leadership roles.

For the most part, Larson is a meat-and-potatoes Democrat. He champions safety-net programs, environmental protection and the concerns of organized labor. When he breaks with a majority of his party, it's to serve local interests. Larson's voting record on national security is partially shaped by Connecticut's defense contractors, and he'll support free-trade deals that stand to benefit manufacturers in the state. He has extensive experience in state and local government, and since 2005 Larson has held a seat on the Ways and Means Committee.

His ability to manage intraparty relationships and stay on message helped propel him into House leadership. Larson counted as a friend and mentor Rep. John P. Murtha of Pennsylvania, who was a close ally of Pelosi. (Murtha died in 2010.) With Murtha's help, Larson was elected vice chairman of the Democratic Caucus in early 2006. He was unopposed in his bid to succeed Illinois Democrat Rahm Emanuel as caucus chairman and took that job in the 111th Congress (2009-10).

Larson became the bridge between leaders and the rest of the party — the friendly face that less-prominent lawmakers were comfortable talking to. He stayed in the background for his first term on the job, winning praise for his patience and persistence with Democratic causes, particularly health care. Larson — whose Hartford district hosts several huge insurance companies — used caucus meetings as an ongoing seminar on health care policy, keeping his party immersed in details en route to the 2010 enactment of its health care overhaul.

Larson stepped forward somewhat in the 112th Congress (2011-12), with Democrats reverting to the minority and reeling from electoral losses. As the party regrouped, Larson helped drive home its talking points heading toward the 2012 elections; he needled Republicans for balking at jobs bills proposed by President Barack Obama, accused the GOP of favoring the wealthy with its tax plans and criticized proposals to overhaul Medicare and Social Security.

Speaking at the Democratic National Convention in 2012, he defended those entitlement programs by describing his mother's reliance on them in dealing with multiple sclerosis and dementia. "Don't ever tell me or any American that's a handout," he said. "It's the insurance they paid for."

But when he reached the party-imposed term limit on his job, he couldn't land a better one — Pelosi, Minority Whip Steny H. Hoyer of Maryland and Assistant Leader James E. Clyburn of South Carolina didn't change or quit their jobs heading into the 113th Congress (2013-14), and Larson resisted entreaties to challenge Hoyer or Clyburn. Pelosi found a new task for him in the 113th — he is coordinating Democrats' efforts to overhaul campaign finance and election laws — but a lot of his leadership clout is now unofficial.

He's also focusing more on Ways and Means, which is considering a comprehensive overhaul of the tax code. Larson sits on the Select Revenue Measures Subcommittee, and he is working with Nebraska Republican Adrian Smith to study parts of the tax code related to financial services.

Larson trumpets common Democratic tax themes. He pushed for a number of credits and tax code adjustments to lessen the burden on small businesses in the 111th Congress, and in the 112th he introduced a package of changes that he said would promote hiring. It included an extension of lower payroll tax rates — which he voted for in a separate bill in early 2012. (The lower rates expired at the end of that year, however.) Larson has also pitched a "carbon tax" on those who produce greenhouse gas emissions, with the revenue going back to the public in the form of a payroll tax rebate.

He has a seat on the Trade Subcommittee. Larson supported free-trade pacts with South Korea and Panama in 2011, saying they would be good for automotive manufacturers and other businesses in Connecticut. He supports the idea of taking stronger punitive measures against China if that country manipulates the value of its currency for a trade advantage, as many have alleged it does.

Larson once sat on the Armed Services Committee, and he is a big congressional supporter of the defense contractor Pratt & Whitney. Larson was raised in East Hartford, and his father was a Pratt & Whitney fireman who moonlighted as an auto mechanic and butcher to support his family.

An influx of cost-cutting Republicans in the 112th Congress helped Larson and others realize a longtime goal: killing a Pentagon program to develop an alternative engine for the F-35 Joint Strike Fighter. Pratt & Whitney is under contract to build one version of the engine, but supporters of a GE-Rolls Royce consortium kept funding going for a second engine for years. The House voted in February 2011 to eliminate the alternative engine funding from the catchall fiscal 2011 spending bill, and the Pentagon canceled the alternative engine program shortly after.

Larson grew up in an East Hartford public housing project originally built for workers of United Aircraft — a precursor to United Technologies Corp., the parent company of Pratt & Whitney. He got an early taste of politics through his mother, a state employee, who served on the town council and was active in Democratic Party organizing.

After graduating from Central Connecticut State University, Larson taught high school history and coached sports for about five years. He then joined an insurance company that he eventually bought. After stints on the school board and town council, he was elected in 1982 to the state Senate, where he served a dozen years, rising to the position of president pro tempore.

Larson ran for governor in 1994, gaining endorsements of party leaders but losing the primary to state Comptroller Bill Curry. In 1996, he led a statewide volunteer drive to wire schools and libraries for the Internet.

When veteran 1st District Democratic Rep. Barbara B. Kennelly announced she was running for governor in 1998, Larson was the first Democrat to file for the race to succeed her. He edged past Connecticut Secretary of State Miles S Rapoport in the primary, rolled to a 17-point victory in the general election and hasn't been seriously threatened since.

Key Votes

2012

Extend a Social Security payroll tax cut and unemployment benefits	YES
Ease securities rules to expand small-business access to capital	YES
Extend for one year subsidized student loan interest rates financed by a cut in health care spending	NO
Cite Attorney General Eric H. Holder Jr. for contempt of Congress	?
Create a visa program for foreign graduates in high-tech fields	NO
Extend most Bush-era income tax rates while allowing rates for top-bracket earners to rise (Jan. 1, 2013)	YES

2011

Strike funding for F-35 alternative engine	YES
Prevent EPA from regulating greenhouse gas emissions to address climate change	NO
Extend certain provisions of Patriot Act for four years	NO
Declare opposition to use of ground troops in Libya	NO
Overhaul patent law	YES
Pass compromise debt limit increase plan and establish future spending limits	NO
Allow consideration of measures to implement three trade agreements	NO

CQ Vote Studies

	PARTY UNITY		PRESIDENTIAL SUPPORT	
	SUPPORT	OPPOSE	SUPPORT	OPPOSE
2012	96%	4%	86%	14%
2011	95%	5%	82%	18%
2010	99%	1%	88%	12%
2009	99%	1%	98%	2%
2008	99%	1%	13%	87%

Interest Groups

	AFL-CIO	ADA	CCUS	ACU
2012	95%	95%	25%	0%
2011	93%	85%	25%	4%
2010	100%	100%	13%	0%
2009	100%	100%	33%	0%
2008	100%	95%	65%	0%

Connecticut 1

Central — Hartford, Bristol

The 1st District, shaped like a backwards "C" centered on the capital city of Hartford and its suburbs, curves through central Connecticut. One arm stretches north and west though sparsely populated towns along the Massachusetts border to part of Torrington, and the other curls south and west to Bristol. Situated midway between Boston and New York — roughly 100 miles from each — the staunchly Democratic district is a commercial center for the Northeast Corridor.

While many capital residents work for the state government, the insurance and financial services industries remain Hartford's foundation. Despite years of layoffs among the region's numerous corporate offices and headquarters and an unemployment rate nearly double the statewide average, incomes remain high in many parts of the greater Hartford area. Aetna, already one of Hartford's largest employers, recently consolidated its operations and welcomed thousands of workers from other locations. The city also is home to the University of Hartford, Trinity College and regional, business and law campuses of the University of Connecticut.

East Hartford is bolstered by the headquarters of United Technologies' Pratt & Whitney, the city's largest employer. Rentschler Field, once an airfield associated with the aircraft engine manufacturer, is the site of the football stadium for the University of Connecticut and the centerpiece of an ongoing mixed-use development project. Further west, Bristol has an industrial past and retains its specialty manufacturing base in clocks and small machine parts. It is perhaps best known for its largest employer: the headquarters of ESPN.

The 1st has a sizable and growing Hispanic population and the state's largest share of black residents, mostly clustered in Hartford and neighboring suburbs, especially Bloomfield.

Major Industry
Insurance, banking, state government, manufacturing

Cities
Hartford, West Hartford, Bristol, Manchester, East Hartford, Southington

Notable
The Hartford Courant, founded in 1764, is the nation's oldest continuously published newspaper, and the Wadsworth Atheneum in Hartford is the nation's oldest public art museum.

Rep. Joe Courtney (D)

Capitol Office
225-2076
courtney.house.gov
2348 Rayburn Bldg. 20515-0702; fax 225-4977

Committees
Agriculture
Armed Services
Education & the Workforce

Residence
Vernon

Born
April 6, 1953; Hartford, Conn.

Religion
Roman Catholic

Family
Wife, Audrey Budarz Courtney; two children

Education
Tufts U., B.A. 1975 (history); U. of Connecticut, J.D. 1978

Career
Lawyer; public defender

Political Highlights
Conn. House, 1987-95; Democratic nominee for lieutenant governor, 1998; Democratic nominee for U.S. House, 2002

ELECTION RESULTS

2012 GENERAL		
Joe Courtney (D)	204,708	68.2%
Paul M. Formica (R)	88,103	29.4%
Colin Bennett (GREEN)	3,638	1.2%
Daniel Reale (LIBERT)	3,511	1.2%
2012 PRIMARY		
Joe Courtney (D)		unopposed
2010 GENERAL		
Joe Courtney (D)	147,748	59.9%
Janet Peckinpaugh (R)	95,671	38.8%
G. Scott Deshefy (GREEN)	3,344	1.4%

Previous Winning Percentages
2008 (66%); 2006 (50%)

Elected 2006; 4th term

Courtney takes an analytical approach as he advocates for his state and its defense-related industries. He mostly operates below the radar, but he has created a few blips in recent years with his work on health care and education.

His popularity in Connecticut makes it easy to forget that he came to Congress by winning one of the closest House races ever. In 2006, Courtney beat Republican Rep. Rob Simmons by just 83 votes. Democrats gave Courtney a leg up in his freshman term by assigning him to the Armed Services Committee, and he uses that post to protect his state's military establishment.

Courtney can cite the exact number of submarines and National Guard units he oversees, and he's intimately aware of challenges facing General Dynamics' Electric Boat facility in Groton — the largest manufacturing plant in his district. As scheduled cuts to defense budgets approached in early 2013, Courtney said that he was following layoff notices "like a box score."

He co-chairs the Congressional Shipbuilding Caucus with Virginia Republican Rob Wittman. Courtney argues that submarines are a vital part of the country's nuclear deterrence strategy, and he wants more of them built. Thanks in part to Courtney's efforts, the fiscal 2013 defense authorization law includes plans to build two submarines in 2014 (as opposed to the one proposed by the Navy), and up to 10 submarines through 2018. A lot of that work goes to Electric Boat.

The Obama administration's desire for an increased military presence in the Pacific warrants continued investment in the New London Naval Submarine Base and the U.S. Coast Guard Academy, Courtney says. And he opposed the administration's call for a new round of military base realignment and closures. The New London submarine base was nearly shuttered in a 2005 round before lawmaker protests saved it.

But Courtney approved of the Obama administration's 2011 cancellation of a second engine for the F-35 Joint Strike Fighter — the primary engine is manufactured at a Pratt & Whitney plant in Connecticut.

Courtney's defense of national security spending is balanced with his willingness to accept some fiscal restraints. He voted for fiscal 2011 and 2012 appropriations bills that shrank discretionary spending, and he supported an August 2011 deficit reduction agreement.

He also walks a line between business and labor. Courtney is a member of the business-friendly New Democrat Coalition, but he's a steady supporter of unions. He returned to the Education and the Workforce Committee for the 113th Congress (2013-14) and serves as the top Democrat on the Workforce Protections Subcommittee, which handles safety issues and legislation regarding the minimum wage.

As a member of the committee in the 111th Congress (2009-10), Courtney tussled with his party on health care overhaul legislation. He led a group of Democrats opposing the excise tax on "Cadillac" insurance plans — high-premium policies often negotiated by established unions. The tax was designed to help pay for the overhaul. The White House cut a deal to delay the excise tax start date, and Courtney was among the last of the holdout Democrats to support the bill.

Courtney has co-sponsored a Republican bill to repeal the Independent Payment Advisory Board, a panel whose recommendations on Medicare cost controls would take effect unless Congress disapproved. He has eschewed proposals to tax employer-sponsored health care benefits; he says doing so would ultimately reduce coverage for Americans and increase long-term federal spending.

A federal takeover of most student lending was packaged with the 2010 health care law, and it made interest rates on those loans into a budget issue — they are set by statute, and changes affect federal revenue. Lower rates set in 2007 were scheduled to double in 2012, which Courtney called a "ticking time bomb for middle-class families." He introduced a bill to make the lower rate permanent, with no budgetary offset; it gathered more than 150 Democratic co-sponsors. A one-year extension was enacted in the summer of 2012.

Courtney encourages increased study of the actual value of college degrees, so students looking to make that investment can better analyze their options. "There really is a gaping need for better transparency and information for students, along the lines of when you buy a house," he said.

His third assignment is to the Agriculture Committee, which he first joined in the 112th Congress (2011-12). He counts a number of small dairy farmers as constituents. In 2009 Courtney successfully lobbied Agriculture Secretary Tom Vilsack to increase government purchases of dairy products in an effort to support prices. He would like to establish a program to offset declines in income for dairy farmers during market downturns.

Courtney grew up as a "political junkie" in West Hartford in the 1960s. "I was an Irish Catholic kid who remembered John F. Kennedy — the nuns actually prayed for him during the election in second grade," he said.

He became a Democrat, even though his father was a moderate Republican. But he followed in his father's footsteps by pursuing a law degree at the University of Connecticut. While in law school, Courtney worked as an aide to Democrat Sam Gejdenson in Connecticut's General Assembly. Gejdenson went on to represent the 2nd District in the U.S. House — his 21-vote victory in 1994 was even closer than Courtney's 2006 win.

Courtney later ran for the state House, where he served from 1987 to 1995; he left after the birth of his second child. His return to electoral politics wasn't triumphant. Courtney lost bids for lieutenant governor in 1998 and for the U.S. House in 2002, when Simmons bested him by 8 points.

But Democrats were having a good year in 2006, and Courtney eked out a win in a rematch. That initial victory margin has shaped his work, he says: "You realize how fragile this opportunity is."

Despite Courtney's narrow victory, Simmons decided not to challenge him in 2008. Courtney raised almost six times as much as his GOP opponent and won with more than 65 percent of the vote. He took 60 percent in 2010, and he faced negligible opposition in 2012.

Courtney defended his state against Hollywood in 2013 — he feuded with screenwriter Tony Kushner, whose script for "Lincoln" inaccurately portrayed Connecticut's House delegation opposing the 13th Amendment.

Key Votes

2012	
Extend a Social Security payroll tax cut and unemployment benefits	YES
Ease securities rules to expand small-business access to capital	YES
Extend for one year subsidized student loan interest rates financed by a cut in health care spending	NO
Cite Attorney General Eric H. Holder Jr. for contempt of Congress	NO
Create a visa program for foreign graduates in high-tech fields	NO
Extend most Bush-era income tax rates while allowing rates for top-bracket earners to rise (Jan. 1, 2013)	YES
2011	
Strike funding for F-35 alternative engine	YES
Prevent EPA from regulating greenhouse gas emissions to address climate change	NO
Extend certain provisions of Patriot Act for four years	NO
Declare opposition to use of ground troops in Libya	NO
Overhaul patent law	YES
Pass compromise debt limit increase plan and establish future spending limits	YES
Allow consideration of measures to implement three trade agreements	NO

CQ Vote Studies

	PARTY UNITY		PRESIDENTIAL SUPPORT	
	SUPPORT	OPPOSE	SUPPORT	OPPOSE
2012	94%	6%	89%	11%
2011	92%	8%	91%	9%
2010	96%	4%	95%	5%
2009	99%	1%	96%	4%
2008	99%	1%	10%	90%

Interest Groups

	AFL-CIO	ADA	CCUS	ACU
2012	95%	90%	25%	4%
2011	100%	80%	31%	0%
2010	100%	90%	25%	0%
2009	100%	95%	33%	0%
2008	100%	95%	50%	8%

Connecticut 2

East — Norwich, New London, Storrs

Connecticut's geographically largest district, the 2nd takes in the eastern half of the state. It borders Massachusetts to the north, Rhode Island to the east, Long Island Sound to the south, and the outskirts of the Hartford and New Haven suburbs to the west. Its population is concentrated to the southeast in the triangle formed by New London, Groton and Norwich.

The southeastern coast has a rich maritime and fishing culture, and military shipbuilding is a major industry in the district. General Dynamics' Electric Boat Corp., which makes submarines for the federal government, has large facilities in Groton and Norwich, while New London is home to a naval submarine base and the U.S. Coast Guard Academy. The University of Connecticut recently completed a marine sciences center at Avery Point. Further north, Storrs is home to the main campus of the University of Connecticut, and Eastern Connecticut State University is in Willimantic.

Unemployment rates in the southeast, while not as high as in the state's largest cities, remain high because of continued layoffs. Pharmaceutical giant Pfizer closed its research headquarters in New London and laid off workers in Groton. Electric Boat shed jobs in the 1990s, but has experienced recent growth. New London faces municipal budget shortfalls.

Windham County is full of small manufacturing and distribution centers, especially in the blue-collar towns of Windham and Killingly. To the northwest, Tolland County contains many of the state's jails.

The Democratic 2nd, which lost Durham and part of Glastonbury after decennial remapping, has the state's highest proportion of white residents. The WNBA's Connecticut Sun, the state's only major league team, plays in the arena at the Mohegan Sun casino.

Major Industry
Defense, shipbuilding, tourism, higher education

Military Bases
New London Naval Submarine Base, 7,500 military, 1,400 civilian

Cities
Enfield, Norwich, Groton, New London

Notable
The Mystic Seaport Museum has the Charles W. Morgan, the last remaining wooden whaleship and oldest surviving American commercial vessel.

Rep. Rosa DeLauro (D)

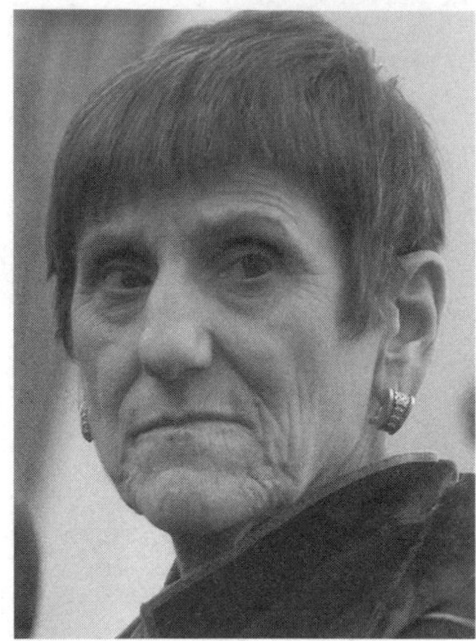

Capitol Office
225-3661
delauro.house.gov
2413 Rayburn Bldg. 20515-0703; fax 225-4890

Committees
Appropriations

Residence
New Haven

Born
March 2, 1943; New Haven, Conn.

Religion
Roman Catholic

Family
Husband, Stanley Greenberg; three children

Education
London School of Economics, attended 1962-63; Marymount College (N.Y.), B.A. 1964; Columbia U., M.A. 1966 (international politics)

Career
Political activist; congressional and mayoral aide

Political Highlights
No previous office

ELECTION RESULTS

2012 GENERAL		
Rosa DeLauro (D)	217,573	74.7%
Wayne Winsley (R)	73,726	25.3%
2012 PRIMARY		
Rosa DeLauro (D)		unopposed
2010 GENERAL		
Rosa DeLauro (D)	143,565	65.1%
Jerry Labriola Jr. (R)	74,107	33.6%
Charles A. Pillsbury (GREEN)	2,984	1.4%

Previous Winning Percentages
2008 (77%); 2006 (76%); 2004 (72%); 2002 (66%); 2000 (72%); 1998 (71%); 1996 (71%); 1994 (63%); 1992 (66%); 1990 (52%)

Elected 1990; 12th term

It's hard not to notice DeLauro on Capitol Hill. She is usually brightly clad, scarved and bespectacled, and she has a demeanor as bold as her attire. When she takes a special interest in a subject — as she has with health care, food safety and wage equality — few people can match her commitment.

DeLauro grew up in Wooster Square, a tight-knit Italian neighborhood in New Haven. Her father, Ted, was an immigrant, and her mother, Luisa, was a factory worker; both served on the New Haven council, and their home was the hub for meetings about schools, jobs and immigration. When her father first ran for the city council, he kept a file box filled with voters' names and their concerns, then walked door-to-door to seek their votes.

In the 1960s, DeLauro was a community organizer for President Lyndon Johnson's War on Poverty legislation. She then worked for the mayor of New Haven. In 1980 she ran Connecticut Democrat Christopher J. Dodd's first Senate campaign, then became his chief of staff for seven years. She also took the helm of EMILY's List, a fundraising group that backs Democratic female political candidates who support abortion rights.

In 1990, DeLauro ran for the seat of Democratic Rep. Bruce Morrison, who was running for governor. She defeated GOP state Sen. Thomas Scott, an energetic conservative. In a 1992 rematch, she defeated him with 66 percent of the vote, and she has been re-elected easily ever since: DeLauro garnered almost 75 percent of the vote in 2012.

Her job security and activist instincts have drawn her into leadership roles in the House Democratic Caucus. In the 107th Congress (2001-02), she ran the party's communications arm as a top assistant of Minority Leader Richard A. Gephardt of Missouri. In the 108th Congress (2003-04), DeLauro lost a race for caucus chairwoman by one vote. But the new minority leader, California's Nancy Pelosi, appointed her co-chairwoman of the Democratic Steering Committee, which makes committee assignments. She still has that job.

DeLauro also has a lot of pull as a senior member of the Appropriations Committee — she is not afraid to mix the panel's traditional fiscal focus with policy initiatives.

Since 2011 she has been the ranking member of the Labor-HHS-Education Subcommittee. DeLauro is not only an advocate for implementation of the 2010 health care overhaul, but also a principal Democratic defender against Republican efforts to neuter it. When Republican appropriators advanced a fiscal 2013 bill that cut out spending for several programs featured in the law, DeLauro was incensed.

"This is wrong for women, wrong for children and wrong for seniors," she said. "Stop pushing an ideological agenda that places the health of our constituents at risk." (The bill was not enacted.)

As the appropriations cycle began in the 113th Congress (2013-14), DeLauro made a plea for expanded funding of public health and research organizations. Slow growth of budgets at the National Institutes of Health, she said, was threatening U.S. leadership in biomedical research.

Many of her favored topics were included in the 2010 overhaul law. Her final comments in the House's floor debate on the measure emphasized its improved coverage and insurance treatment that "will put women's health on an equal footing at last." Her interest in women's health issues stems in part from her own battle with ovarian cancer more than 20 years ago. She has consistently sought funding for medical research and advocates improved breast cancer treatment.

DeLauro in the 111th Congress (2009-10) chaired the Agriculture Subcommittee, where she was integral to an overhaul of the federal food safety regime. DeLauro worked for the final passage of legislation to make the Food and Drug Administration more proactive in preventing contamination; it also allows the agency to order mandatory recalls of potentially tainted products.

At the start of 2013 she was dismayed that regulations mandated by that law had not yet been finalized. "I am deeply concerned that special interests are pressuring the FDA to slow-walk this process and water down these rules that are supposed to protect people," she wrote.

DeLauro is a leading voice for regulation of the food and drug industries, and she weighs in during contamination scares. A fungal meningitis outbreak linked to a compounding pharmacy in New England spurred DeLauro and New York Democrat Nita M. Lowey to action in 2012; their proposed legislation would more clearly define FDA authority over such pharmacies.

She also defends food assistance programs. In 2012, she called proposed cuts to the Supplemental Nutrition Assistance Program "immoral," and she unsuccessfully tried to modify a spending bill to boost international food aid.

DeLauro frequently works on women's issues, whether they relate to her subcommittees or not. In early 2012 she joined with other liberals in supporting the Obama administration's rules requiring religion-affiliated insurance providers to cover women's contraception. And she helped popularize the notion of a Republican "war on women" heading into the 2012 elections.

In the 113th, DeLauro has again introduced her bill to adjust legal recourses in disputes over gender-based pay discrimination. She pitches the bill as a companion to a 2009 law extending the statute of limitations for employees to sue in wage discrimination cases.

DeLauro is very liberal. She was one of just 16 Democrats to oppose the January 2013 "fiscal cliff" deal that increased income tax rates on earnings over $400,000 for individuals — she said that threshold was too high. A longtime member of the Congressional Progressive Caucus, she was the author of the group's 2012 economic stimulus plan, which included infrastructure development proposals. She has proposed that Congress emulate Europe in establishing a public-private partnership called the National Infrastructure Development Bank to attract private investors to critical building projects.

A 2012 tragedy in her state — a mass shooting at an elementary school in Newtown — drew her further into efforts to curtail gun violence. Democrats introduced a host of bills to address mental health programs, gun purchases and more. DeLauro in the 113th has contributed a measure to create a tax credit of $2,000 for those who voluntarily turn in legally owned "assault" weapons defined by the bill.

DeLauro is married to Stanley Greenberg, a prominent Democratic pollster.

Key Votes

2012	
Extend a Social Security payroll tax cut and unemployment benefits	YES
Ease securities rules to expand small-business access to capital	YES
Extend for one year subsidized student loan interest rates financed by a cut in health care spending	NO
Cite Attorney General Eric H. Holder Jr. for contempt of Congress	NO
Create a visa program for foreign graduates in high-tech fields	NO
Extend most Bush-era income tax rates while allowing rates for top-bracket earners to rise (Jan. 1, 2013)	NO
2011	
Strike funding for F-35 alternative engine	YES
Prevent EPA from regulating greenhouse gas emissions to address climate change	NO
Extend certain provisions of Patriot Act for four years	NO
Declare opposition to use of ground troops in Libya	NO
Overhaul patent law	YES
Pass compromise debt limit increase plan and establish future spending limits	NO
Allow consideration of measures to implement three trade agreements	NO

CQ Vote Studies

	PARTY UNITY		PRESIDENTIAL SUPPORT	
	SUPPORT	OPPOSE	SUPPORT	OPPOSE
2012	98%	2%	87%	13%
2011	97%	3%	86%	14%
2010	99%	1%	90%	10%
2009	99%	1%	99%	1%
2008	99%	1%	13%	87%

Interest Groups

	AFL-CIO	ADA	CCUS	ACU
2012	95%	95%	17%	0%
2011	100%	85%	19%	4%
2010	100%	100%	13%	0%
2009	100%	100%	33%	0%
2008	100%	100%	56%	0%

Connecticut 3

South — New Haven, Milford

The 3rd District takes in towns along the central Connecticut coast, including Stratford, Milford and Guilford, as well as the port city of New Haven. Inland, it also includes part of Waterbury and most of Middletown. Suburban professionals in the district commute to jobs throughout the state and as far away as New York City.

The main focus of the district is New Haven, the second-most populous city in the state. Yale University tends to dominate the district's economy as the city's largest employer. In addition to its liberal arts academic community, the Ivy League heavyweight contributes to the region's biomedical research and technology sector, which includes major medical facilities. Tax and labor issues can strain the school's relations with the city — which, as with other cities in the state, is far poorer than its affluent suburbs — and an economic divide is clearly evident between Yale and its publicly funded neighbor, Southern Connecticut State University.

The city has recently embarked on a major redevelopment plan for its downtown, including waterfront renewal projects. Building on a manufacturing history, New Haven is also one of the state's largest wholesale distribution centers, with access to a deep water port, several railroad lines and major interstates.

Defense contractors have a major presence in the district; Stratford-based Sikorsky Aircraft, which builds helicopters such as the Army's Black Hawk and Navy's Seahawk models, employs hundreds of district residents but depends on military contracts for continued viability.

While the district overall is 75 percent white, New Haven and Hamden have among the highest concentrations of black residents in the state. The district's strongly liberal academic populations combined with its blue-collar workforce have created a Democratic stronghold.

Major Industry
Higher education, defense, biotechnology, manufacturing

Cities
New Haven, Hamden, West Haven, Stratford, Milford, Wallingford

Notable
New Haven has the oldest public tree-planting program in the nation, earning it the nickname of Elm City.

Rep. Jim Himes (D)

Capitol Office
225-5541
himes.house.gov
119 Cannon Bldg. 20515-0704; fax 225-9629

Committees
Financial Services
Select Intelligence

Residence
Greenwich

Born
July 5, 1966; Lima, Peru

Religion
Presbyterian

Family
Wife, Mary Himes; two children

Education
Harvard U., A.B. 1988 (social studies); Oxford U., M.Phil. 1990 (Rhodes scholar)

Career
Affordable housing nonprofit executive; investment banker

Political Highlights
Housing Authority of the Town of Greenwich, 2003-06 (chairman, 2003-06); Greenwich Democratic Town Committee chairman, 2004-08; Greenwich Board of Estimate and Taxation, 2006-07

ELECTION RESULTS

2012 GENERAL		
Jim Himes (D)	175,929	60.0%
Steve Obsitnik (R)	117,503	40.0%
2012 PRIMARY		
Jim Himes (D)		unopposed
2010 GENERAL		
Jim Himes (D)	115,351	53.1%
Dan Debicella (R)	102,030	46.9%

Previous Winning Percentages
2008 (51%)

Elected 2008; 3rd term

Himes has a business sensibility and, thanks to a Wall Street career, the technical know-how to back it up. Democrats are tying some of their electoral fortunes to his connections in the finance world — he's heading up the fundraising operation for the Democratic Congressional Campaign Committee.

Himes is a vice chairman of the business-friendly New Democrat Coalition, and each of his House campaigns has featured eye-popping fundraising totals; the finance sector and its workers contribute heavily to his cause. He was involved in campaign operations during the 112th Congress (2011-12), leading the DCCC incumbent retention program. For the 113th Congress (2013-14), he was elevated to the post of finance chairman.

Unsurprisingly, he is seen as having a bright future in the Democratic Party. He is personable, and his Twitter feed, @jahimes, is unusually engaging for a congressman. He can also be feisty and fiscally moderate.

For 12 years, Himes worked as an investment banker at Goldman Sachs. He also led the New York City branch of the affordable-housing nonprofit Enterprise Community Partners. His district is home to many people who work in finance, and it includes Greenwich, the center of the American hedge fund industry. He now sits on the Financial Services Committee, and he makes himself available to colleagues seeking illumination of the often-murky substance of financial regulation.

"I definitely enjoy working on the nitty-gritty and the details of policy," he said. "But I also like to be part of the discussion on larger values issues, the conversation of do we continue to invest in the infrastructure of prosperity and opportunity for everybody, or do we focus our efforts, as the Republicans are doing, on income concentration."

In his first term, the panel labored on the 2010 financial regulatory overhaul known as Dodd-Frank. In his second, it zeroed in on the law's implementation. "We need the industry vibrant and adding to our economy," he said in 2012. "But we need the industry to never do what it did three years ago again."

Himes sits on the Capital Markets and Government Sponsored Enterprises Subcommittee. In 2011, the House passed a bill by Himes and Arkansas Republican Steve Womack meant to increase capital flows to local businesses; it greatly increases the number of shareholders who can invest in a community bank before it must register with the Securities and Exchange Commission. In theory, that allows banks to push more money out to businesses before having to deal with additional federal regulation. The measure was packaged into a 2012 law.

He also sits on the Housing and Insurance Subcommittee. Proximity to New York City makes his district one of the more expensive housing markets in the country, and the city of Bridgeport was hit hard by foreclosures in the financial crisis. Himes still wants Congress to deal with housing giants Fannie Mae and Freddie Mac so "they're not in subprime, they're not running foundations, they're not allowed to lobby," he told The Hour Newspapers in early 2011.

Himes has broader policy interests that have been overshadowed by the demands of the financial crisis. "I didn't decide in 2007, 'I'm gonna run for Congress to help regulate the derivatives market,'" he said. "I just happened to be Johnny-on-the-spot when it happened."

On broader fiscal matters, he often aligns with centrist coalitions. While wary of the spending cuts sought by Republican leaders, he backs a deficit reduction plan based on the work of a 2010 fiscal commission, known as Simpson-Bowles. It would cut deficits by $4 trillion over 10 years through a spending reduction, revenue increases and changes to entitlement programs.

Himes was one of only 38 House members to vote for a fiscal 2013 budget based on the plan. "I was under no illusion that it would pass, but I had expected more votes for it," he told the Stamford Advocate. An amendment to a budget-related bill early in the 113th Congress would have established the Simpson-Bowles guidelines as the basis for federal budget planning; it was rejected, but with 75 votes in support.

He makes a finance-based argument for infrastructure plans favored by Democrats. One of the nation's busiest transportation corridors cuts through his district, and Himes says spending on roads and bridges might be the best way to spur the economy. "We're going to spend the money anyway, I promise you. So why not do it now, when interest rates are zero and all kinds of engineers and electricians and steelworkers are out of work?" he said in 2012.

Several times, he has chimed in on foreign affairs. Himes has advocated the rapid drawdown of American troops in Afghanistan and wants the military to focus almost exclusively on counterterrorism operations. He has a greater say in such matters as a new member of the Intelligence Committee in the 113th Congress.

And Himes, like many New Democrats, is more receptive of free trade than some party colleagues. He was in the minority of his party in 2011 voting for deals with South Korea, Panama and Colombia.

Himes was born in Lima, Peru, where his father worked for the Ford Foundation. He spent his early years there and in Bogota, Colombia. When he was 10, his parents divorced, and he moved to New Jersey with his two sisters and his mother. He later attended Harvard, where he was captain of the lightweight crew team, and was awarded a Rhodes Scholarship to study at Oxford.

Although he thought about working at the State Department, Himes took a job at Goldman Sachs, which was opening a Latin America group. He sold investors on the privatization of Telmex, the Mexican telephone company, until Goldman disbanded the group in 1994. Himes then worked in mergers and acquisitions and the technology group.

When the dot-com boom ended, he decided he'd had enough. Himes served as a commissioner of the Greenwich housing authority, then got into nonprofit housing finance.

In 2008, he raised close to $4 million en route to knocking off 10-term incumbent Christopher Shays, the only House Republican in New England. Himes took 51 percent of the vote.

A similar fundraising effort for 2010 helped him take 53 percent of the vote against state Sen. Dan Debicella, whose campaign sought to tie Himes to the House Democratic leadership. He scored a 20-point win against Republican Steve Obsitnik in 2012.

Key Votes

2012	
Extend a Social Security payroll tax cut and unemployment benefits	YES
Ease securities rules to expand small-business access to capital	YES
Extend for one year subsidized student loan interest rates financed by a cut in health care spending	NO
Cite Attorney General Eric H. Holder Jr. for contempt of Congress	NO
Create a visa program for foreign graduates in high-tech fields	YES
Extend most Bush-era income tax rates while allowing rates for top-bracket earners to rise (Jan. 1, 2013)	YES
2011	
Strike funding for F-35 alternative engine	YES
Prevent EPA from regulating greenhouse gas emissions to address climate change	NO
Extend certain provisions of Patriot Act for four years	NO
Declare opposition to use of ground troops in Libya	YES
Overhaul patent law	YES
Pass compromise debt limit increase plan and establish future spending limits	YES
Allow consideration of measures to implement three trade agreements	YES

CQ Vote Studies

	PARTY UNITY		PRESIDENTIAL SUPPORT	
	SUPPORT	OPPOSE	SUPPORT	OPPOSE
2012	90%	10%	85%	15%
2011	89%	11%	85%	15%
2010	88%	12%	97%	3%
2009	90%	10%	92%	8%

Interest Groups

	AFL-CIO	ADA	CCUS	ACU
2012	80%	80%	42%	4%
2011	90%	80%	44%	0%
2010	93%	90%	29%	13%
2009	95%	95%	40%	4%

Connecticut 4

Southwest — Bridgeport, Stamford

Running up the Long Island Sound from the outskirts of New York City through wealthy "Gold Coast" towns, the 4th District takes in white-collar banking and business hub Stamford, industrial Norwalk, and, in stark contrast to affluence in other parts of the district, Bridgeport, the state's most populous city.

Proximity to New York along commuter rail lines, ferries and Interstate 95 and a lower cost of living than Manhattan long drew wealth from Wall Street to the district's tony suburbs. The district relies on banking and financial services and is home to several of the world's largest hedge funds in Greenwich and Westport. Stamford has a cluster of corporate headquarters and one of the largest financial districts outside of Manhattan, including Swiss banking giant UBS and the Royal Bank of Scotland.

Southwestern Connecticut tops the list nationwide for its proportion of households earning more than $200,000 a year, but housing and luxury-goods markets in Greenwich tumbled during several years of economic downturns. Despite population growth in Bridgeport over the last decade, the city struggles against urban woes common to post-industrial areas. Years of job losses hit the city hard and unemployment remains above statewide and national averages, but Bridgeport's economy still has a diverse workforce at government offices, smaller-scale manufacturers, health care employers and four colleges, as well as the largest regional bank in New England.

While the district, like the rest of the state, is overwhelmingly white, it has the state's largest proportion of Hispanic residents (17 percent), mostly clustered in Bridgeport. The 4th and its economic extremes can be difficult for politicians to navigate. While Bridgeport is overwhelmingly liberal and registered Democrats outnumber Republicans in the district's largest cities, Republican mayors can still win in the suburbs. Barack Obama took 55 percent of the district's vote overall in the 2012 presidential race, but GOP candidate Mitt Romney won some jurisdictions within the 4th.

Major Industry
Banking, manufacturing, health care

Cities
Bridgeport, Stamford, Norwalk, Greenwich, Fairfield

Notable
Norwalk hosts an annual oyster festival with an oyster-slurping contest.

Rep. Elizabeth Esty (D)

Capitol Office
225-4476
esty.house.gov
509 Cannon Bldg. 20515-0705; fax 225-5933

Committees
Science, Space & Technology
Transportation & Infrastructure

Residence
Cheshire

Born
Aug. 25, 1959; Oak Park, Ill.

Religion
Congregationalist

Family
Husband, Dan Esty; three children

Education
Harvard U., A.B. 1981 (government); Yale U., J.D. 1985

Career
Homemaker; lawyer

Political Highlights
Cheshire Town Council, 2005-08; Conn. House, 2009-11; defeated for re-election to Conn. House, 2010

ELECTION RESULTS

2012 GENERAL		
Elizabeth Esty (D)	146,098	51.3%
Andrew Roraback (R)	138,637	48.7%
2012 PRIMARY		
Elizabeth Esty (D)	12,717	44.6%
Chris Donovan (D)	9,216	32.3%
Dan Roberti (D)	6,582	23.1%

Elected 2012; 1st term

Esty says her plans involve the transition of her district's economy toward new opportunities in manufacturing and service. Tragedy also links her to gun control — she represents Newtown, the site of a school shooting in 2012, and she stands behind measures to curb gun violence.

Esty, who is socially liberal but fiscally conservative, belongs to the business-friendly New Democrat Coalition. Some of the biggest businesses in her district are hospitals, and she has professional ties to health care. A lawyer by training, Esty researched health care policy as a scholar at Yale Law School.

She's also interested in the energy sector. During a term in the Connecticut House, she served on its energy and technology committee. She sees high-tech and renewable-energy industries as possible incubators of middle-class jobs. She now sits on the Science, Space and Technology Committee.

She also sits on the Transportation and Infrastructure Committee and its environment panel. Her husband, Dan, taught environmental law at Yale, and in 2011 he was appointed to lead Connecticut's Department of Energy and Environmental Protection.

Esty faults the unintended consequences of government regulations, not the regulations themselves, as the biggest impediment to job creation. She says her experience working at the local level allows her to "see the impact of well-intentioned legislation" — she also served on a town council.

Though she has been vocal regarding gun control, Esty says she prefers to work in the background. "It's a good way to be effective," she says.

Democratic Rep. Christopher S. Murphy left the 5th District open to seek a Senate seat. Esty raised a lot of cash for the primary via her connections to abortion-rights groups, and she needed it to ward off state House Speaker Chris Donovan and public relations executive Dan Roberti. Her victory put her in the general election with moderate GOP state Sen. Andrew Roraback. She won by less than 3 points.

Connecticut 5

West — Danbury, New Britain, most of Waterbury

Settled in bucolic western Connecticut, the 5th District mostly is a mix of midsize former manufacturing towns struggling with the transition to diversified economies and rolling farmland and rivers of the Litchfield Hills. Bordering upstate New York and Massachusetts, it takes in New Britain in the center of the state as well as Danbury and most of Waterbury along Interstate 84.

Danbury, in the district's southwestern corner, has a growing health care sector that includes a large hospital and pharmaceuticals firms. Other major employers include Praxair, which makes industrial gases, and Cartus, a business relocation services and consulting firm. The large white-collar companies are supported by a thriving legal community. A new military reserve training center is expected to be complete by 2014.

Waterbury, the district's largest population hub, has one of the state's highest unemployment rates. The city has begun redeveloping former industrial brownfield sites for commercial and business use, and several state universities and community colleges address local higher education needs.

New Britain, to the east and surrounded on three sides by the 1st District, has been hit by manufacturing job losses, although the Hardware City — so named because of its history of tool manufacturing — is still the headquarters of Stanley Black & Decker. The city has a large population with Polish ancestry and a sizable Hispanic community.

Registered Democrats outnumber Republicans in the district's largest cities, but smaller towns can be friendlier to conservative candidates. The district gave Democrat Barack Obama 54 percent of its presidential vote in 2012; Republican Mitt Romney took Litchfield County in the northwest by 252 votes.

Major Industry
Manufacturing, health care

Cities
Waterbury (pt.), Danbury, New Britain, Meriden, New Milford, Newtown

Notable
Southbury is home to Churaevka, a landmark founded in 1925 by writer George Grebenstchikov and Ilya Tolstoy as a refuge for Russians who fled the Russian Revolution.

DELAWARE

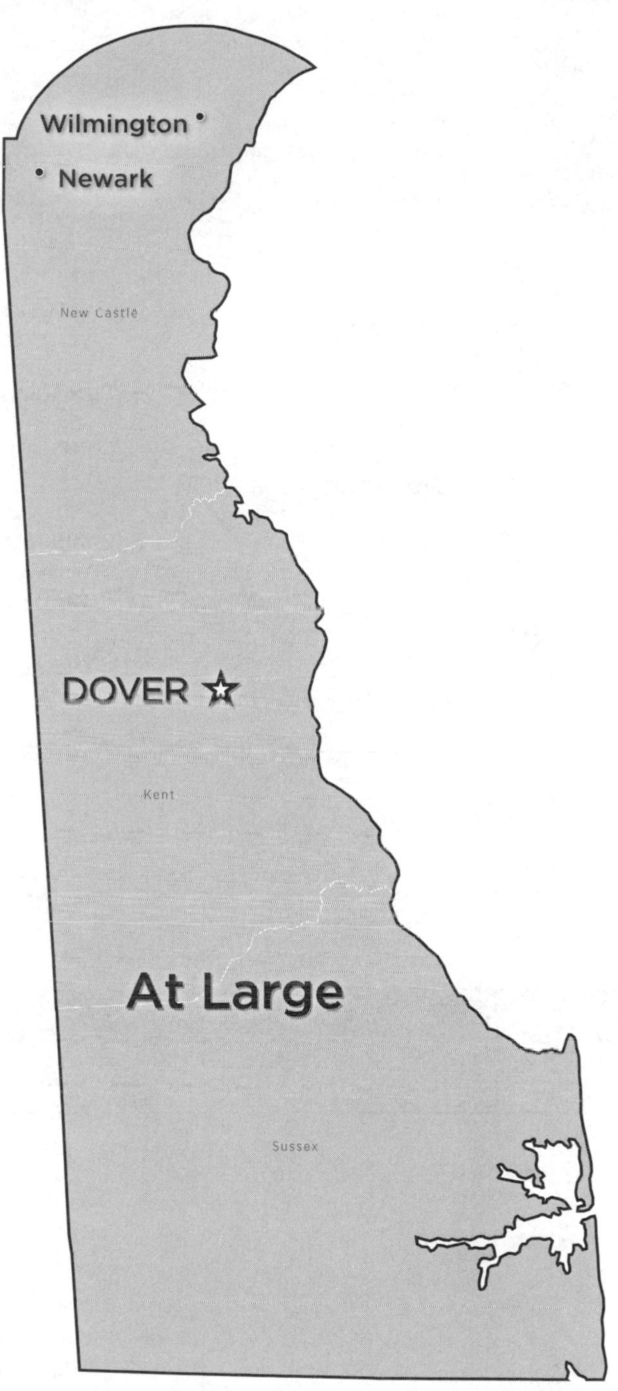

Gov. Jack Markell (D)

First elected: 2008

Length of term: 4 years

Term expires: 1/17

Salary: $171,000

Phone: (302) 739-4101

Residence: Wilmington

Born: Nov. 26, 1960; Newark, Del.

Religion: Jewish

Family: Wife, Carla Markell; two children

Education: Brown U., 1982 B.A. (development studies & economics); U. of Chicago, 1985 M.B.A.

Career: Telecommunications company executive; banker

Political highlights: Del. treasurer, 1999-2009

ELECTION RESULTS

2012 GENERAL

Jack Markell (D)	275,993	69.3%
Jeffrey E. Cragg (R)	113,793	28.6%
Mark Joseph Perri (GREEN)	4,575	1.1%
Jesse McVay (LIBERT)	3,668	0.9%

Lt. Gov. Matthew Denn (D)

First elected: 2008

Length of term: 4 years

Term expires: 1/17

Salary: $78,553

Phone: (302) 744-4333

LEGISLATURE

General Assembly: January-June

Senate: 21 members, 4-year terms

2013 ratios: 13 D, 8 R; 15 men, 6 women

Salary: $44,041

Phone: (302) 744-4129

House: 41 members, 2-year terms

2013 ratios: 27 D, 14 R; 31 men, 10 women

Salary: $44,041

Phone: (302) 744-4351

TERM LIMITS

Governor: 2 terms

Senate: No

House: No

URBAN STATISTICS

CITY	POPULATION
Wilmington	70,851
Dover	36,047
Newark	31,454
Middletown	18,871
Smyrna	10,023

REGISTERED VOTERS

Democrat	47%
Republican	28%
Other	25%

POPULATION

2010 population	897,934
2000 population	783,600
1990 population	666,168
Percent change (2000-2010)	+14.6%
Rank among states (2010)	45
Median age	37.8
Born in state	46.1%
Foreign born	7.5%
Violent crime rate	637/100,000
Poverty level	10.8%
Federal workers	8,846
Military	3,870

ELECTIONS

STATE ELECTION OFFICIAL
(302) 739-4277

DEMOCRATIC PARTY
(302) 328-9036

REPUBLICAN PARTY
(302) 668-1954

MISCELLANEOUS

Web: www.delaware.gov

Capital: Dover

U.S. CONGRESS

Senate: 2 Democrats

House: 1 Democrat

STATISTICS BY DISTRICT

District	2012 Vote for President: Obama	Romney	2008 Vote for President: Obama	McCain	Black	Asian	Hispanic	Median Income	Over 64	Under 20	College Education	Rural	Sq. Miles
AL	59%	40%	62%	37%	21%	3%	8%	$58,814	15%	26%	28%	16%	1,949
STATE	59	40	62	37	21	3	8	58,814	15	26	28	16	1,949
U.S.	51	47	53	46	12	5	17	50,052	13	27	29	21	3,531,905

Sen. Thomas R. Carper (D)

Capitol Office
224-2441
carper.senate.gov
513 Hart Bldg. 20510-0803; fax 228-2190

Committees
Environment & Public Works
(Clean Air & Nuclear Safety - Chairman)
Finance
Homeland Security & Governmental Affairs
- Chairman

Residence
Wilmington

Born
Jan. 23, 1947; Beckley, W.Va.

Religion
Presbyterian

Family
Wife, Martha Carper; two children

Education
Ohio State U., B.A. 1968 (economics); U. of Delaware, M.B.A. 1975

Military Service
Navy, 1968-73; Naval Reserve, 1973-91

Career
State economic development official

Political Highlights
Del. treasurer, 1977-83; U.S. House, 1983-93; governor, 1993-2001

ELECTION RESULTS

2012 GENERAL		
Thomas R. Carper (D)	265,415	66.4%
Kevin Wade (R)	115,700	29.0%
Alexander Pires (I)	15,300	3.8%
2012 PRIMARY		
Thomas R. Carper (D)	43,587	87.8%
Keith Spanarelli (D)	6,028	12.2%

Previous Winning Percentages
2006 (67%); 2000 (56%); 1990 House Election (66%); 1988 House Election (68%); 1986 House Election (66%); 1984 House Election (58%); 1982 House Election (52%)

Elected 2000; 3rd term

Carper wants everyone to get along. Judging by his electoral record, Delawareans seem to agree. The moderate Democrat consciously cultivates personal relationships with colleagues and seeks diverse partners in his efforts to eliminate wasteful government spending. He has an excellent forum for both activities as the chairman of the Homeland Security and Governmental Affairs Committee.

Civility is more than a buzzword to Carper, who in a long career has been Delaware's treasurer, House representative, governor and now senator. He attends a bipartisan, nondenominational Bible study group and leads orientation sessions for freshman senators and their spouses, during which each new senator is assigned both a Republican and a Democratic mentor. He keeps a list of several hundred birthdays of current and former colleagues, staffers and others, calling each of them when their day arrives. And in 2004, he helped to found Third Way, a think tank formed to generate and promote politically moderate policy.

When he has legislative disputes, Carper is more inclined to visit a lawmaker in person than lay out their differences to the media. That tendency could make for an interesting dynamic on the Homeland Security committee. In 2013, when Carper took over for the retired Joseph I. Lieberman of Connecticut, the panel also got a new ranking member. Republican Party term limits forced Susan Collins of Maine from the that spot, and Tom Coburn of Oklahoma took her place. Coburn isn't hostile, but he is famous for his willingness to obstruct Senate proceedings when he dislikes the direction the chamber is headed.

But Carper and Coburn share the goal of getting better results in government for less money. Early in the 113th Congress (2013-14), Carper said improving government efficiency and combating fraud would be at the top of his agenda as chairman. He and Coburn already have collaborated on efforts to crack down on Medicare waste, fraud and abuse. They have worked on legislation to institute stronger penalties for fraud and improve data sharing across government agencies.

Carper claims to be a penny pincher at home — he says he took to heart the lessons he learned as a young state treasurer in the late 1970s, when Delaware's credit rating was abysmal. "I'm very conscious of being pragmatic about spending our own money and about taxpayers' money as well," he said.

The rest of the committee's to-do list includes work that wasn't completed in the 112th Congress (2011-12): overhauls of the nation's cybersecurity defenses and the U.S. Postal Service.

Carper worked on a cybersecurity overhaul in the 112th — his main responsibility was developing provisions to revamp protections for the federal government's own computer networks. The overall bill would have made compliance with new security standards mandatory for private sector entities that own the most-vital computer networks. It was opposed by business groups. Carper eventually supported a version with voluntary compliance, but nothing was enacted.

The cash-strapped Postal Service defaulted in August 2012 on a $5.5 billion loan, after a Senate-passed bill to prevent that outcome died in the House. Carper warned of the consequences of inaction, issuing news releases and giving speeches to publicize the service's situation. "It doesn't send the kind of signal that you want to send," he said of the default. "Businesses like certainty; they like predictability." But senators were far from united on the legislation that passed the chamber. Coburn was among the Republicans who argued that the bill did not go far enough in restructuring the Postal Service.

Carper holds a seat on the Finance Committee, where he worked on the health care overhaul enacted in the 111th Congress (2009-10). He differs from many Democratic colleagues in suggesting that changes to entitlement programs are needed to keep the government solvent. His ideas for the tax code have elements in common with GOP plans. Carper says he favors lowering the top tax rates on businesses and individuals, while eliminating many of the current tax breaks.

He does, however, support tax benefits targeting specific energy resources, namely offshore wind. Carper is the leading supporter of extending an investment tax credit for builders of offshore wind farms, which are being planned off the Delaware coast.

Carper chairs the Environment and Public Works Subcommittee on Clean Air and Nuclear Safety. He has spoken in favor of EPA air regulations, especially with respect to pollution blown across state lines — Delaware is downwind of states that rely on coal to fire their power plants. Carper helped fend off a legislative effort to nullify the agency's cross-state air rule, but an appeals court vacated the regulation in August 2012, sending EPA back to the drawing board. Carper also has supported creation of a cap-and-trade system to limit greenhouse gas emissions.

Carper was raised in Roanoke, Va., and later Columbus, Ohio. As a boy, he was active in the Civil Air Patrol and Boy Scouts and earned an ROTC scholarship to attend Ohio State University. Years later, he told the Columbus Dispatch that until he became governor, the best job he ever had was washing dishes at an Ohio State sorority house.

In college, he underwent a political transformation. Carper at first held the Republican views of his parents, campaigning in 1964 for GOP presidential candidate Barry Goldwater. But by 1968, his skepticism about the Vietnam War led him to volunteer in the anti-war presidential campaign of Democrat Eugene J. McCarthy.

Despite his anti-war sentiments, he joined the Navy that year and wore his uniform to his college graduation. He went on to serve for five years and for another 18 in the Naval Reserve, retiring as a captain in 1991. During his time in the Navy he was smitten by Delaware, flying into Dover aboard a military transport plane and later telling a friend he'd "like to move to a little state where you would not need a lot of money and fame, and maybe run for office."

When he left the Navy, Carper enrolled in the University of Delaware's business school, where he earned a master's degree in business administration. Jim Soles, a favorite professor, ran for Congress in 1974. Carper worked on his campaign, which was unsuccessful.

One day in 1976, he was lying in the sand at Dewey Beach and listening to his transistor radio when he heard a news report that said Democrats could not find a candidate for state treasurer. He entered the race and, at age 29, beat a strongly favored Republican.

In 1982, Carper ran for the House after Democrats again had trouble lining up a candidate. Delaware's economic woes at the time — and revelations that Republican incumbent Thomas B. Evans Jr. was romantically involved with a lobbyist — boosted Carper's campaign, and the state's House seat went Democratic for the first time since 1966.

Carper ran successfully for governor in 1992, swapping jobs with moderate Republican Michael N. Castle. After two terms as governor, in 2000 he took on five-term Republican Sen. William V. Roth Jr. — the Finance Committee chairman whose name was famously attached to a type of individual retirement account.

On paper it was a battle of the titans, but in reality the election was not that close. Carper won by almost 12 points. He took around two-thirds of the vote in his 2006 and 2012 re-election campaigns.

Key Votes

2012	
Prohibit health insurance plans from denying coverage based on the sponsor's religious beliefs	YES
Require approval of the Keystone XL oil pipeline	NO
Ease securities rules to expand small-business access to capital	YES
Reauthorize farm and nutrition programs for five years	YES
Limit debate on a bill that would create private-sector cybersecurity standards	YES
Consent to ratification of a treaty setting global standard for the treatment of people with disabilities	YES
Provide $60.4 billion in disaster relief following Superstorm Sandy	YES
Extend most Bush-era income tax rates while allowing rates for top-bracket earners to rise (Jan. 1, 2013)	NO
2011	
Prevent EPA from regulating greenhouse gas emissions to address climate change	NO
Extend certain provisions of Patriot Act for four years	YES
Clear compromise debt limit increase plan and establish future spending limits	YES
Overhaul patent law	YES
Implement Colombia free trade agreement	YES
Limit debate on confirmation of Caitlin J. Halligan to D.C. Circuit Court of Appeals	YES
Extend payroll tax cut and unemployment benefits for two months	YES

CQ Vote Studies

	PARTY UNITY		PRESIDENTIAL SUPPORT	
	SUPPORT	OPPOSE	SUPPORT	OPPOSE
2012	89%	11%	97%	3%
2011	92%	8%	98%	2%
2010	95%	5%	100%	0%
2009	93%	7%	97%	3%
2008	80%	20%	45%	55%
2007	88%	12%	46%	54%
2006	79%	21%	64%	36%
2005	77%	23%	38%	62%
2004	86%	14%	66%	34%
2003	81%	19%	53%	47%

Interest Groups

	AFL-CIO	ADA	CCUS	ACU
2012	91%	90%	38%	12%
2011	79%	90%	64%	5%
2010	94%	90%	27%	0%
2009	89%	90%	57%	4%
2008	100%	85%	63%	0%
2007	89%	85%	55%	8%
2006	87%	90%	58%	20%
2005	64%	90%	72%	8%
2004	100%	95%	71%	12%
2003	77%	75%	70%	10%

Sen. Chris Coons (D)

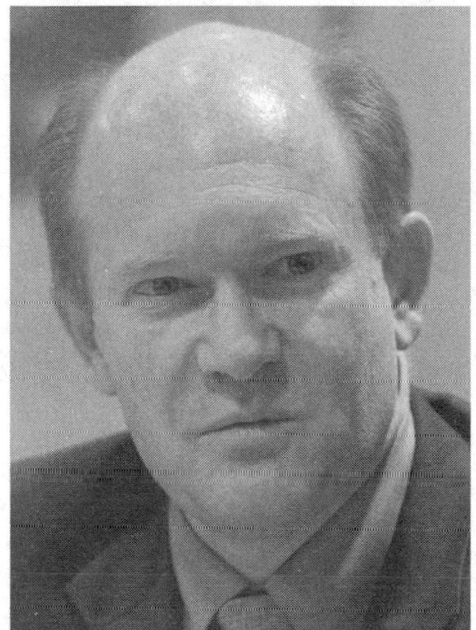

Capitol Office
224-5042
coons.senate.gov
127A Russell Bldg. 20510-0802; fax 228-3075

Committees
Budget
Energy & Natural Resources
Foreign Relations
(African Affairs - Chairman)
Judiciary
(Bankruptcy & Courts - Chairman)

Residence
Wilmington

Born
Sept. 9, 1963; Greenwich, Conn.

Religion
Presbyterian

Family
Wife, Annie Lingenfelter; three children

Education
Amherst College, A.B. 1985 (chemistry & political science); Yale U., J.D. 1992, M.A.R. 1992 (ethics)

Career
Lawyer; education foundation aide; campaign aide

Political Highlights
New Castle County Council president, 2001-05; New Castle County executive, 2005-10

ELECTION RESULTS

2010 SPECIAL		
Chris Coons (D)	174,012	56.6%
Christine O'Donnell (R)	123,053	40.0%
Glenn A. Miller (I)	8,201	2.7%
2010 PRIMARY		
Chris Coons (D)		unopposed

Elected 2010; 1st term

Coons is the most liberal member of his state's congressional delegation. But the state is Delaware, so he still engages in the business-minded policy discussions that are part of its political culture. His diverse range of interests includes the promotion of alternative energy sources and the development of stronger relationships with Africa.

"It is tough to pigeonhole me," says Coons, who prior to his Senate service was the executive of his state's most populous county. In his first years as a senator, he voted reliably for the positions backed by most Democrats, while also seeking bipartisan support for less-contentious economic initiatives.

A member of the Budget Committee, Coons pushes for a combination of federal investments and finding ways to boost national competitiveness. "The formula for our economic success has long been the unstoppable combination of an innovative citizenry and investment in cutting-edge research," he said in his first Senate speech. "This is what generates companies that invent new products, often high-tech and research-driven products, and, along with these, create skilled jobs right here in the United States."

Coons is among the lawmakers pushing for a permanent extension of the research and development tax credit, and he also studies ways to further its reach. He and Wyoming Republican Michael B. Enzi have proposed allowing startup companies to claim the credit against employment taxes instead of income taxes, since startups might not have income to tax. He teamed up with Florida Republican Marco Rubio on a 2011 bill that packaged several business-friendly tax provisions that they said had bipartisan support. "These are ideas that I think ought to be able to pass," he said at the time, and several of them were included in enacted legislation later in the 112th Congress (2011-12).

He advocates federal involvement in alternative-energy research and development from his seat on the Energy and Natural Resources Committee — he works with fellow Delaware Democrat Thomas R. Carper on legislation to create tax incentives for offshore wind farms along Delaware's coast. Coons and Kansas Republican Jerry Moran (another wind energy advocate) are the Senate team leading the charge to allow renewable-energy projects to operate under "master limited partnerships" — a tax structure appealing to private investors that many fossil fuel projects use.

But like many Democrats, Coons is critical of tax provisions advantageous to oil companies. "This isn't picking on one particular industry," he said on the Senate floor in 2011. "This is rationally looking at our immense tax expenditures through the code and saying there is a time here for us to stop."

On the Judiciary Committee, Coons backs a path to legalization for illegal immigrants, though his legislative action has focused on legal immigration, specifically visas for high-tech workers. Rubio and Coons included an expansion of such visas in their measure. Tennessee Republican Lamar Alexander worked with Coons in 2012 on a proposal to create a new class of student visas for graduate students in math and science fields.

For the 113th Congress (2013-14), Coons is chairing the Judiciary subcommittee on bankruptcy, which is not insignificant to the many corporations that call Delaware home (state laws are seen as business-friendly). He describes a crisis in bankruptcy courts, with not enough judges in service to handle the workload.

And he has chaired the Foreign Relations Subcommittee on African Affairs since 2011. Coons studied in Kenya as an undergraduate and later returned to Africa to work for the South African Council of Churches. In his first term he focused attention on "Arab Spring" uprisings, China's inroads on the continent and al-Qaida's presence in Nigeria and Somalia. "I think we're at a place in Africa today where the intersection between security, democracy and economic opportunity are as important as they've ever been," he said.

Coons, who identifies himself as a defense hawk, visited Mali in early 2013 and warned that militants associated with al-Qaida could establish a foothold there. He urged further operational support of French forces fighting there. In his first year in the Senate, he was ambivalent about the Obama administration's Afghanistan strategy, calling for a more significant drawdown of troop levels and a refocus on counterterrorism in other areas.

He's also interested in promoting more commerce with African nations. "We need to shift the U.S. mentality toward Africa from aid to trade," he said in 2012. He supported a 2012 extension of preferential import treatment for Africa-produced garments made from third-country fabrics. Coons also voted for 2011 free-trade agreements with Panama and South Korea, but he cited violence against union workers in Colombia as his reason for opposing a pact with that nation.

He was born in Greenwich, Conn., but grew up in Hockessin, Del., and attended Tower Hill, a private school founded by the du Pont family. His mother taught elementary school. His father worked for a food processing firm and founded his own cabinet and countertop manufacturing company.

In what became a famous bit of youthful writing, he described his path from young Republican to "bearded Marxist," tracing his journey away from his affluent parents' moderate Republicanism. Coons says that the phrase was meant as a joke with his older brother, even as Republicans tried to use it against him in the 2010 election.

He says a period in which his parents' economic fortunes went south, followed by a divorce, caused him to re-evaluate his political outlook. He had helped found a College Republicans group at Amherst College, but within a year Coons switched sides.

He graduated from Amherst with a degree in chemistry and political science. Coons then earned a law degree from Yale Law School and a master's in ethics from Yale Divinity School. He also studied at the University of Nairobi in Kenya, where he says up-close experience with poverty added to his altered ideological leanings.

After college he worked for several nonprofits, including the Investor Responsibility Research Center and the National Coalition for the Homeless. From 1996 to 2004, Coons worked as an attorney for Delaware-based W.L. Gore & Associates, which is owned by his stepfather's family. (Its most famous product is Gore-Tex fabric.)

Elected to the New Castle County Council in 2000, he served as its president for four years before becoming county executive in 2005. The populous county provided Coons with extensive governing experience — he had about 2,000 full-time employees, an executive office staff of about 50 and an operating budget of about $240 million — making the transition to the Senate difficult. "I was able to actually get things done," he said. "I spent much of my last six years focused on balancing budgets, improving services to the community, making difficult choices."

Coons' path to the Senate involved several twists. Joseph R. Biden Jr. left the seat when he was elected vice president, and most observers assumed his son — state Attorney General Beau Biden — would be the Democratic nominee. Ted Kaufman, a Biden aide, was appointed as a seat-warmer.

But when the younger Biden opted not to join the race, Coons jumped in. He was expected to face a difficult challenge from moderate Republican Michael N. Castle, a House veteran in his ninth term, but Castle was upset in his primary by tea party favorite Christine O'Donnell. Coons jumped to an early and big lead in the polls. He defeated O'Donnell by 17 points.

Key Votes

2012	
Prohibit health insurance plans from denying coverage based on the sponsor's religious beliefs	YES
Require approval of the Keystone XL oil pipeline	NO
Ease securities rules to expand small-business access to capital	YES
Reauthorize farm and nutrition programs for five years	YES
Limit debate on a bill that would create private-sector cybersecurity standards	YES
Consent to ratification of a treaty setting global standard for the treatment of people with disabilities	YES
Provide $60.4 billion in disaster relief following Superstorm Sandy	YES
Extend most Bush-era income tax rates while allowing rates for top-bracket earners to rise (Jan. 1, 2013)	YES
2011	
Prevent EPA from regulating greenhouse gas emissions to address climate change	NO
Extend certain provisions of Patriot Act for four years	NO
Clear compromise debt limit increase plan and establish future spending limits	YES
Overhaul patent law	YES
Implement Colombia free trade agreement	NO
Limit debate on confirmation of Caitlin J. Halligan to D.C. Circuit Court of Appeals	YES
Extend payroll tax cut and unemployment benefits for two months	YES

CQ Vote Studies

	PARTY UNITY		PRESIDENTIAL SUPPORT	
	SUPPORT	OPPOSE	SUPPORT	OPPOSE
2012	95%	5%	97%	3%
2011	96%	4%	97%	3%
2010	100%	0%	100%	0%

Interest Groups

	AFL-CIO	ADA	CCUS	ACU
2012	91%	100%	38%	4%
2011	89%	95%	55%	0%
2010	100%		50%	0%

Rep. John Carney (D)

Capitol Office
225-4165
johncarney.house.gov
1406 Longworth Bldg. 20515-0801; fax 225-2291

Committees
Financial Services

Residence
Wilmington

Born
May 20, 1956; Wilmington, Del.

Religion
Roman Catholic

Family
Wife, Tracey Quillen; two children

Education
Dartmouth College, A.B. 1978 (English); U. of Delaware, M.P.A. 1987

Career
Renewable energy company executive; gubernatorial and congressional district aide; county government official; religious youth programs coordinator; high school and college athletics coach

Political Highlights
Del. secretary of finance, 1997-2000; lieutenant governor, 2001-09; sought Democratic nomination for governor, 2008

ELECTION RESULTS

2012 GENERAL		
John Carney (D)	249,933	64.4%
Thomas H. Kovach (R)	129,757	33.4%
Bernard August (GREEN)	4,273	1.1%
Scott Gesty (LIBERT)	4,096	1.1%
2012 PRIMARY		
John Carney (D)		unopposed
2010 GENERAL		
John Carney (D)	173,543	56.8%
Glen Urquhart (R)	125,442	41.0%
Earl R. Lofland (I)	3,704	1.2%

Elected 2010; 2nd term

Carney is a product of what he calls the "pretty civil" politics of Delaware. He aligns himself with business-oriented colleagues of both parties and has been one of the Democrats most active in calling for a balanced approach to fiscal discipline.

"I'm a public service guy," Carney says, and his professional history confirms it. Carney has been a congressional and gubernatorial aide, the state finance director and lieutenant governor. Some of his nonpolitical jobs also have a service element — he coached high school and college sports teams.

A member of the centrist New Democrat Coalition, Carney has an approach to government finance that was nurtured when he served as the secretary of finance for Gov. Thomas R. Carper — who is now the state's senior senator. When Carper served as state treasurer in the late 1970s, his biggest goal was improving Delaware's credit rating, and he has carried that preoccupation with balance sheets throughout his career.

Carney is a kindred spirit. He voted for a 2011 deficit reduction package that also raised the federal debt limit, but he expressed frustration that drawn-out negotiations over the package may have led to a downgrade of the government's credit rating. "Bond ratings mean something to me," he said. "The worst thing that we could do for a fragile economy, coming out of recession, is to give it a body blow to the gut by not raising the debt ceiling and undermining confidence in the market for U.S. debt." He was one of 86 House Democrats to support a short-term suspension of the debt ceiling in January 2013.

That same month, he voted for the "fiscal cliff" package that raised income taxes on higher earners, but had negligible spending cuts. He said his vote was to maintain economic stability and that he again was vexed by the lack of a "long-term 'grand bargain' that would finally put the country on a sustainable deficit reduction trajectory."

Carney was one of 22 Democrats to vote for a fiscal 2013 budget proposal to reduce deficits by $4 trillion over 10 years through a combination of revenue increases, spending cuts and entitlement program changes. He also has supported Democrat-sponsored versions of a balanced-budget amendment to the Constitution, and a bill giving the president line-item veto authority for appropriations bills.

Delaware hosts the headquarters of many financial services companies, and Carney is a member of the Financial Services Committee. As a freshman, he started an informal, bipartisan working group with Republican James B. Renacci of Ohio, also a member of the committee. Typically over weekly breakfasts, they meet with Republicans and Democrats who are "more moderate, more fiscally responsible, business-oriented," Carney said.

Late in 2011, Carney and Republican Stephen Fincher of Tennessee introduced a bill to loosen up regulations on small and medium-sized companies that are making public stock offerings, in theory making it easier for them to access new sources of capital and expand. Their bill became the vessel for several related measures regarding access to capital, and the overall package was enacted in April 2012. It was one of the few overwhelmingly bipartisan laws produced by the 112th Congress (2011-12).

Carney will venture outside of his committee for legislative projects. He worked with Indiana Republican Larry Bucshon on a bill to require a publicly available list of prescription drug shortages and expedited regulatory reviews of critical drugs that are prone to shortages. It was enacted as part of a July 2012 law reauthorizing Food and Drug Administration user fees.

As the sole House member for his state, Carney has extra incentive to pay attention to parochial issues. He wants more federal bonds issued for transportation and infrastructure projects to stimulate the job market. He follows the Delaware congressional tradition of commuting to Washington via Amtrak and is a proponent of rail service. Calling the Northeast Corridor Amtrak's "crown jewel," he supports private investment in the rail service but not complete privatization.

Carney introduced an amendment to the fiscal 2012 authorization of spy programs; it was to require the intelligence community to make rail safety a priority. "Clearly, terrorist organizations around the world have made rail systems a target," he said on the House floor.

Delaware has been hit hard by manufacturing downturns, and in the 112th Carney supported the Democrats' "Make it in America" agenda for manufacturing. He wants to revitalize old manufacturing facilities, and Carney — an executive at a renewable-energy company just before coming to Congress — says investment in alternative energy is crucial. He wants Delaware to get in front of its neighbors.

"There is going to be an offshore wind industry, in my view, in the mid-Atlantic region," he said. "Where they are going to make the turbines, the towers and all that?" Carper is also a big supporter of offshore wind.

Carney picked up one legislative cause from his predecessor, Republican Michael N. Castle: the creation of a national park in Delaware by linking a series of historical sites, instead of designating one large facility. He has twice introduced a bill on the subject. (President Barack Obama declared a national monument incorporating several sites in 2013.)

A Delaware native, Carney comes from a large family with an athletic bent — he is one of nine siblings. He was an All-Ivy League football player at Dartmouth and he continues to coach his sons in lacrosse and basketball. If he weren't in Congress, he would return to coaching or teaching, he said.

While studying for his master's in public administration at the University of Delaware, he served as a staff assistant to Democratic Sen. Joseph R. Biden Jr. He continued that work after getting his degree, and then became deputy chief of staff to Gov. Carper. Carney later took a turn as the state's secretary of finance and was twice elected lieutenant governor. He made an unsuccessful bid for the Democratic nomination for governor in 2008.

In October 2009, after nine terms in the House, Castle announced he was running for the Senate. Carney had a clear field in the primary, then defeated Republican Glen Urquhart with almost 57 percent of the vote.

For the 2012 election, he was again unopposed in the primary. He coasted back to the House against Republican Thomas H. Kovach with more than 64 percent of the vote.

Key Votes

2012	
Extend a Social Security payroll tax cut and unemployment benefits	YES
Ease securities rules to expand small-business access to capital	YES
Extend for one year subsidized student loan interest rates financed by a cut in health care spending	NO
Cite Attorney General Eric H. Holder Jr. for contempt of Congress	?
Create a visa program for foreign graduates in high-tech fields	YES
Extend most Bush-era income tax rates while allowing rates for top-bracket earners to rise (Jan. 1, 2013)	YES
2011	
Strike funding for F-35 alternative engine	NO
Prevent EPA from regulating greenhouse gas emissions to address climate change	NO
Extend certain provisions of Patriot Act for four years	YES
Declare opposition to use of ground troops in Libya	NO
Overhaul patent law	YES
Pass compromise debt limit increase plan and establish future spending limits	YES
Allow consideration of measures to implement three trade agreements	YES

CQ Vote Studies

	PARTY UNITY		PRESIDENTIAL SUPPORT	
	SUPPORT	OPPOSE	SUPPORT	OPPOSE
2012	89%	11%	80%	20%
2011	87%	13%	91%	9%

Interest Groups

	AFL-CIO	ADA	CCUS	ACU
2012	86%	65%	50%	8%
2011	90%	80%	38%	0%

Delaware

At Large

The First State is defined by its coastal terrain, inland agriculture sectors and Wilmington and its suburbs. A string of beach resorts in the state's southeastern corner, from Cape Henlopen State Park and Rehoboth Beach south to Fenwick Island on the Maryland border, draws hordes of visitors to the state, mainly during the summer.

Favorable tax rates and incorporation rules and a specialized business court have combined to attract financial services companies here for decades. Delaware has been the on-paper home to hundreds of Fortune 500 companies. Once known for a strong manufacturing sector, the state continues to lose factory jobs and unemployment hovers around the national average. Even the DuPont Company, the hometown chemical giant, has recently cut jobs. Three gambling and racing facilities contribute to the local tourism industry, in addition to beach and seaside draws.

Still lacking a full-fledged National Park, a designation that local officials have sought for years, several locations together were named a monument in 2013.

Strongly Democratic New Castle County is the state's population center. The county's largest city, Wilmington, is the state's economic engine. Along the Delaware River, redevelopment, including a produce and meats market and luxury condominiums, has made use of public and private funds.

There are some majority-minority communities here, but the state as a whole is 65 percent white and has a median household income close to the national average. Increasingly Democratic-leaning, voters supported Barack Obama and Delaware's favorite son, Joseph R. Biden Jr., in the 2008 and 2012 presidential elections. Democrats also control both chambers of the state legislature. But Sussex County, in the south, gave Republican presidential hopeful Mitt Romney 56 percent in 2012.

Major Industry
Financial services, health care, tourism

Military Bases
Dover Air Force Base, 3,900 military, 1,000 civilian

Cities
Wilmington, Dover

Notable
In 1787, Delaware became the first state to ratify the U.S. Constitution.

FLORIDA

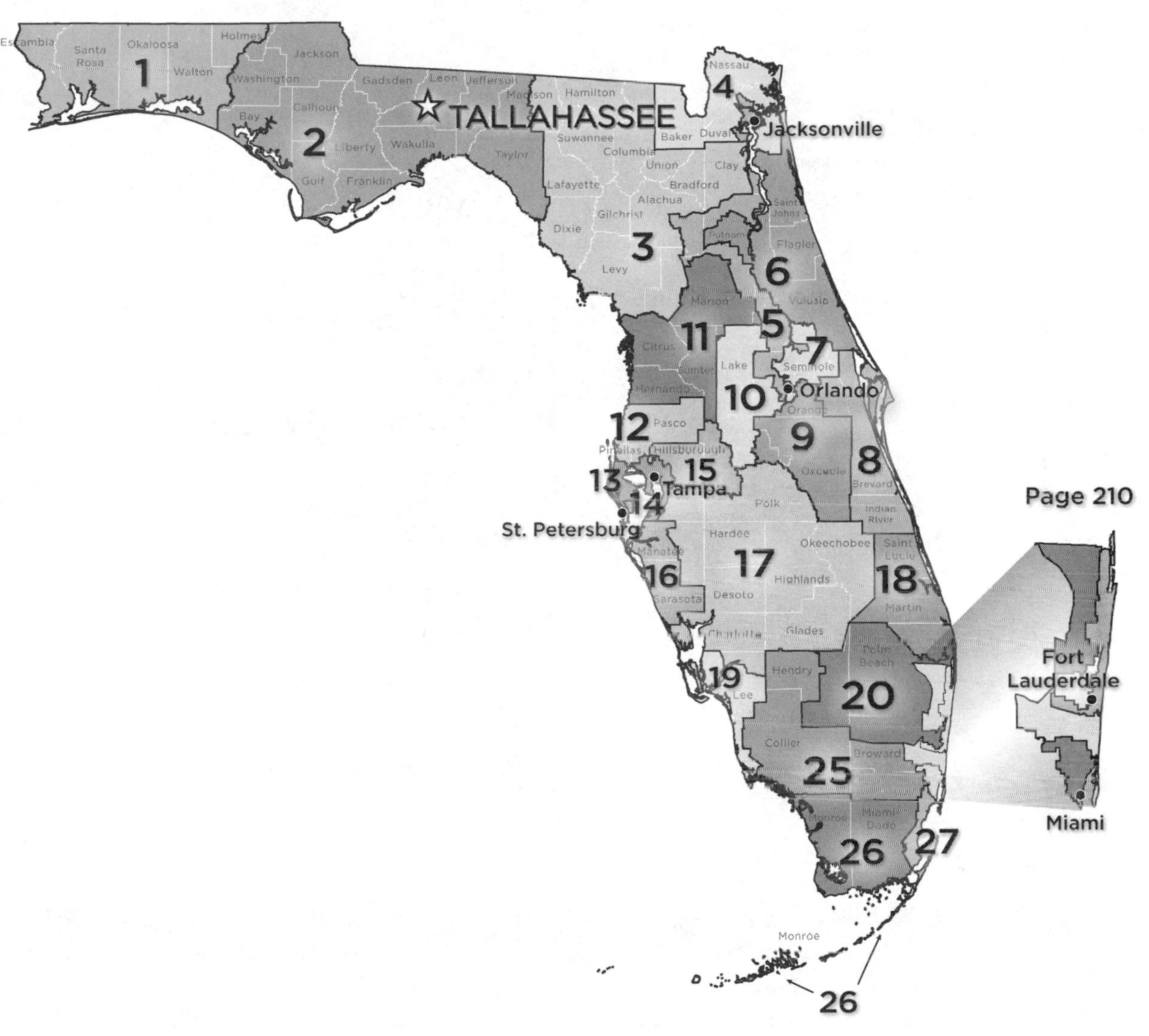

Escambia
Santa Rosa
Okaloosa
Walton
Holmes
Jackson
Washington
1
Gadsden
Leon
Jefferson
Madison
Hamilton
Nassau
4
TALLAHASSEE
Bay
Calhoun
2
Liberty
Wakulla
Gulf
Franklin
Taylor
Suwannee
Columbia
Baker
Duval
Jacksonville
Union
Clay
Bradford
Lafayette
Alachua
Gilchrist
Dixie
Saint Johns
Putnam
Flagler
3
Levy
6
Marion
Volusia
5
7
11
Citrus
Sumter
Lake
Seminole
Hernando
Orlando
10
Orange
12
Pasco
9
Pinellas
Hillsborough
15
Osceola
8
13
Tampa
Brevard
14
Polk
Page 210
St. Petersburg
Indian River
Hardee
Okeechobee
Saint Lucie
17
Manatee
Highlands
18
16
Sarasota
Desoto
Martin
Charlotte
Glades
Palm Beach
Fort Lauderdale
19
Hendry
Lee
20
Collier
Broward
25
Miami
Monroe
Miami-Dade
26
27
Monroe
26

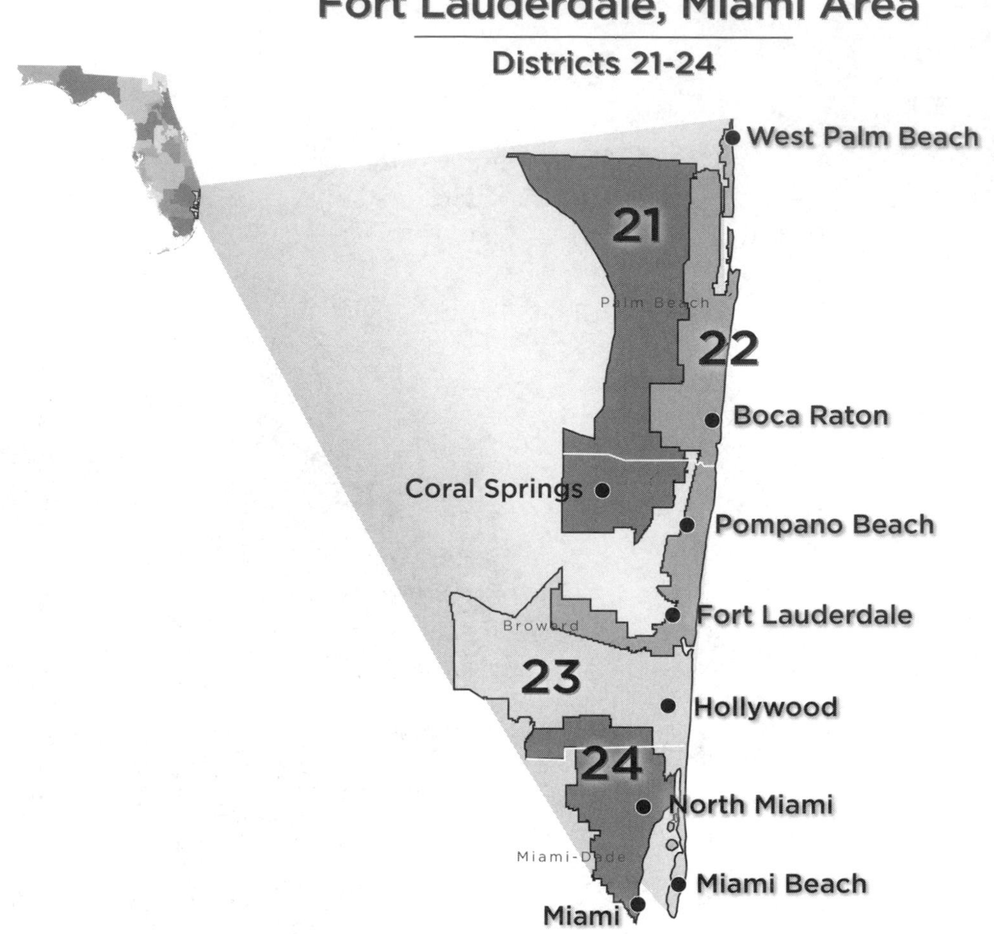

Statistics by District

District	2012 Vote for President Obama	Romney	2008 Vote for President Obama	McCain	Black	Asian	Hispanic	Median Income	Over 64	Under 20	College Education	Rural	Sq. Miles
1	30%	69%	32%	68%	13%	3%	5%	$46,401	14%	25%	26%	19%	4,016
2	47	52	48	52	24	2	5	42,107	13	25	27	34	8,614
3	37	61	40	60	13	3	8	42,966	15	25	23	45	7,306
4	35	64	37	63	13	5	8	53,036	12	24	28	9	1,876
5	70	29	71	29	53	2	12	32,772	11	29	16	9	1,355
6	41	58	46	54	9	2	7	43,375	21	22	25	17	2,507
7	48	51	49.6	50.4	10	4	19	51,007	13	25	33	3	514
8	42	57	44	56	10	2	9	45,366	22	22	26	5	1,752
9	61	38	61	39	11	4	46	41,564	11	27	22	10	1,707
10	46	54	48	52	12	5	16	48,832	16	24	28	7	1,129
11	40	59	44	56	9	1	9	37,885	31	19	17	24	2,510
12	45	54	47	53	5	3	12	46,766	20	23	25	7	884
13	50	49	52	48	5	3	9	42,827	22	19	26	<1	186
14	65	34	66	34	27	3	27	38,036	12	25	24	<1	265
15	46	53	46	54	14	2	17	47,117	13	27	24	6	819

Gov. Rick Scott (R)

First elected: 2010
Length of term: 4 years
Term expires: 1/15
Salary: $130,273
Phone: (850) 488-7146
Residence: Naples
Born: Dec. 1, 1952; Bloomington, Ill.
Religion: Christian
Family: Wife, Ann Scott; two children
Education: U. of Missouri, Kansas City (business administration)
Military service: Navy, 1971-73
Career: Venture capitalist; hospital CEO; lawyer
Political highlights: No previous office

ELECTION RESULTS

2010 GENERAL

Rick Scott (R)	2,619,335	48.9%
Alex Sink (D)	2,557,785	47.7%
Peter Allen (I)	123,831	2.3%

Lt. Gov. (Vacant)

Salary: $124,851
Phone: (850) 488-4711

LEGISLATURE

Legislature: 60 days, March-May
Senate: 40 members, 4-year terms (Note: To accommodate redistricting, 20 Senate seats will have 2-year terms eligible for re-election in 2014.)
2013 ratios: 26 R, 14 D; 28 men, 12 women
Salary: $29,697
Phone: (850) 487-5270
House: 120 members, 2-year terms
2013 ratios: 75 R, 44 D, 1 vacancy; 91 men, 28 women
Salary: $29,697
Phone: (850) 488-1157

TERM LIMITS

Governor: 2 terms
Senate: 2 consecutive terms
House: 4 consecutive terms

URBAN STATISTICS

CITY	POPULATION
Jacksonville	821,784
Miami	399,457
Tampa	335,709
St. Petersburg	244,769
Orlando	238,300

REGISTERED VOTERS

Democrat	40%
Republican	35%
Other	25%

POPULATION

2010 population	18,801,310
2000 population	15,982,378
1990 population	12,937,926
Percent change (2000-2010)	+17.6%
Rank among states (2010)	4
Median age	39.7
Born in state	34.2%
Foreign born	18.1%
Violent crime rate	613/100,000
Poverty level	14.9%
Federal workers	166,903
Military	42,642

ELECTIONS

STATE ELECTION OFFICIAL
(850) 245-6500
DEMOCRATIC PARTY
(850) 222-3411
REPUBLICAN PARTY
(850) 222-7920

MISCELLANEOUS

Web: www.myflorida.gov
Capital: Tallahassee

U.S. CONGRESS

Senate: 1 Democrat, 1 Republican
House: 17 Republicans, 10 Democrats

STATISTICS BY DISTRICT

District	2012 Vote for President		2008 Vote for President		Black	Asian	Hispanic	Median Income	Over 64	Under 20	College Education	Rural	Sq. Miles
	Obama	Romney	Obama	McCain									
16	45%	54%	49%	51%	7%	1%	11%	$45,622	28%	20%	28%	3%	875
17	42	57	44	56	9	1	19	40,162	25	22	18	21	6,370
18	48	52	52	48	12	2	14	47,516	23	22	29	3	1,513
19	39	61	43	57	7	1	17	47,143	27	21	29	5	750
20	83	17	81	19	53	2	21	35,941	13	27	18	1	2,427
21	61	39	64	36	12	3	20	51,757	22	24	34	1	261
22	54	45	57	43	11	2	21	51,227	20	19	36	0	173
23	62	38	62	38	11	4	38	50,581	15	24	37	<1	169
24	87	12	86	14	56	2	30	36,062	11	26	19	0	106
25	49	51	46	54	8	2	70	46,869	14	25	25	6	3,233
26	53	46	50	50	10	1	69	48,899	14	24	26	4	2,099
27	53	46	49	51	8	2	73	38,679	16	23	28	<1	209
STATE	**50**	**49**	**51**	**48**	**16**	**2**	**22**	**44,299**	**18**	**24**	**26**	**9**	**53,625**
US	**51**	**47**	**53**	**46**	**12**	**5**	**17**	**50,052**	**13**	**27**	**29**	**21**	**3,531,905**

Sen. Bill Nelson (D)

Capitol Office
224-5274
billnelson.senate.gov
716 Hart Bldg. 20510-0905; fax 228-2183

Committees
Armed Services
Budget
Commerce, Science & Transportation
(Science & Space - Chairman)
Finance
Special Aging - Chairman

Residence
Orlando

Born
Sept. 29, 1942; Miami, Fla.

Religion
Presbyterian

Family
Wife, Grace C. Nelson; two children

Education
Yale U., B.A. 1965 (political science); U. of Virginia, J.D. 1968

Military Service
Army Reserve, 1965-71

Career
Lawyer

Political Highlights
Fla. House, 1972-78; U.S. House, 1979-91; sought Democratic nomination for governor, 1990; Fla. treasurer and insurance commissioner, 1995-2001

ELECTION RESULTS

2012 GENERAL

Bill Nelson (D)	4,523,451	55.2%
Connie Mack (R)	3,458,267	42.2%
Bill Gaylor (NPA)	126,079	1.5%
Chris Borgia (NPA)	82,089	1.0%

2012 PRIMARY

Bill Nelson (D)	690,112	78.8%
Glenn Burkett (D)	185,629	21.2%

Previous Winning Percentages
2006 (60%); 2000 (51%); 1988 House Election (61%); 1986 House Election (73%); 1984 House Election (61%); 1982 House Election (71%); 1980 House Election (70%); 1978 House Election (61%)

Elected 2000; 3rd term

The low-key Nelson casts himself as a left-leaning centrist and pays extra attention to topics frequently associated with his state: the space program, the military and old people.

Although he can claim to be the only astronaut in Congress, Nelson isn't a particularly flashy lawmaker. His parochial approach to his job and mild demeanor have made him a successful, if not beloved, politician. He's not linked to the drama of leadership battles, and colleagues describe him as both nice and careful. The only Democrat currently holding statewide office in Florida, he has dispatched a string of ineffectual Republican challengers.

Each victory earned him more clout on his Senate committees, and those committees help him tend to Florida's needs. Nelson in the 113th Congress (2013-14) is the chairman of the Special Aging Committee. That panel has no legislative authority but can hold hearings on just about any subject pertaining to older Americans. Nelson has an interest in studying financial scams and other abuses directed at the elderly.

He's also the No. 3 Democrat on the Armed Services Committee — Nelson returned to the panel for the 113th after a two-year absence, giving up a seat on the Intelligence Committee to do so. He indicates broad support for many Obama administration plans, such as the troop withdrawal from Afghanistan. When the Pentagon saw significant budget reductions in the 112th Congress (2011-12), Nelson was his usual diplomatic self. He spoke of the need for overall fiscal restraint, but suggested putting off further defense cuts for a year so Congress could study the issue.

When he allowed himself a rare display of irritation in early 2013, it was to protest another member's perceived bad behavior. As the panel voted to approve the nomination of Chuck Hagel for Defense secretary, he said Texas Republican Ted Cruz had "gone over the line" with his attacks on Hagel.

Florida has its share of military bases, and Nelson's office lists as one of his goals "dispersing our Atlantic nuclear fleet for security reasons." That's another way of saying that Nelson wants carriers and other ships, probably in Virginia, moved to a new home base, probably in Florida. Virginia and Florida lawmakers have been engaged in a battle over aircraft carriers for years, and Virginia has the upper hand for now; the Obama administration in its fiscal 2013 budget request didn't ask for money to move a carrier from Norfolk to Naval Station Mayport in Jacksonville.

The state also has a lot of veterans. Nelson was the primary Senate sponsor of a 2012 law allowing veterans who are transitioning to civilian jobs to use their relevant military training to fulfill federal license requirements. However, Republicans in 2012 blocked a Nelson bill to create a program matching veterans with certain conservation, police and firefighting jobs; they said it was an election year gimmick.

On the Commerce, Science and Transportation Committee, Nelson tries to keep Florida tied to the U.S. space program, and it's not a passing interest. As an undergraduate at Yale University he wrote his senior thesis about the Kennedy Space Center. Nelson served in the U.S. House during the 1980s and chaired a subcommittee with jurisdiction over NASA; in that role he spent six days in 1986 orbiting Earth on the space shuttle Columbia.

He now chairs the Science and Space Subcommittee. Nelson was among the lawmakers who wrestled with the Obama administration after it proposed terminating the Constellation program, the planned successor to the space shuttle program, and shifting to commercial alternatives. He helped broker a deal to continue development of NASA's own rocket and crew vehicle, then steered it to enactment in 2010. During the 112th, Nelson questioned whether NASA was getting enough resources — or spending too much money on projects with private sector developers — to keep the rocket and crew vehicle on schedule.

The full committee has some jurisdiction over surface transportation programs. As Congress considered a two-year reauthorization of such programs in 2012, Nelson was one of the lawmakers fighting for a provision to give Gulf Coast states 80 percent of the Clean Water Act fines related to the 2010 Gulf of Mexico oil spill. It was included in the final law.

Nelson opposes oil drilling off of Florida's coast, citing the potential damage to the state's tourism economy, environment and military installations should a spill occur. He helped negotiate a 2006 deal that banned wells close to the Florida coast. He also sponsored a 2011 bill to prevent oil and gas companies operating in Cuban waters from getting U.S. oil and gas leases — unless they have a response plan and resources to deal with a spill in Cuba that might spread to U.S. waters.

Nelson is no friendlier to oil and gas companies on the Finance Committee, which handles tax matters. Like many Democrats, he has urged an end to credits and other tax advantages enjoyed by that industry, calling them "entitlement spending without accountability."

Finance also looks at many of the entitlement programs that older Americans rely on. As Democrats prepared their health care overhaul in the 111th Congress (2009-10), Nelson, a former state insurance commissioner, called for a bipartisan approach and the creation of state-based insurance pools. But he couldn't drum up support for an amendment to require the pharmaceutical industry to give the government price breaks on drugs sold to "dual eligibles" — people who qualify for both Medicare and Medicaid.

Nelson often steers clear of divisive social issues. In 2010, when the Armed Services Committee considered a repeal of the ban on openly gay servicemembers, Nelson said he wasn't sure about legislating on the issue while the Pentagon was reviewing the matter. He backed a compromise that would have allowed for a repeal after the Defense Department completed a study of its possible effect. After opposing same-sex marriage for most of his career, he announced in April 2013 that he had changed his mind.

Nelson's great-great-grandfather immigrated to America from Denmark in 1829, settling near Chipley in the Florida Panhandle. Much of Nelson's family still lives there. Nelson's father was a lawyer; his mother was a schoolteacher. Nelson majored in political science at Yale, and after law school and a stint in the Army Reserve, he won and held for six years a seat in the state legislature.

In 1978, he won a bid for an open U.S. House seat. He was an early member of the moderate (and now defunct) Democratic Leadership Council that helped boost Bill Clinton to the national stage. Despite a string of re-elections and the publicity attending his adventure as an astronaut, Nelson lost the 1990 Democratic primary for governor to former Sen. Lawton Chiles. It remains his only electoral defeat. Four years later he was elected state insurance commissioner, and he dealt with the aftermath of Hurricane Andrew, which ravaged southern Florida and the state's insurance market in 1992.

Nelson was the front-runner in the 2000 race to succeed retiring Republican Sen. Connie Mack. He portrayed his opponent, 10-term congressman Bill McCollum, as too conservative for Florida, and he won the election with 51 percent of the vote. Republicans had high hopes of defeating him in 2006, but Republican Rep. Katherine Harris ran a muddled campaign and lost by 22 points. Nelson looked vulnerable again heading into 2012. He faced GOP Rep. Connie Mack, his predecessor's son. The younger Mack ran a campaign that many analysts found limp, while Nelson stressed his moderation and attention to Florida. He won by 13 points.

Key Votes

2012

Prohibit health insurance plans from denying coverage based on the sponsor's religious beliefs	YES
Require approval of the Keystone XL oil pipeline	NO
Ease securities rules to expand small-business access to capital	YES
Reauthorize farm and nutrition programs for five years	YES
Limit debate on a bill that would create private-sector cybersecurity standards	YES
Consent to ratification of a treaty setting global standard for the treatment of people with disabilities	YES
Provide $60.4 billion in disaster relief following Superstorm Sandy	YES
Extend most Bush-era income tax rates while allowing rates for top-bracket earners to rise (Jan. 1, 2013)	YES

2011

Prevent EPA from regulating greenhouse gas emissions to address climate change	NO
Extend certain provisions of Patriot Act for four years	YES
Clear compromise debt limit increase plan and establish future spending limits	YES
Overhaul patent law	YES
Implement Colombia free trade agreement	YES
Limit debate on confirmation of Caitlin J. Halligan to D.C. Circuit Court of Appeals	YES
Extend payroll tax cut and unemployment benefits for two months	YES

CQ Vote Studies

	PARTY UNITY		PRESIDENTIAL SUPPORT	
	SUPPORT	OPPOSE	SUPPORT	OPPOSE
2012	91%	9%	99%	1%
2011	90%	10%	97%	3%
2010	89%	11%	98%	2%
2009	93%	7%	97%	3%
2008	89%	11%	42%	58%
2007	90%	10%	42%	58%
2006	76%	24%	60%	40%
2005	84%	16%	47%	53%
2004	92%	8%	62%	38%
2003	90%	10%	56%	44%

Interest Groups

	AFL-CIO	ADA	CCUS	ACU
2012	91%	90%	38%	8%
2011	79%	90%	64%	15%
2010	94%	90%	36%	8%
2009	100%	100%	43%	4%
2008	100%	95%	50%	8%
2007	95%	90%	45%	4%
2006	60%	60%	83%	40%
2005	71%	80%	50%	20%
2004	100%	80%	65%	4%
2003	77%	80%	48%	20%

Sen. Marco Rubio (R)

Capitol Office
224-3041
rubio.senate.gov
284 Russell Bldg. 20510; fax 228-0285

Committees
Commerce, Science & Transportation
Foreign Relations
Small Business & Entrepreneurship
Select Intelligence

Residence
West Miami

Born
May 28, 1971; Miami, Fla.

Religion
Roman Catholic

Family
Wife, Jeanette Rubio; four children

Education
Tarkio College, attended 1989-90; Santa Fe Community College, attended 1990-91; U. of Florida, B.S. 1993 (political science); U. of Miami, J.D. 1996

Career
Lawyer; campaign aide

Political Highlights
West Miami City Commission, 1998-2000; Fla. House, 2000-08 (majority leader, 2003-06; speaker, 2006-08)

ELECTION RESULTS

2010 GENERAL		
Marco Rubio (R)	2,645,743	48.9%
Charlie Crist (I)	1,607,549	29.7%
Kendrick B. Meek (D)	1,092,936	20.2%
2010 PRIMARY		
Marco Rubio (R)	1,069,936	84.6%
William "Billy" Kogut (R)	112,080	8.9%
William Escoffery III (R)	82,426	6.5%

Elected 2010; 1st term

Rubio is seen by many in the Republican Conference as a new face of their party: He's young, telegenic, conservative and willing to step out front on issues of national importance. So far, he has dismissed speculation about an appearance on a national ticket in 2016, but the talk hasn't gone away.

He was vetted as a possible running mate to presidential nominee Mitt Romney in 2012, and Rubio eventually had the honor of introducing Romney during the Republican National Convention in August 2012. He delivered an address saturated with his life story—he's the son of Cuban immigrants—and his vision of the American dream.

"In America, we are all just a generation or two removed from somebody who made our future the purpose of their lives," he said. "To make sure that America is still a place where tomorrow is always better than yesterday, that is what our politics should be about." Rubio also delivered the GOP response to President Barack Obama's State of the Union address in 2013.

Part of the interest in Rubio is clearly linked to his ethnicity. Republicans did not do well with Hispanic voters in the 2012 elections, and Rubio seems to embrace the role of potential ambassador between his party and minorities on issues of immigration and citizenship.

At the start of the 113th Congress (2013-14) he joined a bipartisan group of eight senators that produced a framework for a comprehensive overhaul of immigration law: enhance border security; give those who are in the country illegally an opportunity at "probationary legal status"; create a separate path to citizenship for illegal immigrants who were brought to the U.S. as minors; and expand the use of an electronic employment verification system.

He teamed up with Utah Republican Orrin G. Hatch and Democrats Amy Klobuchar of Minnesota and Chris Coons of Delaware on a bill to update immigration laws for high-skilled jobs. Laws regarding legal immigration "have to move toward merit and skill-based immigration," he told the Wall Street Journal.

"I live this issue on a daily basis," Rubio said on the Senate floor in January 2013. "I live in a family of immigrants, married into a family of immigrants, in a neighborhood of immigrants, in a community of immigrants. I see all the good things legal immigration has done for America, and I see the strain illegal immigration places on our country."

Rubio sits on the Foreign Relations Committee and also the bicameral Commission on Security and Cooperation in Europe (aka the Helsinki Commission). While he is a fiscal conservative, he hasn't called for major reductions in foreign aid. "The central issue of foreign policy today is this balance between making sure we're not trying to do more than we can, and ensuring that we're not doing less than we should," he said at a 2013 hearing.

Rubio has suggested that it's appropriate for the United States to encourage the establishment and development of functioning democracies around the globe. In 2011 he participated in a Republican filibuster against the nominee for ambassador to El Salvador, saying it was to protest the Obama administration's Western Hemisphere policies. When he dropped his opposition, he said he had gotten assurances that the White House would consider a stronger response to allegedly fraudulent elections in Nicaragua.

Like many Cuban-Americans, he is an implacable foe of the Castro regime. The Washington Post reported in 2011 that Rubio might have embellished the details of his family's history; though Rubio had asserted on his Senate website and in other settings that his parents fled the Castro regime, official documents indicated that they came to the United States more than two years before Fidel Castro assumed power. Rubio's office asserted to the Post that the family visited Cuba after Castro's takeover with hopes of returning, then returned to the United States.

Rubio also sits on the Intelligence Committee. He has said the George W. Bush administration was wrong to remove North Korea from the list of state sponsors of terrorism; he also wants less focus on the Israel-Palestine debate and more on Iran's pursuit of nuclear weapons.

From the Commerce, Science and Transportation Committee, he favors offshore oil and gas drilling, despite many Floridians' objections to drilling off the coast of the state.

Spending debates dominated Rubio's freshman term in the 112th Congress (2011-12). He joins many Republicans in the belief that any serious effort to cut federal spending will include an overhaul of entitlement programs. He's open to altering the formula for calculating cost-of-living increases and raising the retirement age.

Rubio opposed a short-term suspension of the government's borrowing limit as one of his first votes of the 113th Congress. He also opposed a December 2012 bill to provide $60 billion in emergency spending for communities hit by Superstorm Sandy. The year before, he opposed a package of appropriations bills providing $915 billion in spending for fiscal 2012. The bill "spends too much, wastes precious taxpayer dollars to fund a menu of job-killing regulations, anti-life provisions and earmarks, and has been ushered through Congress in a highly secretive and nontransparent manner that didn't allow for consideration of even a single amendment," he wrote.

Rubio is a social conservative. He introduced a bill to prohibit requiring organizations to provide coverage for contraception under the 2010 health care law, if such actions would violate religious beliefs.

On leaving Cuba, Rubio's parents settled in Miami. The family moved to Las Vegas and converted to Mormonism when Rubio was 8 years old. But they later returned to both Miami and Catholicism, the established religion of his mother. "We left the Mormon church with nothing but admiration for the place that had been our first spiritual home in Las Vegas and had been so generous to us," Rubio wrote in an autobiography. "I still feel that way."

Rubio's father, Mario, worked as a bartender, a street vendor and a school crossing guard. His mother, Oria, also held a number of jobs, including hotel housekeeper and Kmart stock clerk.

Rubio spent one year at Tarkio College in Missouri on a football scholarship before transferring to a community college in Florida. He eventually earned an undergraduate degree at the University of Florida and a law degree at the University of Miami.

His first foray into electoral politics came as a successful candidate for the West Miami City Commission in 1998. He was elected to the Florida House in 2000, becoming majority leader and then speaker in 2006.

When Rubio announced his Senate candidacy in May 2009, he was given no chance of winning — Republican Gov. Charlie Crist, who had a moderate image and high approval ratings, wanted the nomination. But Crist's lack of devotion to core Republican principles didn't sit well with conservatives. Rubio made good use of Crist's endorsement of Obama's 2009 economic stimulus package. He also got a lift from the tea party movement.

Crist's poll numbers plummeted, and he dropped out of the primary and declared he would run as an independent. Less than two weeks after the primary, Rubio's father died, and Rubio briefly suspended his campaign. Once it resumed, polls showed a seesaw race between Rubio and Crist.

Days before the vote, Crist reportedly asked the Democratic nominee, Rep. Kendrick B. Meek, to withdraw from the race to give him a clear shot at Rubio. Rubio prevailed, winning 49 percent of the vote to Crist's 30 percent and Meek's 20 percent. Late in 2012, Crist registered as a Democrat.

Key Votes

2012	
Prohibit health insurance plans from denying coverage based on the sponsor's religious beliefs	NO
Require approval of the Keystone XL oil pipeline	YES
Ease securities rules to expand small-business access to capital	YES
Reauthorize farm and nutrition programs for five years	NO
Limit debate on a bill that would create private-sector cybersecurity standards	?
Consent to ratification of a treaty setting global standard for the treatment of people with disabilities	NO
Provide $60.4 billion in disaster relief following Superstorm Sandy	NO
Extend most Bush-era income tax rates while allowing rates for top-bracket earners to rise (Jan. 1, 2013)	NO
2011	
Prevent EPA from regulating greenhouse gas emissions to address climate change	YES
Extend certain provisions of Patriot Act for four years	?
Clear compromise debt limit increase plan and establish future spending limits	NO
Overhaul patent law	-
Implement Colombia free trade agreement	YES
Limit debate on confirmation of Caitlin J. Halligan to D.C. Circuit Court of Appeals	NO
Extend payroll tax cut and unemployment benefits for two months	YES

CQ Vote Studies

	PARTY UNITY		PRESIDENTIAL SUPPORT	
	SUPPORT	OPPOSE	SUPPORT	OPPOSE
2012	90%	10%	44%	56%
2011	96%	4%	46%	54%

Interest Groups

	AFL-CIO	ADA	CCUS	ACU
2012	0%	0%	75%	100%
2011	11%	5%	89%	100%

Rep. Jeff Miller (R)

Capitol Office
225-4136
jeffmiller.house.gov
336 Cannon Bldg. 20515-0901; fax 225-3414

Committees
Armed Services
Veterans' Affairs - Chairman
Select Intelligence

Residence
Chumuckla

Born
June 27, 1959; St. Petersburg, Fla.

Religion
Methodist

Family
Wife, Vicki Griswold Miller; two children

Education
U. of Florida, B.A. 1984 (journalism)

Career
Real estate company owner; state agriculture department official; deputy county sheriff

Political Highlights
Fla. House, 1998-2001

ELECTION RESULTS

2012 GENERAL		
Jeff Miller (R)	238,440	69.6%
Jim Bryan (D)	92,961	27.1%
Calen Fretts (LIBERT)	11,176	3.3%
2012 PRIMARY		
Jeff Miller (R)		unopposed
2010 GENERAL		
Jeff Miller (R)	170,821	80.0%
Joe Cantrell (NPA)	23,250	10.9%
John Krause (NPA)	18,253	8.5%

Previous Winning Percentages
2008 (70%); 2006 (69%); 2004 (77%); 2002 (75%); 2001 Special Election (66%)

Elected 2001; 6th full term

Miller is one of the House's most conservative members, although his position as chairman of the less-polarized Veterans' Affairs Committee can obscure that fact. His desire for fiscal discipline and efficiency throughout government is particularly focused when he deals with the bureaucracy of the department he directly oversees.

Miller took up his gavel at the start of the 112th Congress (2011-12) with the intention of taking a closer look at the Department of Veterans Affairs. "We have not had a robust oversight plan for a number of years, and that's our responsibility," he said in 2012.

The VA's health and benefit programs are sprawling, and communication and coordination throughout the organization have been scrutinized by lawmakers. Miller describes a culture devoid of accountability. "A boot, appropriately placed in somebody's backside, is usually a pretty good incentive to be open, honest and transparent," he said. "And, unfortunately, I don't see where that's been done."

He praises the work of Secretary Eric Shinseki but sees breakdowns in "the mid-level bureaucracy." Miller cites a defective incentive structure as a major obstacle, with problems hidden from department leaders "to provide good news so somebody will receive a bonus." His frustration was palpable near the end of 2012, at a hearing on questionable spending at VA conferences. He took offense as a deputy secretary protested that statements by committee members might be disparaging to VA employees. "The truce is over," Miller said, as he gaveled the hearing to a close.

As the top Republican on the Health Subcommittee during the 110th Congress (2007-08), Miller tried to promote quicker, more responsive treatment of veterans. A long backlog of service-connected disability claims led him to call for an overhaul of the VA. After The Washington Post in early 2007 disclosed widespread problems at Walter Reed Army Medical Center, Miller was one of many lawmakers calling for removal of the Army's surgeon general and former commander at Walter Reed, Lt. Gen. Kevin Kiley. Kiley soon retired under pressure.

Miller's stamp was on several laws enacted in the 112th. President Barack Obama in 2011 signed his bill exempting certain veterans who enlisted after the Sept. 11 attacks from a new cap on educational benefits, provided they had enrolled before the cap was in place. Working to address unemployment among Iraq and Afghanistan veterans, Miller combined parts of his measure to promote the hiring of veterans with provisions prepared by his Senate counterpart, Washington Democrat Patty Murray. It was enacted in 2011.

Miller is a fiscal conservative, and in the 112th he voted for most proposals to cut spending or eliminate programs he sees as wasteful. He has cosponsored a measure to replace most federal taxes with a national sales tax.

He tries to shield military accounts from some cuts, however. Miller voted for the August 2011 deal to increase the debt limit and cut spending. But as automatic cuts established by that law approached, he introduced a bill to exempt the Veterans Affairs Department from reductions. Also a member of the Armed Service Committee, Miller has said that large reductions to the defense budget could be "devastating" to national security and the economy. His Panhandle district is home to thousands of active-duty military personnel as well as tens of thousands of military retirees.

Miller is a member of the Republican Study Committee, a group of the House's most conservative members. He voted against the fiscal 2011 defense authorization bill because it included a provision that would repeal the ban on openly gay individuals serving in the military. He opposed stand-alone legislation to do the same that was enacted at the end of 2010.

He's also a strong advocate of gun rights — his office is adorned with a variety of taxidermied animals. The House in 2012 passed his bill to keep public lands open to recreational hunting, fishing and shooting unless federal agencies have certain specific reasons for a prohibition. It didn't move in the Senate.

From the Intelligence Committee, Miller takes an interest in Iran's nuclear program. Miller said in 2012 that the United States should have a defined sense of which Iranian actions will trigger a military response. "There should be red lines," he said. "It does not necessarily mean there should be published red lines. But the [Obama] administration has clearly said there are no red lines. Why would you say that? It doesn't make sense.

"Iran cannot be allowed to obtain a nuclear weapon. And when they get to the point where they have it, it's too late."

Generally speaking, Miller is not a fan of the Obama administration's military or diplomatic policies. "The United States has always led with strength," he said. "This administration has not done that."

A former small-business owner, Miller is close to the business leaders in his community, many of whom rely on a robust tourism economy. He fought the George W. Bush administration's plan to open gas and oil drilling within 20 miles of the coast, complaining it would interfere with military training and weapons testing. He also backed a bill, later rolled into a 2012 surface transportation law, that gives the Gulf Coast states at least 80 percent of the Clean Water Act fines collected in relation to the 2010 oil spill in the gulf.

Miller is a sixth-generation Floridian. His parents sold real estate and operated a cattle ranch near Clearwater.

His own résumé is eclectic. While in high school, Miller was a disc jockey for the local radio station. Later, he had a stint as a deputy county sheriff and held part-time jobs as a stock car racer and auctioneer.

He studied journalism at the University of Florida, where he served as president of the university's education fraternity, Alpha Gamma Rho, and then as president of the school's fraternity system. Subsequently, he was elected president of college fraternities for southeast Florida.

After college, Miller joined the staff of Florida Agriculture Commissioner Doyle Connor. He later served as a state representative for the heavily Republican north Florida area he now represents in Congress.

Miller arrived in Congress in October 2001 after winning a special election to replace Republican Joe Scarborough, who had resigned. (He's now an MSNBC host.) Miller garnered 66 percent of the vote, and his re-elections have not been competitive contests.

Key Votes

2012	
Extend a Social Security payroll tax cut and unemployment benefits	NO
Ease securities rules to expand small-business access to capital	YES
Extend for one year subsidized student loan interest rates financed by a cut in health care spending	NO
Cite Attorney General Eric H. Holder Jr. for contempt of Congress	YES
Create a visa program for foreign graduates in high-tech fields	YES
Extend most Bush-era income tax rates while allowing rates for top-bracket earners to rise (Jan. 1, 2013)	NO
2011	
Strike funding for F-35 alternative engine	YES
Prevent EPA from regulating greenhouse gas emissions to address climate change	YES
Extend certain provisions of Patriot Act for four years	YES
Declare opposition to use of ground troops in Libya	+
Overhaul patent law	NO
Pass compromise debt limit increase plan and establish future spending limits	YES
Allow consideration of measures to implement three trade agreements	YES

CQ Vote Studies

	Party Unity		Presidential Support	
	Support	Oppose	Support	Oppose
2012	97%	3%	17%	83%
2011	97%	3%	16%	84%
2010	98%	2%	33%	67%
2009	98%	2%	11%	89%
2008	99%	1%	85%	15%

Interest Groups

	AFL-CIO	ADA	CCUS	ACU
2012	5%	10%	83%	92%
2011	0%	5%	94%	92%
2010	7%	0%	88%	96%
2009	5%	0%	73%	100%
2008	7%	5%	89%	100%

Florida 1

Panhandle — Pensacola, Fort Walton Beach

Covering the Panhandle border with Alabama, the 1st's Bible Belt culture is more closely tied to the Deep South than to the rest of Florida. Dubbed "lower Alabama," it is peppered with midsize cities, beach towns and nature preserves. The military and the Gulf of Mexico steer its economic course.

The defense presence supports tens of thousands of military, civilian and contractor jobs. Naval Air Station Pensacola is the training base for Navy, Marine Corps and Coast Guard aviators, and Eglin Air Force Base, which sprawls across parts of three counties, has a research and testing focus.

Pensacola, in Escambia County, is the district's population center. Health care and higher-education-based research are key to its economy. The powder-white sands of the 1st's portion of the Emerald Coast, including Fort Walton Beach and Destin in Okaloosa County, support established tourism and retirement sectors. Offshore drilling and regulatory issues remain concerns for residents reliant on the gulf's beaches and seafood industry.

Santa Rosa and Walton counties have experienced significant population growth; the boom is mainly among military families and retirees, and black and Hispanic communities are growing in the majority-white counties.

During decennial redistricting, the 1st lost Washington and parts of Holmes counties while gaining the beaches of Walton County; the district remains deeply conservative. In 2012, Republican Mitt Romney took his statewide high in the presidential contest here with 69 percent of the district's vote.

Major Industry

Defense, tourism, health care

Military Bases

Naval Air Station Pensacola, 17,076 military, 4,029 civilian; Eglin Air Force Base, 8,408 military, 5,353 civilian (2011); Hurlburt Field (Air Force), 3,287 military, 2,334 civilian (2011); Naval Air Station Whiting Field, 1,765 military, 486 civilian (2012)

Cities

Pensacola, Navarre (unincorporated), Ferry Pass (unincorporated)

Notable

The Blue Angels flight demonstration team is stationed at Naval Air Station Pensacola.

Rep. Steve Southerland II (R)

Capitol Office
225-5235
southerland.house.gov
1229 Longworth Bldg. 20515-0902; fax 225-5615

Committees
Natural Resources
Transportation & Infrastructure

Residence
Panama City

Born
Oct. 10, 1965; Nashville, Tenn.

Religion
Southern Baptist

Family
Wife, Susan Southerland; four children

Education
Troy State U., B.S. 1987 (business management); Jefferson State Community College, A.A. 1989 (mortuary science)

Career
Funeral home owner

Political Highlights
Fla. Board of Funeral Directors and Embalmers, 1992-95

ELECTION RESULTS

2012 GENERAL		
Steve Southerland II (R)	175,856	52.7%
Al Lawson (D)	157,634	47.2%
2012 PRIMARY		
Steve Southerland II (R)		unopposed
2010 GENERAL		
Steve Southerland II (R)	136,371	53.6%
Allen Boyd (D)	105,211	41.4%
Paul C. McKain (NPA)	7,135	2.8%
Dianne Berryhill (NPA)	5,705	2.2%

Elected 2010; 2nd term

Southerland says he's more comfortable among fishers and farmers than politicians and pundits. He has a blunt take on Washington's political culture: "I don't like this place."

"When I go home on the weekends and put on my flip flops and my shorts and my John Deere hat, I go to Walmart," he said. "I walk up and down those aisles, and I hear all I need to hear. I don't need to hear from a political prognosticator on what I need to do or how I need to do it. I go to Walmart."

He operated a funeral home and had no legislative experience before joining Congress in 2011. Southerland is one of the more conservative members of the House GOP Conference, and he's not fazed by political brinkmanship.

His concern for the nation's fiscal health was one of his reasons for getting into politics. He wants large and immediate spending cuts, plus structural changes to government spending habits. During deficit reduction debates in July 2011, Southerland was one of 22 Republicans to reject a plan put forth by Speaker John A. Boehner — conservatives felt it didn't have a strong-enough commitment to adding a balanced-budget amendment to the Constitution. Southerland also opposed the fiscal 2012 appropriations bills, which hardliners viewed as spending too much.

"I think tension is a good thing," Southerland said in early 2012. "It's how you grow muscle. Stress and pressure and heat — that's how diamonds are made." He made a good impression on his colleagues in the Republican Class of 2010, who elected him as their representative on the House leadership team in early 2013. He replaced Tim Scott of South Carolina, who was appointed to the Senate.

Southerland views his committee seats as bases from which he can combat federal interference in the economy. As a freshman, he was assigned to the Agriculture, Natural Resources and Transportation and Infrastructure committees. Southerland says that when he was offered the chance to leave the Agriculture and Natural Resources committees for another posting in his first term, "I said thanks, but no thanks. Somebody here needs to fight for farmers. Somebody here needs to fight for fishermen."

However, he did step down from the Agriculture Committee in February 2013 to "dedicate additional focus to my other committee assignments and legislative responsibilities." In addition to being a class liaison, Southerland is active in the Republican Study Committee, heading up an anti-poverty task force for that conservative group. He has co-authored legislation to block the Obama administration from changing work requirements in the 1996 welfare overhaul law.

On Natural Resources, Southerland wants to speed up the permitting process for energy production in the Gulf of Mexico, while maintaining safety reviews — many constituents in his Panhandle district rely on the gulf for their livelihood. However, Southerland in the 112th Congress (2011-12) did vote against several measures to expand offshore drilling. He said he couldn't support drilling near the Panhandle that might interfere with operations at one of the area's many military bases.

In December 2012, he praised the EPA's decision to approve Florida's numeric nutrient standards for water quality. He favors allowing the state to determine its own standards for nitrogen and phosphorus pollutants, which are often linked to farming. He had introduced a bill on the matter.

Southerland served on the conference committee that finalized a two-year reauthorization of surface transportation programs enacted in 2012. He contributed to a bill, which was rolled into that highway law, that gives Gulf Coast states the lion's share of Clean Water Act fines collected in relation to the 2010 gulf oil spill.

He wants to improve Florida's "rate of return" — the amount of federal transportation funding it gets relative to what the state's highway users pay in federal highway taxes. Southerland was pleased with the provisions in the 2012 law meant to streamline regulatory reviews of infrastructure projects.

His departure from the Agriculture Committee lessens his involvement on any potential long-term reauthorization of farm programs in the 113th Congress (2013-14). He calls for greater scrutiny of food assistance programs — the panel-approved version of the 2012 farm bill, which never got a floor vote, had $16.1 billion in cuts to the Supplemental Nutrition Assistance Program. Southerland was one of the 13 panel Republicans supporting an unsuccessful amendment to double that amount.

Born in Tennessee, Southerland has spent most of his life in Florida. The funeral home business started by his grandfather was a constant presence in his life, with four business lines ringing in the house at all hours. "I have a business that is 60 years old, and it has never been closed a day," he said. "We've never signed a death certificate in the history of our family company ... that said 'this individual died from work.' Work is a good thing."

Southerland graduated from Troy State University in 1987 with a degree in business management, then got an associate's degree in mortuary science from Jefferson State Community College in 1989. His business "has allowed me to know every area and every sector of my community," he said. "I bury fishermen, I bury Wall Street tycoons. We serve families in all walks of life. Loggers, fishermen, oystermen, accountants, attorneys, brokers — it doesn't matter. You're coming to a funeral home."

Southerland met his wife, Susan, in the first grade, and they now have four daughters. His only prior political experience came as a member of the Florida Board of Funeral Directors and Embalmers, serving from 1992 to 1995. But he did help establish a Florida tea party group.

Democratic Rep. Allen Boyd, a seven-term incumbent, had never been in a close House election. But he supported the 2010 health care overhaul as he was fending off a primary-election challenge from state Senate Minority Leader Al Lawson. The National Republican Congressional Committee poured money into Southerland's campaign. Democrats answered with financial support for Boyd, but Southerland — a former Democrat, like many Panhandle Republicans — rode the GOP wave to a 12-point victory.

Lawson won the Democratic primary in 2012. He was enough of a threat that the NRCC bought broadcast time in the Panama City and Tallahassee media markets. Southerland won with nearly 53 percent of the vote.

Key Votes

2012	
Extend a Social Security payroll tax cut and unemployment benefits	YES
Ease securities rules to expand small-business access to capital	YES
Extend for one year subsidized student loan interest rates financed by a cut in health care spending	YES
Cite Attorney General Eric H. Holder Jr. for contempt of Congress	YES
Create a visa program for foreign graduates in high-tech fields	YES
Extend most Bush-era income tax rates while allowing rates for top-bracket earners to rise (Jan. 1, 2013)	NO
2011	
Strike funding for F-35 alternative engine	YES
Prevent EPA from regulating greenhouse gas emissions to address climate change	YES
Extend certain provisions of Patriot Act for four years	YES
Declare opposition to use of ground troops in Libya	YES
Overhaul patent law	NO
Pass compromise debt limit increase plan and establish future spending limits	NO
Allow consideration of measures to implement three trade agreements	YES

CQ Vote Studies

	PARTY UNITY		PRESIDENTIAL SUPPORT	
	SUPPORT	OPPOSE	SUPPORT	OPPOSE
2012	96%	4%	18%	82%
2011	97%	3%	19%	81%

Interest Groups

	AFL-CIO	ADA	CCUS	ACU
2012	10%	5%	83%	84%
2011	0%	5%	88%	96%

Florida 2

Panhandle — Tallahassee, Panama City

In the central Panhandle, the 2nd has tourist-driven beach towns, military populations, forests and farms, and the oak-lined streets of the state capital, Tallahassee. While the district takes in all or part of 14 counties, more than 60 percent of its population is clustered in Leon and Bay counties. The 2nd borders Alabama and Georgia to the north and the Gulf of Mexico to the south, sharing cultural ties with the Deep South. Urban Tallahassee is a liberal-leaning outpost in the middle of the conservative rural region.

Tallahassee's economy is stabilized by the presence of government jobs. With nearly 41,000 students, Florida State University is one of the district's largest employers. The capital city is also home to the historically black Florida A&M University. The city accounts for much of the otherwise mainly white district's black population (24 percent). The district's second population hub, Panama City, relies on tourism and Tyndall Air Force Base.

The 2nd takes in large wilderness areas, including Apalachicola National Forest and the Wakulla Springs State Park, which hosts myriad wildlife — including manatees patrolling the natural waterways. Although the district lost some primarily agricultural territory to the 3rd during decennial redistricting, the still-abundant farmland in the 2nd produces cotton, timber, beef cows and peanuts. Oyster farming is predominant along the coast.

Democrats have an edge in voter registration and residents in the capital tend to be more liberal, but the 2nd overall is conservative. In the 2012 presidential race, Republican Mitt Romney's best percentage statewide was 84 percent in Holmes County (shared with the 1st) and Barack Obama's highest was in Gadsden County (70 percent).

Major Industry
State government, higher education; agriculture

Military Bases
Tyndall Air Force Base, 3,256 military, 783 civilian (2011)

Cities
Tallahassee, Panama City, Lynn Haven

Notable
Tallahassee's National High Magnetic Field Laboratory is home to the highest-powered magnet in the world.

Rep. Ted Yoho (R)

Capitol Office
225-5744
yoho.house.gov
511 Cannon Bldg. 20515-0607; fax 225-3973

Committees
Agriculture
Foreign Affairs

Residence
Gainesville

Born
April 13, 1955; Minneapolis, Minn.

Religion
Roman Catholic

Family
Wife, Carolyn Yoho; three children

Education
Broward Community College, A.A. 1977; U. of Florida, B.S.A. 1979 (animal science), D.V.M. 1983

Career
Veterinarian

Political Highlights
No previous office

ELECTION RESULTS

2012 GENERAL		
Ted Yoho (R)	204,331	64.7%
J.R. Gaillot (D)	102,468	32.5%
Philip Dodds (NPA)	8,870	2.8%
2012 PRIMARY		
Ted Yoho (R)	22,273	34.4%
Cliff Stearns (R)	21,398	33.0%
Steve Oelrich (R)	12,329	19.0%
James Jett (R)	8,769	13.5%

Elected 2012; 1st term

Though he arrived in the House in 2013, Yoho is brimming with the anti-establishment spirit of the 2010 elections. He reinforces the ranks of the most conservative Republicans.

Yoho, a veterinarian, registered his displeasure with GOP leaders early on. During the selection of the speaker of the House, he voted for Eric Cantor of Virginia rather than the incumbent, John A. Boehner. He told The Atlantic that he does not find Washington intimidating: "Intimidating is going up to a growling Rottweiler and having to squeeze his anal glands, or going up to a stallion that weighs 1,200 pounds and telling him you're going to take his testicles off," he said. "That's intimidating. I think I can handle Congress."

He described himself to Sunshine State News as a "conservative Christian Republican with a libertarian slant." Yoho touts his political inexperience as a virtue and supports policies with conservative and populist elements: implementation of a consumption tax to replace the personal income tax, term limits for congressmen, a huge reduction in federal regulations and spending and an immigration overhaul that includes national ID cards.

He heavily favors smaller government. Yoho voted against allowing further borrowing for the National Flood Insurance Program to cover Superstorm Sandy claims. "The federal government has no business in the insurance business," he said. He'll be dealing with more insurance programs as a member of the Agriculture Committee.

On the Foreign Affairs Committee, Yoho opposes the deployment of the military for anything other than a direct threat to the United States.

Yoho stunned the political world by knocking off 12-term Rep. Cliff Stearns in a Republican primary in 2012. Yoho had been running a low-budget, grassroots campaign, and Stearns didn't seem to take the challenge seriously until it was too late — he spent very little of his campaign funds. That victory essentially ensured Yoho a term representing the very Republican 3rd District.

Florida 3

North — part of Gainesville

A vast parcel of mostly rural land where Florida's northwestern Panhandle meets the peninsula, the 3rd District takes in sparsely populated northern counties, part of the Jacksonville metro region in the northeast (the city is in the 4th and 5th districts) and a portion of Gainesville. Bordering Georgia and the Gulf of Mexico, much of the 3rd has a rural, socially conservative, Old South feel.

The 3rd's portion of Gainesville, its largest population center, includes the University of Florida's flagship campus. With 50,000 students, it is one of the state's largest schools and a major employer in the district. Although many students and faculty live in the neighboring 5th District, fans congregate in the 3rd on fall weekends for Gator football games. The 3rd's portion of Gainesville also includes the Malcom Randall VA Medical Center, a major veterans' hospital.

Although there are large numbers of highly educated residents in Alachua County near the university, the education levels in the district's rural counties remain some of the lowest in the state. Some of the state's highest poverty rates also plague the district. Heavily agricultural counties in the center of the district — such as Lafayette, Suwannee and Gilchrist counties — produce poultry, dairy, corn, tobacco and grains. With a landscape that includes gently rolling hills, pine forests and magnolia trees, the 3rd lacks the beaches and tourist attractions that many other areas in the state rely on; streams of motorists pass through the district via Interstate 75 on their way to those destinations.

After Florida gained two U.S. House seats as a result of decennial reapportionment, the 3rd was significantly redrawn from areas formerly split among five districts. Although liberal pockets exist, especially near Gainesville, overall it is heavily conservative. Alachua was the only county in the 3rd that backed Democrat Barack Obama in the 2012 presidential contest — he took 54 percent of the vote from the district's portions of the county.

Major Industry
Agriculture, higher education, retail

Cities
Gainesville (pt.), Lake City, Live Oak

Notable
The sports drink Gatorade was developed by University of Florida researchers and named after the school's mascot.

Rep. Ander Crenshaw (R)

Capitol Office
225-2501
crenshaw.house.gov
440 Cannon Bldg. 20515-0904; fax 225-2504

Committees
Appropriations
(Financial Services - Chairman)

Residence
Jacksonville

Born
Sept. 1, 1944; Jacksonville, Fla.

Religion
Episcopalian

Family
Wife, Kitty Crenshaw; two children

Education
U. of Georgia, A.B. 1966 (political science); U. of Florida, J.D. 1969

Career
Investment bank executive; lawyer

Political Highlights
Fla. House, 1972-78; candidate for Fla. secretary of state, 1978; sought Republican nomination for U.S. Senate, 1980; Fla. Senate, 1986-94 (president, 1992-93); sought Republican nomination for governor, 1994

ELECTION RESULTS

2012 GENERAL		
Ander Crenshaw (R)	239,988	76.1%
Jim Klauder (NPA)	75,236	23.8%
2012 PRIMARY		
Ander Crenshaw (R)	46,788	71.9%
Bob Black (R)	11,816	18.1%
Deborah Katz Pueschel (R)	6,505	10.0%
2010 GENERAL		
Ander Crenshaw (R)	178,238	77.2%
Troy Dwayne Stanley (NPA)	52,540	22.8%

Previous Winning Percentages
2008 (65%); 2006 (70%); 2004 (100%); 2002 (100%); 2000 (67%)

Elected 2000; 7th term

Crenshaw says his background in finance — he was an executive at an investment bank — taught him that you can leverage issues with money. The Appropriations Committee is where the money is, and Crenshaw is getting back to his professional roots in the 113th Congress as the chairman of its Financial Services Subcommittee.

Appropriators have opportunities to work on projects quietly and address issues while avoiding political fanfare. "Quiet" can be used to describe much of Crenshaw's legislative style. As he entered the 113th Congress (2013-14), he had introduced fewer than 25 bills during a House career that started in 2001. And, despite serving in the House Republican leadership as a deputy whip, Crenshaw gives only a handful of interviews and is rarely seen on the House floor. In 2011, Roll Call named Crenshaw to its annual "Obscure Caucus," a list of members who avoid the spotlight.

Atop the Financial Services Subcommittee, he is scrutinizing the budgets of Wall Street regulators and various other agencies — a departure from his other Appropriations work, which focuses on defense and foreign policy.

He laments cuts to military budgets. Crenshaw, who sits on the Defense and State-Foreign Operations subcommittees, contends that the military has been "hollowed out," starting with the Carter administration. The United States should not make strategic defense decisions "based purely on budgets," he said. Crenshaw supported a House version of the fiscal 2013 Defense spending bill that would give the Pentagon billions of additional dollars for a variety of new weapons programs — far more than the White House requested and exceeding spending caps set by a 2011 law.

Working on that bill, Crenshaw also fought for spending on 13 military aircraft at Naval Air Station Jacksonville in his district. He previously sat on the Military Construction-VA Subcommittee and was instrumental in pushing for a national veterans' cemetery in Jacksonville that opened in 2009.

He was, however, on the losing end of a long battle in 2012. The Obama administration requested no funding for the relocation of an aircraft carrier from Norfolk, Va., to Jacksonville's Naval Station Mayport. Virginia's congressional delegation strongly opposed the planned move for years, calling it a waste of resources with no practical benefits.

Crenshaw and other supporters tried to highlight the security risks of having multiple carriers at Norfolk. After the Pentagon dropped its funding request, Crenshaw wrote that it was a "shortsighted fiscal decision that is not in the best interest of national security."

Crenshaw was also among the 85 Republicans voting for the "fiscal cliff" deal in January 2013. It raised income tax rates on earnings over $400,000, but Crenshaw said on CNN that it was a "positive step" to make lower rates permanent for income below that threshold. Plus, the bill delayed scheduled cuts to military spending for several months.

He was more fastidious about cutting spending as chairman of the Legislative Branch Subcommittee in the 112th Congress (2011-12). In 2011, the subcommittee reduced funds for congressional offices and Capitol Hill support agencies by approximately 10 percent, to the ire of many of his colleagues. The bill produced for fiscal 2013, which was not enacted, shaved spending a little further, but Democrats were grateful for its smaller cuts. Marcy Kaptur of Ohio called it "the best we could do under the circumstances."

Crenshaw has stood with his party against the major initiatives of the Obama administration, including a 2009 economic stimulus package and a 2010 financial regulatory overhaul law. But near the end of the George W. Bush administration, he broke with most Republicans and voted for a $700 billion rescue package to stabilize financial markets.

Despite his low profile, Crenshaw's career is not devoid of controversy. Some of his foreign trips have raised eyebrows. In 2001, he joined Majority Leader Tom DeLay of Texas on an expenses-paid trip to South Korea, funded by a nonprofit Korean group with ties to a foreign lobbying campaign. Then, in August 2011, Crenshaw and three other House members went on an eco-tourism trip to South Africa and Botswana, also funded by a nonprofit with close ties to corporate lobbying groups. House rules prohibit lawmakers from taking trips financed by lobbyists or foreign agents, and critics argue that non-profits working on behalf of lobbyists should be included in the ban.

Family and community are high priorities in Crenshaw's life, and both shape his legislative interests. Each year, Crenshaw hosts a ceremony honoring veterans in his district, calling it "one of the highlights of my year."

Crenshaw is a leader of the Crohn's and Colitis Caucus; his interest grew from watching friends and family, including his daughter, deal with those conditions. He is also a member of the Congressional Down Syndrome Caucus. For years he has pushed legislation to provide tax-advantaged savings accounts for the care of family members with disabilities. The bill has yet to gain traction, but he says it improves with each new introduction.

Crenshaw's family has been in the Jacksonville area since 1901. A lanky 6 feet 4 inches tall, he went to the University of Georgia on a basketball scholarship and was the third member of his family to letter in a sport for the Bulldogs. The name he uses, Ander, is a shortened version of his given name, Alexander.

He was of draft age during the Vietnam War. Crenshaw served in the ROTC, but a student deferment and a high draft-lottery number kept him from combat. While working on a law degree at the University of Florida, he formed a Campus Crusade for Christ chapter. He eventually found that he wasn't interested in practicing law and turned to investment banking.

Crenshaw said he began thinking about running for political office after he started dating Kitty Kirk, daughter of former Florida Gov. Claude R. Kirk Jr. The two later married. In 1972, Crenshaw won election to the state House, where he served six years. He won a state Senate seat in 1986. In 1993, he became the first Republican to preside over the Florida Senate in 118 years.

Over time, Crenshaw lost three statewide elections: a bid for secretary of state in 1978, the Republican primary for Senate in 1980 and the primary for governor in 1994. After leaving the state Senate in 1994, he stayed out of politics until 2000 — when Republican Rep. Tillie Fowler stuck to a term limit pledge and retired. Crenshaw won the primary easily, ensuring victory in the solidly Republican district. His re-elections have been by wide margins.

Key Votes

2012	
Extend a Social Security payroll tax cut and unemployment benefits	YES
Ease securities rules to expand small-business access to capital	YES
Extend for one year subsidized student loan interest rates financed by a cut in health care spending	YES
Cite Attorney General Eric H. Holder Jr. for contempt of Congress	YES
Create a visa program for foreign graduates in high-tech fields	YES
Extend most Bush-era income tax rates while allowing rates for top-bracket earners to rise (Jan. 1, 2013)	YES
2011	
Strike funding for F-35 alternative engine	NO
Prevent EPA from regulating greenhouse gas emissions to address climate change	YES
Extend certain provisions of Patriot Act for four years	YES
Declare opposition to use of ground troops in Libya	YES
Overhaul patent law	YES
Pass compromise debt limit increase plan and establish future spending limits	YES
Allow consideration of measures to implement three trade agreements	YES

CQ Vote Studies

	PARTY UNITY		PRESIDENTIAL SUPPORT	
	SUPPORT	OPPOSE	SUPPORT	OPPOSE
2012	89%	11%	13%	87%
2011	93%	7%	26%	74%
2010	92%	8%	34%	66%
2009	84%	16%	37%	63%
2008	97%	3%	74%	26%

Interest Groups

	AFL-CIO	ADA	CCUS	ACU
2012	14%	0%	100%	76%
2011	0%	10%	100%	72%
2010	7%	5%	100%	88%
2009	10%	5%	87%	84%
2008	7%	10%	100%	90%

Florida 4

Northeast — part of Jacksonville, Ferandina Beach

Nestled against the Georgia border in the state's northeastern First Coast, the 4th District takes in most of Jacksonville and the beach communities of Duval County, as well as more rural Nassau and Baker counties. More than 85 percent of the district's residents live in Duval, which is nearly conterminous with Jacksonville, the geographically largest city in the lower 48 states.

Served by major commercial and military seaports on the Atlantic coast and the banks of the St. Johns River, Jacksonville's economy depends on shipping, distribution and logistics. Plans to deepen Jacksonville's shipping channels will lure larger vessels following expansion of the Panama Canal. Although the 5th takes in much of downtown Jacksonville, the 4th claims the airport, Naval Air Station Jacksonville and Naval Station Mayport.

The Navy is by far the district's largest employer and the region has one of the largest military presences in the country. The 5th also is strong in health care and includes a Mayo Clinic hospital. Salt marsh nature preserves, home to wildlife and a draw for bird watchers, and quiet towns with serene beaches, like Fernandina Beach, bring tourists to the 4th.

The 4th gained a larger portion of Jacksonville during decennial remapping — and now has all but a central slice of Duval County — while losing several counties along the Georgia border, reducing its rural footprint. The city's downtown and Democratic-voting black neighborhoods are now in the 5th, making the 4th conservative and three-quarters white. Most competition here is intraparty; all counties wholly or partly in the 4th supported Republican presidential nominee Mitt Romney in the 2012 election.

Major Industry
Defense, transportation and distribution, health care

Military Bases
Naval Air Station Jacksonville, 9,995 military, 7,070 civilian; Naval Station Mayport, 8,860 military, 1,247 civilian (2012)

Cities
Jacksonville (pt.), Jacksonville Beach, Atlantic Beach, Fernandina Beach

Notable
Amelia Island is the only part of the current United States to have existed under eight flags: France, Spain (twice), England, local "Patriot," "Green Cross of Florida," Mexico, Confederate States and United States.

Rep. Corrine Brown (D)

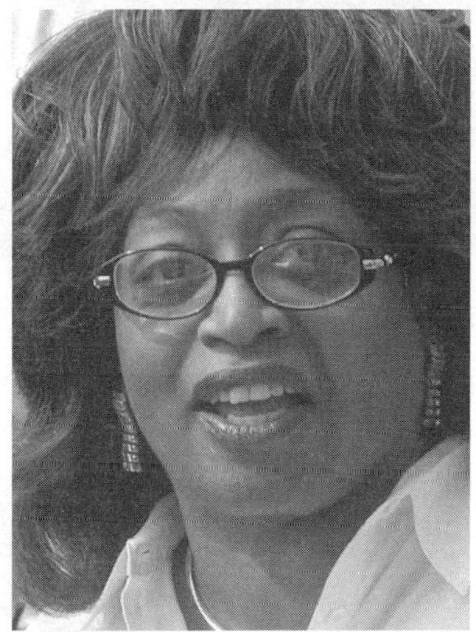

Capitol Office
225-0123
brown.house.gov
2111 Rayburn Bldg. 20515-0903; fax 225-2256

Committees
Transportation & Infrastructure
Veterans' Affairs

Residence
Jacksonville

Born
Nov. 11, 1946; Jacksonville, Fla.

Religion
Baptist

Family
Single; one child

Education
Florida A&M U., B.S. 1969 (sociology), M.A. 1971 (education); U. of Florida, Ed.S. 1974

Career
College guidance counselor; travel agency owner

Political Highlights
Candidate for Fla. House, 1980; Fla. House, 1982-92

ELECTION RESULTS

2012 GENERAL		
Corrine Brown (D)	190,472	70.8%
LeAnne Kolb (R)	70,700	26.3%
Eileen Fleming (NPA)	7,978	3.0%
2012 PRIMARY		
Corrine Brown (D)		unopposed
2010 GENERAL		
Corrine Brown (D)	94,744	63.0%
Michael "Mike" Yost (R)	50,932	33.9%
Terry Martin-Back (NPA)	4,625	3.1%

Previous Winning Percentages
2008 (100%); 2006 (100%); 2004 (99%); 2002 (59%); 2000 (58%); 1998 (55%); 1996 (61%); 1994 (58%); 1992 (59%)

Elected 1992; 11th term

Brown gets national attention for flamboyantly flaying Republicans and roiling racially charged disputes. Florida knows her more as a determined advocate for the specific needs of Jacksonville and the rest of her district.

Brown can be a spectacle on the House floor, sporting eye-catching hair and searingly bright outfits. (She gave a 2009 speech congratulating the University of Florida football team while wearing a high-sheen, orange and blue Gators robe.) Whatever the starting point of a speech, she can get to high dudgeon within seconds, ranting about the "reverse Robin Hood" years of the George W. Bush presidency or other Republican misdeeds.

Those fireworks — and a string of investigations into her finances and possible ethics violations — have not prevented her rise through two House panels important to her constituents. She's a high-ranking member of the Transportation and Infrastructure Committee, which over the years has been her lever for pushing millions of dollars homeward. And she's the No. 2 Democrat on the Veterans' Affairs Committee, which has great relevance to the huge military population in northeast Florida.

Her work on veterans issues has been free from controversy, mostly focusing on employment opportunities, family support and pensions. She introduced a bill in September 2012 to create a jobs corps to fight unemployment among post-9/11 veterans — an idea that President Barack Obama had touted in his 2012 State of the Union address. Chairman Jeff Miller of Florida rebuked the measure, saying it should apply to all veterans. Senate Republicans blocked a similar bill by Florida Democrat Bill Nelson, citing costs.

She's more forceful on the Transportation and Infrastructure Committee. Brown, according to an Orlando Sentinel report, joined that committee as a freshman because a party leader told her, "That's where the pork is." She continues to aggressively seek federal funding for her district.

Brown chaired the subcommittee on railroads and pipelines from 2007 through 2010 when Democrats controlled the House, and she is still its top Democrat. Brown wants more funding for high-speed rail. She was livid when Florida's Republican governor, Rick Scott, declined $2.4 billion in federal funds for a line from Tampa to Orlando. Brown took to the House floor in July 2011 in a near-apoplectic state. "What was he thinking about?" she asked. "I guess he was thinking he didn't want to see those people going to work and making Barack Obama look good."

She was thrilled with the Obama administration's February 2013 release of an $87 million grant for Sun Rail, a Central Florida commuter rail project.

Brown grudgingly approved of a two-year reauthorization of surface transportation programs in 2012, "although I would have preferred a long-term transportation bill with much more funding for infrastructure, and am disappointed we could not include a rail title." Transportation giant CSX Corp. has its headquarters in Jacksonville.

Some of her accomplishments from the 110th Congress (2007-08) are up for review in the 113th Congress (2013-14). As subcommittee chairwoman, Brown was the steward of an Amtrak reauthorization and a rail safety law. The current chairman, California Republican Jeff Denham, opposes high-speed rail funding.

Brown's politics are liberal, and she belongs to the Congressional Progressive Caucus. In a nod to the military presence in her district, however, she will support national security measures opposed by those on the far left.

She describes herself as a district-first lawmaker, but she also makes black identity politics part of her portfolio. Her district was the home of Trayvon

Martin, an African-American teenager shot and killed in early 2012. A self-styled neighborhood watchman said Martin was acting suspiciously, followed him, then claimed to be attacked by Martin. Police initially released the shooter, which incensed members of the community, Brown and other prominent black politicians; she referred to the incident as a "hate crime" and demanded a Justice Department investigation.

She later made a public defense of Marissa Alexander, an African-American woman sentenced for firing a warning shot when she felt her husband was threatening her. The "stand your ground" law that police applied to the man who shot Martin should apply to Alexander, Brown said. "If you are black, the system will treat you differently," she said.

Heading into the 2012 election, Brown accused GOP officials of trying to suppress minority votes by limiting early voting. She and a civil rights group sued Florida Secretary of State Ken Detzner and Duval County Supervisor of Elections Jerry Holland to extend early voting days. "More than any other racial or ethnic group, African-Americans have come to rely on early voting," she wrote. A federal court denied the request. She frequently refers to the infamous 2000 presidential election in Florida as a Republican "coup."

Controversies have entangled Brown for years, several of them related to her hyper-parochial style. Brown's daughter, Shantrel Brown Fields, is a lobbyist, and Brown has secured millions of dollars for clients represented by Fields' employer. Her daughter also once accepted a car from an African businessman who sought help from Brown. Early in her House career, Brown was investigated over the sloppy finances of a travel agency she operated while serving in the Florida legislature.

Brown earned two degrees from Florida A&M University and worked as a community college teacher and guidance counselor. She was steered into politics by one of her sorority sisters at the university, Gwendolyn Sawyer Cherry, who went on to become Florida's first black state representative. Although Brown lost her first state House race in 1980, Cherry kept after her to try again, and Brown won in 1982. She served in the state House for a decade.

When a black-majority 3rd District was created by redistricting for the 1990s, Brown was one of four candidates in the 1992 Democratic primary for the seat. She made it through a runoff election and won 59 percent of the vote in November. Her ethics troubles and occasional GOP challengers sometimes keep her from overwhelming victory margins, but she has never been seriously in trouble.

Her district was renumbered as the 5th for the 2012 election, but it kept the same tortured shape to stretch from Orlando to Jacksonville. Brown defeated Republican LeAnne Kolb with more than 70 percent of the vote.

Key Votes

2012	
Extend a Social Security payroll tax cut and unemployment benefits	+
Ease securities rules to expand small-business access to capital	YES
Extend for one year subsidized student loan interest rates financed by a cut in health care spending	NO
Cite Attorney General Eric H. Holder Jr. for contempt of Congress	?
Create a visa program for foreign graduates in high-tech fields	NO
Extend most Bush-era income tax rates while allowing rates for top-bracket earners to rise (Jan. 1, 2013)	YES
2011	
Strike funding for F-35 alternative engine	YES
Prevent EPA from regulating greenhouse gas emissions to address climate change	NO
Extend certain provisions of Patriot Act for four years	YES
Declare opposition to use of ground troops in Libya	NO
Overhaul patent law	YES
Pass compromise debt limit increase plan and establish future spending limits	NO
Allow consideration of measures to implement three trade agreements	?

CQ Vote Studies

	PARTY UNITY		PRESIDENTIAL SUPPORT	
	SUPPORT	OPPOSE	SUPPORT	OPPOSE
2012	92%	8%	88%	12%
2011	95%	5%	90%	10%
2010	98%	2%	87%	13%
2009	99%	1%	99%	1%
2008	98%	2%	17%	83%

Interest Groups

	AFL-CIO	ADA	CCUS	ACU
2012	90%	80%	25%	8%
2011	100%	90%	19%	8%
2010	93%	100%	13%	0%
2009	100%	100%	40%	0%
2008	100%	95%	69%	0%

Florida 5

North central — parts of Jacksonville, Gainesville, Orlando

The Democratic 5th spirals through parts of north-central Florida's three main cities: Jacksonville, Gainesville and Orlando. About 40 percent of the district's population lives in Duval County (Jacksonville) in the north and another 40 percent lives near Orlando in Orange County to the south. The district tracks the lazy path of the St. Johns River south from Jacksonville before turning west to take in part of the liberal college town of Gainesville. It cuts southeast through forests and swamps until it reaches Orlando.

The 5th takes in downtown Jacksonville, where the economy relies on a busy port, distribution giant CSX Corp., naval military installations (in the 4th District) and the financial services industry. The 5th includes the national headquarters of Fidelity National Financial. Gainesville is dominated by the influence of the University of Florida (in the neighboring 3rd District). And while Orlando overall is reliant on its theme parks and tourist attractions — Walt Disney World and Universal Orlando are in the neighboring 10th District — it also has a growing technology and research sector, supported by the nearby University of Central Florida.

A population boom in central Florida contributed to the addition of two House seats for the state after the 2010 census, but the boundaries of the 5th are nearly identical to the former 3rd District.

A Democratic seat by design, the 5th combines generally liberal voters collected from eight counties and three major but disparate cities. The 5th is one of Florida's majority-minority districts, with blacks making up more than half the population and Hispanics accounting for an additional 12 percent. The 5th also is one of the state's youngest districts, with a median age of 34. In the 2012 presidential contest, the 4th gave Democrat Barack Obama 70 percent of its vote.

Major Industry

Transportation, defense, government, financial services, higher education

Cities

Jacksonville (pt.), Apopka, Gainesville (pt.), Orlando (pt.)

Notable

The Amway Center in Orlando is home to basketball's Magic, and Jacksonville's EverBank field is home to football's Jaguars.

Rep. Ron DeSantis (R)

Capitol Office
225-2706
desantis.house.gov
427 Cannon Bldg 20515-6601; fax 226-6299

Committees
Foreign Affairs
Judiciary
Oversight & Government Reform

Residence
Ponte Vedra Beach

Born
Sept. 14, 1978; Jacksonville, Fla

Religion
Roman Catholic

Family
Wife, Casey Black DeSantis

Education
Yale U., B.A. 2001 (history & political science); Harvard U., J.D. 2005

Military
Navy Reserve, 2010-present; Navy, 2004-10

Career
Lawyer; military prosecutor; high school teacher

Political Highlights
No previous office

ELECTION RESULTS

2012 GENERAL		
Ron DeSantis (R)	195,962	57.2%
Heather Beaven (D)	146,489	42.8%
2012 PRIMARY		
Ron DeSantis (R)	24,132	38.8%
Fred Costello (R)	14,189	22.8%
Beverly Slough (R)	8,229	13.2%
Craig S. Miller (R)	8,113	13.1%
Richard Clark (R)	6,090	9.8%
Alec Pueschel (R)	739	1.2%
William "Billy" Kogut (R)	628	1.0%

Elected 2012; 1st term

DeSantis has little political experience, but as a former military lawyer and author he is no stranger to presenting an argument. He explains conservative philosophy in reasoned tones, making him one of the more viable public faces of the Republican freshman class.

He grew up in Florida, went to Yale University to study history, then earned a law degree at Harvard. He put his training to work for the Navy as a JAG officer. DeSantis was deployed to Iraq in 2007 as an adviser to the Navy SEALs.

Although he says that the Pentagon bureaucracy could be more efficient, DeSantis isn't interested in substantial cuts to defense spending. "I'm somebody who is a Reaganite. I believe in peace through strength," he said on CNN. "I believe that defense spending equates to capability." DeSantis has seats on the Foreign Affairs and Judiciary committees.

DeSantis was the first freshman to join the Fix Congress Now Caucus, a bipartisan group looking to improve the legislature's functionality. But his overall preferences are very conservative. He opposes tax increases, wants to end most federal involvement with education and believes the Obama administration is ignoring the rule of law. His 2011 book on the subject has a title that pokes at the president's memoir: "Dreams From Our Founding Fathers."

He has already enjoyed a victory on fiscal restraint. The House in February 2013 passed a DeSantis bill to extend a pay freeze for federal civilian employees through the end of 2013.

The 6th District, as drawn for the 2012 election, was open — Republican John L. Mica had represented a fair amount of its territory, but he ran in the neighboring 7th District. DeSantis won a seven-way primary and faced Democrat Heather Beaven, who had challenged Mica in 2010. He won easily, with backing from many nationally prominent Republicans.

Republicans are no doubt hoping to see him suit up for CQ Roll Call's annual charity congressional baseball game — he was the captain of the Yale team.

Florida 6

East — Palm Coast, Daytona Beach, St. Augustine

A mix of Atlantic coast cities and farmland, the 6th District travels down Interstate 95 from south of Jacksonville to where Interstate 4 cuts southwest toward Orlando. It includes all of St. Johns and bucolic Flagler counties and most of Volusia and Putnam counties — areas that experienced large population growth between 2000 and 2010. More than half of the district's residents live in Volusia County, which includes Daytona Beach and inland county seat DeLand. The district no longer includes Deltona, Seminole County or the outskirts of Orlando following decennial redistricting.

Tourism is the mainstay here, from resorts and golf courses — including the Tournament Players Club Sawgrass — of Ponte Vedra Beach at the district's north, past the stock car championship speedway at Daytona and spring break destinations at Daytona Beach to the northern tip of the Canaveral National Seashore. Even Florida natives flock to historic St. Augustine, founded by Spanish explorers in the 1600s, but the district's hospitality industry has been susceptible to economic downtowns and swings in gas and air travel prices.

Central Florida's aerospace sector also plays a role in the district's economy. Northrop Grumman has a presence in St. Johns County, and Daytona Beach's Embry-Riddle Aeronautical University campus, which offers aviation and space-related degrees, is one of the 6th's largest employers. Farmland in the district is among the state's top producers of cabbage and potatoes.

The 6th overall has an overwhelmingly white and slightly older population. Although the 6th leans conservative, its elections can be competitive and the GOP holds a slim lead in voter registration. Liberal pockets exist in DeLand and Daytona Beach, but both Volusia and Flagler counties backed Republican Mitt Romney for president in 2012 after favoring Democrat Barack Obama in 2008. Overall, Romney took the district in 2012 with 58 percent of its vote.

Major Industry
Tourism, service, aerospace

Cities
Palm Coast, Daytona Beach, Port Orange, Ormond Beach

Notable
The Castillo de San Marcos in St. Augustine is a 17th century Spanish fort that has survived, in part, because it is made from coquina shells, making it resistant to weather, fire and artillery.

Rep. John L. Mica (R)

Capitol Office
225-4035
mica.house.gov
2187 Rayburn Bldg. 20515-0907; fax 226-0821

Committees
Oversight & Government Reform
(Government Operations - Chairman)
Transportation & Infrastructure

Residence
Winter Park

Born
Jan. 27, 1943; Binghamton, N.Y.

Religion
Episcopalian

Family
Wife, Pat Mica; two children

Education
Miami-Dade Community College, A.A. 1965; U. of Florida, B.A. 1967 (political science & education)

Career
Cellular telephone company executive; lobbyist; trade consultant; real estate investor; congressional aide

Political Highlights
Fla. House, 1976-80; Republican nominee for Fla. Senate, 1980

ELECTION RESULTS

2012 GENERAL		
John L. Mica (R)	185,518	58.7%
Jason H. Kendall (D)	130,479	41.3%
2012 PRIMARY		
John L. Mica (R)	32,119	61.2%
Sandy Adams (R)	20,404	38.8%
2010 GENERAL		
John L. Mica (R)	185,470	69.0%
Heather Beaven (D)	83,206	31.0%

Previous Winning Percentages
2008 (62%); 2006 (63%); 2004 (100%); 2002 (60%); 2000 (63%); 1998 (100%); 1996 (62%); 1994 (73%); 1992 (56%)

Elected 1992; 11th term

Mica likes a good fight, and he had plenty of them in a tumultuous run as chairman of the Transportation and Infrastructure Committee. Republican Party rules forced him out of that job, but he's still battling over transportation policy as a senior member of the panel — and he's eyeing the top spot on the Oversight and Government Reform Committee for 2015.

Conservative and feisty, Mica has an old-school appreciation for the back-and-forth legislative process. When he took the gavel of the transportation panel in the 112th Congress (2011-12), few chairmen faced a tougher task. He had reauthorizations of aviation and surface transportation programs on his plate, his committee was loaded with freshmen, Republican newcomers had been elected after promising to slash federal budgets and the GOP majority had banned earmarked spending — the funding for projects in lawmakers' districts that has helped win many votes for past transportation bills.

It ended up being a productive tenure with lots of headaches. An aviation reauthorization was enacted in early 2012, but not before the Federal Aviation Administration shut down for a few weeks in the summer of 2011.

Mica also shouldered blame for his party not passing a five-year surface transportation bill. The initial plan was a bill using fees from domestic energy production as a funding stream for infrastructure projects. That aspect of the plan pleased some conservatives, but not enough to assuage all concerns about the overall spending levels recommended in the bill. Democrats (and more than a few Republicans) were irked at a provision to divorce federal support for public transit systems from the Highway Trust Fund.

Ranking Democrat Nick J. Rahall II of West Virginia complained that Mica did not include Democratic input in the bill. GOP leaders, reportedly unhappy with Mica's progress, started routing negotiations through Pennsylvania Republican Bill Shuster. Mica did co-chair the conference committee that produced a two-year highway reauthorization, and that law contained a major GOP victory: a significant streamlining of project approval and environmental regulations for road and transit builders.

His persistence and fighting spirit weren't enough to keep him on the job. Republicans limit panel leaders to six years at the top, and Mica, who was the ranking member from 2007 through 2010, wasn't granted a waiver to that rule.

He ultimately endorsed Shuster as his successor and quickly indicated his interest in another gavel — Mica has served on the Oversight and Government Reform Committee longer than any other House Republican, and for now he's the chairman of its Government Operations Subcommittee. Full-committee Chairman Darrell Issa of California will reach his term limit at the end of 2014.

Mica has plenty to keep him busy until then. Passenger rail programs expire in 2013, and Mica wants to significantly rethink the role of the federal government in that sector. He opposes most of the Obama administration's plans for high-speed rail, such as a $68 billion line between Los Angeles and San Francisco. But, in 2011, he dropped his insistence on the privatization of Amtrak's Northeast Corridor. Instead, he suggested that the government should focus all its efforts to develop high-speed passenger rail in that densely populated region. Early in 2013, he began pitching a bill to open up Amtrak-operated intercity and high-speed rail lines to private competition.

Mica finds colorful ways to play up the inefficiencies he perceives in Amtrak operations; to create a contrast with Amtrak's high-cost, money-losing dining operation, he held a 2012 press conference at a Washington McDonald's and highlighted the restaurant's dollar menu.

He wasn't afraid to disagree with the George W. Bush administration, either, though he usually confined his disagreements to the transportation sphere. When Bush was in office, Mica frequently served as the committee's liaison to the administration, more often seeking to persuade Bush to see the committee's point of view rather than the other way around. One such disagreement, over the 2007 water resources bill, resulted in a rare congressional override of a presidential veto.

Mica chaired the Aviation Subcommittee before Democrats took control of Congress in 2007. After the Sept. 11 terrorist attacks, the panel became a hub of security measures that changed the way Americans travel. He helped write the law establishing the Transportation Security Administration, although he has criticized the agency for being unresponsive to local concerns and, eventually, to his requests for information.

He is also invested in his Oversight subcommittee, which looks at federal property. At a February 2013 hearing, he said he was stunned by the overall lack of property management plans. "I was in real estate," he said. "I think the last folks I'd ever give anything to manage would be the federal government."

Like a lot of Floridians, Mica grew up in New York. After years of trips back and forth, the family settled in Florida when Mica was in high school. His father's health was poor, and Mica and his brothers interrupted their schooling to help support the family.

Most members of Mica's family are Democrats, including brother Daniel A. Mica, who served in the House from 1979 to 1989. His other brother worked for Lawton Chiles, a former Democratic U.S. senator and Florida governor. But the first campaign Mica worked on was Richard Nixon's 1960 presidential race against John F. Kennedy.

Mica served two terms in the state House but lost a 1980 bid for the state Senate. He came to Washington as chief of staff for GOP Sen. Paula Hawkins and stayed with her office until 1985. Mica then turned to business ventures, including international trade consulting and the cellular telephone business, becoming a millionaire.

In 1992, GOP Rep. Craig T. James decided not to seek a third term, and Mica went after his seat. He won by 13 points and has been re-elected easily ever since. Redistricting for the 2012 election led to his most notable race. Mica opted to take on tea-party-backed freshman Rep. Sandy Adams in a GOP primary in the redrawn 7th District. He was confident of victory: "I work like an S.O.B.," he said.

Mica defeated Adams by more than 22 points, then took almost 59 percent of the vote to beat self-described "JFK Democrat" Jason H. Kendall.

Mica has no particular recreational interests. "I'm a pretty dull guy," he said. "I don't have a lot of hobby activities. But I love politics."

Key Votes

2012	
Extend a Social Security payroll tax cut and unemployment benefits	NO
Ease securities rules to expand small-business access to capital	YES
Extend for one year subsidized student loan interest rates financed by a cut in health care spending	YES
Cite Attorney General Eric H. Holder Jr. for contempt of Congress	YES
Create a visa program for foreign graduates in high-tech fields	YES
Extend most Bush-era income tax rates while allowing rates for top-bracket earners to rise (Jan. 1, 2013)	NO
2011	
Strike funding for F-35 alternative engine	YES
Prevent EPA from regulating greenhouse gas emissions to address climate change	YES
Extend certain provisions of Patriot Act for four years	YES
Declare opposition to use of ground troops in Libya	YES
Overhaul patent law	YES
Pass compromise debt limit increase plan and establish future spending limits	YES
Allow consideration of measures to implement three trade agreements	YES

CQ Vote Studies

	PARTY UNITY		PRESIDENTIAL SUPPORT	
	SUPPORT	OPPOSE	SUPPORT	OPPOSE
2012	96%	4%	15%	85%
2011	96%	4%	25%	75%
2010	97%	3%	29%	71%
2009	90%	10%	19%	81%
2008	93%	7%	77%	23%

Interest Groups

	AFL-CIO	ADA	CCUS	ACU
2012	19%	0%	100%	92%
2011	0%	5%	100%	83%
2010	7%	0%	88%	96%
2009	10%	0%	80%	100%
2008	0%	10%	94%	100%

Florida 7

Central — most of Seminole County

Centered on the well-to-do suburbs northeast of Orlando, the 7th includes most of Seminole County and parts of Orange and Volusia counties. These residential areas — including Winter Springs, Altamonte Springs and Deltona — have drawn retirees and white-collar commuters for years, contributing to a decades-long population boom amid one of the country's fastest-growing regions.

While Orlando's big-name theme parks and tourist attractions are located in adjacent districts, many hospitality workers live in the 7th. Residents are employed in growing research and technology sectors and at regional health care facilities. The American Automobile Association has its headquarters in Heathrow. The southern edge of the 7th includes the main campus of the University of Central Florida and its more than 56,000 students.

Deltona, the district's largest city, was founded as a retirement community and remains primarily residential. While the state's housing boom helped drive population growth, the recent nationwide financial crisis has depressed economies. Deltona, Altamonte Springs and the district's other suburbs have been hit especially hard, with high rates of foreclosures and widespread unemployment. Local officials have focused on commercial development to broaden tax bases, although growth-management issues remain a priority.

Made up of areas formerly split between four districts, the 7th is more than two-thirds white with a significant Hispanic population. Although it is generally conservative-leaning, the district can be politically competitive because of its changing demographics. The district's edges are more liberal; areas in between — such as Sanford, Altamonte Springs and Oviedo — trend Republican. The GOP leads in voter registration in the district's portions of Seminole and Volusia counties.

Major Industry
Service, retail, higher education, technology

Cities
Deltona, Altamonte Springs, Oviedo, Winter Springs, Winter Park, Orlando (pt.), Sanford (pt.)

Notable
Lake Jessup, one of the largest lakes in Central Florida, has one of the highest concentrations of alligators in North America.

Rep. Bill Posey (R)

Capitol Office
225-3671
posey.house.gov
120 Cannon Bldg. 20515-0915; fax 225-3516

Committees
Financial Services
Science, Space & Technology

Residence
Rockledge

Born
Dec. 18, 1947; Washington, D.C.

Religion
Methodist

Family
Wife, Katie Posey; two children

Education
Brevard Junior College, A.A. 1969

Career
Realtor; insurance claims adjuster; space program engineering inspector

Political Highlights
Rockledge City Council, 1976-86; Fla. House, 1992-2000; Fla. Senate, 2000-08

ELECTION RESULTS

2012 GENERAL		
Bill Posey (R)	205,432	58.9%
Shannon Roberts (D)	130,870	37.5%
Richard H. Gillmor (NPA)	12,607	3.6%
2012 PRIMARY		
Bill Posey (R)		unopposed
2010 GENERAL		
Bill Posey (R)	157,079	64.7%
Shannon Roberts (D)	85,595	35.3%

Previous Winning Percentages
2008 (53%)

Elected 2008; 3rd term

Florida Republicans think of Posey as "the nice guy." His easygoing demeanor belies his political mission: dropping the hammer on those involved with fraud, inefficiency and bloated government.

He earned the nickname "Mr. Accountability" during his 16 years in the state legislature. Posey rooted out cases of insurance fraud, led an overhaul of the state's workers compensation laws and wrote a free book. "Activity Based Total Accountability" outlines a method of full-cost accounting for government programs to better assess what's working. Posey now has a national spin on his ABTA plan, with a bill requiring states to submit certain accounting reports before receiving any federal financial assistance.

Posey, a member of the Republican Study Committee, is a fiscal conservative — he voted against a slew of appropriations and deficit reduction bills in the 112th Congress (2011-12) that didn't control the federal debt as much as he wanted. Accountability colors his thoughts on government spending. While in the state Senate, he had a rule of thumb for keeping government agencies focused: "If you're not going to do it, we're going to get you out of the budget and we'll find somebody who can do the job."

The federal government is tougher to wrangle than a state government, but Posey has had some successes promoting transparency in the House. Republicans in the 112th adopted a 72-hour waiting period before legislation can be brought to the House floor — a rule Posey had first suggested as a freshman.

He sits on the Financial Services Committee, a venue he sees as essential for helping prevent another market collapse like the one that occurred in 2008. Posey had limited chances as a freshman to shape the 2010 financial regulatory overhaul law known as Dodd-Frank. He opposed the measure as offering "zero accountability for government regulators who were asleep at the switch."

"I don't think we stop another crisis from happening by having more agencies that aren't going to do their jobs and aren't going to be accountable," he said. "We're going to stop these crises from happening again ... by holding people accountable and putting some people in jail. That's when people behave." The major actors responsible for the 2008 crash have not been prosecuted, Posey said.

He dislikes the Consumer Financial Protection Bureau created under the Dodd-Frank law, as Congress has no control over its budget.

Posey joined in the Republican campaign against federal regulation in 2012, attaching three amendments to a measure that would prevent most regulations from taking effect until the unemployment rate drops below 6 percent. One Posey amendment would require legal fees from regulation-related lawsuits to be paid out of the budget of the federal office that advanced the rule in question. The bill passed the House but wasn't taken up in the Senate.

Some of Posey's Florida-related interests have a personal tie. His district is on the Space Coast, and his father worked in the aerospace industry for Douglas Aircraft. Posey also went to work for Douglas after high school. "When John Kennedy said we're going to put a man on the moon, and bring him safely back within a decade, at that moment — I was probably a sophomore in high school — I just said, 'Yep, and my fingerprints are going to be on that rocket, too,' " Posey said.

Posey worked as a quality control inspector at the Kennedy Space Center before getting laid off after the Apollo 11 mission. That facility is now in his district. Posey was added to the Science, Space and Technology Committee for the 113th Congress (2013-14).

The fiscal 2013 defense policy law includes Posey's provision allowing greater collaboration between the Defense Department and the private sector on the use and maintenance of space transportation infrastructure. Posey said it would give commercial space companies "an incentive to spend their money here and do business here in Florida and around the U.S., instead of places like Russia and China."

Posey wants human spaceflight to be the focus of NASA, and he says the agency should have the specific goal of returning to the moon. He was one of six Republican co-authors of a 2012 bill to give the director of NASA a 10-year term and create a board of directors for the agency; they argue it needs that kind of structure to facilitate the long-term planning space missions require.

Posey's quest for accountability has led to one instance of media criticism. In March 2009 he proposed a bill to require future presidential candidates to provide copies of their birth certificates. This move made him the target of liberals and drew accusations of catering to a fringe movement.

But Posey said he had received calls daily from constituents concerned about President Barack Obama's place of birth. He said he simply aimed to put the issue to rest and avoid similar problems for future candidates. "If he had filed that the very first day he filed for office, we wouldn't be having any problems right now," Posey told the St. Petersburg Times in 2009.

Born in Washington, D.C., Posey moved with his family to California when he was 2. In 1956, they moved to Orlando before settling in Brevard County. He still recalls the influence of two of his grade-school teachers, Vi Williams and Lucille Quillen, and sends them each Valentine's Day cards every year.

Growing up, Posey was active in Boy Scouts. He bonded with his father through an interest in stock car racing: They worked on cars, attended races and even raced. Later in life, Posey bought a racetrack with a friend and won an award for short-track driver achievement.

He married his high school sweetheart, Katie, and after his stint in the racetrack business he worked in insurance and real estate. His interest in politics came later. "I went to a city council meeting and ... didn't like what I saw," Posey said.

He won a seat on the Rockledge City Council in 1976. In 1992 he ran successfully for the Florida House, and eight years later, for the state Senate.

When Republican Dave Weldon decided to retire in 2008, Posey received the backing of business interests and had little trouble in the GOP primary. He took 53 percent of the vote in the general election against Democratic physician Stephen Blythe. He gave six tickets to the 2009 presidential inauguration to Blythe, who called the move "magnanimous."

He was easily re-elected in 2010, and again in 2012 from the 8th District. He no longer represents Osceola County but has more territory east of Orlando.

Key Votes

2012	
Extend a Social Security payroll tax cut and unemployment benefits	NO
Ease securities rules to expand small-business access to capital	YES
Extend for one year subsidized student loan interest rates financed by a cut in health care spending	YES
Cite Attorney General Eric H. Holder Jr. for contempt of Congress	YES
Create a visa program for foreign graduates in high-tech fields	YES
Extend most Bush-era income tax rates while allowing rates for top-bracket earners to rise (Jan. 1, 2013)	NO
2011	
Strike funding for F-35 alternative engine	YES
Prevent EPA from regulating greenhouse gas emissions to address climate change	YES
Extend certain provisions of Patriot Act for four years	NO
Declare opposition to use of ground troops in Libya	YES
Overhaul patent law	NO
Pass compromise debt limit increase plan and establish future spending limits	NO
Allow consideration of measures to implement three trade agreements	YES

CQ Vote Studies

	PARTY UNITY		PRESIDENTIAL SUPPORT	
	SUPPORT	OPPOSE	SUPPORT	OPPOSE
2012	96%	4%	18%	82%
2011	94%	6%	16%	84%
2010	89%	11%	43%	57%
2009	89%	11%	22%	78%

Interest Groups

	AFL-CIO	ADA	CCUS	ACU
2012	10%	15%	75%	100%
2011	3%	5%	88%	92%
2010	14%	10%	88%	83%
2009	14%	0%	93%	100%

Florida 8

East central — Space Coast

Made up of midsize cities largely populated by out-of-state transplants, the 8th takes in all of Indian River County and Brevard County — known as the Space Coast because NASA's space shuttle program operated out of the Kennedy Space Center at Cape Canaveral — as well as a sparsely populated chunk of Orange County. The majority-white district has a mix of research centers, retirement communities, beach towns and citrus farms.

The Kennedy Space Center long provided the economic thrust in Brevard County, where nearly 80 percent of district residents live. For decades, it supported electronics and aerospace manufacturing and lured tourism. But NASA's budget cuts and the decision to end manned spaceflight and retire the shuttle fleet have resulted in unemployment spikes among shuttle workers and contractors, straining everything from local retail sales to home construction. Commercial spaceflight is the new watchword, as firms look to privatize some of NASA's functions. Military jobs and plans for testing programs at Cape Canaveral's decommissioned launch pads will help.

Like other areas in the state, the 8th's economy has been hurt by declining property values. The region remains a popular retirement destination due in part to its warm climate and sunny beaches; places like Viera's Space Coast Stadium, the home of minor league baseball's Manatees and the spring training site for the Washington Nationals, also offer local entertainment. Indian River County has a more service-oriented and agricultural economy and is one of the state's top citrus-growing counties.

Registered Republicans outnumber Democrats in the 8th. Brevard and Indian River counties both backed Republicans John McCain in the 2008 presidential election, Rick Scott in his successful 2010 gubernatorial race, and Mitt Romney in the 2012 presidential contest.

Major Industry
Aerospace, technology, tourism, agriculture

Military Bases
Patrick Air Force Base, 2,188 military, 2,181 civilian

Cities
Palm Bay, Melbourne, Titusville, Merritt Island (unincorporated), Vero Beach, Rockledge

Notable
A Space Coast-region area code is 321, chosen to mimic the liftoff countdown.

Rep. Alan Grayson (D)

Capitol Office
225-9889
grayson.house.gov
430 Cannon Bldg. 20515-6601; fax 225-9742

Committees
Foreign Affairs
Science, Space & Technology

Residence
Orlando

Born
March 13, 1958; Bronx, N.Y.

Religion
Jewish

Family
Wife, Lolita Grayson; five children

Education
Harvard U., A.B. 1978 (urban studies), M.P.P 1983, J.D. 1983

Career
Lawyer; telecommunications company owner

Political Highlights
Sought Democratic nomination for U.S. House, 2006; U.S. House, 2009-11; defeated for re-election to U.S. House, 2010

ELECTION RESULTS

2012 GENERAL		
Alan Grayson (D)	164,891	62.5%
Todd Long (R)	98,856	37.5%
2012 PRIMARY		
Alan Grayson (D)		unopposed

Previous Winning Percentages
2008 (52%)

Elected 2008; 2nd term

Did not serve 2011-13

Grayson has a lightning-rod style of politics that incorporates strident liberalism and freewheeling insults of Republicans. His polarizing behavior got him noticed as a freshman, but it also contributed to his defeat in 2010. Time away from Congress didn't change him.

"They got rid of me for two years, but now I'm back," he said in February 2013. Grayson said the House historian informed him that his 25-point victory in 2012 marked the biggest comeback in the history of the House — he lost by 18 points to Daniel Webster in 2010.

Of course, his 2012 victory was in a different district — one drawn to safely elect a Democrat. But Grayson, who is known for wearing pinstripe suits, loud ties and cowboy boots, has a habit of calling attention to himself. During debate over the health care overhaul in 2009, he took to the House floor to share his take on the GOP position: "If you get sick, America, the Republican health care plan is this: Die quickly."

Grayson sees himself as a modern-day Huey Long, the Depression-era Louisiana governor and senator who proposed aggressive wealth redistribution policies, challenged President Franklin D. Roosevelt from the left, and was assassinated in 1935. "He illustrated to people in concrete ways that they could organize themselves in a way that was better for the lives of ordinary people," he said. "I find that to be pretty close to what I'm trying to do."

Grayson pins his 2010 loss on political dynamics: He was in a competitive district, and the tea party swamped the Democratic Party that year. He defends his work as a freshman, pointing to his constituent service and passage of what he calls "the only genuinely bipartisan legislation" in the 111th Congress (2009-10) — a bill to require an audit of the Federal Reserve. In that effort, he worked with another unique lawmaker, Texas Rep. Ron Paul. Grayson's participation came fairly late but proved crucial. Their measure was incorporated into the 2010 financial regulatory overhaul law.

Surveying his record, Grayson sees no reason to change methods in the 113th Congress (2013-14). "There's every reason to think that, if people want to see results, that we should continue," he said. His plans include a campaign to force politically treacherous votes for the GOP in committee markups, which he unveiled at the retreat of the liberal Congressional Progressive Caucus in January 2013.

Grayson has returned to the Science, Space and Technology Committee. His district isn't that far removed from the Space Coast, and there is a growing technology sector in Orlando.

He also sits on the Foreign Affairs Committee, where he belongs to the subcommittees handling the Western Hemisphere and the Middle East — areas that are important to his many Hispanic and Jewish constituents. He has an interesting take on Republicans' preferences for foreign policy and the war on terrorism: "They love the taste of blood."

"They're consistently pro-war, consistently pro-killing-foreigners," he said. "They view the entire world as either a massive inconvenience or something they feel is a personal threat."

Grayson's political success stems in part from his effective use of social media, particularly YouTube. He sat on the Financial Services Committee as a freshman, and videos of him facing off with tone-deaf government officials went viral repeatedly.

In one, he laughs at Federal Reserve Chairman Ben S. Bernanke's answers about whether the Fed had the authority to lend money to foreign banks. In another — which has been viewed more than 4 million times — he flummoxes the Federal Reserve's inspector general with seemingly simple questions about who was receiving trillions of dollars in Fed loans.

That success online has translated into gobs of campaign cash, much of it from small donors. "There are only five members who raise more money from small contributions than from large contributions. And we have the highest ratio of anybody on either side of the aisle," Grayson said.

Born in the Bronx in New York City, Grayson worked his way through Harvard University as a janitor and night watchman. He returned to Harvard for his law degree and a master's in public policy from the John F. Kennedy School of Government.

He was a lawyer in Washington in the 1980s, and in the early 1990s he started IDT Corp., a telecom company. Grayson's short stint in business earned him millions of dollars, and he is currently one of the richest members of Congress.

Grayson returned to practicing law. In the early 2000s, he began filing lawsuits alleging waste by contractors in Iraq, utilizing a little-known law that allows whistle-blowers to recoup a portion of the waste they uncover in court. A Wall Street Journal profile described Grayson as "waging a one-man war against contractor fraud in Iraq."

The Iraq War became a political liability for President George W. Bush, and Grayson tried to leverage opposition to the war in 2006 with his first run for political office. Many Democrats were propelled into Congress that year, but Grayson wasn't one of them. He lost a House primary in the 8th District.

Two years later, he rode Barack Obama's coattails to victory over four-term Republican Rep. Ric Keller. Grayson spent almost a year in relative obscurity, but his comments on health care made him a media star. In subsequent television interviews he called Republicans "knuckle-dragging Neanderthals."

According to Grayson, he's just saying what other Democrats think but don't say out loud. "Honestly, I get all sorts of 'atta boys' from people, because I have the chance to appear on TV frequently, and they don't, and I say the things that everyone else is thinking here but nobody else has the chance to say."

His rhetoric came back to bite him in his re-election fight with Webster. Grayson ran an ad that described Webster, a Baptist, as a religious extremist and labeled him "Taliban Dan." The spot included video of a Webster speech that was heavily edited and took Webster's remarks wildly out of context. Disgust over that incident was one factor in Webster's eventual victory.

Redistricting for 2012 created a 9th District with a clear Democratic lean, and there were no Republican incumbents interested in running there. Grayson was unopposed in the primary and easily defeated Republican Todd Long in the general election. Webster was elected in the neighboring 10th District.

CQ Vote Studies

	PARTY UNITY		PRESIDENTIAL SUPPORT	
	SUPPORT	OPPOSE	SUPPORT	OPPOSE
2010	97%	3%	83%	17%
2009	98%	2%	93%	7%

Interest Groups

	AFL-CIO	ADA	CCUS	ACU
2010	100%	100%	13%	4%
2009	100%	100%	33%	0%

Florida 9

Central — Osceola County and part of Orlando

The 9th District takes in central Orange County, all of rapidly growing Osceola County, and a northeastern corner of Polk County. More than half of the district's population lives in the Orange County Orlando suburbs, while to the south, Osceola County is still primarily rural except for Kissimmee and St. Cloud, just south of Orlando.

With fast-growing Hispanic communities in both Orange and Osceola counties, the 9th is the only district outside of South Florida where Hispanics are a plurality of the population, at more than 41 percent. It also has the state's highest percentage of residents who identify ethnically as Puerto Rican, at 25 percent.

Tourism is the district's largest economic sector. Although most of the resort is located in the neighboring 10th District, a corner of the Walt Disney World complex — including Celebration, a planned residential community with direct access to the Magic Kingdom — overlaps into the 9th. Osceola County does include the main entrance to Disney World and the area's largest employers are hotels, resorts and Disney World itself.

The 9th's section of urban Orlando includes Orlando International Airport and the city's growing technology and health care hub, centered on the Medical City at Lake Nona. The developing site includes the University of Central Florida's medical school, which has plans for a teaching hospital, as well as new veterans and children's hospitals and several biomedical research institutes.

South of Orlando, rural farmland and small communities dominate. Osceola County is one of the nation's top sod-harvesting regions and among the state's top producers of cattle, grapefruit and oranges.

The redistricted 9th collects areas formerly split among four districts and is one of the most racially diverse in central Florida. Its younger residents, white-collar professionals and Hispanic voters lean Democratic.

Major Industry

Tourism, health care, service, agriculture

Cities

Orlando (pt.), Kissimmee, St. Cloud, Buenaventura Lakes (unincorporated), Haines City

Notable

The Osceola County Courthouse in Kissimmee, built in 1890, is the oldest courthouse in continuous use in the state of Florida.

Rep. Daniel Webster (R)

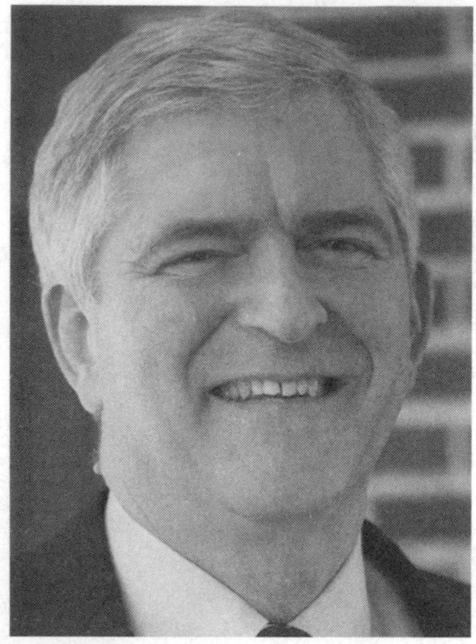

Capitol Office
225-2176
webster.house.gov
1039 Longworth Bldg. 20515-0908; fax 225-0999

Committees
Rules
Transportation & Infrastructure

Residence
Orlando

Born
April 27, 1949; Charleston, W.Va.

Religion
Baptist

Family
Wife, Sandy Webster; six children

Education
Georgia Institute of Technology, B.E.E. 1971

Career
Air conditioning and heating company owner

Political Highlights
Fla. House, 1980-98 (minority leader pro tempore, 1992-94; minority leader, 1994-96; speaker, 1996-98); Fla. Senate, 1998-2008 (majority leader, 2006-08)

ELECTION RESULTS

2012 GENERAL		
Daniel Webster (R)	164,649	51.7%
Val B. Demings (D)	153,574	48.2%
2012 PRIMARY		
Daniel Webster (R)		unopposed
2010 GENERAL		
Daniel Webster (R)	123,586	56.1%
Alan Grayson (D)	84,167	38.2%
Peg Dunmire (TEA)	8,337	3.8%
George L. Metcalfe (NPA)	4,143	1.9%

Elected 2010; 2nd term

Webster has a deal-making mind-set that he developed as a leader in state government. His expertise in the legislative process and his seat on the Rules Committee afford him access to any issue before the House, but he pays extra attention to one of his favorite policy areas: transportation.

He served in the Florida House for 18 years and ended that run as the state's first Republican speaker in more than a century. Webster then moved to the state Senate for a decade and closed out his time there as majority leader.

A devout Baptist, he isn't flashy or particularly divisive. When Webster came to Washington for the 112th Congress (2011-12), he set up short social meetings with all of his neighbors on his floor of the Longworth House Office Building. Ten-minute scheduled chats often turned into 45-minute conversations. "Now they are my friends, and I think that bridges a few gaps," he said in 2011.

Still, Webster is a loyal Republican, and he serves on the most partisan panel in Congress. The Rules Committee sets the terms for House floor debate, so the majority party dictates terms to the minority. Republicans promised more-open floor debate upon regaining the majority in 2011.

Webster likes that notion, as well as relying more on the committee process to develop bills. "I think every member should be a player," he said. "I think the pyramid of power should be pushed down as far as it can so that every member gets a chance."

Ultimately, he fixed blame for legislative gridlock in the 112th on the Democratic Senate. He said in 2011 that stalemates over major legislation "made no sense" to him after years in state government: "We would pass a position, they would pass a position, you get together, you trade tit for tat. That's the way it works." He voted against a tax package on the first day of 2013, describing it as a "last-minute back-room deal that was passed in the dead of night."

But there were also some legislative headaches that started in the House, when rank-and-file members asserted themselves and declined to go along with the plans of Republican leaders.

One notable example was on the Transportation and Infrastructure Committee — Republicans had a hard time coalescing behind a long-term reauthorization of surface transportation programs as conservatives complained about the spending levels in the bill. Congress eventually cleared a two-year reauthorization that expires in 2014. So Webster, as a new member of the transportation committee in the 113th Congress (2013-14), gets to work on the next iteration.

It's a plum assignment for his Orlando-based district, which is a crossroads for tourist traffic and cargo from South Florida ports. His service on the panel also harks back to some of his state government work. State Road 429 in Florida was designated the Daniel Webster Western Beltway in 2005.

Webster has ideas for new approaches to financing infrastructure. He likes the notion of a combination revolving transportation trust fund and infrastructure bank. It would give states a relatively small percentage of a project's cost, with the understanding that toll revenue eventually would repay the loan; the repaid loan would then go to other projects. "It's worked in Florida on a small scale," he said. "It's something that I got a feeling is going to be included in whatever the House does" on transportation programs.

He sees potential savings in the elimination of duplicative transportation programs. Programs providing services for transportation-disadvantaged persons are spread across multiple agencies, and Webster said the system defies auditing. "It's a mess, and nobody is really going to take it on, so I am," he said in 2011.

Webster has tried to develop digestible legislation. He joined a small, bipartisan working group in the 112th with Democrat John Carney of Delaware, Republican James B. Renacci of Ohio, Republican Patrick Meehan of Pennsylvania and Democrat Mike Quigley of Illinois. They introduced a 2011 measure to establish a pre-tax savings account for first-time homebuyers saving for a down payment.

The House in 2012 passed his measure to eliminate a demographic survey from the Census Bureau — Webster said it invades personal privacy and isn't worth funding. The business community immediately objected, saying that the survey data are useful for sales forecasting and lending.

Webster's conservative social values are rooted in his Baptist faith. He and his wife, Sandy, home-schooled their six children. While he was in the state Senate in 2005, Webster tried to move legislation that would have kept alive Terri Schiavo, a brain-damaged Florida woman who was sustained by a feeding tube. Webster opposes abortion in all circumstances and strongly supports gun rights.

An engineer by training, Webster took over his family's air-conditioning and heating business. He says he first entered politics because of a church-zoning issue he encountered while trying to convert a house into a Sunday school. No politician took up his cause, so he stepped up himself. He was elected to the state House in 1980 and served in Tallahassee through 2008.

Webster was briefly a U.S. Senate candidate in 2004. He reluctantly filed for the race — the Orlando Sentinel said he stood "awkwardly" in the shade of a tree with his $9,282 filing fee before jumping into the race. He dropped out before appearing on the GOP primary ballot.

Six years later, he was in the seven-person GOP field seeking to challenge the liberal and abrasive Democratic Rep. Alan Grayson. After Webster won the primary, Grayson ran an ad that compared Webster's religious faith with that of the Afghan Taliban. It used edited video to try to show that Webster was saying the opposite of what he was actually saying. The ad, ripped by FactCheck.org and others, backfired. Webster cruised past the incumbent with 56 percent of the vote.

For the 2012 cycle, Webster ran in the newly drawn 10th District, which collected areas formerly split among six different districts. His Democratic opponent was Orlando Police Chief Val B. Demings.

It was an intense contest. Demings raised more money than Webster, and a super PAC tied to gun-control advocate (and New York mayor) Michael Bloomberg spent more than $2 million to sway voters toward Demings. Webster won by less than 4 points.

At the same time, Grayson was elected in the neighboring 9th District.

Key Votes

2012	
Extend a Social Security payroll tax cut and unemployment benefits	YES
Ease securities rules to expand small-business access to capital	YES
Extend for one year subsidized student loan interest rates financed by a cut in health care spending	YES
Cite Attorney General Eric H. Holder Jr. for contempt of Congress	YES
Create a visa program for foreign graduates in high-tech fields	YES
Extend most Bush-era income tax rates while allowing rates for top-bracket earners to rise (Jan. 1, 2013)	NO
2011	
Strike funding for F-35 alternative engine	YES
Prevent EPA from regulating greenhouse gas emissions to address climate change	YES
Extend certain provisions of Patriot Act for four years	YES
Declare opposition to use of ground troops in Libya	YES
Overhaul patent law	NO
Pass compromise debt limit increase plan and establish future spending limits	YES
Allow consideration of measures to implement three trade agreements	YES

CQ Vote Studies

	Party Unity		Presidential Support	
	SUPPORT	OPPOSE	SUPPORT	OPPOSE
2012	94%	6%	15%	85%
2011	96%	4%	20%	80%

Interest Groups

	AFL-CIO	ADA	CCUS	ACU
2012	14%	5%	92%	88%
2011	10%	15%	94%	83%

Florida 10

Central — part of Orlando, Lake and Polk counties

Nestled in the rapidly growing center of the state, the 10th is dotted with natural lakes, citrus groves and sprawling developments. A hook-shaped tendril on the district's eastern side passes through Orange County's famous theme parks and takes in a heavily populated portion of urban Orlando. The bulk of the district's land area is made up of farmland and suburbs of Lake County, such as Mount Dora and Leesburg, and also includes a chunk of northern Polk County.

Tourism is the economic powerhouse here. The 10th contains the Orlando area's major attractions, including Disney World. With 58,000 employees at its amusement parks, hotels and resorts, Disney is by far the largest single employer here. The region's other prime destinations — Universal Studios and Sea World — are also in the district.

Orlando is also a growing medical and technology hub. The 10th's Orange County slice includes the city's largest hospital, and its portion of downtown has the central business district, which hosts corporate offices and banking services as well as retail, cultural and entertainment venues.

Outside the urban center, Lake County has quieter lakeside communities, farmland and retirement centers. To the south in Polk County, is Winter Haven, a small city with an agricultural past and steady population growth. Situated in the middle of central Florida's all-important citrus industry, the city is building a CSX intermodal transportation center that is expected to create hundreds of jobs.

Redistricting following the 2010 census redrew the boundaries of the 10th to combine areas previously split among six districts. Voters in its portions of Orange County can favor Democrats, but the district overall leans conservative, especially in the suburbs. Republican Mitt Romney took 54 percent here in the 2012 presidential election.

Major Industry
Tourism, service, technology, agriculture

Cities
Orlando (pt.), Ocoee, Winter Garden, Winter Haven

Notable
The Minneola tangelo, a hybrid of grapefruit and tangerine, is named after the city of Minneola in Lake County.

Rep. Rich Nugent (R)

Capitol Office
225-1002
nugent.house.gov
1727 Longworth Bldg. 20515-0905; fax 226-6559

Committees
Armed Services
House Administration
Rules
(Rules & the Organization of the House - Chairman)

Residence
Spring Hill

Born
May 26, 1951; Evergreen Park, Ill.

Religion
United Methodist

Family
Wife, Wendy Nugent; three children

Education
Saint Leo College, B.A. 1991 (criminology); Troy State U., MacDill Air Force Base, M.P.A 1995

Military
Ill. Air National Guard, 1969-75

Career
Deputy county sheriff

Political Highlights
Hernando County sheriff, 2001-10

ELECTION RESULTS

2012 GENERAL		
Rich Nugent (R)	218,360	64.5%
H. David Werder (D)	120,303	35.5%
2012 PRIMARY		
Rich Nugent (R)	unopposed	
2010 GENERAL		
Rich Nugent (R)	208,815	67.4%
James "Jim" Piccillo (D)	100,858	32.6%

Elected 2010; 2nd term

Nugent spent most of his life enforcing laws. Now he conscientiously studies the art of creating them. The former sheriff volunteered for service on the Rules Committee as a freshman, and his training in that legislative boot camp should come in handy in his second term as he sits on the Armed Services Committee.

He has the no-nonsense manner (and moustache, some people would say) of a cop. Nugent was the elected sheriff of Hernando County before riding the tea party wave into Congress in 2010. He values his executive experience from running a police department, but he openly professed a desire to round out his skill set. "I know how to run an organization, but I don't necessarily know how to legislate," he said in 2011.

The Rules Committee, which sets the terms of House floor debate, gave him a crash course. Nugent enjoys when bills come to the floor under open rules, with more chances for members to offer amendments. "I believe that's how our Founding Fathers designed this process," he said. "It was supposed to be messy." He's back on the panel for the 113th Congress (2013-14).

Nugent is also now a member of Armed Services. He served in the Illinois Air National Guard from 1969 to 1975, and all three of his sons are in the Army. Quite a few veterans live in his district, and Nugent has resisted any changes to benefit programs that transfer more service costs to military families.

He was one of 16 Republicans opposing the House version of a fiscal 2013 defense policy bill, and Nugent specifically pinned his vote on a provision increasing the co-payments for prescriptions obtained through Tricare, the military health insurance system. "Anything that affects the troops' readiness and safety or that takes money out of the pockets of military families should be the absolute last thing that we consider going after," he wrote on his congressional website. (His posts there are labeled "SITREPs" — military jargon for situation reports.) Nugent was one of the 31 House Republicans who voted against the enacted version of the bill.

Nugent has said that he supports President Barack Obama's plans for troop withdrawals from Afghanistan and trusts that the decision to leave was based on military realities, not political motives. "What I don't want to see is that we pull out of there prematurely and then we're back there 10 years from now because the Taliban have re-established themselves," he told the St. Petersburg Times in 2011.

He was not thrilled when Obama committed forces to Libya in 2011 without seeking congressional approval. "In my view, both the press and Congress let him get away with it," he wrote in 2012. Nugent supported an unsuccessful 2011 resolution to demand a withdrawal of U.S. forces but opposed a bill to cut off funding to most U.S. military operations in Libya.

Joining most Republicans, Nugent says national defense is the most justifiable budget expense and that recent cuts have left the armed forces dangerously depleted.

Beyond that, he's open to a lot of cost cutting. "This country has a spending addiction," he said on the House floor in 2011. "My 36-plus years in law enforcement told me that when someone has an addiction, you have to first address and admit that you have a problem." Nugent voted for an August 2011 deficit reduction package, but at the beginning of 2013 he was in the majority of House Republicans that opposed a "fiscal cliff" deal centered on tax rates. Conservatives wanted spending cuts included in that package. Nugent is a co-sponsor of a bill to eliminate the IRS and replace most federal taxes with a national sales tax.

Nugent sits on the House Administration Committee, which oversees the Capitol complex and workplace issues for the House. In the 112th Congress (2011-12), he introduced a bill to allow members of Congress to decline certain federal retirement benefits and contributions.

"I was shocked to learn that I was not permitted to decline the congressional pension," he said. "I was able to decline federally funded health insurance, but not the pension. Apparently, under current law, I am required to take it whether I like it or not. In my opinion, my career was in law enforcement—not in Washington."

His earlier career inspired him to get involved with legislation regarding mental health and the criminal justice system. Nugent and Minnesota Democratic Sen. Al Franken are the lead sponsors of bills to extend federal support for mental health courts and programs helping inmates with mental health problems.

Nugent is socially conservative. He's anti-abortion, opposes gay marriage and says he is a "staunch" defender of gun rights.

He was born in Illinois. Nugent's father was a steelworker and his mother a homemaker. He worked as a police officer in Romeoville, Ill., before moving to Hernando County in Florida. Nugent earned a degree in criminology in 1991 from Saint Leo University and a master's in public administration in 1995 from Troy State.

He was first elected sheriff of Hernando County in 2000. Nugent still held that post when four-term GOP Rep. Ginny Brown-Waite announced in April 2010 that she would retire, citing health reasons. Brown-Waite endorsed Nugent in the same announcement, and the timing was paramount—it was the last day of qualifying to get on the ballot, limiting other Republicans from jumping into the race. In the largely Republican 5th District, Nugent took 62 percent of the vote in the primary and surpassed two-thirds of the vote in November against Democrat James Piccillo.

In the 2012 cycle, Nugent ran in the new 11th District, a largely conservative area with the oldest electorate in Florida. Unopposed in the primary, he beat Democrat H. David Werder with almost 65 percent of the vote.

Nugent's wife, Wendy, is a teacher. She decided the summer after her husband was first elected to Congress to remain close—so close that she was in the same building. Wendy, whose personality Nugent describes as "bubbly," served as a tour guide in the Capitol before returning to Florida.

In his spare time, Nugent likes to fish, hike and cook. "The boys love his cooking, and he does Christmas and Thanksgiving," Wendy Nugent told Politico. "In the summer, I like to cook ... healthier. He's like, 'We're having tofu?'"

Key Votes

2012	
Extend a Social Security payroll tax cut and unemployment benefits	NO
Ease securities rules to expand small-business access to capital	YES
Extend for one year subsidized student loan interest rates financed by a cut in health care spending	YES
Cite Attorney General Eric H. Holder Jr. for contempt of Congress	YES
Create a visa program for foreign graduates in high-tech fields	YES
Extend most Bush-era income tax rates while allowing rates for top-bracket earners to rise (Jan. 1, 2013)	NO
2011	
Strike funding for F-35 alternative engine	NO
Prevent EPA from regulating greenhouse gas emissions to address climate change	YES
Extend certain provisions of Patriot Act for four years	YES
Declare opposition to use of ground troops in Libya	YES
Overhaul patent law	YES
Pass compromise debt limit increase plan and establish future spending limits	YES
Allow consideration of measures to implement three trade agreements	YES

CQ Vote Studies

	PARTY UNITY		PRESIDENTIAL SUPPORT	
	SUPPORT	OPPOSE	SUPPORT	OPPOSE
2012	96%	4%	18%	82%
2011	97%	3%	20%	80%

Interest Groups

	AFL-CIO	ADA	CCUS	ACU
2012	10%	0%	83%	88%
2011	0%	5%	100%	84%

Florida 11

Most of Marion County; part of west coast

Starting along central Florida's northwestern coast north of Tampa, the 11th District crosses Interstate 75 into central Marion County. Its largest communities include Ocala in Marion, the retirement community The Villages in Sumter County, and Spring Hill in southern Hernando County. Forested parks, swampland, springs and wildlife refuges make up the 11th's portion of the Nature Coast in Hernando and Citrus counties. The district also takes in a tiny corner of Lake County.

Beach, wilderness and parkland tourism are key to the economy here. Boating, fishing and hunting are popular pastimes, and wildlife preserves offer opportunities to see rare birds, manatees and alligators. The region has long drawn retirees and the "snowbirds" who spend winters here.

The district's farmland produces field and grass seed crops and citrus, as well as pork, horses and livestock. Ocala is a prime horse-breeding region, with terrain similar to Kentucky's bluegrass hills, although it does struggle with high unemployment rates. Several distribution centers and small manufacturers also provide employment throughout the district. The Villages, in otherwise sparsely populated Sumter County, is a booming retirement community where ongoing construction projects bolster an economy dominated by a federal prison and local government jobs.

With a population that is more than 86 percent white, the 11th is one of the least racially diverse in the state. It also has the oldest population statewide, with a median age just shy of 51 years. Like much of Florida's non-urban areas, the 11th is solidly Republican. The counties wholly within the district gave Republican Mitt Romney wide margins of victory in the 2012 presidential contest even as he narrowly lost the state. Fifty-five percent of the registered voters in the 11th are Republicans.

Major Industry

Tourism, service, agriculture, health care

Cities

Spring Hill (unincorporated), Ocala, The Villages (unincorporated), Lady Lake, Crystal River, Inverness, Wildwood

Notable

Weeki Wachee Springs water park is known for its live "mermaid" performances; The Crystal River Wildlife Refuge was established to protect the area's West Indian manatees and is accessible only by boat.

Rep. Gus Bilirakis (R)

Capitol Office
225-5755
bilirakis.house.gov
2313 Rayburn Bldg. 20515-0909; fax 225-4085

Committees
Energy & Commerce
Veterans' Affairs

Residence
Palm Harbor

Born
Feb. 8, 1963; Gainesville, Fla.

Religion
Greek Orthodox

Family
Wife, Eva Bilirakis; four children

Education
St. Petersburg Junior College, attended 1981-83; U. of Florida, B.A. 1986 (political science); Stetson U., J.D. 1989

Career
Lawyer; college instructor

Political Highlights
Fla. House, 1998-2006

ELECTION RESULTS

2012 GENERAL		
Gus Bilirakis (R)	209,604	63.5%
Jonathan Michael Snow (D)	108,770	32.9%
John Russell (NPA)	6,878	2.1%
Paul Sidney Elliott (NPA)	4,915	1.5%
2012 PRIMARY		
Gus Bilirakis (R)		unopposed
2010 GENERAL		
Gus Bilirakis (R)	165,433	71.4%
Anita de Palma (D)	66,158	28.6%

Previous Winning Percentages
2008 (62%); 2006 (56%)

Elected 2006; 4th term

Michael Bilirakis was a 12-term representative with deep involvement in veterans issues and health care policy. His son, Gus, seems intent on building his father's legacy into a family legacy.

Now in his fourth term succeeding his father, the younger Bilirakis (bil-uh-RACK-iss) serves as vice chairman of the Veterans' Affairs Committee — a job his father once held. He sits on both the Energy and Commerce Committee and the Health Subcommittee that his father once chaired. And for good measure, he shares his father's regular-guy personality. Bilirakis mostly avoids the spotlight and advances his priorities by way of amendments to bills and by building friendships with colleagues.

In joining Energy and Commerce for the 113th Congress (2013-14), Bilirakis waded into one of the more partisan environments in the House. It's a definite departure from his earlier work, which focused largely on veterans and homeland security.

Bilirakis isn't the most conservative Republican, but he has joined his party in opposing the 2010 health care overhaul, which he called "a trillion-dollar expansion of the federal government marred with special deals, mandates, tax hikes and Medicare cuts."

His Tampa-area district has lots of retirees and senior citizens, and Bilirakis is protective of Medicare and its benefit levels. He is wary of proposed payment cuts for private insurance plans linked to the Medicare system. "I know that the seniors in my district love their Medicare Advantage," Bilirakis said in 2013. One of the first health care bills he introduced, in 2007, would have required Medicare to cover hearing aids. (Michael Bilirakis was the chairman of the Health Subcommittee when a prescription drug benefit was added to the Medicare program in 2003.)

Bilirakis' support of the GOP's "all of the above" energy policy is tempered by his worries about offshore oil drilling, particularly along the Gulf Coast. In 2012, the House adopted his amendment to a broad-ranging measure promoting fossil fuel development. Bilirakis' provision would have required a study of how Florida's tourism and fishing are affected by energy development within 100 miles of the coast. He was one of 21 Republicans to vote against the underlying bill, which passed the House but died in the Senate.

Bilirakis, whose father is a Korean War veteran, became the vice chairman of the Veterans' Affairs Committee in the 112th Congress (2011-12). He also served as chairman of the Veterans' Affairs Task Force for the Republican Policy Committee. He pursues wide-ranging health, psychological and employment assistance for veterans. President Barack Obama in early 2013 signed a Bilirakis bill meant to provide extra guidance for veterans using GI Bill education benefits.

Under House rules, people serving on Energy and Commerce don't get to sit on any other committees. Bilirakis had to get a waiver to keep his seat on Veterans' Affairs, and he gave up spots on the Homeland Security and Foreign Affairs committees.

In the 112th Congress, he chaired the Homeland Security Subcommittee on Emergency Preparedness, Response and Communications, which touches on the responses to both terrorism and natural disasters. Bilirakis was skeptical of the Obama administration's proposal to consolidate several homeland security grant programs into a single National Preparedness Grant Program; among other things, he worried that grants wouldn't make it through state governments to localities that needed them. Bilirakis wants grants awarded with preference for areas more likely to suffer attacks or disasters.

He has suggested creating a tax credit for those spending to prepare their properties for hurricane or tornado strikes. And the full committee in 2012 approved his bill to modernize public alert and warning systems.

Four times, Bilirakis has introduced his bill to strengthen background checks for student visa applicants. He contends that terrorists could enter the country under the guise of seeking an education, then stay in the country thanks to lax requirements for keeping tabs on such visa holders.

Like his father, Bilirakis takes an interest in foreign affairs that is shaped by his Greek heritage. Bilirakis' ancestors came to Tarpon Springs, which was settled mainly by Greek immigrants who worked as sponge divers, a century ago. In June 2012, he introduced a resolution "to end Turkey's illegal occupation of the Republic of Cyprus, to support Cyprus in its efforts to control all of its territory, and to allow Cyprus to explore its own energy resources without illegal interference by Turkey."

He's a strong supporter of closer ties between Greece and Israel, and has backed sanctions against Iran as it tries to develop its nuclear program.

Bilirakis belongs to the conservative Republican Study Committee, but he isn't beholden to its proposals. He voted against a fiscal 2013 budget prepared by the RSC that was more austere than other GOP budget proposals. He can be fiscally conservative, however. In January 2013, Bilirakis joined most of his party in opposing a $50 billion measure tied to Superstorm Sandy relief, where most of the total was deemed off-budget "emergency" spending. He also endorses a plan to replace federal taxes with a single national sales tax.

Bilirakis says he always wanted to follow his father's example of a career in politics. He attended public schools, then studied at a community college in St. Petersburg before earning his undergraduate degree at the University of Florida with a major in political science. After getting a law degree from Stetson University, he worked in his father's Palm Harbor practice.

His first venture into electoral politics on his own behalf was a successful run in 1998 for the state House seat representing Tampa. His opportunity to move up to the U.S. House came in 2006 with his father's retirement. Bilirakis breezed through the primary, but the general election was tougher. He was helped to victory by his name recognition and public support from a bevy of Republican heavies, including President George W. Bush.

When Florida redrew its electoral map for the 2012 campaign, the closest match to Bilirakis' old 9th District was the new 12th — a more compact district, but one still centered on suburbs north of Tampa. The 12th has a strong GOP lean, and Democrats didn't field an experienced challenger.

Bilirakis won more than 63 percent of the vote to defeat Democrat Jonathan Michael Snow, a 25-year old Walgreens photo technician.

Key Votes

2012	
Extend a Social Security payroll tax cut and unemployment benefits	YES
Ease securities rules to expand small-business access to capital	YES
Extend for one year subsidized student loan interest rates financed by a cut in health care spending	YES
Cite Attorney General Eric H. Holder Jr. for contempt of Congress	YES
Create a visa program for foreign graduates in high-tech fields	YES
Extend most Bush-era income tax rates while allowing rates for top-bracket earners to rise (Jan. 1, 2013)	NO
2011	
Strike funding for F-35 alternative engine	NO
Prevent EPA from regulating greenhouse gas emissions to address climate change	+
Extend certain provisions of Patriot Act for four years	YES
Declare opposition to use of ground troops in Libya	YES
Overhaul patent law	NO
Pass compromise debt limit increase plan and establish future spending limits	YES
Allow consideration of measures to implement three trade agreements	YES

CQ Vote Studies

	Party Unity		Presidential Support	
	SUPPORT	OPPOSE	SUPPORT	OPPOSE
2012	96%	4%	19%	81%
2011	94%	6%	21%	79%
2010	92%	8%	33%	67%
2009	87%	13%	31%	69%
2008	89%	11%	63%	37%

Interest Groups

	AFL-CIO	ADA	CCUS	ACU
2012	15%	0%	91%	84%
2011	0%	5%	94%	76%
2010	14%	15%	75%	88%
2009	10%	5%	73%	100%
2008	13%	30%	83%	88%

Florida 12

West — suburbs north of Tampa

The 12th District takes in suburbs and bedroom communities north of Tampa and St. Petersburg on Florida's west central Gulf Coast. It includes all of Pasco County and the northern Pinellas County communities of Palm Harbor and Tarpon Springs, as well as a small suburban corner of Hillsborough County.

Two-thirds of the district's population lives in booming Pasco County, which has welcomed an influx of both retirees and Hispanic immigrants. Years of growth encouraged a local real estate boom that has since collapsed. Luxury homes and retirement communities popped up in communities such as Wesley Chapel, but an economy still sputtering after the recent nationwide recession is expected to slow growth for years to come. Eastern Pasco County, which includes county seat Dade City, is largely rural and agricultural. Along the Gulf Coast, the county is mostly residential.

Pasco looks to diversify its economy. Baltimore-based financial giant T. Rowe Price plans to build an office complex off State Road 54, bringing more jobs to the county. This boost is needed: Pasco has had among the highest unemployment in the state since the 2008 financial crisis, a problem exacerbated by declining agriculture employment over the past decade. Expansion at local hospitals, generating more high-paying jobs, may bolster the health care sector.

The district's population is overwhelmingly white, but Pasco County's Hispanic population nearly tripled between 2000 and 2010. Tarpon Springs and Palm Harbor both have large Greek Orthodox populations. Overall, conservative older voters — a significant percentage of the population here is retirement age — drive the politics of this Republican-leaning area. Mitt Romney took 54 percent of the district's vote in the 2012 presidential contest.

Major Industry

Health care, government, service

Cities

Palm Harbor (unincorporated), Wesley Chapel (unincorporated), Land O' Lakes (unincorporated), Tarpon Springs, New Port Richey

Notable

Tarpon Springs, still known as the "Sponge Capital of the World," was founded by Greek immigrants who came to dive for natural sponges, and the city's still-active sponge docks are now a tourist destination.

Rep. C.W. Bill Young (R)

Capitol Office
225-5961
young.house.gov
2407 Rayburn Bldg. 20515-0910; fax 225-9764

Committees
Appropriations
(Defense - Chairman)

Residence
Indian Shores

Born
Dec. 16, 1930; Harmarville, Pa.

Religion
Methodist

Family
Wife, Beverly Young; six children

Education
St. Petersburg H.S., graduated 1948

Military
Fla. National Guard, 1948-57

Career
Insurance executive

Political Highlights
Fla. Senate, 1960-70 (minority leader, 1966-70)

ELECTION RESULTS

2012 GENERAL		
C.W. Bill Young (R)	189,605	57.6%
Jessica Ehrlich (D)	139,742	42.4%
2012 PRIMARY		
C.W. Bill Young (R)	39,395	69.1%
Darren Ayres (R)	10,548	18.5%
Madeline Vance (R)	7,049	12.4%
2010 GENERAL		
C.W. Bill Young (R)	137,943	65.9%
Charlie Justice (D)	71,313	34.1%

Previous Winning Percentages
2008 (61%); 2006 (66%); 2004 (69%); 2002 100%); 2000 (76%); 1998 (100%); 1996 (67%); 1994 (100%); 1992 (57%); 1990 (100%); 1988 (73%); 1986 (100%); 1984 (80%); 1982 (100%); 1980 (100%); 1978 (79%); 1976 (65%); 1974 (76%); 1972 (76%); 1970 (67%)

Elected 1970; 22nd term

No current Republican has been in Congress longer than Young, and only two House Democrats can claim more seniority. A month before his 82nd birthday, voters decided to give him a 22nd term. He remains an effective and influential member of the Appropriations Committee, but his occasional admissions of weariness have some people wondering how much longer he'll be on Capitol Hill.

However long it ends up being, it seems likely that Young will retain two seemingly contrary characteristics that, in concert, make him effective: his amiable nature and his ability to fight members of either party.

The 113th Congress (2013-14) began with 46 members who were born after Young was sworn into the House in 1971. He has shown his age more since back surgery in 2010, walking with a cane and periodically relying on aides for help getting around.

Young prefers the nice-guy approach, but he doesn't back down from challenges. He voted for the fiscal 2012 and 2013 budgets prepared by Wisconsin Republican Paul D. Ryan, which included tax code overhauls and changes to entitlement programs. Democrats ran a 2011 ad saying Young had voted to "cut taxes for millionaires and end your Medicare." The Tampa Bay Times reported his response: "I would never quit in the face of vicious attacks like that. It's not me. I keep telling these guys, 'You guys want me to retire, just be nice to me.' "

He also has shown some spunk. Left-leaning activists staged a rally at one of Young's Florida offices in December 2012, and one yelling protester got under Young's skin. The octogenarian lawmaker grabbed the protester's arm and appeared to wave his cane threateningly in the air.

He hasn't been afraid to deviate from his party, either. Late in 2012 he said he'd consider approving tax increases as part of a deficit reduction package, and on the first day of 2013 he voted for the "fiscal cliff" bill that raised income taxes on earnings over $400,000. He bucked GOP colleagues in earlier years by supporting a minimum-wage increase, a ban on certain semiautomatic weapons and federal aid to help protect Florida's beaches from erosion. He opposes offshore drilling close to Florida's coast and introduced a bill to beef up safety standards for offshore platforms.

Young's flexibility is attributable to political experience. He was the only Republican in the Florida Senate when he joined that body in 1960, and he spent 24 years in the U.S. House minority before the GOP victories of 1994. Working with Democrats was necessary to accomplish anything. His mostly non-confrontational style resonates with the culture of the Appropriations Committee, where for years there was a tacit agreement to accede to others' parochial spending projects in exchange for approval of one's own.

When Republicans won the House majority in 1994, Young and two other senior members of Appropriations were passed over for the chairmanship. Young settled for the gavel of the Defense Subcommittee. When he finally took over the full committee in 1999, he allowed conservatives to dominate the early stages of budget negotiations until legislative reality — the need to gain President Bill Clinton's signature — set in.

Republicans usually limit their committee leaders to six years atop a panel, so Young was forced back to the top spot on the Defense Subcommittee in 2005. He was chairman for two years, then served as the ranking member through four years of Democratic control. Young got a waiver from term limits to again become the subcommittee chairman for the 112th Congress (2011-12), and he was granted another waiver for the 113th.

He had a close working relationship with Democrat John P. Murtha of Pennsylvania, the former chairman of the Defense Subcommittee, but it ended with Murtha's death after surgical complications in 2010. In the 113th he's without another Democratic sidekick, as Norm Dicks of Washington retired. Young has outlived the two senators who led their chamber's Defense spending panel for many years: Republican Ted Stevens of Alaska, who perished in a 2010 plane crash two years after leaving the Senate, and Democrat Daniel K. Inouye of Hawaii, who died of respiratory problems in late 2012.

For more than a decade after the terrorist attacks of 2001, that bipartisan and bicameral team oversaw approval of a huge buildup in defense spending, nearly doubling the regular budget and providing several hundred billion dollars for the wars in Iraq and Afghanistan.

Young had supported those U.S. military deployments until September 2012, when — in another act of apostasy against the party line — he told a local newspaper that he felt it was time to bring troops home from Afghanistan. "I just think we're killing kids that don't need to die," he said.

On the Military Construction-VA Subcommittee, Young works to deliver aid to wounded veterans. He found himself on the defensive in 2007, when concerns arose about mismanagement and soldiers' poor living conditions at Walter Reed Army Medical Center in Washington, D.C. Young routinely had visited soldiers there without commenting on the center's conditions.

Young said he knew of the problems as early as 2003 but preferred to confront the hospital commander privately rather than go public or wield his appropriator's clout. The facility closed in 2011 as a result of base realignment.

Young was born into hardscrabble poverty in western Pennsylvania's coal country during the Great Depression. His father, an alcoholic, abandoned the family when Young was a boy. After his mother became ill, the family stayed with relatives in St. Petersburg. Young never went to college but worked his way to success in the insurance business. He entered politics in 1960 when he was elected to the state Senate.

In 1970 he won the state's most dependably Republican U.S. House seat, which opened up after William C. Cramer decided to run for the Senate. Even in years when his district leaned Democratic, Young usually was re-elected with ease. Since 1978, Democrats have fielded a candidate against him only about half the time.

Redistricting for 2012 put him in the new 13th District, and he had a spirited challenger in Democrat Jessica Ehrlich, a 38-year-old lawyer and former congressional aide.

It was Young's closest race since 1992, but he still won by 15 points, even as Barack Obama won the district's presidential vote.

Key Votes

2012	
Extend a Social Security payroll tax cut and unemployment benefits	YES
Ease securities rules to expand small-business access to capital	YES
Extend for one year subsidized student loan interest rates financed by a cut in health care spending	YES
Cite Attorney General Eric H. Holder Jr. for contempt of Congress	YES
Create a visa program for foreign graduates in high-tech fields	YES
Extend most Bush-era income tax rates while allowing rates for top-bracket earners to rise (Jan. 1, 2013)	YES
2011	
Strike funding for F-35 alternative engine	NO
Prevent EPA from regulating greenhouse gas emissions to address climate change	YES
Extend certain provisions of Patriot Act for four years	YES
Declare opposition to use of ground troops in Libya	YES
Overhaul patent law	NO
Pass compromise debt limit increase plan and establish future spending limits	YES
Allow consideration of measures to implement three trade agreements	YES

CQ Vote Studies

	Party Unity		Presidential Support	
	SUPPORT	OPPOSE	SUPPORT	OPPOSE
2012	90%	10%	18%	82%
2011	89%	11%	29%	71%
2010	90%	10%	32%	68%
2009	77%	23%	32%	68%
2008	92%	8%	64%	36%

Interest Groups

	AFL-CIO	ADA	CCUS	ACU
2012	22%	0%	92%	76%
2011	0%	5%	94%	73%
2010	9%	10%	100%	84%
2009	25%	15%	80%	92%
2008	33%	25%	83%	88%

Florida 13

West — most of Pinellas County, St. Petersburg

Nestled between Tampa Bay to the east and the Gulf of Mexico to the west, the 13th District takes in most of the Pinellas County peninsula. It includes most of St. Petersburg's urban core, upscale communities along white-sand beaches and the city of Clearwater.

Three-fourths of Pinellas County's population lives in the 13th. Although the district is majority white, residents are a mix of longtime locals, retired transplants, immigrants and seasonal "snowbirds" who spend their winters enjoying the balmy coastal climate. More than one-fifth of the district's population is 65 or older.

Beach tourism, integral to the economy in cities such as Treasure Island and St. Pete Beach, is vulnerable to economic downturns. And environmental concerns related to the surrounding waters and wildlife areas are as much economic as they are political issues for locals. Another concern for the region is how to recover from foreclosures and downswings in the local housing market. Still, a growing financial services sector and a large health care sector have bolstered the county's white-collar employment.

Downtown St. Petersburg also is home to some corporate headquarters, including the Home Shopping Network. The 13th includes the Old Northeast neighborhood of the city and its stately homes.

During decennial redistricting, the Pinellas-based district gained all of Clearwater, the home to the Church of Scientology's "spiritual headquarters" and a significant Scientology community. Given Pinellas County's cultural diversity, local politics tend to be moderate, but still lean Republican. At the federal level, contests can be more competitive. Democrats hold a slight edge in voter registration in the 13th, but independents can swing the vote. Barack Obama took the 13th by one percentage point in the 2012 presidential election.

Major Industry

Tourism, health care, retail, technology

Cities

St. Petersburg (pt.), Clearwater, Largo, Pinellas Park, Dunedin

Notable

The historic Don CeSar Hotel on St. Pete Beach was built in 1928 to look like a Mediterranean castle and served as an Army hospital during World War II.

Rep. Kathy Castor (D)

Capitol Office
225-3376
castor.house.gov
205 Cannon Bldg. 20515-0911; fax 225-5652

Committees
Budget
Energy & Commerce

Residence
Tampa

Born
Aug. 20, 1966; Miami, Fla.

Religion
Presbyterian

Family
Husband, Bill Lewis; two children

Education
Emory U., B.A. 1988 (political science); Florida State U., J.D. 1991

Career
Lawyer

Political Highlights
Democratic nominee for Fla. Senate, 2000; Hillsborough County Board of Commissioners, 2002-06

ELECTION RESULTS

2012 GENERAL		
Kathy Castor (D)	197,121	70.2%
Evelio "EJ" Otero (R)	83,480	29.8%
2012 PRIMARY		
Kathy Castor (D)		unopposed
2010 GENERAL		
Kathy Castor (D)	91,328	59.6%
Mike Prendergast (R)	61,817	40.4%

Previous Winning Percentages
2008 (72%); 2006 (70%)

Elected 2006; 4th term

Castor comes from a family tradition of public service. Her reliably Democratic voting record and excellent relations with her party's leaders have yielded her opportunities to work on health care and energy, two topics of major importance to her coastal district.

Castor's parents, brother and sister all have run for elected office, and her maternal grandfather was mayor of Glassboro, N.J. After an unsuccessful state Senate run in 2000, Castor was elected in 2002 to the Hillsborough County Board of Commissioners. She had sat in on board meetings as a child when her mother served there.

"I loved the idea of public service from an early age," Castor said. "Being the daughter of a trailblazing female, I was inspired by her, even when confronted with doubts about women in politics" from other people. Betty Castor went on to become a Florida state senator, the state education commissioner, and the 2004 Democratic nominee for the U.S. Senate. She lost that race by 1 point to Republican Mel Martinez.

The younger Castor has been in the good graces of the Democratic Party since arriving in the House in 2007. As a freshman she began a stint on the Democratic Steering Committee, which hands out committee assignments to caucus members; she also sat on the powerful Rules Committee, which sets terms for floor debate. In the 111th Congress (2009-10) she moved to the Energy and Commerce Committee, in time to work on the Democrats' health care overhaul and consumer protection issues.

Castor lost that seat with the GOP takeover in 2011, but returned six months later when there was a vacancy on the panel. "All of the issues that Energy and Commerce considers — energy, health care, Medicaid and Medicare, tourism — are important to Florida," she says.

Castor is an ardent defender of the 2010 health care law and a critic of Florida Gov. Rick Scott, a Republican who refused in 2012 to implement the law's expansion of Medicaid (he announced in February 2013 that he had reconsidered). Scott has "a very narrow vision," Castor said.

She takes a particular interest in children's health issues. Castor, who co-founded the bipartisan Children's Health Care Caucus, led 2008 floor debate on a bill to expand the Children's Health Insurance Program, which helps cover children from low-income families that do not qualify for Medicaid. President Barack Obama signed a later incarnation of the bill in early 2009.

When dealing with energy and the environment, Castor brings a decade of experience practicing environmental law; she also chaired the Environmental Protection Commission for Hillsborough County. Castor promotes both alternative energy and energy efficiency measures.

In the 112th Congress (2011-12), she served as co-chairwoman of a new Gulf Coast Caucus, which successfully pushed for a law that will steer to the Gulf Coast states a large share of fines collected under the Clean Water Act related to the 2010 Deepwater Horizon oil spill.

Castor opposes efforts to drill for oil and gas off the Florida coast — one of the few issues on which she has disagreed with Obama. In March 2010, Obama proposed studying areas in the eastern gulf for expanded leases. Castor countered that a 235-mile buffer zone off the west coast of Florida that was created in 2006 should be maintained. After the spill, Obama retreated on his call for study, and Castor proposed permanently banning drilling off the Gulf Coast and the straits of Florida.

One gulf-related issue where Castor departs from many Democrats is free trade. The Port of Tampa is in her district, and the shipping industry is a big part of the regional economy. Castor was in the minority of Democrats voting for free-trade pacts with Colombia, Panama and South Korea in 2011.

On the Budget Committee, Castor joins in Democratic attacks on the fiscal blueprints of Chairman Paul D. Ryan, a Wisconsin Republican. She is particularly critical of potential cuts to federal health care programs. Castor is close to the committee's top Democrat, Chris Van Hollen of Maryland.

She also has strong working relationships with Florida Democratic Sen. Bill Nelson and several female Democratic lawmakers, including Rep. Jan Schakowsky of Illinois, Rep. Allyson Y. Schwartz of Pennsylvania and Sen. Kirsten Gillibrand of New York. Castor hosted a baby shower for Gillibrand that was open to all congresswomen of both parties. Castor herself has two daughters and says family consumes her time away from work: "People should know I'm a soccer mom."

The work of Castor's parents, who divorced when she was 11, was key to the development of her political philosophy. "You learned about speaking up for people who don't have a voice," she said. Her father, Don, was a Hillsborough County judge and helped found Bay Area Legal Services, a nonprofit group that serves low-income families.

Castor first arrived in Washington as a college intern in the office of Florida Democratic Sen. Lawton Chiles. "I never imagined then that I'd return as a member," she said. After graduating from Emory University in Atlanta and earning a law degree from Florida State, where she met her husband, Bill Lewis, Castor worked in the Department of Community Affairs in Tallahassee enforcing environmental laws.

She returned to Tampa in the mid-1990s to work in a law firm representing the city on zoning issues. On the Hillsborough County board, she was a liberal voice amid the conservative majority. She won support for greater disclosure of commissioners' travel costs and meetings with lobbyists. In 2005, she was the lone dissenting vote when the panel blocked the county government from recognizing gay pride events.

Castor, who has had stints on the Armed Services Committee, cites the "colossal blunder" of the Iraq War as her motivation for her 2006 House campaign — and it didn't hurt that she had a relatively clear path in front of her, as Democratic Rep. Jim Davis made a failed bid for governor that year. She became the early favorite by capitalizing on her name recognition and financial support from EMILY's List, a political committee that backs Democratic women who support abortion rights.

She won the five-way primary with 54 percent of the vote and trounced GOP architect Eddie Adams in the general election. Her three re-elections have been by wide margins.

Key Votes

2012	
Extend a Social Security payroll tax cut and unemployment benefits	YES
Ease securities rules to expand small-business access to capital	YES
Extend for one year subsidized student loan interest rates financed by a cut in health care spending	NO
Cite Attorney General Eric H. Holder Jr. for contempt of Congress	?
Create a visa program for foreign graduates in high-tech fields	NO
Extend most Bush-era income tax rates while allowing rates for top-bracket earners to rise (Jan. 1, 2013)	YES
2011	
Strike funding for F-35 alternative engine	YES
Prevent EPA from regulating greenhouse gas emissions to address climate change	NO
Extend certain provisions of Patriot Act for four years	?
Declare opposition to use of ground troops in Libya	YES
Overhaul patent law	YES
Pass compromise debt limit increase plan and establish future spending limits	YES
Allow consideration of measures to implement three trade agreements	YES

CQ Vote Studies

	Party Unity		Presidential Support	
	Support	Oppose	Support	Oppose
2012	96%	4%	86%	14%
2011	95%	5%	95%	5%
2010	99%	1%	93%	8%
2009	99%	1%	96%	4%
2008	99%	1%	14%	86%

Interest Groups

	AFL-CIO	ADA	CCUS	ACU
2012	90%	70%	33%	4%
2011	88%	75%	47%	0%
2010	100%	95%	25%	0%
2009	100%	100%	33%	0%
2008	100%	95%	63%	9%

Florida 14

Tampa, south St. Petersburg

The 14th is centered on Tampa, the state's third-largest city and a Gulf Coast economic driver. The district cradles the eastern shore of Tampa Bay, including MacDill Air Force Base, and its portion of St. Petersburg (shared with the 13th) includes downtown commercial and entertainment areas.

Founded as a cigar-making town, Tampa (the outskirts of which are in the 15th) has long been the region's economic engine. High-traffic Tampa International Airport and the similarly busy Port of Tampa have become increasingly important; the financial services sector, dominated by Raymond James Financial, provides white-collar employment. The University of South Florida and MacDill Air Force Base each prop up the economy, and the district hosts agribusiness activity. Tampa also remains a cultural and entertainment hub. Ybor City, in the former cigar district, is a well-known night club spot, and the Channelside entertainment complex has offered an economic boost. Like much of the rest of the state, Tampa struggles with declining revenues from falling property values.

To the west, the district's piece of St. Petersburg is dotted with unoccupied condo high-rises and empty retail storefronts. A satellite campus of USF attracts young people downtown. Across the water, the domed Tropicana Field stadium, home to baseball's Tampa Bay Rays, serves as an economic anchor. At the southern tip of the Pinellas County peninsula, the district takes in St. Petersburg's Pink Streets neighborhood, where luxury mansions line streets that were paved pale pink in the 1920s.

One of Florida's few districts where no racial group can claim a majority of the population, the 14th's urban and diverse electorate is mostly Democratic and gives strong support to statewide Democratic candidates.

Major Industry
Transportation, service, health care, financial services

Military Bases
MacDill Air Force Base, 6,914 military, 3,158 civilian (2011)

Cities
Tampa, St. Petersburg (pt.), Town 'n' Country (unincorporated)

Notable
The Salvador Dalí Museum, on the St. Petersburg waterfront, houses the largest collection of art by the Spanish surrealist outside of Europe.

Rep. Dennis A. Ross (R)

Capitol Office
225-1252
dennisross.house.gov
229 Cannon Bldg. 20515-0912; fax 226-0585

Committees
Financial Services

Residence
Lakeland

Born
Oct. 18, 1959; Lakeland, Fla.

Religion
Presbyterian

Family
Wife, Cindy Ross; two children

Education
U. of Florida, attended 1977-78; Auburn U., B.S.B.A. 1981 (organization management); Samford U., J.D. 1987

Career
Lawyer; software sales and marketing representative; state legislative aide

Political Highlights
Polk County Republican Party chairman, 1992-95; Republican nominee for Fla. Senate, 1996; Fla. House, 2000-08

ELECTION RESULTS

2012 GENERAL		
Dennis A. Ross (R)		unopposed
2012 PRIMARY		
Dennis A. Ross (R)		unopposed
2010 GENERAL		
Dennis A. Ross (R)	102,704	48.1%
Lori Edwards (D)	87,769	41.1%
Randy Wilkinson (TEA)	22,857	10.7%

Elected 2010; 2nd term

Ross admires central Florida's cowboy culture, as both an outdoorsman and a politician. His notions of tough-minded self-sufficiency place him among the most conservative members of the House, and he has little patience for government inefficiencies or proposals he sees as detrimental the country's fiscal solvency.

He has considerable political experience, having served as both a county-level GOP chairman and a member of the Florida House before coming to Washington in 2011. But he still emphasizes that he'd rather be hunting. "I can sit in a deer stand for nine hours straight," Ross said. "A committee meeting, maybe about 30 minutes."

In the 113th Congress (2013-14), Ross is getting antsy on a new panel. He traded in his assignments from his freshman term for a seat on the Financial Services Committee. He is almost certain to favor less government regulation and a federal withdrawal from the marketplace.

Ross was the chairman of the Florida House's Insurance Committee for a term, as hurricane damage chased private insurers from the state and drove up insurance premiums. He was against expanding the state's role as a backstop for the insurance industry, and when lawmakers produced a 2007 bill to do so, he was one of only two (out of 158 who voted) to oppose it. Financial Services Chairman Jeb Hensarling, a Texas Republican who has vowed to privatize the flood insurance industry, surely has taken note. (Bill Posey, a Republican state senator who helped write the 2007 package, is also now a member of Financial Services.)

Ross similarly has opposed all federal "bailouts" of corporations, and he wants to eliminate the government-sponsored enterprises involved in the housing sector.

He typically favors a smaller government. He voted against the spending bills for fiscal 2011 and fiscal 2012, as well as a deficit reduction package from August 2011; none of them did enough to control spending for his tastes. His first bill as a freshman was to require "zero-based" federal budgeting, which throws out baseline spending and requires full justification of every item in a department's funding request. Ross also wants to see creation of a "sunset committee" in both the House and Senate to examine agencies and programs that may need elimination.

He has found some creative ways to promote cost-cutting. After learning that a new soccer field and other recreational amenities costing just under $750,000 were being built at the Guantánamo Bay detention facility in Cuba, Ross introduced a bill to cut the Pentagon budget by that amount.

But some of the less-sexy issues before Congress also occupied Ross as a freshman, and one of the biggest was how to modernize the U.S. Postal Service. As chairman of the Oversight and Government Reform subcommittee with jurisdiction over the Postal Service, Ross helped manage an overhaul written by committee Chairman Darrell Issa of California. Differences with Senate plans were not worked out before the start of the 113th Congress, however.

Ross does not mind looking for budget savings in the federal workforce. During the 112th Congress (2011-12) he called for pay freezes for the federal workforce and introduced a bill requiring federal workers to contribute more to their pensions.

Another Ross bill would have reduced travel expenses for federal employees. He said that in a time when people can "text and call from one end of the globe to another," any extra spending on travel "is a luxury that is both no longer necessary and no longer affordable."

Ross was a workers' compensation lawyer, and he once worked for another essential part of central Florida's culture — before starting his own practice, he was an in-house counsel for Disney World.

He no longer holds a seat on the Judiciary Committee, but he does have thoughts on potential immigration law changes that the panel is considering in the 113th Congress. The previous incarnation of his House district included the top citrus-producing county in Florida, and berries and tomatoes are major crops in the area he now represents. Guest workers are important to those agricultural operations, and in January 2013, Ross introduced a bill to create a guest worker program. He supports use of the E-Verify system to determine the immigration status of those seeking work in the United States, but he wants to "make sure my growers, my harvesters, have an adequate labor force from which to choose if they are going to be forced to use an E-Verify program."

Ross was born in Lakeland, the youngest of five children. He once told the local paper that he remembered walking into Richard Nixon's local campaign office as a 9-year-old and plundering it for swag. His family traveled a lot, and Ross now owns a refurbished 1960s Airstream trailer that once belonged to his grandfather. He has visited 49 states, mostly in an RV. Hawaii is the only one missing.

He met his wife in high school, although they didn't date until later in life. He credits her family with getting him into hunting. "They are true Florida crackers," Ross says, affectionately describing his father-in-law as "a game warden's nightmare."

Ross transferred to Auburn University early in his college career and earned a degree in organization management. After working briefly as a state House legislative aide in Florida, he went back to Alabama for law school at Samford University.

He got involved with the Polk County Republican Party and served as its chairman in the early 1990s. After a failed bid for the state Senate in 1996, Ross won election to the state House in 2000. He quickly announced his hope to become speaker in his fourth term (which would be his last under term limit laws), but that job ultimately went to Marco Rubio who is now Florida's junior senator.

Ross' path to the U.S. House opened up when Republican Rep. Adam H. Putnam decided to run for state agriculture commissioner in 2010. Democrats viewed the 12th District as a potential pickup, but Ross held off Democrat Lori Edwards, winning 48 percent of the vote to her 41 percent. A tea party candidate took 11 percent of the vote.

In 2012, running in the newly drawn 15th District, Ross was unopposed in both his primary and general elections.

Key Votes

2012	
Extend a Social Security payroll tax cut and unemployment benefits	NO
Ease securities rules to expand small-business access to capital	YES
Extend for one year subsidized student loan interest rates financed by a cut in health care spending	YES
Cite Attorney General Eric H. Holder Jr. for contempt of Congress	YES
Create a visa program for foreign graduates in high-tech fields	YES
Extend most Bush-era income tax rates while allowing rates for top-bracket earners to rise (Jan. 1, 2013)	NO
2011	
Strike funding for F-35 alternative engine	NO
Prevent EPA from regulating greenhouse gas emissions to address climate change	YES
Extend certain provisions of Patriot Act for four years	YES
Declare opposition to use of ground troops in Libya	YES
Overhaul patent law	YES
Pass compromise debt limit increase plan and establish future spending limits	NO
Allow consideration of measures to implement three trade agreements	YES

CQ Vote Studies

	PARTY UNITY		PRESIDENTIAL SUPPORT	
	SUPPORT	OPPOSE	SUPPORT	OPPOSE
2012	97%	3%	15%	85%
2011	98%	2%	15%	85%

Interest Groups

	AFL-CIO	ADA	CCUS	ACU
2012	10%	5%	83%	96%
2011	0%	5%	94%	100%

Florida 15

West central — Tampa suburbs, Lakeland

Concentrated on a stretch of the Interstate 4 corridor that links Tampa to Orlando, the 15th District covers the northern junction of Hillsborough and Polk counties. Its western half takes in formerly rural areas within the city limits of Tampa, more well-to-do suburbs of Hillsborough County and small-town Plant City. Following the interstate east through pastures and farmland, it heads into Polk County to take in midsize Lakeland.

The Hillsborough County suburbs outside of Tampa include Brandon — east of downtown (in the 14th) — and Temple Terrace. Both cities are primarily residential and retail-oriented suburbs home to many residents who work in Tampa at high-income jobs. Although they have relatively low unemployment rates, the otherwise growing region has experienced declines in construction and property values since 2008 at levels similar to other areas in the state.

Hillsborough County tops the state for land in berries, primarily due to the winter strawberry fields in and around the coincidentally, though aptly, named Plant City (it was named for railroad developer Henry B. Plant). The region also has been a top producer of tomatoes and pork. Areas to the 15th's south also are known for phosphate extraction.

Lakeland, the district's largest incorporated city, is a company town whose economy primarily is supported by the corporate headquarters of Publix Supermarkets, a growing regional chain with locations throughout the South. The city also is home to call centers and distribution centers, as well as Florida Southern College.

The district is roughly 65 percent white, with substantial black and Hispanic populations. The 15th is primarily conservative-leaning, but areas closer to Tampa can be competitive. Republicans hold a slim lead over Democrats in voter registration in the 15th overall, with registered independents accounting for more than the difference between the two parties.

Major Industry

Retail, agriculture, service, distribution

Cities

Tampa (pt.), Lakeland, Brandon (unincorporated) (pt.), Plant City, Temple Terrace, Bartow

Notable

The self-declared winter strawberry capital of the world, Plant City hosts the annual Florida Strawberry Festival.

Rep. Vern Buchanan (R)

Capitol Office
225-5015
buchanan.house.gov
2104 Rayburn Bldg. 20515-0913; fax 226-0828

Committees
Ways & Means

Residence
Longboat Key

Born
May 8, 1951; Detroit, Mich.

Religion
Baptist

Family
Wife, Sandy Buchanan; two children

Education
Cleary College, B.B.A. 1975 (business administration); U. of Detroit, M.B.A. 1986

Military
Mich. Air National Guard, 1970-76

Career
Car dealership owner; copy and printing company owner; marketing representative

Political Highlights
No previous office

ELECTION RESULTS

2012 GENERAL		
Vern Buchanan (R)	187,147	53.6%
Keith Fitzgerald (D)	161,929	46.4%
2012 PRIMARY		
Vern Buchanan (R)		unopposed
2010 GENERAL		
Vern Buchanan (R)	183,811	68.9%
James T. Golden (D)	83,123	31.1%

Previous Winning Percentages
2008 (56%); 2006 (50%)

Elected 2006; 4th term

Ethics inquiries didn't kill Buchanan at the polls in 2012, and he'll find out in the 113th Congress if he emerged any stronger. Connections he made as a top fundraiser for House Republicans could help him when dealing with his own party, and his avoidance of overt partisanship might qualify him as a negotiator as Congress mulls changes to the tax code and entitlement programs.

Buchanan survived multiple congressional and federal ethics snarls to beat back a challenge from Democrat Keith Fitzgerald in Florida's redrawn 16th District. He called the various allegations baseless and politically motivated.

One accusation was that businesses Buchanan owned had illegally reimbursed employees donating to his campaign. The Federal Election Commission rejected those claims in 2011.

In a separate inquiry, the House Ethics Committee concluded that Buchanan failed to report certain income sources on his congressional financial disclosure forms — but the panel took no action because he corrected the errors.

The Justice Department was also said to be investigating Buchanan, who remains tangled in messy legal battles with a former business partner. But the only action taken was against a Buchanan donor, for pass-through contributions that Buchanan said were made without his knowledge.

The whole situation was made more sensitive by Buchanan's role as vice chairman of finance for the National Republican Congressional Committee during the 112th Congress (2011-12) — essentially, he was one of the most important GOP fundraisers in the House. Buchanan has no role with the NRCC in the 113th Congress (2013-14).

"I am honored by your trust in me," Buchanan told supporters on Election Night 2012. He told the Sarasota Herald-Tribune: "I'm getting more seniority, and I think I can have a bigger impact for the country going forward."

He has a seat on the Ways and Means Committee, which is a good place to start. A businessman who made his latest fortune in auto dealerships, Buchanan says the tax code should be reworked. He wrote in a Bradenton Herald op-ed in that "the guiding principle of this effort must be tax simplification."

Ways and Means Republicans have laid out their vision of a simplified code: fewer tax brackets with lower rates (on both the individual and corporate sides) and fewer exemptions and credits. With the Senate and White House still under Democratic control, the details of that vision are up for negotiation, and Buchanan could help.

Buchanan has said that "it is a problem in our country when people are hard-core partisan." His first two terms were in the minority, and his voting record from those years shows some flexibility. He backed a Democrat-written measure allowing the federal government to negotiate prescription drug prices on behalf of Medicare recipients. He subsequently voted with Democrats to override President George W. Bush's veto of a bill to expand the Children's Health Insurance Program, which covers children whose low-income families make too much money to qualify for Medicaid.

He now sits on the Health Subcommittee. Buchanan supports repeal of the 2010 health care law, but he also has worked on legislation with more potential for enactment. He introduced a 2011 bill to crack down on Florida's "pill mill" industry by strengthening state-based monitoring of prescription drugs and toughening the prescription standards for certain addictive pain drugs.

On the Trade Subcommittee, Buchanan endorses exporting goods to China as a path to job creation.

Buchanan backs GOP proposals to increase nuclear energy production and open Alaska's Arctic National Wildlife Refuge to oil drilling. But he opposes expanded drilling in the Gulf of Mexico, and he has supported a permanent ban on drilling within 125 miles of the state's coast. In the 112th Congress he also proposed a bill intended to discourage foreign companies from contracting with Cuba to drill for oil in its waters, which reach within about 50 miles of the Florida coast.

Buchanan isn't in the vanguard of cost-cutting Republicans, but he did make a splash in early 2013 with his bill to freeze U.S. aid to Egypt. "We're drowning in a sea of debt," he said on Fox News. "We can't afford to buy our friends anymore." He has said he wants to reassess all foreign aid.

A former owner of Ford and Dodge dealerships, Buchanan takes pride in having worked more than three decades as a businessman. He likes to say that he has "created jobs, met payrolls and balanced budgets," and that "no issue is more personal" to him than helping small businesses grow.

Like many of the winter residents who flock to the Gulf Coast, Buchanan is a native Midwesterner. He was born into a blue-collar family with five siblings that lived in Inkster, a small city near Detroit. His father was a factory foreman for a computer company, married to a stay-at-home mom. Buchanan earned an MBA from the University of Detroit after working his way through college. He served six years in the Air National Guard.

In his early 20s, Buchanan started American Speedy Printing Centers, which grew to about 750 outlets nationwide. In 1992 he resigned his last duties at the company, which entered bankruptcy. He has since paid millions of dollars to settle allegations of fraud and taking excessive compensation.

In 1990, he moved from Michigan to Florida, where he built his auto dealership empire. He was a top donor to the Republican National Committee, a fundraising chairman to Mel Martinez's successful 2004 Senate campaign, and chairman of the Florida Chamber of Commerce.

In the 2006 general election, he faced Democrat Christine Jennings, his former banker. Buchanan won by 369 votes in the third-closest race of the 2006 election cycle. Jennings contested the results, claiming irregularities and electronic voting machine malfunctions. But in early 2008, the Government Accountability Office concluded that the touch-screen voting machines appeared to have worked properly.

Jennings challenged Buchanan again in 2008. Despite the national Democratic tide across the nation and in Florida, Buchanan cruised to an 18-point victory. He defeated another opponent by 38 points in 2010.

In 2012, Fitzgerald, a former member of the Florida House, tried to make hay out of Buchanan's ethics troubles. But the attacks didn't persuade enough voters to unseat Buchanan, who took more than 53 percent of the vote. For the 113th, Buchanan co-chairs Florida's 27-member House delegation.

Key Votes

2012	
Extend a Social Security payroll tax cut and unemployment benefits	YES
Ease securities rules to expand small-business access to capital	YES
Extend for one year subsidized student loan interest rates financed by a cut in health care spending	YES
Cite Attorney General Eric H. Holder Jr. for contempt of Congress	YES
Create a visa program for foreign graduates in high-tech fields	YES
Extend most Bush-era income tax rates while allowing rates for top-bracket earners to rise (Jan. 1, 2013)	YES
2011	
Strike funding for F-35 alternative engine	YES
Prevent EPA from regulating greenhouse gas emissions to address climate change	YES
Extend certain provisions of Patriot Act for four years	?
Declare opposition to use of ground troops in Libya	YES
Overhaul patent law	YES
Pass compromise debt limit increase plan and establish future spending limits	YES
Allow consideration of measures to implement three trade agreements	YES

CQ Vote Studies

	Party Unity		Presidential Support	
	Support	Oppose	Support	Oppose
2012	94%	0%	23%	77%
2011	94%	6%	21%	79%
2010	89%	11%	39%	61%
2009	82%	18%	41%	59%
2008	80%	20%	44%	56%

Interest Groups

	AFL-CIO	ADA	CCUS	ACU
2012	19%	5%	91%	76%
2011	0%	5%	100%	72%
2010	0%	0%	88%	83%
2009	20%	15%	87%	88%
2008	40%	50%	83%	60%

Florida 16

Central Gulf Coast — Sarasota County; part of Manatee County

Situated along Florida's central Gulf Coast, the 16th District takes in all of Sarasota County and the populated western portions of Manatee County. Retirees and seasonal residents from the north are the backbone of the leisure-driven region. The 16th has one of the oldest and whitest populations in the state, with nearly half of its residents over the age of 50.

Sarasota and Manatee have intertwined economies, but some areas of the counties have markedly different characters. There are luxury mansions in beachside communities — especially along Longboat Key (shared by the two counties) — and museums, theaters and symphony performances in Sarasota, which cultivates a refined image. Away from the water, middle- and working-class neighborhoods dominate. Manatee County has the more working-class character. Its economy depends on service and retail employment, and it is home to light-manufacturing interests as well as a Tropicana citrus processing factory.

The region experienced steady population growth over the past decade, particularly among middle-class Hispanic communities and in planned retirement developments. The financial crisis and subsequent recession left both Sarasota and Manatee reeling as construction and tourism lagged. Tourists and seasonal residents still arrive at midsize Sarasota-Bradenton International Airport, however, and Bradenton is home to the IMG Academies — residential sports-training and academic facilities for top youth athletes in several sports. Local colleges include the Ringling School of Art and Design and the New College of Florida.

Republicans have double-digit voter registration leads in both Sarasota County and the 16th's portion of Manatee County, which lacks most of the county's rural footprint. Republican Mitt Romney took 54 percent of the district's vote in the 2012 presidential contest.

Major Industry
Service, tourism, health care

Cities
North Port, Sarasota, Bradenton, Venice

Notable
The John and Mable Ringling Museum of Art, located on the Sarasota Bay, boasts the mansion once owned by John Ringling.

Rep. Tom Rooney (R)

Capitol Office
225-5792
rooney.house.gov
221 Cannon Bldg. 20515-0916; fax 225-3132

Committees
Appropriations
Select Intelligence

Residence
Okeechobee

Born
Nov. 21, 1970; Philadelphia, Pa.

Religion
Roman Catholic

Family
Wife, Tara Rooney; three children

Education
Syracuse U., attended 1989; Washington & Jefferson College, B.A. 1993 (English literature); U. of Florida, M.A. 1996 (political science); U. of Miami, J.D. 1999

Military
Army, 2000-04

Career
Lawyer; children's services organization director; military and state prosecutor; college instructor; congressional aide

Political Highlights
No previous office

ELECTION RESULTS

2012 GENERAL		
Tom Rooney (R)	165,488	58.6%
William Bronson (D)	116,766	41.4%
2012 PRIMARY		
Tom Rooney (R)	37,881	73.2%
Joe Arnold (R)	13,871	26.8%
2010 GENERAL		
Tom Rooney (R)	162,285	66.8%
Jim Horn (D)	80,327	33.1%

Previous Winning Percentages
2008 (60%)

Elected 2008; 3rd term

Rooney has a competitive nature, but when delivering tough words he does so in a sedate, collected manner. The former Army lawyer lines up with conservatives, has a national security focus and works on the GOP leadership team as a deputy whip.

Competition seems to run in the veins of the Rooney family. Rooney's grandfather, Art, founded the Pittsburgh Steelers in 1933, and the family still runs the team. (Rooney was a teenage water boy.) His father operated horse- and dog-racing tracks, and Rooney played college football. He suits up for the GOP in the Congressional Baseball Game, won the 2012 trap-shooting award at the Congressional Sportsmen's Caucus shootout and has one of the better golf handicaps on Capitol Hill.

Rooney has said that he's looking to leave Congress by the time his kids start playing high school sports, near the end of this decade. "My dad never missed a game of mine in football, basketball or baseball," he said. "I want to be full-time able to do those things."

He's keeping busy until then. Rooney in the 113th Congress (2013-14) continues his service on the Intelligence Committee, and he has also joined the Appropriations Committee. He sits on the spending subcommittees handling military construction, the Justice Department and agriculture.

Rooney put himself in the middle of high-profile scraps during the 112th Congress (2011-12). He made nods to fiscal restraint and parochial politics with his 2011 attempt to kill an alternative engine for the F-35 fighter. For years, lawmakers were bitterly divided over whether the F136 engine was a necessary backup or a waste of money. Rooney — whose district contained a plant of Pratt & Whitney, the maker of the competing F135 engine — called the F136 a "luxury we simply cannot afford," and his amendment to kill $450 million for it was adopted with the help of cost-cutting GOP freshmen. The underlying spending bill wasn't enacted, but the Pentagon canceled the program shortly thereafter.

A few months later, he drew on his legal background to oppose involvement in Libya's civil war. Rooney, who was on the Armed Services Committee at the time, argued that President Barack Obama violated the War Powers act by not getting congressional consent for military action in Libya within 60 days of its commencing. The House rejected his bill to prevent spending on any "hostile" activities in NATO's intervention, but it was a catalyst for a slap at Obama. GOP leaders called up a resolution to authorize the use of force in Libya, which was rejected with considerable help from Democrats.

He opposed, however, the withdrawal deadline Obama set for Afghanistan, arguing that the United States should reassess its mission before deciding to leave.

When it comes to prosecuting the war on terrorism, Rooney wants detainees tried in military settings, not civilian courts. He was indignant when Michigan Republican Justin Amash tried to amend the fiscal 2013 defense policy bill to prevent the military from indefinitely detaining suspected terrorists caught within the United States. The amendment "sacrifices our national security in order to coddle foreign enemy combatants," he said. It was rejected.

He has criticized Republican teamwork more than once. He circulated a letter among colleagues in the summer of 2011 saying that an "intolerant, short-sighted perspective" had become "pervasive" within the Republican Study Committee, the group of conservative House members he left in June 2012. He suggested the RSC staff pushed too hard against those willing to accept compromise measures to reduce the deficit. Rooney was an early supporter of Mitt Romney's campaign, although he noted that some GOP lawmakers did not want to be seen "sympathizing with a moderate."

Rooney in the 112th chaired the Agriculture Subcommittee on Livestock, Dairy and Poultry, but he was relatively hands-off in that role. His panel held few hearings, and Minnesota Democrat Collin C. Peterson handled most of the dairy provisions in the House version of a 2012 reauthorization of farm programs (which was not enacted).

Rooney buys into the notion of "all of the above" energy production and introduced a sweeping bill to expand offshore oil exploration in Florida, nuclear power and renewable energy. As part of that push, he has called for the extension of tax credits for wind energy production, which many conservatives pan as government intervention in the marketplace.

He stays to the right on social issues. Rooney, a Roman Catholic, took to the House floor to protest the Obama administration's 2012 decision to require employers and insurers to provide coverage of contraception in health plans, regardless of religious objections. "I believe that this is a move by the Obama administration to establish secularism over religion," he said.

Many of Rooney's friends in Congress, such as California Republican Duncan Hunter, are fellow veterans. He has tried to improve medical care for veterans with traumatic brain injuries and mental health disorders.

Rooney spent his early years in Pennsylvania, and his family moved to Florida to operate a dog-racing track around the time Rooney began high school. He attended Syracuse University, then transferred to Washington & Jefferson College near Pittsburgh.

He spent a year on Capitol Hill working in the office of GOP Sen. Connie Mack of Florida, where he says he "got the political bug. I subscribed to National Review magazine and really bought into what William Buckley was talking about." Rooney met his wife while attending law school at the University of Miami, and they joined the Army together to serve as JAG officers. After a stint as a prosecutor at Fort Hood in Texas, Rooney taught constitutional law at West Point. Upon leaving the Army, Rooney operated a shelter for abused children for a few years, then went into private practice.

Rooney won a three-way primary in 2008 with 37 percent of the vote to face incumbent Democrat Tim Mahoney. Mahoney was favored to win re-election until late in the campaign, when he admitted to an affair with a former staffer. Rooney trounced him at the polls a few weeks later.

His old 16th District was cut in half when the congressional map was redrawn for the 2012 election. Rooney ran in the newly configured 17th district, which was more friendly to a Republican candidate. He clobbered Democrat William Bronson, taking more than 58 percent of the vote.

Key Votes

2012	
Extend a Social Security payroll tax cut and unemployment benefits	YES
Ease securities rules to expand small-business access to capital	YES
Extend for one year subsidized student loan interest rates financed by a cut in health care spending	YES
Cite Attorney General Eric H. Holder Jr. for contempt of Congress	YES
Create a visa program for foreign graduates in high-tech fields	YES
Extend most Bush-era income tax rates while allowing rates for top-bracket earners to rise (Jan. 1, 2013)	NO
2011	
Strike funding for F-35 alternative engine	YES
Prevent EPA from regulating greenhouse gas emissions to address climate change	YES
Extend certain provisions of Patriot Act for four years	YES
Declare opposition to use of ground troops in Libya	YES
Overhaul patent law	YES
Pass compromise debt limit increase plan and establish future spending limits	YES
Allow consideration of measures to implement three trade agreements	YES

CQ Vote Studies

	Party Unity		Presidential Support	
	Support	Oppose	Support	Oppose
2012	97%	3%	13%	87%
2011	96%	4%	23%	77%
2010	95%	5%	32%	68%
2009	90%	10%	30%	70%

Interest Groups

	AFL-CIO	ADA	CCUS	ACU
2012	14%	0%	92%	96%
2011	0%	5%	100%	88%
2010	8%	0%	88%	100%
2009	10%	5%	87%	96%

Florida 17

South central — southern Polk County, Port Charlotte

The 17th is the heart of Florida's agriculture sector, taking in vast sugarcane fields, citrus groves and vegetable farms. One of the state's geographically largest districts, the mostly inland 17th stretches from sparsely populated areas in Polk County to southern Lee County near Fort Myers. To the east, it takes in part of Lake Okeechobee; to the west, it includes rural outposts near Sarasota and Bradenton, and takes in Charlotte County's gulf coastline. The 17th encompasses six whole counties and parts of four others.

The citrus groves in Polk, Highlands and Hardee counties are among the nation's top producers of oranges, tangerines and grapefruit. The 17th's portion of eastern Manatee County is Florida's top tomato- and cucumber-growing region, although farm land is diminishing. Sugarcane, grown mostly near Lake Okeechobee, can strain the sensitive lake ecosystem and competes for local water resources.

Because of the low-paying and seasonal farm jobs, the region also has the state's highest poverty rates south of the Panhandle, exceeding 30 percent in Hardee and DeSoto counties. Coastal Charlotte County is the exception in the district — a chain of retirement communities draws tourism revenue and wealthy seasonal visitors. Slowed economic growth, however, has had an impact on development in areas such as Babcock Ranch, a master-planned community designed to run on solar energy.

The 17th, a district drawn during decennial remapping to consolidate swathes of rural land, has a mix of inland farmers and retirees on the coast. The population is about 70 percent white, with a growing Hispanic population. Voters are decidedly conservative and back the GOP at the federal level, but some counties in the district (DeSoto, Glades, Hardee, Okeechobee) have more registered Democrats than Republicans; the parts of those counties that are in the 17th still supported GOP candidate Mitt Romney in the 2012 presidential election.

Major Industry
Agriculture, tourism

Cities
Port Charlotte (unincorporated), North Fort Myers (unincorporated) (pt.)

Notable
During the 18th and 19th centuries, Charlotte Harbor was a refuge for pirates and the base for the Spanish pirate José Gaspar, known as Gasparilla, whose ship (Florida Blanca) was sunk in the harbor by the U.S. Navy in 1821.

Rep. Patrick Murphy (D)

Capitol Office
225-3026
patrickmurphy.house.gov
1517 Longworth Bldg. 20515-1004; fax 225-8398

Committees
Financial Services
Small Business

Residence
Jupiter

Born
March 30, 1983; Miami, Fla.

Religion
Roman Catholic

Family
Single

Education
U. of Miami, B.B.A. 2006

Career
Construction company executive; accountant

Political Highlights
No previous office

ELECTION RESULTS

2012 GENERAL		
Patrick Murphy (D)	166,257	50.3%
Allen B. West (R)	164,353	49.7%
2012 PRIMARY		
Patrick Murphy (D)	26,791	79.7%
Jim Horn (D)	3,843	11.4%
Jerry Lee Buechler (D)	2,984	8.9%

Elected 2012; 1st term

Murphy has the eternal gratitude of partisan Democrats — and maybe a few moderate Republicans — as the guy who beat Allen B. West. He's counting on centrist stands to expand his reputation beyond that victory.

Murphy, who was a registered Republican as recently as 2011, had no prior political experience before winning a House seat. He worked in his family's construction business, first as a laborer and then as an accountant. After several years as an auditor at Deloitte and Touche, he came back to the family business. He was a vice president in charge of its division handling disaster relief and environmental cleanup.

He says disgust with the tea party movement turned him into a Democrat, and his 2012 campaign was against one of the movement's biggest stars. West, who was elected in 2010, got national attention as an outspoken, incendiary and black Republican. He was loved by enough supporters to rake in more than $19 million in campaign funds, and hated by enough detractors that Murphy raised almost $5 million. It was an ugly campaign in a competitive district, and Murphy won by fewer than 2,000 votes.

Murphy sits on the Financial Services Committee, which suits both his business background and his fundraising needs. A member of the New Democrat Coalition, he has suggested allowing all companies to "expense all investment for the next three years" to promote job creation. He's also the top Democrat on the Small Business Subcommittee on Agriculture, Energy and Trade.

He has made public displays of political moderation. His first month in office, Murphy helped organize a bipartisan letter from 36 freshmen, urging congressional leaders to "go big" on long-term fiscal changes for the country.

Murphy also speaks of a balance between protecting the environment and promoting industry. "You have to have a long-term plan and long-term goals," he said. "You have to start transitioning to a greener energy economy."

Elected at age 29, Murphy is the youngest member of Congress.

Florida 18

Southeast — St. Lucie and Martin counties; northeast Palm Beach

Fronting the Atlantic Ocean along most of the Treasure Coast in St. Lucie and Martin counties and into the northeastern corner of Palm Beach County, the 18th provides a snapshot of the state since 2000: growing populations, increasing racial diversity, high foreclosure rates and continued reliance on tourism and agriculture. The district's population is focused near the coast while the west is mainly farmland and nature preserves, taking in a section of Lake Okeechobee.

The region's economy relies on tourism and agriculture — the district's citrus groves are among the nation's top producers of grapefruit and oranges — and light manufacturing. But local employment has not kept pace with the population boom driven by Hispanic immigrants and retirees, and the area has yet to recover from a yearslong foreclosure crisis.

St. Lucie County has among the state's highest unemployment rates and a median income below the state average. Martin County has fared better, with higher incomes, lower unemployment and a broader economic base of manufacturing and medical jobs. Jupiter, in the district's portion of Palm Beach County, and Port St. Lucie have had some success in recruiting biotechnology industry.

Although the 18th is mostly white, the Hispanic population here more than doubled between 2000 and 2010. St. Lucie County, which accounts for 40 percent of the district's population, has a larger share of black residents than the less-populous Martin County. Another 40 percent of the 18th lives in more affluent communities in Palm Beach County.

The district is politically competitive, with many independent voters, and generally divided geographically: Republicans outnumber Democrats in older Martin County and vice versa in younger St. Lucie; the GOP has an edge in registration in Palm Beach County. Overall, GOP presidential candidate Mitt Romney took 52 percent here in 2012.

Major Industry
Tourism, health care, agriculture, service

Cities
Port St. Lucie, West Palm Beach (pt.), Jupiter, Palm Beach Gardens

Notable
The Hobe Sound National Wildlife Refuge consists of forest, barrier islands and mangroves, and is home to turtle nesting and wading bird habitats.

Rep. Trey Radel (R)

Capitol Office
225-2536
radel.house.gov
1123 Longworth Bldg. 20515-1305; fax 226-0439

Committees
Foreign Affairs
Transportation & Infrastructure

Residence
Fort Myers

Born
April 20, 1976; Cincinnati, Ohio

Religion
Roman Catholic

Family
Wife, Amy Radel; one child

Education
Loyola U. Chicago, B.A. 1999 (communication)

Career
Radio talk show host; television anchor; public relations and domain registry strategist; newspaper owner

Political Highlights
No previous office

ELECTION RESULTS

2012 GENERAL		
Trey Radel (R)	189,833	62.0%
Jim Roach (D)	109,746	35.8%
Brandon M. Smith (NPA)	6,637	2.2%
2012 PRIMARY		
Trey Radel (R)	22,304	30.0%
Chauncey P. Goss (R)	16,005	21.5%
Paige Kreegel (R)	13,167	17.7%
Gary Aubuchon (R)	11,498	15.5%
Byron Donalds (R)	10,389	14.0%
Joe Davidow (R)	1,028	1.4%

Elected 2012; 1st term

Radel was a conservative radio talk show host and still acts like one. He is provocative, confident in his beliefs and steadfast in defending them. "I'm happy to talk to everyone, to work with everyone," he says. "But I will not compromise ultimately on my conservative values and principles."

Radel grew up in Cincinnati, where his father was a funeral director; he studied communications at Loyola University in Chicago. He spent some time abroad in Italy and has had backpacking adventures on several continents — Radel speaks Italian and Spanish.

He settled on a career in journalism, ending up in Florida as a television reporter. Radel later bought a local newspaper, sold it, became a news anchor, then switched to talk radio. Along the way he married a newscaster. He has said that opinion journalism energized him to run for office.

Most of his rhetoric is conservative. He pledged to never vote for a tax increase, and he says government's core role, "to protect life," applies to unborn children. He has showed some flexibility on immigration, telling Fox News that there's "a moral argument and a fiscal conservative argument" for providing a path to citizenship for children brought to the country illegally.

Radel has a seat on the Transportation and Infrastructure Committee, where he can look out for the maritime needs of his district, which is the southern terminus of the Gulf Coast. He also sits on the Foreign Affairs Committee.

Republican Connie Mack represented most of the territory covered by the 19th District, but he ran for the Senate. Radel's biggest competition in the GOP primary was Chauncey P. Goss, the son of former CIA Director Porter Goss. Radel was endorsed by Mack, while Goss was endorsed by former Gov. Jeb Bush and Wisconsin Republican Rep. Paul D. Ryan.

Radel lent his campaign around $200,000 for an ad blitz just before the primary, and his wife, on leave from her anchor job, appeared in a TV spot on his behalf. He won with 30 percent of the vote, then cruised in November.

Florida 19

Southwest — Cape Coral, Fort Myers, Naples

A haven for retirees flocking to the subtropical climate, shell-abundant beaches and golf courses, the solidly Republican 19th District marks the southern tip of Florida's chain of Gulf Coast barrier islands. The district takes in most of Lee County, including the adjacent cities of Cape Coral and Fort Myers, and snakes along the coastline of Collier County through Naples to Marco Island.

More than three-fourths of the district's population lives in Lee County, mostly between the shore and Interstate 75, which runs south into Collier County to Naples before turning east into the Everglades. Originally a retirement community built on undeveloped rural land, Cape Coral attracted young professionals and the population grew steadily for decades. Lee County long relied on its home construction industry but has been slow to recover from a housing market collapse. But areas such as affluent Naples are experiencing a rise in home values.

The 19th overall depends on tourism revenue and the white sand beaches in places like Sanibel and Captiva Island — areas also susceptible to hurricanes. The Southwest Florida International Airport brings visitors to the district.

The health care and service sectors, catering to the retiree and seasonal resident communities as well as a generally booming population, prop up the economy. About half of the district's population is over the age of 50, and many residents have moved to the area for the warm weather and laid-back lifestyle. Amid the overall population growth, the Hispanic population, which is now 17 percent of the district, has more than doubled since 2000.

Registered Republicans far outnumber Democrats in this strongly conservative district, and voters in the 19th routinely give statewide candidates among their highest vote totals. Environmental issues related to ecotourism, development planning and water resources are top priorities for local leaders.

Major Industry
Tourism, health care, service

Cities
Cape Coral, Lehigh Acres (unincorporated), Fort Myers, Bonita Springs, Naples

Notable
Sanibel Island's curved shaped and west-to-east shoreline makes it an acclaimed location for shelling.

Rep. Alcee L. Hastings (D)

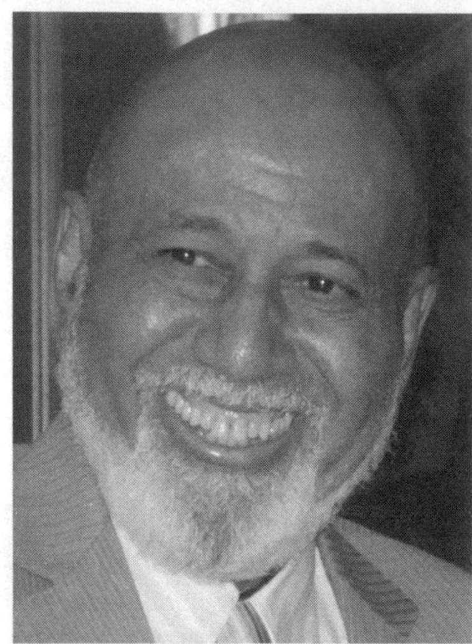

Capitol Office
225-1313
alceehastings.house.gov
2353 Rayburn Bldg. 20515-0923; fax 225-1171

Committees
Rules

Residence
Miramar

Born
Sept. 5, 1936; Altamonte Springs, Fla.

Religion
African Methodist Episcopal

Family
Divorced; three children

Education
Fisk U., B.A. 1958 (biology); Howard U., attended 1958-60 (law); Florida A&M U., J.D. 1963

Career
Judge; lawyer

Political Highlights
Sought Democratic nomination for U.S. Senate, 1970; U.S. District Court judge, 1979-89; removed from U.S. District Court, 1989; Democratic nominee for Fla. secretary of state, 1990

ELECTION RESULTS

2012 GENERAL		
Alcee L. Hastings (D)	214,727	87.9%
Randall Terry (NPA)	29,553	12.1%
2012 PRIMARY		
Alcee L. Hastings (D)		unopposed
2010 GENERAL		
Alcee L. Hastings (D)	100,066	79.1%
Bernard Sansaricq (R)	26,414	20.9%

Previous Winning Percentages
2008 (82%); 2006 (100%); 2004 (100%); 2002 (77%); 2000 (76%); 1998 (100%); 1996 (73%); 1994 (100%); 1992 (59%)

Elected 1992; 11th term

Hastings has overcome potentially career-killing controversies to become an expert on foreign affairs. His loyalty to the Democratic Party and popularity back home have helped him to become influential in his state, but his impeachment as a federal judge in 1988 has effectively blocked him from most leadership roles.

He is comfortable in the realm of international relations. "If you look at South Florida, you will see virtually every congressperson, Republican or Democrat, that comes here serves some time" on the foreign relations committees, he said. "That's the niche I chose."

These days, Hastings does not sit on the Foreign Affairs Committee, nor does he feel the need to do so: The panel "is a debating society, and I'm involved directly with world leaders," he says. In 2007, he was appointed chairman of the Commission on Security and Cooperation in Europe (aka the Helsinki Commission), an independent agency that focuses on democracy and human rights. He was the first African-American to chair the commission since its creation in 1976. In 2009, he handed the gavel to Democratic Sen. Benjamin L. Cardin of Maryland and assumed the role of co-chairman. Now simply a member, he has served on the commission for more than a decade.

Hastings defends the actions of the Obama administration while also laying out his own preferences for foreign policy. At a hearing on the U.S. military detention center at Guantánamo Bay, Cuba, he scolded European governments, complaining that they criticized the United States but refused to take custody of more terrorism suspects.

But he is not a fan of the facility. "These suspects should be tried in federal court," he said in 2012. "People detained there should be detained in prisons in the U.S."

In June 2011, the House rejected his resolution to authorize U.S. participation in NATO efforts in Libya; lawmakers of both parties had accused President Barack Obama of violating the War Powers Act by not getting congressional consent for military actions earlier that spring. "If I had my way, we wouldn't be in Libya at all," Hastings wrote at the time. "But I don't have my way, and here we are, and the solution now is not to cut off all funding and suddenly walk out."

Hastings takes an interest in human rights issues and has cooperated with other lawmakers on human trafficking legislation and getting additional money to combat HIV/AIDS in Africa.

The only congressional panel he sits on is the Rules Committee, which sets the terms for House debate. With Republicans controlling the House, he uses his seat and fiery oratory to protest GOP legislation and floor procedures. He was in form in early 2012, describing two GOP bills to overhaul the budget process: "What Republicans are trying to do is create a Frankenstein budget process: Add a procedure here, sever a rule over there, zap it with electricity, and now you have a budget process that proves tax cuts for the wealthy are the only way to grow our economy. But guess what: It still ain't human, and it certainly isn't humane."

He is well-liked by colleagues, and Hastings calls himself a "member's member" who serves as a resource for fellow lawmakers. Some still refer to him as "Judge" from his days on the U.S. District Court bench.

That job has been the source of some professional headaches. In 1983, a jury acquitted Hastings of charges that he solicited a $150,000 bribe in exchange for granting a lenient sentence. A federal judicial panel later concluded he had lied and made up evidence to secure that verdict. In 1988, by a 413-3 vote, the

House opted to impeach him, and the Senate, a year later, voted 69-26 to remove him from the district court.

After losing a bid for Florida secretary of state in 1990, Hastings in 1992 won a House seat representing the new 23rd District, drawn for the 1990s with a slight black majority. State Rep. Lois Frankel, a liberal white Democrat, took 35 percent of the primary vote to his 28 percent, but Hastings prevailed in a primary runoff with 58 percent. He won that November with 59 percent and has coasted to re-election ever since. (Frankel was elected in 2012 in the 22nd District.)

Hastings is liberal on most issues, but he departs from the Democratic Party position when he sees the need. He opposes some new regulations on for-profit colleges — viewed by many Democrats as predatory — saying those institutions have similar graduation rates as not-for-profit schools. The $787 billion stimulus law passed in 2009 "should have been $3 trillion," he said. And he dislikes the Obama administration's defined date for departure in Afghanistan. He prefers a gradual drawdown of troops.

He was a sharp critic of President George W. Bush's policies both at home and abroad, especially when he was a member of the Intelligence Committee. Hastings bowed out of the race for the Intelligence gavel at the start of the 110th Congress (2007-08) after Republicans raised the issue of the bribery case and his impeachment.

Hastings grew up poor. His parents began as factory workers and then became domestic servants to wealthy families. He earned a degree in biology at Fisk University and was accepted to medical school but chose to pursue a law career instead. He says he practiced "y'all come" law, taking on all manner of cases, from first-degree murder to traffic citations to adoptions: "You walk in my door and I will get you a solution." In 1979, President Jimmy Carter nominated Hastings for a U.S. District Court seat in Miami, and he became the first black federal judge in Florida.

In early 2011, the Ethics Committee, citing "insufficient evidence," closed an investigation of whether Hastings and five other lawmakers had improperly kept excess per diem funds used for official travel. Soon after, a staffer for the Helsinki Commission filed a lawsuit alleging sexual harassment by Hastings, but a federal district court dismissed the allegations early in 2012.

The legal bills related to defending himself against the bribery charges are in the millions. That has given Hastings one dubious distinction: poorest member of Congress. He takes it in stride, saying, "I will leave here in the category that I'm in."

For the 113th Congress (2013-14), Hastings is the co-chairman of the Florida delegation, along with Republican Vern Buchanan.

Key Votes

2012	
Extend a Social Security payroll tax cut and unemployment benefits	NO
Ease securities rules to expand small-business access to capital	YES
Extend for one year subsidized student loan interest rates financed by a cut in health care spending	NO
Cite Attorney General Eric H. Holder Jr. for contempt of Congress	?
Create a visa program for foreign graduates in high-tech fields	?
Extend most Bush-era income tax rates while allowing rates for top-bracket earners to rise (Jan. 1, 2013)	YES
2011	
Strike funding for F-35 alternative engine	YES
Prevent EPA from regulating greenhouse gas emissions to address climate change	NO
Extend certain provisions of Patriot Act for four years	NO
Declare opposition to use of ground troops in Libya	NO
Overhaul patent law	YES
Pass compromise debt limit increase plan and establish future spending limits	NO
Allow consideration of measures to implement three trade agreements	YES

CQ Vote Studies

	PARTY UNITY		PRESIDENTIAL SUPPORT	
	SUPPORT	OPPOSE	SUPPORT	OPPOSE
2012	97%	3%	88%	12%
2011	96%	4%	84%	16%
2010	99%	1%	83%	17%
2009	99%	1%	98%	2%
2008	99%	1%	13%	87%

Interest Groups

	AFL-CIO	ADA	CCUS	ACU
2012	95%	95%	30%	0%
2011	07%	00%	26%	4%
2010	92%	85%	25%	5%
2009	100%	95%	36%	0%
2008	100%	95%	65%	0%

Florida 20

Southeast — Lauderhill and parts of Fort Lauderdale and West Palm Beach

The 20th is one of the state's three black-majority districts, collecting mostly middle-class neighborhoods near the state's southeastern Atlantic coast. Two densely populated arms — one each in Palm Beach and Broward counties — that wrap around most of the neighboring 21st District are connected to the west by rural areas and protected swampland, including a significant portion of the Everglades. The district reaches the southern shores of Lake Okeechobee and into eastern Hendry County.

The 20th takes in black and Hispanic parts of West Palm Beach and Riviera Beach, and cuts past Palm Beach International Airport down the east side of Interstate 95 through Lake Worth and Boynton Beach. To its south, the 20th's Broward County arm, where most residents live, hits Lauderhill and parts of Fort Lauderdale and Pompano Beach. It misses prime beachfront property and marinas, getting instead areas with lower-income workers and middle-class professionals who work in local government, service and retail.

Much of the region saw rapid development between 2000 and 2010 due to an influx of retirees and fast-growing populations of Hispanic and Caribbean immigrants. But a housing market crisis caused property values to plummet and overall growth has stalled significantly.

The district's rural, western chunk is the nation's top producer of sugarcane and bell peppers. Sweet corn, rice and other vegetables are also harvested. Grown in the Everglades muck near Lake Okeechobee, sugarcane has long been the region's most profitable crop, but environmental and water resource issues persist.

The redrawn 20th contains nearly three-quarters of the population of the former 23rd, but the heavily Democratic district's footprint was reduced as decennial remapping accommodated the state's two additional seats.

Major Industry
Agriculture, government, service

Cities
West Palm Beach (pt.), Boynton Beach (pt.), Fort Lauderdale (pt.), Lauderhill

Notable
Lake Okeechobee is the largest lake in Florida and the second-largest freshwater lake wholly in the United States — its name means "big water" in the language of the Seminole Indians.

Rep. Ted Deutch (D)

Capitol Office
225-3001
deutch.house.gov
1024 Longworth Bldg. 20515-0919; fax 225-5974

Committees
Ethics
Foreign Affairs
Judiciary

Residence
Boca Raton

Born
May 7, 1966; Bethlehem, Pa.

Religion
Jewish

Family
Wife, Jill Deutch; three children

Education
U. of Michigan, B.A. 1988 (political science), J.D. 1990

Career
Lawyer

Political Highlights
Fla. Senate, 2006-10

ELECTION RESULTS

2012 GENERAL		
Ted Deutch (D)	221,263	77.8%
W. Michael "Mike" Trout (NPA)	37,776	13.3%
Cesar Henao (NPA)	25,361	8.9%
2012 PRIMARY		
Ted Deutch (D)		unopposed
2010 GENERAL		
Ted Deutch (D)	132,098	62.6%
Joe Budd (R)	78,733	37.3%

Previous Winning Percentages
2010 Special Election (62%)

Elected 2010; 2nd full term

Deutch pairs solid support of Democratic positions with an even-keeled demeanor as he takes on issues paramount to his Florida constituency. The Middle East and Social Security occupy the top spots on his agenda, and he has put himself into the middle of campaign finance debates.

Before running for office, Deutch (DOYTCH) worked as a commercial and real estate lawyer while supporting other people's political campaigns. He became very active in the local Jewish community in Palm Beach County. Through that involvement, he met Democratic Rep. Robert Wexler, a bombastic liberal committed to his work on the Foreign Affairs Committee.

Wexler endorsed Deutch's successful state Senate campaign, then four years later cheered on Deutch in the race to replace him (Wexler resigned from Congress to become president of the S. Daniel Abraham Center for Middle East Peace). Deutch now sits on Foreign Affairs, and in the 113th Congress (2013-14) he serves as the top Democrat on its Middle East and North Africa Subcommittee.

During the 112th Congress (2011-12), many critics said the Obama administration had distanced the United States from Israel, but Deutch stood by the president. "Most telling is what we hear regularly from Israeli officials," he said in 2012 — that in terms of military cooperation and intelligence sharing, "the relationship between the United States and Israel has never been stronger." He and his panel's chairwoman, Republican Ileana Ros-Lehtinen of Florida, introduced a 2013 bill to affirm strategic, security and scientific partnerships between the nations.

As a state senator, Deutch worked to get Florida to divest itself of its economic entanglements with Iran. In Washington, he built on that work as a supporter of sanctions against that nation. Deutch contributed to a package of sanctions, enacted as part of the fiscal 2013 defense policy law, that toughens penalties for those investing in the Iranian energy sector.

Deutch believes that a hard line is necessary with Iran. "Even as the economic pressure is ramped up, the administration's clear policy, that containment is not an option, is the additional piece that's so important in stopping the Iranian nuclear program," he said.

On security issues, Deutch can be close to the political center. He was one of 54 House Democrats to vote for a 2011 extension of expiring surveillance provisions in the anti-terrorism law known as the Patriot Act.

Southeast Florida is known for its retiree population, and Deutch has made a point of chiming in on the future of Social Security. He opposes raising the eligibility age for the benefits program and has proposed adjusting the formula for calculating cost-of-living adjustments to put more emphasis on price increases for goods and services. Deutch wants to phase in an elimination of the cap on wages subject to Social Security taxes.

In late 2010, Deutch reluctantly supported a one-year "holiday" that shaved 2 percentage points from the Social Security payroll tax. "Taxes are easy to cut but hard to restore," he wrote for The Huffington Post. After another extension through 2012, the lower rate expired at the start of 2013.

Deutch also sits on the Judiciary Committee, where he has been a voice for his liberal constituency, backing gun control and abortion rights. Deutch believes that special interests have dominated the committee's work, and he says it inspires him to pursue what he hopes will become a signature issue: a campaign finance overhaul.

Working with a coalition of advocacy groups, Deutch has proposed a constitutional amendment to counteract the Supreme Court's 2010 Citizens

United ruling, which paved the way for super PACs — groups that are independent of official campaigns and that can accept unrestricted donations from individuals or organizations.

Deutch has proposed requiring all political advertisements to be posted online along with the supporting data used to make claims in the ads, and he wants the IRS to examine the tax-exempt status of organizations involved in campaigning.

When Florida's secretary of state moved to purge ineligible voters from the rolls months before the 2012 election, Deutch worked with other members of the state's Democratic congressional delegation to publicize the inclusion of several World War II veterans on the proposed list of 180,000 names. "My fear is, ultimately we'll turn off an awful lot of people to the political process altogether," he said. "And then those outside interests will have won."

Health issues are important to his constituents, and Deutch pressured the Obama administration in early 2013 to finalize rules that would ensure mental-health treatments are covered by insurance. He has also laid some groundwork for less conventional health measures. In the state Senate, he sponsored a dollar-a-pack tax on cigarettes, with the revenue going to cancer research. He drafted a 2012 bill to create a special label for foods and cosmetics that don't contain known carcinogens.

Deutch grew up in Bethlehem, Pa., where his father was a painting contractor and his mother kept the company's books. His father — a World War II veteran with a Purple Heart — fell ill and retired early, and Deutch spent time as a teenager watching CNN and listening to his father's political views. He also dabbled in music and still plays the piano at campaign events.

He earned undergraduate and law degrees at the University of Michigan, where he cut his political teeth in the pro-Israel community and earned the Harry S. Truman scholarship for demonstrated leadership potential and a commitment to public service.

After a brief stop at the Washington law firm known today as Dickstein Shapiro, Deutch moved to Cleveland, closer to his wife's family. He eventually landed in South Florida in 1998 and began work at Broad and Cassel, the law firm where his brother also practiced.

The day after Wexler announced his decision to leave Congress, Deutch joined the race. Potential rivals dropped out as endorsements for Deutch flowed in; his supporters included Reps. Ron Klein and Debbie Wasserman Schultz and former President Bill Clinton, who became a key fundraiser.

Deutch handily won the April 2010 special election and the general election that November, despite the GOP wave that swept four Florida Democratic incumbents, including Klein, from office.

Key Votes

2012	
Extend a Social Security payroll tax cut and unemployment benefits	YES
Ease securities rules to expand small-business access to capital	NO
Extend for one year subsidized student loan interest rates financed by a cut in health care spending	NO
Cite Attorney General Eric H. Holder Jr. for contempt of Congress	NO
Create a visa program for foreign graduates in high-tech fields	NO
Extend most Bush-era income tax rates while allowing rates for top-bracket earners to rise (Jan. 1, 2013)	YES
2011	
Strike funding for F-35 alternative engine	YES
Prevent EPA from regulating greenhouse gas emissions to address climate change	NO
Extend certain provisions of Patriot Act for four years	YES
Declare opposition to use of ground troops in Libya	NO
Overhaul patent law	YES
Pass compromise debt limit increase plan and establish future spending limits	YES
Allow consideration of measures to implement three trade agreements	YES

CQ Vote Studies

	PARTY UNITY		PRESIDENTIAL SUPPORT	
	SUPPORT	OPPOSE	SUPPORT	OPPOSE
2012	98%	2%	93%	7%
2011	96%	4%	92%	8%
2010	98%	2%	97%	3%

Interest Groups

	AFL-CIO	ADA	CCUS	ACU
2012	95%	90%	25%	4%
2011	100%	80%	25%	0%
2010	100%	80%	20%	0%

Florida 21

Southeast — Coral Springs, Wellington

The 21st District takes in a slice of Palm Beach and Broward counties filled with gated communities, subdivisions and country clubs along a portion of the Florida Turnpike. Located inland from the Atlantic beaches without reaching the coast, the district features housing developments and condominiums that replaced previously rural land adjacent to the Everglades protected swampland.

Palm Beach County accounts for more than 60 percent of the district's population, and wealthy communities such as Wellington and Greenacres, as well as suburbs west of Delray Beach and Boca Raton, experienced many years of development. Wellington is particularly well known for its equestrian culture and is home to the International Polo Club Palm Beach. Financial and housing market crises, however, slowed growth and the area is not immune to the high unemployment rates common across the state.

To the south, Broward's more established communities such as Coral Springs and Margate hope to attract more biomedical and technology firms to compensate for stalled construction and financial services sectors.

The district is mostly white, but rapid growth among Hispanic and black communities since 2000 has resulted in a population that is more than one-third minority. There are a large number of affluent and older retirees as well as middle-class professionals who work in the local service and health care sectors.

The redrawn 21st largely follows the lines of the former 19th — although the district lost its portions of Boca Raton to the adjacent 22nd District — and remains a Democratic stronghold. Democrats hold a nearly 2-to-1 voter registration margin over the GOP and there are nearly as many unaffiliated voters as Republicans in the district. Middle East policy and federal assistance for the elderly are especially important issues for the district's Jewish residents and retirees.

Major Industry
Health care, financial services

Cities
Coral Springs, Wellington, Margate (pt.), Greenacres, Deerfield Beach (pt.)

Notable
Wellington's Winter Equestrian Festival hosts competitions for various age ranges as well as qualification trials for the U.S. Olympic teams.

Rep. Lois Frankel (D)

Capitol Office
225-9890
frankel.house.gov
1037 Longworth Bldg. 20515-6601; fax 226-3944

Committees
Foreign Affairs
Transportation & Infrastructure

Residence
West Palm Beach

Born
May 16, 1948; Manhattan, N.Y.

Religion
Jewish

Family
Divorced; one child

Education
Boston U., B.A. 1970 (psychology); Georgetown U., J.D. 1973

Career
Lawyer; county public defender

Political Highlights
Fla. House, 1986-92; sought Democratic nomination for U.S. House, 1992; Fla. House, 1994-2002 (minority leader, 2000-02); West Palm Beach mayor, 2003-11

ELECTION RESULTS

2012 GENERAL		
Lois Frankel (D)	171,021	54.6%
Adam Hasner (R)	142,050	45.4%
2012 PRIMARY		
Lois Frankel (D)	18,483	61.4%
Kristin Jacobs (D)	11,644	38.6%

Elected 2012; 1st term

The coastal communities of southeast Florida are packed with transplants like Frankel who have brought liberal sensibilities to their adopted home. She's a forceful politician who wielded power as the mayor of West Palm Beach — though she also has plenty of experience working in a legislative minority from her days in the Florida House.

Frankel grew up outside New York City, went to college in Boston and got her law degree in Washington; she was immersed in progressive and anti-war politics. She moved to Florida in 1974 to work as a public defender, then branched out into personal injury law.

She served three terms in the Florida House, but in her bid for the U.S. House in 1992, she lost a nasty primary battle to Alcee L. Hastings (who is now her colleague). Returning to the state House, she rose to become its minority leader. When term limits forced her from that job, she won election as mayor.

Frankel, a member of the Congressional Progressive Caucus, still sounds like a mayor when she suggests more federal policies to help small business, which she describes as "the real engine of our economy." She's on the Transportation and Infrastructure Committee — a natural fit, considering her long and recent involvement with local infrastructure needs.

Befitting a district with many Jewish voters (herself included), Frankel says she "will work in a bipartisan manner to fight any and all attempts to delegitimize Israel in the international arena and to ensure the safety and security of the Jewish state." She has a seat on the Foreign Affairs Committee and its panel with jurisdiction over the Middle East.

Frankel originally was poised to run against Rep. Allen B. West, a tea party favorite. But West ran in a neighboring district, and she faced former state Rep. Adam Hasner, whose bid for a Senate nomination had fizzled in early 2012. Frankel won by 9 points. She was named a co-chairwoman of the Democratic Congressional Campaign Committee program to recruit female candidates.

Florida 22

Southeast — Coastal Palm Beach, Broward counties

The 22nd District is a narrow strip of upscale communities along the Atlantic coast of Palm Beach and Broward counties. The district follows Route A1A from Palm Beach south to parts of Fort Lauderdale, where it then curls inland to take in most of the city of Plantation. Along the way it grabs parts of West Palm Beach and Boynton Beach, as well as Delray Beach and Boca Raton.

Much of the region is littered with ritzy resorts and golf courses that cater to tourists and retirees. Shipping is an important economic driver, with the Port of Palm Beach at the northern edge of the district and Port Everglades straddling the southern border with the 23rd District — combined, these ports provide some 13,500 jobs. The district's harbors are also frequented by passenger cruise lines.

Mostly white, the 22nd has a large number of Jewish residents; Hispanic residents make up nearly 20 percent of the population overall, while parts of Plantation are ethinically diverse and the city itself is one-fifth black. Most of the district's neighborhoods are composed of wealthy retirees and professionals who work in the region's health care, development or service sectors; although areas such as Delray Beach are not immune to higher poverty rates.

Security company ADT has its headquarters in Boca Raton, and an American Express call center in Plantation draws workers.

Although the district's boundaries only changed slightly during the decennial remapping process — the 22nd lost areas north of Palm Beach and south of Plantation — its politics shifted from Republican-leaning to Democratic. Registered Democrats have a nearly double-digit voter registration edge over the GOP here. Social Security, the Middle East and port issues top the political agenda for local officials, and residents are concerned about the progress of urban development and addressing transportation infrastructure needs.

Major Industry
Tourism, shipping, health care

Cities
Boca Raton, Plantation (pt.), Fort Lauderdale (pt.), Pompano Beach (pt.), Delray Beach

Notable
The International Swimming Hall of Fame Museum is in Fort Lauderdale.

Rep. Debbie Wasserman Schultz (D)

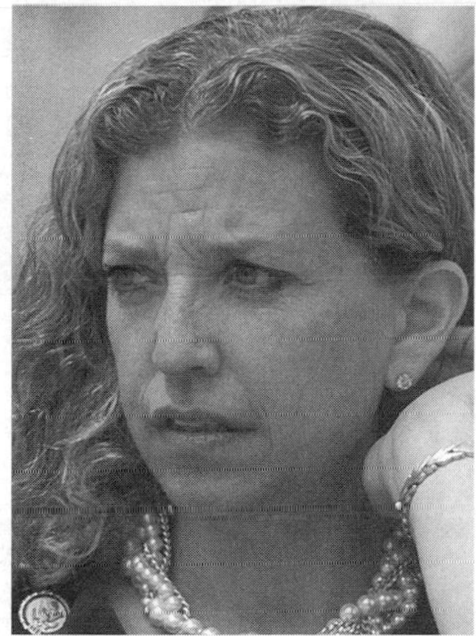

Capitol Office
225-7931
wassermanschultz.house.gov
118 Cannon Bldg. 20515-0920; fax 226-2052

Committees
Appropriations

Residence
Weston

Born
Sept. 27, 1966; Queens, N.Y.

Religion
Jewish

Family
Husband, Steve Schultz; three children

Education
U. of Florida, B.A. 1988 (political science), M.A. 1990 (political science)

Career
University program administrator; college instructor; state legislative aide

Political Highlights
Fla. House, 1992-2000 (Democratic leader pro tempore, 2000); Fla. Senate, 2000-04; Democratic National Committee chairwoman, 2011-present

ELECTION RESULTS

2012 GENERAL

Debbie Wasserman Schultz (D)	174,205	63.2%
Karen Harrington (R)	98,096	35.6%
Ilya Katz (NPA)	3,129	1.1%

2012 PRIMARY

Debbie Wasserman Schultz (D)	unopposed

2010 GENERAL

Debbie Wasserman Schultz (D)	100,787	60.1%
Karen Harrington (R)	63,845	38.1%

Previous Winning Percentages
2008 (77%); 2006 (100%); 2004 (70%)

Elected 2004; 5th term

Americans with functioning televisions are at least aware of Wasserman Schultz. Those who follow politics likely have a strong opinion of her. Since taking over as chairwoman of the Democratic National Committee, she has been a tireless propagandist for her party, receiving both the praise and scorn that go with that partisan job.

Wasserman Schultz once said that she "never really wanted to do anything other than be a member of a legislative body." After 12 years in the Florida Legislature, she won election to the U.S. House at age 38. Democrats quickly appreciated her talents as a fundraiser and campaign operative, as well as her ability to connect with Jewish and women voters. She took on several assignments at the Democratic Congressional Campaign Committee, and in her second term she became a chief deputy whip.

She hoped to lead the DCCC in the 112th Congress (2011-12), but the job went to Steve Israel of New York. Another opportunity came along in April 2011 when DNC Chairman Tim Kaine of Virginia quit to run an ultimately successful Senate campaign. President Barack Obama nominated her to replace Kaine, and on her election she became the first sitting House member to hold the job since Cordell Hull in 1924.

Wasserman Schultz was characteristically energetic, if not as congenial as usual, in performing her duties. She appeared at more than 800 campaign events around the country. Already known as a confident debater, she made scores of appearances on news programs; in addition to carrying water for the Obama campaign, she beat Republicans over the head with the bucket. Wasserman Schultz played up standard attacks, casting the GOP as willing to destroy Medicare, hostile to women and beholden to the rich.

She seemed to get results: Obama was re-elected, carrying her hotly contested home state of Florida, and Democrats gained seats in both chambers. No other leadership opportunities opened up among House Democrats, and Obama nominated Wasserman Schultz for a second term at the DNC. "I'm going to continue to do what I've done from the first day I became a member of Congress, which is help Democrats win their elections," she said.

It wasn't always a smooth ride, however. Wasserman Schultz had a mess on her hands at the 2012 Democratic National Convention when it was observed that the party platform had been changed to remove references to God and the recognition of Jerusalem as the capital of Israel. There were boos from the convention floor when the language was restored, and many people present questioned whether a required two-thirds majority supported the change. Calling the omission a technical error, Wasserman Schultz said on CNN that "there wasn't any discord," which led journalist Anderson Cooper to muse that she was in an "alternate universe."

Reports emerged that the Obama campaign saw Wasserman Schultz as being too partisan to appeal to undecided voters, and she was caught several times contradicting herself or making dubious statements while attacking Republicans. A few conservative pundits welcomed the news of her second term, describing her as a good foil for Republican spokesmen. There's also talk in political circles that the DNC has been marginalized by political organizations controlled more directly by Obama.

Wasserman Schultz has less time for regular congressional business these days, but she keeps a few fires burning. She returned to the Appropriations Committee for the 113th Congress (2013-14) and is the top Democrat on its Legislative Branch panel, which sets spending for congressional operations (she was its chairwoman from 2007 through 2010).

She was once a member of the Judiciary Committee, and she still calls for stricter controls on gun ownership. Her best friend from Congress is Arizona Democrat Gabrielle Giffords, who was shot in the head by a mentally unstable man in Tucson in January 2011. Wasserman Schultz in 2012 read Giffords' resignation letter on the House floor.

She advocates stronger tools to combat the exploitation of children. Obama in 2012 signed a bill by Wasserman Schultz and Texas Republican Lamar Smith to boost the maximum penalties for some child pornography offenses and bolster the efforts of those fighting pornography or online predators.

Wasserman Schultz, who sits on the State-Foreign Operations Appropriations Subcommittee, has many Jewish constituents and favors robust support for Israel. She is fairly hawkish, voting for some anti-terrorism and defense policy measures. She also has business-friendly tendencies and voted for free-trade pacts with Panama, South Korea and Colombia in 2011.

Wasserman Schultz grew up in New York, on the southern shore of Long Island. Her father was the chief financial officer for a girls' clothing company, Roanna Togs; her mother was a horticulturist. She attended the University of Florida, her father's alma mater, earning both undergraduate and graduate degrees in political science.

She stepped into politics when she was an aide to Florida state Rep. Peter Deutsch, a Democrat. She followed in his footsteps, winning Deutsch's seat when he ran successfully for Congress. Local party bosses dismissed her, but she prevailed in a six-way primary and became, at 26, the youngest woman to serve in the Florida House. Eight years later she was elected to the state Senate. After four years there, she won Deutsch's House seat, taking more than 70 percent of the vote in the heavily Democratic district while he waged an unsuccessful Senate campaign. Even before getting elected to the House, she donated $100,000 from her campaign to help other candidates in 2004, exceeding amounts given by many senior House Democrats.

Her rise in politics has coincided with the growth of her family. Wasserman Schultz is married to a banker, Steve Schultz, and they have three school-age children, including a set of twins. Her family lives in Florida.

Wasserman Schultz announced in March 2009 that she had successfully battled breast cancer. She introduced legislation, which was included in the 2010 health care law, to implement an education campaign on breast cancer's threat to young women. In 2009, with Missouri Republican Jo Ann Emerson, she established a charity softball game featuring a team of female members of Congress; the game raises money for a breast cancer nonprofit. It's also another outlet for her competitiveness. Wasserman Schultz broke her leg sliding into second base in the inaugural game.

Key Votes

2012	
Extend a Social Security payroll tax cut and unemployment benefits	YES
Ease securities rules to expand small-business access to capital	YES
Extend for one year subsidized student loan interest rates financed by a cut in health care spending	NO
Cite Attorney General Eric H. Holder Jr. for contempt of Congress	NO
Create a visa program for foreign graduates in high-tech fields	NO
Extend most Bush-era income tax rates while allowing rates for top-bracket earners to rise (Jan. 1, 2013)	YES
2011	
Strike funding for F-35 alternative engine	NO
Prevent EPA from regulating greenhouse gas emissions to address climate change	NO
Extend certain provisions of Patriot Act for four years	YES
Declare opposition to use of ground troops in Libya	NO
Overhaul patent law	YES
Pass compromise debt limit increase plan and establish future spending limits	YES
Allow consideration of measures to implement three trade agreements	?

CQ Vote Studies

	PARTY UNITY		PRESIDENTIAL SUPPORT	
	SUPPORT	OPPOSE	SUPPORT	OPPOSE
2012	97%	3%	93%	7%
2011	94%	6%	92%	8%
2010	99%	1%	95%	5%
2009	99%	1%	97%	3%
2008	99%	1%	13%	87%

Interest Groups

	AFL-CIO	ADA	CCUS	ACU
2012	95%	90%	25%	0%
2011	88%	75%	40%	0%
2010	100%	90%	14%	0%
2009	100%	100%	40%	0%
2008	100%	100%	59%	0%

Florida 23

Southeast — Hollywood, Davie, Miami Beach

The 23rd District captures swanky night clubs and palm tree-lined beaches east of Miami and liberal suburban voters in Broward County. More than three-fourths of the district's population lives in Broward, taking in upscale communities from coastal Hollywood through Davie and part of Pembroke Pines toward the Everglades. The Miami-Dade County leg of the district runs north-to-south along the coast, taking in hotel-lined Miami Beach.

The district's densely populated portion of Broward is located south of Fort Lauderdale and Plantation. Suburbs such as Davie and wealthy subdivisions further west helped drive the state's population boom over the past two decades, but growth has been slowed by recent economic downturns.

Tourism is crucial here, and the economy is bolstered further by related industries. Cargo and passenger travel are important to the district, which hosts the expanding Fort Lauderdale-Hollywood International Airport at its northeastern elbow north of Dania Beach and the nearby Port Everglades, which straddles the border with the 22nd District. Hollywood's section of the port includes the largest cruise ship terminal in the world. Miami Beach is a resort city with a number of retirees and condominiums, as well as an established gay and lesbian community. The trendy South Beach neighborhood is known for its pastel Art Deco architecture, upscale boutiques and exuberant nightclub scene. Hollywood's primary employment sector is health care, with large hospitals that serve the region's retirees.

The district's Hispanic population (38 percent) continues to grow, and the majority-minority 23rd also has a significant black population (11 percent). Overall the area contained within the borders of the 23rd experienced a loss of white inhabitants between 2000 and 2010. Social Security, U.S. relations with Israel and gay rights are prominent issues, and Democrats dominate elections in the district.

Major Industry
Tourism, hospitality, health care

Cities
Hollywood, Pembroke Pines (pt.), Davie, Miami Beach, Weston

Notable
Miami Beach's Art Deco District consists of more than 800 buildings from the 1930s and 1940s, the world's largest collection of Art Deco architecture.

Rep. Frederica S. Wilson (D)

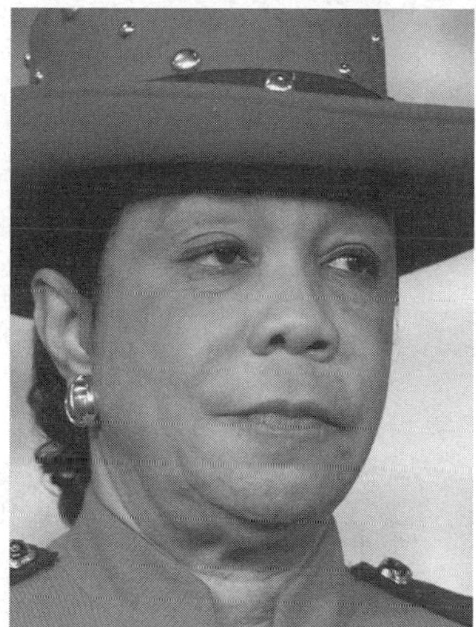

Capitol Office
225-4506
wilson.house.gov
208 Cannon Bldg. 20515-0917; fax 226-0777

Committees
Education & the Workforce
Science, Space & Technology

Residence
Miami Gardens

Born
Nov. 5, 1942; Miami, Fla.

Religion
Episcopalian

Family
Widowed; three children

Education
Fisk U., B.A. 1963 (childhood education); U. of Miami, M.Ed. 1972 (elementary education)

Career
At-risk youth mentorship program founder; elementary school teacher and principal; homemaker

Political Highlights
Miami-Dade County School Board, 1992-98; Fla. House, 1998-2002; Fla. Senate, 2002-10 (minority leader pro tempore, 2006-08)

ELECTION RESULTS

2012 GENERAL		
Frederica S. Wilson (D)		unopposed
2012 PRIMARY		
Frederica S. Wilson (D)	42,807	66.4%
Rudolph "Rudy" Moise (D)	21,680	33.6%
2010 GENERAL		
Frederica S. Wilson (D)	106,361	86.2%
Roderick D. Vereen (NPA)	17,009	13.8%

Elected 2010; 2nd term

Wilson prioritizes the needs of the underprivileged, particularly those in her northern Miami district. "I've always advocated for children, for seniors and for poor people," she says. "Not the middle class. Poor people. And I call it just like that. I don't say that I am trying to strengthen the middle class. I am trying to help people who are poor. The working poor."

While many of her House colleagues have embraced deficit reduction debates, the former educator's agenda features more-traditional Democratic initiatives: boosting employment and economic development through government spending. Wilson said the nation needs more economic recovery, and she does not want cost-cutting until then. "I don't think you can put people to work and make cuts," she said in 2011.

Wilson, a member of both the Congressional Progressive Caucus and the Congressional Black Caucus, was the oldest freshman elected to the House in November 2010. She was also one of the most widely recognized. Her trademark is flamboyant hats, a fashion choice she adopted from her grandmother. (Sadly, they're not allowed on the House floor.) Her legislative style isn't necessarily flamboyant, but she won't hesitate to speak her mind at the lectern.

She'll likely have plenty to say as a member of the Education and the Workforce Committee in the 113th Congress (2013-14). A former elementary school teacher and principal who served on the Miami-Dade County School Board, Wilson wants to play a role in revamping the George W. Bush-era education law known as No Child Left Behind. She says the law has hurt some students with its focus on testing and college preparedness.

As a member of the Science, Space and Technology Committee, she tries to boost federal programs for education in science, technology, engineering and mathematics. "People are losing their jobs not only because of downsizing or outsourcing," she said. "They are not able to blend into the new world of technology." She introduced a bill in the 112th Congress (2011-12) to create a pilot program for grants to local governments or community-based organizations for worker retraining. Wilson is currently the top Democrat on the Science committee's Technology panel.

Wilson sat on the Foreign Affairs Committee during her freshman term, and she still has a parochial interest in foreign policy: Her young, majority-minority district is home to many Haitian-Americans.

Citing reports during the 112th that deportations of Haitians had resumed for the first time since a devastating earthquake struck the country in 2010, Wilson urged the Obama administration to stop that practice. "Current political instability, widespread human rights abuses and the cholera outbreak make conditions on the ground too risky for Haitians to return safely," she told the South Florida Sun Sentinel.

Wilson has visited Haiti a number of times. She expressed concern in November 2011 that Haiti was seeking to build up its army; Wilson said those finances should go elsewhere.

While serving in the Florida Legislature, Wilson sponsored a law requiring the state to have a procedure to report missing foster care children. It is named after Rilya Wilson, a young girl from her community who went missing; Rilya Wilson's foster parent in February 2013 was sentenced to 55 years in prison. Wilson has introduced legislation to replicate her law on a national scale.

She also has introduced a bill to withhold federal transportation funds to states that do not enact laws prohibiting texting or using a cell phone while driving with a minor in the vehicle. "Too many Americans die tragically and needlessly every year due to distracted drivers," she said. She supported a two-year reauthorization of surface transportation programs in July 2012 but wants to see greater federal investment in transportation. Dredging the Port of Miami is also important to her.

Wilson was one of 95 Democrats to vote for the final debt limit agreement in August 2011. "My decision today is ultimately a decision to support President Obama in forging a historic bipartisan compromise to raise the debt ceiling," she said. Shortly after the debt ceiling vote, she introduced three "protection" bills to prevent cuts to Medicare, Medicaid and education programs. Later in the month, Wilson received media attention for stating that the tea party movement's only goal was making Obama a one-term president.

Wilson says her parents were some of the first African-American homeowners in Miami-Dade County. She graduated from Fisk University in 1963 with a degree in childhood education and received her master's degree from the University of Miami.

She worked as a teacher and Head Start coordinator but eventually stepped away from those jobs to raise her three children. When she came back to education, she worked as an assistant principal at an elementary school. She later became the principal. Her first foray into politics was in 1992, when she won a seat on the Miami-Dade school board. One of her initiatives was to incorporate African-American history into teaching curricula.

State Rep. Kendrick B. Meek ran for the Florida Senate in 1998, and Wilson won the race to succeed him. Meek ran for the U.S. House in 2002, and Wilson succeeded him again, serving in the state Senate for eight years. While in the state Legislature, she teamed with Republican Gov. Jeb Bush on criminal justice issues and on removing the Confederate flag from the state Capitol.

Meek opened another door in 2010 by running for the U.S. Senate, leaving the overwhelming Democratic 17th District up for grabs. The primary was crowded, with a number of Haitian-American candidates on the ballot. Wilson won with 34 percent of the vote, which essentially guaranteed her a seat in the 112th Congress.

For the 2012 election cycle, Wilson was named a vice chairwoman for the Florida Democratic Party. She praised a district court decision to issue a permanent injunction on a new state voter registration law. She called the law a "blatant attempt" by Republicans to suppress the vote.

Wilson had no worries about her own re-election. Rudolph Moise, a Haitian-American who worked as an Air Force doctor, had finished second in the 2010 primary. But in a head-to-head matchup with Wilson in 2012, he garnered only a third of the vote.

She was unopposed in the general election for the newly drawn 24th District, which is arguably the most Democratic turf in the state.

Key Votes

2012	
Extend a Social Security payroll tax cut and unemployment benefits	NO
Ease securities rules to expand small-business access to capital	YES
Extend for one year subsidized student loan interest rates financed by a cut in health care spending	NO
Cite Attorney General Eric H. Holder Jr. for contempt of Congress	?
Create a visa program for foreign graduates in high-tech fields	NO
Extend most Bush-era income tax rates while allowing rates for top-bracket earners to rise (Jan. 1, 2013)	YES
2011	
Strike funding for F-35 alternative engine	YES
Prevent EPA from regulating greenhouse gas emissions to address climate change	NO
Extend certain provisions of Patriot Act for four years	NO
Declare opposition to use of ground troops in Libya	NO
Overhaul patent law	YES
Pass compromise debt limit increase plan and establish future spending limits	YES
Allow consideration of measures to implement three trade agreements	?

CQ Vote Studies

	PARTY UNITY		PRESIDENTIAL SUPPORT	
	SUPPORT	OPPOSE	SUPPORT	OPPOSE
2012	98%	2%	90%	10%
2011	97%	3%	89%	11%

Interest Groups

	AFL-CIO	ADA	CCUS	ACU
2012	95%	95%	17%	0%
2011	100%	85%	25%	0%

Florida 24

Southeast — Miami Gardens and part of Miami

The 24th is one of the state's three black-majority districts, reaching north from neon-lit high-rises of downtown Miami into part of Miramar in Broward County. Biscayne Bay forms most of the district's eastern boundary, excluding the ritzy beaches on the region's barrier islands.

Transportation and shipping are key — the district hosts sprawling freeways, a regional airport and the Port of Miami. Miami International Airport is in the neighboring 27th. But the area has struggled with foreclosures, falling property values and job losses in both finance and construction sectors.

The district takes in lower-income communities on both sides of Interstate 95 in Miami Gardens, Opa-Locka and North Miami. Liberty City and Little Haiti — home to many Creole-speaking immigrants — are among Miami's poorest communities. Suburban North Miami has a booming population of young families, while North Miami Beach has long been a retirement destination with an established Jewish community and many new Chinese and Caribbean immigrants. In the district's slice of Broward County, Miramar is more affluent.

White residents have been moving out of the district and black and Hispanic populations have been growing; minorities make up nearly 90 percent of the population here, giving the 24th the smallest proportion of white residents and the largest proportion of black residents statewide. It is also home to a significant Caribbean community, and many residents speak a language other than English at home. With half of its residents under the age of 35, it is one of Florida's youngest districts.

Voter turnout tends to lag behind other districts statewide, but Democrats dominate in elections, routinely giving federal and statewide Democratic candidates more than 80 percent of the vote.

Major Industry

Tourism, service, transportation

Cities

North Miami, Miami (pt.), Miami Gardens, Miramar (pt.), North Miami Beach

Notable

The Sun Life Stadium in Miami Gardens hosts the NFL's Miami Dolphins, college football's University of Miami Hurricanes and the annual Orange Bowl game; Miami's American Airlines Arena is home to basketball's Heat.

Rep. Mario Diaz-Balart (R)

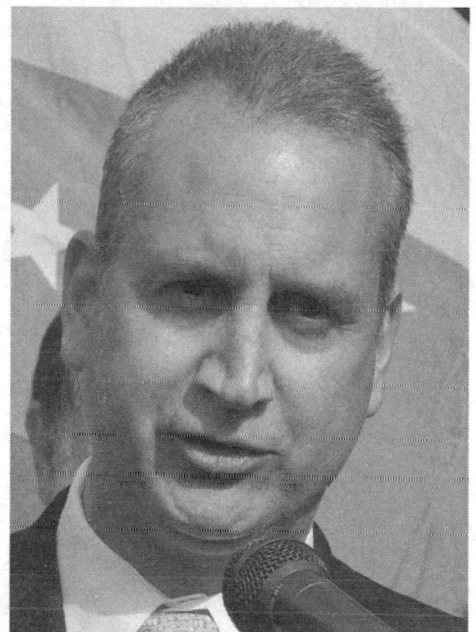

Capitol Office
225-4211
mariodiazbalart.house.gov
436 Cannon Bldg. 20515-0921; fax 225-8576

Committees
Appropriations

Residence
Miami

Born
Sept. 25, 1961; Fort Lauderdale, Fla.

Religion
Roman Catholic

Family
Wife, Tia Diaz-Balart; one child

Education
U. of South Florida, attended 1979-82

Career
Marketing firm executive; mayoral aide

Political Highlights
Fla. House, 1988-92; Fla. Senate, 1992-2000; Fla. House, 2000-02

ELECTION RESULTS

2012 GENERAL

Mario Diaz-Balart (R)	151,466	75.6%
Stanley Blumenthal (NPA)	31,664	15.8%
voteforeddie.com (NPA)	17,099	8.5%

2012 PRIMARY

Mario Diaz-Balart (R)	unopposed

2010 GENERAL

Mario Diaz-Balart (R)	unopposed

Previous Winning Percentages
2008 (53%); 2006 (58%); 2004 (100%); 2002 (65%)

Elected 2002; 6th term

Diaz-Balart has middle-class constituents and an ideological position in the middle of the Republican Party. He has no love for the Obama administration and sees a smaller government as the means to economic growth, but from his seat on the Appropriations Committee, he has backed away from deeper spending cuts proposed by conservatives.

The only issue where he's a hard-liner is the fate of Cuba. Diaz-Balart comes from a famous Cuban political family that flourished under leader Fulgencio Batista, before Fidel Castro and other revolutionaries took over. His father, Rafael Diaz-Balart, was once majority leader of the Cuban House; Mario's brother Lincoln served in the U.S. House for 18 years; and Mario himself served 14 years in the Florida legislature before joining his brother in Congress.

According to Ann Louise Bardach's book "Cuba Confidential," Castro has called the Diaz-Balarts his "most repulsive enemies." Diaz-Balart strongly opposes loosening travel restrictions and bans on economic contacts with Cuba, on the grounds that such engagement props up the communist regime.

Beyond that, Diaz-Balart, a member of the moderate Main Street Partnership, shows flexibility. He supports the GOP's drive to increase domestic energy production, but unlike many conservatives, he's OK with government support of renewable energy and has been wary of offshore drilling near Florida. He's more open to supporting organized labor causes than most Republicans. "I don't represent a wealthy area; I represent working-class, middle-class communities," he said. "So I have a great relationship with working folks. That's who I am."

He has a definite interest in an overhaul of immigration law, and he is part of a secretive House working group on that subject. "We have an immigration system that doesn't work for our national security interests, it doesn't work for our economic interests, it doesn't work for the folks who are here working hard, it doesn't work for the kids who were brought here by their parents," he said in 2012. "It doesn't work for anyone."

When a Senate working group released its principles for an overhaul at the start of the 113th Congress (2013-14) — which included a path to citizenship for those in the country illegally — he said they were "compatible with the discussions in the House."

Diaz-Balart has not been a prolific source of legislation — he introduced one bill in the 112th Congress (2011-12). But he is willing to negotiate or collaborate with either party on immigration measures. In 2010 he backed a bill to create a path to conditional legal status for some illegal immigrants who go to college or join the military. He was one of three Republicans to support the measure, along with his brother Lincoln and fellow Floridian Ileana Ros-Lehtinen.

In 2005, he voted with Democrats against a bill that tightened rules for immigrants trying to obtain asylum, and he sharply criticized Republican legislation that would have made being an illegal immigrant a felony. Diaz-Balart said the idea was "offensive, excessive and demonized hard-working immigrants." He calls his older brother Lincoln a hero for having written a 1997 law that granted legal residency to hundreds of thousands of immigrants who fled war-torn Central American countries.

Diaz-Balart joined the Appropriations Committee at the start of the 112th Congress, and his rhetoric on fiscal matters is mainstream for the GOP. He blames the Obama administration for high unemployment and slow economic growth. "The president's plan, which includes increasing regulations and taxes on job creation, is the primary reason why the economy is as anemic and sluggish as it is," he wrote in mid-2012. Diaz-Balart is a big supporter of free-trade agreements. He said pacts with Colombia, Panama and South Korea in 2011 were "a bright spot, but we had to bring the president along dragging and screaming."

But austerity hasn't been a hallmark of his work. He supported the Democrats' "cash for clunkers" tax credit in the summer of 2009 and was one of 40 Republicans who joined Democrats that same year to pass an expansion of the Children's Health Insurance Program. During the 112th he also opposed GOP amendments to apply across-the-board cuts to appropriations bills.

As a member of the Appropriations State-Foreign Operations Subcommittee, Diaz-Balart has been a voice against Republican calls for deep cuts to foreign aid. He has also used his seat to drum up support for U.S. democracy promotion programs and programs to combat drug trafficking in Mexico and Central America. "Obviously we have to make sure that foreign aid is well spent, but to me that's basically national security spending," Diaz-Balart said in 2012. "We do it for our sake, not for their sake. We do it for our national security interests."

Much of his congressional career has been spent in the shadow of his older brother — at one time critics dismissed him as "Lincoln Lite." But Mario differs from Lincoln. While Lincoln was born in Cuba and lived there until Fidel Castro forced their family into exile, Mario was born in Fort Lauderdale. While Lincoln is reserved, Mario is fast-talking and gregarious.

The youngest of four brothers, Diaz-Balart dropped out of the University of South Florida to work on the campaign of Miami Mayor Xavier Suarez in 1985, the same year he and his brother switched to the Republican Party.

In 1988, he was elected to the Florida House, and four years later he won a seat in the state Senate. Forced out by term limits in 2000, he ran successfully to return to the state House. When Florida got two new seats in Congress, he was appointed to head the panel drawing a new congressional map. He then drew a Hispanic-majority district, the 25th, for himself.

In his first federal election, Diaz-Balart outspent Annie Betancourt, a Cuban-American Democrat, 6-to-1 and won with 65 percent of the vote. He was unopposed in 2004 and won easily in 2006. In 2008, he faced a stronger challenger in Democrat Joe Garcia, the former head of the Cuban American National Foundation. Diaz-Balart won with 53 percent of the vote.

In 2010, he switched from the 25th District to the 21st District, a less competitive area left open by the retirement of his brother. He ran unopposed in 2010. The new congressional map for 2012 renumbered his district as the 25th, but it wasn't any more competitive. He had no Democratic challenger.

The Diaz-Balarts have a family connection to the Castros, despite their enmity. Mario's aunt was Fidel Castro's first wife and mother of Castro's son.

Key Votes

2012	
Extend a Social Security payroll tax cut and unemployment benefits	YES
Ease securities rules to expand small-business access to capital	+
Extend for one year subsidized student loan interest rates financed by a cut in health care spending	YES
Cite Attorney General Eric H. Holder Jr. for contempt of Congress	YES
Create a visa program for foreign graduates in high-tech fields	YES
Extend most Bush-era income tax rates while allowing rates for top-bracket earners to rise (Jan. 1, 2013)	YES
2011	
Strike funding for F-35 alternative engine	NO
Prevent EPA from regulating greenhouse gas emissions to address climate change	YES
Extend certain provisions of Patriot Act for four years	YES
Declare opposition to use of ground troops in Libya	YES
Overhaul patent law	YES
Pass compromise debt limit increase plan and establish future spending limits	YES
Allow consideration of measures to implement three trade agreements	YES

CQ Vote Studies

	PARTY UNITY		PRESIDENTIAL SUPPORT	
	SUPPORT	OPPOSE	SUPPORT	OPPOSE
2012	86%	14%	22%	78%
2011	89%	11%	32%	68%
2010	87%	13%	40%	60%
2009	74%	26%	44%	56%
2008	80%	20%	41%	59%

Interest Groups

	AFL-CIO	ADA	CCUS	ACU
2012	48%	5%	91%	60%
2011	43%	25%	100%	54%
2010	21%	20%	88%	79%
2009	52%	45%	80%	72%
2008	60%	55%	83%	52%

Florida 25

South — Northwest Miami suburbs, part of the Everglades

The Hispanic-majority 25th takes in densely populated suburbs and sprawling bedroom communities northwest of Miami, nature preserves, and a small portion of the Gulf Coast around Everglades City. Although nearly three-fourths of the district's population lives along its easternmost edge in Broward and Miami-Dade counties, the 25th stretches clear across the state via Interstate 75, or "Alligator Alley," to take in huge swathes of the Everglades National Park and the Big Cypress National Preserve.

Tourism is important, and resorts and passenger cruise lines are major employers near Miami. The ecosystems and array of wildlife — including panthers, bears and migratory birds — found in the 25th's national and state parks draw tourists, even if areas are inhospitable and difficult to navigate.

The portions of Broward and Miami-Dade in the district are a mix of upscale suburbs and middle- to working-class areas. Doral, at the southeastern edge of the district, is a residential luxury golfing enclave with a growing population near Miami International Airport (located in the 27th). Miami Lakes is a middle-class community dotted with lakes and golf courses.

Between the two cities is Hialeah, a densely populated, more working-class Spanish-speaking city. The district also takes in part of Miramar, a corporate office cluster with well-educated white-collar workers. Small manufacturing interests and technology companies provide jobs in the 25th.

Most of the district's predominately Hispanic population (70 percent) is of Cuban descent and is concentrated in Miami-Dade County. Many largely Catholic suburbs back Republican candidates, but Democrats have a wide margin in voter registration in Broward County; unaffiliated voters nearly outnumber Republicans in the part of the county in the 25th. Overall, Miami-area and rural Republicans give the GOP an edge in the district, and Mitt Romney took a 2-percentage-point win in the 25th in the 2012 presidential election.

Cities

Doral, Hialeah (pt.), Miramar (pt.), Miami Lakes

Major Industry

Tourism, manufacturing, technology

Notable

The Fakahatchee Strand — swampland, cypress stands, marsh and sawgrass prairie — is one of the region's protected preserves and boasts turtle nesting grounds and manatees, as well as orchids and mangrove forests.

Rep. Joe Garcia (D)

Capitol Office
225-2778
garcia.house.gov
1440 Longworth Bldg. 20515-6601

Committees
Judiciary
Natural Resources

Residence
Miami

Born
Oct. 12, 1963; Miami Beach, Fla.

Religion
Roman Catholic

Family
Divorced, one child

Education
Miami-Dade Community College, attended 1982-84; U. of Miami, B.A. 1987 (politics & public affairs), J.D. 1991

Career
Engineering and design firm executive; political activist; Cuban advocacy organization director

Political Highlights
Candidate for Miami-Dade Commission, 1993; Florida Public Service Commission, 1994-2000 (chairman, 1999-2000); Miami-Dade County Democratic Party chairman, 2007-08; Democratic nominee for U.S. House, 2008; Energy Department director for minority economic impact, 2009-10; Democratic nominee for U.S. House, 2010

ELECTION RESULTS

2012 GENERAL		
Joe Garcia (D)	135,694	53.6%
David Rivera (R)	108,820	43.0%
Angel Fernandez (NPA)	5,726	2.3%
Jose Peixoto (NPA)	2,717	1.1%
2012 PRIMARY		
Joe Garcia (D)	13,927	53.4%
Gloria Romero Roses (D)	8,027	30.8%
Lamar Sternad (D)	2,856	10.9%
Gustavo Marin (D)	1,286	4.9%

Elected 2012; 1st term

The politicized Cuban-American community of South Florida has produced its share of leaders — but on the congressional level, they were all Republicans until Garcia's election.

Garcia's parents were Cuban exiles. In his 20s, he headed up a program that helps Cuban exiles resettle in the United States, and he was later the executive director of the Cuban American National Foundation. Before he started running for office, Garcia led a Hispanic outreach effort at the New Democrat Network, a Washington-based advocacy organization.

He sits on the Judiciary Committee and its immigration panel. Garcia wants any overhaul of immigration law to include a path to citizenship for those in the country illegally. On MSNBC in early 2013, he noted that GOP negotiators had softened on some demands: "For guys who don't believe in evolution, this is really good," he said. He's also on the panel overseeing the regulatory process and antitrust law. Garcia has experience handling both as the former chairman of the Florida Public Service Commission, which regulates power and water utilities. The job also gave him hands-on experience with energy policy, and he has a seat on the Natural Resources Committee. He opposes offshore drilling, which he believes threatens the Everglades — a huge portion of his district — as well as agriculture and commercial fishing in the region.

Regarding Cuba, Garcia envisions a "calibrated" policy that lifts existing bans on people-to-people contact, which he argues will promote American interests and values. A member of the New Democrat Coalition, he also supports greater engagement with Latin America through trade.

Garcia ran for the House in 2008 and 2010, losing the second race to Republican David Rivera. He faced Rivera again in 2012 and capitalized on ethics and criminal investigations swirling around the incumbent. He won easily. In spring 2013, however, Garcia's chief of staff (and lead political strategist) resigned amid allegations of election fraud in the 2012 Democratic primary.

Florida 26

South — western Miami-Dade County, part of the Everglades, Florida Keys

Forming the state's southern tip, the Hispanic-majority 26th includes all of Monroe County and most of inland Miami-Dade County. A vast stretch of the district's land is the protected swamps of the Everglades, and nearly all of the population is settled in the east and along U.S. 1 through the Florida Keys, a 120-mile-long chain of islands between the Gulf of Mexico and the Atlantic Ocean that was added to the district during decennial remapping.

In Miami-Dade, the rapidly developing suburbs south of Miami account for 90 percent of the population of the 26th. Decades of explosive growth in Homestead has been driven by Hispanic immigrants, and new infrastructure and health care facilities support a traditional agriculture economy. Miami-Dade's farmlands produce vegetables and avocados.

Tourism is the major economic driver of the Keys — which are vulnerable to hurricanes — and the economy depends on out-of-state visitors. The haven for diving and fishing has a laid-back and environmentally conscious focus. Key West revels in its independent atmosphere, boasting quirky art galleries, night clubs and an active gay community.

Mainland Monroe County is mostly swampland of the Everglades National Park, an ecosystem teeming with exotic wildlife. Environmental issues — including regulations on animal importation and invasive species, development, and infrastructure — remain top concerns.

The Hispanic population of the district includes a dense concentration of Cubans in suburban Miami-Dade, and has a mix of independent-minded voters who make the 26th politically competitive. While the Cuban population is stridently anti-Castro, support for the trade embargo with Cuba has softened. The GOP has a slight voter registration edge over Democrats, but more than one-fourth of the district's voters are unaffiliated; Barack Obama took the 26th in the 2012 presidential election with 53 percent of its vote.

Major Industry
Tourism, agriculture

Cities
Homestead (pt.), Key West

Notable
Key West is the southernmost city in the continental U.S. and is closer to Cuba, which is about 90 miles south, than to Miami, which is about 160 miles north.

Rep. Ileana Ros-Lehtinen (R)

Capitol Office
225-3931
ros-lehtinen.house.gov
2206 Rayburn Bldg. 20515-0918; fax 225-5620

Committees
Foreign Affairs
(Middle East & North Africa - Chairwoman)
Rules

Residence
Miami

Born
July 15, 1952; Havana, Cuba

Religion
Episcopalian

Family
Husband, Dexter Lehtinen; two children, two stepchildren

Education
Miami-Dade Community College, A.A. 1972 (English); Florida International U., B.A. 1975 (English & education), M.S. 1986 (education); U. of Miami, Ph.D. 2004 (education)

Career
Teacher; private school administrator

Political Highlights
Fla. House, 1982-86; Fla. Senate, 1986-89

ELECTION RESULTS

2012 GENERAL		
Ileana Ros-Lehtinen (R)	138,488	60.2%
Manny Yevancey (D)	85,020	36.9%
Thomas Joe Cruz-Wiggins (NPA)	6,663	2.9%
2012 PRIMARY		
Ileana Ros-Lehtinen (R)		unopposed
2010 GENERAL		
Ileana Ros-Lehtinen (R)	102,360	68.9%
Rolando A. Banciella (D)	46,235	31.1%

Previous Winning Percentages
2008 (58%); 2006 (62%); 2004 (65%); 2002 (69%); 2000 (100%); 1998 (100%); 1996 (100%); 1994 (100%); 1992 (67%); 1990 (60%); 1989 Special Election (53%)

Elected 1989; 12th full term

Lining the wall of Ros-Lehtinen's Washington office are dozens of photographs of her with world leaders — Germany's Angela Merkel, Afghanistan's Hamid Karzai and Israel's Benjamin Netanyahu among them. Catty-corner to that display hangs a row of smaller photos — pictures of the makeshift rafts Cuban émigrés have used to flee across the Gulf of Mexico to the United States.

Born in Havana, Ros-Lehtinen (full name: il-ee-AH-na ross-LAY-tin-nen) was herself a "political refugee," as she calls it, and that experience has formed her identity as a politician and shaped her lens on the world.

Ros-Lehtinen holds an uncompromising view of international relations, believing the difference between freedom and tyranny is stark and American policies should reflect that dichotomy. She espoused that view as chairwoman of the Foreign Affairs Committee in the 112th Congress (2011-12). Republican term limit rules forced her out of that job, but she chairs the Subcommittee on the Middle East and North Africa in the 113th Congress (2013-14). She has also joined the Rules Committee, which sets the terms for floor debate.

In her time as full-committee chairwoman (she was also the ranking Republican from 2007 through 2010), Ros-Lehtinen used her platform to rail against authoritarian regimes in Iran, Russia, China, Cuba and Venezuela. She criticizes Obama administration policies that she says are too accommodating toward such governments. Ros-Lehtinen was adamant as she introduced a 2013 bill to set sanctions for people or entities who contribute to the weapons programs of Iran, Syria or North Korea: "When it comes to these rogue regimes, diplomacy and engagement have not and will not work."

While Ros-Lehtinen's rhetoric can be fierce, her personality is not. The former elementary school principal is warm and voluble, fueled by her daily Cuban coffee and a love for what she does — from campaigning to fundraising to legislating to constituent work. "I like every part about this job," she says.

Little of Ros-Lehtinen's legislative agenda has made it into law, however, given that her stances on foreign affairs are largely at odds with the Democrat-controlled Senate. One top priority has been to overhaul the United Nations, an institution she says is anti-Israel and gives too much voice to bad actors across the globe. But her bill to restructure the U.N. funding system — opponents claim it would wipe out funding for the entire organization — hit a dead end after being marked up in committee.

Ros-Lehtinen did succeed in teaming with other hawks to push through tough rounds of sanctions against Iran in 2010 and 2012. And she helped shepherd legislation through the House that aims to improve sexual assault prevention and response in the Peace Corps. It was enacted in 2011.

Her antipathy toward Iran stems from her unyielding support for Israel, a position she says she developed after spending time engaging with Jewish constituents. The proportion of Jewish voters in her district has ebbed in recent years, thanks to redistricting and demographic changes in South Florida, but that hasn't dampened Ros-Lehtinen's defense of Israel's policies. The ranking Democrat on her subcommittee is Florida's Ted Deutch, who is Jewish and strongly pro-Israel.

She is fiscally conservative and has advocated deep cuts in U.S. foreign aid spending. But outside the foreign policy realm, Ros-Lehtinen is a moderate Republican. On a handful of social issues, Ros-Lehtinen has broken with the GOP, in keeping with the values of her Democratic-leaning district. She has, for example, been an ardent supporter of equal rights for gays and lesbians. In July 2012, she became the first Republican lawmaker to come out in support of gay marriage.

Ros-Lehtinen opposes the GOP's hard line on immigration policy and was one of only six Republicans to vote against construction of a 700-mile fence across the U.S.-Mexico border. She backs proposals to combine enforcement with an expansion of visas and a path to legalization for illegal immigrants. Unlike most of her party, she did not object to the 2012 policy directive by President Barack Obama to halt deportations of young illegal immigrants brought to the United States as children — though she did say Obama should have instead worked with Congress to pass similar legislation that she has co-sponsored every Congress since 2006.

International trade is vital to Florida's economy. Ros-Lehtinen opposed granting President Bill Clinton "fast track" authority — the power to negotiate trade deals that Congress can approve or reject but not amend. But in 2002, she backed such authority for George W. Bush. In 2000, she voted against granting China normal trade status. But she supported the 2005 Central America Free Trade Agreement and the 2011 pacts with Colombia, Panama and South Korea. She voted to normalize trade relations with Russia in 2012, though she said she was voting for human rights provisions in the bill.

Ros-Lehtinen's concern for Cuba and its treatment of political dissidents shaped her rise in politics. In 1999 and 2000, she led the forces arguing that 5-year-old Elián González, who was rescued at sea along with a disabled boat full of refugees, should be allowed to stay with his U.S. relatives. The boy's mother drowned in the crossing.

The Clinton administration favored having him returned to his father in Cuba, which was the eventual outcome. The island's state-run newspaper, Granma, called Ros-Lehtinen a "ferocious wolf disguised as a woman." She took it as a compliment and had "loba feroz" (shortened to "loba frz") stamped on a personalized license plate.

She was 8 when her family fled Cuba for Florida. After growing up in Miami and graduating from college, she became a teacher and ran a bilingual private school in South Florida. She says the experience of working with so many new immigrant families and trying to help with the challenges they faced is what first drove her interest in public policy.

In 1982, at age 30, Ros-Lehtinen became the first Hispanic woman elected to the state legislature after running a heavily grass-roots campaign in which she and family members knocked on every door in the community. In a 1989 special election to replace the late Democratic Rep. Claude Pepper, Ros-Lehtinen unexpectedly defeated three other candidates for the Republican nomination, then beat Democrat Gerald Richman with 53 percent of the vote. She was the first Cuban-American and first Hispanic woman elected to Congress. She has not been seriously challenged since.

Key Votes

2012	
Extend a Social Security payroll tax cut and unemployment benefits	YES
Ease securities rules to expand small-business access to capital	YES
Extend for one year subsidized student loan interest rates financed by a cut in health care spending	YES
Cite Attorney General Eric H. Holder Jr. for contempt of Congress	YES
Create a visa program for foreign graduates in high-tech fields	YES
Extend most Bush-era income tax rates while allowing rates for top-bracket earners to rise (Jan. 1, 2013)	YES
2011	
Strike funding for F-35 alternative engine	NO
Prevent EPA from regulating greenhouse gas emissions to address climate change	YES
Extend certain provisions of Patriot Act for four years	YES
Declare opposition to use of ground troops in Libya	YES
Overhaul patent law	YES
Pass compromise debt limit increase plan and establish future spending limits	YES
Allow consideration of measures to implement three trade agreements	YES

CQ Vote Studies

	PARTY UNITY		PRESIDENTIAL SUPPORT	
	SUPPORT	OPPOSE	SUPPORT	OPPOSE
2012	86%	14%	26%	74%
2011	89%	11%	31%	69%
2010	85%	15%	46%	54%
2009	70%	30%	53%	47%
2008	67%	33%	33%	67%

Interest Groups

	AFL-CIO	ADA	CCUS	ACU
2012	50%	5%	92%	57%
2011	46%	30%	94%	48%
2010	21%	30%	88%	70%
2009	57%	40%	73%	72%
2008	67%	65%	78%	32%

Florida 27

Southeast — Most of Miami, Coral Gables

The 27th has the highest concentration — more than 70 percent — of Hispanics of any district in the state and ranks in the top 10 among districts in the nation. The district takes in parts of Miami south and west of downtown, where Cuban and Central and South American immigrants form the political and cultural base. The 27th edges northwest to take in the Miami International Airport and into more working- and middle-class Miami Springs and part of Hialeah. It also follows Biscayne Bay south to take in the affluent and suburban coastal Coral Gables and Cutler Bay, stopping at the outskirts of Homestead, where the landscape becomes rural.

Little Havana, the spiritual home of Miami's Cuban community, is culturally vibrant but economically downtrodden. Baseball's Florida Marlins relocated to the neighborhood with a new stadium that was expected to be an economic boost, although the team has struggled to fill seats. Outside the urban core, Coral Gables is a well-manicured, wealthy residential area with Mediterranean revival architecture, home to the University of Miami.

Health care and transportation are the economic drivers here. Miami International Airport, a major hub for travel as well as freight shipping, recently completed a significant expansion. The district is home to Miami Children's Hospital and the region's largest hospital, Jackson Memorial, is nearby in the 24th.

The 27th lost the Florida Keys island chain and glitzy Miami Beach during decennial redistricting, but retained its GOP-leaning political base of Hispanic-dominated areas of Miami west of downtown. The district's Cuban population is still anti-Fidel Castro — older Hispanics especially tend to side with Republicans on foreign policy, but the younger generation tends to agree with Democrats on social welfare and the economy. Republicans barely lead Democrats among registered voters here, about 27 percent of voters are independents, and Barack Obama took 53 percent of the district's vote in the 2012 presidential contest.

Major Industry
Transportation, tourism, health care

Cities
Miami (pt.), Coral Gables, Cutler Bay, Homestead (pt.), Hialeah (pt.)

Notable
The Calle Ocho Street Fair in Little Havana is the center of Miami's annual Carnaval celebration.

GEORGIA

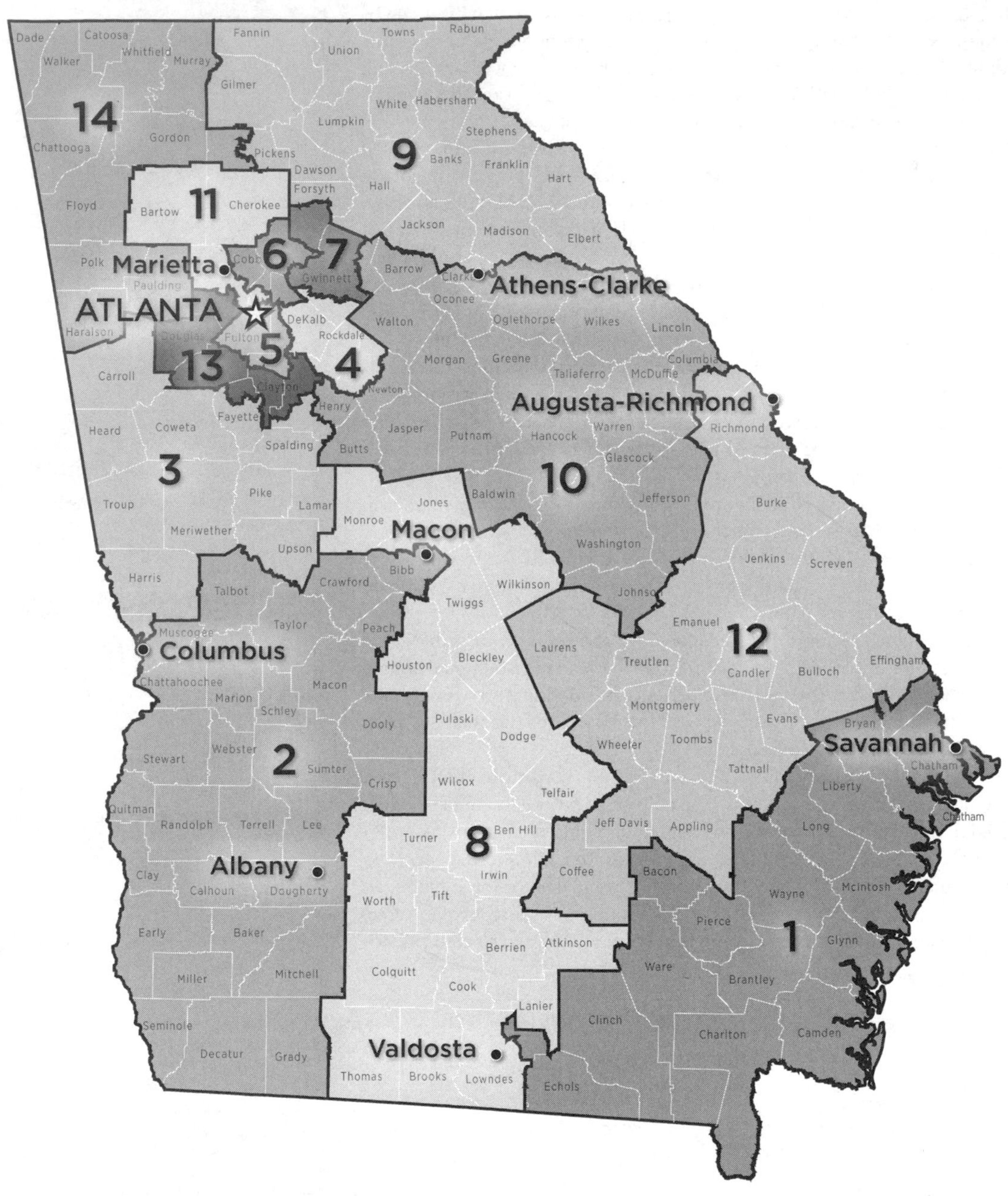

Dade
Catoosa
Whitfield
Murray
Walker
Fannin
Union
Towns
Rabun
Gilmer
White
Habersham
14
Gordon
Lumpkin
Stephens
Chattooga
Pickens
Dawson
9
Banks
Franklin
Hart
Forsyth
Hall
Floyd
Bartow
11
Cherokee
Jackson
Madison
Elbert
Polk
Marietta
Cobb
6
7
Gwinnett
Barrow
Clarke
Athens-Clarke
Paulding
Oconee
ATLANTA
DeKalb
Walton
Oglethorpe
Wilkes
Lincoln
Haralson
Douglas
Fulton
Rockdale
5
4
13
Morgan
Greene
Columbia
Carroll
Taliaferro
McDuffie
Clayton
Newton
Augusta-Richmond
Henry
Fayette
Jasper
Warren
Richmond
Heard
Coweta
Putnam
Hancock
Glascock
Spalding
Butts
3
10
Baldwin
Jones
Jefferson
Burke
Troup
Pike
Lamar
Monroe
Macon
Meriwether
Washington
Upson
Bibb
Jenkins
Screven
Harris
Crawford
Wilkinson
Talbot
Johnson
Twiggs
Taylor
Emanuel
12
Peach
Muscogee
Columbus
Laurens
Houston
Bleckley
Treutlen
Candler
Bulloch
Effingham
Chattahoochee
Macon
Marion
Schley
Montgomery
Evans
Dooly
Pulaski
Bryan
Dodge
Webster
Wheeler
Toombs
Savannah
Stewart
2
Sumter
Tattnall
Chatham
Crisp
Wilcox
Telfair
Liberty
Quitman
Randolph
Terrell
Lee
Jeff Davis
Appling
Chatham
Long
Turner
8
Ben Hill
Albany
Coffee
Bacon
Clay
Calhoun
Dougherty
Irwin
Wayne
Worth
Tift
Mcintosh
Early
Baker
Pierce
Berrien
Atkinson
1
Glynn
Ware
Miller
Mitchell
Colquitt
Brantley
Cook
Lanier
Clinch
Seminole
Charlton
Camden
Decatur
Grady
Valdosta
Thomas
Brooks
Lowndes
Echols

Gov. Nathan Deal (R)

First elected: 2010

Length of term: 4 years

Term expires: 1/15

Salary: $139,339

Phone: (404) 656-1776

Residence: Atlanta

Born: Aug. 25, 1942; Millen, Ga.

Religion: Baptist

Family: Wife, Sandra Dunagan Deal; four children

Education: Mercer U., B.A. 1964, J.D. 1966

Military Service: Army, 1966-68

Career: Lawyer; state prosecutor

Political highlights: Hall County Juvenile Court judge, 1971-72; Hall County attorney, 1977-79; Ga. Senate, 1981-93 (served as a Democrat; president pro tempore, 1991-93); U.S. House, 1993-2010

ELECTION RESULTS

2010 GENERAL		
Nathan Deal (R)	1,365,832	53.0%
Roy E. Barnes (D)	1,107,011	43.0%
John H. Monds (LIBERT)	103,194	4.0%

Lt. Gov. Casey Cagle (R)

First elected: 2006

Length of term: 4 years

Term expires: 1/15

Salary: $91,609

Phone: (404) 656-5030

LEGISLATURE

General Assembly: January-March, limit of 40 days

Senate: 56 members, 2-year terms

2013 ratios: 38 R, 18 D; 48 men, 8 women

Salary: $17,342

Phone: (404) 656-0028

House: 180 members, 2-year terms

2013 ratios: 119 R, 60 D, 1 I; 134 men, 46 women

Salary: $17,342

Phone: (404) 656-5015

TERM LIMITS

Governor: 2 terms

Senate: No

House: No

URBAN STATISTICS

CITY	POPULATION
Atlanta	420,003
Augusta-Richmond	200,549
Columbus	189,885
Savannah	136,286
Athens-Clarke	116,714

REGISTERED VOTERS

Voters do not register by party.

POPULATION

2010 population (est.)	9,687,653
2000 population	8,186,453
1990 population	6,478,216
Percent change (2000-2010)	+18.3%
Rank among states (2010)	9
Median age	34.5
Born in state	55.9%
Foreign born	8.9%
Violent crime rate	426/100,000
Poverty level	16.5%
Federal workers	129,041
Military	73,988

ELECTIONS

STATE ELECTION OFFICIAL
(404) 656-2871

DEMOCRATIC PARTY
(678) 278-2010

REPUBLICAN PARTY
(404) 257-5559

MISCELLANEOUS

Web: www.georgia.gov

Capital: Atlanta

U.S. CONGRESS

Senate: 2 Republicans

House: 9 Republicans, 5 Democrats

STATISTICS BY DISTRICT

District	2012 Vote for President Obama	2012 Vote for President Romney	2008 Vote for President Obama	2008 Vote for President McCain	Black	Asian	Hispanic	Median Income	Over 64	Under 20	College Education	Rural	Sq. Miles
1	43%	56%	44%	55%	29%	2%	6%	$43,077	12%	28%	23%	30%	7,983
2	59	41	56	44	50	1	5	32,049	12	29	14	36	9,626
3	33	66	36	64	24	2	6	50,155	12	29	24	40	3,838
4	74	26	69	30	57	4	10	47,414	9	30	29	4	497
5	83	16	80	20	58	4	9	40,708	9	25	38	<1	265
6	37	61	53	46	13	9	12	72,832	10	27	56	<1	299
7	38	60	39	60	19	12	18	59,843	8	31	38	1	393
8	37	62	39	60	31	1	6	37,232	13	29	19	44	8,712
9	20	78	24	75	8	1	12	41,786	15	28	19	64	5,211
10	36	62	40	59	25	2	5	45,314	12	28	23	47	7,096
11	31	67	36	63	16	3	11	55,813	9	28	38	10	1,071
12	44	55	44	56	35	2	5	39,950	12	29	19	40	8,185
13	69	30	62	38	54	3	10	47,004	8	31	27	6	715
14	25	73	28	71	10	1	10	42,700	12	29	17	41	3,623
STATE	**46**	**53**	**47**	**52**	**30**	**3**	**9**	**46,007**	**11**	**29**	**27**	**26**	**57,513**
US	**51**	**47**	**53**	**46**	**12**	**5**	**17**	**50,052**	**13**	**27**	**29**	**21**	**3,531,905**

Sen. Saxby Chambliss (R)

Capitol Office
224-3521
chambliss.senate.gov
416 Russell Bldg. 20510-1005; fax 224-0103

Committees
Agriculture, Nutrition & Forestry
Armed Services
Rules & Administration
Select Intelligence - Ranking Member
Joint Printing

Residence
Moultrie

Born
Nov. 10, 1943; Warrenton, N.C.

Religion
Episcopalian

Family
Wife, Julianne Chambliss; two children

Education
Louisiana Tech U., attended 1961-62; U. of Georgia, B.B.A. 1966 (business administration); U. of Tennessee, J.D. 1968

Career
Lawyer; hotel owner; firefighter; construction worker

Political Highlights
Sought Republican nomination for U.S. House, 1992; U.S. House, 1995-2003

ELECTION RESULTS

2008 GENERAL RUNOFF

Saxby Chambliss (R)	1,228,033	57.4%
Jim Martin (D)	909,923	42.6%

2008 PRIMARY

Saxby Chambliss (R)	unopposed

Previous Winning Percentages
2002 (53%); 2000 House Election (59%); 1998 House Election (62%); 1996 House Election (53%); 1994 House Election (63%)

Elected 2002; 2nd term

Chambliss won't seek a third term in 2014. He says he's fed up with partisan politics and doesn't expect breakthroughs in the near future. Even if his pessimism proves justified, he has work to do in his final years in the Senate. He's heavily involved with national security and has one last shot at shaping the next iteration of farm programs.

His retirement will close out 20 years in Congress. Chambliss was elected to the House in 1994, then to the Senate in 2002. He announced his departure in January 2013. "The debt ceiling debacle of 2011 and the recent fiscal cliff vote showed Congress at its worst, and, sadly, I don't see the legislative gridlock and partisan posturing improving anytime soon," he said.

By most standards, Chambliss is a solid conservative, but he has been involved in high-profile bipartisan negotiations on fiscal matters. Chambliss was a charter member of the "gang of six," a team of three Republicans and three Democrats that tried to produce deficit reduction legislation based on the work of a 2010 fiscal commission created by President Barack Obama. The group, which later expanded to eight, worked outside the formal committee system. In the 112th Congress (2011-12), it received both praise and veiled scorn from party leaders, but it never produced concrete language to realize its goal: $4 trillion in deficit reduction, achieved through spending reductions, revenue increases and entitlement program changes.

Sterner conservatives have groaned at Chambliss' consideration of revenue increases, and several prominent Georgia Republicans were thinking about challenging him in the 2014 primary election. He said his retirement was not based on those potential challenges.

Chambliss has, for his part, backed some dramatic taxation proposals. He's a leading Senate proponent of a bill to eliminate the IRS and replace most federal taxes with a national sales tax. He's also not a pushover for federal spending — Chambliss was among the lawmakers urging budgetary offsets for any money spent on relief for Superstorm Sandy.

In the 113th Congress (2013-14), Chambliss continues in his role as the top Republican on the Intelligence Committee. He's wary of cybersecurity bills that would increase the government's regulatory authority over privately owned computer networks. Chambliss prefers a voluntary system, where companies share information on threats and security with the government in exchange for liability protections. He has stated that the private sector can be more nimble responding to threats if it isn't bogged down by regulations.

He frequently states that the Obama administration should put less emphasis on targeted killing of terrorists and more emphasis on detaining and interrogating them, in order to improve intelligence gathering. He does not want detainees tried in civilian courts.

On the Armed Services Committee, Chambliss is the latest in a long line of guardians for his state's military installations — almost continuously since World War II, a Georgian has been on the committee. President George W. Bush in 2008 signed into law a Chambliss proposal that reduces the age for receipt of retirement pay by three months for every 90 days that a National Guard or Reserve member spends on active duty.

Chambliss wants to tighten the noose on Iran's economy to dissuade that nation's nuclear weapons program, and he approved of sanctions included in the fiscal 2013 defense policy law. "They're just not paying any attention to us," he said in November 2012. He also handles foreign policy as a member of the Commission on Security and Cooperation in Europe, which is widely known as the Helsinki Commission.

His other big policy interest is agriculture. He came by his expertise as a small-town lawyer in southern Georgia, representing peanut and cotton growers. "No one else in town wanted to take the time to read the regulations and study the law and figure out how the farm bill operates," he said.

Chambliss was the ranking member of the Agriculture, Nutrition and Forestry Committee when it wrote a long-term reauthorization of farm programs in 2008. He hoped that the legislation could benefit peanut farmers, whom he said were wronged in the 2002 farm bill — which ended a peanut subsidy program and guaranteed farmers no more than coverage of their losses for five years. But the 2008 law continued that policy with only modest changes.

He voted against a Senate-passed reauthorization in 2012 that would have ended direct payments to farmers and beefed up crop insurance programs. (It was not enacted.) Chambliss contends that crop insurance is not a particularly useful hedge against long-term price declines in a crop and that it's more favorable to crops grown in the Midwest. He says farmers need a mix of safety net programs, and the panel's current ranking Republican, Thad Cochran of Mississippi, is also sympathetic to Southern farmers.

Chambliss, the son of an Episcopal priest, says his family's frequent moves forced him to learn how to make friends quickly. When he was 5, his father was the announcer for the Rock Hill Chicks, a minor league baseball club in North Carolina. Chambliss dreamed of becoming a baseball star and played second base for the University of Georgia. After getting his undergraduate degree, he worked as a firefighter to pay for law school.

He lost his first bid for public office in 1992, when he sought the Republican nomination to challenge Democratic Rep. J. Roy Rowland in the rural 8th District. But Rowland's retirement left the seat open for the 1994 election. Chambliss was unopposed in the GOP primary and easily defeated Democrat Craig Mathis to capture the seat.

He declined entreaties to run against Democratic Sen. Zell Miller in a 2000 special election, at the urging of GOP Speaker J. Dennis Hastert. Chambliss thought he might get the chairmanship of the Budget Committee as a result, but it didn't materialize. Before long, he decided to challenge Democratic Sen. Max Cleland in 2002.

Three days after the Sept. 11 terrorist attacks, Chambliss got a boost in national prominence when Hastert picked him to chair a new Intelligence Subcommittee on Terrorism and Homeland Security. Chambliss criticized Cleland for opposing portions of President George W. Bush's plans to create a Department of Homeland Security. Democrats charged him with impugning Cleland's patriotism — a significant accusation, as Cleland had lost both legs and one arm while serving in the Army in Vietnam. Chambliss still won by 7 points, as Georgia continued a shift toward Republican dominance.

Democrats had high hopes of defeating him in 2008, and they nominated Jim Martin, a former state representative, Georgia commissioner of human resources and 2006 nominee for lieutenant governor. Chambliss won by 3 points, but he was just shy of an outright majority, which under Georgia law required a December runoff election. In that contest, he won by 15 points.

Chambliss has a long relationship with his state's junior senator, Johnny Isakson; they were business students together at the University of Georgia. They talk often, issue joint news releases and travel the state together. When their stay-at-home wives (who were in the same sorority) are in town, the couples frequently dine together. When they're not, Chambliss and Isakson are part of a group of Republican men who eat out together and gather at each other's homes. The pack has included Sens. Lindsey Graham of South Carolina, Tom Coburn of Oklahoma, John Thune of South Dakota and Richard M. Burr of North Carolina. House Speaker John A. Boehner, one of Chambliss' good friends, occasionally joins in.

Key Votes

2012	
Prohibit health insurance plans from denying coverage based on the sponsor's religious beliefs	NO
Require approval of the Keystone XL oil pipeline	YES
Ease securities rules to expand small-business access to capital	YES
Reauthorize farm and nutrition programs for five years	NO
Limit debate on a bill that would create private-sector cybersecurity standards	NO
Consent to ratification of a treaty setting global standard for the treatment of people with disabilities	NO
Provide $60.4 billion in disaster relief following Superstorm Sandy	NO
Extend most Bush-era income tax rates while allowing rates for top-bracket earners to rise (Jan. 1, 2013)	YES
2011	
Prevent EPA from regulating greenhouse gas emissions to address climate change	YES
Extend certain provisions of Patriot Act for four years	YES
Clear compromise debt limit increase plan and establish future spending limits	NO
Overhaul patent law	YES
Implement Colombia free trade agreement	YES
Limit debate on confirmation of Caitlin J. Halligan to D.C. Circuit Court of Appeals	NO
Extend payroll tax cut and unemployment benefits for two months	YES

CQ Vote Studies

	PARTY UNITY		PRESIDENTIAL SUPPORT	
	SUPPORT	OPPOSE	SUPPORT	OPPOSE
2012	94%	6%	44%	56%
2011	92%	8%	56%	44%
2010	98%	2%	42%	58%
2009	97%	3%	42%	58%
2008	95%	5%	72%	28%
2007	96%	4%	83%	17%
2006	94%	6%	93%	7%
2005	95%	5%	91%	9%
2004	99%	1%	100%	0%
2003	97%	3%	97%	3%

Interest Groups

	AFL-CIO	ADA	CCUS	ACU
2012	9%	0%	100%	84%
2011	16%	20%	82%	80%
2010	6%	0%	100%	100%
2009	17%	10%	71%	92%
2008	30%	25%	100%	76%
2007	11%	10%	82%	92%
2006	13%	0%	92%	96%
2005	21%	5%	94%	96%
2004	0%	5%	93%	96%
2003	15%	5%	91%	90%

Sen. Johnny Isakson (R)

Capitol Office
224-3643
isakson.senate.gov
131 Russell Bldg. 20510-1006; fax 228-0724

Committees
Finance
Health, Education, Labor & Pensions
Veterans' Affairs
Select Ethics - Vice Chairman

Residence
Marietta

Born
Dec. 28, 1944; Atlanta, Ga.

Religion
Methodist

Family
Wife, Dianne Isakson; three children

Education
U. of Georgia, B.B.A. 1966 (real estate)

Military Service
Ga. Air National Guard, 1966-72

Career
Real estate company president

Political Highlights
Candidate for Cobb County Commission, 1974; Ga. House, 1977-90 (Republican leader, 1983-90); Republican nominee for governor, 1990; Ga. Senate, 1993-96; sought Republican nomination for U.S. Senate, 1996; Ga. Board of Education chairman, 1996-99; U.S. House, 1999-2005

ELECTION RESULTS

2010 GENERAL

Johnny Isakson (R)	1,489,904	58.3%
Michael "Mike" Thurmond (D)	996,516	39.0%
Chuck Donovan (LIBERT)	68,750	2.7%

2010 PRIMARY

Johnny Isakson (R)	unopposed

Previous Winning Percentages
2004 (58%); 2002 House Election (80%); 2000 House Election (75%); 1999 Special House Election (65%)

Elected 2004; 2nd term

Isakson has baseline policy positions that are conservative and business-oriented. But he has spent about three-fourths of his legislative career as a member of the minority party, and he bends to meet Democrats when he thinks problems require timely results. That makes him a moderate, at least by the standards of his very Republican home state.

GOP dominance in Georgia is a recent development: Democrats controlled both houses of the General Assembly and the governor's mansion for 130 years, ending in 2002. Isakson, however, got his start in the 1970s.

He was in the state House for 13 years, more than half of those as the Republican leader. He lost a race for governor, but got back into office as a state senator for four years in the 1990s. He then lost a U.S. Senate race, but was resurrected with an appointment to chair the state board of education.

Isakson got his first taste of the majority in 1999, when he successfully ran to succeed House Speaker Newt Gingrich, who resigned. After three terms he won election to the Senate. Two years later, he was back in the minority as Democrats took control of that chamber in the 2006 elections.

So conditions have rarely been ideal for Isakson to win implementation of his policy preferences. He doesn't grumble about it — instead, he tries to meet fellow legislators in the middle. And when dealing with the Obama administration, he is often gentlemanly and willing to give officials the benefit of the doubt in hearings.

He has been increasingly involved in discussions of economic growth and the national debt.

As Congress tried to address the country's troubling finances in the 112th Congress (2011-12), Isakson got behind proposals based on the work of a special 2010 fiscal commission, known as Simpson-Bowles; the framework generally called for at least $4 trillion in deficit reduction through a combination of spending cuts, revenue increases and changes to entitlement programs.

"You've got to have the intestinal fortitude to put everything on the table, and I do mean everything," Isakson told Bloomberg News in late 2012. He offered a few more details in speeches in Georgia in 2011: increasing the Social Security retirement age, creating means-based Medicare and overhauling the tax code. The Finance Committee touches on all those issues, and Isakson was added to its roster for the 113th Congress (2013-14).

Isakson has personal expertise in housing, one of the most vexing sectors of the economy in recent years. His father was a Greyhound bus driver who flipped houses on the side. Isakson followed that early example to get into real estate himself. He is one of the wealthier members of Congress.

At the start of the 111th Congress (2009-10) Isakson won adoption of an amendment to an economic stimulus package to offer homebuyers a $15,000 tax credit in order to spur housing sales. (The amount was cut in half in the enacted version, as Isakson and most other Republicans refused to support the underlying bill.)

Isakson and California Democrat Barbara Boxer in 2011 introduced legislation to allow mortgage giants Fannie Mae and Freddie Mac to let borrowers take advantage of low interest rates and refinance their mortgages — even if they owe far more on their loan than their house is worth. The White House took administrative action later in the year to effectively implement that plan. Throughout the 112th, Isakson insisted that proposed Obama administration regulations requiring 20 percent down payments for many loans would be too restrictive and slow down the housing market.

Isakson also credits his father, a high school dropout, for his interest in education. After Isakson's older sister died as a young child, his father repeatedly told him he was destined to be the first in the family to attend college. The elder Isakson bought season tickets to Georgia Tech football games but deliberately parked two miles away from the stadium, so he could walk his son across the campus while selling him on furthering his education. Isakson eventually got a degree from the University of Georgia.

As a member of the House, Isakson helped write the 2002 education law known as No Child Left Behind. He now sits on the Health, Education, Labor and Pensions Committee. A reauthorization of that law sputtered out in the 112th Congress, but Isakson and three other panel Republicans did introduce a package of bills with their proposed changes, many of which involved increasing the authority of states in setting educational standards or allocating education funds.

Isakson specifically calls for an end to the standardized tests that measure "adequate yearly progress" of schools. "After 10 years of implementation, I believe that AYP has served its purpose in raising expectations and standards," Isakson wrote. "While I believe that schools should still report their progress, it is time for Congress to repeal AYP." He has also indicated that the law should allow more flexibility in assessing and serving non-English-speaking children and students with special education needs.

When dealing with labor and pension issues on the panel, Isakson puts Georgia first. He worked closely in 2006 with the late Edward M. Kennedy, a Massachusetts Democrat, on an overhaul of the law governing private pension plans. He successfully included provisions to give Atlanta-based Delta Air Lines and other financially strapped airlines extra time to fully fund their pension plans.

More recently, he has been a strong critic of the National Labor Relations Board, accusing it of giving organized labor unfair advantages. "The administration is attempting to circumvent the legislative branch of government and tip the scales in favor of unions through rule and regulation," Isakson said on the Senate floor in April 2012. Georgia has a right-to-work law.

Isakson and Washington Democrat Patty Murray are lead negotiators in the 113th Congress on a potential overhaul of worker training programs. A draft they worked on in the 112th would replace a host of smaller programs with one national job training system; it would also create an "innovation fund" to encourage states to form partnerships with business and education groups to train workers for the jobs in greatest demand.

Isakson was a member of the Foreign Relations Committee, but he gave up that assignment when he joined the Finance Committee.

With foreign operations spending on the chopping block, Isakson in 2011 opposed "disproportionate cuts" to development assistance programs. But he has also called for a more business-oriented approach to assistance, introducing a bill to require development programs to coordinate with the private sector in the countries they are helping. "Sustained economic growth through trade and private investment is the only thing that will lift developing countries out of poverty," he said. He still has a forum to work on the issue as the top Republican on the Finance subcommittee for trade.

Isakson lost the 1990 governor's race to moderate Democrat Zell Miller, who later revived Isakson's political career by appointing him to the board of education in 1996. He had a huge advantage in name recognition and campaign funds when he ran to succeed Gingrich, and he took 65 percent of the vote against five opponents in the special election.

Miller went on to serve in the Senate, and his retirement created the open seat that Isakson sought in 2004. He defeated Republicans Herman Cain and Rep. Mac Collins in the primary, then went on to defeat one-term Democratic Rep. Denise L. Majette with 58 percent of the vote. He won re-election by a similar margin in 2010.

Key Votes

2012	
Prohibit health insurance plans from denying coverage based on the sponsor's religious beliefs	NO
Require approval of the Keystone XL oil pipeline	YES
Ease securities rules to expand small-business access to capital	YES
Reauthorize farm and nutrition programs for five years	NO
Limit debate on a bill that would create private-sector cybersecurity standards	NO
Consent to ratification of a treaty setting global standard for the treatment of people with disabilities	NO
Provide $60.4 billion in disaster relief following Superstorm Sandy	NO
Extend most Bush-era income tax rates while allowing rates for top-bracket earners to rise (Jan. 1, 2013)	YES
2011	
Prevent EPA from regulating greenhouse gas emissions to address climate change	YES
Extend certain provisions of Patriot Act for four years	YES
Clear compromise debt limit increase plan and establish future spending limits	YES
Overhaul patent law	YES
Implement Colombia free trade agreement	YES
Limit debate on confirmation of Caitlin J. Halligan to D.C. Circuit Court of Appeals	NO
Extend payroll tax cut and unemployment benefits for two months	YES

CQ Vote Studies

	PARTY UNITY		PRESIDENTIAL SUPPORT	
	SUPPORT	OPPOSE	SUPPORT	OPPOSE
2012	92%	8%	45%	55%
2011	90%	10%	55%	45%
2010	93%	7%	42%	58%
2009	97%	3%	45%	55%
2008	94%	6%	72%	28%
2007	97%	3%	85%	15%
2006	97%	3%	93%	7%
2005	95%	5%	91%	9%
2004	99%	1%	89%	11%
2003	99%	1%	96%	4%

Interest Groups

	AFL-CIO	ADA	CCUS	ACU
2012	9%	0%	100%	80%
2011	16%	25%	91%	75%
2010	0%	5%	100%	91%
2009	17%	5%	86%	96%
2008	20%	25%	88%	76%
2007	11%	10%	82%	96%
2006	13%	0%	92%	96%
2005	21%	5%	94%	100%
2004	8%	5%	100%	95%
2003	0%	5%	100%	84%

Rep. Jack Kingston (R)

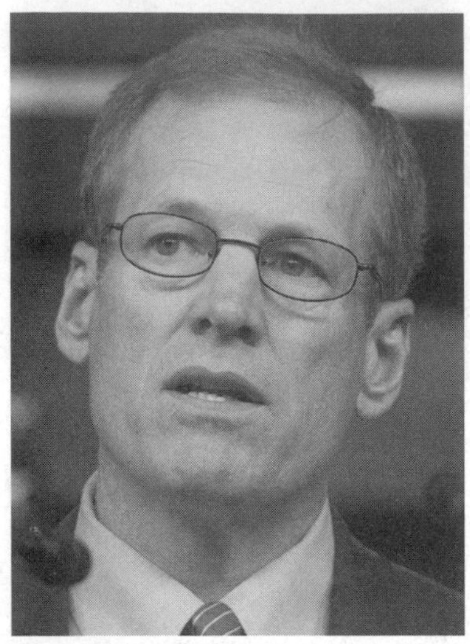

Capitol Office
225-5831
kingston.house.gov
2372 Rayburn Bldg. 20515-1001; fax 226-2269

Committees
Appropriations
(Labor-HHS-Education - Chairman)

Residence
Savannah

Born
April 24, 1955; Bryan, Texas

Religion
Anglican

Family
Wife, Libby Kingston; four children

Education
U. of Georgia, B.A. 1978 (economics)

Career
Insurance broker

Political Highlights
Ga. House, 1984-92

ELECTION RESULTS

2012 GENERAL		
Jack Kingston (R)	157,181	63.0%
Lesli Rae Messinger (D)	92,399	37.0%
2012 PRIMARY		
Jack Kingston (R)		unopposed
2010 GENERAL		
Jack Kingston (R)	117,270	71.6%
Oscar L. Harris II (D)	46,449	28.4%

Previous Winning Percentages
2008 (67%); 2006 (69%); 2004 (100%); 2002 (72%); 2000 (69%); 1998 (100%); 1996 (68%); 1994 (77%); 1992 (58%)

Elected 1992; 11th term

Kingston is the most conservative of the House "cardinals" — the 12 Republicans who lead Appropriations subcommittees. He has an easygoing manner, decent relations with Democratic colleagues and a firm commitment to shrinking federal budgets. "Washington has a spending problem," he wrote in The Atlanta Journal-Constitution in March 2013, "and the only way to solve it is through spending cuts."

Kingston plans to test his brand of conservatism in a statewide contest. Sen. Saxby Chambliss is retiring at the end of the 113th Congress (2013-14), and in May 2013 Kingston announced that he will run for that seat.

For now, he is the chairman of the Labor-HHS-Education Appropriations Subcommittee. He also has a seat on the Defense panel, and between those two assignments he has direct oversight of the biggest pieces of the federal discretionary budget.

Like most Republicans, Kingston hopes for changes to federal entitlement programs, which are widely accepted as the cause of most projected debt in the decades ahead. But he takes his spending cuts where he can get them. An August 2011 deficit reduction law set up about $500 billion in automatic spending cuts and gave Congress until the start of 2013 to settle on an alternative before they kicked in. Kingston in the Journal-Constitution called it a "boneheaded approach," but he wasn't upset when the cuts started taking hold. It "may not be the best approach, but with a White House and Senate that refuse to act, it is our best chance to reduce spending today," he wrote.

His preferences are more austere than those of most appropriators — of either party — but Kingston tries to produce spending bills that can eventually win enough bipartisan support to become law. He takes pride in good relationships with Democratic appropriators, including Rosa DeLauro of Connecticut, one of the House's most passionate liberals. DeLauro is the ranking Democrat on Kingston's subcommittee. It's a reversal of their roles from the 110th and 111th Congresses (2007-10), when DeLauro chaired the Agriculture Subcommittee and Kingston was her ranking member.

Kingston sees a role for federal assistance to people and communities, especially those affected by poverty. His mission is trying to get such services to run more efficiently, and his committee has jurisdiction over most of the biggest social welfare programs. At his first hearing as chairman, he advised agencies to "review programs and propose eliminations" of projects that are duplicative or stray from an agency's mission statement.

He had a similar agenda when chairing the Agriculture Subcommittee in the 112th Congress (2011-12). While moving the fiscal 2012 Agriculture spending bill through the House, he noted that there are about a dozen federal programs that will help feed a child younger than 5, and nine for older children. For people older than 65, there are a handful of programs. "We want to make sure no one falls through the cracks and no one goes hungry. Yet, at the same time, is it possible that some folks are eligible for not just three meals a day but maybe four and five?" Kingston said on the House floor. "Can we enter into that discussion without a lot of finger-pointing and a lot of emotion?"

Kingston encouraged efforts to root out fraud in the administration of food assistance programs, including "common-sense reforms" packaged in his fiscal 2013 spending bill — such as listing fraud hotlines on benefit cards and requiring certification that new vendors and retailers collecting payments have not already been debarred from participating.

He also looked at mandatory benefits for farmers. He allowed the Appropriations Committee to twice adopt an amendment by Arizona Republican

Jeff Flake to end direct payments to those earning more than $250,000 in adjusted gross income. "In any instance that the safety net has become a hammock, we need to reform the system," Kingston has said of farm aid.

Kingston often uses humor to get his point across. At a 2012 hearing on the efficiency of the Agriculture Department's data collection procedures, he produced a questionnaire from the National Agricultural Statistics Service that arrived at his home in suburban Georgia. "If you saw my garden, you would see that I do not qualify as an agriculture guy in any measure," he said.

His wit has made Kingston popular with TV hosts across the political spectrum, including liberal host Bill Maher and conservative Sean Hannity. Kingston was the first congressman to go on "Better Know a District," a recurring segment on "The Colbert Report," comedian Stephen Colbert's fake-news show on Comedy Central.

A popular figure in his own party, he served as vice chairman of the House Republican Conference during the 109th Congress (2005-06). But he fell short in a bid for the conference chairmanship in late 2006, losing to fellow conservative Adam H. Putnam of Florida by nine votes on the third ballot. He also made an underdog bid for the chairmanship of the full Appropriations Committee in the 112th.

Kingston usually votes with a majority of Republicans when they oppose a majority of Democrats. But he will oppose some bills if he feels they aren't meeting his standard of fiscal responsibility. In 2006, he was also the only Georgia Republican to vote for renewal of the 1965 Voting Rights Act, siding with top leaders of both political parties.

Kingston was born in Texas, where his father was an art professor. He and his family spent a few months in Ethiopia — his father was working with the Education Department to help set up schools — before settling in Georgia when Kingston was a toddler. He claims Georgia as his native state, once joking, "If you're potty-trained in a state, I think that gives you native status."

After earning an undergraduate degree in economics, Kingston moved to Savannah to sell insurance. He won election in 1984 to the state House, where he served for eight years.

When Democratic Rep. Lindsay Thomas retired in 1992, Kingston was well-positioned to woo voters into the GOP column; many of them already had been voting Republican for president. Kingston drew minor primary opposition, then dispatched Democrat Barbara Christmas, a school principal. He took 58 percent of the vote that year — and after 10 re-election campaigns, that remains his low-water mark in House races.

Redistricting after the 2000 census put Kingston and Chambliss in the same House district for the 2002 election, but Chambliss ran for the Senate.

Key Votes

2012	
Extend a Social Security payroll tax cut and unemployment benefits	NO
Ease securities rules to expand small-business access to capital	YES
Extend for one year subsidized student loan interest rates financed by a cut in health care spending	?
Cite Attorney General Eric H. Holder Jr. for contempt of Congress	YES
Create a visa program for foreign graduates in high-tech fields	YES
Extend most Bush-era income tax rates while allowing rates for top-bracket earners to rise (Jan. 1, 2013)	NO
2011	
Strike funding for F-35 alternative engine	NO
Prevent EPA from regulating greenhouse gas emissions to address climate change	YES
Extend certain provisions of Patriot Act for four years	YES
Declare opposition to use of ground troops in Libya	YES
Overhaul patent law	NO
Pass compromise debt limit increase plan and establish future spending limits	NO
Allow consideration of measures to implement three trade agreements	YES

CQ Vote Studies

	Party Unity		Presidential Support	
	Support	Oppose	Support	Oppose
2012	95%	5%	12%	88%
2011	96%	4%	17%	83%
2010	97%	3%	26%	74%
2009	95%	5%	17%	83%
2008	93%	7%	68%	32%

Interest Groups

	AFL-CIO	ADA	CCUS	ACU
2012	5%	0%	92%	88%
2011	0%	5%	88%	92%
2010	0%	5%	75%	100%
2009	15%	5%	73%	96%
2008	15%	10%	61%	96%

Georgia 1

Southeast — Savannah, Hinesville

Reclaiming its traditional seat of Savannah after decennial remapping, the 1st District spans 15 whole counties and parts of two others. It sails down the state's coastline and takes in nearly half of Georgia's border with Florida. Population growth across all but one of the counties in the 1st has included rapid expansion of the district's Hispanic population.

The district's economy is anchored by its ports and coastline, making trade and environmental conservation dominant issues. Local officials hope dredging and deepening along the Savannah River will lure larger deep-water ships and traffic to the port, one of the nation's busiest. To the south, the port at Brunswick relies on auto imports and also supports agricultural exports at its terminals.

Historic downtown Savannah and a string of islands off Brunswick known for their golf courses and resorts provide the bulk of the district's tourism revenue. The district's four military installations together employ tens of thousands, and aerospace parts manufacturing offers jobs in the area.

To balance the addition of Savannah to the formerly suburban and rural district, most or all of 10 farming-based counties were ceded to the neighboring 8th and 12th districts. The new borders of the 1st, removing roughly two-thirds of the farmland it held in the last decade — and the subsequent income — give agriculture a much smaller role in the district's economy.

Pockets of Democratic support in counties that have a large proportion of black populations — Chatham, Liberty and McIntosh — cannot counter the 1st's overall GOP-friendly tilt.

Major Industry
Military, tourism, agriculture

Military Bases
Fort Stewart/Hunter Army Airfield, 24,839 military, 4,320 civilian; Kings Bay Naval Submarine Base, 4,732 military, 2,269 civilian; Moody Air Force Base, 5,272 civilian, 653 civilian (2011) (shared with the 8th)

Cities
Savannah, Hinesville, Pooler

Notable
The Okefenokee Swamp — roughly 7,000 years old — covers more than 438,000 acres.

Rep. Sanford D. Bishop Jr. (D)

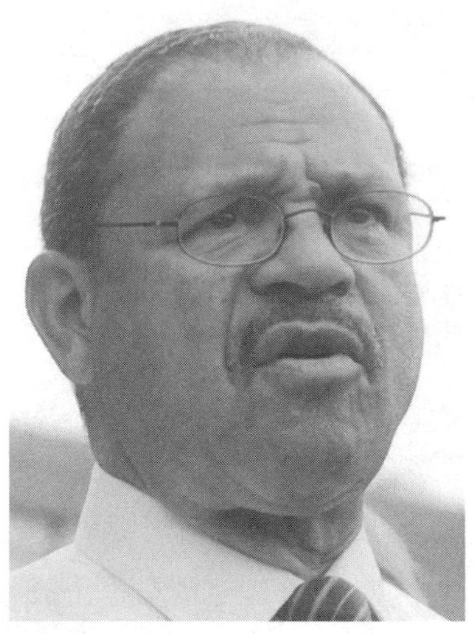

Capitol Office
225-3631
bishop.house.gov
2429 Rayburn Bldg. 20515-1002; fax 225-2203

Committees
Appropriations

Residence
Albany

Born
Feb. 4, 1947; Mobile, Ala.

Religion
Baptist

Family
Wife, Vivian Creighton Bishop; one stepchild

Education
Morehouse College, B.A. 1968 (political science); Emory U., J.D. 1971

Military
Army, 1971

Career
Lawyer

Political Highlights
Ga. House, 1977-91; Ga. Senate, 1991-93

ELECTION RESULTS

2012 GENERAL		
Sanford D. Bishop Jr. (D)	162,751	63.8%
John House (R)	92,410	36.2%
2012 PRIMARY		
Sanford D. Bishop Jr. (D)	unopposed	
2010 GENERAL		
Sanford D. Bishop Jr. (D)	86,520	51.4%
Mike Keown (R)	81,673	48.6%

Previous Winning Percentages
2008 (69%); 2006 (68%); 2004 (67%); 2002 (100%); 2000 (53%); 1998 (57%); 1996 (54%); 1994 (66%); 1992 (64%)

Elected 1992; 11th term

Although Bishop once again represents a black-majority district, he survives in Georgia politics by staying occupied with topics other than race. He's one of the more conservative House Democrats, often voting for fiscal and regulatory constraint. And as a member of the Appropriations Committee, he pays special attention to the agriculture and military interests of his constituents.

Bishop's public career grew out of the civil rights era. He was raised in Mobile, Ala., where his father was a college president — his school was renamed Bishop State Community College after his death in the 1970s. His mother was the college librarian. Bishop was an Eagle Scout and class president in high school, then headed to Morehouse College in the mid-1960s.

Inspired by his school's most famous alumnus, the Rev. Martin Luther King Jr., Bishop decided to get a law degree. "I realized that every time Dr. King got locked up, he had to call a lawyer to get him out," he once told The Atlanta Journal-Constitution. While attending Emory University Law School, Bishop spent a summer interning with the NAACP's Legal Defense Fund in New York. He practiced civil rights law in Columbus, Ga., and represented inmates at a state prison. Their 1972 lawsuit resulted in a Supreme Court decision ordering changes at the facility.

Many of those changes weren't implemented, and Bishop was convinced that running for office was a better way to effect change. He was elected to the state legislature in 1976, serving for 16 years, often in white-majority districts; since joining the U.S. House in 1993, he also has frequently represented a district with a white-majority population. And he has represented his constituents while acting as a fiscal conservative. Bishop and fellow Georgian David Scott are the only black members of the Blue Dog Coalition, the group of fiscally conservative House Democrats.

When his party controlled the House in the 111th Congress (2009-10), Bishop voted for many of its signature legislative efforts: the 2009 stimulus law; the 2010 health care and financial regulatory overhauls; and a failed attempt to create a cap-and-trade system to limit greenhouse gas emissions.

The return of a Republican majority in 2011 has provided Bishop more opportunities for dissent, however. Bishop was one of 25 House Democrats to vote for a balanced-budget amendment to the Constitution in late 2011, and he backed a deficit reduction package in August 2011.

He responded to complaints that the Obama administration was creating a regulatory environment stifling to economic growth. Bishop voted for bills to curtail EPA regulation of farming activities, coal and greenhouse gases. He and 20 other House Democrats voted for a bill (which died in the Senate) to expand offshore drilling and open the Arctic National Wildlife Refuge to energy exploration. At the start of the 113th Congress (2013-14), Democrat Collin C. Peterson of Minnesota was the only House Democrat with a lifetime score from the League of Conservation Voters lower than Bishop's.

Bishop also maintains a fairly conservative social voting record. He has voted for proposed constitutional amendments to ban same-sex marriage and ban desecration of the flag. He aligns with his fellow Democrats in supporting abortion rights but voted in 2011 to ban the use of federal funds for insurance coverage of abortion services.

Whatever his concerns about federal resources, Bishop tries to steer them to his district when possible. He joined the Appropriations Committee in 2003 and sits on the Agriculture and Military Construction-VA panels.

Wheat, cotton, soybeans, pecans, watermelons and tobacco are among the crops grown in southwestern Georgia. It's also home to a huge peanut industry and the nation's most famous peanut farmer, Jimmy Carter. Bishop and Alabama Republican Martha Roby co-chair the House Peanut Caucus.

Livestock, poultry and an ethanol plant play an economic role in the region. Bishop opposed the House's fiscal 2012 Agriculture spending bill because of cuts to agriculture research programs, rural development programs and nutrition assistance. He also expressed concern with the EPA's 2012 decision to not waive the mandate on the use of corn for ethanol production — that mandate, combined with drought in the Midwest, limited corn supplies and drove up feed costs for chicken farmers, according to Bishop.

Bishop argues that farmers in his part of the country require more equipment because of the variety of crops they produce, and that income thresholds tied to federal farming benefits should account for those capital outlays.

Bishop is the top Democrat on the Military Construction-VA panel, which bodes well for Fort Benning in his district. Before earmarking of funds was banned by the GOP majority, Bishop helped direct money to the base for equipment, training, cutting-edge weaponry and research.

Earmarking has caused some headaches for Bishop. In 2009, Georgia investigators looked into earmarks he secured for the Muscogee County Junior Marshal program, based in Columbus. Bishop once worked for the program, which provides mentoring for children before they enter high school. News reports indicated Bishop's stepdaughter and her husband were employed by the program and that paychecks were deposited directly to the account of Bishop's wife, the clerk of the county municipal court. Bishop denied having prior knowledge of the employment situation.

Bishop has been on both ends of the redistricting process in his political career. As a state senator in 1992, he served on the reapportionment committee that drew a new black-majority 2nd District for the U.S. House. Columbus business leaders helped finance his successful challenge to white Democratic Rep. Charles Hatcher.

A federal court found the district lines to be an unconstitutional "racial gerrymander" and handed down a revised map in 1995; the black share of the population in the district dropped to 39 percent. Bishop moved to Albany in the center of the district and weathered a few tough re-elections.

Republicans had a great year in 2010, and Bishop scored less than 52 percent of the vote against GOP state Rep. Mike Keown. But in the reapportionment that followed the 2010 census, Georgia was awarded an extra House seat, and his district was condensed to help make room.

The 2nd District had been a black-plurality region, but on the new map it was once again black-majority. Bishop easily defeated Republican John House, a retired Army colonel.

Key Votes

2012	
Extend a Social Security payroll tax cut and unemployment benefits	YES
Ease securities rules to expand small-business access to capital	YES
Extend for one year subsidized student loan interest rates financed by a cut in health care spending	NO
Cite Attorney General Eric H. Holder Jr. for contempt of Congress	?
Create a visa program for foreign graduates in high-tech fields	NO
Extend most Bush-era income tax rates while allowing rates for top-bracket earners to rise (Jan. 1, 2013)	YES
2011	
Strike funding for F-35 alternative engine	YES
Prevent EPA from regulating greenhouse gas emissions to address climate change	YES
Extend certain provisions of Patriot Act for four years	YES
Declare opposition to use of ground troops in Libya	YES
Overhaul patent law	YES
Pass compromise debt limit increase plan and establish future spending limits	YES
Allow consideration of measures to implement three trade agreements	YES

CQ Vote Studies

	PARTY UNITY		PRESIDENTIAL SUPPORT	
	SUPPORT	OPPOSE	SUPPORT	OPPOSE
2012	75%	25%	53%	47%
2011	77%	23%	73%	27%
2010	96%	4%	90%	10%
2009	96%	4%	94%	6%
2008	98%	2%	21%	79%

Interest Groups

	AFL-CIO	ADA	CCUS	ACU
2012	86%	45%	64%	32%
2011	90%	60%	60%	16%
2010	100%	75%	38%	4%
2009	100%	95%	53%	8%
2008	100%	90%	67%	4%

Georgia 2

Southwest — part of Columbus, most of Macon, Albany

The 2nd reaches from Macon, in the middle of the state, west to Columbus near the Alabama border and south to a portion of the border with Florida. Predominately rural, the district takes in the cities of Albany and Americus, as well as most of Macon and more than half of Columbus. Now a black-majority district, the 2nd has the smallest proportion of Hispanic residents among the state's districts.

The district relies on farming, especially peanuts, wheat, cotton, soybeans and tobacco. But drought has hurt output, particularly in the northern half of the district. Two military bases play a vital role in buffering the local economy. Fort Benning, east and south of Columbus, and the Marine Corps base in Albany host tens of thousands of servicemembers and contractors. Fort Benning — some of which crosses the state line into Russell County, Ala. — is home to the Army's infantry and armor schools.

Continuing layoffs in manufacturing have kept unemployment rates high. Several regional and community colleges offer job training, but poverty remains an issue across the 2nd; Sumter County (Americus) and Dougherty County (Albany) both have higher rates than the statewide average.

The 2nd gained Macon (from the 8th District) and a larger portion of Columbus (from the 3rd District) during the decennial redistricting process. Democratic votes in those cities outweigh the pockets of GOP strength in centrally located Lee County and in southern parts of the district around Bainbridge and Cairo. Sixteen counties in the 2nd supported Democrat Barack Obama in the 2012 presidential contest (13 went for GOP candidate Mitt Romney) including more populous Bibb, Dougherty and Muscogee.

Major Industry
Agriculture, military, health care, manufacturing

Military Bases
Fort Benning (Army), 27,436 military, 3,320 civilian (shared with Alabama's 3rd District); Marine Corps Logistics Base, 477 military, 2,977 civilian (2011)

Cities
Columbus (pt.), Macon (pt.), Albany

Notable
Andersonville National Historic Site, a memorial to all American prisoners of war, is located on the site of the Confederate Army's Camp Sumter military prison.

Rep. Lynn Westmoreland (R)

Capitol Office
225-5901
westmoreland.house.gov
2433 Rayburn Bldg. 20515-1008; fax 225-2515

Committees
Financial Services
Select Intelligence

Residence
Grantville

Born
April 2, 1950; Atlanta, Ga.

Religion
Southern Baptist

Family
Wife, Joan Westmoreland; three children

Education
Georgia State U., attended 1969-70

Career
Construction company owner; real estate developer

Political Highlights
Sought Republican nomination for Ga. Senate, 1988; Republican nominee for Ga. Senate, 1990; Ga. House, 1993-2005 (minority leader, 2001-03)

ELECTION RESULTS

2012 GENERAL		
Lynn Westmoreland (R)	unopposed	
2012 PRIMARY		
Lynn Westmoreland (R)	64,765	71.6%
Chip Flanegan (R)	13,139	14.5%
Kent Kingsley (R)	12,517	13.8%
2010 GENERAL		
Lynn Westmoreland (R)	168,304	69.5%
Frank Saunders (D)	73,932	30.5%

Previous Winning Percentages
2008 (66%); 2006 (68%); 2004 (76%)

Elected 2004; 5th term

Each round of congressional redistricting shapes House politics for the decade that follows. Westmoreland coordinated Republican strategy for redrawing the latest maps, and his labors might have saved his party from an outright debacle on Election Day 2012. He now has even more responsibility for GOP campaign operations as the deputy chairman of the National Republican Congressional Committee.

During the 111th and 112th Congresses (2009-12), Westmoreland was the vice chairman of redistricting for the NRCC, the campaign arm of the House GOP. He helped recruit candidates for his party's wildly successful takeover of the House in 2010, and during the 2012 election cycle he counseled Republican state legislators who were charged with drawing new congressional district boundaries based on data from the 2010 census. Westmoreland emphasized the creation of districts that would account for changing demographics in the decade to come.

Democrats had the better day at the polls in November 2012, keeping control of the White House and increasing their ranks in the Senate. But overall GOP losses in the House were minimal, and Westmoreland thinks his strategy made a difference. "We have a bright future for the House," he said the day after the election. The new NRCC chairman, Greg Walden of Oregon, soon tapped Westmoreland to serve as his second in command.

For his part, Westmoreland is a feisty conservative and a member of the Republican Study Committee. In the 112th Congress he voted against most of the major spending bills before the House, saying they did not cut spending enough. A tax code overhaul is one of his biggest priorities, and he has cosponsored a bill to replace most federal taxes with a national sales tax.

However, Westmoreland has softened his opposition to earmarks — money directed to specific projects in members' districts. Conservatives engineered a ban on that practice, but Westmoreland says the ban has given the White House too much discretion in choosing which projects get federal funds.

A former real estate developer, Westmoreland sits on the Financial Services Committee. For the 113th Congress (2013-14) he was given the curious new role of "committee whip." There are disputes within the Republican Party over long-term plans for the housing sector, monetary policy and the insurance industry. Westmoreland, who is famously blunt, will be hashing out those differences as the committee prepares legislation.

Even though he sometimes takes hard-line conservative stances, he has an appreciation for party discipline. GOP leaders removed several obstinate members from their preferred committees heading into the 113th, and Westmoreland colorfully explained the rationale: "I guess you could say it was an asshole factor."

His biggest parochial concern on Financial Services is the impact of Federal Deposit Insurance Corporation policies on smaller lending institutions. Late in 2011, President Barack Obama signed his bill directing the FDIC and the Government Accountability Office to investigate the causes of hundreds of bank failures during the recent recession — his district had a particularly egregious number of collapses. He reiterated his concerns to Federal Reserve Chairman Ben S. Bernanke in a hearing at the start of the 113th Congress. "I hope that ... as we continue to talk about 'too big to fail,' that we will also look at the banks that are too small to save," he said.

He also sits on the Intelligence Committee. Westmoreland is not a fan of the Obama administration's international dealings. "You can see that our position in the world is deteriorating," he said in 2012. Obama does not have a foreign policy, but "more of an appeasement policy," he added. Westmoreland suggests that countries that regularly oppose the United States through their votes in the United Nations should have their foreign aid slashed.

Westmoreland is almost always combative. He once compared Democrats to "a tick on a fat dog" to criticize their preferences on taxes and spending. In 2010, he said forcing a government shutdown might be necessary to wring spending cuts from the Obama administration. He joined some fellow lawmakers in 2012 to defend Chick-fil-A, an Atlanta-based company, after its CEO was criticized for expressing strong opposition to gay marriage.

His pugnacity — and a propensity for careless word choice — have at times gotten him into trouble. In September 2008, Westmoreland called Obama and his wife "uppity," a racially loaded word. He later said he considered the word akin to "elitism" and that he did not know of the racial overtones. "I think everyone knew I was being as sincere as I could be," he said. "Sometimes it makes you look like a dumbass if you admit things like that. But if it makes me look like a dumbass, then I'm just a dumbass."

Westmoreland's strong views cost him his first leadership post in his own caucus. He was stripped of his position as deputy whip the second day on the job for not supporting a leadership-backed rule governing debate on a bill — a violation of a GOP Conference rule. GOP leaders restored the title to him in the 111th Congress.

Westmoreland comes from a family of Atlanta mill workers. His father was a firefighter in the Atlanta suburbs who died on the job while responding to an early-morning alarm at a warehouse fire in freezing weather. Westmoreland spent one year at Georgia State University, but left to work full time. He was married at the time, and his father-in-law hired him in his home-building business. After a few years, he started his own construction business and later expanded into real estate development and sales in the late 1980s.

He grew up in a family of conservative Democrats but had little interest in politics until the mid-1980s, when he was inspired by another Georgian: Newt Gingrich, the conservative who was emerging as a party leader and later helped Republicans win control of Congress.

Westmoreland made failed bids for the state Senate in 1988 and 1990. He finally broke through with a successful campaign for the state House in 1992. He rose to become the minority leader, and with Georgia's shift to the right he had the chance to become the first Republican speaker of the Georgia House. He decided instead to run for Congress in 2004.

Westmoreland won a GOP primary runoff against a Gingrich-backed candidate, Dylan Glenn, with 55 percent of the vote, then won the general election by a 3-1 margin. He has had no trouble since and ran unopposed in 2012.

Key Votes

2012	
Extend a Social Security payroll tax cut and unemployment benefits	YES
Ease securities rules to expand small-business access to capital	YES
Extend for one year subsidized student loan interest rates financed by a cut in health care spending	NO
Cite Attorney General Eric H. Holder Jr. for contempt of Congress	YES
Create a visa program for foreign graduates in high-tech fields	YES
Extend most Bush-era income tax rates while allowing rates for top-bracket earners to rise (Jan. 1, 2013)	NO
2011	
Strike funding for F-35 alternative engine	YES
Prevent EPA from regulating greenhouse gas emissions to address climate change	YES
Extend certain provisions of Patriot Act for four years	YES
Declare opposition to use of ground troops in Libya	YES
Overhaul patent law	YES
Pass compromise debt limit increase plan and establish future spending limits	NO
Allow consideration of measures to implement three trade agreements	YES

CQ Vote Studies

	PARTY UNITY		PRESIDENTIAL SUPPORT	
	SUPPORT	OPPOSE	SUPPORT	OPPOSE
2012	97%	3%	17%	83%
2011	98%	2%	19%	81%
2010	99%	1%	27%	73%
2009	99%	1%	13%	87%
2008	98%	2%	76%	24%

Interest Groups

	AFL-CIO	ADA	CCUS	ACU
2012	10%	10%	83%	100%
2011	0%	5%	94%	96%
2010	7%	0%	88%	100%
2009	5%	0%	71%	100%
2008	80%	0%	67%	100%

Georgia 3

West central — Atlanta and Columbus suburbs

Solidly Republican, the 3rd District takes in all or part of 13 counties, beginning in Atlanta's outer suburbs and heading south down Interstate 85 to parts of Columbus. Lakes, rivers and forests fill the western, rural counties along the Alabama border.

Atlanta-area Carroll, Coweta and Henry counties in the 3rd's northeast all have experienced years of population growth, with marked increases in the district's portion of Henry County, which is shared with the 10th and 13th. An influx of black and Hispanic residents account for some of the growth, but like most of the district, all three counties remain predominately white.

Atlanta may dominate the region's culture, but the district boasts several established towns recognized for their quality of life and access to the metropolitan area. Peachtree City in Fayette County is a planned community of more than 30,000 residents known for its extensive network of golf cart paths. The small-town charm of the 3rd has also attracted the film industry.

The 3rd's portion of Columbus includes retail centers and the regional airport, as well as residential neighborhoods south of the J.R. Allen Parkway. Although the 3rd lost its part of massive Fort Benning to the 2nd following decennial redistricting, military jobs — for servicemembers and defense contractors — remain important to the district's economy.

In the less-populated former textile towns, aerospace, food processing and biotechnology firms have re-invigorated the manufacturing sector, which already relies on automotive production. Kia Motors, a Caterpillar engine factory and a Yamaha ATV plant all provide jobs. Construction companies and the health care industry are also major employers in the district.

Major Industry

Health care, service, manufacturing, military

Cities

Columbus (pt.), Peachtree City, Newnan

Notable

Franklin D. Roosevelt died April 12, 1945, at his Little White House in Warm Springs while posing for the "Unfinished Portrait," which is on display in the home's museum; Barnesville, once dubbed "The Buggy Capital of the World" for guiding the reins on the industry, still hosts an annual festival.

Rep. Hank Johnson (D)

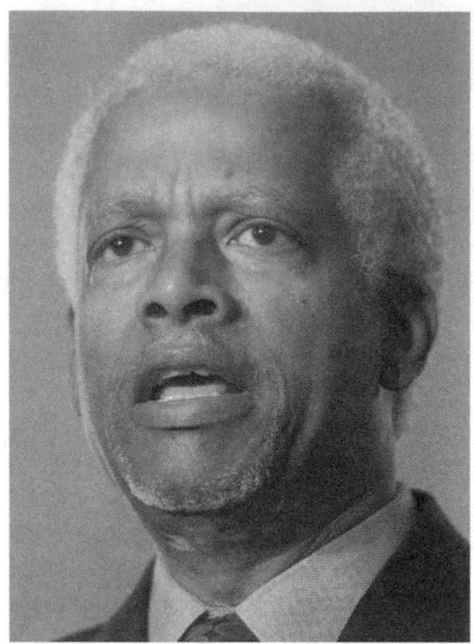

Capitol Office
225-1605
hankjohnson.house.gov
2240 Rayburn Bldg. 20515-1004; fax 226-0691

Committees
Armed Services
Judiciary

Residence
Lithonia

Born
Oct. 2, 1954; Washington, D.C.

Religion
Buddhist

Family
Wife, Mereda Davis Johnson; two children

Education
Clark College, B.A. 1976 (political science); Texas Southern U., J.D. 1979

Career
Lawyer; county judge

Political Highlights
Sought Democratic nomination for Ga. House, 1986; DeKalb County Board of Commissioners, 2001-06

ELECTION RESULTS

2012 GENERAL		
Hank Johnson (D)	208,861	73.6%
J. Chris Vaughn (R)	75,041	26.4%
2012 PRIMARY		
Hank Johnson (D)	52,982	77.0%
Courtney L. Dillard Sr. (D)	13,130	19.1%
Lincoln Nunnally (D)	2,728	4.0%
2010 GENERAL		
Hank Johnson (D)	131,760	74.7%
Lisbeth "Liz" Carter (R)	44,707	25.3%

Previous Winning Percentages
2008 (100%); 2006 (75%)

Elected 2006; 4th term

Johnson has become bolder in articulating his progressive philosophy, prompted by what he sees as an orchestrated movement toward "unregulated and unbridled capitalism" that concentrates wealth and power with a select few. His committees involve him in defense and legal matters, and Johnson takes a special interest when those areas overlap.

Johnson is a member of the Congressional Progressive Caucus, the group of the most liberal House members, and he serves the Democratic Party as a regional whip. He's also one of three Buddhists in Congress — Johnson and Mazie K. Hirono of Hawaii were the first two ever elected, and they were joined by Colleen Hanabusa, another Hawaii Democrat, in 2011.

"We need to emphasize freedom, education, health care, and if we stay at the top in all of those areas, we will continue to lead the world," Johnson said. "America needs to take care of its people instead of just policies for the rich and the trickle-down thinking that seems to be so pervasive." Those same principles can be advanced in other nations, according to Johnson: "We promote that not through military means, but through soft power, diplomacy, sharing, concern, compassion. Those are qualities that are universal."

A former county judge, Johnson speaks slowly and chooses words deliberately. His increased assertiveness is tied in part to a shift to the House minority in the 112th Congress (2011-12). "There's abundant opportunity to criticize and complain," he said, "and so I have taken on that opportunity with the enthusiasm of a courtroom lawyer."

He also has been energized by an improvement in his health. Diagnosed with hepatitis C in 1998, he was undergoing treatment for the disease and related liver and thyroid problems when he came to Congress. "It really took a lot out of me. I'm still reclaiming, physically and mentally, my wits and my endurance, my strength and endurance," he said. Johnson received his last treatment for the disease in January 2012.

Johnson's protests haven't gotten much media exposure, but he carries on. He serves on the Judiciary and Armed Services committees and has turned his attention to the intersection of the military and civil rights. "External threats can have an impact on our internal rights, depending on how we respond to them," he said.

Johnson scrutinized the treatment of Bradley Manning, the Army private arrested in 2010 and accused of leaking classified documents to the WikiLeaks website. Manning was effectively held in solitary confinement at a Marine base, which Johnson considered inhumane. After protests by Johnson and others, Manning was moved to a different facility. (He pleaded guilty to a number of charges in February 2013.)

Johnson also tried in early 2011 to kick start an investigation of an alleged plot to spy on opponents of the U.S. Chamber of Commerce. Johnson said there was evidence indicating that three government contractors and a Chamber-affiliated law firm were planning to use intelligence-gathering tools, developed for the war on terrorism, against U.S. citizens, journalists and progressive organizations. Johnson's request for a probe was ignored.

On matters of defense spending, Johnson questions the necessity of a missile defense shield on the West Coast, asking why Congress would leave out Americans in the Midwest or on the East Coast. He sponsored an amendment to the fiscal 2013 defense policy bill to say the deployment of nuclear weapons to South Korea would destabilize the region. It was rejected.

On the Judiciary Committee, Johnson focuses on civil rights and litigation issues. Johnson has on several occasions sponsored a bill to make discrimination based on employment status a violation of the Civil Rights Act of 1964; he also has suggested that the government might want to address discrimination against the long-term unemployed, arguing that the issue has a disproportionate impact on minorities.

He frets over possible violations of privacy rights. Johnson in 2012 launched "AppRights," a segment of his website that solicits ideas for legislation to protect the privacy of those using mobile communications devices. "Our apps should serve us — not spy on us," the site reads.

President Barack Obama signed a 2011 Johnson measure to clarify when cases against federal officers or agencies can be moved from state court to federal court.

Serving in the House has been a homecoming for Johnson. He was raised in Washington; his mother taught school in Arlington County, Va., and his father was a high-level official with the Federal Bureau of Prisons. He went south for college, first to his mother's alma mater, Clark College (now Clark Atlanta University), and then to Texas Southern University for law school, where he met his wife, Mereda.

He attributes both his career choice and his political path to a much older cousin, Archibald "Tokey" Hill, who graduated from law school when Johnson was young. Johnson read The Washington Post aloud to his mother each day as she washed the dinner dishes, and he frequently passed the Capitol. "Since I wanted to be an attorney, since I wanted to be a public official like my cousin Tokey, the only legislature that I knew was the United States Congress," he said. "So it was always kind of planted in the back of my head that I would be a member of Congress one day."

First, however, he spent nearly three decades practicing law with his wife in Decatur, focusing on criminal and civil litigation. He spent 10 years as an associate judge in DeKalb County. He told the Atlanta Journal-Constitution that his diagnosis with hepatitis C — and the threat of a shorter life that came with it — helped spur him to finally run for office.

Johnson challenged abrasive Democratic Rep. Cynthia A. McKinney, whom he once supported, in the 2006 primary. He held her to less than 50 percent of the vote as a third Democrat in the race captured more than 8 percent. That pushed McKinney into a runoff with Johnson, who won the contest. Winning the primary is tantamount to being elected in the strongly Democratic, black-majority 4th District.

Johnson was held to 55 percent in the Democratic primary in 2010, but he rebounded to claim 77 percent of the vote in 2012. McKinney started a petition drive to make the ballot as a Green Party candidate against Johnson but failed to submit any signatures by the deadline, the Journal-Constitution reported.

Key Votes

2012	
Extend a Social Security payroll tax cut and unemployment benefits	NO
Ease securities rules to expand small-business access to capital	NO
Extend for one year subsidized student loan interest rates financed by a cut in health care spending	NO
Cite Attorney General Eric H. Holder Jr. for contempt of Congress	?
Create a visa program for foreign graduates in high-tech fields	NO
Extend most Bush-era income tax rates while allowing rates for top-bracket earners to rise (Jan. 1, 2013)	YES
2011	
Strike funding for F-35 alternative engine	YES
Prevent EPA from regulating greenhouse gas emissions to address climate change	NO
Extend certain provisions of Patriot Act for four years	NO
Declare opposition to use of ground troops in Libya	?
Overhaul patent law	YES
Pass compromise debt limit increase plan and establish future spending limits	YES
Allow consideration of measures to implement three trade agreements	YES

CQ Vote Studies

	PARTY UNITY		PRESIDENTIAL SUPPORT	
	SUPPORT	OPPOSE	SUPPORT	OPPOSE
2012	98%	2%	84%	16%
2011	96%	4%	89%	11%
2010	98%	2%	90%	10%
2009	99%	1%	96%	4%
2008	99%	1%	12%	88%

Interest Groups

	AFL-CIO	ADA	CCUS	ACU
2012	100%	95%	25%	4%
2011	100%	90%	25%	0%
2010	92%	90%	25%	0%
2009	100%	95%	33%	0%
2008	100%	100%	47%	8%

Georgia 4

Southeast Atlanta suburbs — most of DeKalb and Rockdale counties

The Democratic, suburban and DeKalb County-based 4th District takes in both eastern suburbs of Atlanta and the more-removed and fast-growing counties to the southeast. Many of the district's newest residents have left Atlanta seeking a suburban atmosphere. Two decades of rapid population growth has slowed marginally in DeKalb County, which contains the most-established Atlanta suburbs, while continuing in the new bedroom communities of Rockdale and Newton counties.

Overall growth patterns have been mirrored by shifts in racial and ethnic demographics, as many minority residents have moved from the urban center and established suburbs in counties further afield. The district retained a majority black identity after redistricting, at just shy of 60 percent of the population.

Residential development has transformed previously unpopulated land from Lithonia east past Conyers, in Rockdale County. Many residents rely on jobs in Atlanta or work in service sectors in the district. Emory University and the Centers for Disease Control and Prevention, on the eastern edge of the 5th, employ many 4th District residents who commute from the suburbs. Parts of the 3rd further east, away from Atlanta, struggle with poverty rates higher than the state average.

The bulk of the 4th's residents live in Democratic Party strongholds of DeKalb County, which hosts some wealthy black communities. Democratic voters outnumber Republicans in Newton and Rockdale, as well. The district's portions of southern Gwinnett County are more conservative than the rest of the 4th, although Barack Obama won 54 percent of its 2012 presidential vote. Overall, the 4th backs Democratic candidates at the federal level.

Major Industry

Health care, government, retail

Cities

Redan, Tucker (pt.)

Notable

Stone Mountain Park has a huge granite rock face onto which a sculpture of Robert E. Lee and other Confederate leaders is carved; Conyers is home to a Trappist monastery, established in 1944 and the first American-founded monastery of that order, where about 40 monks live and pray.

Rep. John Lewis (D)

Capitol Office
225-3801
johnlewis.house.gov
343 Cannon Bldg. 20515-1005; fax 225-0351

Committees
Ways & Means

Residence
Atlanta

Born
Feb. 21, 1940; Troy, Ala.

Religion
Baptist

Family
Widowed; one child

Education
American Baptist Theological Seminary, B.A. 1961 (theology); Fisk U., B.A. 1963 (religion & philosophy)

Career
Civil rights activist; U.S. volunteer agency manager

Political Highlights
Sought Democratic nomination for U.S. House (special election), 1977; Atlanta City Council, 1982-86

ELECTION RESULTS

2012 GENERAL		
John Lewis (D)	234,330	84.4%
Howard Stopeck (R)	43,335	15.6%
2012 PRIMARY		
John Lewis (D)	69,985	80.8%
Michael Johnson (D)	16,666	19.2%
2010 GENERAL		
John Lewis (D)	130,782	73.7%
Fenn Little (R)	46,622	26.3%

Previous Winning Percentages
2008 (100%); 2006 (100%); 2004 (100%); 2002 (100%); 2000 (77%); 1998 (79%); 199 (100%); 1994 (69%); 1992 (72%); 1990 (76%); 1988 (78%); 1986 (75%)

Elected 1986; 14th term

Lewis enjoys universal admiration and a degree of authority as a hero of the civil rights movement. He's willing to wield that irreproachable clout in a partisan manner as a lawmaker. He makes liberal arguments in the stark moral tones of the Civil Rights Era, excoriating Republicans and championing federal programs that advance his notions of economic and social justice.

His personal history is closely intertwined with his political persona. In 1961, Lewis became one of the 13 original Freedom Riders seeking to integrate interstate bus travel in the segregated South. He helped form the Student Nonviolent Coordinating Committee, a youth-driven fulcrum of the civil rights movement that focused on civil disobedience. He was named chairman of the group in 1963, with 24 arrests under his belt and more than a dozen to come.

Over the next three years, he led the SNCC's campaign to secure voting rights, and he gained national fame as a leader of the March 7, 1965, protest march from Selma, Ala., to the state Capitol at Montgomery.

State and local police attacked the peaceful marchers on the Edmund Pettus Bridge at the start of their journey in what became known as "Bloody Sunday." The outrage sparked by images of the event inspired enactment of the landmark Voting Rights Act, which President Lyndon Johnson signed into law in August that year.

Lewis shows those who visit his office the poster-sized pictures of him being clubbed over the head by police. He leads members of Congress on a pilgrimage each year to Selma and other major landmarks of the civil rights era. Lewis received the Presidential Medal of Freedom, the nation's highest civilian honor, in February 2011; the image of Lewis at the top of his congressional website in early 2013 showed him wearing the medal.

Now in his 14th term in the House, Lewis is an influential Democrat. He holds the appointed caucus post of senior chief deputy whip and serves on the Ways and Means Committee, which has jurisdiction over many safety net programs. He is a member of the Congressional Progressive Caucus, a group of the most liberal House members.

Lewis frequently declares that "the time is always right to do what is right" — a Martin Luther King Jr. quote that he has deployed in support of legislation to end discrimination against gays and lesbians in the workplace, as well as in support of the 2010 health care overhaul. (He also states in hearings and speeches that health care is a right, "not a privilege.")

Lewis was rhetorically merciless with House Republicans through much of the 112th Congress (2011-12), casting their efforts to reduce federal spending as ill will toward the less affluent. Proposed cuts for some safety net programs in 2012 prompted a stern response from Lewis.

"It seems very clear that sound fiscal policy is not the point of these cuts, no matter what the other side says," he said. "They want to create a society where the rich get richer and the poor get poorer, with no chance that hard work will help them rise out of their circumstances."

At a 2011 hearing on the effect of government workers' pension plans on state budgets, Lewis — the top Democrat on the Ways and Means Subcommittee on Oversight — accused Republicans of painting "teachers, firefighters, librarians and nurses as villains in their quest to widen the gap between the rich and the poor."

His most impassioned arguments in the 112th were on behalf of voting rights. As Republican state legislatures passed laws to toughen standards for voter registration and identification — ostensibly to prevent voter fraud — Lewis saw "a deliberate and systematic attempt" to suppress "minority, seniors, disabled and rural voters," he told The Atlantic. Lewis was the most prominent Democrat pressing these concerns, even airing his accusations in a speech at the 2012 Democratic National Convention.

Earlier in the year, Georgia Republican Paul Broun offered an amendment to block funding for the federal approval of election maps under the Voting Rights Act, a process meant to prevent disenfranchisement of minorities; Broun said the process was no longer needed. Lewis took to the House floor to condemn the proposal as "shameful." Broun withdrew it.

From his Ways and Means perch, Lewis has promoted bills to reduce racial disparities in health care, provide medical services for the poor and the uninsured, and prevent the IRS from using private companies to collect back taxes.

Lewis does not vote for war funding measures and has implied that "defense, homeland security and other conservative favorites" have been protected at the expense of benefit programs; he has proposed that the per-taxpayer cost of the Afghanistan and Iraq wars be posted on a public website. He also balks at many surveillance-related measures, citing the days when the government spied on him and other civil rights leaders.

Lewis has had legislative successes over the years. President George W. Bush in 2003 signed his bill to establish a Smithsonian Institution museum devoted to detailing African-American life, art, history and culture. Construction began in 2012 and is slated for a 2015 completion. A 2012 reauthorization of surface transportation programs included Lewis' bill to strengthen the safety standards for motor coaches and their drivers.

One of 10 children of sharecroppers, Lewis recalls being shy when attending segregated schools in rural Alabama. He was inspired by King's sermons on the radio and developed a sense of outrage at the 1955 lynching in Mississippi of Emmett Till, who was the same age as the then-15-year-old Lewis. Later, as a student at the American Baptist Theological Seminary in Nashville, he attended workshops on non-violent resistance.

Lewis first ran for Congress in 1977, for the seat Andrew Young left to become U.N. ambassador. He lost to Wyche Fowler.

Lewis then went to Washington to head the federal volunteer agency ACTION, under President Jimmy Carter. Returning to Atlanta, he won a seat on the city council in 1981. He made his next bid for the House in 1986, when Fowler ran for the Senate. He beat state Sen. Julian Bond for the Democratic nomination, but the race turned the longtime allies and civil rights icons into bitter rivals.

He won easily that November. Lewis often runs unopposed, and when Republicans do field a candidate, he still coasts.

Lewis' wife of 44 years, Lillian, died on the last day of 2012.

Key Votes

2012	
Extend a Social Security payroll tax cut and unemployment benefits	YES
Ease securities rules to expand small-business access to capital	YES
Extend for one year subsidized student loan interest rates financed by a cut in health care spending	NO
Cite Attorney General Eric H. Holder Jr. for contempt of Congress	?
Create a visa program for foreign graduates in high-tech fields	?
Extend most Bush-era income tax rates while allowing rates for top-bracket earners to rise (Jan. 1, 2013)	?
2011	
Strike funding for F-35 alternative engine	YES
Prevent EPA from regulating greenhouse gas emissions to address climate change	NO
Extend certain provisions of Patriot Act for four years	NO
Declare opposition to use of ground troops in Libya	NO
Overhaul patent law	YES
Pass compromise debt limit increase plan and establish future spending limits	NO
Allow consideration of measures to implement three trade agreements	NO

CQ Vote Studies

	Party Unity		Presidential Support	
	Support	Oppose	Support	Oppose
2012	99%	1%	93%	7%
2011	97%	3%	81%	19%
2010	100%	0%	83%	17%
2009	99%	1%	93%	7%
2008	99%	1%	15%	85%

Interest Groups

	AFL-CIO	ADA	CCUS	ACU
2012	95%	95%	27%	0%
2011	100%	95%	19%	8%
2010	100%	100%	13%	0%
2009	100%	85%	43%	0%
2008	100%	95%	50%	4%

Georgia 5

Atlanta

The 5th is based around the state's capital and largest city, Atlanta, and includes surrounding areas in northern portions of Clayton County and western portions of DeKalb County. The symbolic capital of the New South, Atlanta is the commercial center of the Southeast and boasts corporate headquarters, a bustling downtown and cultural and entertainment venues.

Home to Hartsfield-Jackson Atlanta International Airport and a major and high-volume interstate highway network, Atlanta is a transportation hub for the area. The airport, which remains the nation's busiest for passenger travel, delivers tens of billions of dollars to the region annually. The district also hosts CNN and major American companies, including Coca-Cola, Delta Air Lines and Georgia-Pacific. A skilled and educated labor force in the district supports high-tech manufacturing, aerospace and higher education sectors across the region.

Atlanta's tourist draws include the Georgia World Congress Center and its Centennial Olympic Park and the Georgia Dome; the Woodruff Arts Center; Turner Field, home to baseball's Braves; the World of Coca-Cola, and the Georgia Aquarium. The 5th also hosts Clark Atlanta University, Emory University, the Georgia Institute of Technology, Georgia State University and Morehouse College.

The collapse of the construction and home-building industries, which led to a high rate of residential vacancies, did not curtail overall population growth in the Atlanta metropolitan area over the past decade. But most of the development in Fulton County in particular has been in suburban areas along the interstates in neighboring districts. The addition of well-educated, white residents has resulted in modest overall population growth for the still black-majority city, but most of the growth within the 5th has been in DeKalb suburbs to the east. Despite some Republican voters in affluent outlying areas, the majority-black 5th is a Democratic stronghold and gave Barack Obama his statewide best in the 2012 presidential election with 83 percent of the vote.

Major Industry

Transportation, distribution, higher education, tourism

Cities

Atlanta, East Point

Notable

The Rev. Martin Luther King Jr.'s childhood home and the Ebenezer Baptist Church, where he was a pastor, are in the Sweet Auburn neighborhood.

Rep. Tom Price (R)

Capitol Office
225-4501
tomprice.house.gov
100 Cannon Bldg. 20515-1006; fax 225-4656

Committees
Budget
Education & the Workforce
Ways & Means

Residence
Roswell

Born
Oct. 8, 1954; Lansing, Mich.

Religion
Presbyterian

Family
Wife, Elizabeth Clark Price; one child

Education
U. of Michigan, B.A. 1976 (general studies), M.D. 1979

Career
Surgeon

Political Highlights
Ga. Senate, 1997-2005 (minority whip, 1999-2002; majority leader, 2003)

ELECTION RESULTS

2012 GENERAL		
Tom Price (R)	189,669	64.5%
Jeff Kazanow (D)	104,365	35.5%
2012 PRIMARY		
Tom Price (R)		unopposed
2010 GENERAL		
Tom Price (R)	198,100	99.9%

Previous Winning Percentages
2008 (68%); 2006 (72%); 2004 (100%)

Elected 2004; 5th term

Price strives to direct the course of the conservative movement, although he currently doesn't enjoy the full trappings of leadership. The ambitious doctor wants Republicans to focus on substantial alternatives to Democratic plans on health care, taxes and more.

"The way that you actually attract individuals to a cause is to provide a vision," Price said in late 2012. "As the Good Book says, where there is no vision, the people perish."

In the 111th Congress (2009-10), he headed up the Republican Study Committee, the large bloc of conservative House Republicans. Price helped develop the vision of the GOP majority during the 112th Congress (2011-12) as the elected chairman of the Republican Policy Committee, which formulates legislative proposals — in this case, a spate of bills to roll back regulations, expand domestic energy production, cut spending and repeal the 2010 overhauls of health care and financial sector regulation.

For the 113th Congress (2013-14), however, he's a leader without a major title. Shortly after Republicans lost House and Senate seats in the 2012 election, Price ran for chairman of the Republican Conference, the No. 4 position on the House GOP's leadership team. He was defeated by the moderate Cathy McMorris Rodgers of Washington. She had the backing of Speaker John A. Boehner, who offered Price a graceful exit — the appointed "chairman of the leadership" job — if he agreed to withdraw.

Price opted for a Light Brigade charge, indicating his commitment to confrontational and conservative policy. His decision was probably made easier by his status as a favorite guest of TV talk shows, which gives him a ready outlet for his views, and his seat on the Ways and Means Committee, which keeps him at the center of the most heated policy debates.

And GOP leaders have tried to keep him close. Price was named the vice chairman of the Budget Committee, as well as the vice chairman for policy at the National Republican Congressional Committee, the campaign arm of House Republicans.

Ways and Means has jurisdiction over many health care programs, and Price has invested much of his professional and legislative life in that subject. He grew up in Michigan, the son of a dairy farmer who decided to attend medical school at age 36 to become an emergency room doctor. He recalls going on rounds during his childhood with his grandfather, who was also a doctor. He moved to Atlanta for a residency in orthopedic surgery at Emory University and eventually settled in the area with his anesthesiologist wife. Price says he was drawn to politics because he felt lawmakers wielded too much power over his actions as a doctor.

In the 112th Congress, Price offered a top-to-bottom overhaul of the health care system — a conservative response to the 2010 health care law that would let people opt out of government health plans and shop for private insurance with the help of tax credits. His other, more targeted bills included a measure to limit medical malpractice suits and legislation to exclude pathologists from Medicare and Medicaid incentive payments.

Repeal of the 2010 law is close to impossible with a Democrat in the White House, but Price wants more attempts at full repeal, as well as smaller measures to break off parts of the law unpopular with members of both parties. "As a physician for over 25 years, I cared for patients who bristled at the notion that the federal government ought to be involved in their health care," he said at a 2009 markup.

Ways and Means also covers taxes and many large entitlement programs.

Price is firmly against tax rate increases and has co-sponsored a bill to eliminate the IRS and replace most federal taxes with a national sales tax. "Tax reform is imperative," he said in 2012. "Can't have the current tax code and expect that the economy is going to boom."

Price is a big supporter of spending reductions. In 2011 and 2013, he and Florida Republican Sen. Marco Rubio introduced companion bills to rescind $45 billion in federal funding that has not yet been obligated. Price, who also sits on the Education and the Workforce Committee, unsuccessfully tried to amend a fiscal 2011 spending bill to eliminate all money for the National Labor Relations Board.

In his first term, he introduced a bill requiring more public disclosure for earmarks, funding for special projects in members' districts. In January 2008, he announced that he wouldn't request any new earmarks until the system is overhauled. He is an enthusiastic supporter of the current GOP moratorium on the practice of earmarking.

His persona — which led The Washington Post to dub him a "Republican guerrilla warrior" — has earned Price comparisons to former Speaker Newt Gingrich, a fellow Republican whose suburban-Atlanta district Price now represents. Like Price, Gingrich made a name for himself with his repeated challenges to Democrats.

Price is socially conservative and unbending on what he considers matters of principle. Earlier in his career, he was the only member of the Education panel to vote against a bill that would expand the definition of the word "disabled." He argued that the expanded definition was too broad. "If everyone is disabled, then nobody is actually disabled," he said.

Frustration with government led Price to become increasingly involved in civic organizations, such as the Rotary Club, and in Republican politics as an organizer and fundraiser. When a friend in the state Senate decided to retire in 1996, she urged Price to run.

In the General Assembly, he was known as a quick study on the details of policy and the rules and mechanics of passing bills. Within two years, he was chosen for a leadership position, and when Republicans took control of the state Senate in 2003, he became majority leader.

After Gingrich resigned from Congress, Republican Johnny Isakson succeeded him and held the seat for almost three terms. When Isakson successfully ran for the Senate in 2004, it created an opening for Price.

He finished first in a seven-candidate primary, then won a runoff against fellow GOP state Sen. Robert Lamutt. Lamutt got Gingrich's endorsement, but Price prevailed, 54 percent to 46 percent. He was unopposed in the general election and has been easily re-elected since.

Key Votes

2012	
Extend a Social Security payroll tax cut and unemployment benefits	YES
Ease securities rules to expand small-business access to capital	YES
Extend for one year subsidized student loan interest rates financed by a cut in health care spending	NO
Cite Attorney General Eric H. Holder Jr. for contempt of Congress	YES
Create a visa program for foreign graduates in high-tech fields	YES
Extend most Bush-era income tax rates while allowing rates for top-bracket earners to rise (Jan. 1, 2013)	NO
2011	
Strike funding for F-35 alternative engine	NO
Prevent EPA from regulating greenhouse gas emissions to address climate change	YES
Extend certain provisions of Patriot Act for four years	YES
Declare opposition to use of ground troops in Libya	YES
Overhaul patent law	YES
Pass compromise debt limit increase plan and establish future spending limits	YES
Allow consideration of measures to implement three trade agreements	YES

CQ Vote Studies

	PARTY UNITY		PRESIDENTIAL SUPPORT	
	SUPPORT	OPPOSE	SUPPORT	OPPOSE
2012	97%	3%	20%	80%
2011	98%	2%	18%	82%
2010	99%	1%	26%	74%
2009	98%	2%	11%	89%
2008	99%	1%	76%	24%

Interest Groups

	AFL-CIO	ADA	CCUS	ACU
2012	10%	10%	92%	100%
2011	0%	5%	100%	92%
2010	0%	0%	88%	100%
2009	0%	0%	73%	100%
2008	7%	10%	72%	100%

Georgia 6

North Atlanta suburbs — Roswell, Alpharetta, most of Sandy Springs

As a result of the decennial remapping process that redrew the 6th, the district ceded about half of its footprint in the northern Atlanta suburbs and exurbs, losing all of Cherokee County to the adjacent 11th District. Stretching from the Atlanta city limits to the Appalachian foothills north of Milton, the 6th now consists of chunks of DeKalb, Cobb and Fulton counties.

Before settlement of Atlanta, the land of the 6th was Cherokee and Creek territory and many of the area's natural landmarks are still associated with the American Indian tribes. The Hightower Trail, which serves as the northern border of DeKalb County, was formerly a trading route for the area. Today, the office parks, malls, golf courses and housing subdivisions of established suburbs dominate the region.

Northern Fulton County, the heart of the 6th, hosts various corporate offices: UPS's headquarters are in Sandy Springs, ADP has two offices in Alpharetta, Kimberly-Clark has a corporate office in Roswell, and GE Energy Management has its headquarters in the southern end of the district. Roswell, formerly a cotton-milling center, is now a Fulton County bedroom community with a historic district of landmarks, outdoor recreation and commercial centers.

Between 2000 and 2010, populations in the counties shared by the 6th grew significantly. Most areas in the district experienced overall population growth, and Hispanic and Asian communities had some of the largest changes. The additional residents led to the incorporation of several municipalities among the suburbs, and towns such as Chamblee and Doraville are increasingly home to large foreign-born populations.

The predominately white district is reliably Republican overall, with strong support for the GOP at the federal level in the district's portions of Cobb and Fulton counties. Northern DeKalb County is home to much of the district's minority population, and voters tend to be socially moderate.

MAJOR INDUSTRY
Technology, distribution, finance, health care

CITIES
Roswell, Johns Creek, Sandy Springs (pt.), Alpharetta

NOTABLE
Roswell introduced telephone service in 1901 — all numbers were one digit.

Rep. Rob Woodall (R)

Capitol Office
225-4272
woodall.house.gov
1725 Longworth Bldg. 20515-1007; fax 225-4696

Committees
Budget
Oversight & Government Reform
Rules
(Legislative & Budget Process - Chairman)

Residence
Lawrenceville

Born
Feb. 11, 1970; Athens, Ga.

Religion
Methodist

Family
Single

Education
Furman U., B.A. 1992 (political science); U. of Georgia, J.D. 1997

Career
Congressional aide

Political Highlights
No previous office

ELECTION RESULTS

2012 GENERAL		
Rob Woodall (R)	156,689	62.2%
Steve Reilly (D)	95,377	37.8%
2012 PRIMARY		
Rob Woodall (R)	45,157	71.8%
David Hancock (R)	17,730	28.2%
2010 GENERAL		
Rob Woodall (R)	160,898	67.1%
Doug Heckman (D)	78,996	32.9%

Elected 2010; 2nd term

Woodall calls himself a "true believer in federalism." The former Capitol Hill aide pushes for smaller government and took the tax policy baton from his predecessor and former boss, Republican John Linder, on a bill to replace the federal code with a national sales tax.

Chatting with reporters or speaking on the House floor, Woodall has the energy and optimism of a publicist when it comes to his tax proposals or the GOP's fiscal agenda. His comfort stems from both conviction and experience. Linder hired Woodall in 1994 and promoted him to chief of staff five years later; Woodall left that post only to succeed his boss in the House. GOP leaders put him on the Budget and Rules committees in his first term, and Woodall relishes the opportunity to work on Congress' legislative engine.

Speaking with a Southern twang — it's not uncommon to hear a "golly" — he makes his case for reserving more authority for individual states. "We have the [Environmental Protection Division] in Georgia," he said. "If the EPA went away tomorrow, we're not going to start polluting the Chattahoochee River.... We're environmentalists to the nth degree, and we have a state agency that ensures that rules get followed."

Woodall promotes his fiscal agenda on the Budget Committee, and in the 113th Congress (2013-14) he's also heading up the budget task force for the Republican Study Committee, a large bloc of conservative House members. Entitlement programs consume a huge portion of federal outlays, and Woodall supports program changes to yield greater individual control over benefits across a range of programs. "There's something special about making your own choices," he said. He was added to the Oversight and Government Reform Committee, and its panel on entitlement programs, for the 113th.

He applauded GOP efforts in the fall of 2011 to offset disaster relief funding with spending cuts, rather than declaring it off-budget "emergency" spending. He voted against a $50 billion package of aid tied to Superstorm Sandy in January 2013, most of which was deemed emergency spending.

Woodall also wants an overhaul of the federal budgeting process and the scoring models used to evaluate the costs of various proposals. The House in 2012 passed his bill to stop the Congressional Budget Office from including "automatic inflators" — assumed annual increases in a discretionary program's baseline cost — when calculating budgetary impacts.

He calls a potential balanced-budget amendment to the Constitution a "game-changer" and backs codified consequences, such as flat funding from year to year, should Congress not adopt a budget.

Woodall also tackles budgeting on Rules, where he chairs the Legislative and Budget Process Subcommittee. He worked as a staff director on the full committee when Linder served there.

The committee is the gateway to the House floor, and his first rule was a big one: Woodall shepherded the resolution setting debate terms for a Republican-backed fiscal 2011 spending bill, which led to a flood of amendments from both parties. "We have an open process," he said on the House floor, "for the first time in the history of this House — the best I can tell — an open process on a continuing resolution."

Woodall's work with Linder involved him in a crusade. His first day in office he introduced a bill, dubbed the FairTax Act, that would eliminate the IRS, abolish most federal taxes and create a 23 percent national sales tax. Woodall contributed to Linder's 2005 and 2008 books on the subject, both of which reached No. 1 on The New York Times' nonfiction best-seller list.

He contends that the bill would broaden the tax base, reduce bureaucracy and "abolish all of the power that Congress has today to manipulate you through the tax code." Critics say a national sales tax is regressive and would largely hurt low-income individuals.

The FairTax had arguably its best Congress ever in the 112th (2011-12); the bill garnered 70 co-sponsors and a hearing in the Ways and Means Committee. Woodall continues to make his case in the 113th Congress, and he has a home-state ally on Ways and Means: Republican Tom Price. He said in January 2013 that he would press for a committee vote on his bill.

Woodall stuck with the majority of Republicans throughout the 112th Congress, with a few notable exceptions. He won't back measures if he feels they threaten civil liberties; Woodall was one of 31 in his party to oppose a four-year extension of surveillance provisions in the anti-terrorism law known as the Patriot Act, saying it did not include proper due process protections.

He was also one of two House members to vote against a bill (enacted in 2012) meant to prevent lawmakers or their staffers from using privileged information to gain an advantage in the stock market. Woodall said such insider trading was already illegal and the bill was unnecessary.

Woodall was born in Athens, Ga., where his parents were finishing up their graduate education; the family later moved to Avondale. His mother was a child psychology major — "You can judge for yourself how that sorted itself out," Woodall jokes — and his father earned a Ph.D. in entomology. "So lots of bugs and snakes and rodents of all kinds running around the house growing up," he said. Woodall still enjoys the wildlife: He hikes and has visited many of the major Western national parks.

The family was not political, but "civic-minded," according to Woodall. "When the Avondale park needed cleaning up and reworking, you didn't go and get a Bobcat somewhere. You got all the sons with shovels and you went down there and you did it."

He graduated from Furman University in 1992, then enrolled in law school at the University of Georgia. Woodall's interest in politics was stoked by summer jobs at Washington law firms. He left law school in 1994 to join Linder's staff, but finished his law degree in 1997 by taking night classes.

Linder announced his retirement during his ninth term in the House. He endorsed Woodall, who finished well ahead of seven other candidates in the primary. He won a runoff with talk show host and Baptist minister Jody Hice to win the nomination in the overwhelmingly Republican 7th District district, which had been one of the fastest-growing in the nation in the prior decade. He easily won the general election.

His district was made more compact on the congressional map drawn for the 2012 election, but Woodall still won handily.

Key Votes

2012	
Extend a Social Security payroll tax cut and unemployment benefits	NO
Ease securities rules to expand small-business access to capital	YES
Extend for one year subsidized student loan interest rates financed by a cut in health care spending	NO
Cite Attorney General Eric H. Holder Jr. for contempt of Congress	YES
Create a visa program for foreign graduates in high-tech fields	YES
Extend most Bush-era income tax rates while allowing rates for top-bracket earners to rise (Jan. 1, 2013)	NO
2011	
Strike funding for F-35 alternative engine	NO
Prevent EPA from regulating greenhouse gas emissions to address climate change	YES
Extend certain provisions of Patriot Act for four years	NO
Declare opposition to use of ground troops in Libya	YES
Overhaul patent law	YES
Pass compromise debt limit increase plan and establish future spending limits	YES
Allow consideration of measures to implement three trade agreements	YES

CQ Vote Studies

	PARTY UNITY		PRESIDENTIAL SUPPORT	
	SUPPORT	OPPOSE	SUPPORT	OPPOSE
2012	96%	4%	17%	83%
2011	96%	4%	18%	82%

Interest Groups

	AFL-CIO	ADA	CCUS	ACU
2012	14%	10%	83%	90%
2011	3%	5%	100%	92%

Georgia 7

Northeast of Atlanta — most of Gwinnett County

Located at the northeastern corner of the Atlanta metropolitan area, the 7th District curls around the neighboring 6th's inner suburbs, arcing through Duluth, Lawrenceville and Cumming. Having shed more-rural areas to the east after decennial redistricting, the 7th is now firmly a suburban district. The Interstate 85 corridor cuts through the center of the 7th, offering a prime commuting route into downtown Atlanta. Proximity to the state capital has fueled rapid population growth and transformed quiet towns into bustling bedroom communities.

Several large professional service and technology firms provide economic stability. Primerica, a life insurance and financial services company in Duluth, is one of the largest employers in the region. The district is also home to Scientific Atlanta, a subsidiary of cable and broadband equipment company Cisco Systems.

Packed developments in the south give way to less-densely populated enclaves and some forest land in the northern edge of the district. Forsyth County includes the southern tip of Lake Lanier, home to camping and recreational activities around Lanier Park Beach. Tourism drives the economy in this portion of the district, with hiking, fishing and camping opportunities in and around the Sawnee Mountain Preserve.

An overall population boom that included an influx of minority residents in the greater Atlanta metropolitan area has shifted the district's demographic makeup over the past decade. The number of black and Hispanic residents in Gwinnett County, most of which is in the 7th, more than doubled between 2000 and 2010, while rural areas of the district north of Interstate 85 are predominately white. The district remains a Republican stronghold — the parts of Gwinnett in the 7th gave Republican presidential nominee Mitt Romney 55 percent in 2012 — although the changing demographics could make the southern portion of the district more competitive.

Major Industry

Technology, retail, service

Cities

Lawrenceville, Duluth, Buford

Notable

Norcross hosts the headquarters of Waffle House, the popular roadside diner.

Rep. Austin Scott (R)

Capitol Office
225-6531
austinscott.house.gov
516 Cannon Bldg. 20515-1003; fax 225-3013

Committees
Agriculture
(Horticulture, Research, Biotechnology & Foreign Agriculture - Chairman)
Armed Services

Residence
Tifton

Born
Dec. 10, 1969; Augusta, Ga.

Religion
Baptist

Family
Wife, Vivien Scott; one child

Education
U. of Georgia, B.B.A. 1993 (risk management and insurance)

Career
Insurance agency owner

Political Highlights
Ga. House, 1997-2011

ELECTION RESULTS

2012 GENERAL		
Austin Scott (R)		unopposed
2012 PRIMARY		
Austin Scott (R)		unopposed
2010 GENERAL		
Austin Scott (R)	102,770	52.7%
Jim Marshall (D)	92,250	47.3%

Elected 2010; 2nd term

Scott has operated out of the national spotlight, working in a relatively quiet fashion on the agricultural and military policy relevant to his south Georgia district. He has small-government, pro-business beliefs that are broadly representative of the Republican mainstream.

When he came to the House in 2011, Scott was cast as a high-profile leader: The 87-member GOP freshman class elected him as its president. Many observers expected Scott to be in the thick of intraparty disputes and battles with the Obama administration, given the size of that class, the anti-Washington sentiment of many of its members and Scott's considerable experience as a state legislator.

But Scott didn't take an overly active role as a class spokesman in the 112th Congress (2011-12), either in the media or when dealing with the House Republican leadership team. For their part, the leaders often met directly with the entire freshman class. Describing his role as a go-between in 2011, Scott said, "I don't have to do it much." He instead voted as a solid conservative and plugged away on his committees.

Scott has a seat on the Agriculture Committee, and for the 113th Congress (2013-14) he chairs its Horticulture, Research, Biotechnology and Foreign Agriculture Subcommittee. The 8th District is home to cotton, peanut, peach, pecan and timber growers, and Scott himself once helped his grandfather operate a cattle ranch. He also ran his own insurance agency, which gives him business insight as lawmakers consider shifting the safety net for farmers further toward crop insurance.

As the committee worked on a long-term authorization of farm programs in 2012, Scott was protective of several existing subsidy programs favored by Southern growers. "If it's not broken, don't fix it," he said at a hearing. He voted to approve the bill the committee produced, but he opposed an amendment to alter protections for sugar producers. He also voted against an attempt by Oregon Democrat Kurt Schrader — now the ranking member on Scott's subcommittee — to increase mandatory funding for specialty crop research. The bill never got a vote on the House floor, and Scott supported a similar measure at a May 2013 markup.

Scott sees big potential savings in the Supplemental Nutrition Assistance Program, which is bundled in the farm bill. He says funding for SNAP should be reduced to discourage long-term reliance on the program, and that states should have more options — such as drug testing to determine eligibility — for handling fraud and abuse in low-income assistance programs. "If somebody has got the ability to buy drugs, they have the ability to pay for their own food," he said.

His first bill in 2011 was a measure to block funding for the Legal Services Corporation, which provides civil-litigation assistance to low-income people. Scott filed the legislation several days after the Equal Employment Opportunity Commission announced it was suing Hamilton Growers, a Norman Park, Ga., grower, for allegedly firing 19 U.S. workers and replacing them with foreign guest workers. Georgia Legal Services helped the workers file complaints against the grower, which is the state's largest employer of foreign farm labor.

A Washington Post columnist accused Scott of retaliation; Scott said he was unaware of the lawsuit when he filed his bill and acted because the organization had not been reauthorized by Congress since 1980. He filed the bill again at the start of the 113th Congress.

Scott's other seat is on the Armed Services Committee. Although he favors many spending cuts, Scott spent much of 2012 trying to minimize cuts to the defense budget. He has pledged to protect Robins Air Force Base, a major employer in his district, from reductions; the Air Force in November 2011 announced cuts of more than 500 civilian jobs at Robins, one of three air logistics centers for the service, as part of its efforts to cut overhead.

At a 2011 hearing he lamented the proposed downsizing at military installations in Georgia and elsewhere. "I want to be an ally," he told Air Force officials. "I'm quite honestly embarrassed that we have more discussions in this Congress about cuts to the military than we do about cuts to social programs." Scott sits on the Readiness Subcommittee, which oversees the base closure and realignment process.

A member of the conservative Republican Study Committee, Scott opposed the August 2011 deficit reduction law, saying it did not have enough immediate spending cuts. He's also a social conservative. Scott, a member of the Congressional Sportsmen's Caucus, enjoys turkey hunting and opposes restrictions to gun owners' rights.

Scott grew up in Tifton, a small city about 180 miles south of Atlanta on Interstate 75. His father was an orthopedic surgeon and his mother was a teacher. Scott went to the University of Georgia and got a degree in risk management and insurance; he had a few jobs in the insurance industry before opening his own agency in the late 1990s.

He was just 26 when he was elected to the Georgia House. In the course of 14 years, Scott served on the appropriations and tax-writing committees. He also distinguished himself as the only Republican in that chamber to cosponsor the 2001 bill that removed the huge Confederate battle emblem on the Georgia flag.

Scott started a gubernatorial campaign in 2009, during which he walked 1,000 miles across the state in 64 days. But he was behind other GOP rivals in fundraising, and in April 2010 he changed races to take on four-term Rep. Jim Marshall, a fiscally conservative Democrat. On a campaign swing through Georgia, Minority Leader John A. Boehner promised to give Scott a seat on Armed Services if he won.

There was some drama when a Democratic activist filed to have records from Scott's 2001 divorce unsealed. The records detailed fairly acrimonious proceedings, but they were kept under wraps until February 2011 — and even then, they didn't cause much of a stir on their release. Scott beat Marshall by more than 5 points.

Redistricting for 2012 strengthened the Republican hold on the district, and Scott was unopposed in both the primary and general election. He was able to distribute around $300,000 to the Republican Party and individual campaigns throughout the election cycle.

Key Votes

2012	
Extend a Social Security payroll tax cut and unemployment benefits	NO
Ease securities rules to expand small-business access to capital	YES
Extend for one year subsidized student loan interest rates financed by a cut in health care spending	YES
Cite Attorney General Eric H. Holder Jr. for contempt of Congress	YES
Create a visa program for foreign graduates in high-tech fields	YES
Extend most Bush-era income tax rates while allowing rates for top-bracket earners to rise (Jan. 1, 2013)	NO
2011	
Strike funding for F-35 alternative engine	YES
Prevent EPA from regulating greenhouse gas emissions to address climate change	YES
Extend certain provisions of Patriot Act for four years	YES
Declare opposition to use of ground troops in Libya	YES
Overhaul patent law	NO
Pass compromise debt limit increase plan and establish future spending limits	NO
Allow consideration of measures to implement three trade agreements	YES

CQ Vote Studies

	PARTY UNITY		PRESIDENTIAL SUPPORT	
	SUPPORT	OPPOSE	SUPPORT	OPPOSE
2012	98%	2%	13%	87%
2011	98%	2%	16%	84%

Interest Groups

	AFL-CIO	ADA	CCUS	ACU
2012	14%	5%	83%	96%
2011	0%	5%	87%	92%

Georgia 8

South central — Valdosta, most of Warner Robins

A strip of southern Georgia running from near Macon in the central part of the state to the Florida border, the 8th hosts industrial complexes, suburban communities and rural expanses. Assigned more land to the south following decennial remapping, the district takes in all or part of 24 counties.

The area around Macon, nearly all of which was placed in the adjacent 2nd District during redistricting, relies on Robins Air Force Base. Beyond active-duty military jobs, related industrial production and nearby aerospace firms are economic drivers — there are more than 20,000 civilian and contractor jobs related to aircraft maintenance and manufacturing.

Twiggs County in the geographic center of the state is a distribution center. The rest of the district is largely rural and relies on a large and diverse agricultural base. The southeastern part of the district produces cotton, pecans and peanuts. Most of the state's tobacco is produced in the southwestern part of the 8th, although the sector has been steadily declining statewide.

Thirty percent of the district's population is black. Poverty and low rates of higher education persist across the district. Only two counties — Jones and Houston — have household incomes above the statewide median.

Most voters in the 8th support the GOP in statewide and federal races, but Twiggs County is reliably Democratic. The parts of all other counties in the 8th backed Republican Mitt Romney in the 2012 presidential race.

Major Industry
Aerospace, agriculture, distribution

Military Bases
Robins Air Force Base, 6,614 military, 14,324 civilian (2011); Moody Air Force Base, 5,200 military, 836 civilian (2011) (shared with the 1st)

Cities
Warner Robins, Valdosta, Thomasville

Notable
Macon's Wesleyan College has a vegetarian club dating to the 1830s named after Sylvester Graham, the inventor of the cracker that bears his name; Sylvester holds the Georgia Peanut Festival every October.

Rep. Doug Collins (R)

Capitol Office
225-9893
dougcollins.house.gov
513 Cannon Bldg. 20515-6601; fax 226-1224

Committees
Foreign Affairs
Judiciary
Oversight & Government Reform

Residence
Gainesville

Born
Aug. 16, 1966; Gainesville, Ga.

Religion
Baptist

Family
Wife, Lisa Jordan Collins; three children

Education
North Georgia College, B.S. 1988 (political science); New Orleans Baptist Theological Seminary, M.Div. 1996; John Marshall Law School (Atlanta), J.D. 2008

Military
Air Force Reserve, 2002-present

Career
Lawyer; minister; gas detector manufacturer government relations manager

Political Highlights
Ga. House, 2007-13

ELECTION RESULTS

2012 GENERAL		
Doug Collins (R)	192,101	76.2%
Jody Cooley (D)	60,052	23.8%
2012 PRIMARY RUNOFF		
Doug Collins (R)	39,016	54.6%
Martha Zoller (R)	32,417	45.4%

Elected 2012; 1st term

Collins is a perfect fit for his super-Republican district, holding views on immigration, abortion and federal regulation that largely track with those of his north Georgia constituents.

He has worn many different hats over the years. Collins grew up in Hall County and went to a military college in north Georgia. He held a variety of jobs before getting a master's in divinity from the New Orleans Baptist Theological Seminary. While working as a minister, he also owned a scrapbooking business with his wife. In his mid-30s, he joined the Air Force Reserve, and as his 40s got under way, he won election to the state House and got a law degree.

Collins applies his legal experience on the Judiciary Committee and shares his thoughts on international engagements on the Foreign Affairs Committee — while serving in the state House, he deployed to Iraq as a military chaplain.

Collins quickly identified regulations as one of his chief concerns. Writing with fellow Republican Ted Yoho of Florida in early 2013, he noted that "the administration posted an average of 68 new regulations and notices each day. If our economy doesn't collapse from the sheer weight of these new administrative burdens, it will certainly be crippled by their cost." He sits on the Judiciary subcommittee overseeing the regulatory process.

Regarding immigration, Collins says border security and enforcement must be a big part of any overhaul. He is fiscally conservative, and he has endorsed a plan by fellow Georgia Republican Rob Woodall to eliminate the IRS and replace federal taxes with a single national sales tax.

Georgia got a new House seat in reapportionment after the 2010 census, and by political standards the open 9th District was it. The area is so Republican that the three-way GOP primary was the real contest for the seat. Collins was the early favorite, but conservative talk show host Martha Zoller finished just 734 votes behind him. That forced a runoff, which Collins won by 10 points. He took more than three-fourths of the vote in November.

Georgia 9

Northeast — Blue Ridge Mountains, Gainesville

The hilly 9th District spans northeastern Georgia's forests and newly built subdivisions. The addition of a new district following the 2010 census shifted the 9th east along the Tennessee border. Forests in the northern half and Athens suburbs and the outskirts of the Atlanta metropolitan area to the south, the district now abuts South Carolina in the east. The 9th splits booming Forsyth County near Atlanta with the 7th and Pickens County with the 14th. Interstate 85, which connects Greenville, S.C., to Atlanta, cuts through the district.

The Blue Ridge Mountains and the Chattahoochee-Oconee National Forest account for much of the land in the district's north. The loss of woodland to residential development, logging and recreational trails makes conservation a significant concern for officials and residents. Already a popular vacation home site, the district has attracted large numbers of permanent residents over the last decade.

Blue-collar jobs remain important to the 9th. Gainesville in Hall County has relied on poultry processing since the end of World War II, and major processing plants form the backbone of its economy — the district produces more than one-fourth of the birds in Georgia's multi-billion-dollar poultry industry. Granite deposits support more than 45 quarries producing 2 million cubic feet of the mineral annually, most of which is made into tombstones.

As in much of the state generally, household incomes have fallen across all the 9th's counties since 2000. Communities along Interstates 85 and 985 generally have higher median household incomes than those along the South Carolina border. Public-private investment in high-speed Internet infrastructure should address the needs of counties around the Chattahoochee National Forest.

Republicans thoroughly dominate politics in the 9th. GOP candidates ran unopposed in nearly every 2012 state House and Senate race in districts within the 9th, and Georgian Newt Gingrich won a majority of 2012 Republican presidential primary votes. Mitt Romney took his statewide best here in the 2012 general, with 78 percent of the district's vote.

Major Industry
Poultry processing, mining, tourism

Cities
Martinez (unincorp.), Gainesville, Toccoa

Notable
Springer Mountain is the southern terminus of the 2,175-mile Appalachian National Scenic Trail.

Rep. Paul Broun (R)

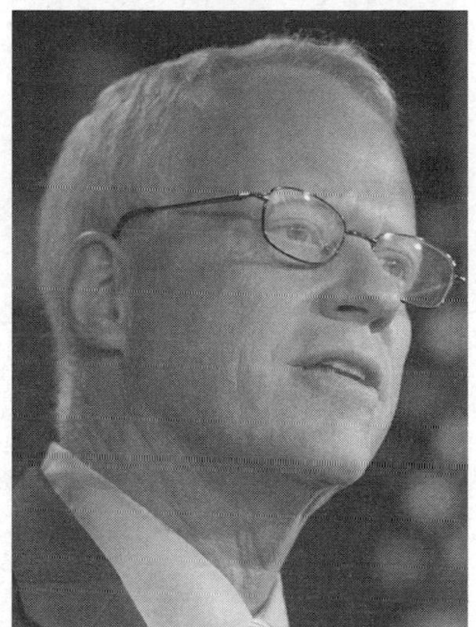

Capitol Office
225-4101
broun.house.gov
2437 Rayburn Bldg. 20515-1009; fax 226-0776

Committees
Homeland Security
Natural Resources
Science, Space & Technology
(Oversight - Chairman)

Residence
Watkinsville

Born
May 14, 1946; Atlanta, Ga.

Religion
Southern Baptist

Family
Wife, Niki Broun; three children

Education
U. of Georgia, B.S. 1967 (chemistry); Medical College of Georgia, M.D. 1971

Military
Marine Corps Reserve, 1964-67; Naval Reserve, 1967-72; Ga. Air National Guard, 1972-73; Navy Reserve Medical Corps, 2010-present

Career
Physician

Political Highlights
Republican nominee for U.S. House, 1990; sought Republican nomination for U.S. House, 1992; sought Republican nomination for U.S. Senate, 1996

ELECTION RESULTS

2012 GENERAL		
Paul Broun (R)		unopposed
2012 PRIMARY		
Paul Broun (R)	58,405	69.0%
Stephen K. Simpson (R)	26,256	31.0%
2010 GENERAL		
Paul Broun (R)	138,062	67.4%
Russell Edwards (D)	66,905	32.6%

Previous Winning Percentages
2008 (61%); 2007 Special Runoff Election (50%)

Elected 2007; 3rd full term

Broun's uncompromising vision of limited government has made him one of his party's most intense fiscal hawks, and he can be just as strident on social issues. He has started his campaign for Georgia's open Senate seat in 2014 — a prospect as exciting to hard-core conservatives as it is frightening to Republican Party strategists.

He does not mince words: "I call it as I see it. With me, what you see is what you get." Broun (BROWN) consistently calls President Barack Obama a socialist and describes global warming as a "hoax." A physician before winning a seat in Congress, he insists that the 2010 health care overhaul is "killing jobs. It's going to be a destroyer of our freedom."

Broun says Congress' authority should be limited to the 18 powers outlined under Article I, Section 8 of the Constitution and that the most frustrating thing he faces is colleagues' poor knowledge of that founding document. He has similarly strong religious convictions: Broun in 2012 was recorded at a sportsman's banquet for a Georgia Baptist church saying that evolution and the Big Bang Theory are "lies straight from the pit of hell."

He had been hinting at a challenge to Sen. Saxby Chambliss in the 2014 Republican primary. Chambliss announced his retirement in early 2013, and Broun was the first in his party to file for the race. The thought of Broun as a statewide candidate has some Republicans worried — intense, socially conservative Senate nominees lost 2012 races in Missouri and Indiana that had been seen as winnable.

Broun isn't fazed by such worries, and he seems unlikely to change his positions to seem more electable. Before every vote, Broun asks whether legislation fits "the Judeo-Christian biblical principles that the nation was founded upon"; whether it's allowed by the "original intent" of the Constitution; whether the nation needs it; and whether the nation can afford it. He rejects any measure that fails even one of those tests.

"I get a lot of encouragement to continue to vote the way I do and be the person I am," Broun says. "I may not be politically correct, but I've never been politically correct, and I don't think America should be, either."

That willingness to engage in third-rail politics has earned him admirers and headaches. In May 2012, Broun attempted to amend a Justice Department spending bill to block any funds related to the federal approval of election maps under the Voting Rights Act. Broun said the law, meant to prevent disenfranchisement of minorities, was outdated and embarrassing to states still forced to comply. Georgia Democrat John Lewis, a civil rights icon, rose to call Broun's proposal an embarrassment. Broun withdrew the amendment.

Broun (who prefers to be called Dr. Broun) has attracted attention for his repudiation of the health care overhaul. Early in 2012, Broun introduced an alternative plan to change Medicare to a voucher system, allow consumers to purchase health insurance across state lines and encourage the use of health savings accounts. Broun has also proposed combining Medicaid and the Children's Health Insurance Program into a single block grant.

He has a seat on the Natural Resources Committee, where he joins most Republicans in calling for more domestic oil and gas exploration. He cheerleads for nuclear power as well — Broun applauded when the Nuclear Regulatory Commission in 2012 approved construction of new reactors in Georgia.

He also serves on the Homeland Security Committee and its panel on Counterterrorism and Intelligence. Broun has been an emphatic critic of the Transportation Security Administration, accusing the agency of practicing "Gestapo-type tactics" that breach civil liberties. In May 2012, citing allegations of corruption and continued lack of security, Broun demanded the resignation of TSA Administrator John S. Pistole. Security efforts should focus on "those entities that want to do us harm," he said at a 2011 Homeland hearing, meaning violent Islamic extremists. "We've got to profile these folks."

Broun's small-government, anti-deficit beliefs led him to reject most of the major spending bills of the 112th Congress (2011-12), even compromise measures backed by the House GOP leadership that reduced overall discretionary spending. Since 2011, Broun has chaired the Science, Space and Technology subcommittee on oversight, and he uses that post to study federal spending that he sees as wasteful — for example, some of the research and science funding from the $787 billion 2009 stimulus law.

He has similarly staunch views on revenues and monetary policy. Broun proposes the elimination of corporate taxes and the capital gains tax, which he says would inject trillions of dollars into the economy. "Who pays for corporate taxes anyway?" he said. "It's not the corporation. It's either the consumer, or it's taken out of the dividends." Broun in 2013 introduced a bill to require a full audit of the Federal Reserve. He inherited the cause from another noted fiscal conservative, retired Texas Rep. Ron Paul.

Broun is the son of a tire dealership owner and a stay-at-home mom. He was 16 when his father was elected to the Georgia Senate, where he served for nearly four decades. The same year, a peanut farmer from Plains named Jimmy Carter was elected to the same chamber. Broun's parents and the Carters became friends, and the future president would use Broun's bed for the night when visiting Athens.

In high school, Broun joined the ROTC. He remained in Athens to attend college, earning a bachelor's degree from the University of Georgia in 1967, and four years later he got his medical degree from the Medical College of Georgia in Augusta. For much of the Vietnam War, he was serving in the Naval Reserve but did not see active duty. He joined the Georgia Air National Guard after completing medical school. He returned to the military in 2010 when he joined the Navy Reserve Medical Corps.

Broun eventually opened a practice in his hometown. At one point, he was in between offices and decided to start visiting patients at their homes or workplaces in the interim. That arrangement "grew very rapidly into a full-time house-call medical practice," he said.

Broun lost three bids for Congress before emerging as the surprising winner of a special election to succeed the late Republican Charlie Norwood. Broun bested Republican Jim Whitehead, a former state senator and friend of Norwood's, by a slim margin. His re-election bids have been much easier, and Broun ran unopposed in the 2012 general election.

Key Votes

2012	
Extend a Social Security payroll tax cut and unemployment benefits	NO
Ease securities rules to expand small-business access to capital	YES
Extend for one year subsidized student loan interest rates financed by a cut in health care spending	NO
Cite Attorney General Eric H. Holder Jr. for contempt of Congress	YES
Create a visa program for foreign graduates in high-tech fields	YES
Extend most Bush-era income tax rates while allowing rates for top-bracket earners to rise (Jan. 1, 2013)	NO
2011	
Strike funding for F-35 alternative engine	YES
Prevent EPA from regulating greenhouse gas emissions to address climate change	YES
Extend certain provisions of Patriot Act for four years	NO
Declare opposition to use of ground troops in Libya	YES
Overhaul patent law	NO
Pass compromise debt limit increase plan and establish future spending limits	NO
Allow consideration of measures to implement three trade agreements	YES

CQ Vote Studies

	PARTY UNITY		PRESIDENTIAL SUPPORT	
	SUPPORT	OPPOSE	SUPPORT	OPPOSE
2012	94%	6%	21%	79%
2011	95%	5%	15%	85%
2010	99%	1%	22%	78%
2009	98%	2%	10%	90%
2008	100%	0%	83%	17%

Interest Groups

	AFL-CIO	ADA	CCUS	ACU
2012	15%	30%	83%	100%
2011	4%	5%	88%	96%
2010	0%	5%	75%	100%
2009	0%	0%	73%	100%
2008	0%	0%	67%	100%

Georgia 10

Eastern piedmont — Athens

Planted between Atlanta and Augusta, the state's two largest cities, the 10th hosts fast-growing suburbs and rural getaways. Exurbs of Atlanta, much of Athens and areas northwest of Augusta populate the district's northern half. To the southeast, it juts into the state's sparsely populated central region.

Colleges and universities are key players in the regional economy. The University of Georgia in Athens is a hub of professional and commercial activity, and a new medical school on the campus is jointly run with Augusta's Georgia Health Sciences University (in the 12th). Milledgeville, in Baldwin County, is home to Georgia College and State University and the Georgia Military College. Monroe's hospital complex adds to the health care sector.

Tourism boosts the 10th's economy. The Oconee National Forest and Lake Sinclair lure visitors for hiking, camping and water sports. Greensboro hosts the Reynolds Plantation — home to several recent PGA tournaments and a draw for golf enthusiasts. Northwest of Augusta along the Savannah River, Georgia's half of Lake Strom Thurmond is a major outdoor recreation site.

The district's southernmost counties rely on agriculture and mining. Jefferson County and the surrounding area is famous for its cotton but also produces timber, wheat and dairy. Neighboring Washington County is known for its abundance of alumina-silicate clay, but the once-thriving industry has declined. Unemployment rates have remained above state and national averages in the southern portion of the district, particularly in black-majority Washington, Jefferson and Hancock counties.

The 10th stayed solidly Republican after decennial remapping, and pockets of Democratic support in the northern suburbs and some of the economically struggling southern small towns cannot boost federal candidates.

Major Industry
Higher education, health care, tourism, mining, agriculture

Military Bases
Fort Gordon (Army), 15,000 military, 8,000 civilian (shared with the 12th)

Cities
Athens, Lawrenceville, Milledgeville

Notable
Sandersville's International Kaolin Festival every October recognizes the mineral's impact on the region.

Rep. Phil Gingrey (R)

Capitol Office
225-2931
gingrey.house.gov
442 Cannon Bldg. 20515-1011; fax 225-2944

Committees
Energy & Commerce
House Administration

Residence
Marietta

Born
July 10, 1942; Augusta, Ga.

Religion
Roman Catholic

Family
Wife, Billie Gingrey; four children

Education
Georgia Institute of Technology, B.S. 1965 (chemistry); Medical College of Georgia, M.D. 1969

Career
Physician

Political Highlights
Marietta Board of Education, 1993-97 (chairman, 1994-97); Ga. Senate, 1999-2003

ELECTION RESULTS

2012 GENERAL		
Phil Gingrey (R)	196,968	68.6%
Patrick Thompson (D)	90,353	31.4%
2012 PRIMARY		
Phil Gingrey (R)	75,697	80.9%
Michael S. Opitz (R)	9,231	9.9%
William Llop (R)	8,604	9.2%
2010 GENERAL		
Phil Gingrey (R)		unopposed

Previous Winning Percentages
2008 (68%); 2006 (71%); 2004 (57%); 2002 (52%)

Elected 2002; 6th term

Gingrey worked as a doctor and thrives on discussions of health care. He's an animated conservative who eagerly participates as Republicans shape their policy positions. And he's hoping to be Georgia's next senator.

Sen. Saxby Chambliss is retiring at the end of the 113th Congress (2013-14), and Gingrey is gearing up for the GOP primary in 2014. Several prominent politicians are expected to join the race, which already includes another conservative doctor — Paul Broun of the 10th District.

Gingrey came to politics after decades as an obstetrician. He has kept his medical license, volunteers at a medical clinic and, even though he's in his 70s, says he may return to clinical practice when his political career ends. A co-founder and co-chairman of the House GOP Doctors Caucus, he says his physician's sensibility provides a perspective that health care experts seldom have.

"What I brought to Congress that they can never have, unless they have been in that situation, was actually practicing medicine and being at the bedside," he said. He wants "to try to make sure that these policy wonks understand this is just not like any other business. You can't put a business model to it.... There's almost a sanctity to it."

Gingrey was added to the Energy and Commerce Committee and its Health panel in the 111th Congress (2009-10), as debate on the eventual 2010 health care law took off. He served within a group of 16 House Republicans who were tapped in 2009 to create a GOP alternative to Democrats' plans.

After the elections of 2012, he acknowledged that a full repeal of the law is unlikely in the current political environment, but he continues trying to chip off parts of it. Gingrey sees bipartisan interest in eliminating the law's long-term-care insurance program; its independent Medicare spending advisory board; and a tax on medical device manufacturers.

In March 2013, only 14 House Republicans opposed the chamber's initial fiscal 2013 spending package, and Gingrey was one of them. He said he couldn't support a bill that provides funding for implementation of the health care law, which "threatens patient access and imposes massive tax increases on Americans, particularly middle-class families and young adults."

Throughout the 112th Congress (2011-12), Gingrey provided colorful criticism of the Obama administration's health care policies. He likened the former head of the Centers for Medicare and Medicaid Services, Donald M. Berwick, to Don Corleone from the "Godfather" movies, and the law itself to Boss Hogg, the crooked Georgia county commissioner from "The Dukes of Hazzard."

Gingrey has a particular interest in limiting medical malpractice suits, and he has cited that cause as one of his initial reasons for running for Congress. In 2012, the House approved his legislation to cap punitive damage awards and establish a time limit by which most claims would have to be filed. The House also passed his bill in 2005. "I feel like I've got the perfect bill, but I know better than that," he said. "Nobody ever has the perfect bill."

His health care concerns extend beyond the 2010 law. Gingrey worries that other recent program changes will overburden state budgets — he opposed a 2009 expansion of the Children's Health Insurance Program, which covers children whose low-income families make too much money to qualify for Medicaid. He and other Republicans said the bill should have focused on a more limited group of low-income people.

A 2012 reauthorization of the Food and Drug Administration's user fee programs included a provision, written in part by Gingrey, to spur development of drugs to treat increasing cases of infections resistant to existing antibiotics.

Gingrey belongs to the Republican Study Committee and frequently shows up on lists of the most conservative lawmakers in the House. He is one of the House's staunchest opponents of abortion, including in cases of rape or incest. He's also a member of the Republican Policy Committee, which helps steer the House GOP agenda. Gingrey unsuccessfully sought the chairmanship of the policy committee in 2006, losing to Adam H. Putnam of Florida.

As Republicans fought to reduce spending levels in the 112th, Gingrey voted against stopgap spending bills to continue funding the government at previous levels. He voted against an August 2011 deal to raise the debt limit, and he supports adding a balanced-budget amendment to the Constitution. "These members that say we don't need a balanced-budget amendment because Congress can take care of that, we're grown men and women — well, we're not," he said.

Gingrey holds a seat on the House Administration Committee. He addresses humanitarian causes and foreign affairs as a member of the Commission on Security and Cooperation in Europe — better known as the Helsinki Commission. Earlier in his career, he was on the Armed Services Committee.

His mother was the daughter of Irish immigrants and grew up in New York City. His father, who grew up in South Carolina, owned a series of small businesses, including a drive-through restaurant, a liquor store and a motel in Augusta, Ga.

Gingrey worked his way through the Georgia Institute of Technology with a factory job. He intended to become an engineer, but after visiting an operating room with a family friend who was a neurosurgeon, he decided to go to medical school. Gingrey served about four years as Marietta school board chairman when his children were in school, then went on to two terms in the Georgia Senate while continuing his medical practice. He became well-known for advocating tighter teen driving laws.

In 2001, he considered challenging Democratic incumbent Max Cleland for a seat in the Senate. But after redistricting gave Georgia two new House seats, he decided to run for that chamber.

The new 11th District had a Democratic tilt, so Republican Bob Barr, who represented a portion of it, chose to run in the 7th District primary against John Linder. With Barr out, Gingrey jumped in and won a primary runoff in the 11th. In November, he took 52 percent of the vote against Roger Kahn, a wholesale liquor distributor who lent his own campaign $2.5 million. Gingrey appealed to religious conservatives and got help from the American Medical Association, which paid for polling and radio ads.

When Georgia's congressional districts were redrawn in 2005, his became more favorable to the GOP. It remained strongly Republican after the latest round of remapping, and Gingrey won easily in 2012.

Key Votes

2012	
Extend a Social Security payroll tax cut and unemployment benefits	NO
Ease securities rules to expand small-business access to capital	YES
Extend for one year subsidized student loan interest rates financed by a cut in health care spending	YES
Cite Attorney General Eric H. Holder Jr. for contempt of Congress	YES
Create a visa program for foreign graduates in high-tech fields	YES
Extend most Bush-era income tax rates while allowing rates for top-bracket earners to rise (Jan. 1, 2013)	NO
2011	
Strike funding for F-35 alternative engine	YES
Prevent EPA from regulating greenhouse gas emissions to address climate change	YES
Extend certain provisions of Patriot Act for four years	YES
Declare opposition to use of ground troops in Libya	YES
Overhaul patent law	+
Pass compromise debt limit increase plan and establish future spending limits	NO
Allow consideration of measures to implement three trade agreements	YES

CQ Vote Studies

	PARTY UNITY		PRESIDENTIAL SUPPORT	
	SUPPORT	OPPOSE	SUPPORT	OPPOSE
2012	99%	1%	12%	88%
2011	95%	5%	22%	78%
2010	99%	1%	25%	75%
2009	95%	5%	20%	80%
2008	99%	1%	72%	28%

Interest Groups

	AFL-CIO	ADA	CCUS	ACU
2012	10%	0%	83%	96%
2011	0%	5%	93%	100%
2010	8%	5%	75%	100%
2009	10%	5%	73%	96%
2008	7%	10%	78%	96%

Georgia 11

Northwest Atlanta suburbs — most of Marietta

The 11th shifted closer to Atlanta during decennial remapping and now is made up of mainly white suburbs and exurbs of the city, picking up commuter towns along Interstates 75 and 575. Home to white-collar, middle-income families, the district is a Republican stronghold — the only significant sources of Democratic votes are in the 11th's part of Cobb County near Atlanta. Farther out, northern Bartow and Cherokee counties remain largely rural even as suburban development has begun to take root.

A high-skilled manufacturing base is still the heart of the swath of Cobb County in the 11th. Marietta (shared with the 6th) still depends on aerospace and military jobs. The local Lockheed Martin plant builds cargo and fighter planes, although production slowdowns have caused recent job losses. A nearby former naval air station now hosts the state National Guard headquarters and multi-service reserve training operations. In Cartersville in Bartow County, the flooring company Shaw Industries is a major employer.

In rural areas outside of Atlanta's immediate orbit, poultry production, which developed in the region as cotton declined, is still important. Outdoor recreation destinations at district lakes and mountains lure visitors.

Areas in the district continued to experience explosive population growth over the past decade, with Cherokee County growing by more than 50 percent between 2000 and 2010. A good school system, low tax rates and proximity to the state's largest city have attracted residents from across the state to the 11th. In its slice of Fulton County, some of the district's most affluent neighborhoods sit along tree-lined lanes. Demands on infrastructure have mirrored the population growth — shopping centers and new area hospitals are planned, and manufacturing and entertainment complexes have expanded.

Major Industry
Defense, manufacturing, poultry processing

Cities
Marietta, Kennesaw, Woodstock

Notable
The nearly 3,000-acre Kennesaw Mountain National Battlefield Park preserves remnants of Confederate fortifications from a successful stand against William Tecumsah Sherman-led Union troops in 1864.

Rep. John Barrow (D)

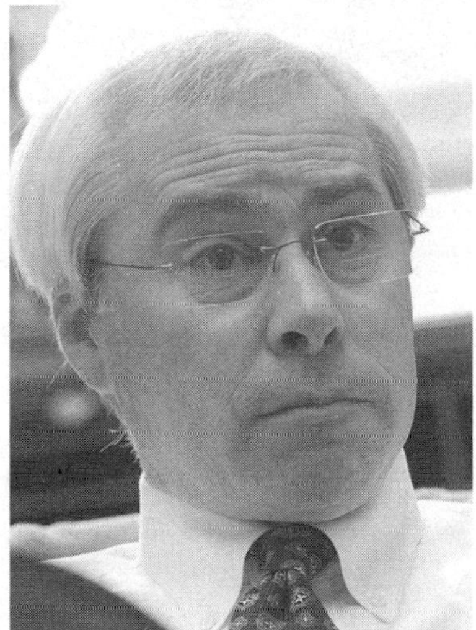

Capitol Office
225-2823
barrow.house.gov
2202 Rayburn Bldg. 20515-1012; fax 225-3377

Committees
Energy & Commerce

Residence
Augusta

Born
Oct. 31, 1955; Athens, Ga.

Religion
Baptist

Family
Divorced; two children

Education
U. of Georgia, B.A. 1976 (history & political science); Harvard U., J.D. 1979

Career
Lawyer

Political Highlights
Sought Democratic nomination for Ga. House, 1986; Athens-Clarke County Commission, 1991-2005

ELECTION RESULTS

2012 GENERAL		
John Barrow (D)	139,148	53.7%
Lee Anderson (R)	119,973	46.3%
2012 PRIMARY		
John Barrow (D)		unopposed
2010 GENERAL		
John Barrow (D)	92,459	56.6%
Raymond McKinney (R)	70,938	43.4%

Previous Winning Percentages
2008 (66%); 2006 (50%); 2004 (52%)

Elected 2004; 5th term

Barrow has one of the most moderate voting records of any Democrat in Congress and a seat on the far-reaching Energy and Commerce Committee. Those factors have helped him survive repeated attempts by Republicans to end his House career.

According to Barrow, Congress needs more centrists and moderates. "We could spend all night talking about what's wrong with Congress, but I'll sum it up in a nutshell: Everybody is trying to pick a fight with the other side," he told The Wall Street Journal in 2012. "Folks come from very partisan districts. They get caught up in the herd instinct."

As the Deep South's only white Democrat in the House, he is a favorite target of the Republican Party. "It don't make any difference in terms of how I do the job," he says. Barrow was first elected in 2004, and during his freshman term, the Georgia legislature redrew congressional lines to cut Barrow's hometown of Athens out of his district. He moved to Savannah and won re-election in 2006 by less than 1 point. Redistricting for 2012 cut out Savannah, so Barrow uprooted, moved to Augusta and won re-election by 7 points. Each time he moves, he takes with him a reputation as a fierce campaigner and fundraiser.

In the 113th Congress (2013-14), Barrow is the co-chairman for administration of the fiscally conservative Blue Dog Coalition. Votes on federal spending often find him siding with Republicans.

He was one of 25 House Democrats to vote in 2011 for a balanced-budget amendment to the Constitution, and he proposed his own version in 2013. "It's one thing to say, 'I support a balanced budget,'" he told an Augusta TV station. "It's another to say, 'Just elect me and we'll get it without any choices, without any ideas to how we're going to do it.'"

Barrow has said that "raising taxes on anyone at a time when our economy is already fragile would be irresponsible," and he was one of just 16 House Democrats to vote against the January 2013 "fiscal cliff" deal, which increased tax rates on earnings over $400,000. A few weeks later, he refused to vote for a suspension of the limit on federal borrowing, saying he would not accept any increase to the debt limit without accompanying deficit reduction.

He has a folksy way of expressing his desire for fiscal discipline. "My great-great-great grandmother said, 'Use it up, wear it out, make do or do without,'" he says. "I think the federal government could use a little of that."

From his seat on Energy and Commerce, Barrow focuses on energy and environment issues, crossing party lines on a regular basis. Barrow says he aims to "break our dependence on foreign oil and come up with solutions that have a lasting impact on our financial security."

He was one of two Democrats on the Energy and Commerce panel to vote in 2012 for a bill to prevent the Energy Department from issuing loan guarantees for renewable-energy projects — a direct response to the failure of Solyndra Inc., a solar panel manufacturer that had used the program. He was one of 19 House Democrats to vote in 2011 for a bill to prevent the EPA from regulating greenhouse gas emissions to address climate change.

And he has worked with Nebraska Republican Lee Terry on attempts to secure the approval of the Keystone XL pipeline, a project opposed by environmentalists that would connect Canada's tar sands to refineries on the Gulf Coast. Their 2013 proposal would eliminate President Barack Obama from the approval process — he denied the permit in early 2012.

He also sat on the Energy and Commerce Committee in the 111th Congress (2009-10) as it helped shape the 2010 health care overhaul. Barrow was one of the few Democrats to vote against the final health care bill (although he voted against repealing it in 2011). He insists that a health care overhaul does not need to be all-or-nothing, and he co-sponsored a bill to repeal the provisions in the law that require employers to provide health coverage to their employees.

Barrow says his record simply reflects his promise to his constituents. "I said I would listen to both sides ... and vote for the one I thought was right," he told the Savannah Morning News. "I've kept that promise."

Despite his tenuous ties to his party, Barrow takes a no-nonsense approach to his job. He has rarely missed a vote since joining Congress in 2005, and in 2012, Barrow sponsored a bill to dock a lawmaker's pay for each and every vote missed. "Millions around the country are looking for work. At the very least, members of Congress can do the work that they're paid to do, or do without the pay," he said.

Barrow is a big booster of the military. Both his parents served in the Army, and both were captains. His father was in a tank destroyer battalion, his mother in military intelligence. "They were pacing each other," he says. "They'd call each other, and Daddy said, 'Well, I just made captain.' And Mama said, 'Me too.'" He sat on the Veterans' Affairs Committee in the 112th Congress (2011-12), and Barrow has long sought to increase the amount veterans are reimbursed for their travel to Veterans Affairs hospitals for medical care.

Barrow is a native of Athens. His parents were civil rights advocates, serving in the 1960s as co-chairmen of the local chapter of Help Our Public Education, or HOPE, which fought for integration. After attending Harvard Law School, he returned to Athens to work as a trial lawyer.

In 1986, he made a failed bid for the state House, losing by 30 votes in a special-election runoff. In 1990, he won a seat on the Athens-Clarke County Commission, where he served for 14 years.

In his first U.S. House race in 2004, he took more than 51 percent of the vote in a four-way primary, then beat Republican Rep. Max Burns by nearly 4 points. The new map for the 2006 election made the district more Republican-friendly, and Burns came back for a rematch. Barrow had raised $2.5 million and built a centrist voting record. He won by 864 votes.

He had easier races in 2008 and 2010, but redistricting for 2012 again undercut some of Barrow's support base. He pulled in around $2.9 million for his campaign and ran aggressive and amusing ads against his opponent, GOP state Rep. Lee Anderson.

Barrow had the endorsement of the National Rifle Association, and the U.S. Chamber of Commerce even spent $100,000 in support of his campaign. The National Republican Congressional Committee and Americans for Tax Reform spent heavily against Barrow, but to no avail.

Key Votes

2012	
Extend a Social Security payroll tax cut and unemployment benefits	YES
Ease securities rules to expand small-business access to capital	YES
Extend for one year subsidized student loan interest rates financed by a cut in health care spending	YES
Cite Attorney General Eric H. Holder Jr. for contempt of Congress	YES
Create a visa program for foreign graduates in high-tech fields	YES
Extend most Bush-era income tax rates while allowing rates for top-bracket earners to rise (Jan. 1, 2013)	NO
2011	
Strike funding for F-35 alternative engine	YES
Prevent EPA from regulating greenhouse gas emissions to address climate change	YES
Extend certain provisions of Patriot Act for four years	YES
Declare opposition to use of ground troops in Libya	YES
Overhaul patent law	YES
Pass compromise debt limit increase plan and establish future spending limits	YES
Allow consideration of measures to implement three trade agreements	NO

CQ Vote Studies

	PARTY UNITY		PRESIDENTIAL SUPPORT	
	SUPPORT	OPPOSE	SUPPORT	OPPOSE
2012	51%	49%	28%	72%
2011	62%	38%	59%	41%
2010	91%	9%	83%	17%
2009	87%	13%	85%	15%
2008	83%	17%	27%	73%

Interest Groups

	AFL-CIO	ADA	CCUS	ACU
2012	67%	20%	100%	60%
2011	76%	60%	75%	20%
2010	71%	65%	75%	17%
2009	86%	75%	64%	17%
2008	87%	75%	67%	24%

Georgia 12

East central — Augusta, Vidalia, Douglas

The 12th District reaches from Augusta to the northern Savannah suburbs along the South Carolina border and heads southwest through rural counties in the center of the state. The loss of Democratic strongholds in the city of Savannah (to the 1st) and Hancock County (to the 10th) during decennial redistricting, as well as the addition of five conservative rural counties in the south, left Augusta as the district's sole Democratic hub.

Augusta, the largest city in the district and second-largest in the state, revolves around government jobs at Fort Gordon and a Department of Energy research facility. The Army base, which is almost entirely in the 12th, has more than $1 billion in annual economic impact on the region. The Department of Energy's 15,000-acre Savannah River Site across the river in South Carolina hosts nuclear weapons and waste research.

The economy in much of the rest of the district is agriculture-driven. Toombs County is home to the sweet Vidalia onion, which was first grown there in the 1930s. The district also has a history of timber production, particularly in Treutlen, Appling, Bulloch and Emanuel counties.

The district overall is white-majority, but black residents make up more than one-third of the residents here. The population in Augusta's Richmond County overall did not show significant growth between 2000 and 2010, but rising numbers of African-American residents as well as the loss of white residents has resulted in a black-majority populace. Adding to the demographic shift in the county, the Hispanic population rose by 48 percent during that decade. Rapid population growth on both sides of Interstate 20 in adjacent Columbia County (shared with the 10th) also included marked increases among black and Hispanic residents. These demographic shifts, and changes after decennial redistricting, made the U.S. House contest here competitive. In the 2012 presidential election, Mitt Romney took 55 percent of the district's vote.

Major Industry
Defense, agriculture, manufacturing, timber

Military Bases
Fort Gordon (Army), 15,000, military, 8,000 civilian (shared with the 10th)

Cities
Augusta-Richmond, Statesboro

Notable
The annual Masters golf tournament is held at Augusta National Golf Club.

Rep. David Scott (D)

Capitol Office
225-2939
davidscott.house.gov
225 Cannon Bldg. 20515-1013; fax 225-4628

Committees
Agriculture
Financial Services

Residence
Atlanta

Born
June 27, 1945; Aynor, S.C.

Religion
Baptist

Family
Wife, Alfredia Scott; two children

Education
Florida A&M U., B.A. 1967 (English & speech); U. of Pennsylvania, M.B.A. 1969

Career
Advertising agency owner; recruiting firm executive; defense contracting company manager

Political Highlights
Ga. House, 1975-83; Ga. Senate, 1983-2003

ELECTION RESULTS

2012 GENERAL		
David Scott (D)	201,988	71.7%
S. Malik (R)	79,550	28.3%
2012 PRIMARY		
David Scott (D)		unopposed
2010 GENERAL		
David Scott (D)	140,294	69.4%
Mike Crane (R)	61,771	30.6%

Previous Winning Percentages
2008 (69%); 2006 (69%); 2004 (100%); 2002 (60%)

Elected 2002; 6th term

As Scott draws close to logging 40 years of legislative service, he still describes bipartisanship as a necessity rather than a burden. He's on the same page with Democrats on most issues, but he'll work with Republicans on defense- and business-related goals. "You can't dance by yourself," he says.

Before his recent decade in the U.S. House, Scott spent 28 years in the Georgia legislature. A Wharton MBA, he belongs to the fiscally conservative Blue Dog Coalition — fellow Georgian Sanford D. Bishop Jr. is the only other black member — the business-friendly New Democrat Coalition and the liberal Congressional Black Caucus.

So he has some flexibility. Scott signed off on some major Democratic measures, such as the 2010 health care law (although he wanted a liberal-favored government-run health care plan included) and the 2009 stimulus law. But he was one of seven Democrats to vote for the tax cuts favored by President George W. Bush in 2003, and he has been a longtime backer of overhauling medical malpractice laws. He joined Georgia Republican Phil Gingrey on legislation to do so in the 112th Congress (2011-12).

Scott sits on the Financial Services Committee, where he considers the concerns of both businesses and those walloped by the 2008 financial crisis.

In the fall of 2008, he initially voted against Bush's $700 billion plan to help the ailing financial services industry. When a second version was in the works, Scott stumped for inclusion of a provision to assist homeowners facing foreclosure — what became known as the "Hardest Hit" fund. Georgia received a portion of the 2012 national settlement with five large banks accused of improper lending practices; Scott urged Georgia Republican Gov. Nathan Deal to use as much as possible for foreclosure prevention.

Scott sits on the panel overseeing government-sponsored enterprises. As Congress mulls the future of Fannie Mae and Freddie Mac, Scott sees a definite role for the federal government in the housing sector. "We're not in a situation where we can just depend exclusively on the private sector to solve our problems," he said in 2012. "There is a very, very strong and needed role for government," from public housing to rental assistance.

A five-year reauthorization of the National Flood Insurance Program enacted in 2012 included Scott's provision to give low-income homeowners the option of paying their premiums in installments.

Scott is the No. 3 Democrat on the Agriculture Committee and the ranking member of its panel on General Farm Commodities and Risk Management. When the panel took up a reauthorization of farm programs in 2012, Scott worked with Virginia Republican Robert W. Goodlatte to oppose a dairy management program that would require a reduction in milk production when there is a surplus. While the dairy industry is "very important" in the rural regions outside of Atlanta, Scott said the provision could cause higher milk prices that would burden consumers. The bill never reached the House floor, and as the panel considered a new version in May 2013, he and Goodlatte again opposed its dairy provisions.

He says direct payments to farmers should be examined closely "to make sure that we're not being overly generous." But he thinks crop insurance is critical, particularly in light of devastating weather patterns. In committee votes on the 2012 farm bill, Scott opposed cuts to school lunch programs and to food stamp benefits, which he said 20 percent of Georgians rely on.

Scott, a former member of the Foreign Affairs Committee, also has a keen interest in international relations. He had hoped to return to Foreign Affairs in the 113th Congress (2013-14), but he still has a spot in the U.S. delegation to the NATO Parliamentary Assembly. In the fall of 2012, he presented a paper to that body on diplomatic efforts to scale down Iran's nuclear program. Amid appeals for a more cautious approach, Scott said the U.S. will stand by Israel in disputes with Iran, "even if this means military means."

A co-founder of the Democrats' national security study group, Scott believes Democrats can again be the party associated with a strong military by returning to the hawkish defense postures of Presidents Franklin D. Roosevelt and John F. Kennedy. But he opposed the Iraq War from the beginning and pushed for a quicker end to U.S. involvement there.

Scott was one of 54 House Democrats to vote for a 2011 extension of expiring surveillance provisions in the anti-terrorism law known as the Patriot Act.

Born in impoverished Aynor, S.C., Scott attended elementary school in Pennsylvania. When he was in sixth grade, his family moved to Scarsdale, N.Y., where his parents worked for a wealthy family as a chauffeur and a maid. He was their only child and the only black student in his school.

Scott says he encountered little overt bigotry among Scarsdale's upper crust, but his racial isolation was nonetheless stressful. "I learned at a very young age how to have confidence in myself and how to get along with people who don't look like me," he said.

Scott finished high school in Daytona Beach, Fla., then attended Florida A&M University before interning with the Labor Department in Washington. While on Capitol Hill, Scott met George W. Taylor, a noted labor management expert who suggested Scott apply to the University of Pennsylvania's Wharton School of Finance, where Taylor was on the faculty.

With a Wharton MBA in hand, in the early 1970s Scott was attracted to Atlanta and its emerging crop of black leaders. He was a volunteer with Democrat Andrew Young's successful campaign for the U.S. House in 1972. Two years later, Scott won his first election to the Georgia House. He later moved over to the state Senate.

When Scott ran for Congress in 2002, establishment Democrats backed a rival in the primary. Over the years, Scott was closely associated with Atlanta's black and liberal leaders — former mayors Young and Maynard Jackson, as well as Jimmy Carter — but he won the nomination and then the general election with strong support from affluent suburbanites and business leaders.

In recent years, he has come under fire from ethics groups for failing to pay taxes on time and putting family members on his campaign payroll. In 2007, the family advertising company in which he was once a principal was revealed to have about 40 tax liens, which local reports said were paid off by June 2008. Regardless, voters have continued to deliver him overwhelming victories.

In a district slightly altered by redistricting for 2012, he won by 43 points.

Key Votes

2012	
Extend a Social Security payroll tax cut and unemployment benefits	YES
Ease securities rules to expand small-business access to capital	YES
Extend for one year subsidized student loan interest rates financed by a cut in health care spending	NO
Cite Attorney General Eric H. Holder Jr. for contempt of Congress	?
Create a visa program for foreign graduates in high-tech fields	NO
Extend most Bush-era income tax rates while allowing rates for top-bracket earners to rise (Jan. 1, 2013)	YES
2011	
Strike funding for F-35 alternative engine	NO
Prevent EPA from regulating greenhouse gas emissions to address climate change	NO
Extend certain provisions of Patriot Act for four years	YES
Declare opposition to use of ground troops in Libya	NO
Overhaul patent law	YES
Pass compromise debt limit increase plan and establish future spending limits	YES
Allow consideration of measures to implement three trade agreements	NO

CQ Vote Studies

	PARTY UNITY		PRESIDENTIAL SUPPORT	
	SUPPORT	OPPOSE	SUPPORT	OPPOSE
2012	93%	7%	87%	13%
2011	91%	9%	88%	12%
2010	98%	2%	95%	5%
2009	97%	3%	93%	7%
2008	98%	2%	18%	82%

Interest Groups

	AFL-CIO	ADA	CCUS	ACU
2012	90%	75%	27%	8%
2011	97%	75%	31%	4%
2010	100%	90%	25%	0%
2009	100%	95%	47%	0%
2008	100%	95%	67%	4%

Georgia 13

Southwest Atlanta suburbs — parts of Cobb, Fulton and Clayton counties, Douglas County

Georgia's 13th District cradles the city of Atlanta, curling southeast through suburbs from Smyrna to Stockbridge. Three of the region's busiest freeway systems — Interstates 20, 85 and 75 — slice through the district, making it a pass-through for commercial and commuter traffic.

The district's economic identity is wrapped up in its proximity to Atlanta. Communities along the district's northern border offer quick commutes to the region's largest employers, including major corporate headquarters. The Hartsfield-Jackson Atlanta International Airport, located in the neighboring 5th District, supports retail and hospitality sectors in northern Clayton County, while aeronautics at defense contractor Lockheed Martin in the nearby 11th District provide other high-paying jobs.

Most residents commute outside the district for work, but local businesses help stabilize the regional economy. The chain restaurant Chick-fil-A has its headquarters in Fulton County. The district is also a popular destination for conventions and corporate events, with the 6,000-square-foot Merle Manders conference center in Stockbridge.

The 13th has been transformed in recent years by a surge in population and a shift in racial demographics. Population in the district grew significantly between 2000 and 2010, as did much of the Atlanta metropolitan region — Henry County's population grew by more than 70 percent. The rapid growth has been fueled, in part, by an increase in the number of black residents. The percentage of black residents has more than doubled in Douglas County and more than tripled in Henry County since 2000.

Despite Republican voters in Douglas County portions of the 13th, as well as in the northern part of Fayette County, the district is safe ground for Democrats.

Major Industry
Aerospace, hospitality, health care, retail

Cities
Smyrna, Mableton, Douglasville

Notable
Jonesboro was the setting for Tara, the plantation in Margaret Mitchell's novel "Gone With the Wind."

Rep. Tom Graves (R)

Capitol Office
225-5211
tomgraves.house.gov
432 Cannon Bldg. 20515-1010; fax 225-8272

Committees
Appropriations

Residence
Ranger

Born
Feb. 3, 1970; St. Petersburg, Fla.

Religion
Southern Baptist

Family
Wife, Julie Graves; three children

Education
U. of Georgia, B.B.A. 1993 (finance)

Career
Commercial property developer; landscape company owner, retail repossessions agent

Political Highlights
Gordon Co. Board of Election and Voter Registration, 2001-02; Ga. House, 2003-10

ELECTION RESULTS

2012 GENERAL		
Tom Graves (R)	159,947	73.0%
Daniel "Danny" Grant (D)	59,245	27.0%
2012 PRIMARY		
Tom Graves (R)		unopposed
2010 GENERAL		
Tom Graves (R)		unopposed

Previous Winning Percentages
2010 Special Runoff Election (56%)

Elected 2010; 2nd full term

Graves has been a conservative anchor in the ideological tug of war, pulling hard enough to win the admiration of many Republicans. Some have expressed worry, however, that he might be yanking his own party off balance in the process.

Youthful, confident and always sporting cowboy boots, Graves dramatically describes the United States as being at a pivotal moment. "Are we going to build upon our greatness, or are we going to drift off into history?" he asks. "That's the decision point where we are."

Speaking at the Conservative Political Action Conference in 2012, he expressed that idea as a warning. "The decision to end the American story looks a little bit like this," Graves said. "We ignore the foundational principles that have set us apart from all others — the principles of less government, lower taxes, personal responsibility and liberty and justice for all — and instead allow the erosion of these pillars to continue." He also offered a prescription: "Common sense will conquer liberal ideology."

His conservative statements have been backed up by his voting record. By almost any definition, Graves is one of the most committed conservatives in the House, rejecting any measure that does not meet his standards for fiscal restraint, a smaller government or civil liberties protection. He has perfect or near-perfect ratings from several conservative advocacy groups.

Graves' commitment has at times put him at odds with his party. He served in the Georgia House and was once stripped of his committee assignments after voting against the speaker's wishes in a state transportation board election. He began his first full term in the U.S. House as a member of the GOP's whipping operation, but before the year was out, he no longer held that post. There were reports that Graves whipped positions favored by the conservative Republican Study Committee, rather than those of the party leadership.

Graves told the Atlanta Journal-Constitution that he left the whip team to pursue a more active role in the RSC. He has called that bloc the "conscience" of the GOP Conference and sees it as having a "solution-oriented focus" and supporting policies that align with his view of a smaller government.

He was the leading candidate to chair the RSC for the 113th Congress (2013-14), having gotten endorsements from outgoing Chairman Jim Jordan of Ohio and the RSC's founders. But Louisiana's Steve Scalise announced his candidacy late, said he wanted to prevent GOP infighting and won the chairmanship in November 2012. A former chief of staff to Speaker John A. Boehner made phone calls to round up support for Scalise.

Graves has a seat on the Appropriations Committee, and in the fiscal battles of 2011 some Republicans called for him to lose it. He was one of 48 Republicans in the House who refused to back a stopgap spending bill to keep the government running through the start of fiscal 2012. The move forced Republican leaders to hold an embarrassing second vote to get it passed. Graves and 23 others refused to budge and opposed the second bill, which narrowly passed. Despite the grousing, he was not punished.

Graves says Appropriations was "the last committee I thought I would ever serve on ... because I didn't want to spend any money." He does not clamor for a return of earmarking, which Republicans effectively banned in 2011. "I have three children, and if they abuse a privilege, you take it away. ... Then they must earn your trust again," he said. "And so I would reverse the question back to any member who wants earmarks and ask them, 'Do you think the American people trust you?'"

The addition of Graves and other like-minded lawmakers has led to "a lot of growing pains" on the Appropriations panel, he said in 2012, but the panel "has been meeting the numbers that have been prescribed by the Republican budget. ... You can't say that about all the other committees."

Graves doesn't introduce many bills, but he has rolled out a few bold proposals. One measure would deauthorize all funding for the implementation of the 2010 health care law; Graves introduced it in both 2011 and 2013.

He also has tried to stir interest in "devolution," or the returning of responsibilities to the states. A 2012 bill on the subject would largely eliminate the federal gas tax and give states responsibility for maintaining transportation infrastructure. "Surely the federal government can entrust the states with these responsibilities that they can handle so much better than we can here," he said.

The older of two sons, Graves grew up in Bartow County in a single-wide trailer. His father worked for Georgia Power in a coal plant, and his mother was a homemaker. "They sure encouraged me to dream big," he said. His father served as his driver for his first U.S. House campaigns, taking him around the district for a year.

Formerly an owner of a landscaping company, Graves also operated as a commercial property developer. That enterprise has caused a few political headaches. Bartow County Bank sued Graves' company for non-payment of a $2.2 million loan on a motel property; Graves filed a counterclaim, saying the bank broke its promise to refinance. The case was settled in 2011.

Church is a central feature of his personal life. Graves met his wife during a singles program at their Baptist church, where he is now a deacon. He traces his civic involvement to the anti-abortion movement. After his family moved to Gordon County, his wife founded the local Right to Life chapter, and through a series of protests and petitions they helped prevent the opening of an abortion facility in the area.

"We realized if you're passionate about something and you believe in various things, then you've got to be engaged more," he recalls.

He won an open seat in the Georgia House in 2002 and served there until 2010. That year, Rep. Nathan Deal resigned to focus on his ultimately successful gubernatorial campaign. Graves and Republican Lee Hawkins, a former state senator, emerged out of an eight-candidate, all-party field in the special election. With tea party support, Graves defeated Hawkins in the runoff to join the 111th Congress (2009-10).

A few weeks later, he defeated Hawkins in the primary and the primary runoff for the 112th Congress. In a very Republican district, Graves was unopposed in the general election. His district retained its strong conservative bent after redistricting for 2012, and that year he won 73 percent of the vote.

Key Votes

2012	
Extend a Social Security payroll tax cut and unemployment benefits	NO
Ease securities rules to expand small-business access to capital	YES
Extend for one year subsidized student loan interest rates financed by a cut in health care spending	NO
Cite Attorney General Eric H. Holder Jr. for contempt of Congress	YES
Create a visa program for foreign graduates in high-tech fields	YES
Extend most Bush-era income tax rates while allowing rates for top-bracket earners to rise (Jan. 1, 2013)	NO
2011	
Strike funding for F-35 alternative engine	YES
Prevent EPA from regulating greenhouse gas emissions to address climate change	YES
Extend certain provisions of Patriot Act for four years	NO
Declare opposition to use of ground troops in Libya	YES
Overhaul patent law	NO
Pass compromise debt limit increase plan and establish future spending limits	NO
Allow consideration of measures to implement three trade agreements	YES

CQ Vote Studies

	PARTY UNITY		PRESIDENTIAL SUPPORT	
	SUPPORT	OPPOSE	SUPPORT	OPPOSE
2012	97%	3%	16%	84%
2011	96%	4%	14%	86%
2010	99%	1%	24%	76%

Interest Groups

	AFL-CIO	ADA	CCUS	ACU
2012	5%	5%	83%	100%
2011	0%	5%	88%	100%
2010	0%	5%	67%	100%

Georgia 14

Northwest — Rome

Nestled in the northwestern corner of the state, the new 14th District stretches from the Tennessee border — where it hosts several Chattanooga bedroom communities — to the edge of the Atlanta metropolitan area. Interstate 75 bisects the district and drives commercial development. Interstate 20 runs along part of the district's southern border.

A strong and diverse manufacturing base is the engine of the region's economy. Dalton, located along the Interstate 75 corridor in Whitfield County, is home to some of the world's largest carpet and flooring manufacturers, although continuing layoffs at some of the industrial sites keep unemployment rates high. Rome also supports several automotive parts manufacturers.

The district is a health care hub for northwestern Georgia and eastern Alabama. Rome hosts three major hospitals that serve a regional population of approximately 500,000 and provide a stable source of employment.

The tourism industry also supports the local economy. Among the district's destinations is Lookout Mountain, where visitors, and hang gliding enthusiasts, can find sweeping views of the Chattanooga Valley. Part of the Chattahoochee National Forest, west of Dalton, and Fort Mountain State Park, on the district's eastern border, offer opportunities for hiking, camping and outdoor activities.

The 14th District has, along with the rest of the state, experienced significant population growth in the past decade. Several counties between Chattanooga and Atlanta — including Catoosa, Whitfield and Pickens — grew by more than 20 percent between 2000 and 2010. Increases in the Dalton area, in particular, have been fueled by an influx of Hispanic residents seeking factory jobs. Paulding County, located west of Atlanta, grew by more than 70 percent; its population of black residents more than tripled. Despite its changing demographics, the district remains safe territory for Republicans.

Major Industry
Manufacturing, health care, tourism, retail

Cities
Rome, Dalton, Calhoun

Notable
Like its namesake, Rome is built on seven hills.

HAWAII

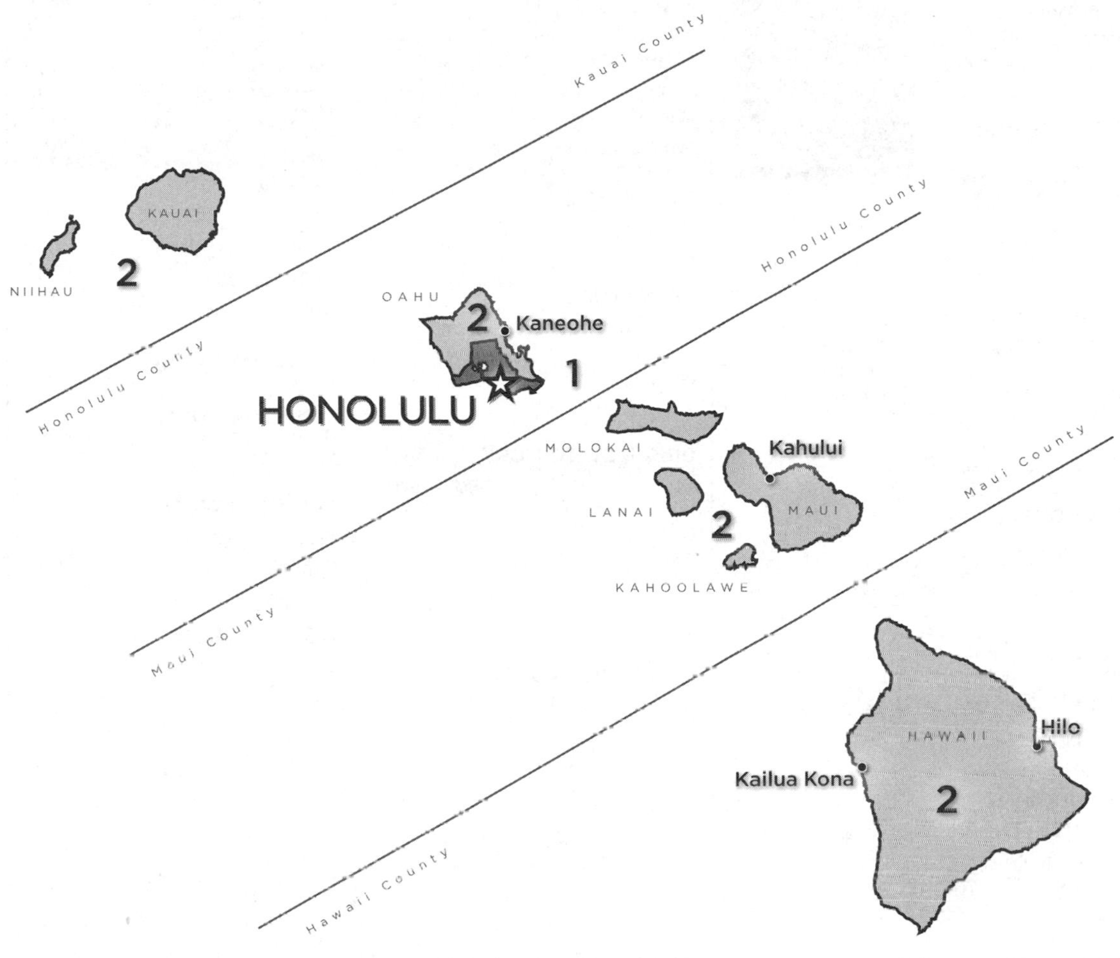
Kauai County
KAUAI
NIIHAU
2
Honolulu County
OAHU
2
Kaneohe
1
HONOLULU
Honolulu County
MOLOKAI
Kahului
LANAI
MAUI
2
KAHOOLAWE
Maui County
Maui County
HAWAII
Hilo
Kailua Kona
2
Hawaii County

Gov. Neil Abercrombie (D)

First elected: 2010
Length of term: 4 years
Term expires: 12/14
Salary: $117,312
Phone: (808) 586-0034
Residence: Honolulu
Born: June 26, 1938; Buffalo, N.Y.
Religion: Unspecified
Family: Wife, Nancie Caraway
Education: Union College (N.Y.), B.A. 1959; U. of Hawaii, M.A. 1964, Ph.D. 1974 (American studies)
Career: Teaching assistant
Political highlights: Sought Democratic nomination for U.S. Senate, 1970; Hawaii House, 1974-78; Hawaii Senate, 1978-86; U.S. House, 1986-87; defeated in primary for re-election to U.S. House, 1986; Honolulu City Council, 1988-90; U.S. House, 1991-2010

ELECTION RESULTS

2010 GENERAL

Neil Abercrombie (D)	222,724	57.8%
Duke Aiona (R)	157,311	40.8%

Lt. Gov. Shan S. Tsutsui (D)

Appointed: 2012
Length of term: 4 years
Term expires: 12/14
Salary: $114,420
Phone: (808) 586-0255

LEGISLATURE

Legislature: 60 days January-May
Senate: 25 members, 4-year terms
2013 ratios: 24 D, 1 R; 17 men, 8 women
Salary: $55,896
Phone: (808) 586-6720
House: 51 members, 2-year terms
2013 ratios: 44 D, 7 R; 35 men, 16 women
Salary: $55,896
Phone: (808) 586-6400

TERM LIMITS

Governor: 2 consecutive terms
Senate: No
House: No

URBAN STATISTICS

CITY	POPULATION
Urban Honolulu	337,256
East Honolulu	49,914
Pearl City	47,698
Hilo	43,263
Kailua	38,635

REGISTERED VOTERS

Voters do not register by party.

POPULATION

2010 population (est.)	1,360,301
2000 population	1,211,537
1990 population	1,108,229
Percent change (2000-2010)	+12.3%
Rank among states (2010)	40
Median age	37.5
Born in state	54.0%
Foreign born	15.8%
Violent crime rate	275/100,000
Poverty level	10.4%
Federal workers	38,378
Military	40,874

ELECTIONS

STATE ELECTION OFFICIAL
(808) 453-8683

DEMOCRATIC PARTY
(808) 596-2980

REPUBLICAN PARTY
(808) 593-8180

MISCELLANEOUS

Web: www.hawaii.gov
Capital: Honolulu

U.S. CONGRESS

Senate: 2 Democrats
House: 2 Democrats

STATISTICS BY DISTRICT

District	2012 Vote for President Obama	2012 Vote for President Romney	2008 Vote for President Obama	2008 Vote for President McCain	Black	Asian	Hispanic	Median Income	Over 64	Under 20	College Education	Rural	Sq. Miles
1	70%	29%	70%	28%	2%	51%	8%	$65,602	16%	23%	32%	<1%	209
2	71	27	73	25	1	25	11	57,492	13	26	26	20	6,213
STATE	**71**	**28**	**72**	**27**	**2**	**39**	**9**	**61,821**	**15**	**25**	**29**	**10**	**6,423**
U.S.	**51**	**47**	**53**	**46**	**12**	**5**	**17**	**50,052**	**13**	**27**	**29**	**21**	**3,531,905**

Sen. Brian Schatz (D)

Capitol Office
224-3934
schatz.senate.gov
722 Hart Bldg. 20510-1102; fax 228-1153

Committees
Commerce, Science & Transportation
Energy & Natural Resources
(Water & Power - Chairman)
Indian Affairs

Residence
Honolulu

Born
Oct. 20, 1972; Ann Arbor, Mich.

Religion
Jewish

Family
Wife, Linda Kwok Schatz; two children

Education
Pomona College, B.A. 1994 (philosophy)

Career
Nonprofit social services organization CEO; nonprofit environmental volunteering organization founder; teacher

Political Highlights
Hawaii House, 1998-2006; sought Democratic nomination for U.S. House, 2006; Hawaii Democratic Party chairman, 2008-10; lieutenant governor, 2010-12

Appointed December 2012; 1st term

Schatz was serving as Hawaii's lieutenant governor in December 2012 when the state lost its iconic congressional leader — Sen. Daniel K. Inouye died in the middle of his ninth term. As Inouye's appointed replacement, Schatz plans to promote renewable energy and make the case for his state's infrastructure needs. His work in the 113th Congress can be seen as an audition, as he tries to convince fellow Democrats that he is worthy of election to the seat he now holds.

Inouye's death came just weeks before the retirement of Daniel K. Akaka, Hawaii's other senator. Many observers wondered how the delegation would handle its sudden drop in seniority in that chamber. Inouye was a deft appropriator who struck countless deals, sending federal money to his state; his efforts helped build up military bases, transportation infrastructure and education programs. Now, neither of Hawaii's senators serves on the Appropriations Committee.

To Schatz, that means they need to work harder. "It's not just about Hawaii having its hand out for appropriations," he said. "It's also demonstrating to international policy makers, to the administration, where Hawaii can be an asset to the nation."

The key to that argument, he said, is showing lawmakers that entities based in Hawaii — such as the Pacific Command and the East-West Center — serve the national interest. The same strategy can be applied, according to Schatz, to promote the state's efforts to move toward an economy run on cleaner forms of energy. "It's all about relationships, and we are off to a good start with respect to our colleagues," he said.

Schatz himself is certainly off to a good start, in terms of building up clout on energy and environmental policy. In early 2013, Oregon Democrat Ron Wyden, who chairs the Energy and Natural Resources Committee, chose Schatz to lead the Subcommittee on Water and Power.

As lieutenant governor, Schatz oversaw the coordination of Hawaii's energy priorities. Hawaii has had to import oil to fuel upwards of 90 percent of its power, but it's an ordeal to transport fossil fuels to the islands, which makes energy far more costly. Schatz began working with state agencies, the private sector and foreign interests on development of "clean" and renewable power sources.

As a member of Energy and Natural Resources, he wants to apply lessons that Hawaii learned from implementing its clean-energy initiative to the committee's work. Hawaii has tripled the percentage of clean energy generated over the last three years, while unemployment simultaneously dropped to just above 5 percent, Schatz said.

"We've been able to do that through a diverse portfolio of energy resources, and we've made real progress in conservation aspects — the efficiency and conservation space," he said.

Even before he joined the Senate, Schatz said that he sees climate change as "the most urgent challenge of our generation." He has repeated that view as President Barack Obama has pursued greater investments in clean-energy technologies during his second term. Schatz has signed on to a bill to create a "carbon tax" as a means to decrease the use of fossil fuels.

"I think we need more senators to say what they know to be true about climate change, which is that it is real, it is human-caused and it is solvable," Schatz said. "There are Republicans who know that, but they need to be able to operate in a political context where they're allowed to say it out loud."

Schatz also holds seats on the Indian Affairs and Commerce, Science and

Transportation committees, which handle significant Hawaiian interests — native populations and shipping. Inouye and Akaka (who was the Indian Affairs chairman when he retired) fought for years to secure federal recognition for the Native Hawaiian population, similar to the status already held by Native Americans and Alaska Natives. Schatz's focuses on the Commerce panel include maritime infrastructure, given the state's dependence on imports, and ways to facilitate tourism from international visitors.

Schatz was a surprise choice to succeed Inouye. While hospitalized with respiratory problems, Inouye wrote a letter in which he requested Rep. Colleen Hanabusa as his replacement. The state Democratic Party presented a list of three candidates to Gov. Neil Abercrombie that included Hanabusa. Given Inouye's 50 years of Senate service, it seemed natural that Abercrombie would take his recommendation and select the congresswoman.

But Abercrombie picked his own 2010 running mate, saying it was "in the overall best interest of the party." Hanabusa has a seat on the House Armed Services Committee, which is important to a state where the military is a huge economic engine. Also, keeping her in the House eliminated the possibility of Republicans capturing her Honolulu-based district in a special election—as they did in 2010 when Abercrombie resigned his House seat to focus on his campaign for governor.

In April 2013, Hanabusa announced that she will challenge Schatz in the special-election primary in 2014.

Schatz was born in Michigan but moved to the islands with his family as a toddler. He attended Punahou School, the private school that also graduated Obama. He went to college in California, getting a degree in philosophy from Pomona College; he spent some time as an undergraduate studying in Kenya. Returning home, Schatz founded a nonprofit focusing on environmental activism. He later worked for eight years as the CEO of Helping Hands Hawaii, a large nonprofit community social services organization.

Schatz won election to the Hawaii House in 1998 at age 26, unseating a Republican incumbent. In four terms he served as majority whip and chairman of the Economic Development Committee. He then pursued a U.S. House seat in 2006 when Democratic Rep. Ed Case decided to run for the Senate. The primary for the 2nd District (which covers every part of the state other than Honolulu) was a free-for-all, with Schatz coming in sixth behind Hanabusa and winner Mazie K. Hirono — a former lieutenant governor who is now Schatz's Senate colleague in the 113th Congress (2013-14).

Schatz worked on the Hawaii campaign of Obama in 2008 and was chosen that year to chair the state Democratic Party. He stepped down from that post in early 2010 to run for lieutenant governor, landing on the eventual winning ticket with Abercrombie.

The No. 2 job in Hawaii has few official responsibilities, but Abercrombie vowed that Schatz wouldn't be a ceremonial figure. In addition to his clean-energy work, he was tasked with assisting the state's preparations for an Asia-Pacific Economic Cooperation conference in November 2011, which went smoothly. In Hawaii's parochial tradition, Schatz worked on state requests for federal grants and other funding.

Above all, Schatz was loyal to Abercrombie. As the governor struggled with low approval ratings, even among Democrats, Schatz did not publicly challenge or criticize his boss. He said several times that he planned to run for governor — but in 2018, when Abercrombie, if re-elected, would be unable to run again due to term limits.

Schatz's career is now on a different track. He has been aggressively raising funds for the 2014 special election, and he reportedly will have the support of the Democratic Senatorial Campaign Committee. Whoever wins the special election would have to defend their seat two years later — Inouye's original term expires at the end of 2016.

Key Votes

2012

Provide $60.4 billion in disaster relief following Superstorm Sandy	YES
Extend most Bush-era income tax rates while allowing rates for top-bracket earners to rise (Jan. 1, 2013)	YES

CQ Vote Studies

	PARTY UNITY		PRESIDENTIAL SUPPORT	
	SUPPORT	OPPOSE	SUPPORT	OPPOSE
2012	100%	0%	80%	20%

Sen. Mazie K. Hirono (D)

Capitol Office
224-6361
hirono.senate.gov
330 Hart Bldg. 20510; fax 224-9549

Committees
Armed Services
Judiciary
Veterans' Affairs

Residence
Honolulu

Born
Nov. 3, 1947; Fukushima, Japan

Religion
Buddhist

Family
Husband, Leighton Kim Oshima; one stepchild

Education
U. of Hawaii, B.A. 1970 (psychology); Georgetown U., J.D. 1978

Career
Lawyer; campaign and state legislative aide

Political Highlights
Hawaii House, 1980-94; lieutenant governor, 1994-2002; Democratic nominee for governor, 2002; U.S. House, 2007-13

ELECTION RESULTS

2012 GENERAL		
Mazie K. Hirono (D)	269,489	62.6%
Linda Lingle (R)	160,994	37.4%
2012 PRIMARY		
Mazie K. Hirono (D)	134,745	57.7%
Ed Case (D)	95,553	40.9%

Previous Winning Percentages
2010 House Election (72%); 2008 House Election (76%); 2006 House Election (61%)

Elected 2012; 1st term

Hawaii's Senate team was completely overturned in 2012 by the November election of Hirono and the December death of Daniel K. Inouye. She nonetheless provides a degree of continuity. Hirono practices politics that the islands have come to love: conventional liberalism accented by aggressive pursuit of federal resources. Education and labor issues have always been on her agenda, but her policy interests are multiplying as she steps into the unexpected role of dean of the state's congressional delegation.

Her predecessor, Democrat Daniel K. Akaka, was one of the more liberal and anonymous senators; he preferred behind-the-scenes work and seldom drew media attention on issues unrelated to Hawaii. Hirono has taken a similar approach. She served six years in the House and showed little inclination to break with Democratic positions or outwardly facilitate deals with Republicans. Hirono is often described as a private individual, and her partisanship isn't combative.

She refined her style during a long career in state government. Hirono broke into politics as a campaign worker and legislative aide. The Honolulu Advertiser in 2002 placed her in the "class of Democrats who came to power in the 1970s and helped build a state government that was unapologetically interventionist and indisputably liberal." Hirono was elected to the state House in 1980 and served 14 years, doting on the labor and feminist movements. Critics accused her of having no signature legislative achievements but weren't able to sway voters. She was elected lieutenant governor twice.

Hirono has described herself as a successor to Hawaii Democratic Rep. Patsy T. Mink, the first non-Caucasian woman elected to Congress. "Patsy fought for working men and women, and she fought for education," she said. "Those are the issues that are really important to me."

But she arranged for committee assignments that are really important to Hawaii. Hirono was set to serve on the Energy and Natural Resources panel in the 113th Congress (2013-14), but the death of Inouye, the chairman of the Defense Appropriations Subcommittee, changed those plans. She was instead given a seat on the Armed Services Committee. Combined with her seat on the Veterans' Affairs Committee, it gives Hirono a base from which to support the large military presence in Hawaii.

Hirono also sits on the Judiciary Committee and its panel on immigration. At a February 2013 hearing, she said any overhaul of immigration law should preserve the goal of keeping families together. Several thousand Filipino soldiers who fought for the United States in World War II were granted U.S. citizenship in 1990, and Hirono's first bill as a senator would exempt their adult children from limits on immigrant visas — effectively removing them from waiting lists. Democrat Colleen Hanabusa, Hirono's Hawaii colleague, sponsored the House version of the bill.

The Senate has a more flexible work environment than the House, and Hirono can still offer input on many of her established policy interests, even without relevant committee seats.

She invests much of her time in early-childhood education. Hirono has promoted universal preschool programs going back to her time as lieutenant governor. In each of her House terms, she introduced bills to bolster preschool programs or require states to revise their early-learning guidelines; a 2007 reauthorization of Head Start included her provision ensuring that preschool teacher training is conducted by people with expertise in infant and toddler development. Her second bill as a senator was to create a grant program for states looking to expand or improve their preschool programs.

The alternative-energy industry has a growing presence in Hawaii, where fossil fuels are unusually expensive because of the cost of transporting them to the islands. Hirono is on board when lawmakers try to expand either production or research of alternative energy. Part of her portfolio as lieutenant governor was chairing a task force studying the role of technology in Hawaii's future, and she pushed hard for a 2011 reauthorization of grant programs to both commercialize research and involve more small businesses in federal research projects.

Before earmarks were effectively banned by House rules in 2011, Hirono worked with state colleagues to steer millions of dollars to projects in Hawaii — Inouye, who tacitly endorsed Hirono's Senate run, was recognized as a master of the practice. After the ban, they continued their efforts by seeking federal grants. Hirono, Inouye, Akaka and Hanabusa secured $250 million in 2012 for a Honolulu rail project.

On most subjects, Hirono is firmly to the left. She has prioritized worker and consumer protections throughout her legislative career and gets high marks from environmental groups. She was a strong supporter of the Democrats' health care overhaul in the 111th Congress (2009-10) as a member of the House Education and Labor Committee.

Hirono was born in 1947 in Fukushima, Japan. She said she never really knew her father, an alcoholic and compulsive gambler. In 1955, her mother, Laura Chie Hirono, decided that life in rural Japan with an abusive husband was "no life for her family." The move to Hawaii took covert plotting, but her mother managed to leave with Hirono and her oldest son. A year later, another son and Hirono's grandparents joined them.

Her mother worked various jobs to support the family and relied on the children to help her learn English. Her mother's struggle inspired Hirono's political career. "I know what it feels like to be discriminated against, to feel powerless, to have landlords who threaten to kick you out, and not having a place to go," she told the Advertiser. To succeed, she immersed herself in school and books and worked hard to learn the language. She eventually graduated from the University of Hawaii with a degree in psychology, thinking she might want to be a social worker to "help people one by one."

In college she met anti-war protester David Hagino, who asked Hirono to run his 1970 campaign for the state House. He lost, but two years later Hirono helped in the successful state House campaign of Democrat Anson Chong. She then went to work in Chong's legislative office. After earning a law degree from Georgetown University, Hirono returned to Hawaii and served as a deputy attorney general before winning a state House seat.

Hirono considered running for mayor of Honolulu in 2002, but after some intraparty jockeying she switched to the governor's race. She narrowly defeated Ed Case in the Democratic primary but ultimately lost to Republican Linda Lingle — voters were venting their frustration with 40 years of Democratic control in Hawaii. Case, meanwhile, won a special election to replace Mink, who had died of pneumonia.

Case mounted an unsuccessful primary challenge to Akaka in 2006, leaving the 2nd District seat open. Hirono won a 10-way primary, then easily defeated a Republican state senator that November to join the House. When Akaka announced his retirement, she quickly entered the race, which was a who's who of Hawaii politics.

Case waged a bitter campaign against Hirono in the primary, accusing her of being a political insider with little initiative. Hirono beat him by 17 points, moving on to face Lingle in the general election.

Hirono had an early lead in the polls. She defended it by casting Lingle as beholden to the GOP's national platform. Lingle repeated the attack that Hirono is not a leader, but it wasn't enough. Hirono won by 25 points. She is the first Buddhist and the first Asian-American woman to serve in the Senate.

Key Votes (while House member)

2012	
Extend a Social Security payroll tax cut and unemployment benefits	YES
Ease securities rules to expand small-business access to capital	YES
Extend for one year subsidized student loan interest rates financed by a cut in health care spending	?
Cite Attorney General Eric H. Holder Jr. for contempt of Congress	NO
Create a visa program for foreign graduates in high-tech fields	NO
Extend most Bush-era income tax rates while allowing rates for top-bracket earners to rise (Jan. 1, 2013)	YES
2011	
Strike funding for F-35 alternative engine	YES
Prevent EPA from regulating greenhouse gas emissions to address climate change	NO
Extend certain provisions of Patriot Act for four years	NO
Declare opposition to use of ground troops in Libya	NO
Overhaul patent law	NO
Pass compromise debt limit increase plan and establish future spending limits	YES
Allow consideration of measures to implement three trade agreements	YES

CQ Vote Studies (while House member)

	PARTY UNITY		PRESIDENTIAL SUPPORT	
	SUPPORT	OPPOSE	SUPPORT	OPPOSE
2012	98%	2%	92%	8%
2011	98%	2%	86%	14%
2010	99%	1%	93%	7%
2009	99%	1%	97%	3%
2008	99%	1%	13%	87%
2007	99%	1%	4%	96%

Interest Groups (while House member)

	AFL-CIO	ADA	CCUS	ACU
2012	94%	75%	30%	0%
2011	100%	90%	19%	0%
2010	100%	95%	13%	0%
2009	100%	100%	33%	0%
2008	100%	100%	56%	4%
2007	96%	100%	45%	0%

Rep. Colleen Hanabusa (D)

Capitol Office
225-2726
hanabusa.house.gov
238 Cannon Bldg. 20515-1101; fax 225-0688

Committees
Armed Services
Natural Resources

Residence
Honolulu

Born
May 4, 1951; Honolulu, Hawaii

Religion
Buddhist

Family
Husband, John Souza

Education
U. of the Pacific, attended 1969-70; U. of Hawaii, B.A. 1973 (economics & sociology); Colorado College, attended 1970-71; U. of Hawaii, M.A. 1975 (sociology), J.D. 1977

Career
Lawyer

Political Highlights
Hawaii Senate, 1999-2010 (majority leader, 2003-07; president, 2007-10); candidate for U.S. House (special election), 2003; sought Democratic nomination for U.S. House, 2006; candidate for U.S. House (special election), 2010

ELECTION RESULTS

2012 GENERAL		
Colleen Hanabusa (D)	116,505	54.6%
Charles K. Djou (R)	96,824	45.4%
2012 PRIMARY		
Colleen Hanabusa (D)	92,136	84.1%
Roy F. "Sky" Wyttenbach (D)	17,369	15.9%
2010 GENERAL		
Colleen Hanabusa (D)	94,140	53.2%
Charles K. Djou (R)	82,723	46.8%

Elected 2010; 2nd term

Hanabusa says her goal is a re-centering of the map. North America is in the middle of current schoolbook charts, but she sees the military and economic future of the United States hinging on the Pacific. Account for that shift in perspective, "and guess what's right smack in the middle?"

For now, she pursues that goal as a member of the House, but she hopes to move across the Capitol. Shortly before Hawaii Sen. Daniel K. Inouye died in December 2012, he requested that Hanabusa be appointed as his replacement. Gov. Neil Abercrombie instead chose Lt. Gov. Brian Schatz — a move which many people in the state saw as a slight to the memory of Inouye, who had served 50 years in the Senate. Hanabusa announced in the spring of 2013 that she would take on Schatz in the primary for the 2014 special election to complete Inouye's term, which expires in 2016.

Hanabusa had decades of experience as a labor attorney before entering politics. She served as majority leader and president of the state Senate. Democrats dominate that body, so her time in the Republican-controlled House has been an adjustment. "I've taken the position that there is nothing wrong with asking," she says.

Many of her requests regard Hawaii's huge military interests. Hanabusa sits on the Armed Services Committee and supports the plan, announced by the Obama administration in 2011, of a strategic "pivot" to the Pacific.

Hanabusa has tried to clarify big-picture issues associated with that pivot. She urges Congress to make a "policy commitment" to define the broader U.S. military role, saying that a clear statement would facilitate long-term planning.

She has her suggestions for what else to include: protection of trade interests in the Pacific and monitoring China's growth. Hanabusa opposed free trade pacts with Colombia and Panama, but she was one of 59 Democrats to back a South Korea deal in 2011. She called that agreement "vital to our country's defense posture." Hanabusa also sees a diplomatic role for the military, writing in Roll Call in 2011 that the armed forces are "our ambassadors to the world and the individuals responsible for embodying and conveying American beliefs, values and strategies."

Hanabusa joined the Seapower and Projection Forces Subcommittee in the 113th Congress (2013-14). She takes a particular interest in units and weapons that have the most flexibility. Marine expeditionary forces can be self-reliant for several months. If that approach can be expanded, "you don't have the expense of building bases," she said. Hanabusa studied the acquisitions process in the 112th Congress (2011-12) as a member of an Armed Services panel examining the problems contractors have when dealing with the Pentagon.

She strongly advocates defense spending in Hawaii. Hanabusa didn't like automatic defense cuts put in place by an August 2011 deficit reduction law. But she didn't turn her back on Democratic priorities to prevent them from taking hold in 2013. She voted against a 2012 Republican bill to reverse some of those cuts by eliminating a preventive care program created by the 2010 health care overhaul.

Whatever her preference for readiness in the Pacific, Hanabusa has opposed conflicts elsewhere. She disliked the invasion of Iraq and applauded President Barack Obama's decision to withdraw troops by the end of 2011. She told The Hill in 2011 that she did not support U.S. involvement in Libya because she was "not sure that there is a real endgame to what they're doing there." She wants to end the mission in Afghanistan as soon as possible.

Hanabusa sits on the Natural Resources Committee, and she is the top Democrat on a subcommittee with wide-ranging implications for her district:

Indian and Alaska Native Affairs. She supports federal recognition of Native Hawaiians, which would allow the formation of sovereign entities similar to those created by American Indians and Alaska Natives. "I think if we could just get to the point of a recognition, let us then battle Congress after Congress after that as to what then it means," Hanabusa said.

She has environmentalist tendencies on many resources issues. In the 112th, she unsuccessfully tried to modify Republican bills on oil production to require companies to prepare worst-case-scenario plans for spills. The House version of the fiscal 2012 Interior-Environment spending bill would have blocked the listing of new plants and animals under the Endangered Species Act; Hanabusa was one author of an unsuccessful amendment to strike that provision.

However, she was one of only 41 Democrats to back a 2011 Republican bill that would have curtailed EPA regulation of emissions from industrial boilers. The cost of complying with such regulations would be too great for sugar mills and other Hawaii businesses, she wrote at the time.

Hanabusa pitches the islands as a laboratory for alternative energy: "I think that research in energy should be funded, and that we are the perfect place to do it." Beyond solar, wind and geothermal power, she is a cheerleader for algae-based biofuel. Hanabusa casts the research in military terms: "Ultimately what we're looking for is a 100 percent sustainable force without fossil fuels in Hawaii."

A Japanese-American whose family has been in Hawaii for four generations, Hanabusa was raised on a sugar plantation, largely by her maternal grandmother; her parents operated a Chevron gas station. In addition to regular schooling, she studied the Japanese language and ikebana, the art of floral arrangement. The friendly Hanabusa is one of two Buddhists in the House and describes her faith as "more of a philosophy than a religion" for her.

After law school, she embarked on a long career as a labor attorney. Hanabusa won election to the state Senate in 1998, and in 2007 she became the first woman to lead either chamber of the Hawaii Legislature.

She was elected to the House on her fourth try. Hanabusa lost a 2003 special election in the 2nd District, and she finished just 844 votes behind winner Mazie K. Hirono in the 2nd District's 2006 Democratic primary.

The 1st District opened up in February 2010 when Abercrombie, then a 10-term Democrat, resigned to run for governor. In the special election that May to determine his replacement, Hanabusa and former Rep. Ed Case split the Democratic vote, handing victory to Republican Charles K. Djou. Case opted not to enter the regular primary that year, and Hanabusa cruised to the nomination. She beat Djou in November with 53 percent of the vote, then defeated him again when she ran for re-election in 2012.

Key Votes

2012	
Extend a Social Security payroll tax cut and unemployment benefits	YES
Ease securities rules to expand small-business access to capital	YES
Extend for one year subsidized student loan interest rates financed by a cut in health care spending	NO
Cite Attorney General Eric H. Holder Jr. for contempt of Congress	?
Create a visa program for foreign graduates in high-tech fields	NO
Extend most Bush-era income tax rates while allowing rates for top-bracket earners to rise (Jan. 1, 2013)	YES
2011	
Strike funding for F-35 alternative engine	YES
Prevent EPA from regulating greenhouse gas emissions to address climate change	NO
Extend certain provisions of Patriot Act for four years	NO
Declare opposition to use of ground troops in Libya	YES
Overhaul patent law	YES
Pass compromise debt limit increase plan and establish future spending limits	YES
Allow consideration of measures to implement three trade agreements	YES

CQ Vote Studies

	PARTY UNITY		PRESIDENTIAL SUPPORT	
	SUPPORT	OPPOSE	SUPPORT	OPPOSE
2012	95%	5%	87%	13%
2011	95%	5%	83%	17%

Interest Groups

	AFL-CIO	ADA	CCUS	ACU
2012	90%	80%	33%	4%
2011	97%	80%	31%	0%

Hawaii 1

Oahu — Honolulu, Aiea, Pearl City

The 1st represents the southern portion of Oahu, the state's center of commerce and tourism. From the island's easternmost point the district follows the Koolau Ridge toward the northwest before cutting due west to Mililani. The district's boundary line turns southward, following Kamehemeha Highway and the H-1 highway past Waipahu to Ko Olina. Honolulu, the state capital, hosts most of Hawaii's business and nearly 30 percent of its people, leading to pervasive traffic congestion throughout the city. Manoa, Moiliili, Kaimuki and Kapahulu are neighborhoods east of downtown.

The district draws most of the more than 4 million tourists who arrive on the island annually. Waikiki Beach is one of the most popular tourist spots in the nation. A new visitors center welcomes the 1.5 million annual visitors to the U.S.S. Arizona Memorial in Pearl Harbor, and Walt Disney Co. recently opened an $850 million resort west of Honolulu in more remote Ko Olina.

The home of the U.S. Pacific Command, the 1st has a large military presence and massive complexes near Pearl Harbor. The local economy benefits from the hundreds of millions of dollars in military construction contracts awarded for installation upgrades.

Honolulu leads the nation as the only majority-Asian county in the U.S., and the district has large Japanese, Chinese and Filipino communities. A sizable proportion of residents have multi-racial backgrounds. A large Mormon community boosted GOP rolls in support of coreligionist Mitt Romney during the 2012 presidential election, but Honolulu-born Barack Obama easily won on the island. The district has a long history of Democratic strength.

Major Industry
Tourism, military, construction

Military Bases
Joint Base Pearl Harbor-Hickam, 19,095 military, 11,986 civilian (2011); Fort Shafter (Army), 3,797 military, 3,186 civilian (2011); Tripler Army Medical Center, 1,427 military, 1,642 civilian (2007); Camp H.M. Smith Marine Corps installation, 1,655 military, 682 civilian (2011)

Cities
Urban Honolulu, East Honolulu, Pearl City, Waipahu

Notable
Iolani Palace, the royal residence of King Kalakaua and Queen Liliuokalani, is in downtown Honolulu.

Rep. Tulsi Gabbard (D)

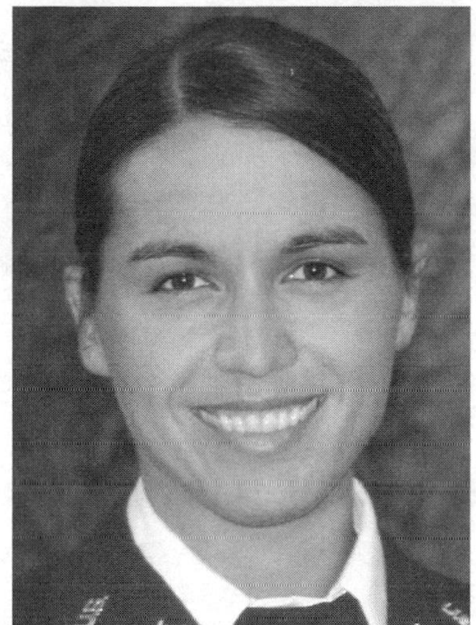

Capitol Office
225-4906
gabbard.house.gov
502 Cannon Bldg. 20515-1102; fax 225-4987

Committees
Foreign Affairs
Homeland Security

Residence
Kailua

Born
April 12, 1981, Leloaloa, A.S.

Religion
Hindu

Family
Divorced

Education
Hawaii Pacific U., B.A. 2009 (international business)

Military
Hawaii National Guard, 2003-present

Career
Media production company owner; congressional aide

Political Highlights
Hawaii House, 2002-04; Honolulu City Council, 2011-12

ELECTION RESULTS

2012 GENERAL		
Tulsi Gabbard (D)	168,503	80.5%
Kawika Crowley (R)	40,707	19.5%
2012 PRIMARY		
Tulsi Gabbard (D)	62,882	55.1%
Mufi F. Hannemann (D)	39,176	34.3%
Esther Kia'aina (D)	6,681	5.8%
Bob Marx (D)	4,327	3.8%

Elected 2012; 1st term

Gabbard's political ascent has been improbable and impressive. She seems aware of her potential star power within the Democratic Party, and ready to work to realize that potential.

She was home-schooled in Hawaii by her civically active parents — her father, Mike, is a state senator and former Republican. As a teenager, she helped her father found and run a nonprofit dedicated to environmental protection and community health. (Mike Gabbard also founded a nonprofit advocating against same-sex marriage and civil unions, a view Tulsi Gabbard says she no longer shares.) Like her mother, Gabbard is a Hindu — she is the first person of that faith to serve in Congress.

At 21, she became the youngest woman ever elected to the Hawaii House. While holding that job, she signed up for the National Guard and volunteered for deployment to the Middle East. After she returned, she worked as a legislative aide to Sen. Daniel K. Akaka. Gabbard then deployed a second time, and on her return she successfully ran for the Honolulu City Council. She says she is guided by the "principle of servant leadership."

Gabbard has seats on the Homeland Security and Foreign Affairs committees, and on the latter she serves on the panel on Asia and the Pacific. Before she had served one month in the House, she was chosen as a vice chairwoman of the Democratic National Committee, giving her a national role promoting the party's platform and candidates.

The 2nd District was left open in 2012 by Democrat Mazie K. Hirono, who ran for the Senate. In the primary, Gabbard was an underdog to Mufi F. Hannemann, a former Honolulu mayor who had the endorsement of Senate Majority Leader Harry Reid. She stunned the establishment, winning by more than 20 points. She scored an easy victory in November.

When Democratic Sen. Daniel K. Inouye died in December 2012, Gabbard made waves when she applied to be the appointee to replace him.

Hawaii 2

Suburban and outer Oahu; 'Neighbor Islands'

Home to a stunning array of tropical flora and fauna, as well as active volcanoes and sandy beaches, the 2nd boasts most of Oahu and all other Hawaiian islands. Residents of the 2nd are spread across the eight major islands of the Hawaiian archipelago. Roughly 40 percent live on Oahu in towns near Army and Marine installations or beach communities along the island's North Shore, a world-famous surfing spot. Ka Lae, on the "Big Island" of Hawaii, is the southernmost point in the U.S.

Maui is the state's second most popular tourist destination, and Hawaii and Kauai draw more than a million tourists annually. Lanai, with two Four Seasons resorts, is preferred by a more exclusive clientele. Kauai offers aerial tours of verdant valley rain forest and kayaking. Whale-watching tours operate in the Auau Channel.

The island of Hawaii, the chain's geologic youngest, has diverse geography of lava field desert, black sand beaches, tropical rainforest and towering waterfalls. The arid summit of Mauna Kea is home to the world's largest astronomical observatory facility. Kilauea on the island's southeastern shore has erupted continuously since 1983, making it one of the most active volcanic sites in the world, and Mauna Loa is the world's largest active volcano.

Most of the state's multibillion-dollar agricultural industry is in the 2nd. The large sugar cane plantations, which attracted the islands' original Japanese and Chinese populations, have dwindled to one, but farmers grow the nation's largest quantities of coffee and macadamia nuts as well as large amounts of algae, which the military uses to make biofuel.

Multi-ethnic residents, Asians and Native Hawaiians give the consistently Democratic 2nd a unique demographic makeup.

Major Industry
Tourism, agriculture, military

Military Bases
Schofield Barracks, 19,362 military, 4,228 civilian (2011); Marine Corps Base Hawaii, 5,792 military, 694 civilian (2009)

Cities
Hilo, Kailua, Kaneohe

Notable
Papahānaumokuākea Marine National Monument is the largest U.S. conservation area and larger than all U.S. national parks combined.

IDAHO

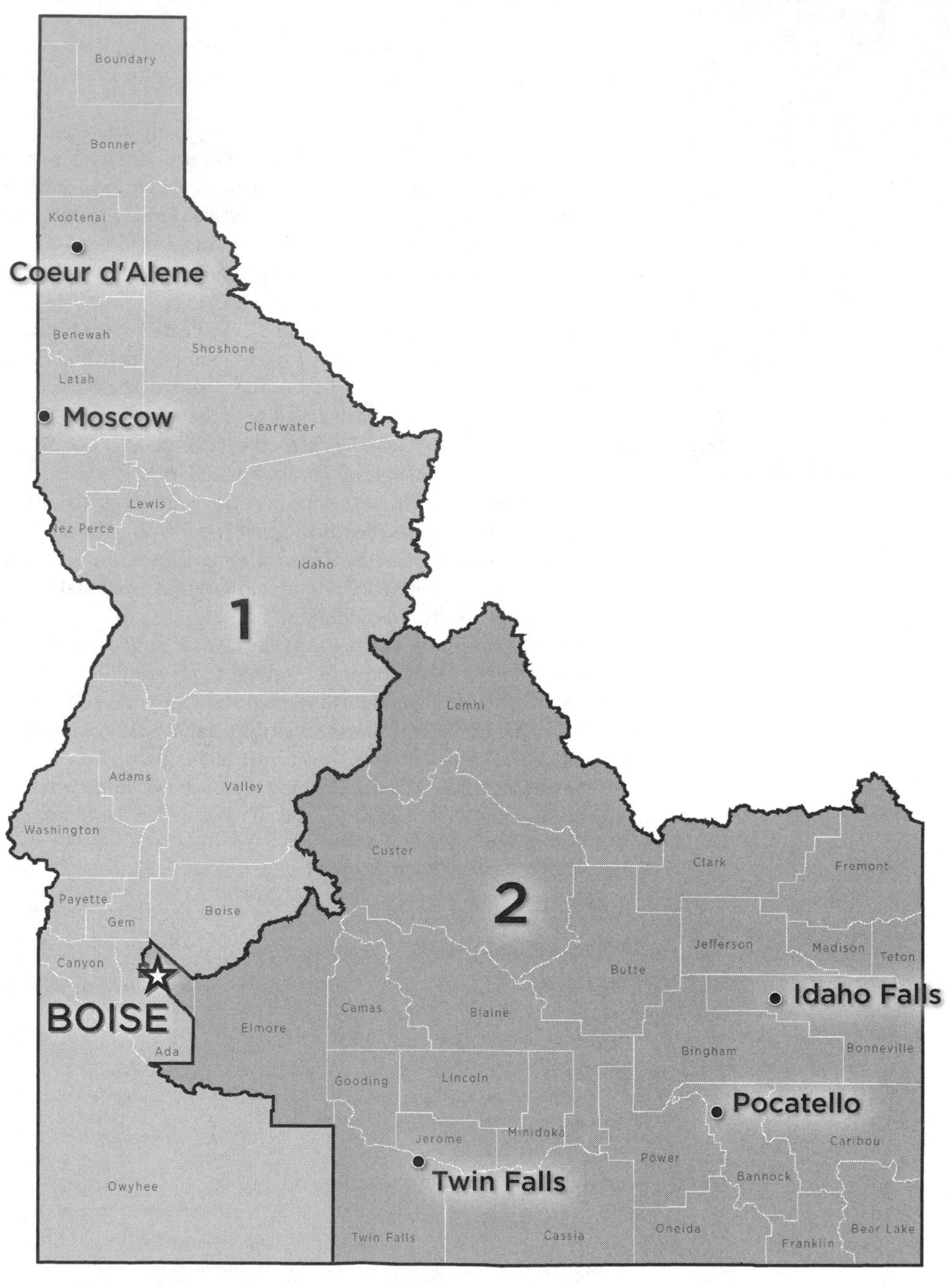

Boundary
Bonner
Kootenai
Coeur d'Alene
Benewah
Shoshone
Latah
Moscow
Clearwater
Lewis
Nez Perce
Idaho
1
Lemhi
Adams
Valley
Washington
Custer
Clark
Fremont
2
Payette
Gem
Boise
Jefferson
Madison
Teton
Canyon
Butte
Idaho Falls
BOISE
Camas
Blaine
Elmore
Ada
Bingham
Bonneville
Gooding
Lincoln
Pocatello
Jerome
Minidoka
Caribou
Power
Twin Falls
Bannock
Owyhee
Oneida
Twin Falls
Cassia
Bear Lake
Franklin

Gov. C.L. 'Butch' Otter (R)

First elected: 2006

Length of term: 4 years

Term expires: 1/15

Salary: $119,000

Phone: (208) 334-2100

Residence: Star

Born: May 3, 1942; Caldwell, Idaho

Religion: Roman Catholic

Family: Wife, Lori Otter; four children

Education: College of Idaho, B.A. 1967 (political science)

Military Service: Idaho National Guard, 1968-73

Career: Agribusiness company executive; oil company partner

Political highlights: Idaho House, 1972-76; sought Republican nomination for governor, 1978; lieutenant governor, 1987-2001; U.S. House, 2001-07

ELECTION RESULTS

2010 GENERAL

C.L. 'Butch' Otter (R)	267,483	59.1%
Keith Allred (D)	148,680	32.9%
Jana M. Kemp (I)	26,655	5.9%
Ted Dunlap (LIBERT)	5,867	1.3%
Pro-Life (I)	3,850	0.9%

Lt. Gov. Brad Little (R)

Assumed Office: 2009

Length of term: 4 years

Term expires: 1/15

Salary: $35,100

Phone: (208) 334-2200

LEGISLATURE

Legislature: January-May

Senate: 35 members, 2-year terms

2013 ratios: 28 R, 7 D; 30 men, 5 women

Salary: $16,116

Phone: (208) 334-2475

House: 70 members; 2-year terms

2013 ratios: 57 R, 13 D; 48 men, 22 women

Salary: $16,116

Phone: (208) 334-2475

TERM LIMITS

Governor: No

Senate: No

House: No

URBAN STATISTICS

CITY	POPULATION
Boise	205,671
Nampa	81,557
Meridian	75,092
Idaho Falls	56,813
Pocatello	54,255

REGISTERED VOTERS

Voters do not register by party.

POPULATION

2010 population (est.)	1,567,582
2000 population	1,293,953
1990 population	1,006,749
Percent change (2000-2010)	+21.1%
Rank among states (2010)	39
Median age	34.0
Born in state	46.0%
Foreign born	5.5%
Violent crime rate	228/100,000
Poverty level	14.3%
Federal workers	20,044
Military	4,967

ELECTIONS

STATE ELECTION OFFICIAL
(208) 334-2852

DEMOCRATIC PARTY
(208) 336-1815

REPUBLICAN PARTY
(208) 343-6405

MISCELLANEOUS

Web: www.idaho.gov

Capital: Boise

U.S. CONGRESS

Senate: 2 Republicans

House: 2 Republicans

STATISTICS BY DISTRICT

District	2012 Vote for President Obama	2012 Vote for President Romney	2008 Vote for President Obama	2008 Vote for President McCain	Black	Asian	Hispanic	Median Income	Over 64	Under 20	College Education	Rural	Sq. Miles
1	32%	65%	35%	63%	<1%	1%	10%	$45,103	14%	29%	24%	36%	39,418
2	33	64	37	61	1	1	13	42,086	12	31	26	30	43,225
STATE	**33**	**65**	**36**	**62**	**1**	**1**	**11**	**43,341**	**13**	**30**	**25**	**33**	**82,643**
U.S.	**51**	**47**	**53**	**46**	**12**	**5**	**17**	**50,052**	**13**	**27**	**29**	**21**	**3,531,905**

Sen. Michael D. Crapo (R)

Capitol Office
224-6142
crapo.senate.gov
239 Dirksen Bldg. 20510-1205; fax 228-1375

Committees
Banking, Housing & Urban Affairs - Ranking Member
Budget
Environment & Public Works
Finance
Indian Affairs

Residence
Idaho Falls

Born
May 20, 1951; Idaho Falls, Idaho

Religion
Mormon

Family
Wife, Susan Crapo; five children

Education
Brigham Young U., B.A. 1973 (political science); Harvard U., J.D. 1977

Career
Lawyer

Political Highlights
Idaho Senate, 1984-92 (president pro tempore, 1988-92); U.S. House, 1993-99

ELECTION RESULTS

2010 GENERAL		
Michael D. Crapo (R)	319,953	71.2%
P. Tom Sullivan (D)	112,057	24.9%
Randy Lynn Bergquist (CNSTP)	17,429	3.9%
2010 PRIMARY		
Michael D. Crapo (R)	127,332	79.3%
Claude M. "Skip" Davis III (R)	33,150	20.7%

Previous Winning Percentages
2004 (99%); 1998 (70%); 1996 House Election (69%); 1994 House Election (75%); 1992 House Election (61%)

Elected 1998; 3rd term

Crapo is now the top Republican on the Banking, Housing and Urban Affairs Committee, a position that solidifies his authority on financial matters. He is invested in a conservative agenda, but as he negotiates to improve the government's fiscal situation, his moderate demeanor is an asset.

Over the years, Crapo (CRAY-poe) has done his share of work on behalf of his party. He was named a deputy whip in the 111th Congress (2009-10), and he became the chief deputy whip at the start of the 113th Congress (2013-14). In 2012 he completed his fourth consecutive two-year term as chairman of the party's Committee on Committees, which matches GOP colleagues with panel assignments.

As the government's fiscal woes have dominated the news, however, the unassuming and well-liked senator has found wider distinction as part of a bipartisan group trying to assemble a package of spending cuts, entitlement program changes and tax code rewrites.

In 2011, the "gang of six" (which later expanded to eight) began its effort to produce legislation based on the work of a 2010 fiscal commission created by President Barack Obama. Crapo was among three GOP senators who served on that commission, which became known as Simpson-Bowles. The gang's initial goal was a package achieving $4 trillion in debt reduction over 10 years.

"My hope is that we will be able to put together a comprehensive fiscal plan," Crapo said in 2012, emphasizing the need for a tax overhaul. "I think if you look at our code right now, we'd be hard-pressed to have created one that is more unfair, more complex, more expensive to comply with and frankly more anti-competitive to U.S. business interests than the one we've got."

Whatever actions Congress takes on fiscal matters, Crapo is positioned to have his opinions heard. A term limit forced Alabama's Richard C. Shelby from the top Republican spot on Banking, allowing Crapo to take over in 2013.

He joined other Republicans in opposing the 2010 financial regulatory overhaul known as Dodd-Frank. He said it would make credit more expensive, discourage capital formation and unreasonably extend government control over the economy.

As regulations required by that law have been written, Crapo has suggested legislative fixes to eliminate their unintended consequences — one major concern is removing new margin requirements for non-financial companies that use derivatives to hedge risks. Crapo took the lead in 2006 on a wide-ranging banking regulation bill aimed at easing restrictions on banks, credit unions and other financial institutions. In October 2008, he opposed a $700 billion measure to rescue the ailing financial services sector, contending it didn't include enough protections for taxpayers.

Crapo can tackle taxes as a member of the Finance Committee. Working from that panel, he took a leading role in the unsuccessful GOP effort to defeat the health care overhaul during the 111th Congress. He offered a motion to prevent the legislation from increasing taxes on upper-income earners. He predicted the law will result in higher costs and an "unprecedented expansion of governmental control over health care."

Crapo wants major fiscal deals to include changes to health care entitlement programs. He says he is open to several options, but that a "premium support" model is "definitely one that I think should be under consideration."

Outside of the "gang" talks, Crapo has a handful of other bipartisan priorities. He worked in 2012 with Judiciary Chairman Patrick J. Leahy, a Vermont Democrat, on a reauthorization of programs to combat domestic violence and help its victims. House conservatives objected to several provisions in the bill and stopped its progress in that chamber, but it was reintroduced in 2013 and quickly enacted.

Another bipartisan effort yielded what Crapo considers one of his proudest moments: Inclusion of the Owyhee initiative in a public lands bill signed by Obama in early 2009. The initiative was the culmination of an eight-year effort to settle a long-running turf battle among conservationists, American Indians, the Air Force, ranchers and off-road-vehicle groups in southwest Idaho. The resulting legislation protects more than 700,000 acres.

In 2010, Obama signed a bill by Crapo and Minnesota Democrat Amy Klobuchar to prohibit composite wood products from containing potentially hazardous levels of formaldehyde.

Crapo frequently goes to bat for Idaho's interests. He joined other senators in objecting to cuts in farm programs proposed by Obama in 2009. A year later he called on the administration to make sure there was a level playing field for Idaho dairy producers in trade agreements. He voted against the Senate's version of a 2012 reauthorization of farm programs, however, saying its proposed spending levels were too high. The bill was not enacted.

On the Environment and Public Works Committee, Crapo promotes development of renewable energy sources, which his state has in abundance. He has proposed a quicker review process for geothermal energy development on federal lands (most of Idaho is owned by the federal government) and more use of biofuels.

As a House member he opposed implementation of the 1993 North American Free Trade Agreement and the 1994 General Agreement on Tariffs and Trade. He was wary of Canada's policies on timber and agricultural trade.

Crapo grew up in Idaho Falls, the youngest of six children of the local postmaster and his homemaker wife. His father also farmed 200 acres of potatoes, grain and cattle pasture, and the children pitched in. The family farm expanded over the years and today is run by Crapo's uncles and cousins.

At Brigham Young University, Crapo earned a degree in political science and indulged a passion for dirt bike racing. He then worked as a Washington intern for Idaho GOP Rep. Orval Hansen. He considered a career in medicine, but changed his mind after gaining admission to Harvard Law School.

Crapo spent a year clerking in San Diego before returning to his hometown to practice law. He has said his experiences in the Mormon church, which gives its lay leaders considerable responsibilities in dealing with personal and community issues, helped prepare him for public office. Crapo suffered a double embarrassment in December 2012 when he was arrested in Virginia for driving under the influence of alcohol — beyond the arrest, practicing Mormons are not supposed to consume alcohol.

He was elected to the Idaho Senate at age 33 and was chosen as its president pro tempore four years later. In 1992 he ran for the U.S. House seat being vacated by Democrat Richard Stallings, who ran unsuccessfully for the Senate. He defeated Democrat J.D. Williams by nearly 26 points. In his first term he landed a sought-after seat on the Energy and Commerce Committee.

Crapo has never faced a tough election. When Republican Sen. Dirk Kempthorne ran for governor in 1998, Crapo quickly became the front-runner to succeed him. His popularity enabled him to crush Bill Mauk, a former Idaho Democratic Party chairman, by more than 40 points. He had token opposition in 2004 and easily defeated businessman Tom Sullivan in 2010.

Crapo's sunny demeanor belies an ambition fueled in part by his dedication to his oldest brother, who was his mentor and law partner. Terry Crapo, a state legislator, died two weeks after being diagnosed with leukemia in 1982. Crapo faced his own trial when doctors diagnosed his prostate cancer in 2000 and operated. The cancer returned in 2005, and Crapo underwent radiation treatments while still in the Senate. He is currently cancer-free.

Key Votes

2012

Prohibit health insurance plans from denying coverage based on the sponsor's religious beliefs	NO
Require approval of the Keystone XL oil pipeline	YES
Ease securities rules to expand small-business access to capital	YES
Reauthorize farm and nutrition programs for five years	NO
Limit debate on a bill that would create private-sector cybersecurity standards	NO
Consent to ratification of a treaty setting global standard for the treatment of people with disabilities	NO
Provide $60.4 billion in disaster relief following Superstorm Sandy	NO
Extend most Bush-era income tax rates while allowing rates for top-bracket earners to rise (Jan. 1, 2013)	YES

2011

Prevent EPA from regulating greenhouse gas emissions to address climate change	YES
Extend certain provisions of Patriot Act for four years	YES
Clear compromise debt limit increase plan and establish future spending limits	YES
Overhaul patent law	YES
Implement Colombia free trade agreement	YES
Limit debate on confirmation of Caitlin J. Halligan to D.C. Circuit Court of Appeals	NO
Extend payroll tax cut and unemployment benefits for two months	YES

CQ Vote Studies

	PARTY UNITY		PRESIDENTIAL SUPPORT	
	SUPPORT	OPPOSE	SUPPORT	OPPOSE
2012	93%	7%	46%	54%
2011	99%	1%	49%	51%
2010	98%	2%	36%	64%
2009	94%	6%	48%	52%
2008	94%	6%	76%	24%
2007	92%	8%	81%	19%
2006	95%	5%	88%	12%
2005	95%	5%	84%	16%
2004	96%	4%	90%	10%
2003	98%	2%	97%	3%

Interest Groups

	AFL-CIO	ADA	CCUS	ACU
2012	0%	10%	75%	88%
2011	11%	10%	100%	95%
2010	6%	0%	100%	100%
2009	17%	10%	71%	92%
2008	20%	15%	75%	88%
2007	5%	15%	82%	88%
2006	7%	0%	83%	88%
2005	21%	10%	94%	100%
2004	8%	10%	94%	92%
2003	15%	5%	91%	89%

Sen. Jim Risch (R)

Capitol Office
224-2752
risch.senate.gov
483 Russell Bldg. 20510; fax 224-2573

Committees
Energy & Natural Resources
Foreign Relations
Small Business & Entrepreneurship - Ranking Member
Select Ethics
Select Intelligence

Residence
Boise

Born
May 3, 1943; Milwaukee, Wis.

Religion
Roman Catholic

Family
Wife, Vicki Risch; three children

Education
U. of Wisconsin, Milwaukee, attended 1961-63; U. of Idaho, B.S. 1965 (forest resources management), J.D. 1968

Career
Lawyer; rancher; trailer company owner; property management company owner; college instructor

Political Highlights
Ada County prosecuting attorney, 1970-74; Idaho Senate, 1974-89 (majority leader, 1976-82; president pro tempore, 1982-89); defeated for re-election to Idaho Senate, 1988; sought Republican nomination for Idaho Senate, 1994; Idaho Senate, 1995-2003 (majority leader, 1997-2003); lieutenant governor, 2003-06; governor, 2006-06; lieutenant governor, 2007-09

ELECTION RESULTS

2008 GENERAL

Jim Risch (R)	371,744	57.6%
Larry LaRocco (D)	219,903	34.1%
Rex Rammell (I)	34,510	5.4%
Kent A. Marmon (LIBERT)	9,958	1.5%
Pro-Life (I)	8,662	1.3%

Elected 2008; 1st term

Risch believes Republicans and Democrats are hard-wired differently, and he's not averse to some colorful generalizations: Conservatives want a hands-off government in the spirit of the Founding Fathers, while Democrats see government as "an enterprise that should be in control of everything."

"These people believe that in America, we should have a government that takes care of everything, and that the government can do it better than the evil, black-hearted, entrepreneurial free-market-system types, who all they want to do is make money," he said. "And so they think that if they can get their hands on all the assets — if they can do the health care system, they can do the banking system, they can do all of these, and do it from Washington, D.C. — we will live in utopia."

His long and wide-ranging career in Idaho state politics was spent mostly in the majority or the executive branch. But as a senator, Risch has been happy to serve as a roadblock, particularly on federal spending. He counts himself among the "12 or 15 of us that believe we're in a crisis situation," and he keeps a three-minute speech handy to convince constituents that the nation's financial condition is "substantially worse than what you think it is."

Risch stumps for a balanced-budget amendment to the Constitution, calls 10-year budgeting "ridiculous" and likes to point out that the federal government borrows more in a day than Idaho spends in a year. "I think it's going to take a crisis to resolve it," he said. "And don't worry, that crisis is coming."

For a man anticipating economic Armageddon, Risch manages to be cheery. He speaks rapidly, smiles broadly and professes no personal animus toward Democratic colleagues.

His energy is well-known in Idaho. Risch was serving as lieutenant governor when Gov. Dirk Kempthorne was chosen as Interior secretary in 2006. Rather than serving as a caretaker after his promotion, Risch called a special legislative session to overhaul the state's tax structure. He also spearheaded a new management plan for millions of roadless acres in the state. The door from his governor's office stands in the reception area of his Senate office.

Risch now tackles issues important to his state (two-thirds of which is federally owned) as a member of the Energy and Natural Resources Committee. He is the top Republican on its Energy panel.

The federal government has few appropriate roles in the energy sector, he says. One is providing loan guarantees for nuclear power plants — "the future of energy in the world is nuclear energy" — and another is investments in researching clean-coal technology.

Most of his efforts on the panel have been to get the government out of the way. When Democrats accused oil market speculators of driving up gas prices, Risch went on cable news programs to defend speculators as part of a free-market system. He sees federal restrictions as decimating the timber and mining industries in Idaho, and he resents the federal reintroduction and protection of gray wolves in his state. Among his many business interests — he is one of the wealthiest congressmen — he owns a ranch, and wolves have killed calves on his property.

Risch wants to streamline permitting for renewable-energy projects on federal land. He worked with fellow Idaho Republican Michael D. Crapo and several House members to include language in a fiscal 2012 spending law to block a court decision allowing the EPA to regulate runoff water from forest roads. Risch has a degree in forest management from the University of Idaho.

When he wants a change of pace, Risch turns to the Foreign Relations and Intelligence committees. He negotiated his way on to Foreign Relations because "I'm so tired of budgets," he joked. Risch is less dogmatic on that panel, believing that many international situations require "a judgment call on a case-by-case basis."

Risch is the top Republican on the Near Eastern and South and Central Asian Affairs Subcommittee. During the 112th Congress (2011-12), he was skeptical of the value of some aid to Pakistan, such as spending on bridge construction. "There's no good will to be bought," he said. After four Americans were killed in an attack on a U.S. consulate in Libya, he gave a blistering critique of the Obama administration's Middle East policy: It is "a foreign policy of apology, it is a foreign policy of appeasement, it is a foreign policy of dithering and looking the other way," he said on the Senate floor.

He urges a hard line on containing Iran's nuclear ambitions. Risch wrote to the Obama administration in 2012 that sanctions shouldn't be relaxed for anything less than sustained suspension of Iran's uranium enrichment program. "We cannot make a mistake on this," he said at a 2011 hearing. Risch called for isolation of Syria's government as that country's civil war escalated in 2012.

Risch helped lead GOP opposition to the strategic arms reduction treaty that the Senate approved in the waning days of the 111th Congress (2009-10).

In the 113th Congress (2013-14), Risch is the top Republican on the Small Business and Entrepreneurship Committee, from which he plans to "protect our nation's job creators from hurtful regulations, tax hikes and government overreach." He also serves on the Ethics Committee.

But he'll jump in on any issue he finds compelling. In 2011, the Obama administration's plans to limit the use of student loans for for-profit colleges struck him as an unfair attack on the private sector. "I made a couple of speeches on it, and all of a sudden I was in the middle of it," he said. "That's the way things happen around here. It makes you more careful about the speeches."

Risch hails from Milwaukee, where his father climbed telephone poles for Wisconsin Bell. "He was really insistent that all of us get up in the morning and go to work," Risch said. The nuns at the Catholic high school he attended gave him a career aptitude test, and Risch was thrilled to learn he would make a fine forest ranger. After two years attending college in his hometown, he headed west to study forestry in Idaho.

He fell in love with Idaho's mountains, but his interest in being a ranger faded. After marrying his wife, Vicki, and graduating from law school, Risch was first elected to office in 1970, as prosecutor for Ada County. When a murderer he convicted went free after serving only 18 months of a life sentence, Risch decided to run for the state Senate.

"The only way you could control the parole board was to get into the state Senate," Risch said. "I started rejecting all the appointments to the parole board real quick, and then the rest of them got mad and quit, and that was just fine by me."

Risch opened a private law practice that would make him wealthy. At the same time, he flourished in the state Senate, beating out Larry E. Craig for the post of majority leader in 1976 and 1978. Risch wasn't afraid to make enemies as he mastered the inside political game, and he lost his seat in 1988 after frequent clashes with the governor. Risch returned to the state Senate in 1995 with a less aggressive style. In 2002, he spent $360,000 of his own money on a successful run for lieutenant governor. After filling out Kempthorne's term, he ran again for the lieutenant's job.

In the early 1980s, Risch recruited Crapo for a slot in the state Senate leadership. Years later, Crapo encouraged Risch to run for the U.S. Senate seat left open by the retirement of Craig. With Crapo serving as his campaign co-chairman, Risch took on former Democratic state Rep. Larry LaRocco in the 2008 Senate campaign. He won easily, taking 58 percent of the vote.

Key Votes

2012	
Prohibit health insurance plans from denying coverage based on the sponsor's religious beliefs	NO
Require approval of the Keystone XL oil pipeline	YES
Ease securities rules to expand small-business access to capital	YES
Reauthorize farm and nutrition programs for five years	NO
Limit debate on a bill that would create private-sector cybersecurity standards	NO
Consent to ratification of a treaty setting global standard for the treatment of people with disabilities	NO
Provide $60.4 billion in disaster relief following Superstorm Sandy	?
Extend most Bush-era income tax rates while allowing rates for top-bracket earners to rise (Jan. 1, 2013)	YES
2011	
Prevent EPA from regulating greenhouse gas emissions to address climate change	YES
Extend certain provisions of Patriot Act for four years	YES
Clear compromise debt limit increase plan and establish future spending limits	YES
Overhaul patent law	YES
Implement Colombia free trade agreement	YES
Limit debate on confirmation of Caitlin J. Halligan to D.C. Circuit Court of Appeals	NO
Extend payroll tax cut and unemployment benefits for two months	YES

CQ Vote Studies

	PARTY UNITY		PRESIDENTIAL SUPPORT	
	SUPPORT	OPPOSE	SUPPORT	OPPOSE
2012	94%	6%	41%	59%
2011	98%	2%	46%	54%
2010	98%	2%	37%	63%
2009	95%	5%	47%	53%

Interest Groups

	AFL-CIO	ADA	CCUS	ACU
2012	0%	5%	75%	96%
2011	11%	10%	100%	95%
2010	6%	0%	100%	100%
2009	17%	10%	71%	96%

Rep. Raúl R. Labrador (R)

Capitol Office
225-6611
labrador.house.gov
1523 Longworth Bldg. 20515-1201; fax 225-3029

Committees
Judiciary
Natural Resources

Residence
Eagle

Born
Dec. 8, 1967; Carolina, P.R.

Religion
Mormon

Family
Wife, Rebecca Johnson Labrador; five children

Education
Brigham Young U., B.A. 1992 (Spanish); U. of Washington, J.D. 1995

Career
Lawyer

Political Highlights
Idaho House, 2006-10

ELECTION RESULTS

2012 GENERAL		
Raúl R. Labrador (R)	199,402	63.0%
Jimmy Farris (D)	97,450	30.8%
Rob Oates (LIBERT)	12,265	3.9%
Pro-Life (I)	7,607	2.4%
2012 PRIMARY		
Raúl R. Labrador (R)	58,003	80.6%
Reed C. McCandless (R)	13,917	19.4%
2010 GENERAL		
Raúl R. Labrador (R)	126,231	51.0%
Walt Minnick (D)	102,135	41.3%
Dave Olson (D)	14,365	5.8%
Mike Washburn (LIBERT)	4,696	1.9%

Elected 2010; 2nd term

Labrador muscles his way toward the front on a variety of issues as a fiscal conservative and a caustic overseer of the executive branch. A former immigration lawyer, he also has designs on reformulating Republican strategies on border issues.

He describes himself as a "passionate legislator," and in both the Idaho House and the U.S. House, Labrador has favored directness over delicacy. His approach endears him to conservatives and agitates many Democrats.

When Labrador is flexible, it's often because policy is moving his preferred direction. In July 2011, as Speaker John A. Boehner prepared his version of a deal to raise the debt limit, Labrador wanted the increase tied to congressional passage of a balanced-budget amendment to the Constitution. He negotiated with the GOP leadership to add that provision and rallied support for the measure, which passed with 218 votes.

"Raúl has done a great job as one of the leaders of the freshman class," Boehner told the Idaho Statesman at the time. "He's sometimes outspoken, but we've built a good relationship." Their relationship got more complicated, however. After the House passed a "fiscal cliff" package with no spending reductions at the end of the 112th Congress (2011-12), Labrador declined to vote for Boehner as speaker in the 113th Congress (2013-14). He reportedly helped organize a campaign attempting to deny Boehner the post.

Labrador opposes all tax increases, but he still wants to scrub from the tax code exceptions and credits for specific industries. He was one of two original co-sponsors of a 2011 bill by Kansas Republican Mike Pompeo to eliminate all tax credits for energy industries. He voted in the 112th Congress for spending cuts to many specific programs, but he has no problem with across-the-board cuts if they're more politically feasible.

One area where Labrador runs against the GOP grain is immigration. "I think the Republican Party should be the party for legal immigration, not the party against illegal immigration," he says. As an lawyer, he represented many illegal immigrants. "My job was to help them get straight," he told Politico in 2011. He joined the Judiciary Committee at the start of the 113th Congress, and he also emerged as a member of an eight-person bipartisan House working group drafting a comprehensive immigration overhaul.

"It's always been odd to me that Republicans will say that everything in government is broken and we want to fix it all, but we're not going to fix the immigration system," Labrador said. He opposes "amnesty" for illegal immigrants, but he supports incentives to make them come forward and enter some legalized status short of citizenship. He rejects the notion that complete border security must precede all immigration changes, arguing that improvements to the immigration system would allow more-targeted border security. He wants the southern border militarized, with both the National Guard and the Border Patrol present.

If Labrador is intense on fiscal and immigration matters, he can be blistering when it comes to oversight. He sat on the Oversight and Government Reform Committee in the 112th Congress. Obama administration officials and panel Democrats were often flustered and infuriated by his questions, which can be sarcastic and abrupt.

Labrador was front-and-center as Republicans investigated Operation Fast and Furious, in which weapons tracked by the Justice Department might have been used in Mexican border violence. Attorney General Eric H. Holder Jr. testified that he had limited knowledge of the program, and Labrador frequently stated that Holder was either lying or grossly incompetent.

At a February 2012 hearing, Labrador showed clips of Holder's comments on unrelated subjects to "establish a pattern" of behavior. Holder retorted on the spot: "That was among the worst things I think I've ever seen in Congress. ... If you don't like me, that's one thing, but you should respect the fact that I hold an office that is deserving of respect."

Investigating allegations of mismanagement at the Nuclear Regulatory Commission in 2011, Labrador told Chairman Gregory B. Jaczko: "I've never seen such self-deluded behavior by any individual in probably my entire life."

Labrador serves on the Natural Resources Committee, dealing with issues that factor heavily in a state where the federal government owns and manages more than half the land. He believes federal restrictions on land use are a major drag on Idaho's economy, and he would like the property ultimately to revert to state or private control. "You look at the federal lands, and they look like they are decaying, they look like they're old, they look like they're diseased," he said. "You look at the state and private lands and they look healthy and vibrant. So we can manage our own lands, and we don't need all the environmental regulations."

In 2012, the House passed an energy bill that included Labrador's provision to expedite exploration for geothermal energy on federal lands. Labrador joins most Republicans in calling for expanded U.S. energy production.

Labrador was born in Puerto Rico and raised by his mother. She worked in the hotel industry and had other pursuits as well, including hosting what Labrador called "one of the first Oprah-like shows" on local television, with 10-minute segments on topics including beauty, fashion and jobs. He was educated in military schools and bilingual schools, spending free time at the beach. When he was 13, his mother's work took them to Las Vegas. Labrador could not speak English well but was comfortable within a few years.

At that age, he also became a Mormon. His mission took him to Santiago, Chile, for two years, and he attended Brigham Young University, where he met his future wife. Rebecca has a master's degree in school psychology, and "she needed it for me" more than for their five children, he says.

His early political influences were Democratic — he remembers his mother taking him to a presidential campaign rally for Edward M. Kennedy in Puerto Rico. But the appeal of Ronald Reagan brought both him and his mother to the Republican side.

Labrador was carried into the House on a wave of tea party support in 2010. He upended Vaughn Ward, the preferred candidate of the national Republican establishment, in the primary. He then defeated one of the most conservative members of the Democratic Caucus, one-term lawmaker Walt Minnick, by more than 9 points. He won a second term in 2012 by 32 points.

Key Votes

2012	
Extend a Social Security payroll tax cut and unemployment benefits	NO
Ease securities rules to expand small-business access to capital	YES
Extend for one year subsidized student loan interest rates financed by a cut in health care spending	NO
Cite Attorney General Eric H. Holder Jr. for contempt of Congress	YES
Create a visa program for foreign graduates in high-tech fields	YES
Extend most Bush-era income tax rates while allowing rates for top-bracket earners to rise (Jan. 1, 2013)	NO
2011	
Strike funding for F-35 alternative engine	YES
Prevent EPA from regulating greenhouse gas emissions to address climate change	YES
Extend certain provisions of Patriot Act for four years	NO
Declare opposition to use of ground troops in Libya	YES
Overhaul patent law	YES
Pass compromise debt limit increase plan and establish future spending limits	NO
Allow consideration of measures to implement three trade agreements	YES

CQ Vote Studies

	Party Unity		Presidential Support	
	Support	Oppose	Support	Oppose
2012	93%	7%	27%	73%
2011	95%	5%	13%	87%

Interest Groups

	AFL-CIO	ADA	CCUS	ACU
2012	18%	20%	83%	96%
2011	3%	15%	94%	95%

Idaho 1

West — Nampa, panhandle, part of Boise

From its smokestack-shaped panhandle that opens into British Columbia in the north, the 1st District stretches 500 miles south to the Nevada state line in the western half of Idaho, bordering both Washington and Oregon. Rural and rugged, the 1st features mountainous, and federally owned, wilderness as well as rivers, canyons and the trails that Lewis and Clark traveled as they sought a route to the Pacific Ocean.

Boise, the state capital and largest city, has traditionally been split between the state's two districts — following decennial remapping that shifted the boundaries, the 1st now takes in only a western sliver of the city and the area near the airport. West of the capital are suburbs Meridian and Nampa. Home to large food processing companies, Nampa had the fastest population growth in the region for several years, but recovery in the home construction industry has been slow. The local technology sector, the major players of which have offices in the 2nd, has rebounded. Nampa also hosts the Idaho Center, a large entertainment complex with indoor and outdoor facilities.

Northern Idaho relied for decades on the timber and mining industries but has begun to focus on tourism, call centers and manufacturing companies. Coeur d'Alene is 33 miles east of Spokane, Wash., where many panhandle residents commute to work. Ski resorts and American Indian casino venues draw tourists. North Idaho College and satellite campuses of Lewis-Clark State College and the University of Idaho — whose flagship is in the middle of the district in Moscow — provide a trained workforce.

Like the rest of the state, the 1st District is a conservative bastion that heavily favors Republicans. Only two Democrats have held the seat since the 1960s, and never for more than two terms. Latah County (Moscow) in the panhandle was one of only two counties in the state to favor Barack Obama for president in 2012.

Major Industry

Technology, manufacturing, timber, government

Cities

Nampa, Meridian, Boise City (pt.), Caldwell, Coeur d'Alene, Lewiston

Notable

The Snake River Canyon, south of Nampa, features petroglyphs painted by indigenous peoples dating back 12,000 years.

Rep. Mike Simpson (R)

Capitol Office
225-5531
simpson.house.gov
2312 Rayburn Bldg. 20515-1202; fax 225-8216

Committees
Appropriations
(Interior-Environment - Chairman)

Residence
Idaho Falls

Born
Sept. 8, 1950; Burley, Idaho

Religion
Mormon

Family
Wife, Kathy Simpson

Education
Utah State U., attended 1968-72 (pre-dentistry); Washington U. (Mo.), D.M.D. 1977; Utah State U., B.S. 2002 (pre-dentistry)

Career
Dentist

Political Highlights
Blackfoot City Council, 1980-84; Idaho House, 1984-98 (speaker, 1992-98)

ELECTION RESULTS

2012 GENERAL		
Mike Simpson (R)	207,412	65.2%
Nicole LeFavour (D)	110,847	34.8%
2012 PRIMARY		
Mike Simpson (R)	50,799	69.6%
Chick Heileson (R)	22,240	30.4%
2010 GENERAL		
Mike Simpson (R)	137,468	68.8%
Mike Crawford (D)	48,749	24.4%
Brian Schad (I)	13,500	6.8%

Previous Winning Percentages
2008 (71%); 2006 (62%); 2004 (71%); 2002 (68%); 2000 (71%); 1998 (53%)

Elected 1998; 8th term

Opinions of Simpson hinge on the viewer. Environmentalists lambaste him as the Republican appropriator charged with keeping the EPA in check, while budget watchers know him as a leader of a broad bipartisan coalition in search of transformative fiscal changes. Many people agree, however, that he is one of the more good-natured souls in Congress.

Early in his House career, Simpson drew notice for attempting to land face-to-face meetings with all 434 of his colleagues; he fell short but chatted with hundreds of lawmakers. Rare is the hearing when Simpson doesn't let out a loud and deep laugh while bantering with the room. Since his days in the Idaho House, which included six years as speaker, he has kept in his office a set of "Simpson's Rules," 12 maxims which include "hear both sides before judging" and "never, never make an enemy needlessly." While generally conservative, particularly on issues important to his Western constituents, he belongs to the centrist Main Street Partnership.

In the 112th Congress (2011-12), Simpson invested some personal capital in forming the Go Big Coalition. The August 2011 law to raise the federal debt limit created a "supercommittee" to devise a deficit reduction plan for Congress to vote on. Working with Minority Whip Steny H. Hoyer of Maryland, Simpson united more than 100 lawmakers in requesting that the panel find at least $4 trillion in reductions over 10 years to improve the nation's long-term fiscal health. Their plea indicated that Democrats would accept changes to entitlement programs, while Republicans could swallow revenue increases.

The supercommittee disbanded without meeting its goal, but Simpson has continued on his quest. His own thoughts for revenue increases run to eliminating all exemptions from the tax code while simultaneously getting rates as low as they can possibly go.

"The tax code should be a simple system intended to raise the necessary revenue for appropriate government functions, not a complex system directing social behavior," he wrote in the Idaho Statesman in 2011.

Simpson sits at the fulcrum of spending debates as a member of the Appropriations Committee. He chairs the Interior-Environment Subcommittee.

He has faulted Republicans as much as Democrats for a "broken" budget process, and he prefers cultural, rather than structural, fixes. "Every legislative body I've ever sat in, there's always the Senate, the House and the appropriators," he said. "It's almost like they don't think we're part of the process."

He urges better communication among budget writers, authorizing committees and the spending panels. Simpson also sees an eventual return of earmarked spending, which was banned in 2011. Strong oversight can address any concerns of corruption or impropriety, he said.

Disputes on his subcommittee have their own flavor, Simpson said: "The division within my bill is not so much Republican and Democrat as it is East and West."

His Western approach to the EPA is what rankles environmentalists. Simpson has long seen the agency as imposing excessive regulations on the industries and vast federal lands of his state. (More than half of Idaho is federal land.) Simpson boasted of cutting the EPA budget by $2 billion, or close to 20 percent, during 2011. He also oversaw the inclusion in spending bills of provisions to curtail enforcement of greenhouse gas regulations and effectively block the extension of the Clean Water Act to runoff from logging roads.

In 2011, the Los Angeles Times placed him at No. 4 on its list of "Congress' 10 biggest enemies of the Earth." Simpson was flattered. "I get applause for that in Idaho," he said.

He is critical of federal land management. For years he has promoted his bill to create three new wilderness areas in Idaho while releasing other federal land for development. He has also sought ways to curtail environmentalists' legal challenges to many economic or recreational uses of federal lands.

Simpson also sits on the Energy-Water spending panel, another prime spot for a Westerner. He advocates expanding nuclear energy and developing a new generation of nuclear reactors, as well as the use of the Yucca Mountain nuclear waste repository that was shuttered by the Obama administration.

He studies some of the biggest pieces of federal spending as a member of the Labor-HHS-Education Subcommittee.

Simpson grew up in the eastern Idaho town of Blackfoot, where his father and uncle had a dental practice. He met his wife in high school — he was on the football team and she was a cheerleader. They both attended Utah State University. He studied political science for a bit but eventually decided to go into the family business. He received a dentistry degree from Washington University in St. Louis. Simpson has introduced several bills to increase access to dental care for low-income people.

His first run for the Blackfoot City Council wasn't issue-driven. "I read the Thursday morning paper at the office one day," he said. "Filing deadline was on Friday. There were two open seats, and only one person had filed. And I say, 'Aha! This is the time to get on the City Council!'" Several other people had the same idea, but Simpson still won — by eight votes.

Simpson says his legislative strategy is "more to prevent bad things from happening" than to rewrite the law books. He won election to the Idaho House in 1984 and started out with a reputation as an occasionally angry maverick. But he mellowed and made a name for himself in Boise.

Simpson thought about seeking the governorship in 1998 but decided against it when Republican Sen. Dirk Kempthorne chose to run. Rep. Michael D. Crapo made a bid for Kempthorne's Senate seat, and Simpson instead eyed the resulting House vacancy.

Social conservatives worried that Simpson was insufficiently ardent about their causes, but he won a four-way GOP primary. He made no effort to hide that he is a lapsed Mormon who once smoked and still drinks occasionally. Those personal details seemed to have little effect on the heavily Mormon and Republican electorate. He defeated Democrat Richard Stallings, who had held the seat from 1985 through 1992, and he has easily won re-election since then.

Simpson is an accomplished painter — his watercolors decorate his office. He is also a good golfer, though he professes to have little time for golfing or painting anymore. Golf Digest reported in 2011 that he still has a handicap of 8, one of the best in Congress.

Key Votes

2012	
Extend a Social Security payroll tax cut and unemployment benefits	NO
Ease securities rules to expand small-business access to capital	YES
Extend for one year subsidized student loan interest rates financed by a cut in health care spending	YES
Cite Attorney General Eric H. Holder Jr. for contempt of Congress	YES
Create a visa program for foreign graduates in high-tech fields	+
Extend most Bush-era income tax rates while allowing rates for top-bracket earners to rise (Jan. 1, 2013)	YES
2011	
Strike funding for F-35 alternative engine	NO
Prevent EPA from regulating greenhouse gas emissions to address climate change	YES
Extend certain provisions of Patriot Act for four years	YES
Declare opposition to use of ground troops in Libya	YES
Overhaul patent law	YES
Pass compromise debt limit increase plan and establish future spending limits	YES
Allow consideration of measures to implement three trade agreements	YES

CQ Vote Studies

	PARTY UNITY		PRESIDENTIAL SUPPORT	
	SUPPORT	OPPOSE	SUPPORT	OPPOSE
2012	88%	12%	15%	85%
2011	91%	9%	24%	76%
2010	90%	10%	29%	71%
2009	79%	21%	32%	68%
2008	92%	8%	62%	38%

Interest Groups

	AFL-CIO	ADA	CCUS	ACU
2012	14%	5%	91%	80%
2011	10%	20%	100%	64%
2010	7%	5%	75%	96%
2009	19%	10%	80%	84%
2008	27%	35%	94%	80%

Idaho 2

East — Pocatello, Idaho Falls, part of Boise

The 2nd District sprawls across the Gem State's eastern and central portions and most of the capital city of Boise. This vast swath of land includes some midsize cities, most of the state's farms and ranches, and mountainous wilderness areas and rivers that support a variety of outdoor tourism and fishing.

Redistricting following the 2010 census shifted the 2nd's border farther west into Boise. It takes in downtown, several urban parks, and Boise State University. Technology firms — including Hewlett-Packard and Micron Technology — state government and jobs at the university shore up the city's economy. The district's portion of Boise is also home to an established Basque population.

South of the city along Interstate 84 is Mountain Home Air Force Base, but most of the district relies on agricultural production, mainly fed by the Snake River. Idaho is the country's leading producer of potatoes, the majority of which are grown in the 2nd — Blackfoot, in Bingham County, is known as the potato producing capital of the world. Seeds, sugar beets, wheat, trout and cattle are also major commodities.

Members of The Church of Jesus Christ of Latter-Day Saints make up the district's largest religious group, and like most Mormon areas, the district is strongly conservative — eastern Idaho has been represented by a Mormon in the U.S. House since 1951. Republican presidential candidates regularly win the district with more than 60 percent of the vote. Blaine County, home to the Sun Valley ski resort, is the only county to reliably vote for Democratic presidential candidates, although Democrats can win state legislature seats from the Boise area.

Major Industry
Agriculture, food processing, tourism, technology

Military Bases
Mountain Home Air Force Base, 4,131 military, 315 civilian (2011)

Cities
Boise City (pt.), Pocatello, Idaho Falls, Twin Falls, Rexburg

Notable
The Idaho National Laboratory near Idaho Falls is the Energy Department nuclear research site; The Pocatello Zoo specializes in animals native to the Mountain West, such as grizzly bears, American bison, pronghorn and lynx.

ILLINOIS

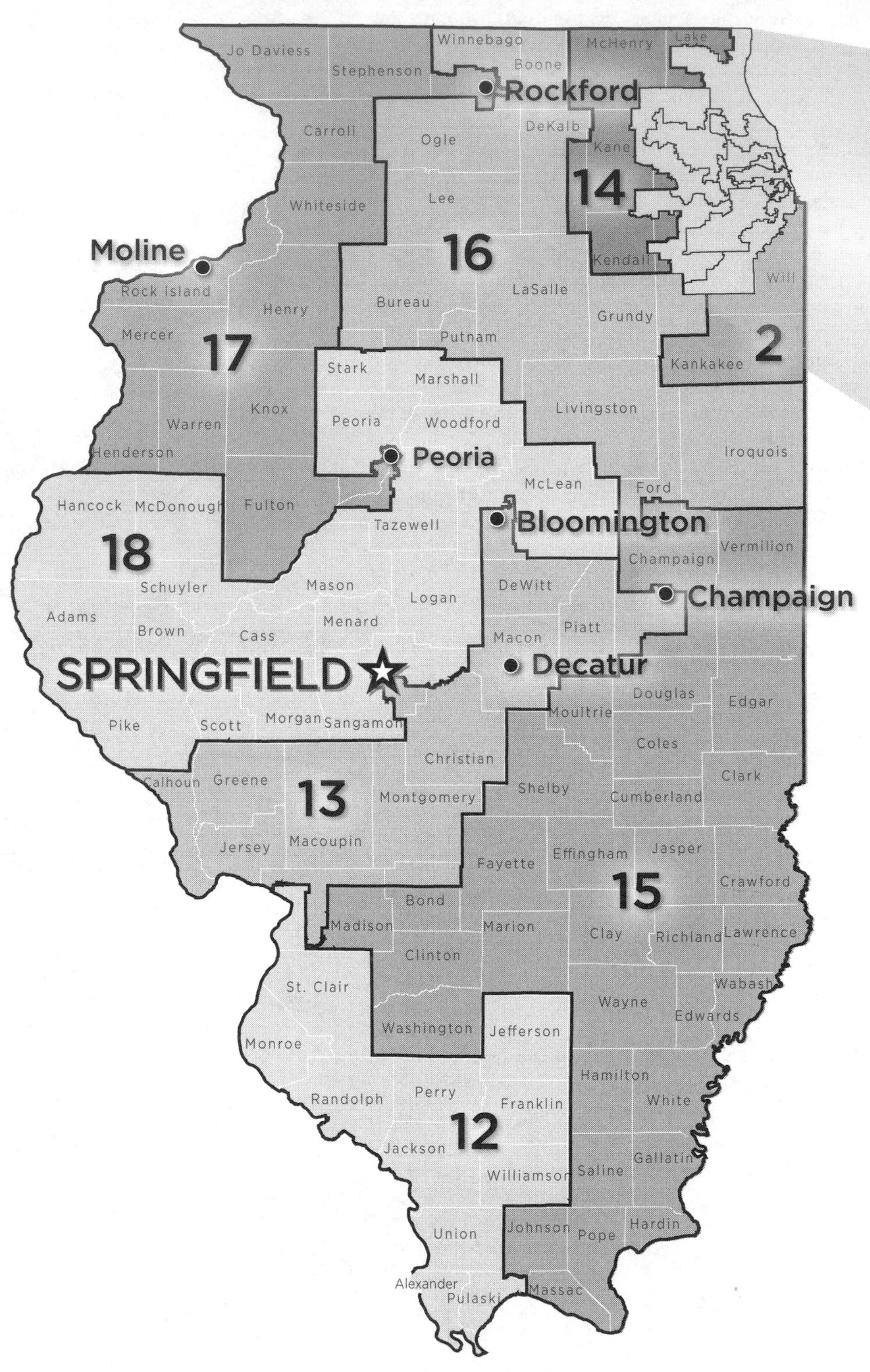
Jo Daviess
Stephenson
Winnebago
Boone
McHenry
Lake
Rockford
Carroll
Ogle
DeKalb
Kane
14
Whiteside
Lee
16
Moline
Rock Island
Henry
Bureau
LaSalle
Kendall
Will
Grundy
Mercer
17
Putnam
Kankakee
2
Stark
Marshall
Knox
Warren
Peoria
Woodford
Livingston
Henderson
Peoria
Iroquois
McLean
Ford
Hancock
McDonough
Fulton
Tazewell
Bloomington
18
Champaign
Vermilion
Schuyler
Mason
DeWitt
Champaign
Adams
Logan
Brown
Cass
Menard
Macon
Piatt
SPRINGFIELD
Decatur
Douglas
Edgar
Moultrie
Pike
Scott
Morgan
Sangamon
Coles
Christian
Clark
Calhoun
Greene
13
Shelby
Cumberland
Montgomery
Jersey
Macoupin
Effingham
Jasper
Fayette
15
Crawford
Bond
Madison
Marion
Clay
Richland
Lawrence
Clinton
St. Clair
Wabash
Wayne
Edwards
Washington
Jefferson
Monroe
Hamilton
Randolph
Perry
Franklin
White
12
Jackson
Gallatin
Williamson
Saline
Union
Johnson
Pope
Hardin
Alexander
Pulaski
Massac

Chicago Area

Districts 1, 3-11

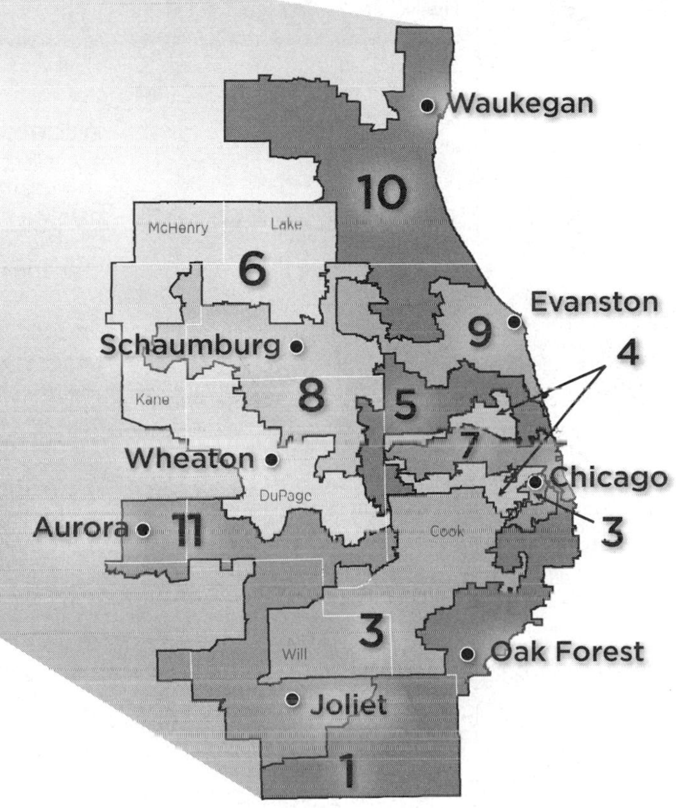

Statistics by District

District	2012 Vote for President		2008 Vote for President										
	Obama	Romney	Obama	McCain	Black	Asian	Hispanic	Median Income	Over 64	Under 20	College Education	Rural	Sq. Miles
1	79%	20%	81%	19%	51%	2%	10%	$46,458	13%	28%	26%	1%	258
2	81	19	81	18	56	1	13	45,572	13	29	21	5	1,081
3	56	43	58	40	4	3	29	56,579	13	28	25	<1	237
4	81	17	81	18	4	2	72	39,744	7	31	17	0	52
5	66	32	70	29	2	7	18	62,632	11	20	51	0	96
6	45	53	51	47	3	8	8	85,655	13	28	50	1	379
7	87	12	89	10	55	5	13	44,535	10	27	37	0	63
8	57	41	62	37	5	13	26	60,073	10	28	33	<1	206
9	65	33	69	30	9	12	11	59,321	16	22	50	0	105
10	58	41	63	36	7	10	22	65,864	12	29	42	<1	300

Gov. Pat Quinn (D)

First elected: 2010
Took office Jan. 29, 2009, due to the impeachment and removal from office of Rod R. Blagojevich.

Length of term: 4 years

Term expires: 1/15

Salary: $177,000

Phone: (217) 782-0244

Residence: Chicago

Born: Dec. 16, 1948; Hinsdale, Ill.

Religion: Roman Catholic

Family: Divorced; two children

Education: Geogetown U., 1971 B.S. (international economics); Northwestern U., 1980 J.D.

Career: Lawyer, college instructor; city government official; political activist; campaign and gubernatorial aide

Political highlights: Cook County Board of Tax Appeals, 1982-86; sought Democratic nomination for Ill. treasurer, 1986; Ill. treasurer, 1991-95; Democratic nominee for Ill. secretary of State, 1994; sought Democratic nomination for U.S. Senate, 1996; lieutenant governor, 2002-09

ELECTION RESULTS

2010 GENERAL

Pat Quinn (D)	1,745,219	46.8%
Bill Brady (R)	1,713,385	45.9%
Scott Lee Cohen (I)	135,705	3.6%
Rich Whitney (GREEN)	100,756	2.7%

Lt. Gov. Sheila Simon (D)

First elected: 2010

Length of term: 4 years

Term expires: 1/15

Salary: $122,109

Phone: (217) 558-3085

LEGISLATURE

General Assembly: January-May; meets in October or November to consider vetoes

Senate: 59 members, rotates between 2- and 4-year terms

2013 ratios: 40 D, 19 R; 44 men, 15 women

Salary: $67,836

Phone: (217) 782-5715

House: 118 members, 2-year terms

2013 ratios: 71 D, 47 R; 76 men, 42 women

Salary: $67,836

Phone: (217) 782-8223

TERM LIMITS

Governor: No

Senate: No

House: No

URBAN STATISTICS

CITY	POPULATION
Chicago	2,695,598
Aurora	197,899
Rockford	152,871
Joliet	147,433
Naperville	141,853

REGISTERED VOTERS

Voters do not register by party.

POPULATION

2010 population	12,830,632
2000 population	12,419,293
1990 population	11,430,602
Percent change (2000-2010)	+3.3%
Rank among states (2010)	5
Median age	35.9
Born in state	66.9%
Foreign born	13.3%
Violent crime rate	497/100,000
Poverty level	13.3%
Federal workers	111,692
Military	10,111

ELECTIONS

STATE ELECTION OFFICIAL
(217) 782-4141

DEMOCRATIC PARTY
(217) 546-7404

REPUBLICAN PARTY
(217) 525-0011

MISCELLANEOUS

Web: www.illinois.gov

Capital: Springfield

U.S. CONGRESS

Senate: 1 Democrat, 1 Republican

House: 12 Democrats, 6 Republicans

STATISTICS BY DISTRICT

	2012 Vote for President		2008 Vote for President										
District	Obama	Romney	Obama	McCain	Black	Asian	Hispanic	Median Income	Over 64	Under 20	College Education	Rural	Sq. Miles
11	58%	41%	61%	37%	11%	7%	27%	$65,938	10%	31%	35%	<1%	281
12	50	48	55	44	17	1	3	42,181	14	26	21	24	5,008
13	49	49	55	44	11	3	3	44,915	14	25	28	21	5,794
14	44	54	51	48	3	4	12	77,758	10	30	37	11	1,598
15	34	64	43	55	5	1	2	45,122	16	25	18	51	14,696
16	45	53	50	48	4	1	9	52,101	15	27	20	30	7,917
17	58	41	60	38	11	1	8	41,194	16	26	17	28	6,933
18	37	61	44	54	4	2	2	54,571	16	25	30	37	10,516
STATE	**58**	**41**	**62**	**37**	**15**	**5**	**16**	**53,234**	**13**	**27**	**31**	**12**	**55,519**
U.S.	**51**	**47**	**53**	**46**	**12**	**5**	**17**	**50,052**	**13**	**27**	**29**	**21**	**3,531,905**

Sen. Richard J. Durbin (D)

Capitol Office
224-2152
durbin.senate.gov
711 Hart Bldg. 20510-1304; fax 228-0400

Committees
Appropriations
(Defense - Chairman)
Foreign Relations
Judiciary
(Constitution, Civil Rights & Human Rights - Chairman)
Rules & Administration
Joint Library

Residence
Springfield

Born
Nov. 21, 1944; East St. Louis, Ill.

Religion
Roman Catholic

Family
Wife, Loretta Durbin; three children (one deceased)

Education
Georgetown U., B.S.F.S. 1966 (international affairs & economics), J.D. 1969

Career
Gubernatorial and state legislative aide; lawyer

Political Highlights
Democratic nominee for Ill. Senate, 1976; Democratic nominee for lieutenant governor, 1978; U.S. House, 1983-97

ELECTION RESULTS

2008 GENERAL		
Richard J. Durbin (D)	3,615,844	67.8%
Steve Sauerberg (R)	1,520,621	28.5%
Kathy Cummings (GREEN)	119,135	2.2%
2008 PRIMARY		
Richard J. Durbin (D)		unopposed

Previous Winning Percentages
2002 (60%); 1996 (56%); 1994 House Election (55%); 1992 House Election (57%); 1990 House Election (66%); 1988 House Election (69%); 1986 House Election (68%); 1984 House Election (61%); 1982 House Election (50%)

Elected 1996; 3rd term

Durbin is a liberal utility player who does a lot of things for the Democratic Party, and he does them well enough to hold the party's No. 2 leadership post in the Senate. He's no longer the presumed favorite to succeed Majority Leader Harry Reid, but his skills as a communicator, negotiator, fundraiser and vote-counter keep him involved in just about every major debate.

Democratic colleagues elected Durbin their whip after the 2004 elections. Partly, it was to balance the elevation of Reid to the No. 1 post. Durbin has stronger ties to the liberal wing of the party than the Nevadan.

He also has a reputation for massaging public opinion. During the last of Durbin's seven terms in the House, Democratic leaders put him in charge of reshaping the party's political messaging. He reprised that role after his election to the Senate. Durbin is an impassioned and combative speaker, equally comfortable with broad themes and policy details. It's nearly impossible to knock him off-message; he was sent to defend President Barack Obama's record as part of the "response team" at the Republican National Convention in August 2012.

Whips are supposed to maintain caucus discipline around floor votes, and Durbin has been effective in that regard. Before his election to Congress, he spent 13 years as the parliamentarian of the Illinois Senate, leaving him well-versed in legislative procedure. He has a friendly Midwestern demeanor off the Senate floor and uses humor to disarm colleagues. Reid, who served with Durbin as a House freshman in 1983, has called him "one of the nicest and kindest members of the Senate."

There were rough moments in the 111th Congress (2009-10), but the leadership team oversaw passage of major bills on health care and financial regulation with little to no Republican support. Durbin often served as an unofficial conduit between the Senate and the Obama administration. The president had been Illinois' junior senator under Durbin.

Even so, some observers say Durbin's star has dimmed. Reid has given many official communications duties to New York's Charles E. Schumer, who serves as the No. 3 Democrat (and shares a Capitol Hill home with Durbin). No one questions Durbin's commitment to the Democratic agenda, but Schumer is more aggressive in the media. Similarly, Durbin is an excellent fundraiser for the party, but Schumer has been even more prodigious. Rank-and-file Democrats sometimes grouse that Durbin gets bogged down in policy discussions instead of galvanizing the party.

When Reid faced a tough re-election in Nevada in 2010, speculation ran rampant that Schumer could leapfrog Durbin to become party leader should Reid lose. And in the 112th Congress (2011-12), Reid sniffed at some of Durbin's policy efforts.

The biggest of those involved the "gang of six" (which later expanded to eight), a bipartisan group of senators working on proposals to reduce deficits. Durbin had served on a 2010 fiscal commission created by Obama, and the work of that group became the framework for the gang's objective: $4 trillion in deficit reduction over 10 years through a mix of spending cuts and revenue increases. The gang produced no legislation, and Reid publicly questioned the value of its meetings.

Durbin finds the time for committee-based priorities. He chaired the Financial Services Appropriations Subcommittee in the 112th, and he urged strong funding of the agencies implementing the 2010 financial regulatory overhaul. When Republicans tried to trim funding for the Commodity Futures Trading Commission, he accused them of "basically saying, let's go back to those thrilling days of yesteryear," the economic collapse of 2008.

He wrote the provision of the overhaul that limited the fees financial institutions can charge retailers to process debit card transactions. He defended that change in the 112th, saying the fees were unreasonable and transferred to consumers as higher prices. He sides with retailers in his attempts to allow states to collect sales taxes on online purchases; online retailers have a competitive advantage under current law, according to Durbin.

In the 113th Congress (2013-14), Durbin chairs the Defense Appropriations Subcommittee, taking the gavel once held by Hawaii Democrat Daniel K. Inouye, who died in late 2012.

On the Judiciary Committee, Durbin is a leading proponent of broad changes to immigration law. He was cheered by a 2012 Obama administration policy directive to halt the deportation of certain illegal immigrants brought to the country as children. Durbin has pursued legislation along those lines and has taken to the Senate floor many times to relate the personal stories of such immigrants. He was part of the bipartisan, eight-person immigration working group that produced a comprehensive immigration overhaul bill in the early months of the 113th Congress. It includes a path to citizenship for those already in the country illegally.

Durbin chairs the Judiciary subcommittee on the Constitution, and he uses that position to vent concerns about super PACs, the groups independent of official political campaigns that can accept unrestricted donations from individuals or organizations. "I have with some hesitation reached the conclusion that a constitutional amendment is necessary to clean up our campaign finance system once and for all," he said at a 2012 hearing.

His subcommittee also covers civil rights. Durbin was the Senate sponsor of the 2010 law reducing the codified disparity in sentencing between crack and powder cocaine offenses — critics called the wide gap an unfair targeting of minorities, who have a higher proportion of crack offenses. He held a 2012 hearing on the effect of solitary confinement on those in U.S. prisons.

He was raised in East St. Louis, Ill., by an Irish-American father who was a railroad night watchman and a Lithuanian-born mother who was a switchboard operator. Durbin, the youngest of three brothers, was 14 when his chain-smoking father died of lung cancer. In the late 1980s, he led the successful effort to ban smoking on domestic airline flights. And in the 110th Congress (2007-08), he helped persuade the Rules and Administration Committee, on which he serves, to ban the sale of tobacco products in the Senate and to close two designated smoking rooms in the Senate office buildings.

Durbin caught the politics bug in college, when he was an intern for Democrat Paul Douglas, whose seat he now holds. He would have long conversations with Douglas, who used to tell Durbin stories as the young intern handed him letters to sign. One of Durbin's sons is named after Douglas.

After completing law school at Georgetown University, Durbin returned home. For about five years in the 1970s, he was co-owner of a bar in Springfield. His early political career included his work as parliamentarian and a stint as an aide to Lt. Gov. Paul Simon, who later became a U.S. senator and presidential candidate. In 1982, Durbin unseated 11-term GOP Rep. Paul Findley by 1,410 votes in a Springfield-based House district.

When Simon announced he would not seek re-election in 1996, Durbin got into the race and won by 15 points against conservative state Rep. Al Salvi. Durbin coasted to a second term in 2002 and a third six years later.

The 2008 election was a high-water mark for Durbin. Obama won the White House and Democrats increased their Senate majority by eight seats. The period, however, was marked by personal tragedy when Durbin's adult daughter, Christine, died three days before Election Day from complications related to a congenital heart condition.

Durbin has said that he will run for a fourth term in 2014.

Key Votes

2012	
Prohibit health insurance plans from denying coverage based on the sponsor's religious beliefs	YES
Require approval of the Keystone XL oil pipeline	NO
Ease securities rules to expand small-business access to capital	NO
Reauthorize farm and nutrition programs for five years	YES
Limit debate on a bill that would create private-sector cybersecurity standards	YES
Consent to ratification of a treaty setting global standard for the treatment of people with disabilities	YES
Provide $60.4 billion in disaster relief following Superstorm Sandy	YES
Extend most Bush-era income tax rates while allowing rates for top-bracket earners to rise (Jan. 1, 2013)	YES
2011	
Prevent EPA from regulating greenhouse gas emissions to address climate change	NO
Extend certain provisions of Patriot Act for four years	NO
Clear compromise debt limit increase plan and establish future spending limits	YES
Overhaul patent law	YES
Implement Colombia free trade agreement	NO
Limit debate on confirmation of Caitlin J. Halligan to D.C. Circuit Court of Appeals	YES
Extend payroll tax cut and unemployment benefits for two months	YES

CQ Vote Studies

	PARTY UNITY		PRESIDENTIAL SUPPORT	
	SUPPORT	OPPOSE	SUPPORT	OPPOSE
2012	97%	3%	96%	4%
2011	98%	2%	97%	3%
2010	99%	1%	100%	0%
2009	100%	0%	100%	0%
2008	98%	2%	31%	69%
2007	98%	2%	36%	64%
2006	98%	2%	47%	53%
2005	99%	1%	33%	67%
2004	96%	4%	54%	46%
2003	97%	3%	46%	54%

Interest Groups

	AFL-CIO	ADA	CCUS	ACU
2012	100%	95%	38%	0%
2011	89%	95%	45%	0%
2010	100%	95%	18%	0%
2009	94%	95%	43%	0%
2008	100%	100%	63%	4%
2007	100%	95%	45%	0%
2006	100%	100%	45%	4%
2005	100%	100%	28%	0%
2004	92%	95%	47%	4%
2003	85%	95%	35%	10%

Sen. Mark S. Kirk (R)

Capitol Office
224-2854
kirk.senate.gov
524 Hart Bldg. 20510-1305; fax 228-4611

Committees
Appropriations
Banking, Housing & Urban Affairs
Health, Education, Labor & Pensions
Special Aging

Residence
Highland Park

Born
Sept. 15, 1959; Champaign, Ill.

Religion
Christian

Family
Divorced

Education
Cornell U., B.A. 1981 (history); London School of Economics, M.S. 1982; Georgetown U., J.D. 1992

Military Service
Navy Reserve, 1989-present

Career
Congressional aide; lawyer; U.S. State Department aide; World Bank officer

Political Highlights
U.S. House, 2001-10

ELECTION RESULTS

2010 GENERAL		
Mark S. Kirk (R)	1,778,698	48.0%
Alexi Giannoulias (D)	1,719,478	46.4%
LeAlan M. Jones (GREEN)	117,914	3.2%
Mike Labno (LIBERT)	87,247	2.4%
2010 SPECIAL		
Mark S. Kirk (R)	1,677,729	47.3%
Alexi Giannoulias (D)	1,641,486	46.3%

Previous Winning Percentages
2008 House Election (53%); 2006 House Election (53%); 2004 House Election (64%); 2002 House Election (69%); 2000 House Election (51%)

Elected 2010; 1st full term

"I was once a pessimist," Kirk wrote in February 2013. "I'm not that man anymore. And that change, brought about by misfortune, is the best thing that ever happened to me."

The misfortune was a January 2012 stroke that dramatically limited Kirk's speech and mobility. His triumph was returning to Washington a year later, to take a symbolic walk up the Capitol steps. Kirk was physically removed from the day-to-day activities of the Senate for a year while recovering; however, he and his staff still tried to advance his legislative goals. He started the 113th Congress (2013-14) at a slow but steady pace, working on the national security, foreign affairs, spending and transportation issues that have shaped his time in Washington.

Kirk served 10 years in the House and was one of its centrist Republicans. Fiscally conservative and socially moderate, he had little trouble merging into the coalition-dependent Senate in late 2010. He upheld an Illinois tradition dating to the 1980s by hosting weekly constituent coffee sessions with the state's senior senator — Democratic Whip Richard J. Durbin. "We agree on a ton of Illinois issues," Kirk said. "We have a very good working relationship."

One of Kirk's first initiatives of 2013 was a bill with New York Democrat Kirsten Gillibrand to establish gun trafficking as a federal crime. Kirk wants stiffer penalties for straw purchasers — those who buy guns legally, then transfer them to a third party without any background check. "Gun trafficking is allowing gangs and violence to flourish in Chicago," he wrote.

Kirk was on the House Appropriations Committee for eight years and now sits on the Senate's version of the panel. He makes overtures toward fiscal restraint and a balanced budget. Kirk and West Virginia Democrat Joe Manchin III — a close friend — introduced a resolution in November 2011 to express that any major deficit reduction measure should achieve at least $4 trillion in reductions over 10 years. Earlier in the year, Kirk introduced a measure to oppose bailouts of states by the federal government — Illinois' finances are, by almost any standard, abysmal.

He criticized a January 2013 law providing a short-term suspension of the government's borrowing limit. "Only a long-term solution to our fiscal problems will give our markets the stability that they need and deserve," he said.

But the moderate in Kirk wants to expand the Small Business Administration, the Agriculture Department and the U.S. Trade Development Agency to help Illinois farmers and small businesses boost exports into growing markets. Kirk has outlined his "Small Business Bill of Rights," as well as a 23-item "Economic Policy Checklist." Both documents include familiar themes of reducing regulations and taxes and promoting domestic energy production.

A self-described "national security hawk," he uses his Appropriations seat to influence spending on foreign operations and his state's military installations. Kirk was commissioned as an intelligence officer in the Navy Reserve at age 29 and continued his service through 2012. He has worked at the State Department and the World Bank.

Iran has been a major focus for Kirk. In December 2012, he and New Jersey Democrat Robert Menendez scored a victory when they amended the fiscal 2013 defense policy bill to blacklist Iran's energy and shipping sectors. Signed into law, the provision is intended to put extra economic pressure on Tehran as it considers a new round of diplomatic negotiations on its nuclear program.

He's also interested in Poland. Chicago has a large Polish population, and in May 2012 Polish President Bronislaw Komorowski awarded Kirk the Commander's Cross of the Order of Merit of the Republic of Poland for his work on U.S.-Poland relations. Kirk and Maryland Democrat Barbara A. Mikulski have introduced measures to add Poland to the Visa Waiver Program, which would make it easier for Polish people to visit the United States.

Kirk sits on the Banking, Housing and Urban Affairs Committee, where he's the top Republican on the subcommittee handling international finance. From the Health, Education, Labor and Pensions Committee, he pursues some of his goals on social policies. He has collaborated on a bill to expand access to, and funding opportunities for, charter schools.

Transportation and infrastructure improvements are also important for Kirk and his state. He has introduced a bill to reduce federal restrictions on public-private partnerships — arrangements often cited as a means to leverage limited federal transportation dollars into encouraging private sector investments in infrastructure.

Kirk is socially liberal on a lot of issues. In late 2010, he was among the Republican senators who voted to repeal the military's ban on openly gay servicemembers. He announced support for same-sex marriage in April 2013. And he's more sympathetic to environmentalist positions than most of his party. According to the legislative scorecard of the League of Conservation Voters, Kirk had the second-strongest environmental record among Senate Republicans at the start of the 113th Congress. As a House member, he was one of eight Republicans to vote for a 2009 measure to create a cap-and-trade system to regulate greenhouse gas emissions.

Kirk grew up in Kenilworth, a wealthy suburb of Chicago. At age 16, he nearly drowned in a boating accident on Lake Michigan. The incident convinced him to do something positive with his life. "To be given a second chance means it has to mean something," he told the Chicago Tribune. "For me, that means making a difference through public service."

He graduated from New Trier High School and followed that up with three university degrees, a stint in Mexico to learn Spanish, and his time in military intelligence. He has traveled in more than 40 countries.

One of his earliest jobs was as a legislative counsel for the House International Relations Committee. He also worked for several years on the staff of his predecessor in the House, fellow GOP centrist John Edward Porter.

When Porter announced his retirement before the 2000 election, Kirk ran in a primary field jammed with 10 other Republicans. With Porter's backing, Kirk defeated his nearest rival by 16 points. In the general election, he prevailed over Democratic state Rep. Lauren Beth Gash by 2 points. He won with ease in 2002 and 2004 before facing tough battles with Democrat Dan Seals in two House elections, when he was a top Democratic target.

In 2008, he won an endorsement from Planned Parenthood and was one of six Republican congressional candidates endorsed by the Sierra Club. He raised more than $5 million — the most of any House incumbent that year — and took 53 percent of the vote.

He ran for an open Senate seat in 2010. Democrat Roland W. Burris, who had been appointed to the seat vacated by Barack Obama, decided not to run. The Democratic primary was won by state Treasurer Alexi Giannoulias. Kirk won the GOP nod easily over a collection of lesser-known opponents.

In a seesaw general election campaign, Giannoulias tried to make hay out of exaggerations Kirk had made in his military record; Kirk highlighted work that Giannoulias' family bank did with mobsters before federal regulators seized the institution.

The president and first lady Michelle Obama campaigned hard for Giannoulias, but in a good year for Republicans, Kirk prevailed by nearly 2 points, winning 48 percent of the vote. He was seated for the last months of the 111th Congress (2009-10), as he simultaneously won a special election to complete the term started in 2005 by Obama.

Key Votes

2012	
Prohibit health insurance plans from denying coverage based on the sponsor's religious beliefs	?
Require approval of the Keystone XL oil pipeline	?
Ease securities rules to expand small-business access to capital	?
Reauthorize farm and nutrition programs for five years	?
Limit debate on a bill that would create private-sector cybersecurity standards	?
Consent to ratification of a treaty setting global standard for the treatment of people with disabilities	?
Provide $60.4 billion in disaster relief following Superstorm Sandy	?
Extend most Bush-era income tax rates while allowing rates for top-bracket earners to rise (Jan. 1, 2013)	?
2011	
Prevent EPA from regulating greenhouse gas emissions to address climate change	YES
Extend certain provisions of Patriot Act for four years	YES
Clear compromise debt limit increase plan and establish future spending limits	YES
Overhaul patent law	YES
Implement Colombia free trade agreement	YES
Limit debate on confirmation of Caitlin J. Halligan to D.C. Circuit Court of Appeals	NO
Extend payroll tax cut and unemployment benefits for two months	NO

CQ Vote Studies

	PARTY UNITY		PRESIDENTIAL SUPPORT	
	SUPPORT	OPPOSE	SUPPORT	OPPOSE
2011	79%	21%	63%	37%
2010	76%	24%	45%	55%
2010	76%	24%	45%	55%
2009	78%	22%	50%	50%
2008	73%	27%	53%	47%
2007	70%	30%	41%	59%
2006	79%	21%	80%	20%
2005	80%	20%	67%	33%
2004	84%	16%	63%	37%
2003	87%	13%	81%	19%

Interest Groups

	AFL-CIO	ADA	CCUS	ACU
2012	0%			
2011	16%	20%	91%	60%
2010	0%	10%	100%	63%
2010	0%	10%	100%	63%
2009	48%	35%	87%	72%
2008	47%	55%	83%	48%
2007	52%	40%	84%	40%
2006	36%	45%	80%	54%
2005	20%	30%	81%	36%
2004	29%	45%	90%	63%

Rep. Bobby L. Rush (D)

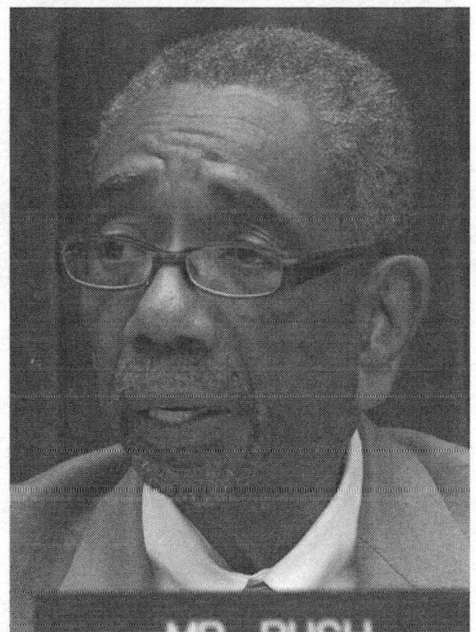

Capitol Office
225-4372
rush.house.gov
2268 Rayburn Bldg. 20515-1301; fax 226-0333

Committees
Energy & Commerce

Residence
Chicago

Born
Nov. 23, 1946; Albany, Ga.

Religion
Protestant

Family
Wife, Carolyn Rush; six children (one deceased)

Education
Roosevelt U., B.A. 1973 (political science); U. of Illinois, Chicago, attended 1975-77 (political science), M.A. 1994 (political science); McCormick Theological Seminary, M.A. 1998 (theological studies)

Military
Army, 1963-68

Career
Insurance broker; political activist

Political Highlights
Candidate for Chicago City Council, 1975; sought Democratic nomination for Ill. House, 1978; Chicago City Council, 1983-93; candidate for mayor of Chicago, 1999

ELECTION RESULTS

2012 GENERAL		
Bobby L. Rush (D)	236,854	73.8%
Donald E. Peloquin (R)	83,989	26.2%
2012 PRIMARY		
Bobby L. Rush (D)	64,533	83.8%
Raymond M. Lodato (D)	3,210	4.2%
Harold L. Bailey (D)	2,598	3.4%
Clifford M. Russell Jr. (D)	2,412	3.1%
Fred Smith (D)	2,232	2.9%
Jordan Sims (D)	1,980	2.6%

Previous Winning Percentages
2010 (80%); 2008 (86%); 2006 (84%); 2004 (85%); 2002 (81%); 2000 (88%); 1998 (87%); 1996 (86%); 1994 (76%); 1992 (83%)

Elected 1992; 11th term

Rush famously called a rival in a 2000 Democratic primary an "educated fool" with an "ivory-tower outlook." That criticism of Barack Obama speaks to Rush's view of his own work: He's a ground-level politician trying to improve the lot of his Chicago-area constituents, and a liberal protester willing to hold the megaphone. As Obama observed at the time, Rush's style makes it tough for him to score legislative victories while serving in the House minority.

Born in southern Georgia, Rush moved to Chicago with his mother and four siblings at age 7 when her marriage ended. The civil rights movement was nearing its peak in his high school years.

Rush dropped out of high school and joined the Army, serving several years at a Chicago-area base. He became disillusioned by a commanding officer he viewed as racist and joined the Student Non-Violent Coordinating Committee. He went AWOL after the assassination of Martin Luther King Jr. but was later honorably discharged.

He joined the Black Panthers and soon helped found the organization's Illinois chapter. Rush, the group's deputy minister of defense, served six months in prison for illegal possession of weapons, but he also coordinated a program that provided free breakfasts for children and a clinic that developed a mass screening effort for sickle cell anemia.

By 1974, Rush had quit the Panthers — he has said the group was "glorifying thuggery and drugs." He sold insurance for a few years, then won election to the city council in 1983. Rush excelled at the retail politicking demanded by that job, and in 1992 he was elected to the House. Along the way, he became an ordained Baptist minister and founded the Beloved Community Christian Church. Nonprofits affiliated with the church provide social services in his district (and have received federal grants).

A lot of Rush's congressional work involves directing federal resources to Chicago; Rush says that in his tenure he has brought more than $1 billion to his district for local municipalities, libraries, museums, police departments, hospitals, schools and programs that support the arts.

He is acutely aware of the consequences of poverty and the crime rates that go with it. Moving away from his militant past, Rush now advocates strict controls on firearms — a position that was strengthened when his son Huey (named after Black Panther leader Huey Newton) was shot and killed in a Chicago sidewalk robbery in 1999. In 2002, Rush's nephew was charged with murder and attempted robbery in the shooting death of a man. Police said it was a drug deal gone bad.

Rush has served on the Energy and Commerce Committee since his second term, and his work there has a constituent service element. He is a big supporter of programs to expand Internet access and upgrade networks in low-income neighborhoods. As chairman of the Subcommittee on Commerce, Trade and Consumer Protection in the 110th Congress (2007-08), Rush introduced and steered to enactment a bill overhauling consumer product safety regulations. And Illinois uses lots of nuclear power, so Rush keeps up on nuclear safety issues.

Since 2011, Rush has been the ranking member of the Energy and Power Subcommittee. That job gives him few opportunities to directly help constituents but plenty of opportunities to defend liberal positions, such as federal support of renewable-energy development. Rush is also co-chairman of the Congressional Black Caucus Energy, Environment and Agriculture Taskforce.

He supports the idea of regulating greenhouse gas emissions to mitigate the effects of climate change. After Superstorm Sandy struck the East Coast in

2012, Rush and California Democrat Henry A. Waxman asked for a hearing on the role of such emissions in creating extreme weather conditions. "Sandy is exactly the type of extreme weather event that climate scientists have said will become more frequent and more severe if we fail to reduce our carbon pollution," they wrote to GOP panel leaders.

Republicans in the 112th Congress (2011-12) preferred calling hearings to criticize the EPA, and by July 2012 Rush was fed up. He used an opening statement to accuse the GOP of "putting on a dog and pony show for the cameras."

Despite voicing that criticism, Rush himself speaks of the importance of protest. The 1st District was the first black-majority district in the nation, and Rush is more than willing to comment on racial matters.

In March 2012, Rush was escorted from the House floor while protesting the racially charged Trayvon Martin case. Martin, a black Florida teenager, was shot to death by a neighborhood watch volunteer while wearing a hooded sweatshirt. Many people, including Rush, alleged that the shooting was racially motivated. To draw attention to the case, Rush donned a hoodie on the House floor, which violated the chamber's ban on hats.

"Racial profiling has to stop," he said. "Just because someone wears a hoodie does not make them a hoodlum." He continued speaking, quoting the Bible, as the presiding officer banged his gavel and ordered Rush to stop.

Rush's rhetoric stoked a good deal of controversy after Obama's election to the presidency. Illinois Democratic Gov. Rod R. Blagojevich had the job of appointing Obama's replacement in the Senate, and he was impeached and removed from office for a series of alleged crimes that included trying to sell the seat. But before his removal, he appointed former Illinois Attorney General Roland W. Burris. Other Illinois lawmakers called on Burris to refuse the appointment, but Rush asked reporters not to "hang or lynch" the man who would be the Senate's only African-American.

To join the House, Rush challenged and defeated Democratic Rep. Charles A. Hayes in the 1992 primary. That win essentially guaranteed his general-election victory in the overwhelmingly Democratic district.

Rush has had no problems running for Congress, but his 1999 bid to oust Chicago Mayor Richard M. Daley was a disaster. He received only 28 percent of the vote in that primary. Following that defeat, Rush faced an emboldened field of primary challengers in 2000, including Obama. He still won easily, and he remains the only person to defeat Obama in an election.

His district grew geographically in the redistricting process for 2012, spreading out to take in more suburbs and rural areas south of Chicago. Rush in 2012 had his worst showing in a general election — and still took around 74 percent of the vote. Obama's Chicago home is still in Rush's district.

Key Votes

2012	
Extend a Social Security payroll tax cut and unemployment benefits	YES
Ease securities rules to expand small-business access to capital	YES
Extend for one year subsidized student loan interest rates financed by a cut in health care spending	NO
Cite Attorney General Eric H. Holder Jr. for contempt of Congress	?
Create a visa program for foreign graduates in high-tech fields	?
Extend most Bush-era income tax rates while allowing rates for top-bracket earners to rise (Jan. 1, 2013)	YES
2011	
Strike funding for F-35 alternative engine	NO
Prevent EPA from regulating greenhouse gas emissions to address climate change	NO
Extend certain provisions of Patriot Act for four years	NO
Declare opposition to use of ground troops in Libya	?
Overhaul patent law	NO
Pass compromise debt limit increase plan and establish future spending limits	YES
Allow consideration of measures to implement three trade agreements	YES

CQ Vote Studies

	PARTY UNITY		PRESIDENTIAL SUPPORT	
	SUPPORT	OPPOSE	SUPPORT	OPPOSE
2012	97%	3%	87%	13%
2011	96%	4%	83%	17%
2010	96%	4%	83%	17%
2009	97%	3%	97%	3%
2008	99%	1%	29%	71%

Interest Groups

	AFL-CIO	ADA	CCUS	ACU
2012	95%	95%	20%	5%
2011	100%	85%	20%	0%
2010	93%	85%	14%	9%
2009	100%	100%	47%	0%
2008	100%	30%	67%	13%

Illinois 1

Chicago — South Side; southwestern Cook County and part of Will County

The nation's first black-majority district, the 1st has retained its African-American heritage despite expansion of the district's borders to pick up growing and white-majority subdivisions and some farmland. Following decennial remapping, the 1st starts at 26th Street in Chicago's historic black hub before branching southwest through residential areas of Cook County and into Will County.

Although areas in the district's urban northern reaches have been losing residents overall for years, most of the population is still concentrated in neighborhoods within the Chicago city limits. The 1st is home to several of the city's subsidized housing projects and high-poverty areas as well as some more affluent neighborhoods such as Hyde Park, home to the University of Chicago. Bronzeville and Douglas work to attract black-owned businesses and young black professionals, marketing the area's jazz and blues traditions. There is a small stretch of Lake Michigan shoreline northeast of Washington and Hyde parks.

Some residents of the middle-class and blue-collar Cook County suburbs commute into Chicago; these areas still support manufacturing, and public-private partnerships are aimed at easing rail gridlock in the highly congested region. Health care and hospital jobs remain key to the district's economy, as does higher education. In Will County, the 1st grabs fast-growing Frankfort — the population in the town grew by more than 70 percent between 2000 and 2010 — where sprawl has become a concern.

Minority, union-backing and liberal voters in the district's Cook County base outnumber the GOP-friendly residents in Will County. The strongly Democratic parts of the district in Chicago have given hometown candidate Barack Obama overwhelming support in elections.

Major Industry
Hospitals, higher education, manufacturing

Cities
Chicago (pt.), Orland Park (pt.), Tinley Park (pt.), Blue Island, Evergreen Park

Notable
The first self-sustaining nuclear reaction took place at the University of Chicago under the stands at Stagg Field in 1942, and the location is marked by a Henry Moore statue.

Rep. Robin Kelly (D)

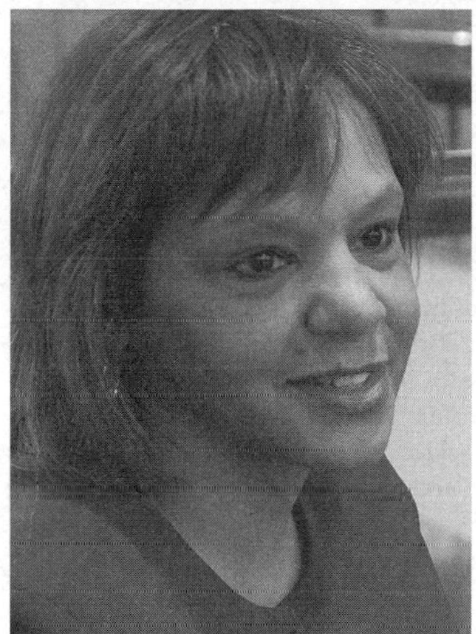

Capitol Office
225-0773
robinkelly.house.gov
2419 Rayburn Bldg. 20515; fax 225-1583

Committees
Oversight & Government Reform
Science, Space & Technology

Residence
Matteson

Born
April 30, 1956; Manhattan, N.Y.

Religion
Non-denominational Christian

Family
Husband, Nathaniel Horn; two children

Education
Bradley U., B.A. 1978 (psychology), M.A. 1982 (counseling); Northern Illinois U., Ph.D. 2004 (political science)

Career
State treasurer aide; city community affairs director; university minority student services director; counseling center director, hospital administrative assistant

Political Highlights
Cook County chief administrative officer, 2011-12; Democratic nominee for Ill. treasurer, 2010; Ill. House, 2003-07

ELECTION RESULTS

2013 SPECIAL		
Robin Kelly (D)	56,979	70.72%
Paul McKinley (R)	17,994	22.1%
Elizabeth "Liz" Pahlke (I)	2,462	3.04%
LeAlan M. Jones (GREEN)	1,487	1.84%
Marcus Lewis (I)	1,330	1.63%
2013 PRIMARY SPECIAL		
Robin Kelly (D)	31,079	50.4%
Debbie Halvorson (D)	14,650	23.8%
Anthony A. Beale (D)	6,457	10.5%
Joyce Washington (D)	2,563	4.2%
Ernest B. Fenton (D)	1,545	2.5%
Anthony W. Williams (D)	641	1.0%

Elected April 2013; 1st term

Kelly has years of experience in public service, quite a few of them as an administrator and right-hand woman. Her knowledge of behind-the-scenes politics should afford her a smooth transition into her new role representing the 2nd District.

Born and raised in New York City, Kelly moved to Illinois to attend Bradley University in Peoria. (Rep. Aaron Schock is also an alumnus.) She earned a master's degree in counseling and spent several years as a social worker, which included a stint as the director of a youth shelter.

Kelly eventually moved to Matteson, a Chicago suburb. She was the director of community affairs for the village for 10 years, then won election to the state House. She served two terms before becoming the chief of staff to Illinois Treasurer Alexi Giannoulias. Both she and her boss had a rough year in 2010. He lost a U.S. Senate race to Republican Mark S. Kirk, and she lost her bid to become the state treasurer herself. In 2011, she was appointed the chief administrative officer of Cook County, putting her in charge of many nuts-and-bolts functions for an area that includes a huge chunk of the state's population.

Kelly's election was made possible by the implosion of Jesse L. Jackson Jr.'s political career. In June 2012, Jackson took a leave of absence from the House to receive treatment for bipolar disorder. He was also under investigation for misuse of campaign funds. He resigned on Nov. 21, two weeks after winning a seat in the 113th Congress (2013-14). He pleaded guilty to fraud in 2013.

A drove of Democrats entered the February 2013 special-election primary. Kelly benefited from her support of gun control — a super PAC spent more than $2 million boosting Kelly and attacking former Rep. Debbie Halvorson for her support of gun rights. Kelly won around half of the vote.

Committee rosters were set by the time Kelly won the April special election. Democrats found spots for her on the Oversight and Government Reform and Science, Space and Technology committees.

Illinois 2

Chicago — far South Side; Chicago Heights; south Chicago exurbs

A decade of population and demographic shifts in Cook and Will counties resulted in a redrawn 2nd District following the 2010 census. Remapping dragged the district's border 30 miles south of its previous territory, and it now runs from Jackson Park on Chicago's South Side through southern Cook County and an arm of Will County to grab all of Kankakee County. The 2nd edges along some of Lake Michigan and 50 miles of the Indiana border.

Much of the population loss within the district's borders occurred north of the Tri-State Tollway, while the suburban and rural southern half of the 2nd gained new residents. Although the 2nd is no longer an urban, Chicagoland-focused district, it still has the state's highest percentage of black residents (56 percent), and a significant portion of the population is Hispanic (13 percent).

The district once was built on the steel business, but Ford Motor Co. is one of the few remaining large manufacturers, with a stamping plant in Chicago Heights and an assembly plant north of Calumet City, which is the company's oldest operating facility. A U.S. Steel plant along the lake closed in 1992, and officials hope that planned mixed development there will boost ailing South Side neighborhoods.

A proposed third Chicago-area airport in Peotone (Will County) could add jobs to the region, and farming still plays a role in less-populated Kankakee County, where Kankakee and Bradley struggle with unemployment.

Despite the addition of Republican voters in Kankakee and Will counties, the 2nd overall is a Democratic stronghold, both at the federal and gubernatorial levels. Established and growing minority communities and working-class voters in areas like Pullman, Dolton and Matteson provide an overwhelming Democratic base in the Cook County portions of the district.

Major Industry
Automotive manufacturing, agriculture, health care

Cities
Chicago (pt.), Calumet City, Chicago Heights, Kankakee

Notable
The Museum of Science and Industry in Jackson Park along Lake Michigan occupies the Fine Arts Building from Chicago's World's Fair, the 1893 Columbian Exposition.

Rep. Daniel Lipinski (D)

Capitol Office
225-5701
lipinski.house.gov
1717 Longworth Bldg. 20515-1303; fax 225-1012

Committees
Science, Space & Technology
Transportation & Infrastructure

Residence
Western Springs

Born
July 15, 1966; Chicago, Ill.

Religion
Roman Catholic

Family
Wife, Judy Lipinski

Education
Northwestern U., B.S. 1988 (mechanical engineering); Stanford U., M.S. 1989 (engineering-economic systems); Duke U., Ph.D. 1998 (political science)

Career
Professor; congressional and campaign aide

Political Highlights
No previous office

ELECTION RESULTS

2012 GENERAL		
Daniel Lipinski (D)	168,738	68.5%
Richard L. Grabowski (R)	77,653	31.5%
2012 PRIMARY		
Daniel Lipinski (D)	44,532	87.3%
Farah Baqai (D)	6,463	12.7%
2010 GENERAL		
Daniel Lipinski (D)	116,120	69.7%
Michael A. Bendas (R)	40,479	24.3%
Laurel Lambert Schmidt (GREEN)	10,028	6.0%

Previous Winning Percentages
2008 (73%); 2006 (77%); 2004 (73%)

Elected 2004; 5th term

Lipinski says his working-class district affords him the luxury of being a "sensible, moderate Democrat," particularly on the transportation, scientific and social issues that have become his focus.

An engineer and political scientist by training, he can be methodical and straightforward as a lawmaker. He avoids cable talk shows and writes much of his own press and campaign material. Lipinski will buck his party leadership if he feels it is in the interests of his south Chicagoland constituents.

He was one of 19 Democrats to support someone other than Nancy Pelosi for party leader in 2011; he cast a vote for Marcy Kaptur of Ohio, praising her anti-abortion views and advocacy for American-Polish relations. He was also the only Illinois Democrat to defy President Barack Obama and vote against the 2010 health care overhaul. The bill's abortion language was his "stumbling block" — Lipinski is Roman Catholic — but he outlined other "serious flaws," including Medicare cuts and a lack of cost controls.

Lipinski does not back full repeal of the law, however. "I don't want to go back to square one and have nothing to replace it with," he said.

During the 112th Congress (2011-12), Lipinski cemented his reputation as a fiscal moderate. He voted in favor of a balanced-budget amendment to the Constitution in 2011, and he called for enactment of a major deficit reduction plan. His preference is based on the work of a 2010 fiscal commission known as Simpson-Bowles; it calls for $4 trillion in deficit reduction through a mix of entitlement program changes, spending cuts and revenue increases. Lipinski in 2013 joined the Blue Dog Coalition of fiscally conservative Democrats.

But he's not averse to some traditional forms of federal spending, such as earmarking: the now-taboo practice of setting aside funding for specific projects in a lawmaker's district. "I never understood why members of Congress are any less able, less clean, in determining where the money should be spent than the administration here in Washington or state legislators back in our home states," he says.

He sits on the Transportation and Infrastructure Committee, one of the former bastions of earmarking. Lipinski works to drive more transportation funding to his district, where he was born and raised. The area is crisscrossed by highways, is a longtime rail hub and holds Midway Airport. Fittingly, from Lipinski's window in his Washington office, planes can be seen landing at Reagan National Airport and train whistles can be heard across Capitol Hill.

He took the mantle of transportation policy champion from his father and congressional predecessor, William O. Lipinski, the old-style urban politician and titan of transportation on Capitol Hill.

Lipinski wants a long-term surface transportation reauthorization, and he bemoaned the version that panel Republicans introduced in early 2012; the majority party did not consult with Democrats and shortchanged mass transit funding for large urban areas, he said. Support for that bill crumbled, and a two-year version was enacted in 2012.

He pushes for grants for the Chicago Region Environmental and Transportation Efficiency Program, a partnership among government and transportation stakeholders in the region. And he was one of only 24 Democrats to vote for a reauthorization of aviation programs in 2012. It included his language to expedite the rollout of the NextGen satellite navigation system.

Also in line with his district's economic concerns, Lipinski calls for a national strategy to boost manufacturing. His bill to develop such a plan passed the House in 2010, and with Illinois Republican Adam Kinzinger as a co-author in 2012, it was passed again. The Senate didn't act on it, however.

Lipinski holds engineering degrees from Northwestern and Stanford, in addition to a doctorate in political science from Duke. He says the United States needs to "do a better job" of yielding marketable products from federally funded research, and he works on that goal as the top Democrat on the Science, Space and Technology Subcommittee on Research.

"What is the future for jobs in America?" he asks. "I think it has to be in innovation." Lipinski pays particular attention to the National Science Foundation's Innovation Corps program, which seeks to move discoveries from laboratories to the business world.

Lipinski and Texas Republican Michael McCaul (who is now the Homeland Security Committee chairman) collaborated on a 2011 bill to map out and coordinate the government's cybersecurity research and training. It was passed overwhelmingly by the House but wasn't acted on by the Senate.

As evidenced by his health care law vote, Lipinski is more socially conservative than many Democratic colleagues. "The first time I ran, I was clear on my position on the life issue" from the beginning, he said. "I figure my time is best spent trying to get things done for my constituents. When that issue would come up, people knew where I was going to stand."

Lipinski's family connections have been a help and a hindrance. His father all but assured that his son would succeed him: William Lipinski filed to run for re-election in 2004, was unopposed in the Democratic primary, then announced during the August recess that he would retire. A committee of 3rd District Democrats, which included the senior Lipinski and his allies, unanimously selected Daniel to fill the ballot slot. The younger Lipinski won easily.

Some Democratic activists were annoyed by what they viewed as nepotistic shenanigans, and they back other candidates each time Lipinski comes up for re-election. Regardless, he has had no problems winning.

Lipinski worked as an associate professor at the University of Tennessee. When he returned to the Chicago area to run for public office after 15 years away, he wasn't a total novice. He had worked on Illinois campaigns, served as an aide to Illinois Rep. Rod R. Blagojevich and earned a fellowship in the office of House Minority Leader Richard A. Gephardt of Missouri.

His academic career was also devoted to politics. He published several papers on how politicians communicate with constituents. The judge of his doctoral thesis at Duke was Democratic Rep. David E. Price, who was between congressional stints.

Lipinski did not express great enthusiasm when the congressional map for 2012 brought U.S. Cellular Field, the home of the White Sox, into his district. "I admit I am a Cubs fan," he said. "What was I gonna do? Change? I always say it just goes to show, I stick with what I believe."

Key Votes

2012	
Extend a Social Security payroll tax cut and unemployment benefits	YES
Ease securities rules to expand small-business access to capital	YES
Extend for one year subsidized student loan interest rates financed by a cut in health care spending	YES
Cite Attorney General Eric H. Holder Jr. for contempt of Congress	P
Create a visa program for foreign graduates in high-tech fields	YES
Extend most Bush-era income tax rates while allowing rates for top-bracket earners to rise (Jan. 1, 2013)	YES
2011	
Strike funding for F-35 alternative engine	NO
Prevent EPA from regulating greenhouse gas emissions to address climate change	NO
Extend certain provisions of Patriot Act for four years	YES
Declare opposition to use of ground troops in Libya	YES
Overhaul patent law	NO
Pass compromise debt limit increase plan and establish future spending limits	YES
Allow consideration of measures to implement three trade agreements	NO

CQ Vote Studies

	PARTY UNITY		PRESIDENTIAL SUPPORT	
	SUPPORT	OPPOSE	SUPPORT	OPPOSE
2012	79%	21%	61%	39%
2011	84%	16%	80%	20%
2010	88%	12%	86%	14%
2009	94%	6%	90%	10%
2008	97%	3%	16%	84%

Interest Groups

	AFL-CIO	ADA	CCUS	ACU
2012	86%	55%	50%	24%
2011	80%	75%	31%	20%
2010	86%	65%	25%	8%
2009	100%	90%	43%	8%
2008	100%	90%	59%	8%

Illinois 3

Chicago — southwest side; Southwestern Cook County and part of Will County

Highways, airways, rail lines and the Chicago Sanitary and Ship Canal put transportation firmly at the focus of the 3rd, which cuts southwest from the junction of interstates 94 and 55 on the South Side of Chicago, through some working-class neighborhoods of the Bungalow Belt, past Midway International Airport and across two more major highways into Will County.

Near Garfield Ridge, Midway and its related transportation, retail and service industries steady the district's economy. Southwest Airlines continues to expand operations there, filling a void left by the departures of other carriers. The 3rd has also historically relied on food processing, distribution and manufacturing linked to the cargo rail hubs in Bridgeview and in adjacent districts. Hundreds of millions of dollars in highway expansion in Will County has mitigated traffic congestion among outer suburbs.

Despite more than a decade of drastic population loss overall in Cook County, especially in Chicago itself, several neighborhoods and villages in the district have gained residents, many of whom are Hispanic and filling in areas that have shed white residents. In particular, the district's northeastern neck, which once was stocked with voters of Irish, Eastern European and Italian descent, now is mainly Hispanic. Asian communities have spread southwest from Chicago's traditional Chinatown neighborhood (in the 7th) into Bridgeport, the historically Irish neighborhood that has been the political base of the powerful Daley family. In Will County, which received much of the population that shifted from urban Cook County, the 3rd becomes less densely populated and less diverse.

Areas in the 3rd have tended to send Democrats to Washington, though not by such wide margins as other Chicago-based districts. Many middle-class voters are more conservative on social issues but will support Democrats running for local offices. Barack Obama took 56 percent of the district's vote in the 2012 presidential election.

Major Industry

Transportation, distribution

Cities

Chicago (pt.), Cicero (pt.) Orland Park (pt.), Oak Lawn, Lockport

Notable

The district is home to both baseball's White Sox, in Chicago, and soccer's Fire, in Bridgeview.

Rep. Luis V. Gutierrez (D)

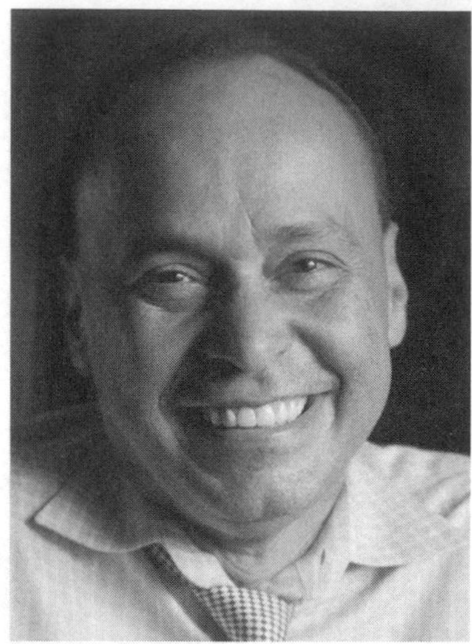

Capitol Office
225-8203
luisgutierrez.house.gov
2408 Rayburn Bldg. 20515-1304; fax 225-7810

Committees
Judiciary
Select Intelligence

Residence
Chicago

Born
Dec. 10, 1953; Chicago, Ill.

Religion
Roman Catholic

Family
Wife, Soraida Arocho Gutierrez; two children

Education
Northeastern Illinois U., B.A. 1975 (liberal arts)

Career
Mayoral aide; teacher; social worker; cab driver

Political Highlights
Chicago City Council, 1986-93

ELECTION RESULTS

2012 GENERAL		
Luis V. Gutierrez (D)	133,226	83.0%
Hector Concepcion (R)	27,279	17.0%
2012 PRIMARY		
Luis V. Gutierrez (D)	30,908	100.0%
2010 GENERAL		
Luis V. Gutierrez (D)	63,273	77.4%
Israel Vasquez (R)	11,711	14.3%
Robert J. Burns (GREEN)	6,808	8.3%

Previous Winning Percentages
2008 (81%); 2006 (86%); 2004 (84%); 2002 (80%); 2000 (89%); 1998 (82%); 1996 (94%); 1994 (75%); 1992 (78%)

Elected 1992; 11th term

Gutierrez earned the nickname "el Gallito" — the little fighting rooster — in the famously combative arena of Chicago politics. He wants a comprehensive overhaul of immigration law, calling it his "unfinished business" in Congress — and for the first time in a long time, there might be a path to his goal.

One advocate called Gutierrez "the closest thing we have to an Al Sharpton figure" in the immigration fight. He started his House career trying to expand citizenship education and English-language proficiency programs for newly arrived immigrants. In 2001, Gutierrez sponsored a bill to establish a path to citizenship for undocumented youths brought to the United States by their parents. The Senate passed a version of that measure in 2006, and the House did the same in 2010, but it was never signed into law.

Gutierrez was named chairman of the Democratic Caucus Immigration Task Force in 2009, and he also chairs the Congressional Hispanic Caucus Immigration Task Force. In the 111th Congress (2009-10), he was the most outspoken House advocate for a broad immigration overhaul that would include a path to legal residency and citizenship for illegal immigrants already in the country, beefed-up border security, changes to the foreign guest worker program and workplace enforcement measures. That effort died well short of enactment.

The issue became intractable, with most Republicans demanding a secure border as a precursor for an overhaul or refusing to accept any "amnesty" for those in the country illegally.

Democratic leaders didn't invest much political capital in the issue in the 111th Congress, when they controlled both chambers of Congress and the White House. Gutierrez did not hide his frustration. In the spring of 2010, he was arrested at a White House sit-in, eventually paying a $100 fine.

He defended President Barack Obama's 2012 policy directive to halt the deportation of some immigrants brought to America illegally as children — a component of his bill from 2001. Critics called the order a sop to Hispanic voters in an election year. "You can't look at his actions in a vacuum," Gutierrez said, calling the order an example of actual progress.

He was critical of a 2012 Supreme Court ruling that upheld part of an Arizona law that allowed local law enforcement officers to check on someone's citizenship status in the course of their duties. Gutierrez said it "will sanction pretextual stops and racial profiling."

The 2012 election started a thaw, however. Republicans had a miserable showing with Hispanic voters, and Obama promised to work toward an overhaul in his second term. Gutierrez had moved off the Judiciary Committee in the 112th Congress (2011-12), but with the blessing of party leaders he returned to both the panel and its immigration subcommittee at the start of the 113th Congress (2013-14). He was quickly in the middle of bipartisan negotiations, and in March 2013 he was optimistic that some form of legislation would pass.

"When you look at so many issues that seem so bound up in partisanship and gridlock, immigration stands out as the one area where the two parties will find a way to get something done this year," he wrote in Roll Call.

In order to get back on Judiciary, Gutierrez gave up his seat on the Financial Services Committee, where he was the No. 3 Democrat. In the 112th Congress he was the ranking member of the Insurance, Housing and Community Opportunity Subcommittee. "We're quick to rush to save the financial institutions from a disaster, which they created with the funds of the people," he said. "But how reluctant we are to help the very people who, through no fault of their own, find disaster and need a helping hand."

In the 111th Congress, he chaired the Financial Institutions and Consumer Credit Subcommittee and contributed several provisions to the 2010 financial regulatory overhaul law, such as a "dissolution fund" to help cover the costs should the government have to dismantle a failing financial institution, and an assessment system that would ensure larger and riskier depository institutions pay more into the Federal Deposit Insurance Corporation.

Gutierrez still serves on the Intelligence Committee. He says he wants to balance the safety of Americans with "the need to know that your government isn't intruding and violating your civil rights."

He was born in Chicago and grew up in the largely blue-collar and immigrant community of Lincoln Park. His mother worked at a manufacturing plant soldering ballasts for light fixtures, while his father transitioned between work as a cab driver and a building superintendent.

"Their working-class background really does shape my values and perspective on what government's priorities should be," he said. He is a member of the Congressional Progressive Caucus, the group of the most-liberal House members.

Gutierrez attended high school in Puerto Rico, then returned to Chicago for college; he participated in protests and served as president of the Union for Puerto Rican Students, even promoting Puerto Rican independence. After another few years in Puerto Rico he came back to the city, this time with a new bride. He worked as a public school teacher and social worker.

His venture into politics began in 1983. Gutierrez saw racial motivations behind Democratic opposition to the agenda of the city's first black mayor, Harold Washington. Gutierrez quit his job with the Illinois Department of Children and Family Services and drove a cab to raise funds in his campaign for 32nd Ward Democratic committeeman.

He was crushed — his opponent was Rep. Dan Rostenkowski, the chairman of the Ways and Means Committee — but Washington took notice and hired Gutierrez for his staff. He subsequently endorsed Gutierrez when he decided to run for the city council in the newly drawn 26th Ward, which contained a largely Latino electorate. Gutierrez won.

Washington died in office in 1987, and Gutierriez mended fences with Richard M. Daley — Washington's opponent in 1983 — who became mayor in 1989. For the 1992 elections, a new U.S. House district was created with a majority of Chicago's Latinos. Gutierrez jumped in, and Daley's endorsement helped him secure an easy victory. All his re-elections have been landslides.

Gutierrez considered a run for mayor himself in 2010 but said he stayed in Congress to keep working on immigration. "History is not written by those who change battles in the middle of the fight," he told supporters.

Key Votes

2012	
Extend a Social Security payroll tax cut and unemployment benefits	NO
Ease securities rules to expand small-business access to capital	YES
Extend for one year subsidized student loan interest rates financed by a cut in health care spending	NO
Cite Attorney General Eric H. Holder Jr. for contempt of Congress	?
Create a visa program for foreign graduates in high-tech fields	NO
Extend most Bush-era income tax rates while allowing rates for top-bracket earners to rise (Jan. 1, 2013)	YES
2011	
Strike funding for F-35 alternative engine	NO
Prevent EPA from regulating greenhouse gas emissions to address climate change	NO
Extend certain provisions of Patriot Act for four years	NO
Declare opposition to use of ground troops in Libya	NO
Overhaul patent law	YES
Pass compromise debt limit increase plan and establish future spending limits	YES
Allow consideration of measures to implement three trade agreements	YES

CQ Vote Studies

	PARTY UNITY		PRESIDENTIAL SUPPORT	
	SUPPORT	OPPOSE	SUPPORT	OPPOSE
2012	98%	2%	89%	11%
2011	96%	4%	81%	19%
2010	95%	5%	82%	18%
2009	98%	2%	93%	7%
2008	99%	1%	16%	84%

Interest Groups

	AFL-CIO	ADA	CCUS	ACU
2012	95%	90%	25%	0%
2011	96%	80%	20%	0%
2010	100%	90%	14%	0%
2009	100%	100%	33%	0%
2008	100%	90%	56%	0%

Illinois 4

Chicago — parts of northwest, lower West Side; Cicero

The horseshoe-shaped 4th District, which surrounds most of the black-majority 7th District, has for decades served to unite the city's Hispanic neighborhoods into one voting bloc. Following remapping after the 2010 census, the 4th retains its Hispanic majority — and its status as the state's only Hispanic-majority district — even as the number of Hispanic Chicagoans overall has increased across the city.

Many recent immigrants live in the district's already established Hispanic neighborhoods or the traditionally Ukrainian and Polish areas of the Bungalow Belt. Some areas in the 4th, such as the parts of Cicero in the southern stretch of the district, claim populations that are more than 80 percent Hispanic.

In its northern arm, the district takes in Logan Square and historically Puerto Rican Hermosa, stretching west through Melrose Park. It cuts south along a narrow strip of highway interchanges to pick up cemeteries, railway lines and some white-majority villages before heading east through Brookfield and Cicero all the way to the Little Italy neighborhood. Brookfield Zoo, a popular tourist destination, is located at the district's southern elbow.

The 4th has a primarily blue-collar workforce — most jobs in the district are in transportation and manufacturing, and the warehouse industry is strong. Officials hope the redevelopment of two southwest side coal-fired power plants will boost the local economy.

The district is young and poor — the district has the state's highest percentage of residents under 35 and lowest household median income (under $40,000) — and many areas have higher poverty rates and lower rates of formal education than statewide averages. The district has the state's second-lowest rate of adults with at least one college degree (17 percent). The 3rd is solidly Democratic, although it is plagued by low voter turnout.

Major Industry
Transportation, light manufacturing, warehouses

Cities
Chicago (pt.), Cicero (pt.), Berwyn (pt.), Melrose Park (pt.)

Notable
Berwyn is home to the World's Largest Laundromat, with roughly 300 washers and dryers combined, and runs on solar power.

Rep. Mike Quigley (D)

Capitol Office
225-4061
quigley.house.gov
1124 Longworth Bldg. 20515-1305; fax 225-5603

Committees
Appropriations

Residence
Chicago

Born
Oct. 17, 1958; Indianapolis, Ind.

Religion
Christian

Family
Wife, Barbara Quigley; two children

Education
Roosevelt U., B.A. 1981 (political science); U. of Chicago, M.P.P 1985; Loyola U. Chicago, J.D. 1989

Career
College instructor; lawyer; legislative aide

Political Highlights
Candidate for Chicago City Council, 1991; Cook County Board of Commissioners, 1998-2009

ELECTION RESULTS

2012 GENERAL		
Mike Quigley (D)	177,729	65.7%
Dan Schmitt (R)	77,289	28.6%
Nancy Wade (GREEN)	15,359	5.7%
2012 PRIMARY		
Mike Quigley (D)		unopposed
2010 GENERAL		
Mike Quigley (D)	108,360	70.6%
David Ratowitz (R)	38,935	25.4%
Matt Reichel (GREEN)	6,140	4.0%

Previous Winning Percentages
2009 Special Election (69%)

Elected 2009; 2nd full term

Quigley is a scrapper in both the hockey rink and the legislative arena. Governmental transparency and oversight have been themes of his public career, going back to his battles with Chicago's political machines.

A former Cook County commissioner and college instructor — and an avid hockey fan and player — Quigley does not shy from grunt work. The motto of his Washington office is "We live in the weeds."

There are plenty of weeds in the federal budget, which Quigley is parsing in the 113th Congress (2013-14) as a new member of the Appropriations Committee. He sits on the Financial Services and General Government Subcommittee, which deals with the regulators who oversee large parts of Chicago's finance sector, as well as some of the agencies and departments integral to day-to-day federal operations. Quigley is also on the Transportation-HUD Subcommittee, which is a big deal for his city's rail and aviation hubs.

Quigley, a member of the New Democrat Coalition, has touted his fiscal moderation. In the 112th Congress (2011-12), he stood up for a federal budget based on the work of a 2010 fiscal commission known as Simpson-Bowles. It would reduce deficits by $4 trillion over a decade through a mix of entitlement program changes, revenue increases and spending cuts.

Quigley says he's particularly interested in the elimination of duplicative and wasteful programs, which is a goal he shares with many conservatives. He wants more-effective delivery of services, and conservatives want smaller government. "If we work together, our common theme there is that it saves money and it makes government more efficient," he said. "It's worthwhile."

In 2010, Quigley joined with Republican Darrell Issa of California in founding the Congressional Transparency Caucus, which he still co-chairs. Though "ethics and transparency and accountability don't poll first or second" as voter concerns, they are crucial in building public trust in Congress, he said. "If everything was more transparent, you'd just have better government overall."

All taxpayers, Quigley says, should get a receipt breaking down how their income taxes are spent. He also wants to improve public access to information on lawmakers' finances, travel, gifts and earmarks.

Quigley claims as one of his first victories the March 2010 declaration of a one-year moratorium on earmarks going to for-profit entities; Quigley had introduced a resolution in July 2009, with Republicans Jeff Flake of Arizona and Mark S. Kirk of Illinois, to require a prohibition. Republicans have now banned earmarks outright.

Citing poor records of the condition of government-held properties and their maintenance costs, he worked with Utah Republican Jason Chaffetz on a bill to create a pilot program to dispose of unneeded federal property. The House passed it in March 2012. Collaborating with Ohio Republican James B. Renacci — they met with other members in an informal bipartisan working group in the 112th — he introduced a 2011 bill to mandate additional reports on the federal budgeting process and move to a two-year budgeting cycle.

Quigley's interest in transparency is grounded in Chicago's sometimes-sordid political history. His district has been represented by two lawmakers who didn't exactly cover themselves in glory — Democrats Dan Rostenkowski, who went to prison on federal charges, and Rod R. Blagojevich, who attempted to profit from a Senate vacancy while governor and was later impeached and imprisoned. But Quigley maintains an optimism about the political process. "I tell people: Save the world, change the world," he said. "And I was in Chicago politics since 1982, so if anyone should be cynical by now, it should be me."

Gun control is also important to his constituents. "I come from Chicago," he said. "That's why we are so interested in corruption; it's why we are interested in guns." A 2013 Quigley bill would ensure that firearms are marked with serial numbers and that the government preserves background check records for 180 days.

Quigley, who was a criminal defense attorney for eight years, gave up his seat on the Judiciary Committee to become an appropriator. He represents a number of Polish-Americans and has introduced bills that would expand a visa waiver program to Polish citizens making temporary visits to the United Sates. He calls the current situation "an insult" to an allied country and has worked on the issue with Kirk (now a senator) and Sen. Barbara A. Mikulski, a Maryland Democrat.

Quigley is socially liberal, and he balks at tying social issues to spending or non-related measures. "However you feel about Planned Parenthood or how everyone feels about NPR, we aren't going to balance the budget zeroing them out," he said. "And it's just bad policy."

He was born in Indianapolis and moved to the Chicago suburbs in second grade. His mother was a schoolteacher, and his father worked for a telephone company. He earned a political science degree from Roosevelt University and worked as an aide to Chicago Alderman Bernard Hansen while attending graduate school.

Quigley obtained a law degree from Loyola University in Chicago in 1989 and eventually became an adjunct professor of political science at both Loyola and Roosevelt. He taught a course on environmental policy at Loyola and said protecting the environment is "the reason I got into this business." He supported the House Democrats' 2009 bill to create a cap-and-trade system to regulate greenhouse gas emissions. Quigley bikes everywhere, and his office features numerous recycling bins.

It also features seats from Wrigley Field. In the 1980s, Quigley was one of the leaders of Citizens United for Baseball in Sunshine, a neighborhood group that unsuccessfully fought the Chicago Cubs over installing lights at Wrigley Field, which is in his district.

Quigley first entered electoral politics in 1991, when he unsuccessfully ran for alderman in Chicago's 46th Ward. Seven years later he was elected to the Cook County Board of Commissioners, where he was an occasional thorn in the side of Mayor Richard M. Daley.

Democrat Rahm Emanuel resigned his House seat in 2009 to become White House chief of staff, and Quigley took 22 percent of the vote in the 12-way Democratic special-election primary to replace him. He then swamped Republican Rosanna Pulido. His re-elections have been by wide margins.

Key Votes

2012	
Extend a Social Security payroll tax cut and unemployment benefits	YES
Ease securities rules to expand small-business access to capital	YES
Extend for one year subsidized student loan interest rates financed by a cut in health care spending	NO
Cite Attorney General Eric H. Holder Jr. for contempt of Congress	NO
Create a visa program for foreign graduates in high-tech fields	NO
Extend most Bush-era income tax rates while allowing rates for top-bracket earners to rise (Jan. 1, 2013)	YES
2011	
Strike funding for F-35 alternative engine	YES
Prevent EPA from regulating greenhouse gas emissions to address climate change	NO
Extend certain provisions of Patriot Act for four years	YES
Declare opposition to use of ground troops in Libya	NO
Overhaul patent law	YES
Pass compromise debt limit increase plan and establish future spending limits	YES
Allow consideration of measures to implement three trade agreements	NO

CQ Vote Studies

	PARTY UNITY		PRESIDENTIAL SUPPORT	
	SUPPORT	OPPOSE	SUPPORT	OPPOSE
2012	96%	4%	92%	8%
2011	93%	7%	87%	13%
2010	95%	5%	88%	12%
2009	96%	4%	97%	3%

Interest Groups

	AFL-CIO	ADA	CCUS	ACU
2012	85%	90%	25%	0%
2011	90%	85%	38%	4%
2010	100%	95%	20%	4%
2009	93%		42%	0%

Illinois 5

Chicago — North Side; O'Hare

The 5th takes in the majority of Chicago's North Side and its rows of brownstones before swinging west to Schiller Park and O'Hare International Airport and then south into a slice of DuPage County suburbs. It also includes one of Chicago's few remaining active industrial sectors, running along the North Branch of the Chicago River and taking in almost all of the Goose Island manufacturing zone.

DePaul University students and "lakefront liberals" inhabit wealthy communities near the lake, such as Lincoln Park. Roscoe Village and Lakeview, which includes the gay community Boystown, have experienced an influx of younger residents; overdevelopment is a concern for locals who want to keep neighborhoods' traditional identities intact. Ethnic restaurants and entertainment spots in eastern parts of the district, especially those along public transportation lines, provide weekend and evening destinations for residents from other parts of the city as well as from close-in suburbs.

From the northwestern corner of the district, O'Hare (a small part of which is in the 8th) is one of the busiest airports in the world and steers much of the economy for the neighboring area. It was moved into the 5th after decennial reapportionment, as the districts ringing Chicago and its inner suburbs were redrawn. Rosemont, just east of O'Hare, hosts an 840,000-square-foot convention center. Hotels and businesses related to the travel industry, and firms seeking airport access, have located in the 5th and in adjacent districts — the 8th and the 9th. As construction to modernize the airport continues, officials hope public-private partnerships will help fund construction of new runways.

Second- and third-generation German and Polish residents still dominate much of the 5th, but an increasing number of Hispanic residents have made the population more diverse. Despite western suburbs aligning more with the GOP, the mix of minority, ethnic and liberal-leaning groups keeps the 5th Democratic. In the 2012 presidential race, residents in its parts of Cook County gave Barack Obama 69 percent of their vote, while DuPage County voters in the 5th gave GOP candidate Mitt Romney 54 percent.

Major Industry
Airport, manufacturing, warehousing

Cities
Chicago (pt.), Elmhurst (pt.), Franklin Park

Notable
Wrigley Field hosts baseball's Chicago Cubs.

Rep. Peter Roskam (R)

Capitol Office
225-4561
roskam.house.gov
227 Cannon Bldg. 20515-1306; fax 225-1166

Committees
Ways & Means

Residence
Wheaton

Born
Sept. 13, 1961; Hinsdale, Ill.

Religion
Anglican

Family
Wife, Elizabeth Roskam; four children

Education
U. of Illinois, B.A. 1983 (political science); Illinois Institute of Technology, J.D. 1989

Career
Lawyer; nonprofit education scholarship executive director; congressional aide; teacher

Political Highlights
Ill. House, 1993-99; Sought Republican nomination for U.S. House, 1998; Ill. Senate, 2000-07

ELECTION RESULTS

2012 GENERAL		
Peter Roskam (R)	193,138	59.2%
Leslie Coolidge (D)	132,991	40.8%
2012 PRIMARY		
Peter Roskam (R)		unopposed
2010 GENERAL		
Peter Roskam (R)	114,456	63.6%
Benjamin S. Lowe (D)	65,379	36.4%

Previous Winning Percentages
2008 (58%); 2006 (51%)

Elected 2006; 4th term

Roskam invites the trust of his party with a steady demeanor and razor-sharp legislative know-how. He describes his position as the Republican chief deputy whip as "listener-in-chief" and says he has learned how to accommodate myriad viewpoints without drying out a message.

"You give good members good information and give them time, and you're going to get to a good result," he said. "Don't drop something on their desk and tell them they are going to vote on it tomorrow. It won't end well."

He has risen quickly in the House. He received a desired post on the Ways and Means Committee in his second term, then became the deputy to Majority Whip Kevin McCarthy of California in his third. Speaking to the Chicago Daily Herald in 2012, Majority Leader Eric Cantor called Roskam "a rock star" and explained: "People like him, he's smart, he's savvy, he understands the policy end and how it relates to the political end."

Georgia's Tom Price, a leader of the GOP's conservative wing, has a different but still positive take: "He's not excitable, which is what you want."

Party elders trusted Roskam to lead the drafting of the "Pledge to America," a document that helped lay the intellectual groundwork for big GOP electoral victories in 2010. He spent much of the 112th Congress (2011-12) working with members first elected in that wave.

During debates over federal spending in 2011, many observers called the new Republicans difficult for leaders to manage; Roskam offered a different view. "The freshman class has taught me that they have come here to do something and not to be somebody," he said. "There is a buoyancy to that; there is a freshness to that."

Legislatively, Roskam gravitates toward tax overhaul measures, hoping to increase American competitiveness by simplifying the tax code. He attributes his vision of "less government is better" to his experiences as a legislative aide for the late Republican Henry J. Hyde — who represented much of the same suburban Chicago territory as Roskam for 16 terms — and on the staff of former GOP Rep. Tom DeLay of Texas in the mid-1980s.

Although a party loyalist, he sees tax changes as a launching point for bipartisanship: "There's no voice in the public square today that can look at the totality of the tax code and say, 'It's terrific. We just love this whole thing.'"

He gathered substantial Democratic support for a 2011 bill to make permanent the IRS Free File Program, which provides low-income taxpayers free online help preparing and filing their taxes. He reintroduced it in 2013.

Roskam has also dabbled in tweaks to entitlement programs, which he deals with as a member of the Ways and Means Health Subcommittee. He teamed with Delaware Democrat John Carney on a bill to reduce fraud in the Medicare payment system by, among other things, incorporating fraud prevention tactics used by the credit card industry.

Like most Republicans, he has been critical of the Obama administration's economic and regulatory agenda. He opposed the 2010 financial-sector regulatory overhaul, saying it ignored the biggest part of the problem. "No true financial reform bill will be complete until it deals with reform of Fannie Mae and Freddie Mac and their $5.4 trillion in liabilities," Roskam wrote in May 2010 on the Heritage Foundation's Foundry blog.

A member of the Financial Services Committee during the 110th Congress (2007-08), Roskam voted against two versions of a $700 billion measure — the second of which became law — to shore up the struggling financial industry. He said it would place too great a burden on taxpayers, while providing no guarantee of success.

Roskam follows in the conservative footsteps of his predecessor on social policy and foreign policy. Like Hyde, whose name is attached to a law that has long barred federal funding of most abortions, Roskam opposes abortion.

He supports a strong U.S. relationship with Israel and vacationed in that country for a week in 2006 with his family. In the Middle East, "Israel is our one friend that we can consistently count on, that has a shared set of values," he said. Roskam is furthering his involvement with foreign affairs in the 113th Congress (2013-14) as a new member of the Ways and Means Trade Subcommittee. He made several shows of public support in 2012 for normalization of trade relations with Russia, which imports a lot of goods from Illinois. A normalization bill was enacted late that year.

Roskam was born into a middle-class family from Glen Ellyn. His mother was a homemaker and later opened a nursery school; his father was a sales manager who had fought in the Korean War. Roskam and Illinois Democrat Daniel Lipinski have urged the establishment of a national Korean War museum in Chicago.

The elder Roskam dropped out of college because he was unable to afford it, but a gift from wealthy farmers enabled him to return. Years later, he started a nonprofit scholarship program, Education Assistance. During much of the 1990s, the son served as executive director of the program, which collects extra inventory from corporations and donates it to colleges. The colleges then grant scholarships in the amounts of the merchandise.

Roskam was a varsity gymnast in high school. He first showed up on a ballot in a successful campaign for student senate president. He went on to earn a bachelor's degree in political science from the University of Illinois, then taught history and government in the U.S. Virgin Islands for a year. He moved to Washington in 1985 and worked for DeLay, who was then a freshman representative. Roskam worked for Hyde before graduating law school in 1989.

Roskam won a state House seat in 1992 and served three terms before losing his first bid for the U.S. House. In that 1998 race in the 13th District, he lost the Republican primary to Judy Biggert. In 2000 he was appointed to the state Senate, where he served until his successful 2006 bid for Congress. For several of those years, he worked alongside Democratic state Sen. Barack Obama.

The 2006 race drew national attention because many saw it as a referendum on the Iraq War. His opponent, Democrat Tammy Duckworth, was a member of the Illinois Army National Guard who lost her legs when a rocket-propelled grenade hit her helicopter in Iraq. Roskam eked out a 3-point win despite a huge fundraising effort by national Democrats on Duckworth's behalf.

Roskam, himself a prodigious fundraiser, has won re-elections comfortably. Duckworth was elected in the neighboring 8th District in 2012.

Key Votes

2012	
Extend a Social Security payroll tax cut and unemployment benefits	YES
Ease securities rules to expand small-business access to capital	YES
Extend for one year subsidized student loan interest rates financed by a cut in health care spending	YES
Cite Attorney General Eric H. Holder Jr. for contempt of Congress	YES
Create a visa program for foreign graduates in high-tech fields	YES
Extend most Bush-era income tax rates while allowing rates for top-bracket earners to rise (Jan. 1, 2013)	NO
2011	
Strike funding for F-35 alternative engine	NO
Prevent EPA from regulating greenhouse gas emissions to address climate change	YES
Extend certain provisions of Patriot Act for four years	YES
Declare opposition to use of ground troops in Libya	YES
Overhaul patent law	YES
Pass compromise debt limit increase plan and establish future spending limits	YES
Allow consideration of measures to implement three trade agreements	YES

CQ Vote Studies

	PARTY UNITY		PRESIDENTIAL SUPPORT	
	SUPPORT	OPPOSE	SUPPORT	OPPOSE
2012	95%	5%	16%	84%
2011	96%	4%	25%	75%
2010	98%	2%	29%	71%
2009	94%	6%	26%	74%
2008	95%	5%	71%	29%

Interest Groups

	AFL-CIO	ADA	CCUS	ACU
2012	38%	0%	100%	80%
2011	28%	15%	100%	76%
2010	8%	5%	86%	100%
2009	10%	0%	80%	100%
2008	13%	10%	94%	96%

Illinois 6

West and far northwest Chicago suburbs — part of Cook County, Wheaton and part of Naperville

The 6th is made up of predominately white-collar and well-to-do north and northwest Chicago suburbs. Redrawn during decennial remapping, the district takes in portions of five counties — a slice of suburban Cook, southwestern Lake, southeastern McHenry, a corner of Kane and a swath of DuPage. The shape consolidates Republican voters, forming a hook around areas that tend to support Democratic candidates. Overall, the 6th District gave Mitt Romney 53 percent of its 2012 presidential vote.

Many district residents commute to Chicago — several cities in the 6th are served by rail lines to downtown — or to well-established satellite cities, such as Downers Grove, Naperville (shared with the 11th) or Schaumburg (in the 8th). Downers Grove has been one of the region's leading suburban business centers, although Sara Lee moved its corporate headquarters to Chicago in 2012. Naperville still hosts the headquarters of OfficeMax, although the company — one of Naperville's largest employers — could relocate if a planned merger with Florida-based Office Depot occurs.

Naperville has experienced years of population growth only slightly stunted by drops in the housing market. Its residents are highly educated — 65 percent have a bachelor's degree or higher — and well-to-do — median household income is more than $100,000, nearly double the statewide average. Closer in to Chicago, upper-middle-class Wheaton is home to many conservative voters as well as the non-denominational Christian liberal-arts Wheaton College. In addition to rapidly filling residential areas, the district also is home to the Morton Arboretum near Naperville and open parkland and lakes to the north.

The majority-white district has sizable Asian communities; the Hispanic population is growing, although at a slower pace than in nearby suburbs.

Major Industry
Corporate offices, higher education

Cities
Naperville (pt.), Elgin (pt.) Downers Grove (pt.), Palatine (pt.)

Notable
Barnes & Noble traces its beginnings to 1873, when Charles M. Barnes sold books from his home in Wheaton.

Rep. Danny K. Davis (D)

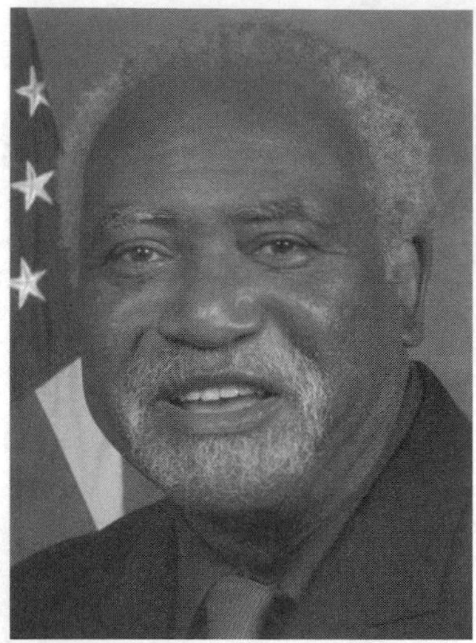

Capitol Office
225-5006
davis.house.gov
2159 Rayburn Bldg. 20515-1307; fax 225-5641

Committees
Oversight & Government Reform
Ways & Means

Residence
Chicago

Born
Sept. 6, 1941; Parkdale, Ark.

Religion
Baptist

Family
Wife, Vera G. Davis; two children

Education
Arkansas AM&N College, B.A. 1961 (history & education); Chicago State U., M.A. 1968 (guidance); Union Institute, Ph.D. 1977 (public administration)

Career
Health care association executive; teacher; postal clerk

Political Highlights
Chicago City Council, 1979-90; sought Democratic nomination for U.S. House, 1984, 1986; Cook County Commission, 1990-97; sought Democratic nomination for mayor of Chicago, 1991

ELECTION RESULTS

2012 GENERAL		
Danny K. Davis (D)	242,439	84.6%
Rita Zak (R)	31,466	11.0%
John H. Monaghan (I)	12,523	4.4%
2012 PRIMARY		
Danny K. Davis (D)	57,896	84.5%
Jacques A. Conway (D)	10,638	15.5%
2010 GENERAL		
Danny K. Davis (D)	149,846	81.5%
Mark M. Weiman (R)	29,575	16.1%
Clarence Desmond Clemons (I)	4,428	2.4%

Previous Winning Percentages
2008 (85%); 2006 (87%); 2004 (86%); 2002 (83%); 2000 (86%); 1998 (93%); 1996 (82%)

Elected 1996; 9th term

Davis has a distinctive baritone voice with glacial qualities — when he speaks, his words seem slow, steady and inevitable. Fittingly, he has a steady approach to governing. In advocating on behalf of the impoverished, he takes a comprehensive, long-term approach. "Change is more evolutionary than it is revolutionary," he says.

He can certainly understand the plight of those he seeks to assist. Davis and his 10 siblings were born to sharecroppers in southeastern Arkansas. The children were sent to a segregated, one-room schoolhouse four or five months of the year, spending the rest of the time doing farm work. Davis credits his voracious reading habits with eventually leading him to Washington.

"I read everything I could get my hands on," he said. "If I saw a piece of paper lying on the ground, I'd probably pick it up and just see what it was. I worked for a guy who let me clear his yard, but every week he would save me his two newspapers."

Although his district takes in some of Chicago's glossier locations — including the Loop, downtown offices of the Chicago Mercantile Exchange and part of the affluent Gold Coast — it is also marked by poor, drug-ravaged neighborhoods. "I'm very conscious of the taxpayers' money, but I'm also conscious of the fact that if there is no investment, there is no return," he said. "I put a lot of emphasis on people who are disadvantaged."

The district also includes several hospitals and clinics, and Davis has been a dedicated supporter of the 2010 health care law, which he helped write as a member of the Ways and Means Committee in the 111th Congress (2009-10). In March 2012, he called the law "the most important thing that has happened to health care in this country since the Indians discovered corn flakes." Davis was also once the president of the National Association of Community Health Centers, and he is the facilities' greatest advocate in Congress, helping to secure a sharp funding increase in the health care law.

Davis returned to Ways and Means in the 113th Congress (2013-14) after a two-year hiatus. He sits on the Human Resources Subcommittee, which oversees welfare, nutrition and unemployment programs. In late 2012, Davis protested the possible expiration of expanded unemployment benefits: "Our economy needs federal unemployment benefits to support its growth," he said. He also sits on the Oversight and Government Reform Committee and its panels on job creation and entitlement programs.

One of Davis' top priorities every year is securing money for a grant program to help former prisoners re-enter society. "We've got to fight like a dog to try to get the little funding" it receives, he said. Congress passed his bill reauthorizing the program in 2008, but Davis wants more money dedicated. "The amount of money that we fund the program with is minuscule in terms of what's actually needed," he said. "It is such a massive problem, it is unimaginable." In 2009, he sponsored a bill that would reduce sentences for criminals who maintain a good record of conduct while in prison.

Davis also repeatedly introduces a bill to ensure funding for grants to promote active participation in family life by fathers and strengthen low-income families. But he is decidedly non-wonky in describing proposals to boost employment and affordable housing, and he's not married to the notion of legislation as the best agent for change: "A lot of people introduce bills, hundreds of them; nothing ever happens with them."

He will sign on to bills that benefit Chicago. Davis is part of a bipartisan, bicameral effort to alter the federal support program for sugar producers. His contention is that government support makes U.S. sugar more expensive, which in turn drives up costs for food and beverage producers — such as the candy companies that used to be far more numerous in his city.

Davis describes himself as a "staunch, hard-nosed Democrat" but not an embittered one when dealing with Republicans. He says he's less bothered by partisanship than many colleagues are. "We're going to always be having the fights, but yet we manage in very civilized kind of ways," he said.

A member of the Congressional Black Caucus, Davis has pushed for a federal review of police brutality and racial profiling. In 2007, he found himself a victim of what he called "driving while being black" when he was given a ticket in Chicago for allegedly crossing over the center line. Davis fought the charge and was ultimately acquitted.

After graduating from college, he accepted $50 from his father and left Arkansas with the intention of heading for California — but he was in Chicago when his money ran out. He stayed with an older sister and got a job teaching language arts and social studies at a high school while moonlighting at the post office. Davis got involved in the community and eventually ran the health centers association. In 1979, he led a committee of neighborhood leaders looking for a candidate to challenge the Democratic machine in a Chicago City Council race, but it failed to turn up anyone. "So I said, 'What the hell' and decided to run myself," he said.

While on the council he made two attempts to unseat Democratic Rep. Cardiss Collins, and in 1991, while on the Cook County Commission, he ran a losing race in a Democratic primary for mayor against incumbent Richard M. Daley. Collins announced plans to retire in 1996. Davis emerged from a crowded primary field and coasted to victory in the general election in the heavily Democratic district.

When Cook County Board President John Stroger suffered a stroke prior to the Democrats winning the House in November 2006, Davis let it be known that he was interested in the post, one of the most powerful jobs in Chicago politics. But the party regulars chose the former board president's son, Todd Stroger. Davis pondered another run for the job in 2010, going so far as to file for the race. But he pulled out in November 2009 and ran for re-election to the House instead.

In December 2008, Davis turned down a chance to take Barack Obama's Senate seat, as the offer came from Democratic Gov. Rod R. Blagojevich, who had just been indicted (and was later impeached and then convicted) for allegedly trying to sell the vacant post. Davis said he does not see a "compelling need" to run for any other office at this point. "I've always been interested, since I can remember, in helping to promote change, and sometimes you can do that just as effectively from the outside."

Key Votes

2012	
Extend a Social Security payroll tax cut and unemployment benefits	NO
Ease securities rules to expand small-business access to capital	YES
Extend for one year subsidized student loan interest rates financed by a cut in health care spending	NO
Cite Attorney General Eric H. Holder Jr. for contempt of Congress	?
Create a visa program for foreign graduates in high-tech fields	NO
Extend most Bush-era income tax rates while allowing rates for top-bracket earners to rise (Jan. 1, 2013)	YES
2011	
Strike funding for F-35 alternative engine	YES
Prevent EPA from regulating greenhouse gas emissions to address climate change	NO
Extend certain provisions of Patriot Act for four years	NO
Declare opposition to use of ground troops in Libya	NO
Overhaul patent law	YES
Pass compromise debt limit increase plan and establish future spending limits	YES
Allow consideration of measures to implement three trade agreements	NO

CQ Vote Studies

	PARTY UNITY		PRESIDENTIAL SUPPORT	
	SUPPORT	OPPOSE	SUPPORT	OPPOSE
2012	97%	3%	87%	13%
2011	97%	3%	82%	18%
2010	96%	4%	83%	17%
2009	99%	1%	97%	3%
2008	99%	1%	16%	84%

Interest Groups

	AFL-CIO	ADA	CCUS	ACU
2012	100%	95%	27%	0%
2011	97%	90%	31%	4%
2010	93%	85%	29%	4%
2009	100%	95%	40%	0%
2008	100%	80%	56%	0%

Illinois 7

Chicago — downtown, West Side, South Side; west suburbs

East to west, the 7th stretches from the Loop, Chicago's iconic downtown business district, almost to the DuPage County line, taking in the wealthy towns of River Forest and Oak Park. North to south, the district runs from parts of the Old Town neighborhood to 71st Street on the South Side.

The eastern end of the 7th holds many of Chicago's gems: the Willis Tower (formerly known as the Sears Tower), several museums and theaters, plush high-rises of River North, nearly a dozen colleges and universities, Printers Row, and the "Magnificent Mile" and its high-end shopping.

Chicago's financial sector is here, with headquarters of companies such as Boeing, United Airlines, Quaker Oats and Hyatt. Tourists and conventions flock to McCormick Place. The 7th is also home to the Illinois Medical District, the nation's largest urban health care and research district. The district hosts basketball's Bulls and hockey's Blackhawks at the United Center and football's Bears at Soldier Field near Lake Michigan.

Once home to Chicago's most notorious public housing projects, some dilapidated areas have transitioned to lofts and galleries, while others continue to struggle. The west and south sides of the city are plagued with gang violence and poverty, as the city works to improve public safety and low-performing schools. In contrast, the far western portion of the 7th features some well-to-do areas. Transportation provides blue-collar jobs at the district's several large train and cargo yards.

The 7th fills with white commuters during the day, but the district is still black-majority. Chicago's traditional Chinatown neighborhood, an Asian-majority area whose population continues to grow, dominates the strip of the 7th that connects the South Loop to the South Side. The 7th is a reliably Democratic district at all levels and gave Barack Obama his highest statewide percentages in both the 2008 and 2012 presidential elections.

Major Industry

Insurance, financial services, health care

Cities

Chicago (pt.), Berwyn (pt.), Oak Park

Notable

As many as 80 WWII planes remain at the bottom of Lake Michigan after wartime pilot training at Navy Pier.

Rep. Tammy Duckworth (D)

Capitol Office
225-3711
duckworth.house.gov
104 Cannon Bldg. 20515-1308; fax 225-7830

Committees
Armed Services
Oversight & Government Reform

Residence
Hoffman Estates

Born
March 12, 1968; Bangkok, Thailand

Religion
Unspecified

Family
Husband, Bryan Bowlsbey

Education
U. of Hawaii, B.A. 1989 (political science); George Washington U., M.A. 1992 (international affairs); Northern Illinois U., attended 1992-2001; Capella U., attending 2009-present

Military
Army Reserve, 1991-96; Ill. National Guard, 1996-present

Career
State veterans affairs director; humanitarian foundation program manager

Political Highlights
Democratic nominee for U.S. House, 2006; Veterans Affairs Department assistant secretary, 2009-11

ELECTION RESULTS

2012 GENERAL

Tammy Duckworth (D)	123,206	54.7%
Joe Walsh (R)	101,860	45.3%

2012 PRIMARY

Tammy Duckworth (D)	17,097	66.2%
Raja Krishnamoorthi (D)	8,736	33.8%

Elected 2012; 1st term

Prominent Democrats have been enamored of Duckworth for several years. She is one of the first female combat veterans in Congress, and she's working on defense policy as a member of the Armed Services Committee.

Duckworth has served in the military since 1991. She lost both of her legs and partial use of her right arm in Iraq in 2004, when her helicopter was shot down. During her recovery she became an advocate for veterans. She was recruited to run for the House in 2006, but lost to Republican Peter Roskam. However, a few weeks after that loss she was appointed director of the Illinois Department of Veterans Affairs. In 2009 she became an assistant secretary of Veterans Affairs in the Obama administration.

She supports withdrawal from Afghanistan and prefers narrower military efforts focusing on terrorism. Duckworth says cuts to defense budgets could be better managed with improvements to the Pentagon's contracting process, and she applauded the announced expansion of combat roles for women. Duckworth, who once worked on humanitarian assistance as an employee of Rotary International, endorses a multilateral approach to foreign affairs.

Duckworth also sits on the Oversight and Government Reform Committee and its panel on energy, health care and entitlement programs. Duckworth, who serves as a whip for Democratic freshmen, sticks to the party line on those subjects. She vows to oppose cuts in Social Security or Medicare benefits and frequently mentions that she wants to end tax breaks for oil companies and large corporations.

In 2006, Duckworth had a fundraising advantage but no campaign experience. She lost by 3 points. In 2012, she had a huge fundraising advantage as she challenged fiery GOP freshman Joe Walsh in the redrawn 8th District. Walsh accused her of playing up her military service for political gain, while Duckworth accused Walsh, who had settled a child support dispute, of being a "deadbeat dad." The district is slightly Democratic, and she won by 9 points.

Illinois 8

Northwest Chicago suburbs — Elgin, Schaumburg

Taking in suburbs in Kane, DuPage and Cook counties, the 8th District is defined by the plotted subdivisions, business parks and major interstate highways crisscrossing from Elk Grove Village in the east toward Carpentersville and Elgin in the northwest and south into parts of Lombard — Interstate 290 (the Eisenhower Expressway) in particular serves as a major artery into central Chicago.

The white-collar workforce across the district is made up mainly of residents who travel to Chicago or other suburbs for work, although there are a number of corporate headquarters located in the 8th. Sears, which has won incentives by state legislators to stay in the area, has its corporate offices in Hoffman Estates.

A large mall in Schaumburg draws shoppers from across the northwestern and western exurbs, and a river boat casino in Elgin boosts the economy there; local officials also hope newly approved video-gambling ventures at bars and restaurants will add revenue.

Carpentersville, which used to be a blue-collar German, Swedish and Polish community, now relies mostly on its retail sector.

Despite Republican-leaning areas in Bloomingdale and the wealthier South Barrington, the 8th has trended Democratic at the federal level following remapping after the 2010 census. A century of a manufacturing tradition and a more diverse population than in neighboring districts — the 8th has the state's highest proportion of Asian residents (13 percent) and is more than one-fourth Hispanic — gives it labor-backing Democratic voters as well as liberal voters.

The fast-growing Hispanic presence in the district is particularly notable in Addison and Elgin.

Major Industry
Retail, health care, gaming

Cities
Elgin (pt.), Schaumburg, Palantine (pt.), Hoffman Estates (pt.), Lombard (pt.)

Notable
Elgin's observatory was built by the Elgin National Watch Company in 1910 as a celestial timing device and is now used, with the original telescope, as a planetarium by the local school district.

Rep. Jan Schakowsky (D)

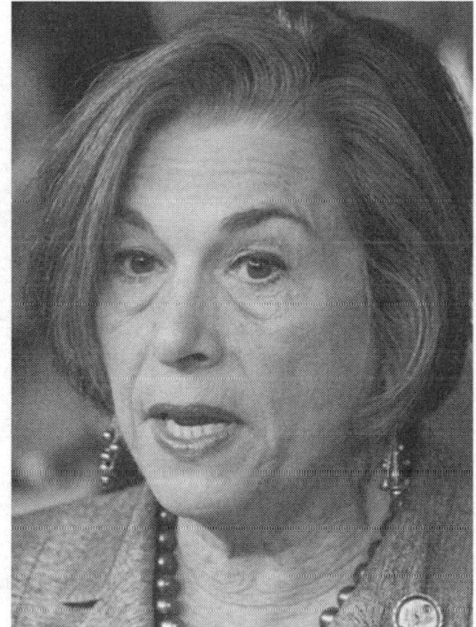

Capitol Office
225-2111
schakowsky.house.gov
2367 Rayburn Bldg. 20515-1309; fax 226-6890

Committees
Energy & Commerce
Select Intelligence

Residence
Evanston

Born
May 26, 1944; Chicago, Ill.

Religion
Jewish

Family
Husband, Robert Creamer; three children

Education
U. of Illinois, B.S. 1965 (elementary education)

Career
Senior citizens group director; consumer advocate; homemaker; teacher

Political Highlights
Candidate for Cook County Commission, 1986; Ill. House, 1991-99 (floor leader, 1994-99)

ELECTION RESULTS

2012 GENERAL		
Jan Schakowsky (D)	194,869	66.3%
Timothy C. Wolfe (R)	98,924	33.7%
2012 PRIMARY		
Jan Schakowsky (D)	48,124	91.8%
Simon Ribeiro (D)	4,270	8.2%
2010 GENERAL		
Jan Schakowsky (D)	117,553	66.3%
Joel Barry Pollak (R)	55,182	31.1%
Simon Ribeiro (GREEN)	4,472	2.5%

Previous Winning Percentages
2008 (75%); 2006 (75%); 2004 (76%); 2002 (70%); 2000 (76%); 1998 (75%)

Elected 1998; 8th term

Schakowsky, a liberal and trailblazing consumer activist, hasn't reached the heights of leadership in the House for which she once seemed destined. But as a close ally of Minority Leader Nancy Pelosi, she remains an influential voice on the left and an irritant to Republicans.

With the GOP controlling the House, Schakowsky (shuh-KOW-ski) has often been relegated to the role of bomb-thrower. But she has taken on the job with relish, accusing Republican leaders of sexism and insensitivity to the needs of children and older Americans.

A prime example: When Republicans unveiled a budget proposal in 2012, she called it "this immoral bill," blasted the GOP for asking "nothing from the wealthiest Americans" and for "taking food and health care away from children and senior citizens." She drew attention to her critiques by, among other things, attempting to rely for a week on the food stamp allotment provided to the poor. In her purse she carries a bar graph illustrating the increase in income experienced by the wealthiest Americans since the 1970s. On the chart, everyone else's pay has stayed flat.

Liberals have clearly embraced Schakowsky. In October 2011, the liberal magazine The Progressive featured her under the headline: "The Fighter." She's a vice chairwoman of the Congressional Progressive Caucus, and she also serves as a chief deputy whip for House Democrats.

Still, it's hard for liberals to get much done in a House run by Republicans, and Schakowsky hasn't fared better than others. In the 112th Congress (2011-12) she continued to introduce bills related to consumer safety — her longtime passion — only to see them gather dust. Legislation to bar certain chemicals in cosmetics did not garner any hearings, nor did a bill to require homes built with federal funds to be more accessible for the disabled.

Pelosi named Schakowsky one of three House Democrats to serve on a special 2010 fiscal commission, which came to be known as Simpson-Bowles. But Schakowsky opposed a deficit reduction outline the commission worked on, saying it threatened both middle-class and lower-income Americans. Her alternative included more tax increases, additional cuts in defense spending and no changes to Social Security.

As the principles of Simpson-Bowles — $4 trillion in deficit reduction over 10 years through spending reductions, revenue increases and entitlement program changes — became accepted as middle ground in the fiscal negotiations of the 112th Congress, Schakowsky put her foot down. "It would not invest in the economy, would not create jobs, does not raise enough in revenues, and doesn't protect Social Security, Medicare and Medicaid," she said at a 2012 Progressive Caucus event.

Schakowsky's seat on the Energy and Commerce Committee enables her to continue the work she began more than three decades ago on behalf of consumers. In 2008 she won enactment of a bill requiring automakers to adopt safety measures to decrease the number of deaths and injuries resulting from children being backed over, asphyxiated by power windows or killed when cars are inadvertently shifted into gear. She complained about the Transportation Department's failure to issue rules implementing the law, a delay rumored to be the result of automakers' complaints about the cost.

She is also committed to legislative action to address climate change, and she pushes for a government-run "public option" health care plan to compete with private insurers. Schakowsky introduced a bill in 2013 to let the secretary of Health and Human Services stop or change "unreasonable" health insurance rate increases in states where regulators don't already have that power.

She had tried to include that proposal in the 2010 health care law.

She uses her seat on the Intelligence Committee to guard against government encroachment into the private lives of Americans. "It seems often to be my role to continually bring up the question of privacy and civil liberties," she said. She preaches against the use of private contractors to do intelligence work, arguing that government employees should hold such jobs.

A community activist for more than 25 years before entering Congress, Schakowsky, along with her husband, Robert Creamer, created a training program for political advocates that has been replicated nationwide. The program brought volunteers to a "campaign school" in Chicago where they were given instruction and political tools and then put to work on several House races.

Schakowsky grew up in the Chicago area. Her father was a furniture salesman and her mother was a public school teacher. Schakowsky followed her into that field after graduating from the University of Illinois with a degree in elementary education. She has described her upbringing as middle-class and idyllic.

Her move into public activism came in the early 1970s when, having left teaching to stay at home with her children, she helped launch a successful nationwide campaign to require freshness dates on food products. She said six women got together and decided they wanted to know how old the food was in their local grocery. She continued as a community activist and was elected to the Illinois House in 1990. She rose to become chairwoman of the Labor and Commerce Committee and Democratic floor leader.

When liberal Democrat Sidney R. Yates, who had held the 9th District seat for 48 years, announced his retirement in 1998, Schakowsky entered the race to succeed him. She bested state Sen. Howard W. Carroll and Hyatt Hotels heir Jay "J.B." Pritzker in the primary and easily won the general election in the heavily Democratic district.

Schakowsky was an early supporter of University of Chicago law professor Barack Obama when he ran for the Illinois Senate in 1996, and she had hoped to be appointed to Obama's U.S. Senate seat after he was elected president. After Roland W. Burris was appointed, Schakowsky considered running for the Senate in 2010. She decided against it, saying she wanted to focus her attention on defending the 2010 health care law from GOP attacks.

Her support for that overhaul prompted Republican Joel Barry Pollak, a recent Harvard Law School graduate and political novice, to challenge her. Still, Schakowsky won with 66 percent of the vote.

Redistricting after the 2010 census made Schakowsky's district less liberal than it had been, but she retained enough of her base. She faced another inexperienced Republican in 2012 and won easily.

Key Votes

2012	
Extend a Social Security payroll tax cut and unemployment benefits	YES
Ease securities rules to expand small-business access to capital	NO
Extend for one year subsidized student loan interest rates financed by a cut in health care spending	NO
Cite Attorney General Eric H. Holder Jr. for contempt of Congress	-
Create a visa program for foreign graduates in high-tech fields	NO
Extend most Bush-era income tax rates while allowing rates for top-bracket earners to rise (Jan. 1, 2013)	YES
2011	
Strike funding for F-35 alternative engine	YES
Prevent EPA from regulating greenhouse gas emissions to address climate change	NO
Extend certain provisions of Patriot Act for four years	NO
Declare opposition to use of ground troops in Libya	NO
Overhaul patent law	YES
Pass compromise debt limit increase plan and establish future spending limits	NO
Allow consideration of measures to implement three trade agreements	NO

CQ Vote Studies

	PARTY UNITY		PRESIDENTIAL SUPPORT	
	SUPPORT	OPPOSE	SUPPORT	OPPOSE
2012	99%	1%	90%	10%
2011	98%	2%	86%	14%
2010	98%	2%	88%	12%
2009	99%	1%	96%	4%
2008	99%	1%	16%	84%

Interest Groups

	AFL-CIO	ADA	CCUS	ACU
2012	100%	100%	25%	0%
2011	100%	95%	13%	8%
2010	100%	95%	25%	0%
2009	100%	100%	33%	0%
2008	100%	100%	61%	0%

Illinois 9

Chicago — North Side lakefront; Evanston

The 9th District takes in upscale lakeshore communities north of Chicago and bends north of O'Hare International Airport (which is split between the neighboring 5th and 8th districts) into parts of middle-class northern Cook County suburbs, such as Arlington Heights and Mount Prospect.

The district skims up some of the northern Chicago beaches and parks and moves north through the city's Uptown neighborhood to the terminus of Lake Shore Drive. This area of Chicago — including Edgewater and Rogers Park, home to Loyola University — was once a destination for Eastern European and Irish immigrants, but now hosts an eclectic mix of Asian, European and African immigrants.

The 9th passes Evanston and Northwestern University on its way into wealthy Winnetka. Many residents who live near the lake commute to white-collar jobs in the city. Several of the suburbs in the eastern half of the district, particularly Skokie and Glenview, have established Jewish communities.

Northfield remains the headquarters of the Kraft foods brand grocery business and corporate management facilities, but the company's renamed snack food branch, Mondelez International, is located in Deerfield in the neighboring 10th District.

A new casino in the 9th's part of Des Plaines next to the Tri-State Tollway near the local forest preserve lured new business and millions of visitors to the suburb, which felt the sting of several years of declining home prices. Area hospitals also provide professional and service jobs, and the district relies on its proximity to O'Hare and the travel- and hospitality-oriented village of Rosemont (in the 5th).

Following decennial remapping, the traditionally Democratic 9th added some Republicans among the northern old-money suburbs as well as some independent-minded voters to the northwest, but Democrats still have an edge in federal races. In the 2012 presidential election, Barack Obama won the 9th with 65 percent of its vote.

Major Industry
Health care, higher education, insurance

Cities
Chicago (pt.), Arlington Heights (pt.), Evanston, Skokie, Des Plaines (pt.)

Notable
Tinkertoy sets were invented by an Evanston stonemason in 1913.

Rep. Brad Schneider (D)

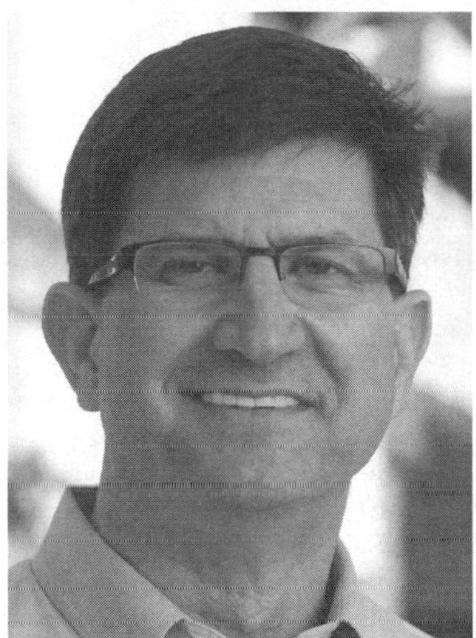

Capitol Office
225-4835
schneider.house.gov
317 Cannon Bldg. 20515-3602; fax 225-0837

Committees
Foreign Affairs
Small Business

Residence
Deerfield

Born
Aug. 20, 1961; Denver, Colo.

Religion
Jewish

Family
Wife, Julie Dann; two children

Education
Northwestern U., B.S. 1983 (industrial engineering), M.B.A. 1988

Career
Business strategy consulting firm executive; management consulting firm owner; insurance agency executive; electric cable manufacturing company marketing director; industrial engineer

Political Highlights
No previous office

ELECTION RESULTS

2012 GENERAL		
Brad Schneider (D)	133,890	50.6%
Robert Dold (R)	130,564	49.4%
2012 PRIMARY		
Brad Schneider (D)	15,530	46.9%
Ilya Sheyman (D)	12,767	38.5%
John Tree (D)	2,938	8.9%
Vivek Bavda (D)	1,881	5.7%

Elected 2012; 1st term

Voters in the well-off communities north of Chicago often sent moderate Republicans to Congress. They're now giving a moderate Democrat a chance. Schneider emphasizes his business experience as he works on economic problems, and he is involved in international relations as a supporter of Israel.

Schneider, a member of the New Democrat Coalition, worked as a business consultant and once owned and managed his own life insurance agency. He has a seat on the Small Business Committee and has spoken in favor of fewer regulations and more "targeted tax incentives" for small businesses. His first bill, a collaboration with Pennsylvania Republican Lou Barletta, would allow federally supported worker training programs to prioritize skill sets that manufacturers identify as in demand.

He held no political office before his election to the House, but Schneider has long been civically active through Jewish charities. He spent a year on an Israeli kibbutz after college, and he was a citizen lobbyist for the American Israel Public Affairs Committee, which describes itself as "America's pro-Israel lobby." Schneider sits on the Foreign Affairs Committee and its panel on the Middle East. He endorses tougher sanctions to stymie Iran's nuclear program, and he wants to add Israel to the U.S. visa waiver program.

As a candidate, Schneider indicated his broad support for a multilateral approach to foreign affairs, with a focus on economic relationships. He also sits on the subcommittee that handles trade.

Schneider had to battle the liberal wing of his party to get the Democratic nomination. He defeated Ilya Sheyman, a 25-year-old activist who had worked for MoveOn. He then faced moderate one-term Republican Robert Dold. As drawn for the 2012 election, more than a third of the 10th District was new to Dold, and the region had a clear Democratic tilt. It was a very expensive race for both men, and national party organizations also spent heavily on advertising. Dold nearly beat the odds — Schneider won by only 3,326 votes.

Illinois 10

Most of Lake County — lakeshore, Waukegan, Mundelein; northeast Cook County

The mostly upscale 10th District hugs Lake Michigan from the northernmost suburban Cook County shoreline to the Wisconsin border, taking in tony lakefront communities of Chicagoland's old-money elite, before dipping west into affluent, well-established suburbs northwest of Chicago.

The 10th is home to well-educated, white-collar workers and to several Fortune 500 companies, including Allstate Insurance in Northbrook and Walgreens in Deerfield. North Chicago hosts medical device company Abbott Laboratories and a Jelly Belly facility. Abbot spun off a pharmaceuticals research division, AbbVie, in North Chicago in 2012.

Military and environmental issues round out the local agenda. The district hosts the Great Lakes naval base, the nation's only naval recruit training command. It also is home to the Illinois State Beach Park and part of the Chain O'Lakes region in the west.

Most of the majority-white district's minority residents live near Waukegan, which has experienced marked growth in its Hispanic population since 2000 and is nearly one-fifth black. North Chicago also is minority-majority, with black residents accounting for nearly 30 percent of the population. The 10th also hosts a large Jewish constituency.

The district, which combines white-collar suburbanites with the working-class population of Waukegan, was drawn following the 2010 census to be more friendly to Democratic candidates on the federal level. The new boundaries of the 10th exclude some of the most expensive residential areas — Wilmette, Kenilworth and Winnetka were all drawn fully into the 9th. Residents tend to be fiscally conservative and lean more to the left on social issues.

Major Industry
Pharmaceutical research, insurance, military

Military Bases
Naval Station Great Lakes, 3,108 military, 3,636 civilian

Cities
Waukegan, Des Plaines (pt.), North Chicago, Mundelein

Notable
Highland Park's Ravinia Festival is the oldest outdoor music festival in North America.

Rep. Bill Foster (D)

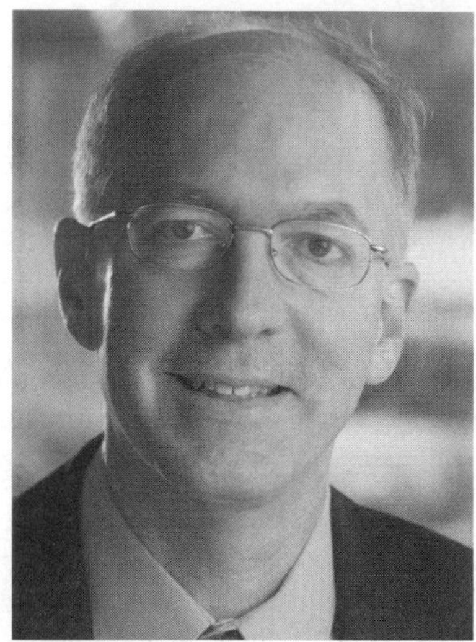

Capitol Office
225-3515
foster.house.gov
1224 Longworth Bldg. 20515-3808; fax 225-9420

Committees
Financial Services

Residence
Naperville

Born
Oct. 7, 1955; Madison, Wis.

Religion
Unspecified

Family
Wife, Aesook Byon; two children

Education
U. of Wisconsin, B.A. 1976 (physics); Harvard U., Ph.D. 1983 (experimental physics)

Career
Physicist; theater lighting company owner

Political Highlights
U.S. House, 2008-11; defeated for re-election to U.S. House, 2010

ELECTION RESULTS

2012 GENERAL		
Bill Foster (D)	148,928	58.6%
Judy Biggert (R)	105,348	41.4%
2012 PRIMARY		
Bill Foster (D)	12,126	58.5%
Juan Thomas (D)	5,212	25.1%
Jim Hickey (D)	3,399	16.4%

Previous Winning Percentages
2008 (58%); 2008 Special Election (53%)

Elected 2008; 2nd full term

Did not serve 2011-13

Foster once won a surprising special-election victory in a northern Illinois district that reached only the outskirts of the state's biggest metropolis — but he lost his seat in the GOP wave of 2010. He's back for a second run in the House, this time representing a swath of suburban Chicago. It's still competitive territory, however, which makes Foster just as likely to cross party lines this time around.

His return to Congress also led him back to the business-friendly New Democrat Coalition and the Financial Services Committee. During his previous tenure on the panel, financial markets were crumbling, and Democrats fashioned the regulatory overhaul known as Dodd-Frank.

Foster, a physicist, says he wants to complete unfinished business and make sure that law is implemented correctly. "I didn't really want to become pigeonholed as Mr. Science," he said in 2013. "The Financial Services Committee was, frankly, a wonderful and terrifying place to be for the three years that I served. I do feel that I have a responsibility coming back to make sure that the endgame on Dodd-Frank is done carefully."

Specifically, Foster is interested in studying the capital requirements for banks, which are also affected by the Basel III international banking standards now taking hold around the world. He also wants to prevent future housing bubbles — an endeavor for which he's reaching across the aisle, even consulting with the conservative American Enterprise Institute.

Foster lists regulation of the housing industry as one of his three top legislative priorities, along with promoting STEM (science, technology, engineering and math) education and advanced manufacturing. "All three of those areas should, in principle, be good areas for bipartisan cooperation," he said.

Immigration is a hot topic for the 113th Congress (2013-14), and it's also an issue Foster worked on in his previous stint in the House. On the campaign trail he touted his earlier support of a bill to create a path to citizenship for some people who were brought to the country illegally as children. He also supports bills to loosen the visa standards for citizens of Poland and Israel — the Chicago area has ethnic populations sympathetic to that cause.

Foster's work on immigration serves both the booming Hispanic population in his district and his own personal interests. "My wife is a first-generation Asian-American, so we have a natural connection in having a non-broken immigration policy in this country," he said.

He also wants to be more involved in transportation policy, as he now represents Joliet, a major hub for the state.

And to some extent, the Mr. Science moniker will still apply. Argonne National Laboratory is partly in his district, and the Fermi National Accelerator Laboratory — the research lab for scientists studying high-energy physics where he used to work — is nearby. Foster has said that he takes a scientific approach to many issues. He told The Hill that he voted against a 2009 bill to create a cap-and-trade system for regulating greenhouse gases because it was making unreasonable assumptions about "carbon capture" technology and the financial impact of such a system.

Foster comes from a family that was active in Democratic politics. His parents met while his mother was an aide to Democratic Illinois Sen. Paul H. Douglas (1949-67) and his father was an aide to Democratic Pennsylvania Sen. Francis J. Myers (1945-51). His father, a trained chemist, eventually worked as a law professor at the University of Wisconsin and a civil rights attorney. He wrote some of the landmark Civil Rights Act of 1964.

Foster was a 19-year-old college sophomore when he and his brother Fred started Electronic Theatre Controls in their basement, using $500 borrowed from their parents. The theater lighting equipment business now provides lighting for 70 percent of the country's theater and entertainment venues.

After earning a physics degree from Wisconsin in 1976, Foster worked with ETC for three years. He then went to Harvard and earned a Ph.D. in 1983 in experimental physics. He retained an advisory role on the company's board until 2007, when he sold his share of the company to prevent any conflict of interest. (Foster is one of the wealthiest members of Congress.)

He moved to the Chicago suburbs in the early 1980s, where he worked at Fermilab. But after nearly 25 years as a physicist, Foster took a leave of absence to step into politics.

"All the time I was in business, and all the time I was in science, ultimately those are things you do for yourself," he said. "There is some fraction of my life that I wanted to spend servicing my fellow man."

He volunteered for the successful campaign of Pennsylvania Rep. Patrick J. Murphy, who in 2006 defeated Republican Rep. Michael G. Fitzpatrick. And he volunteered in Murphy's Capitol Hill office, working for four months as an adviser on science and technology issues.

Foster decided to run for office in 2007 when House Minority Leader J. Dennis Hastert announced his retirement, and later his resignation. Although the district had been in Republican hands for a long time, Foster defeated Republican Jim Oberweis by 5 points in the March 2008 special election. The two candidates spent a combined $8 million on the race, more than $5 million of which came out of their own pockets. He defeated Oberweis a second time in November to win a full term.

However, he couldn't survive the GOP's national resurgence in 2010. Randy Hultgren defeated Foster by 6 points.

In 2011, Illinois Democrats controlled the state's redistricting process and redrew the 11th District as a piece of southwestern Chicagoland. Seven-term Republican Rep. Judy Biggert decided to run there, as it included about half of the district she had represented previously. Foster's old district covered only a quarter of the new one, but he had the upper hand given the district's overall Democratic lean.

The matchup was one of country's most expensive House races. The two campaigns spent more than $6 million between them, and outside groups dumped in millions more. Foster again dipped into his pockets to fund his race, donating about $500,000 of his own money in the final weeks.

Polls showed a very close race heading into the home stretch, but the genteel Biggert struggled to bite back in public debates. Foster won by 17 points, but he says he still views his home turf as "a very swing district."

CQ Vote Studies

	Party Unity		Presidential Support	
	SUPPORT	OPPOSE	SUPPORT	OPPOSE
2010	89%	11%	90%	10%
2009	85%	15%	90%	10%
2008	92%	8%	21%	79%

Interest Groups

	AFL-CIO	ADA	CCUS	ACU
2010	100%	90%	25%	9%
2009	86%	80%	53%	4%
2008	92%	65%	56%	13%

Illinois 11

West and southwest Chicago exurbs — most of Aurora, Joliet

The 11th District snakes through Kane, Kendall, DuPage and Will counties, from Aurora east to Bolingbrook, down part of Interstate 55 and east to Joliet. Aurora, the second-largest city in the state, anchors the northern portion of the 11th and Joliet the south. Significant population growth in the area continued over the past decade, as Illinoisans moved farther from Chicago and began packing these established economic centers.

A mix of a blue-collar manufacturing tradition and scientific research facilities in adjacent districts define the 11th. Many of the 5th's white-collar workers have jobs at the Argonne National Laboratory — which is split with the 3rd along Interstate 55, between Bolingbrook and Burr Ridge — or the Fermi National Accelerator Laboratory just across the district line in the 14th.

Heavy-machinery manufacturer Caterpillar remains a top employer in Aurora, historically a railroad town, and is key to Joliet, which has been working to lure visitors to the Chicagoland Speedway and Route 66 Raceway. Other major employers include medical centers. Officials in the two cities hope that small-business and retail growth, high-tech industries and the local casinos will continue to drive the economy.

East of Aurora, the district picks up portions of Naperville (shared with the 6th), which is a leading business and residential center. Some of the small towns in less densely populated areas, such as Shorewood west of Joliet, have begun to fill in with residents.

The 11th was drawn during decennial redistricting to be friendlier to Democrats and barely resembles its earlier iterations — or any other district from previous congresses. Aurora, which has a large Hispanic population, and Joliet historically have supported Democrats, while the areas around Naperville lean more conservative. The sliver of Cook County in the 11th supported GOP candidate Mitt Romney in the 2012 presidential election, but Barack Obama won the portions of all other counties here.

Major Industry
Farm equipment manufacturing, scientific research, health care

Cities
Aurora (pt.), Joliet (pt.), Bolingbrook, Naperville (pt.)

Notable
The notoriously tough and now-closed Joliet Prison inspired the name of a minor-league independent baseball team, the Slammers.

Rep. Bill Enyart (D)

Capitol Office
225-5661
enyart.house.gov
1722 Longworth Bldg. 20515-1312; fax 225-0285

Committees
Agriculture
Armed Services

Residence
Belleville

Born
Sept. 22, 1949; Pensacola, Fla.

Religion
Christian

Family
Wife, Annette Eckert; two children

Education
U. of Illinois, attended 1967-68; Southern Illinois U., Edwardsville, B.A. 1974 (mass communications); Southern Illinois U., J.D. 1979

Military
Air Force, 1969-73; Air Force Reserve, 1973-75; Ill. National Guard, 1982-2012

Career
State military agency director; lawyer; journalist; retail store clerk; welder

Political Highlights
No previous office

ELECTION RESULTS

2012 GENERAL

Bill Enyart (D)	157,000	51.6%
Jason Plummer (R)	129,902	42.7%
Paula Bradshaw (GREEN)	17,045	5.6%

Elected 2012; 1st term

Enyart's career as a lawyer isn't particularly distinctive for Congress. His service as a major general, however, sets him apart. He has a district-centered approach to politics that could position him as a centrist in many debates.

Enyart grew up in central Illinois. He signed up for the Air Force in 1969 and was stationed as Scott Air Force Base, not far from where he lives today. As he was embarking on a legal career in the 1980s, he enlisted in the National Guard. In 2007, he was appointed the state's adjutant general — the administrator and commanding officer overseeing the entire Illinois National Guard.

That experience landed him on the Armed Services Committee. In February 2013, Enyart said that he was heartened by plans for a speedier withdrawal of troops from Afghanistan, but he vows to protect jobs and missions at Illinois' military installations — particularly Scott AFB.

He has found military matters to deal with on the Agriculture Committee, as well. The armed services have an increasing interest in biodiesel fuels, and the farms of southern Illinois grow a lot of corn and soybeans suitable for that purpose. Enyart represents what he calls the "western coast of Illinois" — land along the Mississippi — and he pushes for water infrastructure improvements to keep crops and manufactured goods moving along the river to markets.

Enyart calls himself a "pragmatist," and he stands opposed to many environmentalists in the Democratic Party as a co-chairman of the Congressional Coal Caucus. He was named a vice chairman of a Democratic task force on gun violence, but he stepped away from that job and said he would rather consult on the matter with his constituents than the party.

The retirement of Democratic Rep. Jerry F. Costello created an open seat in 2012. The winner of the Democratic primary withdrew from the race in May for health reasons, and Enyart was picked by party officials to face Republican Jason Plummer. The district has many socially conservative areas, and Republicans fought hard for the seat, but Enyart won by 9 points.

Illinois 12

Southwest — East St. Louis, Belleville, Carbondale

Settled in the state's southwestern corner, the 12th borders the Mississippi River from Alton to the southern tip of the state where it merges with the Ohio River. Most residents live in one of three population centers: near the St. Louis metro area in the 12th's northwestern corner; around Carbondale near its center; or along Interstate 57 in the easternmost stretch.

East St. Louis, an overwhelmingly black city in St. Clair County, has experienced declining population and some of the state's worst urban blight for years; the city struggles with its municipal finances and high unemployment rates. Crime is of particular concern, drawing attention from statewide legislators. Near East St. Louis, Belleville is primarily dependent upon military and contracting jobs connected to Scott Air Force Base, the area's major employer.

In the northern arm of the district in Madison County, Alton and Granite City still struggle with declining populations. In Alton, where more than 20 percent of residents live in poverty, officials hope to stimulate tourism along the Mississippi and at Civil War-era sites.

Higher education remains a key source of jobs, with Carbondale's Southern Illinois University bolstering Jackson County's economy.

The 12th, with a manufacturing legacy and deep concerns about economic stability as well as a large minority population, has been solid Democratic turf for decades, though there are signs of eroding support. St. Clair County, where East St. Louis is located, has backed the Democratic candidate in every presidential race since 1976. Of the 12 counties wholly or partially in the 12th, Barack Obama won the district's portions of only four of them in the 2012 presidential race.

Major Industry
Manufacturing, higher education, agriculture

Military Bases
Scott Air Force Base, 5,533 military, 5,085 civilian (2011)

Cities
Belleville, Carbondale, East St. Louis

Notable
Cahokia Mounds, a prehistoric civilization, was designated by the United Nations as a World Heritage Site in 1982.

Rep. Rodney Davis (R)

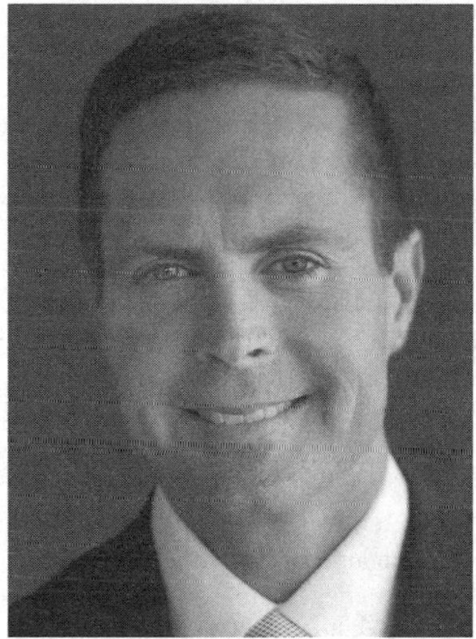

Capitol Office
225-2371
rodneydavis.house.gov
1740 Longworth Bldg. 20515-1313; fax 226-0791

Committees
Agriculture
Transportation & Infrastructure

Residence
Taylorville

Born
Jan. 5, 1970; Des Moines, Iowa

Religion
Roman Catholic

Family
Wife, Shannon Davis; three children

Education
Millikin U., B.A. 1992 (political science)

Career
Congressional district and campaign aide; party voter outreach state director; state government aide

Political Highlights
Republican nominee for Ill. House, 1996; candidate for mayor of Taylorville, 2001

ELECTION RESULTS

2012 GENERAL

Rodney Davis (R)	137,034	46.5%
David Gill (D)	136,032	46.2%
John Hartman (I)	21,319	7.2%

Elected 2012; 1st term

The most famous Republican from the 13th District, Abraham Lincoln, dealt with a few schisms in his day. Davis faces less daunting problems, but he does have to operate in a politically divided district.

Davis has political experience, just not in elected roles. For 15 years, he was an Illinois-based staffer for Rep. John Shimkus (now of the 15th District). He also did organizing and campaign work for the state Republican Party.

He embraces the GOP themes of fiscal restraint and low taxes, but Davis, a member of the Main Street Partnership, is not a staunch conservative. That approach has worked in central Illinois — during the 112th Congress (2011-12), the area now represented by Davis was divided between five Republicans, and all of them were moderates.

One of those five, Timothy V. Johnson, retired. Davis is considered to be his successor, and he sits on the same committees as Johnson: Agriculture, and Transportation and Infrastructure. "Illinois feeds the world," Davis says, and he emphasizes the importance of strong crop insurance programs to the farmers in his district. The western border of his district is the Mississippi River, and Davis has jumped into bipartisan, bicameral efforts to keep river traffic moving. He is on the Transportation subcommittee for water projects.

The husband of a nurse and cancer survivor, Davis supports a health care safety net, but would like to see the 2010 health care law repealed and replaced with a market-based approach.

Johnson won the March 2012 Republican primary, then announced his retirement a month later. Party leaders chose Davis to replace him. The Democratic Congressional Campaign Committee quickly denounced Davis as a "career political hack," and it spent close to $3 million on ads attacking him.

Republican-leaning groups similarly went after Democrat David Gill, an emergency room doctor who had lost to Johnson three times before. Davis won by just 1,002 votes — the closest Republican victory of 2012.

Illinois 13

Central — Decatur, parts of Springfield, Bloomington and Champaign

Rows of corn and soybeans form an agricultural backbone in the heart of Illinois, and the 13th District grabs most of the state capital, Springfield, as well as all or parts of mid-state hubs Champaign, Bloomington and Decatur. It reaches the Mississippi River in the west and slips down to Collinsville east of the St. Louis, Mo., metro area.

Champaign-Urbana is home to the University of Illinois' flagship campus. The university hosts more than 40,000 students as well as research facilities, including a research park that counts Fortune 500 companies and start-ups as tenants. To the northwest, the 13th also brings in the western part of the Bloomington-Normal area, where Illinois State and Illinois Wesleyan are major draws. Many local white-collar workers head into the neighboring 18th District to the State Farm Insurance corporate headquarters in Bloomington.

Archer Daniels Midland is in Decatur, which has struggled with double-digit unemployment rates. The worldwide distributor, which anchors the regional food-processing and agribusiness sectors, announced layoffs in 2012.

Farther west, the 13th is home to all of Springfield except for the city's southwestern corner. The downtown neighborhood includes the state Capitol, the Old State Capitol building, the Lincoln Home National Historic Site and the Lincoln Tomb. The University of Illinois-Springfield is on the western shore of Lake Springfield.

The white-majority 13th was drawn during decennial redistricting to be competitive, taking in the more Democratic-leaning Champaign-Urbana metropolitan region and leaving some GOP-friendly areas of Springfield to the neighboring 18th District. The 2012 presidential vote here was nearly even — Republican nominee Mitt Romney won by 928 votes.

Major Industry
Agriculture, higher education, food processing, insurance

Cities
Springfield (pt.), Decatur, Champaign (pt.), Bloomington (pt.)

Notable
A statue in Decatur marks the location of Abraham Lincoln's first political speech, given in 1830.

Rep. Randy Hultgren (R)

Capitol Office
225-2976
hultgren.house.gov
332 Cannon Bldg. 20515-1314; fax 225-0697

Committees
Financial Services
Science, Space & Technology

Residence
Winfield

Born
March 1, 1966; Park Ridge, Ill.

Religion
Protestant

Family
Wife, Christy Hultgren; four children

Education
Bethel College, B.A. 1988 (communications & political science); Illinois Institute of Technology, J.D. 1993

Career
Securities company executive; financial planning consultant; lawyer; congressional aide

Political Highlights
DuPage County Board, 1994-98; DuPage County Forest Preserve District Board of Commissioners, 1994-98; Ill. House, 1999-2007; Ill. Senate, 2007-11

ELECTION RESULTS

2012 GENERAL		
Randy Hultgren (R)	177,603	58.8%
Dennis Anderson (D)	124,351	41.2%
2012 PRIMARY		
Randy Hultgren (R)		unopposed
2010 GENERAL		
Randy Hultgren (R)	112,369	51.3%
Bill Foster (D)	98,645	45.0%
Daniel J. Kairis (GREEN)	7,949	3.6%

Elected 2010; 2nd term

Hultgren has taken tough, fiscally conservative positions and been thrown into a few awkward contests with fellow Republicans. His likability still shines through, illustrating his skill at managing both the politics and the interpersonal relationships of his job. In his second term, he gets to play to some professional strengths as a new member of the Financial Services Committee.

Hultgren kicked off his political career in his early 20s as an aide to Republican Rep. J. Dennis Hastert—who would later become speaker of the House. He got a law degree and went on to a career as a financial company executive. Along the way, Hultgren became involved in county government and emerged to spend 12 years, all as a member of the minority party, in the Illinois state legislature.

He understands ground game politics. When Hultgren was elected to the Illinois House at age 32, the Chicago Daily Herald noted that even during his own race, he shrewdly had dished out campaign cash to other Republican candidates. He kept the chief of staff of his predecessor, Peter Roskam, who had resigned to run for Congress. (Roskam lost, but in 2006 he was elected in the 6th District and is now the chief deputy whip.) "I'm not coming in looking to be a renegade," Hultgren told the Herald at the time.

Hultgren made similar comments after joining the U.S. House in 2011. "I'm never going to be the national media guy," he said. "I don't think it really helps my district that much." To win his seat, Hultgren had to dispatch Ethan A. Hastert, the son of his former boss, in a primary; his years of supporting fellow conservatives paid off in the form of a fairly comfortable victory. Hultgren also pays close attention to constituent services.

Fiscal conservatism was one of his hallmarks in the 112th Congress (2011-12). Hultgren didn't like the final deals reached on deficit reduction or fiscal 2012 spending; he was one of 48 Republicans to vote against a stopgap measure to keep the government running at the start of that fiscal year, then one of 24 who still opposed it when GOP leaders had to call a second vote. At the end of the 112th he opposed the "fiscal cliff" law that permanently extended lower income tax rates on earnings under $400,000. He said it should have been packaged with more spending cuts.

But Hultgren managed to express his dissent without ruffling feathers. He dished out hundreds of thousands of dollars to colleagues during the campaign season and got his requested seat on the Financial Services Committee for the 113th Congress (2013-14).

He served on similar committees in the state legislature, and Hultgren worked as both a financial planner and a vice president of investment and financial management companies. He's the only Republican from Illinois currently on the committee, which gives him extra incentive to watch out for the Chicago Mercantile Exchange and any regulatory action regarding the huge derivatives industry. He touched on that subject as a freshman from the Agriculture Committee, which also has jurisdiction over commodities markets.

Hultgren is wary of the 2010 financial regulatory law and the agencies spawned by it. "Regulators are using the ambiguity of that legislation to get into some areas that I don't think were ever intended by lawmakers who passed that bill," he said.

He teamed up with Connecticut Democrat Jim Himes on a 2013 bill that would eliminate the law's requirement that banks "push out" some of their derivatives trading from the part of their business that is federally insured. Critics of the provision, including Federal Reserve Chairman Ben S. Bernanke, say it will be costly to financial institutions without reducing systemic risk.

Usually a seat on Financial Services precludes other assignments, but Hultgren got a waiver to keep his seat on the Science, Space and Technology Committee. He represents a renowned scientific research facility: the government's Fermi National Accelerator Lab, which conducts studies on high-energy particle physics. Home to the recently closed Tevatron particle accelerator, the facility is in a state of transition. Hultgren — who takes his sons to bike and jog on the trails of the Fermilab campus — wants to maintain funding for the research done there. "Basic scientific research is something that we should do" as a government, Hultgren says. "We don't even know what we're going to find, but if we don't do it, someone else will."

He is not happy with the Obama administration's scaled-down approach to the space program, calling it a "clear threat to American exceptionalism." At a 2012 hearing on research universities, he called for more science investments: "I feel like we have very little vision as far as science policy goes for our nation from the government, from our leadership. We need to change that."

Hultgren is socially conservative. He supports gun rights and opposes federal funding of abortion.

He grew up in suburban Wheaton — a dry town until 1985 — upstairs from his family's funeral home. His great-grandfather was a doorman at Marshall Field's in downtown Chicago, and a photograph of him hangs in Hultgren's Washington office. He and his wife have home-schooled their four children. (He has introduced a bill to require parental consent to release records of home-schooled students.)

Hultgren graduated from Bethel College in 1988. A paid internship in Hastert's office eventually turned into job as a district aide. He earned a law degree from the Illinois Institute of Technology's Chicago-Kent College of Law.

From 1994 to 1998, he served on the DuPage County Board, and then won a seat in the state House. He moved to the state Senate in 2007 and served there until winning a seat in Congress. Memorabilia connected to the iconic Illinois politician Abraham Lincoln decorates his Washington office.

In the 2010 general election, Hultgren faced Democratic incumbent Bill Foster, a former Fermilab physicist who had won a March 2008 special election to replace the elder Hastert. Hultgren was able to paint Foster, who backed almost all of President Barack Obama's economic initiatives, as too liberal for the district. He won with just over 51 percent of the vote.

Redistricting for 2012 was not kind to Illinois Republicans. Hultgren was drawn into a district with fellow freshman Joe Walsh, a controversial conservative firebrand. Walsh in December 2011 opted to run in the redrawn — and more Democratic — 8th District. He lost, while Hultgren cruised to re-election. At the same time, Foster was sent back to the House in the new 11th District.

Key Votes

2012	
Extend a Social Security payroll tax cut and unemployment benefits	YES
Ease securities rules to expand small-business access to capital	YES
Extend for one year subsidized student loan interest rates financed by a cut in health care spending	YES
Cite Attorney General Eric H. Holder Jr. for contempt of Congress	YES
Create a visa program for foreign graduates in high-tech fields	YES
Extend most Bush-era income tax rates while allowing rates for top-bracket earners to rise (Jan. 1, 2013)	NO
2011	
Strike funding for F-35 alternative engine	NO
Prevent EPA from regulating greenhouse gas emissions to address climate change	YES
Extend certain provisions of Patriot Act for four years	YES
Declare opposition to use of ground troops in Libya	YES
Overhaul patent law	NO
Pass compromise debt limit increase plan and establish future spending limits	NO
Allow consideration of measures to implement three trade agreements	YES

CQ Vote Studies

	PARTY UNITY		PRESIDENTIAL SUPPORT	
	SUPPORT	OPPOSE	SUPPORT	OPPOSE
2012	96%	4%	17%	83%
2011	95%	5%	16%	84%

Interest Groups

	AFL-CIO	ADA	CCUS	ACU
2012	29%	0%	100%	88%
2011	28%	15%	88%	88%

Illinois 14

West and northwest Chicago 'collar' exurbs

The GOP-friendly 14th District was redrawn following the 2010 census, shifting from an east-west slice across the north-central part of the state into a collection of rural communities and established towns — such as Woodstock, Hampshire and Sugar Grove — ringing the compact suburbs and exurbs of Chicago. The district borders Wisconsin to the north and the 16th District along its entire western and southern edges.

The district, which forms a buffer between the more-rural and downstate regions of Illinois and the Chicagoland area, takes in parts of Lake, McHenry, DeKalb, Kane, DuPage, Kendall and Will counties. Most of the district's population is weighted to the east among Chicago exurbs along the Fox River Valley. The western reaches of the district are farther removed from the metropolis.

Kendall County's population has more than doubled since 2000, and Plainfield and Shorewood (shared with the 11th) in Will County also experienced a decade of growth; much of that growth was within a well-educated workforce. Kane County's Batavia, once a manufacturing town, now relies on the Fermi National Accelerator Laboratory. Fermilab's large research campus, which is entirely in the 14th and crosses into DuPage County, is focused on high-energy physics and also hosts bike trails, fishing and cultural events.

In Lake County, the 14th includes parts of the scenic Chain O'Lakes region (shared with the 10th). An agricultural heritage in McHenry County remains with wheat and some soybean production, and a retirement community in Huntley has drawn commercial development. Sycamore in DeKalb County looks west into the 16th toward Northern Illinois University. Light manufacturing is important to the region.

Major Industry
Light manufacturing, agriculture, health care

Cities
Oswego, Geneva, McHenry

Notable
The Illinois Railway Museum in Union boasts restored locomotives, freight cars and trolleys among the several hundred pieces of equipment in its collection.

Rep. John Shimkus (R)

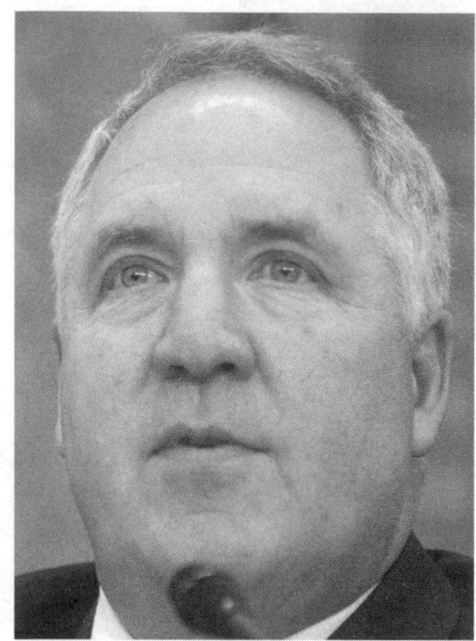

Capitol Office
225-5271
shimkus.house.gov
2452 Rayburn Bldg. 20515-1319; fax 225-5880

Committees
Energy & Commerce
(Environment & the Economy - Chairman)

Residence
Collinsville

Born
Feb. 21, 1958; East St. Louis, Ill.

Religion
Lutheran

Family
Wife, Karen Muth Shimkus; three children

Education
U.S. Military Academy, B.S. 1980; Southern Illinois U., Edwardsville, M.B.A. 1997

Military
Army, 1980-86; Army Reserve, 1986-2008

Career
Teacher

Political Highlights
Candidate for Madison County Board, 1988; Collinsville Township Board of Trustees, 1989-93; Madison County treasurer, 1990-97; Republican nominee for U.S. House, 1992

ELECTION RESULTS

2012 GENERAL		
John Shimkus (R)	205,775	68.6%
Angela Michael (D)	94,162	31.4%
2012 PRIMARY		
John Shimkus (R)		unopposed
2010 GENERAL		
John Shimkus (R)	166,166	71.2%
Tim Bagwell (D)	67,132	28.8%

Previous Winning Percentages
2008 (64%); 2006 (61%); 2004 (69%); 2002 (55%); 2000 (63%); 1998 (61%); 1996 (50%)

Elected 1996; 9th term

Shimkus doesn't apologize for arguing with colleagues, either in Energy and Commerce Committee meetings or on the House floor. "I can be pretty jerky sometimes. I get that," he said. "I am combative when I need to be. I am respectful and kind when I can get away with it."

A retired lieutenant colonel in the Army Reserve, Shimkus now marshals GOP troops as chairman of the Subcommittee on Environment and the Economy. His battles are often with environmentalists whom he feels disregard the negative impact of regulations on businesses and consumers.

Despite occasional frustrations, Shimkus — a devout Christian who tweets Bible verses daily — has kept the faith. "I guess you have to always come to this job with a little naiveté, thinking that you can still change the world and make things right," he said. "Otherwise, why would you put up with this for so long?"

Shimkus has been a member of Energy and Commerce since 1997 and landed his subcommittee gavel in 2011 after an unsuccessful bid to chair the full committee. He said his panel deals with "trash and recyclables," which includes nuclear waste and spent nuclear fuel. It's an issue that hits home: Illinois generates the most nuclear power of any state.

In the 112th Congress (2011-12) he took to the House floor on a weekly basis, using that pulpit for a single purpose: to push for keeping Nevada's Yucca Mountain as the lone facility for housing commercial nuclear waste, as stipulated in a 1987 law. He had employed the strategy before. In mid-2008, when national gas prices averaged $4 per gallon, he spoke on the issue almost daily.

President Barack Obama said in 2009 that he would end the Yucca project and find a new system for storage — a move applauded by Nevada Democrat Harry Reid, the Senate majority leader. "The federal government, Harry Reid and the president refuse to follow the law," Shimkus said. "It's pretty simple."

In May 2011, he accused Energy and Commerce's top Democrat, Henry A. Waxman of California, of sabotaging an investigation into whether the head of the Nuclear Regulatory Commission had acted illegally in closing the facility. In a hearing, Waxman read aloud accusatory emails gathered as part of Shimkus' probe. Shimkus said he had requested secrecy from Waxman, and he left a hearing he was co-chairing to air his complaints in an impromptu press conference.

As co-chairman of the Congressional Coal Caucus, Shimkus also goes to bat for a more traditional energy source. Like many Republicans, he sees the Obama administration as actively trying to kill the coal industry through regulations. He supported a House-passed bill to push regulation of coal ash — a byproduct of coal combustion sometimes used in construction materials — to the states, instead of the EPA.

"The states are by no means junior regulators or the minor leagues of environmental protection," he said at a February 2013 hearing. Shimkus hopes Illinois will set standards for hydraulic fracturing, a method for extracting oil and gas from shale deposits.

He opposes the idea of cap-and-trade systems for regulating greenhouse gas emissions, contending they could be "deadly" to the oil, gas and coal industries. He also has backed attempts to block the EPA from enforcing regulations on the emission of greenhouse gases from stationary sources, such as power plants.

It's not always a combat situation with Shimkus, however. "If you want to be successful, you have to be bipartisan," he said. Citing a need to reduce reliance on oil, he introduced a bill in 2011 to require car manufacturers to build more vehicles capable of running on fuels other than standard gasoline. It garnered more Democratic co-sponsors than Republican.

Though not the staunchest fiscal conservative, Shimkus wants a balanced-budget constitutional amendment and voted for a GOP fiscal 2012 budget that included significant structural changes to Medicare. He's not opposed to cost-saving changes to entitlement programs. He called the Democrats' 2010 health care overhaul law an "unmitigated disaster" and walked out during Obama's September 2009 address to Congress on the issue.

He co-chairs the NG9-1-1 Caucus, which seeks to strengthen the nation's 911 emergency system; his current focus is getting cutting-edge technology in the hands of first-responders. The issue was handed to him by former Energy and Commerce Chairman Billy Tauzin, a Louisiana Republican. "Sometimes people from your district raise an issue, sometimes you have a great passion and claw for it, sometimes things are given to you," he said with a laugh.

Shimkus is of Lithuanian ancestry — he co-founded the House Baltic Caucus — and grew up in Collinsville. His father worked at a local telephone company for 50 years while his mother was raising seven children. Shimkus played junior varsity baseball at West Point. He stays active pitching for the Republicans in the annual charity baseball game against the Democrats (which CQ Roll Call sponsors). He lives in a Capitol Hill home with GOP House teammates: Kevin Brady of Texas, Erik Paulsen of Minnesota and Steve Scalise of Louisiana. "Shimkus tells us how horrible we're playing, how we need to get better, how old and slow we've become," Brady told Roll Call in July 2011. "He's the motivator in this whole thing."

He served in the Army from 1980 to 1986 and is currently a member of the NATO Parliamentary Assembly. He was an unwavering supporter of President George W. Bush's conduct of the Iraq War, but the troop drawdown in 2011 also met his approval. "The sooner we could leave, if things were stable, the better," he said. He has voiced similar sentiments on Afghanistan.

After the Army, he returned to Collinsville to teach high school history and government classes. He now teaches Bible study in his district.

Shimkus won his first election to the Collinsville Township Board of Trustees in 1989 and went on to be Madison County treasurer. In 1992, he challenged Democratic Rep. Richard J. Durbin, who had represented the 20th District for 10 years, and lost. When Durbin was elected to the Senate in 1996, Shimkus was ready to try again. In the general election, he faced state Rep. Jay C. Hoffman and won by 1,238 votes.

Illinois lost a House seat to reapportionment before the 2002 election, and Shimkus beat Democratic Rep. David Phelps in the new 19th District. The state lost another seat 10 years later, and Shimkus won an easy victory in the new 15th District, which had large portions of the old 19th.

Key Votes

2012	
Extend a Social Security payroll tax cut and unemployment benefits	YES
Ease securities rules to expand small-business access to capital	YES
Extend for one year subsidized student loan interest rates financed by a cut in health care spending	YES
Cite Attorney General Eric H. Holder Jr. for contempt of Congress	YES
Create a visa program for foreign graduates in high-tech fields	YES
Extend most Bush-era income tax rates while allowing rates for top-bracket earners to rise (Jan. 1, 2013)	YES
2011	
Strike funding for F-35 alternative engine	NO
Prevent EPA from regulating greenhouse gas emissions to address climate change	YES
Extend certain provisions of Patriot Act for four years	YES
Declare opposition to use of ground troops in Libya	YES
Overhaul patent law	YES
Pass compromise debt limit increase plan and establish future spending limits	YES
Allow consideration of measures to implement three trade agreements	YES

CQ Vote Studies

	PARTY UNITY		PRESIDENTIAL SUPPORT	
	SUPPORT	OPPOSE	SUPPORT	OPPOSE
2012	91%	9%	18%	82%
2011	91%	9%	26%	74%
2010	96%	4%	31%	69%
2009	92%	8%	35%	65%
2008	94%	6%	71%	29%

Interest Groups

	AFL-CIO	ADA	CCUS	ACU
2012	33%	0%	100%	75%
2011	33%	10%	94%	68%
2010	7%	0%	88%	96%
2009	24%	5%	73%	92%
2008	8%	20%	88%	91%

Illinois 15

Danville; Wabash River Valley; Outer St. Louis Suburbs

Decennial reapportionment following the 2010 census stripped a U.S. House seat from Illinois, and the remapping process shifted the 15th south and west to take in new territory from the former 19th District — but the new lines still retain the district's GOP lean.

Geographically the largest district in the state, the 15th ranges across sparsely populated counties from Vermillion and parts of Ford counties in the north down the Indiana border to forests at the state's southern tip across the Ohio River from Kentucky. Interstate 70 bisects the district from the Terre Haute, Ind., region across the state to near East St. Louis in the west.

The district's diversity is in its landscape. The 15th's southern arm looks more like Appalachia than Midwestern prairie, and the hilly counties north of the Shawnee National Forest, which hold rich deposits of coal, once were one of the nation's chief coal mining regions.

Agriculture — notably corn and soybeans — dominates the economy. Areas in the central part of the district, such as Effingham, support a burgeoning wine-making business.

Midsize towns such as Danville, in Vermillion County, and Mattoon, in Coles County, rely on agribusiness and manufacturing; Mattoon is home to a Lender's Bagels factory. Dow Chemicals closed its factory in Charleston, near Matoon east of Interstate 57, in 2012. Eastern Illinois University remains a top employer for the region. In Collinsville, in the 15th's chunk of Madison County to the west, a horse racing track adds jobs as well.

Despite allegiances to manufacturing, this overwhelmingly white district is GOP territory. All of the 29 counties wholly in the district backed Republican presidential nominee Mitt Romney in the 2012 election. There is an Amish presence near Arthur and Arcola.

Major Industry
Agriculture, manufacturing, food products

Cities
Danville, Vandalia, Collinsville (pt.)

Notable
Metropolis was declared the official hometown of Superman in 1972.

Rep. Adam Kinzinger (R)

Capitol Office
225-3635
kinzinger.house.gov
1221 Longworth Bldg. 20515-1311; fax 225-3521

Committees
Energy & Commerce
Foreign Affairs

Residence
Channahon

Born
Feb. 27, 1978; Kankakee, Ill.

Religion
Protestant

Family
Single

Education
Illinois State U., B.A. 2000 (political science)

Military
Ill. Air National Guard, 2001-03; Wis. Air National Guard, 2003-present

Career
Information technology services company account representative

Political Highlights
McLean County Board, 1998-2003

ELECTION RESULTS

2012 GENERAL		
Adam Kinzinger (R)	181,789	61.8%
Wanda Rohl (D)	112,301	38.2%
2012 PRIMARY		
Adam Kinzinger (R)	45,546	53.9%
Donald Manzullo (R)	38,889	46.1%
2010 GENERAL		
Adam Kinzinger (R)	129,108	57.3%
Debbie Halvorson (D)	96,019	42.6%

Elected 2010; 2nd term

Kinzinger was billed as a young GOP star when he came to the House, and the Democrats in charge of Illinois redistricting forced him to prove it — a new electoral map required him to take out a 10-term Republican to secure a return to Congress. He zeroes in on defense and energy issues, equipped with the clear support of some powerful House leaders and a seat on the Energy and Commerce Committee.

Named one of The Hill newspaper's "50 Most Beautiful People," Kinzinger is one of the youngest lawmakers on Capitol Hill and counts political messaging as one of his strengths. "I am a very passionate person, just in general," he says. "You don't see me as someone who is at my desk and writing down every idea that comes to my mind. But a lot of times people come out with very good ideas that I like to champion."

Messaging helped him win a March 2012 primary. The Democrat-controlled Illinois legislature created a map for the 2012 cycle that placed Kinzinger's home in a Democratic district. He opted to run against Donald Manzullo, a low-profile and more-conservative Republican, in a 16th District that included some of his old turf.

It was pegged as a race of youth versus experience, and also a proxy battle between establishment Republican leaders and the tea party movement. When Kinzinger got the endorsement of Majority Leader Eric Cantor, Manzullo was enraged; tea party groups jumped in on his behalf. Kinzinger did a better job with voters in parts of the district new to both men, and he won with 54 percent of the vote.

Kinzinger, a deputy whip, is somewhere on the moderate end of the GOP spectrum. He initially joined the Republican Study Committee but left with a few others members in October 2011; he belongs to the moderate Main Street Partnership and No Labels, a nonpartisan group that seeks ways to improve the functionality of Congress.

He was in the minority of House Republicans voting for the January 2013 "fiscal cliff" deal that extended lower tax rates only for income under $400,000 — though he said it should have contained more spending cuts.

First elected to a county board at 20 years old, Kinzinger likes the GOP youth movement, which includes fellow Illinoisan Aaron Schock. "To move forward, we're going to have to begin to hand the torch over to that next generation," he said in 2011.

Kinzinger trumpets the common theme of energy independence from the Energy and Commerce Committee. He's a devotee of the "all of the above" strategy for domestic energy production, and he particularly liked a sweeping bill from California Republican Devin Nunes in the 112th Congress (2011-12). It would expand offshore energy leasing and plow the proceeds into a trust fund for the development of renewable-energy resources. It would also increase permits for new nuclear reactors and prohibit the regulation of greenhouse gases to mitigate climate change.

Illinois leads the country in nuclear power generation. Kinzinger in 2011 introduced a bill to ensure continuous operation of the Nuclear Regulatory Commission. It would allow commissioners to serve until their successors have been appointed and confirmed, eliminating any prolonged vacancies on the panel. He supports the use of Yucca Mountain in Nevada as a national repository for nuclear waste.

On the commerce side of the committee, Kinzinger and Illinois Democrat Daniel Lipinski in the 112th introduced a bill to develop a national manufacturing strategy; it passed the House but went nowhere in the Senate. Northern

Illinois has been hit hard by downturns in manufacturing.

"At a time when we are on the brink of a new manufacturing renaissance in this country, the only barriers that pose a threat to this recovery would be government-created," he wrote.

Kinzinger is a pilot in the Wisconsin Air National Guard — he flies on the weekends if he has time — and served five tours in Iraq and Afghanistan with both Wisconsin and Illinois Air National Guard units. He worked on defense issues as a freshman and joined the Foreign Affairs Committee for the 113th Congress (2013-14).

Kinzinger opposed the withdrawal of U.S. forces from Iraq in 2011. "You're leaving a nation that now really only has Iran to influence it, a nation that is still young," he said. Nor does he support the withdrawal from Afghanistan. "Wind down under conditions of victory," he told Fox News in May 2011.

He joined Democratic Sen. Mark Warner of Virginia in pushing for the Air Force to investigate cases of oxygen-supply problems encountered by pilots flying F-22 Raptors. In July 2012, the department eased restrictions on F-22s after concluding that the main problem was a faulty valve on a high-pressure vest. The House passed his first bill of the 113th Congress, which allows grants to states to help them streamline the transition process for veterans with military emergency medical training who want to become civilian emergency medical technicians. He supported a deficit reduction package in August 2011, though he said that potential military budget cuts in that deal made him "sick."

Kinzinger was raised in Bloomington. His mother is an elementary school teacher, and his father is a former CEO of two faith-based organizations. He graduated from nearby Illinois State University.

Shortly after the Sept. 11 attacks, Kinzinger signed up for the Air National Guard. He won an Air Force Airman's Medal in Milwaukee for saving a woman whose boyfriend was trying to stab her.

"I said, I'm going to get stabbed and I'm going to die," Kinzinger told the Weekly Standard. "But the second thought that went through my head was, I can't watch this happen to her and live with that memory for the rest of my life. ... I literally would have rather died than to have the thought of saying that I sissied out and ran."

In 2010, challenging one-term Democrat Debbie Halvorson, Kinzinger was outspent — but he won going away, with 57 percent of the vote. After beating Manzullo in the 2012 GOP primary, he defeated Democrat Wanda Rohl, a social worker with no political experience, by more than 23 points.

Kinzinger is serving as one of five regional chairmen for the National Republican Congressional Committee — the campaign arm of House Republicans — for the 2014 election cycle.

Key Votes

2012	
Extend a Social Security payroll tax cut and unemployment benefits	YES
Ease securities rules to expand small-business access to capital	YES
Extend for one year subsidized student loan interest rates financed by a cut in health care spending	YES
Cite Attorney General Eric H. Holder Jr. for contempt of Congress	YES
Create a visa program for foreign graduates in high-tech fields	YES
Extend most Bush-era income tax rates while allowing rates for top-bracket earners to rise (Jan. 1, 2013)	YES
2011	
Strike funding for F-35 alternative engine	NO
Prevent EPA from regulating greenhouse gas emissions to address climate change	YES
Extend certain provisions of Patriot Act for four years	YES
Declare opposition to use of ground troops in Libya	YES
Overhaul patent law	YES
Pass compromise debt limit increase plan and establish future spending limits	YES
Allow consideration of measures to implement three trade agreements	YES

CQ Vote Studies

	PARTY UNITY		PRESIDENTIAL SUPPORT	
	SUPPORT	OPPOSE	SUPPORT	OPPOSE
2012	91%	9%	18%	82%
2011	91%	9%	27%	73%

Interest Groups

	AFL-CIO	ADA	CCUS	ACU
2012	43%	5%	100%	76%
2011	21%	20%	100%	72%

Illinois 16

North and east central — part of Rockford, DeKalb

The 16th District sweeps southeast in a wide arc from the Wisconsin border north of Rockford to the state's line with Indiana in Iroquois County, picking up old manufacturing and farming towns and portions of at least six major interstate highways.

In the north, the district grabs the eastern half of Rockford — the industrial hub was split between the 16th and the 17th districts during decennial redistricting following the 2010 census. Once a center for major machine-tool manufacturing, Rockford suffered a typical Rust Belt decline before transitioning to technology manufacturing and remains a densely populated manufacturing community. Double-digit unemployment rates remain a concern. Local officials look to growth in aerospace, transportation equipment and machinery production. Neighboring Belvidere has a Chrysler assembly plant.

In the north, the district also takes in DeKalb, home to Northern Illinois University, and Utica's Starved Rock State Park.

Agricultural production in the district is varied. Farms in Ogle County in the north grow hay and wheat; central LaSalle produces corn and soybeans; and Livingston and Iroquois counties in the southeast have wheat and soybean harvests.

Some residents in Will County — a small corner of the county surrounding Wilmington is in the 16th — are concerned about a proposed east-west corridor connecting Interstate 55 in the district to Interstate 65 in Indiana. The link could accommodate growth in the developing county and ease traffic on truck routes.

The district is overwhelmingly white and, outside of Rockford and DeKalb, sparsely populated. The 16th was drawn to remain solidly Republican at the federal level.

Major Industry
Manufacturing, agriculture

Cities
DeKalb (pt.), Rockford (pt.)

Notable
President Ronald Reagan's boyhood home is in Dixon.

Rep. Cheri Bustos (D)

Capitol Office
225-5905
bustos.house.gov
1009 Longworth Bldg. 20515-6601

Committees
Agriculture
Transportation & Infrastructure

Residence
East Moline

Born
Oct. 17, 1961; East Moline, Ill.

Religion
Roman Catholic

Family
Husband, Gerry Bustos; three children

Education
Illinois College, attended 1979-81; U. of Maryland, B.A. 1983 (government and politics); U. of Illinois, Springfield, M.A. 1985 (public affairs reporting)

Career
Health care network communications executive; journalist

Political Highlights
East Moline City Council, 2007-11

ELECTION RESULTS

2012 GENERAL		
Cheri Bustos (D)	153,519	53.3%
Bobby Schilling (R)	134,623	46.7%
2012 PRIMARY		
Cheri Bustos (D)	18,652	54.4%
George W. Gaulrapp (D)	8,838	25.8%
Greg Aguilar (D)	6,798	19.8%

Elected 2012; 1st term

Bustos has flourished in many of her family's pursuits: sports, journalism and now politics. She holds standard Democratic positions but says she is happy to work with anyone if the issue is in her constituents' best interests.

She is the daughter of Gene Callahan, a sports nut who couldn't find a job as a sports reporter. Instead, he covered crime and politics, which got him into government. He was an aide to Lt. Gov. Paul Simon and eventually became the chief of staff to Illinois Sen. Alan Dixon. (Later in life, he was the chief lobbyist for Major League Baseball.) Bustos grew up knowing many Illinois Democrats through her father's connections in the party — she was a baby sitter to the children of current Sen. Richard J. Durbin.

A basketball and volleyball star in college, Bustos got a master's in journalism and became an investigative reporter for the Quad-City Times. She later served as a communications director for a health care network, then jumped into politics as a city council member in East Moline.

She sits on the Agriculture Committee, which is big for a district filled with farms and agricultural equipment manufacturers, including Caterpillar. Bustos has urged better coordination among businesses, schools and government to make worker training programs more responsive to employer needs.

Bustos also sits on the Transportation and Infrastructure Committee. She has teamed with Durbin and several Republicans on a bill to explore the use of public-private partnerships for water infrastructure improvements.

Bustos supports the 2010 health care law but says more can be done to lower costs and improve care, including better-coordinated care and wider use of electronic health records in Medicare and Medicaid.

The 17th District was an ugly gerrymandered affair, but a new congressional map for 2012 made it more compact — and Democratic. Bustos was helped in the primary by Durbin, who reportedly asked a few of her competitors to step aside. She beat one-term GOP Rep. Bobby Schilling by more than 6 points.

Illinois 17

Northwest — Moline and Rock Island; parts of Peoria and Rockford

The 17th, which was significantly redrawn during decennial remapping, now takes in the northwestern corner of the state. It stretches east to pick up a chunk of Rockford and south down the Mississippi River through working-class river towns before sweeping inland to downtown Peoria.

The 17th includes rich farmland along the Mississippi, as well as Rock Island and Moline — Illinois' half of the industrial Quad Cities that straddle the river across from Iowa. John Deere's corporate headquarters are in Moline, which depends on the farm implement manufacturer for jobs and the tourism revenue from the John Deere Pavilion and factory tours. The Rock Island Arsenal remains a major regional employer, adding jobs to an otherwise agriculture-dependent area. Local officials look to continue commercial, residential and cultural development in Moline's river district.

In the central part of the state, the 17th heads into Peoria, home of the heavy-machinery manufacturer Caterpillar. The company is taking a leading role in development along the Illinois River. Across the river in East Peoria (shared with the 18th), construction of a central commercial hub is under way. The 17th takes in both the small Peoria and Rockford airports.

North of Moline and Rock Island on the Mississippi, tourists also head to Galena among the rolling hills of Jo Daviess County, which leads the state in beef cattle and hay production. Towns that relied on smaller-scale manufacturing interests have struggled as plants closed.

Although portions of the district remain conservative, the 17th includes minority communities in Peoria and Rockford as well as blue-collar workers who back Democrats. Among the counties wholly or partially in the 17th, 2012 GOP presidential nominee Mitt Romney won only in Stephenson.

Major Industry
Farm equipment manufacturing, agriculture

Military Bases
Rock Island Arsenal (Army), 374 military, 4,868 civilian (2011)

Cities
Rockford (pt.), Moline, Rock Island, Peoria (pt.)

Notable
The Rockford Peaches were three-time champions of the All-American Girls Professional Baseball League.

Rep. Aaron Schock (R)

Capitol Office
225-6201
schock.house.gov
328 Cannon Bldg. 20515-1318; fax 225-9249

Committees
House Administration
Ways & Means

Residence
Peoria

Born
May 28, 1981; Morris, Minn.

Religion
Baptist

Family
Single

Education
Illinois Central College, attended 1999-2002; Bradley U., B.S. 2002 (finance)

Career
Real estate developer; home improvement company owner

Political Highlights
Board of Education of the City of Peoria, 2001-05 (president, 2004-05); Ill. House, 2005-09

ELECTION RESULTS

2012 GENERAL		
Aaron Schock (R)	244,467	74.2%
Steve Waterworth (D)	85,164	25.8%
2012 PRIMARY		
Aaron Schock (R)		unopposed
2010 GENERAL		
Aaron Schock (R)	152,868	69.1%
Deirdre "DK" Hirner (D)	57,046	25.8%
Sheldon Schafer (GREEN)	11,256	5.1%

Previous Winning Percentages
2008 (59%)

Elected 2008; 3rd term

When Schock first joined the House, he was noted for his youth and looks. The novelty has survived, partly through Schock's own efforts. The moderate Republican has used his image to open doors, quickly entering GOP campaign operations and the Ways and Means Committee. "I'm a big believer if you want to change people's minds or get someone to vote for you, either a voter or a colleague, you've got to first get their attention," he said.

He definitely got attention in May 2011, notably or notoriously, for showing his six-pack abs on the cover of Men's Health magazine — under the title "America's Fittest Congressman." In the accompanying article, Schock endorsed personal responsibility for a healthy lifestyle, applauded the anti-childhood-obesity campaign of first lady Michelle Obama and offered a few suggestions for maintaining American competitiveness.

It was an example of Schock embracing the role of a 21st-century spokesman, both for the GOP and a younger generation. (He was the first person born in the 1980s to be elected to the House.) His party has indulged him: He spoke at the 2008 Republican National Convention even before being elected, was named a deputy whip in his first term and has had opportunities to bend the ear of House leaders, sometimes over morning workouts at the House gym.

Devotion to the political ground game has helped his cause. Advising the Class of 2010 early in the 112th Congress (2011-12), Schock said constituent casework was the key to re-election and that lobbyists could be a useful resource. He has contributed hundreds of thousands of dollars to GOP organizations, both nationally and in Illinois.

"The best way for my positions to be advanced, my ideals to be enacted into law, is to ensure that my party maintains the majority," he said. Schock has reportedly been considering a statewide run — possibly for governor — in 2014.

Schock deals with many of the hottest fiscal debates on the Ways and Means Committee. Though a long way from retirement, he focuses in part on Social Security: "I think our biggest challenge right now is just creating awareness that the program's going broke," he says. Schock has supported proposals to raise the retirement age for younger Americans.

The committee continues to consider a tax code overhaul, and Schock offers his definition of a fair code: "It means everybody pays something and that we don't favor certain industries." Reflecting Rust Belt sensibilities, Schock has worked on proposals to cajole companies into hiring. In 2011, he teamed with New York Democrat Charles B. Rangel on an extension of the Work Opportunity Tax Credit for employers who hire adults receiving public aid; a one-year extension for those hiring veterans was enacted as part of a veterans package.

He voted for the January 2013 "fiscal cliff" package, which permanently extended lower income tax rates on earnings under $400,000; it also extended a tax credit for the production of biodiesel, which Schock supported.

From the Trade Subcommittee, Schock pushes a get-tough policy on China's alleged unfair trade practices. "If you're not tough with a bully in the classroom, he's only going to get stronger," he said, adding that those wary of starting a "trade war" with complaints to the World Trade Organization (such as Caterpillar, a large manufacturer important to his district) would hamstring the enforcement of future pacts with countries such as Russia. He has also proposed legislation to allow more low-cost goods to enter the country without some of the regulation and paperwork required by current customs law.

Schock uses his influence on high-profile issues outside the panel's jurisdiction. A member of the moderate Main Street Partnership, he helped sell House leaders on a plan to use federal energy leases as a funding source for infrastructure programs. That idea became a centerpiece of a 2012 GOP proposal for a long-term reauthorization of surface transportation programs.

Because it included expanded energy production favored by Republicans as well as infrastructure spending favored by unions and Democrats, Schock thought the plan could be a winner. "It was trying to find two things that were the art of the possible, things that could actually happen, and marry them together," he said. But environmental groups objected, and most Democrats rejected the combination.

Schock, the self-described "oops child" of a family physician and a homemaker, was born in Morris, Minn. He was five years behind his brother. (Schock also has two older sisters.) The family lived on a farm, and early on he discovered an entrepreneurial bent, working with his siblings to sell strawberries they had picked.

Those habits blossomed when the family moved to Peoria. In junior high school, he managed a database for a local bookstore. He worked for an online ticket brokerage firm and in a gravel pit throughout high school. While his brother was buying dirt bikes, Schock bought rental property.

He was equally industrious in high school, but the local school board wouldn't let him graduate early. Schock later ran for the Peoria board of education at age 19 and eventually became the youngest president in the board's history. He still keeps tabs on education. Schock advocates programs to encourage parental contacts with schools and is a proponent of "experiential learning," which exposes students to business environments they might be considering.

During his senior year of high school, Schock racked up enough credits at a junior college that he was able to graduate from Bradley University in two years. He opened a franchise of a home-improvement company shortly thereafter. From 2005 to 2009, he served in the Illinois House and developed a reputation for constituent service.

Schock jumped into a U.S. House race when Republican Ray LaHood announced his retirement after seven terms. He won 59 percent of the vote in 2008, improved to 69 percent in 2010, and after redistricting for 2012, he took 74 percent.

Some of Schock's campaign spending came under scrutiny in 2011, with reports that he had charged (among other things) a trip to Greece and workout videos to his campaign. Spokesmen maintained that the charges were either related to fundraising or accidents that had been reimbursed. The Ethics Committee also is investigating an allegation that Schock illegally solicited a donation for a super PAC backing the 2012 re-election of his friend and in-state colleague, Adam Kinzinger.

Key Votes

2012	
Extend a Social Security payroll tax cut and unemployment benefits	YES
Ease securities rules to expand small-business access to capital	YES
Extend for one year subsidized student loan interest rates financed by a cut in health care spending	YES
Cite Attorney General Eric H. Holder Jr. for contempt of Congress	YES
Create a visa program for foreign graduates in high-tech fields	YES
Extend most Bush-era income tax rates while allowing rates for top-bracket earners to rise (Jan. 1, 2013)	YES
2011	
Strike funding for F-35 alternative engine	YES
Prevent EPA from regulating greenhouse gas emissions to address climate change	YES
Extend certain provisions of Patriot Act for four years	YES
Declare opposition to use of ground troops in Libya	YES
Overhaul patent law	NO
Pass compromise debt limit increase plan and establish future spending limits	YES
Allow consideration of measures to implement three trade agreements	YES

CQ Vote Studies

	PARTY UNITY		PRESIDENTIAL SUPPORT	
	SUPPORT	OPPOSE	SUPPORT	OPPOSE
2012	89%	11%	19%	81%
2011	92%	8%	31%	69%
2010	93%	7%	33%	67%
2009	84%	16%	36%	64%

Interest Groups

	AFL-CIO	ADA	CCUS	ACU
2012	38%	0%	100%	76%
2011	31%	15%	93%	68%
2010	7%	0%	100%	88%
2009	15%	5%	93%	92%

Illinois 18

West Central — Peoria suburbs and part of Bloomington; Quincy

The 18th District takes in parts of three downstate population centers — Peoria, Bloomington-Normal and Springfield — and swings west across corn and soybean fields to towns along the Mississippi River and the state's borders with Missouri and Iowa. The geographically vast district includes 14 whole counties and parts of five others.

Northern Peoria — most of the city is now in the 17th District following decennial remapping — and the close-in suburbs on most sides of the city, including Peoria Heights and part of East Peoria, have lost population over the last decade. Residents have headed farther out to previously undeveloped areas in Peoria and Woodford counties. Heavy-machinery maker Caterpillar, whose headquarters are downtown in the 17th, dominates the area's economy, and there are biotechnology and agriculture research facilities nearby that draw workers from the district's middle-class suburbs.

To the southeast, the 18th heads into Bloomington-Normal (shared with the 13th), including the eastern portions of the two adjacent cities. State Farm Insurance has its headquarters in the 18th's part of Bloomington.

Southwest of Bloomington, the district reaches Sangamon County near Springfield. Although the bulk of the state capital is in the 13th, wealthier areas around Springfield beyond the city's downtown and historic sites, fall into the 18th. State government jobs are key here.

Small and midsize towns dot otherwise rural counties to the west. Macomb hosts Western Illinois University, and Adams County's Quincy is an established Mississippi River town.

The 18th, which is more than 90 percent white, is reliably Republican, and the district's portions of the major population hubs are less diverse than the cities overall. In the 2012 presidential contest, GOP candidate Mitt Romney easily won the 18th with 61 percent of its vote.

Major Industry
Farm equipment manufacturing, agriculture, insurance

Cities
Peoria (pt.), Normal (pt.), Springfield (pt.)

Notable
Hancock County's Carthage Jail — the site of Mormon religious leader Joseph Smith's incarceration and death — has been restored to its mid-19th-century appearance.

INDIANA

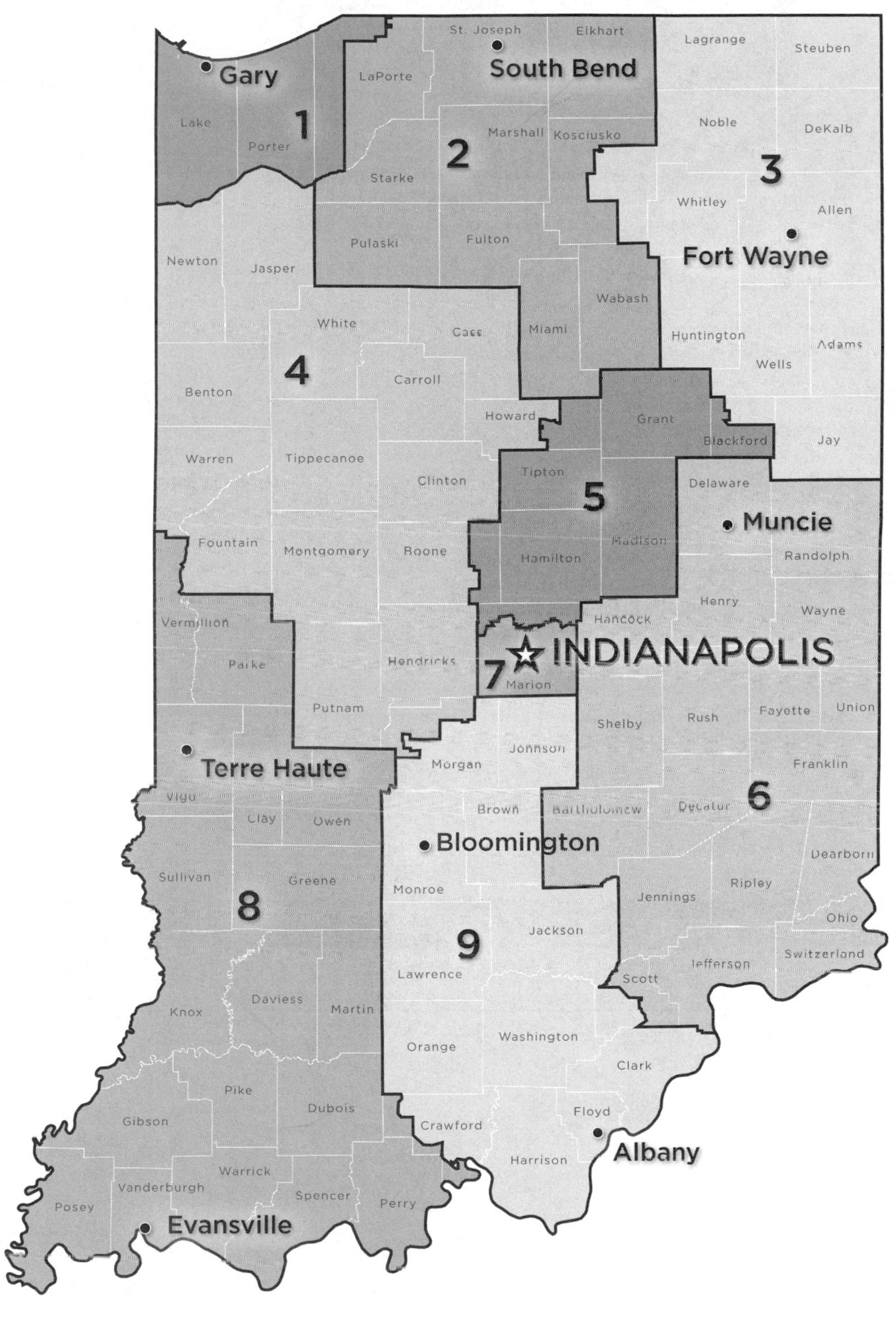

Gary
1
Lake
Porter
LaPorte
St. Joseph
South Bend
Elkhart
2
Marshall
Kosciusko
Starke
Pulaski
Fulton
Lagrange
Steuben
Noble
DeKalb
3
Whitley
Allen
Fort Wayne
Newton
Jasper
White
Cass
Miami
Wabash
Huntington
Wells
Adams
4
Benton
Carroll
Howard
Grant
Blackford
Jay
Warren
Tippecanoe
Clinton
Tipton
5
Delaware
Muncie
Fountain
Montgomery
Boone
Hamilton
Madison
Randolph
Henry
Wayne
Vermillion
Hancock
Parke
Hendricks
7
Marion
INDIANAPOLIS
Putnam
Shelby
Rush
Fayette
Union
Terre Haute
Johnson
Morgan
Franklin
Vigo
Clay
Owen
Brown
Bartholomew
Decatur
6
Bloomington
Dearborn
Sullivan
Greene
Monroe
Ripley
8
Jennings
Ohio
Jackson
9
Switzerland
Lawrence
Jefferson
Scott
Knox
Daviess
Martin
Washington
Orange
Clark
Pike
Dubois
Floyd
Gibson
Crawford
Albany
Harrison
Warrick
Vanderburgh
Spencer
Perry
Posey
Evansville

Gov. Mike Pence (R)

First elected: 2012

Length of term: 4 years

Term expires: 1/17

Salary: $111,687.94

Phone: (317) 232-4567

Residence: Indianapolis

Born: June 7, 1959; Columbus, Ind.

Religion: Christian

Family: Wife, Karen Pence; three children

Education: Hanover College, B.A. 1981 (history); Indiana U., J.D. 1986

Career: Think tank president; lawyer; radio and television broadcaster

Political highlights: Republican nominee for U.S. House, 1988, 1990; U.S. House, 2001-13

ELECTION RESULTS

2012 GENERAL

Mike Pence (R)	1,275,424	49.5%
John R. Gregg (D)	1,200,016	46.5%
Rupert Boneham (LIBERT)	101,868	4.0%

Lt. Gov. Sue Ellspermann (R)

First elected: 2012

Length of term: 4 years

Term expires: 1/17

Salary: $85,880.60

Phone: (317) 232-4545

LEGISLATURE

General Assembly: January-April in odd-numbered years; January-March in even-numbered years

Senate: 50 members, 4-year terms

2013 ratios: 37 R, 13 D; 42 men, 8 women

Salary: $22,616

Phone: (317) 232-9400

House: 100 members, 2-year terms

2013 ratios: 69 R, 31 D; 67 men, 23 women

Salary: $22,616

Phone: (317) 232-9600

TERM LIMITS

Governor: 2 terms

Senate: No

House: No

URBAN STATISTICS

CITY	POPULATION
Indianapolis	829,718
Fort Wayne	253,691
Evansville	117,429
South Bend	101,168
Hammond	80,830

REGISTERED VOTERS

Voters do not register by party.

POPULATION

2010 population	6,483,802
2000 population	6,080,485
1990 population	5,544,159
Percent change (2000-2010)	+6.6%
Rank among states (2010)	15
Median age	36.4
Born in state	68.5%
Foreign born	4.0%
Violent crime	333/100,000
Poverty level	14.4%
Federal workers	46,627
Military	3,108

ELECTIONS

STATE ELECTION OFFICIAL

(317) 232-3939

DEMOCRATIC PARTY

(317) 231-7100

REPUBLICAN PARTY

(317) 635-7561

MISCELLANEOUS

Web: www.indiana.gov

Capital: Indianapolis

U.S. CONGRESS

Senate: 1 Democrat, 1 Republican

House: 7 Republicans, 2 Democrats

STATISTICS BY DISTRICT

District	2012 Vote for President Obama	2012 Vote for President Romney	2008 Vote for President Obama	2008 Vote for President McCain	Black	Asian	Hispanic	Median Income	Over 64	Under 20	College Education	Rural	Sq. Miles
1	61%	37%	63%	36%	20%	1%	14%	$50,669	13%	27%	21%	9%	1,157
2	42	56	50	49	7	1	8	44,494	14	28	20	29	3,959
3	36	63	43	56	6	2	6	46,504	13	29	21	34	4,180
4	37	61	45	54	3	2	5	47,073	13	28	23	36	6,353
5	41	57	47	53	8	3	5	58,115	13	28	43	12	1,925
6	37	60	44	55	2	1	2	42,994	15	26	18	44	6,207
7	63	35	66	33	28	2	10	36,565	10	29	19	1	304
8	40	58	48	51	4	1	2	45,736	15	26	18	41	7,255
9	41	57	46	53	3	2	3	48,522	13	27	23	36	4,487
STATE	**44**	**54**	**50**	**49**	**9**	**2**	**6**	**46,438**	**13**	**28**	**23**	**27**	**35,826**
U.S.	**51**	**47**	**53**	**46**	**12**	**5**	**17**	**50,052**	**13**	**27**	**29**	**21**	**3,531,905**

Sen. Dan Coats (R)

Capitol Office
224-5623
coats.senate.gov
493 Russell Bldg. 20510-1404; fax 228-1820

Committees
Appropriations
Commerce, Science & Transportation
Select Intelligence
Joint Economic

Residence
Indianapolis

Born
May 16, 1943; Jackson, Mich.

Religion
Presbyterian

Family
Wife, Marsha Coats; three children

Education
Wheaton College, B.A. 1965 (political science); Indiana U., Indianapolis, J.D. 1972

Military Service
Army Corps of Engineers, 1966-68

Career
Lobbyist; congressional district aide; lawyer

Political Highlights
U.S. House, 1981-89; U.S. Senate, 1989-99; U.S. ambassador to Germany, 2001-05

ELECTION RESULTS

2010 GENERAL		
Dan Coats (R)	952,116	54.6%
Brad Ellsworth (D)	697,775	40.0%
Rebecca Sink-Burris (LIBERT)	94,330	5.4%
2010 PRIMARY		
Dan Coats (R)	217,225	39.5%
Marlin Stutzman (R)	160,981	29.2%
John Hostettler (R)	124,494	22.6%
Don Bates Jr. (R)	24,664	4.5%
Richard Behney (R)	23,005	4.2%

Previous Winning Percentages
1990 Special Election (54%)

Elected 2010; 2nd full term

Also served 1989-99

Coats says he came back for a second tour in the Senate to bolster the nation's economic and national security. He is fiscally conservative and militarily hawkish, and his conclusion from decades of political service is that crises — whether organic or manufactured — present great opportunities for long-term shifts in the nation's posture.

He started in politics as a district aide for GOP Rep. Dan Quayle, then succeeded him in the House when Quayle was elected to the Senate in 1980. When Quayle was elected vice president in 1988, Coats was appointed to replace him in the Senate. He eventually won a full term, but retired at the end of it to satisfy a self-imposed term limit. Coats stayed involved in international affairs as George W. Bush's ambassador to Germany. He returned to the Senate in 2010, and this time "age is my term limit," he said.

Coats has a clear idea of how he likes to operate. "I'm not an in-the-weeds legislator," he said. "I don't want to be an in-the-weeds legislator. I'm at the point in life where I want to focus on the urgency of dealing with the major issues." The Senate is designed to defeat a "bottom-up approach, where you're trying to fix little things all the way along the line," according to Coats. He didn't shy from the standoffs that defined the 112th Congress (2011-12).

Speaking to economists at a December 2012 hearing of the Joint Economic Committee, he defended the use of the federal debt limit as a bargaining tool. Republicans demanded a deficit reduction package as a condition for allowing the government to borrow more money in August 2011. "Whether you think that was enough or not enough," Coats said, it wouldn't have happened "without the threat of defaulting on our debt." (Coats voted against that deal, saying it fell "significantly short.") He's the top Republican senator on the Joint Economic Committee for the 113th Congress (2013-14).

Coats' ideas for federal finances include all the major themes Republicans have emphasized: spending cuts, tax changes and entitlement program overhauls. He and Oregon Democrat Ron Wyden released a 2011 measure to set the corporate tax rate at 24 percent, reduce the number of individual tax brackets from six to three, repeal the corporate alternative minimum tax and eliminate tax preferences that favor certain businesses or activities.

He co-wrote the Clinton-era line item veto law that the Supreme Court declared unconstitutional. Coats now backs "enhanced rescission authority," which would give Congress the chance to review any spending provisions the president removes from a bill; such an arrangement could get around the earlier constitutional objections. He has voted for a balanced-budget amendment to the Constitution and expresses a willingness to raise the eligibility ages for Social Security and Medicare.

Coats voted for the "fiscal cliff" package at the start of 2013, grudgingly accepting income tax increases on earnings above $400,000 in exchange for maintaining lower tax rates below that threshold. He also liked that the law temporarily averted scheduled cuts to defense budgets.

He tackles both spending and security as a member of the Appropriations Committee. Coats also sits on the Intelligence Committee, reprising an assignment he had in the 1990s.

Coats has criticized what he refers to as the Obama administration's "nice diplomacy" in the Middle East. Tough economic sanctions on Iran have won his approval, and he has indicated that a military strike might be called for if that country doesn't abandon attempts to develop nuclear weapons. Before returning to the Senate, Coats studied Iran's quest for nuclear weapons for the Bipartisan Policy Center, a Washington think tank.

When the United Nations Educational, Scientific and Cultural Organization admitted the Palestinian Authority as a member in 2011, Coats responded with a bill to shut down U.S. funding to any U.N. body recognizing the Palestinian Authority. The next year he amended a State-Foreign Operations spending bill to reroute U.N. funding to global health initiatives. It was not enacted.

Coats doesn't have a reflexive dislike for foreign operations spending, however. After the 2012 attack against the U.S. consulate in Benghazi, Libya, he said he did not support immediately stopping all U.S. aid to Libya, Egypt and Pakistan. "We have a right to be angry, but we must not let our anger dictate our foreign policy," he said.

In May 2011, he voted for a reauthorization of expiring surveillance provisions of the anti-terrorism law known as the Patriot Act, calling the law an "essential security tool." He says it is "imperative" that Congress pass cybersecurity legislation. Coats has a secondary venue to address Internet issues in the 113th Congress as a new member of the Commerce, Science and Transportation Committee.

Coats is socially conservative. Throughout his career, he has been a champion of the anti-abortion movement.

He was born in Jackson, Mich., where his father was a salesman. His mother, a Swedish immigrant, stayed at home with her three children. Coats holds familiar Republican positions on immigration; he favors robust efforts to prosecute illegal immigrants and deny them federal benefits, and he is in a position to do something about it as the top Republican on the Homeland Security Appropriations Subcommittee.

After graduating from college, Coats spent a few years in the Army Corps of Engineers, then studied law at Indiana University's Indianapolis campus. He went to work for an insurance company in Fort Wayne, where he first met Quayle. That launched his political career.

In 1990, running to fill the remainder of Quayle's Senate term, Coats faced state Rep. Baron P. Hill, who at that time was best known in the Hoosier State as a high school basketball star. Hill was an effective campaigner, but Coats was more in tune with the state's Republican leanings. He triumphed with nearly 54 percent of the vote. (Hill eventually won election to the House in 1998, was defeated in 2004, came back in 2006 and lost again in 2010.)

Running for a full term in 1992, Coats bested Indiana Secretary of State Joseph H. Hogsett, a Democrat and close associate of Gov. Evan Bayh. Coats' retirement cleared the field for Bayh himself to run in 1998. He captured the seat that had been held by his father, Birch, until the elder Bayh's defeat by Quayle in 1980.

Coats was named ambassador to Germany in 2001 and served in that role until 2005. His second official day of work as ambassador was Sept. 11. "It changed everything about the job," he said. On leaving that job, Coats worked as a lobbyist, with a client list that included General Electric and Google. He also helped the Bush administration shepherd the Supreme Court nominations of White House counsel Harriet E. Miers (which failed) and Samuel A. Alito Jr.

His entry to the 2010 Senate race was a surprise to many. Days after Coats joined the race, Bayh announced he would not seek re-election, withdrawing too late for Democrats to add a name to the primary ballot. Party leaders selected Rep. Brad Ellsworth, a member of the fiscally conservative Blue Dog Coalition, as their candidate.

Coats had name recognition and superior fundraising, allowing him to best state Sen. Marlin Stutzman—now a member of the House—and former Rep. John Hostettler in the primary. He beat Ellsworth by almost 15 points.

Coats has a love for Wheaten terriers. His first dog was named Hoosier, and his newest family member is named Honey.

Key Votes

2012	
Prohibit health insurance plans from denying coverage based on the sponsor's religious beliefs	NO
Require approval of the Keystone XL oil pipeline	YES
Ease securities rules to expand small-business access to capital	YES
Reauthorize farm and nutrition programs for five years	YES
Limit debate on a bill that would create private-sector cybersecurity standards	YES
Consent to ratification of a treaty setting global standard for the treatment of people with disabilities	NO
Provide $60.4 billion in disaster relief following Superstorm Sandy	NO
Extend most Bush-era income tax rates while allowing rates for top-bracket earners to rise (Jan. 1, 2013)	YES
2011	
Prevent EPA from regulating greenhouse gas emissions to address climate change	YES
Extend certain provisions of Patriot Act for four years	YES
Clear compromise debt limit increase plan and establish future spending limits	NO
Overhaul patent law	YES
Implement Colombia free trade agreement	YES
Limit debate on confirmation of Caitlin J. Halligan to D.C. Circuit Court of Appeals	NO
Extend payroll tax cut and unemployment benefits for two months	YES

CQ Vote Studies

	PARTY UNITY		PRESIDENTIAL SUPPORT	
	SUPPORT	OPPOSE	SUPPORT	OPPOSE
2012	89%	11%	54%	46%
2011	91%	9%	57%	43%

Interest Groups

	AFL-CIO	ADA	CCUS	ACU
2012	0%	10%	88%	80%
2011	16%	10%	91%	90%

Sen. Joe Donnelly (D)

Capitol Office
224-4814
donnelly.senate.gov
720 Hart Bldg. 20510; fax 224-5011

Committees
Agriculture, Nutrition & Forestry
(Commodities & Markets - Chairman)
Armed Services
Special Aging

Residence
Granger

Born
Sept. 29, 1955; Queens, N.Y.

Religion
Roman Catholic

Family
Wife, Jill Donnelly; two children

Education
U. of Notre Dame, B.A. 1977 (government), J.D. 1981

Career
Customized office products company owner; lawyer

Political Highlights
Democratic nominee for Ind. Senate, 1990; Democratic nominee for U.S. House, 2004; U.S. House, 2007-13

ELECTION RESULTS

2012 GENERAL		
Joe Donnelly (D)	1,281,181	50.0%
Richard E. Mourdock (R)	1,133,621	44.3%
Andy Horning (LIBERT)	145,282	5.7%
2012 PRIMARY		
Joe Donnelly (D)		unopposed
2010 HOUSE GENERAL		
Joe Donnelly (D)	91,341	48.2%
Jackie Walorski (R)	88,803	46.8%
Mark Vogel (LIBERT)	9,447	5.0%

Previous Winning Percentages
2008 House Election (67%);
2006 House Election (54%)

Elected 2012; 1st term

Donnelly established himself as a conservative Democrat during three terms in the House, where the shrinking of the ranks of political moderates also squeezed some of his legislative clout. It's a new game as he starts his career in the Senate, where he's a potential swing vote on fiscal measures, national security and government regulation.

First elected to Congress in 2006, Donnelly was a member of the Blue Dog Coalition, the group of the House's most fiscally conservative Democrats. That group had 43 members in his first term, but at the start of the 113th Congress (2013-14) it was down to 15.

Even so, Donnelly stayed the course and looked for ways to reduce federal deficits. In 2011 he voted for a balanced-budget amendment to the Constitution, and in 2012 he supported a version of a line-item veto that the president could use on spending bills. "It is our moral responsibility to get this financial situation squared away," Donnelly said in 2013. "It's intergenerational theft. I will feel as if I had not done everything I needed to do in my time in office if I cannot provide long-term solutions to this problem."

He also takes some Republican-sounding positions on energy. Donnelly was one of 44 Democrats voting against a 2009 measure to create a cap-and-trade system to regulate greenhouse gases, and he voted for several bills in the 112th Congress (2011-12) meant to restrain the regulatory powers of the EPA. The coal industry is big in Indiana. "I'll work toward trying to help make coal cleaner and help provide more opportunities to create those technologies that can do that," he said. "But for the president or anybody else to walk away from coal is ridiculous. It's an American energy source."

Donnelly has a seat on the Armed Services Committee and says national defense is his "first and foremost" obligation as a senator. He was a member of the Veterans' Affairs Committee for all three of his terms in the House, and Donnelly is likely to take a particular interest in personnel issues. During the confirmation hearing for Chuck Hagel as Defense secretary, Donnelly was the only person on the panel to ask the nominee about military suicides. "Our servicemen and women need proper assistance to transition to civilian life," he wrote after the hearing.

Donnelly also sits on the Agriculture, Nutrition and Forestry Committee, where he chairs the panel on Commodities and Markets. In that role, he oversees the Commodity Futures Trading Commission and the derivatives market, a continuation of his six years of work on the House Financial Services Committee.

While on the campaign trail, Donnelly expressed his displeasure that Congress hadn't cleared a long-term reauthorization of farm programs during the 112th Congress. The House Agriculture Committee approved a bill, but most Democrats in the chamber were offended by its $16 billion in reductions to the Supplemental Nutrition Assistance Program. Donnelly wasn't so upset.

"We had folks on the left who were screaming that we were treating our children inappropriately," he told Purdue public radio station WBAA in early 2013. "I love my children; I love everybody's children. But at the same time, we have to reduce spending. So we were able to reduce it by $16 billion and still have an effective program."

Although he's considered a fiscal hawk, Donnelly also is a strong ally of organized labor. He stood with many unions in opposing free-trade deals with Panama, South Korea and Colombia in 2011. One of his chief legislative initiatives is a bill to streamline workforce education to provide workers with in-demand technical skills; it would revise federal training programs to heed the needs of locally approved services and programs.

Donnelly, a Catholic, also takes some socially conservative stances. During the health care debate in the 111th Congress (2009-10), he was among the anti-abortion Democrats who held out for tougher restrictions on the use of federal funds for abortion services. He voted for the final bill, but he has since worked to repeal the medical device tax included in it.

He has opposed creating a path to citizenship for illegal immigrants, and the National Rifle Association has endorsed Donnelly on several occasions. But in April 2013, he and several other senators announced that they would now support same-sex marriage.

Donnelly grew up in Massapequa, N.Y., on Long Island, with one brother and three sisters. His mother died when he was 10, leaving his father, the manager of a printing shop in New York City, to raise five children. "My dad, for probably 50 years, got up in the morning, got on the train — hour and a half into work, hour and a half back from work — he worked like a dog every day. He set a wonderful example for his family and how a person should conduct themselves, and he let us know that we have an obligation to give back as well," he said.

He headed to Indiana to attend Notre Dame University, where he got a bachelor's degree and a law degree and met his wife. Donnelly worked as a lawyer for 15 years, then started a company selling printing-related products — he calls it a spinoff of the family business.

Dealing with rules and regulations, he said, gave him a "natural inclination and natural admiration" for other small-business owners in his state. "My job is to try to make sure I can make their lives easier," he said. In the House, Donnelly introduced several pieces of legislation with Oklahoma Democrat Dan Boren meant to bolster Small Business Administration loan programs.

Donnelly tried to secure the Democratic nomination for Indiana attorney general in 1988 but fell short at the party convention. Two years later, he lost a campaign for state Senate. Still, party officials asked him to run for Congress in 2004 against Rep. Chris Chocola, a very fiscally conservative freshman Republican. Donnelly lost by 10 points.

With the nation growing increasingly wary of President George W. Bush and Republicans in 2006, Donnelly came back for a rematch and took 54 percent of the vote. He easily won re-election two years later.

With the nation growing increasingly wary of President Barack Obama and Democrats in 2010, Donnelly survived an electoral scare. National Republicans targeted him, releasing their first campaign advertisements of the fall in his district. Donnelly had a tough challenger in GOP state Rep. Jackie Walorski, and he won by fewer than 2,600 votes — with a Libertarian candidate taking more than 9,000 votes.

In early 2011, Donnelly started eying the Senate seat. He began as the underdog, raising little money while centrist six-term Sen. Richard G. Lugar took on a GOP primary challenger, the intensely conservative state Treasurer Richard E. Mourdock. A stunning victory by Mourdock quickly changed Donnelly's prospects.

Donnelly and Mourdock traded minuscule leads in public polls throughout most of the campaign. However, the race permanently shifted in mid-October during the final 15 minutes of their last debate. Asked about his position on abortion, Mourdock suggested pregnancy from rape was something "God intended" to happen. After that, wavering independents and former Lugar supporters, especially in the Indianapolis collar counties, flocked to Donnelly. He won by 7 points.

Some of Donnelly's defeated foes have landed on their feet. Chocola is the president of the Club for Growth, a powerhouse political action committee (which backed Mourdock). Walorski in 2012 won the 2nd District seat vacated by Donnelly.

Key Votes (while House member)

2012	
Extend a Social Security payroll tax cut and unemployment benefits	YES
Ease securities rules to expand small-business access to capital	YES
Extend for one year subsidized student loan interest rates financed by a cut in health care spending	YES
Cite Attorney General Eric H. Holder Jr. for contempt of Congress	YES
Create a visa program for foreign graduates in high-tech fields	YES
Extend most Bush-era income tax rates while allowing rates for top-bracket earners to rise (Jan. 1, 2013)	YES
2011	
Strike funding for F-35 alternative engine	NO
Prevent EPA from regulating greenhouse gas emissions to address climate change	YES
Extend certain provisions of Patriot Act for four years	YES
Declare opposition to use of ground troops in Libya	NO
Overhaul patent law	YES
Pass compromise debt limit increase plan and establish future spending limits	YES
Allow consideration of measures to implement three trade agreements	NO

CQ Vote Studies (while House member)

	PARTY UNITY		PRESIDENTIAL SUPPORT	
	SUPPORT	OPPOSE	SUPPORT	OPPOSE
2012	55%	45%	39%	61%
2011	63%	37%	67%	33%
2010	73%	27%	76%	24%
2009	77%	23%	85%	15%
2008	79%	21%	25%	75%
2007	77%	23%	19%	81%

Interest Groups (while House member)

	AFL-CIO	ADA	CCUS	ACU
2012	75%	25%	91%	58%
2011	86%	65%	56%	28%
2010	79%	60%	63%	25%
2009	81%	70%	53%	24%
2008	87%	70%	72%	28%
2007	88%	85%	60%	44%

Rep. Peter J. Visclosky (D)

Capitol Office
225-2461
visclosky.house.gov
2256 Rayburn Bldg. 20515-1401; fax 225-2493

Committees
Appropriations

Residence
Merrillville

Born
Aug. 13, 1949; Gary, Ind.

Religion
Roman Catholic

Family
Wife, Joanne Royce; two children

Education
Indiana U., Northwest, B.S. 1970 (accounting); U. of Notre Dame, J.D. 1973; Georgetown U., LL.M. 1982

Career
Lawyer; congressional aide

Political Highlights
No previous office

ELECTION RESULTS

2012 GENERAL		
Peter J. Visclosky (D)	187,743	67.3%
Joel Phelps (R)	91,291	32.7%
2012 PRIMARY		
Peter J. Visclosky (D)		unopposed
2010 GENERAL		
Peter J. Visclosky (D)	99,387	58.6%
Mark Leyva (R)	65,558	38.6%
Jon Morris (LIBERT)	4,762	2.8%

Previous Winning Percentages
2008 (71%); 2006 (70%); 2004 (68%); 2002 (67%); 2000 (72%); 1998 (73%); 1996 (69%); 1994 (56%); 1992 (69%); 1990 (66%); 1988 (77%); 1986 (73%); 1984 (71%)

Elected 1984; 15th term

Visclosky has spent two decades on the Appropriations Committee, and in 2013 he claimed one of its most coveted assignments: He is the top Democrat on the subcommittee overseeing defense spending. He's also continuing his protection of the steel industry, an effort that has defined much of his career.

The son of an ironworker, Visclosky looks out for northwestern Indiana's shrinking manufacturing base. He has battled with presidents who haven't done enough, in his view, to counteract the impact of foreign competition on the struggling steel industry.

As vice chairman of the Congressional Steel Caucus, he has urged President Barack Obama to press Chinese leaders on illegal trading practices, such as devaluing currency and underpricing goods in foreign markets. He also testified in front of the International Trade Commission about placing pricing duties on Chinese drill pipes to protect American manufacturers. Usually given to nuanced analysis during House floor debates, Visclosky struck a blunt tone in July 2011, declaring, "I don't trust the Chinese."

Visclosky and most other Democrats opposed 2011 free-trade pacts with Colombia, Panama and South Korea that the Obama administration had prioritized. He said on the floor that the agreements would "undermine America's manufacturing sector and allow the continued hemorrhage of our jobs to foreign countries." Visclosky tries to promote "buy American" requirements, whereby various projects that receive federal funds must use iron and steel products produced in the United States.

The military builds a few things out of metal, so Visclosky continues the fight on the Defense Subcommittee. He had not been noted for his defense work prior to the 113th Congress (2013-14), but Visclosky has supported a number of Navy shipbuilding projects and an overall expansion of the fleet.

Visclosky also has opportunities to apply the expertise he developed as the top Democrat on the Energy-Water Subcommittee. He chaired that panel from 2007 through 2010, he was its ranking member in the 112th Congress (2011-12), and he still holds a seat there. It oversees weapons programs run by the Energy Department, and during the 112th Visclosky tried to encourage sharp cuts to various nuclear weapons initiatives.

The Pentagon is a huge consumer of energy and has increasing interest in renewable-energy programs. Visclosky considers himself a pragmatist on the issue. At a March 2012 hearing, he said the country "ought to move from a carbon-based economy." But he has resisted plans to cut funding for coal-based energy technology: "Why not work to get more efficiency out of that ounce of coal we're going to continue to burn till 2035?"

It's a position that sometimes places him at odds with the party line on pollution control standards. Visclosky opposed a 2009 Democratic bill to create a cap-and-trade system for greenhouse gas emissions, citing its likely effect on the steel industry.

Visclosky has also criticized the Obama administration's "green jobs" initiative, a key part of the president's economic agenda. "I'm sick of green jobs," he said in a hearing. "My green job is the United States steel industry using 30 percent less CO_2 since 1990 to make a ton of steel."

Visclosky has taken a relatively moderate stance on fiscal matters in recent years. He voted against an August 2011 deficit reduction law, calling it an "inadequate" solution to long-term fiscal problems. He repeated that argument when he was one of 16 House Democrats to oppose the January 2013 "fiscal cliff" deal, which permanently extended lower income tax rates on earnings under $400,000.

In 2008, he opposed a $700 billion rescue package for the financial sector, saying it was "in essence a blank check" with no concrete plan for how the money would be used. And he has become a supporter of the "Simpson-Bowles" budget framework, which would cut deficits by $4 trillion through spending cuts, revenue increases and entitlement program changes.

Visclosky has capitalized on his Appropriations post to set aside tens of millions of dollars for projects and programs in his district and state. But his proclivity for earmarking prior to 2011, when a ban on the practice went into effect, drew him unwelcome attention. In early 2009, news reports revealed that he was the top recipient of contributions from the family of Paul Magliocchetti, founder of The PMA Group. The now-defunct lobbying group specialized in earning its clients defense contracts but came under investigation for its campaign contributions.

Visclosky said he would return the contributions and stayed quiet during the probe. After a federal grand jury subpoenaed records from Visclosky's congressional and campaign offices, he temporarily stepped aside as the chairman of the Energy-Water Subcommittee.

Magliocchetti was indicted in August 2010 for allegedly coordinating illegal campaign contributions and making false statements. His son, Mark, pleaded guilty to making illegal corporate campaign contributions at his father's behest. Visclosky was cleared by the House Ethics Committee of accusations that he exchanged earmarks for campaign contributions.

As a teenager, Visclosky aspired to the priesthood. But he dropped out of a Roman Catholic seminary at age 15 and instead earned degrees at two Catholic universities, Notre Dame and Georgetown. Despite a passion for history, he made the decision to pursue an accounting degree. After graduating from Notre Dame law school in 1973, he linked his fortunes to those of Adam Benjamin Jr., then a state senator and rising political star in Indiana. Visclosky coordinated Benjamin's successful campaign for Congress in 1976 and served as one of his top aides in Washington for nearly six years.

When Benjamin died in September 1982, Democrats were without a candidate for the November election. The district's Democratic Party chairman chose Katie Hall, a state senator, as the nominee. She won the seat easily.

In 1984, Visclosky challenged Hall in the primary, putting on dozens of $2 "dog and bean" dinners to attract the young, the elderly and the unemployed. His "Slovak kid" background helped, as did the memory that older voters had of his father, John Visclosky, who had served as Gary's comptroller in the 1950s and as its mayor in 1962 and 1963.

Visclosky bested Hall by 2 points, then swamped Republican Joseph B. Grenchik, the mayor of Whiting, in November. He has won handily since.

Key Votes

2012	
Extend a Social Security payroll tax cut and unemployment benefits	NO
Ease securities rules to expand small-business access to capital	NO
Extend for one year subsidized student loan interest rates financed by a cut in health care spending	NO
Cite Attorney General Eric H. Holder Jr. for contempt of Congress	NO
Create a visa program for foreign graduates in high-tech fields	-
Extend most Bush-era income tax rates while allowing rates for top-bracket earners to rise (Jan. 1, 2013)	NO
2011	
Strike funding for F-35 alternative engine	NO
Prevent EPA from regulating greenhouse gas emissions to address climate change	NO
Extend certain provisions of Patriot Act for four years	NO
Declare opposition to use of ground troops in Libya	YES
Overhaul patent law	NO
Pass compromise debt limit increase plan and establish future spending limits	NO
Allow consideration of measures to implement three trade agreements	-

CQ Vote Studies

	PARTY UNITY		PRESIDENTIAL SUPPORT	
	SUPPORT	OPPOSE	SUPPORT	OPPOSE
2012	92%	8%	76%	24%
2011	88%	12%	71%	29%
2010	95%	5%	83%	17%
2009	97%	3%	93%	7%
2008	99%	1%	12%	88%

Interest Groups

	AFL-CIO	ADA	CCUS	ACU
2012	95%	80%	18%	0%
2011	100%	95%	20%	12%
2010	79%	95%	14%	4%
2009	90%	90%	47%	8%
2008	100%	80%	53%	8%

Indiana 1

Northwest — Gary, Hammond

The 1st District covers Indiana's northwestern corner, stretching east from the Rust Belt industrial cities of East Chicago and Gary near the Illinois border along the state's Lake Michigan shoreline. Most of the district's population lives in Lake County.

In contrast to the farming that dominates most of the state, manufacturing remains the key industry here. Gary's U.S. Steel and East Chicago's Arcelor-Mittal factories still employ thousands of workers, as do shipping interests at the lakefront ports in Lake and Porter counties. But decades of job losses in steel production and the heavy manufacturing that relies on steel have hurt overall employment. Local officials have proposed plans to generate lakefront development in East Chicago, where the number of residents below the poverty line is double the statewide average.

Health care and service industries also provide jobs, and regional tourism continues to create revenue for the state. The district has both nature-based destinations at the Indiana Dunes National Lakeshore and casinos in Hammond, East Chicago and Michigan City. Valparaiso is home to a namesake university and several satellite campuses.

In Gary, population drain has mirrored industrial decline for decades. More than 30 percent of families live below the poverty line, and many homes have been left vacant after the nationwide housing market crisis. Although the state's population is predominately white, Gary is nearly 85 percent black and nearby Hammond is home to a growing Hispanic population.

The district is a Democratic stronghold in an otherwise conservative-leaning state. Redistricting after the 2010 census shed strongly Republican counties to the south in favor of parts of Democratic-leaning LaPorte County, east of Porter. Lake gave Barack Obama his statewide best in both the 2008 and 2012 presidential elections. Many of those Democratic votes were based in historically strong unions. Porter County has also tended to support local Democratic candidates for the past decade.

Major Industry
Steel, health care, tourism

Cities
Hammond, Gary, Portage, Michigan City

Notable
Gary elected Karen Freeman-Wilson, Indiana's first black female mayor, in 2011.

Rep. Jackie Walorski (R)

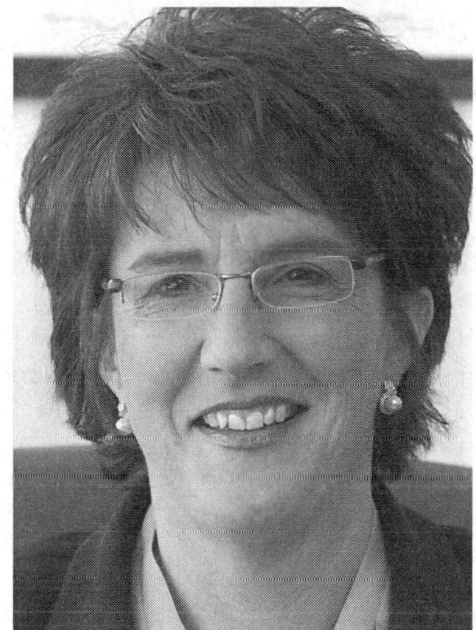

Capitol Office
225-3915
walorski.house.gov
419 Cannon Bldg. 20515-0908; fax 225-6798

Committees
Armed Services
Budget
Veterans' Affairs

Residence
Elkhart

Born
Aug. 17, 1963; South Bend, Ind.

Religion
Evangelical Christian

Family
Husband, Dean Swihart

Education
Liberty Baptist College, attended 1981-83; Taylor U., B.A. 1985 (mass communication)

Career
International humanitarian organization founder; university fundraiser; animal protection organization director; television reporter

Political Highlights
Republican nominee for St. Joseph County Board of Commissioners, 1996; Ind. House, 2005-11; Republican nominee for U.S. House, 2010

ELECTION RESULTS

2012 GENERAL		
Jackie Walorski (R)	134,033	49.0%
Brendan Mullen (D)	130,113	47.6%
Joseph Wayne Ruiz (LIBERT)	9,326	3.4%
2012 PRIMARY		
Jackie Walorski (R)	46,873	72.8%
Greg Andrews (R)	17,522	27.2%

Elected 2012; 1st term

When Walorski first ran for Congress in 2010, she said she was proud to be known as a "pit bull" in the Indiana House. Her rhetoric has softened a bit since then, but her tenacity in supporting conservative policies hasn't changed.

She clearly has the courage of her convictions. Walorski, a native of South Bend, worked as a TV reporter and a college fundraiser. But a few years after getting married in 1995, she and her husband sold most of what they owned and moved to Romania to do humanitarian and missionary work.

After she returned to Indiana, Walorski won election to the state House, where she served three terms. She is a fiscal and social conservative, and in the U.S. House she has joined the Republican Study Committee.

Walorski sits on the Budget Committee, and she heartily endorsed the fiscal 2014 spending blueprint produced by Chairman Paul D. Ryan. President Barack Obama had a question-and-answer session with House Republicans in March 2013, and Walorski, one of the seven questioners, asked him why he thought balanced budgets aren't necessary. "In the state of Indiana where I'm from, Hoosiers sit around the kitchen tables and they have to make their budgets work," she told reporters afterwards.

She's not so keen on many reductions to military spending, however. She sits on the Armed Services and Veterans' Affairs committees, and she maintains that Indiana will lose thousands of jobs if defense cuts continue.

Walorski trumpets many common GOP themes, such as the need to reduce taxes and regulation. She has expressed support for letting younger workers invest a portion of their Social Security taxes the way they choose.

In 2010, she was about 2,500 votes short of unseating Rep. Joe Donnelly, a conservative Democrat. Walorski quickly planned to run again, while Donnelly ran for the Senate. She faced Democrat Brendan Mullen, a 34-year-old Army veteran. Walorski, who was supported by the super PAC tied to GOP strategist Karl Rove, won by fewer than 4,000 votes.

Indiana 2

North central — South Bend, Elkhart

Covering north-central Indiana along the Michigan border, the 2nd District is made up of Elkhart and St. Joseph counties and a constellation of less-populated areas to the west and south. The blue-collar workforce relies on manufacturing, of both consumer and industrial products, but the spiritual and population center of the 2nd is still St. Joseph County.

The district's largest city is South Bend, the St. Joseph County seat and home to the University of Notre Dame. The college attracts a wealthy professional and academic population to the campus, but the largely minority communities on the outskirts of the city have shed residents over the last decade. Neighboring Mishawaka has experienced modest population growth, and the two cities form the economic hub of "Michiana" — the region along the Michigan border.

Elkhart's manufacturing sector remains the district's most significant industry, with the economy outside of Elkhart and St. Joseph propped up by retail and health care. The production of recreational vehicles remains important despite high unemployment rates. Although there has been growth among minority populations, the city of Elkhart has lost residents overall since 2000. The Norfolk Southern rail yard is a transportation hub. Retirement communities rank among major employers along the southern tier of counties.

During decennial remapping, the 2nd lost Democratic-leaning Kokomo — which had helped Democrats hold onto the U.S. House seat — and added the rest of strongly conservative Elkhart County, now the second-most populous county in the district. Redistricting also halved the 2nd's portion of LaPorte County, the district's most reliably liberal-leaning area. The rest of the district's counties vote strongly Republican, including the new additions of Wabash and Miami counties. With a diverse population, South Bend tends to favor liberal candidates, as does St. Joseph County overall. Overall, Mitt Romney took 56 percent of the district's vote in the 2012 presidential contest.

Major Industry
Manufacturing, higher education, health care

Cities
South Bend, Elkhart, Mishawaka, Goshen

Notable
The World Whiffleball Championship is played annually in Mishawaka.

Rep. Marlin Stutzman (R)

Capitol Office
225-4436
stutzman.house.gov
1728 Longworth Bldg. 20515-1403; fax 226-9870

Committees
Financial Services

Residence
Howe

Born
Aug. 31, 1976; Sturgis, Mich.

Religion
Baptist

Family
Wife, Christy Stutzman; two children

Education
Glen Oaks Community College, attended 1999; Tri-State U., attended 2005-07

Career
Farmer; commercial trucking company owner

Political Highlights
Ind. House, 2003-09; Ind. Senate, 2009-10

ELECTION RESULTS

2012 GENERAL		
Marlin Stutzman (R)	187,872	67.0%
Kevin R. Boyd (D)	92,363	33.0%
2012 PRIMARY		
Marlin Stutzman (R)		unopposed
2010 GENERAL		
Marlin Stutzman (R)	116,140	62.8%
Thomas Hayhurst (D)	61,267	33.1%
Scott Wise (D)	7,631	4.1%

Previous Winning Percentages
2010 Special Election (57%)

Elected 2010; 2nd full term

Stutzman is strikingly conservative, both fiscally and socially. As a farmer, he has a natural inclination to work on agriculture policy, but he gave up some clout on those issues for the chance to handle banking, housing and the rest of the financial sector.

In his second full term, Stutzman is already the most senior Indiana Republican in the House, thanks to the departure of some powerful colleagues. He told Howey Politics Indiana that the GOP delegation coordinated its committee requests for the 113th Congress (2013-14) to compensate for the losses. Todd Young ended up on the Ways and Means Committee, and Stutzman landed a seat on the Financial Services Committee.

He supports picking apart the 2010 financial regulatory overhaul known as Dodd-Frank, believing the rule-making triggered by that law has created confusion throughout the financial system: "Especially talking to bankers and insurance folks, savings and loan folks across the state, there's a lot of uncertainty," he told the Fort Wayne Journal Gazette in late 2012.

Stutzman sits on the subcommittee overseeing financial institutions and looks out for the smaller banks that farmers and small businesses in his district rely on. He shares with many Republicans the concern that small banks do not have the resources to comply with Dodd-Frank or its related regulations.

He is also on the monetary policy subcommittee, where he is worried that the Federal Reserve will trigger harmful inflation through "quantitative easing" — the practice of printing new money, then using it to buy financial instruments with the goal of keeping interest rates down. He said that a round of easing announced in 2012 could "weaken the dollar, push commodity prices higher, and put seniors on fixed incomes at risk."

Stutzman is strident about reducing the size of government. He thought the appropriations bills for fiscal 2011 and 2012 didn't do enough to cut spending, and he opposed the January 2013 law that extended lower income tax rates only for earnings under $400,000. "It's time for Washington to get serious and reform our nation's entitlements and tax structure, not just simply raise taxes that will hurt small-business owners and their employees," he wrote after the vote. He's a co-sponsor of a bill to eliminate most federal taxes and replace them with a national sales tax.

His seat on the Financial Services Committee had a price: Stutzman had to give up his seat on the Agriculture Committee. A fourth-generation farmer and former state legislator, he wants to "let the free markets work" by removing government influence in farm policy.

He worked with Republican Sen. Richard G. Lugar in 2011 on a bill meant to influence an eventual long-term reauthorization of agriculture programs. The Lugar-Stutzman bill sought to save $40 billion over a decade by ending direct payments to farmers, streamlining conservation programs and closing certain loopholes in the Supplemental Nutrition Assistance Program (which is more commonly known as food stamps).

The farm bill approved by the panel in 2012 contained some of those elements, but Stutzman voted against it in committee — he said it didn't cut SNAP spending enough. He also criticized its inclusion of programs propping up the sugar industry. "Such stringent controls and artificial barriers should be the antiquated relics of the Eastern bloc, not mainstays of U.S. policy," he wrote in a 2012 opinion piece with Lugar.

He says he would prefer a safety net for farmers built around crop insurance. But the farming operations in his family have received direct federal payments. He got into trouble during the 2010 campaign when he said he had no choice but to accept the payments — the Agriculture Department said that wasn't necessarily the case.

As a freshman, Stutzman chaired the Veterans' Affairs subcommittee on economic opportunity and sought to ease the transition for veterans returning home to find employment. He applauded the final fiscal 2013 defense authorization bill that kept A-10 fighter jets at the Indiana Air National Guard's Fort Wayne facility.

Stutzman is a member of the conservative Republican Study Committee. But he didn't join the Tea Party Caucus, opting instead for the Constitution Caucus, which he co-chairs. "The Constitution will last longer than the tea party will," he said. "I am proud to be associated with [the tea party]. At the same time, even deeper than that, I believe in the Constitution and the founding principles of this country."

A Baptist, Stutzman has traveled extensively on mission trips, including to Russia, Haiti, Guatemala and Mexico. He opposes abortion, and he voted against legislation, signed into law in late 2010, that allowed repeal of the ban on openly gay military servicemembers. He supports gun owners' rights. While in the state House, he won enactment of a 2006 law creating handgun permits that last for a lifetime.

Stutzman was elected to the Indiana House in 2002 at age 26, making him the youngest member of the legislature. He moved to the state Senate in 2009.

To make it to Congress, he ran two campaigns for three races in 2009 and 2010. He first sought to replace retiring Sen. Evan Bayh, a Democrat. He ran a respectable primary campaign against former Sen. Dan Coats and former Rep. John Hostettler, finishing second in the May 2010 election. (Coats won and is now the state's senior senator.)

Days later, Republican Rep. Mark Souder resigned after admitting to an extramarital affair. Souder had already won a primary, so party leaders had to choose his replacement on the ballot. Stutzman bested 14 other contenders — he was helped by name recognition gained from his Senate race.

Stutzman handily defeated Democrat Thomas Hayhurst, a former Fort Wayne city councilman, in November. He simultaneously won a term in the 112th Congress and the special election to finish Souder's term.

He scored another easy victory in 2012. That win, plus the departure of Dan Burton and Mike Pence (who was elected governor) made Stutzman the most senior Indiana Republican in the House — his few extra weeks of service in 2010 put him ahead of other members elected that year.

Stutzman and his wife decided to bring their two sons to Washington during the school year, in part on the advice of Pence. "Mike Pence told me, you will hug me one day when you realize having your family here will help," he said.

Key Votes

2012	
Extend a Social Security payroll tax cut and unemployment benefits	YES
Ease securities rules to expand small-business access to capital	YES
Extend for one year subsidized student loan interest rates financed by a cut in health care spending	YES
Cite Attorney General Eric H. Holder Jr. for contempt of Congress	YES
Create a visa program for foreign graduates in high-tech fields	YES
Extend most Bush-era income tax rates while allowing rates for top-bracket earners to rise (Jan. 1, 2013)	NO
2011	
Strike funding for F-35 alternative engine	NO
Prevent EPA from regulating greenhouse gas emissions to address climate change	YES
Extend certain provisions of Patriot Act for four years	YES
Declare opposition to use of ground troops in Libya	YES
Overhaul patent law	YES
Pass compromise debt limit increase plan and establish future spending limits	NO
Allow consideration of measures to implement three trade agreements	YES

CQ Vote Studies

	PARTY UNITY		PRESIDENTIAL SUPPORT	
	SUPPORT	OPPOSE	SUPPORT	OPPOSE
2012	97%	3%	13%	87%
2011	97%	3%	17%	83%
2010	100%	0%	25%	75%

Interest Groups

	AFL-CIO	ADA	CCUS	ACU
2012	11%	5%	92%	100%
2011	0%	5%	94%	100%
2010	0%		67%	100%

Indiana 3

Northeast — Fort Wayne

The 3rd District covers Indiana's northeastern corner, stretching from the Michigan border past the cities of Fort Wayne and Huntington, as far south as rural Jay County. Most of the district's population lives in Allen County within the orbit of Fort Wayne. Overall, the 3rd is more than 80 percent white and mainly middle-class.

Manufacturing remains the primary industry near Fort Wayne, with General Motors and BF Goodrich employing thousands of workers across Allen County. Growth in high-tech sectors such as telecommunications, defense and aerospace has helped insulate Fort Wayne from the industrial decline common to other Rust Belt communities. Production of orthopedic devices, especially in Warsaw, and the health care sector provide jobs in the district as well. As in the state's other northern districts, the Indiana Toll Road forms a transportation thoroughfare to Ohio and Michigan.

Fort Wayne hosts many of the district's arts venues and museums, including the Embassy Theater, where the Fort Wayne Philharmonic Orchestra plays. The city also is home to a joint regional campus of Indiana University and Purdue University.

In LaGrange County to the northwest, members of a large and well-established Amish community maintain farms and work in local factories. Shipshewana, in particular, attracts tourists to food markets and crafts sellers. Farmland and rural towns cover the area south of Allen County, where crops include soybeans, wheat and alfalfa hay, and where livestock graze.

The newly redrawn 3rd District lost Elkhart and most of Kosciusko counties and added several rural counties south of Fort Wayne. The district, a longtime Republican bastion despite union ties among blue-collar factory communities, retains its socially conservative character. All counties in the 3rd supported Republican presidential nominee Mitt Romney in 2012.

Major Industry

Manufacturing, agriculture, health care

Cities

Fort Wayne, Huntington, New Haven, Auburn

Notable

Fort Wayne hosts an annual Johnny Appleseed Festival in honor of the historical figure who planted apple orchards across Ohio and Indiana; Ligonier hosts an annual marshmallow festival — Kraft Foods produces the treats at a nearby facility.

Rep. Todd Rokita (R)

Capitol Office
225-5037
rokita.house.gov
236 Cannon Bldg. 20515-1404; fax 226-0544

Committees
Budget
Education & the Workforce
(Early Childhood, Elementary & Secondary Education - Chairman)
House Administration

Residence
Indianapolis

Born
Feb. 9, 1970; Chicago, Ill.

Religion
Roman Catholic

Family
Wife, Kathy Rokita; two children

Education
Wabash College, B.A. 1992 (political science); Indiana U., Indianapolis, J.D. 1995

Career
State government official; lawyer

Political Highlights
Ind. secretary of state, 2003-10

ELECTION RESULTS

2012 GENERAL		
Todd Rokita (R)	168,688	62.0%
Tara E. Nelson (D)	93,015	34.2%
Benjamin Gehlhausen (LIBERT)	10,565	3.9%
2012 PRIMARY		
Todd Rokita (R)		unopposed
2010 GENERAL		
Todd Rokita (R)	138,732	68.6%
David Sanders (D)	53,167	26.3%
John Duncan (LIBERT)	10,423	5.2%

Elected 2010; 2nd term

Rokita, a former Indiana secretary of state, wants to see far less federal involvement in state affairs. That underlying principle informs his desire to cut spending on health care, transportation and education — areas where the two levels of government interact.

There's a moral element to Rokita's conservatism. He espouses the belief that entitlement programs and federal involvement can undermine American values. Rokita (ro-KEE-ta) said as much at a 2012 hearing on the proposed loosening of work requirements in the welfare program.

"We always believed that work was a good thing, that as human beings we were created to do good work, to create value with our lives and value in the lives of others," he said. "What this administration is basically saying is that dignity comes, in fact, from the government, at their timing and at their pleasure and not from individuals using their God-given capacity to work."

He tries to practice what he preaches. Rokita has a pilot's license and volunteers with the Veterans Airlift Command, flying active and retired military members pro bono. "I really like this program because we're doing all of this without the federal government," he said. "This is people helping people, like our founders intended."

Rokita tried to help Republican people in 2012, by giving hundreds of thousands of dollars to GOP congressional candidates. He then stumped for a seat on the Ways and Means Committee, but that spot went to fellow Hoosier Todd Young. For the 113th Congress (2013-14), he returned to the Education and the Workforce Committee and was awarded the gavel of the Early Childhood, Elementary and Secondary Education Subcommittee.

The 112th Congress (2011-12) didn't reauthorize the 2002 education law known as No Child Left Behind, so that work is near the top of Rokita's agenda. As Republicans kicked around their version of an overhaul in 2012 (it never got a floor vote), Rokita made clear his distaste for federal involvement. The committee adopted his amendment to eliminate scores of education programs that he said were "duplicative and ineffective." More dramatic than that, Rokita worked with New Jersey Republican Scott Garrett on a proposal to allow states to opt out of federal education requirements. All federal education spending for the state would then be distributed to the state's taxpayers as a tax credit.

In April 2012, he supported an extension of federally subsidized student loan rates, but he wasn't happy about it: "My ultimate goal is to get the federal government out of the student loan business, but in the meantime, we shouldn't hold students hostage," he said.

Rokita is not terribly friendly to the preferences of organized labor. He wants mandatory waiting periods inserted into the union organizing process, and he has introduced a bill to prohibit Transportation Security Administration unions from engaging in collective bargaining. "We do not negotiate collective bargaining agreements with security personnel, and TSA clearly falls within that category," he wrote.

He has argued that some union contracts are sapping the work ethic of employees — Rokita has proposed amending the National Labor Relations Act to allow employers to award merit-based bonuses or raises beyond the ceilings set by union contracts.

Rokita also sits on the House Administration Committee, which has jurisdiction over federal elections. From 2003 to 2010 he was the top elections official for Indiana, and before that he served as deputy secretary and a general counsel to the secretary of state. Rokita oversaw implementation of Indiana's requirement that voters show photo identification at polling places, and he pushed for changes in redistricting that would have made the highly partisan practice slightly less partisan. He told The Washington Post that he also used "heavy doses of technology, furloughs, and pay cuts" to run his office at 1987 budget levels.

In 2012 he joined with Michigan Republican Candice S. Miller — another former secretary of state, who now chairs House Administration — on a bill to require motor vehicle departments to ask new state residents applying for a license if they want to register to vote in the state. If so, the new state would have to notify the state where they had been registered.

Rokita is very conservative on fiscal matters. He opposed the January 2013 "fiscal cliff" deal extending lower income tax rates for earnings under $400,000 — it did not include the spending cuts he wanted. And he wants to replace Medicaid and the Children's Health Insurance Program with block grants issued to states.

He opposed an August 2011 deficit reduction law because it didn't include "permanent and structural reform" of federal spending practices. As a member of the Budget Committee in the 112th Congress, Rokita co-wrote four bills to revamp the budget process: one to establish a biennial budgeting cycle, one to establish binding spending and deficit limits enforced by automatic spending cuts, one to restructure long-term spending plans, and one to require periodic reauthorizations of all federal programs.

Rokita was born in Chicago but grew up near Munster, Ind. He played soccer and served as student body president. He also was active on the speech and debate team — he and New York Rep. Nan Hayworth, who lost her re-election bid in 2012, shared a speech coach. Rokita graduated from Wabash College, an all-male liberal arts school, with a degree in political science. He then earned a law degree at Indiana University.

A few years into his law career, he joined the secretary of state's office as general counsel, and he eventually became deputy secretary of state. The state GOP convention selected him as the nominee for secretary of state in 2002 — he beat out Richard E. Mourdock, who went on to lose the 2012 Senate race in Indiana. Rokita was 32 when he won the office.

Rokita briefly flirted with a Senate candidacy in 2010, but when 4th District Republican Rep. Steve Buyer announced his retirement, Rokita jumped into that race. He easily won a 13-candidate primary, which essentially sealed a November victory in the Republican district.

The 4th District was significantly redrawn for the 2012 election, but it was still very Republican. His Democratic opponent, Tara E. Nelson, raised almost no money for her campaign, allowing Rokita the chance to help out other GOP candidates around the country. He won easily.

Key Votes

2012	
Extend a Social Security payroll tax cut and unemployment benefits	NO
Ease securities rules to expand small-business access to capital	YES
Extend for one year subsidized student loan interest rates financed by a cut in health care spending	YES
Cite Attorney General Eric H. Holder Jr. for contempt of Congress	YES
Create a visa program for foreign graduates in high-tech fields	YES
Extend most Bush-era income tax rates while allowing rates for top-bracket earners to rise (Jan. 1, 2013)	NO
2011	
Strike funding for F-35 alternative engine	NO
Prevent EPA from regulating greenhouse gas emissions to address climate change	YES
Extend certain provisions of Patriot Act for four years	NO
Declare opposition to use of ground troops in Libya	YES
Overhaul patent law	YES
Pass compromise debt limit increase plan and establish future spending limits	NO
Allow consideration of measures to implement three trade agreements	YES

CQ Vote Studies

	PARTY UNITY		PRESIDENTIAL SUPPORT	
	SUPPORT	OPPOSE	SUPPORT	OPPOSE
2012	98%	2%	15%	85%
2011	97%	3%	17%	83%

Interest Groups

	AFL-CIO	ADA	CCUS	ACU
2012	10%	0%	92%	100%
2011	0%	5%	94%	95%

Indiana 4

West central — Kokomo, Indianapolis suburbs

The 4th District was radically redrawn after the 2010 census — more than half of its new area was poached from parts of neighboring districts. Now concentrated in a compact block of west-central Indiana, the district includes a mix of rural farmland, manufacturing communities and midsize cities. Overall, the district has a large agricultural presence and is home to some of the state's highest-producing corn and soybean fields.

Bordering Illinois, the new 4th stretches from farms in Jasper and Newton counties through Lafayette and West Lafayette, and it extends as far east as Kokomo and as far southeast as the suburbs of Indianapolis. The largest population center is in the twin cities of Lafayette and West Lafayette. The Lafayette area revolves around Purdue University but also has a base in manufacturing that has been muddling through the downturn of recent years. Among indications of recovery, Alcoa Inc. is expanding with a new $90 million aluminum plant in Lafayette.

Kokomo, the district's second-largest city, is an auto manufacturing town that has rebounded in the years since the sector bottomed out nationally. Chrysler employs about 5,000 workers at four auto plants in the city; Delphi Electronics has a factory for hybrid car technology. Smaller communities here have suffered typical Rust Belt decline. Bonnell Aluminum, once one of Newton County's major employers, closed its plant there in 2012.

Like most of Indiana, the 4th District has a strongly conservative profile, with the vast majority of its rural and small-town counties comprising Republican strongholds. Likewise, highly populated Hendricks County, including the more affluent western suburbs of Indianapolis, gave Mitt Romney a better than 2-to-1 margin in the 2012 presidential election. Still, there are areas where Democrats are competitive. Kokomo, home to autoworkers, supports Democrats.

Major Industry
Manufacturing, agriculture, higher education, retail

Cities
Lafayette, Kokomo, West Lafayette, Plainfield, Brownsburg

Notable
Then-governor, and later president, William Henry Harrison led troops against an American Indian force at Tippecanoe in 1811.

Rep. Susan W. Brooks (R)

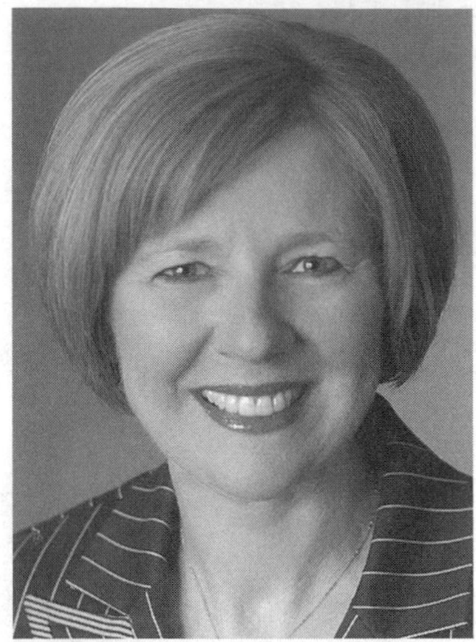

Capitol Office
225-2276
susanwbrooks.house.gov
1505 Longworth Bldg. 20515-1405; fax 225-0016

Committees
Education & the Workforce
Ethics
Homeland Security
(Emergency Preparedness, Response & Communications - Chairwoman)

Residence
Carmel

Born
Aug. 25, 1960; Auburn, Ind.

Religion
Roman Catholic

Family
Husband, David M. Brooks; two children

Education
Miami U. (Ohio), B.A. 1982 (political science & sociology); Indiana U., Indianapolis, J.D. 1985

Career
Community college administrator; lawyer

Political Highlights
Deputy mayor of Indianapolis, 1998-99; U.S. attorney, 2001-07

ELECTION RESULTS

2012 GENERAL		
Susan W. Brooks (R)	194,570	58.4%
Scott Reske (D)	125,347	37.6%
Richard Reid (LIBERT)	13,442	4.0%
2012 PRIMARY		
Susan W. Brooks (R)	31,185	30.0%
David M. McIntosh (R)	30,175	29.0%
John P. McGoff (R)	23,773	22.8%
Wayne Seybold (R)	11,874	11.4%
John R. "Jack" Lugar (R)	4,758	4.6%

Elected 2012; 1st term

Republicans seem to be using Brooks' freshman term as an audition for a bigger role. She is a polished communicator on education and homeland security, and she has management experience that could make her an effective part of the GOP political team.

Brooks spent many years as a lawyer specializing in criminal defense and government services. She helped coordinate public safety and emergency response services as an appointed deputy mayor of Indianapolis. Starting in 2001, she broadened her law enforcement experience as the U.S. attorney for the Southern District of Indiana. On leaving that job, Brooks became a vice president at Indiana's largest public post-secondary educational institution, Ivy Tech Community College.

Her committees provide her opportunities to maximize the use of her professional past. As a member of the Education and the Workforce Committee, Brooks approved of a Republican bill to overhaul and streamline worker-training programs that the House passed in March 2013; it included her provision to allow states to implement pay-for-performance strategies for trainers.

On the Homeland Security Committee, Brooks chairs the panel overseeing emergency response and preparedness programs — another venue to show off her policy expertise. She also has a seat on the Ethics Committee, which is a labor-intensive panel; service there is generally seen as a way to curry favor with party leaders. Brooks belongs to both the conservative Republican Study Committee and the moderate Main Street Partnership.

When Brooks announced her campaign in 2011, she was anticipating a battle with 15-term Rep. Dan Burton, who had endured highly competitive Republican primaries in 2008 and 2010. Burton announced his retirement in early 2012, however. In an eight-way race, Brooks came out 1,010 votes ahead of conservative former Rep. David M. McIntosh. The primary was the hard part — she easily defeated Democrat Scott Reske in November.

Indiana 5

Central — part of Indianapolis and suburbs, Anderson

Dominated by Indianapolis suburbs, the 5th was redrawn into a more compact shape after the 2010 census. The district stretches from the northern areas of the state capital through Hamilton County — the fastest-growing, wealthiest and best-educated county in Indiana — to include all of Madison, Tipton and Grant counties. Part of Boone County and most of Blackford County were added to the 5th during decennial remapping, and the district now takes in only the area east of Kokomo (in the 4th) in Howard County. Overall, the 5th boasts the highest household median income among districts statewide, at more than $58,000.

The district owes much of its relative prosperity to Hamilton's fast-growing population centers of Carmel and Fishers, which are separated by the White River. The cities have a predominately white-collar commuter workforce. Insurance and financial services are major industries in both cities, and Fishers boasts several medical technology firms and is home to an Indiana University medical complex that opened in late 2011. Hamilton County's minority populations, although smaller than those in Indianapolis' Marion County, have grown significantly since 2000.

To the north and east, most areas are losing population, and an economy once dominated by factories now relies on retail centers. Anderson, the Madison County seat, has been particularly hard-hit by population and manufacturing declines and local officials focus on redevelopment of blighted neighborhoods. A Nestlé foods plant now provides some jobs, and local technical colleges provide worker-retraining programs. The new Hoosier Park Racing and Casino has managed to lure visitors from the greater Indianapolis area.

Hamilton County is the state's and the district's most populous Republican stronghold, where suburban professionals have for decades given GOP presidential candidates wide margins of victory; Mitt Romney took 66 percent of the vote there in 2012. But Madison County did give home state Rep. Joe Donnelly 52 percent in his successful bid for U.S. Senate that same year.

Major Industry
Financial services, retail, health care

Cities
Carmel, Fishers, Lawrence, Anderson

Notable
Fairmount hosts an annual James Dean Festival to honor its beloved rebel without a cause.

Rep. Luke Messer (R)

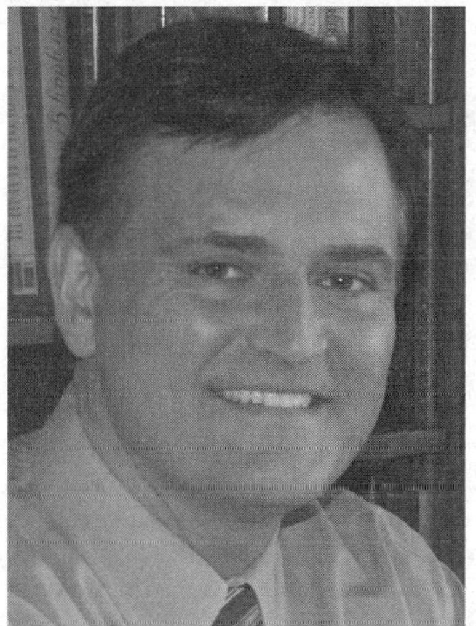

Capitol Office
225-3021
messer.house.gov
508 Cannon Bldg. 20515-2210; fax 225-3382

Committees
Budget
Education & the Workforce
Foreign Affairs

Residence
Shelbyville

Born
Feb. 27, 1969; Evansville, Ind.

Religion
Presbyterian

Family
Wife, Jennifer Messer; three children

Education
Wabash College, B.A. 1991 (speech); Vanderbilt U., J.D. 1994

Career
Education nonprofit president; lobbyist; lawyer; state party executive director; political consultant; congressional aide; campaign aide

Political Highlights
Sought Republican nomination for U.S. House, 2000; Ind. House, 2003-06; sought Republican nomination for U.S. House, 2010

ELECTION RESULTS

2012 GENERAL		
Luke Messer (R)	162,613	59.1%
Bradley T. Bookout (D)	96,678	35.1%
Rex Bell (LIBERT)	15,962	5.8%
2012 PRIMARY		
Luke Messer (R)	32,859	39.4%
Travis Hankins (R)	23,276	27.9%
Don Bates Jr. (R)	10,913	13.1%
William G. Frazier (R)	8,446	10.1%
Joe Sizemore (R)	2,346	2.8%
George Thomas Holland (R)	2,059	2.5%
Allen K. Smith II (R)	1,679	2.0%
Joseph S. Van Wye Sr. (R)	989	1.2%
John Hatter (R)	917	1.1%

Elected 2012; 1st term

Messer has participated in politics as a candidate, a congressional aide, a state legislator, a lobbyist and a functionary for the Indiana Republican Party. The breadth of his experience landed him a leadership role — freshman Republicans elected him their class president — and allowed him to find his place quickly in discussions of federal budgeting and education policy.

His earlier jobs as a committee and staff aide on Capitol Hill were in the 1990s; one former boss, John J. Duncan Jr. of Tennessee, is still in the House. Messer first sought an open House seat in 2000 — Republican Mike Pence won — then became the executive director of the state party. He won election to the state House to replace a lawmaker who died in office.

Messer made his mark despite serving less than two terms. He was the author of an aggressive law meant to shrink the dropout rate at Indiana's high schools; it received national attention. He now has a seat on the Education and the Workforce Committee.

He also participated as the state closed a $600 million budget hole and shrank its government workforce. Messer, a member of the Republican Study Committee, sits on the Budget Committee. In March 2013, the House passed his first bill, which requires future White House budgets to include estimates of the per-taxpayer cost of federal deficits. "Our government does not tax too little," he wrote that month. "It spends too much."

Messer was raised by a single mother who worked for Delta Faucet. He went to the all-male Wabash College, graduating one year before fellow GOP Rep. Todd Rokita. He is a social conservative and co-founded a nonprofit group trying to increase the involvement of faith-based organizations in foster care.

Messer challenged GOP Rep. Dan Burton in the 5th District in 2010, finishing a close second in the primary. The congressional map for 2012 put Messer in the 6th District, where Pence was stepping aside to run for governor. He outclassed eight competitors in the primary and won easily in November.

Indiana 6

Southeast — Muncie

The 6th District has a heartland feel in a Rust Belt region, featuring rural farmland punctuated by manufacturing communities. Redistricting following the 2010 census shifted the 6th into the state's southeastern corner, sweeping from eastern Indianapolis suburbs northeast to Muncie and south to the Ohio River. Corn and soybean fields fill out the rolling hills of the rural counties, where livestock farms dot the landscape.

Muncie, the Delaware County seat and the district's largest city, had been fueled by a now declining manufacturing industry. Steel, auto and turbine parts production, including a Honda plant in Decatur County in Greensburg, remain important to the regional economy even as light manufacturing firms shed jobs. Ball State University and Ball Memorial Hospital help shore up Muncie's economy; home prices, though improving, remain low.

Columbus is a more well-to-do enclave where many residents work at the headquarters of engine parts manufacturers. The city is known for its world-class modernist architecture, with more than 70 buildings and works of art by internationally renowned architects and artists, six of which are listed as national historic landmarks. To the northwest of Columbus is the bulk of a sprawling National Guard training facility.

The district is more than 90 percent white, but Hispanic and black populations have been growing for a decade, especially in the suburbs east of Indianapolis, as well as those near Louisville, Ky., and Cincinnati, Ohio, where the hospitality industry is a top employer.

Those southeast border suburbs, which are new to the redrawn 6th, added some Democratic voters to areas outside of liberal outpost Delaware County, but conservatives remain the dominant force in the region. All but Delaware of the 19 counties wholly or partially in the district preferred GOP presidential candidates John McCain, in the 2008 election, and Mitt Romney, in 2012. But six counties here, mainly at the southern and northern edges, supported Democratic Rep. Joe Donnelly in his successful bid for U.S. Senate in 2012.

Major Industry
Manufacturing, agriculture

Cities
Muncie, Columbus, Richmond, Greenfield

Notable
At 1,257 feet, Hoosier Hill in Wayne County is the state's highest point; The Indiana Basketball Hall of Fame is in New Castle.

Rep. André Carson (D)

Capitol Office
225-4011
carson.house.gov
2453 Rayburn Bldg. 20515-1407; fax 225-5633

Committees
Armed Services
Transportation & Infrastructure

Residence
Indianapolis

Born
Oct. 16, 1974; Indianapolis, Ind.

Religion
Muslim

Family
Wife, Mariama Shaheed-Carson; one child

Education
Concordia U. Wisconsin, Indianapolis, B.A. 2003 (management of criminal justice); Indiana Wesleyan U., M.S. 2005 (management)

Career
Marketing representative; state investigative agency officer

Political Highlights
Indianapolis and Marion County City-County Council, 2007-08

ELECTION RESULTS

2012 GENERAL		
André Carson (D)	162,122	62.8%
Carlos A. May (R)	95,828	37.2%
2012 PRIMARY		
André Carson (D)	34,782	90.3%
Bob Kern (D)	2,048	5.3%
Woodrow Wilcox (D)	1,082	2.8%
Pierre Quincy Pullins (D)	586	1.5%
2010 GENERAL		
André Carson (D)	86,011	58.9%
Marvin B. Scott (R)	55,213	37.8%
Dav Wilson (LIBERT)	4,815	3.3%

Previous Winning Percentages
2008 (65%); 2008 Special Election (54%)

Elected 2008; 3rd full term

For Carson, poverty is both an economic puzzle and the backdrop to his early life. "That experience never left me," he says. "It contributes to my job, and to my fears." He can be both populist and progressive while looking to assist the poor and working-class people of Indianapolis and elsewhere.

Carson's mother earned graduate degrees, but she also struggled with serious mental-health issues. He was a toddler when they moved into a homeless shelter. Carson soon went to live with his maternal grandmother, Julia Carson — a trailblazing African-American state legislator who eventually served in the U.S. House.

Tagging along with his grandmother exposed him to politics. He remembers attending the 1984 Democratic National Convention in San Francisco, months shy of his 10th birthday. After the convention, he knocked on doors in Indiana to register voters and recruit volunteers. In high school, he collected signatures to bring the first black-history class to his school.

The issues Carson watched his grandmother handle during the 1980s — education, child nutrition, national security, poverty and unemployment — are what he focuses on now. They "began to settle into my spirit," he said. He belongs to the Congressional Progressive Caucus, the group of the most liberal House members.

Carson has new panel assignments in the 113th Congress (2013-14). He joined the Armed Services Committee, which he touted as a place to advocate on behalf of military personnel. The fiscal 2012 defense policy law included his provision to expand military counseling programs to include financial planning. "Typically when someone is in the military," Carson said, "they get three square meals a day. They are younger. Their housing is provided. So once they get back into society, they don't have the financial skills to make good financial decisions." Another Carson provision in the law strengthens the mental-health assessments used by the military in making deployment decisions.

He also has a seat on the Transportation and Infrastructure Committee, which he describes as a good venue for promoting job creation.

But so far, committee work hasn't been that integral to Carson's career. He had a relatively low profile on the Financial Services Committee in the 111th and 112th Congresses (2009-12).

He does take an interest in consumer advocacy, and he supports the Consumer Financial Protection Bureau created by the 2010 financial regulatory overhaul. Carson and other members of the Congressional Black Caucus worked to include funding for foreclosure prevention programs in the law. Financial literacy programs are another major interest. He has proposed a grant program to fund "centers of excellence" coordinating financial education for teenagers and young adults.

Carson was raised Baptist, served as an altar boy at Catholic school and converted to Islam in the 1990s. He is one of two Muslims in Congress, and he hasn't shied from that distinction. Carson was criticized for remarks at a 2012 conference of the Islamic Circle of North America.

"America will never tap into educational innovation and ingenuity without looking at the model that we have in our madrassas, in our schools, where innovation is encouraged, where the foundation is the Quran," Carson said at the conference. He defended the comments as part of a broader thesis: that faith-based educational institutions can provide a working model for public schools. Smaller class sizes, innovative teaching methods and financial efficiency contribute to the quality of faith-based education, he said.

And Carson has spoken to New York lawmakers in regards to the New York

City Muslim community and its concerns about police spying. "I have to be a spokesperson for those who have no voice," he said.

Carson supported the 2010 health care overhaul, even though he wanted the law to include a government-run insurance plan to compete with private companies — against the wishes of WellPoint Inc., a huge insurer, and drug-maker Eli Lilly and Co., both of which have headquarters in Indianapolis. When the House voted in early 2011 to repeal the law, Carson called it "political theater at a time when the American people want progress."

Carson is no stranger to political theater, however. As the whip for the Congressional Black Caucus, he helped organize a Democratic walkout during a 2012 vote to hold Attorney General Eric H. Holder Jr. in contempt of Congress for refusing to provide documents in an investigation of a gun-trafficking operation. Republicans "have recklessly moved forward with this resolution for political gain alone," he wrote.

In August 2011, he caused a stir speaking at a Black Caucus event in Florida: "Some of these folks in Congress right now would love to see us as second-class citizens," he said. "Some of them in Congress right now with this tea party movement would love to see you and me ... hanging on a tree."

As a young man, Carson turned to poetry, music and break dancing to escape the crack-cocaine culture sweeping across his Indianapolis neighborhood. He performed at local variety shows, rapping under the stage name Juggernaut, with dreams of becoming a professional singer after graduating from Arsenal Technical High School.

When his musical career didn't result in a major record deal, Carson returned to school to study criminal justice. He worked as a state excise officer, enforcing alcohol, tobacco and gambling laws. Carson graduated from the Indianapolis center of Concordia University Wisconsin in 2003. Three years later, he was named a liaison to the state's homeland security agency, working on such concerns as supremacist groups and terrorism threats.

His political career began in late 2007, when he was chosen to fill an open seat on the Indianapolis and Marion County City-County Council. Less than seven months later, he ran to succeed his grandmother. She had died of lung cancer in December 2007, halfway through her sixth term in the U.S. House.

Carson spent the first few months of 2008 campaigning against Republican state Rep. Jon Elrod, whom he beat by 11 points in a March special election.

The Democratic primary for a full term in the 111th Congress was less than two months later. Carson benefited from his popular last name and an endorsement from presidential candidate Barack Obama and took 47 percent of the vote — nearly double that of any challenger. He crushed a little-known Republican that November and hasn't been seriously challenged since then.

Key Votes

2012

Extend a Social Security payroll tax cut and unemployment benefits	YES
Ease securities rules to expand small-business access to capital	YES
Extend for one year subsidized student loan interest rates financed by a cut in health care spending	NO
Cite Attorney General Eric H. Holder Jr. for contempt of Congress	?
Create a visa program for foreign graduates in high-tech fields	NO
Extend most Bush-era income tax rates while allowing rates for top-bracket earners to rise (Jan. 1, 2013)	YES

2011

Strike funding for F-35 alternative engine	NO
Prevent EPA from regulating greenhouse gas emissions to address climate change	NO
Extend certain provisions of Patriot Act for four years	NO
Declare opposition to use of ground troops in Libya	NO
Overhaul patent law	YES
Pass compromise debt limit increase plan and establish future spending limits	NO
Allow consideration of measures to implement three trade agreements	NO

CQ Vote Studies

	PARTY UNITY		PRESIDENTIAL SUPPORT	
	SUPPORT	OPPOSE	SUPPORT	OPPOSE
2012	94%	6%	88%	12%
2011	94%	6%	84%	16%
2010	99%	1%	93%	8%
2009	99%	1%	97%	3%
2008	99%	1%	12%	88%

Interest Groups

	AFL-CIO	ADA	CCUS	ACU
2012	90%	90%	27%	4%
2011	100%	90%	19%	4%
2010	100%	90%	25%	0%
2009	100%	100%	33%	0%
2008	100%	75%	53%	4%

Indiana 7

Most of Indianapolis

Indianapolis dominates the 7th, Indiana's smallest district in size and entirely confined within Marion County. Although central areas of the city have shed residents over the last decade, the state capital contains more than three times the population of Fort Wayne, the state's second-most populous city. The 7th has the state's most racially diverse population.

Known as Indy by the locals, the capital city has a workforce largely made up of white-collar professionals and state government employees. Health care fields — medical device manufacturing and pharmaceuticals — drive the economy here. Drug maker Eli Lilly & Co. has long been a mainstay of the Indianapolis economy and its largest employer. Aircraft engine-maker Rolls-Royce recently opened a large downtown campus. Insurance and financial services round out the city's diverse economy.

The city also boasts several higher education institutions, the largest of which is the joint campus of Indiana University-Purdue University Indianapolis. Cultural attractions in the district include the Children's Museum of Indianapolis and the Indianapolis Symphony Orchestra at Monument Circle. The city continues redevelopment efforts, particularly in the Fountain Square area. Preparations for the 2012 Super Bowl included hundreds of millions of dollars in infrastructure renewal as well as a new community center in the poverty- and crime-ridden Near Eastside neighborhood.

Despite support for the state's major professional teams — football's Colts and basketball's Pacers and Fever — the 7th's biggest pro sport is auto racing. The Indianapolis Motor Speedway, one of the world's largest spectator sporting facilities, has hosted the annual Indianapolis 500 race for more than a century.

Well-educated young couples and large minority populations combine to create a strong Democratic base in the 7th. While the urban center remains the driver of the district's politics, Franklin Township in the county's southeast corner trends Republican at the local level.

Major Industry
Pharmaceuticals, higher education, state government, tourism

Cities
Indianapolis, Lawrence, Beech Grove

Notable
Indianapolis is home to the national headquarters of The American Legion, the largest veterans' organization in the world.

Rep. Larry Bucshon (R)

Capitol Office
225-4636
bucshon.house.gov
1005 Longworth Bldg. 20515-1408; fax 225-3284

Committees
Education & the Workforce
Science, Space & Technology
(Research - Chairman)
Transportation & Infrastructure

Residence
Newburgh

Born
May 31, 1962; Taylorville, Ill.

Religion
Lutheran

Family
Wife, Kathryn Bucshon; four children

Education
U. of Illinois, B.S. 1984 (chemistry); U. of Illinois, Chicago, M.D. 1988

Military
Naval Reserve, 1989-98

Career
Surgeon

Political Highlights
No previous office

ELECTION RESULTS

2012 GENERAL		
Larry Bucshon (R)	151,533	53.4%
Dave Crooks (D)	122,325	43.1%
Bart Gadau (LIBERT)	10,134	3.6%
2012 PRIMARY		
Larry Bucshon (R)	34,511	58.0%
Kristi Risk (R)	24,960	42.0%
2010 GENERAL		
Larry Bucshon (R)	117,259	57.5%
Trent Van Haaften (D)	76,265	37.4%
John Cunningham (LIBERT)	10,240	5.0%

Elected 2010; 2nd term

Bucshon, a doctor with blue-collar roots, sees shifts in America's culture as contributing to the problems before Congress. He wants people "to get back to taking personal responsibility for their own lives." He values private sector perspectives on government policy and applies his experience as a heart surgeon in discussions on health care.

Bucshon (boo-SHON) is relatively new to government, having held no political office before entering the House in 2011. He says he ran for Congress in part because he wanted more health care professionals on Capitol Hill.

He dislikes much of the 2010 health care law, sharing a common Republican belief that changes to the health care sector should be based on free-market principles, not increased government activity.

He's skeptical that the expansion of insurance coverage in the law will necessarily improve people's health. There is "this assumption that because you have health insurance coverage, all of a sudden you have miraculously developed personal responsibility for your actions," he said at a 2012 hearing. "I've had patients with the best insurance that money can buy, and they take no care of themselves at all."

For the 113th Congress (2013-14), Bucshon continues to address health care from both the Education and the Workforce Committee and the Science, Space and Technology Committee.

Science Chairman Lamar Smith of Texas pointed to Bucshon's medical background when naming him to lead the Research Subcommittee in the 113th. That panel oversees, among other things, university-based programs and health research. Bucshon has a large military research facility to look after — the Naval Surface Warfare Center, Crane Division, is in the 8th District.

Bucshon's first bill in 2011 was to require the Federal Register to publish the scientific studies used in the preparation of proposed federal rules — a nod to the Republican accusation that the Obama administration often regulates based on political ideology. He successfully added a version of his measure to a 2012 bill meant to stop or ease various regulations affecting the coal industry. It passed the House but did not move in the Senate.

On the Education and the Workforce Committee, Bucshon works on health care as it affects employers. He says he wants to expand the use of health savings accounts, and to allow groups of small businesses to pool their employees "so that they can create large buying groups to compete for health insurance." He wants to allow the purchase of health insurance across state lines to foster more competition.

Bucshon lists at least two other ways he'd like to drive down health costs: changes to medical malpractice laws, and increasing price transparency. "If I tell you, 'Go down the street and buy a Chevy,' you kind of in your mind have an idea of how much that is going to cost you, based on your experience," he said. "But if I told you that you needed an open-heart surgery, how much that is going to cost you? You actually have no idea."

Regarding labor issues, Bucshon says he can relate to blue-collar workers. "My dad was a United Mine Worker," he said. "He was a union coal miner for 37 years. I understand that perspective." In the 112th Congress (2011-12), however, Bucshon was suspicious that the National Labor Relations Board was actively favoring unions over employers.

"The appointees of this administration are overreaching," he said in 2011. "In that respect, I'll push back."

Bucshon also has a seat on the Transportation and Infrastructure Committee. He was on the conference committee that finalized a two-year extension of surface transportation programs in 2012. He pushed for changes to the formula for distributions from the Highway Trust Fund, wanting Indiana to get back more of the money that it contributes to the fund in taxes. The rate of return went from 92 percent to 97 percent.

"These funding formulas still aren't perfect, and we have additional work to do," he reported to the Indiana Legislature. Bucshon touted the measure as providing more funds for the extension of Interstate 69 in his state — when completed, it will connect Evansville, on the southern border, to Indianapolis, in the middle of the state.

A member of the conservative Republican Study Committee, Bucshon takes a limited-government, less-taxation approach to most issues. He joined many conservatives in opposing the fiscal 2012 appropriations bills, which were seen as too big. He also opposed the January 2013 measure extending lower income tax rates only for earnings under $400,000. That change should have been accompanied with substantial spending cuts, Bucshon said.

Bucshon was raised in Kincaid, a coal-mining town in central Illinois. While his dad, a former Navy serviceman, worked in the mines, his mother was a nurse. He told the Evansville Courier and Press that she would take him to the hospital, where he "would talk to the doctors and observe surgeries." His family was strongly Democratic, but Bucshon has said that Ronald Reagan's 1980 campaign helped bring him to the Republican Party.

He received his bachelor's and medical degrees at University of Illinois campuses. Bucshon did his residency in Milwaukee, and while there he joined the Naval Reserve. He served until 1998, leaving with the rank of lieutenant commander. Bucshon eventually ended up working as a surgeon in Evansville and became president of a cardiovascular surgery practice in 2003.

By the time Democratic Rep. Brad Ellsworth announced in February 2010 that he was running for the Senate, Bucshon was already in the House race. He won an eight-way primary with almost 33 percent of the vote, then had little trouble topping Democratic state Rep. Trent Van Haaften.

For the 2012 primary, Bucshon squared off with Kristi Risk, who had finished second in the 2010 primary. Risk tried to promote herself as being the more conservative candidate, but Bucshon won 58 percent of the vote.

The 8th District has lots of manufacturing interests and a few college towns, but socially it remains conservative. Bucshon beat Democratic former state Rep. Dave Crooks in the general election with 53 percent of the vote.

Along with politics, Bucshon picked up another hobby later in life: hockey. He plays in a charity congressional hockey game held each year.

"I didn't begin playing hockey until I was 40, and it has been a great way to stay healthy," he said.

Key Votes

2012	
Extend a Social Security payroll tax cut and unemployment benefits	YES
Ease securities rules to expand small-business access to capital	YES
Extend for one year subsidized student loan interest rates financed by a cut in health care spending	YES
Cite Attorney General Eric H. Holder Jr. for contempt of Congress	YES
Create a visa program for foreign graduates in high-tech fields	YES
Extend most Bush-era income tax rates while allowing rates for top-bracket earners to rise (Jan. 1, 2013)	NO
2011	
Strike funding for F-35 alternative engine	NO
Prevent EPA from regulating greenhouse gas emissions to address climate change	YES
Extend certain provisions of Patriot Act for four years	YES
Declare opposition to use of ground troops in Libya	YES
Overhaul patent law	YES
Pass compromise debt limit increase plan and establish future spending limits	YES
Allow consideration of measures to implement three trade agreements	YES

CQ Vote Studies

	Party Unity		Presidential Support	
	Support	Oppose	Support	Oppose
2012	95%	5%	15%	85%
2011	96%	4%	22%	78%

Interest Groups

	AFL-CIO	ADA	CCUS	ACU
2012	14%	0%	100%	88%
2011	3%	10%	100%	84%

Indiana 8

Soutwest — Evansville, Terre Haute

Covering Indiana's southwestern corner, the 8th District is anchored by Evansville, the third-largest city in the state and the industrial and commercial hub of the tri-state region. The district borders Illinois and the Wabash River to the west, with Kentucky and the Ohio River to the south, stretching north through parts of the Wabash Valley to Terre Haute. To the southeast, the 8th includes a sizable chunk of the Hoosier National Forest.

Manufacturing remains the district's largest job base, with factories and port activity in Evansville and manufacturing near Terre Haute farther north. Local officials in Evansville have lured new investment to the area after some major employers cut jobs or moved operations elsewhere during recent economic downturns. Expansion of an interstate between Evansville and the Crane weapons base is part of a project to link the southeastern part of the state to the capital. Evansville has also tried to stimulate tourism to sites like a World War II-era warship and Bosse Field, where "A League of Their Own" was filmed. Rural counties in the Wabash Valley grow corn, soybeans, wheat and fruits and vegetables.

Like much of Indiana, the 8th is overwhelmingly white. This largely lower-middle-class district has a strong socially conservative bent, although the major education hubs of Indiana State University in Terre Haute and the University of Southern Indiana in Evansville offer pockets of liberal support. Moderately competitive at the congressional level, the U.S. House seat changed party hands twice in the 2000s. In the 2012 presidential race, Republican Mitt Romney took 58 percent of the district's vote. During remapping after the 2010 census, the 8th gained areas to the southeast: Democratic Perry County and Republican Spencer, Dubois and part of rural Crawford counties.

Major Industry
Manufacturing, agriculture, higher education

Military Bases
Naval Surface Warfare Center, Crane Division, 20 military, 3,000 civilian

Cities
Evansville, Terre Haute, Vincennes

Notable
Vincennes is the oldest city in Indiana; as determined by the census, the median center of the U.S. population is about 40 miles north of Evansville.

Rep. Todd Young (R)

Capitol Office
225-5315
toddyoung.house.gov
1007 Longworth Bldg. 20515-1409; fax 226-6866

Committees
Ways & Means

Residence
Bloomington

Born
Aug. 24, 1972; Lancaster, Pa.

Religion
Christian

Family
Wife, Jennifer Young; four children

Education
U.S. Naval Academy, B.S. 1995 (political science); U. of London, M.A. 2001 (United States studies); U. of Chicago, M.B.A. 2002; Indiana U., Indianapolis, J.D. 2006

Military
Marine Corps, 1995-2000

Career
Lawyer; congressional aide; conservative think tank aide

Political Highlights
No previous office

ELECTION RESULTS

2012 GENERAL		
Todd Young (R)	165,332	55.4%
Shelli Yoder (D)	132,848	44.6%
2012 PRIMARY		
Todd Young (R)		unopposed
2010 GENERAL		
Todd Young (R)	118,040	52.3%
Baron P. Hill (D)	95,353	42.3%
Greg Knott (LIBERT)	12,070	5.4%

Elected 2010; 2nd term

Young hopes to operate like his old boss and fellow Hoosier, former Sen. Richard G. Lugar: "I aspire to be a statesman," he says. His biggest policy interests are "kitchen table" economic matters affecting every household, and Republicans have granted him a seat on the Ways and Means Committee to deal with them.

He calls himself a "libertarian conservative," and he is on board with plans for cutting spending, streamlining the tax code and reducing federal regulation. Young, a former Marine, "looks over the horizon, at the big issues," he says. In that sense, he is similar to another youthful and detail-oriented Ways and Means member, Wisconsin Republican Paul D. Ryan.

As a member of the Budget Committee in the 112th Congress (2011-12), Young championed the fiscal blueprints prepared by Ryan, the Budget chairman. He applauded their proposed changes to entitlement programs, which included shifting Medicare to a "premium support" model for people under a certain age.

The overall plans were reasonable ways to begin controlling government deficits, according to Young. "We figured out how to do it ... in a gradual and very humane way," he said. The fiscal 2014 budget produced by Ryan got a similar review from Young.

Young supported a number of compromise spending and deficit reduction measures in the 112th Congress, but he couldn't bring himself to vote for a January 2013 deal to extend lower income tax rates only for earnings under $400,000. Young and other conservatives wanted spending reductions and entitlement program changes included in the deal. "The continued refusal to seriously address our largest and most unsustainable programs of government could likely result in further credit rating downgrades, interest rate increases, business failures and job losses," he wrote.

He supports adding a balanced-budget amendment to the Constitution and as a freshman helped prepare a package of proposed changes to the budgeting process. He likes the idea of biennial budgeting and also eliminating inflation adjustments from the budget. Young doesn't want Congress to claim credit for a spending cut after simply eliminating a program's inflationary increase.

In his quest to restrain government, Young has had one cause dropped in his lap. Kentucky Republican Geoff Davis was the longtime sponsor of a bill to require congressional approval of all federal regulations with an annual economic impact exceeding $100 million. The 2011 version accumulated more than 200 co-sponsors. Before resigning from the 112th Congress, Davis anointed Young as the new lead sponsor, calling him one of the "hardest-working and most diligent new members of Congress."

Born in Pennsylvania, Young grew up in Carmel, Ind. Weeks after his high school graduation, he signed up for the Naval Academy's prep school, which led to his eventual enrollment at Annapolis. He played soccer there and has used the sport as an analogy for politics. "The most interesting action occurs far away from the ball," he said. "The most interesting action is not what you're reading in the newspaper; it's certainly not always as a result of the people behind the podiums. It's the players behind the scenes, whether it's staff or quiet members."

He graduated from the Naval Academy in 1995 and was commissioned into the Marine Corps, serving until 2000. Young now takes a particular interest in the Pentagon's spending practices. As a freshman, he sat on the Armed Services Committee and its Defense Financial Management and Auditability

Reform Panel. His goal was to "ensure that every dollar we spend on anything gives us the most bang for the buck," he said. He wants to keep the Defense Department on track for its goal of being audit-ready in 2014.

Young also wants to see contingency plans for the armed forces that account for future spending reductions. "We don't know which strategy changes will be required, and presumably you're the strategic thinkers of our military," he told Pentagon officials at a September 2012 hearing. He said that the lack of such plans "seems most irresponsible."

Young was less harsh than some critics of the Obama administration with regard to the military withdrawal from Iraq; he said internal Iraqi politics may have greatly hampered the negotiations to keep U.S. forces in the country. He did join many Republicans in worrying about Iranian influence in the region. In 2011, he questioned the decision to use U.S. forces in Libya, wanting an explanation of U.S. objectives from the Obama administration.

In 2001, Young briefly attended the University of London, studying U.S. economic theories. He eventually got an MBA from the University of Chicago and a law degree from Indiana University. Young now represents Bloomington, which is the home of Indiana University's flagship campus.

Young worked at the Heritage Foundation, a conservative think tank, for a year. He then served as an energy and economic policy aide for Lugar. He jokes that the Senate is a little quieter than the House.

"It's not as raucous at times as things are over here, and therefore, it's not as fun," he said.

From 2007 until arriving in Congress, he was an attorney at a law firm started by his wife's great-grandfather. He described the work as being a "country lawyer" with a range of business and municipal clients.

In 2010, Democrat Baron P. Hill sought a sixth term in Congress. Although known as a centrist, Hill had cast a number of votes in support of Obama's economic initiatives. Those votes made him a prime GOP target.

Young narrowly won the four-candidate GOP primary, thereby ending a streak of four consecutive general-election contests between Hill and former Republican Rep. Mike Sodrel.

The general election proved to be a battle, and it included a Young advertisement featuring a nationally noted incident in which Hill scolded a college student who was trying to shoot a video during a town hall event. Young prevailed by 10 points.

After decennial redistricting for the 2012 election, the 9th District had a lot of territory new to Young, but it was still fairly conservative. Young was unopposed in his primary and took 55 percent of the vote against Democrat Shelli Yoder, a former Miss Indiana who had worked for a number of nonprofits.

Key Votes

2012	
Extend a Social Security payroll tax cut and unemployment benefits	YES
Ease securities rules to expand small-business access to capital	YES
Extend for one year subsidized student loan interest rates financed by a cut in health care spending	YES
Cite Attorney General Eric H. Holder Jr. for contempt of Congress	YES
Create a visa program for foreign graduates in high-tech fields	YES
Extend most Bush-era income tax rates while allowing rates for top-bracket earners to rise (Jan. 1, 2013)	NO
2011	
Strike funding for F-35 alternative engine	NO
Prevent EPA from regulating greenhouse gas emissions to address climate change	YES
Extend certain provisions of Patriot Act for four years	YES
Declare opposition to use of ground troops in Libya	YES
Overhaul patent law	YES
Pass compromise debt limit increase plan and establish future spending limits	YES
Allow consideration of measures to implement three trade agreements	YES

CQ Vote Studies

	PARTY UNITY		PRESIDENTIAL SUPPORT	
	SUPPORT	OPPOSE	SUPPORT	OPPOSE
2012	97%	3%	13%	87%
2011	97%	3%	22%	78%

Interest Groups

	AFL-CIO	ADA	CCUS	ACU
2012	14%	0%	92%	88%
2011	0%	5%	100%	88%

Indiana 9

South central — Bloomington

Situated among forests and rolling hills of south-central Indiana, the redrawn 9th District stretches from densely populated suburbs south of Indianapolis through Bloomington to Louisville suburbs along the Kentucky border.

Nearly one-fourth of the district is territory added after the 2010 census. The 9th gained Johnson County just south of Indianapolis, as well as part of Morgan County, the rest of Monroe County and limestone-rich Lawrence County. Most of the district's population is in the north; the growing Clark County suburbs of Louisville, Ky., are surrounded by rural counties.

The district's largest city is Bloomington, a bustling college town that's home to Indiana University's more than 40,000 students. Anchored by the university, the city frequently ranks near the top of national quality-of-living surveys. Recent initiatives include the B-Line Trail, a recreational path connecting downtown with the university, known for its bicycle culture. Local officials hope to attract firms to a city-supported technology park.

Manufacturing interests near Greenwood, as well as in areas to the south in the Ohio River Valley, support the regional economy. In Harrison County, to the west of the Louisville metropolitan area, Elizabeth relies on the hospitality industry centered on the riverboat casino and resort.

A decade of population surge in Clark County mirroring that of the greater Louisville region, which remains overwhelmingly white, included considerable growth in Hispanic communities. While youthful Bloomington remains reliably liberal, the Republican state legislature consolidated the conservative-leaning counties of south-central Indiana in redrawing the 9th during the decennial remapping process. The new map carved out the left-leaning swing counties east of Evansville and added the rock-ribbed Republican Johnson County, which strongly supports Republican candidates at the federal level. Overall, the 9th gave Mitt Romney 57 percent of its vote in the 2012 presidential election.

Major Industry
Retail, higher education, agriculture, manufacturing

Cities
Bloomington, Greenwood, Jeffersonville, New Albany

Notable
Indiana University hosts the annual "Little 500," the nation's largest collegiate bike race, modeled after the Indianapolis 500 race car event.

IOWA

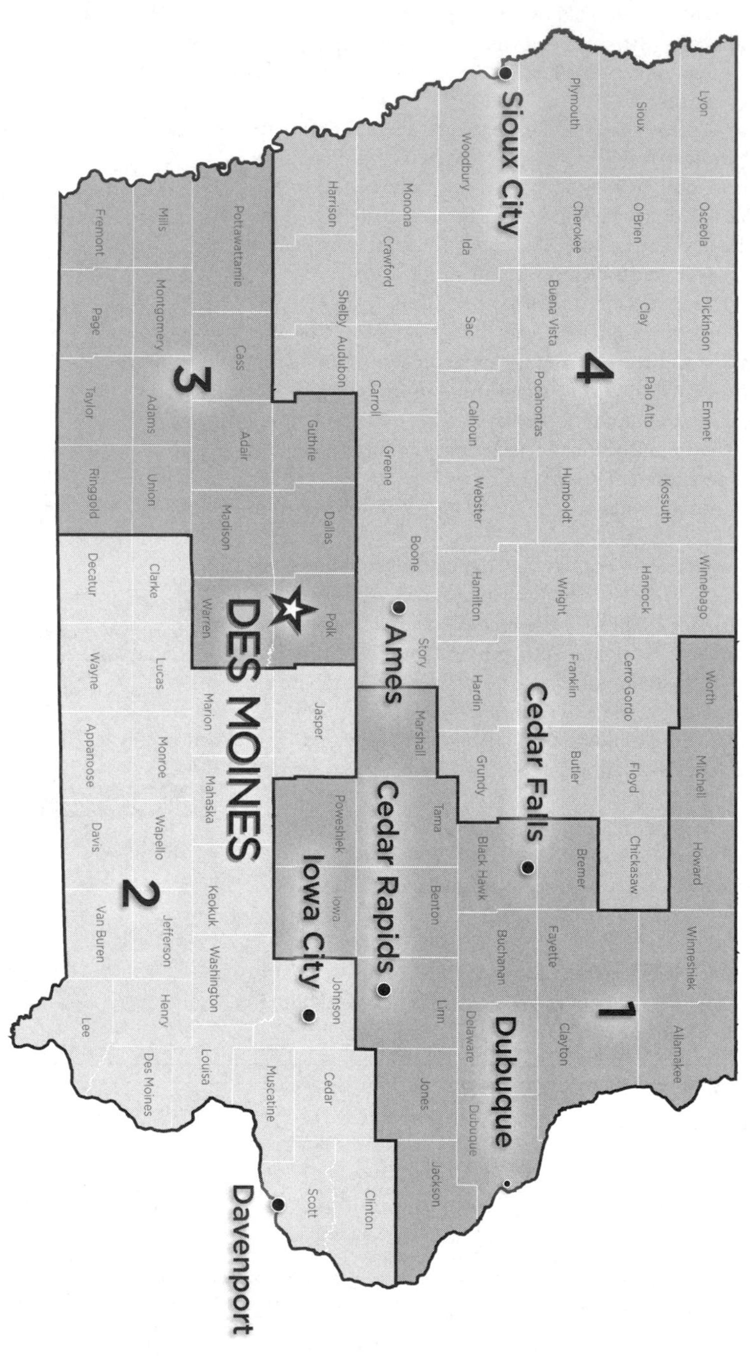
Sioux City
DES MOINES
Ames
Cedar Falls
Cedar Rapids
Iowa City
Dubuque
Davenport
1
2
3
4
Lyon
Osceola
Dickinson
Emmet
Kossuth
Winnebago
Worth
Mitchell
Howard
Winneshiek
Allamakee
Sioux
O'Brien
Clay
Palo Alto
Hancock
Cerro Gordo
Floyd
Chickasaw
Plymouth
Cherokee
Buena Vista
Pocahontas
Humboldt
Wright
Franklin
Butler
Bremer
Fayette
Clayton
Woodbury
Ida
Sac
Calhoun
Webster
Hamilton
Hardin
Grundy
Black Hawk
Buchanan
Delaware
Dubuque
Monona
Crawford
Carroll
Greene
Boone
Story
Marshall
Tama
Benton
Linn
Jones
Jackson
Harrison
Shelby
Audubon
Guthrie
Dallas
Polk
Jasper
Poweshiek
Iowa
Johnson
Cedar
Clinton
Scott
Pottawattamie
Cass
Adair
Madison
Warren
Marion
Mahaska
Keokuk
Washington
Muscatine
Louisa
Mills
Montgomery
Adams
Union
Clarke
Lucas
Monroe
Wapello
Jefferson
Henry
Des Moines
Fremont
Page
Taylor
Ringgold
Decatur
Wayne
Appanoose
Davis
Van Buren
Lee

Gov. Terry E. Branstad (R)

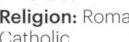

First elected: 2010

Length of term: 4 years

Term expires: 1/15

Salary: $130,000

Phone: (515) 281-5211

Residence: Boone

Born: November 17, 1946; Leland, Iowa

Religion: Roman Catholic

Family: Wife, Chris Branstad; three children

Education: U. of Iowa, B.A. 1969 (political science & sociology); Drake U., J.D. 1974

Military service: Army, 1969-71

Career: University president; business consultant; farm owner

Political highlights: Iowa House, 1973-79; lieutenant governor, 1979-83; governor, 1983-99

ELECTION RESULTS

2010 GENERAL

Terry E. Branstad (R)	592,494	52.9%
Chet Culver (D)	484,708	43.3%
Jonathan Narcisse (I)	20,859	1.8%
Eric Cooper (LIBERT)	14,398	1.3%

Lt. Gov. Kim Reynolds (R)

First elected: 2010

Length of term: 4 years

Term expires: 1/15

Salary: $107,182

Phone: (515) 281-5211

LEGISLATURE

General Assembly: January-May or June

Senate: 50 members, 4-year terms

2013 ratios: 26 D, 24 R; 40 men, 10 women

Salary: $25,000

Phone: (515) 281-3371

House: 100 members, 2-year terms

2013 ratios: 53 R, 47 D; 75 men, 25 women

Salary: $25,000

Phone: (515) 281-3221

TERM LIMITS

Governor: No

Senate: No

House: No

URBAN STATISTICS

CITY	POPULATION
Des Moines	203,433
Cedar Rapids	126,326
Davenport	99,685
Sioux City	82,684
Waterloo	68,406

REGISTERED VOTERS

Other	30%
Democrat	32%
Republican	32%

POPULATION

2010 population	3,046,355
2000 population	2,926,324
1990 population	2,776,755
Percent change (2000-2010)	+4.1%
Rank among states (2010)	30
Median age	37.9
Born in state	72.7%
Foreign born	3.7%
Violent crime rate	279/100,000
Poverty level	11.8%
Federal workers	25,821
Military	1,296

ELECTIONS

STATE ELECTION OFFICIAL
(515) 281-0145

DEMOCRATIC PARTY
(515) 244-7292

REPUBLICAN PARTY
(515) 282-8105

MISCELLANEOUS

Web: www.iowa.gov

Capital: Des Moines

U.S. CONGRESS

Senate: 1 Democrat, 1 Republican

House: 2 Republicans, 2 Democrats

STATISTICS BY DISTRICT

District	2012 Vote for President Obama	2012 Vote for President Romney	2008 Vote for President Obama	2008 Vote for President McCain	Black	Asian	Hispanic	Median Income	Over 64	Under 20	College Education	Rural	Sq. Miles
1	56%	43%	58%	40%	3%	1%	3%	$50,125	16%	26%	25%	37%	12,049
2	56	43	57	42	3	2	5	47,391	15	26	26	36	12,262
3	51	47	52	46	4	3	6	54,641	13	28	31	23	8,790
4	45	53	49	50	1	2	6	45,454	17	27	21	49	22,757
STATE	**52**	**46**	**54**	**45**	**3**	**2**	**5**	**49,427**	**15**	**27**	**25**	**37**	**55,857**
U.S.	**51**	**47**	**53**	**46**	**12**	**5**	**17**	**50,052**	**13**	**27**	**29**	**21**	**3,531,905**

Sen. Charles E. Grassley (R)

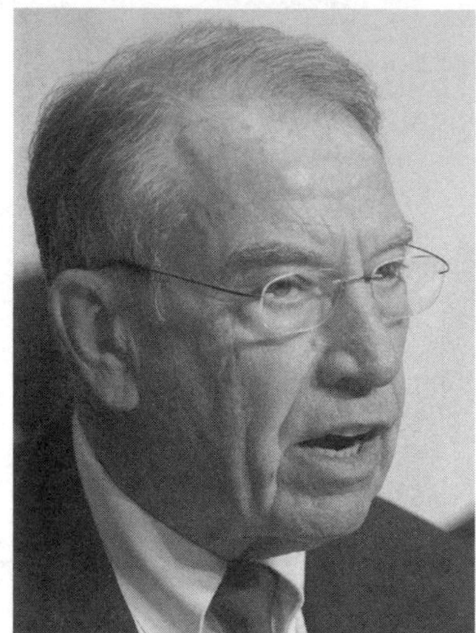

Capitol Office
224-3744
grassley.senate.gov
135 Hart Bldg. 20510; fax 224-6020

Committees
Agriculture, Nutrition & Forestry
Budget
Finance
Judiciary - Ranking Member
Joint Taxation

Residence
New Hartford

Born
Sept. 17, 1933; New Hartford, Iowa

Religion
Baptist

Family
Wife, Barbara Grassley; five children

Education
U. of Northern Iowa, B.A. 1955, M.A. 1956 (political science); U. of Iowa, attended 1957-58 (graduate studies)

Career
Farmer

Political Highlights
Republican nominee for Iowa House, 1956; Iowa House, 1959-75; U.S. House, 1975-81

ELECTION RESULTS

2010 GENERAL		
Charles E. Grassley (R)	718,215	64.4%
Roxanne Conlin (D)	371,686	33.3%
John Heiderscheit (LIBERT)	25,290	2.3%
2010 PRIMARY		
Charles E. Grassley (R)	197,194	98.0%
write-in (R)	3,926	2.0%

Previous Winning Percentages
2004 (70%); 1998 (68%); 1992 (70%); 1986 (66%); 1980 (54%); 1978 House Election (75%); 1976 House Election (57%); 1974 House Election (51%)

Elected 1980; 6th term

Now closing out his fourth decade of service in Congress, Grassley manages to be friendly, cantankerous and inimitable. The independent-minded conservative is a source of aggressive investigations into even the obscure reaches of the federal government.

Grassley has been noted for tenacity in pursuit of his goals, and also for occasional lapses in eloquence. His longevity and political skill have resulted in some prominent leadership roles over the years, most notably as the top Republican on the Finance Committee from 2001 through 2010.

Since 2011 he has been the top Republican on the Judiciary Committee. Grassley doesn't have a law degree and admitted in 2012 that he was more at ease in his previous gig. "Because I'm a non-lawyer, when you get to the highly technical legal questions, I don't feel quite as comfortable as I would with almost any subject that I took up at Finance," he said.

Even so, Grassley already has logged 32 years on the Judiciary Committee, and he has been fully engaged with the issues under its jurisdiction.

As discussions of an immigration law overhaul picked up at the start of the 113th Congress (2013-14), Grassley was firm in his commitment to a strong enforcement regime; he introduced a bill to make it mandatory for employers to use the E-Verify employment verification system.

He has heard out Democratic proposals to curb gun violence, but in March 2013 he was on defense during debate on a bill requiring background checks for all gun purchases. "Criminals will continue to steal guns and buy them illegally to circumvent the requirements," he said. "When that happens, we will be back here debating whether gun registration is needed. And when registration fails, then the next step is gun confiscation."

Grassley also hasn't been a pushover regarding the confirmation of judicial nominees. He claims that Republicans have been more accommodating to President Barack Obama than Democrats were to George W. Bush, and he blames the White House for being slow to nominate judges in the first place.

And then there's one of his favorite jobs: oversight. In the 112th Congress (2011-12), Grassley joined with House Republicans in a high-profile probe of Operation Fast and Furious, a gun-tracking sting run by the Bureau of Alcohol, Tobacco, Firearms and Explosives from 2009 to 2011. Grassley's efforts helped lead to the departures of acting ATF Director Kenneth E. Melson and Dennis K. Burke, a United States attorney in Phoenix. They were accused of knowingly allowing weapons to be sold into Mexico, where they were used by drug cartels. Grassley attempted to link the scandal to high-ranking Obama administration officials, an effort supported by conservative activists.

However, that probe was unrepresentative of most of his oversight work, which is neither partisan nor highly publicized. He has worked many years with Finance Chairman Max Baucus, a Montana Democrat, to uncover fraud against the nation's health care programs. In May 2012, he and Baucus sent letters to pharmaceutical companies, asking about their ties to doctors who have advocated increased use of narcotic painkillers. Grassley often questions whether nonprofit hospitals are providing enough charitable services to merit their standing in the tax code.

Over the years, Grassley has targeted the Food and Drug Administration, the Defense Department, the Smithsonian Institution, nonprofits such as the Nature Conservancy, and televangelists. Oversight achieves results more quickly than legislation, Grassley said, and it avoids political roadblocks: "You need 51 votes to pass a bill, but you only have to have one vote to do oversight."

Grassley is a leading congressional champion of whistle-blowers, both inside and outside government. One of his proudest legislative achievements is a 1986 update of the Civil War-era False Claims Act that allows private citizens to sue government contractors for fraud and share in any money recovered for the government. He said the law has recouped more than $20 billion for taxpayers.

On the Finance Committee, where he continues to serve, Grassley has been key to advancing initiatives on taxes, health care, Social Security, trade and welfare. He has often worked hand in glove with Baucus, who took over the panel's chairmanship from Grassley when Democrats gained control in the 110th Congress (2007-08). Agreements between the two men helped clear the way for some of Bush's biggest victories, beginning with a 10-year, $1.35 trillion tax cut in 2011. They also were central to passage of fast-track trade authority in 2002, which required up-or-down votes on trade deals, and the 2003 Medicare prescription drug benefit. Baucus was unable to get Grassley on board with the Democrats' 2010 health care law, however.

In general, Grassley is not one to shy away from a dispute. He was one of eight senators to oppose the January 2013 "fiscal cliff" deal, which extended the Bush-era tax cuts only for earnings under $400,000 (and extended a wind-production tax credit that he strongly favors). He called it "a fiscal farce to raise taxes and hurt economic growth only to fuel more government spending with record deficits and debt."

At times, Grassley's tendency to talk first and ask questions later has drawn unwanted attention. In 2008, he seemed to disparage victims of Hurricane Katrina while trying to win quick passage of legislation to help flood-stricken areas of the Midwest. Told that the bill would need to be offset by spending cuts or tax increases, Grassley noted that Katrina aid hadn't been subject to that requirement. "Why the double standard?" Grassley asked. "Is it because people aren't on rooftops complaining for helicopters to rescue them and you see it on television for two months? We aren't doing that in Iowa; we're trying to help ourselves in Iowa. We have a can-do attitude."

In 2012, he called Obama "stupid" on Twitter: "Constituents asked why i am not outraged at PresO attack on supreme court independence. Bcause Am ppl r not stupid as this x prof of con law." Twitter, Grassley says, is just the latest way to communicate with constituents and "promote representative government." He expresses some remorse for not using more "diplomatic" language, but "sometimes I think it's legitimate to wake people up, so that's part of my motive too."

Grassley's rebellious streak is cushioned by his disarming candor — the product of a lifetime in small-town Iowa. He grows corn and soybeans on 720 acres near New Hartford with his son and grandson, and, to keep in touch with his staff, he tucks a cellphone set to vibrate under his cap while on a tractor. A member of the Agriculture, Nutrition and Forestry Committee, he looks out for his state's many pork producers and corn growers.

He holds public hearings in each of Iowa's 99 counties every year. His devotion hasn't kept him away from Washington, however. Grassley hasn't missed a vote since July 1993 — the longest streak in the Senate.

Grassley dreamed of a career in politics when he was in high school. After graduating from the University of Northern Iowa, he continued with graduate work there and at another Iowa university while working in a factory, where he was a Machinists union member. A few years later, he and his wife, Barbara, took over his family's grain and livestock operation.

He spent 16 years in the Iowa House and was elected to the U.S. House in 1974, succeeding the retired H.R. Gross, a Republican revered in the state. Six years later, he unseated liberal Democratic Sen. John C. Culver. He has won with ease since. Grassley says he will run for a seventh term only if he stays in good health.

Key Votes

2012	
Prohibit health insurance plans from denying coverage based on the sponsor's religious beliefs	NO
Require approval of the Keystone XL oil pipeline	YES
Ease securities rules to expand small-business access to capital	YES
Reauthorize farm and nutrition programs for five years	YES
Limit debate on a bill that would create private-sector cybersecurity standards	NO
Consent to ratification of a treaty setting global standard for the treatment of people with disabilities	NO
Provide $60.4 billion in disaster relief following Superstorm Sandy	NO
Extend most Bush-era income tax rates while allowing rates for top-bracket earners to rise (Jan. 1, 2013)	NO
2011	
Prevent EPA from regulating greenhouse gas emissions to address climate change	YES
Extend certain provisions of Patriot Act for four years	YES
Clear compromise debt limit increase plan and establish future spending limits	NO
Overhaul patent law	YES
Implement Colombia free trade agreement	YES
Limit debate on confirmation of Caitlin J. Halligan to D.C. Circuit Court of Appeals	NO
Extend payroll tax cut and unemployment benefits for two months	YES

CQ Vote Studies

	PARTY UNITY		PRESIDENTIAL SUPPORT	
	SUPPORT	OPPOSE	SUPPORT	OPPOSE
2012	83%	17%	49%	51%
2011	91%	9%	53%	47%
2010	93%	7%	42%	58%
2009	92%	8%	47%	53%
2008	93%	7%	72%	28%
2007	79%	21%	79%	21%
2006	93%	7%	87%	13%
2005	96%	4%	89%	11%
2004	97%	3%	94%	6%
2003	96%	4%	99%	1%

Interest Groups

	AFL-CIO	ADA	CCUS	ACU
2012	9%	20%	88%	72%
2011	11%	5%	91%	90%
2010	13%	10%	91%	88%
2009	22%	20%	71%	96%
2008	30%	25%	100%	76%
2007	32%	30%	64%	84%
2006	20%	5%	92%	88%
2005	14%	5%	100%	96%
2004	17%	20%	100%	96%
2003	0%	5%	100%	80%

Sen. Tom Harkin (D)

Capitol Office
224-3254
harkin.senate.gov
731 Hart Bldg. 20510-1502; fax 224-9369

Committees
Agriculture, Nutrition & Forestry
Appropriations
(Labor-HHS-Education - Chairman)
Health, Education, Labor & Pensions - Chairman
Small Business & Entrepreneurship

Residence
Cumming

Born
Nov. 19, 1939; Cumming, Iowa

Religion
Roman Catholic

Family
Wife, Ruth Harkin; two children

Education
Iowa State U., B.S. 1962 (government & economics); Catholic U. of America, J.D. 1972

Military Service
Navy, 1962-67; Naval Reserve, 1968-74

Career
Lawyer; congressional aide

Political Highlights
Democratic nominee for U.S. House, 1972; U.S. House, 1975-85; sought Democratic nomination for president, 1992

ELECTION RESULTS

2008 GENERAL

Tom Harkin (D)	941,665	62.7%
Christopher Reed (R)	560,006	37.3%

2008 PRIMARY

Tom Harkin (D)	unopposed

Previous Winning Percentages
2002 (54%); 1996 (52%); 1990 (54%); 1984 (56%); 1982 House Election (59%); 1980 House Election (60%); 1978 House Election (59%); 1976 House Election (65%); 1974 House Election (51%)

Elected 1984; 5th term

Harkin is a product of the populist tradition of Iowa. While respecting the state's conservative leanings, he has been a devoted proponent of spending for the poor, agriculture programs and health care. But the 113th Congress will be his last — he said in early 2013 that "it's somebody else's turn."

A proud old-school progressive, Harkin boasted that during his 1992 presidential candidacy, he was the "only Democrat in the race," tacking to the left of eventual winner Bill Clinton. In January 2013, he was one of only three Democratic senators voting against a measure to extend lower income tax rates on earnings under $450,000 for married couples. Harkin said it didn't bring in enough money to meet the needs of government programs and spared too much income for the wealthy. "If you're making more than $250,000, you're not middle class," he said on the Senate floor.

Harkin is chairman of both the Health, Education, Labor and Pensions Committee and the Labor-HHS-Education Appropriations Subcommittee. Those assignments make him the principal Senate Democratic spokesman for health and education policy. He passed up the opportunity to chair the full Appropriations Committee for the 113th Congress (2013-14) — he said the HELP Committee is "where my passion lies."

"The erosion of the middle class and growing income inequality are among our most pressing issues as a country," he said in late 2012. "To that end, I am committed to doing everything I can to reverse those trends."

Harkin took the gavel of the HELP Committee in 2009, succeeding the late Edward M. Kennedy of Massachusetts just as the Senate was putting the final touches on its version of the Democrats' health care overhaul measure.

He considers the passage of the final health bill one of the defining votes of his career — although he had hoped, like many liberals, for inclusion of a government-run insurance plan in the final package. Harkin was largely responsible for prevention provisions in the law. Harkin in the 112th Congress (2011-12) firmly lectured Obama administration officials that "not one more nickel" will be transferred from funding for enhanced preventive health services outlined in the law. He opened the 113th Congress by introducing a sprawling package of preventive health programs meant to encourage healthier food offerings and increased exercise for schoolchildren, create community gardens, establish new sports programs for the disabled and boost taxes on tobacco, among other things.

For the home stretch of his four-decade congressional career, Harkin is promoting an overhaul of pension law, based on the premise that the retirement system should be "universal and automatic." He says his plan combines the advantages of defined-benefit and defined-contribution plans. It would complement Social Security — for that program, Harkin favors higher benefits and elimination of the cap on income subject to its payroll taxes.

He also will tackle reauthorizations of federal programs for primary, secondary and post-secondary education. Harkin is not averse to applying federal leverage to try to make college education more affordable. He might use a rewrite of the Higher Education Act — which deals with the entire federal student loan system, Pell grants and other scholarship programs — to achieve one of his personal goals: overhauling regulation of for-profit colleges.

Harkin started work in the 112th Congress on a rewrite of the 2002 education law known as No Child Left Behind. He advanced a bipartisan measure out of his committee in 2011 that would remove the much-criticized accountability system that requires all students to be proficient in math and reading by 2014. Instead, it would require states to adopt "college- and career-ready" standards and develop statewide accountability systems to receive federal funding. It went nowhere in the full Senate.

Prior to his leadership of the HELP Committee, Harkin alternated with Republicans for nine years in leading the Agriculture, Nutrition and Forestry Committee. That panel is a natural spot for an Iowa senator, as its major task is the supervision and reauthorization of agricultural production and nutrition support programs. Harkin pressed for increased agricultural conservation incentives and led the committee through difficult bicameral negotiations leading up to the enactment of the 2002 farm bill. The 2008 farm bill provided enhanced biofuel production incentives — Harkin is a big supporter of the ethanol industry — and it was enacted over a veto by President George W. Bush.

Harkin's work on the HELP and Agriculture panels has often been tempered by other committees. The Finance Committee has jurisdiction over taxes, which frequently brings it into discussions of any broad reauthorization measures. Harkin at times has been frustrated by what he views as its interference with his agenda. There were reports that he was "boxed out" of negotiations on the 2008 farm bill, and he complained at the time: "Do the Ag Committee members run the Ag Committee, or does the Finance Committee?" Budget Chairman Kent Conrad, a North Dakota Democrat, shot down a 2002 Harkin effort to add $6 billion to the agriculture budget.

His signature achievement prior to the health care overhaul was the 1990 Americans With Disabilities Act, which gave broad civil rights protections to an estimated 54 million Americans with mental and physical disabilities. At the time of its passage, Harkin said he was inspired by his brother, Frank, who was deaf. He repeated that sentiment in 2008 when Bush signed his bill expanding the number of people who qualify for the law's protections.

The son of a coal miner, Harkin grew up in a small, crowded house in Cumming. His life took a tragic turn at age 10 when his mother, a Slovenian immigrant, died. After working his way through college, Harkin spent five years as a Navy pilot during the 1960s.

Although interested in politics since college — he was president of the Young Democrats at Iowa State — he stumbled into the field as a career. In 1968, out of the Navy and out of work, he was watching TV at a diner when President Lyndon B. Johnson startled him by announcing he would not seek another term. The next morning, a friend working for the Iowa Democratic Party offered him a job. "I thought, 'I'm going broke, I've got no prospects for the future. Why not?'" Harkin recalled.

In 1969, he was hired by Iowa Democratic Rep. Neal Smith as an aide on the House select committee investigating the U.S. military's progress in Vietnam. He made a name for himself with his discovery of South Vietnam's "tiger cages." Outwitting a government official on a guided tour of a prison camp, Harkin found hundreds of men, women and children behind a hidden door and crammed into underground cells, with open grates on top through which guards poured skin-searing doses of the chemical lime. His photographs and story in Life magazine energized the anti-war movement. The move cost the 30-year-old Harkin his Capitol Hill job.

Harkin lost a race for the House in 1972, the same year he earned his law degree. But two years later he defeated Republican incumbent William J. Scherle by a slim margin. He held the seat until winning election to the Senate in 1984, ousting Republican Roger W. Jepsen with 56 percent of the vote.

His Senate campaigns haven't been cakewalks; in the races for his second, third and fourth terms, he won by less than 11 points. In 2008, Harkin eclipsed a 60 percent majority for the first time as senator.

Democratic Rep. Bruce Braley is running to become Harkin's successor. Harkin said he will not get involved in the primary, but he has complimented Braley's work as a lawmaker.

Key Votes

2012	
Prohibit health insurance plans from denying coverage based on the sponsor's religious beliefs	YES
Require approval of the Keystone XL oil pipeline	NO
Ease securities rules to expand small-business access to capital	NO
Reauthorize farm and nutrition programs for five years	YES
Limit debate on a bill that would create private-sector cybersecurity standards	YES
Consent to ratification of a treaty setting global standard for the treatment of people with disabilities	YES
Provide $60.4 billion in disaster relief following Superstorm Sandy	YES
Extend most Bush-era income tax rates while allowing rates for top-bracket earners to rise (Jan. 1, 2013)	NO
2011	
Prevent EPA from regulating greenhouse gas emissions to address climate change	NO
Extend certain provisions of Patriot Act for four years	NO
Clear compromise debt limit increase plan and establish future spending limits	NO
Overhaul patent law	YES
Implement Colombia free trade agreement	NO
Limit debate on confirmation of Caitlin J. Halligan to D.C. Circuit Court of Appeals	YES
Extend payroll tax cut and unemployment benefits for two months	YES

CQ Vote Studies

	PARTY UNITY		PRESIDENTIAL SUPPORT	
	SUPPORT	OPPOSE	SUPPORT	OPPOSE
2012	97%	3%	93%	7%
2011	98%	2%	91%	9%
2010	98%	2%	95%	5%
2009	99%	1%	97%	3%
2008	97%	3%	25%	75%
2007	96%	4%	35%	65%
2006	95%	5%	46%	54%
2005	98%	2%	27%	73%
2004	94%	6%	52%	48%
2003	98%	2%	46%	54%

Interest Groups

	AFL-CIO	ADA	CCUS	ACU
2012	100%	95%	38%	4%
2011	100%	95%	27%	5%
2010	100%	100%	9%	0%
2009	100%	100%	43%	0%
2008	100%	95%	50%	4%
2007	100%	95%	36%	8%
2006	100%	100%	36%	8%
2005	100%	100%	33%	4%
2004	100%	100%	59%	8%
2003	100%	95%	32%	15%

Rep. Bruce Braley (D)

Capitol Office
225-2911
braley.house.gov
2263 Rayburn Bldg. 20515-1501; fax 225-6666

Committees
Energy & Commerce

Residence
Waterloo

Born
Oct. 30, 1957; Grinnell, Iowa

Religion
Presbyterian

Family
Wife, Carolyn Braley; three children

Education
Iowa State U., B.A. 1980 (political science); U. of Iowa, J.D. 1983

Career
Lawyer

Political Highlights
No previous office

ELECTION RESULTS

2012 GENERAL		
Bruce Braley (D)	222,422	56.9%
Benjamin Lange (R)	162,465	41.6%
Gregory James Hughes (NPA)	4,772	1.2%
2012 PRIMARY		
Bruce Braley (D)	11,912	99.2%
2010 GENERAL		
Bruce Braley (D)	104,428	49.5%
Benjamin Lange (R)	100,219	47.5%
Rob J. Petsche (LIBERT)	4,087	1.9%

Previous Winning Percentages
2008 (65%); 2006 (55%)

Elected 2006; 4th term

"I've made my living with my voice," Braley says, first as a trial lawyer and now as a purveyor of liberal and populist policies in the House.

But he hopes to make his living in the Senate. Braley is running for the seat that Democratic Sen. Tom Harkin will vacate at the end of the 113th Congress (2013-14). He is the clear favorite to win the Democratic nomination, at least in the early going — Agriculture Secretary Tom Vilsack, a former Iowa governor, announced that he isn't a candidate, and Braley has already started locking up endorsements.

In the meantime, Braley remains a member of the House Democratic minority and the Energy and Commerce Committee. In those roles, he sees his intense approach to congressional oversight as one of his greatest strengths. Braley prides himself on knowing how to grill witnesses in hearings — a skill he developed as a plaintiff's attorney.

"You have to know what answers you want from that witness, and you have to be able to use leading questions," he said. "And when they answer something else, you have to hold them accountable, and you can't do that unless you are listening intently to what they're saying." Braley several times has gotten government officials or corporate executives to swallow hard and confirm facts they'd rather not publicize, with cameras rolling and YouTube waiting for the clips.

Braley returned to the Energy and Commerce Committee (and its Oversight and Investigations Subcommittee) in 2013 — Democrats had to leave him off the panel for the 112th Congress (2011-12), because their committee rosters shrank after losses in the 2010 elections.

The committee has jurisdiction over a huge range of issues. Braley is eager to oversee implementation of the 2010 health care overhaul, as the insurance "exchanges" in the law come online. He views his contributions to the overhaul during the 111th Congress (2009-10) as some of his most important work. Braley sought commitments for studies on improving Medicare's reimbursement model, and he was part of the group of Democrats trying to level out geographic disparities for physician and hospital reimbursements.

Braley also supports directing more federal resources to the development of "clean" energy and the improvement of telecommunications infrastructure in rural areas.

In the 112th Congress, Braley sat on both the Veterans' Affairs and Oversight and Government Reform committees. The former was the launching pad for enactment of Braley's bill to extend a Veterans Administration housing grant program through 2022. The program provides assistance to injured and disabled veterans to help them retrofit their homes for increased accessibility.

Braley named the law after Andrew Connelly, a constituent who served in Iraq, came back to Iowa with a tumor in his spine, became a wheelchair user and then died. His constituent service request "turned into a bill that is going to provide enhanced benefits for wounded warriors," Braley said.

He introduced several other veterans bills, including one to create a jobs corps to employ veterans as police officers, firefighters and caretakers at national parks, among other jobs. Washington Democrat Patty Murray tried to move the Senate version, but it was blocked by Republicans who said it would exceed federal spending caps.

Braley is not affiliated with any major blocs of House Democrats, but he is the founding chairman of the House Populist Caucus, a group of approximately two dozen pro-union, socially liberal Democrats. Braley supported all of President Barack Obama's major first-term economic initiatives: the health care overhaul, the 2009 economic stimulus law and an energy bill to create a cap-and-trade system for greenhouse gas emissions.

When Braley butts heads with Obama or other Democrats, it's because he feels their spending priorities are off. In 2011 he called for immediate withdrawal from Afghanistan and opposed involvement in Libya because he thought the money spent on those conflicts could be used for addressing domestic problems. He also signed on to Republican-sponsored legislation in 2012 to require annual federal spending to be based on the previous three years of government revenue. "It's a simple concept that would revolutionize the way our government does business," he said. "States must balance their budgets; families must balance their checkbooks. Why shouldn't the federal government?"

Braley's family came to Iowa 150 years ago — his great-great-grandfather walked there from Vermont and staked out a farm. His father worked in a grain elevator and his mother was a fourth-grade teacher. When he was a child, his mother drove back and forth from their home to the University of Iowa in Iowa City to earn her degree. Braley's grandmother and great-grandmother also were teachers. His wife, Carolyn, teaches at Waterloo West High School, which all three of their children attended.

Braley says his blue-collar upbringing in the town of Brooklyn made him a natural advocate for the Democratic Party. His interest in politics began when his father, a moderate Republican, and his mother, a Democrat, routinely talked about the daily news around the dinner table with their four children. Two of the major topics were the Vietnam War and the Watergate scandal.

As a third-grader, Braley landed his first job: paperboy for the Des Moines Tribune. Later he tackled some of the more labor- and sweat-intensive jobs well known to Midwestern teens — baling hay, detasseling corn, working at a grain elevator and driving dump trucks. Braley graduated in 1980 with a degree in political science from Iowa State University, where he also met his wife. After he earned a law degree from the University of Iowa, they settled in Waterloo, where Braley built a legal career.

GOP Rep. Jim Nussle created an open House seat in 2006 with his unsuccessful run for governor. Braley won a close primary, then faced restaurant and hotel entrepreneur Mike Whalen in the general election. The two political novices spent a combined $4.8 million on the race, which Braley won by 12 points. He handily defeated a state senator in 2008.

The Republican wave of 2010 nearly swamped him, but Braley defeated lawyer and former congressional aide Benjamin Lange by 2 points. Redistricting for 2012 significantly altered his constituent base (Iowa went from five districts to four), and in a rematch with Lange he won by about 15 points.

Key Votes

2012	
Extend a Social Security payroll tax cut and unemployment benefits	YES
Ease securities rules to expand small-business access to capital	YES
Extend for one year subsidized student loan interest rates financed by a cut in health care spending	NO
Cite Attorney General Eric H. Holder Jr. for contempt of Congress	NO
Create a visa program for foreign graduates in high-tech fields	NO
Extend most Bush-era income tax rates while allowing rates for top-bracket earners to rise (Jan. 1, 2013)	YES
2011	
Strike funding for F-35 alternative engine	YES
Prevent EPA from regulating greenhouse gas emissions to address climate change	NO
Extend certain provisions of Patriot Act for four years	NO
Declare opposition to use of ground troops in Libya	YES
Overhaul patent law	YES
Pass compromise debt limit increase plan and establish future spending limits	NO
Allow consideration of measures to implement three trade agreements	NO

CQ Vote Studies

	PARTY UNITY		PRESIDENTIAL SUPPORT	
	SUPPORT	OPPOSE	SUPPORT	OPPOSE
2012	94%	6%	84%	16%
2011	94%	6%	75%	25%
2010	98%	2%	93%	7%
2009	99%	1%	97%	3%
2008	98%	2%	13%	87%

Interest Groups

	AFL-CIO	ADA	CCUS	ACU
2012	95%	85%	25%	0%
2011	96%	75%	29%	4%
2010	100%	100%	13%	0%
2009	100%	95%	40%	0%
2008	100%	90%	56%	4%

Iowa 1

Northeast — Cedar Rapids, Waterloo, Dubuque

Expanded after decennial redistricting to encompass Iowa's entire northeastern corner, the 1st District borders Minnesota to the north and Wisconsin and Illinois along the east. Scattered among Mississippi River counties and farmland, the 1st has a few midsize cities with manufacturing technology interests that sustain major employers in the region.

Cedar Rapids, in Linn County, is the state's second-largest city and is home to the headquarters of aerospace electronics giant Rockwell Collins, one of the region's largest employers. Cedar Rapids remains a major food and grain processing hub, with a large Quaker Oats cereal plant; historically, manufacturing has been a mainstay for its economy. The city was ravaged by a 500-year flood in 2008 and total recovery is expected to cost billions. But the city's large-scale rebuilding plan includes a new downtown amphitheater and levees, as well as a new convention and events center.

As elsewhere in the state, John Deere is a strong presence in the 1st, including in Waterloo to the west. In Dubuque along the Mississippi River to the east, John Deere has a nearly 1,500-acre factory where heavy-equipment models are made. A few smaller colleges and universities are in Dubuque, including three theological seminaries. The long-established meatpacking industry in Black Hawk County historically drew in Eastern European and then Latin American immigrants. Corn, soybean and alfalfa fields dominate the rural landscape in the 1st, but recent drought conditions threaten productivity.

The newly drawn 1st can count on a union presence and the 13,000 students at Cedar Fall's University of Northern Iowa to provide a Democratic base. Democrats slightly edge Republicans in voter registration in the district. Of the 12 counties here, only three — Delaware, Benton and Iowa — supported Republican presidential nominee Mitt Romney in 2012.

Major Industry

Food processing, manufacturing, agriculture

Cities

Cedar Rapids, Waterloo, Dubuque, Cedar Falls, Marion

Notable

"Field of Dreams" was filmed 25 miles west of Dubuque in Dyersville, which plans to build multi-field youth tournament facilities on the site.

Rep. Dave Loebsack (D)

Capitol Office
225-6576
loebsack.house.gov
1527 Longworth Bldg. 20515-1502; fax 226-0757

Committees
Armed Services
Education & the Workforce

Residence
Iowa City

Born
Dec. 23, 1952; Sioux City, Iowa

Religion
Methodist

Family
Wife, Teresa Loebsack; four children

Education
Iowa State U., B.S. 1974 (political science), M.A. 1976 (political science); U. of California, Davis, Ph.D. 1985 (political science)

Career
Professor

Political Highlights
No previous office

ELECTION RESULTS

2012 GENERAL		
Dave Loebsack (D)	211,863	55.6%
John Archer (R)	161,977	42.5%
Alan Aversa (NPA)	7,112	1.9%
2012 PRIMARY		
Dave Loebsack (D)	17,467	81.5%
Joe M. Seng (D)	3,913	18.3%
2010 GENERAL		
Dave Loebsack (D)	115,839	51.0%
Mariannette Miller-Meeks (R)	104,319	45.9%
Gary Sicard (LIBERT)	4,356	1.9%
Jon Tack (CNSTP)	2,463	1.1%

Previous Winning Percentages
2008 (57%); 2006 (51%)

Elected 2006; 4th term

The low-key Loebsack works mainly behind the scenes, doing "whatever works" to advance his priorities for education, the National Guard and Iowa's infrastructure.

Loebsack doesn't speak on the floor too often, and he generally stays out of the media. He jokes that he spent his time grandstanding in his earlier career as a college professor. Raised in poverty by a single parent, he worked to put himself through school and is grateful for the role federal support played in him receiving a Ph.D. in political science.

He believes Washington's main goal should be to boost the middle class through access to education and basic support systems. Loebsack is a member of the Congressional Progressive Caucus, the group of the most-liberal House Democrats. But he also belongs to the collaborative Center Aisle and Common Ground caucuses.

"I'm not a Pollyanna about this," he said. "I know the [National Republican Congressional Committee] wants to see me gone. But at the same time, I'm not going to let that stuff get in the way of trying to work on issues."

In 2011, he joined a bipartisan coalition that called for $4 trillion in deficit reduction over 10 years through a mix of spending cuts and revenue increases. Loebsack was also one of 25 House Democrats that year to vote for a balanced-budget amendment to the Constitution.

Most of his life has been spent in Iowa, except for when he was taking classes for his doctorate at the University of California in Davis. He returned to Iowa in 1982 to teach political science at Cornell College in the small town of Mount Vernon. His wife is a retired elementary school teacher.

So Loebsack brings some expertise to the Education and the Workforce Committee. Loebsack wants to boost American competitiveness through investment in science, technology, engineering and math programs and increased Pell grant support. "It's about providing opportunities for folks like me growing up in poverty," he said. "I wouldn't be where I am had it not been for the education I received."

He has questioned the annual testing of public school students to assess progress, as required by the 2002 education law known as No Child Left Behind. There needs to be more flexibility in assessing those measurements, he said, to account for local realities. He pushes for "multiple levels of achievement" in evaluating student progress rather than one high-stakes exam.

Working with Wisconsin Republican Tom Petri in the 112th Congress (2011-12), he introduced a bill to increase emphasis on critical-thinking and problem-solving skills in secondary schools. And he had a measure of his own to boost statistics-related programs and education.

Loebsack also has an interest in workforce training. Three times he has introduced a bill to provide grants for coordination among educators, workers and employers in a region, so that training programs focus on skills that local employers need.

His other committee assignment is on Armed Services. Loebsack taught college-level foreign policy courses for 24 years and traveled extensively overseas. His stepson served in both Iraq and Afghanistan.

Calling the Iraq War "foolhardy," he voted earlier in his tenure for U.S. troop withdrawal deadlines and benchmarks. By 2012 he was ready for an Afghanistan withdrawal. The United States has "done the things that we had to do and that we could do," he said. Loebsack co-sponsored a bill to require funds for Afghanistan to be used only for the withdrawal of troops and contractors.

On the Military Personnel Subcommittee, Loebsack keeps the needs of the

National Guard in the forefront. His 2007 measure to require the National Guard and reserve branches to place mental health counselors at readiness centers during training became law. Mental health issues are of particular importance to Loebsack, whose mother battled mental illness for years.

In February 2012, Loebsack said he was "deeply concerned" about an Air Force decision to reduce the number of Air National Guard forces; officials cited the tight budget climate as the impetus for the proposal.

A new congressional map for the 113th Congress (2013-14) added Davenport to Loebsack's district, which gives him more incentive to look out for the Rock Island Arsenal Joint Manufacturing and Technology Center — that facility is in the Illinois portion of the Mississippi River, but it's an economic boon to Iowa as well. Loebsack and Illinois Republican Bobby Schilling wrote a bill to remove limits on the number of public-private partnerships Army industrial facilities can enter into. It was included in the fiscal 2012 defense policy law.

Loebsack and the rest of the Iowa delegation have continued to work on recovery from severe floods in 2008 and 2010. He has called for homeowners to have greater participation when the federal government redraws flood maps to determine flood insurance needs.

Loebsack, his three siblings and their mother moved into his maternal grandmother's Sioux City home when he was in the fourth grade. At 16, he started working at a waste treatment control plant under a federally funded program providing employment opportunities for poor students. He hardly knew his father, who died while Loebsack was in high school.

To help pay for college he used student loans, Social Security survivor benefits tied to his father's death, and money he saved from working summers as a janitor at his high school, Sioux City East. He entered Iowa State University thinking he would study meteorology, but he eventually earned degrees in political science, en route to his doctorate.

Loebsack decided to challenge 15-term Republican Rep. Jim Leach in 2006. He failed to meet the petition requirements to qualify for the primary, but since no other Democrat filed to run, state law allowed the party to appoint Loebsack as the nominee. In a banner year for Democrats, Loebsack won with 51 percent of the vote. He took 57 percent in 2008 against ophthalmologist and Army veteran Mariannette Miller-Meeks. Though Republicans experienced a resurgence in 2010, Loebsack held on with 51 percent of the vote in a rematch.

Iowa lost one House seat in reapportionment after the 2010 census, and the new congressional map put Loebsack's Mount Vernon home in the 1st District. He moved to Iowa City to avoid a primary contest against fellow Democrat Bruce Braley. Loebsack defeated Republican lawyer John Archer by 13 points, even though the NRCC spent $768,000 to campaign against Loebsack.

Key Votes

2012	
Extend a Social Security payroll tax cut and unemployment benefits	YES
Ease securities rules to expand small-business access to capital	YES
Extend for one year subsidized student loan interest rates financed by a cut in health care spending	NO
Cite Attorney General Eric H. Holder Jr. for contempt of Congress	NO
Create a visa program for foreign graduates in high-tech fields	NO
Extend most Bush-era income tax rates while allowing rates for top-bracket earners to rise (Jan. 1, 2013)	YES
2011	
Strike funding for F-35 alternative engine	NO
Prevent EPA from regulating greenhouse gas emissions to address climate change	NO
Extend certain provisions of Patriot Act for four years	NO
Declare opposition to use of ground troops in Libya	YES
Overhaul patent law	YES
Pass compromise debt limit increase plan and establish future spending limits	NO
Allow consideration of measures to implement three trade agreements	NO

CQ Vote Studies

	PARTY UNITY		PRESIDENTIAL SUPPORT	
	SUPPORT	OPPOSE	SUPPORT	OPPOSE
2012	87%	13%	70%	30%
2011	90%	10%	82%	18%
2010	97%	3%	95%	5%
2009	97%	3%	97%	3%
2008	97%	3%	13%	87%

Interest Groups

	AFL-CIO	ADA	CCUS	ACU
2012	85%	70%	58%	16%
2011	93%	80%	25%	4%
2010	100%	95%	25%	4%
2009	100%	95%	36%	0%
2008	100%	90%	56%	0%

Iowa 2

Southeast — Davenport, Iowa City

The 2nd District, which after decennial remapping takes up the southeastern corner of the state, is quintessential Iowa: large-scale manufacturing, plains covered in farmland and sports-loving college towns.

Davenport and Bettendorf make up Iowa's half of the Quad Cities that straddle the Mississippi River into Illinois. Scott County relies on heavy-equipment manufacturer John Deere — the agricultural giant's headquarters are located across the river in Moline — as well as jobs at the Army's Rock Island Arsenal in Illinois' half of the Mississippi. Health care, aluminum and food manufacturing companies and casinos are also top employers.

Iowa City is home to the University of Iowa, one of the district's largest employers, and includes the nation's largest university-owned teaching hospital. Residents here generally are more educated than the state average and unemployment is low. The area is a cultural hub and boasts the Englert Theatre downtown, the Herbert Hoover Presidential Library east of Iowa City, the turn-of-the-century-themed Johnson County Historical Society Museum in Coralville, and the University of Iowa Museum of Art near the city's general aviation municipal airport.

South and west, the district heads into less-populated counties; farms grow corn, soybeans and alfalfa and produce pork and dairy. Burlington, the namesake of the historic railroad company, draws revenue from its riverboat casino.

The 2nd can be politically competitive, but leans Democratic due to the university in Iowa City and a union presence in manufacturing areas. Davenport has a moderate minority population — more than 10 percent of its residents are black and 7 percent Hispanic. Overall in the 2nd, Democrats outnumber Republicans in terms of voter registration, although a number of voters remain independent. Barack Obama won Johnson County, which includes Iowa City, with 70 percent of the presidential vote in 2008 and 67 percent in 2012, both his best showings in the state.

Major Industry

Food processing, manufacturing, agriculture, higher education

Cities

Davenport, Iowa City, Bettendorf, Clinton, Burlington, Ottumwa

Notable

The Herbert Hoover Presidential Library houses the papers of journalist and biographer Rose Wilder Lane, the daughter of Laura Ingalls Wilder.

Rep. Tom Latham (R)

Capitol Office
225-5476
latham.house.gov
2217 Rayburn Bldg. 20515-1504; fax 225-3301

Committees
Appropriations
(Transportation-HUD - Chairman)

Residence
Clive

Born
July 14, 1948; Hampton, Iowa

Religion
Lutheran

Family
Wife, Kathy Latham; three children

Education
Wartburg College, attended 1967; Iowa State U., attended 1967-70 (agriculture & business)

Career
Seed company executive; insurance agency marketing representative; insurance agent; bank teller

Political Highlights
Franklin County Republican Party chairman, 1984-91

ELECTION RESULTS

2012 GENERAL		
Tom Latham (R)	202,000	52.2%
Leonard L. Boswell (D)	168,632	43.6%
Scott G. Batcher (NPA)	9,352	2.4%
David Rosenfeld (SW)	6,286	1.6%
2012 PRIMARY		
Tom Latham (R)	27,757	99.2%
2010 GENERAL		
Tom Latham (R)	152,588	65.6%
Bill Maske (D)	74,300	32.0%
Dan Lensing (I)	5,499	2.4%

Previous Winning Percentages
2008 (61%); 2006 (57%); 2004 (61%); 2002 (55%); 2000 (69%); 1998 (99%); 1996 (65%); 1994 (61%)

Elected 1994; 10th term

Latham, a seasoned member of the Appropriations Committee, accommodates competing demands. He's happy to tilt federal spending in the direction of his Iowa constituents when he sees the need, but he also tries to serve the Republican Party's increased enthusiasm for fiscal restraint.

"The big issue, obviously, is spending," he said in 2012. "I always step back and look at the situation we're in with $16 trillion in debt. It simply is not sustainable." As he pursues spending reductions, Latham skillfully engages in a political balancing act.

Budgets are one example. Latham has voted for spending blueprints produced by Wisconsin Republican Paul D. Ryan that include changes to entitlement programs. He has repeatedly stated, however, that he opposes privatization of Social Security or Medicare and raising the eligibility age for those programs.

And then there's earmarks. He has no qualms with those spending requests, which direct money to specific local projects. Latham, the No. 2 Republican on the Agriculture Subcommittee, has secured millions of dollars for Iowa's needs over the years, and he says earmarks are particularly appropriate for transportation and infrastructure projects where local knowledge can lead to more-efficient spending. But he still endorsed the ban on earmarks that Republicans imposed in 2011 — he is a close friend of Speaker John A. Boehner, who stands behind the ban.

That's not to say that Latham is always a party-line Republican. He voted against several bills to raise the debt limit in the summer of 2011 — including one engineered by Boehner — saying they didn't do enough to control deficits. He voted against Boehner's preference again in January 2013, opposing a "fiscal cliff" deal that extended lower income tax rates only on earnings under $400,000.

And shortly after taking that conservative stance, Latham showed up on the roster of the moderate Main Street Partnership in the 113th Congress (2013-14).

The balancing act makes perfect sense in the traditional culture of the Appropriations Committee, where parochial concerns intermingle with broad policy debates, often in a bipartisan fashion.

Latham chairs the Transportation-HUD Subcommittee, and in 2012 he was proud that the $51.6 billion bill his panel produced both cut spending (by about $4 billion from the previous year) and had bipartisan support (79 Democrats voted for it, and 55 Republicans opposed it). He is a natural salesman and was once a professional one — Latham sold seeds to farms as part of his family's business.

He was vexed that work on his spending bill in 2012 was essentially negated, as all federal appropriations were rolled into a stopgap measure running through the opening months of the 113th Congress (2013-14). "It's my hope that we could get back to actually accomplishing things rather than to play politics," he said. "That's very frustrating, especially to a lot of appropriators who have to work together every year, across the aisle."

Latham has gravitated toward one specific means of reducing government waste. He is one of the congressional advocates of "Lean Six Sigma," a waste-cutting management philosophy adopted by a number of Fortune 500 companies. (Newt Gingrich, a former speaker of the House and 2012 presidential aspirant, is a big fan.) Latham has introduced a bill to require nearly every federal agency to use Lean Six Sigma and report on the results. He wrote in 2011 that it would create "a unified and consistent method for reducing the duplication and wasted resources."

Latham was born in Iowa, not long after his father, Willard, started a seed company. Latham and his brothers grew up doing farm chores and helping out at the family business. He attended Wartburg College, about 50 miles east of his hometown of Alexander, then went to Iowa State University, about 60 miles south in Ames.

In his early 20s, he headed to Colorado, spurred in part by his father's insistence that his children had to do something on their own before they could take their place in the family business. There, Latham worked as a bank teller, a bookkeeper and an insurance agent. The insurance firm transferred him to Des Moines.

In the mid-1970s, he returned home to start working in the seed business; he and his brothers also co-owned several farms.

Latham chaired the Franklin County Republican Party for several years but rebuffed entreaties to run for the state legislature, because the seasonal nature of the seed business conflicted with legislative sessions.

His interest in elective office was stoked by a trip he took in 1990 as a member of a farm delegation that visited Russia and Poland. Latham was appalled by the primitive agricultural methods and machinery, which he blamed on the totalitarian governments that not only mismanaged the economy, he says, but "destroyed individual freedom and dignity." He remembers a Polish farmer who tearfully told him that farmers hadn't owned their land since the Nazis seized it in World War II.

In 1994, when GOP Rep. Fred Grandy gave up the 5th District seat in an unsuccessful try for the governorship, Latham decided to run. He breezed to election. He was returned to the House easily in three subsequent elections, but in 2002 new district lines drafted by a nonpartisan state agency made the district more competitive. The new map put Latham's home in the 4th District, while more than half his constituents lived in the 5th. He ran in the 4th anyway, and he won by almost 12 points against Democrat John Norris, a former state party chairman.

Redistricting for the 2012 election forced Latham into another tough spot. Reapportionment after the 2010 census took away one of Iowa's congressional districts, and Latham ended up in a general-election race with eight-term Democratic Rep. Leonard L. Boswell. The race attracted negative advertising from big-spending outside groups; despite a past collegial relationship, both candidates were ungentlemanly at times. Latham used a big fundraising advantage to defeat Boswell by more than 8 points. Late in 2012, he buried the hatchet by leading a House floor tribute to Boswell's congressional service.

Latham has said he will not run for the Senate seat being vacated by Democrat Tom Harkin at the end of the 113th Congress.

Key Votes

2012	
Extend a Social Security payroll tax cut and unemployment benefits	YES
Ease securities rules to expand small-business access to capital	YES
Extend for one year subsidized student loan interest rates financed by a cut in health care spending	YES
Cite Attorney General Eric H. Holder Jr. for contempt of Congress	YES
Create a visa program for foreign graduates in high-tech fields	YES
Extend most Bush-era income tax rates while allowing rates for top-bracket earners to rise (Jan. 1, 2013)	NO
2011	
Strike funding for F-35 alternative engine	NO
Prevent EPA from regulating greenhouse gas emissions to address climate change	YES
Extend certain provisions of Patriot Act for four years	YES
Declare opposition to use of ground troops in Libya	YES
Overhaul patent law	YES
Pass compromise debt limit increase plan and establish future spending limits	NO
Allow consideration of measures to implement three trade agreements	YES

CQ Vote Studies

	PARTY UNITY		PRESIDENTIAL SUPPORT	
	SUPPORT	OPPOSE	SUPPORT	OPPOSE
2012	87%	13%	15%	85%
2011	91%	9%	24%	76%
2010	90%	10%	29%	71%
2009	81%	19%	35%	65%
2008	90%	10%	63%	37%

Interest Groups

	AFL-CIO	ADA	CCUS	ACU
2012	19%	0%	100%	71%
2011	3%	15%	94%	70%
2010	0%	0%	88%	91%
2009	14%	5%	80%	80%
2008	20%	30%	89%	88%

Iowa 3

Southwest — Des Moines, Council Bluffs

The 3rd is bookended by Des Moines to the east and Council Bluffs to the west. The district covers Iowa's southwest, and outside of these steadily growing population centers, it is rural and sparsely populated.

Des Moines is the district's most populous city and is among the most ethnically diverse in the Hawkeye State, although its population is still more than three-fourths white overall. Some of the residents have high incomes, but the city's poverty rate is nearly five percentage points higher than the statewide average.

Des Moines, unlike the rest of Iowa's population centers, has a stable economy that is not dependent on farming, although agribusiness companies do employ segments of the workforce. The city is an anchor for insurance and financial companies, with some, like Wells Fargo home mortgage services, having headquarters in the city. Des Moines' skyline includes the Iowa Events Center and four miles of skywalk, allowing residents to move easily among downtown locations. Historical areas, such as East Village, host the state Capitol and museums.

Populations have diminished in the farm counties in northern Iowa, resulting in the loss of a congressional seat following the 2010 census. But more than half of the population growth Iowa did experience occurred around Des Moines as suburban development spread west into formerly agricultural land. Dallas County was the state's fastest growing county, and nation's seventh-fastest growing, between 2000 and 2010.

Across corn and soybean fields, Council Bluffs sits on the Missouri River in the Omaha, Neb., metropolitan area. The main employers are riverboat casinos and food processing companies — Tyson Foods, ConAgra and Oakland Foods. Google recently expanded data center operations here.

The newly drawn 3rd is politically competitive turf with close to equal numbers of registered Democrats, Republicans and non-affiliated voters. But only Polk and Union counties backed Barack Obama for president in 2012.

Major Industry
Agriculture, manufacturing, insurance

Cities
Des Moines, Council Bluffs, West Des Moines, Ankeny, Urbandale

Notable
The Union Pacific Railroad Museum is located in Council Bluffs.

Rep. Steve King (R)

Capitol Office
225-4426
steveking.house.gov
2210 Rayburn Bldg. 20515-1505; fax 225-3193

Committees
Agriculture
(Department Operations, Oversight & Nutrition - Chairman)
Judiciary
Small Business

Residence
Kiron

Born
May 28, 1949; Storm Lake, Iowa

Religion
Roman Catholic

Family
Wife, Marilyn King; three children

Education
Northwest Missouri State U., attended 1967-70

Career
Construction company owner

Political Highlights
Iowa Senate, 1997-2002

ELECTION RESULTS

2012 GENERAL		
Steve King (R)	200,063	52.9%
Christie Vilsack (D)	169,470	44.8%
Martin James Monroe (NPA)	8,124	2.2%
2012 PRIMARY		
Steve King (R)	38,238	98.9%
write-ins (R)	420	1.1%
2010 GENERAL		
Steve King (R)	128,363	65.7%
Matthew Campbell (D)	63,160	32.4%
Martin James Monroe (I)	3,622	1.9%

Previous Winning Percentages
2008 (60%); 2006 (58%); 2004 (63%); 2002 (62%)

Elected 2002; 6th term

King has gone from riding a bulldozer in his construction business to being a bulldozer on behalf of the conservative movement. A leader among tea party Republicans, he is forceful and direct when trying to push policies on health care, immigration and fiscal matters toward the right — often to the vexation of those in his way.

"I'm here to serve God and country, in that order," King said. "There is a map for life, and that is the Bible. And there is a map for our country, and that is the Constitution."

His service to conservatives includes many media appearances covering a wide range of subjects. King is polite and self-deprecating in individual encounters, but capable of delivering a 30-minute stemwinder on the House floor. He doesn't equivocate on policy suggestions or criticisms of Democrats, and he attributes some of that style to his business experiences. "I've done hundreds, probably thousands, of verbal contracts over the years," he said. When communicating, "I want it clear. I don't have time for the vague areas."

He elicits a response. One of his closest friends and colleagues in Congress is Michele Bachmann of Minnesota, and, like Bachmann, King is admired by the like-minded and reviled by opponents on the left.

Some of his sharpest commentary sprouts from his work on the Judiciary Committee. King's father worked for the Iowa state police radio station, and King says his upbringing helped lay the "rule of law" foundation he now builds on. He is a member of the Constitution subcommittee and frequently cites that document as the authority limiting federal reach; King is a member of the Republican Study Committee and its 10th Amendment Task Force, which develops proposals to disperse powers to state and local governments.

He also sits on the Judiciary Subcommittee on Immigration and Border Security. "Most of the immigration laws that we need have been passed and are in place," he said. "They are just being ignored." King vehemently opposed the Obama administration's moves in the 112th Congress (2011-12) to ease the deportations of certain classes of illegal immigrants, such as younger people brought into the country as children. He supports state efforts to enforce federal immigration law.

Many of his introduced bills deal with immigration in some form; King has proposed eliminating the automatic granting of citizenship to those born on U.S. soil to illegal-immigrant parents and making English the official national language. One of his favorite ideas is preventing employers from listing as an expense the wages and benefits paid to illegal immigrants — the increase in tax liability would be an incentive for employers to stay within the law, he said.

King had one of the more fiscally conservative voting records in the House in the 112th Congress. He opposed every final spending bill for fiscal 2011 and fiscal 2012, and he is one of the most prominent promoters of replacing most federal taxes with a single national sales tax.

King's anti-spending rhetoric could heat up the Agriculture Committee in the 113th Congress (2013-14). He has been given the gavel of the subcommittee overseeing nutrition assistance programs. In 2012, a reauthorization of farm programs was held up partly because of objections to cuts to the Supplemental Nutrition Assistance Program in the panel-approved version of the bill. Most Democrats abhorred them, while conservatives wanted them to be bigger.

The farm bill approved by the panel in May 2013 still had large nutrition program cuts, as well as King's amendment barring state and local governments from blocking the sale of agricultural products made in jurisdictions with different rules for production. California's standards for the treatment of chickens shut many Iowa egg producers out of that market. King defends his measure as addressing interstate commerce, one area where Congress has the constitutional authority to act.

King despises the 2010 health care law and first proposed a repeal in the 111th Congress (2009-10). He would be happy to see a full repeal before work starts on replacement proposals. He prefers piece-by-piece changes to the health care industry. Some of his biggest priorities are allowing the selling of insurance across state lines and making sure the self-employed can deduct the full cost of their insurance premiums when calculating their taxes. King has been tweaking his own plan for reducing Medicare rolls: changes to the tax code that would allow Medicare-eligible people with robust health savings accounts to buy their own insurance, then use the leftover balance as a kind of retirement account.

It's arguable that King sometimes fudges on his political philosophy for his district's interests. His is one of the most economically successful farming districts in the country, and some of that agriculture is diverted into the biofuels industry. His opposition to most government intervention in the marketplace has sometimes been checked when federal support of ethanol is involved. (He also backs the tax credit for wind energy producers, another major employer at home.)

King's family has lived in Iowa since his great-grandparents settled there after the Civil War. King is the second of five children; speaking to the Sioux City Journal, he said that "I don't have a family sob story of any kind" — he fondly recalled playing sports and hunting with his father. King started dating Marilyn Kelly in his senior year of high school and married her in 1972.

He dropped out of college before his senior year to pursue construction work, and he eventually took out a loan to buy a bulldozer and start his own company specializing in soil erosion solutions for farmers. King's frustrations with government regulation and taxes influenced his decision to seek public office. In 1996, King was elected to the Iowa Senate and quickly became known for his socially conservative views.

In 2002, when redistricting moved Republican Rep. Tom Latham to another district, King ran in the newly vacant 5th District. After an inconclusive primary, he secured a spot on the ballot at a nominating convention, then won 62 percent of the vote that November.

Iowa lost a House seat going into the 2012 elections, and King ran in the new 4th District. Democrats recruited a big-name opponent in Christie Vilsack — the wife of Tom Vilsack, the Agriculture secretary and former Iowa governor. King and Vilsack were neck and neck in fundraising, but King won by more than 8 points. He has passed on a Senate run for 2014.

Key Votes

2012	
Extend a Social Security payroll tax cut and unemployment benefits	NO
Ease securities rules to expand small-business access to capital	YES
Extend for one year subsidized student loan interest rates financed by a cut in health care spending	YES
Cite Attorney General Eric H. Holder Jr. for contempt of Congress	YES
Create a visa program for foreign graduates in high-tech fields	YES
Extend most Bush-era income tax rates while allowing rates for top-bracket earners to rise (Jan. 1, 2013)	NO
2011	
Strike funding for F-35 alternative engine	NO
Prevent EPA from regulating greenhouse gas emissions to address climate change	YES
Extend certain provisions of Patriot Act for four years	YES
Declare opposition to use of ground troops in Libya	YES
Overhaul patent law	NO
Pass compromise debt limit increase plan and establish future spending limits	NO
Allow consideration of measures to implement three trade agreements	YES

CQ Vote Studies

	PARTY UNITY		PRESIDENTIAL SUPPORT	
	SUPPORT	OPPOSE	SUPPORT	OPPOSE
2012	97%	3%	12%	88%
2011	94%	6%	29%	71%
2010	98%	2%	22%	78%
2009	99%	1%	13%	87%
2008	97%	3%	77%	23%

Interest Groups

	AFL-CIO	ADA	CCUS	ACU
2012	5%	0%	92%	88%
2011	0%	5%	88%	92%
2010	0%	5%	75%	96%
2009	5%	0%	73%	96%
2008	0%	5%	83%	96%

Iowa 4

Northwest — Sioux City, Ames

Sweeping up 39 counties, the 4th District is adjacent to South Dakota and Nebraska in the Siouxland region to the west and Minnesota in the north. Much of the district is manufacturing and fertile farming counties, and some areas have experienced years of population loss.

Sioux City, the district's largest population center and a hub of the tri-state metropolitan area, has a rich link to America's history: Lewis and Clark passed through on their way to the Pacific Northwest. Home of the original annual "Corn Palaces" in the late 19th century, Sioux City is now a distribution center for the state's primary crop. Other food processing facilities and health care jobs are economic mainstays.

In contrast to steady population loss in several centrally located counties, Ames and surrounding Story County have welcomed new residents in the last decade. Ames' proximity to state government — the college town is just 30 miles north of Des Moines — and its agricultural engineering research centers near Iowa State University attract educated professionals and provide a stable economy. The city is home to several state and federal government facilities, including the National Animal Disease Center and National Veterinary Services Laboratories.

Rural farmland and small communities blanket the rest of the district. The region is heavy in corn and soybean fields, as well as cattle ranching. The Iowa Great Lakes lie in the north and generate tourism revenue, and investors have eyed the expansive region for greater wind energy development.

Long a rock-ribbed Republican region, the newly drawn district became slightly more politically competitive with the additions of liberal-leaning Story County and some north-central counties during decennial remapping. Republicans hold an edge in voter registration here, and traditionally Dutch areas in the northwest are strongly conservative — Sioux County regularly gives Republicans their highest margins of victory in the state.

Major Industry
Agriculture, food processing, distribution, research

Cities
Sioux City, Ames, Mason City, Fort Dodge

Notable
In 1959, after playing a last concert, Buddy Holly, Ritchie Valens and J.P. "The Big Bopper" Richardson died in a plane crash near Clear Lake.

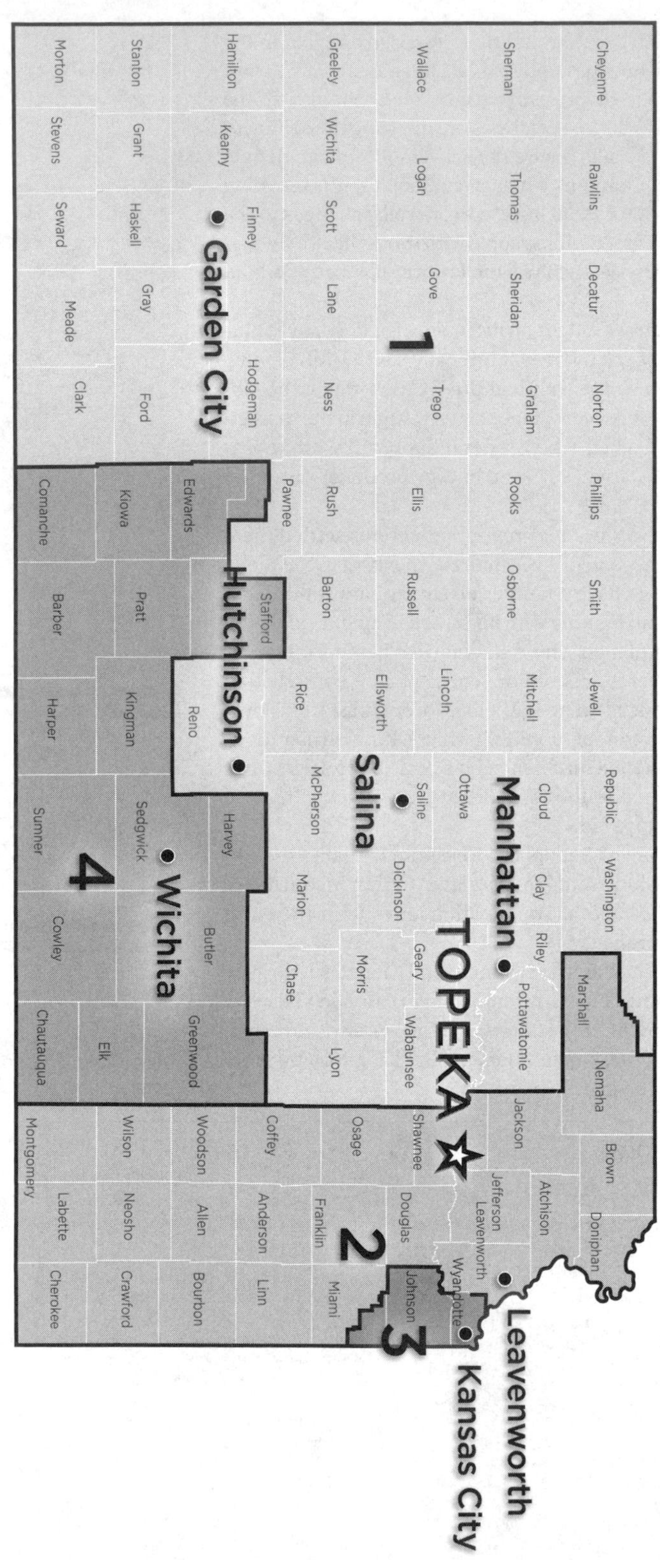
1
2
3
4
Garden City
Hutchinson
Salina
Manhattan
TOPEKA
Wichita
Leavenworth
Kansas City
Cheyenne
Rawlins
Decatur
Norton
Phillips
Smith
Jewell
Republic
Washington
Marshall
Nemaha
Brown
Doniphan
Sherman
Thomas
Sheridan
Graham
Rooks
Osborne
Mitchell
Cloud
Clay
Riley
Pottawatomie
Jackson
Atchison
Jefferson
Leavenworth
Wyandotte
Wallace
Logan
Gove
Trego
Ellis
Russell
Lincoln
Ottawa
Saline
Dickinson
Geary
Wabaunsee
Shawnee
Douglas
Johnson
Greeley
Wichita
Scott
Lane
Ness
Rush
Barton
Ellsworth
McPherson
Marion
Morris
Chase
Lyon
Osage
Franklin
Miami
Hamilton
Kearny
Finney
Hodgeman
Pawnee
Stafford
Rice
Reno
Harvey
Butler
Greenwood
Coffey
Anderson
Linn
Edwards
Pratt
Kingman
Sedgwick
Woodson
Allen
Bourbon
Stanton
Grant
Haskell
Gray
Ford
Kiowa
Barber
Harper
Sumner
Cowley
Elk
Wilson
Neosho
Crawford
Morton
Stevens
Seward
Meade
Clark
Comanche
Chautauqua
Montgomery
Labette
Cherokee

Gov. Sam Brownback (R)

First elected: 2010
Length of term: 4 years
Term expires: 1/15
Salary: $109,000
Phone: (785) 296-3232
Residence: Topeka
Born: Sept. 12, 1956; Garnett, Kan.
Religion: Roman Catholic
Family: Wife, Mary Brownback; five children
Education: Kansas State U., B.S. 1979 (agricultural economics); U. of Kansas, J.D. 1982
Career: College instructor; lawyer; White House fellow
Political highlights: Kan. secretary of agriculture, 1986-93; U.S. House, 1995-96; U.S. Senate, 1996-2011

ELECTION RESULTS

2010 GENERAL

Sam Brownback (R)	530,760	63.2%
Tom Holland (D)	270,166	32.2%
Andrew Grey (LIBERT)	22,460	2.6%
Kenneth Cannon (REF)	15,397	1.8%

Lt. Gov. Jeff Colyer (R)

First elected: 2010
Length of term: 4 years
Term expires: 1/15
Salary: $31,301
Phone: (785) 296-2214

LEGISLATURE

Legislature: January to spring, limit of 90 days in even-numbered years
Senate: 40 members, 4-year terms
2013 ratios: 32 R, 8 D; 28 men, 12 women
Salary: $26,132
Phone: (785) 296-2456
House: 125 members, 2-year terms
2013 ratios: 92 R, 33 D; 98 men, 27 women
Salary: $26,132
Phone: (785) 296-7633

TERM LIMITS

Governor: 2 terms
Senate: No
House: No

URBAN STATISTICS

CITY	POPULATION
Wichita	382,368
Overland Park	173,372
Kansas City	145,786
Topeka	127,473
Olathe	125,872

REGISTERED VOTERS

Republican	45%
Democrat	25%
Other	30%

POPULATION

2010 population	2,853,118
2000 population	2,688,418
1990 population	2,477,574
Percent change (2000-2010)	+6.1%
Rank among states (2010)	33
Median age	35.9
Born in state	59.1%
Foreign born	5.8%
Violent crime rate	400/100,000
Poverty level	13.4%
Federal workers	35,148
Military	25,482

ELECTIONS

STATE ELECTION OFFICIAL
(785) 296-4561
DEMOCRATIC PARTY
(785) 234-0425
REPUBLICAN PARTY
(785) 234-3456

MISCELLANEOUS

Web: www.kansas.gov
Capital: Topeka

U.S. CONGRESS

Senate: 2 Republicans
House: 4 Republicans

STATISTICS BY DISTRICT

District	2012 Vote for President: Obama	Romney	2008 Vote for President: Obama	McCain	Black	Asian	Hispanic	Median Income	Over 64	Under 20	College Education	Rural	Sq. Miles
1	28%	70%	31%	67%	3%	2%	14%	$43,340	15%	28%	23%	44%	52,542
2	42	55	45	53	5	1	6	45,008	14	27	27	37	14,143
3	44	54	49	50	9	4	11	61,380	11	29	43	5	757
4	36	62	40	59	6	3	11	48,100	13	29	27	21	14,316
STATE	**38**	**60**	**42**	**57**	**6**	**2**	**11**	**48,964**	**13**	**28**	**30**	**27**	**81,759**
U.S.	**51**	**47**	**53**	**46**	**12**	**5**	**17**	**50,052**	**13**	**27**	**29**	**21**	**3,531,905**

Sen. Pat Roberts (R)

Capitol Office
224-4774
roberts.senate.gov
109 Hart Bldg. 20510-1605; fax 224-3514

Committees
Agriculture, Nutrition & Forestry
Finance
Health, Education, Labor & Pensions
Rules & Administration - Ranking Member
Select Ethics
Joint Library
Joint Printing

Residence
Dodge City

Born
April 20, 1936; Topeka, Kan.

Religion
Methodist

Family
Wife, Franki Roberts; three children

Education
Kansas State U., B.A. 1958 (journalism)

Military Service
Marine Corps, 1958-62

Career
Congressional aide; newspaper owner; reporter

Political Highlights
U.S. House, 1981-97

ELECTION RESULTS

2008 GENERAL

Pat Roberts (R)	727,121	60.1%
Jim Slattery (D)	441,399	36.5%
Randall L. Hodgkinson (LIBERT)	25,727	2.1%
Joseph L. Martin (REF)	16,443	1.4%

2008 PRIMARY

Pat Roberts (R)	unopposed

Previous Winning Percentages
2002 (83%); 1996 (62%); 1994 House Election (77%); 1992 House Election (68%); 1990 House Election (63%); 1988 House Election (100%); 1986 House Election (77%); 1984 House Election (76%); 1982 House Election (68%); 1980 House Election (62%)

Elected 1996; 3rd term

The political culture of Kansas has moved further to the right in recent years, but Roberts hasn't changed. He is a conservative in the mold of fellow Kansan Bob Dole, committed to basic ideological principles but strongly valuing legislative results.

Like Dole, Roberts also has a homespun and pithy humor — though he has been less hesitant to showcase it. More than once, Washingtonian magazine's survey of Capitol Hill staffers has identified Roberts as the "funniest senator." When a reporter asked if he had concerns about the Senate farm bill, Roberts replied, "I think we can pay it."

However, Roberts couldn't have found it amusing when he was deposed as the ranking member of the Agriculture, Nutrition and Forestry Committee at the start of the 113th Congress (2013-14). Republican Party rules barred Mississippi's Thad Cochran from continuing as the ranking member of the Appropriations Committee, so Cochran asserted his seniority and bumped Roberts aside. Roberts was publicly gracious and promised his state's farmers that "I will continue to be your voice and your champion at every turn."

Roberts frequently says that he wants the market, not the government, to shape farming decisions. He was the chairman of the House Agriculture Committee during the writing of the 1996 law reauthorizing farm programs. It replaced traditional crop subsidies with a system of fixed but declining payments to farmers — a program meant to smooth the transition into a world without subsidies. But the 2002 farm law, which Roberts voted against as a senator, made direct payments a linchpin of farm policy.

During the 112th Congress (2011-12), Roberts helped develop a five-year reauthorization that passed the Senate in June 2012. That bill would have ended direct payments, replacing them with "shallow loss" coverage — a program that makes up part of the difference when revenues from a crop yield fall below the average level from the last five years. Roberts and Michigan Democrat Debbie Stabenow, the panel's chairwoman, formed a working relationship that enabled them and their House counterparts to set a deficit reduction target of $23 billion over 10 years for farm bill programs. "It is not the best possible bill, but it is the best bill possible," Roberts said.

The House never voted on its version, however, and Roberts battled Cochran as work continued in the 113th Congress. According to Cochran, the 2012 bill was not fair to Southern farmers. When the panel approved a new version in May 2013, it included a "target price" program that pays out when commodity prices fall below levels set by the government — something that Southerners had clamored for. Roberts panned it as another government subsidy, and he urged the committee to get back to the "risk-oriented and market-based approach."

Roberts continues to look for savings in farm and food programs. He has introduced a bill to trim $36 billion from the Supplemental Nutrition Assistance Program over a decade, mostly via changes to program eligibility.

He also participates in the GOP push to limit federal regulations. He worked with Stabenow in 2011 to approve a House-passed bill that prevents the EPA from implementing new permitting requirements for commercial pesticide users who spray over rivers and other bodies of water. Roberts said the requirements constituted an unnecessary burden on farmers. Democrats on the Environment and Public Works Committee blocked the measure from further consideration, however.

Outside of agriculture, Roberts is interested in reducing regulations related to the 2010 health care overhaul law. He sits on the Finance Committee and the Health, Education, Labor and Pensions Committee, which have jurisdiction over health care. "I think the overregulation in virtually every economic sector that we have out there is a result of very comprehensive legislation back here," he said. "We are drowning in regulations."

Roberts is concerned about how rural health care facilities will fare under new rules required by the health care law and said he would work "to stop this Katrina of regulations on our health care delivery system."

He also worked with fellow Kansan Jerry Moran in 2011 to force the White House to withdraw the nomination of Democrat Steve N. Six for the 10th U.S. Circuit Court of Appeals. When Six was the Kansas attorney general, he concluded that the federal health care law was not constitutionally deficient, and he did not file a lawsuit against it. Roberts was not pleased.

Still, Roberts hasn't been an intractable partisan. Rep. Barney Frank, a liberal Massachusetts Democrat who is now retired, once told the Kansas City Star that Roberts was "not one of the impossible ideologues." In the 110th Congress (2007-08), only seven Republican senators voted against President George W. Bush's stated preferences more often than Roberts.

He considers Health and Human Services Secretary Kathleen Sebelius a friend. She is the daughter-in-law of former Republican Rep. Keith G. Sebelius of Kansas. Roberts was an aide to the older Sebelius, and he succeeded him in the House when he retired.

Roberts also has held thankless jobs. "I'm the longest-serving member in the history of the Senate on the Ethics Committee," he jokes. "I don't know why I've been treated that way. I can't get off. I've resigned twice."

Earlier in his career, Roberts had a deeper involvement with national security issues. He chaired the Intelligence Committee from 2003 through 2006. Documents released in early 2010 suggested that Roberts had raised no objection to the CIA's plan to destroy videotapes that allegedly showed agents waterboarding terror suspects; Roberts denied approving the plan.

As the first chairman of the Armed Services Subcommittee on Emerging Threats and Capabilities in 1999, Roberts pressed the Pentagon and Congress to move beyond a Cold War mentality and prepare for attacks on civilian populations and computer networks. Roberts gave up his slot on Armed Services but still defends Kansas' military installations and aviation industry.

Roberts lobbied successfully for the Homeland Security Department to recommend Manhattan, Kan., as the new location for the National Bio and Agro-Defense Facility. He now finds himself fighting for the federal funding to complete the move.

A fourth-generation Kansan, Roberts earned a journalism degree from Kansas State University, intending to follow a family tradition in the news business. His great-grandfather, J.W. Roberts, founded the Oskaloosa Independent, the second-oldest newspaper in Kansas. Politics ran in the family, too. Roberts' father, Wes, was chairman of the Republican National Committee under President Dwight D. Eisenhower.

After graduation, Roberts was drafted and served in the Marines, as his father had. His office is decorated with Corps regalia. On leaving the military, Roberts worked as a reporter and then co-owned a weekly newspaper. He began working as a congressional aide in Washington in 1967.

His first run for office was his 1980 bid to succeed Sebelius in the "Big First," the sprawling rural district that covers most of the state. He took 62 percent of the vote.

Roberts initially balked at running for the Senate in 1996 when Republican Nancy Landon Kassebaum retired. He said he wanted to focus on shepherding the farm bill into law. When he eventually entered the race, he handily won the GOP nod and then the general election. His worst showing in any congressional race was in 2008 — he still took 60 percent of the vote.

Roberts has indicated that he plans to seek a fourth term in 2014.

Key Votes

2012

Prohibit health insurance plans from denying coverage based on the sponsor's religious beliefs	NO
Require approval of the Keystone XL oil pipeline	YES
Ease securities rules to expand small-business access to capital	YES
Reauthorize farm and nutrition programs for five years	YES
Limit debate on a bill that would create private-sector cybersecurity standards	NO
Consent to ratification of a treaty setting global standard for the treatment of people with disabilities	NO
Provide $60.4 billion in disaster relief following Superstorm Sandy	NO
Extend most Bush-era income tax rates while allowing rates for top-bracket earners to rise (Jan. 1, 2013)	YES

2011

Prevent EPA from regulating greenhouse gas emissions to address climate change	YES
Extend certain provisions of Patriot Act for four years	?
Clear compromise debt limit increase plan and establish future spending limits	YES
Overhaul patent law	YES
Implement Colombia free trade agreement	YES
Limit debate on confirmation of Caitlin J. Halligan to D.C. Circuit Court of Appeals	NO
Extend payroll tax cut and unemployment benefits for two months	YES

CQ Vote Studies

	PARTY UNITY		PRESIDENTIAL SUPPORT	
	SUPPORT	OPPOSE	SUPPORT	OPPOSE
2012	86%	14%	47%	53%
2011	90%	10%	53%	47%
2010	99%	1%	29%	71%
2009	90%	10%	51%	49%
2008	87%	13%	65%	35%
2007	84%	16%	81%	19%
2006	94%	6%	88%	12%
2005	94%	6%	93%	7%
2004	99%	1%	92%	8%
2003	96%	4%	97%	3%

Interest Groups

	AFL-CIO	ADA	CCUS	ACU
2012	9%	15%	100%	72%
2011	16%	15%	100%	80%
2010	7%	0%	100%	96%
2009	11%	5%	67%	96%
2008	30%	20%	88%	72%
2007	26%	20%	73%	92%
2006	27%	5%	92%	84%
2005	8%	0%	100%	88%
2004	17%	15%	100%	92%
2003	0%	15%	100%	90%

Sen. Jerry Moran (R)

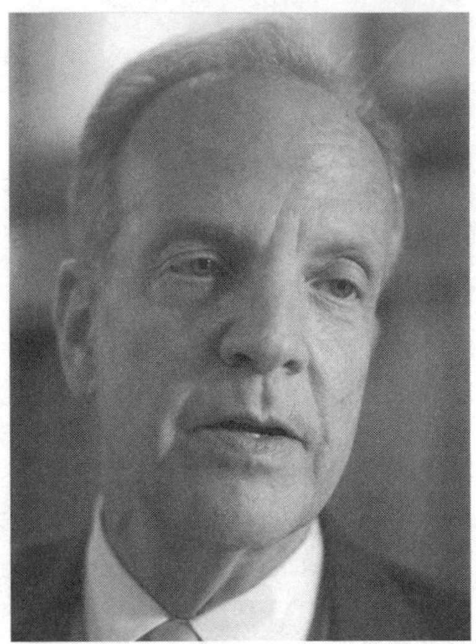

Capitol Office
224-6521
moran.senate.gov
361A Russell Bldg. 20510; fax 228-6966

Committees
Appropriations
Banking, Housing & Urban Affairs
Veterans' Affairs

Residence
Hays

Born
May 29, 1954; Great Bend, Kan.

Religion
Christian

Family
Wife, Robba Moran; two children

Education
Fort Hays Kansas State College, attended 1972-73; U. of Kansas, B.S. 1976 (economics), J.D. 1981

Career
Lawyer; banker

Political Highlights
Kan. Senate, 1989-97 (vice president, 1993-95; majority leader, 1995-97); U.S. House, 1997-2011

ELECTION RESULTS

2010 GENERAL		
Jerry Moran (R)	587,175	70.1%
Lisa Johnston (D)	220,971	26.4%
Michael Wm. Dann (LIBERT)	17,922	2.1%
Joe Bellis (D)	11,624	1.4%
2010 PRIMARY		
Jerry Moran (R)	163,483	49.7%
Todd Tiahrt (R)	146,702	44.6%
Tom Little (R)	10,256	3.1%
Robert "Bob" Londerholm (R)	8,278	2.5%

Previous Winning Percentages
2008 House Election (82%); 2006 House Election (79%); 2004 House Election (91%); 2002 House Election (91%); 2000 House Election (89%); 1998 House Election (81%); 1996 House Election (73%)

Elected 2010; 1st term

Moran sticks with a combination that serves him well: small-government conservatism; a respectful demeanor; and flexibility when his constituents demand it. He is now testing his methods on a national scale as the head of campaign operations for Senate Republicans.

Moran was elected chairman of the National Republican Senatorial Committee in November 2012, shortly after Republicans were disheartened by the loss of two Senate seats in the general election. Some observers considered Moran an odd choice, given his low profile and lack of experience as a national fundraiser, but he ran unopposed.

He assuaged some worries (and demonstrated his flexibility) by agreeing to work with two deputies. Rob Portman of Ohio is helping him with fundraising, and Ted Cruz of Texas is focusing on grass-roots outreach efforts. And as he coordinates his team, Moran can point to his success working with all parts of the Republican Party in Kansas.

Moderates and conservatives have battled for control of the Kansas GOP going back to the 1980s. Moran has flourished while straddling the divide between them. A native of the "Big First" — the agriculture-dominated district covering most of the state — Moran worked as a banker and lawyer before hopping into electoral politics. A run of eight years in the state Senate, the last two as majority leader, ended with a move to the U.S. House.

His 14 years in that chamber were marked by dominance at the polls and a few prominent splits with GOP leaders. Citing desires for limited government and less spending, he opposed the 2003 Medicare prescription drug benefit law and the 2002 education law known as No Child Left Behind. He was more forgiving of interventions on behalf of farmers or rural residents.

Conservatives currently control the Kansas government and have a tea-party-backed governor in Sam Brownback, whom Moran succeeded in the Senate. To win his Senate seat in 2010, Moran played up his conservative credentials and slipped by Rep. Todd Tiahrt in the Republican primary.

In the 112th Congress (2011-12), he emphasized fiscal themes in line with tea party thinking. On the Appropriations Committee, Moran and Wisconsin Republican Ron Johnson were the only members opposing an increase in annual spending caps for fiscal 2013. He supports replacing most taxes with a national sales tax and complains of a stifling regulatory environment.

Moran served on the Agriculture Committee in the House, but his colleague Pat Roberts has the state well represented on the Senate panel. His early Senate career has seen much of his committee focus shift to financial matters. He sits on the Banking, Housing and Urban Affairs Committee, as well as the Financial Services Appropriations Subcommittee.

True to form, Moran has sought ways to oversee implementation of the 2010 financial regulatory overhaul law without seeming partisan. In 2012, he pleaded with banking panel colleagues to spare each other allegations that "we're carrying water for some particular financial institution or segment of the financial industry" whenever a change to the law is suggested.

Moran has homed in on the Commodity Futures Trading Commission. Under the 2010 law, the CFTC is tasked with devising new regulations for derivatives, the risk-hedging financial instruments used by many industries, including agriculture. In the 112th Congress, Moran criticized the CFTC as botching its rule-writing duties and creating uncertainty in markets.

MF Global went bankrupt in 2011 because of questionable trading practices, and the Peregrine Financial Group collapsed in 2012 amid outright fraud. Moran questioned whether the CFTC could handle its workload and demanded the resignation of Chairman Gary Gensler. "On two occasions, the most basic requirement to protect the sanctity of customer accounts has been neglected," he said.

In 2013, Moran introduced a bill to alter the Consumer Financial Protection Bureau, which was created by the 2010 law. He wants its director replaced with a five-person commission, and he dislikes that the CFPB doesn't rely on congressional appropriations for its operating budget.

Moran's desire to help startup companies has led to a collaboration with Virginia Democrat Mark Warner. They wrote a 2011 bill that included a tax credit for certain startups and elimination of capital gains taxes on investments in small businesses that are held at least five years. Moran stumped for the measure at every opportunity, including the South by Southwest Interactive Festival in Austin, Texas. Warner and Moran later combined their plan with a bill by Delaware Democrat Chris Coons and Florida Republican Marco Rubio meant to get more visas to highly educated workers in technical fields. Rubio was replaced by Missouri Republican Roy Blunt in 2013 as the latest version of the bill was unveiled.

Moran makes time for issues with a direct effect on Kansas. He pursues commitments to build the National Bio and Agro-Defense Facility in Manhattan, and as a member of the Veterans' Affairs Committee, he emphasizes the needs of veterans in rural areas far from VA facilities. He has tried to attract more aviation business to the state, as the Boeing Co. pulled up stakes in 2012. He departs from conservatives in his support of the tax credit for the wind energy industry — Kansas derives more than 8 percent of its electricity from wind.

He also tries to influence some farm policies. Moran wants Cuba opened to agricultural exports, against the wishes of many Republicans. With drought affecting all of Kansas in 2012, he formed the Water Caucus with Arkansas Democrat Mark Pryor.

When Moran was 5, his family moved from the country to Plainville, population 2,000. His father was a laborer in the oil fields, and his mother worked as a secretary at an electric utility. As a student government officer at his high school, Moran was in charge of inviting the local congressman, Republican Keith G. Sebelius, to speak at a fundraising dinner.

In the summer of 1974, Moran went to Washington to work as an intern for Sebelius — he was on a staff with Roberts, who was an aide to Sebelius. Moran attended almost every House Judiciary Committee hearing on President Richard Nixon's impeachment.

After graduating from college with a degree in economics in 1976, Moran took a job as a banker. He earned his law degree five years later and opened his own practice in Hays. He made a long-shot run for the state Senate in 1988 against an 18-year incumbent. He won by a couple hundred votes in a historically Democratic district. Moran went on to become chairman of the chamber's Judiciary Committee, then ascended to majority leader in 1995.

Roberts was occupying the 1st District seat in 1996, but he decided to run for the Senate. Moran won the House race with more than 73 percent of the vote against Democrat John Divine, a former Salina mayor. Moran adopted the tradition, started by Sebelius, of a summer "listening tour," driving through all the counties in his district. His attention to constituents paid off. He has never won less than 70 percent of the vote in a general election for Congress.

Moran saved up for a statewide campaign, and when Brownback announced his 2010 gubernatorial run, he had his chance. In the primary, Tiahrt attacked Moran as not reliably conservative. Moran countered that he has been "a conservative even when Republicans are in charge and are doing things we can't afford." He won by 5 points and had no problem in November — Kansas hasn't elected a Democrat to the Senate since 1932.

Key Votes

2012	
Prohibit health insurance plans from denying coverage based on the sponsor's religious beliefs	NO
Require approval of the Keystone XL oil pipeline	YES
Ease securities rules to expand small-business access to capital	YES
Reauthorize farm and nutrition programs for five years	YES
Limit debate on a bill that would create private-sector cybersecurity standards	NO
Consent to ratification of a treaty setting global standard for the treatment of people with disabilities	NO
Provide $60.4 billion in disaster relief following Superstorm Sandy	NO
Extend most Bush-era income tax rates while allowing rates for top bracket earners to rise (Jan. 1, 2013)	YES
2011	
Prevent EPA from regulating greenhouse gas emissions to address climate change	YES
Extend certain provisions of Patriot Act for four years	YES
Clear compromise debt limit increase plan and establish future spending limits	NO
Overhaul patent law	YES
Implement Colombia free trade agreement	YES
Limit debate on confirmation of Caitlin J. Halligan to D.C. Circuit Court of Appeals	NO
Extend payroll tax cut and unemployment benefits for two months	NO

CQ Vote Studies

	PARTY UNITY		PRESIDENTIAL SUPPORT	
	SUPPORT	OPPOSE	SUPPORT	OPPOSE
2012	81%	19%	52%	48%
2011	88%	12%	57%	43%
2010	99%	1%	18%	82%
2009	96%	4%	21%	79%
2008	90%	10%	69%	31%
2007	87%	13%	71%	29%
2006	87%	13%	70%	30%
2005	92%	8%	76%	24%
2004	92%	8%	68%	32%
2003	92%	8%	82%	18%

Interest Groups

	AFL-CIO	ADA	CCUS	ACU
2012	9%	15%	88%	64%
2011	11%	10%	91%	85%
2010	8%	5%	71%	100%
2009	19%	5%	80%	96%
2008	14%	15%	89%	92%
2007	21%	30%	80%	88%
2006	29%	5%	93%	84%
2005	29%	15%	93%	96%
2004	21%	10%	95%	92%
2003	27%	25%	90%	92%

Rep. Tim Huelskamp (R)

Capitol Office
225-2715
huelskamp.house.gov
129 Cannon Bldg. 20515-1601; fax 225-5124

Committees
Small Business
Veterans' Affairs

Residence
Fowler

Born
Nov. 11, 1968; Fowler, Kan.

Religion
Roman Catholic

Family
Wife, Angela Huelskamp; four children

Education
College of Santa Fe, B.A. 1991 (education); American U., Ph.D. 1995 (political science)

Career
Farmer

Political Highlights
Kan. Senate, 1997-2011

ELECTION RESULTS

2012 GENERAL		
Tim Huelskamp (R)		unopposed
2012 PRIMARY		
Tim Huelskamp (R)		unopposed
2010 GENERAL		
Tim Huelskamp (R)	142,281	73.8%
Alan Jilka (D)	44,068	22.8%
Jack Warner (D)	6,537	3.4%

Elected 2010; 2nd term

Huelskamp represents Eisenhower country, and he's borrowing a page from the general by creating a second front in his personal war. After furiously attacking government spending in his first term, he has started open hostilities with House Republican leaders, whom he accuses of betraying conservative principles.

A small-town farmer who served more than a decade in the Kansas Senate, Huelskamp (HYOOLS-camp) always has presented himself as deeply conservative — someone who sees government as contributing to "the fiscal and cultural crises facing our nation," as he wrote in 2012. He has strong support from the tea party movement (which is ascendant in Kansas politics) and the anti-tax Club for Growth. He's also an agricultural policy expert in an immense rural district. If he never becomes a supreme commander of the Republican Party, Huelskamp has the potential to survive as a conservative warlord.

Huelskamp compiled one of the most fiscally conservative voting records in the 112th Congress (2011-12), repeatedly rejecting spending and deficit reduction measures as being inadequately austere. As a member of the Budget Committee, he was one of two panel Republicans to vote against the fiscal 2013 budget of Chairman Paul D. Ryan; he was then one of 10 in his party to oppose it on the House floor.

He is sharply against tax increases. When Democrats rallied behind statements by billionaire Warren Buffett that he should have to pay more taxes, Huelskamp helped write a bill to add a line to tax forms where people could voluntarily contribute to reduce the national debt. (He wrote a similar bill as a state senator.) He wants significant changes to entitlement programs. He worked on an overhaul of Kansas' Medicaid system as a state senator, and he was an original co-sponsor of a 2012 bill to convert federal Medicaid spending into a block grant.

Huelskamp as a freshman was generally irritated by the institution of Congress, and he wasn't afraid to voice his discontent. "There was a race on to see if the freshman class could change the system before the system changed them, and I think as a whole we are losing that race," Huelskamp said. He was livid that several major pieces of legislation were negotiated by small groups and not shaped on the House floor, and he was caustic when publicly expressing his disappointment with GOP leaders.

The leaders noticed. After the 2012 elections, the GOP Steering Committee removed Huelskamp from the Budget and Agriculture committees, making him one of four Republicans punished in that manner. Defending the decision to a group of conservatives, Steering member Lynn Westmoreland of Georgia said it was based on refusal to work constructively within the system: "I guess you could say it was an asshole factor." Other rank-and-file Republicans have been vexed by Huelskamp's behavior.

Huelskamp unleashed a series of angry missives at GOP leaders, vowing that conservatives would not roll over. "This is clearly a vindictive move, and a sure sign that the GOP establishment cannot handle disagreement," he wrote. He participated in an unsuccessful campaign to deny John A. Boehner a second term as speaker in the 113th Congress (2013-14). He was photographed on the House floor looking at a list of lawmakers who might have been willing to join him. After voting against Boehner, he issued a fundraising letter that said, "They will punish me. They will attack my family."

It will be tough for Huelskamp to jump into legislative debates in the 113th. He now sits on the Small Business and Veterans' Affairs committees, which are not due to take up any major reauthorizations.

His removal from the Agriculture Committee could smart the most, as the panel will still be working on a long-term reauthorization of farm and nutrition programs. In 1995, Huelskamp attained a doctorate in political science, and his thesis is titled "Congressional Change: Committees on Agriculture in the United States Congress." It deals with past farm bills.

Huelskamp has proposed major changes to that legislative package. He wants federal nutrition programs split off into their own bill and converted into a block grant. In 2011 he introduced a measure to add a regulatory section to the farm bill, including provisions to prohibit regulation of farm dust, delay derivatives regulations under the 2010 financial services overhaul law, restrict the expansion of EPA water regulations and prohibit regulation of greenhouse gas emissions under the Clean Air Act.

The 1st District is behind only North Dakota's at-large district in the receipt of direct federal farm subsidies. Huelskamp, however, is among the lawmakers expecting that system to disappear. The Washington Post reported that Huelskamp delivered the message personally to rural constituents in June 2011. "If you're a farmer like me, you're going to expect less," he said. "The direct payments are going to go away."

He is just as conservative socially as he is fiscally. Huelskamp is committed to seeking a ban on abortion. In the Kansas Senate, he pushed for amendments to the state constitution to guarantee individual gun rights and to ban gay marriage, and in January 2012 he introduced a bill to both protect military chaplains who refuse to perform gay marriages and prevent the use of Defense Department facilities for such functions.

A native of Fowler, Huelskamp attended Catholic seminary for two years in Santa Fe, then pursued his bachelor's degree in education at the College of Santa Fe. He worked as a budget and legislative analyst for the state of New Mexico while in college.

He earned his Ph.D. at American University, where he met his wife, Angela. Together they were active in assisting women in crisis pregnancies. The couple now has four adopted children: Natasha, Rebecca, Athan and Alexander, two of whom were born in Haiti.

Huelskamp opened a federal campaign account in 2006 when Rep. Jerry Moran, a Republican, was mulling a gubernatorial bid. Moran announced in 2008 that he would make a bid two years later for a Senate seat. Huelskamp entered the race to succeed him in the House.

He won the endorsement of the Club for Growth and raised the most money, taking nearly 35 percent of the vote in a six-way primary. He then crushed the Democratic nominee, former Salina Mayor Alan Jilka. He was unopposed in 2012.

Key Votes

2012	
Extend a Social Security payroll tax cut and unemployment benefits	YES
Ease securities rules to expand small-business access to capital	YES
Extend for one year subsidized student loan interest rates financed by a cut in health care spending	NO
Cite Attorney General Eric H. Holder Jr. for contempt of Congress	YES
Create a visa program for foreign graduates in high-tech fields	YES
Extend most Bush-era income tax rates while allowing rates for top-bracket earners to rise (Jan. 1, 2013)	NO
2011	
Strike funding for F-35 alternative engine	YES
Prevent EPA from regulating greenhouse gas emissions to address climate change	YES
Extend certain provisions of Patriot Act for four years	+
Declare opposition to use of ground troops in Libya	NO
Overhaul patent law	NO
Pass compromise debt limit increase plan and establish future spending limits	NO
Allow consideration of measures to implement three trade agreements	YES

CQ Vote Studies

	Party Unity		Presidential Support	
	SUPPORT	OPPOSE	SUPPORT	OPPOSE
2012	95%	5%	28%	72%
2011	96%	4%	20%	80%

Interest Groups

	AFL-CIO	ADA	CCUS	ACU
2012	19%	35%	83%	92%
2011	0%	5%	88%	92%

Kansas 1

Central and west — Manhattan, Salina, Hutchinson, Garden City

In the 1960s, Truman Capote described western Kansas as a "lonesome area that other Kansans call 'out there.'" The conservative Big 1st takes in nearly all of rural western Kansas and reaches east past Manhattan, avoiding the state's major population centers.

Many counties in the 1st shed residents between 2000 and 2010 while the state's larger cities grew. During decennial remapping, the district ceded some rural counties in the south to the Wichita-based 4th and added Manhattan and Pottawatomie County. The new areas, which include Kansas State University and the massive active-duty and military retiree populations near Fort Riley (both in Manhattan), solidified the district's GOP advantage.

The ongoing population shift from the western counties to the east has depleted the region west of Barton County to the Colorado border. The district overall is overwhelmingly white, although three counties in the southwest — Finney, Ford and Seward — are home to large Hispanic populations drawn to the meatpacking and cattle-ranching industries.

The manufacturing, health care and construction industries are key to the eastern portion of the 1st. Food processor Schwan has operations in Salina, as does battery maker Exide and bus maker ElDorado National. The west still relies on cattle, farming and oil and gas production.

The district is comfortably Republican. Voters backed the GOP candidate for U.S. Senate and governor in 2010. Republican presidential nominee Mitt Romney won many counties in the 1st by wide margins in 2012 and some sparsely populated areas gave him more than 80 percent of the vote, but he had less support in Riley County (Manhattan), as well as near some of the 1st's other population centers — Salina and Garden City.

Major Industry
Agriculture, defense, construction, manufacturing

Military Bases
Fort Riley (Army), 19,468 military, 6,279 civilian

Cities
Manhattan, Salina, Dodge City

Notable
Dwight D. Eisenhower's burial place and presidential library are in Abilene.

Rep. Lynn Jenkins (R)

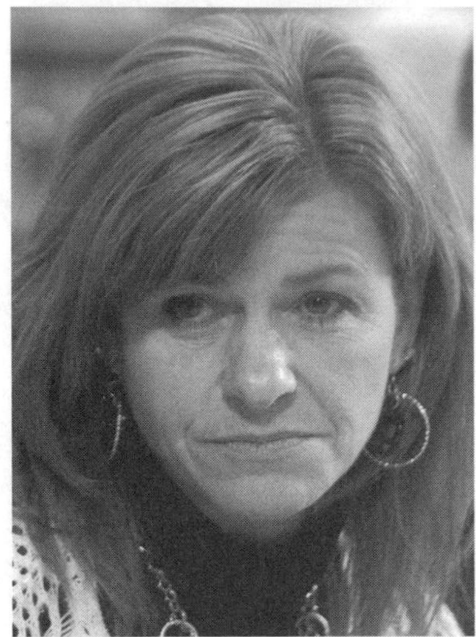

Capitol Office
225-6601
lynnjenkins.house.gov
1027 Longworth Bldg. 20515-1602; fax 225-7986

Committees
Ways & Means

Residence
Topeka

Born
June 10, 1963; Topeka, Kan.

Religion
United Methodist

Family
Divorced; two children

Education
Kansas State U., A.A. 1985 (business administration); Weber State College, B.S. 1985 (accounting)

Career
Accountant; homemaker

Political Highlights
Kan. House, 1999-2001; Kan. Senate, 2001-03; Kan. treasurer, 2003-09

ELECTION RESULTS

2012 GENERAL		
Lynn Jenkins (R)	167,463	57.0%
Tobias Schlingensiepen (D)	113,735	38.7%
Ira Dennis "Dennis" Hawver (LIBERT)	12,520	4.3%
2012 PRIMARY		
Lynn Jenkins (R)		unopposed
2010 GENERAL		
Lynn Jenkins (R)	130,034	63.1%
Cheryl Hudspeth (D)	66,588	32.3%
Robert Garrard (D)	9,353	4.5%

Previous Winning Percentages
2008 (51%)

Elected 2008; 3rd term

Not that long ago, Jenkins said she was content to serve as an anonymous wonk on the Ways and Means Committee. "I'd be happy if I never did an interview," she commented in the spring of 2012. "I don't need to see my name in print, ever."

Things have changed. In the 113th Congress (2013-14), Jenkins is the vice chairwoman of the Republican Conference. She told The Topeka Capital-Journal that she sought the job because GOP leaders in the 112th Congress (2011-12) were failing to connect with a huge segment of their constituency: "They weren't talking to women's hearts."

In her new role, Jenkins is an occasional spokeswoman in the media and a liaison between rank-and-file Republicans and the House leadership team. She has connections throughout the party. Jenkins belongs to the conservative Republican Study Committee and the moderate Main Street Partnership. In early 2013, she joined No Labels, a bipartisan group with the goal of increasing the overall productivity of Congress.

She retains her interest in fiscal policy. As an accountant and former state treasurer, Jenkins is a numbers person. And as a small-government conservative, she wants the government's numbers, whether for tax rates or spending, to go way down.

Jenkins found her natural habitat in 2011 when she joined Ways and Means. At a 2012 hearing on tax policy and financial accounting, she told witnesses, "I'm not sure I've had this much fun in the year that I've been on the panel." Chairman Dave Camp of Michigan teased her for redefining fun.

She says her interest in financial planning probably goes back to her early life. The youngest of three children, she was raised on a dairy farm near Holton; the town square was essentially "Mayberry R.F.D.," she said. The whole family worked — there are no family vacations on a dairy farm — and money was tight. "People shouldn't have to lay awake at night worrying if they can make the bills," and that also applies to government, she said.

Jenkins sees an overhaul of the tax code as one of her best opportunities to effect large-scale change, and she subscribes to the "simpler, flatter, fairer" standard used by many lawmakers. To Jenkins, a fair code means "lower rates with less subsidies." It would take in at least some money from the half of U.S. earners currently not paying income taxes. "We're using our tax code to subsidize certain industries and certain people," she said. "I think that's where the calls of crony capitalism come in."

Jenkins has introduced bills to expand tax credits for hiring National Guard members and for railroad track maintenance. She teamed with Wisconsin Democrat Ron Kind on a bill to expand the uses of "529" college savings plans. She said those initiatives would disappear in the tax code she envisions. "I think we shouldn't be trying to do social policy through the tax code," though things like the home mortgage interest deduction might survive, Jenkins said.

She speculates that she is one of the last members of Congress to file her own tax returns, and she says compliance costs are far too high for both individuals and businesses. Accountants are all for simplicity, she said: "They'd rather be doing the planning and some of the higher-level work than dealing with compliance work."

She has advocated lowering corporate tax rates and making other changes that she says will keep the United States internationally competitive. From the Trade Subcommittee, she strongly endorsed free-trade agreements with South Korea, Panama and Colombia in 2011.

Jenkins has been intrigued by dramatic tax changes. She is a co-sponsor of the "FairTax" bill, which would replace most taxes with a national sales tax — but she said it's an idea that likely has to wait for now.

The same goes for changes to the government's accounting methods. "We have no idea what the balance sheet looks like," she said. "We don't know where our assets are at. We don't fully account for what our liabilities are. Any CPA up here would be shocked and appalled. ... But again, that's a battle that's going to take a long time."

On the spending side of the balance sheet, Jenkins is very much in tune with the tea party sensibilities that Kansas has favored in recent years. She wants the federal government stripped back to core missions such as defense and infrastructure development and rejects the notion that states couldn't handle a federal withdrawal. As Kansas treasurer, "I wished the federal government had just gone away." The responsibility for Medicare and Social Security should stay in Washington, but Kansas would do just about everything else better and more efficiently than the federal government, Jenkins maintains.

In fact, she concurs with most reductions in the federal role, as long as there is enough lead time for financial planning. Agriculture is an example. Jenkins says Kansas farmers are fine with the elimination of direct federal payments, as long as they have "a year or two to respond" and plan for it. They would like crop insurance programs to survive as a safety net, however, and they wouldn't mind funding of the National Bio and Agro-Defense Facility being built at Kansas State University in the 1st District.

The energetic Jenkins puts a premium on constituent service, traveling back to Kansas every week; she has been criticized in the past for the costs of mailings and other communications with her district. Her family has been in the state for six generations — President James Buchanan signed the deed held by her ancestors. Her parents were always active in GOP politics, and she remembers marching in 4-H Club parades while wearing sandwich boards for Bob Dole. She served as student body president at her high school.

After a decade as a CPA and homemaker, friends drafted her into a special election for a vacant state House seat. Party officials chose the winner, and Jenkins lost by a single vote — a "bad experience" she remedied by winning the regular election the next year. Jenkins quickly moved to the state Senate, then won two statewide races for treasurer.

In 2008, Jenkins set her sights on first-term Democrat Nancy Boyda, who had upset Republican Rep. Jim Ryun in 2006. She edged past Ryun in the GOP primary. Her race against Boyda was an acrimonious campaign to which both national parties devoted serious attention, with Jenkins winning by 4 points. Three days after the election, Jenkins' husband filed for divorce.

Her two re-elections were by wide margins.

Key Votes

2012	
Extend a Social Security payroll tax cut and unemployment benefits	YES
Ease securities rules to expand small-business access to capital	YES
Extend for one year subsidized student loan interest rates financed by a cut in health care spending	?
Cite Attorney General Eric H. Holder Jr. for contempt of Congress	YES
Create a visa program for foreign graduates in high-tech fields	YES
Extend most Bush-era income tax rates while allowing rates for top-bracket earners to rise (Jan. 1, 2013)	NO
2011	
Strike funding for F-35 alternative engine	YES
Prevent EPA from regulating greenhouse gas emissions to address climate change	YES
Extend certain provisions of Patriot Act for four years	YES
Declare opposition to use of ground troops in Libya	YES
Overhaul patent law	YES
Pass compromise debt limit increase plan and establish future spending limits	YES
Allow consideration of measures to implement three trade agreements	YES

CQ Vote Studies

	PARTY UNITY		PRESIDENTIAL SUPPORT	
	SUPPORT	OPPOSE	SUPPORT	OPPOSE
2012	99%	1%	16%	84%
2011	97%	3%	23%	77%
2010	97%	3%	26%	74%
2009	95%	5%	22%	78%

Interest Groups

	AFL-CIO	ADA	CCUS	ACU
2012	10%	0%	82%	100%
2011	0%	5%	100%	84%
2010	0%	0%	88%	100%
2009	10%	5%	87%	92%

Kansas 2

East — Topeka, Leavenworth

The vertical 2nd runs the length of east Kansas from Nebraska to Oklahoma, passing west of Kansas City. It combines rural farm communities and urbanized areas, including the state capital of Topeka and the city of Lawrence. Statewide population shifts, especially in the last decade, have brought new residents to the outer Kansas City suburbs and Topeka.

Following decennial remapping, the new 2nd lost Manhattan, home to Kansas State University and Fort Riley, to the 1st. But it gained areas outside of Kansas City in Douglas County (including the University of Kansas), Montgomery County to the southwest and parts of Marshall and Nemaha counties to the north.

Topeka and the surrounding areas of Shawnee County rely on state government jobs, but the city also will host a Mars Chocolate factory by the end of 2013. The Army's Fort Leavenworth, the oldest active U.S. Army post west of Washington, D.C., is known as the "intellectual center of the Army." The base provides support functions for the U.S. Army Combined Arms Center, including the Army Command and General Staff College and the Foreign Military Studies Office.

A conservative district, the redrawn 2nd has more registered Democrats than it did in the last decade, but nearly as many voters are unaffiliated. Democrats have success in the capital, Kansas City suburbs and Lawrence, but the rural areas are strongly Republican and the district overall backs the GOP at the federal level. Although the Democratic U.S. House candidate won in Shawnee and Douglas counties in 2012, Barack Obama only won in Douglas in the presidential contest. The district is overwhelmingly white, and the Hispanic population is the smallest in the state. The 2nd also hosts three American Indian reservations, all in the northern counties.

Major Industry
Agriculture, higher education, state government

Military Bases
Fort Leavenworth (Army), 4,063 military, 4,612 civilian

Cities
Topeka, Lawrence

Notable
Amelia Earhart was from Atchison, which hosts an annual festival in her honor; Pleasanton's Mine Creek Battlefield was the site of Kansas' only Civil War battle.

Rep. Kevin Yoder (R)

Capitol Office
225-2865
yoder.house.gov
215 Cannon Bldg. 20515-1603

Committees
Appropriations

Residence
Overland Park

Born
Jan. 8, 1976; Hutchinson, Kan.

Religion
Christian

Family
Wife, Brooke Robinson Yoder

Education
U. of Kansas, B.A. 1999 (political science & English), J.D. 2002

Career
Lawyer

Political Highlights
Kan. House, 2003-11

ELECTION RESULTS

2012 GENERAL		
Kevin Yoder (R)	201,087	68.4%
Joel Balam (LIBERT)	92,675	31.5%
2012 PRIMARY		
Kevin Yoder (R)		unopposed
2010 GENERAL		
Kevin Yoder (R)	136,246	58.4%
Stephene Moore (D)	90,193	38.7%
Jasmin Talbert (LIBERT)	6,846	2.9%

Elected 2010; 2nd term

Yoder typifies the new breed of Republican appropriators — he's young, energetic and mostly interested in cutting spending. But he has urged his party to stay flexible, should opportunities for transformative fiscal change present themselves.

Despite his age, Yoder has been immersed in budget politics for a long time. He was elected to the Kansas House at 26 and served eight years, the last two as chairman of its Appropriations Committee.

His freshman term in Washington was marked by flashes of exuberance; Yoder is personable and seems to enjoy being in Congress. At an April 2011 hearing, he asked Anthony M. Kennedy a question, then immediately interrupted his answer — "because as a young lawyer, it's always been my dream to interrupt a Supreme Court justice." He showed geeky enthusiasm for presiding over the House floor, advertising those appearances on his Facebook page.

In the one flash he'd rather forget, Yoder swam in the Sea of Galilee — a holy site to many people — during a congressional trip to Israel in 2011. Many lawmakers joined in the late-night dip, but only Yoder stripped naked. He was chastised by Majority Leader Eric Cantor of Virginia at the time, but when the story leaked a year later, Democrats tried to make it an international incident. GOP presidential nominee Mitt Romney went on record to call Yoder's actions reprehensible. Yoder apologized.

That incident was a minor distraction, though, from Yoder's work on fiscal matters. Just six House Republicans in the 112th Congress (2011-12) declined to sign the anti-tax-increase pledge of activist Grover Norquist, and Yoder was one of them. "I can't foresee every scenario," he explained to The New York Times in 2011. A few months later, he told The Washington Post that Republicans erred in abandoning a "grand compromise" on deficit reduction with President Barack Obama. "It's going to hurt us with independents," he said.

Still, it's clear that deals acceptable to Yoder would lean in the direction of fiscal conservatism. He voted against the fiscal 2011 spending package and a stopgap measure to keep the government running through the first half of fiscal 2013; both spent too much money for his tastes. He argues for reducing the size of government, even if "we're talking about social services and education and things that none of us wants to reduce."

Yoder rejects the idea that spending cuts will seriously derail government services. Writing in Roll Call in 2011 about his state House days, he said "the overblown statements of public spending advocates were not based in reality."

A member of the conservative Republican Study Committee, he supports the GOP's ban on earmarks, calling them "sort of a gateway drug to greater federal spending" when used to entice lawmakers to vote for larger measures. He voted in early 2013 against a $50 billion package of aid related to Superstorm Sandy — he explained that it was "far greater than the amount that could be spent this year," and that he couldn't countenance that much "emergency" spending, which isn't offset by budget reductions elsewhere.

Yoder can be persuaded to expand federal investments in science and research. "If we're going to spend federal dollars, we ought to spend those federal dollars in a way that has the greatest impact on the economy and that has the greatest impact on the future prosperity of the country," he said in 2012. "I can think of really no better way to do that than investment in research."

He has some say in federal research spending as the vice chairman of the Agriculture Appropriations Subcommittee in the 113th Congress (2013-14). Yoder has defended funding for the National Bio and Agro-Defense Facility in Manhattan, Kan.

In February 2013, Yoder teamed up with Democrats Mike Doyle of Pennsylvania and Zoe Lofgren of California on a bill to make publicly funded research more readily available. It requires agencies with an "extramural research budget of $100 million or more" to put published results online, free of charge, within six months of publication.

Yoder's interest in science extends to his leisure time. He volunteers that he's a science fiction fan — "Doctor Who," in particular.

His voting record as a freshman put Yoder in line with a majority of House Republicans most of the time. He supports repeal of the 2010 health care and financial regulatory overhaul laws, and he introduced a resolution calling for a one-year postponement of the implementation of all major federal rules — including rules created by those laws.

Yoder was involved in education debates at the state level, and he calls for a repeal of the 2002 federal education law known as No Child Left Behind. Federal involvement in education should be focused on early-childhood education programs such as Head Start, he said. In August 2011, he was appointed to the board of trustees of Gallaudet University, the federally chartered university for the education of students who are deaf and hard of hearing.

He represents the least rural district in Kansas, but he grew up on a grain and livestock farm near the town that carries his family name. He's the youngest of three children. His father worked the farm, and his mother worked at a medical center. She later earned a master's in social work from the University of Kansas, while having occasional lunches with her freshman son.

Yoder was part of a state champion debate team his senior year of high school — the topic was health care — and competed in Student Congress. In college he ran for the student Senate, eventually rising to student body president. He also served as his fraternity's president and interned in the Kansas Legislature. Yoder was a Democrat then, but switched parties before running for the state House; he said the move to the right was a natural progression.

He stuck with the university for law school and met his future wife in Washington while working as a summer law clerk at the Pentagon; though from Kentucky, she also went to Kansas' law school. "I think I've got her fully converted to a Jayhawk," Yoder says. An avid basketball fan, he sometimes relaxes by playing in the congressional gym.

Six-term Democratic Rep. Dennis Moore announced in November 2009 that he was retiring. Yoder won 44 percent of the vote in a nine-candidate Republican primary for the open seat. He then had an easy time defeating Moore's wife, Stephene, who sought to succeed her husband in what was considered the only swing district in Kansas.

Democrats did not run a candidate against Yoder in 2012.

Key Votes

2012	
Extend a Social Security payroll tax cut and unemployment benefits	YES
Ease securities rules to expand small-business access to capital	YES
Extend for one year subsidized student loan interest rates financed by a cut in health care spending	YES
Cite Attorney General Eric H. Holder Jr. for contempt of Congress	YES
Create a visa program for foreign graduates in high-tech fields	YES
Extend most Bush-era income tax rates while allowing rates for top-bracket earners to rise (Jan. 1, 2013)	NO
2011	
Strike funding for F-35 alternative engine	YES
Prevent EPA from regulating greenhouse gas emissions to address climate change	YES
Extend certain provisions of Patriot Act for four years	YES
Declare opposition to use of ground troops in Libya	YES
Overhaul patent law	YES
Pass compromise debt limit increase plan and establish future spending limits	NO
Allow consideration of measures to implement three trade agreements	YES

CQ Vote Studies

	PARTY UNITY		PRESIDENTIAL SUPPORT	
	SUPPORT	OPPOSE	SUPPORT	OPPOSE
2012	97%	3%	13%	87%
2011	97%	3%	20%	80%

Interest Groups

	AFL-CIO	ADA	CCUS	ACU
2012	10%	0%	92%	96%
2011	0%	5%	94%	84%

Kansas 3

Kansas City region — Overland Park, Olathe

The 3rd District differs markedly from the state's other districts — compact, it grabs all of Kansas City, Kan., and its populous suburbs, including Overland Park and Olathe. It hugs the Missouri River on its eastern border, while the Kansas River winds through its heart, nearly parallel to the interstates and railways that lead into the Kansas City hub.

Suburban areas in the Kansas City, Mo., orbit have experienced sustained population growth since 2000. Decennial remapping realigned all of more-liberal Douglas County into the 2nd District and added a portion of conservative Miami County, including Louisburg, to the 3rd's southern edge.

While the district is predominately white (roughly four-fifths of the population), it has the highest percentage of minority residents of any district in the state. Many black residents left Wyandotte for Johnson County over the last 10 years, and racial and ethnic minorities have contributed more than half of that mainly suburban county's population growth in the last decade. Johnson boasts an unemployment rate lower than the state average and a median household income higher than $70,000.

The area's economy mainly revolves around professional services in the city and its immediate suburbs — the tax-preparation service H&R Block has its headquarters in Kansas City. Local leaders hope more high-tech, high-paying jobs relocate after Google's selection of Kansas City to lead its pilot program installing super-high-speed fiber internet connections in the city. Blue-collar construction adds jobs in exurban Miami County.

The 3rd may have Democratic voters, but it is still largely conservative — no Democrat challenged Rep. Kevin Yoder in his 2012 U.S. House re-election contest. Wyandotte County (Kansas City) accounts for a bulk of the Democratic votes here, and Barack Obama took double the number of votes in Wyandotte that Republican nominee Mitt Romney did in the 2012 presidential race.

Major Industry
Professional services, health care, construction

Cities
Overland Park, Kansas City, Olathe

Notable
The Mahaffie Stagecoach in Olathe is the last remaining stagecoach stop on the Santa Fe Trail that is still open to the public.

Rep. Mike Pompeo (R)

Capitol Office
225-6216
pompeo.house.gov
107 Cannon Bldg. 20515-1604; fax 225-3489

Committees
Energy & Commerce
Select Intelligence

Residence
Wichita

Born
Dec. 30, 1963; Orange, Calif.

Religion
Presbyterian

Family
Wife, Susan Pompeo; one child

Education
U.S. Military Academy, B.S. 1986 (engineering management); Harvard U., J.D. 1994

Military
Army, 1986-91

Career
Oilfield equipment company president; aerospace parts manufacturing company president; lawyer

Political Highlights
Republican National Committee, 2008-11

ELECTION RESULTS

2012 GENERAL		
Mike Pompeo (R)	161,094	62.2%
Robert Leon Tillman (D)	81,770	31.6%
Thomas Jefferson (LIBERT)	16,058	6.2%
2012 PRIMARY		
Mike Pompeo (R)		unopposed
2010 GENERAL		
Mike Pompeo (R)	119,575	58.8%
Raj Goyle (D)	74,143	36.4%
Susan G. Ducey (REF)	5,041	2.5%
Shawn Smith (LIBERT)	4,624	2.3%

Elected 2010; 2nd term

Pompeo projects a serene confidence in business and a dislike for government involvement in free markets. His signature initiative is an attempt to end all federal tax subsidies related to energy, and he's also an advocate for the aviation industry in his district.

His professional career matches up very well with his congressional work. Pompeo (pom-PAY-oh) was the president of an aerospace parts manufacturing company for a decade, then took the helm at an oil field equipment business. As a freshman he secured a seat on the Energy and Commerce Committee, as well as spots on the subcommittees handling manufacturing and energy. For the 113th Congress (2013-14), he joined the panel covering the communications industry.

Pompeo champions a number of conservative causes, but he has made the most noise with his effort to kill all the incentives for energy production contained in the tax code.

His bill, first introduced in 2011, ends tax subsidies for electric vehicles, biofuels, wind, solar, nuclear, coal, oil and gas production. It offsets the resulting increase in federal revenue by lowering corporate tax rates. The measure is enthusiastically supported by conservative groups. (The targeting of the wind tax credit puts Pompeo at odds with many Kansas Republicans — the state has both manufacturing and production interests in that industry.)

The House didn't act on the bill in the 112th Congress (2011-12), but when Pompeo rolled out a slightly modified version in January 2013, he said it had spurred a debate on the need for tax credits: "It's already a sea change in the way this House thinks about these things."

Pompeo describes the bill as a starting point, as he would also like to end the Energy Department's loan guarantee program — he wants alternative-energy producers to stand on their own. "The way we've always found the next great energy technology is through somebody out there trying to make money and innovate and grow their little world," he said. "The solution is in somebody's garage who's tinkering today on something I don't even know about, who's never been to Washington, D.C., and who has no desire to come here."

In 2011, Pompeo told Politico that a lot of his time is spent trying to "spank back the EPA." Many regulations are now "unmoored from science," he said, and Pompeo contends that some rules — a particular target is tougher standards on emissions from utility plants — will cause economic hardships with health effects far worse than those of the pollution they aim to reduce.

The aviation industry defines the 4th District, with Wichita known as the "Air Capital of the World." The Boeing Co. deflated that title when it announced in early 2012 that it would be closing operations there. An irate Pompeo accused the company of breaking "years and years of promises" to stay in the region.

He's similarly irked by perceived smears of corporate jet owners. Democrats "believe it is corporate fat cats having fun and drinking champagne on airplanes, and so they badmouth it," Pompeo said. "Who it really impacts are welders, riveters, purchasing clerks, people that build these airplanes."

Wichita is also home to Koch Industries, a conglomerate whose owners give lots of money to conservative causes. The Koch brothers have bogeyman status in some liberal circles, and Pompeo — who has received campaign donations from Koch Industries — has publicly defended the company.

Writing in Politico in 2012, he said that "the Democrats' obsession with the Kochs as a political target is, indeed, additional evidence of a truly Nixonian approach to politics."

Pompeo is a fiscal conservative, and as a freshman he set his sights on wiping out at least one government agency. The House in 2012 rejected a Pompeo amendment to zero out funding for the Economic Development Administration. That agency provides grants for what Pompeo called "quintessentially local projects — that in most instances would go forward" without federal assistance.

Along with his business background, Pompeo has military experience. He graduated first in his class from West Point and served as a tank commander in Germany near the end of the Cold War. He was added to the Intelligence Committee for the 113th Congress.

He's less troubled than many Republicans by potential cuts to defense spending. "If my choices were defense cuts or tax increases, I would avoid the tax increases," he said in 2011. The key, according to Pompeo, is giving defense leaders enough time to adjust to budget reductions: "They don't want us to go from 'X' to 'X minus a whole lot' really fast."

Pompeo's connection to Kansas runs through his mother, who grew up as one of nine brothers and sisters in Wellington — Pompeo has a solid voting base of more than 100 cousins in the 4th District. She landed a job as a purchasing clerk with the Boeing Co. after high school. In that job, she fielded regular sales calls from a persistent man at a California manufacturer of fasteners, screws and bolts. After a year, he suggested they meet for a long weekend. That trip resulted in an engagement, and they were married until her death. Pompeo remembers that she regularly advised her children against a similar stunt.

The family set up in California's Orange County, where Pompeo did "typical kid stuff." He also landed his "first real corporate job" at Baskin Robbins. "I was the head scooper, and I moved all the way up to assistant manager." He applied to West Point because he was drawn by both its egalitarian environment and the possibility of a free education. On leaving the Army he attended Harvard Law School, and as an attorney he did mostly white-collar criminal defense litigation.

He moved to Kansas in 1996 to start Thayer Aerospace. He was also active in state politics. At the time of his 2010 election, he was a member of the Republican National Committee.

Republican Rep. Todd Tiahrt made bid for the Senate in 2010, which opened up the 4th District for a newcomer. In a sometimes nasty GOP primary, Pompeo topped state Sen. Jean Kurtis Schodorf and businessman Wink Hartman. He then defeated Democratic state Rep. Raj Goyle with 59 percent of the vote.

Kansas didn't get any less Republican in 2012. Pompeo won the general election by more than 30 points.

Key Votes

2012	
Extend a Social Security payroll tax cut and unemployment benefits	NO
Ease securities rules to expand small-business access to capital	YES
Extend for one year subsidized student loan interest rates financed by a cut in health care spending	YES
Cite Attorney General Eric H. Holder Jr. for contempt of Congress	YES
Create a visa program for foreign graduates in high-tech fields	YES
Extend most Bush-era income tax rates while allowing rates for top-bracket earners to rise (Jan. 1, 2013)	NO
2011	
Strike funding for F-35 alternative engine	YES
Prevent EPA from regulating greenhouse gas emissions to address climate change	YES
Extend certain provisions of Patriot Act for four years	+
Declare opposition to use of ground troops in Libya	YES
Overhaul patent law	YES
Pass compromise debt limit increase plan and establish future spending limits	YES
Allow consideration of measures to implement three trade agreements	YES

CQ Vote Studies

	PARTY UNITY		PRESIDENTIAL SUPPORT	
	SUPPORT	OPPOSE	SUPPORT	OPPOSE
2012	99%	1%	13%	87%
2011	98%	2%	19%	81%

Interest Groups

	AFL-CIO	ADA	CCUS	ACU
2012	5%	5%	83%	100%
2011	0%	5%	100%	88%

Kansas 4

South central — Wichita

The 4th District is settled in south central Kansas and takes in both the Wichita area and rural counties. Following decennial remapping, six rural counties and a portion of Pawnee County were added to the western reaches of the district, while Montgomery County and part of Greenwood County to the east were moved into the 2nd.

Wichita (Sedgwick County) is the state's most populous city. The metropolitan area has experienced modest population growth since 2000, outpacing statewide and nationwide rates. Known for decades as the "Air Capital of the World" because of its general aviation aircraft production industry, Wichita has faced recent uncertainty in the aerospace and commercial airline sectors. Boeing announced that it will close its facilities in the city by the end of 2013, but Bombardier Learjet broke ground on a jet manufacturing plant. McConnell Air Force base, tasked with air refueling and airlifting operations, is south of Wichita. Beyond aviation, the region is also home to robust health care and construction industries.

Outside of Wichita, much of the rest of the district is farmland. Butler County, to the east, raises a significant portion of the area's cattle, while the stretches west and south of Wichita hold prime wheat-producing land key not only to the state but also on a national scale.

The 4th is overwhelmingly white, and Hispanic residents make up the largest minority group in the district (11 percent). While still small as a proportion overall, the Hispanic population here has grown rapidly in some counties. The district is a conservative stronghold and GOP candidates earn wide margins at the federal level, even in more urban Sedgwick County: Republican presidential nominee Mitt Romney took 58 percent of the vote in Sedgwick in 2012.

Major Industry
Aviation, agriculture, defense, health care

Military Bases
McConnell Air Force Base, 3,066 military, 427 civilian (2012)

Cities
Wichita

Notable
Wichita hosts the Museum of World Treasures, among which are a four-and-a-half-ton section of the Berlin Wall and the pitchfork from "The Wizard of Oz."

KENTUCKY

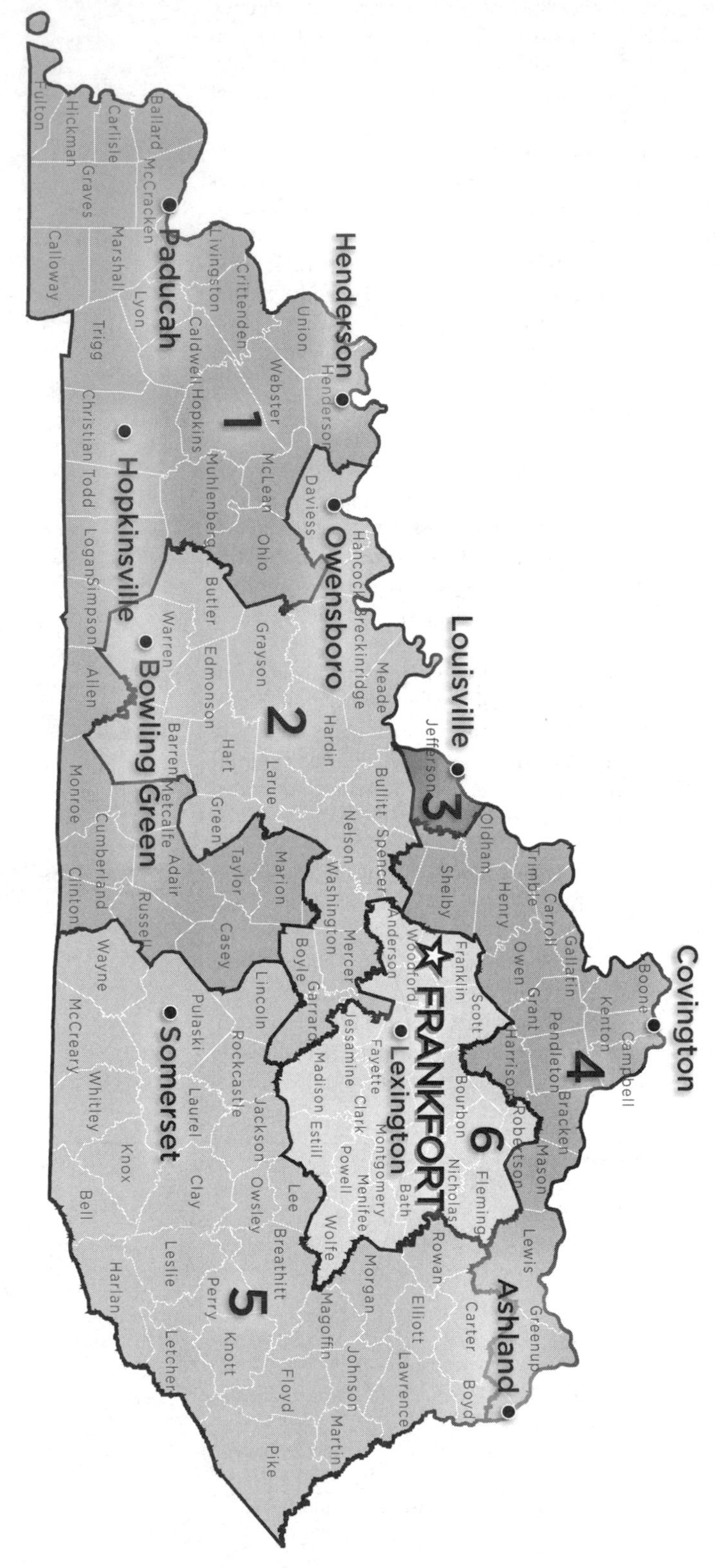

Fulton
Hickman
Carlisle
Ballard
McCracken
Graves
Calloway
Marshall
Paducah
Livingston
Lyon
Crittenden
Caldwell
Trigg
Union
Webster
Hopkins
Henderson
Henderson
1
Christian
Hopkinsville
Todd
McLean
Muhlenberg
Daviess
Owensboro
Ohio
Logan
Simpson
Butler
Hancock
Breckinridge
Warren
Grayson
Edmonson
Bowling Green
Allen
Meade
2
Louisville
Jefferson
Hardin
Barren
Hart
Larue
3
Monroe
Metcalfe
Green
Bullitt
Nelson
Spencer
Oldham
Cumberland
Adair
Taylor
Marion
Washington
Shelby
Henry
Trimble
Carroll
Clinton
Russell
Casey
Anderson
Mercer
Woodford
Franklin
Owen
Gallatin
Boone
Covington
Kenton
Wayne
Boyle
Lincoln
Pulaski
Somerset
Garrard
Jessamine
FRANKFORT
Scott
Grant
Pendleton
Campbell
4
Harrison
Fayette
Lexington
McCreary
Whitley
Rockcastle
Madison
Clark
Bourbon
6
Laurel
Jackson
Estill
Powell
Montgomery
Nicholas
Robertson
Bracken
Mason
Fleming
Knox
Clay
Owsley
Lee
Menifee
Bath
Bell
Wolfe
Breathitt
Morgan
Rowan
Lewis
Leslie
Harlan
Perry
5
Magoffin
Elliott
Carter
Ashland
Greenup
Knott
Letcher
Floyd
Johnson
Lawrence
Boyd
Martin
Pike

Gov. Steven L. Beshear (D)

First elected: 2007
Length of term: 4 years
Term expires: 1/16
Salary: $135,971
Phone: (502) 564-2611
Residence: Lexington
Born: Sept. 21, 1944; Dawson Springs, Ky.
Religion: Disciples of Christ
Family: Wife, Jane Beshear; two children
Education: U. of Kentucky, B.A. 1966 (history), J.D. 1968
Military service: Army Reserve, 1969-75
Career: Lawyer
Political highlights: Ky. House, 1975-79; attorney general, 1979-83; lieutenant governor, 1983-87; sought Democratic nomination for governor, 1987; Democratic nominee for U.S. Senate, 1996

ELECTION RESULTS

2011 GENERAL

Steven L. Beshear (D)	464,245	55.7%
David L. Williams (R)	294,034	35.3%
Gatewood Galbraith (I)	74,860	9.0%

Lt. Gov. Jerry Abramson (D)

First elected: 2011
Length of term: 4 years
Term expires: 1/16
Salary: $115,594
Phone: (502) 564-2611

LEGISLATURE

General Assembly: January-April in even-numbered years, limit of 60 days; January-March in odd-numbered years, limit of 30 days
Senate: 38 members, 4-year terms
2013 ratios: 23 R, 14 D, 1 I; 31 men, 7 women
Salary: $188 per day in session
Phone: (502) 564-8100
House: 100 members, 2-year terms
2013 ratios: 54 D, 45 R, 1 vacancy; 81 men, 18 women
Salary: $188 per day in session
Phone: (502) 564-8100

TERM LIMITS

Governor: 2 terms
Senate: No
House: No

URBAN STATISTICS

CITY	POPULATION
Louisville Metro	741,096
Lexington-Fayette	295,803
Bowling Green	58,067
Owensboro	57,265
Covington	40,640

REGISTERED VOTERS

Democrat	55%
Republican	38%
Other	7%

POPULATION

2010 population	4,339,367
2000 population	4,041,769
1990 population	3,685,296
Percent change (2000-2010)	+7.4%
Rank among states (2010)	26
Median age	37.3
Born in state	71.1%
Foreign born	2.7%
Violent crime rate	259/100,000
Poverty level	18.6%
Federal workers	42,823
Military	43,138

ELECTIONS

STATE ELECTION OFFICIAL
(502) 573-7100
DEMOCRATIC PARTY
(502) 695-4828
REPUBLICAN PARTY
(502) 875-5130

MISCELLANEOUS

Web: www.kentucky.gov
Capital: Frankfort

U.S. CONGRESS

Senate: 2 Republicans
House: 5 Republicans, 1 Democrat

STATISTICS BY DISTRICT

	2012 Vote for President		2008 Vote for President										
District	Obama	Romney	Obama	McCain	Black	Asian	Hispanic	Median Income	Over 64	Under 20	College Education	Rural	Sq. Miles
1	32%	66%	37%	62%	7%	1%	2%	$37,011	16%	26%	15%	64%	12,080
2	35	63	37	61	6	1	3	41,857	13	28	18	51	7,177
3	56	43	56	43	21	2	5	44,407	14	25	29	1	319
4	35	63	37	61	4	1	3	51,881	12	28	25	32	4,382
5	23	75	32	67	1	<1	1	29,627	14	25	11	77	11,235
6	42	56	45	54	9	2	4	43,399	12	26	29	27	4,293
STATE	**38**	**60**	**41**	**57**	**8**	**1**	**3**	**41,141**	**14**	**26**	**21**	**42**	**39,486**
U.S.	**51**	**47**	**53**	**46**	**12**	**5**	**17**	**50,052**	**13**	**27**	**29**	**21**	**3,531,905**

Sen. Mitch McConnell (R)

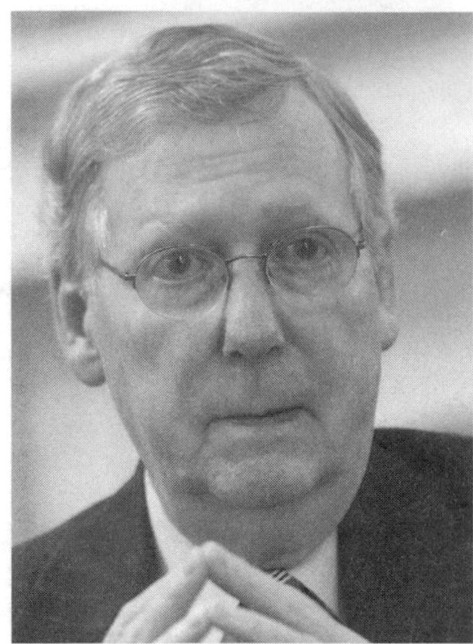

Capitol Office
224-2541
mcconnell.senate.gov
317 Russell Bldg. 20510-1702; fax 224-2499

Committees
Agriculture, Nutrition & Forestry
Appropriations
Rules & Administration

Residence
Louisville

Born
Feb. 20, 1942; Sheffield, Ala.

Religion
Baptist

Family
Wife, Elaine L. Chao; three children

Education
U. of Louisville, B.A. 1964; U. of Kentucky, J.D. 1967

Career
Lawyer; U.S. Justice Department official; congressional aide

Political Highlights
Jefferson County judge-executive, 1978-85

ELECTION RESULTS

2008 GENERAL		
Mitch McConnell (R)	953,816	53.0%
Bruce Lunsford (D)	847,005	47.0%
2008 PRIMARY		
Mitch McConnell (R)	168,127	86.1%
Daniel Essek (R)	27,170	13.9%

Previous Winning Percentages
2002 (65%); 1996 (55%); 1990 (52%); 1984 (50%)

Elected 1984; 5th term

Republicans fumbled a chance to take control of the Senate in the 2012 elections, leaving McConnell to face two more years as the chamber's minority leader. It's not the job he hoped for, but his position atop the GOP Conference ensures his party's effective opposition to the plans of Majority Leader Harry Reid.

McConnell and the Nevada Democrat, who assumed their respective posts in 2007, are two of the shrewdest operators in the Senate. They come from a pragmatic legislative tradition (they once served together on the deal-happy Appropriations Committee) and have an excellent grasp of how to exploit the Senate's procedural rules. Each man is somewhere in the middle of the political spectrum for his party; Reid isn't a die-hard liberal, nor is McConnell a die-hard conservative.

They have each done reasonably good jobs keeping their teams unified as they try to win legislative battles and sway public opinion.

When going on offense, McConnell uses the work of the Republican House as his cudgel. In the 112th Congress (2011-12), he pushed for votes on the Republican-backed bills coming from across the Capitol. He tried to depict Democrats as ignoring the public's will, as expressed in the 2010 election that created the House majority.

When on defense, he relies on procedural votes, his most powerful tool for blocking Democratic plans or forcing concessions. Most Senate action requires the consent of 60 senators, and McConnell has kept his party together to prevent Reid from reaching that threshold when he deems it necessary. Moderates, the most likely defectors, are sympathetic to his argument that Republicans don't get enough chances to offer amendments to legislation moving through the chamber.

McConnell and Reid agreed on rule changes at the start of the 113th Congress (2013-14) so that Republicans would be able to offer a minimum number of amendments on bills while giving up some power to force procedural votes. The changes weren't insignificant, but they did not neuter the power of either leader.

In general, McConnell has the standing within his conference to negotiate on its behalf. He attributes some of his success to his willingness to hear out all parts of the Republican Party. He has said that in the Senate, "the only way to be effective is to be a good listener."

In the summer of 2011, McConnell produced a "fallback" plan for a deal to raise the federal debt limit. His idea, included in the final agreement, was to allow "disapproval" votes for increases to the debt limit, thereby forcing Democratic senators to go on the record on a sensitive fiscal issue without creating any serious threat of a government default.

He was also an eleventh-hour architect of the "fiscal cliff" deal enacted in January 2013. Automatic spending cuts put in place by the 2011 debt limit deal were about to take hold, and tax cuts enacted in the George W. Bush era were about to expire. Negotiations between Obama and House Republican leaders imploded, so McConnell and Vice President Joseph R. Biden Jr. worked out a framework to delay the automatic cuts and allow tax rates to increase on earnings over $400,000. McConnell sold it as a strategic victory that would make it harder for Democrats to demand more tax increases in the future.

Even though he has led opposition to Obama's agenda, McConnell has never been a favorite of conservatives. A veteran appropriator, he used to advertise his ability to bring federal money back to Kentucky through earmarks. He could have a difficult campaign in 2014, with potentially strong challengers in both the primary and the general election.

But McConnell does adjust to changing political dynamics. Recently, that has meant a sometimes awkward embrace of the tea party movement. Kentucky's activists are far more enthusiastic about the state's junior senator, Rand Paul, who in a 2010 primary defeated McConnell's close ally, Kentucky Secretary of State Trey Grayson. McConnell hired Jesse Benton, a longtime adviser to the Paul family, to run his 2014 campaign. Benton wrote on the Daily Caller website that he wasn't worried about McConnell's history: "The job of leader by definition does not accommodate ideological purity, but Sen. McConnell's conservative record is very clear," he said.

One fact is indisputably clear: When McConnell takes personal interest in an issue, he pursues it relentlessly.

He's very interested in First Amendment rights. He blocked a rewrite of campaign finance rules for 15 years, mounting more than 20 filibusters against various iterations of the legislation. When a measure was enacted in 2002, he took the battle to the Supreme Court, which narrowly upheld the law in 2003. (A subsequent ruling in 2010 overturned parts of it.) McConnell serves on the Rules and Administration Committee, which handles both campaign finance measures and many of his own procedural powers.

Predating his time as Republican leader, he led efforts to impose sanctions against Myanmar and the repressive military junta that rules it. He visited there in January 2012, meeting for the first time with pro-democracy leader Aung San Suu Kyi. After consultation with the White House, he announced in May 2013 that he would not seek another extension of sanctions, as "enough progress has been made."

McConnell gained clout with Republicans in part by doing a lot of grunt work for the party. He chaired the Senate Ethics Committee in 1995 when it voted to expel Oregon Republican Bob Packwood over charges of sexual misconduct. (Packwood subsequently resigned.) During the 1998 and 2000 election cycles, he led the National Republican Senatorial Committee.

He was unanimously elected Republican whip for the 108th Congress (2003-04) and kept the job for four years. When Republican leader Bill Frist of Tennessee resigned, McConnell was the natural choice to replace him.

An only child, McConnell was born in Alabama. He lived in Georgia for part of his childhood and moved to Kentucky at age 13. His father, an Army officer who fought in World War II, became a civilian Army employee after the war and then a human resources director for DuPont in Louisville.

While the family was living in Alabama, McConnell, at age 2, was stricken with polio. His mother administered a physical therapy regimen and took him to specialists in Warm Springs, Ga. At their urging, she kept her child from walking until he was 4, a seemingly impossible task that saved him from permanent damage to his afflicted left leg.

McConnell showed an early taste for politics. He was a student body president in high school and college. At the University of Kentucky, he was president of his law school class. After law school he worked for GOP Sen. Marlow W. Cook of Kentucky, then as a deputy assistant attorney general in the Ford administration.

He served two terms as the chief executive of Jefferson County, essentially metropolitan Louisville, before ousting two-term Democratic Sen. Walter D. Huddleston in a close race in 1984. He was assisted by Ronald Reagan's crushing defeat of Walter F. Mondale in the state's presidential tally.

In 1990, McConnell was re-elected with 52 percent of the vote. His margin of victory got more comfortable in his next two races. In 2008, he faced wealthy Democratic businessman Bruce Lunsford amid a hostile national political climate for the GOP, but McConnell captured 53 percent of the vote.

McConnell's wife, Elaine L. Chao, served as secretary of Labor for all eight years of the George W. Bush administration.

Key Votes

2012	
Prohibit health insurance plans from denying coverage based on the sponsor's religious beliefs	NO
Require approval of the Keystone XL oil pipeline	YES
Ease securities rules to expand small-business access to capital	YES
Reauthorize farm and nutrition programs for five years	NO
Limit debate on a bill that would create private-sector cybersecurity standards	NO
Consent to ratification of a treaty setting global standard for the treatment of people with disabilities	NO
Provide $60.4 billion in disaster relief following Superstorm Sandy	NO
Extend most Bush-era income tax rates while allowing rates for top-bracket earners to rise (Jan. 1, 2013)	YES
2011	
Prevent EPA from regulating greenhouse gas emissions to address climate change	YES
Extend certain provisions of Patriot Act for four years	YES
Clear compromise debt limit increase plan and establish future spending limits	YES
Overhaul patent law	YES
Implement Colombia free trade agreement	YES
Limit debate on confirmation of Caitlin J. Halligan to D.C. Circuit Court of Appeals	NO
Extend payroll tax cut and unemployment benefits for two months	YES

CQ Vote Studies

	PARTY UNITY		PRESIDENTIAL SUPPORT	
	SUPPORT	OPPOSE	SUPPORT	OPPOSE
2012	93%	7%	48%	52%
2011	97%	3%	51%	49%
2010	98%	2%	41%	59%
2009	95%	5%	46%	54%
2008	97%	3%	76%	24%
2007	95%	5%	86%	14%
2006	96%	4%	91%	9%
2005	99%	1%	93%	7%
2004	99%	1%	98%	2%
2003	99%	1%	100%	0%

Interest Groups

	AFL-CIO	ADA	CCUS	ACU
2012	0%	0%	88%	100%
2011	11%	10%	100%	85%
2010	6%	0%	100%	96%
2009	22%	10%	71%	96%
2008	20%	20%	100%	80%
2007	11%	10%	82%	92%
2006	13%	5%	100%	84%
2005	14%	5%	94%	100%
2004	8%	15%	94%	96%
2003	0%	10%	100%	84%

Sen. Rand Paul (R)

Capitol Office
224-4343
paul.senate.gov
208 Russell Bldg. 20510; fax 228-6917

Committees
Foreign Relations
Health, Education, Labor & Pensions
Homeland Security & Governmental Affairs
Small Business & Entrepreneurship

Residence
Bowling Green

Born
Jan. 7, 1963; Pittsburgh, Pa.

Religion
Presbyterian

Family
Wife, Kelley Paul; three children

Education
Baylor U., attended 1981-84; Duke U., M.D. 1988

Career
Ophthalmologist

Political Highlights
No previous office

ELECTION RESULTS

2010 GENERAL		
Rand Paul (R)	755,411	55.7%
Jack Conway (D)	599,843	44.2%
2010 PRIMARY		
Rand Paul (R)	206,986	58.8%
Trey Grayson (R)	124,864	35.4%
Bill Johnson (R)	7,861	2.2%
John Stephenson (R)	6,885	2.0%

Elected 2010; 1st term

Paul assertively advertises a philosophy of government that's a hybrid of libertarian and conservative principles. He is clearly positioning himself as a leader — but opinions vary as to what exactly he is leading.

His detractors describe him as the public face of a fringe movement. Paul was elected in 2010, and in the 112th Congress (2011-12) he made some of the most impassioned demands for a smaller, less-intrusive federal government. Democrats mocked the severity of Paul's proposals — for example, he suggested $500 billion in spending cuts for fiscal 2011, when most Senate Republicans had proposed $50 billion. A few well-known Republicans, such as Arizona Sen. John McCain, repeatedly complained when Paul brought Senate business to a halt while trying to force votes on his own proposals.

The notion of Paul as an outsider is boosted by his association with his father. Rep. Ron Paul of Texas, who retired at the end of the 112th Congress, sought the presidency as a Libertarian in 1988 and as a Republican in 2008 and 2012. The elder Paul's denunciations of U.S. monetary policy and military policy attracted an enthusiastic group of followers — who, as they try to take over GOP organizations at the state level, have caused headaches for mainstream Republicans.

Fans of the younger Paul describe him as an ideological standard-bearer with the passion to march the Republican Party into a new era. In the opening months of 2013, Paul gave a dizzying array of speeches that outlined various principles and policy goals.

He gave the "tea party response" to President Barack Obama's State of the Union address. Paul repeated his call for a balanced-budget amendment to the Constitution. He spoke of how government programs interfere with market forces and drive up prices paid by the working class: "The president offers you free stuff, but his policies keep you poor." And he once again suggested steep reductions in defense spending and foreign aid, starting with "aid to countries that are burning our flag."

Paul told the Conservative Political Action Conference that the GOP "has grown stale and moss-covered" and must change "by going forward to the classical and timeless ideas enshrined in our Constitution." He gave highlights of his five-year budget plan, which would eliminate the Education Department, aim to give more overall power back to the states and create a flat income tax of 17 percent.

Speaking to the U.S. Hispanic Chamber of Commerce, Paul said that conservatives should be open to an overhaul of immigration law that includes an opportunity for immigrants already in the country illegally to get some kind of legal status. "We aren't going to deport 12 million illegal immigrants," he said. "If you wish to work, if you wish to live and work in America, then we will find a place for you."

Most famously, he held the Senate floor for 13 hours on March 6, conducting a "talking filibuster" to delay a confirmation vote on Obama's nominee for CIA director. Paul wanted the White House to give a clear answer on whether the president has the authority to use a weaponized drone to kill a U.S. citizen on U.S. soil. He got his answer — no — the next day, along with a good deal of applause from people who view the expansion of presidential power as a threat to civil liberties.

Paul hasn't dismissed speculation that he might run for president in 2016, but he says he won't make that decision until 2014. For now, he continues to defend his positions in the Senate. His approach there can be described as principled, but not completely obstructionist — he wants votes on his proposals, and he lets legislation move once he gets them.

A few eyebrows were raised when Paul was added to the Foreign Relations Committee for the 113th Congress (2013-14) — along with McCain. (In a 2013 interview with the Huffington Post, McCain called Paul a "wacko bird.") Paul's thoughts on international relations and national security are a big departure from those of most Republicans.

Paul maintains that participation in organizations such as the United Nations threatens the nation's sovereignty. He has proposed dramatic reductions to foreign aid, particularly to Pakistan, Libya and Egypt. He says the 2001 invasion of Afghanistan was warranted, but he opposes military interventions where there isn't a direct threat to the United States.

He addresses some of his concerns about executive power and civil liberties on the Homeland Security and Governmental Affairs Committee. In 2011, Paul opposed the extension of expiring surveillance provisions of the anti-terrorism law known as the Patriot Act. He says Fourth Amendment protections against unreasonable searches and seizures should be explicitly extended to Internet history, email, telephone records, text messages, credit card statements and all other forms of information given to third parties.

Paul also sits on the Health, Education, Labor and Pensions Committee. He calls the 2010 health care overhaul unconstitutional, and the 2012 Supreme Court ruling to the contrary did not dissuade him. "Just because a couple people on the Supreme Court declare something to be 'constitutional' does not make it so," he wrote shortly after the decision was announced. "The whole thing remains unconstitutional."

As a conservative and a Kentuckian, Paul is "absolutely opposed to cap-and-trade, absolutely opposed to any carbon tax." He calls himself "a great friend of coal." Paul also is opposed to abortion. He has proposed a bill to extend the 14th Amendment's guarantee of equal protection under the law to "each born and preborn human person."

Growing up in the Texas home of a libertarian, Paul was not given an allowance, which his parents viewed as equivalent to being on the dole, according to a New York Times profile.

He attended Baylor University and later received a degree from Duke Medical School, following his father into medicine. Ron Paul is an obstetrician, and Rand Paul is an ophthalmologist. He moved to Kentucky in 1993 to open a practice and quickly got involved in political activism. He founded Kentucky Taxpayers United, a watchdog group.

When Paul entered the Senate race to succeed retiring Republican Jim Bunning, he was considered the underdog. Kentucky Secretary of State Trey Grayson had the backing of most party officials in the state and was considered the protégé of Senate Minority Leader Mitch McConnell.

But Paul was among the earliest candidates to get a boost from the tea party movement. He easily defeated Grayson in the May primary. McConnell and Paul appear to have put aside campaign differences to work together. McConnell even hired one of Paul's advisers to run his 2014 campaign.

The general election, in which he faced state Attorney General Jack Conway, was bitterly contested. Paul got into hot water during the campaign when he cited some aspects of the Civil Rights Act of 1964 as an example of government overreach. In an interview on MSNBC, Paul questioned the constitutional foundation of provisions in the law that barred discrimination by private companies. The substance of his argument wasn't disputed, but Democrats pounced on the remarks as racially insensitive.

A month before the election, he credited his campaign successes to his father. The Lexington Herald-Leader quoted Paul as saying that "my father's fame helps me quite a bit. It helps me in raising money, it helps me get started, it helps the media pay attention to me. Without that, I couldn't do it."

On Election Day, Paul took 56 percent of the vote to Conway's 44 percent.

Key Votes

2012	
Prohibit health insurance plans from denying coverage based on the sponsor's religious beliefs	NO
Require approval of the Keystone XL oil pipeline	YES
Ease securities rules to expand small-business access to capital	YES
Reauthorize farm and nutrition programs for five years	NO
Limit debate on a bill that would create private-sector cybersecurity standards	NO
Consent to ratification of a treaty setting global standard for the treatment of people with disabilities	NO
Provide $60.4 billion in disaster relief following Superstorm Sandy	NO
Extend most Bush-era income tax rates while allowing rates for top-bracket earners to rise (Jan. 1, 2013)	NO

2011	
Prevent EPA from regulating greenhouse gas emissions to address climate change	YES
Extend certain provisions of Patriot Act for four years	NO
Clear compromise debt limit increase plan and establish future spending limits	NO
Overhaul patent law	NO
Implement Colombia free trade agreement	YES
Limit debate on confirmation of Caitlin J. Halligan to D.C. Circuit Court of Appeals	NO
Extend payroll tax cut and unemployment benefits for two months	?

CQ Vote Studies

	PARTY UNITY		PRESIDENTIAL SUPPORT	
	SUPPORT	OPPOSE	SUPPORT	OPPOSE
2012	92%	8%	34%	66%
2011	89%	11%	41%	59%

Interest Groups

	AFL-CIO	ADA	CCUS	ACU
2012	0%	10%	75%	100%
2011	11%	15%	73%	100%

Rep. Edward Whitfield (R)

Capitol Office
225-3115
whitfield.house.gov
2184 Rayburn Bldg. 20515-1701; fax 225-3547

Committees
Energy & Commerce
(Energy & Power - Chairman)

Residence
Hopkinsville

Born
May 25, 1943; Hopkinsville, Ky.

Religion
Methodist

Family
Wife, Constance Harriman Whitfield; one child

Education
U. of Kentucky, B.S. 1965 (business); Wesley Theological Seminary, attended 1966; U. of Kentucky, J.D. 1969

Military
Army Reserve, 1967-73

Career
Lawyer; oil distributor; railroad executive

Political Highlights
Ky. House, 1974-75 (served as a Democrat)

ELECTION RESULTS

2012 GENERAL		
Edward Whitfield (R)	199,956	69.6%
Charles Kendall Hatchett (D)	87,199	30.4%
2012 PRIMARY		
Edward Whitfield (R)		unopposed
2010 GENERAL		
Edward Whitfield (R)	153,519	71.2%
Charles Kendall Hatchett (D)	61,960	28.8%

Previous Winning Percentages
2008 (64%); 2006 (60%); 2004 (67%); 2002 (65%); 2000 (58%); 1998 (55%); 1996 (54%); 1994 (51%)

Elected 1994; 10th term

Whitfield vociferously defends Kentucky's coal industry, and those efforts go hand-in-glove with his criticism of the EPA's air policies. He has signaled a willingness, however, to work across the aisle and across the Capitol to get energy legislation to the president's desk.

Whitfield is in his second term chairing the Energy and Commerce Subcommittee on Energy and Power. The panel's expansive jurisdiction covers everything from fossil fuels and renewable resources to the Clean Air Act, which was its chief focus during Whitfield's first term at the helm.

Committee Republicans produced a stream of bills in the 112th Congress (2011-12) designed to block or pre-empt EPA air pollution rules, and the campaign didn't put Democrats in the mood to compromise. They blasted many GOP members as "science deniers" due to their questioning of whether human activity contributes to changes in the Earth's climate.

Whitfield is hopeful for bipartisan and bicameral cooperation on energy legislation in the 113th Congress (2013-14). The Senate Energy and Natural Resources Committee has a new chairman — Oregon Democrat Ron Wyden — who was once a neighbor of Whitfield's in Washington. Whitfield sees a chance to cooperate with Wyden and the panel's ranking Republican, Lisa Murkowski of Alaska.

"I would think there would be a lot of areas of common ground," Whitfield said in 2012. "We have one of the very significant issues out there."

But more likely than not, Whitfield will have a hard time convincing the Senate to strip the EPA of its authority to regulate greenhouse gas emissions — a power that he and many other Republicans say Congress did not intend to bestow upon the agency when writing the 1990 iteration of the Clean Air Act. No votes on such a measure have succeeded in the Democratic Senate since Republicans took control of the House in 2011. Whitfield also is strongly against Democratic plans to enact a cap-and-trade system for greenhouse gas emissions.

Whitfield is a proponent of clean-coal technology, saying its widespread use would reduce energy costs. However, he opposes using regulations to compel companies to adopt the technology. In fact, he has been intrigued by a proposal to choke off a great deal of federal support for all kinds of energy. He is a co-sponsor of a bill by Kansas Republican Mike Pompeo that would end tax subsidies related to biofuels, wind power, solar power, nuclear power, coal, oil and gas. It offsets the resulting increase in federal revenue by lowering corporate tax rates.

Whitfield is a member of the moderate Main Street Partnership. He supports most tenets of the current GOP agenda but makes exceptions to defend policies and programs favored by his older and working-class constituents.

He was one of 10 House Republicans who voted against Budget Chairman Paul D. Ryan's fiscal 2013 budget — he said that none of the proposals put forth in the House would do enough to balance the country's ledger and "provide the needed reform to preserve Medicare, Medicaid and Social Security."

He is also an advocate for a biennial budgeting and appropriations process, which he says would offer members more time and flexibility to flag wasteful programs. "It really is not necessary for Congress to initiate a budget each year for the federal government, because the president submits a budget and Congress has the responsibility of adopting or changing his budget, rather than wasting time developing its own budget," he said.

But Whitfield, a member of the Energy and Commerce Subcommittee on Health, holds the party line on the 2010 health care overhaul. He opposed the bill as it worked its way through Congress in 2009 and 2010 and voted to repeal it in 2011. He opposed a measure, signed into law by President Barack Obama in 2009, that expanded a program that provides health insurance for children in lower-income families that make too much money to qualify for Medicaid.

Whitfield and his wife, Constance, a senior adviser to the Humane Society of the United States, have worked to curb the slaughter of horses. They were motivated to do so after witnessing a sick horse at a 2004 auction in Pennsylvania being loaded onto a trailer for a 1,500-mile trip to Texas to be killed. With the last horse slaughter plants shuttered in 2007, he is now pushing legislation to ban the use of performance-enhancing drugs in horse racing.

He joined Energy and Commerce in his first term, when Republicans took control of the House following the 1994 elections. An influential Republican from another tobacco state, Thomas J. Bliley Jr. of Virginia, became chairman and sought to bring friends of the industry onto the panel. In the latter half of the 1990s, Whitfield fought Clinton administration attempts to sue tobacco companies for selling hazardous products. In 2004, he pushed for provisions in a comprehensive corporate tax bill giving tobacco farmers a 10-year, $10 billion buyout. Congress passed the measure and George W. Bush signed it.

Born in Hopkinsville, near the Tennessee border, Whitfield is the son of a railroad conductor. His mother worked in finance at a local hospital. Whitfield got a degree from the University of Kentucky. He then spent a year at Wesley Theological Seminary in Washington, D.C., before going back to Kentucky for law school.

He was a Democrat in those days, and he served for two years in the state House in the mid-1970s. Like many other Southern Democrats, he switched parties during the 1980s.

Whitfield spent much of his early career doing regulatory and legislative work for major railroads. He lived many of those years in Washington and in the early 1990s was a lawyer for the Interstate Commerce Commission.

In 1994, Kentucky Republican Sen. Mitch McConnell recruited Whitfield to challenge Democratic Rep. Tom Barlow. Whitfield had not lived in the state for a dozen years — to be eligible for the race, he moved from CSX Corp. headquarters in Jacksonville, Fla.

Efforts to paint him as a carpetbagger were offset by the strength of his roots in the 1st District, where his extended family had been farming since 1799. Whitfield won with 51 percent of the vote, becoming the first Republican to represent the district. He easily survived the anti-Republican tide of 2006, taking 60 percent of the vote in a rematch with Barlow, and won handily in 2008. Whitfield scored whopping victories in 2010 and 2012 against Democrat Charles Kendall Hatchett.

Key Votes

2012	
Extend a Social Security payroll tax cut and unemployment benefits	NO
Ease securities rules to expand small-business access to capital	YES
Extend for one year subsidized student loan interest rates financed by a cut in health care spending	YES
Cite Attorney General Eric H. Holder Jr. for contempt of Congress	YES
Create a visa program for foreign graduates in high-tech fields	YES
Extend most Bush-era income tax rates while allowing rates for top-bracket earners to rise (Jan. 1, 2013)	NO
2011	
Strike funding for F-35 alternative engine	NO
Prevent EPA from regulating greenhouse gas emissions to address climate change	YES
Extend certain provisions of Patriot Act for four years	YES
Declare opposition to use of ground troops in Libya	YES
Overhaul patent law	YES
Pass compromise debt limit increase plan and establish future spending limits	YES
Allow consideration of measures to implement three trade agreements	YES

CQ Vote Studies

	PARTY UNITY		PRESIDENTIAL SUPPORT	
	SUPPORT	OPPOSE	SUPPORT	OPPOSE
2012	91%	9%	17%	83%
2011	92%	8%	24%	76%
2010	90%	10%	39%	61%
2009	81%	19%	30%	70%
2008	89%	11%	56%	44%

Interest Groups

	AFL-CIO	ADA	CCUS	ACU
2012	40%	10%	100%	79%
2011	24%	10%	100%	72%
2010	14%	15%	88%	77%
2009	19%	0%	93%	88%
2008	29%	35%	72%	78%

Kentucky 1

West — Hopkinsville, Henderson, Paducah

The mostly rural 1st takes up the state's western wedge and includes land around the Green River. It hosts some of the state's most prolific mining and agriculture regions.

Along the Ohio River, the district is home to oil drilling, and although eastern Kentucky boasts more, the 1st has some of the state's most productive coal mines — Hopkins County produces the most in the state. The region's farmland includes the state's top producers of soybeans, corn and wheat. Meat processing is also big business — Tyson Foods, Perdue Farms and Pilgrim's Pride employ thousands in their chicken processing plants. To the east, the district has charcoal, limestone, wood and parts manufacturing, but poverty rates remain high. Elsewhere in the 1st, prominent employers are manufacturers of plastics, metals, textiles and processed foods. Carhartt Inc. has clothing factories in Hopkins and Metcalfe counties.

Hopkinsville, the district's largest city, has a proportion of black residents four times higher than the state average as well as high poverty rates; the economy relies on Fort Campbell, which crosses into Tennessee.

Paducah is home to Western Kentucky Community and Technical College, a key resource for job training as the local economy has shifted from manufacturing to the service sector. Similarly, Taylor County has transitioned from metal, auto, and clothing manufacturing to service-oriented commerce driven by an Amazon.com shipping facility and Intelenet center.

Registered Democrats outnumber Republicans here, yet the 1st increasingly backs GOP candidates in federal races: four counties here supported Al Gore for president in 2000, but none backed Barack Obama in 2012.

Major Industries

Agriculture, manufacturing, coal

Military Bases

Fort Campbell, 34,600 military, 3,300 civilian (shared with Tennessee's 7th District)

Cities

Hopkinsville, Henderson, Paducah

Notable

Hopkinsville hosts the Trail of Tears Commemorative Park, recognizing the path taken by American Indians displaced by the government in the 1800s.

Rep. Brett Guthrie (R)

Capitol Office
225-3501
guthrie.house.gov
308 Cannon Bldg. 20515-1702; fax 226-2019

Committees
Education & the Workforce
Energy & Commerce

Residence
Bowling Green

Born
Feb. 18, 1964; Florence, Ala.

Religion
Church of Christ

Family
Wife, Beth Guthrie; three children

Education
U.S. Military Academy, B.S. 1987 (mathematical economics); Yale U., M.P.P.M 1997

Military
Army, 1987-90; Army Reserve, 1990-2002

Career
Automotive supply company executive

Political Highlights
Ky. Senate, 1999-2009

ELECTION RESULTS

2012 GENERAL		
Brett Guthrie (R)	181,508	64.3%
David Lynn Williams (D)	89,541	31.7%
Andrew Beacham (I)	6,304	2.2%
Craig R. Astor (LIBERT)	4,914	1.7%
2012 PRIMARY		
Brett Guthrie (R)		unopposed
2010 GENERAL		
Brett Guthrie (R)	155,906	67.9%
Ed Marksberry (D)	73,749	32.1%

Previous Winning Percentages
2008 (53%)

Elected 2008; 3rd term

Guthrie spends his legislative energies on two areas with personal significance: looking out for manufacturers and creating training opportunities for workers. On most other topics he is unassuming, happily operating in the background with a minimum amount of fuss.

A decade in the Kentucky Senate taught him that "you can't be an expert in everything," he says. Guthrie knows manufacturing, however. After leaving the Army, he became a jack-of-all-trades at the automobile die-casting company founded by his father. His last position there was in human resources, but he also served as a production manager and a quality engineer, among other roles.

He now sits on the Energy and Commerce Subcommittee on Commerce, Manufacturing and Trade. In the 113th Congress (2013-14), Guthrie is again on the Education and the Workforce Committee, where he served as a freshman. He has a seat on its workforce training panel.

Guthrie tries to keep open lines of communication with manufacturing-sector stakeholders, and he says an overhaul of the federal tax structure is the No. 1 way to rev up the industry. A lower corporate tax rate and a switch to "territorial" taxation — a system under which business income is taxed only in the country where it is earned — would boost the economy, according to Guthrie.

He wants to eliminate many corporate tax breaks as a means of increasing competition. Younger, growing companies are the creators of many new jobs, but "our tax code favors mature businesses," Guthrie says. Larger companies can spread around losses or depreciations from various divisions or plants to drop into lower tax brackets, but single-site companies can't take advantage of such tactics.

Guthrie's commitment to worker training goes back to his high school years in Alabama. When Ford closed the plant where his father worked, the whole town was "devastated by being dependent on one industry," he says. Guthrie's father had availed himself of educational opportunities over the years and was able to open his new company in Kentucky. Other families were crushed.

Perhaps with that experience in mind, Guthrie broke with most Republicans on providing federal aid to the ailing automobile industry in 2009. He backed creation of the "cash for clunkers" vehicle trade-in program and voted to pour an additional $2 billion into it after the initial $1 billion in rebates were spent.

And he has kept a close watch on federal assistance for worker-training programs. Even with current unemployment levels, companies cannot find the skilled workers they want, he says. Guthrie believes unemployment insurance should be modified to include more training components.

He supported a bill, passed by the House in March 2013, to consolidate most federally run workforce development programs into a single system funded by a block grant. It would also give employers more input to the kinds of training needed in their markets. Democrats panned the measure, claiming that the consolidation would hurt specific populations that are targeted by the existing range of programs.

Guthrie likes local control for all kinds of education. He is OK with broad policies — "I mean, we're competing globally, so we need to have federal goals and federal views of what kids should be learning" — but he wants implementation of those goals and standards left largely to the states.

He even brings a workforce perspective to the Energy and Commerce Health Subcommittee. In his view, the 2010 health care overhaul law and its coverage requirements will hurt workers. The more routine care that insurers must cover, the higher premiums will get, he says, and the more employers will compensate by cutting wages. Guthrie would rather see workers get higher salaries and less-comprehensive coverage; they could use the extra cash to supplement policies as they see fit.

His other business interests have local roots. Coal and oil are big for Kentucky, and Guthrie joins many Republicans in describing the Obama administration as being openly hostile to the fossil fuel industry. The EPA demands protections with little health benefit and massive costs to businesses, he says, and the resulting higher energy prices will "wreck the economy."

As co-chairman of the Congressional Horse Caucus in the 112th Congress (2011-12), Guthrie tried to spotlight the effect of online gaming on Kentucky's horse racing industry. "We cannot ignore this important industry as we consider changes to online gaming," he said at an Energy and Commerce hearing in October 2011.

Drawing on his military past, Guthrie sometimes kicks the tires on defense issues. He advocates mission-driven defense budgeting, whereby clear parameters for the military are established, then spending is set to accommodate the force required. And he has introduced several measures meant to help veterans. He has sponsored a bill to increase the study of urotrauma issues among servicemembers. That injury is commonly caused by improvised explosive devices, such as those used against troops in Afghanistan.

Guthrie grew up in Florence, Ala., and his drawl hints at those origins. His mother looked after him and his three brothers while his father worked. He played football, as "everybody growing up in northwest Alabama wanted to play football for Bear Bryant." He also enjoyed water sports along the Tennessee River.

Guthrie broke his shoulder playing high school football, "so I was laid up for the fall of 1980 watching Ronald Reagan campaign for president." He was stirred by talk of the Cold War — an uncle had been killed in Korea, and his grandparents were strongly anti-Communist — and ended up going to West Point. He served as a field artillery officer in the 101st Airborne Division until 1990. Opting for a family life with less travel, he then moved over to the Army Reserve and joined his father's business in Bowling Green.

Drawn to his military and business experience, friends recruited him for his first state Senate race. He had served for a decade when seven-term Republican Ron Lewis announced his retirement — on the last day to file for the May 2008 primary, ostensibly to hand a victory to his chief of staff. But Guthrie also filed, and he chased out the opposition. He dispatched a Democratic state senator in the general election with 53 percent of the vote, then scored easy victories in 2010 and 2012.

Key Votes

2012	
Extend a Social Security payroll tax cut and unemployment benefits	YES
Ease securities rules to expand small-business access to capital	YES
Extend for one year subsidized student loan interest rates financed by a cut in health care spending	YES
Cite Attorney General Eric H. Holder Jr. for contempt of Congress	YES
Create a visa program for foreign graduates in high-tech fields	YES
Extend most Bush-era income tax rates while allowing rates for top-bracket earners to rise (Jan. 1, 2013)	NO
2011	
Strike funding for F-35 alternative engine	NO
Prevent EPA from regulating greenhouse gas emissions to address climate change	YES
Extend certain provisions of Patriot Act for four years	YES
Declare opposition to use of ground troops in Libya	+
Overhaul patent law	YES
Pass compromise debt limit increase plan and establish future spending limits	YES
Allow consideration of measures to implement three trade agreements	YES

CQ Vote Studies

	PARTY UNITY		PRESIDENTIAL SUPPORT	
	SUPPORT	OPPOSE	SUPPORT	OPPOSE
2012	95%	5%	15%	85%
2011	95%	5%	23%	77%
2010	96%	4%	29%	71%
2009	85%	15%	32%	68%

Interest Groups

	AFL-CIO	ADA	CCUS	ACU
2012	19%	0%	100%	80%
2011	0%	10%	100%	76%
2010	8%	0%	88%	95%
2009	14%	10%	80%	88%

Kentucky 2

West central — Bowling Green, Owensboro

From Owensboro on the Ohio River, east through tobacco country and the hilly Green River Valley, the conservative 2nd has small manufacturing towns and distribution, tourism, agriculture and military-related jobs.

Fast-growing Bowling Green is the district's largest city and third-largest in the state. The college town's largest employer is Western Kentucky University. While still mainly white, Bowling Green's minority populations are about twice as populous as state averages. Auto parts manufacturing is prominent in surrounding Warren County, as it is throughout the 2nd. Bullitt County, near Interstate 65, is a shipping hub for online retailer Zappos.

Owensboro, the Daviess County seat, hosts an inland port for steel, aluminum, copper and fertilizer along the Ohio River. Daviess, one of Kentucky's most productive agricultural counties, is rich in corn and soybeans. It also sits on the edge of Western Kentucky's oil and coal fields. Barren County, in the southeastern corner, is the state's top burly tobacco producer.

Fort Knox, famous for the gold depository run by the Treasury Department, covers land in Bullitt, Hardin and Meade counties. Many civilian jobs at the fort are with the Army's Human Resources Center. Mammoth Caves, the world's longest known cave system, lures tourists, as does, the region's iconic Kentucky Bourbon Trail tourism — Jim Beam is distilled in the 2nd.

Registered Democrats outnumber Republicans in the 2nd, but it leans strongly Republican in federal elections. Conservative Democrats win some local elections, and counties like Daviess, Mercer and Garrard have supported Democratic congressional candidates. Every county wholly or partly within the 2nd backed Republican nominee Mitt Romney in 2012.

Major Industries
Manufacturing, agriculture and tobacco, tourism

Military Bases
Fort Knox, 9,300 military, 8,000 civilian

Cities
Bowling Green, Owensboro, Elizabethtown

Notable
The International Bluegrass Music Museum is in Owensboro.

Rep. John Yarmuth (D)

Capitol Office
225-5401
yarmuth.house.gov
403 Cannon Bldg. 20515-1703; fax 225-5776

Committees
Budget
Education & the Workforce

Residence
Louisville

Born
Nov. 4, 1947; Louisville, Ky.

Religion
Jewish

Family
Wife, Cathy Yarmuth; one child

Education
Yale U., B.A. 1969 (American studies); Georgetown U. Law School, attended 1971-72

Career
Periodical publisher and columnist; television commentator; public relations executive; congressional aide; stockbroker

Political Highlights
Republican nominee for Louisville Board of Aldermen, 1975; Republican nominee for Jefferson County Board of Commissioners, 1981

ELECTION RESULTS

2012 GENERAL		
John Yarmuth (D)	206,385	64.0%
Brooks Wicker (R)	111,452	34.5%
Bob DeVore Jr. (I)	4,819	1.5%
2012 PRIMARY		
John Yarmuth (D)	43,635	86.7%
Burrel Charles Farnsley (D)	6,716	13.3%
2010 GENERAL		
John Yarmuth (D)	139,940	54.7%
Todd Lally (R)	112,627	44.0%

Previous Winning Percentages
2008 (59%); 2006 (51%)

Elected 2006; 4th term

Yarmuth excelled at rhetorical exercises while building careers in journalism and politics. He now says the partisan posturing in Washington is "very frustrating. ... It's not how I would prefer to spend my time in Congress." But he hasn't ended his fealty to Democratic positions or his jabs at Republicans while promoting plans on manufacturing, education and more.

Yarmuth's father founded National Industries, which at one time was the second-largest public company in Kentucky. It had holdings in retail business, manufacturing, transportation, oil and services. His maternal grandfather was a prominent Louisville banker.

The family fortune helped Yarmuth begin a career in publishing. In 1976, he founded Louisville Today magazine, which he published until 1982, along with an alternative newspaper, City Paper. After a stint in public relations in the 1980s, he founded and edited the weekly Louisville Eccentric Observer in the 1990s. He also appeared as a radio and TV commentator.

He now offers commentaries in the House, usually on the deficiencies of Republicans. Yarmuth sits on the Budget Committee. In 2012, the panel's Democrats let him make closing remarks on the GOP's fiscal 2013 budget. "For all the detail they've provided in this budget, where they'll get their revenue, they might as well have written their budget on a cocktail napkin," Yarmuth said. "But I saved them the trouble. I did it for them. Here's their budget plan: tax cuts for the rich, slash spending, shift health care costs to the seniors, and pray for incredible growth."

For the 112th Congress (2011-12) he also had a seat on the highly partisan Oversight and Government Reform Committee. Yarmuth asked his share of pointed questions but also said he's "up for those battles" when Democrats push back against Republican investigations.

Even with his colorful criticism, Yarmuth seems to come from the "happy warrior" mold; he generally avoids personal hostility. And while he seldom votes against the majority of Democrats, he belongs to no major moderate or liberal caucus. In the opening months of the 113th Congress (2013-14), some of his more bipartisan work came to light—he has been part of an eight-person House working group trying to assemble compromise proposals for an overhaul of immigration law.

Manufacturing is a major policy interest for Yarmuth and the city of Louisville, and at the start of the 113th Congress he returned to the Education and the Workforce Committee. He has championed several plans for strengthening the nation's manufacturing base. In the 111th Congress (2009-10) he fought for extension of tax credits to manufacturers of energy-efficient appliances—such as the General Electric Co., which operates its Appliance Park in Louisville.

Yarmuth likes providing financial incentives for companies to bring work back to the United States, as GE did when it moved 430 jobs from China to Louisville. "The Chinese are implementing policies in their own best interest. We need to do the same," he said. Yarmuth has not been a backer of free-trade deals: He voted against pacts with South Korea, Colombia and Panama in 2011.

Yarmuth supported the major Democratic initiatives of the 111th Congress, and "I don't back away or get cowed by shifting winds," he says. He'd rather have a government-run "single payer" health care system, but he continues to defend the 2010 health care overhaul.

Despite representing coal-rich Kentucky, he voted in 2009 for energy legislation to create a cap-and-trade system aimed at reducing greenhouse gas emissions. Yarmuth lamented that the policy was "not very easy to explain in

9.8 seconds, which is the average sound bite." He opposes mountaintop-removal coal mining and sponsored a 2013 bill to put a moratorium on permitting for such projects until the federal government conducts studies on their health effects.

Kentucky voters also generally oppose restrictions on gun ownership, but a tragic shooting at a Connecticut school in December 2012 strengthened Yarmuth's resolve to support measures to curb gun violence. "I have been largely silent on the issue of gun violence over the past six years, and I am now as sorry for that as I am for what happened to the families who lost so much in this most recent, but sadly not isolated, tragedy," he wrote.

In the months leading up to the 2012 election, Yarmuth called for changes to campaign finance law, objecting particularly to the rules for super PACs. He proposed a constitutional amendment stating that campaign expenditures do not constitute protected speech and giving Congress the power to enact a mandatory public campaign financing system. When such changes come, "it will be because the public demands it," he said. At the start of 2013, he introduced a bill to start a public financing system for congressional campaigns.

Yarmuth grew up in a Republican family; his father had been a fundraiser for President Richard Nixon. Yarmuth was drawn more to the moderate wing of the party, embodied by New York's Nelson Rockefeller.

While an undergraduate at Yale University, Yarmuth spent his summers working for Jefferson County Judge-Executive Marlow W. Cook. When Cook was elected to the Senate, Yarmuth joined his office as a legislative aide from 1971 to 1974.

He ran unsuccessfully for office twice as a Republican. The first race was for the Louisville Board of Aldermen in 1975. Six years later, at the suggestion of a county judge named Mitch McConnell, he ran for the Jefferson County Board of Commissioners. McConnell is now the Senate minority leader, and Yarmuth has been highly critical of him in recent years. He tried to recruit another Democrat — actress Ashley Judd — to challenge McConnell in 2014.

It was not until 1985 that Yarmuth became a Democrat, deciding the party more closely reflected his views. He was a late entrant into the 2006 House race. Some of his suggestions as a columnist — such as removing "under God" from the Pledge of Allegiance — provided fodder for attack ads. But he won the primary handily and went on to beat Republican Rep. Anne M. Northup by more than 2 points.

Northup came back for a rematch in 2008, but the Democratic tide swamped her — the 3rd District was the only one President Barack Obama carried in Kentucky. Yarmuth won with 59 percent of the vote. In 2012, he took 64 percent against GOP candidate Brooks Wicker.

Key Votes

2012

Extend a Social Security payroll tax cut and unemployment benefits	YES
Ease securities rules to expand small-business access to capital	YES
Extend for one year subsidized student loan interest rates financed by a cut in health care spending	NO
Cite Attorney General Eric H. Holder Jr. for contempt of Congress	?
Create a visa program for foreign graduates in high-tech fields	NO
Extend most Bush-era income tax rates while allowing rates for top-bracket earners to rise (Jan. 1, 2013)	YES

2011

Strike funding for F-35 alternative engine	NO
Prevent EPA from regulating greenhouse gas emissions to address climate change	NO
Extend certain provisions of Patriot Act for four years	NO
Declare opposition to use of ground troops in Libya	YES
Overhaul patent law	YES
Pass compromise debt limit increase plan and establish future spending limits	NO
Allow consideration of measures to implement three trade agreements	NO

CQ Vote Studies

	PARTY UNITY		PRESIDENTIAL SUPPORT	
	SUPPORT	OPPOSE	SUPPORT	OPPOSE
2012	97%	3%	93%	7%
2011	96%	4%	88%	12%
2010	99%	1%	90%	10%
2009	99%	1%	97%	3%
2008	98%	2%	13%	87%

Interest Groups

	AFL-CIO	ADA	CCUS	ACU
2012	95%	90%	18%	0%
2011	100%	90%	27%	4%
2010	100%	100%	13%	0%
2009	100%	100%	40%	0%
2008	100%	95%	61%	4%

Kentucky 3

Louisville Metro

The only district in the state contained within one county, the 3rd centers on Louisville, a Democratic-leaning city with a diverse economy and heritage. Louisville and surrounding Jefferson County suburbs merged in 2003 to become the state's largest municipality. The Ohio River, the district's northern border, draws a line between Southern and Midwestern cultures.

While the rest of Kentucky's economy has relied on mining and agriculture, Louisville built an economic base aided by its central location and inland shipping port. The city's manufacturing sector is anchored by GE's home appliance division and Ford Motor Co. Health care is now one of the city's ascendant industries: Headquarters for insurance giant Humana are here. Other corporate headquarters in the city include UPS, the district's largest single employer, and Yum! Brands. Louisville International Airport is home to the Kentucky Air National Guard and UPS's international shipping hub. The University of Louisville is one of the state's largest schools.

The city's cultural landscape includes Churchill Downs, which hosts the world-famous Kentucky Derby horse race in the shadow of its twin spires. Old-fashioned riverboat casinos also are a draw. While central Louisville has seen some decline, it offers lower-cost housing for students and young professionals, and the Old Louisville neighborhood near downtown has one of the largest collections of Victorian architecture in the United States. A thriving independent music and art scene supports a number of annual festivals.

With its combination of Kentucky's largest black community, a large student population, a well-established union presence and a professional workforce, the Louisville Metro region is the state's most reliable source of Democratic votes. Republican Sen. Rand Paul lost the county by an 11-point margin in 2010, and Democratic presidential candidates have won the county for decades.

Major Industry

Health care, shipping, manufacturing, tourism

Cities

Louisville

Notable

Hillerich & Bradsby, makers of the famous Louisville Slugger baseball bat, have had their headquarters in the city since the 1880s — the factory and museum building features a gigantic baseball bat at the entrance.

Rep. Thomas Massie (R)

Capitol Office
225-3465
massie.house.gov
314 Cannon Bldg. 20515-1704; fax 225-0003

Committees
Oversight & Government Reform
Science, Space & Technology
(Technology - Chairman)
Transportation & Infrastructure

Residence
Garrison

Born
Jan. 13, 1971; Huntington, W.Va.

Religion
Methodist

Family
Wife, Rhonda Massie; four children

Education
Massachusetts Institute of Technology, S.B. 1993 (electrical science and engineering), S.M. 1996 (mechanical engineering)

Career
Farmer; technology company executive

Political Highlights
Lewis County judge-executive, 2010-12

ELECTION RESULTS

2012 SPECIAL		
Thomas Massie (R)	174,092	59.9%
William R. "Bill" Adkins (D)	106,598	36.7%
David Lewis (I)	9,987	3.4%
2012 GENERAL		
Thomas Massie (R)	186,036	62.1%
William R. "Bill" Adkins (D)	104,734	35.0%
David Lewis (I)	8,674	2.9%
2012 PRIMARY		
Thomas Massie (R)	19,689	44.8%
Alecia Webb-Edgington (R)	12,557	28.6%
Gary Moore (R)	6,521	14.8%
Walter Christian Schumm (R)	3,514	8.0%
Marc Carey (R)	783	1.8%
Tom Wurtz (R)	598	1.4%

Elected 2012; 1st full term

Massie is deeply inquisitive, but he is already sure of his thoughts regarding government — he wants it to be smaller, more efficient and paid for. An engineer by training, he has libertarian leanings and few qualms about going against the Republican team when he sees the need.

Of the congressmen first elected in 2012, Massie is one of the most intriguing. He founded a company to sell technology that he designed; he left that life behind to operate a farm with his family; and he built a timber-frame home out of lumber he cut and milled himself, blogging about the whole experience. For good measure, he plays the banjo.

He's an unusual mix of earnestly wonkish scientist and charismatic schmoozer. Massie laughs often and tells stories with verve, charm and a slight northern Kentucky twang.

However, he's not a go-along-to-get-along politician. Massie has been compared to former Texas Rep. Ron Paul and his son, Kentucky Sen. Rand Paul — outsider Republicans who are sometimes strident in expressing free-market, civil-libertarian beliefs.

On the campaign trail, Massie said "out-of-control spending" was his biggest worry. He was seated to fill a vacancy in the final months of the 112th Congress (2011-12) and voted against a bill that raised income tax rates on annual earnings over $400,000. Massie was irked that the measure wasn't packaged with spending cuts and that it postponed automatic "sequestration" cuts put in place by a 2011 law.

At the start of the 113th Congress (2013-14), he was one of a dozen Republicans who opted not to support John A. Boehner for speaker of the House. Instead of backing Boehner, who had been a key figure in the late 2012 fiscal negotiations, Massie voted for Michigan Republican Justin Amash, another libertarian darling.

A few weeks later, Massie was one of 33 House Republicans who opposed a temporary increase in the government's borrowing limit. "I couldn't get there, on principle," he said. Massie wants the federal budget to be balanced within 10 years. Early in 2013, he said pressure from fiscal conservatives was "already changing the dialogue" toward that goal. Massie sees many domestic programs as having no basis in the Constitution and has suggested eliminating the Education and Energy departments.

Despite his early disagreements with the GOP leadership, Massie chairs the Science, Space and Technology Subcommittee on Technology. "I assume it's not the most powerful position here if they have let me have it," he joked.

He's interested in improving the overall efficiency of technology programs. Massie told Reason magazine that Republicans sometimes run the risk of seeming anti-technology, particularly in terms of alternative energy. "There is no reason we should be against solar panels," he said. "We can be against subsidies for them, but there is no reason to hate solar panels. ... There is no reason to hate electric cars; we can despise the fact that they are subsidized."

Massie's own house is "off the grid," relying on solar, geothermal and other natural power sources.

He sits on the Transportation and Infrastructure Committee, where he's looking out for infrastructure along the Ohio River, which forms the northern border of his district. Massie told Reason that he'd prefer to limit federal infrastructure spending to projects with interstate aspects.

His third panel is the Oversight and Government Reform Committee. Massie says there is plenty of government waste to target for cuts, and he is skeptical of much government regulation. He co-sponsored a bill to require congressional approval of any new regulation that is estimated to have $100 million or more in cumulative economic impact.

Massie is socially conservative. He opposes federal funding of abortion and believes life begins at conception. He also adheres to many civil libertarian principles — he opposed the fiscal 2013 defense policy law over provisions that he said would allow indefinite detention of U.S. citizens without trial.

Growing up in Kentucky, Massie would take appliances completely apart and keep the pieces strewn about his room. His parents pushed him to clean up the mess. "I thought, 'I'll build a robot that can clean the room out of all of this junk,'" he said. "It's kind of recursive, if you think about it."

An android was beyond his abilities, but he did build a robot arm. He kept on building them in middle school and high school, entering science fairs along the way. For college, he headed to the Massachusetts Institute of Technology; his high school sweetheart, Rhonda, followed him there two years later. They're now married with four children.

As a senior, Massie designed a device to allow computer users — designers, engineers, doctors or whoever — to have the physical sensation of touching virtual objects. He and Rhonda founded SensAble Technologies and operated it for a decade. Massie holds 24 technology-related patents.

When they sold the company, they bought the 1,200-acre farm where Rhonda grew up. Massie set about building them a new house, raised his family and tended 50 head of cattle. He got involved in politics by fighting agricultural zoning changes and small tax initiatives in his home county. Massie participated in tea party events and campaigned for Rand Paul, who was seeking a Senate seat in 2010. That year, Massie defeated a Republican incumbent en route to winning election as Lewis County judge-executive — in effect, the mayor of the county. According to several accounts, he clashed with other county officials while emphasizing spending reductions.

Rep. Geoff Davis announced in late 2011 that he would be retiring. His resignation in July 2012 was a surprise — he cited a family health issue as the reason. Massie entered the race to succeed him with the backing of tea party groups and support from free-market, libertarian-leaning organizations. He was endorsed and mentored by Rand Paul. Massie won 45 percent of the vote in a seven-way primary. The district is heavily Republican, and Massie easily won both a full term and the special election to complete Davis' term in the 112th Congress. He hired several former Ron Paul staffers for his office.

Massie wasn't into politics in college, but he notes that his first macroeconomics teacher was liberal Nobel laureate Paul Krugman. Massie aced the course, but Krugman's version of things "didn't make sense then, and it doesn't make sense now," he says.

Key Votes

2012	
Create a visa program for foreign graduates in high-tech fields	YES
Extend most Bush-era income tax rates while allowing rates for top-bracket earners to rise (Jan. 1, 2013)	NO

CQ Vote Studies

	PARTY UNITY		PRESIDENTIAL SUPPORT	
	SUPPORT	OPPOSE	SUPPORT	OPPOSE
2012	87%	13%	40%	60%

Interest Groups

	AFL-CIO	ADA	CCUS	ACU
2012			100%	

Kentucky 4

North — Covington, Florence, Ashland

The 4th District stretches wide across northern Kentucky, tracing a portion of the state's border with Indiana and its entire border with Ohio. A mix of small cities, midsize suburbs and the Appalachian northeast, the district's main population centers are in the state's northernmost counties — home to suburbs across the Ohio River from Cincinnati — and to the west in the Louisville suburbs.

Boone, Kenton and Campbell in the Cincinnati area are home to suburban commuters as well as manufacturing interests and large corporate headquarters, although some businesses have departed for Cincinnati. The Cincinnati-Northern Kentucky International Airport, located outside Covington, is an important regional economic driver, hosting major operations for international shipping company DHL. The St. Elizabeth Medical Center is a major regional health care hub and one of the district's largest employers, and Northern Kentucky University, outside Covington, is one of the state's fastest-growing schools. Newport on the Levee is a popular entertainment district, including the first authentic Hofbräuhaus in the U.S., modeled after the establishment in Munich.

Outside of the metro area, the district includes some portions of the Bluegrass region, where farming and horse breeding are important to the culture as well as the economy. The Appalachian section of the district has struggled with high poverty rates and a stagnant economy. Local officials have sought ways to attract more industrial firms to the tri-state area.

The 4th is extremely friendly to Republicans. Redistricting following the 2010 census consolidated the district among Kentucky's conservative northernmost counties; remapping shaved off six swing counties along its southern border and added areas on the outskirts of the Louisville Metro region. In the 2012 presidential election, Republican Mitt Romney took well over 50 percent in each of the counties in the 4th.

Major Industry

Transportation, manufacturing, health care, service

Cities

Covington, Florence, Independence, Ashland

Notable

During the 19th century, Campbell County produced about one-third of all U.S. wine, and the region continues to host vineyards.

Rep. Harold Rogers (R)

Capitol Office
225-4601
halrogers.house.gov
2406 Rayburn Bldg. 20515-1705; fax 225-0940

Committees
Appropriations - Chairman

Residence
Somerset

Born
Dec. 31, 1937; Barrier, Ky.

Religion
Baptist

Family
Wife, Cynthia Doyle Rogers; three children

Education
Western Kentucky U., attended 1956-57; U. of Kentucky, B.A. 1962, LL.B. 1964

Military
Ky. National Guard, 1956-57; N.C. National Guard, 1957-58; Ky. National Guard, 1958-63

Career
Lawyer

Political Highlights
Pulaski and Rockcastle counties commonwealth attorney, 1969-80; Republican nominee for lieutenant governor, 1979

ELECTION RESULTS

2012 GENERAL		
Harold Rogers (R)	195,408	77.9%
Kenneth Stepp (D)	55,447	22.1%
2012 PRIMARY		
Harold Rogers (R)		unopposed
2010 GENERAL		
Harold Rogers (R)	151,019	77.4%
Jim Holbert (D)	44,034	22.6%

Previous Winning Percentages
2008 (84%); 2006 (74%); 2004 (100%); 2002 (78%); 2000 (74%); 1998 (78%); 1996 (100%); 1994 (79%); 1992 (55%); 1990 (100%); 1988 (100%); 1986 (100%); 1984 (76%); 1982 (65%); 1980 (68%)

Elected 1980; 17th term

Rogers waited almost three decades to chair what had been one of the most powerful panels in Congress — only to find that the job atop the Appropriations Committee had radically changed.

He frequently jokes that his panel now should be called the "Disappropriations Committee," as its focus is wringing money out of the budget. Once a key distributor of perks to fellow lawmakers, the Appropriations chairman now decides which of their favored programs will take the deepest cuts. Since Rogers took the post in 2011, he has sliced tens of billions of dollars from what amounts to the federal government's basic operating expenses — its regular discretionary budget.

A veteran lawmaker long noted for his skill as a deal-maker, Rogers has taken the reversal in stride. He often says he tells Speaker John A. Boehner that while he "ran to be chief chef, you've got me in charge of the latrines."

The 112th Congress (2011-12), with its influx of conservative freshmen, was not the first time Rogers had to contend with demands for deep cuts in federal spending. As a senior appropriator in the 1990s, Rogers faced another group of fiery GOP freshmen, many of whom had little patience for party oldtimers. In the 1980s, Rogers worked against the Ronald Reagan administration's efforts to kill the Appalachian Regional Commission and trim black-lung benefits, which are important to his coal-dependent district.

Despite now serving in what many consider one of the tougher assignments in the House, Rogers has no immediate plans to retire. "I don't walk away from a challenge," he said in a September 2012 C-SPAN interview.

Rogers had a somewhat satisfying finish to his first year as chairman in 2011. He finished two sets of annual spending bills in that time. One set, the fiscal 2012 measures, moved through something close to "regular order," the increasingly rare process of both chambers advancing their annual bills to the floor, holding conferences on the measures and clearing them.

But in his second year, congressional leaders decided to cover the first half of fiscal 2013 with a six-month continuing resolution. Rogers began the 113th Congress (2013-14) working out a continuing resolution to cover the second half. House appropriators had approved 11 of the 12 spending bills for fiscal 2013, and the CRs obviated a good deal of their work.

Many fiscal decisions have been routed away from appropriators in recent years, as congressional leaders and the White House have negotiated directly over deficit reduction. A 2011 deficit reduction law created $1.2 trillion in spending cuts, known as sequestration, that would take hold in 2013 if Congress found no alternatives.

Rogers was on damage control as those cuts started to go into effect. "Sequestration is about not making choices," he said, calling it "terrible politics and a terrible policy."

For Rogers, passing annual appropriations bills means more than simply sorting out spending levels for agencies. The bills also are one of Congress' best tools for trying to compel federal agencies to change their operations. While serving as chairman of the Subcommittee on Homeland Security, Rogers threatened to slash fiscal 2006 funding for the Coast Guard's troubled Deepwater program by almost half, to $500 million, before relenting and allowing $933 million to be appropriated.

Once called a "Prince of Pork," Rogers had been one of the most ardent defenders of earmarks, the spending provisions that direct money to specific projects in lawmakers' districts. In 2009, Rogers came to the aid of fellow GOP appropriator John Culberson of Texas, who was fighting a bid by budget hawk

Jeff Flake of Arizona to strip a Culberson earmark from the Homeland Security bill. Rogers told Culberson on the floor that he "would be derelict in his duties to the Congress and to the people of his district and the country if he didn't make these efforts to help the people that he represents."

In 2006, Rogers fought Flake over a bid to eliminate money that Rogers himself wanted earmarked to boost tourism in impoverished southern Kentucky. Rogers was quick to note that federal investment had aided Flake's home state. "The federal government over the years earmarked hundreds of millions of dollars to provide water out of the Colorado River so that Arizona in the desert would bloom," Rogers said.

But earmarks have gone out of favor, and Rogers faced some criticism for his, even back in his home state. In a 2010 editorial criticizing the appropriator's earmarking, the Lexington Herald-Leader said that it was "no coincidence that Rogers' district has remained mired in an economic nowhere land while a favored few have benefited from the congressman's position."

Republicans banned the practice in 2011, which puts Rogers in the awkward role of enforcing the moratorium. At the Appropriations Committee's organizational meeting for the 113th Congress, Virginia Democrat James P. Moran asked the chairman to consider creating a panel to look at whether earmarks could be revived. Rogers didn't respond at all to the request, and moved to other committee business.

Still, Rogers takes particular pride in having steered money home to fight the drug problem in southern and eastern Kentucky. According to his website, Rogers has directed tens of millions of dollars to Operation UNITE (Unlawful Narcotics Investigations, Treatment and Education), which serves 29 Kentucky counties. For years, Rogers has been aggressively seeking federal help in fighting abuse of painkillers such as oxycodone.

After graduating from high school in rural Kentucky in 1955, Rogers left home in search of work in Cincinnati. He returned to earn undergraduate and law degrees at the University of Kentucky.

Rogers made his name locally in the 1960s as a civic activist promoting industrial development in Somerset. He took over as a commonwealth's attorney in 1969, continuing to play a conspicuous role in politics as the prosecutor for Pulaski and Rockcastle counties. He was unsuccessful as the GOP nominee for lieutenant governor in 1979, but the race helped him build name recognition. That paid off in his first House campaign in 1980.

He ran to succeed retiring Republican Tim Lee Carter. Rogers was the victor in a 10-person GOP primary, then took 68 percent of the vote in November. It was the first in a long series of decisive victories. He took almost 78 percent of the vote to beat Democrat Kenneth Stepp in 2012.

Key Votes

2012	
Extend a Social Security payroll tax cut and unemployment benefits	YES
Ease securities rules to expand small-business access to capital	YES
Extend for one year subsidized student loan interest rates financed by a cut in health care spending	YES
Cite Attorney General Eric H. Holder Jr. for contempt of Congress	YES
Create a visa program for foreign graduates in high-tech fields	YES
Extend most Bush-era income tax rates while allowing rates for top-bracket earners to rise (Jan. 1, 2013)	YES
2011	
Strike funding for F-35 alternative engine	NO
Prevent EPA from regulating greenhouse gas emissions to address climate change	YES
Extend certain provisions of Patriot Act for four years	YES
Declare opposition to use of ground troops in Libya	YES
Overhaul patent law	YES
Pass compromise debt limit increase plan and establish future spending limits	YES
Allow consideration of measures to implement three trade agreements	YES

CQ Vote Studies

	PARTY UNITY		PRESIDENTIAL SUPPORT	
	SUPPORT	OPPOSE	SUPPORT	OPPOSE
2012	80%	11%	16%	84%
2011	93%	7%	27%	73%
2010	97%	3%	26%	74%
2009	82%	18%	35%	65%
2008	96%	4%	69%	31%

Interest Groups

	AFL-CIO	ADA	CCUS	ACU
2012	19%	0%	100%	72%
2011	0%	10%	100%	72%
2010	7%	0%	88%	96%
2009	14%	0%	87%	88%
2008	13%	20%	94%	84%

Kentucky 5

East and southeast — Somerset, Middleboro

Covering rural southeastern Kentucky, the 5th District borders Tennessee, Virginia and West Virginia in hardscrabble Appalachian coal country that has experienced the state's most concentrated population loss since 2000. Composed of small manufacturing and mining communities with overwhelmingly white populations, every county in the 5th has poverty rates higher than the state average.

The region's economy still depends on energy production, as it did through much of the 20th century, but the district is reeling from the decline in coal industry jobs over the past several decades as extraction methods have changed. The Devonian Black Shale is the state's densest natural gas drilling area. Pike County is by far the state's top natural gas producer, while Lee County has oil wells. Kentucky has been one of the nation's top three coal producers for the past 50 years, and Harlan and Pike counties are among the state's most productive counties.

Pulaski and Warren counties have some cattle and dairy production, but the 5th overall has less farmland than other districts in the state. Data support and customer service call-in centers and small manufacturing plants provide other jobs in the district.

Bell County has turned to outdoors and adventure tourism, capitalizing on its proximity to the Pine Mountain State Park and Daniel Boone National Forest. Pulaski County has also recently pursued winery tourism. Lake Cumberland is split with the 1st District near Somerset, the 5th's largest city. Recent renovation projects at Wolf Dam by the Army Corps of Engineers are expected to stunt the lake's tourism draw through about 2014.

Despite a Democratic majority in voter registration, the 5th has increasingly trended conservative and prefers Republicans in federal elections. Elliott was the only county in the 5th not to support Republican nominee Mitt Romney the 2012 presidential election.

Major Industry

Coal, oil, tourism, data processing

Cities

Somerset, Middlesboro

Notable

In 2012, Bell County opened a countywide community garden, the first of its kind in the United States.

Rep. Andy Barr (R)

Capitol Office
225-4706
barr.house.gov
1432 Longworth Bldg. 20515-1706; fax 225-2122

Committees
Financial Services

Residence
Lexington

Born
July 24, 1973; Lexington, Ky.

Religion
Episcopalian

Family
Wife, Carol Leavell Barr; two children

Education
U. of Virginia, B.A. 1996 (government); U. of Kentucky, J.D. 2001

Career
Lobbyist; lawyer; gubernatorial and state agency aide; congressional aide

Political Highlights
Republican nominee for U.S. House, 2010

ELECTION RESULTS

2012 GENERAL		
Andy Barr (R)	153,222	50.6%
Ben Chandler (D)	141,438	46.7%
Randolph S. Vance (I)	8,340	2.8%
2012 PRIMARY		
Andy Barr (R)	20,104	82.8%
Patrick J. Kelly II (R)	2,823	11.6%
Curtis Kenimer (R)	1,354	5.6%

Elected 2012; 1st term

Barr stands firmly upon the Republican Party platform, promoting an anti-tax, small-government agenda. He puts extra emphasis on defense of the coal industry, which has a significant economic bearing on his home state.

Barr grew up in Lexington, where his family has lived for several generations. His father ran an accounting practice and his mother was an Episcopal deacon. Barr got an undergraduate degree in Virginia, then worked as an aide to Rep. Jim Talent of Missouri in the 1990s. He went back home to Kentucky to attend law school, and after several years as an attorney he was added to the staff of Republican Gov. Ernie Fletcher. Barr started as a speechwriter and ended up as Fletcher's general counsel.

He ran for the House in 2010 and lost by 647 votes to Rep. Ben Chandler, a conservative Democrat. Barr ran again in 2012, and even though a new congressional map packed more Democrats into the 6th District, he beat Chandler by close to 12,000 votes. Barr didn't change his positions — he is fairly conservative and joined the Republican Study Committee — but he convinced voters that Chandler was too close the Obama administration and its alleged "war on coal." (Mitt Romney easily won the state.)

Barr vows to push back against regulations that he sees as stifling energy production. He supports coal gasification, development of natural gas deposits and the proposed Keystone XL pipeline.

He doesn't have an energy-related committee assignment, however. Barr sits on the Financial Services Committee, where he says he'll try to relieve regulatory burdens on smaller community banks.

Barr says the 2010 health care law weighed down employment growth by saddling the economy with $675 billion in prospective tax increases. He favors an overhaul of the tax code to increase the overall number of taxpayers and cut marginal rates. He would end the alternative minimum tax and estate tax, but expand tax-free savings accounts such as 401(k) plans.

Kentucky 6

East central — Lexington, Frankfort

The 6th embodies the culture and economic pursuits that most outsiders associate with Kentucky. This is the heart of the Bluegrass region, home to Lexington and capital Frankfort. A patchwork of urban, suburban and rural, the district — which hosts government and universities — has produced Kentucky Derby winners, tons of tobacco and casks of liquor.

The 6th has one of the nation's densest hubs of horse and pony farms, and Lexington touts itself as the "Horse Capital of the World." It also takes in the mostly agricultural Bourbon County, but the namesake whiskey is now produced in distilleries to the southwest. Lexington officials have planned a Distillery District in the city to connect with the "Bourbon Trail" tourism, shared with the neighboring 2nd.

Lexington and surrounding Fayette County are home to major printers, including Xerox, as well as corporate headquarters for Lexmark International. An Amazon.com distribution center and a branch of defense contractor Lockheed Martin are also top employers. Most of Frankfort's workers are employed by the state or local government. The capital's economy is buttressed by auto parts factories. Poverty rates are high near Appalachia. Several universities are located here, including the University of Kentucky in Lexington — the state's largest school and the district's largest employer. Frankfort hosts historically black Kentucky State University.

The 6th was the focus of Kentucky's most intense partisan debates during decennial redistricting. It gained several counties to the northeast and lost areas in the southwest to increase the Democratic voter registration edge. Voters are socially conservative and will support candidates of either party. Although Fayette and Franklin counties narrowly backed Barack Obama and Rep. Ben Chandler in 2012, Democrats lost their hold on the U.S. House seat.

Major Industry
Manufacturing, government, higher education, horse breeding

Military Bases
Blue Grass Army Depot, 139 military, 1,114 civilian (2009)

Cities
Lexington, Frankfort, Richmond, Winchester

Notable
Lexington's Kentucky Horse Park hosted the first world championships held outside Europe.

LOUISIANA

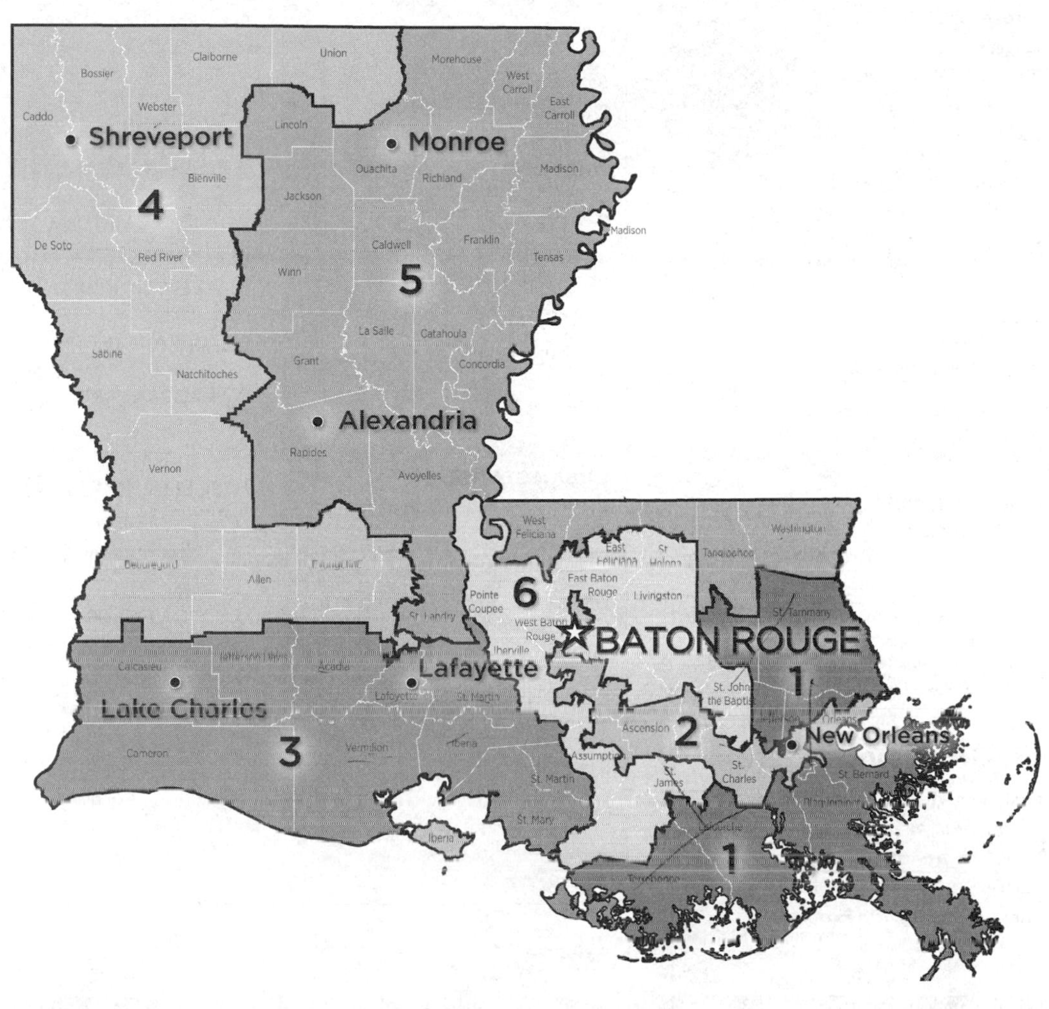

Shreveport
Monroe
Alexandria
Lafayette
Lake Charles
BATON ROUGE
New Orleans
1
2
3
4
5
6
Caddo
Bossier
Claiborne
Union
Morehouse
West Carroll
East Carroll
Webster
Lincoln
Ouachita
Richland
Madison
Bienville
Jackson
Caldwell
Franklin
Tensas
De Soto
Red River
Winn
La Salle
Catahoula
Sabine
Natchitoches
Grant
Concordia
Rapides
Vernon
Avoyelles
West Feliciana
Washington
Allen
Pointe Coupee
East Baton Rouge
Livingston
St. Tammany
West Baton Rouge
Iberville
Calcasieu
Acadia
Ascension
Cameron
Vermilion
Iberia
St. Martin
St. Mary
St. Charles
St. Bernard

Gov. Bobby Jindal (R)

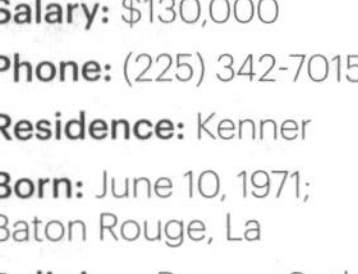

Pronounced: JIN-dle

First elected: 2007

Length of term: 4 years

Term expires: 1/16

Salary: $130,000

Phone: (225) 342-7015

Residence: Kenner

Born: June 10, 1971; Baton Rouge, La

Religion: Roman Catholic

Family: Wife, Supriya Jindal; three children

Education: Brown U., Sc.B. 1991 (biology & public policy); Oxford U., M.Litt. 1994 (Rhodes scholar)

Career: State university system president; management consultant

Political highlights: La. Health and Hospitals Department secretary, 1996-98; U.S. Health and Human Services assistant secretary for planning and evaluation, 2001-03; candidate for governor, 2003; U.S. House, 2005-08

ELECTION RESULTS

2011 GENERAL

Bobby Jindal (R)	673,239	65.8%
Tara Hollis (D)	182,925	17.9%
Cary J. Deaton (D)	50,071	4.9%
Ivo "Trey" Roberts (D)	33,280	3.3%
David Blanchard (NON)	26,705	2.6%
Androniki Papazoglakis (D)	21,885	2.1%
Scott Lewis (LIBERT)	12,528	1.2%

Lt. Gov. Jay Dardenne (R)

First elected: 2010

Length of term: 4 years

Term expires: 1/16

Salary: $115,000

Phone: (225) 342-7009

LEGISLATURE

Legislature: March-June in odd-numbered years; April-June in even-numbered years

Senate: 39 members, 4-year terms

2013 ratios: 24 R, 15 D; 35 men, 4 women

Salary: $16,800

Phone: (225) 342-2040

House: 105 members, 4-year terms

2013 ratios: 58 R, 45 D, 2 I; 92 men, 13 women

Salary: $16,800

Phone: (225) 342-6945

TERM LIMITS

Governor: 2 terms

Senate: No

House: No

URBAN STATISTICS

CITY	POPULATION
New Orleans	343,829
Baton Rouge	229,493
Shreveport	199,311
Lafayette	120,623
Lake Charles	71,993

REGISTERED VOTERS

Democrat	48%
Republican	28%
Other	24%

POPULATION

2010 population	4,533,372
2000 population	4,468,976
1990 population	4,219,973
Percent change (2000-2010)	+1.4%
Rank among states (2010)	25
Median age	35.5
Born in state	79.2%
Foreign born	3.0%
Violent crime rate	620/100,000
Poverty level	17.3%
Federal workers	44,533
Military	17,398

ELECTIONS

STATE ELECTION OFFICIAL
(225) 922-0900

DEMOCRATIC PARTY
(225) 336-4155

REPUBLICAN PARTY
(225) 928-2998

MISCELLANEOUS

Web: www.louisiana.gov

Capital: Baton Rouge

U.S. CONGRESS

Senate: 1 Democrat, 1 Republican

House: 5 Republicans, 1 Democrat

STATISTICS BY DISTRICT

	2012 Vote for President		2008 Vote for President										
District	Obama	Romney	Obama	McCain	Black	Asian	Hispanic	Median Income	Over 64	Under 20	College Education	Rural	Sq. Miles
1	28%	70%	26%	72%	13%	2%	8%	$50,979	13%	26%	26%	14%	4,030
2	73	25	71	27	63	3	6	34,603	11	27	20	4	1,268
3	32	66	34	64	25	1	3	41,022	12	28	18	26	6,983
4	40	59	40	59	34	1	3	40,569	14	28	20	43	12,435
5	38	61	37	62	36	<1	2	32,854	14	28	15	53	14,453
6	34	65	32	66	22	2	4	54,406	11	28	28	22	4,034
STATE	**41**	**58**	**40**	**59**	**32**	**2**	**4**	**41,734**	**13**	**27**	**21**	**27**	**43,204**
U.S.	**51**	**47**	**53**	**46**	**12**	**5**	**17**	**50,052**	**13**	**27**	**29**	**21**	**3,531,905**

Sen. Mary L. Landrieu (D)

Capitol Office
224-5824
landrieu.senate.gov
703 Hart Bldg. 20510-1804; fax 224-9735

Committees
Appropriations
(Homeland Security - Chairwoman)
Energy & Natural Resources
Homeland Security & Governmental Affairs
Small Business & Entrepreneurship - Chairwoman

Residence
New Orleans

Born
Nov. 23, 1955; Arlington, Va.

Religion
Roman Catholic

Family
Husband, Frank Snellings; two children

Education
Louisiana State U., B.A. 1977 (sociology)

Career
Realtor

Political Highlights
La. House, 1980-88; La. treasurer, 1988-96; candidate for governor, 1995

ELECTION RESULTS

2008 GENERAL		
Mary L. Landrieu (D)	988,298	52.1%
John Kennedy (R)	867,177	45.7%
2008 PRIMARY		
Mary L. Landrieu (D)		unopposed
2002 GENERAL RUNOFF		
Mary L. Landrieu (D)	638,654	51.7%
Suzanne Haik Terrell (R)	867,177	48.3%

Previous Winning Percentages
1996 (50%)

Elected 1996; 3rd term

Landrieu is one of the most experienced hands in the Senate when it comes to debating domestic energy policy, disaster relief and the economy. That puts her in her comfort zone for the 113th Congress, where all three of those issues are likely to factor heavily into the legislative workload.

Although Hurricane Katrina hit in 2005, the storm is very much a part of Landrieu's daily life. She uses her position as chairwoman of the Homeland Security Appropriations Subcommittee, which oversees the Federal Emergency Management Agency, to direct any available support to the Gulf Coast. Landrieu also holds a seat on the Homeland Security and Governmental Affairs subcommittee that handles disaster recovery. She continues to tout any Katrina-related money the federal government releases.

But there's a new disaster on Landrieu's agenda: Superstorm Sandy, which struck New York, New Jersey, Connecticut and West Virginia with such ferocity that state officials have predicted the need for Katrina-level spending on recovery efforts.

Landrieu said the process for figuring out that price tag will take years, but she started it early in the 113th Congress (2013-14). Congress quickly cleared bills to increase the borrowing authority of the federal flood insurance program and provide $50 billion in spending for various agencies and programs working on short- and long-term Sandy recovery.

The second bill included provisions altering the rules on how disaster aid can be spent and increasing the flexibility of response efforts — Landrieu had been contributing to that push for years.

She emphasizes that "tools" and "money" aren't synonymous. "Throwing money at the situation without the right tools is useless," Landrieu said. She notes that prior to Katrina, the federal government had no laws directing the dispute process for FEMA-issued rebuilding funds. In 2009, she authored language that Congress passed creating an expedited arbitration process for projects stemming from Hurricanes Katrina and Rita.

Landrieu looks to remove similar roadblocks as chairwoman of the Small Business and Entrepreneurship Committee. She also wants to look at ways to overhaul the Army Corps of Engineers, a group heavily involved with storm preparation that she calls overworked and under-resourced.

Landrieu is hoping to close the books on another disaster tied to her work on energy: the 2010 oil spill in the Gulf of Mexico. BP decided in 2012 to plead guilty, settle claims with the federal government and pay $4.5 billion for felony counts related to the spill, which was caused by an explosion on a BP oil rig. Landrieu has taken campaign contributions from BP and is seen as a friend to the offshore drilling industry, but she hopes BP will settle a civil case that went to trial in early 2013. "For the people I represent, getting a few billion dollars now is important, instead of waiting 20 years," she said.

Her work on energy policy has resulted in a complicated relationship with the White House. Landrieu says she wants to see oil and gas serve as "transition fuels," but when it comes to cutting down on the use of foreign oil, she says producing more domestically can be beneficial.

She often criticizes the Obama administration's regulations on oil drilling. She laid into the Interior Department in 2010 for a post-BP spill announcement that it would not expand offshore oil exploration into the eastern Gulf of Mexico and along the Atlantic Coast. She supports opening Alaska's Arctic National Wildlife Refuge to oil drilling, and in 2006 George W. Bush signed a bill including her language to open new areas of the Gulf of Mexico to offshore drilling, which promised billions in royalties to her state.

As a member of the Energy and Natural Resources Committee, she pushes for more oil exploration and wants to secure a larger portion of energy royalties for Louisiana and its neighbors. Landrieu has teamed up with Lisa Murkowski of Alaska, the panel's top Republican, on a bill that would steer 27.5 percent of revenue from all kinds of offshore energy development — including wind and other renewable sources — to coastal states. A state could get another 10 percent for setting up a "clean" energy or conservation fund. Rolling out the bill in March 2013, Landrieu said that states could use that money to build up coastal infrastructure, which could prevent Katrina-style disasters in the future.

Reauthorizations of small-business research and technology programs in the 112th Congress (2011-12) have left Landrieu with no banner legislation to tackle on the Small Business Committee, but she has led discussions on ways to encourage startups and keep regulations from impeding small-business development.

Landrieu was a known wild card on supporting Democratic Party causes. Each year of the Bush administration, she broke ranks on roughly one-quarter of the votes where majorities of Republicans and Democrats diverged. She was one of nine Democrats to oppose a $700 billion rescue plan for the financial services industry that became law in fall 2008. Under President Barack Obama, she has voted more reliably with her party. She sided with Democrats and the president in the 112th Congress on bills to address the deficit and preserve expanded unemployment insurance.

However, on energy-related bills, she still often lines up with Republicans. In 2010, she backed a joint resolution disapproving of an EPA finding that greenhouse gases qualify as dangerous pollutants under the Clean Air Act. The following year, she supported a bill trying to block the EPA from regulating greenhouse gas emissions.

Landrieu says her energy stances and moderate leanings are advantages as both parties clamor for increased cooperation. "That's the position where I'm most comfortable, my caucus depends on me to do that, and I'm happy to do it, because it reflects where the politics of Louisiana are," she said.

Landrieu has two adopted children at home and serves as co-chairwoman of the Congressional Coalition on Adoption. She is the daughter of Moon Landrieu, who was mayor of New Orleans for eight years and secretary of Housing and Urban Development in the Carter administration. Her brother, Mitch, served as lieutenant governor and is now mayor of New Orleans.

That lineage aided Landrieu's swift political rise. She was elected to the Louisiana House at age 23, went on to become state treasurer, then made an unsuccessful run for governor in 1995. A year later, in a race to fill the seat of retiring Democrat J. Bennett Johnston, she won by the slimmest margin ever in a Senate race in Louisiana — 5,788 votes out of 1.7 million cast. The loser, conservative Louis "Woody" Jenkins, alleged voter fraud. Landrieu was seated, but the Senate Rules Committee, run by Republicans, conducted a lengthy probe; it eventually ruled there was no "quantum level of fraud."

She ran again in 2002 and was forced into a runoff after falling short of the 50 percent needed to claim victory under Louisiana's election laws. She had finished first with 46 percent in the nine-candidate field, which included three well-known Republicans: state Elections Commissioner Suzanne Haik Terrell, Rep. John Cooksey and state Rep. Tony Perkins. In the runoff, she won by 42,012 votes.

Republican strategists were confident they could thwart her quest for a third term in 2008, given her previous tight races and the overall difficulty Democrats face in the Deep South. But Landrieu had little trouble winning, even as Republican Sen. John McCain easily prevailed in Louisiana over Obama in the presidential election. By early 2013 she already had a well-known challenger lined up against her in GOP Rep. Bill Cassidy.

Key Votes

2012

Prohibit health insurance plans from denying coverage based on the sponsor's religious beliefs	YES
Require approval of the Keystone XL oil pipeline	YES
Ease securities rules to expand small-business access to capital	NO
Reauthorize farm and nutrition programs for five years	NO
Limit debate on a bill that would create private-sector cybersecurity standards	YES
Consent to ratification of a treaty setting global standard for the treatment of people with disabilities	YES
Provide $60.4 billion in disaster relief following Superstorm Sandy	YES
Extend most Bush-era income tax rates while allowing rates for top-bracket earners to rise (Jan. 1, 2013)	YES

2011

Prevent EPA from regulating greenhouse gas emissions to address climate change	YES
Extend certain provisions of Patriot Act for four years	YES
Clear compromise debt limit increase plan and establish future spending limits	YES
Overhaul patent law	YES
Implement Colombia free trade agreement	YES
Limit debate on confirmation of Caitlin J. Halligan to D.C. Circuit Court of Appeals	YES
Extend payroll tax cut and unemployment benefits for two months	YES

CQ Vote Studies

	PARTY UNITY		PRESIDENTIAL SUPPORT	
	SUPPORT	OPPOSE	SUPPORT	OPPOSE
2012	87%	13%	90%	10%
2011	91%	9%	95%	5%
2010	93%	7%	98%	2%
2009	90%	10%	97%	3%
2008	69%	31%	53%	47%
2007	78%	22%	47%	53%
2006	75%	25%	71%	29%
2005	76%	24%	64%	36%
2004	81%	19%	68%	32%
2003	78%	22%	58%	42%

Interest Groups

	AFL-CIO	ADA	CCUS	ACU
2012	100%	75%	75%	16%
2011	84%	85%	64%	10%
2010	93%	75%	36%	8%
2009	89%	90%	60%	16%
2008	100%	65%	75%	32%
2007	95%	80%	73%	40%
2006	73%	65%	75%	24%
2005	86%	95%	76%	44%
2004	100%	85%	71%	32%
2003	77%	60%	78%	20%

Sen. David Vitter (R)

Capitol Office
224-4623
vitter.senate.gov
516 Hart Bldg. 20510-1803; fax 228-5061

Committees
Armed Services
Banking, Housing & Urban Affairs
Environment & Public Works - Ranking Member
Small Business & Entrepreneurship

Residence
Metairie

Born
May 3, 1961; New Orleans, La.

Religion
Roman Catholic

Family
Wife, Wendy Baldwin Vitter; four children

Education
Harvard U., A.B. 1983; Oxford U., B.A. 1985 (Rhodes scholar); Tulane U., J.D. 1988

Career
Lawyer; professor

Political Highlights
La. House, 1992-99; U.S. House, 1999-2005

ELECTION RESULTS

2010 GENERAL		
David Vitter (R)	715,415	56.6%
Charlie Melancon (D)	476,572	37.7%
Randall Todd Hayes (LIBERT)	13,957	1.1%
2010 PRIMARY		
David Vitter (R)	85,225	87.6%
Chet D. Traylor (R)	6,841	7.0%
Nick J. Accardo (R)	5,232	5.4%

Previous Winning Percentages
2004 (51%); 2002 House Election (81%); 2000 House Election (80%); 1999 Special Runoff Election (51%)

Elected 2004; 2nd term

Vitter has become a marquee member of the GOP's conservative wing, and he is now the party's lead Senate negotiator on infrastructure and environmental policy. He disparages many plans of the Obama administration, particularly when they reach into Louisiana.

Vitter serves on four committees cutting across a range of subjects, while also helping Republican leaders keep the conference in line as a deputy whip. He has increasingly availed himself of a lone senator's ability to slow the chamber's operations to a crawl. In many ways, his party has shifted to meet him — the 2010 election that saw him win a second term also reinforced the ranks of conservatives in both chambers.

But he was a strident critic of President Barack Obama well before that. Many of his beefs with the administration stem from the 2010 BP oil spill in the Gulf of Mexico. Vitter, the son of a petroleum engineer, complained that the White House was too slow to reopen many potential drilling areas. That grievance served as a springboard for touting a broader energy agenda, one focused largely on increasing oil and gas drilling opportunities, particularly those in the gulf that would benefit Louisiana.

Instead of a ban on drilling, he called for immediate rig safety inspections. In the 112th Congress (2011-12), Vitter teamed up with Republican Dan Coats of Indiana on another plan: redirecting energy lease approvals from the Interior Department to the Energy Department, in hopes of speeding up production cycles for energy development companies. In 2013, he introduced a bill to raise the cap on revenues that states receive from offshore energy leases.

He has worked to direct more money to states affected by the spill. Vitter sat on the conference committee for a 27-month surface transportation reauthorization measure enacted in 2012. The law included a provision to steer at least 80 percent of the fines collected under the Clean Water Act in relation to the spill toward Gulf Coast states. Some legislators saw that provision as an unnecessary hitch, but Vitter got his way.

At the start of the 113th Congress (2013-14), Vitter became the ranking Republican on the Environment and Public Works Committee. That spot strengthens his position as he combats environmental regulations that he describes as unnecessary and detrimental to economic activity. It also puts him opposite Chairwoman Barbara Boxer, a liberal California Democrat. He stands firmly against one of Boxer's priorities, the creation of a "carbon tax" meant to discourage the use of fossil fuels. "It's not just energy prices that would skyrocket from a carbon tax; the cost of nearly everything built in America would go up," Vitter said.

But Vitter and Boxer have already worked together on infrastructure. In May 2013, the Senate overwhelmingly passed a bill to authorize water development projects that was produced by their committee. The measure includes a provision the eventually requires all fees collected for the Harbor Maintenance Trust Fund to be spent on dredging and other improvements, rather than diverted to other spending needs. States with shipping interests (such as Louisiana) have long demanded that change.

It also contains language designed to speed up the environmental permitting process for water projects — similar to streamlining provisions in the 2012 surface transportation law. Vitter and Boxer will address highway programs in the 113th Congress, as that law expires in 2014.

Vitter's commitment to a conservative agenda seems to have repaired the damage from a sex scandal that broke in 2007. His use of an escort service was exposed when his phone number showed up in the records of "D.C.

Madam" Deborah Jeane Palfrey, who was arrested on charges of running a prostitution ring. His phone number appeared five times between 1999 and 2001, when he was in the U.S. House.

Vitter apologized for the indiscretion and redoubled his legislative efforts. At the start of the 111th Congress (2009-10) he filed more than 30 measures, establishing conservative positions on a range of subjects. He repeated that performance in the 112th and 113th Congresses.

One of Vitter's passions is securing the borders, particularly as a precursor to changes in immigration law. He chairs the Border Security and Enforcement First Immigration Caucus; it includes other right-leaning senators such as Jeff Sessions of Alabama and Roger Wicker of Mississippi.

Sessions and Wicker — along with Oklahoma's James M. Inhofe — also have worked with Vitter on the Armed Services Committee to protect and expand missile defense programs. Vitter has said that Obama will "walk away from missile defense and helping protect our close allies in Europe."

Vitter also sits on the Banking, Housing and Urban Affairs Committee. He voted against the $700 billion financial sector rescue law from 2008, and he wants unspent money from that law diverted to paying down the national debt. His advocacy for amendments to that effect has held up several major bills. He introduced a 2012 bill to halt the Financial Stability Oversight Council's ability to designate financial institutions as "too big to fail."

He wants to overhaul federal involvement in the housing sector, and he wants to do it soon. Vitter joined with a bipartisan group of panel members on a 2013 bill meant to force the issue. It would block the use of guarantee fees on federally backed mortgages as budgetary offsets for other federal spending — thereby limiting the political complications of housing changes.

Vitter has a somewhat cool relationship with his Louisiana colleague, Democrat Mary L. Landrieu, and they don't always work well together. After Hurricane Katrina devastated their state in 2005, Vitter and Landrieu offered competing measures aimed at helping cash-strapped local governments pay workers. The conflict led to a confrontation on the Senate floor that ended when Vitter walked out of the chamber.

His first experience with congressional politics was as a college intern for Joe Moakley, a liberal House member from Massachusetts. Vitter graduated from Harvard University and later got a law degree from Tulane University. He is also a Rhodes Scholar. Early in his career, Vitter practiced law and taught at Tulane and Loyola universities.

In 1991, he ran for state office, saying he wanted to do something about the low reputation of Louisiana politics. He won the state House seat vacated by former Ku Klux Klan leader David Duke, who ran for governor.

Brash and willing to ruffle some feathers, Vitter made a name for himself by winning passage of term limits for state lawmakers and taking hawkish stances on legislative ethics. Some people accused him of grandstanding, but Vitter wasn't fazed. He still introduces term limit proposals.

When Republican Robert L. Livingston announced in 1998 that he would leave the U.S. House six months later — spurred by the revelation of an extramarital affair — Vitter was one of nine candidates who jumped into the 1999 special election to replace him. He finished second in the initial round of voting, then won the runoff by less than 2 points.

In 2004, Vitter ran for the seat held by retiring Sen. John B. Breaux. He beat Breaux's protégé, Democratic Rep. Chris John, to become Louisiana's first Republican senator since Reconstruction.

By the time of the 2010 election, his sex scandal was becoming a distant memory. Vitter said the only people who continued to bring it up were reporters and "political hacks." Vitter concentrated on tying his challenger, Democratic Rep. Charlie Melancon, to policies of the Obama administration. He defeated Melancon by 19 points.

Key Votes

2012	
Prohibit health insurance plans from denying coverage based on the sponsor's religious beliefs	NO
Require approval of the Keystone XL oil pipeline	YES
Ease securities rules to expand small-business access to capital	YES
Reauthorize farm and nutrition programs for five years	NO
Limit debate on a bill that would create private-sector cybersecurity standards	NO
Consent to ratification of a treaty setting global standard for the treatment of people with disabilities	NO
Provide $60.4 billion in disaster relief following Superstorm Sandy	YES
Extend most Bush-era income tax rates while allowing rates for top-bracket earners to rise (Jan. 1, 2013)	YES
2011	
Prevent EPA from regulating greenhouse gas emissions to address climate change	YES
Extend certain provisions of Patriot Act for four years	YES
Clear compromise debt limit increase plan and establish future spending limits	NO
Overhaul patent law	YES
Implement Colombia free trade agreement	YES
Limit debate on confirmation of Caitlin J. Halligan to D.C. Circuit Court of Appeals	NO
Extend payroll tax cut and unemployment benefits for two months	YES

CQ Vote Studies

	PARTY UNITY		PRESIDENTIAL SUPPORT	
	SUPPORT	OPPOSE	SUPPORT	OPPOSE
2012	89%	11%	41%	59%
2011	94%	6%	43%	57%
2010	94%	6%	37%	63%
2009	96%	4%	42%	58%
2008	98%	2%	76%	24%
2007	93%	7%	85%	15%
2006	94%	6%	87%	13%
2005	94%	6%	89%	11%
2004	98%	2%	94%	6%
2003	99%	1%	96%	4%

Interest Groups

	AFL-CIO	ADA	CCUS	ACU
2012	18%	5%	88%	80%
2011	11%	5%	91%	100%
2010	8%	5%	100%	95%
2009	17%	10%	86%	100%
2008	20%	5%	88%	84%
2007	21%	10%	73%	96%
2006	20%	0%	92%	92%
2005	29%	15%	83%	96%
2004	7%	5%	100%	96%
2003	0%	10%	97%	88%

Rep. Steve Scalise (R)

Capitol Office
225-3015
scalise.house.gov
2338 Rayburn Bldg. 20515-1801; fax 226-0380

Committees
Energy & Commerce

Residence
Jefferson

Born
Oct. 6, 1965; Baton Rouge, La.

Religion
Roman Catholic

Family
Wife, Jennifer Scalise; two children

Education
Louisiana State U., B.S. 1989 (computer science)

Career
Software engineer; technology company marketing executive

Political Highlights
La. House, 1996-2008; La. Senate, 2008

ELECTION RESULTS

2012 GENERAL		
Steve Scalise (R)	193,496	66.6%
M.V. "Vinny" Mendoza (D)	61,703	21.2%
Gary King (R)	24,844	8.6%
David "Turk" Turknett (NOP)	6,079	2.1%
Arden Wells (NOP)	4,288	1.5%
2010 GENERAL		
Steve Scalise (R)	157,182	78.5%
Myron Katz (D)	38,416	19.2%
Arden Wells (I)	4,578	2.3%

Previous Winning Percentages
2008 (66%); 2008 Special Election (75%)

Elected 2008; 3rd full term

Scalise thinks big on the national stage, trying to facilitate an ascendancy of conservative policy and values. For Louisiana, he tries to help coastal recovery and boost the energy sector from the Energy and Commerce Committee.

Scalise (skuh-LEASE) puts a pleasant face on a combative agenda. "We've got to fight for conservative principles," he said. After more than a decade of battling in the Louisiana state government, "I think I've been very active in doing that since I came to Washington."

His quest has taken an intriguing turn in the 113th Congress (2013-14). He is serving as chairman of the Republican Study Committee, the bloc of conservative House members. Throughout the 112th Congress (2011-12), the RSC often seemed at odds with the House's Republican leadership team, particularly regarding federal spending. The RSC supported legislative positions that had virtually no chance of passing the Senate and panned many deals negotiated with Democrats.

Scalise started his run for the chairmanship a few weeks before the 2012 elections, and he emphasized that he would be a pragmatic leader. "It's not enough just to talk about conservative values," he said. "We need to pass conservative policy." Republicans lost seats on Election Day, and talk immediately turned to the need for less intraparty conflict. A few weeks later, Scalise defeated Tom Graves of Georgia, who had been endorsed by the RSC's former leaders. A former aide to Speaker John A. Boehner whipped up support on Scalise's behalf.

Relationships between GOP leaders and conservatives seemed friendlier in the opening months of 2013. Scalise joined a five-man working group that included Budget Chairman Paul D. Ryan of Wisconsin. He secured commitments from leaders to pursue further spending cuts, and he laid groundwork to demand changes to entitlement programs in future fiscal fights.

Scalise has worked within the Republican Party structure in the past. He has served on the GOP Policy and Steering committees, which set legislative strategies and committee assignments. And he was in charge of candidate recruitment for the National Republican Congressional Committee, the campaign organization for House Republicans, during the 2012 cycle.

That job gave him plenty of opportunities to criticize President Barack Obama, and Scalise didn't pass them up. Obama "campaigns on divisiveness while imposing a radical agenda," Scalise wrote in Roll Call in June 2012. His provision to block federal spending on several executive-branch "czars" was incorporated into the fiscal 2011 spending law. Obama largely ignored the ban.

Many of his clashes — and his bipartisan parochial efforts — originate on the Energy and Commerce Committee. Scalise spent much of 2010 responding to the largest oil spill in U.S. history, caused by the explosion of a BP oil rig in the Gulf of Mexico. He was hardly complimentary of BP, but he also accused Obama of "trying to exploit this disaster." The temporary shutdown of deepwater drilling after the spill was devastating to the economy, he said.

Scalise was the House sponsor of a bill to give most of the Clean Water Act fines related to the spill to Gulf Coast states. The Louisiana delegation won inclusion of that language in a two-year extension of surface transportation programs enacted in 2012. They didn't like the budgetary offset — a reduction of more than $650 million in Louisiana's Medicaid funding — but Scalise still called it "probably the most significant legislation that's been passed for Louisiana's coast in the history of the state of Louisiana."

Going back to his Louisiana House days, Scalise has been friends with Democrat Cedric L. Richmond, who is now the representative from New

Orleans. "We don't agree on a lot, but we put Louisiana first," Richmond said.

In the 112th Congress, the House adopted spending bill amendments by Scalise and Richmond to secure at least some funding for ecosystem restoration along the coasts. The duo also pushed for funding to continue dredging operations in the gulf and on the Mississippi River.

Scalise brings a guiding principle to the Communications and Technology Subcommittee: "The less government is involved, the more successful the technology industry is." He introduced a 2011 bill to deregulate the television industry by repealing Federal Communications Commission broadcast and media ownership rules and requirements for service providers to carry certain broadcast signals. He opposes regulation of the Internet.

Social issues also find Scalise in the conservative camp. He is a supporter of gun owners' rights and a member of the National Rifle Association. As a state legislator he led a fight in 1999 against former New Orleans Mayor Marc Morial, a Democrat who sued a group of gun manufacturers to reimburse the city for expenses related to its efforts to stem violent crime. Scalise drafted a bill that prohibited municipalities from suing companies for what customers did with their products. The Supreme Court upheld the legislation in 2000.

He is an opponent of abortion and the original sponsor of Louisiana's constitutional amendment that defines marriage as a union between a man and a woman. Voters approved it in 2004.

The middle of three children, Scalise grew up in Metairie, a suburb of New Orleans. His father sold real estate while his mother was a homemaker and a volunteer in senior citizens programs. As a child, Scalise roamed his local streets on a patriotic-bunted bicycle, speaking into a battery-powered microphone and encouraging his neighbors to visit the polls at election time. He became a registered Republican the day he turned 18.

While attending Louisiana State University he got involved in student government and with the College Republicans. After college, he worked in computer engineering while volunteering for several campaigns, including George Bush's 1988 run for president. Scalise was elected to the state House in 1995 and served 12 years before being elected to the state Senate in 2007.

He considered running for the U.S. House in 1999, when a special election was held to replace Republican Robert L. Livingston. He changed his mind after party leaders favored David Vitter. When Vitter left the House for the Senate in 2004, Scalise was overlooked again, with party support this time going to Bobby Jindal.

In the May 2008 special election to succeed Jindal, who had been elected governor, Scalise beat Democrat Gilda Reed. He took more than 65 percent of the vote that November for a full term. He won easily in 2010 and 2012.

Key Votes

2012	
Extend a Social Security payroll tax cut and unemployment benefits	YES
Ease securities rules to expand small-business access to capital	YES
Extend for one year subsidized student loan interest rates financed by a cut in health care spending	YES
Cite Attorney General Eric H. Holder Jr. for contempt of Congress	YES
Create a visa program for foreign graduates in high-tech fields	YES
Extend most Bush-era income tax rates while allowing rates for top-bracket earners to rise (Jan. 1, 2013)	NO
2011	
Strike funding for F-35 alternative engine	NO
Prevent EPA from regulating greenhouse gas emissions to address climate change	YES
Extend certain provisions of Patriot Act for four years	YES
Declare opposition to use of ground troops in Libya	YES
Overhaul patent law	YES
Pass compromise debt limit increase plan and establish future spending limits	NO
Allow consideration of measures to implement three trade agreements	YES

CQ Vote Studies

	PARTY UNITY		PRESIDENTIAL SUPPORT	
	SUPPORT	OPPOSE	SUPPORT	OPPOSE
2012	98%	2%	15%	85%
2011	97%	3%	22%	78%
2010	97%	3%	31%	69%
2009	98%	2%	23%	77%
2008	99%	1%	79%	21%

Interest Groups

	AFL-CIO	ADA	CCUS	ACU
2012	5%	0%	92%	100%
2011	0%	5%	93%	92%
2010	0%	0%	88%	96%
2009	0%	0%	80%	100%
2008	0%	5%	94%	100%

Louisiana 1

East — coastal parishes and Lake Pontchartrain

When Louisiana lost a seat during reapportionment after the 2010 census, the 1st was drawn to take up the state's southeastern tip, gathering areas formerly spread among three districts while excluding most of the city of New Orleans, which it surrounds. A region wracked by hurricanes over the past decade and the disastrous Deepwater Horizon oil spill in 2010, recovery and reconstruction have been residents' main focus for years.

The district's population centers are along the shores of Lake Pontchartrain. North shore and St. Tammany Parish bedroom communities have become home to an influx of New Orleans and Mississippi residents displaced by Hurricane Katrina in 2005, accelerating a two-decade trend in St. Tammany. A retail and service-based economy is boosted by the oil industry, including affiliated shipbuilding and offshore equipment sectors. In contrast, coastal St. Bernard Parish had the largest population decline in the state between 2000 and 2010 (nearly 50 percent) due largely to Katrina. Gulf Coast bayous are lined with small shrimp and oyster businesses.

On Lake Pontchartrain's south shore, the 1st includes Metairie, one of the most populous unincorporated communities in the nation, a suburb of New Orleans where once-residential neighborhoods are giving way to mixed-use centers. The district also takes in mainly white neighborhoods of New Orleans, including Lakeview, and Tulane and Loyola universities.

The new 1st — which has the state's largest Hispanic population (8 percent) — is only slightly more competitive than its reliably Republican predecessors in the former 1st and 3rd. Democrats and Republicans run even in voter registration, but GOP-leaning independents make up more than one-fourth of voters.

Major Industry
Petrochemicals, shipbuilding, agriculture, fishing

Military Bases
Naval Air Station Joint Reserve Base New Orleans, 3,240 military, 1,854 civilian

Cities
Metairie (unincorporated), Kenner (pt.), New Orleans (pt.), Houma, Slidell

Notable
Most of Metairie's nightclubs are in a district dubbed "Fat City," after the local Mardi Gras celebrations.

Rep. Cedric L. Richmond (D)

Capitol Office
225-6636
richmond.house.gov
240 Cannon Bldg. 20515-1002; fax 225-1088

Committees
Homeland Security
Judiciary

Residence
New Orleans

Born
Sept. 13, 1973; New Orleans, La.

Religion
Baptist

Family
Single

Education
Morehouse College, B.A. 1995 (business administration); Tulane U., J.D. 1998

Career
Lawyer

Political Highlights
La. House, 2000-11; sought Democratic nomination for U.S. House, 2008

ELECTION RESULTS

2012 GENERAL		
Cedric L. Richmond (D)	158,501	55.2%
Gary Landrieu (D)	71,916	25.0%
Dwayne Bailey (R)	38,801	13.5%
Josue Larose (R)	11,345	3.9%
Caleb Trotter (LIBERT)	6,791	2.4%
2010 GENERAL		
Cedric L. Richmond (D)	83,705	64.6%
Anh "Joseph" Cao (R)	43,378	33.5%
Anthony Marquize (NPA)	1,876	1.4%

Elected 2010; 2nd term

Richmond isn't bashful about his allegiance to the Democratic Party, but he is influenced just as strongly by the evolving needs of New Orleans. His policy pitches are tailored to suit his home town, sometimes demanding more federal assistance, other times favoring private sector industries that could drive economic growth.

Richmond is young, serious and occasionally scrappy — a few times, he has criticized Republican political tactics as "sinful." He counts Barack Obama as one of his heroes, and a copy of the famous Shepard Fairey print of the president hangs in his Washington office. In a decade in the Louisiana House — he was first elected at 26 — Richmond shared the president's love of oration.

"I was the person you would go get if you needed an argument made on the House floor," he said. "But up here, you don't have a captive audience to really do the great floor speech or the moving floor speech, because no one is paying attention."

Which isn't to say that Richmond hasn't been noticed by his party. He was named a senior whip for the 113th Congress (2013-14) and given a seat on the Judiciary Committee. The Times-Picayune reported in 2012 that Richmond is a regular dinner companion of James E. Clyburn of South Carolina and Bennie Thompson of Mississippi — respectively, the No. 3 House Democrat and the ranking member of the Homeland Security Committee, on which Richmond also sits.

But as the only Democrat in the Louisiana House delegation, he has a strong incentive to work with Republicans on local concerns. Richmond has a good relationship with Steve Scalise, whom he served with in the state House. In the 112th Congress (2011-12) they worked on amendments to direct funds toward ecological restoration programs for the Louisiana coast, which has been damaged by both Hurricane Katrina in 2005 and a Gulf of Mexico oil spill in 2010.

They also have tried to win money and attention for dredging the Mississippi River — a project that Richmond has called his top priority. "For the long-term future of the country, you have to do it," he said.

Dredging to 55 feet in harbors and rivers is necessary to accommodate larger cargo and oil vessels, which keeps the country competitive on global markets, Richmond said. New Orleans is a shipping hub, and Richmond split from most Democrats to support 2011 free-trade agreements with South Korea and Panama. (He opposed a Colombia pact, citing violence against Colombian labor leaders.)

Richmond, a member of the New Democrat Coalition, has been open to more offshore oil and gas drilling. While sympathetic to worries spurred by the 2010 oil spill, he wants to expedite the review of permits for drilling. He was one of just 21 House Democrats to support a 2012 bill to expand offshore energy production, open up parts of the Arctic National Wildlife Refuge to oil and gas exploration, and establish a trust fund for Gulf Coast restoration.

The recovery from Katrina factors heavily into Richmond's work. "We will not get full recovery without more federal help," he said. Richmond urges forgiveness of many federal disaster loans to local institutions.

He oversees the Federal Emergency Management Agency from the Homeland Security Committee, and in 2012 he introduced a plan to overhaul its disaster response plans. Richmond wants money distributed to local governments faster, as well as a mandate to hire local workers for rebuilding efforts. "That would have made a tremendous difference in New Orleans," he said, in terms of employment and community morale. He liked the disaster response changes included in the 2013 aid package tied to Superstorm Sandy.

Richmond is the ranking member of the Transportation Security Subcommittee for the 113th. At a 2012 hearing, he suggested that the Transportation Security Administration may have gotten too large: "Any entity can run a little bit leaner and smarter," he said.

On the Judiciary Committee, he sits on the panel that handles terrorism and homeland security. Richmond had public disputes in 2011 with Homeland Security Chairman Peter T. King of New York, over hearings into radicalization in the American Muslim community. "If we keep looking at Muslims, while we're doing that, somebody else is plotting just as much," he said. "The blinders, I think, are dangerous to us."

Richmond was born in New Orleans, the younger of two boys. His father died when he was 7, and his mother worked as a special education teacher. She later helped run an electrical contracting business with Richmond's stepfather.

Sports were Richmond's passion in childhood, and also the starting point for public life. He coached youth baseball starting at 16, then played on the baseball team at Morehouse College. He coached both baseball and basketball on his return to New Orleans for law school at Tulane. In 2011 and 2012 he pitched complete games to lead the Democrats to victory in the annual Congressional Baseball Game (which CQ Roll Call sponsors).

His first run for the Louisiana House was inspired in part, he said, by frustration that funding for his teams was mostly coming from him or his family. "We should really invest in kids," he said. Bolstered by the connections he made as a Little League director, he was victorious.

Richmond first ran for the House in 2008, losing the Democratic nomination to incumbent William J. Jefferson, who had been indicted on bribery and racketeering charges in 2007. Republican Anh "Joseph" Cao beat Jefferson in the general election. (Jefferson was convicted in 2009.) But the district was heavily Democratic, and the party quickly got behind Richmond for his 2010 campaign. He cruised to a primary election victory, then took almost 65 percent of the vote to beat Cao.

The exodus caused by Katrina factored into the reapportionment process that followed the 2010 census — Louisiana's House delegation shrank by one seat. Richmond's district had been fairly compact, but as drawn for the 2012 election it stretches from New Orleans to Baton Rouge, about 100 miles up the Mississippi River.

Richmond had no dedicated challengers; no one else in the race raised more than $10,000 for their campaign. He won with 55 percent of the vote, which is a deceptively low share. Under Louisiana's unusual election rules for 2012, there was an "open primary" on the day of the general election, so four other candidates, including one Democrat, split the remaining vote.

Key Votes

2012	
Extend a Social Security payroll tax cut and unemployment benefits	YES
Ease securities rules to expand small-business access to capital	YES
Extend for one year subsidized student loan interest rates financed by a cut in health care spending	NO
Cite Attorney General Eric H. Holder Jr. for contempt of Congress	?
Create a visa program for foreign graduates in high-tech fields	NO
Extend most Bush-era income tax rates while allowing rates for top-bracket earners to rise (Jan. 1, 2013)	YES
2011	
Strike funding for F-35 alternative engine	NO
Prevent EPA from regulating greenhouse gas emissions to address climate change	NO
Extend certain provisions of Patriot Act for four years	NO
Declare opposition to use of ground troops in Libya	NO
Overhaul patent law	YES
Pass compromise debt limit increase plan and establish future spending limits	YES
Allow consideration of measures to implement three trade agreements	NO

CQ Vote Studies

	PARTY UNITY		PRESIDENTIAL SUPPORT	
	SUPPORT	OPPOSE	SUPPORT	OPPOSE
2012	94%	6%	89%	11%
2011	91%	9%	86%	14%

Interest Groups

	AFL-CIO	ADA	CCUS	ACU
2012	90%	80%	33%	13%
2011	93%	95%	38%	0%

Louisiana 2

New Orleans and most of Baton Rouge

The 2nd District contains most of culturally rich New Orleans, a city still trudging the road to recovery after Hurricane Katrina in 2005. When Louisiana lost a seat during decennial reapportionment, the 2nd stretched westward to grab a portion of Baton Rouge, linking the state's two largest cities and funneling liberal voters into an already strongly Democratic district.

The oil and petrochemical industry is an economic driver in both New Orleans and Baton Rouge. The state's capital region has the highest concentration of chemical industry employment in Louisiana and is home one of the largest refineries in the United States. New Orleans' diversified economy also includes shipbuilding and logistics firms, as well as aerospace and industrial manufacturing. The scheduled 2013 closing of the Avondale shipyard is expected to leave thousands unemployed, and discussions regarding the site's future use are ongoing.

Tourism is a major draw to the Big Easy, which offers Mississippi riverboat gaming, jazz festivals, the colorful nightlife of the French Quarter and the epicenter of famous Mardi Gras celebrations. Neighboring Jefferson Parish has had some success in courting the movie and film industry. The district also includes Louis Armstrong New Orleans airport.

Although a slow population decline had been in process for decades, New Orleans lost about 30 percent of its residents after Katrina and has only gradually recovered. The city continues to receive recovery grants from the federal government — politicians and locals are concerned about the status of rebuilding as emergency funds begin to peter out.

The 2nd is Louisiana's only black-majority district, at more than 60 percent of the population, and nearly all of the newly added Baton Rouge residents are black. Registered Democrats far outnumber Republicans districtwide.

Major Industry

Oil and petrochemicals, shipbuilding, tourism, manufacturing

Cities

New Orleans (pt.), Marrero (unincorporated), Kenner (pt.), Baton Rouge (pt.)

Notable

The first New Orleans Jazz & Heritage Festival in 1970 had performances by Duke Ellington and city native Mahalia Jackson — the 10-day festival now draws 400,000 visitors and features a wide range of styles, including jazz, zydeco, blues, Cajun, bluegrass, gospel, Afro-Caribbean, rap and country.

Rep. Charles Boustany Jr. (R)

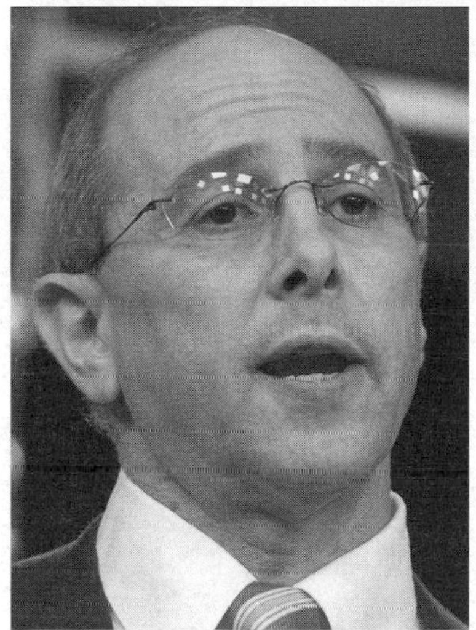

Capitol Office
225-2031
boustany.house.gov
1431 Longworth Bldg. 20515-1807; fax 225-5724

Committees
Ways & Means
(Oversight - Chairman)

Residence
Lafayette

Born
Feb. 21, 1956; Lafayette, La.

Religion
Episcopalian

Family
Wife, Bridget Boustany; two children

Education
U. of Southwestern Louisiana, B.S. 1978 (biology); Louisiana State U., M.D. 1982

Career
Surgeon

Political Highlights
No previous office

ELECTION RESULTS

2012 GENERAL RUNOFF		
Charles Boustany Jr. (R)	58,820	60.9%
Jeff Landry (R)	37,767	39.1%
2012 GENERAL		
Charles Boustany Jr. (R)	139,123	44.7%
Jeff Landry (R)	93,527	30.0%
Ron Richard (D)	67,070	21.5%
Bryan Barrilleaux (R)	7,908	2.5%
Jim Stark (LIBERT)	3,765	1.2%
2010 GENERAL		
Charles Boustany Jr. (R)		unopposed

Previous Winning Percentages
2008 (62%); 2006 (71%); 2004 (55%)

Elected 2004; 5th term

Competence, not commotion, typifies Boustany's work. A former thoracic surgeon, he chairs the Ways and Means Subcommittee on Oversight and employs the kind of focus that he honed in the operating room. He looks to become a more prominent voice on taxes and trade.

Boustany's district has produced some flamboyant pols, such as former Democratic Gov. Edwin W. Edwards — the uncle of Boustany's wife. His style is not personality-driven, however. One of his childhood heroes was quarterback Bart Starr, the strong-but-silent quarterback. And while other boys venerated military heroes such as George S. Patton, Boustany preferred George C. Marshall. "He was the consummate master planner," he said.

Boustany (boo-STAN-knee) has been the top Republican on the Oversight Subcommittee since 2009, which means he's up against his party's three-term limit for panel leaders. Since becoming chairman at the start of the 112th Congress (2011-12), he has used hearings to seek out instances of fraud and abuse in Medicare and Social Security programs.

He also studies many of the tax provisions tied to the 2010 health care law and its implementation. Boustany continues to call for repeal of the law, saying he favors more competition among insurers and providers and less emphasis on expanding insurance coverage. He said he is particularly concerned about employers dropping insurance coverage and how comparative-effectiveness research might lead to a "cookbook approach" that could undermine the doctor-patient relationship.

Boustany has a parochial interest in the tax used to fill the Harbor Maintenance Trust Fund — shipping is a big deal for the Gulf Coast. In the 113th Congress (2013-14), Boustany reintroduced his bill to require that money collected for the trust fund is used exclusively for dredging and maintenance of ports and waterways and not diverted to other purposes. The 2011 version of the bill had 196 co-sponsors.

He's expanding his involvement in shipping matters as a new member of the Trade Subcommittee in the 113th. He and Louisiana Democrat Cedric L. Richmond have introduced a bill meant to strengthen the ability of Customs and Border Protection officials to prevent importers from illegally circumventing duties.

China is an important market for Louisiana's agricultural products, farm machinery and chemicals. Boustany co-chairs the U.S.-China Working Group with Washington Democrat Rick Larsen and has met with a number of high-ranking Chinese officials. He told The Advocate newspaper that "the U.S.-China relationship will define how our 21st centuries go," adding that "it is the most important geopolitical relationship in the world today."

Boustany voted against a 2010 bill that would have encouraged countervailing duties as a response to China's undervaluation of its currency. In the 112th Congress, he publicly campaigned for a bilateral investment treaty with China to smooth private sector investments between the countries.

Coastal Louisiana bore the brunt of major hurricanes in 2005 and 2008, as well as the Deepwater Horizon oil spill in 2010. Constituent service and disaster response have therefore been a big part of Boustany's job. Nine months into his first term in 2005, and less than a month after Hurricane Katrina, he won enactment of a bill giving the Labor Department more flexibility in providing temporary work and training in disaster areas.

Boustany's voting record indicates fairly strong fiscal conservatism, but in January 2013 he was one of 49 Republicans to vote for a $50 billion spending measure tied to Superstorm Sandy recovery — most of the spending was deemed "emergency" and therefore outside federal spending limits.

On social issues, Boustany almost always takes a conservative position. But in 2008 he sided with Democrats — and President George W. Bush — in moving a bill expanding U.S. funding for global AIDS programs. And he joined with Democrats that July in voting for a law aimed at helping homeowners struggling to pay their mortgages. Late in the year, he was one of 25 Republicans to switch his vote from "no" to "yes" on a $700 billion package to rescue the financial sector, helping Bush and Democratic leaders pass the final bill.

Boustany's Maronite Christian grandparents emigrated from Lebanon to Louisiana in the early 20th century, partly because of the region's French connection. Today, Lafayette and New Iberia have significant Lebanese populations. He grew up in Lafayette, the son of a longtime coroner for Lafayette Parish. His mother, a homemaker with 10 children, did charitable work in the community. His family was staunchly Democratic, but Boustany early on was influenced by columnist George Will and other conservative thinkers. The political split with his father "created friction," he said.

In 2001, Boustany developed severe arthritis in his neck and hands, forcing him to close his Lafayette medical practice. "It was devastating, because I was at the peak of my career," he said.

As he pondered what to do next, Boustany began paying more attention to politics. "The common denominator here was a lack of good political leadership for the state," he said. In 2004, after Democratic Rep. Chris John launched a bid for the Senate, Boustany decided to run for John's seat.

He finished first that November with 39 percent of the vote. Boustany cruised to a 10-point win in the runoff with state Sen. Willie Landry Mount, a Democrat who'd run afoul of the area's sizable black community. Boustany was the first Republican elected from the area since 1884.

Boustany was expected to have a difficult race in 2012. Louisiana lost a congressional district in reapportionment following the 2010 census, which left seven incumbents vying for six seats. Republican freshman Jeff Landry, a tea party favorite, ran against Boustany in the new 3rd District. National conservative groups supported Landry, who criticized Boustany and GOP leaders for eventually accepting an increase in the federal debt limit in August 2011. Landry also tried to portray Boustany as insufficiently supportive of Israel.

But voters seemed to value Boustany's ties to Speaker John A. Boehner, as well as his family's roots in the area. Boustany ran well ahead of Landry and three other candidates on Election Day (Louisiana's unusual system has no primaries). In a runoff against Landry a month later, he picked up African-American and union votes in Democratic-leaning Lake Charles and won by almost 22 points.

Key Votes

2012	
Extend a Social Security payroll tax cut and unemployment benefits	NO
Ease securities rules to expand small-business access to capital	YES
Extend for one year subsidized student loan interest rates financed by a cut in health care spending	YES
Cite Attorney General Eric H. Holder Jr. for contempt of Congress	YES
Create a visa program for foreign graduates in high-tech fields	YES
Extend most Bush-era income tax rates while allowing rates for top-bracket earners to rise (Jan. 1, 2013)	NO
2011	
Strike funding for F-35 alternative engine	YES
Prevent EPA from regulating greenhouse gas emissions to address climate change	YES
Extend certain provisions of Patriot Act for four years	+
Declare opposition to use of ground troops in Libya	YES
Overhaul patent law	YES
Pass compromise debt limit increase plan and establish future spending limits	YES
Allow consideration of measures to implement three trade agreements	YES

CQ Vote Studies

	PARTY UNITY		PRESIDENTIAL SUPPORT	
	SUPPORT	OPPOSE	SUPPORT	OPPOSE
2012	97%	3%	15%	85%
2011	96%	4%	21%	79%
2010	96%	4%	33%	67%
2009	97%	3%	23%	77%
2008	94%	6%	68%	32%

Interest Groups

	AFL-CIO	ADA	CCUS	ACU
2012	14%	5%	100%	92%
2011	0%	5%	100%	83%
2010	0%	0%	88%	100%
2009	14%	5%	80%	96%
2008	8%	20%	94%	83%

Louisiana 3

Southwest coast; Lafayette, Lake Charles

The heel of Louisiana's boot, the 3rd District stretches along the Gulf of Mexico from the Texas border east to the Atchafalaya Delta. These low marshlands and bayous constitute the southwestern band of the historic Acadiana region, or Cajun country, which radiates north and east beyond the district's borders. The 3rd's population is mostly white, one-fourth black and has a median household income lower than the state average.

Lafayette, the district's largest city, is a transportation hub where Interstates 10 and 49 intersect with the terminus of the U.S. Route 90 "Energy Corridor" that runs through oil towns to New Orleans. The oil and petrochemical industry shapes the business climate of the 3rd well beyond Lafayette, including fabricators in Vermilion Parish and drilling platform manufacturers in New Iberia. In deep-water port Lake Charles, petrochemical-connected industries have dominated the economy since the 1940s.

Oil and natural gas industries often clash with the interests of the district's other major enterprise: commercial seafood. The 2010 Deepwater Horizon oil spill hit the 3rd's harvesters hard, forcing the closure of oyster beds and fisheries. Even without the obstacles created by natural or manmade disasters, local fishermen often battle with regulators over catch limits.

More than two-thirds of Jefferson Davis Parish is farmland, much of it devoted to rice cultivation. St. Mary and Iberia parishes are the state's top two producers of sugar cane; Calcasieu Parish is its top cattle producer.

Population losses in Acadiana, notably after Hurricane Rita in 2005, played a significant role in Louisiana losing a congressional seat during reapportionment following the 2010 census. The socially conservative and largely Catholic area nevertheless sent Democrats to the U.S. House from 1884 to 2004. GOP-backing now, the district has provided recent Republican presidential candidates strong showings, although ticket-splitting between state and federal races remains.

Major Industry
Oil and petrochemicals, agriculture, aquaculture

Cities
Lafayette, Lake Charles, New Iberia

Notable
Atchafalaya Basin is the nation's largest swamp, with 885,000 acres of forested wetlands and 517,000 acres of marshland.

Rep. John Fleming (R)

Capitol Office
225-2777
fleming.house.gov
416 Cannon Bldg. 20515-1804; fax 225-0000

Committees
Armed Services
Natural Resources
(Fisheries, Wildlife, Oceans & Insular Affairs - Chairman)

Residence
Minden

Born
July 5, 1951; Meridian, Miss.

Religion
Southern Baptist

Family
Wife, Cindy Fleming; four children

Education
U. of Mississippi, B.S. 1973 (medicine), M.D. 1976

Military
Navy Medical Corps, 1976-82

Career
Physician; sandwich store owner

Political Highlights
Webster Parish coroner, 1996-2000

ELECTION RESULTS

2012 GENERAL		
John Fleming (R)	187,894	75.3%
Randall Lord (LIBERT)	61,637	24.7%
2010 GENERAL		
John Fleming (R)	105,223	62.3%
David Melville (D)	54,609	32.4%
Artis "Doc" Cash (I)	8,962	5.3%

Previous Winning Percentages
2008 (48%)

Elected 2008; 3rd term

Fleming is one of the most conservative members of the House and a voluble critic of Democratic policies. He relates his small-government views to his experiences as a businessman and physician, and his committee work involves him in military and energy debates.

He calls himself a Reagan Republican, although his convictions aren't all rooted in 1980s politics. As he was growing up in the South, his family, schools and churches kept him "constantly immersed in a very strong Christian-oriented value system," he said.

Fleming cultivates relationships with several branches of the House GOP. He belongs to both the conservative Republican Study Committee and the Tea Party Caucus, and in the 113th Congress (2013-14) he is serving on the Republican Policy Committee.

Fiscal policy proposals dominated debates in 2011, and Fleming voted as one of the most die-hard budget cutters. He opposed all the final spending bills for fiscal 2011 and fiscal 2012, and he opposed an agreement to raise the federal debt limit. They did not do enough to impose fiscal restraint, by his standards. Before voting for a balanced-budget amendment to the Constitution, he said on the House floor that Washington was "hopelessly addicted" to spending. For Fleming, that's not an empty metaphor; his medical career includes extensive experience treating substance abuse.

Fleming ties some of his cost-cutting rhetoric to health care — especially when it comes to Democrats' 2010 health care overhaul. Claims that the law would cut the budget deficit are "a Disney fantasy of accounting," he once said on Fox News. He has advocated a private insurance system in which people would have health savings accounts and government would help pay premiums on a sliding scale.

His medical background and clear partisan viewpoint made Fleming a much-sought media commentator during the health care debate in the 111th Congress (2009-10). He cites government intrusion in the health care sector as his reason for getting into politics. Dating to the 1980s, Fleming said, regulations on the use of lab equipment and reimbursement rates were "destructive" to his own practice.

In March 2013, he became an original co-sponsor of a bill to protect health care "conscience rights." It states that employers and religious institutions do not have to provide access to insurance plans that cover abortion or contraception if they have a moral or religious objection.

Fleming sits on the Natural Resources Committee. He questions the value of many conservation and environmental rules and paints them as hurting economic growth. He supports increased oil and gas exploration on the outer continental shelf. More to his district's benefit — it has no coastline — he promotes development of the Haynesville Shale, a source of natural gas.

He chairs the Subcommittee on Fisheries, Wildlife, Oceans and Insular Affairs. That panel handles the U.S. territories, and Fleming lived in Guam for two years while in the Navy Medical Corps. Territorial governments often rely heavily on federal funding, and even with his preferences for cost-cutting, Fleming has been sympathetic to their needs.

He also sits on the Armed Services Committee. Air Force and Army bases in his district hold together large parts of the local economy. Fleming said he believes in "peace through strength": He has defended funding for long-range bombers, fought against the retirement of Air Force A-10s and criticized cuts to nuclear weapons programs. He co-founded the Long-Range Strike Caucus to support the replacement of the nation's aging bomber fleet.

Fleming said he could swallow some military spending cuts, with the Iraq War ended and the Afghanistan War winding down. But he opposed the cuts to the defense budget that were put in place by the 2011 debt limit law. Those reductions, which started taking effect in 2013, "will reduce the readiness of our military and the ability to extend our presence around the world," he said.

When Fleming criticizes Democratic policies, he is pointed and confident — although not overly animated. The liberal blogosphere has pounced gleefully on Fleming when opportunities arise. Fleming is a strong social conservative and opposes abortion. In early 2012, his Facebook page included a link to a satirical article in The Onion about an $8 billion abortion facility opened by Planned Parenthood. The posting included the comment: "More on Planned Parenthood. Abortion by the wholesale." The post was quickly removed, but Fleming was ridiculed for not knowing the story was made up.

Outside of his medical practice, Fleming owns a number of Subway sandwich franchises and is a sub-franchisor of The UPS Store. Appearing on MSNBC in 2011 to argue that tax increases could force businessmen such as himself to fire employees, he said that "by the time I feed my family, I have maybe $400,000 left over" — a sound bite many cited as evidence that Republicans are out of touch with the middle class.

Fleming comes from the middle class, however. He was raised in Meridian, Miss. His father was a World War II veteran and power company lineman who switched to a desk job after breaking his back falling from a pole. He died of a heart attack while Fleming was in high school. His mother worked low-wage white-collar jobs until becoming disabled.

His grandmother worked as a nurse and inspired him at age 11 to become a doctor. Halfway through his first year of medical school, Fleming ran out of money and signed up for a Navy scholarship program. He went on to serve six years in the Navy Medical Corps, practicing family medicine and working on drug and alcohol treatment programs.

After leaving the Navy he set up a practice in Minden, La. Fleming volunteered as a deacon and Sunday school teacher at the First Baptist Church of Minden, and he started his small-business enterprises.

In late 2007, Republican Rep. Jim McCrery announced his retirement. Fleming won both the initial primary and a runoff to set up a race against Democrat Paul J. Carmouche, the former Caddo Parish district attorney. Fleming lent his campaign more than $1 million and paid his own corporation advertising fees to have Subway workers stuff sandwich bags with campaign literature. In a banner year for Democrats, Fleming won by 350 votes.

Shifting political winds and better name recognition made his re-election a breeze in 2010, and Democrats fielded no candidate against him in 2012.

Key Votes

2012	
Extend a Social Security payroll tax cut and unemployment benefits	NO
Ease securities rules to expand small-business access to capital	YES
Extend for one year subsidized student loan interest rates financed by a cut in health care spending	YES
Cite Attorney General Eric H. Holder Jr. for contempt of Congress	YES
Create a visa program for foreign graduates in high-tech fields	YES
Extend most Bush-era income tax rates while allowing rates for top-bracket earners to rise (Jan. 1, 2013)	NO
2011	
Strike funding for F-35 alternative engine	NO
Prevent EPA from regulating greenhouse gas emissions to address climate change	YES
Extend certain provisions of Patriot Act for four years	YES
Declare opposition to use of ground troops in Libya	YES
Overhaul patent law	YES
Pass compromise debt limit increase plan and establish future spending limits	NO
Allow consideration of measures to implement three trade agreements	YES

CQ Vote Studies

	PARTY UNITY		PRESIDENTIAL SUPPORT	
	SUPPORT	OPPOSE	SUPPORT	OPPOSE
2012	98%	2%	15%	85%
2011	98%	2%	16%	84%
2010	98%	2%	24%	76%
2009	97%	3%	26%	74%

Interest Groups

	AFL-CIO	ADA	CCUS	ACU
2012	5%	10%	83%	100%
2011	0%	5%	94%	100%
2010	0%	5%	75%	96%
2009	10%	0%	80%	100%

Louisiana 4

Northwest — Shreveport, Bossier City

The 4th District forms a "C" along Louisiana's northern and western borders. Decennial redistricting extended its reach into the "Sportsman's Paradise" region by adding Union Parish in the north of the state. The redrawn 4th also pushes eastward into Allen and Evangeline parishes and a sliver of St. Landry Parish in its southeastern arm.

Majority-black Shreveport is tucked in the northwest near the Arkansas and Texas borders on the west bank of the Red River. Anchored by the Louisiana State University Health Sciences Center, the city is an emerging regional health care hub. Smaller Bossier City sits across the river, as does Barksdale Air Force Base, part of the Air Force Global Strike Command. The base is a major employer for residents of both cities.

The military also has a large presence farther south in the district. Leesville in Vernon Parish is home to the Army's Fort Polk, a major training base and the second-largest employer in Louisiana.

Gaming helps float the economy of the 4th. Riverboat casinos dock on the Red River near Shreveport, although competition from American Indian gambling venues in Oklahoma has sapped some revenue. Allen Parish is the site of the large Coushatta Resort and Casino.

Louisiana still relies on timber, much of which comes from the district's northern forests. Red River Parish exports lumber, while wood products and paper are manufactured in Natchitoches, Bienville, St. Landry and Sabine. The district's farmland boasts cattle, sorghum and rice.

Republican candidates do well in this conservative district. Only Caddo Parish (Shreveport) supported Barack Obama in either 2008 or 2012.

Major Industry
Military, timber, agriculture and ranching, gaming, health care

Military Bases
Fort Polk, 9,792 military, 2,882 civilian (2009); Barksdale Air Force Base, 6,960 military, 1,786 civilian

Cities
Shreveport, Bossier City, Natchitoches

Notable
The City of Natchitoches is the oldest permanent settlement in the area covered by the Louisiana Purchase.

Rep. Rodney Alexander (R)

Capitol Office
225-8490
alexander.house.gov
316 Cannon Bldg. 20515-1005; fax 225-5639

Committees
Appropriations
(Legislative Branch - Chairman)

Residence
Quitman

Born
Dec. 5, 1946; Quitman, La.

Religion
Baptist

Family
Wife, Nancy Alexander; three children

Education
Louisiana Tech U., attended 1965; U. of Louisiana, Monroe, B.A. 2009 (general studies)

Military
Air Force Reserve, 1965-71

Career
Insurance agent; road construction contractor

Political Highlights
Jackson Parish Police Jury, 1972-87 (president, 1980-87); La. House, 1988-2002 (served as a Democrat)

ELECTION RESULTS

2012 GENERAL		
Rodney Alexander (R)	202,536	77.8%
Ron Ceasar (NOP)	37,486	14.4%
Clay Steven Grant (LIBERT)	20,194	7.8%
2010 GENERAL		
Rodney Alexander (R)	122,033	78.6%
Tom Gibbs (NPA)	33,279	21.4%

Previous Winning Percentages
2008 (100%); 2006 (68%); 2004 (59%); 2002 (50%)*
*Elected as a Democrat in 2002

Elected 2002; 6th term

One of the last conservative Dixiecrats to defect to the Republican Party, Alexander has kept constituents happy by keeping local priorities such as flood insurance high on his agenda. He'd like the ability to do even more: Alexander is among the ranks of appropriators ready for the return of earmarks.

Alexander reluctantly supported his House colleagues in 2011 when they decided to ban the member-directed funding set-asides for specific projects, denying members of the Appropriations Committee a traditional means of control over federal funding. Many conservative Republicans describe earmarks as wasteful and, in some cases, corrupt.

But Alexander has grown increasingly skeptical of the ban. "I think appropriators should have more say-so about where money is being spent," he said in 2012. "It's unfair for the administration to make all the decisions." As his ability to send funds back to his district has declined, his constituents — among the country's poorest — have suffered, Alexander said. He has sought other ways to fight for their interests.

To that end, in the 112th Congress (2011-12) he was heavily involved in debates on federal flood insurance. Levees protect much of his district, and new federal flood maps had the potential to place more of his constituents in flood zones, obligating them to pay more for insurance.

Alexander sits on the panel for water and energy spending. He badgered the Obama administration, drafted letters and introduced bills to force the Federal Emergency Management Agency to reconsider the mapping. FEMA backed off, but not Alexander. He contends that the levees, built by the Army Corps of Engineers, are a federal responsibility and that Louisianans don't have the money to fix them.

It caused some problems with his colleagues. When Republicans tried in February 2012 to revive the line-item veto, which would have given the president the ability to eliminate specific programs in an appropriations bill without vetoing the entire bill, Alexander was one of only 41 Republicans to object, on the grounds that the line-item veto would give the executive branch too much control over spending. Alexander offered an amendment to exempt Army Corps funding from rescissions, but his fellow Republicans rejected it. The measure stalled in the Senate.

In January 2013, Alexander was one of 49 Republicans to vote for a $50 billion spending package tied to Superstorm Sandy, which included some funding for corps operations.

He is more in concert with his GOP colleagues in fighting President Barack Obama's agenda. In 2010, he voted "no" on the health care overhaul and the rewrite of financial services regulations. In 2011, Alexander, who is vice chairman of the panel overseeing health care spending, was chosen to lead the floor debate on a House bill to block implementation of the health care overhaul.

The law "is devastating to businesses, and it's going to be devastating to the state of Louisiana," he said, in large part because it would allow lower-middle-income people to receive Medicaid, the federal health insurance program for the poor. Because the states and federal government share costs associated with Medicaid, it's a huge burden on state budgets, he said. The Senate rejected the bill.

He has not taken the hardest line on spending reductions, however, often rejecting deeper cuts proposed by more-conservative colleagues. Alexander doesn't consider himself partisan. He reached across the aisle after Hurricane Katrina devastated the Gulf Coast in 2005, asking the federal government to contribute funding.

One of Alexander's main responsibilities in the 113th Congress (2013-14) has relatively little to do with his constituents — he is chairing the Legislative Branch Subcommittee. The announcement of smaller budgets for House offices in early 2013 didn't faze Alexander; he said it was incumbent on House members to "lead by example" in response to unsustainable federal spending.

Stylistically, Alexander is a social conservative who prefers the constituent service side of his job. He most enjoys spending time with his children — he helped build homes for his two daughters near his own in Quitman, a small town in the north-central part of the state — and grandchildren. His son also lives nearby.

Alexander's family has been in Louisiana for generations. His father ran a road construction business and also sat on the Jackson Parish Police Jury, the Louisiana equivalent of a county board of supervisors. His mother was a preacher and school bus driver. Alexander dropped out of Louisiana Tech University to join his father's business, but he was skeptical about politics. "When I was a young man watching my dad in politics, it was something I didn't want to participate in," he said. "I saw my dad struggling to provide family income. I saw him working around the clock."

Ultimately, he grew to respect his father's service. He won a seat on the police jury at age 25, the year after he left the Air Force Reserve. He served there for 15 years, eight of those with his father, then went on to serve 14 years in the state House before running for Congress.

Alexander was still a Democrat when he decided to run for the House in 2002 — GOP incumbent John Cooksey announced he was seeking a Senate seat. Alexander led a field of seven candidates in the state's all-party "open" primary, but he didn't get the majority needed under state law to avoid a runoff. He was considered the underdog in the weeks leading up to the runoff, behind Republican Lee Fletcher, a former top aide to Cooksey.

Fletcher outspent Alexander 2-to-1, but Alexander benefited from a surge in Democratic voting in support of Mary L. Landrieu's Senate re-election campaign. He beat Fletcher by 974 votes.

That close call might have been on his mind two years later when Alexander switched parties just minutes before the filing deadline, preventing Democrats from recruiting a strong challenger. He sailed to victory, and Republicans rewarded him with a seat on Appropriations in the 109th Congress (2005-06). Alexander said he didn't switch parties to win perks. "I'm pro-life, pro-family, pro-gun," he said. "That's why I was uncomfortable being a Democrat."

The district is clearly comfortable with a Republican representative, as he has won easily in every election since then. In 2009, he finally got his college degree from the University of Louisiana at Monroe.

Key Votes

2012	
Extend a Social Security payroll tax cut and unemployment benefits	YES
Ease securities rules to expand small-business access to capital	YES
Extend for one year subsidized student loan interest rates financed by a cut in health care spending	YES
Cite Attorney General Eric H. Holder Jr. for contempt of Congress	YES
Create a visa program for foreign graduates in high-tech fields	YES
Extend most Bush-era income tax rates while allowing rates for top-bracket earners to rise (Jan. 1, 2013)	YES
2011	
Strike funding for F-35 alternative engine	NO
Prevent EPA from regulating greenhouse gas emissions to address climate change	YES
Extend certain provisions of Patriot Act for four years	YES
Declare opposition to use of ground troops in Libya	YES
Overhaul patent law	YES
Pass compromise debt limit increase plan and establish future spending limits	YES
Allow consideration of measures to implement three trade agreements	YES

CQ Vote Studies

	PARTY UNITY		PRESIDENTIAL SUPPORT	
	SUPPORT	OPPOSE	SUPPORT	OPPOSE
2012	91%	9%	17%	83%
2011	92%	8%	25%	75%
2010	97%	3%	26%	74%
2009	87%	13%	27%	73%
2008	95%	5%	70%	30%

Interest Groups

	AFL-CIO	ADA	CCUS	ACU
2012	29%	0%	100%	75%
2011	21%	10%	100%	68%
2010	0%	5%	88%	100%
2009	19%	0%	80%	88%
2008	20%	25%	94%	84%

Louisiana 5

Northeast and central — Monroe, Alexandria,

The 5th District takes up Louisiana's northeastern corner, stretching along the Arkansas and Mississippi borders, including northern sections of the so-called Florida Parishes in the east. Interstate 20 slices across the district to the north; the Mississippi River defines much of the east. With only two midsize urban areas, the region is mostly rural and marked by persistently high poverty rates. High rates of out-migration in this region was a key contributor to the state's loss of a congressional seat after the 2010 census: Tensas Parish, for example, experienced a more than 20 percent drop in population from 2000 to 2010.

Pulp and paper mills are big business in Monroe. The city also boasts a healthy financial services sector for processing insurance claims and mortgages and is home to broadband and telecommunications company CenturyLink. Alexandria has more of a manufacturing base with a large Procter & Gamble chemical plant, among others. The site of England Air Force Base, which closed in the early 1990s, is now an industrial park hosting manufacturing and technology companies.

The northeastern region, bordered by the Mississippi River, is among Louisiana's top-producing farmland for cotton, corn, sorghum and other grains. East Carroll, Tensas and Catahoula parishes have farm-heavy economies. Poverty remains high, and unemployment in the region is the highest in the state — it hits double-digit percentages in some parishes.

Politically, the 5th District was relatively unchanged by decennial redistricting. Registered Democrats outnumber Republicans by nearly 2-to-1, but voters favor conservatives of either party and tend to support Republicans at the federal level.

Major Industry

Wood and paper products, agriculture, financial services, health care

Cities

Monroe, Alexandria, Bastrop, Opelousas, Ruston

Notable

Kisatchie National Forest, the state's only national forest, has more than 604,000 acres of bayous, cypress groves and pine trees spread among seven central Louisiana parishes; Opelousas claims the title of spice capital of Louisiana and is home to spice production facilities.

Rep. Bill Cassidy (R)

Capitol Office
225-3901
cassidy.house.gov
1131 Longworth Bldg. 20515-1806; fax 225-7313

Committees
Energy & Commerce

Residence
Baton Rouge

Born
Sept. 28, 1957; Highland Park, Ill.

Religion
Christian

Family
Wife, Laura Layden Cassidy; three children

Education
Louisiana State U., B.S. 1979 (biochemistry), M.D. 1983

Career
Physician

Political Highlights
La. Senate, 2006-08

ELECTION RESULTS

2012 GENERAL		
Bill Cassidy (R)	243,553	79.4%
Rufus Holt Craig Jr. (LIBERT)	32,185	10.5%
Richard "RPT" Torregano (NOP)	30,975	10.1%
2010 GENERAL		
Bill Cassidy (R)	138,607	65.6%
Merritt E. McDonald Sr. (D)	72,577	34.4%

Previous Winning Percentages
2008 (48%)

Elected 2008; 3rd term

Cassidy works as a team player on the Energy and Commerce Committee, helping promote GOP plans for health care and energy. He also chips in policy ideas of his own that reflect his professional expertise as a doctor.

He is hoping that the combination of party loyalty and policy finesse makes him a viable statewide candidate. In April 2013, Cassidy announced that he is running for the Senate seat currently held by Democrat Mary L. Landrieu.

Republicans placed him on Energy and Commerce and its Subcommittee on Health in the 112th Congress (2011-12), in a nod to both his professional background and his good standing within the party. Cassidy is a member of the GOP whip team.

He also belongs to the GOP Doctors Caucus, a group of health professionals in the House. In his down time, he often keeps up with fellow doctors Michael C. Burgess of Texas, Tom Price and Phil Gingrey of Georgia, and Phil Roe of Tennessee. And Cassidy, a gastroenterologist, has been front and center in attempts to repeal the 2010 health care law.

He voices support for health care concepts regularly mentioned by Republicans, such as greater use of Health Savings Accounts (HSAs), permitting the sale of insurance across state lines, new "pooling mechanisms" to improve the bargaining power of patients and an overhaul of medical liability law.

"Containing costs step by step — not expanding government in one fell swoop — is the right approach to health care reform," he said in a June 2012 Republican response to President Barack Obama's weekly radio address.

His contributions to health care debates have drawn the attention of his colleagues and stakeholders in the private sector, and Cassidy is revisiting the issue in the 113th Congress (2013-14).

The 2010 law's expansion of coverage relies in large part on an expansion of Medicaid, the federal-state partnership providing insurance for the poor and disabled. Republicans contend that states can't handle the new budget demands or bureaucracy.

In 2012, Cassidy rolled out his plan to restructure Medicaid's financing mechanism. The current system ties the federal share of each state's Medicaid budget to a state's per capita income; Cassidy would instead tie the federal payment to the number of Medicaid enrollees in the state, with different payout levels for the elderly, the disabled, children and adults. His proposal would shift a greater percentage of Medicaid spending to the federal government.

Another Cassidy idea is to encourage HSAs to cover pregnancy expenses without a deductible — an arrangement that would allow more women to keep high-deductible (and lower-premium) insurance plans. Since the health care law won't be repealed anytime soon, he has proposed using HSAs as a way to defray its costs. Cassidy wants an HSA option included in the health insurance "exchanges" set up under the law, so that premium subsidies could be deposited in those accounts rather than used toward insurance purchases.

He has a personal interest in one particular health issue. As the father of a daughter with dyslexia, Cassidy joined forces with California Democrat Pete Stark to form the Congressional Dyslexia Caucus in 2012. "We have heard numerous examples of bright, hardworking dyslexic young men and women who, with accommodations, have succeeded in school only to be stopped in their tracks because they're refused accommodations on tests," they wrote in Roll Call. Stark was defeated in 2012, and freshman Democrat Julia Brownley of California became co-chairwoman in 2013. Cassidy's wife, Laura, is in the process of establishing the Louisiana Key Academy, a charter school in Baton Rouge that will serve financially insecure youths with dyslexia.

Energy and Commerce is also a plum assignment for those hoping to bolster Louisiana's energy sector, and Cassidy avails himself of the opportunity.

Cassidy denounced what he perceived to be political overreach after the 2010 BP oil spill in the Gulf of Mexico — oil production in the gulf was effectively halted for months. He has since refocused his efforts on moving past the disaster. Cassidy joined the rest of the Louisiana delegation in backing a provision in a 2012 transportation law to send at least 80 percent of the spill-related fines collected from BP under the Clean Water Act to Gulf Coast states.

The Republicans' "all of the above" energy policy has his blessing. Cassidy urges increases in fossil fuel, nuclear and renewable-energy production. He proposes tweaks to restrictions on natural gas production to allow the creation of more natural-gas-based products for use as automotive fuel.

Cassidy is a social conservative who opposes both abortion and proscriptions of gun rights. Fiscally, he is not among his party's hard-line cost-cutters, but he supports significant reductions to the federal budget and backs the GOP's ban on earmarked spending.

Cassidy was born in Highland Park, Ill., but raised in Baton Rouge, where his father sold life insurance. His interest in medicine was sparked during his senior year in high school, when doctors thought he had cancer but eventually diagnosed him with swollen lymph nodes. "I saw all these doctors and said, 'Wow, this is a fulfilling field,'" he said.

He holds a bachelor's degree in biochemistry from Louisiana State University and earned a medical degree in 1983 from the university's medical school. That's where he met his wife, who also is a physician.

In addition to his medical practice, Cassidy taught medical students at LSU and worked with uninsured patients at the Earl K. Long Hospital. He helped found the Greater Baton Rouge Community Clinic, which provides free dental and health care to uninsured workers. After Hurricane Katrina hit, he directed the conversion of an empty Kmart into an emergency medical facility for hurricane evacuees. He served as chairman of the East Baton Rouge Parish Medical Society's health care overhaul committee until 1998 and raised concerns then about the future of the Medicaid program.

As a special-election candidate to fill a state Senate seat in 2006, he advocated using surplus state funds to improve health care. He suggested a redesign of the health care system to make it more affordable and accessible, and he called for the creation of a statewide electronic medical records system.

After starting his second term in the state Senate, he decided to run for a U.S. House seat. He challenged incumbent Democratic Rep. Don Cazayoux in 2008 and took back what had been a reliably Republican seat, scoring 48 percent of the vote. Cassidy enjoyed easy re-elections in 2010 and 2012.

Key Votes

2012	
Extend a Social Security payroll tax cut and unemployment benefits	NO
Ease securities rules to expand small-business access to capital	YES
Extend for one year subsidized student loan interest rates financed by a cut in health care spending	?
Cite Attorney General Eric H. Holder Jr. for contempt of Congress	YES
Create a visa program for foreign graduates in high-tech fields	YES
Extend most Bush-era income tax rates while allowing rates for top-bracket earners to rise (Jan. 1, 2013)	NO
2011	
Strike funding for F-35 alternative engine	YES
Prevent EPA from regulating greenhouse gas emissions to address climate change	YES
Extend certain provisions of Patriot Act for four years	YES
Declare opposition to use of ground troops in Libya	YES
Overhaul patent law	YES
Pass compromise debt limit increase plan and establish future spending limits	YES
Allow consideration of measures to implement three trade agreements	YES

CQ Vote Studies

	PARTY UNITY		PRESIDENTIAL SUPPORT	
	SUPPORT	OPPOSE	SUPPORT	OPPOSE
2012	96%	4%	17%	83%
2011	94%	6%	24%	76%
2010	92%	8%	35%	65%
2009	92%	8%	37%	63%

Interest Groups

	AFL-CIO	ADA	CCUS	ACU
2012	15%	10%	100%	92%
2011	0%	5%	100%	76%
2010	14%	5%	100%	91%
2009	20%	20%	87%	88%

Louisiana 6

Part of Baton Rouge; central bayou

The horseshoe-shaped 6th District is centered on Baton Rouge, the state capital and its second-largest city. It also includes parts of the more sparsely populated surrounding parishes, stretching southeast to the outskirts of Houma and stopping outside the New Orleans suburbs. Areas west of Baton Rouge were among the only regions in the state that experienced notable population growth between 2000 and 2010.

A stretch of the New Orleans-based 2nd District cuts through the core of the 6th and splits Baton Rouge awkwardly. The state capitol lies within the 6th, but the Louisiana governor's mansion, just across Capitol Lake, is in the 2nd. The city's downtown district and Louisiana State University are also within the boundaries of the 6th.

The presence of state government, by far Baton Rouge's largest employer, provides the northern portion of the 6th a relatively stable economy. Industry related to lucrative offshore drilling in the Gulf of Mexico trickles wealth up to district households. The capital region has the highest concentration of chemical industry jobs in the state and is home to one of ExxonMobil's largest refineries. Several industrial manufacturing, engineering and construction firms throughout the region bolster the sector.

Outside of the capital and the district's manufacturing facilities, scenic rivers, forests and bayous support boating and fishing. The 6th contains almost all of Lake Maurepas and the western edge of Lake Pontchartrain.

Decennial redistricting carved out some of Baton Rouge's black population, making the 6th roughly three-fourths white. Democrats account for the largest segment of registered voters in the 6th, although conservative-leaning independents can make races competitive. Barack Obama eked out a 50.5 percent win in East Baton Rouge Parish in 2008 and a 5-point margin in 2012, but surrounding parishes can be extremely conservative.

Major Industry
Oil and petrochemicals, state government, manufacturing, construction

Cities
Baton Rouge (pt.), Prairieville (unincorp.), Thibodaux, Denham Springs

Notable
Louisiana has the tallest state capitol in the U.S., at 450 feet and 34 stories high — former Gov. Huey P. Long, who was assassinated there in 1935, is buried on the capitol grounds.

MAINE

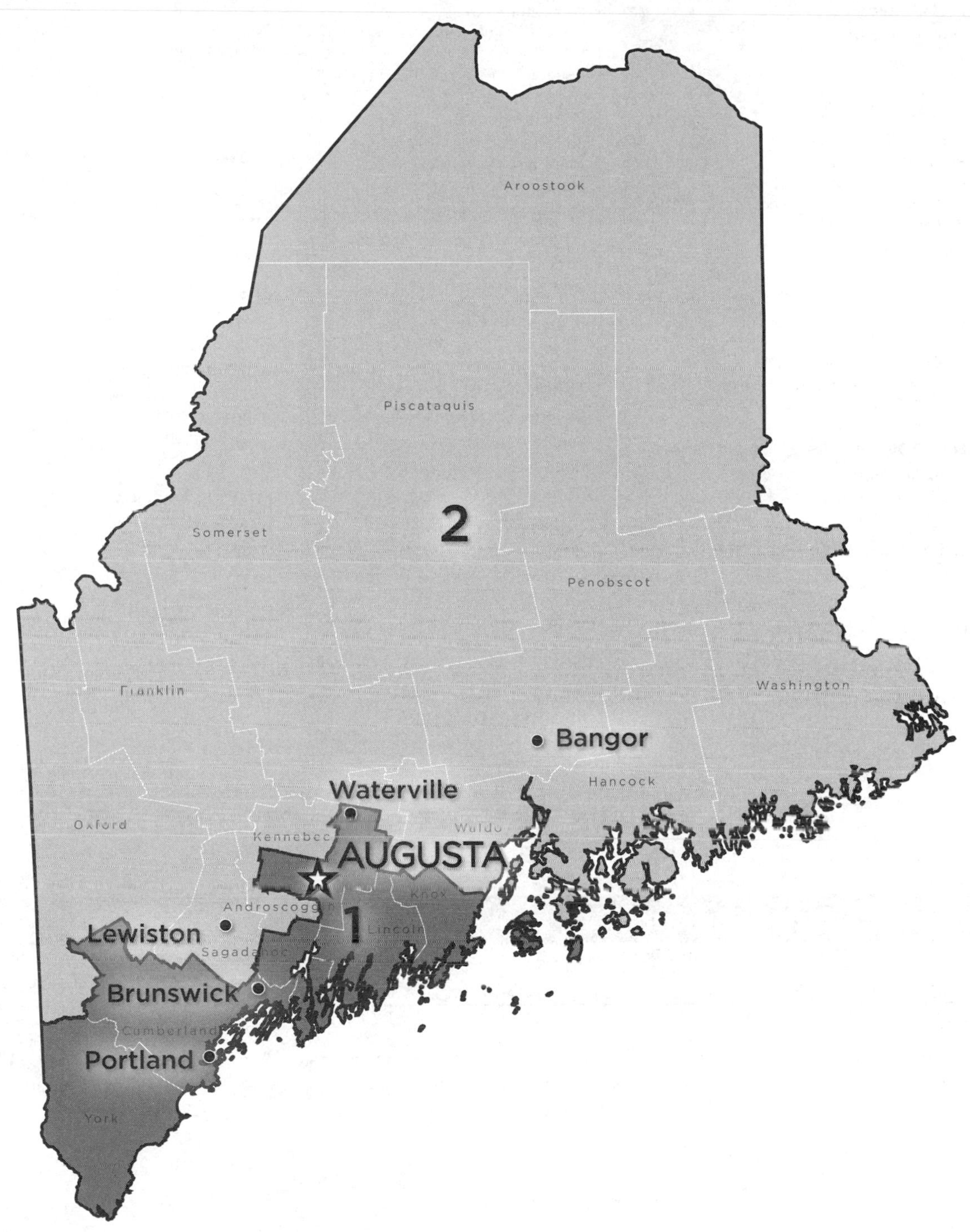
Aroostook
Piscataquis
2
Somerset
Penobscot
Franklin
Washington
Bangor
Hancock
Waterville
Oxford
Kennebec
Waldo
AUGUSTA
Knox
Androscoggin
1
Lincoln
Lewiston
Sagadahoc
Brunswick
Cumberland
Portland
York

Gov. Paul R. LePage (R)

First elected: 2010
Length of term: 4 years
Term expires: 1/15
Salary: $70,000
Phone: (207) 287-3531
Residence: Waterville
Born: Oct. 9, 1948; Lewiston, Maine
Religion: Roman Catholic
Family: Wife, Ann LePage; five children
Education: Husson College, B.S. 1971 (business administration); U. of Maine, M.B.A. 1975
Career: Store manager; business consultant; forestry products company executive; state housing department officer
Political highlights: Waterville City Council, 1999-2003; mayor of Waterville, 2002-11

ELECTION RESULTS

2010 GENERAL

Paul LePage (R)	218,065	37.6%
Eliot R. Cutler (I)	208,270	35.9%
Libby Mitchell (D)	109,387	18.8%
Shawn H. Moody (I)	28,756	5.0%
Kevin L. Scott (I)	5,664	1.0%

Senate President Justin Alfond (D)

(no lieutenant governor)
Phone: (207) 287-1500

LEGISLATURE

Legislature: January-June in odd-numbered years; January-April in even-numbered years.
Senate: 35 members, 2-year terms
2013 ratios: 19 D, 15 R, 1 other; 28 men, 7 women
Salary: $13,852 first year of term; $9,661 second year of term
Phone: (207) 287-1540
House: 151 members, 2-year terms
2013 ratios: 89 D, 58 R, 2 I, 2 other; 105 men, 46 women
Salary: $13,852 first year of term; $9,661 second year of term
Phone: (207) 287-1400

TERM LIMITS

Governor: 2 consecutive terms
Senate: 4 consecutive terms
House: 4 consecutive terms

URBAN STATISTICS

CITY	POPULATION
Portland	66,194
Lewiston	36,592
Bangor	33,039
South Portland	25,002
Auburn	23,055

REGISTERED VOTERS

Other	40%
Democrat	33%
Republican	27%

POPULATION

2010 population	1,328,361
2000 population	1,274,923
1990 population	1,227,928
Percent change (2000-2010)	+4.2%
Rank among states (2010)	41
Median age	41.4
Born in state	64.0%
Foreign born	3.3%
Violent crime rate	120/100,000
Poverty level	12.3%
Federal workers	16,159
Military	730

ELECTIONS

STATE ELECTION OFFICIAL
(207) 626-8400
DEMOCRATIC PARTY
(207) 622-6233
REPUBLICAN PARTY
(207) 622-6247

MISCELLANEOUS

Web: www.maine.gov
Capital: Augusta

U.S. CONGRESS

Senate: 1 Independent, 1 Republican
House: 2 Democrats

STATISTICS BY DISTRICT

District	2012 Vote for President: Obama	Romney	2008 Vote for President: Obama	McCain	Black	Asian	Hispanic	Median Income	Over 64	Under 20	College Education	Rural	Sq. Miles
1	60%	38%	61%	37%	1%	1%	2%	$52,323	16%	23%	35%	53%	3,286
2	53	44	54	44	1	1	1	40,518	17	23	22	77	27,557
STATE	56	41	58	40	1	1	1	46,033	16	23	28	65	30,843
U.S.	51	47	53	46	12	5	17	50,052	13	27	29	21	3,531,905

Sen. Susan Collins (R)

Capitol Office
224-2523
collins.senate.gov
413 Dirksen Bldg. 20510-1904; fax 224-2693

Committees
Appropriations
Select Intelligence
Special Aging - Ranking Member

Residence
Bangor

Born
Dec. 7, 1952; Caribou, Maine

Religion
Roman Catholic

Family
Husband, Thomas Daffron

Education
St. Lawrence U., B.A. 1975 (government)

Career
Business center director; congressional aide

Political Highlights
Maine Department of Professional and Financial Regulation commissioner, 1987-91; Small Business Administration official, 1992-93; Maine deputy treasurer, 1993; Republican nominee for governor, 1994

ELECTION RESULTS

2008 GENERAL		
Susan Collins (R)	444,300	61.3%
Tom Allen (D)	279,510	38.6%
2008 PRIMARY		
Susan Collins (R)		unopposed

Previous Winning Percentages
2002 (58%); 1996 (49%)

Elected 1996; 3rd term

As Collins closes out her third term in the Senate, her circumstances have changed. Some of her closest allies have left the chamber, and she no longer sits on the Homeland Security and Governmental Affairs Committee, where she was the top Republican for 10 years. What's unchanged is her status as the most moderate member of her party — and that keeps her intimately involved in just about every major policy debate.

All other contenders for the GOP moderation title are gone: Scott P. Brown of Massachusetts was defeated, and Olympia J. Snowe of Maine has retired. In 2012, when majorities of Republicans and Democrats voted against each other, Collins split with her party more than 60 percent of the time. No one on the Republican roster in the 113th Congress (2013-14) comes close to that mark. Many times, she has cast the swing vote allowing Democrats to take up their favored legislation.

Her state loves her — a Republican consultant told Roll Call that Collins "has become a political rock star in Maine." And moderation does have its benefits. The tug of war for her vote allows her to serve as a negotiator and peacekeeper on controversial bills and oversight efforts.

She has done some notable work over the past decade. Teaming up with her close friend Joseph I. Lieberman, an independent from Connecticut, Collins shaped a 2004 rewrite of intelligence laws to create a more centralized spy infrastructure. She and Snowe used their swing-vote status to chop chunks of funding off the 2009 economic stimulus law. And she led bipartisan investigations of the federal responses to Hurricane Katrina and a 2012 attack on a U.S. consulate in Libya.

Several of those efforts originated from the Homeland Security and Governmental Affairs Committee, where Collins worked closely with Lieberman — who has also retired. Collins lost her spot as the panel's ranking member because of a term limit rule, and she also departed the Armed Services Committee. But she still has venues to work on security concerns. She sits on the Defense Appropriations Subcommittee, and in 2013 she was added to the Intelligence Committee.

Collins has worked to assuage concerns that attention to homeland security is flagging as the Sept. 11 attack recedes into the past. A series of high-profile threats in 2009 and 2010 — including the shooting at Fort Hood, Texas; a plot to attack New York City's transit system; the Christmas Day attempt to blow up a Northwest Airlines flight; and the failed Times Square car bombing — brought terrorism back to the forefront. Collins says she and Lieberman pushed the Obama administration "to pay more attention to homegrown terrorism."

She was highly critical of the FBI and the Defense Department for their handling of the 2009 Fort Hood shooting, saying they had ample evidence of the growing radicalization of suspect Army Maj. Nidal Malik Hasan but failed to curb it. The incident, which resulted in 13 deaths and 32 injured servicemembers and civilians, could have been prevented if investigators had linked all of the information they had on Hasan, Collins said.

Her final investigation with Lieberman looked at the 2012 Libya incident. Collins said she was perplexed by the White House's hesitance to describe it as a terrorist attack perpetrated by Islamist extremists. "The administration repeatedly has refused to name the threat that we face."

In 2012, Collins and Lieberman put forth their plan for improving cybersecurity; the bill, which had White House backing, would allow DHS to set mandatory standards for tech infrastructure deemed critical. To overcome some Republican opposition, they modified the bill so the standards would be voluntary and the government would provide incentives for compliance. But the bill bogged down, and work continues in the 113th Congress.

The drawback of moderation is that Collins has the potential to irritate people all along the political spectrum.

When she worked to pare the stimulus legislation in 2009, liberal groups went after her for scrapping funding for things like education and energy efficiency efforts. She was dubbed "Swine Flu Sue" by bloggers who were upset about reductions for pandemic flu preparations. House Appropriations Chairman David R. Obey of Wisconsin called Collins and Snowe the "crown princesses of Maine" in disapproving of their cuts.

She has angered Republicans by declining to support the budgets written by House Budget Chairman Paul D. Ryan of Wisconsin. Collins also has considered legislative action to curtail greenhouse gas emissions. In 2010, she and Washington Democrat Maria Cantwell devised a "cap and dividend" proposal, whereby fossil fuel producers must buy "carbon shares" and the proceeds go to both clean-energy research and taxpayers' pockets.

She irked social conservatives by backing repeal of the military's "don't ask, don't tell" policy on openly gay servicemembers. Collins stuck with Republicans to block the addition of the repeal to a defense policy bill in 2010 — she accused Democrats of trying to limit GOP amendments — but she supported a stand-alone measure a few months later.

But Collins also has been a hero of the GOP in many instances. During debate on the health care overhaul in 2010, she joined in keeping Democrats from securing a single Republican vote for the package.

Collins goes to bat for constituents from the Appropriations Committee, where she is the top Republican on the Transportation-HUD Subcommittee. It's tougher to steer federal funding to Maine now that earmarks are effectively banned, but Collins does what she can to help the state and one of its largest industrial employers, Bath Iron Works. That shipyard builds destroyers, which face perennial funding threats. In 2006, she worked with Mississippi lawmakers to block a proposed Navy strategy to build the ships in only one of the two states.

Collins hails from a political family; each of her parents served as Caribou's mayor. Her father, grandfather, great-grandfather and great-great-grandfather served as Maine legislators. Collins visited the U.S. Capitol as a high school senior and spent two hours talking with a Republican woman trailblazer, Maine Sen. Margaret Chase Smith. "It really was in some ways a transformational experience," Collins has said. Inspired by Smith, who showed up for every Senate vote for nearly 20 years, Collins has maintained a perfect voting attendance record.

After graduating from St. Lawrence University in 1975, she moved to Washington to work as an aide to William S. Cohen, another moderate Republican senator from Maine who became her mentor. She then returned to Maine to serve as commissioner of the state's Department of Professional and Financial Regulation.

In 1994, Collins won the Republican nomination for governor but finished a disappointing third behind Democratic nominee Joseph E. Brennan and independent Angus King, who won the contest. (King is now the state's junior senator.) In 1996, when Cohen announced his retirement, Collins regrouped and took the race by 5 points. She won handily in 2002, beating Democratic challenger Chellie Pingree (who is now a House member).

In 2008, Collins faced an experienced opponent in Democratic Rep. Tom Allen, with Barack Obama on the ticket. She still won by more than 22 points.

Collins got married in 2012 to Thomas Daffron, a consultant in his 70s who worked most of his career as a Senate aide. He met Collins four decades earlier when they both worked for Cohen. The marriage is a first for Collins.

Key Votes

2012	
Prohibit health insurance plans from denying coverage based on the sponsor's religious beliefs	NO
Require approval of the Keystone XL oil pipeline	YES
Ease securities rules to expand small-business access to capital	YES
Reauthorize farm and nutrition programs for five years	YES
Limit debate on a bill that would create private-sector cybersecurity standards	YES
Consent to ratification of a treaty setting global standard for the treatment of people with disabilities	YES
Provide $60.4 billion in disaster relief following Superstorm Sandy	YES
Extend most Bush-era income tax rates while allowing rates for top-bracket earners to rise (Jan. 1, 2013)	YES
2011	
Prevent EPA from regulating greenhouse gas emissions to address climate change	NO
Extend certain provisions of Patriot Act for four years	YES
Clear compromise debt limit increase plan and establish future spending limits	YES
Overhaul patent law	YES
Implement Colombia free trade agreement	NO
Limit debate on confirmation of Caitlin J. Halligan to D.C. Circuit Court of Appeals	NO
Extend payroll tax cut and unemployment benefits for two months	YES

CQ Vote Studies

	PARTY UNITY		PRESIDENTIAL SUPPORT	
	SUPPORT	OPPOSE	SUPPORT	OPPOSE
2012	39%	61%	78%	22%
2011	48%	52%	72%	28%
2010	69%	31%	69%	31%
2009	48%	52%	85%	15%
2008	46%	54%	59%	41%
2007	50%	50%	61%	39%
2006	66%	34%	79%	21%
2005	59%	41%	62%	38%
2004	78%	22%	82%	18%
2003	78%	22%	87%	13%

Interest Groups

	AFL-CIO	ADA	CCUS	ACU
2012	45%	50%	75%	20%
2011	26%	45%	82%	55%
2010	44%	40%	82%	64%
2009	61%	65%	86%	48%
2008	100%	75%	75%	20%
2007	68%	55%	64%	36%
2006	47%	45%	92%	48%
2005	64%	65%	78%	32%
2004	50%	45%	94%	68%
2003	31%	45%	78%	35%

Sen. Angus King (I)

Capitol Office
224-5344
king.senate.gov
188 Russell Bldg. 20510-1903; fax 224-1946

Committees
Armed Services
Budget
Rules & Administration
Select Intelligence

Residence
Brunswick

Born
March 31, 1944; Alexandria, Va.

Religion
Episcopalian

Family
Wife, Mary J. Herman; five children

Education
Dartmouth College, A.B. 1966 (government); U. of Virginia, J.D. 1969

Career
Management consultant; alternative energy company executive; energy conservation company owner; television program host; lawyer; congressional aide

Political Highlights
Governor, 1995-2003

ELECTION RESULTS

2012 GENERAL

Angus King (I)	370,580	52.9%
Charlie Summers (R)	215,399	30.7%
Cynthia Ann Dill (D)	92,900	13.3%
Stephen M. Woods (I)	10,289	1.5%

Elected 2012; 1st term

King represents not just Maine, but a political brand. The former governor casts himself as a true independent who is interested in repairing damaged political relationships in the Senate.

King has won three statewide elections running with no party affiliation, and he is very good at selling the concept of political independence. He has a stockpile of quotes, anecdotes and jokes that frame his stated philosophy; he does not ask the party affiliation of the hires for his office. His maiden speech on the Senate floor was a plea for cooperation, and he offered 10 examples from American history of conflicts between "traditional Democrats and a Republican party largely driven by the antifederalist sentiments of the tea party."

"There's no right answer" to the question of activist versus limited government, he said. "The tension is hard-wired into our system, but I think it helps us find balanced policy."

King caucuses with Democrats, and Republican critics have wondered if his paeans to nonpartisanship are a voter-pleasing gimmick. King has not been rattled by the speculation. "This business of party alignment — somebody said, 'Aren't you closer to the Democrats?' And I said, 'When?' If this were 1988, I'd be closer to the Republicans. But the Republican Party has changed. And so I'm sort of still where I am, where I always have been."

In the parlance of Maine, King is "from away." He was born in Alexandria, Va., in 1944. His parents were teachers, and his father (whom he is named after) went on to become a lawyer and a federal magistrate. He has described his parents as Roosevelt Democrats, and he once told the Bangor Daily News that growing up in history- and politics-rich Northern Virginia shaped his interest in government. He played football at Hammond High School, which was racially integrated his freshman year.

King went to Dartmouth College in New Hampshire, where he was involved in student government and called play-by-play for football broadcasts. The summer after graduating, he took a motorcycle tour across communist Eastern Europe. (He still rides bikes, and a centerpiece of his 2012 campaign was a 600-mile trip around the state.)

After getting a law degree at the University of Virginia, King moved to Maine with his first wife to work for a nonprofit providing legal assistance to low-income people. He worked on the 1972 Senate campaign of Democratic Rep. William D. Hathaway, who won an upset over Republican incumbent Margaret Chase Smith. He moved to Washington for a few years to work as an aide to Hathaway.

In 1975, He returned to Maine and continued practicing law. That year, he also started deepening his connections in the state by hosting public affairs programs on Maine public television — he was a TV host for 18 years. He took a job with a renewable-energy company in 1983, and in 1989 he started his own company that contracted with Central Maine Power Co. on energy-efficiency projects.

When he sold that business, he made $8 million, which helped him self-fund a good portion of his first gubernatorial campaign in 1994. He emphasized how his business experiences had moved him away from some standard Democratic positions. "I don't consider that my goals have changed at all," he told the Daily News that year. "I still want to help people in a just society. I've come to the conclusion that the best engine for that is free enterprise." He beat a Democrat and a Republican (current senator Susan Collins) with 35 percent of the vote.

In eight years, King protected a decent-sized chunk of land from development and engineered a program to provide laptop computers to middle school students. He touted his efforts to move Maine toward a more modern economy and reduce some business taxes — although the state still ranked fairly high in terms of tax burdens (and provision of social services) as he departed. A decline in state revenue tied to the stock market collapse also created a budget crisis in 2002.

King now deals with big economic questions on the Budget Committee. He supported the Democrats' fiscal 2014 budget resolution, but he has been firm in stating that almost all future deficit woes are tied to health care. He is wary of plans to "squeeze and change Medicare," and he has suggested in hearings that the government isn't using its sway as "a very big customer" to force changes in health care delivery. "We need to pay for health," he told the Portland Press Herald. "But I don't think we should pass a law. I think you do it by having employers take control of their health care costs."

Maine uses biennial budgeting, and King wouldn't mind seeing that process introduced at the federal level. He also wants the Office of Management and Budget more involved in reviewing the costs of regulations — an area where he expects to cooperate with Republicans. "My sense is that there are a lot of regulations that are outmoded and overly onerous and don't have a benefit that is close to what the cost is," he said. King has suggested that he would have voted against the 2010 financial regulatory overhaul law.

He also sits on the Armed Services and Intelligence committees, and his early lines of inquiry on those panels have made him hard to categorize. In February 2013, he proposed establishing a court for reviewing targeted killings using drones. At a meeting two months later, he was wary of arming Syrian rebels: "We only want to arm the good guys, if only we could tell for sure who they are." And he has questioned whether sanctions on countries such as Iran and North Korea actually affect the decisions of their leaders.

But he also shows some support for a robust military. He criticized plans to hold off on maintenance for weapons systems to save money. It "isn't a savings. It's simply deferring the cost to a later date," he said. He wants multiyear procurement authority for shipbuilding programs (which is important to New England shipyards) and said an East Coast missile shield might be needed.

For the most part, King is socially liberal. As governor, he unsuccessfully tried to persuade voters to defeat a referendum to repeal legal protections for gay people. (Maine voters did legalize gay marriage in 2012, however.) He backed some gun control measures in April 2013, but declined to support a proposed ban on "assault" weapons.

After leaving the governor's office, King went on a six-month RV trip with his second wife and their two kids; he wrote about his experiences in the book "Governor's Travels." In 2007, he became a founding partner of Independence Wind, an energy company that received a federal loan guarantee. He also lectured at Bowdoin College, in his current hometown of Brunswick. King is an admirer of Joshua Chamberlain, a hero of the Battle of Gettysburg who later became Bowdoin's president.

King entered the 2012 Senate race after Republican Sen. Olympia J. Snowe, a noted moderate, announced her retirement and proclaimed that she was fed up with partisan politics. He was immediately the favorite, thanks to his popularity as governor and his name recognition.

Republicans had outside hopes that King and Democratic state Sen. Cynthia Dill would compete for the same voters, allowing Maine Secretary of State Charlie Summers to claim victory with a plurality. In 2010, the presence of an independent candidate had allowed Republican Paul R. LePage to win the governor's race in that fashion. But King's appeal across the political spectrum was too strong. He won almost 53 percent of the vote.

Rep. Chellie Pingree (D)

Capitol Office
225-6116
pingree.house.gov
1318 Longworth Bldg 20515-1901; fax 225-5590

Committees
Appropriations

Residence
North Haven

Born
April 2, 1955; Minneapolis, Minn.

Religion
Lutheran

Family
Husband, Donald Sussman; three children

Education
U. of Southern Maine, attended 1973; College of the Atlantic, B.A. 1979 (human ecology)

Career
Inn owner; Common Cause president; knitting company owner; farmer

Political Highlights
North Haven Board of Assessors, 1981-87 (chairwoman, 1982-83, 1984-87); North Haven Planning Board, 1981-91; Maine School Administrative District #7 Board of Directors, 1990-93 (chairwoman, 1991-93); Maine Senate, 1992-2000 (majority leader, 1996-2000); Democratic nominee for U.S. Senate, 2002

ELECTION RESULTS

2012 GENERAL		
Chellie Pingree (D)	236,363	64.8%
Jonathan T.E. Courtney (R)	128,440	35.2%
2012 PRIMARY		
Chellie Pingree (D)		unopposed
2010 GENERAL		
Chellie Pingree (D)	169,114	56.8%
Dean Scontras (R)	128,501	43.2%

Previous Winning Percentages
2008 (55%)

Elected 2008; 3rd term

Pingree has pursued liberal causes in a variety of roles, always with the commitment of an activist — she is unafraid, she says, of getting her hands dirty "either in politics or on the farm."

She was an anti-war protester as a teenager, then participated in the 1970s back-to-the-land movement. During the 1990s, Pingree (her first name is pronounced "Shelley") gained prominence as a state legislator. She followed that work with a turn as president of the campaign watchdog Common Cause before coming to the U.S. House.

Pingree is interested in a number of issues, but when it comes to Maine, she still gets back to the land.

Originally from Minnesota, Pingree moved to a cabin on North Haven, an island in Maine's Penobscot Bay, with her high school boyfriend. She returned there after earning a degree in human ecology from the College of the Atlantic in Bar Harbor. She set up a farming operation; sheep from that endeavor helped supply materials for a knitting and yarn business. More recently, she opened an inn and restaurant supplied with locally grown vegetables.

"I'm probably one of the most engaged caucus members on this issue of local food," she says. "It just happens to be my area of interest, and it's a huge issue for my home state."

In the 113th Congress (2013-14), Pingree became a member of the Appropriations Committee and its Agriculture Subcommittee. She also sits on the Interior-Environment Subcommittee, which deals with the EPA — an agency that can profoundly affect farms and fisheries.

To get those assignments, Pingree gave up a seat on the Agriculture Committee. In the 112th Congress (2011-12) she suggested adding a "local foods" title to multi-year reauthorizations of farm and nutrition programs. In 2011, Pingree and Ohio Democratic Sen. Sherrod Brown introduced their plans to encourage the use of local foods, such as facilitating the use of Supplemental Nutrition Assistance Program benefits at farmers' markets and a pilot program to help schools buy local food. The Senate-passed 2012 farm bill (which was not enacted) included those provisions.

She sells her plans as having health benefits. "We all acknowledge that we're not eating enough healthy food," she said. "That's not a partisan issue."

Health issues have always interested Pingree. She first garnered national attention when, as the state Senate majority leader, she shepherded to passage Maine Rx, a 2000 law that allows the state to negotiate with drug companies and offer lower prices to the uninsured. She was part of the unsuccessful push to include a government-run insurance plan in the 2010 health care law, and in 2012 she feuded publicly with Republican Gov. Paul R. LePage over his proposal to balance the state budget in part with Medicaid cuts.

Pingree's voting record places her among the most liberal members of the House — she is a former vice chairwoman of the Congressional Progressive Caucus. She is still anti-war in many cases — for example, she opposed U.S. intervention in Libya in 2011. But her district contains the Portsmouth Naval Shipyard, and Bath Iron Works is one of its biggest employers. Pingree resisted Defense Secretary Robert M. Gates' 2010 calls for trimmed shipbuilding budgets, suggesting that ending the wars in Iraq and Afghanistan would be a better way to reduce costs.

Pingree has stayed involved with campaign finance issues while in Congress. She co-sponsored a 2009 bill to create a public financing system for House candidates and a 2011 resolution proposing a constitutional amendment to strip corporations of any rights the Constitution reserves for "natural persons." The latter was a response to a Supreme Court ruling that allowed super PACs — advocacy groups independent of official campaigns that can accept unrestricted donations from individuals or organizations.

Ironically, Pingree is an accomplished fundraiser. In her 2002 campaign against Republican Sen. Susan Collins, she and the Democratic Senatorial Campaign Committee established a joint fundraising committee and received several large donations from individuals. Pingree in 2011 married one of those donors, hedge fund manager Donald Sussman.

Sussman is also a major donor to a Democratic super PAC. Pingree supports that practice until the law can be changed. "I'm working as hard as I possibly can for the day when this is a fairer system of elections, but until then I respect the fact, for my husband or anyone else who chooses to donate, that this is what they have to do," she said. Pingree's daughter, former Maine House Speaker Hannah Pingree, testified before Congress about Maine's publicly financed campaign system.

Pingree is continuing her involvement with the campaign system in the 2014 cycle as a co-chairwoman of Women LEAD, a program at the Democratic Congressional Campaign Committee that recruits female candidates.

Pingree grew up in a Republican family. Her mother was a nurse and her father was an accountant. While living in North Haven, Pingree won local, nonpartisan races for tax assessor and school board. When she ran for state Senate in 1992, she didn't take long to decide she was a Democrat. Her role as owner of North Island Designs — a mail-order knitting company that sold pattern books and yarn — helped get her campaign off the ground. When she knocked on doors, women would announce, "Oh, my gosh, you're the knitting lady!" Pingree won that race and four years later became majority leader.

Term-limited at the state level, Pingree considered a 2002 gubernatorial bid, but stepped aside for the ultimately successful campaign of Democratic Rep. John Baldacci. She instead challenged Collins. Pingree raised almost as much money as Collins, but won only 42 percent of the vote.

Six-term Democrat Tom Allen decided to give up his House seat to run against Collins in 2008, and Pingree won a six-way primary for the chance to succeed him. Republicans nominated former state Sen. Charlie Summers, a Navy Reserve lieutenant commander who had deployed to Iraq during the campaign. Pingree won with 55 percent of the vote, and she improved on that performance in each of her re-elections.

Sussman bought a 5 percent equity stake in Maine's largest newspaper company in 2012, raising questions about how the newspapers would cover his wife. "I think it's safe to say that the newspaper used to criticize me for things in the past, and it still does," Pingree said.

Key Votes

2012	
Extend a Social Security payroll tax cut and unemployment benefits	NO
Ease securities rules to expand small-business access to capital	NO
Extend for one year subsidized student loan interest rates financed by a cut in health care spending	NO
Cite Attorney General Eric H. Holder Jr. for contempt of Congress	?
Create a visa program for foreign graduates in high-tech fields	NO
Extend most Bush-era income tax rates while allowing rates for top-bracket earners to rise (Jan. 1, 2013)	YES
2011	
Strike funding for F-35 alternative engine	YES
Prevent EPA from regulating greenhouse gas emissions to address climate change	NO
Extend certain provisions of Patriot Act for four years	NO
Declare opposition to use of ground troops in Libya	YES
Overhaul patent law	NO
Pass compromise debt limit increase plan and establish future spending limits	NO
Allow consideration of measures to implement three trade agreements	NO

CQ Vote Studies

	PARTY UNITY		PRESIDENTIAL SUPPORT	
	SUPPORT	OPPOSE	SUPPORT	OPPOSE
2012	99%	1%	86%	14%
2011	96%	4%	78%	22%
2010	99%	1%	83%	17%
2009	99%	1%	90%	10%

Interest Groups

	AFL-CIO	ADA	CCUS	ACU
2012	100%	95%	17%	0%
2011	100%	85%	19%	8%
2010	100%	100%	13%	0%
2009	100%	100%	33%	0%

Maine 1

South — Portland, Augusta

Taking in picturesque college towns, oceanfront villages and the capital, the 1st represents the Pine Tree State's southern tip. The district is dominated by the Portland area, which contains roughly one-third of Maine's population and accounts for nearly half of its economy. More plugged in to the rest of New England, communities in the 1st differ from the more rural portions of the state.

The district plays up Maine's rustic and salty charms as it grabs the lion's share of the state's multibillion-dollar tourism industry. Portland touts its culinary culture, particularly local seafood, and is well known as a haven for outdoor enthusiasts. A huge hunting boot greets shoppers at L.L. Bean's flagship store in Freeport. The beaches of York County draw New Englander and Canadian day trippers and those looking for secluded getaways.

While the 1st's lobster fleets draw the gourmands, heavy-duty seafaring remains a vital component of the district's economy. The Portsmouth Naval Shipyard, just across the border from New Hampshire, maintains nuclear submarines. Bath Iron Works, now owned by General Dynamics, has built destroyers for the Navy since the early 20th century, and Portland's commercial port is the largest in New England. The former Brunswick Naval Air Station used to provide more military and contractor jobs, but now awaits plans for redevelopment.

Although the 1st is more solidly Democratic than Maine's other district, it shares the ornery streak that runs through the state's political culture, and independents slightly outnumber registered Democrats. Electoral results out of the 1st also illustrate Mainers' peculiar disinclination to adhere to party slates: In 2012, Barack Obama won every county in the district, as did independent Angus King as he swept the U.S. Senate race.

Major Industry
Military shipbuilding, tourism, financial services, retail

Military Bases
Portsmouth Naval Shipyard, 100 military, 4,700 civilian

Cities
Portland, South Portland, Biddeford, Augusta

Notable
Poet Henry Wadsworth Longfellow was born in Portland and taught at his alma mater, Bowdoin College in Brunswick.

Rep. Michael H. Michaud (D)

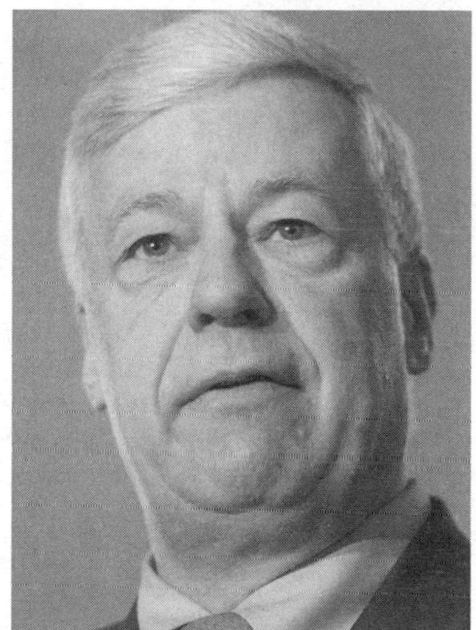

Capitol Office
225-6306
michaud.house.gov
1724 Longworth Bldg. 20515-1902; fax 225-2943

Committees
Transportation & Infrastructure
Veterans' Affairs - Ranking Member

Residence
East Millinocket

Born
Jan. 18, 1955; Millinocket, Maine

Religion
Roman Catholic

Family
Single

Education
Schenck H.S., graduated 1973

Career
Paper mill worker

Political Highlights
Maine House, 1981-94; Maine Senate, 1995-2002 (president, 2001)

ELECTION RESULTS

2012 GENERAL

Michael H. Michaud (D)	191,456	58.2%
Kevin L. Raye (R)	137,542	41.8%

2012 PRIMARY

Michael H. Michaud (D)	unopposed

2010 GENERAL

Michael H. Michaud (D)	147,042	55.1%
Jason J. Levesque (R)	119,669	44.9%

Previous Winning Percentages
2008 (67%); 2006 (71%); 2004 (58%); 2002 (52%)

Elected 2002; 6th term

Michaud, a former mill employee, sides with the blue-collar workers he used to call colleagues. He is also heavily involved in helping another large Maine constituency as the top Democrat on the Veterans' Affairs Committee.

Michaud (ME-shoo) grew up in Medway, close to the Great Northern Paper Co. mill. Like his father and grandfather, he went to work at the mill after high school. He never went to college and still remains affiliated with what is now United Steelworkers Local 4-00037.

During his 29 years at the mill he also built a political career. Elected to the state House in 1980, he took advantage of a clause in his union contract that allowed workers to keep their jobs while serving in the legislature. (Maine doesn't have a full-time legislature, but service can require long absences from other jobs.)

After seven terms, he was elected to the Maine Senate in 1994. Two years later, he became chairman of its Appropriations Committee, and in 2000 he was elected state Senate president. His campaigns have always benefited from the electoral and financial support of organized labor.

In Washington, he works to promote economic development in his district, taking aim at trade deals. He says they have hurt manufacturers such as his former employer. Three days after he was sworn in to the U.S. House in 2003, Great Northern filed for bankruptcy and closed the mill where he had worked. Michaud blamed the North American Free Trade Agreement for putting U.S. manufacturers "at a competitive disadvantage."

Michaud in the 110th Congress (2007-08) co-founded the House Trade Working Group, an informal collection of lawmakers dubious of international trade agreements. He routinely votes against such pacts. In 2011, he opposed pacts with Korea, Panama and especially Colombia, which Michaud said ignores human rights and labor rights violations. President Barack Obama supported the agreements, a stance Michaud chalked up to giving in "to the Washington elites, once again."

When in the House majority, Michaud introduced legislation that would radically alter current and future U.S. trade deals. His bill called for a review and renegotiation of major trade agreements, including NAFTA, and would have established labor, environmental, food and product safety standards that he says should be a part of all U.S. trade pacts.

In the GOP-controlled 112th Congress (2011-12), he set his sights lower. As negotiations continued on the Trans-Pacific Partnership, a multilateral agreement for the Asia-Pacific region, Michaud teamed with shoemaker New Balance to lobby against using the TPP to eliminate tariffs — doing so would threaten American workers, including 900 who work in the company's three plants in his district, he said. Michaud has strongly urged enforcement actions against China for what he calls unfair trade practices.

His ascent to the top of the Veterans' Affairs Committee at the start of the 113th Congress (2013-14) followed six years as the top Democrat on its Health Subcommittee. His bill to increase reimbursement rates for veterans homes that treat the severely disabled and elderly was included in a 2012 package of veterans bills signed into law. Like Chairman Jeff Miller of Florida, Michaud has identified the benefit claims backlog at the Department of Veterans Affairs as one of his biggest concerns.

He helped pass legislation in 2009 that allows the VA to receive appropriations for medical care a year in advance, thereby avoiding shortfalls when Congress does not pass appropriations bills before the start of the fiscal year. In 2013, Michaud and Miller proposed extending that arrangement to the rest of the VA budget — among other things, it would allow for smoother technology upgrades that could speed the processing of benefit claims, they said.

Michaud also sits on the Transportation and Infrastructure Committee, and he secured a modest increase is Maine's highway funding in a two-year reauthorization of surface transportation programs enacted in 2012. He was also able to include provisions promoting research in University of Maine-developed bridge repair technology.

Michaud is the only New Englander affiliated with the fiscally conservative Blue Dog Coalition, and during the 112th Congress he often voted for cost-cutting spending bills opposed by more-liberal members.

Which isn't to say he's a standard moderate. Michaud's qualms with the 2010 health care law reflected those of liberal critics — he wanted inclusion of a government-run "public option" insurance plan. But he also backed an amendment to the overhaul that would have ensured that no federal funds were used to pay for abortion coverage. In the end, he supported the final version of the measure, which did not include either the abortion or public option provisions.

He also opposes many military interventions. Michaud was against the Iraq War, and he also opposed Obama's 2009 decision to increase troop levels in Afghanistan. He was one of 26 House Democrats to vote against the fiscal 2011 defense policy bill, which authorized more than $159 billion for the Iraq and Afghanistan wars; in June 2011 he was one of 36 Democrats to support a bill to prohibit Pentagon spending on the NATO mission in Libya.

Michaud says he decided to run for the state House because he was concerned about pollution in the Penobscot River — a lot of it caused by the mill where he worked. He chaired the Environment Committee and wrote bills to clean up the river. Sometimes he would put in a long day in Augusta, the state capital, then hurry home to work a midnight shift. He eventually took a leave of absence from the mill after he was elected Senate president.

In the 2002 race for the seat of Democratic Rep. John Baldacci, who was running for governor, support from organized labor helped Michaud eke out a narrow victory over Republican Kevin L. Raye, former chief of staff for GOP Sen. Olympia J. Snowe. Michaud won his next three terms by wide margins.

As Baldacci neared the end of his second term, there was speculation that Michaud would again follow in his footsteps. But Michaud demurred and was re-elected in 2010 with 55 percent of the vote. Snowe announced her retirement in 2012, and Michaud toyed with the idea of running to succeed her. But he backed off again and won a sixth term in the House.

Michaud is reportedly giving serious consideration to a 2014 gubernatorial campaign, which would likely pit him against GOP incumbent Paul R. LePage.

Key Votes

2012	
Extend a Social Security payroll tax cut and unemployment benefits	YES
Ease securities rules to expand small-business access to capital	YES
Extend for one year subsidized student loan interest rates financed by a cut in health care spending	NO
Cite Attorney General Eric H. Holder Jr. for contempt of Congress	NO
Create a visa program for foreign graduates in high-tech fields	YES
Extend most Bush-era income tax rates while allowing rates for top-bracket earners to rise (Jan. 1, 2013)	YES
2011	
Strike funding for F-35 alternative engine	YES
Prevent EPA from regulating greenhouse gas emissions to address climate change	NO
Extend certain provisions of Patriot Act for four years	NO
Declare opposition to use of ground troops in Libya	YES
Overhaul patent law	YES
Pass compromise debt limit increase plan and establish future spending limits	YES
Allow consideration of measures to implement three trade agreements	NO

CQ Vote Studies

	PARTY UNITY		PRESIDENTIAL SUPPORT	
	SUPPORT	OPPOSE	SUPPORT	OPPOSE
2012	91%	9%	83%	17%
2011	87%	13%	75%	25%
2010	91%	9%	88%	12%
2009	92%	8%	92%	8%
2008	94%	6%	13%	87%

Interest Groups

	AFL-CIO	ADA	CCUS	ACU
2012	95%	85%	33%	8%
2011	100%	90%	25%	4%
2010	93%	90%	13%	0%
2009	100%	90%	40%	8%
2008	100%	90%	50%	12%

Maine 2

North — Lewiston, Bangor, Presque Isle

Millions of acres of trees surround the small towns of northern Maine's 2nd. The largest district in a state east of the Mississippi River, the 2nd attracts millions of visitors "from away" — local lingo for out of state — to Acadia National Park, Baxter State Park and the many lakes and ski slopes. The 2nd runs along the state's entire border with Canada.

Maine's North Woods, a 16,000-square-mile area, is the backbone of the state's multibillion-dollar forestry industry. Free-trade agreements and increased global competition, however, have shuttered many paper and lumber mills. A recent trade pact with Canada and recovery in the domestic-construction sector offer glimmers of hope for the industry.

The more rural of Maine's districts, the 2nd does not have a diversified economy. Timber reigns inland, lobstering dominates the coast and agricultural production includes potatoes and blueberries. Small towns long relied on paper mill jobs, some of which are returning, and textile factory jobs. New Balance operates three shoe factories in the 2nd.

Lacking a major city, the district derives its political slant from the concerns of hundreds of small towns that traditionally have enjoyed considerable autonomy from the capital. Its far-flung communities' geographic and cultural isolation from southern Maine reinforces a political culture defined by local control and voter independence. Although voters here are more conservative on such issues as gun rights and abortion than those in the Portland area, elections typically hinge on perceptions of candidates' capabilities and personal connection to their communities, not partisan ideology.

In contrast to the state's demographics — the second-highest percentage of white residents of any nationwide — Lewiston is recently home to thousands of immigrants from Somalia, Sudan and the Congo. The former mill town is the 2nd's largest population center at less than 40,000 residents.

Major Industry
Logging, agriculture, fishing, tourism

Cities
Lewiston, Bangor, Auburn

Notable
Margaret Chase Smith, who represented the district from 1940 to 1949, was the first woman elected to both the U.S. House and Senate; established in 1919, Acadia National Park was the first national park east of the Mississippi River.

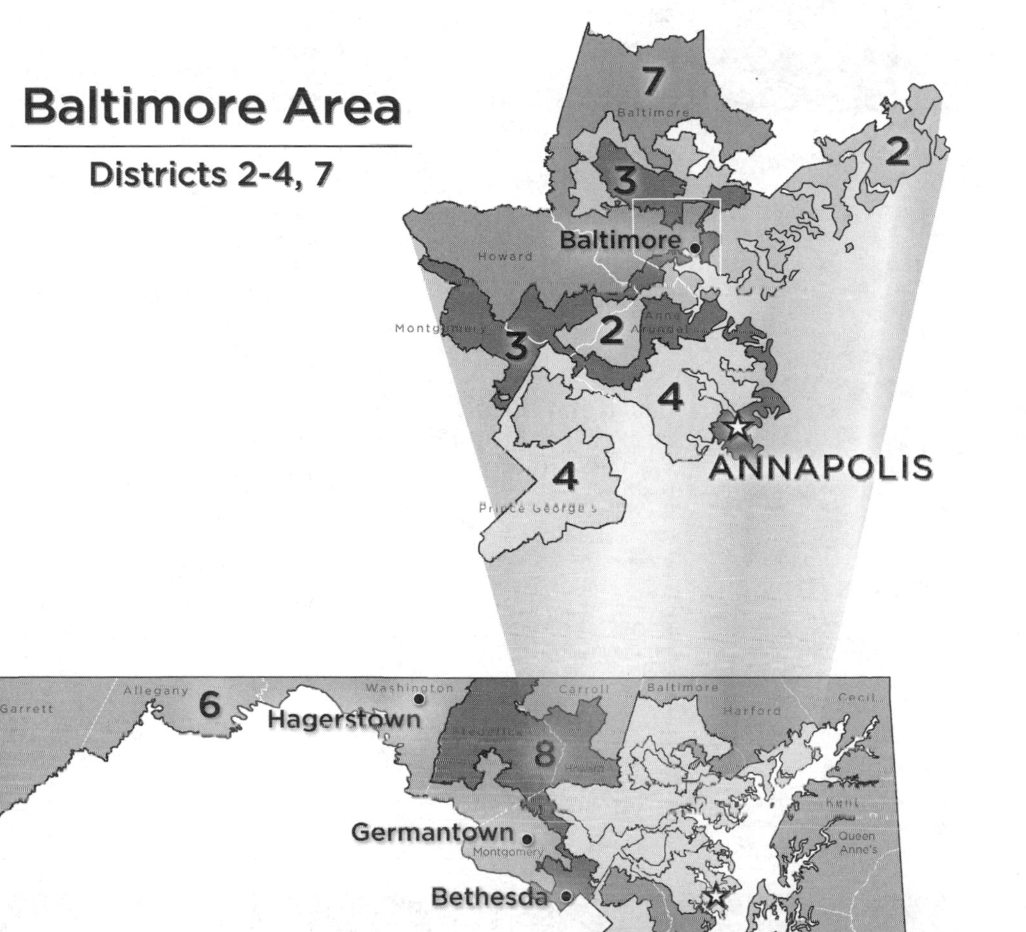
Baltimore Area
Districts 2-4, 7
7
Baltimore
2
3
Baltimore
Howard
Montgomery
3
2
Anne Arundel
4
ANNAPOLIS
4
Prince George's
Garrett
Allegany
6
Hagerstown
Washington
Carroll
Baltimore
Harford
Cecil
8
Howard
Kent
Germantown
Montgomery
Queen Anne's
Bethesda
Anne Arundel
Talbot
Caroline
Prince George's
Calvert
Charles
5
1
Dorchester
St. Marys
Wicomico
Salisbury
Worcester
Somerset
Chesapeake Bay

Gov. Martin O'Malley (D)

First elected: 2006
Length of term: 4 years
Term expires: 1/15
Salary: $150,000
Phone: (410) 974-3901
Residence: Baltimore
Born: Jan. 18, 1963; Washington, D.C.
Religion: Roman Catholic
Family: Wife, Catherine Curran O'Malley; four children
Education: Catholic U., B.A. 1985 (political science); U. of Maryland, Baltimore, J.D. 1988
Career: Lawyer; city prosecutor; campaign aide
Political highlights: Democratic nominee for Md. Senate, 1990; Baltimore City Council, 1991-99; mayor of Baltimore, 1999-2007

ELECTION RESULTS

2010 GENERAL

Martin O'Malley (D)	1,044,961	56.2%
Robert Ehrlich (R)	776,319	41.8%

Lt. Gov. Anthony G. Brown (D)

First elected: 2006
Length of term: 4 years
Term expires: 1/15
Salary: $125,000
Phone: (410) 974-2804

LEGISLATURE

General Assembly: 90 days January-April
Senate: 47 members, 4-year terms
2013 ratios: 35 D, 12 R; 36 men, 11 women
Salary: $43,500
Phone: (410) 841-3700
House: 141 members, 4-year terms
2013 ratios: 98 D, 43 R; 95 men; 46 women
Salary: $43,500
Phone: (800) 492-7122

TERM LIMITS

Governor: 2 consecutive terms
Senate: No
House: No

URBAN STATISTICS

CITY	POPULATION
Baltimore	620,961
Frederick	65,239
Rockville	61,209
Gaithersburg	59,933
Bowie	54,727

REGISTERED VOTERS

Democrat	56%
Republican	26%
Other	18%

POPULATION

2010 population	5,773,552
2000 population	5,296,486
1990 population	4,781,468
Percent change (2000-2010)	+9.0%
Rank among states (2010)	19
Median age	37.3
Born in state	48.0%
Foreign born	12.0%
Violent crime rate	590/100,000
Poverty level	9.1%
Federal workers	280,658
Military	29,160

ELECTIONS

STATE ELECTION OFFICIAL
(410) 269-2840
DEMOCRATIC PARTY
(410) 269-8818
REPUBLICAN PARTY
(410) 263-2125

MISCELLANEOUS

Web: www.maryland.gov
Capital: Annapolis

U.S. CONGRESS

Senate: 2 Democrats
House: 7 Democrats, 1 Republican

STATISTICS BY DISTRICT

	2012 Vote for President		2008 Vote for President										
District	Obama	Romney	Obama	McCain	Black	Asian	Hispanic	Median Income	Over 64	Under 20	College Education	Rural	Sq. Miles
1	39%	59%	39%	60%	12%	2%	3%	$64,151	16%	26%	29%	39%	3,977
2	62	36	61	38	32	5	7	58,345	12	25	28	1	349
3	61	37	61	38	21	8	7	73,053	13	24	45	1	304
4	78	21	77	22	54	3	16	71,135	10	27	32	1	298
5	67	32	66	33	37	4	6	87,457	11	28	32	23	1,481
6	56	42	57	42	14	11	11	68,361	12	26	40	18	1,950
7	75	23	76	23	55	5	3	51,018	13	27	36	7	488
8	62	36	63	36	12	8	14	90,959	14	25	53	11	860
STATE	**62**	**36**	**62**	**37**	**29**	**6**	**8**	**70,004**	**13**	**26**	**36**	**13**	**9,707**
U.S.	**51**	**47**	**53**	**46**	**12**	**5**	**17**	**50,052**	**13**	**27**	**29**	**21**	**3,531,905**

Sen. Barbara A. Mikulski (D)

Capitol Office
224-4654
mikulski.senate.gov
503 Hart Bldg. 20510-2003; fax 224-8858

Committees
Appropriations - Chairwoman
(Commerce-Justice-Science - Chairwoman)
Health, Education, Labor & Pensions
Select Intelligence

Residence
Baltimore

Born
July 20, 1936; Baltimore, Md.

Religion
Roman Catholic

Family
Single

Education
Mount Saint Agnes College, B.A. 1958 (sociology); U. of Maryland, M.S.W. 1965

Career
Social worker

Political Highlights
Baltimore City Council, 1971-77; Democratic nominee for U.S. Senate, 1974; U.S. House, 1977-87

ELECTION RESULTS

2010 GENERAL		
Barbara A. Mikulski (D)	1,140,531	62.2%
Eric Wargotz (R)	655,666	35.8%
Kenniss Henry (GREEN)	20,717	1.1%

2010 PRIMARY		
Barbara A. Mikulski (D)	396,252	82.3%
Christopher J. Garner (D)	36,194	7.5%
Anthony "Billy Bob" Jaworski (D)	15,335	3.2%
Blaine Taylor (D)	11,049	2.3%
Theresa C. Scaldaferri (D)	8,092	1.7%
Sanquetta Taylor (D)	7,684	1.6%
Lih Young (D)	6,911	1.4%

Previous Winning Percentages
2004 (65%); 1998 (71%); 1992 (71%); 1986 (61%); 1984 House Election (68%); 1982 House Election (74%); 1980 House Election (76%); 1978 House Election (100%); 1976 House Election (75%)

Elected 1986; 5th term

Mikulski fiercely defends her belief that government should be an engine of social justice, whether it drives access to health care or strengthens national security. The longest-serving woman in congressional history, she does not shy from a fight.

"I feel that I am my brother's keeper and my sister's keeper," says Mikulski, a Roman Catholic. "I think that's why I am shaped by the words of Jesus himself: 'Love thy neighbor.' And I took it seriously."

She relishes her role as dean of the Senate women and owns many historic distinctions: first woman elevated to a leadership post in the Senate; first female Democrat to serve in both chambers; only current member of Congress in the National Women's Hall of Fame; and one of the first women to wear pants on the Senate floor. In March 2012 she surpassed Republican Rep. Edith Nourse Rogers of Massachusetts for the title of longest-serving woman. Appropriations Chairman Daniel K. Inouye died in December 2012, and Mikulski succeeded him to become the first woman in either chamber to lead a full spending panel.

Mikulski offers new women in Congress introductory seminars and dispenses advice on everything from organizing offices to setting long-range goals. "The political bosses would still have me making pierogies in the basement of the church," she said, referring to her roots in Baltimore politics.

In addition to serving as Appropriations chairwoman, Mikulski continues to lead the panel's subcommittee overseeing the Commerce and Justice departments, as well as space and science programs. Mikulski loved science as a girl, idolizing Nobel winner Marie Skłodowska-Curie, and she looks to protect the research assets in her home state.

That includes NASA. The Obama administration drew her ire with its 2010 decision to end the moon-bound Constellation program and favor a plan to work with the private sector to ferry astronauts into space. In April 2012, her support of space research was recognized: The Space Telescope Science Institute in Baltimore dubbed an exploding star "Supernova Mikulski." (Some people might see it as a comment on Mikulski's personality — in Washingtonian magazine's surveys of congressional aides, she has won the title of "meanest senator" several times.)

In another technology niche, Mikulski wants to make Maryland the "global epicenter of cybersecurity." The National Security Agency, the eavesdropping arm of the spy community, has its headquarters in her state; so, too, does the National Institute of Standards and Technology and its cybersecurity center. Mikulski has a seat on the Intelligence Committee.

She was one of 19 Democrats to side with a majority of Republicans in clearing a 2008 measure updating laws regarding warrantless surveillance. Mikulski said the revisions to the Foreign Intelligence Surveillance Act would help law enforcement officials keep up with increasingly sophisticated terrorists. "Terrorists remain on the hunt for U.S. vulnerabilities, using disposable phone cards, laptop computers and hundreds of different email addresses, all in efforts to evade detection by our intelligence professionals," Mikulski said. The older version of the FISA law "made it nearly impossible for the U.S. to engage in 'techno-hot-pursuit' of terrorists overseas." She supported a 2011 extension of surveillance provisions in the anti-terrorism law known as the Patriot Act and a 2012 extension of FISA.

Mikulski has sought other ways to give Maryland a leg up. When Florida's Republican governor said in early 2011 that he didn't want federal funds for a high-speed rail project in his state, Mikulski was one of 10 senators who asked the Transportation Department to redirect the money to Maryland and other states in the Northeast Corridor. An ally of organized labor, she put language in a fiscal 2012 spending law to delay a Labor Department requirement to increase the hourly wages of certain temporary foreign workers; it could have harmed those picking crab meat and shucking oysters in Maryland.

A social worker by trade, Mikulski resists spending cuts that would lessen assistance from entitlement programs. She blasted the fiscal 2014 budget adopted by House Republicans, calling it "unkind" to women and children and criticizing its proposed changes to Medicare. "I cannot believe that we're going to replace Medicare with a voucher and a promise," she said on the Senate floor.

Mikulski is similarly skeptical of deficit reduction proposals that might reduce Social Security benefits. "Social Security did not cause our debt," she said. "It did not cause our deficit."

Mikulski is the No. 2 Democrat on the Health, Education, Labor and Pensions Committee. She is an outspoken advocate of improving health care for women and children. She won a battle in 2009 to bar insurers from charging copayments for many preventive services for women. "We organized the women of the Senate. We suited up in our pink jackets. The good men joined us," Mikulski said after her win.

She was a sharp critic of a defeated 2012 proposal by Missouri Republican Roy Blunt that would have allowed employers or religious groups with a moral or religious objection to a medical service, such as contraception or abortion, to opt out of the requirement to provide insurance that covers it. She called it "politics masquerading as morality."

Mikulski's father suffered from Alzheimer's disease, and she wants to see more research for chronic diseases and a speeding up of drug development.

She served for a decade as caucus secretary, the No. 3 Democratic leadership post, before stepping down in 2004 to give another woman, Michigan's Debbie Stabenow, a boost onto the leadership ladder.

Mikulski's roots are in working-class east Baltimore. Her parents ran a grocery store called Willy's Market, across the street from their row house. The store opened early every morning so steelworkers could buy lunch before their morning shift. Nearby, her Polish immigrant grandmother operated a bakery legendary for its jelly doughnuts and raisin bread. (Mikulski herself is known for her crab cake recipe.) She's the Senate sponsor of a bill to extend a visa waiver program to Poland.

She earned a master's degree in social work at the University of Maryland in 1965. When parts of her neighborhood were set ablaze after the 1968 assassination of Martin Luther King Jr., Mikulski delivered food to families, sometimes by riding atop a tank.

In the early 1970s, she jumped into a neighborhood battle to stop a highway project that would have leveled some Baltimore neighborhoods. At one point, she recalls, she jumped on a table and gave a fiery speech, saying, "The British couldn't take Fells Point, the termites couldn't take Fells Point and goddamn if we'll let the State Roads Commission take Fells Point!" to wild cheers from her audience. The battle against the highway project was successful, and Mikulski went on to win a city council seat in 1971.

She seized on the public backlash against Republicans in the post-Watergate election of 1974 by challenging Sen. Charles McC. Mathias Jr. She lost, but two years later Democrat Paul S. Sarbanes gave up his seat as Baltimore's representative in the House to run for the Senate.

Mikulski won the race to succeed him and went on to serve five terms in the House, becoming a champion of consumer causes. When Mathias retired in 1986, Mikulski won the race to succeed him, besting Republican Linda Chavez by 22 points. She has not been seriously challenged since.

Key Votes

2012	
Prohibit health insurance plans from denying coverage based on the sponsor's religious beliefs	YES
Require approval of the Keystone XL oil pipeline	NO
Ease securities rules to expand small-business access to capital	NO
Reauthorize farm and nutrition programs for five years	YES
Limit debate on a bill that would create private-sector cybersecurity standards	YES
Consent to ratification of a treaty setting global standard for the treatment of people with disabilities	YES
Provide $60.4 billion in disaster relief following Superstorm Sandy	YES
Extend most Bush-era income tax rates while allowing rates for top-bracket earners to rise (Jan. 1, 2013)	YES
2011	
Prevent EPA from regulating greenhouse gas emissions to address climate change	NO
Extend certain provisions of Patriot Act for four years	YES
Clear compromise debt limit increase plan and establish future spending limits	YES
Overhaul patent law	YES
Implement Colombia free trade agreement	NO
Limit debate on confirmation of Caitlin J. Halligan to D.C. Circuit Court of Appeals	YES
Extend payroll tax cut and unemployment benefits for two months	YES

CQ Vote Studies

	PARTY UNITY		PRESIDENTIAL SUPPORT	
	SUPPORT	OPPOSE	SUPPORT	OPPOSE
2012	95%	5%	95%	5%
2011	97%	3%	97%	3%
2010	99%	1%	98%	2%
2009	99%	1%	99%	1%
2008	88%	12%	42%	58%
2007	94%	6%	42%	58%
2006	96%	4%	49%	51%
2005	98%	2%	35%	65%
2004	96%	4%	61%	39%
2003	97%	3%	44%	56%

Interest Groups

	AFL-CIO	ADA	CCUS	ACU
2012	100%	95%	38%	0%
2011	95%	95%	45%	0%
2010	100%	90%	27%	0%
2009	94%	95%	43%	0%
2008	100%	90%	63%	0%
2007	94%	85%	55%	0%
2006	93%	100%	42%	0%
2005	100%	90%	41%	5%
2004	100%	100%	56%	8%
2003	100%	90%	39%	15%

Sen. Benjamin L. Cardin (D)

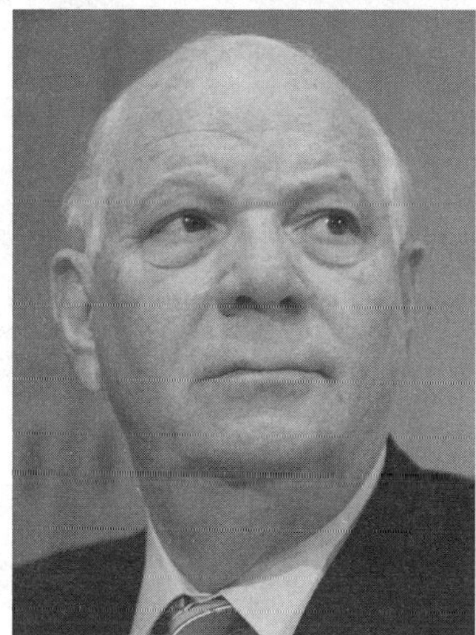

Capitol Office
224-4524
cardin.senate.gov
509 Hart Bldg. 20510-2002; fax 224-1651

Committees
Environment & Public Works
(Water & Wildlife - Chairman)
Finance
Foreign Relations
(East Asian & Pacific Affairs - Chairman)
Small Business & Entrepreneurship

Residence
Baltimore

Born
Oct. 5, 1943; Baltimore, Md.

Religion
Jewish

Family
Wife, Myrna Edelman Cardin; two children (one deceased)

Education
U. of Pittsburgh, B.A. 1964 (economics); U. of Maryland, Baltimore, LL.B. 1967

Career
Lawyer

Political Highlights
Md. House, 1967-87 (speaker, 1979-87); U.S. House, 1987-2007

ELECTION RESULTS

2012 GENERAL

Benjamin L. Cardin (D)	1,474,028	56.0%
Daniel John Bongino (R)	693,291	26.3%
S. Rob Sobhani (UNA)	430,934	16.4%
Dean Ahmad (LIBERT)	32,252	1.2%
	3,313	1.0%

Previous Winning Percentages
2006 (54%); 2004 House Election (63%); 2002 House Election (66%); 2000 House Election (76%); 1998 House Election (78%); 1996 House Election (67%); 1994 House Election (71%); 1992 House Election (74%); 1990 House Election (70%); 1988 House Election (73%); 1986 House Election (79%)

Elected 2006; 2nd term

Cardin is repeating patterns he established during 20 years in state government and 20 years in the U.S. House. As colleagues come to appreciate his work ethic, nice-guy persona and dedication to the legislative process, he puts his liberal stamp on more and more policy.

Aides have described Cardin, a Baltimore native who speaks with the city's accent, as obsessed with legislating. One of his political heroes is President John F. Kennedy; another is Theodore R. McKeldin, a GOP mayor of Baltimore and Maryland governor who was among the first politicians to court the state's Jewish voters. And a third is his father—the son of Russian Jewish immigrants, Meyer Cardin served as a Baltimore judge.

The younger Cardin entered the Maryland House of Delegates at age 23, before he graduated from the University of Maryland's law school. He was elected to a seat that had been held by his father and his uncle, and he became the youngest House speaker in Maryland in 100 years. In 1986, he won a Baltimore-area seat in the U.S. House.

His talents were paying dividends by the early 1990s. Cardin nabbed a seat on the Ways and Means Committee, where he often focused on pension and retirement issues. Democrats trusted him to lead their transition team when the party shifted to the minority after 1994. And he was the lead Democrat investigating ethics charges against Speaker Newt Gingrich in 1996.

But he relished the chance to jump to the Senate in 2006. His current home "gives me the opportunity to play a meaningful role in many more issues than I could in the House," he told Washington Jewish Week in 2012.

Cardin has a seat on the Foreign Relations Committee, which complements his role as chairman of the Commission on Security and Cooperation in Europe (aka the Helsinki Commission). Already a prominent voice on trade —Baltimore has a large port, and Cardin also sits on the Finance Committee, which handles the issue—in the 112th Congress (2011-12) he stepped up his attempts to tie human rights protections to trade agreements.

Cardin drew attention to the case of Sergei Magnitsky, a lawyer who died in Russian police custody after exposing a case of expansive tax fraud. Russia joined the World Trade Organization in 2012, and when Congress cleared a bill "normalizing" trade relations with that nation, it included Cardin's provision to freeze assets and block visas of Russians who commit human rights violations. Cardin's original bill wasn't limited to Russia, but he eventually supported the narrower version, saying it "sets a precedent for future trade and other bilateral agreements."

For the 113th Congress (2013-14), Cardin took the gavel of the Subcommittee on East Asian and Pacific Affairs. His expertise in foreign affairs still rests with Europe, but the Pacific is where the action is—for example, negotiations are under way on the Trans-Pacific Partnership. At a March 2013 hearing of the Finance Committee, Cardin urged trade officials to be "bolder" in pressing environmental and labor standards as they work on that pact.

Cardin promotes the use of foreign assistance as a way to improve the United States' international standing. Examining aid to Afghanistan at a 2011 hearing, he said that "when done correctly, foreign assistance can fundamentally change countries for the better and is a vital tool in our national security toolbox. When misspent, it fuels corruption, distorts markets, undermines the host government's ability to exert control over resources and contributes to insecurity and instability."

On the Environment and Public Works Committee, Cardin chairs the Water and Wildlife panel. He frequently pursues grants and protections for the

Chesapeake Bay, but his work on the panel reflects broader environmental concerns. The Senate Agriculture Committee approved a 2011 bill to stop the EPA from using the Clean Water Act to require permits for various pesticides regulated under another law. Cardin put a hold on the bill, saying it needed further consideration; it never saw floor action.

Cardin, a charter member of the Oceans Caucus, opposes energy exploration off Maryland's coast. He likes tax credits for the production of "clean" energy, but wants to eliminate tax provisions favoring fossil fuels. During debate on climate change legislation in the 110th Congress (2007-08), he successfully appended $171 million for public transportation projects, including new rail transit systems. His intent was to curb greenhouse gas emissions from automobiles and provide relief to the car-choked Baltimore-Washington suburbs. The bill was pulled from the floor before a final vote.

Given Maryland's proximity to the nation's capital, Cardin is very involved with debates on the federal workforce and contracting. On the Small Business and Entrepreneurship Committee, he has tried to permanently increase the size of "surety bonds" that the Small Business Administration can help companies obtain — bigger bonds allow the companies to pursue larger federal contracts.

Cardin wants to stop lawmakers from finding budgetary savings in the compensation of federal workers. A 2012 extension of lower payroll taxes and expanded unemployment benefits was paid for in part by requiring federal workers to contribute more to their pension plans. Cardin and Democratic Rep. Chris Van Hollen of Maryland were on the conference committee and tried to block the change altogether; they eventually let the bill proceed after securing a "grandfather" clause to exempt current workers.

His seat on the Finance Committee could put him in the middle of major fiscal talks in the 113th Congress (2013-14). He has been open to negotiations in the past. As a member of the Ways and Means Committee, he developed a close relationship with Ohio Republican Rob Portman, who later became George W. Bush's budget director — and now is Cardin's Senate colleague. In the 108th Congress (2003-04), the two men developed an alternative to Bush's plan to restructure Social Security and allow younger workers to divert a share of their payroll taxes into personal retirement accounts. Cardin had proposed adding an investment component to the program as early as the Clinton administration.

Cardin was a vocal supporter of including a government-run insurance program in the health care overhaul enacted in 2010. He lost that fight, but he won inclusion of funding for oral health care and an amendment establishing the National Institute on Minority Health and Health Disparities.

Cardin was in his 10th term in the House when Democratic Sen. Paul S. Sarbanes announced his retirement. Hoping to succeed him, Cardin ran in a 2006 primary that included more than a dozen candidates. His chief competition was former Democratic Rep. Kweisi Mfume, a past NAACP president and longtime friend. Cardin won, 44 percent to 41 percent.

In the general election, he was up against another tough competitor — Lt. Gov. Michael S. Steele, Maryland's first black statewide elected official. The Republican tailored his TV and radio ads to black voters and brought in endorsements from several prominent black Democrats. But Cardin succeeded in tying Steele to Bush and won with 54 percent of the vote. In 2012 he easily defeated former Secret Service agent Daniel John Bongino.

Cardin's family is close-knit and shares his interests — Myrna, his wife of more than 40 years, is among his most trusted advisers. The couple endured tragedy in 1998 when their son Michael, 30, who worked as a volunteer with low-income Baltimoreans, committed suicide. "I look at what he was able to accomplish in a few years as a challenge to all of us to make the most of what we have," Cardin said.

Key Votes

2012	
Prohibit health insurance plans from denying coverage based on the sponsor's religious beliefs	YES
Require approval of the Keystone XL oil pipeline	NO
Ease securities rules to expand small-business access to capital	NO
Reauthorize farm and nutrition programs for five years	YES
Limit debate on a bill that would create private-sector cybersecurity standards	YES
Consent to ratification of a treaty setting global standard for the treatment of people with disabilities	YES
Provide $60.4 billion in disaster relief following Superstorm Sandy	YES
Extend most Bush-era income tax rates while allowing rates for top-bracket earners to rise (Jan. 1, 2013)	YES
2011	
Prevent EPA from regulating greenhouse gas emissions to address climate change	NO
Extend certain provisions of Patriot Act for four years	YES
Clear compromise debt limit increase plan and establish future spending limits	YES
Overhaul patent law	YES
Implement Colombia free trade agreement	NO
Limit debate on confirmation of Caitlin J. Halligan to D.C. Circuit Court of Appeals	YES
Extend payroll tax cut and unemployment benefits for two months	YES

CQ Vote Studies

	PARTY UNITY		PRESIDENTIAL SUPPORT	
	SUPPORT	OPPOSE	SUPPORT	OPPOSE
2012	99%	1%	96%	4%
2011	100%	0%	97%	3%
2010	99%	1%	98%	2%
2009	99%	1%	99%	1%
2008	97%	3%	31%	69%
2007	97%	3%	37%	63%
2006	95%	5%	25%	75%
2005	95%	5%	22%	78%
2004	94%	6%	35%	65%
2003	93%	7%	24%	76%

Interest Groups

	AFL-CIO	ADA	CCUS	ACU
2012	100%	95%	38%	0%
2011	95%	100%	45%	0%
2010	100%	90%	27%	0%
2009	94%	95%	43%	0%
2008	100%	100%	63%	8%
2007	95%	95%	45%	0%
2006	100%	90%	40%	8%
2005	92%	95%	40%	0%
2004	100%	95%	43%	0%
2003	87%	90%	37%	20%

Rep. Andy Harris (R)

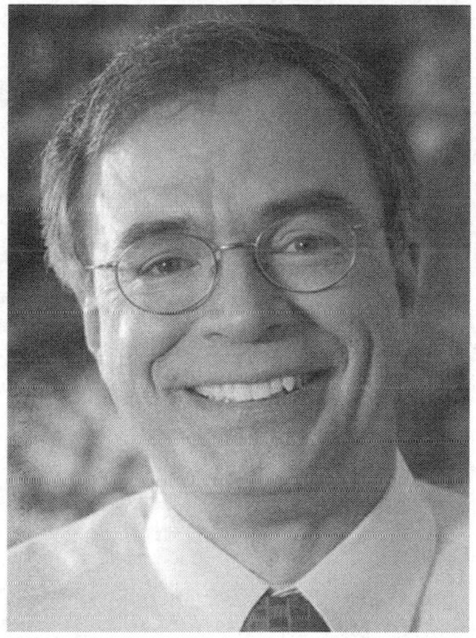

Capitol Office
225-5311
harris.house.gov
1533 Longworth Bldg. 20515-2001; fax 225-0254

Committees
Appropriations

Residence
Cockeysville

Born
Jan. 25, 1957; Brooklyn, N.Y.

Religion
Roman Catholic

Family
Wife, Sylvia "Cookie" Harris; five children

Education
U. of Pennsylvania, attended 1973-75; Johns Hopkins U., B.A. 1977 (human biology), M.D. 1980, M.H.S. 1995 (health finance & management)

Military
Navy Reserve, 1988-2005

Career
Physician

Political Highlights
Md. Senate, 1999-2010 (Republican whip, 2003-06); Republican nominee for U.S. House, 2008

ELECTION RESULTS

2012 GENERAL		
Andy Harris (R)	214,204	63.4%
Wendy Rosen (D)	92,812	27.5%
John LaFerla (D)	14,858	4.4%
Muir Wayne Boda (LIBERT)	12,857	3.8%
2012 PRIMARY		
Andy Harris (R)		unopposed
2010 GENERAL		
Andy Harris (R)	155,118	54.1%
Frank Kratovil Jr. (D)	120,400	42.0%
Richard Davis (LIBERT)	10,876	3.8%

Elected 2010; 2nd term

Harris' status as the only Republican in the Maryland delegation doesn't stop him from being very Republican. He champions spending cuts and wants to reduce federal regulation, particularly regarding energy production.

He didn't come by his conservatism casually. His father spent two years in a Siberian gulag, and his parents left Eastern Europe to flee communism after World War II. "They believed that we had a true gift in America of being able to be involved in a really democratic process," he said. "I am a firm believer that what this country does ... better than any other place in the world, is provide equal opportunity. It doesn't provide equal outcome. That's up to the individual."

An earlier career as an anesthesiologist gives Harris a "scientific way of looking at things," and he can be clinical in explaining his votes. In early 2013, he was one of 67 Republicans to oppose a bill to give $9.7 billion in additional borrowing authority to the federal flood insurance program — an installment of aid for states damaged by Superstorm Sandy, which had walloped parts of his district months before. Harris said the bill did "nothing to ensure the long-term stability" of the insurance program "so that it does not need another multibillion-dollar bailout when the next storm hits."

Harris often interprets facts as pointing to the need for smaller government and balanced budgets. He opposed a January 2013 law extending lower tax rates on earnings under $400,000, because the extension wasn't bundled with spending cuts. He opposed fiscal 2011 and 2012 appropriations laws, which he felt spent too much.

In February 2013, Harris jumped at the chance to handle spending more directly. A spot opened up on the Appropriations Committee, and Harris gave up all his other panel assignments — including a subcommittee chairmanship — to fill it. He now sits on the Commerce-Justice-Science and Labor-HHS-Education spending subcommittees.

The gavel he relinquished was for the Science, Space and Technology Subcommittee on Environment. A major Harris priority is oversight of the EPA "to make sure they use sound science and are transparent."

Harris is incensed by possible federal regulation of hydraulic fracturing, a method of extracting gas and oil deposits. Environmentalists say it threatens to contaminate ground water, while the energy industry touts several studies of "fracking" that found no problems. At a February 2012 hearing, Harris decried President Barack Obama's "remarkable display of arrogance and disregard for the plain facts" in proclaiming support for natural gas production "while at the same time allowing every part of his administration to attack these practices through scientific innuendo and regulatory straitjacketing."

He takes a keen interest in the efficiency of federal research programs, and he cites National Institutes of Health grants as a model for nonpolitical, nonpartisan funding. Harris is also a fan of ARPA-E — the Advanced Research Projects Agency-Energy.

"The program focuses on truly cutting-edge technology advances that otherwise would probably not be funded by a private company," he said in 2011. "There are programs that are 10 times that size ... that I think don't use money sufficiently." He raised some eyebrows at a December 2012 hearing when he questioned whether NASA should pursue manned spaceflight, because those missions "just don't deliver the bang for the buck."

His district includes Maryland's portion of the Eastern Shore of the Chesapeake Bay, so he has the delicate task of balancing environmental stewardship with the economic activity that depends on the bay. His first bill as a freshman was to address the problem of algal blooms; it advanced through the Science Committee in July 2011. Harris also tackled the issue when he served in the Maryland Senate. The measure would authorize research, including an interagency task force, on harmful algae in water. Algal blooms can become toxic and create "red tides."

As a freshman, Harris also served on the Natural Resources Committee, and the Transportation and Infrastructure Committee. In May 2011, he was upset by planned Maryland toll increases that he said unfairly targeted rural areas. Harris said Congress should consider withholding federal transportation money from states unless they demonstrate they will spend it equitably.

Harris is sensitive about possible infringements of civil liberties. He was one of 31 House Republicans who voted against a 2011 extension of surveillance provisions in the 2002 anti-terrorism law know as the Patriot Act. He opposed a fiscal 2012 defense policy law over his concern that a provision might allow indefinite military detention of American citizens suspected of terrorism.

Harris was born in Brooklyn and grew up in a small Cape Cod-style house. He skipped his last year of high school, briefly attended the University of Pennsylvania, then entered Johns Hopkins University, where he graduated with a degree in human biology. He got his medical degree three years later.

He started as an anesthesiologist in 1984 and worked at Johns Hopkins Hospital. He entered the Navy Reserve in 1988, and reached the rank of commander before leaving the service in 2005.

A state Senate bid in 1998 was his first run for office. He won, and he served in that chamber until he was elected to Congress on his second try.

In his first bid, in 2008, he defeated nine-term incumbent Wayne T. Gilchrest in the Republican primary with the backing of the fiscally conservative Club for Growth. Gilchrest then endorsed Democrat Frank Kratovil Jr., who defeated Harris by less than 1 point. In the 2010 rematch, Harris topped Kratovil with 54 percent of the vote, becoming the first person from the Chesapeake Bay's Western Shore to win the 1st District in two decades.

For the 2012 cycle, his Democratic opponent, Wendy Rosen, dropped out of the race after allegations of voting improprieties — she was later charged with illegally voting in Maryland, as she was registered in Florida and had voted there.

Rosen still appeared on the ballot, and John LaFerla, the Democratic write-in candidate, got only 4 percent of the vote. Harris won easily. He made headlines in the heart of campaign season for stopping along Route 50 and saving the life of a 2-year-old whose family had pulled over after the child had stopped breathing.

Key Votes

2012	
Extend a Social Security payroll tax cut and unemployment benefits	NO
Ease securities rules to expand small-business access to capital	YES
Extend for one year subsidized student loan interest rates financed by a cut in health care spending	YES
Cite Attorney General Eric H. Holder Jr. for contempt of Congress	YES
Create a visa program for foreign graduates in high-tech fields	YES
Extend most Bush-era income tax rates while allowing rates for top-bracket earners to rise (Jan. 1, 2013)	NO
2011	
Strike funding for F-35 alternative engine	YES
Prevent EPA from regulating greenhouse gas emissions to address climate change	YES
Extend certain provisions of Patriot Act for four years	NO
Declare opposition to use of ground troops in Libya	YES
Overhaul patent law	YES
Pass compromise debt limit increase plan and establish future spending limits	NO
Allow consideration of measures to implement three trade agreements	YES

CQ Vote Studies

	PARTY UNITY		PRESIDENTIAL SUPPORT	
	SUPPORT	OPPOSE	SUPPORT	OPPOSE
2012	95%	5%	12%	88%
2011	91%	9%	20%	80%

Interest Groups

	AFL-CIO	ADA	CCUS	ACU
2012	10%	0%	83%	92%
2011	0%	15%	94%	88%

Maryland 1

Northeast and Eastern Shore

The 1st District contains the entirety of Maryland's Eastern Shore and its Atlantic beaches on the Delmarva Peninsula. At the state's northeastern corner, the district hooks west at the Pennsylvania border to include most of Harford County and northern chunks of more rural areas in Baltimore and Carroll counties — new additions to the district after decennial redistricting removed parts of Anne Arundel County.

The rural Eastern Shore is home to some of Maryland's most robust agriculture, including corn, soybeans, wheat and chickens. Perdue Farms runs a processing plant in Wicomico County. Plastics manufacturing plants — Gore-Tex, Solo Cups and medical supply companies — also dot these counties. Water quality and pollution remain pressing concerns for residents near the Chesapeake Bay.

In Harford, Carroll and Cecil counties, engineering and construction firms are economic drivers, as are processing and distribution centers for consumer goods. Cecil County residents commute to plants in Harford and the Amazon.com distribution center across the Delaware border. The Army's Aberdeen Proving Ground, in the 2nd District, employs more people in Harford County than the next five largest employers combined.

Salisbury, the largest city on the Eastern Shore, is home to Salisbury University. Farther east are beach resort towns such as Ocean City, which has been a mid-Atlantic tourism hub for half a century.

Land use and regulation can be hot-button issues in semi-rural counties like Carroll, where residents protect their small residential communities from development and have loudly protested development proposals. Politically, the 1st has favored conservatives, strongly supporting Republican presidential candidates and unsuccessful Republican gubernatorial candidates in recent years. Socially conservative, every county wholly or partly in the district except Baltimore voted against the state's successful 2012 referendum to allow same-sex marriage.

Major Industry
Agriculture, manufacturing, distribution

Cities
Bel Air South, Salisbury

Notable
Wild ponies roam Assateauge Island, a barrier island on the Atlantic Ocean.

Rep. C.A. Dutch Ruppersberger (D)

Capitol Office
225-3061
dutch.house.gov
2416 Rayburn Bldg. 20515-2002; fax 225-3094

Committees
Select Intelligence - Ranking Member

Residence
Cockeysville

Born
Jan. 31, 1946; Baltimore, Md.

Religion
Methodist

Family
Wife, Kay Ruppersberger; two children

Education
U. of Maryland, attended 1963-67; U. of Baltimore, J.D. 1970

Career
Collection agency owner; lawyer; county prosecutor

Political Highlights
Democratic nominee for Md. Senate, 1978; Baltimore County Council, 1985-94; Baltimore County executive, 1994-2002

ELECTION RESULTS

2012 GENERAL

C.A. Dutch Ruppersberger (D)	194,088	65.6%
Nancy C. Jacobs (R)	92,071	31.1%
Leo Wayne Dymowski (LIBERT)	9,344	3.2%

2012 PRIMARY

C.A. Dutch Ruppersberger (D)	unopposed

2010 GENERAL

C.A. Dutch Ruppersberger (D)	134,133	64.2%
Marcelo Cardarelli (R)	69,523	33.3%
Lorenzo Gaztanaga (LIBERT)	5,090	2.4%

Previous Winning Percentages
2008 (72%); 2006 (69%); 2004 (67%); 2002 (54%)

Elected 2002; 6th term

Ruppersberger, like many a congressman, caters to the parochial interests of his constituents. What's unusual is that he does so as the top Democrat on the Intelligence Committee.

For most lawmakers, service on that panel provides a chance to burnish national security credentials. But Ruppersberger's specialization in spying matters is vital to his district. It is home to the National Security Agency, U.S. Cyber Command and related industries along the Interstate 95 corridor. He describes his home turf as the "cyber capital of the world."

He is at his most moderate when dealing with national security. That fact irritates some Democrats who feel he works too closely with Intelligence Chairman Mike Rogers, a Michigan Republican. "My philosophy is, during elections, you roll with your party," he said. "When the election's over, you work together."

An affable former Baltimore County executive, Ruppersberger is at ease with the back-slapping nature of the business, and his kinship with Rogers is furthered by their law enforcement pasts. Rogers served as an FBI agent, and Ruppersberger worked as a prosecutor. They crack jokes about their unusual alliance on a panel that was plagued by partisan rifts for years.

Ruppersberger has cut deals with Rogers on several intelligence policy bills since becoming the panel's top Democrat in 2011. They restored the practice of passing an annual measure reauthorizing spy agencies, largely by removing politically radioactive topics from the legislation. With those bills, the committee has walked a fine line between backing cuts to intelligence spending and trying to shield spy agencies from bigger reductions.

Their most controversial work was a bill to foster the sharing of information regarding cybersecurity threats between businesses that own the majority of the nation's most important computer networks and the federal agencies that monitor those threats and have access to classified data.

Privacy advocates attacked the measure before it came to the House floor in the spring of 2012, arguing that businesses would be allowed to deliver too much information about average citizens to the federal government. The Obama administration threatened a veto, repeating the arguments of many privacy advocates and saying the bill didn't do enough to protect networks overall — since it was voluntary and had no requirements for businesses to shore up defenses. Ruppersberger and Rogers tweaked some language and argued that passing the measure was better than not acting. They prevailed, with support from most Republicans and 42 Democrats. Efforts on a similar measure petered out in the Senate, and the House duo reintroduced their bill early in the 113th Congress (2013-14). With a few modifications, they picked up 50 additional Democratic votes when it passed the House in April 2013.

Ruppersberger was pleased that the fiscal 2013 defense policy law reclassified satellites and their components for purposes of international trade — they had been considered weapons, which hampered exports by U.S. manufacturers. He had sought the change for years, saying it would strengthen the domestic satellite industry and, by extension, national security.

A former member of the Armed Services Committee, Ruppersberger still looks out for his district's military installations — Fort Meade and Aberdeen Proving Ground — as a co-chairman of the House Army Caucus.

During the Democratic majority in the 110th and 111th Congresses (2007-10), he sat on the Appropriations Committee, but as one of the more junior members of the panel he lost his seat after the 2010 elections. Getting the Intelligence panel ranking member assignment eased the blow, but Ruppersberger has said he wants to return to the spending panel in the future. His fast-growing district, like many suburban areas in the Baltimore-Washington region, has pressing infrastructure needs.

Although Ruppersberger focuses heavily on national security, he misses local government and enjoys working on some of the same issues as city officials. "I come from local government," he said. "I like the old-style grass-roots politics where you can meet with people."

He is the son of a Baltimore manufacturing salesman and a schoolteacher. He was born Charles Albert Ruppersberger III, but goes by Dutch — he says the doctor who delivered him described him as a "big, blond Dutchman." His hair has since turned black. As practical a politician as they come, Ruppersberger adopted the nickname legally when he realized his last name was too long for a bumper sticker.

A good athlete as a youth, he played lacrosse at the University of Maryland and made the U.S. national team in 1967. During college summers, he was a lifeguard in Ocean City, Md., then worked his way through law school as an insurance claims adjuster.

Ruppersberger began his government career as a Baltimore County assistant state's attorney. While investigating a drug trafficking case in 1975, he was in a near-fatal car crash. He devoted himself to public service, at the urging of the doctor who saved his life at the University of Maryland's renowned Shock Trauma Center. He remains an avid supporter of the hospital, serving on the trauma center's board of visitors.

He lost a state Senate bid in 1978, but in 1985 he was appointed to finish a term on the Baltimore County Council. He was elected to the seat the following year. In 1994, he was elected county executive. He steered the county to triple-A bond ratings while building new schools, roads and parks.

Ruppersberger planned to run for governor in 2002, but he was dogged by events from two years earlier. In 2000, he had aggressively pushed a bill to allow the county to condemn private property for urban revitalization. People in the affected areas fought back with a referendum that passed by a 2-to-1 ratio. Then in November 2000, The Baltimore Sun reported that he had steered government grants to an apartment rental company with which he had personal business dealings. Ruppersberger called the report flawed and said he had broken no laws.

But he was too weakened politically for a competitive Democratic primary. Rep. Steny H. Hoyer of Maryland, who was then the Democratic Caucus chairman, urged him to run instead in the newly redrawn 2nd District. He defeated former Republican Rep. Helen Delich Bentley by almost 9 points and hasn't been seriously challenged since.

Key Votes

2012	
Extend a Social Security payroll tax cut and unemployment benefits	YES
Ease securities rules to expand small-business access to capital	YES
Extend for one year subsidized student loan interest rates financed by a cut in health care spending	NO
Cite Attorney General Eric H. Holder Jr. for contempt of Congress	?
Create a visa program for foreign graduates in high-tech fields	YES
Extend most Bush-era income tax rates while allowing rates for top-bracket earners to rise (Jan. 1, 2013)	YES
2011	
Strike funding for F-35 alternative engine	NO
Prevent EPA from regulating greenhouse gas emissions to address climate change	NO
Extend certain provisions of Patriot Act for four years	YES
Declare opposition to use of ground troops in Libya	NO
Overhaul patent law	YES
Pass compromise debt limit increase plan and establish future spending limits	YES
Allow consideration of measures to implement three trade agreements	NO

CQ Vote Studies

	PARTY UNITY		PRESIDENTIAL SUPPORT	
	SUPPORT	OPPOSE	SUPPORT	OPPOSE
2012	88%	12%	74%	26%
2011	89%	11%	89%	11%
2010	97%	3%	93%	7%
2009	97%	3%	96%	4%
2008	97%	3%	21%	79%

Interest Groups

	AFL-CIO	ADA	CCUS	ACU
2012	86%	55%	50%	8%
2011	100%	90%	44%	4%
2010	100%	80%	25%	0%
2009	100%	90%	40%	4%
2008	100%	90%	67%	4%

Maryland 2

Parts of Baltimore and Towson, Dundalk

The 2nd is a collection of struggling urban and working-class suburban communities fortified by two major military bases. The district hugs the upper northwestern shore of the Chesapeake Bay near the Aberdeen Proving Ground, cuts through portions of Baltimore and encompasses Fort George G. Meade to the south. It curls north around the city of Baltimore into the well-established and densely populated suburbs of Baltimore County.

The military looms large here. Developed as an artillery testing site, the Aberdeen Proving Ground has made the transition to a communications and electronic-warfare center, luring military contractors and technology firms. In the southwest, Fort Meade, the largest employer in the state, is home to the National Security Agency and the U.S. Cyber Command. Despite the military presence, voters here reliably back Democrats.

About 60 percent of the population lives in GOP-leaning Baltimore County suburbs to the north and largely African-American areas to the west of the city. The Sparrows Point steel mill, once a key employer in working-class eastern suburbs, was shuttered in 2012 and is expected to be dismantled.

The population of the 2nd's portion of Baltimore City is two-thirds black.

The district includes the city's southern and eastern edges, a mix of poor and working-class residential communities and industrial areas along the waterfront, where exporters make use of the major seaport. On the city's outskirts, in predominately black neighborhoods such as Cherry Hill, rates of poverty and unemployment are well above the citywide average, and violent crime is a persistent problem. The city has targeted the nearby Westport neighborhood for redevelopment, wooing new residents and businesses related to growth at Aberdeen and Fort Meade.

Major Industry
Defense, manufacturing, distribution

Military Bases
Fort George G. Meade, 14,000 military and 27,800 civilian (shared with the 3rd); Aberdeen Proving Ground, 3,900 military and 7,500 civilian

Cities
Baltimore (pt.), Dundalk (unincorp.), Essex, Randallstown (unincorp.)

Notable
Aberdeen is home to Cal Ripken Baseball, a youth division of the amateur Babe Ruth League.

Rep. John Sarbanes (D)

Capitol Office
225-4016
sarbanes.house.gov
2444 Rayburn Bldg. 20515-2003; fax 225-9219

Committees
Energy & Commerce

Residence
Towson

Born
May 22, 1962; Baltimore, Md.

Religion
Greek Orthodox

Family
Wife, Dina Sarbanes; three children

Education
Princeton U., A.B. 1984 (public & international affairs); Harvard U., J.D. 1988

Career
Lawyer; state education consultant

Political Highlights
No previous office

ELECTION RESULTS

2012 GENERAL		
John Sarbanes (D)	213,747	66.8%
Eric Delano Knowles (R)	94,549	29.6%
Paul W. Drgos Jr. (LIBERT)	11,028	3.4%
2012 PRIMARY		
John Sarbanes (D)	32,527	86.4%
David H. Lockwood (D)	5,111	13.6%
2010 GENERAL		
John Sarbanes (D)	147,448	61.1%
Jim Wilhelm (R)	86,947	36.0%
Jerry McKinley (LIBERT)	5,212	2.2%

Previous Winning Percentages
2008 (70%); 2006 (64%)

Elected 2006; 4th term

Sarbanes is laying the groundwork for long-term involvement with health care and environmental policy, while also testing out some ambitious plans for promoting public service and overhauling campaign finance. "If you have a broad set of interests," he said of holding public office, "in some ways there is no better job."

His father, Paul S. Sarbanes, represented Maryland in the House and Senate for 36 years, making his most lasting mark in financial regulation. The younger Sarbanes — a loyal Democrat like his father — has focused on the Energy and Commerce Committee. After losing his seat on the panel at the start of the 112th Congress (2011-12) due to Democratic losses in the 2010 elections, he rejoined in early 2012 when a vacancy opened up. Sarbanes is "not looking to move."

The panel's broad jurisdiction includes health care, and Sarbanes has a seat on the Health Subcommittee. He spent 18 years representing health care practitioners with the law firm Venable, and for six of those years he was chairman of the health care practice. During the health care debate of the 111th Congress (2009-10), he pushed for a provision authorizing a grant program for school-based health clinics to provide primary care to medically underserved children and families.

While championing access to preventive and primary care, Sarbanes takes a particular interest in the supply side of the system: "You have to have the practitioners to provide the services," specifically primary care doctors and nurses, he said. The 2010 health care law includes a Sarbanes plan creating a national commission to identify health care workforce shortages, but its work has been delayed due to a lack of appropriated funds.

Sarbanes has proposed legislation that would create a grant program for hospitals, medical schools and other medical institutions that re-train physicians who have left their practices for various reasons. In return, the practitioners would serve at public health care providers.

That idea shares the same ethic as a 2007 law that Sarbanes considers his greatest legislative success thus far. Feeling that student loan debt was too burdensome, Sarbanes wrote a bill to forgive debt for graduates — if they become government or nonprofit group employees for 10 years and make regular loan payments. It was rolled into an enacted student aid measure. He also collaborated on two pieces of a 2009 law overhauling public service programs, one creating a service corps of veterans and the other a service corps for clean-energy projects.

On environmental issues, Sarbanes again shows an interest in planting the seeds of grass-roots involvement. Several times, he has introduced a bill to establish grant programs for environmental education at all grade levels. "The only way you can save the environment is by developing habits that millions of people exercise every day," he said. The measure passed the House in his first term but was never taken up by the Senate.

Sarbanes has had a hand in education in the past — for seven years, he was a liaison to Baltimore public schools for Maryland's superintendent of schools. He believes science education should be placed on closer footing with math and reading programs when setting federal education standards.

Sarbanes, a Baltimore native, is an advocate for the Chesapeake Bay — he remembers crabbing and beach trips as a kid. He has proposed a bill to reauthorize and increase funding for the Chesapeake Bay Gateways Network, which educates locals about how to protect the bay and enhance water trails. Sarbanes served on the Natural Resources Committee from the start of his

House career up to March 2012, when he rejoined Energy and Commerce.

Committees aside, Sarbanes in the 112th Congress adopted a new cause: campaign finance reform. Like many Democrats, he is a critic of the Supreme Court's 2010 Citizens United ruling, which allowed the creation of "super PACs" — advocacy groups independent of official campaigns that can accept unrestricted donations from individuals or organizations. Interest groups "have undue influence over the way policy gets made," Sarbanes said, and he laments the constant need for campaign fundraising.

Sarbanes calls for public financing of congressional campaigns and outlines a system where candidates have financial incentives to focus on donors who give less than $100 — public funds would be provided in proportion to the number of smaller donations collected. Sarbanes set up his 2012 campaign finances along those lines as a demonstration project, with funds from larger donors substituting for public funding; he "unlocked" his access to the larger funds as he hit certain targets for small donations.

Sarbanes is a purebred Baltimorean. Some of his earliest memories are of attending Orioles games at Memorial Stadium, just a few blocks from his childhood home in the Guilford neighborhood, a comfortable middle-class enclave. His father was elected to the state legislature when John was 4 and entered Congress when John was 8.

Like his father, whose old House seat he now occupies, Sarbanes attended Princeton University and Harvard Law School. Sarbanes studied law and politics in Greece on a Fulbright scholarship, and he stays connected with the Greek community. On the wall of his House office is the ship manifest from when his grandfather immigrated from Greece to the United States in 1909.

After graduating law school, Sarbanes returned to Baltimore to clerk for U.S. District Judge J. Frederick Motz before representing hospitals and other medical providers at Venable. He also served for 15 years as a board member for the Public Justice Center, a Baltimore organization providing legal assistance to the poor, and in his school liaison post.

Sarbanes got his shot at the 3rd District House seat in 2006, when Democratic Rep. Benjamin L. Cardin launched his successful bid to succeed the senior Sarbanes in the Senate.

Eight candidates contested the primary, but the family name trumped all; Sarbanes appeared alongside his father in ads and used his father's longtime motto of "fairness and opportunity" on his campaign literature.

In the November election, Sarbanes easily defeated Republican John White, an Annapolis marketing executive, with 64 percent of the vote. Even in the strong Republican year of 2010, he won by 25 points, and his 2012 victory over Republican Eric Delano Knowles was even more lopsided.

Key Votes

2012	
Extend a Social Security payroll tax cut and unemployment benefits	NO
Ease securities rules to expand small-business access to capital	NO
Extend for one year subsidized student loan interest rates financed by a cut in health care spending	NO
Cite Attorney General Eric H. Holder Jr. for contempt of Congress	?
Create a visa program for foreign graduates in high-tech fields	NO
Extend most Bush-era income tax rates while allowing rates for top-bracket earners to rise (Jan. 1, 2013)	YES
2011	
Strike funding for F-35 alternative engine	NO
Prevent EPA from regulating greenhouse gas emissions to address climate change	NO
Extend certain provisions of Patriot Act for four years	NO
Declare opposition to use of ground troops in Libya	NO
Overhaul patent law	YES
Pass compromise debt limit increase plan and establish future spending limits	NO
Allow consideration of measures to implement three trade agreements	NO

CQ Vote Studies

	PARTY UNITY		PRESIDENTIAL SUPPORT	
	SUPPORT	OPPOSE	SUPPORT	OPPOSE
2012	98%	2%	85%	15%
2011	97%	3%	87%	13%
2010	99%	1%	95%	5%
2009	99%	1%	99%	1%
2008	99%	1%	16%	84%

Interest Groups

	AFL-CIO	ADA	CCUS	ACU
2012	100%	90%	25%	4%
2011	100%	90%	19%	4%
2010	100%	95%	25%	0%
2009	100%	100%	33%	0%
2008	100%	100%	61%	0%

Maryland 3

Part of Baltimore; Olney; Annapolis

A contorted district in a state with several tortuous boundaries, the 3rd has tendrils snaking through three major cities: Baltimore, Columbia and Annapolis. It includes some traditionally Jewish suburbs north of Baltimore; northern and central sections of the city; suburbs between Baltimore and Washington; and a long stretch of well-to-do communities on the western shore of the Chesapeake Bay, including Annapolis, the state capital.

Government is the prime employer here; federal offices, military sites and related high-tech firms dot the 3rd. Annapolis hosts the U.S. Naval Academy and naval complex; many residents work at Fort George G. Meade (shared with the 2nd). Radar and electronics manufacturers are in Annapolis, an important harbor and agricultural shipping center. The Baltimore/Washington International Thurgood Marshall Airport is a commercial hub.

The 3rd includes affluent northern Baltimore as well as the nightlife and central shopping areas around Fells Point. It crosses the neck of the Inner Harbor to grab the stadiums for football's Ravens and baseball's Orioles. With the decline of the steel industry, Baltimore has established itself as a hub for research. The 3rd also takes in liberal areas of Montgomery County and a section of southern Columbia in Howard County that is home to several major white-collar employers, such as Blue Cross Blue Shield, Honeywell and Johns Hopkins University Applied Physics Laboratory.

Anne Arundel County can lean conservative but liberal voters in Baltimore city and suburbs, with liberal areas outside Washington, account for more than half of district's population — keeping the 3rd Democratic.

Major Industry

Government, technology, defense, research

Military Bases

Fort George G. Meade, 14,000 military, 27,800 civilian (shared with the 2nd); U.S. Naval Academy/Naval Support Activity Annapolis, 662 military, 1,410 civilian; Adelphi Army Research Laboratory, 95 military, 956 civilian (shared with the 4th)

Cities

Baltimore (pt.), Columbia (unincorp.) (pt.), Glen Burnie (unincorp.), Annapolis

Notable

The Annapolis Historic District has more than 100 buildings from the 18th century — including the campus of St. John's College — and the City Dock.

Rep. Donna Edwards (D)

Capitol Office
225-8699
donnaedwards.house.gov
2445 Rayburn Bldg. 20515-2004; fax 225-8714

Committees
Science, Space & Technology
Transportation & Infrastructure

Residence
Oxon Hill

Born
June 28, 1958; Yanceyville, N.C.

Religion
Baptist

Family
Divorced; one child

Education
Wake Forest U., B.A. 1980 (English); Franklin Pierce Law Center, J.D. 1989

Career
Nonprofit executive director; lobbyist; lawyer; aeronautical company project manager; United Nations publication editor

Political Highlights
Sought Democratic nomination for U.S. House, 2006

ELECTION RESULTS

2012 GENERAL		
Donna Edwards (D)	240,385	77.2%
Faith M. Loudon (R)	64,560	20.7%
Scott Soffen (LIBERT)	6,204	2.0%
2012 PRIMARY		
Donna Edwards (D)	42,815	91.8%
George McDermott (D)	2,359	5.1%
Ian Garner (D)	1,464	3.1%
2010 GENERAL		
Donna Edwards (D)	160,228	83.4%
Robert "Bro" Broadus (R)	31,467	16.4%

Previous Winning Percentages
2008 (86%), 2008 Special Election (81%)

Elected 2008; 3rd full term

Edwards is a liberal Democrat with a reputation for being ambitious, and she has absorbed any criticism that comes with that reputation. Transportation and science are the core of her committee work, but in her pursuit of influence within the Democratic Party she is liable to step into any debate.

When making the case for a progressive federal government, Edwards weaves in her personal story. She defended the 2010 health care overhaul by relating her struggle to pay hospital bills as a young, uninsured single mother. Speaking at the Democratic National Convention in 2012, she said that "no one should end up in an emergency room facing financial ruin and the loss of middle-class life, my middle-class life, just because they can't afford a doctor's visit and a $20 dollar batch of antibiotics."

Edwards has spoken of the embarrassment of needing to use food pantries as a struggling lawyer. On issues such as campaign finance and domestic violence, she invokes her work experience at a number of nonprofits.

She attributes her openness in part to her childhood: Edwards is the second of six children raised by an Air Force officer and a stay-at-home mom, and frequent relocations forced her to adapt quickly. "There's not a room I go in where I feel like a stranger," she once told The Washington Post.

Her partisan and personality-driven messaging has drawn attention. Esquire Magazine in 2010 said she possessed "an uncommon intelligence and legislative savvy." In the 112th Congress (2011-12), she and Colorado Democrat Jared Polis headed the "Red to Blue" program of the Democratic Congressional Campaign Committee, which offers financial and logistical support to non-incumbent candidates. In the 113th Congress (2013-14), she is heading up candidate recruitment for the DCCC, and she is the co-chairwoman of the Congressional Caucus for Women's Issues. And she aspired to even more authority: At the end of her first full term, Edwards ran unsuccessfully for chairwoman of the Congressional Progressive Caucus.

Some in her party, particularly in Maryland, have chafed at her aggression. Edwards came to the House after taking out Rep. Albert R. Wynn in a 2008 Democratic primary. She touted her opposition to the wars in Iraq and Afghanistan and ran to the left of Wynn, who had the support of many members of the Congressional Black Caucus. When the House was considering deficit reduction plans in the summer of 2011, Edwards reportedly tore into Minority Whip Steny H. Hoyer at a party meeting as she insisted that cuts to Social Security and Medicare should be off the table. She panned Maryland's congressional map for the 2012 elections — which was adopted by an overwhelmingly Democratic state government, then endorsed by voters in a 2012 referendum — as slighting minority voters.

Edwards sits on the Transportation and Infrastructure Committee, where she tries to address the needs of her suburban Washington district. Even before coming to the House, Edwards supported the notion of the Purple Line, a light-rail corridor through Maryland that would cross several branches of the capital region's existing hub-and-spoke mass transit system. The project entered an advanced planning stage in 2011.

She was disappointed with a 2012 reauthorization of surface transportation programs, suggesting that it could have done more to spur job creation; she did not agree with provisions to streamline the environmental review process for many infrastructure projects. Edwards in 2011 introduced a bill to create grants for state and local governments working on "green infrastructure" to manage storm runoff and other water issues.

Edwards once worked as a manager on the Spacelab program for Lockheed

Martin Corp. at the Goddard Space Flight Center—which is located in Hoyer's 5th District. She is now the top Democrat on the Science, Space and Technology Subcommittee on Space. She is a frequent questioner at Science hearings, especially when the space program is involved. Edwards has expressed concern that the shift of human spaceflight capabilities to the private sector could gut NASA's overall capabilities. She criticized the Obama administration in 2012 for doubling its budget request for commercial programs without laying out measurable goals for that spending.

She is a strong supporter of education programs for science, technology, engineering and math. Edwards proposes making the tax credit for research permanent. "It is important to use the tax code to incentivize things you want," she said. "Something like research-and-development tax credits, coupled with science and technology tax credits, actually put us on a pathway to stronger economic success."

Edwards also worked as a lobbyist for Public Citizen, a nonprofit that advocates changes in the campaign finance system. Like many Democrats, she described a "complete meltdown" in that system after the Supreme Court's 2010 ruling that allowed the creation of "super PACs," advocacy groups independent of official campaigns that can accept unrestricted donations from individuals or organizations. Three times, Edwards has proposed a constitutional amendment to permit restrictions on corporate spending on political activities—though not on spending by unions, which also are empowered by the 2010 ruling.

As a child, Edwards bounced around the country with her family. They settled in the D.C. suburbs during her senior year of high school. She had some political involvement during college and in her early professional career; Edwards volunteered on Jimmy Carter's 1976 presidential campaign and Jesse Jackson's 1984 and 1988 runs. She worked for a U.N. publication and Lockheed Martin before attending Franklin Pierce Law Center in New Hampshire.

After finishing law school in 1989, Edwards worked for several nonprofit groups. She co-founded the National Network to End Domestic Violence in 1990 and was its first executive director, pushing for the 1994 law that expanded resources for the prosecution of such crimes and services for victims.

Her first attempt at electoral politics came in 2006, as she challenged Wynn in a Democratic primary. Edwards had worked for Wynn after her second year in law school, when he was a state senator, and she also campaigned for one of Wynn's early congressional races. Edwards lost a close race, but prevailed in the 2008 rematch. Wynn resigned from Congress to join a lobbying firm after that defeat, and Edwards cruised in both the special election to finish Wynn's term and the general election in November.

Key Votes

2012	
Extend a Social Security payroll tax cut and unemployment benefits	NO
Ease securities rules to expand small-business access to capital	NO
Extend for one year subsidized student loan interest rates financed by a cut in health care spending	NO
Cite Attorney General Eric H. Holder Jr. for contempt of Congress	?
Create a visa program for foreign graduates in high-tech fields	-
Extend most Bush-era income tax rates while allowing rates for top-bracket earners to rise (Jan. 1, 2013)	YES
2011	
Strike funding for F-35 alternative engine	YES
Prevent EPA from regulating greenhouse gas emissions to address climate change	NO
Extend certain provisions of Patriot Act for four years	NO
Declare opposition to use of ground troops in Libya	NO
Overhaul patent law	NO
Pass compromise debt limit increase plan and establish future spending limits	NO
Allow consideration of measures to implement three trade agreements	NO

CQ Vote Studies

	PARTY UNITY		PRESIDENTIAL SUPPORT	
	SUPPORT	OPPOSE	SUPPORT	OPPOSE
2012	97%	3%	88%	12%
2011	97%	3%	83%	17%
2010	98%	2%	77%	23%
2009	99%	1%	94%	6%
2008	99%	1%	17%	83%

Interest Groups

	AFL-CIO	ADA	CCUS	ACU
2012	100%	95%	27%	0%
2011	100%	95%	6%	4%
2010	93%	95%	25%	5%
2009	100%	100%	33%	0%
2008	100%		58%	7%

Maryland 4

Inner Prince George's County; Severna Park

A sprawling suburban district with a black-majority population, the 4th stretches from the eastern and southern borders of Washington, D.C., to the outskirts of Annapolis. Its west side takes in about two-thirds of the population of suburban Prince George's County with large populations of working-class and black residents. Skirting up part of the Montgomery County line, the district turns east to close in on Annapolis.

Most of the population lives in Prince George's County. Proximity to the state and federal capitals makes government an economic driver and primary job source for residents. The 4th includes the Andrews Air Force Base main runways and buildings. Part of the Patuxent Research Refuge — the only National Wildlife Refuge dedicated to research — bridges the Prince George's and Anne Arundel portions of the district. Jobs at Fort George G. Meade in the 2nd and 3rd districts are important, as are the range of professional services and high-tech firms that support government agencies. The 4th's technology industries are bolstered by the University of Maryland and NASA's Goddard Space Flight Center (both in the 5th).

Decennial remapping following the 2010 census removed a large chunk of suburban Montgomery County north of Washington, including Silver Spring, and turned the northern arm of the district east into Anne Arundel County to take in some wealthy gated communities outside of Annapolis. While these shifts slightly increased the 4th's share of white residents and decreased its share of liberal voters, the district's black population is still the second-largest in the state, after the 7th, and registered Democrats maintain a large majority.

Major Industry
Retail, technology, defense, professional services

Military Bases
Andrews Air Force Base (shared with the 5th), 7,000 military, 925 civilian; Adelphi Army Research Laboratory, 25 military, 956 civilian (shared with the 3rd)

Cities
Laurel, Landover (unincorp.), Bowie (pt.), Suitland (unincorp.)

Notable
Air Force One is kept at Andrews Air Force Base.

Rep. Steny H. Hoyer (D)

Capitol Office
225-4131
hoyer.house.gov
1705 Longworth Bldg. 20515-2005; fax 225-4300

Committees
No committee assignments

Residence
Mechanicsville

Born
June 14, 1939; Manhattan, NY

Religion
Baptist

Family
Widowed; three children

Education
U. of Maryland, B.S. 1963 (political science); Georgetown U., J.D. 1966

Career
Lawyer

Political Highlights
Md. Senate, 1967-79 (president, 1975-79); sought Democratic nomination for lieutenant governor, 1978; Md. Board of Higher Education, 1978-81

ELECTION RESULTS

2012 GENERAL		
Steny H. Hoyer (D)	236,618	69.2%
Tony O'Donnell (R)	95,271	27.9%
Bob S. Auerbach (GREEN)	5,040	1.5%
Arvin Vohra (LIBERT)	4,503	1.3%
2012 PRIMARY		
Steny H. Hoyer (D)	36,961	84.7%
Cathy Johnson Pendleton (D)	6,688	15.3%
2010 GENERAL		
Steny H. Hoyer (D)	155,110	64.3%
Charles J. Lollar (R)	83,575	34.6%
H. Gavin Shickle (LIBERT)	2,578	1.1%

Previous Winning Percentages
2008 (74%); 2006 (83%); 2004 (69%); 2002 (69%); 2000 (65%); 1998 (65%); 1996 (57%); 1994 (59%); 1992 (53%); 1990 (81%); 1988 (79%); 1986 (82%); 1984 (72%); 1982 (80%); 1981 Special Election (55%)

Elected 1981; 16th full term

As the most moderate member of the House Democratic leadership, the silver-haired Hoyer serves as a tactician and unifying figure for his caucus. The unanswered question is whether he'll get the chance to lead it.

Hoyer is the Democratic whip, and in the twilight of his career he continues to wait on his boss and rival, Minority Leader Nancy Pelosi. Her absence would, in all likelihood, leave the party's top spot for Hoyer.

The tension between Hoyer and Pelosi is downplayed by both lawmakers. "There is no breach between Nancy and I," Hoyer said in 2012. "Do we always agree on every issue? We do not. But that can be said of a lot of Democrats, not just Nancy and me."

Even so, Democrats privately describe the Hoyer-Pelosi relationship as a major factor in the politics of their caucus, with important committee assignments and leadership roles often hinging on loyalty to Hoyer or Pelosi. The two leaders are almost the same age and have held a succession of similar jobs as congressional aides, appropriators and caucus leaders. Pelosi, a Maryland native, first met Hoyer in the early 1960s, when they both interned for their state's Democratic senator, Daniel B. Brewster.

Almost 40 years later, Hoyer was serving as the Democratic Caucus chairman when Pelosi defeated him in the 2001 election to choose the Democratic whip. When Pelosi was elected minority leader after the 2002 elections, Hoyer succeeded her as minority whip.

Pelosi was promoted to speaker of the House after Democrats won control in the 2006 elections. In the race to replace her as minority leader, she vigorously supported John P. Murtha of Pennsylvania, but Hoyer won easily. Since that race, Hoyer has worked to show his loyalty to Pelosi.

When they put their differences aside, Pelosi and Hoyer can operate as a powerful team — his sway with fiscally and socially moderate Democrats complements her grip on liberals. They kept House Democrats united in the 111th Congress (2009-10) to pass overhauls of health care and financial sector regulation with no Republican support.

They mostly maintained that unity in the 112th Congress (2011-12) as a new Republican majority tried to dismantle those laws.

But Hoyer still retains the ability to deal with the opposition. He condemns Republican policies at weekly sessions with reporters, but Hoyer is a natural Democratic emissary to the GOP. Well-liked and respected, he enjoys a warm relationship with Speaker John A. Boehner and other high ranking members of the Republican Party.

"Even when I was president of the Maryland Senate," where Democrats outnumbered Republicans by more than 3-1, "essentially I could have ignored the Republicans altogether. I did not do that," Hoyer said in 2012.

The dynamics of the 112th Congress produced few chances for collaboration, but Hoyer did what he could. He is an aggressive promoter of international trade, and he kept his party in line to pass a 2012 reauthorization of the Export-Import Bank — easily overcoming a swell of opposition from conservative Republicans.

Hoyer also took a crack at shaping the nation's fiscal future. Working with Idaho Republican Mike Simpson, in late 2011 he organized the "go big" movement, a bipartisan collection of 100 House members that announced its support for at least $4 trillion in deficit reduction over 10 years.

He did move further to the left on one social issue during the 112th Congress. Hoyer had supported the 1996 law that prevented the federal government from recognizing same-sex marriages, and for a long time he was the only member of the Democratic leadership team who opposed allowing same-sex marriage — he said that civil unions were a sufficient means to equality for gay couples.

But in May 2012, he announced a change of heart, stating that there was "much more in the word [marriage] in terms of the implications for respect and support for the relationship." A month later, his daughter Stefany Hoyer Hemmer announced that she is gay.

Hoyer and Pelosi have challenged each other in recent years, but never directly — their conflicts haven't disrupted the operations of the Democratic Party. When Pelosi ally Henry A. Waxman of California tried to displace John D. Dingell of Michigan at the top of the Energy and Commerce Committee in 2008, Hoyer stood by Dingell. Waxman won, but Hoyer still worked for 2009 passage of a bill to create a cap-and-trade system to regulate greenhouse gases — a major priority of Waxman and other liberals. The House passed the bill with virtually no Republican support, but it died in the Senate.

The Democratic electoral disaster of 2010 inspired a rump rebellion against Pelosi, but Hoyer deflected suggestions that he should try to overthrow his boss — he backed Pelosi's decision to stay on as minority leader. South Carolina Democrat James E. Clyburn considered challenging Hoyer for the whip post, but Pelosi intervened, appointing Clyburn to a newly created "assistant leader" position.

Hoyer was born in New York City, the son of a Danish immigrant who abandoned his family when Hoyer was 9. His stepfather was in the Air Force, and his mother worked at the Navy Federal Credit Union. He spent much of his childhood in Florida, but his stepfather's transfer to Andrews Air Force Base brought the family to Maryland when Hoyer was in high school.

In 1959, Hoyer was a public relations major at the University of Maryland. He went to hear Sen. John F. Kennedy speak, and he says he was moved toward politics by hearing Kennedy tell the crowd that public service is a noble calling. He switched his major to political science, and he was selected "outstanding male graduate" in 1963.

Hoyer then went to law school at Georgetown University and landed an internship with Brewster. In 1966, at age 27, he was elected to the Maryland Senate. Two terms later he became that chamber's youngest president.

Hoyer lost a 1978 primary race for lieutenant governor. Three years later, he revived his career in elective politics by claiming the 5th District seat in a special election after Democratic Rep. Gladys Noon Spellman fell ill.

He held the seat easily until redistricting in the 1990s added a conservative swath of southern Maryland to his home turf. He won only 53 percent of the vote in 1992, but he has not fallen below 64 percent since 1996.

Key Votes

2012	
Extend a Social Security payroll tax cut and unemployment benefits	NO
Ease securities rules to expand small-business access to capital	YES
Extend for one year subsidized student loan interest rates financed by a cut in health care spending	NO
Cite Attorney General Eric H. Holder Jr. for contempt of Congress	?
Create a visa program for foreign graduates in high-tech fields	NO
Extend most Bush-era income tax rates while allowing rates for top-bracket earners to rise (Jan. 1, 2013)	YES
2011	
Strike funding for F-35 alternative engine	YES
Prevent EPA from regulating greenhouse gas emissions to address climate change	NO
Extend certain provisions of Patriot Act for four years	YES
Declare opposition to use of ground troops in Libya	?
Overhaul patent law	YES
Pass compromise debt limit increase plan and establish future spending limits	YES
Allow consideration of measures to implement three trade agreements	YES

CQ Vote Studies

	PARTY UNITY		PRESIDENTIAL SUPPORT	
	SUPPORT	OPPOSE	SUPPORT	OPPOSE
2012	94%	6%	88%	12%
2011	94%	6%	97%	3%
2010	99%	1%	98%	2%
2009	99%	1%	97%	3%
2008	99%	1%	18%	82%

Interest Groups

	AFL-CIO	ADA	CCUS	ACU
2012	95%	80%	25%	4%
2011	90%	75%	40%	4%
2010	100%	90%	14%	0%
2009	100%	100%	40%	0%
2008	100%	90%	67%	0%

Maryland 5

Outer Prince George's County; southern Maryland

Some of the state's largest population growth since 2000 took place among areas in the 5th, yet its borders were the least altered during decennial remapping. Redistricting removed some liberal voters in Laurel, but the 5th remains a Democratic stronghold: Southern Maryland's conservative voters are outnumbered by the liberal suburban professionals and working-class black populations of Prince George's County.

The district's northern tip takes in some of the suburbs northeast of Washington, D.C., including College Park and such end-of-the-line Metro stops as Greenbelt and New Carrollton. From there it snakes east through outer Prince George's County, excluding the poorest suburbs directly east and southeast of Washington, and spreads south to include all of the more rural Calvert, Charles and St. Mary's counties.

Forty-five percent of the district's population lives in Prince George's — mainly suburban professionals who commute to work in Washington and most of the 5th's liberal black population. To the northwest is the University of Maryland. Contracting and professional firms support the state and federal governments in nearby Washington and Annapolis and provide steady white-collar employment. The district is home to naval facilities and defense contractors as well as the NASA Goddard Space Flight Center.

The district's south is bounded by the Chesapeake Bay on the east and the Potomac River on the west, making environmental issues important. Traditional tobacco farming has faded, but production in southern Maryland has shifted to vegetables, wine grapes, corn, soybeans and barley, although much of the land has given way to housing subdivisions.

Major Industry
Defense, technology, agriculture

Military Bases
Naval Air Station Patuxent River, 1,850 military, 9,400 civilian; Naval Support Facility Indian Head, 670 military, 2,106 civilian (2012)

Cities
Waldorf (unincorp.), Bowie (pt.), Clinton (unincorp.), College Park

Notable
College Park Airport, established in 1909, is the world's oldest continuously operating airport.

Rep. John Delaney (D)

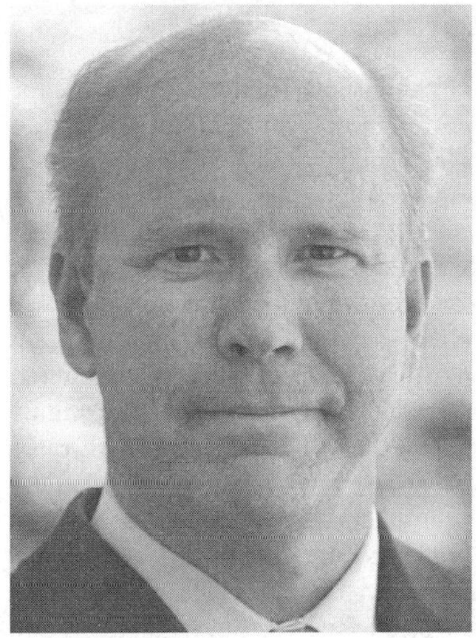

Capitol Office
225-2721
delaney.house.gov
1632 Longworth Bldg. 20515-2006; fax 225-1203

Committees
Financial Services
Joint Economic

Residence
Potomac

Born
April 16, 1963; Wood-Ridge, N.J.

Religion
Roman Catholic

Family
Wife, April McClain Delaney; four children

Education
Columbia U., B.S. 1985 (biology); Georgetown U., J.D. 1988

Career
Nonprofit economic development organization founder; private equity investment executive; medical services company owner; lawyer

Political Highlights
No previous office

ELECTION RESULTS

2012 GENERAL		
John Delaney (D)	181,921	58.8%
Roscoe G. Bartlett (R)	117,313	37.9%
Nickolaus Mueller (LIBERT)	9,916	3.2%
2012 PRIMARY		
John Delaney (D)	20,414	54.2%
Rob Garagiola (D)	10,981	29.1%
Milad Pooran (D)	3,590	9.5%
Charles Bailey (D)	1,572	4.2%
Ron Little (D)	1,131	3.0%

Elected 2012; 1st term

Delaney was a successful businessman and financier, and his favorite buzzword is "competitiveness." He hammers that theme with varying results — sometimes he sees government as helping people to compete, and other times he sees it interfering with competitive dynamics in the private sector.

Delaney comes from a blue-collar New Jersey family. He went to Georgetown Law School but quickly abandoned a legal career. He and a few friends bought a small medical services company in the D.C. area and sold it for a profit a few years later. They started a business specializing in the financing of small health care firms and eventually took it public; that business sold for half a billion dollars in 1999. He then started CapitalSource, which lends money to small and midsized businesses.

A member of the New Democrat Coalition, Delaney sits on the Financial Services Committee. He supports the 2010 financial regulatory overhaul and says the law's increased capital requirements are a good way to go. His priority on the panel is housing, and he explicitly states that the government needs to let the private sector take the lead on housing finance. He told American Banker that Fannie Mae and Freddie Mac could be eliminated.

But he wants the government to take an active role in shaping the workforce and infrastructure that the private sector uses. Delaney's first big legislative project is a new national system to finance public-private partnerships for infrastructure development. In March 2013, he applauded a Democratic fiscal 2014 budget proposal for its "investments in education and infrastructure" — but in a nod to his fiscal moderation, he added that "I look forward to it being improved with appropriate entitlement reform and deficit reduction."

The 6th District was represented by 10-term Republican Roscoe G. Bartlett, but Democrats redrew its borders in 2012 to favor their party. Delaney was a political unknown, but he used his personal fortune to sweep past a party-backed state senator in the primary. He defeated Bartlett by almost 21 points.

Maryland 6

Panhandle; Frederick; western Montgomery County

The 6th District takes in Maryland's northwest panhandle, bordered by Pennsylvania to the north and the Potomac River and the Virginias to the west. In the state's most contentious redistricting outcome, the 6th transitioned from Maryland's most Republican-leaning district to majority Democratic. Remapping removed the conservative-leaning, mostly white counties east of Frederick and replaced them with liberal, racially diverse voters in the Montgomery County suburbs of Washington, D.C.

Technology and data companies are key to the economy here. Data processing firms are among the largest employers in Washington County, and the military data center at the Allegany Ballistics Lab, across the border in West Virginia, employs residents throughout the tri-state region. Hagerstown has long been known as a hub for railroads and highways; rail giant CSX is a major employer in nearby Allegany County.

Garrett, Allegany and Washington counties have higher poverty rates and less racially diverse populations than the state overall.

Natural gas in the Marcellus Shale has brought an energy boom to Appalachia, and officials in the 6th back the extraction technique known as fracking.

The redistricted 6th lost the rural northern half of Frederick County but retained the city of Frederick. The local economy relies on high-skilled technology jobs, thanks in large part to Fort Detrick and its bioscience labs.

New to the 6th are some northwestern Montgomery County suburbs and exurbs, including Gaithersburg, Germantown and the northeastern section of Potomac. This addition to the 6th — densely populated areas with prominent Asian and Latino populations as well as mainly liberal upper-middle-class white enclaves — added a jolt of Democratic voters to a district that had supported the GOP at all levels.

Major Industry
Technology, manufacturing

Military Bases
Fort Detrick, 1,971 military, 4,015 civilian (2012)

Cities
Cumberland, Hagerstown, Frederick

Notable
The Antietam National Battlefield marks the bloodiest single-day battle in American history.

Rep. Elijah E. Cummings (D)

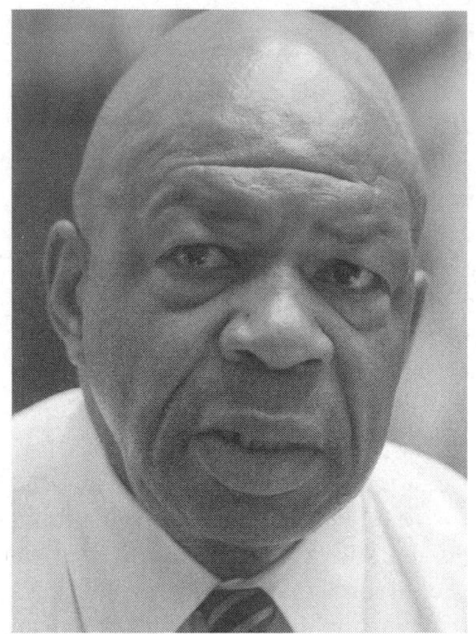

Capitol Office
225-4741
cummings.house.gov
2235 Rayburn Bldg. 20515-2007; fax 225-3178

Committees
Oversight & Government Reform - Ranking Member
Transportation & Infrastructure
Joint Economic

Residence
Baltimore

Born
Jan. 18, 1951; Baltimore, Md.

Religion
Baptist

Family
Wife, Maya Rockeymoore Cummings; three children

Education
Howard U., B.A. 1973 (political science); U. of Maryland, J.D. 1976

Career
Lawyer

Political Highlights
Md. House, 1983-96 (speaker pro tempore, 1995)

ELECTION RESULTS

2012 GENERAL		
Elijah E. Cummings (D)	247,770	76.5%
Frank Mirabile Jr. (R)	67,405	20.8%
Ronald M. Owens-Bey (LIBERT)	8,211	2.5%
2012 PRIMARY		
Elijah E. Cummings (D)	49,625	92.8%
Charles U. Smith (D)	2,438	4.6%
Ty Glen Busch (D)	1,396	2.6%
2010 GENERAL		
Elijah E. Cummings (D)	152,669	75.2%
Frank Mirabile Jr. (R)	46,375	22.8%
Scott Spencer (LIBERT)	3,814	1.9%

Previous Winning Percentages
2008 (80%); 2006 (98%); 2004 (73%); 2002 (74%); 2000 (87%); 1998 (86%); 1996 (83%); 1996 Special Election (81%)

Elected 1996; 9th full term

Cummings relishes opportunities to exercise his legal muscles as the top Democrat on the Oversight and Government Reform Committee. "Once a lawyer, always a lawyer," he says. His own vision for the panel is stymied by the Republican majority, so he offers spirited defenses when he thinks GOP investigations go too far afield.

Dealing with committee business or appearing on news shows, Cummings is usually assertive but contained. However, when whipping up a crowd or speaking from the House floor about Democratic priorities, he sometimes breaks into a forceful shout — displaying a personality large enough to counterbalance that of California Republican Darrell Issa, the Oversight chairman.

Cummings beat out New York Democrat Carolyn B. Maloney for the ranking member post in the 112th Congress (2011-12), with the backing of House Democratic leaders. He is viewed as a contender for a future leadership post, although he says the Oversight gavel is all he's interested in.

He took issue with Issa's agenda in the 112th Congress, describing many investigations and hearings, such as those on the effects of regulations, as a waste of energy. "You could stick them in the microwave, warm them up and serve them again," he said. "We're doing the same things over and over and over again. ... This is the one committee that could have a tremendous impact on the lives of Americans, and I just don't think we're doing that."

Cummings sees it as his duty to make sure the Obama administration is "treated fairly" when Issa looks its way. He was exasperated by the probe of the Justice Department operation known as Fast and Furious, which tried to build cases against drug cartels by allowing gun traffickers to smuggle weapons into Mexico. Some of those weapons were recouped at the crime scene of a murdered American patrol agent in 2010.

Issa investigated who in the chain of command knew of the controversial tactics. Attorney General Eric H. Holder Jr. claimed ignorance, but President Barack Obama invoked executive privilege to block the release of information that Issa subpoenaed. The standoff resulted in lawmakers finding Holder in contempt of Congress in June 2012.

Cummings derided the Justice Department tactics while also defending the administration. He issued a 95-page minority report that concluded the "gunwalking" program began on President George W. Bush's watch. He criticized Issa for refusing to question Democrat-recommended witnesses. Cummings and many other Democrats refused to vote on the contempt resolution, which he called "the culmination of one of the most highly politicized and reckless congressional investigations in decades."

In September 2012, the Justice Department's inspector general recommended disciplinary action against senior officials at the Bureau of Alcohol, Tobacco, Firearms and Explosives, but he said Holder had no advance knowledge of the operation.

Cummings and Issa reached a detente in late 2012, agreeing to collaborate on more oversight efforts. Under GOP rules, Issa's run as chairman should end at the conclusion of the 113th Congress (2013-14).

Cummings' preference for oversight is "focusing more on the things that go to the center of people's lives." He says home foreclosures fit that description, and he has repeatedly urged Issa to investigate foreclosures that occurred after the 2008 credit crisis.

The 2010 financial regulatory overhaul law included a Cummings proposal to establish a $1 billion fund from which struggling homeowners could apply for low-interest bridge loans to help them stay current on their mortgage payments. Cummings won inclusion of a provision requiring lenders to notify borrowers of the consequences of refinancing or purchasing a home equity loan. It also requires creditors to disclose their policies on partial payments for a residential mortgage loan, and the Treasury Department to provide state-by-state breakdowns of the conditions that banks require struggling borrowers to meet when they want to modify their existing loans.

Cummings begrudgingly supported the $700 billion plan to rescue the faltering financial system in 2008. He spent much of the 111th Congress (2009-10) grilling corporate executives and federal regulators at panel hearings about why the financial markets had veered off a cliff.

"Gray markets" for pharmaceuticals have also captured his interest. Cummings introduced 2012 legislation to curb the practice, whereby wholesalers snap up supplies of drugs that are in short supply, then sell them to hospitals at much higher prices. His bill would have prohibited wholesalers from purchasing drugs from pharmacies and created a nationwide database to identify such suspicious activities. Cummings worked on the gray markets issue with Democratic Sen. Tom Harkin of Iowa, and he also shares Harkin's concerns about the potentially abusive practices of for-profit colleges.

Cummings has held onto his seat on the Transportation and Infrastructure Committee, where in the 111th Congress he chaired the Coast Guard and Maritime Transportation Subcommittee. Baltimore's bustling port has a significant economic impact on his district.

Born in Baltimore, Cummings was one of seven children of former sharecroppers who migrated from South Carolina. "We did not have many opportunities," he recalled of his childhood. "We did not play on grass. We played on asphalt." But his "two very strong parents" set him on a productive course and saved to buy their own home in a city neighborhood that was integrating.

He graduated from Howard University in Washington, D.C., where he was student government president. He said his mother was hesitant about attending his graduation ceremony because she did not want to embarrass her son in front of "all those sophisticated people" at Howard. Cummings told her he would be honored to have her there.

He then earned a law degree from the University of Maryland. Six years later, he was elected to the state House. He rose to the chamber's second-ranking position, at the time the highest state office ever held by an African American.

Rep. Kweisi Mfume resigned from the House in 1996 to become president of the NAACP, and Cummings scored more than 37 percent of the vote in a special-election primary that featured 26 other Democrats. He easily dispatched his Republican opposition and has won re-elections easily.

Key Votes

2012

Extend a Social Security payroll tax cut and unemployment benefits	NO
Ease securities rules to expand small-business access to capital	NO
Extend for one year subsidized student loan interest rates financed by a cut in health care spending	NO
Cite Attorney General Eric H. Holder Jr. for contempt of Congress	?
Create a visa program for foreign graduates in high-tech fields	NO
Extend most Bush-era income tax rates while allowing rates for top-bracket earners to rise (Jan. 1, 2013)	YES

2011

Strike funding for F-35 alternative engine	YES
Prevent EPA from regulating greenhouse gas emissions to address climate change	NO
Extend certain provisions of Patriot Act for four years	NO
Declare opposition to use of ground troops in Libya	NO
Overhaul patent law	YES
Pass compromise debt limit increase plan and establish future spending limits	NO
Allow consideration of measures to implement three trade agreements	NO

CQ Vote Studies

	PARTY UNITY		PRESIDENTIAL SUPPORT	
	SUPPORT	OPPOSE	SUPPORT	OPPOSE
2012	97%	3%	86%	14%
2011	97%	3%	81%	19%
2010	99%	1%	90%	10%
2009	98%	2%	97%	3%
2008	99%	1%	12%	88%

Interest Groups

	AFL-CIO	ADA	CCUS	ACU
2012	95%	95%	25%	0%
2011	100%	100%	10%	4%
2010	100%	95%	13%	0%
2009	100%	100%	40%	0%
2008	100%	100%	50%	5%

Maryland 7

Central — most of Baltimore, Ellicott City

The Democratic 7th includes main metropolitan Baltimore — downtown and West Baltimore — and has the largest black population among the state's eight districts, at 55 percent. Sailboat-shaped, the 7th takes in the northern and western parts of Baltimore County and the northern half of Howard County.

Research and technology facilities are gradually replacing the steel industry that drove Baltimore's economy in the 20th century. The University of Maryland Medical Center, Johns Hopkins University and affiliated medical institutions — including the Bloomberg School of Public Health and Kennedy Krieger Institute — are among the area's largest employers. Loyola University Maryland (in the 3rd) and the University of Maryland, Baltimore County, are other major employers. Some of the district's residents take advantage of lower cost of living and commuter transit options in Baltimore while working in Washington, D.C.

Baltimore's cultural institutions are in the 7th, including renowned museums, the National Aquarium, the historic Lyric Opera House and the Peabody Institute, a classical music and dance conservatory. The 7th is also home to the Maryland Institute College of Art. However, the city continues to struggle with crime, ranking among the most dangerous in the country; public health initiatives are under way to reduce violence, particularly gun violence, which is a major source of ongoing concern.

The 7th District gained a large and conservative swath of rural Baltimore County during remapping after the 2010 census. Still, more than half of the 7th's population lives in strongly liberal Baltimore city and keeps the district in the Democratic column. Democratic candidates for president regularly win more than 70 percent of the vote in the district. The NAACP national headquarters is in the northwestern corner of the city.

Major Industry

Health care, research, higher education, technology

Cities

Baltimore (pt.), Ellicott City (unincorporated)

Notable

Edgar Allen Poe is buried at the Westminster Hall Burying Ground, where devotees have paid annual tribute at his grave — Baltimore is also home to the Edgar Allen Poe Society.

Rep. Chris Van Hollen (D)

Capitol Office
225-5341
vanhollen.house.gov
1707 Longworth Bldg. 20515-2008; fax 225-0375

Committees
Budget - Ranking Member

Residence
Kensington

Born
Jan. 10, 1959; Karachi, Pakistan

Religion
Episcopalian

Family
Wife, Katherine Wilkens Van Hollen; three children

Education
Swarthmore College, B.A. 1983 (philosophy); Harvard U., M.P.P. 1985; Georgetown U., J.D. 1990

Career
Lawyer; gubernatorial aide; congressional aide

Political Highlights
Md. House, 1991-95; Md. Senate, 1995-2003

ELECTION RESULTS

2012 GENERAL		
Chris Van Hollen (D)	217,531	63.4%
Kenneth R. Timmerman (R)	113,033	32.9%
Mark Grannis (LIBERT)	7,235	2.1%
George Gluck (GREEN)	5,064	1.5%
2012 PRIMARY		
Chris Van Hollen (D)	35,989	92.2%
George T. English (D)	3,041	7.8%
2010 GENERAL		
Chris Van Hollen (D)	153,613	73.3%
Michael Lee Philips (R)	52,421	25.0%
Mark Grannis (LIBERT)	2,713	1.3%

Previous Winning Percentages
2008 (75%); 2006 (77%); 2004 (75%); 2002 (52%)

Elected 2002; 6th term

Van Hollen wants a bigger role in the Democratic Party, and he has the implicit blessing of some of its most powerful members. What's been missing in recent years is a high-profile position to publicly validate his high reputation among his peers — but even without one, Van Hollen continues to operate as part of the House Democratic leadership team.

Van Hollen had lots of political experience as a state lawmaker and a congressional aide by the time he got to the House in 2003. In his second term he became an integral part of campaign operations, recruiting candidates for the 2006 election.

Democrats won the House that year, and Van Hollen took over as chairman of the Democratic Congressional Campaign Committee for the 2008 and 2010 elections. As "assistant to the speaker," he was a White House liaison for Nancy Pelosi in the 111th Congress (2009-10), when Democrats enacted overhauls of the health care and financial regulatory systems.

He improved his reputation with Democratic leaders by avoiding awkward intraparty battles. Van Hollen stayed out of a 2006 Senate race to clear the way for fellow House Democrat Benjamin L. Cardin. He then backed off a run for Democratic Caucus chairman after the 2008 election, letting Pelosi ally John B. Larson of Connecticut have that job.

But his job as assistant to the speaker disappeared when Democrats lost the House majority in 2010, and Van Hollen stepped down at the DCCC after that Republican landslide. Democratic committee rosters shrank, and Van Hollen lost his seat on the Ways and Means Committee. Still, few in the party seemed to blame Van Hollen for their losses — he continued serving as an unofficial campaign strategist in the 2012 cycle. And Pelosi helped install Van Hollen as the top Democrat on the Budget Committee in 2011. He continues to hold that job in the 113th Congress (2013-14).

While waiting for his next major opportunity, Van Hollen gets to serve as the Democrats' foil to Wisconsin Republican Paul D. Ryan, the Budget chairman and 2012 vice presidential candidate. The role suits him. Both men are wonky and bright with nice-guy demeanors. (Van Hollen is 11 years older, but still youthful.) When Vice President Joseph R. Biden Jr. was preparing to debate Ryan in 2012, Van Hollen played Ryan in the practice sessions.

House Republicans heartily endorsed Ryan's budgets for fiscal 2012, 2013 and 2014, effectively making them the framework for the GOP's economic agenda. Those plans have included spending cuts, a tax code overhaul and structural changes to entitlement programs. Van Hollen — one of the most frequent Democratic guests on television news programs — does his best to pick them apart.

He propagated the idea that Ryan's "premium support" model for Medicare would turn the program into a voucher system bad for seniors. Van Hollen argues that Ryan's tax plans run counter to the idea that everyone should pay a fair share. "[Ryan] presents a plan that's bad for the country with a smile, so I think the challenge is dealing with presentation of the plan, explaining why the plan is bad for the country," he said. After Ryan joined the presidential ticket in 2012, Van Hollen also tied the GOP budget to Mitt Romney.

Van Hollen leans toward the middle on some economic matters. He was one of 81 House Democrats to vote for a fiscal 2011 spending deal that cut about $40 billion from 2010 levels, and he voted for a 2011 deficit reduction package that raised the federal debt limit. He has supported free-trade deals, and he voted for 2011 pacts with South Korea, Colombia and Panama. Van Hollen likes the idea of "enhanced rescission," which would let the president cross out specific items in a spending bill without vetoing the whole thing.

In most cases, however, Van Hollen is in line with the Democratic leadership. He has a close-to-perfect lifetime rating from the League of Conservation Voters and is liberal on most social issues. Van Hollen favors abortion rights and restrictions on gun owners' rights.

He also waves the party's banner on campaign finance issues. A 2010 Supreme Court ruling eliminated restrictions on campaign spending by unions and corporations, if the spending isn't directly coordinated with a candidate. Van Hollen sponsored a bill, which the House passed, to set stricter disclosure requirements to reveal which groups paid for an ad. The bill was not enacted, and versions Van Hollen introduced in 2012 and 2013 went nowhere in the Republican-controlled House.

Well-educated and well-traveled, Van Hollen is a good match for his district, which is mainly defined by a swath of demographically elite suburbs just outside Washington. Many of his constituents work for the federal government, contractors or lobbyists; many others are engaged in biomedical research and technology. A 2012 extension of lower payroll taxes and expanded unemployment benefits was paid for in part by requiring federal workers to contribute more to their pension plans. Van Hollen and Cardin altered it to include a "grandfather" clause to exempt current workers.

The son of a Foreign Service officer, Van Hollen was born in Karachi, Pakistan, and lived in Turkey, India and Sri Lanka, where his father was ambassador. His mother was an expert on Russia. He earned a graduate degree in public policy and national security studies from Harvard's Kennedy School of Government, where he met his wife, Katherine. He then joined the staff of Maryland Sen. Charles McC. Mathias Jr., a Republican moderate, as a legislative assistant for defense and foreign policy.

When Mathias retired in 1986, Van Hollen went to work for the Senate Foreign Relations Committee as an arms control and NATO specialist, while Katherine worked for the House Foreign Affairs Committee. He won election to the Maryland House in 1990, and four years later he went after a state Senate seat. He took on the incumbent Democrat in the primary, even though she had helped him win his House seat. He won and went on to serve eight years.

Van Hollen saw his chance to move up to Congress when redistricting after the 2000 census packed more Democrats into Maryland's 8th District, where liberal Republican Constance A. Morella regularly won re-election. First, he had to survive a five-way primary, narrowly edging out state Rep. Mark K. Shriver, a nephew of President John F. Kennedy. He and Morella then waged one of the costliest and most-watched contests of the 2002 election. Van Hollen eked out a 4-point win and has sailed to re-election ever since.

Key Votes

2012	
Extend a Social Security payroll tax cut and unemployment benefits	NO
Ease securities rules to expand small-business access to capital	YES
Extend for one year subsidized student loan interest rates financed by a cut in health care spending	NO
Cite Attorney General Eric H. Holder Jr. for contempt of Congress	?
Create a visa program for foreign graduates in high-tech fields	NO
Extend most Bush-era income tax rates while allowing rates for top-bracket earners to rise (Jan. 1, 2013)	YES
2011	
Strike funding for F-35 alternative engine	YES
Prevent EPA from regulating greenhouse gas emissions to address climate change	NO
Extend certain provisions of Patriot Act for four years	NO
Declare opposition to use of ground troops in Libya	NO
Overhaul patent law	YES
Pass compromise debt limit increase plan and establish future spending limits	YES
Allow consideration of measures to implement three trade agreements	NO

CQ Vote Studies

	PARTY UNITY		PRESIDENTIAL SUPPORT	
	SUPPORT	OPPOSE	SUPPORT	OPPOSE
2012	97%	3%	91%	9%
2011	96%	4%	96%	4%
2010	100%	0%	95%	5%
2009	99%	1%	97%	3%
2008	99%	1%	14%	86%

Interest Groups

	AFL-CIO	ADA	CCUS	ACU
2012	95%	90%	25%	4%
2011	90%	[illegible]	[illegible]	0%
2010	100%	100%	13%	0%
2009	100%	100%	33%	0%
2008	100%	100%	61%	0%

Maryland 8

Part of Montgomery County; Westminster

Stretching from Washington, D.C., to the Pennsylvania border, the 8th is a mix of highly educated suburban professionals in the south and conservative-leaning populations in rural Carroll and Frederick counties to the north. The population is concentrated in racially diverse suburban hubs — Bethesda, Rockville, Silver Spring and Takoma Park.

Most of the district's population lives in the affluent Montgomery County suburbs, where federal agencies are major employers and health care, research and technology companies rely on proximity to the federal government and agency funding. Bethesda hosts the National Institutes of Health and the Walter Reed National Military Medical Center, the world's largest military hospital. Aerospace giant Lockheed Martin also has its corporate headquarters in Bethesda. Major non-defense interests include a Microsoft regional office in Chevy Chase and the Discovery Channel in Silver Spring.

To the north, Frederick is Maryland's largest agricultural county — growing vegetables, wine grapes and Christmas trees — and is the state's top producer of dairy. The 8th's share of Carroll includes small-town Westminster and its 19th-century architecture and budding arts scene.

The 8th's Montgomery County footprint was reduced during decennial remapping as liberal voters were shifted into the conservative-leaning 6th. In exchange, the 8th gained GOP-leaning rural areas in Frederick and Carroll counties. Concentrations of liberal voters still outnumber Republicans, however, keeping the 8th safely Democratic. While the district is predominately white overall, the portion of Montgomery County in the 8th is home to large black, Asian and Hispanic communities.

Major Industry

Government, technology, research, retail, agriculture

Military Bases

Walter Reed National Military Medical Center, 3,069 military, 2,531 civilian (2012); Naval Surface Warfare Center, Carderock Division, 1 military, 1,369 civilian

Cities

Silver Spring (unincorp.), Rockville, Bethesda (unincorp.)

Notable

Glen Echo Park has a working Dentzel Carousel in the menagerie style with an original Wurlitzer band organ, one of only 11 that still exist.

MASSACHUSETTS

Boston Area

Districts 5, 7, 8

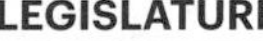

Gov. Deval Patrick (D)

First elected: 2006
Length of term: 4 years
Term expires: 1/15
Salary: $139,832
Phone: (617) 725-4000
Residence: Milton
Born: July 31, 1956; Chicago
Religion: Presbyterian
Family: Wife, Diane Patrick; two children
Education: Harvard U., A.B. 1978 (English & American literature), J.D. 1982
Career: Lawyer; beverage company executive
Political highlights: Assistant attorney general, Civil Rights Division, 1994-97

ELECTION RESULTS

2010 GENERAL

Deval Patrick (D)	1,112,283	47.9%
Charles Baker (R)	964,866	41.6%
Tim Cahill (I)	184,395	7.9%
Jill Stein (GREEN)	32,895	1.4%

Lt. Gov. (Vacant)

Length of term: 4 years
Term expires: 1/15
Salary: $122,058
Phone: (617) 725-4005

LEGISLATURE

General Court: Usually year-round, but meeting times vary.
Senate: 40 members, 2-year terms
2013 ratios: 35 D, 4 R, 1 vacancy; 27 men, 12 women
Salary: $61,133
Phone: (617) 722-1276
House: 160 members, 2-year terms
2013 ratios: 127 D, 30 R, 3 vacancies; 118 men, 39 women
Salary: $61,133
Phone: (617) 722-2356

TERM LIMITS

Governor: 2 terms
Senate: No
House: No

URBAN STATISTICS

CITY	POPULATION
Boston	617,594
Worcester	181,045
Springfield	153,060
Lowell	106,519
Cambridge	105,162

REGISTERED VOTERS

Other	52%
Democrat	37%
Republican	11%

POPULATION

2010 population	6,547,629
2000 population	6,349,097
1990 population	6,016,425
Percent change (2000-2010)	+3.1%
Rank among states (2010)	14
Median age	38.5
Born in state	63.8%
Foreign born	14.1%
Violent crime rate	457/100,000
Poverty level	10.3%
Federal workers	60,027
Military	3,205

ELECTIONS

STATE ELECTION OFFICIAL
(617) 727-2828
DEMOCRATIC PARTY
(617) 939-0800
REPUBLICAN PARTY
(617) 523-5005

MISCELLANEOUS

Web: www.mass.gov
Capital: Boston

U.S. CONGRESS

Senate: 2 Democrats
House: 9 Democrats

STATISTICS BY DISTRICT

	2012 Vote for President		2008 Vote for President										
District	Obama	Romney	Obama	McCain	Black	Asian	Hispanic	Median Income	Over 64	Under 20	College Education	Rural	Sq. Miles
1	64%	34%	64%	34%	6%	2%	15%	$49,270	15%	25%	27%	21%	2,350
2	59	39	60	37	4	5	8	58,439	13	26	36	18	1,628
3	57	41	59	39	3	6	16	63,270	12	26	35	9	758
4	57	41	60	38	2	6	4	81,131	13	26	49	6	668
5	65	33	66	32	5	10	7	75,564	14	23	52	1	265
6	55	44	57	41	3	4	8	76,130	15	25	40	4	527
7	82	16	82	17	27	10	20	48,034	10	23	40	0	63
8	58	41	58	41	9	7	5	70,420	15	23	42	1	326
9	56	43	58	41	3	1	4	57,517	18	23	32	14	1,215
STATE	**61**	**38**	**62**	**36**	**7**	**5**	**10**	**62,859**	**14**	**24**	**39**	**9**	**7,800**
U.S.	**51**	**47**	**53**	**46**	**12**	**5**	**17**	**50,052**	**13**	**27**	**29**	**21**	**3,531,905**

Sen. Elizabeth Warren (D)

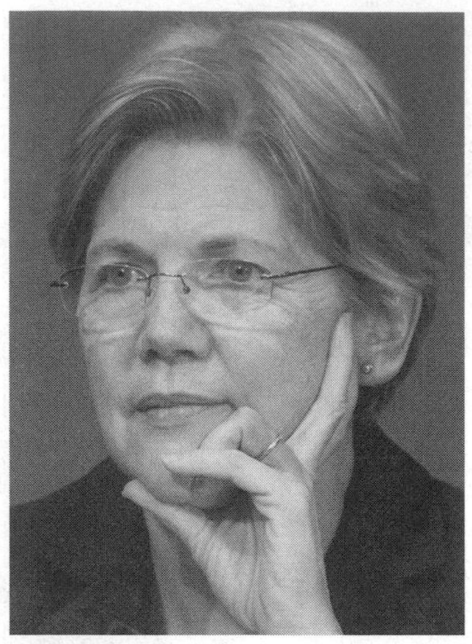

Capitol Office
224-4543
warren.senate.gov
2 Courtyard Russell Bldg. 20510-2101; fax 228-2071

Committees
Banking, Housing & Urban Affairs
Health, Education, Labor & Pensions
Special Aging

Residence
Cambridge

Born
June 22, 1949; Oklahoma City, Okla.

Religion
Methodist

Family
Husband, Bruce Mann; two children

Education
George Washington U., attended 1966-68; U. of Houston, B.S. 1970 (speech pathology & audiology); Rutgers U., J.D. 1976

Career
Law professor; White House consumer protection adviser; financial markets oversight panel chairwoman; bankruptcy analyst; lawyer; homemaker; elementary school speech pathologist

Political Highlights
No previous office

ELECTION RESULTS

2012 GENERAL		
Elizabeth Warren (D)	1,696,346	53.7%
Scott P. Brown (R)	1,458,048	46.2%
2012 PRIMARY		
Elizabeth Warren (D)		unopposed

Elected 2012; 1st term

Warren helped develop the Obama administration's plans for financial-sector regulation, and her work made her a national figure even before she was a candidate for office. She was celebrated by Democrats as a champion of the little guy and despised by Republicans as an avatar of intrusive government. Those prejudices follow her into the Senate, where her professed agenda is solidly liberal.

She made a name for herself as an academic. Warren was a tenured law professor at Harvard, specializing in bankruptcy; her research and writing often focused on the economic challenges facing the middle class. Warren made a number of documentary film and television appearances commenting on financial matters.

The economic crisis of 2008 led to a $700 billion rescue package for the finance industry, as Congress tried to prevent the chaotic collapse of many private sector companies. Senate Majority Leader Harry Reid appointed Warren to chair a five-person panel overseeing the Troubled Asset Relief Program, as it was called. Warren's expertise in bankruptcy law gave her the background to become a crusader for consumer protections while she served in that capacity. "I went to Washington in the middle of the financial crisis to try to put some accountability into the bank bailout system," Warren said. "While I was there I had the chance to work on another idea I had."

That idea was realized in the form of the Consumer Financial Protection Bureau, which was created by the 2010 financial regulatory overhaul — a bill that was enacted with practically no Republican support. The CFPB is meant to serve as a watchdog for borrowers seeking mortgages, credit cards and other financial products.

"The way I saw it, there was nobody in Washington who was really looking out for consumers," Warren said. "We needed just a fair game, just a level playing field here. It was a tough fight, but we got it."

Republicans and the banking industry did not like the bureau from the start; they describe it as being unaccountable to Congress and having too much power to meddle with the private sector. They were livid at the thought of Warren running it, believing her to be biased against Wall Street and prone to creating regulatory sclerosis in the marketplace. A filibuster was threatened, and President Barack Obama never nominated Warren to become the first director of the CFPB. Instead, she was named an adviser to oversee its creation.

Warren's travails propelled her to stardom in the Democratic Party and led to her 2012 Senate campaign, in which she defeated the moderate Republican incumbent, Scott P. Brown. She now gets to oversee the CFPB as a member of the Banking, Housing and Urban Affairs Committee.

Also a member of the Health, Education, Labor and Pensions Committee, she has said she will press for government action to hold corporations accountable.

Beyond that, she espouses positions that resonate with the liberal wing of her party. Warren calls for a job creation program that begins with more federal spending on infrastructure and education. "In the short run, we can put people back to work repairing roads and bridges, upgrading communications and making sure we have teachers in the classroom and firefighters in the fire station," she said.

She wants Congress to address the growing burden of student loans on consumers. And she will push her colleagues to invest in renewable-energy technology, which she says is vital not only to protecting the environment, but also to the country's health and national security.

Warren has said she is "a big Teddy Roosevelt fan," citing his work to rein in trusts, his record on conservation issues and his signing of the Food and Drug Act. "He fought hard to create a level playing field for working families," she says.

Warren's biggest challenge in her first term might be adapting to life as a legislator. She was a liberal firebrand on the campaign trail, but she appeared reluctant to make media appearances after her victory; a news conference several days after the election was stilted, with Warren giving abrupt answers and stumbling over questions outside of her policy wheelhouse. A month later she told the Boston Globe that her job "is to be effective on behalf of Massachusetts" and that she was parsing the best ways to go about it in the Senate, where freshmen are traditionally expected to be deferential.

She might have a model in Minnesota Democrat Al Franken. Elected in 2008, the famous comedian and brazen radio host has been relatively anonymous as a lawmaker, declining television appearances and seldom talking to media outlets not based in his home state.

Warren told the Globe that she will be quiet when it suits her purposes, but that "I'm not patient." Case in point: She advocates changing Senate rules to make it more difficult to maintain a filibuster.

"I want to fight for jobs for people who want to work. I want millionaires and billionaires and big oil companies to pay their fair share. And I want to hold Wall Street accountable," Warren wrote in a Huffington Post opinion piece. "But here's the honest truth: we'll never do any of that if we can't get up-or-down votes in the Senate."

Warren was raised in Oklahoma, the youngest of four children and the only daughter. Her father had a number of jobs, including maintenance man. As Warren was entering her teen years, he had a heart attack, and during his recuperation her mother took a job doing catalog sales for Sears. Warren graduated high school at 16 and got a debate scholarship to George Washington University. In her book "The Two-Income Trap," Warren wrote that both parents kept working to help pay for her college education.

She married at age 19 and moved to Texas with her husband, a NASA engineer; Warren completed a degree in speech pathology at the University of Houston and worked in that field briefly before becoming a homemaker. When the family moved to New Jersey, she got a law degree at Rutgers, and when they moved back to Texas she got a non-tenured position at the law school at her alma mater. Warren divorced, remarried and worked at several other schools before landing at Harvard.

According to the Boston Globe, Warren spent a long time as an anomaly at Harvard, having public school credentials rather than a degree from an Ivy League school. It became an issue in her Senate campaign, when Brown questioned whether Warren had gotten a tenured position because she claimed to have Native American heritage — based on family lore that has not been verified.

Academics knowledgeable of her hiring at Harvard insisted to the Globe that Warren's claim did not help her get the tenure-track job.

Warren's contest against Brown proved to be the most expensive congressional race in the country during the 2012 cycle, with a total cost of more than $85 million, according to calculations by CQ Roll Call. Democrats wanted the seat badly, as Brown had been an upset winner of the 2010 special election to succeed the deceased Democratic Sen. Edward M. Kennedy.

Brown promoted his moderate stances and blue-collar appeal, while Warren worked to spread her name recognition outside of Boston. The polls showed an even race for much of the campaign, but Warren ultimately didn't leave Brown any openings to overcome the state's clearly Democratic lean. She won by nearly 8 points.

Sen. William 'Mo' Cowan (D)

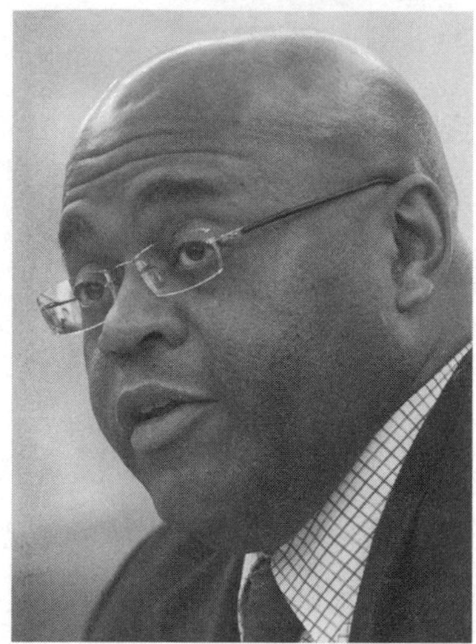

Capitol Office
224-2742
cowan.senate.gov
218 Russell Bldg. 20510-2102; fax 224-8525

Committees
Agriculture, Nutrition & Forestry
(Nutrition, Specialty Crops, Food & Agricultural Research - Chairman)
Commerce, Science & Transportation
Small Business & Entrepreneurship

Residence
Stoughton

Born
April 4, 1969; Yadkinville, N.C.

Religion
Christian

Family
Wife, Stacy Cowan; two children

Education
Duke U., B.A. 1991 (sociology); Northeastern U., J.D. 1994

Career
Gubernatorial aide; lawyer; county prosecutor

Political Highlights
No previous office

Appointed February 2013; 1st term

There's an excellent chance that Cowan will no longer be a senator by the time you read these words. He is serving as a placeholder in this book — in the same way that he served as a placeholder in Congress.

Cowan was appointed in February 2013 to fill the seat vacated by Democrat John Kerry, who became the secretary of State. He is not a candidate in the June 25 special election that determines who will complete Kerry's term.

So if you're looking for information on the junior senator from Massachusetts, you could try reading the profile of Rep. Edward J. Markey of the 5th District. He won the Democratic special-election primary on April 30, and the state is generally friendly to Democrats. He has a good chance of winning.

The term concludes at the same time as the 113th Congress (2013-14), so whoever holds the seat will have to run again in 2014 if he wants to keep it.

For his part, Cowan embraced his role as an interim senator. At the news conference to announce his appointment, he said he would retain Kerry's staff, that he was in agreement with Kerry on policy matters and that he wouldn't seek political office in the future.

The selection of Cowan was a little surprising. When it became clear that Kerry was departing the Senate, well-known Democrats were mentioned as possible placeholders. Rep. Barney Frank, who retired at the end of the 112th Congress (2011-12), publicly stumped for the job; Victoria Reggie Kennedy, the widow of Sen. Edward M. Kennedy, was another possibility. Gov. Deval Patrick instead chose his former chief of staff, who had resigned just weeks earlier with the intention of returning to the private sector.

Cowan couldn't pass up a brief run in the Senate, however. His appointment instantly made him a distinguished footnote in the history of Congress. He is the eighth black person to serve in the Senate, and the second to come from Massachusetts. Edward W. Brooke, a Republican, was elected to two terms, serving from 1967 to 1979.

Cowan has been described as an "insider" in Massachusetts politics, but he hasn't been inside for all that long.

He grew up in Yadkinville, N.C., a rural town west of Winston-Salem. His father died when Cowan was 16, and his seamstress mother took care of Cowan and his sisters while making little more than minimum wage, he told The Boston Globe in 2010. Cowan got a degree in sociology from Duke University — he was the first in his family to get a college degree — and then headed to Boston in the early 1990s to attend law school at Northeastern University.

He had been working for a few years when he landed a job at Mintz Levin, a prominent law firm in the city. He served as president of the Massachusetts Black Lawyers Association and chaired the board of a Boston charter school.

Patrick was something of a mentor to Cowan — Cowan once told the Globe that he "essentially cold-called" Patrick after hearing him speak at a legal event two decades ago, and their conversation led to a friendship. In 2008, Patrick named Cowan to the board that oversees Massachusetts convention centers. (The wife of Democratic Rep. Michael E. Capuano was also on the board.) The next year, Cowan left Mintz to become Patrick's chief legal counsel. In 2011, he became Patrick's chief of staff.

Cowan was assigned to three Senate committees, and he was even named the chairman of the Agriculture, Nutrition and Forestry Subcommittee on Nutrition, Specialty Crops, Food and Agricultural Research. It remains to be seen whether those assignments are transferred to the winner of the special election or a committee shuffle ensues as Cowan departs.

Rep. Richard E. Neal (D)

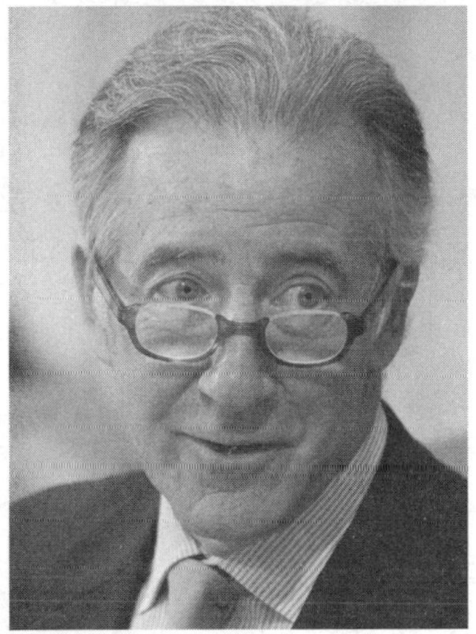

Capitol Office
225-5601
neal.house.gov
2208 Rayburn Bldg. 20515-2101; fax 225-8112

Committees
Ways & Means

Residence
Springfield

Born
Feb. 14, 1949; Worcester, Mass.

Religion
Roman Catholic

Family
Wife, Maureen Neal; four children

Education
American International College, B.A. 1972 (political science); U. of Hartford, M.P.A. 1976

Career
College lecturer; teacher; mayoral aide

Political Highlights
Springfield City Council, 1978-84 (president, 1979); mayor of Springfield, 1984-89

ELECTION RESULTS

2012 GENERAL		
Richard E. Neal (D)	261,936	98.4%
Write Ins (WRI)	4,197	1.6%
2012 PRIMARY		
Richard E. Neal (D)	40,295	65.5%
Andrea Nuciforo (D)	15,159	24.6%
Bill Shein (D)	6,059	9.8%
2010 GENERAL		
Richard E. Neal (D)	122,751	57.3%
Tom Wesley (R)	91,209	42.6%

Previous Winning Percentages
2008 (98%); 2006 (99%); 2004 (99%); 2002 (99%); 2000 (99%); 1998 (99%); 1996 (72%); 1994 (59%); 1992 (53%); 1990 (100%); 1988 (80%)

Elected 1988; 13th term

Neal is a highly regarded expert on tax policy, a subject that in many ways matches his political style. "It's not glitzy," he said.

A former high school history and government teacher, Neal has served since 1993 on the Ways and Means Committee — which he still considers "the premier committee in Congress by far." He missed out on becoming the panel's top Democrat for the 112th Congress (2011-12); Neal narrowly won the endorsement of the Democratic Policy and Steering Committee, but the full Democratic Caucus selected Michigan's Sander M. Levin, who positioned himself as the liberal choice.

Instead, Neal became the ranking member of the Select Revenue Measures Subcommittee, which he chaired from 2007 through 2010 when his party controlled the House. He still holds that post in the 113th Congress (2013-14).

"I think I've earned a reputation for a pretty judicious approach to tax policy," Neal said. He acknowledges, however, that Democratic priorities have had rough going in the Republican House. "It's not like the committee I joined 20 years ago," he said. "Once Republicans started to buy the theology about tax cuts, I think that was transformative."

That "theology," according to Neal, is that tax cuts don't contribute to federal deficits. He sees it as the primary obstacle to an overhaul of the tax code. Neal agrees with the assertion that the current code is making the United States less competitive in the global economy, but if the GOP starts with tax cuts, "it's going to be very hard to get anything done," he said in 2012.

It took a legislative ordeal to accomplish a few of Neal's tax goals at the end of the 112th Congress. In the January 2013 law to address the "fiscal cliff" — a combination of expiring tax rates and scheduled spending cuts — Congress made a permanent change to the alternative minimum tax, the levy intended to ensure that the highest earners don't use deductions to eliminate most of their tax liability.

The earnings thresholds that trigger the AMT weren't indexed for inflation, and Congress had to enact regular "patches" to keep many middle-class taxpayers from getting hit by the AMT. Neal began working on plans to permanently modify the rule in 2007. When the fiscal cliff law was finalized, he told the Berkshire Eagle that "I am declaring victory."

That law also permanently extended lower income tax rates on earnings less than $400,000. More than half a year earlier, Neal had said that such a change "makes some sense."

Neal has worked on "building confidence" in the tax code as a precursor to bigger changes. In the 110th Congress (2007-08), he introduced legislation aimed at barring reduced-rate treatment of dividends from certain companies that avoid paying either U.S. or foreign income taxes, and he has continued to take aim at corporations that establish offshore operations to avoid U.S. taxation. "I've been consistent about arguing against bank secrecy, hiding money offshore, trying to shut down the Bermuda loophole," he said.

Neal also sits on the Trade Subcommittee. He sometimes splits with a majority of Democrats to support free-trade deals that he feels have adequate protections for laborers and the environment. In 2011, he voted for agreements with South Korea and Panama.

Generally, though, Neal has supported party positions. Each year since 2007, he has stuck with Democrats on at least 98 percent of the votes where majorities of the two parties diverged.

One area of Ways and Means' jurisdiction has personal significance for Neal. Both of his parents died when he was a teenager, and Neal and his two younger sisters received Social Security survivor benefits while living with relatives. He compares the benefits to jumping on a trampoline: "You hit it and you bounce back up." In 2005, he worked against President George W. Bush's plan to create private accounts in the Social Security system.

Tax policy is Neal's focus, but he is extremely proud of his work to help broker peace in Northern Ireland. Neal has Northern Irish roots. His grandmother lived there when it was "a very hostile place to live."

Neal, a Catholic, is the current leader of the Friends of Ireland, a congressional group that helped facilitate both the 1998 Good Friday Agreement between the British and Irish governments and subsequent negotiations.

When he spoke at Trinity College on a 2012 trip to Ireland, students "were talking to me as if I was a historian, because they have now had generations grow up in Northern Ireland not knowing any of the violence that had onetime been a state of life," Neal said. "I look at this as a legacy issue, a real accomplishment that's been heralded."

In February 2013, President Barack Obama called for a new free-trade pact with the European Union during his State of the Union address. Neal soon issued a press release that showed some Irish pride. "With Ireland currently holding the European Union presidency, I am confident these negotiations will be successful," he wrote.

Like many of his generation, Neal attributes his interest in politics to President John F. Kennedy. His first role in electoral politics came as co-chairman of Democrat George McGovern's 1972 presidential campaign in western Massachusetts. As it turned out, Massachusetts was the only state McGovern won. Neal still calls the opportunity to work on the race his "big break."

That was also the year Neal graduated from American International College in Springfield. A year later he became an aide to the mayor of Springfield. In 1978, he was elected to serve on the city council, and the next year he became council president.

In 1983, Neal won the first of three terms as Springfield mayor. In that job, he drew praise for stimulating downtown rehabilitation. When Democratic Rep. Edward P. Boland announced his retirement in 1988 after 36 years in the House, Neal hit the ground running, winning the nomination unopposed and handily defeating his Republican opponent.

In the big Republican year of 1994, he faced criticism for 87 overdrafts at the now-defunct House bank, but he still won easily. Since then, he has faced a GOP challenger only twice.

Early in 2013, Neal was named a vice chairman of finance for the Democratic Congressional Campaign Committee for the 2014 cycle — essentially making him one of his party's top fundraisers.

Key Votes

2012	
Extend a Social Security payroll tax cut and unemployment benefits	YES
Ease securities rules to expand small-business access to capital	?
Extend for one year subsidized student loan interest rates financed by a cut in health care spending	NO
Cite Attorney General Eric H. Holder Jr. for contempt of Congress	?
Create a visa program for foreign graduates in high-tech fields	NO
Extend most Bush-era income tax rates while allowing rates for top-bracket earners to rise (Jan. 1, 2013)	YES
2011	
Strike funding for F-35 alternative engine	YES
Prevent EPA from regulating greenhouse gas emissions to address climate change	NO
Extend certain provisions of Patriot Act for four years	NO
Declare opposition to use of ground troops in Libya	?
Overhaul patent law	YES
Pass compromise debt limit increase plan and establish future spending limits	NO
Allow consideration of measures to implement three trade agreements	NO

CQ Vote Studies

	PARTY UNITY		PRESIDENTIAL SUPPORT	
	SUPPORT	OPPOSE	SUPPORT	OPPOSE
2012	99%	1%	93%	7%
2011	98%	2%	88%	12%
2010	99%	1%	88%	12%
2009	99%	1%	96%	4%
2008	100%	0%	14%	86%

Interest Groups

	AFL-CIO	ADA	CCUS	ACU
2012	95%	90%	25%	0%
2011	92%	80%	27%	4%
2010	100%	95%	0%	0%
2009	100%	95%	40%	4%
2008	100%	100%	61%	0%

Massachusetts 1

West — Springfield, Chicopee, Pittsfield

The 1st District takes up western Massachusetts, known for its rolling hills, vibrant foliage and New England charm. The serene countryside and towns in the Berkshires are popular vacation spots. Decennial redistricting stripped the state of one congressional seat after the 2010 census, and the redrawn 1st expanded in the south to include Springfield, the district's most populous city. Although the reach of the 1st in north-central Massachusetts was scaled back, it remains the state's geographically largest district.

Once home to factories and textile mills, the cities and small towns here now rely on white-collar jobs in engineering, health care and financial services. Springfield — a traditional precision manufacturing center since the 1777 founding of the U.S. Armory and still home to Smith & Wesson — hosts the headquarters of MassMutual Insurance, and Baystate Health Care ranks among the largest employers here. The region's traditional manufacturing towns such as Pittsfield have struggled with sustained layoffs, but defense contractor General Dynamics provides engineering jobs and a focal point for western Massachusetts' science and technology education programs.

The Springfield area also boasts several colleges: The 1st is home to all-women Mount Holyoke College, Western New England University and Baystate Medical Center, Tufts University medical school's western campus.

Although the district is overwhelmingly white, Springfield is a minority-majority city with a substantial Hispanic population and is home to a growing gay and lesbian community. Some GOP supporters remain in the district's south, particularly in sparsely populated areas near the Connecticut border. But liberal voters in and around Springfield as well as the northwest make the 1st a strongly Democratic district.

Major Industry
Financial services, health care, manufacturing

Cities
Springfield, Chicopee, Pittsfield, Westfield, Holyoke

Notable
Springfield, the birthplace of basketball in 1891, and Holyoke, where volleyball was invented four years later, host the sports' respective halls of fame; Theodor Geisel, better known by his pen name, was born in Springfield, whose museum grounds include the Dr. Seuss National Memorial Sculpture Garden.

Rep. Jim McGovern (D)

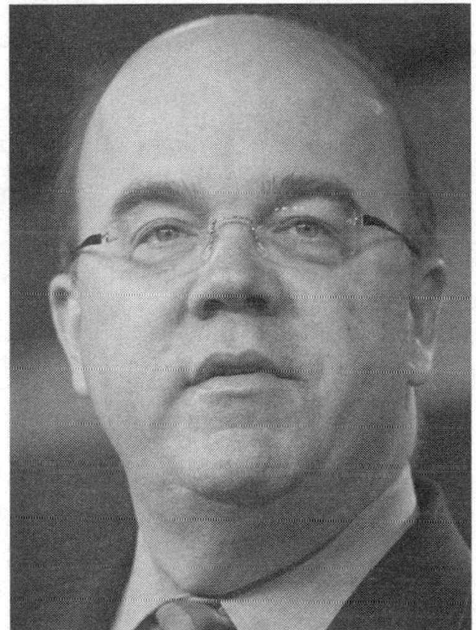

Capitol Office
225-6101
mcgovern.house.gov
438 Cannon Bldg. 20515-2103; fax 225-5759

Committees
Agriculture
Rules

Residence
Worcester

Born
Nov. 20, 1959; Worcester, Mass.

Religion
Roman Catholic

Family
Wife, Lisa McGovern; two children

Education
American U., B.A. 1981 (history), M.P.A. 1984

Career
Congressional aide, campaign aide

Political Highlights
Sought Democratic nomination for U.S. House, 1994

ELECTION RESULTS

2012 GENERAL		
Jim McGovern (D)	259,257	98.4%
Write Ins (WRI)	4,078	1.5%
2012 PRIMARY		
Jim McGovern (D)	24,375	91.5%
William Feegbeh (D)	2,265	8.5%
2010 GENERAL		
Jim McGovern (D)	122,708	56.5%
Marty Lamb (R)	85,124	39.2%
Patrick Barron (I)	9,388	4.3%

Previous Winning Percentages
2008 (98%); 2006 (99%); 2004 (71%); 2002 (99%); 2000 (99%); 1998 (57%); 1996 (53%)

Elected 1996; 9th term

McGovern is a devoted liberal with a pragmatic bent, in the tradition of his political hero and friend — presidential candidate and former South Dakota Sen. George McGovern. Although a party loyalist, he laments the lack of civility in Congress.

Sen. McGovern and former House Rules Chairman Joe Moakley of Massachusetts are the major influences in his political life. "I wouldn't be in politics if not for McGovern," he said. "I wouldn't have stayed if not for Moakley."

Before George McGovern's October 2012 death, Jim McGovern spoke often with his namesake. He believes the caricature of George as a radical to be wrong. "He's a family man, war hero, man of deep faith and one of the most decent human beings I know," the congressman said in the spring of 2012.

He recalls fondly his days working for Moakley, an old-fashioned pol who was his mentor in politics. Before Moakley died, he helped engineer McGovern's move to the Rules Committee, where he is now the No. 2 Democrat. "McGovern taught me it was OK to be an idealist," he once told The Boston Globe. "Moakley taught me how to get things done."

The Rules Committee sets the parameters for floor debate, and in partisan disputes McGovern can get scrappy. In May 2012, panel Republicans refused to make in order a McGovern amendment that would have expedited the withdrawal of U.S. forces from Afghanistan. Incensed, McGovern demanded votes in committee on 86 separate amendments.

"I'm sorry my friends didn't like the roll call votes," McGovern said. "But there has to be a consequence to the fact we weren't going to have a serious debate on the House floor. We can't debate serious issues anymore."

McGovern says there is a general unwillingness in Congress to examine what constitutes national security: "I want a tough military second to none, but excessive military spending does not lead to more security." In 2007, McGovern co-sponsored legislation with Democrats John P. Murtha of Pennsylvania and David R. Obey of Wisconsin that would have raised taxes specifically to pay for the war in Iraq. "If you want to go to war, you ought to pay for it," he said. The bill went nowhere.

In part at his behest, President Bill Clinton created a pilot program that in 2002 became the McGovern-Dole International Food for Education and Child Nutrition Program (named for George McGovern and Kansas Republican Sen. Bob Dole). It has fed millions of children in the developing world. "There are a lot of problems you can't solve, but hunger isn't one of them," McGovern has said. He co-chairs the House Hunger Caucus.

Since 2011, McGovern has held a seat on the Agriculture Committee, which he has used to defend nutrition programs. The agriculture panels in both the House and Senate have considered billions of dollars in cuts to the Supplemental Nutrition Assistance Program as they work on reauthorizations of farm programs. McGovern is appalled by those plans. At a March 2013 hearing, he urged the Obama administration to "stand up and fight for this program. ... As we talk about balancing budgets, SNAP has become kind of the convenient ATM machine." In 2012, he called a proposal to slice $16.5 billion from SNAP funding "unconscionable" and "immoral." During the markup of the 2013 version of the farm bill, he unsuccessfully tried to erase SNAP cuts.

McGovern was named co-chairman of the Congressional Human Rights Caucus in 2008, after the death of longtime Chairman Tom Lantos of California. He later became the first chairman of the Lantos Human Rights Commission. McGovern has been known to take his commitment to the street. He has been arrested twice outside the Sudanese Embassy in Washington, most recently in 2012 with actor George Clooney, in order to publicize the killing of civilians in the Darfur region.

With a longtime interest in Latin America, he has worked tirelessly to shut down the School of the Americas, now named the Western Hemisphere Institute for Security Cooperation, which provides U.S. training to Latin American militaries. As a Moakley aide, he led an investigation of the 1989 murders of six Jesuit priests and two women in El Salvador. U.S. military assistance became tied to the country's record on human rights when the investigation determined the murders had been committed by Salvadoran SOA graduates. He successfully offered an amendment to the fiscal 2010 defense policy bill requiring the Pentagon to release information about the school's students.

In 2012, McGovern injected himself into campaign finance debates, proposing a constitutional amendment to exclude corporations from any rights the Constitution outlines for people — a response to a 2010 Supreme Court ruling that allowed advocacy groups independent of official campaigns to accept unrestricted donations from individuals or organizations (such as unions or companies). Writing on The Huffington Post, he said such donations were "drowning out the voices of individual citizens." Conservative commentators blasted his amendment as a trampling of the First Amendment.

During his childhood in working-class Worcester — his father ran a liquor store and his mother taught dance — the McGoverns were not politically active. But they were devoted to the Kennedys. "We used to drive by the Kennedy compound in Hyannisport when we went to the Cape," he said. When Sen. Robert F. Kennedy of New York was assassinated in 1968, "my father gathered us around the kitchen table and we wrote sympathy cards to [Kennedy's widow] Ethel."

McGovern had his first brush with politics as a junior high school student in 1972, when he became involved in George McGovern's presidential campaign. "My school was primarily Republican and I had to defend my namesake," he said. Later, he tried to get an internship in Sen. McGovern's office. After being turned down by an assistant, the young student bumped into the senator on the way out. Within the hour, the senator asked his office to make room for one more intern. From then on, the two were close friends. In 1984, he served as the Massachusetts campaign manager when McGovern made another presidential bid and delivered a nominating speech at the Democratic National Convention.

Jim McGovern had made an unsuccessful bid in 1994 for the 3rd District seat, but in 1996 he upset two-term Republican Peter I. Blute. He has won easily since then, and Republicans often do not field a candidate to oppose him in the general election.

Key Votes

2012	
Extend a Social Security payroll tax cut and unemployment benefits	YES
Ease securities rules to expand small-business access to capital	YES
Extend for one year subsidized student loan interest rates financed by a cut in health care spending	NO
Cite Attorney General Eric H. Holder Jr. for contempt of Congress	?
Create a visa program for foreign graduates in high-tech fields	NO
Extend most Bush-era income tax rates while allowing rates for top-bracket earners to rise (Jan. 1, 2013)	YES
2011	
Strike funding for F-35 alternative engine	NO
Prevent EPA from regulating greenhouse gas emissions to address climate change	NO
Extend certain provisions of Patriot Act for four years	NO
Declare opposition to use of ground troops in Libya	NO
Overhaul patent law	YES
Pass compromise debt limit increase plan and establish future spending limits	NO
Allow consideration of measures to implement three trade agreements	NO

CQ Vote Studies

	PARTY UNITY		PRESIDENTIAL SUPPORT	
	SUPPORT	OPPOSE	SUPPORT	OPPOSE
2012	99%	1%	92%	8%
2011	97%	3%	80%	20%
2010	99%	1%	85%	15%
2009	99%	1%	94%	6%
2008	99%	1%	13%	87%

Interest Groups

	AFL-CIO	ADA	CCUS	ACU
2012	95%	100%	25%	0%
2011	100%	95%	19%	4%
2010	100%	100%	13%	0%
2009	100%	100%	33%	0%
2008	100%	100%	50%	0%

Massachusetts 2

Central — Worcester, Leominster, Northampton

The 2nd District, redrawn to accommodate the state's loss of one congressional seat following the 2010 census, now stretches through parts of central and western Massachusetts. It borders New Hampshire and a few miles of Vermont to the north, while the southeastern leg touches Connecticut and Rhode Island. It includes most of Worcester County — nearly one-fourth of the population lives in the city of Worcester in the east. In the west, it takes in Amherst, Northampton and other liberal towns north of Springfield in the Pioneer Valley along the Connecticut River, and travels north along Interstate 91 to Greenfield.

Health care, biotechnology and service sector jobs have gradually been replacing the traditional manufacturing base in Worcester, the state's second-largest city. The University of Massachusetts Medical School is one of Worcester's several medical and research facilities. High residential foreclosure rates are expected to come down; long-delayed downtown development projects focusing on entertainment and health care have begun moving forward and are expected to provide an economic boost. Rail company CSX is shifting freight operations to a yard in the city and it is expected to free up more lines for commuter trains to Boston. Although mostly white, Worcester has minority populations higher than state averages.

In the west, the district includes liberal college and manufacturing towns north of Springfield. Amherst is an important higher-education hub, home to the state's flagship campus of the University of Massachusetts, as well as Amherst College. Smith College, a private women's liberal arts college, is located in neighboring Northampton.

Smaller towns and suburbs in Worcester County retain some pockets of moderate conservatism, but the district's politics are dominated by Democratic-leaning Worcester and liberal strongholds in the Pioneer Valley.

Major Industry
Higher education, health care, biotechnology, manufacturing

Cities
Worcester, Leominster, Amherst, Shrewsbury

Notable
The annual Worcester Music Festival began in 1858.

Rep. Niki Tsongas (D)

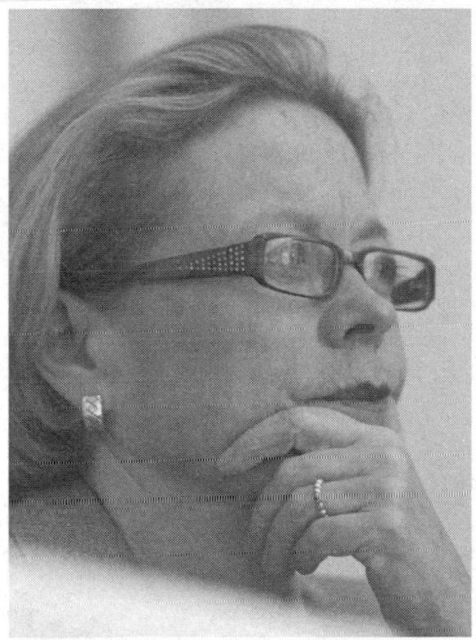

Capitol Office
225-3411
tsongas.house.gov
1607 Longworth Bldg. 20515-2105; fax 226-0771

Committees
Armed Services
Natural Resources

Residence
Lowell

Born
April 26, 1946; Chico, Calif.

Religion
Episcopalian

Family
Widowed; three children

Education
Michigan State U., attended 1964-65; Smith College, B.A. 1968 (religion); Boston U., J.D. 1988

Career
College public affairs official; lawyer; homemaker; paralegal; social worker

Political Highlights
No previous office

ELECTION RESULTS

2012 GENERAL		
Niki Tsongas (D)	212,119	65.9%
Jon Golnik (R)	109,372	34.0%
2012 PRIMARY		
Niki Tsongas (D)		unopposed
2010 GENERAL		
Niki Tsongas (D)	122,858	54.8%
Jon Golnik (R)	94,646	42.2%
Dale E. Brown (I)	4,387	2.0%

Previous Winning Percentages
2008 (99%); 2007 Special Election (51%)

Elected 2007; 3rd full term

Even with her white-collar résumé, Tsongas is at home in the blue-collar city of Lowell, the historic industrial center that anchors her district. She goes along with Democrats on most votes, with occasional defections to address the needs of the region's manufacturers or reflect her concerns about the government's finances.

Tsongas (SONG-gus) has worked as a lawyer and a college official. She also experienced the family side of politics. Her late husband, Paul E. Tsongas, was a two-term House member, one-term senator and presidential candidate before he died of cancer.

She is the only Massachusetts representative on the House Armed Services Committee — and she experienced the family side of the military, as well. The daughter of an Air Force engineer, Tsongas was born in the foothills of California's Cascade Range, but after five years in Chico she rarely stayed any place for long. Her father, who survived the attack on Pearl Harbor, moved frequently in his job, with stops in Germany, Japan, Texas and Virginia. (Her mother was a painter and also worked as a copywriter.)

Tsongas sees some of her biggest responsibilities and legislative successes stemming from military matters, and she takes particular interest in the Military Personnel Subcommittee. Working with Ohio Republican Michael R. Turner, Tsongas added language to the fiscal 2011 defense policy law to expand the legal rights of military members who are sexually assaulted.

"It put a lot of tools in the toolbox" to better train soldiers and encourage victims to seek justice, she said, and more of her sexual assault provisions were included in the fiscal 2013 defense policy law.

Tsongas and Turner co-chair the Military Sexual Assault Prevention Caucus. She says changing the culture of the military is an important aspect of reducing sexual assaults. In the 113th Congress (2013-14), she can further pursue the matter as the ranking member of the Armed Services Oversight and Investigations Subcommittee.

Tsongas has taken several approaches to facilitating the steady increase of women in the armed forces — for example, the fiscal 2013 defense policy law includes a provision requiring the Pentagon to develop body armor for women.

A number of military contractors reside in her district and state. Tsongas keeps them in mind: "It's going to be very important going forward to make the case for Hanscom [Air Force Base] and Lincoln Labs and Natick Soldier Systems," she said in late 2012. "We know the Defense Department has to absorb more cuts ... and there's still room for them to be part of the challenge on cutting back on our debt and deficit."

Tsongas' voting record was almost perfectly in step with the majority of her party when Democrats controlled the House, but several high-profile fiscal votes in the 112th Congress (2011-12) found Tsongas on the side of greater restraint. She was one of 81 Democrats to vote for a cost-cutting fiscal 2011 spending bill, and she backed an August 2011 deal to raise the debt limit and make more spending cuts, saying she didn't want the government to default on its debts.

She also voted to repeal a piece of the 2010 health care law, the overhaul she backed in the 111th Congress (2009-10). She said a tax on medical device manufacturers would hurt businesses in her district. "For small companies it poses a great threat," she said. "It's a tax on sales. It's not a tax on profits. And many of these companies are startup companies."

Tsongas sits on the Natural Resources Committee, where she takes a liberal stance on environmental issues. She voted for 2009 Democratic legislation to create a cap-and-trade system for limiting carbon emissions, calling the measure "one of the most important pieces of legislation we have considered to safeguard the future of our children and grandchildren."

Legislation the House passed in July 2010 in response to that spring's Gulf of Mexico oil spill included language by Tsongas that would require oil companies to submit plans on containing and cleaning up worst-case spills. She introduced a similar measure in 2011.

Her views on social issues are liberal. She supports gay marriage and backed the 2010 repeal of the ban on openly gay military servicemembers.

Tsongas has voted for defense policy bills that liberals oppose, but she is not hawkish. She took up the withdraw-from-Iraq mantle on Armed Services from her Democratic predecessor, Martin T. Meehan. The first bill she introduced as a member of the House would have set deadlines for a withdrawal.

Tsongas was 14 when she became interested in politics, inspired by Democrat John F. Kennedy's presidential campaign.

During the summer between her junior and senior years at Smith College, she interned at a Washington, D.C., investment banking company. That's when she met her future husband, who was interning for Republican Rep. F. Bradford Morse of Massachusetts.

In 1968, Tsongas volunteered for the presidential campaign of Minnesota Sen. Eugene McCarthy, who opposed the Vietnam War policies of President Lyndon B. Johnson, his fellow Democrat. Tsongas helped her husband get elected in 1974 to the U.S. House, where he served two terms before winning a Senate seat. She was a stay-at-home mother until Paul was diagnosed with cancer and retired from Congress in 1985. For years, she had attended law school at night, and she earned a degree from Boston University in 1988. She then co-founded the first all-female law firm in Lowell.

Her husband made a brief return to politics in 1991, losing a bid for the Democratic presidential nomination. He died in 1997 at age 55.

Tsongas' name recognition helped her in the race to succeed Meehan, an eight-term Democrat who resigned in 2007 to become chancellor of the University of Massachusetts at Lowell. Her Republican opponent, retired Air Force officer Jim Ogonowski, drew attention for his connection to the Sept. 11 attacks. His brother was the pilot of the first airplane to be hijacked and flown into the World Trade Center. Tsongas prevailed, 51 percent to 45 percent, and ran unopposed in 2008. She won by nearly 13 points in 2010 over Republican Jon Golnik.

The decennial redistricting process was excellent for Tsongas, who got her wish to keep most of the Merrimack Valley region — including Lowell — in the district. She beat Golnik by almost 32 points in a 2012 rematch.

Key Votes

2012	
Extend a Social Security payroll tax cut and unemployment benefits	YES
Ease securities rules to expand small-business access to capital	YES
Extend for one year subsidized student loan interest rates financed by a cut in health care spending	NO
Cite Attorney General Eric H. Holder Jr. for contempt of Congress	NO
Create a visa program for foreign graduates in high-tech fields	NO
Extend most Bush-era income tax rates while allowing rates for top-bracket earners to rise (Jan. 1, 2013)	YES
2011	
Strike funding for F-35 alternative engine	NO
Prevent EPA from regulating greenhouse gas emissions to address climate change	NO
Extend certain provisions of Patriot Act for four years	YES
Declare opposition to use of ground troops in Libya	YES
Overhaul patent law	NO
Pass compromise debt limit increase plan and establish future spending limits	YES
Allow consideration of measures to implement three trade agreements	NO

CQ Vote Studies

	PARTY UNITY		PRESIDENTIAL SUPPORT	
	SUPPORT	OPPOSE	SUPPORT	OPPOSE
2012	97%	3%	88%	12%
2011	95%	5%	87%	13%
2010	99%	1%	88%	12%
2009	99%	1%	94%	6%
2008	99%	1%	15%	85%

Interest Groups

	AFL-CIO	ADA	CCUS	ACU
2012	95%	95%	33%	0%
2011	96%	90%	19%	0%
2010	100%	95%	25%	0%
2009	100%	95%	29%	0%
2008	100%	100%	56%	0%

Massachusetts 3

North central — Lowell, Lawrence, Fitchburg

The 3rd District is focused on the prominent manufacturing towns of the Merrimack Valley in north-central Massachusetts. It hugs much of the state's border with New Hampshire, taking in former mill communities such as Haverhill, Lowell and Lawrence in the east and stretching as far west as blue-collar Fitchburg. At its center, the district dips southward to take in wealthier regions near Marlborough.

Textile mills and factories made the Merrimack region a booming powerhouse of the Industrial Revolution. While manufacturing remains important, the industry's long, slow decline has only been intensified by the recent financial crisis and recession — unemployment rates in former mill towns Lowell and Lawrence hover around double digits. Those struggling have shifted focus to redeveloping mill and factory buildings for mixed office, residential and commercial uses, finding some success in luring software, technology and financial services companies.

Aside from the minority-majority 7th in Boston, the 3rd is the most demographically diverse district in the state. Still nearly three-fourths white, it has prominent and growing Hispanic communities — especially in Lawrence, where Hispanics make up more than 70 percent of the population.

The newly redrawn 3rd is made up of concentrated Democratic blocs. Blue-collar Lawrence is reliably Democratic, voting by wide margins for Democrat Elizabeth Warren in the 2012 U.S. Senate race; Republican Sen. Scott P. Brown took many of the smaller towns in his unsuccessful re-election bid. Lowell narrowly preferred Brown in the 2010 special election, but gave Warren a nearly 20-point margin two years later.

Major Industry
Manufacturing, technology

Military Bases
Hanscom Air Force Base, 922 military, 2,614 civilian (shared with the 5th and 6th districts)

Cities
Lowell, Lawrence, Haverhill, Methuen Town, Fitchburg, Marlborough

Notable
Concord was the site of the first day of fighting in the Revolutionary War on April 19, 1775 (now celebrated as Patriots Day).

Rep. Joseph P. Kennedy III (D)

Capitol Office
225-5931
kennedy.house.gov
1218 Longworth Bldg. 20515-2901; fax 225-0182

Committees
Foreign Affairs
Science, Space & Technology

Residence
Brookline

Born
Oct. 4, 1980; Brighton, Mass.

Religion
Roman Catholic

Family
Wife, Lauren Birchfield Kennedy

Education
Stanford U., B.S. 2003 (management science and engineering); Harvard U., J.D. 2009

Career
County prosecutor; Peace Corps volunteer; United Nations research analyst

Political Highlights
No previous office

ELECTION RESULTS

2012 GENERAL		
Joseph P. Kennedy III (D)	221,303	61.1%
Sean Bielat (R)	129,936	35.9%
David Rosa (I)	10,741	3.0%
2012 PRIMARY		
Joseph P. Kennedy III (D)	36,557	90.1%
Rachel Brown (D)	2,635	6.5%
Herb Robinson (D)	1,373	3.4%

Elected 2012; 1st term

Kennedy is the latest member of his famous family to serve in Congress, and many of his political beliefs carry on the liberal and progressive traditions established by his relatives. He has not, however, been associated with the personal drama that often swirls around the family.

Kennedy is the grandson of New York Sen. Robert F. Kennedy and the son of Massachusetts Rep. Joseph Patrick Kennedy II. He and his twin brother grew up outside of Boston and attended a prestigious private school; they also went to Stanford University together. After getting his degree, Kennedy joined the Peace Corps, which was established by his great-uncle, and spent two years in the Dominican Republic helping locals establish an ecotourism business in a national park. He has also worked as an analyst for a United Nations development program.

On his return to the United States, he earned a law degree at Harvard. He did some pro bono work while serving as an assistant district attorney in two different Massachusetts jurisdictions.

Kennedy, a member of the liberal Congressional Progressive Caucus, holds a seat on the Foreign Affairs Committee. He was notably one of the few congressmen who did not heap scorn on the legacy of Venezuelan President Hugo Chavez, who died in March 2013. Some people (including Kennedy's father) considered Chavez to be a champion of the poor.

Kennedy has known many members of the Massachusetts delegation for quite some time, both through his family connections and his personal experiences. One of his professors at Harvard was current Sen. Elizabeth Warren.

The impending retirement of 16-term Democratic Rep. Barney Frank left the 4th District open for the 2012 election. Kennedy announced his candidacy in February, and his name helped him raise more than $4.2 million for the race. His Republican opponent, Sean Bielat, had made a respectable showing challenging Frank in 2010, but he had no realistic chance against a Kennedy.

Massachusetts 4

Newton and Brookline; Attleboro; part of Fall River

Crisscrossed by major interstates, the 4th takes in rural communities, onetime industrial centers and historic colonial towns but does not reach the Buzzards Bay shore following remapping. It has a heavily populated northern arm that stretches into the affluent Boston suburbs of Newton, Brookline and Wellesley.

The 4th's suburbs southwest of Boston are wealthy residential communities lined with stately colonial homes that house professionals who work in Boston's academic, technology and health care sectors. Household incomes in Brookline, Newton and Wellesley are well above the statewide and national averages: In Wellesley, the median household income is more than $145,000. Brookline, the district's second-largest city, has maintained its own identity while surrounded on three sides by Boston; it is home to the nation's oldest private country club.

Local officials hope expansion of industrial parks in several parts of the district — notably in Taunton and the much-smaller Hopedale — and funding for job creation programs will boost the economy. Franklin touts itself as close to the three job sectors of Providence, Boston, and Worcester.

Smaller communities along the Rhode Island border are more middle-class and have higher rates of unemployment. Fall River (shared with the 9th) has long been a bastion of white, blue-collar Democrats with a traditional manufacturing past.

The district's population is Democratic and nearly 90 percent white, with a sizable Asian population in the Boston suburbs. In the 2012 presidential race, Barack Obama easily won the towns nearest Boston — Brookline, Newton, Needham and Wellesley — and the blue-collar population centers, although Republican nominee Mitt Romney won in Hopkinton and a stretch of towns from Dover to North Attleboro. GOP Sen. Scott P. Brown took his highest margin statewide in Wrentham in his unsuccessful re-election bid in 2012.

Major Industry
Service, technology

Cities
Newton, Brookline, Taunton, Attleboro, Fall River (pt.)

Notable
John F. Kennedy's birthplace and childhood home in Brookline is a National Historic Site.

Rep. Edward J. Markey (D)

Capitol Office
225-2836
markey.house.gov
2108 Rayburn Bldg. 20515-2107; fax 226-0092

Committees
Energy & Commerce
Natural Resources - Ranking Member

Residence
Malden

Born
July 11, 1946; Malden, Mass.

Religion
Roman Catholic

Family
Wife, Susan Blumenthal

Education
Boston College, B.A. 1968, J.D. 1972

Military
Army Reserve, 1968-73

Career
Lawyer

Political Highlights
Mass. House, 1973-77

ELECTION RESULTS

2013 PRIMARY SPECIAL		
Edward J. Markey (D)	309,487	57.4%
Stephen F. Lynch (D)	229,594	42.6%
2012 GENERAL		
Edward J. Markey (D)	257,490	75.5%
Thomas P. Tierney (R)	82,944	24.3%
2012 PRIMARY		
Edward J. Markey (D)		unopposed
2010 GENERAL		
Edward J. Markey (D)	145,696	66.4%
Gerry Dembrowski (R)	73,467	33.5%

Previous Winning Percentages
2008 (76%); 2006 (98%); 2004 (74%); 2002 (98%); 2000 (99%); 1998 (71%); 1996 (70%); 1994 (64%); 1992 (62%); 1990 (100%); 1988 (100%); 1986 (100%); 1984 (71%); 1982 (78%); 1980 (100%); 1978 (85%); 1976 (77%)

Elected 1976; 19th full term

It is likely that Markey will become a senator in a June 2013 special election, within days of this book's publication. He defeated fellow Democratic Rep. Stephen F. Lynch in an April primary, and it would be somewhat surprising if Massachusetts — a very blue state — chose the Republican nominee to complete the term of John Kerry, who resigned to become secretary of State.

Markey has held elective office for 40 straight years, championing liberal causes all the way. In the later stages of his House career, he has been a policy leader for the Democrats — a contrast from his early years, when clashes with presidents of either party were not uncommon.

Markey has a broad portfolio. He has been heavily involved with energy policy, privacy rights and telecommunications. He urges continued support of biomedical research and pushes nuclear nonproliferation policies.

His loyalty to his caucus does not waver; every year for the past decade, he has voted with his party on at least 98 percent of the votes where Democrats and Republicans were split along partisan lines. Unsurprisingly, he has had the backing of key Democrats, including Minority Leader Nancy Pelosi. In 2007, Pelosi named Markey the chairman of the new Select Committee on Energy Independence and Global Warming.

Republicans disbanded that panel in 2011 when they regained control of the House, so Markey instead became the ranking member on the Natural Resources Committee, where he has opposed Republican efforts to expand oil and gas production.

He is also a member of the Energy and Commerce Committee, where he is a close ally of ranking Democrat Henry A. Waxman of California. In 2009, he helped write a bill that would have created a cap-and-trade system for regulating greenhouse gas emissions. The House passed the measure, but it died in the Senate — and became a major debating point in the 2010 elections.

Markey has tried to address high energy prices through his committee work. In the 112th Congress (2011-12), he led failed attempts by House Democrats to end tax benefits to oil companies and require them to pay higher royalty fees. He opposes expanded offshore drilling and energy exploration in Alaska's Arctic National Wildlife Refuge, and in July 2011 he bristled at GOP legislation to expedite energy production there. Companies were abandoning leases in the region because of economic factors, Markey said at a committee markup: "It has nothing to do with a bunch of granola-chomping environmentalists opposing it up there."

Most notably, he fought GOP attempts to reverse the Obama administration's denial of a permit for construction of the Keystone XL pipeline, which would bring oil from Canada's tar sands to the United States. In a late 2011 hearing, high-level officials from project contractor TransCanada would not give Markey a commitment that fuel from the pipeline would go only to U.S. refineries. Markey responded with several legislative attempts — all rejected — to require oil or gas originating from the pipeline to be sold domestically.

The Energy and Commerce panel has allowed Markey to indulge in his abiding interest in communications technology. His signature legislative achievement is a 1996 telecommunications law that opened up local phone markets to competition, established guidelines for the regional "Baby Bell" companies to enter new markets and imposed competition regulations between cable and telephone companies.

He is a strong proponent of "network neutrality" rules, which prohibit broadband providers from placing restrictions on access to Internet services. In late 2010, Markey pressed the Federal Communications Commission to include broad guidelines in its proposed "Open Internet Order." New rules went into effect in late 2011, although they were challenged by Republicans as an unprecedented expansion of the FCC's regulatory powers.

Markey and Texas Republican Joe L. Barton are the co-chairmen of the Congressional Privacy Caucus. Markey has been holding technology giants like Google and Facebook accountable over their data-sharing and privacy-protection policies, and he has a particular interest in ensuring data privacy for children and teenagers. "It's only going to get more and more dangerous for kids if we don't put these safeguards in place," he warned at a 2011 hearing.

In 2012, Markey took up a new health care cause when a deadly fungal meningitis outbreak was traced back to a compounding pharmacy in his district. He has proposed giving the Food and Drug Administration clear regulatory authority over such entities.

Markey grew up in Malden, a working-class suburb of Boston. Some of his critics have questioned whether Markey really still lives there — he also has a home in suburban Washington — but he has brushed those comments aside. "I've lived in the same house for 64 years," he said on MSNBC in 2013.

He was influenced by a fellow Irish Catholic: President John F. Kennedy. As a student at Malden Catholic High School, he listened to interviews with the Rev. Martin Luther King Jr. and Malcolm X on a nighttime radio talk show. However, at the height of the Vietnam War, he campaigned for anti-war Sen. Eugene J. McCarthy of Minnesota instead of the slain president's brother, Robert, then a Democratic senator from New York.

After earning a law degree, Markey won a race for a state House seat and quickly became a thorn in the side of establishment Democrats. He picked a fight in 1976 with party leaders over judicial reform, successfully pushing legislation to force judges to give up their law practices while in office. The Massachusetts bar endorsed the bill, but the House speaker kicked him off the Judiciary Committee. When he showed up for work the next day, his office was cleaned out. That notoriety helped Markey prevail in a Democratic primary for an open U.S. House seat involving a dozen aspirants. Once elected, his early tenure was highlighted by his staunch opposition to nuclear power and nuclear proliferation. In 1982, he documented his activities with the publication of "Nuclear Peril: The Politics of Proliferation."

Markey quickly jumped into the special election when Kerry resigned, and he was endorsed by many leading Democrats. Lynch came to the race later and had far less campaign cash than Markey. The campaigns were put on hold for a week after the April 15 bombing at the Boston Marathon, but the interruption did not affect Markey's lead in the polls. If he wins on June 25, a special election will be held to fill his House seat, possibly in the fall of 2013.

Key Votes

2012	
Extend a Social Security payroll tax cut and unemployment benefits	YES
Ease securities rules to expand small-business access to capital	NO
Extend for one year subsidized student loan interest rates financed by a cut in health care spending	NO
Cite Attorney General Eric H. Holder Jr. for contempt of Congress	?
Create a visa program for foreign graduates in high-tech fields	NO
Extend most Bush-era income tax rates while allowing rates for top-bracket earners to rise (Jan. 1, 2013)	YES
2011	
Strike funding for F-35 alternative engine	NO
Prevent EPA from regulating greenhouse gas emissions to address climate change	NO
Extend certain provisions of Patriot Act for four years	NO
Declare opposition to use of ground troops in Libya	NO
Overhaul patent law	NO
Pass compromise debt limit increase plan and establish future spending limits	NO
Allow consideration of measures to implement three trade agreements	NO

CQ Vote Studies

	PARTY UNITY		PRESIDENTIAL SUPPORT	
	SUPPORT	OPPOSE	SUPPORT	OPPOSE
2012	99%	1%	90%	10%
2011	98%	2%	79%	21%
2010	99%	1%	86%	14%
2009	99%	1%	97%	3%
2008	99%	1%	14%	86%

Interest Groups

	AFL-CIO	ADA	CCUS	ACU
2012	100%	100%	25%	0%
2011	100%	95%	13%	8%
2010	100%	100%	13%	0%
2009	100%	100%	33%	0%
2008	100%	100%	56%	0%

Massachusetts 5

North and west Boston suburbs; Framingham

The renumbered 5th is known for its high-tech industry along Route 128, the state's technology corridor that rings Boston. The district takes in suburbs north and west of Boston — including Waltham, Malden and Medford, as well as the middle-class coastal town of Revere — then stretches southwest to Framingham, an urban retail and service hub located between Boston and Worcester. The area takes pride in its history: Each year, Lexington re-enacts Paul Revere's ride and the first Revolutionary War battles (which took place in the 5th and 3rd districts) on Patriot's Day in April.

A strong software and technology-based economy is the backbone of the 5th. Most of the district's population is clustered among the outskirts of Boston, where the suburbs are home to many commuting workers. The district's portion of Cambridge includes Harvard University, and the world-renowned Massachusetts Institute of Technology is nearby in the 7th. Framingham developed as a manufacturing hub and has a strong biotechnology, medical and professional services sector. The easternmost tip of the district grabs some of the runways for Logan International Airport.

The 5th's political roots are a mix of Protestant Yankee Republicans and Irish Democrats; support for the GOP is dwindling at the presidential level. The 5th also has growing Asian — particularly notable closer to Boston in Cambridge and Malden — and Hispanic populations. Wealthy sections of the district vary from moderate Weston to liberal Lincoln. Barack Obama won every one of the district's towns in both the 2008 and 2012 presidential races, and Democrat Elizabeth Warren took more than 60 percent in towns close to Boston in the 2012 U.S. Senate contest.

Major Industry
Technology, telecommunications, higher education

Military Bases
Hanscom Air Force Base, 922 military, 2,614 civilian (shared with the 3rd and 6th districts); Army Soldier Systems Center (Natick), 75 military, 1,500 civilian

Cities
Cambridge (pt.), Framingham, Waltham, Malden, Medford

Notable
The New England Confectionary Co. (NECCO), the oldest multiline candy company in the United States, is located in Revere.

Rep. John F. Tierney (D)

Capitol Office
225-8020
tierney.house.gov
2238 Rayburn Bldg. 20515-2106; fax 225-5915

Committees
Education & the Workforce
Oversight & Government Reform

Residence
Salem

Born
Sept. 18, 1951; Salem, Mass.

Religion
Unspecified

Family
Wife, Patrice Tierney

Education
Salem State College, B.A. 1973 (political science); Suffolk U., J.D. 1976

Career
Lawyer; chamber of commerce official

Political Highlights
Democratic nominee for U.S. House, 1994

ELECTION RESULTS

2012 GENERAL		
John F. Tierney (D)	180,942	48.3%
Richard Tisei (R)	176,612	47.1%
Daniel Fishman (LIBERT)	16,739	4.5%
2012 PRIMARY		
John F. Tierney (D)		unopposed
2010 GENERAL		
John F. Tierney (D)	142,732	56.8%
Bill John Hudak Jr. (R)	107,930	43.0%

Previous Winning Percentages
2008 (70%); 2006 (70%); 2004 (70%); 2002 (68%); 2000 (71%); 1998 (55%); 1996 (48%)

Elected 1996; 9th term

The last time a Democrat lost a House race in Massachusetts was 1994. Tierney came shockingly close to ending that streak in 2012, when he was dogged by legal troubles surrounding his family. As he works to regain his electoral footing, the sometimes pugnacious liberal is continuing his involvement in debates on education, labor and national security.

Throughout 2012, Tierney had to deal with a lingering fraud scandal involving his wife, Patrice, and her brothers, Robert and Daniel Eremian. Patrice Tierney pleaded guilty in October 2010 to aiding and abetting the filing of false tax returns for Robert, a fugitive who had been indicted on charges of illegal gambling and money laundering. She served a month in prison, then testified at her brother's trial in late 2011.

Tierney has said he had no idea of his wife's financial dealings, but Daniel Eremian, right after being sentenced in 2012 to three years in prison for his role in the gambling operation, said Tierney "knew everything."

The Boston Globe endorsed his Republican opponent, Richard Tisei — a socially liberal, fiscally conservative former state senator — and wrote that Tierney's claim of ignorance "strains credulity." Outside groups spent several million dollars on advertisements attacking Tierney. On top of all that, a redrawn congressional map forced Tierney to compete for 50,000 new voters in Tewksbury, Billerica and Andover, areas that lean more Republican.

But thanks to a strong turnout effort, Tierney took 48 percent of the vote, enough for a 1-point win.

Tierney has gotten right back to business in the 113th Congress (2013-14), proceeding with his combative oratorical style and showing willingness to shoulder tough bills. A member of the Congressional Progressive Caucus, he has long been a lieutenant for Minority Leader Nancy Pelosi — whose daughter once served as his chief of staff. He articulates the liberal position on issues from health care to military contracting.

Tierney is the top Democrat on the Oversight and Government Reform Subcommittee on National Security — he chaired an earlier iteration of the panel when Democrats controlled the House. As chairman, he led a tenacious and rigorous oversight of U.S. operations in Afghanistan and Pakistan. In the 111th Congress (2009-10) he released a well-publicized report showing that poorly traced contracting dollars in Afghanistan had gone to corrupt officials, warlords and possible insurgents.

The issue of defense contracting has been a frequent topic for Tierney. He successfully amended the 2008 defense authorization legislation to create a Wartime Contracting Commission to audit contracts, and he blasted the George W. Bush administration for resisting its implementation.

He has supported a quicker withdrawal of U.S. forces from Afghanistan, preferring a more targeted counterterrorism campaign attacking the al-Qaida network in Pakistan and other countries where it operates. In 2011, he was one of 61 House Democrats backing a resolution directing an end to U.S. involvement in Libya's civil war.

He worked to beef up oversight provisions in the fiscal 2013 defense policy law. One Tierney amendment requires the Pentagon to brief Congress on its efforts to reduce energy consumption; another requires the Pentagon to assess the U.S. manufacturing sector's ability to meet the military's needs.

As a member of the Education and the Workforce Committee, he has tried to advance Democrats' plans for workforce training programs. In 2012, he joined Democrats George Miller of California and Rubén Hinojosa of Texas to sponsor a bill to consolidate workforce training programs, provide money to community colleges to offer courses in high-growth areas to laid-off workers, and track how many participants receive postsecondary credentials.

They rolled out an updated version in 2013, but Republicans weren't interested—instead, they passed their own bill to fold many training programs into a single Workforce Investment Fund, with cash provided via a block grant to the states. Tierney and other Democrats walked out of the March markup of the GOP bill and accused Republicans of refusing to negotiate.

In 2010, he was part of a successful effort to make the government the sole provider of federally backed student loans—a provision included in the Democrats' health care overhaul. Tierney then waded into one of the more bitter policy battles of 2012 by introducing the Democrats' version of a student loan bill. Barring congressional action, interest rates on those loans were set to climb to 6.8 percent in July 2012.

Tierney's measure would have kept them at 3.4 percent, where they had been for five years, and paid for that one-year extension by ending tax advantages for oil and gas companies. Republicans wanted the money to come from a preventive health fund created by the 2010 overhaul. Tierney went to the House floor to accuse them of trying to "attack women's health and children's health." A one-year extension of the lower rate was packaged in a transportation law, with a different offset.

Despite his interest in national and international affairs, Tierney has tried not to lose sight of district concerns. He has joined other Massachusetts lawmakers in asking the National Oceanic and Atmospheric Administration to lift catch limits available to fishing fleets off the New England coast.

Hometown pride was behind one of his more popular legislative efforts in the 112th Congress. Tierney, who grew up in Salem and still lives there, introduced a measure celebrating that city as the birthplace of the National Guard, in recognition of the creation of three militia regiments beginning in 1629. It was signed into law, which yielded Tierney positive coverage in hometown newspapers. It also caused friction with Virginia Republican Morgan Griffith, a history buff who asserts that the country's first guard regiment was founded in Virginia in 1624.

Tierney's interest in politics dates from his childhood, when he helped his uncle campaign to be a ward councilor in Peabody. After earning a political science degree from Salem State College and a law degree from Suffolk University, he worked as a partner in the law firm of Tierney, Kalis and Lucas for two decades. Running for the House in 1994, Tierney almost knocked off freshman Republican Peter G. Torkildsen. Their rematch two years later ended in a 371-vote win for Tierney. In a third face-off in 1998, Tierney won by 12 points. He had relatively easy re-elections from that point up to 2012.

Key Votes

2012	
Extend a Social Security payroll tax cut and unemployment benefits	YES
Ease securities rules to expand small-business access to capital	NO
Extend for one year subsidized student loan interest rates financed by a cut in health care spending	NO
Cite Attorney General Eric H. Holder Jr. for contempt of Congress	NO
Create a visa program for foreign graduates in high-tech fields	NO
Extend most Bush-era income tax rates while allowing rates for top-bracket earners to rise (Jan. 1, 2013)	YES
2011	
Strike funding for F-35 alternative engine	NO
Prevent EPA from regulating greenhouse gas emissions to address climate change	NO
Extend certain provisions of Patriot Act for four years	NO
Declare opposition to use of ground troops in Libya	NO
Overhaul patent law	YES
Pass compromise debt limit increase plan and establish future spending limits	NO
Allow consideration of measures to implement three trade agreements	NO

CQ Vote Studies

	PARTY UNITY		PRESIDENTIAL SUPPORT	
	SUPPORT	OPPOSE	SUPPORT	OPPOSE
2012	98%	2%	85%	15%
2011	97%	3%	81%	19%
2010	99%	1%	83%	17%
2009	98%	2%	94%	6%
2008	98%	2%	12%	88%

Interest Groups

	AFL-CIO	ADA	CCUS	ACU
2012	95%	90%	17%	0%
2011	100%	95%	19%	4%
2010	100%	95%	13%	0%
2009	95%	95%	33%	0%
2008	100%	95%	59%	4%

Massachusetts 6

North Shore — Lynn, Peabody

Pristine beaches line the cool ocean of Boston's North Shore, where working-class fishing towns are scattered among communities filled with stately mansions. Country clubs, fox hunting and polo provide popular diversions for residents of the inland portions of the district, where the population is more sparse but wealthy.

The 6th District is more heavily populated south of Route 128, where the cities of Lynn and Peabody have a middle-class, suburban flavor. Arising as leather-tanning towns when the nation was young, these cities now rely on technology and defense manufacturing in a corridor from Burlington to Gloucester. Boston's major universities, just south of the 6th, help anchor technology firms here, and Lynn is home to General Electric's jet engine plant, which is a major employer. Bedford, in the district's southwest, is home to part of Hanscom Air Force Base, which provides a range of defense and technology-related jobs to the region.

Gloucester's traditional fishing industry has declined, struggling to compensate for smaller catches and stringent federal regulations. Salem is a popular tourist destination because of its sites relating to the infamous witch trials of the late 17th century. Beverly — locals describe it as the birthplace of the Navy because the first ship commissioned by the Continental Congress sailed from its harbor in 1775 — is another population center.

The 6th overall is predominately white and one of the state's least racially diverse districts, but Lynn has a growing Hispanic population. The district's southern and coastal cities, particularly Lynn, Salem and Gloucester, tend to back Democratic presidential candidates, while smaller, wealthier enclaves are more conservative, and Beverly is competitive.

Major Industry

Technology, defense, fishing

Military Bases

Hanscom Air Force Base, 922 military, 2,614 civilian (shared with the 3rd and 5th districts)

Cities

Lynn, Peabody, Salem, Beverly

Notable

The first jet engine was tested by General Electric in Lynn in 1941.

Rep. Michael E. Capuano (D)

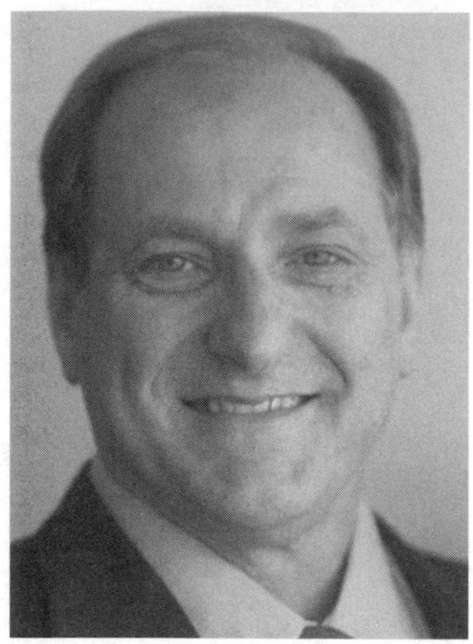

Capitol Office
225-5111
house.gov/capuano
1414 Longworth Bldg. 20515-2108; fax 225-9322

Committees
Ethics
Financial Services
Transportation & Infrastructure

Residence
Somerville

Born
Jan. 9, 1952; Somerville, Mass.

Religion
Roman Catholic

Family
Wife, Barbara Teebagy Capuano; two children

Education
Dartmouth College, B.A. 1973 (psychology); Boston College, J.D. 1977

Career
Lawyer; state legislative aide

Political Highlights
Somerville Board of Aldermen, 1977-79; candidate for mayor of Somerville, 1979, 1981; Somerville Board of Aldermen, 1985-89; mayor of Somerville, 1990-99; sought Democratic nomination for Mass. secretary of state, 1994; sought Democratic nomination for U.S. Senate (special election), 2009

ELECTION RESULTS

2012 GENERAL		
Michael E. Capuano (D)	210,794	83.4%
Karla Romero (I)	41,199	16.3%
2012 PRIMARY		
Michael E. Capuano (D)		unopposed
2010 GENERAL		
Michael E. Capuano (D)	134,974	98.0%
write-ins (WRI)	2,686	2.0%

Previous Winning Percentages
2008 (99%); 2006 (91%); 2004 (99%); 2002 (100%); 2000 (99%); 1998 (82%)

Elected 1998; 8th term

Capuano is more of an old-time city pol than a left-wing talking head. He works closely with Democratic leaders, sits on key House committees and believes strongly in the efficacy of activist government.

He started in politics as an alderman and mayor of the traditionally blue-collar Boston suburb of Somerville. He now represents the historic Boston district that produced both the Kennedy dynasty and House Speaker Thomas P. O'Neill Jr.

Capuano's views are at least as liberal as those of his better-known predecessors. On votes that divide a majority of Democrats and a majority of Republicans, he hardly ever breaks with his party. A Bay State blogger has written that Capuano (KAP-you-AH-no) is "the bluest congressman from the bluest district of the bluest state in the Union."

But while Capuano can deliver a pro-labor stemwinder to a union crowd, you won't find him on MSNBC screaming about a progressive vision for America. "To be the person out there, publicly pushing for an idealistic approach to anything—it's awfully hard to do that when you're also willing to compromise with the very people you're kicking," he said.

On the Financial Services Committee, he gets to act as both a hard-nosed public advocate and a policy wonk. In the 112th Congress (2011-12), Capuano, a former tax attorney, was paired up with Texas Republican Randy Neugebauer, a former real estate developer, atop the Subcommittee on Oversight and Investigations.

Among their oversight efforts, they conducted a feisty investigation of failed investment company MF Global. But Capuano eventually lamented that members of the subcommittee were not "as aggressive as we should have been," and he issued an addendum to Neugebauer's report on the MF Global collapse. To improve coordination among the regulators charged with preventing such failures, Capuano recommended merging the Securities and Exchange Commission and the Commodity Futures Trading Commission.

For the 113th Congress (2013-14), Capuano and Neugebauer hold the top spots on the Housing and Insurance Subcommittee, which is studying a possible federal withdrawal from the housing finance sector. Capuano is not sold on the need to end government involvement in housing. "I like the housing market that we had for 40 years," he said at a March 2013 hearing. "Granted, it got out of whack and we need to put it back in whack. But I don't want to go overboard and completely disincentivize the entire middle class from ever being able to purchase a home."

Capuano has urged the Federal Housing Finance Agency to allow more "principal write-downs" on loans held by the government — reducing the amount owed by borrowers whose homes are worth less than what they owe.

He also sits on the Transportation and Infrastructure Committee. His signature achievement, as far as Bostonians are concerned, is reversing the decline in grants to Massachusetts in reaction to the "Big Dig," the over-budget, scandal-ridden tunnel project that had made many in Congress leery of the state's management of transportation funds. When a concrete slab in a Big Dig tunnel fell in 2006 and killed a motorist, Capuano led the state's congressional delegation in demanding a federal probe.

Capuano is close with House Democratic leaders—he led the party's transition team when Democrats won control of the House in the 2006 election. At the start of the 110th Congress (2007-08), Speaker Nancy Pelosi asked Capuano to shoulder a task few lawmakers would relish: pushing for a rules change to allow outsiders to judge the ethical lapses of House members. His task force's report was first delayed and then widely criticized, but a hard push by Pelosi in March 2008 secured passage of its key recommendation: the creation of an independent Office of Congressional Ethics. Capuano is serving on the Ethics Committee in the 113th Congress.

Outside of his committee work, Capuano is a leading voice on human rights. He remains engaged on the issues plaguing the African nations of Sudan and South Sudan. Despite a 2005 peace accord and a 2011 referendum that split South Sudan into an independent nation, the countries are still roiled by violent conflict. Adding to the misery is the ongoing humanitarian crisis in the Darfur region, the site of genocide in the last decade.

Capuano calls the situation "a lot messier" than it once was and says he is trying to keep a spotlight on it. Capuano and British politician Glenys Kinnock wrote an opinion pieced that ran in The Guardian in 2013; they accused the U.N. Security Council of "failing to back up its own resolutions on this conflict and not putting its political muscle behind African Union plans to end the suffering."

Capuano hails from a modest political dynasty — his father was the first Italian-American elected to local office in Somerville. He graduated from Dartmouth College with a degree in psychology, and in 1977 he got a law degree at Boston College. That same year, he began his first stint as an alderman. He was elected mayor on his third try and held that job for a decade starting in 1990. His detractors called him "tyrannical" and said he managed the city like a ward boss — hiring friends and relatives and running enemies out of public agencies.

The retirement of a more prominent scion opened his path to the House in 1998. Six-term Democrat Joseph P. Kennedy II, the son of Robert F. Kennedy and the nephew of President John F. Kennedy, decided to give up his 8th District seat. (The district was renumbered as the 7th after redistricting for 2012.)

The presumed front-runner in the primary to succeed Kennedy was Raymond L. Flynn, a former Boston mayor and ambassador to the Vatican who had abandoned a flagging run for governor. But Capuano and other candidates in the 10-person race ganged up on Flynn. Although greatly outspent by two other candidates, Capuano was lifted to victory by a strong turnout in Somerville and a second-place finish in other municipalities. He breezed past a Republican opponent that November, and the GOP has not fielded a candidate against him since then.

Capuano tried to win a Senate seat in 2009. Pelosi endorsed him as he entered the Democratic primary for the special election to succeed the late Sen. Edward M. Kennedy. He lost by almost 20 points to state Attorney General Martha Coakley, who in turn lost to Republican state Sen. Scott P. Brown.

Key Votes

2012	
Extend a Social Security payroll tax cut and unemployment benefits	NO
Ease securities rules to expand small-business access to capital	NO
Extend for one year subsidized student loan interest rates financed by a cut in health care spending	NO
Cite Attorney General Eric H. Holder Jr. for contempt of Congress	?
Create a visa program for foreign graduates in high-tech fields	NO
Extend most Bush-era income tax rates while allowing rates for top-bracket earners to rise (Jan. 1, 2013)	YES
2011	
Strike funding for F-35 alternative engine	NO
Prevent EPA from regulating greenhouse gas emissions to address climate change	NO
Extend certain provisions of Patriot Act for four years	NO
Declare opposition to use of ground troops in Libya	NO
Overhaul patent law	YES
Pass compromise debt limit increase plan and establish future spending limits	NO
Allow consideration of measures to implement three trade agreements	NO

CQ Vote Studies

	PARTY UNITY		PRESIDENTIAL SUPPORT	
	SUPPORT	OPPOSE	SUPPORT	OPPOSE
2012	99%	1%	83%	17%
2011	97%	3%	78%	22%
2010	98%	2%	85%	15%
2009	99%	1%	96%	4%
2008	99%	1%	22%	78%

Interest Groups

	AFL-CIO	ADA	CCUS	ACU
2012	100%	100%	17%	0%
2011	100%	95%	19%	8%
2010	93%	95%	13%	0%
2009	100%	95%	29%	0%
2008	100%	95%	67%	4%

Massachusetts 7

Part of Boston and inner suburbs

The liberal 7th cuts through Boston's residential neighborhoods and its surrounding suburbs to pick up large Hispanic, black and Asian populations; it was drawn as the state's only minority-majority district during remapping after the 2010 census. New generations of Hispanic immigrants and young professionals have begun to change the face of the city's traditionally Irish neighborhoods, such as Charlestown. Nearly 80 percent of Boston's population lives in the 7th, which also takes in the suburbs of Somerville, Everett, Chelsea and part of Cambridge.

While excluding most of downtown and the harbor, the 7th includes almost all of Logan International Airport — some of its runways are in the 5th District — and some of Boston's most famous locations: Bunker Hill, Fenway Park (home of baseball's Red Sox), Chinatown and the USS Constitution, also known as Old Ironsides. The Back Bay area is a bustling retail and business center. The city has a thriving medical and biotechnology sector as well as a large student population in attendance at Boston's several colleges and universities. The district's portion of Cambridge includes the world-renowned Massachusetts Institute of Technology, one of the most important anchors of the state's higher-education and technology cluster.

The 7th was intended to be a minority-majority district based on demographic statistics from 2010, but estimates still put the white population at around 50 percent; no single minority group is dominant in the cultural patchwork. Boston's Hispanic population helped the city grow faster than the state overall since 2000. Chelsea is about 60 percent Hispanic and home to many lower-income residents. Roxbury is the traditional heart of black culture in Boston, while Mission Hill has a vibrant multicultural flavor.

Typifying the district's monolithically liberal politics, Somerville gave Barack Obama 85 percent of its presidential vote and Elizabeth Warren 80 percent of its U.S. Senate vote in 2012.

Major Industry

Biotechnology, higher education, health care, tourism

Cities

Boston (pt.), Cambridge (pt.), Somerville, Everett, Chelsea

Notable

The Shirley Eustis House in Roxbury, built in the mid-1700s, is the only remaining country house in the United States built by a Royal British colonial governor; The Prudential Center and the John Hancock Tower, both located in the Back Bay neighborhood, are Boston's two tallest buildings.

Rep. Stephen F. Lynch (D)

Capitol Office
225-8273
lynch.house.gov
2133 Rayburn Bldg. 20515-2109; fax 225-3984

Committees
Financial Services
Oversight & Government Reform

Residence
Boston

Born
March 31, 1955; Boston, Mass.

Religion
Roman Catholic

Family
Wife, Margaret Lynch; two children

Education
Wentworth Institute of Technology, B.S. 1988 (construction management); Boston College, J.D. 1991; Harvard U., M.A. 1998 (public administration)

Career
Lawyer; ironworker

Political Highlights
Mass. House, 1995-96; Mass. Senate, 1996-2001; sought Democratic nominiation for U.S. Senate in a special election, 2013

ELECTION RESULTS

2012 GENERAL		
Stephen F. Lynch (D)	263,999	76.1%
Joe Selvaggi (R)	82,242	23.7%
2012 PRIMARY		
Stephen F. Lynch (D)		unopposed
2010 GENERAL		
Stephen F. Lynch (D)	157,071	68.3%
Vernon Harrison (R)	59,965	26.1%
Phil Dunkelbarger (I)	12,572	5.5%

Previous Winning Percentages
2008 (99%); 2006 (78%); 2004 (99%); 2002 (99%); 2001 Special Election (65%)

Elected October 2001; 6th full term

Lynch fell short in his 2013 bid for the Senate, finishing second in a special-election primary on the last day of April. The race put a dent in his campaign coffers and might have bruised a few working relationships, as the winner was fellow Rep. Edward J. Markey. But the timing of the election allowed him to return safely to the House.

Lynch sits on the Financial Services Committee and the Oversight and Government Reform Committee. Those assignments put him alongside many of the outsize personalities in Congress, but his own work is usually marked by reserved, measured rhetoric. He often seems to be thinking out his positions — and, given that he's changed a few significant ones, that's likely the reality.

He once made the transition from ironworker to lawyer, so evolution has been a fact of life for Lynch. Many of his public stands have resonated with the blue-collar, socially conservative Democrats from the South Boston neighborhood where he grew up, but some of them have morphed over time.

Lynch won the special-election primary that propelled him to the House on Sept. 11, 2001, and he was more hawkish than most Democrats during the George W. Bush administration. He voted to authorize the Iraq War in 2002 and backed a 2006 Republican resolution supporting Bush's policies there. Over a decade, Lynch visited both Iraq and Afghanistan at least 10 times.

His support for the Afghanistan War has waned, however. "I think it is entirely right and appropriate that we reassess and look at the possibility of getting out at the end of 2013 instead of 2014," he said at an Oversight hearing in September 2012. Lynch is increasingly skeptical of Pakistan as an ally in the region. He was one of the few Democrats to vote in favor of withdrawing U.S. forces from Libya in 2011 and blocking funding for most military activities there. He told the Boston Herald there was no compelling national security interest for U.S. involvement; he said on the House floor that Obama had acted illegally in committing forces without congressional consent.

The change of heart on Afghanistan was one of several in recent years. Lynch is socially conservative; he opposes abortion and was on record as opposing same-sex marriage. But over the years he backed away from efforts to codify bans on same-sex marriage. In the 111th Congress (2009-10), he supported House legislation intended to grant same-sex partners of federal employees access to federal health care benefits.

Lynch's shifts have put kinks in his relationship with organized labor. His father was an ironworker for 40 years, and his mother was a World War II welder who worked as a post office clerk. Lynch was an ironworker for 18 years, and at age 30 he became the youngest president in the history of Ironworkers Local 7. But as House Democrats assembled a health care overhaul in 2009, Lynch refused to endorse several union-backed priorities for the bill. When he considered running for the Senate that September (to succeed the late Edward M. Kennedy), a lack of union support led him to withdraw quickly from the race.

He has had chances to mend fences with unions, and they have continued to be the largest source of his campaign donations from interest groups. In the 112th Congress (2011-12), he became the top Democrat on the Oversight panel handling the federal workforce, which has huge union contingents.

Lynch has pushed for an overhaul of the struggling Postal Service, working with Elijah E. Cummings of Maryland, the ranking member of the full committee. He wants to authorize the agency to find new sources of revenue, such as check-cashing services or leasing its facilities. He has proposed downsizing the agency by offering early retirements and streamlining operations. Those proposals have gone nowhere, as Republicans have favored their own plans.

Even so, Lynch showed flashes of independence on workforce issues in the 112th Congress: He was one of 19 House Democrats to vote for a Republican measure to reverse Obama administration changes to welfare-to-work requirements.

Lynch's district has white-collar and blue-collar elements side by side; in addition to Southie, he represents Boston's financial district. On the Financial Services Committee, he has lost an ally in Massachusetts Democrat Barney Frank — the former chairman retired at the end of the 112th. Lynch and Frank attributed Standard & Poor's 2011 downgrade of the U.S. credit rating to tea party Republicans stretching out negotiations on raising the federal debt limit. They also criticized S&P for going through with the downgrade, saying it was undeserved.

Among Lynch's top priorities is increasing the funding of drug courts — alternatives to the normal criminal justice system that are geared toward getting nonviolent offenders into a structured system of testing, treatment and possible punishment. Lynch has said he wants to see federal support for drug courts go up by $4 million, enough to enroll 3,000 people in treatment programs over three years. He authored an amendment to that effect for the fiscal 2013 Commerce-Justice-Science spending bill, which the House adopted. He joined with Republican Harold Rogers of Kentucky to resurrect the bipartisan Congressional Caucus on Prescription Drug Abuse.

Lynch started as an ironworker, but he earned a law degree from Boston College in his 30s. He joined a law firm and continued representing housing project residents for free, a practice he had begun in law school. Lynch grew up in one of Southie's poorest projects.

In 1994, he beat Democrat Paul Gannon to claim a seat in the Massachusetts House; two years later, he won a special election for a state Senate seat. Lynch ran in 2001 to succeed Rep. Joe Moakley, a Democrat who died of leukemia. He benefited from his up-by-the-bootstraps personal story, as well as publicity from his decision to donate 60 percent of his liver to his brother-in-law, who had liver cancer. He won the primary with 39 percent of the vote and cruised after that.

The 2013 special election was triggered by the resignation of John Kerry, who became secretary of State. Markey, a more liberal Democrat, entered the race first, lined up endorsements throughout the party and spent far more money on his campaign. The campaigns of both men were temporarily suspended after the April 15 bombing at the Boston Marathon. Lynch tried to challenge Markey's commitment to homeland security in the closing debates, but he couldn't catch up.

Key Votes

2012	
Extend a Social Security payroll tax cut and unemployment benefits	NO
Ease securities rules to expand small-business access to capital	YES
Extend for one year subsidized student loan interest rates financed by a cut in health care spending	NO
Cite Attorney General Eric H. Holder Jr. for contempt of Congress	NO
Create a visa program for foreign graduates in high-tech fields	NO
Extend most Bush-era income tax rates while allowing rates for top-bracket earners to rise (Jan. 1, 2013)	YES
2011	
Strike funding for F-35 alternative engine	YES
Prevent EPA from regulating greenhouse gas emissions to address climate change	NO
Extend certain provisions of Patriot Act for four years	NO
Declare opposition to use of ground troops in Libya	YES
Overhaul patent law	YES
Pass compromise debt limit increase plan and establish future spending limits	YES
Allow consideration of measures to implement three trade agreements	NO

CQ Vote Studies

	PARTY UNITY		PRESIDENTIAL SUPPORT	
	SUPPORT	OPPOSE	SUPPORT	OPPOSE
2012	91%	9%	85%	15%
2011	93%	7%	84%	16%
2010	95%	5%	88%	12%
2009	98%	2%	96%	4%
2008	98%	2%	10%	90%

Interest Groups

	AFL-CIO	ADA	CCUS	ACU
2012	95%	80%	25%	16%
2011	100%	90%	31%	0%
2010	93%	95%	13%	0%
2009	100%	90%	36%	4%
2008	100%	95%	53%	8%

Massachusetts 8

Part of Boston; Quincy; Brockton

The 8th District includes the core of downtown Boston and mostly white communities along the city's southern waterfront, including the working-class Irish Catholic neighborhood known as Southie. The district sweeps down through Quincy and Braintree and as far south as Bridgewater before curving back up through Brockton to West Roxbury.

At the district's northern tip, the downtown financial district is home to one of the world's largest centers for mutual-fund investing. State and city government offices and tourist destinations — such as Beacon Hill, Boston Common and the Old North Church — keep Boston bustling, and Faneuil Hall Marketplace anchors a stable retail industry. The 8th includes the John F. Kennedy Presidential Library and Museum and the newly built Edward M. Kennedy Institute for the United States Senate, which stand adjacent to each other on the Columbia Point waterfront near the University of Massachusetts, Boston, campus and the state archives.

Downtown's wealthy neighborhoods stand in contrast to the lower-income residential areas across the Fort Point Channel in Southie and the commuter suburbs farther south. While Boston's minority communities were carved out of the primarily white 8th District, the majority of the population of middle-class Brockton is a racial or ethnic minority. The city has an industrial history as a shoe manufacturing center and is especially proud of its sports heroes, including boxer Rocky Marciano. Quincy, a suburb linked to Boston by rapid transit, has a fast-growing Asian community that now accounts for nearly one-fourth of the city's population.

The liberal 8th heavily favors Democrats, although areas farther from Boston tend to be more conservative and ethnic tensions can be prominent. In the 2012 U.S. Senate race, incumbent Republican Scott P. Brown did well in Bridgewater and Braintree, while Brockton favored Democrat Elizabeth Warren by a 2-to-1 margin.

Major Industry
Financial services, government, tourism

Cities
Boston (pt.), Brockton, Quincy, Weymouth Town, Braintree Town

Notable
The Boston neighborhood of West Roxbury in the 19th century was home to an experimental utopian community frequented by Ralph Waldo Emerson, Nathaniel Hawthorne and Henry David Thoreau.

Rep. William Keating (D)

Capitol Office
225-3111
keating.house.gov
315 Cannon Bldg. 20515-2110; fax 225-5658

Committees
Foreign Affairs
Homeland Security

Residence
Bourne

Born
Sept. 6, 1952; Norwood, Mass.

Religion
Roman Catholic

Family
Wife, Tevis Keating; two children

Education
Boston College, B.A. 1974 (political science), M.B.A. 1982; Suffolk U., J.D. 1985

Career
Lawyer

Political Highlights
Mass. House, 1977-85; Mass. Senate, 1985-99; Norfolk County district attorney, 1999-2011

ELECTION RESULTS

2012 GENERAL		
William Keating (D)	212,754	58.7%
Christopher Sheldon (R)	116,531	32.2%
Daniel S. Botelho (I)	32,655	9.0%
2012 PRIMARY		
William Keating (D)	31,366	56.0%
Sam Sutter (D)	24,675	44.0%
2010 GENERAL		
William Keating (D)	132,743	46.9%
Jeff Perry (R)	120,029	42.4%
Maryanne Lewis (I)	16,705	5.9%
James Sheets (I)	10,445	3.7%
Joe Van Nes (I)	3,084	1.1%

Elected 2010; 2nd term

Keating boasts more than three decades in Massachusetts politics and espouses energy and social policies that play well in that very Democratic state. When he reaches across the aisle, it's usually to work on law-and-order issues or congressional oversight.

He made his first run for political office at 23, capitalizing on the recognition he built up working a postal route to pay his way through Boston College. Keating says he was well prepared, coming from a "very robust, politically oriented household," headed by a father who was "everyone's local campaign manager." After eight years in the state House, he spent 14 in the state Senate and 12 as a district attorney in Norfolk County, southwest of Boston.

Keating isn't a fire-breathing liberal, however. He was elected in 2010 in the most Republican House district in the state, with only 47 percent of the vote. After reapportionment stripped a seat from the state's delegation for the 113th Congress (2013-14), he jumped to the new 9th District, which is demographically more Democratic. But the opening years of his House tenure have featured centrist moments.

He worked with New York Republican Richard Hanna to promote a package of small-business tax deductions, and he had GOP partners on a bill to require brand-name painkillers currently on the market to switch to a tamper-resistant formula. Keating voted in 2011 for spending cuts and a deficit reduction package that many liberals refused to swallow.

In May of that year, Republicans called a floor vote on a "no strings attached" increase in the federal debt limit, to get Democrats on record as supporting more government borrowing. Keating was the only House member from his state to oppose it. "I was trying to be pragmatic," he said; his hope was to "roll our sleeves up, see if we can do something together ... but it went way too far." He called the Republican tactics "a case of putting personal ideology ahead of commitment to your country."

Keating finds the bipartisanship on the Homeland Security Committee more to his liking. In the 112th Congress (2011-12) he was the top Democrat on the oversight and investigations subcommittee, opposite Republican Michael McCaul of Texas — who now runs the full committee. "We work as well as any two people you'll find in the whole place," Keating said.

The House in 2012 passed a bill by Keating and McCaul to establish an advisory panel assessing the management practices of the Department of Homeland Security. Keating said it could identify "duplicative and obsolete programs" in the sprawling department.

He chimed in on cybersecurity in the 112th, emphasizing that new laws can't infringe on individual privacy. He voted against a 2012 bill to promote information sharing between the intelligence community and the private sector, saying it might allow the government to collect personal data. Keating wants more federal support for cybersecurity research centers based at universities; he wrote in a Roll Call opinion piece that they could provide immediate solutions and serve as "training grounds" for future security experts.

Keating also takes an interest in airport perimeter security — a holdover issue from his district attorney days. Toward the end of his tenure, a North Carolina teenager was killed while stowing away on a flight bound for Boston's Logan International Airport — he had climbed into a plane's wheel well, then fell out on the approach to Boston. The incident raised questions about lax security on tarmacs and runways.

Keating sits on the Foreign Affairs Committee, and in the 113th Congress he is the top Democrat on the subcommittee covering Europe, Eurasia and

Emerging Threats. That's another good spot to talk about security, as well as look out for the large Portuguese and Irish communities in his district.

He focused on the Middle East as a freshman, and Keating says the United States should reduce its military footprint in the region while maintaining a robust counterterrorism capability. Though he was one of 61 Democrats to vote for a 2011 resolution calling for the withdrawal of American troops from Libya, he backs a multilateral approach to foreign affairs. "There's gonna be no stomach ... for a go-it-alone U.S. approach anymore," he said.

Keating is skeptical of the Pakistani government and its possible ties to organizations fighting U.S. forces in Afghanistan. He was one of 15 Democrats voting for a failed amendment to a fiscal 2013 defense policy bill that would have blocked Pentagon assistance to Pakistan. The amendment was sponsored by Dana Rohrabacher, the California Republican now chairing the emerging threats subcommittee.

As a longtime Massachusetts pol, Keating has his share of blue-meat issues. He wants to end tax policies benefiting the oil and gas industry, and in 2011 he introduced two amendments on the House floor seeking greater disclosure of executive compensation at oil companies. He says federal investment in "clean" energy is a win-win-win: "You're getting jobs. You're helping our environment. And you're helping our national security because we're less dependent on oil," he said.

Representing Cape Cod, Keating is also a point man for his state's fishing industry. After Superstorm Sandy, Keating called for more disaster relief to go toward fisheries.

Keating's earliest political memory was a clam bake hosted by a Massachusetts Republican: former House Speaker Joseph W. Martin Jr. His political heritage now decorates his office walls in Washington. On display in striking black-and-white are a number of photos of a young John F. Kennedy that belonged to Keating's aunt. A Roman Catholic, he says Kennedy's 1960 election was a galvanizing moment: "My extended family were so excited with the candidacy of John Kennedy, and going back, Al Smith — it was just some kind of dream, that that could ever happen in this country."

The 10th District seat opened up in 2010 thanks to the retirement of seven-term Democrat Bill Delahunt. Keating won a close primary against a state senator, then squeezed past Republican Jeff Perry, a former state representative, in November.

The new 9th District was home to no incumbent in 2012. Keating quickly announced that he was moving to his Cape Cod vacation home (the Cape was in his old district, as well) and running there. He beat Sam Sutter, the Bristol County district attorney, in the primary and easily won the general election.

Key Votes

2012	
Extend a Social Security payroll tax cut and unemployment benefits	YES
Ease securities rules to expand small-business access to capital	YES
Extend for one year subsidized student loan interest rates financed by a cut in health care spending	NO
Cite Attorney General Eric H. Holder Jr. for contempt of Congress	?
Create a visa program for foreign graduates in high-tech fields	NO
Extend most Bush-era income tax rates while allowing rates for top-bracket earners to rise (Jan. 1, 2013)	YES
2011	
Strike funding for F-35 alternative engine	NO
Prevent EPA from regulating greenhouse gas emissions to address climate change	NO
Extend certain provisions of Patriot Act for four years	YES
Declare opposition to use of ground troops in Libya	NO
Overhaul patent law	YES
Pass compromise debt limit increase plan and establish future spending limits	YES
Allow consideration of measures to implement three trade agreements	NO

CQ Vote Studies

	PARTY UNITY		PRESIDENTIAL SUPPORT	
	SUPPORT	OPPOSE	SUPPORT	OPPOSE
2012	96%	4%	83%	17%
2011	94%	6%	89%	11%

Interest Groups

	AFL-CIO	ADA	CCUS	ACU
2012	90%	85%	25%	0%
2011	100%	85%	31%	0%

Massachusetts 9

South Shore — New Bedford, Cape Cod, islands

One of the most-changed districts following Massachusetts' loss of a seat during decennial reapportionment, the 9th combines tourism-heavy Cape Cod with working-class New Bedford and the Buzzards Bay coast. It reaches up the South Shore, stopping outside of Boston, going only as far north as Rockland and Norwell. The southeast has a rich maritime culture and agricultural land; conservative small towns mix with Democratic cities.

New Bedford has a median income well below the state average. Once a whaling hub in the 19th century, its economy today has a manufacturing and health care base, although fishing remains prominent throughout the region. The city also hopes to build on wind turbine production. Technology and research are economic pillars in the 9th; Woods Hole is home to world-renowned scientific institutions specializing in marine biology.

Tourism is important throughout the district, especially along Cape Cod, where visitors flock to the beaches and sailing slips in the summer. The islands of Nantucket and Martha's Vineyard are lined with upscale boutiques and craft galleries popular with well-to-do vacationers. Further inland, the region is home to cranberry bogs, which produce the state's top crop and attract their share of tourism. In the fall, Plymouth draws modern-day pilgrims to the site of the first Thanksgiving.

The 9th is Massachusetts' least racially diverse district, with a population that is 90 percent white. New Bedford and Fall River (shared with the 4th) have large Portuguese populations. Cape Cod hosts a significant gay and lesbian community, especially in reliably liberal Provincetown. Most of the district's smaller towns are Republican, while New Bedford, Fall River and parts of the Cape are Democratic strongholds. Barack Obama won the district with a 13-point margin in the 2012 presidential election.

Major Industry

Technology, tourism, health care, fishing

Cities

New Bedford, Fall River (pt.), Barnstable Town

Notable

New Bedford is home to the New Bedford Whaling Museum — Herman Melville sailed from the port in 1841 and featured the city in his novel "Moby-Dick;" New Bedford's annual Feast of the Blessed Sacrament boasts being the largest celebration of Portuguese culture in the United States.

MICHIGAN

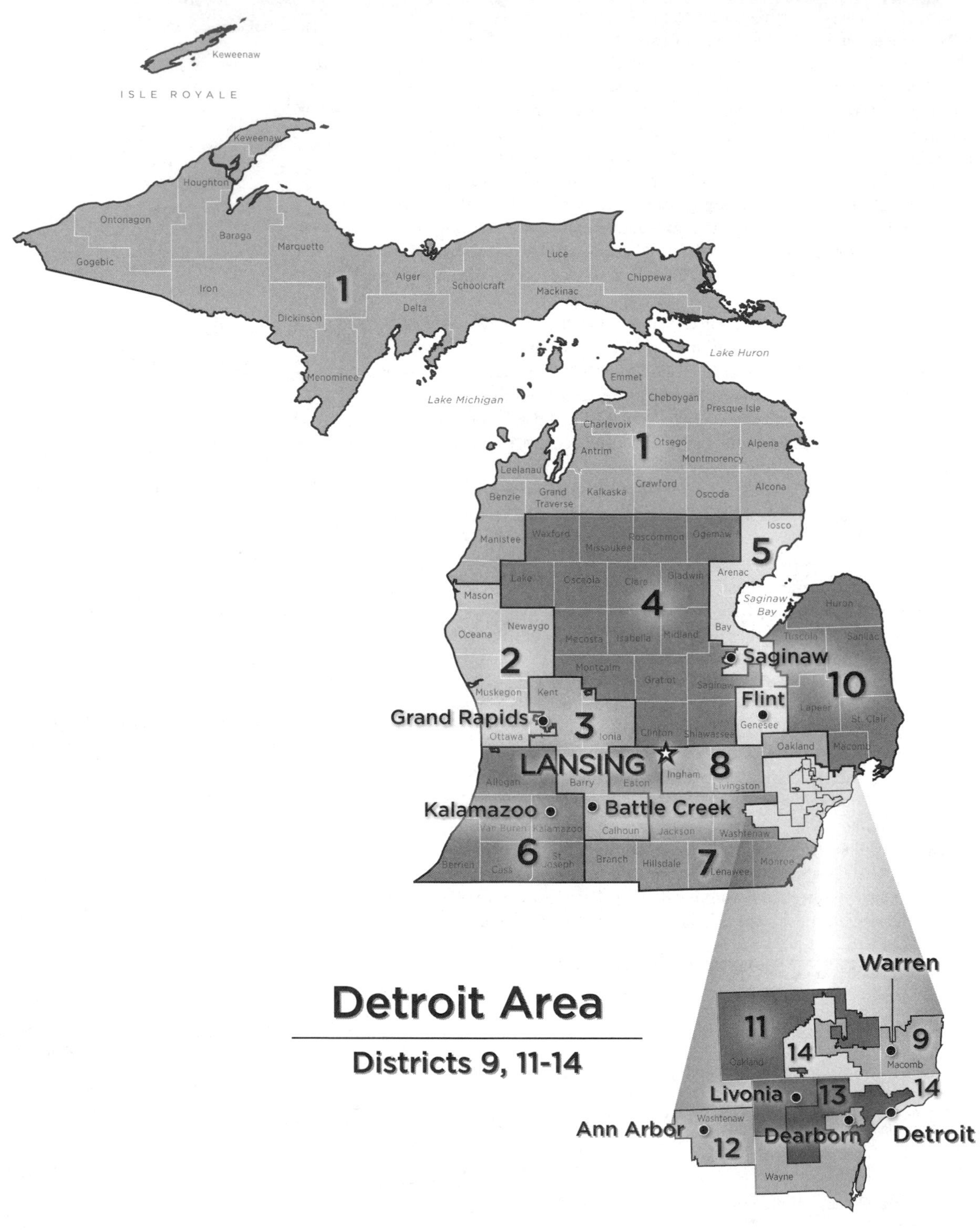

ISLE ROYALE
Keweenaw
Houghton
Ontonagon
Gogebic
Baraga
Marquette
Iron
Dickinson
Menominee
Alger
Delta
Schoolcraft
Luce
Mackinac
Chippewa
Lake Huron
Lake Michigan
Emmet
Cheboygan
Presque Isle
Charlevoix
Antrim
Otsego
Montmorency
Alpena
Leelanau
Benzie
Grand Traverse
Kalkaska
Crawford
Oscoda
Alcona
Manistee
Wexford
Missaukee
Roscommon
Ogemaw
Iosco
Lake
Osceola
Clare
Gladwin
Arenac
Mason
Oceana
Newaygo
Mecosta
Isabella
Midland
Bay
Saginaw Bay
Huron
Tuscola
Sanilac
Saginaw
Montcalm
Gratiot
Muskegon
Kent
Grand Rapids
Ottawa
Ionia
Clinton
Shiawassee
Flint
Genesee
Lapeer
St. Clair
Oakland
Macomb
LANSING
Ingham
Livingston
Allegan
Barry
Eaton
Kalamazoo
Battle Creek
Van Buren
Calhoun
Jackson
Washtenaw
Berrien
Cass
St. Joseph
Branch
Hillsdale
Lenawee
Monroe
1
2
3
4
5
6
7
8
10
Detroit Area
Districts 9, 11-14
Warren
11
14
9
Oakland
Macomb
Livonia
13
14
Washtenaw
Ann Arbor
12
Dearborn
Detroit
Wayne

Gov. Rick Snyder (R)

First elected: 2010

Length of term: 4 years

Term expires: 1/15

Salary: $159,300

Phone: (517) 373-3400

Residence: Ann Arbor

Born: Aug. 19, 1958; Battle Creek, Mich.

Religion: Presbyterian

Family: Wife, Sue Snyder; three children

Education: U. of Michigan, B.A. 1977 (general studies), M.B.A. 1979, J.D. 1982

Career: Venture capitalist; computer company executive; tax and acquisitions firm manager

Political highlights: No previous office

ELECTION RESULTS

2010 GENERAL

Rick Snyder (R)	1,874,834	58.1%
Virg Bernero (D)	1,287,320	39.9%
Others	63,907	2.0%

Lt. Gov. Brian Calley (R)

First elected: 2010

Length of term: 4 years

Term expires: 1/15

Salary: $111,510

Phone: (517) 373-6800

LEGISLATURE

Legislature: Year-round with recess

Senate: 38 members, 4-year terms

2013 ratios: 26 R, 12 D; 34 men, 4 women

Salary: $71,685

Phone: (517) 373-2400

House: 110 members, 2-year terms

2013 ratios: 59 R, 50 D, 1 vacancy; 85 men, 24 women

Salary: $71,685

Phone: (517) 373-0135

TERM LIMITS

Governor: 2 terms

Senate: 2 terms

House: 3 terms

URBAN STATISTICS

CITY	POPULATION
Detroit	713,777
Grand Rapids	188,040
Warren	134,056
Sterling Heights	129,699
Lansing	114,297

REGISTERED VOTERS

Voters do not register by party.

POPULATION

2010 population	9,883,640
2000 population	9,938,444
1990 population	9,295,297
Percent change (2000-2010)	-0.6%
Rank among states (2010)	8
Median age	37.7
Born in state	76.0%
Foreign born	6.1%
Violent crime rate	497/100,000
Poverty level	16.2%
Federal workers	65,360
Military	2,858

ELECTIONS

STATE ELECTION OFFICIAL
(517) 373-2540

DEMOCRATIC PARTY
(517) 371-5410

REPUBLICAN PARTY
(517) 487-5413

MISCELLANEOUS

Web: www.michigan.gov

Capital: Lansing

U.S. CONGRESS

Senate: 2 Democrats

House: 9 Republicans, 5 Democrats

STATISTICS BY DISTRICT

District	2012 Vote for President		2008 Vote for President		Black	Asian	Hispanic	Median Income	Over 64	Under 20	College Education	Rural	Sq. Miles
	Obama	Romney	Obama	McCain									
1	45%	54%	50%	48%	2%	1%	1%	$40,765	19%	22%	21%	72%	25,028
2	43	56	48	50	6	2	9	45,712	13	28	23	30	3,281
3	46	53	50	49	9	1	7	48,010	13	28	27	31	2,629
4	45	53	50	49	2	1	3	42,586	16	26	20	67	8,458
5	61	38	63	35	18	1	5	39,783	15	26	18	23	2,349
6	49	50	53	45	9	1	6	44,376	14	27	25	42	3,547
7	48	51	51	47	4	1	4	49,475	14	26	21	46	4,228
8	48	51	52	46	6	4	5	57,241	12	27	37	19	1,503
9	57	42	58	40	11	4	2	47,777	15	23	27	0	184
10	44	55	48	50	3	2	3	53,121	14	26	21	38	4,140
11	47	52	50	48	5	7	4	69,397	13	26	44	2	419
12	66	33	67	31	10	5	5	48,575	12	26	32	3	403
13	85	14	85	14	57	1	7	29,003	12	29	13	0	185
14	81	19	82	17	57	4	5	38,315	14	27	29	0	186
STATE	**54**	**45**	**57**	**41**	**14**	**2**	**4**	**45,981**	**14**	**26**	**25**	**28**	**56,539**
U.S.	**51**	**47**	**53**	**46**	**12**	**5**	**17**	**50,052**	**13**	**27**	**29**	**21**	**3,531,905**

Sen. Carl Levin (D)

Capitol Office
224-6221
levin.senate.gov
269 Russell Bldg. 20510-2202; fax 224-1388

Committees
Armed Services - Chairman
Homeland Security & Governmental Affairs
(Permanent Investigations - Chairman)
Small Business & Entrepreneurship

Residence
Detroit

Born
June 28, 1934; Detroit, Mich.

Religion
Jewish

Family
Wife, Barbara H. Levin; three children

Education
Swarthmore College, B.A. 1956 (political science); Harvard U., LL.B. 1959

Career
Lawyer

Political Highlights
Michigan Civil Rights Commission general counsel, 1964-67; Detroit chief appellate defender, 1968-69; Detroit City Council, 1970-77 (president, 1974-77)

ELECTION RESULTS

2008 GENERAL

Carl Levin (D)	3,038,386	62.7%
Jack Hoogendyk Jr. (R)	1,641,070	33.8%
Scotty Boman (LIBERT)	76,347	1.6%

2008 PRIMARY

Carl Levin (D)	unopposed

Previous Winning Percentages
2002 (61%); 1996 (58%); 1990 (57%); 1984 (52%); 1978 (52%)

Elected 1978; 6th term

Congressional Democrats will soon need a new go-to guy for national security issues. Levin has decided to retire at the end of the 113th Congress, opting for one last flurry of legislative activity rather than the rigors of a sixth re-election campaign.

Levin, the chairman of the Armed Services Committee, is responsible for passage each year of the defense authorization bill. His achievements in recent years include repeal of the controversial rules that prevented openly gay people from serving in the military, and a 2009 acquisitions law that changed the way the military buys its weapons. As fiscal pressures have affected defense budgets, he has defended large blocks of military spending, while continuing to question the ways the armed forces are used.

After regaining the Armed Services chairmanship in 2007 (he had served as chairman from June 2001 to January 2003), Levin was determined to assert a stronger congressional hand in war policy. He led hearings on issues including interrogation techniques, detainee treatment and the conduct of U.S. contractors in Iraq. In 2009, Levin reacted to President Barack Obama's decision to reduce the U.S. commitment in Iraq by declaring that his own calculations showed an even smaller residual presence was feasible.

More recently, he has pressed for a steady drawdown of troops in Afghanistan. Levin backed the invasion of that country in 2001, but his support for further intervention has waned.

He was a skeptic of Obama's decision in late 2009 to temporarily boost troop levels in Afghanistan by 30,000 — but he quickly pressured the administration to use the surge as an opportunity to increase training and equipping of Afghan forces. He seizes any opportunity to compel the transition of security duties to Afghans, so that most U.S. troops can depart Afghanistan by the end of 2014.

"I think we have got to continue reductions of troops in Afghanistan, because one, it is the way we keep pressing Afghans to take responsibility for their security, and two, because of the huge costs to us in terms of blood and treasure," Levin said. "It is the right thing to do in terms of success; it's the necessary thing in terms of the budget situation and the risk to our troops."

He does see positives in U.S. military interventions, however. Speaking to the Council on Foreign Relations in March 2013, Levin accused the media of ignoring the overall improvements to Afghan society and security since the U.S. invasion. And he suggested that the Obama administration should be pursuing some kind of military operations in Syria, as rebels there work to overthrow President Bashar al-Assad — not necessarily a ground war, but perhaps limited strikes against air defenses "to send Assad a message."

"It's important that we be at the table where the post-Assad decisions are made," he said.

Levin's work in the 113th Congress (2013-14) is complicated by shifting dynamics on his committee. For many years, Levin reveled in his strong working relationship with the panel's ranking member, Republican John McCain of Arizona. They worked together on the procurement overhaul, and in the 112th Congress (2011-12) they tried to minimize the defense spending cuts created by a 2011 deficit reduction law.

But McCain reached a term limit in 2013 and yielded the top spot to Oklahoma Republican James M. Inhofe, a conservative stalwart. The transition was not smooth. It opened with a bitter confirmation fight — Republicans were highly critical of Chuck Hagel, Obama's nominee for Defense secretary. Levin denied several GOP requests to delay the panel's vote on Hagel.

Most people consider defense to be Levin's signature issue, but he says investigation and oversight "are what I'm all about." With his rumpled suits and reading glasses, Levin looks like a professor — but he has the spirit of a litigator. He chairs the Homeland Security and Governmental Affairs Permanent Subcommittee on Investigations, and he has used that panel to probe issues such as counterfeit parts in weapons and the vulnerabilities of the U.S. financial system.

His tenacity was on display in April 2010, as he investigated the role of investment banks in the 2008 financial meltdown. His panel examined millions of pages of documents, interviewed hundreds of witnesses and conducted four hearings with more than 30 hours of testimony. Some of the problems Levin's investigation exposed were addressed in the 2010 financial regulatory overhaul known as Dodd-Frank.

Levin has been "very active" studying the ways companies get privileged treatment in the tax code or avoid taxes. "We have gone after the offshore tax haven loopholes," he said. In 2012, Levin urged changes to Dodd-Frank to prevent banks from engaging in hedge-fund-like activities; he said companies such as JPMorgan Chase were labeling such activity "portfolio hedging" to get around regulatory restrictions. He also was critical of tax provisions that allowed Facebook to take tax deductions on shares sold early to investors before its 2012 initial public offering.

In February 2013, Levin and Rhode Island Democrat Sheldon Whitehouse rolled out their bill to eliminate a number of corporate tax-avoidance techniques. When he announced his retirement, Levin mentioned that effort as one of the biggest priorities for his final years in Congress.

Levin still devotes time to his state's interests. Like many Michigan politicians, he advocates frequently on behalf of the auto industry. He also worked with Michigan Democrat Debbie Stabenow to reach a 2006 agreement with Canadian officials to reduce the amount of trash entering Michigan landfills from Canada. In the 112th Congress, they tried to further discourage such dumping, introducing a bill to establish fees on waste-shipping companies to pay for security inspections of trash trucks.

Levin's older brother, Sander M. Levin, represents Michigan's 9th District in the House and has the top Democratic spot on the Ways and Means Committee. They have collaborated on trade issues, focusing particularly on relations with China. Although Carl made it to the Senate four years before Sander won his House seat, he says he has always looked up to his older brother. Both men absorbed a passion for politics from their father, a lawyer active in liberal causes in Detroit.

As a teenager, Levin worked the assembly line at a Chrysler DeSoto plant, and he still carries a fading United Auto Workers membership card in his wallet. Later, while in law school, Levin drove a taxi, an experience he said helped him deal with people of all backgrounds.

In the 1960s, he was the general counsel to the Michigan Civil Rights Commission. He had no plans to run for office until riots destroyed parts of Detroit in 1967.

Three years later, he was elected to the Detroit City Council and worked to rebuild the city. He butted heads with federal housing officials and said he decided to run for the Senate in 1978 in part to try to make federal agents "more responsive to local communities."

Levin often has an avuncular manner, but he can play political hardball. In 1984, he aired an ad showing his GOP opponent, former astronaut Jack Lousma, telling an audience about the Toyota he owned — a faux pas in a state where the phrase "Japanese car" translates as joblessness. President Ronald Reagan carried Michigan with 59 percent of the vote that year, but Levin held on to win with 52 percent. In his four succeeding re-election efforts, Levin's margin of victory steadily increased.

Key Votes

2012	
Prohibit health insurance plans from denying coverage based on the sponsor's religious beliefs	YES
Require approval of the Keystone XL oil pipeline	NO
Ease securities rules to expand small-business access to capital	NO
Reauthorize farm and nutrition programs for five years	YES
Limit debate on a bill that would create private-sector cybersecurity standards	YES
Consent to ratification of a treaty setting global standard for the treatment of people with disabilities	YES
Provide $60.4 billion in disaster relief following Superstorm Sandy	YES
Extend most Bush-era income tax rates while allowing rates for top-bracket earners to rise (Jan. 1, 2013)	YES
2011	
Prevent EPA from regulating greenhouse gas emissions to address climate change	NO
Extend certain provisions of Patriot Act for four years	YES
Clear compromise debt limit increase plan and establish future spending limits	YES
Overhaul patent law	YES
Implement Colombia free trade agreement	NO
Limit debate on confirmation of Caitlin J. Halligan to D.C. Circuit Court of Appeals	YES
Extend payroll tax cut and unemployment benefits for two months	YES

CQ Vote Studies

	PARTY UNITY		PRESIDENTIAL SUPPORT	
	SUPPORT	OPPOSE	SUPPORT	OPPOSE
2012	96%	4%	96%	4%
2011	95%	5%	95%	5%
2010	99%	1%	98%	2%
2009	99%	1%	99%	1%
2008	97%	3%	31%	69%
2007	95%	5%	39%	61%
2006	94%	6%	56%	44%
2005	97%	3%	41%	59%
2004	96%	4%	60%	40%
2003	98%	2%	50%	50%

Interest Groups

	AFL-CIO	ADA	CCUS	ACU
2012	100%	95%	25%	8%
2011	89%	95%	45%	0%
2010	100%	95%	9%	0%
2009	94%	95%	43%	0%
2008	100%	100%	63%	0%
2007	100%	95%	45%	4%
2006	100%	100%	50%	8%
2005	93%	100%	39%	17%
2004	100%	100%	41%	0%
2003	85%	100%	39%	25%

Sen. Debbie Stabenow (D)

Capitol Office
224-4822
stabenow.senate.gov
133 Hart Bldg. 20510-2204; fax 228-0325

Committees
Agriculture, Nutrition & Forestry - Chairwoman
Budget
Energy & Natural Resources
Finance
(Energy, Natural Resources & Infrastructure - Chairwoman)

Residence
Lansing

Born
April 29, 1950; Clare, Mich.

Religion
United Methodist

Family
Divorced; two children

Education
Michigan State U., B.A. 1972 (social science), M.S.W. 1975

Career
Leadership training consultant

Political Highlights
Ingham County Commission, 1975-78 (chairwoman, 1977-1978); Mich. House, 1979-91; Mich. Senate, 1991-94; sought Democratic nomination for governor, 1994; Democratic nominee for lieutenant governor, 1994; U.S. House, 1997-2001

ELECTION RESULTS

2012 GENERAL

Debbie Stabenow (D)	2,735,826	58.8%
Peter Hoekstra (R)	1,767,386	38.0%
Scotty Boman (LIBERT)	84,480	1.8%

2012 PRIMARY

Debbie Stabenow (D)	unopposed

Previous Winning Percentages
2006 (57%); 2000 (49%); 1998 House Election (57%); 1996 House Election (54%)

Elected 2000; 3rd term

Stabenow has a polished style appreciated by both Republicans and her fellow Democrats. She is relentlessly upbeat about her legislative endeavors in public, willing to strike deals in private, and firm once she sets boundaries. She applies that formula to agriculture and health care, as well as energy and manufacturing policies tailored to Michigan's industrial base.

Stabenow has proved her abilities as a political operator several times. Her 25-year journey to the U.S. Senate had stops in county government, the state House, the state Senate and the U.S. House.

As a senator, she has deftly worked her way into several positions of influence. She was once the Democratic Conference secretary — the No. 4 leadership post. But she yielded that job in exchange for a seat on the Finance Committee, where she indulges her interests in health care and manufacturing. She still has a connection to the leadership team as vice chairwoman of the Democratic Policy and Communications Committee, which dishes out research and policy ideas to lawmakers.

Most prominently, she now chairs the Agriculture, Nutrition and Forestry Committee. Stabenow was largely unknown to agriculture groups beyond her state when she took the gavel in 2011; she was more associated with Detroit and manufacturing than the diverse array of farmers in Michigan.

Stabenow stressed that she had been raised in a small town and that her mother's family hailed from a tiny Oklahoma town (which is coincidentally in the district of Republican House Agriculture Chairman Frank D. Lucas). She established a working relationship with Kansas Republican Pat Roberts, the ranking member, and held her ground with senior committee Democrats.

As Congress pondered deficit reduction in the fall of 2011, Stabenow, Roberts and their House counterparts pulled together a package of potential cuts to farm and nutrition programs for negotiators to consider. The deficit talks fell apart, but their recommendations became the starting point for a 2012 farm bill, which the Senate easily passed in June. It had a 10-year savings of $23 billion, including a $4.5 billion reduction to the Supplemental Nutrition Assistance Program. The measure would have ended annual direct payments to growers, shifting federal support toward insurance-like offerings more favorable to corn and soybean producers in the Midwest. Southerners on her committee opposed the bill as hurting growers in their region, but they praised Stabenow for hearing them out.

House conservatives, however, wanted a steeper SNAP reduction, and that chamber did not vote on its own measure. The existing authorization for farm programs expired in the fall, but no one blamed Stabenow. She worked to get the farm programs included in another round of fiscal talks after the 2012 election. "If it is humanly possible to get to the finish line, Debbie's gonna get it done," Lucas said in late November.

Apparently, it wasn't humanly possible, and a one-year extension of farm programs was bundled into another bill at the close of the 112th Congress (2011-12). Stabenow is trying again, only this time she has a new ranking member to deal with — Thad Cochran of Mississippi. The farm bill approved by the panel in May 2013 included "target price" programs favored by peanut and rice farmers from the South.

With the 2010 health care overhaul in the rearview mirror, Stabenow's focus on the Finance Committee has shifted to defending that law and federal entitlement programs. She has tried several times to eliminate the "sustainable growth rate" formula that determines reimbursements for Medicare physicians. Congress routinely overrides the formula to prevent steep reimbursement cuts, which in turn puts extra debts on Medicare's balance sheets; Republicans in 2009 blocked her effort to eliminate the formula and tweak accounting rules to eliminate the debt obligation. Stabenow also opposes raising the eligibility age for Medicare as a means to achieve budget savings.

The Finance Committee is studying broad tax issues in the 113th Congress (2013-14). Stabenow has thus far tried to leverage the tax code to the advantage of people and industries in Michigan. The state is particularly hard hit by home foreclosures, and Stabenow wrote a 2007 law that prevents the IRS from treating as income the amounts saved when struggling homeowners get loan modifications. She proposes more tax benefits for companies that transfer jobs from overseas facilities to the United States.

She also helped create a tax credit for advanced energy manufacturing, such as the production of next-generation car batteries. Stabenow co-chairs the Senate Manufacturing Caucus with South Carolina Republican Lindsey Graham. She grabbed the gavel of the Finance Subcommittee on Energy, Natural Resources and Infrastructure in 2013, saying it "fits well with what I want to do on manufacturing."

The daughter of an Oldsmobile dealer, Stabenow blames free-trade agreements for many of the struggles of the automotive industry and Michigan in general. When the Obama administration announced that Japan was joining negotiations on the Trans-Pacific Partnership, she said she would fight the final agreement unless Japan allows the importation of more U.S.-made cars and car parts. She voted for a free-trade pact with South Korea in 2011, pegging her support to the addition of protections for U.S. automakers.

Stabenow sits on the Energy and Natural Resources Committee, and she champions an Energy Department loan program for the production of advanced-technology vehicles and components. Her manufacturing concerns have steered her away from the cause of regulating greenhouse gas emissions. She is wary of plans for a cap-and-trade emissions credits system, and she has proposed delaying EPA regulation of greenhouse gases.

Stabenow was born and raised in the small town of Clare, known as the gateway to Michigan's "Up North." The eldest of three children, she says her parents urged her to aim high. "In high school, I would hear 'nurse' or 'teacher' as career options," she told the Detroit News in 2005. "But dad would say, 'No, doctor or engineer.' He gave me confidence to take risks, to push limits."

After graduating from Michigan State University, she got involved in politics. A social worker, she was angered by the closing of a local nursing home. She successfully challenged an incumbent to get a seat on the Ingham County Commission in 1975. She went on to serve 12 years in the Michigan House and a term in the state Senate.

In 1994, she lost the Democratic gubernatorial primary to veteran Democratic Rep. Howard Wolpe. She subsequently lost in the general election as Wolpe's running mate for lieutenant governor. But she made a comeback in 1996, ending Republican Rep. Dick Chrysler's one-term tenure in the politically competitive 8th District. She was easily re-elected to the seat in 1998.

That set up Stabenow's 2000 challenge to Spencer Abraham, a longtime GOP operative and one-term senator. Stabenow had a campaign war chest of $8 million and was the top recipient of funds from EMILY's List, a political action committee that backs Democratic female candidates who support abortion rights. She won by less than 2 points. In typical Stabenow fashion, one of her first acts as a senator was helping Abraham win confirmation as President George W. Bush's secretary of Energy.

Stabenow handily defeated Oakland County Sheriff Mike Bouchard in 2006. Republicans thought they might have a shot at unseating her in 2012, given voters' frustrations with the Michigan economy. But Stabenow won a decisive victory over former Republican Rep. Peter Hoekstra, garnering more votes statewide than President Barack Obama.

Key Votes

2012

Prohibit health insurance plans from denying coverage based on the sponsor's religious beliefs	YES
Require approval of the Keystone XL oil pipeline	NO
Ease securities rules to expand small-business access to capital	YES
Reauthorize farm and nutrition programs for five years	YES
Limit debate on a bill that would create private-sector cybersecurity standards	YES
Consent to ratification of a treaty setting global standard for the treatment of people with disabilities	YES
Provide $60.4 billion in disaster relief following Superstorm Sandy	YES
Extend most Bush-era income tax rates while allowing rates for top-bracket earners to rise (Jan. 1, 2013)	YES

2011

Prevent EPA from regulating greenhouse gas emissions to address climate change	NO
Extend certain provisions of Patriot Act for four years	YES
Clear compromise debt limit increase plan and establish future spending limits	YES
Overhaul patent law	YES
Implement Colombia free trade agreement	NO
Limit debate on confirmation of Caitlin J. Halligan to D.C. Circuit Court of Appeals	YES
Extend payroll tax cut and unemployment benefits for two months	YES

CQ Vote Studies

	PARTY UNITY		PRESIDENTIAL SUPPORT	
	SUPPORT	OPPOSE	SUPPORT	OPPOSE
2012	91%	9%	96%	4%
2011	94%	6%	94%	6%
2010	99%	1%	98%	2%
2009	97%	3%	96%	4%
2008	98%	2%	31%	69%
2007	94%	6%	32%	68%
2006	88%	12%	51%	49%
2005	95%	5%	33%	67%
2004	96%	4%	58%	42%
2003	97%	3%	49%	51%

Interest Groups

	AFL-CIO	ADA	CCUS	ACU
2012	91%	90%	50%	16%
2011	89%	90%	55%	0%
2010	100%	90%	36%	0%
2009	100%	100%	43%	0%
2008	100%	100%	50%	4%
2007	100%	100%	27%	8%
2006	100%	90%	50%	16%
2005	93%	100%	44%	12%
2004	100%	100%	65%	8%
2003	85%	95%	39%	20%

Rep. Dan Benishek (R)

Capitol Office
225-4735
benishek.house.gov
514 Cannon Bldg. 20515-2201; fax 225-4710

Committees
Agriculture
Natural Resources
Veterans' Affairs
(Health - Chairman)

Residence
Crystal Falls

Born
April 20, 1952; Iron River, Mich.

Religion
Roman Catholic

Family
Wife, Judy Benishek; five children

Education
U. of Michigan, B.S. 1974 (biology); Wayne State U., M.D. 1978

Career
Surgeon

Political Highlights
No previous office

ELECTION RESULTS

2012 GENERAL		
Dan Benishek (R)	167,060	48.1%
Gary McDowell (D)	165,179	47.6%
Emily Salvette (LIBERT)	10,630	3.1%
Ellis Boal (GREEN)	4,168	1.2%
2012 PRIMARY		
Dan Benishek (R)		unopposed
2010 GENERAL		
Dan Benishek (R)	120,523	51.9%
Gary McDowell (D)	94,824	40.9%
Glenn Wilson (I)	7,847	3.4%
Patrick Lambert (USTAX)	4,200	1.8%
Keith Shelton (LIBERT)	2,571	1.1%

Elected 2010; 2nd term

Time is of the essence for Benishek, a proudly novice legislator who has pledged to serve no more than three terms in the House. He approves of Republican efforts to rework federal budgets, but his best bets for signature policy changes are tied to personal interests: veterans' health care and the natural resources in his district.

A surgeon by trade, Benishek never held political office before the 112th Congress (2011-12). He campaigns as "Dr. Dan," and in both of his House races his usual attack against his two-time Democratic opponent was calling him a "career politician." Unassuming and affable in person, Benishek expresses frustrations with Washington — particularly with the Senate.

"I'm a general surgeon," he said. "I'm used to making a decision and then having to live with it. ... The Senate hasn't done anything." He's one of the few House Republicans to call for changes to Senate filibuster rules.

Benishek favors a conservative fiscal agenda and significant alterations to the 2010 health care law. (He wants the health sector transformed into "a true marketplace situation where the patient is the purchaser of the services.") However, President Barack Obama will likely be in office through the end of Benishek's tenure, assuming Benishek reaches his term limit and sticks to it. Legislatively speaking, those goals are long shots.

Still, Benishek has opportunities to work on less-partisan policy. In the 113th Congress (2013-14), he chairs the Veterans' Affairs Subcommittee on Health. Benishek worked as a consulting surgeon at the Iron Mountain VA hospital. He cites the facility's high turnover of directors as a "pet peeve" and wants longer tenures for administrative positions, saying it would improve overall performance. "The VA could do what they do more efficiently," he said in 2011.

In 2012, Benishek outlined policies that he said would greatly reduce the backlog in processing benefit claims. Under his framework, veterans would be automatically enrolled in the VA system before moving to civilian life, and they would get training on how to navigate that system. The VA would have a complete medical history on file before that transition. Claims for "simple disabilities" filed with the help of a certified service officer would get automatic disbursements, and video conferencing and other technology would be used to expedite hearings on complex claims.

He also supports efforts to bolster employment of veterans by offering tax credits to employers who hire them. "I think these guys deserve a little help," he said.

Benishek isn't as enthusiastic about other military-related spending. During a 2011 trip to Afghanistan, he "didn't see anything over there that made me feel we have an effective strategy." He voted for an unsuccessful amendment to the fiscal 2013 Defense spending bill that would have limited Afghanistan funding, so that it could be spent only on an orderly troop withdrawal. And he wasn't thrilled about U.S. involvement in Libya in 2011. "I think we have to be very hesitant getting involved in these overseas adventures," he said.

At the end of the 112th Congress, Benishek was in the minority of House Republicans voting for a bill that extended lower income tax rates only for earnings under $400,000. But leading up to that vote, he signed onto a letter requesting more defense cuts as part of deficit reduction plans.

The forests, mines and lakes of the 1st District have been Benishek's other major concern. He has a seat on the Natural Resources Committee, and in the 113th Congress he also joined the Agriculture Committee — which has jurisdiction over the Forest Service. "I want to have a healthy forest and a sustainable forest, but I don't think that some of these environmental people want us to touch the forest at all," Benishek says. He introduced a 2011 bill to prevent the use of lawsuits to block a Forest Service sale late in the sales process.

Benishek blamed EPA regulations for Michigan's denial of a permit for a road project in Marquette County in early 2013. The road would have facilitated mining development near Big Bay, which Benishek has called "a huge employment opportunity." When considering a 2012 bill to ease regulation of the coal industry, the House adopted a Benishek amendment; postulating that the unemployed have poorer health, it would have required federal analysis of regulatory costs to include health costs associated with any jobs lost because of a regulation. The underlying bill was not taken up by the Senate.

Benishek keeps a hunting camp in the Ottawa National Forest — he calls it one of his favorite spots to visit when he can get away from Washington — and he defends the use of public lands for recreational uses. On social issues, he matches the conservatism of many of his constituents. He is strongly in favor of gun rights and opposes abortion.

Benishek grew up in Iron River. He was 5 years old when his father died in an iron mine accident, and he spent his childhood working alongside his mother at the Iron River Hotel — which was owned by his grandmother. It was a "working man's hotel," like a college dorm, he said. "A couple of guys lived there for 20 years."

Sports didn't fit into the work schedule, so "I was sort of a nerd," Benishek said. He earned $10 a week mopping floors, hauling beer and doing odd jobs. The hotel closed when his grandmother died, and Benishek's savings took him over the Mackinac Bridge to the University of Michigan. He did his medical studies at Wayne State and returned to the Upper Peninsula in the early 1980s.

He called the 2009 stimulus law his reason for getting into politics. "I see it as spending a trillion dollars of money we didn't have on a bill they didn't read," he said. After some consideration, "I said to my wife, 'You mind if I run for Congress?' And she said, 'Yeah, sure, go ahead.'"

The 1st District race became a priority for both parties after nine-term Democrat Bart Stupak announced he wouldn't seek re-election. Benishek won the GOP primary by just 15 votes, then focused on Democratic state Rep. Gary McDowell, a farmer and UPS delivery man. Benishek won by 11 points.

The 2012 campaign was a rematch in a reconfigured district — the Lower Peninsula portion of the 1st District now runs clear across the top of Michigan's "mitten," but the district lost its southernmost counties.

It was a hotly contested race with plenty of spending by both the candidates and national party organizations. Benishek prevailed by 1,881 votes, and his victory was one of the few bright spots for Republicans on Election Day.

Key Votes

2012	
Extend a Social Security payroll tax cut and unemployment benefits	YES
Ease securities rules to expand small-business access to capital	YES
Extend for one year subsidized student loan interest rates financed by a cut in health care spending	YES
Cite Attorney General Eric H. Holder Jr. for contempt of Congress	YES
Create a visa program for foreign graduates in high-tech fields	YES
Extend most Bush-era income tax rates while allowing rates for top-bracket earners to rise (Jan. 1, 2013)	YES
2011	
Strike funding for F-35 alternative engine	YES
Prevent EPA from regulating greenhouse gas emissions to address climate change	YES
Extend certain provisions of Patriot Act for four years	YES
Declare opposition to use of ground troops in Libya	YES
Overhaul patent law	NO
Pass compromise debt limit increase plan and establish future spending limits	YES
Allow consideration of measures to implement three trade agreements	YES

CQ Vote Studies

	PARTY UNITY		PRESIDENTIAL SUPPORT	
	SUPPORT	OPPOSE	SUPPORT	OPPOSE
2012	95%	5%	18%	82%
2011	95%	5%	18%	82%

Interest Groups

	AFL-CIO	ADA	CCUS	ACU
2012	14%	5%	100%	80%
2011	0%	5%	94%	88%

Michigan 1

Upper Peninsula; northern Lower Michigan

Forested state parks, hundreds of miles of Great Lakes shoreline, harsh winters and remote cabins: The 1st looks like iconic Michigan. The district is made up of the sparsely populated areas from Michigan's northern Lower Peninsula — no city population in the 1st exceeds 22,000 — and encompasses the entire Upper Peninsula. Self-proclaimed "Yoopers" (residents of the U.P.) are connected to the rest of the district only by the Mackinac Bridge; isolated from the rest of their state, Yoopers tend to identify culturally with nearby Wisconsinites or Canadians.

Tourism is vital to the district. Touching three of the Great Lakes — Superior, Huron and Michigan — and covered by state and national parks, the 1st boasts many outdoor-recreation destinations. Isle Royale, the state's northernmost outpost, draws backpackers. Mackinac Island, known for its prohibition on cars and for its Victorian-style houses and its fudge, is a popular seasonal vacation spot. Traverse City boasts cool lakeside summers and an abundance of sweet cherries. Casinos are a growing business as well. The area of the Upper Peninsula nearest to downstate Michigan features a number of American Indian-run gaming locations that draw tourists from nearby states and Canada.

Although the district has been hit hard by the recession, it is somewhat insulated from the more drastic downturns in the auto-industry-reliant areas of the state closer to Detroit. A long tradition of mining and logging on the U.P. is dwindling but still important.

The district has a GOP lean, but Democratic votes make for competitive elections, and environmental issues remain important to voters. Barack Obama took only two counties in the district in the 2012 presidential contest — sparsely populated Gogebic, at the state's western tip, and Marquette, home of Northern Michigan University — and Republican nominee Mitt Romney won by 9 points in the district overall.

Major Industry
Tourism, mining

Cities
Marquette, Traverse City, Sault Ste. Marie

Notable
The National Ski and Snowboard Hall of Fame is in Ishpeming.

Rep. Bill Huizenga (R)

Capitol Office
225-4401
huizenga.house.gov
1217 Longworth Bldg. 20515-2202; fax 226-0779

Committees
Financial Services

Residence
Zeeland

Born
Jan. 31, 1969; Zeeland, Mich.

Religion
Christian Reformed

Family
Wife, Natalie Huizenga; five children

Education
Calvin College, B.A. 1992 (political science)

Career
Private school fundraiser; congressional district aide; Realtor

Political Highlights
Mich. House, 2003-09

ELECTION RESULTS

2012 GENERAL		
Bill Huizenga (R)	194,653	61.2%
Willie German Jr. (D)	108,973	34.2%
Mary Buzuma (LIBERT)	8,750	2.7%
Ronald E. Graeser (USTAX)	3,176	1.0%
2012 PRIMARY		
Bill Huizenga (R)		unopposed
2010 GENERAL		
Bill Huizenga (R)	148,864	65.3%
Fred Johnson (D)	72,118	31.6%
Joseph Gillotte (LIBERT)	2,701	1.2%
Ronald E. Graeser (USTAX)	2,379	1.0%

Elected 2010; 2nd term

Huizenga has strong convictions but an unobtrusive manner. He promotes both his preferences for fiscal restraint and the Republican agenda on the Financial Services Committee.

Huizenga (HI-zing-uh) can claim to have a finger on the political pulse of his constituents — he has served as a district aide for Republican Rep. Peter Hoekstra and as a member of the Michigan House. He is also culturally attuned to most of the people he represents. "The people in my district are very conservative, Calvinist, religious, humble and face harsh winters," he told the Netherlands National News Agency in 2011. That description fits him, too.

He was born and raised in Zeeland, where his family operated concrete and gravel companies. He attended Calvin College, a Grand Rapids school tied to his church that "promotes lifelong Christian service."

"We have a strong belief that you have to be involved with your community with your time, energy and your treasure," Huizenga once told the Grand Rapids Press. He met his wife in college, and they now live in Zeeland with their five children.

Huizenga started investing in real estate while in college. He went on to become a Realtor, as well as a co-owner of the family gravel business. He was hired by Hoekstra in 1997, and he held that job until winning election to the state House in 2002. Before term limits ended his run, he served as chairman of the Commerce Committee. One of his signature achievements was a 2007 law creating tax incentives to lure the film industry to shoot in Michigan.

In the U.S. House, Huizenga has voted as one of the more fiscally conservative Republicans, but without the fanfare of other cost-cutters. He opposed the final spending bills for fiscal 2011 and 2012, as well as a January 2013 tax package that, according to Huizenga, needed to include spending cuts. In speaking of the need for a balanced-budget amendment to the Constitution, he has Calvinist overtones: "We need institutional spending controls put in place because we, as an entity, don't have the self-discipline to say no," he said.

Huizenga touts the value of his small-business and real estate experience as a member of the Financial Services Committee. As a freshman, he also drew on his years as Hoekstra's liaison to business leaders. Huizenga organized trips to New York and Chicago with fellow panel freshmen to discuss legislative priorities with organizations such as the Board of Trade and the U.S. Chamber of Commerce.

He is skeptical of the 2010 financial regulatory law known as Dodd-Frank and the agencies created by it. "There seems to be this belief that somehow Dodd-Frank came down on this holy writ, and not a jot or tittle shall be changed or altered," Huizenga said in 2011. He wants it to be "workable. ... I don't see how they are realistically able to loosen credit and service the needs that people have."

In late 2012, President Barack Obama signed Huizenga's bill to clarify that privileged information sent by financial institutions to the Consumer Financial Protection Bureau is protected as confidential and is not subject to third-party subpoenas. That distinction was not originally included in the portion of Dodd-Frank that created the CFPB.

Huizenga shares the common Republican fear that the bureau is largely unaccountable to Congress and has too much authority to interfere in the marketplace. "It's not the nature of an agency to leave things alone, whether they're good or whether they're bad," he said at a 2012 hearing.

Huizenga keeps a close eye on global markets and monetary policy. He didn't directly criticize a 2012 round of "quantitative easing," in which the

Federal Reserve orders the printing of money, then uses it to buy financial assets to keep long-term interest rates down. But he did say on CNBC that "having these artificially low rates really just underscores the bad economic policies coming out of this administration and the uncertainty that's out there."

A few of Huizenga's parochial issues were inherited from Hoekstra. The first bill he introduced was to designate the Sleeping Bear Dunes National Lakeshore in Michigan as wilderness. The designation would help protect the land and, possibly, a fragile tourism industry in his district. He first worked on the issue as Hoekstra's aide.

Michigan's sagging manufacturing economy could benefit from changes to federal prison manufacturing rules, according to Huizenga (and Hoekstra before him). Private companies have long claimed that UNICOR, the trade name for the business sector of Federal Prison Industries, has benefited unfairly from cheap prison labor and a "mandatory source" status that requires the Defense Department and other federal agencies to purchase inmate-made products.

Huizenga supports eliminating the mandatory-source status entirely, and he was not pleased when UNICOR in 2011 began competing with the private sector for an expanded list of products. Huizenga had a bipartisan collection of co-sponsors for his bill to subject the prison workforce to the same rules and costs as private employers — it included an increase in prison wages.

Like most of the people of Dutch heritage in his district, Huizenga is a social conservative. He told the Netherlands National News Agency that he was puzzled by the prevailing social attitudes of his ancestral homeland. "There are lots of people in the Netherlands offering the liberal positions in regard to gay marriage, abortion, guns, drugs or euthanasia, but it's hard to understand," he said. "I can still not quite fully understand how the Netherlands so rapidly changed from its conservative origin."

Huizenga's path to Congress opened up when Hoekstra decided to end his House career after 18 years and run for governor in 2010. Seven Republicans entered the contest to succeed him. Huizenga was the upset winner in the primary, using his well-developed network of contacts to defeat former NFL player Jay Riemersma by fewer than 700 votes. (Hoekstra, meanwhile, lost his gubernatorial primary.) In the strongly Republican district, Huizenga beat Democrat Fred Johnson, who had lost to Hoekstra in 2008, by a better than 2-to-1 margin.

In 2012, Huizenga was unopposed in the primary and easily won a second term, defeating Democrat Willie German by 27 points. Hoekstra, meanwhile, lost a Senate race to Democrat Debbie Stabenow.

Key Votes

Vote	
2012	
Extend a Social Security payroll tax cut and unemployment benefits	YES
Ease securities rules to expand small-business access to capital	YES
Extend for one year subsidized student loan interest rates financed by a cut in health care spending	NO
Cite Attorney General Eric H. Holder Jr. for contempt of Congress	YES
Create a visa program for foreign graduates in high-tech fields	YES
Extend most Bush-era income tax rates while allowing rates for top-bracket earners to rise (Jan. 1, 2013)	NO
2011	
Strike funding for F-35 alternative engine	YES
Prevent EPA from regulating greenhouse gas emissions to address climate change	YES
Extend certain provisions of Patriot Act for four years	YES
Declare opposition to use of ground troops in Libya	YES
Overhaul patent law	YES
Pass compromise debt limit increase plan and establish future spending limits	YES
Allow consideration of measures to implement three trade agreements	YES

CQ Vote Studies

	Party Unity		Presidential Support	
	Support	Oppose	Support	Oppose
2012	97%	3%	17%	83%
2011	97%	3%	21%	79%

Interest Groups

	AFL-CIO	ADA	CCUS	ACU
2012	10%	5%	83%	96%
2011	0%	5%	100%	92%

Michigan 2

West — Muskegon, most of Holland

Many of the scenic communities in the 2nd District planted their early roots in the fur trade and timber industry. In addition to the Lake Michigan shoreline, the 2nd takes in most of Manistee National Park and more populous towns to the south, including the western suburbs of Grand Rapids and part of Holland, shared with the 6th District.

The sparsely populated areas north of Muskegon — known for fishing, camping, boating and hunting — rely largely on tourism to survive, and the recent economic downturn has hit this area hard. Once home to many commercial fishing interests, including the Lake Michigan perch, the industry here has been declining in recent years due to overfishing, pollution and the introduction of invasive species.

The 2nd's southern reaches are transitioning from a manufacturing economy focused on the auto industry and the logging operations that once thrived here. South of Muskegon, there are new jobs in hybrid-vehicle research and manufacturing — particularly in the lithium-ion battery sector. Even the renowned local furniture-making industry has experienced contraction.

Largely white, the district does have a small minority population in its southern counties; there is a fast-growing Hispanic population in Ottawa and Kent counties, particularly in suburban Wyoming. Muskegon County has a black population of slightly less than 15 percent, and Lake County in the northeast has the only other sizable black population here (9 percent).

One of the state's most conservative districts, the 2nd backs Republicans consistently. Muskegon and Lake were the district's only counties to back Barack Obama in the 2012 presidential race, and Oceana County switched to Michigan-born Mitt Romney after having backed Obama over Republican John McCain in 2008 — the 2nd gave Romney his highest percentage of any district statewide (56 percent).

Major Industry
Manufacturing, timber, furniture, tourism

Cities
Wyoming, Kentwood, Muskegon, Norton Shores

Notable
Holland, a Dutch-settled port town, hosts the Dutch Village Theme Park and an annual tulip festival.

Rep. Justin Amash (R)

Capitol Office
225-3831
amash.house.gov
114 Cannon Bldg. 20515-2203; fax 225-5144

Committees
Oversight & Government Reform
Joint Economic

Residence
Cascade Township

Born
April 18, 1980; Grand Rapids, Mich.

Religion
Eastern Orthodox

Family
Wife, Kara Amash; three children

Education
U. of Michigan, B.A. 2002 (economics), J.D. 2005

Career
Marketing consultant; lawyer

Political Highlights
Mich. House, 2009-10

ELECTION RESULTS

2012 GENERAL		
Justin Amash (R)	171,675	52.6%
Steve Pestka (D)	144,108	44.2%
Bill Gelineau (LIBERT)	10,498	3.2%
2012 PRIMARY		
Justin Amash (R)		unopposed
2010 GENERAL		
Justin Amash (R)	133,714	59.7%
Pat Miles (D)	83,953	37.5%
James Rogers (LIBERT)	2,677	1.2%

Elected 2010; 2nd term

Amash is often described as the ideological successor to Texas Rep. Ron Paul, the libertarian-leaning presidential candidate who retired from the House after the 112th Congress. But Paul's national stature afforded him some leeway when he disagreed with Republican leaders, whereas Amash is taking his lumps for his dissent.

Young and brainy, Amash (ah-MAHSH) calls himself a "classic liberal," which he defines as someone with a "strong belief in limited government, economic freedom and individual liberty." He keeps a picture of economist Friedrich Hayek on his office wall, abhors the use of government funds to prop up private enterprise — including through tax subsidies — and wants lower overall corporate and income tax rates.

He makes a point of explaining all his votes on Facebook, a practice he started during his one term in the Michigan House. "The Constitution is the first thing you have to look at," he said. "It's not something you look to just to find a justification to defeat legislation. You have to look to it even when it might be a subject matter that you want to support."

Amash is not particularly enamored of NPR, strongly opposes abortion and pushes hard for spending cuts. Yet in the 112th Congress (2011-12), he opposed Republican attempts to cut federal funding for the radio network and Planned Parenthood, a nonprofit that provides counseling on reproductive health issues. In his view, Article 1, Section 9 of the Constitution prohibits laws that single out any one company or group.

But when it is philosophically feasible, he opposes most government spending. "We don't need any more revenue in Washington," he said on Fox News in December 2012. "We have enough revenue to run all of our constitutional functions."

Amash voted against all the major enacted spending and deficit reduction measures of the 112th Congress, believing that they did too little to reduce the national debt or shrink government. On the Budget Committee, Amash and Tim Huelskamp of Kansas were the only Republicans to oppose the fiscal 2013 budget of Chairman Paul D. Ryan, and they were among the 10 Republicans voting against it on the House floor. Amash blamed GOP leaders for not seriously pursuing a plan Democrats would accept and suggested that more defense cuts were needed.

He was also one of four House Republicans to vote against a proposed balanced-budget amendment to the Constitution in November 2011. He favored his version, which would balance yearly spending with the average tax revenues of the previous three years, adjusted for population growth and inflation. Trying to match spending to estimated revenues "makes it difficult for policymakers to determine what kind of appropriations to make," he said.

His devotion to his personal principles has hasn't always sat well with other Republicans. Not long after the 2012 election, the GOP Steering Committee voted to remove Amash from the Budget Committee, while also punishing Huelskamp and two other lawmakers in a similar fashion. At the start of the 113th Congress (2013-14), his only committee assignment was to the Oversight and Government Reform panel. (He was later granted a second term on the Joint Economic Committee, which produces no legislation.)

Amash quickly went public with his displeasure, demanding a public explanation from GOP leaders. When it came time to elect the speaker of the House for the 113th Congress, Amash participated in a failed campaign to deny John A. Boehner a second term, and some reports identified him as the leader of the effort. He voted for Rep. Raúl R. Labrador of Idaho.

With his widely touted devotion to transparency and his well-known philosophy on voting, Amash doesn't have an easy path to the good graces of House leaders — which could explain why he is reportedly considering a 2014 bid for the Senate seat left open by the retirement of Democrat Carl Levin.

On civil liberties and foreign policy, Amash sometimes has the tendencies of a libertarian, and he is comfortable with that label. In 2011, he was one of 31 House Republicans to oppose an extension of certain surveillance powers in the anti-terrorism law known as the Patriot Act.

Amash also voted against defense policy bills in the 112th Congress, worrying that they would allow the president to hold U.S. citizens without trial if they are suspected of associating with terrorists. He and Washington Democrat Adam Smith tried to amend a 2012 bill with the goal of eliminating the military's authority to indefinitely detain individuals suspected of being terrorists, if they are caught within the United States. That effort evoked a stern response from Florida Republican Tom Rooney, a former military prosecutor, who accused Amash of wanting to "coddle foreign enemy combatants."

Amash has called for the withdrawal of U.S. forces from Afghanistan. An Arab-American who considers himself well versed on the politics of the Middle East, he favors a two-state solution to the Israel-Palestine conflict. "We should not be quick to intervene," he said. "We should really focus our efforts on ensuring that we have peaceful, good relations with as many countries as possible and that we have trade with as many countries as possible."

Social conservatism sometimes carries Amash away from conventional libertarianism. He opposes abortion — he says fetuses become human at the moment of conception, which means their civil liberties must be protected.

Amash's father, a former refugee, emigrated from Palestine as a teenager and went on to found a tool company; his mother came from Syria. Amash is Eastern Orthodox. He was born in Grand Rapids, a Republican bastion for decades; his district's borders have moved somewhat over the years, but it is essentially the same one that Gerald R. Ford once represented.

Amash was valedictorian of his high school, then went on to get economics and law degrees at the University of Michigan. He worked as a business lawyer for several years, as well as having a position in his father's tool company.

He was elected to the state House in 2008 and launched his run for Congress in February 2010. Incumbent Republican Vernon J. Ehlers announced the next day that he would retire. Amash beat four other candidates in the primary and defeated Democrat Pat Miles in November with almost 60 percent of the vote.

Redistricting for the 2012 election made his seat tougher to defend, but Amash beat Democrat Steve Pestka, a former state House member, by more than 8 points.

Key Votes

2012	
Extend a Social Security payroll tax cut and unemployment benefits	NO
Ease securities rules to expand small-business access to capital	YES
Extend for one year subsidized student loan interest rates financed by a cut in health care spending	NO
Cite Attorney General Eric H. Holder Jr. for contempt of Congress	YES
Create a visa program for foreign graduates in high-tech fields	YES
Extend most Bush-era income tax rates while allowing rates for top-bracket earners to rise (Jan. 1, 2013)	NO
2011	
Strike funding for F-35 alternative engine	YES
Prevent EPA from regulating greenhouse gas emissions to address climate change	YES
Extend certain provisions of Patriot Act for four years	NO
Declare opposition to use of ground troops in Libya	YES
Overhaul patent law	NO
Pass compromise debt limit increase plan and establish future spending limits	NO
Allow consideration of measures to implement three trade agreements	YES

CQ Vote Studies

	PARTY UNITY		PRESIDENTIAL SUPPORT	
	SUPPORT	OPPOSE	SUPPORT	OPPOSE
2012	85%	15%	51%	49%
2011	89%	11%	21%	79%

Interest Groups

	AFL-CIO	ADA	CCUS	ACU
2012	24%	65%	75%	84%
2011	7%	15%	80%	91%

Michigan 3

West central — Grand Rapids, Battle Creek

From Grand Rapids to Battle Creek, the 3rd District takes in three whole counties and parts of two others. A mix of cities and rural areas, the district includes parts of several thoroughfares that stretch toward Lake Michigan to the west and the state's other major hubs — Detroit and Lansing — to the east. Kent County is home to Grand Rapids, the state's second-most populous city, and Battle Creek is in Calhoun County.

The district has been hurt by recent economic downturns, and poverty rates have risen markedly. But the 3rd is not as reliant on the auto industry as some other parts of the state, and local officials cite public-private cooperation and local philanthropic efforts for luring professionals and keeping jobs in the district's cities. In Grand Rapids, traditionally a furniture-making town, Michigan State University has a community medical campus along the city's "Medical Mile," and tourism officials tout convention facilities. Kellogg's Tony the Tiger makes his home in Battle Creek, where the cereal giant is the largest employer and a philanthropic backer of development and education. A Defense Department logistics facility is also in Battle Creek.

There is still an industrial base in the district, but it is shrinking. Footwear manufacturer Wolverine World Wide and appliance manufacturer Bissell each have a large presence. Direct-sales company Alticor is based in Ada. Farming remains important in the 3rd, especially in the areas east of Grand Rapids; Ionia County is known for its poultry and dairy products.

The district is strongly Republican — Gerald R. Ford made his way to the U.S. House and then the Oval Office from Grand Rapids, and area roads, buildings and an airport are named for the 38th president — and Grand Rapids and its suburbs have a large conservative Christian population of Dutch heritage. The 3rd is largely white outside of Grand Rapids, which has a sizable African-American population, at 20 percent.

Major Industry
Food processing, manufacturing, health care, agriculture

Cities
Grand Rapids, Battle Creek

Notable
The annual Cereal City Festival in Battle Creek features the world's longest breakfast table.

Rep. Dave Camp (R)

Capitol Office
225-3561
camp.house.gov
341 Cannon Bldg. 20515-2204; fax 225-9679

Committees
Ways & Means - Chairman
Joint Taxation - Chairman

Residence
Midland

Born
July 9, 1953; Midland, Mich.

Religion
Roman Catholic

Family
Wife, Nancy Camp; three children

Education
Albion College, B.A. 1975 (economics); U. of San Diego, J.D. 1978

Career
Lawyer; congressional aide

Political Highlights
Mich. House, 1989-91

ELECTION RESULTS

2012 GENERAL		
Dave Camp (R)	197,386	63.1%
Debra Freidell Wirth (D)	104,996	33.6%
John Gelineau (LIBERT)	4,285	1.4%
George M. Zimmer (USTAX)	3,506	1.1%
2012 PRIMARY		
Dave Camp (R)		unopposed
2010 GENERAL		
Dave Camp (R)	148,531	66.2%
Jerry M. Campbell (D)	68,458	30.5%
John Emerick (USTAX)	3,861	1.7%
Clint Foster (LIBERT)	3,504	1.6%

Previous Winning Percentages
2008 (62%); 2006 (61%); 2004 (64%); 2002 (68%); 2000 (68%); 1998 (91%); 1996 (65%); 1994 (73%); 1992 (63%); 1990 (65%)

Elected 1990; 12th term

The 113th Congress is Camp's best opportunity to shine after years of keeping a low profile. He is hoping that his tenure as chairman of the Ways and Means Committee will culminate in the first major tax overhaul in a quarter-century.

Camp has been a member of Ways and Means for most of his House career. He credits his initial appointment to the late President Gerald R. Ford, a fellow Michigander who contacted key legislators in 1992 to help Camp secure the spot. His reputation over the years was that of an unassuming wonk, but he was also a game participant in GOP fundraising efforts, which might have given him the inside track to becoming the panel's top Republican in the 111th Congress (2009-10).

The GOP takeover of the House in 2011 made him the chairman and put him out front as the party's chief guide for tax, health and trade legislation. He sponsored and led debate on nearly every major piece of tax legislation in the 112th Congress (2011-12), while also laying groundwork for a sweeping overhaul of tax policy. Democrats and Republicans have their disputes, but by the end of 2012, few of them disagreed that the tax code is overly complicated and internationally uncompetitive.

Camp told The Wall Street Journal that an overhaul "is my absolute highest priority" and that he wants any overhaul to last for years. He started out the 113th Congress (2013-14) by establishing 11 bipartisan working groups studying different parts of the tax code, and he promised that Ways and Means would approve an overhaul by the end of 2013.

Some of Camp's personal preferences are already on the table: consolidating the current six income tax brackets for individuals into two brackets of 10 percent and no more than 25 percent; reducing the corporate tax rate to no more than 25 percent; maintaining revenue levels between 18 percent and 19 percent of gross domestic product; and changing business taxes from a worldwide to a territorial system.

He often pitches his ideas in terms of job creation and laments that the United States has the highest combined federal-state corporate tax rate in the world. He has repeatedly claimed that his vision for a tax overhaul would quickly add 1 million jobs to the economy. Camp criticizes most Democratic legislation aimed at creating jobs and spurring economic growth, instead favoring reductions in tax rates for businesses.

Although enactment of an overhaul will not be easy, Camp might have helped his cause by supporting the January 2013 "fiscal cliff" deal. It permanently extended lower tax rates on earnings under $400,000, which solidifies budget projections, while also increasing taxes on earnings over that threshold — thereby blunting some Democratic demands for tax increases.

And Camp is highly motivated to succeed. Unless Republicans grant him a waiver to their term limits for committee leaders, he will have to step aside at the end of the 113th Congress.

In addition to taxes, the Ways and Means Committee handles many safety net programs. Camp has endorsed the idea of rolling back recent extensions of unemployment insurance. In 2012, he sponsored a one-year extension of lower payroll tax rates, but packaged it with a provision cutting the maximum benefit by 26 weeks and requiring beneficiaries to actively seek work. It was enacted in early 2012.

He has also sponsored bills to prohibit the Health and Human Services Department from permitting states to waive statutory work requirements for welfare recipients — responding to a 2012 executive order by President Barack

Obama. Camp helped win enactment of the requirements during the Clinton administration.

Camp is a member of the moderate Main Street Partnership. "I'm a conservative on fiscal policy, but a moderate on some other issues," he has said. He broke with his party in March 2010 to support a fully offset $17 billion jobs measure that included tax incentives for businesses that hire unemployed workers. In addition, he has supported Democratic legislation in recent years to boost the Big Three automakers in his state.

Camp was named to the "supercommittee" created by the August 2011 law raising the federal debt ceiling. That bicameral, bipartisan panel was tasked with proposing ways to reduce the deficit by more than $1 trillion. The panel disbanded without achieving that goal, but Camp used the negotiations to talk about a tax overhaul with his Democratic counterparts. It was "deeply regrettable that my Democrat colleagues could not see their way to addressing these much-needed reforms without at least $1 trillion in job-killing tax increases on families and employers," he said.

Trade policy, however, has been one major area of bipartisanship during his chairmanship. In 2012, Obama signed his bill allowing the imposition of countervailing duties against non-market economies, such as China, that may be manipulating trade markets. He heralded the 2011 approval of free-trade agreements with Colombia, Panama and South Korea, and Camp says he is willing to grant Obama "fast track" authority, which prevents Congress from altering trade agreements before voting on their approval.

Camp remains a vocal critic of the health care overhaul enacted in 2010. GOP repeal efforts have fallen short, but some of Camp's bills to peel back tax provisions in the overhaul have been signed into law.

Camp's interest in politics began during law school, and he eventually got involved in GOP campaigns at the local and state levels. After practicing law for five years, he became the chief of staff for Republican Rep. Bill Schuette, a childhood friend. He returned to Michigan in 1986 to manage Schuette's re-election campaign, and two years later Camp won an open state House seat based in Midland, his hometown.

When Schuette ran for the Senate against Democrat Carl Levin in 1990, Camp went after his mentor's House seat. With Schuette's endorsement, Camp eked out a primary victory. He went on to win the general election with 65 percent of the vote and has won re-election easily since then. Camp has been mentioned as a possible Senate candidate for 2014 (Levin is retiring), but in April 2013 he emphasized that he was focusing on his tax efforts.

Camp's office announced in July 2012 that he was being treated for non-Hodgkins' lymphoma. By December, doctors had declared him cancer-free.

Key Votes

2012	
Extend a Social Security payroll tax cut and unemployment benefits	YES
Ease securities rules to expand small-business access to capital	YES
Extend for one year subsidized student loan interest rates financed by a cut in health care spending	?
Cite Attorney General Eric H. Holder Jr. for contempt of Congress	YES
Create a visa program for foreign graduates in high-tech fields	YES
Extend most Bush-era income tax rates while allowing rates for top-bracket earners to rise (Jan. 1, 2013)	YES
2011	
Strike funding for F-35 alternative engine	YES
Prevent EPA from regulating greenhouse gas emissions to address climate change	YES
Extend certain provisions of Patriot Act for four years	YES
Declare opposition to use of ground troops in Libya	YES
Overhaul patent law	YES
Pass compromise debt limit increase plan and establish future spending limits	YES
Allow consideration of measures to implement three trade agreements	YES

CQ Vote Studies

	PARTY UNITY		PRESIDENTIAL SUPPORT	
	SUPPORT	OPPOSE	SUPPORT	OPPOSE
2012	94%	6%	17%	83%
2011	93%	7%	27%	73%
2010	96%	4%	37%	63%
2009	85%	15%	36%	64%
2008	95%	5%	72%	28%

Interest Groups

	AFL-CIO	ADA	CCUS	ACU
2012	14%	0%	100%	84%
2011	3%	10%	100%	72%
2010	14%	0%	100%	92%
2009	15%	15%	93%	88%
2008	20%	20%	94%	83%

Michigan 4

Central — Midland, Mt. Pleasant

The second-largest district in the state by area, the 4th takes in all or part of 15 counties in Michigan's rural center. The district misses Lansing and Saginaw to the south and east, and includes a number of state forests and lakes in the northern tier. The largest population center is Midland, home of Dow Chemical.

Midland relies on Dow's payroll and philanthropy — churches, schools, libraries and a local minor league baseball stadium have been built by its fortune — but the company has cut jobs in recent years. Thirty miles west of Midland, Mount Pleasant is the home of Central Michigan University, the fourth-largest college in the state. The university's new medical school opened in 2012 with a goal of alleviating Michigan's physician shortage.

Many areas in the 4th were once known for their logging operations, but the small towns dotting the landscape now rely on manufacturing in industrial parks. Cadillac in Woxford County has many large manufacturers in the business of making auto parts, household appliances and defense industry products. Tourists come from across the state to the lakes, woods and small towns in the northern 4th every summer.

Much of the rest of the district is agrarian. West and south of Midland and Mount Pleasant, farmers till fields of sugar beets, dry beans, corn, wheat and oats. Christmas tree production is especially high in Missaukee County.

Free trade, price supports and crop insurance are perennial political issues. Conservative rural and small-town residents give Republicans an edge in the district. Only three counties wholly or partially in the district — Isabella, Saginaw and Shiawassee — supported Democrat Barack Obama in his 2012 presidential bid. Mitt Romney took 66 percent of the vote in Missaukee County in 2012, his second-highest percentage of any county statewide.

Major Industry
Agriculture, tourism, chemicals, plastics manufacturing

Cities
Midland, Mount Pleasant

Notable
Chesaning's Showboat Music Festival, which began during the Depression with hopes of aiding an ailing economy, has pumped millions of dollars into the community.

Rep. Dan Kildee (D)

Capitol Office
225-3611
kildee.house.gov
327 Cannon Bldg. 20515-4320; fax 225-6393

Committees
Financial Services

Residence
Flint Township

Born
Aug. 11, 1958; Flint, Mich.

Religion
Roman Catholic

Family
Wife, Jennifer Kildee; three children

Education
U. of Michigan, Flint, attended 1976-82; Central Michigan U., B.S. 2011 (community development & public administration)

Career
Land use think tank president; children's services organization program director

Political Highlights
Flint Board of Education, 1977-85; Genesee County Board of Commissioners, 1986-96; candidate for mayor of Flint, 1991; Genesee County treasurer, 1997-2009

ELECTION RESULTS

2012 GENERAL		
Dan Kildee (D)	214,531	65.0%
Jim Slezak (R)	103,931	31.5%
David Davenport (NPA)	6,694	2.0%
Gregory Creswell (LIBERT)	4,990	1.5%
2012 PRIMARY		
Dan Kildee (D)		unopposed

Elected 2012; 1st term

Every congressman frets over the consequences of the sluggish economy and the pressures on America's industrial base. Kildee got up close and personal with those issues as a longtime official for Genesee County, the home to Flint — a city that has become synonymous with urban decline.

"My passion is rebuilding America's old industrial cities and pursuing policies in terms of infrastructure investment, education, transportation, the whole range of activities that affect development patterns, and making sure that we're reinvesting and rebuilding the great cities that have been so important to the American economy," he says.

Kildee sits on the Financial Services Committee — a good spot for him, as his most prominent work thus far has focused on housing. Kildee was the Genesee County treasurer for 12 years, and in that role he ran the local "land bank," which he helped develop. It seizes delinquent or abandoned properties, then sells, rents or demolishes them as part of a broader strategy to reduce urban blight. His approach was widely copied. Kildee left his post in 2009 to become the president of the Center for Community Progress, a think tank that tackles land use problems.

He is continuing that work in the House, while also studying the financial woes of many municipalities. He sees falling bond ratings as evidence of "a structural failure." At one of the first hearings Kildee participated in, he asked Federal Reserve Chairman Ben S. Bernanke to ponder "how the federal government might intervene" if more cities go bankrupt.

Kildee is the successor to his uncle, Dale E. Kildee, who retired from the House after 18 terms. (Unlike Dale, he favors abortion rights.) Dan worked on some of Dale's campaigns; he says he strives to carry on his uncle's "personal civility." He was unopposed in the Democratic primary, and he easily defeated Republican Jim Slezak, who had served one term in the Michigan House as a Democrat.

Michigan 5

Flint; Saginaw; western Saginaw Bay

From Genesee County and its county seat of Flint north through Saginaw and Bay City, capturing the western shore of Saginaw Bay and into part of the Huron National Forest, the 5th District is full of declining industrial cities and remote wilderness. Nowhere other than Detroit has symbolized the ups and downs of the U.S. auto industry quite like the 5th — every county here lost population between 2000 and 2010.

Car manufacturers and suppliers were responsible for the area's boom in the 20th century and likewise for its periods of economic vulnerability in the past several decades. But recent rebounds at General Motors production facilities have supported jobs and lured parts suppliers back to the region. Flint now builds GM's new electric car, the Chevy Volt, as well as full-size pickup trucks. Saginaw's tradition of blue-collar industrial economy — factory and logging — also left it struggling in the last decade.

Despite a recently stablized factory sector, local officials hope to move away from the region's reliance on manufacturing and develop health care and education hubs. Saginaw looks to draw more medical manufacturers and affiliated industries to its city. Flint hosts a campus of the University of Michigan as well as the engineering-focused Kettering University. Farming, particularly the production of sugar beets in Bay County, remains key.

The district is predominately white, but the southern half of the 5th is more diverse than the sparsely populated northern tier and areas around the bay. Flint and Saginaw both have significant black populations. The district has seen an increase in its Hispanic population since 2000, and many of the newly arrived Latino residents work in the area's agricultural sector. The area's strong union ties and large minority population from the auto industry make the district strongly Democratic. Although the more-rural counties along the bay lean Republican and can make some elections competitive, Barack Obama took 61 percent of the district's presidential vote in 2012.

Major Industry
Agriculture, auto and parts manufacturing

Cities
Flint, Saginaw, Bay City

Notable
Bay City's Antique Toy and Firehouse Museum features the largest collection of fire trucks in the world.

Rep. Fred Upton (R)

Capitol Office
225-3761
upton.house.gov
2183 Rayburn Bldg. 20515-2206; fax 225-4986

Committees
Energy & Commerce - Chairman

Residence
St. Joseph

Born
April 23, 1953; St. Joseph, Mich.

Religion
Protestant

Family
Wife, Amey Upton; two children

Education
U. of Michigan, B.A. 1975 (journalism)

Career
Congressional aide; White House budget analyst

Political Highlights
No previous office

ELECTION RESULTS

2012 GENERAL		
Fred Upton (R)	174,955	54.6%
Mike O'Brien (D)	136,563	42.6%
Christie Gelineau (LIBERT)	6,366	2.0%
2012 PRIMARY		
Fred Upton (R)	45,919	66.6%
Jack Hoogendyk Jr. (R)	23,072	33.4%
2010 GENERAL		
Fred Upton (R)	123,142	62.0%
Don Cooney (D)	66,729	33.6%
Melvin D. Valkner (USTAX)	3,672	1.8%
Fred Strand (LIBERT)	3,369	1.7%

Previous Winning Percentages
2008 (59%); 2006 (61%); 2004 (65%); 2002 (69%); 2000 (68%); 1998 (70%); 1996 (68%); 1994 (73%); 1992 (62%); 1990 (58%); 1988 (71%); 1986 (62%)

Elected 1986; 14th term

Upton climbed the ranks of the Energy and Commerce Committee as a Republican with moderate tendencies. He is still far from a staunch conservative, but as chairman, he has dutifully executed the agenda of House GOP leaders and managed his panel as a staging ground for battles with the Obama administration.

The committee's jurisdiction includes health care, energy policy, communications, the environment and manufacturing. Republicans went on the offensive on all those fronts in the 112th Congress (2011-12) — Upton's first as chairman. His panel produced bills to repeal the 2010 health care law, constrain the EPA, remove barriers to domestic energy production and block regulation of the Internet.

Nearly all those measures died a quick death in the Democratic Senate, but heading into the 2012 election, the panel served as a megaphone for those members insisting that overregulation and government expansion were squelching economic growth.

Upton put his personal stamp on some of those efforts. He has expressed concern over global warming in the past, but the House passed his 2011 bill to block EPA regulation of greenhouse gases. In a Wall Street Journal opinion piece, he called the EPA's actions on that score "an unconstitutional power grab that will kill millions of jobs." With Florida Republican Cliff Stearns, he introduced a bill to phase out an Energy Department's loan guarantee program, which was the focus of oversight investigations into the failure of solar-panel manufacturer Solyndra Inc.

Still, Upton's party loyalty hasn't endeared him to the full range of conservative activists. A few groups denounced his initial selection as chairman, and there were further fits in 2011 when he was named to the "supercommittee," a bicameral, bipartisan special panel tasked with proposing ways to reduce the deficit by more than $1 trillion. Upton, a White House budget analyst during the Reagan administration, was seen by conservatives as a weak link who might accede to tax increases.

The panel disbanded without making any recommendations, but Upton did eventually vote for a tax increase — he was one of 85 House Republicans to back the January 2013 "fiscal cliff" deal, which allowed tax rates to rise on earnings over $400,000 (while also permanently extending lower rates below that threshold).

The Club for Growth ran ads against Upton in the 2012 GOP primary, and some media outlets dubbed it a race to watch. But with a huge fundraising advantage, Upton crushed former state Rep. Jack Hoogendyk Jr. Just before the primary, the Weekly Standard called his tenure "a pleasant surprise."

Upton, a member of the moderate Main Street Partnership, has had high-profile departures from the party line in the past. As the Iraq War ground on, he voted for a 2007 resolution to disapprove of an increase in troop levels there. He has supported an increase in federal funds for stem cell research and some restrictions on gun rights.

He worked with Democrats on various energy issues, teaming up with Edward J. Markey of Massachusetts in 2005 on a proposal to extend daylight saving time for eight weeks. Congress ultimately cleared a version providing a one-month extension, beginning in 2007, which the pair said could help conserve energy used for lighting.

Most famously, he co-wrote a 2007 measure with California Democrat Jane Harman to establish minimum efficiency standards for light bulbs. The provision was hailed by efficiency advocates, but it was a sore point for many conservatives who viewed it as a de facto ban on the incandescent light bulb. During his campaign for the chairmanship, he promised to revisit the issue and ultimately supported efforts to repeal the provision he helped write.

Even in the acrimonious 112th Congress, Upton did work across the aisle on a handful of issues. He and California's Henry A. Waxman, the panel's top Democrat, helped arrange a 2012 reauthorization of the Food and Drug Administration's user fee program for drug and medical-device approval; it included a House provision to shorten the approval process for generic drugs. As the measure was sent to President Barack Obama for his signature, Waxman called it a "significant bipartisan and bicameral achievement."

Despite his independent streak, Upton has generally been a reliable Republican vote on social issues such as same-sex marriage and abortion. After singer Janet Jackson's "wardrobe malfunction" during the 2004 Super Bowl halftime show, Upton sought to stiffen the fines the Federal Communications Commission could levy for broadcast indecency.

He also has a long history of pushing to reduce the deficit, which stems from the nearly 10 years he spent working for Michigan Republican David A. Stockman. Upton served on Stockman's staff when Stockman was a member of the House, and he stuck with his boss when he became President Ronald Reagan's budget director. Upton voted for the major deficit reduction and spending measures of the 112th Congress.

Upton comes from a wealthy Michigan family. His grandfather helped found Whirlpool Corp., which is based in his district. Despite his many years in Congress, Upton has a boyish appearance, and he is an avid tennis player.

After college, Upton began his alliance with Stockman by working on his 1976 congressional campaign. In 1986, Upton was the only Republican to unseat an incumbent in a House primary. His victory over Rep. Mark D. Siljander was not a total shock. Much of the local GOP establishment had long disliked Siljander, a Christian conservative activist whose efforts to link religion and politics had stirred controversy. Upton got a break late in the campaign, when Siljander taped an appeal to fundamentalist ministers, implying that the challenge to him was linked to evil forces and calling on voters to "break the back of Satan."

Upton topped Siljander by 10 points, and he won that November with 62 percent of the vote. He became a deputy to Rep. Newt Gingrich when the Georgia Republican was elected GOP whip in 1989, and the next year he joined Gingrich in castigating President George Bush for agreeing to raise taxes as part of a deal to reduce the deficit. But Upton resigned as a deputy whip in 1993 because he said he disliked Gingrich's confrontational style.

His re-elections have been relatively easy.

Key Votes

2012	
Extend a Social Security payroll tax cut and unemployment benefits	YES
Ease securities rules to expand small-business access to capital	YES
Extend for one year subsidized student loan interest rates financed by a cut in health care spending	YES
Cite Attorney General Eric H. Holder Jr. for contempt of Congress	YES
Create a visa program for foreign graduates in high-tech fields	YES
Extend most Bush-era income tax rates while allowing rates for top-bracket earners to rise (Jan. 1, 2013)	YES
2011	
Strike funding for F-35 alternative engine	YES
Prevent EPA from regulating greenhouse gas emissions to address climate change	YES
Extend certain provisions of Patriot Act for four years	YES
Declare opposition to use of ground troops in Libya	YES
Overhaul patent law	YES
Pass compromise debt limit increase plan and establish future spending limits	YES
Allow consideration of measures to implement three trade agreements	YES

CQ Vote Studies

	PARTY UNITY		PRESIDENTIAL SUPPORT	
	SUPPORT	OPPOSE	SUPPORT	OPPOSE
2012	93%	7%	15%	85%
2011	91%	9%	23%	77%
2010	94%	6%	36%	64%
2009	80%	20%	53%	47%
2008	84%	16%	47%	53%

Interest Groups

	AFL-CIO	ADA	CCUS	ACU
2012	33%	0%	83%	76%
2011	21%	10%	100%	64%
2010	14%	10%	88%	92%
2009	38%	30%	93%	72%
2008	73%	60%	89%	44%

Michigan 6

Southwest — Kalamazoo, Portage, Benton Harbor

Forests, fertile soil and front-row seats to Lake Michigan make the 6th, in the state's southwestern corner, a prime spot for tourists in every season. Apples, blueberries and peaches grow in a fruit belt that extends north from St. Joseph and Benton Harbor through Van Buren County. The wooded shoreline north of the Indiana border boasts miles of sandy beaches where affluent Chicagoans have kept second homes. Local vineyards produce a strong crop of juice grapes, and the area accounts for a significant percentage of the state's wine grapes.

Kalamazoo has not struggled with the population loss common in other parts of the district and the state. A strong local education program known as the "Kalamazoo Promise" pays tuition to any Michigan public college for graduates of the city's school system, and Western Michigan University is home to more than 24,000 students. Orthopedic-device manufacturer Stryker is in Kalamazoo, where local officials lured pharmaceutical start-ups to complement Pfizer's local facilities. Elsewhere in the 6th, Benton Harbor hosts a $66 million downtown office park built by appliance manufacturer Whirlpool Corp., whose headquarters are in the town.

Largely white, the district does have significant minority populations in Kalamazoo and Benton Harbor. The Hispanic population has risen steadily in the last few years in the district, owing in part to a large seasonal migrant worker population on area farms.

A conservative Dutch tradition is steady throughout the district and combines with a working class set of Reagan Democrats to allow Republicans to do well here. Barack Obama won four of the six counties wholly or partly in the current 6th in the 2008 presidential contest, but only two in 2012. Overall, 2012 Republican presidential nominee Mitt Romney eked out a 1-percentage-point victory in the 6th.

Major Industry
Health care, manufacturing, higher education, agriculture, tourism

Cities
Kalamazoo, Portage, Benton Harbor

Notable
Colon, home to magic-trick manufacturers and an annual exposition, calls itself the "Magic Capital of the World."

Rep. Tim Walberg (R)

Capitol Office
225-6276
walberg.house.gov
2436 Rayburn Bldg. 20515-2207; fax 225-6281

Committees
Education & the Workforce
(Workforce Protections - Chairman)
Oversight & Government Reform

Residence
Tipton

Born
April 12, 1951; Chicago, Ill.

Religion
Christian

Family
Wife, Sue Walberg; three children

Education
Western Illinois U., attended 1969-70 (forestry); Fort Wayne Bible College, B.S. 1975 (Christian education); Wheaton College (Ill.), M.A. 1978 (communications)

Career
Religious school fundraiser; education think tank president; minister

Political Highlights
Candidate for Onsted Community Schools Board of Education, 1981; Mich. House, 1983-98; sought Republican nomination for U.S. House, 2004; U.S. House, 2007-09; defeated for re-election to U.S. House, 2008

ELECTION RESULTS

2012 GENERAL		
Tim Walberg (R)	169,668	53.3%
Kurt Richard Haskell (D)	136,849	43.0%
Ken Proctor (LIBERT)	8,088	2.5%
Richard Wunsch (GREEN)	3,464	1.1%
2012 PRIMARY		
Tim Walberg (R)	45,592	76.0%
Dan Davis (R)	14,386	24.0%

Previous Winning Percentages
2010 (50%); 2006 (50%)

Elected 2006; 3rd term

Did not serve 2009-11

A former pastor who served 16 years in the Michigan Legislature, Walberg is a rock-solid social and fiscal conservative. He has friends on both sides of the aisle, thanks to a gracious and even grandfatherly charm, and he is tasked with beating back workplace regulations that Republicans find onerous.

Walberg is serving his second stint in the House. He was a freshman in the 110th Congress (2007-08), lost his re-election bid, then rode a national wave of Republican support to return to Washington two years later. He came back with his Protestant faith and wry sense of humor intact. "I come in not only knowing where the bathroom is, but knowing the process" for getting things done, he said in 2011.

He likes to say that he "was tea party before the tea party," and he updated his office decor to reflect his view that the nation stands at a philosophical and political crossroads. One wall features super-sized prints of the Declaration of Independence and the Bill of Rights; another holds the Gadsden flag. He joined the Tea Party Caucus on his return to the House, and he is also part of the conservative Republican Study Committee.

Walberg sits on the Education and the Workforce Committee and has chaired its Workforce Protections panel since 2011.

In the 112th Congress (2011-12), he challenged Labor Department officials over an "adversarial approach to enforcement," suggesting that the Obama administration is fishing for labor law violations and saddling employers with baseless and costly investigations.

"The bureaucracy is growing, with more staff dedicated to punitive enforcement activities and drafting burdensome regulations, which means employers will have fewer resources to help follow the law and face an ever-growing bureaucracy ready to catch them when they don't," he said at a 2011 hearing. Walberg asserts that state agencies often do a better job both devising and implementing workplace safety rules appropriate to state economies, and that requiring state rules to meet a federal standard often is cumbersome.

Walberg also hasn't been thrilled with new workplace regulations. He protested when the administration floated restrictions on the jobs that young people can do on farms. "While farmers and parents need the help, kids rely on these jobs to pay for college," Walberg wrote in a 2012 opinion piece. That proposal was withdrawn, but another possible rule — to extend minimum wage and overtime protections to many in-home health care workers — is still under consideration.

"The likely result of this new rule is reduced hours for home care workers and higher costs for taxpayers," he wrote in a joint statement with John Kline of Minnesota, the chairman of the full committee.

Walberg also sits on the subcommittee for higher education and workforce training. He dislikes the federal takeover of the student loan industry that was part of the 2010 health care law, and he has accused Democrats of manipulating student loan rates to generate federal revenue to pay for that overhaul's programs. In regards to elementary and secondary education, he wants to end most federal involvement and "turn decision-making back to local parents and teachers."

He sees his spot on the Oversight and Government Reform Committee as an opportunity to "hold the federal bureaucracy accountable to the people." Walberg sits on the Oversight subcommittee that covers the federal workforce, as well as the panel covering energy policy. His most popular measure of the 112th Congress — it had more than 100 co-sponsors, but saw no committee action — was to ban the EPA from regulating greenhouse gases.

Walberg wants to cut federal spending substantially and quickly. In 2011, he made two attempts to slash the budget for the National Endowment for the Arts, but neither reduction was enacted. He voted against the fiscal 2012 appropriations bills, saying they did not do enough to reduce spending. He approves of the idea of restructuring Medicare and has suggested creating personal investment accounts in the Social Security program.

On the revenue side of the ledger, Walberg has co-sponsored a bill to end most federal taxes and replace them with a national sales tax. As a freshman, he wrote a bill to make permanent the income tax rates enacted in 2001 and 2003. But he opposed the January 2013 "fiscal cliff" agreement that locked in those rates for earnings under $400,000 — he wanted spending cuts included in the deal.

Walberg is equally conservative on social issues. He opposes abortion and gay marriage, and he has been associated with the "birther" movement that challenged President Barack Obama's citizenship.

Walberg grew up on Chicago's South Side. As a young man, he worked as a farm and steel mill laborer, and also with the U.S. Forest Service. In his 20s, he earned degrees from Fort Wayne Bible College and Wheaton College, while also working as a pastor.

He won election to the state House in 1982 and stayed there for 16 years — he was forced out by a term limit law enacted in 1992. He then served as president of the Warren Reuther Center for Education and Community Impact. He was also a fundraiser for the Moody Bible Institute of Chicago.

He made his first bid for a U.S. House seat in 2004, losing the GOP primary to a moderate, Joe Schwarz, in the race to succeed retiring Republican Rep. Nick Smith. Walberg challenged Schwarz again in 2006, labeling him a "RINO" — Republican in Name Only — and getting generous support from the anti-tax Club for Growth. He won 53 percent of the vote in the primary, then outraised his Democratic opponent, organic farmer Sharon Marie Renier, by 20-to-1. He beat Renier by about 4 points.

Two years later, when Obama carried the district by 6 points, Walberg lost a close race to Democratic state Sen. Mark Schauer. He announced in 2009 that he wanted a rematch, then won the 2010 primary handily. Both parties' campaign committees and independent groups poured money into the race. For the fourth time in four elections the seat changed hands, with Walberg winning just a little more than half the votes.

Democrats tried to recruit Schwarz to oppose Walberg in 2012, but he declined. Lawyer Kurt Richard Haskell, who had no political experience, won the nomination. He tried to paint Walberg as too extreme for the district, but Walberg had a 15-to-1 fundraising advantage and won by 10 points.

Key Votes

2012	
Extend a Social Security payroll tax cut and unemployment benefits	NO
Ease securities rules to expand small-business access to capital	YES
Extend for one year subsidized student loan interest rates financed by a cut in health care spending	NO
Cite Attorney General Eric H. Holder Jr. for contempt of Congress	YES
Create a visa program for foreign graduates in high-tech fields	YES
Extend most Bush-era income tax rates while allowing rates for top-bracket earners to rise (Jan. 1, 2013)	NO
2011	
Strike funding for F-35 alternative engine	NO
Prevent EPA from regulating greenhouse gas emissions to address climate change	YES
Extend certain provisions of Patriot Act for four years	YES
Declare opposition to use of ground troops in Libya	YES
Overhaul patent law	YES
Pass compromise debt limit increase plan and establish future spending limits	YES
Allow consideration of measures to implement three trade agreements	YES

CQ Vote Studies

	PARTY UNITY		PRESIDENTIAL SUPPORT	
	SUPPORT	OPPOSE	SUPPORT	OPPOSE
2012	98%	2%	15%	85%
2011	97%	3%	18%	82%
2008	92%	8%	68%	32%
2007	96%	4%	84%	16%

Interest Groups

	AFL-CIO	ADA	CCUS	ACU
2012	14%	5%	83%	96%
2011	3%	10%	100%	96%
2008	21%	20%	88%	96%
2007	13%	0%	90%	100%

Michigan 7

Southeast — Jackson, western Lansing suburbs

Taking up the eastern half of the state's southern tier — bordering Indiana, Ohio and Lake Erie — and skirting around western Ann Arbor to snag a tiny slice of Lansing in the central part of Michigan, the 7th District has farms, suburbs and small towns. Shrinking populations and a diminishing industrial base have had an impact on many towns, including Jackson, the largest city in the 7th. Crossed and bounded by major highways — Interstates 69, 75 and 94, as well as nearby Interstate 80 in Ohio — the district has an identity as a regional thoroughfare.

The southeastern portion of the 7th is rural, with soybeans and cornfields dominating the landscape. Lenawee County is the third-largest county in the state in terms of agricultural acreage and leads the state in the number of farms for both crops. Recently, farmers have been turning to renewable energy, and wind turbines and solar cells have gone up in the district. Rural poverty rates remain high in the region; in cities such as Adrian, more than 30 percent of the population lives below the poverty line.

Decennial rempaiing added Monroe County, and Monroe, on Interstate 75 between Toledo and Detroit along Lake Erie, is home to the La-Z-Boy, corporate headquarters. The Port of Monroe is Michigan's only port on Lake Erie.

A predominately white district, the area does have minority populations in Jackson and is becoming more racially diverse as more Hispanics move into the 7th. Part of the district is in the area near liberal Ann Arbor (in the neighboring 12th), and Eaton County in the Lansing orbit is competitive. Independent voters have been able to influence federal races in the past decade, and Monroe County backs Democrats, but the rural character tends to outweigh any non-GOP pockets. Overall, Republican presidential nominee Mitt Romney took 51 percent of the district's vote in 2012.

Major Industry
Agriculture, manufacturing

Cities
Jackson, Waverly (unincorporated), Adrian, Monroe

Notable
Jackson's Ella Sharp Museum features the table used at the founding of Republican Party in 1854 at the convention known as "Under the Oaks."

Rep. Mike Rogers (R)

Capitol Office
225-4872
mikerogers.house.gov
2112 Rayburn Bldg. 20515-2208; fax 225-5820

Committees
Energy & Commerce
Select Intelligence - Chairman

Residence
Howell

Born
June 2, 1963; Livonia, Mich.

Religion
Methodist

Family
Wife, Kristi Clemons Rogers; two children

Education
Adrian College, B.A. 1985 (sociology & criminal justice)

Military
Army, 1985-88

Career
Home construction company owner; FBI agent

Political Highlights
Mich. Senate, 1995-2000 (majority floor leader, 1999-2000)

ELECTION RESULTS

2012 GENERAL		
Mike Rogers (R)	202,217	58.6%
Lance Enderle (D)	128,657	37.3%
Daniel Goebel (LIBERT)	8,083	2.3%
Preston Brooks (NPA)	6,097	1.8%
2012 PRIMARY		
Mike Rogers (R)	56,208	85.7%
Brian Hetrick (R)	6,098	9.3%
Vernon Molnar (R)	3,257	5.0%
2010 GENERAL		
Mike Rogers (R)	156,931	64.1%
Lance Enderle (D)	84,069	34.3%
Bhagwan Dashairya (LIBERT)	3,881	1.6%

Previous Winning Percentages
2008 (57%); 2006 (55%); 2004 (61%); 2002 (68%); 2000 (49%)

Elected 2000; 7th term

Rogers is a Republican leader on national security. He has used his job as chairman of the Intelligence Committee to become a TV staple, and to revive a panel once afflicted with partisan sclerosis.

A former FBI agent, Rogers became the Intelligence chairman in 2011. The committee was paralyzed by battles between Democrats and Republicans in many of the years after the 2001 terrorist attacks, and on paper, Rogers seemed unlikely to reverse that partisan trend — he has been closely involved with the GOP leadership team for years.

Rogers was considered for the job of chief deputy whip for the 108th Congress (2003-04), and he flirted with a run for the GOP whip post in 2006. He has been a generous provider of campaign funds: His leadership political action committee has distributed more than $3 million over the past six campaign cycles. Rogers was the finance chairman of the National Republican Congressional Committee for the 2004 elections, and in 2010 he headed the NRCC's incumbent retention effort.

He has won widespread praise for his work as chairman. Rogers maintains a close working relationship with his committee's top Democrat, C.A. Dutch Ruppersberger of Maryland, whose moderate bent on national security has made it easier to reach compromises. Ruppersberger and Rogers also hit it off because of their similar backgrounds: Rogers comes from law enforcement and Ruppersberger was a prosecutor.

Working with Ruppersberger and their Senate counterparts, Rogers ended a six-year drought during which Congress had not gotten an intelligence authorization bill signed into law. In the 112th Congress (2011-12) he oversaw enactment of authorizations for fiscal 2011, 2012 and 2013.

"Some people come here to be a happy warrior. I came here to actually try to accomplish something," Rogers said. "I don't begrudge the other. And sometimes in a partisan fight you stand up for what you believe in, and it comes across as fairly partisan because one side believes one thing and another side believes another thing. But this is national security. It's important that we get it right and important we try to do as much together as we possibly can."

Rogers, who served in the Army for three years and worked at the FBI for six, joined the Intelligence Committee in 2005. As chairman, he has been quick to praise the intelligence services when he sees grounds to do so. In early 2011, when critics questioned how much spy agencies knew about the uprising in Egypt, Rogers leapt to their defense.

However, he has criticized President Barack Obama's approach to the Middle East as being insufficiently muscular, and he is wary of attempts to try terrorism suspects in civilian courts. In March 2013, he said the United States should send military personnel into Syria to train and equip forces trying to bring down President Bashar al-Assad.

Rogers backs some spy agency cuts. Most details of intelligence spending are classified, but Rogers said he has tried to prune wasteful and redundant programs. He has opposed deep cuts, such as those put in place by the deficit reduction law enacted in August 2011.

Rogers and Ruppersberger sponsored the House's most significant cybersecurity bill of the 112th Congress. It was written to break down barriers to information sharing between the federal government and businesses whose computer networks are coming under attack. The bill was intensely unpopular with civil liberties groups that feared it would jeopardize the privacy of U.S. citizens. But the support of 42 Democrats more than offset the 28 Republicans who opposed the measure. It passed the House in spring 2012.

They reintroduced their bill in the 113th Congress (2013-14), and with some adjustments to assuage the worries of privacy advocates, it passed with the support of 92 Democrats in April 2013. Rogers also is working on legislation to punish nations that steal U.S. intellectual property via cyber-espionage.

Rogers has campaigned against national security leaks. In response to the summer 2010 leak of thousands of pages of classified documents related to the Afghanistan War, Rogers blasted what he called the "culture of disclosure" and said the Army private suspected of leaking the material should face the death penalty if convicted. He collaborated with the Senate Intelligence Committee to include provisions in the fiscal 2013 intelligence authorization bill to crack down on leaks.

Although Rogers mostly works on Intelligence matters these days, he also sits on the Energy and Commerce Committee, where health care is the focus of his work. He has been part of the GOP campaign to repeal or modify the 2010 health care law, and the committee in 2012 approved his bill to take expenditures on insurance agents and brokers out of calculations for the medical-loss ratio — the amount that insurers must spend on actual care. Supporters of the bill said thousands of agent and broker jobs are threatened by the need to stay within those spending parameters.

Like most Michigan lawmakers, Rogers calls for federal support of the U.S. automotive industry. He has proposed providing auto companies with up to $20 billion in federally backed loan guarantees to develop new technology.

Rogers grew up in Livingston County, west of Detroit. His father was a high school vice principal, football coach and town supervisor. His mother ran the local Chamber of Commerce and served on the county commission.

Rogers knew as a teenager that he wanted to be an FBI agent. After graduating from college and leaving the Army, he attended the FBI Academy, finishing first in his class. He won a coveted assignment to the Chicago field office, where he unraveled a major case that involved public officials in Cicero. Handcuffs and headlines from the case are framed in his Capitol Hill office.

In the 1990s, Rogers and his then-wife returned to Michigan to raise their family. With his father and brothers, he ran a modular-home-assembly company. He also entered state politics. When a longtime GOP incumbent retired from the state Senate, Rogers won the Republican district. Re-elected in 1998, he served as majority floor leader during his second, and last, term.

When Democrat Debbie Stabenow opted to give up her House seat to run for the Senate in 2000, Rogers made a bid to succeed her. He beat Democratic state Senate colleague Dianne Byrum by 111 votes. After redistricting added thousands of GOP voters to the district, he was easily re-elected. None of his re-elections since then have been particularly close.

Key Votes

2012	
Extend a Social Security payroll tax cut and unemployment benefits	YES
Ease securities rules to expand small-business access to capital	YES
Extend for one year subsidized student loan interest rates financed by a cut in health care spending	YES
Cite Attorney General Eric H. Holder Jr. for contempt of Congress	YES
Create a visa program for foreign graduates in high-tech fields	YES
Extend most Bush-era income tax rates while allowing rates for top-bracket earners to rise (Jan. 1, 2013)	YES
2011	
Strike funding for F-35 alternative engine	NO
Prevent EPA from regulating greenhouse gas emissions to address climate change	YES
Extend certain provisions of Patriot Act for four years	YES
Declare opposition to use of ground troops in Libya	YES
Overhaul patent law	YES
Pass compromise debt limit increase plan and establish future spending limits	YES
Allow consideration of measures to implement three trade agreements	YES

CQ Vote Studies

	PARTY UNITY		PRESIDENTIAL SUPPORT	
	SUPPORT	OPPOSE	SUPPORT	OPPOSE
2012	96%	4%	15%	85%
2011	95%	5%	27%	73%
2010	94%	6%	35%	65%
2009	90%	10%	31%	69%
2008	91%	9%	68%	32%

Interest Groups

	AFL-CIO	ADA	CCUS	ACU
2012	14%	0%	92%	88%
2011	3%	10%	100%	80%
2010	14%	10%	86%	91%
2009	11%	10%	93%	92%
2008	33%	25%	89%	84%

Michigan 8

Lansing; northern Oakland County

Stamped with the state seal, the 8th, Michigan's capital district, used to be dominated by various manufacturing facilities for the influential auto industry. The district, once home to Olds Motor Vehicle Co., includes Lansing, East Lansing and agricultural communities to the east. It also takes in exurbs between Flint and Detroit in Oakland County that are dotted with country clubs and lakes. The district is steadily emerging from its agrarian and industrial past toward a suburban future.

Lansing's reliance on automobile and parts manufacturing has diminished in the decade since General Motors' Oldsmobile line was eliminated. Now the city depends on state government jobs and employment related to Michigan State University, just down the road in East Lansing. The economic contraction that resulted from repeated auto industry cutbacks has slowed, and residential, commercial and entertainment development continues in downtown Lansing.

While many areas in the district have lost population since 2000, East Lansing did experience modest growth. A relatively young population and a focus on developing livable neighborhoods have lured a steady stream of new residents. Michigan State, the nation's pioneer land-grant college, has invested in further development of some of its renowned programs, including nuclear research. The university as well as state incentives have pushed the growth of health care and biotechnology research sectors.

The 8th's powerful agricultural vote rests in Livingston County, which has become a commuter sanctuary for residents who work in Lansing, Detroit and Flint. Ingham County's traditional Democratic lean, centered on Lansing and East Lansing, resulted in a wide margin of victory in the county for Barack Obama in his 2012 re-election bid. The combination of Ingham with the politically competitive areas of Oakland County is not enough to sway the U.S. House race, and the district has remained Republican.

Major Industry
Higher education, health care, manufacturing

Cities
Lansing (pt.), Rochester Hills (pt.), East Lansing

Notable
The Eli and Edythe Broad Art Museum on the campus of Michigan State University was designed by Pritzker Prize-winning architect Zaha Hadid.

Rep. Sander M. Levin (D)

Capitol Office
225-4961
levin.house.gov
1236 Longworth Bldg. 20515-2212; fax 226-1033

Committees
Ways & Means - Ranking Member
Joint Taxation

Residence
Royal Oak

Born
Sept. 6, 1931; Detroit, Mich.

Religion
Jewish

Family
Wife, Pamela Cole; four children

Education
U. of Chicago, A.B. 1952; Columbia U., M.A. 1954 (international relations); Harvard U., LL.B. 1957

Career
Lawyer; U.S. Agency for International Development official

Political Highlights
Oakland Board of Supervisors, 1961-64; Mich. Senate, 1965-71 (minority leader, 1969-70); Mich. Democratic Party chairman, 1968-69; Democratic nominee for governor, 1970, 1974

ELECTION RESULTS

2012 GENERAL

Sander M. Levin (D)	208,846	61.9%
Don Volaric (R)	114,760	34.0%
Jim Fulner (LIBERT)	6,100	1.8%
Julia Williams (GREEN)	4,708	1.4%

2012 PRIMARY

Sander M. Levin (D)	unopposed

Previous Winning Percentages
2010 (61%); 2008 (72%); 2006 (70%); 2004 (69%); 2002 (68%); 2000 (64%); 1998 (56%); 1996 (57%); 1994 (52%); 1992 (53%); 1990 (70%); 1988 (70%); 1986 (76%); 1984 (100%); 1982 (67%)

Elected 1982; 16th term

Levin employs his considerable intellect when handling the tax and trade matters before the Ways and Means Committee. Often rumpled and usually carrying a sheaf of papers under his arm, the Democrat never seems quite comfortable in front of TV cameras — but with a tax overhaul in the works for the 113th Congress, he's sure to receive plenty of attention.

Levin once chaired Ways and Means, and he fended off the younger, more business-friendly Richard E. Neal of Massachusetts to stay on as the panel's top Democrat in the 112th Congress (2011-12). He still holds that job in the 113th Congress (2013-14).

Republicans under Chairman Dave Camp (a fellow Michigander) laid the foundation for a tax code overhaul during the 112th Congress, and Camp vowed to move a bill through the committee before the end of 2013. Near the start of the year, Camp and Levin formed 11 bipartisan working groups, each one studying a different area of the tax code — Levin had protested earlier that Democrats weren't consulted enough in the 112th Congress. But even with the increased collaboration, Levin has been wary of the overall effort.

He is skeptical of a common GOP formulation: lower rates for corporations and individuals, with the elimination of many credits and deductions to make up lost revenue. He describes some deductions, such as those for mortgage interest and health insurance costs, as integral to the development of the middle class, and he says the middle class would be loath to end them. Likewise, he opposes elimination of tax breaks for manufacturers in the corporate code, such as the credit for spending on research and development.

Levin — who despite his professorial demeanor will throw the occasional partisan elbow — subscribes to his party's creeds on taxing the affluent. He favors raising taxes on private-equity and hedge fund managers, as well as eliminating tax breaks for oil companies.

But there are some areas where he finds common ground with Republicans. Levin chaired the Trade Subcommittee before taking the gavel of the full committee in 2010, and few people dispute his expertise in that subject. Like most Democrats, he wants more worker protections in trade pacts; unlike more-liberal colleagues, he is not reflexively suspicious of free trade.

In 2011, he wouldn't support a deal with Colombia, arguing that its government hadn't done enough to protect labor union leaders from harassment and violence. When Mexico joined talks for the Trans-Pacific Partnership trade agreement in 2012, Levin applauded it as a chance to correct the "flaws on labor and environmental standards" in the 1994 North American Free Trade Agreement. (He vehemently opposes the 2012 Michigan law that makes it a "right to work" state.)

He was the only Michigan Democrat to vote for pacts with South Korea and Panama in 2011, after contributing to adjustments that would make the agreements more palatable to labor unions. In general, he likes trade deals that help his state's auto industry expand into new markets. In regard to the South Korea deal, he told colleagues that he wanted "to be clear what is really at stake here: It is the automotive industry of this country."

Levin is hesitant about Japan's participation in the Trans-Pacific Partnership talks, as that country has traditionally closed off its markets to U.S. cars and car parts. He also came to the aid of the state's automakers in 2011, when the Obama administration proposed a new requirement that cars and light trucks average 56.2 miles per gallon by 2025. Levin called that goal "overly aggressive and not reasonably feasible." When the rules were finalized a year later, the administration budged a little, setting a 54.5 mpg standard.

For years, Levin has kept an eye on the United States' trading relationship with China. He argues that China should be punished with tariffs and duties for artificially depressing the value of its currency, which is believed to hurt U.S. manufacturers.

Levin became the Ways and Means chairman in 2010, when Democrat Charles B. Rangel of New York stepped down during an ethics inquiry. Levin faced immediate challenges, as worries about the national debt clashed with liberals' insistence that the government should continue to pump money into the economy. He tried to move a bill to extend unemployment insurance, revive expired tax breaks and plug state budget holes, but opposition from fiscally conservative Democrats shrank the size of the House proposal. Senate Republicans blocked action on the measure in their chamber.

At the end of that year, Levin reluctantly backed a two-year extension of the George W. Bush-era income tax cuts in order to secure GOP support for an extension of unemployment benefits.

Born and raised in Detroit, Levin now represents the Macomb County suburbs, where the term "Reagan Democrat" was coined and where the auto industry is a major employer. As a youth, Levin worked in a Dodge plant.

Known as "Sandy," he is the older brother of Michigan Sen. Carl Levin. Both men absorbed a passion for politics from their father, who was a lawyer active in liberal causes. The brothers shared a bedroom until Sander left for college.

Levin completed law studies at Harvard and established a private practice. He spent four years as an appointed supervisor in Oakland County, then won a state Senate seat in 1964. He was the minority leader in Lansing and served as state Democratic Party chairman in the late 1960s. Though viewed as a rising star, he lost both the 1970 and 1974 gubernatorial races.

He worked as an assistant administrator in the U.S. Agency for International Development, then ran for the House seat of retiring Democrat William M. Brodhead in 1982. With support from the party establishment, Levin overcame five primary opponents and went on to win the general election easily. Redistricting after the 1990 census made the district more competitive, but Levin won a series of close races. Another redrawing of district lines following the 2000 census made the seat more Democratic again.

Michigan's Republican legislature wasn't so kind following the 2010 census — reapportionment caused Michigan to lose a seat, and parts of Levin's 12th District were combined with Democrat Gary Peters' 9th District. Levin dodged an intraparty battle when Peters opted to run in the 14th District. He easily won re-election in the new 9th. (Peters also won a return to the House.)

Levin's wife of 50 years, Vicki, died of breast cancer in 2008. He married Penn State University psychology professor Pamela Cole in 2012.

Key Votes

2012	
Extend a Social Security payroll tax cut and unemployment benefits	YES
Ease securities rules to expand small-business access to capital	YES
Extend for one year subsidized student loan interest rates financed by a cut in health care spending	NO
Cite Attorney General Eric H. Holder Jr. for contempt of Congress	?
Create a visa program for foreign graduates in high-tech fields	NO
Extend most Bush-era income tax rates while allowing rates for top-bracket earners to rise (Jan. 1, 2013)	YES
2011	
Strike funding for F-35 alternative engine	NO
Prevent EPA from regulating greenhouse gas emissions to address climate change	NO
Extend certain provisions of Patriot Act for four years	YES
Declare opposition to use of ground troops in Libya	NO
Overhaul patent law	YES
Pass compromise debt limit increase plan and establish future spending limits	YES
Allow consideration of measures to implement three trade agreements	YES

CQ Vote Studies

	PARTY UNITY		PRESIDENTIAL SUPPORT	
	SUPPORT	OPPOSE	SUPPORT	OPPOSE
2012	97%	3%	90%	10%
2011	95%	5%	95%	5%
2010	99%	1%	98%	2%
2009	99%	1%	96%	4%
2008	99%	1%	16%	84%

Interest Groups

	AFL-CIO	ADA	CCUS	ACU
2012	95%	80%	25%	4%
2011	93%	80%	31%	0%
2010	100%	90%	25%	0%
2009	100%	90%	43%	0%
2008	100%	95%	59%	0%

Michigan 9

Suburban Detroit — Warren, Clinton

The mainly suburban 9th District sits north of Detroit, borders Lake St. Clair to the east and stops short of Pontiac in its northwest, taking in well-settled outer suburbs between Pontiac and Detroit. Unsurprisingly, the district historically has been, and still is, heavily dependent on the auto industry. Taking in southern Macomb and southeastern Oakland counties north of 8 Mile Road, which is Detroit's northern boundary, the district includes current and former auto industry facilities that contributed to Detroit's status as an auto hub.

Warren, which is the district's most populous city and the state's third-most populous, is home to General Motors' Technical Center design and engineering campus as well as the Army's Tank-automotive and Armaments Command. Wayne State University created an advanced technology education center in Warren linked to a local community college for residents seeking technical, engineering and computer-based jobs.

St. Clair Shores, the self-described "leisure boat capital of the world," is heavily reliant on the tourists who come to visit its miles of waterfront. Northeast of Warren, Clinton Township, at nearly 100,000 residents, claims to be the most populous township in Michigan.

During decennial redistricting following the 2010 census, several heavily Democratic communities with large black populations — including Southfield, Lathrup Village and Oak Park — were removed from the 9th. Overall, the district is more than 80 percent white; between 2000 and 2010, however, racial and ethnic minorities were the only groups in 9th to experience population growth.

To the west, the 9th takes in several southern Oakland County communities near the Detroit boundary that are Democratic-leaning overall but less so than the district's Macomb County portions, which give the party a nearly 2-to-1 advantage. Barack Obama took 57 percent of the district's 2012 presidential vote.

Major Industry

Auto manufacturing, auto and tank research and design

Cities

Warren, Sterling Heights (pt.)

Notable

The Detroit Zoo is in Royal Oak, which received its name in 1819 when Gov. Lewis Cass and his companions christened a large tree.

Rep. Candice S. Miller (R)

Capitol Office
225-2106
candicemiller.house.gov
320 Cannon Bldg. 20515-2210; fax 226-1169

Committees
Homeland Security
(Border & Maritime Security - Chairwoman)
House Administration - Chairwoman
Transportation & Infrastructure

Residence
Harrison Township

Born
May 7, 1954; Detroit, Mich.

Religion
Presbyterian

Family
Husband, Donald Miller; one child

Education
Macomb Community College, attended 1973-74; Northwood Institute, attended 1974

Career
Boat saleswoman

Political Highlights
Harrison Township Board of Trustees, 1979-80; Harrison Township supervisor, 1980-92; Republican nominee for U.S. House, 1986; Macomb County treasurer, 1993-95; Mich. secretary of state, 1995-2002

ELECTION RESULTS

2012 GENERAL		
Candice S. Miller (R)	226,075	68.8%
Chuck Stadler (D)	97,734	29.7%
Bhagwan Dashairya (LIBERT)	4,803	1.5%
2012 PRIMARY		
Candice S. Miller (R)		unopposed
2010 GENERAL		
Candice S. Miller (R)	168,364	72.0%
Henry Yanez (D)	58,530	25.0%
Claude Beavers (LIBERT)	3,750	1.6%
Candace R. Caveny (GREEN)	3,286	1.4%

Previous Winning Percentages
2008 (66%); 2006 (66%); 2004 (69%); 2002 (63%)

Elected 2002; 6th term

Miller practices politics at full sail. When the winds are blowing from her district, that means support for the auto industry, the Great Lakes and infrastructure projects. When they blow from Washington, she assertively pursues her vision of a comprehensive strategy for homeland security.

Her approach has made her a popular figure back home. She grew up in 1960s suburban Detroit, where her father owned a marina. In 1970, she sailed as a member of the first all-woman crew to compete in a 300-mile race across Lake Huron — after she and the other women beat back the local yacht club's effort to bar them. Upon completing the race a 25th time, she earned the title of "Old Goat."

Miller attended a community college, but dropped out to sell boats for the family business. By age 25, she was a divorced single mother with a toddler. (She later remarried.) When the local township board proposed a tax increase on marinas, she became a "noisy activist"; that role grew into a political career. Miller has been considered a trailblazer since 1994, when she was elected Michigan's first female secretary of state, and she consistently wins around two-thirds of the vote in her House re-election bids.

Republicans have taken note. In the 112th Congress (2011-12), Miller became the chairwoman of the Homeland Security Subcommittee on Border and Maritime Security. She fell just short in a bid to chair the full committee for the 113th Congress (2013-14), so she continues to hold her subcommittee gavel. She also was appointed to lead the House Administration Committee.

During the 112th, she led an exhaustive series of hearings promoting interdepartmental synergies and technology as cost-effective means for improving border security. "You're never going to have enough resources for all the people that you would optimally like to have, which is why technology is such a critical component," she said. "It's such a tremendous force multiplier if used effectively."

Miller thinks resources and personnel once employed in Iraq and Afghanistan can have applications for the Department of Homeland Security; she sees great potential in unmanned aerial vehicles. The Pentagon and the DHS should collaborate on procurement projects to find technologies or vehicle platforms useful to both organizations, she said.

That collaboration can extend to facilities as well. "I'm a believer that we should have regional headquarters for the Department of Homeland Security around the nation, particularly along the border areas," she said.

She points to Selfridge Air National Guard Base in her district as a prime spot for monitoring the northern border. Miller's husband, a pilot during the Vietnam War, ended his military career in the Michigan Air National Guard as a base commander at Selfridge. Working with West Virginia Democrat Nick J. Rahall II, Miller secured an amendment in the fiscal 2012 defense policy law elevating the head of the National Guard to a seat on the Joint Chiefs of Staff.

Border security factors into most discussions of immigration. In 2012, the House passed her bill directing the DHS to create a plan for achieving "operational control" — preventing unlawful entries — along the Mexico and Canada borders. Miller also has conducted considerable oversight of visa overstays. She maintains that a huge number of illegal immigrants, including several suspected terrorists, "walked in through the front door."

Another House-passed bill of Miller's would have required the search for efficiencies and broader strategies in port security. The goal of scanning 100 percent of incoming cargo — set by a 2007 law — is "probably not" realistic, she said. Miller has urged DHS to present a plan for "risk-based" scanning.

She supports increased cooperation with security agencies in foreign ports that scan cargo en route to the United States.

Miller addresses some district-centric border issues, such as the maintenance and expansion of the Blue Water Bridge to Canada, from the Transportation and Infrastructure Committee. In February 2013, she accused the Obama administration of reneging on a promise to commit federal resources to the bridge expansion project. On the Water Resources and Environment panel, she has tried to impede the harmful invasion of Asian carp into the Great Lakes, and in 2011 she applauded new standards for the treatment of ships' ballast water (which can contain invasive organisms) before it can be released in the lakes.

But her biggest parochial concern — and the subject that most often puts her at odds with fellow Republicans — is the auto industry. "I play for the home team," she said. Miller stands firmly behind Michigan's Big Three automakers and will sometimes vote for the interests of organized labor. She supported the George W. Bush administration's $14 billion loan to struggling domestic automakers in late 2008. "I know many on my side said that government should never have intervened, that [auto companies] should have just gone through the normal channels," she said. "There was no money. The credit market just dried up everywhere."

She is a lonely voice, however, fighting against one particular government intervention in the marketplace. As Congress worked on a reauthorization of the National Flood Insurance Program in 2011 and 2012, Miller said it was "a typical Washington boondoggle with an endless bureaucracy overseeing out-of-control spending. ... The federal government is a bad insurance company." She has introduced a bill to terminate the program.

Miller already has cut spending as the House Administration chairwoman — House committees on average took an 11 percent budget reduction for the 113th Congress. Miller also has jurisdiction over election law, and she received favorable reviews for her work smoothing out voting problems as secretary of state. Miller says one of her top priorities is making it easier for military servicemembers to vote in U.S. elections while deployed overseas, and to make sure that those votes are counted.

Miller was elected to the Harrison Township board in 1979, and a year later she unseated its supervisor. In her two terms as secretary of state, she was recognized for making the office more efficient and for instituting fraud-proof driver's licenses.

The Republican-controlled legislature redrew a congressional district in 2002 to include several GOP-leaning counties and Miller's base in Macomb County, and she captured it with 63 percent of the vote.

Key Votes

2012	
Extend a Social Security payroll tax cut and unemployment benefits	YES
Ease securities rules to expand small-business access to capital	YES
Extend for one year subsidized student loan interest rates financed by a cut in health care spending	YES
Cite Attorney General Eric H. Holder Jr. for contempt of Congress	YES
Create a visa program for foreign graduates in high-tech fields	YES
Extend most Bush-era income tax rates while allowing rates for top-bracket earners to rise (Jan. 1, 2013)	YES
2011	
Strike funding for F-35 alternative engine	YES
Prevent EPA from regulating greenhouse gas emissions to address climate change	YES
Extend certain provisions of Patriot Act for four years	YES
Declare opposition to use of ground troops in Libya	YES
Overhaul patent law	YES
Pass compromise debt limit increase plan and establish future spending limits	YES
Allow consideration of measures to implement three trade agreements	YES

CQ Vote Studies

	PARTY UNITY		PRESIDENTIAL SUPPORT	
	SUPPORT	OPPOSE	SUPPORT	OPPOSE
2012	93%	7%	18%	82%
2011	92%	8%	23%	77%
2010	94%	6%	31%	69%
2009	77%	23%	56%	44%
2008	83%	17%	44%	56%

Interest Groups

	AFL-CIO	ADA	CCUS	ACU
2012	33%	0%	100%	72%
2011	28%	15%	100%	68%
2010	14%	5%	88%	88%
2009	38%	25%	93%	80%
2008	67%	50%	78%	63%

Michigan 10

Northern Macomb County; most of Michigan 'Thumb'

Grabbing Michigan's "Thumb," the 10th captures part or all of six counties, and shares a border with Canada. The population is anchored in Detroit's outer suburbs; the district also takes in farmland and lakefront towns.

Exurbs sprang up in Macomb County as residents left the crime, congestion and economic contraction in Detroit, resulting in modest population growth in contrast to much of the greater metro area during the past decade. Lapeer County, to the northwest of Macomb County, became a landing spot for upwardly mobile residents drifting farther from the region's urban hubs. But the housing market and municipal budgets in the southern part of the 10th suffered during the recent economic downturn.

St. Clair County's Port Huron is the U.S. terminus of the Blue Water bridges, a connector to Ontario that accommodates up to 20,000 vehicles daily. In an effort to protect waterways on the nation's northern border, a $30 million base for U.S. Customs and Border Protection and Department of Homeland Security operations opened at the nearby Selfridge Air National Guard Base in 2011. Port Huron also hosts a Carnegie Library.

Huron County's border rides along more than 90 miles of Lake Huron shoreline, providing kayaking and fishing to Thumb visitors. Wind turbines have begun sprouting here, as renewable energy companies try to capitalize on gusts off the water; research into offshore projects is ongoing. These communities also depend on agriculture, including corn, the state's famous navy beans, sugar beets and top-producing dairy farms.

Macomb County — home to mainly white, blue-collar voters — was once unfriendly territory for the GOP. During the 1970s, Macomb was regarded as the most Democratic suburb in the nation, but many residents abandoned the party in the 1980s; today they are key swing voters. Rural territory gives the district a GOP lean, and Mitt Romney took an 11-point win here in the 2012 presidential race.

Major Industry
Manufacturing, defense, agriculture, tourism

Cities
Sterling Heights (pt.), Port Huron

Notable
The U.S. Senate's famous navy bean soup uses only Michigan navy beans.

Rep. Kerry Bentivolio (R)

Capitol Office
225-8171
bentivolio.house.gov
226 Cannon Bldg. 20515-6601; fax 225-2667

Committees
Oversight & Government Reform
Small Business

Residence
Milford

Born
Oct. 6, 1951; Royal Oak, Mich.

Religion
Roman Catholic

Family
Wife, Karen Bentivolio; two children

Education
Oakland Community College, attended 1971-83; Michigan State U., attended 1972-75, attended 1989; St. Mary's College (Michigan), B.A. 1999 (social science); Marygrove College, M.A. 2001 (education)

Military
Army, 1970-71; Mich. National Guard, 1974; Mich. National Guard, 1990-2009

Career
Teacher; farmer; homebuilder; auto worker

Political Highlights
Sought Republican nomination for Mich. Senate, 2010

ELECTION RESULTS

2012 GENERAL		
Kerry Bentivolio (R)	181,788	50.8%
Syed S. Taj (D)	158,879	44.4%
John Tatar (LIBERT)	9,637	2.7%
Steven Paul Duke (GREEN)	4,568	1.3%
2012 PRIMARY SPECIAL		
Kerry Bentivolio (R)	10,280	41.7%
Nancy Cassis (R)	8,803	35.7%
Carolyn Kavanagh (R)	2,653	10.8%
Steve King (R)	1,715	7.0%
Kenneth Crider (R)	1,208	4.9%
2012 PRIMARY		
Kerry Bentivolio (R)	42,470	65.4%
write-ins (R)	22,490	34.6%

Elected 2012; 1st term

The eccentric Bentivolio impersonates Santa Claus, is a veteran of three wars, taught high school and has acted in independent films. He comes to his latest job with a goal of ending what he calls the federal "spending problem."

Bentivolio has said that he was inspired by the tea party movement and that he has libertarian sympathies. The first measure he introduced was a proposed constitutional amendment that would bar the government from "using the power of taxation to compel someone to engage in commercial activity" — basically, undercutting the "individual mandate" in the 2010 health care law.

He sits on the Oversight and Government Reform Committee and its panel on National Security. Bentivolio has taken an active interest in Middle East policy, introducing a bill to restrict the sale of military equipment to Egypt until its government is "promoting democracy and stability" in the region.

Bentivolio also sits on the Small Business Committee. Republicans gave a warm reception to his proposal to ease the enforcement of some federal regulations; it would grant a business six months to correct a violation without any penalties if the violation is not imminently life-threatening.

Bentivolio is the proprietor of Old Fashion Santa and Co.; he raises reindeer that are featured in local Christmas events, where he impersonates Santa. He worked as a teacher as well, and reports have surfaced that he was reprimanded for intimidating students — accusations he denies.

The events that led to his election are as curious as his resume. Bentivolio entered a GOP primary to face five-term Rep. Thaddeus McCotter (another noted eccentric), but the state's attorney general disqualified McCotter. There were irregularities with the signatures on his petition to get on the ballot, and an election fraud investigation was opened. McCotter soon resigned.

Bentivolio won the GOP nominations for the general election and a special election to complete McCotter's term. He defeated Democratic physician Syed Taj in the former but lost to Democrat David Curson in the latter.

Michigan 11

Southeast — Livonia, Canton, Troy

Carved from suburbs in western Oakland and Wayne counties, the 11th District was designed to give the GOP an advantage in a region known for its pro-labor Democrats. Starting in the district's south, the 11th moves from Canton Township into some Farmington neighborhoods. The district continues north through lakes, parks and suburbs, and turns east through Waterford Township and hooks to include Troy and Bloomfield Hills.

White-collar and affluent Troy in Oakland County is a major office center and home to much of Michigan's banking industry. Routinely ranked the safest city in Michigan, Troy is a suburban retail center. North of Troy, in Rochester, Oakland University (shared with the 8th) has expanded its medical school and has plans for more campus growth.

Auburn Hills is still the U.S. headquarters for Chrysler, but the demolition of a historic Ford plant in Wixom has cost the 11th factory jobs. Other manufacturing sector interests in the district include telematics and a diesel-engine plant in Novi. Canton Township is embarking on a plan to lure new business activity, including in the film industry.

Upper-middle-class communities in the district include Livonia in Wayne County. The city's blue-collar base diminished with the closure of auto and parts manufacturing facilities. Many residents still commute to jobs in nearby population centers — Livonia is midway between Detroit and Ann Arbor.

Rolling forests, wetlands and chains of lakes cover the terrain in the northwest corner of the district. Trails accommodate equestrian riders, mountain bikers, hikers and skiers.

Competitive for years at the presidential level, the 11th was redrawn during decennial remapping to be friendlier to Republicans and to consolidate conservative residents. Troy and Canton Township have significant minority and immigrant populations and pull in liberal votes; Birmingham and Bloomfield Hills are GOP-friendly enclaves. Republican Mitt Romney won 52 percent of the district's 2012 presidential vote.

Major Industry
Auto manufacturing, technology, health care

Cities
Livonia, Troy, Novi, Auburn Hills, Birmingham

Notable
Auburn Hills hosts the arena for basketball's Pistons.

Rep. John D. Dingell (D)

Capitol Office
225-4071
dingell.house.gov
2328 Rayburn Bldg. 20515-2215; fax 226-0371

Committees
Energy & Commerce

Residence
Dearborn

Born
July 8, 1926; Colorado Springs, Colo.

Religion
Roman Catholic

Family
Wife, Debbie Dingell; four children

Education
Georgetown U., B.S. 1949 (chemistry), J.D. 1952

Military
Army, 1944-46

Career
County prosecutor; lawyer; park ranger

Political Highlights
No previous office

ELECTION RESULTS

2012 GENERAL		
John D. Dingell (D)	206,884	66.9%
Cynthia Kallgren (R)	92,472	29.9%
Richard J. Secula (LIBERT)	9,867	3.2%
2012 PRIMARY		
John D. Dingell (D)	41,116	78.6%
Daniel Marcin (D)	11,226	21.4%
2010 GENERAL		
John D. Dingell (D)	118,336	56.8%
Rob Steele (R)	83,488	40.1%
Aimee Smith (GREEN)	2,686	1.3%

Previous Winning Percentages
2008 (71%); 2006 (88%); 2004 (71%); 2002 (72%); 2000 (71%); 1998 (67%); 1996 (62%); 1994 (59%); 1992 (65%); 1990 (67%); 1988 (97%); 1986 (78%); 1984 (64%); 1982 (74%); 1980 (70%); 1978 (77%); 1976 (76%); 1974 (78%); 1972 (68%); 1970 (79%); 1968 (74%); 1966 (63%); 1964 (73%); 1962 (83%); 1960 (79%); 1958 (79%); 1956 (74%);
1955 Special Election (76%)

Elected 1955; 29th full term

No other congressman carries around more history than Dingell, the dean of the House. With Republicans in charge — after Dingell administered the oath of office to Speaker John A. Boehner in 2011 — he has been fighting to protect much of his legislative legacy, from the Clean Air Act to the 2010 health care law.

He also has been fighting, and mostly losing, a battle against partisan gridlock. "You're talking to a guy who is really sad, but also who is really angry," he said in 2011. If a version of himself from 20 or 30 years ago were transported to the modern day to witness politics at the Capitol, "I'd probably want to go and vomit."

Dingell spreads the blame around, faulting the tea party movement and President Barack Obama, whom Dingell said needs to engage with the public. He accuses the press of a "gotcha" mentality since Watergate.

These are not passing laments. For years he has been urging members to work together, remembering a time when major bills would get 400 votes or more. In a letter to The Washington Post in September 2011 on the congressional battle over raising the debt ceiling, Dingell wrote: "I am ashamed of our performance — of us all, on both sides of the aisle."

Dingell led Democrats in their unsuccessful opposition to the June 2012 House vote holding Attorney General Eric H. Holder Jr. in contempt of Congress. Republicans complained that Holder refused to provide requested documents in an investigation of a gun-tracking sting known as Fast and Furious. One of Dingell's constituents, border agent Brian Terry, was found dead, with two of the guns from Fast and Furious at the scene. "Brian Terry's family wants the truth, and with God as my judge, they deserve it, and they shall have it," but not with a partisan contempt resolution, he said.

In a House career that has spanned almost six decades, Dingell has worked on transformational legislation, from the Civil Rights Act to the Endangered Species Act. Long before the enactment of the 2010 health care law, Dingell called for the creation of a universal system of health insurance.

He introduced universal health care bills at the start of every Congress, from the time he was first elected in 1955 up to 2009. It was a cause he inherited from his father, John Dingell Sr., whom he succeeded in the House.

The 2010 law fell short of the "single payer" system Dingell proposed, but he wasn't unhappy with the result. The Associated Press reported his reaction when the Supreme Court upheld the law in 2012: "Well, I'll be damned," he said. "We did it."

He marked another achievement in February 2009, when he became the longest-serving House member, surpassing the record of Mississippi Democrat Jamie L. Whitten. On June 8, 2013, he will pass West Virginia Democratic Sen. Robert C. Byrd to become the longest-serving member in the history of Congress.

However, Dingell no longer holds the position that earned him his formidable reputation. In November 2008, a longtime Democratic colleague and rival, Henry A. Waxman of California, ousted him as chairman of the Energy and Commerce Committee. Waxman is now the panel's ranking Democrat.

In challenging Dingell, Waxman emphasized his own ties to Obama and Dingell's uncompromising protection of Michigan's automobile industry — which he said was hampering a liberal agenda for energy, climate change and more. Dingell had clashed with Democratic Speaker Nancy Pelosi in 2007 over an energy bill, urging her to let him produce a bipartisan measure. She kept a tight rein on the bill, and the dust-up contributed to Waxman's victory.

Waxman and Pelosi ushered a cap-and-trade climate change bill through the House in 2009 — Dingell voted for it — but it picked up only a smattering of GOP support and died in the Senate. That measure provoked a backlash that became a theme for many successful GOP House campaigns in 2010.

Dingell served as Energy and Commerce chairman from 1981 through 1994. He then became the ranking member until 2007, when his party retook control of Congress and he regained the gavel. He built what scholars consider one of the most expansive congressional power centers of the post-World War II era, with jurisdiction on issues as diverse as energy, health care and telecommunications.

"He will be remembered as one of the most influential members of Congress not to have served as president," said Texas Republican Joe L. Barton, who has served on the panel with Dingell for two decades.

Dingell stands with liberals on most issues but opposes abortion rights and gun control. He inherited his political philosophy from his father, who entered the House in 1933 with Franklin D. Roosevelt's New Deal generation. The younger Dingell grew up in Washington, first stepping onto the House floor at the age of 6. He became a House page at 12 and was in the chamber in 1941 when Roosevelt gave the "Date of Infamy" speech following the Japanese attack on Pearl Harbor.

Less than three years later, Dingell was drafted into the Army. A meningitis infection put Dingell in the hospital as the rest of his 210-person unit was sent to the Battle of the Bulge — he was one of 10 people in the unit to live through the war. Following his military service, he earned chemistry and law degrees from Georgetown University. He worked as a park ranger — trapping bears, blowing up beaver dams and fighting forest fires — during the summers and after law school.

He opened a private law practice and was an assistant county prosecutor in Dearborn, Mich., when his father died. Dingell easily won the special election to complete his father's term.

Dingell has drawn less than 60 percent of the vote in a general election only twice — in 1994 and 2010, the last two times Republicans won control of the House. Age has slowed Dingell, who leans on a cane and no longer towers over colleagues.

But despite talk that he could soon be replaced by another Dingell — his wife, Debbie, or one of his four children — he has not yet shown interest in retirement. "There's an old Polish saying: Before you sell the bear's hide, you first have to shoot the bear," he said in 2009. "This bear's doing pretty good."

Debbie Dingell had toyed with the idea of running for the Senate in 2014, but she dropped those plans in the spring of 2013.

Key Votes

2012	
Extend a Social Security payroll tax cut and unemployment benefits	YES
Ease securities rules to expand small-business access to capital	NO
Extend for one year subsidized student loan interest rates financed by a cut in health care spending	NO
Cite Attorney General Eric H. Holder Jr. for contempt of Congress	NO
Create a visa program for foreign graduates in high-tech fields	NO
Extend most Bush-era income tax rates while allowing rates for top-bracket earners to rise (Jan. 1, 2013)	YES
2011	
Strike funding for F-35 alternative engine	NO
Prevent EPA from regulating greenhouse gas emissions to address climate change	NO
Extend certain provisions of Patriot Act for four years	?
Declare opposition to use of ground troops in Libya	NO
Overhaul patent law	YES
Pass compromise debt limit increase plan and establish future spending limits	YES
Allow consideration of measures to implement three trade agreements	YES

CQ Vote Studies

	PARTY UNITY		PRESIDENTIAL SUPPORT	
	SUPPORT	OPPOSE	SUPPORT	OPPOSE
2012	93%	7%	85%	15%
2011	91%	9%	89%	11%
2010	99%	1%	95%	5%
2009	99%	1%	96%	4%
2008	99%	1%	15%	85%

Interest Groups

	AFL-CIO	ADA	CCUS	ACU
2012	100%	70%	25%	4%
2011	100%	90%	31%	4%
2010	100%	85%	25%	0%
2009	100%	95%	33%	0%
2008	100%	90%	56%	4%

Michigan 12

Southeast — Ann Arbor, Dearborn, Ypsilanti

West and south of Detroit, the redrawn 12th contains a mix of academics, engineers and auto workers: Blue-collar bastions and an overwhelmingly liberal university-based community have created a strongly Democratic district. Barack Obama took 66 percent of the district's vote in the 2012 presidential election.

Residents of Ann Arbor in the district's western reaches hail the impact of the University of Michigan on the politically progressive city. A high standard of living, a strong medical research sector and a highly educated workforce make Ann Arbor a gem in an ailing state, despite major losses from Pfizer's departure and cuts and financial woes at bookselling behemoth Borders. Expansion at the university and in the private sector — such as at AdWords, Google's advertising vehicle — provides employment, and sporting events at the campus draw millions of tourism dollars annually.

Ypsilanti, the liberal working-class town southeast of Ann Arbor, is home to Eastern Michigan University. Engineering and robotics firms in the area near the cities work on computerized auto manufacturing. Just east of Ypsilanti, the Willow Run Airport, which began as a manufacturing plant for bombers during World War II, is a major cargo hub.

Near Detroit, the auto manufacturing industry drives Dearborn's economy. Home to Ford Motor Co. and its Rouge Center factory, Dearborn has maintained its population even as residents have fled the metro area, a trend aided in part by a large Arab-American population that continued to grow in the past decade. Other jobs are provided by work apparel manufacturer Carhartt and steelmaker Severstal.

South of Dearborn, the 12th includes a border with Canada on the Detroit River. Grosse Ile, the largest island in the river, is one of the more affluent townships and is home to the nation's first International Wildlife Refuge.

Major Industry
Higher education, auto manufacturing, steel

Cities
Ann Arbor, Dearborn, Taylor, Lincoln Park, Southgate, Allen Park

Notable
The National Oceanic and Atmospheric Administration's Great Lakes Environmental Research Laboratory is in Ann Arbor.

Rep. John Conyers Jr. (D)

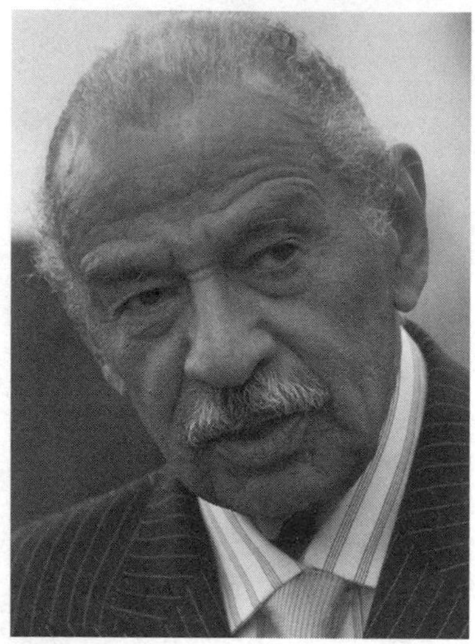

Capitol Office
225-5126
conyers.house.gov
2426 Rayburn Bldg. 20515-2214; fax 225-0072

Committees
Judiciary - Ranking Member

Residence
Detroit

Born
May 16, 1929; Detroit, Mich.

Religion
Baptist

Family
Wife, Monica Conyers; two children

Education
Wayne State U., B.A. 1957, LL.B. 1958

Military
Mich. National Guard, 1948-50; Army, 1950-54; Army Reserve, 1954-57

Career
Lawyer; congressional district aide

Political Highlights
Candidate for mayor of Detroit, 1989, 1993

ELECTION RESULTS

2012 GENERAL		
John Conyers Jr. (D)	235,336	82.8%
Harry T. Sawicki (R)	38,769	13.6%
Chris Sharer (LIBERT)	6,076	2.1%
Martin Gray (USTAX)	4,089	1.4%
2012 PRIMARY		
John Conyers Jr. (D)	38,371	55.4%
Glenn Anderson (D)	12,586	18.2%
Shanelle Jackson (D)	8,708	12.6%
Bert Johnson (D)	6,928	10.0%
John Goci (D)	2,664	3.8%

Previous Winning Percentages
2010 (77%); 2008 (92%); 2006 (85%); 2004 (84%); 2002 (83%); 2000 (89%); 1998 (87%); 1996 (86%); 1994 (81%); 1992 (82%); 1990 (89%); 1988 (91%); 1986 (89%); 1984 (89%); 1982 (97%); 1980 (95%); 1978 (93%); 1976 (92%); 1974 (91%); 1972 (88%); 1970 (88%); 1968 (100%); 1966 (84%); 1964 (84%)

Elected 1964; 25th term

Age hasn't weakened Conyers' passion for, or insistence on, liberal policy solutions. He still holds a position of respect as a civil rights leader and the top Democrat on the Judiciary Committee. However, even some supporters now question his viability as a day-to-day lawmaker.

The Detroit Free Press has endorsed Conyers in almost every election going back to 1964, but in 2012 its editorial board was lugubrious in indicating its support: "Our backing of Conyers has reflected the arc of his career: first enthusiastic, then ambivalent, and now nearly agitated as his energy and effectiveness are clearly on a downward slope."

At the start of that career, he was a Korean War veteran with a law degree. He had experience working for Democratic Rep. John D. Dingell (the only current House member with more seniority), and he had served on a panel of lawyers picked by President John F. Kennedy to look for ways of easing racial tensions in the South. As a freshman, Conyers hired Rosa Parks to his congressional staff and helped pass the Voting Rights Act. He went on to become a prominent figure in the turbulent civil rights era.

Conyers has enjoyed his share of legislative successes. He was the key figure behind recognizing Martin Luther King Jr.'s birthday as a federal holiday.

"He influenced my activity and my political views: jobs, justice and peace," Conyers says. That was the slogan Conyers ran on in 1964, when a second black-majority district was created in Detroit.

He touts his part in enactment of the 1993 "motor voter" law that allows citizens to register to vote at motor vehicle departments and other social service agencies, and the 1994 law authorizing federal programs to prevent violence against women and aid victims.

Recent years have not been as fruitful, however. Conyers co-founded the Congressional Black Caucus, but he also identifies very strongly with the Congressional Progressive Caucus, the group of the most-liberal Democrats. His far-left politics might have marginalized him in legislative efforts throughout the George W. Bush administration. He was a stern critic of Bush, once calling for his impeachment over the handling of the Iraq War.

The return to a Democratic majority in the 110th and 111th Congresses (2007-10) — when Conyers chaired the Judiciary Committee — also wasn't particularly productive by his liberal standards. He was disappointed that the 2010 health care overhaul didn't transition to a "single payer" system, a longtime goal. The House passsed a Conyers bill to allow bankruptcy court judges to rewrite home mortgage terms to help homeowners, but it died in the Senate.

He did win enactment of broader federal hate crime laws in 2009, but a rewrite of patent laws wasn't in the offing. When Republicans again took control of the House in the 112th Congress (2011-12), GOP panel leaders negotiated a patent overhaul with the Senate, and it was enacted over Conyers' objections. Conyers is a fierce defender of privacy rights, and he calls for updates to privacy protections to account for the Internet era. But in 2011, he couldn't stop a four-year extension of surveillance provisions in the anti-terrorism law known as the Patriot Act.

Conyers also has an odd relationship with the nation's first black president. He said the re-election of Barack Obama in 2012 was a "ratification of the policies of the 44th president and a tilt toward more progressive legislation." However, several times in Obama's first term, Conyers expressed frustration that Obama wasn't aggressive or progressive enough. In 2009, he told reporters that Obama called him to ask why Conyers had been "demeaning" him.

Generally, though, Conyers has a low-key bearing. As the 113th Congress

(2013-14) started, he complimented the new Judiciary chairman, Robert W. Goodlatte of Virginia. "He has a very definite philosophy about things, but he does it in a way that is not offensive or hostile," Conyers told The Hill.

Conyers still has bold-sounding initiatives on his to-do list, including the push for a single-payer system to make "health care a fundamental right for every American." He says it doesn't matter whether the payer is an existing insurance agency, an amalgamation of them or the federal government.

He wants to work toward a "full-employment society," with his bill to allow state and local governments to apply for Labor Department grants to put people to work on infrastructure projects and in human services jobs, such as tutoring children or working as home health aides. It would be paid for by a tax on financial transactions.

Conyers pushes bills to aid the poor and minorities, and he frequently works with the other members of the Progressive Caucus. He introduced a bill in the 112th Congress to ban racial profiling, and he proposes establishing a commission to study paying reparations to descendants of African-American slaves. He opposes most military involvements and has called for the fastest possible withdrawal from Afghanistan.

He is also working on a possible overhaul of immigration law. At a February 2013 hearing, he protested the use of the term "illegal immigrant," saying that "the people in this country are not illegal, they are out of status."

Conyers served in the Army in Korea, then went home to Detroit. While in law school, he became involved in the Democratic Party before his 1964 run. He won a primary race against accountant Richard H. Austin by 108 votes. He won the Democratic district in a rout that November.

Although Conyers made ineffectual bids to become mayor of Detroit in 1989 and 1993, he has not been seriously challenged for re-election to the House. The 2012 primary campaign was the closest he came to a scare in ages. Conyers' district was redrawn during decennial redistricting to include more of Detroit's suburbs, away from his power base in the city. He had primary challengers for the first time since 1994, including state Sen. Glenn Anderson, who came from the new part of the district, and two urban challengers. They held Conyers to 55 percent of the vote, but he cruised to re-election in November with almost 83 percent.

Several personal problems and allegations of ethics violations have plagued Conyers in recent years. He was investigated by the ethics committee after complaints that he compelled his official staff to do campaign work and personal chores; he promised in 2006 not to use his staff for campaign work. And in 2009, his wife, Monica, a Detroit City Council member, was sentenced to three years in federal prison after pleading guilty to bribery charges.

Key Votes

2012	
Extend a Social Security payroll tax cut and unemployment benefits	YES
Ease securities rules to expand small-business access to capital	YES
Extend for one year subsidized student loan interest rates financed by a cut in health care spending	NO
Cite Attorney General Eric H. Holder Jr. for contempt of Congress	?
Create a visa program for foreign graduates in high-tech fields	NO
Extend most Bush-era income tax rates while allowing rates for top-bracket earners to rise (Jan. 1, 2013)	YES
2011	
Strike funding for F-35 alternative engine	YES
Prevent EPA from regulating greenhouse gas emissions to address climate change	NO
Extend certain provisions of Patriot Act for four years	-
Declare opposition to use of ground troops in Libya	NO
Overhaul patent law	NO
Pass compromise debt limit increase plan and establish future spending limits	NO
Allow consideration of measures to implement three trade agreements	NO

CQ Vote Studies

	PARTY UNITY		PRESIDENTIAL SUPPORT	
	SUPPORT	OPPOSE	SUPPORT	OPPOSE
2012	99%	1%	88%	12%
2011	95%	5%	78%	22%
2010	99%	1%	92%	8%
2009	98%	2%	91%	9%
2008	98%	2%	12%	88%

Interest Groups

	AFL-CIO	ADA	CCUS	ACU
2012	100%	95%	25%	0%
2011	100%	95%	19%	4%
2010	92%	90%	13%	0%
2009	100%	85%	33%	0%
2008	100%	100%	50%	9%

Michigan 13

Part of Detroit and most of Dearborn Heights

The 13th takes in nearly half of Detroit, including part of its resurgent downtown, and dips into industrial River Rouge south on the Detroit River. It heads west through part of Dearborn Heights before dropping across Interstate 94 to grab Detroit Metro Airport, which is Delta Air Lines' second-largest hub and its primary Asian departure location. One of the state's two minority-majority districts following decennial redistricting, the 13th's population is 56 percent black and overwhelmingly Democratic.

Crime, poverty, population loss and residential blight plague Detroit. Through economic recession and auto production declines, the city has struggled to balance its budget, and the state appointed an emergency financial manager. But a new class of young, college-educated residents lives in Midtown, luring trendy bars and restaurants to once-empty streets. Technology start-ups have begun to move into downtown office buildings, supported by partnerships with Wayne State University and firms offering financial incentives to entrepreneurs willing to base their businesses in Detroit. Some of the most blighted neighborhoods have been denied federal funding in an attempt to filter resources to more populated areas that planners believe are better equipped for recovery.

Although the famed Motown Records building has been demolished, the 13th includes the popular Motown Historical Museum, or "Hitsville USA." The New Center neighborhood also contains the 30-story art deco Fisher Building and the racks of Dittrich Furs, one of the city's oldest family-owned businesses. Economic hardship is not limited to urban Detroit; two blue-collar suburbs — Westland, the largest suburb in the district, and Wayne — have been forced to combine parts of their budgets. The overwhelmingly black and poor Highland Park is an enclave completely surrounded by Detroit.

Major Industry

Government, auto manufacturing, health care, technology

Cities

Detroit (pt.), Westland, Dearborn Heights (pt.), Garden City, Inkster

Notable

The Detroit Institute of Arts, Comerica Park (home to baseball's Tigers), Ford Field (football's Lions) and the city's famed Eastern Market are in the 13th.

Rep. Gary Peters (D)

Capitol Office
225-5802
peters.house.gov
1609 Longworth Bldg. 20515-2209; fax 226-2356

Committees
Financial Services

Residence
Bloomfield Township

Born
Dec. 1, 1958; Pontiac, Mich.

Religion
Episcopalian

Family
Wife, Colleen Ochoa Peters; three children

Education
Alma College, B.A. 1980 (political science); U. of Detroit, M.B.A. 1984; Wayne State U., J.D. 1989; Michigan State U., M.A. 2007 (philosophy)

Military
Naval Reserve, 1993-2000; Navy Reserve, 2001-05

Career
College instructor; investment firm branch executive

Political Highlights
Democratic nominee for Mich. Senate, 1990; Rochester Hills City Council, 1991-93; Mich. Senate, 1995-2002; Democratic nominee for Mich. attorney general, 2002; Mich. Lottery Bureau commissioner, 2003-07

ELECTION RESULTS

2012 GENERAL		
Gary Peters (D)	270,450	82.3%
John Hauler (R)	51,395	15.6%
Leonard Schwartz (LIBERT)	3,968	1.2%
2012 PRIMARY		
Gary Peters (D)	41,230	47.0%
Hansen Clarke (D)	30,847	35.2%
Brenda Lawrence (D)	11,644	13.3%
Mary Waters (D)	2,919	3.3%
Bob Costello (D)	1,027	1.2%

Previous Winning Percentages
2010 (50%); 2008 (52%)

Elected 2008; 3rd term

Peters clearly enjoys the nuts and bolts of policy, especially when it comes to housing, manufacturing and other issues salient to the Detroit area. The former financial executive also shows a deft political touch — he won a 2012 primary in a new black-majority district, running against a half-black House colleague — that has Democrats talking up his potential as a party leader.

He will try to realize that potential in 2014. Democratic Sen. Carl Levin is retiring, and in the spring of 2013, Peters entered the race to succeed him.

Like many lawmakers of both parties, he considers the domestic economy his main focus. Peters homes in on efforts to promote the manufacturing sector and to reshape the American mortgage industry, which is still recovering from the 2008 financial crisis.

Peters displays in his office one of the pens President Barack Obama used to sign a 2010 bill providing loan incentives and tax cuts for small businesses. He was the author of an amendment that created a collateral support program for small businesses struggling to get loans because the capital they owned had decreased in value during the recession. "A major focus since the day I've been here is making sure funding is available for small business and small manufacturers that they need to grow," he said.

A lot of the manufacturing concerns in his district are tied to car companies or their parts suppliers. Peters has introduced a bill to fund Energy Department research and development for automobile technologies, such as those needed to make electric cars. It passed the Democratic House in 2009, but the 2011 version went nowhere with Republicans in charge. He introduced it again in 2013, with Democrat Debbie Stabenow of Michigan sponsoring the Senate version.

"Without a strong and vibrant auto industry, a country simply can't have ... a vibrant manufacturing sector," Peters said. "And I'm a passionate believer that if you don't actually make something, you can't be a strong country."

He belongs to the New Democrat Coalition, which often supports free trade, but Peters see some pacts as hurting the automotive industry and other manufacturers. He voted against agreements with South Korea, Panama and Colombia in 2011. Peters also supports organized labor. He co-sponsored a bill to make union organizing easier by not requiring a secret-ballot election to put a union in place. He won the endorsement of the major labor unions over his 2012 Democratic opponent, freshman Rep. Hansen Clarke.

Peters sits on the Financial Services Committee, where overhauling the mortgage system is a priority. He has worked with California Republican John Campbell on legislation to replace the government-sponsored mortgage giants Fannie Mae and Freddie Mac with private companies whose mortgage-backed securities are girded by government guarantees.

"We get rid of Freddie and Fannie, bring in ... substantial private capital, but still have a government role as a final backstop," Peters said in 2012. Campbell and Peters have contended that without a government guarantee, the traditional 30-year mortgage will disappear from the marketplace.

Some Republicans prefer to completely privatize the mortgage industry, but Peters hopes to get a hearing on the bill in the 113th Congress (2013-14), then build momentum from there. Peters also is backing legislation with Campbell that would forgive some mortgage debt of qualifying "underwater" homeowners whose loans are larger than the value of their homes.

Campbell and Peters are also the co-chairmen of the House Automotive Caucus in the 113th Congress.

Before deciding on a Senate campaign, Peters spent the opening months of

2013 deepening his involvement with the House Democratic Caucus. "I've had tough races to get here and to stay here," he said in late 2012. "Now is the time where I can spend more time helping the caucus and being involved in some of the big, broader public policy debates."

He had agreed to serve as vice chairman for candidate recruiting at the Democratic Congressional Campaign Committee, the campaign arm of House Democrats. He was also chairing the political action committee of the New Democrat Coalition.

Peters grew up in the Detroit suburb of Rochester, where his family has lived since the 1840s. His father was a World War II veteran and taught in the public school system. His mother worked as a nurse's aid.

Peters' interest in politics was sparked when, as a college student, he interned for a local union organizer. He majored in political science but went into the financial industry straight after graduating, working for nine years at Merrill Lynch, where he became an assistant vice president. He then moved to Paine Webber, where he became vice president of investments. Along the way he picked up an MBA and a law degree.

Issues facing the Rochester community drew him into local politics in the 1990s. After a two-year stint on the Rochester Hills City Council, he served for eight years in the state Senate. In 2002, he ran for Michigan attorney general, losing by around 5,000 votes.

Peters says he "didn't plan to get involved in politics again" after that loss. He did serve as Michigan's lottery commissioner, but he also began pursuing a Ph.D. in philosophy at Michigan State University. Entreaties from the Democratic Party convinced him to take on eight-term GOP Rep. Joe Knollenberg in 2008. Peters won by more than 9 points. In 2010, he squeaked by Republican Rocky Raczkowski with just under 50 percent of the vote.

Redistricting for 2012 erased the old suburban 9th District, so Peters and Clarke jumped into the race for the redrawn 14th District, even though neither man initially lived there. The narrow, winding 14th stretches along the iconic 8 Mile Road, taking in parts of inner-city Detroit as well as some of its wealthiest suburbs. Its creation marked the first time in decades that a district crossed 8 Mile, which is seen as a boundary between Detroit's haves and have-nots.

Votes Peters took that could have hurt him in his old district — like supporting Obama's 2009 economic stimulus package and 2010 health care overhaul — became assets in the new, more liberal district. Peters ran a strong campaign, courting both suburban voters and Detroit's black community; Clarke was oddly inept, at one point declining to participate in a debate with Peters and other candidates, then showing up to watch. Peters won the primary with 47 percent of the vote and the general election with more than 82 percent.

Key Votes

2012	
Extend a Social Security payroll tax cut and unemployment benefits	YES
Ease securities rules to expand small-business access to capital	YES
Extend for one year subsidized student loan interest rates financed by a cut in health care spending	NO
Cite Attorney General Eric H. Holder Jr. for contempt of Congress	?
Create a visa program for foreign graduates in high-tech fields	NO
Extend most Bush-era income tax rates while allowing rates for top-bracket earners to rise (Jan. 1, 2013)	YES
2011	
Strike funding for F-35 alternative engine	NO
Prevent EPA from regulating greenhouse gas emissions to address climate change	NO
Extend certain provisions of Patriot Act for four years	YES
Declare opposition to use of ground troops in Libya	YES
Overhaul patent law	YES
Pass compromise debt limit increase plan and establish future spending limits	NO
Allow consideration of measures to implement three trade agreements	NO

CQ Vote Studies

	PARTY UNITY		PRESIDENTIAL SUPPORT	
	SUPPORT	OPPOSE	SUPPORT	OPPOSE
2012	95%	5%	90%	10%
2011	89%	11%	90%	10%
2010	83%	17%	83%	17%
2009	91%	9%	87%	13%

Interest Groups

	AFL-CIO	ADA	CCUS	ACU
2012	90%	80%	25%	8%
2011	100%	75%	27%	4%
2010	100%	90%	25%	8%
2009	95%	95%	40%	8%

Michigan 14

Part of Detroit and northwestern suburbs

Snaking from Pontiac into northern and northwestern Detroit suburbs, and then east to Lake St. Clair before sliding down the Detroit River into the state's largest metropolitan hub, the 14th combines parts of suburban Oakland County — the richest in the state — with destitute urban neighborhoods in Wayne County. 8 Mile Road serves as a dividing line between the two counties.

Widespread blight and crime, especially on the city's east side, is a problem in Detroit, although the 14th's downtown section of the city along the river includes headquarters for General Motors and Quicken Loans. "Green" redevelopment of the riverfront and the Joe Louis Arena, home to hockey's Red Wings, provide bright spots. Crossing the bridge to Belle Isle's scenic beaches, a conservatory and Dossin Great Lakes Museum are popular escapes for locals and visitors. The five affluent communities of Grosse Pointe, upriver of Detroit, are known for lakefront parks, tree-lined streets and gated mansions, but home values have declined here as foreclosure and unemployment rates have risen.

Oakland County's major suburbs long relied on the auto industry, and the sector's decline devastated Pontiac's economy. Investments in new technology have put workers back on the assembly line at its General Motors plant and the company has plans for expansions.

Several heavily Democratic southern Oakland communities that have large black populations were moved into the 14th during decennial remapping. Southfield, which is home to many black urban professionals, Lathrup Village and Oak Park are in the district. Hamtramck, an ethnically diverse enclave originally settled by Polish immigrants, is a city surrounded entirely by Detroit. Overall the 14th provided Barack Obama his second-highest percentage statewide in the 2012 presidential race — the district's 81 percent was lower only than the other Detroit-based district, the 13th.

Major Industry
Auto manufacturing, health care, government

Cities
Detroit (pt.), Farmington Hills, Southfield, Pontiac, Oak Park, Hamtramck

Notable
Woodward Avenue, between 6 Mile and 7 Mile roads, was the nation's first paved street in 1909; the Holocaust Memorial Center, the first free-standing Holocaust museum built in the United States, is in Farmington Hills.

MINNESOTA

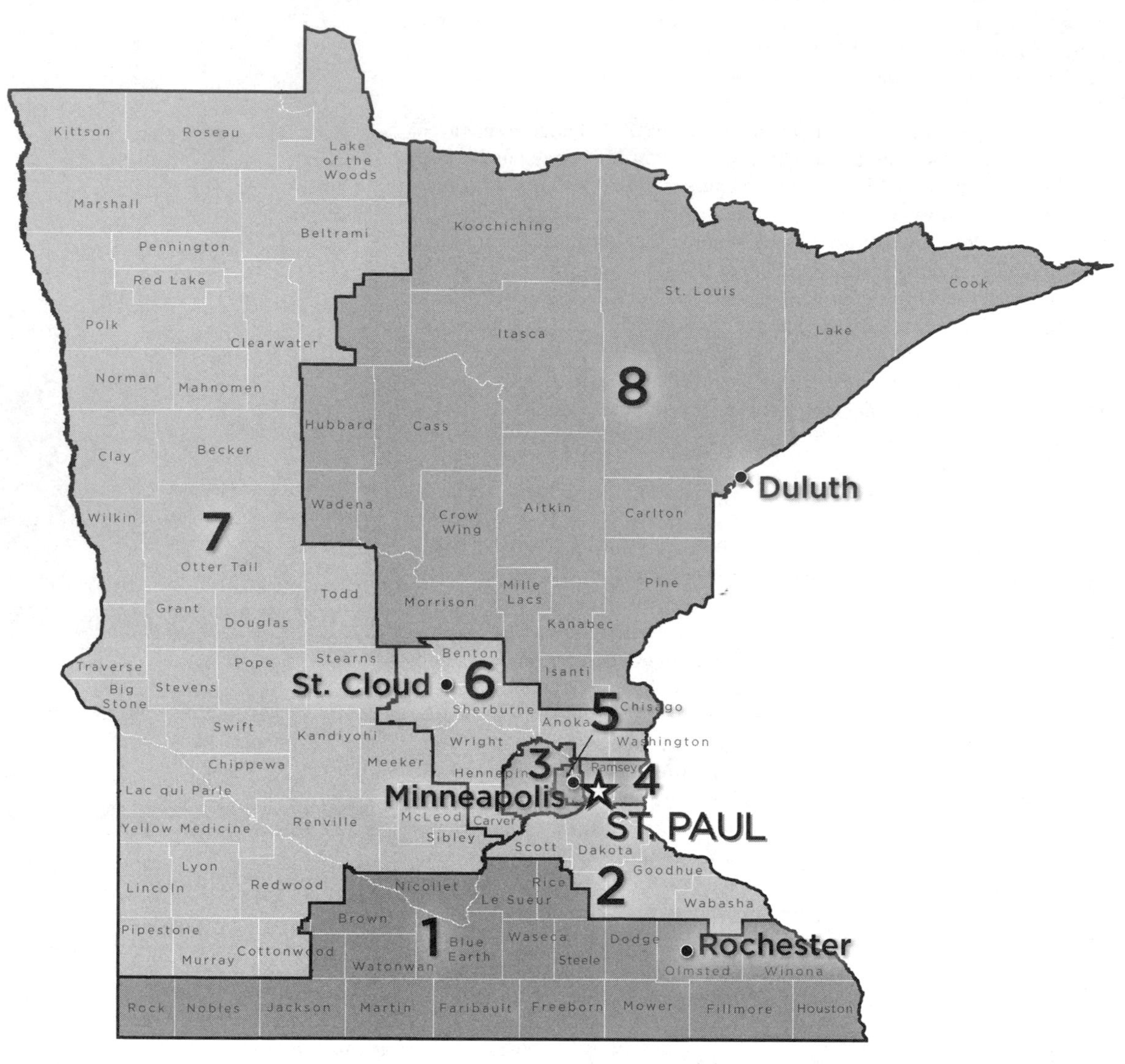
Kittson
Roseau
Lake of the Woods
Marshall
Beltrami
Pennington
Red Lake
Koochiching
St. Louis
Cook
Polk
Clearwater
Itasca
Lake
Norman
Mahnomen
8
Hubbard
Cass
Clay
Becker
Duluth
Wadena
Crow Wing
Aitkin
Carlton
Wilkin
7
Otter Tail
Pine
Todd
Mille Lacs
Grant
Morrison
Douglas
Kanabec
Stearns
Benton
Traverse
Pope
Isanti
St. Cloud
6
Big Stone
Stevens
Sherburne
5
Chisago
Anoka
Swift
Kandiyohi
Wright
Washington
3
Chippewa
Meeker
Ramsey
Hennepin
4
Lac qui Parle
Minneapolis
Yellow Medicine
Renville
McLeod
Carver
ST. PAUL
Sibley
Scott
Dakota
Lyon
Goodhue
Lincoln
Redwood
Nicollet
Rice
2
Le Sueur
Wabasha
Brown
Pipestone
1
Blue Earth
Waseca
Dodge
Rochester
Murray
Cottonwood
Watonwan
Steele
Olmsted
Winona
Rock
Nobles
Jackson
Martin
Faribault
Freeborn
Mower
Fillmore
Houston

Gov. Mark Dayton (D)

First elected: 2010
Length of term: 4 years
Term expires: 1/15
Salary: $120,311
Phone: (651) 201-3400
Residence: St. Paul
Born: Jan. 26, 1947; Minneapolis, Minn.
Religion: Presbyterian
Family: Divorced; two children
Education: Yale U., B.A. 1969 (psychology)
Career: Investment company president; runaway youth home director; congressional and gubernatorial aide; social worker; teacher
Political highlights: Minn. commissioner of economic development, 1978; Democratic nominee for U.S. Senate, 1982; Minn. commissioner of energy and economic development, 1983-86; Minn. auditor, 1991-95; sought Democratic nomination for governor, 1998; U.S. Senate, 2001-07

ELECTION RESULTS

2010 GENERAL

Mark Dayton (D)	919,232	43.6%
Tom Emmer (R)	910,462	43.2%
Tom Horner (I)	251,487	11.9%

Lt. Gov. Yvonne Prettner Solon (D)

First elected: 2010
Length of term: 4 years
Term expires: 1/15
Salary: $78,196
Phone: (651) 201-3400

LEGISLATURE

Legislature: January-May in odd-numbered years; February-May in even-numbered years

Senate: 67 members, 4-year terms (2-year terms in redistricting years)

2013 ratios: 39 D, 28 R; 44 men, 23 women

Salary: $31,140

Phone: (651) 296-7198

House: 134 members, 2-year terms

2013 ratios: 73 D, 61 R; 89 men, 45 women

Salary: $31,140

Phone: (651) 296-2146

TERM LIMITS

Governor: No
Senate: No
House: No

URBAN STATISTICS

CITY	POPULATION
Minneapolis	382,578
St. Paul	285,068
Rochester	106,769
Duluth	86,265
Bloomington	82,893

REGISTERED VOTERS

Voters do not register by party.

POPULATION

2010 population	5,303,925
2000 population	4,919,479
1990 population	4,375,099
Percent change (2000-2010)	+7.8%
Rank among states (2010)	21
Median age	37
Born in state	69.0%
Foreign born	6.4%
Violent crime rate	244/100,000
Poverty level	11.0%
Federal workers	38,265
Military	1,897

ELECTIONS

STATE ELECTION OFFICIAL
(651) 215-1440

DEMOCRATIC PARTY
(651) 293-1200

REPUBLICAN PARTY
(651) 222-0022

MISCELLANEOUS

Web: www.state.mn.us
Capital: St. Paul

U.S. CONGRESS

Senate: 2 Democrats
House: 5 Democrats, 3 Republicans

STATISTICS BY DISTRICT

District	2012 Vote for President: Obama	Romney	2008 Vote for President: Obama	McCain	Black	Asian	Hispanic	Median Income	Over 64	Under 20	College Education	Rural	Sq. Miles
1	50%	48%	51%	47%	2%	2%	6%	$52,335	15%	27%	26%	38%	11,974
2	49.1	49.0	51	48	4	4	5	70,095	10	29	36	13	2,438
3	50	49	51	48	6	6	4	73,468	12	27	46	4	527
4	62	35	63	36	9	10	6	57,791	12	27	39	2	332
5	74	24	73	25	16	6	10	50,923	12	24	42	0	136
6	42	56	43	55	2	2	3	65,461	10	30	28	31	2,882
7	44	54	47	51	1	1	4	47,739	18	26	21	67	33,429
8	52	46	53	45	1	1	1	46,692	17	25	21	69	27,908
STATE	**53**	**45**	**54**	**44**	**5**	**4**	**5**	**56,954**	**13**	**27**	**32**	**30**	**79,627**
U.S.	**51**	**47**	**53**	**46**	**12**	**5**	**17**	**50,052**	**13**	**27**	**29**	**21**	**3,531,905**

Sen. Amy Klobuchar (D)

Capitol Office
224-3244
klobuchar.senate.gov
302 Hart Bldg. 20510-2305; fax 228-2186

Committees
Agriculture, Nutrition & Forestry
Commerce, Science & Transportation
Judiciary
(Antitrust, Competition Policy & Consumer Rights - Chairwoman)
Rules & Administration
Joint Economic - Vice Chairwoman

Residence
Minneapolis

Born
May 25, 1960; Plymouth, Minn.

Religion
Congregationalist

Family
Husband, John Bessler; one child

Education
Yale U., B.A. 1982 (political science); U. of Chicago, J.D. 1985

Career
Lawyer; lobbyist

Political Highlights
Hennepin County attorney, 1999-2007

ELECTION RESULTS

2012 GENERAL		
Amy Klobuchar (D)	1,854,595	65.2%
Kurt Bills (R)	867,974	30.5%
Stephen Williams (INDC)	73,539	2.6%
Tim Davis (GR)	30,531	1.1%
2012 PRIMARY		
Amy Klobuchar (D)	183,766	90.8%
Dick Franson (D)	6,837	3.4%
Jack Edward Shepard (D)	6,632	3.3%
Darryl Stanton (D)	5,155	2.5%

Previous Winning Percentages
2006 (58%)

Elected 2006; 2nd term

During her first term, Klobuchar pursued many center-left, consumer-focused policies and became a well-liked colleague. Now firmly ensconced in the Senate, she is expanding her influence over larger economic matters.

In committee markups, passing conversations and speeches, Klobuchar (KLO-buh-shar) — who has a disarming Midwestern monotone — makes fellow senators laugh with an unassuming charm. She has had success, particularly when handling smaller-bore issues, at recruiting bipartisan groups of allies to help her achieve her goals. "It's just getting to know people, and treating them with respect, and seeing where you agree," she said.

Klobuchar is studying some of the bigger issues before Congress as the top Democrat on the Joint Economic Committee in the 113th Congress (2013-14). The panel has no legislative authority, but it serves as an idea mill for policymakers in both parties. Klobuchar started her tenure by highlighting some common Democratic plans, but in her usual collegial manner.

In regard to debt reduction, "I think there are ways that we could add revenue into this mix without setting the recovery on its back," Klobuchar said at a 2013 hearing. She suggested a cap on the home mortgage tax deduction and an end to some oil company tax breaks. In 2010, Klobuchar was one of about a dozen Democratic moderates who rallied behind a 2010 bill to create a fiscal commission to address the deficit. President Barack Obama created one (known as Simpson-Bowles) by executive order when the measure died in the Senate.

"Our financial industry is important, but it cannot be the basis of our economy," she said at another hearing. "We need to be a country that makes jobs, that invents things, that exports to the world."

Democrats often link infrastructure to employment, but Klobuchar was less successful as a consensus-builder when she was promoting Obama's infrastructure plans in the 112th Congress (2011-12). She was the sponsor of a 2011 bill that tracked with several White House proposals; it would have put $50 billion toward infrastructure projects and created a $10 billion national infrastructure bank. The costs would have been covered by a surtax on people making more than $1 million a year. The measure got no Republican votes and died in the Senate. Klobuchar, who sits on the Commerce, Science and Transportation Committee, stayed upbeat, saying that ideas such as the infrastructure bank "will gain bipartisan support and ultimately pass."

Meanwhile, she has been optimistic about the state of economic recovery, and she says Minnesota relied on "innovation and exports" to make it through the recent prolonged recession. She is a member of the Commerce panel on Competitiveness, Innovation and Export Promotion. In February 2013, she joined with a bipartisan team of senators to introduce a bill that might quadruple the number of temporary H-1B visas, which allow companies to bring in foreign workers for specialized jobs.

Klobuchar seems to be cornering the market on competitiveness — in 2013, she became the chairwoman of the Judiciary Subcommittee on Antitrust, Competition Policy and Consumer Rights. She immediately began studying the merger between American Airlines and US Airways, eyeing potential price increases, shrinking service options and the effect on consumers.

Klobuchar, a former county attorney, has taken an interest in consumer protection throughout her career, and her seats on the Commerce and Justice committees are ideal for indulging that interest.

She sponsored a bill, signed into law in 2007 by President George W. Bush, that bolstered safety standards for pool drains. She also made successful pushes to restrict formaldehyde in wood products and prohibit lead in children's toys. "I've always believed that the first responsibility of government is to protect its citizens," she has said.

In the 112th Congress, she turned her focus to consumer electronics, urging the Federal Trade Commission to strengthen its oversight of cellphone billing. In 2013, she signed on to a bill to allow cell phone owners to "unlock" their phones, so that they can use them with the wireless carrier of their choosing. Klobuchar also joined Connecticut Democrat Richard Blumenthal in introducing a 2012 bill that would prohibit employers from requiring prospective employees to turn over passwords to their Facebook, Twitter and other online profiles.

"We need to ensure that our laws keep up with advances in technology and respect fundamental values like the right to privacy," she said.

From the Agriculture, Nutrition and Forestry Committee, she helped write a 2010 overhaul of the food safety regime in the United States. (Klobuchar also uses that post to help the ethanol industry in her state, and she has worked with South Dakota Republican John Thune to promote biofuels.)

Her work on consumer protection has boosted her popularity, but it has drawn criticism from Democrats and interest groups on her left, who have accused her of focusing on small, politically popular issues while staying clear of more-controversial policy debates. "Dealing with swimming pools is good and important to families, but it doesn't change the big drivers in our society," said Steve Morse of the Minnesota Environmental Partnership to the Minneapolis Star Tribune.

Klobuchar grew up in the Minneapolis suburb of Plymouth. Her mother taught second grade, and her father, Jim Klobuchar, was a columnist for the Star Tribune. She attended Yale, where her senior thesis detailed the 10-year political debate over the building of the Hubert H. Humphrey Metrodome in Minneapolis. Published as a book, "Uncovering the Dome" has been used as a text in college courses.

After graduating from the University of Chicago's law school, Klobuchar returned to Minnesota to practice law. She also worked as a legal adviser to Walter F. Mondale, who provided her first Washington experience through an internship in his office when he was the vice president.

She also helped her father recover from alcoholism, a battle he subsequently chronicled in a book. The challenge gave her thick skin, which came in handy during her first Senate run. "Growing up with my dad being in the public eye was also very helpful," she said. His three DWI arrests "were all very prominent and well-known."

The events that propelled her into big-league politics came in 1995. Her daughter Abigail was born with a frozen palate that prevented her from swallowing. While the baby stayed at the hospital, Klobuchar was discharged after 24 hours because it was all her health insurance plan would cover. Outraged, she successfully lobbied state lawmakers for a law to guarantee new mothers 48 hours at the hospital.

Klobuchar entered the Hennepin County attorney's race in 1998 and defeated Sheryl Ramstad, sister of Republican Rep. Jim Ramstad. Klobuchar was re-elected in 2002 without opposition.

When Democrat Mark Dayton announced his retirement from the Senate in early 2005, Klobuchar was recognized as an early favorite to secure the Democratic-Farmer-Labor Party nomination, and her three leading opponents dropped out of the race during the primary campaign. In the general election, she topped Republican Rep. Mark Kennedy, with 58 percent of the vote to Kennedy's 38 percent. It was the largest margin of victory in a U.S. Senate race in the state since 1978.

She broke her own record in 2012. Klobuchar beat GOP state Rep. Kurt Bills by almost 35 points.

Key Votes

2012	
Prohibit health insurance plans from denying coverage based on the sponsor's religious beliefs	YES
Require approval of the Keystone XL oil pipeline	NO
Ease securities rules to expand small-business access to capital	YES
Reauthorize farm and nutrition programs for five years	YES
Limit debate on a bill that would create private-sector cybersecurity standards	YES
Consent to ratification of a treaty setting global standard for the treatment of people with disabilities	YES
Provide $60.4 billion in disaster relief following Superstorm Sandy	YES
Extend most Bush-era income tax rates while allowing rates for top-bracket earners to rise (Jan. 1, 2013)	YES
2011	
Prevent EPA from regulating greenhouse gas emissions to address climate change	NO
Extend certain provisions of Patriot Act for four years	YES
Clear compromise debt limit increase plan and establish future spending limits	YES
Overhaul patent law	YES
Implement Colombia free trade agreement	NO
Limit debate on confirmation of Caitlin J. Halligan to D.C. Circuit Court of Appeals	YES
Extend payroll tax cut and unemployment benefits for two months	YES

CQ Vote Studies

	PARTY UNITY		PRESIDENTIAL SUPPORT	
	SUPPORT	OPPOSE	SUPPORT	OPPOSE
2012	93%	7%	99%	1%
2011	92%	8%	95%	5%
2010	90%	10%	100%	0%
2009	89%	11%	97%	3%
2008	94%	6%	31%	69%
2007	93%	7%	38%	62%

Interest Groups

	AFL-CIO	ADA	CCUS	ACU
2012	91%	90%	38%	4%
2011	79%	85%	55%	0%
2010	93%	90%	36%	4%
2009	100%	100%	43%	12%
2008	100%	100%	57%	16%
2007	95%	100%	45%	4%

Sen. Al Franken (D)

Capitol Office
224-5641
franken.senate.gov
309 Hart Bldg. 20510-2303; fax 224-0044

Committees
Energy & Natural Resources
(Energy - Chairman)
Health, Education, Labor & Pensions
Indian Affairs
Judiciary
(Privacy, Technology & the Law - Chairman)

Residence
Minneapolis

Born
May 21, 1951; Manhattan, N.Y.

Religion
Jewish

Family
Wife, Franni Franken; two children

Education
Harvard U., A.B. 1973 (general studies)

Career
Author; radio talk show host; screenwriter; comedian

Political Highlights
No previous office

ELECTION RESULTS

2008 GENERAL		
Al Franken (D)	1,212,629	41.5%
Norm Coleman (R)	1,212,317	41.5%
Others	496,109	17.0%
2008 PRIMARY		
Al Franken (D)	164,136	65.3%
Priscilla Lord Faris (D)	74,655	29.7%
Dick Franson (D)	3,923	1.6%
Bob Larson (D)	3,152	1.2%
Rob Fitzgerald (D)	3,095	1.2%

Elected 2008; 1st term

Franken is partisan and progressive, and he used those qualities to great effect during his career as a political commentator and satirist. As a senator, he has kept his political philosophy, while smoothing out his rhetoric and impressing many people with his dedication to policy work. If he wins re-election uneventfully in 2014, it would arguably complete his transition from showman to statesman.

Franken was born in New York City and raised in St. Louis Park, a suburb of Minneapolis. His mother was a homemaker and sold real estate. His father owned a fabric factory and also worked as a printing agent. Franken went to college at Harvard University.

In 1975, Franken and his high school friend Tom Davis were hired to write for the then-fledgling "Saturday Night Live." He has also written for and appeared in movies such as "Stuart Saves His Family" and "Trading Places." Over the course of his comedy career, Franken won several Emmy Awards.

Franken appeared on CNN to provide commentary for the 1988 Democratic National Convention, and he anchored Comedy Central's 1992 and 1996 election coverage. In 2004, Franken began broadcasting a daily radio show on the now-defunct Air America Radio. "The O'Franken Factor," later renamed "The Al Franken Show," tackled political issues from Franken's liberal perspective.

Throughout his performance and punditry career, Franken pushed boundaries. His book "Rush Limbaugh is a Big Fat Idiot" attacked not only the popular talk show host but also House Speaker Newt Gingrich and ex-United Nations ambassador Jeane Kirkpatrick. In a subsequent book, "Lies and the Lying Liars Who Tell Them," Franken blasted the George W. Bush administration and Fox News commentator Bill O'Reilly.

Since becoming a senator in 2009, Franken has let that part of his persona recede. He has declined national media interviews for much of his first term, and most of his overt support for the Democratic Party has been in quieter settings. During the 2012 campaign, he addressed state Democratic Party dinners all over the country, penned multiple emails for the Democratic Senatorial Campaign Committee and raised money for Democratic candidates, all while avoiding controversy.

His political idol and inspiration is the late Minnesota Democratic Sen. Paul Wellstone, who died in a plane crash in 2002. In 2012, Franken choked up on the Senate floor as he spoke of Wellstone and his wife, Sheila.

Like his hero, Franken boasts a solidly liberal voting record and a seat on the Health, Education, Labor and Pensions Committee. He can claim credit for shaping the 2010 health care overhaul. Franken took Minnesota's "medical loss ratio" law and adapted it for the national overhaul. His original proposal would have required 90 percent of premiums collected by insurers to be spent on clinical services and quality of care. The percentages were nudged down in the final version of the law, but insurers that did not hit the target started providing rebates in 2012.

Franken also worked with fellow Minnesota Democrat Amy Klobuchar to reduce the overhaul's new tax on medical device manufacturers. In the 113th Congress (2013-14) they are pressing for its repeal—many device companies are in their state. He is an advocate of allowing Medicare to negotiate with drug companies to lower prescription costs, and of speeding the rate at which "generic" drugs can enter the market.

Franken has stepped up his involvement with education. In early 2013, he and three other Democrats rolled out a plan to create a grant program for states looking to expand or improve their preschool programs.

He also wants more school-based mental-health programs. Franken has personal reasons for working on mental-health policy. First, it was a major interest of Wellstone: The 2008 law requiring insurance companies to treat mental health the same as physical health bears Wellstone's name. Beyond that, Franken's wife struggled with alcoholism, and many of his friends in show business had addiction problems. His work on mental health extends to the Judiciary Committee. Franken and Florida Republican Rep. Rich Nugent are the lead sponsors of bills to extend federal support for mental-health courts and programs helping inmates with mental-health problems.

Franken chairs the Judiciary Subcommittee on Privacy, Technology and the Law. His most vigorous efforts as the leader of that panel have involved "location privacy." The full Judiciary Committee approved a 2012 Franken bill that would have banned companies from using applications on mobile devices to track a consumer without the consumer's consent.

He also has been outspoken in defending "net neutrality" rules, the 2011 regulations that bar broadband providers from blocking certain Web traffic or establishing tiered pathways for Internet content. Republicans describe the rules as a gateway to severe regulation of the Internet, but Franken has called net neutrality "the First Amendment issue of our time."

Democrats expanded Franken's portfolio in 2013, choosing him as the chairman of the Energy and Natural Resources Subcommittee on Energy. At the first hearing of the full committee in 2013, Franken tried to undercut GOP resistance to federal support of renewable-energy development. He pointed out that the "hydraulic fracturing" technique that has led to a natural-gas boom was developed in part through government programs. "This abundance of natural gas came from the expenditure of federal dollars," he said. "We need to do the same thing when it comes to renewables."

As successful as Franken has been at avoiding unwanted attention, his old habits sometimes surface. In 2010 he was scolded for making faces and gesticulating while presiding in the chair during a speech by Minority Leader Mitch McConnell of Kentucky. When McConnell was finished speaking, he approached Franken in the presiding officer's chair and reportedly told him, "This is not 'Saturday Night Live,' Al." Franken later sent a note of apology.

But, by most accounts, he has been a fairly pleasant colleague. In 2011 he immediately struck up a friendship with his ideological opposite, freshman Republican Rand Paul of Kentucky, and agreed to serve as his Senate mentor; that same year he told a magazine that he likes Rep. Michele Bachmann, a tea party firebrand from Minnesota. In 2012, he worked with Arizona Republican John McCain on legislative language to legalize the purchase of prescription drugs from Canada.

Franken also encourages bipartisanship by initiating new social traditions on Capitol Hill. He is Jewish, but he organized the Senate's first Secret Santa gift exchange, with a $10 price limit — he gave Arkansas Republican John Boozman a mahnomin porridge kit from a Minneapolis restaurant. He started a baking contest for the Minnesota delegation, which he won the second time around. Franken's wife, Franni, plays an outsized role in many of his extracurricular activities.

In fact, the most controversial aspect of his Senate career to date is his 2008 election. At the end of the final episode of his radio show in 2007, he announced that he would challenge Republican incumbent Norm Coleman.

Following a lengthy recount, Franken defeated Coleman by a 312-vote margin out of 2.9 million cast. It became clear in the months after Election Day that Franken would win, but Republicans stalled his seating with legal proceedings that lasted six months.

In June 2009, the Minnesota Supreme Court declared Franken the winner, and Coleman conceded.

Key Votes

2012	
Prohibit health insurance plans from denying coverage based on the sponsor's religious beliefs	YES
Require approval of the Keystone XL oil pipeline	NO
Ease securities rules to expand small-business access to capital	NO
Reauthorize farm and nutrition programs for five years	YES
Limit debate on a bill that would create private-sector cybersecurity standards	YES
Consent to ratification of a treaty setting global standard for the treatment of people with disabilities	YES
Provide $60.4 billion in disaster relief following Superstorm Sandy	YES
Extend most Bush-era income tax rates while allowing rates for top-bracket earners to rise (Jan. 1, 2013)	YES
2011	
Prevent EPA from regulating greenhouse gas emissions to address climate change	NO
Extend certain provisions of Patriot Act for four years	NO
Clear compromise debt limit increase plan and establish future spending limits	YES
Overhaul patent law	YES
Implement Colombia free trade agreement	NO
Limit debate on confirmation of Caitlin J. Halligan to D.C. Circuit Court of Appeals	YES
Extend payroll tax cut and unemployment benefits for two months	YES

CQ Vote Studies

	PARTY UNITY		PRESIDENTIAL SUPPORT	
	SUPPORT	OPPOSE	SUPPORT	OPPOSE
2012	98%	2%	96%	4%
2011	98%	2%	94%	6%
2010	99%	1%	98%	2%
2009	98%	2%	97%	3%

Interest Groups

	AFL-CIO	ADA	CCUS	ACU
2012	100%	95%	38%	0%
2011	95%	95%	55%	0%
2010	100%	90%	18%	0%
2009	100%		50%	0%

Rep. Tim Walz (D)

Capitol Office
225-2472
walz.house.gov
1034 Longworth Bldg. 20515-2301; fax 225-3433

Committees
Agriculture
Transportation & Infrastructure
Veterans' Affairs

Residence
Mankato

Born
April 6, 1964; West Point, Neb.

Religion
Lutheran

Family
Wife, Gwen Walz; two children

Education
Chadron State College, B.S. 1989 (social science education); Minnesota State U., Mankato, M.S. 2001 (educational leadership); Saint Mary's U. of Minnesota, attending

Military
Neb. National Guard, 1981-96; Minn. National Guard, 1996-2005

Career
Teacher; mortgage processor

Political Highlights
No previous office

ELECTION RESULTS

2012 GENERAL		
Tim Walz (D)	193,211	57.5%
Allen Quist (R)	142,164	42.3%
2012 PRIMARY		
Tim Walz (D)		unopposed
2010 GENERAL		
Tim Walz (D)	122,365	49.3%
Randy Demmer (R)	109,242	44.0%
Steven Wilson (INDC)	13,242	5.3%
Lars Johnson (PTF)	3,054	1.2%

Previous Winning Percentages
2008 (63%); 2006 (53%)

Elected 2006; 4th term

Walz was once a football coach, and he seems to have a playbook for surviving as a moderate Democrat. He scores points with nonpartisan measures on veterans' issues and congressional ethics, while trying to address his district's agriculture and infrastructure needs.

Walz (WALLS) grew up in Nebraska and studied education in college — he was part of the first government-sanctioned group of American educators to teach in China. (He speaks Mandarin and serves on the Congressional-Executive Commission on China.) He eventually ended up at Mankato West High School in Minnesota, where he taught geography and served as the defensive coordinator for two state championship runs.

Plus, he's the highest-ranking enlisted soldier to ever serve in Congress. Walz joined the Army National Guard to help pay for college and served 24 years, achieving the position of command sergeant major. He was deployed to Italy in 2003 to oversee supply shipments to troops in Afghanistan.

He had no experience as an elected official when he won a House seat in 2006. Now in his fourth term, he can no longer claim to be an outsider — but he still laments the environment of Congress. At a 2012 campaign debate he complained of lawmakers seeking "perfect" bills. "Perfect is what you get in heaven," he said. "The U.S. House of Representatives is closer to hell."

And he continues to champion outsider causes. His biggest success is a 2012 law to prevent congressmen, Capitol Hill staffers and federal employees from using privileged information when making stock trades. Walz and New York Democrat Louise M. Slaughter had introduced bills on the subject since his freshman term, but public interest spiked after "60 Minutes" aired a 2011 segment on the superior investment returns of lawmakers. A version of their proposal, which sets tougher disclosure standards for trading activities, was quickly enacted.

Some lawmakers grumbled that insider trading was already illegal and that the bill seemed like an admission of wrongdoing. Walz was undeterred: "This law will work to hold Washington accountable and restore the American people's faith in democracy," he wrote after the bill signing. He and Slaughter continue to pursue disclosure and reporting requirements for the "political intelligence" industry.

Walz engages in many bipartisan efforts on the Veterans' Affairs Committee. He takes a particular interest in veterans' employment. In 2012, President Barack Obama signed a bill by Walz and California Republican Jeff Denham; it lets military training satisfy certification requirements for federal licenses that are useful in the civilian workforce. A few months later, Obama signed a Walz bill requiring the Transportation Security Administration to comply with existing rules protecting the jobs of TSA employees called to active duty.

His other committees are where he attends to parochial needs.

The 1st District has lots of high-value farming operations, as well as a thriving food-processing industry. Walz sits on the Agriculture Committee, where he has a powerful ally in ranking member Collin C. Peterson, another moderate Minnesota Democrat.

The law governing federal farming programs expired in the fall of 2012, as Congress did not finish a long-term reauthorization. Walz blamed the GOP: "I am absolutely appalled by how the extreme tea party wing of the House Republicans has gummed up the workings of the legislative process yet again and prevented compromise and progress," he said. A short-term extension was eventually enacted, and work continues in the 113th Congress (2013-14).

Walz worked on number of provisions in the long-term reauthorization the

Agriculture Committee approved in 2012. One was to ensure that young or beginning farmers would have access to federal assistance programs; another, worked on with Vermont Democrat Peter Welch, was to reduce some of the regulations in a program providing grants and loan guarantees to farmers who engage in energy efficiency or renewable-energy projects on their land.

Walz and South Dakota Republican Kristi Noem introduced a 2012 "sod-saver" bill, which would reduce the federal subsidies paid to insure or grow on lower-quality, previously uncultivated land; they touted the measure as an incentive for land conservation and a cost-saver for the government. In 2013, Walz became the top Democrat on the Conservation, Energy and Forestry Subcommittee, and he and Noem re-introduced their bill.

On the Transportation and Infrastructure Committee, Walz has a number of local concerns. The Mississippi River marks the eastern border of his district, and it is a shipping route for the farms and factories of Minnesota. In 2013 he became a co-chairman of the bicameral Mississippi River Caucus.

Walz grew up in a middle-class family from the Sandhills region of north-central Nebraska. His mother was a homemaker; his father was a superintendent. Walz was in high school when his father was diagnosed with cancer and his family moved to his mother's hometown of Butte. Walz, his mother and his 8-year-old brother soon found themselves living off of Social Security survivor benefits. "If there wouldn't have been a safety net, it would have been different," he said.

At 17, Walz joined the Nebraska National Guard to help pay for his studies at Chadron State College, a public university nestled along the bluffs in the state's northwest. He earned a degree in social science education and headed to China shortly after. On his return he taught in Nebraska, then moved to Mankato in 1996. Walz retired from the military in 2005.

Walz's only venture into politics prior to his 2006 campaign consisted of some community organizing for Massachusetts Sen. John Kerry's 2004 presidential campaign. But in a very good year for Democrats, he defeated six-term Republican Rep. Gil Gutknecht by more than 5 points, capitalizing in part on Gutknecht's retraction of an earlier pledge to serve no more than 12 years.

He won by almost 30 points in 2008, but when the political tide reversed in 2010, Republican state Rep. Randy Demmer became a formidable opponent. He tried to paint Walz as too liberal for the district. Walz won by 5 points, but with less than 50 percent of the vote.

He had no problems holding the seat in 2012, defeating former state Rep. Allen Quist by 15 points. For the 2014 cycle, Walz is in charge of the Frontline Program of the Democratic Congressional Campaign Committee — its goal is to aid incumbents in competitive districts.

Key Votes

2012	
Extend a Social Security payroll tax cut and unemployment benefits	YES
Ease securities rules to expand small-business access to capital	YES
Extend for one year subsidized student loan interest rates financed by a cut in health care spending	YES
Cite Attorney General Eric H. Holder Jr. for contempt of Congress	YES
Create a visa program for foreign graduates in high-tech fields	NO
Extend most Bush-era income tax rates while allowing rates for top-bracket earners to rise (Jan. 1, 2013)	YES
2011	
Strike funding for F-35 alternative engine	YES
Prevent EPA from regulating greenhouse gas emissions to address climate change	NO
Extend certain provisions of Patriot Act for four years	NO
Declare opposition to use of ground troops in Libya	YES
Overhaul patent law	YES
Pass compromise debt limit increase plan and establish future spending limits	YES
Allow consideration of measures to implement three trade agreements	NO

CQ Vote Studies

	PARTY UNITY		PRESIDENTIAL SUPPORT	
	SUPPORT	OPPOSE	SUPPORT	OPPOSE
2012	85%	15%	71%	29%
2011	87%	13%	80%	20%
2010	97%	3%	95%	5%
2009	94%	6%	96%	4%
2008	96%	4%	14%	86%

Interest Groups

	AFL-CIO	ADA	CCUS	ACU
2012	76%	70%	42%	13%
2011	93%	80%	44%	8%
2010	100%	90%	25%	4%
2009	100%	100%	47%	4%
2008	93%	85%	50%	20%

Minnesota 1

South — Rochester, Mankato

Stretching from the flat plains at the South Dakota border to the towering bluffs overlooking the Mississippi River, Minnesota's rural 1st District is cut horizontally by Interstate 90 and vertically by Interstate 35. Rural areas continue to lose population to the Twin Cities, but new residents have moved to Mankato and Rochester, home to the Mayo Clinic.

Agriculture and food processing still drive the local economy. Corn, soybeans, sugar beets, hogs and dairy are staples here. The 1st has among the highest agricultural market values of any district in the country; more than 20,000 farms dot the 1st's landscape. Food processing — from fresh turkey to canned soup — dominates areas west of Rochester. West of Mankato, no town has more than 15,000 residents, and most counties have experienced a steady drop in population during the past decade.

The regional economy depends heavily on the Mayo Clinic in Rochester. Consistently ranked one of the best hospitals in the nation, the facility draws patients from all over the world. The clinic employs more than 33,000 physicians, scientists and health care staff. Rochester has a highly educated populace: 42 percent of the city's residents hold at least a bachelor's degree. The district has also established itself as a regional leader in wind energy production. The Buffalo Ridge — in the southwestern part of the state — spins out wind turbines and renewable energy companies. Sulzon Wind Energy Corporation operates a blade-manufacturing facility in Pipestone. EnXco and Xcel Energy also opened a 201-megawatt wind farm in nearby Nobles County.

The 1st is roughly 90 percent white, but minority residents have arrived to work in factories, on farms and at Rochester's hospitals. Worthington in particular has a large immigrant population and a significant proportion of non-English-speaking children in its schools. The 1st is politically moderate; the GOP tends to have success at the state level, but Barack Obama eked out slim majorities here in the 2008 and 2012 presidential races.

Major Industry
Health care, agriculture, food processing, renewable energy

Cities
Rochester, Mankato, Winona

Notable
The birthplace of SPAM, Austin is home to the SPAM Museum.

Rep. John Kline (R)

Capitol Office
225-2271
kline.house.gov
2439 Rayburn Bldg. 20515-2302; fax 225-2595

Committees
Armed Services
Education & the Workforce - Chairman

Residence
Burnsville

Born
Sept. 6, 1947; Allentown, Pa.

Religion
Methodist

Family
Wife, Vicky Kline; two children

Education
Rice U., B.A. 1969 (biology); Shippensburg U., M.S. 1988 (public administration)

Military
Marine Corps, 1969-94

Career
Think tank executive; farmer; management consultant; Marine officer

Political Highlights
Republican nominee for U.S. House, 1998, 2000

ELECTION RESULTS

2012 GENERAL		
John Kline (R)	193,587	54.0%
Mike Obermueller (D)	164,338	45.8%
2012 PRIMARY		
John Kline (R)	15,859	85.1%
David Gerson (R)	2,772	14.9%
2010 GENERAL		
John Kline (R)	181,341	63.3%
Shelley Madore (D)	104,809	36.6%

Previous Winning Percentages
2008 (57%); 2006 (56%); 2004 (56%); 2002 (53%)

Elected 2002; 6th term

Republicans have put Kline's military efficiency to use on the Education and the Workforce Committee, one of the busier House panels. But one of the chairman's more effective weapons — a personable demeanor — has been neutralized in partisan battles over health care, education and union labor.

Kline, a 25-year Marine Corps veteran, took the top Republican slot on his committee in June 2009, then ascended to the chairmanship in 2011. His dealings with the opposition are often cordial; during hearings he usually can been seen whispering and exchanging grins with California's George Miller, the panel's top Democrat.

"It has been hard," Kline said in 2012. "Mr. Miller and I get along really, really well on a personal level. Politics has gotten in the way of us being able to get together to do things."

The committee's agenda for the 112th Congress (2011-12) — which is largely repeated in the 113th Congress (2013-14) — made politics almost impossible to avoid. From the first week, the panel was one of the forums for the Republican effort to repeal, dismantle and block funding for Democrats' 2010 health care overhaul law. Kline was involved in the health care debate during the 111th Congress (2009-10), when he recommended an emphasis on health insurance providers and businesses working together to reduce the cost of plans.

In 2012, party divisions sank the effort that Kline invested the most time in: a reauthorization of the 2002 education law known as No Child Left Behind. With no agreement on a broad overhaul, Kline shepherded two smaller GOP bills out of committee on party-line votes in March. Miller accused the GOP of a "highly partisan process," while Kline said, "Democrats decided not to participate in it. Their effort was not really engaging."

The bills centered on the school and teacher accountability standards in the law, which are often criticized as overly burdensome to many schools. They also emphasized the GOP call for greater local control of education. Kline supports a mandate for schools to measure progress, but would leave it to states or localities to design the system. "We need to see what you're doing, but we're not going to tell you how to do it," he said.

Although less vitriolic toward the National Labor Relations Board than some colleagues, Kline lent his clout when Republicans accused the NLRB of increasingly favoring unions over employers during the Obama administration. He similarly questioned regulations meant to curtail allegedly deceptive marketing practices by for-profit colleges. "It is an assault on students' ability to find an institution that best fits their needs," he said in early 2011.

The early months of 2013 did not indicate a changed dynamic on the committee. Many people, including President Barack Obama, had cited workforce investment programs as an example of duplicative government operations. Kline quickly advanced a bill to consolidate 35 employment and training programs into a single Workforce Investment Fund; money for the programs would come from a block grant to the states. Panel Democrats walked out of the markup for the bill, alleging that Republicans had refused to negotiate. The full House passed the bill in March.

Kline also was skeptical of a Democratic call to expand early-childhood education. "Before we spend more taxpayer dollars on new programs, we must first review what is and is not working in existing initiatives, such as Head Start," he said.

Some of the work most personally important to Kline occurs outside his role as chairman, on the Armed Services Committee. "I will always stay engaged in that," Kline said of his work on behalf of servicemembers and their families.

"That's the reason I came to Congress." Kline is particularly dedicated to the National Guard's reintegration program, which assists soldiers returning to civilian life. He successfully included an expansion of the program in the fiscal 2012 defense authorization law.

He is one of the few members of Congress with a child who served in both the Iraq and Afghanistan conflicts. Kline insists that politicians need to listen to the judgments of the military leaders on the ground when deciding on a course of action.

Kline belongs to the Republican Study Committee, although he is not the staunchest fiscal conservative in that group. He is a social conservative. He opposes abortion and fought the 2010 law that allowed repeal of the "don't ask, don't tell" policy for gay servicemembers. In 2011, he won the Republican "Top Gun" title at the Congressional Sportsmen's Foundation's annual shootout, where lawmakers compete on trap, skeet and sporting clay ranges.

Born in Pennsylvania, Kline spent most of his childhood in Corpus Christi, Texas, near where his father had bought a newspaper business. His mother managed the Corpus Christi Symphony Orchestra for 40 years. He joined the ROTC at Rice University in Houston, and he later earned a master's degree in public administration at Shippensburg University in Pennsylvania.

While in the military, Kline piloted helicopters in Vietnam, commanded aviation forces in Somalia, and flew the presidential helicopter, Marine One. He did stints carrying the "football" — a briefcase containing the nation's nuclear attack codes — for Jimmy Carter and Ronald Reagan. He also worked at Marine Corps headquarters as a program development officer, responsible for formulating a long-range spending plan. After retiring in 1994 as a colonel, Kline settled in Lakeville, Minn., where he helped his father-in-law manage the family farm in Houston County.

In 1998, he decided to run for the U.S. House. He won the GOP nomination at an old-fashioned, traditional Minnesota convention, but he lost the general election to Democratic incumbent Bill Luther. He tried again in 2000, getting help from national Republican groups the second time around. He lost by about 5,500 votes.

Redistricting paired Luther with GOP Rep. Mark Kennedy in the new 6th District in 2002. Luther moved to the redrawn 2nd District, which was far more Republican than before, and Kline challenged him again. Luther tried to portray Kline as an "extremist," but Kline's message of lower taxes, smaller government and a strong military prevailed.

After another round of redistricting following the 2010 census, Kline scored only 54 percent of the vote in 2012, his smallest share since his first victory. Democrats announced early on that they would be targeting him in 2014.

Key Votes

2012

Extend a Social Security payroll tax cut and unemployment benefits	YES
Ease securities rules to expand small-business access to capital	YES
Extend for one year subsidized student loan interest rates financed by a cut in health care spending	YES
Cite Attorney General Eric H. Holder Jr. for contempt of Congress	YES
Create a visa program for foreign graduates in high-tech fields	YES
Extend most Bush-era income tax rates while allowing rates for top-bracket earners to rise (Jan. 1, 2013)	YES

2011

Strike funding for F-35 alternative engine	NO
Prevent EPA from regulating greenhouse gas emissions to address climate change	YES
Extend certain provisions of Patriot Act for four years	YES
Declare opposition to use of ground troops in Libya	YES
Overhaul patent law	YES
Pass compromise debt limit increase plan and establish future spending limits	YES
Allow consideration of measures to implement three trade agreements	YES

CQ Vote Studies

	PARTY UNITY		PRESIDENTIAL SUPPORT	
	SUPPORT	OPPOSE	SUPPORT	OPPOSE
2012	99%	1%	18%	82%
2011	98%	2%	25%	75%
2010	94%	6%	27%	73%
2009	98%	2%	17%	83%
2008	97%	3%	77%	23%

Interest Groups

	AFL-CIO	ADA	CCUS	ACU
2012	14%	0%	100%	96%
2011	3%	10%	100%	88%
2010	0%	0%	88%	96%
2009	10%	5%	80%	100%
2008	13%	15%	94%	88%

Minnesota 2

Southern Twin Cities suburbs

The 2nd is made up of suburbs from the southern and southwestern portions of the Minneapolis-St. Paul metropolitan area between the Mississippi and Minnesota rivers. It extends southeast to include rural Rice, Goodhue and Wabasha counties.

Scott and Dakota counties directly south of the Twin Cities continue decades of population growth as suburbs spread south of Burnsville down Interstate 35 and around the river city of Hastings. The district, while mostly white, has become more diverse since 2000. Parts of Eagan, West St. Paul, Burnsville and Apple Valley have experienced growth in Asian and Hispanic populations.

The district's southern tier of counties, however, remain agricultural. Nearly two-thirds of the land in the 2nd is farmed, with corn and dairy production dominant. In Northfield, 45 miles south of Minneapolis, top employers are in cereal processing and grocery distribution.

Professionals seeking the feel of suburban life near jobs in a big city have settled in the district in large numbers. The area also supports construction jobs and health care management services — Blue Cross and Blue Shield of Minnesota has its headquarters in Eagan, a middle- to upper-class suburb south of the twin cities. Red Wing produces the famed shoes that bear its name — the factory there boasts a 16-foot tall boot. Indian gaming has taken off in the area and a number of casinos are located in the district. Mystic Lake and Little Six casinos are both in Prior Lake, and Treasure Island Casino is in Welch.

Decennial redistricting after the 2010 census made the 2nd highly competitive at the presidential level. Sen. John McCain of Arizona, the Republican presidential nominee, won a narrow victory in 2008 under the old lines, but would have lost by 3 points in the newly drawn district; Barack Obama beat Mitt Romney by 226 votes in 2012.

Major Industry
Professional services, agriculture, health care

Cities
Eagan, Burnsville, Lakeville

Notable
Students from Carleton College in Northfield decorated the campus observatory as a giant R2-D2 so it would seem the "Star Wars" droid's head would track the movement of the nighttime sky.

Rep. Erik Paulsen (R)

Capitol Office
225-2871
paulsen.house.gov
127 Cannon Bldg. 20515-2303; fax 225-6351

Committees
Ways & Means
Joint Economic

Residence
Eden Prairie

Born
May 14, 1965; Bakersfield, Calif.

Religion
Lutheran

Family
Wife, Kelly Paulsen; four children

Education
St. Olaf College, B.A. 1987 (mathematics)

Career
Business strategies analyst; congressional aide

Political Highlights
Minn. House, 1995-2009 (majority leader, 2003-07)

ELECTION RESULTS

2012 GENERAL		
Erik Paulsen (R)	222,335	58.1%
Brian Barnes (D)	159,937	41.8%
2012 PRIMARY		
Erik Paulsen (R)	18,672	90.2%
John W. Howard III (R)	2,032	9.8%
2010 GENERAL		
Erik Paulsen (R)	161,177	58.8%
Jim Meffert (D)	100,240	36.6%
Jon Oleson (INDC)	12,508	4.6%

Previous Winning Percentages
2008 (48%)

Elected 2008; 3rd term

Paulsen espouses free-market principles, but he colors them with a touch of Midwestern populism. That combination puts him closer to the moderate end of the Republican spectrum.

He sits on the Ways and Means Committee, where economic growth is the unifying theme for most of his work — whether it's for Minnesota businesses or the nation at large. "Those engineers, those doctors, those entrepreneurs, you know, they get up in the morning, they're excited about something, they want to create something, they want to hire people, they want to invent, they want to grow," he said. "I want to keep that dream alive."

Paulsen himself worked a stint in marketing. Deciding that he wanted to do something more meaningful with his career, he took an internship in the office of Sen. Rudy Boschwitz, a Minnesota Republican. From there Paulsen moved to the D.C. office of Republican Rep. Jim Ramstad, and then back to Minnesota to become Ramstad's state director.

Paulsen was elected to the state House in 1994 and served there until the start of 2009, when he joined the U.S. House. Four of those years, he was majority leader. Legislating is a part-time gig in Minnesota, so Paulsen also worked as a business analyst at Target Corp.

His most visible legislative effort thus far is his quest to repeal a tax on medical devices that was included in the 2010 health care overhaul. The tax, which took effect at the start of 2013, strikes close to home — a number of device manufacturers operate out of Minnesota. Paulsen says it will cost the country jobs and reduce access to life-saving technologies, threatening what he calls "a great American success story."

His bill to repeal the tax passed the House in the 112th Congress (2011-12) with support from 37 Democrats. The measure also included a provision pushed by Paulsen that would repeal the overhaul's restrictions on using tax-preferred accounts to pay for over-the-counter drugs. It died in the Senate.

Paulsen, who co-chairs the Medical Technology Caucus, re-introduced the device tax repeal at the start the of 113th Congress (2013-14), while splitting out the provisions on tax-preferred accounts into a separate bill. Minnesota Sens. Al Franken and Amy Klobuchar — both Democrats — are pressing from their side of the Capitol to eliminate the device tax. Paulsen voted for full repeal of the overhaul law in the 112th Congress, but he says that "in the past, Republicans were wrong to ignore the need for health care reform."

Paulsen praised a five-year reauthorization of the Food and Drug Administration's user fee programs that was enacted in July 2012 as a positive for medical devices. He was the lead author of a provision reauthorizing a program that allows third parties to conduct reviews of some devices as part of the approval process — those reviews free up resources at the FDA so it can get innovative devices to the market faster, according to Paulsen.

His deep interest in trade stems from his state's export-driven economy, and in the 112th Congress he attended most of the Trade Subcommittee's hearings despite not having a seat on the panel. He describes his approach as "selling American" and was active in the discussions on the trade agreements that made their way through Congress in 2011.

Paulsen served on the Financial Services Committee in his freshman term, during debate on the financial regulatory overhaul that was enacted in 2010. He argued that the legislation didn't do enough to address problems presented by institutions deemed "too big to fail" and put up hurdles for community banks. "I'll meet with these small banks, and rather than having more loan officers now looking at where loan opportunities are, they have more compliance officers just following some of these new regulations," he said in 2012. "It's getting too complicated."

Paulsen introduced bills in 2009 and 2010 that would terminate the Troubled Asset Relief Program, the Treasury Department-run initiative that Congress approved in fall 2008 to strengthen the financial sector. In September 2009, he won House passage of his bill to require the TARP special inspector general to study the effect of the program on small businesses and small financial institutions. And amid public outrage over bonuses paid out by insurance giant American International Group Inc., which had received money from the rescue package, he sponsored a measure that would have required the Treasury secretary to recoup the bonus payments.

Paulsen avoids harsh rhetoric but has criticized the Obama administration for what he characterizes as "misguided" economic policies. (In 2013, Paulsen was added to the Joint Economic Committee.) He opposed the 2009 stimulus package and energy legislation that would have created a cap-and-trade system aimed at reducing greenhouse gas emissions.

Still, he associates with the Main Street Partnership, a moderate bloc. He was one of two Republicans on Ways and Means to oppose panel approval of the revenue portion of a five-year surface transportation bill in February 2012. Paulsen objected to language in the overall bill that would open up Alaska's Arctic National Wildlife Refuge to drilling — he said it got thrown in "out of nowhere." He was one of just 40 House Republicans to vote for a 2009 bill expanding the Children's Health Insurance Program, which covers children from low-income families that make too much money to qualify for Medicaid.

Paulsen tends to downplay social issues. His district sent the centrist Ramstad to Congress nine times, and Paulsen has said that he and Ramstad are "cut from the same cloth on many issues."

Paulsen was born in Bakersfield, Calif., and his family moved about a year later to Chanhassen, a western Minneapolis suburb. He said he grew up in a "regular" suburban Minnesota home before studying mathematics at St. Olaf College, a small Lutheran liberal arts school in Northfield, Minn. From there he went into the business world and on to politics.

When Ramstad announced his retirement in 2007, Paulsen was the consensus Republican choice to succeed him. Democrats saw the open seat in a swing district as an opportunity, but Paulsen won by 8 points against newcomer Ashwin Madia. He had very comfortable re-elections in 2010 and 2012.

Paulsen enjoys camping and canoeing with his family — he has a full-size, Minnesota-made Wenonah canoe on display in his office. He also plays in congressional baseball and hockey games, and he competes with some of his old college friends in broomball in the winter.

Key Votes

2012

Extend a Social Security payroll tax cut and unemployment benefits	**YES**
Ease securities rules to expand small-business access to capital	**YES**
Extend for one year subsidized student loan interest rates financed by a cut in health care spending	**YES**
Cite Attorney General Eric H. Holder Jr. for contempt of Congress	**YES**
Create a visa program for foreign graduates in high-tech fields	**YES**
Extend most Bush-era income tax rates while allowing rates for top-bracket earners to rise (Jan. 1, 2013)	**NO**

2011

Strike funding for F-35 alternative engine	**YES**
Prevent EPA from regulating greenhouse gas emissions to address climate change	**YES**
Extend certain provisions of Patriot Act for four years	**YES**
Declare opposition to use of ground troops in Libya	**YES**
Overhaul patent law	**YES**
Pass compromise debt limit increase plan and establish future spending limits	**YES**
Allow consideration of measures to implement three trade agreements	**YES**

CQ Vote Studies

	PARTY UNITY		PRESIDENTIAL SUPPORT	
	SUPPORT	OPPOSE	SUPPORT	OPPOSE
2012	95%	5%	17%	83%
2011	92%	8%	25%	75%
2010	89%	11%	33%	67%
2009	89%	11%	32%	68%

Interest Groups

	AFL-CIO	ADA	CCUS	ACU
2012	15%	0%	83%	84%
2011	0%	5%	100%	84%
2010	0%	0%	88%	92%
2009	14%	10%	87%	88%

Minnesota 3

Hennepin County suburbs

The 3rd District wraps around Minneapolis from Coon Rapids to Bloomington and includes the suburban towns along Interstate 494. It stretches west through Hennepin County and Lake Minnetonka and covers the northeastern corner of Carver County.

The area, relatively well-off and established, is home to a diverse economic base. While not as agrarian as the rest of the state, the areas of the district further from the Twin Cities have more of an agricultural feel. Closer to the metropolitan hubs, the 3rd is home to some large corporations, such as Cargill, grocer Supervalu and logistics and transportation provider C. H. Robinson. Some of these enclaves are successfully moving beyond their roots as bedroom communities of Minneapolis-St. Paul. Much of the district's population works in financial services, professional services, manufacturing, health care and entertainment.

The 3rd is continuing to experience a rise in minority populations with marked growth among black and Hispanic communities — many minority residents take jobs in the area's agricultural sector — but these numbers remain below the national average for diversity. Some of this growth in the black population stems from resettled Somali immigrants in small towns in Hennepin County. Slightly higher than the state's average, the district is home to a minority population of about 17 percent.

The district has conservative leanings that were shifted slightly farther to the right during decennial remapping, but the 3rd remains competitive up and down the ballot. Barack Obama would have carried the 3rd in 2008, and he won it again in 2012, although his second victory was by fewer than 4,000 votes. The area has sent Republicans to the U.S. House for decades. The farther from Minneapolis — which is in the 5th District's portion of Hennepin County — the district gets, the more conservative the 3rd becomes.

Major Industry

Retail, professional services, transportation

Cities

Bloomington, Brooklyn Park, Plymouth

Notable

The humongous Mall of America in Bloomington contains a LEGO play area for children from which more than 170,000 of the toy bricks have been lost since it opened.

Rep. Betty McCollum (D)

Capitol Office
225-6631
mccollum.house.gov
1714 Longworth Bldg. 20515-2304; fax 225-1968

Committees
Appropriations

Residence
St. Paul

Born
July 12, 1954; Minneapolis, Minn.

Religion
Roman Catholic

Family
Divorced; two children

Education
Inver Hills Community College, A.A. 1980; College of St. Catherine, B.A. 1987 (education)

Career
Teacher; retail saleswoman

Political Highlights
Candidate for North St. Paul City Council, 1984; North St. Paul City Council, 1987-92; Minn. House, 1993-2001

ELECTION RESULTS

2012 GENERAL		
Betty McCollum (D)	216,685	62.3%
Tony Hernandez (R)	109,659	31.5%
Steve Carlson (INDC)	21,135	6.1%
2012 PRIMARY		
Betty McCollum (D)	27,291	84.2%
Diana Longrie (D)	3,212	9.9%
Brian Stalboerger (D)	1,913	5.9%
2010 GENERAL		
Betty McCollum (D)	136,746	59.1%
Teresa Collett (R)	80,141	34.6%
Steve Carlson (INDC)	14,207	6.1%

Previous Winning Percentages
2008 (68%); 2006 (70%); 2004 (57%); 2002 (62%); 2000 (48%)

Elected 2000; 7th term

Pleasant, partisan and liberal, McCollum stands up for the priorities of President Barack Obama from her post on the Appropriations Committee. She takes a keen interest in implementation of the 2010 health care overhaul and a revisit of federal education law.

McCollum hopes that, using Minnesota as a model, she can promote ideas to further increase access to health care and speed the implementation of the Democrats' health care law. She touts her work on the overhaul during the 111th Congress (2009-10), when she fought for inclusion of provisions to address geographic disparities in Medicare reimbursements. Several large health facilities and teaching hospitals are in her district.

She is open to tweaking the law — McCollum has supported a bill to repeal its tax on medical device manufacturers, of which there are many in Minnesota — but she says most Republican-led repeal efforts "will deny Americans life-saving care." Every American, according to McCollum, has a "fundamental right to access quality, affordable health services."

McCollum, a former member of the Foreign Affairs Committee, is very engaged in international health and women's rights issues. She sponsored legislation aimed at preventing child marriage, and in 2005 she founded the Congressional Global Health Caucus. In early 2013 she visited South Sudan to inspect the progress of U.S. efforts to bolster agricultural development and fight poverty in the fledgling nation.

McCollum also once sat on the Education and the Workforce Committee. Her district contains a number of colleges and universities, and McCollum spent time at the front of classrooms as a teacher before entering politics.

The 2002 education law known as No Child Left Behind is still up for reauthorization in the 113th Congress (2013-14). McCollum would like to see more coordination between the states and the federal government on education policy, and more federal funding for education.

The education standards of the states should be unified, McCollum says — not by federal edict, but via governor-level discussions to develop standards that are adaptable to individual state needs. McCollum believes the intent of Obama's Race to the Top program is good; it encourages states to change their education policies so that they are eligible for competitive grants issued by the Education Department. But she adds that the program might be a costly distraction, given the limited funding available for education.

As an appropriator, McCollum vigorously opposes Republicans' priorities and their favored spending cuts. Her own suggestions for cost-cutting include eliminating military advertisements and sponsorships, such as those seen on race cars. "If we can't cut some of the icing off the programs in the Pentagon, how are we going to get our house in order?" she asked in 2012. In the 113th Congress (2013-14), she joined the Defense Appropriations Subcommittee and made sure to mention that "now is the time for tough choices, smart cuts, and real deficit reduction that includes cuts to defense spending."

She also returned as a member of the Interior-Environment Subcommittee, which handles Indian affairs. In 2013 she was chosen as the Democratic co-chairwoman of the Congressional Native American Caucus.

McCollum wants an end to the GOP-imposed ban on earmarked spending, provided that earmark requests are suitably transparent. She makes the increasingly bipartisan argument that the ban reduces public access to the budgeting process and stifles targeted community and research investments.

One of McCollum's more distinctive ideas for spurring economic growth is to include nonprofit organizations within the purview of the Small Business

Committee. Like small businesses, nonprofits "are vital employers working to keep families and communities strong and successful," McCollum said. She cites Minnesota's large number of nonprofits — and the large number of people working at them — as evidence of the sector's strength and says congressional attention could encourage innovation and efficiency.

McCollum was born in Minneapolis and raised in the Twin Cities area in what she describes as a frugal middle-class household. Her father was a veteran of the Army Air Corps. She says that family discussions, which often included references to far-off places, spurred her interest in global affairs. "My father served in India, Burma and China during World War II, so we always had the atlas open at home, talking about countries and food and geography and culture and climate," she said. St. Paul has a large number of faith-based and immigrant communities.

Her interest in civic participation picked up in high school. The Vietnam War was affecting friends, classmates and local families, and the adoption of the 26th Amendment in 1971 empowered her to vote as an 18-year-old in the 1972 presidential election. She backed George McGovern and his opposition to the war. McCollum ardently opposed the Iraq War and has called for a more rapid withdrawal from Afghanistan.

McCollum studied at a community college and worked as a sales clerk at JC Penney, a department manager at Sears department stores and a substitute teacher while raising two children.

She got her bachelor's degree at 32, about the time she was venturing into politics. After being rebuffed by the city of North St. Paul in her quest to get immediate repairs at a local playground after her daughter was injured, McCollum ran for the city council. She lost that bid but won in a second attempt. She moved to the state legislature six years later, beating two incumbents thrown into the same district by redistricting.

With 14 years in elected office under her belt, McCollum in 2000 jumped into the primary race for the House seat being vacated by Democrat Bruce F. Vento, who announced he had lung cancer and wouldn't run again. Three other Democrats ran, but McCollum gained an important edge when she was endorsed by the state party. McCollum took 48 percent of the vote that November — which was still enough to give her a 17-point win over Republican state Sen. Linda Runbeck. Her re-elections have not been difficult.

Redistricting for the 2012 election pushed the eastern edge of McCollum's district to the Wisconsin border. The change put the home of Republican Rep. Michele Bachmann on McCollum's turf, but Bachmann ran in the redrawn 6th District.

McCollum, meanwhile, overwhelmed Republican Tony Hernandez.

Key Votes

2012

Extend a Social Security payroll tax cut and unemployment benefits	YES
Ease securities rules to expand small-business access to capital	NO
Extend for one year subsidized student loan interest rates financed by a cut in health care spending	NO
Cite Attorney General Eric H. Holder Jr. for contempt of Congress	?
Create a visa program for foreign graduates in high-tech fields	NO
Extend most Bush-era income tax rates while allowing rates for top-bracket earners to rise (Jan. 1, 2013)	YES

2011

Strike funding for F-35 alternative engine	YES
Prevent EPA from regulating greenhouse gas emissions to address climate change	NO
Extend certain provisions of Patriot Act for four years	NO
Declare opposition to use of ground troops in Libya	NO
Overhaul patent law	YES
Pass compromise debt limit increase plan and establish future spending limits	NO
Allow consideration of measures to implement three trade agreements	NO

CQ Vote Studies

	PARTY UNITY		PRESIDENTIAL SUPPORT	
	SUPPORT	OPPOSE	SUPPORT	OPPOSE
2012	98%	2%	86%	14%
2011	96%	4%	87%	13%
2010	98%	2%	90%	10%
2009	99%	1%	96%	4%
2008	99%	1%	13%	87%

Interest Groups

	AFL-CIO	ADA	CCUS	ACU
2012	95%	95%	25%	4%
2011	100%	75%	20%	5%
2010	100%	100%	13%	0%
2009	100%	100%	33%	0%
2008	100%	100%	56%	0%

Minnesota 4

St. Paul and suburbs

The 4th includes all of St. Paul and its eastern and northern suburbs in Ramsey and Washington counties. While the old district focused almost entirely around St. Paul, remapping following the 2010 census added wealthier areas of Washington County due east of the state capital.

The smaller of the Twin Cities, St. Paul is a collection of distinct neighborhoods, which include residential areas, liberal university communities, labor populations and state government workers. St. Paul developed as a major port and railroad center and still has a strong labor tradition, but the district boasts a relatively strong and diverse economic base. Large corporations such as 3M and Ecolab have headquarters in the district and draw from the well-educated local population. Dairy producer Land O'Lakes has a corporate office in Arden Hills, in the district's northwest.

Like most urban centers in the United States, the district has seen a shift in population growth back into the cities from the suburbs over the last decade, and officials hope to spur more downtown residential and retail development. With a 26 percent minority population, the 4th is the second-most diverse district statewide. Blacks and Hispanics together make up about 15 percent of the district's population, and the district's minority population is growing at a faster rate than rates for the nation as a whole — by the next census Ramsey County is expected to match the nation's overall racial diversity. There's also a large Hmong community in the Twin Cities.

The 4th is still a stronghold for Democrats, even after decennial redistricting changed the lines to include more conservative areas from Washington County and move liberal areas south of the Mississippi River into the 2nd District. Barack Obama would have won the new district by 27 percentage points in 2008, the same margin he took over Republican Mitt Romney in the 2012 presidential election. Obama won both counties in 2012, although he only eked out a win by less than 1 point in Washington.

Major Industry
Professional services, health care, government

Cities
St. Paul, Woodbury

Notable
Hockey's Minnesota Wild play in St. Paul's Xcel Energy Center.

Rep. Keith Ellison (D)

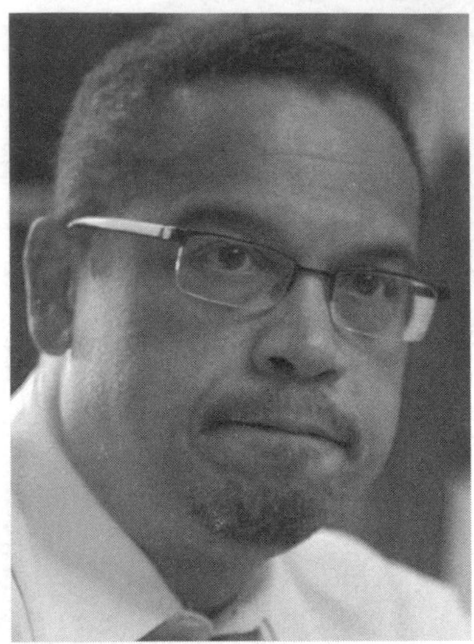

Capitol Office
225-4755
ellison.house.gov
2244 Rayburn Bldg. 20515-2305; fax 225-4886

Committees
Financial Services

Residence
Minneapolis

Born
Aug. 4, 1963; Detroit, Mich.

Religion
Muslim

Family
Divorced; four children

Education
Wayne State U., B.A. 1986 (economics), attended 1986-87 (economics); U. of Minnesota, J.D. 1990

Career
Lawyer; nonprofit law firm executive director

Political Highlights
Minn. House, 2003-06

ELECTION RESULTS

2012 GENERAL		
Keith Ellison (D)	262,102	74.5%
Chris Fields (R)	88,753	25.2%
2012 PRIMARY		
Keith Ellison (D)	30,609	89.6%
Gregg A. Iverson (D)	2,143	6.3%
Gary Boisclair (D)	1,397	4.1%
2010 GENERAL		
Keith Ellison (D)	154,833	67.7%
Joel Demos (R)	55,222	24.1%
Lynne Torgerson (I)	8,548	3.7%
Tom Schrunk (INDC)	7,446	3.3%
Michael Cavlan (IDP)	2,468	1.1%

Previous Winning Percentages
2008 (71%); 2006 (56%)

Elected 2006; 4th term

Ellison packages his beliefs as the "politics of generosity and inclusion," and he advocates societal change that leads to "real human solidarity." He is one of the most liberal — and visible — members of the House.

He co-chairs the Congressional Progressive Caucus and serves as a chief deputy whip for House Democrats in the 113th Congress (2013-14). Ellison takes to the House floor often and appears regularly on cable news shows of every ideological stripe, commenting confidently on the economy, foreign affairs and parochial issues. Unpacking his philosophy, he identifies four priority areas: civil and human rights, "prosperity for working people," environmental sustainability and peace.

Ellison's family roots extend to the civil rights movement. His maternal grandfather, Frank Martinez, worked with the NAACP in the 1950s, organizing black voters in Louisiana amid racial tension and violence. He died before Ellison was born, but Ellison's mother shared memories that made Martinez a big influence on Ellison's life. "We have successfully defeated Jim Crow segregation," Ellison said. "But you still have an entrenched disparity that is, in many ways, as damaging to people's opportunity."

Ellison worked for several years as executive director of the Legal Rights Center in Minneapolis, a nonprofit that represents, per its website, "low-income people and people of color who have legal problems associated with the juvenile justice, criminal justice and child welfare systems." His efforts included the establishment of a civilian review board for police activities. In Washington, Ellison has worked to reduce the disparity in sentencing requirements between crack and powder cocaine offenses; proponents argue the harsher penalties for crack disproportionately affect poor blacks.

He puts in time for a lot of different demographics. He serves as a vice chairman of the LGBT Equality Caucus; he favors a comprehensive overhaul of immigration laws; he urges the restoration of habeas corpus rights to enemy combatants held as part of the war on terrorism; and he wants a ban on racial profiling by law enforcement. Ellison, the first Muslim elected to Congress, opposed 2011 hearings by the Homeland Security Committee on radicalization among American Muslims.

His efforts on behalf of working people often take place on the Financial Services Committee. A "bill of rights" for credit card users enacted in 2009 contained an Ellison provision prohibiting "universal default," whereby a late payment for one card could result in higher interest rates for other cards held by the same person. Ellison defends the 2010 financial regulatory overhaul law, as well as the Consumer Financial Protection Bureau it created.

In the 113th Congress, he rolled out a proposal meant to help poorer people afford housing. It would convert the mortgage interest tax deduction into a tax credit, which would open it up to people who do not itemize their deductions. It would cut in half the amount of mortgage debt that can be factored into calculating the credit, which would create more federal revenue. That revenue would be plowed into rental assistance programs.

In a 2011 MSNBC interview, Ellison called for "direct job creation from the government," in the style of the Depression-era Works Progress Administration. The fiscal 2013 budget offered by the Progressive Caucus included substantial investments in on-the-job training programs for teachers, firefighters, construction workers and others. The fiscal 2014 budget is dubbed the "Back to Work" budget, and it includes job corps for students, child care and public works projects.

Much of Ellison's environmental work focuses on atrazine. Several times, he has introduced a bill to ban that herbicide, which is often used to kill weeds in corn crops. Ellison insists that the substance — which has been approved by the EPA — has a slew of detrimental health effects for humans.

Ellison joins many liberals in opposing tax provisions used by fossil fuel companies. "I want to take away the coal, oil and fossil fuel industries' loopholes and giveaways," he said, "and do some equalization with renewable energy." The fiscal 2014 CPC budget also includes a carbon tax.

Ellison defines his peace efforts as "getting out of wars, promoting dialogue and diplomacy and development." He supported President Barack Obama's decision to intervene in the Libyan civil war in 2011, but Ellison has often demanded a faster withdrawal of troops from Afghanistan — he voted against the fiscal 2013 defense policy law in part because it authorizes funds for continuing operations there. Ellison has pushed for closer ties between Islamic countries and the United States and a tougher line with Israel. His resolution on a "Global Marshall Plan" would ask leading industrialized nations "to give up a small percentage of their GDP to help alleviate global poverty."

Born and raised in Detroit, Ellison is the third of five sons. His mother was a social worker and his father a psychiatrist. Ellison and three of his siblings became lawyers while one became a doctor. He credits his parents with emphasizing hard work, education and "standing for what you believe in."

Ellison converted to Islam at age 19 while studying at Wayne State University. He moved to Minnesota for law school, and on graduating he worked for three years at a private law firm handling commercial and real estate litigation. After his five-year stint at the Legal Rights Center, he returned to private practice to support a growing family. He successfully ran for the Minnesota House in 2002.

Democrat Martin Olav Sabo chose to end his House career after 28 years, and Ellison won the 2006 primary for the race to succeed him with 41 percent of the vote. Republican candidate Alan Fine, a Jewish business consultant, criticized Ellison for articles he had written in law school defending Nation of Islam leader Louis Farrakhan against charges of anti-Semitism. American Jewish World, a Jewish newspaper in Minneapolis, still endorsed Ellison, who took 56 percent of the vote.

At a ceremonial swearing-in, Ellison took his oath on a copy of the Koran once owned by Thomas Jefferson, drawing some criticism from a handful of conservative politicians and commentators.

"Honestly, I never really understood myself as making any historical points by being elected to Congress," Ellison said. "To me, the most important thing would be to just serve well."

Ellison has won his re-elections by wide margins.

Key Votes

2012	
Extend a Social Security payroll tax cut and unemployment benefits	NO
Ease securities rules to expand small-business access to capital	YES
Extend for one year subsidized student loan interest rates financed by a cut in health care spending	NO
Cite Attorney General Eric H. Holder Jr. for contempt of Congress	?
Create a visa program for foreign graduates in high-tech fields	NO
Extend most Bush-era income tax rates while allowing rates for top-bracket earners to rise (Jan. 1, 2013)	YES
2011	
Strike funding for F-35 alternative engine	YES
Prevent EPA from regulating greenhouse gas emissions to address climate change	NO
Extend certain provisions of Patriot Act for four years	NO
Declare opposition to use of ground troops in Libya	NO
Overhaul patent law	YES
Pass compromise debt limit increase plan and establish future spending limits	NO
Allow consideration of measures to implement three trade agreements	NO

CQ Vote Studies

	PARTY UNITY		PRESIDENTIAL SUPPORT	
	SUPPORT	OPPOSE	SUPPORT	OPPOSE
2012	99%	1%	91%	9%
2011	99%	1%	84%	16%
2010	97%	3%	83%	17%
2009	99%	1%	95%	5%
2008	99%	1%	13%	87%

Interest Groups

	AFL-CIO	ADA	CCUS	ACU
2012	95%	100%	33%	0%
2011	100%	90%	20%	8%
2010	100%	100%	13%	0%
2009	100%	95%	40%	0%
2008	100%	100%	56%	0%

Minnesota 5

Minneapolis and suburbs

A metropolitan hub in a mostly suburban and rural state, the 5th District includes the city of Minneapolis and some of the city's near-in suburbs to the west. Very similar to the map from before decennial redistricting after the 2010 census, the current 5th is located almost entirely within Hennepin County, with some of the district stretching north in Anoka County and east in Ramsey County.

Even though Minneapolis is known for its Scandinavian heritage, the district is the most racially and ethnically diverse district in the state, with a 30 percent minority population. Blacks comprise about 16 percent of the residents, while Hispanics make up about 10 percent — their largest representation of any district statewide. Hmong, Tibetans and Somalis account for more distinct subsets of the population here.

The population of central Minneapolis has grown since 2000 as residents from surrounding suburbs have returned to the urban core. A number of high-culture attractions — including the University of Minnesota, the Guthrie Theater and the Walker Art Center — draw residents to downtown neighborhoods along the Mississippi River. Minneapolis boasts the second-most theaters per capita, trailing only New York City.

During the recent economic recession, Minneapolis fared better than many Midwestern cities. The district benefits from a well-educated population, several large corporations — including Target, Ameriprise Financial and U.S. Bancorp — and Minneapolis-St. Paul International Airport, a major hub for Delta Air Lines.

The 5th is one of the state's reliably Democratic districts. Barack Obama won the district with nearly three fourths of the vote in the last two presidential contests, and Democratic candidates dominate elections for state offices.

Major Industry
Professional services, finance, health care, higher education

Cities
Minneapolis, St. Louis Park, Richfield

Notable
The "Jucy Lucy" burger — an inside out cheeseburger — was created in the district at a Minneapolis bar, although exactly which one remains in dispute; The Depot ice skating rink was once a Milwaukee Road train shed.

Rep. Michele Bachmann (R)

Capitol Office
225-2331
bachmann.house.gov
2417 Rayburn Bldg. 20515-2306; fax 225-6475

Committees
Financial Services
Select Intelligence

Residence
Stillwater

Born
April 6, 1956; Waterloo, Iowa

Religion
Non-denominational Christian

Family
Husband, Marcus Bachmann; five children

Education
Winona State U., B.A. 1978 (political science & English); Oral Roberts U., J.D. 1986; College of William & Mary, LL.M. 1988 (tax law)

Career
Homemaker; U.S. Treasury Department lawyer

Political Highlights
Candidate for Stillwater Area School District Board, 1999; Minn. Senate, 2001-07; sought Republican nomination for president, 2012

ELECTION RESULTS

2012 GENERAL		
Michele Bachmann (R)	179,240	50.5%
Jim Graves (D)	174,944	49.3%
2012 PRIMARY		
Michele Bachmann (R)	14,569	80.3%
Stephen Thompson (R)	2,322	12.8%
Aubrey Immelman (R)	1,242	6.8%
2010 GENERAL		
Michele Bachmann (R)	159,476	52.5%
Tarryl Clark (D)	120,846	39.8%
Bob Anderson (INDC)	17,698	5.8%
Aubrey Immelman (I)	5,490	1.8%

Previous Winning Percentages
2008 (46%); 2006 (50%)

Elected 2006; 4th term

Bachmann's political identity has been only loosely tied to Congress. She is instead a national conservative figure, riding a whirlwind of publicity that has been energetic, elevating, chaotic and destructive. But her time in the House seems to be ending — she announced in May 2013 that she will not seek a fifth term.

Bachmann (BOCK-man) was a relatively unknown freshman when a 2008 appearance on MSNBC brought her to the nation's attention. At the not-so-subtle goading of "Hardball" host Chris Matthews, she said that presidential candidate Barack Obama "may have anti-American views." Bachmann expressed regret for her phrasing, but her comments resulted in a huge spike in campaign donations for Bachmann's opponent — and Bachmann herself. "She's a self-created figure, but she was created by accident," Oklahoma Republican Rep. Tom Cole said in 2011.

Bachmann made use of social media and judiciously chosen television appearances to become a mouthpiece for those frustrated with Democratic policies. In the 111th Congress (2009-10), she made appeals to the public for populist-style protests of the health care overhaul. Her small-government beliefs led her in 2010 to form the House Tea Party Caucus, a group of about 50 Republicans dedicated to "fiscal responsibility, adherence to the Constitution and limited government." She used a tea party group's website to give a response to Obama's 2011 State of the Union address.

Her possible apex was a bid during the 112th Congress (2011-12) for the GOP presidential nomination. Bachmann won a straw poll in Iowa in 2011 and had respectable showings in debates showcasing a large field of GOP contenders.

But more-conventional Republicans gave Bachmann a wide berth. Her penchant for questionable statements when criticizing Democrats opened her to attacks — fact-checkers have had several field days vetting Bachmann's media appearances. Reports surfaced that Bachmann sometimes suffers debilitating migraines and has high turnover for key posts on her congressional staff. She finished sixth in the January 2012 Iowa caucuses and withdrew from the race.

Meanwhile, critics questioned her work in the House. Bachmann has a short list of legislative achievements, and she was resoundingly defeated in her bid to become chairwoman of the House Republican Conference for the 112th Congress. The activities of the Tea Party Caucus have been relatively meager under her leadership.

And redistricting following the 2010 census almost ended her House career. She accused mapmakers of having a "liberal bias" as they put her home in a district with Democratic Rep. Betty McCollum. Bachmann opted to avoid McCollum and ran in the redrawn 6th District, turning her attention to that race after ending her presidential bid. A ridiculously huge fundraising advantage helped her defeat Democratic businessman Jim Graves — by 1 point.

Bachmann had a lower profile in the early months of the 113th Congress (2013-14) before announcing her retirement. She said eight years was enough, while denying that she was motivated by a possible rematch with Graves in 2014 or investigations into the fundraising for her presidential campaign.

Although Bachmann is a divisive figure, colleagues often describe her as authentic and pleasant. Minnesota Sen. Al Franken, one of the most liberal Democrats, said in a 2011 magazine interview that he likes Bachmann, if not her politics.

She is a social and fiscal conservative and a defense hawk. She sits on the Financial Services Committee, where she has proposed outright repeal of the 2010 financial regulatory overhaul. In the 112th Congress, she cast votes against several spending bills and fiscal packages that she said did not do enough to contain the deficit. Her only unwavering support of spending is for veterans and active-duty troops; she has proposed a freeze on the costs paid by those in the military's health care system.

Bachmann was added to the Intelligence Committee in 2011. She was skeptical of the newly elected government of Egypt, which was led by the Muslim Brotherhood; in 2012, Bachmann joined in letters to several federal departments saying the group is bent on "destroying the Western civilization from within." She was rebuked by Arizona Republican Sen. John McCain when she suggested that Huma Abedin — a top aide to Secretary of State Hillary Rodham Clinton — could be connected to the organization. "These attacks have no logic, no basis and no merit, and they need to stop," McCain said on the Senate floor. He called the accusations "specious and degrading."

She did enjoy a bipartisan success in the 112th Congress. In 2012, Obama signed a bill, championed by Bachmann and Minnesota Democratic Sen. Amy Klobuchar, to eliminate regulatory hurdles for construction of a bridge over the St. Croix River between Wisconsin and Minnesota.

Bachmann was born in Waterloo, Iowa. Her mother worked in a factory before staying home to raise four children. Her father was an engineer. When Bachmann was a teenager, her father accepted a job with Honeywell in the Twin Cities. A few years later, her parents divorced.

After working for Jimmy Carter's 1976 campaign, Bachmann made her first trek to Washington to attend Carter's inauguration. She says that while reading Gore Vidal's "Burr" during the train ride home, she realized she was no longer a Democrat. She said she thought the book — a novel about Aaron Burr, a Revolutionary War hero and suspected traitor — was mocking the Founding Fathers. Bachmann and her husband, Marcus, a clinical therapist, married in 1978. They later settled in St. Paul, where Bachmann was a federal tax litigation attorney.

She became a local activist after objecting to the state's performance-based Profile of Learning program; she favors local control of schools. Bachmann was encouraged to enter politics but lost a race in 1999 for the Stillwater Area School District Board. A year later, she won a campaign to unseat 28-year Republican incumbent Gary Laidig in the state Senate.

When Republican Rep. Mark Kennedy decided to run for the U.S. Senate in 2006, Bachmann entered the race to succeed him. She called herself a "woman on a mission" and defeated Democrat Patty Wetterling by 8 points. She eked out a 3-point win over Democrat El Tinklenberg in 2008, after her "Hardball" controversy. Capitalizing on her new status as a fundraising juggernaut, she spent $8.5 million on her successful 2010 campaign.

Key Votes

2012	
Extend a Social Security payroll tax cut and unemployment benefits	NO
Ease securities rules to expand small-business access to capital	YES
Extend for one year subsidized student loan interest rates financed by a cut in health care spending	YES
Cite Attorney General Eric H. Holder Jr. for contempt of Congress	YES
Create a visa program for foreign graduates in high-tech fields	YES
Extend most Bush-era income tax rates while allowing rates for top-bracket earners to rise (Jan. 1, 2013)	NO
2011	
Strike funding for F-35 alternative engine	NO
Prevent EPA from regulating greenhouse gas emissions to address climate change	YES
Extend certain provisions of Patriot Act for four years	YES
Declare opposition to use of ground troops in Libya	YES
Overhaul patent law	NO
Pass compromise debt limit increase plan and establish future spending limits	NO
Allow consideration of measures to implement three trade agreements	?

CQ Vote Studies

	PARTY UNITY		PRESIDENTIAL SUPPORT	
	SUPPORT	OPPOSE	SUPPORT	OPPOSE
2012	97%	3%	15%	85%
2011	94%	6%	23%	77%
2010	98%	2%	26%	74%
2009	98%	2%	14%	86%
2008	96%	4%	75%	25%

Interest Groups

	AFL-CIO	ADA	CCUS	ACU
2012	5%	5%	91%	100%
2011	5%	0%	80%	95%
2010	0%	5%	75%	100%
2009	5%	0%	73%	100%
2008	7%	0%	94%	100%

Minnesota 6

Outer Twin Cities suburbs; St. Cloud

The 6th comprises an arc of far Twin Cities suburbs sweeping from the Interstate 35 East-West split around the 3rd District to the Minnesota River. It then extends to the northwest to St. Cloud in Stearns County. Taking in portions of Benton, Carver, Stearns, Sherburne, Hennepin, Wright, Anoka and Washington counties, the district is very similar to its predecessor prior to decennial redistricting. The 6th did lose parts of western Stearns County and a portion of Washington County to the east of St. Paul while adding a piece of Carver County in the west.

The second-least diverse district in the state, the 6th has small black and Asian populations — less than 10 percent of the district's residents are minorities. Overall, the area's population is growing rapidly, which required the remapping process to cut more than 96,000 residents out of the 6th for the 2012 elections. Wright County, in particular, grew by 39 percent between 2000 and 2010.

The district's business interests are diverse, ranging from financial services to industrial production. St. Cloud, a city historically rooted in granite mining and trade interests, hosts companies such as ING Direct, Xcel Energy and Gold N' Plump poultry, and many businesses gravitate to the state's Interstate 94 thoroughfare, which cuts through the 6th. St. Cloud is also home to its namesake St. Cloud State University and its more than 17,000 students.

Agriculture is a large part of life here, especially amid high-quality farmland west of Minneapolis. Corn and soybeans are major crops. Benton County, in the district's north, is largely agrarian, with German Catholic roots.

The 6th is a reliably conservative district. John McCain would have won the new 6th with 55 percent in the 2008 presidential election, and Mitt Romney took 56 percent in 2012 — both of those percentages were the Republicans' statewide bests. The city of St. Cloud and the border region with Wisconsin east of St. Paul provide some Democratic votes.

Major Industry
Professional services, finance, agriculture

Cities
St. Cloud, Blaine

Notable
"A Prairie Home Companion" host Garrison Keillor was born in Anoka.

Rep. Collin C. Peterson (D)

Capitol Office
225-2165
collinpeterson.house.gov
2109 Rayburn Bldg. 20515-2307; fax 225-1593

Committees
Agriculture - Ranking Member

Residence
Detroit Lakes

Born
June 29, 1944; Fargo, N.D.

Religion
Lutheran

Family
Divorced; three children

Education
Moorhead State College, B.A. 1966 (accounting)

Military
Minn. National Guard, 1963-69

Career
Accountant

Political Highlights
Minn. Senate, 1977-87; sought Democratic nomination for U.S. House, 1982; Democratic nominee for U.S. House, 1984, 1986; sought Democratic nomination for U.S. House, 1988

ELECTION RESULTS

2012 GENERAL		
Collin C. Peterson (D)	197,791	60.4%
Lee Byberg (R)	114,151	34.8%
Adam Steele (INDC)	15,298	4.7%
2012 PRIMARY		
Collin C. Peterson (D)		unopposed
2010 GENERAL		
Collin C. Peterson (D)	133,096	55.2%
Lee Byberg (R)	90,652	37.6%
Gene Waldorf (I)	9,317	3.9%
Glen Menze (INDC)	7,839	3.2%

Previous Winning Percentages
2008 (72%); 2006 (70%); 2004 (66%); 2002 (65%); 2000 (69%); 1998 (72%); 1996 (68%); 1994 (51%); 1992 (50%); 1990 (54%)

Elected 1990; 12th term

Peterson is a straightforward operator whose overriding concern is the farm economy. Often going his own way rather than voting with his party's leaders, he serves as a bellwether for moderates in the Democratic Caucus.

His centrist legislative style was more common when he first came to the House in 1991. Peterson is happy to give up ground in committee, get measures through the House and let conference committees meet in the middle. "I'm too old to retrain," he says.

He held the gavel of the Agriculture Committee when Democrats were in the majority from 2007 through 2010, and Peterson shepherded the 2008 reauthorization of agriculture and nutrition programs (known as the farm bill) to enactment, overcoming a veto from President George W. Bush.

Peterson set aside thoughts of retirement in hopes of working on the next iteration of the farm bill — but the 2012 edition turned out to be a tough row to hoe. No long-term extension was enacted, and Peterson is back for another term as the ranking member of the Agriculture Committee in the 113th Congress (2013-14).

Peterson and Chairman Frank D. Lucas of Oklahoma did move a bipartisan bill through their committee in the 112th Congress (2011-12). There were significant differences with a Senate-passed version, but both bills included an end to direct payments to farmers and a bolstering of crop insurance programs. The House bill had projected savings running into the tens of billions of dollars (much if it from nutrition assistance programs), because "we're willing to do our part," Peterson said.

GOP leaders, however, declined to bring the House bill to the floor in the months before the 2012 election, fearing a messy debate pitting some farm-state Republicans against fiscal conservatives looking to shrink the bill further. The 2008 farm law expired for a few months, before a one-year extension was agreed to in the final moments of the 112th Congress. "I'm not all that upset about that," Peterson said in 2013, since he was in charge of the 2008 law.

Peterson pays extra attention to the safety net for dairy farmers and policies protecting sugar producers. He wrote the dairy language that made it into both chambers' 2012 bills and has said the industry is in "the most danger" if a full reauthorization is not enacted. A farm bill approved by the panel in May 2013 included both extensions of sugar provisions and Peterson's preferred "stabilization" program to prevent overproduction of milk.

Peterson sees political parties and voters as increasingly captive to the "take-no-prisoners attitude" of their more extreme factions. "A lot of the electorate just believes that they can have it their way and to hell with everybody else," he said. "It just doesn't work that way. You've got to be practical."

A founder of the fiscally conservative Blue Dog Coalition, he sees recent budgetary battles as symptomatic of that extremism. In 2011, Peterson voted for a balanced-budget amendment to the Constitution. He has shown interest in budgets based on the ideas of a 2010 special fiscal commission, which is known as Simpson-Bowles. Generally, they proposed to cut deficits by $4 trillion over 10 years through a mix of spending reduction, revenue increases and entitlement program changes.

Peterson has been sympathetic to the notion that some regulation stifles economic growth, and he prefers regulations to be "principle-based" rather than disciplinary. "It's not about convicting people," he said. "It's about discovering when something goes out of whack in the marketplace and having enough information." He cites the Commodity Futures Trading Commission as an example for other agencies to follow.

The EPA has been a frequent target of Peterson's, and he says that rules under the Obama administration have been unnecessarily complex and tinged with ideology. After winning concessions that he felt helped protect farmers, he reluctantly supported Democrats' 2009 bill to regulate greenhouse gas emissions through a cap-and-trade system. However, in 2011 he was one of three Democratic co-sponsors of legislation to block the EPA from regulating greenhouse gases without congressional approval. Of all current House Democrats, Peterson has the lowest lifetime rating on the scorecard of the League of Conservation Voters.

In the 111th Congress (2009-10), Peterson sat on the conference committee that produced the final version of the 2010 financial regulatory law. He offered a key compromise that required banks to set up firewalls between their deposit banking operations and their most risky financial products. Peterson has said he originally wanted to ban credit default swaps outright, likening the financial instruments to casino gambling.

Peterson was not on board with his party as it assembled an overhaul of the health care system in the 111th Congress. He voted against both the House version and the final version of the measure, faulting the legislation for not addressing regional imbalances in the hospital and doctor reimbursements made by Medicare. But he did not vote to repeal the law in 2011 or 2012.

Peterson is a pilot and avid sportsman. He has earned high marks from the National Rifle Association; he once boasted that he has "more dead animals on my wall than anybody in this Congress, except for [Alaska Republican] Don Young." He gets along well enough with Republicans that he was the lone Democrat in a now-defunct five-lawmaker country rock band called the Second Amendments. Their gigs included performances for U.S. troops overseas.

He grew up on his family's farm near the North Dakota border and learned self-sufficiency at an early age. Peterson used money he earned on the farm to buy a guitar, and at 16 he joined a touring band. He gave up his dream of stardom when it became clear that he would have to quit college to pursue it. He chose accounting as a career.

He got his start in politics with 10 years in the state Senate. In the 1980s, he made four unsuccessful bids for a U.S. House seat. He finally broke through in 1990 against Republican incumbent Arlan Stangeland, who was under scrutiny for misuse of his House credit card. He has won with relative ease since scratching out close victories in 1992 and 1994.

Peterson has indicated that he might not seek re-election in 2014. "I'm not one of these guys that they'll be pushing around in a wheelchair," he said. Republicans are targeting his district, as Republican Mitt Romney defeated Barack Obama there by 10 points in the 2012 presidential race.

Key Votes

2012	
Extend a Social Security payroll tax cut and unemployment benefits	NO
Ease securities rules to expand small-business access to capital	YES
Extend for one year subsidized student loan interest rates financed by a cut in health care spending	YES
Cite Attorney General Eric H. Holder Jr. for contempt of Congress	YES
Create a visa program for foreign graduates in high-tech fields	YES
Extend most Bush-era income tax rates while allowing rates for top-bracket earners to rise (Jan. 1, 2013)	NO
2011	
Strike funding for F-35 alternative engine	YES
Prevent EPA from regulating greenhouse gas emissions to address climate change	YES
Extend certain provisions of Patriot Act for four years	YES
Declare opposition to use of ground troops in Libya	YES
Overhaul patent law	YES
Pass compromise debt limit increase plan and establish future spending limits	YES
Allow consideration of measures to implement three trade agreements	YES

CQ Vote Studies

	Party Unity		Presidential Support	
	Support	Oppose	Support	Oppose
2012	46%	54%	25%	75%
2011	47%	53%	57%	43%
2010	81%	19%	69%	31%
2009	87%	13%	83%	17%
2008	91%	9%	21%	79%

Interest Groups

	AFL-CIO	ADA	CCUS	ACU
2012	67%	20%	100%	52%
2011	79%	60%	63%	40%
2010	64%	40%	88%	21%
2009	71%	55%	40%	24%
2008	80%	80%	50%	20%

Minnesota 7

West — Moorhead, Willmar

Minnesota's 7th District stretches nearly the entire length of the state from the Canada border to Rock County near Iowa. Primarily rural, the 7th includes some of the state's most popular lake resorts and most productive farmland. Interstate 94 bisects the region, connecting Fargo-Moorhead with the Twin Cities. Predominately white, the 7th also includes the White Earth Indian Reservation in Mahnomen, Becker and Clearwater counties.

Agriculture drives the regional economy. Farmers in the southern portion of the district primarily harvest a rotation of corn and soybeans. An increase in worldwide demand for corn, along with a robust renewable energy sector, has driven up the price of land in the area and made corn a profitable crop. Sugar beets, wheat and sunflower seeds also are grown.

The district also benefits from agriculture-affiliated business. Jennie-O Turkeys, a subsidiary of Hormel foods, operates a processing plant in Willmar. The R.D. Offutt Company — the largest potato grower in the nation — has a significant investment in the area's agricultural sector.

To the north, from Douglas County up through Beltrami County, the economy relies heavily on tourism and recreation. Resorts along the region's many lakes offer popular getaways for families in the Upper Midwest. Itasca State Park and the Two Inlets State Forest offer year-round opportunities for outdoor recreation, including hiking, fishing and camping. The fall hunting seasons also bring outdoor enthusiasts to the area. Manufacturing stabilizes the economy in the north as well. Polaris Industries, which manufactures snowmobiles and all-terrain vehicles, operates an assembly plant in Roseau, and Marvin Windows operates a plant in nearby Warroad.

The 7th is politically competitive. Rep. Collin C. Peterson — a moderate Democrat — has sailed to victory since first being elected in 1990. Republicans, however, have carried recent presidential and gubernatorial elections: Mitt Romney took 54 percent of the presidential vote here in 2012.

Major Industry
Agriculture, poultry processing, light manufacturing, tourism

Cities
Moorhead, Willmar

Notable
Winona LaDuke — one-time vice presidential candidate for the Green Party, American Indian activist and member of the Anishinabe tribe — lives on the White Earth Reservation.

Rep. Rick Nolan (D)

Capitol Office
225-6211
nolan.house.gov
2447 Rayburn Bldg. 20515-2308; fax 225-0699

Committees
Agriculture
Transportation & Infrastructure

Residence
Crosby

Born
Dec. 17, 1943; Brainerd, Minn.

Religion
Roman Catholic

Family
Wife, Mary Nolan; four children

Education
Saint John's U., attended 1962-64; U. of Minnesota, B.A. 1966 (political science); U. of Maryland, attended 1967; St. Cloud State U., attended 1969

Career
Real estate broker; sawmill owner; international business consultant; state export official; export management company owner; catalog sales company executive; teacher; congressional aide

Political Highlights
Democratic nominee for U.S. House, 1972; Minn. House, 1969-73; U.S. House, 1975-81

ELECTION RESULTS

2012 GENERAL		
Rick Nolan (D)	191,976	54.3%
Chip Cravaack (R)	160,520	45.4%
2012 PRIMARY		
Rick Nolan (D)	20,840	38.3%
Tarryl Clark (D)	17,554	32.2%
Jeff Anderson (D)	16,035	29.5%

Previous Winning Percentages
1978 (55%); 1976 (60%); 1974 (55%)

Elected 2012; 4th term

Also served 1975-81

Nolan started a promising House career in the 1970s, then walked away from Congress as the Reagan era was beginning. His personal odyssey took him through a series of jobs in the public and private sectors and brought him back to the House 32 years later — with his liberal beliefs largely unchanged.

He grew up in the Minnesota lake country, raised by his postal worker father and homemaker mother. After getting a degree in political science from the University of Minnesota in 1966, he worked in Washington as a staffer to Minnesota Sen. Walter F. Mondale.

Nolan returned to Minnesota after a few years and taught social studies at the high school level. And he embarked on his own public career, getting elected at the age of 24 to the state House. He served two terms, then lost a 1972 campaign for the U.S. House.

The post-Watergate election in 1974 was friendlier to Democrats, and Nolan defeated Republican Jon Grunseth to win an open seat in the 6th District. The same year, Democrat James L. Oberstar won the first of 18 terms in the 8th District.

Nolan was recognized as a committed liberal in the first phase of his career. He strongly opposed the Vietnam War and backed robust welfare programs.

He was particularly outspoken when trying to direct federal assistance to farmers — in some cases, a lot more assistance than Democratic colleagues preferred. Nolan served on the Agriculture Committee his first three terms and was the primary House sponsor of two major measures: a 1980 law expanding the Agriculture Department's resources for rural development initiatives, and the 1977 resolution encouraging creation of a presidential commission on world hunger, on which Nolan later served. He tried to make it a federal priority to preserve farmland.

His decision to voluntarily depart Washington after three terms surprised many people, given Nolan's youth and relative success as a lawmaker. But he told The Washington Post that the job had strained his personal life, leading to a divorce, and that he was fed up with the institution.

"Congress is relatively impotent to make the changes the country needs: mandatory wage and price controls, drastic tax reform, national health insurance, arms cutbacks, new directions in energy, mandatory conservation, a redirection of agriculture," he said.

Nolan also told the Post that his service had made him more "liberal and radicalized." In his third term, he led a campaign to "draft" Democratic Sen. Edward M. Kennedy for the 1980 presidential race, to the detriment of President Jimmy Carter and his vice president — Mondale.

On leaving Congress in 1981, Nolan helped found a political action committee to promote rural causes, saying that rural America "has been severely and grossly neglected." He also started a small export management company that worked in the agriculture sector.

He later worked on exports on a state level, as the head of the Minnesota World Trade Center Corp., a state-supported entity helping Minnesota businesses that were active in global markets. For a time he owned and operated a sawmill, which is now owned by his daughter and son-in-law.

Nolan's politics haven't changed dramatically since his first run in the House. In 2013, he joined the Congressional Progressive Caucus. He outlined priorities such as defending Social Security, Medicare and Medicaid from budget cuts and ending all "wars of choice."

Nolan is back on the Agriculture Committee, as well as its subcommittee on forestry. The economy of the 8th District has a lot of ties to timber. He says he's particularly interested in helping small and medium-size family farms as Congress again tries to write a long-term reauthorization of farm programs.

He also has a seat on the Transportation and Infrastructure Committee. Nolan requested and received four subcommittee assignments on that panel. For his district, "surface and water transportation are critically important arteries that support our taconite-timber-tourism-based economy," he said. He would like to see more federal spending on infrastructure programs.

Nolan has said that he is more prepared than ever to contribute effectively to Congress. But he has panned some developments in national politics since his departure. He spent the first few weeks of his fourth term railing against the state of campaign finance law. In February 2013, he teamed with Wisconsin Democrat Mark Pocan to propose a constitutional amendment that would eliminate First Amendment protections for campaign spending and declare that "artificial entities," such as corporations, do not have constitutional rights.

Nolan's victory in 2012 came against one of the most surprising members of the 112th Congress (2011-12). Republican Chip Cravaack, a former airline pilot who held no prior elected office, stunned the political world in 2010 by defeating Oberstar, the chairman of the Transportation and Infrastructure Committee. It was a strong year for Republicans overall, and conservative elements in the 8th District weren't pleased with Oberstar's votes for President Barack Obama's agenda.

Democrats saw the victory as a fluke, and Nolan decided in July 2011 to seek the party's nomination for 2012. In an expensive primary election, Nolan received the official endorsement of the Democratic-Farmer-Labor Party (he is a former DFL vice chairman). He won 38 percent of the vote, enough to best former state Sen. Tarryl Clark and former Duluth City Council President Jeff Anderson.

As he faced off with Cravaack, Nolan campaigned against the House Republican agenda from the 112th Congress. Cravaack emphasized some of his ties to organized labor — he walked picket lines as a pilot. But he also had a slight image problem, as his family had moved to New Hampshire to be closer to his wife's new job in Boston. Cravaack was splitting his time between two states and Washington.

Outside groups spent heavily against each of the candidates: $3.7 million against Nolan and $4.7 million against Cravaack. Republican-leaning groups criticized Nolan's record as ultra-liberal, but his experience as a politician paid off. Former St. Paul Mayor George Latimer, who worked with Nolan on the World Trade Center project, told the Star Tribune that "the guy had this positive energy that comes out of him, and it's still there."

Nolan opened up a lead in the polls and won by almost 9 points.

Minnesota 8

Northeast — Duluth, Iron Range

Minnesota's 8th District covers the northeastern corner of the state, stretching from the Canada border to outer-ring Twin Cities suburbs in the south. Bluffs overlooking the Lake Superior shoreline run along the district's eastern border. Dense forestland in the northern Arrowhead region gives way to open plains and farmland in the central part of the state.

The district is best known as home to the Iron Range — the once-prosperous iron ore and taconite mining region just northwest of Duluth. A booming mining industry at the turn of the 20th century attracted Finnish, Swedish and Croatian immigrants, who formed small, closely knit communities in Hibbing, Cloquet and Virginia. The industry peaked in the 1950s and in recent decades has declined along with the domestic demand for steel. Recent investments by Chinese companies, however, have revived a few local communities.

The logging and forestry sectors provide employment throughout the district. St. Louis and Itasca counties lead the state in timber harvesting. Paper mills also support small towns in the area, even though the industry has experienced layoffs in recent years. UPM Bland Paper Mill in Grand Rapids, which produces coated magazine paper, remains one of the largest employers in the region. Other local mills have switched from producing paper pulp to cellulose pulp, which is used in textiles.

The region relies on tourism to stabilize the local economy. The North Shore along Lake Superior provides opportunities for hiking and camping in the summer. Steep hillsides in the state's Arrowhead region also provide boast prime locations for skiing and snowboarding in the winter.

Once considered safe territory for Democrats, the district sent a Republican to the U.S. House in 2010 at the expense of 18-term Rep. James L. Oberstar. However in 2012, GOP Rep. Chip Cravaack lost to a Democrat returning to the House after a long hiatus, and the district gave Barack Obama 52 percent of its presidential vote.

Major Industry
Mining, timber, recreation

Cities
Duluth, Hibbing

Notable
The U.S. Hockey Hall of Fame is in Eveleth.

MISSISSIPPI

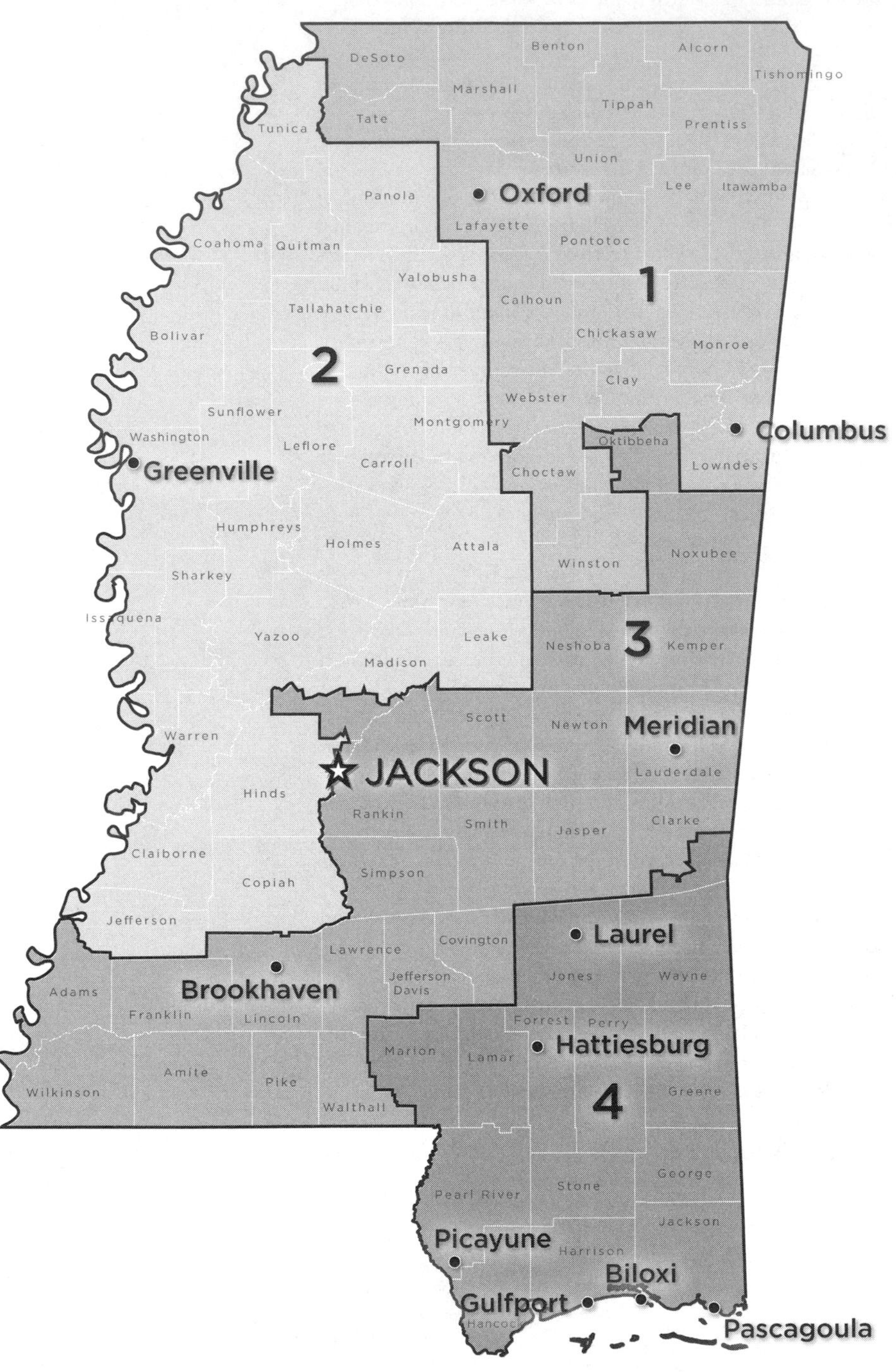

Gov. Phil Bryant (R)

First elected: 2011

Length of term: 4 years

Term expires: 1/16

Salary: $122,160

Phone: (601) 359-3150

Residence: Brandon

Born: Dec. 9, 1954; Moorhead, Miss.

Religion: Methodist

Family: Wife, Deborah Bryant; two children

Education: Hinds Junior College, A.A. 1975 (police science); U. of Southern Mississippi, B.A. 1977 (criminal justice); Mississippi College, M.S. 1988 (political science)

Career: Insurance claims investigator; police officer

Political highlights: Sought Republican nomination for Rankin County Board of Supervisors, 1988; Miss. House, 1992-96; Miss. auditor, 1996-2008; lieutenant governor, 2008-11

ELECTION RESULTS

2011 GENERAL

Phil Bryant (R)	544,851	61%
Johnny L. DuPree (D)	348,617	39%

Lt. Gov. Tate Reeves (R)

First elected: 2011

Length of term: 4 years

Term expires: 1/16

Salary: $60,000

Phone: (601) 359-3200

LEGISLATURE

Legislature: 90 days January-April

Senate: 52 members, 4-year terms

2013 ratios: 32 R, 20 D; 44 men, 8 women

Salary: $10,000

Phone: (601) 359-3202

House: 122 members, 4-year terms

2013 ratios: 64 R, 57 D, 1 vacancy; 100 men, 21 women

Salary: $10,000

Phone: (601) 359-3360

TERM LIMITS

Governor: 2 terms

Senate: No

House: No

URBAN STATISTICS

CITY	POPULATION
Jackson	173,514
Gulfport	67,793
Southaven	48,982
Hattiesburg	45,989
Biloxi	44,054

REGISTERED VOTERS

Voters do not register by party.

POPULATION

2010 population	2,967,297
2000 population	2,844,658
1990 population	2,573,216
Percent change (2000-2010)	+4.3%
Rank among states (2010)	31
Median age	35
Born in state	71.8%
Foreign born	1.9%
Violent crime rate	281/100,000
Poverty level	21.9%
Federal workers	37,510
Military	9,895

ELECTIONS

STATE ELECTION OFFICIAL
(601) 359-6360

DEMOCRATIC PARTY
(601) 969-2913

REPUBLICAN PARTY
(601) 948-5191

MISCELLANEOUS

Web: www.ms.gov

Capital: Jackson

U.S. CONGRESS

Senate: 2 Republicans

House: 3 Republicans, 1 Democrat

STATISTICS BY DISTRICT

District	2012 Vote for President: Obama	Romney	2008 Vote for President: Obama	McCain	Black	Asian	Hispanic	Median Income	Over 64	Under 20	College Education	Rural	Sq. Miles
1	37%	62%	37%	62%	26%	<1%	3%	$39,353	13%	29%	17%	59%	10,573
2	66	33	64	35	65	<1	2	31,084	12	30	19	45	15,552
3	39	60	38	61	35	1	2	38,630	13	28	24	57	12,754
4	31	68	31	68	23	2	4	39,095	13	28	20	42	8,044
STATE	**44**	**55**	**43**	**56**	**37**	**1**	**3**	**36,919**	**13**	**29**	**20**	**51**	**46,923**
U.S.	**51**	**47**	**53**	**46**	**12**	**5**	**17**	**50,052**	**13**	**27**	**29**	**21**	**3,531,905**

Sen. Thad Cochran (R)

Capitol Office
224-5054
cochran.senate.gov
113 Dirksen Bldg. 20510-2402; fax 224-9450

Committees
Agriculture, Nutrition & Forestry - Ranking Member
Appropriations
Rules & Administration

Residence
Oxford

Born
Dec. 7, 1937; Pontotoc, Miss.

Religion
Baptist

Family
Wife, Rose Cochran; two children

Education
U. of Mississippi, B.A. 1959 (psychology), J.D. 1965

Military Service
Navy, 1959-61

Career
Lawyer

Political Highlights
U.S. House, 1973-78

ELECTION RESULTS

2008 GENERAL

Thad Cochran (R)	766,111	61.4%
Erik Fleming (D)	480,915	38.6%

2008 PRIMARY

Thad Cochran (R) unopposed

Previous Winning Percentages
2002 (85%); 1996 (71%); 1990 (100%); 1984 (61%); 1978 (45%); 1976 House Election (76%); 1974 House Election (70%); 1972 House Election (48%)

Elected 1978; 6th term

Cordial and soft-spoken, Cochran practices a style of politics that has gone out of vogue in recent years. He remains an effective behind-the-scenes power broker and steers whatever funds he can to Mississippi. Although he is no longer the top Republican appropriator, he is looking out for Southern farmers as the ranking member of the Agriculture, Nutrition and Forestry Committee.

Cochran came to Congress in a different era. He was elected to the House before the Watergate scandal and joined the Senate during the Carter administration. He's a defender of Senate procedure and works politely with fellow lawmakers regardless of their political beliefs.

In 2005, Cochran became the chairman of the Appropriations Committee, and he stayed on as the ranking member when Democrats took control of the Senate in 2007. The panel's Democratic leader was Daniel K. Inouye of Hawaii, a kindred spirit and friend to Cochran.

Inouye died in December 2012, and Cochran stepped aside as ranking member weeks later — the GOP has term limits for panel leaders. But in the 113th Congress (2013-14), he still has considerable sway as a senior member of the committee and the ranking member of its Defense Subcommittee.

Cochran laments the collapse of regular order in recent appropriations cycles. As chairman, he made a priority of getting all 12 annual spending bills through the Senate in his first year, rather than relying on a catchall measure to wrap up overdue work. With opponents of government spending increasingly questioning federal funding as the annual budget deficit has hovered above $1 trillion, it has been nearly impossible to achieve that goal, however.

He criticized the 2012 deal struck by congressional leaders to pass a six-month stopgap measure funding the government through the first half of fiscal 2013. "Agreeing to put the government on autopilot for six months is no great achievement," Cochran wrote. At the start of the 113th Congress, he worked on the bill to delineate spending for the remainder of the year, emphasizing that Congress needed to express its priorities for defense spending. The thought of operating on stopgap measures "is unconscionable during a time of war," he wrote.

Cochran has also been cramped by a ban on earmarks that has been in place since 2011. He grudgingly accepted the ban, which was forced by conservatives and is intended to reduce spending and eliminate the potential for corruption, but he has shown unwavering support for the constitutional right of lawmakers to direct funding back to their states. He continues to work his connections with federal agencies to get projects funded and grants steered home.

His efforts have been criticized by small-government advocates. Taxpayers for Common Sense placed him among the most prolific earmarkers in Congress for several years running. Cochran has maintained that his earmarks always receive his colleagues' blessings and greatly benefit his poor, rural state. Among the chief recipients of his earmarks have been universities and communities ravaged by Hurricane Katrina and other storms.

Cochran nabbed the top spot on the Defense Subcommittee in 2008, when Alaska Republican Ted Stevens was entangled in an ethics controversy and was forced to relinquish the post. Cochran has long obtained money for Huntington Ingalls' naval shipyard in Pascagoula and the state's other military installations.

Farming is a major concern for Mississippi, and Cochran looks out for cotton, peanut, rice and sugar farmers as both an appropriator and the ranking member of the Agriculture Committee — on losing his Appropriations post, he asserted his seniority and took that job from Pat Roberts of Kansas.

Cochran and other Southerners voted against the Senate's 2012 attempt at a long-term reauthorization of farm programs, contending that the bill would hurt the safety net for crops grown mostly in Southern states, such as peanuts and cotton. It would have eliminated direct payments to farmers and many "target price" protections.

"Unfortunately, farmers across the South will suffer a disproportionate loss of support under the bill the Senate adopted," Cochran wrote. "The one-size-fits-all approach in the Senate bill places unfair burdens on some crops and regions, and puts them at a distinct disadvantage for investing in rural infrastructure and agriculture-related jobs." The bill was not enacted, as the House did not pass its version.

When work resumed in 2013, Cochran clearly had the ear of Michigan Democrat Debbie Stabenow, the panel chairwoman — the farm bill approved by the committee in May 2013 contained target prices.

Cochran was a major player in the 2002 rewrite of the farm law, but his short run as Agriculture chairman in 2003 and 2004 was uneventful. He held few meetings to debate bills, in part to prevent Iowa Republican Charles E. Grassley, a panel member, from offering amendments to reduce the maximum federal payments a farmer could receive. Grassley wanted to free up money for other farm programs, while Cochran opposed lower limits.

He is also on the Rules and Administration Committee, where the jurisdiction includes election laws. Cochran played a pivotal role in the drive to curb the large individual donations to political parties (aka soft money). His 2001 announcement that he would support a campaign finance overhaul bill by Arizona Republican John McCain began an erosion of GOP opposition. The law was enacted 14 months later.

Cochran's father was a school principal, and his mother was a math teacher. He was a standout in high school: valedictorian of his class, a Boy Scout leader, a member of the 4-H Club, and an athlete lettering in football, basketball, baseball and tennis.

At the University of Mississippi, Cochran was a fraternity president and cheerleader who was four years ahead of Trent Lott. The men were later congressional colleagues and political rivals. In law school, Cochran got a Rotary fellowship to study international law at Trinity College in Dublin. He joined a Jackson law firm after finishing up his law degree at Ole Miss and made partner in less than three years.

Cochran was active in local party politics during his law career and was a key state figure in Richard Nixon's 1968 presidential campaign. In 1972, when Democratic Rep. Charles H. Griffin retired, Cochran narrowly won the open seat. Lott was elected to the House the same year, and the two soon led warring factions within the state party. The pragmatists, led by Cochran, and the ideologues, led by Lott, feuded with increasing intensity for nearly two decades.

Cochran became Mississippi's first GOP senator in a century when long-serving Democrat James O. Eastland retired in 1978. Cochran won with 45 percent of the vote, as an independent black candidate drew much of the black vote away from Democrat Maurice Dantin, a former Columbia mayor. All of Cochran's Senate re-elections have been cakewalks.

He won election to the Senate a decade before Lott, but by 1995, Lott had zipped ahead of Cochran to become the Republican whip. When Majority Leader Bob Dole resigned to focus on his 1996 presidential campaign, the two Mississippians battled each other for the job; Lott won easily, 44-8.

Cochran is up for re-election in 2014, and there has been speculation in Mississippi circles that the 113th Congress will be his last. He said he wouldn't make that decision at least until late 2013.

Key Votes

2012	
Prohibit health insurance plans from denying coverage based on the sponsor's religious beliefs	NO
Require approval of the Keystone XL oil pipeline	YES
Ease securities rules to expand small-business access to capital	YES
Reauthorize farm and nutrition programs for five years	NO
Limit debate on a bill that would create private-sector cybersecurity standards	NO
Consent to ratification of a treaty setting global standard for the treatment of people with disabilities	NO
Provide $60.4 billion in disaster relief following Superstorm Sandy	YES
Extend most Bush-era income tax rates while allowing rates for top-bracket earners to rise (Jan. 1, 2013)	YES
2011	
Prevent EPA from regulating greenhouse gas emissions to address climate change	YES
Extend certain provisions of Patriot Act for four years	YES
Clear compromise debt limit increase plan and establish future spending limits	YES
Overhaul patent law	YES
Implement Colombia free trade agreement	YES
Limit debate on confirmation of Caitlin J. Halligan to D.C. Circuit Court of Appeals	NO
Extend payroll tax cut and unemployment benefits for two months	YES

CQ Vote Studies

	PARTY UNITY		PRESIDENTIAL SUPPORT	
	SUPPORT	OPPOSE	SUPPORT	OPPOSE
2012	72%	28%	54%	46%
2011	76%	24%	57%	43%
2010	89%	11%	47%	53%
2009	75%	25%	62%	38%
2008	85%	15%	74%	26%
2007	85%	15%	82%	18%
2006	87%	13%	89%	11%
2005	97%	3%	96%	4%
2004	98%	2%	92%	8%
2003	98%	2%	98%	2%

Interest Groups

	AFL-CIO	ADA	CCUS	ACU
2012	18%	20%	100%	52%
2011	11%	20%	100%	70%
2010	6%	5%	100%	88%
2009	28%	10%	86%	84%
2008	10%	15%	88%	68%
2007	11%	15%	82%	83%
2006	15%	10%	92%	67%
2005	21%	0%	100%	88%
2004	8%	15%	100%	92%
2003	0%	5%	100%	85%

Sen. Roger Wicker (R)

Capitol Office
224-6253
wicker.senate.gov
555 Dirksen Bldg. 20510-2403; fax 228-0378

Committees
Armed Services
Budget
Commerce, Science & Transportation
Environment & Public Works
Joint Economic

Residence
Tupelo

Born
July 5, 1951; Pontotoc, Miss.

Religion
Southern Baptist

Family
Wife, Gayle Wicker; three children

Education
U. of Mississippi, B.A. 1973 (political science & journalism), J.D. 1975

Military Service
Air Force, 1976-80; Air Force Reserve, 1980-2004

Career
County public defender; lawyer; military prosecutor; congressional aide

Political Highlights
Miss. Senate, 1988-94; U.S. House, 1995-2007

ELECTION RESULTS

2012 GENERAL		
Roger Wicker (R)	709,626	57.2%
Albert N. Gore Jr. (D)	503,467	40.6%
Thomas Cramer (CNSTP)	15,281	1.2%
Shawn O'Hara (REF)	13,194	1.1%
2012 PRIMARY		
Roger Wicker (R)	254,669	89.2%
Robert Maloney (R)	18,822	6.6%
E. Allen Hathcock (R)	12,094	4.2%

Previous Winning Percentages
2008 Special Senate Election (55%); 2006 House Election (66%); 2004 House Election (79%); 2002 House Election (71%); 2000 House Election (70%); 1998 House Election (67%); 1996 House Election (68%); 1994 House Election (63%)

Elected 2008; 1st full term

Appointed 2007

Thad Cochran and Trent Lott waged a back-and-forth battle for supremacy in the Mississippi Republican Party dating back to the 1970s. Lott became a media-loving and highly partisan Senate majority leader; Cochran rose to the top of the Senate Appropriations Committee by being quieter and more accommodating. Wicker is a next-generation senator who has employed a hybrid of those approaches.

Like his predecessor, Lott, Wicker commits to the institution of the Republican Party. Like his current colleague, Cochran, he gravitates to behind-the-scenes legislative work. And like both men, Wicker scours the federal government for resources to direct to Mississippi.

Wicker, who has a courteous demeanor and speaks in a slow, rolling cadence, credits his early devotion to the GOP to his stint as a congressional page in 1967. Assigned to the Republican page desk, he "got to observe up close people like Gerald Ford and Melvin Laird and the Republican leadership, so I guess I returned from my short stay as a Republican page a committed Republican," he remembers.

He was the first Republican elected as student body president at the University of Mississippi (which is also the alma mater of Cochran and Lott) and went on to serve as a delegate to the 1972 Republican National Convention. While there, he became acquainted with Lott, who was making his first run for Congress. After law school and four years on active duty in the Air Force, Wicker went to work for Lott in Washington in 1980.

Wicker returned home after a few years and worked as a public defender. In 1987, he won a state Senate seat. He helped write Mississippi's strict abortion law and push through an education overhaul that included a school choice provision.

Wicker was elected to the U.S. House as part of the 1994 Republican Revolution, but he "didn't come to Washington to burn all the buildings down," he once said.

He served on the back-scratching Appropriations Committee and grew to enjoy sending federal dollars to Mississippi, which has one of the highest poverty rates in the nation. Wicker contributed significantly as Congress assembled a relief package after Hurricane Katrina hit the Gulf Coast in 2005. When Lott resigned from the Senate in 2007 and Wicker was chosen to fill the vacancy, he joined Cochran, an undisputed master of parochial politics.

Now in his first full term, Wicker emphasizes an overall conservative outlook. He became a deputy whip in 2011 and was happy to blame Democrats for legislative gridlock in the 112th Congress (2011-12). Late in 2012 he took to the Senate floor to complain that Democratic leaders were not allowing Republicans to offer amendments to bills. "I am deprived from the ability that I think a representative of several states should have," he said.

Wicker, who joined the Budget and Joint Economic committees in 2013, also tried to put the country's fiscal situation in folksier terms — a not uncommon strategy for Southern conservatives. "What we need to do is approach it as a family does that has fallen on hard times," he told the Memphis Commercial Appeal. "They sit around the table and they say, 'we can't afford this anymore — we can't afford this much anymore.' And I just don't see the willingness. ... It is absolutely a mathematical impossibility to get anywhere near where we need to be unless we address the growth of entitlements."

But Wicker is far from a slash-and-burn conservative, and he continues to seek federal assistance related to recovery from hurricanes and the 2010 Gulf of Mexico oil spill. At the end of the 111th Congress (2009-10), he helped win extension of tax incentives for rebuilding in the Gulf Coast. A five-year reauthorization of the National Flood Insurance Program enacted in 2012 included Wicker's provision to provide the NFIP with more data from other federal entities when it tries to determine if wind or water damaged a property.

Wicker's seat on the Armed Services committee has allowed him to continue his effort to turn Mississippi into a magnet for defense jobs. He was the ranking member of the Seapower Subcommittee in the 112th — the Pascagoula region has Huntington Ingalls Industries shipbuilding facilities — and in the 113th Congress (2013-14) he switched over to take the top Republican spot on the Airland Subcommittee.

He says he's open to ways to reduce Pentagon spending, but Wicker opposed across-the-board "sequestration" defense cuts that Congress wrote into a 2011 deficit reduction package.

"A strong maritime presence is critical to America's ability to project power," he said after a November 2012 attack by Iranian jets on a U.S. unmanned aerial vehicle over the Persian Gulf. "Sequestration's arbitrary 9.4 percent cuts to defense spending would reduce our aircraft carrier fleet from 11 ships to 10 ships and reduce our Navy's fleet size to the smallest it has been since World War I."

Wicker also has seats on two panels that handle infrastructure: Commerce, Science and Transportation, where he is the No. 2 Republican, and Environment and Public Works, which he joined in 2013.

He is the top Republican on the Commerce subcommittee covering technology and the Internet, and on assuming that post he said he wanted to "ensure quality broadband access to all corners of America, particularly in rural areas like my home state of Mississippi." He touted his seat on the Environment panel as a chance to promote infrastructure in the state, and he applauded the authorization of water infrastructure programs that the committee produced in early 2013.

Wicker is conservative on social issues and is adamantly opposed to abortion. He has co-sponsored a number of bills that seek to limit taxpayer dollars from even indirectly funding the procedure. The fiscal 2012 defense policy bill included a Wicker amendment to clarify that military chaplains are not required to perform marriages that they have a moral objection to, such as same-sex unions. But the provision was removed before the bill was enacted.

Wicker grew up in Pontotoc, 20 miles west of Tupelo in northeastern Mississippi. The grandson of sharecroppers from Benton, he said his father's humble upbringing makes his ascension to Congress "a pretty powerful statement of the American dream." His father lived in a small farmhouse with his parents and four siblings before becoming a county attorney, a state senator and then a circuit judge for 20 years. Wicker's father was a Democrat, but that didn't stop his son from organizing the local teenage Republican club in high school.

Democrat Jamie L. Whitten opted to retire at the end of the 1994, after 53 years in the House. The conservative 1st District was ripe for a Republican takeover. Wicker emphasized his legislative experience and edged out Grant Fox, a former Senate aide, for the GOP nomination. He won easily in November and was never seriously challenged in a re-election campaign. (Republican Alan Nunnelee worked on Wicker's 1994 campaign, succeeded him in the state Senate and now represents the 1st District.)

Wicker joined the Senate on New Year's Eve 2007, when Mississippi Republican Gov. Haley Barbour appointed him to replace Lott. In a 2008 special election for the right to complete Lott's term, Wicker beat former Democratic Gov. Ronnie Musgrove — who once roomed with Wicker when both were in the state Senate — by 10 points.

In 2012, he easily earned a full term over his 82-year-old Democratic opponent, Albert N. Gore Jr., a retired Methodist minister and Army veteran.

Key Votes

2012

Prohibit health insurance plans from denying coverage based on the sponsor's religious beliefs	NO
Require approval of the Keystone XL oil pipeline	YES
Ease securities rules to expand small-business access to capital	YES
Reauthorize farm and nutrition programs for five years	NO
Limit debate on a bill that would create private-sector cybersecurity standards	NO
Consent to ratification of a treaty setting global standard for the treatment of people with disabilities	NO
Provide $60.4 billion in disaster relief following Superstorm Sandy	YES
Extend most Bush-era income tax rates while allowing rates for top-bracket earners to rise (Jan. 1, 2013)	YES

2011

Prevent EPA from regulating greenhouse gas emissions to address climate change	YES
Extend certain provisions of Patriot Act for four years	YES
Clear compromise debt limit increase plan and establish future spending limits	YES
Overhaul patent law	YES
Implement Colombia free trade agreement	YES
Limit debate on confirmation of Caitlin J. Halligan to D.C. Circuit Court of Appeals	NO
Extend payroll tax cut and unemployment benefits for two months	YES

CQ Vote Studies

	PARTY UNITY		PRESIDENTIAL SUPPORT	
	SUPPORT	OPPOSE	SUPPORT	OPPOSE
2012	85%	15%	50%	50%
2011	88%	12%	51%	49%
2010	96%	4%	41%	59%
2009	88%	12%	49%	51%
2008	94%	6%	70%	30%
2007	89%	11%	81%	19%
2006	97%	3%	97%	3%
2005	97%	3%	84%	16%
2004	95%	5%	86%	14%
2003	97%	3%	96%	4%

Interest Groups

	AFL-CIO	ADA	CCUS	ACU
2012	18%	10%	100%	64%
2011	11%	15%	100%	75%
2010	0%	0%	100%	96%
2009	22%	15%	86%	88%
2008	20%	10%	88%	80%
2007	0%	5%	84%	96%
2006	7%	0%	100%	88%
2005	20%	5%	93%	96%
2004	8%	0%	100%	87%
2003	0%	10%	97%	88%

Rep. Alan Nunnelee (R)

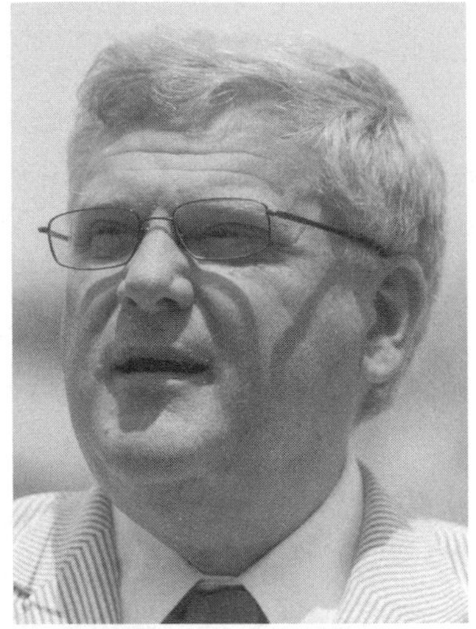

Capitol Office
225-4306
nunnelee.house.gov
1427 Rayburn Bldg. 20515-2401; fax 225-3549

Committees
Appropriations
Budget

Residence
Tupelo

Born
Oct. 9, 1958; Tupelo, Miss.

Religion
Baptist

Family
Wife, Tori Nunnelee; three children

Education
Mississippi State U., B.S. 1980 (marketing)

Career
Insurance company owner

Political Highlights
Miss. Senate, 1995-2010

ELECTION RESULTS

2012 GENERAL		
Alan Nunnelee (R)	186,760	60.4%
Brad Morris (D)	114,076	36.9%
Danny Bedwell (LIBERT)	3,584	1.2%
2012 PRIMARY		
Alan Nunnelee (R)	43,487	57.4%
Henry Ross (R)	21,944	28.9%
Robert Estes (R)	10,390	13.7%
2010 GENERAL		
Alan Nunnelee (R)	121,074	55.3%
Travis W. Childers (D)	89,388	40.8%
Wally Pang (I)	2,180	1.0%

Elected 2010; 2nd term

Nunnelee is a cost-cutting appropriator with a social-conservative bent. He says he approaches the federal budget like he does a family budget: "The principles stay the same, the governmental budget just adds a string of zeros."

His spending philosophy was tested in the fall of 2011, as the House debated whether extra funding for disaster relief should be offset by reductions elsewhere. The 1st District town of Smithville had been devastated by a tornado, but Nunnelee favored requiring offsets for disaster relief.

"Those families don't have the option of cranking up a printing press and churning out new money just to pay for the disaster," he said. "I think it's appropriate that government make critical choices just like families and businesses in Smithville make."

Nunnelee once served as the chairman of the appropriations committee in the Mississippi Senate, and most of his professional life focused on financial planning — he spent three decades selling life insurance. A member of the conservative Republican Study Committee, he has been open to raising eligibility ages for federal entitlement programs to keep them solvent, and he told a Mississippi newspaper in 2011 that "the worst thing we could do in a tough economy is to raise taxes on anybody."

That said, he hasn't taken the hardest line on spending. Nunnelee joined the majority of House Republicans in supporting the major fiscal measures of the 112th Congress (2011-12), even as some party colleagues opposed them as not austere enough. Budgetary earmarks for special projects in lawmakers' districts were banned starting in 2011, but Nunnelee said greater transparency could eliminate ethics concerns and allow the return of the practice.

A member of the Agriculture Appropriations Subcommittee, Nunnelee is wary of appropriators setting farm policy. "We need to come up with a farm bill ... and then live with the rules established in that farm bill during its tenure" to allow long-term planning for the agriculture sector, he said. He voted for a proposed 5 percent reduction to discretionary accounts in the fiscal 2012 Agriculture spending bill, but he opposed an attempt to remove research spending from the bill. Both amendments were defeated.

Nunnelee, who also sits on the Military Construction-VA Subcommittee, opposes cuts to defense programs that would compromise national security. He emphasized, however, that "it would be naïve to say that we cannot save any money in the defense budget, whether it's on the construction side or the operations side."

The Energy-Water Subcommittee gives him a direct avenue to the energy issues important to his district. Nunnelee focuses on supporting Mississippi's natural gas industry and the lignite coal mine in his district. He said the first job of the government in promoting energy should be "to get the environmental extremists out of the way," and he calls for expansion of nuclear power and alternative sources of energy. The government should support energy research, but not private sector manufacturing of energy technology, he said.

He wants a national energy goal akin to John F. Kennedy's plans for a moon landing. "It's time for a new challenge, that by the end of this decade we be energy secure," Nunnelee said.

Nunnelee had first-term success with a policy rider to the Energy-Water bill; in both 2011 and 2012 he attached language banning agencies funded by the bill from hiring an employee who has not been cleared through E-Verify, the verification system to screen out illegal immigrants.

Nunnelee pushed social conservative causes in the state Senate, but in the U.S. House those issues "have been overshadowed by our commitment on the economy and jobs," he admitted in 2011. "What I've seen as a result of the Great Society is that there are those who feel that government programs can take the place of a family," he said. "That'll never happen."

He opposes abortion. The Appropriations Committee adopted a Nunnelee amendment to the fiscal 2013 Financial Services bill that would restrict federally administered plans in the "exchanges" created by the 2010 health care law from using federal funds to pay for administrative costs associated with abortions. (The underlying bill was not enacted.)

In 2003, he spearheaded a successful effort to amend the Mississippi Constitution to ban same-sex marriage, and in 2001 he backed legislation to place the national motto, "In God We Trust," on the walls of school classrooms.

The first of four children, Nunnelee was born in Tupelo to teenage parents. Shortly after Nunnelee was born, his father took a job with a life insurance company. He eventually worked his way up to the executive level.

Nunnelee's mother started community college during his teen years; he remembers working on his math homework while she worked on hers. She became a pediatric nurse.

A degenerative eye disease he had since birth made him legally blind while he was at Mississippi State University. "During that period in my life I did a lot of speaking — civic clubs, churches — about that personal experience," he said. His eyesight was restored by cornea transplants. Being a baseball fan, he recalls going to a college game shortly thereafter just to watch a curveball: "To that day, I had never seen a ball break." He cheers for both Mississippi State and Ole Miss, which is in the 1st District. (He says he never attends a game when they play each other.)

After completing his studies, Nunnelee was ready to go into life insurance. A first job fell through over concern about his eyes, but he landed at his father's company. Nunnelee opened branches throughout the South, eventually becoming a vice president.

He was involved with the Republican Party in northern Mississippi for years. After a corporate merger soured his work experience, he signed on as the finance director for the successful 1994 House campaign of state Sen. Roger Wicker — who now serves in the U.S. Senate. Nunnelee ran to replace Wicker in the state Senate and remained there through 2010.

Nunnelee won a three-way GOP primary in 2010, avoiding a runoff by taking 52 percent of the vote. The general-election race against Democratic incumbent Travis W. Childers cast one of the most conservative Democrats in the House against an even more conservative Republican. Nunnelee won by 14 points. Childers' former chief of staff Brad Morris tried to avenge the defeat in 2012, but Nunnelee took 60 percent of the vote.

Key Votes

2012	
Extend a Social Security payroll tax cut and unemployment benefits	YES
Ease securities rules to expand small-business access to capital	YES
Extend for one year subsidized student loan interest rates financed by a cut in health care spending	YES
Cite Attorney General Eric H. Holder Jr. for contempt of Congress	YES
Create a visa program for foreign graduates in high-tech fields	YES
Extend most Bush-era income tax rates while allowing rates for top-bracket earners to rise (Jan. 1, 2013)	NO
2011	
Strike funding for F-35 alternative engine	NO
Prevent EPA from regulating greenhouse gas emissions to address climate change	YES
Extend certain provisions of Patriot Act for four years	YES
Declare opposition to use of ground troops in Libya	YES
Overhaul patent law	NO
Pass compromise debt limit increase plan and establish future spending limits	YES
Allow consideration of measures to implement three trade agreements	?

CQ Vote Studies

	Party Unity		Presidential Support	
	Support	Oppose	Support	Oppose
2012	97%	3%	13%	87%
2011	96%	4%	24%	76%

Interest Groups

	AFL-CIO	ADA	CCUS	ACU
2012	14%	0%	92%	96%
2011	0%	5%	94%	83%

Mississippi 1

North — Tupelo, Southaven, Columbus

The northeastern Hill Country supports an agricultural economy in the 1st, while manufacturing dominates in Lee County (Tupelo) and surrounding areas. Decennial redistricting moved rich farmland on the edge of the Delta region in northwestern Mississippi from the 1st District into the 2nd — Panola, Yalobusha and Grenada counties were traded for parts of Winston and Webster counties, as well as parts of Oktibbeha County, from the 3rd. A history of backing Democrats for the U.S. House was broken in 1994, and voters now regularly support the GOP in all federal races.

Tupelo has long been a major producer of upholstered furniture, but the city has struggled in a weak national economy and with competition from China. Skilled manufacturing has brought some new jobs — a nearby Toyota plant opened in 2011 and hired 2,000 employees to produce as many as 150,000 sedans a year. Columbus is home to a million-square-foot steel fabrication facility owned by the Russian Severstal Group and a production site for American Eurocopter, a subsidiary of EADS North America. Oxford is home to the University of Mississippi (Ole Miss).

DeSoto County is the 1st's most populous and the state's fastest-growing. Many residents commute over the Tennessee border into Memphis. Southaven and Olive Branch are distribution hubs for large manufacturing firms. Most of the black residents in this white-majority district come from the population hubs in DeSoto, Lee and Lowndes counties; more-rural Marshall County also has a significant black population.

The district includes Mississippi's entire portion of the planned Interstate 22 (currently Highway 78), which will connect Memphis to Birmingham. Tourism in Tupelo includes the visitor center for the 444-mile Natchez Trace Parkway, and the birthplace of Elvis Presley.

Major Industry
Manufacturing, agriculture

Military Bases
Columbus Air Force Base, 1,447 military, 615 civilian

Cities
Southaven, Tupelo, Olive Branch, Horn Lake

Notable
Columbus lures visitors to its historic antebellum home tours.

Rep. Bennie Thompson (D)

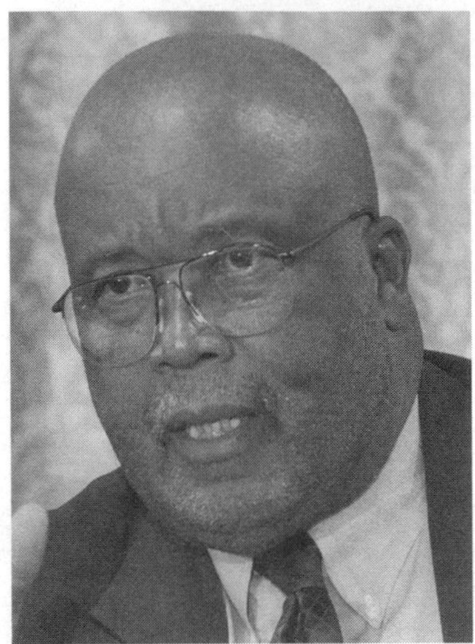

Capitol Office
225-5876
benniethompson.house.gov
2466 Rayburn Bldg. 20515-2402; fax 225-5898

Committees
Homeland Security - Ranking Member

Residence
Bolton

Born
Jan. 28, 1948; Bolton, Miss.

Religion
United Methodist

Family
Wife, London Thompson; one child

Education
Tougaloo College, B.A. 1968 (political science); Jackson State College, M.S. 1972 (educational administration)

Career
Teacher

Political Highlights
Bolton Board of Aldermen, 1969-73; mayor of Bolton, 1973-79; Hinds County Board of Supervisors, 1980-93

ELECTION RESULTS

2012 GENERAL		
Bennie Thompson (D)	214,978	67.1%
Bill Marcy (R)	99,160	31.0%
Cobby Mondale Williams (I)	4,605	1.4%
2012 PRIMARY		
Bennie Thompson (D)	49,083	87.5%
Heather McTeer (D)	7,040	12.5%
2010 GENERAL		
Bennie Thompson (D)	105,327	61.5%
Bill Marcy (R)	64,499	37.6%

Previous Winning Percentages
2008 (69%); 2006 (64%); 2004 (58%); 2002 (55%); 2000 (65%); 1998 (71%); 1996 (60%); 1994 (54%); 1993 Special Runoff Election (55%)

Elected 1993; 10th full term

Thompson still speaks in the same low tones and deliberate cadence that have carried him through two decades in office — even at a time when rifts have opened between him and Republican leaders on the homeland security issues that dominate his agenda.

He attributes his demeanor to his upbringing in a largely poor district, saying he uses his time there to center himself. "I go home every week," he said. "I live in a community of 500 people, and I've lived there all my life. I'm told that people judge you by what you do, rather than how loudly you do it."

Thompson has been the top Democrat on the Homeland Security Committee since its creation in 2005. Despite splitting with Republicans on most major homeland security issues in the 112th Congress (2011-12), such as chemical facility regulations and cybersecurity, he says he is convinced that domestic security is still an area where lawmakers can put aside party affiliation.

For most of Thompson's tenure, the panel's top Republican was Peter T. King of New York. The two spent the 112th Congress in a high-profile conflict over hearings King had set up to explore the possibility of radicalization within Muslim communities in the United States. Thompson said the hearings were unfairly focused on a single population and called on King to add other potentially threatening groups, such as neo-Nazis and environmental terrorists, to the inquiry. King refused.

King had to step aside at the start of 2013 due to the term limits Republicans impose on their panel leaders. Thompson's new counterpart is Michael McCaul of Texas, a less bombastic but more conservative lawmaker. Thompson used their first hearing together to lament the lack of major legislation coming out of the panel in recent years.

Thompson supports many aspects of the Obama administration's management of the Department of Homeland Security. He dislikes GOP proposals to replace much of the Transportation Security Administration's airport screening workforce with contractors, and he applauded a 2011 administration decision to allow collective bargaining for airport security officers — he had pushed for the change for years.

His support is hardly unqualified, though. Thompson is a critic of the TSA's "behavior detection" initiatives; he said test programs saw screeners target minorities rather than look out for suspicious behavior. In 2013, when the TSA suddenly announced that it would again allow passengers to take small knives on planes, Thompson wrote that "policies that impact millions of passengers and thousands of front-line workers must not be created in a vacuum."

He also questions the department's development of a secure identification card for port security workers, arguing that the process of obtaining and renewing cards is overly burdensome for workers. And, because the department missed by more than two years its scheduled date to deploy authentication machines that confirm workers' identities, Thompson has said the IDs have been merely serving as expensive badges.

Thompson has led calls in the House to grant DHS new powers to oversee cybersecurity at critical-infrastructure facilities such as power plants, and to increase its regulatory reach over chemical plants considered vulnerable to terrorist attacks. Both notions proved unpopular with the House's Republican majority in the 112th Congress.

The inability of Congress to pass legislation addressing those threats is troubling, Thompson said in 2012, noting that they have been on the table for multiple sessions. In the area of cybersecurity, lawmakers have received briefing upon briefing stating that the problem is real and growing, both from criminals and state-sponsored hackers. "I can have all the priorities in the world, but if we can't translate those priorities into meaningful legislation, then nothing happens," he said. McCaul has identified cybersecurity as one of his top priorities for the 113th Congress (2013-14). Thompson's concerns about critical infrastructure go beyond cybersecurity, though; he has called the U.S. electric grid weak, and he backs the development of new technology to supplant it.

Thompson's own district seems an unlikely target for terrorists, but with its proximity to the Gulf of Mexico it is touched by the natural disasters that DHS also handles. Hurricane Katrina in 2005 "opened the eyes of a lot of people, including me, as to how the system works versus how it should work," he said. "The fact that American citizens were left abandoned by their government will forever be embedded in my mind."

He says that the economy is the top concern of his constituents and that the rural hospitals that serve them are worried about keeping their doors open. Farming supports much of his district. Thompson, who left the Agriculture Committee to serve on the Homeland panel, said he'll be watching the next reauthorization of farm programs closely. "Unlike a lot of the members here from urban areas who might be looking at the nutrition sections of the farm bill — which are important — I'm looking at the conservation sections of it and the sections about actually raising crops," he said in 2012.

Thompson is a member of the Congressional Progressive Caucus, the group of the most-liberal House Democrats. But he will break with most Democrats to oppose some regulatory measures, especially those that could be economically damaging to his district — for example, he voted for a 2011 GOP measure to prevent EPA regulation of dust produced by farm activities.

Born in 1948, Thompson was educated in segregated elementary and secondary schools. His father, a mechanic, died when Thompson was in the 10th grade. At Tougaloo College in Jackson, he met civil rights activist Fannie Lou Hamer, who inspired him to pursue politics. He graduated in 1968, the year he made his first run for public office.

He was elected alderman in his hometown of Bolton, but the town's whites didn't want a black man on the board, so they barred him from City Hall. He got a court order forcing them to back down and let him claim his seat. Thompson says those experiences helped shape him into a champion for civil rights.

Four years later he was elected mayor. At 32, he was elected to the board of supervisors for Hinds County, which includes the capital city, Jackson. He ran for the House in a 1993 special election after Democrat Mike Espy resigned to become President Bill Clinton's Agriculture secretary. Thompson triumphed in a runoff, with 55 percent of the vote. In his 1994 bid for a full term, he won by 15 points, and he has won handily ever since.

Key Votes

2012

Extend a Social Security payroll tax cut and unemployment benefits	YES
Ease securities rules to expand small-business access to capital	YES
Extend for one year subsidized student loan interest rates financed by a cut in health care spending	NO
Cite Attorney General Eric H. Holder Jr. for contempt of Congress	?
Create a visa program for foreign graduates in high-tech fields	NO
Extend most Bush-era income tax rates while allowing rates for top-bracket earners to rise (Jan. 1, 2013)	YES

2011

Strike funding for F-35 alternative engine	NO
Prevent EPA from regulating greenhouse gas emissions to address climate change	NO
Extend certain provisions of Patriot Act for four years	NO
Declare opposition to use of ground troops in Libya	NO
Overhaul patent law	YES
Pass compromise debt limit increase plan and establish future spending limits	NO
Allow consideration of measures to implement three trade agreements	NO

CQ Vote Studies

	PARTY UNITY		PRESIDENTIAL SUPPORT	
	SUPPORT	OPPOSE	SUPPORT	OPPOSE
2012	92%	8%	85%	15%
2011	92%	8%	77%	23%
2010	98%	2%	83%	17%
2009	99%	1%	97%	3%
2008	99%	1%	13%	87%

Interest Groups

	AFL-CIO	ADA	CCUS	ACU
2012	95%	85%	17%	8%
2011	100%	95%	25%	8%
2010	93%	95%	25%	4%
2009	100%	95%	43%	0%
2008	100%	90%	50%	8%

Mississippi 2

West central — most of Jackson, Mississippi Delta

Lying mostly west of Interstate 55 and north of Interstate 20, the 2nd combines most of Jackson — the state's capital and largest city — with Vicksburg and the nutrient-rich flatlands of the Mississippi Delta. Population loss in this region resulted in the addition of three Delta counties during decennial redistricting following the 2010 census — Panola, Yalobusha and Grenada counties were shifted from the 1st — along with the remainder of Leake County, which had been shared with the 3rd.

Agriculture and aquaculture are pivotal here, and the 2nd supports catfish-raising, cotton, rice and soybeans. The Delta's rural economy has promoted landowner/tenant relationships that have made the 2nd one of the nation's poorest districts — median household income is just higher than $30,000.

In Vicksburg, a mixture of tourism, casinos and a Mississippi River port has brought some local prosperity. Outside Canton, a Nissan assembly plant north of Jackson has expanded to employ more than 5,000 workers.

Government, service and small-scale manufacturing have long kept unemployment in check in Jackson, although nationwide economic downturns have hurt the capital and unemployment rates have reached double digits. The city is working to revitalize its downtown and opened a new convention center in 2009. Jackson also hosts the State Fair and annual rodeo.

Some low-income white residents live in the 2nd, but it is the state's only black-majority district — it also has the highest proportion of black residents of any district in the nation (65 percent). Despite a Republican foothold in some areas near Jackson and to the northeast, and the addition of Republican-leaning counties during remapping, the 2nd remains overwhelmingly Democratic and the only district statewide to back Democrats in federal races; in 2012, Barack Obama won here by a 2-to-1 margin.

Major Industry
Agriculture, government, gaming

Cities
Jackson, Greenville, Clinton

Notable
Norris Bookbinding, based in Greenwood, is the largest Bible rebinding plant in the nation.

Rep. Gregg Harper (R)

Capitol Office
225-5031
harper.house.gov
307 Cannon Bldg. 20515-2403; fax 225-5797

Committees
Energy & Commerce
House Administration
Joint Library - Chairman
Joint Printing - Vice Chairman

Residence
Pearl

Born
June 1, 1956; Jackson, Miss.

Religion
Southern Baptist

Family
Wife, Sidney Harper; two children

Education
Mississippi College, B.S. 1978 (chemistry); U. of Mississippi, J.D. 1981

Career
Lawyer; city prosecutor

Political Highlights
Rankin County Republican Party chairman, 2000-07

ELECTION RESULTS

2012 GENERAL		
Gregg Harper (R)	234,717	80.0%
John "Luke" Pannell (REF)	58,605	20.0%
2012 PRIMARY		
Gregg Harper (R)	78,667	91.8%
Robert J. Allen (R)	7,025	8.2%
2010 GENERAL		
Gregg Harper (R)	132,393	68.0%
Joel L. Gill (D)	60,737	31.2%

Previous Winning Percentages
2008 (63%)

Elected 2008; 3rd term

Harper has taken on more than his share of grunt work for the GOP and promoted the Republican energy platform. His more collaborative efforts stem from his personal experiences helping those with intellectual disabilities.

Harper, a good-natured partisan, was a county GOP chairman before winning a seat in Congress. He served as an election observer in Florida in 2000, a legal volunteer for President George W. Bush in Ohio in 2004 and a volunteer for a Senate campaign in Missouri in 2006. "When you work for free, your friends always call you," he said. "I was a highly unpaid political volunteer." He had a leadership political action committee even before he was elected to the House in 2008.

That involvement in nuts-and-bolts operations continues in Washington. Harper sits on the House Administration Committee; he has served on the Republican Steering Committee, which determines panel assignments; and six months into Harper's first term, Minority Leader John A. Boehner put him on the seldom-sought Ethics Committee.

Many of those jobs are seen as ways to get ahead in a political party, but a leadership position eluded Harper at the end of the 112th Congress (2011-12). He started a bid to become GOP Conference secretary but withdrew shortly after the 2012 election. The speculation was that Harper was hoping to become the House Administration chairman instead, but Candice S. Miller of Michigan was awarded that post.

Harper, a member of the conservative Republican Study Committee, still has a choice assignment on the Energy and Commerce Committee. He reliably talks up the GOP's "all of the above" energy strategy and was unimpressed when President Barack Obama sounded similar sentiments in 2012. "Nobody that fluent with the issue buys that," he said. "Almost every decision he's made has had a negative impact on [the price of] gas at the pump."

He says the administration overreacted in shutting down oil production in the Gulf of Mexico after the 2010 explosion of BP's Deepwater Horizon rig and the subsequent oil spill — and that sentiment is shared by several families of people from his district who were killed in the explosion, according to Harper.

He saw election year politics as the reason for the denial of a permit for the Keystone XL pipeline to carry oil from Canada's oil sands as far as Texas refineries. Rural areas must have cheaper gas, Harper said, since "it's nothing for someone to drive 50 to 100 miles a day to and from work."

Harper often says the EPA is out of control, with regulations slowing the development of nuclear power, clean-coal technology and more. An agency plan to regulate coal ash, a byproduct of coal combustion, as a hazardous material was "another decision by the agency to regulate business without the use of facts, science or common sense," Harper said on the House floor in 2011.

He also has an interest in election law, which falls under the jurisdiction of the House Administration Committee.

One of Harper's pet projects is a bill to eliminate the Election Assistance Commission, an organization that has its origins in the Florida presidential recount Harper observed. "The butterfly ballot was not the greatest invention known to man," he noted.

The EAC was created to administer grants to states to modernize voting equipment. Harper said its three-year mission was fulfilled, noted in 2012 that it currently has no commissioners and said its other election-monitoring duties can be transferred to the Federal Election Commission. If spending for the EAC can't be eliminated, Harper asked, "how do you cut anything?"

Democrats attacked the 2011 version of Harper's bill as a GOP effort to make voting more difficult for Democratic constituencies, but the House passed it; the bill would also terminate taxpayer financing of presidential election campaigns through check-off donations on income tax returns.

Harper pounced when the Obama administration floated a possible executive order to require federal contractors to disclose all their campaign donations, saying it "would grant Washington bureaucrats the flexibility to approve or deny federal contracts for purely political purposes." The plan was more or less abandoned in 2012.

Harper's father was a petroleum engineer and a World War II veteran. "Mississippi was always home," he said, though he attended 10 different schools in four states as the family moved for his father's work. Harper's older brother was an Air Force pilot for decades and later became a civilian employee in the Defense Department.

A Southern Baptist, Harper made faith and family values themes of his 2008 campaign. He opposes abortion rights and gay marriage. He had his religious awakening after 10th grade, and he started dating his future wife when he was 17 and she was 15. They were married a little over five years later.

Their son, Livingston, has factored into his congressional work: He has Fragile X syndrome, a genetic disorder that causes behavioral, developmental and language disabilities and autistic-like behaviors. Harper is a co-chairman in the Fragile X Caucus and established an internship program bringing people with intellectual disabilities to work in congressional offices.

"So many of these kids, when they get out of high school, they drop off the educational face of the Earth," Harper said. He has introduced a series of bills to improve coordination of federal efforts to move the intellectually disabled into real-world working opportunities.

During his legal career, Harper worked for a few banks, was a board attorney for the Mississippi Baptist Children's Village and served as a city prosecutor. A friend got him to work on a phone bank for a 1978 Senate primary, then left Harper in charge when he quit. Harper really enjoyed the work, and over the years he connected with the GOP grass-roots organization.

The retirement of Rep. Charles W. "Chip" Pickering Jr. created an open 3rd District seat in 2008. Though relatively anonymous, Harper avoided the mudslinging in a nasty seven-way GOP primary, triumphed over a state legislator in the runoff and then easily won the general election.

Harper has participated in congressional charity baseball and basketball games and loves college football weekends. His D.C. office features some remarkable mementos — "the worse the athlete, the more the memorabilia," he says — including Jesse Owens' signature and 11 baseballs signed by members of baseball's 500-home-run club.

Key Votes

2012	
Extend a Social Security payroll tax cut and unemployment benefits	YES
Ease securities rules to expand small-business access to capital	YES
Extend for one year subsidized student loan interest rates financed by a cut in health care spending	YES
Cite Attorney General Eric H. Holder Jr. for contempt of Congress	YES
Create a visa program for foreign graduates in high-tech fields	YES
Extend most Bush-era income tax rates while allowing rates for top-bracket earners to rise (Jan. 1, 2013)	NO
2011	
Strike funding for F-35 alternative engine	NO
Prevent EPA from regulating greenhouse gas emissions to address climate change	YES
Extend certain provisions of Patriot Act for four years	YES
Declare opposition to use of ground troops in Libya	YES
Overhaul patent law	YES
Pass compromise debt limit increase plan and establish future spending limits	YES
Allow consideration of measures to implement three trade agreements	YES

CQ Vote Studies

	PARTY UNITY		PRESIDENTIAL SUPPORT	
	SUPPORT	OPPOSE	SUPPORT	OPPOSE
2012	92%	8%	16%	84%
2011	96%	4%	26%	74%
2010	97%	3%	26%	74%
2009	93%	7%	[illegible]	[illegible]

Interest Groups

	AFL-CIO	ADA	CCUS	ACU
2012	14%	0%	100%	80%
2011	0%	10%	100%	79%
2010	7%	0%	[illegible]	90%
2009	6%	0%	80%	96%

Mississippi 3

East central to southwest — Meridian, Jackson suburbs

The 3rd picks up Jackson's northeastern corner and some of its mostly white northern and eastern suburbs as it sprawls across 24 counties, moving from Oktibbeha and Noxubee counties in the east-central part of the state to the Mississippi River in its southwestern corner.

Rankin County's growth over the past two decades has been spurred by an influx of nearby Jackson residents moving out of the city. The district's white-collar and relatively well-educated workforce provides some economic stability, but unemployment rates have hovered above national averages in many counties outside Jackson's sphere.

Health care and defense are important sectors. Meridian is home to medical centers, a Naval Air Station, an Air National Guard base and Peavey Electronics, one of the world's largest guitar and amplifier manufacturers.

Timber is key to the economy, although prices depend on demand from construction sectors nationwide; poultry and dairy farms abound across the district. Pearl's minor league baseball stadium and a Bass Pro Shop outdoor store anchor an entertainment complex. Natchez, on the Mississippi River in Adams County, relies on tourism and draws nearly 700,000 visitors annually to antebellum homes and dockside casinos. Mississippi State University, the state's largest, is in Starkville at the district's northeastern tip.

Republicans now dominate federal races in the 3rd, as Democrats did for most of the 20th century. Black-majority and sparsely populated counties will still back Democrats, but Republicans win in the district's population centers. The 3rd has the state's highest percentage of black residents (35 percent) in a white-majority district.

Major Industry
Timber, poultry, agriculture, defense

Military Bases
Naval Air Station Meridian, 1,500 military, 600 civilian (2012)

Cities
Jackson (pt.), Meridian, Pearl

Notable
Mississippi State University is home to a large collection of papers from author and alumnus John Grisham.

Rep. Steven M. Palazzo (R)

Capitol Office
225-5772
palazzo.house.gov
331 Cannon Bldg. 20515-2404; fax 225-7074

Committees
Armed Services
Homeland Security
Science, Space & Technology
(Space - Chairman)

Residence
Biloxi

Born
Feb. 21, 1970; Gulfport, Miss.

Religion
Roman Catholic

Family
Wife, Lisa Palazzo; three children

Education
U. of Southern Mississippi, B.S.B.A. 1994 (accounting), M.B.A. 1996

Military
Miss. National Guard, 1997-present; Marine Corps Reserve, 1988-96

Career
Accountant; defense contracting company financial manager; oil rig inventory supervisor

Political Highlights
Miss. House, 2007-10

ELECTION RESULTS

2012 GENERAL		
Steven M. Palazzo (R)	182,998	64.1%
Matt Moore (D)	82,344	28.8%
Ron Williams (LIBERT)	17,982	6.3%
2012 PRIMARY		
Steven M. Palazzo (R)	60,722	73.9%
Ron Vincent (R)	15,378	18.7%
Cindy Burleson (R)	6,081	7.4%
2010 GENERAL		
Steven M. Palazzo (R)	105,613	51.9%
Gene Taylor (D)	95,243	46.8%

Elected 2010; 2nd term

When Palazzo puts his district first, there are national implications: He calls for strong federal investment in defense and space programs, which have a big economic impact on southeast Mississippi. On most subjects he is a party-line Republican, endorsing overall fiscal restraint and the social conservatism that is common among his party's Southern contingent.

His first years in the House are practically a how-to guide for establishing a long career in Congress. A former Marine reservist, Palazzo (puh-LAZZ-oh) holds a seat on the Armed Services Committee, where he is an advocate for the shipyards and military bases that employ thousands of his constituents. He also represents the John C. Stennis Space Center, NASA's primary facility for rocket testing — and as a freshman, he was named chairman of the Science, Space and Technology subcommittee overseeing the space program. He kept his gavel for the 113th Congress (2013-14).

There have been rough patches, however. In early 2013, Palazzo voted against a $9.7 billion increase in the borrowing authority of the National Flood Insurance Program to cover claims related to Superstorm Sandy. He was horsewhipped by national and local media outlets, as his own district had been hit by Hurricane Katrina in 2005. Some people noted that Palazzo, working for the Biloxi Housing Authority at that time, had requested federal aid.

Palazzo said his vote — which didn't threaten the bill's passage — was to highlight the national debt and flaws in federal disaster response. (Palazzo had just been added to the Homeland Security Committee at the start of 2013.) The Sun Herald of Biloxi rendered harsh judgment: "Seldom has a single vote in Congress appeared as cold-blooded and hard-headed." Palazzo took a trip to New Jersey and New York to tour damaged areas, and a week later he was one of 49 Republicans to vote for a $50 billion package of disaster aid.

The incident evoked memories of minor stumbles in 2011. Allegations were raised that Palazzo and his wife had used aides as baby sitters and to help the family move into a D.C. apartment. He was on his third chief of staff by August, and he fired two aides who had rented an Annapolis house for a weekend, then allegedly impersonated Palazzo on the phone while trying to smooth over a dispute with the owner.

Still, growing pains haven't slowed his committee work.

He urges faster development of a government-owned system to carry people and cargo into space. When the Obama administration in 2011 announced plans to proceed with the Space Launch System for deep-space missions, Palazzo wrote that it was overdue: "This administration's lack of commitment for human space exploration has frustrated and angered many of us in Congress who are committed to American leadership in space." Such a system will be a needed backup, Palazzo argued, should commercial companies falter in developing the capability to carry passengers and cargo into low Earth orbit.

He does support that private sector development. The president signed his 2012 bill to extend a program that lets the government share the cost of damages suffered by the public should something go wrong with a commercial space launch. Without the program, the potential costs of a disaster would scare companies away from the industry, Palazzo said. And he has prodded federal aviation authorities to quickly set up the regulatory regime governing commercial launches so companies can account for safety standards as they develop their systems.

Palazzo wants a long-term commitment for NASA on planetary exploration — likely Mars. "I am deeply worried that NASA will be viewed by our international partners as an unreliable, schizophrenic agency," he said at a 2011 hearing.

"The administration appears to be interfering with the agency's efforts to reach out and engage foreign governments in future flagship missions," and fluctuating budgets could scare off potential cost-sharing partners, he said.

Palazzo was an accountant, and his experience in that regard comes into play on Armed Services. He swapped jargon with witnesses while serving on a short-term panel (created in July 2011) overseeing the Defense Department's financial management. Palazzo has floated the idea of providing enticements, such as higher starting salary levels, to lure top-notch civilian CPAs to work for the Pentagon.

He joins many Republicans who say the defense budget is suffering too many reductions. Shipbuilding is a big business in the 4th District. Palazzo calls the Navy "the world's greatest power projection force" and says the fleet should be bigger. He has pitched multiyear procurement allowances for the DDG-51 destroyer — built in Pascagoula by Huntington Ingalls Industries — saying that such arrangements are cost-effective and create "stability for the defense industrial base."

Palazzo is socially conservative. The House-passed fiscal 2013 defense policy bill included his provision banning same-sex marriages from taking place on military property, but it was stripped from the enacted version.

Palazzo was born in Gulfport. After high school he entered the Marine Corps Reserve and served in the Persian Gulf War. While in the reserve he attended the University of Southern Mississippi and earned an accounting degree and an MBA. As a CPA, he specialized in tax returns for Americans living abroad. He served four years in the Mississippi House and was a strong states' rights advocate, spurning the acceptance of funds from the 2009 stimulus law. "Every time we take a federal dollar from the government, there are strings attached, and as a citizenry, we lose certain rights," he said at the time.

Democratic Rep. Gene Taylor represented the 4th District for more than 20 years, even as its voters consistently backed Republican candidates for president. Arguably the most conservative Democrat in the House, Taylor fell below 60 percent of the vote in a re-election race only once until meeting Palazzo in 2010.

Palazzo was able to tie Taylor to the Democratic leadership he so often opposed. Aided by a late financial boost from the National Republican Congressional Committee, Palazzo won with 52 percent of the vote.

Democratic plans to challenge Palazzo in 2012 never clicked. The winner of the Democratic primary, Michael Herrington, withdrew from the race in September, citing personal reasons. He was replaced on the ballot by Matt Moore, a 36-year-old community college student. Palazzo cruised with 64 percent of the vote.

Key Votes

2012	
Extend a Social Security payroll tax cut and unemployment benefits	YES
Ease securities rules to expand small-business access to capital	YES
Extend for one year subsidized student loan interest rates financed by a cut in health care spending	YES
Cite Attorney General Eric H. Holder Jr. for contempt of Congress	YES
Create a visa program for foreign graduates in high-tech fields	YES
Extend most Bush-era income tax rates while allowing rates for top-bracket earners to rise (Jan. 1, 2013)	NO
2011	
Strike funding for F-35 alternative engine	NO
Prevent EPA from regulating greenhouse gas emissions to address climate change	YES
Extend certain provisions of Patriot Act for four years	YES
Declare opposition to use of ground troops in Libya	YES
Overhaul patent law	YES
Pass compromise debt limit increase plan and establish future spending limits	YES
Allow consideration of measures to implement three trade agreements	YES

CQ Vote Studies

	PARTY UNITY		PRESIDENTIAL SUPPORT	
	SUPPORT	OPPOSE	SUPPORT	OPPOSE
2012	96%	4%	11%	89%
2011	96%	4%	24%	76%

Interest Groups

	AFL-CIO	ADA	CCUS	ACU
2012	14%	0%	92%	84%
2011	0%	5%	100%	84%

Mississippi 4

Southeast — Gulf Coast, Hattiesburg

Mississippi's only Gulf Coast district, the 4th relies on shipbuilding, casinos, petrochemicals and government jobs to fuel the economies in Hancock, Harrison and Jackson counties, the more densely populated areas on the district's southern edge. The University of Southern Mississippi and Camp Shelby, a large military reserves training site, are in Hattiesburg, the other population center to the north.

The coastal counties suffered catastrophic damage in 2005 when Hurricane Katrina displaced 100,000 residents, but populations there now surpass pre-Katrina levels. Harrison County again draws tourists to its nine casinos, and Gulfport has restored some 80 downtown buildings since 2005. National Wildlife Refuge designations near the coast preserve some areas amid development. Tourism revenue, property values and wildlife populations along the district's coast took a hit following the 2010 Deepwater Horizon oil spill. The rural north supports poultry and berry farms, and the large De Soto National Forest sprawls over several counties.

Huntington Ingalls Industries' shipbuilding facilities in the district employ more than 11,000 residents, and the district has become a hub for the U.S. aerospace industry. NASA's John C. Stennis Space Center in Hancock hosts Lockheed Martin, Pratt & Whitney Rocketdyne and federal agencies.

Residents here are fiscally conservative and support the GOP. In the last two decades, the Gulf Coast district has given Republican presidential candidates among their highest percentages statewide. During redistricting after the 2010 census, the 4th District lost parts of three rural counties to the 3rd, but the shifts in the map did not change the political outlook.

Major Industry
Military, shipbuilding, casinos, tourism

Military Bases
Keesler Air Force Base, 8,000 military, 1,859 civilian (2011); Naval Construction Training Center Gulfport, 3,664 military, 799 civilian; Naval Oceanographic Office, 23 military, 867 civilian

Cities
Gulfport, Hattiesburg

Notable
Black Creek is the state's only National Scenic River.

MISSOURI

Atchison
Worth
Mercer
Putnam
Schuyler
Scotland
Clark
Nodaway
Harrison
Gentry
Sullivan
Grundy
Adair
Knox
Lewis
Holt
Andrew
6
Daviess
Dekalb
Livingston
Macon
Shelby
Marion
Linn
St. Joseph
Buchanan
Caldwell
Clinton
Ralls
Chariton
Platte
Monroe
Ray
Carroll
Randolph
Pike
Clay
5
Audrain
Saline
Howard
Lincoln
Boone
1
Kansas City
Lafayette
Montgomery
Columbia
Jackson
Callaway
St. Charles
Warren
Cooper
2
St. Louis
3
Cass
Johnson
Pettis
Moniteau
Osage
Cole
Gasconade
St. Louis
4
Morgan
Henry
JEFFERSON CITY
Bates
Franklin
Benton
Miller
Maries
Jefferson
St. Clair
Crawford
Hickory
Washington
Ste. Genevieve
Camden
Phelps
Vernon
St. Francois
Cedar
Pulaski
Iron
Perry
Polk
Dallas
Laclede
Dent
Barton
Dade
Reynolds
Madison
Cape Girardeau
Greene
Webster
Jasper
Wright
Texas
Cape Girardeau
Springfield
8
Bollinger
Shannon
Wayne
Christian
Lawrence
Carter
Scott
Douglas
Stoddard
Newton
Howell
Mississippi
7
Butler
McDonald
Barry
Stone
Taney
Ozark
Oregon
Ripley
New Madrid
Pemiscot
Dunklin

Gov. Jay Nixon (D)

First elected: 2008
Length of term: 4 years
Term expires: 1/17
Salary: $133,821
Phone: (573) 751-3222
Residence: Jefferson City
Born: Feb. 13, 1956; DeSoto, Mo.
Religion: Methodist
Family: Wife, Georganne Wheeler Nixon; two children
Education: U. of Missouri, B.A. 1978 (political science), J.D. 1981
Career: Lawyer
Political highlights: Mo. Senate, 1987-93; Democratic nominee for U.S. Senate, 1988; Mo. attorney general, 1993-2009; Democratic nominee for U.S. Senate, 1998

ELECTION RESULTS

2012 GENERAL

Jay Nixon (D)	1,494,056	54.8%
David Spence (R)	1,160,265	42.5%
James Higgins (LIBERT)	73,509	2.7%

Lt. Gov. Peter Kinder (R)

First elected: 2004
Length of term: 4 years
Term expires: 1/17
Salary: $86,484
Phone: (573) 751-4727

LEGISLATURE

General Assembly: January-May
Senate: 34 members, 4-year terms
2013 ratios: 24 R, 10 D; 29 men, 5 women
Salary: $35,915
Phone: (573) 751-3766
House: 163 members, 2-year terms
2013 ratios: 109 R, 53 D, 1 vacancy; 124 men, 38 women
Salary: $35,915
Phone: (573) 751-3659

TERM LIMITS

Governor: 2 terms
Senate: 2 terms
House: 4 terms

URBAN STATISTICS

CITY	POPULATION
Kansas City	459,787
St. Louis	319,294
Springfield	159,498
Independence	116,830
Columbia	108,500

REGISTERED VOTERS

Voters do not register by party.

POPULATION

2010 population	5,988,927
2000 population	5,595,211
1990 population	5,117,073
Percent change (2000-2010)	+7.0%
Rank among states (2010)	18
Median age	37.3
Born in state	66.4%
Foreign born	3.5%
Violent crime rate	492/100,000
Poverty level	14.6%
Federal workers	64,362
Military	17,925

ELECTIONS

STATE ELECTION OFFICIAL
(573) 751-2301

DEMOCRATIC PARTY
(573) 636-5241

REPUBLICAN PARTY
(573) 636-3146

MISCELLANEOUS

Web: www.mo.gov
Capital: Jefferson City

U.S. CONGRESS

Senate: 1 Democrat, 1 Republican
House: 6 Republicans, 2 Democrats

STATISTICS BY DISTRICT

District	2012 Vote for President Obama	2012 Vote for President Romney	2008 Vote for President Obama	2008 Vote for President McCain	Black	Asian	Hispanic	Median Income	Over 64	Under 20	College Education	Rural	Sq. Miles
1	80%	19%	80%	19%	49%	2%	3%	$37,115	12%	26%	28%	<1%	225
2	41	57	46	53	4	4	2	71,239	16	25	46	1	466
3	36	62	43	56	3	1	2	51,769	13	27	24	41	6,852
4	36	61	42	57	5	1	3	42,910	14	27	23	53	14,401
5	59	39	62	37	21	2	9	42,572	14	26	25	8	2,425
6	38	60	43	55	4	1	3	49,367	14	27	25	42	18,199
7	30	68	35	63	2	1	4	40,796	15	26	23	38	6,273
8	32	66	38	60	5	1	2	35,965	16	26	14	63	19,901
STATE	**44**	**54**	**49.3**	**49.4**	**12**	**2**	**4**	**45,247**	**14**	**26**	**26**	**31**	**68,742**
U.S.	**51**	**47**	**53**	**46**	**12**	**5**	**17**	**50,052**	**13**	**27**	**29**	**21**	**3,531,905**

Sen. Claire McCaskill (D)

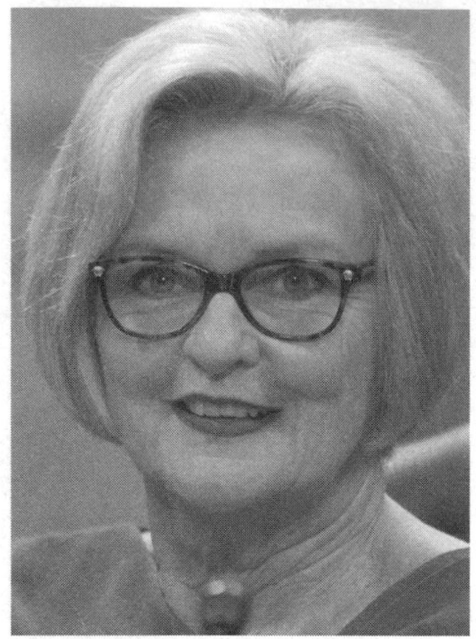

Capitol Office
224-6154
mccaskill.senate.gov
506 Hart Bldg. 20510-2505; fax 228-6326

Committees
Armed Services
Commerce, Science & Transportation
(Consumer Protection, Product Safety & Insurance - Chairwoman)
Homeland Security & Governmental Affairs
(Financial & Contracting Oversight - Chairwoman)
Special Aging

Residence
Kirkwood

Born
July 24, 1953; Rolla, Mo.

Religion
Roman Catholic

Family
Husband, Joseph Shepard; seven children

Education
U. of Missouri, B.A. 1975 (political science), J.D. 1978

Career
Lawyer; city prosecutor

Political Highlights
Mo. House, 1983-89; sought Democratic nomination for Jackson County prosecutor, 1988; Jackson County Legislature, 1991-93; Jackson County prosecutor, 1993-99; Mo. auditor, 1999-2007; Democratic nominee for governor, 2004

ELECTION RESULTS

2012 GENERAL		
Claire McCaskill (D)	1,494,125	54.8%
Todd Akin (R)	1,066,159	39.1%
Jonathan Dine (LIBERT)	165,468	6.1%
2012 PRIMARY		
Claire McCaskill (D)		unopposed

Previous Winning Percentages
2006 (50%)

Elected 2006; 2nd term

Republicans have the clear advantage in Missouri these days, so McCaskill stays relevant by promoting bipartisan efforts on fiscal restraint and seeking out nonpartisan oversight roles. The former auditor and prosecutor spends much of her energy searching for government waste and wrongdoers.

McCaskill comes from a politically active family. Her father served as state insurance director, and her mother was the first woman to serve on the Columbia City Council. She recalls going to political events wearing sashes and "those obnoxious foam little bowler hats" to advertise candidates' campaigns. She caught the political bug, particularly after a teacher urged her to become a lawyer, noting that she was better at arguing than she was in subjects that had obvious right and wrong answers.

After graduating from the University of Missouri and its law school, she clerked for the Missouri Court of Appeals and soon got a job as an assistant prosecutor in Kansas City. In 1982, she won a seat in the Missouri House, where she wrote the state's first minimum-sentencing law for repeat offenders. McCaskill was elected Jackson County prosecutor on her second try in 1992. Six years later, she was elected state auditor.

In 2004, McCaskill took on the Democratic Party establishment by defeating the incumbent governor, Bob Holden, in the primary. She lost the general election to Republican Matt Blunt, the son of House Majority Whip Roy Blunt, by 3 points. (The father is now her Senate colleague.) Two years later, she scored a 2-point victory over Republican incumbent Jim Talent to join the Senate.

In her 2012 campaign for a second term, McCaskill got some electoral help from her GOP opponent. Conservative Rep. Todd Akin set off an explosion of unfavorable national publicity in August with awkward comments about rape victims and pregnancy. Republicans pleaded with him to step aside for another candidate, but Akin refused. What was expected to be a nail-biter of a race turned into a 15-point win for McCaskill.

But even before that electoral windfall, McCaskill was competitively positioned as a fairly independent Democrat. "There's a number of times I have parted with [President Barack Obama]," McCaskill said during a 2012 interview on MSNBC. "And I think if the president were asked about me, he'd say I can be a real pain."

Senators are considering a comprehensive immigration overhaul in the 113th Congress (2013-14), and McCaskill is one of the few Senate Democrats who has publicly opposed "amnesty" for illegal immigrants. She voted against a 2007 bill to stop the deportation of some illegal immigrants brought to the country as children. (She did support a narrower version of the bill in 2010, however.)

In the 112th Congress (2011-12), McCaskill urged Obama to support a federal spending cap — she wrote a bill to create one, working with Tennessee Republican Bob Corker. She called for approval of the proposed Keystone XL pipeline from Canada to Gulf Coast refineries (Obama denied a permit in 2012) and asked Obama to stop pursuing a cap-and-trade system for reducing greenhouse gas emissions. She similarly fought for an end to EPA regulations of some farming operations. She said the rules were costly and redundant.

The government isn't tremendously popular with voters of either party, and McCaskill makes a point of finding and correcting its inefficiencies. She had chaired the Homeland Security and Governmental Affairs Subcommittee on Contracting Oversight, and for the 113th Congress, the jurisdiction of her panel has been expanded to include the finances of every federal agency and department. McCaskill was revved up when she announced the change. "I'm putting every federal agency on notice —any employee or contractor who wastes taxpayer money, or acts inappropriately on the taxpayer dime, will have this committee to answer to," she said.

She introduced a raft of government-focused bills in the 112th Congress, including proposals to cap federal agency expenditures for conferences; to expand whistle-blower protections for non-federal workers whose disclosures involve misuse of federal funds; to create an inspector general's office to audit and investigate Senate programs and operations; and to tighten restrictions on foreign trips lawmakers and aides take for work.

McCaskill also sits on the Armed Services Committee. After reading a report that as much as $60 billion spent on federal contracts in Iraq and Afghanistan had been wasted, McCaskill began pushing legislation in 2012 that would create a lead inspector general in charge of investigating waste and abuse during each overseas contingency. The fiscal 2013 defense law includes her provisions that overhaul rules for wartime contracting.

McCaskill has some ties to Obama, who as a senator campaigned for her in 2006. They worked together in the Senate on ethics rules and correcting problems at Walter Reed Army Medical Center. And she was the first Democratic woman in the Senate to back him in the 2008 primaries against New York Sen. Hillary Rodham Clinton.

But oversight is oversight, and McCaskill teamed with Ohio Republican Rob Portman in 2012 to launch an investigation into the administration's spending on public relations and advertising.

Further cementing her status as one of the chief watchdogs in the Senate, McCaskill in 2013 became the chairwoman of the Commerce, Science and Transportation Subcommittee on Consumer Protection, Product Safety and Insurance.

She has broken from the majority of her Democratic peers on the issue of earmarking. McCaskill and Pennsylvania Republican Patrick J. Toomey have tried to pass a legislative ban on that practice. McCaskill succeeded in limiting the practice of senators putting "secret holds" on nominations and bills, which block floor consideration without any public acknowledgement. She co-sponsored legislation requiring holds to be made public within one legislative day, and the Senate changed its rules in the 112th Congress to require that members who place holds be identified.

Even with her independent streak, McCaskill has voted with Democrats on major bills of recent years. She consistently reiterates her position that critics of the 2010 health care law use scare tactics to drive public opposition. "We have had a lot of Chicken Little around this building over the last few months: 'The sky is falling, the sky is falling,'" she said in March 2010 on the Senate floor. "As time goes on, people in America are going to realize this bill is not full of booby traps, it is full of good things that will reform health care."

When Akin's comments put women's issues in the spotlight, McCaskill defended an Obama administration decision under the health care law to require insurance plans to cover contraception. Republicans protested that entities with religious or moral objections should get exemptions.

The national Republican Party pulled its support of Akin shortly after his controversial remarks, and he never recovered. McCaskill took a break from the campaign when her 84-year-old mother died of kidney and heart complications, but still won easily.

In March 2011, the Missouri Republican Party filed two complaints with the Senate Ethics Committee, asking the panel to investigate McCaskill's use of an airplane, owned by her family, for Senate- and campaign-related activities. McCaskill has since paid the U.S. Treasury $88,000 to cover her use of the plane for official business, and she and her husband paid $287,000 in back taxes on the plane.

Key Votes

2012	
Prohibit health insurance plans from denying coverage based on the sponsor's religious beliefs	YES
Require approval of the Keystone XL oil pipeline	YES
Ease securities rules to expand small-business access to capital	YES
Reauthorize farm and nutrition programs for five years	YES
Limit debate on a bill that would create private-sector cybersecurity standards	YES
Consent to ratification of a treaty setting global standard for the treatment of people with disabilities	YES
Provide $60.4 billion in disaster relief following Superstorm Sandy	YES
Extend most Bush-era income tax rates while allowing rates for top-bracket earners to rise (Jan. 1, 2013)	YES
2011	
Prevent EPA from regulating greenhouse gas emissions to address climate change	NO
Extend certain provisions of Patriot Act for four years	YES
Clear compromise debt limit increase plan and establish future spending limits	YES
Overhaul patent law	NO
Implement Colombia free trade agreement	NO
Limit debate on confirmation of Caitlin J. Halligan to D.C. Circuit Court of Appeals	YES
Extend payroll tax cut and unemployment benefits for two months	YES

CQ Vote Studies

	PARTY UNITY		PRESIDENTIAL SUPPORT	
	SUPPORT	OPPOSE	SUPPORT	OPPOSE
2012	78%	22%	96%	4%
2011	80%	20%	92%	8%
2010	85%	15%	98%	2%
2009	72%	28%	80%	20%
2008	81%	19%	45%	55%
2007	81%	19%	41%	59%

Interest Groups

	AFL-CIO	ADA	CCUS	ACU
2012	91%	80%	63%	20%
2011	84%	85%	45%	0%
2010	94%	90%	27%	17%
2009	89%	95%	43%	28%
2008	90%	80%	75%	20%
2007	95%	90%	9%	8%

Sen. Roy Blunt (R)

Capitol Office
224-5721
blunt.senate.gov
B40C Dirksen Bldg. 20510-2503; fax 224-8149

Committees
Appropriations
Armed Services
Commerce, Science & Transportation
Rules & Administration
Joint Library

Residence
Springfield

Born
Jan. 10, 1950; Niangua, Mo.

Religion
Baptist

Family
Wife, Abigail Blunt; four children

Education
Southwest Baptist U., B.A. 1970 (history); Southwest Missouri State U., M.A. 1972 (history & government)

Career
University president; teacher

Political Highlights
Greene County clerk, 1973-84; Republican nominee for lieutenant governor, 1980; Mo. secretary of state, 1985-93; sought Republican nomination for governor, 1992; U.S. House, 1997-2011

ELECTION RESULTS

2010 GENERAL

Roy Blunt (R)	1,054,160	54.2%
Robin Carnahan (D)	789,736	40.6%
Jonathan Dine (LIBERT)	58,663	3.0%
Jerry Beck (CNSTP)	41,309	2.1%

Previous Winning Percentages
2008 House Election (68%); 2006 House Election (67%); 2004 House Election (70%); 2002 House Election (75%); 2000 House Election (74%); 1998 House Election (73%); 1996 House Election (65%)

Elected 2010; 1st term

Blunt willingly plays the role of a coordinator for the Republican Party. His 14-year run in the House included orchestration of GOP messaging and strategy during most of the George W. Bush administration. Since coming to the Senate, he hasn't missed a beat — colleagues use him as a conduit for communications with each other, the House and the business community.

Blunt was first elected to the House in 1996, after a 20-year career in Missouri state politics. In only his second term, he landed the job of chief deputy whip. Four years later, he was promoted to the whip post. Blunt kept close ties to the Bush administration, carefully coordinating political strategies with the White House and keeping Republicans in line for big votes.

He is somewhat conservative, but his style is mostly non-combative — it plays well in Missouri, which was long considered a battleground state. Blunt maximized his leverage by cultivating relationships with lobbyists. His strategy as whip, he once said, was to make House legislation as conservative as possible, then count on negotiations with the Senate to bring the final versions of bills closer to what the president had in mind.

In hindsight, Blunt says, Republicans might have been a little too close to the White House. As Bush's approval ratings fell, so did Blunt's political stock. He came up short in a bid to become the majority leader in February 2006 (losing to John A. Boehner of Ohio), and he stepped down as whip after Republicans were drubbed in the 2008 elections.

But his popularity at home was untarnished — Blunt easily won a Senate seat in 2010. Republicans also hadn't soured on his potential as a leader. He started out his Senate career as a deputy whip, and at the end of 2011, his Senate colleagues elected him to the No. 5 leadership post of Republican Conference vice chairman. It's a vague job, and Blunt decided to dedicate himself to improving communications between House and Senate Republicans as the 2012 elections approached. Blunt was also the chief Senate liaison for the presidential campaign of Mitt Romney.

Given the range of his connections and his interest in political strategy, Blunt can get involved in just about any policy debate; he is cool under fire and often serves as a media spokesman for the party. He also has a seat on the wide-ranging Appropriation Committee. Blunt is the top Republican on the Agriculture Subcommittee, and in the 113th Congress (2013-14) he touted his addition to the Defense Subcommittee.

At the same time, he joined the Armed Services Committee. In a time of shrinking defense budgets, his new posts are particularly suited to protecting military installations and personnel in his state. The fiscal 2012 defense authorization law included an amendment by Blunt and New York Democrat Kirsten Gillibrand. Active-duty personnel returning from deployments are granted certain employment protections; their provision extends those protections to National Guard troops mobilized for domestic emergency missions, such as natural disasters.

Blunt also sits on the Commerce, Science and Transportation Committee, and in the 113th Congress he is the top Republican on the subcommittee that handles surface transportation and infrastructure security. Blunt noted its jurisdiction over pipelines — unsurprisingly, as energy has been a longtime interest for him. (He was a member of the Energy and Commerce Committee in the House.) Blunt is strongly opposed to cap-and-trade proposals for addressing greenhouse gas emissions. During the 110th Congress (2007-08), Blunt chaired a GOP energy task force that pushed for more oil and gas drilling and incentives for alternative energy.

As a freshman senator, Blunt was the top Republican on the Subcommittee on Competitiveness, Innovation and Export Promotion. He backed passage of trade agreements with Panama, Colombia and South Korea, with agribusiness and industries in his state looking to expand their export markets. When serving in the House, he regularly conducted an agricultural tour of his district, visiting farms and ranches and bringing along trade representatives from Asia.

Blunt was also one of 17 Republican senators to support the revival of expanded federal assistance for workers displaced by international trade — a Democratic demand for considering the three trade pacts. He joined the majority of Republicans, however, in opposing a Democratic bill targeting China that would allow sanctions against trade partners who manipulate their currency's value for an advantage. Blunt told reporters the bill would have a negligible benefit to American businesses and risk a trade war.

Given Blunt's experience as a legislative tactician, he is a natural fit on the Rules and Administration Committee. Late in 2012, he organized resistance to possible changes of the Senate's filibuster rules, which were mostly sought by Democrats who hoped to limit the ability of Republicans to slow or block consideration of various bills. Senate leaders worked out a deal that limited some obstructionist tactics while preserving the option of a filibuster.

For most of his career, Blunt has not been noted as a social conservative. In 2012, however, he was the Senate champion of a proposal to undo a rule established by the 2010 health care law. The Obama administration issued a requirement that insurance providers have to cover contraception. Blunt rolled out a proposal to nullify coverage requirements when employers, insurers or organizations have moral or religious objections to a medical service. Democrats were incensed by the proposal — they said it would effectively allow groups to opt out of covering anything — and used it as alleged evidence of a Republican "war on women" in their political campaigns. When the proposal was offered as an amendment to another bill, the Senate voted to table it.

The son of a dairy farmer and a state legislator, Blunt was raised on a farm near Springfield. After college, he became a high school government and history teacher. But he was active in politics at an early age, working in 1972 on an unsuccessful congressional bid by Republican John Ashcroft. A year later, Blunt was appointed the Greene County clerk by Republican Gov. Christopher S. Bond.

Blunt won the first of two terms as Missouri secretary of state in 1984. After losing the gubernatorial primary in 1992, Blunt accepted the presidency of his alma mater, Southwest Baptist University. He jumped back into public life when GOP Rep. Mel Hancock announced his retirement in 1996. Blunt cruised to victory and was easily re-elected in succeeding years.

When Bond, who had moved to the Senate, announced his retirement, Blunt entered the race as the favorite. Missouri Secretary of State Robin Carnahan was her party's nominee. She tried to paint Blunt as a Washington insider, while Blunt tried to tie her to the policies of congressional Democrats, highlighting her support for the 2009 stimulus law and the health care overhaul. Blunt took more than 54 percent of the vote, enough to win by more than 13 points. On switching chambers, he took over the Senate floor desk and old offices of a storied Missouri senator, Democrat Harry S. Truman.

Blunt's ties to lobbyists have raised eyebrows in the past. In 2002, he tried to slip a provision benefiting Philip Morris USA into a homeland security bill at a time when he was romantically involved with a Philip Morris lobbyist, Abigail Perlman, whom he later married after divorcing his first wife.

Blunt's son Matt was the governor of Missouri from 2005 through 2008. He is now the president of the American Automotive Policy Council, a lobbying group for the "Big Three" U.S. automakers.

Key Votes

2012	
Prohibit health insurance plans from denying coverage based on the sponsor's religious beliefs	NO
Require approval of the Keystone XL oil pipeline	YES
Ease securities rules to expand small-business access to capital	YES
Reauthorize farm and nutrition programs for five years	YES
Limit debate on a bill that would create private-sector cybersecurity standards	NO
Consent to ratification of a treaty setting global standard for the treatment of people with disabilities	NO
Provide $60.4 billion in disaster relief following Superstorm Sandy	NO
Extend most Bush-era income tax rates while allowing rates for top-bracket earners to rise (Jan. 1, 2013)	YES
2011	
Prevent EPA from regulating greenhouse gas emissions to address climate change	YES
Extend certain provisions of Patriot Act for four years	YES
Clear compromise debt limit increase plan and establish future spending limits	YES
Overhaul patent law	YES
Implement Colombia free trade agreement	YES
Limit debate on confirmation of Caitlin J. Halligan to D.C. Circuit Court of Appeals	NO
Extend payroll tax cut and unemployment benefits for two months	YES

CQ Vote Studies

	PARTY UNITY		PRESIDENTIAL SUPPORT	
	SUPPORT	OPPOSE	SUPPORT	OPPOSE
2012	79%	21%	47%	53%
2011	81%	19%	54%	46%
2010	96%	4%	29%	71%
2009	91%	9%	24%	76%
2008	97%	3%	80%	20%
2007	98%	2%	90%	10%
2006	98%	2%	97%	3%
2005	98%	2%	91%	9%
2004	97%	3%	100%	0%
2003	98%	2%	100%	0%

Interest Groups

	AFL-CIO	ADA	CCUS	ACU
2012	9%	10%	100%	72%
2011	16%	20%	100%	70%
2010	0%	0%	80%	100%
2009	14%	5%	87%	92%
2008	7%	15%	83%	88%
2007	13%	10%	79%	96%
2006	7%	0%	100%	88%
2005	14%	0%	93%	96%
2004	7%	0%	100%	96%
2003	0%	5%	97%	88%

Rep. William Lacy Clay (D)

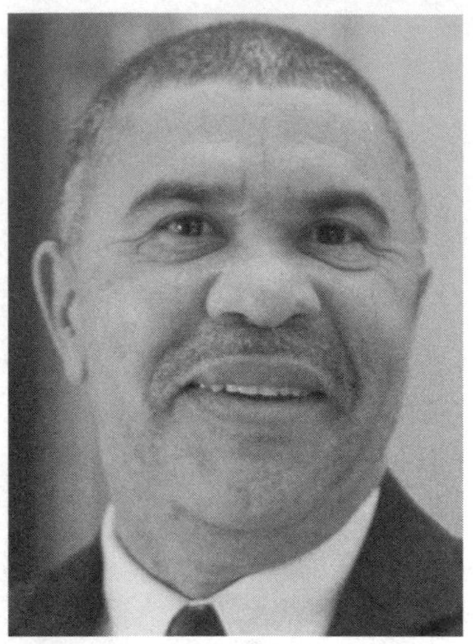

Capitol Office
225-2406
lacyclay.house.gov
2418 Rayburn Bldg. 20515-2501; fax 226-3717

Committees
Financial Services
Oversight & Government Reform

Residence
St. Louis

Born
July 27, 1956; St. Louis, Mo.

Religion
Roman Catholic

Family
Divorced; two children

Education
U. of Maryland, B.S. 1983 (government & politics)

Career
Paralegal; real estate agent; congressional aide

Political Highlights
Mo. House, 1983-91; Mo. Senate, 1991-2000

ELECTION RESULTS

2012 GENERAL		
William Lacy Clay (D)	267,927	78.7%
Robyn Hamlin (R)	60,832	17.9%
Robb E. Cunningham (LIBERT)	11,824	3.5%
2012 PRIMARY		
William Lacy Clay (D)	57,791	63.3%
Russ Carnahan (D)	30,943	33.9%
Candice Britton (D)	2,570	2.8%
2010 GENERAL		
William Lacy Clay (D)	135,907	73.6%
Robyn Hamlin (R)	43,649	23.6%
Julie Stone (LIBERT)	5,223	2.8%

Previous Winning Percentages
2008 (87%); 2006 (73%); 2004 (75%); 2002 (70%); 2000 (75%)

Elected 2000; 7th term

Clay's critics have accused him of riding the coattails of his famous father: William L. Clay, an African-American political pioneer who served in the House for 32 years. When Clay struggled in college, his father's connections helped him land a job in the House documents room. Later, the younger Clay tapped his dad's powerful political network in St. Louis to help secure seats in the state House and Senate, and ultimately to succeed his father in Congress.

But no one can accuse Clay of coasting anymore. Missouri lost a district in the reapportionment process before the 2012 election, and when House incumbents settled on their re-election plans, Clay was facing a primary challenge from another political scion — Russ Carnahan, the son of former Missouri Democratic Gov. Mel Carnahan. Clay took more than 63 percent of the vote. Old friendships and political alliances were destroyed in the process, but Clay proved he could stand on his own.

The general election was an afterthought in the heavily Democratic district, so after dispatching Carnahan, Clay turned his attention to helping President Barack Obama's campaign in Missouri. It was a familiar role for Clay, who has spent recent years defending the administration from GOP attacks.

In the 112th Congress (2011-12), for example, he used his seat on the Oversight and Government Reform Committee to berate Republicans for what he called a "disgraceful political witch hunt" against Attorney General Eric H. Holder Jr. The GOP majority voted to hold Holder in contempt of Congress in June 2012 for failing to turn over documents related to a sting operation that ended with government-supplied guns in the hands of Mexican drug cartels.

When Democrats controlled the House, Clay pushed open-government initiatives on the panel. In March 2007, he won House passage of legislation to stop former presidents and vice presidents from shielding their records from the public. It would have upended President George W. Bush's executive order of 2001, aimed at protecting some of his father's White House records, that allowed former Oval Office occupants and their successors to keep certain documents secret. It failed to move in the Senate, but Obama instituted the law's provisions by executive order in 2009.

Clay also made a splash in 2011 when he used his seat on the Financial Services Committee to defend the Federal Reserve. Some Republicans accuse the Fed of slowing economic recovery. Longtime Fed critic Ron Paul, a Texas Republican, held a February hearing of the monetary policy subcommittee to excoriate the agency. As the panel's top Democrat, Clay tried to spoil the day for him. "There is no doubt that the Fed's prudent actions to carefully expand the money supply were appropriate, and they are helping put Americans back to work," he said.

The panel's jurisdiction shifted somewhat at the start of the 113th Congress (2013-14) — it now includes trade — but Clay remains its top Democrat. At hearings in early 2013, he again defended "quantitative easing" as keeping interest rates low and aiding the recovery of the housing market.

Much of Clay's work is on topics less abstract than monetary policy. He is a member of the Congressional Black Caucus and the Congressional Progressive Caucus, the group of the most-liberal Democrats. Clay frequently chimes in on housing or employment policies that stand to benefit his district, which is the only minority-majority district in the state.

He joined other prominent black politicians in 2012 to protest new voting laws put in place by many Republican state governments — Clay and others described new standards for registration and identification as voter suppression efforts targeting minorities.

Clay — who goes by his middle name, Lacy — is an avid cook and a golf fanatic, but his mother told a local newspaper that politics "has been his life." He was 12 when his father was elected to Congress, and he spent his teenage years in suburban Maryland, attending high school in Silver Spring and college at the University of Maryland.

He was placed on academic probation in his freshman year, prompting his father to encourage him to find a job. He landed in the House's documents room, where he spent two years before finding work as a House doorman. He took seven years to earn his degree. But it was during that time that Clay says he decided to follow in his father's footsteps.

He was starting law school when an opening in the Missouri House led him back to St. Louis to run in a special election. He spent 17 years in the General Assembly, serving eight years in the House before winning a 1991 special election for a state Senate vacancy. He supplemented his part-time legislator's salary by working in real estate and as a paralegal.

Clay was the presumed heir to the 1st District seat from the moment his father announced his retirement in 1999. He won easily in 2000 with 75 percent of the vote.

His 2012 primary battle was set up when Missouri's Republican-controlled legislature pushed through its redistricting plan over the veto of Democratic Gov. Jay Nixon. It merged Clay's old 1st District with Carnahan's 3rd. The new 1st District covers all of St. Louis.

The race was ugly from the start. After the new map came out, Carnahan approached Clay on the House floor and cursed at him for, in Carnahan's view, not doing enough to protect Carnahan's district. Clay and state Democrats urged Carnahan to run for a suburban seat vacated by Republican Todd Akin, who was running for the Senate.

Clay painted Carnahan as a puppet of Wall Street, citing his vote in 2008 for a $700 billion rescue package for banks. And Clay consolidated his support in the black community, arguing that keeping an African-American in the seat was crucial to the Missouri Democratic Party's cohesion. If he were to lose to Carnahan, Clay told the St. Louis Post-Dispatch, "it would be viewed as setting back the black community, for sure."

Carnahan accused Clay of siding with rent-to-own companies in their bid to escape regulation. He argued that the companies victimized minority communities disproportionately and that customers usually paid more than the original list price of the items they rented, such as televisions and furniture.

In the end, Clay dominated in the city's black wards; Carnahan, who spent a lot more money on the campaign than Clay did, was nearly as strong in the white ones. Neither candidate would say race was a factor.

Key Votes

2012

Extend a Social Security payroll tax cut and unemployment benefits	NO
Ease securities rules to expand small-business access to capital	NO
Extend for one year subsidized student loan interest rates financed by a cut in health care spending	NO
Cite Attorney General Eric H. Holder Jr. for contempt of Congress	?
Create a visa program for foreign graduates in high-tech fields	NO
Extend most Bush-era income tax rates while allowing rates for top-bracket earners to rise (Jan. 1, 2013)	YES

2011

Strike funding for F-35 alternative engine	YES
Prevent EPA from regulating greenhouse gas emissions to address climate change	NO
Extend certain provisions of Patriot Act for four years	NO
Declare opposition to use of ground troops in Libya	NO
Overhaul patent law	YES
Pass compromise debt limit increase plan and establish future spending limits	YES
Allow consideration of measures to implement three trade agreements	NO

CQ Vote Studies

	PARTY UNITY		PRESIDENTIAL SUPPORT	
	SUPPORT	OPPOSE	SUPPORT	OPPOSE
2012	97%	3%	89%	11%
2011	96%	4%	80%	20%
2010	97%	3%	80%	20%
2009	99%	1%	96%	4%
2008	97%	3%	11%	89%

Interest Groups

	AFL-CIO	ADA	CCUS	ACU
2012	94%	95%	25%	0%
2011	100%	90%	25%	0%
2010	92%	85%	25%	0%
2009	100%	100%	33%	4%
2008	100%	100%	47%	8%

Missouri 1

St. Louis; eastern St. Louis County

Framed by the Mississippi and Missouri rivers to the east and north, the St. Louis-based 1st District is a mixture of middle-class suburbs west and north of the city, a downtown business district, colleges and universities, and poor urban areas. The 1st is relatively young and diverse compared with other Missouri districts, and a decades-long population decline in St. Louis, especially among whites, has not reversed. The loss of a congressional district in the state during decennial reapportionment gathered all of St. Louis together in one district; the inclusion of suburban areas added some Republican votes, but the 1st remains solidly Democratic overall.

High-tech manufacturing jobs at Boeing and other plants remain important to the regional economy, but many of the district's warehouses sit vacant. State officials hope to spur job growth at Lambert St. Louis International Airport to the northwest in St. Louis County suburbs. In an effort to turn St. Louis into a new hub for international trade, the airport began receiving cargo flights from China in late 2011.

Health care and life sciences are also strong industries in the 1st. St. Louis-based hospital network BJC HealthCare supports medical research endeavors at the nonprofit life-sciences campus in Forest Park. The Anheuser-Busch brewery in the southern part of the city remains a St. Louis icon, but the beer-maker maintains a significantly smaller workforce since merging with Belgian InBev in 2008. The local craft beer sector — including brewing at Maplewood's Schlafly Bottleworks — has expanded.

The Gateway Arch, urban Forest Park — which is about 500 acres larger than New York's Central Park — and quirky destinations like the City Museum help attract tourists to the city. Billions of dollars in downtown renovation over the last decade — including at Busch Stadium, home to baseball's Cardinals — is expected to continue with renovations to the Edward Jones Dome, where the Rams play football.

Major Industry

Aircraft manufacturing, health care, beer manufacturing, higher education

Cities

St. Louis, Florissant, University City, Hazelwood, Spanish Lake (unincorp.)

Notable

The first suit filed by Dred Scott was tried in St. Louis' historic Old Courthouse, now part of Jefferson National Expansion Memorial Park; The 1904 Olympics were held at Washington University's Francis Field.

Rep. Ann Wagner (R)

Capitol Office
225-1621
wagner.house.gov
435 Cannon Bldg. 20515-4312; fax 225-2563

Committees
Financial Services

Residence
Ballwin

Born
Sept. 13, 1962; St. Louis, Mo.

Religion
Roman Catholic

Family
Husband, Ray Wagner; three children

Education
U. of Missouri, B.S.B.A. 1984

Career
Party official; homemaker; supply chain and customer service manager

Political Highlights
Lafayette Township Committee, 1996-2005; Mo. Republican Party chairwoman, 1999-2005; U.S. ambassador to Luxembourg, 2005-09; sought Republican National Committee chairwoman, 2011

ELECTION RESULTS

2012 GENERAL		
Ann Wagner (R)	236,971	60.1%
Glenn Koenen (D)	146,272	37.1%
Bill Slantz (LIBERT)	9,193	2.3%
2012 PRIMARY		
Ann Wagner (R)	53,583	65.8%
Randy Jotte (R)	18,644	22.9%
John Morris (R)	6,041	7.4%
James O. Baker (R)	3,185	3.9%

Elected 2012; 1st term

Wagner was a formidable political figure even before she got elected to the House — she has an impressive record as a Republican Party official and fundraiser. GOP freshmen chose her as their liaison to the House leadership team.

Wagner grew up in St. Louis, where her parents operated carpet and flooring stores; she met her husband, Ray, when he was working for her parents. She has said that her husband drew her into politics. They moved to Jefferson City when he got a job as an aide to Gov. John Ashcroft, and "in a state with a small capital, you either work in government or you do party politics," she told the St. Louis Business Journal.

Choosing the latter, she rose through the ranks of the Missouri Republican Party, and in 1999 she became its chairwoman. Wagner oversaw a stark turnaround of GOP fortunes in the Show Me State. She was also a co-chairwoman of the Republican National Committee during George W. Bush's first term, and in 2005 Bush appointed her ambassador to Luxembourg. She made a bid to become the RNC chairwoman in 2011. (Ray Wagner, meanwhile, is in charge of government relations for Enterprise Rent-A-Car.)

Wagner, a member of the conservative Republican Study Committee, was placed on the Financial Services Committee and its panel on government-sponsored enterprises. She has called for the end of Fannie Mae and Freddie Mac, once the government establishes "market guidelines that provide transparency and legal certainty for private investors," so that the private sector can take the reins of the housing finance sector. She is also on the Oversight and Investigations Subcommittee; her time in Luxembourg, a nation that has been criticized for its banking secrecy laws, could be useful in that venue.

Wagner had no trouble winning the 2nd District seat, which was left open by Rep. Todd Akin as he made a disastrous bid for the Senate.

The energetic Wagner has musical talents, as well. She had a vocal performance scholarship to the University of Missouri.

Missouri 2

Western St Louis County; part of St. Charles County

Fanning west from an inner ring of suburbs just outside St. Louis to the Ozark Mountain foothills, the 2nd contains roughly half of St. Louis County, a portion of fast-growing St. Charles County and a small corner of Jefferson County in the district's southeast. Missouri lost a congressional seat in reapportionment following the 2010 census: The newly drawn 2nd District acquired some areas that had formerly belonged to one of the St. Louis-based seats.

Decades of city-to-county residential and commercial migration led to the urbanization of St. Louis County. Wealthy residents have followed white-collar jobs to Chesterfield in western St. Louis County and O'Fallon (shared with the 3rd) in St. Charles County, while working-class neighborhoods decline. Some of the state's wealthiest zip codes and strongest public schools are found in the 2nd in places such as Ladue.

Two of the area's largest employers are SSM Health Care and Monsanto. The regional hospital system and the international agribusiness giant both have headquarters in Creve Coeur. Other large private sector employers include Enterprise Rent-a-Car. The National Geospatial-Intelligence Agency and the St. Louis VA Medical Center-Jefferson Barracks are both in the southeastern corner of the 2nd.

Completing major highway refurbishment projects, especially on the bridges crossing the Missouri River from St. Louis County into St. Charles County, is a key goal for local officials hoping to ease commuting woes. Several retail hubs near the St. Louis city limits and in wealthy areas farther out draw urban and suburban crowds.

The district strongly backs Republicans, sending Ann Wagner to the U.S. House by a wide margin. Republican Mitt Romney won 57 percent of the district's 2012 presidential vote, 4 percentage points higher than John McCain would have taken from the area within the new 2nd in the 2008 presidential contest.

Major Industry
Health care, financial services, retail

Cities
O'Fallon (pt.), St. Charles (pt.), Chesterfield

Notable
The Spirit of St. Louis Airport in Chesterfield was named in honor of the custom-built, single-engine monoplane that St. Louis native Charles Lindbergh flew in 1927 on the first solo nonstop trans-Atlantic flight.

Rep. Blaine Luetkemeyer (R)

Capitol Office
225-2956
luetkemeyer.house.gov
2440 Rayburn Bldg. 20515-2509; fax 225-5712

Committees
Financial Services
Small Business

Residence
St. Elizabeth

Born
May 7, 1952; Jefferson City, Mo.

Religion
Roman Catholic

Family
Wife, Jackie Luetkemeyer; three children

Education
Lincoln U. (Mo.), B.A. 1974 (political science)

Career
Insurance agency owner; rancher; banker; state finance examiner

Political Highlights
Village of St. Elizabeth Board of Trustees, 1978-87; Mo. House, 1999-2005; sought Republican nomination for Mo. Treasurer, 2004; Mo. Tourism Commission director, 2006-08

ELECTION RESULTS

2012 GENERAL		
Blaine Luetkemeyer (R)	214,843	63.5%
Eric C. Mayer (D)	111,189	32.9%
Steve Wilson (LIBERT)	12,353	3.6%
2012 PRIMARY		
Blaine Luetkemeyer (R)		unopposed
2010 GENERAL		
Blaine Luetkemeyer (R)	162,724	77.4%
Christopher W. Dwyer (LIBERT)	46,817	22.3%

Previous Winning Percentages
2008 (50%)

Elected 2008; 3rd term

Luetkemeyer describes the regulatory system as spinning out of control, burdening businesses and keeping regular folks from pursuing the American dream. The "onslaught" has become his office's primary focus, he says: "This is all we spend our time on almost every day."

He grew up raising hogs and cattle, while also cultivating dreams of a baseball career. But he followed his father into finance. Luetkemeyer (LUTE-ka-myer) is a former banker and state banking regulator. Since 2011 he has served on the Financial Services Committee, and he once chaired Missouri's version of that panel in the state House.

"We have to improve the burdensome regulatory environment that we're in, and we've got to fix the punitive tax code that we've got right now," he said. During the 112th Congress (2011-12), Luetkemeyer joined much of his panel in taking a hard look at the 2010 financial regulatory overhaul known as Dodd-Frank.

He sees a role for some regulations, to provide structure and to dissuade bad actors. But Luetkemeyer calls Dodd-Frank a perfect example of policy trying to fix problems that don't exist. The law's rules rope in all sorts of financial institutions — such as community banks, payday lenders and insurance companies — that did not contribute to the financial collapse of 2008, he said.

"You impugn their integrity by saying they're part of the problem when they weren't," he said. "How can a payday lender be a systemic risk to the financial system? I mean, it's absurd. How can a small community bank in the middle of my district in Missouri be a financial systemic risk?"

In 2011, he introduced a bill to exempt small banks from certain regulations, including some set out by both Dodd-Frank and the 2002 accounting overhaul known as Sarbanes-Oxley. Luetkemeyer maintains that many federal regulators don't understand how audits and examinations of smaller banks actually transpire: "I can tell you from having been in that situation, both sides of the table, the guys in D.C. haven't got a clue."

He espouses a gentle approach from Washington, with harsher remedies reserved for repeat offenders. For institutions with a history of good behavior, "there's no reason to go in there and rip them a new one."

Luetkemeyer's voting has mostly followed the party line; he almost always sides with a majority of House Republicans when they oppose a majority of Democrats. He has long been a staunch social conservative; Luetkemeyer opposes abortion and same-sex marriage. He belongs to the conservative Republican Study Committee.

He will work with Democrats on some issues, however. In 2012, Luetkemeyer and Georgia Democrat David Scott introduced a bill to eliminate the requirement that ATMs carry a sticker or other external sign disclosing their fees — a mandate they said is outdated, since fees are disclosed on the screen during transactions. President Barack Obama signed their bill that December.

"We've got some rather enterprising folks that go in and tear the sticker off," Luetkemeyer said. "Then they turn around and they threaten a class-action suit for the institution.'"

In 2013, the House passed his bipartisan bill to exempt financial institutions from requirements to send customers annual notices about their privacy policies, if those policies haven't changed. He touts the measure as a way for the institutions to save paper and money.

Luetkemeyer rejoined the Small Business Committee in 2013, where he is the vice chairman to fellow Missouri Republican Sam Graves. That panel's work on business lending and capital formation overlaps with the work of the

Financial Services Committee.

His ties to Missouri run deep. Luetkemeyer grew up in St. Elizabeth, and his family raised cattle and hogs on his great-grandfather's nearby farm. He purchased his own cattle ranch after high school, and that business helped him pay for college. Luetkemeyer was strongly critical of an Obama administration proposal, withdrawn in 2012, to ban children under 16 from using power-driven farm equipment. Whoever prepared the proposal "probably doesn't know the difference between a horse and a cow," he said.

Luetkemeyer's mother was a teacher, and his father was an insurance agent. He and his wife, Jackie, now live two houses away from his family home. After college, he became a bank examiner for the state of Missouri. He later followed in his father's footsteps to work for the family-owned Bank of St. Elizabeth, serving as a loan officer and vice president. In 1988, he started the Luetkemeyer Insurance Agency, which he sold after 20 years.

Neither banking nor politics may have been his first-choice career. He played baseball in college and tried out unsuccessfully for the Kansas City Royals and the Pittsburgh Pirates. A shoulder injury is a legacy of that pursuit, but he is still a huge baseball fan. He follows the Royals, but his heart is often in St. Louis: "We sort of live and breathe Cardinals baseball."

He considers Missouri colleague Roy Blunt, the former House GOP whip who is now a senator, to be his mentor. And his work in politics is also shaped by his religious views. Raised in a family with strong Catholic values, he taught Sunday school and served on the board of St. Lawrence Catholic Church.

His political career began when he landed a seat on the Village of St. Elizabeth Board of Trustees, where he served for nine years. In 1998, he won election to the Missouri House. He ran unsuccessfully for the Republican nomination for state treasurer in 2004, but two years later Republican Gov. Matt Blunt — the son of Roy Blunt — appointed him director of the Missouri Tourism Commission.

When six-term Republican Kenny Hulshof decided to run for governor in 2008, Luetkemeyer jumped into the race to succeed him, campaigning as a social and fiscal conservative. In a five-way primary, Luetkemeyer won with nearly 40 percent of the vote.

That November, he faced Democratic state Rep. Judy Baker, a former health care consultant. Luetkemeyer, citing Baker's support of abortion rights, said she was too liberal to represent the district. Using $1.8 million of his own money, he won by less than 3 points — far short of the 11-point margin by which Republican Sen. John McCain of Arizona won the district's presidential vote. Democrats did not field an opponent against him in 2010, however. He won easily in 2012.

Key Votes

2012	
Extend a Social Security payroll tax cut and unemployment benefits	YES
Ease securities rules to expand small-business access to capital	YES
Extend for one year subsidized student loan interest rates financed by a cut in health care spending	YES
Cite Attorney General Eric H. Holder Jr. for contempt of Congress	YES
Create a visa program for foreign graduates in high-tech fields	YES
Extend most Bush-era income tax rates while allowing rates for top-bracket earners to rise (Jan. 1, 2013)	YES
2011	
Strike funding for F-35 alternative engine	NO
Prevent EPA from regulating greenhouse gas emissions to address climate change	YES
Extend certain provisions of Patriot Act for four years	YES
Declare opposition to use of ground troops in Libya	YES
Overhaul patent law	YES
Pass compromise debt limit increase plan and establish future spending limits	YES
Allow consideration of measures to implement three trade agreements	YES

CQ Vote Studies

	PARTY UNITY		PRESIDENTIAL SUPPORT	
	SUPPORT	OPPOSE	SUPPORT	OPPOSE
2012	96%	4%	18%	82%
2011	97%	3%	24%	76%
2010	96%	4%	29%	71%
2009	97%	3%	27%	73%

Interest Groups

	AFL-CIO	ADA	CCUS	ACU
2012	14%	0%	100%	80%
2011	0%	5%	100%	76%
2010	7%	0%	88%	100%
2009	10%	5%	80%	96%

Missouri 3

East central — Jefferson City and St. Louis exurbs

The 3rd, which borders five other Missouri districts and Illinois, takes in the state capital — Jefferson City — and most of St. Charles County near St. Louis, as well as the grape-growing "Rhineland" wine region that stretches between the two. Part of the Lake of the Ozarks creeps into the district's southwestern corner.

The district's eastern arms curl north and south around St. Louis suburbs, capturing more-removed communities that continue to gain residents as the city loses population. Although General Motors employs a significant workforce and has begun expansion at its Wentzville plant, St. Charles County (shared with the 2nd), has a mainly white-collar workforce employed in the financial services and telecommunications industries.

Many residents in these bedroom communities commute to jobs in O'Fallon (shared with the 2nd) or travel to the city over congested highways. Jefferson County residents in the southern St. Louis suburbs face similarly heavy commutes into the city on Interstate 55. Overall, as the population of metropolitan St. Louis has spread outward, millions of dollars are being invested into the region's transportation infrastructure.

Manufacturing and agriculture dominate the forested hills and Missouri River valley towns between St. Louis and the state capital. Ameren's Callaway Nuclear Generating Station provides energy and more than 1,000 jobs. State government is the main employer in Jefferson City and nearby.

Missouri lost a U.S. House seat in reapportionment after the 2010 census, and the new 3rd eats up some of the shifted areas near St. Louis and takes in much of the former 9th. The 3rd is GOP territory — Mitt Romney won the district's portion of every county wholly or partly in the 3rd in the 2012 presidential race — although Democratic Sen. Claire McCaskill eked out a victory in Franklin County in her successful 2012 Senate re-election bid.

Major Industry

Financial services, telecommunications, manufacturing, government

Cities

O'Fallon (pt.), St. Charles (pt.), St. Peters (pt.), Jefferson City, Wentzville

Notable

Winston Churchill gave his famous "Iron Curtain" speech after World War II at Westminster College in Fulton, which now hosts the National Churchill Museum.

Rep. Vicky Hartzler (R)

Capitol Office
225-2876
hartzler.house.gov
1023 Longworth Bldg. 20515-2504; fax 225-0148

Committees
Agriculture
Armed Services
Budget

Residence
Harrisonville

Born
Oct. 13, 1960; Archie, Mo.

Religion
Evangelical Christian

Family
Husband, Lowell Hartzler; one child

Education
U. of Missouri, B.S. 1983 (home economics & education); Central Missouri State U., M.S. 1992 (education)

Career
Farmer; rancher; farm equipment dealership owner; homemaker; teacher

Political Highlights
Mo. House, 1995-2001

ELECTION RESULTS

2012 GENERAL		
Vicky Hartzler (R)	192,237	60.3%
Teresa Hensley (D)	113,120	35.5%
Thomas Holbrook (LIBERT)	10,407	3.3%
2012 PRIMARY		
Vicky Hartzler (R)	71,615	84.0%
Bernie Mowinski (R)	13,645	16.0%
2010 GENERAL		
Vicky Hartzler (R)	113,489	50.4%
Ike Skelton (D)	101,532	45.1%
Jason Michael Braun (LIBERT)	6,123	2.7%
Greg Cowan (CNSTP)	3,912	1.7%

Elected 2010; 2nd term

Hartzler has taken a meat-and-potatoes approach in the House, staying close to the Republican line and doting on the agricultural and military interests in her district. When she makes national news, it usually has to do with her conservative Christian views.

Hartzler has said that "public service is a ministry," and she wrote the book on waging faith-based campaigns. "Running God's Way" is based on her election to the Missouri House in the mid-1990s. More than a few Democratic strategists took the Lord's name in vain when she was elected in 2010 — she defeated 17-term incumbent Ike Skelton, the sitting chairman of the Armed Services Committee.

Religious convictions have spurred some of her most noted political stands. Hartzler was at the forefront of a successful 2004 campaign in favor of a state constitutional amendment banning gay marriage. She supports a federal constitutional amendment to give civil rights protections to the unborn from the point of fertilization. In 2011, after the Obama administration announced that it would no longer defend in court the 1996 law allowing states not to recognize same-sex unions from other states, Hartzler found more than 120 co-sponsors for her resolution condemning the decision.

Hartzler has other policy interests, and some of them are just as informed by her personal story. A lifetime in farming landed her on the Agriculture Committee. She grew up driving tractors and cleaning the hog barns on her parents' farm, and Hartzler says the experience helped shape her work habits, as well as her faith: "You can't control the weather, so you do a lot of praying as a farmer."

Hartzler and her husband own a farm three miles away from the one still operated by her parents and sister. They also sell combines, tractors and other large farm equipment at three locations in the area. One store is near the Lamar birthplace of another political Missouri farmer, Harry S. Truman.

Federal farm programs lapsed in the fall of 2012 — the House never voted on a long-term reauthorization. But Hartzler did sign off on a bill that was approved by the Agriculture Committee. It eliminated direct payments to farmers — Hartzler has received them in the past — while shifting the safety net for farmers to crop insurance programs. "It's a win-win for the taxpayer," she said. "It prevents the large disaster payments that used to be the case in the past."

A short-term extension of farm programs was agreed upon in the closing moments of the 112th Congress (2011-12).

Citing a need to "feed the world," Hartzler supports spending on agriculture research. In 2011, she voted several times against attempts on the House floor to reduce discretionary funding in the agriculture spending bill. Hartzler calls estate taxes, a perennial issue among small farmers, "highway robbery." She wants them kept low, if not eliminated.

The Agriculture panel has jurisdiction over commodities markets, and Hartzler has joined in the Republican effort to roll back the 2010 financial regulatory overhaul known as Dodd-Frank. In 2012, the House passed her bill to exempt small banks, credit unions and farm credit banks from many of the law's regulations. They do not have the resources to comply, she said.

Hartzler belongs to both the Tea Party Caucus and the Republican Study Committee, and she says government agencies are "running amok over the rights of individuals." But one agency she defends is the Pentagon, and she does so from the Armed Services Committee. Hartzler calls national defense the most important function of the government required by the Constitution.

She advocates expanding the operations at Fort Leonard Wood and Whiteman Air Force Base in her district, and she has vehemently opposed cuts to defense spending, calling them a threat to readiness. Hartzler voted against a deficit reduction deal in August 2011, citing its defense spending cuts.

Her religious values also are reflected in her Armed Services work. Hartzler unsuccessfully pleaded with military service chiefs in April 2011 not to certify the repeal of the "don't ask, don't tell" policy on openly gay servicemembers. "You are the last force to be able to stop this onerous policy," she said.

In March 2011, Hartzler told Politico that the United States had a "moral obligation" in Libya "for people wanting freedom who are being slaughtered by a dictator." She voted against a resolution calling for a U.S. withdrawal.

Hartzler joined the Budget Committee for the 113th Congress (2013-14), giving her another forum for her fiscal priorities.

Before her first run for the Missouri House, Hartzler was a home economics teacher. She said she sees little need for federal involvement in education outside of "some funding through different grants like Carl Perkins grants" for vocational education students.

Hartzler's working life started early, as she helped out on the family farm. Her parents were on the board of the local Farm Bureau and served in other agricultural organizations. There were 38 students in her graduating class at Archie High School, and Hartzler said she enjoyed being a "big duck in a little puddle." She was a standout athlete, editor of the yearbook and president of the Future Homemakers of America.

After graduating from the University of Missouri, she spent a decade as a teacher and sports coach while also working the farm of her husband's family, which she and her husband have since purchased. She met her husband during her senior year of college, although they grew up three miles apart, going to different high schools.

Hartzler served three terms in the Missouri House and touts an overhaul of Missouri's adoption laws as one of her proudest achievements. She left that chamber to raise her own adopted daughter, Tiffany.

Skelton had not faced a competitive election since 1982. But Hartzler was able to tap into voter discontent with Congress, the economy and the Democratic agenda to become one of three Republicans to unseat a committee chairman in 2010. She won with 50 percent of the vote to Skelton's 45 percent.

When Missouri redrew its electoral map for the 2012 election, Hartzler picked up Democratic turf near Columbia. Cass County prosecutor Teresa Hensley got the Democratic nomination and tried to blame Hartzler for the farm bill's expiration. Hartzler kept her focus on the economy, built a significant fundraising advantage and won by almost 25 points.

Key Votes

2012	
Extend a Social Security payroll tax cut and unemployment benefits	YES
Ease securities rules to expand small-business access to capital	YES
Extend for one year subsidized student loan interest rates financed by a cut in health care spending	YES
Cite Attorney General Eric H. Holder Jr. for contempt of Congress	YES
Create a visa program for foreign graduates in high-tech fields	YES
Extend most Bush-era income tax rates while allowing rates for top-bracket earners to rise (Jan. 1, 2013)	NO
2011	
Strike funding for F-35 alternative engine	NO
Prevent EPA from regulating greenhouse gas emissions to address climate change	YES
Extend certain provisions of Patriot Act for four years	YES
Declare opposition to use of ground troops in Libya	YES
Overhaul patent law	NO
Pass compromise debt limit increase plan and establish future spending limits	NO
Allow consideration of measures to implement three trade agreements	YES

CQ Vote Studies

	PARTY UNITY		PRESIDENTIAL SUPPORT	
	SUPPORT	OPPOSE	SUPPORT	OPPOSE
2012	97%	3%	13%	87%
2011	97%	3%	22%	78%

Interest Groups

	AFL-CIO	ADA	CCUS	ACU
2012	14%	0%	100%	80%
2011	0%	10%	87%	88%

Missouri 4

West central — Columbia, southern Kansas City suburbs

Lakes and rivers, small-scale farming and sparsely populated prairie cover much of the 4th, with the population clustered in two corners of this west central district. To the northeast is Columbia, the district's most populous city and home to the University of Missouri's flagship campus, while the Kansas City metropolitan area provides manufacturing jobs in the west. The 4th stretches across 21 whole counties and parts of three others.

Columbia relies on higher education, health care and the insurance industry. The University of Missouri and its hospitals employ more than 15,000 people. IBM also plays a key role in local economic development. Growing suburbs south of Kansas City boosted Cass County's population between 2000 and 2010; retail superstores are the county's biggest employers and many residents commute to jobs in Jackson County (in the 5th).

Median household incomes in the central part of the district are low; more than one-fifth of the population in Dade and Vernon counties lives in poverty. The landscape offers outdoor recreation in the Lake of the Ozarks region. Henry, St. Clair, Benton and Hickory counties lure hunters to the forested hills bordering the 56,000-acre Harry S. Truman Reservoir. Trout fishers cast their lines in Bennett Spring State Park.

The 4th has veteran populations — Whiteman Air Force Base is in Johnson County and Pulaski County has Fort Leonard Wood — and a nearly uniform conservative bent. White-collar and university-centric Boone County provides liberal votes — it was the only county in the 4th to back Barack Obama in 2012 — and some counties in the west and north supported incumbent Democratic Sen. Claire McCaskill in her 2012 re-election.

Major Industry
Higher education, agriculture, defense, manufacturing

Military Bases
Fort Leonard Wood, 7,000 military, 9,500 civilian (2012); Whiteman Air Force Base, 3,300 military, 2,800 civilian (2012)

Cities
Columbia, Belton, Sedalia, Raymore

Notable
The University of Missouri was the first state university established in the Louisiana Purchase territory.

Rep. Emanuel Cleaver II (D)

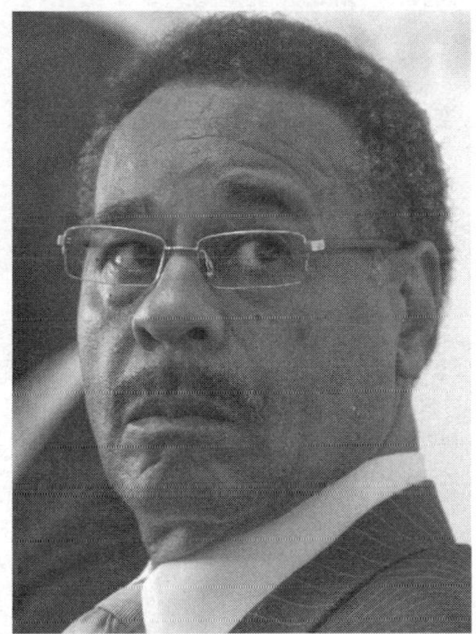

Capitol Office
225-4535
cleaver.house.gov
2335 Rayburn Bldg. 20515-2505; fax 225-4403

Committees
Financial Services

Residence
Kansas City

Born
Oct. 26, 1944; Waxahachie, Texas

Religion
Methodist

Family
Wife, Dianne Cleaver; four children

Education
Murray State College (Okla.), attended 1963-64; Prairie View A&M College, B.S. 1972 (sociology); Saint Paul School of Theology, M.Div. 1974

Career
Minister; radio talk show host; car wash owner; civil rights group chapter founder; charitable group manager

Political Highlights
Sought Democratic nomination for Mo. House, 1970; sought Democratic nomination for Kansas City Council, 1975; Kansas City Council, 1979-91; mayor of Kansas City, 1991-99

ELECTION RESULTS

2012 GENERAL		
Emanuel Cleaver II (D)	200,290	60.5%
Jacob Turk (R)	122,149	36.9%
Randall Langkraehr (LIBERT)	8,497	2.6%
2012 PRIMARY		
Emanuel Cleaver II (D)		unopposed
2010 GENERAL		
Emanuel Cleaver II (D)	102,076	53.3%
Jacob Turk (R)	84,578	44.2%
Randall Langkraehr (LIBERT)	3,077	1.6%

Previous Winning Percentages
2008 (64%); 2006 (64%); 2004 (55%)

Elected 2004; 5th term

Cleaver's pursuit of pleasant discourse across racial and political lines has been tested in recent years, but he has stuck to his message. "Civility creates legislative bipartisanship," he says. "It's infinitely easier to compromise with someone you like than someone you consider to be the enemy."

As the chairman of the Congressional Black Caucus in the 112th Congress (2011-12), Cleaver was a man in the middle. He was an enthusiastic supporter of Barack Obama and a national co-chairman of the president's re-election campaign. But, like much of the Black Caucus, he was frustrated by the pace of economic recovery. As such, he became adept at gingerly managing policy disagreements between his largely liberal caucus and the president who was once a member.

"We have on a number of occasions suppressed our feelings. That has been a challenge," Cleaver said in 2012. "There is almost universal belief that fortuitously I was chosen as the chair at this time because of my tendency to quiet discord." He has yielded the chairmanship to Marcia L. Fudge of Ohio but remains active in the CBC.

Civility is not a political gimmick for Cleaver, who is an ordained Methodist minister. In the weeks before his first term in the House, he talked of reviving a Civility Caucus. His chief collaborator has been West Virginia Republican Shelley Moore Capito, and they have taken to the House floor to debate issues they differ on. Cleaver sends weekly notes to all of his House colleagues with a meditation on civility.

During the debt and deficit debates of 2011, Cleaver signed on to the bipartisan "Go Big" letter, in which 100 representatives urged $4 trillion in deficit reduction via a combination of revenue increases and spending cuts — he considered it an impressive show of cooperation. In June 2012, he bemoaned the "divisive posturing" of House Republicans in voting to hold Attorney General Eric H. Holder Jr. in contempt for refusing to turn over documents in an investigation of a gun-tracking program. Cleaver led a walkout of dozens of Democrats in protest of the move.

Cleaver was reportedly a victim of uncivil behavior during debate on the 2010 health care overhaul. He said a tea party protester spit on him as he walked to the House chamber to vote for the measure. Still, he maintains that most opposition to Obama is not based on race, and that the tea party, "though misguided, is a group of patriotic Americans who believe that the government can't be a force for equality in the country, particularly economic equality."

His civility does not guarantee political moderation. Cleaver is a loyal Democrat, almost always voting with a majority of the party when it diverges from a majority of Republicans.

He criticized Republicans during the summer of 2011 for refusing to support an increase in the country's debt limit absent major spending cuts. Cleaver made waves when he tweeted that a final deal to lift the debt ceiling was "a sugar-coated Satan sandwich."

Should Republicans one day succeed in implementing their budget proposals from the 112th Congress — which included structural changes to several entitlement programs — the backlash "might be the best thing that happened to the Democratic Party since FDR," he said.

Cleaver disdains efforts by his colleagues to mix religion and politics. In 2011, he was one of nine House members who went on the record opposing a resolution reaffirming "In God We Trust" as the national motto.

On the other hand, in 2007, Speaker Nancy Pelosi appointed Cleaver to a panel on energy independence and global warming with the specific charge to reach out to his fellow ministers to get them engaged on the issue. Cleaver is a passionate spokesman for energy independence — he uses a 1998 Ford Econoline van, converted to run on vegetable oil as well as diesel fuel, as an office-on-wheels in his district.

Cleaver also aims to transform his district into a model of sustainability. His "Green Impact Zone" is a 150-square-block area of urban Kansas City that will feature weatherized homes, a job-training program and an electric smart grid. The initiative was largely funded by the 2009 economic stimulus law. At Cleaver's insistence, a report detailing all expenditures is released every 45 days. "It might be the biggest and the best thing I've ever done," he said.

Though relatively quiet on the Financial Services Committee, Cleaver has proposed requiring "energy audits" for homes purchased with federal loans, to identify possible improvements to energy efficiency.

The most prominent item in Cleaver's congressional office is a framed photo of the shack in Waxahachie, Texas, where he grew up with his father, mother and three sisters. Cleaver's description of the dwelling as a "slave shanty" is no rhetorical exercise: It housed slaves in the 1800s.

Cleaver lived there until he was almost 8, when the family moved to public housing. Eventually, Cleaver's father, a maître d' at an exclusive club, saved enough money to buy a home in a predominately white part of town. But the reality of segregation soon led the family to move to the black district on the east side.

When Cleaver was young, he had a bad temper and a penchant for fighting. He wears a mustache to cover up stitches on his upper lip, where he was hit with a brick. He eventually learned to control his anger with the help of his college football coach.

Cleaver has served as a pastor at St. James United Methodist Church in Kansas City since 1972 and still delivers the occasional sermon there; he founded Harmony in a World of Difference, an organization that promotes interfaith dialogue.

He was elected to the Kansas City Council in 1979 and became the city's mayor in 1991. In eight years in office, he helped bring new businesses to the region and oversaw the rejuvenation of the historic 18th and Vine jazz district. But he said he was most proud of averting strife at a time when racial disturbances occurred in other urban areas.

In 2004, Cleaver sought to succeed retiring Democratic Rep. Karen McCarthy. Emphasizing his mayoral record, he defeated Republican businesswoman Jeanne Patterson by 13 points.

In each of his re-elections campaigns, he has squared off against Republican Jacob Turk. Their closest contest was Cleaver's 9-point victory in 2010.

Key Votes

2012	
Extend a Social Security payroll tax cut and unemployment benefits	NO
Ease securities rules to expand small-business access to capital	YES
Extend for one year subsidized student loan interest rates financed by a cut in health care spending	NO
Cite Attorney General Eric H. Holder Jr. for contempt of Congress	?
Create a visa program for foreign graduates in high-tech fields	NO
Extend most Bush-era income tax rates while allowing rates for top-bracket earners to rise (Jan. 1, 2013)	YES
2011	
Strike funding for F-35 alternative engine	NO
Prevent EPA from regulating greenhouse gas emissions to address climate change	NO
Extend certain provisions of Patriot Act for four years	NO
Declare opposition to use of ground troops in Libya	NO
Overhaul patent law	YES
Pass compromise debt limit increase plan and establish future spending limits	NO
Allow consideration of measures to implement three trade agreements	NO

CQ Vote Studies

	PARTY UNITY		PRESIDENTIAL SUPPORT	
	SUPPORT	OPPOSE	SUPPORT	OPPOSE
2012	95%	5%	89%	11%
2011	95%	5%	78%	22%
2010	98%	2%	81%	19%
2009	99%	1%	96%	4%
2008	99%	1%	13%	87%

Interest Groups

	AFL-CIO	ADA	CCUS	ACU
2012	95%	95%	27%	0%
2011	100%	90%	19%	8%
2010	92%	100%	13%	0%
2009	100%	95%	36%	0%
2008	100%	90%	61%	4%

Missouri 5

Kansas City and suburbs

Kansas City has a signature taste — its namesake barbecue — and a signature sound — a bluesy style of jazz; Missouri's most populous city anchors the 5th. Nearly 90 percent of the district's population lives in Jackson County and a few close-in areas of Clay County, both of which are shared with the 6th.

Beyond Kansas City's minority and lower-income neighborhoods, central business district and high-end downtown lofts, the district stretches east to take in most of Independence and other Jackson County suburbs and then into three sparsely populated counties.

One of the nation's largest rail hubs, Kansas City is served by four major railroads and remains a center for logistics and warehousing despite slow recovery from nationwide shipping declines. Financial firms, including tax preparation service H&R Block, have headquarters in the 5th. Across greater Kansas City, telecommunications jobs, a life sciences research industry and the federal government support a white-collar workforce. Luxury condos have sprung up in renovated office buildings in Kansas City's River Market and Crown Center neighborhoods, and plans are in the works for a downtown streetcar system. The city is also engaged in a renovation of its impoverished Center City neighborhood.

Kansas City's Hispanic population has grown significantly since 2000 and is largely concentrated northeast of downtown; the 5th includes all of Kansas City's black-majority neighborhoods. Wealthier residents live in the suburban communities of Blue Springs and growing Lee's Summit (split with the 6th). Further east, the population thins in Ray, Lafayette and Saline counties, which do not have the racial and ethnic diversity of Kansas City.

Jackson County's voters largely back Democratic candidates, but Lee's Summit and the district's rural counties lean decidedly Republican at the state and federal levels.

Major Industry
Transportation, financial services, telecommunications, agriculture

Cities
Kansas City (pt.), Independence (pt.), Lee's Summit (pt.)

Notable
The Negro Leagues Baseball Museum is in the 18th & Vine Historic Jazz District in Kansas City.

Rep. Sam Graves (R)

Capitol Office
225-7041
graves.house.gov
1415 Longworth Bldg. 20515-2506; fax 225-8221

Committees
Small Business - Chairman
Transportation & Infrastructure

Residence
Tarkio

Born
Nov. 7, 1963; Fairfax, Mo.

Religion
Baptist

Family
Separated, three children

Education
U. of Missouri, B.S. 1986 (agronomy)

Career
Farmer

Political Highlights
Mo. House, 1993-95; Mo. Senate, 1995-2000

ELECTION RESULTS

2012 GENERAL		
Sam Graves (R)	216,906	65.0%
Kyle Yarber (D)	108,503	32.5%
Russ Lee Monchil (LIBERT)	8,279	2.5%
2012 PRIMARY		
Sam Graves (R)	59,388	80.3%
Christopher Ryan (R)	9,945	13.4%
Bob Gough (R)	4,598	6.2%
2010 GENERAL		
Sam Graves (R)	154,103	69.4%
Clint Hylton (D)	67,762	30.5%

Previous Winning Percentages
2008 (59%); 2006 (62%); 2004 (64%); 2002 (63%); 2000 (51%)

Elected 2000; 7th term

Small businesses have been touted by both Republicans and Democrats as a key to economic recovery, and Graves sits atop the House committee charged with tending to their health. He is a staunch opponent of federal regulation and an ally of Republican leaders. As a chairman, he has painted the Obama administration as an impediment to entrepreneurs' success.

For six generations, the business of Graves' family has been farming. A lifelong resident of tiny Tarkio, he returned to the family farm after graduating from the University of Missouri in 1986 with a degree in agronomy. Now his younger brother and his father run the farm, raising corn, soybeans and cattle. He still waxes rhapsodic about the many uses of baling wire and his memories of climbing up on the 1968 John Deere 4020 tractor that his grandfather bought new. When he's in his district, Graves sometimes helps out on the farm.

He became the ranking member of the Small Business Committee in 2009, then its chairman in 2011. Under current House GOP rules, he can hold the gavel through the end of the 113th Congress (2013-14).

Graves contributed to some legislative victories in his first term as chairman. From his committee, he railed against two provisions of the 2010 health care law. One required businesses to file reports with the IRS on any vendor paid more than $600 in a year, while the other required federal, state and local governments to begin withholding 3 percent of their payments to contractors. Both provisions were designed to frustrate tax cheats (and thereby raise revenue), but businesses and Graves complained about the compliance burden they imposed. Repeals of both provisions were enacted.

At the end of 2011, President Barack Obama signed a six-year reauthorization of a grant program to help small companies participate in federally funded research. Graves insisted on including a provision to increase incentives for research that could be commercialized, and he agreed to increase the size of the grants. He said he hoped the program would spur job growth. For the most part, however, Graves sticks with the GOP's budget-cutting agenda. He has proposed big budget cuts for the Small Business Administration, saying it spends too much on duplicative and ineffective programs.

Other efforts by Graves during the 112th Congress (2011-12) also fit into Republican themes. He condemned the health care law and EPA regulation as impediments to hiring and economic recovery. And he held hearings to warn the new Consumer Financial Protection Bureau, created as part of the 2010 financial regulatory overhaul, to steer clear of new regulations on small companies.

When the Obama administration proposed a reorganization of federal agencies charged with promoting trade, Graves offered his own plan that would give Congress more oversight authority. The administration, in turn, disliked his proposals to expand the percentage of federal contracts going to small companies and to limit the government's ability to bundle contracts together in a way that makes it more difficult for small companies to compete.

A number of bills moved through the Small Business Committee and the House, then died in the Democratic Senate.

With an overhaul of the tax code on the agenda for 2013, Graves has insisted that changes include both the corporate and individual income tax code, as many small companies file taxes using the individual code. Graves has also co-sponsored a bill to replace most federal taxes with a national sales tax.

Graves is sometimes willing to let the government take a more active role when it will benefit the rural parts of his district. In 2011, his amendment to an energy and water appropriations bill shifted $1 million away from environmental conservation programs to levee maintenance. Levee breaches in Graves' home county had caused flooding along the Missouri River.

He also sits on the Transportation and Infrastructure Committee. He counts as one of his most significant legislative accomplishments a provision in the 2005 highway law that banned a legal avenue for people injured by a rental car to sue the rental car company as well as the driver of the vehicle. He played a small role in the 2012 reauthorization of highway spending: A Graves amendment ensured that farmers transporting their goods to market would not be affected by new Transportation Department rules governing how long truckers can spend behind the wheel.

Graves is a former member of the Agriculture Committee and hopes to return there as chairman — current Chairman Frank D. Lucas of Oklahoma will hit the GOP-imposed term limit at the end of 2014.

As an Eagle Scout, Graves is a supporter of the Boy Scouts of America, often praising the organization from the House floor.

Graves' involvement in politics was a natural fit, given his family's long history in northwest Missouri government. His great-grandfather, also named Sam, was a Democrat who served on the Atchison County Commission. Graves' brother Todd was the U.S. attorney for western Missouri.

Graves became civically involved through the Missouri Farm Bureau, and he once was named the national organization's outstanding young farmer. He spent two years in the Missouri House and six in the state Senate.

Six months before the 2000 election, Democratic Rep. Pat Danner announced her retirement, citing a battle with breast cancer. Graves jumped into the primary contest and quickly overshadowed several less-known Republican hopefuls. Democrats nominated Danner's son, Steve, but Graves ran an assertive campaign and secured a victory.

His relatively easy re-elections include a 2008 besting of Kay Barnes, a former Democratic mayor of Kansas City. Missouri lost a House seat in reapportionment after the 2010 census, and heading into the 2012 elections, the 6th District expanded from 26 mostly rural counties to 37 counties encompassing all of northern Missouri. The change did not seem to hamper Graves, who won easily.

Graves was the subject of an anonymous ethics complaint in 2009 after he invited a business partner of his wife's to testify before the Small Business Committee during a hearing on renewable fuels. Neither Graves nor the witness acknowledged the relationship publicly at the hearing, but the Ethics Committee exonerated Graves several months later, saying that no House rule prohibited such an invitation.

In April 2012, Graves and his wife announced that they planned to divorce.

Key Votes

2012	
Extend a Social Security payroll tax cut and unemployment benefits	NO
Ease securities rules to expand small-business access to capital	YES
Extend for one year subsidized student loan interest rates financed by a cut in health care spending	YES
Cite Attorney General Eric H. Holder Jr. for contempt of Congress	YES
Create a visa program for foreign graduates in high-tech fields	YES
Extend most Bush-era income tax rates while allowing rates for top-bracket earners to rise (Jan. 1, 2013)	-
2011	
Strike funding for F-35 alternative engine	YES
Prevent EPA from regulating greenhouse gas emissions to address climate change	YES
Extend certain provisions of Patriot Act for four years	YES
Declare opposition to use of ground troops in Libya	YES
Overhaul patent law	YES
Pass compromise debt limit increase plan and establish future spending limits	YES
Allow consideration of measures to implement three trade agreements	+

CQ Vote Studies

	PARTY UNITY		PRESIDENTIAL SUPPORT	
	SUPPORT	OPPOSE	SUPPORT	OPPOSE
2012	99%	1%	13%	87%
2011	96%	4%	23%	77%
2010	95%	5%	28%	72%
2009	98%	2%	19%	81%
2008	89%	11%	54%	46%

Interest Groups

	AFL-CIO	ADA	CCUS	ACU
2012	10%	0%	100%	84%
2011	21%	25%	100%	76%
2010	8%	0%	88%	100%
2009	11%	0%	79%	96%
2008	47%	40%	83%	88%

Missouri 6

North — St. Joseph and part of Kansas City, Hannibal

Running across the entire northern tier of Missouri along the Iowa border, and from the Missouri River in the west to the Mississippi River in the east, the 6th District covers nearly three dozen counties, many of them rural. To the southwest, the 6th dips into Kansas City and parts of some Jackson County suburbs. The district's only population center is along the Missouri River from St. Joseph in Buchanan County south to Kansas City.

Platte, Clay and eastern Jackson counties surround portions of Kansas City, which the 6th splits with the neighboring 5th. Platte County's Kansas City International Airport is a hub for travel and aviation employment. Manufacturing jobs are tied to production at Claycomo's Ford factory and a Harley Davidson plant near the airport.

The state's largest city north of Kansas City — about an hour's drive — is St. Joseph, which was the Pony Express terminus for riders carrying mail to and from California 150 years ago. It remains a distribution center and an economic hub, with veterinary pharmaceutical jobs and food-processing plants in Buchanan County.

The roughly 18,000-sqaure-mile district is the state's top producer of corn, soybeans and hogs. Agricultural production supports food and biofuel processing here. Plans to develop wind farms in the district's sparsely populated center have been met by concerns over market sustainability.

Kirksville is home to Truman University, and to the east in Marion County, a modest tourism industry is sustained in Hannibal along the shores of the Mississippi, where sites commemorate Mark Twain's boyhood home.

The new 6th, which was extended to the east during decennial remapping, is politically and demographically homogenous. Minorities make up less than 10 percent of the population, and residents across the district have strongly conservative leanings.

Major Industry
Aviation, agriculture and food processing, manufacturing, health care

Cities
Kansas City (pt.), Independence (pt.), Lee's Summit (pt.), St. Joseph

Notable
The Jesse James Home in St. Joseph is where the outlaw was shot and killed in 1882.

Rep. Billy Long (R)

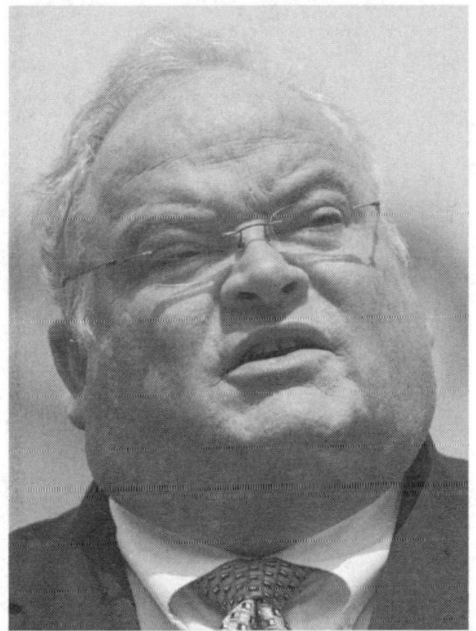

Capitol Office
225-6536
long.house.gov
1541 Longworth Bldg 20515-2507; fax 225-5604

Committees
Energy & Commerce

Residence
Springfield

Born
Aug. 11, 1955, Springfield, Mo.

Religion
Presbyterian

Family
Wife, Barbara Long; two children

Education
U. of Missouri, attended 1973-74

Career
Auction company owner; Realtor; radio talk show host

Political Highlights
No previous office

ELECTION RESULTS

2012 GENERAL		
Billy Long (R)	203,565	63.9%
Jim Evans (D)	98,498	30.9%
Kevin Craig (LIBERT)	16,668	5.2%
2012 PRIMARY		
Billy Long (R)	62,917	59.7%
Mike Moon (R)	22,860	21.7%
Tom Stilson (R)	19,666	18.6%
2010 GENERAL		
Billy Long (R)	141,010	63.4%
Scott Eckersley (D)	67,545	30.4%
Kevin Craig (LIBERT)	13,866	6.2%

Elected 2010; 2nd term

Long has said that he's "fed up" with career politicians, but he has a post that many career politicians would envy. After establishing himself as a non-disruptive conservative in his freshman term, Long finds himself on the roster of the Energy and Commerce Committee.

Most people trying to describe Long eventually settle on "colorful." He's an auctioneer, Realtor, avid bass fisherman, former radio host and wearer of cowboy hats. Long gets wrapped up in anecdotes, has a crowd-pleasing sense of humor and dashes off the occasional one-liner on his Twitter account. After winning election in 2010, he told Gannett News Service that he disagreed with a newspaper story that called him a "smack-talking auctioneer."

"I'm not a smack-talker. I'm more of a colloquial talker," Long told Gannett. "I've got a lot of Ozark sayings. I use a lot of Billyisms, as I call them. But I'm sure not a smack-talker."

That bore out in the 112th Congress (2011-12). Long is on board with Republican Party plans to reduce federal spending and shrink government involvement in health care and other areas. But he isn't a national spokesman for those causes, and even with his professed animus toward Washington, he hasn't given Republican leaders many headaches, as some anti-establishment conservatives have.

Early in his first term, Long voted against a final spending package for fiscal 2011 that was bigger than the Republican version he supported. After that, however, he almost always voted with a majority of Republicans when they opposed a majority of Democrats. Long isn't a prolific author of legislation; Georgia Republican Lynn Westmoreland in 2011 described Long as "not a detail person." (To handle details, Long hired a former Westmoreland aide as his chief of staff.)

He left the Homeland Security and Transportation and Infrastructure committees to join Energy and Commerce in the 113th Congress (2013-14). Long has seats on the subcommittees on Commerce, Manufacturing and Trade; Communications and Technology; and Oversight and Investigations.

Long has made a point of promoting free trade, which he sees as opening markets to the farmers and manufacturers in his district. He voted for pacts with Colombia, Panama and South Korea, and he was among the half of House Republicans that supported expanded federal assistance for workers displaced by international trade. In 2012, Long helped organize the support of fellow GOP freshmen for normalizing trade relations with Russia. President Barack Obama signed a bill to do so a few months later.

Long took some interest in technology issues during cybersecurity debates on the Homeland Security Committee in the 112th Congress. He supports the sharing of information between the private sector and the government to bolster network safety, but he wants regular reports to Congress in order to ensure that the privacy of regular citizens isn't violated when information is shared.

Energy and Commerce handles a lot of health care legislation, and Long has called the 2010 health care law an "unmitigated disaster."

He wants small businesses to have more leeway to join together to allow them to negotiate stronger coverage. He favors programs that entice health care providers to work in rural areas, by forgiving portions of their student loans. And Long adamantly opposes any federal spending that can be seen as promoting abortion.

But he pointed to the fiscal debates of 2011 as the most important accomplishment of his early career. He maintains that Republicans "completely changed the conversation" in Washington by forcing Democrats to accept tens of billions of dollars in cuts to government spending. Early in 2013, Long wrote to constituents that "every government agency should get a haircut. ... I support across-the-board spending cuts for all agencies." He has co-sponsored a bill to eliminate most federal taxes and replace them with a national sales tax.

Long hasn't hesitated to call himself a member of the tea party movement. "You remember that old Barbara Mandrell song, 'I was country before country was cool?' We've been tea partying in the 7th District of Missouri before the tea party was cool," he said to the McClatchy-Tribune News Service.

However, the tea party movement hasn't always been enamored of Long. In May 2011, a tornado leveled large parts of Joplin in his district, killing 161 people. Long was quick to thank the federal government for coming to Joplin's aid, praising Obama and embracing Minority Leader Nancy Pelosi on the House floor. He lauded the work of the Federal Emergency Management Agency. Some conservative commentators accused Long of "shedding his tea party stripes" in asking for more federal assistance.

In his one term on the Transportation and Infrastructure Committee, he focused on streamlining government activity. He introduced a 2011 bill to shield from judicial review any federal decision to issue a permit or license for a surface transportation project. Long wrote that the measure would prevent delays and cost increases caused by "frivolous lawsuits."

The panel was also referred a Long bill to block the EPA from classifying livestock manure as a hazardous substance. He said "environmental extremists" were proposing just that. In the summer of 2011, Long adopted a practice of the career politician whom he replaced by embarking on a tour of his district's farms. Republican Roy Blunt, who was elected to the Senate in 2010, had done such tours for years.

Long grew up in Missouri. His father was in the furniture business but had other interests as well, including a miniature golf course that Long helped manage as a teenager. He went to the University of Missouri for a few years but dropped out and went into the real estate business. He thought he might have some success auctioning homes, and that led to him opening his own auction company in 1983. He has served as president of the Missouri Professional Auctioneers Association.

He later took a job as a morning talk show host on a radio station reaching much of the district he now represents. He has described his show as "a poor man's cross between Paul Harvey and Rush Limbaugh."

Blunt's Senate campaign in 2010 opened up the House seat he had held since 1997. Long won a crowded and competitive GOP primary with almost 37 percent of the vote. He easily defeated Democrat Scott Eckersley in the solidly Republican district and had no problems winning re-election in 2012.

Key Votes

2012	
Extend a Social Security payroll tax cut and unemployment benefits	YES
Ease securities rules to expand small-business access to capital	YES
Extend for one year subsidized student loan interest rates financed by a cut in health care spending	YES
Cite Attorney General Eric H. Holder Jr. for contempt of Congress	YES
Create a visa program for foreign graduates in high-tech fields	YES
Extend most Bush-era income tax rates while allowing rates for top-bracket earners to rise (Jan. 1, 2013)	NO
2011	
Strike funding for F-35 alternative engine	YES
Prevent EPA from regulating greenhouse gas emissions to address climate change	YES
Extend certain provisions of Patriot Act for four years	+
Declare opposition to use of ground troops in Libya	YES
Overhaul patent law	YES
Pass compromise debt limit increase plan and establish future spending limits	YES
Allow consideration of measures to implement three trade agreements	YES

CQ Vote Studies

	Party Unity		Presidential Support	
	SUPPORT	OPPOSE	SUPPORT	OPPOSE
2012	97%	3%	13%	87%
2011	97%	3%	19%	81%

Interest Groups

	AFL-CIO	ADA	CCUS	ACU
2012	14%	0%	100%	96%
2011	0%	5%	100%	92%

Missouri 7

Southwest — Springfield, Joplin

Located in the state's fast-growing southwestern corner, the 7th includes Missouri's third-largest city, Springfield in Greene County, as well as the regional getaway destination Branson. Its borders take in 10 GOP-heavy southwestern Missouri counties as well as a corner of Webster County. Agriculture, tourism revenue and an expansive health care industry keep the region's economy afloat, as some areas battle high poverty rates.

Roughly half of the 7th's population lives in Greene or neighboring Christian County in the eastern half of the district. Springfield has a strong health care industry anchored by several major hospitals and clinics. Missouri State University is in Springfield, and national retail giants Bass Pro Shops and O'Reilly Auto Parts both have headquarters there. The district's other population center, Joplin in Jasper County on the state's western edge, continues to rebuild following a catastrophic tornado in 2011.

Hotels, museums and family attractions — from country music shows to Christian-themed musical theater — make Branson, a town of 11,000 people and 50 entertainment venues, another hub of cultural and economic activity. Visitors also stay at resorts around Taneycomo and Table Rock lakes. Springfield-Branson National Airport serves four major airlines. Much of a two-decade improvement project for U.S. Highway 71, part of which winds south of Joplin on a route linking Kansas City to Arkansas, was finished in 2012; the road will be renamed Interstate 49.

The Ozark Mountain region has experienced significant growth in black and Hispanic populations, but remains overwhelmingly white overall. McDonald County, with an 11 percent Hispanic population, has the highest proportion of minority residents in the district. The Assemblies of God, based in Springfield, is among the religious groups that reflect the area's devout, conservative population; the region has been represented by Republicans in the U.S. House for decades.

Major Industry
Agriculture, tourism, health care, transportation

Cities
Springfield, Joplin

Notable
George Washington Carver's boyhood home in Diamond (Newton County) is a national monument.

Rep. Jason Smith (R)

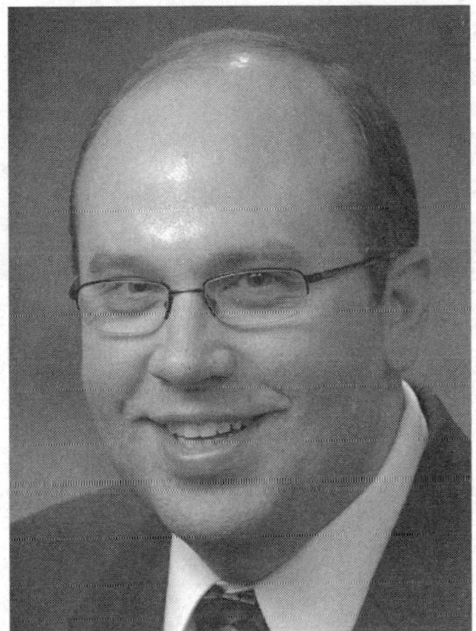

Capitol Office
225-4404
2230 Rayburn Bldg., Washington, DC 20515

Committees
Has not been assigned committees

Residence
Salem

Born
June 16, 1980; St. Louis, Mo.

Religion
Assemblies of God

Family
Single

Education
U. of Missouri, B.S. 2001 (agricultural economics & business administration); Oklahoma City U., J.D. 2004

Career
Real estate company owner; Realtor; farm owner; lawyer

Political Highlights
Missouri House, 2006-13 (speaker pro tempore, 2013)

ELECTION RESULTS

2013 SPECIAL ELECTION*		
Jason Smith (R)	42,145	67.1%
Steve Hodges (D)	17,203	27.4%
Doug Enyart (CNSTP)	2,265	3.6%
Bill Slantz (LIBERT)	968	1.5%

* Results were not certified as of press time.

Elected June 2013; 1st term

Although Republicans have held the 8th District since 1981, the election of Smith marked a change for the region — he is much younger and significantly more conservative than his predecessor, noted moderate Jo Ann Emerson.

Smith grew up in rural southern Missouri. His parents worked in an auto shop, and his family has long been involved with agriculture. He now owns the family farm. Smith got degrees in agricultural economics and business administration from the University of Missouri, and he completed a law degree at Oklahoma City University in 2004. He then returned home to start his legal career. He also operates his own real estate development business.

His political career got rolling in 2005 when he won a special election and became one of the youngest members in the history of the Missouri House. The state has term limits for its lawmakers, which allows assertive politicians to move quickly into leadership roles. Smith was selected as the majority whip after the 2010 election, and two years later he became the speaker pro tem.

Smith is conservative, both fiscally and socially. He told The Missouri Times that he has a "passion for agriculture," and he speaks frequently of the need to reduce regulations on farmers. In 2013, he proposed an amendment to the state Constitution to block any law that "abridges the right of farmers and ranchers to employ agricultural technology and modern livestock production and ranching practices." It also would prevent rules and regulations that "unreasonably restrict hunting, fishing and harvesting wildlife." In 2012, Democratic Gov. Jay Nixon signed Smith's bill to require periodic review of administrative rules to determine whether they are still needed.

Emerson resigned in January 2013 to become the president of the National Rural Electric Cooperative Association. Smith was aggressive in seeking the nomination for the June special election to fill the vacancy, driving thousands of miles for face-to-face meetings with scores of GOP functionaries. Once they placed him on the ballot, he had little trouble in the solidly Republican district.

Missouri 8

Southeast — Cape Girardeau, Ozark Plateau

The 8th is an expansive district, stretching north up the Mississippi Valley from the state's "bootheel" tip to exurban St. Louis sprawl in parts of Jefferson County's Festus and Crystal City, then west across national forests and bountiful farmland. The landscape includes most of the 1.5 million-acre Mark Twain National Forest as well as the 80,000-acre Ozark National Scenic Riverways.

Cape Girardeau, on the shores of the Mississippi River, is the region's most populous city and its economy relies on health care and manufacturing. Population is heavily concentrated in the northern portion of the 8th, which includes half of Jefferson County. In recent years, Rolla, a onetime manufacturing stronghold, has attracted technology start-ups to the area near Missouri University of Science and Technology.

The 8th has the lowest median household income of any district statewide and high unemployment rates. Years of declines in the manufacturing, mining and lumber industries hurt small factories, lead and lime production, and logging interests. But job growth is expected in The Old Lead Belt, a region of the eastern Ozarks where mining has been a mainstay, and increased construction demand could help timber producers. Landowners in the southeastern portion of the 8th continue recovery after a 130,000-acre flood swamped the region in 2011. Tens of millions of dollars in crop damage keep federal funding of levees a top priority for local farmers.

The 8th trends conservative in federal elections, having sent Republicans to Congress since the 1980s and backing recent GOP presidential candidates. Democrats can win local and state legislative races in the bootheel, where blacks make up one-fourth of the population. They also hold sway with blue-collar voters in Washington and Iron counties and voters near St. Louis who tend to be less socially conservative than the district's rural residents.

Major Industry
Agriculture, manufacturing, mining, lumber

Cities
Cape Girardeau, Rolla, Poplar Bluff

Notable
The nation's mean center of population is northeast of Plato in Texas County.

MONTANA

Lincoln
Sanders
Mineral
Flathead
Lake
Kalispell
Missoula
Missoula
Ravalli
Granite
Powell
Glacier
Deer Lodge
Beaverhead
Silver Bow
Butte
Lewis and Clark
Teton
Pondera
Jefferson
HELENA
Madison
Toole
Cascade
Broadwater
Meagher
Gallatin
Great Falls
Liberty
Park
Bozeman
Chouteau
Judith Basin
Hill
Sweet Grass
Wheatland
Stillwater
Golden Valley
Fergus
Carbon
Blaine
Musselshell
Petroleum
Yellowstone
Billings
At Large
Phillips
Big Horn
Treasure
Garfield
Rosebud
Valley
McCone
Powder River
Custer
Prairie
Daniels
Roosevelt
Dawson
Carter
Fallon
Wibaux
Richland
Sheridan

Gov. Steve Bullock (D)

First elected: 2012
Length of term: 4 years
Term expires: 1/17
Salary: $108,167
Phone: (406) 444-3111
Residence: Helena
Born: April 11, 1966
Religion: Roman Catholic
Family: Wife, Lisa Bullock; three children
Education: Claremont McKenna College, B.A. 1988 (economics & philosophy); Columbia U., J.D. 1994
Career: Lawyer; state justice department acting chief deputy; campaign aide; truck safety nonprofit director; business analyst
Political highlights: Sought Democratic nomination for Mont. attorney general, 2000; Mont. attorney general, 2009-13

ELECTION RESULTS

2012 GENERAL

Steve Bullock (D)	236,450	48.9%
Rick Hill (R)	228,879	47.3%
Ron Vandevender (LIBERT)	18,160	3.8%

Lt. Governor John Walsh (D)

First elected: 2012
Length of term: 4 years
Term expires: 1/17
Salary: $86,362
Phone: (406) 444-5665

LEGISLATURE

Legislature: January-April in odd-numbered years, limit of 90 days
Senate: 50 members, 4-year terms
2013 ratios: 29 R, 21 D; 40 men, 10 women
Salary: $83 per legislative day
Phone: (406) 444-4801
House: 100 members; 2-year terms
2013 ratios: 61 R, 39 D; 68 men, 32 women
Salary: $83 per legislative day
Phone: (406) 444-4819

TERM LIMITS

Governor: 8 years in a 16-year period
Senate: 8 years in a 16-year period
House: 8 years in a 16-year period

URBAN STATISTICS

CITY	POPULATION
Billings	104,170
Missoula	66,788
Great Falls	58,505
Bozeman	37,280
Butte-Silver Bow	34,200

REGISTERED VOTERS

Voters do not register by party.

POPULATION

2010 population	989,415
2000 population	902,195
1990 population	799,065
Percent change (2000-2010)	+9.7%
Rank among states (2010)	44
Median age	39
Born in state	54.4%
Foreign born	1.9%
Violent crime rate	254/100,000
Poverty level	15.1%
Federal workers	19,130
Military	3,623

ELECTIONS

STATE ELECTION OFFICIAL
(406) 444-4732

DEMOCRATIC PARTY
(406) 442-9520

REPUBLICAN PARTY
(406) 442-6469

MISCELLANEOUS

Web: www.mt.gov
Capital: Helena

U.S. CONGRESS

Senate: 2 Democrats
House: 1 Republican

STATISTICS BY DISTRICT

District	2012 Vote for President Obama	Romney	2008 Vote for President Obama	McCain	Black	Asian	Hispanic	Median Income	Over 64	Under 20	College Education	Rural	Sq. Miles
AL	42%	55%	47%	50%	<1%	1%	3%	$44,222	15%	25%	28%	48%	145,546
STATE	42	55	47	50	<1	1	3	44,222	15	25	28	48	145,546
U.S.	51	47	53	46	12	5	17	50,052	13	27	29	21	3,531,905

Sen. Max Baucus (D)

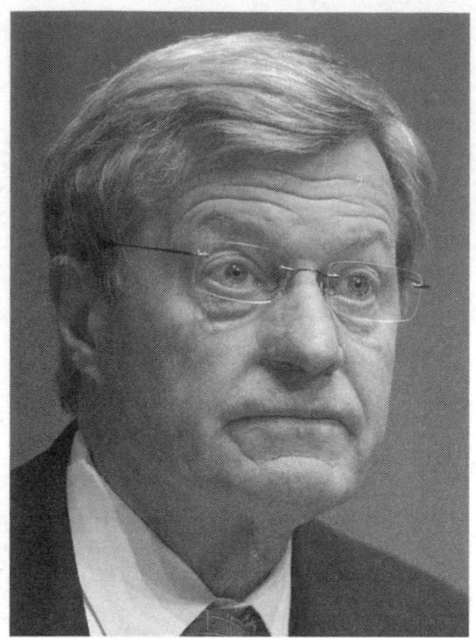

Capitol Office
224-2651
baucus.senate.gov
511 Hart Bldg. 20510-2602; fax 224-9412

Committees
Agriculture, Nutrition & Forestry
Environment & Public Works
(Transportation & Infrastructure - Chairman)
Finance - Chairman
Joint Taxation - Vice Chairman

Residence
Helena

Born
Dec. 11, 1941; Helena, Mont.

Religion
Protestant

Family
Wife, Melodee Hanes; one child

Education
Stanford U., A.B. 1964 (economics), LL.B. 1967

Career
Lawyer

Political Highlights
Mont. House, 1973-75; U.S. House, 1975-78

ELECTION RESULTS

2008 GENERAL

Max Baucus (D)	348,289	72.9%
Bob Kelleher (R)	129,369	27.1%

2008 PRIMARY

Max Baucus (D)	unopposed

Previous Winning Percentages
2002 (63%); 1996 (50%); 1990 (68%); 1984 (57%); 1978 (56%); 1976 House Election (66%); 1974 House Election (55%)

Elected 1978; 6th term

With his fingerprints on the major tax and health care laws of the last decade, Baucus is easily Montana's most influential politician since Mike Mansfield, the storied Senate majority leader.

But as he wraps up his congressional career — he will retire at the end of the 113th Congress (2013-14) — the Finance Committee chairman remains a controversial figure within the Democratic Party. Baucus is still hard to pin down almost four decades after winning election to the House in the "Watergate baby" Class of 1974. He's a lawyer by trade, but he traveled with Roma during a college term in Europe. He can be inscrutable, pragmatic and cautious — sometimes to a fault, say friends and foes alike.

The blessing and curse of the Finance Committee is that it contemplates many of the nation's most profound economic issues. So no matter what Baucus does, he offends somebody in his independent-minded state.

During the writing of the 2010 health care overhaul, Baucus refused to fight for a single-payer system, a longtime goal of liberals. It put him sharply at odds with popular Montana Gov. Brian Schweitzer — who hit a term limit at the start of 2013 and is now the early favorite to win the 2014 Democratic primary. But his role as a key negotiator of the overhaul, which is despised by conservatives, dragged down his approval ratings.

Baucus nonetheless continues to deal. In the 113th Congress, the potential blockbuster is a reworking of the tax code. House Ways and Means Chairman Dave Camp, a Michigan Republican, has been testing out his plans for an overhaul, and Baucus has worked with him in the past. They are the leaders of the Joint Taxation Committee, and they served on the "supercommittee" created by an August 2011 deficit reduction law. That bicameral, bipartisan panel was tasked with proposing ways to reduce the deficit by more than $1 trillion over 10 years. Baucus worked with Camp until the final hours, but the panel dissolved without accomplishing that goal.

Details are up for negotiation, but Baucus and Camp have spoken in favor of a code with fewer tax breaks and lower tax rates aimed at spurring economic growth. In March 2013, Baucus was one of four Democrats to vote against the budget prepared by his party, which directs his panel to propose legislation that would increase revenue by $975 billion over 10 years. "It was too lopsided," Baucus said. "I think $1 trillion in tax increases is too much."

Baucus and Camp have also used their panels to promote trade. In 2011, they finalized pacts with Colombia, South Korea and Panama — key export markets for Montana's farmers and ranchers. Baucus wants to give President Barack Obama "trade promotion authority," which allows him to submit trade agreements to Congress that cannot be amended; he also welcomed the addition of Japan to the Trans-Pacific Partnership trade negotiations that are currently under way. Japan opened its markets to more beef imports in 2013, a change Baucus had sought for years — he is also a member of the Agriculture, Nutrition and Forestry Committee.

Stylistically, Baucus stands in contrast to previous high-profile Finance chairmen, such as Republican Bob Dole of Kansas and Democrats Lloyd Bentsen of Texas and Daniel Patrick Moynihan of New York. Neither a glad-handing deal-maker nor a fixture on the talk show circuit, Baucus has an approach to negotiation — consulting at length with individual lawmakers and groups before going public — that is frustrating to many people. Still, it has yielded a long list of laws.

Many liberals won't forgive Baucus for breaking with the party to support President George W. Bush's first tax cut package in 2001. Dubbed "K Street's favorite Democrat" by The Nation, Baucus was one of two Democrats whom Republicans allowed to participate in drafting the 2003 Medicare prescription drug law. "I think he's more reasonable than some of the others that control his party," said Utah's Orrin G. Hatch, the top Republican on Finance.

Baucus has served on the committee since 1979; at the end of his career he will have been on the panel longer than any senator in history. He had an unusually strong working relationship with Hatch's predecessor, Republican Charles E. Grassley of Iowa. Baucus takes seriously the Senate's history of consensus-building, epitomized by Mansfield. "You don't understand Max Baucus" if you don't understand Mansfield, Grassley said.

Which isn't to say that he's not a party loyalist on most issues. Baucus helped kill Bush's 2005 push to create private investment accounts in Social Security, and he has been a leading opponent of Republican plans to restructure Medicare.

Baucus staked his claim to the health care debate early, releasing his own blueprint just after Obama was elected president in 2008. Edward M. Kennedy, the Massachusetts Democrat who chaired the Health, Education, Labor and Pensions Committee, was ailing and absent — he later died of a brain tumor — so Baucus took the lead role. He resisted efforts to fast-track the health care bill using special budget procedures, and he met behind the scenes for months with a small group of negotiators. His decision to leave a government-run insurance plan out of his proposal yielded negligible GOP support, but the final law was largely Baucus' handiwork, including the mandate for individuals to have insurance or pay a penalty.

On the Environment and Public Works Committee, where he chairs the Transportation and Infrastructure Subcommittee, he must balance competing interests in his state. As chairman of the full committee in the early 1990s, he was a key player on several major environmental laws. But over the years he has drawn the ire of environmentalists for seeking to protect miners and ranchers from tougher regulations. In 2012, he was one of 11 Senate Democrats to vote for an unsuccessful Republican proposal to approve the Keystone XL pipeline that would carry oil from Canada to Texas.

Baucus' ancestors emigrated from Germany in the late 1800s and settled in Montana. His great-grandfather Henry Sieben was named to the Hall of Great Westerners at the National Cowboy and Western Heritage Museum. Baucus' brother and sister-in-law now run the Sieben Ranch north of Helena, and Baucus has done his part to uphold the state's tradition of ruggedness. In recent years, he has suffered a motorcycle accident and a major head injury when he fell during a 50-mile ultramarathon.

He spent part of his junior year in college at an exchange program in France; he then went to England before traveling the world. He was in the Congo when he had an "epiphany" to undertake a career in public service.

After finishing Stanford Law School in 1967, he was a lawyer for the Securities and Exchange Commission for three years. He returned to Montana in 1971 to coordinate the state's constitutional convention, and in 1972 he won a seat in the state legislature.

He captured a U.S. House seat in 1974, ousting a two-term GOP incumbent. Four years later, he arrived in the Senate. Although he had just won a six-year term starting in January 1979, he was appointed to the seat in December 1978 after Democrat Paul G. Hatfield resigned. Hatfield had been appointed earlier in the year after the death of Sen. Lee Metcalf, but Baucus defeated him in the Democratic primary.

Baucus faced conflict-of-interest accusations related to the revelation in late 2009 that he was having a romantic relationship with Melodee Hanes, his former state office director, when he recommended her to be the U.S. attorney for Montana. Hanes eventually withdrew from consideration, and the couple married in 2011.

Key Votes

2012

Prohibit health insurance plans from denying coverage based on the sponsor's religious beliefs	YES
Require approval of the Keystone XL oil pipeline	YES
Ease securities rules to expand small-business access to capital	NO
Reauthorize farm and nutrition programs for five years	YES
Limit debate on a bill that would create private-sector cybersecurity standards	NO
Consent to ratification of a treaty setting global standard for the treatment of people with disabilities	YES
Provide $60.4 billion in disaster relief following Superstorm Sandy	YES
Extend most Bush-era income tax rates while allowing rates for top-bracket earners to rise (Jan. 1, 2013)	YES

2011

Prevent EPA from regulating greenhouse gas emissions to address climate change	NO
Extend certain provisions of Patriot Act for four years	NO
Clear compromise debt limit increase plan and establish future spending limits	YES
Overhaul patent law	YES
Implement Colombia free trade agreement	YES
Limit debate on confirmation of Caitlin J. Halligan to D.C. Circuit Court of Appeals	YES
Extend payroll tax cut and unemployment benefits for two months	YES

CQ Vote Studies

	PARTY UNITY		PRESIDENTIAL SUPPORT	
	SUPPORT	OPPOSE	SUPPORT	OPPOSE
2012	91%	9%	92%	8%
2011	91%	9%	95%	5%
2010	93%	7%	97%	3%
2009	92%	8%	96%	4%
2008	89%	11%	35%	65%
2007	83%	17%	41%	59%
2006	79%	21%	61%	39%
2005	74%	26%	45%	55%
2004	72%	28%	57%	43%
2003	74%	26%	54%	46%

Interest Groups

	AFL-CIO	ADA	CCUS	ACU
2012	100%	90%	63%	12%
2011	79%	85%	64%	5%
2010	81%	85%	27%	12%
2009	83%	85%	57%	20%
2008	90%	80%	75%	8%
2007	89%	80%	55%	20%
2006	71%	70%	70%	8%
2005	85%	95%	71%	24%
2004	92%	85%	71%	29%
2003	62%	85%	74%	15%

Sen. Jon Tester (D)

Capitol Office
224-2644
tester.senate.gov
706 Hart Bldg. 20510-2603; fax 224-8594

Committees
Appropriations
Banking, Housing & Urban Affairs
(Securities, Insurance & Investment - Chairman)
Homeland Security & Governmental Affairs
(Efficiency of Federal Programs - Chairman)
Indian Affairs
Veterans' Affairs

Residence
Big Sandy

Born
Aug. 21, 1956; Havre, Mont.

Religion
Church of God

Family
Wife, Sharla Tester; two children

Education
College of Great Falls, B.A. 1978 (music education & secondary education)

Career
Farmer; teacher

Political Highlights
Big Sandy School Board of Trustees, 1983-92 (chairman, 1986-91); Mont. Senate, 1999-2007 (minority whip, 2001-03; minority leader, 2003-05; president, 2005-07)

ELECTION RESULTS

2012 GENERAL

Jon Tester (D)	236,123	48.6%
Denny Rehberg (R)	218,051	44.9%
Dan Cox (LIBERT)	31,892	6.6%

2012 PRIMARY

Jon Tester (D)	unopposed

Previous Winning Percentages
2006 (49%)

Elected 2006; 2nd term

Even millionaires strive to be regular guys in Montana, so Tester's greatest political asset might be his earthy authenticity. The burly farmer claims a hands-on understanding of the lifestyle of his sparsely populated state, and he sells big-government Democratic ideas as populist ways to give average folks a little help.

"I put Montanans first in every decision that I make," Tester said while campaigning in 2012. He often says he wants D.C. to be more like Montana, though his Democratic colleagues probably want a scenario more tilted to the left. Montanans don't reject federal involvement — it's a fact of life in the state's agriculture and mining industries, on Indian reservations and across vast public lands — but they also have a Western culture of self-reliance. Both Democrats and Republicans have been successful statewide.

Tester won both of his Senate campaigns with less than 50 percent of the vote, and each time a libertarian candidate racked up vote totals much larger than his margin of victory over the losing Republican.

Personality can be the difference in close races, and Tester has that covered. He grew up on an 1,800-acre farm near Big Sandy. Tester and his brothers were put to work at an early age; grinding meat as a child, he lost three fingers on his left hand.

After graduating from college, he taught music for a couple of years at his hometown elementary school (he has said his accident forced him to switch from saxophone to trumpet). Tester gave up teaching to concentrate on the farm, where the family also operated a custom butcher shop his parents had started in the 1960s. They went organic in 1987 and now grow wheat, barley, lentils, peas, millet, buckwheat, alfalfa and hay.

In 2007, Tester's daughter and son-in-law moved back to the farm to run it in his absence. He still relishes chances to do farm work, calling the long rides on his tractor ideal times to think through the issues before Congress.

Tester served as chairman of the Big Sandy school board and of the local Soil Conservation Service Committee before winning election to the state Senate in 1998. He has said that he ran because he was "fed up with huge rate hikes following the disastrous deregulation of Montana's energy industry." He was one of the chamber's more conservative Democrats, with a strong record of supporting gun rights.

He rose to minority whip and minority leader before becoming president of the state Senate in 2005. The next year, he ran for the U.S. Senate and beat Republican incumbent Conrad Burns by less than 1 point.

In Washington, Tester has stood with Democrats on big-ticket bills such as the 2009 stimulus package and the 2010 overhauls of health insurance and financial-sector regulations.

But Tester, who considers Theodore Roosevelt a political role model, quickly points out his differences with his party, especially when they appeal to working-class Montanans. Tester hasn't been eager to create a path to citizenship for illegal immigrants, and he is more supportive than the average Democrat of efforts to increase fossil fuel production. In the 110th Congress (2007-08), he voted against what he and other opponents called bailouts for the financial services and auto industries.

Senate Democrats have tried to boost Tester's electoral standing, most notably by adding him to the Appropriations Committee in 2009. In 2012, party leaders promised a vote on Tester's bill to open more federal land to hunting and fishing. The measure had broad bipartisan support, but Republicans raised a point of order when it headed to the floor after the election, because it would let the Interior Department raise the fee for duck stamps on hunting licenses. Tester is working to resolve those differences.

Tester sits on the Banking, Housing and Urban Affairs Committee, where he looks at the problems of consumers and smaller financial institutions. He won adoption of an amendment to the 2010 financial regulatory overhaul to direct the Federal Deposit Insurance Corporation to charge banks premiums based on the risk of their activity. He said community banks were paying 30 percent of FDIC premiums while holding only 20 percent of the nation's banking assets. "They don't deserve to be left holding the bag for risky behavior of the big banks," he said on the Senate floor.

In 2011, Tester and Tennessee Republican Bob Corker fell short in their bid to delay for a year new limits on swipe fees that banks charge retailers for processing transactions using debit cards. "Main Street banks and credit unions will not be OK if these rules are implemented," he said. The fee limits were inserted into the 2010 overhaul by Illinois Democrat Richard J. Durbin, the majority whip.

In the 113th Congress (2013-14), Tester chairs the Subcommittee on Securities, Insurance and Investment. He and the ranking member, Nebraska Republican Mike Johanns, have introduced a bill to create a single licensing standard for agents and brokers who operate across state lines.

The Indian Affairs and Veterans' Affairs committees offer lots of chances for Tester to put Montanans first. In 2007, President George W. Bush signed into law a Tester provision to increase the mileage reimbursement rate for veterans traveling to government health clinics. He has pushed for better prosecution of crimes committed on Indian reservations. "Businesses have told me that because of a lack of law enforcement, customers never come through the door, and it is hard for them to find good employees," Tester said at a 2011 hearing. "Hospital directors have told me they can't find docs. They can't find nurses because their families don't want to live in communities that are dangerous."

He also sits on the Homeland Security and Governmental Affairs Committee. Tester voted against a 2011 extension of surveillance provisions in the anti-terrorism law known as the Patriot Act, emphasizing his concern about federal access to private records. "When we give up our rights, we give way to exactly what the terrorists wanted for us — fewer freedoms and invasion of privacy," he said. "It is not acceptable in Montana, and I am sure it is not acceptable anywhere else."

On the government side of the panel, Tester chairs the subcommittee on efficiency of federal programs. He also emphasizes transparency. He has introduced legislation to require federal agencies to post all public documents and records in a searchable online clearinghouse and co-sponsored a bill to forbid members of Congress from ever working as lobbyists. He posts his daily public schedule on his website, listing all appointments and activities. He also prohibits gifts, meals and travel from lobbyists to him or his staff.

Tester knew early in the 2012 election cycle that he was in for a fight. Six-term Republican Rep. Denny Rehberg announced his campaign in 2011, and the multimillionaire rancher and real estate developer has the same regular-guy appeal as Tester — it was the only Senate race pitting a man with a flat-top haircut against a man with a mustache. Liberal Democratic activists who had contributed heavily to Tester's win in 2006 were also grumbling about his more-moderate votes.

Tester played up his political independence and Montana-first attitude, while Rehberg tried to tie Tester to the Obama administration. The state backed GOP presidential challenger Mitt Romney and a Republican candidate for the House, but Tester won his race by less than 4 points. Libertarian Dan Cox might have spoiled the GOP's night by taking more than 6 percent of the vote.

Key Votes

2012	
Prohibit health insurance plans from denying coverage based on the sponsor's religious beliefs	YES
Require approval of the Keystone XL oil pipeline	YES
Ease securities rules to expand small-business access to capital	YES
Reauthorize farm and nutrition programs for five years	YES
Limit debate on a bill that would create private-sector cybersecurity standards	NO
Consent to ratification of a treaty setting global standard for the treatment of people with disabilities	YES
Provide $60.4 billion in disaster relief following Superstorm Sandy	YES
Extend most Bush-era income tax rates while allowing rates for top-bracket earners to rise (Jan. 1, 2013)	YES
2011	
Prevent EPA from regulating greenhouse gas emissions to address climate change	NO
Extend certain provisions of Patriot Act for four years	NO
Clear compromise debt limit increase plan and establish future spending limits	YES
Overhaul patent law	YES
Implement Colombia free trade agreement	NO
Limit debate on confirmation of Caitlin J. Halligan to D.C. Circuit Court of Appeals	YES
Extend payroll tax cut and unemployment benefits for two months	YES

CQ Vote Studies

	PARTY UNITY		PRESIDENTIAL SUPPORT	
	SUPPORT	OPPOSE	SUPPORT	OPPOSE
2012	92%	8%	95%	5%
2011	87%	13%	90%	10%
2010	89%	11%	97%	3%
2009	92%	8%	97%	3%
2008	92%	8%	30%	70%
2007	84%	16%	37%	63%

Interest Groups

	AFL-CIO	ADA	CCUS	ACU
2012	91%	90%	63%	4%
2011	84%	80%	45%	10%
2010	81%	85%	36%	20%
2009	89%	90%	57%	16%
2008	90%	85%	63%	16%
2007	95%	95%	30%	16%

Rep. Steve Daines (R)

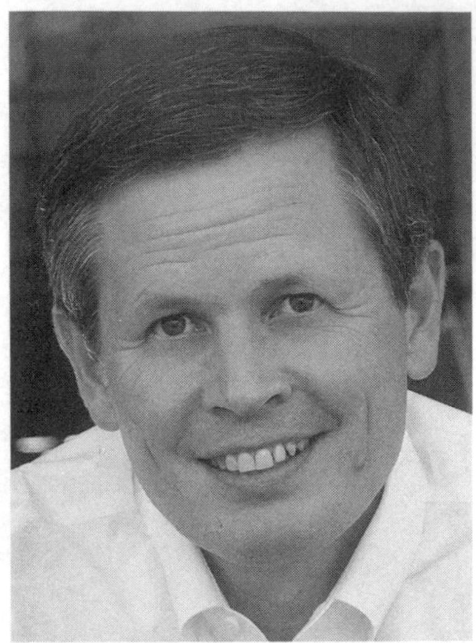

Capitol Office
225-3211
daines.house.gov
206 Cannon Bldg. 20515; fax 225-5687

Committees
Homeland Security
Natural Resources
Transportation & Infrastructure

Residence
Bozeman

Born
Aug. 20, 1962; Van Nuys, Calif.

Religion
Presbyterian

Family
Wife, Cindy Daines; four children

Education
Montana State U., B.S. 1984 (chemical engineering)

Career
Software company executive; construction company project manager; supply chain operations manager

Political Highlights
Republican nominee for lieutenant governor, 2008

ELECTION RESULTS

2012 GENERAL		
Steve Daines (R)	255,468	53.2%
Kim Gillan (D)	204,939	42.7%
David Kaiser (LIBERT)	19,333	4.0%
2012 PRIMARY		
Steve Daines (R)	82,843	71.2%
Eric Brosten (R)	21,012	18.1%
Vincent Melkus (R)	12,420	10.7%

Elected 2012; 1st term

Daines ran on a slogan of "more jobs, less government." His thoughts on the economy, taxes and the nation's regulatory environment are in sync with a majority of the Republican Conference.

Daines grew up in Bozeman and stayed there through his college years at Montana State. After getting a degree in chemical engineering, he left the state to take a job with Procter & Gamble; he accrued managerial experience in jobs in the United States and overseas. Daines returned home in 1997 and worked a few years for his family's construction business. He then became an executive at RightNow Technologies, a software company. Oracle Corp. bought it for $1.5 billion in 2011 — Daines is a millionaire several times over.

He invokes his business experience when discussing fiscal matters. He says his primary goal is simplifying the tax code. That includes the elimination of subsidies for all industries, even those for the oil and gas sector.

Daines, a member of the conservative Republican Study Committee, has great spots to promote energy development in his state. He sits on the Natural Resources Committee, as well as the Transportation and Infrastructure Subcommittee on Water Resources and Environment.

He was also assigned to the Homeland Security Committee. His experiences as an executive could come in handy on the subcommittee overseeing the management of the sprawling Department of Homeland Security, and his knowledge of the tech industry will be helpful in cybersecurity debates.

Daines, who had run for lieutenant governor in 2008, planned for a Senate bid in 2012. But when GOP Rep. Denny Rehberg entered that race, Daines set his sights on the House. He easily won the primary. Democrat Kim Gillan, the state Senate minority whip, didn't have the financial resources or name recognition to keep up. Daines won by more than 10 points.

For the 2014 cycle, Daines was named one of the five regional chairmen for the National Republican Congressional Committee.

Montana

At Large

Montana's Big Sky country was explored by fur trappers and miners and settled by farmers and ranchers able to outlast harsh winters. Now known as "The Last Best Place," Montana has also become home to communities of writers, artists and celebrities in recent years.

The economy is supported by natural resources, forcing Montana to find a balance between exploiting its terrain and protecting it, especially in the face of increased global demand for energy resources. Wind, solar and biofuel industries are growing, and alternative-energy companies are responsible for increasing numbers of jobs.

Unemployment rates in the northwestern counties have soared well above national and state averages, but the statewide economy remains stable. Butte, once the site of decades of copper mining, is now the site of a massive superfund toxic-runoff containment effort. In Helena, the state capital, the loss of government jobs raises concerns.

The state's economy also is sustained by tourism, with three of the five entrances to Yellowstone National Park in southern Montana and Glacier National Park located in the northwestern part of the state.

Political ideology used to split the state geographically. The western, mountainous half of the state, with an environmental base and a union tradition in mining and lumber mills, leaned Democratic, while the eastern half, a flat plain where wheat and cattle are raised, followed a tradition of rural Republicanism.

Now Democrats find support in main population centers such as Billings, Great Falls and Butte — although not necessarily in the counties surrounding them — as well as state capital Helena and Missoula, which is home to a sizable university community. Voters here will split their tickets: In 2012, Mitt Romney took 55 percent of the state's presidential vote and Steve Daines won the U.S. House seat, but Democrats Steve Bullock and Rep. Jon Tester won the gubernatorial and U.S. Senate races.

Major Industry
Agriculture, tourism, forestry

Military Bases
Malmstrom Air Force Base, 3,310 military, 3,330 civilian (2012)

Cities
Billings, Missoula, Great Falls, Bozeman

Notable
Montana elected Jeannette Rankin, the first woman in Congress, in 1916.

NEBRASKA

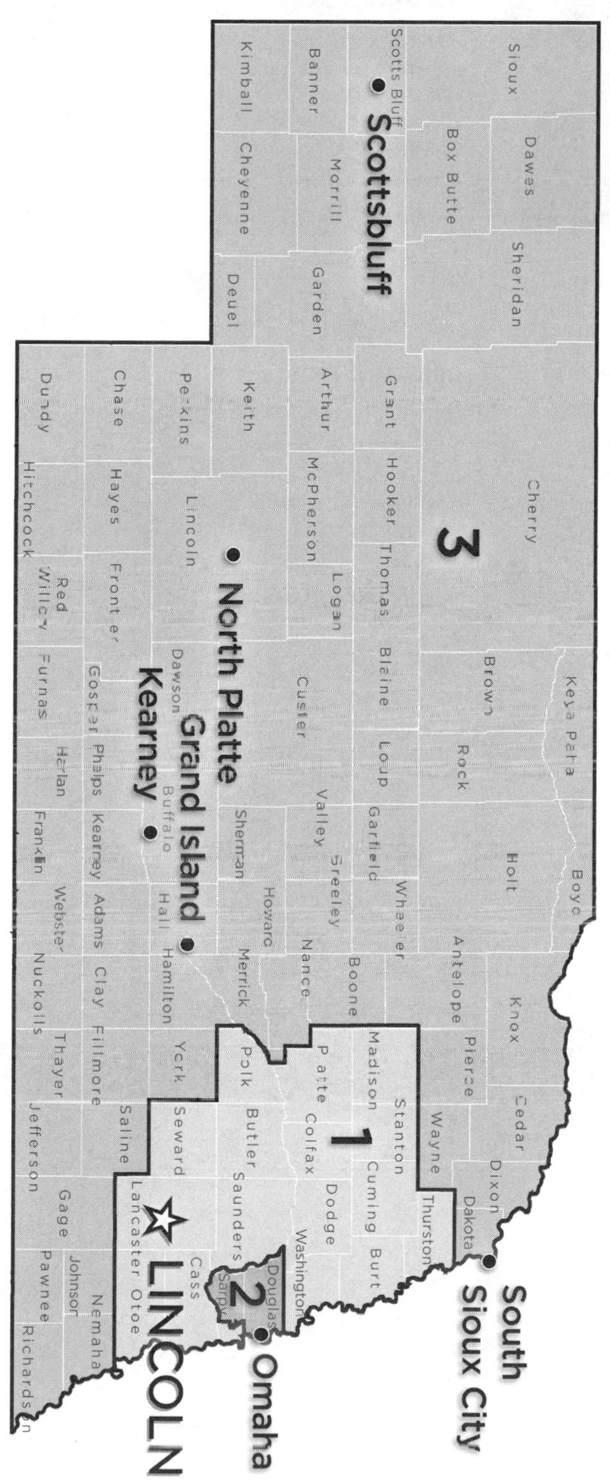

Sioux
Dawes
Scotts Bluff
Scottsbluff
Banner
Kimball
Box Butte
Sheridan
Morrill
Cheyenne
Garden
Deuel
Cherry
3
Grant
Arthur
Keith
Perkins
Chase
Dundy
Hooker
McPherson
Lincoln
North Platte
Hayes
Hitchcock
Thomas
Logan
Frontier
Red Willow
Keya Paha
Brown
Blaine
Custer
Dawson
Gosper
Furnas
Rock
Loup
Boyd
Holt
Garfield
Valley
Sherman
Buffalo
Kearney
Phelps
Harlan
Wheeler
Greeley
Howard
Hall
Grand Island
Adams
Webster
Franklin
Antelope
Knox
Boone
Nance
Merrick
Hamilton
Clay
Nuckolls
Pierce
Madison
Platte
Polk
York
Fillmore
Thayer
Cedar
Dixon
Wayne
Stanton
1
Colfax
Butler
Seward
Saline
Jefferson
Dakota
Thurston
Cuming
Dodge
Saunders
Lancaster
Gage
Burt
Washington
Douglas
Sarpy
2
Cass
Otoe
Johnson
Pawnee
Nemaha
Richardson
South Sioux City
Omaha
LINCOLN

Gov. Dave Heineman (R)

First elected: 2006; assumed office Jan. 20, 2005, following appointment of Mike Johanns, R, to be Agriculture secretary

Length of term: 4 years

Term expires: 1/15

Salary: $105,000

Phone: (402) 471-2244

Residence: Lincoln

Born: May 12, 1948; Falls City, Neb.

Religion: Methodist

Family: Wife, Sally Ganem; one child

Education: U.S. Military Academy, B.S. 1970 (economics)

Military: Army, 1970-75

Career: Congressional aide; health and beauty products company salesman

Political highlights: Neb. Republican Party executive director, 1979-81; Fremont City Council, 1990-94; Neb. treasurer, 1995-2001; lieutenant governor, 2001-05

ELECTION RESULTS

2010 GENERAL

Dave Heineman (R)	360,645	73.9%
Mike Meister (D)	127,343	26.1%

Lt. Gov. Lavon Heidemann (R)

Appointed: 2013

Length of term: 4 years

Term expires: 1/15

Salary: $75,000

Phone: (402) 471-2256

LEGISLATURE

Unicameral Legislature: 90 days in odd-numbered years; 60 days in even-numbered years

Legislature: 49 nonpartisan members, 4-year terms

2013 ratios: 39 men, 10 women

Salary: $12,000

Phone: (402) 471-2271

TERM LIMITS

Governor: 2 consecutive terms

Legislature: 2 consecutive terms

URBAN STATISTICS

CITY	POPULATION
Omaha	408,958
Lincoln	258,379
Bellevue	50,137
Grand Island	48,520
Kearney	30,787

REGISTERED VOTERS

Republican	48%
Democrat	32%
Other	20%

POPULATION

2010 population (est.)	1,826,341
2000 population	1,711,263
1990 population	1,578,385
Percent change (2000-2010)	+6.7%
Rank among states (2010)	38
Median age	35.9
Born in state	66.1%
Foreign born	5.4%
Violent crime rate	282/100,000
Poverty level	12.3%
Federal workers	18,284
Military	6,845

ELECTIONS

STATE ELECTION OFFICIAL
(402) 471-2555

DEMOCRATIC PARTY
(402) 434-2180

REPUBLICAN PARTY
(402) 475-2122

MISCELLANEOUS

Web: www.nebraska.gov

Capital: Lincoln

U.S. CONGRESS

Senate: 2 Republicans

House: 3 Republicans

STATISTICS BY DISTRICT

District	2012 Vote for President: Obama	Romney	2008 Vote for President: Obama	McCain	Black	Asian	Hispanic	Median Income	Over 64	Under 20	College Education	Rural	Sq. Miles
1	41%	57%	44%	54%	3%	2%	8%	$51,306	13%	28%	29%	26%	8,879
2	46	53	50	49	10	3	10	55,114	10	29	36	3	510
3	28	70	31	67	1	1	10	44,995	17	27	20	55	67,435
STATE	**38**	**60**	**42**	**57**	**5**	**2**	**9**	**50,296**	**14**	**28**	**28**	**29**	**76,824**
U.S.	**51**	**47**	**53**	**46**	**12**	**5**	**17**	**50,052**	**13**	**27**	**29**	**21**	**3,531,905**

Sen. Mike Johanns (R)

Capitol Office
224-4224
johanns.senate.gov
404 Russell Bldg. 20510; fax 228-0436

Committees
Agriculture, Nutrition & Forestry
Appropriations
Banking, Housing & Urban Affairs
Veterans' Affairs

Residence
Omaha

Born
June 18, 1950; Osage, Iowa

Religion
Roman Catholic

Family
Wife, Stephanie Johanns; two children

Education
St. Mary's College (Minn.), B.A. 1971 (communication arts); Creighton U., J.D. 1974

Career
Lawyer

Political Highlights
Lancaster County Board of Commissioners, 1983-87 (served as a Democrat); Lincoln City Council, 1989-91; mayor of Lincoln, 1991-98; governor, 1999-2005; Agriculture secretary, 2005-07

ELECTION RESULTS

2008 GENERAL		
Mike Johanns (R)	455,854	57.5%
Scott Kleeb (D)	317,456	40.1%
Kelly Renee Rosberg (NEB)	11,438	1.4%
2008 PRIMARY		
Mike Johanns (R)	112,191	78.0%
Pat Flynn (R)	31,560	22.0%

Elected 2008; 1st term

Johanns passed through city hall, the governor's mansion and the Cabinet en route to the Senate, carrying with him an unflappable demeanor and a desire for tangible results. He now says that he's ready for a new direction. In February 2013 he announced that he won't seek a second term, saying that his family had decided it was "time to close this chapter of our lives."

He grew up on a dairy farm and raised hogs as a teen, and he still has some of his farm habits. Johanns (JOE-hanns, rhymes with cans) starts his days before sunrise and, flouting Capitol Hill custom, shows up a few minutes early for most hearings and appointments. He's fastidiously organized, right down to an unyielding hairstyle, and he has demonstrated long-term focus — his campaign for governor in the late 1990s stretched over three years and helped him outpace better-known GOP candidates in the primary.

Johanns turned his focus to the government's finances during the 112th Congress (2011-12), joining a group of senators seeking a starting point for deficit reduction. He takes cues from the political culture of his state, which features a unicameral, nonpartisan legislature. "Nebraskans put a tremendous premium on somebody who is a problem-solver," he said. If there are attempts "to resolve issues in a give-and-take sort of way, then I hope I'm asked to be at the table."

Early in 2011, Johanns and Colorado Democrat Michael Bennet gathered 64 signatures on a letter to President Barack Obama, urging him to support a deficit reduction package containing spending cuts, tax code revisions and changes to entitlement programs. Their efforts brought them into talks with an informal bipartisan group — with their addition, it was known as the "gang of eight" — that sought the middle ground in spending disputes. It aimed to reduce deficits by at least $4 trillion over a decade. "I don't look at this as a problem for my children and grandchildren anymore," Johanns said. "I will live to see this become a very serious problem."

Johanns echoes the familiar Republican call for a tax code with fewer brackets and lower rates; he has supported means testing for programs such as Medicare. When contemplating health care spending, he is less than complimentary of Democrats' 2010 health care law. "I'm open to a whole range of possibilities, but not this idiotic stuff that we ended up with," he said. "You can almost set out to do the opposite and get better policy."

Not long after the law's enactment, Johanns introduced a bill to repeal its provision requiring the filing of a 1099 tax form any time a business pays a vendor more than $600 in a year. Predicting an avalanche of paperwork and expenses for small businesses, he continued to be the leading GOP advocate for repeal in the Senate, and in April 2011 the House version of a repeal was signed by Obama.

Johanns had experience refereeing major policy debates before coming to the Senate. During his nearly three-year tenure as Agriculture secretary, he was the George W. Bush administration's point man on a five-year reauthorization of farm programs. He won praise from congressional leaders for his directness and willingness to listen to all sides. But he also drew criticism for leaving before the $289 billion bill was completed — he resigned from office in September 2007 to launch his candidacy for the Senate seat being vacated by Republican Chuck Hagel.

As a member of the Agriculture, Nutrition and Forestry Committee, he got involved with the next iteration of the farm bill in 2012. He helped steer the Senate-passed version toward a "risk management" approach. Farmers are fine, he said, with the end of direct and countercyclical payments. "They know there's a budget problem. They're not bothered by this," he explained. Johanns approved of the bolstering of crop insurance programs, and he applauded the consolidation of 23 conservation programs into 13 — a move he encouraged while heading the USDA.

However, that bill was not enacted, and he did not like the version the panel approved in May 2013. The addition of a "target price" program to the bill "took us a step back towards 1980s farm policy," he wrote.

Johanns backs free-trade pacts, particularly when they open markets to Nebraska's farmers and ranchers. While in the Cabinet, he cultivated support for a 2005 free-trade agreement with five Central American countries and the Dominican Republic, and in the Senate he pushed for the 2011 ratification of deals with South Korea, Colombia and Panama.

The ethanol industry (fueled in part by Nebraska corn) has also enjoyed his support over the years. While "I have not been impressed with the grant programs" for energy producers, Johanns said, he has found accelerated depreciation and other "very targeted things" to be appropriate ways for the federal government to encourage energy production.

A lot of other government intervention he can do without. Having dealt with the impact of regulations as a governor and mayor, Johanns says "the federal government interferes more than it helps."

He is particularly critical of rules handed down by the Obama administration: "I've never seen a bunch like this, and I think they're all reading off the same memo, that basically says 'take your authority and push it to the limits.'" As Agriculture secretary, he said, he wouldn't take any action where his legal authority was in doubt.

On the Banking, Housing and Urban Affairs Committee, Johanns questions whether any other nation subjects its financial sector to rules as complex as those allowed by the 2010 financial regulatory overhaul. He has some input into the operating budget of financial regulators. He joined the Appropriations Committee for the 113th Congress and is the top Republican on its Financial Services Subcommittee.

Johanns was raised in Osage, Iowa, just south of the Minnesota border. Although his parents were not very interested in politics, their living room displayed pictures of the pope and President John F. Kennedy. Johanns is a Catholic and a social conservative who opposes federal funding of abortion and defines marriage as being between a man and a woman.

The money Johanns and his brother earned raising hogs helped him pay for his college education. He considered a career in farming but headed to law school at Creighton University in Omaha. He worked as a lawyer, doing "whatever the partners didn't want to do," before starting his political career in 1983 on the Lancaster County Board of Commissioners — as a Democrat.

Johanns mulled a 1986 run for mayor of Lincoln, but he became disenchanted with local Democrats; he dropped his bid in December and that Christmas Eve married Stephanie Armitage, a Republican he met while they both served on the county board. It was the second marriage for both. Johanns switched his party affiliation shortly thereafter, then returned to politics in 1989 by winning election to the city council in Lincoln.

He was elected mayor two years later. During much of his second term, he traveled the state building a support network for his successful 1998 bid to succeed the term-limited governor, Democrat Ben Nelson. He resigned that job in January 2005, midway through his second four-year term, after Bush tapped him to be Agriculture secretary.

Hagel's 2007 retirement announcement led Johanns to take a shot at the Senate. He faced Democrat Scott Kleeb, a Yale-educated rancher and educator who in 2006 took 45 percent of the vote against Republican Rep. Adrian Smith in the overwhelmingly Republican 3rd District. Though Democrats surged nationwide, Johanns won easily.

Key Votes

2012	
Prohibit health insurance plans from denying coverage based on the sponsor's religious beliefs	NO
Require approval of the Keystone XL oil pipeline	YES
Ease securities rules to expand small-business access to capital	YES
Reauthorize farm and nutrition programs for five years	YES
Limit debate on a bill that would create private-sector cybersecurity standards	NO
Consent to ratification of a treaty setting global standard for the treatment of people with disabilities	NO
Provide $60.4 billion in disaster relief following Superstorm Sandy	NO
Extend most Bush-era income tax rates while allowing rates for top-bracket earners to rise (Jan. 1, 2013)	YES
2011	
Prevent EPA from regulating greenhouse gas emissions to address climate change	YES
Extend certain provisions of Patriot Act for four years	YES
Clear compromise debt limit increase plan and establish future spending limits	YES
Overhaul patent law	YES
Implement Colombia free trade agreement	YES
Limit debate on confirmation of Caitlin J. Halligan to D.C. Circuit Court of Appeals	NO
Extend payroll tax cut and unemployment benefits for two months	YES

CQ Vote Studies

	PARTY UNITY		PRESIDENTIAL SUPPORT	
	SUPPORT	OPPOSE	SUPPORT	OPPOSE
2012	81%	19%	52%	48%
2011	87%	13%	61%	39%
2010	93%	7%	48%	52%
2009	94%	6%	52%	48%

Interest Groups

	AFL-CIO	ADA	CCUS	ACU
2012	9%	15%	100%	80%
2011	21%	20%	100%	70%
2010	13%	10%	100%	80%
2009	25%	15%	83%	95%

Sen. Deb Fischer (R)

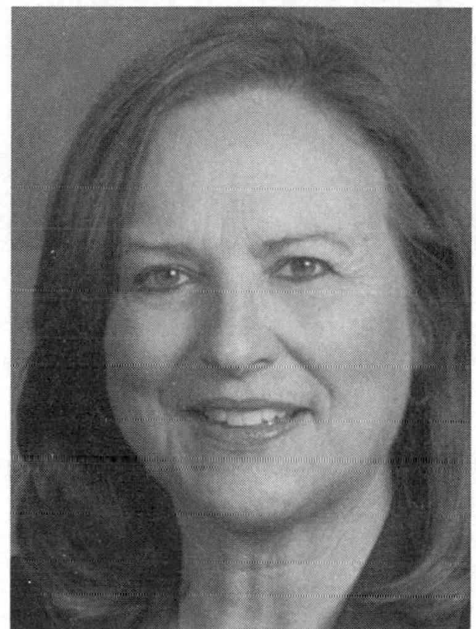

Capitol Office
224-6551
fischer.senate.gov
825B Hart Bldg. 20510-2706; fax 228-1325

Committees
Armed Services
Commerce, Science & Transportation
Environment & Public Works
Indian Affairs
Small Business & Entrepreneurship

Residence
Valentine

Born
March 1, 1951, Lincoln, Neb.

Religion
Presbyterian

Family
Husband, Bruce Fischer; three children

Education
U. of Nebraska, B.S. 1988 (education)

Career
Rancher

Political Highlights
Valentine Rural High School Board of Education, 1990-2004; Neb. Coordinating Commission for Postsecondary Education, 2000-04; Neb. Legislature, 2005-13

ELECTION RESULTS

2012 GENERAL		
Deb Fischer (R)	449,240	58.1%
Bob Kerrey (D)	323,753	41.9%
2012 PRIMARY		
Deb Fischer (R)	79,941	41.0%
Jon Bruning (R)	70,067	35.9%
Don Stenberg (R)	36,727	18.8%
Pat Flynn (R)	5,413	2.8%

Elected 2012; 1st term

Fischer had several nicknames as a member of the Nebraska Legislature. Friends and foes knew her as The General, for her ability to keep her allies in line. She was also called The Velvet Hammer. "If I was opposed to policy on a bill — sometimes you have to kill it," she said. "But I would do so in a very gracious way, of course."

She is well aware of her reputation as an intimidating conservative, and she seems modestly tickled by it. Fischer is both confident and composed. As a state legislator, she relied on a combination of resolve and preparation when launching a policy offensive. When she headed to floor debates with evidence to support her position, "it would usually take two people carrying all the binders," she said. "That seemed to forestall any questioning of me on any legislation whatsoever — because we had all the information."

Fischer grew up in Lincoln. Her father worked for the Nebraska Department of Roads for more than four decades — he became the head of the department under Gov. Kay Orr. Her mother was an elementary school teacher. Fischer has two older brothers, and she describes her upbringing as a pleasant middle-class affair.

She was a news junkie at a young age and had designs on a career in public service, but romance put those plans on hold. While attending the University of Nebraska, she met Bruce Fischer, who came from a ranching family. She fell in love, got married, and left school before graduating. Fischer moved 300 miles away to Valentine, in north central Nebraska. She worked the Sunny Slope Ranch — which covers thousands of acres — and raised a family.

A few years after moving to Valentine, she got civically involved through the local school board, although "local" seems like a misnomer. The rural school district for Valentine is bigger than some states. When people say she came out of nowhere to win a Senate race, she emphasizes that she came out of "the middle of nowhere." In her 30s, she went back to college to complete an education degree; her mother filled in for her at the ranch, while she lived with her father in Lincoln for a few months. Fischer ended up serving as the president of the Nebraska Association of School Boards.

When her three sons were grown (they all work on the ranch), she ran for the state legislature in 2004, driving thousands of miles to make face-to-face connections with the people of her state legislative district, which was about the size of New Jersey. She won by 128 votes.

As a state legislator, Fischer acknowledged only four core duties of state government: "Public education, public safety, public infrastructure and taking care of those who truly can't care for themselves." She would not cosponsor bills unless she co-wrote them or entirely agreed with them. And she was notoriously tough. A friend of Fischer's described her to the Kearney Hub in 2012: "At her core she's made of steel."

Fischer sees only a few principal duties for the federal government. One is national defense, and she sits on the Armed Services Committee.

It's a relatively new policy area for Fischer, but she has jumped into it. She is the ranking member of the Emerging Threats and Capabilities Subcommittee, and she also sits on the Strategic Forces panel. Both of those subcommittees are good places to address the country's nuclear arsenal. The U.S. Strategic Command (aka Stratcom) is based near Omaha.

Fischer emphasizes the importance of nuclear deterrence. "I think we need to have respect from people who are not our friends," she says. And she agrees with the notion that the Obama administration has not lived up to its promises to modernize the nuclear stockpile.

Her subcommittees touch on cybersecurity, and Fischer advocates outlining clear consequences for nations, such as China, that regularly engage in cyberattacks.

She is generally critical of the Obama administration's military posturing. In early 2013, when the president announced a more-rapid drawdown of troops in Afghanistan, she told the Omaha World-Herald that "what the White House is saying is they're giving up on Afghanistan and don't care."

Fischer sees infrastructure as another responsibility of the federal government. States are "pretty good at doing roads and bridges," but ports, dams and transmission lines require federal guidance, she said. She sits on both the Environment and Public Works Committee and the Commerce, Science and Transportation Committee.

In the Nebraska Legislature, Fischer chaired the Transportation and Telecommunications Committee for six years. Her signature initiative, which takes effect in 2013, was a law that dedicates a portion of the state sales tax toward infrastructure projects . Fischer touted it as a way to "prioritize and fund" without increasing tax rates, which also provided the long-term certainty needed to plan such projects.

"You can do it with existing revenue if you make those tough decisions ... and you're able to say, this is a duty of government, this is what we need to fund," she said. "We can't be everything to everyone. We can't keep implementing new programs, especially when we aren't able to fund the current ones." Fischer opposes tax increases.

A 2012 surface transportation law included provisions to streamline regulatory reviews of infrastructure projects, and Fischer says more efficiency "would be fabulous." She is incredulous of the value of many environmental rules. "A crisis comes, and we can waive them?" she asked. "Why can't we waive them all the time? Why are they there? They need to be gone."

Fischer supports federal efforts to increase the availability of broadband service in rural areas. She and Minnesota Democrat Al Franken amended the Senate's fiscal 2014 budget proposal to indicate a commitment to such spending.

She also sits on the Small Business and Indian Affairs committees. Despite her longtime involvement with education, she does not anticipate getting involved in education debates at the federal level. She prefers to leave that subject to states and localities. "I think government is always best the more local it is, the more in touch it is with citizens," she said.

Fischer had no farming experience when she ended up on the ranch. It was a trial by fire. "We were married and calving started right away," she remembers. Her sons were out working in the hay fields when they were 8 years old, she said. She still likes pitching in on the ranch when she has the chance to do so.

Fischer was not well known throughout the state when she decided to run for the Senate. But she was a tireless candidate, with experience campaigning in Nebraska's rural areas. She ran on a conservative, small-government platform, and she beat out two Republicans who had won statewide elections before: Attorney General Jon Bruning and Treasurer Don Stenberg. A few days before the primary, she was endorsed by Sarah Palin.

In the general election, she faced Democrat Bob Kerrey, a former governor and two-term senator. When Kerrey retired from the Senate at the end of the 106th Congress (1999-2000), he moved to New York and spent a decade as president of the New School. He was recruited by Democrats to run for the open seat (Democratic Sen. Ben Nelson was retiring) and moved back to the state in 2012 — to accusations of being a carpetbagger.

Fischer left Kerrey no openings, and Nebraska continued its recent trend of support for Republicans. Fischer won a decisive 16-point victory. She has vowed to serve no more than two terms.

Rep. Jeff Fortenberry (R)

Capitol Office
225-4806
fortenberry.house.gov
1514 Longworth Bldg. 20515-2701; fax 225-5686

Committees
Appropriations

Residence
Lincoln

Born
Dec. 27, 1960; Baton Rouge, La.

Religion
Roman Catholic

Family
Wife, Celeste Fortenberry; five children

Education
Louisiana State U., B.A. 1982 (economics); Georgetown U., M.P.P. 1986; Franciscan U. of Steubenville, M.Div. 1996 (theology)

Career
Publishing firm public relations manager and sales representative; economist; congressional aide

Political Highlights
Lincoln City Council, 1997-2001

ELECTION RESULTS

2012 GENERAL		
Jeff Fortenberry (R)	173,473	68.3%
Korey L. Reiman (D)	80,412	31.7%
2012 PRIMARY		
Jeff Fortenberry (R)	55,658	86.4%
Jessica L. Turek (R)	5,255	8.2%
Dennis L. Parker (R)	3,511	5.4%
2010 GENERAL		
Jeff Fortenberry (R)	116,871	71.3%
Ivy Harper (D)	47,106	28.7%

Previous Winning Percentages
2008 (70%); 2006 (58%); 2004 (54%)

Elected 2004; 5th term

William Jennings Bryan once represented Nebraska's 1st District. He and Fortenberry have little in common in terms of policy, but they share something in terms of spirit. Like his populist Democratic predecessor, the Republican speaks of the values of the common man and seeks universal context for his work — he often connects efforts on foreign affairs, agriculture and social issues to the nurturing of fundamental rights. In the 113th Congress, he gets to use the Appropriations Committee as his rostrum.

His quest to understand the big picture started early. As a college student, Fortenberry traveled in Egypt and immersed himself in Arab history, culture and religion. After earning a master's degree in public policy at Georgetown University, he interned for the Agriculture Department and worked for a Senate subcommittee. But "I had a real deep nagging of the heart to really go into the deeper questions of life," Fortenberry told the Lincoln Journal Star in 2006. He enrolled at Franciscan University in Ohio, earning a master's degree in theology.

His new seat on Appropriations lets him deal with anything the government spends money on, which includes just about everything. He's also open to a variety of political approaches, belonging to both the conservative Republican Study Committee and the moderate Main Street Partnership.

But his earlier congressional work was built around some clearly defined interests. Fortenberry shared a number of thoughtful arguments on the Foreign Affairs Committee, where he served in the 112th Congress (2011-12) as vice chairman of the Africa, Global Health and Human Rights panel. He says "every person has inherent dignity and, therefore, rights." While America's political culture is founded on that principle, it is not uniquely American — "it's a call of the human heart," according to Fortenberry. He encourages the active use of diplomacy, development and (as a last resort) defense in the promotion of human rights internationally.

Some of his efforts are legislatively focused. A 2008 law included his provisions to stem aid to governments that use child soldiers, and he helped win enactment of a 2007 law granting special visas to Iraqi translators, who helped the U.S. government at great personal risk.

He says economic liberalization does not necessarily lead to advances in human rights. Countries such as China have introduced some free-market principles, he said, but without the expansion of human rights that growing markets can bring. He would like the United States to be more deliberate in leveraging cultural exchanges, trade deals and other engagements in a "holistic approach" toward promoting "the well-being of all persons."

"We cannot carry the entire weight of international stability anymore," Fortenberry said. He believes the defining movement of the 21st century will be the enrollment of other actors, including Western allies, in the defense of human rights. "They are living off of the benefits that we primarily have provided to the international community — in terms of stability, so that free commerce can take place — without the corresponding responsibility," he said.

Fortenberry's signature foreign affairs issue is nuclear non-proliferation. He co-founded the Congressional Nuclear Security Caucus with California Democrat Adam B. Schiff, and he introduces bills and amendments to bolster non-proliferation programs.

On the domestic side, Fortenberry waxes philosophical about how values that come from working the land — "hard work, personal responsibility, community life, neighbor helping neighbor" — have shaped Nebraska's character. Fortenberry once chaired the Agriculture Subcommittee on Department

Operations, Oversight and Credit, and he now sits on the Agriculture Appropriations Subcommittee.

Noting that the average age for farmers is now in the high 50s, he promotes credit programs to help next-generation farmers enter the capital-intensive industry. A 2012 panel-approved version of a bill to reauthorize farm programs included his amendments to expand some credit programs and provide microloans with new farmers in mind. Fortenberry has worked to promote some of the business practices of startup farms, including local distribution via farmers markets, growth of specialty crops and direct-to-consumer sales. "It is an emerging field that is actually traditional," he said. "It's the way we used to do agriculture."

Fortenberry is a strong backer of federal support for the ethanol industry and for the development of renewable sources of energy in general.

He is a social conservative, believing that an overreaching government can stymie the efforts of other institutions that address society's ills. Family, faith groups and civic clubs "beautifully teach natural virtues," he said.

After enactment of the 2010 health care law, Fortenberry introduced a bill to prevent new rules requiring the insurance coverage of services, such as contraception, that might conflict with religious "rights of conscience." He brought that measure back early in the 112th Congress, even before the Obama administration issued a contraception-coverage mandate that put the issue in the national spotlight. House action on the measure stalled in 2012 because of Senate opposition.

Fortenberry was born and raised in Baton Rouge, La. His father died in a car accident when Fortenberry was 12; he has said that the tragedy instilled in him a feeling of responsibility. He was interested in politics and international affairs from a young age. As a fifth-grader, he wrote a letter to Richard Nixon about the president's 1972 trip to China. At 17, Fortenberry served as a page to a Democratic state senator in Louisiana. He switched parties in 1982, citing the influence of President Ronald Reagan.

He met his wife, Celeste (with whom he has five daughters), while studying at Franciscan. The couple headed west to Lincoln, where Fortenberry became public relations director for what is now Sandhills Publishing. He won a seat on the Lincoln City Council, serving from 1997 to 2001.

When 13-term Republican Doug Bereuter, a prominent voice on foreign affairs, announced his retirement, a free-for-all ensued in the 2004 primary. In the seven-candidate field, Fortenberry ran as a social conservative and won with 39 percent of the vote. He took 54 percent of the vote that November, which remains his worst showing to date.

Fortenberry has opted not to seek Nebraska's open Senate seat in 2014.

Key Votes

2012	
Extend a Social Security payroll tax cut and unemployment benefits	NO
Ease securities rules to expand small-business access to capital	YES
Extend for one year subsidized student loan interest rates financed by a cut in health care spending	YES
Cite Attorney General Eric H. Holder Jr. for contempt of Congress	YES
Create a visa program for foreign graduates in high-tech fields	YES
Extend most Bush-era income tax rates while allowing rates for top-bracket earners to rise (Jan. 1, 2013)	YES
2011	
Strike funding for F-35 alternative engine	NO
Prevent EPA from regulating greenhouse gas emissions to address climate change	YES
Extend certain provisions of Patriot Act for four years	YES
Declare opposition to use of ground troops in Libya	YES
Overhaul patent law	NO
Pass compromise debt limit increase plan and establish future spending limits	YES
Allow consideration of measures to implement three trade agreements	YES

CQ Vote Studies

	PARTY UNITY		PRESIDENTIAL SUPPORT	
	SUPPORT	OPPOSE	SUPPORT	OPPOSE
2012	90%	10%	19%	81%
2011	86%	14%	30%	70%
2010	87%	13%	29%	71%
2009	81%	19%	46%	54%
2008	82%	18%	56%	44%

Interest Groups

	AFL-CIO	ADA	CCUS	ACU
2012	26%	5%	100%	73%
2011	7%	10%	88%	72%
2010	7%	15%	75%	96%
2009	14%	5%	87%	88%
2008	27%	40%	72%	84%

Nebraska 1

East — Lincoln, Fremont, Norfolk

The 1st District includes state capital Lincoln and much of the area outside Omaha — the state's largest city and most of its immediate suburbs are in the 2nd. Made up of 16 whole counties and parts of two others, the 1st was made more compact following decennial remapping that shifted rural counties to the north and south into the 3rd District. The 1st is nestled in an arc between the Omaha-based 2nd and the rest of the state.

Unsurprisingly, agriculture is important to the economy here. But government jobs, as well as the military, health care industries and higher education, also play key roles in keeping communities stable. South of Omaha, Offutt Air Force Base was moved from the 2nd District to the 1st during redistricting as the district boundary shifted west; that shift added more of Sarpy County to the 1st. The base, which serves as the economic foundation of the Omaha region, contributes more than a billion dollars annually to the economy.

The flagship campus of the University of Nebraska is in Lincoln. On football game days in the fall, the university's Memorial Stadium could qualify as the third-largest city in the state, seating more than 80,000 football fans. The stadium is expected to be completely renovated by the start of the 2013 season to hold more than 91,000.

The district overall is overwhelmingly Republican despite some Democratic pockets, and the GOP has a voter registration edge in every county wholly within the 1st except Thurston County. Thurston, which is made up entirely of the Omaha and Winnebago American Indian reservations, is one of the poorer regions of the state and has the highest unemployment rate statewide.

Major Industry
Government, higher education, agriculture

Military Bases
Offutt Air Force Base, 6,023 military, 2,830 civilian (2012)

Cities
Lincoln, Bellevue

Notable
The skeleton of a 14-foot male elephant, found in 1922 in Lincoln County (in the 3rd District) by a rancher and his wife, is on display at the University of Nebraska State Museum in Lincoln.

Rep. Lee Terry (R)

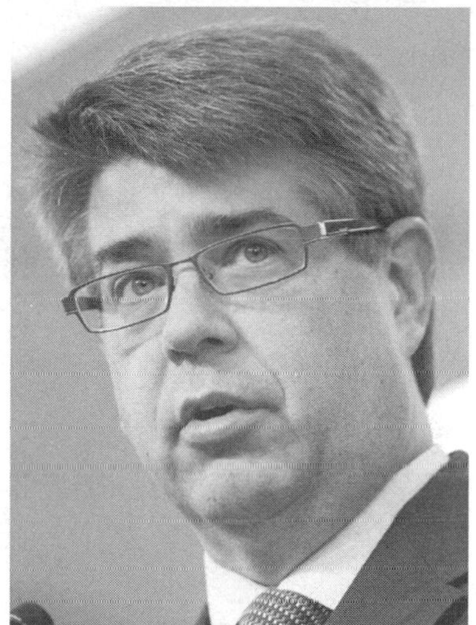

Capitol Office
225-4155
leeterry.house.gov
2266 Rayburn Bldg. 20515-2702; fax 226-5452

Committees
Energy & Commerce
(Commerce, Manufacturing & Trade - Chairman)

Residence
Omaha

Born
Jan. 29, 1962; Omaha, Neb.

Religion
Protestant

Family
Wife, Robyn Terry; three children

Education
U. of Nebraska, B.S. 1984 (political science); Creighton U., J.D. 1987

Career
Lawyer

Political Highlights
Omaha City Council, 1991-99 (president, 1994-95)

ELECTION RESULTS

2012 GENERAL		
Lee Terry (R)	128,307	51.2%
John W. Ewing Jr. (D)	122,452	48.8%

2012 PRIMARY		
Lee Terry (R)	27,998	59.4%
Brett Lindstrom (R)	10,753	22.8%
Jack Heidel (R)	5,406	11.5%
Glenn M. Freeman (R)	1,885	4.0%
Paul Anderson (R)	1,051	2.2%

2010 GENERAL		
Lee Terry (R)	93,840	60.8%
Tom White (D)	60,486	39.2%

Previous Winning Percentages
2008 (52%); 2006 (55%); 2004 (61%); 2002 (63%); 2000 (66%); 1998 (66%)

Elected 1998; 8th term

Terry has been a student of politics most of his life, and he constantly faces the challenge of balancing his personal enthusiasm for policy work with the type of soft-pedaled conservatism his constituents relate to.

He grew up in a Republican household with three sisters. Terry's father anchored the nightly news for Omaha's ABC affiliate, and he took his son along for Saturday tapings of an interview show. Politicians regularly met the young Terry off-camera. For reasons he can't quite remember, Terry kept an autographed photo of Nebraska Sen. Roman L. Hruska on his bedroom wall.

Politics often dominated dinner conversation, and his dad ran for the House in 1976. He is "further to the right than I am," said Terry, who belongs to the centrist Main Street Partnership. The campaign was unsuccessful, but it inspired Terry to plan on civic life. He studied political science, went to law school, and then focused on personal injury, workers' compensation and negligence cases. At 29, he was elected to the Omaha City Council.

Since the 107th Congress (2001-02), Terry has brought his love of politics — and his measured baritone — to the Energy and Commerce Committee. The panel allows him to negotiate and nudge tech issues; sometimes he admits to being a poor publicist for the more esoteric parts of his portfolio. He has a great opportunity for some chest thumping in the 113th Congress (2013-14), however, as the new chairman of the Commerce, Manufacturing and Trade Subcommittee. He has jurisdiction over some front-page economic issues, such as the effects of federal regulations on the business environment and a possible expansion of trade with the European Union.

But he still has a strong interest in the Communications and Technology Subcommittee. Terry has long wanted changes to the Universal Service Fund, which is meant to spread telecom services to rural areas. Requirements that companies use USF funds to maintain their current system were blocking them from upgrading, he said. Terry considers "getting high-speed broadband ubiquitously available" to be a big tech priority, and he notes that the Federal Communications Commission's 2011 plan for USF changes included many features of bipartisan legislation he had previously introduced.

Terry joins most Republicans in opposing the FCC's "network neutrality" rules, which were adopted in 2011 and meant to keep Internet service providers from restricting access to various kinds of content. The success of the Internet, Terry says, is attributable largely to decisions not to regulate it.

But he thinks most Internet issues are too complex to allow for simple political polarization. He supports protection of copyrights, but says attempts to stop online piracy might trample the rights of some businesses. Cybersecurity is similarly sticky; Terry said a good place to start is tweaking antitrust law to make sure companies can collaborate on best practices to prevent breaches. Liability protections for diligent companies might help, as well as allowing the government to share classified information with companies under attack.

Terry has been more demonstrative in recent energy debates. He is the face of the House campaign to approve the Keystone XL oil pipeline from Canada to the Gulf of Mexico. Environmentalists oppose the pipeline, which was planned to pass through Nebraska's Sand Hills region, over a major aquifer. (The proposed route has been changed.) In 2011, the House passed a Terry bill directing the president to expedite review of the project. The White House denied the permit, saying it did not have enough time to consider it. Terry came back with another House-passed provision to transfer the decision to the Federal Energy Regulatory Commission. In 2013, he produced a bill that would cut out the executive branch and legislatively approve the project.

When the Obama administration canceled the Yucca Mountain project, in which a Nevada site would serve as the nation's nuclear waste repository, Republicans criticized the Nuclear Regulatory Commission as slow-walking appeals of the decision. Responding to allegations that Chairman Gregory B. Jaczko had withheld information from fellow commissioners to influence the decision, Terry wrote a bill to constrain the powers of the chairman.

In 2012, Terry was even willing to stop federal assistance for ethanol — the corn-based fuel he has often promoted in the past. "They're mature enough now," he said. "They can compete." He is OK with federal funding of research for less-developed technologies, such as batteries for hybrid or electric cars. Terry teamed with Democrat Baron P. Hill of Indiana in 2007 as key negotiators on a law to increase the fuel efficiency of cars, small trucks and SUVs.

One long-term interest of Terry's has a personal origin. For several congresses, he has introduced bills to improve planning for, and access to, hospice and long-term health care. He was inspired by his mother's bout with cancer: "Keeping people out of nursing homes is really important." Medicaid-based nursing facilities are woeful, and tax credits for the purchase of private care would be one way to help consumers, he said.

But generally, he would like the tax code simplified to remove most credits. He also strongly supports a balanced-budget amendment to the Constitution, citing his local government days as proof that such requirements can work.

His eight years as a councilman pushed him out front in the race for an open House seat in 1998. Terry won the five-way primary by 10 points and then triumphed by 31 points over Democrat Michael Scott, a newscaster. Terry announced a three-term limit but later backed off that promise. Voters didn't seem to mind, and Terry coasted to easy re-election wins until 2006.

That year, with Republicans facing a backlash from voters upset over ethics scandals on Capitol Hill and the Iraq War, Terry spent nearly $1 million to hold off Democrat Jim Esch. In an attempt to raise his profile, he put up pictures of himself on 17 large billboards in and around Omaha. The billboards said, "Thank you for your trust." Esch again questioned Terry's accomplishments in 2008, but Terry pulled out a 4-point win.

He had a surprisingly close race against Democratic Douglas County treasurer John W. Ewing Jr. in 2012. The Omaha World-Herald endorsed Terry's opponent for the first time ever, and even with a huge fundraising advantage Terry won by less than 3 points. He told the World-Herald that "we're going to take a hard look at this campaign."

Terry watches sports for fun, particularly Husker football. But he also co-founded the Hockey Caucus. He cheers for college teams at home and the Washington Capitals on the professional level.

Key Votes

2012	
Extend a Social Security payroll tax cut and unemployment benefits	NO
Ease securities rules to expand small-business access to capital	YES
Extend for one year subsidized student loan interest rates financed by a cut in health care spending	YES
Cite Attorney General Eric H. Holder Jr. for contempt of Congress	YES
Create a visa program for foreign graduates in high-tech fields	YES
Extend most Bush-era income tax rates while allowing rates for top-bracket earners to rise (Jan. 1, 2013)	NO
2011	
Strike funding for F-35 alternative engine	NO
Prevent EPA from regulating greenhouse gas emissions to address climate change	YES
Extend certain provisions of Patriot Act for four years	YES
Declare opposition to use of ground troops in Libya	YES
Overhaul patent law	NO
Pass compromise debt limit increase plan and establish future spending limits	YES
Allow consideration of measures to implement three trade agreements	YES

CQ Vote Studies

	PARTY UNITY		PRESIDENTIAL SUPPORT	
	SUPPORT	OPPOSE	SUPPORT	OPPOSE
2012	93%	7%	16%	84%
2011	93%	7%	20%	80%
2010	92%	8%	29%	71%
2009	90%	10%	41%	59%
2008	90%	10%	68%	32%

Interest Groups

	AFL-CIO	ADA	CCUS	ACU
2012	29%	5%	100%	72%
2011	14%	10%	94%	88%
2010	7%	5%	88%	92%
2009	14%	15%	93%	88%
2008	13%	15%	100%	92%

Nebraska 2

East — Omaha and suburbs

Omaha, which served as a departure point westward for the Union Pacific Railroad, has replaced its dusty cowboy image — a railroad junction and Missouri River port where cattle became steaks — with downtown skyscrapers and white-collar jobs in agribusiness and insurance.

Omaha, which is the largest city in the state and the center of the 2nd District, continues to focus on revitalization of former industrial areas and serves as a regional arts and culture hub. Officials from Omaha and parts of surrounding Douglas County have considered merging into a single municipality to address continued growth.

Many of the jobs in Omaha revolve around insurance and 1-800 call centers for telemarketing, credit processing and customer service operations. A decade of growth and downtown redevelopment projects has attracted new technology-based companies, such as online payment processing giant PayPal, to the city that already is home to Fortune 500 companies — Berkshire Hathaway, Union Pacific Railroad, ConAgra Foods, Kiewit Corp., and Mutual of Omaha.

The rest of Douglas County outside Omaha and roughly half of Sarpy County to the south fill in the 2nd, but all of Bellevue and Offutt Air Force Base moved into the neighboring 1st District during decennial remapping. Sarpy County remains a top destination for retired military personnel, and the Omaha area overall touts low unemployment rates and high quality of life rankings.

The 2nd's increasingly conservative lean is more pronounced as a result of redistricting. Douglas County has some of the few pockets of Democratic strength in the entire state, but Barack Obama lost the county by 3 percentage points in the 2012 presidential election after winning there in 2008. In 2012, Republican Mitt Romney won by an 18-point margin in the district's portion of Sarpy.

Major Industry
Call centers, insurance

Cities
Omaha

Notable
Billionaire investor Warren Buffett lives in Omaha — his father, Republican Howard H. Buffett, represented Omaha in the House from 1943-49 and 51-53; The College World Series for NCAA baseball is held in Omaha every year.

Rep. Adrian Smith (R)

Capitol Office
225-6435
adriansmith.house.gov
2241 Rayburn Bldg. 20515-2703; fax 225-0207

Committees
Ways & Means

Residence
Gering

Born
Dec. 19, 1970; Scottsbluff, Neb.

Religion
Christian

Family
Single

Education
Liberty U., attended 1989-90; U. of Nebraska, B.S. 1993 (secondary education)

Career
Storage company owner; Realtor; education workshop coordinator; substitute teacher

Political Highlights
Gering City Council, 1994-98; Neb. Legislature, 1999-2006

ELECTION RESULTS

2012 GENERAL		
Adrian Smith (R)	187,496	74.2%
Mark Sullivan (D)	65,026	25.8%
2012 PRIMARY		
Adrian Smith (R)	62,645	81.4%
Bob Lingenfelter (R)	14,297	18.6%
2010 GENERAL		
Adrian Smith (R)	117,275	70.1%
Rebekah Davis (D)	29,932	17.9%
Dan Hill (I)	20,036	12.0%

Previous Winning Percentages
2008 (77%); 2006 (55%)

Elected 2006; 4th term

By design, the youthful Smith is one of the more anonymous House Republicans: He relies on scarcity to drive up the value of his words, then spends them almost exclusively on the concerns of his vast rural district.

Smith introduces very few bills, and he rarely speaks on the House floor for more than a minute at a time — although he did go out of his way to honor the centennial of Ronald Reagan's birth in 2011. "I rely on the same principles he championed," Smith said. "Facing deep economic challenges, like we are today, President Reagan championed solutions to reduce the size of government, promote free enterprise and empower individuals."

In hearings he is unerringly polite and reserved. His preferred way of getting things done is through member-to-member contact, which he feels cuts out interest group pressure. Smith's primary goal is to raise awareness of how national policies will affect his district, and he says his constituents' primary request is for government to leave them alone. "I'm all over that one," he says.

Smith, the co-chairman of the Congressional Rural Caucus, has long tried to highlight parts of the tax code that neglect rural realities, and in 2011 he joined the tax-writing Ways and Means Committee.

He maintains that complexity is the biggest problem with the tax code, and he advocates a system with lower rates and fewer preferences for specific groups. "Broad-based" preferences are acceptable, however, and he says tax incentives for homeownership meet that standard: "We expect everyone to benefit from that."

Tax deductions for health insurance premiums could also be broader, Smith says — current rules favor those who get insurance through an employer over those who purchase it themselves (a not-uncommon practice among farmers). He joined the Health Subcommittee for the 113th Congress (2013-14).

And like many Republicans, he says failure to repeal the estate tax will devastate family-owned farms and small businesses. Ways and Means continued work on a major tax overhaul proposal in 2013, and Smith teamed up with Connecticut Democrat John B. Larson to gather stakeholder input on taxes affecting the financial services sector.

Smith has a seat on the Trade Subcommittee, where he seeks to increase Nebraska's agricultural exports — the entrance to his D.C. office features a dry erase board with the day's commodity prices. He was vocal in supporting trade deals with South Korea, Colombia and Panama in 2011, often mentioning that Korea's tariff on red meat would be eliminated as part of the agreement. The state's popcorn industry saw a surge in business from those deals.

The Trans-Pacific Partnership is under negotiation, and a potential deal with the European Union is on the horizon. Smith emphasizes the need for strong sanitary and phytosanitary measures in those trade pacts — without consistent health standards for food imports, nations can jerry-rig their requirements to effectively deny goods from another nation, he said.

When Smith favors federal action, it's often to benefit rural America. He'd like investment in research into biodiesel fuels — including corn-based ethanol — and their byproducts. "The most important aspect of biofuel is that it's not oil," Smith said. "Biofuels are part of my all-of-the-above approach to energy supplies." He supports subsidies to help keep rural airports open, as well as various initiatives to help rural areas attract or retain younger professionals.

When he wants government out of the way, it's often to benefit rural America. In 2011, he opposed potential regulations on child farm labor and on the dust kicked up by agricultural activities. He produced a bill in both the 111th and 112th Congresses (2009-12) to exempt small hydropower projects from federal licensing requirements. The environmental impact on the fast-moving irrigation canals he has in mind is negligible, but regulatory costs currently make the projects non-viable, Smith said. The electricity generated, he suggests, could go into the electric grid, but could also power farms' center-pivot irrigation systems (which are manufactured in his district). Similar language was included in a bill passed by the House in February 2013.

When Smith parts with Republicans, it's often to benefit rural America. In 2007, he was one of 19 Republicans to support the Democrats' five-year rewrite of farm and nutrition policy, and he voted to override President George W. Bush's veto of the bill.

He should be in tune with his district, as his family has lived there for generations. Smith has spent his life in Gering, near the state's western border. The town was put on the map, Smith jokes, by the victory of local teenager Teresa Scanlan in the 2011 Miss America pageant.

Both his parents were teachers, though his father later became an insurance agent. They built a house outside of town so that Smith and his older brother could go to a country school through 8th grade, when his class was just six students. Smith said the experience helped him appreciate the value of locally controlled education.

Smith worked in a retail education supply store operated by his mother, among other places. He did many jobs for his mom, but he particularly enjoyed the challenge of collecting on the occasional bad check. Working retail in a small town paid dividends. "That's kind of how I got to meet so many people and then run for office," he said. At age 23, he was elected to the city council.

But his political interest goes further back. Smith remembers being starstruck when Republican Rep. Virginia Smith came through town. His parents were Reagan Democrats, and at his request they walked him through the issues of the 1980 election; he ended up putting Reagan signs on his desk at school. At the University of Nebraska, he got involved with the College Republicans, and over time his activism pulled his parents into the GOP. Both have been involved in the Nebraska Republican Party.

After earning a degree in secondary education, he returned to western Nebraska and briefly worked as a substitute teacher. Envisioning a political future, he settled on a career in real estate, which gave him a more flexible schedule. He moved from the city council to the Nebraska Legislature, where he was known as an anti-abortion, anti-bureaucracy Christian conservative.

Smith's door to the U.S. House opened when Republican Tom Osborne made an unsuccessful bid for governor in 2006. Smith outpaced four rivals for the GOP nomination and coasted to a 10-point win in the heavily Republican district. His re-election campaigns have been romps.

Key Votes

2012	
Extend a Social Security payroll tax cut and unemployment benefits	YES
Ease securities rules to expand small-business access to capital	YES
Extend for one year subsidized student loan interest rates financed by a cut in health care spending	YES
Cite Attorney General Eric H. Holder Jr. for contempt of Congress	YES
Create a visa program for foreign graduates in high-tech fields	YES
Extend most Bush-era income tax rates while allowing rates for top-bracket earners to rise (Jan. 1, 2013)	NO
2011	
Strike funding for F-35 alternative engine	NO
Prevent EPA from regulating greenhouse gas emissions to address climate change	YES
Extend certain provisions of Patriot Act for four years	YES
Declare opposition to use of ground troops in Libya	YES
Overhaul patent law	NO
Pass compromise debt limit increase plan and establish future spending limits	YES
Allow consideration of measures to implement three trade agreements	YES

CQ Vote Studies

	PARTY UNITY		PRESIDENTIAL SUPPORT	
	SUPPORT	OPPOSE	SUPPORT	OPPOSE
2012	98%	2%	15%	85%
2011	96%	4%	25%	75%
2010	97%	3%	26%	74%
2009	97%	3%	15%	85%
2008	98%	2%	74%	26%

Interest Groups

	AFL-CIO	ADA	CCUS	ACU
2012	14%	0%	100%	84%
2011	0%	5%	94%	88%
2010	0%	0%	88%	100%
2009	5%	0%	80%	100%
2008	7%	15%	89%	96%

Nebraska 3

West — Grand Island, North Platte, Scottsbluff

Scouting what would later become the Oregon Trail, early-19th-century explorers described this section of the country as the "Great American Desert." The district is home to both the Sandhills region, which is the largest sand dune formation in the Western hemisphere, and the Ogallala Aquifer, which supplies Nebraska with much of its water.

Most of the 3rd is arid, and most of the district's population lives along the Platte River. Grand Island and Kearney are the district's two largest cities and serve primarily as regional centers for health care and retail needs along Interstate 80, as does Scottsbluff to the west on the North Platte River near the Wyoming border.

One of the geographically largest districts in the country, the 3rd is made up of 75 counties, most of which are devoted to cattle ranches, corn, soybeans and hog farms. Four of the state's top five agriculture producing counties — Custer, Dawson, Phelps and Lincoln — are within the district, and the agrarian economy is susceptible to changes in the region's weather. Droughts remain a matter of particular urgency to residents in the 3rd, which contains several counties that depend almost entirely on agricultural production.

The district's agricultural output also supports seed processing and other biotechnology. Several cities in the 3rd host Monsanto facilities, including a processing plant in Kearney. Expansion of wind farms across the district add to the energy portfolio here, which also includes biofuel production and may eventually include part of the Keystone XL oil pipeline.

The 3rd is strongly conservative and tends to favor Republicans by wide margins at the statewide and federal levels, but there are areas of Democratic strength, including parts of Greeley, Saline and Sherman counties.

Major Industry

Agriculture, biotechnology, transportation

Cities

Grand Island, Kearney, Hastings

Notable

Union Pacific's Bailey Yard in North Platte is the world's largest railroad classification yard; The Naval Ammunition Depot in Hastings output more than 40 percent of the ammunitions used by the United States during World War II.

NEVADA

Humboldt
Elko
Washoe
Elko
2
Pershing
Lander
Churchill
Reno
Eureka
White Pine
Storey
CARSON CITY
Lyon
Nye
Mineral
Esmeralda
4
Lincoln
1
Clark
Las Vegas
Henderson
3

Gov. Brian Sandoval (R)

First elected: 2010
Length of term: 4 years
Term expires: 1/15
Salary: $149,573
Phone: (775) 684-5670
Residence: Reno
Born: Aug. 5, 1963; Redding, Calif.
Religion: Roman Catholic
Family: Wife, Kathleen Sandoval; three children
Education: U. of Nevada, B.A. 1986 (English & economics); Ohio State U., J.D. 1989
Career: State gaming commission official; lawyer
Political highlights: Nev. House, 1994-97; Nev. attorney general, 2003-05; U.S. District Court judge, 2005-09

ELECTION RESULTS

2010 GENERAL

Brian Sandoval (R)	382,350	53.4%
Rory Reid (D)	298,171	41.6%
Other	23,777	3.3%
None of these candidates	12,231	1.7%

Lt. Gov. Brian R. Krolicki (R)

First elected: 2006
Length of term: 4 years
Term expires: 1/15
Salary: $63,648
Phone: (775) 684-5637

LEGISLATURE

Legislature: February-June in odd-numbered years, limit of 120 days
Senate: 21 members, 4-year terms
2013 ratios: 11 D, 10 R; 17 men, 4 women
Salary: $8,777
Phone: (775) 684-1400
Assembly: 42 members, 2-year terms
2013 ratios: 27 D, 15 R; 28 men, 14 women
Salary: $8,777
Phone: (775) 684-8555

TERM LIMITS

Governor: 2 terms
Senate: 3 terms
House: 6 terms

URBAN STATISTICS

CITY	POPULATION
Las Vegas	583,756
Henderson	257,729
Reno	225,221
North Las Vegas	216,961
Sparks	90,264

REGISTERED VOTERS

Democrat	42%
Republican	34%
Other	24%

POPULATION

2010 population	2,700,551
2000 population	1,998,257
1990 population	1,201,833
Percent change (2000-2010)	+35.1%
Rank among states (2010)	35
Median age	35.3
Born in state	23.2%
Foreign born	17.6%
Violent crime rate	702/100,000
Poverty level	12.4%
Federal workers	24,586
Military	10,034

ELECTIONS

STATE ELECTION OFFICIAL
(775) 684-5705
DEMOCRATIC PARTY
(702) 737-8683
REPUBLICAN PARTY
(702) 258-9182

MISCELLANEOUS

Web: www.nv.gov
Capital: Carson City

U.S. CONGRESS

Senate: 1 Democrat, 1 Republican
House: 2 Republicans, 2 Democrats

STATISTICS BY DISTRICT

District	2012 Vote for President: Obama	Romney	2008 Vote for President: Obama	McCain	Black	Asian	Hispanic	Median Income	Over 64	Under 20	College Education	Rural	Sq. Miles
1	66%	32%	65%	33%	9%	9%	43%	$36,447	12%	26%	15%	0%	105
2	45	53	49	48	2	4	21	51,505	14	26	25	15	55,830
3	50	49	54	45	8	12	15	61,286	13	25	32	2	2,849
4	54	44	56	41	14	4	30	50,134	12	30	17	9	50,998
STATE	**53**	**46**	**55**	**43**	**8**	**7**	**27**	**48,927**	**13**	**27**	**22**	**6**	**109,781**
U.S.	**51**	**47**	**53**	**46**	**12**	**5**	**17**	**50,052**	**13**	**27**	**29**	**21**	**3,531,905**

Sen. Harry Reid (D)

Capitol Office
224-3542
reid.senate.gov
522 Hart Bldg. 20510-2803; fax 224-7327

Committees
No committee assignments

Residence
Searchlight

Born
Dec. 2, 1939; Searchlight, Nev.

Religion
Mormon

Family
Wife, Landra Reid; five children

Education
Southern Utah State College, A.S. 1959; Utah State U., B.A. 1961 (history & political science); George Washington U., J.D. 1964; U. of Nevada, Las Vegas, attended 1969-70

Career
Lawyer

Political Highlights
Nev. Assembly, 1969-71; lieutenant governor, 1971-75; Democratic nominee for U.S. Senate, 1974; candidate for mayor of Las Vegas, 1975; Nevada Gaming Commission chairman, 1977-81; U.S. House, 1983-87

ELECTION RESULTS

2010 GENERAL		
Harry Reid (D)	362,785	50.3%
Sharron Angle (R)	321,361	44.5%
None of these candidates (WRI)	16,197	2.2%
2010 PRIMARY		
Harry Reid (D)	87,401	75.3%
None of these candidates (D)	12,341	10.6%
Alex Miller (D)	9,717	8.4%
Eduardo "Mr. Clean" Hamilton (D)	4,645	4.0%
Carlo Poliak (D)	1,938	1.7%

Previous Winning Percentages
2004 (61%); 1998 (48%); 1992 (51%); 1986 (50%); 1984 House Election (56%); 1982 House Election (58%)

Elected 1986; 5th term

Reid took over as Senate majority leader in 2007, when he enjoyed the cooperation of a Democratic House. He picked up a Democratic president in 2009. Success was defined by holding his party together, and there were impressive results: Using procedural tools and his talents for horse-trading, Reid helped engineer a stimulus package and overhauls of the health care system and financial sector regulation.

The switch to a Republican House in 2011 changed the dynamics of the Capitol and sharpened perceptions of Reid. To Democrats, he is a bulwark protecting their recent successes, and to Republicans he is an obstructionist boogeyman — the nebulous figure thwarting their preferred plans for fiscal stability and for shrinking the size of government.

Reid often doesn't bother to define himself in any explicit way. He is a mediocre public speaker and lets vocal lieutenants — Charles E. Schumer of New York and Richard J. Durbin of Illinois — take Democratic messages to the media. On major issues, he usually lets committee chairmen take the lead in shaping bills.

But Reid is a fighter. The son of an alcoholic miner and a high-school dropout mother, he grew up in Searchlight, a small mining town in Nevada. Reid was an amateur middleweight boxer before scrapping his way through college and law school, and his early political career included tangling with the mob as chairman of the state gaming commission.

In the 112th Congress (2011-12), his most prominent strategy was a rope-a-dope battle with House Republicans on fiscal matters. Reid consciously sidelined the Senate in budget and spending talks. As Republicans liked to point out, Reid didn't push for passage of a Senate budget; the chamber didn't take up regular spending bills in 2012; and negotiations on major fiscal issues often took place between the White House and House Republicans. Spending cuts (and their consequences) could arguably be associated almost entirely with the House GOP, and Republicans had a bad election season in 2012.

There were a few deals to emerge from the Senate in the 112th. The House eventually had to accept a two-year reauthorization of surface transportation programs, after the Senate passed one with bipartisan support. Senate Republicans and Democrats reached agreement on a reauthorization of farm programs, while the House could not. But Reid mostly refused to call up House-passed energy and regulatory bills, accusing Republicans of trying to ram through an extremist agenda.

Reid can be brutally blunt in assessing GOP opponents — he once called President George W. Bush a "loser" and "the worst president we've ever had." In late 2012, while Reid again mostly kept the Senate out of major fiscal negotiations, he accused House Speaker John A. Boehner of running a "dictatorship" and refusing to compromise. At a White House meeting the next day, Boehner suggested that Reid do something to himself that would be anatomically difficult.

In the 2012 election cycle he mixed it up on behalf of Democratic Senate candidates. He is not an enthusiastic fundraiser himself, but Reid deployed his operatives to a well-funded pair of super PACs. He also went after GOP presidential nominee (and fellow Mormon) Mitt Romney, publicly criticizing the candidate for his hesitance to release comprehensive tax returns. At the start of the 113th Congress (2013-14), he initially avoided votes on gun control that could haunt moderate Democrats up for re-election in 2014. After a few months, he went with public opinion and allowed a series of votes on gun proposals in April — all of which were defeated.

Reid has a mostly cordial relationship with GOP leader Mitch McConnell, but a "gentlemen's agreement" they struck early in 2011 didn't hold. Republicans continued to filibuster procedural motions to slow down bills, and Reid often "filled the amendment tree" — a procedure that prevents the minority from proposing changes to bills on the Senate floor. At the start of the 113th, they agreed on rule changes so that Republicans would be able to offer a minimum number of amendments on bills while giving up some of their power to force procedural votes.

As far as his personal politics, Reid backs New Deal-style policies aimed at lifting up the working class. But he sits closer to the middle of the Democratic spectrum than the liberal end. (Durbin, the No. 2 Senate Democrat, is further to the left.) One parochial issue Reid always makes time for is Yucca Mountain. He has spent most of his quarter-century in Congress leading the opposition to that proposed nuclear waste repository in his state.

Reid was his party's second-in-command for six years, serving under Tom Daschle of South Dakota. When Daschle was defeated for re-election in 2004, Reid, in a matter of hours, lined up the votes he needed to move up from whip. When Democrats won control in 2006, there was no question Reid would make the transition from minority to majority leader.

He still keeps a home in Searchlight, but as a young man he wanted out, so he applied himself to his studies. Reid boarded with families 40 miles away in Henderson to attend Basic High School, where he served as student body president. It was there that history teacher and boxing coach Mike O'Callaghan — who was also the local Democratic chairman — took notice of Reid and helped arrange a scholarship for him at Utah State University. Reid later earned a law degree at George Washington University while moonlighting as a U.S. Capitol Police officer.

Reid returned to Henderson and won election to the Nevada Legislature at age 28. In 1970, he ran successfully for lieutenant governor on a ticket with O'Callaghan, who was elected governor. After one term on the job, Reid came within 625 votes of election to the U.S. Senate. It was 1974, and the Watergate scandal almost lifted Reid past Paul Laxalt, a former Republican governor. The next year, Reid lost his bid to be mayor of Las Vegas.

O'Callaghan got him rolling again with an appointment to the Nevada Gaming Commission, giving Reid oversight of the state's top industry at a time it was tainted by organized crime. In 1982, Reid won his first of two House terms. He tried again for the Senate in 1986 and won with 50 percent of the vote over Republican Rep. Jim Santini.

Nevada's enduring conservative element has made Reid's re-election campaigns an adventure. In 1992, Reid outspent GOP rancher Demar Dahl 5-to-1 to prevail with 51 percent of the vote. In his 1998 campaign, Reid won by only 428 votes over John Ensign, who was then a House member from Las Vegas. He was looking vulnerable in 2010, as there was a national surge of enthusiasm for Republicans. Reid ramped up his campaign operation early and attacked the GOP primary candidate who seemed the most threatening, former state Republican Party Chairwoman Sue Lowden. Reid crippled her campaign by homing in on a comment she made at a campaign event that people could pay for health care on a barter system.

Lowden's demise cleared the way for former Assemblywoman Sharron Angle, a tea party favorite whom Reid thought he could easily caricature as a right-wing zealot. He tried, but Angle proved no pushover, raising more than $21 million to Reid's $17 million. Independent groups spent millions more on behalf of both candidates. In the end, Angle's army of enthusiasts was no match for Reid's get-out-the-vote operation, and he pulled out a surprisingly solid 6-point win.

There is speculation that Reid will retire after his current term, but he has said that he is preparing for another re-election campaign in 2016.

Key Votes

2012	
Prohibit health insurance plans from denying coverage based on the sponsor's religious beliefs	YES
Require approval of the Keystone XL oil pipeline	NO
Ease securities rules to expand small-business access to capital	YES
Reauthorize farm and nutrition programs for five years	YES
Limit debate on a bill that would create private-sector cybersecurity standards	NO
Consent to ratification of a treaty setting global standard for the treatment of people with disabilities	YES
Provide $60.4 billion in disaster relief following Superstorm Sandy	YES
Extend most Bush-era income tax rates while allowing rates for top-bracket earners to rise (Jan. 1, 2013)	YES
2011	
Prevent EPA from regulating greenhouse gas emissions to address climate change	NO
Extend certain provisions of Patriot Act for four years	YES
Clear compromise debt limit increase plan and establish future spending limits	YES
Overhaul patent law	YES
Implement Colombia free trade agreement	NO
Limit debate on confirmation of Caitlin J. Halligan to D.C. Circuit Court of Appeals	YES
Extend payroll tax cut and unemployment benefits for two months	YES

CQ Vote Studies

	PARTY UNITY		PRESIDENTIAL SUPPORT	
	SUPPORT	OPPOSE	SUPPORT	OPPOSE
2012	94%	6%	95%	5%
2011	93%	7%	93%	7%
2010	95%	5%	97%	3%
2009	96%	4%	99%	1%
2008	84%	16%	43%	57%
2007	95%	5%	39%	61%
2006	93%	7%	57%	43%
2005	92%	8%	38%	62%
2004	83%	17%	61%	39%
2003	95%	5%	53%	47%

Interest Groups

	AFL-CIO	ADA	CCUS	ACU
2012	90%	90%	38%	0%
2011	95%	95%	36%	0%
2010	100%	75%	18%	0%
2009	94%	95%	43%	8%
2008	50%	70%	75%	16%
2007	89%	85%	45%	0%
2006	93%	90%	50%	12%
2005	93%	100%	50%	4%
2004	100%	90%	53%	21%
2003	100%	70%	35%	21%

Sen. Dean Heller (R)

Capitol Office
225-6224
heller.senate.gov
324 Hart Bldg. 20510; fax 228-6753

Committees
Banking, Housing & Urban Affairs
Commerce, Science & Transportation
Energy & Natural Resources
Veterans' Affairs
Special Aging

Residence
Carson City

Born
May 10, 1960; Castro Valley, Calif.

Religion
Mormon

Family
Wife, Lynne Heller; four children

Education
U. of Southern California, B.S. 1985 (business administration)

Career
Commercial banker; stockbroker; chief deputy state treasurer

Political Highlights
Nev. Assembly, 1990-94; Nev. secretary of state, 1995-2007; U.S. House, 2007-11

ELECTION RESULTS

2012 GENERAL		
Dean Heller (R)	457,656	45.9%
Shelley Berkley (D)	446,080	44.7%
David Lory VanderBeek (IA)	48,792	4.9%
2012 PRIMARY		
Dean Heller (R)	88,958	86.3%
Sherry Brooks (R)	5,356	5.2%
Eddie Hamilton (R)	2,628	2.5%
Richard Charles (R)	2,295	2.2%
Carlo Poliak (R)	512	.5%

Previous Winning Percentages
2010 House Election (63%); 2008 House Election (52%); 2006 House Election (50%)

Elected 2012; 1st full term

Appointed 2011

Heller won a full term in the Senate by emphasizing a commitment to ending legislative gridlock, not his often conservative record. That survival tactic could position him to thrive. Republicans will be courting him to keep the Democratic majority in check, while Democrats will look to him as a potential swing vote who can keep bills moving.

He is a product of the state capital of Carson City. Heller was elected three times to the U.S. House to represent every part of Nevada that isn't Las Vegas or its suburbs. He was appointed to the Senate in May 2011 — Republican Sen. John Ensign had resigned after failing to shake the repercussions of an extramarital affair — and started working immediately toward election in 2012. Heller had won statewide office before, serving three terms as secretary of state, but Democrats have a definite registration edge and more sway in the populous southeast corner of the state.

Heller quickly became a louder voice for cooperation between the parties, and he reached out to independent voters. It was not so much a change in course as an amplification of his anti-establishment tendencies from his days in the House, where he occasionally scolded GOP leaders. Heller several times joined some of the most recognized Senate GOP moderates to vote against procedural delays that were stalling action on Democrat-favored bills and amendments.

Late in 2011, he was the only Republican to support a Democratic proposal for a balanced-budget amendment to the Constitution, as well as a GOP version. He became the Senate standard-bearer for "No Budget, No Pay," a bill to withhold congressional salaries if lawmakers don't adopt a budget by a certain deadline. The measure was touted by No Labels, a nonpartisan group devoted to making Congress more productive.

Heller also voted against the fiscal 2013 budget of Republican Rep. Paul D. Ryan of Wisconsin. He voted for the fiscal 2012 version, both in the House and the Senate. But when Democrats called the fiscal 2013 budget up for a vote, Heller voted "no" — he said he was protesting a process never meant to produce a federal budget.

"I want to be a little bit more pragmatic about the way to get work done here," Heller said in 2011. "The problem isn't as much policy around here as it is process." His approach paid off. Facing liberal Democratic Rep. Shelley Berkley in the 2012 election, he secured 46 percent of the vote, which was enough for a 1-point win. His victory was one of the few bright spots for Republicans in a largely miserable slate of Senate contests.

And Heller didn't change course after the election. At the start of the 113th Congress (2013-14) he strengthened his affiliation with No Labels, and a House version of "No Budget, No Pay" was enacted. When Ryan's fiscal 2014 budget came up for a Senate vote, Heller opposed it — he said he wanted to start with a more moderate budget framework.

If Heller's flexibility on procedural matters gives him leverage in the 113th Congress, he's still likely to use it to move some conservative causes. Heller takes a smaller-government, free-market approach to most problems.

A former stockbroker, he opposed the $700 billion rescue package for the financial services industry in 2008. "That is Wall Street arrogance," he told the Las Vegas Review-Journal. "They created their problems and they want someone else to bail them out." He joined the Banking, Housing and Urban Affairs Committee in 2013, and he is the top Republican on its Economic Policy Subcommittee.

Heller is socially conservative. He defines marriage as between a man and a woman and votes against federal funding of abortion. He strongly backs gun rights — Heller in 2012 blocked consideration of Elissa F. Cadish for district court judge in Nevada, citing her statements on the Second Amendment. Cadish, who withdrew herself from consideration in 2013, was recommended by Nevada's senior senator, Democratic leader Harry Reid.

When Heller breaks with Republicans on policy, it's usually over Nevada-centric issues. He sits on the Energy and Natural Resources Committee, where he backs an "all of the above" energy strategy but opposes the use of Yucca Mountain as a nuclear waste depository. "I believe Nevadans have the right to be safe in their own backyards," he said at a 2012 hearing.

He's also on the Commerce, Science and Transportation Committee, a good venue to promote Nevada's tourism industry. Heller has called for stronger regulation of online gambling, a position favored by the casinos that bring visitors to the state. Even while running against Berkley, he teamed with her on a 2012 bill to eliminate any "blacklist" preventing federal agencies from holding conferences in certain cities. Reports of a gaudy General Services Administration conference in Las Vegas had spurred congressional hearings.

Heller has also supported expanded unemployment insurance and changes to the tax code to help "underwater" homeowners whose mortgage balance exceeds the worth of their house. Nevada was one of the states hit hardest by the 2008 financial crisis.

Heller is the son of an auto mechanic whose customers included a number of state legislators. As a boy, he rode his bike from his father's shop to play with the children of Paul Laxalt, the Nevada governor who went on to become a U.S. senator (by defeating Reid in 1974). Heller was a star basketball player at Carson High School. As an adult, he played 17 consecutive years in the same recreational basketball league in Carson City. He also enjoys stock car racing, a hobby he shares with his father.

At the University of Southern California, Heller studied business administration, specializing in finance and securities analysis. He put himself through college by working on the Pacific Stock Exchange. After graduation, he worked as a stockbroker and trader in Los Angeles.

In 1989, Heller returned to Carson City to become the deputy to Nevada Treasurer Ken Santor, a Republican. On Heller's first day on the job, Santor had a falling out with the state Assembly's powerful Ways and Means chairman, and Heller was asked to substitute for his boss at committee meetings. The minority leader, a Republican, took notice and suggested Heller run for public office himself. The following year, he was elected to the Assembly with the help of his father and his father's reputation.

Heller was elected Nevada secretary of state in 1994. In his three terms, he became known for making Nevada the first state to implement an auditable paper trail for electronic voting machines.

Republican Rep. Jim Gibbons ran for governor in 2006, and Heller won a five-way primary for the chance to succeed him, besting Assemblywoman Sharron Angle by 421 votes. He won by 5 points in November and enjoyed larger victory margins in his two re-election bids.

His 2012 campaign against Berkley, who represented Las Vegas, looked to be a tossup from the start. Heller made the most of an ethics inquiry that Berkeley had improperly intervened as a lawmaker to boost her husband's medical practice. He also highlighted her husband's financial stake in a business that flipped homes in foreclosure. He ran a TV ad calling her one of the most corrupt members of Congress.

Berkley accused Heller of having no credibility on middle-class issues, but statewide polling showed Berkley suffering from high disapproval ratings statewide. Heller won by around 12,000 votes, even as President Barack Obama carried the state by more than 6 points.

Key Votes

2012	
Prohibit health insurance plans from denying coverage based on the sponsor's religious beliefs	NO
Require approval of the Keystone XL oil pipeline	YES
Ease securities rules to expand small-business access to capital	YES
Reauthorize farm and nutrition programs for five years	NO
Limit debate on a bill that would create private-sector cybersecurity standards	NO
Consent to ratification of a treaty setting global standard for the treatment of people with disabilities	NO
Provide $60.4 billion in disaster relief following Superstorm Sandy	YES
Extend most Bush-era income tax rates while allowing rates for top-bracket earners to rise (Jan. 1, 2013)	YES
2011	
Prevent EPA from regulating greenhouse gas emissions to address climate change	YES
Extend certain provisions of Patriot Act for four years	NO
Clear compromise debt limit increase plan and establish future spending limits	NO
Overhaul patent law	YES
Implement Colombia free trade agreement	YES
Limit debate on confirmation of Caitlin J. Halligan to D.C. Circuit Court of Appeals	NO
Extend payroll tax cut and unemployment benefits for two months	YES

CQ Vote Studies

	PARTY UNITY		PRESIDENTIAL SUPPORT	
	SUPPORT	OPPOSE	SUPPORT	OPPOSE
2012	65%	35%	54%	46%
2011	84%	16%	45%	55%
2010	92%	8%	33%	67%
2009	91%	9%	22%	78%
2008	92%	8%	68%	32%
2007	94%	6%	75%	25%

Interest Groups

	AFL-CIO	ADA	CCUS	ACU
2012	27%	20%	100%	71%
2011	7%		88%	92%
2010	7%	10%	100%	88%
2009	5%	5%	87%	92%
2008	36%	25%	89%	80%
2007	13%	15%	80%	96%

;tudies

PARTY UNITY		PRESIDENTIAL SUPPORT	
ORT	OPPOSE	SUPPORT	OPPOSE
%	8%	88%	12%
%	5%	94%	6%

;roups

CIO	ADA	CCUS	ACU
%	85%	50%	0%
0%	95%	33%	4%

has a popular hospitality manage-

s of property value declines, high
residential neighborhoods and at
he economic uncertainty. Some local
ing market recoveries.

d a tremendous influx of Hispanic
reflected employment opportunities,
r the recession began. The 1st gives
c candidates; it is the only district
ority of registered voters.

er education

as Vegas Boulevard has a drive-

; 2nd term

3

ent of politics and a longtime practitioner. The former Nevada as a tough and brainy Democratic partisan, and ence serving in a legislative minority. For 16 years, she he state Senate.

dignified and genteel — far from the caricature of her f Las Vegas. She analyzed politics for years as a political l she laments the "dumbing down" of political discourse of courtesy" and the fact that "no one can write a letter

peeches and see how eloquent they were," she says. "He wn, even though there were fewer people with educa- should be more literate, but foreign policy has been "

eciates the frontier mentality of her state. "I wouldn't hat I have if I had stayed in Georgia. Things there are so traditional," she says. "Nevada has an entrepreneurial od idea, you can get people to go along with you."

nts include 20 years of service as a state senator. In her vas the minority leader. Described by Nevada political nt, combative and ambitious, she has taken on some of hts, including U.S. Senate Majority Leader Harry Reid. most of the Nevada Democratic establishment report- un in the 3rd District, which she represented in the 111th before losing to Republican Joe Heck. Reid wanted a senator, Ruben Kihuen, to run for the 1st District seat mocrat Shelley Berkley (who lost a Senate campaign). ht, could drive up Hispanic turnout in statewide races; an 40 percent Latino.

spect of a safe Democratic seat, Titus undid those plans. campaign war chest, partly with the help of groups such former colleagues such as Democratic Whip Steny H. he commissioned polls showing her with a huge lead over worked, as Kihuen decided to forgo the race. Titus eas- eneral election over former naval officer Chris Edwards. ngress representing a redrawn district that is more urban, rse, more dependent on tourism and more Democratic represented. "The issues have shifted a bit," Titus says, ause her new district includes the Las Vegas Strip, she tourism.

Transportation and Infrastructure Committee. "Devel- d rail is a challenge we must take on," she testified to the 1 2013. Titus is pushing for a high-speed rail line connect- hern California. She's interested in speeding the develop- a planned highway linking Las Vegas to Phoenix.

er of the Veterans' Affairs Committee. Titus bucked most ats in March 2013 when she voted for the House's initial g resolution that funded government operations through — although it had spending cuts she disliked, she said ns in the law were acceptable.

hetoric usually match up with those of most Democrats. a hundred mostly liberal Democrats in a February 2013 letter to President Barack Obama urging him to oppose any reductions to entitlement programs — including higher eligibility ages for Medicare or Social Security, or the use of a "chained" consumer price index to calculate benefit increases. Titus calls for federal support of renewable-energy development, and she has said that Nevada has the potential to become "the Saudi Arabia of solar power."

During her state Senate tenure, Titus had a reputation as a fierce partisan, but she was open to collaborative efforts. She formed a coalition to help protect Red Rock Canyon from encroaching development, championed legislation to provide tax breaks for renewable-energy development and authored a bill that requires insurance companies to cover the costs of the HPV vaccine.

Titus' maternal grandfather immigrated to America from Greece in 1911, eventually settling in West Point, Ga. (Titus speaks with a Southern drawl.) Like many of his countrymen, her grandfather ran a small restaurant. He once delivered food to President Franklin D. Roosevelt during one of his therapeutic stays at nearby Warm Springs. "There was no Greek church or school," and he had to go all the way to Jacksonville, Fla., to get olive oil and cheese, Titus said. "But he helped us retain our Greek roots."

As a young girl, she would listen in on the local politicos who drank coffee at her grandfather's restaurant, which was across from the courthouse. Her father ran the city planning and building department; his great-grandfather, James Seward, served in the House in the 33rd through 35th Congresses (1853-59). Her interest in politics was sealed when she went to hear Hubert H. Humphrey speak in 1968. "I grew up a Democrat. I've always been for the underdog; it's who I fight for," she says.

Titus didn't like high school, and before graduating she was accepted to the College of William and Mary — the alma mater of Thomas Jefferson. She studied government there, then got her advanced degrees in political science at the University of Georgia and Florida State University. She's a rare Ph.D. without a high school diploma. In 1977 she took a teaching post at UNLV, where she remained for more than three decades.

She joined the state Senate in 1988. Apparently fed up with life in a legislative minority, she thought about running to become a Clark County commissioner in 2002. She scuttled those plans when Rory Reid, the son of Harry Reid, decided to run. Four years later, Titus lost to Republican Jim Gibbons when she ran for governor.

Titus was initially hesitant to wage another high-profile campaign, but she opted to challenge GOP Rep. Jon Porter in the 3rd District in 2008. Porter had a big fundraising edge, but Titus was helped by increased Democratic registration in a presidential year. She prevailed by 5 points. Heck successfully tied her to the policies of the Obama administration and narrowly defeated her in 2010.

CQ Vote	
	SUF
2010	9
2009	9

Interest	
	AF
2010	9
2009	1(

Nevada 1

Las Vegas

Neon lights along the Strip and the chance of easy money lure pleasure seekers to the 1st, which includes part of Las Vegas as well as many of the famous casinos, convention halls and restaurants south of the city. Guests from around the country and the world fly into newly expanded McCarran International Airport (which is split with the 3rd) to visit — and try their luck.

Decennial reapportionment called for the addition of one U.S. House seat to the state's delegation after the 2010 census. Most of the Las Vegas region's population growth was farther out of the urban core south and west of the city in the 3rd District, but overall growth in the area shrank the 1st's footprint to a compact square of densely populated neighborhoods inside the Las Vegas Beltway.

The Las Vegas area depends on revenue from tourism, a sector that has been notoriously volatile in recent years. Ups and downs in the economies of convention-hosting can have dramatic effects on the service industry workforce: Unemployment rates overall remain high, and close to 15 percent of the population of Las Vegas is below the poverty line. Outside of the glitz of the casinos, the University of Nevada-Las Vegas, whose campus is near the airport and unsurprisingl ment program, is a major employer.

Regional budget issues linked to yea rates of foreclosures and vacancies commercial centers have not eased officials are optimistic regarding hou

In the last decade, the 1st experienc residents; Hispanic population grow however, and stagnated not long aft wide margins of victory to Democra statewide where Democrats are a m

Major Industry
Tourism, gambling, conventions, hig

Cities
Las Vegas

Notable
The Little White Wedding Chapel on through window for weddings.

Rep. Mark Amodei (R)

Capitol Office
225-6155
amodei.house.gov
222 Cannon Bldg. 20515-2802; fax 225-5079

Committees
Judiciary
Natural Resources
Veterans' Affairs

Residence
Carson City

Born
June 12, 1958; Carson City, Nev.

Religion
Christian

Family
Divorced; two children

Education
U. of Nevada, B.A. 1980 (political science), U. of the Pacific, J.D. 1983

Military
Army, 1983-87

Career
Mining association president; lawyer

Political Highlights
Republican nominee for Nev. System of Higher Education Board of Regents, 1994; Nev. Assembly, 1996-98; Nev. Senate, 1998-2010 (president pro tempore, 2003-08); Nev. Republican Party Chairman, 2010-11

ELECTION RESULTS

2012 GENERAL		
Mark Amodei (R)	162,213	57.6%
Samuel Koepnick (D)	102,019	36.2%
Michael L. Haines (I)	11,166	4.0%
Russell Best (IA)	6,051	2.2%
2012 PRIMARY		
Mark Amodei (R)		unopposed
2011 SPECIAL		
Mark Amodei (R)	75,180	57.9%
Kate Marshall (D)	46,818	36.1%
Helmuth Lehmann (I)	5,372	4.1%
Tim Fasano (IA)	2,421	1.9%

Elected 2011; 1st full term

Amodei is a "face-time guy" working to get as much face time as possible with his district's biggest landlord — the federal government. Given his long professional and political involvement with Nevada's water and land-use issues, they have plenty to talk about.

Amodei (AM-uh-day) is chatty, personable and happy to crack wise. Joining the House in September 2011 after a special election, he spoke two sentences in his inaugural floor speech before taking it home: "I was told that the longer you talk, the less popular you are; so I yield back my time." He says he prefers to work quietly, but "if it's time to tell the story, I'm comfortable telling the story."

On the Natural Resources Committee, some of that comfort comes from experience. During 12 years in the state Senate, Amodei served on the Public Lands Committee and spent 16 months as president of the Nevada Mining Association. After leaving the Senate he sat on the state's Colorado River Commission. Much of his private law practice focused on zoning and resource issues. Amodei is a native and current resident of Carson City, and he easily rattles off the names of the capital's water and land management officials.

What's more, his father was a wildland firefighter — "he was kind of the Smokey the Bear guy for the Nevada Division of Forestry" — and Amodei spent a few summers cleaning bathrooms and putting up cattle guards for the Bureau of Land Management.

Amodei sees himself as a facilitator between federal and local stakeholders, and when it comes to public lands policy, "I'm a firm believer in multiple use," he says. People hoping to expand mining and grazing operations have an interest in preserving lands — and their reputations as good-faith stewards — for future economic opportunities, he argues.

Speaking on the House floor in late 2011, he blamed underuse of public lands for contributing to Nevada's high unemployment rate. "We are trying to generate economic development, and it's taking years to get a permit because of regulatory regimes," he said. "There is no one that will indicate that that is not the case."

In 2012, the House passed his bill to expedite permits for mining critical minerals on public lands, over Democratic objections that the bill would cover nearly all mines and weaken environmental reviews. He reintroduced the bill in 2013, along with four other measures tied to specific parcels of Nevada land.

With the federal government controlling many surface water resources in the state, Amodei wants to defend state control of ground water, at the very least as a bargaining chip: "When you're in the Great Basin and you're talking about land use, and we have kind of the exclusive control over ground water, that's pretty much our only lever."

Battles over the state's most contentious plot of land find Amodei in the political center. Prominent Nevadans — including Senate Majority Leader Harry Reid — oppose the use of Yucca Mountain as a nuclear waste depository, but given the widespread national support for the site, "I don't know how you can ... say that a responsible policy course is to continue to say, 'Well, we have the majority leader of the United States Senate, and he says no, and so too bad for you.' " Amodei argues that the facility can be used as a reprocessing or research center. "Give us something to talk about other than just a dump," he said.

Amodei has a seat on the Judiciary Committee, and he once chaired the equivalent panel in the Nevada Senate. He nabbed a seat on the immigration subcommittee for the 113th Congress (2013-14). In early 2013, Amodei told an

Elko television station that "there's not going to be an amnesty element" in any overhaul of immigration law, but that it would have "some sort of status element." He panned the idea of a mass deportation of illegal immigrants.

On the Veterans' Affairs Committee, he has the perspective of both a veteran (Amodei was a JAG officer in the Army after finishing law school) and the father of a veteran. His oldest daughter served in the Navy and deployed to the Persian Gulf three times.

Amodei has a distinctive state record on fiscal matters. He cites as one of his proudest political moments the 2003 defeat of a proposal to restructure state business taxes around gross receipts.

He took heat from some conservatives for proposing an alternative package of service and sin taxes to raise $900 million over two years, and in 2009 he told the Las Vegas Review-Journal that it is "an act of cowardice" for lawmakers to reject taxes but approve spending.

Amodei had a standard suburban upbringing in a Carson City subdivision, complete with Little League, a little sister, Schwinn bikes and "running wild on the hills outside of town." While his dad fought fires, his mother was a bookkeeper and a receptionist for a surgeon from the 1960s until her retirement. It wasn't a particularly political household; his dad's reaction to his first state Assembly race was, "Dammit, you were raised better than that."

He majored in political science at the University of Nevada, interning in the state legislature, then in the Washington office of Republican Sen. Paul Laxalt. His freshman year, he enjoyed mandatory ROTC participation enough to sign on for a bigger commitment, and after getting his law degree he fulfilled his service commitment as a JAG.

Amodei won an Assembly race in 1996, then moved to the state Senate in 1998. Toward the end of his tenure there (thanks to term limits) he took the mining association position, but resigned 16 months later amid some protests that his political job created a conflict of interest. Amodei briefly entertained a challenge to Reid in the 2010 Senate election, but pulled the plug after six months due to lackluster fundraising. He was chosen in 2010 as the chairman of the Nevada Republican Party.

Rep. Dean Heller was appointed to the Senate in 2011 after an ethics scandal led to the resignation of Republican Sen. John Ensign. Party organizations picked their candidates for the special election to fill Heller's seat: Amodei and Democratic state Treasurer Kate Marshall.

The election centered on federal programs such as Medicare, the federal budget and plans to invigorate Nevada's economy. But the wide voter registration advantage in the district took the drama out of the result. Amodei won with nearly 58 percent of the vote. He easily secured a full term in 2012.

Key Votes

2012	
Extend a Social Security payroll tax cut and unemployment benefits	YES
Ease securities rules to expand small-business access to capital	YES
Extend for one year subsidized student loan interest rates financed by a cut in health care spending	YES
Cite Attorney General Eric H. Holder Jr. for contempt of Congress	YES
Create a visa program for foreign graduates in high-tech fields	YES
Extend most Bush-era income tax rates while allowing rates for top-bracket earners to rise (Jan. 1, 2013)	NO
2011	
Allow consideration of measures to implement three trade agreements	YES

CQ Vote Studies

	PARTY UNITY		PRESIDENTIAL SUPPORT	
	SUPPORT	OPPOSE	SUPPORT	OPPOSE
2012	95%	5%	20%	80%
2011	99%	1%	23%	77%

Interest Groups

	AFL-CIO	ADA	CCUS	ACU
2012	17%	60%	100%	86%
2011	0%		100%	

Nevada 2

North — Reno, Carson City, Elko

The drastically shrunk, newly drawn 2nd District sits in the northern third of the state, from Reno and Carson City east to the Utah border, but for the first time since it was created in 1982, it does not reach south of Douglas County. Previously gathering in nearly the whole state outside of Las Vegas and its suburbs, the 2nd lost almost half of its land area, mostly to the new 4th District, during decennial redistricting.

The 2nd includes nine full counties, half of Lyon County and independent Carson City. Outside of the cluster between Reno and Carson City —which includes Lake Tahoe — the 2nd is rural. The federal government owns more than 80 percent of the land in Nevada, and much of the 2nd. The district is majority white, with some notable Hispanic communities.

More than half of the district's population lives in Washoe County, which includes Lake Tahoe and Reno and which experienced a decade of marked population growth. This area, particularly Reno, struggled during the recent housing market crash. Tourism continues to be vital to the economy: Casino-goers and outdoor enthusiasts flock to Lake Tahoe. Government work is a source of jobs in Carson City, the state capital.

The rest of the 2nd is rural — Pershing, Lander, Storey and Eureka counties each have fewer than 7,000 residents. Mining and agriculture are prominent, and much of the north and east is known as the "Cow Counties."

The 2nd is considered safe for the GOP in federal races: Sharron Angle won only among areas now in the 2nd in her unsuccessful 2010 U.S. Senate bid, and Mitt Romney took 53 percent of the district's 2012 presidential vote — his only winning margin statewide. The U.S. House seat for northern Nevada has never been held by a Democrat.

Major Industry
Gambling, government, agriculture, mining

Military Bases
Naval Air Station Fallon, 1,100 military, 700 civilian (2012)

Cities
Reno, Sparks, Carson City

Notable
The University of Nevada was founded as the State University of Nevada in Elko in 1874 — officials moved the flagship campus to Reno 11 years later because the northeastern part of the state was, and is, so sparsely populated.

Rep. Joe Heck (R)

Capitol Office
225-3252
heck.house.gov
132 Cannon Bldg. 20515-2803; fax 225-2185

Committees
Armed Services
Education & the Workforce
Select Intelligence

Residence
Henderson

Born
Oct. 30, 1961; Queens, N.Y.

Religion
Roman Catholic

Family
Wife, Lisa Heck; three children

Education
Pennsylvania State U., B.S. 1984 (health education); Philadelphia College of Osteopathic Medicine, D.O. 1988

Military
Army Reserve, 1991-present

Career
Physician; medical response training consultant; U.S. Defense Department medical school administrator

Political Highlights
Nev. Senate, 2004-08; defeated for re-election to Nev. Senate, 2008

ELECTION RESULTS

2012 GENERAL		
Joe Heck (R)	137,244	50.4%
John Oceguera (D)	116,823	42.9%
Jim Murphy (IA)	12,856	4.7%
Tom Jones (IA)	5,600	2.0%
2012 PRIMARY		
Joe Heck (R)	20,798	90.0%
Chris Dyer (R)	2,298	10.0%
2010 GENERAL		
Joe Heck (R)	128,916	48.1%
Dina Titus (D)	127,168	47.5%
Barry Michaels (I)	6,473	2.4%
Joseph P. Silvestri (LIBERT)	4,026	1.5%

Elected 2010; 2nd term

Habits that Heck learned from stints as an emergency room doctor carry over to his work on Capitol Hill. He works quickly, keeps cool and seems remarkably efficient at producing policy results. Triage principles contribute to his status as a moderate Republican — he often puts party labels aside when trying to improve the ailing Las Vegas-area economy.

The 3rd District went from a population boom to an economic bust in recent years. The region's downturn mirrored that of the national economy "in the worst sense of every one of the indicators," Heck said in 2011. "We're No. 1 in personal bankruptcies, No. 1 in foreclosures, No. 1 in unemployment."

Heck is an osteopathic physician, and he took a whole-body approach to treating the local economy in the 112th Congress (2011-12). "I'm not very out there on a lot of issues," he says, but he prefers to have supporters lined up "before we come out with the fanfare."

Though he doesn't sit on the Natural Resources Committee, Heck engineered the 2011 enactment of a bill to extend electricity allocations from the Hoover Dam until 2067; he called the law "critically important" to providing stability for the region's economic recovery. The House passed his bill to require the government to sell an abandoned mine site in Henderson to local entities at a reduced price, with the understanding that developers would pay for environmental cleanup. It was reintroduced in 2013.

Though he doesn't sit on the Judiciary or Foreign Affairs committees, Heck promoted his 2011 bill to require the State Department to accelerate the visa evaluation process for visitors from China, India and Brazil; four months later President Barack Obama ordered such a change for China and Brazil.

Heck does sit on the Education and the Workforce Committee. He was the co-author of a 2011 bill to streamline federal job training programs, which many Republicans criticize as duplicative and ineffective. The measure would, among other things, consolidate many of the programs into one large block grant and increase coordination with local employers to determine what skills to teach. "We've got to make sure that the unemployed are prepared to take the jobs that will exist, not the job that they may have had previously that they lost," he said. Democrats criticized the plan as an attempt to cut the programs' funding, and they walked out of a markup of the 2013 version of the bill — which the House passed in March.

His other committee work matches up with his military experience. Heck holds the rank of colonel in the Army Reserve and spends one weekend a month in San Pablo, Calif., where his medical readiness support group is stationed. (In spring 2013, he was nominated for promotion to brigadier general, which requires Senate approval.) He was deployed to Iraq in 2008 and worked in a combat support hospital. Even his leisure time has a military bent — he enjoys the novels of W.E.B. Griffin and World War II history.

Heck is a member of the Intelligence Committee and chaired the Technical and Tactical Intelligence Subcommittee in the 112th — covering "all the whiz-bang gadgets," including selection of a new constellation of spy satellites. He also sits on the Armed Services Committee, and he expresses concern that cuts to defense accounts could "hollow out" the military. From the personnel subcommittee, he opposes reductions to military pay or benefits.

The Reserve presents a cost-effective means of maintaining a fighting force, according to Heck. "We spend a lot of time investing in these individuals, and so you don't want somebody coming in, spending four to eight years, then letting them go." Transitioning people into the Reserve keeps them in uniform at "about one-quarter the cost," he said.

Heck's interests in health care and military policy intersected in the 112th Congress, as he and Pennsylvania Democrat Allyson Y. Schwartz sought a bipartisan change to Medicare physician reimbursement rates. The current formula for determining the rates dictates huge payment cuts for doctors; Congress regularly overrides them, which puts a large hole in the budget. Their plan would repeal the formula and set up a five-year transition period during which the administration would test new payment models, from which doctors could choose. Originally, they planned to pay the cost of implementation with savings from winding down military operations in Iraq and Afghanistan, but they removed that controversial offset from the 2013 version of their bill.

Heck splits with the GOP on a few Nevada-related issues. He was the only one in his party to vote against a 2011 bill to terminate a Federal Housing Administration program to help "underwater" homeowners refinance their loans. Heck also opposes the use of Yucca Mountain as a nuclear waste repository, calling it a "20th-century solution." He was one of 10 House Republicans to vote against the GOP's fiscal 2014 budget, saying the cuts it outlined would hurt his state too much.

Heck was born in Queens, N.Y., the first of three children. His mother was a homemaker; his father worked in the retail grocery business, starting as a stock boy and working his way up to supervisor. The family moved to northeastern Pennsylvania when Heck was a teenager.

At Penn State, Heck worked as a student athletic trainer for the Nittany Lions football team during their 1982 championship season. He had plans to be a teacher, but following a student-teaching stint in front of 10th graders, "I decided to go do something less stressful, so I went into medicine." He completed medical school and a residency in Philadelphia.

Heck was recruited to a hospital in Las Vegas and moved west, but he headed back east in the late 1990s to work as a civilian employee at the Uniformed Services University of the Health Sciences in Bethesda, Md. A few years later he was back in Nevada, operating a business providing medical consulting, training and operational support. He served one four-year term in the Nevada Senate, losing his re-election bid in 2008.

He returned to politics in 2010 and nipped one-term Democrat Dina Titus in one of the year's closest House races. Democrats were pulling for a rematch in 2012, but Titus ran (successfully) in the 1st District. John Oceguera, the speaker of the Nevada Assembly, challenged Heck. Both candidates cast themselves as centrists, but Heck had a fundraising edge and a respectable body of work to run on. He won by more than 7 points.

Heck met his wife, Lisa, a nurse and fellow Penn State graduate, working in an emergency department.

Key Votes

2012	
Extend a Social Security payroll tax cut and unemployment benefits	YES
Ease securities rules to expand small-business access to capital	YES
Extend for one year subsidized student loan interest rates financed by a cut in health care spending	YES
Cite Attorney General Eric H. Holder Jr. for contempt of Congress	YES
Create a visa program for foreign graduates in high-tech fields	YES
Extend most Bush-era income tax rates while allowing rates for top-bracket earners to rise (Jan. 1, 2013)	YES
2011	
Strike funding for F-35 alternative engine	NO
Prevent EPA from regulating greenhouse gas emissions to address climate change	YES
Extend certain provisions of Patriot Act for four years	YES
Declare opposition to use of ground troops in Libya	YES
Overhaul patent law	YES
Pass compromise debt limit increase plan and establish future spending limits	YES
Allow consideration of measures to implement three trade agreements	YES

CQ Vote Studies

	PARTY UNITY		PRESIDENTIAL SUPPORT	
	SUPPORT	OPPOSE	SUPPORT	OPPOSE
2012	89%	11%	18%	82%
2011	90%	10%	25%	75%

Interest Groups

	AFL-CIO	ADA	CCUS	ACU
2012	24%	10%	92%	72%
2011	21%	20%	100%	60%

Nevada 3

Southern Clark County

Deserts and mountains between California and Arizona dominate the 3rd's landscape after decennial remapping, but most of the district's population is packed together near Las Vegas. The district sits in the southern half of Clark County (shared with the 1st and 4th), stretching from a corner of Las Vegas and its western and southern suburbs to the states' southern tip.

Decades of explosive population growth drove residential development in the district, especially in Henderson — which is the second-largest city in the state and the largest city in the district — and planned subdivisions in Enterprise and Summerlin. Henderson grew up as a mining town in the middle of the 20th century, and there are still mines nearby. The city's economy also now includes large hospitals and pharmaceutical companies in addition to the regional foundation of gaming, hotels and golfing.

Natural tourist magnets in the district include state parks, wildlife refuges and national forests, as well as Lake Mead Recreational Area, which follows the Colorado River from Lake Mead to north of Laughlin as the district's eastern border, and is shared with both Nevada's 4th District and Arizona's 4th District. About 30 miles southeast of Las Vegas, the 3rd's part of the river includes the Hoover Dam, which provides hydroelectric power for more than 1 million Nevada, California and Arizona residents — the demand on the river for fresh water, a valuable commodity in the 3rd's hot, desert communities, is a perennial issue here.

The district, whose population grew across all ethnic groups from 2000 to 2010, remains majority white, but there are sizable Asian and Hispanic populations here, especially in Henderson and south of the Las Vegas Beltway in Enterprise. Democrats have a narrow voter registration advantage in the district, but the largest proportion of unaffiliated voters of any district in the state can make federal contests close. Barack Obama won the district's 2012 presidential vote by roughly 2,200 votes.

Major Industry
Health care, tourism, gambling

Cities
Henderson, Las Vegas (pt.), Enterprise (unincorporated)

Notable
Put up for sale by the federal government as "war surplus property" when the local magnesium plant was no longer required after the end of World War II, the land for Henderson was purchased by the state.

Rep. Steven Horsford (D)

Capitol Office
225-9894
horsford.house.gov
1330 Longworth Bldg. 20515-6601; fax 225-9783

Committees
Homeland Security
Natural Resources
Oversight & Government Reform

Residence
Las Vegas

Born
April 29, 1973; Las Vegas, Nev.

Religion
Baptist

Family
Wife, Sonya Horsford; three children

Education
U. of Nevada, B.A. 2013 (political science)

Career
Nonprofit job training program executive; lobbyist

Political Highlights
Nev. Senate, 2004-12 (minority leader, 2008-09; majority leader, 2009-12)

ELECTION RESULTS

2012 GENERAL		
Steven Horsford (D)	120,501	50.1%
Danny Tarkanian (R)	101,261	42.1%
Floyd Fitzgibbons (IA)	9,389	3.9%
Joseph P. Silvestri (LIBERT)	9,341	3.9%
2012 PRIMARY		
Steven Horsford (D)		unopposed

Elected 2012; 1st term

Horsford impressed a lot of people as he climbed the political ladder in Nevada. He is now the first black person to represent the state in Congress.

Born in Las Vegas to a teenage mother, Horsford faced hardships growing up — his mother had addiction problems and his father was shot and killed when Horsford was 19. He helped raise his younger siblings.

While attending college, Horsford landed an internship with the state Assembly. He got involved with various campaigns and worked several years as a lobbyist; he left that industry to lead a nonprofit job training program that prepares students for careers in the hospitality industry. He stayed involved in politics as a Democratic National Committeeman for Nevada.

In 2004, he won election to the state Senate. When the minority leader, Dina Titus, ran for the House in 2008, Horsford replaced her. Just months later, Democrats captured a majority, making Horsford the youngest Senate leader in the history of the chamber. He also chaired the Finance Committee. In 2011, he vowed to block the state budget proposed by Republican Gov. Brian Sandoval, ultimately helping to change the spending plan to provide more money for education and other services.

In addition to Las Vegas, he represents a big rural swath in the middle of the state. He sits on the Natural Resources Committee, which is a decent spot to work on mining and energy development concerns of those counties. He also sits on the Homeland Security and Oversight and Government Reform panels.

Nevada's steady population growth led to the creation of a fourth House district for the 2012 election. Horsford was unopposed in the primary, and Democrats have a clear advantage in the new 4th. But he had his hands full when facing Republican Danny Tarkanian, the son of UNLV's famous former basketball coach. Tarkanian tried to call Horsford's ethics into question, and the Crossroads GPS super PAC spent heavily against Horsford. He won by 8 points, but he barely cleared 50 percent of the vote.

Nevada 4

Part of Las Vegas, North Las Vegas and central 'Cow Counties'

Population growth, particularly in Clark County areas such as North Las Vegas, demanded a new district following the 2010 census. The 4th District includes the northern half of Clark County as well as five other whole counties and part of a sixth. Federally owned land — national parks, mountains, desert and military ranges — and ranching and mining operations contrast with the densely populated planned development in the Las Vegas orbit.

The most populous of Nevada's 16 counties, Clark is split with the 1st and 3rd. North Las Vegas continues to add residents, even as the largely blue-collar and minority-majority city recovers from a housing market collapse and sustained high unemployment rates. Budget shortfalls, foreclosures and residential vacancies still plague the populated areas of the 4th.

East of North Las Vegas, Nellis Air Force Base is an air combat training program location and is one of the region's largest employers. Sprawling across parts of Clark, Nye and Lincoln counties, the Nellis air ranges and Creech Air Force Base near Indian Springs host unmanned vehicle testing and operations centers.

Outside of Clark County, the rest of the district is rural, and mining is an important source of jobs. Counter to the decades-long trend statewide, mountainous Esmeralda County continues to shed residents. Nye County grew by more than 35 percent from 2000 to 2010, but struggles with high poverty rates.

The 4th is majority white with a growing Hispanic population, and there is a sizable black population in North Las Vegas. Barack Obama's wide margin of victory in the district's portion of Clark County in the 2012 presidential race was enough to overcome every other county's support of Republican Mitt Romney.

Major Industry
Tourism, defense, mining

Military Bases
Nellis Air Force Base, 9,748 military, 967 civilian (2011); Creech Air Force Base, 1,913 military, 868 civilian (2012)

Cities
Las Vegas (pt.), North Las Vegas

Notable
The Desert National Wildlife Range (1.5 million acres) is the largest in the contiguous U.S.

NEW HAMPSHIRE

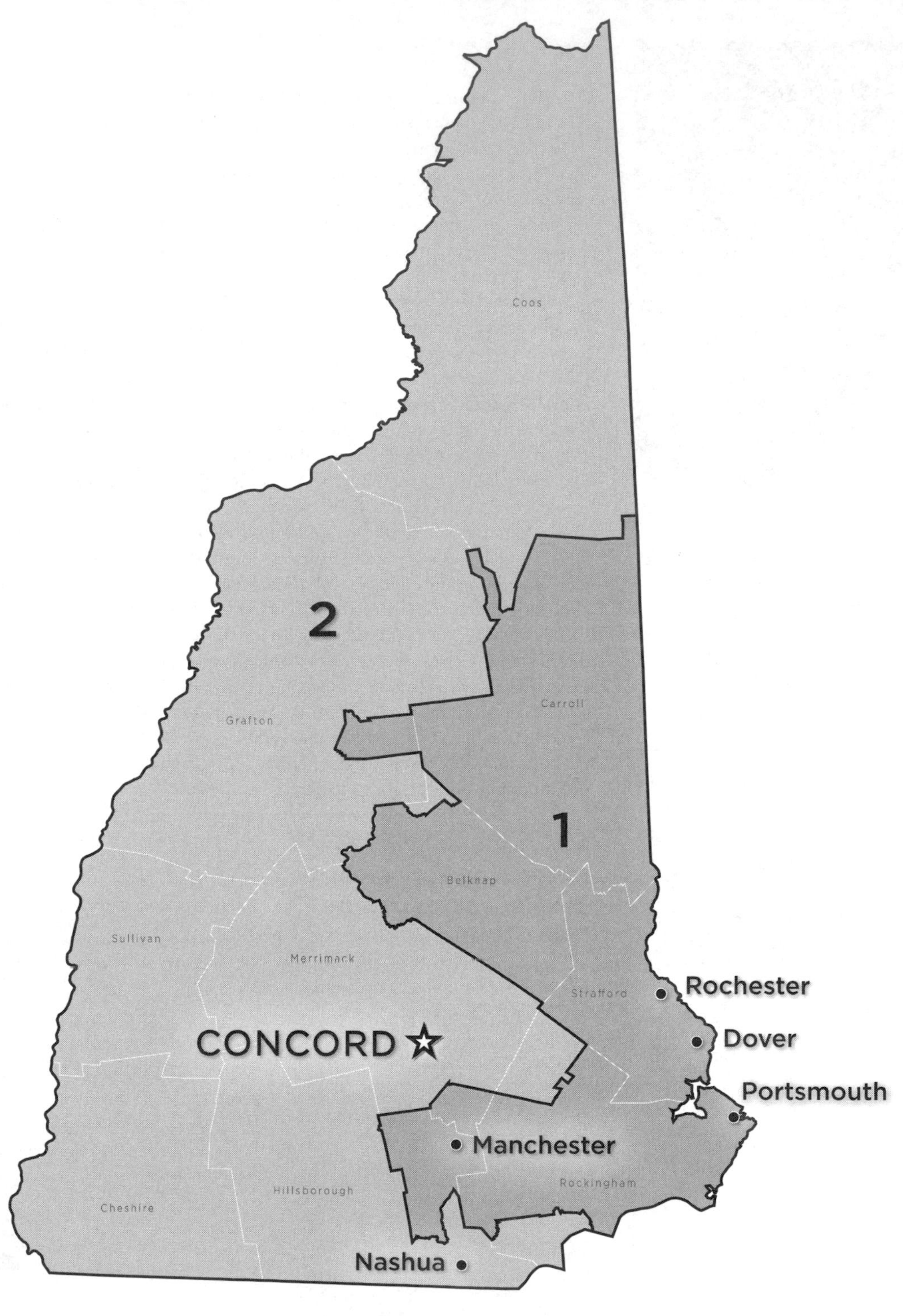

Gov. Maggie Hassan (D)

First elected: 2012
Length of term: 2 years
Term expires: 1/15
Salary: $110,418
Phone: (603) 271-2121
Residence: Exeter
Born: Feb. 27, 1958; Boston, Mass.
Religion: Church of Christ
Family: Husband, Thomas E. Hassan; two children
Education: Brown U., A.B. 1980 (history); Northeastern U., J.D. 1985
Career: Lawyer; state public information officer
Political highlights: Democratic nominee for N.H. Senate, 2002; N.H. Senate, 2004-10 (majority leader, 2009-10); defeated for re-election to N.H. Senate, 2010

ELECTION RESULTS

2012 GENERAL

Maggie Hassan (D)	378,934	54.6%
Ovide Lamontagne (R)	295,026	42.5%
John Babiarz (LIBERT)	19,251	2.8%

Senate President Peter Bragdon (R)

(no lieutenant governor)
Phone: (603) 271-2675

LEGISLATURE

General Court: January-June
Senate: 24 members, 2-year terms
2013 ratios: 13 R, 11 D; 15 men, 9 women
Salary: $200/2-year term
Phone: (603) 271-2111
House: 400 members, 2-year terms
2013 ratios: 218 D, 179 R, 1 other, 2 vacancies; 267 men, 131 women
Salary: $200/2 year term
Phone: (603) 271-3661

TERM LIMITS

Governor: No
Senate: No
House: No

URBAN STATISTICS

CITY	POPULATION
Manchester	109,565
Nashua	86,494
Concord	42,695
Derry	33,109
Dover	29,987

REGISTERED VOTERS

Other	42%
Democrat	27%
Republican	31%

POPULATION

2010 population	1,316,470
2000 population	1,235,786
1990 population	1,109,252
Percent change (2000-2010)	+9.7%
Rank among states (2010)	42
Median age	39.6
Born in state	41.9%
Foreign born	5.17%
Violent crime rate	160/100,000
Poverty level	7.5%
Federal workers	19,130
Military	675

ELECTIONS

STATE ELECTION OFFICIAL
(603) 271-3242
DEMOCRATIC PARTY
(603)225-6899
REPUBLICAN PARTY
(603) 225-9341

MISCELLANEOUS

Web: www.nh.gov
Capital: Concord

U.S. CONGRESS

Senate: 1 Democrat, 1 Republican
House: 2 Democrats

STATISTICS BY DISTRICT

District	2012 Vote for President Obama	2012 Vote for President Romney	2008 Vote for President Obama	2008 Vote for President McCain	Black	Asian	Hispanic	Median Income	Over 64	Under 20	College Education	Rural	Sq. Miles
1	50%	49%	53%	46%	1%	2%	3%	$63,587	14%	24%	33%	35%	2,464
2	54	45	56	43	1	2	3	61,832	14	25	34	53	6,489
STATE	**52**	**47**	**54**	**45**	**1**	**2**	**3**	**62,647**	**14**	**24**	**33**	**44**	**8,953**
U.S.	**51**	**47**	**53**	**46**	**12**	**5**	**17**	**50,052**	**13**	**27**	**29**	**21**	**3,531,905**

Sen. Jeanne Shaheen (D)

Capitol Office
224-2841
shaheen.senate.gov
520 Hart Bldg. 20510; fax 228-3194

Committees
Appropriations
(Legislative Branch - Chairman)
Armed Services
(Readiness & Management Support - Chairwoman)
Foreign Relations
Small Business & Entrepreneurship

Residence
Madbury

Born
Jan. 28, 1947; St. Charles, Mo.

Religion
Protestant

Family
Husband, Bill Shaheen; three children

Education
Shippensburg State College, B.A. 1969 (English); U. of Mississippi, M.S.S. 1973 (political science)

Career
University public affairs institute director; campaign aide; jewelry store owner; teacher

Political Highlights
Democratic nominee for N.H. Senate, 1978; Madbury Zoning Board of Adjustment, 1983-96 (chairwoman, 1987-96); N.H. Senate, 1990-96; governor, 1997-2003; Democratic nominee for U.S. Senate, 2002

ELECTION RESULTS

2008 GENERAL		
Jeanne Shaheen (D)	358,438	51.6%
John E. Sununu (R)	314,403	45.3%
Ken Blevens (LIBERT)	21,516	3.1%
2008 PRIMARY		
Jeanne Shaheen (D)	42,968	88.3%
Raymond Stebbins (D)	5,281	10.8%

Elected 2008; 1st term

Shaheen honed her political skills over three decades in famously iconoclastic New Hampshire — she started out doing groundwork for the Jimmy Carter campaign in 1976, entered the governor's mansion in 1997 and won a Senate seat in 2008. Her core principles make her very sympathetic to the Democratic Party agenda, but she is savvy enough to tout her nonpartisan efforts when circumstances allow.

"If we can't compromise, if we can't all sit down at the table and figure out how we can agree to move this country forward, then our democracy is in danger," she told New Hampshire Public Radio.

Some of her more public efforts have been on issues with fewer partisan considerations. Shaheen and Georgia Republican Johnny Isakson are leading proponents of biennial budgeting. She cites the success New Hampshire has had with that practice, and she told the Concord Monitor that the change is "a critical tool for improving legislative and agency review of government programs, so that we're not just spending blindly, but analyzing what works and what doesn't." When the Senate adopted a fiscal 2014 budget, it included their provision advocating the change.

She works with Ohio Republican Rob Portman to promote energy efficiency. In the 112th Congress (2011-12) they introduced a bill to use Energy Department funds to incentivize the retrofitting of homes and commercial buildings and to establish efficiency standards for outdoor lighting, heating, ventilation, air conditioning and household appliances. A few of the bill's lesser provisions were included in a 2012 law.

As a member of the Armed Services Committee, Shaheen protects contractors and defense facilities in New England. She favors retrofitting the Navy's Virginia-class submarines to carry more cruise missiles, thereby solidifying a continued role for the Portsmouth Naval Shipyard. (The shipyard is across the border from Portsmouth in Maine.) For the 113th Congress (2013-14), she grabbed the gavel of the Readiness and Management Support Subcommittee, which oversees shipyards and the base realignment process. Shaheen panned a Pentagon proposal to close bases in 2013 and 2015. Her ranking member is New Hampshire Republican Kelly Ayotte; the pair provides their state a strong congressional bulwark around its defense interests.

But Shaheen has also waved many traditional Democratic banners. She was one of 35 co-chairmen of President Barack Obama's 2012 re-election campaign. She made headlines in early 2012 when she and fellow co-chairman Russ Feingold, a former senator from Wisconsin, called on Democrats to adopt a plank in the party platform to support same-sex marriage.

She rates highly with environmentalists, and she has blamed speculators in commodity markets for higher energy costs. In 2012, Shaheen faulted the Commodity Futures Trading Commission for failing to establish limits on speculation for crude oil, home heating oil and gasoline. Shaheen gave up her seat on the Energy and Natural Resources Committee, but only so she could join the Appropriations Committee in the 113th Congress.

She has also been a solid backer of Democrats' 2010 health care law. Republicans have objected to requirements under that law for insurers to cover female contraception, arguing that entities with religious objections should be exempt. Shaheen joined most Democrats to kill an amendment containing the "conscience clause."

"Improving access to birth control is good health policy and good economic policy," she wrote in a Wall Street Journal op-ed with Democrats Patty Murray and Barbara Boxer. "It will save money for businesses and consumers. ... Our nation will be better for it."

Shaheen sits on the Foreign Relations Committee. She is a former chairwoman of the European Affairs Subcommittee, and she currently serves on the Commission on Security and Cooperation in Europe, which is also known as the Helsinki Commission.

Speaking to the Carnegie Endowment for International Peace, she said that 2012 saw the "worst deterioration in Russia's human rights record since the breakup of the Soviet Union." She approved of a 2012 law that freezes the U.S. assets of human rights abusers in Russia and blocks them from obtaining visas.

She has been a staunch supporter of continued U.S. involvement in NATO and wrote in Foreign Affairs magazine that the 2011 intervention in Libya — orchestrated in large part by Obama — was proof of the alliance's ability for effective and decisive action. She also approves of Obama's timeline for troop withdrawal from Afghanistan.

Shaheen is a former small-business owner, having operated a family jewelry business for eight years early in her marriage. She serves on the Small Business and Entrepreneurship Committee, where she has backed tax breaks for small businesses to encourage hiring.

She also once taught at a public high school in Mississippi, while her husband attended law school. Expanding access to kindergarten was a central issue in her 1996 campaign for governor, and she spent much of her time in the statehouse wrestling with New Hampshire's school funding difficulties. In April 2011, she introduced a bill to create a matching grant program to fund science, technology, engineering and mathematics (STEM) programs in public schools.

Born in Missouri to a traditionally Republican family, Shaheen cast her first presidential vote for Richard Nixon in 1968. She became more politically active while attending Shippensburg State College in Pennsylvania, where she registered as a Democrat and protested a campus curfew that applied only to women.

She met her husband, Bill, while working in York, Maine, the summer after graduating. In an uncharacteristically impractical moment, she agreed to marry him only six weeks after telling him to "drop dead" when he first asked for her phone number. After her brief stay in Mississippi, where she also received a master's degree in political science, the couple settled in Bill's home state of New Hampshire.

Shaheen worked as a regional organizer for Carter's successful 1976 presidential campaign. She managed Gary Hart's insurgent 1984 New Hampshire primary campaign, as well as several other state races throughout the 1980s. In 1990, Shaheen was elected to the state Senate. In 1996, running on a platform of affordable health care, access to education and lower electric rates, she became New Hampshire's first Democratic governor in nearly 15 years.

Her first try for the Senate came up short. Despite being the sitting governor, she lost by 4 points to Republican Rep. John E. Sununu in 2002. She later blamed the defeat on her support of a state sales tax and a political environment favorable to the GOP. In her time out of office, Shaheen served as national chairwoman for Sen. John Kerry's 2004 presidential campaign. In 2005, she became director of the Institute of Politics at Harvard's John F. Kennedy School of Government.

After much speculation, Shaheen re-entered electoral politics in September 2007 by announcing she would challenge Sununu. Republicans were slumping all across the nation, and polls had shown her leading Sununu even prior to her announcement. She took the rematch by 6 points, becoming the first woman in U.S. history to win elections for governor and the Senate.

Sununu announced in April 2013 that he would not try to recapture the seat in 2014.

Key Votes

2012	
Prohibit health insurance plans from denying coverage based on the sponsor's religious beliefs	YES
Require approval of the Keystone XL oil pipeline	NO
Ease securities rules to expand small-business access to capital	YES
Reauthorize farm and nutrition programs for five years	YES
Limit debate on a bill that would create private-sector cybersecurity standards	YES
Consent to ratification of a treaty setting global standard for the treatment of people with disabilities	YES
Provide $60.4 billion in disaster relief following Superstorm Sandy	YES
Extend most Bush-era income tax rates while allowing rates for top-bracket earners to rise (Jan. 1, 2013)	YES

2011	
Prevent EPA from regulating greenhouse gas emissions to address climate change	NO
Extend certain provisions of Patriot Act for four years	YES
Clear compromise debt limit increase plan and establish future spending limits	YES
Overhaul patent law	YES
Implement Colombia free trade agreement	YES
Limit debate on confirmation of Caitlin J. Halligan to D.C. Circuit Court of Appeals	YES
Extend payroll tax cut and unemployment benefits for two months	YES

CQ Vote Studies

	PARTY UNITY		PRESIDENTIAL SUPPORT	
	SUPPORT	OPPOSE	SUPPORT	OPPOSE
2012	97%	3%	99%	1%
2011	93%	7%	98%	2%
2010	94%	6%	100%	0%
2009	95%	5%	95%	5%

Interest Groups

	AFL-CIO	ADA	CCUS	ACU
2012	91%	95%	38%	0%
2011	79%	90%	64%	10%
2010	94%	90%	18%	0%
2009	100%	100%	43%	8%

Sen. Kelly Ayotte (R)

Capitol Office
224-3324
ayotte.senate.gov
144 Russell Bldg. 20510-2904; fax 224-4952

Committees
Armed Services
Budget
Commerce, Science & Transportation
Homeland Security & Governmental Affairs
Special Aging

Residence
Nashua

Born
June 27, 1968; Nashua, N.H.

Religion
Roman Catholic

Family
Husband, Joseph Daley; two children

Education
Pennsylvania State U., B.A. 1990 (political science); Villanova U., J.D. 1993

Career
State deputy attorney general; gubernatorial aide; state prosecutor; lawyer

Political Highlights
N.H. attorney general, 2004-09

ELECTION RESULTS

2010 GENERAL		
Kelly Ayotte (R)	273,218	60.0%
Paul W. Hodes (D)	167,545	36.8%
Chris Booth (I)	9,194	2.0%
Ken Blevens (LIBERT)	4,753	1.0%
2010 PRIMARY		
Kelly Ayotte (R)	53,056	38.2%
Ovide M. Lamontagne (R)	51,397	37.0%
Bill Binnie (R)	19,508	14.0%
Jim Bender (R)	12,611	9.1%
Dennis Lamare (R)	1,388	1.0%

Elected 2010; 1st term

Veteran senators have warmed to Ayotte, a former attorney general who arguably has become the most prominent Republican in her state. She has described herself as a "mainstream conservative" and made national security a clear priority in the opening stages of her legislative career.

Prominent Republicans haven't hidden their interest in Ayotte's demographic characteristics. "What Kelly brings to our caucus is the diversity of being a mother of two young children, the wife of a small-businessman, she's a woman and she's from the Northeast," said Lamar Alexander of Tennessee. Minority Leader Mitch McConnell added Ayotte (EYH-ott) to his informal group of advisers at the start of 2013, touting her insight on "issues that affect American families." She has also been named a deputy whip for the 113th Congress (2013-14).

She has contributed to discussions of domestic policy, but Ayotte has received the most notice for her efforts on the Armed Services Committee. Her work there features calls for fiscal responsibility and hawkish uses of the military. "If we don't restore fiscal sanity to Washington and reduce our national debt, I'm concerned that rising debt payments will begin to significantly crowd out the finances we have to protect our nation and its interests," she said at a 2011 hearing.

In 2012, Ayotte teamed up with Republicans John McCain of Arizona and Lindsey Graham of South Carolina to campaign against "sequestration" reductions in the defense budget—more than $500 billion in automatic cuts put in place by an August 2011 deficit reduction law. Those cuts began taking hold across the board in 2013, and Ayotte has produced several proposals for alternative spending reductions to take their place.

In studying the defense budget, she looks for money that can be reassigned for purposes she considers more useful. Ayotte has aggressively tried to zero out the Medium Extended Air Defense System, missile defense technology that the military is not planning to procure; its advocates argue that development should be completed to satisfy international partners and advance overall research. The fiscal 2012 defense policy law included a provision by Ayotte and Rhode Island Democrat Jack Reed to allow the Air Force to reduce its fleet of strategic airlift aircraft—military leaders said they didn't need all the planes that the law had required them to maintain.

Ayotte and Jeanne Shaheen, her Democratic colleague from New Hampshire, are the leaders of the Subcommittee on Readiness and Management Support in the 113th Congress.

Ayotte generally has not been a fan of the Obama administration's foreign policy or military decisions. Speaking at the Conservative Political Action Conference in 2013, she said the president "has undercut his commanders time and time again," allowed a resurgence of Islamic radicalism by avoiding military engagements, and "repeatedly undercut Israel."

"We sat on the sidelines while over 70,000 Syrians were slaughtered, ceding our policy to the vetoes of the Russians and the Chinese in the United Nations," she added. Ayotte also is involved in foreign affairs as a member of the Commission on Security and Cooperation in Europe, also known as the Helsinki Commission.

Drawing on her authority as a prosecutor, Ayotte has become one of the most vocal Senate critics of the Obama administration's policies for detaining and trying alleged terrorists. She contends that the president has an "ad hoc" structure with little idea of which suspects should be detained where and by whom. Where he does have a policy, Ayotte said, it has been too oriented toward civilian courts. She became a member of the Homeland Security and Governmental Affairs Committee in 2013.

Ayotte hasn't served in the military, but her husband did. Joseph Daley flew missions over Iraq and recently retired from the Air National Guard.

Like most of the Republicans elected in 2010, Ayotte speaks of a need to reduce federal deficits. She won a seat on the Budget Committee in May 2011, and near the end of that year she voted for a Republican proposal to add a balanced-budget amendment to the Constitution. She also supports the current moratorium on earmarks, the spending set-asides for projects in a member's home state or district. She says that spending vital to her state, such as funding for projects at the Portsmouth Naval Shipyard, should go through the regular appropriations process.

She has tried to use her seat on the Commerce, Science and Transportation Committee to New Hampshire's advantage. A growing number of lawmakers in both parties are interested in requiring the collection of sales taxes when purchases are made online, even when the buyer is in a different state than the seller — states could use the money, they say, and it would eliminate a competitive advantage for online retailers. Ayotte is strongly against the idea. New Hampshire has no sales tax, and she says requiring its online retailers to collect taxes for other states would be a "bureaucratic nightmare" that slows business growth.

Ayotte takes conservative stands on social issues. She opposes abortion and same-sex marriage and defends gun owners' rights. A school shooting in Connecticut prompted a flurry of gun-related legislation in early 2013, but Ayotte told the Nashua Telegraph that she preferred to focus on expanding mental health services and training as a way to curb mass shootings.

Ayotte was born in Nashua, but she attended college and law school in Pennsylvania. She earned a bachelor's degree in political science at Penn State, where she was a competitive skier, and a law degree from Villanova, where she served as executive editor of the Environmental Law Journal.

She spent a year clerking for a justice of the New Hampshire Supreme Court before working in private practice.

Ayotte then joined the state attorney general's office as a prosecutor, where she handled a number of gruesome murder cases. According to a profile in the Manchester Union Leader, "to read accounts of Ayotte's work over the next couple years is to descend the depths of human depravity."

She briefly served as legal counsel to Republican Gov. Craig Benson before returning to the attorney general's office as deputy. She was in the No. 2 spot for about a year when her boss resigned. She took over as attorney general.

In her most celebrated case, she defended the state's parental notification law, which required minors to inform their parents before obtaining an abortion. Having lost in two lower courts, she appealed to the Supreme Court, against the wishes of incoming Democratic Gov. John Lynch. The high court vacated the lower court's judgment but did not rule on the substance of the challenge to the law's constitutionality. The law was repealed in 2007.

Republican Sen. Judd Gregg announced in 2009 that he would not seek re-election — after deciding against joining the Obama administration as Commerce secretary. Ayotte resigned as attorney general to run for the seat. Her opponent in the primary, Ovide M. Lamontagne, was the favorite among conservatives. She was able to balance the wings of the party just enough, besting Lamontagne by less than 2 points.

Her opponent in the general election was two-term Democratic Rep. Paul W. Hodes. He was swamped by a banner Republican year in New Hampshire — the GOP also captured both U.S. House seats and both chambers of the state legislature. Ayotte defeated Hodes with 60 percent of the vote.

Circumstances in the state quickly changed — the 2012 election saw the GOP lose both House seats.

Key Votes

2012

Prohibit health insurance plans from denying coverage based on the sponsor's religious beliefs	NO
Require approval of the Keystone XL oil pipeline	YES
Ease securities rules to expand small-business access to capital	YES
Reauthorize farm and nutrition programs for five years	NO
Limit debate on a bill that would create private-sector cybersecurity standards	NO
Consent to ratification of a treaty setting global standard for the treatment of people with disabilities	YES
Provide $60.4 billion in disaster relief following Superstorm Sandy	NO
Extend most Bush-era income tax rates while allowing rates for top-bracket earners to rise (Jan. 1, 2013)	YES

2011

Prevent EPA from regulating greenhouse gas emissions to address climate change	YES
Extend certain provisions of Patriot Act for four years	YES
Clear compromise debt limit increase plan and establish future spending limits	NO
Overhaul patent law	YES
Implement Colombia free trade agreement	YES
Limit debate on confirmation of Caitlin J. Halligan to D.C. Circuit Court of Appeals	NO
Extend payroll tax cut and unemployment benefits for two months	YES

CQ Vote Studies

	PARTY UNITY		PRESIDENTIAL SUPPORT	
	SUPPORT	OPPOSE	SUPPORT	OPPOSE
2012	86%	14%	56%	44%
2011	97%	3%	57%	43%

Interest Groups

	AFL-CIO	ADA	CCUS	ACU
2012	0%	10%	88%	76%
2011	11%	10%	91%	95%

Rep. Carol Shea-Porter (D)

Capitol Office
225-5456
shea-porter.house.gov
1530 Longworth Bldg. 20515-2901; fax 225-5822

Committees
Armed Services
Natural Resources

Residence
Rochester

Born
Dec. 1952; Brooklyn, N.Y.

Religion
Roman Catholic

Family
Husband, Gene Porter; two children

Education
U. of New Hampshire, B.A. 1975 (social services), M.P.A. 1979

Career
Community college instructor; social worker

Political Highlights
U.S. House, 2007-11; defeated for re-election to U.S. House, 2010

ELECTION RESULTS

2012 GENERAL

Carol Shea-Porter (D)	171,650	49.8%
Frank Guinta (R)	158,659	46.0%
B. Kelly (LIBERT)	14,521	4.2%

2012 PRIMARY

Carol Shea-Porter (D)	unopposed

Previous Winning Percentages
2008 (52%); 2006 (51%)

Elected 2006; 3rd term

Did not serve 2011-13

Shea-Porter's political career has thus far floated on national tides — she has risen and fallen along with the Democratic Party. But through it all, her support of populist and liberal causes hasn't waned.

She was first elected in 2006, thanks in large part to her opposition to the Iraq War. Shea-Porter was a little-known activist, but grass-roots support helped her beat a Democratic establishment candidate in the primary. Riding a national swell of anti-Republican sentiment, she beat GOP Rep. Jeb Bradley by less than 3 points. With Barack Obama at the top of the Democratic ticket in 2008, she beat Bradley by 6 points in their rematch.

Her gains were wiped out in 2010 as the independent-minded electorate of New Hampshire turned against a federal government entirely controlled by Democrats. She lost by more than 11 points to Republican Frank Guinta.

But Obama was back on the ballot two years later, and Republicans were losing steam. Shea-Porter returned to the House, defeating Guinta by almost 4 points. She has little margin for error in the campaign for 2014 — Republicans started running ads against her just months into 2013.

For her part, Shea-Porter is picking up where she left off in the 111th Congress (2009-10). She is back on the Armed Services and Natural Resources committees, and she has renewed her commitment to earlier causes.

Her first bill of the 113th Congress (2013-14) was a version of a measure she introduced twice before. It would require the Department of Veterans Affairs to ensure that every state has a full-service veterans hospital, or that similar services are made available through contracts with hospitals in the state. She frequently points out that New Hampshire is the only state without such an arrangement.

She also plans to pursue the creation of a veterans jobs corps that would help servicemembers transition into the civilian workforce. Shea-Porter sits on the Armed Services Subcommittee on Military Personnel, and her husband is a retired Army officer. Despite her involvement in the anti-war movement, she has been an advocate for military contractors and National Guard facilities in and near her state.

On the Natural Resources Committee, Shea-Porter has environmentalist tendencies. In February 2013, she joined in a letter calling for a new presidential permit and full environmental impact statement before a pipeline between Montreal and Portland, Maine, could be used to move crude oil from Canada's tar sands. "New Hampshire's natural resources are critical to our state's economy and our future," she said. "We must preserve our state and national resources and deal with global climate change." She voted for a 2009 bill to create a cap-and-trade system to regulate greenhouse gases, and she likes the idea of a coordinated scientific effort, similar to the one that resulted in the moon landing, to advance renewable energy.

On most issues Shea-Porter is a liberal Democrat — for example, during debate on the 2010 health care overhaul, she supported efforts to create a government-run "public option" insurance plan to compete with private insurers. But she embraces the "populist" label as she supports initiatives to aid low- and middle-income families. She has proposed allowing income tax rates to increase for those making more than $300,000. She would bolster Social Security's financial foundation by increasing the amount of income subject to the payroll tax. And she wants further restrictions on campaign activity by super PACs and advocacy organizations.

In 2013, the rest of her state delegation was slow to react to gun control proposals by Obama that were issued after a tragic shooting at a Connecticut elementary school. Shea-Porter was quick to endorse them. "I support President Obama's call to close loopholes in gun trafficking laws, and to beef up law enforcement in communities," she said. "Let's also step up mental health services, and work together to encourage a reduction of violence in video games and television and movies."

There are currently no state licensing requirements for the purchase of any rifle, shotgun or handgun in New Hampshire, which is home to two big gun makers — Sig Sauer and Sturm, Ruger & Co. — and where hunting is a popular recreational activity.

Shea-Porter was born in Brooklyn and moved to Durham as a teenager. Her father served in World War II and used GI benefits to become a lawyer. Her mother did various jobs, including watching over a household that included Shea-Porter, her six siblings, a great-uncle, a grandmother and often local children who were facing difficult times in their lives.

"My dad, who was born and died a Republican, never forgot the power of good government to transform lives," she said.

Shea-Porter graduated from Oyster River High School in Durham, then earned her bachelor's and master's degrees from the University of New Hampshire. After college, she worked as a social worker while moving around the country with her husband.

She later taught current affairs and American history at a community college in Maryland, then lectured to retired diplomats, federal employees and other professionals in the Washington area. She and her husband returned to New Hampshire in the 1990s.

She says she decided to seek elected office after making two visits to New Orleans as a volunteer after it was hit by Hurricane Katrina in August 2005. She was concerned about the slow federal response. But it was her activism against the Iraq War that gained her the most attention in her district and pushed her past Jim Craig, a Democratic leader in the state House, in the 2006 primary.

For much of the 2012 cycle, Shea-Porter was an underdog to Guinta, due to her lackluster fundraising. Her hopes were very much tied to Obama's electoral performance in the state, and even some Democrats were dubious of her chances of returning to Congress.

Although she won, Shea-Porter took less than 50 percent of the vote, and her margin of victory was likely padded by the presence of a Libertarian candidate on the ballot who drew off some votes from Guinta. The National Republican Congressional Committee attacked Shea-Porter in its first television advertisement of the 2014 cycle, criticizing her vote against a bill to withhold lawmakers' salaries if they do not adopt a budget.

CQ Vote Studies

	PARTY UNITY		PRESIDENTIAL SUPPORT	
	SUPPORT	OPPOSE	SUPPORT	OPPOSE
2010	97%	3%	88%	12%
2009	97%	3%	91%	9%
2008	97%	3%	14%	86%
2007	98%	2%	5%	95%

Interest Groups

	AFL-CIO	ADA	CCUS	ACU
2010	100%	95%	13%	0%
2009	100%	95%	36%	0%
2008	100%	90%	50%	12%
2007	96%	95%	50%	0%

New Hampshire 1

East — Manchester, Rochester, Dover

New Hampshire's 1st District comprises about one-fourth of the state's land, primarily in the southeast, including Manchester, the state's most populous city; the coastal town of Portsmouth; and the border areas near Maine surrounding Rochester and Dover. It takes in the tourism-heavy coast, a chunk of the Interstate 95 corridor, and to the north, some of the White Mountains. Decennial redistricting following the 2010 census moved the small towns of Sanbornton, Tilton and Campton into the 1st.

In Manchester, education, health care and trade provide jobs. A decade of diversification helped stabilize the city after years of slow growth, and the city has built up a high-end manufacturing base. Manchester is also home to the University of Southern New Hampshire, a campus of the University of New Hampshire and several smaller liberal arts colleges.

Maine's Portsmouth Naval Shipyard, just across the border from namesake Portsmouth, N.H., is one of four remaining yards in the country and employs about 5,000, many of whom live in the 1st. Expansion to service the Navy's nuclear submarine fleet is expected to boost the local economy, although locals fear the impact of defense spending cuts. Beyond the military, Portsmouth also hosts theaters, whale-watching excursion companies and art museums.

About half of the Portsmouth and Rochester-Dover areas' residents are employed on farms, many known for producing berries and apples. An increasing interest in "farm-to-table" restaurants hopes to further support small-scale agriculture in the state.

Races in the 1st District are competitive. In 2012, Carroll County as well as Belknap and Rockingham counties (both of which fall primarily into the 1st) backed Republican Mitt Romney in the presidential contest and Democrat Maggie Hassan in her successful gubernatorial bid. Overall, Barack Obama won the district's 2012 presidential vote, but his margin was less than 2 percentage points.

Major Industry
Health care, manufacturing, agriculture

Cities
Manchester, Dover

Notable
Poet Robert Frost operated a farm in Derry that is now a state historic site.

Rep. Ann McLane Kuster (D)

Capitol Office
225-5206
kuster.house.gov
137 Cannon Bldg. 20515-5206; fax 225-2946

Committees
Agriculture
Small Business
Veterans' Affairs

Residence
Hopkinton

Born
Sept. 5, 1956; Concord, N.H.

Religion
Christian

Family
Husband, Brad Kuster; two children

Education
Dartmouth College, A.B. 1978 (environmental policy studies); Georgetown U., J.D. 1984

Career
Lawyer; lobbyist; congressional aide

Political Highlights
Democratic nominee for U.S. House, 2010

ELECTION RESULTS

2012 GENERAL		
Ann McLane Kuster (D)	169,275	50.2%
Charles Bass (R)	152,977	45.4%
H. Macia (LIBERT)	14,936	4.4%
2012 PRIMARY		
Ann McLane Kuster (D)		unopposed

Elected 2012; 1st term

Kuster is new to elected office, but not to politics. For many years, she was a lobbyist and advocate representing a wide range of interests throughout her state, with a particular focus on education and health care. She was also active in Democratic Party politics, working on a number of presidential campaigns.

She has a family history rich with political figures. Her great-grandfather was a governor, her father was a mayor of Concord, and her mother served in the state Senate. But they were Republicans, whereas Kuster is a member of the liberal Congressional Progressive Caucus. Still, she vows to work across party lines. "I was born bipartisan," she says — and while she panned the fiscal 2014 Republican budget, she also voted against the CPC version.

Renewable energy is a big industry in her district, which has three wind farms, a growing residential solar market and a $275 million, 75-megawatt bioenergy plant in the northern town of Berlin.

Kuster didn't get a seat on the Energy and Commerce Committee, but she was assigned to the Agriculture Committee and its panels handing biotechnology, energy and forestry. She is the first New Hampshire House member to serve on the committee in decades.

She also serves on the Veterans' Affairs and Small Business panels. She can coordinate her work on behalf of veterans with the three other women of the New Hampshire delegation, who serve on the House and Senate Armed Services committees.

Kuster first sought the 2nd District seat in 2010, when Democratic Rep. Paul W. Hodes left it open to pursue a Senate bid. She lost a close race to Republican Charles Bass, who was making a comeback. He held the seat for 12 years before losing it in 2006. Kuster quickly decided on a rematch and raised oodles of campaign cash — $1 million more than Bass. Democratic groups also spent heavily on her behalf, and she targeted regions where Bass had bested her in their first contest. Kuster ended up winning by almost 5 points.

New Hampshire 2

West — Nashua, Concord

The 2nd, the larger of the state's two districts, encompasses the western half of state, stretching from the scenic mountains and forests of the vast "North Country" to the white-collar territory surrounding the towns of Nashua and Salem on the state's border with Massachusetts. During decennial remapping, Deerfield, Northwood and Center Harbor were moved into the 2nd.

Many residents of the southern towns of Salem, Windham and Atkinson are former Massachusetts residents who fled higher tax rates. Some of them work for high-tech and government contracting companies such as the state's largest manufacturing employer — BAE Systems is based in Nashua. Once a textile town, Nashua emerged into a computer and high-tech manufacturing base reliant on maintaining a relatively well-educated populace.

To the sparsely populated and scenic northern part of the state, the White Mountain National Forest, ski resorts, maple syrup and lakes drive the tourism industry. The densely forested North Country has long relied on wood products even as local officials work to diversify industrial sectors. Near Concord, granite quarrying has been key to the local economy for more than a century — rocks from the region were used in building the Library of Congress.

Historically Republican — voters to the north, in particular, have long rejected government interference and valued self-sufficiency — the 2nd District now trends Democratic. The party is helped by votes in the capital city, Concord, and liberal college towns of Hanover (Dartmouth College) and Keene (home to the state's public liberal arts college). In 2012, Grafton County, nearly all of which is in the 2nd, gave Democrat Barack Obama his highest percentage statewide, at just more than 61 percent. The district as a whole backed Obama with 54 percent of its vote and sent a Democrat to the U.S. House as the seat changed party hands for the second time in successive elections.

Major Industry
Technology, manufacturing, timber, tourism

Cities
Nashua, Concord

Notable
The most expansive township in the contiguous U.S., Pittsburg covers more than 300,000 acres of forests, lakes and mountains; The privately run Mount Washington Observatory, which opened in 1870, gathers weather data at the highest peak in the Northeast.

NEW JERSEY

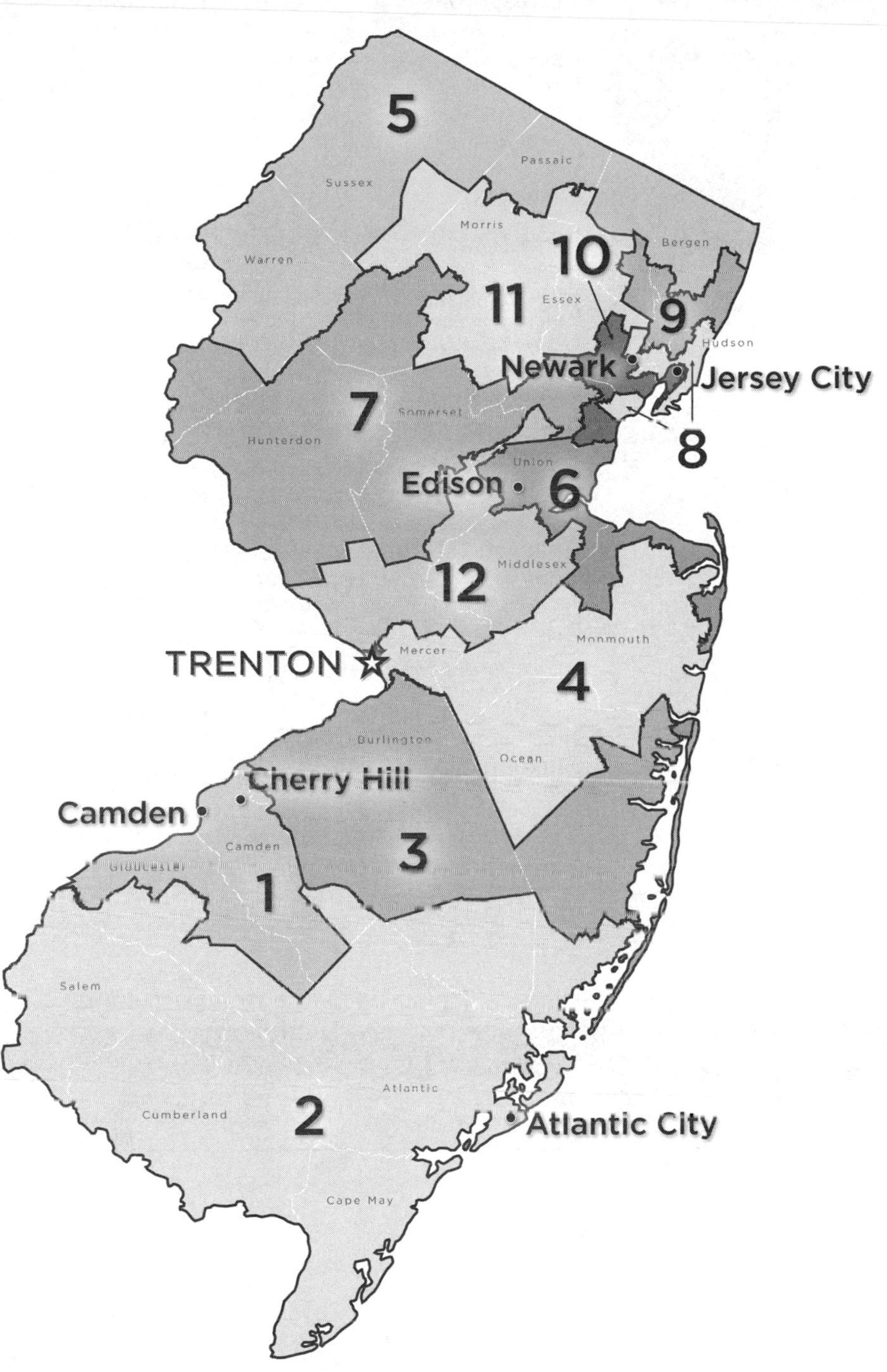
5
Sussex
Passaic
Morris
Warren
Bergen
10
11
Essex
9
Hudson
Newark
Jersey City
7
Somerset
Hunterdon
8
Union
Edison
6
Middlesex
12
Mercer
TRENTON
Monmouth
4
Burlington
Ocean
Cherry Hill
Camden
Camden
3
1
Salem
Atlantic
Cumberland
2
Atlantic City
Cape May

Gov. Chris Christie (R)

First elected: 2009
Length of term: 4 years
Term expires: 1/14
Salary: $175,000
Phone: (609) 292-6000
Residence: Mendham
Born: Sept. 6, 1962; Newark, N.J.
Religion: Roman Catholic
Family: Wife, Mary Pat Christie; four children
Education: U. of Delaware, B.A. 1984 (political science); Seton Hall U., J.D. 1987
Career: Lawyer; lobbyist
Political highlights: Morris County Board of Freeholders, 1995-97; sought Republican nomination for N.J. Assembly, 1995; defeated in primary for re-election to Morris County Board of Freeholders, 1997; U.S. attorney, 2002-08

ELECTION RESULTS

2009 GENERAL

Chris Christie (R)	1,174,445	48.5%
Jon Corzine (D)	1,087,731	44.8%
Christopher J. Daggett (I)	139,579	5.8%

Lt. Governor Kim Guadagno (R)

First elected: 2009
Length of term: 4 years
Term expires: 1/14
Salary: $141,000
Phone: (609) 777-2581

LEGISLATURE

Legislature: Year-round with recess
Senate: 40 members, 4-year terms
2013 ratios: 24 D, 16 R; 29 men, 11 women
Salary: $49,000
Phone: (609) 292-4840
Assembly: 80 members, 2-year terms
2013 ratios: 48 D, 32 R; 56 men, 24 women
Salary: $49,000
Phone: (609) 292-4840

TERM LIMITS

Governor: 2 consecutive terms
Senate: No
House: No

URBAN STATISTICS

CITY	POPULATION
Newark	277,140
Jersey City	247,597
Paterson	146,199
Elizabeth	124,969
Edison	99,967

REGISTERED VOTERS

Other	47%
Democrat	33%
Republican	20%

POPULATION

2010 population	8,791,894
2000 population	8,414,350
1990 population	7,730,188
Percent change (2000-2010)	+4.5%
Rank among states (2010)	11
Median age	38.3
Born in state	52.6%
Foreign born	19.3%
Violent crime rate	312/100,000
Poverty level	9.4%
Federal workers	83,107
Military	6,673

ELECTIONS

STATE ELECTION OFFICIAL
(609) 292-3760
DEMOCRATIC PARTY
(609) 392-3367
REPUBLICAN PARTY
(609) 989-7300

MISCELLANEOUS

Web: www.nj.gov
Capital: Trenton

U.S. CONGRESS

Senate: 1 Democrat, 1 vacancy
House: 6 Republicans, 6 Democrats

STATISTICS BY DISTRICT

District	2012 Vote for President: Obama	Romney	2008 Vote for President: Obama	McCain	Black	Asian	Hispanic	Median Income	Over 64	Under 20	College Education	Rural	Sq. Miles
1	65%	34%	65%	34%	16%	5%	12%	$61,225	13%	26%	28%	2%	350
2	54	45	53	45	14	4	15	55,032	15	25	24	15	2,092
3	52	47	51	48	11	3	8	68,300	17	23	30	4	900
4	45	54	45	53	7	4	9	71,084	17	28	36	4	692
5	48	51	49	50	5	8	13	86,213	15	26	44	13	991
6	61	37	58	41	10	17	21	70,878	12	26	35	0	216
7	47	52	48	51	4	8	12	95,189	13	27	48	14	970
8	79	20	75	24	10	8	54	51,416	9	25	29	0	55
9	68	31	64	35	11	13	34	55,907	13	26	31	0	95
10	86	13	82	17	53	7	17	45,270	11	27	25	0	76
11	47	52	47	52	4	9	9	93,655	16	24	50	4	505
12	66	32	66	33	18	15	15	75,649	13	26	42	2	412
STATE	**58**	**41**	**57**	**42**	**14**	**8**	**18**	**67,458**	**14**	**26**	**35**	**5**	**7,354**
U.S.	**51**	**47**	**53**	**46**	**12**	**5**	**17**	**50,052**	**13**	**27**	**29**	**21**	**3,531,905**

Sen. Robert Menendez (D)

Capitol Office
224-4744
menendez.senate.gov
528 Hart Bldg. 20510-3004; fax 228-2197

Committees
Banking, Housing & Urban Affairs
(Housing, Transportation & Community Development - Chairman)
Finance
Foreign Relations - Chairman

Residence
North Bergen

Born
Jan. 1, 1954; Manhattan, N.Y.

Religion
Roman Catholic

Family
Divorced; two children

Education
Saint Peter's College, B.A. 1976 (political science & urban studies); Rutgers U., J.D. 1979

Career
Lawyer

Political Highlights
Union City Board of Education, 1974-82; mayor of Union City, 1986-92; N.J. Assembly, 1987-91; N.J. Senate, 1991-93; U.S. House, 1993-2006

ELECTION RESULTS

2012 GENERAL

Robert Menendez (D)	1,987,680	58.9%
Joseph M. Kyrillos (R)	1,329,534	39.4%

2012 PRIMARY

Robert Menendez (D)	unopposed

Previous Winning Percentages
2006 (53%); 2004 House Election (76%); 2002 House Election (78%); 2000 House Election (79%); 1998 House Election (80%); 1996 House Election (79%); 1994 House Election (71%); 1992 House Election (64%)

Elected 2006; 2nd full term

Appointed 2006

Menendez says he was a shy introvert while growing up in a Union City tenement. Things have changed: Nearing the end of his fourth decade in politics, he is one of the more outspoken senators, a formidable fundraiser and a defender of a liberal vision of government.

The son of Cuban immigrants, he attributes some of his personal success to government assistance. Menendez is a reliable purveyor of talking points for the Democrats, and in 2012 he took umbrage at comments by GOP presidential nominee Mitt Romney about the dependence of poorer people on government assistance.

"I wouldn't be sitting here without the Pell grants and Perkins loans that helped me attend St. Peter's College and Rutgers Law School," Menendez told Politicker NJ in September 2012. "I wouldn't be a U.S. senator. To suggest the power of the federal government is something that makes them part of an entitled victim class, that's tough."

Democrats have put Menendez's boisterousness and enthusiasm to work in leadership, campaign and committee roles. As a House member, he was the first Hispanic of either party to secure a leadership post when he was elected Democratic Caucus chairman in 2003. He ran the Democratic Senatorial Campaign Committee during the 2010 election cycle, outraising GOP counterparts despite a big year for Republicans.

His is now the chairman of the Foreign Relations Committee. He rose to that post in 2013 when the former chairman, John Kerry of Massachusetts, became secretary of State.

Menendez's Cuban heritage comes into play on Foreign Relations. In the 112th Congress (2012-12) he chaired the Western Hemisphere subcommittee. (He served as the top Democrat on the corresponding panel when he served in the House.) His parents moved to New York from Cuba because of their opposition to the government of Fulgencio Batista, but Menendez has no love for the Castro regime that replaced that strongman.

He opposes a thaw in the relationship with Cuba's government. As proponents of opening up American travel to Cuba pushed legislation in the House in 2010, Menendez said he would use his power as a senator to block such action. "I want to make it absolutely clear that I will oppose — and filibuster if need be — any effort to ease regulations that stand to enrich a regime that denies its own people basic human rights," he said on the Senate floor.

Menendez has similarly backed economic sanctions against Iran. But as a House member, he opposed the 2002 resolution granting President George W. Bush the authority to invade Iraq, and he wants U.S. troops out of Afghanistan "as soon as possible."

He also has taken a close look at the global narcotics trade. Menendez calls for more international coordination in developing a hemispherewide strategy to fight drug production and trafficking.

On other committees, Menendez has been in the middle of Democrats' biggest legislative victories of recent years. From the Finance Committee he helped shape the 2010 health care law, and on the Banking, Housing and Urban Affairs Committee he had a hand in the 2010 overhaul of financial regulations, known as Dodd-Frank. The health care law includes a provision he wrote that increases customers' ability to protest when their insurance companies deny claims. Dodd-Frank includes his provision requiring derivatives traders to disclose their actions and investment advisers to disclose potential conflicts of interest to their clients.

Menendez has chaired the Banking panel on Housing, Transportation and

Community Development since 2009. He pays extra attention to the housing needs of the poor or struggling. Menendez is a backer of foreclosure mitigation programs and defends Section 8 rental assistance. The latter enables "millions of low-income Americans to live in safe and affordable homes," he said at an August 2012 hearing. "It's critical that we make these programs more efficient and place them on a stable footing."

He has championed legislation that would make it easier for homeowners to refinance their mortgages, and he touts his involvement in the development of a 2009 law bolstering consumer protections for credit card users.

Menendez is the only Hispanic Democrat in the Senate, and his efforts at overhauling immigration law fared no better than those of other lawmakers in recent years. He issued a sweeping proposal in October 2010 that would allow illegal immigrants to register with the federal government, then require them to pay all their taxes and learn English—en route to possible citizenship. It went nowhere. But in the 113th Congress (2013-14), he was back at it as part of a bipartisan eight-man working group negotiating another proposal for a comprehensive immigration overhaul, with similar elements.

Among his home-state projects is health aid for first-responders to the Sept. 11 terrorist attacks, many of whom live in New Jersey. He also spearheaded Foreign Relations investigations into the 2009 release of a convicted Libyan terrorist involved in the 1988 bombing of Pan Am Flight 103 over Lockerbie, Scotland. Thirty-four New Jerseyans died in that attack.

According to Menendez, a public-speaking course taken in his senior year of high school taught him the skills that transformed him into an outspoken politician. He got an early taste for elective office at age 20. While attending college in Jersey City, he won a seat on the school board.

He became the mayor of Union City in 1986 and won a seat in the state legislature in 1987, serving in both offices simultaneously. In 1991, he was named to fill a vacancy in the state Senate, where he served until winning a U.S. House seat in 1992—redistricting before that election nearly doubled the Hispanic population of the 13th District.

While making his mark in the House, Menendez kept an eye on the Senate, raising millions of dollars for a future campaign. But he passed on chances to run in 2000 and 2002.

When Democratic Sen. Jon Corzine ran for governor in 2005, Menendez spotted an opportunity. He rallied fundraising networks and national Hispanic groups in support of Corzine, while also adding to his own campaign coffers. When Corzine became governor, he appointed Menendez as his replacement. "Is he aggressive? Yeah," Corzine told The Bergen Record. "But I believe in competency and people who get things done, and Bob is one of those people."

His campaign in 2006 for a full term was noisy, bitter and marked by a federal probe—his opponent charged that he steered federal funds to a nonprofit group that rented property from him. Menendez denied wrongdoing and won by 9 points over Republican Thomas H. Kean Jr., the son of a popular former governor. Menendez had an easier time winning a second full term in 2012. He had an enormous fundraising advantage over Republican state Sen. Joseph M. Kyrillos and cruised to victory.

The only time the race got national attention was a few days before the election, when a conservative website reported allegations that Menendez solicited prostitutes in the Dominican Republic during trips with Salomon Melgen, a Florida ophthalmologist who is a friend and campaign donor. Media investigations poked holes in the prostitution story, but it didn't end there. The Washington Post reported in March 2013 that a Miami-based grand jury is scrutinizing Menendez's ties to his campaign donors over the years, in search of possible quid pro quos. Menendez did reimburse Melgen for two 2010 plane trips that he had not reported on earlier disclosure forms.

Key Votes

2012	
Prohibit health insurance plans from denying coverage based on the sponsor's religious beliefs	YES
Require approval of the Keystone XL oil pipeline	NO
Ease securities rules to expand small-business access to capital	YES
Reauthorize farm and nutrition programs for five years	YES
Limit debate on a bill that would create private-sector cybersecurity standards	YES
Consent to ratification of a treaty setting global standard for the treatment of people with disabilities	YES
Provide $60.4 billion in disaster relief following Superstorm Sandy	YES
Extend most Bush-era income tax rates while allowing rates for top-bracket earners to rise (Jan. 1, 2013)	YES
2011	
Prevent EPA from regulating greenhouse gas emissions to address climate change	NO
Extend certain provisions of Patriot Act for four years	?
Clear compromise debt limit increase plan and establish future spending limits	NO
Overhaul patent law	YES
Implement Colombia free trade agreement	NO
Limit debate on confirmation of Caitlin J. Halligan to D.C. Circuit Court of Appeals	YES
Extend payroll tax cut and unemployment benefits for two months	YES

CQ Vote Studies

	PARTY UNITY		PRESIDENTIAL SUPPORT	
	SUPPORT	OPPOSE	SUPPORT	OPPOSE
2012	97%	3%	97%	3%
2011	96%	4%	95%	5%
2010	97%	3%	100%	0%
2009	98%	2%	99%	1%
2008	98%	2%	28%	72%
2007	97%	3%	38%	62%
2006	95%	5%	50%	50%
2005	93%	7%	24%	76%
2004	93%	8%	34%	66%
2003	93%	7%	24%	76%

Interest Groups

	AFL-CIO	ADA	CCUS	ACU
2012	91%	95%	38%	8%
2011	89%	90%	45%	15%
2010	94%	90%	36%	0%
2009	94%	90%	43%	0%
2008	100%	100%	63%	4%
2007	95%	95%	55%	0%
2006	93%	90%	55%	4%
2005	93%	100%	40%	4%
2004	93%	85%	35%	8%
2003	93%	90%	37%	20%

Sen. Frank R. Lautenberg (D)

Capitol Office
224-3224
lautenberg.senate.gov
141 Russell Bldg. 20510-3003; fax 228-4054

Committees
Appropriations
(Financial Services - Chairman)
Commerce, Science & Transportation
(Surface Transportation and Merchant Marine - Chairman)
Environment & Public Works

Residence
Cliffside Park

Born
Jan. 23, 1924; Paterson, N.J.

Religion
Jewish

Family
Wife, Bonnie Lautenberg; four children

Education
Columbia U., B.S. 1949 (economics)

Military Service
Army, 1942-46

Career
Paycheck processing firm founder

Political Highlights
No previous office

ELECTION RESULTS

2008 GENERAL

Frank R. Lautenberg (D)	1,951,218	56.0%
Dick Zimmer (R)	1,461,025	42.0%

2008 PRIMARY

Frank R. Lautenberg (D)	203,012	58.9%
Robert E. Andrews (D)	121,777	35.3%
Donald Cresitello (D)	19,743	5.7%

Previous Winning Percentages
2002 (54%); 1994 (50%); 1988 (54%); 1982 (51%)

Died June 2013

Elected 1982; did not serve 2001-03

New Jersey politicians were preparing for a changing of the guard in 2014, as Democrat Frank R. Lautenberg had announced his intention to retire when his fifth term concluded at the end of the 113th Congress.

But on June 3, 2013, the 89-year-old Lautenberg died of viral pneumonia. Even before the funeral, political observers couldn't help but notice that his death had significantly altered the political dynamics of the race to become the state's next elected senator. The day after Lautenberg died, Republican Gov. Chris Christie announced that an Oct. 16 special election would determine who completes the term, with primaries held on Aug. 13. Whoever wins will have to face voters again in 2014 to retain the seat.

At first glance, Democrats have a pronounced advantage — the last time an elected Republican represented New Jersey in the Senate was the 95th Congress (1977-78). The Democratic contenders include Rep. Frank Pallone Jr. of the 6th District.

Christie also announced that he would appoint an interim senator to serve until the special election — however, he had not chosen that person by the time "Politics in America" went to press.

Looking beyond New Jersey, Lautenberg's death created openings at the top of several important panels. At the start of the 113th Congress (2013-14), he had taken over as the chairman of the Financial Services Appropriations Subcommittee, which sets spending levels for the scandal-plagued IRS, the Consumer Product Safety Commission, and the regulatory agencies that oversee Wall Street. He died in the middle of the appropriations season for fiscal 2014.

He was also the chairman of the Commerce, Science and Transportation panel with jurisdiction over surface transportation. Programs on passenger rail and rail safety are up for reauthorization in 2013, and the law governing highway programs expires in 2014.

Other senators will pick up those gavels, but in some ways, Lautenberg can't be replaced. At the time of his death, he was the longest-serving senator in New Jersey's history. He was a proud and feisty liberal, and even as his health began to falter, he fended off suggestions that he make way for someone younger. "I'm playing pretty much at the top of my game," he said in 2012. "It falls on me to get up to the plate and take a few swings." When Newark Mayor Cory Booker said that he would seek the Democratic nomination in 2014, Lautenberg suggested to the Philadelphia Inquirer that Booker might need a "spanking" for being "disrespectful."

However, illness and weakness kept him from Washington for long periods starting in late 2012, and in February 2013 he decided to wrap up his career. In characteristic fashion, he declined to announce it as a retirement — instead, he called it "the beginning of a two-year mission" to help working families, write gun-safety laws and overhaul regulation of toxic chemicals.

Born in Paterson, Lautenberg was the son of Polish and Russian immigrants. His parents moved their family a dozen times in their search for work. His father, Sam, worked in silk mills, sold coal and once ran a tavern. When his father died of cancer, Lautenberg, then a teenager, worked nights and weekends to help the family stay afloat.

After high school, Lautenberg enlisted and served in the Army Signal Corps in Europe during World War II. When he returned, he enrolled in Columbia University on the GI Bill, graduating with an economics degree in 1949. With two boyhood friends from his old neighborhood, he started a payroll services company. Automatic Data Processing turned into one of the world's largest computing services companies. Lautenberg was one of the wealthiest members of Congress.

He dabbled in politics as a Democratic activist and fundraiser, and his $90,000 contribution to George McGovern's 1972 presidential campaign earned him a place on President Richard Nixon's enemies list. In 1982, he ran for the Senate seat opened by the conviction of Democratic incumbent Harrison A. Williams Jr. in the Abscam corruption probe. Lautenberg spent $4 million of his own money on the race and took 51 percent of the vote to defeat GOP Rep. Millicent Fenwick.

He retired from the Senate at the end of the 106th Congress (1999-2000). But Democratic Sen. Robert G. Torricelli dropped off the ballot five weeks before the 2002 general election amid revelations of improper dealings with a campaign donor. The party furiously courted replacement candidates, but they declined, and Democrats feared losing the seat to GOP businessman Doug Forrester. Age 78 at the time, Lautenberg was an older candidate than party leaders would have preferred, but he was widely known. He won by 10 points. Democrats were grateful, but did not restore the seniority he had accrued during his first stint in the Senate.

He drew a Democratic opponent in 2008 — Rep. Robert E. Andrews, who had long been known to harbor ambitions for statewide office. But in the June primary, Lautenberg defeated Andrews with 59 percent of the vote and breezed past former GOP Rep. Dick Zimmer in November.

His agenda in the final years of his career was not notably different from earlier in his career: Lautenberg took care of home-state appropriations needs while also pushing social and environmental priorities.

When considering the role of government in society, Lautenberg was indisputably liberal and aggressive in promoting his views. He used his recovery in 2010 from a cancerous tumor in his stomach as a testimonial for the 2010 health care overhaul. He told The Star-Ledger that he had learned the importance of "having a card" to get hospital care.

He attacked Republicans for what he called their war on revenue. "You have to work on the fundamentals," Lautenberg said. "Do you believe we are a society that puts humanity first, or puts accounting first?"

Superstorm Sandy devastated parts of New Jersey in 2012, and Lautenberg spent some of his final months overseeing recovery efforts. He was indignant at Republicans who balked at long-term infrastructure funding included in a $50 billion emergency appropriations package enacted in early 2013. The aid package wasn't "any kind of a gift," he said at a press conference. "It's an obligation of our country."

Lautenberg also tried to shore up plans for a commuter rail tunnel from New Jersey to Manhattan — he clashed with Christie in 2010 when the governor canceled the project. Lautenberg then pivoted to focus on funding for new Amtrak tunnels that are expected to have a commuter rail component.

To boost employment, Lautenberg called for the creation of a new Works Progress Administration, funded by a surtax on income over $1 million. In late 2010, he was one of 10 members of the Senate Democratic caucus who tried to block a vote on the deal struck by President Barack Obama to extend the George W. Bush-era tax cuts for two years. "Windfalls for the wealthiest of us do not benefit our economy or create jobs — and they are what got us into this fiscal mess to begin with," he said on the Senate floor.

And he also wanted tougher gun safety laws. He scolded the White House for the "administration's silence" on gun control after the January 2011 attack that wounded Arizona Democratic Rep. Gabrielle Giffords and killed six others. He repeated his pleas for action after mass shootings in Colorado and Connecticut in 2012.

Despite relying on a wheelchair, he made sure to show up for votes on various gun proposals in April 2013, even though they were all defeated.

Key Votes

2012

Prohibit health insurance plans from denying coverage based on the sponsor's religious beliefs	YES
Require approval of the Keystone XL oil pipeline	NO
Ease securities rules to expand small-business access to capital	NO
Reauthorize farm and nutrition programs for five years	NO
Limit debate on a bill that would create private-sector cybersecurity standards	YES
Consent to ratification of a treaty setting global standard for the treatment of people with disabilities	YES
Provide $60.4 billion in disaster relief following Superstorm Sandy	?
Extend most Bush-era income tax rates while allowing rates for top-bracket earners to rise (Jan. 1, 2013)	?

2011

Prevent EPA from regulating greenhouse gas emissions to address climate change	NO
Extend certain provisions of Patriot Act for four years	NO
Clear compromise debt limit increase plan and establish future spending limits	NO
Overhaul patent law	YES
Implement Colombia free trade agreement	NO
Limit debate on confirmation of Caitlin J. Halligan to D.C. Circuit Court of Appeals	YES
Extend payroll tax cut and unemployment benefits for two months	YES

CQ Vote Studies

	PARTY UNITY		PRESIDENTIAL SUPPORT	
	SUPPORT	OPPOSE	SUPPORT	OPPOSE
2012	97%	3%	95%	5%
2011	98%	2%	94%	6%
2010	99%	1%	97%	3%
2009	99%	1%	97%	3%
2008	99%	1%	30%	70%
2007	98%	2%	37%	63%
2006	97%	3%	46%	54%
2005	98%	2%	27%	73%
2004	96%	4%	57%	43%
2003	97%	3%	44%	56%

Interest Groups

	AFL-CIO	ADA	CCUS	ACU
2012	100%	90%	38%	0%
2011	89%	90%	36%	10%
2010	93%	95%	9%	0%
2009	94%	95%	43%	0%
2008	100%	100%	63%	4%
2007	100%	90%	55%	0%
2006	93%	100%	42%	0%
2005	93%	100%	29%	0%
2004	100%	100%	38%	0%
2003	100%	95%	26%	15%

Rep. Robert E. Andrews (D)

Capitol Office
225-6501
andrews.house.gov
2265 Rayburn Bldg. 20515-3001; fax 225-6583

Committees
Armed Services
Education & the Workforce

Residence
Haddon Heights

Born
Aug. 4, 1957; Camden, N.J.

Religion
Episcopalian

Family
Wife, Camille Spinello Andrews; two children

Education
Bucknell U., B.A. 1979 (political science); Cornell U., J.D. 1982

Career
Lawyer; professor

Political Highlights
Camden County Board of Freeholders, 1987-90 (director, 1988-90); sought Democratic nomination for governor, 1997; sought Democratic nomination for U.S. Senate, 2008

ELECTION RESULTS

2012 GENERAL		
Robert E. Andrews (D)	210,470	68.2%
Gregory W. Horton (R)	92,459	30.0%
John William Reitter (GREEN)	4,413	1.4%
2012 PRIMARY		
Robert E. Andrews (D)	21,318	88.4%
Francis X. Tenaglio (D)	2,797	11.6%
2010 GENERAL		
Robert E. Andrews (D)	106,334	63.2%
Dale M. Glading (R)	58,562	34.8%

Previous Winning Percentages
2008 (72%); 2006 (100%); 2004 (75%); 2002 (93%); 2000 (76%); 1998 (73%); 1996 (76%); 1994 (72%); 1992 (67%); 1990 (54%); 1990 Special Election (55%)

Elected 1990; 12th full term

At the start of his House career, Andrews was known as a ladder-climbing workaholic. His Democratic colleagues, particularly within the New Jersey delegation, were sometimes put off by his ambition — they frowned on his gubernatorial bid in 1997 and his challenge to Democratic Sen. Frank R. Lautenberg in 2008. Andrews still had powerful allies and a decent amount of seniority; he resolved "to be the most effective member of the House that I can be." But investigations into alleged misuses of his campaign funds started to dog him during the 112th Congress.

And then, suddenly, he was granted a position of influence within his party. California's George Miller stepped down after 10 years as the policy chairman of the Democratic Steering and Policy Committee. Minority Leader Nancy Pelosi nominated Andrews as his replacement, giving him a strong hand in shaping the agenda of the Democratic Caucus in the 113th Congress (2013-14).

At first glance, Andrews was a surprising choice, if only because of the appearance of hypocrisy. Pelosi famously vowed to "drain the swamp" when Democrats ran the House, and the Ethics Committee has created an investigative panel to probe Andrews' finances — he is accused of spending thousands of campaign dollars on a family trip to Scotland, a trip for his daughter and a large party.

But Pelosi also stands by her inner circle, and Andrews has been close to her for years, taking on a number of behind-the-scenes tasks for the caucus. He has been unfazed by the investigation. "I follow rules and certainly followed these," Andrews said in 2012. "It's an occupational hazard of modern politics that people will attempt to attack you."

Andrews is also a logical successor to Miller. The Californian is the top Democrat on the Education and the Workforce Committee, and Andrews is right below him on the panel's seniority list.

He is currently the ranking member of the Health, Employment, Labor and Pensions Subcommittee, which he chaired from 2007 through 2010. He was a facilitator for the party during the health care debates of the 111th Congress (2009-10), explaining legislative developments to his colleagues and trying to sell Democratic overhaul plans via media appearances.

In the 112th Congress (2011-12), Andrews dismissed GOP attempts to repeal the law as political theater, and he offered rhetorical defenses of the National Labor Relations Board as Republicans accused it of a pro-union bias.

Andrews is also the No. 5 Democrat on the Armed Services Committee. In the 111th Congress, he chaired the Defense Acquisition Reform Panel, with K. Michael Conaway of Texas as the ranking Republican. The panel offered ways to improve the Pentagon's buying practices.

Andrews sees improvement on that front. "We seem to have few Nunn-McCurdy breaches, which is a good sign," he said in 2012, referring to a provision in a 1982 defense policy law that terminates defense programs that go over budget by more than 25 percent.

He and Conaway swapped jobs in the 112th Congress on the short-term Defense Financial Management and Auditability Reform Panel. "If you have to make hard decisions about cutting spending, you want to know where you're spending your money right now," he said.

Andrews has been more open to defense spending cuts than many Armed Services members, seeing little material gain in equipment or force size despite "a 40 percent real-dollar increase in the core defense budget over a six- or seven-year period." He also backs requirements for more Pentagon reliance on renewable energy sources, claiming it would lead to jobs in the alternative-fuel sector and that such sources are more reliable in the long run.

Andrews has sometimes been hawkish on foreign policy. He supported the U.S. invasion of Iraq. But in early 2007 he spoke out against the "surge" of troops to the region, and in recent years he has raised concerns during hearings about the role of U.S. troops in Afghanistan.

He is also occasionally near the middle on fiscal policy. After the Republican Revolution of 1994, Andrews teamed with New Hampshire Republican Bill Zeliff on an "A to Z" plan for deficit reduction, whereby the House would set aside 56 hours of debate time for amendments to cut spending. It garnered both favorable headlines and derision from New Jersey colleagues. Democrat Donald M. Payne called Andrews a "political opportunist," the Philadelphia Inquirer reported.

Andrews voted for a fiscal 2013 budget based on the work of the 2010 special fiscal commission known as Simpson-Bowles: The plan would cut deficits by $4 trillion over 10 years through a mix of spending reduction, revenue increases and entitlement changes. Only 37 House members joined Andrews in supporting it.

The son and grandson of shipyard workers, Andrews grew up in Bellmawr. At 14, he worked for a local paper chain, hoping to cover sports. Instead, he was assigned to write about local government for $6 an article.

"The experience covering government and what went on in the local scene made me want to be a part of it," he said. The first in his family to go to college, Andrews was a teaching assistant during his senior year at Bucknell University. He wrote one question to serve as the entire final exam for an introductory political science class: "Politics is everything. Explain."

After law school and five years of legal practice, Andrews won a seat on the Camden County governing board. He was a protégé of Democratic Rep. James J. Florio, and when Florio was elected governor in 1989, Andrews won the special election to replace him. His campaign staff included a young Rahm Emanuel, who went on to become a House member, White House chief of staff and now mayor of Chicago. Andrews' House re-election campaigns have not been competitive.

Democrats in the state's House delegation frowned on his 1997 gubernatorial bid, and Andrews was narrowly upset in the primary by state Sen. James E. McGreevey. He offered harsh words for party leaders and the political system. "People who control vast sums of money have undue leverage," he told reporters. Every Democratic member of the House delegation endorsed Lautenberg in the 2008 Senate primary, and Andrews lost by a wide margin.

His wife had won the Democratic primary for the 1st District. She withdrew from the race, and party officials named Andrews to replace her on the ballot.

Key Votes

2012	
Extend a Social Security payroll tax cut and unemployment benefits	YES
Ease securities rules to expand small-business access to capital	YES
Extend for one year subsidized student loan interest rates financed by a cut in health care spending	NO
Cite Attorney General Eric H. Holder Jr. for contempt of Congress	?
Create a visa program for foreign graduates in high-tech fields	NO
Extend most Bush-era income tax rates while allowing rates for top-bracket earners to rise (Jan. 1, 2013)	YES
2011	
Strike funding for F-35 alternative engine	NO
Prevent EPA from regulating greenhouse gas emissions to address climate change	NO
Extend certain provisions of Patriot Act for four years	YES
Declare opposition to use of ground troops in Libya	NO
Overhaul patent law	NO
Pass compromise debt limit increase plan and establish future spending limits	YES
Allow consideration of measures to implement three trade agreements	NO

CQ Vote Studies

	PARTY UNITY		PRESIDENTIAL SUPPORT	
	SUPPORT	OPPOSE	SUPPORT	OPPOSE
2012	94%	6%	85%	15%
2011	94%	6%	88%	12%
2010	98%	2%	93%	7%
2009	99%	1%	96%	4%
2008	100%	0%	17%	83%

Interest Groups

	AFL-CIO	ADA	CCUS	ACU
2012	86%	85%	25%	4%
2011	100%	80%	25%	0%
2010	100%	90%	25%	0%
2009	100%	100%	33%	0%
2008	100%	85%	63%	0%

New Jersey 1

Southwest — Camden, Cherry Hill

The 1st is crisscrossed by interstates, waterways and train tracks. It takes in the city and county of Camden and a large chunk of Gloucester County, across the Delaware River from Philadelphia. Decennial redistricting shifted suburban Cherry Hill into the 1st, solidifying the district's Democratic lean.

Many residents commute daily over the Delaware by car or rail into Philadelphia, making transit and infrastructure on both sides of the river a concern. Several commuter rail systems serve district residents on the New Jersey side, although progress has been stop-and-go on a proposed extension of a light-rail line from Camden south to Glassboro. Significant farmland remains at the district's southeastern edges, where growers produce melons, potatoes and sod.

The 1st is about two-thirds white. Much of its minority population is concentrated within Camden, which is itself racially divided, with black residents living mainly in the city center, Parkside and Gateway neighborhoods; Hispanic-majority communities take up neighborhoods northeast of downtown. The Hispanic population across Camden County has grown by 50 percent since 2000.

Camden's financial troubles have required years of state aid. With funds drying up, and in order to save millions of dollars in labor costs, the city disbanded its police force in the fall of 2012 and relies on county-level service. The city has a reputation as one of the most dangerous in the nation. Redevelopment efforts, some supported by the hometown Campbell's Soup Co., have sprouted up in the Gateway district. Projects along the riverfront — including a minor league baseball park and an aquarium — may spur some economic upswing, but the city still has an unemployment rate higher than 18 percent.

Camden's inner-ring suburbs tend to be working-class, while those closer to the New Jersey Turnpike, such as Haddonfield and Voorhees, are affluent and boast median household incomes above $100,000.

Major Industry
Shipping, manufacturing, health care

Cities
Camden, Glassboro, Cherry Hill

Notable
The first phonograph records were manufactured in Camden.

Rep. Frank A. LoBiondo (R)

Capitol Office
225-6572
lobiondo.house.gov
2724 Rayburn Bldg. 20515-3002; fax 225-3318

Committees
Armed Services
Transportation & Infrastructure
(Aviation - Chairman)
Select Intelligence

Residence
Ventnor

Born
May 12, 1946; Bridgeton, N.J.

Religion
Roman Catholic

Family
Wife, Tina Ercole; two children

Education
Saint Joseph's U., B.S. 1968 (business administration)

Career
Trucking company operations manager

Political Highlights
Cumberland County Board of Freeholders, 1985-87; N.J. Assembly, 1988-94; Republican nominee for U.S. House, 1992

ELECTION RESULTS

2012 GENERAL		
Frank A. LoBiondo (R)	166,677	57.7%
Cassandra Shober (D)	116,462	40.3%
2012 PRIMARY		
Frank A. LoBiondo (R)	20,551	87.6%
Mike Assad (R)	2,914	12.4%
2010 GENERAL		
Frank A. LoBiondo (R)	109,460	65.5%
Gary Stein (D)	51,690	30.9%
Peter F. Boyce (CNSTP)	4,120	2.5%

Previous Winning Percentages
2008 (59%); 2006 (62%); 2004 (65%); 2002 (69%); 2000 (66%); 1998 (66%); 1996 (60%); 1994 (65%)

Elected 1994; 10th term

LoBiondo puts his district first, and his district often steers him well to the left of his fellow Republicans. But even when standing apart from his party, LoBiondo mostly avoids attention.

"I don't think there is anything wrong with a Beltway agenda, but that has certain implications and realities that do not allow you to pursue a district agenda, at least the way I view it," he said. "It was clear to me from the beginning that I did not want a Beltway agenda."

The beginning for LoBiondo was the election of 1994, which carried him into a seat left open by the retirement of 10-term Democrat William J. Hughes. LoBiondo joined many fellow Republican candidates that year in vowing to serve no more than six terms. But as he reaped the benefits of congressional seniority, he decided to stick around. Voters haven't punished him — his worst showing at the polls was in 2012, and he still won close to 58 percent of the vote.

In the 113th Congress (2013-14), a lot of his work undoubtedly will involve the ongoing recovery from Superstorm Sandy, which devastated large parts his South Jersey district in 2012. LoBiondo was livid at Republicans who were reluctant to support the $50 billion aid measure enacted in January 2013, especially those from disaster-prone states. "Florida, good luck with no more hurricanes," he said on the House floor. "California, congratulations. Did you get rid of the San Andreas Fault? The Mississippi is in a drought. Do you think you're not going to have a flood again? Who are you going to come to when you have these things?"

South Jersey draws tourists to the beaches, the bays and Atlantic City's casinos. Seeking to protect the first two, LoBiondo strongly opposes oil drilling off the state's coast, fearing spills that could despoil local beaches and fishing. He has introduced legislation to block any such exploration in every Congress of the past decade. "We want gambling in Atlantic City; we don't want gambling in our environment," he once said. LoBiondo was critical of the Department of Homeland Security over its response to the 2010 Gulf of Mexico oil spill; he accused DHS leaders of failing to commit adequate resources and attention to the training programs for oil spill response.

LoBiondo and fellow New Jerseyan Christopher H. Smith are the two House Republicans with the highest lifetime rankings from the League of Conservation Voters. He was one of eight GOP House members who voted for Democrats' 2009 bill to create a cap-and-trade system regulating greenhouse gas emissions — though he did support a 2011 bill to prevent the EPA from regulating greenhouse gases.

Looking out for the gambling industry, LoBiondo has introduced a bill to allow states to seek exemptions from a federal sports-betting ban, which would be a boon to Atlantic City.

LoBiondo has garnered support from labor unions, which figure prominently in the manufacturing sector in his district. When authorization for many Federal Aviation Administration activities lapsed amid political disputes in 2011, LoBiondo introduced a bill to provide back pay to furloughed workers who went two weeks without wages. He was one of 10 House Republicans to vote against a 2013 bill to extend a freeze on federal salary levels. A member of the Intelligence Committee, he said his vote was in support of Foreign Service officers and intel analysts — but federal freezes also affect a lot of unionized workers.

And LoBiondo opposed 2011 free-trade pacts with Colombia, Panama and South Korea; only five other House Republicans voted against all three. Political action committees affiliated with organized labor are among the largest contributors to LoBiondo's campaign coffers.

His disagreements with his party haven't stopped LoBiondo from wielding some influence. In the 113th Congress he became the chairman of the Transportation and Infrastructure Subcommittee on Aviation. His district has several training facilities for air travel security workers, as well as the FAA William J. Hughes Technical Center, which tests and develops the NextGen air traffic control system. His panel also looks at unmanned aerial vehicles, which sometimes come up on the Intelligence Committee.

The White House planned closures of a number of air traffic control towers in 2013, citing "sequestration" cuts put in place by a 2011 deficit reduction law. LoBiondo wondered whether the decision was meant to make cost-cutting Republicans look bad. "It is my concern that the Obama administration's decision to close these towers is merely to fit their public relations narrative about sequestration rather than sound policy and management practices," he said.

In the 112th Congress (2011-12), he chaired the Coast Guard and Maritime Transportation Subcommittee. The only recruit training center for the Coast Guard is located in his district. LoBiondo and his ranking member, Democrat Rick Larsen of Washington, worked with Senate counterparts to produce a two-year reauthorization of Coast Guard spending; the version that was enacted in December 2012 included LoBiondo's provisions to help maritime vessels defend themselves against pirates.

Larsen is also the new ranking member on the Aviation panel. He said in 2013 that he and LoBiondo have "forged a strong bipartisan relationship."

LoBiondo sits on the Armed Services Committee and lists support of local facilities, such as the 177th Fighter Wing of the New Jersey Air National Guard, among his proudest achievements.

LoBiondo's grandparents arrived in South Jersey from Sicily and established a vegetable farm, where he grew up. In the 1920s, his father bought a used truck to take his produce to market. Soon he was carrying his neighbors' produce as well, and the enterprise grew into LoBiondo Brothers Motor Express Inc., where the younger LoBiondo worked for 26 years.

His father was mayor of Deerfield Township, president of the school board and an active member of the Kiwanis. LoBiondo credits his father with kickstarting his own political career.

LoBiondo was elected to a county office in 1984, not intending to go further. But his state assemblyman, who was retiring because he had cancer, urged him to run for the seat. He won that race and served in the state House for almost seven years.

In 1992, he challenged Hughes but won only 41 percent of the vote. When Hughes stepped aside two years later, LoBiondo won easily.

Key Votes

2012	
Extend a Social Security payroll tax cut and unemployment benefits	YES
Ease securities rules to expand small-business access to capital	YES
Extend for one year subsidized student loan interest rates financed by a cut in health care spending	YES
Cite Attorney General Eric H. Holder Jr. for contempt of Congress	YES
Create a visa program for foreign graduates in high-tech fields	YES
Extend most Bush-era income tax rates while allowing rates for top-bracket earners to rise (Jan. 1, 2013)	YES
2011	
Strike funding for F-35 alternative engine	NO
Prevent EPA from regulating greenhouse gas emissions to address climate change	YES
Extend certain provisions of Patriot Act for four years	YES
Declare opposition to use of ground troops in Libya	YES
Overhaul patent law	YES
Pass compromise debt limit increase plan and establish future spending limits	YES
Allow consideration of measures to implement three trade agreements	YES

CQ Vote Studies

	PARTY UNITY		PRESIDENTIAL SUPPORT	
	SUPPORT	OPPOSE	SUPPORT	OPPOSE
2012	80%	20%	25%	75%
2011	81%	19%	26%	74%
2010	86%	14%	40%	60%
2009	66%	34%	68%	32%
2008	73%	27%	39%	61%

Interest Groups

	AFL-CIO	ADA	CCUS	ACU
2012	52%	15%	75%	52%
2011	59%	40%	81%	44%
2010	29%	15%	88%	67%
2009	57%	35%	87%	60%
2008	67%	60%	72%	52%

New Jersey 2

South — Atlantic City, Vineland, Cape May

One of the Garden State's most politically and economically diverse districts, the 2nd stretches from the Philadelphia suburbs in Gloucester County to the popular oceanfront communities on Long Beach Island.

Cumberland and Atlantic counties contain New Jersey's most productive farmlands, while Salem County on the 2nd's western edge has large swaths of preserved land. Tomatoes, soybeans, sod and hothouse plants are grown here, with cranberry bogs and blueberry farms covering Atlantic County's Pine Barrens. Glass and plastics manufacturing are vital to Cumberland County, particularly around Millville and Vineland. Salem County has a large nuclear power plant operated by PSEG.

Tourism is a multibillion-dollar industry here. Superstorm Sandy took a tremendous toll on the shoreline of the 2nd in late 2012, flooding coastal towns from Atlantic City to the northern end of Long Beach Island and washing beach sand out to sea. The storm spared some popular attractions such as Cape May's Victorian homes and the Wildwood amusement park, as well as much of the 2nd's commercial fishing fleets. The storm likely complicated ongoing efforts to restore oysters in Delaware Bay.

The casinos of Atlantic City make hospitality a major economic sector for the 2nd. The gaming industry, however, has struggled in recent years. New investment from the Mohegan Indian tribe and interest spurred by the popular HBO series "Boardwalk Empire," set in Prohibition-era Atlantic City, may encourage a rebound; new online gambling laws with preferences for New Jersey casinos should also give a boost.

The 2nd has no problem sending a Republican to the U.S. House, but Democrats fare well in statewide elections around Atlantic City and its industrial towns. Cape May and Ocean were the only counties in the 2nd to support Republican nominee Mitt Romney in his 2012 presidential bid; Barack Obama took 54 percent of the district's presidential vote overall.

Major Industry
Tourism, gambling, agriculture, manufacturing

Cities
Vineland, Atlantic City, Millville

Notable
Millville's Museum of American Glass features the most comprehensive exhibit of American glass in the world.

Rep. Jon Runyan (R)

Capitol Office
225-4765
runyan.house.gov
1239 Longworth Bldg. 20515-3003; fax 225-0778

Committees
Armed Services
Natural Resources
Veterans' Affairs
(Disability Assistance & Memorial Affairs - Chairman)

Residence
Mt. Laurel

Born
Nov. 27, 1973; Flint, Mich.

Religion
Roman Catholic

Family
Wife, Loretta Runyan; three children

Education
U. of Michigan, attended 1992-95 (movement science)

Career
Professional football player; professional arena football team owner

Political Highlights
No previous office

ELECTION RESULTS

2012 GENERAL		
Jon Runyan (R)	174,253	53.7%
Shelley Adler (D)	145,506	44.8%
2012 PRIMARY		
Jon Runyan (R)		unopposed
2010 GENERAL		
Jon Runyan (R)	110,215	50.0%
John Adler (D)	104,252	47.3%
Peter DeStefano (TEA)	3,284	1.5%

Elected 2010; 2nd term

Given Runyan's huge physical size, it seems incongruous to describe him as a moderate. But that's what he is: The former football star pulls to the middle of the ideological spectrum, backs up the Republican leadership team and keeps his feet moving with parochial and veterans issues.

For a 6-foot-7-inch lawmaker, he keeps a relatively low profile. Runyan, an All-Pro offensive tackle in the NFL, spent most of his career playing for the Philadelphia Eagles. (Many Philly athletes live in South Jersey.) He still loves his sports metaphors. "If you're out there winning games with good policy," he says, "the people are going to show up in the stands."

Runyan has shared football lessons in the House. When some Republicans publicly criticized Speaker John A. Boehner's leadership in 2011, Runyan told the GOP Conference that sticking together was important, The New York Times reported. "It only takes one guy to bring down a locker room," he said.

His only public rift with Republican leaders came at the close of the 112th Congress (2011-12), when Boehner declined to schedule a vote on a Superstorm Sandy relief package. Parts of Runyan's district were severely damaged by the storm — he represents Seaside Heights, which produced the iconic image of a roller coaster washed into the ocean. "I think everybody, bipartisan-wise, would say this is going to happen," Runyan said on MSNBC. "Why are we delaying it?" The vote was soon squeezed into the schedule at the start of the 113th Congress (2013-14).

A member of the moderate Main Street Partnership, Runyan supports spending cuts, but not the more-severe reductions favored by conservatives. He is a little more friendly to organized labor and takes a nuanced approach to social issues — Runyan accepts abortion rights but opposes federal funding of abortion. He opposes gay marriage but has been open to civil unions. Many Republicans balked at a 2012 reauthorization of programs to combat domestic violence, objecting to provisions providing services to illegal immigrants and gay, lesbian, transgender and bisexual people. Runyan marshaled support for the version that was enacted in 2013.

The 3rd District has a large population of veterans, and Runyan chairs the Veterans' Affairs Subcommittee on Disability Assistance and Memorial Affairs. In 2012, he steered to enactment his bill to provide a cost-of-living increase to disabled veterans' benefit payments. He also proposed making that annual increase automatic. The House passed his 2011 bill to create a pilot program to improve claims processing training for Veterans Affairs Department employees.

He urges the VA to place more emphasis on the issue of traumatic brain injury among veterans of Iraq and Afghanistan. Football experiences helped shape his concern, given recent discoveries that players who suffered multiple concussions have a much higher rate of developing neurological diseases. "I've seen guys that played — you see them all the time — that they're not the same person they were," he said.

Runyan's main interest on the Armed Services Committee is promoting Joint Base McGuire-Dix-Lakehurst, located partly in his district; he tries to use defense policy bills to multiply missions and resources at the base. Runyan was quoted early in 2011 as saying everything — including defense — should be on the table for spending reductions, but by the fall he told a New Jersey radio call-in show that the defense budget had been cut enough.

His third committee is Natural Resources. Runyan supports increased domestic energy production, but as Republicans pushed a July 2012 bill to expand leasing areas for offshore drilling, Runyan proposed giving New Jersey the chance to opt out of the leasing program via a public referendum. "I think it goes back to the states' rights issue and allowing the people to have their voice," he said at a markup. His amendment was defeated, and Runyan was the only committee Republican to vote against approving the underlying bill.

To support the fishing industry in his district, Runyan wants federal officials to account for the economic impact of the management plans they devise for fisheries. "If you want to say fish are a resource, you can only use the term resource if you can use it and conserve it at the same time," Runyan said. "If you're conserving everything, it's not a resource."

Born in Flint, Mich., Runyan was the first member of his family to attend college when he headed off to play football at the University of Michigan. His father worked as a plant mechanic for General Motors for 30 years. (Tom Runyan needed experimental surgery to reattach a severed thumb when Jon was young.) When he was laid off, the family briefly went on food stamps. One of his uncles also worked in the plant, while two others were truck drivers.

From that working-class background, Runyan says, he inherited a strong work ethic. "You go put your time in, do your job, take care of your family, that type of thing, which carries over into any aspect of your life — whether it's academics, athletics, professional, whatever you want. You can carry that stuff around with you, and that's kind of how you're wired."

Runyan moved to South Jersey in 2000, when he signed the richest contract ever for an NFL offensive lineman (at that time, at least). He retired in 2009 after rehabilitation following knee surgery for a microfracture.

His personality and competitiveness off the field paved the way for his political career. With strong name recognition and deep pockets, he was an attractive recruit to Republican leaders in Burlington and Ocean counties who were eyeing the 2010 elections. After winning the GOP nomination, Runyan trailed one-term Democrat John Adler into the fall. But conservatives swung support to Runyan when reports surfaced that Adler had helped get a Tea Party candidate on the ballot to split the Republican vote. Runyan won by nearly 6,000 votes. Five months later, Adler died after emergency heart surgery made necessary by a bacterial infection.

A new congressional map for 2012 removed Cherry Hill, a Democratic-leaning suburb of Philadelphia, from Runyan's district, making it a little safer. Democrat Shelley Adler, a former Cherry Hill town councilwoman — and his first opponent's widow — ran against him. The national political parties earmarked a lot of money for ads in the Philadelphia media market, anticipating some tight races. Adler ran an aggressive campaign, but Runyan made no mistakes. He won by 9 points.

Runyan has said that he will limit himself to four terms in the House.

Key Votes

2012	
Extend a Social Security payroll tax cut and unemployment benefits	YES
Ease securities rules to expand small-business access to capital	YES
Extend for one year subsidized student loan interest rates financed by a cut in health care spending	YES
Cite Attorney General Eric H. Holder Jr. for contempt of Congress	YES
Create a visa program for foreign graduates in high-tech fields	YES
Extend most Bush-era income tax rates while allowing rates for top-bracket earners to rise (Jan. 1, 2013)	YES
2011	
Strike funding for F-35 alternative engine	NO
Prevent EPA from regulating greenhouse gas emissions to address climate change	YES
Extend certain provisions of Patriot Act for four years	YES
Declare opposition to use of ground troops in Libya	YES
Overhaul patent law	YES
Pass compromise debt limit increase plan and establish future spending limits	YES
Allow consideration of measures to implement three trade agreements	YES

CQ Vote Studies

	PARTY UNITY		PRESIDENTIAL SUPPORT	
	SUPPORT	OPPOSE	SUPPORT	OPPOSE
2012	85%	15%	20%	80%
2011	91%	9%	31%	69%

Interest Groups

	AFL-CIO	ADA	CCUS	ACU
2012	48%	5%	100%	56%
2011	34%	25%	94%	64%

New Jersey 3

South central — Toms River

The 3rd District takes in part of south-central New Jersey, including some Jersey Shore beaches along the Atlantic Ocean as well as commuter towns near the New Jersey Turnpike to the west.

Residents in towns in the western portion of the district rely on white-collar jobs in commercial centers up and down the state. Joint Base McGuire-Dix-Lakehurst (shared with the 4th) sits at the center of the district, attracting defense contractors and providing the state with 42,000 jobs affiliated with the base. Agriculture also plays a key role in the district's economy; Burlington County farmers produce the second-largest cranberry crop in the nation and boast sweet corn and other fruits.

Superstorm Sandy ravaged the coastline of the 3rd District in October 2012, destroying huge swaths of popular vacation towns and damaging tens of thousands of structures that make up local property tax bases. Shops, homes and restaurants along the shore were demolished; locals planned to re-open some locations in late 2013 and the summer of 2014. Gov. Chris Christie has vowed to rebuild the boardwalk and attractions at Seaside Heights, where he and his family have vacationed over the years.

Redistricting after the 2010 census added Republican-leaning Brick Township north of Toms River while losing solidly Democratic Cherry Hill to the 1st. Ocean County was one of seven of the state's 21 counties to back GOP nominee Mitt Romney over Barack Obama in the 2012 presidential election and is a Republican bastion in state politics. Burlington County, which contains most of the district's population, trends Democratic in federal elections.

Major Industry
Health care, defense, tourism, agriculture

Military Bases
Joint Base McGuire-Dix-Lakehurst (shared with the 4th), 5,700 military, 1,500 civilian

Cities
Toms River (unincorporated)

Notable
Double Trouble State Park is on the site of the former Double Trouble Village, a cranberry and timber company town — farmers maintain a cranberry bog at the park.

Rep. Christopher H. Smith (R)

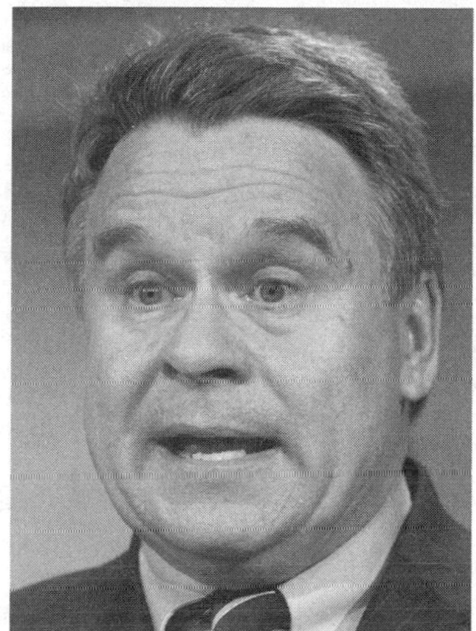

Capitol Office
225-3765
chrissmith.house.gov
2373 Rayburn Bldg. 20515-3004; fax 225-7768

Committees
Foreign Affairs
(Africa, Global Health, Global Human Rights & International Organizations - Chairman)

Residence
Robbinsville

Born
March 4, 1953; Rahway, N.J.

Religion
Roman Catholic

Family
Wife, Marie Smith; four children

Education
Trenton State College, B.A. 1975 (business)

Career
Sporting goods executive; state anti-abortion group director

Political Highlights
Republican nominee for U.S. House, 1978

ELECTION RESULTS

2012 GENERAL		
Christopher H. Smith (R)	195,145	63.7%
Brian P. Froelich (D)	107,991	35.3%
Leonard P. Marshall (NJC)	3,111	1.0%
2012 PRIMARY		
Christopher H. Smith (R)	21,520	83.6%
Terrence McGowan (R)	4,209	16.4%
2010 GENERAL		
Christopher H. Smith (R)	129,752	69.4%
Howard Kleinhendler (D)	52,118	27.9%
Joseph A. Siano (LIBERT)	2,912	1.6%

Previous Winning Percentages
2008 (66%); 2006 (66%); 2004 (67%); 2002 (66%); 2000 (63%); 1998 (62%); 1996 (64%); 1994 (68%); 1992 (62%); 1990 (63%); 1988 (66%); 1986 (61%); 1984 (61%); 1982 (53%); 1980 (57%)

Elected 1980; 17th term

Smith is a leading humanitarian in Congress, striving to offer assistance to the groups he sees as vulnerable. Decades of tenacious advocacy and legislating have made him one of the most prominent lawmakers combating human rights violations, opposing abortion and steering aid to veterans.

At the core of Smith's work is a belief that all life is "incredibly sacred." As a college student assigned to discuss abortion in a public speaking class, he read a news story about a child who had survived a late-term abortion and was later adopted. "It all started with the right-to-life issue of the unborn child, and the more I worked on that issue ... the more I became convinced that the vulnerable and disadvantaged need real advocates," he said.

His causes trump any allegiance to the Republican agenda, and Smith's voting record consistently places him among the most independent House Republicans — for example, he sees labor causes as a "human rights issue" and has backed allowing unions to organize workplaces without secret-ballot votes. Among House Republicans, he also has the highest lifetime score from the League of Conservation Voters. His flexibility, his willingness to devote long hours to his work and a scandal-free reputation have kept him popular.

Smith also runs one of the most effective constituent service operations in the House, and many of his initiatives grow out of casework. Inspired by the parents of two autistic children in his district, Smith worked to include provisions expanding autism research in a 2000 children's health law. He sponsored a 2011 reauthorization of autism programs that President Barack Obama signed into law. Smith values his work for the disabled because "God doesn't make junk," he said.

Superstorm Sandy ravaged parts of his district in 2012. Smith joined with the rest of the New Jersey delegation to secure the January 2013 enactment of a $50 billion package tied to Sandy recovery. A month later, the House passed Smith's bill to explicitly make houses of worship eligible for federal disaster aid on the same terms as other nonprofit institutions.

Abortion debates put him in the news more than any other issue. Voting mostly along party lines, the House passed his 2011 bill to ban federal funding of abortions in almost all cases, as well as prohibit tax credits to employers offering health insurance that includes abortion coverage. Supporters said the measure would codify a series of policy riders that have long been attached to annual appropriation bills. Democrats said it would go beyond current law.

In the 108th Congress (2003-04), Smith spearheaded the drive that led to enactment of a ban on a procedure that opponents call "partial birth" abortion.

Smith has served on the Foreign Affairs Committee since the 1980s. He hoped to serve as its chairman in the 113th Congress (2013-14), but Republican colleagues selected a conservative, Ed Royce of California. Still, there are few parts of the globe that Smith doesn't reach. He chairs the Subcommittee on Africa, Global Health, Global Human Rights and International Organizations. He sits on the Western Hemisphere panel. And he co-chairs governmental organizations that monitor human rights: the Congressional-Executive Commission on China, and the Commission on Security and Cooperation in Europe (which is known as the Helsinki Commission).

Smith pushed hard in 2012 to expedite the release of Chinese dissident and human rights activist Chen Guangcheng to the United States. Chen is known for exposing alleged abuses of China's family-planning policy, including forced abortions and sterilizations. Chen testified by phone to Smith's panel on several occasions. "We will be unceasing in our efforts to secure your freedom," Smith told him. Chen was released in late May.

In assessing the Obama administration's approach to foreign assistance, "I am concerned that this president has tipped his hand, that he does want to integrate abortion into foreign policy and foreign aid," Smith said.

In 2011, his opposition to abortion became tangled with his fight against human trafficking. The Health and Human Services Department decided not to renew its contract with the U.S. Conference of Catholic Bishops for trafficking victims' services, due to the bishops' refusal to cover reproductive health expenses. The introduction of abortion politics to the issue sapped bipartisan support for a reauthorization of one of Smith's prides: an anti-trafficking law enacted in 2000. The reauthorization was eventually tacked to a 2013 measure renewing programs to combat domestic violence. Smith voted against it.

Smith has been a champion of anti-trafficking initiatives since the 1990s, and he served as a special representative on human trafficking on the Helsinki Commission. Smith also has tried to steer the commission to address anti-Semitism, and he thinks the United States should have a zero-tolerance policy for anti-Semitism in the international community.

Smith believes that peacekeeping forces are the best defenders of human rights on a global scale, and that the United States working in conjunction with NATO has been the best peacekeeper. Abuses can be deterred, he said, by the military's reputation for strength and capability.

He calls for continued investments to fight AIDS and other diseases in Africa, as well as a more cohesive plan for expanding trade with the continent, as economic growth can benefit public health. "We do not have a strategy for Africa," he said. "We have good people at the USAID, and others who want to do more at the Export-Import Bank. ... It's not unlike the way our intelligence gathering was before 9/11. It's all stovepiped."

Smith's independence hasn't always pleased party leaders. He was stripped of the Veterans' Affairs Committee gavel at the start of the 109th Congress (2005-06), after he called for increases in veterans' health care spending despite demands from GOP leaders for leaner budgets. Smith said the 2007 disclosures of severe problems at Walter Reed Army Medical Center in Washington and veterans' hospitals around the country vindicated his stance.

Smith, whose parents owned a New Jersey wholesale sporting goods business, studied business at Trenton State College. But after an internship with a state senator, he was hooked on politics. He ran the campaign of an unsuccessful Democratic Senate candidate in 1976, then lost his own race for the House two years later. He was executive director of the New Jersey Right to Life Committee before winning election to Congress at age 27. He defeated 13-term Democrat Frank Thompson, who was tainted by a bribery scandal. The last time he took less than 60 percent of the vote was 1982.

Key Votes

2012	
Extend a Social Security payroll tax cut and unemployment benefits	YES
Ease securities rules to expand small-business access to capital	YES
Extend for one year subsidized student loan interest rates financed by a cut in health care spending	YES
Cite Attorney General Eric H. Holder Jr. for contempt of Congress	YES
Create a visa program for foreign graduates in high-tech fields	YES
Extend most Bush-era income tax rates while allowing rates for top-bracket earners to rise (Jan. 1, 2013)	YES
2011	
Strike funding for F-35 alternative engine	NO
Prevent EPA from regulating greenhouse gas emissions to address climate change	YES
Extend certain provisions of Patriot Act for four years	YES
Declare opposition to use of ground troops in Libya	YES
Overhaul patent law	YES
Pass compromise debt limit increase plan and establish future spending limits	YES
Allow consideration of measures to implement three trade agreements	YES

CQ Vote Studies

	PARTY UNITY		PRESIDENTIAL SUPPORT	
	SUPPORT	OPPOSE	SUPPORT	OPPOSE
2012	81%	19%	23%	77%
2011	80%	20%	29%	71%
2010	84%	16%	40%	60%
2009	65%	35%	65%	35%
2008	68%	32%	32%	68%

Interest Groups

	AFL-CIO	ADA	CCUS	ACU
2012	48%	10%	83%	52%
2011	59%	35%	81%	44%
2010	29%	15%	100%	67%
2009	57%	30%	80%	64%
2008	80%	65%	67%	28%

New Jersey 4

Central — part of Trenton, Lakewood

The 4th District begins just outside Trenton, following Interstate 195 across the state to the Atlantic Ocean. It takes a large cut of Monmouth County from its southwestern point through Lakewood Township and up the Garden State Parkway to Holmdel. Redistricting after the 2010 census shifted wealthy towns near the Navesink River into the 4th while giving much of the Burlington County suburbs to the 3rd.

Lakewood Township in the southern part of the district is New Jersey's fastest-growing town. It has attracted an unusual combination of Mexican immigrants, seniors and Orthodox Jews and is now the Garden State's seventh-most-populous municipality. Overall, however, the 4th is the state's least racially diverse district.

Joint Base McGuire-Dix-Lakehurst (shared with the 3rd) anchors a strong defense sector for the district; Naval Weapons Station Earle provides ordnance for the Navy's Atlantic fleet. The beaches in Monmouth County rely heavily on tourism, making recovery from Superstorm Sandy — which damaged boardwalks and homes and shifted sand dunes — a vital interest to the district. Major medical facilities in Neptune and Freehold are large employers. A diverse range of businesses are supported in the Trenton suburbs, and horse farms and croplands dot the rural areas.

As the 4th District lost part of Trenton during the decennial redistricting process, the area has moved further to the right politically. John McCain won the old 4th with 52 percent of the 2008 presidential vote, and the district's new boundaries gave Mitt Romney 54 percent in 2012. Barack Obama won the district's portion of less-populous Mercer County, but Romney dominated in Ocean and won easily in Monmouth.

Major Industry
Tourism, agriculture, defense

Military Bases
Joint Base McGuire-Dix-Lakehurst (shared with the 3rd), 5,700 military, 1,500 civilian; Naval Weapons Station Earle, 150 military, 450 civilian

Cities
Lakewood (unincorporated), Hamilton (unincorporated)

Notable
Supreme Court justice Samuel A. Alito Jr. was raised in Hamilton and attended Hamilton East-Steinert High School — a local street is named after him.

Rep. Scott Garrett (R)

Capitol Office
225-4465
garrett.house.gov
2232 Rayburn Bldg. 20515-3005; fax 225-9048

Committees
Budget
Financial Services
(Capital Markets & Government Sponsored Enterprises Chairman)

Residence
Wantage

Born
July 9, 1959; Englewood, N.J.

Religion
Protestant

Family
Wife, Mary Ellen Garrett; two children

Education
Montclair State College, B.A. 1981 (political science); Rutgers U., J.D. 1984

Career
Lawyer

Political Highlights
N.J. Assembly, 1990-2003; sought Republican nomination for U.S. House, 1998, 2000

ELECTION RESULTS

2012 GENERAL		
Scott Garrett (R)	167,501	55.0%
Adam Gussen (D)	130,100	42.7%
Patricia Alessandrini (GREEN)	6,770	2.2%
2012 PRIMARY		
Scott Garrett (R)	24,709	87.2%
Michael J. Cino (R)	2,107	7.4%
Bonnie Somer (R)	1,511	5.3%
2010 GENERAL		
Scott Garrett (R)	124,030	64.9%
Tod Theise (D)	62,634	32.8%
Ed Fanning (GREEN)	2,347	1.2%

Previous Winning Percentages
2008 (56%); 2006 (55%); 2004 (58%); 2002 (59%)

Elected 2002; 6th term

Garrett spends his time wading through some of the most complex issues confronting the federal government, all the while looking for ways to simplify its role. He is a prominent conservative thinker on budgeting and financial regulation, and his overall vision is a stripped-down bureaucracy bound by the Constitution.

He looks like a man who knows his way around a spreadsheet. Garrett speaks quickly, often with a machine-gun cadence. He seldom minces words, making his dry sense of humor easy to miss. However, his expansive bandwidth for processing information has made him a trusted Republican spokesman when numbers are involved, as well as a leader on the Financial Services Committee.

Garrett has chaired the Capital Markets and Government Sponsored Enterprises Subcommittee since 2011. He is trying to pave the way for a federal withdrawal from the housing sector. In the 112th Congress (2011-12), Garrett oversaw approval of more than a dozen bills to reshape or chip away at Fannie Mae and Freddie Mac, the mortgage giants held in conservatorship by the government since the market collapse in 2008.

He repeatedly emphasizes that taxpayers should not be responsible for more bailouts, and at a 2013 hearing he blamed government for causing the spate of bad mortgages tied to the collapse, "by systematically reducing underwriting standards" to increase homeownership.

Anticipating an eventual demise of the GSEs, Garrett in 2011 presented his plan for facilitating the growth of a private housing mortgage market. "Bank balance sheets are not large enough to provide for the financing for housing to the level that this country has grown accustomed to," Garrett says. He calls for a "restart" of securitization — the bundling of loans for sale to various investors. In his plan, a federal agency would standardize regulations for securitization while adding beefed-up protections for investors. The federal guarantee for home mortgages would go away.

Garrett dismisses critics who say the end of such guarantees would collapse the housing market. "Even after the day comes that the GSEs are no longer here, you will still have a litany of federal support," he said, including interventions by the Federal Housing Administration, Federal Reserve monetary policy and the mortgage interest tax deduction.

Garrett dislikes the 2010 financial regulatory law known as Dodd-Frank. Speaking on the 2011 anniversary of its enactment, he was characteristically blunt: "We now know after a year of Dodd-Frank that [Democrats] had absolutely no idea what they were doing." He sees the law as a substantial overreach, addressing issues having nothing to do with the 2008 collapse. He says the confusion caused by new agencies and regulations taking effect at the same time halted economic recovery.

On the Budget Committee, Garrett is the No. 2 Republican. In 2012, the House passed his bill to, among other things, account for GSEs in the federal budget. He is also a fan of zero-based budgeting, which requires every agency to justify its full budget each year.

He also has a hand in setting spending priorities. In the 112th Congress, Democrats lambasted the blueprints offered by House Budget Chairman Paul D. Ryan of Wisconsin, who proposed significantly reducing spending and restructuring entitlement programs. Garrett, who chaired the Budget and Spending Task Force of the conservative Republican Study Committee, prepared RSC budget proposals that cut even further. "It's the right thing to do," he said. Garrett opposed the fiscal 2011 and 2012 spending laws, saying they did not reducing spending enough.

Garrett believes one way to cut spending would be shrinking the government to the size that he says was dictated by the Constitution. He co-founded the Constitution Caucus, which organizes events to educate lawmakers and their staff on various interpretations of the founding document. Garrett also co-founded the 10th Amendment Task Force, which aims to restore to the states powers that critics say have been stripped away by the federal government. For example, Garrett has proposed a "devolution" of infrastructure responsibilities to the states and an end to federal involvement in education.

But in January 2013, he did vote for a $50 billion package of aid tied to Superstorm Sandy recovery. He also sponsored the law that increased the borrowing authority of the National Flood Insurance Program so it could pay out claims related to the storm.

Garrett, a devout evangelical Christian, is consistently conservative on social issues. He opposes abortion and same-sex marriage. Spurred by both constituents and national security concerns, Garrett takes some interest in international affairs. He regularly expresses support for Taiwan's government and promotes its inclusion in international organizations.

The youngest son of a Uniroyal executive, Garrett represents both Wall Street commuters and family farm operators. When he was a kid, his family moved from Bergen County's suburbs to a 100-acre farm in Wantage, where they grew greenhouse tomatoes and Christmas trees, in addition to raising Yorkshire pigs. Garrett is a lawyer with an interest in environmental law, and he occasionally tilts to the center on conservation matters. He pushed for the 2006 law that designated parts of the Musconetcong River for protection as a wild and scenic river.

He took an early interest in civics, publishing an alternative high school newspaper that questioned the school administration's spending practices and getting elected student government treasurer. After earning his law degree, he worked in insurance and jumped into politics. He served more than a decade in the New Jersey Legislature, where he belonged to a group of maverick, conservative Republicans called the "mountain men."

In 1998, Garrett launched a campaign to unseat moderate Republican Rep. Marge Roukema. Although he lost the primary, he got the attention of the Club for Growth, an influential anti-tax group that spent more than $250,000 on his behalf two years later — when he lost again, by around 2,000 votes. By 2002, Roukema had lost a bid to chair Financial Services and was ready to retire. Garrett won easily. Democrats and moderate Republicans have viewed Garrett as too conservative for New Jersey politics, but he has had relatively little difficulty fending off challengers in a series of well-financed campaigns.

Key Votes

2012	
Extend a Social Security payroll tax cut and unemployment benefits	NO
Ease securities rules to expand small-business access to capital	YES
Extend for one year subsidized student loan interest rates financed by a cut in health care spending	NO
Cite Attorney General Eric H. Holder Jr. for contempt of Congress	YES
Create a visa program for foreign graduates in high-tech fields	YES
Extend most Bush-era income tax rates while allowing rates for top-bracket earners to rise (Jan. 1, 2013)	NO
2011	
Strike funding for F-35 alternative engine	YES
Prevent EPA from regulating greenhouse gas emissions to address climate change	YES
Extend certain provisions of Patriot Act for four years	YES
Declare opposition to use of ground troops in Libya	YES
Overhaul patent law	NO
Pass compromise debt limit increase plan and establish future spending limits	NO
Allow consideration of measures to implement three trade agreements	YES

CQ Vote Studies

	PARTY UNITY		PRESIDENTIAL SUPPORT	
	SUPPORT	OPPOSE	SUPPORT	OPPOSE
2012	98%	2%	20%	80%
2011	96%	4%	16%	84%
2010	97%	3%	24%	76%
2009	98%	2%	18%	82%
2008	97%	3%	77%	23%

Interest Groups

	AFL-CIO	ADA	CCUS	ACU
2012	10%	15%	82%	100%
2011	3%	5%	88%	96%
2010	0%	5%	71%	100%
2009	0%	0%	73%	100%
2008	0%	5%	78%	100%

New Jersey 5

North — Hackensack, Paramus

The 5th District is shaped like an upside down "V" sitting on top of northern New Jersey, boomeranging from the Delaware Water Gap to the Palisades along the Hudson River. Most of the district's constituents live in a cluster of affluent New York City suburbs in northeastern Bergen County.

The 5th's Bergen County suburbs are home to some of the wealthiest zip codes in the nation, such as Alpine, which celebrities Jay-Z, Chris Rock and Stevie Wonder call home. At the intersection of the Garden State Parkway and heavily traveled Route 17, the Garden State Plaza in Paramus hosts one of the oldest (and largest) suburban retail malls in the nation.

Hackensack University Medical Center to the south has one of the nation's largest cancer treatment centers. The top employers in Bergen County are health systems or health related, including pharmaceutical companies and research labs.

Further west the district becomes more rural, rugged, scenic and hilly. The small portion of the Appalachian Trail that passes through the state runs through the 5th, and High Point State Park sits in the district's northwestern corner.

As young New York City commuters are forced further out into Sussex and Warren counties, they have challenged the small town feel of many communities at the edges of the district. Local officials have taken an interest in preserving agricultural land against continued large-scale residential development.

Although Bergen County is politically competitive, wipeout margins of victory for Republicans in Warren, Sussex, and Passaic counties tilt this district to the GOP. Republican Mitt Romney took 52 percent of the district's presidential vote in 2012.

Major Industry
Pharmaceuticals, electronics, shipping, agriculture

Cities
Hackensack, Bergenfield, Paramus

Notable
Mars Chocolate has its North American headquarters and M&M manufacturing center in Hackettstown — the building features the largest solar garden installed by a food manufacturer.

Rep. Frank Pallone Jr. (D)

Capitol Office
225-4671
pallone.house.gov
237 Cannon Bldg. 20515-3006; fax 225-9665

Committees
Energy & Commerce
Natural Resources

Residence
Long Branch

Born
Oct. 30, 1951; Long Branch, N.J.

Religion
Roman Catholic

Family
Wife, Sarah Hospodor-Pallone; three children

Education
Middlebury College, B.A. 1973 (history & French); Tufts U., M.A. 1974 (international relations); Rutgers U., J.D. 1978

Career
Lawyer

Political Highlights
Long Branch City Council, 1982-88; N.J. Senate, 1984-88

ELECTION RESULTS

2012 GENERAL		
Frank Pallone Jr. (D)	151,782	63.3%
Anna C. Little (R)	84,360	35.2%
2012 PRIMARY		
Frank Pallone Jr. (D)		unopposed
2010 GENERAL		
Frank Pallone Jr. (D)	81,933	54.7%
Anna C. Little (R)	65,413	43.7%

Previous Winning Percentages
2008 (67%); 2006 (69%); 2004 (67%); 2002 (66%); 2000 (68%); 1998 (57%); 1996 (61%); 1994 (60%); 1992 (52%); 1990 (49%); 1988 (52%); 1988 Special Election (52%)

Elected 1988; 13th full term

Pallone has plenty on his plate as a key Democratic negotiator on health care and a defender of the environment. But he would like to be a senator, and in the opening months of 2013, he tried to drum up support within his party for a possible run — Democratic Sen. Frank R. Lautenberg had announced that he would retire at the end of the 113th Congress.

Any hesitance was swept away in June 2013 when Lautenberg died of viral pneumonia. Republican Gov. Chris Christie quickly scheduled a special election for Oct. 16, with primaries on Aug. 13. Within hours of that announcement, Pallone informed various New Jersey Democrats that he would be a candidate.

Pallone has been eyeing the other side of the Capitol for some time. He formed an exploratory committee in 1999, when Lautenberg made his first retirement announcement. He was offered a spot on the ballot in 2002, when scandal-plagued Democrat Robert G. Torricelli ended his re-election bid five weeks before Election Day. Worried that he didn't have the resources to compete, Pallone declined that opportunity — Lautenberg replaced Torricelli and won a return to Congress. Pallone tried but failed to secure appointment to the Senate in 2006, when Democratic Sen. Jon Corzine became governor.

His decision to run in 2013 was almost certainly helped by the timing of the special election. Should he lose, he can still seek re-election in 2014.

Pallone's most daunting Democratic foe would be Newark Mayor Cory Booker, who has national recognition and excellent fundraising connections. Pallone has superior ties to party organizations in the state, which can make all the difference in a primary. The two men also have opposing personalities. Whereas Booker is considered charismatic, Pallone is often reserved and laconic — The Star-Ledger has said that his "idea of a smile is a mild grimace."

If he stays in the House, he'll still have a lot of influence. Pallone sits on the Energy and Commerce Committee, and he is the top Democrat on its Health Subcommittee. He knew little of the details of health policy before taking the gavel of that panel in 2007, but he quickly got up to speed.

Pallone was the House sponsor of the enacted 2009 bill to expand the Children's Health Insurance Program. He was also at the center of negotiations on the 2010 health care overhaul. He fielded the concerns of both Republicans and moderate Democrats — though many in the GOP later said they were shut out of the process.

As the ranking member of the Health Subcommittee in the 112th Congress (2011-12), Pallone was on the defensive. When the panel considered bills to convert mandatory spending in the 2010 law to discretionary spending that is subject to congressional review, Pallone called it "an effort to dismantle the health care reform block by block, by cherry-picking the provisions." Even though most Democrats admitted the financial difficulties of implementing a long-term-care program in the law, Pallone trashed a bill to eliminate it: "Repealing it at this point accomplishes nothing other than to send a very negative message to the disabled community and those who are supportive of trying to come up" with a solution, he said.

He did agree with a 2011 GOP effort to repeal the Independent Payment Advisory Board, which under the 2010 law is tasked with recommending Medicare cost controls that go into effect unless Congress disapproves. Pallone dislikes that cession of power — but he voted against the final bill on the House floor, because changes to medical malpractice law were attached.

New Jersey is a hub for pharmaceutical companies, and Pallone urges the Food and Drug Administration to prioritize generic drugs. A reauthorization of FDA user-fee programs enacted in 2012 included a new fee program for generic drugs and provisions meant to speed up the drug approval process.

Pallone's other major legislative concern is the environment, which he addresses from both Energy and Commerce and the Natural Resources Committee. His wife, Sarah Hospodor-Pallone, is a deputy associate administrator of congressional and intergovernmental relations at the EPA.

He opposes offshore drilling for oil and gas. He has introduced a bill to ban all new drilling in U.S. waters, as well as a measure to permanently ban drilling in all states from Maine to Virginia. He has opposed all major trade agreements, in part because of his concerns that an expansion of global trade would damage the environment. He regularly introduces bills to change water pollution laws to effectively outlaw mountaintop-removal mining.

Pallone is a member of the Congressional Progressive Caucus, the group of the most-liberal House members. His voting record over the course of his career has put him increasingly in line with a majority of the Democratic Party.

Over the years, he has represented a sizable Indian-American community, and he is a founder of the House Caucus on India and Indian-Americans. He supported the 2006 U.S.-India nuclear pact allowing shipments of civilian nuclear fuel to India, saying it would help keep the country a strategic ally in the increasingly unstable region.

He also has many Armenian constituents. As co-chairman of the House Armenian Caucus, he co-sponsored a resolution condemning as genocide the mass killings of Armenians in Ottoman Turkey in 1915.

Pallone's father, who inspired him to pursue public life, was a cop in the central Jersey town of Long Branch. He was also a longtime activist in local Democratic affairs, including the campaigns of former Rep. James J. Howard.

After graduating from Middlebury College in Vermont, Pallone went to Tufts University's Fletcher School, where he earned an international relations degree. He was accepted into a program that would have allowed him to spend a year in Switzerland. He opted for New Jersey instead, heading to Rutgers University to pursue law.

In 1982, Howard urged Pallone to run for the Long Branch City Council. A year later, Pallone won a state Senate seat. In March 1988, Howard died of a heart attack. Many Democratic insiders, including Howard's widow, backed Pallone. He won two elections on the same day, each by 5 points: a special election to fill the vacancy and a general election for a full term. His first re-election was close, but after that his victory margins widened.

Several rounds of redistricting have kept his district relatively safe for a Democratic candidate. In 2010, he defeated Republican Anna C. Little, then the mayor of the Borough of Highlands, by 11 points. After more redistricting, he beat her by 28 points in 2012.

Key Votes

2012	
Extend a Social Security payroll tax cut and unemployment benefits	YES
Ease securities rules to expand small-business access to capital	YES
Extend for one year subsidized student loan interest rates financed by a cut in health care spending	NO
Cite Attorney General Eric H. Holder Jr. for contempt of Congress	?
Create a visa program for foreign graduates in high-tech fields	NO
Extend most Bush-era income tax rates while allowing rates for top-bracket earners to rise (Jan. 1, 2013)	YES
2011	
Strike funding for F-35 alternative engine	YES
Prevent EPA from regulating greenhouse gas emissions to address climate change	NO
Extend certain provisions of Patriot Act for four years	NO
Declare opposition to use of ground troops in Libya	YES
Overhaul patent law	YES
Pass compromise debt limit increase plan and establish future spending limits	NO
Allow consideration of measures to implement three trade agreements	NO

CQ Vote Studies

	PARTY UNITY		PRESIDENTIAL SUPPORT	
	SUPPORT	OPPOSE	SUPPORT	OPPOSE
2012	99%	1%	88%	12%
2011	98%	2%	85%	15%
2010	99%	1%	93%	7%
2009	99%	1%	97%	3%
2008	99%	1%	17%	83%

Interest Groups

	AFL-CIO	ADA	CCUS	ACU
2012	95%	100%	17%	0%
2011	100%	95%	19%	4%
2010	100%	95%	25%	0%
2009	100%	95%	36%	0%
2008	100%	100%	67%	0%

New Jersey 6

East central — Edison, Perth Amboy

The 6th District follows the New Jersey coastline from Raritan Bay around Sandy Hook and down to Asbury Park. It takes in townships north of the Raritan River and New Brunswick at its western tip and dives into Marlboro in northwestern Monmouth County.

The 6th is one of the most diverse districts in the state. Several Middlesex County municipalities have large populations of Asian residents, mainly of Indian, Pakistani and Chinese descent. Populous Hispanic communities make up much of Perth Amboy and New Brunswick, while Asbury Park is majority black.

Edison — renamed in 1954 to honor Thomas Edison's "invention factory" here — is a major business and distribution hub. Its Raritan Center Business Park is one of the largest on the East Coast, with 13 million square feet of office, warehouse, and industrial space. Pharmaceutical giant Johnson & Johnson has its headquarters in New Brunswick, and Robert Wood Johnson University Hospital boosts the city's health care industry profile. New owners plan to expand and modernize the sprawling Perth Amboy oil refinery on the Arthur Kill. The 6th also covers most of the large Rutgers University's campuses in New Brunswick and Piscataway Township.

The home of Asbury Park — perhaps the most famous of all Jersey Shore towns thanks to the eponymous album by Bruce Springsteen — and other Atlantic Ocean beaches, the 6th relies heavily on the tourism industry to support its economy. Superstorm Sandy took a heavy toll on coastal communities here in October 2012.

Decennial redistricting shifted heavily Democratic Plainfield out of the 6th but only slightly diminished party strength, at least in federal elections. GOP support exists in pockets —Republican Chris Christie took Edison and Sayreville in the 2009 gubernatorial race — but Barack Obama won the district overall in 2012 with 61 percent of its presidential vote.

Major Industry
Higher education, distribution, health care, pharmaceuticals

Cities
New Brunswick, Old Bridge (unincorp.), Woodbridge (unincorp.) (pt.)

Notable
Sandy Hook Lighthouse is the oldest lighthouse in the United States, completed in 1764.

Rep. Leonard Lance (R)

Capitol Office
225-5361
lance.house.gov
133 Cannon Bldg. 20515-3007; fax 225-9460

Committees
Energy & Commerce

Residence
Lebanon

Born
June 25, 1952; Easton, Pa.

Religion
Roman Catholic

Family
Wife, Heidi A. Rohrbach; one stepchild

Education
Lehigh U., B.A. 1974 (American studies); Vanderbilt U., J.D. 1977; Princeton U., M.P.A. 1982

Career
Lawyer; gubernatorial aide

Political Highlights
N.J. Assembly, 1991-2002; sought Republican nomination for U.S. House, 1996; N.J. Senate, 2002-09 (minority leader, 2004-09)

ELECTION RESULTS

2012 GENERAL		
Leonard Lance (R)	175,662	57.2%
Upendra J. Chivukula (D)	123,057	40.1%
Dennis A. Breen (IRFM)	4,078	1.3%
Patrick McKnight (LIBERT)	4,078	1.3%
2012 PRIMARY		
Leonard Lance (R)	23,432	60.6%
David Larsen (R)	15,253	39.4%
2010 GENERAL		
Leonard Lance (R)	105,084	59.4%
Ed Potosnak (D)	71,902	40.6%

Previous Winning Percentages
2008 (50%)

Elected 2008; 3rd term

Lance's moderate demeanor matches his moderate politics. He is studious and unfailingly polite, joining the GOP call for fiscal restraint while harboring centrist views on the environment and social issues.

Over the course of 18 years in the New Jersey Legislature, Lance earned the respect of both parties for his efforts to balance the state budget, and he proved willing to accept compromises. In its 2008 endorsement of Lance, The New York Times praised his "leadership qualities and his voice of moderation."

Lance has had notable departures from the Republican Conference while in the House. In the 111th Congress (2009-10), he supported a bill to create a cap-and-trade system to regulate greenhouse gas emissions. He hasn't been bothered by federal efforts to increase renewable-energy production, and he doesn't join efforts to chip away at benefits enjoyed by organized labor. Although he told the Newark Star-Ledger that he sometimes fantasizes about debt reduction while in the shower, in 2011 Lance balked at many GOP amendments meant to wipe out funding for specific programs.

Even so, in the 112th Congress (2011-12) he joined one of the most heated partisan battlegrounds: the Energy and Commerce Committee. "It is without a doubt the committee that's most important to the district," he said. That's because his district has huge pharmaceutical and manufacturing concerns. Lance sits on the Health Subcommittee and the Commerce, Manufacturing and Trade Subcommittee.

He opposed the health care overhaul enacted in 2010, and the legislative process that formed it. Lance said that Democrats gave short shrift to Republican input, including an alternative proposal by the moderate Tuesday Group, to which he belongs. (He is also a member of the Main Street Partnership.) The medical device tax included in the law will be "very harmful" to manufacturers in his district, he said, and he supports efforts to repeal it.

Other health issues have caught his eye. In 2011, Lance and New York Democrat Joseph Crowley re-established the Rare Disease Caucus. He teamed with Democrats Anna G. Eshoo of California and Sen. Sheldon Whitehouse of Rhode Island in 2012 on a bipartisan measure to boost funding for pancreatic cancer and lung cancer research at the National Institutes of Health. It was signed into law at the start of 2013.

His stated hope for the economy and employers is "greater certainty" through, among other things, an overhaul of the tax code: He favors lower individual and corporate tax rates with fewer targeted preferences for specific groups or industries. Meanwhile, Lance is on board with at least some Republican attempts to check the regulatory power of the EPA. He voted for a 2011 House bill to prevent the agency from regulating greenhouse gases without congressional approval.

Lance intends to stay on Energy and Commerce, even though his state legislative career often focused on budgeting. He served for a time as chairman of the New Jersey Assembly's appropriations committee, and he was the ranking Republican on the state Senate's version of the panel.

Lance's reputation in the state legislature was that of a fiscal conservative. He opposed Republican Gov. Christine Todd Whitman's 1997 proposal to fund a state pension system with borrowed money, a stance that irked the GOP establishment. In November 2008, voters approved a proposal by Lance to amend the state constitution to require voter approval for the government to borrow money.

The House-passed budgets of 2011 and 2012 were "not perfect," Lance said, but "legitimate and honest" attempts to address the national debt.

Lance did join the rest of the New Jersey delegation to fight for a package of recovery assistance related to Superstorm Sandy, which devastated the state in 2012. Most of the $50 billion in the January 2013 law was deemed "emergency" spending, putting it outside of regular budgeting rules, but Lance and 48 other House Republicans voted for it.

A bit of a traditionalist, Lance admits that he didn't even begin using a cellphone until he was elected state Senate minority leader in 2004. He has, however, become quite fond of holding telephone town hall meetings, where he's able to connect with thousands of his constituents from his Washington office. "I get to hear the concerns of the people I represent, and I would hope that my constituents benefit from interactions with me," he says.

Lance's family has lived in Hunterdon County since 1710; the house that he lives in was built in 1780. Lance has said that he grew up in "an adult-centered, not child-centered, household," where politics and policy were discussed. His father helped shape the New Jersey Constitution as state Senate president.

Long interested in a career in public service, Lance wasn't sure whether he'd enter politics when he graduated from Lehigh University with a degree in American studies in 1974. He went to law school at Vanderbilt University, where he met Heidi A. Rohrbach, whom he married in 1996. She is a corporate lawyer.

Lance worked as a court clerk and later received a master's degree in public administration from Princeton University. He studied under Fred Greenstein, a noted scholar on Dwight D. Eisenhower. Lance calls himself both a "student of history" and an "Eisenhower Republican." The general "was a moderate who brought people together," he said.

After serving as assistant counsel for New Jersey Republican Gov. Thomas H. Kean for seven years, Lance successfully ran for the Assembly in 1991. His victory carried on a family tradition: Great-uncle H. Kiefer Lance and his father, Wesley L. Lance, also served in the New Jersey Legislature.

He first sought a seat in Congress in 1996, when he unsuccessfully ran in the Republican primary for the state's 12th district. When Republican Rep. Mike Ferguson announced that he would retire from the 7th District at the end of the 110th Congress (2007-08), Lance decided to run. He defeated six other candidates in the GOP primary, then beat Democratic state Rep. Linda Stender by 8 points, even as Barack Obama carried the district's presidential vote.

Lance faced opposition from tea-party-backed candidate David Larsen in both the 2010 and 2012 Republican primaries, but he secured well over 50 percent of the vote in each race. Redistricting made his seat a little safer for a Republican heading into 2012, and he easily beat Democratic Assemblyman Upendra J. Chivukula that November.

Key Votes

2012	
Extend a Social Security payroll tax cut and unemployment benefits	YES
Ease securities rules to expand small-business access to capital	YES
Extend for one year subsidized student loan interest rates financed by a cut in health care spending	YES
Cite Attorney General Eric H. Holder Jr. for contempt of Congress	YES
Create a visa program for foreign graduates in high-tech fields	YES
Extend most Bush-era income tax rates while allowing rates for top-bracket earners to rise (Jan. 1, 2013)	YES
2011	
Strike funding for F-35 alternative engine	YES
Prevent EPA from regulating greenhouse gas emissions to address climate change	YES
Extend certain provisions of Patriot Act for four years	YES
Declare opposition to use of ground troops in Libya	YES
Overhaul patent law	YES
Pass compromise debt limit increase plan and establish future spending limits	YES
Allow consideration of measures to implement three trade agreements	YES

CQ Vote Studies

	PARTY UNITY		PRESIDENTIAL SUPPORT	
	SUPPORT	OPPOSE	SUPPORT	OPPOSE
2012	93%	7%	16%	84%
2011	85%	15%	34%	66%
2010	91%	9%	31%	69%
2009	78%	22%	47%	53%

Interest Groups

	AFL-CIO	ADA	CCUS	ACU
2012	33%	5%	92%	76%
2011	34%	25%	100%	44%
2010	7%	5%	88%	88%
2009	48%	40%	87%	68%

New Jersey 7

North central — Bridgewater, Roxbury Township

The 7th sits in the outer suburbs of New York City in Essex, Union, Somerset and Morris counties. Interstate 78 runs though the center of the district, which widens as it runs west to the Delaware River. The 7th includes all of Hunterdon County and the southwestern corner of Warren County, and it is mainly wealthy and white-collar, with the highest median household income of any district statewide and fifth-highest nationwide ($95,000).

Stopping just short of the industrial grit by the Arthur Kill, the 7th covers affluent communities in eastern and northern Union County, such as Summit and Westfield where median household incomes are near $120,000, as well as Milburn in Essex County. Bending around Peapack and Gladstone, the district gathers up the hilly, tony suburbs of Morris County up to Interstate 80. The 7th also snags Hispanic-majority, working-class Dover.

Pharmaceutical office parks and production facilities line Interstate 78 and U.S. Route 202, particularly near Raritan and Bridgewater. The headquarters of Merck & Co. is here, while Roche Molecular Systems makes blood screening supplies in Branchburg. Business service provider USI Services Group is based in Union and is the county's third-largest private employer.

Telecommunications, once a local economic strength, has suffered through the most recent recession. AT&T and Alcatel-Lucent have both downsized at their Somerset County facilities.

Although less populous, the western counties of the district provide a base of support for Republicans. Hunterdon County sends some of the most conservative members of the New Jersey Legislature to Trenton. Union County is Democratic-leaning as a whole, but the voters captured by the 7th are split relatively evenly between the parties. In the 2012 presidential race, Mitt Romney won the district as redrawn following decennial remapping by 5 percentage points; Barack Obama had eked out a 1-point win on the previous map in 2008.

Major Industry
Pharmaceuticals, manufacturing

Cities
Plainfield (pt.), Westfield, Summit, Dover

Notable
The United States Golf Association Museum is located in Far Hills.

Rep. Albio Sires (D)

Capitol Office
225-7919
sires.house.gov
2342 Rayburn Bldg. 20515-3013; fax 226-0792

Committees
Foreign Affairs
Transportation & Infrastructure

Residence
West New York

Born
Jan. 26, 1951; Bejucal, Cuba

Religion
Roman Catholic

Family
Wife, Adrienne Sires; one stepchild

Education
Saint Peter's College, B.A. 1974 (Spanish & marketing); Middlebury College, M.A. 1985 (Spanish)

Career
Property title insurance firm owner; state community affairs agency aide; teacher

Political Highlights
Candidate for West New York Town Commission, 1983; Republican nominee for U.S. House, 1986; Republican nominee for Hudson County Board of Chosen Freeholders, 1987; candidate for West New York Town Commission, 1991; candidate for West New York Town Commission (recall election), 1993; West New York Town Commission, 1995-2006 (mayor, 1995-2006); N.J. Assembly, 2000-06 (speaker, 2002-06)

ELECTION RESULTS

2012 GENERAL		
Albio Sires (D)	130,853	78.0%
Maria Karczewski (R)	31,763	18.9%
Herbert H. Shaw (PAC)	1,839	1.1%
Stephen Deluca (RAP)	1,710	1.0%
2012 PRIMARY		
Albio Sires (D)	30,840	89.0%
Michael J. Shurin (D)	3,808	11.0%

Previous Winning Percentages
2010 (74%); 2008 (75%); 2006 (78%); 2006 Special Election (97%)

Elected 2006; 4th full term

Sires has been active in New Jersey politics for nearly 30 years. A former mayor of West New York and speaker of the state Assembly, he stays relatively quiet as a congressman. Back home, he is a power broker with influence over state Democratic politics.

His experience affords Sires (SEAR-eez) the ability to engage friends and foes. Colleagues praise his party loyalty, but he spent a decade as a Republican and aims for bipartisan support on policies regarding homeland security, transportation and education, which are all concerns of Hudson County.

He has shown a particular ability for engineering momentum around a variety of causes, such as pushing for unemployment benefits and disaster relief for states. Superstorm Sandy caused dreadful flooding in parts of his district in 2012, and Sires was part of the bipartisan effort by the state's delegation to secure emergency relief funding. In 2013, he began promoting a bill to create a public-private "national catastrophe fund" that he said would speed up both disaster response and preventive maintenance projects.

Sires, a member of the Transportation and Infrastructure Committee, often calls on colleagues to support road improvements and other development projects that are popular in his district. A two-year surface transportation bill enacted in 2012 required the development of a national freight strategy for the nation's highway system; Sires has proposed expanding that strategy to incorporate railroads, waterways, airports and other channels.

A lot of his other work also caters to local concerns. He is a frequent advocate for the recommendations of the panel that investigated the Sept. 11 attacks. Sires is also the vice chairman of the Congressional Hispanic Caucus Immigration Task Force, at a time when serious discussions of an immigration law overhaul are under way.

From the Foreign Affairs Committee, Sires reminds colleagues about Cuba's human rights violations and economic oppression of its people. In January 1962, Sires and his family fled Cuba during the socialist revolution and settled in Brooklyn before moving to what was then the mostly Italian city of West New York. "I experienced at the age of 11 how to take apart and put together a Czechoslovakian machine gun. I experienced the people knocking on my house door because they thought my father was carrying contraband into the black market. I remember the military coming into my house and taking inventory before I left," Sires said at a 2009 hearing. He is the ranking member on the Western Hemisphere Subcommittee in the 113th Congress (2013-14).

When his family arrived in America, his father worked in a foam rubber factory earning $1.39 an hour, and his mother was a seamstress. The family eventually saved enough money to move out of his aunt's house and into a $45-a-month cold-water flat. Sires struggled to learn English and was held back following his first year in his new school. Tall for his age, he established himself as a prolific basketball player, earning statewide accolades during his days at West New York's Memorial High School.

He went on to play at Saint Peter's College in Jersey City. After graduating with a bachelor's degree, he returned to his high school to teach Spanish and coach basketball. Meanwhile, West New York began transforming from an Italian enclave to a city consisting predominately of Cuban families.

Ethnic differences boiled over into the political scene, which in the 1980s was controlled by Anthony DeFino, a large man known as "the Mountain" who was West New York's mayor for more than two decades. DeFino worked tirelessly to crush Sires' bid for the town commission in 1983. Disillusioned with politics, Sires retreated to Vermont to earn a master's degree in Spanish from Middlebury College.

When he returned, he was recruited by state Republicans who hoped to break up Hudson County's Democratic machine. Sires had complained of nepotism and corruption among longtime officeholders.

He switched his allegiance and in 1986 ran as the GOP candidate for the House seat held by Democrat Frank J. Guarini. He got less than 30 percent of the vote in a humiliating defeat. (Once in office, though, Sires had a post office in Jersey City named for Guarini, with whom he'd developed a friendship.)

No longer teaching and once again on the losing end of a campaign, he spent a year coordinating outreach to the Hispanic community for Republican Gov. Thomas H. Kean. Although Sires ultimately left the Republican Party, claiming he always had Democratic priorities, he cites Kean as a mentor.

After working with Kean, Sires started a title insurance business and lost two bids for nonpartisan local office. When DeFino opted not to run for re-election to the town commission in 1995, Sires jumped into the race and won the mayoral slot. In 1999, he was overwhelmingly re-elected and rejoined the Democratic Party in order to set up a run for the New Jersey Legislature. He teamed up with Weehawken Mayor Richard Turner, a driving force in Hudson County Democratic circles. (Turner would serve in Sires' administration in West New York and is now his district director.)

Sires served two years in the legislature when Gov.-elect James E. McGreevey backed him to serve as speaker. A scandal involving Sires' top fundraiser, Rene Abreu, threatened to derail his political career. But while Abreu was convicted of bank fraud and spent seven years in prison, authorities couldn't link Sires to a crime. "If I did anything wrong, don't you think they would have charged me?" he asked the New York Times.

Sires spent almost four years as speaker, then ran for the House seat vacated when Robert Menendez was appointed to the Senate. Sires beat Perth Amboy Mayor Joseph Vas in 2006 in a primary marked by venomous negative ads, then easily took the very Democratic district. Even with his popularity, critics argue he has engaged in the same type of patronage he fought against three decades ago — for example, Sires' wife, Adrienne, is president of the West New York board of education, whose members are frequent contributors to his campaigns.

Sires made headlines after the Democrats lost the majority in 2010 when he publicly called for the ouster of California's Nancy Pelosi as party leader. "We need some new direction, and I think the best way is for her to move on," he said. While he opposed Pelosi's re-election as minority leader, he was not among the 18 Democratic defectors who voted for representatives other than Pelosi in the election for speaker at the start of the 112th Congress (2011-12).

Key Votes

2012	
Extend a Social Security payroll tax cut and unemployment benefits	YES
Ease securities rules to expand small-business access to capital	YES
Extend for one year subsidized student loan interest rates financed by a cut in health care spending	?
Cite Attorney General Eric H. Holder Jr. for contempt of Congress	?
Create a visa program for foreign graduates in high-tech fields	NO
Extend most Bush-era income tax rates while allowing rates for top-bracket earners to rise (Jan. 1, 2013)	YES
2011	
Strike funding for F-35 alternative engine	YES
Prevent EPA from regulating greenhouse gas emissions to address climate change	NO
Extend certain provisions of Patriot Act for four years	?
Declare opposition to use of ground troops in Libya	NO
Overhaul patent law	YES
Pass compromise debt limit increase plan and establish future spending limits	YES
Allow consideration of measures to implement three trade agreements	YES

CQ Vote Studies

	PARTY UNITY		PRESIDENTIAL SUPPORT	
	SUPPORT	OPPOSE	SUPPORT	OPPOSE
2012	95%	5%	86%	14%
2011	94%	6%	91%	9%
2010	98%	2%	86%	14%
2009	98%	2%	97%	3%
2008	99%	1%	16%	84%

Interest Groups

	AFL-CIO	ADA	CCUS	ACU
2012	90%	80%	27%	0%
2011	93%	90%	44%	0%
2010	100%	90%	14%	0%
2009	100%	100%	33%	0%
2008	100%	90%	71%	0%

New Jersey 8

Northeast — Elizabeth, Bayonne, Hoboken, parts of Jersey City and Newark

Decennial redistricting confined the 8th to a ribbon of densely populated cities and towns along the New Jersey's Hudson River waterfront, mixing both blue- and white-collar interests. The district represents downtown Elizabeth, parts of Bayonne, Jersey City and Secaucus. At Hoboken, it turns west to follow the Passaic River around a portion of Newark and into Harrison and Kearny. The district has a decidedly liberal tilt with Democratic strength among younger, minority voters.

Immigration is ingrained into the identity of the 8th. The district includes Liberty State Park, which provides spectacular views of the Statue of Liberty and Ellis Island. Nearly half of Elizabeth and more than half of West New York and Union City's populations are foreign-born, having emigrated overwhelmingly from Latin America. Substantial numbers of Indians live in the portion of Jersey City represented by the 8th. Overall, the 8th is more than two-fifths minority.

Newcomers of a different sort have flocked to Weehawken and Hoboken, as these communities have become popular enclaves for affluent young professionals commuting daily to Manhattan via the Lincoln Tunnel, PATH train or ferry.

The area has seen fits and starts of development. Harrison, north of Newark, is the site of a 25,000-seat soccer stadium complex that also includes new residential units. Some financial companies, too, have relocated to the district out of New York's financial district and midtown Manhattan. Massive Harborside Financial sits directly on the Hudson, while work has begun on the largest mixed-use development on the East Coast in the Newport neighborhood.

Newark's Liberty International Airport, shared with the 10th District, is the second-largest airport in the New York metropolitan area and is a hub for United Airlines.

Major Industry
Financial services, transportation and shipping

Cities
Newark (pt.), Jersey City (pt.), Elizabeth, Union City, West New York

Notable
The first organized game of baseball was played in Hoboken in 1846.

Rep. Bill Pascrell Jr. (D)

Capitol Office
225-5751
pascrell.house.gov
2370 Rayburn Bldg. 20515-3008; fax 225-5782

Committees
Budget
Ways & Means

Residence
Paterson

Born
Jan. 25, 1937; Paterson, N.J.

Religion
Roman Catholic

Family
Wife, Elsie Marie Pascrell; three children

Education
Fordham U., B.A. 1959 (journalism), M.A. 1961 (philosophy)

Military
Army 1961; Army Reserve, 1962-67

Career
City planning official; teacher

Political Highlights
Paterson Board of Education, 1977-81 (president, 1981); N.J. Assembly, 1988-97; mayor of Paterson, 1990-97

ELECTION RESULTS

2012 GENERAL		
Bill Pascrell Jr. (D)	162,822	74.0%
Shmuley Boteach (R)	55,091	25.0%
2012 PRIMARY		
Bill Pascrell Jr. (D)	31,435	61.2%
Steven R. Rothman (D)	19,947	38.8%
2010 GENERAL		
Bill Pascrell Jr. (D)	88,478	62.7%
Roland Straten (R)	51,023	36.1%
Raymond Giangrasso (I)	1,707	1.2%

Previous Winning Percentages
2008 (71%); 2006 (71%); 2004 (69%); 2002 (67%); 2000 (67%); 1998 (62%); 1996 (51%)

Elected 1996; 9th term

Pascrell is a fighter, and he has blue-collar Democrats in his corner. More of a neighborhood politician than a wonk, the former mayor of Paterson nonetheless has one of the more-coveted policy portfolios in Congress as a member of the Ways and Means Committee.

Although he usually saves his punches for Republicans, Pascrell won an ugly fight with another Democrat in the 112th Congress (2011-12). Eight-term Rep. Steven R. Rothman studied the electoral map created after the 2010 census and decided to take on Pascrell in the primary for the redrawn 9th District. On paper, it was blue-collar versus white-collar. Pascrell walloped Rothman by 22 points. At his victory party he gave "a special shout-out to organized labor, for police officers, teachers and our firefighters. Thank you. Thank you."

Months after that victory, Pascrell said cooperation was on his mind: "Reaching across the aisle has got to be a priority on my agenda." He said the partisanship of recent years "really stinks" and that when it comes to ideologues, Republicans "seem to have a monopoly on it lately, but probably not." Lawmakers need to "step back once in a while to see if we're contributing to it," he said.

On occasion, he has contributed. Pascrell will shoot barbs across the aisle during floor debates, and he enjoys arguing with the hosts of conservative-leaning news programs. According to The Record of Bergen County, Minority Leader Nancy Pelosi put him on the Budget Committee in the 112th Congress so he could get in the face of members with tea party sympathies. In 2013, he tore into Republicans who complained that a $50 billion disaster relief bill tied to Superstorm Sandy was full of pork projects.

Toughness comes naturally to Pascrell. He was born in Paterson, where his Italian immigrant grandparents settled. His father worked for the railroad, and Pascrell was the first member of his family to go to high school — pals razzed him when he went to college at Fordham. Years later, as mayor, he promoted a law-and-order agenda, even interfering with the communications of drug dealers by personally ripping out the lines and receivers of pay telephones that had not been issued a city permit.

Still, if he can find Republican partners, Pascrell should have opportunities to collaborate in the 113th Congress (2013-14) as the Ways and Means Committee works on a tax code overhaul.

Pascrell, who first joined the committee in 2007, agrees with Republicans that comprehensive changes are required, if only to avoid the political pitfalls of tweaking smaller portions of the tax code. He intends to be a staunch advocate for the middle class in the debate, and his past tax code proposals often had workers in mind. He introduced a measure in 2012 to improve tax incentives for "insourcing," when companies reclaim some business functions from contractors. (Pascrell has also tried to maintain tax credits and eliminate trade duties to benefit New Jersey's chemical, pharmaceutical and manufacturing interests.)

He is less likely to budge on Social Security and Medicare. In a December 2010 interview on Fox News, Pascrell argued against raising the eligibility age of Social Security. "If you extend the years ... you are hurting the very poor and the middle class," he said.

The middle class crops up in much of Pascrell's rhetoric. Should it suffer, "we're going to turn into much less than we think we are," he said. "We're still the greatest country in the world, but we can't treat it as a given." Pascrell plans to push for more government investments in education and transportation, and he is a big proponent of federal assistance for first-responders.

He did not, however, dig in against all spending cuts in the 112th Congress. Pascrell voted for a fiscal 2011 spending package with substantial cuts, as well as a deficit reduction package in August 2011.

A former member of the Homeland Security Committee, he was more willing than many House Democrats to back defense and homeland policy bills. Pascrell was one of 54 in the caucus to support a 2011 law extending surveillance provisions of the 2001 anti-terrorism law known as the Patriot Act.

Outside of his committee work, one long-standing cause has been research on, and treatment of, brain injuries. Inspired by the plight of a constituent, he was a co-founder in 2001 of the Congressional Brain Injury Task Force. In April 2008, he helped steer into law the reauthorization of a traumatic-brain-injury treatment program that offers research and rehabilitation grants to states. In 2010, the House passed a Pascrell bill that would establish new guidelines for handling concussions among school-aged athletes.

After finishing his schooling in the early 1960s, Pascrell worked as a high school history teacher in nearby Paramus. In 1974, he became director of public works for Paterson, then headed up the planning and development office. At the same time, he worked as a campaign volunteer for Democratic Rep. Robert A. Roe and others. He was appointed to the Paterson Board of Education and later was elected its president. Pascrell won a seat in the state Assembly in 1987, and starting in 1990 he simultaneously served as Paterson's mayor.

He was his party's choice to take on Rep. Bill Martini in 1996, two years after the freshman Republican's narrow victory had ended 34 years of Democratic hegemony in the 8th District. Pascrell won by less than 6,300 votes, then raised enough campaign cash to dissuade Martini from attempting a rematch.

He cruised along until 2012's bitter primary. Rothman's former home base was put in a Republican-leaning district, spurring his challenge to Pascrell, who previously represented less than half of the new 9th District. The campaign split the state and national Democratic Party. President Bill Clinton swung through the district with an endorsement for Pascrell; Rothman, who portrayed himself as more reliably liberal, got the tacit support of President Barack Obama during a White House visit. After beating Rothman, Pascrell crushed his Republican opponent in November.

Pascrell sometimes shows a soft side. He loves reading and writing poetry. And in 2009, he won a bittersweet enactment of legislation he had promoted for years to include the Great Falls in Paterson in the National Park System. As a catcher on his high school baseball team, Pascrell always walked by the falls with his mother on their way home from games. It was a place they both cherished. His 95-year-old mother, Roffie, died two days before Obama signed the proposal into law.

Key Votes

2012	
Extend a Social Security payroll tax cut and unemployment benefits	YES
Ease securities rules to expand small-business access to capital	YES
Extend for one year subsidized student loan interest rates financed by a cut in health care spending	NO
Cite Attorney General Eric H. Holder Jr. for contempt of Congress	?
Create a visa program for foreign graduates in high-tech fields	NO
Extend most Bush-era income tax rates while allowing rates for top-bracket earners to rise (Jan. 1, 2013)	YES
2011	
Strike funding for F-35 alternative engine	YES
Prevent EPA from regulating greenhouse gas emissions to address climate change	NO
Extend certain provisions of Patriot Act for four years	YES
Declare opposition to use of ground troops in Libya	YES
Overhaul patent law	YES
Pass compromise debt limit increase plan and establish future spending limits	YES
Allow consideration of measures to implement three trade agreements	NO

CQ Vote Studies

	PARTY UNITY		PRESIDENTIAL SUPPORT	
	SUPPORT	OPPOSE	SUPPORT	OPPOSE
2012	97%	3%	85%	15%
2011	94%	6%	94%	6%
2010	99%	1%	95%	5%
2009	98%	2%	97%	3%
2008	99%	1%	13%	87%

Interest Groups

	AFL-CIO	ADA	CCUS	ACU
2012	94%	95%	25%	0%
2011	96%	85%	33%	0%
2010	100%	95%	25%	4%
2009	100%	90%	36%	0%
2008	100%	95%	56%	4%

New Jersey 9

Northeast — Paterson, Clifton, Passaic

The 9th, across the Hudson River from the northern half of Manhattan and part of the Bronx, takes in New York City suburbs and a major stadium complex. It includes affluent and predominately Asian-American areas along the Hudson — Englewood Cliffs and Fort Lee — as well as ethnically diverse and lower-income Paterson, inland in Passaic County near Interstate 80 and north of the Garden State Parkway. East Rutherford, at the district's southern elbow, is home to the Meadowlands Sports Complex.

Many district residents commute to New York City and rely on the region's congested roads or mass transit. Local leaders had hoped a proposed rail tunnel connecting the area's commuters into the city would shorten travel times, but the plan was halted by the governor. New light-rail connections link the Meadowlands — which hosts football's Giants and Jets at Metlife Stadium — with Manhattan and other areas in New Jersey. The sports and entertainment hub's reputation has suffered because of a much-delayed and over-budget retail and recreation project expected to be completed in 2014. And some of the area's professional teams have left the complex: hockey's Devils have moved south to Newark (in the 10th), and soccer's Red Bulls have a stadium in Harrison (in the 8th). Across the Hackensack River from East Rutherford is Seacaucus, a mainly commercial center with some residential areas amid transit lines and light manufacturing sectors.

Drawn during decennial redistricting as a minority-majority district, the 9th is 34 percent Hispanic, 13 percent Asian and 11 percent black. The Hispanic population has grown rapidly in the last decade, especially in Clifton and Paterson in the western arm of the district. Paterson has a significant community of Dominican newcomers.

The 9th is Democratic turf and much competition here is intraparty. In the 2012 presidential election, Barack Obama won by wide margins in Fort Lee (Bergen County) and Passaic (Passaic County) and by a greater than 2-to-1 margin in the district overall.

Major Industry

Manufacturing, stadium events, transportation

Cities

Paterson, Clifton, Passaic

Notable

Teterboro Airport hosts the Aviation Hall of Fame and Museum of New Jersey and has helicopters, model airplanes and the first American hovercraft.

Rep. Donald M. Payne Jr. (D)

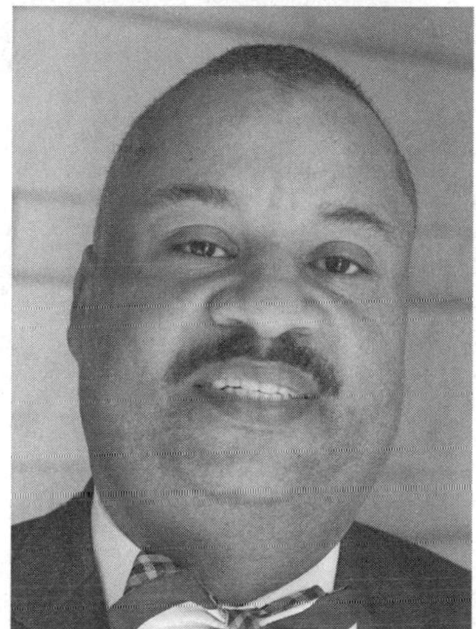

Capitol Office
225-3436
payne.house.gov
103 Cannon Bldg. 20515-3010; fax 225-4160

Committees
Homeland Security
Small Business

Residence
Newark

Born
Dec. 16, 1958; Newark, N.J.

Religion
Baptist

Family
Wife, Beatrice Payne; three children

Education
Kean College, attended 1976-78

Career
County education transportation director; state highway toll collector; computer forms company manager

Political Highlights
Essex County Board of Freeholders, 2006-12; Newark Municipal Council, 2006-12 (president, 2010-12)

ELECTION RESULTS

2012 SPECIAL		
Donald M. Payne Jr. (D)	166,413	97.4%
Joanne Miller (CHA)	4,500	2.6%
2012 GENERAL		
Donald M. Payne Jr. (D)	201,435	87.6%
Brian C. Kelemen (R)	24,271	10.6%
Joanne Miller (CHA)	3,127	1.4%
2012 PRIMARY		
Donald M. Payne Jr. (D)	36,576	59.6%
Ronald C. Rice (D)	11,939	19.5%
Nia H. Gill (D)	10,207	16.6%
Wayne Smith (D)	1,356	2.2%
Dennis R. Flynn (D)	779	1.3%
2012 PRIMARY SPECIAL		
Donald M. Payne Jr. (D)	34,358	70.7%
Ronald C. Rice (D)	11,935	24.6%
Wayne Smith (D)	2,318	4.8%

Elected 2012; 1st full term

Payne operates in the liberal Democratic tradition of his family — most notably his late father, who served in the House for more than two decades. He draws on his own experience as a member and president of the Newark city council in developing his legislative priorities.

Donald M. Payne Sr. was known as a quiet legislator who steadily looked out for his working-class constituents and, through the Foreign Affairs Committee, the people of Africa. He died in March 2012 of colon cancer, in the middle of his 24th year in Congress.

Shortly after, his son announced his intention to run for the seat, and was all but assured of winning that November. Payne secured a term in the 113th Congress (2013-14), and he simultaneously won a special election to complete the final weeks of his father's term in the 112th Congress (2011-12).

Payne has already had many opportunities to stake out his position in the Democratic Caucus, and he appears to be a reliable vote for his party. He opposed bills to freeze the salaries of federal workers and block possible changes to the work requirements in welfare programs. Studying the fiscal 2014 budget put forth by Republicans, Payne said it "destroys the safety net for working families and seniors."

At the start of the 113th Congress, he quickly joined Democrats' push for legislation to curb gun violence. Payne's first bill would create a program to provide federal money to states, local communities and approved gun dealers, for the purpose of establishing gun buy-back programs to remove handguns and semi-automatic weapons from the streets.

"The types of guns that are in my legislation are the types of guns that I have heard about on the streets of Newark, Chicago and across this nation, that are made for no other reason than to totally destroy people, kill them, cut their bodies in half," Payne said. As the father of teenage triplets (a girl and two boys), he said he is especially concerned about gun violence and its effect on youths. "As a member of the Newark city council, I witnessed countless young people suffer from this kind of violence."

Payne also pledges to defend abortion rights, support the 2010 health care overhaul, and work to end the 2002 education law known as No Child Left Behind. He says that standards set by that law are unrealistic, and that it needlessly punishes public schools that can't hope to meet them.

Like his father, he also takes an interest in Africa. Payne has advocated on behalf of Liberian refugees in his district. When civil war erupted in Liberia in the 1990s, the federal government allowed Liberians who met certain criteria to remain in the United States, even if they did not have permanent residency. That "deferred enforced departure" status was set to expire, but in March 2013 the Obama administration announced an 18-month extension — at an event hosted by Payne.

Payne sits on the Small Business Committee and says job creation, particularly in his district, is a top priority — he mentions access to capital as one of the biggest concerns of the businesses in his district. He dealt with jobs issues at the city level, as well. Payne was part of the team persuading Panasonic to move its U.S. headquarters from Secaucus to Newark. He also worked on a job-training program tailored to produce 100 job-ready residents to take a range of positions at two new major hotels in the city.

His other assignment is to the Homeland Security Committee, where he is the top Democrat on the emergency preparedness subcommittee. Payne's district includes what is sometimes called the "most dangerous two miles" in America. "We have chemical installations. We have the airport. We have the port. It's a very attractive target," he said. "I thought with that being in my district and my backyard — I live five minutes away from the airport — that it was something I felt I should be involved in."

Payne worries about the effect of smaller budgets on the Transportation Security Administration and its workers at Newark Liberty International Airport — many of them have relied on overtime pay, which is increasingly restricted or eliminated. An understaffed or tired TSA might encourage more terrorists, he said. At a March 2013 hearing, Payne criticized the TSA decision to again allow passengers to carry small knives onto planes. "Why give anyone the opportunity?" he asked. The plan was dropped in June 2013.

In the early going, Congress has been a mix of the familiar and unfamiliar, Payne said. He knew members of the Congressional Black Caucus well before he was a member of the group, and he is adjusting to the idea of them as colleagues. "They continue to try to get me to understand I am one of them, as opposed to my father's son," he said.

His father, a former Black Caucus chairman, is fondly remembered by the group. "I get stories of how he helped so many of them when they got here, the first person to reach out to them, and always had words of encouragement or some guidance," he said. Payne retained most of his father's staff when he joined the House.

Payne's mother died when he was 4, which made his father a particularly big presence in his life. Politics was always a family concern. One of his early childhood memories is being in a van, with its sound system blaring a city council campaign announcement for his uncle, William Payne (who would later serve in the state Assembly).

He was a teenager when his father started out in county government. Payne began his own political activity as a student, when he helped form the Newark South Ward Junior Democrats.

Payne left college after a few years and worked at Urban Data Systems, a computer forms company founded by his uncle William. He later held jobs as a toll collector and a student busing coordinator for Essex County, which includes Newark. He describes his political activity in those years as "doing a lot of the foot work, the grunt work, the political nuance" in support of his father's agenda.

In late 2005, he was elected to the Essex County Board of Freeholders (essentially a county council), and half a year later he was also elected to the Newark city council. He became the city council president in 2010.

Payne believes his father's death might have been averted with an earlier cancer screening. He introduced a resolution to support the designation of March as National Colorectal Cancer Awareness Month.

Key Votes

2012	
Create a visa program for foreign graduates in high-tech fields	NO
Extend most Bush-era income tax rates while allowing rates for top-bracket earners to rise (Jan. 1, 2013)	YES

CQ Vote Studies

	PARTY UNITY		PRESIDENTIAL SUPPORT	
	SUPPORT	OPPOSE	SUPPORT	OPPOSE
2012	100%	0%	100%	0%

Interest Groups

	AFL-CIO	ADA	CCUS	ACU
2012		80%	50%	

New Jersey 10

Northeast — parts of Newark, Jersey City and East Orange

The black-majority 10th heads from Montclair and the Oranges — several adjacent and directionally named townships in Essex County — in the northwest through parts of Newark before splitting to cross the Newark Bay into Jersey City and skirt Elizabeth (in the 8th District) to reach as far south as Rahway. The district provides a solid base for Democrats.

The district's portion of Newark is made up of the largely black central, south and west wards of the city. Years of urban decay, high crime and poverty have been countered by recent population growth and plans to revitalize parts of downtown. Development, aided by state subsidies, has included a new hotel, and Panasonic moved its North American headquarters to the city. The 10th's part of Newark also is home to University Heights Science Park, a collaboration among local universities and startup technology companies. The district hosts the University of Medicine and Dentistry of New Jersey, the New Jersey Institute of Technology, Essex County College and part of Rutgers University.

Newark's Liberty International Airport (shared with the 8th District) is a hub for United Airlines, and Newark's Penn Station (also shared with the 8th) is the state's busiest rail station. The station connects Amtrak, PATH and New Jersey Transit services. Port Newark-Elizabeth provides shipping jobs to the region. Many of Jersey City's residents commute into New York City or the neighboring 8th for jobs.

The state's most racially and ethnically diverse district, the 10th is home to concentrated black populations in Newark and Jersey City and Hispanic communities scattered among the 10th's townships. In the 2012 presidential contest, Barack Obama won by overwhelming margins in the district's portion of each of the counties it shares: 77 percent in Union, 84 percent in Hudson, and 91 percent in Essex, the district's most populous jurisdiction.

Major Industry
Aviation, shipping, financial services, higher education

Cities
Newark (pt.), Jersey City (pt.), East Orange

Notable
The University of Medicine and Dentistry of New Jersey is the nation's largest public university of the health sciences; The Jersey City and Harsimus Cemetery is one of the first garden-style landscape cemeteries.

Rep. Rodney Frelinghuysen (R)

Capitol Office
225-5034
frelinghuysen.house.gov
2306 Rayburn Bldg. 20515-3011; fax 225-3186

Committees
Appropriations
(Energy-Water Chairman)

Residence
Harding

Born
April 29, 1946; Manhattan, N.Y.

Religion
Episcopalian

Family
Wife, Virginia Robinson; two children

Education
Hobart College, B.A. 1969; Trinity College (Conn.), attended 1971 (American history)

Military
Army, 1969-71

Career
County board aide

Political Highlights
Morris County Board of Freeholders, 1974-83 (director, 1980); sought Republican nomination for U.S. House, 1982; N.J. Assembly, 1983-94; sought Republican nomination for U.S. House, 1990

ELECTION RESULTS

2012 GENERAL		
Rodney Frelinghuysen (R)	182,237	58.8%
John Arvanites (D)	123,897	40.0%
Barry Berlin (OCG)	3,725	1.2%
2012 PRIMARY		
Rodney Frelinghuysen (R)		unopposed
2010 GENERAL		
Rodney Frelinghuysen (R)	122,149	67.2%
Douglas Herbert (D)	55,472	30.5%
Jim Gawron (LIBERT)	4,179	2.3%

Previous Winning Percentages
2008 (62%); 2006 (72%); 2004 (68%); 2002 (72%); 2000 (68%); 1998 (68%); 1996 (66%); 1994 (71%)

Elected 1994; 10th term

Frelinghuysen is a shrewd Republican moderate. On the Appropriations Committee, he neatly stakes out centrist positions on social issues and the environment, while accommodating Republican demands for cost-cutting when he can. His low-key approach has spared him the grief heaped on other moderates in recent years.

Based on lineage alone, he should know how to be an effective lawmaker. Frelinghuysen (FREE-ling-high-zen) is the sixth member of his family to serve New Jersey in Congress. A Frelinghuysen served in the Continental Congress; three were senators, including one who later served as secretary of State and one who was Henry Clay's vice presidential running mate on the Whig ticket in 1844. His father, Peter H.B. Frelinghuysen, served in the House for 22 years, until 1975. (He died in 2011 at age 95.)

After serving in the Army in Vietnam, Frelinghuysen had extended runs in county and state government, which included time spent as the chairman of the Appropriations Committee in the New Jersey Assembly. When he came to Capitol Hill in 1995 as a freshman, he was assigned to the House's spending panel. He has been there ever since.

In the 111th Congress (2009-10), his seniority helped him land the top Republican spot on the Energy-Water Subcommittee, and he became chairman in 2011 when the GOP regained the majority. He reportedly has designs on claiming the gavel of the Defense Subcommittee, but his state is happy to see him in his current job for now — he has jurisdiction over the Army Corps of Engineers, which has a part to play in the recovery from Superstorm Sandy. (He also sits on the Homeland Security Subcommittee, which sets funding for the Federal Emergency Management Agency.)

The original relief package for Sandy was $17 billion and mostly covered immediate recovery needs. Frelinghuysen prepared an amendment adding $33 billion to the total, much of it for long-term repairs and infrastructure improvements to mitigate future disasters. Conservatives said the long-term spending could be meted out in a more fiscally responsible manner, but he held firm; 37 other House Republicans voted for his amendment, which was enough to secure adoption. The law was enacted in January 2013.

He has had other conflicts with conservatives in the past. Frelinghuysen has stronger environmental sympathies than most of his party. He opposes oil exploration off New Jersey's coast or in Alaska's Arctic National Wildlife Refuge and backs a number of land and water conservation programs. Frelinghuysen has tried to expand the Garden State's Great Swamp National Wildlife Refuge. His father sponsored the bill that established it.

But Frelinghuysen hasn't dwelled on the differences. He criticized President Barack Obama's fiscal 2013 budget for concentrating spending increases on still-developing renewable-energy programs, instead of nuclear power and fossil fuels — "the two most important energy sources for the economic recovery of our country," he said at a 2012 hearing.

Frelinghuysen supports investments in alternative-energy research, but he spoke of tough budget choices in the 112th Congress (2011-12) and produced a fiscal 2013 Energy-Water bill that would beef up fossil fuel energy research and development. It preserved funding for Yucca Mountain, the planned nuclear waste depository that the Obama administration has tried to shutter. And Frelinghuysen (well before Sandy) tried to enforce a "no new starts" policy for the Army Corps of Engineers. Completing existing projects was a better use of resources, he said. The spending bills was not enacted, however.

He did not fight Republicans who targeted the Energy Department's loan guarantee program. The 2011 bankruptcy of solar panel maker Solyndra Inc. — it had received a loan of more than $500 million — spurred complaints of government interference in the marketplace. Frelinghuysen expressed regret: "It's unfortunate that the water has sort of been poisoned here." Still, he voted in 2012 for a bill to block new guarantees for renewable-energy projects.

Frelinghuysen makes a point of acknowledging fiscal restraints on defense spending. "I tell my colleagues who have pledged to support a strong national defense that recent budgets represent the high-water mark for defense funding," he wrote on his website. "It's all downhill from here."

But in 2012, he was among the Republicans arguing that defense accounts had been cut enough. When South Carolina Republican Mick Mulvaney tried to amend an appropriations bill to freeze Pentagon spending at the previous year's level, Frelinghuysen ticked off a list of costly challenges facing the United States. "Russia wants to reclaim its former glory," he said. "China is on the fast track to a stronger military. Iran is working night and day to acquire nuclear weapons. Al-Qaida, Hezbollah and other terrorist groups continue to plot and plan. Obviously the future is challenging." Despite his efforts, the amendment was adopted.

Frelinghuysen is a leading proponent of "risk-based" allocations of homeland security funding. Such formulas favor states like New Jersey, which has high population density and many ports.

Frelinghuysen belongs to the Main Street Partnership, a bloc of moderates. Though not out front on social issues, he has voted to protect federal funding of family-planning organizations both domestically and internationally.

Some of Frelinghuysen's youth was spent in Washington. With his dad in Congress, he attended St. Albans prep school at the same time as future Vice President Albert Gore Jr.

Frelinghuysen entered politics after college and his Army service. He went to work for Dean A. Gallo, a Republican Morris County freeholder (akin to a county councilman) who later was elected to the House. Frelinghuysen became a freeholder in 1974. He lost the primary for the 12th District House seat in 1982 but won a state Assembly seat the next year. In 1990, he fell short in another attempt at nabbing the 12th District nomination.

He eventually won his House seat in 1994, but the victory was bittersweet. He took the seat of his mentor and friend Gallo, who had become ill. Gallo designated Frelinghuysen as his successor, and Frelinghuysen won easily.

Frelinghuysen is one of the wealthiest members of Congress, thanks to a number of stock and real estate holdings. A sizable chunk of his portfolio is Procter & Gamble stock. His mother, born Beatrice Sterling Procter, came from the family that founded that company.

Key Votes

2012	
Extend a Social Security payroll tax cut and unemployment benefits	YES
Ease securities rules to expand small-business access to capital	YES
Extend for one year subsidized student loan interest rates financed by a cut in health care spending	YES
Cite Attorney General Eric H. Holder Jr. for contempt of Congress	YES
Create a visa program for foreign graduates in high-tech fields	+
Extend most Bush-era income tax rates while allowing rates for top-bracket earners to rise (Jan. 1, 2013)	YES
2011	
Strike funding for F-35 alternative engine	NO
Prevent EPA from regulating greenhouse gas emissions to address climate change	+
Extend certain provisions of Patriot Act for four years	YES
Declare opposition to use of ground troops in Libya	?
Overhaul patent law	YES
Pass compromise debt limit increase plan and establish future spending limits	YES
Allow consideration of measures to implement three trade agreements	YES

CQ Vote Studies

	PARTY UNITY		PRESIDENTIAL SUPPORT	
	SUPPORT	OPPOSE	SUPPORT	OPPOSE
2012	87%	13%	22%	78%
2011	90%	10%	31%	69%
2010	91%	9%	29%	71%
2009	77%	23%	42%	58%
2008	87%	13%	73%	27%

Interest Groups

	AFL-CIO	ADA	CCUS	ACU
2012	19%	100%	91%	72%
2011	0%	20%	100%	60%
2010	7%	5%	88%	88%
2009	19%	15%	93%	68%
2008	13%	15%	100%	80%

New Jersey 11

North central — eastern Morris County, Wayne

Located in northern New Jersey, mostly within Morris County — home to exclusive pastoral estates and Fortune 500 firms — the 11th District also takes in affluent areas of Essex, Passaic and Sussex counties. The district is predominately white, wealthy and well-educated.

Residents here bring home among the nation's highest median household incomes ($94,000) to mainly small and midsize bedroom communities connected by interstate highways and state routes amid parks, country clubs and nature preserves. Population growth in the district has been driven by couples and families moving in to get away from the region's large cities; suburban sprawl is a concern for longtime residents.

Much of the white-collar workforce, especially in the eastern half of the district, commutes to New York City, but the 11th also hosts its own large international corporations. Novartis in East Hanover and Atlantic Health in Morristown are the two largest employers in the district, providing stability to the regional health care sector since the decline of Morris Plains-based Pfizer pharmaceuticals. Toys "R" Us is based in Wayne, and Honeywell has its corporate headquarters in Morristown. In all, nearly 50 Fortune 500 companies have headquarters or major facilities in the 11th.

The new boundaries of the 11th following decennial redistricting include many Hispanic residents, with large concentrations in Morristown, but most of the region's minority populations were drawn into the adjacent 7th and 9th districts. Fiscally conservative, the 11th leans Republican, and Mitt Romney won 52 percent of the district's 2012 presidential vote.

Major Industry
Health care, professional services, telecommunications

Military Bases
Picatinny Arsenal (Army), 100 military, 3,900 civilian

Cities
Morristown, Madison, Rockaway

Notable
Morristown's Frelinghuysen Arboretum is a mansion bequeathed to the town by the Frelinghuysen family and today serves as the headquarters of the Morris County Park Commission — Rodney Frelinghuysen, a distant cousin of the home's original occupant, represents the 11th in the U.S. House.

Rep. Rush D. Holt (D)

Capitol Office
225-5801
holt.house.gov
1214 Longworth Bldg. 20515-3012; fax 225-6025

Committees
Education & the Workforce
Natural Resources

Residence
Hopewell Township

Born
Oct. 15, 1948; Weston, W.Va.

Religion
Quaker

Family
Wife, Margaret Lancefield; three children

Education
Carleton College, B.A. 1970 (physics); New York U., M.S. 1980 (physics), Ph.D. 1981 (physics)

Career
University research assistant director; U.S. State Department strategic science official; physics professor

Political Highlights
Sought Democratic nomination for U.S. House, 1996

ELECTION RESULTS

2012 GENERAL		
Rush D. Holt (D)	189,926	69.2%
Eric A. Beck (R)	80,906	29.5%
2012 PRIMARY		
Rush D. Holt (D)		unopposed
2010 GENERAL		
Rush D. Holt (D)	108,214	53.0%
Scott Sipprelle (R)	93,634	45.9%
Kenneth J. Cody (TVH)	2,154	1.1%

Previous Winning Percentages
2008 (63%); 2006 (66%); 2004 (59%); 2002 (61%); 2000 (49%); 1998 (50%)

Elected 1998; 8th term

Holt's father was a senator, but his own background as a physicist has just as much bearing on his approach to politics. He sees his very liberal positions as standing on an analytical foundation. "We need, in this country, to return to a scientific frame of mind," he said. "If we were more evidence-based in our thinking, we would do things differently."

On leaving Princeton University's Plasma Physics Laboratory in 1997, Holt aspired either to write a book on his father, Rush Dew Holt, or to serve in Congress. "From my earliest memories, I've been interested in how people get along — that's politics — and how the world works — that's science," he said.

The elder Holt was elected to the U.S. Senate in 1934 from West Virginia; at 29, he was the youngest person elected to the chamber, and he had to wait six months to take office in order to meet the Constitution's age requirement for the job. Although he started as an ardent supporter of President Franklin D. Roosevelt, Holt shifted to the right, becoming a critic of the New Deal and a staunch isolationist. He lost his re-election bid and died shortly after a 1952 run for governor — on the Republican ticket.

The younger Holt, however, has been a solid Democrat during the past decade. He belongs to the New Democrat Coalition, traditionally a more business-friendly faction, but he is also a member of the liberal Congressional Progressive Caucus. Holt sides with most of his party on the overwhelming majority of votes where they oppose a majority of Republicans.

He brings that record — and a nearly perfect lifetime score from the League of Conservation Voters — to the Natural Resources Committee. Since 2011, he has been the ranking member of the Subcommittee on Energy and Mineral Resources.

Holt has tried to serve as a foil to Republican efforts to expand oil and gas production on private and public lands. He is an opponent of hydraulic fracturing, or "fracking," which involves injecting pressurized water mixed with sand and chemicals deep underground to release natural gas and petroleum embedded in rock seams. Its defenders have cited decades of fracking regulated by the states, while Holt and others have called for tighter EPA regulation because of concerns that groundwater may be contaminated by the process.

"Extracting natural gas should not threaten public health or pollute our water," Holt wrote in early 2011. "Our loyalties shouldn't be with oil and gas companies — our loyalties should be with families affected by fracking."

Holt opposes new drilling on the outer continental shelf and opening the Arctic National Wildlife Refuge to oil and gas development. He supports legislative efforts to regulate or curtail greenhouse gas emissions; he also favors tax credits and other federal investments to encourage the production of energy from renewable sources.

He has been at the forefront of trying to slow suburban sprawl and has worked to replenish the Land and Water Conservation Fund, a federal program providing funds to governments to purchase land, water and wetlands with the goal of preserving open spaces. He has repeatedly fought against cuts to the program and helped restore its state-side grant portion early in his career.

From his post on the Education and the Workforce Committee, Holt has actively promoted math and science education. Holt wrote several science and technology provisions in a 2008 higher education law, including a program providing loan forgiveness for students committed to serve in science, technology, engineering or math (STEM) fields after graduation.

Holt appreciated the theory of the 2002 federal education law known as No

Child Left Behind, if not the practice. The law's central premises — that every student make adequate progress and that schools be held accountable for student advancement — were reasonable, but the implementation "has been close to a disaster. ... It ended up being formulaic in the testing that needed to be done, which, in many cases, is not very relevant to the students' progress."

More federal attention should go to professional development programs for teachers, Holt said. When panel Republicans pushed two bills in 2012 as part of an attempted education law rewrite, Holt said they "ignored science education altogether." He introduced legislation in 2011 and 2013 to provide certain full-time school teachers of STEM courses with a tax credit for 10 percent of their undergraduate tuition.

Holt can be scathing when venting frustrations. He called fiscally conservative Republicans "hostage-takers" for using a possible breach of the federal debt limit to force spending reductions in August 2011; he rejects what he calls the "inane premise of the tea party ... that our nation is defined by its debt."

Outside of his congressional accomplishments, Holt's claim to fame might be his five wins on the TV quiz show "Jeopardy!" In 2011, he beat the IBM Watson computer in a round of the game show. "I didn't expect to win," Holt said. "This Watson software is a really pretty important step, and it was an opportunity to highlight research."

Holt developed his interest in science at an early age from his mother, who taught science at a junior college. She was also a West Virginia state legislator and secretary of state. When Holt's father died, he and his mother moved to Washington, D.C., where he went to high school and she worked for the Department of Housing and Urban Development.

Holt earned a doctorate in physics after completing a dissertation about the outer layer of the sun. He holds a patent for improving the efficiency of solar ponds, a source of thermal energy. After school, he worked at the State Department on arms control and space activities before becoming assistant director of the Princeton laboratory. While working there, he ran for Congress in 1996, losing in the Democratic primary to David M. Del Vecchio, who in turn lost a close race to Republican Michael Pappas.

Less than two years later, Holt quit the lab and focused on his campaign. He portrayed Pappas as too conservative for the district, and his 5,000-vote victory placed Holt high on the GOP's list of targeted incumbents in 2000. His campaign against moderate Republican Dick Zimmer, who had held the House seat for three terms ending in 1996, was bitter. The outcome was in doubt for three weeks after Election Day. Holt eventually was declared the victor by 651 votes. His district's borders were shifted substantially for the 2012 election, and Holt took 69 percent of the vote — his best showing to date.

Key Votes

2012	
Extend a Social Security payroll tax cut and unemployment benefits	YES
Ease securities rules to expand small-business access to capital	NO
Extend for one year subsidized student loan interest rates financed by a cut in health care spending	NO
Cite Attorney General Eric H. Holder Jr. for contempt of Congress	NO
Create a visa program for foreign graduates in high-tech fields	NO
Extend most Bush-era income tax rates while allowing rates for top-bracket earners to rise (Jan. 1, 2013)	YES
2011	
Strike funding for F-35 alternative engine	YES
Prevent EPA from regulating greenhouse gas emissions to address climate change	NO
Extend certain provisions of Patriot Act for four years	NO
Declare opposition to use of ground troops in Libya	NO
Overhaul patent law	YES
Pass compromise debt limit increase plan and establish future spending limits	NO
Allow consideration of measures to implement three trade agreements	NO

CQ Vote Studies

	PARTY UNITY		PRESIDENTIAL SUPPORT	
	SUPPORT	OPPOSE	SUPPORT	OPPOSE
2012	98%	2%	87%	13%
2011	97%	3%	83%	17%
2010	99%	1%	90%	10%
2009	99%	1%	97%	3%
2008	98%	2%	15%	85%

Interest Groups

	AFL-CIO	ADA	CCUS	ACU
2012	100%	100%	18%	0%
2011	100%	95%	19%	4%
2010	100%	100%	13%	0%
2009	100%	100%	33%	0%
2008	100%	100%	61%	0%

New Jersey 12

Central — Trenton, Princeton, East Brunswick, Plainfield

The 12th sits in the middle of the state in Mercer, Middlesex and Somerset counties with a slice of Union County to the northeast. It takes in parts of Trenton, Princeton and areas outside New Brunswick (in the 6th) before crossing a thin stretch of Interstate 287 to head north to Plainfield. Decennial reapportionment cost New Jersey one of its U.S. House seats, and the district lost its portions of Hunterdon County, including some wealthy townships along the Delaware River, as well as the eastern reaches near the Atlantic Ocean during the remapping process.

Almost half of the district's population is made up of minority residents, with nearly even splits among blacks (18 percent), Hispanics (15 percent) and Asians (15 percent). The district splits Trenton with the 4th, placing most of the city's African-American population in the 12th. The district's largely blue-collar section of Trenton includes the state Capitol, as well as the governor's official residence, the stately and imposing Drumthwacket. Some midsize communities, such as Ewing in Mercer County, have had to contend with the effects of suburban sprawl, but many areas along the Delaware River retain a small-town charm.

Princeton University is central New Jersey's largest employer and helps drive the regional economy. University-related jobs keep a stable, educated workforce in the district, and the well-established health care sector revolves around the medical center and serves a significant local elderly population. Part of a Rutgers University campus near New Brunswick and several large hospitals in neighboring districts are other key employers.

The Ivy League academics at Princeton anchor a solidly Democratic constituency in Mercer County, once an old-money and suburban haven. Liberal-leaning independent voters also tend to erode any historical Republican strength here.

Major Industry
Higher education, health care

Cities
Trenton (pt.), Old Bridge (unincorporated), South River

Notable
The New Jersey State Museum in Trenton boasts four venues: archeology, fine arts, cultural history and natural history museums.

NEW MEXICO

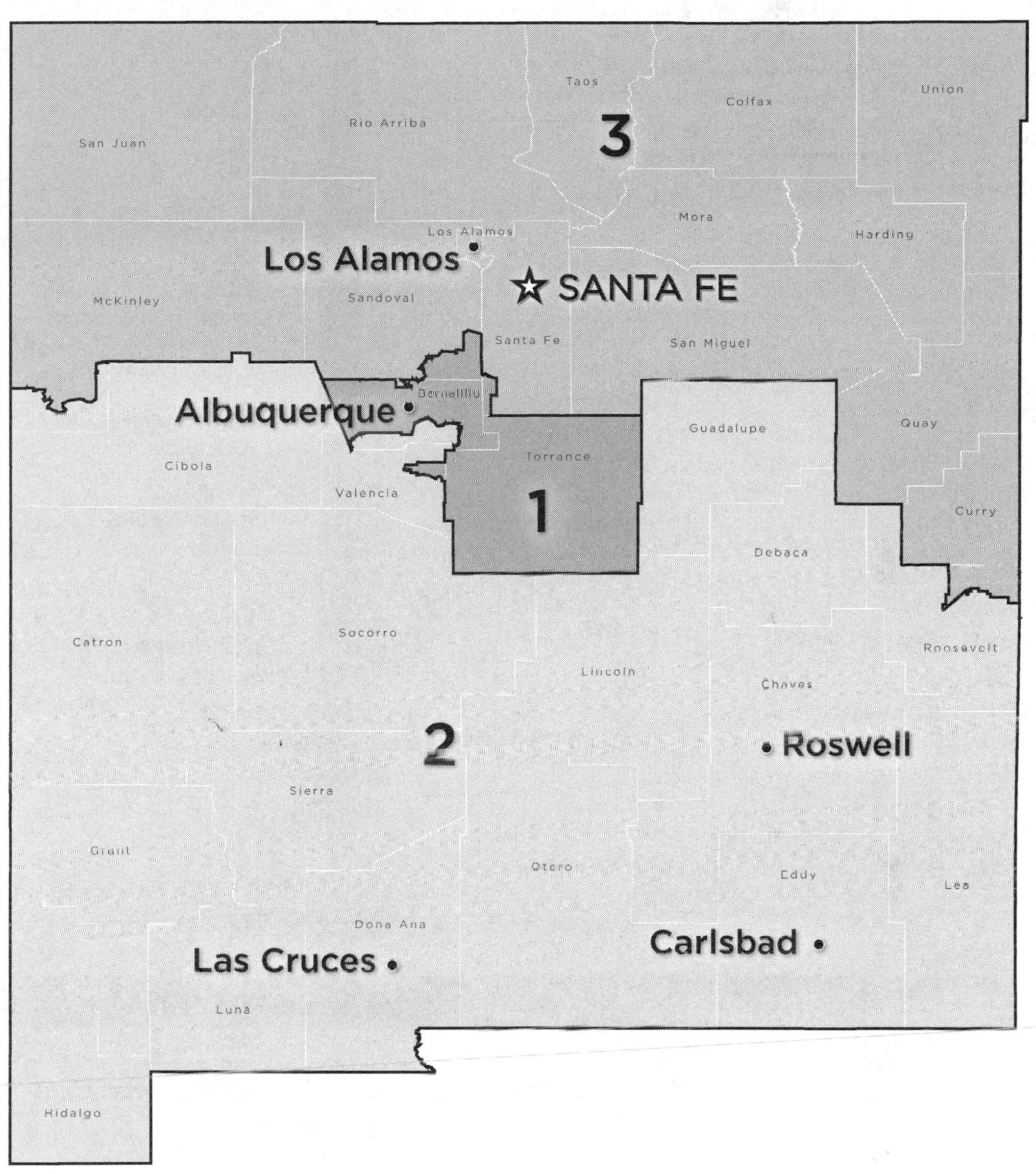
Taos
Colfax
Union
Rio Arriba
San Juan
3
Mora
Harding
Los Alamos
Los Alamos
SANTA FE
McKinley
Sandoval
Santa Fe
San Miguel
Albuquerque
Guadalupe
Quay
Cibola
Torrance
Valencia
1
Curry
Debaca
Catron
Socorro
Roosevelt
Lincoln
Chaves
2
Roswell
Sierra
Grant
Otero
Eddy
Lea
Dona Ana
Carlsbad
Las Cruces
Luna
Hidalgo

Gov. Susana Martinez (R)

First elected: 2010

Length of term: 4 years

Term expires: 1/15

Salary: $110,000

Phone: (505) 476-2200

Residence: Las Cruces

Born: July 14, 1959; El Paso, Texas

Religion: Roman Catholic

Family: Husband, Chuck Franco; one step-child

Education: U. of Texas, El Paso, B.A. 1981 (criminal justice); U. of Oklahoma, J.D. 1986

Career: County prosecutor; state government agency lawyer

Political highlights: N.M. 3rd Judicial Circuit district attorney, 1996-2010

ELECTION RESULTS

2010 GENERAL

Susana Martinez (R)	321,219	53.3%
Diane D. Denish (D)	280,614	46.7%

Lt. Gov. John A. Sanchez (R)

First elected: 2010

Length of term: 4 years

Term expires: 1/15

Salary: $85,000

Phone: (505) 476-2250

LEGISLATURE

Legislature: 60 days January-March in odd-numbered years; 30 days January-February in even-numbered years

Senate: 42 members, 4-year terms

2013 ratios: 25 D, 17 R; 36 men, 6 women

Salary: $154/day

Phone: (505) 986-4714

House: 70 members, 2-year terms

2013 ratios: 38 D, 32 R; 45 men, 25 women

Salary: $154/day

Phone: (505) 986-4751

TERM LIMITS

Governor: 2 consecutive terms

Senate: No

House: No

URBAN STATISTICS

CITY	POPULATION
Albuquerque	545,852
Las Cruces	97,618
Rio Rancho	87,521
Santa Fe	67,947
Roswell	48,366

REGISTERED VOTERS

Democrat	47%
Republican	31%
Others	22%

POPULATION

2010 population	2,059,179
2000 population	1,819,046
1990 population	1,515,069
Percent change (2000-2010)	+13.2%
Rank among states (2010)	36
Median age	35.5
Born in state	51.7%
Foreign born	9.1%
Violent crime rate	619/100,000
Poverty level	18.0%
Federal workers	50,045
Military	11,038

ELECTIONS

STATE ELECTION OFFICIAL
(505) 827-3600

DEMOCRATIC PARTY
(505) 830-3650

REPUBLICAN PARTY
(505) 298-3662

MISCELLANEOUS

Web: www.newmexico.gov

Capital: Santa Fe

U.S. CONGRESS

Senate: 2 Democrats

House: 2 Democrats, 1 Republican

STATISTICS BY DISTRICT

District	2012 Vote for President Obama	2012 Vote for President Romney	2008 Vote for President Obama	2008 Vote for President McCain	Black	Asian	Hispanic	Median Income	Over 64	Under 20	College Education	Rural	Sq. Miles
1	55%	40%	60%	39%	3%	2%	48%	$43,618	13%	26%	31%	8%	4,600
2	45	52	48	50	2	1	52	37,252	14	29	20	31	71,739
3	58	39	61	38	2	1	40	44,467	13	28	26	35	44,959
STATE	**53**	**43**	**57**	**42**	**2**	**1**	**46**	**41,963**	**14**	**28**	**25**	**25**	**121,298**
U.S.	**51**	**47**	**53**	**46**	**12**	**5**	**17**	**50,052**	**13**	**27**	**29**	**21**	**3,531,905**

Sen. Tom Udall (D)

Capitol Office
224-6621
tomudall.senate.gov
110 Hart Bldg. 20510; fax 228-3261

Committees
Appropriations
Environment & Public Works
(Superfund, Toxics & Environmental Health - Chairman)
Foreign Relations
(Western Hemisphere & Global Narcotics Affairs - Chairman)
Indian Affairs
Rules & Administration
Joint Printing

Residence
Santa Fe

Born
May 18, 1948; Tucson, Ariz.

Religion
Mormon

Family
Wife, Jill Z. Cooper; one child

Education
Prescott College, B.A. 1970 (government & political science); Cambridge U., B.L.L. 1975; U. of New Mexico, J.D. 1977

Career
Lawyer; congressional aide

Political Highlights
Assistant U.S. attorney, 1978-81; sought Democratic nomination for U.S. House, 1982; Democratic nominee for U.S. House, 1988; N.M. attorney general, 1991-99; U.S. House, 1999-2009

ELECTION RESULTS

2008 GENERAL

Tom Udall (D)	505,128	61.3%
Steve Pearce (R)	318,522	38.7%

2008 PRIMARY

Tom Udall (D)	unopposed

Previous Winning Percentages
2006 House Election (75%); 2004 House Election (69%); 2002 House Election (100%); 2000 House Election (67%); 1998 House Election (53%)

Elected 2008; 1st term

Udall's first term has been a mix of traditional and radical. As major bills have passed through his committees, he has often kept his head down and let senior Democrats take the lead. His campaign against some of the Senate's established procedures, however, demonstrates his interest in a more free-wheeling chamber.

The retirement of Democrat Jeff Bingaman has made Udall his state's senior senator in just his fifth year on the job. Still, he is no stranger to Congress. Udall served 10 years in the House and has a long political bloodline. His father, Stewart L. Udall, represented Arizona in the House and was secretary of Interior under presidents John F. Kennedy and Lyndon B. Johnson. His uncle, Morris K. Udall, succeeded Stewart in the House in 1961 and was a well-known leader on environmental protection for 30 years. (He also made a presidential bid in 1976.)

Udall sits on the Environment and Public Works Committee but hasn't gained much attention for environmentalism thus far. Instead, the media has noted his efforts to change Senate rules and tighten campaign finance laws. Udall and several other relatively junior Democrats, including Mark Begich of Alaska and Jeff Merkley of Oregon, stumped at the start of the 112th Congress (2011-12) for a change to filibuster rules: namely, reducing the 60-vote threshold needed to cut off debate and force votes.

His seat on the Rules and Administration Committee made Udall a big player in the effort, which fell short; the chamber adopted only a ban on secret holds on nominations. He was back on the case as the start of the 113th Congress (2013-14) approached, writing in USA Today that a senator delaying a nomination or bill "should be required to hold the floor and explain the reasons why to the American people."

A few more rules changes meant to limit filibusters were approved in January 2013, and Udall has already vowed to renew his efforts in the 114th Congress (2015-16), assuming he wins a second term. He quoted his uncle Morris: "Reform is not for the short-winded."

With the blessing of Democrats, he is also aggressive when it comes to campaign finance law. Udall has backed measures to undo the Supreme Court's 2010 Citizens United ruling, which allowed the creation of super PACs — advocacy groups independent of official campaigns that can accept unrestricted donations from individuals or organizations. "What campaigns were about was the candidate with the best idea," Udall said at a news conference announcing the 2012 legislation. "We're now in an auction situation, in my mind."

Outside of those subjects, a lot of Udall's initiatives have been small-bore. But the departure of Bingaman made him the dean of the New Mexico delegation, and he also took a seat on the Appropriations Committee in 2013 — as well as its Energy-Water and Interior-Environment panels. He is positioned to lead on issues of great importance to his state, which has Los Alamos and Sandia national laboratories, huge tracts of federal land and a stake in the renewable-energy industry.

Udall has a track record in that regard. As a member of the House Natural Resources Committee, he backed new wilderness designations for the West; as a senator in 2009, he supported a law giving 16,000 acres that designation. In 2010, he sought an active role in striking a deal on curbing carbon dioxide emissions, and he supports the idea that the EPA can use regulations to achieve what congressional Democrats cannot.

He balances support for alternative energy with New Mexico's position as a major oil and natural gas producer. Udall is a leading proponent of requiring states to obtain a certain portion of their electricity from renewable sources. (New Mexico already has such a standard.) In 2007, the House passed as part of an energy package his language for a 15 percent national mandate for retail electricity production from renewable sources by 2020. The proposal died in the Senate, but Udall has still pursued it.

Udall also holds the gavel of the Environment and Public Works Subcommittee on Superfund, Toxics and Environmental Health. He has looked for ways to expedite the cleanup of old uranium mines in his state.

On the Foreign Relations Committee, Udall has stood to the left. He is skeptical of continued U.S. involvement in Afghanistan, and he called NATO airstrikes on Libya in 2011 a "slippery path." He sides with civil liberties advocates in pressing for privacy protections in national security laws. He chairs the panel on the Western Hemisphere and drug trafficking — relations with Mexico are very important to his state. He is also a member of the Commission on Security and Cooperation in Europe.

He looks out for the numerous American Indian tribes in his state as a member of the Indian Affairs Committee. He successfully incorporated a permanent authorization of various Indian health care initiatives in the 2010 health care law. A 2013 reauthorization of programs to fight and prosecute violence against women contained provisions he favored to address domestic violence in tribal communities. Udall's wife was a New Mexico officer of cultural affairs and works at the Smithsonian Institution's National Museum of the American Indian.

Udall was elected to the Senate at the same time as his cousin Mark, a Democrat from Colorado. (Mark also served five terms in the House.) Tom Udall's voting record is a tad more liberal and loyal than his cousin's: In 2011 and 2012, he never voted against a majority of Democrats when they opposed a majority of Republicans. Mark is more outgoing than Tom and has positioned himself more prominently on debt discussions, while New Mexico's stronger Democratic lean makes that issue less pressing for Tom.

He staked out one of the more liberal positions on health care in the 111th Congress (2009-10), calling for the creation of a government-run "public option" insurance plan. It was not included in the overhaul law. There are times he'll go with his state's Western culture, though — Udall will vote against some proscriptions of gun owners' rights.

Udall was born in Arizona, the state where the Udall clan is centered. After earning degrees from both Prescott College and England's Cambridge University, he entered law school at the University of New Mexico, graduating in 1977. He stayed in the state as an appeals court law clerk, then worked as an assistant U.S. attorney and chief counsel to the state Department of Health and Environment before going into private practice.

Udall made two unsuccessful runs for the House: He lost the 1982 Democratic primary to Bill Richardson, who went on to serve as governor, and the 1988 election to Republican Steven H. Schiff. He became attorney general in 1991. He made a third try for the House in 1998, winning an eight-candidate primary, then handily beating the incumbent, Republican Bill Redmond. He regularly won re-election with at least two-thirds of the vote and seemed a natural favorite to succeed Pete V. Domenici when the veteran Republican senator announced in 2007 that he would not seek a seventh term.

But Udall initially turned down a chance to run, saying his seat on the House Appropriations Committee was his best opportunity to serve his state. He eventually bowed to pressure from the national Democratic Party.

His opponent in the race was House colleague Steve Pearce, a conservative from the state's southeastern corner. Pearce sought to portray Udall as too liberal for New Mexico, but it was an ill-timed message in a state that gave 57 percent of the presidential vote to Barack Obama. Udall won easily.

Key Votes

2012	
Prohibit health insurance plans from denying coverage based on the sponsor's religious beliefs	YES
Require approval of the Keystone XL oil pipeline	NO
Ease securities rules to expand small-business access to capital	NO
Reauthorize farm and nutrition programs for five years	YES
Limit debate on a bill that would create private-sector cybersecurity standards	YES
Consent to ratification of a treaty setting global standard for the treatment of people with disabilities	YES
Provide $60.4 billion in disaster relief following Superstorm Sandy	YES
Extend most Bush-era income tax rates while allowing rates for top-bracket earners to rise (Jan. 1, 2013)	YES
2011	
Prevent EPA from regulating greenhouse gas emissions to address climate change	NO
Extend certain provisions of Patriot Act for four years	NO
Clear compromise debt limit increase plan and establish future spending limits	YES
Overhaul patent law	YES
Implement Colombia free trade agreement	NO
Limit debate on confirmation of Caitlin J. Halligan to D.C. Circuit Court of Appeals	YES
Extend payroll tax cut and unemployment benefits for two months	YES

CQ Vote Studies

	PARTY UNITY		PRESIDENTIAL SUPPORT	
	SUPPORT	OPPOSE	SUPPORT	OPPOSE
2012	100%	0%	96%	4%
2011	100%	0%	94%	6%
2010	98%	2%	97%	3%
2009	96%	4%	96%	4%
2008	96%	4%	14%	86%
2007	98%	2%	3%	97%
2006	96%	4%	10%	90%
2005	97%	3%	11%	89%
2004	95%	5%	21%	79%
2003	97%	3%	18%	82%

Interest Groups

	AFL-CIO	ADA	CCUS	ACU
2012	100%	100%	38%	0%
2011	95%	95%	55%	5%
2010	100%	95%	18%	0%
2009	100%	100%	43%	8%
2008	100%	90%	47%	12%
2007	96%	100%	47%	0%
2006	100%	95%	29%	4%
2005	100%	95%	41%	0%
2004	93%	100%	29%	8%
2003	100%	100%	23%	12%

Sen. Martin Heinrich (D)

Capitol Office
224-5521
heinrich.senate.gov
702 Hart Bldg 20510; fax 228-0832

Committees
Energy & Natural Resources
Select Intelligence
Joint Economic

Residence
Albuquerque

Born
Oct. 17, 1971; Fallon, Nev.

Religion
Lutheran

Family
Wife, Julie Heinrich; two children

Education
U. of Missouri, B.S. 1995 (mechanical engineering); U. of New Mexico, attended 2001-02

Career
State natural resources director; community advocacy consultant; outdoor education nonprofit director; AmeriCorps volunteer; mechanical engineering draftsman

Political Highlights
Albuquerque City Council, 2003-07 (president, 2005-06); U.S. House, 2009-13

ELECTION RESULTS

2012 GENERAL		
Martin Heinrich (D)	395,717	51.0%
Heather A. Wilson (R)	351,260	45.3%
Jon R. Barrie (IA)	28,199	3.6%
2012 PRIMARY		
Martin Heinrich (D)	83,432	58.9%
Hector Balderas (D)	58,128	41.1%
2010 HOUSE GENERAL		
Martin Heinrich (D)	112,010	51.8%
Jon Barela (R)	104,215	48.2%

Previous winning percentages
2008 House Election (56%)

Elected 2012; 1st term

Heinrich is most known for his efforts to protect the environment. Elected to the Senate in 2012 after two terms representing Albuquerque in the House, he figures to continue that work, particularly through the formulation of energy policy.

He is generally supportive of energy strategies the Democratic Party has pursued in recent years: attempting to nurture "clean" energy by granting incentives for solar and wind producers, and making it more expensive to produce energy through the burning of fossil fuels. He supported a 2009 bill to create a cap-and-trade system to regulate greenhouse gas emissions. It passed the House but died in the Senate.

Heinrich (HINE-rick) can pursue those objectives from the Energy and Natural Resources Committee, where he steps into the shoes of its retired former chairman, New Mexico Democrat Jeff Bingaman.

Heinrich built up his own energy track record in four years on the House Natural Resources Committee. He proposed an "Apollo Project" for energy independence, reminiscent of the 1960s space exploration initiative. His plan called for an "everything" agenda incorporating the efforts of government, industry, labor, nonprofits and academics. He favors the continued use of nuclear power, and he co-sponsored legislation to require a percentage of electricity sold to be generated from renewable sources.

He also promoted legislation to give the Bureau of Land Management dedicated funding to process a backlog in alternative-energy project applications and facilitate future projects on public lands. The economic use of federal property is a hot topic in Western states, with Republicans taking a far more permissive stance than most Democrats. Heinrich has tried to split the difference between development and conservation.

Heinrich is an outdoorsman who feeds his children the elk and deer he kills hunting in the New Mexico wilderness — he favors the use of public lands for such activities. He is open to other economic uses, such as mining, but says that it's appropriate to put restrictions on many parcels. "Not every use should happen on every acre," he says. "Then you lose some of the very special places that drive our economy in Western states."

He continues to spend a lot of his free time hunting. Heinrich and his wife enjoy experimenting with different game recipes. "Some people have trophies on their wall. Mine are in the freezer," he says.

In the House, Heinrich served on the Armed Services Committee, and he sought a seat on the Senate's equivalent. Democrats couldn't find room there, but Heinrich was assigned to the Intelligence and Joint Economic panels. He says the Intelligence Committee was a good fallback, since it also has a say in funding and policies related to his state's national laboratories, Sandia and Los Alamos.

On economic issues, Heinrich leans to the left but is willing to meet the opposition in the middle. In 2011, he voted for compromise spending and deficit reduction packages that split House Democrats. During the budget talks that dominated the end of 2012, he opposed efforts to cut Social Security and raise the Medicare eligibility age. But he said he was open to greater means testing of Medicare benefits. He supported President Barack Obama's push for higher tax rates on the wealthy.

Heinrich has followed a twisting path that took him from origins as a Midwestern farm boy — he grew up on his parents' cattle ranch in central Missouri — to his job as a Western senator. His father, a German immigrant whose support for Franklin D. Roosevelt inspired Heinrich's interest in politics, was a utility lineman. His mother sewed Levis and later worked in a factory that made wheel rims for cars. On the side, they bred calves for sale.

After graduating from the University of Missouri in 1995 with a degree in mechanical engineering, Heinrich pursued work in St. Louis. But his wife, Julie, whom he'd met at the university, was intrigued by the New Mexico portrayed in Rudolfo Anaya's classic novel "Bless Me, Ultima," a coming-of-age tale set in the state's rural Chicano culture. "It just started a conversation where she said to me, 'If this job you are looking at in St. Louis doesn't work out, what do you think of New Mexico?'" he recalled. The job in St. Louis never materialized, and "the more we talked about it, we just talked ourselves into packing up the car and driving out there."

He had no job lined up, but he eventually landed with a contractor doing mechanical drawings at Kirtland Air Force Base. Less than a year later, he left to join AmeriCorps, the national service program started in the Clinton administration. He worked on a Mexican wolf recovery project sponsored by the Interior Department. Heinrich remains the only member of Congress to have served as an AmeriCorps volunteer.

Heinrich kept stockpiling good will with the environmental community. He took a job as executive director of the Cottonwood Gulch Foundation, which enrolls children in wilderness education programs. He left that post in 2001, and in 2003 he launched a bid for the Albuquerque City Council, running on a conservation platform. He won, and his fundraising prowess caught the attention of Democratic operatives. In 2006, Gov. Bill Richardson named him to a state post overseeing the restoration of areas contaminated by hazardous materials, a job he held concurrently with his council seat.

As a councilman, Heinrich helped establish a federal wilderness area northwest of Albuquerque and pushed for the city to acquire open-space land while supporting new green-building codes, curbside recycling and incentives for hybrid vehicles.

When 1st District Republican Rep. Heather A. Wilson opted to run for the Senate in 2008, Heinrich decided to make a bid for Congress. The Democratic tide that year helped Heinrich take nearly 56 percent of the vote against Republican Darren White, the Bernalillo County sheriff.

The tide reversed in 2010, helping Republican businessman Jon Barela tie Heinrich to unpopular Democratic policies, such as the 2010 health care law. But Heinrich struck back, attacking his opponent for favoring lax Wall Street regulation and President George W. Bush's policies. He rode strong fundraising to victory, with nearly 52 percent of the vote.

Bingaman's retirement cleared a path to the Senate. After securing the Democratic nomination, he faced Wilson, an Air Force veteran and Rhodes scholar who made her name on national security issues during five terms in the House. She had been out of politics since losing in 2008. Wilson criticized Heinrich for supporting a 2011 budget deal that threatened big defense cuts, potentially hurting New Mexico's Kirtland Air Force Base and its laboratories. Heinrich touted his work on the Armed Services panel to protect the budgets of those facilities.

Meanwhile, environmental groups swung into action, paying for close to $2 million in ads criticizing Wilson's environmental positions.

Heinrich appealed to the state's large Hispanic population by calling for legislation to create a path to citizenship for illegal immigrants brought to the country as children. Wilson declined to state a position. And Heinrich won over the state's American Indian population by pursuing legislation, signed by Obama in 2012, to make it easier for American Indians to buy homes on tribal land.

He had a strong showing among Hispanics and in the state's biggest cities. Wilson ran several points ahead of GOP presidential nominee Mitt Romney, but Heinrich still secured 51 percent of the vote.

Key Votes (while House member)

2012	
Extend a Social Security payroll tax cut and unemployment benefits	YES
Ease securities rules to expand small-business access to capital	YES
Extend for one year subsidized student loan interest rates financed by a cut in health care spending	NO
Cite Attorney General Eric H. Holder Jr. for contempt of Congress	NO
Create a visa program for foreign graduates in high-tech fields	NO
Extend most Bush-era income tax rates while allowing rates for top-bracket earners to rise (Jan. 1, 2013)	YES
2011	
Strike funding for F-35 alternative engine	YES
Prevent EPA from regulating greenhouse gas emissions to address climate change	NO
Extend certain provisions of Patriot Act for four years	NO
Declare opposition to use of ground troops in Libya	NO
Overhaul patent law	YES
Pass compromise debt limit increase plan and establish future spending limits	YES
Allow consideration of measures to implement three trade agreements	NO

CQ Vote Studies (while House member)

	PARTY UNITY		PRESIDENTIAL SUPPORT	
	SUPPORT	OPPOSE	SUPPORT	OPPOSE
2012	91%	9%	85%	15%
2011	90%	10%	91%	9%
2010	97%	3%	95%	5%
2009	94%	6%	87%	13%

Interest Groups (while House member)

	AFL-CIO	ADA	CCUS	ACU
2012	95%	75%	18%	8%
2011	100%	85%	31%	4%
2010	100%	100%	13%	0%
2009	100%	100%	40%	4%

Rep. Michelle Lujan Grisham (D)

Capitol Office
225-6316
lujangrisham.house.gov
214 Cannon Bldg. 20515-3007; fax 225-4975

Committees
Agriculture
Budget
Oversight & Government Reform

Residence
Albuquerque

Born
Oct. 24, 1959; Los Alamos, N.M.

Religion
Roman Catholic

Family
Widowed; two children

Education
U. of New Mexico, B.U.S. 1982, J.D. 1987

Career
Health consulting firm owner; state aging agency director; state legal association program director; lawyer; energy company staff assistant

Political Highlights
N.M. Aging and Long-term Services Department secretary, 2004; N.M. Health Department secretary, 2004-07; sought Democratic nomination for U.S. House, 2008; Bernalillo County Board of Commissioners, 2011-12

ELECTION RESULTS

2012 GENERAL		
Michelle Lujan Grisham (D)	162,924	59.1%
Janice E. Arnold-Jones (R)	112,473	40.8%
2012 PRIMARY		
Michelle Lujan Grisham (D)	19,111	40.1%
Eric G. Griego (D)	16,702	35.0%
Martin J. Chavez (D)	11,895	24.9%

Elected 2012; 1st term

Public health has been at the center of Lujan Grisham's professional life. She ran the New Mexico Agency on Aging for more than a decade, and she followed that job with a few years leading the state Health Department.

She demonstrated a clear commitment to her work. Early in her tenure at the Agency on Aging, she went undercover at a senior care facility for three days, pretending to be a stroke victim; the experience shaped her efforts to overhaul regulation of such facilities. "I am a hard-charging, aggressive advocate for people who do not otherwise have a voice in government," she says.

Just as the agency became a Cabinet-level department, she was appointed to lead the Health Department. (The day after her appointment, she experienced a personal tragedy as her husband died of a brain aneurysm.)

Lujan Grisham sits on the Oversight and Government Reform Committee and its panel handling health care and entitlement programs. She also sits on the Agriculture Committee. Her Albuquerque district doesn't have much in the way of farms, but it does have a high percentage of people who use federal nutrition programs. She has a seat on the relevant subcommittee. As a state official, she worked to remove junk food from schools.

She describes herself "a strong progressive Democrat who is able to work effectively in a bipartisan manner without compromising my core values."

Lujan Grisham ran for the 1st District seat in 2008, when Republican Rep. Heather A. Wilson ran for the Senate. She finished third in the primary, and Democrat Martin Heinrich went on to win the seat. He ran for the Senate in 2012, so Lujan Grisham tried again. She was the third Democrat to enter the race, but she caught up in fundraising. In a sometimes nasty primary, she defeated Martin J. Chavez, a former mayor of Albuquerque, and state Sen. Eric G. Griego, a favorite of liberal activists. She won easily in November.

Lujan Grisham is one of the class presidents for Democratic freshmen and a whip in the Congressional Hispanic Caucus.

New Mexico 1

Central — Albuquerque

Representing Albuquerque, where more than one-fourth of New Mexico's population lives, the 1st is the only urban district in the state. It includes Torrance County at the state's center, most of Bernalillo County, and small portions of Sandoval, Santa Fe and Valencia counties.

Defense spending has driven Albuquerque's growth since the 1940s, when it blossomed from a town of 35,000 into a major research center. From 2000 to 2010, the city added almost 100,000 new residents. Sandia National Laboratory, established in the 1940s to aid the Manhattan Project, designed nuclear weapons during the Cold War. It remains a leading high-tech research and computing facility. Its scientists and engineers collaborate with other researchers at the Air Force Research Lab at Kirtland Air Force Base (shared with the 2nd) and at the University of New Mexico, both of which employ more than 10,000 local residents.

Private-sector technology firms also have attracted a highly educated workforce. Despite layoffs during the most recent recession, Intel's Rio Rancho plant (located in the 3rd) is metro Albuquerque's largest private employer. The area also supports many solar technology manufacturing firms.

The 1st has the largest foreign-born population in New Mexico, with more than 70,000 immigrants living in Bernalillo County. Hispanics are a 48 percent plurality of the district's population.

Although Democrats currently hold a solid lead in voter registration and occupy most local offices, the 1st is competitive. Republicans draw support from the mainly white, affluent Northeast Heights section of Albuquerque, while Democrats rely on the district's large number of state workers and Hispanic voters. The district's highly populated Bernalillo County portion gave Democrat Barack Obama a 17-point edge in the 2012 presidential contest — he won the district overall with 55 percent.

Major Industry
Defense, research, higher education, government

Military Bases
Kirtland Air Force Base, 3,535 military, 3,748 civilian (shared with the 2nd)

Cities
Albuquerque (pt.), South Valley (unincorp.)

Notable
The Anderson-Abruzzo Albuquerque International Balloon Museum presents historical artifacts and art work related to ballooning and the annual balloon fiesta hosted by the city.

Rep. Steve Pearce (R)

Capitol Office
225-2365
pearce.house.gov
2432 Rayburn Bldg. 20515-3102; fax 225-9599

Committees
Financial Services

Residence
Hobbs

Born
Aug. 24, 1947; Lamesa, Texas

Religion
Baptist

Family
Wife, Cynthia Pearce; one child

Education
New Mexico State U., B.B.A. 1970 (economics); Eastern New Mexico U., M.B.A. 1991

Military
Air Force, 1970-76

Career
Oil well services company owner; pilot

Political Highlights
Sought Republican nomination for U.S. Senate, 2000; N.M. House, 1997-2000; U.S. House, 2003-09; Republican nominee for U.S. Senate, 2008

ELECTION RESULTS

2012 GENERAL		
Steve Pearce (R)	133,180	59.1%
Evelyn Madrid Erhard (D)	92,162	40.9%
2012 PRIMARY		
Steve Pearce (R)		unopposed
2010 GENERAL		
Steve Pearce (R)	94,053	55.4%
Harry Teague (D)	75,708	44.6%

Previous Winning Percentages
2006 (59%); 2004 (60%); 2002 (56%)

Elected 2002; 5th term

Did not serve 2009-11

Pearce maintains a controlled hostility toward big government and the Obama administration, and he frequently vents it as a spokesman for Western Republicans. His second stint in the House has also been marked by frustration with his own party for a perceived lack of urgency with the conservative economic agenda.

Raised in Hobbs, Pearce has long been tied to the energy industry in New Mexico. His father worked as an oilfield roustabout, while also selling vegetables on the side of the road to make extra money to support his six children. Pearce joined the Air Force coming out of college and served as a combat pilot in Vietnam. After that, he ran his own oil services company with his wife. He ranks among the wealthier members of Congress.

His interest in energy and land use issues makes him highly suited to chair the Congressional Western Caucus, a group of conservative Republicans dedicated to reducing federal regulation and leaving more land use decisions in the hands of local authorities.

Pearce delivers that message in a matter-of-fact tone that sometimes gives way to chippy criticisms of government actions. "We're getting eaten up in the West by federal rules that are not constitutional," he says.

The 113th Congress (2013-14) marks Pearce's second term as chairman, a job he shares with Wyoming's Cynthia M. Lummis. In the 112th Congress (2011-12), Pearce called for more energy development, including on federal land. He was publicly critical as the Obama administration kicked the tires on new federal regulation of hydraulic fracturing, a process for oil and gas extraction that many environmentalists dislike. When deficit reduction talks were revived at the end of 2012, Pearce recommended (to no avail) using an increase in energy leasing and the divestment of federal landholdings as ways to increase revenues and decrease government overhead.

Looking out for his state's logging industry in 2011, Pearce picked up a chainsaw and cut down a Douglas fir to kick off a demonstration in central New Mexico. The event was meant to pressure the U.S. Forest Service into deferring to the local officials' plan to fell more trees than the federal agency had allowed, with the county arguing that it would reduce risk of fires while aiding the economy.

In the 112th Congress, Pearce and Texas Sen. John Cornyn were leaders of the effort to keep the dune sagebrush lizard off the endangered species list. Pearce alleged that federal protection of the lizard's habitat would destroy thousands of jobs in the New Mexico oil fields.

The listing was averted by a June 2012 conservation agreement between the Interior Department and landowners in the region, but news broke months later that the lesser prairie chicken might go on the list. Pearce issued a missive under the title, "Here we go again."

Pearce thinks of himself as "very conservative," and his voting record backs him up. He found the August 2011 deficit reduction deal too weak and stumped against the Senate version of a 2012 extension of surface transportation programs — he wrote to GOP leaders that transportation programs should be in the hands of the states.

He was put off by the January 2013 law extending lower income tax rates only for earnings under $400,000, with no major spending cuts attached. During the selection of the speaker of the 113th Congress, Pearce voted for Majority Leader Eric Cantor, rather than incumbent Speaker John A. Boehner. "I'm saying, 'Let's wake up and change direction,' " he said. "We're doing nothing to solve the problems."

Pearce also had a problem with GOP messaging in 2006, when he unsuccessfully sought the vice chairmanship of the GOP Conference; he wrote to colleagues that the party "talked too much about things in the wrong way."

Pearce sits on the Financial Services Committee and has been part of the GOP effort to dismantle housing giants Fannie Mae and Freddie Mac. A subcommittee approved his 2011 measure to require the approval of the Treasury secretary before those entities could issue new debt.

He hasn't been thrilled with the monetary policy of the Federal Reserve. Pearce said the fall 2012 announcement of more quantitative easing, in which the Fed prints money and uses it to buy financial assets, was driving down interest rates and punishing responsible savers.

On several occasions, Pearce has suggested that financial market regulators in the Obama administration are beholden to large financial institutions. He was livid at the decision to treat derivatives broker MF Global as an equities firm for its 2011 bankruptcy, which put customers behind creditors in the order for repayment.

"I just wonder about this administration, which constantly talks about the 99 percent," he said at a 2012 hearing. "When it comes down to the rub, it protected the 2 percent. It didn't protect the small guys. It didn't protect the hog farmers."

Pearce is a social conservative on many issues. He opposes abortion and restrictions on gun rights, and he wants to amend the Constitution to prohibit same-sex marriage. He says he rises at 4:30 a.m. daily to read the Bible.

After winning two terms in the New Mexico House, Pearce made a bid for the U.S. Senate in 2000. He got swamped in the GOP primary. He jumped into the 2002 U.S. House race after Republican Joe Skeen's failing health led to his retirement announcement. Pressing a fundraising advantage, he defeated Democratic state Sen. John Arthur Smith by 12 points. In 2004, Pearce faced Gary King, a businessman, lawyer and state legislator whose father, Bruce, was the longest-serving governor in state history. Pearce won with 60 percent of the vote.

He gave up his seat in 2008 for a second try at the Senate. Pearce beat fellow Rep. Heather A. Wilson in the GOP primary, but he was crushed in November by Democrat Tom Udall, 61 percent to 39 percent.

In 2010, with the national climate more favorable to Republicans, Pearce attacked the Democrat who replaced him in the House, Harry Teague, for his support of President Barack Obama's "big government" agenda. Outside groups and both party campaign committees targeted the district. Pearce won by more than 10 points.

He had no trouble holding the seat in 2012.

Key Votes

2012	
Extend a Social Security payroll tax cut and unemployment benefits	NO
Ease securities rules to expand small-business access to capital	YES
Extend for one year subsidized student loan interest rates financed by a cut in health care spending	YES
Cite Attorney General Eric H. Holder Jr. for contempt of Congress	YES
Create a visa program for foreign graduates in high-tech fields	YES
Extend most Bush-era income tax rates while allowing rates for top-bracket earners to rise (Jan. 1, 2013)	NO
2011	
Strike funding for F-35 alternative engine	YES
Prevent EPA from regulating greenhouse gas emissions to address climate change	YES
Extend certain provisions of Patriot Act for four years	YES
Declare opposition to use of ground troops in Libya	NO
Overhaul patent law	NO
Pass compromise debt limit increase plan and establish future spending limits	NO
Allow consideration of measures to implement three trade agreements	YES

CQ Vote Studies

	PARTY UNITY		PRESIDENTIAL SUPPORT	
	SUPPORT	OPPOSE	SUPPORT	OPPOSE
2012	94%	6%	18%	82%
2011	96%	4%	19%	81%
2008	94%	6%	70%	30%
2007	96%	4%	81%	19%
2006	98%	2%	97%	3%

Interest Groups

	AFL-CIO	ADA	CCUS	ACU
2012	10%	10%	91%	88%
2011	0%	10%	88%	92%
2008	13%	20%	89%	92%
2007	13%	5%	80%	96%
2006	14%	5%	100%	92%

New Mexico 2

South — Las Cruces, Roswell, Little Texas

Taking up the southern half of the state, the 2nd is arid and sparsely populated. Employers, including the federal government, have brought nuclear research and waste facilities to its remote deserts and deep salt beds. Near Albuquerque, the 2nd takes in the southern edge of Bernalillo County and most of Valencia County, including part of Kirtland Air Force Base.

The 3,200-square-mile White Sands Missile Range runs up the center of the 2nd from the Mexico border. This facility was the site of the first atomic bomb test in 1945 and since has been shared by the military and NASA. Holloman Air Force Base is within the boundaries of the range. Las Cruces, the largest city nearby, relies on White Sands for jobs. New Mexico State University is also a major employer.

The 2nd also has sites of extraterrestrial interest. Spaceport America, an 18,000-acre facility for commercial spaceflight ventures, is under construction near Truth or Consequences. Virgin Galactic plans to fly passengers into space — for $200,000 per ticket. Across the state in Roswell, the site of a 1947 crash of an alleged alien craft draws UFO enthusiasts.

Although the Rio Grande runs through the center of the 2nd, the Chihuahua Desert prevents much agriculture beyond ranching and pecans. Many towns have built their economies on traditional Western industries, such as mining. Counties to the southeast sit on a natural gas basin.

The 2nd is the state's only Hispanic-majority district. Democrats lead in voter registration, but Republicans remain competitive in federal elections with strong support in the district's southeast. Republican Mitt Romney took the 2nd in the 2012 presidential race with 52 percent of the vote.

Major Industry
Defense, oil and gas, mining

Military Bases
Kirtland Air Force Base, 3,535 military, 3,748 civilian (shared with the 1st); Holloman Air Force Base, 4,037 military, 1,078 civilian (2010); White Sands Missile Range, 768 military, 2,620 civilian

Cities
Las Cruces, Roswell, Hobbs, Alamogordo

Notable
The Gila Wilderness is the world's oldest designated wilderness area (1924) — it has no roads and visitors must enter on foot or horseback.

Rep. Ben Ray Luján (D)

Capitol Office
225-6190
lujan.house.gov
2446 Rayburn Bldg. 20515-3708; fax 226-1528

Committees
Energy & Commerce

Residence
Nambe

Born
June 7, 1972; Santa Fe, N.M.

Religion
Roman Catholic

Family
Single

Education
U. of New Mexico, attended 1990-95; New Mexico Highlands U., B.B.A. 2007 (business administration)

Career
State government aide; human resources manager; legislative publication marketing director; casino services supervisor

Political Highlights
N.M. Public Regulation Commission, 2005-09 (chairman, 2005-07)

ELECTION RESULTS

2012 GENERAL		
Ben Ray Luján (D)	167,103	63.1%
Jefferson L. Byrd (R)	97,616	36.9%
2012 PRIMARY		
Ben Ray Luján (D)		unopposed
2010 GENERAL		
Ben Ray Luján (D)	120,048	57.0%
Tom Mullins (R)	90,617	43.0%

Previous Winning Percentages
2008 (57%)

Elected 2008; 3rd term

Luján says heartfelt passion fuels his liberal beliefs. Legislatively, he channels that emotion into a polished energy-and-technology agenda. Politically, it has established him as a leader in the Congressional Hispanic Caucus.

He credits his personal style to his father, the longtime speaker of the New Mexico House of Representatives. Ben Luján died of lung cancer in December 2012. "I was able to learn from dad the importance of talking to people and treating everyone with respect," Luján said. In the sometimes surly world of New Mexico politics, opponents accused the elder Luján of nepotism when his son landed a state government job in 2002; they accused the younger Luján of riding coattails in his various election campaigns.

Luján keeps in his Washington office a photo of himself and his father working on the family farm, as a joking reminder of those slights. "I told my dad, 'One day, they're going to say that the reason you represented the people of New Mexico is that you're the father of the congressman.' This picture was kind of a reminder to say, 'Dad's still in charge.' " In the photo, his dad is wielding a chainsaw.

Some people see the younger Luján in charge one day. He has a reputation for being ambitious, a proficient fundraiser, and good at staying on message. He is the first vice chairman of the CHC for the 113th Congress (2013-14), and he was also named a chief deputy whip for the Democratic Caucus. Not only that, Luján was granted a seat on the Energy and Commerce Committee, where he can continue his campaign to bolster his state's energy sector.

As a member of the New Mexico Public Regulation Commission, he helped implement the state's standard for renewable energy, which requires 20 percent of production to come from such sources by 2020. Luján outlines three ways government should promote renewable energy: the extension of production tax credits; adoption of a national renewables standard; and maximizing the use of national laboratories — such as Los Alamos, in his district, and Sandia, in Albuquerque.

The White House, he said, should direct labs to work on improvements to energy transmission and storage: "Whatever nation wins the race to solving the storage issue is going to lead the world for a decade." He also wants labs to have a mandate to work more closely with private industry in developing and testing technology to get it to the market. Luján and Virginia Republican Frank R. Wolf formed the Technology Transfer Caucus in 2011.

Luján would like a renaissance for Cooperative Research and Development Agreements, which partner businesses with federal labs; though popular in the 1990s, CRDAs now require too much investment from the private sector, meaning only deep-pocketed companies can use them, he said.

The contention that renewable energy isn't affordable to consumers isn't fair, according to Luján, because established nuclear or coal plants depreciated for 20 or 30 years, driving down production costs. He sees an energy bonanza in the future, if major private and federal investment in renewable-energy infrastructure happens today: "What happens if you have buildup of electricity generation in the country, and you get to a point where all those assets are depreciated and the cost of the fuel is free?"

He gives extra attention to solar power, as New Mexico is particularly suited for it. Luján has twice introduced a bill to set national standards for connecting small rooftop solar arrays to larger power grids. Water is also a concern in the West, and Luján sees a role for the national labs in advancing water recycling technology. A former member of the Natural Resources Committee, he has tried to alert the government to the needs of acequias, small irrigation channels that in many cases predate the United States. When their headwaters are on federal land, some jurisdiction problems have arisen; several of them run through the Luján family farm.

Luján sits on the Oversight and Investigations Subcommittee, and also the Communications and Technology Subcommittee. He defends federal programs to expand broadband into rural areas. The Public Regulation Commission oversaw utilities, telecommunications, motor carriers and insurance companies, so Luján also has some experience in the consumer protection issues that come before the Energy and Commerce Committee.

When Luján has turned to Hispanic issues, it has often been in the context of his other work. In 2009, he tried to advance provisions to give special consideration to Hispanic and American Indian colleges in creating "energy innovation hubs," consisting of academic and private research groups. Education is a particularly pressing concern for Latino populations, he said, and Luján thinks K-12 schooling should have a greater emphasis on developing entrepreneurial skills and personal fiscal discipline.

Luján and Texas Democrat Henry Cuellar are helping the Democratic Congressional Campaign Committee recruit Latino candidates and campaign donors for the 2014 House races.

An eighth-generation New Mexican, Luján grew up in the small farming community of Nambe, just north of Santa Fe. His great-grandparents, grandparents and parents all lived in his current home. Luján's grandfather was a sheep herder, and the family still raises sheep on the land.

His father entered the state House in 1975, and Luján remembers wandering the halls of the New Mexico Legislature and attending political events from an early age. After high school, Luján took classes at the University of New Mexico, though he did not receive a college degree until 2007, when he completed his course work at New Mexico Highlands University. In between, he worked a series of jobs, including stints as a dealer at a casino and in human resources at a horse racetrack.

He entered government in 2002 as deputy state treasurer. Two years later, he was elected to the Public Regulation Commission.

In the 2008 House race to succeed Democrat Tom Udall (who successfully ran for the Senate), Luján campaigned energetically while taking advantage of his family connections — the Albuquerque Journal reported that more than two dozen lobbyists and other campaign contributors who gave to the elder Luján also donated to his. He beat five other primary candidates, taking more than 41 percent of the vote. The primary was the hard part. In November, Luján took 57 percent in the heavily Democratic district. He hasn't been seriously challenged since then.

Key Votes

2012	
Extend a Social Security payroll tax cut and unemployment benefits	YES
Ease securities rules to expand small-business access to capital	YES
Extend for one year subsidized student loan interest rates financed by a cut in health care spending	NO
Cite Attorney General Eric H. Holder Jr. for contempt of Congress	NO
Create a visa program for foreign graduates in high-tech fields	NO
Extend most Bush-era income tax rates while allowing rates for top-bracket earners to rise (Jan. 1, 2013)	YES
2011	
Strike funding for F-35 alternative engine	YES
Prevent EPA from regulating greenhouse gas emissions to address climate change	NO
Extend certain provisions of Patriot Act for four years	NO
Declare opposition to use of ground troops in Libya	NO
Overhaul patent law	NO
Pass compromise debt limit increase plan and establish future spending limits	NO
Allow consideration of measures to implement three trade agreements	NO

CQ Vote Studies

	PARTY UNITY		PRESIDENTIAL SUPPORT	
	SUPPORT	OPPOSE	SUPPORT	OPPOSE
2012	93%	7%	89%	11%
2011	94%	6%	84%	16%
2010	99%	1%	95%	5%
2009	99%	1%	93%	7%

Interest Groups

	AFL-CIO	ADA	CCUS	ACU
2012	95%	80%	25%	4%
2011	100%	85%	13%	8%
2010	100%	100%	13%	0%
2009	100%	100%	40%	0%

New Mexico 3

North — Santa Fe, Rio Rancho, Farmington

Since Georgia O'Keeffe first painted northern New Mexico in 1929, the 3rd District's breathtaking scenery and Spanish and American Indian history have attracted thousands of artists and tourists. The district's current residents range from celebrated artists and science Ph.D.s to impoverished Native American farmers.

Running across the upper tier of the state, the 3rd includes the Sangre de Cristo Mountains at its center and the mesas of the Colorado Plateau to the west. Galleries and studios remain a major draw in Taos and Santa Fe. The state capital's zoning laws mandate Pueblo-style architecture in the 400-year-old city. Nearby luxury resorts and ski slopes also cater to well-to-do visitors.

Scientists at Los Alamos National Laboratory, 40 miles northwest of Santa Fe, developed the atomic bomb during World War II. The facility continues to maintain the nation's nuclear stockpile and generates $3 billion annually for the state's economy. Rio Rancho, where Intel operates a large plant, also has a highly skilled workforce.

More than 17 percent of the 3rd's residents are American Indian. A large Navajo Indian reservation to the district's west is in territory once inhabited by the Anasazi. Some Native American residents rely on selling crafts at roadside shops, such as those in Gallup along the former Route 66. Natural gas deposits in San Juan and Rio Arriba counties have created wealth, but roughly one-third of nearby McKinley County residents live in poverty.

Santa Fe's wealthy, liberal base gives Democrats an overwhelming lead in voter registration in the 3rd, although conservative pockets exist in San Juan County and in the district's southeastern arm.

Major Industry
Government, defense, ranching

Military Bases
Cannon Air Force Base, 4,189 military, 533 civilian (2011)

Cities
Rio Rancho (pt.), Santa Fe, Farmington

Notable
The town of Clovis became a major archeological touchstone in 1929, when the oldest North American manmade prehistoric stone tools were uncovered — 13,000 years old, they helped date human arrival on the continent.

NEW YORK

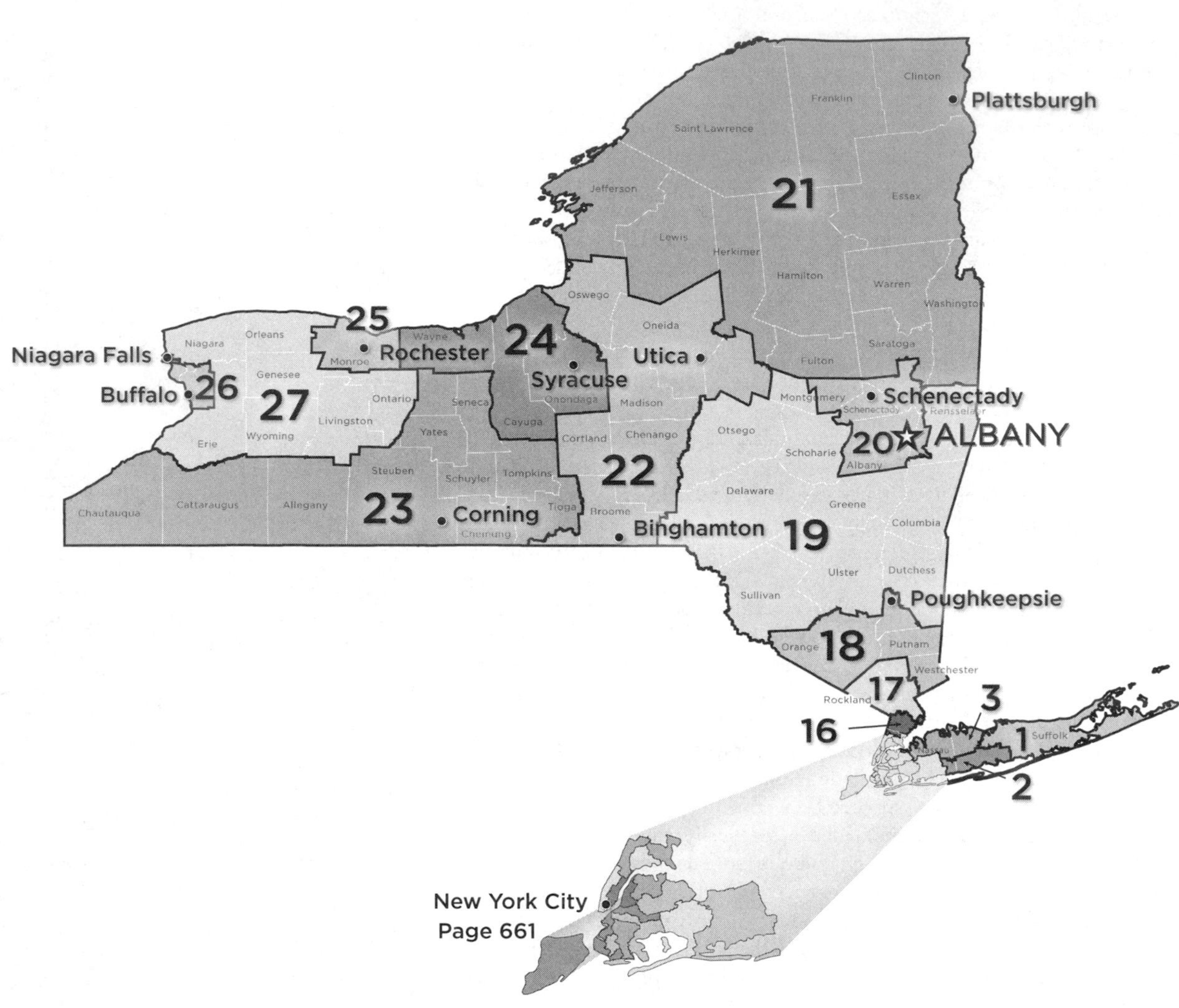

Plattsburgh
Clinton
Franklin
Saint Lawrence
21
Jefferson
Essex
Lewis
Herkimer
Hamilton
Warren
Washington
Oswego
Oneida
Saratoga
25
24
Niagara Falls
Niagara
Orleans
Rochester
Utica
Fulton
Wayne
Monroe
Syracuse
Buffalo
26
Genesee
27
Onondaga
Schenectady
Montgomery
Schenectady
Rensselaer
Ontario
Seneca
Madison
ALBANY
Livingston
Cayuga
Otsego
Yates
Cortland
Chenango
20
Erie
Wyoming
Schoharie
Albany
Steuben
Schuyler
Tompkins
22
Delaware
Greene
Chautauqua
Cattaraugus
Allegany
23
Corning
Tioga
Broome
Binghamton
19
Columbia
Chemung
Ulster
Dutchess
Sullivan
Poughkeepsie
18
Orange
Putnam
Westchester
17
Rockland
3
16
1
Suffolk
Nassau
2
New York City
Page 661

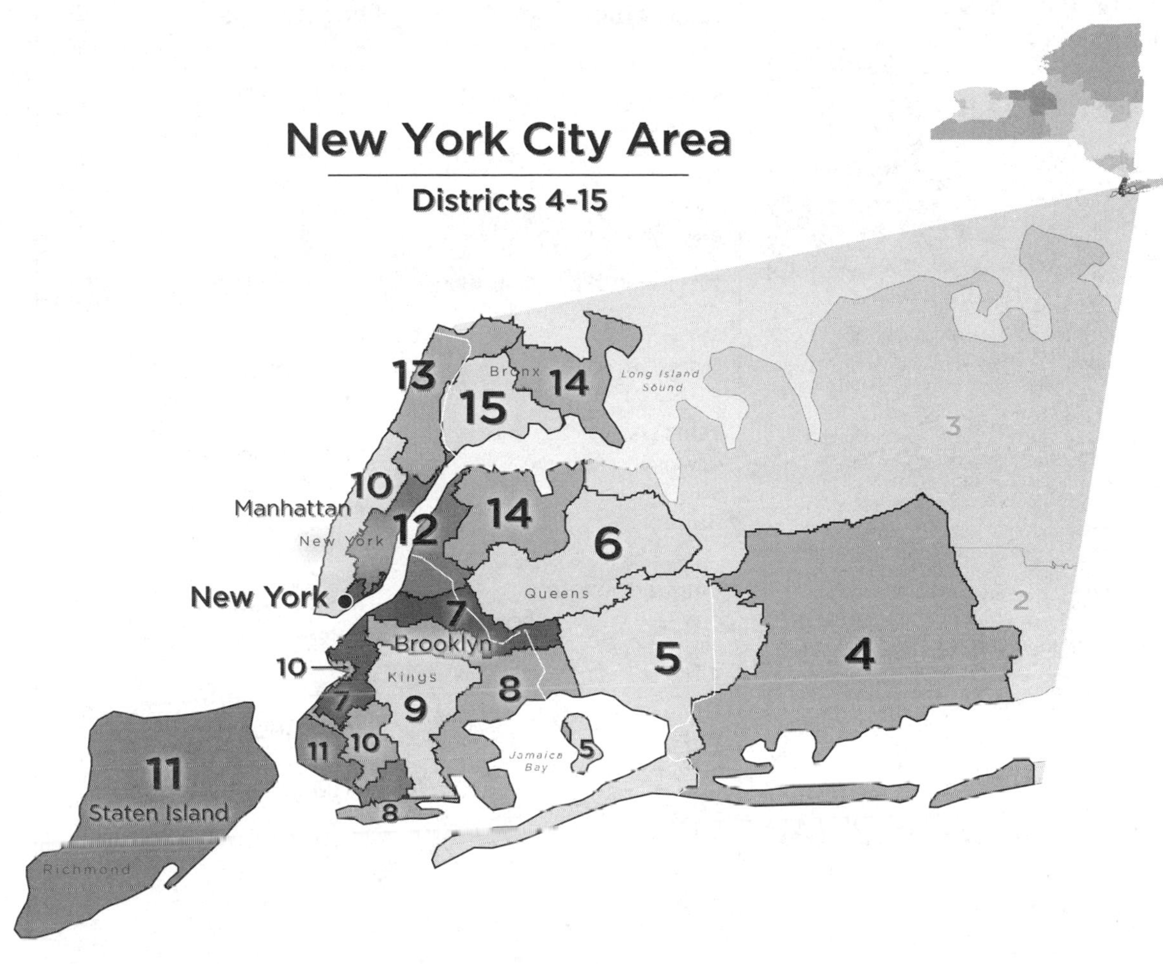

Statistics by District

District	2012 Vote for President Obama	2012 Vote for President Romney	2008 Vote for President Obama	2008 Vote for President McCain	Black	Asian	Hispanic	Median Income	Over 64	Under 20	College Education	Rural	Sq. Miles
1	50%	49%	52%	48%	5%	4%	13%	$83,144	15%	25%	34%	12%	650
2	52	47	52	48	10	3	23	82,197	13	26	27	1	182
3	51	48	54	46	3	13	9	95,699	17	26	51	1	255
4	56	43	56	44	15	6	18	87,860	14	26	38	0	111
5	90	10	86	14	51	13	20	57,485	12	26	24	0	52
6	68	31	64	36	4	36	17	55,043	15	21	38	0	30
7	88	10	85	15	10	18	44	40,554	9	27	27	0	16
8	89	10	86	14	56	4	18	39,912	13	25	27	0	30
9	85	14	85	15	53	7	12	44,029	12	26	32	0	16
10	74	25	76	24	4	16	13	70,270	13	22	57	0	14
11	52	47	49	51	8	13	16	62,045	14	24	30	0	66
12	77	22	81	19	5	12	14	82,360	14	14	69	0	15
13	95	5	94	6	31	5	53	34,360	11	24	27	0	10
14	81	18	77	23	11	16	47	46,990	11	23	25	0	28
15	97	3	95	5	34	1	66	23,894	9	33	11	0	15

Gov. Andrew M. Cuomo (D)

First elected: 2010

Length of term: 4 years

Term expires: 1/15

Salary: $179,000

Phone: (518) 474-7516

Residence: Queens

Born: Dec. 6, 1957; Queens, N.Y.

Religion: Roman Catholic

Family: Divorced; three children

Education: Fordham U., B.A. 1979; Albany Law School, J.D. 1982

Career: Real estate investor; U.S. Housing and Urban Development Department official; city homeless commission director; alternative housing nonprofit founder; lawyer; city prosecutor; gubernatorial and campaign aide

Political highlights: U.S. Department of Housing and Urban Development secretary, 1997-2001; Liberal Party candidate for governor, 2002; N.Y. attorney general, 2007-10

ELECTION RESULTS

2010 GENERAL

Andrew M. Cuomo (D)	2,911,721	62.6%
Carl Paladino (R)	1,548,184	33.3%
Howie Hawkins (GREEN)	59,929	1.3%
Others	134,518	2.8%

Lt. Gov. Robert Duffy (D)

First elected: 2010

Length of term: 4 years

Term expires: 1/15

Salary: $151,500

Phone: (518) 474-8390

LEGISLATURE

Legislature: Year-round; main session January-June

Senate: 63 members, 2-year terms

2013 ratios: 33 D, 30 R; 52 men, 11 women

Salary: $79,500

Phone: (518) 455-3216

Assembly: 150 members, 2-year terms

2013 ratios: 103 D, 42 R, 1 I, 1 INDC, 3 vacancies; 111 men, 36 women

Salary: $79,500

Phone: (518) 455-4218

TERM LIMITS

Governor: No

Senate: No

House: No

URBAN STATISTICS

CITY	POPULATION
New York City	8,175,133
Buffalo	261,310
Rochester	210,565
Yonkers	195,976
Syracuse	145,170

REGISTERED VOTERS

Democrat	50%
Republican	24%
Other	26%

POPULATION

2010 population	19,378,102
2000 population	18,976,457
1990 population	17,990,455
Percent change (2000-2010)	+2.1%
Rank among states (2010)	3
Median age	37.7
Born in state	64.5%
Foreign born	21.4%
Violent crime rate	385/100,000
Poverty level	14.2%
Federal workers	168,197
Military	29,553

ELECTIONS

STATE ELECTION OFFICIAL
(518) 474-6220

DEMOCRATIC PARTY
(212) 725-8825

REPUBLICAN PARTY
(518) 462-2601

MISCELLANEOUS

Web: www.ny.gov

Capital: Albany

U.S. CONGRESS

Senate: 2 Democrats

House: 21 Democrats, 6 Republicans

STATISTICS BY DISTRICT

	2012 Vote for President		2008 Vote for President										
District	Obama	Romney	Obama	McCain	Black	Asian	Hispanic	Median Income	Over 64	Under 20	College Education	Rural	Sq. Miles
16	74%	26%	73%	27%	32%	5%	23%	$59,849	15%	26%	37%	0%	78
17	57	42	58	42	11	6	21	84,664	14	28	44	2	383
18	51	47	53	47	9	3	15	71,399	13	28	34	19	1,353
19	52	46	54	46	4	1	7	53,769	16	23	26	70	7,937
20	59	39	59	41	9	4	6	56,811	14	25	36	11	1,231
21	52	46	53	47	3	1	3	48,759	15	25	22	65	15,115
22	48.8	49.2	49.97	50	3	2	3	45,578	16	25	24	43	5,077
23	48	50	50.4	49.6	3	2	3	44,518	15	25	23	55	7,372
24	57	41	57	43	8	2	4	51,724	14	26	28	27	2,389
25	59	39	60	40	16	3	8	49,343	14	26	35	4	510
26	64	34	64	36	18	3	5	41,018	15	24	29	<1	219
27	43	55	45	55	2	1	3	55,340	16	25	27	42	3,973
STATE	**63**	**36**	**63**	**36**	**16**	**7**	**18**	**55,246**	**14**	**25**	**33**	**14**	**47,126**
U.S.	**51**	**47**	**53**	**46**	**12**	**5**	**17**	**50,052**	**13**	**27**	**29**	**21**	**3,531,905**

Sen. Charles E. Schumer (D)

Capitol Office
224-6542
schumer.senate.gov
322 Hart Bldg. 20510 3203; fax 228-3027

Committees
Banking, Housing & Urban Affairs
Finance
Judiciary
(Immigration, Refugees & Border Security - Chairman)
Rules & Administration - Chairman
Joint Library
Joint Printing - Chairman

Residence
Brooklyn

Born
Nov. 23, 1950; Brooklyn, N.Y.

Religion
Jewish

Family
Wife, Iris Weinshall; two children

Education
Harvard U., A.B. 1971, J.D. 1974

Career
None

Political Highlights
N.Y. Assembly, 1975-81; U.S. House, 1981-99

ELECTION RESULTS

2010 GENERAL

Schumer (D)	3,047,775	66.3%
Jay Townsend (R)	1,480,337	32.2%

2010 PRIMARY

Schumer (D, INDC, WFM)	unopposed

Previous Winning Percentages
2004 (71%); 1998 (55%); 1996 House Election (75%); 1994 House Election (73%); 1992 House Election (89%); 1990 House Election (80%); 1988 House Election (78%); 1986 House Election (93%); 1984 House Election (72%); 1982 House Election (79%); 1980 House Election (77%)

Elected 1998; 3rd term

Schumer has nearly complete control over Senate Democrats' messaging operations, and the omnipresent New Yorker doesn't mind pulling double duty as the actual messenger. His steady accumulation of crucial party responsibilities and his willingness to jump into almost any policy battle have positioned him as a potential successor to Majority Leader Harry Reid.

He already holds the title of Democratic Conference vice chairman — the No. 3 leadership post that Reid created in late 2006 as a reward for Schumer's wildly successful first term as chairman of the Democratic Senatorial Campaign Committee. He turned in another solid fundraising performance as DSCC chairman in the 110th Congress (2007-08), and he has advised his successors in more recent election cycles.

Since 2009, he has held the gavel of the Rules and Administration Committee, which wields internal power over the chamber and is responsible for the Senate's day-to-day operations. And in 2011, Reid tapped him to run the Democratic Policy and Communications Center, which pushes out policy information and legislative research to senators and their staff members.

When his spate of media appearances is factored in, one gets the impression that Schumer is building the set, working behind the scenes and standing in the spotlight simultaneously. "God has blessed me with a lot of energy," he has said.

As the DPCC chairman, Schumer was an architect of the "Winning the Future" agenda in the 112th Congress (2011-12), which called for more spending on education, energy and highways, as well as targeted tax cuts. He constantly attacked the policies of House Republicans. Schumer called GOP spending plans for fiscal 2011 and beyond "a road map to disaster." The following year, when Republicans unveiled their fiscal 2013 blueprint, Schumer called it "a smoke-and-mirrors budget."

He also adhered to one of his personal creeds for political communications: tailoring presentations to appeal to the middle class. As Democrats promoted the idea of a surtax on higher earnings, Schumer persuaded the White House to set the boundary at $1 million, as opposed to lower earnings, to sharpen the political debate. In October 2012, he said no fiscal deal with Republicans should lower the top two tax brackets.

Schumer's committees cover a wide range of jurisdictions. He was able to participate at the panel level on the 2010 health care and financial regulatory overhauls, as a member of both the Finance and the Banking, Housing and Urban Affairs committees. On the Judiciary Committee, he weighs in on high-profile issues from abortion to the war on terrorism, and helps President Barack Obama move Democratic judicial nominees. For Supreme Court Justice Sonia Sotomayor (a fellow New Yorker), he served as a "sherpa," or guide, during her Senate confirmation process.

He has put himself in the negotiating room on big issues. At the conclusion of the 112th Congress, Schumer led the Senate effort to assemble and pass a $60 billion measure tied to recovery from Superstorm Sandy, which slammed into New York City. (He also led attempts to publicly shame Republicans who, for various reasons, delayed enactment of Sandy relief until January 2013.)

As the chairman of the Judiciary subcommittee on immigration, Schumer became part of an eight-man, bipartisan working group that produced a comprehensive immigration overhaul proposal in the spring of 2013. He was simultaneously involved in attempts to produce a bill to set stricter requirements for background checks before any gun purchase — although Schumer's preferred language was criticized by privacy advocates such as the American

Civil Liberties Union. A less stringent version by other senators was still defeated in April 2013, however.

At a 2013 event organized by Politico, Arizona Republican John McCain compared Schumer to a well-known deal-maker, the late Sen. Edward M. Kennedy of Massachusetts. "The trait that Sen. Schumer and Sen. Kennedy share is, one, you know exactly where they stand," McCain said. "And number two, they will never change. They will never go back on their word."

As a House member, Schumer helped broker deals on several major bills, including the 1994 anti-crime law that helped fund 100,000 state and local police jobs, banned certain classes of semi-automatic weapons, and created a "three strikes" mandatory life sentence for repeat violent offenders. He was the chief sponsor of the 1993 Brady law requiring background checks for handgun buyers and of a 2006 bill requiring that stolen guns be reported in every state. When the National Rifle Association called him "the criminal's best friend," Schumer retorted, "I wear this like a badge of honor."

But he'll also spend political capital and airtime on smaller measures, such as banning text messaging by drivers, investigating the health hazards of metal grill brushes or trying to impose strict penalties on those who denounce U.S. citizenship to avoid taxes.

Schumer has gone on the record on so many subjects over the years — sometimes with his own positions, other times with his party's — that there is occasionally the appearance of self-promotion and self-contradiction. Early in his Senate career, Schumer supported legislation that broke down barriers between commercial banks and investment banks. While still in the House, he backed liability protections for firms facing securities fraud charges. But in 2010, some New Yorkers questioned Schumer's push to increase financial regulation rather than defend a home-state industry. He has defended the financial regulatory overhaul as "necessary."

He is one of the most prominent Jewish members of Congress and a staunch backer of Israel. Schumer was critical of Obama's efforts to publicly pressure Israel to stop expanding Jewish neighborhoods in east Jerusalem — but during the 2012 campaign, he defended Obama's policies toward Iran. When GOP presidential candidate Mitt Romney said Iran would succeed in building a nuclear weapon if Obama were re-elected, Schumer pounced. "If you care about Israel more than you care about politics, you would never make that statement, even if you believe it," he said in March 2012.

Schumer was born and raised in the Kings Highway section of Brooklyn. His father, Abe, owned a pest extermination business, and his mother, Selma, stayed at home with Schumer and his two siblings. He said he "didn't have a political bone" in his body until, as a freshman at Harvard, he worked on Eugene J. McCarthy's 1968 presidential primary campaign. Schumer decided to become a lawyer with the goal of getting into politics.

After law school, he declined a job at a prominent law firm to run for the state Assembly (which is a full-time legislature). His parents argued with his decision, but he was steadfast. Schumer won the seat at age 23. Six years later, Schumer easily won the Brooklyn-based House seat of Democrat Elizabeth Holtzman, who was running for the Senate.

In 1998, after 18 years in the House, Schumer took aim at Republican Sen. Alfonse M. D'Amato, winning the Democratic nomination with almost 51 percent of the vote against former Rep. Geraldine A. Ferraro, the Democrats' 1984 vice presidential nominee, and New York City Public Advocate Mark Green. Schumer, pointing to his anti-crime and gun control efforts in the House and recounting D'Amato's ethics problems, won in November with nearly 55 percent of the vote. In 2004, he lost in only one county — Hamilton County, in the Adirondacks. At times he has been rumored to have an eye on the governorship, but he passed up the 2006 gubernatorial primary. He was re-elected to the Senate with almost two-thirds of the vote in 2010.

Key Votes

2012	
Prohibit health insurance plans from denying coverage based on the sponsor's religious beliefs	YES
Require approval of the Keystone XL oil pipeline	NO
Ease securities rules to expand small-business access to capital	YES
Reauthorize farm and nutrition programs for five years	YES
Limit debate on a bill that would create private-sector cybersecurity standards	YES
Consent to ratification of a treaty setting global standard for the treatment of people with disabilities	YES
Provide $60.4 billion in disaster relief following Superstorm Sandy	YES
Extend most Bush-era income tax rates while allowing rates for top-bracket earners to rise (Jan. 1, 2013)	YES
2011	
Prevent EPA from regulating greenhouse gas emissions to address climate change	NO
Extend certain provisions of Patriot Act for four years	+
Clear compromise debt limit increase plan and establish future spending limits	YES
Overhaul patent law	YES
Implement Colombia free trade agreement	NO
Limit debate on confirmation of Caitlin J. Halligan to D.C. Circuit Court of Appeals	YES
Extend payroll tax cut and unemployment benefits for two months	YES

CQ Vote Studies

	PARTY UNITY		PRESIDENTIAL SUPPORT	
	SUPPORT	OPPOSE	SUPPORT	OPPOSE
2012	97%	3%	99%	1%
2011	97%	3%	98%	2%
2010	99%	1%	100%	0%
2009	99%	1%	99%	1%
2008	98%	2%	30%	70%
2007	97%	3%	35%	65%
2006	93%	7%	52%	48%
2005	93%	7%	31%	69%
2004	91%	9%	62%	38%
2003	96%	4%	47%	53%

Interest Groups

	AFL-CIO	ADA	CCUS	ACU
2012	91%	95%	38%	0%
2011	89%	90%	45%	0%
2010	94%	95%	27%	0%
2009	94%	95%	43%	0%
2008	100%	100%	63%	4%
2007	100%	90%	55%	0%
2006	100%	100%	64%	4%
2005	86%	100%	39%	8%
2004	100%	100%	65%	12%
2003	85%	95%	39%	10%

Sen. Kirsten Gillibrand (D)

Capitol Office
224-4451
gillibrand.senate.gov
478 Russell Bldg. 20510-3204; fax 228-0282

Committees
Agriculture, Nutrition & Forestry
(Livestock and Dairy - Chairwoman)
Armed Services
(Personnel - Chairwoman)
Environment & Public Works
Special Aging

Residence
Brunswick

Born
Dec. 9, 1966; Albany, N.Y.

Religion
Roman Catholic

Family
Husband, Jonathan Gillibrand; two children

Education
Dartmouth College, A.B. 1988 (Asian studies); U. of California, Los Angeles, J.D. 1991

Career
Lawyer; U.S. Housing and Urban Development Department aide

Political Highlights
U.S. House, 2007-09

ELECTION RESULTS

2012 GENERAL

Gillibrand (D, WFM, INDC)	4,816,880	72.2%
Wendy Long (R, C)	1,758,089	26.4%

2012 PRIMARY

Gillibrand (D)		unopposed

2010 SPECIAL

Gillibrand (D, WFM, INDC)	2,837,589	62.9%
Joseph J. DioGuardi (R, C)	1,582,603	35.1%

Previous Winning Percentages
2008 House Election (62%); 2006 House Election (53%)

Elected 2012; 1st full term

Appointed 2009

The 113th Congress marks the first time that Gillibrand doesn't have to worry about a re-election campaign. Given the chance to stretch her legs as a senator, she has her choice of paths to walk: the conservative route from her brief House career, the liberal route from her early Senate career, or something in between.

Gillibrand (full name: KEER-sten JILL-uh-brand) won election to the House in 2006, in a competitive district near her hometown of Albany. She had been practicing corporate law in New York City, but she moved upstate a few years before her campaign with a run for Congress in mind, she told New York magazine. She toppled a four-term Republican incumbent through a combination of aggressive campaigning, fundraising and appeals to conservative elements in the region. She touted her support of gun rights and fiscal restraint. She joined the Blue Dog Coalition of fiscally conservative Democrats in the 110th Congress (2007-08) and easily won re-election.

When Sen. Hillary Rodham Clinton resigned to become secretary of State in early 2009, Gillibrand was the relatively obscure pick of Democratic Gov. David A. Paterson to replace her. "She is dynamic, she is articulate, she is perceptive, she is courageous, she is outspoken," Paterson said.

She's also well-connected. Gillibrand had put her fundraising skills to work for other Democrats, including Clinton, and she has a political pedigree. Her father is prominent attorney and lobbyist Doug Rutnik, who, despite being a registered Democrat, has close ties to a pair of leading New York Republicans, former Gov. George Pataki and former Sen. Alfonse D'Amato. Her grandmother, Polly Noonan, founded Albany's first Democratic women's club.

Democratic critics looked at Gillibrand's House record and fretted that she would be too conservative for the statewide constituency. Her opposition to gun control was a major sticking point, and she didn't do herself any favors when, weeks after her appointment, she disclosed in a Newsday interview that she and her husband stored two rifles under their bed.

Gillibrand's voting record as a senator has silenced most of those critics. She still opposes some gun control measures, but in April 2013 she voted for a ban on "assault" weapons that was defeated by a wide margin. She had supported civil unions for same-sex couples while in the House, but she shifted as a senator to back gay marriage; and in the 111th Congress (2009-10) she helped lead the successful effort to repeal the ban on openly gay military servicemembers.

Her committee assignments are friendly to the upstate region, making her a good complement to fellow Democratic Sen. Charles E. Schumer, who has New York City's financial sector covered.

Gillibrand joined the Armed Services Committee in 2011. She sponsored a package of bills in 2012 to direct the Defense Department to combat hazing, as well as ensure gender equality and take steps to further integrate military leadership. "No soldier should have to mentally or physically fear another soldier," she said. As the chairwoman of the Personnel Subcommittee in the 113th Congress (2013-14), the first hearing she called was to examine sexual assault in the military.

Her seat on the Environment and Public Works Committee became more valuable to the state in late 2012, when Superstorm Sandy caused tremendous amounts of damage. Schumer and Gillibrand helped lead the preparation of a $60 billion aid package, which included money for infrastructure programs. Republicans criticized the bill as containing too much spending for projects unrelated to Sandy, but $60 billion in aid was enacted in January 2013.

Gillibrand also uses the panel for efforts to reduce carbon dioxide emissions and improve energy efficiency on upstate farms. She introduced a measure to award grants to manufacturers to produce clean-energy technology and provide a tax credit for investments in value-added agriculture, such as organic farms.

Gillibrand sits on the Agriculture, Nutrition and Forestry Committee. In 2012, the committee worked on a long-term reauthorization of farm programs. She fought to include provisions for crop insurance for fruit and vegetable farmers, rural broadband access and expanded resources for developing value-added crops.

But she opposed the bill at the committee level, because it would have cut $4.5 billion from the Supplemental Nutrition Assistance Program. She subsequently offered an amendment that would have restored the funding and offset the costs with subsidy reductions to crop insurance companies. "We should all be able to agree that the last thing we should be doing is protecting subsidies for insurance companies making huge profits at the expense of the most vulnerable in our society, particularly hungry children," she said. The bill was not enacted, and a reauthorization is still under consideration.

Gillibrand chairs the Livestock and Dairy Subcommittee. In response to the "dairy crisis" — in which New York dairy farmers have been forced to reduce labor costs as a result of a disproportionately low revenue-to-cost milk market — Gillibrand introduced bills to extend the Milk Income Loss Contract program and establish a dairy market stabilization program. In 2013, she and Maine Republican Susan Collins introduced their plan to overhaul the dairy pricing system.

Gillibrand has a degree in Asian studies and is fluent in Mandarin Chinese. She studied abroad in China and Taiwan, and while attending Dartmouth College she spent a month in India on a fellowship, during which she interviewed the Dalai Lama and Tibetan refugees for a senior project. During law school, she worked one summer for D'Amato.

As a lawyer for Davis, Polk & Wardwell during the 1990s, Gillibrand spent five years representing tobacco giant Philip Morris USA as it endured civil lawsuits and criminal investigations. She told the Albany Times-Union that her work focused on assembling information sought by federal investigators checking out claims that the company was involved in crimes against consumers. She also concentrated on securities litigation.

Near the end of the Bill Clinton administration, she served as a special counsel to Secretary of Housing and Urban Development Andrew M. Cuomo, who is now governor of New York. Gillibrand returned to corporate law after that job, then transferred upstate. In 2006, she took 53 percent of the vote to topple Republican Rep. John E. Sweeney and help Democrats take control of the House.

At the time of her 2009 appointment, Gillibrand shared a significant political network with her Senate predecessor. Many of Clinton's top advisers, including her political, financial and state directors, joined Gillibrand's 2010 special election campaign almost immediately after she was appointed.

Gillibrand won the Democratic nomination for the 2010 special election to finish out Clinton's term. Early in Gillibrand's Senate tenure, Democratic Reps. Carolyn McCarthy and Carolyn B. Maloney each vowed to challenge her due to conflicting views on gun control, immigration and the economy, but they ultimately backed off. Gillibrand coasted to victory over former Republican Rep. Joseph DioGuardi with 63 percent of the vote.

In 2012, she won a full term in the Senate in a romp. She took more than 72 percent of the vote against Republican Wendy Long, a lawyer and activist.

Gillibrand posts her daily schedule on her website so constituents can see which lobbyists she meets and which fundraisers she attends. "I can defend anything I spend congressional time doing," she says.

Key Votes

2012

Prohibit health insurance plans from denying coverage based on the sponsor's religious beliefs	YES
Require approval of the Keystone XL oil pipeline	NO
Ease securities rules to expand small-business access to capital	NO
Reauthorize farm and nutrition programs for five years	YES
Limit debate on a bill that would create private-sector cybersecurity standards	YES
Consent to ratification of a treaty setting global standard for the treatment of people with disabilities	YES
Provide $60.4 billion in disaster relief following Superstorm Sandy	YES
Extend most Bush-era income tax rates while allowing rates for top-bracket earners to rise (Jan. 1, 2013)	YES

2011

Prevent EPA from regulating greenhouse gas emissions to address climate change	NO
Extend certain provisions of Patriot Act for four years	YES
Clear compromise debt limit increase plan and establish future spending limits	NO
Overhaul patent law	YES
Implement Colombia free trade agreement	NO
Limit debate on confirmation of Caitlin J. Halligan to D.C. Circuit Court of Appeals	YES
Extend payroll tax cut and unemployment benefits for two months	YES

CQ Vote Studies

	PARTY UNITY		PRESIDENTIAL SUPPORT	
	SUPPORT	OPPOSE	SUPPORT	OPPOSE
2012	97%	3%	97%	3%
2011	98%	2%	94%	6%
2010	99%	1%	98%	2%
2009	99%	1%	97%	100%
2008	91%	9%	22%	78%
2007	90%	10%	6%	94%

Interest Groups

	AFL-CIO	ADA	CCUS	ACU
2012	100%	95%	38%	0%
2011	89%	85%	45%	5%
2010	94%	100%	9%	0%
2009	93%	90%	50%	0%
2008	100%	70%	69%	23%
2007	96%	95%	60%	8%

Rep. Timothy H. Bishop (D)

Capitol Office
225-3826
timbishop.house.gov
306 Cannon Bldg. 20515-3201; fax 225-3143

Committees
Education & the Workforce
Transportation & Infrastructure

Residence
Southampton

Born
June 1, 1950; Southampton, N.Y.

Religion
Roman Catholic

Family
Wife, Kathryn Bishop; two children

Education
College of the Holy Cross, A.B. 1972; Long Island U., M.P.A. 1981

Career
College provost and administrator

Political Highlights
No previous office

ELECTION RESULTS

2012 GENERAL		
Bishop (D, WFM)	146,179	52.4%
Randy Altschuler (R, C, INDC)	132,304	47.6%
2012 PRIMARY		
Bishop (D)		unopposed
2010 GENERAL		
Bishop (D, WFM, INDC)	98,316	50.1%
Randy Altschuler (R, C)	97,723	49.8%

Previous Winning Percentages
2008 (58%); 2006 (62%); 2004 (56%); 2002 (50%)

Elected 2002; 6th term

Bishop comes from working-class roots and survived decades of campus politics before jumping to Congress. That history sets the table for much of his left-leaning policy work — and maybe provides some seasoning as he tries to hold a politically competitive district for the Democratic Party.

His father's family has lived in Southampton, N.Y., for 12 generations — ever since they emigrated in 1643 from Southampton, England. His great-great-grandfather was mayor of the town. Bishop grew up there, and he now lives a block away from the house where he was raised.

Bishop's father was a lineman for the New York Telephone Company. He often worked 80-hour weeks, and he used overtime wages to put his five kids through college. The father's experience taught the son about the value of unions: "It was in effect worth my father's while to work that much, because of the protections my father's collective bargaining agreement gave him."

Bishop sits on the Education and the Workforce Committee, and he has been a consistent supporter of organized labor.

In his first term, Bishop pushed a proposal to increase the minimum wage from $5.15 to $7 an hour, and another to require company pension boards to have employee representation. He actively opposed the George W. Bush administration's plan to scale back regulations dictating the need for overtime pay. In the 112th Congress (2011-12), he and North Carolina Republican Walter B. Jones continued their effort to end federal programs that train foreign workers for jobs that arguably could go to Americans.

On the education side of the panel, Bishop draws on his own professional experience. He spent 29 years working at Southampton College, where he served as an admissions counselor, director of financial aid and, with a promotion in 1986, provost. (A few years after he left, in 2005, the school closed amid severe budget deficits.) Education has been a family business: His wife is the founder and director of a school for early-childhood development.

"My whole adult life has been about enhancing the dual goals of access and affordability for higher education," Bishop said.

The financing side, he said, requires cooperation among family, the government and the institution, "and families right now ... are having a very hard time meeting their piece of that compact between the three parties. I think that makes the argument that the other two pieces, the other two legs of the stool, have to be willing to step up to the plate."

Bishop has supported legislation to facilitate government and school assistance for struggling families. In August 2011, he sponsored a bill to allow students with loans under the Federal Family Educational Loan program to convert them to lower-interest, direct federal loans without penalty. That October, President Barack Obama announced administrative changes to essentially achieve that goal.

And in early 2012, Bishop was one of 13 House Democrats to vote for a Republican bill to prevent an increase in interest rates on federally backed student loans. He did not like the bill's budgetary offset to pay for that change — cuts to a preventive health fund from the 2010 health care law — but still supported the measure. A compromise version with a different offset was enacted two months later.

He also sits on the Transportation and Infrastructure Committee. In 2011, he became the top Democrat on the Water Resources and Environment Subcommittee. That assignment became far more important to New York in 2012, when Superstorm Sandy buffeted the state. Bishop is now on the front lines, requesting more long-term authorizations of coastal restoration projects for the Army Corps of Engineers. At a 2013 hearing, he said it was essential to "strengthen our lines of defense to withstand the onslaught of future storms that are becoming all too frequent."

Bishop also promotes his plan to create "a toolbox of things that would help us to begin to attack the $300 billion backlog of wastewater infrastructure needs that we have in this country." A version he introduced in 2011 gathered a smattering of GOP support; it would have authorized close to $14 billion for such projects over five years.

As negotiations over a long-term reauthorization of surface transportation programs came to a standstill in March 2012, Bishop became the House sponsor of a two-year extension that had passed the Senate. Negotiators eventually shaped a modified two-year extension (packaged with the cuts to student loan rates) that was enacted in July.

Through a coalition of pediatricians, insurance companies and families affected by roadway accidents, Bishop has worked to incorporate an incentive-based safety agenda into federal highway legislation that would prepare teens for responsible driving.

Bishop occasionally breaks with a majority of his party when it opposes defense policy or intelligence measures. In general, however, he has been supportive of the House Democratic leadership's positions over the years. Because Republicans have a voter registration edge in his district, his support sometimes causes him headaches.

When he took on incumbent Republican Felix J. Grucci in 2002, Bishop's only prior civic experience was on the Southampton Town Board of Ethics. He had a powerful ally, though, in Robert F.X. Sillerman, a longtime friend and entertainment mogul who also served as chancellor of Southampton College. Sillerman was chairman of Bishop's campaign and helped his fundraising efforts in the Hamptons and in Hollywood, while Grucci ran an awkward and gaffe-filled campaign. Bishop prevailed with 50 percent of the vote.

In his first three re-election campaigns, Bishop had stronger showings. But in 2010, Republican businessman Randy Altschuler spent more than $4 million of his personal wealth trying to knock off Bishop — who set his own personal fundraising record, pulling in around $3 million. Bishop was up after the initial tally, down after a re-reading of electronic voting machines, then up again when absentee ballots were sorted out. He prevailed by 593 votes.

Early in 2011, the Democratic Congressional Campaign Committee added Bishop to its Frontline Program, which directs fundraising and organizational assistance to incumbents facing tough re-election bids. Altschuler came back for a rematch, but this time Bishop won by almost 5 points. He is also a member of the Frontline Program for the 2014 cycle.

Key Votes

2012	
Extend a Social Security payroll tax cut and unemployment benefits	YES
Ease securities rules to expand small-business access to capital	YES
Extend for one year subsidized student loan interest rates financed by a cut in health care spending	YES
Cite Attorney General Eric H. Holder Jr. for contempt of Congress	NO
Create a visa program for foreign graduates in high-tech fields	NO
Extend most Bush-era income tax rates while allowing rates for top-bracket earners to rise (Jan. 1, 2013)	YES
2011	
Strike funding for F-35 alternative engine	YES
Prevent EPA from regulating greenhouse gas emissions to address climate change	NO
Extend certain provisions of Patriot Act for four years	YES
Declare opposition to use of ground troops in Libya	NO
Overhaul patent law	YES
Pass compromise debt limit increase plan and establish future spending limits	YES
Allow consideration of measures to implement three trade agreements	NO

CQ Vote Studies

	PARTY UNITY		PRESIDENTIAL SUPPORT	
	SUPPORT	OPPOSE	SUPPORT	OPPOSE
2012	93%	7%	78%	22%
2011	95%	5%	91%	9%
2010	96%	4%	95%	5%
2009	96%	4%	97%	3%
2008	99%	1%	16%	84%

Interest Groups

	AFL-CIO	ADA	CCUS	ACU
2012	90%	60%	50%	8%
2011	100%	85%	31%	0%
2010	100%	95%	25%	0%
2009	100%	100%	33%	0%
2008	100%	85%	71%	0%

New York 1

Eastern Suffolk County — Hamptons, Smithtown, Brookhaven

The 1st covers the eastern two-thirds of Suffolk County, from Smithtown and Hauppauge to Long Island's tip at Montauk. This swing district collects small fishing villages, oceanfront vacation towns and affluent suburbs.

Decennial redistricting changed the 1st's boundaries little, trading the Kings Park area of Smithtown for the hamlet of Hauppauge. Both areas solidly back Republicans, ensuring this district remains competitive. It flipped between parties in the presidential elections between 2000 and 2008 before voting for Democrat Barack Obama a second time in 2012. Republicans win county legislative seats, sometimes without opposition, but the district overall trends slightly Democratic.

Stony Brook University is the largest single-site employer in the district and on Long Island. Along with Brookhaven National Laboratory, the university sustains significant research communities in information technology, health care, energy, computing and other high-tech sectors. Stony Brook ranks among the top of U.S. universities in producing computer science graduates.

At the eastern end of the district, beachfront estates and vacation villages stretch through the Hamptons down the South Fork of Long Island along Route 27. The area is the summer playground of Wall Street titans and big-name entertainers. The North Fork of Long Island is home to some 47 wineries among the area's established agricultural sector. Local golf clubs have hosted numerous major PGA Tournaments.

Small fishing villages coexist among this largesse, and hostility toward federal regulations on catches drives some of local politics. The district's part-time celebrity residents participate in local politics, too, often through campaign contributions to candidates. Hedge fund founders who have homes in the district are some of the biggest donors.

Major Industry
Health care, research, retail, tourism

Cities
Coram (unincorp.), Centereach (unincorp.), Shirley (unincorp.)

Notable
The Montauk Point Lighthouse, constructed in 1796, was the first lighthouse built in New York.

Rep. Peter T. King (R)

Capitol Office
225-7896
peteking.house.gov
339 Cannon Bldg. 20515-3203; fax 226-2279

Committees
Financial Services
Homeland Security
(Counterterrorism & Intelligence - Chairman)
Select Intelligence

Residence
Seaford

Born
April 5, 1944; Manhattan, N.Y.

Religion
Roman Catholic

Family
Wife, Rosemary King; two children

Education
St. Francis College, B.A. 1965 (history); U. of Notre Dame, J.D. 1968

Military
N.Y. National Guard, 1968-73

Career
Lawyer; deputy county attorney; county government aide

Political Highlights
Hempstead Town Council, 1978-81; Nassau County comptroller, 1981-93; Republican nominee for N.Y. attorney general, 1986

ELECTION RESULTS

2012 GENERAL		
King (R, C, INDC)	142,309	58.6%
Vivianne C. Falcone (D, WFM)	100,505	41.4%
2012 PRIMARY		
King (R)		unopposed
2010 GENERAL		
King (R, C, INDC)	131,674	71.9%
Howard A. Kudler (D)	51,346	28.0%

Previous Winning Percentages
2008 (64%); 2006 (56%); 2004 (63%); 2002 (72%); 2000 (60%); 1998 (64%); 1996 (55%); 1994 (59%); 1992 (50%)

Elected 1992; 11th term

Despite his standing as one of the more independent House Republicans, the pugnacious King has been one of the most polarizing members of his party, thanks to a relentless focus and unfiltered commentary on national security matters. "I'm not that nice of a guy, so it's not like I run around trying to make friends," he said.

King became chairman of the Homeland Security Committee in September 2005. He served four years as its ranking Republican, then took the gavel again for the 112th Congress (2011-12). He wanted to stay on as chairman, but GOP term limits for panel leaders forced him out of the job — in the 113th Congress (2013-14), he chairs the Counterterrorism and Intelligence Subcommittee.

He has stated his belief that the primary job of the full panel is to oversee the Department of Homeland Security "to combat Islamist extremism." King is known for spurring a debate more divisive than even he expected, by holding hearings on the threat of radicalization in Muslim communities in the United States. King started scheduling witnesses — including a number of Muslims — to testify on the topic in 2011, and Democrats quickly accused him of being racist and blind to threats posed by other groups. Few in his own party offered a public defense of King.

"The reaction is the reaction," he said in August 2012. "I don't care. ... Believe it or not, I do think through what I do before I do it. And I feel that I'm doing the right thing, so I do it."

Controversy at least whips up attention, which King says is important as the public's attention to terrorist threats wanes. "The idea is to try to keep people focused on it, to try to keep from too many cuts being made into homeland security, but not sound like I'm paranoid about it," he said.

He used controversy to tremendous effect at the start of 2013. Superstorm Sandy hit the East Coast in October 2012, and King thought that a large package of federal assistance was the right thing. Republican leaders did not schedule a House vote on an aid package before the conclusion of the 112th Congress (2011-12), and King nearly exploded. He unleashed a torrent of criticism in the media, calling the decision a "disgrace" and "immoral." It was soon announced that votes would be held in early 2013.

Many Republicans, including some from disaster-prone states, voted against two bills tied to Sandy recovery, complaining that they were loaded with unrelated spending. An MSNBC host later asked King if he could forgive those votes. "No, I won't," he said. "And I never will."

During the 112th Congress, King voted to preserve or expand grant programs for first responders. He has supported a "risk-based" allocation of homeland security resources, with preferences for regions (such as New York City) deemed more likely to be targeted by terrorists.

King sits on the Financial Services Committee, where he championed a bill that extended for seven years the Terrorism Risk Insurance Act, which obligates the government to help pay for financial losses from future attacks. The measure was signed into law in December 2007. He also joined the Intelligence Committee in 2011.

King attributes some of his style to growing up in Queens, where there were many ethnic groups and "nobody cared about anybody else's feelings." His blue-collar Irish upbringing also has something to do with it: "No one thinks they're better than the other guy and you know everybody has an angle, including yourself, so you don't take yourself too seriously."

His political toughness hasn't resulted in overt partisanship over the years. He worked with Bill and Hillary Rodham Clinton to promote peace efforts in

Northern Ireland, held bipartisan hearings with his Senate counterparts and turned a rocky relationship with Homeland Security Secretary Janet Napolitano into a friendship. He once called Speaker Newt Gingrich of Georgia "road kill on the highway of American politics."

King is more sympathetic than most Republicans to the concerns of union labor. He is not an ardent cost-cutter, and he has described legislation requiring background checks for every gun purchase as a "no-brainer."

He hasn't flirted with a party switch, however. King declined an offer to become ambassador to Ireland at the start of the Obama administration. He said in 2012 that he couldn't see himself "sitting around with a bunch of Irish guys saying some bullshit about how evil the United States is and how [George W.] Bush is a terrible president."

King once kept a closer watch on the peace process with Northern Ireland and had a close relationship with Gerry Adams, the leader of Sinn Fein, the political wing of the Irish Republican Army. His enthusiasm has flagged. He was especially turned off, he said, by a prominent Irish official telling him how important it was to close the Guantánamo Bay detention facility in Cuba. "They'd still be killing each other if it wasn't for the U.S., and they're worried about a few guys who got waterboarded," King said. "They were acquiring a European sophistication that annoyed me."

King's father was a New York City police officer, heading the physical fitness training for the force. That gave King early exposure to boxing, which he has pursued as a hobby over the last decade.

Another major hobby is fiction writing. In his 2004 novel "Vale of Tears," the protagonist, a congressman, faces radical Islamists in cahoots with the IRA. In the earlier "Deliver Us From Evil," another thinly disguised congressman seeks an end to fighting in Northern Ireland. He sees his writing style as a cross between that of journalists Jimmy Breslin and Pete Hamill, with influence from the late sports writer Jimmy Cannon.

King borrowed money to attend Notre Dame's law school. Afterward he interned (along with Rudy Giuliani, who later became mayor of New York) at Richard Nixon's New York law firm. He entered public life in 1972 as a deputy Nassau County attorney and eventually became the county comptroller, serving three terms. He lost a 1986 run for New York attorney general.

When veteran GOP Rep. Norman F. Lent stepped down in 1992, King moved quickly to claim the seat. After coasting through the primary, he edged the better-funded Democrat, Steve A. Orlins.

Running in a reconfigured and renumbered district in 2012, King took almost 59 percent of the vote — while Barack Obama carried the district's presidential vote.

Key Votes

2012	
Extend a Social Security payroll tax cut and unemployment benefits	YES
Ease securities rules to expand small-business access to capital	YES
Extend for one year subsidized student loan interest rates financed by a cut in health care spending	YES
Cite Attorney General Eric H. Holder Jr. for contempt of Congress	YES
Create a visa program for foreign graduates in high-tech fields	YES
Extend most Bush-era income tax rates while allowing rates for top-bracket earners to rise (Jan. 1, 2013)	YES
2011	
Strike funding for F-35 alternative engine	YES
Prevent EPA from regulating greenhouse gas emissions to address climate change	YES
Extend certain provisions of Patriot Act for four years	YES
Declare opposition to use of ground troops in Libya	YES
Overhaul patent law	YES
Pass compromise debt limit increase plan and establish future spending limits	YES
Allow consideration of measures to implement three trade agreements	YES

CQ Vote Studies

	PARTY UNITY		PRESIDENTIAL SUPPORT	
	SUPPORT	OPPOSE	SUPPORT	OPPOSE
2012	86%	14%	15%	85%
2011	88%	12%	31%	69%
2010	89%	11%	33%	67%
2009	74%	26%	54%	46%
2008	87%	13%	67%	33%

Interest Groups

	AFL-CIO	ADA	CCUS	ACU
2012	38%	0%	100%	60%
2011	41%	30%	93%	56%
2010	7%	10%	100%	92%
2009	38%	20%	93%	88%
2008	53%	45%	94%	50%

New York 2

Southwestern Suffolk County and part of Nassau County

The redrawn 2nd District spans part of the Atlantic Coast of Long Island, from Massapequa in Nassau County east to Bayport in Suffolk County. Drawn during remapping after the 2010 census, the 2nd and adjacent 3rd reflect the island's traditional divide between North Shore and South Shore communities.

The new map erased the complicated shape of the former 3rd and divides the two new districts roughly along the Long Island Expressway. Much of Islip, North Amityville, and the Wyandanch portion of Babylon now fall into the 2nd, as do the Deer Park and Brentwood areas of Suffolk County.

Pulling the lines of the former 3rd to the south and east doubled its Hispanic population. Suffolk County communities of Islip and Brentwood are home to thousands of Central American and Puerto Rican immigrants. Towns on the western edge of the district are overwhelmingly white and wealthy, and the district as a whole has a median household income of $82,000.

Although more famous spots to the east and west get more visitors, Babylon has three municipally owned ocean beaches. The district shares a sliver of serene Fire Island with the 1st. State parks and country clubs are scattered throughout the 2nd's bedroom communities. White-collar industries in nearby towns on Long Island employ many district residents. Parts of the 2nd experienced severe flooding and debris-based damage from Superstorm Sandy in 2012.

The new 2nd contains Democratic-leaning portions of Suffolk County, making slightly more competitive what had been two safe U.S. House seats — one each for Democrats and Republicans. The new 2nd, however, trends overall to the Democrats; Barack Obama won the district's 2012 presidential vote with 55 percent, with a slightly larger margin in more-populous Suffolk County.

Major Industry
Professional services, financial services, information technology, retail

Cities
Brentwood (unincorp.), Levittown (unincorp.), West Babylon (unincorp.)

Notable
Between 1947 and 1951, William Levitt & Sons constructed more than 17,000 homes in Levittown, a pace of 30 homes completed a day.

Rep. Steve Israel (D)

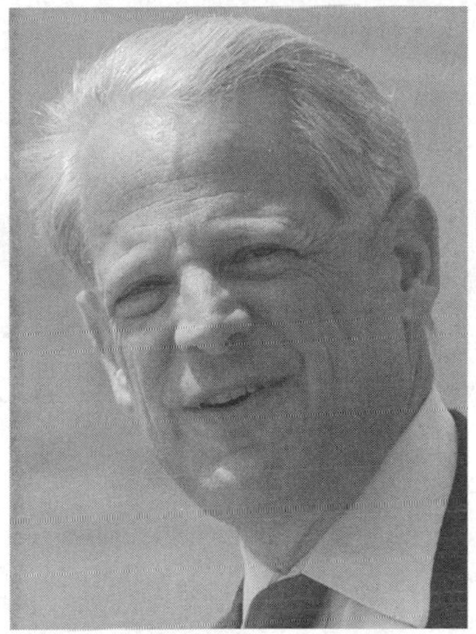

Capitol Office
225-3335
israel.house.gov
2457 Rayburn Bldg. 20515-3202; fax 225-4669

Committees
No committee assignments

Residence
Huntington

Born
May 30, 1958, Brooklyn, N.Y.

Religion
Jewish

Family
Separated; two children

Education
Nassau Community College, A.A. 1978 (liberal arts); Syracuse U., attended 1978-79; George Washington U., B.A. 1982 (political science)

Career
Public relations and marketing firm manager; assistant county executive; university fundraising director; Jewish advocacy group county director; congressional aide

Political Highlights
Democratic nominee for Suffolk County Legislature, 1987; Huntington Town Board, 1993-2001 (majority leader, 1997-2001)

ELECTION RESULTS

2012 GENERAL		
Israel (D, WFM, INDC)	157,880	57.8%
Stephen A. Labate (R, C)	113,203	41.5%
2012 PRIMARY		
Israel (D)		unopposed
2010 GENERAL		
Israel (D, WFM, INDC)	94,594	56.3%
John Gomez (R, C)	72,029	42.9%

Previous Winning Percentages
2008 (67%); 2006 (70%); 2004 (67%); 2002 (58%); 2000 (48%)

Elected 2000; 7th term

Israel wears two very different hats. He's a pragmatic centrist representing a wealthy Long Island district, and a hard-charging partisan determined to put Democrats back in the majority.

He says there is no contradiction. As chairman of the Democratic Congressional Campaign Committee, Israel has not shied from attacking Republicans and their agenda, and he regularly huddles with senior Democratic Party officials. But he likes to point out that when Democratic leader Nancy Pelosi tapped him to head the DCCC — shortly after Republicans gained more than 60 House seats in the 2010 elections — she touted his "practical experience in running and winning in difficult districts."

A workaholic — he says he sleeps only four hours a night — Israel threw himself into the job with characteristic energy in the 2012 election cycle. He raised more money than his Republican counterparts, encouraged the use of sophisticated data analysis and research tools, and played the role of eternal optimist, touting his party's chances of retaking the House.

In the spring of 2012, Israel said that his greatest worry was super PACs — independent advocacy groups that can accept unrestricted donations from individuals or organizations. They "are going to come in and spend tens of millions of dollars in stealth money, supported by corporate interests, and try to steal this election away from us," he said in the spring of 2012. Democrats repeated that narrative, over and over.

His biggest foe, however, was the redistricting process. Republicans were in charge of many statehouses after 2010, and the congressional maps they produced for the 2012 elections made Democratic gains all the more difficult. Democrats picked up eight seats on Election Day, which was 17 fewer than they needed to regain the majority.

Israel began looking toward 2014 almost immediately, calling around to recruit candidates. And he seems to have a powerful new person on his team. President Barack Obama committed to appear at several DCCC fundraisers, and his campaign team agreed to share its voter data with Israel's staff. "We will make 2014 a referendum on the tea party, and we will win that referendum by recruiting, deploying and fielding candidates who run as solutionists and problem solvers," Israel said in 2013.

Israel urges Democrats to focus on solutions rather than on ideology — a philosophy he has put into practice since winning his first House race in 2000 with just 48 percent of the vote. (That amount was good enough for a 13-point win, however.)

He has moderate views on energy and foreign affairs, and he focuses attentively on constituent service — a necessity, since Israel sits on no committees as he focuses on his DCCC work. Israel says his proudest achievement as a lawmaker is securing $5 million in back pay for military veterans.

A self-described "policy wonk on the middle class," he broke with the White House on taxes during the 112th Congress (2011-12). Israel argued that the George W. Bush-era tax cuts should be extended for families making $250,000 or more — an income level that isn't considered that high in his upper-crust district. He got his wish in January 2013, when the "fiscal cliff" agreement increased tax rates only on joint-filer income above $450,000.

Israel joined the fiscally conservative Blue Dog Coalition upon arriving in the House in 2001, and he created the bipartisan Center Aisle Caucus in 2005. He started the group after a particularly busy day, when he was racing to catch a flight home and flung open a House door with such force that it struck the man in front of him, Illinois Republican Timothy V. Johnson. Israel introduced himself, and the caucus was born. Its membership was greatly reduced, however, as lawmakers left during the 2010 campaign season. Israel himself left the Blue Dog Coalition.

Before taking over the DCCC, Israel sat on the Appropriations Committee, where he dedicated himself to becoming a leader on energy policy.

He proposed expanded tax credits for families to offset the costs of alternative fuel and energy-efficient technologies, as well as tax and investment incentives for businesses to encourage development of wind power, solar power and other renewable-energy sources. In 2009, Israel joined Democrat Betty Sutton of Ohio in sponsoring a bill to create a "cash for clunkers" program to encourage consumers to trade in older cars for more fuel-efficient models. Their bill was supplanted by a less stringent version that became law.

Israel keeps pictures of his maternal grandparents and their immigration certificates — they grew up in czarist Russia — in his Washington office. He says that he often thinks about their experiences and calls them "my best political consultants."

Israel became interested in politics at an early age. He started reading newspapers after hearing in his Levittown, N.Y., elementary school that Sen. Robert F. Kennedy of New York had been assassinated.

In high school, he rode his bicycle after classes to the campaign headquarters of Democrat Franklin Ornstein, who in 1974 waged an unsuccessful challenge to GOP Rep. Norman F. Lent. As a political science student at George Washington University, Israel worked part-time for California Democratic Rep. Robert T. Matsui, then spent three years with Rep. Richard L. Ottinger, a New York Democrat. He returned to Long Island in 1983, where he worked as a fundraiser for Touro College, a Jewish-sponsored institution. In 1987, he lost a bid for the Suffolk County Legislature.

Israel formed his own fundraising and public relations firm and was director of the Institute on the Holocaust and the Law, which is affiliated with Touro and the American Jewish Congress. He stayed active in local politics, winning a seat on the Huntington Town Board in a 1993 special election.

During his years in Long Island politics, he always had in mind a return to Washington. His chance came in 2000. New York Mayor Rudy Giuliani announced that he had prostate cancer and dropped a bid for the Senate. The 2nd District's four-term congressman, Republican Rick A. Lazio, stepped in to take the GOP Senate nomination, and Israel immediately launched a campaign for the open seat.

He won the primary by 555 votes en route to a November victory. His subsequent races have turned out to be easy wins. His district changed significantly in the latest round of redistricting and now extends into part of New York City.

Key Votes

2012	
Extend a Social Security payroll tax cut and unemployment benefits	YES
Ease securities rules to expand small-business access to capital	YES
Extend for one year subsidized student loan interest rates financed by a cut in health care spending	NO
Cite Attorney General Eric H. Holder Jr. for contempt of Congress	?
Create a visa program for foreign graduates in high-tech fields	NO
Extend most Bush-era income tax rates while allowing rates for top-bracket earners to rise (Jan. 1, 2013)	YES
2011	
Strike funding for F-35 alternative engine	NO
Prevent EPA from regulating greenhouse gas emissions to address climate change	NO
Extend certain provisions of Patriot Act for four years	YES
Declare opposition to use of ground troops in Libya	NO
Overhaul patent law	YES
Pass compromise debt limit increase plan and establish future spending limits	YES
Allow consideration of measures to implement three trade agreements	NO

CQ Vote Studies

	PARTY UNITY		PRESIDENTIAL SUPPORT	
	SUPPORT	OPPOSE	SUPPORT	OPPOSE
2012	95%	5%	86%	14%
2011	94%	6%	93%	7%
2010	98%	2%	93%	7%
2009	99%	1%	97%	3%
2008	99%	1%	15%	85%

Interest Groups

	AFL-CIO	ADA	CCUS	ACU
2012	90%	80%	33%	8%
2011	100%	85%	31%	0%
2010	100%	90%	25%	0%
2009	100%	95%	33%	0%
2008	100%	95%	61%	0%

New York 3

Part of Queens; northern Nassau County; northwest Suffolk County

One of two central Long Island districts completely remapped following the 2010 census, the new 3rd tracks the island's North Shore from the Queens terminus entrance of the Whitestone Bridge to Smithtown Bay. With reapportionment eliminating one of Long Island's U.S. House seats, the former 3rd's constituents were divided among four different districts.

The new 3rd was given affluent parts of northeastern Suffolk County from the old 2nd District, including Northport, Dix Hills, Melville and Huntington. Its boundaries extend into the tony communities of Nassau County's Gold Coast, the setting for "The Great Gatsby" and still home to some of the wealthiest zip codes in the nation — the Americana Manhasset shopping plaza provides high-end shopping destinations to match.

The Little Neck section of Queens, where single-family homes dominate, has a suburban feel within New York City. Similarly residential, Whitestone had been filled with older homes, many of which were razed to make way for larger, modern residences — local officials relied on zoning law changes to halt the transformation of the traditionally blue-collar area.

The new 3rd is politically competitive, and one of the GOP's only New York City Council seats is in the district. Despite losing the voting strength of southern Suffolk County, the strong lean of Queens and Democratic voters in Nassau County are enough for Democratic candidates at the federal level. Barack Obama won with a 7-percentage-point margin here in the 2012 presidential election.

Although the district remains close to 80 percent white, the addition of several Asian-majority areas of Queens diversified the 3rd's population. Asians make up nearly 13 percent of residents, while Hispanics account for almost 9 percent; the 3rd has the smallest proportion of black residents of any district that includes a part of New York City.

Major Industry
Financial services, retail, telecommunications

Cities
New York (pt.), Hicksville (unincorp.), Commack (unincorp.)

Notable
Bethpage State Park has five public golf courses, including Bethpage Black, the only public course on the PGA Tour; The Queens County Farm Museum is New York City's largest tract of farmland.

Rep. Carolyn McCarthy (D)

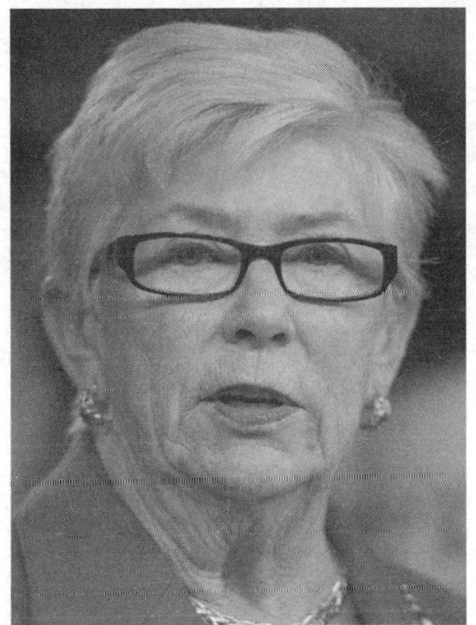

Capitol Office
225-5516
carolynmccarthy.house.gov
2346 Rayburn Bldg. 20515 3204, fax 225-5758

Committees
Education & the Workforce
Financial Services

Residence
Mineola

Born
Jan. 5, 1944; Brooklyn, N.Y.

Religion
Roman Catholic

Family
Widowed; one child

Education
Glen Cove Nursing School, L.P.N. 1964

Career
Nurse

Political Highlights
No previous office

ELECTION RESULTS

2012 GENERAL		
McCarthy (D, WFM, INDC)	163,955	61.8%
Fran Becker (R)	85,693	32.3%
Frank Scaturro (CNSTP)	15,603	5.9%
2012 PRIMARY		
McCarthy (D)		unopposed
2010 GENERAL		
McCarthy (D, WFM)	94,483	53.6%
Fran Becker (R, C, INDC)	81,718	46.4%

Previous Winning Percentages
2008 (64%); 2006 (65%); 2004 (63%); 2002 (56%); 2000 (61%); 1998 (53%); 1996 (57%)

Elected 1996; 9th term

McCarthy always will be identified with gun control, but she also takes a keen interest in financial sector oversight and improving the public education system. "Most of my experience comes from nursing," she said. "I'm there to protect those that need the most help, and right now, my middle-income families need help."

Born into a blue-collar Brooklyn household, McCarthy moved to Long Island when she was 8. In high school, her boyfriend was in a serious car accident; the private-duty nurse who cared for him before he died of his injuries inspired her to apply to nursing school, she once told Good Housekeeping magazine. McCarthy monitored terminally ill patients for 30 years.

Another tragedy put her on a political path. In December 1993, her husband and son were shot by a deranged gunman on the Long Island Railroad. Her husband did not survive. McCarthy became a gun control activist, which led to her 1996 House campaign.

She was a registered Republican but ran as a Democrat, and throughout her House career McCarthy has generally stuck with the Democratic Party. Still, as a member of the business-oriented New Democrat Coalition, she seeks out the middle ground on some spending, budgetary and trade measures. As a member of the New York delegation wary of further terrorist attacks, she has backed expansions of surveillance authority and defense measures that more-liberal Democrats oppose.

"I've always looked to see that the majority of the bill is good," she said. "If there are things in there I don't like, I will still vote for it."

Her gun control work can be seen as starting from the middle ground. The problem is not the Second Amendment, according to McCarthy, but the ways people take advantage of it without proper supervision.

In the 112th Congress (2011-12), she introduced bills to require background checks for every firearm sale. Every U.S. governor received a letter from her denouncing a 2011 House-passed bill to allow people with concealed-carry permits from one state to bring weapons to most other states, regardless of their laws. McCarthy called it an infringement of states' rights.

She also proposed a ban on the use of high-capacity ammo magazines, similar to language included in the Clinton-era ban on certain semiautomatic weapons that expired in 2004. Such a device was used in the shooting that killed her husband, and in the 2011 shooting of Arizona Democrat Gabrielle Giffords. Both of those incidents, as well as a mass shooting at Virginia Tech in 2007, were followed by flurries of activity by McCarthy.

She redoubled her efforts after two more tragedies in 2012: mass shootings at a Colorado movie theater and a Connecticut elementary school. In the 113th Congress (2013-14), McCarthy is the House sponsor of an assault weapons ban proposed by California Democratic Sen. Dianne Feinstein. She also revived her slate of bills on background checks, magazines and ammunition sales.

McCarthy says the pro-gun lobby makes it hard for such bills to advance: "When you're working here in Congress and you see the odds and the strong hold the NRA and gun manufacturers have on members — basically threatening that they're not going to win re-election — I think it's tough."

On the Financial Services Committee, McCarthy is sympathetic to concerns that the 2010 financial regulatory overhaul could be harming institutions that weren't responsible for the 2008 financial collapse, as regulators impose rules outside of lawmakers' original intent. "I do not believe that businesses are evil," she said. "I don't believe that everybody out there is trying to pull the wool over someone's eyes." However, she says the 2010 law and its newly created Consumer Financial Protection Bureau have been helping the average consumer.

She has a parochial interest in the recovery of the financial services sector, as many Wall Street employees make their home on Long Island. Her district was also hit hard by Superstorm Sandy in 2012. McCarthy is a co-sponsor of a bipartisan bill to slow the rate of flood insurance premium increases for people living in disaster areas.

McCarthy strongly supported a 2012 reauthorization of the Export-Import Bank, which helps businesses export products overseas. She looks to serve as an educator to both constituents and fellow lawmakers on the vagaries of the global economy; she says her own knowledge has evolved substantially since her freshman term.

As a member of the Education and the Workforce Committee, she tries to draw attention to students. In 2013, McCarthy became the top Democrat on the Early Childhood, Elementary and Secondary Education Subcommittee. She supported the 2002 law known as No Child Left Behind, but said its requirements for measured progress pressured educators to "teach to the test."

"I hate mandates," said McCarthy, who wants rewrites of the law to focus on increased flexibility for states and local entities to reach targets set at the federal level. Requirements for special-needs students with physical or intellectual disabilities are particularly tough for schools to meet under current constraints, she said. Having grown up with dyslexia, McCarthy cares deeply about special-needs education. She has professed a dislike of charter schools that avoid enrolling students with disabilities.

President Barack Obama proposed expanding early-childhood education programs in his 2013 State of the Union address. Weeks later, McCarthy and Hawaii Democratic Sen. Mazie K. Hirono introduced bills to create a grant program for states looking to expand or improve their preschool programs.

McCarthy and her stockbroker husband purchased her childhood home in Mineola from her parents, and they lived there together for 27 years until his death. Her son was paralyzed in the 1993 shooting, but with McCarthy's care, he was able to resume his commute to work in Manhattan.

Three years after the shootings, McCarthy was incensed when freshman Republican Daniel Frisa voted in 1996 to eliminate the ban on semiautomatic weapons. Republican officials tried to discourage her from running, so she launched a campaign as a Democrat to unseat him and won with more than 57 percent of the vote. Most of her re-election campaigns have been fairly easy, including a nearly 30-point victory over Republican Fran Becker in 2012.

McCarthy announced in June 2013 that she had been diagnosed with lung cancer and would miss some congressional activities during her treatment.

Key Votes

2012	
Extend a Social Security payroll tax cut and unemployment benefits	YES
Ease securities rules to expand small-business access to capital	YES
Extend for one year subsidized student loan interest rates financed by a cut in health care spending	NO
Cite Attorney General Eric H. Holder Jr. for contempt of Congress	?
Create a visa program for foreign graduates in high-tech fields	NO
Extend most Bush-era income tax rates while allowing rates for top-bracket earners to rise (Jan. 1, 2013)	YES
2011	
Strike funding for F-35 alternative engine	YES
Prevent EPA from regulating greenhouse gas emissions to address climate change	NO
Extend certain provisions of Patriot Act for four years	?
Declare opposition to use of ground troops in Libya	YES
Overhaul patent law	YES
Pass compromise debt limit increase plan and establish future spending limits	YES
Allow consideration of measures to implement three trade agreements	NO

CQ Vote Studies

	PARTY UNITY		PRESIDENTIAL SUPPORT	
	SUPPORT	OPPOSE	SUPPORT	OPPOSE
2012	91%	9%	81%	19%
2011	91%	9%	95%	5%
2010	96%	4%	93%	8%
2009	97%	3%	97%	3%
2008	99%	1%	16%	84%

Interest Groups

	AFL-CIO	ADA	CCUS	ACU
2012	90%	65%	42%	8%
2011	96%	75%	44%	0%
2010	100%	80%	17%	4%
2009	100%	95%	40%	0%
2008	100%	95%	65%	0%

New York 4

Southern Nassau County — Hempstead

The 4th District unites low-key suburban towns and beach villages with working-class enclaves and is centered on most of the town of Hempstead, in the southwestern corner of Nassau County on Long Island.

Decennial redistricting added significant stretches of South Shore coastline to the 4th, including popular Jones Beach State Park, site of an annual summertime concert series. The seaside town of Long Beach is the terminus for a branch of the Long Island Rail Road. Wantagh, a Baby Boom-era suburb of dual-income families north of Jones Beach, also joined the 4th.

With aging town centers, redevelopment — and the related environmental and traffic impact — is a major factor in local politics in the 4th. Hockey's New York Islanders moved to Brooklyn following drawn-out negotiations for a $3 billion multipurpose development and public-funding debates regarding a possible $400 million replacement for Nassau Veterans Memorial Coliseum.

Hempstead, meanwhile, has approved a $2 billion revitalization plan for downtown and hosts Hofstra University, the state's largest private college and a pillar of the district's economy. The university opened a medical school with North Shore-LIJ Health System, located in the 3rd District, in 2011. Like its neighbors along the coast, the 4th District suffered damage from Superstorm Sandy in late 2012, particularly in Long Beach.

The 4th is the most ethnically and racially diverse of the four Long Island-based districts. Large African-American and Hispanic communities populate Hempstead, as well as Uniondale and areas south to Freeport. The 4th is home to four of the so-called "Five Towns" of sizable Orthodox Jewish communities in the southwestern corner of Nassau County. Hispanics make up 18 percent of the district overall. These demographics contribute to a Democratic base in the 4th, and Barack Obama won 53 percent of the district's presidential vote in 2012.

Major Industry

Health care, higher education, technology, service

Cities

Hempstead Village, Freeport, East Meadow (unincorp.)

Notable

In 1957, Adelphi University in Garden City hosted the first National Wheelchair Games.

Rep. Gregory W. Meeks (D)

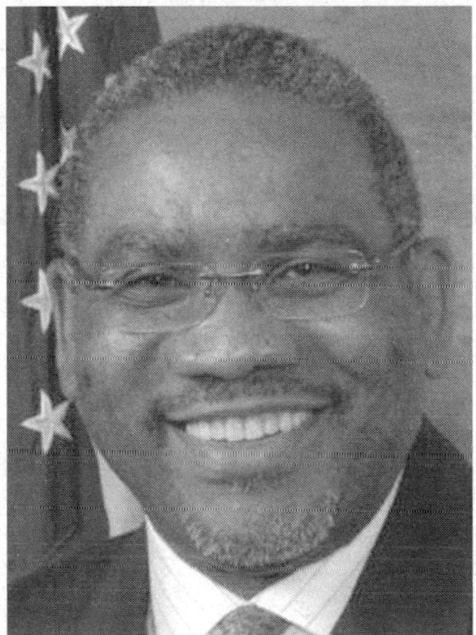

Capitol Office
225-3461
meeks.house.gov
2234 Rayburn Bldg. 20515-3206; fax 226-4169

Committees
Financial Services
Foreign Affairs

Residence
Queens

Born
Sept. 25, 1953; Manhattan, N.Y.

Religion
African Methodist Episcopal

Family
Wife, Simone-Marie Meeks; three children

Education
Adelphi U., B.A. 1975; Howard U., J.D. 1978

Career
Workers' compensation board judge; lawyer; city prosecutor

Political Highlights
N.Y. Assembly, 1993-98

ELECTION RESULTS

2012 GENERAL		
Meeks (D)	167,836	89.7%
Allan W. Jennings Jr. (R)	17,875	9.6%
2012 PRIMARY		
Meeks (D)	9,920	66.5%
Allan W. Jennings Jr. (D)	1,972	13.2%
Mike Scala (D)	1,694	11.4%
Joseph R. Marthone (D)	1,327	8.9%
2010 GENERAL		
Meeks (D)	85,096	87.7%
Asher Taub (R)	11,826	12.2%

Previous Winning Percentages
2008 (100%); 2006 (100%); 2004 (100%); 2002 (97%); 2000 (100%); 1998 (100%); 1998 Special Election (56%)

Elected 1998; 8th full term

Meeks often plays the part of a New York City liberal, but his focus on financial issues and his support for free trade distinguish him from some of his more ideological colleagues on the Democratic left.

A member of the Financial Services Committee and the business-friendly New Democrat Coalition, Meeks spends much of his time working on domestic economic policy and consumer finance issues that affect his mostly middle-class, African-American district in Queens.

He is particularly interested in the banking and investment industry, which dominates the New York economy, and he helped develop the 2010 overhaul of financial regulations, known as Dodd-Frank. While he enthusiastically supported the legislation, he opposed elements that might pose a threat to the financial sector, including provisions in the enacted version that allowed regulators to break up firms that become so large and interconnected that their failure could threaten the broader economy.

In the 112th Congress (2011-12), he turned to protecting the legislation from Republican efforts to chip away at it. "We worked very hard on Dodd-Frank and in fact put a lot of ideas in it that were from the other side," Meeks said. "It's been a fight on the committee just to preserve what we did."

For the 113th Congress (2013-14), Meeks is the top Democrat on the Financial Institutions and Consumer Credit Subcommittee. Early in 2013, he told a trade association that he supports regulatory changes that would more than double the amount of capital that credit unions can loan to small businesses.

When Democrats controlled the House, Meeks chaired the committee's International Monetary Policy and Trade panel, where he staked out centrist positions on trade issues. Although many Democrats are wary of free trade, Meeks' district is home to John F. Kennedy International Airport, and he has been an advocate for boosting cargo traffic there. "The more cargo coming in and out of the JFK Airport ... the more jobs it creates in my district," he said.

He is also interested in a diverse set of trade partners. "When you start talking about trade agreements with emerging countries, that's where the problems are" politically, he said. "But that's exactly who we want to trade with. ... It helps improve and raise their level of living," which Meeks sees as improving global stability.

He voted in favor of free-trade agreements with South Korea, Panama and Colombia in 2011, and he favored granting Russia preferential trade status to coincide with its entry into the World Trade Organization. "The only one that loses if we don't do that would be us," he said. Congress approved that change in December 2012.

Meeks backs the current efforts to produce a Trans-Pacific Partnership trade agreement, which the United States is negotiating with nearly a dozen other countries that border the Pacific Ocean. He welcomed Japan as it petitioned to join that group in 2013. Many of his Democratic colleagues remain skeptical of the pact, given domestic industry and labor opposition. Meeks co-founded the Services Caucus, with the goals of boosting trade in services such as banking, insurance, express delivery and information technology and of breaking down barriers for U.S. companies to invest in places such as India and China.

He also pursues trade goals on the Foreign Affairs Committee. On almost all foreign affairs issues, Meeks is squarely behind President Barack Obama's agenda, including the speedier withdrawal from Afghanistan and the withdrawal from Iraq. He has countered GOP calls for deep cuts in foreign assistance programs, something he calls "penny-wise and pound-foolish." As anti-

American protests swept the Muslim world in September 2012, he wrote on The Hill website that aid to Libya and Egypt should not be cut.

Meeks was one of the official representatives of the U.S. government at the funeral of Venezuelan President Hugo Chavez in March 2013. He was diplomatic in describing the trip to the Politicker website, saying that as controversial as Chavez was, "he did have his heart on the poor."

On social issues, Meeks is a staunch liberal, supporting gun control laws and gay rights and opposing restrictions on abortion.

Raised in public housing in East Harlem, Meeks traces his interest in public affairs to his mother, who resumed her education when her four children were in their teens. She frequently got her kids involved in community improvement projects. "From the time that I could remember, I wanted to be a lawyer," Meeks told Newsday. "I always admired Thurgood Marshall, and I learned from my parents what he was doing to make life better for people of color."

After graduating from Howard University Law School, Meeks began his career as a Queens County assistant district attorney prosecuting narcotics crimes. In 1992, he ran for and won the first of three terms to the state Assembly. In his years in Albany, he had seats on committees that oversaw state codes, the judiciary and insurance.

When six-term Democratic Rep. Floyd H. Flake resigned in late 1997 to lead an influential African Methodist Episcopal church in Jamaica, Queens, he endorsed Meeks as his successor. Meeks captured 56 percent of the vote in a five-way contest in the February 1998 special election. He was unopposed for a full term that November and has not been seriously challenged in subsequent elections.

But he has faced a series of questions about ethics. Early in 2008, Meeks agreed to pay a $63,000 fine and to reimburse his campaign committee after the Federal Election Commission found that he had illegally used campaign cash from the 2004 election for a personal trainer and had leased cars for personal use. Meeks blamed sloppy bookkeeping by his treasurer.

In 2010, The New York Times took him to task for buying a home built for him by a campaign contributor and for expenditures on fundraising trips. Never charged with wrongdoing, he said he had to travel to where the donors are. In 2007, Meeks accepted a $40,000 loan from a personal friend in his district. It did not show up on his disclosure forms. When the New York Daily News reported on the loan a few years later, he quickly repaid it.

Meeks says the infraction was an oversight — he failed to "disclose a loan that I had, and when I realized that it was not disclosed, I disclosed it." The Ethics Committee ended its investigation in December 2012, saying there was no way of determining if the loan was an impermissible gift.

Key Votes

2012	
Extend a Social Security payroll tax cut and unemployment benefits	YES
Ease securities rules to expand small-business access to capital	YES
Extend for one year subsidized student loan interest rates financed by a cut in health care spending	NO
Cite Attorney General Eric H. Holder Jr. for contempt of Congress	?
Create a visa program for foreign graduates in high-tech fields	NO
Extend most Bush-era income tax rates while allowing rates for top-bracket earners to rise (Jan. 1, 2013)	YES
2011	
Strike funding for F-35 alternative engine	YES
Prevent EPA from regulating greenhouse gas emissions to address climate change	NO
Extend certain provisions of Patriot Act for four years	NO
Declare opposition to use of ground troops in Libya	NO
Overhaul patent law	?
Pass compromise debt limit increase plan and establish future spending limits	YES
Allow consideration of measures to implement three trade agreements	YES

CQ Vote Studies

	PARTY UNITY		PRESIDENTIAL SUPPORT	
	SUPPORT	OPPOSE	SUPPORT	OPPOSE
2012	96%	4%	89%	11%
2011	95%	5%	89%	11%
2010	99%	1%	95%	5%
2009	98%	2%	97%	3%
2008	99%	1%	19%	81%

Interest Groups

	AFL-CIO	ADA	CCUS	ACU
2012	94%	85%	30%	0%
2011	89%	70%	36%	0%
2010	100%	90%	25%	0%
2009	100%	100%	40%	0%
2008	100%	90%	65%	0%

New York 5

South Queens — Jamaica, St. Albans, Rockaways

Almost wholly within the borders of Queens, the majority-black 5th District stretches from Belmont Park — home of the last leg of horse-racing's Triple Crown series — to the tip of the Rockaway Peninsula. Most of its constituents live in a cluster of middle-class areas north of John F. Kennedy International Airport. Decennial redistricting added the campus of St. John's University to the north, Inwood in Nassau County in the southeast, and all of the Rockaways down to the gated beach bungalows of Breezy Point.

Jamaica has been one of New York's major middle-class black districts for generations. Recent decades have seen thousands of immigrants arrive annually, especially from India, Bangladesh, El Salvador and the Dominican Republic. Nearby neighborhoods such as Hollis, St. Albans and Ozone Park also have large Ecuadoran and Puerto Rican communities. The Richmond Hill neighborhood is known as "Little Guyana."

JFK Airport is a major economic dynamo, employing nearly 58,000 residents of the 5th and other parts of the region. It is the nation's leading hub of international commercial flights as well as a primary cargo airport. A $350 million rail hub in the center of Jamaica connects airport travelers to commuter trains and subways.

Despite a relatively strong economic foundation overall, the downturn in the housing market hit the 5th District hard. Foreclosures surged in southeastern Queens in 2010, accelerated by widespread loan fraud. The number of residents on government income assistance programs more than doubled from 2000 to 2010.

Union members, residents of established though shrinking middle-class black communities and recent immigrants give Democrats a 6-to-1 voter registration lead in the district. Barack Obama took 86 percent of the district's 2012 presidential vote.

Major Industry
Transportation, government, health care

Cities
New York (pt.), Valley Stream, Elmont (unincorp.)

Notable
Hollis is the hometown of many legendary hip-hop figures, including Russell Simmons, the members of Run-DMC and LL Cool J.

Rep. Grace Meng (D)

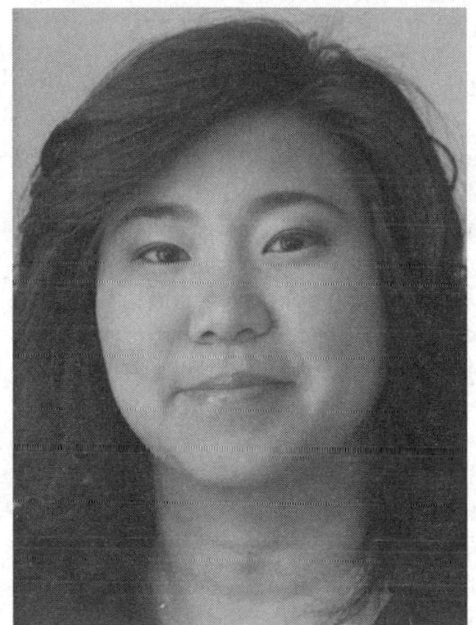

Capitol Office
225-2601
meng.house.gov
1317 Longworth Bldg. 20515-2110; fax 225-1500

Committees
Foreign Affairs
Small Business

Residence
Queens

Born
Oct. 1, 1975; Queens, N.Y.

Religion
Christian

Family
Husband, Wayne Kye; two children

Education
U. of Michigan, B.A. 1997 (Chinese & history); Yeshiva U., J.D. 2002

Career
Lawyer; campaign aide; communications firm aide

Political Highlights
N.Y. Assembly, 2009-13

ELECTION RESULTS

2012 GENERAL		
Meng (D, WFM)	111,501	67.9%
Daniel J. Halloran (R, C)	50,846	31.0%
Evergreen C. Chou (GREEN)	1,913	1.2%
2012 PRIMARY		
Meng (D)	14,825	53.0%
Rory I. Lancman (D)	7,089	25.3%
Elizabeth S. Crowley (D)	4,606	16.5%
Robert Mittman (D)	1,462	5.2%

Elected 2012; 1st term

An influx of Asian-Americans and immigrants has dramatically reshaped many communities in Queens. Meng represents not just her district, but the growing clout of that demographic — she is the first Asian-American in the history of New York's congressional delegation.

Meng is the oldest child of Taiwanese immigrants. Her father, Jimmy K. Meng, owned a lumber company and was the first Asian-American member of the New York Assembly. She grew up in Queens, went to the University of Michigan for college, then returned to New York to get a law degree.

She stepped up her involvement in politics by managing her father's 2004 Assembly campaign. He didn't seek a second term, and Meng hoped to succeed him — but a court found that she did not meet the residency requirement for the district. She tried again in 2008 and won. Constituent service took up huge amounts of her time — she told The Empire blog that in her first term, "I barely physically left the boundaries of my district."

Meng still touts a district-focused agenda, wanting to create more jobs at home. She is the top Democrat on the Small Business Subcommittee on Contracting and Workforce, and she favors more tax credits for small businesses. She is also on the Foreign Affairs Committee and its panel on the Middle East — her district has a sizable Jewish community.

Meng has two young sons. Her husband, who was her high school sweetheart, is a Korean-American dentist.

The 6th District was cobbled together from pieces of several old districts, but the incumbents from the old districts cleared out for the 2012 election. Republican Bob Turner ran for the Senate, and Democrat Gary L. Ackerman retired. Meng got the endorsement of Rep. Joe Crowley, who chairs the Queens County Democratic Party, and easily won the very Democratic district.

Jimmy Meng was convicted of wire fraud in November 2012, for offering to bribe prosecutors on behalf of a businessman charged with tax fraud.

New York 6

North Queens — Forest Hills, part of Flushing, Bayside

Quiet, tree-lined neighborhoods of northern and central Queens make up the new 6th District, which brings together long-established working-class communities and burgeoning immigrant enclaves.

The 6th is the crossroads of a redistricted Long Island, combining former constituents of five different U.S. House seats. It stretches from Ridgewood and Glendale at the Brooklyn border through Rego Park and Forest Hills, swinging north along the Whitestone Expressway to include Flushing and Murray Hill. Bayside, a tony neighborhood, and Oakland Gardens form its easternmost limits.

Stringent zoning restrictions have preserved much of the district's older, often pre-war housing stock of Tudor, cape and Romanesque-revival homes. Residents and visitors enjoy the Frederick Law Olmsted-designed Forest Park as well as the Queens Botanical Garden.

The district's portion of Flushing is home to New York City's second major Chinatown, and Chinese and Korean immigrant communities have spread eastward down the Long Island Expressway to Bayside and near Rego Park. Asians and whites each make up large proportions of the district's residents, mixing with a sizable Hispanic population. Within the 6th's racial demographics is a dizzying array of ethnic diversity, among which are Indian-Americans and a community of Bukharian Jews — immigrants from Central Asia — in Forest Hills, Rego Park and Kew Gardens. Religious diversity abounds here, mirroring the mix of nationalities in the district. The district's communities host churches, synagogues and temples. Queens College, part of the City College of New York system, also reflects the 6th's diversity — more than half of its 20,000 students were born in one of 130 foreign countries.

The 6th is solid Democratic territory. In the 2012 presidential election, Barack Obama took 68 percent of the district's vote.

Major Industry
Service, health care

Cities
New York (pt.)

Notable
Gangsters Lucky Luciano and John Gotti are buried at St. John's Cemetery in Middle Village.

Rep. Nydia M. Velázquez (D)

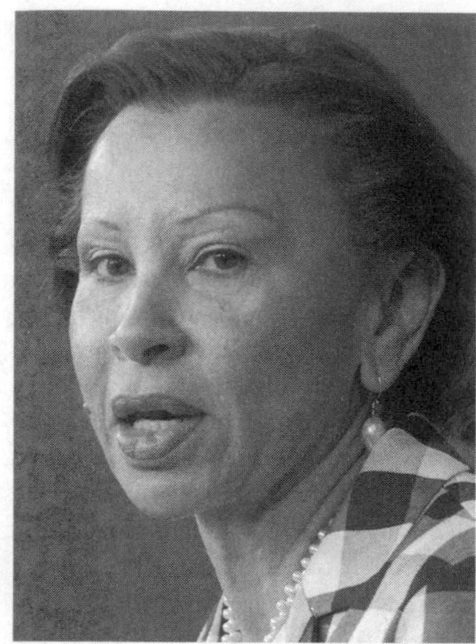

Capitol Office
225-2361
velazquez.house.gov
2302 Rayburn Bldg. 20515-3212; fax 226-0327

Committees
Financial Services
Small Business - Ranking Member

Residence
Brooklyn

Born
March 28, 1953; Yabucoa, P.R.

Religion
Roman Catholic

Family
Divorced

Education
U. of Puerto Rico, B.A. 1974 (political science); New York U., M.A. 1976 (political science)

Career
Puerto Rican Community Affairs Department director; congressional aide; professor

Political Highlights
New York City Council, 1984-85; defeated for election to New York City Council, 1984

ELECTION RESULTS

2012 GENERAL		
Velázquez (D, WFM)	141,359	94.8%
James Murray (C)	7,816	5.2%
2012 PRIMARY		
Velázquez (D)	17,208	57.9%
Erik Martin Dilan (D)	10,408	35.0%
Daniel J. O'Connor (D)	1,351	4.5%
George Martinez (D)	745	2.5%
2010 GENERAL		
Velázquez (D, WFM)	68,624	93.8%
Alice Gaffney (C)	4,482	6.1%

Previous Winning Percentages
2008 (90%); 2006 (90%); 2004 (86%); 2002 (96%); 2000 (86%); 1998 (84%); 1996 (85%); 1994 (92%); 1992 (77%)

Elected 1992; 11th term

Throughout her House career, Velázquez has subscribed to the notion that small businesses are an engine of economic growth, and her desire to tune that engine tempers her otherwise uncompromising brand of liberalism. She is considered a pioneer among female Hispanic politicians and operates with some degree of independence from the Democratic Party establishment.

Born in Puerto Rico, she grew up in the territory and first moved to New York City for graduate school in the 1970s. As an appointee, she became the first Hispanic woman on the City Council. Velázquez later returned to Puerto Rico for a time to work for the territorial government but went back to the city to oversee Puerto Rico's community relations office there. A new, heavily Hispanic district drawn for the 1992 elections made her the first Puerto Rican woman elected to the House.

Velázquez has said she won her seat without the support of the local Democratic Party; critics noted that she ran a Hispanic voter registration effort financed by the Puerto Rican government just before the election, and they accused her of targeting potential constituents. The New York Times and other publications have over the years noted her clashes with Brooklyn party bosses, and she has stuck to liberal positions even when Democratic presidents have tried to rally votes around centrist bills.

She has still managed to hold positions of leadership. She chaired the Congressional Hispanic Caucus in the 111th Congress (2009-10), and since 2005 she has been the top Democrat on the Small Business Committee. Her four-year stint as chairwoman of that panel marked the first time a Hispanic woman led a House committee.

Velázquez can be pointed and partisan in hearings and on the House floor. She does not regularly appear in headlines, however. The Small Business Administration was marginalized under the George W. Bush administration, and her committee has a lower profile than most panels.

But she has tried to enhance federal support for small businesses, while also making some nods to reducing regulatory burdens. Velázquez publicizes reports on whether federal agencies are meeting their requirements for contracting with small businesses. (They aren't.) In the 112th Congress (2011-12), she suggested that cuts to small-business loan programs were slowing economic recovery; she also stated that start-up businesses, as the most prolific creators of new jobs, deserve extra attention and support.

She has used her pulpit to badger a company widely perceived as a destroyer of small businesses. In a 2011 opinion piece in New York's Daily News, Velázquez and New York City Council Speaker Christine Quinn mused how the opening of a Walmart could turn a neighborhood into a "deserted, economic crater, with Walmart at the epicenter."

That rhetoric aside, Velázquez made some bipartisan overtures in the 112th Congress. When she was chairwoman, she fought to change the Small Business Innovation Research program, which steers federal research grants and contracts to smaller companies, so that businesses owned primarily by venture capital firms would be eligible. Some business associations argued that large venture capital firms don't need the help, but Chairman Sam Graves of Missouri agreed with Velázquez, and a six-year reauthorization enacted in 2011 included the change.

She also endorsed the successful repeal of a provision in the 2010 health care law requiring businesses to report to the IRS every vendor paid more than $600 in a year. The requirement was meant to stop tax cheats, but Velázquez agreed that compliance costs were too much for small businesses.

She walks a more partisan line as a member of the Financial Services Committee. Republicans contend that Democrats' 2010 financial regulatory law restricts capital flows, particularly to small businesses. Velázquez counters that the new agencies and regulators created by the law have mandates to consider their effect on small business. At a 2012 hearing on the Consumer Financial Protection Bureau, she said: "If done properly, this agency can make the entire financial system and the economy more stable without constricting our nation's entrepreneurs."

Velázquez touts to her constituents her seat on the Financial Services Committee's housing panel, and she has urged more federal attempts to mitigate foreclosures.

Her business-friendly impulses sometimes clash with her progressive tendencies. Velázquez backed a 2012 reauthorization of the Export-Import Bank, which helps many small businesses sell goods overseas. But in 2011, she voted against free-trade agreements with Colombia, Panama and South Korea.

She is a member of the Congressional Progressive Caucus, the group of the most-liberal Democrats, and her stances jibe with those of her constituents, a majority of whom are working-class minorities. She is critical of the 1996 welfare overhaul law for being too harsh on the poor, and she favors more-liberal immigration policies.

Velázquez was raised in Yabucoa, in the sugar cane region in southeastern Puerto Rico, with her twin sister and seven other siblings. Her father cut cane and her mother helped make ends meet by selling food to other cane workers. Her father also made cinder blocks and owned a cockfighting pit. He had only a third-grade education but was a community leader and founded a political party in their hometown.

She entered the University of Puerto Rico at age 16 and was the first in her family to receive a college diploma. After grad school on the mainland, she taught Puerto Rican Studies at Hunter College and became a special assistant to Democratic Rep. Edolphus Towns.

In 1984, city council members appointed her, at 31, to replace a member who had been convicted of corruption. She served a short time before losing her attempt to hold the seat in an election.

Her second try for elective office was a success. Nine-term Democrat Stephen J. Solarz had his district largely broken up by redistricting, and Velázquez defeated him and four other Democrats in the 1992 primary. In the general election, she took 77 percent of the vote. Her re-elections have been easy.

State leaders made minor tweaks to Velázquez's district during redistricting for 2012, which inspired Councilman Erik Martin Dilan to challenge Velázquez in the primary. She defeated him by almost 23 points.

Key Votes

2012	
Extend a Social Security payroll tax cut and unemployment benefits	YES
Ease securities rules to expand small-business access to capital	YES
Extend for one year subsidized student loan interest rates financed by a cut in health care spending	NO
Cite Attorney General Eric H. Holder Jr. for contempt of Congress	?
Create a visa program for foreign graduates in high-tech fields	-
Extend most Bush-era income tax rates while allowing rates for top-bracket earners to rise (Jan. 1, 2013)	YES
2011	
Strike funding for F-35 alternative engine	YES
Prevent EPA from regulating greenhouse gas emissions to address climate change	NO
Extend certain provisions of Patriot Act for four years	NO
Declare opposition to use of ground troops in Libya	NO
Overhaul patent law	NO
Pass compromise debt limit increase plan and establish future spending limits	NO
Allow consideration of measures to implement three trade agreements	NO

CQ Vote Studies

	PARTY UNITY		PRESIDENTIAL SUPPORT	
	SUPPORT	OPPOSE	SUPPORT	OPPOSE
2012	99%	1%	93%	7%
2011	97%	3%	78%	22%
2010	96%	4%	79%	21%
2009	99%	1%	94%	6%
2008	100%	0%	14%	86%

Interest Groups

	AFL-CIO	ADA	CCUS	ACU
2012	95%	90%	18%	0%
2011	100%	90%	19%	8%
2010	100%	100%	13%	0%
2009	100%	100%	33%	0%
2008	100%	100%	50%	0%

New York 7

Lower East Side of Manhattan; part of Brooklyn — Brooklyn Heights, Williamsburg, Bushwick

The boomerang-shaped 7th District encapsulates New York City's past century of immigration history, as it traces through the ethnically diverse neighborhoods of western Brooklyn, lower Manhattan and western Queens.

The southern edge of the overwhelmingly Democratic 7th starts in Brooklyn's Sunset Park, an area divided between a Chinese community to the east and Mexican, Puerto Rican and Dominican pockets to the west. It then runs north through part of affluent Park Slope and gentrifying areas in Red Hook, Carroll Gardens and Cobble Hill, home to professionals and creative types priced out of Manhattan. Major commercial and residential redevelopment projects for downtown Brooklyn — basketball's Nets have moved from New Jersey into the new Barclays Center at Atlantic Yards in the neighboring 9th — will have an impact on the economy here.

Crossing the East River, the district pivots in southeastern Manhattan. It includes Chinatown, which, with the arrival of Fujianese and Taiwanese newcomers, has spread into nearby historic Little Italy. The district covers the Lower East Side, an enclave of Eastern European immigrants a century ago and now heavily Chinese and Puerto Rican. Although popular with young singles, it remains among the poorest neighborhoods in the city.

From Manhattan, the 7th shoots east through the redevelopment hotspots at the Brooklyn Navy Yard and Williamsburg into Hispanic-majority Bushwick, where rent tends to be unusually low. The district bends through heavily Puerto Rican and Dominican Cypress Hills, another neighborhood popular with first-home owners, before reaching its easternmost extent in the Queens neighborhood of Woodhaven.

Major Industry
Health care, service

Cities
New York (pt.)

Notable
Green-Wood Cemetery near Sunset Park has more than 560,000 interred, including abolitionist Henry Ward Beecher, Tammany Hall's William "Boss" Tweed and conductor Leonard Bernstein.

Rep. Hakeem Jeffries (D)

Capitol Office
225-5936
jeffries.house.gov
1339 Longworth Bldg. 20515-1202; fax 225-1018

Committees
Budget
Judiciary

Residence
Brooklyn

Born
Aug. 4, 1970; Brooklyn, N.Y.

Religion
Baptist

Family
Wife, Kennisandra Jeffries; two children

Education
State U. of New York, Binghamton, B.A. 1992 (African studies & political science); Georgetown U., M.P.P. 1994; New York U., J.D. 1997

Career
Lawyer

Political Highlights
Sought Democratic nomination for N.Y. Assembly, 2000; Independence and Libertarian nominee for N.Y. Assembly, 2000; sought Democratic nomination for N.Y. Assembly, 2002; N.Y. Assembly, 2007-13

ELECTION RESULTS

2012 GENERAL		
Jeffries (D, WFM)	184,039	90.2%
Alan S. Bellone (R, C)	17,650	8.6%
Colin M. Beavan (GREEN)	2,441	1.2%
2012 PRIMARY		
Jeffries (D)	27,504	71.4%
Charles Barron (D)	11,035	28.6%

Elected 2012; 1st term

Jeffries has been dubbed "Brooklyn's Barack," and his career path does have similarities with that of the president. He is a lawyer, he is ambitious, he has navigated big-city Democratic politics, and his public career took off in his mid-30s. The New York Times noted his ability to "talk to the gentrifiers in Clinton Hill and Fort Greene and to the Hasidim in Crown Heights," as well as his district's large black community.

Jeffries (first name: HA-keem) was born and raised in Brooklyn. He left town for college and grad school, then returned to work on his law degree at New York University. A few years into his legal career, he was hired as a counsel for Viacom Inc. and CBS. Before turning 30, he launched an unsuccessful primary challenge to Democratic state Assemblyman Roger Green. Two years later, he tried again — and failed again. Green stepped aside to run for the U.S. House in 2006, and Jeffries won the election to succeed him. While serving in the Assembly, he wrote the 2010 law to stop the New York Police Department from keeping a database of information on people detained, then released under its "stop and frisk" policy. Mayor Michael Bloomberg was not pleased.

Jeffries, a member of the liberal Congressional Progressive Caucus, vows to assist distressed homeowners in his district — he said that federal interventions to preserve and create affordable housing are "absolutely critical." He worked on the issue in the state legislature and established a legal clinic that offers free advice and services to residents facing displacement.

He supports liberal spending priorities from the Budget Committee. He also sits on the Judiciary Committee and its Commercial and Antitrust Law Subcommittee, where he can draw on his experience as a corporate lawyer.

In early 2012, Jeffries filed to run in the heavily Democratic 8th District, setting up a primary battle with 15-term Rep. Edolphus Towns. A few months later, Towns opted to retire. The only other Democrat in the race was New York Councilman Charles Barron, a former Black Panther. Jeffries won easily.

New York 8

Brooklyn — most of Bedford-Stuyvesant, East New York, Canarsie, Coney Island

The 8th District cuts a broad arc through Brooklyn and catches a slice of western Queens — now reaching from Sea Gate toward John F. Kennedy International Airport (in the 5th) and back west to Fort Greene. Majority-black and overwhelmingly Democratic, the 8th combines some of Brooklyn's most pervasively impoverished neighborhoods with rapidly redeveloping areas.

Decennial redistricting significantly widened the geographic reach of the former 10th District to the south and east. The new 8th clips Howard Beach and part of Ozone Park from Queens. It hugs the Belt Parkway tightly around Sheepshead Bay and bends toward new reaches beyond Coney Island. The 8th now also contains half of Jamaica Bay, part of which is a national wildlife refuge.

Race divides the communities at the 8th's elbow. Howard Beach is overwhelmingly white, while nearby Ozone Park and East New York are heavily Hispanic and African-American, respectively. Predominately Jewish and Italian a generation ago, Canarsie to the south is also mostly black, home to many immigrants from Haiti and the West Indies.

Made famous by the gritty depictions of artists such as Spike Lee, Jay-Z and the Notorious B.I.G., Bedford Stuyvesant — or Bed-Stuy — is rapidly turning over as new arrivals snatch up Brooklyn's iconic brownstones. To the west, Clinton Hill and Fort Greene's historic housing stock has attracted professionals priced out of Park Slope. Long Island University and Pratt Institute are landmarks here, and redevelopment plans — including entertainment, shopping, technology and cultural districts — are under way in the 8th and adjacent districts.

With rock-solid Democratic credentials, the 8th District's main political competition occurs in intraparty contests. The district gave Barack Obama 89 percent of its vote in the 2012 presidential election.

Major Industry
Retail, construction, government

Cities
New York (pt.)

Notable
Commodore Barry Park, originally named City Park, was bought by the city in 1836 and is the oldest park in Brooklyn.

Rep. Yvette D. Clarke (D)

Capitol Office
225-6231
clarke.house.gov
2351 Rayburn Bldg. 20515-3211; fax 226-0112

Committees
Ethics
Homeland Security
Small Business

Residence
Brooklyn

Born
Nov. 21, 1964; Brooklyn, N.Y.

Religion
Christian

Family
Single

Education
Oberlin College, attended 1982-86 (Black studies)

Career
Local economic development director; day care and youth program coordinator; state agency aide; state legislative aide

Political Highlights
New York City Council, 2002-07; sought Democratic nomination for U.S. House, 2004

ELECTION RESULTS

2012 GENERAL		
Clarke (D, WFM)	186,141	87.3%
Daniel J. Cavanagh (R, C)	24,164	11.3%
Vivia Morgan (GREEN)	2,991	1.4%
2012 PRIMARY		
Clarke (D)	15,069	88.3%
Sylvia G. Kinard (D)	1,993	11.7%
2010 GENERAL		
Clarke (D, WFM)	104,297	90.5%
Hugh C. Carr (R, C)	10,858	9.4%

Previous Winning Percentages
2008 (93%); 2006 (90%)

Elected 2006; 4th term

Clarke is a partisan Democrat who looks to her Jamaican heritage, Brooklyn upbringing and ethnically diverse district to guide her in Congress. Liberal and often outspoken, she focuses on civil rights, immigration and homeland security.

She clearly has decent standing within her party. In the 113th Congress (2013-14), Clarke is the only Democrat in the House serving as the ranking member on two subcommittees. She also joined the Ethics Committee, where service is often considered a favor to party leaders.

Clarke became the top Democrat on the Homeland Security Subcommittee on Cybersecurity, Infrastructure Protection and Security Technologies in 2011 — she had chaired the Emerging Threats Subcommittee, a panel with similar jurisdiction, in the 111th Congress (2009-10). Now working with Chairman Patrick Meehan of Pennsylvania, Clarke keeps a sharp focus on cybersecurity in particular.

She has tried to position the Department of Homeland Security as the lead federal agency for cybersecurity, urging Congress to codify that role. She is supportive of greater information sharing between the federal government and the private sector as they fight off cyberattacks, but she voted against a 2012 bill to boost such cooperation — she said it needed more guarantees that companies couldn't give customer data to the government. An April 2013 version with added protections won her support.

Republicans are hesitant to create mandatory cybersecurity standards for the private sector, but Clarke has written that "a more proactive approach" is merited for systems tied to "critical infrastructure," such as power and water utilities. And at a March 2013 hearing, she said it was essential to start calling out nations engaging in cyberattacks: "Foreign actors can no longer be permitted to commit industrial-strength espionage against our government and businesses without being brought to account."

In general, Clarke sees most homeland security efforts as under-resourced. "If we treated our armed services the way we treat homeland security, other nations would be eating our lunch," she said at a February 2013 hearing.

As a member of the Small Business Committee, Clarke takes cues from the ethnic diversity of her district. She has introduced bills to increase the number of federal contracts given to minority business owners, increase funding for minority-owned business development and create grant and mentorship programs for small construction firms owned by women, veterans and minorities. In 2013, she was named the top Democrat on the Investigations, Oversight and Regulations Subcommittee.

Immigration weighs heavily on the minds of the black and Latino residents throughout her district. It is also a driving issue for Clarke, who, as the daughter of Jamaican immigrants, takes it personally. "When people say immigration, they think Spanish-speaking Latinos," she said. "I'm an English-speaking 'sista' born in Brooklyn, but, you know, I am a part of the immigrant experience." As discussions of a comprehensive immigration law overhaul began in the 113th Congress, Clarke urged lawmakers to remember African immigrants. "This debate cannot solely rest on the shoulders of our Latino brothers and sisters," she wrote.

Clarke's first bill in 2007 was meant to expedite FBI background checks on immigrants awaiting determination of their legal status; a 2009 Clarke measure would have criminalized the exploitation of people seeking immigration assistance.

She is keenly interested in the interactions between the minority communities in her district and law enforcement. Particularly, she has urged the Justice Department to investigate the New York Police Department's "stop and frisk" policy, which allows police officers to detain a suspicious individual and search his or her body for any illegal possessions. In a Huffington Post op-ed, Clarke argued that the policy illegally targets minorities and "jeopardizes the constitutional rights of those who are stopped, questioned and searched with very limited cause."

Clarke is a member of both the Congressional Black Caucus and the liberal Congressional Progressive Caucus.

Speaking to a Democratic group in Brooklyn in 2012, Clarke described some tea party protesters from the health care debate of the 111th Congress (2009-10), saying that they "had no problems with racial epithets, they had no problem with cursing, spitting and everything else" and that they "really just showed the ugliest sides of the United States of America." An edited video of her comments posted on the Internet resulted in threatening phone calls to her offices and prompted Clarke to notify the U.S. Capitol Police.

Born in Brooklyn, Clarke resides in the same Flatbush neighborhood where she grew up. Her father, Leslie L. Clarke Sr., was a civil engineer for the Port Authority of New York and New Jersey. Her mother, Una S.T. Clarke, worked as an accountant, early-childhood educator and education consultant before being elected to the New York City Council in 1991.

After attending New York City public schools, Clarke received a scholarship to Oberlin College, where she majored in black studies. She later served as business development director for the Bronx Empowerment Zone and the first director of the Bronx branch of the New York City Empowerment Zone.

When her mother stepped down from the city council in 2001 because of term limits, Clarke was her successor. She won adoption of an ordinance requiring city government buildings to have twice as many restroom stalls for women as for men. In 2007, once in Congress, she co-sponsored a bill by her New York Democratic colleague Edolphus Towns that would apply the same requirement to federal buildings. In the 111th Congress, she backed a version requiring at least a 1-to-1 ratio.

In 2000, Una Clarke lost a primary contest to incumbent House Democrat Major R. Owens. Four years later, the younger Clarke took her turn against Owens and lost, drawing 29 percent of the vote in a four-way primary that Owens won with a plurality. When Owens announced he would step down at the end of the 109th Congress (2005-06), Clarke decided to try again. She bested a trio of other hopefuls, including the congressman's son, Chris, to claim the nomination — tantamount to election in the heavily Democratic district. She sailed to re-election in three subsequent races.

Key Votes

2012	
Extend a Social Security payroll tax cut and unemployment benefits	NO
Ease securities rules to expand small-business access to capital	NO
Extend for one year subsidized student loan interest rates financed by a cut in health care spending	NO
Cite Attorney General Eric H. Holder Jr. for contempt of Congress	?
Create a visa program for foreign graduates in high-tech fields	NO
Extend most Bush-era income tax rates while allowing rates for top-bracket earners to rise (Jan. 1, 2013)	YES
2011	
Strike funding for F-35 alternative engine	NO
Prevent EPA from regulating greenhouse gas emissions to address climate change	NO
Extend certain provisions of Patriot Act for four years	NO
Declare opposition to use of ground troops in Libya	NO
Overhaul patent law	YES
Pass compromise debt limit increase plan and establish future spending limits	NO
Allow consideration of measures to implement three trade agreements	NO

CQ Vote Studies

	PARTY UNITY		PRESIDENTIAL SUPPORT	
	SUPPORT	OPPOSE	SUPPORT	OPPOSE
2012	98%	2%	88%	12%
2011	97%	3%	77%	23%
2010	98%	2%	76%	24%
2009	99%	1%	96%	4%
2008	99%	1%	16%	84%

Interest Groups

	AFL-CIO	ADA	CCUS	ACU
2012	95%	95%	17%	0%
2011	100%	95%	13%	8%
2010	93%	95%	25%	4%
2009	100%	100%	33%	0%
2008	100%	100%	56%	0%

New York 9

Brooklyn — Flatbush, Crown Heights, Brownsville, Sheepshead Bay

The 9th cuts through the heart of Brooklyn. Ethnically and economically diverse, this district contains many of the borough's cultural treasures and iconic neighborhoods. Minorities make up more than 70 percent of the population. Heavily Democratic, those neighborhoods gave Barack Obama more than 80 percent of the vote in the past two presidential contests.

The top of the 9th runs across neighborhoods south of Atlantic Avenue. At its northwestern corner are some of the tree-lined streets of Park Slope, arguably the most desirable area in Brooklyn. Nearby is slightly scruffier Prospect Heights, which blends brownstone walk-ups and modern residential towers. Those neighborhoods wrap around Prospect Park, home to many of Brooklyn's major attractions, including the Brooklyn Museum of Art and the borough's central library, Botanic Garden and zoo.

A large Hasidic Jewish community lives in Crown Heights, south of Eastern Parkway. Tensions between the orthodox sect and Caribbean neighbors north of the parkway have eased since the famous 1991 riots; the Jewish Children's Museum is a destination in the neighborhood. Midwood, another Orthodox Jewish enclave, is the site of Brooklyn College's Georgian-style campus.

Brownsville, on the 9th's northeastern edge, has high-rise housing projects and a serious gang problem. Flatbush, where the iconic Ebbets Field once stood, is in the district's center; home to various ethnicities, more than half of its residents are of West Indian, Latin American or South Asian descent.

Several hospitals in the district — including Kings County Hospital and the State University of New York Downstate Medical Center in East Flatbush — provide jobs. Sheepshead Bay forms the lower tier of the district, just north of Belt Parkway, and hosts large Chinese, Russian and Ukrainian communities.

Major Industry
Health care, retail, service

Cities
New York (pt.)

Notable
The West Indian Day Carnival Parade in Crown Heights and Prospect Park attracts millions of visitors each year on Labor Day.

Rep. Jerrold Nadler (D)

Capitol Office
225-5635
nadler.house.gov
2110 Rayburn Bldg. 20515-0200; fax 225-6923

Committees
Judiciary
Transportation & Infrastructure

Residence
Manhattan

Born
June 13, 1947; Brooklyn, N.Y.

Religion
Jewish

Family
Wife, Joyce L. Miller; one child

Education
Columbia U., A.B. 1969 (government); Fordham U., J.D. 1978

Career
State legislative aide

Political Highlights
N.Y. Assembly, 1976-92; candidate for Manhattan borough president, 1985; candidate for New York City comptroller, 1989

ELECTION RESULTS

2012 GENERAL		
Nadler (D, WFM)	165,743	80.8%
Michael W. Chan (R, C)	39,413	19.2%
2012 PRIMARY		
Nadler (D)		unopposed
2010 GENERAL		
Nadler (D, WFM)	88,758	73.4%
Susan Kone (R, C)	31,996	26.5%

Previous Winning Percentages
2008 (80%); 2006 (85%); 2004 (81%); 2002 (76%); 2000 (81%); 1998 (86%); 1996 (82%); 1994 (82%); 1992 (81%); 1992 Special Election (100%)

Elected 1992; 11th full term

Nadler has a New Yorker's sense of civility when he shares his thoughts on civil liberties and civil rights. Loud and very liberal, he distinguishes himself by championing gay rights, women's rights and Jewish causes. And despite representing the district that bore the brunt of the Sept. 11 attacks, he doggedly monitors the use of executive power in the war on terrorism.

Nadler (NAD-ler) was born in Brooklyn, but he spent his early years in New Jersey. Once he returned to New York City, he was there for good. He got a degree in government from Columbia University, where he organized a group of students, dubbed the "West Side Kids," to advance a liberal and anti-war agenda in New York politics.

He then worked at an off-track betting office and as a legislative aide for a state senator while attending Fordham University at night to get a law degree. In 1976, even before he completed law school, he won a seat in the state Assembly. He held it until 1992, when he was elected to the House.

The causes Nadler has adopted over his career resonate with his district, which includes large numbers of liberal Jewish voters and gay and lesbian political activists. In 2012, Nadler lauded the success of ballot initiatives for same-sex marriage in Maine, Maryland and Washington. He praised the election of Wisconsin Democrat Tammy Baldwin as the first openly gay senator. "Our nation is truly changing," he wrote.

Nadler works to facilitate that change. He helped lead the repeal of the ban on openly gay military servicemembers, which was completed in 2011. Nadler has tried several times to repeal the 1996 law that directs the federal government to recognize only marriages between one man and one woman. (The Supreme Court reviewed the law in March 2013.) When President Barack Obama endorsed same-sex marriage in May 2012, Nadler said it was a "brave and honest step. ... The course toward marriage equality and justice is the correct and inevitable path."

He is also an advocate for women's rights. He introduced a 2012 bill to require employers to make reasonable accommodations for pregnant workers and ban employers from using an employee's pregnancy to deny her employment opportunities.

From 2007 through 2010, Nadler chaired the Judiciary Subcommittee on the Constitution, Civil Rights and Civil Liberties. Since 2011, he has been the ranking member on its renamed equivalent. He describes, often in stark terms, an undue growth of presidential power. Nadler was a strident critic of President George W. Bush's prosecution of the war on terrorism. During the 110th Congress (2007-08), he used his oversight powers to test the waters on impeaching the president.

Several times, Nadler has pushed bills to rein in the use of the "state secrets" privilege, which allows the executive branch to bar evidence and even entire cases from court if it could expose sensitive national security information. In 2012 he rolled out a bill to prohibit the detention of any person without charge. "The notion that the United States ought to conduct itself according to the Constitution and the law of war should not be controversial," Nadler wrote. He supported Obama's decision (which was later reversed) to hold civilian trials for five individuals accused of conspiring in the Sept. 11 attacks.

Nadler is a vigorous opponent of the 2001 anti-terrorism law known as the Patriot Act, taking every opportunity to insist on its review. In 2012, he urged greater oversight of the government's electronic surveillance activities.

In a Judiciary Committee hearing in June 2012, Nadler demanded that the Justice Department release to Congress a memo that explains the legal rationale for targeted killings overseas of U.S. citizens suspected of terrorism. He repeatedly pressed Attorney General Eric H. Holder Jr. to provide the memo.

Nadler also has a seat on the Transportation and Infrastructure Committee. According to Newsday, during his time in the state Assembly, Nadler was the body's "reigning expert on transportation."

He is a longtime proponent of expanding freight rail capacity in New York City, partly as a means to reduce truck traffic. A two-year surface transportation bill was enacted in 2012, but Nadler was unable to secure commitments for a freight rail tunnel under New York Harbor, connecting Brooklyn with Bayonne, N.J. He says the tunnel would foster economic development, reduce air pollution and lower consumer costs in the city.

The Port of New York and New Jersey is another major local infrastructure concern. Since the creation of the Homeland Security Department in 2003, Nadler has criticized it for not doing enough on port security. When DHS failed to meet a July 2012 goal of screening 100 percent of cargo entering U.S. ports, Nadler and two colleagues took their displeasure to the New York Times. "Cost and technology have never been the primary obstacles to meeting this mandate," they wrote. "What is missing is a sense of urgency and determination."

Nadler is one of the most liberal House Democrats, and he is not always polite in assessing the GOP. Discussing Republican opposition to the 2010 health care law on MSNBC in 2012, Nadler said, "Their calculation has been from the very beginning of this debate that most Americans have insurance, and they don't care about those who don't." The GOP attitude, Nadler said, was to "let them die."

Nadler was raised in an Orthodox Jewish household. He spent his early years on a New Jersey poultry farm. He said he was drawn to public service, in part, after watching his father rail against President Dwight D. Eisenhower and Agriculture Secretary Ezra Taft Benson, blaming them for policies that made it impossible for Nadler's family to keep the farm. His family moved back to New York City after the farm failed.

Liberal Democratic Rep. Ted Weiss died on the eve of the 1992 Democratic primary, but voters renominated him anyway, giving party officials the right to pick a successor. That set off a scramble, with six candidates competing in the nine-day race for the nomination. Other aspirants were better known to the public, but Nadler had ties to the party insiders who would cast the votes. He got the nomination and won the special election, as well as the general election for a full term; his subsequent re-elections have been a breeze.

In 2002, Nadler underwent gastric bypass surgery to tackle obesity issues that had pushed the 5-foot-4-inch-tall lawmaker's weight as high as 338 pounds. Years later, the weight loss is still significant.

Key Votes

2012	
Extend a Social Security payroll tax cut and unemployment benefits	YES
Ease securities rules to expand small-business access to capital	NO
Extend for one year subsidized student loan interest rates financed by a cut in health care spending	NO
Cite Attorney General Eric H. Holder Jr. for contempt of Congress	NO
Create a visa program for foreign graduates in high-tech fields	NO
Extend most Bush-era income tax rates while allowing rates for top-bracket earners to rise (Jan. 1, 2013)	YES
2011	
Strike funding for F-35 alternative engine	YES
Prevent EPA from regulating greenhouse gas emissions to address climate change	NO
Extend certain provisions of Patriot Act for four years	NO
Declare opposition to use of ground troops in Libya	NO
Overhaul patent law	YES
Pass compromise debt limit increase plan and establish future spending limits	NO
Allow consideration of measures to implement three trade agreements	NO

CQ Vote Studies

	PARTY UNITY		PRESIDENTIAL SUPPORT	
	SUPPORT	OPPOSE	SUPPORT	OPPOSE
2012	99%	1%	88%	12%
2011	96%	4%	78%	22%
2010	98%	2%	86%	14%
2009	98%	2%	97%	3%
2008	99%	1%	14%	86%

Interest Groups

	AFL-CIO	ADA	CCUS	ACU
2012	95%	100%	17%	0%
2011	100%	95%	20%	4%
2010	100%	100%	14%	0%
2009	100%	95%	36%	0%
2008	100%	95%	53%	0%

New York 10

West Side of Manhattan; Borough Park, Bensonhurst

From tip to tail, the newly redrawn 10th District measures roughly 15 miles in length from West 122nd Street down the West Side of Manhattan, through the Brooklyn-Battery Tunnel, along the Brooklyn waterfront and into Bensonhurst. Along the way, it grabs many of the Big Apple's most famous landmarks and commercial centers.

Decennial redistricting stretched this district — the former 8th — north up Manhattan's West Side about 35 blocks through the campuses of Columbia University and Barnard College in Morningside Heights. It now also takes in about three-fourths of Central Park, including the Metropolitan Museum of Art, and the American Museum of Natural History is located on Central Park West. From Columbus Circle, the 10th roughly follows 8th Avenue through Hell's Kitchen and Chelsea. It widens at the West Village and takes in SoHo, Tribeca and the rest of Lower Manhattan.

The 8th crosses the East River and snags Governors Island and some of the Brooklyn waterfront. At its southeastern end it gathers heavily Hungarian and Polish Borough Park and most of Bensonhurst, where a traditionally Italian community is giving way to Chinese immigrants. These Brooklyn neighborhoods are the only reliable source of Republican votes in the district, which is a Democratic stronghold overall, combining academics, numerous ethnic backgrounds and liberal urbanites.

With the support of government funding and private developers, Lower Manhattan is experiencing a boom in residential construction. A new 76-story, Frank Gehry-designed apartment building and a number of other large towers around the World Trade Center site are in the works. New York's financial sector, an enormous force in the 10th's economic health, continues to stagger out of the recent recession — Wall Street firms no longer rent the most commercial space in Manhattan.

Major Industry
Finance, retail, tourism

Cities
New York (pt.)

Notable
The 10th is home to the Statue of Liberty, Ellis Island and the South Street Seaport; The Stonewall Inn, the site of a police raid and riot that touched off the Gay Rights movement in 1969, is still open in Greenwich Village.

Rep. Michael G. Grimm (R)

Capitol Office
225-3371
grimm.house.gov
512 Cannon Bldg. 20515-3213; fax 226-1272

Committees
Financial Services

Residence
Staten Island

Born
Feb. 7, 1970; Brooklyn, N.Y.

Religion
Roman Catholic

Family
Divorced

Education
Baruch College, B.B.A. 1994; New York Law School, J.D. 2002

Military
Marine Corps, 1989-90, Marine Corps Reserve, 1990-97

Career
Health food store owner; FBI agent; stockbroker

Political Highlights
No previous office

ELECTION RESULTS

2012 GENERAL		
Grimm (R, C)	103,118	52.2%
Mark S. Murphy (D, WFM)	92,430	46.8%
2012 PRIMARY		
Grimm (R)		unopposed
2010 GENERAL		
Grimm (R, C)	65,024	51.3%
Michael E. McMahon (D, INDC)	60,773	47.9%

Elected 2010; 2nd term

Grimm is the only congressional Republican representing New York City. He is one of his party's most moderate members and, early in his career, a magnet for controversy. He generates a flurry of legislation regarding the financial sector and a host of other subjects.

His story reads like a mash-up of movie plots. Grimm dropped out of college when he was 19 to join the Marine Corps, served in the Persian Gulf War, then switched to active reserve status as he completed his college studies.

While still in school, he began working as a clerk for the FBI on the midnight shift. He did a stint as an analyst and trader on Wall Street, then returned to the bureau. Grimm became a special agent investigating the Gambino crime family, before switching to fighting financial crimes. He went undercover, posing as a hedge fund manager in Operation Wooden Nickel, which resulted in wire fraud and money-laundering charges against dozens of traders. For good measure, he earned a law degree in 2002.

Drama has followed him to Congress, and not always in a positive way. The Justice Department is investigating Grimm's fundraising from his 2010 campaign, and in August 2012 it arrested one of his fundraisers on an immigration charge. Several people have alleged that Grimm used straw donors to exceed donation limits and promised to help the fundraiser, an Israeli national, get a green card in exchange for donations solicited from a New York synagogue. The Ethics Committee announced in November 2012 that it would start an investigation once the Justice Department wraps up.

Federal prosecutors also have alleged that a business partner of Grimm's — they owned a health food restaurant together after Grimm retired from the FBI — has ties to the Gambino family.

The allegations haven't affected Grimm's way of doing business. Like his nearby colleague in the state delegation, Long Island Republican Peter T. King, Grimm is moderate in politics, but not in demeanor.

He says he is "just right of center," and three months after he took office in 2011, he blasted members of the tea party movement — which he called an "extreme wing of the Republican Party" — for opposing a continuing resolution to keep the government operating. Grimm said it was important to give leaders more time to work out a spending deal. "I'm showing leadership here, and I'm stepping up and making some bold statements, but that's because of what I truly believe," he said at the time.

At the end of his first term, Grimm was livid that GOP leaders did not schedule a vote on a relief package tied to Superstorm Sandy, which had devastated parts of his Staten Island-based district. "I am here tonight saying to myself for the first time that I am not proud of the decision that my team has made," he said on the House floor.

During the 112th Congress (2011-12), Grimm voted for spending cuts, but he did not support many amendments targeting various grant and assistance programs. He also opposed efforts to limit the powers of the National Labor Relations Board and loosen rules on carrying guns across state lines. Interest group scorecards for his freshman term suggest that Grimm is one of the least conservative Republicans in Congress.

Grimm pumps out a lot of bills on a variety of subjects. In the 112th Congress, the House passed his bill to create a national "Blue Alert" system, to aid in the capture of people who seriously injure or kill law enforcement officers. It also passed a Grimm bill to clarify that states and localities could create programs to give residents discounts on toll roads — a major concern for Staten Islanders who regularly cross the Verrazano-Narrows Bridge. President Barack Obama signed bills by Grimm to allow a natural gas pipeline for New York City to run through some federally owned land, and to limit the regulatory penalties for hospital labs that make small administrative errors.

He sits on the Financial Services Committee. Grimm would like a full repeal of the 2010 financial regulatory overhaul known as Dodd-Frank, but in the meantime, he is working to modify pieces of the law.

Grimm won House passage of his 2011 bill to tweak derivatives regulations. It would exempt nonfinancial companies that use derivatives to hedge risk from having to meet the margin requirements in the law. Grimm said doing so would allow businesses to mitigate risk without tying up too much capital; he argued that derivatives let producers keep their supply costs stable, which in turn leads to more-stable prices for consumers.

Another Grimm measure would modify the incentives for whistle-blowers to report misconduct in financial services companies. Contending that the Securities and Exchange Commission cannot process reports quickly enough, he wants whistle-blowers to use a company's internal reporting systems first.

Grimm has been a little less assertive regarding housing. He agrees with the idea that Fannie Mae and Freddie Mac must be reduced and restructured, and that the private sector should be encouraged to fill the void as the government-sponsored enterprises retreat from the mortgage industry. But he has not committed to their elimination. "I know that they did a good job as secondary market providers in the past, and if they are able to do that job well, then maybe we don't have to disband them," he told MarketWatch in September 2012.

The Financial Services Committee handles flood insurance programs, and in 2013 Grimm introduced a bill to slow down the rate of premium increases for people living in disaster areas. Meant to ease the financial burdens on New Yorkers affected by Superstorm Sandy, the bill has bipartisan support.

Born in Brooklyn and raised in Queens, Grimm says his upbringing in New York City helped prepare him for the rigors of Congress: "The best and brightest go to New York City. That naturally makes me competitive."

Grimm defeated Michael A. Allegretti, a former aide to New York Mayor Michael Bloomberg, by more than 2-1 in the 2010 Republican primary. He took on one-term Democrat Michael E. McMahon in the general election and rode the national Republican wave to a 3-point victory.

Democrats thought they had a great shot at recapturing the seat in 2012, but they did not have a top-tier candidate in Mark S. Murphy, a former congressional aide and the son of former Rep. John Murphy. Grimm raised more than twice as much money as Murphy and took 52 percent of the vote. McMahon is pondering a challenge to Grimm in 2014, and New York City Councilman Domenic Recchia has already announced his candidacy.

Key Votes

2012	
Extend a Social Security payroll tax cut and unemployment benefits	YES
Ease securities rules to expand small-business access to capital	YES
Extend for one year subsidized student loan interest rates financed by a cut in health care spending	YES
Cite Attorney General Eric H. Holder Jr. for contempt of Congress	YES
Create a visa program for foreign graduates in high-tech fields	YES
Extend most Bush-era income tax rates while allowing rates for top-bracket earners to rise (Jan. 1, 2013)	YES
2011	
Strike funding for F-35 alternative engine	NO
Prevent EPA from regulating greenhouse gas emissions to address climate change	YES
Extend certain provisions of Patriot Act for four years	YES
Declare opposition to use of ground troops in Libya	YES
Overhaul patent law	YES
Pass compromise debt limit increase plan and establish future spending limits	YES
Allow consideration of measures to implement three trade agreements	YES

CQ Vote Studies

	PARTY UNITY		PRESIDENTIAL SUPPORT	
	SUPPORT	OPPOSE	SUPPORT	OPPOSE
2012	87%	13%	18%	82%
2011	88%	12%	30%	70%

Interest Groups

	AFL-CIO	ADA	CCUS	ACU
2012	43%	0%	100%	64%
2011	45%	30%	93%	52%

New York 11

Staten Island; Bay Ridge, Gravesend

The 11th District, which takes in all of Staten Island, spans the Verrazano Narrows into a southwestern corner of Brooklyn. Decennial redistricting swapped most of Bensonhurst into the 10th for much of eastern Sheepshead Bay, a move that gave the district a bit more of a Russian accent.

The 11th is the only one of the three majority-white New York City districts that does not represent any of Manhattan. Most constituents live on Staten Island, which is three-fourths white. Sizable Puerto Rican and Mexican communities live on its north shore, but much of the southern half of the island is of Italian, Irish and Eastern European descent.

The Brooklyn precincts of the 11th include heavily Italian sections such as Bay Ridge and Dyker Heights. Nearly 10,000 residents of Arab descent now live there as well, and the changing demographics have caused some tension.

The only New York City U.S. House seat represented by a Republican, the 11th has been held by the GOP in nearly every Congress for a generation. Its largely Catholic voting base is socially conservative. The southern third of Staten Island, its most affluent portion, is particularly fertile Republican territory. Its north shore is the only Democratic stronghold.

Staten Island residents endure 90-minute round-trip commutes, some of the worst nationwide for decades. More than 65,000 passengers take the 25-minute ride from the Staten Island Ferry's St. George Terminal to Lower Manhattan daily, and three bridges connect the borough to New Jersey. Locally, employment relies on retail and the health care sector. The 11th was hit hard by Superstorm Sandy in 2012, and rebuilding efforts continue; construction near the ferry terminal of the New York Wheel, planned to be the world's tallest Ferris wheel, is set to be complete by 2015.

Major Industry
Health care, retail, service

Military Bases
Fort Hamilton (Army), 267 military, 731 civilian

Cities
New York (pt.)

Notable
From 1948 to March 2001, the Fresh Kills landfill received New York City's waste — it briefly reopened to process wreckage from the Sept. 11, 2001, attacks on the World Trade Center — and is now a nature preserve.

Rep. Carolyn B. Maloney (D)

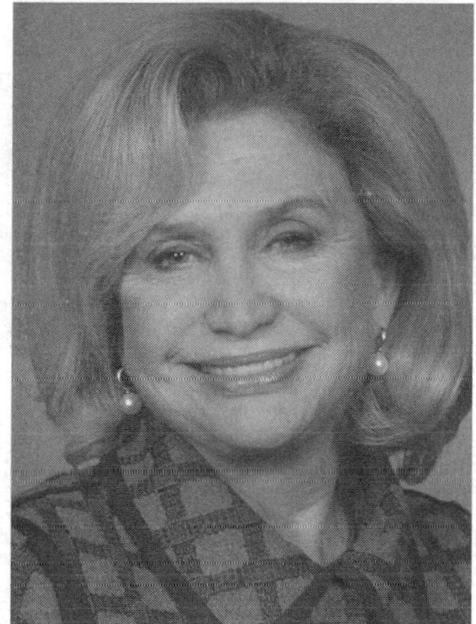

Capitol Office
225-7944
maloney.house.gov
2308 Rayburn Bldg. 20515-3214; fax 225-4709

Committees
Financial Services
Oversight & Government Reform
Joint Economic

Residence
Manhattan

Born
Feb. 19, 1946; Greensboro, N.C.

Religion
Presbyterian

Family
Widowed; two children

Education
Greensboro College, A.B. 1968; University of North Carolina, attended 1968-69

Career
State legislative aide; city board of education program coordinator; teacher

Political Highlights
New York City Council, 1982-93

ELECTION RESULTS

2012 GENERAL		
Maloney (D, WFM)	194,370	80.6%
Christopher Wight (R, C, INDC)	46,841	19.4%
2012 PRIMARY		
Maloney (D)		unopposed
2010 GENERAL		
Maloney (D, WFM)	107,327	75.0%
Ryan Brumberg (R)	32,065	22.4%
Tim Healy (C)	1,891	1.3%
Dino LaVerghetta (INDC)	1,617	1.1%

Previous Winning Percentages
2008 (80%); 2006 (84%); 2004 (81%); 2002 (75%); 2000 (74%); 1998 (77%); 1996 (72%); 1994 (64%); 1992 (50%)

Elected 1992; 11th term

Once Maloney chooses a cause to support, she won't drop it until she achieves her goals. "I am best when I take an issue and just push and push it," she says.

Over the years, Maloney has picked up a wide range of causes, usually promoting a liberal position. She is an unrelenting advocate for her constituents, women's rights and consumers; she has a long history overseeing the financial services industry; and she is especially passionate about helping the survivors of, first-responders to and families affected by the Sept. 11 terrorist attacks.

In the 113th Congress (2013-14), she is the top Democrat on the Financial Services Subcommittee on Capital Markets and Government Sponsored Enterprises, which is studying the long-term future of housing finance. The panel's chairman, Republican Scott Garrett of New Jersey, strongly endorses an end to federally guaranteed mortgages and the eventual death of Fannie Mae and Freddie Mac.

Early in 2013, Maloney agreed that the system would one day change, but she wasn't keen on a big reduction in the federal role. "Homeownership has played a critical role in the American dream in our country," she said at a hearing. "Nowhere in the world are mortgage products like the 30-year fixed-rate mortgage available without some form of government involvement." She said she firmly supports "the policy goal of affordable housing" — which many Republicans see as the root cause of the financial crisis of 2008.

Not all of Maloney's efforts are strictly partisan. She was the chairwoman of the Financial Institutions and Consumer Credit Subcommittee from 2007 through 2010. She wrote a "Bill of Rights" for credit card users, prohibiting certain interest rate hikes and billing practices. It passed the House with overwhelming support in 2008 and 2009, with the second version becoming law.

Maloney and other New York members of Financial Services have been actively looking for ways to expedite recovery efforts following Superstorm Sandy, which caused heavy damage to the city in October 2012. She announced her plan for a bill to loosen up some lending restrictions on credit unions if they are issuing loans in recent disaster areas. Maloney was livid when Republican leaders did not schedule a vote on a Sandy relief package at the end of the 112th Congress (2011-12). She called it an "act of spiteful indifference that will go down in history as a low point in a low era." A package was enacted in January 2013.

Maloney is the No. 2 Democrat on the Oversight and Government Reform Committee. She lost a bid to be the top Democrat on that panel in the 112th Congress — the job went to Elijah E. Cummings of Maryland.

As a member of the Oversight committee, Maloney helped win the 2004 enactment of a reorganization of U.S. intelligence operations in response to the recommendations of the commission that investigated the Sept. 11 attacks. She still calls it the "most important work I've done in Congress."

Maloney, who wears a silver bracelet with "9-11-01" engraved on it, formed a bipartisan caucus on the 9/11 terrorist attacks. She spearheaded a legislative effort backed by members of both parties to provide health care, monitoring and treatment for first-responders and community members exposed to deadly toxins in the aftermath of the World Trade Center collapse. The measure was stalled for months by concerns about the cost. The chambers didn't send the bill to the president until three days before Christmas 2010, when the House cleared it in its last roll call of the 111th Congress (2009-10).

She also holds a seat on the Joint Economic Committee, which she chaired in the 111th Congress.

Maloney is a former co-chairwoman of the Caucus for Women's Issues, and she has made very public demonstrations of her views. In 2012, the Oversight committee held a hearing on rules to require contraceptive coverage under the 2010 health care law. The first panel was all men. "Where are the women?" Maloney asked, before she walked out of the hearing.

To win support for human rights funding in Afghanistan, Maloney spoke on the House floor in October 2001 wearing a blue burqa. For Mother's Day 2012 she visited troops in Afghanistan, where she again promoted women's education and rights. In 2006, she and Republican Deborah Pryce of Ohio saw their bill to address sex trafficking enacted as part of a broader measure.

And the 2010 health care overhaul contained two Maloney provisions: one that requires large employers to provide private nursing areas for hourly employees, and another that created offices of women's health in five health-related government agencies.

Maloney's socially liberal stances extend beyond women's issues. She has long angled for stricter gun control measures, but in 2013 she took a new approach, introducing a bill to require gun buyers to have liability insurance coverage before making their purchase. She said interns in her office fielded death threats after the bill was introduced.

Maloney hails from Greensboro, N.C., where her mother was a homemaker and her father sold real estate — he also started a retirement community in Edenton. She thought about becoming a lawyer, but on a visit to New York in her early 20s, she fell in love with the city and decided to stay. She married her husband, investment banker Clifton Maloney, in 1976. (They were married until his death during a 2009 mountain climbing expedition in the Himalayas.)

She worked as a teacher before taking on administrative roles for the Board of Education. Maloney then took a position as an aide in the state legislature. In 1982, she won a seat on the New York City Council, and she held it for a decade. Some of her colleagues told the New York Times that she initially came across as "a little spacey," but proved to be remarkably tenacious once she found issues she wanted to pursue.

Maloney saw federal aid to the city scaled back during the administrations of Presidents Ronald Reagan and George Bush. Eager to change the trend, in 1992 she announced her intention to run against seven-term Republican Rep. Bill Green.

Media hype about the "Year of the Woman" lent momentum to her underdog challenge. She also benefited from redistricting, which forced Green to campaign on some unfamiliar turf. She won narrowly — her margin of victory was less than 5,000 votes — but her election victories since have been runaways in the overwhelmingly Democratic district.

Key Votes

2012	
Extend a Social Security payroll tax cut and unemployment benefits	YES
Ease securities rules to expand small-business access to capital	YES
Extend for one year subsidized student loan interest rates financed by a cut in health care spending	NO
Cite Attorney General Eric H. Holder Jr. for contempt of Congress	?
Create a visa program for foreign graduates in high-tech fields	NO
Extend most Bush-era income tax rates while allowing rates for top-bracket earners to rise (Jan. 1, 2013)	YES

2011	
Strike funding for F-35 alternative engine	YES
Prevent EPA from regulating greenhouse gas emissions to address climate change	NO
Extend certain provisions of Patriot Act for four years	NO
Declare opposition to use of ground troops in Libya	NO
Overhaul patent law	YES
Pass compromise debt limit increase plan and establish future spending limits	NO
Allow consideration of measures to implement three trade agreements	NO

CQ Vote Studies

	PARTY UNITY		PRESIDENTIAL SUPPORT	
	SUPPORT	OPPOSE	SUPPORT	OPPOSE
2012	98%	2%	86%	14%
2011	96%	4%	83%	17%
2010	98%	2%	87%	13%
2009	99%	1%	97%	3%
2008	99%	1%	17%	83%

Interest Groups

	AFL-CIO	ADA	CCUS	ACU
2012	100%	85%	20%	0%
2011	93%	80%	31%	4%
2010	100%	95%	25%	0%
2009	100%	95%	36%	0%
2008	100%	95%	65%	0%

New York 12

East Side of Manhattan; western Queens and northern Brooklyn

Straddling the East River, the 12th takes in some of Manhattan's most famous sights and exclusive neighborhoods as well as traditionally blue-collar sections of Queens, Brooklyn and Randalls and Roosevelt islands.

Redistricting following the 2010 census expanded this district — the former 14th — into western Maspeth and across Newton Creek into Brooklyn's Greenpoint section. Young hipsters fleeing the high rents of Williamsburg have enlivened this largely Polish, formerly industrial area that is as yet untouched by high-rise development.

In Manhattan, the 12th also spread into NoHo, the Flatiron District and the entire Theater District, including Times Square, one of the world's most popular tourist attractions. Redistricting also placed the Empire State Building and Madison Square Garden in the 12th, adding to the district's already-impressive roster of destinations, including: the Museum of Modern Art, United Nations Plaza, the 5th Avenue shopping hub, Rockefeller Plaza, the Guggenheim Museum and Carnegie Hall.

Wealthy, well-educated professionals call the Upper East Side home, and can have an outsize impact on politics through campaign donations, ensuring the 12th remains squarely Democratic.

Crossing over Roosevelt Island, the 12th covers Long Island City, an industrial center that is undergoing a major transformation. Vacant factories have been converted into office space, lofts and studios, while new office and apartment towers have risen along the waterfront. Silvercup Studios is home to a number of television shows, including "30 Rock," "Person of Interest" and "Girls." Astoria is the quintessential New York melting pot: A historically Greek community, it has attracted immigrants from Southeast Asia, Eastern Europe, South America and the Caribbean.

Major Industry

Finance, health care, tourism, advertising, publishing, construction

Cities

New York (pt.)

Notable

Steinway Pianos have been built in Long Island City since 1870; Workers at Greenpoint's Continental Iron Works constructed the U.S.S. Monitor during the Civil War.

Rep. Charles B. Rangel (D)

Capitol Office
225-4365
rangel.house.gov
2354 Rayburn Bldg. 20515-3215; fax 225-0816

Committees
Ways & Means
Joint Taxation

Residence
Manhattan

Born
June 11, 1930; Manhattan, N.Y.

Religion
Roman Catholic

Family
Wife, Alma Rangel; two children

Education
New York U., B.S. 1957; St. John's U., LL.B. 1960

Military
Army, 1948-52

Career
Lawyer

Political Highlights
Assistant U.S. attorney, 1961-62; N.Y. Assembly, 1967-71; sought Democratic nomination for N.Y. City Council president, 1969

ELECTION RESULTS

2012 GENERAL		
Rangel (D, WFM)	175,016	90.8%
Craig Schley (R)	12,147	6.3%
Deborah O. Liatos (SW)	5,548	2.9%
2012 PRIMARY		
Rangel (D)	19,187	44.4%
Adriano Espaillat (D)	18,101	41.9%
Clyde Edward Williams Jr. (D)	4,266	9.9%
Joyce S. Johnson (D)	1,018	2.4%
Craig Schley (D)	598	1.4%

Previous Winning Percentages
2010 (80%); 2008 (89%); 2006 (94%); 2004 (91%); 2002 (88%); 2000 (92%); 1998 (93%); 1996 (91%); 1994 (97%); 1992 (95%); 1990 (97%); 1988 (97%); 1986 (96%); 1984 (97%); 1982 (97%); 1980 (96%); 1978 (96%); 1976 (97%); 1974 (97%); 1972 (96%); 1970 (87%)

Elected 1970; 22nd term

At the start of the 113th Congress, Rangel became the longest-serving member of the legislative body's oldest committee. The joy in that accomplishment was muted by the ethics problems and electoral woes that have marked the precipitous decline in his influence.

Seats on the Ways and Means Committee have been sought by House members since the 18th century, and Rangel got his in 1975. With its jurisdiction over taxes, trade and several entitlement programs, the panel is crucial to the agendas of both Republicans and Democrats. In 2007, Rangel became the first black chairman of the committee.

But his reign was marred by investigations into his finances and conduct. Rangel stepped aside as chairman in the 111th Congress (2009-10) as the House ethics committee pursued 13 charges against him on a variety of matters, including using a rent-stabilized Harlem apartment for a campaign office, under-reporting rental income on a vacation property in the Dominican Republic, failing to disclose personal assets and using congressional letterhead as part of a fundraising campaign.

In 2010, the House (while still under Democratic control) voted for an official censure of Rangel, the first such action against a House member in 27 years. Rangel maintained that he had not intentionally abused his office for personal gain.

"I truly feel good," he told colleagues at the time, according to a Wall Street Journal report. "A lot of it has to do with the fact that I know in my heart that I am not going to be judged by this Congress, but I am going to be judged by my life." (Still, Rangel filed a lawsuit in 2013 attempting to overturn the censure; he alleged numerous violations of his due process rights.)

Redistricting heading into the 2012 election changed the group of voters judging him. Rangel has long represented Harlem, but he ran in 2012 in a district that also included a chunk of the Bronx that he had never represented. The racial makeup of his constituents shifted from nearly three-quarters black when he was first elected to a Hispanic majority. His most prominent challenger in the Democratic primary, Adriano Espaillat, would have become the first Dominican-born member of Congress had he won.

Rangel was also targeted by a political action committee working to defeat incumbents, and he was recovering from a back injury that kept him away from Capitol Hill for long stretches. He squeaked out a win in the primary, which effectively guaranteed him a 22nd term. "If they didn't think after 42 years that I was the best-qualified, I promise them that in the next two years they'll have no question about the fact that we elected the best," he told supporters.

Some aspects of Rangel's routine haven't changed. He is still a frequent and favorite guest on cable news shows, delivering both policy diatribes and zingers in his unmistakable raspy voice. Rangel defends the Obama administration and makes the occasional scorching partisan comment. "If you're familiar with the Bible and you're familiar with Matthew and you're familiar with the Torah ... the other side of whatever good they say, that's the new Republican program," he said at a May 2012 news conference. "The hell with the poor, the vulnerable, the sick; if they're naked, find clothes somewhere. If you're in trouble, then you just have to pray and work your way out of it."

However, his scandals and the minority status of his party have kept him on the outskirts of recent big-time policy debates.

Rangel has long defied easy classification on policy matters. He has taken an interest in safety-net and economic-growth programs for low-income communities. He wrote the 1993 "empowerment zones" law that provided tax credits to businesses that moved into blighted areas, as well as the 1986 tax credit for developers of low-income housing. Rangel was a critic of the 1996 law adding work requirements to the welfare program.

But business lobbyists and many Republicans know a different Rangel. As Ways and Means chairman at the start of the 110th Congress (2007-08), he worked with the top Republican, Jim McCrery of Louisiana, to advance legislation providing small-business tax breaks, relief for Hurricane Katrina victims, taxpayer identity protections and a ban on genetic discrimination by health insurers.

Rangel struck several other important agreements later in the 110th Congress. He negotiated with the George W. Bush administration on a trade framework that strengthened labor and environmental standards, allowing a free-trade deal with Peru to become law. He paired a minimum-wage increase with tax breaks and pushed an economic stimulus package through Congress that provided tax rebates to individuals and investment incentives to businesses.

Rangel voted for trade pacts with Panama and South Korea in 2011, and he was a lead Democratic sponsor on a 2012 extension of trade preferences for Africa-produced garments made from third-country fabrics; Rangel had been a key supporter of the 2000 law that created the preferences.

In 2013, he recovered at least some degree of authority when he became the top Democrat on the Trade Subcommittee — a panel that will be busy as the Trans-Pacific Partnership and a possible pact with the European Union continue to take shape. (Rangel, despite his seniority, was not the ranking member of any subcommittees in the previous Congress.)

Quite a few of his constituents are of Caribbean descent, and Rangel has tried to promote economic development in that region. He irked Brazil in 2011 by trying to extend a tariff on imported ethanol; his hope was to steer more business to ethanol processing plants in Caribbean nations with a partial exemption from the tariff. The tariff expired. He has proposed an end to the embargo on Cuba.

Rangel grew up in Harlem, where he was raised by his seamstress mother and her family. He dropped out of high school at 16, joined the Army and won a Purple Heart and Bronze Star in the Korean War, surviving firefights that killed much of his unit. The experience provided the title of his autobiography: "And I Haven't Had a Bad Day Since." After returning home, he finished high school and then college, landing an internship with the local district attorney.

After four years in the state Assembly, he set his sights on the U.S. House and ousted the incumbent in his district, Adam Clayton Powell Jr., in the 1970 Democratic primary. He won his first general election with 87 percent of the vote and amassed even larger wins for most of his career.

Key Votes

2012	
Extend a Social Security payroll tax cut and unemployment benefits	?
Ease securities rules to expand small-business access to capital	?
Extend for one year subsidized student loan interest rates financed by a cut in health care spending	?
Cite Attorney General Eric H. Holder Jr. for contempt of Congress	?
Create a visa program for foreign graduates in high-tech fields	NO
Extend most Bush-era income tax rates while allowing rates for top-bracket earners to rise (Jan. 1, 2013)	YES
2011	
Strike funding for F-35 alternative engine	YES
Prevent EPA from regulating greenhouse gas emissions to address climate change	NO
Extend certain provisions of Patriot Act for four years	NO
Declare opposition to use of ground troops in Libya	NO
Overhaul patent law	?
Pass compromise debt limit increase plan and establish future spending limits	NO
Allow consideration of measures to implement three trade agreements	YES

CQ Vote Studies

	PARTY UNITY		PRESIDENTIAL SUPPORT	
	SUPPORT	OPPOSE	SUPPORT	OPPOSE
2012	97%	3%	87%	13%
2011	97%	3%	83%	17%
2010	98%	2%	85%	15%
2009	99%	1%	96%	4%
2008	100%	0%	16%	84%

Interest Groups

	AFL-CIO	ADA	CCUS	ACU
2012	100%	60%	33%	0%
2011	93%	85%	21%	8%
2010	100%	100%	13%	0%
2009	100%	95%	43%	0%
2008	100%	85%	61%	0%

New York 13

Northern Manhattan — Harlem; part of the Bronx

The nation's geographically smallest district, the 13th represents a narrow strip of Upper Manhattan and a corner of the Bronx. It runs from East Harlem and Central Park's North Meadow up through downtown Harlem, Washington Heights and Inwood. Crossing the Bronx River, the 13th follows the Major Deegan Expressway north from the Cross Bronx Expressway to Van Courtland Park. Riverdale Avenue and the campus of Fordham University roughly form its eastern and western boundaries.

The district includes the Bronx neighborhoods of Marble Hill, Norwood and Jerome Park. Decennial redistricting trimmed the district's borders on the west side of Manhattan: Portions of the Upper West Side and Morningside Heights, including Columbia University, that had been in the district when it was the 15th are now represented by the 10th; Randalls Island shifted to the 12th. Because of these geographic changes, the 13th is a new Hispanic-majority district; its white constituency shrank to about 12 percent.

Immigration transformed this district from majority-black when it was created in the 1940s to less than one-third black. Many constituents are foreign-born, more than half of whom are from the Dominican Republic. A large Dominican community settled in Washington Heights, where local pride for hometown hero Manny Ramirez and Dominican-native David Ortiz has created an awkwardly large fan base for the Boston Red Sox across the river from Yankee Stadium. A Puerto Rican constituency lives in East Harlem. Decades of redevelopment in long-blighted Harlem have lured commercial and retail tenants as well as thousands of new white residents. Columbia University began a multibillion-dollar expansion into Manhattanville.

Barack Obama has received nearly unchallenged support among voters here, taking 95 percent of the 2012 presidential vote.

Major Industry
Health care, retail, government, higher education

Cities
New York (pt.)

Notable
Columbia University demolished most of the Audubon Ballroom, the site of Malcolm X's 1965 assassination, in the 1990s — but the ballroom's façade and the section of the stage where he was shot were preserved.

Rep. Joseph Crowley (D)

Capitol Office
225-3965
crowley.house.gov
1436 Longworth Bldg. 20515-3207; fax 225-1909

Committees
Ways & Means

Residence
Queens

Born
March 16, 1962; Queens, N.Y.

Religion
Roman Catholic

Family
Wife, Kasey Crowley; three children

Education
Queens College, B.A. 1985 (communications & political science)

Career
None

Political Highlights
N.Y. Assembly, 1987-99

ELECTION RESULTS

2012 GENERAL		
Crowley (D, WFM)	120,761	83.2%
William F. Gibbons Jr. (R, C)	21,755	15.0%
Anthony Gronowicz (GREEN)	2,570	1.8%
2012 PRIMARY		
Crowley (D)		unopposed
2010 GENERAL		
Crowley (D, WFM)	71,247	80.5%
Ken Reynolds (R, C)	16,145	18.2%
Anthony Gronowicz (GREEN)	1,038	1.2%

Previous Winning Percentages
2008 (85%); 2006 (84%); 2004 (81%); 2002 (73%); 2000 (72%); 1998 (69%)

Elected 1998; 8th term

Crowley matches the city he represents: He is soundly Democratic with an eye for business. Equipped with an outsize personality and a 6-foot-4-inch frame to match, he hovered around the House leadership for years before getting elected vice chairman of the Democratic Caucus in late 2012.

Politics has been his only career. Crowley was elected to the New York Legislature one year out of college and served there until his election to the House. His familiarity with the political process has led to a diverse set of responsibilities on Capitol Hill.

In the 112th Congress (2011-12), Crowley chaired the business-friendly New Democrat Coalition; he served as a chief deputy whip; he sat on the Democratic Steering Committee, which sets panel assignments; and he was chairman of finance for the Democratic Congressional Campaign Committee.

In addition to holding his new leadership role, he continues to serve as one of the DCCC finance chairmen in the 113th Congress (2013-14). At home, he is still the head of the Queens Democratic Party, one of the most powerful political machines in New York.

Crowley was named "a rising star" in the Democratic Caucus in 2012 by the National Journal, but it hasn't been a rapid or flawless ascent. In 2004, he was a top contender to chair the DCCC, but the job was given to Rahm Emanuel, a close ally of Minority Leader Nancy Pelosi. When the Democratic Caucus vice chairmanship opened up in 2006, Crowley actively campaigned for it. He won a plurality of votes on the first ballot, but support eventually drifted to another Pelosi ally, John B. Larson of Connecticut. Six years later, Democrats finally elected Crowley to that job by a unanimous vote.

Some observers said that Pelosi held Crowley down — and noted that Crowley supported Steny H. Hoyer of Maryland for party whip, when Pelosi defeated Hoyer for that job in 2002. If there are hard feelings, Crowley has kept them out of the public eye. He is a prodigious fundraiser; Crowley, through his campaign and political action committee, doled out hundreds of thousands of dollars to various Democratic campaigns in the 2012 election cycle.

He has also sought a more prominent messaging role, sometimes with creative flair. Imitating Bob Dylan's video for "Subterranean Homesick Blues," Crowley in April 2011 made a floor speech with no words — just phrases criticizing Republicans' economic agenda, torn off a large white pad. The stunt got significant attention on social media platforms. (Coincidentally, Crowley can play the guitar and has been known to sing in public.)

Crowley serves on the Ways and Means Committee, where he heralds the interests of both his middle-class district and the prominent financial industry that employs so many New Yorkers. He does not see those constituencies as necessarily opposed. "It's about trying to find a balance," he said. "It's about educating people that what keeps the light bulbs on in this city is the industries — finance and health."

He supported the $700 billion bailout of Wall Street in 2008, screaming across the House floor at Republicans after an initial version of the bill was rejected. But he was among the first members of Congress to question the insurer American International Group Inc. for attempting to distribute bonuses when it was on the brink of failure. Crowley toes the Democratic line of shifting the tax burden toward high-income earners. He speaks passionately on a gamut of middle-class issues, including stabilizing student loan rates, expanding health care coverage and providing tax credits for working families.

Trade is one area where he will depart from Democrats. In 2003, he split with his party to back free-trade pacts with Chile and Singapore. In 2011, he voted in favor of agreements with Colombia, Panama and South Korea that a majority of Democrats opposed. He has said that he wants to be a voice for "reasonable, fair trade agreements" that incorporate labor and environmental standards.

Crowley served on the Foreign Affairs Committee every term of his House career before the 112th Congress, and his Irish roots and New York's diversity factor heavily into his work.

The son of an Irish immigrant mother and first-generation Irish-American father, Crowley closely followed the Ireland peace process throughout his career and co-chairs the Ad Hoc Committee on Irish Affairs. He actively supported the implementation of the Good Friday peace accords throughout all of Ireland and met with Northern Ireland Deputy First Minister Martin McGuinness when McGuinness announced the Irish Republican Army was committed to nonviolence in 2005.

He created the Bangladesh Caucus and is a co-chairman of the Congressional Caucus on India and Indian-Americans. In 2010, he spearheaded efforts to renew sanctions against Myanmar, and in 2012 he became the first House member in 12 years to visit the strife-torn area. He also sponsored a bill, which was signed into law in 2008, to award a congressional gold medal to Aung San Suu Kyi in recognition of her work on civil rights in Myanmar.

Crowley comes from a close-knit family. For years, he, his siblings and his mother all lived within three miles of one another in Queens, where Crowley was born and raised. (Crowley's children now attend school in Virginia.) His mother emigrated from County Armagh in Northern Ireland and his father was a city police officer who earned a law degree at night.

His surname has prominence in New York, as his uncle, Walter Crowley, served on the City Council. Crowley's uncle drew inspiration from the Kennedy family, an icon of both the Democratic Party and Irish-American immigrants. Growing up, Crowley worked on his uncle's campaign and attributes his political adroitness to that early tutelage.

Crowley flourished under the mentoring of Democrat Thomas J. Manton, his predecessor in the House, whom he once considered an enemy. In 1984, Manton beat Crowley's uncle in a four-way primary for the House seat. But in 1986, Manton tapped Crowley on the shoulder at an Irish dinner dance and asked whether he'd thought about running for an open Assembly seat.

He won the seat at age 24. During his 12 years in Albany he developed a close friendship with Manton. In 1998, Manton picked Crowley as his successor in the House by announcing his retirement several days after the filing deadline, then joining with other party officials in nominating him. Crowley trounced the Republican candidate in the general election. He has won handily since.

Key Votes

2012	
Extend a Social Security payroll tax cut and unemployment benefits	YES
Ease securities rules to expand small-business access to capital	YES
Extend for one year subsidized student loan interest rates financed by a cut in health care spending	NO
Cite Attorney General Eric H. Holder Jr. for contempt of Congress	?
Create a visa program for foreign graduates in high-tech fields	NO
Extend most Bush-era income tax rates while allowing rates for top-bracket earners to rise (Jan. 1, 2013)	YES
2011	
Strike funding for F-35 alternative engine	NO
Prevent EPA from regulating greenhouse gas emissions to address climate change	NO
Extend certain provisions of Patriot Act for four years	NO
Declare opposition to use of ground troops in Libya	NO
Overhaul patent law	YES
Pass compromise debt limit increase plan and establish future spending limits	NO
Allow consideration of measures to implement three trade agreements	NO

CQ Vote Studies

	PARTY UNITY		PRESIDENTIAL SUPPORT	
	SUPPORT	OPPOSE	SUPPORT	OPPOSE
2012	97%	3%	90%	10%
2011	97%	3%	87%	13%
2010	99%	1%	87%	13%
2009	99%	1%	99%	1%
2008	98%	2%	19%	81%

Interest Groups

	AFL-CIO	ADA	CCUS	ACU
2012	90%	95%	25%	0%
2011	89%	75%	33%	4%
2010	100%	95%	25%	0%
2009	100%	100%	40%	0%
2008	100%	100%	67%	0%

New York 14

Northwest Queens and East Bronx

The 14th is home to a wide contrast of landscapes — it stretches from industrial districts in Queens to high-rise apartment towers and bayside parkland in the Bronx. A diverse constituency resides in between.

Formerly the 7th District, the new 14th expanded its former reaches in Queens significantly following decennial redistricting. It added most of industrial Maspeth on its southern edge and the Ditmars-Steinway neighborhood north of Astoria, which some residents have dubbed "Asthma Alley" because of its proximity to several power plants and LaGuardia Airport.

Southeast of the airport, the 14th added Corona and Flushing Meadows, home to Arthur Ashe Stadium and baseball's Mets at Citi Field. The 14th also now includes Rikers Island, the city's main jail.

Redistricting shifted Bronx neighborhoods west of the Whitestone Bridge and Cross Bronx Expressway, as well as the Bronx Zoo, to the 15th. Pelham Bay Park sits at the 14th's northeastern corner along Long Island Sound. Three times larger than Central Park, it has 13 miles of salt marsh coastline and acres of meadow. East Bronx is being eyed as a location for passenger rail service extensions.

Redistricting shifted about 9 percent of the old 7th's black population, and the new 14th is slightly more white, while Hispanics make up a near-majority of 47 percent. Hispanic communities vary widely by ethnicity: Corona and Jackson Heights have large Mexican, Ecuadoran and Dominican neighborhoods, while Puerto Rican areas are common on the Bronx side of the district. Large Italian populations also live in Bronx districts such as Morris Park. Thousands of South and East Asians live in Woodside and fast-growing College Point, Queens.

Like the neighboring New York City districts to the south, the 14th is a Democratic stronghold: The district gave Barack Obama 81 percent of its vote in the 2012 presidential election.

Major Industry
Transportation, health care, service

Cities
New York (pt.)

Notable
The Maritime Industry Museum and SUNY Maritime College are at Fort Schuyler in Throgs Neck, where the East River hits Long Island Sound.

Rep. José E. Serrano (D)

Capitol Office
225-4361
serrano.house.gov
2227 Rayburn Bldg. 20515-3216; fax 225-6001

Committees
Appropriations

Residence
Bronx

Born
Oct. 24, 1943; Mayaguez, P.R.

Religion
Roman Catholic

Family
Divorced; five children

Education
Lehman College, attended 1979-80

Military
Army Medical Corps, 1964-66

Career
School district administrator; banker

Political Highlights
N.Y. Assembly, 1975-90; sought Democratic nomination for Bronx borough president, 1985

ELECTION RESULTS

2012 GENERAL		
Serrano (D, WFM)	152,661	97.2%
Frank DellaValle (R, C)	4,427	2.8%
2012 PRIMARY		
Serrano (D)		unopposed
2010 GENERAL		
Serrano (D, WFM)	61,642	95.7%
Frank DellaValle (R, C)	2,758	4.3%

Previous Winning Percentages
2008 (97%); 2006 (95%); 2004 (95%); 2002 (92%); 2000 (96%); 1998 (95%); 1996 (96%); 1994 (96%); 1992 (91%); 1990 (93%); 1990 Special Election (92%)

Elected 1990; 12th full term

Serrano, who came from poverty, has no qualms about leveraging government resources to benefit those further down the economic ladder — a group that includes many of his constituents. He is gregarious, liberal and attuned to the concerns of the Hispanic community.

His family started out in Puerto Rico; at a 2009 appearance in New York he spoke of being born in a "one-room flat with a latrine." When Serrano was 7, he and his family moved to the Bronx. He grew up in the Millbrook Houses, a public housing project. For years, he has represented one of the poorest, least-educated and least-white districts in the country.

All that factors into his congressional work, most notably on the Appropriations Committee, where Serrano has served since 1993. He promotes and defends spending on the social safety net, as well as programs and agencies meant to protect consumers or assist small businesses.

During the Democratic majority of the 110th and 111th Congresses (2007-10), Serrano chaired the Financial Services Appropriations Subcommittee. In 2011, he became its ranking member, a role he still holds in the 113th Congress (2013-14) alongside Chairman Ander Crenshaw of Florida.

The financial services sector is crucial to New York's economy, but Serrano in 2008 opposed the $700 billion package to shore up the industry. "I was speaking for the people in the Bronx and people across the nation who are stuck without any help from our government," he said.

Government entities under the subcommittee's jurisdiction are largely responsible for implementing and enforcing the 2010 law that overhauled financial sector regulation. The panel also funds the IRS. Serrano argued against budget cuts as the subcommittee considered its fiscal 2013 bill: "We should not be underfunding the very agencies that protect Americans from abusive practices, ensure a fair playing field and collect revenue."

He called for increased funding for the Securities and Exchange Commission, saying "we need a strong cop on the beat to prevent the financial meltdown of 2008 from occurring again." In his time as chairman, he highlighted budget increases for the Consumer Product Safety Commission, the Federal Trade Commission and other agencies with consumer protection duties.

Serrano also sits on the Commerce-Justice-Science and Interior-Environment subcommittees. From the latter he has helped obtain federal money to clean up the Bronx River, plant trees in the borough and reduce air pollution from trucks, which is believed to be a contributing factor in the high incidence of asthma among his constituents. His district contains and is close to a number of major highways.

Serrano is a member of the Congressional Progressive Caucus, the group of the most-liberal House members. Thanks to his trademark black mustache, he is one of the most recognizable lawmakers on Capitol Hill. He is also reputed to be one of the most humorous, although he is decidedly serious when addressing any topic important to his district.

Immigration is one such topic. Serrano was livid at a 2010 Arizona law cracking down on illegal immigration; he made sports headlines in 2010 when he asked Major League Baseball to move the 2011 All-Star Game, slated to take place in Phoenix. "It is important that everyone who believes in justice and our national spirit of decency speak out against this measure," he said at the time. "MLB has a very loud megaphone." The game was not moved.

Serrano wasn't satisfied by a 2012 Supreme Court ruling that struck down part of the law, but left intact a provision allowing law enforcement officers to check on the documentation of people they stop while performing their duties.

"I can't consider [the decision] something that I would jump up and down about when there's still that provision that allows you to stop me and ask me for my papers," he told Capital New York, an online news publication.

Serrano cheered President Barack Obama's 2012 policy directive to defer the deportation of children and young adults who were brought into the country illegally as minors. "Today is a joyous day in our community," he wrote, "as thousands of children and young adults who have been living in fear and suspense can finally begin to lead full lives without fear of deportation."

Nearly 200,000 of his constituents share Serrano's Puerto Rican heritage. He was a strong supporter of a House-passed 2010 bill to give residents of the island a chance to vote on its political status. In 2013, the White House asked for $2.5 million to pay for a plebiscite.

He has long been an advocate of easing restrictions on travel to Cuba. The 2009 catchall spending law included his provision to allow Americans with family members living in Cuba more-expansive travel rights. Several times, he has introduced a bill to lift the trade embargo on Cuba. In 2009 and 2011, Serrano introduced legislation to ease prohibitions on Cubans coming to the United States to play professional baseball.

His advocacy for the poor led to a highly criticized alliance with the late Venezuelan President Hugo Chavez, an authoritarian, anti-American leader. Serrano invited Chavez to his district in 2005, and Chavez established a program of development grants for the South Bronx. When Chavez died in 2013, Serrano praised him in the media, to the consternation of many people.

Serrano has also been noted for his seemingly unusual quest to repeal the 22nd Amendment, which sets term limits on the president. He first introduced his proposal in 1997 and has brought it back every two years since then.

Serrano said he learned English by listening to the Frank Sinatra records his father brought back from the Army. Serrano remained a big fan of the crooner, amassing a large collection of Sinatra records and even sponsoring the 1997 measure to award the singer a Congressional Gold Medal. In 2008, he helped the U.S. Postal Service introduce a commemorative Sinatra stamp.

He graduated from a vocational high school, served in the Army, took a job in a New York City bank and began making political contacts, which helped him win a state Assembly seat in 1974.

After Democratic Rep. Robert Garcia resigned in 1990, following a conviction for defense contract extortion, Serrano moved quickly to stake his claim to the seat. He breezed to victory with 92 percent of the vote in the special election and won a full term with 93 percent that November.

He has never taken less than 90 percent of the vote in a re-election race, and he barely has to bother with campaign fundraising.

Key Votes

2012	
Extend a Social Security payroll tax cut and unemployment benefits	YES
Ease securities rules to expand small-business access to capital	YES
Extend for one year subsidized student loan interest rates financed by a cut in health care spending	NO
Cite Attorney General Eric H. Holder Jr. for contempt of Congress	?
Create a visa program for foreign graduates in high-tech fields	NO
Extend most Bush-era income tax rates while allowing rates for top-bracket earners to rise (Jan. 1, 2013)	YES
2011	
Strike funding for F-35 alternative engine	NO
Prevent EPA from regulating greenhouse gas emissions to address climate change	NO
Extend certain provisions of Patriot Act for four years	NO
Declare opposition to use of ground troops in Libya	NO
Overhaul patent law	YES
Pass compromise debt limit increase plan and establish future spending limits	NO
Allow consideration of measures to implement three trade agreements	NO

CQ Vote Studies

	PARTY UNITY		PRESIDENTIAL SUPPORT	
	SUPPORT	OPPOSE	SUPPORT	OPPOSE
2012	98%	2%	91%	9%
2011	97%	3%	76%	24%
2010	99%	1%	81%	19%
2009	99%	1%	94%	6%
2008	99%	1%	13%	87%

Interest Groups

	AFL-CIO	ADA	CCUS	ACU
2012	95%	100%	17%	0%
2011	100%	95%	19%	4%
2010	100%	100%	13%	0%
2009	100%	100%	33%	0%
2008	100%	100%	39%	8%

New York 15

South Bronx

Representing the South Bronx, the renumbered 15th is the poorest and one of the least educated districts in the nation. The New York Yankees have played here since 1923; when the new Yankee Stadium opened in 2009, it was the most expensive sports arena ever built in the United States. Hunts Point on the district's southeastern edge is a major food distribution center and has been home to the city's famous Fulton Fish Market since 2005.

The neighborhoods of the 15th became symbols of urban decay in the 1970s, when a wave of insurance fraud-motivated arson reduced many blocks to ruins. In the 1990s, nonprofits and a federal empowerment zone program kicked off a slow redevelopment process. New condominiums and co-op apartments dot the cityscape or are in the works, with district residents often leading efforts to encourage affordable and environmentally sustainable housing.

Nevertheless, roughly 60 percent of district residents receive some form of government income assistance and homeownership rates for most neighborhoods in the district are in the single digits. The Bronx's last independent bookstore closed in December 2011 in Longwood.

Two-thirds of 15th constituents are Hispanic. Neighborhoods on the western edge of the district, such as Highbridge, Morris Heights and Mount Hope, are heavily Dominican, while Puerto Ricans dominate in eastern and southern areas such as Soundview, Mott Haven, Port Morris and Melrose. The rest of the district's population is largely black.

The 15th's strong Puerto Rican presence began with a post-World War II immigration boom and led to the community's dominance in local politics. The district has elected individuals of Puerto Rican descent to Congress since 1970. Residents in the district give universally strong support for Democratic candidates; Barack Obama took 97 percent here in the 2012 presidential election, his highest percentage nationwide.

Major Industry
Health care, food distribution, light manufacturing

Cities
New York (pt.)

Notable
In 2010, developers named a new 50-unit co-op building in Longwood for former secretary of state Gen. Colin L. Powell, who grew up a few blocks away.

Rep. Eliot L. Engel (D)

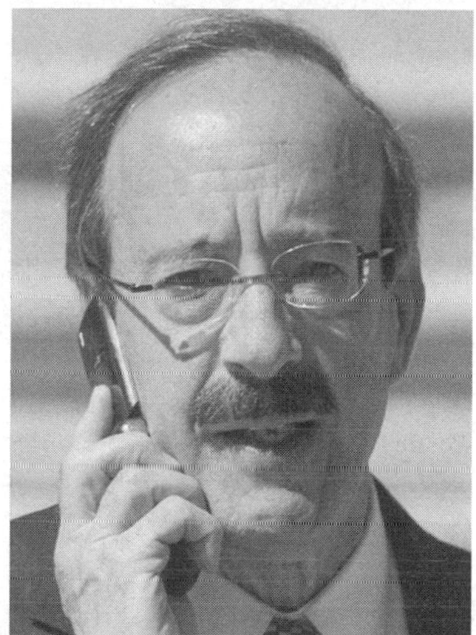

Capitol Office
225-2464
engel.house.gov
2161 Rayburn Bldg. 20515-3217; fax 225-5513

Committees
Energy & Commerce
Foreign Affairs - Ranking Member

Residence
Bronx

Born
Feb. 18, 1947; Bronx, N.Y.

Religion
Jewish

Family
Wife, Patricia Ennis Engel; three children

Education
Hunter-Lehman College, B.A. 1969 (history); City U. of New York, Lehman College, M.A. 1973 (guidance & counseling); New York Law School, J.D. 1987

Career
Teacher; guidance counselor

Political Highlights
Bronx Democratic district leader, 1974-77; N.Y. Assembly, 1977-88

ELECTION RESULTS

2012 GENERAL		
Engel (D, WFM)	179,562	75.9%
Joseph McLaughlin (R)	53,935	22.8%
Joseph Diaferia (GREEN)	2,974	1.3%
2012 PRIMARY		
Engel (D)	12,856	87.3%
Aniello V. Grimaldi (D)	1,864	12.7%
2010 GENERAL		
Engel (D, WFM)	95,346	72.8%
Anthony Mele (R)	29,792	22.8%
York Kleinhandler (C)	5,661	4.3%

Previous Winning Percentages
2008 (80%); 2006 (76%); 2004 (76%); 2002 (63%); 2000 (90%); 1998 (88%); 1996 (85%); 1994 (78%); 1992 (80%); 1990 (61%); 1988 (56%)

Elected 1988; 13th term

Engel often mentions the importance of constituent service. His electoral success suggests he is good at it — the lifelong Bronx resident has represented one of the most racially and ethnically diverse districts and found ways to connect with voters of many backgrounds. And it's not always via regular casework: He is the top Democrat on the Foreign Affairs Committee and a senior member of the Energy and Commerce Committee.

Hispanics and blacks are the bulk of his constituents, and lots of the whites he represents have strong ethnic or religious identities — for example, many of them, like Engel, are Jewish. Most parts of the world interest someone in his district, and Engel has been involved in policy and diplomacy regarding the Americas, Eastern Europe, Africa and the Middle East. He began serving as the ranking member of Foreign Affairs in the 113th Congress (2013-14).

Some observers describe him as an interventionist. Engel supports using the military to stop humanitarian crises and doesn't mind when the United States directly shapes global affairs. In early 2011, he backed limited U.S. involvement in Libya to assist rebels fighting Muammar el-Qaddafi. Engel was an early proponent of U.S. intervention in Yugoslavia's civil war, and in 1993 he urged the Clinton administration to side against the Bosnian Serbs, who were accused of forcing the removal of Muslims.

Engel was the top Democrat on the Western Hemisphere Subcommittee from 2007 through 2012. As chairman, he encouraged assistance for Haiti to address food shortages and hurricane damage long before a devastating earthquake brought the nation to the forefront of legislators' minds in January 2010. He supported aid for Mexico and Latin America to fight the illegal drug trade.

Many Republicans on the Foreign Affairs Committee see multilateral organizations as infringing on U.S. sovereignty. In the 112th Congress (2011-12), Engel defended the Organization of American States to his colleagues and said he wants it to actively foster democratic governments.

Speaking to the OAS in March 2012, he said that "this organization is the best hope for us to make this hemisphere better and to enhance our cooperation so that the lives of all of our peoples can be improved." Engel, a member of the business-friendly New Democrat Coalition, broke with most House Democrats in 2011 to support trade pacts with Panama and Colombia. At a 2012 hearing, he said he did so because it is "important that we let our friends know that there is an upside to being allies with the United States."

Engel supports the embargo on Cuba. He also backs economic punishments for wayward regimes in the Middle East. During the 108th Congress (2003-04), he teamed with Republican Ileana Ros-Lehtinen of Florida to win passage of a sanctions bill targeting Syria. In 2013, Engel and Chairman Ed Royce of California proposed tougher sanctions on Iran, to further cut it off from the global economy if it continues its nuclear weapons program.

Engel sees Syria and Iran as existential threats to Israel, and when it comes to Israel, he is as hawkish as they come. He has delicately criticized some of the Obama administration's Middle East policies. Engel called the 2010 decision to send an ambassador to Syria a mistake, and in May 2011 he said President Barack Obama was wrong to suggest that negotiations on Israel's borders could begin with the 1967 lines. Engel wants Jerusalem recognized as the capital of Israel, and in the 112th Congress he successfully pushed amendments in committee to block aid to the Palestinian Authority if it declares independence or seeks United Nations recognition.

He was less delicate with other presidents. He said if he knew how "incompetent" the George W. Bush administration would be in executing the Iraq

War, he would not have voted in 2002 to authorize it.

Engel ties some of his Energy and Commerce work to foreign affairs. He sits on the Energy and Power Subcommittee and says a move away from oil as an energy source is crucial to national security. Engel is among the opponents of tax advantages used by oil companies, and he has proposed requiring that all new cars be capable of running on a fuel other than gasoline. Although he does not "dismiss nuclear power summarily," he is critical of federal support for that industry.

On the Health Subcommittee, Engel has enjoyed some victories on bills targeting specific illnesses or conditions. His measures to provide for research on muscular dystrophy and establish a national registry to study data on amyotrophic lateral sclerosis were enacted in 2008; the latter disease killed his grandmother. That year, his bill to increase U.S. assistance in the global fight against tuberculosis was rolled into a larger measure concerning AIDS and malaria, which was enacted.

Outside of his Foreign Affairs work, Engel mostly falls in line with Democratic Party positions, unless he feels New York is threatened. He organized a New York delegation meeting with Minority Leader Nancy Pelosi in 2011 to discuss a proposed compromise to raise the debt ceiling, saying the state's teaching hospitals would be adversely affected by budget cuts in the deal. Engel called on Obama to raise the debt limit without congressional approval. When that did not happen, he voted against the deal altogether.

Engel grew up in the Democratic clubs of the Bronx and walked the picket lines with his father, a welder who was active in his union. He attended New York City public schools, where he later worked as a teacher and guidance counselor. He was elected in 1976 to the state Assembly, where he took up a portfolio on housing and substance abuse issues. In 1988, he successfully challenged Democratic Rep. Mario Biaggi, who resigned after being convicted of bribery, conspiracy and extortion but remained on the ballot. Engel easily rebuffed a Biaggi comeback attempt in 1992, and he has faced no serious opposition since.

Recent redistricting significantly altered his district — large chunks of real estate were swapped between the neighboring districts held by Engel and Nita M. Lowey, another Jewish Democrat who is now the party's top House appropriator. His district remains one of the most diverse in the country.

The Ethics Committee in 2011 said it would not pursue allegations that Engel and five other lawmakers inappropriately spent per diem funds issued for official travel. He has since taken flak from local newspapers for an apartment he bought with money borrowed from a friend and campaign donor, but his spokesman said the committee pre-approved the arrangement.

Key Votes

2012	
Extend a Social Security payroll tax cut and unemployment benefits	YES
Ease securities rules to expand small-business access to capital	?
Extend for one year subsidized student loan interest rates financed by a cut in health care spending	NO
Cite Attorney General Eric H. Holder Jr. for contempt of Congress	?
Create a visa program for foreign graduates in high-tech fields	NO
Extend most Bush-era income tax rates while allowing rates for top-bracket earners to rise (Jan. 1, 2013)	YES
2011	
Strike funding for F-35 alternative engine	NO
Prevent EPA from regulating greenhouse gas emissions to address climate change	NO
Extend certain provisions of Patriot Act for four years	NO
Declare opposition to use of ground troops in Libya	NO
Overhaul patent law	YES
Pass compromise debt limit increase plan and establish future spending limits	NO
Allow consideration of measures to implement three trade agreements	NO

CQ Vote Studies

	PARTY UNITY		PRESIDENTIAL SUPPORT	
	SUPPORT	OPPOSE	SUPPORT	OPPOSE
2012	94%	6%	86%	14%
2011	95%	5%	87%	13%
2010	99%	1%	90%	10%
2009	99%	1%	97%	3%
2008	98%	2%	17%	83%

Interest Groups

	AFL-CIO	ADA	CCUS	ACU
2012	95%	85%	25%	4%
2011	92%	85%	27%	4%
2010	100%	100%	13%	0%
2009	100%	100%	40%	0%
2008	100%	95%	65%	0%

New York 16

Southern Westchester County — Yonkers, New Rochelle; North Bronx

Although the boundaries of the remapped and renumbered 16th changed significantly during decennial redistricting, the Democratic district's demographic and economic diversity remain; no single racial group constitutes a majority in what had been the 17th. It includes affluent residential villages, working-class high-rises and several liberal arts colleges.

The district added a broad expanse of southern Westchester County to existing territory at the northern edge of New York City. Riverdale, one of New York City's most affluent areas and one where many school-age residents attend top-tier college preparatory academies, sits in the southwestern corner of the district. To the south and east, on the other side of Van Cortlandt Park and Woodlawn Cemetery, there is a large black population, in Williamsbridge and Laconia. The 16th also takes in the huge Co-op City complex, a cluster of 35 apartment towers.

North of Riverdale, the district follows the Hudson River to Hastings-on-Hudson. It takes in exclusive Westchester towns and some of the nation's wealthiest ZIP codes, including those in Ardsley and Scarsdale, and, along the Long Island Sound, Rye through Mamaroneck to Pelham Manor, just north of the New York City line. Many of the 16th's black residents — who account for more than 30 percent of the district's population overall — live in Westchester's Mount Vernon. A large hospital and nursing school anchor Mount Vernon's economy.

Yonkers, the state's fourth-largest city, is a diverse mix of old Italian and Irish neighborhoods to the north and Hispanic districts to the south. The city's Hispanic population has grown during the past decade, a pattern that coincided with the departure of many white residents. The city is in the middle of a multibillion-dollar redevelopment of its formerly industrial waterfront, in the hope of luring more residents to the urban core.

Major Industry

Health care, professional services, government

Cities

New York (pt.), Yonkers, Mount Vernon

Notable

Elisha Graves Otis opened a factory in Yonkers to produce his new invention, the modern elevator, in 1853.

Rep. Nita M. Lowey (D)

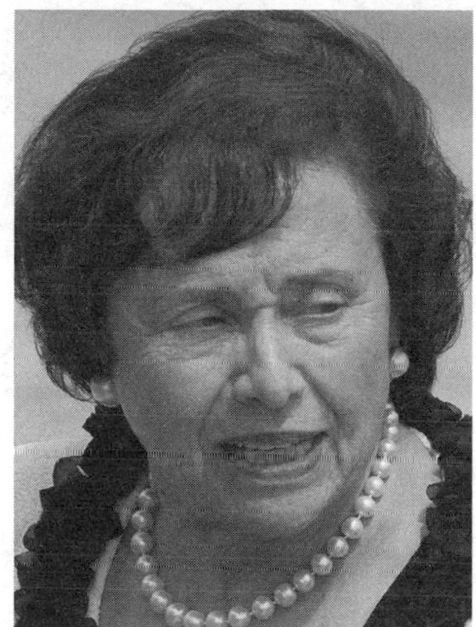

Capitol Office
225-6506
lowey.house.gov
2365 Longworth Bldg. 20515-3210, fax 225-0546

Committees
Appropriations - Ranking Member

Residence
Harrison

Born
July 5, 1937; Bronx, N.Y.

Religion
Jewish

Family
Husband, Stephen Lowey; three children

Education
Mount Holyoke College, B.A. 1959 (political science)

Career
State government aide; homemaker

Political Highlights
N.Y. assistant secretary of state, 1985-87

ELECTION RESULTS

2012 GENERAL

Lowey (D, WFM)	171,417	64.4%
Joe Carvin (R)	91,899	34.5%
Francis E. Morganthaler (WTP)	2,771	1.0%

2012 PRIMARY

Lowey (D)		unopposed

2010 GENERAL

Lowey (D, WFM, INDC)	104,836	63.4%
Jim Russell (R, C)	60,513	36.6%

Previous Winning Percentages
2008 (68%); 2006 (71%); 2004 (70%); 2002 (92%); 2000 (67%); 1998 (83%); 1996 (64%); 1994 (57%); 1992 (56%); 1990 (63%); 1988 (50%)

Elected 1988; 13th term

In her pursuit of greater influence, Lowey once considered seeking a seat in the Senate. She stuck with the House, and that bet has paid off in a big way. She is now the top Democratic member of the Appropriations Committee — a prominent platform from which to promote her liberal views.

Her public career started out simply. Lowey served as a leader in the PTA and other neighborhood groups. She cites her family and Jewish traditions as important factors in her involvement in service: "I believe in tikkun olam — to make it a better world — and tzedakah, which is charity," she said. Her measure of personal warmth is complemented by a willingness to be pushy on policy debates.

Lowey's ascent of the Appropriations Committee began when she joined the panel in 1993. She successfully lobbied GOP leaders to keep her seat after the 1994 Republican Revolution eliminated some Democratic slots on the panel. As a result, she was fourth on the depth chart of committee Democrats by the start of the 112th Congress (2011-12). Ranking member Norm Dicks of Washington retired, and colleagues chose Lowey over Marcy Kaptur of Ohio as his replacement for the 113th Congress (2013-14). She is the first woman to hold a top spot on the full committee.

For Lowey, it might be the outcome she had in mind when she shut down a possible Senate run in 2000. She also took her name out of consideration for an appointment to the Senate after Hillary Rodham Clinton became secretary of State in 2009.

Lowey has a record of being a workhorse for her party and its message. In 2002, she served as chairwoman of the Democratic Congressional Campaign Committee, the campaign arm for House Democrats. She tenaciously presses Democratic talking points, pinning congressional inertia on Republicans, speaking of a GOP agenda against women, resisting structural changes to Social Security and Medicare and defending public broadcasting.

In addition to being the ranking member of the full committee, Lowey continues as the top Democrat on the State-Foreign Operations panel. (She chaired it from 2007 through 2010.) In the 112th Congress, she fought what she saw as GOP efforts to undermine assistance to foreign countries. Early in 2011, she panned a proposal by Majority Leader Eric Cantor of Virginia to separate money for Israel from the general foreign aid pool; she said it was a ploy to "make it easier" for Republican members to reject foreign aid legislation while maintaining a pro-Israel stance.

Lowey has a good relationship with the Republican chairwoman of the subcommittee, Kay Granger of Texas: "We're respectful of each other, and we still write the bill together, respecting differences," she said in 2012. But she criticized the spending bill their panel produced in 2012, saying it "shortchanges our diplomatic and development efforts and could weaken America's standing in the world," leading to a future security crisis. Lowey has proposed some expansive plans for aid, including a measure to authorize billions of dollars for education initiatives in developing countries.

Lowey gets her dander up when social policy is involved, in foreign aid debates or elsewhere. For more than a decade she sought a codified end to the "Mexico City policy" — a ban on sending U.S. dollars to non-governmental organizations that perform or promote abortions in other countries.

She was similarly aggressive on reproductive health issues on the Labor-HHS-Education Subcommittee. During the 1998 appropriations cycle, Lowey secured for the first time mandatory contraceptive coverage for federal employees. Earlier in her House career, Lowey chaired the Congressional

Caucus for Women's Issues and the House Pro-Choice Caucus, and in the 112th Congress she railed against attempts to cut funding to Planned Parenthood. "It's outrageous that rather than focusing on job creation, the House Republican majority has been targeting women's health," she said. In 2013, Lowey ultimately supported the "continuing resolution" that set funding levels for the remainder of fiscal 2013, but she complained that it did not provide enough money for implementation of the 2010 health care overhaul law.

Lowey isn't a hard-liner for increased spending; she says she is open to finding ways to reduce the federal deficit and debt. She voted for a fiscal 2011 package that cut spending by $40 billion, as well as the August 2011 compromise that raised the debt limit and locked in further spending reductions. Like most New York lawmakers, however, she does push for more spending on homeland security.

Lowey says her biggest goal is job creation, and that carefully vetted earmarks — spending directed to specific projects in a lawmaker's district — are one way to reach it. (Republicans have currently banned the practice.) She calls for bigger federal investments in science and math education, and she is more receptive to free trade than many Democrats. In 2010, President Barack Obama signed into law a Lowey provision increasing the maximum size of loans available through several Small Business Administration programs. She called the change "vital in high-cost-of-living areas like my district."

Lowey was a homemaker in Queens. In 1974, she volunteered for a neighbor's campaign for lieutenant governor. The neighbor was Mario M. Cuomo. Though Cuomo lost the primary race, new Democratic Gov. Hugh L. Carey appointed him secretary of state, and Cuomo hired Lowey to work in the anti-poverty division.

By the mid-1980s, Cuomo was governor and Lowey was the top aide to New York Secretary of State Gail Shaffer. Lowey made an impressive debut in electoral politics in 1988. She first survived a primary against Hamilton Fish V, publisher of The Nation magazine and scion of a famous Republican family in New York, and businessman Dennis Mehiel. She then unseated two-term GOP Rep. Joseph J. DioGuardi.

For that cycle she raised $1.3 million, a huge sum for a challenger at the time, and won the general election with 50 percent of the vote. Since then, she has outdistanced all competition. Lowey is one of the wealthiest members of Congress; she and her lawyer husband have substantial investments and real estate holdings.

She has not garnered less than 60 percent of the vote in a general election in her suburban district since 1994. Her district was substantially altered by redistricting heading into the 2012 election, but she still won easily.

Key Votes

2012	
Extend a Social Security payroll tax cut and unemployment benefits	YES
Ease securities rules to expand small-business access to capital	YES
Extend for one year subsidized student loan interest rates financed by a cut in health care spending	NO
Cite Attorney General Eric H. Holder Jr. for contempt of Congress	?
Create a visa program for foreign graduates in high-tech fields	NO
Extend most Bush-era income tax rates while allowing rates for top-bracket earners to rise (Jan. 1, 2013)	YES
2011	
Strike funding for F-35 alternative engine	YES
Prevent EPA from regulating greenhouse gas emissions to address climate change	NO
Extend certain provisions of Patriot Act for four years	YES
Declare opposition to use of ground troops in Libya	NO
Overhaul patent law	YES
Pass compromise debt limit increase plan and establish future spending limits	YES
Allow consideration of measures to implement three trade agreements	NO

CQ Vote Studies

	PARTY UNITY		PRESIDENTIAL SUPPORT	
	SUPPORT	OPPOSE	SUPPORT	OPPOSE
2012	97%	3%	89%	11%
2011	95%	5%	95%	5%
2010	98%	2%	95%	5%
2009	99%	1%	97%	3%
2008	99%	1%	14%	86%

Interest Groups

	AFL-CIO	ADA	CCUS	ACU
2012	95%	80%	25%	4%
2011	93%	80%	31%	0%
2010	100%	90%	25%	0%
2009	100%	100%	33%	0%
2008	100%	100%	67%	0%

New York 17

Rockland and part of Westchester counties — White Plains, Peekskill

Many white-collar, well-educated commuters take advantage of the 17th's proximity to New York City and Connecticut. Following decennial remapping, the district takes in all of Rockland County as well as portions of Westchester County across the Hudson River. Commuters use the Tappan Zee Bridge to cross the river toward New York City, and many members of the Westchester workforce ride commuter rail lines to midtown Manhattan; others take major routes into Greenwich and Stamford in Connecticut. The district is predominately white, but roughly one-fifth of the population is Hispanic. Barack Obama won in both counties in the district in the 2012 presidential contest, but by smaller margins than his victories to the south.

Largely wealthy and suburban Rockland County has good schools, large Jewish and Irish populations and many residents in professional occupations. Boutique retail centers draw shoppers from the across the region.

Across the Hudson River is Westchester County, which remains one of the wealthiest counties in the state although it has not fully recovered from the recent economic crisis. Home to Fortune 500 companies decades ago and midsize companies in business parks more recently, the county has had to focus on creating a more diverse economic base. The 17th also has working-class areas, such as parts of Sleepy Hollow, Port Chester and growing White Plains and New Rochelle. Westchester County's largest retail hub is in White Plains, as are the City Center complex and Renaissance Square hotel, shopping and residential buildings.

Rockland and Westchester counties both have major pharmaceutical and biotech employers, as well as several colleges, the PepsiCo headquarters in Purchase, the Indian Point Energy Center in Buchanan and Sing Sing prison in Ossining — its location north of the city on the Hudson River led New Yorkers to refer to prison-bound convicts as being "sent up the river."

Major Industry
Health care, retail, biotechnology

Cities
White Plains, Spring Valley

Notable
North Tarrytown was renamed Sleepy Hollow in honor of the Washington Irving story set there.

Rep. Sean Patrick Maloney (D)

Capitol Office
225-5441
seanmaloney.house.gov
1529 Longworth Bldg. 20515-3218; fax 225-3289

Committees
Agriculture
Transportation & Infrastructure

Residence
Cold Spring

Born
July 30, 1966; Sherbrooke, Canada

Religion
Roman Catholic

Family
Partner, Randy Florke; three children

Education
Georgetown U., attended 1986; U. of Virginia, B.A. 1988 (foreign affairs), J.D. 1992

Career
Lawyer; gubernatorial aide; financial management software company executive; White House and presidential campaign aide

Political Highlights
Sought Democratic nomination for N.Y. attorney general, 2006

ELECTION RESULTS

2012 GENERAL		
Maloney (D, WFM)	143,845	51.9%
Nan Hayworth (R, C)	133,049	48.0%
2012 PRIMARY		
Maloney (D)	7,493	48.3%
Richard H. Becker (D)	5,036	32.4%
Matthew C. Alexander (D)	1,857	12.0%
Duane Jackson (D)	780	5.0%
Thomas Wilson (D)	356	2.3%

Elected 2012; 1st term

Maloney calls himself a "Bill Clinton Democrat" — which is no big surprise, considering he was an adviser and assistant in the Clinton White House. An energetic member of the New Democrat Coalition, he is focusing on farming and infrastructure as he tries to hold on to a competitive district.

Maloney grew up in New Hampshire, but he headed to the University of Virginia for college. In 1992, he completed his law degree at UVA and went to work for Clinton's first presidential campaign. While doing advance work in New York City, he met Randy Florke, who is still his partner today — they have three children. Florke, a real estate and design maven, starred in "My Flipp'n Brother," a cable-TV reality show that made its debut in December 2012.

After the campaign, Maloney moved to New York and worked as a lawyer. His work on Clinton's re-election bid segued into a job in the West Wing. By the end of the administration, Maloney was staff secretary. He later served as a deputy secretary in the New York governor's office.

For his first term, Maloney sought and got a seat on the Transportation and Infrastructure Committee. He touts his work in New York government, where he helped create a public-private partnership commission to study ways of financing infrastructure development. "I want people working on projects like the Tappan Zee Bridge tomorrow," he says. Maloney expressed early interest in reauthorizing the National Dam Safety Program.

He also sits on the Agriculture Committee, where he is looking out for the specialty crop growers of the Hudson Valley. He has said that existing crop insurance programs often are not suited to specialty crops.

Maloney was living in New York City, so he did a little forum shopping before settling on a race in the 18th District in 2012. It was held by one-term Republican Nan Hayworth, and redistricting did not make it any easier for her to defend. After a hotly contested campaign, Maloney won by 4 points — a smaller margin of victory than President Barack Obama enjoyed in the district.

New York 18

Hudson Valley — Poughkeepsie, West Point

Snug between Connecticut and New Jersey, with a small border shared with Pennsylvania, the 18th District forms an arc between New York City's suburbs and upstate New York. It takes in all of Putnam and Orange counties and parts of Westchester and Dutchess. The Hudson River cuts through the middle of the district, from West Point to Poughkeepsie.

The landscape is a mix of rural areas and population hubs, with well-to-do enclaves along the river. Containing much of what had been the 19th District, the new 18th was stretched further north by decennial remapping to pick up Walden, in Orange County, and lost areas in Westchester to the south, such as wealthy Croton-on-Hudson.

The district's northernmost stretch of the Hudson is in Poughkeepsie, the 18th's most-populous city and home to Vassar College and Marist College. The United States Military Academy is in West Point, sitting along the steep embankments of the Hudson. Technology and research firms provide jobs in the mid-Hudson region, with IBM facilities in Poughkeepsie. An expansion of Stewart International Airport, near Newburgh, is planned.

Commuter rail lots fill early each day, as district residents commute to white-collar jobs in New York City or southern Westchester County. East of the river are commuter exurbs and well-settled suburbs, while the west has forests, rural towns and farmland.

The district — which is predominately white, with pockets of Hispanic communities — is politically competitive, particularly at the federal level, and constituents here tend to be middle-of-the-road. Poughkeepsie is more Democratic than the rest of Dutchess County overall. The second-most-populous county in the district, Orange, is slightly less Democratic than the parts of Westchester in the 18th, and Newburgh is competitive. In the 2012 presidential election, Barack Obama won 51 percent of the district's vote.

Major Industry
Health care, technology, agriculture

Military Bases
U.S. Military Academy, 1,521 military, 2,348 civilian

Cities
Poughkeepsie, Newburgh, Middletown

Notable
The home and farm of John Jay, first chief justice of the United States, is in Katonah.

Rep. Chris Gibson (R)

Capitol Office
225-5614
gibson.house.gov
1708 Longworth Bldg. 20515-3220; fax 225-1168

Committees
Agriculture
Armed Services

Residence
Kinderhook

Born
May 13, 1964; Rockville Centre, N.Y.

Religion
Roman Catholic

Family
Wife, Mary Jo Gibson; three children

Education
Siena College, B.A. 1986 (history); Cornell U., M.P.A. 1995, Ph.D. 1998 (government)

Military
Army, 1986-2010

Career
Army officer; college instructor

Political Highlights
No previous office

ELECTION RESULTS

2012 GENERAL		
Gibson (R, C, INDC)	150,245	52.8%
Julian Schreibman (D, WFM)	134,295	47.2%
2012 PRIMARY		
Gibson (R)		unopposed
2010 GENERAL		
Gibson (R, C)	130,178	54.8%
Scott Murphy (D, WFM, INDC)	107,075	45.1%

Elected 2010; 2nd term

Gibson was a career soldier, but he doesn't take marching orders from the leaders of the Republican Party. He broke ranks more than any other member of the House GOP Conference in 2012, defining himself as a moderate in a district that seems to demand it.

He joined the Army National Guard while still in high school and later took officer training while attending Siena College. During 24 years in the Army, Gibson rose to the rank of colonel and was deployed seven times, including four combat tours in Iraq; he also taught at West Point. His last assignment was in Haiti, where he commanded a team providing humanitarian relief after the 2010 earthquake. Gibson retired to run for office, and when he won he said he was treating his first term as "a deployment."

Politically, his district is tricky terrain. It is mostly rural and middle-class, and strong Democratic constituencies have fanned out from Albany and New York City to inhabit parts of it.

Hard-line liberal or conservative stances on fiscal or social issues generally are not well received by the electorate. Gibson charts a moderate course and pays close attention to constituent demands.

As a freshman in the 112th Congress (2011-12), he was a cautious participant in the Republican campaign for spending reductions. Gibson backed the finished versions of spending packages, but he balked at proposed cuts to a number of programs. When House appropriators moved to reduce subsidies for home heating oil, Gibson said it "would cause a significant hardship for New York families." He defended funding for public broadcasting, job training and high-speed railroads, saying cuts should be spread more widely.

In 2011, Gibson split with a majority of House Republicans more than 20 percent of the time when they opposed a majority of Democrats — the second highest rate in the party.

He ran that number up to 38 percent in 2012. Most notably, Gibson was one of 10 in his party to oppose the fiscal 2013 budget of Wisconsin's Paul D. Ryan — he said it proposed too much spending for the military. Gibson supported a budget plan to reduce deficits by $4 trillion over 10 years through a mix of spending cuts, revenue increases and changes to entitlement programs. When the fiscal 2014 budget came up for a vote in the 113th Congress (2013-14), 10 Republicans voted against it, and Gibson was again a part of that group.

Gibson started in the House as a member of the conservative Republican Study Committee, but he isn't listed on its roster for the 113th Congress. He does belong to the Main Street Partnership, a group of centrists.

Gibson has a seat on the Armed Services Committee and clearly is comfortable trading lingo with the military leaders who show up at hearings. His thoughts on the military set him apart from many Republicans.

He calls for a retrenching and restructuring of the military, and part of that plan is accepting large budget reductions for the Pentagon. "We still have a framework that our posture around the world still reflects the threats that were present during the Cold War," he told the Albany Times-Union. "We've tinkered around the edges. We've never fundamentally restructured."

The national security apparatus could be "flatter" and more efficient, he said, and Gibson has suggested a closer look at the Quadrennial Defense Review process, to make sure it is accounting for enough perspectives. During his military career, Gibson wrote a book, "Securing the State," that made the case for greater cooperation between the country's military and civilian authorities.

His thoughts on security also seem to be tempered by concerns about civil liberties. Gibson opposed the 2011 extension of certain surveillance provisions in the anti-terrorism law known as the Patriot Act. The next year, he was one of 28 Republicans opposing a bill to increase information sharing between the government and the private sector to help cybersecurity. Many opponents of the cybersecurity bill said it did not have safeguards to stop private companies from giving the government personal information about customers. Gibson also voted against a 2013 version.

A seat on the Agriculture Committee afforded Gibson the chance to stump for New York farmers swamped by heavy rains in 2011 and 2012. Gibson urged more disaster aid for those affected by the storms and introduced a measure to extend certain Agriculture Department disaster programs to cover some of the farmers of upstate New York.

Gibson wants crop insurance programs strengthened and is an advocate of several land conservation initiatives, such as the Environmental Quality Incentives Program. He touts his support of a proposal to allow schools to opt out of an existing Agriculture Department produce program and instead buy local produce. He tried to scale down conservative-favored reductions to food assistance programs in a long-term authorization of farm and nutrition programs that the committee worked on in 2012. (The bill was not enacted.)

Gibson grew up in Kinderhook — Martin Van Buren's hometown — and still lives there. (He also represents Hyde Park, the home of Franklin D. Roosevelt.) He was the eldest of four children and was the point guard for the basketball team at Ichabod Crane High School. His family members were working-class Democrats. Gibson's father was an elevator repairman and union member, but when the economy sagged in the late 1970s, he turned to selling cars and managing a store, and he was on unemployment for a time. Gibson says watching his dad's struggles opened him to Ronald Reagan's message in 1980.

Democrat Kirsten Gillibrand held the 20th District seat and had just begun her second term when she was appointed to the Senate in 2009. Scott Murphy barely kept the seat in Democratic hands in a March special election. Gibson decided early that year to challenge him. He retired from the military in 2010 and called on powerful friends with connections to the state Republican Party. Weeks after entering the race, Gibson won the endorsement of GOP officials in the district, which cleared out all challengers. Riding the Republican wave, he beat Murphy by almost 10 points.

A redrawing of the congressional map for 2012 took away the northern arm of his district, added territory to the southwest and changed its number to the 19th. Democrat Julian Schreibman, a federal prosecutor, raised a fair amount of cash, and the battle between him and Gibson got ugly at times. Gibson's early lead in the polls shrank, but he held on to win by less than 6 points.

Key Votes

2012	
Extend a Social Security payroll tax cut and unemployment benefits	YES
Ease securities rules to expand small-business access to capital	YES
Extend for one year subsidized student loan interest rates financed by a cut in health care spending	YES
Cite Attorney General Eric H. Holder Jr. for contempt of Congress	YES
Create a visa program for foreign graduates in high-tech fields	YES
Extend most Bush-era income tax rates while allowing rates for top-bracket earners to rise (Jan. 1, 2013)	YES
2011	
Strike funding for F-35 alternative engine	YES
Prevent EPA from regulating greenhouse gas emissions to address climate change	YES
Extend certain provisions of Patriot Act for four years	NO
Declare opposition to use of ground troops in Libya	YES
Overhaul patent law	NO
Pass compromise debt limit increase plan and establish future spending limits	YES
Allow consideration of measures to implement three trade agreements	YES

CQ Vote Studies

	PARTY UNITY		PRESIDENTIAL SUPPORT	
	SUPPORT	OPPOSE	SUPPORT	OPPOSE
2012	62%	38%	38%	62%
2011	78%	22%	28%	72%

Interest Groups

	AFL-CIO	ADA	CCUS	ACU
2012	57%	20%	83%	40%
2011	38%	30%	94%	52%

New York 19

Hudson Valley and Catskill Mountains

The Catskill Mountains, farmland and swathes of forest define the landscape west of the residential Hudson River Valley, along which most of the 19th District's population centers are found. Four major interstate routes fan out from the Albany area, which is just north of the district in the 20th, toward New York City and major hubs in upstate New York, the state's southern tier and Massachusetts. After decennial redistricting, the new 19th District was drawn to include parts of four former districts, combining much of the areas that previously had fallen in the 22nd and 20th.

The district still relies on traditional agricultural production, including dairy farms and apple orchards; the district's primary crop produces McIntosh, Cortland, Empire and other varieties. Ulster County is fertile territory for computer-manufacturing firms as well as orchards — the site of a former IBM plant in Kingston now hosts electronics and solar-energy companies. And two towns in the 19th host State University of New York campuses: New Paltz near Interstate 87 next to the Hudson, and Oneonta in the west.

The Catskills and the Leatherstocking Region, including Oneonta and Cooperstown, draw tourists. Once a prominent Jewish resort area, the Catskills' Borscht Belt has focused on modernizing its hospitality industry. The mountain peaks less than two hours north of New York City are a draw, as is the Baseball Hall of Fame in Cooperstown. Fishing, camping and outdoor recreation are important in Greene, Delaware and Ostego counties.

The district is predominately white, with pockets of minority residents in Dutchess and Sullivan counties. The district's residents are largely middle class, but poverty is a problem in areas, including New Palz and Monticello.

The district has had a slight Republican lean, and independent voters tend to back the GOP in federal races. Republican Mitt Romney won Broome, Schoharie, Greene and Delaware, and the part of Montgomery in the 19th, by wide margins in the 2012 presidential election, but Barack Obama competed well elsewhere and took 52 percent of the district's vote overall.

Major Industry

Agriculture, tourism, health care

Cities

Kingston, Oneonta, New Paltz

Notable

Bethel was the site of the marathon Woodstock rock concert in 1969.

Rep. Paul Tonko (D)

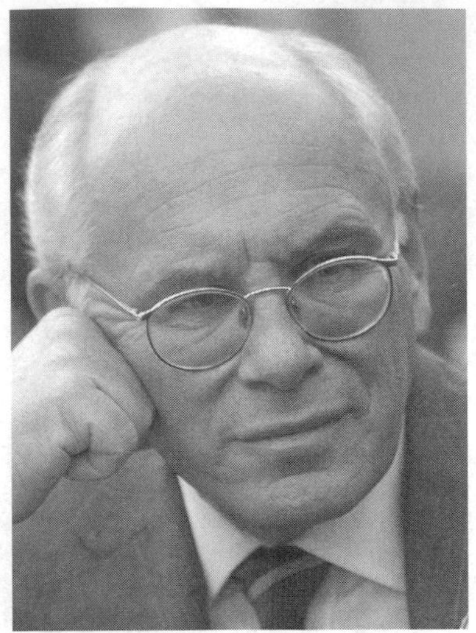

Capitol Office
225-5076
tonko.house.gov
2463 Rayburn Bldg. 20515-3221; fax 225-5077

Committees
Energy & Commerce

Residence
Amsterdam

Born
June 18, 1949; Amsterdam, N.Y.

Religion
Roman Catholic

Family
Single

Education
Clarkson U., B.S. 1971 (mechanical and industrial engineering)

Career
State public works engineer; state transportation agency employee

Political Highlights
Montgomery County Board of Supervisors, 1976-83 (chairman, 1981); N.Y. Assembly, 1983-2007; New York State Energy Research Development Authority president, 2007-08

ELECTION RESULTS

2012 GENERAL		
Tonko (D, WFM, INDC)	203,401	68.4%
Robert J. Dieterich (R, C)	93,778	31.6%
2012 PRIMARY		
Tonko (D)		unopposed
2010 GENERAL		
Tonko (D, WFM, INDC)	124,889	59.2%
Theodore J. Danz Jr. (R, C)	85,752	40.7%

Previous Winning Percentages
2008 (62%)

Elected 2008; 3rd term

The friendly Tonko enjoys being seen as the "energy guy" by fellow lawmakers, having established that reputation — and a solidly liberal political record — with more than 30 years of policy experience at the state and local levels. In his third term, Democrats finally found room for him on the Energy and Commerce Committee.

Tonko trained as a mechanical and industrial engineer in college. He got involved in county government while working as a public works engineer for the state of New York. His 24-year run in the state Assembly included 15 years chairing its Energy Committee; Tonko followed that tenure with a year heading a state agency focused on energy efficiency and affordability.

Discussing energy, he invokes the spirit of one of his Democratic inspirations, President John F. Kennedy: Tonko describes the transition from fossil fuels to a more comprehensive energy sector as the new space race. "We came off the defeat of the Sputnik moment, dusted off our backsides and said, 'Never again,'" and the same can be done with energy, he contends.

Tonko's preferred strategy has many facets. He would incorporate engineering into the curricula of elementary and secondary schools, create a "smart grid" to improve long-distance transmission of power, and provide tax breaks to foster growth in the renewable-energy sector. On the transportation side, Tonko supports further development of hybrid-powered commercial vehicles and the expansion of high-speed rail.

Success on those fronts would bode well for his Albany-region district, which Tonko has supported as a hub for technology and renewable-energy businesses. The area hosts advanced battery manufacturing, nanotechnology companies, one of the largest chipset manufacturing operations in the country and General Electric's wind turbine operation. While in the Assembly, Tonko sponsored one of the first laws in the country mandating a statewide target for the use of renewable energy, and he has backed the idea of a cap-and-trade system to regulate greenhouse gas emissions.

In addition to joining Energy and Commerce in the 113th Congress (2013-14), Tonko was named the top Democrat on its Environment and the Economy Subcommittee. He also sits on the Energy and Power Subcommittee.

For part of the 112th Congress (2011-12), Tonko served on the Natural Resources Committee. He railed against the efforts of Republicans, particularly those from the West, to open public lands to energy exploration and ease environmental protections in the name of energy independence. Such efforts "dull our competitiveness as a country" in the energy sectors that would lead to infrastructure improvement and job growth, Tonko says.

In 2013, he panned the Republican effort to secure approval of the Keystone XL pipeline, which would run from Canada's tar sands to U.S. refineries. "This project is not about jobs," he said at a hearing. "It's about committing us to an oil-based economy for another 50 years or more."

Tonko takes a parochial interest in the waterways within the Hudson-Mohawk River Basin. He helped create the Mighty Waters Task Force, a consortium of state, local and private entities to promote conservation, as well as educational and economic development around the waterfront. The basin encompasses a large portion of the Great Lakes.

The task force became more active after floods ravaged the area in 2011. Tonko introduced legislation to establish a commission, similar to those that have been created for the Delaware River Basin and the Colorado River, to devise a comprehensive development strategy for the Hudson-Mohawk basin.

Most issues outside of energy and the environment still find Tonko in the liberal camp. Whether serving in the minority or the majority, he rarely votes against a majority of Democrats when they oppose most Republicans. Tonko also relishes the chance to chime in on a variety of liberal and local causes; he is one of the more frequent speakers on the House floor.

He does have a few other specific interests, however, such as extending mental-health coverage. Tonko pushed to include language in the 2010 health care overhaul to expand access to mental-health and substance abuse services. Tonko did similar work in the Assembly, leading an effort to require health insurers to cover mental-health treatment. That law was named after Timothy O'Clair, a Schenectady 12-year-old who hanged himself in 2001; Tonko said the boy was a constituent, but also someone "who I knew, who I loved." He cites the law as one of his proudest accomplishments.

The two-year authorization of surface transportation programs enacted in 2012 included his provision authorizing funds for states to improve trucker rest areas. Tonko dedicated his initial bill to a New York trucker who was killed during a robbery when he pulled over to rest at an abandoned gas station.

Tonko still lives in his native Amsterdam, N.Y. His grandparents were Eastern European immigrants who settled in the area. Tonko graduated from Amsterdam High School and studied engineering at Clarkson University in Potsdam.

It was shortly after graduating that Tonko became interested in politics. He cites Kennedy's call to service, made when Tonko was approaching his teen years, as his initial inspiration. It was "a time of hope, change and potential" that spoke to him in his youth. He says the civil rights movement and the space race inspired him to volunteer with his local Democratic Committee.

His desire to "give it a try" rapidly evolved into a candidacy for the Montgomery County Democratic Committee, and he was elected at age 22. Four years later, while working as an engineer with the state Department of Public Service, Tonko became the youngest person elected to the Montgomery County Board of Supervisors.

In 1983, he was elected to the state Assembly, where he served for 24 years. He resigned in 2007 to become president and chief executive of the New York State Energy Research and Development Authority.

Tonko resigned that post after 10 months to focus on the House race to replace retiring 10-term Democrat Michael R. McNulty. He defeated four other Democrats in the September primary and then breezed past GOP businessman James Buhrmaster in the general election with 62 percent of the vote.

In 2010 he easily bested Republican Theodore J. Danz, owner of a heating and air conditioning company, taking 59 percent of the vote. After redistricting for the 2012 election, he scored his biggest win to date, with 68 percent.

Key Votes

2012	
Extend a Social Security payroll tax cut and unemployment benefits	YES
Ease securities rules to expand small-business access to capital	YES
Extend for one year subsidized student loan interest rates financed by a cut in health care spending	NO
Cite Attorney General Eric H. Holder Jr. for contempt of Congress	?
Create a visa program for foreign graduates in high-tech fields	YES
Extend most Bush-era income tax rates while allowing rates for top-bracket earners to rise (Jan. 1, 2013)	YES
2011	
Strike funding for F-35 alternative engine	NO
Prevent EPA from regulating greenhouse gas emissions to address climate change	NO
Extend certain provisions of Patriot Act for four years	NO
Declare opposition to use of ground troops in Libya	YES
Overhaul patent law	YES
Pass compromise debt limit increase plan and establish future spending limits	NO
Allow consideration of measures to implement three trade agreements	NO

CQ Vote Studies

	PARTY UNITY		PRESIDENTIAL SUPPORT	
	SUPPORT	OPPOSE	SUPPORT	OPPOSE
2012	98%	2%	86%	14%
2011	98%	2%	83%	17%
2010	97%	3%	86%	14%
2009	99%	1%	97%	3%

Interest Groups

	AFL-CIO	ADA	CCUS	ACU
2012	95%	95%	42%	0%
2011	100%	95%	19%	4%
2010	100%	100%	0%	0%
2009	100%	100%	33%	0%

New York 20

Capital District — Albany, Schenectady, Troy, Saratoga Springs

As the terminus of the Erie Canal, which connects the Great Lakes to the Hudson River, New York's Capital District was one of the state's earliest industrial centers. Blue-collar workers and state employees give the Albany-Schenectady-Troy area a substantial union population and a solidly Democratic vote. Outside the capital-area tri-cities, the 20th is home to Saratoga Springs and its well-known horse racetracks.

The county seat as well as the state capital, Albany relies on government work, although budget cuts have led to some layoffs. Beyond government-related employment, health care research and high-tech manufacturing are key cogs in the economy here.

Albany's medical center is the second-largest employer in the region, and the College of Nanoscale Science and Engineering uses federal grants to study nanotech research and the development of solar-energy technology. GlobalFoundries, a manufacturing and technology company in Malta, is a major player in the capital region. Schenectady hosts GE, and Saratoga Springs and Malta have software and alternative-energy business clusters. Rensselaer Polytechnic Institute and Sienna College are both in the 20th.

The district is small in comparison to some of the other upstate districts but generally more diverse demographically. White residents remain the majority, but the 20th has notable black (9 percent), Hispanic (6 percent) and Asian populations (4 percent) for a district outside New York City. The 20th favors Democrats, although the southern portions of Saratoga County and the district's part of Montgomery County back the GOP.

Major Industry

Government, technology, manufacturing

Military Bases

Watervliet Arsenal (Army), 1 military, 650 civilian

Cities

Albany, Schenectady, Troy

Notable

Samuel Wilson, a meat packer who provided the Army with much of its rations during the War of 1812 and who is believed to have been the inspiration of "Uncle Sam," is buried in Troy; The Proctors Theatre in Schenectady hosted the first public demonstration of television in 1930.

Rep. Bill Owens (D)

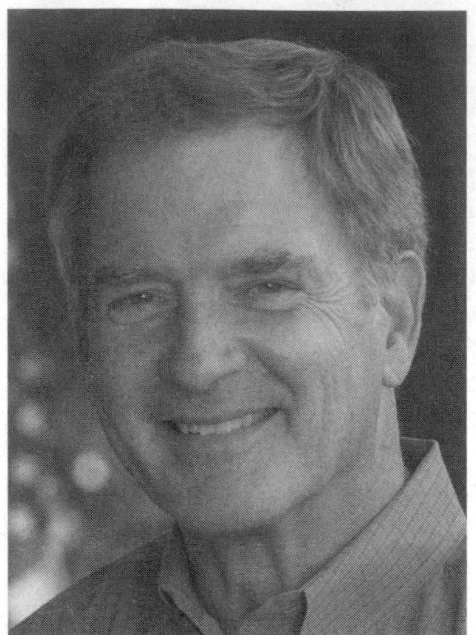

Capitol Office
225-4611
owens.house.gov
405 Cannon Bldg. 20515-3223; fax 226-0621

Committees
Appropriations

Residence
Plattsburgh

Born
Jan. 20, 1949; Brooklyn, N.Y.

Religion
Roman Catholic

Family
Wife, Jane Owens; three children

Education
Manhattan College, B.S.B.A. 1971 (economics); Fordham U., J.D. 1974

Military
Air Force Reserve, 1971-75; Air Force, 1975-79; Air Force Reserve, 1979-82

Career
Lawyer; college instructor

Political Highlights
No previous office

ELECTION RESULTS

2012 GENERAL		
Owens (D, WFM)	126,631	50.2%
Matt Doheny (R, C, INDC)	121,646	48.2%
Donald L. Hassig (GREEN)	4,174	1.6%
2012 PRIMARY		
Owens (D)		unopposed
2010 GENERAL		
Owens (D, WFM)	82,232	47.5%
Matt Doheny (R, INDC)	80,237	46.4%
Doug Hoffman (C)	10,507	6.1%

Previous Winning Percentages
2009 Special Election (48%)

Elected 2009; 2nd full term

Owens has led a charmed political life, capturing and holding a district where the odds often favor Republicans. His approach as a lawmaker has been to make his own luck. Owens owns one of the most centrist voting records in the Democratic Caucus, and the farm, business and military interests of his upstate New York district are the foundation of his work.

The military brought Owens to the area. He was born in Brooklyn and raised on Long Island. After college and law school in New York City, he enlisted in the Air Force and served as a JAG officer. Within a few years, he was stationed at Plattsburgh Air Force Base in the northeastern corner of the state. When he left the service, Owens and his wife decided to stay in the region. He started a successful tax and business law practice.

He cultivated an active civic life, if not a political one. His most notable engagement was with the formation of the Plattsburgh Airbase Redevelopment Corp. — the base closed in 1995, and PARC lures businesses to set up shop on the old property. Owens had never held an elective office when Democrats put him on the ballot for the November 2009 special election to replace Republican Rep. John M. McHugh. At the time, Owens wasn't even a registered member of the party.

A Democrat hadn't represented the region since the Millard Fillmore administration, but dissent in the GOP ranks resulted in a conservative and a moderate splitting the vote. Owens sneaked through and joined the 111th Congress (2009-10), and the same GOP divisions helped him return for the 112th Congress (2011-12).

Owens served on the Agriculture, Small Business and Armed Services committees, but he gave up those seats in the 113th Congress (2013-14) to take an assignment on the Appropriations Committee. He sits on the Defense and Homeland Security subcommittees.

He operates as a man in the middle, ruffling few feathers with a disciplined public demeanor. Owens is a member of the business-friendly New Democrat Coalition, and he has been sympathetic to some Republican stances on economic growth and federal spending. A former member of a bank board, he voted against the 2010 overhaul of financial regulations, saying it would be too burdensome for small-town institutions.

During the 112th Congress, he was one of just 19 Democrats to vote for a 2012 bill to extend the George W. Bush-era tax cuts for all income levels; only 20 other Democrats joined Owens to support a GOP bill that would expand the potential for oil and gas exploration on public lands. He approved of measures meant to constrain EPA regulation of farm dust and the emissions from industrial boilers.

When taking the initiative, Owens zeroes in on the economic concerns of his district, and that often means dealing with Canada. His district has several border crossings, and Owens urges colleagues to support the "Beyond the Border" action plan, a joint U.S.-Canadian effort to find cost-efficient and secure ways to keep people and goods moving between the countries. In early 2011, President Barack Obama signed Owens' bill requiring a northern border counternarcotics strategy. He is the co-chairman of the House Northern Border Caucus.

Farming is an economic driver in his district, and Owens tries to lower the costs of, and expand the services for, entrepreneurs. The Agriculture Committee's version of a 2012 bill to reauthorize farm programs contained three Owens provisions: one to make more family farms eligible for Farm Service Agency loans; one to stop U.S. inspections of apples shipping to Canada (they are inspected when they get there); and one to encourage maple syrup production. He backs price supports for dairy farmers — and he and other lawmakers have requested an end to Canadian tariffs on dairy and poultry products from the United States. (The farm bill was not enacted.)

Fort Drum and military contractors employ many of Owens' constituents — in fact, McHugh resigned his House seat to become secretary of the Army. Owens has tried to defend the projects of local contractors from budget cuts.

He takes a special interest in veterans with post-traumatic stress disorder or traumatic brain injury. Owens cited such veterans when introducing his bill to automatically enroll those leaving combat zones in veterans health programs. Getting them into the health care system quickly would improve early screening, he said.

Owens can credit some of his legislative output to cooperation with Republicans. He and Utah's Jason Chaffetz produced a bill to eliminate a cap on the fees banks can charge businesses for processing debit card transactions. They said banks would charge higher fees to consumers to compensate. Obama signed a bill by Owens and Mississippi's Gregg Harper to eliminate a requirement for auto dealers to provide customers with a booklet on insurance costs.

When Owens got into the 2009 special election, Republicans nominated Dede Scozzafava, a moderate Republican state assemblywoman. Grass-roots conservatives revolted, backing a challenge by accountant Doug Hoffman. In a remarkable turn of events, Scozzafava dropped out less than a week before the election and endorsed Owens. Her name stayed on the ballot, and her vote total was more than twice Owens' margin of victory over Hoffman.

Hoffman ran again in 2010, but GOP leaders backed Matt Doheny, a Wall Street banker who was capable of funding his own campaign as needed. Doheny bested Hoffman in a September primary and immediately set out to paint Owens as a liberal. Owens' campaign spent $3 million, and Doheny's spent $3.4 million, but Hoffman was the spoiler. He appeared on the ballot for the Conservative Party and got more than 10,000 votes. Owens beat Doheny by only 2,000.

Remapping for the 2012 election seemed to increase the Republican lean of the district, and Doheny came back for a rematch. Owens ran an aggressive and organized campaign, and Doheny also suffered a scandal. Weeks before his June 2012 wedding, photos and videos surfaced where Doheny appeared to be kissing a campaign consultant at a Washington steakhouse.

Even without the benefit of a vote-splitting candidate — and with several Republican-leaning groups spending heavily against him — Owens cleared 50 percent of the vote for the first time and beat Doheny by 2 points. Obama carried the district's presidential vote by a wider margin.

Key Votes

2012	
Extend a Social Security payroll tax cut and unemployment benefits	YES
Ease securities rules to expand small-business access to capital	YES
Extend for one year subsidized student loan interest rates financed by a cut in health care spending	YES
Cite Attorney General Eric H. Holder Jr. for contempt of Congress	YES
Create a visa program for foreign graduates in high-tech fields	-
Extend most Bush-era income tax rates while allowing rates for top-bracket earners to rise (Jan. 1, 2013)	YES
2011	
Strike funding for F-35 alternative engine	YES
Prevent EPA from regulating greenhouse gas emissions to address climate change	NO
Extend certain provisions of Patriot Act for four years	?
Declare opposition to use of ground troops in Libya	YES
Overhaul patent law	YES
Pass compromise debt limit increase plan and establish future spending limits	YES
Allow consideration of measures to implement three trade agreements	YES

CQ Vote Studies

	PARTY UNITY		PRESIDENTIAL SUPPORT	
	SUPPORT	OPPOSE	SUPPORT	OPPOSE
2012	68%	32%	48%	52%
2011	65%	35%	73%	27%
2010	83%	17%	83%	17%
2009	87%	13%	86%	14%

Interest Groups

	AFL-CIO	ADA	CCUS	ACU
2012	67%	35%	91%	36%
2011	90%	75%	69%	8%
2010	79%	70%	50%	21%
2009	100%		43%	14%

New York 21

North — Watertown, Plattsburgh, Glens Falls

The majority of the sprawling, rural 21st — expanded and renumbered during decennial remapping — is covered by Adirondack Park, and its lakes, mountains and waterfalls. The Canada border forms the northern and northwestern edges of the district — the cargo-heavy St. Lawrence River runs from Lake Ontario west of Watertown to a series of island state parks, where the international border tracks east to Interstate 87 north of Plattsburgh. Vermont abuts the district's eastern border.

Fort Drum, just outside of Watertown, is one of the largest and most modern Army facilities on the East Coast. It has survived rounds of base realignment and the more-than-100,000-acre base is home to the 10th Mountain Division and a major training center. For decades Watertown was a paper mill town, but as the mills closed, the city's economy stuttered. Now it relies on favorable exchange rates to lure Canadian tourists.

The local economy also depends on several community colleges, State University of New York branches and private colleges. Many small communities swell with vacationers during the summer months. A controversial plan to develop the Adirondack Club and Resort in Tupper Lake was approved in early 2012. Unemployment is major concern; tourists only prop up the economy part of the year, much of the district is remote and winters can be harsh. Lake Placid was home to the 1932 and 1980 Olympics and hopes to host the 2022 Olympics jointly with Plattsburgh.

The district historically was a GOP stronghold, and the northeastern corner of the state sent Republicans to the U.S. House from 1873 until 2009. Despite a sizable voter registration edge for the GOP, a break between moderates and conservatives has put this House seat in Democratic hands. Barack Obama took 52 percent of the district's 2012 presidential vote..

Major Industry
Defense, tourism

Military Bases
Fort Drum, 19,605 military, 4,739 civilian (2012)

Cities
Watertown, Plattsburgh

Notable
Adirondack Park, first established in 1882, is larger than Yellowstone, Yosemite, Glacier, Grand Canyon and the Great Smokies parks combined.

Rep. Richard Hanna (R)

Capitol Office
225-3665
hanna.house.gov
319 Cannon Bldg. 20515-3224; fax 225-1891

Committees
Small Business
(Contracting & Workforce - Chairman)
Transportation & Infrastructure
Joint Economic

Residence
Barneveld

Born
Jan. 25, 1951; Utica, N.Y.

Religion
Roman Catholic

Family
Wife Kim Hanna; two children

Education
Reed College, B.A. 1976 (economics and political science)

Career
Construction company owner; property development company manager

Political Highlights
Republican nominee for U.S. House, 2008

ELECTION RESULTS

2012 GENERAL		
Hanna (R, INDC)	157,941	60.7%
Dan Lamb (D)	102,080	39.3%
2012 PRIMARY		
Hanna (R)	10,627	71.1%
Michael J. Kicinski Sr. (R)	4,314	28.9%
2010 GENERAL		
Hanna (R, C, INDC)	101,599	53.0%
Michael Arcuri (D, MOD)	89,809	46.8%

Elected 2010; 2nd term

Hanna is a moderate Republican with a libertarian streak. He knows the construction industry and how to operate a business, and GOP leaders clearly like it when he plays to his strengths: He has influential positions on committees handling infrastructure and federal contracting.

Hanna came to the House in 2011 with no legislative experience. A self-described "practical guy," he says he runs his office as a customer-oriented business: "I don't live in a world where ideology helps you."

His congressional paycheck is the first he has received from someone other than himself. His father died when Hanna was 20, leaving him and his sister to provide for the family. He put himself through college during the next several years and afterward founded Hanna Construction, which handled a wide variety of jobs. He ran the company for three decades.

"I started from nothing, so I kind of have this whole from-the-bottom-up sense" about business, he said. Hanna ranks as one of the wealthiest members of Congress.

He is not the most eloquent purveyor of political philosophy, but Hanna is in his element when talking about the business world. He sits on the Small Business Committee, which he says "is like watching your life on replay." For the 113th Congress (2013-14), he chairs the Subcommittee on Contracting and Workforce.

Hanna used to bid on public contracts, and he would like to change the rules for surety bonds, the collateral that bidders agree to forfeit should they fail to deliver. In 2012, the House passed his bill to require "individual sureties" — organizations or persons who assume responsibility for paying a debt — to list specific and stable assets as collateral for federal construction contracts. Hanna said the use of fraudulent or shaky sureties can put unsuspecting contractors at risk of financial ruin, or allow less-qualified contractors to compete unfairly for contracts they can't fulfill.

He wants the contracting process to be as efficient as possible, but Hanna isn't sentimental about competitive bidding. When a witness at a 2012 hearing posited a scenario where a company spends $100,000 preparing a unsuccessful bid, Hanna responded, "That's life."

Many small businesses in his district are farms. Hanna has been involved with the effort to expand the visa program for temporary agriculture workers to include dairy workers. He co-chairs both the Northeast Agriculture Caucus and the Congressional Organic Caucus.

Hanna, a longtime member of the International Union of Operating Engineers, also sits on the Transportation and Infrastructure Committee. As a freshman, he was vice chairman of the Highways and Transit Subcommittee; he helped pitch an unsuccessful GOP plan to expand the revenue stream for transportation projects by adding lease revenue from new domestic energy production.

He was on the conference committee that finalized a two-year reauthorization of surface transportation programs in 2012. Hanna was pleased with provisions of that law that streamline regulatory reviews of projects, and in final negotiations he defended the ability of local planning organizations to assist in the selection of infrastructure projects.

In 2013, he became the vice chairman of the subcommittee handling railroads and pipelines, as Congress considers reauthorizations of Amtrak and rail safety laws. Hanna has said that he opposes ending federal support for Amtrak, but he is interested in modifying the passenger rail service. He seems keen on the use of public-private partnerships to further develop or maintain the Northeast Corridor, Amtrak's busiest service area.

Early in 2011, Hanna said he wasn't interested in high-speed rail development outside of the Northeast Corridor. He told the Watertown Daily Times that he didn't see the economic benefit in a high-speed line for the Empire Corridor, which runs from Buffalo to Albany to New York City.

Hanna describes himself as a fiscal conservative and a social moderate. In 2013, he was among the first House Republicans to openly support same-sex marriage. He also supports abortion rights. He and Judy Biggert of Illinois were the only House Republicans to vote against a 2011 bill to ban outright the use of federal money for abortion services.

Still, Hanna says that many social issues "are really a diversion from the desperate need we have to regrow our economy."

He belongs to both the conservative Republican Study Committee and the moderate Main Street Partnership. He voted for fiscal 2012, 2013 and 2014 budgets produced by Wisconsin Republican Paul D. Ryan, who proposed a fundamental restructuring of Medicare. However, Hanna opposes privatization of Social Security and raising the retirement age.

Hanna has worked extensively as a philanthropist, serving on numerous boards and charities. He joined with a local organization in his district in 2004 to found Annie's Fund, which offers monetary intervention to women in temporary crisis.

He also was a "sustaining member" of the libertarian Cato Institute, and his ties to the organization resulted in a slap on the wrist early in 2011. Hanna was one of 31 Republicans to vote against a four-year reauthorization of expiring surveillance provisions of the anti-terrorism law known as the Patriot Act. Explaining his opposition in a Syracuse Post-Standard opinion piece — Hanna was concerned the provisions infringed on civil liberties — he copied passages from a Cato scholar.

Hanna said he had permission to do so, but a Post-Standard editorial scolded him for "near plagiarism."

Hanna first made a bid for office in 2008, challenging first-term Democratic Rep. Michael Arcuri in the 24th District. He lost by 4 points. Republicans were experiencing a resurgence when Hanna challenged Arcuri again in 2010, and he won by 6 points.

The congressional map for upstate New York saw major changes in redistricting for 2012. Hanna ran in the 22nd District, which included the big population centers from the old 24th. His opponent was Dan Lamb, the longtime district director for Democratic Rep. Maurice D. Hinchey, who was retiring. Hanna brought in more than three times the campaign cash that Lamb did, and he won by more than 21 points.

Key Votes

2012	
Extend a Social Security payroll tax cut and unemployment benefits	YES
Ease securities rules to expand small-business access to capital	YES
Extend for one year subsidized student loan interest rates financed by a cut in health care spending	YES
Cite Attorney General Eric H. Holder Jr. for contempt of Congress	YES
Create a visa program for foreign graduates in high-tech fields	YES
Extend most Bush-era income tax rates while allowing rates for top-bracket earners to rise (Jan. 1, 2013)	YES
2011	
Strike funding for F-35 alternative engine	NO
Prevent EPA from regulating greenhouse gas emissions to address climate change	YES
Extend certain provisions of Patriot Act for four years	NO
Declare opposition to use of ground troops in Libya	YES
Overhaul patent law	YES
Pass compromise debt limit increase plan and establish future spending limits	YES
Allow consideration of measures to implement three trade agreements	YES

CQ Vote Studies

	PARTY UNITY		PRESIDENTIAL SUPPORT	
	SUPPORT	OPPOSE	SUPPORT	OPPOSE
2012	85%	15%	21%	79%
2011	83%	17%	26%	74%

Interest Groups

	AFL-CIO	ADA	CCUS	ACU
2012	33%	5%	92%	64%
2011	21%	25%	100%	40%

New York 22

Central — Utica, Binghamton, Rome

The 22nd District now stretches from the Pennsylvania border to the shores of Lake Ontario. The region that once was dominated by manufacturing and farms has been hurting economically since before the most recent economic downturn. It is filled with state forests, small towns and midsize cities. Interstate 81, a major transportation route to and from Canada, cuts through the district at various points, as does the New York State Thruway (Interstate 90). Binghamton and Utica are the predominately white district's population centers.

Binghamton University, a regional public college, is a major employer. The city and surrounding area is home to many white-collar employers, including technology firms. Local and school officials are planning a business incubator to help develop and maintain additional high-skilled jobs. The other points of the Broome County tri-cities, Johnson City and Endicott, also sit along the Southern Tier Expressway (Interstate 86).

Oneida's Utica and Rome are aging industrial cities on the Mohawk River. Utica is now a haven for immigrants, partially offsetting population losses elsewhere in the district. Nearly one in six residents is foreign-born, from African and Southeast Asian immigrants to a large Bosnian community.

Environmental issues are key here. The base of the Adirondacks is in the northern part of Oneida County, and the Marcellus Shale sits under the southern portion of the district. Neighboring Pennsylvania has seen an economic windfall as a result of its natural gas exploration, but local residents are concerned about the environmental impact of extraction.

Republicans hold a voter registration edge in every county wholly or partly in the district, with a wide margin in Oswego and Chenango, except for Broome County. It can be competitive on the national scale: In 2008, Republican John McCain won the areas within the current district's boundaries by about 150 votes; in 2012, Barack Obama won here by less than 1,500.

Major Industry
Higher education, government, technology

Cities
Utica, Binghamton, Rome

Notable
"The Wizard of Oz" was written by Chittenango native L. Frank Baum — the Oz-Stravaganza is held every year to celebrate his books.

Rep. Tom Reed (R)

Capitol Office
225-3161
reed.house.gov
1504 Longworth Bldg. 20515-3229; fax 226-6599

Committees
Ways & Means

Residence
Corning

Born
Nov. 18, 1971; Joliet, Ill.

Religion
Roman Catholic

Family
Wife, Jean Reed; two children

Education
Alfred U., B.A. 1993 (political science); Ohio Northern U., J.D. 1996

Career
Lawyer; real estate company owner

Political Highlights
Mayor of Corning, 2008-09

ELECTION RESULTS

2012 GENERAL		
Reed (R, C, INDC)	137,669	51.9%
Nate Shinagawa (D, WFM)	127,535	48.1%
2012 PRIMARY		
Reed (R)		unopposed
2010 GENERAL		
Reed (R, C, INDC)	112,314	56.5%
Matthew Zeller (D, WFM)	86,099	43.3%

Previous Winning Percentages
2010 Special Election (57%)

Elected 2010; 2nd full term

Reed likes tackling big fiscal issues, and his seat on the Ways and Means Committee lets him do so. The relatively moderate Republican has worked with his party's leadership team, promoting many of their strategies on tax policy, entitlement programs and spending reductions.

A former mayor of Corning, Reed sees himself as a workhorse. "There are some members who come here and they want to have their five minutes in the press, their five minutes of glory, so to speak," he says. "I came here to do something." Reed belongs to both the conservative Republican Study Committee and the moderate Main Street Partnership.

He caught the eye of GOP leaders early in his House career. Reed was part of the Republican Policy Committee in the 112th Congress (2011-12), and a few months into his first full term he was moving up. Reed departed the Transportation and Infrastructure Committee to join the Rules Committee, a panel where service is specifically at the invitation of party leaders. A few months later, he moved to an open spot on Ways and Means.

Reed cites the state of the nation's finances as his inspiration for seeking a House seat — he said he knew the country was headed down the wrong path when he saw President Barack Obama's agenda, including the $787 billion stimulus law of 2009, which he calls a "horrible mistake." He introduced a bill to place a real-time display of the country's national debt in the House chamber, and in hearings he has gotten analysts to flatly state that current federal spending is not sustainable.

He likes the changes to Medicare proposed in the budgets by Wisconsin Republican Paul D. Ryan, and he says he is open to modifying Social Security (but opposes its privatization). Reed was also one of 38 House members who voted for a fiscal 2013 budget proposal based on the work of the 2010 fiscal commission known as Simpson-Bowles. It would cut deficits by $4 trillion over 10 years through a mix of spending reduction and revenue increases.

At the end of the 112th Congress, Reed wanted spending cuts included in a bill to extend expiring income tax rates. The final measure permanently extended lower tax rates only for income under $400,000, with negligible cuts. But Reed voted for it anyway, as a matter of strategy — making the lower rates permanent solidified the long-term budget baseline. "Permanency was critical," Reed said. "It's a bridge to comprehensive tax reform. It allows that debate to start."

Reed has worked well with Dave Camp of Michigan, the Ways and Means chairman. In 2012, he gathered signatures from scores of freshman lawmakers for a letter expressing support of tariff suspensions — relatively narrow bills meant to lower the costs of specific supplies for manufacturers and other businesses. Some conservatives think of suspensions as earmarks, which have been banned by the Republican majority. Camp supported Reed's effort as a way to head off dissent. Congress did not get around to considering a tariff bill in the 112th, however.

On the Human Resources Subcommittee, Reed has called for an end to extensions of unemployment benefits, saying states cannot continue to keep up their end of the federal-state program.

One area where Reed sees a role for government is on transportation spending. He said his experience as mayor made him aware of the importance of infrastructure to economic development. "I am an outspoken advocate for limited government," he wrote in Roll Call in early 2011. "Government should only do what individuals cannot. Making transportation and infrastructure investments is one of the legitimate roles of government."

Reed praised Obama for making infrastructure investment a priority in job creation efforts but said determining the funding for such work is a "critical debate." A two-year reauthorization of surface transportation programs enacted in 2012 had regulatory streamlining provisions, which Reed approves of; he introduced a 2011 bill to exclude certain highway construction projects from environmental assessment requirements. A 2012 Reed bill would require a study of ways to use federally owned land along the highway system to generate energy or revenue.

Energy is a big issue in his upstate New York district, which sits atop the Marcellus Shale. Environmentalists contend that hydraulic fracturing, a means of extracting oil and gas from shale formations, can contaminate groundwater. Reed has said that states are doing a good job of studying and regulating the practice and that further federal intervention isn't needed.

Reed is one of 12 children. His father, a career Army officer who served in both World War II and the Korean War, died when he was 2. His mother moved the family to Corning to live in the house built by Reed's grandfather — the same house Reed now occupies with his wife and two children.

He earned a political science degree at Alfred University, where he was an All-American swimmer. He says the discipline and setting of personal goals from his swimming days influence him today: "That mind-set has really paid off for me."

Reed went on to earn a law degree and started practicing law in Rochester. He returned to Corning in 1999 and continued his law practice; he also started several businesses dealing with real estate. He was elected mayor of Corning in 2007 and served one two-year term. After it ended, he set his sights on the House. He declared his plans to challenge freshman Democrat Eric Massa.

His road got a lot easier in March 2010, when Massa resigned after being accused of sexually harassing male staff members. Reed defeated Democrat Matthew Zeller with 57 percent of the vote in November, while simultaneously winning a special election to complete Massa's term in the 111th Congress (2009-10).

Redistricting for the 113th Congress (2013-14) substantially transformed districts in upstate New York. Reed ran in the new 23rd, which contained about half of his old constituents. His Democratic opponent was Nate Shinagawa, a 28-year-old hospital administrator who also served on the Tompkins County Legislature. Shinagawa accused Reed of neglecting the middle class; he also touted his opposition to hydraulic fracturing. Reed had a huge fundraising advantage, but the result was close — he won by less than 4 points.

For the 2014 election cycle, Reed is serving as one of five regional chairmen of the National Republican Congressional Committee.

Key Votes

2012	
Extend a Social Security payroll tax cut and unemployment benefits	YES
Ease securities rules to expand small-business access to capital	YES
Extend for one year subsidized student loan interest rates financed by a cut in health care spending	YES
Cite Attorney General Eric H. Holder Jr. for contempt of Congress	YES
Create a visa program for foreign graduates in high-tech fields	YES
Extend most Bush-era income tax rates while allowing rates for top-bracket earners to rise (Jan. 1, 2013)	YES
2011	
Strike funding for F-35 alternative engine	YES
Prevent EPA from regulating greenhouse gas emissions to address climate change	YES
Extend certain provisions of Patriot Act for four years	YES
Declare opposition to use of ground troops in Libya	YES
Overhaul patent law	YES
Pass compromise debt limit increase plan and establish future spending limits	YES
Allow consideration of measures to implement three trade agreements	YES

CQ Vote Studies

	PARTY UNITY		PRESIDENTIAL SUPPORT	
	SUPPORT	OPPOSE	SUPPORT	OPPOSE
2012	89%	11%	18%	82%
2011	93%	7%	22%	78%
2010	92%	8%	29%	71%

Interest Groups

	AFL-CIO	ADA	CCUS	ACU
2012	10%	0%	100%	80%
2011	7%	10%	100%	76%
2010	0%		100%	100%

New York 23

Southern Tier — Elmira, Corning; part of the Finger Lakes

Laid along much of the state's Southern Tier and rising into part of the Finger Lakes region, the 23rd District is rural and wide. Near Binghamton in the east to Lake Erie in the west, the district runs along a large stretch of the Pennsylvania border.

The 23rd is a mix of forests, lakes, farms and small towns; agriculture helps drive the economy. The Seneca Lake Wine Trail, the largest and most active in the New York State Finger Lakes wine region, is here — New York is the second-largest wine-producing state behind California. The vineyards and wineries lure tourists, and outdoor enthusiasts come for the water activities and hiking.

Other parts of the district are also dependent on tourism. Fishing and hunting are crucial to places such as Steuben County in the southwest. Watkins Glen International race track ("The Glen") is just south of Seneca Lake.

Corporate headquarters in the district include Corning, a Fortune 500 company still located in its namesake city, and CUTCO in Olean. White-collar jobs in the southeastern corner of the district revolve around Lockheed Martin in Owego. Corning is also known for its optics industry, and the stretch of the Chemung River toward Elmira is still home to some heavy manufacturing sites.

The predominately white district is in Republican hands, with the GOP boasting a solid lead in voter registration. Progressive voters have a hold near Ithaca — home of Cornell University and Ithaca College — but Steuben County (Corning) has a nearly 2-to-1 voter registration preference for Republicans. A key issue here is whether the state will allow natural gas exploration of the Marcellus Shale, which lies under a large portion of the Southern Tier. Hydrofracturing to remove the natural gas could bring jobs, but opponents cite environmental concerns.

Major Industry
Agriculture, tourism, manufacturing

Cities
Jamestown, Ithaca, Elmira

Notable
The first convention for women's rights was held in Seneca Falls in 1848.

Rep. Dan Maffei (D)

Capitol Office
225-3701
maffei.house.gov
422 Cannon Bldg. 20515-6601; fax 225-4042

Committees
Armed Services
Science, Space & Technology

Residence
DeWitt

Born
July 4, 1968; Syracuse, N.Y.

Religion
Roman Catholic

Family
Wife, Abby Davidson Maffei

Education
Brown U., A.B. 1990 (history); Columbia U., M.S. 1991 (journalism); Harvard U., M.P.P. 1995

Career
Economic think tank analyst; investment firm executive; political consultant; congressional aide; television reporter and producer

Political Highlights
Democratic nominee for U.S. House, 2006; U.S. House, 2009-11; defeated for re-election to U.S. House, 2010

ELECTION RESULTS

2012 GENERAL

Maffei (D, WFM)	143,044	48.9%
Ann Marie Buerkle (R, C, INDC)	127,054	43.4%
Ursula E. Rozum (GREEN)	22,670	7.7%

2012 PRIMARY

Maffei (D)	unopposed

Previous Winning Percentages
2008 (55%)

Elected 2008; 2nd term

Did not serve 2011-13

Maffei has run for the House four times, alternating between losing and winning. He hopes to break that pattern with a victory in 2014, and he says the lessons he learned from the 111th Congress will help him do so.

"I have become better at picking my fights," he says. "And I really understand the value of persistence, that if you can't get something done one way, there may be alternatives."

A former Capitol Hill press aide, Maffei (muh-FAY) can come across as wonkish. On several occasions, he has described the younger version of himself as a nerd. "I may not have been the cool kid in high school, but you embrace your own personality," he said. "I am a little nerdy, but as long as my wife is OK with it, then that's all that matters."

Maffei has lifelong ties to the city that anchors his district. The oldest of three children, he grew up in Syracuse, where his parents were social workers.

A history buff, Maffei made that subject his major at Brown University. He still studies up on his district, and he sponsored legislation to create a national historical park in Auburn for abolitionist Harriet Tubman, who lived and is buried there. (He touts the bill as a way to boost tourism.) He earned a master's degree in journalism from Columbia University, then started a career as a television journalist back home in Syracuse. "I liked the excitement of TV, the immediacy of it," he said.

But he became restless, yearning to be more of an advocate. Maffei earned a master's in public policy from Harvard's Kennedy School of Government, then got a job in Washington as a press aide to Democratic Sen. Bill Bradley of New Jersey. When Bradley retired, he moved over to the office of Sen. Daniel Patrick Moynihan of New York. He eventually spent several years as an aide to the House Ways and Means Committee, serving under New York Democrat Charles B. Rangel.

Maffei moved back home in 2005, and the next year he ran for the House against nine-term Republican Rep. James T. Walsh. He lost by 3,417 votes — a small enough margin to keep him on the radar of national Democrats. Two years later, Walsh retired and Maffei tried again. He beat Republican Dale A. Sweetland by 13 points to earn a seat in the 111th Congress (2009-10).

After a voter-forced hiatus during the 112th Congress (2011-12), he returned to the House in 2013 and immediately began outlining and studying plans for economic growth, both in the urban center of his district and the surrounding countryside.

Maffei belongs to the New Democrat Coalition, a bloc of House Democrats that is seen as more centrist and friendly to business interests. He says he wants to remove "needless regulations" on small businesses, and that he is "for public-private partnerships all the time."

But he is not opposed to solid federal investments in worker training programs or various infrastructure projects. He likes the idea of a high-speed rail line running through upstate New York. "It's been 50 years since we had any new infrastructure" upstate, he said. "We are sort of cut off. ... We need a 21st-century Erie Canal." While campaigning, he was skeptical of free-trade pacts, saying they had hurt manufacturers in the area.

Maffei took a seat on the Armed Services Committee, filling a void left when his upstate Democratic colleague Bill Owens moved to the Appropriations Committee. From that seat, he will look out for the 174th Air National Guard at Syracuse's Hancock Airport and Fort Drum (in the 21st District). He says the "defense budget is in need of trimming," but he did not like the across-the-board cuts put in place by an August 2011 deficit reduction law.

He also sits on the Science, Space and Technology Committee, and he is the top Democrat on its Oversight Subcommittee. Maffei has always had an interest in science, and he represents numerous universities and companies that focus on scientific research and development, including clean-energy and sustainability practices. He recently worked as a part-time instructor on the environment and politics at the SUNY College of Environmental Science and Forestry.

On both of his committees, he intends to be an advocate for cybersecurity research and the Air Force Research Laboratory in Rome, in the neighboring 22nd District.

He says science, technology, engineering and mathematics education programs should incorporate creative aspects. And his support of public-private partnerships extends to government interests such as the space program. "I don't think it should be one big government enterprise," he said. "Maybe that makes me a bit conservative."

Fiscally, Maffei is just a little bit conservative. He says he dislikes raising the debt ceiling and would like to shrink federal deficits by targeting waste, fraud and abuse.

He pushes for a lower corporate tax rate, and he suggests that there "may need to be some reform" of unemployment insurance and nutrition programs. He has sponsored legislation to repeal the excise tax on medical devices that was created by the 2010 health care overhaul. But he would offset the loss of revenue by eliminating tax breaks for oil and gas companies — a favorite Democratic position.

As a freshman, Maffei sat on the Financial Services and Judiciary committees. One of his major focuses was trying to save automobile dealerships in his district that were threatened with closure. He had one bill signed into law during his first go-round as a legislator; it delayed the date by which retailers had to start printing new consumer protection information on gift cards, per a 2009 law. Maffei sought the change so that old cards would not have to be thrown out heading into the 2010 holiday season.

Maffei was involved in one of the closest elections of 2010 — with Republicans surging nationwide, nurse Ann Marie Buerkle defeated him by just 648 votes. That narrow margin, and changes to the district's borders that seemed to favor Democrats, encouraged Maffei to seek a rematch in 2012. He was unopposed in the primary.

The competing campaigns combined to spend more than $4 million on the race, and outside groups added millions more. Maffei took 49 percent of the vote, beating Buerkle by more than 5 points. A Green Party candidate took almost 8 percent.

CQ Vote Studies

	PARTY UNITY		PRESIDENTIAL SUPPORT	
	SUPPORT	OPPOSE	SUPPORT	OPPOSE
2010	93%	7%	79%	21%
2009	94%	6%	94%	6%

Interest Groups

	AFL-CIO	ADA	CCUS	ACU
2010	100%	90%	25%	4%
2009	100%	100%	40%	0%

New York 24

North central — Syracuse

The 24th District is predominately rural and filled with farms, lakes and hills. It includes all of Onondaga County — including the city of Syracuse — and Cayuga County, as well as all of Wayne County and the easternmost suburbs of Rochester. Western portions of Oswego County are to the north.

The economic engine of the district is Syracuse, the 24th's largest city, with higher education as the fuel. Syracuse University, LeMoyne College, the State University of New York Upstate Medical University and the SUNY College of Environmental Science and Forestry are all within the city limits. The medical university is undergoing a multimillion-dollar expansion. The city is also home to the state fair, minor league hockey and baseball teams, and the Onondaga Reservation. Unlike many other Native American tribes in the northeast, the Onondaga Nation does not operate casinos.

Oswego, along Lake Ontario, hosts outdoor enthusiasts and activities during the summer months, including the regional festival Harborfest. Cayuga County includes the northeastern section of the Finger Lakes region. These lakes and their wineries help spur tens of millions of dollars annually in tourism revenue. Non-vineyard agriculture is also crucial to the county, which ranks first in corn and soybeans and second in milk production statewide.

Local Republican stronghold Wayne County is in the western portion of the district and, although it is considered part of suburban Rochester, it is mainly dotted with small towns. While manufacturing remains important here, farming is the primary industry, with apples leading the way — Wayne is the top apple-producing county in the state.

Barack Obama did well in the district in the 2012 presidential election, easily taking Onondaga, the 24th's most-populous county, by more than 20 percentage points and Cayuga by double-digits.

Major Industry
Higher education, agriculture, tourism

Cities
Syracuse

Notable
Fort Ontario in Oswego was home to the only camp in the United States for "displaced persons," many of them Jewish survivors of concentration camps, as a result of World War II.

Rep. Louise M. Slaughter (D)

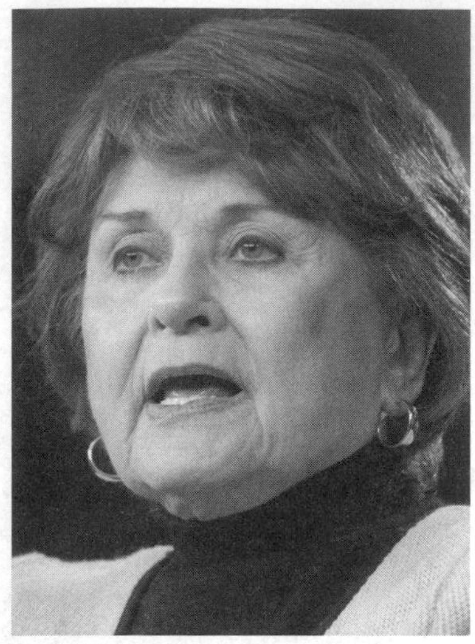

Capitol Office
225-3615
louise.house.gov
2469 Rayburn Bldg. 20515-3228; fax 225-7822

Committees
Rules - Ranking Member

Residence
Fairport

Born
Aug. 14, 1929; Harlan County, Ky.

Religion
Episcopalian

Family
Husband, Robert Slaughter; three children

Education
U. of Kentucky, B.S. 1951 (microbiology), M.P.H. 1953

Career
State government aide; market researcher; microbiologist

Political Highlights
Monroe County Legislature, 1975-79; N.Y. Assembly, 1983-87

ELECTION RESULTS

2012 GENERAL

Slaughter (D, WFM)	179,810	57.4%
Maggie Brooks (R, C, INDC)	133,389	42.6%

2012 PRIMARY

Slaughter (D)	unopposed

2010 GENERAL

Slaughter (D, WFM, INDC)	102,514	64.9%
Jill A. Rowland (R, C)	55,392	35.1%

Previous Winning Percentages
2008 (78%); 2006 (73%); 2004 (73%); 2002 (62%); 2000 (66%); 1998 (65%); 1996 (57%); 1994 (57%); 1992 (55%); 1990 (59%); 1988 (57%); 1986 (51%)

Elected 1986; 14th term

Colleagues of all persuasions have been charmed by Slaughter. Democrats, however, are particularly taken with her vigorous partisanship. Her influence as a legislative tactician is muted while serving in the minority, but that hasn't kept her from attacking Republican proposals and aggressively pursuing health causes and other issues adopted as her own.

The oldest woman in Congress, Slaughter has spent most of her adult life in a suburb of Rochester. But she was brought up in the mountains of Kentucky's Harlan County — her father was a blacksmith in a coal mine — and her Southern accent has survived. When she came to Congress in 1987, House Democratic leaders quickly took a liking to her warmth, grit and liberal views. In her second term she was given a seat on the Rules Committee, which sets the terms for floor debate. She lost the seat when Republicans took over in the 104th Congress (1995-96), then returned in 1997.

Slaughter became the panel's first chairwoman in 2007 and showed unswerving loyalty to her party, helping steer to passage several major Democratic initiatives with little or no Republican support.

During the 2010 health care debate, she was accused of bending the rules. Some House Democrats were reluctant to go on the record supporting a Senate version of the overhaul bill. Leaders floated the idea of a rule that would deem the bill passed once the House voted only on some minor corrections. Republicans called it "the Slaughter solution" and blasted it as possibly unconstitutional. It was eventually scrapped.

Slaughter had no qualms about returning the criticism. In 2012, Republicans put forth a bill to create an expedited process for considering a possible tax code overhaul in the 113th Congress (2013-14). As the ranking member on Rules, Slaughter attacked. "House Republicans want special procedures that allow them to force their right-wing legislative agenda through the Senate," she said on the House floor. "Why are we wasting time in trying to change the rules of the Senate — trying to force the other body to accept partisan Republican priorities — rather than just sitting down together and working out a bipartisan path forward?"

Words are her primary weapon on the Rules Committee; its lopsided party ratios effectively neuter the minority party. Given her diminished power, her age and a competitive election in 2012 — redistricting after the 2010 census added a number of Republican areas to her home turf — some people asked whether Slaughter might retire. She missed a substantial number of votes to attend to an unspecified "family matter" in 2011, and in April 2012 she tripped and broke her leg crossing a New York City street.

Speaking to reporters from a Rochester hospital that April, she was adamant about her health and determination: "I would not be running for office if I was about to die," she said. "I never start something I don't intend to finish."

That has certainly been her attitude when working on her pet causes. By Slaughter's account, a newspaper article is all it takes to get her started. She read a Wall Street Journal piece about congressional staffers using information gleaned from their official duties to make stock trades, and that prompted her to introduce a 2006 measure tightening restrictions on the practice.

Slaughter and Democrat Tim Walz of Minnesota kept introducing the bill, but they gained little traction until "60 Minutes" reported on the superior stock market returns of lawmakers in 2011. Slaughter made another push, and a version was enacted in 2012. She then followed up with more proposals to tack on provisions that the GOP majority had removed over her objections.

Stories on flawed body armor used by the military inspired her campaign for improved testing of equipment. Slaughter pushed for a series of reports and audits on the body armor contracts, leading to a 2009 recall and continued re-examination of existing contracts.

Before her political career, Slaughter worked as a microbiologist, and she has a master's degree in public health. In the 109th Congress (2005-06), President George W. Bush signed a version of her bill barring employers and insurers from discriminating against people based on their genetic profile. She had pressed the legislation for years, and at enactment she called it "the most important thing I have done in my life."

One battle still in progress is over routine antibiotic use. Slaughter is the leading congressional opponent of antibiotic use in farm animals, believing it is "the root cause" of the development of antibiotic-resistant "superbugs." In 2007, she began introducing legislation to restrict such use, and she has said the Food and Drug Administration "ignored the threat of antibiotic resistance for well over 30 years."

Slaughter is on the Democratic Steering and Policy Committee, and she is also a member of the liberal Congressional Progressive Caucus. She holds liberal views on taxes, the Afghanistan War and a host of other subjects. She is particularly pointed on women's issues, joining in the accusations that Republicans are waging a "war on women." She called a 2011 bill to block federal funding of any health plan that covers abortion "one of the biggest invasions into the private lives of Americans that our nation has ever seen." Slaughter co-wrote the 1994 law establishing increased protections of, and assistance for, victims of domestic violence.

Slaughter moved to New York in the 1950s, when her husband went to work as an executive with a local company. Her first brush with public policy came in 1971, when she joined with some neighbors to try to save a stand of trees from development. "I thought in my best Kentucky fashion that if I would put on my best dress and go and be very nice and polite and ask them to save this forest that they would say, 'Well, why not?'" she later told The Associated Press. "And they just handed me my hat."

The episode sparked an interest in politics. She served as a Monroe County legislator and as an assistant to Mario M. Cuomo, New York's secretary of state. In 1982, she ousted a Republican incumbent to join the state Assembly. She served four years before winning her seat in the House with 51 percent of the vote against first-term Republican Fred J. Eckert.

Reapportionment after the 2000 census placed Slaughter in the same district as 14-term Democrat John J. LaFalce, who retired rather than face Slaughter in a primary. Republicans hoped for a redistricting-assisted upset in 2012, but Slaughter still easily bested Monroe County Executive Maggie Brooks.

Key Votes

2012	
Extend a Social Security payroll tax cut and unemployment benefits	YES
Ease securities rules to expand small-business access to capital	YES
Extend for one year subsidized student loan interest rates financed by a cut in health care spending	-
Cite Attorney General Eric H. Holder Jr. for contempt of Congress	NO
Create a visa program for foreign graduates in high-tech fields	-
Extend most Bush-era income tax rates while allowing rates for top-bracket earners to rise (Jan. 1, 2013)	YES
2011	
Strike funding for F-35 alternative engine	NO
Prevent EPA from regulating greenhouse gas emissions to address climate change	NO
Extend certain provisions of Patriot Act for four years	NO
Declare opposition to use of ground troops in Libya	NO
Overhaul patent law	NO
Pass compromise debt limit increase plan and establish future spending limits	NO
Allow consideration of measures to implement three trade agreements	NO

CQ Vote Studies

	PARTY UNITY		PRESIDENTIAL SUPPORT	
	SUPPORT	OPPOSE	SUPPORT	OPPOSE
2012	99%	1%	92%	8%
2011	97%	3%	82%	18%
2010	100%	0%	89%	11%
2009	99%	1%	95%	5%
2008	100%	0%	12%	88%

Interest Groups

	AFL-CIO	ADA	CCUS	ACU
2012	90%	60%	25%	0%
2011	100%	90%	21%	4%
2010	100%	100%	13%	0%
2009	100%	90%	45%	4%
2008	100%	95%	47%	0%

New York 25

Rochester and suburbs

Decennial remapping consolidated Rochester, which is the state's third-largest city, and most of its suburbs into one district. The 25th District is made up of parts of four previous U.S. House districts, and it now includes almost all of Monroe County on the shores of Lake Ontario.

Rochester is a relatively diverse city, with nearly equal white (38 percent) and black (42 percent) populations and a significant Hispanic population (16 percent). Education and income levels are low for many residents of the city and the proportion of those below the poverty level (31 percent) is nearly double the statewide average. Unlike the city, the rest of Monroe County is predominately white and has income levels on par with the state average.

White-collar industries host health care and visual technology sectors. Although Kodak has downsized in recent years, it is still a major player in the city. The University of Rochester, the city's largest employer, and the Rochester Institute of Technology also support the high-skill field. The university is home to the renowned Institute of Optics, and RIT has a top-tier imaging-science department. Xerox and Bausch + Lomb are here as well.

Despite some struggling areas, unemployment rates overall have remained relatively low during the recent economic downturn, especially compared with other parts of upstate New York. Traditional manufacturing and the region's industrial diversification have kept goods moving out of the district. Just outside Rochester in Gates, the headquarters of Wegmans, which began as a small neighborhood grocery in 1930, is the second-largest employer in the region.

Overall the district is more than 70 percent white and the median household income is just less than $50,000. Democrats have an edge in voter registration, but constituents still harbor conservative sentiments. In 2012, Democrat Barack Obama took 59 percent of the district's presidential vote.

Major Industry

Technology, higher education, health care

Cities

Rochester

Notable

Women's rights activist Susan B. Anthony and abolitionist Frederick Douglass are both buried in Rochester's Mount Hope Cemetery.

Rep. Brian Higgins (D)

Capitol Office
225-3306
higgins.house.gov
2459 Rayburn Bldg. 20515-3227; fax 226-0347

Committees
Foreign Affairs
Homeland Security

Residence
Buffalo

Born
Oct. 6, 1959; Buffalo, N.Y.

Religion
Roman Catholic

Family
Wife, Mary Jane Hannon; two children

Education
State U. of New York, Buffalo State, B.A. 1984 (political science), M.A. 1985 (history); Harvard U., M.P.A. 1996

Career
State and county legislative aide

Political Highlights
Democratic nominee for Erie County comptroller, 1993; Buffalo Common Council, 1988-94; N.Y. Assembly, 1999-2004

ELECTION RESULTS

2012 GENERAL		
Higgins (D, WFM)	212,588	74.8%
Michael Madigan (R, C, INDC)	71,666	25.2%
2012 PRIMARY		
Higgins (D)		unopposed
2010 GENERAL		
Higgins (D, WFM)	119,085	60.9%
Leonard A. Roberto (R)	76,320	39.1%

Previous Winning Percentages
2008 (74%); 2006 (79%); 2004 (51%)

Elected 2004; 5th term

Higgins has bounced around committees while maintaining a consistent style and focus: He keeps a low profile while advocating on behalf of Buffalo, which he calls "one of the great industrial centers" of the United States.

His blue-collar background is exactly the kind many people would associate with his hometown. Higgins' father was a union bricklayer, and all five of his children helped lay bricks. Higgins has fond memories of playing hockey as a kid and participates in annual charity games pitting a team of lawmakers and staff against a team of lobbyists.

But his education and career have been more white-collar. Higgins earned two master's degrees, worked as a legislative aide and served in city and state government before arriving in the House.

Western New York is on his mind much of the time. In the 112th Congress (2011-12), Higgins became a member of the Homeland Security and Foreign Affairs committees, and he immediately put their overlapping jurisdictions to work in trying to direct attention to his city's border crossing to Canada.

At a February 2011 hearing, Higgins questioned Homeland Security Department officials about the future of the Peace Bridge, which opened to traffic in 1927 and connects Buffalo and Fort Erie, Ontario. He frequently emphasizes the economic value of trade and visitors crossing over the bridge, and he lauded a border agreement with Canada that, among other things, seeks to reduce wait times at the border and develop a five-year infrastructure investment plan for the bridge.

Higgins also pushed for the opening of a new passport office in Buffalo to "make travel abroad easier for residents in Western New York." The Buffalo region has a significant Polish-American population, and Higgins belongs to the Congressional Poland Caucus; he has backed adding Poland to the Visa Waiver Program, which would allow the country's citizens to travel to the United States using their passport without obtaining a special visa.

Higgins has more clout on international relations in the 113th Congress (2013-14). He is the top Democrat on the Homeland Security Subcommittee on Counterterrorism and Intelligence, and he sits on the Foreign Affairs subcommittee handling the Middle East.

One of Higgins' Homeland Security Committee priorities is Urban Areas Security Initiative grant funding. Cuts to that program during the 112th Congress resulted in the elimination of grants for many midsize cities, including Buffalo. Higgins helped create the UASI Caucus late in 2011 to coordinate House members from such cities in their efforts to restore and modernize the program for their districts.

Higgins took a roundabout path to his current committees. His first two terms, he sat on the Transportation and Infrastructure panel, where he steered $42 million to his district in the 2005 reauthorization of surface transportation programs. He also helped negotiate a 50-year license for the Niagara Power Project, demanding that the State Power Authority help finance waterfront development projects as part of the deal.

He gave up that assignment in the 111th Congress (2009-10) for a seat on the powerful Ways and Means Committee, just as it was gearing up for debate on the health care overhaul. Higgins supported the inclusion of a government-run "public option," which he said would provide competition to private plans and drive down prices. The provision did not make it into the final version of the bill, but Higgins voted for it anyway. A shift in committee ratios after the Republican takeover in 2011 knocked him off Ways and Means, and Democrats didn't find a spot for him to return in the 113th Congress.

Higgins was a strong supporter of the 2009 economic stimulus bill and has highlighted projects in his district that have benefited from federal spending. An ally of labor unions, he is skeptical of free-trade deals, even though he was once a member of the business-friendly New Democrat Coalition. He voted against the Central America Free Trade Agreement in 2005, as well as 2011 pacts with Panama, Colombia and South Korea.

On social issues, Higgins is a reliable Democrat. He voted in 2010 to repeal the military's "don't ask, don't tell" policy. He made local headlines in 2007 when, during a Sunday Mass in the church where he was baptized and married, a lay deacon rebuked him for supporting federal funding of embryonic stem cell research. Higgins walked out of the service and later got an apology from the pastor.

The Higgins family has been in Buffalo since his grandfather emigrated from Ireland as a 12-year-old orphan. His grandfather was a bricklayer, and he handed the trade down to Higgins' father and uncles. Higgins' father served on the Buffalo Common Council and later was a commissioner of the state workers' compensation board.

Higgins earned an undergraduate degree in political science from Buffalo State in 1984, followed by a master's degree in history a year later. He was elected to the Buffalo Common Council in 1987 at the age of 28.

Six years later, after losing a bid to become Erie County's comptroller, Higgins left upstate New York for Harvard's Kennedy School of Government, where he earned a master's degree. Upon graduation, he returned home to work as a legislative aide in the Erie County legislature before being elected to the New York State Assembly in 1998.

In 2004, six-term Republican Rep. Jack Quinn announced that he would not seek re-election. Higgins entered the race to succeed him. He emerged the winner in a five-way Democratic primary. In the general election, he won by 3,774 votes over Republican Nancy Naples—who had defeated him in the 1993 race for Erie County comptroller. He won easily in 2006, 2008 and 2010.

New York's redrawn congressional map for the 2012 election shifted his district from potentially competitive to staunchly Democratic. He beat Republican Michael H. Madigan by almost 50 points.

In late 2008, he was among the people considered to fill the Senate seat of New York Democrat Hillary Rodham Clinton, who became secretary of State. Leonard Lenihan, the Democratic chairman in Erie County, backed Higgins, saying his appointment would blunt criticism that state Democrats are too New York City-centric. Ultimately, Democratic Gov. David A. Paterson went for an even newer face — Rep. Kirsten Gillibrand, who had just won her first re-election.

Key Votes

2012	
Extend a Social Security payroll tax cut and unemployment benefits	YES
Ease securities rules to expand small-business access to capital	YES
Extend for one year subsidized student loan interest rates financed by a cut in health care spending	YES
Cite Attorney General Eric H. Holder Jr. for contempt of Congress	NO
Create a visa program for foreign graduates in high-tech fields	NO
Extend most Bush-era income tax rates while allowing rates for top-bracket earners to rise (Jan. 1, 2013)	YES
2011	
Strike funding for F-35 alternative engine	NO
Prevent EPA from regulating greenhouse gas emissions to address climate change	NO
Extend certain provisions of Patriot Act for four years	YES
Declare opposition to use of ground troops in Libya	YES
Overhaul patent law	YES
Pass compromise debt limit increase plan and establish future spending limits	YES
Allow consideration of measures to implement three trade agreements	NO

CQ Vote Studies

	PARTY UNITY		PRESIDENTIAL SUPPORT	
	SUPPORT	OPPOSE	SUPPORT	OPPOSE
2012	95%	5%	80%	20%
2011	93%	7%	91%	9%
2010	98%	2%	90%	10%
2009	98%	2%	97%	3%
2008	99%	1%	20%	80%

Interest Groups

	AFL-CIO	ADA	CCUS	ACU
2012	90%	80%	42%	0%
2011	100%	90%	38%	4%
2010	93%	90%	25%	4%
2009	100%	100%	36%	0%
2008	100%	80%	65%	4%

New York 26

Buffalo and suburbs

Buffalo — the state's largest city outside of New York City — and international tourist attraction Niagara Falls are the anchors of the 26th District. The district is overwhelmingly Democratic, and has one of the largest minority populations of any district statewide outside of New York City. During decennial redistricting, Buffalo and its suburbs were consolidated into a compact district.

Railways and seaways were the engines for Buffalo for decades, and the city has transitioned from an industrial powerhouse to a health care hub. A new medical school affiliated with the University of Buffalo is in the works, and the Buffalo Niagara Medical Campus employs more than 8,500 people. The University of Buffalo, the largest of the State University of New York schools, and Buffalo State are here as well, and General Mills still operates in the city. Still largely a white-collar city, some communities struggle with poverty, and nearly 30 percent of the city's population lives below the poverty line.

Buffalo was one of the final stops of the Underground Railroad and has always had a sizable black population; today it is a minority-majority city. While many blacks and other minorities remain in the city, a significant number have moved to suburbs including Amherst and Cheektowaga. There also remains a strong community of the descendents of the original Polish, Irish and Italian settlers. The downtown area is still active, mainly due to a tradition of catering to the late-shift workers who used to stream out of the now-mostly-closed local factories.

Niagara Falls is the oldest state park in the nation. In addition to tourism revenue, the area's economy is aided by Canadian shoppers lured by beneficial exchange rates. Local officials market the scenic location as a wedding and honeymoon destination, particularly to the gay and lesbian community.

Major Industry
Health care, higher education, tourism

Cities
Buffalo, Niagara Falls

Notable
The Michigan Street Baptist Church was an important stop on the Underground Railroad.

Rep. Chris Collins (R)

Capitol Office
225-5265
chriscollins.house.gov
1117 Longworth Bldg. 20515-6601; fax 225-5910

Committees
Agriculture
Small Business
(Health and Technology - Chairman)

Residence
Clarence

Born
May 20, 1950; Schenectady, N.Y.

Religion
Roman Catholic

Family
Wife, Mary Collins; three children

Education
North Carolina State U., B.S. 1972 (mechanical engineering); U. of Alabama, Birmingham, M.B.A. 1975

Career
Private equity investor; gear manufacturing business owner

Political Highlights
Republican nominee for U.S. House, 1998; Erie County executive, 2007-11; defeated for re-election to Erie County executive, 2011

ELECTION RESULTS

2012 GENERAL		
Collins (R, C)	161,220	50.8%
Kathy Hochul (D, WFM)	156,219	49.2%
2012 PRIMARY		
Collins (R)	11,677	59.9%
David G. Bellavia (R)	7,830	40.1%

Elected 2012; 1st term

As Erie County executive, Collins had a sign in his office: "In God we trust — all others bring data." The intense, business-minded Republican was chosen as the chairman of a Small Business subcommittee, and he has the chance to shore up support in his competitive, heavily rural district through his seat on the Agriculture Committee.

Collins made a great living by creating and revitalizing companies. In his early 30s, he quit his job at the Westinghouse Electric Corp. — so that he and some partners could buy the gear manufacturing division he had managed. As that business flourished and expanded, Collins purchased and invested in several other companies. He is a huge fan of Lean Six Sigma, a metrics-driven management methodology, and in several hearings he has urged government officials to bring in more of the system's "master black belts."

He ran as a businessman in his campaign for Erie County executive in 2006, and when he won he embarked on a dramatic cost-cutting campaign. It turned around the county's fiscal outlook, but it might have cost him some political support — he fell short in his 2010 bid for a second term.

Collins chairs the Small Business Subcommittee on Health and Technology, which oversees the implementation of the 2010 health care law as it pertains to small businesses. His congressional website features an "ObamaCare" complaint form for small businesses and employees.

A member of both the conservative Republican Study Committee and the moderate Main Street Partnership, Collins took a few independent-minded positions early in his House tenure. On the Agriculture Committee, he indicated that he might support an immigration overhaul if it gives dairy farmers access to the guest workers they need.

In 2012, Collins took on Democratic freshman Kathy Hochul in a newly drawn 27th District that was fairly conservative, particularly by New York standards. Hochul was a strong candidate, but Collins prevailed by 5,000 votes.

New York 27

Rural West

The conservative 27th is primarily rural and bisected by the New York State Thruway (Interstate 90). The shoreline of Lake Ontario makes up the district's northern border, and Lake Erie is to the far southwest, with suburbs of Buffalo — the city is in the 26th, which is surrounded on three sides by the 27th — between them. Redistricting following the 2010 census did not dramatically alter the 27th's boundaries beyond adding the lakes' shores, and it contains much of the former 26th District.

The district is made up of four whole counties — Genesee, Livingston, Orleans and Wyoming — and parts of Erie, Monroe, Niagara and Ontario. State parks dot the district's beachfronts and occupy its more forested central areas.

Agriculture and manufacturing are the key economic drivers for the 27th. Genesee County has cabbage and sweet corn, and New York's prized apples are big commodities in Monroe, Niagara, Orleans and Wayne counties. Wyoming County is the state's top producer of milk, and Genesee County's Batavia will host a major yogurt processing plant. State government is a major employer as well here, with jobs at the prisons throughout the district. Although tourism related to nearby attractions in Niagara, Buffalo and the Finger Lakes region is important, as a whole it does not play as vital a role in the district's economy as elsewhere in the region.

Nearly 40 percent of the district population is in the suburbs of Buffalo and Niagara Falls. Buffalo Niagara International Airport is in the adjacent 26th District, and there are several smaller regional airports in the 27th. Potential downsizing at the Niagara Falls Air Station would hasten the decline of an already diminishing military impact in the western New York region.

Republicans have substantial voter registration leads in most of the district's counties. In the 2012 presidential race, Mitt Romney won in every whole or partial county in the district and took a 12-point win overall.

Major industry
Agriculture, manufacturing, government

Cities
Lockport, Batavia

Notable
A group of women opened Hamburg's free library in 1897.

NORTH CAROLINA

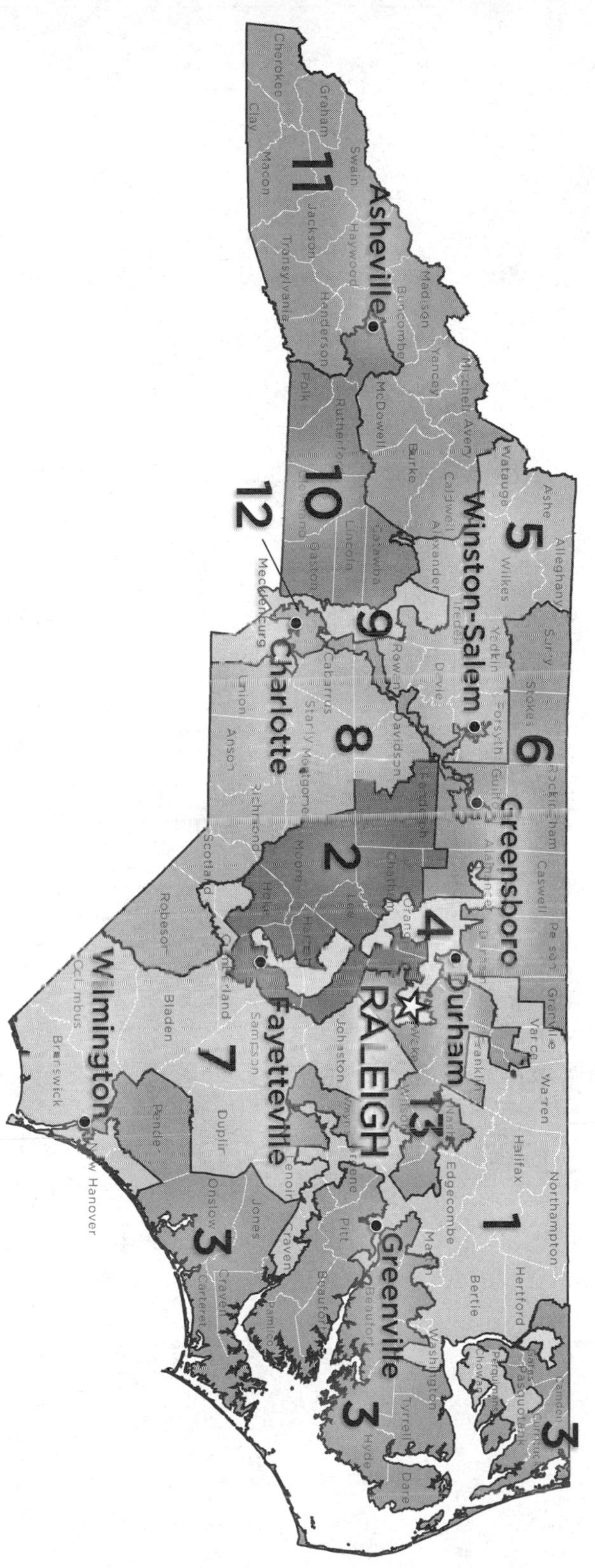

Gov. Pat McCrory (R)

First elected: 2012

Length of term: 4 years

Term expires: 1/17

Salary: $141,265

Phone: (919) 814-2000

Residence: Charlotte

Born: Oct. 17, 1956; Columbus, Ohio

Religion: Presbyterian

Family: Wife, Ann McCrory

Education: Catawba College, B.A. 1978 (political science)

Career: Economic development and policy consultant; energy company manager

Political highlights: Charlotte City Council, 1989-95; mayor of Charlotte, 1995-2009; Republican nominee for governor, 2008

ELECTION RESULTS

2012 GENERAL

Pat McCrory (R)	2,440,707	54.6%
Walter H. Dalton (D)	1,931,580	43.2%
Barbara J. Howe (LIBERT)	94652	2.1%

Lt. Gov. Dan Forest (R)

First elected: 2012

Length of term: 4 years

Term expires: 1/17

Salary: $123,198

Phone: (919) 733-7350

LEGISLATURE

General Assembly: Convenes in January in odd-numbered years; May in even-numbered. There is no statutory or constitutional requirement for when session must end.

Senate: 50 members, 2-year terms

2013 ratios: 33 R, 17 D; 42 men, 8 women

Salary: $13,951

Phone: (919) 733-7928

House: 120 members, 2-year terms

2013 ratios: 77 R, 43 D; 89 men, 31 women

Salary: $13,951

Phone: (919) 733-7928

TERM LIMITS

Governor: 2 consecutive terms

Senate: No

House: No

URBAN STATISTICS

CITY	POPULATION
Charlotte	731,424
Raleigh	403,892
Greensboro	269,666
Winston-Salem	229,617
Durham	228,330

REGISTERED VOTERS

Democrat	43%
Republican	31%
Other	26%

POPULATION

2010 population	9,535,483
2000 population	8,049,313
1990 population	6,628,637
Percent change (2000-2010)	+18.5%
Rank among states (2010)	10
Median age	36.6
Born in state	59.2%
Foreign born	6.5%
Violent crime rate	404/100,000
Poverty level	16.3%
Federal workers	86,244
Military	116,073

ELECTIONS

STATE ELECTION OFFICIAL
(919) 733-7173

DEMOCRATIC PARTY
(919) 821-2777

REPUBLICAN PARTY
(919) 828-6423

MISCELLANEOUS

Web: www.ncgov.com

Capital: Raleigh

U.S. CONGRESS

Senate: 1 Democrat, 1 Republican

House: 9 Republicans, 4 Democrats

Statistics by District

District	2012 Vote for President Obama	2012 Vote for President Romney	2008 Vote for President Obama	2008 Vote for President McCain	Black	Asian	Hispanic	Median Income	Over 64	Under 20	College Education	Rural	Sq. Miles
1	71%	28%	71%	29%	52%	1%	8%	$32,009	14%	27%	18%	37%	5,494
2	42	57	43	56	16	4	11	48,077	13	29	27	35	3,247
3	41	58	43	56	21	1	6	44,871	13	26	22	44	7,810
4	71	27	72	27	33	5	12	47,242	9	27	39	10	1,045
5	40	59	42	57	13	1	9	41,781	15	25	25	43	3,572
6	41	58	43	56	16	2	6	46,927	15	25	29	43	3,675
7	40	59	42	58	18	<1	10	41,935	15	26	22	50	6,162
8	41	58	42	58	19	1	9	38,549	12	28	16	48	4,513
9	43	56	46	54	14	4	7	65,681	11	28	48	9	857
10	41	58	42	57	12	2	6	41,582	15	25	23	37	2,575
11	38	61	41	58	3	1	6	39,322	20	23	21	61	6,838
12	78	21	78	21	49	4	15	33,891	9	29	22	4	550
13	44	55	45	54	17	2	8	61,234	12	28	38	32	2,281
STATE	**48**	**51**	**50**	**49**	**21**	**2**	**8**	**43,916**	**13**	**27**	**27**	**36**	**48,618**
U.S.	**51**	**47**	**53**	**46**	**12**	**5**	**17**	**50,052**	**13**	**27**	**29**	**21**	**3,531,905**

Sen. Richard M. Burr (R)

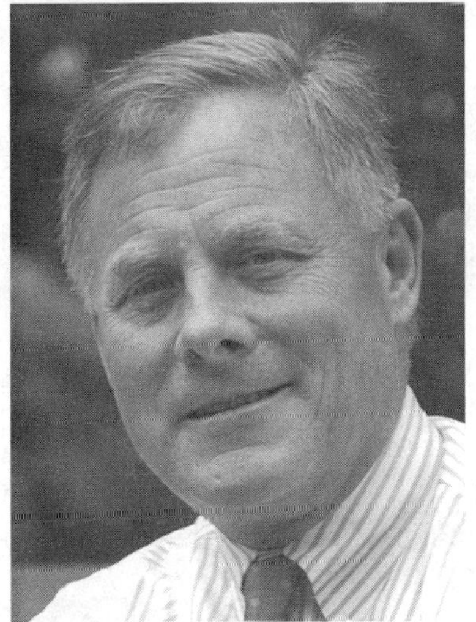

Capitol Office
224-3154
burr.senate.gov
217 Russell Bldg. 20510-3306; fax 228-2981

Committees
Finance
Health, Education, Labor & Pensions
Veterans' Affairs - Ranking Member
Select Intelligence

Residence
Winston-Salem

Born
Nov. 30, 1955; Charlottesville, Va.

Religion
Methodist

Family
Wife, Brooke Burr; two children

Education
Wake Forest U., B.A. 1978 (communications)

Career
Marketing manager; kitchen appliance salesman

Political Highlights
Republican nominee for U.S. House, 1992; U.S. House, 1995-2005

ELECTION RESULTS

2010 GENERAL		
Richard M. Burr (R)	1,458,046	54.8%
Elaine Marshall (D)	1,145,074	43.0%
Mike Beitler (LIBERT)	55,687	2.1%
2010 PRIMARY		
Richard M. Burr (R)	297,993	80.1%
Brad Jones (R)	37,616	10.1%
Eddie Burks (R)	22,111	5.9%
Larry Linney (R)	14,248	3.8%

Previous Winning Percentages
2004 (52%); 2002 House Election (70%); 2000 House Election (93%); 1998 House Election (68%); 1996 House Election (62%); 1994 House Election (57%)

Elected 2004; 2nd term

Burr caught the attention of Republican leaders through diligent policy work, and for a time he wanted to move up the leadership ranks. In 2012, he had a change of heart. "The legislative side of my job is too important to let that be overshadowed by some meaningless leadership role," he said.

Burr joined the Senate in 2005 after serving five terms in the House. In 2007, he lost a bid to become the Republican Conference chairman. Two years later he was named the chief deputy whip for his party. The job of whip was coming open in 2013, thanks to the retirement of Arizona's Jon Kyl. Burr was a candidate, but in March 2012 he dropped out, saying he wanted to focus on advancing his own policy proposals.

He has no leadership jobs in the 113th Congress (2013-14), and he says he wants to use that freedom to "stir up the hornets' nest" on subjects such as health care.

Burr sits on the Health, Education, Labor and Pensions Committee, as well as the Finance Committee. Together, those panels account for most of the Senate's health care jurisdiction. He sees Medicare as a government obligation, and its solvency is one of his biggest concerns. Working with frequent partner Tom Coburn of Oklahoma — who regularly sets the hornets' nest on fire — he introduced a 2012 proposal to convert Medicare to a program providing means-tested amounts of money to help beneficiaries pay for insurance plans of their choosing.

In 2009, Burr, Coburn and Rep. Paul D. Ryan of Wisconsin pitched a similar plan as an alternative to the Democrats' health care overhaul. It would have provided a tax credit to individuals for the purchase of health insurance.

Burr also addresses health care as the ranking member of the Veterans' Affairs Committee. (Barring a waiver from GOP term limit rules, the 113th Congress will be his last in that job.) One of Burr's contentions is that plans to improve health care for veterans are "hung up with process and not with outcome." He questions whether increases in personnel and technology automatically lead to better service or faster processing of benefit claims.

In 2012, he introduced legislation to reorganize the Veterans Health Administration by cutting almost in half the number of regional networks it operates and increasing oversight. As the panel examined mental health care for veterans in 2013, he said that the Veterans Affairs Department "needs to look outside the box for answers and engage the private sector and charitable organizations for help in treating veterans in need of mental health services."

Burr often looks for ways to involve the private sector in policy solutions, rather than simply provide direct benefits. He is among the lawmakers interested in improving "credentialing" for servicemembers — essentially, creating standards that allow them to easily apply their military skills toward obtaining licenses and certifications that are useful in seeking private sector employment.

The Finance Committee handles taxes, and the conservative anti-tax movement was Burr's entry point to politics. He is a former co-chairman of North Carolina Taxpayers United. He says a simpler tax code would create an environment hospitable to private sector investment. He is even open to dramatic rewrites, including the "FairTax" plan to replace most federal taxes with a national sales tax. Burr is close friends with its Senate sponsor, Georgia Republican Saxby Chambliss.

It's plausible that Burr could succeed Chambliss as top Republican on the Intelligence Committee after Chambliss retires at the end of the 113th Congress. Burr is currently the No. 2 Republican on the panel. In 2012, President

Barack Obama signed Burr's bill requiring the State Department to either designate the Taliban-affiliated Haqqani network as a terrorist organization or issue a report explaining why not. The network is seen as having ties to the Pakistani government, so the designation complicates the relationship with Pakistan — but the State Department acceded.

Dovetailing with his work on the HELP Committee, Burr has also been a key negotiator on laws meant to improve national preparedness for a biological or chemical attack. A reauthorization of preparedness programs was enacted in 2013.

Burr generally votes with the GOP on defense issues, and he consistently votes in support of military activities in Iraq and Afghanistan. But he was one of eight Senate Republicans to side with Democrats in a 2010 vote to repeal the military's "don't ask, don't tell" policy. "Given the generational transition that has taken place in our nation, I feel that this policy is outdated and repeal is inevitable," he wrote.

Burr has a longtime interest in energy policy and is a former member of the Energy and Natural Resources Committee. He likes the "all of the above" energy strategy, and he is particularly fond of natural gas, calling it "the only flexible mobile fuel we've got." In November 2011, he teamed with Democrats Harry Reid of Nevada and Robert Menendez of New Jersey on a bill to increase domestic production of natural gas vehicles and the building of refueling infrastructure by extending tax credits.

He also looks out for his state's tobacco companies and farmers. He opposed legislation directing the Food and Drug Administration to regulate tobacco, arguing in a 2008 opinion column in USA Today that giving the FDA control over tobacco would "severely impede the FDA's core mission" by taking its focus away from existing problems such as food and drug safety.

In 2009, he joined North Carolina Democrat Kay Hagan to propose a less stringent alternative that would impose limits on marketing tobacco. (It failed, and the FDA was granted new regulatory powers that year.) In 2004, he helped win passage of a popular tobacco buyout that steered $3.8 billion to his state's farmers. Burr himself quit smoking in 1998 after making a televised vow to do so, but he remains close with one of Washington's most famous smokers: House Speaker John A. Boehner.

Burr is a true-blue North Carolinian, having grown up in Winston-Salem. His minister father, head of the city's 3,000-member First Presbyterian Church, was often gone, tending to his large flock. Burr graduated from Wake Forest University in 1978, where he lettered for three seasons on the football team. Still a season ticket holder, he attends as many games as he can.

He took a job with Carswell Distributing, selling appliances and teaching housewives how to cook with their newfangled microwave ovens. He rose to national sales manager. Along the way, Burr became politically active in the anti-tax movement. One day in 1991, Burr came home from his job and surprised his wife by announcing he wanted to run for Congress, even though he had no political experience. He lost his first bid in 1992. Two years later, he won an open seat with 57 percent of the vote.

Encouraged by state party officials to run for governor in 2000, Burr declined. He then deferred to Republican Elizabeth Dole and stayed out of a 2002 race for an open Senate seat. Instead, he prepared for a 2004 challenge to Democrat John Edwards — who later decided not to seek re-election.

Burr weathered criticism for an initially lackluster campaign against Democrat Erskine Bowles, a former chief of staff to President Bill Clinton. But aided by President George W. Bush's strong showing in the state, Burr won with 52 percent of the vote. In 2010, he defeated North Carolina Secretary of State Elaine Marshall, 55 percent to 43 percent.

Around the Capitol complex, Burr might be best known for his car: a primer-gray Volkswagen Thing plastered with political bumper stickers.

Key Votes

2012	
Prohibit health insurance plans from denying coverage based on the sponsor's religious beliefs	NO
Require approval of the Keystone XL oil pipeline	YES
Ease securities rules to expand small-business access to capital	YES
Reauthorize farm and nutrition programs for five years	NO
Limit debate on a bill that would create private-sector cybersecurity standards	NO
Consent to ratification of a treaty setting global standard for the treatment of people with disabilities	NO
Provide $60.4 billion in disaster relief following Superstorm Sandy	NO
Extend most Bush-era income tax rates while allowing rates for top-bracket earners to rise (Jan. 1, 2013)	YES
2011	
Prevent EPA from regulating greenhouse gas emissions to address climate change	YES
Extend certain provisions of Patriot Act for four years	YES
Clear compromise debt limit increase plan and establish future spending limits	YES
Overhaul patent law	YES
Implement Colombia free trade agreement	YES
Limit debate on confirmation of Caitlin J. Halligan to D.C. Circuit Court of Appeals	NO
Extend payroll tax cut and unemployment benefits for two months	YES

CQ Vote Studies

	PARTY UNITY		PRESIDENTIAL SUPPORT	
	SUPPORT	OPPOSE	SUPPORT	OPPOSE
2012	94%	6%	45%	55%
2011	94%	6%	51%	49%
2010	96%	4%	43%	57%
2009	97%	3%	39%	61%
2008	99%	1%	81%	19%
2007	97%	3%	89%	11%
2006	94%	6%	88%	12%
2005	95%	5%	89%	11%
2004	92%	8%	79%	21%
2003	94%	6%	96%	4%

Interest Groups

	AFL-CIO	ADA	CCUS	ACU
2012	0%	0%	100%	88%
2011	16%	10%	100%	94%
2010	7%	5%	100%	92%
2009	6%	10%	71%	100%
2008	10%	5%	100%	79%
2007	5%	0%	73%	92%
2006	20%	10%	67%	92%
2005	29%	5%	94%	92%
2004	33%	10%	94%	87%
2003	27%	15%	93%	84%

Sen. Kay Hagan (D)

Capitol Office
224-6342
hagan.senate.gov
521 Dirksen Bldg. 20510; fax 228-2563

Committees
Armed Services
(Emerging Threats & Capabilities - Chairwoman)
Banking, Housing & Urban Affairs
Health, Education, Labor & Pensions
(Children & Families - Chairwoman)
Small Business & Entrepreneurship

Residence
Greensboro

Born
May 26, 1953; Shelby, N.C.

Religion
Presbyterian

Family
Husband, Chip Hagan; three children

Education
Florida State U., B.A. 1975 (American studies); Wake Forest U., J.D. 1978

Career
Homemaker; bank executive

Political Highlights
N.C. Senate, 1999-2009

ELECTION RESULTS

2008 GENERAL		
Kay Hagan (D)	2,249,311	52.6%
Elizabeth Dole (R)	1,887,510	44.2%
Christopher Cole (LIBERT)	133,430	3.1%
2008 PRIMARY		
Kay Hagan (D)	801,920	60.1%
Jim Neal (D)	239,623	17.9%
Marcus W. Williams (D)	170,970	12.8%
Duskin C. Lassiter (D)	62,136	4.6%
Howard Staley (D)	60,403	4.5%

Elected 2008; 1st term

Republicans are eager to knock off Hagan in the 2014 elections, but her actions as a first-term senator have set her up for a spirited defense. She casts herself as a pragmatic Democrat, and she takes many of her political cues from North Carolina's economy and culture.

Her state has a huge banking hub in Charlotte, and Hagan holds a seat on the Banking, Housing and Urban Affairs Committee. Professionally, she worked as an attorney and then as a vice president in the estates and trust division for North Carolina National Bank (now Bank of America). She left after 10 years to raise her family.

Hagan stood with her party to pass a 2010 overhaul of financial regulations, but in the 112th Congress (2011-12) she was open to revisiting some of its provisions. She co-sponsored a bill to delay a ban, opposed by the industry, on proprietary trading by banks. She joined Democratic moderates and Republicans to vote for legislation to delay the law's restrictions on fees that banks charge for debit card transactions.

She works to protect tobacco, which is linked to more than 250,000 North Carolina jobs, according to the state's Department of Agriculture and Consumer Services. Hagan has lobbied to include tobacco in the vast trade deal known as the Trans-Pacific Partnership, noting that the crop hasn't been excluded from other recent trade agreements.

In June 2009, she was the only Democrat to vote against a bill to allow the Food and Drug Administration to regulate the manufacture, sale, and promotion of tobacco products. Hagan, who helped harvest the crop on her grandparents' farm as a child, backed a proposal from North Carolina Republican Richard M. Burr to create a separate regulatory entity that could test only for nicotine levels and require that products be labeled accordingly. They were unable to keep the FDA bill from enactment.

Like many of her Southern Democratic colleagues, Hagan supports Second Amendment rights. Her Senate website describes gun ownership as "part of the fabric of North Carolina." In February 2009, she joined 40 Republicans and 21 other Democrats in voting to repeal the District of Columbia's firearms prohibitions and gun registration laws. In April 2013, however, Hagan voted for an expansion of the federal background check system as part of a compromise gun policy bill.

Hagan sits on the Health, Education, Labor and Pensions Committee. In 2011, she and Michael Bennet of Colorado led a group of moderate Democrats to set out principles for a reauthorization of the 2002 education law known as No Child Left Behind. Their suggestions included competitive grants to fund teacher training programs; better reporting of how schools use federal funds; and requiring the worst-performing schools in each state to adopt one of four turnaround models.

She has laid groundwork for a reauthorization of higher education law in 2013. During the 112th, she introduced one bill to prevent all colleges and universities from using federal student aid to pay for recruiting and marketing, and another to prohibit using the phrase "GI Bill" in the marketing of for-profit colleges, saying the schools were taking advantage of veterans.

In the 113th Congress (2013-14), Hagan is chairing the HELP Subcommittee on Children and Families, which oversees early-childhood education. Early in 2013 she expressed interest in a reauthorization of the Child Care and Development Block Grant.

Hagan also sits on the Armed Services Committee, where she chairs the Emerging Threats and Capabilities Subcommittee. Her panel studies cybersecurity, which is of no small concern to the financial institutions she also looks after on the Banking committee.

North Carolina has a lot of economic ties to the military, and Hagan has been wary of reductions to defense spending. When she voted against the Senate's fiscal 2014 budget — which was written by Democrats — she said its proposed $240 billion in cuts to the military were too much.

She has addressed some local concerns on the panel. She and Burr won 2012 enactment of a bill to provide health care to those previously afflicted by water contamination at North Carolina's Camp Lejeune, the largest Marine Corps base on the East Coast.

Though she never served, Hagan has connections to the military. Her father-in-law was a two-star Marine general, her brother and father both served in the Navy, and her husband is a Vietnam veteran who used the GI Bill to help pay for law school. She applauded the announcement of expanded combat roles for women, and she voted to repeal the ban on openly gay servicemembers. "Anybody who's qualified should be able to serve," she said. (In March 2013, she announced her support for same-sex marriage.)

A member of the Small Business and Entrepreneurship Committee, she cited savings in energy costs as a way to boost small businesses. She introduced a bill in February 2011 to increase domestic production of lithium. Two companies capable of doing such work are located in North Carolina.

Hagan usually backs up Democratic positions on the biggest issues before Congress. She defends the 2010 health care overhaul, and she supports increasing taxes on high-income earners. She opposed a two-year extension of the George W. Bush-era tax cuts that was enacted in late 2010 because it included the highest-income groups. She voted for the January 2013 "fiscal cliff" deal that allowed rate increases on earnings over $400,000.

Hagan credits her appreciation for local causes to a family history rich in politics. She was born in Shelby, N.C., and her family later moved to Lakeland, Fla., where her father became the city's mayor. She attended college at Florida State University, then spent six months interning in Washington for her uncle, Democratic Florida Sen. Lawton Chiles. Hagan learned the literal ups and downs of the Capitol; she operated a senators-only elevator.

Hagan returned to North Carolina to attend Wake Forest University's law school, where she met her husband, Chip. The couple settled in Greensboro.

She was recruited into politics by four-term Democratic Gov. James B. Hunt, who selected her to lead his Guilford County organization in his 1992 and 1996 campaigns. In 1998, Hunt and state Sen. Marc Basnight recruited Hagan to challenge a GOP state senator. She won and served five terms.

She was uncertain at first about the 2008 U.S. Senate race against Republican Elizabeth Dole, announcing in October 2007 that she would not be a candidate, then changing her mind a short time later. Hagan won 60 percent of the vote in the Democratic primary and blanketed the state with campaign appearances as the national Democratic Party spent heavily in support of her. Emphasizing her North Carolina roots, she frequently jabbed Dole — wife of 1996 GOP presidential nominee Bob Dole — for a life spent largely in Kansas and Washington. Hagan also benefited from Barack Obama's name at the top of the ticket.

Late in the campaign, as polls began to indicate a Hagan victory, Dole ran television ads suggesting Hagan was an atheist. Hagan, a Sunday school teacher and elder at her church, fired back with an ad, declaring "I believe in God," and a lawsuit, charging Dole with defamation. Hagan withdrew the lawsuit after winning by more than 8 points.

The swing-state status of North Carolina — and a strong GOP showing there in the 2012 elections — made Hagan an early target of Republicans. She hired campaign manager Preston Elliott, who helped orchestrate the reelection of Montana Democrat Jon Tester in 2012.

Key Votes

2012	
Prohibit health insurance plans from denying coverage based on the sponsor's religious beliefs	YES
Require approval of the Keystone XL oil pipeline	YES
Ease securities rules to expand small-business access to capital	YES
Reauthorize farm and nutrition programs for five years	YES
Limit debate on a bill that would create private-sector cybersecurity standards	YES
Consent to ratification of a treaty setting global standard for the treatment of people with disabilities	YES
Provide $60.4 billion in disaster relief following Superstorm Sandy	YES
Extend most Bush-era income tax rates while allowing rates for top-bracket earners to rise (Jan. 1, 2013)	YES
2011	
Prevent EPA from regulating greenhouse gas emissions to address climate change	NO
Extend certain provisions of Patriot Act for four years	YES
Clear compromise debt limit increase plan and establish future spending limits	YES
Overhaul patent law	YES
Implement Colombia free trade agreement	NO
Limit debate on confirmation of Caitlin J. Halligan to D.C. Circuit Court of Appeals	YES
Extend payroll tax cut and unemployment benefits for two months	YES

CQ Vote Studies

	PARTY UNITY		PRESIDENTIAL SUPPORT	
	SUPPORT	OPPOSE	SUPPORT	OPPOSE
2012	87%	13%	96%	4%
2011	90%	10%	90%	10%
2010	88%	12%	95%	5%
2009	91%	9%	96%	4%

Interest Groups

	AFL-CIO	ADA	CCUS	ACU
2012	91%	85%	50%	12%
2011	95%	95%	40%	5%
2010	81%	85%	18%	4%
2009	94%	95%	43%	16%

Rep. G.K. Butterfield (D)

Capitol Office
225-3101
butterfield.house.gov
2305 Rayburn Bldg. 20515-3301; fax 225-3354

Committees
Energy & Commerce

Residence
Wilson

Born
April 27, 1947; Wilson, N.C.

Religion
Baptist

Family
Divorced; two children

Education
North Carolina Central U., B.A. 1971 (political science & sociology), J.D. 1974

Military
Army, 1968-70

Career
Lawyer; child care center owner

Political Highlights
Candidate for Wilson City Council, 1976; N.C. Superior Court judge, 1989-2001; N.C. Supreme Court, 2001-02; defeated for election to N.C. Supreme Court, 2002; N.C. Superior Court judge, 2003-04

ELECTION RESULTS

2012 GENERAL		
G.K. Butterfield (D)	254,644	75.3%
Pete DiLauro (R)	77,288	22.9%
Darryl Holloman (LIBERT)	6,134	1.8%
2012 PRIMARY		
G.K. Butterfield (D)	89,531	81.1%
Daniel-Lynn Whittacre (D)	20,822	18.9%
2010 GENERAL		
G.K. Butterfield (D)	103,294	59.3%
Ashley Woolard (R)	70,867	40.7%

Previous Winning Percentages
2008 (70%); 2006 (100%); 2004 (64%); 2004 Special Election (71%)

Elected 2004; 5th full term

Butterfield is a low-key liberal with solid connections in the Democratic Party. When he outwardly uses his clout, it's for causes favorable to his district, which is one of the poorest in the nation.

His family history is compelling. Butterfield's great-grandfather was a white slaveholder who conceived a child with one of his slaves. The child, Butterfield's maternal grandfather, was born in the final days of slavery and became a minister. Butterfield's father was a native of Bermuda; he came to the United States at age 16 and became a dentist. He also became a civic leader, organizing black voters in North Carolina in the 1940s and 1950s.

Butterfield himself has an assured speaking style, a penetrating voice and a legal career that includes years as a state judge. But he generally opts not to draw attention his way. "I can say in two minutes what some people say in 20," he has said. "And I say it just as well." Given a turn at the microphone at the 2012 Democratic National Convention — in his home state, no less — he kept his remarks under 150 words.

Still, Butterfield has some pull. He has called James E. Clyburn of South Carolina, the No. 3 House Democrat, "my very best friend in the U.S. Congress." He has been a chief deputy whip for House Democrats since 2007, and he is the first vice chairman of the Congressional Black Caucus in the 113th Congress (2013-14).

Butterfield also has a seat on the Energy and Commerce Committee. In 2013, he joined its Health Subcommittee, and in doing so he vowed to protect the 2010 health care law and hospitals throughout his district.

In the 112th Congress (2011-12), he was the top Democrat on the Commerce, Manufacturing and Trade Subcommittee. There wasn't much legislative action in the 112th, but Butterfield made efforts at cooperation with Republican Chairwoman Mary Bono Mack of California. In December 2012, President Barack Obama signed a bill that they ushered through their committee. It reauthorized through 2020 the tools used by the Federal Trade Commission to fight online fraud across international borders.

Butterfield has pursued ways to bring high-tech training and equipment to poor rural areas. In 2011, he re-introduced legislation to require federal agencies to donate excess computers to "educational recipients," particularly in poorer and smaller communities.

He stuck with House Democrats in 2009 when they passed a bill to create a cap-and-trade system to regulate greenhouse gas emissions. But Butterfield kept his constituents in mind, proposing that a portion of the money collected from the sale of pollution credits under such a system go to poorer customers of electric utilities, who might be hit by higher power costs.

Continuing in that vein, Butterfield worked with Virginia Republican Morgan Griffith on a 2011 bill to nullify new EPA standards for emissions from industrial and commercial boilers. They said businesses and other entities using such boilers did not have enough time to comply with the upgrades needed and predicted the rules would cause job losses. The bill was introduced after the Obama administration had put the rules on hold in May, and it was passed by the House in October. It was never considered by the Senate, but revised final standards issued in December 2012 were narrower and had a longer compliance window.

Butterfield supports the development of energy sources other than fossil fuels, though he diverges from environmentalists in his party by supporting nuclear power. "The South is positioned to lead the way in development of nuclear energy," he said to a nuclear industry trade group in 2012. "North

Carolina is ready, willing and able to become a hub for nuclear energy."

Agriculture is a big part of the economy in Butterfield's district, and in 2012 he tried to prevent the closure of Farm Service Agency offices in his district. Writing to Agriculture Secretary Tom Vilsack, Butterfield said the closures "will severely limit access to USDA services for black farmers in eastern North Carolina, which is a step in the wrong direction."

Butterfield had a brief stay on the Ethics Committee in the 111th Congress (2009-10). He was the only member of the committee to oppose the 2010 censure of New York Democrat Charles B. Rangel, who had been accused of irregularities in his personal and campaign finances. He pleaded unsuccessfully on the House floor for a reduction in Rangel's penalty.

Butterfield grew up in Wilson. He told the Charlotte Observer that when his father first moved there, only 40 or so blacks in town were registered to vote. His father was able to register unimpeded, but when he encouraged other blacks to follow suit, they asked him to stop, fearing reprisals from whites.

He resumed the effort after the Great Depression. When literacy tests were introduced to discourage blacks from voting, Butterfield's father began teaching people to read. He then ran for the city council, winning narrowly in 1953.

In 1957, while the family was vacationing out of town, local officials called an emergency meeting and replaced ward-by-ward elections — which had allowed the elder Butterfield to win among a black-majority constituency — with at-large elections.

Those childhood events spurred Butterfield to get involved politically. In 1968, he was a student at North Carolina Central University in Durham. Inspired by a crop of black candidates running for office, he led a voter registration march to Wilson. The Rev. Martin Luther King Jr. was scheduled to appear at a voter registration event in the state a few days later, and Butterfield hoped to meet him. But King postponed his visit, heading to Memphis, Tenn., to support striking sanitation workers. He was assassinated during that visit.

Butterfield went on to get a law degree, as well as the last word in his father's long fight. He handled several voting-rights lawsuits in eastern North Carolina counties, resulting in the court-ordered implementation of district elections for local officials.

Butterfield's first run for office was a losing city council bid in 1976. But he was elected a Superior Court judge in 1988, and he held that job until Democratic Gov. Michael F. Easley elevated him to the state Supreme Court in 2001. After Butterfield lost a 2002 election for the seat, Easley reinstated him on the lower court. In 2004, when Democratic Rep. Frank W. Ballance Jr. resigned, party officials tapped Butterfield as their choice to succeed him. He won the special election by 44 points, and subsequent elections have been a breeze.

Key Votes

2012	
Extend a Social Security payroll tax cut and unemployment benefits	YES
Ease securities rules to expand small-business access to capital	YES
Extend for one year subsidized student loan interest rates financed by a cut in health care spending	NO
Cite Attorney General Eric H. Holder Jr. for contempt of Congress	?
Create a visa program for foreign graduates in high-tech fields	NO
Extend most Bush-era income tax rates while allowing rates for top-bracket earners to rise (Jan. 1, 2013)	YES
2011	
Strike funding for F-35 alternative engine	YES
Prevent EPA from regulating greenhouse gas emissions to address climate change	NO
Extend certain provisions of Patriot Act for four years	YES
Declare opposition to use of ground troops in Libya	NO
Overhaul patent law	YES
Pass compromise debt limit increase plan and establish future spending limits	NO
Allow consideration of measures to implement three trade agreements	YES

CQ Vote Studies

	PARTY UNITY		PRESIDENTIAL SUPPORT	
	SUPPORT	OPPOSE	SUPPORT	OPPOSE
2012	95%	5%	88%	12%
2011	91%	9%	91%	9%
2010	98%	2%	90%	10%
2009	99%	1%	97%	3%
2008	98%	2%	11%	89%

Interest Groups

	AFL-CIO	ADA	CCUS	ACU
2012	90%	75%	33%	5%
2011	100%	85%	27%	4%
2010	100%	90%	25%	5%
2009	100%	95%	40%	0%
2008	93%	100%	56%	12%

North Carolina 1

Northeast — parts of Durham, Goldsboro, Rocky Mount

The 1st District represents the heart of North Carolina's tobacco country in the state's northeast. It shoots out tentacles to gather far-flung, largely black communities in Durham, Goldsboro and Elizabeth City. Mainly rural and poor, the 1st has the state's lowest education and income levels.

Many of the 1st's rural counties have black-majority populations. Cotton is the main crop for the district's northern farms; sweet potatoes, soybeans and poultry are also important. To the south are some of the largest flue-cured tobacco harvests in the nation but falling tobacco prices have hurt the district, which has some of the highest unemployment rates in the state. Median household income for the district overall is $32,000 and, in some areas, more than 20 percent of the population lives in poverty.

Durham, the home of Duke University and North Carolina Central University, has a stable base of professional and service jobs. Duke, including its medical center, is one of the largest employers in the state. Seymour Johnson Air Force Base, a major source of jobs in Goldsboro, hosts the only F-15E Strike Eagle training squadron. New Bern is close enough to Marine Corps Air Station Cherry Point and Camp Lejeune (both in the 3rd) to reap some economic benefit from military and contractor jobs.

In the small towns scattered throughout the district, manufacturing includes appliances, pharmaceuticals and paper. Hatteras Yachts builds fishing boats and luxury craft in New Bern at the mouth of the Neuse River. Dominion Power operates a number of power stations near Virginia.

Registered Democrats significantly outnumber Republicans, and the district has a long history of electing Democrats to Congress — decennial remapping added Durham to the 1st, strengthening the district's Democratic lean.

Major Industry
Agriculture, higher education, manufacturing, defense

Military Bases
Seymour Johnson Air Force Base, 5,213 military, 987 civilian (2012)

Cities
Durham (pt.), Greenville (pt.), Rocky Mount (pt.), Wilson (pt.)

Notable
Wilbur Hardee opened the first Hardee's drive-in restaurant in Greenville.

Rep. Renee Ellmers (R)

Capitol Office
225-4531
ellmers.house.gov
426 Cannon Bldg. 20515-3302; fax 225-5662

Committees
Energy & Commerce

Residence
Dunn

Born
Feb. 9, 1964; Ironwood, Mich.

Religion
Roman Catholic

Family
Husband, Brent Ellmers; one child

Education
Oakland U., B.S. 1990 (nursing)

Career
Hospital administrator; nurse

Political Highlights
Dunn Planning Board, 2006-11 (chairwoman, 2008-09)

ELECTION RESULTS

2012 GENERAL		
Renee Ellmers (R)	174,066	55.9%
Steve Wilkins (D)	128,973	41.4%
Brian Irving (LIBERT)	8,358	2.7%
2012 PRIMARY		
Renee Ellmers (R)	37,661	56.0%
Richard Speer (R)	20,099	29.9%
Sonya Holmes (R)	6,535	9.7%
Clement F. Munno (R)	2,982	4.4%
2010 GENERAL		
Renee Ellmers (R)	93,876	49.5%
Bob Etheridge (D)	92,393	48.7%
Tom Rose (LIBERT)	3,505	1.8%

Elected 2010; 2nd term

Health care is the issue that propelled Ellmers to Washington, but some powerful Republicans also like her approach to other big issues. The former nurse is a friend and proxy of the GOP leadership team.

Ellmers is married to a surgeon, and they operated a small medical practice together. She was active in the business community as a leader of the Dunn Chamber of Commerce, and she often says that the 2010 health care overhaul and its potential effect on small businesses are what compelled her to run for office.

One of the more vexing things about government, according to Ellmers, is that it moves even slower than the pace of life in her small Southern town. "I like to fix the problems," she said, "and you know, it's a lot of hurry up and wait." As a freshman, she tried to keep the campaign against the overhaul moving. Ellmers was given the gavel of the Small Business Subcommittee on Healthcare and Technology, and she used her position to highlight disadvantages small businesses might suffer under the new health care regime.

Ellmers maintains that small insurers might be unable to meet the spending and service requirements for participating in state-based "exchanges" created by the law; they would then be effectively excluded from the marketplace. In 2011, she introduced a bill to ease penalties on doctors and hospitals that lack the technology required to submit electronic prescriptions, per Medicare's E-prescribe mandate. The bill would leave in place incentives for doctors and hospitals to upgrade their technology, without punishing smaller medical practices that may find such upgrades too costly.

She celebrated every time Republicans managed to knock off a chunk of funding for the law. Ellmers sat on the conference committee for a 2012 extension of lower payroll taxes; the final measure sliced $5 billion from the Prevention and Public Health Fund created by the overhaul. Ellmers called it a "dramatic blow."

Ellmers dislikes mandated insurance coverage, and she was defiant when the Supreme Court upheld the overhaul's "individual mandate" in 2012. "We are and will remain committed to this," Ellmers said at a news conference. "We will repeal Obamacare."

Her work helped earn her a spot on the Energy and Commerce Committee and its Health panel in the 113th Congress (2013-14).

Ellmers supports "free-market-based" changes to the health care system, such as allowing the purchase of health plans across state lines. Changes should focus on increasing accessibility, lowering costs and improving technology, she said. In April 2013, Ellmers and Tennessee Republican Marsha Blackburn issued a set of seven general ideas for modernizing and changing Medicare; it included means testing for benefits and an overhaul of medical malpractice laws.

The addition of Ellmers to the Energy and Commerce Committee is indicative of her good relationship with Republican leaders. During deficit reduction talks in the summer of 2011, some conservative Republicans chafed at the proposals of the GOP leadership team. Ellmers, on the other hand, was recruited to rally support for Speaker John A. Boehner's plan to raise the debt ceiling. She appeared with the leadership team at a number of media events during the 112th Congress (2011-12), and she has called Majority Whip Kevin McCarthy of California "a great friend and a great mentor."

As the GOP looked to soften its image following a disappointing showing in the 2012 elections, Ellmers got behind leadership candidates who suited that purpose. A member of the Republican Study Committee, she whipped votes for Louisiana's Steve Scalise in his bid to chair the group. Scalise, who promised a less combative RSC, won.

Ellmers also speaks openly of wanting to reclaim the "feminist" label for conservatives. "It's the women that understand what's happening out there," she said. "We're the ones who are writing the bills, making out the check, paying the mortgage. ... We're watching the prices of food go up. ... It's not so much about the politics as just trying to solve the problems."

When Ellmers parts from a majority of her party, it's usually in support of a local interest. She was one of 21 House Republicans to oppose a free-trade agreement with South Korea in 2011; she later said that parts of that deal "throw the textile industry under the bus."

Ellmers shares many of the socially conservative views of her constituents. She is against the use of federal funds to pay for abortions, and she introduced a bill to block funding to the U.N. Population Fund — she said UNPF money has been used in connection with China's one-child policy to pay for abortions.

She supports gun rights and has a concealed-carry permit. In January 2013, when President Barack Obama unveiled several executive orders regarding guns — on the heels of a mass shooting at a Connecticut elementary school — Ellmers wrote that he was "exploiting a tragedy for political gain and eroding our constitutional rights for the sake of an extreme liberal agenda."

In a break with some social conservatives, however, Ellmers supports civil unions between same-sex couples.

Ellmers grew up in Michigan and graduated from Oakland University in 1990 with a nursing degree. She and her husband, Brent, moved to North Carolina after their son was born. They opened a small medical practice. When she is back in North Carolina, Ellmers likes going to Topsail Beach with her family. She's also likely to pop in to Wal-Mart to look for a pet Snuggie or the latest meatloaf pan advertised on the Home Shopping Network — novelty gadgets are her guilty pleasure.

She was stirred to political action at a town hall meeting on health care that featured her predecessor, seven-term Democrat Bob Etheridge. Her 2010 challenge to Etheridge was one of the tightest races in the country. It got national attention when Etheridge was videotaped grabbing a young man trying to interview him. Ellmers held a slim lead on election night, but Etheridge didn't concede for a few weeks. Ellmers won by just less than 1,500 votes.

Redistricting was friendly to North Carolina Republicans heading into the 2012 elections. Ellmers faced Democrat Steve Wilkins, a retired Army Special Forces officer. Her fundraising effort swamped that of Wilkins, and Ellmers won by more than 14 points. She is considering a bid for the Senate in 2014 and said she hoped to make that decision by June 2013.

Key Votes

2012	
Extend a Social Security payroll tax cut and unemployment benefits	YES
Ease securities rules to expand small-business access to capital	YES
Extend for one year subsidized student loan interest rates financed by a cut in health care spending	YES
Cite Attorney General Eric H. Holder Jr. for contempt of Congress	YES
Create a visa program for foreign graduates in high-tech fields	YES
Extend most Bush-era income tax rates while allowing rates for top-bracket earners to rise (Jan. 1, 2013)	NO
2011	
Strike funding for F-35 alternative engine	YES
Prevent EPA from regulating greenhouse gas emissions to address climate change	YES
Extend certain provisions of Patriot Act for four years	YES
Declare opposition to use of ground troops in Libya	YES
Overhaul patent law	YES
Pass compromise debt limit increase plan and establish future spending limits	YES
Allow consideration of measures to implement three trade agreements	YES

CQ Vote Studies

	PARTY UNITY		PRESIDENTIAL SUPPORT	
	SUPPORT	OPPOSE	SUPPORT	OPPOSE
2012	97%	3%	16%	84%
2011	96%	4%	26%	74%

Interest Groups

	AFL-CIO	ADA	CCUS	ACU
2012	14%	0%	100%	91%
2011	3%	10%	94%	84%

North Carolina 2

Central — parts of Cary and Fayetteville, Asheboro

No district changed more during North Carolina's decennial redistricting process than the 2nd. Less than 30 percent of its original constituency remains from its previous iteration in the state's center. The new district resembles an elephant's head and trunk as it stretches from the outskirts of Raleigh south to Fayetteville, then through Fort Bragg into parts of rural Moore and Randolph counties. Its new shape is appropriate, as the 2nd's footprint makes it lean much more strongly toward the GOP.

Taking up a portion of the Research Triangle Region in Cary (shared with the 4th) and part of Apex (shared with the 13th), the 2nd plugs into the state's technology and computing sector. The northern tip of the district's trunk is between the state capital Raleigh and college town Chapel Hill.

The 2nd gained a major economic and political plum when remapping drew all of Fort Bragg into its boundaries. The massive base was previously shared with two other districts. The former Pope Air Force Base was realigned into an Army airfield, boosting the base's employment power. Many defense contractors operate out of nearby Fayetteville (shared with the 4th).

Once North Carolina's definitive crop, flue-cured tobacco still plays a role in some of the area's rural towns, but years of falling demand have left many farmers struggling. Nearly one in 10 residents is out of work in the district's western counties. Some manufacturing jobs producing batteries, furniture and roofing materials help. Sanford calls itself the nation's brick capital.

Republicans have an edge in voter registration in Randolph and Moore counties. Black-majority neighborhoods near Fayetteville provide some Democratic votes. But this is a Republican-friendly district and it gave GOP presidential nominee Mitt Romney 57 percent of its vote in 2012.

Major Industry
Technology, military, agriculture

Military Bases
Fort Bragg (Army), 54,359 military, 7,022 civilian (2011)

Cities
Fayetteville (pt.), Cary (pt.), Apex (pt.), Sanford, Asheboro

Notable
A completed section of US Bike Route 1, a planned bicycle trail from Maine to Florida, runs through Cary.

Rep. Walter B. Jones (R)

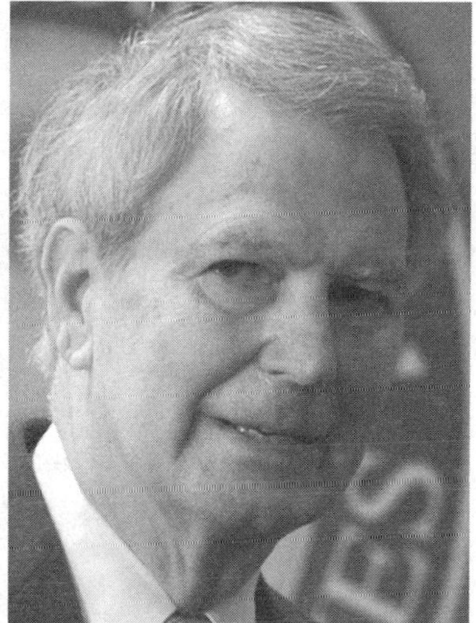

Capitol Office
225-3415
jones.house.gov
2333 Rayburn Bldg. 20515-3303; fax 225-3286

Committees
Armed Services

Residence
Farmville

Born
Feb. 10, 1943; Farmville, N.C.

Religion
Roman Catholic

Family
Wife, Joe Anne Jones; one child

Education
North Carolina State U., attended 1962-65 (history); Atlantic Christian College, B.A. 1968 (history)

Military
N.C. National Guard, 1967-71

Career
Lighting company executive; insurance benefits company executive; office supply company executive; wine broker

Political Highlights
N.C. House, 1983-92 (served as a Democrat); sought Democratic nomination for U.S. House, 1992

ELECTION RESULTS

2012 GENERAL		
Walter B. Jones (R)	195,571	63.1%
Erik Anderson (D)	114,314	36.9%
2012 PRIMARY		
Walter B. Jones (R)	42,644	69.0%
Frank Palombo (R)	19,166	31.0%
2010 GENERAL		
Walter B. Jones (R)	143,225	71.9%
Johnny Rouse (D)	51,317	25.7%
Darryl Holloman (LIBERT)	4,762	2.4%

Previous Winning Percentages
2008 (66%); 2006 (69%); 2004 (71%); 2002 (91%); 2000 (61%); 1998 (62%); 1996 (63%); 1994 (53%)

Elected 1994; 10th term

In a House that has tended toward polarization in recent years, Jones is an anomaly. He was once a reliable supporter of Republican Party leaders, but his dismay over the handling of the Iraq War accelerated a dramatic shift away from GOP orthodoxy. "My heart dictates my thinking many, many times," he has said.

In 2011, Jones was the House Republican most likely to break with a majority of the party when they opposed a majority of Democrats. In 2012, he was No. 2 in that regard. And Jones doesn't save his dissent for inconsequential matters — he defies GOP leaders on some of the most high-profile votes.

Republicans took a political risk by presenting a fiscal 2012 budget that included a restructuring of Medicare, and those Medicare plans cost them Jones' support. He was one of four in his party to oppose that budget, and he didn't flinch in opposing a similar one for fiscal 2013.

He rejected the August 2011 deal to raise the government's borrowing authority while cutting spending; Jones said that the cuts were both too small and too heavily tilted toward the Defense Department. His district is home to Camp Lejeune, the Marines' East Coast headquarters, and he says that any threat to Navy funding would hurt his constituents. Plus, he hates the notion of adding to the national debt — at a 2013 hearing, he said the American people "do not fully understand the deficit and the debt problems facing our country."

Jones' refusal to go along extended to many issues. Long an opponent of trade deals, in 2011 he was the only Republican to vote against the rule that would allow three pacts to be debated on the House floor. Earlier that year, in May, he voted against extending certain surveillance provisions of the anti-terrorism law known as the Patriot Act.

In December 2012, he paid a political price. The Republican Steering Committee removed Jones and three other obstinate lawmakers from prized panel assignments — in Jones' case, the Financial Services Committee. The decision incensed conservative activists, but it stood.

Jones registered his displeasure by voting against John A. Boehner in the selection of the speaker of the House for the 113th Congress (2013-14). He voted for David Walker, a former comptroller general of the United States.

And he kept on dissenting. He was the only Republican to vote against the rules package for the 113th Congress, and when the party's fiscal 2014 budget was presented, he voted against that, too. He said he liked some parts of the budget, but "when you're running trillion [dollar] deficits, the first thing you should do is stop foreign aid," he wrote.

Jones' break with his party dates to his 2005 decision to oppose the Iraq War. It was a serious change of heart. Jones had voted in 2002 to authorize President George W. Bush to use force to topple Saddam Hussein. But three years later, Jones said he had a spiritual awakening at the funeral of a Marine named Michael Bitz. After the funeral, Jones decided the war was wrong.

His office writes every family that has lost someone in Iraq or Afghanistan, and he has photos, letters and military paraphernalia from the casualties' families. But he says he cannot read their letters because he becomes too emotional. He intends to write a book about the letters because, he says, "God wants me to." In 2013, he said that military servicemembers "deserve better than what they get from an administration and a Congress that want to send them around the world and change the culture of countries that could care less about freedom."

His rift with Republicans widened in 2006 as he quit the conservative Republican Study Committee because he felt it was too willing to compromise on illegal immigration. Jones strongly opposes creating a path to citizenship for those in the county illegally, and in the 112th Congress (2011-12) he introduced a measure to require federal reporting of all crimes committed by such immigrants.

Even before the 2012 committee purge, Jones suffered for his independence. In 2007, when he was up for the top Republican spot on one of the Armed Services subcommittees, he was told it would go to a more junior member. He is now the No. 3 Republican on Armed Services, and he still holds no gavel. "I'll put it this way: There's a price to pay for anyone," he told Roll Call. "And I am at peace with that."

Jones' heresies in Washington have hardly affected his standing back home. He has maintained his popularity in his district by paying assiduous attention to issues of local concern, like fishing rights and beach access — he represents the state's famous Outer Banks — and to Camp Lejeune.

In addition to his striking stands on federal spending and foreign policy, Jones has become the leading Republican advocate in the House for new rules requiring more disclosure of campaign spending by outside interest groups and corporations. "The American people are crying out for sunshine and reform in the electoral process," he said at the introduction of a 2010 bill — by Maryland Democrat Chris Van Hollen — meant to roll back a Supreme Court decision allowing more spending by groups unaffiliated with campaigns.

As a member of the Financial Services Committee, he was a critic of Wall Street. He was one of three House Republicans to vote for the financial regulatory overhaul that Democrats pushed to enactment in 2010. Jones is unapologetic, saying he wants to combat the influence of the big banks.

Jones grew up around politics and government. His father was Democratic Rep. Walter B. Jones Sr., a pragmatist who was a bit more liberal than his son. Jones attended Virginia's Hargrave Military Academy, which emphasized Christian values, and became a standout basketball player there. He graduated from Atlantic Christian College in 1968, did a stint in the National Guard, then took a job as a wine broker with a region covering North Carolina and Virginia. Raised a Baptist, he converted to Catholicism when he was 29.

Jones was almost 40 when he followed his father into politics. In 1982, the local Democratic Party asked him to finish the term of a state representative who had died in office. Jones wound up staying for a decade.

In 1992, the senior Jones fell ill and retired from the House. Jones ran for his father's 1st District seat as a Democrat, but lost a primary runoff. The next year, he registered as a Republican, feeling he had more in common with the GOP. He ran in the 3rd District in 1994 and was swept into office by the strong Republican tide that year, winning with just less than 53 percent of the vote.

Key Votes

2012	
Extend a Social Security payroll tax cut and unemployment benefits	YES
Ease securities rules to expand small-business access to capital	YES
Extend for one year subsidized student loan interest rates financed by a cut in health care spending	YES
Cite Attorney General Eric H. Holder Jr. for contempt of Congress	YES
Create a visa program for foreign graduates in high-tech fields	NO
Extend most Bush-era income tax rates while allowing rates for top-bracket earners to rise (Jan. 1, 2013)	NO
2011	
Strike funding for F-35 alternative engine	YES
Prevent EPA from regulating greenhouse gas emissions to address climate change	YES
Extend certain provisions of Patriot Act for four years	NO
Declare opposition to use of ground troops in Libya	NO
Overhaul patent law	NO
Pass compromise debt limit increase plan and establish future spending limits	NO
Allow consideration of measures to implement three trade agreements	NO

CQ Vote Studies

	PARTY UNITY		PRESIDENTIAL SUPPORT	
	SUPPORT	OPPOSE	SUPPORT	OPPOSE
2012	65%	35%	36%	64%
2011	65%	35%	30%	70%
2010	72%	28%	51%	49%
2009	71%	29%	36%	64%
2008	77%	23%	37%	63%

Interest Groups

	AFL-CIO	ADA	CCUS	ACU
2012	38%	45%	67%	67%
2011	34%	40%	50%	60%
2010	50%	30%	71%	65%
2009	22%	15%	71%	83%
2008	53%	50%	59%	58%

North Carolina 3

East — Jacksonville, part of Wilmington, Outer Banks

The iconic Cape Hatteras Lighthouse rises from eastern edge of the 3rd in the Outer Banks, protecting ships from some of the Atlantic Ocean's most treacherous shores. Encompassing all or part of 22 counties, the 3rd, following decennial remapping, reaches from the Virginia border south to parts of Wilmington. The GOP-leaning district is nearly three-fourths white, with a mix of farmland, vacation destinations and midsize inland cities.

Three Marine Corps facilities — Camp Lejeune and air stations New River and Cherry Point — are home to nearly 60,000 military personnel. Jacksonville and the rest of eastern North Carolina benefit to the tune of nearly $7 billion in economic activity, but military life makes many residents transient.

Island tourism brings more than $800 million in annual revenue for Dare County, which hosts beachfront properties in Kitty Hawk, Kill Devil Hills and Duck, as well as the tall, sandy dunes of Nags Head. To the south, the 3rd snags downtown Wilmington and its sea port, as well as the University of North Carolina at Wilmington campus.

Farmers harvest flue-cured tobacco, cotton and peanuts in the sandy soil of the coastal plains. Hog farming has become popular in the district's south, stoking concerns about waste pollution in waterways. Education and life sciences are leading employment sectors in Greenville, where the 3rd grabs 62 percent of the population and East Carolina University. The city has evolved from a rural tobacco processing center to a cultural hub.

Major Industry

Military, tourism, agriculture, higher education

Military Bases

Camp Lejeune Marine Corps Base, 42,700 military, 6,200 civilian (2012); Marine Corps Air Station New River, 7,000 military, 300 civilian (2011); Marine Corps Air Station Cherry Point, 9,554 military, 4,578 civilian (2011)

Cities

Wilmington (pt.), Greenville (pt.), Jacksonville, Havelock

Notable

Wilbur and Orville Wright completed four flights at Kill Devil Hills, now a part of the Wright Brothers National Memorial; The infamous pirate Edward Teach, better known as Blackbeard, lived in Hammock House in Beaufort.

Rep. David E. Price (D)

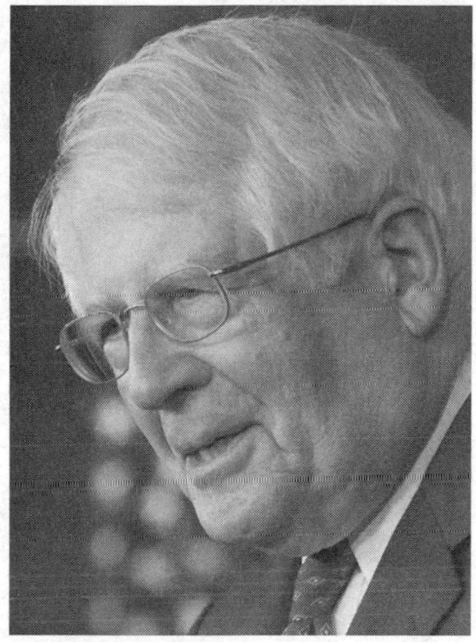

Capitol Office
225-1784
price.house.gov
2162 Rayburn Bldg. 20515-3304; fax 225-2014

Committees
Appropriations

Residence
Chapel Hill

Born
Aug. 17, 1940; Erwin, Tenn.

Religion
Baptist

Family
Wife, Lisa Price; two children

Education
Mars Hill College, attended 1957-59; U. of North Carolina, B.A. 1961 (American history & math); Yale U., B.D. 1964 (theology), Ph.D. 1969 (political science)

Career
Professor

Political Highlights
N.C. Democratic Party chairman, 1983-84; U.S. House, 1987-95; defeated for re-election to U.S. House, 1994

ELECTION RESULTS

2012 GENERAL		
David E. Price (D)	259,534	74.5%
Tim D'Annunzio (R)	88,951	25.5%
2012 PRIMARY		
David E. Price (D)		unopposed
2010 GENERAL		
David E. Price (D)	155,384	57.2%
William "B.J." Lawson (R)	116,448	42.8%

Previous Winning Percentages
2008 (63%); 2006 (65%); 2004 (64%); 2002 (61%); 2000 (62%); 1998 (57%); 1996 (54%); 1992 (65%); 1990 (58%); 1988 (58%); 1986 (56%)

Elected 1986; 13th term

Did not serve 1995-97

Few have studied congressional trends as intently as Price, a former political science professor with a seat on the Appropriations Committee. His take on recent years lines up with the armchair analysis of many fellow Democrats: He blames "the extreme ideology that seems to have taken over the Republican Party" for breakdowns in the legislative process.

Price's up-close study of Washington started in the 1960s. During summers in graduate school, he worked as an aide to Alaska Democratic Sen. Bob Bartlett, and with his boss opening doors, he interviewed a third of the Senate. His doctoral dissertation was about legislative initiative in that chamber. Price settled in as a professor at Duke University in the 1970s and became increasingly involved in party politics. He eventually chaired the North Carolina Democratic Party in the 1980s and won election to the House in 1986.

In 1992 he published "The Congressional Experience," his book describing working conditions and political realities facing lawmakers. He has updated it several times since, offering his interpretation of the shifting balance of power between committees and party leaders.

Price seemed ready for another update in the 112th Congress (2011-12). He chaired the Homeland Security Appropriations Subcommittee in the 110th and 111th Congresses (2007-10) and he has stayed on as its top Democrat. Spending panels are reputed as being less partisan than other committees, but Price said policy provisions that conservative Republicans attached to the fiscal 2013 homeland bill spoiled the end product.

"It hit the floor, and a bunch of highly irresponsible immigration amendments were added to the bill," he said. "Instead of rolling their eyes, leadership actually carried the amendments. In two or three hours' time, they wrecked many months of work and ended up with a partisan division." Only 17 House Democrats voted for the bill, and Price wasn't among them.

Price has shown concern for securing the border. In 2010, he shepherded through Congress a law that provided $600 million to beef up patrol activity along the Mexico border with new personnel and equipment. In an oversight capacity, he highlighted the ways that various agencies interact in trying to prevent gun smuggling across the border. But he also supports the Obama administration's discretionary enforcement of immigration law, defending as cost-effective the directives to slow or stop prosecutions of certain classes of illegal immigrants.

He resisted attempts by Republican leaders in 2011 to put additions to the Federal Emergency Management Agency's Disaster Relief Fund on budget. The "emergency spending" designation for such bills eliminates the need to find budgetary offsets under pay-as-you-go spending rules; requiring an offset would be a "radical departure" from past practice, he said on the floor in 2011. Price also protested any cuts to FEMA grants for first-responders.

As lawmakers studied spending related to Superstorm Sandy recovery in 2013, Price made the case for boosting infrastructure projects meant to mitigate damage from storms and other disasters. "We can't continue just to make investments in rebuilding after an event occurs, we must pay equal attention to preventing damage from occurring in the first place," he said.

There was no Homeland Security Subcommittee when Price joined the Appropriations panel in his third term. Most of his attention back then went to education and science, two areas of importance to the Research Triangle constituents in his district. Over the years he has steered tens of millions of dollars to research centers back home. He also helped secure $40 million in the 2009 stimulus law for North Carolina's new National Guard Headquarters and State Emergency Operations Center in Raleigh.

Price says congressional discord is linked in part to the Supreme Court's 2010 Citizens United ruling, which paved the way for super PACs — advocacy groups independent of campaigns that can accept unrestricted donations from individuals or organizations. Price introduced a bill in the 112th Congress to require super PACs to list their top five donors in broadcast advertisements. It was Price who worked on the "stand by your ad" provision in the 2002 campaign finance overhaul law. It requires candidates to include their approval of a message in broadcast advertisements.

Price supports public financing of campaigns, and he introduced bills in 2012 and 2013 to establish such a system. He also sponsored 2011 legislation meant to make the Presidential Election Campaign Fund program more attractive to candidates.

His interest in the workings of government has an international component. Price and California Republican David Dreier participated in a 1990s task force assisting legislatures in new European democracies. In 2005 they oversaw creation of what is now the House Democracy Partnership, which assists legislatures in emerging democracies through peer-to-peer relationships.

Price was born and raised in the town of Erwin in eastern Tennessee. His father was the local high school principal, while his mother was an English teacher. He earned an undergraduate degree from the University of North Carolina, then went to Yale University for more study, earning political science and divinity degrees.

In addition to his state party work, in 1985 he was a founding member of the national Democratic Leadership Council, a now-defunct group of moderates trying to steer the party toward the center of the political spectrum. (Price does not belong to any major House faction, but he consistently backs abortion rights, environmental protection and other standard party positions.)

The contacts Price made helped him raise money and attract supporters for a successful House race in 1986. He beat out three opponents for the Democratic nomination, then ousted freshman Republican Bill Cobey by 12 points.

He won re-election three times by comfortable margins, but he lost to former Raleigh Police Chief Fred Heineman by 1,215 votes in the GOP landslide of 1994. Price avenged that defeat in 1996, waging an aggressive campaign that emphasized door-to-door canvassing. He won by almost 11 points and has prevailed easily in subsequent elections.

A new congressional map for 2012 substantially altered the 4th District — it now has all of Raleigh, but none of Durham. The changes posed no problems for Price, who secured his most commanding victory to date.

Key Votes

2012	
Extend a Social Security payroll tax cut and unemployment benefits	YES
Ease securities rules to expand small-business access to capital	YES
Extend for one year subsidized student loan interest rates financed by a cut in health care spending	NO
Cite Attorney General Eric H. Holder Jr. for contempt of Congress	?
Create a visa program for foreign graduates in high-tech fields	NO
Extend most Bush-era income tax rates while allowing rates for top-bracket earners to rise (Jan. 1, 2013)	YES
2011	
Strike funding for F-35 alternative engine	NO
Prevent EPA from regulating greenhouse gas emissions to address climate change	NO
Extend certain provisions of Patriot Act for four years	NO
Declare opposition to use of ground troops in Libya	NO
Overhaul patent law	YES
Pass compromise debt limit increase plan and establish future spending limits	NO
Allow consideration of measures to implement three trade agreements	NO

CQ Vote Studies

	PARTY UNITY		PRESIDENTIAL SUPPORT	
	SUPPORT	OPPOSE	SUPPORT	OPPOSE
2012	97%	3%	90%	10%
2011	96%	4%	91%	9%
2010	99%	1%	95%	5%
2009	100%	0%	97%	3%
2008	99%	1%	14%	86%

Interest Groups

	AFL-CIO	ADA	CCUS	ACU
2012	95%	90%	25%	4%
2011	90%	80%	38%	4%
2010	100%	95%	25%	0%
2009	100%	100%	33%	0%
2008	100%	100%	61%	0%

North Carolina 4

Central — parts of Raleigh, Chapel Hill and Fayetteville

The 4th District links part of the technology and research corridor of Interstate 40 with defense-centered Fayetteville, grabbing a few piedmont manufacturing towns along the way.

The district's economic epicenter runs along the stretch of highway that connects Raleigh, Durham and Chapel Hill. The 4th includes Research Triangle Park, a medical and technological research park created in the 1950s to diversify the state's economy beyond the traditional tobacco and textile industries. Spread over 7,000 acres, the park employs about 38,000 at companies such as IBM, Cisco and GlaxoSmithKline.

The University of North Carolina at Chapel Hill and North Carolina State University in Raleigh add to the district's brain trust, although it lost Tobacco Road rival Duke University to the 1st during decennial remapping. In addition to its 29,000 student body, UNC pumps up the district's economy with a large hospital system that includes the university's medical school.

The state capital, Raleigh, nearly doubled in population from 2000 to 2010 on the strength of its health care and professional services industries. The state government employs nearly 25,000.

Burlington (shared with the 6th), at the district's far western edge, includes manufacturing plants. Part of Fayetteville is connected to the district by a long tail to the south that winds through the piedmont forests and farms. Fort Bragg in the nearby 2nd brings defense contractors to the city.

Although Durham's large black population was shifted into the 1st District, the 4th remains one of the strongest Democratic seats in the Tar Heel State. In the 2012 presidential race, Barack Obama gathered more votes in the 4th than in any other district statewide and bested GOP nominee Mitt Romney by 44 percentage points.

Major Industry
Higher education, health care, technology, government

Cities
Raleigh (pt.), Fayetteville (pt.), Chapel Hill, Burlington (pt.)

Notable
The Morehead Planetarium and Science Center in Chapel Hill trained early astronauts in celestial navigation.

Rep. Virginia Foxx (R)

Capitol Office
225-2071
foxx.house.gov
2350 Rayburn Bldg. 20515-3305; fax 225-2995

Committees
Education & the Workforce
(Higher Education & Workforce Training - Chairwoman)
Rules

Residence
Watauga County

Born
June 29, 1943; Bronx, N.Y.

Religion
Roman Catholic

Family
Husband, Tom Foxx; one child

Education
Lees-McRae College, attended 1961; Appalachian State Teachers' College, attended 1962-63; U. of North Carolina, B.A. 1968 (English), M.A.C.T. 1972 (sociology); U. of North Carolina, Greensboro, Ed.D. 1985 (curriculum and teaching/higher education)

Career
Community college president; nursery and landscaping company owner; state government official; professor; secretary

Political Highlights
Candidate for Watauga County Board of Education, 1974; Watauga County Board of Education, 1977-89; N.C. Senate, 1995-2004

ELECTION RESULTS

2012 GENERAL		
Virginia Foxx (R)	200,945	57.5%
Elisabeth Motsinger (D)	148,252	42.5%
2012 PRIMARY		
Virginia Foxx (R)		unopposed
2010 GENERAL		
Virginia Foxx (R)	140,525	65.9%
Billy Kennedy (D)	72,762	34.1%

Previous Winning Percentages
2008 (58%); 2006 (57%); 2004 (59%)

Elected 2004; 5th term

What the Bible says about industriousness, Foxx takes to heart. Her hands-on approach to the legislative process, conservative messaging and campaign operations makes her highly visible and a target of liberal commentators.

Foxx shows few signs of slowing down as she enters her eighth decade, and she credits her faith. "I do believe that God has led me to where I am," said Foxx, who attends weekly bipartisan prayer meetings and Bible study sessions when in Washington. "I get great strength from my faith, and I feel really nourished in this job. I frankly don't understand how people who don't have a strong faith can operate."

Republicans looked to capitalize on her energy by making her vice chairwoman of grass-roots development for the National Republican Congressional Committee in the 2012 campaign cycle. And late in 2012, Foxx was chosen by colleagues as GOP Conference secretary for the 113th Congress (2013-14), making her No. 6 on the party's leadership team.

Foxx also has faith in government, stating that reports of dysfunction are overblown. "One of the things that I wish people understood is that the system works," she said. Since the 111th Congress (2009-10), Foxx has served on the Rules Committee, which sets the parameters for floor debate.

That assignment offers opportunities to comment on almost any issue, and Foxx hasn't been bashful. In a speech about the health care overhaul bill in late 2009, Foxx said the legislation was a greater threat than terrorism. In April that same year, she said Democrats had a "tar baby on their hands," as their 2009 stimulus law apparently allowed bonuses for executives of corporations that had received government bailouts. "We have to be careful how we say things," Foxx says. "But certainly I feel very strongly about my beliefs."

Foxx is a member of the Education and the Workforce Committee, where her beliefs are informed by professional experience. Her political career began with a dozen years on the Watauga County Board of Education. She worked as an assistant dean of Appalachian State University, a college instructor and president of Mayland Community College. Since 2011, she has been the chairwoman of the Subcommittee on Higher Education and Workforce Training.

In that role she has overseen development of a reauthorization of worker training programs. In 2012, the full committee approved her bill to update the 1998 law governing such programs. It would have consolidated a number of the programs into one large jobs-training block grant and given local stakeholders more input into the skills and training those programs should try to deliver. Democrats said the changes would divert funding from underserved populations, such as the homeless or veterans.

Foxx introduced an updated version of that bill in 2013 — after President Barack Obama used his State of the Union address to criticize a confusing web of job training programs. The bill was quickly marked up, approved and passed by the House, but not without controversy. Democrats on the Education and the Workforce panel publicly accused Foxx and other Republicans of denying requests for bipartisan negotiations on the measure, and they walked out of a markup. The White House also panned the bill.

Foxx figures to have a hand in reauthorizing higher education programs, which expire at the end of 2013. "We put more and more resources in, but now we have to focus on the other side, and that's how you hold down the cost," she said. Foxx wants to provide incentives for colleges and universities to keep tuition lower and to stabilize the federal student loan program and Pell grants, the latter of which face a $6 billion shortfall in fiscal 2014.

By Foxx's estimation, community colleges and for-profit colleges can be a big part of the solution. She believes such schools, unlike public universities, have the flexibility to innovate and quickly adapt to local needs.

To that end, Foxx has been a leader in efforts to roll back regulations designed to put a tighter leash on for-profit colleges, some of which have come under intense scrutiny for deceitful marketing and recr=uiting practices, as well high student loan debt and dropout rates.

In 2012, the House passed a Foxx bill to rescind the Education Department's regulation defining credit hours and its rules on granting a college or university permission to operate within a state. She has also backed amendments to block "gainful employment" regulations that eliminate federal financial aid for programs in which high proportions of graduates are not repaying their student loans or end up with excessive debt loads relative to their salaries.

Appearing on a syndicated radio show in April 2012, Foxx said she had "very little tolerance for people who tell me that they graduate with $200,000 of debt or even $80,000 of debt, because there's no reason for that." She recounted her own experience of working her way through school over seven years. Democrats, including Obama, tore into the remarks as callous.

Foxx has found bipartisan support for her effort to eliminate "unfunded mandates," regulations that ultimately impose compliance costs on states, local governments and individuals. California Democrat Loretta Sanchez cosponsored Foxx's 2013 bill to require all federal agencies to report on the potential costs of their new rules.

Foxx belongs to the conservative Republican Study Committee and almost always votes with a majority of her party — although she opposes trade agreements if she feels they threaten industries in her district, such as textile plants. She is a staunch social conservative.

The granddaughter of Italian immigrants, Foxx grew up poor. Her family's home had no running water or electricity until she was a teenager. She took an after-school job as a janitor at her high school. As she was sweeping floors one day, a teacher told her she was smart and needed to go to college, marry a college man and get out of town.

Foxx did all three. She earned her bachelor's and advanced degrees from the University of North Carolina. In addition to her work in education, she and her husband, Tom Foxx, started a successful nursery and landscaping business. Foxx served for a decade in the state Senate after leaving Mayland.

When Republican Rep. Richard M. Burr decided to run for the Senate in 2004, Foxx entered the race to succeed him. She prevailed over seven other Republicans in the primary and went on to beat Democrat Jim A. Harrell in November. At age 61, she was one of the oldest members of the freshman class. Her re-elections have been fairly easy.

Key Votes

2012	
Extend a Social Security payroll tax cut and unemployment benefits	NO
Ease securities rules to expand small-business access to capital	YES
Extend for one year subsidized student loan interest rates financed by a cut in health care spending	NO
Cite Attorney General Eric H. Holder Jr. for contempt of Congress	YES
Create a visa program for foreign graduates in high-tech fields	YES
Extend most Bush-era income tax rates while allowing rates for top-bracket earners to rise (Jan. 1, 2013)	NO
2011	
Strike funding for F-35 alternative engine	NO
Prevent EPA from regulating greenhouse gas emissions to address climate change	YES
Extend certain provisions of Patriot Act for four years	YES
Declare opposition to use of ground troops in Libya	YES
Overhaul patent law	YES
Pass compromise debt limit increase plan and establish future spending limits	YES
Allow consideration of measures to implement three trade agreements	YES

CQ Vote Studies

	PARTY UNITY		PRESIDENTIAL SUPPORT	
	SUPPORT	OPPOSE	SUPPORT	OPPOSE
2012	97%	3%	11%	89%
2011	96%	4%	15%	85%
2010	99%	1%	26%	74%
2009	99%	1%	10%	90%
2008	97%	3%	84%	16%

Interest Groups

	AFL-CIO	ADA	CCUS	ACU
2012	10%	5%	83%	92%
2011	3%	10%	94%	88%
2010	7%	5%	75%	100%
2009	5%	0%	73%	100%
2008	7%	5%	78%	100%

North Carolina 5

Northwest — Winston-Salem suburbs, Hickory, Statesville

The 5th sweeps west from Winston-Salem and the piedmont's rolling hills to the Tennessee border and the Blue Ridge Mountains. The district is largely rural and includes some small manufacturing towns.

Much of the 5th revolves around Winston-Salem and its suburbs, where tobacco once was an economic driver. R.J. Reynolds Tobacco still calls the area home — its largest plant is in Tobaccoville and the headquarters is in the 12th — but the region now relies more heavily on banking and health care. BB&T and Wells Fargo have corporate offices in Winston-Salem; Wake Forest University's medical center is a major employer.

Several towns surrounding Winston-Salem are more dependent on manufacturing and distribution — tires, food products and textiles are made here — and were hit hard by years of economic downturn. Unemployment in Forsyth County hovers around 9 percent.

With the decline of the tobacco industry, some tobacco producers have converted their farms into vineyards. The Yadkin Valley wine region, which includes more than 30 wineries, has become a tourist destination. Christmas tree farming is also popular in the district's western towns. The Fraser fir is native to North Carolina's southern Appalachian Mountains. Boone is home to Appalachian State University, and education and entertainment industries provide employment here, but local officials hope to designate a stretch of woodlands near Blowing Rock as the Grandfather National Scenic Area to draw more tourists.

The 5th is solid GOP territory. After decennial remapping, the 5th took in more land near Winston-Salem considered friendly to Democrats, but in 2012 every county here supported Republican Pat McCrory for governor and all but one (Catawba County) backed Mitt Romney for president.

Major Industry
Health care, finance, manufacturing

Cities
Winston-Salem (pt.), Statesville, Kernersville

Notable
First organized in 1924, Union Grove's Old Time Fiddlers' Convention (now called the Ole Time Fiddlers' and Bluegrass Festival) is the nation's longest-running bluegrass festival.

Rep. Howard Coble (R)

Capitol Office
225-3065
coble.house.gov
2188 Rayburn Bldg. 20515-3306, fax 225-8611

Committees
Judiciary
(Courts, Intellectual Property & the Internet - Chairman)
Transportation & Infrastructure

Residence
Greensboro

Born
March 18, 1931; Greensboro, N.C.

Religion
Presbyterian

Family
Single

Education
Appalachian State Teachers' College, attended 1949-50 (history); Guilford College, A.B. 1958 (history); U. of North Carolina, J.D. 1962

Military
Coast Guard, 1952-56; Coast Guard Reserve, 1960-82; Coast Guard, 1977-78

Career
Lawyer; insurance claims supervisor

Political Highlights
N.C. House, 1969-70; assistant U.S. attorney, 1969-73; N.C. Department of Revenue secretary, 1973-77; Republican nominee for N.C. treasurer, 1976; N.C. House, 1979-84

ELECTION RESULTS

2012 GENERAL		
Howard Coble (R)	222,116	60.9%
Tony Foriest (D)	142,467	39.1%
2012 PRIMARY		
Howard Coble (R)	50,701	57.3%
Bill Flynn (R)	19,741	22.3%
Billy Yow (R)	18,057	20.4%

Previous Winning Percentages
2010 (75%); 2008 (67%); 2006 (71%); 2004 (73%); 2002 (90%); 2000 (91%); 1998 (89%); 1996 (73%); 1994 (100%); 1992 (71%); 1990 (67%); 1988 (62%); 1986 (50%); 1984 (51%)

Elected 1984; 15th term

Coble zestfully chaired the Judiciary panel on intellectual property from 1997 through 2002. As his reign was ending, a Hollywood Reporter columnist wrote that "more significant legislation with a direct impact on Hollywood moved through his subcommittee than at any time since 1976." He is back on the job a decade later, as the Internet and digital media have produced a new set of challenges to address.

On the surface, Coble doesn't seem like someone who would have a particular interest in technology-fueled disputes. He is in his 80s, and he has a persona like Ben Matlock, if Ben Matlock were a prosecutor. Still, he loves debating IP law. In his first run as chairman, he oversaw enactment of a landmark measure to augment copyright protection for digital works — and shield Internet service providers from liability for copyright violations committed by their customers. Another law extended the length of copyrights.

Coble's detractors from that era cast him as favoring corporate interests, and he has backed strong copyright protections, which are anathema to many people raised in the Internet era. In 2013, he and California Democrat Judy Chu formed the Creative Rights Caucus, and in doing so Coble praised the film industry for creating jobs in North Carolina.

But Coble also has a deep respect for artists, particularly musicians. The walls of his D.C. office hold requisite political snapshots, but also the mugs of bluegrass and country stars like Earl Scruggs, Grandpa Jones, Lyle Lovett and Garth Brooks. If he could select a different career, he'd pick a banjo or play the fiddle in a bluegrass band. "I can't play anything but the radio," he laments. Coble met Scruggs during his earlier run as chairman, and he says that one of the highlights of his congressional career was helping to present Scruggs with a lifetime achievement award at the 2008 Grammys.

A provision inserted into a 1999 law under Coble's watch classified recordings as "work for hire," which eliminated the ability of artists to eventually take control of original master recordings. Musicians were incensed, but they later applauded Coble for working to reverse the change the next year.

Coble also is charged with overseeing implementation of a 2011 overhaul of patent law. His first hearing in 2013 examined "patent trolls," the people or companies who allegedly use patent litigation to stifle competition.

Coble has served on the Judiciary Committee his entire House career. In the 112th Congress (2011-12) he chaired the Courts, Commercial and Administrative Law panel. The House passed his bill to prevent states from collecting income taxes from people who work fewer than 30 days a year in their jurisdiction; he said it was needed to eliminate a web of filing requirements for the mobile, modern workforce. The measure was re-introduced in 2013.

He has been on the Transportation and Infrastructure Committee since 1995. He has gladly steered tens of millions of dollars to his district over the years for various infrastructure projects. "Earmarks that are properly handled, I find them not offensive at all," he said. But the practice has been excoriated by some conservatives and banned by the House GOP.

Other kinds of federal spending have brought out the skeptic in Coble. In his first term — during the Reagan administration — he started a crusade against congressional and executive branch pensions. He has called them a "taxpayer rip-off" and declined the pension for himself. "It may have been naive on my part," he said in 2012. Coble has seen estimates that declining the pension may have cost him $1 million, and he called the decision the "biggest regret" of his career.

Despite the cost to his bank account, that campaign and its underlying ethic helped earn him the rating of "Taxpayer Hero" for 16 years from the Council for Citizens Against Government Waste, a group that fights federal spending. Coble has sponsored and voted for numerous measures that tried to scale back his colleagues' pensions, and he has taken his message everywhere from congressional committee rooms to a segment on the news show "20/20."

"All of these past efforts died quickly and quietly," he testified to a House panel in 2012, but he continues to try. Coble joined the Tea Party Caucus in 2010, and the American Conservative Union has given him high marks in its legislative scoring throughout his career.

But the tea party movement, with its anti-establishment undertones, has sometimes picked on Coble. He was elected for years from his strongly Republican district with no challengers in primary elections, but upstarts filed to run against him in 2010 and 2012.

Coble proudly describes himself as "old school" but has adapted to the times, somewhat. He allowed his campaign staff to launch a Facebook page in 2010 but drew the line at Twitter. "I'm too long in the tooth to tweet," he told the High Point Enterprise. He also isn't wrapped up in the perceived death match between Republicans and Democrats: "We live in a republic with only two major parties," he said. "There's going to be partisanship." He doesn't do much fundraising for the GOP, saying it takes away from his district time.

That reluctance to fill the party coffers, according to Coble, is what keeps him from holding the gavel of the Judiciary Committee. High-profile dissents with Republican positions might have contributed as well. Coble consistently supports federal funding for stem cell research; he urged a speedier withdrawal of troops from Iraq; and he votes against trade deals that he thinks might threaten the textile or manufacturing industries in his district (most recently a South Korea pact in 2011).

He was born in Greensboro to parents who had little formal education. His father spent 44 years working at the Belk department store chain, starting as a floor sweeper and working his way up to manager of the Greensboro store.

Coble built a career as a federal prosecutor before being appointed the state's chief tax collector in the mid-1970s. In 1984, after four years as a state representative, he earned a 164-vote GOP primary victory and the right to face freshman Democratic Rep. Robin Britt. Coble stressed his fiscal conservatism while painting Britt as an extravagant liberal. Coble won by 2,662 votes.

There was speculation that Coble might step aside after the 112th Congress, given his age and tea party challengers. "When it comes time to retire, I'd like to voluntarily retire rather than get kicked out," he said. In early 2013, Coble missed some votes when he was hospitalized following a series of dizzy spells. He vowed to improve his eating habits.

Key Votes

2012	
Extend a Social Security payroll tax cut and unemployment benefits	YES
Ease securities rules to expand small-business access to capital	YES
Extend for one year subsidized student loan interest rates financed by a cut in health care spending	NO
Cite Attorney General Eric H. Holder Jr. for contempt of Congress	YES
Create a visa program for foreign graduates in high-tech fields	YES
Extend most Bush-era income tax rates while allowing rates for top-bracket earners to rise (Jan. 1, 2013)	YES
2011	
Strike funding for F-35 alternative engine	YES
Prevent EPA from regulating greenhouse gas emissions to address climate change	YES
Extend certain provisions of Patriot Act for four years	YES
Declare opposition to use of ground troops in Libya	YES
Overhaul patent law	YES
Pass compromise debt limit increase plan and establish future spending limits	YES
Allow consideration of measures to implement three trade agreements	YES

CQ Vote Studies

	PARTY UNITY		PRESIDENTIAL SUPPORT	
	SUPPORT	OPPOSE	SUPPORT	OPPOSE
2012	96%	4%	22%	78%
2011	93%	7%	17%	83%
2010	97%	3%	27%	73%
2009	95%	5%	23%	77%
2008	96%	4%	65%	35%

Interest Groups

	AFL-CIO	ADA	CCUS	ACU
2012	21%	5%	100%	91%
2011	4%	15%	93%	87%
2010	7%	5%	100%	96%
2009	10%	5%	80%	96%
2008	13%	20%	89%	88%

North Carolina 6

North central — parts of Greensboro, High Point and Burlington

The Piedmont Triad, a distribution and manufacturing region around Greensboro and High Point, remains the focal point of the 6th. Decennial redistricting, however, flipped its footprint out of central North Carolina and into several rural counties along the Virginia border. It now runs through tobacco country from Kerr Lake to Mount Airy, the childhood home of Andy Griffith and the inspiration for television's Mayberry.

A wealth of transportation resources in the southern part of the district — including several interstate highways, freight rail and the Piedmont Triad International Airport — has helped the area grow as a logistics center. FedEx, with air and ground hubs near Greensboro, is a major employer. Although industrial manufacturing remains important in this part of the district — buses, airplanes and tractor-trailers are built here — health care has made inroads in the workforce and helped diversify the economy.

The traditional industries of tobacco and textiles continue to play a role in Greensboro, the state's third-most populous city. Lorillard Tobacco, the nation's third-largest tobacco company, and International Textile Group, a fabrics conglomerate, are located here, but their ability to prop up the economy has waned. High Point, which the 6th shares with the 12th District, remains a furniture manufacturing center; foreign competition, however, has shrunk its profile.

Greensboro and High Point each have large minority populations, but the 6th was drawn to exclude them and is roughly three-fourths white. Three counties partially in the 6th — Durham, Guilford and Orange — supported Democrat Walter H. Dalton in the 2012 gubernatorial race, and portions of Durham and Granville counties backed Barack Obama in the presidential race; the district overall is conservative and gave GOP presidential nominee Mitt Romney a 17-percentage-point win in the 2012 election.

Major Industry
Distribution, health care, manufacturing, tobacco

Cities
Greensboro (pt.), High Point (pt.), Burlington (pt.)

Notable
The last battle of the War of Regulation, a failed rebellion of North Carolina farmers against colonial officials, took place in Alamance in 1771.

Rep. Mike McIntyre (D)

Capitol Office
225-2731
mcintyre.house.gov
2428 Rayburn Bldg. 20515-3307; fax 225-5773

Committees
Agriculture
Armed Services

Residence
Lumberton

Born
Aug. 6, 1956; Lumberton, N.C.

Religion
Presbyterian

Family
Wife, Dee McIntyre; two children

Education
U. of North Carolina, B.A. 1978 (political science), J.D. 1981

Career
Lawyer

Political Highlights
No previous office

ELECTION RESULTS

2012 GENERAL		
Mike McIntyre (D)	168,695	50.1%
David Rouzer (R)	168,041	49.9%
2012 PRIMARY		
Mike McIntyre (D)		unopposed
2010 GENERAL		
Mike McIntyre (D)	113,957	53.7%
Ilario Pantano (R)	98,328	46.3%

Previous Winning Percentages
2008 (69%); 2006 (73%); 2004 (73%); 2002 (71%); 2000 (70%); 1998 (91%); 1996 (53%)

Elected 1996; 9th term

It's safe to call McIntyre a conservative Southern Democrat. However, he chooses to describe his record in nonpartisan terms. "My votes have continued to be reflective of judging the issues on their merit and being right down the middle," he says.

McIntyre has always been a moderate, but now it's a matter of survival. With control of North Carolina's redistricting process, the GOP targeted McIntyre in 2012 by packing the redrawn 7th District with Republicans and cutting out most of McIntyre's home county. GOP state Sen. David Rouzer did his best, but McIntyre had a strong showing with independent voters. He won by 654 votes, even as Republican Mitt Romney won the district's presidential vote by 19 points.

If McIntyre can't hold on to the seat in 2014 — Rouzer is angling for a rematch — it's hard to imagine a Democrat who could. He holds senior positions on committees of crucial interest to the state's economy, he is culturally attuned to his constituents, and he makes efforts to reach across the aisle.

On matters of national defense, agriculture and the regulatory environment, McIntyre often agrees with the Republican point of view. He'll stand with Democrats on education policy, labor causes and protecting Social Security and Medicare. "My first and last question on any issue has always been, 'How will this affect the folks back home?'" he says.

The folks back home are fiscally and socially conservative, and McIntyre has them covered on both counts. Since his first days in Congress, he has belonged to the fiscally conservative Blue Dog Coalition. In 2011, he was one of 25 Democrats in the House to vote for a balanced budget amendment to the Constitution, and one of four to vote for a resolution of disapproval when President Barack Obama requested an increase to the federal debt limit.

McIntyre opposes abortion and has voted to restrict federal funding of insurance plans that cover it. The National Rifle Association endorsed him in 2012, and he opposes the idea of providing a path to citizenship for illegal immigrants. He also has a spiritual side — McIntyre co-chairs the Congressional Prayer Caucus with Virginia Republican J. Randy Forbes. The group's prayer sessions are "one of the things that helps deal with the polarization" in Congress, according to McIntyre.

Democratic leaders have accepted that McIntyre won't be on board for a lot of their biggest priorities. He voted against the 2010 overhauls of the health care system and financial regulations. He did support the 2009 economic stimulus law, but only after urging that more money be directed to rural areas for water, wastewater and community facilities projects.

Even so, McIntyre has been loyal on a fundamental level. Republicans have asked him about switching sides, but McIntyre has deep roots in the Democratic Party. He was chairman of the Teen Democrats in high school and spent the summer after his junior year at a congressional seminar program in Washington. When he was 16, his father, a city council member, took him to a 1972 victory party for newly elected Rep. Charlie Rose. (He commented at that event that he wanted to be in Congress one day.)

McIntyre was standing at the back of the room when White House lawyer John Dean testified before the Senate Watergate Committee, which was chaired by North Carolina's legendary Democrat Sam J. Ervin Jr. The next summer, he worked as an intern in Rose's office. At the University of North Carolina, he was vice president of the campus chapter of college Democrats. He later was an organizer of the Robeson County Young Democrats.

For the 113th Congress (2013-14), McIntyre is the No. 2 Democrat on the

Agriculture Committee and No. 3 on Armed Services. Both panels are important to his district; many constituents have ties to farming or the military.

He is the top Democrat on the Armed Services Subcommittee on Seapower and Projection Forces, and in the 113th Congress he is serving alongside a new chairman — Forbes. McIntyre says the Pentagon has already taken enough hits in the recent spate of budget cuts, and he expresses the concern that the country's shipbuilding capacity has been hollowed out by unsteady production. McIntyre fights for multiyear procurement authority for new submarines and destroyers.

He no longer has a major military installation in his district, but Fort Bragg and Camp Lejeune are both nearby.

On the Agriculture Committee, McIntyre has tried to limit the regulatory burden on farmers. He joined with Republicans in the 112th Congress (2011-12) on legislation to prevent both new EPA regulation of farm dust and new permitting requirements for pesticides. As the panel considered a reauthorization of federal farm programs in 2012, McIntyre focused on keeping crop insurance programs favorable for the growers in his district.

In the early 2000s, McIntyre developed a plan to buy out tobacco growers. From 2003 through 2006, he was the top Democrat on the Agriculture panel with jurisdiction over tobacco programs, and he helped push a $10 billion tobacco buyout bill to enactment in 2004. But he opposed the 2009 law giving the Food and Drug Administration power to regulate tobacco.

Some agriculture-minded lawmakers tout free-trade agreements as a way to open markets to U.S. farmers, but McIntyre is not among them. He has business-friendly impulses and belongs to the New Democrat Coalition, but he watched the area's textile industry crumble following implementation of the North American Free Trade Agreement. McIntyre votes against free-trade agreements before Congress and has introduced a quixotic bill to withdraw the United States from NAFTA.

McIntyre was born and raised in Lumberton. His father was an optometrist and his mother was a bank branch manager. After graduating from law school at UNC, he was involved in community, church, civic and professional activities as he built a law practice. Among those activities was coaching his sons. The co-chair of the Congressional Caucus on Youth Sports, McIntyre in 2012 was chosen for induction into the Robeson County Sports Hall of Fame.

When Rose announced his retirement in 1996, McIntyre was one of seven Democrats to enter the primary. He took 23 percent of the vote, finishing second, then won the runoff. He beat Bill Caster, a Republican New Hanover County commissioner, in the general election. He had fairly easy re-elections until the strong Republican year of 2010.

Key Votes

2012	
Extend a Social Security payroll tax cut and unemployment benefits	YES
Ease securities rules to expand small-business access to capital	YES
Extend for one year subsidized student loan interest rates financed by a cut in health care spending	YES
Cite Attorney General Eric H. Holder Jr. for contempt of Congress	YES
Create a visa program for foreign graduates in high-tech fields	YES
Extend most Bush-era income tax rates while allowing rates for top-bracket earners to rise (Jan. 1, 2013)	NO
2011	
Strike funding for F-35 alternative engine	NO
Prevent EPA from regulating greenhouse gas emissions to address climate change	YES
Extend certain provisions of Patriot Act for four years	YES
Declare opposition to use of ground troops in Libya	YES
Overhaul patent law	YES
Pass compromise debt limit increase plan and establish future spending limits	NO
Allow consideration of measures to implement three trade agreements	NO

CQ Vote Studies

	PARTY UNITY		PRESIDENTIAL SUPPORT	
	SUPPORT	OPPOSE	SUPPORT	OPPOSE
2012	48%	52%	18%	82%
2011	66%	34%	50%	50%
2010	70%	30%	64%	36%
2009	83%	17%	82%	18%
2008	89%	11%	17%	83%

Interest Groups

	AFL-CIO	ADA	CCUS	ACU
2012	60%	10%	100%	60%
2011	62%	50%	75%	40%
2010	57%	35%	75%	38%
2009	76%	50%	80%	38%
2008	93%	85%	61%	32%

North Carolina 7

Southeast — most of Wilmington, Smithfield

The 7th expands north from the Cape Fear region in the state's southeastern corner and takes in farmland and a few small manufacturing towns. It is largely dominated by Wilmington, a historic port city, and a surrounding group of fast-growing coastal communities.

While the 3rd District covers Wilmington's historic downtown, the 7th represents its beach-oriented communities that are increasingly popular retirement spots. Health care is an important industry here, as is the entertainment sector. Studios located in the neighboring 3rd have filmed a number of television series and movies in the area, giving the regional economy a cut of hundreds of millions of dollars in revenue.

Towns dotting the district's Atlantic coast depend on tourism and commercial fishing. A pre-recession housing boom gobbled up prime real estate and forced the closure of some waterfront seafood wholesalers, but a state tax break and growing demand for locally caught seafood has eased some pressures on fisherman. Local marshes are known for high-quality oysters.

Agriculture and manufacturing remain dominant in the 7th's rural counties. Here, farmers grow tobacco, soybeans, sweet potatoes and peanuts. Food processing is also a major employer. Sampson and Columbus counties have some of the highest poverty rates in the state, but the district's northernmost residents are relatively well off and highly educated. Many commute to work to technology jobs in the nearby Research Triangle Park.

During decennial remapping, the 7th was drawn with an expected GOP lean, but it has divided tendencies: In one of the closest U.S. House races in 2012, the 7th re-elected Democratic Rep. Mike McIntyre, but also backed GOP presidential nominee Mitt Romney with 59 percent. Columbus, Bladen, Robeson and Hoke counties provide most of the Democratic votes.

Major Industry
Health care, manufacturing, tourism

Cities
Wilmington (pt.), Raeford (pt.), Clayton

Notable
After the wooden structure was destroyed by Hurricane Fran in 1996, Johnnie Mercer's Pier in Wrightsville Beach was rebuilt with concrete — it is the only such structure in the state.

Rep. Richard Hudson (R)

Capitol Office
225-3715
hudson.house.gov
429 Cannon Bldg. 20515-3308; fax 225-4036

Committees
Agriculture
Education & the Workforce
Homeland Security
(Transportation Security - Chairman)

Residence
Concord

Born
Nov. 4, 1971; Franklin, Va.

Religion
Christian

Family
Wife, Renee Hudson

Education
U. of North Carolina, Charlotte, B.A. 1996 (history & political science)

Career
Communications consulting company president; congressional aide; state party aide; gubernatorial campaign aide

Political Highlights
Rowan-Cabarrus Community College Board of Trustees, 2001-05

ELECTION RESULTS

2012 GENERAL		
Richard Hudson (R)	160,695	53.2%
Larry Kissell (D)	137,139	45.4%
Antonio Blue (WRI)	3,990	1.3%
2012 PRIMARY RUNOFF		
Richard Hudson (R)	10,699	63.6%
Scott Keadle (R)	6,118	36.4%

Elected 2012; 1st term

Hudson was a known commodity to House Republicans, having served as a chief of staff to three of his current colleagues. He apparently made a good impression — he sits on three committees prone to complex policy debates, and he holds the gavel of a panel overseeing one of the most visible functions of government.

Born in Virginia, Hudson grew up in North Carolina. From the time he graduated from UNC Charlotte, he was involved in politics; his first long-term job was as communications director for the state Republican Party. Hudson spent six years as the district director for Rep. Robin Hayes, then headed to Washington to become the chief of staff for Virginia Foxx. He went on to work for Texas Republicans John Carter and K. Michael Conaway. He moved back to North Carolina in 2011.

So the Capitol holds no mysteries for Hudson. He was named the chairman of the Homeland Security Subcommittee on Transportation Security. In his first hearing he outlined several goals, including advancing "risk-based" policies, studying the procurement of security technology, and increasing collaboration with the private sector. He defended a Transportation Security Administration decision to allow passengers to once again carry small knives on planes, but he urged the TSA to be more transparent as it formulates its rules, to avoid public backlash. (The plan was dropped in June 2013.)

Hudson was also placed on the Agriculture and Education and the Workforce committees. He joined the conservative Republican Study Committee.

Redistricting made Democrat Larry Kissell one of the most vulnerable incumbents in 2012, and five Republicans lined up hoping to take him on. Hudson, who knew most of the district from his time working for Hayes, ran 10 points ahead of the nearest challenger in the primary, then easily won the runoff. GOP campaign groups eagerly unleashed attack ads on Kissell, and Hudson won by almost 8 points — avenging Hayes, who lost to Kissell in 2008.

North Carolina 8

South central — Kannapolis, eastern Charlotte suburbs, Lumberton

Redistricting following the 2010 census pushed the 8th northward all the way to the outskirts of High Point. Most of the redesigned district is wedged between Interstates 85 and 74, with a tail extending along the South Carolina border past Lumberton.

The 8th is predominately white, although a large Lumbee Indian population lives in overwhelmingly Democratic Robeson County. Republicans enjoy voter registration advantages in Cabarrus and Union counties near Charlotte. As a whole, the 8th supports the GOP and gave Republican Mitt Romney 58 percent of its presidential vote in 2012.

Once heavily reliant on the textile industry, the neighboring towns of Concord and Kannapolis have been forced to diversify their economies. Pharmaceuticals and glass are now made here, and the Charlotte Motor Speedway brings NASCAR fans to the area. Tourists, who injected more than $300 million into the local economy in 2012, have helped keep unemployment rates in Cabarrus County below the state average. Further north on Interstate 85, Thomasville, known locally as Chair City, retains the legacy of furniture and cabinet making even as the industry has declined across much of the state.

The 8th becomes poorer and more rural to the south, where tobacco and soybean farming are key. Scotland and Robeson counties have some of the lowest education rates and household incomes in the state. Closer to Charlotte, however, Monroe's diverse economy has helped it withstand some of the job losses seen nearby, with health care, construction and metal alloy production providing stable economic sectors.

Redistricting also moved massive Fort Bragg entirely into the 2nd District, although the southern edge of the 8th remains close enough to feel the base's economic and cultural impact.

Major Industry
Manufacturing, agriculture, tourism

Cities
Concord (pt.), Kannapolis, Monroe

Notable
Reed Gold Mine near Midland is the site of the first documented gold discovery in the U.S.

Rep. Robert Pittenger (R)

Capitol Office
225-1976
pittenger.house.gov
224 Cannon Bldg. 20515-3815; fax 225-3389

Committees
Financial Services

Residence
Charlotte

Born
Aug. 15, 1948; Dallas, Texas

Religion
Protestant

Family
Wife, Suzanne Pittenger; four children

Education
U. of Texas, B.A. 1970 (government)

Career
Real estate investor; conservative policy organization fundraiser; youth ministry organization manager

Political Highlights
N.C. Senate, 2003-08; Republican nominee for lieutenant governor, 2008

ELECTION RESULTS

2012 GENERAL		
Robert Pittenger (R)	194,537	51.8%
Jennifer Roberts (D)	171,503	45.6%
Curtis Campbell (LIBERT)	9,650	2.6%
2012 PRIMARY RUNOFF		
Robert Pittenger (R)	18,982	52.9%
James Pendergraph (R)	16,902	47.1%

Elected 2012; 1st term

Pittenger is a deeply spiritual man and an able publicist for political causes. He sits on the Financial Services Committee, which is a boon to the large finance sector in his adopted hometown of Charlotte.

Pittenger grew up in Austin, Texas, and had a religious awakening while attending the University of Texas. During the 1970s, he was a key organizer of Campus Crusade for Christ, an international evangelical movement. In the early 1980s, he found himself in the Washington area as the executive director of the STEP Foundation, a nonprofit attempting to fight inner-city poverty by enlisting the aid of the private sector. He moved to Charlotte in the middle of that decade and established a real estate investment company; as his connections in the business world grew, so did his ties to the Republican Party.

He was elected to the state Senate in 2002, and he established himself as a skillful promoter of his conservative agenda. When he put out the call for doctors to lobby the legislature on tort reform in 2003, more than 3,000 of them showed up. He was not known as a negotiator; in 2008, the Senate's Democratic leader told the Charlotte Observer that Pittenger was "flying solo." He resigned from the Senate to make a bid for the lieutenant governorship.

Pittenger, a member of the Republican Study Committee, favors smaller government: "Those in government are proficient in adding," he says. "They never learned to subtract." He is skeptical of the 2010 financial regulatory overhaul and would like to repeal it; early in 2013, he suggested that the overhaul is stopping community banks from recovering. He also said the economy was being "spoon-fed by the Federal Reserve" and needed to stand on its own.

The retirement of Republican Sue Myrick left the 9th District open in 2012. Eleven people entered the GOP primary. Myrick endorsed former Mecklenburg County sheriff James Pendergraph, but Pittenger had deep pockets (he spent more than $2.2 million on his own campaign) and name recognition. He edged out Pendergraph, then beat Democrat Jennifer Roberts by 6 points.

North Carolina 9

West central — part of Charlotte

The 9th District centers on Charlotte, particularly the mostly white neighborhoods south of downtown. Decennial redistricting dropped much of the 9th's presence in Gaston County, stretching it instead northward along Interstate 77 into most of Iredell County. The 9th also traces Union County down along the South Carolina border. Nearly all the regions in the 9th experienced population growth, among all racial and ethnic groups, between 2000 and 2010.

Most of the district's population lives in well-to-do Mecklenburg County, which has an above-average median household income and the fourth-highest percentage of college graduates in the state, at more than 40 percent. Many residents in this part of the 9th work in downtown Charlotte (called "Uptown," and located in the 12th District) in the financial services and health care industries. The recent recession even hit white-collar workers with layoffs as the banking sector faltered. A billion-dollar lawsuit brought by the federal government against Bank of America continues to cast a shadow over the district.

Lake Norman, the state's largest man-made lake, lies between Huntersville and Mooresville. The former is a wealthy bedroom community that has increased its population by a multiple of 10 since 1990. The massive growth has brought traffic issues, but residents hope a project to widen the interstate will help relieve congestion. National hardware chain Lowe's is based in Mooresville.

Despite the explosive growth of new housing developments, Iredell County remains the state's top producer of cattle and milk cows.

Republicans dominate politics in the 9th. Since the district became oriented around Charlotte prior to the 1968 election, it has been represented in the U.S. House only by Republicans. In the 2012 presidential election, Republican Mitt Romney bested Democrat Barack Obama by 13 percentage points in the 9th, although the race was much closer in the portion of Mecklenburg County in the district.

Major Industry
Finance, retail, manufacturing

Cities
Charlotte (pt.), Huntersville, Mooresville, Matthews

Notable
Mooresville is home to several NASCAR teams and the North Carolina Auto Racing Hall of Fame, which services as the official visitors' center for the town.

Rep. Patrick T. McHenry (R)

Capitol Office
225-2576
mchenry.house.gov
2334 Rayburn Bldg. 20515-3310; fax 225-0316

Committees
Financial Services
(Oversight & Investigations - Chairman)
Oversight & Government Reform

Residence
Cherryville

Born
Oct. 22, 1975; Charlotte, N.C.

Religion
Roman Catholic

Family
Wife, Giulia McHenry

Education
North Carolina State U., attended 1994-97; Belmont Abbey College, B.A. 2000 (history)

Career
Real estate broker; U.S. Labor Department special assistant, campaign aide and political consultant

Political Highlights
Republican nominee for N.C. House, 1998; N.C. House, 2003-04

ELECTION RESULTS

2012 GENERAL		
Patrick T. McHenry (R)	190,826	57.0%
Patsy Keever (D)	144,023	43.0%
2012 PRIMARY		
Patrick T. McHenry (R)	58,844	72.5%
Ken H. Fortenberry (R)	15,936	19.6%
Don Peterson (R)	6,337	7.8%
2010 GENERAL		
Patrick T. McHenry (R)	130,813	71.2%
Jeff Gregory (D)	52,972	28.8%

Previous Winning Percentages
2008 (58%); 2006 (62%); 2004 (64%)

Elected 2004; 5th term

McHenry's early career was a study in partisanship, but in recent years he has become more of a policy specialist sticking to fiscal and financial issues. His politics are as conservative as ever, and echoes of his old incendiary self are sometimes heard — but his labors on behalf of the Republican Party have been quieter.

A congressional veteran at age 37, McHenry once boasted of a "combative style" and went toe to toe on the House floor with Democrats who were far senior. Critics accused him of naked ambition; Republican leaders gave him a deputy whip position at the start of his second term.

That job and some self-reflection inspired him to narrow his focus, he says — he learned "how to actually have a fruitful engagement that actually achieves some fairly decent results, versus some of the early battles that I had. I was engaged in a broader attack on the Democrat majority in 2007, and I've left those battles up to other folks." His theatrics on the House floor have tapered off.

At the same time, he has stepped up his involvement when Congress considers the federal role in the financial sector. McHenry is a member of the Financial Services Committee, and in the 113th Congress (2013-14) he chairs its Oversight and Investigations Subcommittee. He moved to that assignment after chairing the Oversight and Government Reform subcommittee on financial services and government bailouts in the 112th Congress (2011-12).

McHenry shares the concerns most Republicans express about the 2010 financial regulatory overhaul known as Dodd-Frank. "I don't believe it will prevent the next crisis," he said. He frequently states his belief that overregulation is stifling the creation or expansion of businesses.

He had some success loosening regulations in the 112th. McHenry says he has an affinity for startup companies; his father and a business partner started a roadside mowing business in Gastonia, N.C., that eventually grew to employ a few hundred people. McHenry, his two brothers and two sisters pitched in, and their mother kept the books. "I saw what my father's small business did ... and how it put the five of us through college," he said.

A 2012 law to expand small-business access to capital included a "crowd funding" title contributed by McHenry. His language allows entrepreneurs to raise capital from a large pool of small investors, with fewer requirements to report to the Securities and Exchange Commission. McHenry called the overall law "a big bipartisan step."

McHenry's commitment to that law brought out some of his bombast, however. He used his Oversight subcommittee to follow up on its implementation, and later in 2012 he was highly displeased with the SEC's progress in issuing rules relevant to crowdfunding. In a letter to SEC Chairwoman Mary L. Schapiro, he accused her of "ideological opposition to a bipartisan effort by Congress and the president to improve the conditions for capital formation."

He was also vexed by several regulatory agencies created by Dodd-Frank, such as the Consumer Financial Protection Bureau, whose budgets are not set by Congress. McHenry and other Republicans on his panel were accused of being short with Elizabeth Warren, the Obama administration official orchestrating the CFPB's creation, at a May 2011 hearing. When Warren (who is now a Massachusetts senator) tried to leave the hearing after one hour, McHenry accused her of "making up" a pre-arranged time limit for her testimony.

McHenry, a licensed real estate broker, has an interest in housing issues. In 2011, the House passed his bill to eliminate the Home Affordable Modification Program, which is meant to help homeowners avoid foreclosures. Conservatives pointed to reports that the program was assisting far fewer homeowners than initial estimates and still had the potential to spend tens of billions more dollars. McHenry said the government should get out of the housing refinancing market altogether.

McHenry also backs the position — held by Financial Services Chairman Jeb Hensarling of Texas — that the government-sponsored enterprises Fannie Mae and Freddie Mac should be dismantled. "I think we'll be taking a strong lead to make sure we can pass the right policy that gets federal housing finance back into the private sector rather than funded by the taxpayer," he said.

For the most part, McHenry is a party-line Republican. He did go against the wishes of party leaders to oppose the fiscal 2011 and 2012 spending bills — like other conservative opponents, he worried that they were spending too much. He voted with his district in opposing a free-trade pact with South Korea in 2011. Many western North Carolina residents blame trade liberalization policies for the loss of thousands of textile industry jobs.

McHenry was raised outside Charlotte, the youngest of five siblings. Once the youngest member of the House, he says it was tougher being the youngest child. "I've got fewer bruises from serving in Congress," McHenry said.

He graduated from Belmont Abbey College in his hometown, and while there he founded the school's College Republican chapter. He chaired the North Carolina Federation of College Republicans, and his allies and connections from that group became a support network for his political campaigns.

His first race was an unsuccessful bid for the state House, while he was still in college. McHenry expanded his contacts while working in Washington at the DCI Group, a conservative communications company, and as a special assistant to Labor Secretary Elaine L. Chao, the wife of current Senate Minority Leader Mitch McConnell.

McHenry returned home and won election to the state House. Within a few months, he jumped into the 2004 race to replace Republican Rep. Cass Ballenger, who had announced his retirement. McHenry was a relative unknown, but he finished second in a four-way primary, then took the runoff by 85 votes. The strongly Republican district gave him a 28-point victory in November.

Redistricting for the 2012 election gave McHenry a significant amount of new turf to defend: All of Gastonia was added to the 10th District, as well as portions of the liberal city of Asheville. It was not a surprise to McHenry, who was heavily involved in the redistricting process and trying to guarantee a large GOP advantage in the House delegation. Republicans picked up three seats in the state as McHenry won his race by 14 points.

For the 2014 election cycle, McHenry is the vice chairman for candidate recruitment at the National Republican Congressional Committee.

Key Votes

2012	
Extend a Social Security payroll tax cut and unemployment benefits	YES
Ease securities rules to expand small-business access to capital	YES
Extend for one year subsidized student loan interest rates financed by a cut in health care spending	?
Cite Attorney General Eric H. Holder Jr. for contempt of Congress	YES
Create a visa program for foreign graduates in high-tech fields	YES
Extend most Bush-era income tax rates while allowing rates for top-bracket earners to rise (Jan. 1, 2013)	NO
2011	
Strike funding for F-35 alternative engine	NO
Prevent EPA from regulating greenhouse gas emissions to address climate change	YES
Extend certain provisions of Patriot Act for four years	YES
Declare opposition to use of ground troops in Libya	YES
Overhaul patent law	YES
Pass compromise debt limit increase plan and establish future spending limits	YES
Allow consideration of measures to implement three trade agreements	YES

CQ Vote Studies

	PARTY UNITY		PRESIDENTIAL SUPPORT	
	SUPPORT	OPPOSE	SUPPORT	OPPOSE
2012	98%	2%	15%	85%
2011	97%	3%	17%	83%
2010	98%	2%	29%	71%
2009	99%	1%	11%	89%
2008	98%	2%	78%	22%

Interest Groups

	AFL-CIO	ADA	CCUS	ACU
2012	14%	0%	82%	100%
2011	3%	10%	94%	96%
2010	7%	0%	88%	96%
2009	5%	0%	73%	100%
2008	13%	10%	78%	100%

North Carolina 10

West — Asheville, Gastonia

More than half of the voters of the 10th are newly represented by the district — the decennial redistricting process slid its boundaries away from the Tennessee border south into three counties along the South Carolina border and west to Asheville. East of Hickory, the Catawba River forms its boundary. Redistricting linked small towns nestled in the foothills of the Blue Ridge Mountains with old textile mill towns still struggling with plant closures. In the east, Highway 321, known as the "Furniture Corridor," connects furniture manufacturers and retail outlets in Lincolnton and Hickory.

Gastonia is the largest city wholly represented by this district. A large portion of the district's black population lives in surrounding Gaston County. Preceding decades have witnessed many plant closings, as competition with overseas manufacturers has pressed wages down and forced firms out of business. Parkdale, the world's leading cotton yarn supplier, maintains its international headquarters and manufacturing facilities in the city. Cotton farmers in neighboring Cleveland County supply the textile industry. Internet companies, including Facebook, have descended on the district, repurposing shuttered textile plants into server-hosting facilities; Apple is building a solar-powered data center outside of Maiden.

Proximity to Charlotte has driven rapid growth in Lincoln and Gaston counties. A new bypass project on U.S. Route 74 aims to ease traffic congestion but will not be completed until 2030.

The 10th gained most of scenic Asheville, home to well-preserved Art Deco architecture, performing arts venues, breweries and mountain-living crafters. With dozens of art galleries and the Gilded Age-era Biltmore Estate nearby, the city draws more than 3 million visitors annually. The National Climatic Data Center, the world's largest weather data archive, is in Asheville.

Even though Asheville harbors some liberal votes, this is one of the most conservative districts in the state: Voters here have elected Republicans to Congress for 40 years.

Major Industry
Manufacturing, textiles, tourism, agriculture, data processing

Cities
Asheville (pt.), Gastonia, Hickory (pt.), Shelby

Notable
Shelby pays tribute to a popular local fried meat dish during its annual Livermush Festival.

Rep. Mark Meadows (R)

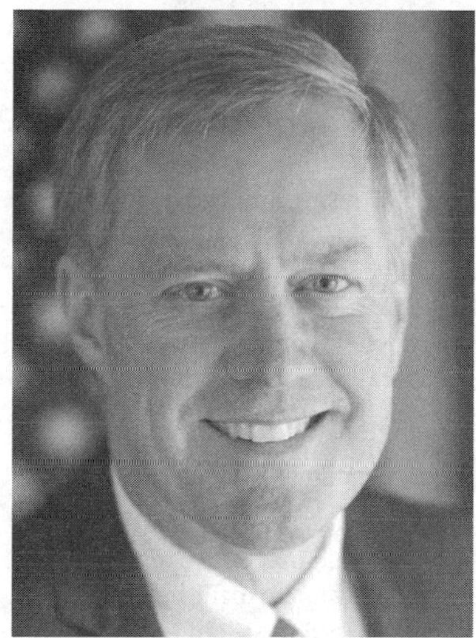

Capitol Office
225-6401
meadows.house.gov
1516 Longworth Bldg. 20515-0905; fax 226-6422

Committees
Foreign Affairs
Oversight & Government Reform
Transportation & Infrastructure

Residence
Cashiers

Born
July 28, 1959; Maginot Barracks (Army), Verdun, France

Religion
Christian

Family
Wife, Debbie Meadows; two children

Education
U. of South Florida, A.A. 1980

Career
Real estate developer; restaurateur; energy company customer relations director

Political Highlights
Macon County Republican Party chairman, 2001-02

ELECTION RESULTS

2012 GENERAL		
Mark Meadows (R)	190,319	57.4%
Hayden Rogers (D)	141,107	42.6%
2012 PRIMARY RUNOFF		
Mark Meadows (R)	17,520	76.2%
Vance Patterson (R)	5,471	23.8%

Elected 2012; 1st term

Meadows emphasizes that he is a Christian, a conservative and a "small-business guy." Most of his positions line up nicely with the GOP platform. He has been active in the Republican Party for a long time, but his service in the House is his first experience as a legislator.

He was born in France, where his father was stationed with the Army. The family settled in Tampa, Fla. Meadows told the Smoky Mountain News that he was a "fat nerd" in his early years, though he worked hard to lose weight in high school — and he caught the attention of his future wife. They completed their college studies at the University of South Florida. The couple visited western North Carolina on their honeymoon, and they were so taken with the region that they moved there in the mid-1980s. They operated a small restaurant for several years, then sold that business as Meadows got into real estate. He also got involved with the Republican Party, and for a time he was the chairman of the Macon County GOP.

Meadows has a seat on the Transportation and Infrastructure Committee and its panel on economic development — which oversees the Appalachian Regional Commission, a federal-state partnership devoted to economic growth in the region. On the Water Resources and Environment Subcommittee, he is chasing down regulations, which he blames for high unemployment in his district. He also sits on the Foreign Affairs subcommittee on global human rights, which is chaired by another devout Christian Republican, New Jersey's Christopher H. Smith.

Democratic Rep. Heath Shuler, a leader of the fiscally conservative Blue Dog Coalition, decided to retire at the end of the 112th Congress (2011-12) — Republicans controlled redistricting in the state, and the redrawn 11th District was going to be very difficult to hold. Meadows prevailed in an eight-person primary, then easily won a runoff. In the general election, he defeated Shuler's former chief of staff, Hayden Rogers, by almost 15 points.

North Carolina 11

Western tip — Great Smoky Mountains

Spanning 17 counties in the western end of North Carolina, the 11th boasts the natural beauty of the Great Smoky Mountains in the Blue Ridge range. Much of its western territory along the Tennessee, Georgia and South Carolina borders is national forest.

Containing the Tar Heel State's share of Great Smoky Mountains National Park, the nation's most-visited wilderness, the district relies on outdoor recreational tourism. Revenue in this sector has been on the rise in recent years. In the district's northeast, which is still picturesque but lacks much parkland, High Country tourism proponents have pushed for the designation of a new national scenic area and expanded hiking and mountain biking trails.

Asheville (split with the 10th) is the only city within the district that has more than 41,000 people. The 11th captures about one-fourth of its population within a southeastern curve of neighborhoods. Visitors often head northwest from its tourist sites on the scenic Blue Ridge Parkway for day trips to Mount Mitchell, the highest peak east of the Mississippi River.

Counties in the southwestern tip of the district — Swain, Graham and Cherokee — struggle with some of the highest unemployment rates in the state. Tracts of land in these rural hollows were parceled out generations ago, and many families descend from the land's earliest inhabitants.

The East Bend Cherokee Indians, whose ancestors avoided the "Trail of Tears" by hiding in the mountains, operate a casino that is undergoing expansion. Native Americans, however, account for only 1.4 percent of the population overall in this overwhelmingly white district.

Federal support programs are politically important here because of the district's large numbers of retirees and poor households. Once a Blue Dog Democrat district, the 11th's newly crafted borders shifted it dramatically in Republicans' favor, and the newly drawn district gave Republican Mitt Romney 61 percent of its vote in the 2012 presidential race; he had particularly strong support in the far western counties.

Major Industry
Tourism, forest products, retail

Cities
Asheville (pt.), Lenoir

Notable
The Nantahala Gorge is named "land of the noon day sun" in Cherokee — sunlight only reaches the valley's floor at midday.

Rep. Melvin Watt (D)

Capitol Office
225-1510
watt.house.gov
2304 Rayburn Bldg. 20515-3312; fax 225-1512

Committees
Financial Services
Judiciary

Residence
Charlotte

Born
Aug. 26, 1945; Charlotte, N.C.

Religion
Presbyterian

Family
Wife, Eulada Watt; two children

Education
U. of North Carolina, B.S. 1967 (business administration); Yale U., J.D. 1970

Career
Nursing home owner; campaign aide; lawyer

Political Highlights
N.C. Senate, 1985-86

ELECTION RESULTS

2012 GENERAL		
Melvin Watt (D)	247,591	79.6%
Jack Brosch (R)	63,317	20.4%
2012 PRIMARY		
Melvin Watt (D)	52,968	80.9%
Matt Newton (D)	12,495	19.1%
2010 GENERAL		
Melvin Watt (D)	103,495	63.9%
Greg Dority (R)	55,315	34.1%
Lon Cecil (LIBERT)	3,197	2.0%

Previous Winning Percentages
2008 (72%); 2006 (67%); 2004 (67%); 2002 (65%); 2000 (65%); 1998 (56%); 1996 (71%); 1994 (66%); 1992 (70%)

Elected 1992; 11th term

Watt is a longtime member of the Financial Services Committee, but when Republicans took control of the House in 2011, his name mostly disappeared from business headlines. That changed in May 2013 — President Barack Obama nominated Watt to lead the Federal Housing Finance Agency, which oversees mortgage giants Fannie Mae and Freddie Mac.

Many Democrats were happy; they had been eager to replace Edward J. DeMarco, the acting director of the FHFA since August 2009. DeMarco resisted calls to implement principal reduction policies — forgiving portions of loans for struggling homeowners —whereas Watt is receptive to that plan. Many conservatives were upset; National Review dubbed him "Wall Street's favorite racist," accusing him of practicing racial-identity politics and being cozy with the large banks in his Charlotte-based district.

Some Senate Republicans vowed to oppose Watt, and the battle over his confirmation — regardless of the outcome — could mark the opening of hostilities as Congress considers future federal involvement in the housing sector.

Much of Watt's work on Financial Services is in the mold of a consumer advocate. In 2008, he joined panel Democrats in calling on mortgage holders to postpone foreclosing on any homes until the law to aid the housing industry went into effect. In early 2009, he urged colleagues to support a bill to permit mortgage write-downs by bankruptcy judges. That year he also backed a bill to ban several credit card billing practices, siding with consumer groups over Wachovia and Bank of America, two of his district's largest employers.

But he opposed a 2011 measure to suspend already-approved compensation packages for Fannie Mae and Freddie Mac executives, arguing that slicing executive pay will have a negative effect on the companies in the future.

Watt was heavily involved in negotiations on the financial regulatory overhaul known as Dodd-Frank during the 111th Congress (2009-10). In fact, he has spent much of his House career at the negotiating table, even though his voting record is liberal. "I just do my job and try to keep moving," he said.

During the 112th Congress (2011-12), he invested a lot of his energy on the Judiciary Committee. Watt spent two decades as an attorney specializing in minority business and economic development law. Since 2011, he has been the top Democrat on the subcommittee handling intellectual property and the Internet. At a 2011 hearing on a patent system overhaul — something Watt had worked on for years — he reflected on his House career. "One important lesson that has been reinforced for me throughout my time in Congress: Progress requires compromise," he said.

The patent overhaul was enacted with Watt's support, though his efforts to allow the Patent and Trademark Office to keep and spend all the fees it collects were unsuccessful. Watt and his allies argued that the funds could help the office work through its substantial backlog of applications without having to wait on federal appropriators each year.

Watt also worked with Republicans on a 2011 online piracy bill, which among other things would have allowed law enforcement agencies to get court orders shutting down websites that illegally post copyrighted material. The bill was scrapped after a huge backlash from the tech community and civil liberties advocates worried about potential abuse.

Watt joined the battle against "the high-tech bandits roving the Internet" because he wanted to strengthen penalties for online theft and address the impact that piracy has on consumers. "Maybe we didn't find the appropriate solution for it, but everybody acknowledges that there's a serious problem," he said. The new chairman of the IP subcommittee for the 113th Congress

(2013-14) is Watt's North Carolina colleague, Republican Howard Coble.

In 2006, Watt was the chief Democratic negotiator on an extension of the 1965 Voting Rights Act. He produced a bill that was praised by leaders of both parties. Watt got heavily involved because the bill dealt with redistricting. "I've been the poster child of redistricting. My district was changed five times in a 10-year period, so people knew that I understood that issue," he said.

Watt is a member of the Congressional Black Caucus; he chaired the CBC in the 109th Congress (2005-06) and has been very loyal to its members over the years. He also belongs to the Congressional Progressive Caucus, a group of the most-liberal Democrats. But he joined the bipartisan "Go Big" coalition in 2011, which called for $4 trillion in deficit reduction over 10 years through a mix of spending cuts and revenue increases; Watt was one of only 22 House Democrats to vote for a fiscal 2013 budget based on those parameters.

Watt found himself in the middle of an Office of Congressional Ethics investigation of his fundraising activities that coincided with key votes on Dodd-Frank. Watt, among eight Republican and Democratic lawmakers under investigation, was cleared of wrongdoing by the end of summer 2010. The next year, he proposed a 40 percent cut to OCE's budget, saying that he figured that limiting the office's funds would "get them back to their mission."

"I actually voted for the OCE being set up," he said, "but I never thought I was voting to give them the right to initiate actions themselves."

Underpinning Watt's success is the determination he developed during a difficult early life. He grew up in rural Mecklenburg County in a tin-roofed shack that lacked running water and electricity. His mother raised him and his two brothers while working as a maid, and he earned money by shining shoes at a barbershop where he could not get his own hair cut until it was night-time.

"People look at you in a suit as a member of Congress, and they think you've always been in a suit and always been a member of Congress," he once said. "I came out of a different kind of history."

After attending a segregated high school, he went on to graduate from the University of North Carolina. Watt didn't get a chance to play baseball for the Tar Heels, but he had the chance to "live out that dream" as the Democrats' starting pitcher for 11 consecutive years in the Roll Call Congressional Baseball Game. He retired from the baseball field in 2006 and took up golf.

While practicing law, Watt had a two-year stint in the North Carolina Senate, and he managed the unsuccessful 1990 Senate campaign of Democrat Harvey Gantt, who lost to Jesse Helms. He won his first House election in 1992 in a newly created black-majority district. Court challenges kept changing the shape of his district, but not Watt's re-election prospects. Prior to his nomination, there was speculation that Watt might retire at the end of the 113th.

Key Votes

2012	
Extend a Social Security payroll tax cut and unemployment benefits	**YES**
Ease securities rules to expand small-business access to capital	**YES**
Extend for one year subsidized student loan interest rates financed by a cut in health care spending	**NO**
Cite Attorney General Eric H. Holder Jr. for contempt of Congress	**?**
Create a visa program for foreign graduates in high-tech fields	**?**
Extend most Bush-era income tax rates while allowing rates for top-bracket earners to rise (Jan. 1, 2013)	**YES**
2011	
Strike funding for F-35 alternative engine	**P**
Prevent EPA from regulating greenhouse gas emissions to address climate change	**NO**
Extend certain provisions of Patriot Act for four years	**NO**
Declare opposition to use of ground troops in Libya	**NO**
Overhaul patent law	**YES**
Pass compromise debt limit increase plan and establish future spending limits	**NO**
Allow consideration of measures to implement three trade agreements	**NO**

CQ Vote Studies

	PARTY UNITY		PRESIDENTIAL SUPPORT	
	SUPPORT	OPPOSE	SUPPORT	OPPOSE
2012	97%	3%	90%	10%
2011	96%	4%	86%	14%
2010	95%	5%	90%	10%
2009	99%	1%	97%	3%
2008	99%	1%	15%	85%

Interest Groups

	AFL-CIO	ADA	CCUS	ACU
2012	95%	90%	27%	0%
2011	97%	95%	19%	4%
2010	92%	85%	38%	4%
2009	100%	95%	36%	0%
2008	100%	100%	61%	0%

North Carolina 12

Central — parts of Charlotte, Winston-Salem and Greensboro

Winding its way northeast from Charlotte, the narrow 12th picks up parts of Salisbury and Lexington before splitting west into Winston-Salem and curving east into a portion of Greensboro. The district's traditionally serpentine shape landed it before the Supreme Court four times in the 1990s amid allegations of racial gerrymandering. The heavily Democratic minority-majority district, which routinely gives Democratic nominees their best showings in the state, is about half black, one-third white and one-seventh Hispanic.

Half of the district's population lives in Charlotte in an arc that runs from Interstate 77 southwest of the city to U.S. Highway 74 to its southeast. The 12th covers the skyscrapers of Uptown, home to the nation's largest banking center outside of New York. Bank of America maintains its headquarters here but recently sold off a second downtown skyscraper. The homes of the city's professional football and basketball franchises are nearby. Outside the business district sit the historically African-American Wilmore, Cary and Biddleville neighborhoods, including historically black Johnson C. Smith University.

As it snakes out of Charlotte, the 12th is cut by the major interstates of the Piedmont Triad and absorbs much of the Interstate 85 corridor. Highway infrastructure, major distribution and packaging centers and the Charlotte Douglas International Airport make transportation key to the economy.

Greensboro is the other population hub, where nearly one-fifth of the district's residents live. Poverty rates have risen in the city, and East Side residents complain of a lack of access to affordable retail options.

High Point hosts more than 50 retail furniture outlets, and its furnishings industry trade show draws more than 75,000 people every six months. The district takes in one-fifth of Winston-Salem, including the skyline-dominating tower that formerly served as Wachovia's world headquarters.

Major Industry
Finance, transportation, manufacturing, retail, health care

Cities
Charlotte (pt.), Greensboro (pt.), Winston-Salem (pt.), High Point (pt.)

Notable
Charlotte is home to the library and museum dedicated to the personal and pastoral history of Christian evangelist Billy Graham.

Rep. George Holding (R)

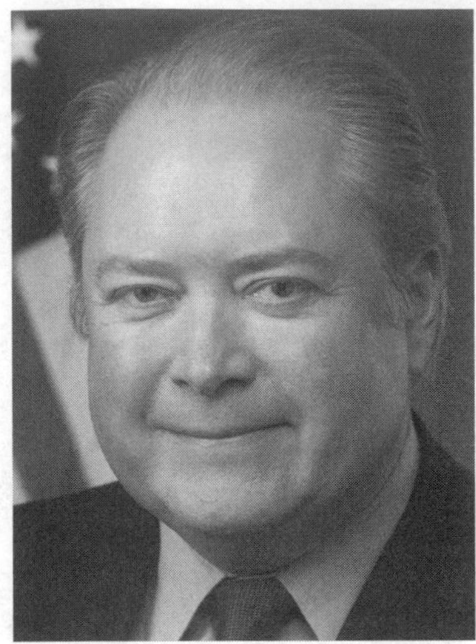

Capitol Office
225-3032
holding.house.gov
507 Cannon Bldg. 20515-3313; fax 225-0181

Committees
Foreign Affairs
Judiciary

Residence
Raleigh

Born
April 17, 1968; Raleigh, N.C.

Religion
Baptist

Family
Wife, Lucy E. Holding; four children

Education
Wake Forest U., B.A. 1991 (classical studies); U. of St. Andrews (Scotland) , attended 1991-92; Wake Forest U., J.D 1996

Career
Lawyer; congressional aide

Political Highlights
Assistant U.S. attorney, 2002-06; U.S. attorney, 2006-11

ELECTION RESULTS

2012 GENERAL		
George Holding (R)	210,495	56.8%
Charles Malone (D)	160,115	43.2%
2012 PRIMARY		
George Holding (R)	37,341	43.5%
Paul Y. Coble (R)	29,354	34.2%
William Randall (R)	19,119	22.3%

Elected 2012; 1st term

After a decade of prosecuting politicians, Holding has joined their ranks. The former U.S. attorney has an agenda that should make him a reliable vote for the Republican majority.

Holding has spent most of his life in Raleigh; he was born there, grew up there, and returned there after completing law school at Wake Forest (which was only about 100 miles away). His family controls the parent company of First Citizens Bank. In 1998, he left private practice to become a Washington-based aide to iconic Republican Sen. Jesse Helms. A few years later, he returned to Raleigh, and in 2002 he was hired as an assistant U.S. attorney.

He was appointed to head up the office for the Eastern District of North Carolina in 2006. While serving in the office, he participated in high-profile prosecutions of public officials, including former Sen. John Edwards; Holding stayed in his job through the opening years of the Obama administration, resigning after Edwards was indicted on charges of conspiracy and campaign finance violations. (The case ended in mistrial in 2012.)

Holding now sits on the Judiciary Committee, as well as its subcommittees on immigration, commercial law and the Internet. He urges strong enforcement of existing laws, whether regarding illegal immigrants or the alleged theft of intellectual property by nations such as China. He is also a member of the Foreign Affairs Committee. Holding, a member of the Republican Study Committee, is a fiscal conservative. He has called for the end of the Education and Energy departments.

The 13th District was represented by Democrat Brad Miller, but he opted to retire after surveying changes that Republicans made through the redistricting process for 2012. Holding won the primary with help from his family. Several of them formed a super PAC that boosted him in a testy campaign against Paul Y. Coble, the former mayor of Raleigh. He ran a mistake-free campaign to defeat Democrat Charles Malone by more than 13 points.

North Carolina 13

East central — parts of Raleigh and Goldsboro

The jagged 13th is focused on Raleigh, surrounding the city on three sides. Little of the district's old footprint remains after decennial redistricting pushed its boundaries out of the Raleigh city center and into its suburbs; instead of hugging the Virginia border northwest of Raleigh, the district now bends eastward to Wilson and sprawls around Rocky Mount to the north and Goldsboro to the south. It takes in nine counties, but none sit wholly within the 13th.

Changes to the 13th's map shifted black-majority portions of inner Raleigh into the 4th and replaced them with white-majority suburbs. Overall, the 13th is about three-fourths white and has one of the highest median household incomes in the state ($61,000).

Holly Springs and Apex, which the 13th splits with the 2nd, are among the fastest-growing suburbs, among nearly all ethnic groups, in the nation. Wake Forest is to the northeast of Raleigh. Technology and energy companies have moved into these communities, which are, overall, well-educated enclaves: More than half of the residents of Holly Springs hold at least a bachelor's degree.

Further east, the 13th is more dependent on manufacturing, and the region has suffered after years of decline in the tobacco industry. Tires and food products are still made in Wilson, but more than one in 10 are unemployed in the area. Wilson County as a whole has about 30 truck terminals and tries to leverage its proximity to the Interstate 95 corridor, Raleigh and the Atlantic coast.

Although Democrats enjoy a voter registration advantage within the Research Triangle region of the district, their strength is limited overall and the 13th is safe for Republicans. In 2012, Mitt Romney took a comfortable 55 percent of the district's vote in the presidential contest, one percentage point better than 2008 Republican nominee John McCain would have won within the new boundaries.

Major Industry
Health care, technology, government

Cities
Raleigh (pt.), Rocky Mount (pt.), Wilson (pt.)

Notable
Apex hosts an annual barbecue cooking competition called Pig Fest.

NORTH DAKOTA

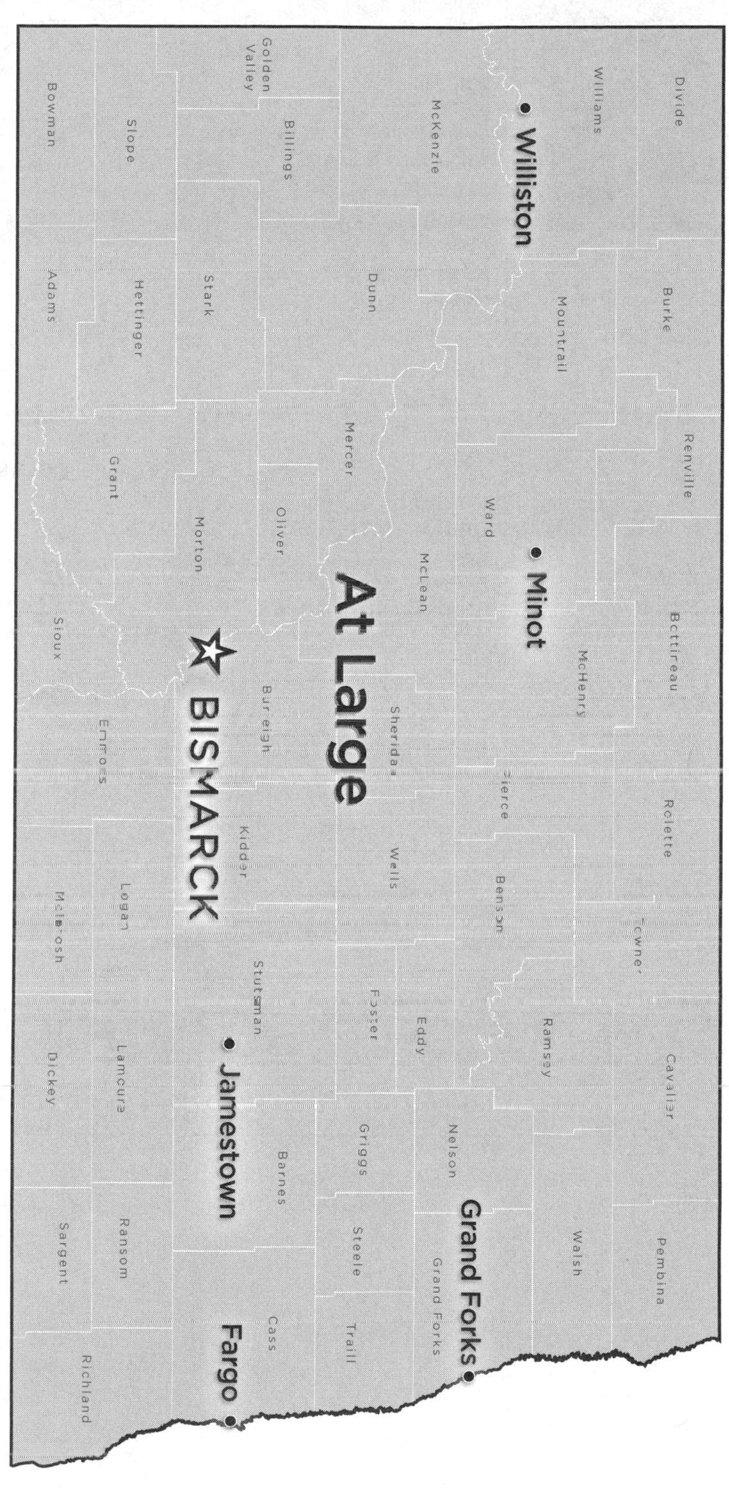

Gov. Jack Dalrymple (R)

First elected: 2012; Assumed office Dec. 7, 2010, due to the election of John Hoeven to the U.S. Senate.

Length of term: 4 years

Term expires: 12/16

Salary: $116,999

Phone: (701) 328-2200

Residence: Casselton

Born: Oct. 16, 1948; Minneapolis, Minn.

Religion: Presbyterian

Family: Wife, Betsy Dalrymple; four children

Education: Yale U., B.A. 1970 (American studies)

Career: Farmer

Political highlights: N.D. House, 1985-2000; lieutenant governor, 2000-10

ELECTION RESULTS

2012 GENERAL

Jack Dalrymple (R)	200,525	63.1%
Ryan M. Taylor (D)	109,048	34.3%
Paul Sorum (I)	5,356	1.7%

Lt. Gov. Drew Wrigley (R)

Elected: 2012

Length of term: 4 years

Term expires: 12/16

Salary: $85,615

Phone: (701) 328-2200

LEGISLATURE

Legislative Assembly: January-April in odd-numbered years

Senate: 47 members, 4-year terms

2013 ratios: 33 R, 14 D; 39 men, 8 women

Salary: $5,280; $157/day in session

Phone: (701) 328-2916

House: 94 members, 4-year terms

2013 ratios: 71 R, 23 D; 78 men, 16 women

Salary: $5,280; $157/day in session

Phone: (701) 328-2916

TERM LIMITS

Governor: No

Senate: No

House: No

URBAN STATISTICS

CITY	POPULATION
Fargo	105,549
Bismarck	61,272
Grand Forks	52,838
Minot	40,888
West Fargo	25,830

REGISTERED VOTERS

Voters do not register by party.

POPULATION

2010 population	672,591
2000 population	642,200
1990 population	638,800
Percent change (2000-2010)	+4.7%
Rank among states (2010)	48
Median age	36.6
Born in state	69.8%
Foreign born	2.1%
Violent crime rate	201/100,000
Poverty level	11.7%
Federal workers	11,919
Military	7,209

ELECTIONS

STATE ELECTION OFFICIAL
(701) 328-4146

DEMOCRATIC PARTY
(701) 255-0460

REPUBLICAN PARTY
(701) 255-0030

MISCELLANEOUS

Web: www.nd.gov

Capital: Bismarck

U.S. CONGRESS

Senate: 1 Democrat, 1 Republican

House: 1 Republican

STATISTICS BY DISTRICT

District	2012 Vote for President: Obama	Romney	2008 Vote for President: Obama	McCain	Black	Asian	Hispanic	Median Income	Over 64	Under 20	College Education	Rural	Sq. Miles
AL	39%	58%	45%	53%	1%	1%	2%	$51,704	14%	25%	27%	43%	69,001
STATE	39	58	45	53	1	1	2	51,704	14	25	27	43	69,001
U.S.	51	47	53	46	12	5	17	50,052	13	27	29	21	3,531,905

Sen. John Hoeven (R)

Capitol Office
224-2551
hoeven.senate.gov
338 Russell Bldg. 20510; fax 224-7999

Committees
Agriculture, Nutrition & Forestry
Appropriations
Energy & Natural Resources
Indian Affairs

Residence
Bismarck

Born
March 13, 1957; Bismarck, N.D.

Religion
Roman Catholic

Family
Wife, Mical "Mikey" Hoeven; two children

Education
Dartmouth College, B.A. 1979 (history & economics); Northwestern U., M.B.A. 1981

Career
Bank CEO

Political Highlights
Governor, 2000-10

ELECTION RESULTS

2010 GENERAL		
John Hoeven (R)	181,689	76.1%
Tracy Potter (D)	52,955	22.2%
Keith J. Hanson (LIBERT)	3,890	1.6%
2010 PRIMARY		
John Hoeven (R)	65,075	99.8%

Elected 2010; 1st term

Hoeven, a moderate Republican, was the governor of North Dakota for a decade. At the end of his tenure, he enjoyed approval ratings in the range usually reserved for dictators. He has a different set of tools at his disposal in the Senate but the same message for economic growth. "I fundamentally believe in empowering people — in creating a forum, and then people achieve," he says.

North Dakota defied national trends as the country slipped into recession late in the George W. Bush administration. The state's once-shrinking population grew, its unemployment rate never drifted much higher than 4 percent and the government enjoyed budget surpluses.

Critics chalked up Hoeven's popularity to an energy sector boom, which they said was not his doing. But Hoeven describes a conscious effort to create a hospitable environment for business. In a Republican radio address early in 2012, Hoeven (HO-ven) said his state had succeeded by "empowering the private sector — by building the kind of legal, tax and regulatory climate that encourages private investment and spurs economic growth." That mantra matched up almost perfectly with the talking points of GOP leaders throughout the 112th Congress (2011-12), Hoeven's first as a senator.

Hard-line conservatives might quibble with Hoeven's style, as his state's growth was accomplished with a degree of bipartisanship. "Governors have to work with people from both sides of the aisle," he said. Hoeven himself was a Democrat until four years before becoming governor, and among his allies in the Senate is West Virginia Democrat Joe Manchin III, another former governor from a state with strong ties to the energy sector.

Hoeven likes to point out that his state's economy grew in several sectors, but he still has a heavy focus on energy as a member of the Energy and Natural Resources Committee. He believes that with the right environment, domestic energy production can exceed U.S. energy demands "in five to seven years."

His state's comprehensive energy plan promotes fossil fuel development (largely in the Bakken Shale formation) and renewable sources such as wind. The state created an oil and gas research fund and a pipeline authority, used tax incentives to lure companies and coordinated with higher education institutions to meet employers' needs. Hoeven emphasizes that regulatory certainty is necessary, and he opposes cap-and-trade systems to regulate greenhouse gas emissions.

In 2012, Hoeven tried unsuccessfully to amend a two-year reauthorization of surface transportation programs so that it would effectively approve a permit for the Keystone XL pipeline, which would carry oil from Canada's tar sands as far as Texas refineries. He introduced a bill to block further EPA regulation of coal ash, a byproduct of coal combustion sometimes used in road construction. Hoeven has continued working on Keystone XL in the 113th Congress (2013-14); the Senate-approved budget for fiscal 2014 includes his amendment calling for approval of the pipeline, and he also introduced a stand-alone bill allowing Congress to approve the project.

Energy aside, agriculture has the biggest share of North Dakota's economy. Hoeven sits on both the Agriculture, Nutrition and Forestry Committee and the Agriculture Appropriations Subcommittee. "I've been around agriculture all my life," he says — his grandfather had a cattle ranch.

Hoeven said the Senate-passed 2012 reauthorization of farm programs was a model of bipartisanship that "lines up with what farmers asked for." That bill would have eliminated direct payments to farmers while expanding crop insurance programs. Some criticized the measure's $23 billion in spending reductions as illusory, as severe crop losses might trigger huge insurance payouts. Hoeven called it "cost-effective" and more of a "market-driven solution" to risk management. (It was not enacted, and work on a long-term reauthorization continues in the 113th Congress.)

Market-based changes are a frequent theme with Hoeven, on topics including health care and transportation. In 2011, he teamed up with Democrats Ron Wyden of Oregon and Mark Begich of Alaska to propose a new bond program to increase private investment in infrastructure projects. It would allow states or state infrastructure banks to issue tax-credit bonds. The plan would allow investors to get a federal tax credit equal to the average yield on an outstanding corporate bond instead of interest payments.

Hoeven looks for other savings on the Appropriations Committee, though he was not as zealous as conservative Republicans in seeking discretionary spending cuts during the 112th Congress.

As ranking Republican on the Legislative Branch spending panel, Hoeven in 2011 proposed cutting the Senate's own budget by 7 percent, beyond the target set by the chamber, and he opposed the panel's 2012 spending bill because it increased spending for the Senate. "I think we should look at making sure we do at least as much [cutting] as the House did," he told Roll Call. He also sits on the Interior-Environment Subcommittee.

Hoeven opposes the current ban on earmarks, saying that with proper oversight and transparency such directed spending is acceptable. He supports a balanced-budget amendment to the Constitution.

On social issues, Hoeven is conservative. He opposes abortion, same-sex marriage and many proscriptions of gun owners' rights.

Hoeven was born in Bismarck. His dad was a banker; his mother was trained as a teacher but primarily was a homemaker. Hoeven went east for his education, earning a bachelor's degree from Dartmouth College in New Hampshire and a master's degree in business administration from Northwestern University in Illinois.

He returned to North Dakota in the early 1980s as executive vice president of First Western Bank in Minot, and he found his home state languishing economically. "What led me to public service was recognizing the need in my state to really get the economy growing and diversified," he said. Hoeven initially was active in civic affairs, but not electoral politics.

In 1993, he became president and CEO of Bank of North Dakota, the only state-owned and state-run financial institution in the nation. The bank almost doubled in size during his seven years at the helm.

He had never run for political office before seeking the governorship in 2000. He defeated Democratic state Attorney General Heidi Heitkamp (who is now his Senate colleague), pulling away at the end to claim a 10-point win. He was easily re-elected in 2004 and 2008.

Heading into the 2010 Senate race, Hoeven was one of the most popular state executives. A December 2009 Rasmussen poll showed him with an 87 percent approval rating. His popularity made him the obvious target for Republican recruiters, and in hypothetical matchups in late 2009 he led Democrat Byron L. Dorgan by more than 20 points. Soon after the first of the year, Dorgan announced he would not seek re-election.

During the campaign, Hoeven attended a February tea party rally in Bismarck featuring GOP Rep. Michele Bachmann of Minnesota, a conservative favorite. "We're a big-tent party and we need to include all kinds of people. This is us reaching out and getting people involved," Hoeven told the Bismarck Tribune.

His Democratic opponent, state Sen. Tracy Potter, was overmatched from the start. Charges that Hoeven was moving too far to the right largely fell on deaf ears, and Hoeven took 76 percent of the vote in November.

Key Votes

2012	
Prohibit health insurance plans from denying coverage based on the sponsor's religious beliefs	NO
Require approval of the Keystone XL oil pipeline	YES
Ease securities rules to expand small-business access to capital	YES
Reauthorize farm and nutrition programs for five years	YES
Limit debate on a bill that would create private-sector cybersecurity standards	NO
Consent to ratification of a treaty setting global standard for the treatment of people with disabilities	NO
Provide $60.4 billion in disaster relief following Superstorm Sandy	YES
Extend most Bush-era income tax rates while allowing rates for top-bracket earners to rise (Jan. 1, 2013)	YES
2011	
Prevent EPA from regulating greenhouse gas emissions to address climate change	YES
Extend certain provisions of Patriot Act for four years	YES
Clear compromise debt limit increase plan and establish future spending limits	YES
Overhaul patent law	YES
Implement Colombia free trade agreement	YES
Limit debate on confirmation of Caitlin J. Halligan to D.C. Circuit Court of Appeals	NO
Extend payroll tax cut and unemployment benefits for two months	YES

CQ Vote Studies

	PARTY UNITY		PRESIDENTIAL SUPPORT	
	SUPPORT	OPPOSE	SUPPORT	OPPOSE
2012	67%	33%	60%	40%
2011	81%	19%	55%	45%

Interest Groups

	AFL-CIO	ADA	CCUS	ACU
2012	18%	30%	100%	48%
2011	11%	15%	100%	80%

Sen. Heidi Heitkamp (D)

Capitol Office
224-2043
heitkamp.senate.gov
G55 Dirksen Bldg 20510-3403; fax 224-7776

Committees
Agriculture, Nutrition & Forestry
(Jobs, Rural Economic Growth & Energy Innovation - Chairwoman)
Banking, Housing & Urban Affairs
Homeland Security & Governmental Affairs
Indian Affairs
Small Business & Entrepreneurship

Residence
Mandan

Born
Oct. 30, 1955; Breckenridge, Minn.

Religion
Roman Catholic

Family
Husband, Darwin Lange; two children

Education
U. of North Dakota, B.A. 1977 (political science); Lewis & Clark College, J.D. 1980

Career
Lawyer; homemaker; state tax commission lawyer; assistant state attorney general; EPA lawyer

Political Highlights
Democratic nominee for N.D. auditor, 1984; N.D. tax commissioner, 1986-92; N.D. attorney general, 1993-2000; Democratic nominee for governor, 2000

ELECTION RESULTS

2012 GENERAL		
Heidi Heitkamp (D)	161,337	50.2%
Rick Berg (R)	158,401	49.3%
2012 PRIMARY		
Heidi Heitkamp (D)	57,246	99.8%

Elected 2012; 1st term

According to Heitkamp, North Dakota values include compromise and "getting the job done." A surprising and hard-fought victory brought her to the Senate, where she is taking on the job of a Democratic centrist.

Prior to joining the Senate, her highest-profile political position was as North Dakota's attorney general; she also served as the state tax commissioner. Heitkamp's electoral fortunes have been helped throughout her career by her outwardly warm personality and humor. Speaking at a Washington Press Club function in early 2013, she acknowledged the odds against her 2012 triumph in a Republican-leaning state.

"You're asking yourself, 'How did this middle-aged, red-headed Democrat win a United States Senate seat in a red state that the president lost by 21 points?'" she said. "To you, I'm like a unicorn. You guys don't think I exist. You just wanted to tell your family that you saw me in person and I am the last of my species."

Heitkamp expresses disdain for partisanship and "one size fits all" federal policies, which can put her at odds with Democratic colleagues at times. One of the most obvious areas of disagreement is energy: North Dakota has used the growth of its energy sector to become perhaps the greatest economic success story among the states in recent years.

She opposes plans to expand federal regulation of hydraulic fracturing, a method of extracting oil and gas from shale deposits that is disliked by environmentalists. Heitkamp is skeptical of claims that it can lead to groundwater contamination. "I'm not convinced that they've seen evidence where they say there's evidence," she said.

She espouses a Democratic-tinged version of an "all of the above" energy policy. Heitkamp is fine with continued development of fossil fuels — she was a board member for the Dakota Gasification Company, which works with lignite coal, and she calls for construction of the Keystone XL pipeline. But she also doesn't mind federal incentives for supporting the development of renewable-energy sources such as biofuels, wind and geothermal power.

Heitkamp supports the 2010 health care overhaul, although she didn't like its requirement for individuals to get insurance. "I think that the focus should've been on incentives to get people into the health care system, as opposed to mandates," she said. Mandates gave the law "a big black eye." She wants further progress on driving down health care costs, including allowing the Medicare system to directly negotiate drug prices with manufacturers.

And she cautioned against sweeping federal gun-control legislation in early 2013, calling it potentially "a one-size-fits-all that violates the Second Amendment rights of law-abiding Americans." She endorsed the idea of a Commission on Mass Violence that was proposed by West Virginia Democrat Joe Manchin III, and she supports the expansion of mental health services as a response to recent gun violence.

Heitkamp sits on the Agriculture, Nutrition and Forestry Committee and chairs its panel on Jobs, Rural Economic Growth and Energy Innovation.

She says enactment of a long-term reauthorization of farm programs is her top legislative priority. The Senate passed such a bill in 2012, but it wasn't enacted; when it was reintroduced at the start of the 113th Congress (2013-14), Heitkamp signed on as a co-sponsor. Heitkamp said the farm bill should have a fuels title that "deals with renewable-fuel standards and that recognizes the importance of biofuels."

Her work as an attorney general included lots of consumer protection efforts, and her work as a tax commissioner had her overseeing banking in her state. A spot on the Banking, Housing and Urban Affairs Committee gives Heitkamp the opportunity to continue her work as a consumer advocate.

She also sits on the Small Business and Entrepreneurship Committee and says she wants to make sure that the federal government does not impose excessive regulations on small "Main Street" banks and credit unions as it implements the 2010 financial regulatory overhaul law. North Dakota's housing shortage, a partial result of the recent oil and gas boom in the state, is another problem that she hopes to address.

Heitkamp, as a senator from a Western state where Native Americans are more than 5 percent of the population, went after a seat on the Indian Affairs Committee. She expresses a particular interest in helping military veterans in the Indian population, and she co-sponsored a 2013 reauthorization of federal programs to combat domestic violence. It included some provisions, opposed by conservative Republicans, that affected the prosecuting powers of tribal governments. Anyone who wanted to pass the bill "without protecting Native American women and children, or families, really should spend some time in states like North Dakota or do the work that I did as attorney general," she said.

On fiscal issues, Heitkamp says she has an aversion to debt: "In my personal life I don't like paying interest unless I absolutely have to, and I don't want to spend the taxpayers' money paying interest unless we absolutely have to." She supports amending the Constitution to require a balanced budget and says plans to reduce unemployment should factor into federal budgeting. "Underemployment and unemployment in this country costs us double, because it costs us revenue and it costs us services," she said. "So getting people back to work is a two-for-one deal for us in the budget."

Heitkamp grew up in Mantador, one of seven children in a working-class family. Her father was a seasonal construction worker, and her mother was a school cook. Her brother, Joel Heitkamp, served as a state senator in North Dakota from 1994 to 2008. He is now a radio talk show host, having replaced fellow North Dakotan Ed Schultz (currently of MSNBC) as host of the program News and Views. Heitkamp has occasionally filled in for her brother.

After graduating from the University of North Dakota, Heitkamp got a law degree in Portland, Ore., at Lewis and Clark College. She worked in the Office of the State Tax Commissioner during the early 1980s, serving under Democrat Kent Conrad. Heitkamp was elected to succeed Conrad in 1986, as he successfully ran for the U.S. Senate. She won her campaign for attorney general in 1992.

Heitkamp ran for governor of North Dakota in 2000, losing by 10 points to Republican John Hoeven, who is now the state's senior senator. During the campaign, Heitkamp was diagnosed with breast cancer and, with the encouragement of cancer patients and survivors, decided to continue running. "I had a lot of cancer survivors and women who were going through breast cancer write me," Heitkamp said. "I mean, just boxes and boxes of letters encouraging me to stay in the race and encouraging me to continue to kind of live my life."

After her defeat, she served as a director with Dakota Gas. Conrad's retirement brought her back into politics. She was unopposed in the Democratic primary, and her Republican opponent was Rick Berg, a 25-year veteran of the North Dakota House who had been elected to the state's lone U.S. House seat in 2010.

When Berg announced his candidacy in May 2011, it was a foregone conclusion to many people that he'd be the victor. But Heitkamp had a winning personality and more experience in statewide campaigns. She effectively ran against the dysfunction of Congress while promoting her moderate record.

Berg, meanwhile, was a bit lackluster. Heitkamp scored one of the upset victories of the 2012 cycle, winning by fewer than 3,000 votes.

Rep. Kevin Cramer (R)

Capitol Office
225-2611
cramer.house.gov
1032 Longworth Bldg. 20515-3401; fax 226 0893

Committees
Natural Resources
Science, Space & Technology

Residence
Bismarck

Born
Jan. 21, 1961; Rolette, N.D.

Religion
Evangelical Christian

Family
Wife, Kris Cramer; five children

Education
Concordia College, B.A. 1983 (social work); U. of Mary, M.M 2003

Career
University fundraiser; state economic development and finance director; state tourism director; state party official; campaign aide

Political Highlights
N.D. Republican Party chairman, 1992-93; Republican nominee for U.S. House, 1996, 1998; N.D. Public Service Commission, 2003-12

ELECTION RESULTS

2012 GENERAL		
Kevin Cramer (R)	173,585	54.9%
Pam Gulleson (D)	131,870	41.7%
Eric Olson (LIBERT)	10,216	3.2%
2012 PRIMARY		
Kevin Cramer (R)	54,405	54.4%
Brian P. Kalk (R)	45,415	45.4%

Elected 2012; 1st term

Cramer, an evangelical Christian, describes himself as a "joyful, optimistic conservative" out to cut spending while building interparty and intraparty relationships. "I hope I can be a bridge-builder," he says. "I love Democrats, and I care about them and I pray for them."

Cramer has been active in GOP politics for a long time. After college, he worked as a campaign aide. By his early 30s, he was the chairman of the North Dakota Republican Party. Gov. Ed Schafer named him the state's tourism director in 1993, and in 1997 he became the economic development director. He made unsuccessful bids for the U.S. House in 1996 and 1998.

He left politics behind for a little while, becoming a fundraiser and foundation director at the University of Mary in Bismarck. But Gov. John Hoeven appointed him to the state Public Service Commission in 2003, and he served there until his election to the House. (Hoeven is now the state's senior senator.)

The position had him overseeing rapid growth in the energy sector, much of it tied to development of the Bakken Shale. Cramer cites his state as an economic example for the rest of the country, and he wants to see the government, particularly the EPA, ease off regulations. Federal land management policies could also be less stringent, he says: "They were hard to deal with when the Republicans were in charge, and they're impossible now." He sits on the Natural Resources Committee and its panels on Energy and Mineral Resources, and Public Lands and Environmental Regulations. He also sits on the Science, Space and Technology Subcommittee on Energy.

In 2010, Cramer sought the GOP nomination for the House race, but Rick Berg beat him out at the party convention en route to capturing the seat. Berg ran for the Senate in 2012, and this time Cramer skipped the convention, running directly in the primary. He defeated the party-endorsed candidate, fellow Public Service Commissioner Brian P. Kalk, by 10 points. He easily won the general election.

North Dakota

At Large

North Dakota includes fertile eastern Red River farmlands, wheat-covered plains, arid grasslands and Theodore Roosevelt's beloved ranches near the western border.

The state's agriculture-based economy must withstand extreme weather conditions, including severe droughts to the west and flooding along the Red River. Wind energy, biofuels, coal, gas and oil are key to the west, and technology has emerged as a significant economic contributor in the eastern part of the state. Fargo hosts a Microsoft campus.

The Bakken oil formation in the west has made North Dakota second among U.S. states in domestic production and has transformed nearly empty parts of the prairie, bringing in temporary workers who need permanent infrastructure — roads and homes — to operate. Residents fear a boom-bust energy cycle and there are environmental concerns about the impact of extraction.

Economic trends have intensified migration of the state's young people away from rural farming communities and into the cities of Fargo and Grand Forks, where a diversified economy, health care facilities and several universities provide greater job choice. Grand Forks has a low unemployment rate and ranks high in quality of life indicators.

After two decades of sending an entirely Democratic delegation to Congress, the state elected Republican Gov. John Hoeven to the U.S. Senate and Republican Rick Berg to the U.S. House in 2010. Berg was beaten in the 2012 Senate race by Democrat Heidi Heitkamp, although a Republican succeeded him in the House. Eastern communities around Grand Forks and Fargo and American Indian reservations are more likely to back Democrats, but Republican roots are strong throughout the state — the state legislature and governorship are both GOP-controlled. Mitt Romney carried the state by 20 percentage points in the 2012 presidential election, losing in only 6 of the state's 53 counties.

Major Industry
Agriculture, energy, technology, health care, higher education

Military Bases
Minot Air Force Base, 5,569 military, 1,185 civilian; Grand Forks Air Force Base, 1,204 military, 373 civilian (2011)

Cities
Fargo, Bismarck, Grand Forks, Minot

Notable
The National Buffalo Museum is in Jamestown.

OHIO

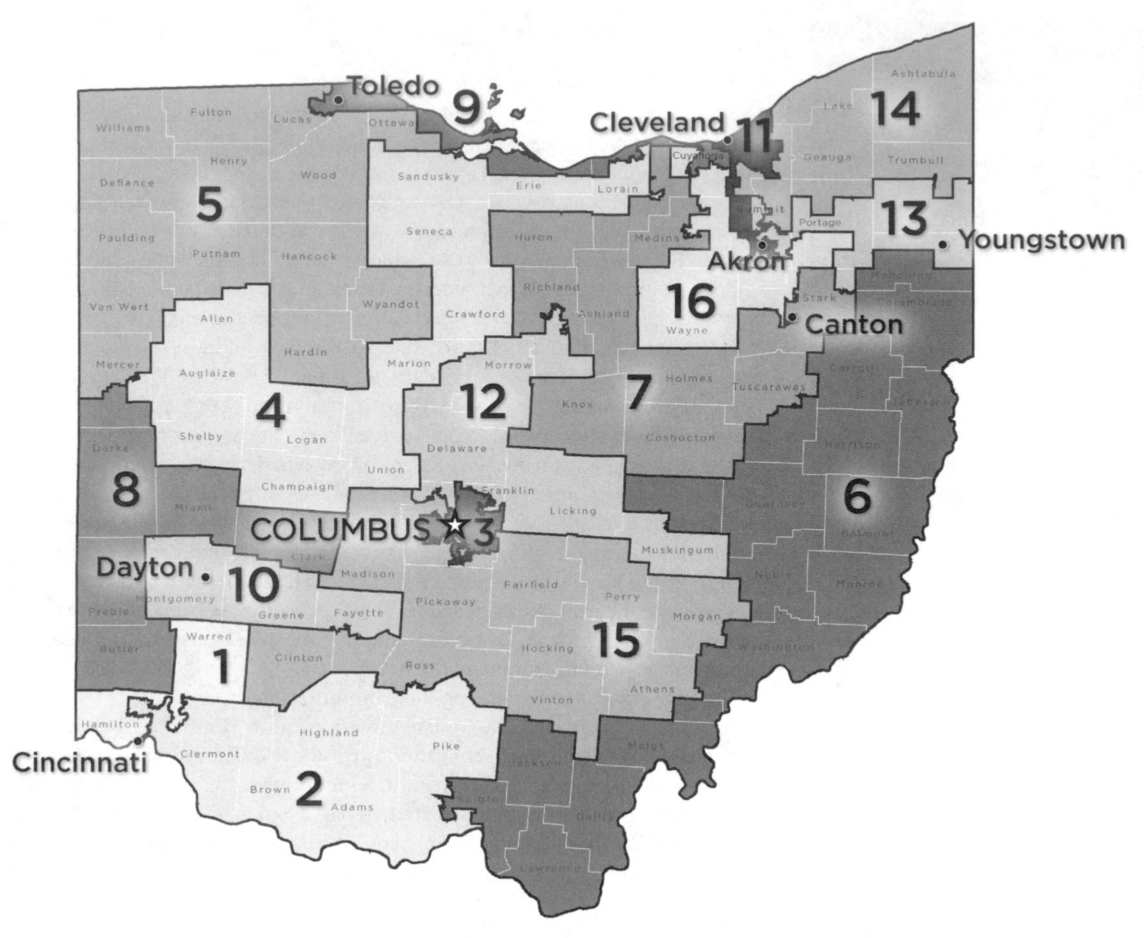

Toledo
9
Cleveland
11
14
Ashtabula
Lake
Geauga
Trumbull
13
Youngstown
Portage
Summit
Akron
Cuyahoga
16
Wayne
Stark
Canton
Mahoning
Columbiana
Williams
Fulton
Lucas
Ottawa
Defiance
Henry
Wood
5
Sandusky
Erie
Lorain
Paulding
Putnam
Hancock
Seneca
Huron
Medina
Van Wert
Allen
Wyandot
Crawford
Richland
Ashland
Mercer
Auglaize
Hardin
Marion
Morrow
Holmes
Tuscarawas
Carroll
Jefferson
4
12
Knox
7
Shelby
Logan
Delaware
Coshocton
Harrison
Darke
Union
8
Champaign
Miami
Franklin
Licking
Guernsey
6
Belmont
COLUMBUS
3
Clark
Muskingum
Dayton
10
Madison
Fairfield
Noble
Monroe
Montgomery
Preble
Greene
Fayette
Pickaway
Perry
Morgan
Warren
Butler
1
Clinton
15
Hocking
Washington
Ross
Athens
Vinton
Hamilton
Highland
Pike
Meigs
Cincinnati
Clermont
Jackson
Brown
2
Adams
Gallia
Lawrence

Gov. John R. Kasich (R)

First elected: 2010
Length of term: 4 years
Term expires: 1/15
Salary: $148,304
Phone: (614) 466-3555
Residence: Westerville
Born: May 13, 1952; McKees Rocks, Pa.
Religion: Christian
Family: Wife, Karen Kasich; two children
Education: Ohio State U., B.A. 1974 (political science)
Career: Television show host; investment banker; state legislative aide
Political highlights: Ohio Senate, 1979-83; U.S. House, 1983-2001

ELECTION RESULTS

2010 GENERAL

John R. Kasich (R)	1,889,186	49.0%
Ted Strickland (D)	1,812,059	47.0%
Ken Matesz (LIBERT)	92,116	2.4%
Dennis Spisak (GREEN)	58,475	1.5%

Lt. Gov. Mary Taylor (R)

First elected: 2010
Length of term: 4 years
Term expires: 1/15
Salary: $78,041
Phone: (614) 644-0935

LEGISLATURE

General Assembly: Year-round with recess

Senate: 33 members, 4-year terms

2013 ratios: 23 R, 10 D; 25 men, 8 women

Salary: $60,584

Phone: (614) 466-4900

House: 99 members, 2-year terms

2013 ratios: 60 R, 39 D; 76 men, 23 women

Salary: $60,584

Phone: (614) 466-3357

TERM LIMITS

Governor: 2 terms

Senate: 2 consecutive terms

House: 4 consecutive terms

URBAN STATISTICS

CITY	POPULATION
Columbus	787,033
Cleveland	396,815
Cincinnati	296,943
Toledo	287,208
Akron	199,110

REGISTERED VOTERS

Voters do not register by party.

POPULATION

2010 population	11,536,504
2000 population	11,353,140
1990 population	10,847,115
Percent change (2000-2010)	+1.6%
Rank among states (2010)	7
Median age	37.9
Born in state	75.1%
Foreign born	3.6%
Violent crime rate	332/100,000
Poverty level	15.2%
Federal workers	93,577
Military	8,261

ELECTIONS

STATE ELECTION OFFICIAL
(614) 466-2585

DEMOCRATIC PARTY
(614) 221-6563

REPUBLICAN PARTY
(614) 228-2481

MISCELLANEOUS

Web: www.ohio.gov

Capital: Columbus

U.S. CONGRESS

Senate: 1 Democrat, 1 Republican

House: 12 Republicans, 4 Democrats

STATISTICS BY DISTRICT

	2012 Vote for President		2008 Vote for President										
District	Obama	Romney	Obama	McCain	Black	Asian	Hispanic	Median Income	Over 64	Under 20	College Education	Rural	Sq. Miles
1	46%	52%	47%	52%	22%	2%	3%	$49,645	12%	28%	30%	7%	687
2	44	55	44	54	8	1	2	48,066	14	26	29	25	3,222
3	70	29	67	31	32	3	6	37,667	9	28	25	<1	228
4	42	56	44	54	6	1	3	45,326	15	26	16	35	4,665
5	44	54	46	52	3	1	4	48,211	15	26	23	36	5,626
6	43	55	45	53	2	<1	1	41,355	17	24	15	56	7,215
7	44	54	47	51	4	1	2	45,910	15	27	18	38	3,865
8	36	62	38	60	6	2	3	48,452	14	28	21	23	2,450
9	68	31	67	32	15	2	10	37,749	14	26	20	4	465
10	48	50	49.1	49.4	17	2	2	42,813	15	26	26	7	1,130
11	83	17	82	17	54	2	4	32,014	15	26	25	1	244
12	44	54	45	54	5	3	2	61,304	13	27	37	23	2,272
13	63	35	62	36	12	1	3	38,697	16	24	20	9	894
14	48	51	49	49	4	2	2	56,506	16	25	31	22	1,953
15	46	52	46	52	3	2	2	53,239	13	26	28	37	4,739
16	45	53	47	51	2	2	2	56,251	17	25	31	14	1,205
STATE	**51**	**48**	**52**	**47**	**12**	**2**	**3**	**45,749**	**14**	**26**	**25**	**21**	**40,861**
U.S.	**51**	**47**	**53**	**46**	**12**	**5**	**17**	**50,052**	**13**	**27**	**29**	**21**	**3,531,905**

Sen. Sherrod Brown (D)

Capitol Office
224-2315
brown.senate.gov
713 Hart Bldg. 20510-3503; fax 228-6321

Committees
Agriculture, Nutrition & Forestry
Banking, Housing & Urban Affairs
(Financial Institutions & Consumer Protection - Chairman)
Finance
(Social Security, Pensions & Family Policy - Chairman)
Veterans' Affairs
Select Ethics

Residence
Avon

Born
Nov. 9, 1952; Mansfield, Ohio

Religion
Lutheran

Family
Wife, Connie Schultz; two children, two stepchildren

Education
Yale U., B.A. 1974 (Russian & East European studies); Ohio State U., M.A. 1979 (education), M.A. 1981 (public administration)

Career
College instructor

Political Highlights
Ohio House, 1975-83; Ohio secretary of state, 1983-91; defeated for re-election as Ohio secretary of state, 1990; U.S. House, 1993-2007

ELECTION RESULTS

2012 GENERAL

Sherrod Brown (D)	2,762,690	50.7%
Josh Mandel (R)	2,435,712	44.7%
Scott A. Rupert (I)	250,616	4.6%

2012 PRIMARY

Sherrod Brown (D)	unopposed

Previous Winning Percentages
2006 (56%); 2004 House Election (67%); 2002 House Election (69%); 2000 House Election (65%); 1998 House Election (62%); 1996 House Election (60%); 1994 House Election (49%); 1992 House Election (53%)

Elected 2006; 2nd term

Brown heartily supports an interventionist government, begging off only when he feels his working-class constituents are threatened. He is a staunch critic of free trade, a champion of organized labor and one of the Senate Democrats most reviled by free-market conservatives.

Right-leaning and corporate-backed organizations spent tens of millions of dollars in the 2012 election cycle trying to deny Brown a second term. All of that outside money could motivate him in pursuit of another liberal goal — overhauling campaign finance law — but Brown said new causes won't interfere with his top priority: boosting manufacturing in his Rust Belt state.

"We need to grow our way out of this," Brown said. "I'll keep focusing on manufacturing. To me, it's as important as the fiscal issues." In the 112th Congress (2011-12), Brown and Illinois Republican Mark S. Kirk were the sponsors of a bill requiring the development of a national manufacturing strategy. The House passed its version in 2012, but the Senate did not take it up.

Brown has a working-class persona, if not working-class roots. His father was a doctor, and Brown — who has an unruly mop of hair and loves baseball — was a college instructor. He became interested in politics as a teenager in the late 1960s, went to Yale University and was barely 22 when he started his political career in the Ohio House.

No one questions his sincerity on blue-collar issues, however. Brown wrote a 2004 book on a topic about which he cares fervently: "Myths of Free Trade: Why American Trade Policy Has Failed." He served 14 years in the U.S. House before joining the Senate, and in that time he fought free-trade agreements tooth and nail. Brown maintains that pacts such as the North American Free Trade Agreement have harmed the manufacturing industry in his state and across the nation and exacerbated the trade deficit. He wants trade pacts revamped to include incentives for corporations to create jobs in this country rather than outsource them.

"There's nothing I feel stronger about than how this country has sold out the middle class on trade issues," he said. Brown now has an even closer connection to trade issues — he joined the Finance Committee, and its subcommittee on trade, for the 113th Congress (2013-14).

During the 112th Congress, Brown criticized President Barack Obama for not labeling China a currency manipulator. (It is widely believed that China manipulates the value of its currency to give its exports an advantage in global markets.)

"This president has done better than his predecessors on trade rules and trade law," Brown said in 2012. "But I'm concerned about new trade agreements that don't serve our country. I will continue to work on that." He was not thrilled when Japan joined talks for the Trans-Pacific Partnership in 2013, worrying that it might "undermine the impressive gains made by the American auto industry." Japan has mostly closed its markets to American cars and car parts.

Brown could be involved in efforts to change campaign finance laws in the 113th Congress. He wants more restrictions on spending by outside groups; the U.S. Chamber of Commerce and Crossroads GPS invested heavily in his Republican opponent for 2012, Ohio State Treasurer Josh Mandel. It was a generally nasty campaign, and Brown described some of the most "cynical politics I've ever seen. ... Out-of-state interest groups, oil companies that outsource jobs, Wall Street and billionaires were trying to buy the election."

While Brown wants to curb the influence of corporate interests on elections, he does not call for similar restraints on unions' political work. He told the Columbus Dispatch that he bristles at the "false equivalency" between corporate and union political expenditures, saying unions pale in comparison.

The majority of his years in Congress, Brown has received a 100 percent annual score from the AFL-CIO for his voting record. Brown calls the inability of workers to receive a bigger share of the wealth they help create "the most fundamental problem in our economy." He is chairing the Finance subcommittee with jurisdiction over pensions. It also covers Social Security, and Brown opposes changes that would reduce benefits from that program.

His support for fighting global warming is tempered by his concern for Ohio's industries. Brown was one of four Democrats to vote in June 2008 against proceeding to a vote on a bill to cap greenhouse gas emissions; he said it could hurt his state's economy. He has called for clean-energy legislation to include considerations of manufacturing competitiveness.

From his spot on the Banking, Housing and Urban Affairs Committee, Brown keeps an eye on Wall Street. Brown chairs the Financial Institutions and Consumer Protection Subcommittee, and he backed a successful $700 billion bill in fall 2008 to assist the ailing financial services industry — because the failure of financial institutions would harm average Americans, he said. He wants tougher requirements for banks to keep capital reserves, which he says would keep banks from growing too large and spare the government from having to provide more bailouts.

He also sits on the Agriculture, Nutrition and Forestry Committee. In 2011, Brown and Maine Democratic Rep. Chellie Pingree introduced their plans to encourage the use of local foods, such as facilitating the use of Supplemental Nutrition Assistance Program benefits at farmers' markets and a pilot program to help schools buy local food. The Senate-passed 2012 farm bill (which was not enacted) included those provisions, and Brown introduced a similar measure in 2013.

Brown's liberalism extends to social issues and infuses both his public and private lives. Long divorced, he had become an enthusiastic reader of a local newspaper writer's columns about Cleveland's poor. Brown sent an admiring note to the writer, future Pulitzer Prize winner Connie Schultz. That led to a meeting; less than a year after their first date in 2003, they were married.

To avoid a conflict of interest, Schultz gave up her column once Brown's Senate campaign got under way. She did, however, pen a 2007 book, "... and His Lovely Wife: A Memoir from the Woman Beside the Man," about her experience working for Brown's Senate campaign.

Raised in Mansfield, in the north-central part of the state, Brown's first taste of elective office came as student council president in high school. His interest in politics was sparked by the Vietnam War, the civil rights movement and the 1968 presidential candidacy of Robert F. Kennedy.

Brown earned a degree in Russian from Yale University in 1974, the same year that he was elected to the Ohio House for the first time. He served in that chamber for eight years, then spent eight more as Ohio secretary of state. He was defeated for re-election in 1990 by Republican Bob Taft, who would later serve two terms as governor.

In 1992, Brown won a seat in the House and focused on trade issues, particularly his strong opposition to NAFTA, which President Bill Clinton supported. He held a seat on the Energy and Commerce Committee.

Brown narrowly won re-election in the Republican wave of 1994. But he won subsequent elections with ease, and in the process he amassed a huge campaign treasury in preparation for a bid for governor or senator.

Brown beat incumbent Republican Sen. Mike DeWine by 12 points in 2006, racking up large percentages in the counties around Cleveland and Mahoning Valley — traditionally the most unionized part of Ohio. In 2012, he beat Mandel by 6 points, even as Obama won the state by only 2 points.

Key Votes

2012	
Prohibit health insurance plans from denying coverage based on the sponsor's religious beliefs	YES
Require approval of the Keystone XL oil pipeline	NO
Ease securities rules to expand small-business access to capital	NO
Reauthorize farm and nutrition programs for five years	YES
Limit debate on a bill that would create private-sector cybersecurity standards	YES
Consent to ratification of a treaty setting global standard for the treatment of people with disabilities	YES
Provide $60.4 billion in disaster relief following Superstorm Sandy	YES
Extend most Bush-era income tax rates while allowing rates for top-bracket earners to rise (Jan. 1, 2013)	YES
2011	
Prevent EPA from regulating greenhouse gas emissions to address climate change	NO
Extend certain provisions of Patriot Act for four years	NO
Clear compromise debt limit increase plan and establish future spending limits	YES
Overhaul patent law	YES
Implement Colombia free trade agreement	NO
Limit debate on confirmation of Caitlin J. Halligan to D.C. Circuit Court of Appeals	YES
Extend payroll tax cut and unemployment benefits for two months	YES

CQ Vote Studies

	PARTY UNITY		PRESIDENTIAL SUPPORT	
	SUPPORT	OPPOSE	SUPPORT	OPPOSE
2012	97%	3%	96%	4%
2011	98%	2%	92%	8%
2010	99%	1%	98%	2%
2009	99%	1%	96%	4%
2008	97%	3%	30%	70%
2007	97%	3%	35%	65%
2006	92%	8%	36%	64%
2005	97%	3%	7%	93%
2004	98%	2%	26%	74%
2003	99%	1%	11%	89%

Interest Groups

	AFL-CIO	ADA	CCUS	ACU
2012	100%	100%	38%	0%
2011	95%	95%	45%	0%
2010	100%	95%	9%	0%
2009	100%	100%	43%	0%
2008	100%	95%	63%	8%
2007	100%	95%	36%	0%
2006	93%	75%	40%	25%
2005	93%	100%	33%	4%
2004	100%	95%	24%	4%
2003	100%	100%	25%	16%

Sen. Rob Portman (R)

Capitol Office
224-3353
portman.senate.gov
448 Russell Bldg. 20510-3504; fax 224-9075

Committees
Budget
Energy & Natural Resources
Finance
Homeland Security & Governmental Affairs

Residence
Terrace Park

Born
Dec. 19, 1955; Cincinnati, Ohio

Religion
Methodist

Family
Wife, Jane Portman; three children

Education
Dartmouth College, B.A. 1978 (anthropology); U. of Michigan, J.D. 1984

Career
Lawyer

Political Highlights
White House associate counsel, 1989; White House Legislative Affairs director, 1989-91; U.S. House, 1993-2005; U.S. trade representative, 2005-06; Office of Management and Budget director, 2006-07

ELECTION RESULTS

2010 GENERAL

Rob Portman (R)	2,168,736	56.8%
Lee Fisher (D)	1,503,286	39.4%
Eric Deaton (CNSTP)	65,856	1.7%
Michael L. Pryce (I)	50,100	1.3%

2010 PRIMARY

Rob Portman (R)	unopposed

Previous Winning Percentages
2004 House Election (72%); 2002 House Election (74%); 2000 House Election (74%); 1998 House Election (76%); 1996 House Election (72%); 1994 House Election (77%); 1993 Special House Election (70%)

Elected 2010; 1st term

Portman brings plenty of political and fiscal expertise to the Senate, as well as a centrist approach to policymaking. He is definitely conservative in regards to budgeting, however, believing that cutting federal spending is paramount.

His involvement with Washington started in the 1980s as a young lawyer at Patton, Boggs and Blow; Portman was, among other things, a specialist in trade law. He eventually ended up working in the White House legislative affairs office for President George Bush.

Portman was elected to the House in 1993 and was soon added to the Ways and Means Committee, which handles trade, taxes and entitlement programs. During the George W. Bush administration, he was chosen by House GOP leaders as their liaison to the White House. The White House then named Portman the U.S. trade representative in 2005. He became Bush's budget director the next year.

Portman, who returned to Congress as a senator in 2011, doesn't shy from the "Washington insider" label, using it to his advantage when pushing legislation or trying to sway opinions. For the 113th Congress (2013-14), he was named a deputy whip.

The National Republican Senatorial Committee also created a new position for Portman, vice chairman of finance, which involves him in the party's fundraising for the 2014 election cycle. His familiarity with the financial world and its political donors is seen as a big help to NRSC Chairman Jerry Moran of Kansas, who is less connected.

Portman's friendly style, command of substance and reputation as a fair dealer have brought him praise from both major parties. Because of his budgeting and policy experience, he was selected in 2011 to serve on the Joint Select Committee on Deficit Reduction. The 12-member temporary panel was given the goal of generating a plan to reduce the federal deficit by at least $1.2 trillion through fiscal 2021.

"It's not something that I sought, but when I was asked I accepted it, and I did so knowing that it would be very tough to reach consensus," he told the American Enterprise Institute in November 2011. "It was too critical for us not to try."

The panel didn't succeed, but Portman said he would build on its efforts. He opposed a short-term increase to the federal government's borrowing limit in January 2013. "The bills are too high, and it would be irresponsible to merely pay our past obligations without having a real debate about Washington's reckless spending habits and how to avoid this situation in the future," he wrote. He has introduced a bill to require increases in the debt limit to be offset by spending cuts of an equivalent amount.

But Portman, who sits on the Budget Committee, has also shown some weariness of brinkmanship. In 2012 and again in 2013, he proposed a bill to eliminate the possibility of government shutdowns when spending laws expire. His bill would create a series of short "continuing resolutions" to keep government running at progressively lower spending levels until a regular spending law is put in place.

His influence over fiscal issues increased in the 113th Congress as he joined the Finance Committee, which is basically the Senate equivalent of the Ways and Means Committee.

Portman still relishes the role of advocate for free trade. As the U.S. trade representative, he helped negotiate pacts with South Korea, Colombia and Panama that were finally approved in 2011; as the deals were finalized, Portman wrote on The Daily Caller website that trade negotiations had been stagnating under the Obama administration. He likes trade promotion authority, which lets presidents submit agreements to Congress for up-or-down votes with no amendments. He also favors more-aggressive enforcement of intellectual property law and stronger rebukes of China for currency manipulation. He said that a 2012 law normalizing trade relations with Russia "has teeth and brings Russia into a rules-based trading system."

He has sought structural changes to entitlement programs to reduce the growth of their costs. As a House member, he was credited with a successful push to include tax incentives for retirement savings in the $1.35 trillion tax cut package enacted in 2001 — the only major component that was not proposed by Bush. Portman attributed the victory to "five years of blood, sweat and tears" with his Democratic ally, Benjamin L. Cardin of Maryland, who is now a Senate colleague.

Portman also holds seats on the Energy and Natural Resources Committee and the Homeland Security and Governmental Affairs Committee. He says he wants to "aggressively pursue domestic energy sources" and worked with New Hampshire Democrat Jeanne Shaheen on a measure to promote energy savings in residential and commercial buildings. He suggests creating an International Conservation Strategy, with benchmarks and goals for working with other nations.

A social conservative, Portman has signed on to anti-abortion legislation and wants to make it a federal offense to move a minor across state lines for an abortion in order to skirt another state's abortion laws. He married his wife, Jane, in 1986. As the story goes, before their marriage, he agreed to become a Methodist and she agreed to become a Republican. Portman surprised many people in March 2013 when he announced his support for gay marriage; he said his change of heart was inspired by his son, who came out to his parents in 2011.

Portman's family has deep roots in Ohio. His mother's parents bought and refurbished the Golden Lamb, a landmark Lebanon hotel that once hosted Mark Twain and Daniel Webster. (It now has a George W. Bush suite.)

Portman grew up in Cincinnati. His father founded the Portman Equipment Company, a forklift truck dealership that grew substantially; Portman and his siblings worked there while growing up.

After getting a law degree, Portman headed to Washington. He volunteered on the 1988 Bush campaign, then worked in the White House. When he left that job, he returned to Cincinnati to work in business law.

The resignation of Republican Rep. Bill Gradison opened Portman's path to the House. He won a tight Republican primary, then took the special election in the solidly conservative suburban district with 70 percent of the vote.

He left the George W. Bush administration late in 2007 and again returned to Cincinnati to practice law. When Republican Sen. George V. Voinovich announced plans to retire, Portman quickly entered the race and ran unopposed for the Republican nomination in 2010.

On the Democratic side, Lt. Gov. Lee Fisher won a testy primary and started out the general election campaign in good position in most polls. Fisher tried, without much success, to blame Portman for the growth of spending under Bush and a Republican Congress.

Portman pointed to Fisher's role as the state's "job czar" during a time when Ohio lost hundreds of thousands of jobs. Portman began pulling ahead by the end of June and led by double digits in most polls heading into October. He won by nearly 18 points.

Portman is an avid hunter and told USA Today that his great-grandfather "went out into a duck blind on a frozen lake, and he never came back" — according to family lore, he had died of a heart attack "with his gun over his lap and with a smile on his face." Portman now owns the gun.

Key Votes

2012

Prohibit health insurance plans from denying coverage based on the sponsor's religious beliefs	NO
Require approval of the Keystone XL oil pipeline	YES
Ease securities rules to expand small-business access to capital	YES
Reauthorize farm and nutrition programs for five years	NO
Limit debate on a bill that would create private-sector cybersecurity standards	NO
Consent to ratification of a treaty setting global standard for the treatment of people with disabilities	NO
Provide $60.4 billion in disaster relief following Superstorm Sandy	NO
Extend most Bush-era income tax rates while allowing rates for top-bracket earners to rise (Jan. 1, 2013)	YES

2011

Prevent EPA from regulating greenhouse gas emissions to address climate change	YES
Extend certain provisions of Patriot Act for four years	YES
Clear compromise debt limit increase plan and establish future spending limits	YES
Overhaul patent law	YES
Implement Colombia free trade agreement	YES
Limit debate on confirmation of Caitlin J. Halligan to D.C. Circuit Court of Appeals	NO
Extend payroll tax cut and unemployment benefits for two months	YES

CQ Vote Studies

	PARTY UNITY		PRESIDENTIAL SUPPORT	
	SUPPORT	OPPOSE	SUPPORT	OPPOSE
2012	86%	14%	49%	51%
2011	92%	8%	59%	41%
2005	99%	1%	100%	0%
2004	95%	5%	94%	6%
2003	95%	5%	98%	2%

Interest Groups

	AFL-CIO	ADA	CCUS	ACU
2012	0%	10%	88%	76%
2011	11%	15%	100%	75%
2005	0%	0%	100%	
2004	20%	10%	100%	88%
2003	13%	5%	97%	84%

Rep. Steve Chabot (R)

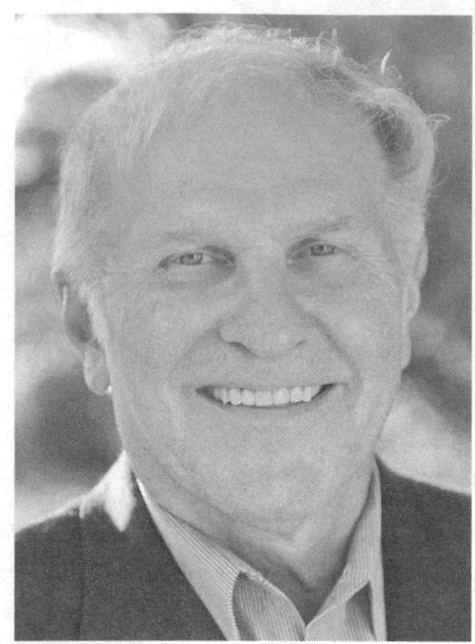

Capitol Office
225-2216
chabot.house.gov
2371 Rayburn Bldg. 20515-3501; fax 225-3012

Committees
Foreign Affairs
(Asia & the Pacific - Chairman)
Judiciary
Small Business

Residence
Cincinnati

Born
Jan. 22, 1953; Cincinnati, Ohio

Religion
Roman Catholic

Family
Wife, Donna Chabot; two children

Education
College of William & Mary, A.B. 1975 (history); Northern Kentucky U., J.D. 1978

Career
Lawyer; teacher

Political Highlights
Independent candidate for Cincinnati City Council, 1979; Republican candidate for Cincinnati City Council, 1983; Cincinnati City Council, 1985-90; Republican nominee for U.S. House, 1988; Hamilton County Board of Commissioners, 1990-95; U.S. House, 1995-2009; defeated for re-election to U.S. House, 2008

ELECTION RESULTS

2012 GENERAL		
Steve Chabot (R)	201,907	57.7%
Jeff Sinnard (D)	131,490	37.6%
Jim Berns (LIBERT)	9,674	2.8%
Rich Stevenson (GREEN)	6,645	1.9%
2012 PRIMARY		
Steve Chabot (R)		unopposed

Previous Winning Percentages
2010 (52%); 2006 (52%); 2004 (60%); 2002 (65%); 2000 (53%); 1998 (53%); 1996 (54%); 1994 (56%)

Elected 1994; 9th term

Did not serve 2009-11

Chabot is a frank and consistent conservative. A long House career hasn't dulled his verve for restraining government, while his climb up committee rosters has made him an authority on international relations, legal affairs and small businesses.

The voters of southern Ohio made Chabot (SHAB-it) a part of two GOP waves. He was swept into office with the 1994 Republican Revolution, and after what he calls a "two-year involuntary sabbatical," he returned to the House with the Class of 2010. He is still a strong believer in the Contract With America, a creed of transparency and cost-cutting that helped carry Republicans to power in 1994. Chabot carried a copy of that document in his pocket during that campaign — he had it framed, and it now sits on his desk.

Chabot rarely raises his voice, but he is blunt in expressing his beliefs. He maintained a lively blog on his campaign website for 2012 and gave his interpretation of nationwide election results. "We should look at and treat people equally, without regard to skin color or ethnicity," he wrote. "The reality is that African-Americans vote overwhelmingly for Democrats (even more so for Barack Obama), and Hispanics and Asians are trending strongly in the same direction. This is something that absolutely must be addressed by Republicans, or we will go the way of the Whig Party, and America is doomed."

Throughout his House tenure, Chabot has stuck with the three committee assignments he received as a freshman. His accumulation of seniority has paid off in leadership roles. Chabot chaired the Judiciary Subcommittee on the Constitution from 2001 through 2006, served as the ranking Republican on the Small Business Committee in 2007 and 2008, and took the gavel of the Foreign Affairs Subcommittee on the Middle East and South Asia in the 112th Congress (2011-12).

For the 113th Congress (2013-14), Chabot is running the show at the Foreign Affairs Subcommittee on Asia and the Pacific. In his first House tour, he was a founding member and co-chairman of the Congressional Taiwan Caucus. He pushes for stronger links with Taiwan and supporting democracy in the Asia-Pacific region. Those goals go hand in hand with his get-tough stance on China. Chabot says the United States should be more willing to confront that nation over its manipulation of its currency and certain trade deals.

Chabot is similarly unimpressed with the Obama administration's approach to North Korea. Speaking at a Washington forum, he said a North Korean nuclear test in February 2013 was "further evidence that President Obama's policies of ineffective sanctions and empty threats towards North Korea have failed. ... The administration needs to take a different strategy that stops offering carrot-and-stick deals."

Chabot blogged in early 2012 that he could support Obama's plans to commit more military resources to the Pacific — but not if it means reducing the U.S. presence in the Middle East. He called the early response to Libya's 2011 civil war "tepid"; he supported U.S. intervention when it came, though he was miffed that Congress wasn't consulted on the matter.

When unrest started in Egypt in early 2011, Chabot quickly warned about "the rise of the Muslim Brotherhood and their Islamic jihadist allies to power." Late in 2012, with the brotherhood in power, he said the U.S. should consider suspending aid to Egypt if Islamists continued to dominate the government.

Chabot has used his spot on the Judiciary Committee to promote fiscal restraint, via a balanced-budget amendment to the Constitution. He remembers voting for a such a measure as a freshman, walking over to the Senate and watching the measure fail by one vote. He was "devastated," he said. Chabot often voted against Republican-written spending bills during his earlier tenure, and he voted for every additional spending cut offered on the floor when the House passed a catchall spending bill that would trim fiscal 2011 spending by $58 billion. He opposed a less-austere package that was eventually enacted. "In my view, we shouldn't be raising taxes on anyone, period," he wrote in early 2013. "We should be cutting spending."

As a social conservative, Chabot has called for constitutional amendments to ban flag desecration, outlaw same-sex marriage, protect crime victims' rights and allow people to pray and display religious symbols on public property. He was the principal House sponsor of a 2003 law outlawing the procedure known by opponents as "partial birth" abortion.

Chabot often says that the nation is being brought low by "rogue" federal judges. He has pushed to allow media cameras in federal courtrooms, again introducing a bill to that effect in the 112th Congress.

He tries to increase the availability of capital for small businesses from his third committee. Chabot hoped to chair the Small Business Committee in the 112th Congress, but that job went to Sam Graves of Missouri. Graves will hit GOP term limits (per the Contract With America) at the end of 2014 — positioning Chabot as a possible successor, should he return to the House for another term.

Chabot was born and raised in Cincinnati. His father was an optician, and Chabot lived in a trailer, working part-time jobs to help with tuition at his parochial high school. In college, he majored in history. He taught elementary school in Cincinnati while attending law school at night across the river at Northern Kentucky University. A few years after earning his law degree, he opened a neighborhood law practice.

Chabot's political career began on the Cincinnati City Council. After two failed attempts to join the council, the first at age 26, Chabot won a seat in 1985.

He lost a congressional bid against Democrat Thomas A. Luken in 1988. The 1994 campaign was his second attempt, and he was up against first-term Democrat David Mann. Chabot campaigned on a platform of lower taxes, less government and change in Washington. With national trends favoring the GOP, he won with 56 percent of the vote.

In 2008, Steve Driehaus, a member of a well-known Cincinnati political family, touted his experience as a grass-roots organizer and state legislator. Driehaus bested Chabot by 5 points. Chabot got right to work, announcing his candidacy in February 2009. With the political winds blowing from the other direction in 2010, Chabot upended the one-term Democrat, winning by more than 5 points. His district was slightly altered in redistricting for the 2012 election, and Chabot beat Democrat Jeff Sinnard by 20 points.

Key Votes

2012

Extend a Social Security payroll tax cut and unemployment benefits	NO
Ease securities rules to expand small-business access to capital	YES
Extend for one year subsidized student loan interest rates financed by a cut in health care spending	YES
Cite Attorney General Eric H. Holder Jr. for contempt of Congress	YES
Create a visa program for foreign graduates in high-tech fields	YES
Extend most Bush-era income tax rates while allowing rates for top-bracket earners to rise (Jan. 1, 2013)	NO

2011

Strike funding for F-35 alternative engine	NO
Prevent EPA from regulating greenhouse gas emissions to address climate change	YES
Extend certain provisions of Patriot Act for four years	YES
Declare opposition to use of ground troops in Libya	YES
Overhaul patent law	YES
Pass compromise debt limit increase plan and establish future spending limits	YES
Allow consideration of measures to implement three trade agreements	YES

CQ Vote Studies

	PARTY UNITY		PRESIDENTIAL SUPPORT	
	SUPPORT	OPPOSE	SUPPORT	OPPOSE
2012	97%	3%	15%	85%
2011	97%	3%	21%	79%
2008	94%	6%	64%	36%
2007	94%	6%	80%	20%
2006	89%	11%	95%	5%

Interest Groups

	AFL-CIO	ADA	CCUS	ACU
2012	14%	10%	83%	96%
2011	0%	5%	100%	96%
2008	13%	15%	83%	100%
2007	13%	10%	70%	100%
2006	21%	10%	93%	96%

Ohio 1

Western Cincinnati and suburbs; Warren County

The 1st takes in western Cincinnati and most of surrounding Hamilton County in Ohio's southwestern corner, as well as all of fast-growing Warren County to the northeast. Nestled on the banks of the Ohio River, Cincinnati is Ohio's third-largest city and forms a metropolitan area with parts of Kentucky and Indiana — an industrial manufacturing region with German Catholic roots.

The city's diverse economy has included auto and aviation manufacturing, metalworking, chemicals, insurance and financial services. Corporate headquarters for companies including Procter & Gamble, Kroger groceries and Macy's Inc. have fed a marketing research sector. Sporting and concert arenas and nightlife venues have lured single professionals and families to the central downtown district, even after years of population shifts to the suburbs. A new $400 million casino complex is expected to boost tourism and revenue. Two colleges support the workforce: the University of Cincinnati includes a renowned music conservatory and major medical center, and the smaller Xavier University (shared with the 2nd) is a Jesuit school.

Suburban and rural Warren County is about 20 miles north of Cincinnati and 15 miles south of Dayton. Added to the 1st during decennial redistricting, Warren is the second-fastest-growing county statewide — most of that growth has been fueled by affluent families moving into new suburban communities on what was once farmland. The county is full of antique stores and historic small towns, and it hosts Kings Island Amusement Park.

Some of Cincinnati's northern Hamilton County suburbs were shifted into the 2nd during remapping, while the city's black-majority neighborhoods were kept within the 1st. Overall, the region is conservative, although Democrats can do well among the urban areas and student populations. In 2012, GOP presidential nominee Mitt Romney took 52 percent of the district's vote.

Major Industry

Manufacturing, consumer products, higher education, financial services

Cities

Cincinnati (pt.), Middletown (pt.), Fairfield, Mason, Lebanon, Forest Park

Notable

The National Underground Railroad Freedom Center is in the downtown Cincinnati corridor between Paul Brown Stadium — home of football's Bengals — and the Great American Ballpark — home of baseball's Reds.

Rep. Brad Wenstrup (R)

Capitol Office
225-3164
wenstrup.house.gov
1223 Longworth Bldg. 20515-3810; fax 225-1992

Committees
Armed Services
Veterans' Affairs

Residence
Cincinnati

Born
June 17, 1958; Cincinnati, Ohio

Religion
Roman Catholic

Family
Wife, Monica Wenstrup

Education
U. of Cincinnati, B.A. 1980 (psychology); William M. Scholl College of Podiatric Medicine, B.S. 1985 (biological sciences), D.P.M. 1985

Military
Army Reserve Medical Corps, 1998-present

Career
Surgeon

Political Highlights
Republican nominee for mayor of Cincinnati, 2009; Cincinnati Board of Health, 2009-12

ELECTION RESULTS

2012 GENERAL		
Brad Wenstrup (R)	194,296	58.6%
William R. Smith (D)	137,077	41.4%
2012 PRIMARY		
Brad Wenstrup (R)	42,482	48.7%
Jean Schmidt (R)	37,383	42.9%
Tony Brush (R)	4,275	4.9%
Fred Kundrata (R)	2,999	3.4%

Elected 2012; 1st term

Much of Wenstrup's public identity is tied to his military service. In 1998, he enlisted in the Army Reserve. He deployed to Iraq in 2005 and was the chief of surgery at the Abu Ghraib complex (the prisoner abuse scandal had already passed), tending to both soldiers and detainees. "It was the worst thing I ever had to do but the best thing I ever got to do," he says. "The people that you serve with are outstanding."

Wenstrup, the third of five children, was born and raised in Cincinnati. His father was an optician, and his mother was a homemaker. He remembers watching the shows "Combat" and "Medical Center" with his dad; "I knew at an early age I wanted to be a doctor," he says. A podiatrist, he did his medical training and residency in Chicago.

When he returned from Iraq, he caught the eye of Republican insiders while speaking about his service to various groups in Ohio. He was recruited for the Cincinnati mayoral race in 2009, then appointed to the city's Board of Health by the Democrat who beat him, Mark Mallory.

Wenstrup brings his military experience to the Armed Services Committee. He also sits on the Veterans' Affairs Committee and its Health panel. At hearings early in 2013, he asked officials about ways to cut back on some of the administrative duties of doctors at veterans hospitals — anything that "takes them away from patient care." A member of the Republican Study Committee, he dislikes the 2010 health care law and generally positions himself as a small-government conservative.

Wenstrup's March 2012 victory in a Republican primary was the first stunner of the campaign season. An anti-incumbent super PAC helped push him past Rep. Jean Schmidt in a solidly GOP district. Wenstrup ran a disciplined campaign while waiting for November, and he beat Democrat William R. Smith by 17 points. His 2012 was momentous on several fronts: Two months after the primary election, he got married.

Ohio 2

Eastern Cincinnati and suburbs; Portsmouth

Roughly 100 miles of the Ohio River separate the 2nd's portion of Cincinnati to the west and declining industrial Portsmouth to its east. The mostly conservative small towns of Ohio's western Appalachian region that fill the space between highlight the distinction between affluent suburbs and struggling rural communities.

Remapping after the 2010 census expanded the 2nd's share of eastern Cincinnati and Hamilton County, including wealthy areas east of Interstate 71, such as Hyde Park and Mount Lookout, where young professionals jog tree-lined streets filled with trendy restaurants, large old homes and new condos. Farther north is Blue Ash, a suburb where some of the region's major corporations occupy satellite office buildings. Pharmaceutical research is a growing sector here, with the recent relocation and promised expansion of Medpace Inc. in Madisonville expected to bring more jobs.

Further east of Cincinnati, the district quickly becomes rural Appalachian hollows. Adams, Highland and Pike counties have among the highest poverty and unemployment rates in the state. To the 2nd's east are Portsmouth and Chillicothe. Portsmouth produces castings, concrete, paper products and trucks. The city includes Shawnee State University, which focuses on emerging technologies. Chillicothe, which was added to the 2nd, hosts a large truck manufacturer and a paper plant that were hit hard by the recession. Health care has been the city's largest growth sector, with a regional medical center (in the 15th) and a Veterans Administration hospital as the city's two largest and fastest-growing employers.

Conservatives do well in this district, although areas around the cities can be competitive. Barack Obama took the district's portion of Hamilton County in the 2012 presidential election, but Republican Mitt Romney won by wide margins in Clermont County and some less-populous counties — and took 55 percent overall in the 2nd.

Major Industry
Manufacturing, consumer products, agriculture

Cities
Cincinnati (pt.), Chillicothe, Portsmouth

Notable
The city of Chillicothe, which touts itself as the first capital of Ohio, served as the state's capital twice, from 1803 to 1810 and from 1812 to 1816.

Rep. Joyce Beatty (D)

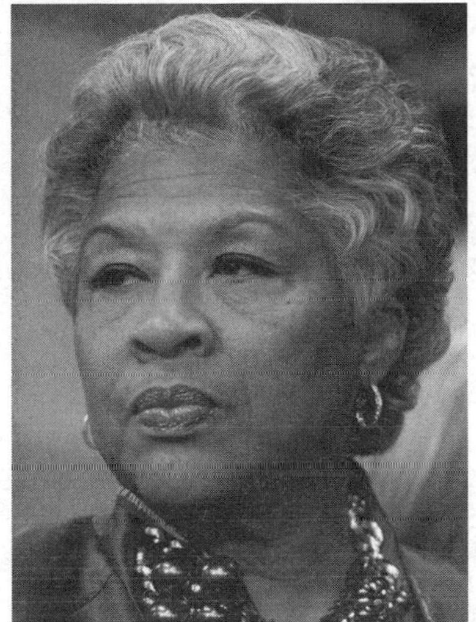

Capitol Office
225-4324
beatty.house.gov
417 Cannon Bldg. 20515-6601; fax 225-1984

Committees
Financial Services

Residence
Columbus

Born
March 12, 1950; Dayton, Ohio

Religion
Baptist

Family
Husband, Otto Beatty Jr.; two stepchildren

Education
Central State U., B.A. 1972 (drama), Wright State U., M.S. 1975 (mental health counseling); U. of Cincinnati, attended 1975-79

Career
Clothing store owner; management consulting company owner; university community outreach administrator; county health services department director; professor

Political Highlights
Ohio House, 1999-2008 (minority leader, 2006-08)

ELECTION RESULTS

2012 GENERAL		
Joyce Beatty (D)	201,897	68.3%
Chris Long (R)	77,901	26.3%
Richard Ehrbar (LIBERT)	9,462	3.2%
Bob Fitrakis (GREEN)	6,387	2.2%
2012 PRIMARY		
Joyce Beatty (D)	15,848	38.3%
Mary Jo Kilroy (D)	14,369	34.7%
Priscilla R. Tyson (D)	6,244	15.1%
Ted Celeste (D)	4,895	11.8%

Elected 2012; 1st term

Beatty has been in constant contact with the public throughout her adult life. She was a social worker, a college professor, the director of a county health department and the owner of a consulting firm. Her crowning achievement was becoming the first female Democratic leader in the history of the Ohio House — until she was elected to the U.S. House.

She grew up in Dayton but moved to Columbus in the early 1990s to start her consulting firm. Around that time, she married Otto Beatty, a prominent lawyer and member of the Ohio House. When he resigned — he was facing term limits and said he had business opportunities to pursue — she was appointed as his successor. She easily held the seat, eventually becoming minority leader; when she reached her term limit, she went to work for Ohio State University in 2009 as a vice president for outreach. Beatty also owns a clothing boutique in downtown Columbus; it started as a hobby but keeps her tapped into small-business concerns, she says.

Beatty sits on the Financial Services Committee, as well as its Housing and Insurance Subcommittee. She served on the equivalent committee in the Ohio House and supports government efforts to mitigate foreclosures. (Her consulting firm often helped the city of Columbus with public-housing relocations.) Beatty also wants to continue her work promoting financial literacy. Young people, she says, need more guidance: "If you take their calculator away, if the cash register doesn't tell you the change, they are lost," she says.

Beatty, who suffered a cerebral brain stem stroke in 2000, is a defender of the 2010 health care law.

The 3rd District as drawn for the 2012 elections was one of the few clearly Democratic districts in Ohio. In a four-way primary, Beatty prevailed by less than 4 points over Mary Jo Kilroy, who had served in the 111th Congress (2009-10). The general election was a formality: Beatty beat Republican Chris Long by 42 points.

Ohio 3

Most of Columbus and suburbs

Following decennial redistricting, the 3rd District now centers on the capital city of Columbus, extending east through the metro area within Franklin County, to Reynoldsburg and Whitehall, middle- and working-class suburbs with black populations double the state average. Drawn to gather a growing urban population with a large university and young professionals, the 3rd is one of Ohio's few collections of decidedly Democratic voters. In 2012, Barack Obama received his second-highest percentage statewide in the 3rd, with 70 percent of the presidential vote.

Previously, Columbus was sliced up among three districts; now a strong majority of the city sits in the 3rd, including economically depressed areas to the east with urban decay and some immigrant populations. Absent from the redistricted 3rd are upscale northwestern suburbs such as Upper Arlington and Dublin.

Several of the downtown draws are in the 3rd, though, including the Ohio Statehouse, city hall, the stadium for soccer's Crew and a full-scale replica of one of Christopher Columbus' ships, the Santa Maria, on the Scioto riverfront.

State government is the economic force in Columbus, and Ohio State University (shared with the 15th) is the largest single employer. With 10,000 employees and 56,000 students on nearly 1,800 acres, the campus looms large in the city, as does its sports culture.

Professional services provide supporting industries; JP Morgan Chase and Nationwide Insurance both keep corporate offices in the area, as do retail chains The Limited and Bath and Body Works. A large service and hospitality sector rounds out the city's economy, and the airport is east of the city past residential Bexley.

While population growth statewide was sluggish enough to cause Ohio to lose two seats after the 2010 census, Columbus grew by nearly 11 percent between 2000 and 2010. Nearly one-third of newcomers to the area are immigrants.

Major Industry
State government, higher education, service

Cities
Columbus (pt.), Reynoldsburg

Notable
Ohio State University's Billy Ireland Cartoon Library & Museum is the largest and most comprehensive academic research facility documenting printed cartoon art.

Rep. Jim Jordan (R)

Capitol Office
225-2676
jordan.house.gov
1524 Longworth Bldg. 20515-3504; fax 226-0577

Committees
Judiciary
Oversight & Government Reform
(Economic Growth, Job Creation and Regulatory Affairs - Chairman)

Residence
Urbana

Born
Feb. 17, 1964; Troy, Ohio

Religion
Christian

Family
Wife, Polly Jordan; four children

Education
U. of Wisconsin, B.S. 1986 (economics); Ohio State U., M.A. 1991 (education); Capital U., J.D. 2001

Career
College wrestling coach

Political Highlights
Ohio House, 1995-2000; Ohio Senate, 2001-06

ELECTION RESULTS

2012 GENERAL		
Jim Jordan (R)	182,643	58.4%
Jim Slone (D)	114,214	36.5%
Chris Kalla (LIBERT)	16,141	5.2%
2012 PRIMARY		
Jim Jordan (R)		unopposed
2010 GENERAL		
Jim Jordan (R)	146,029	71.5%
Doug Litt (D)	50,533	24.7%
Donald Charles Kissick (LIBERT)	7,708	3.8%

Previous Winning Percentages
2008 (65%); 2006 (60%)

Elected 2006; 4th term

Intensity comes naturally to Jordan, who moved to politics from the world of wrestling. He was a four-time Ohio state champion in high school and won two national college championships at the University of Wisconsin. He then went into coaching before his successful transition to state politics. "You get married, you have kids, you get tired of government taking your money and insulting your values, and you said, you know what, I'm going to run and see if I can make a difference," he said.

Jordan is a central figure as Republicans contemplate their ideological positioning and messaging. His competitive tactics have made him a leader among the most conservative lawmakers, but they also might have damaged his standing with the party at large.

He arrived in the U.S. House after 12 years in state government, and in his second term he led the budget and spending task force of the Republican Study Committee, the caucus of conservative House members. He was elected RSC chairman for the 112th Congress (2011-12), as a huge influx of tea-party-inspired members gave Republicans control of the House — and cemented the 170-member RSC as the most powerful bloc in the party.

His term at the top was marked by conflict. Jordan and the RSC were a thorn in the side of Speaker John A. Boehner. In 2011, they urged spending cuts much steeper than Boehner and the party leadership team were willing to risk. Polls showed the public souring on Republicans as the standoffs produced a string of threatened government shutdowns or defaults.

RSC aides even enlisted outside conservative groups to undercut support for a debt reduction deal Boehner was negotiating with the White House in 2011. When emails from that effort were revealed, many rank-and-file Republicans were aghast and asked whether the RSC was out of control. Jordan apologized in a closed-door meeting of the Republican Conference, but with a redrawing of Ohio's congressional map under way, leaders considered altering Jordan's district to make his re-election tougher. That idea was ultimately dropped.

The next year, conflicts between conservatives and moderates stalled or slowed action on reauthorizations of surface transportation and agriculture programs. Jordan said his task in 2012 was to show that "there's a difference between [the GOP nominee] and President Obama."

Jordan endorsed Tom Graves of Georgia as his successor. Like Jordan, Graves had perfect or near-perfect lifetime ratings from groups such as the American Conservative Union and the Club for Growth. In an upset, Graves was defeated by Louisiana's Steve Scalise, who promised to be a more pragmatic leader. A former top aide for Boehner whipped votes for Scalise.

Even without control of the RSC, Jordan has some pull in the 113th Congress (2013-14). In the 112th, he chaired the Oversight and Government Reform subcommittee on federal spending and regulations; after some tweaks to jurisdiction, he chairs the Economic Growth, Job Creation and Regulatory Affairs Subcommittee in the 113th. Jordan has used his panel to support a number of mainstream GOP lines of attack. He has called hearings to scrutinize "green" energy programs, upticks in federal regulations and the Obama administration's bailout of the automotive industry.

From his seat on the Judiciary Committee, he has backed efforts to improve border security while opposing the creation of a path to citizenship for illegal immigrants.

Jordan comments frequently on fiscal matters. In 2013, he joined a five-man working group trying to find middle ground between Boehner and conservatives. Its other members are Paul D. Ryan of Wisconsin, Tom Price of Georgia, Jeb Hensarling of Texas, and Scalise.

He split with most Republicans in October 2012 by offering some support for cuts to defense budgets put in place by an August 2011 law. "I would say the only thing that's worse than cutting national defense is not having any scheduled cuts at all take place," he told C-SPAN.

Jordan also sees potential savings in his proposal to convert federal nutrition programs (such as the Supplemental Nutrition Assistance Program, formerly known as food stamps) into a block grant for states.

Jordan is socially conservative as well. In his first three terms, he introduced a bill to require abortion providers to perform an ultrasound on a pregnant woman and show her the images before she consents to an abortion. He has also introduced a bill to extend 14th Amendment rights to each "each born and preborn human."

Jordan grew up in the rural community of St. Paris, about an hour west of Columbus. His father worked at the local General Motors plant from his teens until he retired. His mother, who cared for Jordan and two younger siblings, supplemented the family income by running a cleaning business.

In junior high, Jordan took an interest in wrestling, influenced by several relatives who were amateur wrestlers. His father built him a wrestling room so he could practice. While winning state championships at Graham High School, he lost only one match. That led to a scholarship at Wisconsin. He was inducted into the University of Wisconsin Athletic Hall of Fame in 2005.

Between his junior and senior years, Jordan married his high school sweetheart. He returned to Ohio, where he went to graduate school at Ohio State University and began a career in coaching. His wife had just given birth to their fourth child in 1994 when Jordan decided to get into the contest to succeed a longtime GOP incumbent in the state House.

During six years in the Ohio House and six more in the state Senate, Jordan routinely bucked Republican leaders, often voting against proposals he said weren't conservative enough. He attended Capital University while serving in the legislature and earned a law degree in 2001.

When Republican Rep. Michael G. Oxley announced his retirement in 2006, Jordan was part of a six-candidate Republican field hoping to succeed him. His time in the legislature gave him a clear record to run on, and he took more than 50 percent of the primary vote.

In November, he cruised to victory over Democratic lawyer Richard E. Siferd. The strong GOP tilt of his district helped him easily win re-election in 2008, even as Democrats were surging nationally. After redistricting, he still won by 22 points in 2012.

Key Votes

2012	
Extend a Social Security payroll tax cut and unemployment benefits	NO
Ease securities rules to expand small-business access to capital	YES
Extend for one year subsidized student loan interest rates financed by a cut in health care spending	YES
Cite Attorney General Eric H. Holder Jr. for contempt of Congress	YES
Create a visa program for foreign graduates in high-tech fields	YES
Extend most Bush-era income tax rates while allowing rates for top-bracket earners to rise (Jan. 1, 2013)	NO
2011	
Strike funding for F-35 alternative engine	NO
Prevent EPA from regulating greenhouse gas emissions to address climate change	YES
Extend certain provisions of Patriot Act for four years	YES
Declare opposition to use of ground troops in Libya	YES
Overhaul patent law	YES
Pass compromise debt limit increase plan and establish future spending limits	NO
Allow consideration of measures to implement three trade agreements	YES

CQ Vote Studies

	PARTY UNITY		PRESIDENTIAL SUPPORT	
	SUPPORT	OPPOSE	SUPPORT	OPPOSE
2012	97%	3%	15%	85%
2011	97%	3%	17%	83%
2010	99%	1%	22%	78%
2009	99%	1%	13%	87%
2008	95%	5%	85%	15%

Interest Groups

	AFL-CIO	ADA	CCUS	ACU
2012	5%	5%	83%	100%
2011	0%	5%	93%	100%
2010	0%	5%	75%	100%
2009	5%	0%	73%	100%
2008	0%	0%	83%	100%

Ohio 4

North and west central — Elyria, Lima

Stretching from a corner of Mercer County in the western part of the state near the Indiana border, through all or parts of 12 other counties on the way east to part of Lorain County, the mainly rural S-shaped 4th is one of the least compact districts in the state following decennial remapping. A stretch of the Ohio Turnpike runs through the northern arm in Sandusky, Erie and Lorain counties, and Interstate 75, which connects Dayton to Toledo, cuts through Shelby, Auglaize and Allen counties in the southwest.

In the central and western portions of the district, small industrial companies and large assembly plants aid the economy. The Joint Systems Manufacturing Center in Lima is responsible for the Army's Abrams tank; the General Dynamics-run factory is a leading job provider in the area, although potential defense funding cuts could endanger production. Lima also hosts a Ford engine plant. Union County, which experienced explosive population growth during the last decade, is home to a Honda manufacturing facility.

Agriculture is also important: Corn and soybeans dominate the landscape, and poultry and vegetables round out the production. In the city of Marion, educational facilities and manufacturing companies have teamed up to establish an industrial robotics and advanced manufacturing center.

Heading north, the district includes suburban portions of Erie and Lorain counties, as well as all of Sandusky County. Oberlin College — the first co-educational institution of higher learning in the United States — is located in the city of the same name in Lorain County and adds reliably liberal votes.

The safely Republican district includes Allen County, which last voted for a Democratic presidential candidate in the Roosevelt-Landon contest of 1936. Democratic strength in the northern tier of the district is not enough to balance out the strongly conservative Republican edge elsewhere — Auglaize and Shelby were among the top-five margins of victory statewide for unsuccessful Republican candidates Mitt Romney and Josh Mandel in the 2012 presidential and U.S. Senate races.

Major Industry
Manufacturing, agriculture

Cities
Elyria, Lima, Marion, Sidney

Notable
Astronaut Neil Armstrong's hometown of Wapakoneta has a museum in his honor.

Rep. Bob Latta (R)

Capitol Office
225-6405
latta.house.gov
2448 Rayburn Bldg. 20515-3505; fax 225-1985

Committees
Energy & Commerce

Residence
Bowling Green

Born
April 18, 1956; Bluffton, Ohio

Religion
Roman Catholic

Family
Wife, Marcia Latta; two children

Education
Ohio Northern U., attended 1974-75; Bowling Green State U., B.A. 1978 (history); Ohio Northern U., attended 1978-79 (law); U. of Toledo, J.D. 1981

Career
Lawyer

Political Highlights
Ohio Republican Central Committee, 1986-88; sought Republican nomination for U.S. House, 1988; Ohio Republican Central Committee, 1990—92; Wood County Commission, 1990-96; Ohio Senate, 1997-2000; Ohio House, 2001-07

ELECTION RESULTS

2012 GENERAL		
Bob Latta (R)	201,514	57.3%
Angela Zimmann (D)	137,806	39.2%
Eric Eberly (LIBERT)	12,558	3.6%
2012 PRIMARY		
Bob Latta (R)	76,477	82.6%
Robert Wallis (R)	16,135	17.4%
2010 GENERAL		
Bob Latta (R)	140,703	67.8%
Caleb Finkenbiner (D)	54,919	26.5%
Brian L. Smith (LIBERT)	11,831	5.7%

Previous Winning Percentages
2008 (64%); 2007 Special Election (57%)

Elected 2007; 3rd full term

Latta spends his weekends behind the wheel, crisscrossing his western Ohio district; he says the needs of the manufacturers, farmers and small businesses back home take priority. It's a concept that was instilled in him when he worked for his father, Delbert L. Latta, a budget hawk who held the same seat for 30 years.

"I have to see it," he said. "If you just get letters all the time from people, that's not going to work. You have to be out on the plant floor, you have to be out in the agricultural field, to understand exactly what they are doing."

Latta is meticulous: He reviews and signs each piece of mail that goes out to his constituents. A history buff, when he wanted to "brush up" on the Civil War, he read 31 books.

He is also a loyal Republican. In 2011, Latta voted with the GOP 99.3 percent of the time when majorities of the parties opposed each other — the highest rate in the House. Since 2010 he has been a part of the party's whip team, and he is a member of the Republican Study Committee. He rarely bends his pro-business and small-government principles, and he uses his seat on the Energy and Commerce Committee to push for a reduction in federal regulations on energy and agricultural concerns.

The GOP's "all of the above" energy platform resonates with Latta. He wants more gas and oil exploration, both onshore and offshore. He supports development of the Utica and Marcellus shale depositories, which stretch into eastern Ohio. Coal production should be protected, he said, while alternative energy sources are developed.

He bristles at EPA regulations he views as burdensome. Latta has actively opposed the regulation of coal ash (a byproduct of coal combustion sometimes used in construction materials), as well as tougher emissions standards for backup diesel generators at various facilities. In the 111th Congress (2009-10), he opposed Democrats' bill to create a cap-and-trade system for regulating greenhouse gas emissions, saying it would destroy jobs.

Latta feels states are often better suited to manage their own environments. "Our forefathers meant for states to be laboratories for experimentation with the right governance," he wrote in Politico in 2011. "Regulation of hydraulic fracturing is the perfect example of a process better left to state governments, which have the best, firsthand knowledge of how to deal with their specific circumstances." That process is often used in natural gas extraction. Environmentalists allege that it runs the risk of contaminating ground water and releasing methane gas into the environment.

Telecommunications work also draws his interest. He is the vice chairman of the Communications and Technology Subcommittee in the 113th Congress (2013-14). His approach to technology lines up with his approach to energy. He introduced a 2013 resolution to state that for continued growth of the telecom and tech sectors, the government should "get out of the way and stay out of the way."

The wireless broadband industry needs dedicated broadcast spectrum to expand, and Latta was an early proponent of the "incentive auctions" now being organized by the Federal Communications Commission, per a 2012 law. They allow current license-holders to give up part of all of their bandwidth in exchange for a part of the auction proceeds. More wireless means a better, more productive business environment, Latta has written.

He has made some use of the spectrum himself, communicating with constituents through platforms including Twitter, Facebook and Amplify. A founder of the Republican New Media Caucus, Latta said Republicans have been successful in getting information to constituents via multimedia. At the start of the 112th Congress (2011-12), he was named to the House Technology Operations Team, tasked with making the chamber a friendlier online environment, starting with the house.gov website.

Latta cites the health care overhaul debate in the 111th Congress as an example of the GOP effectively using multimedia to convey its priorities. He was a sharp critic of the package, lamenting its "devastating effects" on seniors and small businesses. He calls it "anti-business to the point that people are not going to hire because of it."

On fiscal matters, he supports a balanced-budget constitutional amendment and giving presidents a line-item veto. He wants to see the estate tax repealed, citing its effect on his district's farmers. He likened the 2009 stimulus law to socialism, and in 2008 he said the law providing $700 billion in aid for the financial services industry was too expensive.

Latta did side with constituents in supporting an override of George W. Bush's veto of a 2008 reauthorization of farm programs, He said the legislation would keep Ohio farmers employed.

A Roman Catholic, Latta is socially conservative and anti-abortion.

Latta was 2 years old when his father won a seat in Congress in 1958. The family split time between residences in Bowling Green and Washington. By the time Latta entered fifth grade, he was enrolled in Virginia schools full time, though he returned to Ohio for high school. He often spent days off with his father on Capitol Hill. When his father served on the Rules Committee, which governs floor debate on legislation, Latta often sat behind Massachusetts Democrat Thomas P. O'Neill Jr., who later became speaker.

As a teenager, Latta helped his father by answering phone calls from district residents and taking shifts driving his father to and from airports. Latta worked for a Wood County judge while earning a history degree from Bowling Green State University. In 1981, he earned a law degree from the University of Toledo. He worked for a corporate law firm and in private practice before joining the Toledo Bank Trust Co.

Latta made a run for his father's seat in 1988 but lost to Paul E. Gillmor in the GOP primary by 27 votes. In 1990, he defeated a Democratic incumbent to become a Wood County commissioner; six years later, he was elected to the Ohio Legislature. He served four years in the Senate and six in the House.

When Gillmor died in 2007, Latta made another run for the seat. He won the primary after an unruly campaign in which Latta and his chief opponent accused each other of lying about their respective legislative records. He defeated Democrat Robin Weirauch with 57 percent of the vote in the December 2007 special election, and he has been re-elected easily since.

Key Votes

2012	
Extend a Social Security payroll tax cut and unemployment benefits	YES
Ease securities rules to expand small-business access to capital	YES
Extend for one year subsidized student loan interest rates financed by a cut in health care spending	YES
Cite Attorney General Eric H. Holder Jr. for contempt of Congress	YES
Create a visa program for foreign graduates in high-tech fields	YES
Extend most Bush-era income tax rates while allowing rates for top-bracket earners to rise (Jan. 1, 2013)	YES
2011	
Strike funding for F 35 alternative engine	NO
Prevent EPA from regulating greenhouse gas emissions to address climate change	YES
Extend certain provisions of Patriot Act for four years	YES
Declare opposition to use of ground troops in Libya	YES
Overhaul patent law	YES
Pass compromise debt limit increase plan and establish future spending limits	YES
Allow consideration of measures to implement three trade agreements	YES

CQ Vote Studies

	PARTY UNITY		PRESIDENTIAL SUPPORT	
	SUPPORT	OPPOSE	SUPPORT	OPPOSE
2012	96%	4%	16%	84%
2011	99%	1%	19%	81%
2010	99%	1%	25%	75%
2009	98%	2%	13%	87%
2008	99%	1%	73%	27%

Interest Groups

	AFL-CIO	ADA	CCUS	ACU
2012	14%	5%	92%	84%
2011	0%	5%	100%	88%
2010	0%	0%	88%	100%
2009	5%	0%	80%	100%
2008	7%	15%	89%	96%

Ohio 5

Northwest — Bowling Green, Perrysburg

Bordering Indiana and Michigan in the northwestern corner of the state, the 5th cuts south of Toledo into the north-central portion of Ohio. The most-populous jurisdiction in the 5th is the district's chunk of Lucas County west and south of Toledo; other than Wood County south of Lucas, most of the population is spread out amid flat farmland born from the once-impervious Great Black Swamp that covers the middle of the district. During decennial redistricting, the 5th was consolidated and pushed to the west, losing counties, such as Huron, to the east; its overall character was not altered during line redrawing.

Wood County hosts Bowling Green and the eponymous university there. The school is one of the largest employers in the county and has a significant impact on the regional economy. Although wheat, tomatoes, soybeans and corn dominate most of the landscape in Wood, manufacturing remains a key economic cog, as it does across the district. To the south in Hancock County, Findlay is home to the international headquarters of Cooper Tire & Rubber, one of the largest manufacturers of tires in the world, and a Whirlpool dishwasher plant.

Retail outlets, particularly big-box stores, provide a job base in the district's small towns, but unemployment rates remain high in many areas.

The district is overwhelmingly white, and Republicans have a solid grasp on it. The southwestern corner of the 5th — Mercer (shared with the 4th), Van Wert and Putnam counties — gave Mitt Romney particularly high margins of victory even as he lost the state in the 2012 presidential contest. Wood and the part of Lucas County in the 5th are more competitive in federal and statewide races. Overall, the 5th gave Romney 54 percent of its 2012 presidential vote, 2 points higher than what Republican John McCain would have received in the new 5th in the 2008 contest.

Major Industry
Manufacturing, agriculture

Cities
Findlay, Bowling Green, Perrysburg

Notable
Perrysburg, named to honor Commodore Oliver Hazard Perry's victory over the British in the 1813 Battle of Lake Erie, is one of only two U.S. cities to have been planned by the federal government.

Rep. Bill Johnson (R)

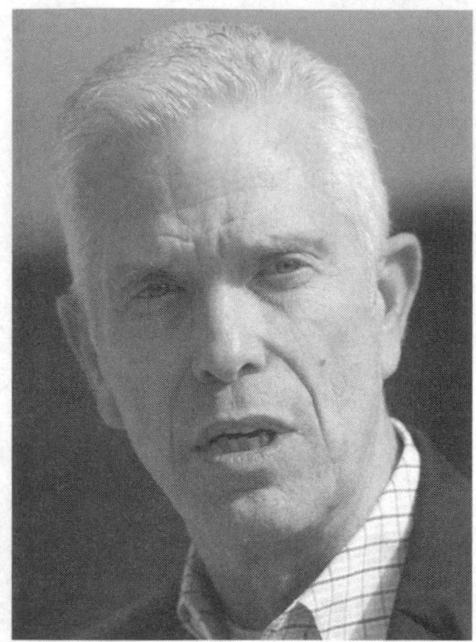

Capitol Office
225-5705
billjohnson.house.gov
1710 Longworth Bldg. 20515-3506; fax 225-5907

Committees
Energy & Commerce

Residence
Marietta

Born
Nov. 10, 1954; Roseboro, N.C.

Religion
Protestant

Family
Wife, LeeAnn Johnson; four children

Education
Troy U., B.S. 1979 (computer science); Georgia Institute of Technology, M.S. 1984 (computer science)

Military
Air Force, 1973-78; Air Force, 1979-99

Career
Air Force officer; information technology executive

Political Highlights
No previous office

ELECTION RESULTS

2012 GENERAL		
Bill Johnson (R)	164,536	53.2%
Charlie Wilson (D)	144,444	46.7%
2012 PRIMARY		
Bill Johnson (R)	56,905	83.9%
Victor Smith (R)	10,888	16.1%
2010 GENERAL		
Bill Johnson (R)	103,170	50.2%
Charlie Wilson (D)	92,823	45.2%
Richard E. Cadle (CNSTP)	5,077	2.5%
Martin J. Elsass (LIBERT)	4,505	2.2%

Elected 2010; 2nd term

Johnson is a pertinacious questioner in committee rooms, seldom mincing words when it comes to federal regulation of energy, agriculture or other issues relevant to his southeastern Ohio district.

His constituents live in portions of rugged Appalachia and have been hit hard by slumps in manufacturing. New energy development, he believes, will stimulate the economy of both his district and the country at large. Johnson also sells such development as a chance to return to the idea of American exceptionalism. "Americans can do anything," he says. "We've always been able to do anything. ... Think about what happens when we unleash the innovative engine of American ingenuity."

Johnson is a retired Air Force officer with a background in computer science and information technology. He had not served in an elective office before he won his seat in 2010. As a freshman, he stridently opposed the Obama administration's energy policies and worked on veterans issues, and for his second term he was added to the Energy and Commerce Committee.

Johnson buys into the "all of the above" energy strategy that Republicans have touted in recent years. He supports wind and solar production, as well as offshore drilling; he has called nuclear power the "cleanest, safest form of energy known to man."

The Marcellus and Utica shale formations are actively drilled in his district, and Johnson is fine with using hydraulic fracturing, or "fracking," to tap them. He wants local control of those projects paired with increased training for workers. "We do not need bureaucrats from Washington, D.C., telling Ohio's regulators how to do the job they've already been doing responsibly for decades," he says.

Johnson is at his loudest when protesting what he calls the "war on coal." President Barack Obama "made it very clear in his campaign that he was going to make it economically unfeasible to start up or to operate coal-fired power plants," Johnson said to Fox News in September 2012. "That's one promise that he has kept."

In the 112th Congress (2011-12), Johnson introduced a bill to limit through the end of 2013 the secretary of the Interior's authority to issue coal regulations. "The farm that I was raised on, we cooked and heated with coal," he said. "We didn't have indoor plumbing; we didn't have central air and heat. And I went to the coal pile many, many mornings and brought in buckets of coal from my uncle's and my grandparents' to put in a potbellied stove."

He joined most House Republicans in opposing the Obama administration's work toward rewriting a rule that requires a buffer zone around streams to prevent mine operators from dumping into water sources. The George W. Bush administration modified the rule in 2008 to allow for exemptions, and Johnson told Fox News that Obama's rewrite will "virtually shut down underground coal mining in America."

Johnson worked as an information technology executive and calls himself an "IT geek." He sat on the Natural Resources Committee during his first term, and that panel approved his 2011 bill to expand a Bureau of Land Management pilot program allowing the Interior Department to conduct Internet-based live sales for onshore oil and gas leases. "Much of the federal government still needs to be dragged — sometimes kicking and screaming — into the 21st century," he wrote at the time.

He also sat on the Veterans' Affairs Committee during his first term. He wants the Veterans Affairs Department to improve its technology infrastructure, in part to accelerate the processing of benefits claims. He introduced a bill, supported by the VA, to authorize the department to use electronic communication to provide notices to veterans claiming medical benefits. In 2011, Obama signed a Johnson bill to authorize certain projects and leases for VA medical facilities.

Johnson is socially conservative, opposing abortion and restrictions on gun rights. He introduced a bill to install on the World War II Memorial in Washington the text of the prayer President Franklin D. Roosevelt shared with the nation on June 6, 1944, when Allied forces landed at Normandy. Johnson opposed repeal of the "don't ask, don't tell" policy that barred openly gay servicemembers and said the controversy was a result of agitation by "the radical homosexual lobby," not problems in the military.

On fiscal matters, Johnson usually voted with the majority of House Republicans during the 112th Congress. He supported a deficit reduction package in August 2011 and a balanced-budget amendment to the Constitution.

He found himself in the GOP minority when he voted for the January 2013 "fiscal cliff" package to extend lower income tax rates only for earnings under $400,000. Johnson supported free-trade pacts with Colombia, Panama and South Korea, but he was also in the half of the GOP Conference that voted for expanded federal assistance to workers displaced by international trade. He belongs to both the conservative Republican Study Committee and the moderate Main Street Partnership.

Born in Roseboro, N.C., Johnson graduated from Troy University in Alabama with a degree in computer science in 1979. He was an Air Force ROTC cadet in college, continued in the service and retired in 1999. While still in the Air Force, Johnson got a master's degree in computer science, and when he entered the private sector he worked in information technology positions at various companies. He also operated his own consulting business.

Johnson carefully chose his district when running for the House in 2010, deciding that the 6th was better suited to a Republican. He criticized two-term Democratic Rep. Charlie Wilson for supporting the 2009 economic stimulus and the 2010 health care law. The contest originally wasn't on the national radar, but Johnson got an October boost from a National Republican Congressional Committee ad campaign when polls tightened. He won with 50 percent of the vote, to Wilson's 45 percent.

In the 2012 cycle, redistricting made the 6th more conservative by subtracting liberal regions near Athens. But it remained competitive, and Wilson announced late in 2011 that he would run again. The race was one of the more expensive matchups in the state, with outside groups and national parties contributing heavily. Johnson prevailed with 53 percent of the vote.

Wilson died in April 2013 of complications from a stroke.

Key Votes

2012	
Extend a Social Security payroll tax cut and unemployment benefits	YES
Ease securities rules to expand small-business access to capital	YES
Extend for one year subsidized student loan interest rates financed by a cut in health care spending	YES
Cite Attorney General Eric H. Holder Jr. for contempt of Congress	YES
Create a visa program for foreign graduates in high-tech fields	YES
Extend most Bush-era income tax rates while allowing rates for top-bracket earners to rise (Jan. 1, 2013)	YES
2011	
Strike funding for F-35 alternative engine	NO
Prevent EPA from regulating greenhouse gas emissions to address climate change	YES
Extend certain provisions of Patriot Act for four years	YES
Declare opposition to use of ground troops in Libya	YES
Overhaul patent law	YES
Pass compromise debt limit increase plan and establish future spending limits	YES
Allow consideration of measures to implement three trade agreements	YES

CQ Vote Studies

	PARTY UNITY		PRESIDENTIAL SUPPORT	
	SUPPORT	OPPOSE	SUPPORT	OPPOSE
2012	95%	5%	18%	82%
2011	96%	4%	26%	74%

Interest Groups

	AFL-CIO	ADA	CCUS	ACU
2012	19%	0%	100%	80%
2011	4%	10%	100%	92%

Ohio 6

South and east — Steubenville, Cambridge

The 6th District parallels the Ohio River for nearly 300 miles, touching three states and taking in hardscrabble areas from Appalachia to the Mahoning Valley near Youngstown. Communities throughout the 6th have large elderly populations, white majorities, struggling economies and often high rates of poverty, as their former industrial mainstays have faded away.

Manufacturing is the touchstone for the 6th, particularly in industrial construction materials, clay, rubber, polymers and lumber. Steel towns in the north are still coping with the industry's decline, although energy sector activity has given some boost to steel production. The discovery of oil and natural gas deposits in the Marcellus and Utica shales beneath Appalachia have created an energy boom in eastern Ohio — four counties in the 6th now rank among the state's most actively drilled. Belmont County is the state's historic leader in coal mining production, although the coal industry has diminished in recent decades and environmental regulations can have a strong impact on employers here.

Some areas have turned to tourism to fill economic gaps. Columbiana County, situated along the river and served by highways between Pittsburgh and Cleveland, has set its hopes on becoming an industrial distribution hub; the county's economy depends on agriculture and is unusually productive for eastern Ohio, where corn and soybean farms are less dense than in the state's west.

While the district can be politically competitive, it generally leans conservative. During decennial remapping, the 6th lost the liberal college town of Athens and gained all or parts of several conservative counties. This region has supported U.S. Senate and gubernatorial candidates of both parties and elected two different Democratic congressmen in the past decade, but it increasingly prefers Republican presidential candidates — the district gave Mitt Romney 55 percent of its vote in 2012.

Major Industry
Manufacturing, energy, health care

Cities
Steubenville, Marietta, East Liverpool

Notable
Gallipolis, in Gallia County, was founded in 1790 by a group of 500 French immigrants.

Rep. Bob Gibbs (R)

Capitol Office
225-6265
gibbs.house.gov
329 Cannon Bldg. 20515-3518; fax 225-3394

Committees
Agriculture
Transportation & Infrastructure
(Water Resources & Environment - Chairman)

Residence
Lakeville

Born
June 14, 1954; Peru, Ind.

Religion
Methodist

Family
Wife, Jody Gibbs; three children

Education
Ohio State U., A.A.S. 1974 (animal husbandry)

Career
Property management company owner; hog farmer

Political Highlights
Ohio House, 2003-09; Ohio Senate, 2009-10

ELECTION RESULTS

2012 GENERAL		
Bob Gibbs (R)	178,104	56.4%
Joyce R. Healy-Abrams (D)	137,708	43.6%
2012 PRIMARY		
Bob Gibbs (R)	54,067	79.9%
Hombre M. Liggett (R)	13,621	20.1%
2010 GENERAL		
Bob Gibbs (R)	107,426	53.9%
Zack Space (D)	80,756	40.5%
Lindsey Sutton (CNSTP)	11,246	5.6%

Elected 2010; 2nd term

A hog farmer turned legislator, Gibbs has taken a yeomanlike approach to committee work since his days in state government. Republicans have given him control of a panel where he can direct the conversation on environmental regulation and water-based infrastructure development.

Gibbs burnished his political skills while rising through the Ohio Farm Bureau, starting out as a volunteer on the membership team and ending up as the president of the state-level organization.

He won election to the Ohio House, where an unexpected sales tax issue tied to his district drew him into tax policy; a few years later, he was chairman of the Ways and Means Committee. When Gibbs moved to the state Senate in 2009, he was named Ways and Means chairman of that chamber, as well as the No. 2 Republican on its Agriculture Committee.

House Republicans put him right to work as a freshman, handing him the gavel of the Transportation and Infrastructure Subcommittee on Water Resources and Environment. Gibbs is reprising that role in the 113th Congress (2013-14). His panel is the showroom floor for arguments that over-regulation is hurting agricultural and energy production. It also has jurisdiction over an anticipated reauthorization of water infrastructure projects.

Gibbs zestfully used hearings to go after regulators in the 112th Congress (2011-12). He called EPA Administrator Lisa P. Jackson "the biggest stumbling block to American job creation," and he says the Obama administration's EPA is using "mission creep" to expand its regulatory authority and burden local governments. In a 2011 opinion piece, he said the agency "is now implementing the personal agendas of radical environmentalists."

That is a common Republican refrain, particularly in regard to hydraulic fracturing, the injection of high-pressure fluids into rock layers to allow access to new deposits of gas and oil. Environmentalists say it threatens to contaminate groundwater, and the Obama administration has mulled more federal regulation of fracking. Gibbs says "states are doing a good job" of overseeing it already. His corner of Ohio has seen an increase in energy development in recent years.

In the 112th Congress, he was pleased with a bill shepherded through his panel that would have restricted the EPA's authority under the Clean Water Act to reject state water pollution plans and enforce stricter standards. The House also passed a Gibbs bill to prohibit the EPA or states from requiring a permit for the use of registered pesticides in or near navigable waters. He said fear of litigation and increased administrative costs prohibited abatement spraying for the West Nile Virus. Gibbs sits on the Agriculture Committee, and provisions from his bill were included in a panel-approved reauthorization of farm programs in 2012. Neither bill was enacted.

Water infrastructure can be a tricky issue for cost-cutting Republicans, as it pits substantial federal spending against aiding the flow of commerce. Gibbs said in an April 2012 hearing that he supports alternative financing for such projects, mainly via public-private partnerships. "When it comes to inland waterway systems, we have been investing too slowly for too long," he said.

Gibbs casts water infrastructure as necessary for sustaining trade, which makes things such as port dredging "the kind of investments that taxpayers ought to be investing in." He has said that the Harbor Maintenance Trust Fund should be dedicated exclusively to harbors and not diverted elsewhere.

On most fiscal matters, Gibbs lines up with mainstream Republicans. He signed off on slimmed-down spending bills for fiscal 2011 and fiscal 2012. He opposed a January 2013 "fiscal cliff" measure to extend lower income tax rates only for earnings under $400,000 — he wanted spending cuts included as well. "This country's deficit spending is unsustainable," he wrote. "Passing a bill without addressing it is downright irresponsible."

His cost-cutting and parochial interests intermingle on the Agriculture Committee. Gibbs opposed the farm bill approved by the committee in 2012, saying it had "too much potential to move agriculture away from market-driven planting decisions." He criticized the measure's target prices — the price points for various commodities at which federal farm subsidies kick in. Many Midwestern lawmakers argued that the targets in the bill were too generous for Southern crops and would encourage people to "farm for the program." When the panel voted on a similar farm bill in May 2013, Gibbs was one of two Republicans who did not support it.

Gibbs has no problem with ending direct payments to farmers, but he wants to make sure crop insurance stays viable. "I am a strong proponent to maintain a safety net program," he said, as a safeguard against drought, floods or unforeseen problems with global supplies. "You can have a market distortion event that could bankrupt farmers that you have no control over."

In 1974, Gibbs graduated from Ohio State University with a degree in animal husbandry. "I didn't grow up on the farm," he said. "I grew up in a Cleveland suburb. I became a farmer. So I'm either crazy or stupid." While working as a hog farmer, he also developed the hobby of building and restoring homes, doing the plumbing and electric work himself. When he got rid of the hogs, around the time that he started in state government, he continued working as a property manager.

He served three terms in the Ohio House and won a seat in the state Senate in 2009. Running in the 18th District in 2010, Gibbs earned the Republican nomination by taking 21 percent of the vote, which was just enough to finish atop the eight-candidate field. He beat the runner-up by fewer than 200 votes.

Incumbent Democrat Zack Space won by comfortable margins in 2006 and 2008. He opposed the 2010 health care overhaul and won the endorsement of the National Rifle Association. But Gibbs was able to appeal to the district's conservative lean. He took advantage of a bad year for Democrats nationally — and a worse year for Democrats in Ohio — winning nearly 54 percent of the vote to 40 percent for Space.

Decennial reapportionment cost Ohio two House seats heading into the 2012 election. Gibbs ran in the newly drawn 7th District, which took in more land to the north and less of Appalachia. Overall, the district is GOP friendly. Gibbs went up against Democrat Joyce R. Healy-Abrams, a longtime Ohioan who operated a file management business with her husband. He took more than 56 percent of the vote.

Key Votes

2012	
Extend a Social Security payroll tax cut and unemployment benefits	YES
Ease securities rules to expand small-business access to capital	YES
Extend for one year subsidized student loan interest rates financed by a cut in health care spending	YES
Cite Attorney General Eric H. Holder Jr. for contempt of Congress	YES
Create a visa program for foreign graduates in high-tech fields	YES
Extend most Bush-era income tax rates while allowing rates for top-bracket earners to rise (Jan. 1, 2013)	NO
2011	
Strike funding for F-35 alternative engine	NO
Prevent EPA from regulating greenhouse gas emissions to address climate change	YES
Extend certain provisions of Patriot Act for four years	YES
Declare opposition to use of ground troops in Libya	YES
Overhaul patent law	YES
Pass compromise debt limit increase plan and establish future spending limits	YES
Allow consideration of measures to implement three trade agreements	YES

CQ Vote Studies

	Party Unity		Presidential Support	
	Support	Oppose	Support	Oppose
2012	95%	5%	16%	84%
2011	97%	3%	21%	79%

Interest Groups

	AFL-CIO	ADA	CCUS	ACU
2012	14%	0%	100%	80%
2011	3%	5%	100%	79%

Ohio 7

Outer Cleveland suburbs; most of Canton

Curling counterclockwise from near the Lake Erie shoreline in Lorain County across Interstate 71 in Richland and Ashland counties to Knox, Coshocton and Holmes counties, the 7th crosses Interstate 77 and heads northeast past Canton. Much of the district is filled with forests, lakes and farmland and is made up of small, rural communities.

Ohio lost two congressional seats during reapportionment after the 2010 census and the new 7th District was created in the center and north-center of the state — the previously numbered 7th hugged counties south of Columbus, and the 16th did not reach Cuyahoga County — and was drawn to be GOP-friendly.

Canton, the district's largest city, is shared with the 16th, but almost all of the urban area falls in the 7th. The city has a manufacturing and steel tradition and has retained a high-skill manufacturing base. Local officials have emphasized growth in retail and service-based sectors, and hospitals also provide jobs. Canton was hit hard when Hoover closed its facilities there. The city has struggled with population loss — it dropped roughly 10 percent between 2000 and 2010 — and low rates of educational attainment.

Outside of Canton and Massillon, the second largest city in the district, the 7th becomes increasingly remote, and manufacturing is key. Kraft Foods is a leading employer in Coshocton County. Much of Holmes County is taken up by forests, and the county is a top producer of multiple crops, including Christmas trees. Knox County is the leading producer of sheep and goats in the state. Ashland County does host some white-collar employers, including product-safety company WIL Research Laboratories.

The district tends to favor Republicans overall, but the 7th's portion of Lorain County is competitive and Stark County can back Democrats. Ohio treasurer Josh Mandel won every county wholly within the 7th in his unsuccessful bid to unseat Democratic Sen. Sherrod Brown in 2012.

Major Industry
Health care, agriculture, steel

Cities
Canton (pt.), Massillon, North Ridgefield

Notable
Canton is home to both the Professional Football Hall of Fame and William McKinley's tomb.

Rep. John A. Boehner (R)

Capitol Office
225-6205
johnboehner.house.gov
1011 Longworth Bldg. 20515-3508; fax 225-0704

Committees
No committee assignments

Residence
West Chester Township

Born
Nov. 17, 1949; Cincinnati, Ohio

Religion
Roman Catholic

Family
Wife, Debbie Boehner; two children

Education
Xavier U., B.S. 1977

Military
Navy, 1968

Career
Plastics and packaging executive

Political Highlights
Union Township Board of Trustees, 1982-84; Ohio House, 1985-91

ELECTION RESULTS

2012 GENERAL		
John A. Boehner (R)	246,378	99.2%
2012 PRIMARY		
John A. Boehner (R)	71,120	83.8%
David Lewis (R)	13,733	16.2%
2010 GENERAL		
John A. Boehner (R)	142,731	65.6%
Justin A. Coussoule (D)	65,883	30.3%
David A. Harlow (LIBERT)	5,121	2.4%
James J. Condit Jr. (CNSTP)	3,701	1.7%

Previous Winning Percentages
2008 (68%); 2006 (64%); 2004 (69%); 2002 (71%); 2000 (71%); 1998 (71%); 1996 (70%); 1994 (100%); 1992 (74%); 1990 (61%)

Elected 1990; 12th term

On a business-style Republican leadership team, Boehner operates like a chairman of the board. He relies on his instincts and collaborative decisions to resolve disputes while working with select allies to rally his caucus and expand its appeal. His methods as speaker of the House have encouraged Republicans of all stripes to express themselves — and made it tougher to keep the party unified behind his preferred policies.

Since rising to the speakership at the start of the 112th Congress (2011-12), Boehner (BAY-ner) has regularly dealt with some of the biggest names in Washington. His leadership team features young conservative heroes in Majority Leader Eric Cantor of Virginia and Budget Chairman Paul D. Ryan of Wisconsin, the 2012 GOP vice presidential nominee. He established a rough working relationship with President Barack Obama through direct, hard-nosed negotiations and occasional agreements on stopgap fiscal measures.

In his first term as speaker, Boehner also had to deal with lawmakers who refused to collaborate. Small-government conservatives in the House sank his plans for long-term reauthorizations of surface transportation and farming programs. The Democratic Senate routinely ignored regulatory, energy and health care bills that House Republicans passed enthusiastically.

He survived his party's loss of a handful of seats in the 2012 election by emphasizing his intent to broaden the GOP's appeal in the 113th Congress (2013-14). Boehner supported several moderates and fresher faces seeking bigger roles — such as Cathy McMorris Rodgers of Washington, who was elected conference chairwoman.

The 2012 election created "a mandate for us to find a way to work together," he said. Boehner offered agenda items for the 113th: repealing some components of the 2010 health care law (as opposed to the whole thing); and taking a "common sense, step-by-step approach" to secure the nation's borders and "fix a broken immigration system." He suggested working with Obama on a tax code overhaul and changes to entitlement programs.

But when Boehner tried to tweak his trademark laissez-faire management style to give himself a little more authority, there were uneven results. Several GOP dissidents had broken ranks on major votes in the 112th Congress, and Republican leaders oversaw their removal from key committees. The push to promote party loyalty angered some conservatives.

Several weeks later, he suffered a public defeat while trying to negotiate a deficit reduction package with Obama. Hoping to give his party some political cover, he proposed an extension of expiring tax cuts, except for income over $1 million. Conservatives shot the plan down. As he pulled the plug on the tax measure in a caucus meeting, Boehner acknowledged that he did not have the votes and recited the Serenity Prayer. He then left negotiations in the hands of senators and the White House.

A rich baritone and a bantering style made Boehner a popular figure among Republicans; he has an easy sense of humor and rolls with the punches when people joke about his tanned good looks, chain smoking and devotion to golf. His tendency to get teary-eyed at emotional moments gives a glimpse of the passion below his cool surface. He encourages frank talk in closed-door meetings with members and has frequent huddles to plot strategy with Cantor — his top lieutenant and, by some accounts, biggest rival within the party.

After a long career in Congress, Boehner is more a creature of the institution than are the next-wave Republicans in his caucus. Still, he scored points with his party's right wing by walking away from deficit reduction negotiations with Obama in 2011 because of proposed tax increases. Boehner's insistence on pairing an increase in the government's borrowing limit with spending cuts was ultimately accommodated in the bill Obama signed that August.

He also regained some footing in the early stages of the 113th Congress — he coordinated with conservative leaders on strategies for upcoming debates on taxes and spending. There was minimal dissent as fiscal 2013 spending laws were enacted in the early spring.

Soon after Republicans regained the majority in the 2010 elections, Boehner promoted changes aimed at reducing spending and emphasizing a regular-order process on the floor and in committees. He pressed for a "cut-go" requirement to bar new spending initiatives from coming to the House floor under suspension of the rules unless they were offset by spending cuts. He also backed an end to many votes on commemorative resolutions that celebrate civic achievements or name post offices.

Such changes reflected his penchant for bold gestures, which dates back to his freshman term in the 102nd Congress (1991-92). Then, he pushed for full disclosure during the 1992 scandal involving members who overdrew their House checking accounts. His zeal made him a favorite of the new breed of confrontational Republicans led by Newt Gingrich of Georgia, and four years later he became GOP Conference chairman. After Republican setbacks in the 1998 election, Boehner lost his post. He focused on serving as chairman of the Education and the Workforce Committee, where he promoted the 2002 education law known as No Child Left Behind.

His rehabilitation was completed when he was elected majority leader in February 2006, replacing Tom DeLay of Texas. After Republicans lost their majority that November, Boehner served four years as minority leader. He was the easy choice for speaker when Republicans surged back into the majority.

Boehner's story is as good as any politician's rags-to-riches tale. He grew up in western Ohio's Rust Belt with 11 siblings. As a kid, Boehner rose at 5 a.m. to help his father, Earl, sort bottles and mop floors at Andy's Cafe restaurant and bar. He was a linebacker on his high school football team.

Boehner worked his way through Xavier College as a janitor. After graduating, he and a partner bought a small plastics and packaging firm, Nucite Sales Inc., and built it into a multimillion-dollar business. In his first political race he won a seat on a township board.

He went on to serve six years in the Ohio House. In 1990, he joined the primary field challenging Rep. Donald E. "Buz" Lukens, who had been convicted of having sex with a teenage girl. Boehner outspent the front-runner, former Rep. Thomas N. Kindness, and won with 49 percent of the vote. That November, he bested Democrat Gregory V. Jolivette, a former mayor of Hamilton. His re-elections have not been particularly difficult.

Key Votes

2012	
Extend a Social Security payroll tax cut and unemployment benefits	
Ease securities rules to expand small-business access to capital	
Extend for one year subsidized student loan interest rates financed by a cut in health care spending	YES
Cite Attorney General Eric H. Holder Jr. for contempt of Congress	
Create a visa program for foreign graduates in high-tech fields	
Extend most Bush-era income tax rates while allowing rates for top-bracket earners to rise (Jan. 1, 2013)	YES
2011	
Strike funding for F-35 alternative engine	
Prevent EPA from regulating greenhouse gas emissions to address climate change	
Extend certain provisions of Patriot Act for four years	
Declare opposition to use of ground troops in Libya	
Overhaul patent law	
Pass compromise debt limit increase plan and establish future spending limits	YES
Allow consideration of measures to implement three trade agreements	

CQ Vote Studies

	Party Unity		Presidential Support	
	SUPPORT	OPPOSE	SUPPORT	OPPOSE
2012	67%	33%	33%	67%
2011	100%	0%	25%	75%
2010	99%	1%	23%	77%
2009	98%	2%	12%	88%
2008	99%	1%	85%	15%

Interest Groups

	AFL-CIO	ADA	CCUS	ACU
2012	0%	0%	100%	
2011	0%		100%	
2010	0%	0%	100%	100%
2009	5%	0%	80%	96%
2008	0%	0%	94%	92%

Ohio 8

West — Hamilton, Springfield

The 8th District takes in a portion of southwestern Ohio north of the Cincinnati area along the Indiana border, as well as Miami and Clark counties north and northeast of Dayton. It is a collection of midsize industrial cities in a manufacturing-dependent region that also includes some of the state's most productive farmland and a major undergraduate university.

Most of the district's cities have relied on manufacturing. AK Steel is still a top employer, but the region has been hit hard by job losses, especially at a former division of BAE Systems. Butler County includes some of the district's most populous cities and most active industrial centers; West Chester Township is one of the state's fastest-growing residential areas.

Miami University, one of the region's largest employers, is in Oxford. Butler Tech, the county's vocational training school, is now the largest career-technical school in Ohio, with diverse courses including digital media, biotechnology and network technology.

Newly added to the 8th District as a result of decennial remapping is Clark County, which includes the city of Springfield. Historically a farm equipment manufacturing hub — and the birthplace of the modern combine — Springfield is transitioning to a technology and service-based economy. The region also benefits from proximity to Dayton's aerospace sector: The Springfield Air National Guard shares some jobs with the much larger Wright Patterson Air Force Base, located 20 miles away in the 10th District.

Remapping cut out the 8th's more liberal portion of Dayton and extended east into Clark County. Republicans do well across the district, especially in Darke and Preble counties: The two gave Mitt Romney among his top-10 winning percentages statewide in 2012. Democrats can be competitive at the local level in the college town of Oxford. Presidential elections are frequently close in conservative-leaning Clark County, with margins of victory typically less than 5 percentage points, but Republicans regularly win more than 60 percent of the vote in all of the district's other counties.

Major Industry

Manufacturing, agriculture, higher education

Cities

Hamilton, Springfield, Middletown, Fairfield, Troy

Notable

The international 4-H program began in 1902 when a Springfield teacher, A.B. Graham, had a group of students conduct agricultural experiments.

Rep. Marcy Kaptur (D)

Capitol Office
225-4146
kaptur.house.gov
2186 Rayburn Bldg. 20515-3509; fax 225-7711

Committees
Appropriations

Residence
Toledo

Born
June 17, 1946; Toledo, Ohio

Religion
Roman Catholic

Family
Single

Education
U. of Wisconsin, B.A. 1968 (history); U. of Michigan, M.U.P. 1974 (urban planning); Massachusetts Institute of Technology, attended 1981 (urban planning)

Career
White House aide; urban planner

Political Highlights
No previous office

ELECTION RESULTS

2012 GENERAL		
Marcy Kaptur (D)	217,771	73.0%
Samuel J. Wurzelbacher (R)	68,668	23.0%
Sean P. Stipe (LIBERT)	11,725	3.9%
2012 PRIMARY		
Marcy Kaptur (D)	42,902	56.2%
Dennis J. Kucinich (D)	30,564	40.0%
Graham Veysey (D)	2,900	3.8%
2010 GENERAL		
Marcy Kaptur (D)	121,819	59.4%
Rich Iott (R)	83,423	40.6%

Previous Winning Percentages
2008 (74%); 2006 (74%); 2004 (68%); 2002 (74%); 2000 (75%); 1998 (81%); 1996 (77%); 1994 (75%); 1992 (74%); 1990 (78%); 1988 (81%); 1986 (78%); 1984 (55%); 1982 (58%)

Elected 1982; 16th term

Kaptur rejects many of the Machiavellian aspects of congressional politics and bluntly pursues the interests of her blue-collar district. Her methods make her popular with voters, even if they haven't helped her secure the leadership roles usually associated with lawmakers who have her degree of seniority.

She stays in tune with her constituents by sharing their lifestyle. Most weekends, Kaptur returns to the small Toledo house she grew up in, which she shares with her brother. She grows vegetables, paints watercolors and makes Polish coffee cakes and sausages at the holidays. Kaptur doesn't like campaign fundraising and makes it palatable by organizing bake sales.

And like many of the ethnic, working-class voters who back her, Kaptur is a devout Catholic — she attends Mass at the church where she was baptized. The Plain Dealer reported in 2012 that when visiting areas of Cleveland that would belong to the 9th District in the 113th Congress (2013-14), Kaptur sometimes crashed overnight with a congregation of nuns. She opposes abortion and has steered clear of supporting gay marriage.

The whole package has contributed to Kaptur's electoral success. She has more House seniority than any other woman, and she has served on the Appropriations Committee longer than any other Democrat — she joined the panel in 1990. But entering her fourth decade in Congress, she has never held a major chairmanship or leadership job.

Her 2012 bid to become the ranking member on Appropriations was telling. Given her seniority, Kaptur had a reasonable expectation of succeeding Norm Dicks of Washington, who retired at the end of the 112th Congress (2011-12). The job went to Nita M. Lowey of New York, the committee's No. 4 Democrat and a longtime ally of Minority Leader Nancy Pelosi of California.

Kaptur undermined her chances with her 2005 decision to trade the ranking member spot on the Agriculture Subcommittee for a seat on the Defense panel; she saw the Defense seat as means to steer more federal money to her district. When Democrats gained the House majority in the 2006 elections, Kaptur was no longer in line to be a subcommittee chairwoman. Lowey, on the other hand, ran the State-Foreign Operations panel.

Regional battles also played a part, according to former Republican appropriator David L. Hobson. "On the Democratic side, if you put the California mafia and the New York mafia together, you don't have much of a chance," he told The Plain Dealer. When Kaptur ran for vice chairwoman of the Democratic Caucus in 2008, she lost to California's Xavier Becerra.

With or without a fancier title, Kaptur plugs away on behalf of her district. On winning re-election in 2012, she said her agenda is "always jobs and economic growth, continuing the recovery of the automotive industry and many related sectors, and working hard on energy independence."

She did become the ranking member on the Energy-Water Subcommittee in 2013. Kaptur returned to the Defense Subcommittee, and she grabbed a seat on the Financial Services Subcommittee as well.

A member of the liberal Congressional Progressive Caucus, Kaptur challenges policies that she says benefit corporations and the rich at the expense of the middle class and poor. Her admirers include former independent presidential candidate Ross Perot, who sought to have Kaptur, a fellow critic of the North American Free Trade Agreement, as his running mate in 1996.

She bristles at connections between federal officials and top Wall Street firms, particularly Goldman Sachs. In 2012, she took offense when Gary Gensler, chairman of the Commodity Futures Trading Commission, told appropriators that he was not participating in the investigation of the MF

Global bankruptcy. Former Sen. Jon Corzine, the CEO of MF Global, once worked with Gensler at Goldman Sachs.

At a 2010 hearing, Kaptur asked Treasury Secretary Timothy F. Geithner about why he made more than 100 phone calls to a Goldman official around the time of the government bailout of American International Group Inc., a move that benefited the firm's creditors, including Goldman. At another 2010 hearing, Kaptur blamed the financial crisis on a "revolving door of influence-peddling of extraordinary proportions."

She has proposed amending the Constitution to allow regulation of the campaign expenditures of "corporations and other business organizations."

Kaptur has introduced numerous bills to assist homeowners facing foreclosure. She said she was angered to hear of constituents who had been frightened by initial foreclosure notices and simply walked away from their homes without seeking help. She went on cable news shows and the House floor in 2009 to urge those facing foreclosure to get adequate legal representation and to make sure that the banks had the papers needed to prove their cases.

Kaptur's paternal grandparents were from western Poland, and her maternal ones were from eastern Poland, in an area that is now part of Ukraine. Her father ran a grocery store in Rossford and later took a job at a Jeep factory. Her mother worked for Champion Spark Plug and helped organize a union at its Toledo plant. After the 1997 death of her mother, Kaptur and her brother founded the nonprofit Anastasia Fund, which has helped support democracy movements in Ukraine, China and Mexico. Kaptur also has established the Kaptur Community Fund, which makes charitable donations in Toledo; she regularly contributes her congressional pay raise to the fund.

Kaptur was the first in her family to attend college. She went to work for a regional planning commission and worked on some Democratic campaigns. After studying urban planning, she took on projects in several cities, including one effort to save a Polish neighborhood in Chicago. That led to a job in the Carter administration as an adviser on urban policy.

She was studying for her doctorate in urban planning at the Massachusetts Institute of Technology when she was recruited to challenge first-term GOP Rep. Ed Weber in 1982. With northwestern Ohio in a deep recession, Weber's support for President Ronald Reagan's economic policies proved politically fatal. Kaptur won by 19 points.

Ohio lost two districts for the 2012 election, and as a result Kaptur squared off with fellow Democratic Rep. Dennis J. Kucinich in a primary. Kucinich's anti-war views had won him a national recognition and celebrity admirers, but the new 9th District favored Kaptur. Kaptur beat Kucinich by 16 points and easily won the general election.

Key Votes

2012	
Extend a Social Security payroll tax cut and unemployment benefits	YES
Ease securities rules to expand small-business access to capital	YES
Extend for one year subsidized student loan interest rates financed by a cut in health care spending	NO
Cite Attorney General Eric H. Holder Jr. for contempt of Congress	?
Create a visa program for foreign graduates in high-tech fields	NO
Extend most Bush-era income tax rates while allowing rates for top-bracket earners to rise (Jan. 1, 2013)	YES
2011	
Strike funding for F-35 alternative engine	NO
Prevent EPA from regulating greenhouse gas emissions to address climate change	NO
Extend certain provisions of Patriot Act for four years	NO
Declare opposition to use of ground troops in Libya	?
Overhaul patent law	NO
Pass compromise debt limit increase plan and establish future spending limits	NO
Allow consideration of measures to implement three trade agreements	NO

CQ Vote Studies

	PARTY UNITY		PRESIDENTIAL SUPPORT	
	SUPPORT	OPPOSE	SUPPORT	OPPOSE
2012	94%	6%	84%	16%
2011	93%	7%	76%	24%
2010	95%	5%	86%	14%
2009	94%	6%	90%	10%
2008	95%	5%	9%	91%

Interest Groups

	AFL-CIO	ADA	CCUS	ACU
2012	95%	85%	17%	0%
2011	100%	85%	13%	4%
2010	86%	85%	25%	8%
2009	95%	85%	40%	17%
2008	100%	100%	47%	13%

Ohio 9

North — Toledo, Sandusky, western Cleveland suburbs

Stretching more than 100 miles along Lake Erie, the traditionally Democratic 9th moves east from Lucas County and Toledo along a strip of shoreline into western Cleveland in Cuyahoga County. Auto workers and ethnic enclaves of Irish, Puerto Rican and Eastern Europeans fill in the district.

At the mouth of the Maumee River, the largest river flowing into the Great Lakes, Toledo accounts for much of the district's population despite a decade of residents moving out of the city. Once nicknamed the "Glass City" because of its history in that industry, Toledo long relied on auto manufacturing. There are major auto factories in the district — including an expanding Jeep sport utility plant in Toledo — in addition to numerous other car plants, facilities and suppliers. Cars drive the economy outside of Toledo, as well, and Ford employs about 1,900 workers at an Avon Lake plant.

The portion of Cleveland in the 9th includes one-time manufacturing strongholds now dependent on service-economy jobs. The Cleveland Hopkins International Airport is nestled in the 9th's southeastern corner.

Vacation spots put tourism at the fore here. Sandusky's Cedar Point amusement park, the top employer for Erie County, is consistently ranked as home to the best roller coasters in the world and attracts more than 3 million visitors annually. Millions of visitors travel to Lake Erie's Bass Islands each year, and Toledo hosts a Penn National Gaming casino. Health care is a vital part of the economy, and the University of Toledo Medical Center provides a base for the sector.

There are numerous blue-collar ethnic neighborhoods throughout the overwhelmingly Democratic district. There is a strong concentration of Polish and other Eastern European residents in Parma and Cleveland, and Lorain has a large concentration of Puerto Ricans. The western Cleveland suburbs are also home to many Irish communities.

Major Industry

Manufacturing, health care, tourism

Cities

Cleveland (pt.), Toledo (pt.), Parma, Lorain, Sandusky

Notable

The glacial grooves on the north side of Kelleys Island were scoured into limestone bedrock by ice sheets about 18,000 years ago.

Rep. Michael R. Turner (R)

Capitol Office
225-6465
turner.house.gov
2239 Rayburn Bldg. 20515-3503; fax 225-6754

Committees
Armed Services
(Tactical Air & Land Forces - Chairman)
Oversight & Government Reform

Residence
Dayton

Born
Jan. 11, 1960; Dayton, Ohio

Religion
Protestant

Family
Divorced; two children

Education
Ohio Northern U., B.A. 1982 (political science); Case Western Reserve U., J.D. 1985; U. of Dayton, M.B.A. 1992

Career
Real estate developer; lawyer

Political Highlights
Mayor of Dayton, 1994-2002; defeated for re-election as mayor of Dayton, 2001

ELECTION RESULTS

2012 GENERAL		
Michael R. Turner (R)	208,201	59.5%
Sharen Swartz Neuhardt (D)	131,097	37.5%
David A. Harlow (LIBERT)	10,373	3.0%
2012 PRIMARY		
Michael R. Turner (R)	65,574	80.1%
John D. Anderson (R)	14,435	17.6%
Edward Focke Breen (R)	1,839	2.2%
2010 GENERAL		
Michael R. Turner (R)	152,629	68.1%
Joe Roberts (D)	71,455	31.9%

Previous Winning Percentages
2008 (63%); 2006 (59%); 2004 (62%); 2002 (59%)

Elected 2002; 6th term

Turner, a former mayor of Dayton, was known early on as a moderate Republican with voter-friendly ideas to address urban and working-class problems. That image has since been supplemented by a reputation as an advocate for a robust military.

The planes the Wright brothers designed in Dayton were a tad less sophisticated than the multibillion-dollar marvels Turner now oversees. In the 113th Congress (2013-14), Turner is chairing the Armed Services Subcommittee on Tactical Air and Land Forces, which has jurisdiction over the purchase, research and development of jet fighters, drones, tanks and a host of other weapons. Many vehicles and systems have deteriorated over a decade of war, and tighter budgets are forcing more-selective investments. A lot of the panel's efforts will hinge on differences between Turner's vision for the Pentagon's future needs and the vision of President Barack Obama.

Turner doesn't have a military past — just a black belt in taekwondo — but he supports programs that keep the defense and manufacturing businesses of Ohio humming. Wright-Patterson Air Force Base is in his district, and the Lima Army Tank Plant is 70 miles up the road. Earlier in his House career, Turner was involved in efforts to secure almost $700 million for research and development at Wright-Patterson; he fought for an expansion of the base's workforce during the 2005 round of military base realignments; and a 2012 House-passed bill included his amendment to designate the base's Air Force Institute of Technology as a cybersecurity training site for federal employees.

He has resisted some attempts to end military programs. In 2011, he voted against the amendment that killed an alternative engine for the F-35 fighter — a redundancy that conservatives held up as an example of wasteful defense spending. Turner objected to the Pentagon's cancellation of the Marine Corps' Expeditionary Fighting Vehicle, which would have been built in Ohio.

Flourishing weapons programs suit Turner's strategic thinking as well as Ohio's economy. He expresses grave concerns about potential threats from China and North Korea and believes in a peace-through-strength military strategy. In the 112th Congress (2011-12), he led the Strategic Forces Subcommittee, which oversees missile defense and the nuclear stockpile. Turner frequently accused the Obama administration of ignoring commitments to modernize nuclear weapons while reducing their number under a 2010 treaty with Russia. "We cannot have a credible nuclear deterrent if we allow them to decay," he said.

Turner unsuccessfully pushed legislation to make modernization a condition of arms reductions. He also has led the fight for construction of an East Coast missile defense site, which he says would defend against intercontinental missiles from states such as Iran and North Korea. The fiscal 2013 defense authorization law included a provision requiring environmental studies of at least three possible locations, two of which must be on the East Coast. Turner continued criticizing the Obama administration in 2013, in light of a nuclear test and displays of aggressive behavior by North Korea.

Turner belongs to both the conservative Republican Study Committee and the moderate Main Street Partnership. His moderate side comes out when tackling urban policy and Rust Belt concerns. Raised in Dayton, he attended public schools and has working-class roots. His father worked for more than 40 years at a General Motors Corp. plant and was a member of the electrical workers union. His mother was an elementary school teacher. Turner supports labor union positions more often than the average Republican.

A group of non-union workers has gotten a lot of attention from Turner, however. He is among the Republicans advocating on behalf of Delphi Corp. employees who lost the bulk of their pensions when the government bailed out General Motors. Delphi contributes parts to build GM vehicles and was already in bankruptcy when the government stepped in. The Pension Benefit Guaranty Corporation terminated the pension plans. GM helped cover the losses of Delphi members of the United Auto Workers union, but not those of non-union workers. Turner calls the situation an "absolute injustice" and wants the pensions of the non-union workers restored.

Before winning his first term as mayor in 1993, Turner practiced law and worked with nonprofit groups in Dayton dealing with low-income housing, homelessness and community development. "Growing up in the inner city and having served as mayor, I understand the importance of the community being active," Turner said. "It typically takes a coalition of people working at the state and local and federal level and the business community."

As mayor, he spurred several development projects in downtown Dayton. In the House, he has pressed for tax incentives to encourage the cleanup of industrial brownfields and the rehabilitation of old homes and old schools. He's a fan of the Community Development Block Grant program and was one of its defenders when the George W. Bush administration tried to shrink it dramatically in 2005.

Turner also has Democratic partners on military personnel issues. He and Niki Tsongas of Massachusetts have worked together to fight sexual assault in the military, introducing legislation and amendments to expand services available to victims. Turner was inspired by a constituent, Lance Cpl. Maria Lauterbach, who was attacked and killed by a senior member of her unit in 2007. "We still have progress that needs to be made," Turner said. "This requires a cultural shift in the military."

In 2001, Turner lost his bid for a third term as mayor to a popular Democratic state senator, but his bipartisan appeal caught the eye of GOP recruiters. When Bush tapped 12-term Democratic Rep. Tony P. Hall to serve as the ambassador to three world hunger relief organizations, Turner became a favorite to run for the seat. He first defeated newspaper publisher Roy E. Brown, son and grandson of former members of Congress, in the primary, then took 59 percent of the vote to defeat Democrat Rick Carne, Hall's former chief of staff.

His re-elections have been by comfortable margins. Redistricting for 2012 placed him in the 10th District with fellow Republican Rep. Steve Austria, but Austria opted to retire from Congress at the end of his second term.

Turner announced in November 2012 that he was separating from his wife. The divorce was finalized in the spring of 2013.

Key Votes

2012

Extend a Social Security payroll tax cut and unemployment benefits	**YES**
Ease securities rules to expand small-business access to capital	**YES**
Extend for one year subsidized student loan interest rates financed by a cut in health care spending	**YES**
Cite Attorney General Eric H. Holder Jr. for contempt of Congress	**YES**
Create a visa program for foreign graduates in high-tech fields	**YES**
Extend most Bush-era income tax rates while allowing rates for top-bracket earners to rise (Jan. 1, 2013)	**NO**

2011

Strike funding for F-35 alternative engine	**NO**
Prevent EPA from regulating greenhouse gas emissions to address climate change	**YES**
Extend certain provisions of Patriot Act for four years	**YES**
Declare opposition to use of ground troops in Libya	**YES**
Overhaul patent law	**NO**
Pass compromise debt limit increase plan and establish future spending limits	**NO**
Allow consideration of measures to implement three trade agreements	**YES**

CQ Vote Studies

	PARTY UNITY		PRESIDENTIAL SUPPORT	
	SUPPORT	OPPOSE	SUPPORT	OPPOSE
2012	88%	12%	13%	87%
2011	89%	11%	24%	76%
2010	89%	11%	36%	64%
2009	71%	29%	61%	39%
2008	85%	15%	58%	42%

Interest Groups

	AFL-CIO	ADA	CCUS	ACU
2012	43%	0%	100%	64%
2011	38%	15%	88%	72%
2010	14%	10%	88%	82%
2009	33%	35%	80%	72%
2008	57%	55%	81%	63%

Ohio 10

Dayton and suburbs

The new 10th takes in all of Montgomery and Greene counties and part of Fayette, collecting areas formerly split among three districts. Dayton, hometown of the Wright brothers, rightly stakes its claim as a key city in aviation history and hosts Wright-Patterson Air Force Base and a multitude of supporting aerospace-related businesses.

Dayton's strong auto industry has faded in recent years, following the trend of typical Rust Belt decline. The region has increasingly depended on aviation and technology industries linked to Wright-Patterson. The base, which was already the region's largest single employer, absorbed hundreds of jobs after the latest BRAC round. The city also has an international airport.

Tech firms make use of the 1,250-acre Miami Valley Research Park, and LexisNexis has an office in the area. These companies are served by higher education communities, notably Wright State University and Catholic-run University of Dayton, Ohio's largest private university. Health care is also a major industry here. Dayton's medical centers provide regional service, and the National Center for Medical Readiness, affiliated with Wright State, has a public health disaster training site known as Calamityville.

Balanced by liberal voters in the city and conservatives in the suburbs, this southwestern district is one of the state's most politically competitive. Democrats can do well near Dayton, frequently eking out wins at the presidential and statewide levels. Several neighborhoods in the west of the city are black-majority. Barack Obama won Montgomery in the 2008 and 2012 presidential contests. The suburbs, however, trend conservative enough to swing elections — unsuccessful Republican candidates Mitt Romney for president and state treasurer Josh Mandel for U.S. Senate each won neighboring Greene County by roughly 20 percentage points.

Major Industry

Aviation and aerospace, technology, research, health care, higher education

Military Bases

Wright-Patterson Air Force Base, 7,197 military, 13,231 civilian (2011)

Cities

Dayton, Kettering, Beavercreek, Fairborn, Xenia

Notable

The National Museum of the U.S. Air Force at Wright-Patterson Air Force Base is the largest and oldest military aviation museum in the world.

Rep. Marcia L. Fudge (D)

Capitol Office
225-7032
fudge.house.gov
2344 Rayburn Bldg. 20515-3511; fax 225-1339

Committees
Agriculture
Education & the Workforce

Residence
Warrensville Heights

Born
Oct. 29, 1952; Cleveland, Ohio

Religion
Baptist

Family
Single

Education
Ohio State U., B.S. 1975 (business administration); Cleveland State U., J.D. 1983

Career
Congressional aide; county government finance administrator; law clerk; sales and marketing representative

Political Highlights
Mayor of Warrensville Heights, 2000-08

ELECTION RESULTS

2012 GENERAL		
Marcia L. Fudge (D)		unopposed
2012 PRIMARY		
Marcia L. Fudge (D)	65,333	89.4%
Gerald C. Henley (D)	4,570	6.2%
Isaac Powell (D)	3,169	4.3%
2010 GENERAL		
Marcia L. Fudge (D)	139,684	82.9%
Thomas Pekarek (R)	28,752	17.1%

Previous Winning Percentages
2008 (85%); 2008 Special Election (100%)

Elected 2008; 3rd full term

Fudge takes ownership of health and education causes near and dear to her constituents, always with a progressive philosophy in mind. "If you can't take care of people at the most basic level — that being a level of housing, a safe neighborhood, a decent school, food on the table — then you've failed as a government," she says.

Her confidence in delivering her message has placed her on a prominent stage. Fudge chairs the Congressional Black Caucus in the 113th Congress (2013-14), and she vows to present the CBC agenda in economic terms, working to "heighten awareness" of unemployment and other woes in African-American communities.

As to whether the CBC will take a closer look at her signature issue of nutrition? "No doubt about it," Fudge said. "It is something that affects every single one of our communities." She expresses hopes of stronger coordination with the Obama administration on CBC priorities, and in the opening months of 2013 she aggressively urged the president to appoint more African-Americans to Cabinet positions and other prominent roles.

Administrative know-how underpins Fudge's political career. While in law school, she served as a clerk to Municipal Judge Stephanie Tubbs Jones, and she later became the budget director for Cuyahoga County. After Tubbs Jones became county prosecutor, she hired Fudge in 1991 to manage her office. When Tubbs Jones was elected to the U.S. House in 1998, she brought Fudge along as her chief of staff. Fudge quit that Washington job to run for mayor of Warrensville Heights, a Cleveland suburb, and her hard-nosed budgeting in that job won applause from many quarters.

So she speaks authoritatively about the intersection of federal and local finances, particularly when it comes to schools. Fudge sat on the Education and the Workforce Committee in her first full term and returned there midway through her second. She focuses on providing all children "the same opportunity to a quality education" — an opportunity not currently enjoyed by poorer and minority populations, she says.

She criticizes plans, Democratic or Republican, that she sees running counter to that goal. In the 112th Congress (2011-12), Fudge scrutinized the Obama administration's Race to the Top competitive grant program, saying it steers funds to too few states and eliminates potential gains for the vast majority of communities. She appreciates Republicans' desire for state control of federal education funding, but she says block grants should go to municipalities or counties, which would spend the money more quickly and effectively.

Fudge wants national uniformity when evaluating school performance, but she has also called for special consideration of the ability of poorer schools to implement federal mandates without major budget problems.

Childhood health has been a major issue for Fudge. She promotes a comprehensive approach to fighting obesity that includes educational programs, spending on nutrition and funding of youth sports programs. (Fudge herself was a standout student athlete and her school's fencing champion.) She puts the issue in budgetary terms, touting reduced health care costs if healthy habits are started early. She describes the threat of "a generation of people who do not learn well because they are not well." She and Ohio Republican Steve Stivers introduced a 2013 bill to permanently remove a protein and grain limit on school-provided meals.

Fudge joined the Agriculture Committee in the 112th Congress and serves as the top Democrat on its Department Operations, Oversight, and Nutrition panel. She has attacked Republican budgets and spending bills that include reductions to the Supplemental Nutrition Assistance Program. "There is a cold and cruel war being waged on the poor and hungry in America," she said in criticizing a GOP fiscal 2013 budget on the House floor.

If nutrition programs must shrink, Fudge says, there are ways to fill the void. She is the leading House proponent of "urban agriculture," the development of city plots into farms or gardens. The practice creates both economic uses for abandoned or vacant lots (of which Cleveland has many) and fresh food for communities where fruits and vegetables can be scarce. In 2012, the Agriculture Committee approved a farm bill that included her provisions to extend credit programs to smaller urban operations.

Heading into the 2012 election, Fudge was one of the loudest voices against perceived efforts at voter suppression. She repeatedly appeared on news programs and the House floor to describe a concerted effort by Republican governors and state legislatures to take Democratic constituencies off voting rolls through new laws and regulations. She called the efforts "an all-out assault, really, on the rights of voters, most of whom are people who have no voice."

Fudge grew up in Cleveland, living with her mother, Marian Saffold, after her parents divorced. Saffold was a lab technician at a hospital and a union organizer for the American Federation of State, County and Municipal Employees. Fudge credits her mother and maternal grandmother with getting her interested in public service. When she was 10, Fudge went with a neighbor to see the Rev. Martin Luther King Jr. speak at the 1963 march on Washington. As a teenager she worked on the 1967 Cleveland mayoral bid of Carl Stokes, who became the first black mayor of a major U.S. city.

She earned a business administration degree from Ohio State University in 1975 and eight years later earned a law degree from Cleveland State University. In conversation, Fudge often talks about her allegiance to Delta Sigma Theta, a sorority whose members are predominantly black college-educated women. It was through the Cleveland chapter that she met Tubbs Jones, and Fudge also served as a national president of the organization.

Tubbs Jones won her 2008 primary but died that August after suffering a cerebral aneurysm. Fudge was endorsed by Cleveland Mayor Frank Jackson and former Democratic Rep. Louis Stokes, and the Cuyahoga County Democratic Party put her on the ballot. She won both the special election to finish the remainder of Tubbs Jones' term and the general election to serve in the 111th Congress (2009-10). She easily won re-election in 2010.

Democratic state Sen. Nina Turner, a liberal firebrand, filed to run against Fudge in a redrawn 11th District that included new turf stretching down to Akron. But Turner dropped her bid late in 2011, handing Fudge an easy primary win in 2012. She was unopposed in November.

Key Votes

2012	
Extend a Social Security payroll tax cut and unemployment benefits	NO
Ease securities rules to expand small-business access to capital	NO
Extend for one year subsidized student loan interest rates financed by a cut in health care spending	NO
Cite Attorney General Eric H. Holder Jr. for contempt of Congress	?
Create a visa program for foreign graduates in high-tech fields	NO
Extend most Bush-era income tax rates while allowing rates for top-bracket earners to rise (Jan. 1, 2013)	YES
2011	
Strike funding for F-35 alternative engine	NO
Prevent EPA from regulating greenhouse gas emissions to address climate change	NO
Extend certain provisions of Patriot Act for four years	NO
Declare opposition to use of ground troops in Libya	NO
Overhaul patent law	YES
Pass compromise debt limit increase plan and establish future spending limits	NO
Allow consideration of measures to implement three trade agreements	NO

CQ Vote Studies

	PARTY UNITY		PRESIDENTIAL SUPPORT	
	SUPPORT	OPPOSE	SUPPORT	OPPOSE
2012	96%	4%	88%	12%
2011	97%	3%	78%	22%
2010	98%	2%	83%	17%
2009	99%	1%	98%	2%
2008	100%	0%	100%	0%

Interest Groups

	AFL-CIO	ADA	CCUS	ACU
2012	95%	100%	17%	0%
2011	100%	90%	13%	8%
2010	93%	95%	25%	4%
2009	100%	100%	33%	0%
2008	100%			0%

Ohio 11

Most of Cleveland and eastern suburbs; part of Akron

Cleveland is the focal point of this district, but the 11th also stretches south near Interstate 77, to take in racially diverse portions of Akron. It is a minority-majority district and is home to contrasting areas: both affluent neighborhoods and areas that are ravaged by poverty. In addition to its African-American majority, the district also includes a substantial Jewish population and Asian communities.

The 11th's portion of Cleveland (shared with the 9th District) takes in poor, inner-city areas of the East Side as well as the city's downtown destinations, and extends east into various historic neighborhoods such as Little Italy. University Circle is Cleveland's cultural center and home to Case Western Reserve University, the Cleveland Orchestra and the Cleveland Museum of Art. The Circle is also the heart of Cleveland's health care industry, taking in the University Hospitals of Cleveland, Cleveland Clinic and Louis Stokes Veterans Affairs Medical Center. Economic stability here will depend on medical and biotechnology firms based in the Cleveland Health-Tech Corridor. Downtown is also home to the Rock and Roll Hall of Fame along the lake, as well as football's Cleveland Browns Stadium and Progressive Field, where baseball's Indians play. Cleveland State University downtown and John Carroll University in University Heights are also in the district.

Like Cleveland, Akron, once known as the world's rubber capital, relies on health care and higher education. The portion of the University of Akron (shared with the 13th) that is in the 11th includes the College of Polymer Science and Polymer Engineering. The adjacent National Inventors Hall of Fame-affiliated public school focuses on science and technology. Akron General and the children's hospital round out the health care influence.

The 11th District gave Barack Obama his highest percentages statewide — more than 80 percent — in both the 2008 and 2012 presidential races.

Major Industry
Health care, research, higher education, manufacturing

Cities
Cleveland (pt.), Euclid, Cleveland Heights, Akron (pt.)

Notable
A landmark 1926 case brought by the city of Euclid was the first U.S. Supreme Court decision to uphold city zoning ordinances.

Rep. Pat Tiberi (R)

Capitol Office
225-5355
tiberi.house.gov
106 Cannon Bldg. 20515-3512; fax 226-4523

Committees
Ways & Means
(Select Revenue Measures - Chairman)

Residence
Genoa Township

Born
Oct. 21, 1962; Columbus, Ohio

Religion
Roman Catholic

Family
Wife, Denice Tiberi; four children

Education
Ohio State U., B.A. 1985 (journalism)

Career
Realtor; congressional district aide

Political Highlights
Ohio House, 1993-2001 (majority leader, 1999-2001)

ELECTION RESULTS

2012 GENERAL		
Pat Tiberi (R)	233,869	63.5%
Jim Reese (D)	134,605	36.5%
2012 PRIMARY		
Pat Tiberi (R)	72,560	77.9%
Bill Yarbrough (R)	20,610	22.1%
2010 GENERAL		
Pat Tiberi (R)	150,163	55.8%
Paula Brooks (D)	110,307	41.0%
Travis M. Irvine (LIBERT)	8,710	3.2%

Previous Winning Percentages
2008 (55%); 2006 (57%); 2004 (62%); 2002 (64%); 2000 (53%)

Elected 2000; 7th term

Republicans have been itching for a major tax code overhaul, and Tiberi should be in the middle of things if and when the legislative effort reaches critical mass. Quietly, he has become one of the most powerfully placed figures in Congress, using his connections and skills to land the top spot on the Ways and Means subcommittee that deals with tax issues.

His goals were once a little more modest. The son of Italian immigrants in a blue-collar neighborhood of Columbus, Tiberi (TEA-berry) wanted to be the first member of his family to go to college. Another goal was to be a part of the Ohio State University marching band, which he viewed as the next best thing to playing on the school's football team.

Now, he could conceivably become chairman or ranking Republican on Ways and Means — perhaps as early as 2015, when GOP term limits would force his friend, current Chairman Dave Camp of Michigan, to step down from his post. Tiberi said in 2012 that he wasn't thinking that far ahead: "It's never been my style to chart out a path. I'm elected for a term, and I work hard that term, and I run to get re-elected and work hard the next term."

His work as chairman of the Select Revenue Measures panel in the 112th Congress (2011-12) was to build support for a structural overhaul of the tax code, one that would reduce the number of provisions with expiration dates, the number of exemptions and credits targeted to specific groups, and the rates paid by both individuals and businesses. He called the process "educationally invigorating" but "really frustrating"; hearings and bills did not appear to significantly engage the Obama administration or Senate Democrats.

There could be a thaw in the 113th Congress (2013-14). Camp has pledged to move a major tax overhaul by the end of 2013, and Senate Finance Chairman Max Baucus of Montana began gearing up for legislative action as well.

Like almost all House Republicans, Tiberi has signed a pledge to never raise taxes. He also has endorsed the idea of preserving some tax breaks, such as the deduction for home mortgage interest.

Partly because of his sober temperament and partly because of the location of his district, Tiberi is one of the most trusted allies of a fellow Ohioan, House Speaker John A. Boehner. Easygoing and accessible, he is also something of a spokesman for Camp, spending more time talking about tax policy with reporters than perhaps any other lawmaker. Tiberi himself was once majority leader of the Ohio House.

Even with those ties to the leadership team, Tiberi has taken quite a few centrist positions over his career. He grew up in a Democratic household — he switched to the Republican Party in the 1980s — and he represented a district that Barack Obama won by 10 points in the 2008 presidential race. (When the congressional map was redrawn for 2012, however, Obama lost the district.) Tiberi belongs to the moderate Main Street Partnership.

During President George W. Bush's second term, Tiberi expressed skepticism about Bush's proposal to create private investment accounts in Social Security. He is also more sympathetic to union labor positions than many Republicans. In the 110th Congress (2007-08), he voted for a few major Democratic bills, including a measure to boost fuel efficiency standards for vehicles. He was one of 35 House Republicans to support a bill that sought to outlaw employment discrimination based on sexual orientation, and one of 40 to support the children's health insurance expansion that Obama signed early in his first term.

Tactics favored by tea-party-backed House members in the 112th Congress clashed with Tiberi's preferred style. He rejected the tactic of letting the government breach the federal debt ceiling, a course urged by conservatives who wanted to hold out for more spending reductions. "I believe in governing," he said during a constituent meeting organized by a tea party group in August 2011. "Some of my colleagues don't, and maybe some people in this room don't. There are people who I serve with who'd rather just let it all fall apart.... I guess I'm not pure enough to say, 'I don't care what the consequences are, I'm not raising the debt ceiling.'"

Tiberi has supported Republican budgets that would significantly cut spending on Medicare and Medicaid, but in the same meeting he said that even discretionary spending cuts usually cause "real pain" for people.

Tiberi is the eldest of three children. His parents arrived in the United States three years before he was born. His mother was a seamstress; his father was a machinist who lost his job and his pension when his company restructured.

He met his wife, Denice, at a Northland High School marching band alumni gathering. He played trumpet; she played flute. They have four daughters, including triplets born in 2009.

Tiberi had no interest in politics as a career until a political science class he took in college led to an internship in the Columbus office of Republican Rep. John R. Kasich. At that point, he became a Republican. He spent eight years handling constituent casework for Kasich, who is now Ohio's governor.

In 1992, state legislative district remapping created an open seat in his neighborhood. He won that election and spent four terms in the state House, rising to majority leader in 1999 and earning a reputation as a conservative willing to work with Democrats. He wrote a law to establish a DNA database to track violent criminals and was a prime mover behind a state law that, for a time, limited large jury awards. (It was ruled unconstitutional.) From 1995 to 2000, Tiberi supplemented his income by working as a Realtor.

Barred by term limits from seeking re-election to the state House in 2000, Tiberi was considering a career change when Kasich announced he was leaving the U.S. House. Support from Kasich and Boehner helped Tiberi cruise to an easy primary victory over three rivals. Democrats put up Columbus City Councilwoman Maryellen O'Shaughnessy, but Tiberi racked up big margins in the suburban GOP strongholds of Delaware and Licking counties and won by 9 points.

In 2005, Tiberi helped Ohio Republicans defeat a ballot initiative that would have changed the redistricting process in a way that could have cost the GOP seats. As a token of gratitude, Thomas M. Reynolds of New York, then the chairman of the National Republican Congressional Committee, gave Tiberi a framed map of the state signed by Ohio's GOP lawmakers. Every Ohio Republican incumbent on the November ballot won re-election in 2006.

Key Votes

2012	
Extend a Social Security payroll tax cut and unemployment benefits	YES
Ease securities rules to expand small-business access to capital	YES
Extend for one year subsidized student loan interest rates financed by a cut in health care spending	YES
Cite Attorney General Eric H. Holder Jr. for contempt of Congress	YES
Create a visa program for foreign graduates in high-tech fields	YES
Extend most Bush-era income tax rates while allowing rates for top-bracket earners to rise (Jan. 1, 2013)	YES
2011	
Strike funding for F-35 alternative engine	NO
Prevent EPA from regulating greenhouse gas emissions to address climate change	YES
Extend certain provisions of Patriot Act for four years	YES
Declare opposition to use of ground troops in Libya	YES
Overhaul patent law	YES
Pass compromise debt limit increase plan and establish future spending limits	YES
Allow consideration of measures to implement three trade agreements	YES

CQ Vote Studies

	PARTY UNITY		PRESIDENTIAL SUPPORT	
	SUPPORT	OPPOSE	SUPPORT	OPPOSE
2012	89%	11%	16%	84%
2011	92%	8%	25%	75%
2010	91%	9%	33%	67%
2009	90%	10%	41%	59%
2008	92%	8%	60%	40%

Interest Groups

	AFL-CIO	ADA	CCUS	ACU
2012	25%	0%	100%	76%
2011	24%	15%	100%	72%
2010	7%	0%	88%	96%
2009	24%	15%	87%	83%
2008	40%	35%	94%	72%

Ohio 12

Central — northern and eastern Columbus suburbs

Radiating in two directions from the Columbus suburbs — north along Interstate 71 to Mansfield and east along Interstate 70 to Zanesville — the crescent-shaped 12th District includes white-collar urban populations and rural manufacturing towns, as well as fertile farmland.

Newark, the district's largest city, produces plastics, metals and building materials. The Central Ohio Aerospace & Technology Center in nearby Heath — on the site of a former Air Force base — helps drive a modest aerospace and defense industry, with Boeing repair facilities and Meritor military vehicle parts manufacturing. Factories have replaced farmland in Licking County, yet it is still one of the state's most productive agricultural counties and is among Ohio's most active counties in oil and gas drilling.

Dublin lies in the district's jigsawed southwestern corner near Columbus. An affluent suburb, it has a population that is 15 percent Asian, a proportion nine times larger than the statewide average; the wealth and ethnic diversity are both anomalous traits in the largely white, working-class 12th. Financial services firms and telecommunications companies rate among Dublin's biggest employers. Fast-food chain Wendy's recently consolidated its world headquarters in Dublin, as well. Delaware County's population grew by nearly 60 percent from 2000 to 2010, but nearly half of its land remains farmland. Retail and manufacturing distribution centers provide jobs in Muskingum County. The 12th also hosts Ohio Wesleyan University, Ohio University-Zanesville and popular rentals for Ohio State University students.

The newly remapped 12th mainly takes in reliably Republican territory. Mansfield provides some Democratic voters, but in statewide races, the GOP wins by wide margins in Richland County overall and in all the district's counties, except for Franklin, only a sliver of which is in the 12th. Mitt Romney took 54 percent of the district's vote in the 2012 presidential race.

Major Industry

Finance, telecommunications, manufacturing, distribution, agriculture

Cities

Newark, Mansfield, Dublin, Westerville, Delaware

Notable

The headquarters for clothing manufacturer Abercrombie & Fitch in New Albany was designed to mimic lakeside summer lodges with sheds, timber-frame structures and wooded paths.

Rep. Tim Ryan (D)

Capitol Office
225-5261
timryan.house.gov
1421 Longworth Bldg. 20515-3517; fax 225-3719

Committees
Appropriations
Budget

Residence
Niles

Born
July 16, 1973; Niles, Ohio

Religion
Roman Catholic

Family
Wife, Andrea Ryan; two children

Education
Youngstown State U., attended 1991-92; Bowling Green State U., B.A. 1995 (political science); Franklin Pierce Law Center, J.D. 2000

Career
Congressional aide

Political Highlights
Ohio Senate, 2001-02

ELECTION RESULTS

2012 GENERAL		
Tim Ryan (D)	235,492	72.8%
Marisha G. Agana (R)	88,120	27.2%
2012 PRIMARY		
Tim Ryan (D)		unopposed
2010 GENERAL		
Tim Ryan (D)	102,758	53.9%
Jim Graham (R)	57,352	30.1%
James A. Traficant Jr. (I)	30,556	16.0%

Previous Winning Percentages
2008 (78%); 2006 (80%); 2004 (77%); 2002 (51%)

Elected 2002; 6th term

Ryan's politics are rooted in traditional Midwestern manufacturing and labor issues. His passions, however, center on the potential of the human mind. His unusual focus is helping Americans pay attention at school and on the job.

He is an advocate of "mindfulness," a meditation practice meant to improve adherents' awareness and attention. Ryan published "A Mindful Nation" in 2012, winning famous fans such as NBA coaching legend Phil Jackson and hip-hop magnate Russell Simmons. "It's basically a stress reduction technique, a performance-enhancing technique that the Marines are starting to use, that many corporations are starting to use," he said. "There's some good studies coming online about the benefits for improved health, boosting your immune system, reducing your stress levels."

Ryan calls for further study of the practice and would like it included in national health and education initiatives. In a world overrun by distractions, he said, teaching children how to pay attention is vital to their learning.

Ryan also has more-immediate concerns, mostly involving the revitalization of his district's economy. There's a natural-gas boom in northeastern Ohio, and Ryan splits with many Democrats to support the practice of hydraulic fracturing, or "fracking," which involves injecting pressurized fluid into the ground to release oil or gas. The country should transition from an oil-based economy to one where natural gas plays a larger role, he said.

Unlike Republican fracking supporters, though, Ryan urges heavy federal oversight of the practice, as opposed to relying on state-level regulation. The EPA should monitor site selection of wells and disposal of the chemical-laden fluids used, he said.

The natural-gas boom has revamped his district's manufacturing sector, particularly for the steel tubing used in fracking operations. Ryan hopes more next-generation industries will supplant the Rust Belt's older technologies.

Manufacturing is also at the top of his defense-related concerns. He wants to see the U.S. focus on rebuilding an industrial base for the military, and using the armed forces to bolster the economy. In the 113th Congress (2013-14), Ryan returned to the Appropriations Committee — and its Defense Subcommittee — after a two-year hiatus forced by Democratic electoral losses in 2010. He lists cybersecurity as another defense priority.

Ryan also sits on the Transportation-HUD Subcommittee, and he returned as a member of the Budget Committee in 2013.

Ryan's interest in manufacturing keeps him involved in all its ancillary issues. He is known as a friend of organized labor and said in 2012 that unions could see a turnaround from recent declines: "I really think there's an opportunity to revitalize the labor movement, really because of the way the economy has been."

He is skeptical of many free-trade pacts, and he is particularly critical of China's trade policies. For years, Ryan has called for punitive measures against China should it manipulate the value of its currency for a trading advantage, and in 2011 he said it was the No. 1 issue before Congress. (He is not the most prominent protectionist born in Niles, Ohio. William McKinley gets that honor.)

Ryan supported the Occupy Wall Street movement, and he spoke on several occasions in the 112th Congress about income inequality in America. "It was only a matter of time before the American people realized what gave rise to the highest level of income inequality since the Great Depression: a runaway economic system devoid of compassion or patriotism and a political system that would rather fight ideological battles than pragmatically fix the problem," he said in 2011.

Like many colleagues from socially conservative, working-class districts, he supports gun ownership rights and opposes abortion — although he backed the Democrats' 2010 health care overhaul, which critics said would allow federal dollars to be spent on abortion coverage. He hailed the Supreme Court decision that upheld most of that law as "a victory for the American people."

After Democratic losses in 2004, he said the party suffered from unreasonable absolutism on social issues. But he has voted twice against amending the Constitution to ban same-sex marriage. When the ban on openly gay servicemembers was lifted in 2011, Ryan called it "a new era of equality in America."

A sizable portion of his work in the 112th Congress was focused on getting Brazil to hand over Claudia Hoerig, who is accused of killing her husband, an Iraq war veteran living in Ohio, then fleeing to South America in 2007. Ryan has accused Brazil of not honoring a 1961 extradition treaty. He put forward three measures to penalize the country by either cutting off $14 million in foreign aid or denying an estimated 1.8 million visas to its citizens. None of the measures passed.

Ryan's parents divorced when he was in grade school, and he and his older brother were raised by their mother and grandparents. His mother was a chief deputy clerk of Trumbull County. His grandmother worked for the county clerk of courts, his grandfather was a steelworker and both were union members. Ryan was a football player in high school and college until he ruined his knee. He studied political science at Ohio's Bowling Green State University and earned a law degree from New Hampshire's Franklin Pierce Law Center. His studies included a stint in an international law program in Florence, Italy.

In the mid-1990s, he worked as an aide for the colorful Democratic Rep. James A. Traficant Jr. of Ohio. Ryan won election to the Ohio Senate in 2000, the year he completed law school. In 2002, with Traficant facing jail on bribery and racketeering charges (he was eventually expelled from the House), Ryan entered a competitive primary for the seat. He faced eight-term Democratic Rep. Tom Sawyer, who was thrown into the contest by redistricting. Sawyer outspent him 10-to-1, but Ryan prevailed and went on to easily defeat GOP state Sen. Ann Womer Benjamin.

He was re-elected with ease until 2010, when he was held to 54 percent against Republican Jim Graham and Traficant, who polled 16 percent running as an independent. Another round of redistricting made his seat much safer for 2012, and he won 73 percent of the vote. Ryan has considered a bid for statewide office, but he has already announced that he does not plan to enter Ohio's gubernatorial race in 2014.

Key Votes

2012	
Extend a Social Security payroll tax cut and unemployment benefits	NO
Ease securities rules to expand small-business access to capital	YES
Extend for one year subsidized student loan interest rates financed by a cut in health care spending	NO
Cite Attorney General Eric H. Holder Jr. for contempt of Congress	NO
Create a visa program for foreign graduates in high-tech fields	NO
Extend most Bush-era income tax rates while allowing rates for top-bracket earners to rise (Jan. 1, 2013)	YES
2011	
Strike funding for F-35 alternative engine	NO
Prevent EPA from regulating greenhouse gas emissions to address climate change	NO
Extend certain provisions of Patriot Act for four years	NO
Declare opposition to use of ground troops in Libya	NO
Overhaul patent law	NO
Pass compromise debt limit increase plan and establish future spending limits	NO
Allow consideration of measures to implement three trade agreements	NO

CQ Vote Studies

	PARTY UNITY		PRESIDENTIAL SUPPORT	
	SUPPORT	OPPOSE	SUPPORT	OPPOSE
2012	92%	8%	85%	15%
2011	92%	8%	81%	19%
2010	98%	2%	93%	7%
2009	99%	1%	97%	3%
2008	[illegible]	2%	20%	[illegible]

Interest Groups

	AFL-CIO	ADA	CCUS	ACU
2012	95%	90%	17%	12%
2011	100%	85%	13%	12%
2010	93%	90%	38%	0%
2009	100%	95%	33%	4%
2008	100%	90%	61%	4%

Ohio 13

Northeast — Youngstown, part of Akron

Bordering Pennsylvania in part of northeastern Ohio's Mahoning Valley, including Youngstown, the 13th is a Democratic bastion. Once a leading steel producer, the valley now symbolizes industrial decline; most of the mills that have not been torn down are either silent or abandoned. Recent energy development in the state spurs hope for increased steel production in the region, which struggles with high rates of unemployment. The district takes in parts of five different counties: Mahoning, Portage, Stark, Summit — including parts of the city of Akron — and Trumbull.

Youngstown is the only employment hub in Mahoning County and has struggled with population loss and widespread unemployment; one-third of the city's residents live in poverty. The population of Youngstown hovered around 170,000 from the 1930s through the 1960s; the 2010 census counted just 67,000 people. Youngstown's economic devastation and population loss have forced officials to plan for a smaller city, converting vacant homes and commercial and industrial sites into open space. To the west, Cuyahoga Falls is a solid middle-class city, with nearly 50 percent of its land in residential use; its income rates are at the statewide average.

Manufacturing is still important to areas of the district. Goodyear Tire & Rubber Co.'s corporate headquarters in the 13th District's portion of Akron is a leading employer in Summit County, and General Motors has a plant in Lordstown. Other job sources in the district include the Youngstown-Warren Regional Airport in Trumbull County and colleges: Youngstown State University, Kent State University and portions of the University of Akron.

Ohio lost two U.S. House seats during reapportionment after the 2010 census, and the new 13th roughly models the old 17th District. Still reliably Democratic, combining traditional union values and some minority votes, the 13th gave Barack Obama 63 percent of its vote in the 2012 presidential contest.

Major Industry
Manufacturing, health care, higher education

Cities
Youngstown, Warren, Akron (pt.)

Notable
The Butler Institute of American Art in Youngstown, dedicated in 1919, was one of the first museums to display only American art.

Rep. David Joyce (R)

Capitol Office
225-5731
joyce.house.gov
1535 Longworth Bldg. 20515-1410; fax 225-3307

Committees
Appropriations

Residence
Russell Township

Born
March 17, 1957; Cleveland, Ohio

Religion
Roman Catholic

Family
Wife, Kelly Joyce; three children

Education
U. of Dayton, B.S. 1979 (accounting), J.D. 1982

Career
County public defender

Political Highlights
Geauga County prosecutor, 1988-2013

ELECTION RESULTS

2012 GENERAL		
David Joyce (R)	183,657	54.0%
Dale Virgil Blanchard (D)	131,637	38.7%
Elaine R. Mastromatteo (GREEN)	13,038	3.8%
David Macko (LIBERT)	11,536	3.4%

Elected 2012; 1st term

Joyce was relatively unknown when he joined the House, thanks to the odd circumstances of his election. He is establishing himself as a legislator, but he is doing so as a marked man — Democrats are targeting him in 2014.

Joyce grew up in northeastern Ohio, then went to the University of Dayton to get undergraduate and law degrees. He soon became the top public defender in Geauga County, east of Cleveland. In 1988, he was appointed the county's prosecutor, and he kept that job in a string of elections over two decades. Early in his tenure, he teamed with the prosecutor of neighboring Lake County, Steven C. LaTourette, on cases and the management of their offices.

He made connections in the Republican Party and was recommended to the George W. Bush administration for a U.S. attorney job. But the nomination stalled, and Joyce eventually withdrew. Explaining the incident to the Cleveland Plain Dealer in 2012, Joyce said, "I got out-politicked."

LaTourette won a U.S. House seat in 1994 and was a leading moderate among Republicans. He won the 2012 primary but stunningly announced his retirement a few months later, saying he was tired of partisan politics. Joyce was chosen by party officials as his replacement on the ballot, and Democrats had basically conceded the seat to LaTourette. Joyce won in November with no difficulty. However, the district is politically competitive — Mitt Romney won its presidential vote by only 3 points. Democrats have already started lining up for the 2014 race.

Joyce has indicated that he is further to the right than LaTourette, but he joined both the conservative Republican Study Committee and the moderate Main Street Partnership. He sits on the Appropriations Committee, where it's easier to avoid overt partisanship. And he took up one of LaTourette's old bipartisan causes, trying to find new ways to finance the demolition of blighted and abandoned properties from neighborhoods. Joyce describes himself as a fiscal conservative.

Ohio 14

Northeast — Cleveland and Akron suburbs

The 14th District moves east along the Lake Erie shoreline, tracked by Interstate 90, from just outside Cleveland to the Pennsylvania border in the state's northeastern tip. It includes all of Ashtabula, Lake and Geauga counties, as well as portions of Cuyahoga, Trumbull, Portage and Summit counties. These depressed far northeastern communities remain reliant on the ailing steel, chemical and auto-manufacturing industries. Some Cleveland residents have moved out of the city and into Lake and Geauga counties, where there are wealthy suburban enclaves.

The 14th's portion of Cuyahoga County includes the upscale and Republican-leaning villages of Bentleyville and Moreland Hills in the east. Mayfield Village is home to Progressive Insurance, and the city boasts a fiber-optics network that helps alleviate technical costs to local businesses. The lakeshore region in Lake and Ashtabula counties produces fruit farms and much of Ohio's wine-grape acreage, with resorts and country clubs catering to wine enthusiasts. Lake County leads the state in sales of nursery and greenhouse products.

Closer to Cleveland, communities are more ethnically diverse, but overall the 14th is more than 90 percent white, and about 23 percent of the district is over 60 years of age. Many of the counties have traditional Scandinavian roots, and Finns have a base in Ashtabula County.

In Lake, Republicans perform well in areas south of Mentor, such as Kirtland and Kirtland Hills, which are overwhelmingly wealthy and white. Democrats can do well in Painesville, where nearly half of Lake's blacks and Hispanics live. Democratic votes in Ashtabula and Lake for federal and statewide offices are not sufficient to sway Trumbull, Geauga and Summit's Republican leans. In the 2012 presidential race, GOP candidate Mitt Romney won Lake County by roughly 1,000 votes and the part of Cuyahoga in the district by about 600; he took wide margins in Geauga and the district's portion of Portage. Barack Obama won only in Ashtabula. Overall, the 14th gave Romney a 3-percentage-point win in the election.

Major Industry
Agriculture, health care, manufacturing, retail

Cities
Mentor, Willoughby, Painesville

Notable
Twinsburg calls its annual August gathering of twins the world's largest.

Rep. Steve Stivers (R)

Capitol Office
225-2015
stivers.house.gov
1022 Longworth Bldg. 20515-3515; fax 225-3529

Committees
Financial Services

Residence
Columbus

Born
March 24, 1965; Cincinnati, Ohio

Religion
United Methodist

Family
Wife, Karen Stivers; two children

Education
Ohio State U., B.A. 1989 (international studies), M.B.A. 1996

Military
Ohio Army National Guard, 1988-present

Career
Lobbyist; securities company executive; county party official; campaign aide

Political Highlights
Ohio Senate, 2003-08; Republican nominee for U.S. House, 2008

ELECTION RESULTS

2012 GENERAL		
Steve Stivers (R)	205,274	61.6%
Pat Lang (D)	128,188	38.4%
2012 PRIMARY		
Steve Stivers (R)	70,191	89.3%
Charles Chope (R)	8,404	10.7%
2010 GENERAL		
Steve Stivers (R)	119,471	54.2%
Mary Jo Kilroy (D)	91,077	41.3%
William J. Kammerer (LIBERT)	6,116	2.8%
David Ryon (CNSTP)	3,887	1.8%

Elected 2010; 2nd term

Stivers fits the description of a moderate Rust Belt Republican, with a few distinguishing qualities. His experience in the financial sector informs his committee work; his service as a National Guardsman gives him gravitas on military matters; and he has the attention of GOP leaders.

Modest and pleasant, Stivers supports the Republican agenda and avoids hard-line stances. On the Financial Services Committee, he contributes to the campaign for a looser regulatory environment for businesses. He made a point in the 112th Congress (2011-12) of promoting expansion of domestic energy production and accepting compromise measures to reduce federal spending and deficits.

Stivers, who belongs to the conservative Republican Study Committee and the centrist Main Street Partnership, was one of the 85 House Republicans to vote for the January 2013 fiscal cliff deal to allow income tax increases on earnings higher than $400,000. Conservatives wanted it bundled with spending cuts, but Stivers said the permanent extension of lower rates on income below that threshold made it worthwhile.

In casting that vote, he stood with Speaker John A. Boehner, the embattled Ohio Republican who personally recruited Stivers in 2008 for his first House campaign. Stivers has no high-profile leadership posts in the Republican Party, but he does have a history of working for the GOP.

He was heavily involved with the Franklin County Republican Party. Stivers served a turn as its finance director and has been described as a "prolific" fundraiser. A few insiders have mentioned him as a possible future chairman of the National Republican Congressional Committee. For the 113th Congress (2013-14), he is serving as the NRCCs' vice chairman for finance.

Stivers worked as a lobbyist for Bank One, which was later swallowed in a merger, and spent a few years at an Ohio securities company. His work on the Financial Services Committee has dealt with the financial sector and the ways in which it intersects with various Republican policies.

In 2012, the House passed a bill by Stivers and Ohio Democrat Marcia L. Fudge to narrow the application of derivatives regulations in the 2010 financial regulatory overhaul known as Dodd-Frank. Their bill would block clearing, margin and collateral rules (and their compliance costs) for "swap" contracts between entities controlled by the same parent company. Stivers says the rules were meant for contracts between unaffiliated entities and that inter-affiliate swaps don't add risk to the overall financial system. The Senate didn't act on the bill, and it was reintroduced in 2013.

Stivers wants to eliminate a Dodd-Frank provision giving credit-rating agencies increased exposure to lawsuits. Many experts claimed that inaccurate ratings of mortgage-backed securities contributed to the 2008 financial crisis, but Stivers said the provision froze the market for asset-backed securities — which in turn hurt manufacturers that use them to generate cash flow.

The Securities and Exchange Commission voluntarily halted enforcement, but Stivers introduced a bill to codify the change. It stalled after winning committee approval.

He contributes to the finance portions of other GOP bills. In the 112th, Stivers helped formulate a Republican plan to tie domestic-energy production to infrastructure funding; revenue from new energy leases would be used to pay off government-issued infrastructure bonds. Democrats panned that idea, and it was not included in a two-year reauthorization of surface transportation programs enacted in 2012.

Stivers also participated as Republicans generated plans for cybersecurity legislation in 2011. He wants clearer rules for legal liability when computer networks are breached, saying that clarity will facilitate development of a cybersecurity insurance market.

Security issues in general hold Stivers' interest. He joined the Ohio Army National Guard in 1988, deployed overseas as a battalion commander for most of 2005 and is still an active National Guardsman. His undergraduate degree is in international studies, and his master's work at the U.S. Army War College — completed during his first term in the House — focused on strategic studies. Stivers said in 2011 that budget pressures on the military "mean we will have to transform the force."

Stivers has found Democratic partners for bills to boost the employment prospects of veterans. Some of his employment bills have been more partisan, however. The expansion of unemployment insurance since the 2008 financial crisis has gone too far, according to Stivers, and he would rather see a shorter benefits window followed by opportunities to enroll in job training or public service programs. "We need to give people an incentive to get out and work as soon as possible," he said in 2011. "I'm not blaming the people that are unemployed. It's the fault of the program. We've created a perverse incentive. We need to fix it."

Stivers grew up in Ripley, a small town southeast of Cincinnati and just across the Ohio River from Kentucky. He headed to Columbus to attended Ohio State University. He was in a pickle in June 2011 when he obtained some memorabilia signed by Jim Tressel, the scandal-plagued former football coach, to give to troops at Walter Reed National Military Medical Center. He still distributed the items. "I figured, if you're an OSU fan, it'll be OK," he told the Columbus Dispatch.

Before working for the Franklin County GOP and the finance sector, Stivers in college was an aide to state Sen. H. Cooper Snyder. His Republican Party connections helped him win caucus approval to fill a vacancy in the state Senate in 2003. He was something of a surprise choice, and some conservatives weren't thrilled. Sen. Jim Jordan, who is now a House colleague, voted against Stivers' appointment because of his views on abortion. (Stivers supports abortion rights but has voted to bar federal funding of the procedure.)

Boehner recruited Stivers in 2008 as a possible successor to retiring eight-term Republican Rep. Deborah Pryce. After a bitter campaign, Stivers came up about 2,300 votes short of Democrat Mary Jo Kilroy. Republicans had a great year in 2010, and Stivers won the rematch by 13 points.

His district was dramatically altered for the 2012 election. Although it still has parts of Columbus, most of it is suburban, rural and far more Republican. Stivers beat Democrat Pat Lang by 23 points to secure a second term.

Key Votes

2012	
Extend a Social Security payroll tax cut and unemployment benefits	YES
Ease securities rules to expand small-business access to capital	YES
Extend for one year subsidized student loan interest rates financed by a cut in health care spending	YES
Cite Attorney General Eric H. Holder Jr. for contempt of Congress	YES
Create a visa program for foreign graduates in high-tech fields	YES
Extend most Bush-era income tax rates while allowing rates for top-bracket earners to rise (Jan. 1, 2013)	YES
2011	
Strike funding for F-35 alternative engine	NO
Prevent EPA from regulating greenhouse gas emissions to address climate change	YES
Extend certain provisions of Patriot Act for four years	YES
Declare opposition to use of ground troops in Libya	YES
Overhaul patent law	?
Pass compromise debt limit increase plan and establish future spending limits	YES
Allow consideration of measures to implement three trade agreements	YES

CQ Vote Studies

	PARTY UNITY		PRESIDENTIAL SUPPORT	
	SUPPORT	OPPOSE	SUPPORT	OPPOSE
2012	91%	9%	20%	80%
2011	90%	10%	28%	72%

Interest Groups

	AFL-CIO	ADA	CCUS	ACU
2012	26%	0%	100%	73%
2011	22%	15%	100%	66%

Ohio 15

Parts of Columbus and suburbs; Athens

Ohio lost two U.S. House seats during reapportionment following the 2010 census, and the 15th District was redrawn to include areas formerly split among four separate districts. The new 15th now takes in part of the capital city and some of its growing upscale suburbs and country clubs as well as the liberal college town of Athens, with a wide swath of conservative manufacturing towns and farmland in between. The district's southwestern arm picks up part of Fayette County and all of Clinton County.

Higher education looms large in the district. The Ohio State University flagship campus (shared with the 3rd) hosts 56,000 students. The school's Buckeyes sports games draw huge crowds to a city not generally regarded as a tourist destination. At the eastern edge of the 15th is Ohio University in Athens; with more than 21,000 students it is now the largest employer in Athens County, which used to rely on mining and manufacturing.

The district includes the affluent — and overwhelmingly white — residential suburbs neighboring OSU northwest of Columbus, including the mansions of tony Upper Arlington and Hilliard's planned communities. South is Grove City, a fast-growing suburb with a prominent service sector that has had some success in attracting new businesses to its industrial and commercial parks. About 30 miles southeast of Columbus is Lancaster, whose industrial heritage is evident in glass factories and EPA-funded brownfield sites. The city has a burgeoning small-town arts scene, with galleries and museums.

Farmland and light manufacturing dominate the district's center. Mostly rural Pickaway County is a top producer of corn and soybeans. The district's east edges into Appalachian Ohio, where coal mining was once big.

Some areas around Columbus and the college town of Athens are Democratic. Athens is the only county in the 15th to back Rep. Steve Stivers' Democratic opponent in the 2012 U.S. House race; it also gave Barack Obama a more than 2-to-1 margin over Republican Mitt Romney in the presidential contest. Overall, the 15th gave Romney 52 percent of its vote.

Major Industry
Higher education, manufacturing, professional services, agriculture

Cities
Columbus (pt.), Lancaster, Grove City, Hilliard, Athens

Notable
The Fairfield County Fair, dating back to 1850, is the oldest continuously operating fair in Ohio.

Rep. James B. Renacci (R)

Capitol Office
225-3876
renacci.house.gov
130 Cannon Bldg. 20515-3516; fax 225-3059

Committees
Ways & Means

Residence
Wadsworth

Born
Dec. 3, 1958; Monongahela, Pa.

Religion
Roman Catholic

Family
Wife, Tina Renacci; three children

Education
Indiana U. of Pennsylvania, B.S. 1980 (accounting)

Career
Business management consultant; professional arena football team executive; nursing homes owner; accountant

Political Highlights
Wadsworth Board of Zoning Appeals, 1994-95; Wadsworth City Council president, 2000-03; mayor of Wadsworth, 2004-07

ELECTION RESULTS

2012 GENERAL		
James B. Renacci (R)	185,165	52.0%
Betty Sutton (D)	170,600	48.0%
2012 PRIMARY		
James B. Renacci (R)		unopposed
2010 GENERAL		
James B. Renacci (R)	114,652	52.1%
John Boccieri (D)	90,833	41.3%
Jeffrey J. Blevins (LIBERT)	14,585	6.6%

Elected 2010; 2nd term

Renacci has scads of executive experience from time spent as a mayor and a highly successful business owner. The moderate Republican freely admits it isn't always useful in the working environment of Congress.

"Nothing ever starts on time ... no matter what the numbers you see are, it's actually much worse ... and it is very political," he told a service organization in his district in 2012. "You can't get things done right away. You have to get people to know and trust you."

Renacci (reh-NAY-see) spent a good deal of his time in the 112th Congress (2011-12) building a network to achieve those results, despite a polarized House and his freshman status. He joined both the Republican Study Committee, the bloc of conservative House members, and the Main Street Partnership, a more-moderate caucus. He was granted a seat on the Republican Policy Committee, which sets the tone for many House GOP initiatives.

More notably, he and Delaware Democrat John Carney organized an informal, bipartisan "breakfast club" to kick around legislative ideas every few weeks. Several media outlets took notice of the group, often mentioning it as a contrast to the usual dynamics of the House. Carney called those attending "more moderate, more fiscally responsible, business oriented." Speaking to a Republican group in Washington, Renacci described its principles: "You can talk about anything you want to talk about as long as you don't demonize the other side."

The club scored a legislative success in early 2012 when President Barack Obama signed an extension of reduced payroll tax rates. That law contained a proposal, originally sponsored by Renacci, allowing demonstration projects whereby states pay employers a portion of a person's unemployment benefits when they hire an unemployed person.

He stood behind other bills generated by the club: a measure to establish a pre-tax savings account for first-time homebuyers saving for a down payment; a measure to require an up-or-down vote every four years on a package to cut or update various regulations; a measure allowing a lower tax on corporate profits brought back to the United States from overseas, if those profits are used for hiring or business investments in the United States; and a measure requiring extensive new reports on the federal budget, as well as switching the government to a two-year budgeting cycle.

Throughout his career, Renacci has been a numbers guy. A 1980 graduate of the Indiana University of Pennsylvania, he got his start in business as an accountant for a large firm in Pittsburgh, where he kept the books for nursing-home companies. He left for Ohio in 1984 and started his own nursing home, which grew into a chain of more than 20 facilities. Fifteen years later he sold the chain and launched an accounting business. His other investments have included sports teams — from 2003 to 2009 he co-owned the Columbus Destroyers, an Arena Football League team, and he has a stake in the Lancaster JetHawks, a minor league baseball franchise in California. He is one of the wealthiest members of Congress.

He has stated that numbers got him into politics, as he thought government budgets could be better drafted and executed. Renacci served as city council president for Wadsworth, Ohio, before becoming the town's mayor from 2004 to 2007. "We not only cut spending, we came up with a surplus without a single tax increase," he told Human Events magazine. He also lured commercial development to the area and touted his pro-growth, limited spending, low-tax policies. Renacci adhered to the GOP line on tax increases in 2011, insisting that spending cuts had to be the government's priority.

Republicans have provided him with committee assignments suited to his talents. As a freshman, he was a member of the Financial Services Committee, and one month into the 113th Congress (2013-14) he was named to fill the last unassigned spot on the tax-writing Ways and Means Committee.

In his first term, he was vice chairman of the Financial Services Subcommittee on Financial Institutions and Consumer Credit, which had a key role overseeing the implementation of the 2010 financial regulatory overhaul known as Dodd-Frank. Renacci questioned whether the new Consumer Financial Protection Bureau was given too much power to interfere in financial markets, and he introduced a bill to remove the director of the CFPB from the board of the Federal Deposit Insurance Corporation. He also examined the effect of new regulations on credit unions and smaller lending institutions, often stating that the law could be drying up capital for small businesses.

Renacci touts his conservative social values — he opposes abortion — but fiscal issues are what spurred his 2010 campaign. He had purchased a failing Chevrolet dealership in Wadsworth in 2007, and during the 2009 government reorganization of General Motors, he was told that his dealership would be closed. He unsuccessfully fought that decision, but Renacci cites the battle as his inspiration to run for the House.

Traditionally a GOP district, the Canton-based 16th was carried by Republican John McCain in the 2008 presidential race while the House seat — vacated by Republican Ralph Regula, who retired after 36 years — was won by Democrat John Boccieri. During the 2010 campaign, Democrats highlighted the story of a woman who died in one of the nursing facilities Renacci owned. He filed court papers against a labor union for defamation in an advertising campaign. He won the election by almost 11 points.

Ohio lost two House seats after reapportionment following the 2010 census, and Renacci was pushed into a highly competitive 2012 race with three-term Democrat Betty Sutton. The redrawn 16th was about half new to Renacci, while Sutton had represented only a fifth of district.

His fundraising came under scrutiny when federal prosecutors began a probe of donations from employees of the Suarez Foundation, a Canton-based direct marketing company whose owner often supports GOP causes. Several employees who had never given to campaigns before were reported to have made the maximum allowable contribution to Renacci and Senate candidate Josh Mandel. Renacci was not under investigation, but he returned the money.

Interest groups and party organizations poured huge sums into negative campaigning — more than $4 million against each candidate. Renacci did not dip into his personal fortune to fund his campaign, however. He pulled out a 4-point win over Sutton.

Key Votes

2012	
Extend a Social Security payroll tax cut and unemployment benefits	YES
Ease securities rules to expand small-business access to capital	YES
Extend for one year subsidized student loan interest rates financed by a cut in health care spending	YES
Cite Attorney General Eric H. Holder Jr. for contempt of Congress	YES
Create a visa program for foreign graduates in high-tech fields	YES
Extend most Bush-era income tax rates while allowing rates for top-bracket earners to rise (Jan. 1, 2013)	NO
2011	
Strike funding for F-35 alternative engine	NO
Prevent EPA from regulating greenhouse gas emissions to address climate change	YES
Extend certain provisions of Patriot Act for four years	YES
Declare opposition to use of ground troops in Libya	YES
Overhaul patent law	YES
Pass compromise debt limit increase plan and establish future spending limits	YES
Allow consideration of measures to implement three trade agreements	YES

CQ Vote Studies

	PARTY UNITY		PRESIDENTIAL SUPPORT	
	SUPPORT	OPPOSE	SUPPORT	OPPOSE
2012	92%	8%	20%	80%
2011	93%	7%	22%	78%

Interest Groups

	AFL-CIO	ADA	CCUS	ACU
2012	24%	0%	100%	72%
2011	3%	5%	100%	80%

Ohio 16

North Central — western Cleveland suburbs, North Canton

The 16th stretches from just south of Lake Erie's shores inland to North Canton. It includes all of Wayne County and portions of Summit, Stark, Cuyahoga, Portage and Medina counties. It is largely rural, but also includes some Cleveland and Canton suburbs.

The northern part of the district is suburban and white collar. Residents of Rocky River, Westlake, Fairview Park and North Olmsted commute to jobs in downtown Cleveland. Automotive and metal manufacturing and agriculture dominate in Wayne County. Food processing in Wayne includes the headquarters of Smucker's; the county also hosts the liberal arts College of Wooster. Stark County, which hosts steel manufacturer Timken, was added to the 16th during decennial remapping. A few large manufacturing interests in Medina County employ hundreds of residents in the region and in Cuyahoga County, faucet company Moen maintains corporate headquarters in North Olmsted.

Farmland in the district, particularly in Wayne County, produces fruits, tree nuts, berries, hay, milk and corn. Portage, which is a heavily wooded county, is a leading producer of Christmas trees. Some of the wide open space in the district is kept as wildlife preserves and parks.

The district is Republican overall, and Democratic votes in the 16th's portions of Cuyahoga (Cleveland) and Summit counties cannot overcome GOP strength in overwhelmingly Republican Wayne County — which also has a significant Amish community — and Stark and Medina counties. In the 2012 presidential election, Barack Obama eked out a narrow win in the district's portion of Cuyahoga — he won by fewer than 600 votes — but lost in every other county in the district. Republican Mitt Romney won Wayne County by more than 20 percentage points and took 53 percent of the district's presidential vote.

Major Industry
Manufacturing, agriculture

Cities
Strongsville, Westlake, North Olmstead

Notable
In addition to founding his food products company in Orrville, J.M. Smucker at one time taught evening courses in penmanship.

OKLAHOMA

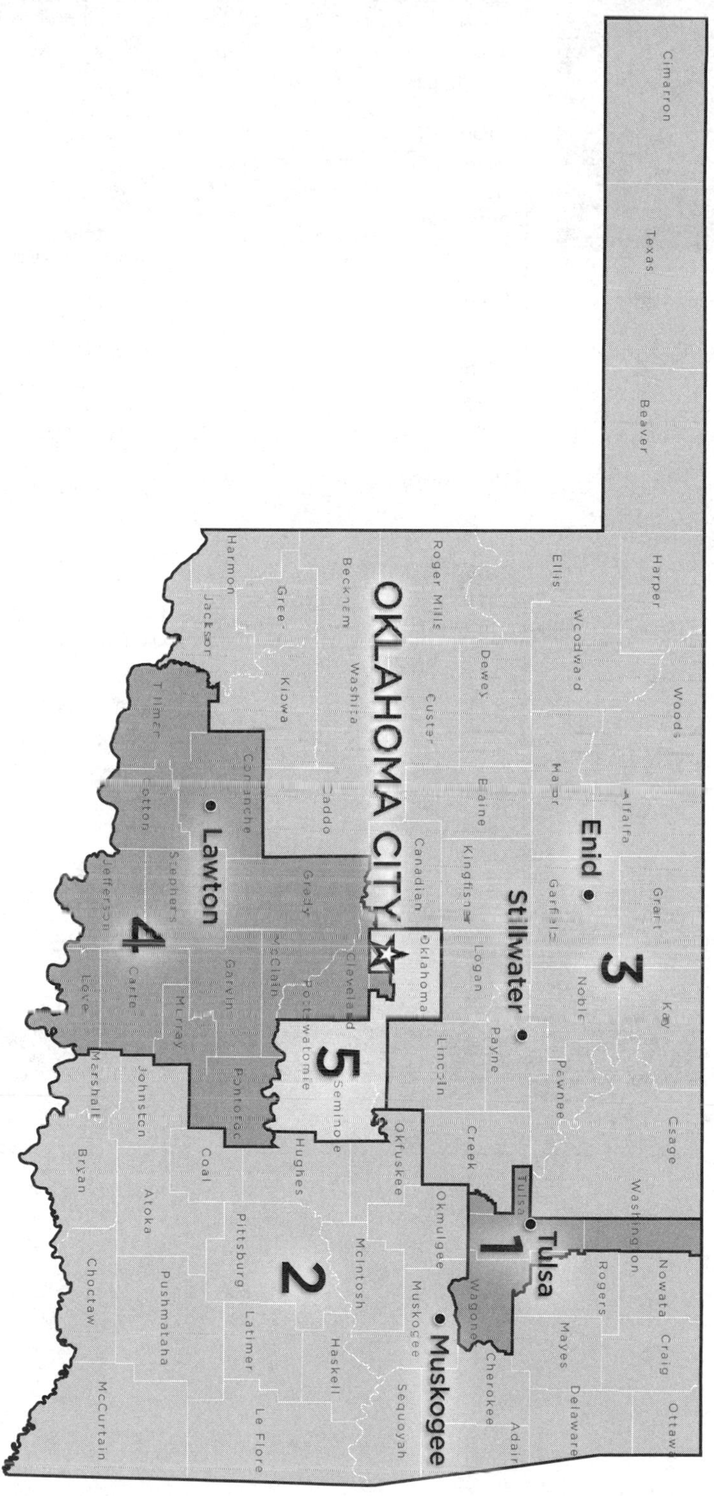

OKLAHOMA CITY
Lawton
Enid
Stillwater
Tulsa
Muskogee
1
2
3
4
5
Cimarron
Texas
Beaver
Harper
Woods
Ellis
Woodward
Roger Mills
Dewey
Custer
Washita
Kiowa
Harmon
Jackson
Tillman
Comanche
Caddo
Cotton
Stephens
Jefferson
Grady
Canadian
Kingfisher
Major
Alfalfa
Grant
Kay
Noble
Logan
Oklahoma
Cleveland
McClain
Garvin
Carter
Love
Murray
Pottawatomie
Lincoln
Payne
Pawnee
Osage
Creek
Seminole
Marshall
Johnston
Coal
Hughes
Okfuskee
Okmulgee
Tulsa
Washington
Nowata
Rogers
Wagoner
Muskogee
Mayes
Craig
Ottawa
Delaware
Cherokee
Adair
Sequoyah
Haskell
McIntosh
Pittsburg
Latimer
Le Flore
Atoka
Bryan
Choctaw
Pushmataha
McCurtain

Gov. Mary Fallin (R)

First elected: 2010

Length of term: 4 years

Term expires: 1/15

Salary: $147,000

Phone: (405) 521-2342

Residence: Endmond

Born: Dec. 9, 1954; Warrensburg, Mo.

Religion: Christian non-denominational

Family: Husband, Wade Christensen; two children, four stepchildren

Education: Oklahoma Baptist U., attended 1973-75; Oklaboma State U., B.S. 1977 (family relations and child development); U. of Central Oklahoma, attended 1979-81 (business administration)

Career: Real estate broker; hotel properties manager; state tourism agency official

Political highlights: Okla. House, 1990-94; lieutenant governor, 1995-2007; U.S. House, 2007-11

ELECTION RESULTS

2010 GENERAL

Mary Fallin (R)	625,506	60.4%
Jari Askins (D)	409,261	39.6%

Lt. Gov. Todd Lamb (R)

First elected: 2010

Length of term: 4 years

Term expires: 1/15

Salary: $109,900

Phone: (405) 521-2161

LEGISLATURE

Legislature: February-May

Senate: 48 members, 4-year terms

2013 ratios: 36 R, 12 D; 44 men, 4 women

Salary: $38,400

Phone: (405) 524-0126

House: 101 members, 2-year terms

2013 ratios: 72 R, 29 D; 85 men, 16 women

Salary: $38,400

Phone: (405) 521-2711

TERM LIMITS

Governor: 2 terms

Senate: No more than 12 years combined

House: No more than 12 years combined

URBAN STATISTICS

CITY	POPULATION
Oklahoma City	579,999
Tulsa	391,906
Norman	110,925
Broken Arrow	98,850
Lawton	96,867

REGISTERED VOTERS

Democrat	45%
Republican	42%
Other	13%

POPULATION

2010 population	3,751,351
2000 population	3,450,654
1990 population	3,145,585
Percent change (2000-2010)	+8.7%
Rank among states (2010)	28
Median age	35.9
Born in state	61.4%
Foreign born	4.8%
Violent crime rate	501/100,000
Poverty level	16.2%
Federal workers	59,013
Military	21,673

ELECTIONS

STATE ELECTION OFFICIAL
(405) 521-2391

DEMOCRATIC PARTY
(405) 427-3366

REPUBLICAN PARTY
(405) 528-3501

MISCELLANEOUS

Web: www.ok.gov

Capital: Oklahoma City

U.S. CONGRESS

Senate: 2 Republicans

House: 5 Republicans

STATISTICS BY DISTRICT

District	2012 Vote for President		2008 Vote for President										
	Obama	Romney	Obama	McCain	Black	Asian	Hispanic	Median Income	Over 64	Under 20	College Education	Rural	Sq. Miles
1	34%	66%	36%	64%	9%	2%	10%	$47,211	13%	28%	29%	9%	1,632
2	32	68	34	66	3	<1	5	37,364	16	27	16	67	20,995
3	26	74	27	73	4	1	8	42,953	14	27	20	49	34,117
4	33	67	34	66	6	2	8	47,170	13	27	24	33	9,777
5	41	59	41	59	14	3	15	42,029	12	28	29	11	2,074
STATE	**33**	**67**	**34**	**66**	**7**	**2**	**9**	**43,225**	**14**	**28**	**23**	**34**	**68,595**
U.S.	**51**	**47**	**53**	**46**	**12**	**5**	**17**	**50,052**	**13**	**27**	**29**	**21**	**3,531,905**

Sen. James M. Inhofe (R)

Capitol Office
224-4721
inhofe.senate.gov
205 Russell Bldg. 20510-3603; fax 228-0380

Committees
Armed Services - Ranking Member
Environment & Public Works

Residence
Tulsa

Born
Nov. 17, 1934; Des Moines, Iowa

Religion
Presbyterian

Family
Wife, Kay Inhofe; four children

Education
U. of Tulsa, B.A. 1973

Military Service
Army, 1957-58

Career
Real estate developer; insurance executive

Political Highlights
Okla. House, 1967-69; Okla. Senate, 1969-77; Republican nominee for governor, 1974; Republican nominee for U.S. House, 1976; mayor of Tulsa, 1978-84; defeated for re-election as mayor of Tulsa, 1984; U.S. House, 1987-94

ELECTION RESULTS

2008 GENERAL		
James M. Inhofe (R)	763,375	56.7%
Andrew Rice (D)	527,736	39.2%
Stephen P. Wallace (I)	55,708	4.1%
2008 PRIMARY		
James M. Inhofe (R)	116,371	84.2%
Evelyn L. Rogers (R)	10,770	7.8%
Ted Ryals (R)	7,306	5.3%
Dennis Lopez (R)	3,800	2.7%

Previous Winning Percentages
2002 (57%); 1996 (57%); 1994 Special Election (55%); 1992 House Election (53%); 1990 House Election (56%); 1988 House Election (53%); 1986 House Election (55%)

Elected 1994; 3rd full term

Inhofe is one of the most partisan senators, if not the most partisan. He's a die-hard conservative who is adamantly opposed to most federal regulation of the environment, and he is willing to indulge conspiracy theories about the motives of his opponents. But he also can be an effective facilitator of Senate action when he thinks more federal spending makes sense.

Oklahomans find Inhofe's stubborn nature to be endearing, and he isn't lacking in personality: After buying a stunt airplane months before his 78th birthday, Inhofe (IN-hoff) told the Tulsa Rotary Club that he would quit running for re-election only "when I can no longer fly an airplane upside down."

For the 113th Congress (2013-14), he's the new top Republican on the Armed Services Committee. On getting the job, he vowed to focus on missile defense, modernizing the nuclear stockpile, overhauling the Pentagon's acquisition programs and avoiding substantial cuts to military budgets. He wants to speed up purchases of the F-35, the next-generation fighter jet.

Some observers have wondered if Inhofe's ascension will substantially change the bipartisan atmosphere on the committee, and the early months of 2013 were filled with tense debate.

Inhofe issued stern criticisms of Chuck Hagel, who was nominated for secretary of Defense; he said Hagel was "cozy" with Iran, and he did not discourage even harsher criticisms by other Republicans on the panel. Inhofe said the White House was engaging in a "cover-up" of the true nature of a 2012 attack on a U.S. consulate in Libya.

He continued to criticize the Obama administration's military posturing, stating at a hearing that the president was on a "misguided search for a peace dividend that I don't believe exists." He opposed the withdrawal from Iraq and is wary of a rapid withdrawal from Afghanistan.

But he also dismissed worries about dysfunction, saying that current events were the reason for the early discord. "They have to put on their show. We have to put on our show," he said during an event at the Center for Strategic and International Studies. "But we get along fine." Inhofe has said he will work with Chairman Carl Levin, a Michigan Democrat, whenever he can.

His track record suggests he means it. In a 2012 session dominated by gridlock, Inhofe helped shepherd one of the year's only legislative accomplishments: a 27-month reauthorization of federal transportation programs. He did it by working closely with one of the most liberal senators, Democrat Barbara Boxer of California.

Inhofe, then the top Republican on the Environment and Public Works Committee, had to convince colleagues not only that passing the $120 billion measure made policy sense, but also that it would aid the GOP in November's elections. He worked through thorny policy issues, such as Republicans' desire to force the Obama administration to allow construction of the Keystone XL pipeline connecting Canada's tar sands to refineries in Texas.

It wasn't an easy sell. House conservatives upset with the price tag of a reauthorization had slowed work to a crawl in their chamber. Inhofe called them out, blaming the impasse on "Republicans who are not conservative wanting to look conservative." He says it's an essential role of government to build and maintain infrastructure.

Inhofe made the case that a new bill would give conservatives a greater say over transportation policy than extensions of the previous transportation law would. To keep things moving, the pipeline provision was scrapped. But the final version did include language to streamline regulatory reviews of infrastructure projects, which Inhofe strongly supported — similar provisions were included in a water resources bill approved by the panel in early 2013.

His cooperation with Boxer was remarkable, given how strongly the two disagree over environmental regulatory policy. Boxer, the Environment chairwoman, says the government needs to do more to stop climate change. In 2012, Inhofe published a book, "The Greatest Hoax," explaining his theory that climate change science is part of a broader conspiracy by liberals to increase regulations and taxes. When Inhofe proposed a resolution in June 2012 to strike new EPA rules on power plant emissions, Boxer was among those who voted to kill it; Inhofe has used his clout to block or tone down environmental legislation sponsored by Democrats.

Inhofe shares many conservative views with his home-state colleague, Republican Tom Coburn. They denounced the 2010 laws overhauling health care and financial sector regulations.

But one area where they disagree is earmarking, the practice of adding directed spending for hometown projects to government funding bills. Coburn supported a successful ban on the practice during the 112th Congress (2011-12). Inhofe said it was another Democratic conspiracy that stripped Congress of some of its power to direct government spending and handed it to the Obama administration.

Inhofe attends weekly prayer meetings held by the Fellowship Foundation, an evangelical Christian network that sponsors housing for members of Congress, as well as the annual National Prayer Breakfast. He has traveled regularly to Africa to do humanitarian work, calling it a "Jesus thing." He teamed with Democratic Sen. Russ Feingold of Wisconsin on legislation, signed into law by President Barack Obama in 2010, that required the president to develop a plan for providing support to regions affected by the Lord's Resistance Army, a rebel group that has wreaked havoc in Uganda, Sudan and Congo. Inhofe is a former member of the Foreign Relations Committee.

Inhofe has about 50 years of experience as a pilot, and he has never lost his love of flying despite nearly losing his life on more than one occasion. In 2010, he landed his twin-engine Cessna 340 on a runway that was closed for repairs on a trip to his vacation home on South Padre Island in Texas. After he was forced to take remedial training by the Federal Aviation Administration, Inhofe pushed a bill through Congress giving pilots whom the agency accuses of wrongdoing more authority to review the evidence against them. Obama signed it in 2012.

Inhofe was born in Des Moines, Iowa, but his parents moved to Tulsa in 1942 in search of jobs in the insurance industry. Inhofe inherited their penchant for business; at 15, he worked as a door-to-door salesman. He lives just three houses away from the one in which he was raised.

After two years as an Army private in the late 1950s, Inhofe followed his parents into insurance, then became a real estate developer. As a businessman, he became frustrated with an "over-regulated society," which launched him into a 10-year career in the Oklahoma Legislature. "I once had to go to 26 government agencies to get a document," he said. "I thought, 'Wait a minute, the government is supposed to be on our side.'"

Inhofe lost a 1974 campaign for governor to Democrat David L. Boren. Elected mayor of Tulsa in 1978, Inhofe was defeated for re-election in 1984. He bounced back two years later and picked up a House seat, taking 55 percent of the vote to succeed Democrat James R. Jones. He never cracked 56 percent in four elections despite being in the state's most Republican district.

Meanwhile, Boren had become a senator. He resigned in 1994 to become the president of the University of Oklahoma, and Inhofe made a run for the seat. He faced Rep. Dave McCurdy, a pro-business Democrat who was favored to win. McCurdy was closely associated with President Bill Clinton, whom he introduced at the 1992 Democratic National Convention. Inhofe won by 15 points. He hasn't had a tough race since.

Key Votes

2012

Prohibit health insurance plans from denying coverage based on the sponsor's religious beliefs	NO
Require approval of the Keystone XL oil pipeline	YES
Ease securities rules to expand small-business access to capital	YES
Reauthorize farm and nutrition programs for five years	NO
Limit debate on a bill that would create private-sector cybersecurity standards	NO
Consent to ratification of a treaty setting global standard for the treatment of people with disabilities	NO
Provide $60.4 billion in disaster relief following Superstorm Sandy	NO
Extend most Bush-era income tax rates while allowing rates for top-bracket earners to rise (Jan. 1, 2013)	YES

2011

Prevent EPA from regulating greenhouse gas emissions to address climate change	YES
Extend certain provisions of Patriot Act for four years	YES
Clear compromise debt limit increase plan and establish future spending limits	NO
Overhaul patent law	YES
Implement Colombia free trade agreement	YES
Limit debate on confirmation of Caitlin J. Halligan to D.C. Circuit Court of Appeals	NO
Extend payroll tax cut and unemployment benefits for two months	YES

CQ Vote Studies

	PARTY UNITY		PRESIDENTIAL SUPPORT	
	SUPPORT	OPPOSE	SUPPORT	OPPOSE
2012	92%	8%	44%	56%
2011	97%	3%	48%	52%
2010	96%	4%	39%	61%
2009	98%	2%	35%	65%
2008	99%	1%	75%	25%
2007	98%	2%	87%	13%
2006	94%	6%	88%	12%
2005	94%	6%	91%	9%
2004	98%	2%	92%	8%
2003	98%	2%	97%	3%

Interest Groups

	AFL-CIO	ADA	CCUS	ACU
2012	9%	0%	88%	80%
2011	16%	5%	91%	100%
2010	6%	0%	100%	96%
2009	11%	5%	71%	100%
2008	22%	5%	63%	96%
2007	5%	10%	80%	100%
2006	20%	0%	91%	100%
2005	21%	5%	83%	100%
2004	17%	10%	100%	100%
2003	0%	5%	100%	84%

Sen. Tom Coburn (R)

Capitol Office
224-5754
coburn.senate.gov
172 Russell Bldg. 20510-3602; fax 224-6008

Committees
Banking, Housing & Urban Affairs
Homeland Security & Governmental Affairs
- Ranking Member
Select Intelligence

Residence
Muskogee

Born
March 14, 1948; Casper, Wyo.

Religion
Baptist

Family
Wife, Carolyn Coburn; three children

Education
Oklahoma State U., B.S. 1970 (accounting); U. of Oklahoma, M.D. 1983

Career
Physician; optical firm manager

Political Highlights
U.S. House, 1995-2001

ELECTION RESULTS

2010 GENERAL		
Tom Coburn (R)	718,482	70.6%
Jim Rogers (D)	265,814	26.1%
Stephen P. Wallace (I)	25,048	2.5%
2010 PRIMARY		
Tom Coburn (R)	223,997	90.4%
Evelyn L. Rogers (R)	15,093	6.1%
Lewis Kelly Spring (R)	8,812	3.6%

Previous Winning Percentages
2004 (53%); 1998 House Election (58%); 1996 House Election (55%); 1994 House Election (52%)

Elected 2004; 2nd term

Coburn champions small-government causes and notoriously uses any procedural tool at his disposal while doing so. Colleagues of both parties can find his consistency either exasperating or heroic, depending on the circumstances. But none doubt his sincerity as a negotiator for deficit reduction, in part because he has already forsworn any run for a third term.

His dedication to fiscal restraint has yielded, among other things, a 2012 book. In "The Debt Bomb," Coburn blames elected officials in Washington for the government's balance sheet, contending that they have willfully ignored a worsening financial outlook to continue with business as usual.

The book outlines his objections to duplicative programs and his opposition to earmarks; an appendix lists votes that demonstrate, according to Coburn, the Senate's willingness to engage in pork-barrel politics.

Republican leaders have tried to harness Coburn's discontent when possible. At the start of the 113th Congress (2013-14), Coburn secured his party's top spot on the Homeland Security and Governmental Affairs Committee. That panel's new chairman, Thomas R. Carper of Delaware, has indicated that he is amenable to Coburn's campaign to improve government efficiency.

And in the 111th Congress (2009-10), Minority Leader Mitch McConnell appointed Coburn to serve on a fiscal commission, eventually known as Simpson-Bowles, that President Barack Obama established by executive order. The commission developed (but never approved) an outline to reduce deficits by $4 trillion over 10 years.

Coburn has tried to shape parts of that outline into laws. He particularly likes the idea of coupling discretionary spending cuts and changes in entitlement programs with ending preferences in the tax code. "The code is loaded with spending programs masquerading as tax cuts," Coburn wrote in his book. "Spending in the tax code is stimulus for the tax compliance industry that produces nothing of real economic value."

During the summer of 2011, congressional Republicans resisted an increase in the federal debt limit, insisting that it needed to be tied to spending reductions. Coburn was an on-again, off-again member of the "gang of six," a bipartisan, informal group of senators that attempted to produce legislation based on the Simpson-Bowles plans. He also chipped in his own plan, which offered up to $9 trillion in deficit reduction over a decade.

Coburn often emphasizes that he is not necessarily against the specific programs that Congress is debating — but he wants to figure out ways to pay for them. He has repeatedly forced roll call votes on amendments to spending bills, trying to cut what he identifies as unnecessary government programs. The amendments generally lose, but not by much. Every year, the Government Accountability Office issues a report on overlapping federal programs; it effectively pours gasoline on Coburn's fire.

An obstetrician by trade, Coburn made an infamous attempt to hold up the health care overhaul bill in the 111th Congress. As work on the bill was nearing completion in early 2010, Coburn offered an amendment to prohibit convicted sex offenders from getting erectile-dysfunction drugs through the insurance markets the bill would establish. Adoption of the amendment would have forced the Senate to return the bill to the House for further (and possibly fatal) debate, so Democrats held their noses and voted against it. Montana Democrat Max Baucus, a key negotiator on the health care law, called Coburn's gambit "a crass political stunt."

The year before, Coburn, Richard M. Burr of North Carolina and Rep. Paul D. Ryan of Wisconsin pitched an alternative to the Democrats' health care overhaul; it would have provided a tax credit to individuals for the purchase of health insurance. Working with Burr in 2012, he introduced a proposal to convert Medicare to a program where beneficiaries get means-tested amounts of money to help pay for the insurance plan of their choosing.

While he was harshly critical of the 2010 overhaul, he offered suggestions to combat fraud, such as engaging medical professionals in "random, undercover investigations of health care providers" receiving payments from federal programs.

Coburn departed the Finance and Judiciary committees at the start of the 113th Congress, taking seats on the Intelligence Committee and the Banking, Housing and Urban Affairs Committee instead. But he takes advantage of the flexibility offered by the Senate to participate in any debate that intrigues him. In 2013, he negotiated with West Virginia Democrat Joe Manchin III, trying to produce an expanded system of background checks for gun purchases; he ultimately said gun control advocates wanted requirements that were too rigorous to pass the Senate. He was right — a proposal by Manchin and Pennsylvania Republican Patrick J. Toomey was defeated weeks later.

Coburn frequently places procedural holds on pending nominations and legislative business to address concerns or get answers from nominees. Unlike many senators, however, he has always disclosed his objections.

When he hasn't budged, Democratic leaders have painted him as a poster boy for Republican obstructionism or gone to great lengths to get around him. Coburn prevented Senate consideration of a slew of lands bills in the 110th Congress (2007-08). So at the outset of the 111th, Majority Leader Harry Reid quickly brought to the floor an omnibus lands measure that came to be known as the "Tomnibus." The Senate passed the bill, but it took more than two months of procedural finagling by the majority before it was cleared by Congress and enacted.

Coburn has had a few encounters with the Senate Ethics Committee over the years. He clashed with the panel when he wanted to continue practicing medicine while the Senate is not in session. In 2005, the committee refused to modify a ban on senators receiving outside payment for professional services. Coburn wanted to keep collecting just enough fees from his obstetrics practice in Muskogee to cover his costs. The House had allowed him to do so; the Senate did not. He said he would keep on seeing patients anyway whenever he was home.

Coburn was born in Wyoming but grew up in Muskogee. He had a strained relationship with his father, an alcoholic optician who founded a successful business. (They reconciled six months before his father's death.) His father's company made equipment to process optical lenses and eventually became Muskogee's biggest employer.

After his junior year at Oklahoma State, Coburn married Carolyn Denton, a former Miss Oklahoma he'd had a crush on since elementary school. He went to work for his father at age 22, and for several years he managed a Virginia branch of the business, Coburn Optical Products. He built it into a $40 million venture, which Revlon bought in 1975. Coburn moved back to Oklahoma and, at 31, decided to go to medical school.

He was a first-time candidate for public office when he ran for the House in the big Republican year of 1994. Incumbent Mike Synar, a Democrat, lost in the primary, and Coburn went on to beat Virgil R. Cooper, a 71-year-old retired middle school principal.

Coburn stuck to a term limit pledge, serving six years in the House and then leaving. But he missed the fray, and in 2004 he ran for the seat of retiring GOP Sen. Don Nickles. Coburn defeated moderate Democratic Rep. Brad Carson by more than 11 points. He won re-election in 2010 by 44 points.

Coburn has overcome multiple bouts with cancer, undergoing surgery for prostate cancer in 2011.

Key Votes

2012	
Prohibit health insurance plans from denying coverage based on the sponsor's religious beliefs	NO
Require approval of the Keystone XL oil pipeline	YES
Ease securities rules to expand small-business access to capital	YES
Reauthorize farm and nutrition programs for five years	NO
Limit debate on a bill that would create private-sector cybersecurity standards	NO
Consent to ratification of a treaty setting global standard for the treatment of people with disabilities	NO
Provide $60.4 billion in disaster relief following Superstorm Sandy	NO
Extend most Bush-era income tax rates while allowing rates for top-bracket earners to rise (Jan. 1, 2013)	YES

2011	
Prevent EPA from regulating greenhouse gas emissions to address climate change	YES
Extend certain provisions of Patriot Act for four years	YES
Clear compromise debt limit increase plan and establish future spending limits	NO
Overhaul patent law	NO
Implement Colombia free trade agreement	?
Limit debate on confirmation of Caitlin J. Halligan to D.C. Circuit Court of Appeals	NO
Extend payroll tax cut and unemployment benefits for two months	YES

CQ Vote Studies

	PARTY UNITY		PRESIDENTIAL SUPPORT	
	SUPPORT	OPPOSE	SUPPORT	OPPOSE
2012	92%	8%	41%	59%
2011	99%	1%	52%	48%
2010	98%	2%	33%	67%
2009	99%	1%	27%	73%
2008	99%	1%	85%	15%
2007	96%	4%	89%	11%
2006	92%	8%	88%	12%
2005	93%	7%	91%	9%

Interest Groups

	AFL-CIO	ADA	CCUS	ACU
2012	0%	0%	100%	92%
2011	21%	5%	63%	100%
2010	13%	5%	82%	100%
2009	11%	5%	71%	100%
2008	0%	0%	75%	96%
2007	17%	5%	50%	100%
2006	27%	5%	64%	100%
2005	21%	5%	89%	100%

Rep. Jim Bridenstine (R)

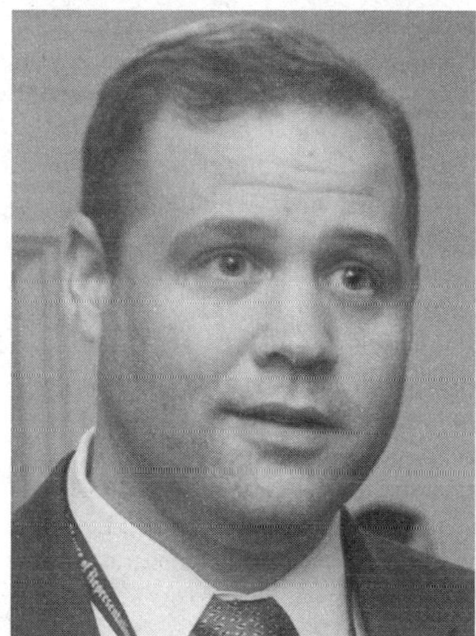

Capitol Office
225-2211
bridenstine.house.gov
216 Cannon Bldg. 20515-3601; fax 225-9187

Committees
Armed Services
Science, Space & Technology

Residence
Tulsa

Born
June 15, 1975; Ann Arbor, Mich.

Religion
Baptist

Family
Wife, Michelle Bridenstine; three children

Education
Rice U., B.A. 1997 (economics, managerial studies & psychology); Cornell U., M.B.A. 2009

Military
Navy, 1998-2007; Navy Reserve, 2010-present

Career
Marketing and defense consultant; museum director

Political Highlights
No previous office

ELECTION RESULTS

2012 GENERAL		
Jim Bridenstine (R)	181,084	63.5%
John Olson (D)	91,421	32.0%
Craig Allen (I)	12,807	4.5%
2012 PRIMARY		
Jim Bridenstine (R)	28,055	53.8%
John Sullivan (R)	24,058	46.2%

Elected 2012; 1st term

Bridenstine is a fiscal conservative who takes confrontational stances against both Democrats and fellow Republicans. His policy positions are often rooted in his interpretation of the Constitution.

Bridenstine's family moved to the Tulsa region when he was in his late teens. An excellent swimmer, he was given a scholarship to Rice University in Houston; after suffering a shoulder injury, he focused on studying business and economics. He joined the Navy and became a pilot, flying combat missions in Afghanistan and Iraq and serving as an instructor. He also became an investor in the Rocket Racing League, which is tied to the development of commercial spaceflight. On leaving the Navy he earned an MBA, and he was hired as the executive director of the Tulsa Air and Space Museum. He later joined the Navy Reserve.

He did not have any political experience to speak of, but he said frustrations over federal spending compelled him to challenge five-term Republican John Sullivan. The race got ugly once it was clear that it might be competitive, and Sullivan criticized Bridenstine's financial management of the museum. He still pulled off the upset in the heavily Republican district.

One of his first acts as a congressman was to vote against John A. Boehner for re-election as the speaker for the 113th Congress (2013-14). Bridenstine is staunchly against raising the federal debt limit or increasing mandatory spending, and he wants a full repeal of the 2010 health care law. He takes an enforcement-first approach to immigration changes. "We cannot reward people who broke our laws," he wrote on his congressional website.

Bridenstine sits on the Armed Services Committee, where he has defended drug interdiction efforts — he has participated in such missions as a reservist. "We can prevent people from becoming addicted by driving down the access" to cocaine, he said at a hearing. He also sits on the Science, Space and Technology Committee, and its subcommittees on space and technology.

Oklahoma 1

Tulsa; Wagoner and Washington counties

Wooden homes on small plots of land in the city's outskirts contrast with the skyscrapers of downtown Tulsa, the heart of the 1st. Tulsa — the state's second-largest city and friendly rival to its largest, the state capital Oklahoma City — is a cultural hub, and Tulsans like to distinguish themselves from the "dust-on-their-boots" stereotype of the state.

Once the "oil capital of the world," Tulsa's economy remains tied to the energy industry; dozens of corporate headquarters are in or near the city, and the sector extends beyond oil to natural gas extraction and stakes in solar projects, biofuels and the maintenance of high-efficiency transmission systems. Tulsa also relies on white-collar and manufacturing jobs affiliated with energy firms.

The district is home to aerospace parts manufacturers and support facilities. Tribal gaming sites are also increasingly important to the economy, although continued expansion of resorts and casinos has its detractors. American Airlines employs thousands in the city, and struggled with downsizing following a 2012 bankruptcy, but a likely merger with US Airways provides stability. About 20 minutes outside of Tulsa, Broken Arrow is a bedroom community working to establish more local manufacturing and retail job sources. It is home to a Blue Bell Creameries facility.

The 1st is nearly three-fourths white, but Hispanic residents account for more than for 10 percent of the district's residents. The counties in the 1st each experienced significant population growth overall between 2000 and 2010, and the Hispanic population more than doubled in some areas.

Although Democrats can hold their own in local elections, the socially conservative voters here tend to vote Republican, particularly in federal elections. The region has voted for a Democratic presidential candidate only twice since 1920. In the 2012 presidential race, Republican Mitt Romney enjoyed a nearly 2-to-1 margin of victory, with percentages above 70 percent in the counties outside Tulsa.

Major Industry
Energy, aerospace

Cities
Tulsa, Broken Arrow, Bartlesville

Notable
Oral Roberts University is known for its 200-foot Prayer Tower and the "Praying Hands" sculpture at the campus' main entrance.

Rep. Markwayne Mullin (R)

Capitol Office
225-2701
mullin.house.gov
1113 Longworth Bldg. 20515-0401; fax 225-3038

Committees
Natural Resources
Transportation & Infrastructure

Residence
Westville

Born
July 26, 1977; Tulsa, Okla.

Religion
Pentecostal

Family
Wife, Christie Mullin; three children

Education
Missouri Valley College, attended 1996; Oklahoma State U. Institute of Technology, A.A.S. 2010 (construction technology)

Career
Plumbing company owner; rancher

Political Highlights
No previous office

ELECTION RESULTS

2012 GENERAL		
Markwayne Mullin (R)	143,701	57.3%
Rob Wallace (D)	96,081	38.3%
Michael G. Fulks (I)	10,830	4.3%
2012 PRIMARY RUNOFF		
Markwayne Mullin (R)	12,059	56.8%
George Faught (R)	9,167	43.2%

Elected 2012; 1st term

Mullin took over his father's plumbing company, expanded it, then branched into other business areas. His diversification into politics has largely been based on fighting regulations that he sees as stifling economic growth.

The youngest of seven children, Mullin grew up in Westville, just a few miles from the Arkansas border. He went to college on a wrestling scholarship, but he left school and took the reins of Mullin Plumbing when his father fell ill. The business expanded to more than 100 employees, and Mullin started related companies dealing with septic systems and HVAC services; he also owns ranching operations and a martial-arts studio called Oklahoma Fight Club. He became something of a public figure by hosting a local radio show about home improvement.

Mullin, who has promised to serve no more than six years in the House, has singled out the EPA in particular as a source of frustration. He told Environment and Energy Daily that his district has coal, water, timber, natural gas and oil, but "we can't get to it because of all the red tape it takes to get to products that should be ours." He has a seat on the Natural Resources Committee, and he also belongs to the Transportation and Infrastructure Subcommittee on Water Resources and Environment. His first introduced bills dealt with regulations affecting oilfield workers and wind energy development.

A social and fiscal conservative, Mullin joined the Republican Study Committee. He is a registered member of the Cherokee Nation, and he sits on the Natural Resources panel on Indian affairs.

Four-term Rep. Dan Boren, one of the most conservative House Democrats, decided to retire rather than go through another election. No one doubted that a Republican would take the seat; it was just a matter of which Republican. Mullin raised far more money than his competitors (and contributed some of his own) and won the initial primary; he then beat state Rep. George Faught in a runoff. He won handily in November.

Oklahoma 2

East — Muskogee, 'Little Dixie'

Covering the eastern region of Oklahoma, the 2nd District borders four states: Kansas to the north; Missouri and Arkansas to the east; and Texas to the south. Made up of mostly working-class rural communities, the district's northeastern corner hosts a large American Indian population, particularly in the northeastern Ozark foothills and its southeastern stretches are home to an Old South and Baptist-influenced culture in the "Little Dixie" region.

The district's largest population center is Muskogee, a sleepy city southeast of Tulsa. It has a paper mill, small manufacturing companies, a regional veterans' hospital and a federal district court. Oil wells dot the district's landscape and are clustered along its western border; Claremore is home to an oil field equipment plant. In McAlester, an army munitions plant is a major employer.

Agriculture is also important to the rural 2nd, which is full of cattle ranches and vegetable farms. Green peas and beans are grown in the southeast, with big harvests in LeFlore County, while pecans are a popular crop in the district's southwest.

The district includes several American Indian tribes. Since 2000, Native Americans have become the largest ethnic group in Stilwell, home to a large and entrepreneurial Cherokee community. The Cherokee and Choctaw nations do significant business in the district, operating casinos and contracting on professional services and in defense manufacturing. The Choctaw Nation recently partnered with Southeastern Oklahoma State University to establish Choctaw University.

Once competitive at the local level and the last bastion of the state's beleaguered Democratic Party, the 2nd followed statewide trends and gave wide margins to GOP U.S. House and presidential candidates in 2012.

Major Industry
Ranching, timber, oil and gas, agriculture

Military Bases
McAlester Army Ammunition Plant, 31 military, 1,968 civilian

Cities
Muskogee, Claremore, McAlester

Notable
The American Indian "Trail of Tears" of 1838-39 ended in Tahlequah — about one-fourth of the Cherokee Nation died en route.

Rep. Frank D. Lucas (R)

Capitol Office
225-5565
lucas.house.gov
2311 Rayburn Bldg. 20515-3603; fax 225-8698

Committees
Agriculture - Chairman
Financial Services
Science, Space & Technology

Residence
Cheyenne

Born
Jan. 6, 1960; Cheyenne, Okla.

Religion
Baptist

Family
Wife, Lynda Lucas; three children

Education
Oklahoma State U., B.S. 1982 (agricultural economics)

Career
Farmer; rancher

Political Highlights
Republican nominee for Okla. House, 1984, 1986; Okla. House, 1989-94

ELECTION RESULTS

2012 GENERAL		
Frank D. Lucas (R)	201,744	75.3%
Timothy Ray Murray (D)	53,472	20.0%
William M. Sanders (I)	12,787	4.8%
2012 PRIMARY		
Frank D. Lucas (R)	33,454	88.2%
William Craig Stump (R)	4,492	11.8%
2010 GENERAL		
Frank D. Lucas (R)	161,927	78.0%
Frankie Robbins (D)	45,689	22.0%

Previous Winning Percentages
2008 (70%); 2006 (67%); 2004 (82%); 2002 (76%); 2000 (59%); 1998 (65%); 1996 (64%); 1994 (70%); 1994 Special Election (54%)

Elected 1994; 10th full term

Lucas learned about politics and agriculture in western Oklahoma. Born and raised on a farm that has been in his family since 1912, he tagged along when his father went to Republican political events. He listened to his grandparents' stories about life during the Great Depression and the Dust Bowl. His home was in a "super, uber-Democratic county," and his mother is a conservative Southern Baptist Democrat from Texas. While Lucas works in Washington, his wife runs their beef cattle and wheat operation.

Those forces shape his views on government and farm policy, as well as his style as chairman of the Agriculture Committee.

Lucas fears the ways that bad policy can affect rural Oklahoma, citing the decisions that contributed to the Dust Bowl and the agricultural and energy industry collapses of the 1980s. Much of the state — the jumping-off point for "The Grapes of Wrath" — is a sparsely populated area of farms, ranches and small towns. "I do not intend to allow the process I am a part of to set a chain of events into motion that creates those kinds of hardships on another generation," he said.

Lucas took the gavel of the Agriculture Committee in the 112th Congress (2011-12). He spent much of the term navigating regional and political obstacles to move a five-year reauthorization of farm, nutrition, conservation and other programs.

He worked closely with ranking Democrat and former chairman Collin C. Peterson of Minnesota to produce a farm bill with a net savings of $35 billion over the coming decade. They got the bill out of their committee with a bipartisan vote. Remembering his mother and his home county, "I work very hard to incorporate my Democrat committee members' perspective into things," Lucas says.

However, the bill's path to the House floor was blocked by GOP leaders, who said they did not have the votes to pass it. One sticking point was $16 billion in spending cuts to the Supplemental Nutrition Assistance Program. Conservatives in the caucus wanted larger reductions, while most Democrats opposed any cuts. A Senate-passed version with savings of $23 billion and a $4.5 billion SNAP reduction was unacceptable to Republican leaders. The 2008 farm law expired as lawmakers went home for the 2012 election recess; it was later extended for another year as part of the January 2013 "fiscal cliff" agreement.

Lucas, who had a hand in drafting the 2008 farm bill as the ranking Republican on the Subcommittee on Conservation, Credit, Energy and Research, was philosophical about the setback. He said he tried to be "very careful, very methodical in trying to maintain that balance of doing good committee work and trying to make sure my elected leadership understood what I was doing and how it would fit in with the agenda of the whole House."

The proposed savings in the House bill, Lucas said, reflected the work of people knowledgeable about agriculture and constituted a fair contribution to GOP efforts to reduce the budget deficit. He successfully fought ad hoc efforts, such as a proposal to cap commodity support payments that was offered during debate on a catchall spending measure the House passed in early 2011.

When he resumed work on a farm bill in the 113th Congress (2013-14), Lucas used the 2012 bill as the starting point for discussion. A version approved by the committee in May 2013 had most of the same elements — an end to direct payments, a bolstering of crop insurance, a "target price" program to protect farm revenue, and substantial reductions in nutrition assistance spending.

Lucas is a member of the Republican Study Committee and has a fairly conservative voting record. He will on occasion take a more permissive stance toward federal promotion of renewable energy. He is a promoter of wind and solar power, and during the 110th Congress (2007-08) he introduced legislation to provide tax breaks to farmers who install wind turbines on their land.

But he balked at an EPA proposal in late 2009 that he worried would impose unnecessary fees on farmers. The agency had indicated it planned to establish a nationwide system for reporting greenhouse gas emissions that would include animal feed operations. He proposed legislation to bar the program from requiring livestock producers to obtain an operating permit under the Clean Air Act. Lucas called the EPA plan "an underhanded way of imposing cap-and-tax regulations on the American people." In the 112th Congress, Lucas frequently offered the EPA as an example of an overly aggressive regulator.

Lucas, as Agriculture chairman and a senior member of the Financial Services panel, also challenges the financial regulatory overhaul that became law in 2010. The statute gives the Commodity Futures Trading Commission, which falls under Agriculture Committee jurisdiction, shared authority with the Securities and Exchange Commission to regulate the market for derivatives. Those contracts among private parties are traditionally used to hedge against business risks, but their unregulated use grew rapidly in the early 21st century to include high-risk mortgages and financial deals. They are considered a contributor to the 2008 financial crisis.

Lucas called CFTC Chairman Gary Gensler before the Agriculture Committee several times to express concern about the scope and cost of proposed rules required under the 2010 law. In late 2012, he signed on to a letter asking Treasury Secretary Timothy F. Geithner to intervene in his role as chairman of the Financial Stability Oversight Committee and delay CFTC rule-making pertaining to non-banks and derivatives trades by foreign subsidiaries of U.S. companies.

Lucas' father was the Republican Party chairman for Roger Mills County, and Lucas got interested in politics while trekking to GOP functions with his dad. He became a student senator at Oklahoma State University, president of the College Republicans and a volunteer in local campaigns. In keeping with his family's business, he majored in agricultural economics.

He made two unsuccessful bids for a state House seat in what was then a mostly Democratic area, and he eventually captured a seat in 1988.

Lucas made a run for Congress when 10-term Democratic Rep. Glenn English resigned in early 1994. He won the nomination over four other Republicans. Stressing his work in agriculture and his lifelong residency in the district, he won 54 percent of the vote in the special election against Democrat Dan Webber Jr., a former aide to Oklahoma Democratic Sen. David L. Boren. That was Lucas' closest election.

Key Votes

2012	
Extend a Social Security payroll tax cut and unemployment benefits	YES
Ease securities rules to expand small-business access to capital	YES
Extend for one year subsidized student loan interest rates financed by a cut in health care spending	YES
Cite Attorney General Eric H. Holder Jr. for contempt of Congress	YES
Create a visa program for foreign graduates in high-tech fields	YES
Extend most Bush-era income tax rates while allowing rates for top-bracket earners to rise (Jan. 1, 2013)	YES
2011	
Strike funding for F-35 alternative engine	NO
Prevent EPA from regulating greenhouse gas emissions to address climate change	YES
Extend certain provisions of Patriot Act for four years	YES
Declare opposition to use of ground troops in Libya	YES
Overhaul patent law	YES
Pass compromise debt limit increase plan and establish future spending limits	YES
Allow consideration of measures to implement three trade agreements	YES

CQ Vote Studies

	PARTY UNITY		PRESIDENTIAL SUPPORT	
	SUPPORT	OPPOSE	SUPPORT	OPPOSE
2012	89%	11%	18%	82%
2011	94%	6%	26%	74%
2010	96%	4%	26%	74%
2009	89%	11%	17%	83%
2008	96%	4%	66%	34%

Interest Groups

	AFL-CIO	ADA	CCUS	ACU
2012	19%	0%	100%	64%
2011	0%	5%	100%	80%
2010	7%	0%	88%	100%
2009	5%	0%	80%	91%
2008	14%	15%	89%	96%

Oklahoma 3

Panhandle; west and north-central

Nothing stops the constant wind that forces its way across the plains of this sprawling, rural district in western and north-central Oklahoma, the area that was devastated by the Dust Bowl in the 1930s. Energy and agriculture are the name of the game here, but few regions have suffered the vacillations of the oil industry more than the 3rd; oil busts chased residents away over the years and blunted the region's prosperity.

During decennial remapping, the 3rd expanded slightly to absorb parts of the Oklahoma City suburbs in fast-growing Canadian County as well as some Creek County outskirts of Tulsa. It also has several American Indian lands, including all of the Osage Nation reservation.

Made up of dry prairies in the west and parts of "Tornado Alley" in the east, the 3rd has the state's most productive wheat and cattle farms. Hog farms have a large presence in the panhandle; cotton is key in the southwest.

Enid is a population center and Garfield County seat. Once known as the Wheat Capital of Oklahoma, it has one of the highest grain storage capacities in the nation. The city's growth has been sluggish, and local officials have emphasized infrastructure upgrades, including a downtown revitalization project. Faster-growing Stillwater is the district's second-largest city, anchored by Oklahoma State University — Boone Pickens Stadium, home to the school's football team, is a focal point of the region's culture. A focus on research and technology has boosted Stillwater, which already has a specialty manufacturing base.

The 3rd is overwhelmingly Republican, thanks to strong Bible Belt conservatism. While there are pockets of support for conservative Democrats in local races near the southwestern border, the district votes overwhelmingly for Republicans at the federal level.

Major Industry

Oil and gas, agriculture, construction, higher education

Military Bases

Vance Air Force Base, 1,248 military, 284 civilian; Altus Air Force Base, 1,192 military, 1,131 civilian (2012)

Cities:

Enid, Stillwater, Ponca City, Yukon, Altus

Notable

Roger Mills County was named in 1892 by referendum in honor of then-U.S. Rep. Roger Q. Mills from Texas.

Rep. Tom Cole (R)

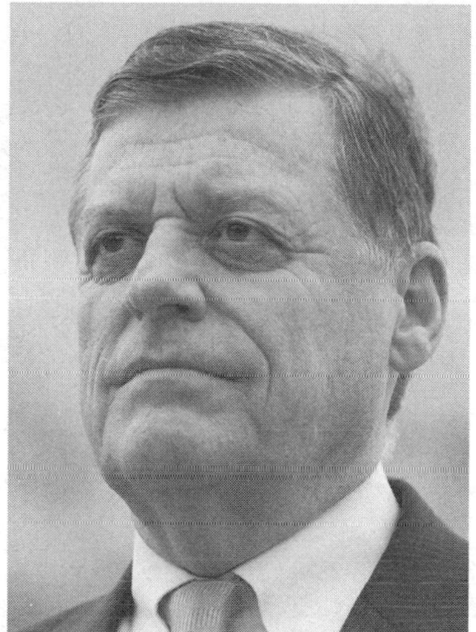

Capitol Office
225-6165
cole.house.gov
2458 Rayburn Bldg. 20515-6165; fax 225-3512

Committees
Appropriations
Budget
Rules

Residence
Moore

Born
April 28, 1949; Shreveport, La.

Religion
Methodist

Family
Wife, Ellen Cole; one child

Education
Grinnell College, B.A. 1971 (history); Yale U., M.A. 1974 (British history); U. of Oklahoma, Ph.D. 1984 (19th Century British history)

Career
Political consultant; party official; congressional district director; professor

Political Highlights
Okla. Republican Party chairman, 1985-89; Okla. Senate, 1989-91; Okla. secretary of state, 1995-99

ELECTION RESULTS

2012 GENERAL		
Tom Cole (R)	176,740	67.9%
Donna Marie Bebo (D)	71,846	27.6%
R. J. Harris (I)	11,745	4.5%
2012 PRIMARY		
Tom Cole (R)	22,840	87.7%
Gary D. Caissie (R)	3,195	12.3%
2010 GENERAL		
Tom Cole (R)		unopposed

Previous Winning Percentages
2008 (66%); 2006 (65%); 2004 (78%); 2002 (54%)

Elected 2002; 6th term

Cole started in politics as a graduate student managing a campaign for his mother. Thirty years later, he was running campaign operations for House Republicans. The current crop of GOP leaders doesn't always agree with his political strategies, but Cole stays involved in their conversations thanks to his experience, conservatism and straightforward style.

Few congressmen can claim connections or a background in political operations comparable to Cole's. He chaired the Oklahoma Republican Party, served as Oklahoma secretary of state, worked as the chief of staff on the Republican National Committee in the 2000 election cycle and was a partner in a successful political consulting firm.

The impetus for it all was a loss. Cole's mother, a bank teller, ran for the state House in 1976, when Cole was working on a Ph.D. in British history. (His dissertation is on a working-class neighborhood in East London.) "Like all graduate students, I was incredibly self-absorbed, and I didn't do anything to help my mother," Cole said. "She lost a very close election. The worst place on the planet to be is your mother's watch party on the night she loses and you haven't done anything."

He atoned in the next race, coming home from a Fulbright fellowship in London and thoroughly enjoying the chance to manage her to a win. Helen Cole went on to become Oklahoma's first Native American state senator — she was a Chickasaw. Cole and fellow Oklahoman Markwayne Mullin are the only Native Americans in Congress.

Since coming to Congress in 2003, Cole has endured a few rough patches operating on the national level. His fundraising abilities and connections to GOP leaders helped him win election as chairman of the National Republican Congressional Committee for the 110th Congress (2007-08). But when he took over, the NRCC was already in debt and disarray. Many rank-and-file Republicans weren't thrilled with his performance; others saw Cole as facing an impossible situation. Democrats expanded their majority by 21 seats. The next chairman, Pete Sessions of Texas, significantly reorganized the NRCC.

Cole ruffled conservative feathers in late 2012 with his suggestions during touchy fiscal talks with Democrats. He has frequently denounced tax increases, but he said the GOP should acquiesce to demands to raise taxes on the top 2 percent of earners — to take the issue off the negotiating table. Speaker John A. Boehner initially shot down that plan, but later tried to rally support behind a plan to raise taxes on earnings above $1 million. The final "fiscal cliff" deal, enacted in January 2013, raised taxes on earnings above $400,000.

Cole later said that he was fighting "political immaturity" from some members of the right wing of the conference. "This isn't a pickup game of football where you draw the plays in the sand and then go run 'em," he said. GOP leaders put him on the Rules Committee for the 113th Congress (2013-14).

He has the latitude to speak up. He served as a deputy whip in the 112th Congress (2011-12) and stayed on message: He advocated fewer regulations, more domestic energy production, less spending and a restructuring of entitlement programs. He had helped develop that overall agenda heading into the 2010 election, under the title of the "Pledge to America."

He promoted the GOP's overall fiscal agenda as a member of both the Appropriations and Budget committees. Cole voted for the plans of Budget Chairman Paul D. Ryan of Wisconsin, which included changes to Medicare. "No other previous Republican majority, certainly not one that I was a part of, would have the courage to pass anything like the Ryan budget," he said.

Cole proudly touted the reductions to discretionary spending that House

Republicans engineered for fiscal 2011 and 2012, as well as GOP success in curtailing funding for some parts of the 2010 health care overhaul. The House passed his bills to end public financing of political party conventions and presidential campaigns.

Not every proposed spending cut won his approval, however. Cole supports federal education programs highly favored by his district (which hosts the University of Oklahoma). A member of the Defense Appropriations Subcommittee, he has described potential further cuts to security spending as disastrous. Fort Sill and Tinker Air Force Base are in his district.

Cole, who chairs the Congressional Native American Caucus, also prioritizes the needs of Indian tribes over spending reductions when he feels the need. He sits on the Interior-Environment Appropriations Subcommittee — the panel that handles Indian affairs.

A 2012 reauthorization of federal programs to combat violence against women stalled out when House conservatives objected to Senate provisions expanding the programs to gay, lesbian, bisexual and transgender victims, as well as illegal immigrants. Cole was OK, however, with Senate provisions regarding Native Americans. He helped quell some of the House resistance in early 2013, and a Senate version of the reauthorization was enacted.

Cole is a fifth-generation Oklahoman. His father, John, was an Air Force veteran who later worked as a civilian at Tinker Air Force Base. To marry Helen, John agreed to her terms that their children would be raised as Chickasaws. "He said that was a good deal," Cole remembers. His great aunt Te Ata was an award-winning storyteller and trained actress. His great-grandfather, Thomas Benjamin Thompson, was the last elected treasurer of the Chickasaw Nation before Oklahoma statehood.

Cole attended Yale and the University of Oklahoma for his graduate work, teaching both history and politics along the way. His success helping his mother's campaign led to participation in other local races, a stint as district director for GOP Rep. Mickey Edwards, then the chairmanship of the Oklahoma Republican Party. He followed that job with a run in the state Senate.

His political consulting group, Cole, Hargrave, Snodgrass and Associates, had a hand in numerous races in 1994. Many were in Oklahoma. Cole contributed to the successful House campaigns of Tom Coburn and Frank D. Lucas and Mary Fallin's bid for lieutenant governor. Coburn is now a senator, Lucas chairs the Agriculture Committee and Fallin is governor.

That year, Cole also ran the House campaign of J.C. Watts Jr. When Watts decided to retire at the end of 2002, he endorsed Cole as his replacement. Cole beat Democrat Darryl Roberts that November with 54 percent of the vote, and that remains his worst showing in any House campaign.

Key Votes

2012	
Extend a Social Security payroll tax cut and unemployment benefits	YES
Ease securities rules to expand small-business access to capital	YES
Extend for one year subsidized student loan interest rates financed by a cut in health care spending	YES
Cite Attorney General Eric H. Holder Jr. for contempt of Congress	YES
Create a visa program for foreign graduates in high-tech fields	YES
Extend most Bush-era income tax rates while allowing rates for top-bracket earners to rise (Jan. 1, 2013)	YES
2011	
Strike funding for F-35 alternative engine	YES
Prevent EPA from regulating greenhouse gas emissions to address climate change	YES
Extend certain provisions of Patriot Act for four years	YES
Declare opposition to use of ground troops in Libya	YES
Overhaul patent law	YES
Pass compromise debt limit increase plan and establish future spending limits	YES
Allow consideration of measures to implement three trade agreements	YES

CQ Vote Studies

	PARTY UNITY		PRESIDENTIAL SUPPORT	
	SUPPORT	OPPOSE	SUPPORT	OPPOSE
2012	89%	11%	16%	84%
2011	93%	7%	25%	75%
2010	89%	11%	29%	71%
2009	86%	14%	22%	78%
2008	95%	5%	73%	27%

Interest Groups

	AFL-CIO	ADA	CCUS	ACU
2012	19%	0%	100%	72%
2011	3%	5%	100%	80%
2010	7%	0%	88%	96%
2009	5%	0%	80%	92%
2008	7%	10%	94%	88%

Oklahoma 4

South central — Norman, Lawton, part of Oklahoma City

A mix of cities, farmland, oil fields and protected wilderness, the 4th covers the state's south-central region. The district's vibrant feel is rooted in its parts of Oklahoma City and the city's expanding suburbs, the University of Oklahoma and the Sooners football team, and two military bases.

Population growth since 2000 resulted in a smaller footprint for the 4th following decennial remapping. Growth was most robust in Cleveland and McClain counties (south of Oklahoma City), and the Hispanic population near the state capital is the district's fastest-growing demographic.

The population centers here are two military bases and the state's largest university. Tinker Air Force Base in Midwest City is one of the district's key employers, hosting tens of thousands of military personnel, civilians and contractors. Aerospace companies, including Boeing, support base functions and the local workforce. Southwest in Lawton, Fort Sill provides an Army presence near Wichita Mountains Wildlife Refuge, where bison, elk and longhorn cattle graze. Norman is dominated by the University of Oklahoma.

As in much of the state, the oil and gas industry has a major impact in the 4th, especially in Carter and Stephens counties. Halliburton Energy Services produces oil field and automotive equipment in Duncan. The 4th is also sprinkled with manufacturing firms, grain and cattle farms and pecan crops. Jefferson County on the Texas border produces watermelons. A massive tornado hit towns here in 2013, demolishing much of Moore.

A deeply conservative Bible Belt disposition defines the district's political leanings, and Democrats have lost ground even in local elections. Republicans dominate the district at the federal level.

Major Industry

Oil and gas, agriculture, military, higher education

Military Bases

Tinker Air Force Base, 7,000 military, 26,600 civilian; Fort Sill (Army), 8,831 military, 3,951 civilian (2011)

Cities

Oklahoma City (pt.), Norman, Lawton, Moore, Midwest City, Duncan

Notable

Fort Sill, a National Historic Landmark, was the base for frontier scouts such as "Wild Bill" Hickok, "Buffalo Bill" Cody and the African-American Buffalo Soldiers.

Rep. James Lankford (R)

Capitol Office
225-2132
lankford.house.gov
228 Cannon Bldg. 20515-3605; fax 226-1463

Committees
Budget
Oversight & Government Reform
(Energy Policy, Health Care and Entitlements - Chairman)

Residence
Oklahoma City

Born
March 4, 1968; Dallas, Texas

Religion
Baptist

Family
Wife, Cindy Lankford; two children

Education
U. of Texas, B.S.Ed. 1990 (secondary education history); Southwestern Theological Baptist Seminary, M.Div. 1994 (biblical languages)

Career
Religious youth camp director

Political Highlights
No previous office

ELECTION RESULTS

2012 GENERAL		
James Lankford (R)	153,603	58.7%
Tom Guild (D)	97,504	37.3%
Pat Martin (I)	5,394	2.1%
Robert T. Murphy (I)	5,176	2.0%
2012 PRIMARY		
James Lankford (R)		unopposed
2010 GENERAL		
James Lankford (R)	123,236	62.5%
Billy Coyle (D)	68,074	34.5%
Clark Duffe (LIBERT)	3,067	1.6%
Dave White (I)	2,728	1.4%

Elected 2010; 2nd term

Lankford's faith led him to Congress, but as a lawmaker his wonkish approach has been far more defining than his social conservatism. He embraces the GOP effort to shrink government and is a remarkably quick study on legislative matters — enough so to head House Republicans' policy operations.

He was a political newcomer when he was elected in 2010, but Lankford, a cordial, baby-faced and deep-voiced redhead, could point to some administrative experience. He spent more than a decade running the Falls Creek Baptist youth camp, which accommodates as many as 51,000 visitors each summer. Early in his first term, he quipped to Fox News that it was relevant experience, because "there are a lot of congressmen that act pretty juvenile."

Joking aside, Lankford and Congress have developed a healthy mutual respect. He has stayed close to Republican leaders when voting and done his homework on committees. For the 113th Congress (2013-14), GOP colleagues chose him to chair the Republican Policy Committee, putting him in charge of crystallizing the party's small-government agenda. He also has a complementary position as the chairman of the Oversight and Government Reform subcommittee on energy, health care and entitlement programs.

Lankford has won praise for his attentive demeanor and his attempts to hear out all parts of the Republican Conference. He has emphasized to leaders the importance of bringing major legislation through committees, rather than closed-door negotiations. "Process is a very big deal," he said. "People have to be heard. People were elected here to be legislators, not just voters. And so they have to be involved in the process."

Lankford built his reputation in his freshman term as chairman of the Oversight subcommittee on government procurement and intergovernmental relations. He sees the federal contracting process as needlessly difficult; he also calls for an overhaul of the grants process, maintaining that agencies have turned to grants as a simpler alternative to contracting. In 2011, he introduced a bill requiring the creation of standards for how agencies announce, award and disclose grants; it also would create a website for the posting of performance reports at the conclusion of a grant.

One of his favorite themes is regulatory burdens. He is particularly supportive of a bill by North Carolina Republican Virginia Foxx requiring reports on the compliance costs to businesses or state and local governments when a federal rule is created. Lankford is critical of the 2010 financial regulatory overhaul, calling it "death by a thousand cuts" for community banks and other small lending institutions.

He's also wary of EPA regulation of hydraulic fracturing, the practice of shooting high-pressure fluid into the ground to recover oil and natural gas deposits. In the 112th Congress (2011-12), he addressed the matter from both his Oversight panel and as a member of the Transportation and Infrastructure Subcommittee on Water Resources and Environment.

Environmentalists have said that "fracking" can contaminate ground water or affect air quality, but Lankford called that stance "paranoia." Fracking is "not new to Oklahoma," he said. "We've done hydraulic fracking since 1949. ... Our water is clean, our air is clean, it's a beautiful state."

As part of his first-term success, Lankford served on the conference committee assembling the final version of a 2012 two-year reauthorization of surface transportation programs; he worked to secure consolidations of several highway programs.

He has proposed a significant restructuring of transportation funding, whereby states would get the option of having their contributions to the

Highway Trust Fund returned to them. Projects using the returned money would not be subject to federal spending requirements or construction regulations. Lankford said such a system would give states greater flexibility to deal with their pressing infrastructure needs, as well as speed up the pace of construction projects. Oklahoma Republican Tom Coburn introduced a companion measure in the Senate in the 112th Congress.

Lankford also sits on the Budget Committee, where he is interested in new approaches to the appropriations process. He calls a potential balanced-budget amendment to the Constitution "the parent in the room," and in July 2011, he quoted the Bible on the House floor in calling for one: "Proverbs 22:7 states, 'The borrower is a slave to the lender.' Proverbs 22 applies to families, and Proverbs 22 applies to nations."

He opposes tax increases and has co-sponsored a measure to eliminate most federal taxes and replace them with a national sales tax. Lankford cites the 1996 welfare overhaul, with its emphasis on work requirements, as a model for other social-welfare spending.

Lankford's religious outlook informs his social conservatism. He opposes same-sex marriage and abortion. He also opposes restrictions on gun rights — among other hobbies, he sometimes shoots clay pigeons to unwind.

The younger of two sons, Lankford grew up in Dallas. He lived with his mother, a public school library director, after his parents divorced; she remarried when Lankford was 12. Religion was always a part of his life. "I accepted Christ when I was 8 years old," he said.

In the fourth grade, he got involved with speech-and-debate teams; in high school, he served as the drum captain for the marching band. After taking courses in history and speech at the University of Texas, he worked as a youth pastor, which eventually led to his work at Falls Creek.

He credits his faith with bringing him to politics. "In 2008, I really sensed a calling to do this," he said. "It was about a seven-month prayer journey for my wife and I, just to be able to struggle through this, and the insanity of leaving what we loved and what we were doing."

Lankford's predecessor, Republican Mary Fallin, left the 5th District seat open as she made a successful run for governor. His 13 years at Falls Creek helped him develop a network that proved invaluable to his grass-roots mobilization effort. He finished first in a seven-candidate GOP primary, then won the runoff by an almost 2-to-1 margin. He had no trouble besting Democrat Billy Coyle in the strongly Republican district, winning 63 percent of the vote to Coyle's 35 percent.

He was unopposed in the 2012 primary and easily dispatched Democrat Tom Guild, a college professor.

Key Votes

2012	
Extend a Social Security payroll tax cut and unemployment benefits	NO
Ease securities rules to expand small-business access to capital	YES
Extend for one year subsidized student loan interest rates financed by a cut in health care spending	YES
Cite Attorney General Eric H. Holder Jr. for contempt of Congress	YES
Create a visa program for foreign graduates in high-tech fields	YES
Extend most Bush-era income tax rates while allowing rates for top-bracket earners to rise (Jan. 1, 2013)	NO
2011	
Strike funding for F-35 alternative engine	YES
Prevent EPA from regulating greenhouse gas emissions to address climate change	YES
Extend certain provisions of Patriot Act for four years	YES
Declare opposition to use of ground troops in Libya	YES
Overhaul patent law	YES
Pass compromise debt limit increase plan and establish future spending limits	YES
Allow consideration of measures to implement three trade agreements	YES

CQ Vote Studies

	PARTY UNITY		PRESIDENTIAL SUPPORT	
	SUPPORT	OPPOSE	SUPPORT	OPPOSE
2012	97%	3%	11%	89%
2011	97%	3%	20%	80%

Interest Groups

	AFL-CIO	ADA	CCUS	ACU
2012	14%	0%	92%	84%
2011	0%	5%	100%	84%

Oklahoma 5

Most of Oklahoma City; Pottawatomie and Seminole counties

A large urban center among the desolate plains, downtown Oklahoma City — including the governor's mansion and the state Capitol — is the hub of the 5th District, which takes in most of Oklahoma County and all of Pottawatomie and Seminole counties to the southeast.

Professional, scientific and technical services employ large portions of the workforce in Oklahoma County, and the state government provides a stable source of jobs. Oil giants such as Chesapeake Energy have corporate offices in the city, while drilling and extraction is a key industry for Seminole County's rural population. Oklahoma University's Health Sciences Center supports the medical industry in the region, which also includes defense contractors and a major airport. Although Tinker Air Force Base itself has been carved out of the district to the south, many people commute from the 5th to the base.

Farms and agriculture remain important to the 5th. Numerous horse and livestock expos cater to Oklahoma City's Western tradition, providing a major source of tourism revenue throughout the year.

Greater Oklahoma City has had higher population growth than many other metropolitan areas in the nation since 2000. With a rapidly growing Hispanic population and several American Indian lands in Seminole and Pottawatomie, the 5th is the state's most racially and ethnically diverse district.

Oklahoma City, and the district as a whole, is a Republican stronghold, although some conservative Democratic sympathies can be found at the local level. Bill Clinton managed to win Seminole County in the 1990s, but Republican candidate Mitt Romney won in Seminole by 30 points in the 2012 presidential race. Romney took 59 percent of the district's overall presidential vote.

Major Industry

Oil and gas, technology, health care, government, education, agriculture

Cities

Oklahoma City (pt.), Edmond, Shawnee

Notable

The Oklahoma City National Memorial Museum and the Institute for the Prevention of Terrorism now stands on the 3.3-acre site damaged by the 1995 bombing of the Alfred P. Murrah Federal Building.

OREGON

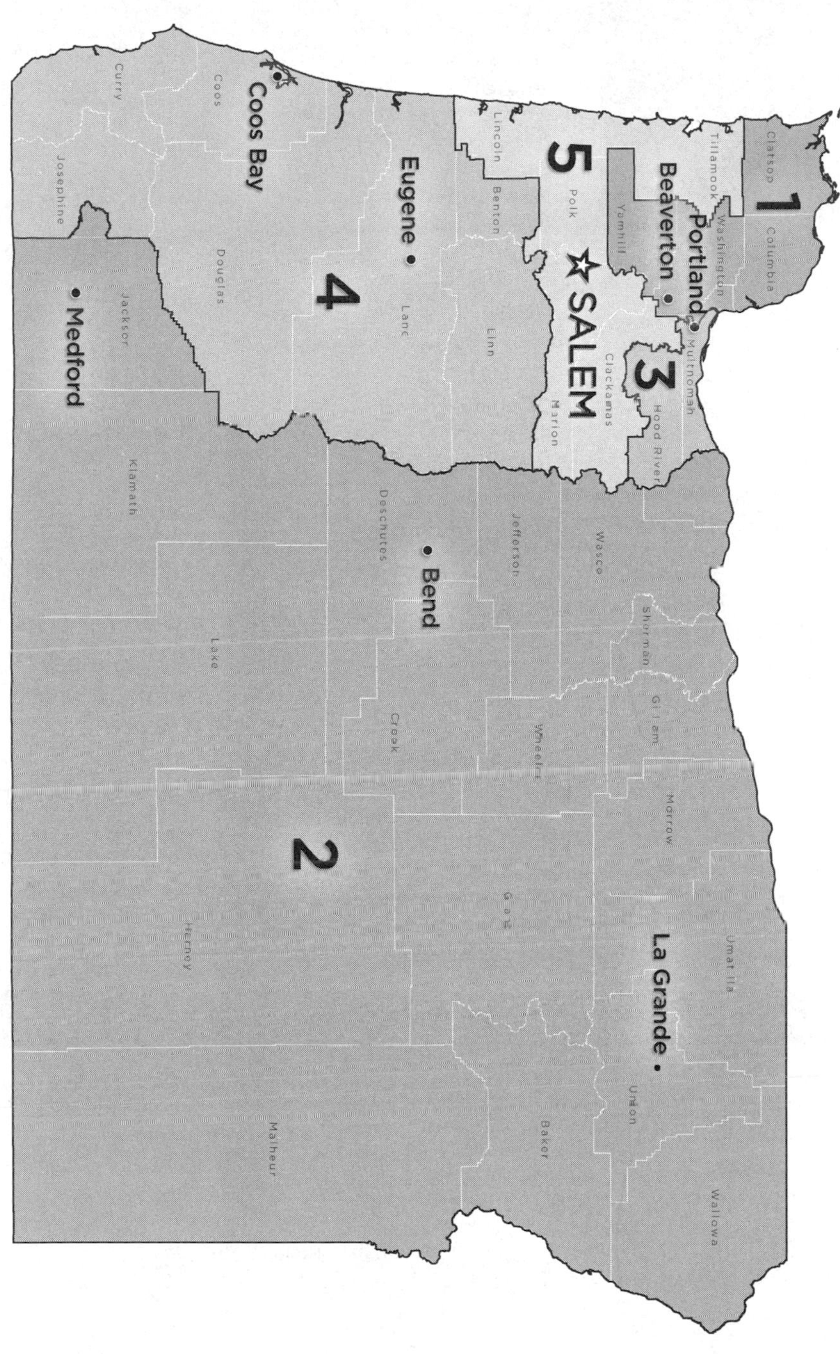

Curry
Coos
Coos Bay
Josephine
Eugene
Lincoln
5
Tillamook
Clatsop
1
Portland
Beaverton
Washington
Columbia
Yamhill
Polk
Benton
Douglas
4
Lane
Linn
SALEM
Clackamas
3
Multnomah
Hood River
Marion
Jackson
Medford
Klamath
Deschutes
Bend
Jefferson
Wasco
Sherman
Lake
Crook
Wheeler
Gilliam
2
Morrow
Grant
Harney
Umatilla
La Grande
Union
Baker
Malheur
Wallowa

Gov. John Kitzhaber (D)

First elected: 2010
Length of term: 4 years
Term expires: 1/15
Salary: $93,600
Phone: (503) 378-6827
Residence: Portland
Born: March 5, 1947; Colfax, Wash.
Religion: Unspecified
Family: Partner, Cylvia Hayes; one child
Education: Dartmouth College, A.B. 1969; U. of Oregon, M.D. 1973
Career: Physician
Political highlights: Ore. House, 1979-81; Ore. Senate, 1981-93 (president, 1985-93); governor, 1995-2003

ELECTION RESULTS

2010 GENERAL

John Kitzhaber (D)	716,525	49.3%
Chris Dudley (R)	694,287	47.8%
Greg Kord (CNSTP)	20,475	1.4%
Wes Wagner (LIBERT)	19,048	1.3%

Secretary of State Kate Brown (D)

(no lieutenant governor)
Phone: (503) 986-1523

LEGISLATURE

Legislative Assembly: January-June in odd-numbered years, February-March in even-numbered years
Senate: 30 members, 4-year terms
2013 ratios: 16 D, 14 R; 22 men, 8 women
Salary: $1,855 per month
Phone: (503) 986-1187
House: 60 members, 2-year terms
2013 ratios: 34 D, 26 R; 42 men, 18 women
Salary: $21,612
Phone: (503) 986-1187

TERM LIMITS

Governor: 2 terms
Senate: No
House: No

URBAN STATISTICS

CITY	POPULATION
Portland	583, 776
Eugene	156,185
Salem	154,637
Gresham	105,594
Hillsboro	91,611

REGISTERED VOTERS

Democrat	39%
Republican	31%
Other	30%

POPULATION

2010 population	3,831,074
2000 population	3,421,399
1990 population	2,842,321
Percent change (2000-2010)	+12.0%
Rank among states (2010)	27
Median age	37.7
Born in state	45.5%
Foreign born	9.2%
Violent crime rate	255/100,000
Poverty level	14.3%
Federal workers	34,234
Military	1,615

ELECTIONS

STATE ELECTION OFFICIAL
(503) 986-1518
DEMOCRATIC PARTY
(503) 224-8200
REPUBLICAN PARTY
(503) 595-8881

MISCELLANEOUS

Web: www.oregon.gov
Capital: Salem

U.S. CONGRESS

Senate: 2 Democrats
House: 4 Democrats, 1 Republican

STATISTICS BY DISTRICT

District	2012 Vote for President		2008 Vote for President										
	Obama	Romney	Obama	McCain	Black	Asian	Hispanic	Median Income	Over 64	Under 20	College Education	Rural	Sq. Miles
1	57%	40%	60%	38%	2%	7%	14%	$60,868	12%	26%	37%	13%	3,007
2	40	57	44	54	1	1	13	40,670	17	25	23	36	69,443
3	72	25	73	24	5	7	11	47,378	11	23	35	6	1,074
4	52	45	55	43	1	2	7	40,197	17	23	24	29	17,274
5	50	47	53	45	1	3	16	49,677	15	26	28	18	5,190
STATE	**55**	**42**	**57**	**40**	**2**	**4**	**12**	**46,816**	**14**	**25**	**29**	**21**	**95,988**
U.S.	**51**	**47**	**53**	**46**	**12**	**5**	**17**	**50,052**	**13**	**27**	**29**	**21**	**3,531,905**

Sen. Ron Wyden (D)

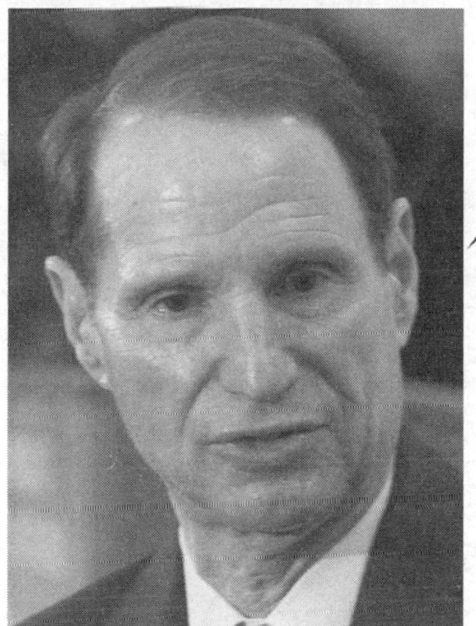

Capitol Office
224-5244
wyden.senate.gov
221 Dirksen Bldg. 20510-3703; fax 228-2717

Committees
Budget
Energy & Natural Resources - Chairman
Finance
(International Trade, Customs & Global Competitiveness - Chairman)
Select Intelligence
Special Aging
Joint Taxation

Residence
Portland

Born
May 3, 1949; Wichita, Kan.

Religion
Jewish

Family
Wife, Nancy Bass-Wyden; five children

Education
U. of California, Santa Barbara, attended 1967-69; Stanford U., A.B. 1971 (political science); U. of Oregon, J.D. 1974

Career
Senior citizen advocacy group state director; lawyer; professor

Political Highlights
U.S. House, 1981-96

ELECTION RESULTS

2010 GENERAL

Ron Wyden (D)	825,507	57.2%
Jim Huffman (R)	566,199	39.2%
Bruce Cronk (WFM)	18,940	1.3%
Marc Delphine (LIBERT)	16,028	1.1%
Rick Staggenborg (PRO)	14,466	1.0%

Previous Winning Percentages
2004 (63%); 1998 (61%); 1996 Special Election (48%); 1994 House Election (73%); 1992 House Election (77%); 1990 House Election (81%); 1988 House Election (99%); 1986 House Election (86%); 1984 House Election (72%); 1982 House Election (78%); 1980 House Election (72%)

Elected 1996; 3rd full term

Wyden has liberal leanings, but they have not kept him from collaborating with GOP colleagues on big ideas. Some of his most noted work in recent years has been the development of policy blueprints with an unlikely cast of Republican characters in both chambers.

He sometimes makes those arrangements independent of his party's broader political strategy. As the 112th Congress (2011-12) battled over the sustainability of federal entitlement programs, Wyden teamed with House Budget Chairman Paul D. Ryan of Wisconsin — the public face of the GOP effort to, in the words of many a Democrat, "end Medicare as we know it."

Their plan, unveiled in a December 2011 policy paper, combined elements of Ryan's fiscal 2012 budget proposal with structures of the 2010 health care law. It would give beneficiaries fixed amounts to purchase insurance but allow for a regulated insurance "exchange" in which traditional Medicare was an option.

"Before the partisan attacks begin to escalate and the 2012 election ads start to air, we are outlining a plan for how Democrats and Republicans can work together to ensure that American retirees — now and forever — have quality, affordable health insurance," Ryan and Wyden wrote. Many publications hailed it as one of the most interesting policy ideas of the year, and a possible undercutting of campaign talking points for both parties.

Politics eventually overtook policy, however. Ryan's fiscal 2013 budget deviated enough from the Wyden-Ryan plan that Wyden declined to show his support.

When GOP presidential nominee Mitt Romney chose Ryan as his running mate and touted Ryan's effort to "co-lead a piece of legislation" on Medicare with a Democrat, Wyden accused Romney of misrepresenting the paper as a formal bill. "Several months after the paper came out, I spoke and voted against the Medicare provisions in the Ryan budget," Wyden said.

Wyden will have lots of chances to cut deals in the 113th Congress (2013-14), particularly on energy — he is the new chairman of the Energy and Natural Resources Committee. He used part of the August recess in 2012 to take an "energy tour" of Alaska with Lisa Murkowski, the panel's top Republican.

Murkowski and Democratic ally Mary L. Landrieu of Louisiana pushed in the 112th for states to get a greater share of the revenue from energy production off their shores, whether it involved fossil fuels, wind or waves. Wyden expressed interest in the idea once Murkowski suggested directing some of the money the federal government makes from offshore production into a clean-energy trust fund. Wyden has been open to discussions as Landrieu and Murkowski have updated their plan in the 113th Congress — whereas the former chairman, Jeff Bingaman of New Mexico, was strongly opposed.

Wyden has also been receptive to attempts to streamline the approval and regulation of smaller hydropower projects — at an April 2013 hearing, he called hydropower and geothermal power the "forgotten renewables."

But he has some deal breakers when it comes to energy. Murkowski is a proponent of exporting liquefied natural gas (LNG) from Alaska's abundant North Slope reserves. Wyden is less sure that such exports are in the best interest of the country. He has joined a chorus of Democrats concerned that selling LNG overseas would lead to much higher prices domestically, counteracting the historically low prices being enjoyed now.

Wyden sits on the Budget Committee and is a backer of simplifying the tax code. A 2011 tax plan he devised with Indiana Republican Dan Coats proposed lowering rates and eliminating deductions. However, tax benefits tailored toward clean-energy resources would have remained untouched.

He also sits on the Finance Committee — and with the impending retirement of Montana Democrat Max Baucus, Wyden might become its top Democrat in the 114th Congress (2015-16).

For now, he chairs the Subcommittee on International Trade, Customs and Global Competitiveness. He has been vocal in his opposition to secrecy in international trade negotiations, which often feature significant input from corporations. He has introduced a bill to ensure that lawmakers and staff have access to closely shielded documents about the Trans-Pacific Partnership trade agreement. While many experts view the framework from that agreement as an essential limitation on China's economic influence in the region, some technology and communications groups have raised fears that negotiations could lead to an outcome that would undercut domestic intellectual property protections.

Wyden has a history of combating secrecy in legislating, as well: He teamed with Republican Charles E. Grassley of Iowa for years to try to require senators who place secret holds on legislation to identify themselves. That effort bore fruit at the beginning of the 112th Congress, as a change in Senate rules barred the practice.

Wyden works for greater openness from the Intelligence Committee, pushing to declassify the amount of spending on spy programs. He has placed holds on several intelligence-related bills, citing his worries that attempts to fight intelligence leaks are trampling civil liberties and freedom of the press. In 2012, he slowed up consideration of a reauthorization of the Foreign Intelligence Surveillance Act, eventually getting a vote on an amendment to require a report to Congress on whether FISA had been used to collect any domestic email or phone communications. Without that information, he said, Congress could not conduct "real oversight" of the program. The amendment was defeated.

In March 2013, he was the one Democrat to contribute to a "talking filibuster" of a confirmation vote for a new CIA director. The effort, led by Kentucky Republican Rand Paul, was meant to compel the White House to clarify its policies on the use of drones in targeted killings.

Wyden's parents were Jewish refugees from Nazi Germany. His mother spent part of her youth in Baghdad, where the family had fled. Wyden was born in Wichita, Kan., and steadily moved west as his father's journalism career advanced. He attended college on a basketball scholarship and retains his obsession with the game — he holds the unofficial congressional free-throw record (47 out of 50 in the House gym). Wyden counts UCLA and Portland Trailblazer great Bill Walton as a good friend. After abandoning his dream of playing professionally, Wyden received his bachelor's degree from Stanford, then followed a girlfriend to Oregon, where he earned a law degree at the University of Oregon.

Wyden was executive director for the Oregon Gray Panthers, an organization promoting senior citizens' interests, when he ran for the House in 1980. He ousted Democratic Rep. Robert B. Duncan in the primary and won with 72 percent of the vote in November in a Democratic, Portland-based district.

When Republican Sen. Bob Packwood resigned in disgrace in 1995 after a sexual-harassment controversy, Wyden jumped into the special-election race. He edged out fellow Democratic Rep. Peter A. DeFazio in the primary, then narrowly defeated Republican Gordon H. Smith (who subsequently won election to Oregon's other Senate seat and became a close ally of Wyden). Wyden has won his three re-elections with ease.

Wyden underwent surgery in December 2010 for early-stage prostate cancer and was back at work when the Senate reconvened for votes in late January 2011. He became a father for the fifth time in late 2012. Scarlett Willa Wyden is his third child with his second wife, Nancy.

Key Votes

2012	
Prohibit health insurance plans from denying coverage based on the sponsor's religious beliefs	YES
Require approval of the Keystone XL oil pipeline	NO
Ease securities rules to expand small-business access to capital	YES
Reauthorize farm and nutrition programs for five years	YES
Limit debate on a bill that would create private-sector cybersecurity standards	NO
Consent to ratification of a treaty setting global standard for the treatment of people with disabilities	YES
Provide $60.4 billion in disaster relief following Superstorm Sandy	YES
Extend most Bush-era income tax rates while allowing rates for top-bracket earners to rise (Jan. 1, 2013)	YES
2011	
Prevent EPA from regulating greenhouse gas emissions to address climate change	NO
Extend certain provisions of Patriot Act for four years	NO
Clear compromise debt limit increase plan and establish future spending limits	YES
Overhaul patent law	YES
Implement Colombia free trade agreement	YES
Limit debate on confirmation of Caitlin J. Halligan to D.C. Circuit Court of Appeals	YES
Extend payroll tax cut and unemployment benefits for two months	YES

CQ Vote Studies

	PARTY UNITY		PRESIDENTIAL SUPPORT	
	SUPPORT	OPPOSE	SUPPORT	OPPOSE
2012	95%	5%	96%	4%
2011	98%	2%	98%	2%
2010	95%	5%	95%	5%
2009	98%	2%	97%	3%
2008	97%	3%	28%	72%
2007	95%	5%	39%	61%
2006	94%	6%	51%	49%
2005	94%	6%	26%	74%
2004	93%	7%	62%	38%
2003	93%	7%	47%	53%

Interest Groups

	AFL-CIO	ADA	CCUS	ACU
2012	91%	95%	50%	0%
2011	79%	90%	64%	5%
2010	100%	100%	0%	12%
2009	100%	100%	43%	4%
2008	100%	95%	50%	8%
2007	94%	95%	55%	4%
2006	100%	100%	42%	8%
2005	79%	95%	33%	4%
2004	100%	100%	59%	4%
2003	92%	90%	43%	15%

Sen. Jeff Merkley (D)

Capitol Office
224-3753
merkley.senate.gov
313 Hart Bldg. 20510; fax 228-3997

Committees
Appropriations
Banking, Housing & Urban Affairs
(Economic Policy - Chairman)
Budget
Environment & Public Works
(Green Jobs & the New Economy - Chairman)

Residence
Portland

Born
Oct. 24, 1956; Eugene, Ore.

Religion
Lutheran

Family
Wife, Mary Sorteberg; two children

Education
Stanford U., B.A. 1979 (international relations); Princeton U., M.P.A. 1982

Career
Nonprofit executive; computer repair company owner; Congressional Budget Office analyst

Political Highlights
Ore. House, 1999-2009 (minority leader, 2003-07; speaker, 2007-09)

ELECTION RESULTS

2008 GENERAL		
Jeff Merkley (D)	864,392	48.9%
Gordon H. Smith (R)	805,159	45.6%
David Brownlow (CNSTP)	92,565	5.2%
2008 PRIMARY		
Jeff Merkley (D)	246,482	44.8%
Steve Novick (D)	230,889	42.0%
Candy Neville (D)	38,367	7.0%
Roger S. Obrist (D)	12,647	2.3%
Pavel Goberman (D)	12,056	2.2%
David Loera (D)	6,127	1.1%

Elected 2008; 1st term

Merkley is one of the most committed liberals in the Senate. In a divided Congress, that distinction raises the degree of difficulty for achieving his legislative goals, but he has continued to fight for his priorities on banking, housing, education and the environment.

Merkley has been parsing policy and societal problems for most of his adult life. He was an intern in the 1970s for Oregon's Republican Sen. Mark O. Hatfield. He followed that job with a stint as a presidential fellow at the Defense Department in the 1980s before becoming a Congressional Budget Office analyst, writing reports on weapons systems.

After returning to Oregon, Merkley served as director of the Portland chapter of Habitat for Humanity and became executive director of the World Affairs Council, an education group focused on international politics and culture. He spent a decade in the Oregon House and was its speaker when he left for the U.S. Senate in 2009.

His political intensity notwithstanding, Merkley is a polite, almost folksy presence in the Senate — he offers constituents the opportunity to meet him for coffee should they visit D.C., and he has taken to YouTube to explain the details of his economic policies on a whiteboard.

Many of those policies have a common thread: government doing the utmost to help those on the middle and lower portions of the economic spectrum, by creating new consumer protections and expanding assistance programs. And many of them have been stuck at the proposal phase thus far.

A member of the Banking, Housing and Urban Affairs Committee, he introduced his plan to aid the housing sector in July 2012. A government trust would buy "underwater" mortgages — those where borrowers owe more than the current value of their home, but still keep up on their payments. The government would then allow refinancing of those mortgages. Merkley argued that the government would ultimately recoup its initial costs by collecting interest payments.

Merkley sits on the Budget Committee and was a critic of the August 2011 agreement to raise the federal debt limit. His opposition centered on cuts to education and environmental protection programs and the potential job losses from those cuts. "While our children in Head Start and our children headed for college and our citizens seeking job training are going to take these blows, the wealthy and well-connected don't contribute one slim dime," he said on the Senate floor. Merkley called the negotiations leading to the law a "process of extortion."

Merkley has blamed war spending for diverting resources from education and proposes increasing the number of school days per year. "We are overinvesting in the overseas wars and underinvesting in education and infrastructure," he told the Oregon Area Jewish Committee in an October 2012 speech. "We are becoming the first generation of parents whose children are getting less education than we've got. That is unacceptable."

In the 113th Congress (2013-14), Merkley can try to rejigger federal investments as a junior Democrat on the Appropriations Committee. His seat there came at a price — he lost a seat on the Health, Education, Labor and Pensions Committee — but he proudly pointed out that he was the first Oregonian on the panel since Hatfield, who was the Appropriations chairman when he retired at the end of the 104th Congress (1995-96).

Merkley represents a rather eco-minded state, and he holds a seat on the Environment and Public Works Committee. Whereas many Western lawmakers chafe at the federal management of land and wilderness protections in their states, Merkley wants more of Oregon to get wilderness designations.

He wants statutory caps on greenhouse gas emissions and a national standard for the production of electricity from renewable sources. His plan for energy independence, rolled out in 2010, leans heavily on slashing oil consumption by moving travelers to mass transit and electric cars. The Senate-passed version of a 2012 reauthorization of farm programs (which was not enacted) had a Merkley provision to provide loans for energy efficiency renovations of homes and businesses in rural areas. Merkley chairs the Subcommittee on Green Jobs and the New Economy.

Democrats had full control of Congress when Merkley joined the Senate in the 111th Congress (2009-10). He came on the scene urging his party to press its advantage, rather than take a conciliatory approach. Some of his biggest legislative successes to date came from that period.

Merkley and Michigan Democrat Carl Levin wrote the provision in the 2010 financial regulatory overhaul that requires creation of a "Volcker rule" — regulations, named after a former Federal Reserve chairman, to separate the banking and investment arms of financial services companies. The regulations were supposed to be in place by July 2012, but the five agencies developing them missed that deadline. "In the years since the law was passed, we have all seen a series of high-profile trading losses at banks and non-bank financial companies — instances where the Volcker rule, if properly implemented, could have prevented significant losses," Merkley and Levin wrote to Federal Reserve Chairman Ben S. Bernanke in October 2012.

Merkley continues to call for forceful tactics; he was one of the senators agitating for changes to filibuster rules at the start of the 112th Congress (2011-12) to curtail the ability of the minority party to obstruct advancement of bills and nominations. He pressed for such changes again in 2013.

Merkley spent part of his childhood in rural southwestern Oregon, where his father worked in a wood mill. Troubles in the timber industry prompted the family to move to Portland, where his father worked as an equipment mechanic and Merkley went to high school. He was the first in his family to attend college.

While in Washington in the early part of his career, Merkley met his future wife, Mary Sorteberg, who was working for the Lutheran Volunteer Corps at a homeless shelter. He also bought a house in the city.

Merkley began five terms as a state legislator in 1999, and he moved up the ladder rapidly. As speaker in 2007 and 2008, he won enactment of a cap on consumer loan interest rates, a ban on junk food in schools and new civil contracts, called domestic partnerships, to lock in legal rights for same-sex couples.

In 2008, Merkley gave up his safe seat to take on Republican Sen. Gordon H. Smith, while potential rivals such as Democratic Reps. Peter A. DeFazio and Earl Blumenauer took a pass. His campaign got off to a rough start; he survived an accident when a Toyota Prius he was riding in rolled over on an icy highway.

He took a $250,000 mortgage out on his Washington house to finance his campaign and edged out Steve Novick, a Portland lawyer and political consultant, in the primary. Merkley got a big boost when he was endorsed by Montana Democratic Sen. Jon Tester, to whom Novick had compared himself. In the general election, Merkley criticized the moderate Smith for neutralizing the liberal votes of Oregon Sen. Ron Wyden. He also attacked Smith for supporting President George W. Bush's economic policies and for coming late to the campaign to end the Iraq War.

Smith raised $9.2 million for the campaign, close to $3 million more than Merkley. But the challenger got help from an ad blitz by the Democratic Senatorial Campaign Committee. Merkley won 49 percent of the vote to beat Smith by 3 points.

Key Votes

2012	
Prohibit health insurance plans from denying coverage based on the sponsor's religious beliefs	YES
Require approval of the Keystone XL oil pipeline	NO
Ease securities rules to expand small-business access to capital	NO
Reauthorize farm and nutrition programs for five years	YES
Limit debate on a bill that would create private-sector cybersecurity standards	NO
Consent to ratification of a treaty setting global standard for the treatment of people with disabilities	YES
Provide $60.4 billion in disaster relief following Superstorm Sandy	YES
Extend most Bush-era income tax rates while allowing rates for top-bracket earners to rise (Jan. 1, 2013)	YES
2011	
Prevent EPA from regulating greenhouse gas emissions to address climate change	NO
Extend certain provisions of Patriot Act for four years	NO
Clear compromise debt limit increase plan and establish future spending limits	NO
Overhaul patent law	YES
Implement Colombia free trade agreement	NO
Limit debate on confirmation of Caitlin J. Halligan to D.C. Circuit Court of Appeals	YES
Extend payroll tax cut and unemployment benefits for two months	YES

CQ Vote Studies

	PARTY UNITY		PRESIDENTIAL SUPPORT	
	SUPPORT	OPPOSE	SUPPORT	OPPOSE
2012	95%	5%	95%	5%
2011	98%	2%	92%	8%
2010	97%	3%	95%	5%
2009	98%	2%	96%	4%

Interest Groups

	AFL-CIO	ADA	CCUS	ACU
2012	100%	100%	50%	0%
2011	100%	95%	36%	5%
2010	100%	100%	0%	4%
2009	100%	100%	43%	4%

Rep. Suzanne Bonamici (D)

Capitol Office
225-0855
bonamici.house.gov
439 Cannon Bldg. 20515-3701; fax 225-9497

Committees
Education & the Workforce
Science, Space & Technology

Residence
Portland

Born
Oct. 14, 1954; Detroit, Mich.

Religion
Unspecified

Family
Husband, Michael H. Simon; two children

Education
Lane Community College, A.A. 1978 (paralegal); U of Oregon, B.A. 1980 (journalism), J.D. 1983

Career
State legislative aide; homemaker; lawyer

Political Highlights
Ore. House, 2007-08; Ore. Senate, 2008-11

ELECTION RESULTS

2012 GENERAL		
Suzanne Bonamici (D)	197,845	59.6%
Delinda Morgan (R)	109,699	33.0%
Steven Reynolds (PRO)	15,009	4.5%
Bob Ekstrom (CNSTP)	8,918	2.7%
2012 PRIMARY		
Suzanne Bonamici (D)	57,146	98.9%
write-ins (D)	608	1.0%
2012 SPECIAL		
Suzanne Bonamici (D)	113,404	53.8%
Rob Cornilles (R)	83,396	39.6%
Steven Reynolds (PRO)	6,798	3.2%
James Foster (LIBERT)	6,618	3.1%
2011 PRIMARY SPECIAL		
Suzanne Bonamici (D)	49,721	65.2%
Brad Avakian (D)	16,963	22.2%
Brad Witt (D)	6,003	7.9%
Dan Strite (D)	1,212	1.6%
Dominic Hammon (D)	923	1.2%

Elected 2012; 1st full term

Bonamici has an inclination to hash out political differences in an amicable fashion. She is both straightforward and methodical as she works on environmental, education and labor policy.

A lawyer and former state legislator, Bonamici (bon-a-ME-chee) belongs to the Congressional Progressive Caucus, the group of the most-liberal House members. But she is also part of the House Civility Caucus. It "wouldn't cost any money" to change some simple things, she said, like divided seating assignments on committees that make members feel as though they're on "separate teams."

She aligns with most of her Democratic colleagues on energy and environmental matters. Bonamici opposes the Keystone XL pipeline project and drilling off the coast of Oregon. She says climate change is a man-made problem and wants more focus on alternative power sources, such as solar energy and wind. Bonamici also supports EPA regulation of greenhouse gas emissions.

When she came to the House after a 2012 special election, Bonamici was assigned to the Science, Space and Technology Committee. She kept that seat for the 113th Congress (2013-14) and became the top Democrat on the Environment Subcommittee.

Her district has logging and fishing interests, as well as a tourism industry tied to its coasts — Haystack Rock and the city of Astoria, both featured in "The Goonies," are represented by Bonamici. She introduced a bill in 2012 to expedite grants to communities with marine debris emergencies — large debris from the 2011 Japanese tsunami was washing ashore in the Pacific Northwest.

Regarding scientific research, she wants to maintain funding levels for the Advanced Research Projects Agency-Energy.

In 2013, Bonamici joined the Education and the Workforce Committee, a panel she had requested when she first joined Congress. Its jurisdiction overlaps with some of her work on the science committee. She suggests integrating art and design into the discussion of STEM education (science, technology, engineering and math), saying that all those fields use the same creative-thinking and problem-solving skills.

Even in a struggling economy, Bonamici says, there should be federal spending on education. "Education is not a budget item that can be cut when times are tough," she said during her campaign. "Now is the time when improving our schools, community colleges and universities is critical to economic recovery." She wants to encourage coordination between community colleges and businesses that are looking for workers. It's a personal cause for Bonamici, who received her first degree from a community college in Oregon.

Interest rates on federally subsidized student loans are set by law, and Bonamici wants to keep those rates low: "Continued access to these financial aid programs will help prepare our next generation of workers for their careers in the next-generation technologies," she said. Many technology companies are in her district.

But maintaining low rates is a budget issue — by statute, interest rates are supposed to jump to 6.8 percent, and every extension of lower rates cuts into projected federal revenue. Bonamici didn't support a 2012 Republican bill to extend lower interest rates for a year, because it would have offset the lost revenue by eliminating a preventive health program created by the 2010 health care law. The extension was later packaged with a transportation bill.

Bonamici plays defense in spending debates, trying to protect social services block grants and other support programs from budget cuts. She opposed the Republicans' fiscal 2013 budget, calling its proposals "devastating" to the middle class and Medicare. She voted for the January 2013 measure that extended lower income tax rates only for earnings under $400,000.

Bonamici is socially liberal and defends abortion rights. She applauded a package of gun regulations proposed by President Barack Obama in January 2013 and wants to see a ban on large ammunition clips.

Raised in Michigan, Bonamici moved to Oregon after high school, put herself through community college and earned undergraduate and law degrees from the University of Oregon.

In her first job after law school in the 1980s, Bonamici worked as a consumer protection lawyer at the Federal Trade Commission in Washington. She is still interested in the subject. In 2012, she and Democratic Sen. Jeff Merkley proposed legislation to strengthen protections for customers of offshore and online lending services. Among its provisions, the bill would allow consumers to cancel a debit charge in the same way they would cancel a check.

While in Washington, Bonamici met her husband, Michael H. Simon. They moved back to Oregon in 1986, and Bonamici entered into private law practice. Simon, who is also a lawyer, was confirmed as a U.S. District Court judge in 2011. Bonamici, who was raised Protestant, now attends synagogue with her husband.

Bonamici quit practicing law to raise her two children, then later got back into the game on the legislative side as an aide in the Oregon Legislature. She was successful in her first bid for public office, winning election to the state House in 2006. After a year, she was appointed to the state Senate. She remained in that chamber until resigning in November 2011 to seek the vacant 1st District seat.

Bonamici's predecessor, Democrat David Wu, resigned from the House in August 2011 after reports of alleged sexual misconduct with a young woman. He also acknowledged having mental-health problems. As Bonamici won the Democratic nomination, Republicans chose Rob Cornilles, a sports-marketing company owner who had challenged Wu in 2010.

The Democratic Congressional Campaign Committee put $1.3 million into the race; the National Republican Congressional Committee gave $85,000 to Cornilles for a coordinated ad campaign. In the January 2012 special election, Bonamici took almost 54 percent of the vote, enough for a 14-point win.

Her race for a full term was less competitive. Republicans nominated Delinda Morgan, who had garnered less than 1,000 votes when seeking the GOP nomination for the special election. Bonamici won by more than 26 points.

She helped set the borders of the district she now represents. As a state senator, Bonamici chaired a committee that in 2011 helped produce new maps for Oregon's legislative and congressional districts. The two previous rounds of redistricting had been resolved in the courts.

Key Votes

2012	
Extend a Social Security payroll tax cut and unemployment benefits	YES
Ease securities rules to expand small-business access to capital	YES
Extend for one year subsidized student loan interest rates financed by a cut in health care spending	NO
Cite Attorney General Eric H. Holder Jr. for contempt of Congress	NO
Create a visa program for foreign graduates in high-tech fields	NO
Extend most Bush-era income tax rates while allowing rates for top-bracket earners to rise (Jan. 1, 2013)	YES

CQ Vote Studies

	PARTY UNITY		PRESIDENTIAL SUPPORT	
	SUPPORT	OPPOSE	SUPPORT	OPPOSE
2012	98%	2%	91%	9%

Interest Groups

	AFL-CIO	ADA	CCUS	ACU
2012	95%	95%	27%	0%

Oregon 1

Northwest and Portland suburbs; Beaverton

Centered on the "Silicon Forest," the 1st is home to educated and tech-savvy suburbanites in the leafy communities west of Portland. The Columbia River snakes along a border with Washington State, from Portland to a deepwater port at Astoria on the Pacific Coast. Southwest of the Portland area, the district traces part of the Willamette River in Yamhill County.

In one of Oregon's biggest changes during decennial redistricting, legislators removed downtown Portland from the 1st in exchange for more residential communities northwest of the city, giving the district a more suburban and less liberal character. The district's clout is now firmly held by Washington County, where population growth has been among the highest statewide since 2000. Beaverton in particular experienced an influx of immigrants — the city is 10 percent Asian and 16 percent Hispanic.

The 1st takes in the Pearl District north of downtown Portland. Warehouses have been turned into galleries, offices and condos. The corridor through Beaverton to Hillsboro has long been home to computer and electronics firms, developing satellite communities into full-fledged cities. Although the state's technology sector has been affected by economic downturns, it is rebounding — Intel, a major employer, has begun adding jobs. Beaverton is home to the world headquarters of sports apparel giant Nike.

Logging and fishing are key outside of Portland's orbit. Coastal tourism is a draw to the small towns in the northwest, while orchards and vineyards of the Northern Willamette Valley region are further south. To the southwest is the Grand Ronde American Indian reservation and casino.

Democrats have dominated in northern Oregon, although the loss of downtown Portland, one of the most liberal cities in the country, might make the 1st District more competitive. The rural farmland of Yamhill County is the district's only conservative outpost, and the 1st gave Barack Obama 57 percent of its vote in the 2012 presidential election.

Major Industry

Electronics, computer manufacturing, wine and agriculture production

Cities

Portland (pt.), Hillsboro, Beaverton, Tigard

Notable

The famous Powell's City of Books, the chain's headquarters with more than 1 million books, is on the north side of Burnside Street in the Pearl District.

Rep. Greg Walden (R)

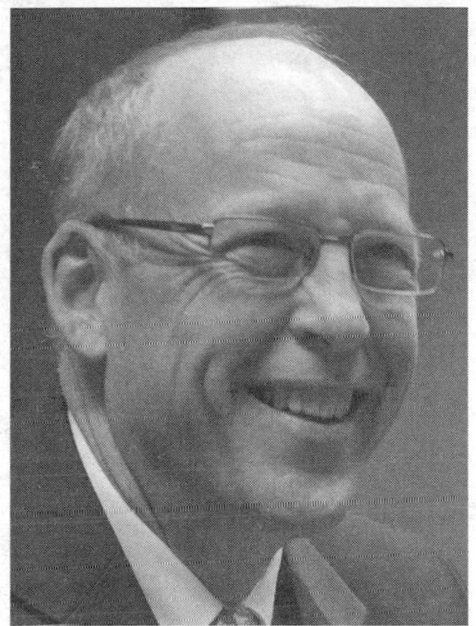

Capitol Office
225-6730
walden.house.gov
2182 Rayburn Bldg. 20515-3702; fax 225-5774

Committees
Energy & Commerce
(Communications & Technology - Chairman)

Residence
Hood River

Born
Jan. 10, 1957; The Dalles, Ore.

Religion
Episcopalian

Family
Wife, Mylene Walden; two children (one deceased)

Education
U. of Alaska, attended 1974-75; U. of Oregon, B.S. 1981 (journalism)

Career
Radio station owner; congressional aide

Political Highlights
Ore. House, 1989-95 (majority leader, 1991-93); Ore. Senate, 1995-97 (assistant majority leader, 1995-97)

ELECTION RESULTS

2012 GENERAL		
Greg Walden (R)	228,043	68.6%
Joyce B. Segers (D)	96,741	29.1%
Joe Tabor (LIBERT)	7,025	2.1%
2012 PRIMARY		
Greg Walden (R)	77,498	99.3%
2010 GENERAL		
Greg Walden (R)	206,245	73.9%
Joyce B. Segers (D)	72,173	25.9%

Previous Winning Percentages
2008 (70%); 2006 (67%); 2004 (72%); 2002 (72%); 2000 (74%); 1998 (61%)

Elected 1998; 8th term

House Republicans put Walden in charge of their campaign operations, ending whatever claim he had to political obscurity. His reputation for being thoughtful and unflappable has helped him flourish in a conservative party despite his relative moderation.

In the 113th Congress (2013-14), Walden is the chairman of the National Republican Congressional Committee, after serving four years as the deputy of his close friend, Pete Sessions of Texas. "Pete's been this transformational figure ... transforming this organization into something it's never been before," Walden said in late 2012. "My goal is to build on that foundation." Walden — an Eagle Scout, like Sessions — said he believes in "leaving your campsite better than you find it."

His strategy is to continue the member-oriented, metric-driven model the NRCC adopted after tough elections in 2006 and 2008. It often requires candidates to meet organizational and fundraising benchmarks when receiving assistance. "Giving more members more responsibility has helped GOP lawmakers have a sense of ownership and connection to the NRCC," he said.

At a GOP retreat in early 2013, he said it was also important to improve minority outreach and communications. "We recognize that Republicans have good answers," he said. "We just have bad communications in many cases." That is Walden's wheelhouse — a former congressional press secretary, he is known as an able and affable messenger who can bridge differences among GOP factions. (He associates with the moderate Main Street Partnership.)

His rise was portended by the attention he received from GOP leaders. He was on the NRCC and serving as a deputy whip when Minority Leader John A. Boehner named him chairman of the Republican leadership in February 2010. Watchers outside Congress were puzzled by the revival of that dormant position — especially for someone little-known outside his district — but it confirmed Walden's status as a trusted party man.

Walden has a seat on the Energy and Commerce Committee, and since 2011 he has chaired its Subcommittee on Communications and Technology.

The full committee quickly moved his 2011 measure to nullify new Federal Communications Commission rules governing how broadband providers allow content to move through their networks — aka "network neutrality" regulations. Walden contends that the FCC lacks the authority to institute such rules. The measure died in the Senate, but Walden continues to oppose most attempts at imposing regulations regarding the Internet.

Walden and his ranking member, California Democrat Anna G. Eshoo, agree on the need for some rearrangement of how broadcast spectrum is allocated. A 2012 law included provisions Walden helped negotiate with Senate counterparts to set aside part of the spectrum for a public safety network; it also allows current license holders to voluntarily put their rights up for auction.

Walden is a congressional ally of traditional over-the-air broadcasters. He earned a degree in journalism from the University of Oregon and worked at his father's radio station in Hood River as both a disc jockey and a talk show host. He and his wife later bought the business, and their company, Columbia Gorge Broadcasters Inc., operated five radio stations.

Although he now heads a highly partisan organization, Walden has good relations with Democrats. In an interview with the Mail Tribune of Medford, Ore., he said Congress and the White House need to work in a more collegial fashion. "Not only are people hoping we will work together, but they are expecting it and they deserve it," he said. "This isn't about changing core values or compromising principles, this is about building better personal relations with each other, seeing the world through another person's eyes."

Bipartisanship is a necessity when Walden wants help from the Oregon congressional delegation, as he is its only Republican. Representing a district that includes all or part of 10 national forests, he shares his constituents' dislike of federal intrusion into land use and environmental management. But he aims for bipartisan solutions for limiting wildfires and helping rural counties hurt by cutbacks in logging.

In 2009, he was one of 38 Republicans who joined the majority of Democrats to pass a land conservation bill designating millions of acres in nine states for preservation. Walden helped ensure that the measure protected a vast swath in the Mount Hood National Forest. At the signing ceremony, Walden handed President Barack Obama a letter urging him to allow more timber to be cut in national forests to prevent future fires.

In 2003, he worked with Oregon Democratic Sen. Ron Wyden to win enactment of a "healthy forests" law that reversed decades of policy and authorized logging and other steps to thin forests.

And in the 113th Congress, he is continuing to push for creation of a public trust to manage almost 1.5 million acres of Oregon forests. It would have the job of accelerating timber production and protecting old-growth trees, and the generated revenue would fund local services in the affected counties. Walden devised the plan in the 112th Congress with Democrats Peter A. DeFazio and Kurt Schrader. They got a hearing on their bill in April 2013.

He has adopted a middle-ground position on abortion. He opposes federal funding for abortions and voted to outlaw a procedure that opponents call "partial birth" abortion. But he doesn't support a reversal of the Supreme Court's 1973 Roe v. Wade decision. He says his views on the issue were shaped when he and his wife considered but rejected an abortion when the child she was carrying was diagnosed with a congenital heart defect. The baby boy was born prematurely and died.

Walden was raised on an 80-acre cherry orchard property in The Dalles, east of Portland. His father served in the Oregon legislature and his mother volunteered for the Red Cross. He worked as an aide to Republican Rep. Denny Smith for five years in the 1980s, before serving eight years in the state legislature, including three as House majority leader and two as assistant Senate majority leader.

Republican Bob Smith decided to retire in 1998, and Walden easily bested Democrat Kevin M. Campbell, a former county judge, in the race to succeed him. In a state that eschews political polarization (the tea party is virtually absent), Walden seldom expects serious opposition in his re-elections.

He defeated Democrat Joyce B. Segers by almost 40 points in 2012.

Key Votes

2012	
Extend a Social Security payroll tax cut and unemployment benefits	YES
Ease securities rules to expand small-business access to capital	YES
Extend for one year subsidized student loan interest rates financed by a cut in health care spending	YES
Cite Attorney General Eric H. Holder Jr. for contempt of Congress	YES
Create a visa program for foreign graduates in high-tech fields	YES
Extend most Bush-era income tax rates while allowing rates for top-bracket earners to rise (Jan. 1, 2013)	YES
2011	
Strike funding for F-35 alternative engine	YES
Prevent EPA from regulating greenhouse gas emissions to address climate change	YES
Extend certain provisions of Patriot Act for four years	YES
Declare opposition to use of ground troops in Libya	YES
Overhaul patent law	YES
Pass compromise debt limit increase plan and establish future spending limits	YES
Allow consideration of measures to implement three trade agreements	YES

CQ Vote Studies

	PARTY UNITY		PRESIDENTIAL SUPPORT	
	SUPPORT	OPPOSE	SUPPORT	OPPOSE
2012	92%	8%	16%	84%
2011	91%	9%	29%	71%
2010	93%	7%	33%	67%
2009	83%	17%	44%	56%
2008	93%	7%	63%	37%

Interest Groups

	AFL-CIO	ADA	CCUS	ACU
2012	29%	0%	100%	72%
2011	21%	15%	100%	68%
2010	0%	0%	88%	96%
2009	25%	15%	86%	80%
2008	20%	30%	89%	75%

Oregon 2

East — Bend; Medford

The rural and rugged 2nd is Oregon's most reliably Republican district. Covering the state's eastern two-thirds, the district encompasses 19 whole counties and part of a 20th. The federal government owns most of the forested land, primarily east of the Cascade Mountains in a dry region known for agriculture and low-income communities. The 2nd has been hit by the housing crash and has some of the state's highest unemployment rates.

Technology firms, more concentrated in the "Silicon Forest" west of Portland, are expanding into rural areas. High-tech data centers are among the newest, attracted by relatively low property taxes and cheap hydropower to run massive server farms. The 2nd is already home to three facilities for the Internet's biggest names: Google in The Dalles, Facebook in Prineville and Amazon in Morrow County. Although the farms are not big employers, they do provide a revenue bump for the region.

Agricultural counties are home to proportionally large populations of Hispanic residents. Umatilla is the district's largest farming county and the state's second-most productive, ranking No. 1 for wheat and potatoes. Casinos on tribal reservations have also boosted economies. Umatilla is also notorious for its role in the statewide crystal meth industry.

Unlike elsewhere in the state, counties in the 2nd District have experienced population declines over the past 10 years. Deschutes County had the district's largest population increase, coinciding with the housing boom in Bend, which has since gone bust. Bend's small-scale aerospace manufacturing industry has wobbled in recent years.

The 2nd consistently backs Republicans — in the 2012 presidential race, the 13 best counties by percentage statewide for GOP nominee Mitt Romney were in the 2nd. Hood River County, which abuts the 3rd District's liberal enclave of Multnomah County, backed Barack Obama in 2012; Wasco County is competitive as well. Both counties have gotten an influx of liberal urbanites from the northwest looking for quiet country living.

Major Industry
Agriculture, forestry, data processing, tourism

Cities
Bend, Medford, Ashland

Notable
Obsidian, crystal, agate and geodes lure rockhounds to Crook County.

Rep. Earl Blumenauer (D)

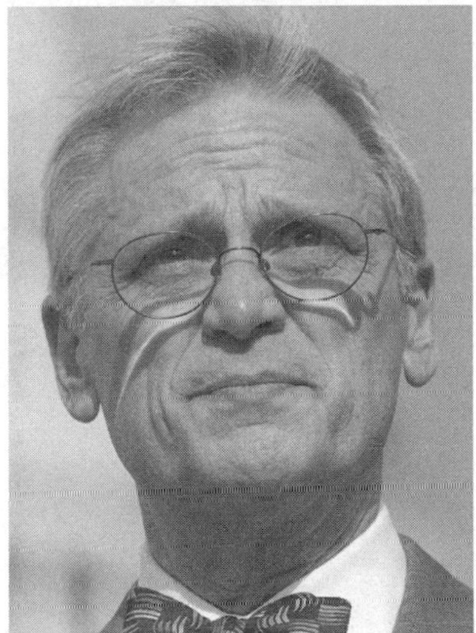

Capitol Office
225-4811
blumenauer.house.gov
1111 Longworth Bldg. 20515-3703; fax 225-8941

Committees
Budget
Ways & Means

Residence
Portland

Born
Aug. 16, 1948; Portland, Ore.

Religion
Unspecified

Family
Wife, Margaret Kirkpatrick; two children, two stepchildren

Education
Lewis & Clark College, B.A. 1970 (political science), J.D. 1976

Career
None

Political Highlights
Ore. House, 1973-77; Multnomah County Commission, 1978-86; candidate for Portland City Council, 1980; Portland City Council, 1986-96; candidate for mayor of Portland, 1992

ELECTION RESULTS

2012 GENERAL		
Earl Blumenauer (D)	264,979	74.5%
Ronald Green (R)	70,325	19.8%
Woodrow Broadnax (PACGRN)	13,159	3.7%
Michael Cline (LIBERT)	6,640	1.9%
2012 PRIMARY		
Earl Blumenauer (D)	84,628	98.9%
write-ins (D)	969	1.1%
2010 GENERAL		
Earl Blumenauer (D)	193,104	70.0%
Delia Lopez (R)	67,714	24.6%
Jeffrey T. Lawrence (LIBERT)	8,380	3.0%
Michael Meo (PACGRN)	6,197	2.2%

Previous Winning Percentages
2008 (75%); 2006 (73%); 2004 (71%); 2002 (67%); 2000 (67%); 1998 (84%); 1996 (67%); 1996 Special Election (70%)

Elected 1996; 9th full term

Blumenauer has plans to move the world, and his considerable political skills serve as a lever. He describes his 40-year career, organized in the framework of "livable communities," as creating a place to stand.

A lot of his work goes beyond Congress. Blumenauer has national stature (among wonks, at least) as a polished and optimistic spokesman for renewable energy, smart growth, environmentalism and multi-modal transportation systems. Many of his weekends are spent advising municipalities on how to finance such things as transit systems. He has gained extensive practical knowledge of the development process as a state representative, a Portland official overseeing public works, and a congressman.

He is equally active in Washington, where he chairs the Democratic Livable Communities Task Force. Blumenauer keeps tabs on taxes, transportation, environmental regulation and anything else that conceivably could affect "livability" at the community level. His goal is to improve coordination among government, civic organizations and private entities on those issues while injecting conservationist principles into their discussions.

Most of his adult life has been spent as a public official, and he has both a strategy and a philosophy for politics. The strategy dates to the early 1970s, when he was a leader in the successful movement to lower the voting age to 18. Though he has his share of liberal initiatives, Blumenauer seeks out what he calls "common-sense, high-impact, low-cost" proposals that attract nontraditional alliances — for example, the coalition supporting a lower voting age included Republicans, Democrats, labor, business and education groups. The relationships established through those efforts facilitate future work on bigger issues: "Everything is long-term, and nothing is small," he says.

His political philosophy centers on being "all about taking advantage of opportunities." In the 112th Congress (2011-12), he saw opportunity everywhere. "All these things that we've been talking about since I've been in Congress and before, they all come crashing down this decade," he said. "Health care, transportation funding, defense, the leaky tax system that's inefficient and expensive. You're not gonna get through another decade."

Blumenauer was disappointed by the output of the 112th Congress. He was one of 16 House Democrats to vote against the "fiscal cliff" package of tax provisions in January 2013. It "represents absolutely the least we could have done under these circumstances and tragically institutionalizes for the next Congress the madness of short-term frenzy around artificial deadlines," he said. He also panned a two-year reauthorization of surface transportation programs enacted in 2012, saying it had "no national vision, no national goals."

But Blumenauer has more opportunities in the 113th Congress (2013-14). He works on the tax system, health care and trade as a member of the Ways and Means Committee. He maintains that the American public is willing to pay more if tax code changes are done fairly, especially if changes are coupled with a decrease in the complexity of the tax code. He would use boosts in revenue to, among other things, provide a more stable Medicare payment system for physicians.

Blumenauer has worked on health care before — in 2009, he wrote language in the House-passed health care overhaul allowing Medicare to cover end-of-life consultations. "I'm the death-panel guy," he jokes, referring to the slang Alaska Gov. Sarah Palin hung on the provision, which was later removed from the bill. He still sees room for bipartisan agreement on the issue.

Blumenauer is more receptive to free trade than many Democrats; Portland is a major hub. But he touts livability goals when working on the issue. A rewrite of the tax code, he said, should scrub the tariff schedule in order to make consumer goods such as Nike shoes more affordable.

He is happy to use the tax code to promote his clean-energy and transportation goals. In 2011, he worked with Washington Republican Dave Reichert in an attempt to extend credits for renewable-energy production through 2016; earlier in the year, he was the lead House Democrat on a widely publicized bill to eliminate tax breaks for the oil and gas industry. He also continued his efforts to extend transit benefits to workers who commute by bicycle rather than use energy-demanding modes.

Though no longer on the Transportation and Infrastructure Committee, Blumenauer stays involved. "It is critical that transportation policy treat all modes of transportation equally," he wrote in Roll Call in 2011. In 2007, he successfully pressed to block rules that slanted transit funding to municipalities that rely on buses; cities turning back to streetcars, such as Portland, were losing out, he said. He is well-known as the founder of the Bicycle Caucus—he bikes everywhere, and the bicycle pins on his jackets are as distinctive as his bow ties. Over the course of his House career he has steered millions of dollars to his district for bike trails, pedestrian facilities and mass-transit systems.

He is not alone in thinking that a new revenue stream for infrastructure is needed to replace the federal gasoline tax. He says the way to go is a tax based on how far each driver travels, and that Oregon's pilot program to do so has shown promise.

Blumenauer is socially liberal. He and Colorado Democrat Jared Polis introduced bills in 2013 that they touted as creating a framework for the de-criminalization and taxation of marijuana under federal law.

Blumenauer grew up in Portland, the older of two sons. His father was in construction and his mother worked in a bank. He always had an interest in civic affairs, "but it really galvanized for me in college," he said, "where I was intensively studying United States foreign policy and could clearly see that our leaders were not squaring with us on the war in Vietnam."

That led directly to his campaign for lowering the voting age, and the political connections he made inspired him to run for the Oregon House at age 24. A few years later, he switched over to the Multnomah County Commission, then spent 10 years on the Portland City Council. His public-works portfolio came with that job, and it gave him "a sense of how you actually fashion a community consensus and implement it."

He ran unsuccessfully for mayor of Portland in 1992, but Democrat Ron Wyden vacated a House seat after winning a special election to the Senate in 1996. Blumenauer easily took the primary and special election to replace Wyden, and he has cruised to re-election ever since.

Key Votes

2012	
Extend a Social Security payroll tax cut and unemployment benefits	YES
Ease securities rules to expand small-business access to capital	YES
Extend for one year subsidized student loan interest rates financed by a cut in health care spending	?
Cite Attorney General Eric H. Holder Jr. for contempt of Congress	NO
Create a visa program for foreign graduates in high-tech fields	YES
Extend most Bush-era income tax rates while allowing rates for top-bracket earners to rise (Jan. 1, 2013)	NO
2011	
Strike funding for F-35 alternative engine	YES
Prevent EPA from regulating greenhouse gas emissions to address climate change	NO
Extend certain provisions of Patriot Act for four years	NO
Declare opposition to use of ground troops in Libya	NO
Overhaul patent law	YES
Pass compromise debt limit increase plan and establish future spending limits	NO
Allow consideration of measures to implement three trade agreements	YES

CQ Vote Studies

	Party Unity		Presidential Support	
	SUPPORT	OPPOSE	SUPPORT	OPPOSE
2012	97%	3%	89%	11%
2011	95%	5%	89%	11%
2010	98%	2%	88%	12%
2009	99%	1%	93%	7%
2008	98%	2%	15%	85%

Interest Groups

	AFL-CIO	ADA	CCUS	ACU
2012	95%	85%	45%	0%
2011	93%	80%	27%	4%
2010	100%	100%	0%	5%
2009	95%	90%	40%	0%
2008	100%	95%	53%	12%

Oregon 3

Portland and eastern suburbs

Split by the Willamette River, the city of Portland has two personalities. The east still depends on blue-collar jobs, while computers and cappuccino fuel the west. Redistricting following the 2010 census pushed the borders of the 3rd westward to include more of the city, including all of eco-friendly and liberal downtown Portland, making it the state's most urban and reliably Democratic district. The 3rd lost suburbs northwest of Portland while expanding into sparsely populated northern Clackamas County.

Portland was the first U.S. city to enact a comprehensive plan to reduce carbon emissions and has pushed several building programs focused on sustainability. Known as a model of urban planning, the city has set growth boundaries to limit sprawl and invested in light rail and a network of bicycle paths to reduce traffic. This emphasis on sustainability has lured "green" architecture firms and alternative-energy startups.

The district includes major colleges and universities, including the Oregon Health & Science University, Portland State University, Reed College and Lewis & Clark College.

The city's older economic driver, the namesake Port of Portland, is the nation's largest shipper of wheat; international trade issues are important to the 3rd. It is also home to the headquarters of Adidas America, part of a cluster of sportswear design and manufacturing firms in the region.

The redrawn 3rd is racially diverse and the largest minority population is Hispanic (11 percent); about 19 percent of Portland's population speaks a language other than English at home. With the addition of downtown and the loss of the northwestern suburbs, the 3rd has gained many reliably liberal voters in Multnomah County, which overwhelms the more conservative lean in Clackamas County. Portland, and Multnomah County overall, are dominated by Democrats: Primaries are the real contests here.

Major Industry
Distribution, higher education, health care, technology, service

Cities
Portland (pt.), Gresham

Notable
"Portlandia," the satirical television show that lampoons the city's über-liberal hipster culture, gets its name from a statue at the entrance to the Portland Building on Fifth Avenue; Soccer's Timbers play at Jeld-Wen Field in Portland's Goose Hollow neighborhood.

Rep. Peter A. DeFazio (D)

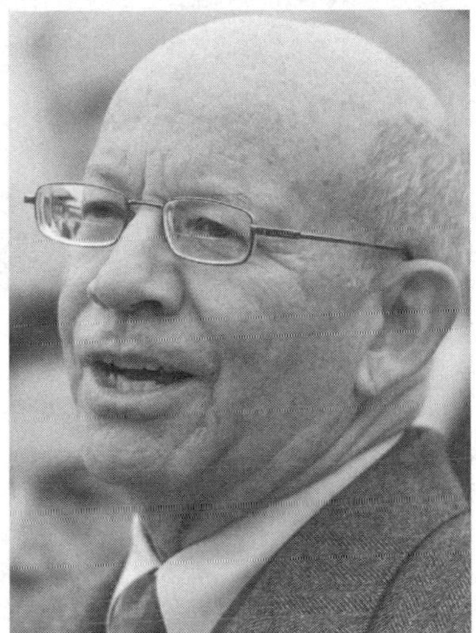

Capitol Office
225-6416
defazio.house.gov
2134 Rayburn Bldg. 20515-3704; fax 226-3493

Committees
Natural Resources
Transportation & Infrastructure

Residence
Springfield

Born
May 27, 1947; Needham, Mass.

Religion
Roman Catholic

Family
Wife, Myrnie L. Daut

Education
Tufts U., B.A. 1969 (economics & political science); U. of Oregon, attended 1969-71 (international studies), M.S. 1977 (public administration & gerontology)

Military
Air Force, 1967-71

Career
Congressional aide; state senior citizens service program director

Political Highlights
Lane County Commission, 1982-86; sought Democratic nomination for U.S. Senate (special election), 1996

ELECTION RESULTS

2012 GENERAL

Peter A. DeFazio (D)	212,866	59.1%
Art Robinson (R)	140,549	39.0%
Chuck Huntting (LIBERT)	6,205	1.7%

2012 PRIMARY

Peter A. DeFazio (D)	69,864	89.9%
Matthew L. Robinson (D)	7,665	9.9%

Previous Winning Percentages
2010 (55%); 2008 (82%); 2006 (62%); 2004 (61%); 2002 (64%); 2000 (68%); 1998 (70%); 1996 (66%); 1994 (67%); 1992 (71%); 1990 (86%); 1988 (72%); 1986 (54%)

Elected 1986; 14th term

A persistent populist progressive, DeFazio has a willful and sarcastic style that has earned him a reputation for being one of the House's most aggressive debaters. He balances generally liberal political beliefs with an insistence on better management of the national debt.

DeFazio is a leading Democratic proponent of a balanced-budget amendment to the Constitution. He was one of 72 House Democrats to vote for such a proposal in 1995, and one of 25 in 2011. He and Dave Loebsack of Iowa were the only members of the liberal Congressional Progressive Caucus to vote "yes" in 2011.

His preferred means for achieving balance, however, line up with the plans of most Democrats. DeFazio wants higher tax rates on the upper-income brackets and the elimination of deductions or "loopholes" used by the wealthy. He was one of 16 House Democrats to vote against the January 2013 "fiscal cliff" deal, which increased income tax rates only on earnings over $400,000 and avoided dramatic increases to the estate tax. He said it didn't increase revenue enough and would put Democrats in a tough spot during future fiscal negotiations.

He has proposed a tax on trades of financial securities, which he says would raise a lot of money and discourage "high-frequency trading" and market speculation. "The first step on the long path to recovery happens when we rein in the excessive speculative activity that has destabilized our financial system," he said in 2011.

DeFazio is trained as a gerontologist, and he puts his fiscal concerns in the context of sustaining entitlement programs for the elderly. "If we want to save Social Security and Medicare, and if we want to make the necessary investments that will put people back to work, we must get our debt and deficit under control," he said. In the 113th Congress (2013-14), he reintroduced a package of bills that would increase the amount high earners pay in Social Security taxes and prohibit the Treasury from borrowing from the Social Security Trust Fund to cover unrelated costs.

DeFazio threatened to vote against the 2010 health care overhaul until language was included to address regional disparities in Medicare reimbursement rates for doctors. It was not the first time that he took issue with one of President Barack Obama's major initiatives. He opposed the 2009 economic stimulus package on the grounds that it prioritized temporary relief in the form of tax cuts over long-term relief in infrastructure spending.

Obama noticed. During a subsequent meeting with House Democrats on the White House's 2010 budget proposal, DeFazio asked the president about increasing infrastructure spending. Obama responded, "I know you think we need more for that because you voted against [the stimulus]. Don't think we're not keeping score, brother." A satisfied DeFazio supported the budget. "At least I got his attention," he later said.

As the 113th Congress began, DeFazio was No. 12 in seniority among House Democrats. He was also the No. 2 Democrat on both the Natural Resources Committee and the Transportation and Infrastructure Committee. If Edward J. Markey of Massachusetts wins a special election to the Senate in June 2013, DeFazio has a chance of taking his place as the top Democrat on the Natural Resources Committee within days of the publication of this book.

He opened the 113th as the top Democrat on the Transportation panel's Highways and Transit Subcommittee — he was the chairman from 2007 through 2010, and he became the ranking member in 2011. DeFazio has had a hand in several multibillion-dollar surface transportation reauthorization bills and, through those bills, directing funds to his district.

He was a House-Senate conferee on the two-year highway bill enacted in 2012. During a heated late-night debate on the measure, Georgia Republican Rep. Paul Broun moved to instruct the conferees to cut roughly $17 billion from infrastructure spending. DeFazio asked Broun, "Why do you hate this country so much?" Broun later said that DeFazio was "not man enough" to apologize.

For several terms, DeFazio served on the Homeland Security Committee, which handles some transportation concerns. He counts among his most important accomplishments a successful push in a post-Sept. 11 aviation and transportation security measure to federalize airport security screening and offer commercial pilots the option to be certified and armed.

DeFazio's seat on Natural Resources puts him in an important but tricky position on forest issues. He has to juggle the interests of logging — one of his district's most vital and vulnerable industries — and environmentalists. He notes that he has been blasted, on a case-by-case basis, by both the timber industry and environmentalists. The committee held an April 2013 hearing on a forest management plan for huge swaths of Oregon devised by DeFazio, fellow Democrat Kurt Schrader and Republican Greg Walden. It would create a public trust with the job of accelerating timber production and protecting old-growth trees. Revenue would fund local services in the affected counties.

DeFazio is a particularly outspoken critic of free-trade agreements, arguing that they have led to "the withering of the U.S. manufacturing base" and "the erosion of U.S. sovereignty." He was a leading opponent of 2011 trade agreements with South Korea, Panama and Colombia.

DeFazio grew up in Massachusetts. His first taste of politics came as a boy at the knee of his great-uncle, a classic Boston pol who followed the word Republican with a Boston-accented epithet so often that young DeFazio thought it was one word: "Republicanbastuhd."

After graduating from Tufts University outside Boston, DeFazio attended graduate school at the University of Oregon. While a student there, he established an employment program for seniors that is still in existence. After earning his graduate degree, he ran a senior citizens' program for a time, then landed a job as a specialist on elder issues with Oregon Democratic Rep. James Weaver, a hot-tempered populist.

In 1982, DeFazio struck out on his own, getting elected to the Lane County Commission. When Weaver announced he would not seek re-election in 1986, DeFazio stepped in. Casting himself as heir to Weaver's populist mantle, he squeaked by in the primary and then won the seat with 54 percent of the vote.

A strong Republican year in 2010 saw him take less than 55 percent of the vote against Art Robinson, but he beat Robinson by 20 points in 2012.

Key Votes

2012	
Extend a Social Security payroll tax cut and unemployment benefits	NO
Ease securities rules to expand small-business access to capital	YES
Extend for one year subsidized student loan interest rates financed by a cut in health care spending	NO
Cite Attorney General Eric H. Holder Jr. for contempt of Congress	NO
Create a visa program for foreign graduates in high-tech fields	YES
Extend most Bush-era income tax rates while allowing rates for top-bracket earners to rise (Jan. 1, 2013)	NO
2011	
Strike funding for F-35 alternative engine	YES
Prevent EPA from regulating greenhouse gas emissions to address climate change	NO
Extend certain provisions of Patriot Act for four years	NO
Declare opposition to use of ground troops in Libya	YES
Overhaul patent law	NO
Pass compromise debt limit increase plan and establish future spending limits	NO
Allow consideration of measures to implement three trade agreements	NO

CQ Vote Studies

	PARTY UNITY		PRESIDENTIAL SUPPORT	
	SUPPORT	OPPOSE	SUPPORT	OPPOSE
2012	91%	9%	77%	23%
2011	89%	11%	67%	33%
2010	95%	5%	85%	15%
2009	97%	3%	90%	10%
2008	93%	7%	13%	87%

Interest Groups

	AFL-CIO	ADA	CCUS	ACU
2012	95%	90%	42%	4%
2011	97%	80%	25%	12%
2010	93%	95%	13%	0%
2009	95%	95%	40%	12%
2008	100%	90%	50%	20%

Oregon 4

Southwest — Eugene, Springfield, Corvallis

The 4th District covers the southern half of Oregon's Pacific coastline and crosses Interstate 5 into the Cascade Mountains. It is home to the liberal college towns of Corvallis and Eugene, as well as conservative areas of southwestern Oregon and communities left struggling since the timber industry's decline. The economy depends on natural resources: Environmentalists, loggers and fishermen combine in a potentially combustible mix.

Several decades of changing regulations and subsidies have hurt the timber counties of Coos, Curry, Josephine and Douglas; local officials have renewed calls to reopen federal land for logging. Coastal areas fall back on tourism to shore up the economy, and a revamped regional freight rail has connected Coos with Oregon's central shipping hubs. Wood products remain the most profitable industry, although the sector's presence has shrunk. Livestock, dairy, fishing and wine grape harvests are also important. As jobs have left timber and fishing areas, so have the young people. Curry County has twice the statewide average of residents over the age of 65.

In contrast to the southern counties is liberal Lane County, home to Eugene, the University of Oregon and more than 24,000 students. Eugene's youthful liberalism and environmental conservationism sometimes clash with the district's rural industrial interests. Eugene's technology industry has shrunk as companies have closed or outsourced, but smaller companies like Symantec remain nearby. Throughout the district, incomes are below the state average, even in the more-educated Eugene and Corvallis.

Redistricting after the 2010 census added a bigger chunk of liberal-leaning Benton County and the entirety of Corvallis — home of Oregon State University — to the 4th. Lane County backs liberal candidates and is three times larger in population than either of the next two most-populous counties. Much of the rest of the district has supported Republican presidential candidates for the past decade.

Major Industry
Timber, agriculture, higher education, technology

Cities
Eugene, Springfield, Corvallis, Albany

Notable
The International Port of Coos Bay is the world's largest forest products shipping port.

Rep. Kurt Schrader (D)

Capitol Office
225-5711
schrader.house.gov
108 Cannon Bldg. 20515-3705; fax 225-5699

Committees
Agriculture
Budget
Small Business

Residence
Canby

Born
Oct. 19, 1951; Bridgeport, Conn.

Religion
Episcopalian

Family
Divorced; five children

Education
Cornell U., B.A. 1973 (government), U. of Illinois, B.S. 1975 (veterinary medicine), D.V.M. 1977

Career
Veterinarian; farmer

Political Highlights
Democratic nominee for Ore. House, 1994; Ore. House, 1997-2003; Ore. Senate, 2003-08

ELECTION RESULTS

2012 GENERAL		
Kurt Schrader (D)	177,229	54.0%
Fred Thompson (R)	139,223	42.4%
Christina Jean Lugo (PACGRN)	7,516	2.3%
Raymond Baldwin (CNSTP)	3,600	1.1%
2012 PRIMARY		
Kurt Schrader (D)	51,652	98.5%
write-ins (D)	805	1.5%
2010 GENERAL		
Kurt Schrader (D)	145,319	51.2%
Scott Bruun (R)	130,313	46.0%
Christina Jean Lugo (PACGRN)	7,557	2.7%

Previous Winning Percentages
2008 (54%)

Elected 2008; 3rd term

Schrader, a veterinarian, is not quite a cowboy — but from his salty and straight-talking demeanor, you can see why they'd trust him with their horses. His fiscal conservatism and business-minded proposals position him as one of the more independent House Democrats.

He has no patience for the work environment in Washington. "The issues are not as overwhelming as the lack of bipartisanship," Schrader said. He blames the leadership of both parties for squashing cooperative efforts, and he has worked with colleagues of both parties "to reform how Congress does things, because we're upset and irritated and mad as hell."

Fiscal discourse in the 112th Congress (2011-12) was especially rankling, with neither party leveling with voters on the demographics driving the nation's deficits, he said in spring 2012: "We pretend people are stupid, and I just don't think people are stupid. They may be uninformed, but if you give them some information, they generally make good decisions. They elected me twice."

His spending priorities line up with those of most Democrats, but Schrader has been a fiscal hawk since his time in the Oregon Legislature. He belongs to the Blue Dog Coalition, and in the 113th Congress (2013-14) he is its co-chairman for communications and outreach. Without overhauls of Medicare and the tax code, "this country is doomed to be like Greece in another seven, eight years," he said. In early 2012 he co-sponsored a budget based on the work of the 2010 White House fiscal commission known as Simpson-Bowles, and he wants deficits cut by at least $4 trillion over a decade through a mix of spending cuts and increased revenues. Bold actions are necessary, Schrader said, to show businesses that "this is the best place in the world to invest." He joined the Budget Committee in 2013.

He also sits on the Small Business and Agriculture committees, which line up with his professional background; in addition to owning his own veterinary practice, he also ran an organic fruit and vegetable farm (most of it is now leased to neighbors).

Schrader's interest in tax changes ties directly to his work on Small Business. His priority is getting rid of "all the goddamn tax breaks" while lowering rates for businesses and individuals — he says any business would take that trade.

Schrader has introduced bills to facilitate the granting of federal contracts to small businesses and to encourage credit unions to lend to small businesses. The fiscal 2013 defense policy law includes a provision by Schrader and Washington Republican Jaime Herrera Beutler to increase the role of Small Business Administration advocates as the government prepares to open a contract for bidding.

On the Agriculture Committee, he wants to end "indefensible 1930s concepts" like direct payments to farmers, believing that they sour public perceptions of the industry. "Agriculture gets a bad rap as this huge agribusiness that enslaves poor workers and pollutes the environment for their own evil, ill-gotten corporate gain," he said. "I think most farmers are down-home, regular family guys" — essentially, small businessmen.

The key to keeping farms humming, he says, is to out-innovate foreign competitors. Schrader wants robust federal investment in agricultural research, noting that farming commissions are likely to multiply the benefits by matching federal dollars with their own. He likes that notion for any industry, believing every grant program should require "skin in the game" from recipients. In 2013, Schrader became the top Democrat on the Horticulture, Research, Biotechnology and Foreign Agriculture Subcommittee.

He has a colorful distaste for government forestry policies, which the Agriculture Committee considers. Management and use of federal forest lands has been awful, he says. "The federal government's attitude is that of libertarianism. ... Let it all burn up, get eaten up by bugs and pests, and slowly but surely what used to be great carbon sink will sink into the abyss of a mossy swamp."

Along with Democrat Peter A. DeFazio and Republican Greg Walden, Schrader has devised a plan to create a public trust to run almost 1.5 million acres of Oregon forests; it would be charged with accelerating timber production and protecting old-growth trees, and revenues would fund local services in the affected counties. Schrader said those opposing the land use are mired in the 1970s timber wars, "or frankly, some of the kids are believing the drivel that comes out of some liberal establishment institution they go to school at, and they get misled."

He feels strongly that EPA bureaucrats are not responsive to the day-to-day needs of Americans, and he has called for mandatory analysis of the economic impact of new regulations. He voted for a 2009 measure to create a cap-and-trade system to regulate greenhouse gas emissions, but also supported a 2011 bill to keep the EPA from imposing greenhouse gas regulations.

Everyone else in Schrader's family is a conservative Republican. His early years were spent outside Philadelphia (he cheers for the city's sports teams), as his dad worked in nearby Delaware as a chemical plant engineer. They moved to Illinois in his teen years. Even as a kid, he was a "huge animal guy."

At Cornell University, he considered a few careers before settling on veterinary medicine, which he went on to study at the University of Illinois. He also hitchhiked all over the place, doing odd jobs and seeing huge swaths of the country. Schrader once raced a buddy to Alaska, with a six-pack of beer as the prize. He won. The Kent State shootings in 1971 raised his civic interest, and he credits Richard Nixon with making him a Democrat. He met his future wife at a Cornell zoology class, and they moved to Oregon in 1978.

His first public service gig was on a local planning commission: "No one wanted to be on it, so it was easy to get on." For 16 years, he worked on smart-growth development of his community. Schrader won a seat in the Oregon House on his second try in 1996 and moved to the state Senate in 2003.

When six-term Democratic Rep. Darlene Hooley announced she would retire at the end of the 110th Congress (2007-08), Schrader easily won a five-person primary. He won the general election by 16 points. Democrats had a rough year in 2010, but Schrader scored a 5-point win over state Rep. Scott Bruun. He beat a woefully funded Republican by more than 11 points in 2012.

Schrader tries to be a straight shooter in his spare time — he visits shooting ranges and competes in cowboy action shooting competitions.

Key Votes

2012	
Extend a Social Security payroll tax cut and unemployment benefits	NO
Ease securities rules to expand small-business access to capital	YES
Extend for one year subsidized student loan interest rates financed by a cut in health care spending	NO
Cite Attorney General Eric H. Holder Jr. for contempt of Congress	NO
Create a visa program for foreign graduates in high-tech fields	YES
Extend most Bush-era income tax rates while allowing rates for top-bracket earners to rise (Jan. 1, 2013)	NO
2011	
Strike funding for F-35 alternative engine	YES
Prevent EPA from regulating greenhouse gas emissions to address climate change	YES
Extend certain provisions of Patriot Act for four years	NO
Declare opposition to use of ground troops in Libya	YES
Overhaul patent law	YES
Pass compromise debt limit increase plan and establish future spending limits	YES
Allow consideration of measures to implement three trade agreements	YES

CQ Vote Studies

	PARTY UNITY		PRESIDENTIAL SUPPORT	
	SUPPORT	OPPOSE	SUPPORT	OPPOSE
2012	82%	18%	74%	26%
2011	76%	24%	71%	29%
2010	94%	6%	78%	22%
2009	95%	5%	92%	8%

Interest Groups

	AFL-CIO	ADA	CCUS	ACU
2012	81%	75%	58%	4%
2011	86%	65%	50%	8%
2010	86%	85%	13%	17%
2009	81%	80%	53%	8%

Oregon 5

Central Willamette Valley — Salem; southern Portland suburbs

Planted in the fertile soil of the Willamette Valley, the 5th has a strong agricultural heritage. Centered on Salem, the state capital, the 5th mixes midsize cities, some suburbs of Portland and farm communities.

Nestled between coastal mountains to the west and the Cascade Mountains to the east, the Willamette Valley is lined with dairy farms, orchards and the vineyards of the Willamette wine region. Acres of wheat fields stretch from Salem to the coast, providing hops for beer brewers, and food processing is a major industry in Salem. American Indian reservations dot the Lincoln County coast; the Spirit Mountain Casino is a major employer.

State government is the largest employer in Salem, which has a diverse workforce of white-collar professionals and technology manufacturing employees. Universities provide a draw for young people. A major T-Mobile call center in Salem has seen some post-recession growth; the city's solar manufacturers have largely weathered turmoil in the industry.

Seemingly minor changes to the 5th's borders following decennial remapping may, over time, result in shifts in the district's demographics. The 5th shed Corvallis, home to Oregon State University, in return for northern parts of Albany, mainly an agricultural and manufacturing town. The district no longer includes Portland's southern riverfront, except for a small bit of the city's southwestern corner and the Mt. Scott neighborhood. Another new addition is the blue-collar Portland suburb of Milwaukie.

The 5th is the state's most politically competitive district. The district lost some of its strongest Democratic areas to decennial remapping, including Corvallis and southwestern Portland. Republicans do well in Polk County, and Marion County, which includes Salem. Overall, the new 5th District gave Barack Obama 50 percent of its vote in the 2012 presidential contest.

Major Industry

Agriculture, timber, food processing, government, manufacturing

Cities

Portland (pt.), Salem, Lake Oswego, Keizer, Oregon City, West Linn

Notable

Dark Horse Comics, one of the first comic book publishers to give artists ownership of their creations, has its headquarters in Milwaukie.

PENNSYLVANIA

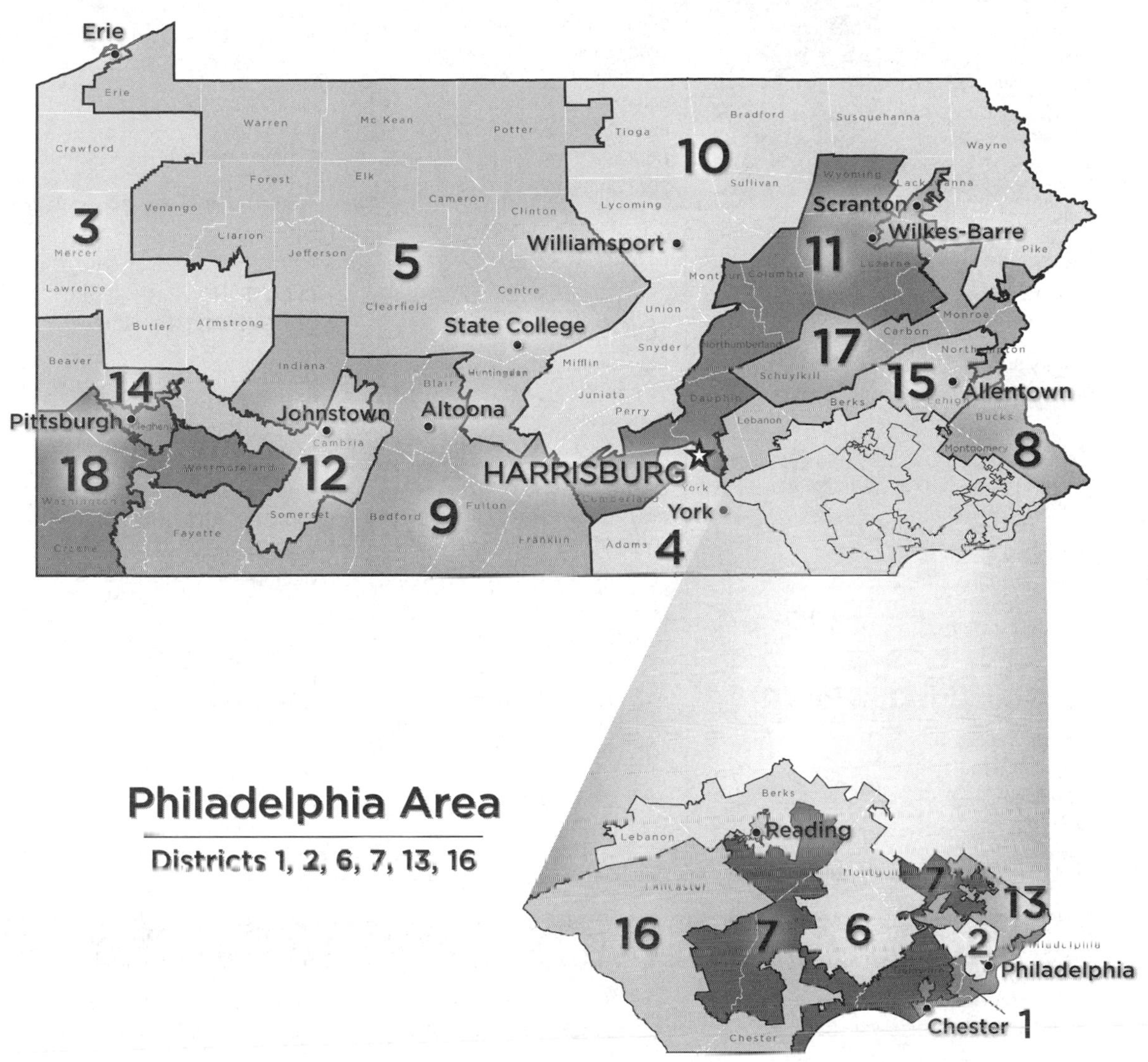

Gov. Tom Corbett (R)

First elected: 2010

Length of term: 4 years

Term expires: 1/15

Salary: $187,256

Phone: (717) 787-2500

Residence: Shaler Township

Born: June 17, 1949; Philadelphia, Pa.

Religion: Roman Catholic

Family: Wife, Susan Corbett; two children

Education: Lebanon Valley College, B.A. 1971 (political science); St. Mary's U. (Texas), J.D. 1975

Military Service: Pa. National Guard, 1971-84

Career: Lawyer; presidential and gubernatorial campaign aide; county prosecutor; teacher

Political highlights: Assistant U.S. attorney, 1980-83; Shaler Township Commission, 1988-89; U.S. attorney, 1989-93; Pa. attorney general, 1995-97, 2005-11

ELECTION RESULTS

2010 GENERAL

Tom Corbett (R)	2,172,763	54.5%
Dam Onorato (D)	1,814,788	45.5%

Lt. Gov. Jim Cawley (R)

First elected: 2010

Length of term: 4 years

Term expires: 1/15

Salary: $157,293

Phone: (717) 787-3300

LEGISLATURE

General Assembly: Year-round with recess

Senate: 50 members, 4-year terms

2013 ratios: 27 R, 23 D; 42 men, 8 women

Salary: $83,801

Phone: (717) 787-5920

House: 203 members, 2-year terms

2013 ratios: 111 R, 92 D; 166 men, 37 women

Salary: $83,801

Phone: (717) 787-2372

TERM LIMITS

Governor: 2 consecutive terms

Senate: No

House: No

URBAN STATISTICS

CITY	POPULATION
Philadelphia	1,526,006
Pittsburgh	305,704
Allentown	118,032
Erie	101,786
Reading	88,082

REGISTERED VOTERS

Democrat	50%
Republican	37%
Other	13%

POPULATION

2010 population	12,702,379
2000 population	12,281,054
1990 population	11,881,643
Percent change (2000-2010)	+3.4%
Rank among states (2010)	6
Median age	39.6
Born in state	75.2%
Foreign born	5.2%
Violent crime rate	381/100,000
Poverty level	12.5%
Federal workers	124,382
Military	5,215

ELECTIONS

STATE ELECTION OFFICIAL
(717) 787-5280

DEMOCRATIC PARTY
(717) 920-8470

REPUBLICAN PARTY
(717) 234-4901

MISCELLANEOUS

Web: www.pa.gov

Capital: Harrisburg

U.S. CONGRESS

Senate: 1 Democrat, 1 Republican

House: 13 Republicans, 5 Democrats

STATISTICS BY DISTRICT

District	2012 Vote for President: Obama	Romney	2008 Vote for President: Obama	McCain	Black	Asian	Hispanic	Median Income	Over 64	Under 20	College Education	Rural	Sq. Miles
1	82%	17%	79%	21%	34%	7%	16%	$35,702	11%	26%	22%	0%	78
2	90	9	91	9	59	5	6	33,543	13	25	32	0	74
3	43	56	46	52	5	1	2	44,092	16	25	23	41	3,851
4	41	57	45	54	8	2	6	54,291	15	25	25	23	1,518
5	41	57	47	51	2	2	2	43,583	16	23	21	56	10,711
6	48	51	53	46	4	4	5	69,570	14	27	41	11	860
7	49	50	51	48	6	4	3	73,638	16	26	39	11	863
8	49.3	49.4	53	46	4	4	4	71,404	15	25	35	10	707
9	36	63	41	58	3	1	2	42,277	18	24	17	47	5,730
10	38	60	42	56	3	1	4	46,590	17	24	20	65	8,378
11	45	54	47	52	5	1	5	49,085	16	24	21	35	3,356
12	41	58	45	54	3	1	1	53,080	18	23	29	25	2,163
13	66	33	65	34	18	8	11	56,222	14	26	32	0	155
14	68	31	67	32	22	3	2	37,307	16	22	27	<1	209
15	48	51	52	47	4	2	13	54,470	15	25	27	17	1,285
16	46	53	50	49	6	2	17	49,910	15	28	22	13	998
17	55	43	57	42	6	2	8	46,722	17	24	20	21	1,733
18	41	58	44	55	2	2	1	55,553	18	23	33	19	2,073
STATE	**52**	**47**	**55**	**44**	**11**	**3**	**6**	**50,228**	**16**	**25**	**27**	**22**	**44,743**
U.S.	**51**	**47**	**53**	**46**	**12**	**5**	**17**	**50,052**	**13**	**27**	**29**	**21**	**3,531,905**

Sen. Bob Casey (D)

Capitol Office
224-6324
casey.senate.gov
393 Russell Bldg. 20510-3804; fax 228-0604

Committees
Finance
(Fiscal Responsibility & Economic Growth - Chairman)
Foreign Relations
(Near Eastern & South & Central Asian Affairs - Chairman)
Health, Education, Labor & Pensions
(Employment & Workplace Safety - Chairman)
Special Aging
Joint Economic

Residence
Scranton

Born
April 13, 1960, Scranton, Pa.

Religion
Roman Catholic

Family
Wife, Terese Casey; four children

Education
College of the Holy Cross, A.B. 1982 (English); Catholic U. of America, J.D. 1988

Career
Lawyer; campaign aide

Political Highlights
Pa. auditor general, 1997-2005; sought Democratic nomination for governor, 2002; Pa. treasurer, 2005-07

ELECTION RESULTS

2012 GENERAL		
Bob Casey (D)	3,021,364	53.7%
Tom Smith (R)	2,509,132	44.6%
Rayburn Smith (LIBERT)	96,926	1.7%

2012 PRIMARY		
Bob Casey (D)	565,488	80.9%
Joseph Vodvarka (D)	133,683	19.1%

Previous Winning Percentages
2006 (59%)

Elected 2006; 2nd term

Casey straddles the divide between conventional liberal politics and the working-class values of northeastern Pennsylvania. In his first term he enjoyed modest success as a good-natured negotiator when those interests clashed. Now secure in his job through 2018 and facing a divided Congress, he might have lots more opportunities to sway debate in the years ahead.

Casey lives with his wife and children in Scranton, where he grew up as the fourth of eight children. His grandfather worked in the coal mines; his father, also known as Bob Casey, became a lawyer before entering politics. The family's finances were sometimes volatile, given his father's numerous political campaigns and the vicissitudes of his employment. But Casey recalls a happy upbringing. His dad "provided a good example for how to handle adversity," he told the Pittsburgh Post-Gazette. The elder Casey was elected governor on his fourth try, in 1986.

The younger Casey followed his father into statewide politics. He graduated from the College of the Holy Cross in 1982, then spent a year teaching fifth grade in Philadelphia with the Jesuits. He got his law degree and practiced in Scranton until he won his first election, for state auditor general, in 1996. He lost the Democratic primary for governor in 2002, but was elected state treasurer two years later. His won his first Senate race in 2006.

In politically "purple" Pennsylvania, Democratic cities to the east and west bracket Republican territory in between. Statewide success can require finesse, and Casey was more of a facilitator than an idea man early in his first term. He was on the 2012 House-Senate conference committee that finalized an extension of expanded unemployment benefits and reduced payroll taxes, and in that role he emphasized private, face-to-face discussions "to better understand what the other side is proposing or what's preventing them from agreeing with you."

He'll have some choice opportunities to shape legislation in the 113th Congress (2013-14). Casey sits on the Health, Education, Labor and Pensions Committee, which is due to reauthorize the 2002 federal education law known as No Child Left Behind. He has proposed altering block grant programs to make more funds available for early-childhood education; he also suggests creating a grant program to increase low-income students' access to courses in arts, civics, economics, environmental education, financial literacy and foreign languages.

On the health side, Casey seeks expanded federal funding of medical research, particularly at the National Institutes of Health. Pennsylvania is one of the leading recipients of NIH funding, with grants supporting research and jobs at higher education institutions such as the University of Pennsylvania and the University of Pittsburgh.

Casey was added to the Finance Committee in 2013, filling the vacancy created when John Kerry of Massachusetts resigned to become secretary of State. He chairs the Subcommittee on Fiscal Responsibility and Economic Growth, and he has seats on the panels covering health care and taxes. The full committee is studying a tax code overhaul in the 113th Congress.

His experience as a state treasurer gives him credibility on fiscal matters. In the 112th Congress (2011-12), Casey chaired the Joint Economic Committee, which holds hearings, conducts research and makes recommendations to the House and Senate on economic policy. However, he is not admired by some free-market advocates. At the start of 2013, Casey had one of the lowest lifetime Senate ratings from the Club for Growth.

Casey's personal beliefs and his political inheritance make him a natural negotiator on abortion issues. His father led the anti-abortion wing of the Democratic Party, famously defending state abortion laws in 1992 against a lawsuit by Planned Parenthood that reached the Supreme Court. (Justices declined to overturn Roe v. Wade.)

Casey is anti-abortion, though less tied to the issue than his father. Even so, when lawmakers debated in late 2009 whether health care overhaul legislation would allow federal dollars to subsidize insurance plans that cover abortion, Majority Leader Harry Reid tasked Casey with producing a compromise acceptable to enough senators on both sides of the abortion debate.

His proposal — requiring insurance plans to "segregate" federal subsidies from the pool of money that would cover abortion services — was panned by leading anti-abortion groups. But it provided the crucial votes necessary to push the bill on toward enactment.

In April 2011, anti-abortion groups criticized Casey for opposing a spending measure that would have blocked federal funding for Planned Parenthood. He said the family planning services the organization provides ultimately decrease the number of abortions. He also went against some social conservatives by announcing support for same-sex marriage in April 2013.

A few issues find Casey walking a line between Democratic preferences and the desires of his state. Though Pennsylvania is a coal state, Casey has supported the creation of a cap-and-trade system to regulate greenhouse gas emissions. But he also calls for the approval of the planned Keystone XL pipeline, and he is a big supporter of extending tax credits for natural gas production, which has boomed in western Pennsylvania.

He often has the state's economy in mind as a member of the Foreign Relations Committee. Casey keeps an eye on international trade practices that could threaten manufacturers in Pennsylvania. He voted for 2011 legislation to allow sanctions against China if the Treasury Department determined that the value of China's currency has been manipulated to create a trading advantage.

Casey has also proved to be a hawk on nuclear proliferation. In 2012, he teamed up with South Carolina Republican Lindsey Graham and Connecticut independent Joseph I. Lieberman on a resolution stating that "containment" was not an option for handling Iran — meaning that Iran would not be allowed to develop or obtain any nuclear weapons. It was adopted.

He chairs the Subcommittee on Near Eastern and South and Central Asian Affairs, and in 2012 he called for the creation of a democratic regime in Syria; in early 2013, Casey and Florida Republican Marco Rubio introduced a bill to authorize humanitarian and non-lethal assistance for Syrian rebels, as well as military training for vetted members of the Free Syrian Army.

Casey's success in Pennsylvania politics attracted the eye of national Democrats, who were gearing up for a challenge to Rick Santorum in 2006. The conservative senator, who at the time was the chamber's third-ranking GOP leader, was viewed as vulnerable in a state that had voted Democratic in the four previous presidential elections. Casey easily defeated two lesser-known candidates to secure the Democratic nomination, then prepared for what was widely anticipated to be a close contest.

Casey ran a low-key, careful campaign, declining a series of debates with Santorum. The perception of Casey as a social conservative helped, and with Democrats enjoying a strong year nationwide, he won by 17 points.

He had an early lead in 2012 against Republican Tom Smith, a relatively unknown former coal company executive who poured a lot of his own money into the race. Smith criticized Casey as being "Senator Zero" — an allusion to the fact that none of Casey's sponsored bills had become law — and a rubber-stamp for President Barack Obama's policies. Casey's huge lead in the polls shrank, but national Republicans kept their resources out of Pennsylvania until late in the race. Casey won by almost 9 points.

Key Votes

2012	
Prohibit health insurance plans from denying coverage based on the sponsor's religious beliefs	NO
Require approval of the Keystone XL oil pipeline	YES
Ease securities rules to expand small-business access to capital	YES
Reauthorize farm and nutrition programs for five years	YES
Limit debate on a bill that would create private-sector cybersecurity standards	YES
Consent to ratification of a treaty setting global standard for the treatment of people with disabilities	YES
Provide $60.4 billion in disaster relief following Superstorm Sandy	YES
Extend most Bush-era income tax rates while allowing rates for top-bracket earners to rise (Jan. 1, 2013)	YES
2011	
Prevent EPA from regulating greenhouse gas emissions to address climate change	NO
Extend certain provisions of Patriot Act for four years	YES
Clear compromise debt limit increase plan and establish future spending limits	YES
Overhaul patent law	YES
Implement Colombia free trade agreement	NO
Limit debate on confirmation of Caitlin J. Halligan to D.C. Circuit Court of Appeals	YES
Extend payroll tax cut and unemployment benefits for two months	YES

CQ Vote Studies

	PARTY UNITY		PRESIDENTIAL SUPPORT	
	SUPPORT	OPPOSE	SUPPORT	OPPOSE
2012	91%	9%	95%	5%
2011	94%	6%	93%	7%
2010	99%	1%	98%	2%
2009	95%	5%	97%	3%
2008	93%	7%	35%	65%
2007	93%	7%	44%	56%

Interest Groups

	AFL-CIO	ADA	CCUS	ACU
2012	91%	85%	63%	12%
2011	95%	95%	45%	0%
2010	100%	90%	27%	0%
2009	94%	90%	43%	12%
2008	100%	90%	63%	8%
2007	100%	100%	36%	8%

Sen. Patrick J. Toomey (R)

Capitol Office
224-4254
toomey.senate.gov
248 Russell Bldg. 20510-3802; fax 228-0284

Committees
Banking, Housing & Urban Affairs
Budget
Finance
Joint Economic

Residence
Zionsville

Born
Nov. 17, 1961; Providence, R.I.

Religion
Roman Catholic

Family
Wife, Kris Toomey; three children

Education
Harvard U., A.B. 1984 (political philosophy)

Career
Club for Growth president; restaurateur; investment banker

Political Highlights
Allentown Government Study Commission, 1994-96; U.S. House, 1999-2005; sought Republican nomination for U.S. Senate, 2004

ELECTION RESULTS

2010 GENERAL		
Patrick J. Toomey (R)	2,028,945	51.0%
Joe Sestak (D)	1,948,716	49.0%
2010 PRIMARY		
Patrick J. Toomey (R)	671,591	81.4%
Peg Luksik (R)	153,154	18.6%

Previous Winning Percentages
2002 House Election (57%); 2000 House Election (53%); 1998 House Election (55%)

Elected 2010; 1st term

Toomey is very interested in reshaping the nation's fiscal outlook, and he is very good at presenting his conservative ideas in matter-of-fact, reasoned tones. He's a prominent figure in the small-government movement, but he has made a few conspicuous attempts at working with Democrats.

His economic agenda reflects the philosophy of the Club for Growth, the low-tax, free-market advocacy group he once led. Toomey supports easing the regulatory burden on businesses; he also wants an overhaul of the tax code and a restructuring of the entitlement programs that he says are responsible for unsustainable deficits.

In September 2012, he took over as chairman of the Senate Steering Committee, a caucus of conservative senators; its previous chairman, Jim DeMint of South Carolina, now runs the conservative Heritage Foundation. When he served as a House member, Toomey was among the lawmakers who reinvigorated the Conservative Action Team and renamed it the Republican Study Group, turning it into an influential segment of the GOP Conference.

He sees Republicans as failing to articulate their message of fiscal restraint. "The policies that got us into this mess were the policies of a big government, liberal policies of failed monetary policy and encouraging lending to people who couldn't pay loans back," he told the Conservative Political Action Conference in 2013. "But we never had an alternative, compelling narrative that explained that. And as a result, I think we lost a lot of ground."

Toomey has great panel assignments for promoting his agenda. He sits on the Budget Committee; the Banking, Housing and Urban Affairs Committee; and the Joint Economic Committee. In the 113th Congress (2013-14), he was awarded a seat on the Finance Committee, which is studying a possible overhaul of the tax code.

He also has the implied blessing of Republican leaders. In 2011, he was named to the "supercommittee," a bicameral, bipartisan deficit reduction panel created by the August 2011 law raising the federal debt limit. That 12-member panel was tasked with proposing a way to reduce deficits by $1.2 trillion over 10 years.

The panel never issued a plan, but Toomey made a compromise proposal notable for a conservative Republican. It included an estimated $750 billion in spending cuts and a purported $500 billion in new revenues. To raise a net $250 billion, his plan would have retained existing capital gains and estate tax rates, lowered corporate and individual tax rates, and limited tax deductions for taxpayers whose incomes fall in the top two brackets. The other $250 billion in revenue would have come from what Toomey described as "noncontroversial" sources such as user fees and asset sales.

From the Banking panel, he contributed several provisions to a 2012 law meant to reduce regulations on, and improve the flow of capital to, small businesses. One, written with Democrat Thomas R. Carper of Delaware, increases the number of shareholders allowed for privately held companies; another, written with Democrat Charles E. Schumer of New York, cuts back on regulatory requirements for small businesses that go public.

Toomey has also worked with Missouri Democrat Claire McCaskill on an effort to permanently ban spending earmarks. They introduced legislation to do so in both 2011 and 2013.

Collaborations aside, Toomey is not a moderate. He rejected the August 2011 deal that created the deficit committee on which he served. He helped write a GOP-backed proposed constitutional amendment that would cap federal spending at 18 percent of the gross domestic product and require a two-thirds vote of both chambers to raise taxes.

He also raised several points of order on the Senate floor to block or alter various measures in the 112th Congress (2011-12). Most notably, he altered a 2012 version of a Superstorm Sandy relief bill, so that $3.4 billion intended for the Army Corps of Engineers to mitigate the effect of future storms was no longer "emergency" spending and would have to be offset by other spending reductions. Democrats said disaster aid had never been offset; Toomey said long-term projects hardly qualified as an emergency.

While he made a name for himself on tax and budget issues, Toomey is also a social conservative. He opposes abortion and same-sex marriage, and he defends gun owners' rights. He surprised a few people in 2013 by negotiating a proposal with West Virginia Democrat Joe Manchin III that would have expanded the system of background checks for gun purchases. "The common ground rests on a simple proposition, and that is that criminals and the dangerously mentally ill shouldn't have guns," he told reporters. " I don't know anyone who disagrees with that premise." The bill was defeated in April 2013, and Toomey said it was "time to move on."

Toomey was born in Providence, R.I. His father laid cable for the Narragansett Electric Co.; his mother was a part-time secretary for their local Roman Catholic church.

After graduating from Harvard, Toomey spent seven years in the high-pressure world of international finance, trading futures contracts, swaps and other often-volatile financial instruments while living in New York, London and Hong Kong. In 1990, he switched his business focus, investing in a chain of sports-themed restaurants in Allentown and Lancaster called Rookies.

Toomey had little political experience prior to his first House bid other than a summer internship in the office of liberal Republican Sen. John H. Chafee of Rhode Island. But he said the 1994 elections convinced him that there was an "opportunity to change the direction of government" and make it more responsive to the citizenry. That year, he was elected to a two-year stint on the Allentown Government Study Commission, where he won enactment of a plan making it harder for the city council to raise taxes.

In 1998, Toomey jumped into the open-seat race created by the retirement of three-term moderate Democrat Paul McHale. He won a six-candidate primary, then bested veteran Democratic state Sen. Roy C. Afflerbach.

The next two elections, he fended off challenges from former United Steelworkers local president Edward J. O'Brien, who depicted him as too conservative. In 2004, Toomey challenged incumbent Arlen Specter in the Senate Republican primary. Making the case that Specter was too liberal, Toomey attracted support from many movement conservatives. But the state party apparatus—including Specter's colleague, conservative stalwart Rick Santorum—and national Republicans rallied around Specter. He held off Toomey's challenge by less than 2 points, then won re-election.

Toomey went on to serve as president of the Club for Growth, enhancing his reputation among activists. He considered a campaign for governor, but decided to take one more shot at Specter. Again, the national Republican Party lined up behind the incumbent. But early polls showed Toomey well ahead of Specter, and two weeks after Toomey formally entered the race, Specter announced he was switching parties.

The Democratic Senatorial Campaign Committee backed Specter, but two-term Rep. Joe Sestak, a former Navy admiral, had already entered the Democratic primary. Despite alleged pleas from the White House to drop out, Sestak stayed in and topped Specter on primary day by 8 points.

The general election was a bare-knuckle affair, with polls rarely separating the two candidates by more than a few points. Toomey benefited from tea party support, his years of activism and President Barack Obama's unpopularity in the state. He prevailed with 51 percent of the vote.

Key Votes

2012	
Prohibit health insurance plans from denying coverage based on the sponsor's religious beliefs	NO
Require approval of the Keystone XL oil pipeline	YES
Ease securities rules to expand small-business access to capital	YES
Reauthorize farm and nutrition programs for five years	NO
Limit debate on a bill that would create private-sector cybersecurity standards	NO
Consent to ratification of a treaty setting global standard for the treatment of people with disabilities	NO
Provide $60.4 billion in disaster relief following Superstorm Sandy	NO
Extend most Bush-era income tax rates while allowing rates for top-bracket earners to rise (Jan. 1, 2013)	YES
2011	
Prevent EPA from regulating greenhouse gas emissions to address climate change	YES
Extend certain provisions of Patriot Act for four years	YES
Clear compromise debt limit increase plan and establish future spending limits	NO
Overhaul patent law	YES
Implement Colombia free trade agreement	YES
Limit debate on confirmation of Caitlin J. Halligan to D.C. Circuit Court of Appeals	NO
Extend payroll tax cut and unemployment benefits for two months	YES

CQ Vote Studies

	PARTY UNITY		PRESIDENTIAL SUPPORT	
	SUPPORT	OPPOSE	SUPPORT	OPPOSE
2012	93%	7%	42%	58%
2011	95%	5%	58%	42%
2004	98%	2%	94%	6%
2003	94%	6%	93%	7%

Interest Groups

	AFL-CIO	ADA	CCUS	ACU
2012	0%	5%	75%	100%
2011	16%	10%	82%	90%
2004	0%	0%	100%	100%
2003	13%	20%	90%	92%

Rep. Robert A. Brady (D)

Capitol Office
225-4731
brady.house.gov
102 Cannon Bldg. 20515-3801; fax 225-0088

Committees
Armed Services
House Administration - Ranking Member
Joint Library
Joint Printing

Residence
Philadelphia

Born
April 7, 1945; Philadelphia, Pa.

Religion
Roman Catholic

Family
Wife, Debra Brady; two children

Education
St. Thomas More H.S., graduated 1963

Career
Union lobbyist; local government official; carpenter

Political Highlights
34th Ward Democratic Executive Committee, 1967-present (leader, 1980-present); candidate for Philadelphia City Council, 1983; Philadelphia Democratic Party chairman, 1986-present; sought Democratic nomination for mayor of Philadelphia, 2007

ELECTION RESULTS

2012 GENERAL		
Robert A. Brady (D)	235,394	84.9%
John J. Featherman (R)	41,708	15.0%
2012 PRIMARY		
Robert A. Brady (D)		unopposed
2010 GENERAL		
Robert A. Brady (D)		unopposed

Previous Winning Percentages
2008 (91%); 2006 (100%); 2004 (86%); 2002 (86%); 2000 (88%); 1998 (81%); 1998 Special Election (74%)

Elected 1998; 8th full term

Brady personifies machine politics — he's the kind of guy who keeps the trains running on time, to places he represents, while staffed with union labor whenever possible. He has worked to duplicate that operational influence on Capitol Hill, but Philadelphia is his No. 1 priority.

Stout, loud and blue-collar, he started out as a union carpenter in the Overbrook neighborhood. Brady credits his decision to get into politics to a broken streetlight. Worried about his mother walking home from her food market job at night, Brady asked his local ward boss to fix it. When the committeeman failed to follow through, Brady ran for a local party post and won.

Swapping favors and keeping close to the city's politicians, Brady eventually was hired as a deputy mayor for labor in the 1980s; he became chairman of the Democratic City Committee in 1986 and still holds that post today.

Brady has served many times as an arbitrator. He has helped end walkouts by Teamsters, teachers and transportation workers. In 2010, he intervened in a dispute between nurses and Temple University Hospital. "I don't negotiate," he told the Philadelphia Inquirer. "I tell everybody the same thing: I don't want to know what you want. Tell me what you need to make a deal."

His critics have accused him of thuggish tactics on behalf of labor unions, but no one can deny his ability to pull strings in either Washington or Philadelphia. In 2012, he was recognized as a mastermind of a deal that prevented the loss of hundreds of jobs in South Philadelphia.

Sunoco had announced plans to close its refinery in the city, and Brady pulled off a nifty bit of politicking to keep the facility open. He wooed Sunoco into a joint venture with the Carlyle Group, a private equity firm, to redevelop the refinery as a hub for processing natural gas and oil from the Marcellus and Bakken shales. He helped convince the EPA to forgo an expensive and lengthy permitting review of the project.

Observers have also credited him with smoothing over racial and ethnic political divides in a diverse city, and his clout in statewide elections has been considerable.

He sticks to a behind-the-scenes approach in Washington. Brady rarely sounds off on the House floor or news shows. Since the 108th Congress (2003-04) he has served on the House Administration Committee, which handles office assignments, parking spots and other day-to-day functions. With the help of another Pennsylvania power broker, Rep. John P. Murtha, he secured the gavel in 2007, becoming the unofficial "mayor of Capitol Hill" for the four years of the Democratic majority.

As chairman, Brady settled a 4-year-old debate by moving legislation to merge the previously separate Library of Congress and Capitol police forces. A member of the Armed Services Committee since his first term, Brady also pushes to employ more wounded veterans in administrative and support positions in the House complex.

Since becoming the ranking member of House Administration in 2011, his legislative output has dwindled and dealt mostly with Philadelphia. Brady introduced only a handful of bills in the 112th Congress (2011-12) — including one for a stamp in recognition of basketball legend Wilt Chamberlain (with whom Brady once played a pickup game).

When he does engage on issues, they are issues important to his working-class, Democratic constituents, such as health care, abortion rights and wage increases. House Administration has jurisdiction over election law, and Brady expressed concern with state, municipal and federal bills that Democrats described as limiting voter access to the polls. When Pennsylvania enacted a

2012 law requiring voters to present photo ID, Brady said it burdened elderly voters who don't drive and have no license — such as his mother.

He has co-sponsored bills to restrict contributions to super PACs, advocacy groups independent of official campaigns that can accept unrestricted donations from individuals or organizations. Labor unions were the single largest category of contributors to Brady's 2012 campaign, and in a 2012 opinion piece he suggested that unions were a key to reducing wage inequality.

Despite Brady's attention to local concerns, he has had some stumbles in the past. He lost in the Democratic primary for the Philadelphia mayoral race in 2007. In the 2010 U.S. Senate primary, he was unable to deliver the city's vote for Arlen Specter, the candidate backed by the party establishment.

Republicans redrew Pennsylvania's electoral map after the 2010 census, and Brady took heat for endorsing the final version, which endangered several Democratic House incumbents. Brady said he simply backed the option that was least bad for the party.

Brady grew up in Overbrook and still lives there with his second wife, a former cheerleader for the Philadelphia Eagles. The neighborhood, which was Catholic and white when Brady was a child, is now mostly black. Brady has worked to secure African-American support through the years, and he calls Georgia Democratic Rep. John Lewis — a civil rights leader beaten during the 1965 march on Selma, Ala. — his hero.

His father was a policeman who died young, and his mother was a supermarket checker. Brady had college scholarship offers but went to work as a carpenter to help support his family. After 12 years in the trade, he moved into a full-time post with the carpenters' union. Brady still carries a union card and until 2012 had a lifetime score of 100 percent in the AFL-CIO's rating of congressional voting records. The blemish was his vote for the House version of a bill to ease regulation of some small businesses. (Most Democrats voted for the measure.)

Once he became part of the Democratic organization, Brady hit it off with then-City Council President George X. Schwartz, securing his patronage by fixing up Schwartz's basement, gratis. When Schwartz was convicted in the 1980 Abscam scandal, in which undercover FBI agents offered money to members of Congress and some local and state officials for government contracts, Schwartz cleared the way for Brady to succeed him as the local Democratic ward leader. Brady made an unsuccessful bid for the city council in 1983 but continued to be a key player in city politics.

When Democratic Rep. Thomas M. Foglietta resigned to become ambassador to Italy, Brady easily won a 1998 special election to succeed him. All his re-elections have come with at least 80 percent of the vote.

Key Votes

2012

Extend a Social Security payroll tax cut and unemployment benefits	YES
Ease securities rules to expand small-business access to capital	NO
Extend for one year subsidized student loan interest rates financed by a cut in health care spending	NO
Cite Attorney General Eric H. Holder Jr. for contempt of Congress	?
Create a visa program for foreign graduates in high-tech fields	NO
Extend most Bush-era income tax rates while allowing rates for top-bracket earners to rise (Jan. 1, 2013)	YES

2011

Strike funding for F-35 alternative engine	YES
Prevent EPA from regulating greenhouse gas emissions to address climate change	NO
Extend certain provisions of Patriot Act for four years	NO
Declare opposition to use of ground troops in Libya	NO
Overhaul patent law	NO
Pass compromise debt limit increase plan and establish future spending limits	YES
Allow consideration of measures to implement three trade agreements	NO

CQ Vote Studies

	PARTY UNITY		PRESIDENTIAL SUPPORT	
	SUPPORT	OPPOSE	SUPPORT	OPPOSE
2012	97%	3%	83%	17%
2011	96%	4%	84%	16%
2010	99%	1%	95%	5%
2009	99%	1%	96%	4%
2008	99%	1%	14%	86%

Interest Groups

	AFL-CIO	ADA	CCUS	ACU
2012	95%	100%	18%	0%
2011	100%	95%	25%	0%
2010	100%	95%	25%	0%
2009	100%	100%	33%	0%
2008	100%	100%	56%	0%

Pennsylvania 1

South and central Philadelphia; Chester

Cobblestone streets and patches of urban decay mark the historic 1st, the birthplace of the Constitution and home of such recognizable icons as the Liberty Bell and the Philly cheesesteak. From working-class areas in northeastern Philadelphia through Chinatown and the heart of the city's Hispanic population to Chester, the district follows the curves of the Delaware River. Ethnically diverse populations and a union presence make the 1st a Democratic stronghold.

Despite cutbacks in the public sector, the federal government remains the district's most notable employer, with a Federal Reserve Bank, the U.S. Mint and bureaus of FEMA, the FBI and the Federal Transit Administration in the 1st. Rebounds at Philadelphia's Navy Yard have been boosted by investments from the city and state to attract shipbuilding, manufacturing and warehousing jobs; pharmaceutical giant GlaxoSmithKline recently moved its headquarters to the complex. Airline unions are fighting cuts at Philadelphia International Airport, a large U.S. Airways hub. History buffs flock to the National Constitution Center and Independence Hall. Sports fans gather at games for football's Eagles, baseball's Phillies, basketball's 76ers and hockey's Flyers — venues for the four teams line Broad Street.

High crime and unemployment rates have hit many neighborhoods. Property values have declined, blight has taken hold in some areas and the city hopes to address academic recovery in overburdened city schools.

Casinos in the Fishtown neighborhood of Philadelphia and in Chester compete with those in nearby states. Chester, a suburb where nearly one in three residents lives in poverty, is also home to soccer's Union near the Commodore Barry Bridge.

The district is 34 percent black, and Fairhill and Juniata Park host a large Puerto Rican community. Many immigrants have arrived from Vietnam and Indonesia. The city's traditional Italian-American neighborhood supports one of the nation's largest and oldest open-air food markets.

Major Industry

Government, health care, airports, shipbuilding, tourism

Cities

Philadelphia (pt), Chester

Notable

In 1776, Thomas Jefferson penned the Declaration of Independence in rented rooms at the Graff House, which has been restored as a historic exhibit.

Rep. Chaka Fattah (D)

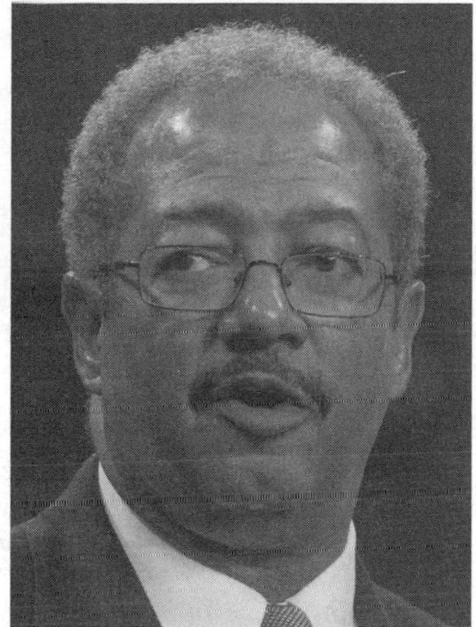

Capitol Office
225-4001
fattah.house.gov
2301 Rayburn Bldg. 20515-3802; fax 225-5392

Committees
Appropriations

Residence
Philadelphia

Born
Nov. 21, 1956; Philadelphia, Pa.

Religion
Baptist

Family
Wife, Renee Chenault-Fattah; four children

Education
Community College of Philadelphia, attended 1976 (political science); U. of Pennsylvania, M.A. 1986 (government administration)

Career
Youth voter registration organization director

Political Highlights
Democratic candidate for Philadelphia City Commission, 1979; Pa. House, 1983-89; Pa. Senate, 1989-95; Consumer Party nominee for U.S. House (special election), 1991; sought Democratic nomination for mayor of Philadelphia, 2007

ELECTION RESULTS

2012 GENERAL		
Chaka Fattah (D)	318,176	89.3%
Robert Mansfield Jr. (R)	33,381	9.4%
James Foster (I)	4,829	1.4%
2012 PRIMARY		
Chaka Fattah (D)		unopposed
2010 GENERAL		
Chaka Fattah (D)	182,800	89.3%
Rick Hellberg (R)	21,907	10.7%

Previous Winning Percentages
2008 (89%); 2006 (89%); 2004 (88%); 2002 (88%); 2000 (98%); 1998 (87%); 1996 (88%); 1994 (86%)

Elected 1994; 10th term

Fattah's House career started off with 12 years in the minority, and in that time he perfected long-haul strategies that resulted in some notable legislative achievements. Once again in the minority, the genial appropriator defends his earlier victories while laying down markers on education, taxation and more.

"I learned from my parents that if you had a desire to make a change, that sometimes it required a total commitment," he said.

For decades, Falaka and David Fattah have been community activists in Philadelphia; spurred in part by concern over gang violence, they opened their home as a shelter for young men. During the late 1960s, the teenaged Fattah often could be found discussing "every subject under the sun" with some of the 20 or so men in residence at any given time. "I think it prepared me well for the Congress," he said.

Fattah (full name: SHOCK-ah fa-TAH) pops up regularly on Al Sharpton's MSNBC program, but he just as often spars with Neil Cavuto on Fox News Channel. You must "have the ability to negotiate some acceptance of ideas" over the long term, he said.

Many of Fattah's negotiations are about education — specifically, the distribution of resources to schools in low-income areas. The federal government, he said, should be a "referee saying that states need to make sure that no matter what the circumstances of birth, that young people get a fair shot at the ladders of opportunity." He beats the drum for his Student Bill of Rights, an oft-introduced measure to guarantee students from any school district access to adequate technology, teachers and other resources. Another Fattah bill would require districts to demonstrate that all their schools receive comparable funding before receiving federal aid.

His most prominent success has been GEAR UP — Gaining Early Awareness and Readiness for Undergraduate Programs — which was enacted in 1998 and updated in 2008. It aids low-income students in preparing for college. The 2009 economic stimulus bill included a Fattah-authored tax credit of up to $2,500 for higher-education expenses incurred by low- to middle-income families. The January 2013 "fiscal cliff" law extended the credit through 2017.

As the top Democrat on the Commerce-Justice-Science Appropriations Subcommittee, he often tries to place education issues in a broader economic context. In the competitive global economy, "we have people chasing at our heels, so that the country has to make a decision that education is a national imperative" and not merely a local prerogative. In early 2012, Fattah applauded as President Barack Obama laid out the goal that every child should graduate from high school career- or college-ready.

Fattah landed the top spot on the C-J-S panel after making a long-shot bid to be the top Democrat on the full committee for the 112th Congress (2011-12). He has tried to defend funding for several programs, including the Legal Services Corporation — which provides civil-case legal aid for low-income Americans — and Clinton-era grants to hire police officers.

He is very interested in the study of the brain, and he packages his efforts as the "Fattah Neuroscience Initiative," a campaign to coordinate federally funded research and engage more public-private partnerships. A fiscal 2012 spending law included his provision creating a working group to coordinate federal investments in neuroscience research. A fiscal 2013 spending law directs the executive branch to ponder what kind of incentives could speed up the development of new treatments for neurological diseases and disorders. He speaks regularly to stakeholder groups on the subject.

Fattah is also a promoter of the Manufacturing Extension Partnership, which attempts to help small- and medium-size manufacturers coordinate with customers and other entrepreneurs. A member of the Energy-Water spending panel, he worked to include language in fiscal 2012 measures that requires the Energy Department to create a "shopping list" of energy-related equipment and products that are not produced by domestic manufacturers.

When it comes to raising revenue, Fattah has gone big. He regularly introduces his plan to dramatically revamp the tax code — and to wipe out the entire national debt within 10 years. First revealed in 2004, the plan abolishes the individual income tax and replaces it with a 1 percent tax on most retail and financial transactions occurring in the United States. "I think we need fundamental tax reform," he said. "I think when we get there — and we will, as a country — that it's going to look very much like what I proposed."

Amid the fiscal angst of the 112th Congress, he touted his idea as the only one to actually eliminate the debt, not just slow its growth: "The entire discussion has been limited to how little more water will go into the basement, and no discussion of getting the water out of the basement."

Born Arthur Davenport, Fattah was renamed as a teen when his mother married his stepfather. He once counseled Barack Obama on the advantages of a distinctive moniker: "Once people get the name, they never forget it," he said. "It has its challenges ... but once people get it, it works."

He dropped out of high school in early 1974 and earned a GED later that year. He went on to enroll in classes at a Philadelphia community college, but never graduated. In 1986, however, while serving as a state lawmaker, he received a master's degree from the University of Pennsylvania.

Fattah met Democratic Rep. William H. Gray III and worked on one of his campaigns. In 1982, he successfully challenged a Democratic Party-backed incumbent for a state House seat, becoming, at 25, the youngest person ever elected to the state legislature. He moved to the state Senate six years later.

Fattah entered the 1991 special election to succeed Gray. But the Democratic Party backed longtime City Councilman Lucien E. Blackwell, so Fattah temporarily quit the party, and ran on the Consumer Party ticket. He lost, but returned to defeat Blackwell in the 1994 primary, this time in a redrawn district he had helped approve as a member of the state Senate. Fattah has not been seriously challenged since, though he did run unsuccessfully for mayor of Philadelphia in 2007, coming in fourth in the Democratic primary.

In early 2012, it was reported that Fattah's son Chaka Fattah Jr. was under Justice Department investigation for his work at a for-profit school that receives funding from the city of Philadelphia. The elder Fattah passed along a 2009 request for federal funding from the school, and he said that his son was uninvolved in that request. No allegations have been made against Fattah.

Key Votes

2012	
Extend a Social Security payroll tax cut and unemployment benefits	YES
Ease securities rules to expand small-business access to capital	YES
Extend for one year subsidized student loan interest rates financed by a cut in health care spending	NO
Cite Attorney General Eric H. Holder Jr. for contempt of Congress	?
Create a visa program for foreign graduates in high-tech fields	?
Extend most Bush-era income tax rates while allowing rates for top-bracket earners to rise (Jan. 1, 2013)	YES
2011	
Strike funding for F-35 alternative engine	YES
Prevent EPA from regulating greenhouse gas emissions to address climate change	NO
Extend certain provisions of Patriot Act for four years	NO
Declare opposition to use of ground troops in Libya	NO
Overhaul patent law	YES
Pass compromise debt limit increase plan and establish future spending limits	YES
Allow consideration of measures to implement three trade agreements	NO

CQ Vote Studies

	PARTY UNITY		PRESIDENTIAL SUPPORT	
	SUPPORT	OPPOSE	SUPPORT	OPPOSE
2012	96%	4%	84%	16%
2011	96%	4%	87%	13%
2010	99%	1%	95%	5%
2009	99%	1%	97%	3%
2008	99%	1%	13%	87%

Interest Groups

	AFL-CIO	ADA	CCUS	ACU
2012	90%	80%	27%	0%
2011	96%	95%	38%	0%
2010	100%	95%	25%	0%
2009	100%	100%	33%	0%
2008	100%	95%	53%	0%

Pennsylvania 2

West Philadelphia; Chestnut Hill

From the vantage point of the William Penn statue atop the imposing City Hall, one can see the 2nd stretching west and north over long-established neighborhoods. It encompasses Center City skyscrapers, then moves west across the Schuylkill River past the University of Pennsylvania and Drexel University. West Philadelphia, once Irish, Greek and Jewish, is now nearly all black and features both poor and middle-class communities.

Philadelphia's Center City is home to the Comcast Center, One Liberty Place, Two Liberty Place and the Bell Atlantic Tower. Home prices here are some of the highest in the city, especially among condos in Rittenhouse Square. Ongoing economic development projects, rising populations and steady white-collar office jobs are projected to help the neighborhood maintain growth, despite declines in the city as a whole.

In addition to Drexel and UPenn near the Schuylkill, most of Temple University is in the 2nd north of Center City; the district is also home to several other colleges, as well as Mercy Philadelphia Hospital, the Children's Hospital of Philadelphia, university research laboratories and the Albert Einstein Medical Center.

The largely residential northeastern reaches of the 2nd include Germantown and Nicetown neighborhoods. The area is home to Underground Railroad houses that once hid escaping slaves and was settled by blacks migrating north in the 20th century. Housing prices have declined in West Philadelphia, and the city has targeted the area for redevelopment.

The 2nd extends beyond overwhelmingly Democratic Philadelphia into a residential corner of Montgomery County, including parts of Lower Merion Township and Narberth. The district's portion of Philadelphia provided a more than 15-to-1 margin for Barack Obama in the 2012 presidential election, and he won the district overall with 90 percent, his highest percentage statewide.

Major Industry
Government, health care, higher education

Cities
Philadelphia (pt.)

Notable
Philadelphia's lavish City Hall is the largest municipal building in the nation, containing more than 14.5 acres of floor space; The steps of the Philadelphia Museum of Art were immortalized in the movie "Rocky."

Rep. Mike Kelly (R)

Capitol Office
225-5406
kelly.house.gov
1519 Longworth Bldg. 20515-3803; fax 225-3103

Committees
Ways & Means

Residence
Butler

Born
May 10, 1948; Pittsburgh, Pa.

Religion
Roman Catholic

Family
Wife, Victoria Kelly; four children

Education
U. of Notre Dame, B.A. 1970 (sociology)

Career
Car dealership owner

Political Highlights
Butler Area School Board, 1982-90; Butler City Council, 2006-09

ELECTION RESULTS

2012 GENERAL		
Mike Kelly (R)	165,826	54.8%
Missa Eaton (D)	123,933	41.0%
Steven Porter (I)	12,755	4.2%
2012 PRIMARY		
Mike Kelly (R)		unopposed
2010 GENERAL		
Mike Kelly (R)	111,909	55.7%
Kathy Dahlkemper (D)	88,924	44.3%

Elected 2010; 2nd term

Blue-collar, back-slapping affability served Kelly well as a car dealer, and he brings that personal charm to the House. Sometimes irritated and always animated, he paints the federal government as a drag on economic recovery.

Kelly speaks rapidly, asking and answering his own questions as he goes; he also projects a jovial enjoyment of his job. "This is all fun for me," he says. His voting record has put him near the ideological middle of his party, but his sense of team spirit helped him emerge as a motivational figure for the GOP Conference in the 112th Congress (2011-12).

His first big pep talk came as Republicans pondered deficit reduction plans in the summer of 2011. Hard-line conservatives weren't happy with a proposal by Speaker John A. Boehner, and their dissent was threatening its passage. At a meeting before the vote, Kelly handed out signs that read "Play Like a Champion Today" — copies of the one hanging in the locker room tunnel at the University of Notre Dame, where Kelly once played football. He exhorted the party to knock the stuffing out of its opponent, only in less polite terms. The Boehner plan passed.

A year later, Kelly took to the House floor to inveigh against the costs of federal regulations on businesses, building in intensity over the course of a five-minute speech. "Take the heavy boot off the throat of America's job creators and let them breathe," he said, and Republican colleagues in the chamber gave him a standing ovation. The video was widely distributed in conservative circles.

And in December 2012, when conservatives scuttled Boehner's plans in another round of deficit reduction talks with the White House, Kelly was furious. After Boehner announced at a GOP Conference meeting that he was accepting defeat, Kelly took the microphone and yelled at dissenters: "How the hell can you do this?"

At the start of the 113th Congress (2013-14), Kelly joined the Ways and Means Committee, and that assignment gives him the opportunity to work on health care, trade, taxes and entitlement programs. As a freshman, Kelly approached those subjects — and many others — by talking about problems caused by regulations and what he describes as an oversized, money-eating government. By the time appropriated money reaches its intended destination, "there's only one or two drops for the people who need it," he says. "It's all absorbed in the bureaucracy."

The energy-rich Marcellus Shale runs under his district, and Kelly sees that natural-gas resource as a key to an economic turnaround. Like many Republicans, he blames EPA intervention in the permitting process for stalling energy development.

According to Kelly, the protracted implementation of the 2010 overhaul of financial regulations has paralyzed banks: "I sell cars off the shelf, they sell money off the shelf, right? That's what they do. They don't know what they're allowed to sell anymore. ... That shuts down the local economy."

He also laments that federal regulations seem to unduly disrupt small businesses. In May 2011, he told Fox Business News that it was harder for him "to change five quarts of oil in my shop back in Butler than it was for BP to sink a hole in the Gulf [of Mexico]. So I don't want to hear about regulations and how they're helping us and how they're saving us money."

Kelly likes to draw on his automotive experience. In the 112th Congress, he targeted federal subsidies for "green"-energy technology — especially electric cars. Kelly called for an end to federal tax credits to consumers who purchase electric cars, saying that the technology was not yet practical and that the credits mostly benefit the wealthy, who can afford the expensive vehicles. He cited his own difficulties trying to move a Chevy Volt off the lot. "The market's not ready for it, so why push it?" he asked.

As a freshman, he sat on the Foreign Affairs Committee, where trade was one of his favorite subjects. He stumped for the free-trade pact with South Korea that was ratified in 2011; in 2013, Kelly became the co-chairman of the Congressional Caucus on Korea. He similarly pushed for the normalization of trade relations with Russia, a status that was codified in late 2012. Kelly said it will greatly increase export opportunities for Pennsylvania businesses.

A practicing Roman Catholic, Kelly is against abortion rights. He also opposes restrictions on gun ownership. In March 2013, he and Kansas Republican Sen. Jerry Moran introduced companion resolutions to oppose the United Nations Arms Trade Treaty, which they described as a threat to both to U.S. sovereignty and Second Amendment rights.

Kelly's childhood started out in Verona, near Pittsburgh. His father excelled as a parts picker at a General Motors warehouse — an ability to roller skate gave him an advantage over slower co-workers — and after serving in World War II he started operating a car dealership. Kelly was one of five children, and the family moved to the blue-collar town of Butler when he was 8.

Football was a passion for the young Kelly, and as a freshman at Notre Dame in 1966, he practiced with that year's eventual national champion. An offensive lineman in high school, "I just wanted to play defense so badly" in college, he said. "That's exactly the way I played it. Badly." Knee injuries ended his football career as a sophomore, and he went into the family business after graduation, eventually buying his father's dealership in the 1990s. Kelly's son runs it today, and he wants to keep it in the family "as long as somebody in the family wants it."

Kelly had some civic involvement, with stints on both the city council and the Butler school board. (His wife and daughter are teachers.) But he traces his current political involvement to 2009. After the federal government bailed out General Motors and installed a new CEO, the company attempted to close Kelly's Cadillac dealership as part of its restructuring. Kelly fought the decision and had his franchise restored, but the incident inspired him to run for office. "There are times in your life when you realize things have gone so badly off track that you've got to get involved," he told The Hill in June 2011.

Early in the 2010 cycle, the GOP targeted the Erie-based 3rd District seat held by freshman Democrat Kathy Dahlkemper. Kelly won a six-candidate GOP primary and defeated Dahlkemper by 11 points. He raised more than four times as much campaign cash as his 2012 Democratic opponent, college professor Missa Eaton, and won by almost 14 points.

Key Votes

2012	
Extend a Social Security payroll tax cut and unemployment benefits	**YES**
Ease securities rules to expand small-business access to capital	**YES**
Extend for one year subsidized student loan interest rates financed by a cut in health care spending	**YES**
Cite Attorney General Eric H. Holder Jr. for contempt of Congress	**YES**
Create a visa program for foreign graduates in high-tech fields	**YES**
Extend most Bush-era income tax rates while allowing rates for top-bracket earners to rise (Jan. 1, 2013)	**YES**
2011	
Strike funding for F-35 alternative engine	**NO**
Prevent EPA from regulating greenhouse gas emissions to address climate change	**YES**
Extend certain provisions of Patriot Act for four years	**YES**
Declare opposition to use of ground troops in Libya	**YES**
Overhaul patent law	**YES**
Pass compromise debt limit increase plan and establish future spending limits	**YES**
Allow consideration of measures to implement three trade agreements	**YES**

CQ Vote Studies

	PARTY UNITY		PRESIDENTIAL SUPPORT	
	SUPPORT	OPPOSE	SUPPORT	OPPOSE
2012	91%	9%	18%	82%
2011	93%	7%	26%	74%

Interest Groups

	AFL-CIO	ADA	CCUS	ACU
2012	29%	0%	100%	76%
2011	21%	15%	100%	80%

Pennsylvania 3

Northwest — Erie

Lake Erie laps at the northern border the of 3rd, while the Kiskiminetas River — a tributary of the Allegheny, which cuts through the district on its way out of Pittsburgh — forms its southern border in Armstrong County, 35 minutes northeast of Pittsburgh. The city of Erie's port is Pennsylvania's only Great Lakes shipping base, and it played a major role in statewide industrial growth. Manufacturing still plays an important role, but the workforce is increasingly dependent on insurance, health care and tourism.

Since the 1970s, Erie's population — traditionally a melting pot of Irish, Italian, Polish, German and Russian settlers — has been migrating to suburban townships. GE Transportation's 2012 announcement that it would relocate its corporate headquarters to Chicago was the most recent in a string of blows to the town's industrial identity, although it still hosts some of the nation's top plastics manufacturers. Meanwhile, hospitals and schools have expanded, and Erie International Airport is a landing point for tourists enjoying the beaches, casino and racing at Presque Isle.

Erie County also sits atop parts of the Marcellus and Utica shale formations — oil and gas drilling could mean a boom for the region. Outside Erie, median household incomes tend to be higher but still below state averages. But major health care providers and the headquarters of Westinghouse Electric have pushed job growth in Butler County.

The population of the 3rd is overwhelmingly white with a concentration of black residents in Erie County. Before decennial redistricting, the 3rd was friendlier to Democrats, and Republican John McCain eked out a win in the area by less than two dozen votes in the 2008 presidential race. After remapping, the 3rd takes in more of GOP-friendly Crawford County, dropping some of Democratic-leaning Erie; Mercer County trends Democratic. GOP presidential nominee Mitt Romney took 56 percent of the district's 2012 presidential vote.

Major Industry
Health care, manufacturing, tourism, shipping

Cities
Erie, New Castle, Hermitage, Butler, Meadville

Notable
Italian-American immigrants in New Castle, the "Fireworks Capital of America," launched the nation's pyrotechnic industry.

Rep. Scott Perry (R)

Capitol Office
225-5836
perry.house.gov
126 Cannon Bldg. 20515-5401; fax 226-1000

Committees
Foreign Affairs
Homeland Security
Transportation & Infrastructure

Residence
Dillsburg

Born
May 27, 1962; San Diego, Calif.

Religion
Christian

Family
Wife, Christy Perry; two children

Education
Pennsylvania State U., Harrisburg, B.S. 1991 (management)

Military
Pa. National Guard, 1980-present

Career
Utility contracting firm owner; draftsman; insurance agent; dock worker

Political Highlights
Pa. House, 2007-12

ELECTION RESULTS

2012 GENERAL		
Scott Perry (R)	181,603	59.7%
Harry Perkinson (D)	104,643	34.4%
Wayne W. Wolff (I)	11,524	3.8%
Michael Koffenberger (LIBERT)	6,210	2.0%
2012 PRIMARY		
Scott Perry (R)	34,881	53.5%
Christopher Reilly (R)	12,143	18.6%
Sean Summers (R)	9,316	14.3%
Theodore Waga (R)	3,086	4.7%
Eric Martin (R)	2,159	3.3%
Mark Swomley (R)	2,150	3.3%
Kevin Downs (R)	1,451	2.2%

Elected 2012; 1st term

The thoroughly conservative Perry has thoughts on federal spending and regulations that mesh well with those of his colleagues in the Republican Study Committee. His three decades of experience in the National Guard help him stand out when he discusses national security.

Perry was born in California, but early in his life his family moved to central Pennsylvania. He joined the Army National Guard not too long after graduating from high school in 1980; he eventually became the commander of a unit that deployed to Iraq for a year in January 2009. Among other roles, Perry has served as a helicopter pilot, and he was promoted to colonel in 2011.

Outside of the guard, Perry founded a mechanical contracting company in 1993 that provides construction and maintenance services to municipal and privately owned utilities. He was also active in Republican politics, heading up the Pennsylvania Young Republicans and helping out for several campaigns. He was elected to the state House in 2007 and pursued a small-government agenda by promoting spending cuts.

Perry sits on the Foreign Affairs and Homeland Security committees, which play to his military background. He is also a member of the Transportation and Infrastructure subcommittee on emergency management, which speaks to another role of the National Guard. His conservatism extends to social issues: He is a defender of Second Amendment rights and opposes abortion.

Six-term Rep. Todd Platts was ostensibly the incumbent in the 4th District created for the 2012 election, but he abided by the 12-year limit he favors for all federal lawmakers. Perry's political experience made him a likely successor. Opponents in the primary tried to make hay of a 2002 incident where Perry was charged with falsifying reports to the state Department of Environmental Protection as part of his business dealings — he blames the incident on an overzealous bureaucrat. Voters were not concerned, as Perry easily won both the primary and the general election.

Pennsylvania 4

South central — York, Harrisburg, Gettysburg

With the exception of state capital Harrisburg, the renumbered 4th sits west of the Susquehanna River and mostly east of the South Mountain ridge in south central Pennsylvania. Historic sites here include the York County Courthouse, where the Articles of Confederation were drafted and adopted, and a Civil War battlefield in Gettysburg. State government, manufacturing and agriculture are the economic drivers.

A Capitol Dome inspired by Michelangelo's design for St. Peter's Basilica in Rome dominates the skyline in Harrisburg (shared with the 11th). The city has been hit by public sector cutbacks on the federal and state level, and its schools are scraping by on reduced budgets.

Major highways and the presence of Capital City Airport make the district a transportation and distribution hub for the Mid-Atlantic region. A strong manufacturing base, including Harley-Davidson assembly lines in York, helps York County market itself as the "Factory Tour Capital of the World." The job market has attracted migration from Maryland, and boosted population growth since 2000. Home construction to accommodate the growth has included lower-income units to address pockets of poverty.

The national cemetery and war memorials at Gettysburg draw 3 million people to Adams County each year, tourism that supports some 7,000 jobs. A National Park Service program aimed at restoring battlefields to their Civil War-condition could enhance the venue.

Although the district is overwhelmingly white, blacks and Hispanics combined account for the majority of the population in York and Harrisburg. The cities harbor Democratic tendencies — the portion of Dauphin County in the 4th strongly supports Democrats — but overall, the district is GOP territory and it gave Republican Mitt Romney 57 percent in the 2012 presidential race.

Major Industry
Government, manufacturing, agriculture, health care

Military Bases
Defense Distribution Depot Susquehanna, 383 military, 3,980 civilians

Cities
Harrisburg (pt.), York

Notable
Rather than dropping a ball at midnight each New Year's Eve, Red Lion raises an 8-foot-long fiberglass cigar to salute its cigar-making history.

Rep. Glenn Thompson (R)

Capitol Office
225-5121
thompson.house.gov
124 Cannon Bldg. 20515-3805; fax 225-5796

Committees
Agriculture
(Conservation, Energy & Forestry - Chairman)
Education & the Workforce
Natural Resources

Residence
Howard Township

Born
July 27, 1959; Bellefonte, Pa.

Religion
Protestant

Family
Wife, Penny Ammerman-Thompson; three children

Education
Pennsylvania State U., B.S. 1981 (recreation & parks); Temple U., M.Ed. 1998 (sports management & leisure studies)

Career
Rehabilitation therapist

Political Highlights
Bald Eagle Area School Board, 1990-95; Republican nominee for Pa. House, 1998, 2000; Centre County Republican Party chairman, 2002-08

ELECTION RESULTS

2012 GENERAL		
Glenn Thompson (R)	177,740	62.9%
Charles Dumas (D)	104,725	37.1%
2012 PRIMARY		
Glenn Thompson (R)		unopposed
2010 GENERAL		
Glenn Thompson (R)	127,427	68.7%
Michael Pipe (D)	52,375	28.2%
Vernon L. Etzel (LIBERT)	5,710	3.1%

Previous Winning Percentages
2008 (57%)

Elected 2008; 3rd term

The unflashy Thompson has a background in health care but a vested interest in energy: His district rests atop massive natural gas deposits. He blends in with rank-and-file Republicans while working on legislation to help his rural constituents.

Thompson spent 26 years in various positions in the regional Susquehanna Health System, most recently as a rehabilitation services manager. He cites frustration over health care debates as his reason for running in 2008: "It was very obvious to me that these legislators were clueless," he said.

The Marcellus Shale, however, has dictated much of his Washington work. Like many Pennsylvanians, he thinks the gas reserve could be "an incredibly important job creator." Thompson works the issue through his seat on the Natural Resources Subcommittee on Energy and Mineral Resources; he also chairs the Agriculture panel for Conservation, Energy and Forestry.

Millions of dollars in federal grants related to energy production have flowed to his district, including a $10 million grant in October 2010 for transportation improvements needed to accommodate Marcellus development. Thompson has been a defender of hydraulic fracturing — the use of high-pressure water and chemicals to extract gas and oil from rock — against critics who say it risks contaminating water supplies.

Thompson was an original co-sponsor of a 2011 bill that contained $5 billion in incentives for natural-gas-powered vehicles — though he and a few other lawmakers later withdrew their support following pressure from conservatives wary of new energy subsidies. In the 113th Congress (2013-14), he is one of the leaders of the Natural Gas Caucus.

Throughout the 112th Congress (2011-12), House Republicans voted to restrict EPA regulatory authority, saying the agency was eyeing standards with minimal health benefits and crushing economic effects. Thompson joined in. He vigorously opposed 2009 legislation to create a cap-and-trade system for regulating greenhouse gas emissions, calling it "a $646 billion tax that will hit almost every American family, small business and family farm."

Thompson has criticized the Obama administration for its stewardship of resources on federal lands. He said in May 2011 that the Forest Service's land management proposal "does not go far enough to ensure and promote active land management practices, or to guarantee the economic viability of timber production."

At a 2013 hearing, Thompson called for increased timber sales out of the National Forest System. He and Oregon Democrat Kurt Schrader have also introduced a measure to include forest products among those covered by the Agriculture Department's BioPreferred Program, which is meant to promote bio-based goods.

A former school board member and county GOP chairman, Thompson says the Boy Scouts gave him his first electoral victory: "The very first elected office I ever held was assistant patrol leader." He is an Eagle Scout and former local Boy Scout Council president, and he continues to have an active role in scouting. Thompson says he tries to uphold the Scouts' values by not demonizing those with whom he disagrees — even as he opposes the Democratic agenda.

And he has worked with Democrats from his state on some education and health care legislation. He is a former co-chairman of the Congressional Health Care Caucus and a former vice chairman of the Congressional Rural Caucus. Thompson tries to keep lawmakers from urban districts aware of rural health issues. "Rural America is certainly outnumbered, which presents a special challenge," he said.

Thompson scored a legislative victory with a provision in the fiscal 2012 defense policy law to speed care to veterans from rural towns; it allows doctors and health professionals to use telemedicine and e-health technology to treat out-of-state patients. In 2011, Thompson worked with Pennsylvania Democrat Jason Altmire in an effort to repeal Medicare's competitive bidding program for durable medical equipment and services; the current system forces smaller providers out of the market, they said.

From the Education and the Workforce Committee, he has backed bills to remove "adequate yearly progress" requirements and change teacher evaluation provisions in the federal education law known as No Child Left Behind. In 2011, Thompson and Pennsylvania Sen. Bob Casey, a Democrat, introduced companion bills to allow schools seeking grants to help low-achieving students the flexibility to incorporate career and technical education into their curricula. The language was included as part of a panel-approved version of an education law rewrite, which was not enacted.

The committee rejected his amendment to change the federal funding formula for impoverished districts. Thompson wants more money distributed to districts with a high percentage of students in poverty, as opposed to districts with high numbers of poor students. Rural districts have complained that they usually lose out to urban districts under the current formula.

Thompson has lived in his district his entire life. He was born in Bellefonte and grew up in Howard; he and his younger brother and sister all live within walking distance of one another. His relatives had been dairy farmers in the area for generations, but his father owned a sporting goods store. Thompson and his wife, Penny, have been together since high school.

After graduating from Penn State in 1981 — he now represents the main campus — Thompson entered the health care field, working for a year at a group home for the disabled before joining Susquehanna Health. In 1998, he received his master's degree in education from Temple University.

He served five years as a member of the Bald Eagle Area School Board before mounting unsuccessful challenges to Democratic state Rep. Mike Hanna in 1998 and 2000. He subsequently became chairman of the Centre County Republican Party. As he and his wife were about to become empty-nesters, with their three children leaving home, he decided it was worth entering the 2008 congressional race.

The contacts Thompson built as a local GOP chairman helped him prevail over eight opponents in the primary. He then easily beat Democrat Mark B. McCracken in the general election. He also won easily in 2010 and 2012.

A new congressional map for 2012 expanded his district; he now represents part of the Lake Erie shoreline and the outskirts of the city of Erie.

Key Votes

2012	
Extend a Social Security payroll tax cut and unemployment benefits	YES
Ease securities rules to expand small-business access to capital	YES
Extend for one year subsidized student loan interest rates financed by a cut in health care spending	YES
Cite Attorney General Eric H. Holder Jr. for contempt of Congress	YES
Create a visa program for foreign graduates in high-tech fields	YES
Extend most Bush-era income tax rates while allowing rates for top-bracket earners to rise (Jan. 1, 2013)	YES
2011	
Strike funding for F-35 alternative engine	YES
Prevent EPA from regulating greenhouse gas emissions to address climate change	YES
Extend certain provisions of Patriot Act for four years	YES
Declare opposition to use of ground troops in Libya	YES
Overhaul patent law	NO
Pass compromise debt limit increase plan and establish future spending limits	YES
Allow consideration of measures to implement three trade agreements	YES

CQ Vote Studies

	PARTY UNITY		PRESIDENTIAL SUPPORT	
	SUPPORT	OPPOSE	SUPPORT	OPPOSE
2012	87%	13%	16%	84%
2011	93%	7%	24%	76%
2010	93%	7%	31%	69%
2009	85%	15%	27%	73%

Interest Groups

	AFL-CIO	ADA	CCUS	ACU
2012	10%	0%	100%	76%
2011	0%	10%	94%	68%
2010	7%	0%	88%	100%
2009	19%	15%	87%	88%

Pennsylvania 5

North central — State College, Erie suburbs,

Sprawling across all or part of 16 counties, the 5th stretches east from Erie County suburbs to the edge of Marcellus Shale territory in Tioga County. Bordering New York, this broad expanse of central Pennsylvania swoops into Centre County, home to Pennsylvania State University — the state's largest college campus. It is the state's geographically largest district and contains the smallest population of minorities.

State College, the 5th's most populous city, abuts Penn State in Centre County and is referred to by locals as "Happy Valley." Centre has one of the state's lowest rates of unemployment and hosts the global headquarters for AccuWeather and an expanding technology sector.

Erie County's Northwest Harborcreek, a fast-growing suburban community, is also an outlier in the spread of small towns clustered between state and national parks. Strong community programs and Penn State's Behrend College help drive growth.

The 5th's other counties are tied to manufacturing, logging and tourism. McKean County's Bradford Oil Field, which produced 83 percent of the nation's oil output at its peak, commemorates the industry with a museum. Quehanna Trail hikers can see the largest stand of white birch trees in the eastern U.S. Massive herds of free-roaming elk can be hunted in Elk Country. Jefferson County is the home of Punxsutawney Phil, the famous groundhog. Tourists flock to Allegheny National Forest's rugged plateau for scenic overlooks and angling opportunities in its 12,000-acre reservoir.

Protecting rural schools and expanding broadband and mobile-phone coverage throughout isolated, mountainous parts of the region are important issues in the 5th. Republicans have represented the district in Congress since the 1970s, and Mitt Romney took 57 percent of its 2012 presidential vote.

Major Industry

Higher education, technology, manufacturing, timber, tourism

Cities

State College, Northwest Harborcreek (unincorp.)

Notable

In 1859, Edwin L. Drake drilled the oil well that launched the modern petroleum industry in Titusville.

Rep. Jim Gerlach (R)

Capitol Office
225-4315
gerlach.house.gov
2442 Rayburn Bldg. 20515-3806; fax 225-8440

Committees
Ways & Means

Residence
West Pikeland Township

Born
Feb. 25, 1955; Ellwood City, Pa.

Religion
Protestant

Family
Wife, Karen Gerlach; three children, three stepchildren

Education
Dickinson College, B.A. 1977 (political science); Dickinson School of Law, J.D. 1980

Career
Lawyer

Political Highlights
Republican nominee for Pa. House, 1986; Pa. House, 1991-95; Pa. Senate, 1995-2003

ELECTION RESULTS

2012 GENERAL		
Jim Gerlach (R)	191,725	57.1%
Manan Trivedi (D)	143,803	42.9%
2012 PRIMARY		
Jim Gerlach (R)		unopposed
2010 GENERAL		
Jim Gerlach (R)	133,770	57.1%
Manan Trivedi (D)	100,493	42.9%

Previous Winning Percentages
2008 (52%); 2006 (51%); 2004 (51%); 2002 (51%)

Elected 2002; 6th term

Gerlach often works with Democrats to introduce popular, narrowly tailored legislation, but he can also be a sharp voice for the priorities of GOP leaders. As a member of the Ways and Means Committee, he has opportunities to perfect that dual approach, seeking tweaks to the tax code and health care laws while also promoting Republican plans for major overhauls.

Gerlach's inclusive politics have helped him ride out the decline of moderate Republicans in the northeast. He became a member of Ways and Means at the start of the 112th Congress (2011-12), after enjoying his first comfortable re-election victory.

He has some of the tendencies common to Philadelphia-area Republicans. Gerlach (GUR-lock) pays more heed to the environmental movement and organized labor, and he doesn't hang his reputation on social issues. He is a member of the moderate Main Street Partnership.

Gerlach built his policy record with a special focus on energy. In the 112th Congress, he and Oregon Democrat Earl Blumenauer introduced a bill to eliminate an excise tax on the purchase of large trucks, to encourage trucking companies to purchase newer, more-efficient vehicles. He voted to preserve funding for renewable-energy programs — a favorite target of cost-cutting conservatives — and has supported the extension of tax credits for renewable-energy production.

Renewable energy likely needs government support to develop into a vibrant part of an "all of the above" energy strategy, Gerlach said, and "some of that may need support for a long period."

But he also criticized the Obama administration for its handling of loan guarantees to failed solar panel manufacturer Solyndra Inc., and he voted for a bill to prohibit new loan guarantees to renewable-energy companies. Guarantees for specific companies are a more "problematic approach," he said. "Creating general opportunities for industries, if they need temporary support from the tax code — that's a little different."

Gerlach is on the Select Revenue Measures and Health subcommittees of Ways and Means. He has worked with Senate partners and Democrats on legislation to extend the research-and-development tax credit to tech startup companies.

He opposes the excise tax on medical devices in the 2010 health care law and wrote a bill to repeal it. "The tax hits well-established companies and startup businesses that are suffering losses in their initial years while they invest heavily in the research and development of their first innovation for patients," he wrote in Roll Call with Minnesota Republican Erik Paulsen.

Even while looking for adjustments to the tax code, Gerlach has stood behind Republican plans to overhaul the code in the 113th Congress (2013-14). He endorsed many of the pieces outlined by Ways and Means Chairman Dave Camp of Michigan over the course of the 112th: two tax brackets of 10 percent and 25 percent for individuals; fewer exemptions and deductions; and lower corporate tax rates.

He doesn't have a seat on the Ways and Means Trade Subcommittee, but the manufacturers in his district are interested in finding outlets for their products. In 2012, Speaker John A. Boehner appointed Gerlach to the President's Export Council, which advises the White House on trade matters.

Gerlach is a champion of open-space preservation and co-founded the House Land Trust Caucus, now called the Land Conservation Caucus. The House passed his 2006 bill to encourage the purchase of conservation easements.

Gerlach's voting record has largely mirrored the ebb and flow of power in Washington. In 2003, on House votes where President George W. Bush had staked out a preference, Gerlach supported him 91 percent of the time. By the end of Bush's second term, that number plummeted to 44 percent.

When President Barack Obama took office, Gerlach stuck with his party on major economic initiatives — he called the 2009 stimulus law an "orgy of spending" — but found some issues to support on the Democratic agenda. He voted for an extension of unemployment benefits without a budgetary offset and backed an expansion of the Children's Health Insurance Program.

Back in the majority in the 112th Congress, he criticized spending under the Obama administration, saying Obama's agenda "threatens to take a wrecking ball to a sputtering recovery." He voted to repeal the 2010 health care law.

Gerlach was born and raised in Ellwood City, a small steel town north of Pittsburgh. His mother raised him and his two sisters on her own after his father was killed by a drunken driver. Gerlach was 5 at the time of the accident. His mother "was just a terrific role model," he said.

He earned undergraduate and law degrees at Dickinson, not too far west of the state capital in Harrisburg. While studying, he also worked summers for a state senator from the Philadelphia suburbs. Gerlach initially settled near Philadelphia to start his legal career, but in 1986 he briefly returned home to Ellwood City to seek a state House seat there. He lost, and not long after, he moved back across the state to Chester County.

In 1990, he waged a door-to-door campaign that yielded him a 23-vote win in his second try for a state House seat. He won a state Senate seat four years later. He was the lead sponsor of Pennsylvania's 1996 welfare overhaul.

Gerlach won his congressional seat in 2002 in a newly drawn district that overlapped with much of his state Senate territory. He beat Democratic lawyer Dan Wofford, the son of former U.S. Sen. Harris Wofford, by 5,520 votes. Each of his first three re-elections was won by less than 5 points.

In February 2009, Gerlach filed paperwork to form an exploratory committee to seek Pennsylvania's governorship in 2010. But he dropped out of the Republican primary race in January, saying he didn't think he could get the fundraising levels to be as competitive as he needed to be. Gerlach turned his attention back to the House and won with 57 percent of the vote in 2010 over Democrat Manan Trivedi, a physician and Iraq War veteran.

Redistricting after the 2010 census gave Pennsylvania Republicans the chance to make Gerlach's district safer. They peeled off some Democratic-leaning areas and added more rural territory. Gerlach chose to defend his House seat rather than run for the Senate, and he again beat Trivedi — once again taking 57 percent of the vote.

Key Votes

2012	
Extend a Social Security payroll tax cut and unemployment benefits	YES
Ease securities rules to expand small-business access to capital	YES
Extend for one year subsidized student loan interest rates financed by a cut in health care spending	YES
Cite Attorney General Eric H. Holder Jr. for contempt of Congress	YES
Create a visa program for foreign graduates in high-tech fields	YES
Extend most Bush-era income tax rates while allowing rates for top-bracket earners to rise (Jan. 1, 2013)	YES
2011	
Strike funding for F-35 alternative engine	NO
Prevent EPA from regulating greenhouse gas emissions to address climate change	YES
Extend certain provisions of Patriot Act for four years	YES
Declare opposition to use of ground troops in Libya	YES
Overhaul patent law	YES
Pass compromise debt limit increase plan and establish future spending limits	YES
Allow consideration of measures to implement three trade agreements	YES

CQ Vote Studies

	PARTY UNITY		PRESIDENTIAL SUPPORT	
	SUPPORT	OPPOSE	SUPPORT	OPPOSE
2012	82%	18%	16%	84%
2011	84%	16%	27%	73%
2010	83%	17%	43%	57%
2009	73%	27%	51%	49%
2008	75%	25%	44%	56%

Interest Groups

	AFL-CIO	ADA	CCUS	ACU
2012	38%	0%	100%	68%
2011	25%	20%	100%	52%
2010	14%	10%	100%	67%
2009	52%	20%	87%	76%
2008	64%	60%	81%	48%

Pennsylvania 6

East central — northern Chester County, Lebanon

The 6th stretches from the Lebanon Valley through the suburbs of Reading and south into West Chester. Its hilly terrain captures portions of four southeastern counties and includes Blue Marsh Lake, portions of Neversink Mountain and a slice of the Schuylkill River Heritage Corridor. Fields of corn, barley and soybeans, logging sites and stone quarries cover areas between sparsely populated towns, with the Reading suburbs in Berks County serving as a population hub.

For generations of workers, the Reading Railroad's coal and freight lines built working class communities in the region. Since the rail line's bankruptcy in 1971, manufacturing and health care have absorbed the workforce here; Lebanon County's Veterans Affairs Medical Center and Reading Hospital are major employers. Factories that produce batteries and construction supplies have survived industrial declines.

The headquarters of investment firm Vanguard, near Valley Forge, and the West Chester campus of pharmaceutical giant Pfizer provide white-collar jobs. The district is also home to Exelon's Limerick Generating Station, a nuclear energy plant in southwestern Montgomery County. Transportation along Route 422, which carries commuters into Philadelphia, is a major issue for the district. Local officials have proposed tolls to pay for upgrades and an extension of commuter rail to ease congestion.

The 6th's population is nearly 90 percent white. Hispanics are the largest and fastest-growing minority group, particularly immigrants from Puerto Rico and the Dominican Republic.

On the state level, voters here tend to elect Republicans and fiscally conservative Democrats. Federal elections are competitive and trending Republican: Mitt Romney won the district in 2012 with 51 percent of the presidential vote, but Barack Obama would have won this territory in 2008 by 7 percentage points.

Major Industry
Health care, manufacturing, pharmaceuticals, financial services

Cities
Reading (pt.), Lebanon (pt.), Pottstown

Notable
Televised home shopping network QVC has its studio in West Chester.

Rep. Patrick Meehan (R)

Capitol Office
225-2011
meehan.house.gov
204 Cannon Bldg. 20515-3807; fax 226-0280

Committees
Ethics
Homeland Security
(Cybersecurity, Infrastructure Protection & Security Technologies - Chairman)
Oversight & Government Reform
Transportation & Infrastructure

Residence
Drexel Hill

Born
Oct. 20, 1955; Cheltenham, Pa.

Religion
Roman Catholic

Family
Wife, Carolyn Meehan; three children

Education
Bowdoin College, B.A. 1978 (classics & government); Temple U., J.D. 1986

Career
Lawyer; congressional district and campaign aide; professional hockey referee

Political Highlights
Delaware County district attorney, 1996-2001; U.S. attorney, 2001-08

ELECTION RESULTS

2012 GENERAL		
Patrick Meehan (R)	209,942	59.4%
George Badey (D)	143,509	40.6%
2012 PRIMARY		
Patrick Meehan (R)		unopposed
2010 GENERAL		
Patrick Meehan (R)	137,825	54.9%
Bryan Lentz (D)	110,314	44.0%
Jim Schneller (I)	2,708	1.1%

Elected 2010; 2nd term

Meehan is a veteran political operator from the moderate camp of the Republican Party. When not tending to the economic needs of southeastern Pennsylvania, the former prosecutor aggressively studies potential threats to homeland security.

In the early 1990s, he worked on the staff of a Pennsylvania Republican so moderate that he eventually became a Democrat: Sen. Arlen Specter. Meehan moved on to become the district attorney for Delaware County, and during much of the George W. Bush administration he served as a U.S. attorney. In that role, he established an anti-terrorism advisory council for the region and famously rooted out corruption in the Philadelphia and state governments.

Those years of investigative and law enforcement experience are now put to use on the Homeland Security Committee. He chaired the Counterterrorism and Intelligence Subcommittee as a freshman, and for the 113th Congress (2013-14) he is leading the Cybersecurity, Infrastructure Protection and Security Technologies Subcommittee.

Meehan emphasizes that he wants to work on bills that can pass the Democratic Senate, and he has proved adept at working with stakeholders in the private sector. Those factors could shape cybersecurity legislation — efforts to set new standards stalled in the 112th Congress (2011-12), in part over disputes about how much authority the government should have over privately owned network infrastructure.

He had a narrower focus on cybersecurity as a freshman, holding a hearing on Iran's attempts to improve its capability for cyberattacks. Meehan said his goal on the counterterrorism panel was to identify "where the next threats are coming from and what we ought to be doing about it," and he saw Iran as the greatest threat. There were reports in 2011 that the Iranian government tried to orchestrate an assassination on U.S. soil, and Meehan said that having that capability would give Iran leverage to resist attempts to defang its nuclear weapons program. "Our government risks a failure of imagination and may not fully be considering the gravity of the Iranian threat," he warned.

Meehan similarly questions whether the Obama administration is paying enough attention to "an emerging worldwide network of al-Qaida affiliates that is increasing in capability, intent and lethality," as he wrote in the Washington Examiner in late 2012. He urges the State Department to designate the Nigerian group Boko Haram as a terrorist organization.

In 2012, the House passed Meehan's bill to formalize information-sharing practices about weapons of mass destruction among intelligence organizations; the Department of Homeland Security needs to maintain technical expertise regarding such threats, he said. He reintroduced it in 2013.

Meehan's work on infrastructure protection started in 2011 with a local concern. Refineries in his district and nearby Philadelphia closed, and Meehan quickly started to probe "the extent to which there can be national security implications to having all our oil-refining capacity focused in just a couple of places." He was one of the lawmakers serving as a facilitator in the effort to keep the sites running — Democrat Robert A. Brady was the key figure — and a series of business deals, labor agreements and promises of expedited regulatory reviews were in place before the end of 2012.

On the Transportation and Infrastructure Committee, Meehan calls for robust federal investment in infrastructure and sees the energy industry as a means to fund it. He was an active promoter of a GOP proposal to expand offshore energy leasing, then dedicate large portions of the lease revenue to both infrastructure projects and the development of "green" technology. "This isn't one of these pie-in-the-sky ideas," he said in 2011.

Meehan voted for a two-year reauthorization of surface transportation programs in 2012, but he wanted a longer and more targeted bill. "Federal policy should focus on our urgent, highest-priority needs and leave the bike paths to local authorities," he wrote in early 2012.

Meehan also has a seat on the Oversight and Government Reform Committee, and he was added to the Ethics Committee for the 113th.

A member of the moderate Main Street Partnership, Meehan has supported overall spending reductions while declining to go after some of the grant programs and agencies targeted by conservatives. He was one of only 16 House Republicans to support a fiscal 2013 budget proposal, widely viewed as middle ground, that would cut deficits by $4 trillion over 10 years through revenue increases, spending cuts and entitlement program changes.

Meehan's occasional support of organized labor also sets him apart from many in the GOP. He was one of seven Republicans to oppose a 2011 bill curtailing the enforcement powers of the National Labor Relations Board.

One of four children, Meehan was born in Cheltenham, a township north of Philadelphia. His father was a Navy veteran and a construction estimator; his mother was a secretary. Meehan went to work at a young age, spending summers as a caddy and lifeguard and doing stints in a rubber factory and on a street construction crew.

He also got an early start in law enforcement, by refereeing ice hockey games for extra cash. Meehan started skating when he was 6 and was a defenseman at Bowdoin College in Maine; he says his job as a player was to "get in the way of the other guys." After college he joined the National Hockey League officiating staff for a few years, working primarily minor league games.

Meehan's first political involvement was volunteering for a state Senate campaign in northeastern Philadelphia, and "I didn't even know what a ward was in those days," he said. He learned quickly. While embarking on a legal career, Meehan worked for several state and local politicians, including Specter; he managed the successful 1994 Senate campaign of Rick Santorum.

He was considered a prize recruit in the 2010 contest to succeed Democrat Joe Sestak, who ran unsuccessfully for the Senate. Democrats put up state Rep. Bryan Lentz, an Iraq War veteran. Sestak had won by double digits twice, but Meehan rode the national GOP wave and a strong Republican ticket above him to an 11-point victory.

GOP officials made some overtures to Meehan about challenging Democratic Sen. Bob Casey in 2012, but he stuck with the 7th District, which became more Republican-friendly after redistricting. He easily defeated Democratic lawyer George Badey.

Key Votes

2012	
Extend a Social Security payroll tax cut and unemployment benefits	YES
Ease securities rules to expand small-business access to capital	YES
Extend for one year subsidized student loan interest rates financed by a cut in health care spending	YES
Cite Attorney General Eric H. Holder Jr. for contempt of Congress	YES
Create a visa program for foreign graduates in high-tech fields	YES
Extend most Bush-era income tax rates while allowing rates for top-bracket earners to rise (Jan. 1, 2013)	YES
2011	
Strike funding for F-35 alternative engine	YES
Prevent EPA from regulating greenhouse gas emissions to address climate change	YES
Extend certain provisions of Patriot Act for four years	YES
Declare opposition to use of ground troops in Libya	YES
Overhaul patent law	YES
Pass compromise debt limit increase plan and establish future spending limits	YES
Allow consideration of measures to implement three trade agreements	YES

CQ Vote Studies

	PARTY UNITY		PRESIDENTIAL SUPPORT	
	SUPPORT	OPPOSE	SUPPORT	OPPOSE
2012	83%	17%	21%	79%
2011	85%	15%	31%	69%

Interest Groups

	AFL-CIO	ADA	CCUS	ACU
2012	45%	5%	100%	56%
2011	28%	20%	100%	52%

Pennsylvania 7

Western Philadelphia suburbs — most of Delaware County and parts of Chester and Berks counties

Located in southeastern Pennsylvania, the 7th is a mix of urban, suburban and agricultural territory. In its jagged splash of communities, it cobbles together parts of King of Prussia and Blue Bell northwest of Philadelphia, Pennsylvania Dutch Country and the Schuylkill Highlands. It includes the state's entire small border with Delaware as well as a cut of the Delaware River across from New Jersey.

Pharmaceutical and technology firms are growing in the largely white-collar center of Montgomery County, with developers competing for corporate park tenants. Retail and tourism also drive the economy: Pennsylvania's newest casino opened in Valley Forge near established historic sites, and the massive King of Prussia mall is in the 13th District.

High foreclosure rates have plagued Marcus Hook since the 2009 closing of Sunoco's oil refinery, but officials hope to revive the area as a storage and processing site for products from the Marcellus Shale region. Layoffs in the health care industry also hurt the economy west of Philadelphia. About 40 percent of Delaware County residents leave its bedroom communities for work.

Nearly half of the land in the western region of the 7th is pastoral or forested, with French Creek State Park encompassing the largest block of contiguous forest between Washington, D.C., and New York City. Farms in Lancaster County rank high nationally for production of milk and eggs.

The majority-white 7th combines conservative Amish culture with more socially moderate suburbs near the city. Republican nominee Mitt Romney eked out a win in 2012 with 50 percent of the district's presidential vote.

Major Industry
Pharmaceuticals, health care, retail, manufacturing, agriculture

Cities
Norristown (pt.), King of Prussia (unincorp.) (pt.)

Notable
A preserved blast furnace and ironmaster's mansion from a 19th-century iron plantation stand at the Hopewell Furnace National Historic Site in eastern Berks County as a testament to the area's industrial past.

Rep. Michael G. Fitzpatrick (R)

Capitol Office
225-4276
fitzpatrick.house.gov
2400 Rayburn Bldg. 20515-3808; fax 225-9511

Committees
Financial Services

Residence
Levittown

Born
June 28, 1963; Philadelphia, Pa.

Religion
Roman Catholic

Family
Wife, Kathy Fitzpatrick; six children

Education
St. Thomas U. (Fla.), B.A. 1985 (political science); Dickinson School of Law, J.D. 1988

Career
Lawyer

Political Highlights
Republican nominee for Pa. House, 1990, 1994; Bucks County Board of Commissioners, 1995-2005; U.S. House, 2005-07; defeated for re-election to U.S. House, 2006

ELECTION RESULTS

2012 GENERAL		
Michael G. Fitzpatrick (R)	199,379	56.6%
Kathy Boockvar (D)	152,859	43.4%
2012 PRIMARY		
Michael G. Fitzpatrick (R)		unopposed
2010 GENERAL		
Michael G. Fitzpatrick (R)	130,759	53.5%
Patrick J. Murphy (D)	113,547	46.5%

Previous Winning Percentages
2004 (55%)

Elected 2010; 3rd term

Also served 2005-07

Fitzpatrick has gotten more conservative over the course of his House career, yet he still ranks as one of the most independent Republicans in the chamber. He operates out of the Financial Services Committee but works on a variety of subjects, sometimes siding with Democrats as they try to defeat spending cuts and anti-regulatory GOP policies.

He started his House service in the 109th Congress (2005-06) and had a moderate voting record — in 2006, he bucked his party on a third of the votes when majorities of Republicans and Democrats diverged. It wasn't enough for his fiscally conservative, socially liberal district. Defeated after one term, he went back to work as a lawyer. When the national mood favored Republicans in 2010, he won his return to Washington. Reflecting on his first term, Fitzpatrick told the Allentown Morning Call that "I wish we had slowed the growth [of the deficit] a little quicker or cut a little deeper. ... I wish we had been more aggressive in reducing government spending."

Fitzpatrick was more fiscally conservative in the 112th Congress (2011-12). He voted for fiscal blueprints produced by the Budget Committee, cost-cutting appropriations bills and a 2011 deficit reduction package.

When opportunities arose, however, he defended grant programs favored by local governments — Fitzpatrick was a Bucks County commissioner for a decade. "If you believe in federalism, if you believe that the best solutions are provided at the local level," then programs such as Community Development Block Grants are worth preserving, he said.

Fitzpatrick is also friendlier to labor and environmental causes than most of his party. He was one of seven Republicans to oppose a 2011 House bill limiting the enforcement powers of the National Labor Relations Board. Several times in the 112th, he rejected attempts to limit the EPA's regulatory authority or alter land and water conservation and restoration programs. He has long expressed reservations about mountaintop removal coal mining, and he was one of 13 Republicans voting against a 2012 bill to ease regulations on the coal industry.

His voting record for his second term put him on the list of top 10 House Republicans who break with their party, and he continued to sound independent themes at the start of the 113th Congress (2013-14). Advocates of stricter gun control look at Fitzpatrick as a possible Republican ally. He introduced a bill in January 2013 to give states incentives to strengthen the criminal background check system used for gun purchases.

Fitzpatrick also promotes a package of bills that he describes as improvements to the federal government. It includes an end to congressional pensions, a pay freeze for lawmakers and a longer ban on lobbying by former lawmakers. On the first day of 2013, the House passed Fitzpatrick's bill to undo a pay raise for federal employees that President Barack Obama ordered a few days before.

On the Financial Services Committee, Fitzpatrick has called for a repeal of the 2010 financial services overhaul known as Dodd-Frank, and he has said that taxpayer investment in mortgage giants Fannie Mae and Freddie Mac should be capped at $200 billion.

Credit rating agencies are also still on his agenda. Fitzpatrick was the House sponsor of a 2006 law meant to increase competition and transparency among the agencies, amid concerns that Standard & Poor's and Moody's Investors Service held too much sway over markets and made dubious assessments.

"It didn't have an opportunity" to take hold before the financial crises of 2007 and 2008, Fitzpatrick maintained. He probed the fall 2011 collapse of the derivatives trader MF Global as vice chairman of the Financial Services subcommittee on oversight. The company's investment-grade ranking days before its bankruptcy suggests a further need to evaluate the rating agencies, Fitzpatrick said.

Fitzpatrick's support of increased flexibility in local governments' spending of federal aid includes natural disaster response. When Hurricane Floyd ravaged the area in 1999, Fitzpatrick aggressively pursued his county's "fair share" of federal disaster funds. Hurricane Irene flooded parts of his district in 2011, and Fitzpatrick gave the Federal Emergency Management Agency excellent reviews.

He had been less kind to FEMA in 2005. The "top-down response" to Hurricane Katrina did not work, he said. President George W. Bush signed his bill to temporarily increase FEMA's borrowing authority to cover flood insurance claims. He endorsed a bipartisan five-year reauthorization of the National Flood Insurance Program that was enacted in 2012.

Fitzpatrick was born in Philadelphia and resides in Levittown; he and his wife have six children. He received his bachelor's degree in political science from St. Thomas University in Florida, then his law degree from Dickinson School of Law in 1988. He made two unsuccessful bids for the Pennsylvania House in the early 1990s, then won a seat on the Bucks County Board of Commissioners in 1995.

In 2004, the surprise retirement of six-term Republican James C. Greenwood created an opportunity in the 8th District. Because Greenwood had already won the primary when he announced he was leaving Congress to take a lobbying job, party leaders picked the nominee. Fitzpatrick — the favorite of leaders in Bucks County, the district's dominant jurisdiction — got the nod. Democratic presidential candidate John Kerry carried the district by 3 points, but Fitzpatrick won 55 percent of the vote.

In 2006, Fitzpatrick was hurt by the unpopularity of Bush. Democrat Patrick J. Murphy beat him by about 1,500 votes. Fitzpatrick went back to practicing law and also dealt successfully with a case of colon cancer. He came back to challenge Murphy in 2010, when the district was unhappy with Democratic policies such as the 2010 health care overhaul. He won by 7 points.

The new congressional map for 2012 didn't change Fitzpatrick's district much, and Democrats targeted him early. Attorney Kathy Boockvar won the Democratic nomination and attacked Fitzpatrick's voting record; she was aided by national campaign organizations and spending by outside groups — including the hyper-liberal Credo super PAC, which curiously tried to brand Fitzpatrick as a tea party extremist. Fitzpatrick won by 13 points, but Democratic groups quickly listed him as a target for 2014.

Fitzpatrick has stated that he won't serve more than four terms in the House.

Key Votes

2012	
Extend a Social Security payroll tax cut and unemployment benefits	YES
Ease securities rules to expand small-business access to capital	YES
Extend for one year subsidized student loan interest rates financed by a cut in health care spending	YES
Cite Attorney General Eric H. Holder Jr. for contempt of Congress	YES
Create a visa program for foreign graduates in high-tech fields	YES
Extend most Bush-era income tax rates while allowing rates for top-bracket earners to rise (Jan. 1, 2013)	YES
2011	
Strike funding for F-35 alternative engine	YES
Prevent EPA from regulating greenhouse gas emissions to address climate change	YES
Extend certain provisions of Patriot Act for four years	NO
Declare opposition to use of ground troops in Libya	YES
Overhaul patent law	YES
Pass compromise debt limit increase plan and establish future spending limits	YES
Allow consideration of measures to implement three trade agreements	YES

CQ Vote Studies

	Party Unity		Presidential Support	
	Support	Oppose	Support	Oppose
2012	77%	23%	27%	73%
2011	79%	21%	22%	78%
2006	66%	34%	65%	35%
2005	76%	24%	61%	39%

Interest Groups

	AFL-CIO	ADA	CCUS	ACU
2012	40%	10%	91%	52%
2011	31%	20%	100%	64%
2006	57%	40%	64%	46%
2005	47%	30%	74%	60%

Pennsylvania 8

Northern Philadelphia suburbs — Bucks County

Creeks and valleys crisscross the 8th, north of Philadelphia. The district borders New Jersey and takes in all of Bucks County and a sliver of northeastern Montgomery County. Its small towns and suburban enclaves support the second-highest median income among districts in the state.

Steel, once a major employer in Bucks, has suffered long-term decline and sustained loss of blue-collar jobs. Propping up the economy are small businesses and health care sector employment. Jobs here also depend on the fledgling alternative-energy industry. Spanish wind turbine manufacturer Gamesa operates a facility in a former steel plant in Bucks County, although uncertainty about a project off the Virginia coast and the future of federal tax credits have led to layoffs. A solar-cell producer closed its doors, citing a vulnerable market.

The district's commuters will benefit from an upgrade to Amtrak's Northeast Corridor, which connects workers to Philadelphia and New Jersey. About half of Bucks County residents commute outside the district for work — many depend upon SEPTA trains from stations in the central and southern portions of the county.

Plans have been implemented to protect the region from flooding along the Neshaminy Creek Watershed. Agriculture, fishing, hunting and forestry dominate in the north.

The 8th is overwhelmingly white, with growing Asian and Hispanic populations. Both political parties have represented the fiscally conservative area in Congress during the past decade. Locally, southern manufacturing regions go for Democrats, while the rest of the district is Republican turf. In the 2012 presidential election, GOP nominee Mitt Romney won the district by 255 votes.

Major Industry
Health care, retail, manufacturing

Cities
Levittown (unincorp.)

Notable
The famous 1776 trip across the Delaware River ahead of the battles of Trenton and Princeton in New Jersey is re-enacted at Washington Crossing each Christmas Day.

Rep. Bill Shuster (R)

Capitol Office
225-2431
shuster.house.gov
2209 Rayburn Bldg. 20515-3809; fax 225-2486

Committees
Armed Services
Transportation & Infrastructure - Chairman

Residence
Hollidaysburg

Born
Jan. 10, 1961; McKeesport, Pa.

Religion
Lutheran

Family
Wife, Rebecca Shuster; two children

Education
Dickinson College, B.A. 1983 (political science & history); American U., M.B.A. 1987

Career
Car dealer; tire company manager

Political Highlights
No previous office

ELECTION RESULTS

2012 GENERAL		
Bill Shuster (R)	169,177	61.7%
Karen Ramsburg (D)	105,128	38.3%
2012 PRIMARY		
Bill Shuster (R)		unopposed
2010 GENERAL		
Bill Shuster (R)	141,904	73.1%
Tom Conners (D)	52,322	26.9%

Previous Winning Percentages
2008 (64%); 2006 (60%); 2004 (70%); 2002 (71%); 2001 Special Election (52%)

Elected 2001; 6th full term

Shuster has gone from selling cars to quarterbacking national transportation policy in a little over a decade. That ascent speaks to natural political skills, loyalty to the Republican Party and the lessons learned from his father, Bud Shuster — the "King of Asphalt," whom he has followed as chairman of the Transportation and Infrastructure Committee.

The younger Shuster held no prior political offices when he was elected to succeed his father, who resigned shortly after starting his 15th term. But selling cars is "a great proving ground for people to be in public life," he said. "You're convincing people to buy things; you're convincing people to vote for you."

Republicans saved him Bud's seat on Transportation and Infrastructure, and (before the House GOP instituted a ban on earmarks) Shuster proved adept at steering funding to projects in his district.

He also worked closely enough with Republican leaders to start holding positions of influence. He has been a part of the National Republican Congressional Committee since his first term, and he serves as a deputy whip. He became the top Republican on the subcommittee for railroads and pipelines in 2007, then its chairman in 2011.

His climb accelerated in the 112th Congress (2011-12). Republican leaders were unhappy with a multiyear surface transportation bill being prepared by Transportation and Infrastructure Chairman John L. Mica, as conservatives grumbled over spending levels and other provisions. Speaker John A. Boehner reportedly took Mica off the project, routing most negotiations through Shuster in March 2012. The move bypassed several more-senior Republicans.

Mica regained traction during a conference with the Senate, but Shuster was a key player in selling the Republican Conference on the bill. Their efforts helped produce a 27-month reauthorization that included provisions to streamline the permitting and review process for infrastructure projects. It also included parts of a Shuster measure to improve bus safety standards.

Mica reached the Republican-imposed term limit for his chairmanship at the end of 2012, and he ultimately endorsed Shuster as his successor.

With the highway law expiring in 2014, Shuster will have another crack at it, and he'll be facing some of the same problems as Mica. Shuster said early in 2013 that he was open to suggestions for new funding mechanisms for infrastructure, as few people see the current federal gasoline tax as a reliable source. He also doesn't have earmarks to help sell the highway bill — or a pending reauthorization of water infrastructure projects — to reluctant lawmakers.

Amtrak is up for reauthorization in 2013, and Shuster supported an abortive 2012 campaign by Mica to privatize the passenger rail service. Rather than condone broad investments in high-speed rail, as proposed by the Obama administration, Shuster has said such investments should first be proved worthwhile in the densely populated Northeast. "We need to find one place in the country to do it right," Shuster said. (Bud Shuster has served as a railroad lobbyist since 2007.)

Shuster scored a legislative victory with the January 2012 enactment of his bill to update federal safety standards for pipeline infrastructure. It doubled the maximum fine for violations and requires automatic shut-off valves on pipelines "where economically, technically and operationally feasible." The measure had broad bipartisan support, and Shuster said it provided the regulatory certainty the pipeline industry needed for growth.

He was also a negotiator for the final version of a reauthorization of federal aviation programs in 2012. Shuster stepped back in that case, withdrawing a provision to require the Federal Aviation Administration to consider how proposed regulations would affect segments of the aviation industry and tailor the rules to address those effects. Critics said the amendment could stop a rule aimed at reducing pilot fatigue issues and increasing training requirements.

Shuster sits on the Armed Services Committee. In the 112th Congress, he chaired the short-term Panel on Business Challenges Within the Defense Industry. He and Washington Democrat Rick Larsen (who also pitched in on the pipeline bill) led a host of hearings in 2011 to study possible improvements to the Pentagon's small-business contracting and procurement policies.

He likes the notion of special panels enough that he created one for the Transportation committee. In April 2013, he tapped his vice chairman, John J. Duncan Jr. of Tennessee, to lead a panel formulating an intermodal freight plan that will tie together infrastructure planning and policy for shipping via roads, rails, planes, ports and inland waterways.

Shuster worked with the Pennsylvania delegation to make it difficult to shut down the 911th Airlift Wing based in Pittsburgh. The Air Force had planned to close the base as part of a plan to save about $354 million by 2018. Shuster was a conferee on the fiscal 2013 defense policy bill, but the law didn't include a House-passed provision to require congressional approval for the closure. However, the Air Force announced in 2013 that the base would stay open at least through 2014. Shuster also supports missile defense programs while looking out for Letterkenny Army Depot, a missile facility in the southeastern part of his district.

Shanksville, where United Airlines Flight 93 crashed after passengers fought hijackers on Sept. 11, is in Shuster's district. In 2008, he secured $4.9 million to build a memorial at the crash site.

Shuster grew up on a farm near Everett, where his father, a computer salesman turned executive, had settled the family. He was 11 when Bud Shuster won election to the House in 1972. As Bud expanded his clout and secured stunning amounts of federal funding to benefit his constituents, Bill studied political science and history at Dickinson College (the alma mater of Pennsylvania's only president, James Buchanan). He went on to get a master's of business administration at American University in Washington, D.C.

He worked for two tire companies, Goodyear and Bandag, and opened his car dealership in East Freedom.

In the special election to succeed his father, Shuster won with 52 percent of the vote, defeating Democrat Scott Conklin, a Centre County commissioner. He was easily re-elected in 2002 but faced a tough campaign in 2004, after one of his aides was accused of spying on his political opponent at home and at fundraising events. Shuster won the GOP primary by less than 3 points. But he won easily in November, and his elections since then have been a breeze.

Key Votes

2012

Extend a Social Security payroll tax cut and unemployment benefits	YES
Ease securities rules to expand small-business access to capital	YES
Extend for one year subsidized student loan interest rates financed by a cut in health care spending	YES
Cite Attorney General Eric H. Holder Jr. for contempt of Congress	YES
Create a visa program for foreign graduates in high-tech fields	YES
Extend most Bush-era income tax rates while allowing rates for top-bracket earners to rise (Jan. 1, 2013)	YES

2011

Strike funding for F-35 alternative engine	NO
Prevent EPA from regulating greenhouse gas emissions to address climate change	YES
Extend certain provisions of Patriot Act for four years	YES
Declare opposition to use of ground troops in Libya	YES
Overhaul patent law	YES
Pass compromise debt limit increase plan and establish future spending limits	YES
Allow consideration of measures to implement three trade agreements	YES

CQ Vote Studies

	PARTY UNITY		PRESIDENTIAL SUPPORT	
	SUPPORT	OPPOSE	SUPPORT	OPPOSE
2012	91%	9%	13%	87%
2011	94%	6%	25%	75%
2010	98%	2%	27%	73%
2009	86%	14%	27%	73%
2008	94%	6%	67%	33%

Interest Groups

	AFL-CIO	ADA	CCUS	ACU
2012	38%	0%	100%	76%
2011	12%	15%	100%	75%
2010	7%	0%	88%	100%
2009	14%	5%	87%	88%
2008	13%	20%	94%	92%

Pennsylvania 9

South central — Altoona

Set in south-central Pennsylvania, the 9th contains the state's highest peak, Mt. Davis, and its deepest river gorge, but no significant metropolis. It is made up of small towns tucked in the Allegheny Mountains and its foothills, state parks and open land bordering Maryland and West Virginia.

Altoona's early growth was due to the Pennsylvania Railroad; its Horseshoe Curve enabled completion of a trans-state rail line and has given its name to the current minor league baseball team. Dependent on transportation industries for centuries — first rail and later interstate highway — Altoona is also home to the headquarters of the Sheetz chain of gas stations. It has promoted light manufacturing and office parks in recent economic-development efforts. To the south, Breezewood is the self-proclaimed "Travelers' Oasis" and continues to lure road-weary drivers to hotels and fast-food restaurants with its garish display of signs at the interchange of the Pennsylvania Turnpike and Interstate 70.

Small towns that developed around natural resources, steel production and railroads in the 18th and 19th centuries are now slow-growth, low-income areas attempting to diversify. Coal mining was integral to the area economy from colonial times through World War II, and coal towns still dot the landscape while environmental problems related to strip mining and bituminous coal processing remain. Fayette County officials are pinning their hopes for economic revival on natural-gas extraction. Farms cover much of the 9th. Wind turbines dot southeastern Somerset County. The picturesque Laurel Highlands have drawn tourists to resorts and spas.

Most voters of the 9th are socially and fiscally conservative and strongly oppose gun control. Republican nominee Mitt Romney won 63 percent of the district's presidential vote in 2012.

Major Industry

Agriculture, manufacturing, service, energy

Military Bases

Letterkenny Army Depot, 33 military, 1,743 civilian

Cities

Altoona, Chambersburg

Notable

A memorial to United Airlines Flight 93 is in Shanksville, where the hijacked airplane crashed in a field Sept. 11, 2001.

Rep. Tom Marino (R)

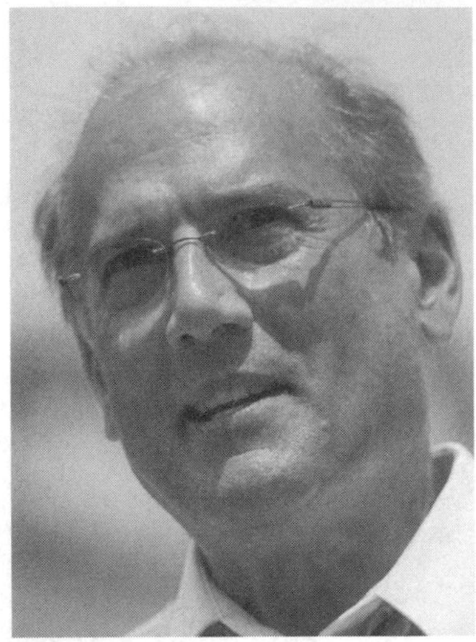

Capitol Office
225-3731
marino.house.gov
410 Cannon Bldg. 20515-3810; fax 225-9594

Committees
Foreign Affairs
Homeland Security
Judiciary

Residence
Lycoming Township

Born
Aug. 13, 1952; Williamsport, Pa.

Religion
Roman Catholic

Family
Wife, Edie Marino; two children

Education
Williamsport Area Community College, A.A. 1983; Lycoming College, B.A. 1985 (political science & secondary education); Dickenson School of Law, J.D. 1988

Career
Lawyer; bakery worker

Political Highlights
Lycoming County district attorney, 1992-2002; U.S. attorney, 2002-07

ELECTION RESULTS

2012 GENERAL		
Tom Marino (R)	179,563	65.6%
Philip Scollo (D)	94,227	34.4%
2012 PRIMARY		
Tom Marino (R)		unopposed
2010 GENERAL		
Tom Marino (R)	110,599	55.2%
Christopher Carney (D)	89,846	44.8%

Elected 2010; 2nd term

Marino was a blue-collar factory worker, then switched to a legal career later in life. As a congressman, he combines the ethic of the former job with the law-and-order agenda of the latter. "I'm pretty much an independent maverick," he says. "I deal with what has to be dealt with."

He got his law degree in his mid-30s, and within a few years he was the elected district attorney of his home county. He held that post for a decade before serving as the George W. Bush administration's top federal prosecutor in a mostly rural region that stretches from Harrisburg to Scranton. The work habits of prosecutors often carry over to congressional service, and Marino isn't an exception — he is methodical, he works on focused legislation, and he is very interested in law enforcement.

Marino has seats on both the Judiciary and Homeland Security committees. Combined, they give him a say in both border and immigration issues. He calls for increased border security — as a U.S. attorney, he often focused on drug-trafficking cases — and wants the guidance of local stakeholders on allocation of resources. "We have to do more, so we have to sit down and talk with the actual border agents," he said. "We have to talk to the communities that are affected by this, and let's hear what they have to say."

Marino opposes a path to citizenship for illegal immigrants and applauds state enforcement of immigration laws "if the federal government for whatever reason is unable to protect our borders."

He introduced a bill in 2012 to change standards for prosecuting drug traffickers; Marino wants offenders punished more severely if they have even a "reasonable cause to believe" that an illegal shipment will reach the United States. Organizations that use intermediaries for distribution can avoid the brunt of the law by claiming ignorance of a shipment's destination, Marino says. That year he also pursued a five-year reauthorization of the grant program providing federal criminal-justice funding to state and local jurisdictions. It passed the House, but the Senate didn't take it up in the 112th Congress (2011-12).

Marino is the vice chairman of the Judiciary subcommittee on intellectual property. He also addresses that topic as a member of the Foreign Affairs Committee. Marino says that Russia and China in particular are subsidizing the theft and copying of American products and that they are not afraid of an American response. "China reminds me a little bit of my 8-year-old," he said at a 2012 hearing, "when Dad says, 'Don't do this,' and he says, 'OK, Dad, I won't,' and then continues to do it." Tariffs must be levied if the practice does not stop, Marino says.

Cybersecurity is part of protecting intellectual property, and he chimed in as the House considered a cybersecurity overhaul in 2012. Marino wrote in Roll Call that he favors a voluntary and incentive-based system to encourage the private sector owners of computer networks to beef up their security. "We must avoid a bureaucratically directed regulatory heavy hand, which will be slow and ineffective given how rapidly threats change and adapt," he said.

He also sits on the Judiciary subcommittee on antitrust issues. He opposed the 2012 merger of Express Scripts and Medco, two of the largest companies that process and pay prescription drug claims. Marino said it could muscle smaller community pharmacies out of business. In 2011, he introduced a bill to exempt independent pharmacies from antitrust laws should they band together to negotiate with health insurers. Working with California Democrat Judy Chu, he brought the measure back in 2013.

In backing smaller pharmacies, Marino cites the needs of his daughter, who has cystic fibrosis. He maintains that a personal connection with a local pharmacist has been essential in emergency situations.

Marino himself has lost one kidney to cancer, and in April 2012 he had surgery to remove several small tumors on his remaining kidney. He voted to repeal the 2010 health care law but emphasizes that parts of it are necessary, including coverage for those with pre-existing conditions — he said he couldn't find an insurance company to cover him during his illness.

On the Foreign Affairs Committee, Marino has a seat on the subcommittee handling international organizations and Africa. He urges stricter oversight of, and conditions on, foreign aid. "The days of sending a bag full of money over and not accounting for it are over," he said. "If I hear of one more dictator who has left office and is living on a tropical island somewhere with billions of our dollars, I want to take my own squad and go after him."

Marino's voting record puts him pretty much in the Republican mainstream. He backs spending cuts but wasn't as draconian as some conservatives in that regard during the 112th Congress. In both of his terms, he has introduced a bill to freeze most federal hiring until the budget is balanced.

All of Marino's grandparents emigrated from Italy. His father was a firefighter and janitor, and his mother was a homemaker. Marino married his high school sweetheart and went to work at factory bakeries after graduating, ending up in middle management after 13 years.

He decided to go back to school when he was passed over for a promotion because he hadn't gone to college — but was still asked to train the person hired. "We sold everything we had" to help finance his education, and five years later he had a law degree, he said. "It's the best move I ever made."

Marino took on two-term Democratic Rep. Christopher Carney in 2010 and tried to tie his opponent to unpopular Democratic policies, such as the health care overhaul.

Carney tried to capitalize on an incident from Marino's past: While serving as a U.S. attorney, he appeared as a reference on a casino application of businessman Louis DeNaples, who had a decades-old felony conviction on his record and was investigated for alleged ties to organized crime. Marino resigned a few weeks after the Allentown Morning Call reported on the reference in August 2007, then took a job working for DeNaples.

The Democratic Congressional Campaign Committee spent more than a half-million dollars on Carney's behalf, but the Republican tide was too strong. Marino won with 55 percent of the vote.

A redrawn congressional map for 2012 made Marino's district more safely Republican. He beat Democrat Philip Scollo, a management consultant, by more than 30 points.

Key Votes

2012

Extend a Social Security payroll tax cut and unemployment benefits	YES
Ease securities rules to expand small-business access to capital	YES
Extend for one year subsidized student loan interest rates financed by a cut in health care spending	?
Cite Attorney General Eric H. Holder Jr. for contempt of Congress	YES
Create a visa program for foreign graduates in high-tech fields	YES
Extend most Bush-era income tax rates while allowing rates for top-bracket earners to rise (Jan. 1, 2013)	YES

2011

Strike funding for F-35 alternative engine	NO
Prevent EPA from regulating greenhouse gas emissions to address climate change	YES
Extend certain provisions of Patriot Act for four years	YES
Declare opposition to use of ground troops in Libya	YES
Overhaul patent law	YES
Pass compromise debt limit increase plan and establish future spending limits	YES
Allow consideration of measures to implement three trade agreements	YES

CQ Vote Studies

	PARTY UNITY		PRESIDENTIAL SUPPORT	
	SUPPORT	OPPOSE	SUPPORT	OPPOSE
2012	93%	7%	19%	81%
2011	95%	5%	27%	73%

Interest Groups

	AFL-CIO	ADA	CCUS	ACU
2012	10%	0%	100%	75%
2011	4%	10%	100%	84%

Pennsylvania 10

Northeast and central — part of the Pocono Mountains, Williamsport

The 10th is Pennsylvania's second-largest district, composed of 10 rural counties and parts of five others. Bordering New York and New Jersey in the northeast, it sprawls southwest through the Susquehanna Valley across U.S. Route 22 to Tuscarora Mountain.

The district's northern counties lie atop the natural-gas-rich Marcellus Shale formation. Bradford County has become ground zero for natural gas drilling in northeastern Pennsylvania, clogging roads and shocking the real estate markets of small towns. The natural gas boom has led to new jobs and local revenue streams, but the industry's use of hydraulic fracturing — or fracking — to extract the gas has raised environmental concerns that have occasionally stalled production. Local officials also complain that state legislation-initiated impact fees removed their ability to control gas drilling operations.

The district grabs a stretch of commercial space in eastern Scranton and the borough of Clark's Summit. Williamsport, in Lycoming County, is a center for state government and health care jobs. Timber logging, dairy farming and other agriculture remain important to the 10th's economy.

Wayne, Pike and Monroe counties along the district's eastern edge are home to several Pocono Mountain recreation areas, which draw visitors year-round. Commuters into New York and New Jersey have moved into booming Pike County for cheaper real estate and less congestion.

A large Catholic population helps edge the 10th toward social conservatism and Republican candidates in federal elections. Conservative Democrats can win here, but the region tends to swing for the GOP. Barack Obama won the parts of Lackawanna and Monroe counties in the district, while Republican nominee Mitt Romney won in every other jurisdiction and took 60 percent of the district's vote overall.

Major Industry

Natural gas, agriculture, transportation, health care, government

Cities

Scranton (pt.), Williamsport

Notable

The Little League World Series tournament is played annually in South Williamsport's stadium complex.

Rep. Lou Barletta (R)

Capitol Office
225-6511
barletta.house.gov
115 Cannon Bldg. 20515-3811; fax 226-6250

Committees
Education & the Workforce
Homeland Security
Transportation & Infrastructure
(Economic Development, Public Buildings & Emergency Management - Chairman)

Residence
Hazleton

Born
Jan. 28, 1956; Hazleton, Pa.

Religion
Roman Catholic

Family
Wife, MaryGrace Barletta; four children

Education
Bloomsburg State College, attended 1973-76; Luzerne County Community College, attended 1976-77

Career
Pavement marking company owner

Political Highlights
Republican nominee for Hazleton City Council, 1996; Hazleton City Council, 1998-2000; Republican nominee for U.S. House, 2002, 2008; mayor of Hazleton, 2000-10

ELECTION RESULTS

2012 GENERAL		
Lou Barletta (R)	166,967	58.5%
Gene Stilp (D)	118,231	41.5%
2012 PRIMARY		
Lou Barletta (R)		unopposed
2010 GENERAL		
Lou Barletta (R)	102,179	54.7%
Paul E. Kanjorski (D)	84,618	45.3%

Elected 2010; 2nd term

Barletta became a national figure fighting illegal immigration on the local level, and his mantra of greater local control extends to education, transportation and economic development. But his support for some federal spending, especially regarding community-based programs, places him closer to the center of the political spectrum.

He has a blinding smile, a confident manner and impeccable suits; Barletta carries himself like a mayor, but for a place much larger than Hazleton — a city of 25,000 in Pennsylvania's mountainous northeast. As mayor, Barletta brought his concerns about illegal immigrants and their economic and social effects to the Justice Department in 2005.

He says he came away from Washington with a lapel pin, the Immigration and Customs Enforcement coffee mug now on display in his office and "zero confidence" that the federal government would enforce immigration laws. In 2006, a Hazleton ordinance would have penalized anyone doing business with illegal immigrants. Lower courts struck it down, but an Arizona law similar to Hazleton's was upheld by the U.S. Supreme Court in May 2011.

Barletta joined the Homeland Security Committee for the 113th Congress (2013-14) and vows to press for better border security and enforcement of existing laws. Even without an immigration-relevant committee as a freshman, he was active on the subject. His first bill was to restrict federal funding to state or local governments that refuse to share information on illegal immigrants with federal authorities; a version was included as an amendment to a fiscal 2013 Homeland Security spending bill that never saw enactment.

He opposed a 2011 measure to require use of a federal employment verification system. Barletta's concern: a clause that he said would prevent states from enforcing verification until the federal government does. "We're really at the crossroads where states are getting the right to defend themselves, and we're going to take that away from them," he said.

He isn't unsympathetic to those who come through the system legally. Three of his grandparents were Italian immigrants. The family built up business interests in Pennsylvania, including a grocery store, a concrete business and an amusement park. "They usually started you at the amusement park until you were old enough to handle a shovel," Barletta remembers. His first job involved pumping sodas and folding pizza boxes at Angela Park. Barletta later operated a highway-line-painting business of his own.

Barletta brings a personal interest to the Education and the Workforce Committee. He studied education in college, and his wife and three of his daughters are teachers or studying to become one. "I hear about No Child Left Behind quite frequently," he said, referring to the 2002 federal education law. "On paper it looks good, but in the classroom it doesn't work." He urges greater local control over the spending of federal education dollars and more flexibility for teachers in setting curriculums.

On the Transportation and Infrastructure Committee, Barletta is a strong supporter of public-private partnerships. Those types of programs, where private entities are the largest stakeholder in a development project, are often floated as cost-effective ways to build out infrastructure in a time of reduced government spending. Barletta's time as mayor made him a fan of such arrangements.

He was disappointed that a five-year reauthorization of surface transportation programs wasn't enacted in the 112th Congress (2011-12). But a two-year version was, and Barletta secured removal of a provision that gave states more leeway to allow heavier trucks on interstate highways. It went against his usual calls for local control, but "our interstate highways should not be a patchwork transportation system," he said.

For Barletta, local flexibility in spending can be a higher priority than cutting spending. "Sometimes I've had to part from my party because of my experience as a mayor," he said. Barletta has opposed cuts to a number of programs that channel money to municipalities, and he is a supporter of Community Development Block Grants, Community Services Block Grants and police and firefighter grants.

In the 113th Congress, Barletta chairs the Transportation and Infrastructure subcommittee that oversees emergency management, which fits nicely with his work on Homeland Security and some of his experiences as a freshman. He devoted many hours to disaster response after severe flooding hit northeastern Pennsylvania in the summer of 2011. In 2012, the House passed his bill to greatly reduce the interest rates on disaster loans provided by the Small Business Administration. "We gave Pakistan $215 million for flood disaster relief, no interest and no payback," Barletta said. "Yet Americans, we'll give you a 6 percent loan." The Senate did not act on the bill.

In hearings, Barletta suggested Congress look for ways to accelerate the delivery of disaster relief to municipalities. He voted against the initial version of a measure to keep the government running at the start of fiscal 2012, saying it did not have enough funding for disaster assistance.

Barletta's father was the Democratic Party chairman in Hazleton. Barletta himself was a Democrat until switching parties while helping a friend with a mayoral race. Ronald Reagan made him into a "believer," he said.

He was a standout baseball player (Barletta is a lifelong Yankees fan) and left college for a chance to try out with the Cincinnati Reds. But competition was stiff, and when he didn't get signed, he headed back to Pennsylvania to work in his father's construction company and take care of his growing family. Inspired by a postcard that said he could start his own business for $29.95, Barletta launched his highway line-painting company. It grew into the largest such business in the state.

Concern over the business environment inspired his first bid for Hazleton's city council. He got in on his second try, then was elected mayor two years later.

Barletta made it into the U.S. House on his third try. He challenged longtime Democratic incumbent Paul E. Kanjorski in 2002, losing by about 13 points. He tried again in 2008 and narrowed the gap to about 3 points. In 2010, Kanjorski, chairman of a Financial Services subcommittee, was at the center of unpopular efforts to respond to the 2008 financial crisis. Barletta took 55 percent of the vote. Redistricting for 2012 strengthened the Republican lean of the district, and Barletta beat Democratic activist Gene Stilp by 17 points.

Key Votes

2012	
Extend a Social Security payroll tax cut and unemployment benefits	YES
Ease securities rules to expand small-business access to capital	YES
Extend for one year subsidized student loan interest rates financed by a cut in health care spending	YES
Cite Attorney General Eric H. Holder Jr. for contempt of Congress	YES
Create a visa program for foreign graduates in high-tech fields	NO
Extend most Bush-era income tax rates while allowing rates for top-bracket earners to rise (Jan. 1, 2013)	YES
2011	
Strike funding for F-35 alternative engine	NO
Prevent EPA from regulating greenhouse gas emissions to address climate change	YES
Extend certain provisions of Patriot Act for four years	YES
Declare opposition to use of ground troops in Libya	YES
Overhaul patent law	YES
Pass compromise debt limit increase plan and establish future spending limits	YES
Allow consideration of measures to implement three trade agreements	YES

CQ Vote Studies

	PARTY UNITY		PRESIDENTIAL SUPPORT	
	SUPPORT	OPPOSE	SUPPORT	OPPOSE
2012	89%	11%	20%	80%
2011	91%	9%	29%	71%

Interest Groups

	AFL-CIO	ADA	CCUS	ACU
2012	29%	6%	92%	72%
2011	25%	20%	100%	76%

Pennsylvania 11

East central — central Susquehanna Valley

Place names like Steelton, Coal Township and Carbon County echo with the 11th District's industrial past. Rusting mill towns, however, represent only one slice of this economically diverse central Pennsylvanian district that encompasses all or part of nine counties. The 11th reaches into northeastern Marcellus Shale country in Wyoming County, and skims the Pocono Mountains in Carbon County. After decennial redistricting, the new 11th stretches to the southwest all the way to Cumberland County up to the Harrisburg city line.

The congested neighborhoods of Colonial Park and Paxtang east of the state capital form the district's population hub. The 4th District takes in the Pennsylvania Capitol in Harrisburg while the 11th snags residential areas just outside the city as well as Harrisburg International Airport.

Pennsylvania State University's Harrisburg campus, along with Shippensburg University and Dickinson College in Cumberland County, make higher education a key component of the southern portion of the district. Carlisle is also the site of the U.S. Army War College.

With new wells in Wyoming County, the 11th has a stake in the natural-gas boom taking place across the state. Montour County's nature preserves and game lands, including more than 22 waterfalls in Ricketts Glen State Park, attract hunters, fishermen and hikers.

Redistricting removed Lackawanna County, the only Democratic bastion, from the 11th District and added several central Pennsylvania counties that went solidly for Mitt Romney in 2012. Overall, Romney won 54 percent of the district's vote.

Major Industry
Retail, transportation, higher education, natural gas

Military Bases
Carlisle Barracks, 700 military, 800 civilian

Cities
Wilkes-Barre (pt.), Hazleton, Carlisle

Notable
Shamokin's St. Edward's Church became the first church in America to be lit by electricity, after Thomas Edison established the Edison Electrical Illuminating Company in the town.

Rep. Keith Rothfus (R)

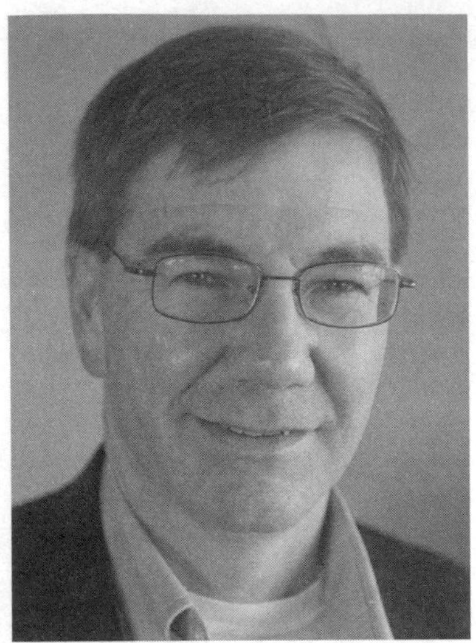

Capitol Office
225-2065
rothfus.house.gov
503 Cannon Bldg. 20515-0518; fax 225-5709

Committees
Financial Services

Residence
Sewickley

Born
April 25, 1962; Endicott, N.Y.

Religion
Roman Catholic

Family
Wife, Elsie Rothfus; six children

Education
State U. of New York, Buffalo, attended 1980-82; State U. of New York, Buffalo State, B.S. 1984 (information systems management); U. of Notre Dame, J.D. 1990

Career
Lawyer; U.S. agency faith-based initiative official; university administrator; computer programmer

Political Highlights
Republican nominee for U.S. House, 2010

ELECTION RESULTS

2012 GENERAL		
Keith Rothfus (R)	175,352	51.7%
Mark Critz (D)	163,589	48.3%
2012 PRIMARY		
Keith Rothfus (R)		unopposed

Elected 2012; 1st term

Rothfus has the hallmarks of a loyal Republican. He joined the conservative Republican Study Committee, and he also sits on the GOP Policy Committee, which helps frame the party's legislative agenda in the House.

After graduating college in Buffalo, he moved to the Washington area to work for IBM. In D.C., he met his wife, an Allegheny County native. He got a law degree from Notre Dame in 1990, settled near Pittsburgh and started in private law practice. After a few years, he took a job as an administrator at Regent University, a Christian college in Virginia Beach, and helped prop up its law school. He then went back to his legal career in western Pennsylvania.

Rothfus volunteered for a few campaigns, and his involvement helped him land a job in the George W. Bush administration; he worked at the Department of Homeland Security, coordinating with faith-based groups trying to contribute to disaster relief efforts. He left that job after being diagnosed with a rare form of cancer. Treatments for that disease in 2007 were successful. At the Republican National Convention in 2012, he spoke of his illness as he emphasized the importance of repealing the 2010 health care law.

He initially had seats on the Judiciary and Homeland Security committees, but he gave them up in April 2013 for a seat on the Financial Services Committee. Much of Rothfus' legal practice dealt with business law, and that panel is as good a spot as any to achieve one of his stated goals: a reduction in federal regulations. (It's also traditionally viewed as a panel that helps candidates raise campaign cash.)

Rothfus first ran for the House in 2010, taking on Democratic Rep. Jason Altmire and losing by less than 4,000 votes. Redistricting for 2012 put the homes of Altmire and Democratic Rep. Mark Critz in the 12th District, and Critz beat Altmire in the primary. The Rothfus-Critz race was hotly contested — lots of the territory was new to both men, and outside groups spent millions on each side of the race. Rothfus won by less than 4 points.

Pennsylvania 12

West — northern Pittsburgh suburbs, Johnstown

Decennial redistricting reoriented the 12th District, shifting it out of Pennsylvania's southwestern corner to its western boundary in Lawrence and Beaver counties. The hammer-shaped 12th now sweeps through northern Allegheny and Westmoreland counties and runs a wide swath along state Highway 219 at its east. Persistent population loss out of the 12th's previous territory necessitated the change.

Once dominated by steel and coal, the region's economy now looks to natural gas in the Marcellus Shale formation for renewal. Its workforce produces pipelines for drilling sites in the booming northeast and southwest regions. Beaver County has lured high-tech job growth from chemical-processing companies, including at a Shell Oil Co. plant.

Coal-producing towns in the eastern portion of the district, meanwhile, have struggled to maintain their dominance in Pennsylvania's energy market as cheap natural gas and more stringent environmental regulations have closed some coal-fired power plants throughout the state. Cambria County's Johnstown has diversified its economic base by attracting health care and technology companies.

Bedroom communities in the Upper Allegheny Valley have some of the district's highest home values, but also contain pockets of suburban poverty. In McCandless Township, more than half of residents have a bachelor's degree. Plum, a suburb east of Pittsburgh, is among the state's fastest-growing municipalities. A $350 million investment in the Allegheny Valley Commuter Rail project may help maintain the white-collar workforce base.

Conservative Democrats who oppose abortion rights and support gun control court votes here, but white working-class areas within the district trend Republican. Energy regulation issues are key to constituents. Republican presidential nominee Mitt Romney won by a 17-point margin here in 2012 and took at least 53 percent of the parts of any county wholly or partially in the district.

Major Industry
Manufacturing, health care, mining

Cities
Allison Park (unincorp.), Johnstown

Notable
Quecreek has erected a Monument for Life to commemorate the rescue of nine miners trapped underground for three days in 2002.

Rep. Allyson Y. Schwartz (D)

Capitol Office
225-6111
schwartz.house.gov
1227 Longworth Bldg. 20515-3813; fax 226-0611

Committees
Budget
Ways & Means

Residence
Jenkintown

Born
Oct. 3, 1948; Queens, N.Y.

Religion
Jewish

Family
Husband, David Schwartz; two children

Education
Simmons College, B.A. 1970 (sociology); Bryn Mawr College, M.S.W. 1972

Career
Municipal child and elderly welfare official; women's health center founder; nonprofit health plan assistant director

Political Highlights
Sought Democratic nomination for U.S. Senate, 2000; Pa. Senate, 1991-2004

ELECTION RESULTS

2012 GENERAL		
Allyson Y. Schwartz (D)	209,901	69.1%
Joseph Rooney (R)	93,918	30.9%
2012 PRIMARY		
Allyson Y. Schwartz (D)		unopposed
2010 GENERAL		
Allyson Y. Schwartz (D)	118,710	56.3%
Dee Adcock (R)	91,987	43.7%

Previous Winning Percentages
2008 (63%); 2006 (66%); 2004 (56%)

Elected 2004; 5th term

Schwartz is running for governor in 2014, and the demands of that race will almost certainly affect her congressional work. Fortunately for Schwartz, her policy expertise is in health care — a topic relevant to just about any political campaign these days.

She made her candidacy official in April 2013, just as she was cementing herself as a power player in the Democratic Caucus. She has the technical know-how to influence legislation, and her political acumen and stature among her peers led to increasingly prominent roles within her party.

Schwartz spent the 2012 election cycle heading up recruitment and candidate services for the Democratic Congressional Campaign Committee, and she had been named the DCCC's lead fundraiser for the 2014 cycle. (She stepped down from the post to focus on her campaign.) At the start of the 113th Congress (2013-14), she also returned to the Ways and Means Committee — she had lost her seat there in 2011 when Democrats' panel rosters shrank after losses in the 2010 elections.

Although Schwartz does not sit on the Health Subcommittee, few people doubt her expertise on the subject. She contributed to several provisions of the 2010 health care overhaul, which she claims as her greatest legislative achievement. The most prominent were to bar insurers from denying coverage to children with pre-existing conditions, and to increase the number of primary care physicians.

Schwartz's family is deeply involved with the health industry. Her husband is a cardiologist and her brother is a physician. She said during the 2010 health care debate that she felt it was important to talk with her husband to get an inside view of the health care sector. "It was helpful to talk to him to see what it was really like," she said.

During the 112th Congress (2011-12), she pushed for a permanent replacement to the formula that dictates how much Medicare reimburses physicians — Congress has passed "doc fix" bills for a decade to prevent reductions in payment rates. She and Nevada Republican Joe Heck, a physician, introduced a 2012 bill to eliminate the current formula after a five-year period of testing potential new models. They introduced a modified version of their bill in February 2013.

Schwartz has been one of the strongest Democratic opponents of the Independent Payment Advisory Board established by the 2010 law — it is charged with devising ways to control the growth of Medicare spending, and its recommendations take effect if not explicitly disapproved by Congress. Republican critics painted it as a cession of authority to unelected bureaucrats. Schwartz co-sponsored legislation to eliminate the board, but voted against the bill after Republicans bundled it with a provision to cap medical malpractice awards. She and Tennessee Republican Phil Roe, another physician Schwartz has teamed up with, are the lead sponsors of the 2013 version of the repeal bill.

"Repealing IPAB, while preserving essential health reforms ... enables providers to focus on innovations that will achieve cost savings by incentivizing efficient, high-quality health care," Schwartz has said.

She sits on the Budget Committee and has attacked the budget blueprints put forth by Republican Chairman Paul D. Ryan of Wisconsin; those plans would convert Medicare into a "premium support" program. Schwartz said savings should instead come from efficiencies in health care delivery and payment systems and a focus on preventive care.

Schwartz is a vice chairwoman of the business-friendly New Democrat Coalition. On select issues, she stakes out pro-business positions that don't always square with Democratic priorities. During the health care debate in the 111th Congress (2009-10), she pushed for tax cuts for the biotechnology sector — not a frontline point of contention — and her work led to the inclusion of up to $1 billion in tax credits for biotech investments.

Schwartz broke from the majority of New Democrats, however, to vote against a bill to repeal a provision of the 2010 health care overhaul that required businesses to notify the IRS of every vendor paid more than $600 in a year. The repeal bill was signed by President Barack Obama in 2011.

Although Schwartz was born and raised in Queens, N.Y., her parents met in Philadelphia, where her father was a dental student and her mother had been sent by a group helping Jewish refugees escape from Europe in the early days of World War II. A former member of the Foreign Affairs Committee, Schwartz supports strong military and political alliances with Israel; she also backs any number of means to prevent Iran from acquiring nuclear weapons.

Her maternal grandmother committed suicide shortly before Schwartz's mother, as a teenager, escaped to the United States. "My mother was very clear that painful experiences in childhood don't necessarily make you stronger, which is maybe where my interest in children and family comes from," she said. Schwartz's mother could not overcome the pain; she committed suicide when Schwartz was 26. "These experiences stay with you. You just don't get past them by saying so," she said of her mother's traumas.

Schwartz moved to Philadelphia in the 1970s so her husband, David, could attend Jefferson Medical College. She earned a master's in social work at Bryn Mawr, then caught public attention in 1975 as the co-founder and first director of a women's health clinic. She had spent a year at the Philadelphia Health Department as a graduate student and then worked for a fledgling HMO for three years before helping to start the Elizabeth Blackwell women's clinic, which offered a full range of health services, including abortions.

In 1983, Schwartz wrote health care position papers for Wilson Goode, who was running for mayor. He won, and during Goode's second term Schwartz became a deputy commissioner of Philadelphia's Department of Human Services, serving until her 1990 election to the state Senate. She defeated a 12-year incumbent to claim that seat, then stayed for 14 years.

Schwartz finished second in the 2000 Democratic primary to run against GOP Sen. Rick Santorum. A long-shot bid by Democrat Joseph M. Hoeffel to unseat then-Republican Sen. Arlen Specter in 2004 gave Schwartz an opening for a second try at Congress. She won a hard-fought primary, then trounced ophthalmologist Melissa Brown, a three-time GOP candidate for the House.

She was not seriously threatened in any of her re-election bids — she won by 38 points in a safely Democratic district in 2012.

Key Votes

2012	
Extend a Social Security payroll tax cut and unemployment benefits	YES
Ease securities rules to expand small-business access to capital	YES
Extend for one year subsidized student loan interest rates financed by a cut in health care spending	NO
Cite Attorney General Eric H. Holder Jr. for contempt of Congress	NO
Create a visa program for foreign graduates in high-tech fields	+
Extend most Bush-era income tax rates while allowing rates for top-bracket earners to rise (Jan. 1, 2013)	YES
2011	
Strike funding for F-35 alternative engine	YES
Prevent EPA from regulating greenhouse gas emissions to address climate change	NO
Extend certain provisions of Patriot Act for four years	YES
Declare opposition to use of ground troops in Libya	?
Overhaul patent law	YES
Pass compromise debt limit increase plan and establish future spending limits	YES
Allow consideration of measures to implement three trade agreements	YES

CQ Vote Studies

	PARTY UNITY		PRESIDENTIAL SUPPORT	
	SUPPORT	OPPOSE	SUPPORT	OPPOSE
2012	95%	5%	91%	9%
2011	93%	7%	95%	5%
2010	98%	2%	95%	5%
2009	98%	2%	96%	4%
2008	99%	1%	15%	85%

Interest Groups

	AFL-CIO	ADA	CCUS	ACU
2012	85%	75%	27%	4%
2011	92%	75%	33%	0%
2010	100%	90%	25%	0%
2009	100%	100%	40%	0%
2008	100%	90%	56%	0%

Pennsylvania 13

East — Northeast Philadelphia, part of Montgomery County

Split between northeastern Philadelphia and Montgomery County, the 13th blends largely blue-collar city neighborhoods with white-collar suburbs. The district's northeastern section runs the Bucks County border to Lansdale. To the west along several interstates, it extends from Conshohocken into parts of Norristown and King of Prussia. To the south, it nearly reaches the Delaware Expressway.

Many residents commute out of the district to jobs in Philadelphia. Towns in the 13th's northwestern corner have experienced rapid growth. Montgomery County seat Norristown has absorbed population shifts, especially of Hispanic and black residents, from Philadelphia over the last decade.

Major area employers in these suburban boroughs include GlaxoSmithKline, Teva Pharmaceuticals, Abington Memorial Hospital and Aria Health's Torresdale campus and Lockheed Martin. Health care is also crucial for the aging population of second- and third-wave Jewish Americans and Russian-speaking immigrants from the Soviet Union who formed communities in Northeast Philadelphia. Overall, 14 percent of the 13th's residents are 65 years of age or older.

Vietnamese and Indonesian refugees account for the latest wave of immigrants in Northeast Philadelphia. Indian-Americans have established communities in Oxford Circle and Somerton. Some are white-collar professionals with advanced degrees, while others work low-income service-economy jobs. These trends give the 13th the largest concentration of Asian residents of any district statewide.

Decennial remapping created a more strongly Democratic district. The Philadelphia portions of the 13th are solidly Democratic, and liberal portions of Montgomery County aided Barack Obama's win in the district in the 2012 presidential contest — he took 66 percent of the vote here.

Major Industry

Health care, pharmaceuticals, retail

Cities

Philadelphia (pt.), Norristown (pt.), King of Prussia (unincorp.) (pt.)

Notable

Pennypack Park, known as the green heart of Northeast Philadelphia, is home to the stone Pennypack Bridge, which has been in use since 1697.

Rep. Mike Doyle (D)

Capitol Office
225-2135
doyle.house.gov
239 Cannon Bldg. 20515-3814; fax 225-3084

Committees
Energy & Commerce

Residence
Forest Hills

Born
Aug. 5, 1953; Pittsburgh, Pa.

Religion
Roman Catholic

Family
Wife, Susan Doyle; four children

Education
Pennsylvania State U., B.S. 1975 (community development)

Career
Insurance company executive; state legislative aide

Political Highlights
Swissvale Borough Council, 1977-81 (served as a Republican)

ELECTION RESULTS

2012 GENERAL		
Mike Doyle (D)	251,932	76.9%
Hans Lessmann (R)	75,702	23.1%
2012 PRIMARY		
Mike Doyle (D)	50,323	80.1%
Janis Brooks (D)	12,484	19.9%
2010 GENERAL		
Mike Doyle (D)	122,073	68.8%
Melissa Haluszczak (R)	49,997	28.2%
Ed Bortz (GREEN)	5,400	3.0%

Previous Winning Percentages
2008 (91%); 2006 (90%); 2004 (100%); 2002 (100%); 2000 (69%); 1998 (68%); 1996 (56%); 1994 (55%)

Elected 1994; 10th term

Doyle has strong ties to Pittsburgh's industrial past, but his recent congressional work includes attempts to diversify his hometown's economy with more high-tech employers. "I see our city as an energy center," he said. "We really do everything in Pittsburgh that's energy related."

The son and grandson of steelworkers, Doyle supports organized labor, opposes free-trade deals and backs a host of Democratic priorities. He keeps a relatively low profile in Washington, despite a definite competitive streak — for seven straight years, Doyle has managed his party's team in the annual CQ Roll Call Congressional Baseball Game.

Doyle's early morning practices have contributed to four straight wins. "Once a year, you play hardball," he said. "You get one shot to win, Democrats versus Republicans, bragging rights for a year." Doyle is a fervent fan of the Pittsburgh Pirates (though he also has season tickets for the Steelers).

Away from the diamond, Doyle uses his seat on the Energy and Commerce Committee to address Pittsburgh's heritage and future prospects. With a nod to the past, he offered a 2012 amendment, ultimately rejected, to ensure that 75 percent of the steel in the proposed Keystone XL pipeline from Canada would come from the United States.

Steel doesn't dominate the city anymore, however. In 2009, Doyle took a stance unpopular in some parts of the Rust Belt by helping write legislation to create a cap-and-trade system to regulate greenhouse gas emissions. The Democratic effort died in the Senate and became a major campaign talking point for Republicans, but "I think a lot of people are now regretting that we didn't go in that direction," he said in 2012.

He has had more success on the Communications and Technology Subcommittee. Doyle was the House sponsor of the 2008 law that made the federal "Do Not Call" registry permanent. Doyle and Nebraska Republican Lee Terry were the House champions of a 2011 law to allow the licensing of more low-power FM radio stations. "I was able to overcome the broadcasters lobby," he said, and allow "small community radio stations to have a voice."

In the 113th Congress (2013-14), Republicans continued to criticize a grant program to expand broadband Internet access that was included in the 2009 economic stimulus law. Doyle came to its defense: "I don't really understand how any of my colleagues can argue that providing better, faster Internet and more digital literacy training to unserved and underserved areas of this country is something we should criticize," he said at a February 2013 hearing.

Pittsburgh hosts a number of universities, and Doyle has proposed that federal agencies provide online access to taxpayer-funded research within six months of its publication. In 2013, he introduced a bill to make that change, teaming up with Republican Kevin Yoder of Kansas. Doyle chairs the Congressional Robotics Caucus — his district is home to the Robotics Institute at Carnegie Mellon University.

Doyle has become more of a party loyalist over his tenure. First elected during the Republican Revolution in 1994, in his early years he split with a majority of his party on around 30 percent of the votes where they opposed a majority of Republicans. Since 2004, he has not diverged on more than 10 percent of such votes in any year. It was Doyle who nominated Nancy Pelosi for minority leader after the drubbing of Democrats in 2010 deposed her as speaker. He voted for a balanced-budget amendment to the Constitution in 1995 but stuck with Democrats to oppose a 2011 version.

He sometimes breaks ranks on abortion. In 2009, Doyle supported the effort led by Michigan Democrat Bart Stupak to restrict federally funded insurance coverage for abortions in the Democrats' health care overhaul. But when the House voted in March 2010 on the final version of the legislation without the Stupak language, he supported the bill.

In the 112th Congress (2011-12), House Republicans instituted a ban on earmarks. Prior to that, Doyle had considerable success directing federal funding to projects in his district. In fiscal 2010, he sponsored or co-sponsored 29 earmarks totaling more than $29 million, according to figures compiled by the Center for Responsive Politics.

Part of his effort to bring more industries to southwestern Pennsylvania was the establishment of the Doyle Center for Manufacturing Technology, a federally funded nonprofit group Doyle launched in 2003. He secured several million dollars in government funds to create the center, which he said would provide "small, local manufacturers with the tools they need to participate in the military contracts with big defense contractors like Boeing, Lockheed Martin and Raytheon." After receiving some criticism, Doyle removed his name from the center, changing it in 2008 to DSN Innovations.

Doyle has a grab-bag of other legislative interests. He founded and co-chairs the Coalition for Autism Research and Education. Doyle and New Jersey Republican Christopher H. Smith ushered to enactment a 2011 reauthorization of federal autism programs. His interest in the issue stems from his time as an aide in the state Senate, where he worked with the parent of an autistic child.

A fervent believer in animal rights, he has tried to shut down puppy mills and some kinds of animal research. Doyle owns two golden retrievers.

As a young adult, Doyle never envisioned a future in government. "Growing up in Swissvale, when your dad's a steelworker, you don't think you're going to be a congressman," he said. His interest in politics was piqued by the 1972 race between President Richard Nixon and Democratic Sen. George McGovern. While studying community development at Penn State, Doyle volunteered for the South Dakotan's losing campaign.

Doyle supported himself in college partly by working in the steel mills. After graduating in 1975, he began work in a multi-line insurance agency before he was elected to the Swissvale Borough Council in 1977. Shortly after, Doyle began working for Republican state Sen. Frank A. Pecora and switched to the GOP out of deference to his boss. He switched back to the Democratic Party when Pecora changed parties in 1992 to mount an unsuccessful challenge against Republican Rep. Rick Santorum.

When Santorum ran successfully for the Senate in 1994, Doyle sought the open 18th District seat, winning a hotly contested seven-person primary with almost 20 percent of the vote. He won in November by nearly 10 points, and that remains the closest of any of his House campaigns.

Key Votes

2012	
Extend a Social Security payroll tax cut and unemployment benefits	YES
Ease securities rules to expand small-business access to capital	NO
Extend for one year subsidized student loan interest rates financed by a cut in health care spending	NO
Cite Attorney General Eric H. Holder Jr. for contempt of Congress	?
Create a visa program for foreign graduates in high-tech fields	NO
Extend most Bush-era income tax rates while allowing rates for top-bracket earners to rise (Jan. 1, 2013)	YES
2011	
Strike funding for F-35 alternative engine	YES
Prevent EPA from regulating greenhouse gas emissions to address climate change	NO
Extend certain provisions of Patriot Act for four years	NO
Declare opposition to use of ground troops in Libya	NO
Overhaul patent law	YES
Pass compromise debt limit increase plan and establish future spending limits	NO
Allow consideration of measures to implement three trade agreements	NO

CQ Vote Studies

	PARTY UNITY		PRESIDENTIAL SUPPORT	
	SUPPORT	OPPOSE	SUPPORT	OPPOSE
2012	95%	5%	88%	12%
2011	95%	5%	81%	19%
2010	99%	1%	90%	10%
2009	99%	1%	97%	3%
2008	99%	1%	16%	84%

Interest Groups

	AFL-CIO	ADA	CCUS	ACU
2012	89%	100%	17%	0%
2011	100%	100%	25%	8%
2010	100%	90%	14%	0%
2009	100%	95%	33%	4%
2008	100%	95%	56%	0%

Pennsylvania 14

Pittsburgh and close-in suburbs

The Allegheny and Monongahela rivers converge to form the Ohio River in the 14th, where medical research labs and office buildings have replaced steel plant smokestacks in downtown Pittsburgh. Representing much of the metropolitan area, the 14th is a model for economic transformation in the Rust Belt.

About 1 in 5 workers in Pittsburgh's private sector are employed in hospitals or other health care service jobs. With locations throughout the city, the University of Pittsburgh Medical Center is the district's top employer. It dominates Pittsburgh's Golden Triangle business center along with several major banks, paint-maker PPG and the iconic H.J. Heinz Co. The renovated Market Square — and the municipality's free Wi-Fi service — lures members of the local workforce at lunchtime.

Nearby Consol Energy Center, home to the NHL's Penguins, opened in 2010. Major League Baseball's Pirates and the NFL's Steelers play across the Allegheny, also in modern stadiums. Hotels and restaurants benefit from the hordes of sports fans who crisscross the city's bridges to attend games.

The Oakland district teems with intellectual energy from the University of Pittsburgh, Carnegie Mellon University and multiple museums. However, K-12 classrooms here have been socked by budget deficits as a result of declining enrollment and competition from charter schools. Many towns surrounding the city center lost double-digit percentages of their populations between 2000 and 2010, and decennial remapping added Allegheny River towns up to Natrona Heights to make up for losses.

More than one-fifth of the district's population is black. Reflecting a larger immigration trend, historically Jewish Squirrel Hill has lost white residents and gained Asian-Indians and Hispanics.

The district remains a strong Democratic bastion. Union strength translates into lopsided margins as registered Democrats far outnumber Republicans. Barack Obama took 68 percent of the 2012 presidential vote here.

Major Industry
Health care, financial services, higher education, service

Cities
Pittsburgh, McKeesport

Notable
The Andy Warhol Museum celebrates Pittsburgh's native son.

Rep. Charlie Dent (R)

Capitol Office
225-6411
dent.house.gov
2455 Rayburn Bldg. 20515-3815; fax 226-0778

Committees
Appropriations
Ethics

Residence
Allentown

Born
May 24, 1960; Allentown, Pa.

Religion
Presbyterian

Family
Wife, Pamela Dent; three children

Education
Pennsylvania State U., B.A. 1982 (foreign service & international politics); Lehigh U., M.P.A. 1993

Career
College fundraiser; electronics salesman; hotel clerk; congressional aide

Political Highlights
Pa. House, 1991-99; Pa. Senate, 1999-2005

ELECTION RESULTS

2012 GENERAL		
Charlie Dent (R)	168,960	56.8%
Rick Daugherty (D)	128,764	43.2%
2012 PRIMARY		
Charlie Dent (R)		unopposed
2010 GENERAL		
Charlie Dent (R)	109,534	53.5%
John Callahan (D)	79,766	39.0%
Jake Towne (I)	15,248	7.4%

Previous Winning Percentages
2008 (59%); 2006 (54%); 2004 (59%)

Elected 2004; 5th term

Dent is an expert in the studied moderation of many eastern Pennsylvania Republicans. He is fiscally conservative and socially moderate, he seeks out Democratic collaborators, and he mostly stays off the soapbox.

That formula got him re-elected in a district that favored Democratic presidential candidates in 2004 and 2008. It also positions him as a broker in the 113th Congress (2013-14), where he co-chairs the Tuesday Group, an informal caucus of moderate Republicans. "Some might call it a governance wing of the party," Dent said. He prefers to call it a "center-right" group.

Dent is also affiliated with No Labels, a nonpartisan group dedicated to improving the functionality of Congress, and he has been open to cooperating with the Blue Dog Coalition, a group of fiscally conservative House Democrats.

Practicality seems to run in his family. Dent's uncles were engineers; his brother and sister are chemical engineers; and his dad worked for years at Bethlehem Steel in the industrial engineering program — not as an engineer, though he was a science major. Dent is a lifelong resident of Allentown, and his family has been in Pennsylvania since colonial times. His great-grandfather started a well-known hardware business in his district.

Dent took a different career path. He interned with one of his predecessors in Congress, Republican Rep. Don Ritter. He went on to work as a salesman in the electronics industry and as a development officer for Lehigh University. Dent says his experience at the university, where he helped win state funding for the school, sparked his interest in running for the state House.

In Washington, he now deals with funding as a member of the Appropriations Committee. Dent joined the panel in 2011 after stints on the Homeland Security and Transportation and Infrastructure committees, and he now sits on the Appropriations subcommittees covering those jurisdictions.

On homeland issues, he favors tight restrictions on illegal immigration and a tough line on terrorism. In 2011, he joined with Pennsylvania Democrat Jason Altmire on a bill to authorize the revocation of citizenship for Americans who engage in acts of terrorism against the United States. He shows enthusiasm for expanding security screening capabilities for transportation systems.

In January 2013, Dent was one of the 49 House Republicans who voted for a $50 billion spending package tied to Superstorm Sandy recovery efforts (his district was hit by the storm). He is keeping an eye on the distribution of that money, however. At a Transportation-HUD Subcommittee hearing in March, he expressed the worry that local governments sometimes "misappropriate" Community Development Block Grant funding — and such grants were bolstered as part of the recovery package.

Dent also sits on the State-Foreign Operations Subcommittee. His mother might have spurred his interest in foreign affairs. Before she was married, she worked for the State Department in West Berlin in the 1950s. Dent became a student of the Cold War and majored in foreign service at Penn State.

"This world demands American leadership, whether we like it or not," he said. "In a more multi-polar world, I suspect there would be more opportunities for tension and conflict than one where we as a nation tend to be more predominant." He wants greater transparency in international development institutions receiving U.S. funding, and he was highly critical when Palestine was admitted in 2011 to the United Nations Educational, Scientific and Cultural Organization. "Maneuvers like this provide no incentive for the Palestinians to negotiate with Israel and global partners in good faith," he wrote.

Spending cuts for security and diplomacy will be necessary, Dent said, until major changes are made to entitlement programs to curb the growth of mandatory spending. He has stood against most of the major legislative initiatives of the Obama administration, including the $787 billion economic stimulus law and the health care overhaul — "a new trillion-dollar entitlement program that the bill does not realistically address how we will afford."

Dent is much more liberal than most Republicans on issues such as abortion and gay rights. He was one of 15 House Republicans to back a 2010 law to repeal the statutory ban on openly gay military servicemembers. He was one of seven Republicans to oppose a 2011 provision added to a catchall spending bill to block federal funding for Planned Parenthood. There is family history there, as well: Mary Dent Crisp, his father's sister and a longtime GOP activist in Arizona, resigned her post as co-chairwoman of the Republican National Convention in 1980 to protest the party's anti-abortion platform plank.

Dent supports federal funding of stem cell research. In 2011 he introduced a bill with Colorado Democrat Diana DeGette to codify President Barack Obama's executive order allowing such funding.

His other interests are eclectic or district-related. A 2012 law reauthorizing certain Food and Drug Administration programs included language by Dent to ban the possession and sale of synthetic drugs that imitate various properties of marijuana, cocaine or methamphetamines. Representing a major hydrogen producer, he co-founded the Hydrogen Fuel Cell Caucus and has urged a "level playing field" when the Energy Department is looking for industries to back. Large cement plants are an economic force in the region, and he joined in as the House passed a 2011 bill to delay new EPA regulations on cement production; the industry needed more time to comply, Dent said.

Charlie also has chocolate factories to worry about. Large confectioners are in his district, and it was expanded in 2013 to take in Hershey.

In 1990, Dent ran for the state House, defeating a Democratic incumbent. He credits his upset win to knocking "on over 20,000 doors" and running a "door-to-door, grass-roots, shoe-leather campaign." Eight years later, he won an open state Senate seat, serving there for six years.

When conservative Republican Patrick J. Toomey gave up his House seat to launch a 2004 primary challenge to Sen. Arlen Specter, Dent ran for the open seat and won easily with 59 percent of the vote. Despite some Democratic tendencies in his district and rough years for Republicans in 2006 and 2008, Dent used significant fundraising advantages to dispatch Democrats trumpeting national party themes.

The new congressional map for 2012 greatly enlarged his district, pushing it out to the west. It is more favorable to Republicans, but not by too much — Dent won by less than 14 points against a basically unfunded Democrat.

Key Votes

2012	
Extend a Social Security payroll tax cut and unemployment benefits	YES
Ease securities rules to expand small-business access to capital	YES
Extend for one year subsidized student loan interest rates financed by a cut in health care spending	YES
Cite Attorney General Eric H. Holder Jr. for contempt of Congress	YES
Create a visa program for foreign graduates in high-tech fields	YES
Extend most Bush-era income tax rates while allowing rates for top-bracket earners to rise (Jan. 1, 2013)	YES
2011	
Strike funding for F-35 alternative engine	YES
Prevent EPA from regulating greenhouse gas emissions to address climate change	YES
Extend certain provisions of Patriot Act for four years	YES
Declare opposition to use of ground troops in Libya	YES
Overhaul patent law	YES
Pass compromise debt limit increase plan and establish future spending limits	YES
Allow consideration of measures to implement three trade agreements	YES

CQ Vote Studies

	PARTY UNITY		PRESIDENTIAL SUPPORT	
	SUPPORT	OPPOSE	SUPPORT	OPPOSE
2012	83%	17%	20%	80%
2011	85%	15%	31%	69%
2010	76%	24%	43%	57%
2009	73%	27%	46%	54%
2008	78%	22%	49%	51%

Interest Groups

	AFL-CIO	ADA	CCUS	ACU
2012	14%	0%	100%	80%
2011	10%	15%	100%	52%
2010	21%	25%	100%	61%
2009	43%	20%	87%	72%
2008	60%	55%	83%	56%

Pennsylvania 15

East central — Allentown, most of Bethlehem, Hershey

Pennsylvania's 15th expanded dramatically during decennial redistricting. From the banks of the Delaware River south of Easton, it now follows Interstate 78 all the way to the outskirts of Harrisburg and the shores of the Susquehanna River southwest of Hershey. The historic steel stronghold of Bethlehem and neighboring Allentown continue to anchor its population.

The dominant manufacturing industry that Billy Joel immortalized in "Allentown," his 1982 tribute to the area's Rust Belt blues, has been replaced by service-sector employment. Continued expansion at two major hospital networks located on the eastern side of the district has bolstered white-collar employment and encouraged migration, especially among Hispanics, from New York and New Jersey. Leisure and hospitality jobs are also on the rise, following the opening of the Sands Casino Resort on the former Bethlehem Steel site, although the area's blue-collar core continues to struggle.

This economic picture is remarkably similar in the western reaches of the district. In Hershey, the hometown of the iconic chocolate company, hundreds of workers were laid off in advance of the opening of a new plant with a smaller workforce. Meanwhile the Penn State Milton S. Hershey Medical Center, which employs about 9,000, constructed a new children's hospital.

Olympus America, electric utility PPL and chemical company Air Products have their headquarters in the 15th in Allentown. The presence of Interstate 78 and the Pennsylvania Turnpike Northeast Extension has made the district an attractive destination for warehouse and distribution centers. Its midsection, in northern Berks County, is primarily agricultural.

Lehigh County, home to half the district's population, is politically competitive, supporting both Republicans and Democrats at the federal level. The 15th's portions of Lebanon and Dauphin counties are GOP strongholds.

Major Industry
Health care, warehousing, manufacturing, service

Cities
Allentown, Bethlehem, Lebanon (pt.), Hershey (unincorp.)

Notable
The Valley Preferred Cycling Center, a premier site for track cycling, has hosted Olympic trial, Junior World Championship and World Cup races.

Rep. Joe Pitts (R)

Capitol Office
225-2411
pitts.house.gov
420 Cannon Bldg 20515-3816; fax 225-2013

Committees
Energy & Commerce
(Health - Chairman)

Residence
Kennett Square

Born
Oct. 10, 1939; Lexington, Ky.

Religion
Protestant

Family
Wife, Virginia M. "Ginny" Pitts; three children

Education
Asbury College, A.B. 1961 (philosophy & religion); West Chester State College, M.Ed. 1972 (comprehensive sciences)

Military
Air Force, 1963-69

Career
Nursery and landscaping business owner, teacher

Political Highlights
Pa. House, 1973-97

ELECTION RESULTS

2012 GENERAL		
Joe Pitts (R)	156,192	54.8%
Aryanna Strader (D)	111,185	39.0%
John A. Murphy (I)	12,250	4.3%
James F. Bednarski (BFC)	5,154	1.8%
2012 PRIMARY		
Joe Pitts (R)		unopposed
2010 GENERAL		
Joe Pitts (R)	134,113	65.4%
Lois K. Herr (D)	70,994	34.6%

Previous Winning Percentages
2008 (56%); 2006 (57%); 2004 (64%); 2002 (88%); 2000 (67%); 1998 (71%); 1996 (59%)

Elected 1996; 9th term

Pitts chairs the Energy and Commerce Subcommittee on Health, which makes him the steward of some of the most partisan bills moving through the House. He represents a culturally diverse district and is firmly to the right on social issues.

Pitts spent 24 years in the Pennsylvania House, and at the start of his 15th year in the U.S. House he found himself holding the Health gavel. Throughout the 112th Congress (2011-12) he helped steer to passage a number of bills targeting the 2010 health care overhaul, provision by provision. He has called that law "shockingly irresponsible."

The panel advanced measures to block funding for the law or eliminate parts of it. Among those were bills to repeal a long-term-care program and an independent board tasked with curbing Medicare spending growth. Both proposals won House passage.

The House also passed Pitts' 2011 bill to eliminate the Prevention and Public Health Fund, which Pitts and other Republicans dubbed a "slush fund." He reintroduced the bill in the 113th Congress (2013-14) — and he also rolled out another plan, to shift money from the prevention fund to high-risk insurance pools created by the law. The Obama administration closed enrollment in those pools, which are meant to provide temporary insurance coverage for people with pre-existing conditions until they can get coverage through the law's insurance exchanges in 2014. It was conservatives that stalled action on that bill in April 2013 — several prominent interest groups said the House should focus on repeal efforts.

Health care battles have been partisan, but Pitts says he enjoys a good working relationship with his subcommittee's ranking Democrat, Frank Pallone Jr. of New Jersey. They have helped shepherd several bipartisan bills through the House. Perhaps the most significant was a five-year reauthorization of the Food and Drug Administration's user fee programs that President Barack Obama signed in July 2012. The law includes provisions to accelerate the FDA approval process for new drugs. Pitts called it "a model of bipartisanship."

Pitts and Pallone also teamed up on bill to reauthorize a program that supports medical residency programs at children's hospitals. The Obama administration has proposed eliminating or shrinking the program, but Pitts said it has a "proven track record." The House passed their bill in 2011 and 2013.

Pitts co-chairs the House Values Action Team, a group of about 80 conservatives who work with advocacy groups on the religious right. His efforts there often involve health care. When Obama signed an executive order reinstating federal funding for embryonic stem cell research, Pitts said the president had "chosen to force American taxpayers to fund research that destroys human life against the objections of their conscience."

Working with Michigan Democrat Bart Stupak in the 111th Congress (2009-10), Pitts proposed an amendment to the health care bill to ban the use of federal funds for insurance plans covering abortion. Stupak accepted a deal with Obama for an executive order affirming the existing ban against federal funding for abortion; Pitts said he was "disappointed."

Outside of the health arena, Pitts concentrates on issues of particular concern to his constituents. His district has one of the nation's largest Amish communities, and he battled across multiple Congresses for a relaxation of child labor laws to ensure Amish teens could enter apprenticeships once their formal education was complete. It was included in a 2004 catchall spending law.

He tries to find ways to encourage farmland preservation and has favored capital gains tax breaks to provide an incentive for farmers to protect their land from development. He formed the Land Conservation Caucus with fellow Pennsylvania Republican Jim Gerlach and Democrat Christopher S. Murphy of Connecticut to promote and support land preservation measures.

Pitts also has a deep interest in foreign policy and humanitarian work, stemming from his time in the Philippines as the son of missionaries. An advocate for religious freedom abroad, he sits on the Commission on Security and Cooperation in Europe — an independent U.S. government agency that focuses on democracy and human rights — and is an executive committee member of the Tom Lantos Human Rights Commission.

But unlike many lawmakers with strong human rights agendas, he favored the 2000 law normalizing trade with China, arguing that increased engagement would spur the communist government to improve its human rights record. He consistently sides with the majority of his party on trade deals.

Pitts rejoined the Energy and Power Subcommittee in 2013, and he is also a member of the Environment and the Economy Subcommittee. He voted against a 2009 bill to create a cap-and-trade system for greenhouse gas emissions. Pitts explained his opposition in a lengthy memorandum to his constituents — a practice he began in 2008, when he laid out his objections to a $700 billion bailout package for the financial services industry. When a debate seems momentous enough, Pitts puts forth a new memo describing his preferences and concerns. For example, he said the 2009 stimulus law was based on "the faulty notion that massive government spending will create prosperity."

After living in the Philippines for much of his youth, Pitts attended Asbury College in Kentucky, where he met his wife, Ginny. He earned degrees in philosophy and religion, and the two of them embarked on teaching careers. Pitts later joined the Air Force and served for five and a half years, including three tours of duty in Southeast Asia and 116 combat missions.

The family then moved to Pennsylvania, where Pitts taught high school math and science. He eventually started his own landscape nursery business. In 1972, he won an open state House seat. His time in that chamber included eight years as chairman of the Appropriations Committee.

Republican Robert S. Walker decided to retire from the U.S. House in 1996. Pitts prevailed in a five-way primary for the open seat and won easily in November. He initially said he would serve no more than 10 years, but announced before the 2002 election that he had changed his mind, explaining that term limits diminish a "lame duck" lawmaker's effectiveness. He has been re-elected by wide margins.

Pitts likes to spend his Sunday afternoons painting — finished works decorate the walls of his D.C. office. He also writes and illustrates children's books for his grandchildren.

Key Votes

2012	
Extend a Social Security payroll tax cut and unemployment benefits	YES
Ease securities rules to expand small-business access to capital	YES
Extend for one year subsidized student loan interest rates financed by a cut in health care spending	YES
Cite Attorney General Eric H. Holder Jr. for contempt of Congress	YES
Create a visa program for foreign graduates in high-tech fields	YES
Extend most Bush-era income tax rates while allowing rates for top-bracket earners to rise (Jan. 1, 2013)	YES
2011	
Strike funding for F-35 alternative engine	NO
Prevent EPA from regulating greenhouse gas emissions to address climate change	YES
Extend certain provisions of Patriot Act for four years	YES
Declare opposition to use of ground troops in Libya	YES
Overhaul patent law	?
Pass compromise debt limit increase plan and establish future spending limits	YES
Allow consideration of measures to implement three trade agreements	YES

CQ Vote Studies

	PARTY UNITY		PRESIDENTIAL SUPPORT	
	SUPPORT	OPPOSE	SUPPORT	OPPOSE
2012	95%	5%	20%	80%
2011	97%	3%	20%	80%
2010	98%	2%	25%	75%
2009	96%	4%	22%	78%
2008	98%	2%	76%	24%

Interest Groups

	AFL-CIO	ADA	CCUS	ACU
2012	19%	5%	100%	79%
2011	0%	5%	100%	84%
2010	7%	0%	88%	100%
2009	10%	5%	87%	96%
2008	0%	5%	88%	100%

Pennsylvania 16

Southeast — Lancaster, Reading

The 16th contains most of fertile Lancaster County, the commonwealth's top agricultural producer, as well as the rural southern portion of Chester County, which makes farming big business here. The district's northern tip captures the city of Reading.

About 10 million visitors flock to the picturesque Pennsylvania Dutch communities of Lancaster County each year to stay at bed and breakfasts, browse quilt shops, admire artisan woodworking and enjoy kid-friendly amusement parks. The county is home to the second-largest Amish community in the nation. Tourism officials are pushing for a controversial hike in the hotel tax to ease construction costs for the Lancaster County Convention Center and continue promoting the region as a travel destination.

District farms produce a wide array of crops. Kennett Square in Chester County supplies almost 50 percent of the mushrooms eaten nationwide, and it calls itself the "Mushroom Capital of the World." Lancaster County is among the nation's leaders in tobacco, livestock feed and corn harvests as well as in milk and egg production.

For Reading (shared with the 7th), an exodus of high-paying manufacturing jobs has left four of every 10 residents in poverty. The city's middle class has migrated away and has been replaced with an influx of Hispanic residents, many working in lower-paying service jobs — Reading is 58 percent Hispanic and 13 percent black. Overall in the 15th, Hispanics account for 17 percent of the population in the majority-white district.

The 16th remains politically competitive, despite a long history of Republican representation in the U.S. House for the region. In the population hub of Reading, voters elect Democrats. South of the city, the Amish residents set a socially conservative tone, though traditionally they have had a low voter turnout. In 2012, Republican nominee Mitt Romney took 53 percent of the 16th's presidential vote despite losing the district's portion of Berks County by a wide margin and it's portion of Chester by 1 percentage point.

Major Industry
Agriculture, transportation, tourism

Cities
Reading (pt.), Lancaster

Notable
The original five-and-dime store that started the Woolworth chain opened in Lancaster in 1879.

Rep. Matt Cartwright (D)

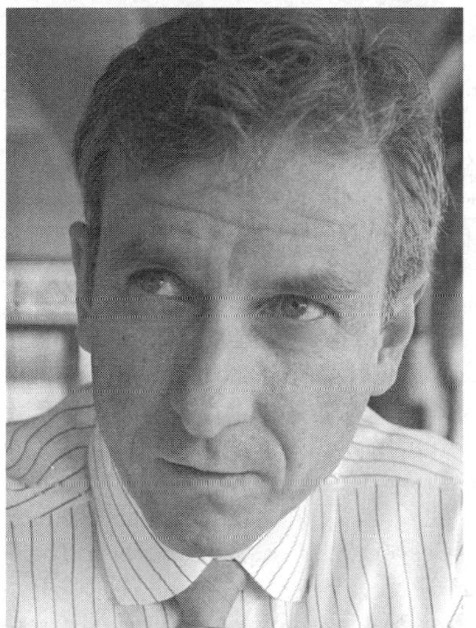

Capitol Office
225-5546
cartwright.house.gov
1419 Longworth Bldg. 20515-3817; fax 226-0996

Committees
Natural Resources
Oversight & Government Reform

Residence
Moosic

Born
May 1, 1961; Erie, Pa.

Religion
Roman Catholic

Family
Wife, Marion Munley Cartwright; two children

Education
Hamilton College, A.B. 1983 (history); Temple U. School of Law, attended 1984; U. of Pennsylvania, J.D. 1986

Career
Lawyer

Political Highlights
No previous office

ELECTION RESULTS

2012 GENERAL		
Matt Cartwright (D)	161,393	60.3%
Laureen Cummings (R)	106,208	39.7%
2012 PRIMARY		
Matt Cartwright (D)	33,255	57.1%
Tim Holden (D)	24,953	42.9%

Elected 2012; 1st term

Cartwright wears his progressive politics on his sleeve, and he has started his House career by being more assertive than the average freshman.

Before he was a politician, Cartwright was known in his district as a lawyer. Like many firms that specialize in personal injury cases, Munley, Munley & Cartwright ran lots of television ads. Cartwright also starred in a popular segment on a local evening news program, where he answered viewers' questions about their legal rights. (His wife, Marion Munley Cartwright, is still a lawyer at the renamed Munley Law.)

Cartwright still has the zeal of a plaintiff's attorney. He belongs to the Congressional Progressive Caucus, a bloc of the most-liberal House members, and he has denounced Republican budget plans and policy proposals. Freshman Democrats made him one of their class presidents for 2013.

He campaigned on a number of environmental causes, and he now sits on the Natural Resources Committee. He opposes hydraulic fracturing, a technique for extracting natural gas and oil from shale deposits — he contends that it contaminates ground water. His first bill was to eliminate a statutory exemption that prevents the EPA from applying certain regulations to "fracking."

On the Oversight and Government Reform Committee, Cartwright is the ranking member of the Economic Growth, Job Creation and Regulatory Affairs panel. He favors major federal investments in infrastructure (such as rail service for his district) as a means to spur the economy.

Cartwright elbowed past a 10-term Democratic incumbent to capture his seat. Tim Holden, a fiscal conservative, had survived tough elections before, but the congressional map for 2012 made most of the 17th District new to him. Cartwright had strong name recognition from his legal career, and he used his personal fortune to bolster his primary campaign; the League of Conservation Voters and an anti-incumbent super PAC also made ad buys against Holden. Cartwright easily won both the primary and the general election.

Pennsylvania 17

East central — Scranton, Wilkes-Barre

Trading the Lebanon Valley for the Lehigh Valley, the redrawn 17th retains only one county (Schuylkill) from the iteration prior to decennial reapportionment and now extends into Scranton-Wilkes-Barre. It shares borders with three neighboring districts and New Jersey. Some of the state's highest rates of unemployment are found in an area that was once central to the nation's coal industry. Labor unions and Democrats have solid bases here, especially in Scranton and Easton.

Four massive stone blast iron furnaces from the Lackawanna Iron and Steel Co. and the Steamtown National Historic Site stand near Scranton's City Hall. Remnants of its industrial heritage are located blocks from economic redevelopment projects, including plans for downtown. Retail, manufacturing and financial sectors continue to struggle, despite millions of dollars of investment in construction projects and infrastructure.

The Wilkes-Barre/Scranton International Airport serves visitors to the Pocono Mountains, and the renovated Sno Mountain Ski Area boasts some of the area's steepest slopes.

The 17th has several defense-related assets. The Wilkes-Barre VA Medical Center employs thousands in the region. The Tobyhanna Army Depot in Monroe County is the military's largest full-service electronics maintenance facility and provides 5,800 jobs, although contracting job layoffs have been announced.

Fertile regions of Schuylkill County, between the Susquehanna River and the Blue Mountain range, produce corn, wheat and Christmas trees. In Pottsville, manufacturing and mine-related businesses support the economy, in addition to brewing — the city is home to Yuengling, the nation's oldest brewery. The district also includes some manufacturing interests in the Lehigh Valley, including the Crayola corporate headquarters in Easton.

Major Industry
Manufacturing, retail, tourism, agriculture

Military Bases
Tobyhanna Army Depot, 30 military, 3,747 civilian

Cities
Scranton, Bethlehem (pt.),Wilkes-Barre (pt.), Easton

Notable
In 1877, nine suspected members of the Molly Maguires, a secret society of Irish-American coal miners, were hanged in Pottsville's prison yard after testimony from agents of the union-busting Pinkerton Detective Agency.

Rep. Tim Murphy (R)

Capitol Office
225-2301
murphy.house.gov
2332 Rayburn Bldg. 20515-3818; fax 225-1844

Committees
Energy & Commerce
(Oversight & Investigations - Chairman)

Residence
Upper St. Clair

Born
Sept. 11, 1952; Cleveland, Ohio

Religion
Roman Catholic

Family
Wife, Nan Missig Murphy; one child

Education
Wheeling College, B.S. 1974 (psychology); Cleveland State U., M.A. 1976 (psychology); U. of Pittsburgh, Ph.D. 1979 (psychology)

Military
Navy Reserve, 2009-present

Career
Psychologist; professor

Political Highlights
Pa. Senate, 1997-2003

ELECTION RESULTS

2012 GENERAL		
Tim Murphy (R)	216,727	64.0%
Larry Maggi (D)	122,146	36.0%
2012 PRIMARY		
Tim Murphy (R)	32,854	63.4%
Evan Feinberg (R)	18,937	36.6%
2010 GENERAL		
Tim Murphy (R)	161,888	67.3%
Dan Connolly (D)	78,558	32.7%

Previous Winning Percentages
2008 (64%); 2006 (58%); 2004 (63%); 2002 (60%)

Elected 2002; 6th term

Health care, manufacturing and the energy potential of the Marcellus Shale are tremendously important to the Pittsburgh-area economy. Murphy, a moderate Republican on the Energy and Commerce Committee, stays in the good graces of constituents by paying close attention to all three. He has more tools to do so in the 113th Congress as chairman of the Oversight and Investigations Subcommittee.

"You really have to know the people" of the district to protect their interests, Murphy says. He knows them well enough that they forgive him for growing up in Cleveland — a fact a GOP primary challenger tried to use against him in 2012. For the record, Murphy is a Steelers fan.

He has some quirks. One of 11 children, he paid his way through school by cleaning out horse stalls and digging graves. He taught himself to play guitar and performed in acoustic bands in high school, college and graduate school. (Murphy occasionally jammed with the eccentric Michigan Republican Thaddeus McCotter, who resigned in 2012.)

He came to Pittsburgh to earn a doctorate in psychology and worked in several hospitals in western Pennsylvania. Murphy eventually opened his own practice, taught at the University of Pittsburgh and gave medical advice as "Dr. Tim" on Pittsburgh radio and television. In 2001, Murphy co-wrote a book on the sources of anger in children and ways parents could respond.

Murphy's professional background gives him a keen interest in health issues. As the 113th Congress (2013-14) began, he decided to focus a lot of his subcommittee's efforts on federal mental-health programs. A number of mass shootings by mentally ill assailants in 2012 led to calls for expansions of such programs.

Murphy said it was important to not just throw money at the problem: "I am going to be relentless in embarking on a meaningful effort to gather information, determine the causes, identify the treatments and make sure all federal dollars on mental health are spent effectively," he said.

He has worked with Democrats on some expansions of care. He supported a 2009 law that increased the reach of the Children's Health Insurance Program, and Murphy and Democrat Gene Green of Texas introduced a 2010 bill to address the shortage of health care providers in community health centers.

But the 2010 health care overhaul went too far for his tastes. "While I thought elected officials were well-intended, they were not well-informed," he said. Murphy has voted to repeal the law and block funding for its implementation. He agrees that the managed care system is in need of an overhaul, but "I know we can do better," he said.

Tackling some narrower health issues, Murphy wrote a 2012 bill to reduce the backlog of generic-drug approval tests at the Food and Drug Administration by collecting $1.5 billion in user fees from the drugs' makers. It was enacted as part of a 2012 reauthorization of FDA user fee programs. He also sponsored a bill to provide free medical malpractice insurance to professionals working at community health care centers, but it died in the Senate.

Murphy opposes abortion. When the Health Subcommittee approved legislation in early 2011 to bar federal funds from being used to cover the costs of any health insurance plan that includes coverage of abortion services, Murphy was blunt: "This is about killing babies and using federal money to do it."

Murphy belongs to the moderate Main Street Partnership, but many of his positions on energy are in the GOP mainstream. He has a seat on the Environment and the Economy Subcommittee, and he defends hydraulic fracturing, the injection of high-pressure fluids into rock layers to allow access to new deposits of gas and oil. "Fracking" is used to access natural gas deposits in the Marcellus Shale, the huge underground formation covering a large part of Pennsylvania. Environmentalists have called for tighter regulation of fracking, saying it could contaminate groundwater. Murphy, a former co-chairman of the Natural Gas Caucus, has asked the Obama administration to hold off on new regulations for fracking.

He supports increased use of nuclear power and more domestic oil drilling. In 2011, he introduced legislation to speed approval of offshore drilling permits. He introduced legislation in the 111th Congress (2009-10) to expand oil and gas exploration on federal lands, with the revenue generated used to expand renewable-energy and conservation programs.

Murphy finds common ground with Democrats on preserving the steel industry. As chairman of the Congressional Steel Caucus, he introduced legislation in 2011 that would require the departments of Transportation, Defense and Homeland Security to use only steel and iron made domestically.

Motivated in part by a desire to help steel and manufacturing exports, Murphy tries to combat allegedly unfair trade practices by China. He and Ohio Democrat Tim Ryan were the lead sponsors on a 2010 bill to require the Commerce Department to impose duties on China, to retaliate for that nation's manipulation of the value of its currency. It passed the House but was not enacted, and Murphy supported a similar measure in the 112th Congress (2011-12). He says stopping currency manipulation is "critically important for southwestern Pennsylvania and manufacturing around the country."

Murphy entered elective politics by winning a state Senate seat in 1996. Pennsylvania lost two House seats in reapportionment after the 2000 census, and the Republican General Assembly drew an 18th District south of Pittsburgh configured to favor Murphy. The incumbent, four-term Democrat Frank R. Mascara, decided to mount what proved to be an unsuccessful primary challenge to Democrat John P. Murtha in the 12th District. Murphy took 60 percent of the vote to defeat Democrat Jack M. Machek.

Some conservatives wanted to find a challenger for Murphy in the 2012 GOP primary. But his eventual opponent, Evan Feinberg — a former aide to Sens. Tom Coburn of Oklahoma and Rand Paul of Kentucky — never raised enough money for a serious bid. Murphy won by almost 27 points.

Democrats tried to take down Murphy with a familiar face: Washington County Commissioner Larry Maggi, who had lost the 2002 Democratic primary. Murphy defeated Maggi by 28 points.

Murphy joined the Navy Reserve in 2009 and has worked as a psychologist at Walter Reed National Military Medical Center, helping soldiers with post-traumatic stress disorder.

Key Votes

2012	
Extend a Social Security payroll tax cut and unemployment benefits	YES
Ease securities rules to expand small-business access to capital	YES
Extend for one year subsidized student loan interest rates financed by a cut in health care spending	NO
Cite Attorney General Eric H. Holder Jr. for contempt of Congress	YES
Create a visa program for foreign graduates in high-tech fields	YES
Extend most Bush-era income tax rates while allowing rates for top-bracket earners to rise (Jan. 1, 2013)	YES
2011	
Strike funding for F-35 alternative engine	NO
Prevent EPA from regulating greenhouse gas emissions to address climate change	YES
Extend certain provisions of Patriot Act for four years	YES
Declare opposition to use of ground troops in Libya	YES
Overhaul patent law	YES
Pass compromise debt limit increase plan and establish future spending limits	YES
Allow consideration of measures to implement three trade agreements	YES

CQ Vote Studies

	PARTY UNITY		PRESIDENTIAL SUPPORT	
	SUPPORT	OPPOSE	SUPPORT	OPPOSE
2012	93%	7%	18%	82%
2011	93%	7%	23%	77%
2010	81%	19%	52%	48%
2009	68%	32%	66%	34%
2008	76%	24%	45%	55%

Interest Groups

	AFL-CIO	ADA	CCUS	ACU
2012	48%	5%	100%	76%
2011	38%	20%	100%	76%
2010	43%	15%	88%	50%
2009	52%	15%	93%	68%
2008	73%	60%	81%	48%

Pennsylvania 18

Southwest — Pittsburgh suburbs, Washington

The 18th takes in the southern portion of Allegheny County and, following decennial redistricting, extends into new territory in the southwestern corner of Pennsylvania. It encompasses most of Greene, Washington and Westmoreland counties, where rich bituminous coal deposits were key to earlier industry and mining continues to shape the economy.

Most of the district's population is concentrated in suburban neighborhoods around Pittsburgh. But decline has plagued established communities such as Carnegie, founded by the steel giant, and Bethel Park. Mount Lebanon has struggled to finance its award-winning schools.

Newer western suburbs in Allegheny County are growing rapidly. Nearby Pittsburgh International Airport is a hub that accommodates more than 8 million travelers each year. City officials are considering plans for expansion to ease travel for businesspeople in the natural-gas sector.

The nation's first Marcellus Shale well was drilled in Washington County's Mt. Pleasant Township in 2004. Extraction operations attracted $200 million in energy industry development projects to the county in 2011 and made it a national leader in job and wage growth. Doctors near heavily drilled areas, however, are concerned some patients' health problems may be related to natural gas. The country's largest underground-coal-mining company, Consol Energy Inc., also has its global headquarters in Canonsburg. Greene County leads the state in bituminous coal production; two of its mines rank among the top 15 for U.S. production. Natural gas, timber production and agriculture are also important to this rural county.

The district's working-class heritage makes good relations with labor crucial to winning elections here. Conservative voters tend to favor moderate Republicans and back the GOP on the federal level. Mitt Romney won 58 percent of the district's 2012 presidential vote.

Major Industry
Transportation, natural gas, mining, timber

Cities
Bethel Park; Greensburg; Washington

Notable
The Meadowcroft Village at the Museum of Rural Life, near Avella in Washington County, preserves the history of mid-19th-century rural life in western Pennsylvania.

RHODE ISLAND

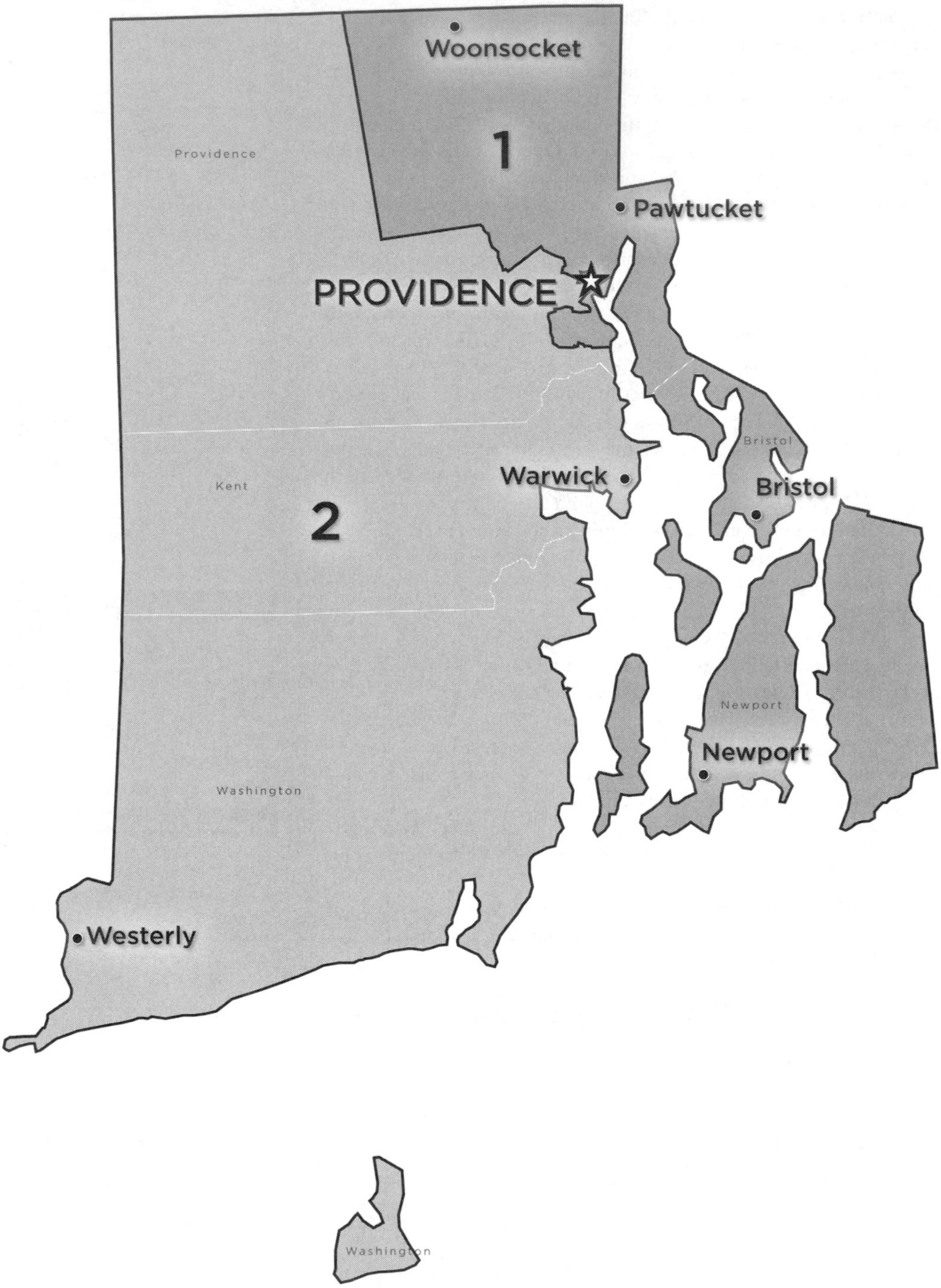

Woonsocket

1

Providence

Pawtucket

PROVIDENCE

Bristol

Warwick

Kent

Bristol

2

Newport

Newport

Washington

Westerly

Gov. Lincoln Chafee (D)

First elected: 2010

Length of term: 4 years

Term expires: 1/15

Salary: $129,210

Phone: (410) 222-2080

Residence: Exeter

Born: March 26, 1953; Warwick, R.I.

Religion: Episcopalian

Family: Wife, Stephanie Chafee; three children

Education: Brown U., A.B. 1975 (classics)

Career: Defense company machine shop planner; blacksmith

Political highlights: Warwick City Council, 1986-91; Republican nominee for mayor of Warwick, 1990; mayor of Warwick, 1992-99; U.S. Senate, 1999-2007; defeated for re-election to U.S. Senate, 2006

ELECTION RESULTS

2010 GENERAL

Lincoln Chafee (I)	123,571	36.1%
John F. Robitaille (R)	114,911	33.6%
Frank T. Caprio (D)	78,896	23.0%
Kenneth J. Block (MDE)	22,146	6.5%

Lt. Gov. Elizabeth Roberts (D)

First elected: 2006

Length of term: 4 years

Term expires: 1/15

Salary: $108,808

Phone: (401) 222-2371

LEGISLATURE

General Assembly: January-June

Senate: 38 members, 2-year terms

2013 ratios: 32 D, 5 R, 1 I; 29 men, 9 women

Salary: $14,640

Phone: (401) 222-6655

House: 75 members, 2-year terms

2013 ratios: 69 D, 6 R; 53 men, 22 women

Salary: $14,640

Phone: (401) 222-2466

TERM LIMITS

Governor: 2 terms

Senate: No

House: No

URBAN STATISTICS

CITY	POPULATION
Providence	178,042
Warwick	82,672
Cranston	80,387
Pawtucket	71,148
East Providence	47,037

REGISTERED VOTERS

Other	48%
Democrat	41%
Republican	11%

POPULATION

2010 population	1,052,567
2000 population	1,048,319
1990 population	1,003,464
Percent change (2000-2010)	+0.4%
Rank among states (2010)	43
Median age	38.6
Born in state	59.2%
Foreign born	12.6
Violent crime rate	253/100,000
Poverty level	11.5%
Federal workers	11,398
Military	1,490

ELECTIONS

STATE ELECTION OFFICIAL
(401) 222-2345

DEMOCRATIC PARTY
(401) 272-3367

REPUBLICAN PARTY
(401) 732-8282

MISCELLANEOUS

Web: www.ri.gov

Capital: Providence

U.S. CONGRESS

Senate: 2 Democrats

House: 2 Democrats

STATISTICS BY DISTRICT

District	2012 Vote for President		2008 Vote for President										
	Obama	Romney	Obama	McCain	Black	Asian	Hispanic	Median Income	Over 64	Under 20	College Education	Rural	Sq. Miles
1	66%	32%	66%	32%	8%	4%	15%	$50,672	15%	24%	32%	4%	268
2	60	38	61	38	4	3	11	57,448	14	24	31	16	765
STATE	**63**	**35**	**63**	**35**	**6**	**3**	**12**	**53,636**	**15**	**24**	**31**	**10**	**1,034**
U.S.	**51**	**47**	**53**	**46**	**12**	**5**	**17**	**50,052**	**13**	**27**	**29**	**21**	**3,531,905**

Sen. Jack Reed (D)

Capitol Office
224-4642
reed.senate.gov
728 Hart Bldg. 20510-3903; fax 224-4680

Committees
Appropriations
(Interior-Environment - Chairman)
Armed Services
(Seapower - Chairman)
Banking, Housing & Urban Affairs

Residence
Jamestown

Born
Nov. 12, 1949; Providence, R.I.

Religion
Roman Catholic

Family
Wife, Julia Reed; one child

Education
U.S. Military Academy, B.S. 1971 (engineering); Harvard U., M.P.P. 1973, J.D. 1982

Military Service
Army, 1971-79; Army Reserve, 1979-91

Career
Lawyer; college instructor

Political Highlights
R.I. Senate, 1985-91; U.S. House, 1991-97

ELECTION RESULTS

2008 GENERAL		
Jack Reed (D)	320,644	73.4%
Robert G. Tingle (R)	116,174	26.6%
2008 PRIMARY		
Jack Reed (D)	48,038	86.8%
Christopher F. Young (D)	7,277	13.2%

Previous Winning Percentages
2002 (78%); 1996 (63%); 1994 House Election (68%); 1992 House Election (71%); 1990 House Election (59%)

Elected 1996; 3rd term

Reed has the voting record of a Democratic partisan but no reputation for enmity. His serious and respectful demeanor has earned him the admiration of Senate colleagues, particularly when he focuses on national security and financial issues.

Reed grew up in a working-class family in Cranston. His father, Joseph Reed, was a school custodian, and his mother, Mary Monahan, was a factory worker. His earliest political memory is of his mother watching the 1960 presidential election returns and reciting the rosary in hopes of a victory for fellow Catholic New Englander John F. Kennedy.

At age 12, Reed told his parents that he wanted to go to a military service academy. He was inspired in part by Army football heroes of that era and seeing other family members serve in uniform. Reed was eventually admitted, barely meeting the height requirement (he is under 5 feet 7 inches tall). After graduation, the Army put him through a master's program at the John F. Kennedy School of Government at Harvard University. Reed commanded a company of the 82nd Airborne and taught at West Point.

After attaining the rank of captain, he left the Army at age 29 to attend Harvard Law School. He returned home to a job in Rhode Island's biggest corporate law firm. In 1984, he won a seat in the state Senate. Six years later, Reed took 59 percent of the vote to win the U.S. House seat that Republican Claudine Schneider gave up to run for the Senate. Six years after that, he was elected to the U.S. Senate.

Reed is more likely to address legislation in quiet negotiations or committee hearings than through the media. He has only three committee assignments — Appropriations, Armed Services, and Banking, Housing and Urban Affairs — but he has influential positions on each of them.

Some of Reed's most notable successes have been on financial matters, going back to his state-level service. He is not averse to government-centered solutions when it comes to stabilizing markets or helping lower-income people.

Reed is the No. 2 Democrat on the Banking committee, where he champions a number of housing programs. He was the chief Senate supporter of the National Housing Trust Fund created in 2008 to help low-income renters, but the challenge since then has been capitalizing the fund. Reed has tried several times to designate revenue streams for the program.

President Barack Obama signed a 2009 bill by Reed and Missouri Republican Christopher S. Bond to consolidate homeless assistance programs and authorize new emergency grants for those nearing homelessness. As the housing sector continues a sluggish recovery from the 2008 financial crisis, Reed has urged the Federal Housing Finance Agency to cut mortgage balances for struggling homeowners with federally held loans.

Reed is also a fan of empowering the regulatory agencies overseeing financial markets. He fought for the creation of the Office of Financial Research in the 2010 financial regulatory overhaul law, envisioning "a world-class institution that can go toe to toe with the top Wall Street banks" by analyzing reams of data to identify problems with markets. (Republicans have called some of those data-collection plans too intrusive.) When Congress considered a 2012 bill to help capital flows to small businesses, Reed unsuccessfully tried to add a provision to increase the number of companies that have to register with the Securities and Exchange Commission.

Reed scored a victory in 2012 when an extension of lower payroll taxes was signed into law; the bill included his plan, based on a Rhode Island program, to reduce layoffs. It allows companies to cut hours rather than fire a worker, with federal unemployment insurance making up some of the difference in lost salary.

Reed is also the No. 2 Democrat on the Armed Services Committee. His military credentials made him a leader of the Democratic opposition to the Iraq War during the George W. Bush administration — he voted against the authorization to use military force in 2002.

He initially opposed sending more combat forces to Afghanistan. But when Obama announced a troop buildup in a 2009 speech at West Point, Reed went with him to back the policy. Reed now supports Obama's plans for troop reductions in Afghanistan in 2014, while encouraging a careful but accelerated pace. He endorsed Obama's decision to intervene (along with NATO) in the Libyan civil war in 2011, and he shared the president's reluctance to aid rebel forces in Syria's civil war in 2012.

Several of the top military leaders in Iraq and Afghanistan were his contemporaries at West Point, and Reed and Gen. John P. Abizaid, the former head of U.S. Central Command, were in the same parachute brigade in the 82nd Airborne Division. Though Reed never served in combat, he said his training and service give him an appreciation for the military's power — and its limits. "It's very impressive when you're lighting up the night sky pretty quickly," he once said. "But decisive action usually involves political, economic, social and cultural action as well."

Reed gets to the Middle East fairly often, and his lengthy trip reports have become must-reads among Armed Services Committee members.

He chairs the Seapower Subcommittee, which puts him in the sometimes tenuous position of calling for restraint in military spending while also promoting Rhode Island's shipbuilders. He supports the Rhode Island-based Naval Undersea Warfare Center and Naval Education Training Center, and he champions funding that goes to Rhode Island contractors such as Textron Systems and Raytheon Co.

He works to protect federal contracts for the building of attack submarines at the General Dynamics Electric Boat Corp. in Rhode Island and nearby Groton, Conn. Reed helped write a provision in the fiscal 2013 defense authorization law that authorizes the secretary of the Navy to buy Virginia-class submarines under a multiyear procurement contract.

Reed also works to send money home as a member of the Appropriations Committee. In the 112th Congress (2011-12), he assumed the chairmanship of the Interior-Environment Subcommittee. Reed has secured hundreds of millions of dollars in federal funding for infrastructure and community development projects for his home state, with added focus after huge storms tore up local communities in 2011 and 2012.

Should Reed win re-election in 2014 — which seems like a near certainty — he would be a candidate for the top Democratic spot on either the Banking or Armed Services committees. The chairmen of those panels, Tim Johnson of South Dakota and Carl Levin of Michigan, are retiring.

Reed is socially liberal. In recent years he voted against banning a procedure opponents call "partial birth" abortion. He also opposed amending the Constitution to prohibit same-sex marriage and supported the late 2010 repeal of the statutory ban on openly gay individuals serving in the military.

When Democratic Sen. Claiborne Pell decided to retire in 1996 after 36 years in office, Reed was ready. He captured the seat with 63 percent of the vote against Republican state Treasurer Nancy J. Mayer. He won re-election in 2002 with 78 percent, and six years later took 73 percent.

In 2005, at age 55, Reed married. He and Julia Hart, then 39, an employee of the Senate office that arranges international travel for senators, wed in West Point's Catholic chapel. It was the first marriage for both Reed and Hart. Their daughter was born in January 2007.

Key Votes

2012	
Prohibit health insurance plans from denying coverage based on the sponsor's religious beliefs	YES
Require approval of the Keystone XL oil pipeline	NO
Ease securities rules to expand small-business access to capital	NO
Reauthorize farm and nutrition programs for five years	NO
Limit debate on a bill that would create private-sector cybersecurity standards	YES
Consent to ratification of a treaty setting global standard for the treatment of people with disabilities	YES
Provide $60.4 billion in disaster relief following Superstorm Sandy	YES
Extend most Bush-era income tax rates while allowing rates for top-bracket earners to rise (Jan. 1, 2013)	YES
2011	
Prevent EPA from regulating greenhouse gas emissions to address climate change	NO
Extend certain provisions of Patriot Act for four years	YES
Clear compromise debt limit increase plan and establish future spending limits	YES
Overhaul patent law	YES
Implement Colombia free trade agreement	NO
Limit debate on confirmation of Caitlin J. Halligan to D.C. Circuit Court of Appeals	YES
Extend payroll tax cut and unemployment benefits for two months	YES

CQ Vote Studies

	PARTY UNITY		PRESIDENTIAL SUPPORT	
	SUPPORT	OPPOSE	SUPPORT	OPPOSE
2012	97%	3%	95%	5%
2011	97%	3%	94%	6%
2010	98%	2%	98%	2%
2009	99%	1%	100%	0%
2008	99%	1%	35%	65%
2007	97%	3%	41%	59%
2006	96%	4%	53%	47%
2005	98%	2%	29%	71%
2004	98%	2%	60%	40%
2003	98%	2%	45%	55%

Interest Groups

	AFL-CIO	ADA	CCUS	ACU
2012	100%	90%	25%	0%
2011	100%	100%	45%	0%
2010	94%	90%	18%	0%
2009	94%	95%	43%	0%
2008	100%	95%	50%	4%
2007	100%	95%	40%	0%
2006	100%	100%	42%	4%
2005	93%	100%	33%	0%
2004	100%	100%	35%	0%
2003	100%	100%	26%	20%

Sen. Sheldon Whitehouse (D)

Capitol Office
224-2921
whitehouse.senate.gov
530 Hart Bldg. 20510-3904; fax 228-6362

Committees
Budget
Environment & Public Works
(Oversight - Chairman)
Health, Education, Labor & Pensions
Judiciary
(Crime & Terrorism - Chairman)
Special Aging

Residence
Newport

Born
Oct. 20, 1955; Manhattan, N.Y.

Religion
Episcopalian

Family
Wife, Sandra Whitehouse; two children

Education
Yale U., B.A. 1978 (architecture); U. of Virginia, J.D. 1982

Career
Lawyer; gubernatorial aide

Political Highlights
R.I. Department of Business Regulation director, 1992-94; U.S. attorney, 1994-98; sought Democratic nomination for governor, 2002; R.I. attorney general, 1999-2003

ELECTION RESULTS

2012 GENERAL

Sheldon Whitehouse (D)	271,034	64.8%
B. Barrett Hinckley (R)	146,222	35.0%

2012 PRIMARY

Sheldon Whitehouse (D)	unopposed

Previous Winning Percentages
2006 (54%)

Elected 2006; 2nd term

Whitehouse is a liberal frontman for several Democratic causes, including a few politically minded proposals the party has used to club Republicans. A former state attorney general, he stays on top of the law-and-order questions swirling around the war on terrorism. And he presses for an aggressive federal response to climate change.

Rhode Island has plenty of working-class Democrats, but Whitehouse comes from Newport, which was the summer playground of obscenely wealthy Americans in the Gilded Age. He's not a Vanderbilt figure, but he had a blue-blood upbringing. Whitehouse's father, Charles, was a wealthy ambassador who worked for the CIA and the State Department.

Charles Whitehouse roomed at Yale with John H. Chafee, who later became a Republican senator. He was also the father of Lincoln Chafee — who in turn became the Republican senator that Whitehouse defeated in 2006. (He is now the Democratic governor of Rhode Island.)

Whitehouse was educated at St. Paul's, a New Hampshire boarding school, and he lived part of the time with his parents in Cambodia, France, Laos, South Africa and Vietnam. He isn't unaware of his WASP image. At a 1999 event, after his election as attorney general, Whitehouse joked that "three times I tried to throw my hat into the ring before I ran. Each time the damn valet brought the hat back."

In the 112th Congress (2011-12), however, Whitehouse wasn't squeamish in promoting fiscal proposals targeting the wealthy. During the 2012 election season, he led the Senate charge for the "Buffett Rule" (named after billionaire Warren Buffett, who supported it). The plan was to impose a 30 percent minimum tax on income over $1 million, which would surpass the current 15 percent rate on capital gains — the primary category of income for many of the nation's wealthiest citizens. Republicans dismissed his bill as class warfare, and it died in the Senate. But it was highly touted by President Barack Obama and Democrats in general.

Whitehouse also went after big-money political donors. A 2010 Supreme Court ruling permitted companies and unions to contribute unlimited amounts to super PACs, campaign organizations unaffiliated with candidates' official campaigns. Whitehouse prepared a bill to require top executives and big donors to super PACs to appear in, or place their names on, ads the groups produce. "No more hiding behind shadow organizations with phony names," Whitehouse wrote in Roll Call.

That measure met the same fate as the Buffett Rule, but Whitehouse remains hopeful that a high-profile Republican, Arizona Sen. John McCain, might sign on to the cause. McCain has expressed reservations that Whitehouse's bill unfairly favors the political influence of Democratic-leaning unions while trying to curb corporate money.

Whitehouse finds occasional Republican partners, but he blames recent Senate inaction mostly on the GOP. "For the last couple of years, the tea party tail has been wagging the Republican dog," he said in 2012. "You have this little group of bitter partisans that has a very outsized effect." Whitehouse describes a conflict between "what you might call the reality-based Republicans and the tea party extremists" and says the business community "has to make some decisions about what way it wants to direct" the GOP.

He'll also grouse if he thinks Democrats aren't doing enough. A member of the Environment and Public Works Committee, Whitehouse wants legislative action to address the Earth's changing climate. "It is incumbent on us to be more active on climate change, whether or not the White House is going to show a lot of leadership in this area," he said in late 2012. He noted that from previous experience with Obama, "if past is prologue, then prologue hasn't been all that great." A member of the Budget Committee, he proposed an amendment to the Senate's fiscal 2014 budget resolution to endorse a tax on carbon emissions. It was resoundingly defeated.

Whitehouse is a co-chairman of the Senate Oceans Caucus, and in the 112th Congress he called for establishment of a National Endowment for the Oceans, Coasts and Great Lakes. His plan would fund the endowment via interest accumulated on Clean Water Act fines related to the 2010 Gulf of Mexico oil spill; funds would then be distributed as grants to states and regional planning commissions to support habitat restoration, fisheries, preservation and more. The provision was included in the Senate version of a 2012 transportation bill, but it was cut out in a House-Senate conference.

Whitehouse and fellow Rhode Island Democrat Jack Reed have worked together trying to secure flood relief and infrastructure funding for their state, particularly in light of major storms in 2011 and 2012.

On the Health, Education, Labor and Pensions Committee, Whitehouse is a salesman for the 2010 health care law, even though it fell short of his standards. Whitehouse helped write a provision to include a government-run insurance program known as the public option, a system that many liberals strongly prefer. It was dropped from the bill in final negotiations.

A more personal health cause for Whitehouse is the battle against pancreatic cancer, which killed his mother. The fiscal 2013 defense policy law includes a provision by Whitehouse and several other partners to direct the National Cancer Institute to advance research on cancers with five-year survival rates below 50 percent — essentially, pancreatic and lung cancers.

Whitehouse gets to wear his old attorney general hat on the Judiciary Committee, where he chairs the Subcommittee on Crime and Terrorism.

He was a strident critic of the George W. Bush administration's use of interrogation techniques that could be construed as torture. He sponsored an amendment to the fiscal 2008 intelligence authorization bill that limited CIA and other executive branch interrogation tactics to those contained in the 2006 Army field manual, which banned waterboarding and other harsh tactics. A modified version of the amendment made it into the final bill, drawing a veto from Bush.

He has also been involved in cybersecurity debates. Whitehouse emphasizes working with businesses — he was one of the few Democrats to support granting immunity to telecommunications companies that had participated in a Bush-era warrantless surveillance program. "I've run wiretap investigations," he said. "I've come to recognize the importance of cooperation with the private sector." Whitehouse and Arizona Republican Jon Kyl helped broker a compromise on a cybersecurity bill floating through the Senate in 2012; instead of putting new mandates on private sector computer networks, their plan would create incentives for businesses to make their networks more secure. The issue is still under debate in the 113th Congress (2013-14).

Whitehouse majored in architecture at Yale and got his law degree from the University of Virginia. After law school, he clerked for the West Virginia Supreme Court, then worked in the Rhode Island attorney general's office. President Bill Clinton appointed him U.S. attorney in 1994. In that role, he launched an investigation into Vincent A. "Buddy" Cianci Jr., the Providence mayor. The corruption investigation came to be known in local media by its code name, "Operation Plunder Dome," and led to Cianci's conviction for racketeering and other charges.

Whitehouse was elected Rhode Island attorney general in 1998. In 2002 he made an unsuccessful bid for governor, but he defeated the moderate Chafee in 2006. He was re-elected in 2012 with 65 percent of the vote against entrepreneur B. Barrett Hinckley.

Key Votes

2012	
Prohibit health insurance plans from denying coverage based on the sponsor's religious beliefs	YES
Require approval of the Keystone XL oil pipeline	NO
Ease securities rules to expand small-business access to capital	NO
Reauthorize farm and nutrition programs for five years	NO
Limit debate on a bill that would create private-sector cybersecurity standards	YES
Consent to ratification of a treaty setting global standard for the treatment of people with disabilities	YES
Provide $60.4 billion in disaster relief following Superstorm Sandy	YES
Extend most Bush-era income tax rates while allowing rates for top-bracket earners to rise (Jan. 1, 2013)	YES
2011	
Prevent EPA from regulating greenhouse gas emissions to address climate change	NO
Extend certain provisions of Patriot Act for four years	YES
Clear compromise debt limit increase plan and establish future spending limits	YES
Overhaul patent law	YES
Implement Colombia free trade agreement	NO
Limit debate on confirmation of Caitlin J. Halligan to D.C. Circuit Court of Appeals	YES
Extend payroll tax cut and unemployment benefits for two months	YES

CQ Vote Studies

	PARTY UNITY		PRESIDENTIAL SUPPORT	
	SUPPORT	OPPOSE	SUPPORT	OPPOSE
2012	95%	5%	95%	5%
2011	97%	3%	94%	6%
2010	99%	1%	97%	3%
2009	99%	1%	100%	0%
2008	95%	5%	41%	59%
2007	98%	2%	35%	65%

Interest Groups

	AFL-CIO	ADA	CCUS	ACU
2012	100%	90%	25%	0%
2011	100%	100%	45%	0%
2010	100%	90%	18%	0%
2009	94%	95%	43%	0%
2008	100%	90%	50%	8%
2007	100%	95%	36%	0%

Rep. David Cicilline (D)

Capitol Office
225-4911
cicilline.house.gov
128 Cannon Bldg. 20515-3901; fax 225-3290

Committees
Budget
Foreign Affairs

Residence
Providence

Born
July 15, 1961; Providence, R.I.

Religion
Jewish

Family
Single

Education
Brown U., A.B. 1983 (political science); Georgetown U., J.D. 1986

Career
Lawyer; public defender

Political Highlights
Sought Democratic nomination for R.I. Senate, 1992; R.I. House, 1995-2003; mayor of Providence, 2003-11

ELECTION RESULTS

2012 GENERAL		
David Cicilline (D)	108,612	53.0%
Brendan Doherty (R)	83,737	40.8%
David S. Vogel (I)	12,504	6.1%
2012 PRIMARY		
David Cicilline (D)	30,203	62.1%
Anthony Gemma (D)	14,702	30.2%
Christopher F. Young (D)	3,701	7.6%
2010 GENERAL		
David Cicilline (D)	81,269	50.6%
John Loughlin (R)	71,542	44.6%
Kenneth A. Capalbo (I)	6,424	4.0%

Elected 2010; 2nd term

Cicilline is a fast-talking and sharp liberal — someone who both bemoans the partisanship of Congress and cheerily denounces the Republican agenda. The former mayor of Providence champions programs that direct funds to local entities, as well as federal leverage that helps the manufacturing sector.

Cicilline (sis-uh-LEE-nee) says he values results above all, because as a mayor "you still see every day the urgency of solving problems and developing practical solutions." He is affiliated with No Labels, a nonpartisan group intent on increasing the legislative output of Congress.

But he has clear opinions on what that output should be. Cicilline is a vice chairman of the Congressional Progressive Caucus, the group of the most-liberal House members. He is aggressive in introducing legislation in order to "begin building a case with my colleagues." He also likes building cases on the House floor: In the 112th Congress (2011-12), C-SPAN credited Cicilline with more appearances than any other freshman.

In his second term, he is promoting Democratic priorities — and bashing Republican ones — as a member of the Budget Committee.

Cicilline was unimpressed with GOP budgets in the 112th Congress. When Budget Chairman Paul D. Ryan was chosen as the Republican vice presidential nominee in 2012, Cicilline issued his backhanded congratulations, which concluded: "I strongly opposed Mr. Ryan's budget proposal that would have ended the Medicare guarantee, slashed funding for Pell grants, and extended more tax breaks for millionaires and corporations that ship American jobs overseas."

Medicare and Social Security are "earned benefits, they're not entitlements," Cicilline says, and he wants Congress to consider raising the limit on income subject to Social Security payroll taxes.

Cicilline is a big supporter of the Democrats' "Make It in America" agenda, which includes his plans for boosting manufacturing. Cicilline and New York Sen. Kirsten Gillibrand introduced companion bills in 2011 to create a competitive grant program, then refined their proposal at the start of the 113th Congress (2013-14). States and regional partnerships could apply for funds, which could be used for upgrading manufacturers' equipment, diversifying business plans, improving energy efficiency or training workers.

Grant programs in general are appealing to Cicilline, who emphasizes their importance to local leaders. He tried to amend the fiscal 2012 Homeland Security spending bill to add $337 million for homeland and firefighter grants to state and local governments. His effort — which would have freed up those funds by cutting border security spending — was rebuffed.

He has some sympathy with the sentiment that local governments need more flexibility in using federal aid. "There are some restrictions on workforce investment funds, or on Community Development Block Grant funds, which sometimes are challenging or don't make a lot of sense," he said.

He is also a fan of public-private partnerships, in which small businesses and other private entities partner with governments in providing services. He says such arrangements are cost-effective ways to stretch federal dollars, especially on infrastructure projects — "because we really don't have a sustainable funding stream for infrastructure in this country." Cicilline supports the creation of a National Infrastructure Bank.

Cicilline has a seat on the Foreign Affairs Committee. He criticizes China's alleged manipulation of its currency, which many people believe gives Chinese exports an advantage.

"The notion that we can't enforce trade agreements ... because they might be mean to us — to me, that is an absolutely unacceptable position," he said.

"China needs the United States as much as the United States needs China."

U.S. troops are scheduled to withdraw from Afghanistan by the end of 2014, but that's not fast enough for Cicilline, who says U.S. resources would be better used at home. In both 2011 and 2012, the House rejected his amendments to eliminate funds for infrastructure improvements in Afghanistan. Cicilline also opposed U.S. involvement in Libya's civil war in 2011.

Cicilline, who is gay, has said he will work to promote the rights of the gay, lesbian, bisexual and transgender communities in other nations.

Cicilline is the middle of five children. His father works as a criminal defense attorney, and his mother spent a few years as a high school guidance counselor while also raising her kids.

He showed an interest in civic engagement at a young age, having his parents shuttle him to school board and town council meetings. "I acknowledge there was something wrong with me," he says. He had some early success: He used a provision in Rhode Island law to force his high school to hire someone to teach Italian, and as a teenager he created an organization that helped block a real estate developer — who was a friend of his father — from building condos on a scenic Narragansett shoreline.

After attending law school at Georgetown, he worked as a public defender in the District of Columbia before returning home to work as a criminal defense and civil rights attorney. He made a failed bid for the state Senate, then spent four terms in the state House. As mayor, he succeeded Buddy Cianci, who had been convicted of racketeering conspiracy.

In 2010, Cicilline emerged from a rough-and-tumble four-way primary, winning 37 percent of the vote in the race to succeed Democrat Patrick J. Kennedy, who retired from Congress. Republican state Rep. John Loughlin ran a respectable campaign but couldn't overcome the district's Democratic lean, as Cicilline took nearly 51 percent of the vote.

The 2012 election cycle was also bumpy. Cicilline touted his financial stewardship of Providence during his 2010 campaign, but reports in 2011 showed the city government in economic distress. City officials criticized Cicilline's accounting practices as mayor, and Fitch Ratings downgraded Providence's bond rating and accused Cicilline's administration of "imprudent budgeting decisions and failure to implement recurring budget solutions." He had some of the lowest approval ratings of any sitting House member.

Anthony Gemma, a self-funding candidate who finished second in the 2010 Democratic primary, forced Cicilline to spend some campaign cash on the primary. Republicans fielded Brendan Doherty, a former state police superintendent. It seemed like Cicilline was in trouble a few weeks before the election, but he ended up with a 12-point victory.

Key Votes

2012	
Extend a Social Security payroll tax cut and unemployment benefits	YES
Ease securities rules to expand small-business access to capital	YES
Extend for one year subsidized student loan interest rates financed by a cut in health care spending	NO
Cite Attorney General Eric H. Holder Jr. for contempt of Congress	?
Create a visa program for foreign graduates in high-tech fields	NO
Extend most Bush-era income tax rates while allowing rates for top-bracket earners to rise (Jan. 1, 2013)	YES
2011	
Strike funding for F-35 alternative engine	YES
Prevent EPA from regulating greenhouse gas emissions to address climate change	NO
Extend certain provisions of Patriot Act for four years	NO
Declare opposition to use of ground troops in Libya	NO
Overhaul patent law	YES
Pass compromise debt limit increase plan and establish future spending limits	YES
Allow consideration of measures to implement three trade agreements	NO

CQ Vote Studies

	Party Unity		Presidential Support	
	Support	Oppose	Support	Oppose
2012	98%	2%	91%	9%
2011	97%	3%	80%	20%

Interest Groups

	AFL-CIO	ADA	CCUS	ACU
2012	95%	90%	17%	0%
2011	100%	95%	31%	0%

Rhode Island 1

East — Pawtucket, part of Providence, Newport

The urban, Democratic 1st runs down a sliver of the eastern part of the state south from former mill towns in the Blackstone Valley along the east bank of the Narragansett Bay, including Newport and part of Providence. Home to a once-thriving manufacturing sector that drove the economy for a century, the region struggles with economic stagnation.

Much of Providence's picturesque East Side neighborhood east of Interstate 95, including Brown University and the Rhode Island School of Design campus, is in the 1st, as is the state Capitol. The state's economy relies on the capital, which has struggled with municipal budget shortfalls and government layoffs, but the health care industry provides jobs.

Woonsocket and Central Falls have not recovered from nationwide economic downturns and decadeslong manufacturing dips. Woonsocket has turned to the arts and government grants to change its course. Pawtucket is home to Hasbro, one of the largest toy manufacturers in the world.

In the southeastern portion of the district outside the population centers along Interstate 95, the region becomes more affluent and more sparsely populated. Newport is home to stately mansions that draw tourists and a maritime defense industry connected to a large naval base and Portsmouth-based contractors. Both the Naval War College and the Naval Academy Preparatory School are based here.

The population of the district is eclectic. Pawtucket has large minority populations of ethnic French-Canadians as well as Portuguese and Cape Verdean communities. Many refugees fleeing Liberia have settled here as well. South Providence has a large Hispanic population.

Major Industry
Health care, government, education, tourism

Military Bases
Naval Station Newport, 1,117 military, 4,220 civilian (2012)

Cities
Providence (pt.); Pawtucket; Woonsocket; Newport

Notable
Touro Synagogue in Newport, dedicated in 1762, is the oldest synagogue in the country.

Rep. Jim Langevin (D)

Capitol Office
225-2735
langevin.house.gov
109 Cannon Bldg. 20515-3902; fax 225-5976

Committees
Armed Services
Select Intelligence

Residence
Warwick

Born
April 22, 1964; Warwick, R.I.

Religion
Roman Catholic

Family
Single

Education
Rhode Island College, B.A. 1990 (political science & public administration); Harvard U., M.P.A. 1994

Career
None

Political Highlights
R.I. House, 1989-95; R.I. secretary of state, 1995-2001

ELECTION RESULTS

2012 GENERAL		
Jim Langevin (D)	124,067	55.7%
Michael G. Riley (R)	78,189	35.1%
Abel G. Collins (I)	20,212	9.1%
2012 PRIMARY		
Jim Langevin (D)	22,161	74.1%
John O. Matson (D)	7,748	25.9%
2010 GENERAL		
Jim Langevin (D)	104,442	59.9%
Mark Zaccaria (R)	55,409	31.8%
John O. Matson (I)	14,584	8.4%

Previous Winning Percentages
2008 (70%); 2006 (73%); 2004 (75%); 2002 (76%); 2000 (62%)

Elected 2000; 7th term

As a member of the House minority, Langevin uses civility and personal relationships to work toward his policy goals. He is a notable voice on national defense, cybersecurity and health care issues.

The first quadriplegic to serve in the House, Langevin (LAN-juh-vin) has been a public official for nearly his entire professional life — his injury as a young man prompted him to go into politics, and he entered the Rhode Island House at 24. While consistently voting with Democrats throughout his career, he has paid particular attention to the interests of the fishing, education and defense interests in his district.

In recent years, he has become a key figure on cybersecurity. The issue caught his attention during his service on the Homeland Security panel; now he sits on the Intelligence Committee. Even on Capitol Hill, people were less receptive to the topic in 2006 and 2007. "Their eyes would glaze over," Langevin said. "Now, many more people are taking note and are recognizing the threat that we face, the challenges that we face."

Langevin has stated that there will need to be some mandatory regulations in place to protect the computer networks for "critical infrastructure" such as power grids and water plants. But he generally favors a light touch in federal regulation of the Internet, and he has been supportive of efforts to facilitate information sharing between the federal government and the operators of sensitive networks to ward off cyberattacks. He successfully amended a 2013 version of a bill on information sharing, to make sure that utility districts could participate. It was passed by the House in April.

He maintains that boosting cybersecurity can boost employment: He sees a demand for more cybersecurity professionals and urges greater federal involvement in encouraging job training in technical fields. He's active in both the Cybersecurity Caucus, which he founded with Texas Republican Michael McCaul — who now chairs the Homeland Security Committee — and the Career and Technical Education Caucus.

Langevin has also worked the issue from the Armed Services Committee, where he is the top Democrat on the Intelligence, Emerging Threats and Capabilities panel. Several times, he has tried to modify defense policy bills to create a National Office for Cyberspace in the White House.

His other defense interests include Virginia-class submarine purchases (which affect contractors in Rhode Island and neighboring Connecticut) and shipbuilding in general: "I want us to have the greatest number of ships possible that meet our national security challenges and needs," he said.

He opposed engagement in Iraq from the onset in 2002. He supported President Barack Obama's increase of troop levels in Afghanistan, but after receiving an update on turmoil in that country in early 2012, he called officials' assessments of progress a "little rosy and maybe too optimistic."

Langevin has also used his Armed Services seat to bolster federal employee unions. The fiscal 2011 defense authorization law included a Langevin amendment — aimed at turning back a contrary effort by Republicans — to ensure that the Pentagon could continue to replace private sector contractors with unionized federal workers.

Langevin rarely votes against the wishes of party leaders. But as a Roman Catholic who opposes abortion in most cases, he backed language in the House's 2009 health care overhaul to bar the use of federal funding for abortion. When the language was later expunged from the final version, Langevin's support for the measure was in question. Ultimately he voted for it, saying that existing restrictions on abortion funding were adequate.

He supports the notion of a universal health care system, and he has long been an advocate of federal funding for embryonic stem cell research — he believes the research could hold promise for the treatment of spinal cord injuries like the one that left him paralyzed from the waist down at age 16. "Being pro-life isn't just about protecting life in the womb," Langevin said. "It has to be about protecting and extending the quality of life for people who are living among us."

As a boy, Langevin dreamed of being a police officer or an FBI agent. He enrolled in a police department cadet program in his hometown of Warwick. On Aug. 22, 1980, he was in the police locker room when a SWAT team member inadvertently pulled the trigger of a gun, discharging a bullet that ricocheted off a locker and hit Langevin in the neck. It severed his spinal cord, leaving him unable to move his legs and with only minimal use of his arms and hands.

Langevin embraces his symbolic importance to people with disabilities. In July 2010, he became the first person in a wheelchair to preside over the House, marking the 20th anniversary of the passage of Americans With Disabilities Act. After the Capitol was evacuated following the Sept. 11 terrorist attacks, with no protocol for how to help people with disabilities get out, Langevin helped develop one. He campaigned for Senate approval of the United Nations Convention on the Rights of Persons with Disabilities, but that effort fell short in December 2012.

In the 109th Congress (2005-06), he helped win enactment of a bill authorizing federal grants to agencies that recruit and train people to provide a respite to families caring for a disabled or ailing person at home. He continually pushes for increased funding for the program.

Langevin says it was the tremendous outpouring of support from the Warwick community after his injury that prompted him to go into politics. Four years after the accident, he volunteered in Frank Flaherty's campaign for mayor. Flaherty recalled being amazed at Langevin's tenacity; later, when Flaherty was still mayor and Langevin was in the state legislature, "he'd come in looking for something for his area of the city and he'd drive me crazy, chase me around. I used to threaten to unplug the battery on his wheelchair so I wouldn't have to listen," Flaherty told the Providence Journal.

While still in college, Langevin was elected as a delegate to the Rhode Island Constitutional Convention. In 1988, he won the first of three terms in the Rhode Island House. In 1994, he was elected secretary of state, and six years later, when Democratic Rep. Bob Weygand ran for the Senate, Langevin made a bid for his 2nd District seat. He took 62 percent of the vote. All his re-elections have been by wide margins.

Key Votes

2012

Extend a Social Security payroll tax cut and unemployment benefits	YES
Ease securities rules to expand small-business access to capital	YES
Extend for one year subsidized student loan interest rates financed by a cut in health care spending	NO
Cite Attorney General Eric H. Holder Jr. for contempt of Congress	NO
Create a visa program for foreign graduates in high-tech fields	NO
Extend most Bush-era income tax rates while allowing rates for top-bracket earners to rise (Jan. 1, 2013)	YES

2011

Strike funding for F-35 alternative engine	YES
Prevent EPA from regulating greenhouse gas emissions to address climate change	NO
Extend certain provisions of Patriot Act for four years	YES
Declare opposition to use of ground troops in Libya	NO
Overhaul patent law	YES
Pass compromise debt limit increase plan and establish future spending limits	YES
Allow consideration of measures to implement three trade agreements	NO

CQ Vote Studies

	PARTY UNITY		PRESIDENTIAL SUPPORT	
	SUPPORT	OPPOSE	SUPPORT	OPPOSE
2012	95%	5%	90%	10%
2011	95%	5%	94%	6%
2010	97%	3%	93%	7%
2009	99%	1%	97%	3%
2008	99%	1%	15%	85%

Interest Groups

	AFL-CIO	ADA	CCUS	ACU
2012	90%	80%	33%	4%
2011	100%	80%	31%	0%
2010	100%	85%	25%	0%
2009	100%	95%	33%	4%
2008	100%	100%	61%	0%

Rhode Island 2

West — part of Providence, Warwick, Cranston

The 2nd takes in a mix of countryside, city life and shoreline that makes up the western two-thirds of the nation's smallest state. Interstate 95 cuts through small towns on its way to Providence, which is shared with the 1st.

The 2nd includes the state's border with Connecticut and roughly half of its northern border with Massachusetts, taking in idyllic beaches and lakes to the south and rolling hills to the north. The main population clusters in the state — Providence, Warwick and Cranston — are all at least partly in the district.

Education and health care have become key to the state's economy: The district hosts Providence College, Rhode Island College and the University of Rhode Island, as well as Roger Williams Medical Center, Rhode Island Hospital, and Women and Infants Hospital. Rhode Island Hospital is a research center.

Defense contracting provides thousands of jobs in the region. Maritime contractors, including General Dynamics' Electric Boat submarine facility at Quonset Point, rely on major military projects and defense spending. Aviation company Textron Systems has its international headquarters in downtown Providence. Other economic drivers include T.F. Green Airport in Warwick, which serves as an alternative to Boston's Logan Airport for New England travel.

The working- and middle-class towns in the district, which remains overwhelmingly white despite population growth in black and Latino communities, have substantial and Democratic-leaning union presences. The large Catholic population makes abortion a key issue, and voters here also can break from national Democrats on gay rights and immigration. The 2nd is slightly less Democratic than the 1st — voters here gave Barack Obama a 6-point-lower win in the 2012 presidential race than voters in the 1st.

Major Industry

Defense, health care, higher education

Cities

Providence (pt.), Warwick, Cranston

Notable

Block Island National Wildlife Refuge is 12 miles off the southern coast.

SOUTH CAROLINA

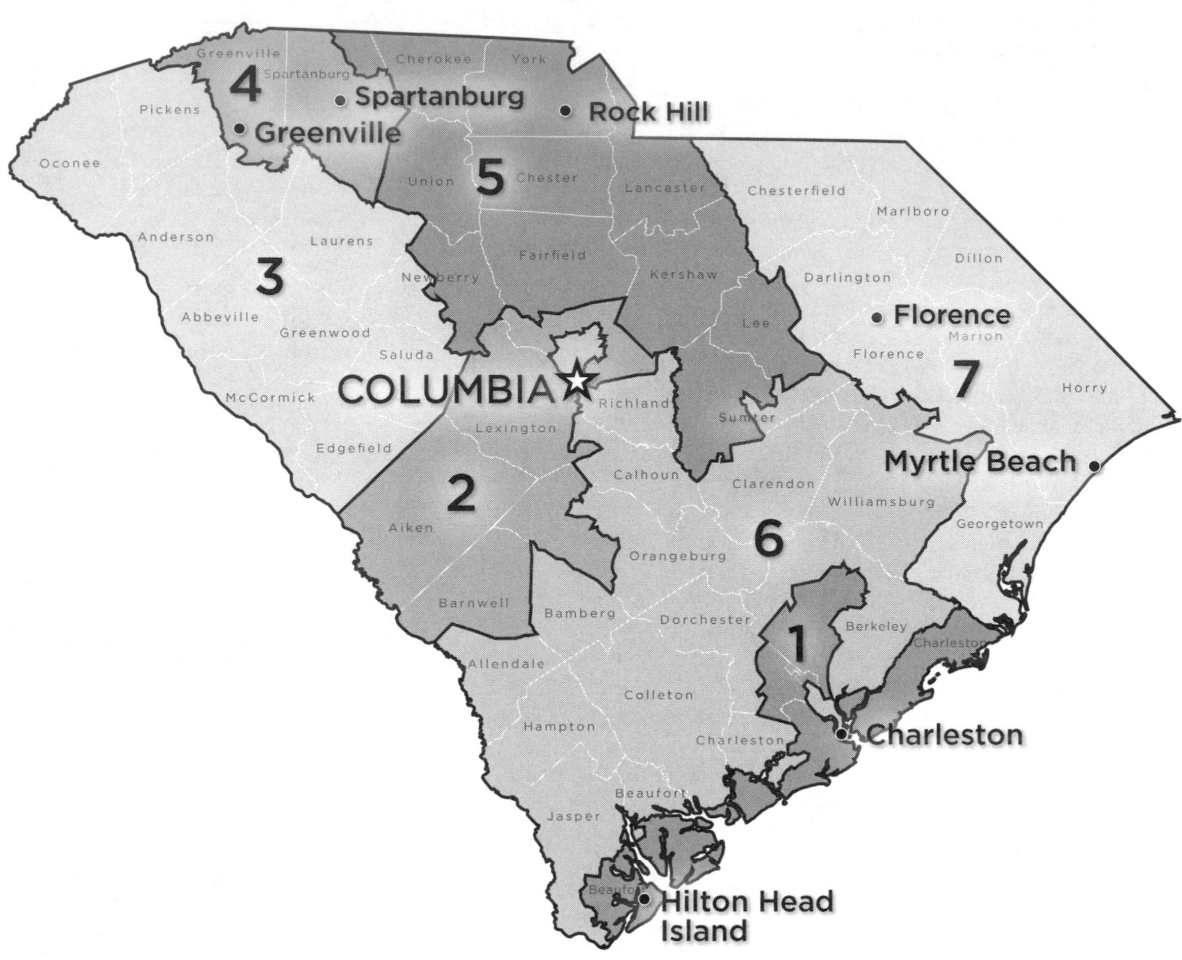

 www.cqpress.com

Gov. Nikki R. Haley (R)

First elected: 2010
Length of term: 4 years
Term expires: 1/15
Salary: $106,078
Phone: (803) 734-2100
Residence: Lexington
Born: January 20, 1972; Bamberg, S.C.
Religion: Methodist
Family: Husband, Michael Haley; two children
Education: Clemson U., B.S. 1994 (accounting)
Career: Accountant
Political highlights: S.C. House, 2005-10 (majority whip, 2006-07)

ELECTION RESULTS

2010 GENERAL

Nikki R. Haley (R)	690,525	51.4%
Vincent A. Sheheen (D)	630,534	46.9%
Others	20,114	1.5%

Lt. Gov. Glenn McConnell (R)

Took office: 2013; assumed office due to the resignation of Ken Ard, R.
Length of term: 4 years
Term expires: 1/15
Salary: $46,545
Phone: (803) 734-2080

LEGISLATURE

General Assembly: January-June
Senate: 46 members, 4-year terms
2013 ratios: 28 R, 18 D; 45 men, 1 woman
Salary: $10,400
Phone: (803) 212-6200
House: 124 members, 2-year terms
2013 ratios: 78 R, 46 D; 103 men, 21 women
Salary: $10,400
Phone: (803) 734-2010

TERM LIMITS

Governor: 2 consecutive terms
Senate: No
House: No

URBAN STATISTICS

CITY	POPULATION
Columbia	129,272
Charleston	120,083
North Charleston	97,471
Mount Pleasant	67,843
Rock Hill	66,154

REGISTERED VOTERS

Voters do not register by party.

POPULATION

2010 population	4,625,364
2000 population	4,012,012
1990 population	3,486,703
Percent change (2000-2010)	+15.3%
Rank among states (2010)	24
Median age	37.2
Born in state	60.1%
Foreign born	4.2%
Violent crime rate	671/100,000
Poverty level	17.1%
Federal workers	45,152
Military	32,518

ELECTIONS

STATE ELECTION OFFICIAL
(803) 734-9060

DEMOCRATIC PARTY
(803) 799-7798

REPUBLICAN PARTY
(803) 988-8440

MISCELLANEOUS

Web: www.sc.gov
Capital: Columbia

U.S. CONGRESS

Senate: 2 Republicans
House: 6 Republicans, 1 Democrat

STATISTICS BY DISTRICT

	2012 Vote for President		2008 Vote for President										
District	Obama	Romney	Obama	McCain	Black	Asian	Hispanic	Median Income	Over 64	Under 20	College Education	Rural	Sq. Miles
1	41%	57%	44%	55%	19%	2%	7%	$56,079	14%	25%	35%	15%	1,548
2	40	59	40	59	25	2	5	50,575	13	27	29	27	3,022
3	34	65	35	64	18	1	4	39,922	15	26	19	52	5,268
4	36	62	38	61	20	2	7	45,108	13	27	28	15	1,299
5	44	55	44	55	28	1	4	41,942	14	27	21	45	5,506
6	69	30	68	31	57	1	5	31,313	13	26	16	46	8,063
7	45	54	45	54	30	1	4	36,940	16	25	20	35	5,355
STATE	**44**	**55**	**45**	**54**	**28**	**1**	**5**	**42,367**	**14**	**26**	**24**	**33**	**30,061**
U.S.	**51**	**47**	**53**	**46**	**12**	**5**	**17**	**50,052**	**13**	**27**	**29**	**21**	**3,531,905**

Sen. Lindsey Graham (R)

Capitol Office
224-5972
lgraham.senate.gov
290 Russell Bldg. 20510-4001; fax 224-3808

Committees
Appropriations
Armed Services
Budget
Judiciary

Residence
Seneca

Born
July 9, 1955; Seneca, S.C.

Religion
Southern Baptist

Family
Single

Education
U. of South Carolina, B.A. 1977 (psychology), attended 1977-78 (public administration), J.D. 1981

Military Service
Air Force, 1982-88; Air Force Reserve, 1988-89; S.C. Air National Guard, 1989-96; Air Force Reserve, 2003-present

Career
Lawyer; military prosecutor

Political Highlights
S.C. House, 1993-95; U.S. House, 1995-2003

ELECTION RESULTS

2008 GENERAL		
Lindsey Graham (R)	1,076,534	57.5%
Bob Conley (D)	790,621	42.2%
2008 PRIMARY		
Lindsey Graham (R)	187,736	66.8%
Buddy Witherspoon (R)	93,125	33.2%

Previous Winning Percentages
2002 (54%); 2000 House Election (68%); 1998 House Election (100%); 1996 House Election (60%); 1994 House Election (60%)

Elected 2002; 2nd term

Graham has a take-charge approach to foreign policy and hawkish instincts regarding national security. On many issues, he'll consider subjugating his conservative principles to his desire for congressional output, and in the 113th Congress he is itching to make deals. "A lot of us are getting tired of just sitting around looking at each other," he said in 2012.

Capitol Hill reporters flock to Graham for his candor. A lawyer by trade, he goes on the record early and often to explain his positions — not unlike his close colleague, Arizona Republican John McCain. He has had some controversial positions to explain.

During the George W. Bush administration, Graham organized talks on overhauling Social Security and did his best to keep judicial nominations moving through the Senate. Deferring to President Barack Obama's judgment, he was the only Judiciary Committee Republican to vote in committee for Supreme Court nominees Elena Kagan and Sonia Sotomayor. In the 113th Congress (2013-14), Graham has negotiated plans to comprehensively reshape immigration law and also indicated that he could accept revenue increases as a trade-off for overhauling entitlement programs. He even once floated his own cap-and-trade plan to regulate greenhouse gas emissions.

Those stances would raise Republican eyebrows in most states, but in Graham's native South Carolina they raise hell. Graham has found himself to the left of his state's other congressional Republicans in recent years; activist groups such as the Club for Growth have complained that Graham is not conservative enough, and he will likely face a well-supported challenger in the 2014 GOP primary. Graham has poked the bear on occasion — in 2010, he famously told The New York Times that the tea party movement "will die out" because "they can never come up with a coherent vision for governing the country."

Graham didn't have many opportunities to cut deals in the 112th Congress (2011-12), so his most frequent role was that of a critic when his preferences on defense and foreign policy were threatened.

Graham has a military background. He joined the Air Force after law school and later transferred to Germany as a prosecutor. He served on active duty in 1991 and 2007, during the Persian Gulf War and the U.S. occupation of Iraq. He now sits on the Armed Services Committee and the Appropriations subcommittees covering the Defense and State departments.

He favors aggressive uses of the military, including a continued presence in Afghanistan. Graham backed the initial 2011 NATO mission in Libya to protect protesters from military retaliation, but he wanted a more explicit goal of deposing Muammar el-Qaddafi. "We used to relish leading the free world," he lamented in a March 2011 interview on Fox News Channel.

In 2012 he called for the U.S. government to arm rebels in Syria, and he has continued that call in 2013. He is also a stinging critic of the Obama administration's handling of Iran. The Senate adopted his 2012 resolution stating that economic or diplomatic containment would not be a strong enough response should Iran obtain nuclear weapons. In 2013, he produced a resolution to indicate that the United States would provide military support should Israel "take military action in self-defense."

Graham isn't keen on most cuts to defense spending. He voted against the August 2011 deficit reduction deal, citing as his main reason its hundreds of billions of dollars in budget cuts for national security.

Working with McCain and New Hampshire Republican Kelly Ayotte, he campaigned against the cuts in 2012, and he has described the cuts as "destroying the Defense Department" and "gutting the military."

Graham also ties foreign assistance to U.S. strength. During the 112th Congress, he vocally supported the Obama administration's plans to provide economic assistance to Arab democracies. In September 2012, Graham got into a public dispute with tea party favorite Rand Paul of Kentucky, who pushed a proposal to cut off foreign aid to Egypt, Libya and Pakistan. "If you want to empower the terrorists that exist in this world, pass this amendment, because they will go crazy with hope and excitement," Graham said on the Senate floor.

He scoffed at Paul again in 2013, when Paul conducted a "talking filibuster" to force the White House to clarify its position on possible drone strikes on U.S. soil. Graham said it was preposterous to suggest that a president would murder a noncombatant, and that the filibuster took the debate "into the absurd." Graham is the top Republican on the Judiciary subcommittee on crime and terrorism, and after a bombing attack in Boston in April 2013, he said the country should be prepared for more of the same: "This is the future. Get ready for it."

He did find an area of agreement with Paul in 2011 — along with Utah Republican Mike Lee, they proposed an increase in the Social Security retirement age and means-testing for the program's benefits. A member of the Budget Committee, Graham wants increases in federal revenue to come from the elimination of tax code preferences for certain industries.

Graham's independence makes headlines, but on most issues he is a conservative at heart. He typically favors limiting the scope of the federal government. He is an opponent of gun control, and he has voted to amend the Constitution to outlaw flag desecration and ban same-sex marriage. Graham has backed legislation to make it a federal crime to harm a fetus in the course of committing any one of 68 federal offenses. He introduced a bill to allow states to opt out of the Medicaid expansion in the 2010 health care overhaul — months before the Supreme Court ruled that they could.

As his state's senior senator, Graham also has a number of parochial concerns on his agenda. The biggest is securing federal assistance to get the Port of Charleston ready to accommodate the larger ships that will soon be traveling through an enlarged Panama Canal.

He is an advocate of allowing oil and gas exploration off the coast of South Carolina. And defending his state's right-to-work philosophy, he has been a regular opponent of National Labor Relations Board rules that could make it easier for unions to organize.

Graham is the son of a tavern owner. He grew up racking billiard balls in his parents' bar in the textile town of Central. The death of both parents from illness when he was not yet out of college left him to care for his 13-year-old sister, Darline, whom he legally adopted. "It changes your world, and you have to grow up a lot quicker," he said. He attended college and law school at the University of South Carolina, then entered the military.

Graham won a state House seat in 1992 and saw an opportunity for advancement early in 1994, when 10-term Democratic Rep. Butler Derrick decided to retire from the U.S. House. Graham won easily that fall with 60 percent of the vote to become the first Republican to represent his district since 1877. He was less interested in compromise back then. Graham was a leader of a 1997 effort by conservatives to oust GOP Speaker Newt Gingrich of Georgia, who they felt was working too closely with President Bill Clinton. There weren't too many hard feelings; the next year, Graham was one of the 13 House managers in the impeachment case against Clinton.

He began planning for a Senate run after Republican Strom Thurmond made it clear that his seventh full term would be his last. By 2002, Graham was unopposed for his party's nomination. He easily won the seat and had no problems holding it in 2008.

Key Votes

2012	
Prohibit health insurance plans from denying coverage based on the sponsor's religious beliefs	NO
Require approval of the Keystone XL oil pipeline	YES
Ease securities rules to expand small-business access to capital	YES
Reauthorize farm and nutrition programs for five years	NO
Limit debate on a bill that would create private-sector cybersecurity standards	NO
Consent to ratification of a treaty setting global standard for the treatment of people with disabilities	NO
Provide $60.4 billion in disaster relief following Superstorm Sandy	NO
Extend most Bush-era income tax rates while allowing rates for top-bracket earners to rise (Jan. 1, 2013)	YES
2011	
Prevent EPA from regulating greenhouse gas emissions to address climate change	YES
Extend certain provisions of Patriot Act for four years	YES
Clear compromise debt limit increase plan and establish future spending limits	NO
Overhaul patent law	YES
Implement Colombia free trade agreement	YES
Limit debate on confirmation of Caitlin J. Halligan to D.C. Circuit Court of Appeals	NO
Extend payroll tax cut and unemployment benefits for two months	YES

CQ Vote Studies

	PARTY UNITY		PRESIDENTIAL SUPPORT	
	SUPPORT	OPPOSE	SUPPORT	OPPOSE
2012	86%	14%	57%	43%
2011	80%	20%	63%	37%
2010	95%	5%	47%	53%
2009	94%	6%	49%	51%
2008	97%	3%	72%	28%
2007	92%	8%	87%	13%
2006	82%	18%	91%	9%
2005	92%	8%	89%	11%
2004	92%	8%	92%	8%
2003	96%	4%	95%	5%

Interest Groups

	AFL-CIO	ADA	CCUS	ACU
2012	0%	0%	88%	92%
2011	16%	25%	82%	75%
2010	14%	5%	100%	92%
2009	28%	15%	86%	88%
2008	14%	15%	100%	82%
2007	0%	20%	100%	88%
2006	7%	0%	92%	83%
2005	29%	20%	83%	96%
2004	8%	25%	88%	92%
2003	17%	15%	83%	90%

Sen. Tim Scott (R)

Capitol Office
224-6121
scott.senate.gov
167 Russell Bldg. 20510-4002; fax 228-5143

Committees
Commerce, Science & Transportation
Energy & Natural Resources
Health, Education, Labor & Pensions
Small Business & Entrepreneurship
Special Aging

Residence
North Charleston

Born
Sept. 19, 1965; North Charleston, S.C.

Religion
Christian

Family
Single

Education
Presbyterian College, attended 1983-84; Charleston Southern U., B.S. 1988 (political science)

Career
Insurance agency owner; financial adviser

Political Highlights
Charleston County Council, 1995-2008 (chairman, 2002-03, 2007-08); Republican nominee for S.C. Senate, 1996; S.C. House, 2009-10; U.S. House, 2011-13

ELECTION RESULTS

Previous Winning Percentages
2012 House Election (62%);
2010 House Election (65%)

Appointed January 2013; 1st term

As a young man, Scott adopted a personal mission statement including an ambitious goal: "to positively impact the lives of a billion people before I die." Democrats might quibble with his definition of "positive," but he is arguably in a position to complete his mission. His appointment to the Senate confirmed his status as a Republican star and gives him a bigger forum for his message of conservatism and personal responsibility.

He was already on the way up when he was chosen to replace Sen. Jim DeMint, who resigned at the start of 2013 to lead a conservative think tank. After more than a decade on the Charleston County Council, Scott served one term in the state House. In 2010, he became the first black Republican elected to the U.S. House from the South in more than a century. His historic victory and up-from-poverty story drew the attention of party colleagues. Scott easily won a second term in the House, and six weeks later, Gov. Nikki R. Haley named him as DeMint's successor. When he was sworn in, he was the only black senator and the first one from the South since the Rutherford B. Hayes administration.

Scott does not dwell on race, however — he did not join the Congressional Black Caucus as a House member. He owned an insurance agency in his non-political life, and Haley touted his understanding of the business environment when announcing his appointment. His politics are solidly conservative, and he takes special interest in the labor and tax issues shaping South Carolina's economy.

He also tries to operate as a facilitator within the GOP, which could make him a valuable addition to the Senate.

As a House member in the 112th Congress (2011-12), he manned the lines of communication between party leaders and the small-government bloc that swelled Republican ranks in 2010. Freshmen chose him as one of two class liaisons to GOP leaders — he called the job both "fantastic" and "excruciating." Before his Senate appointment he ran unopposed to represent the sophomore class at the leadership table in the 113th Congress (2013-14). At the behest of Speaker John A. Boehner, Scott served on the Rules Committee, which is a hub for information on all major legislation.

Scott positions himself as a political catalyst at home. In the run-up to his state's January 2012 presidential primary, he introduced GOP candidates to constituents at "Tim's Town Halls." When the dust settled from that contest, he organized "Revitalizing America" conferences in his district — panels of CEOs and political leaders discussing the economy and entrepreneurship.

But Scott maintained a conservative voting record, even while acting as a moderator. In July 2011, he voted against Boehner's proposal for raising the federal debt limit; he also opposed the final version enacted in August. Scott wanted the packages to include larger spending reductions and a stronger commitment to a balanced-budget amendment to the Constitution.

He envisions a smaller federal government in general. "Across-the-board cuts are probably the simplest way to do it, [and] probably the least effective way to do it as well," he said. Scott points to the Energy and Education departments as particularly ineffective federal agencies, and he is now a member of committees that oversee them: Energy and Natural Resources; and Health, Education, Labor and Pensions.

Scott's ideas for improving the business environment often involve streamlining regulations. In May 2012, he and California Democrat Loretta Sanchez formed the Congressional Regulatory Review Caucus. Tax changes are his other prescription for fiscal health. In 2011, he introduced a bill to cut tax rates for corporations by a third and facilitate repatriation — the process companies use to bring profits earned overseas back to the United States.

Scott is mindful of South Carolina's status as a right-to-work state. The House passed his 2011 bill to eliminate some powers of the National Labor Relations Board. The NLRB had pursued a complaint against Boeing Co., which was alleged to have opened a plant in Scott's district to punish union workers in Washington state. The Boeing dispute was settled through non-legislative means, but Scott calls the NLRB "an ally not of employees, but of labor unions," and says its activities are driving corporate business overseas.

On the Commerce, Science and Transportation Committee, Scott will be looking out for the Port of Charleston, which he calls "the economic engine of South Carolina." The expansion of the Panama Canal, due for completion in 2015, figures to increase freight traffic to Atlantic Coast ports. Scott, the top Republican on the Subcommittee for Competitiveness, Innovation and Export Promotion, pushes for funding of harbor dredging to accommodate larger ships. "Understanding the necessity of our port," he backed a 2011 free-trade pact with South Korea despite concerns that it would hurt his state's textile industry.

He has another parochial interest to look after on the Energy and Natural Resources Committee — a processing center under construction at the Savannah River Site that would turn weapons-grade plutonium into fuel for nuclear reactors. The Obama administration has proposed funding cuts for the over-budget facility. In 2013, Scott was the only panel member to vote against recommending the confirmation of Ernest J. Moniz as Energy secretary, saying he wanted clarification of the plans for the facility.

Scott is a cultural conservative, opposing gun control and abortion.

He was born in North Charleston. His parents divorced when he was 7, and Scott and his siblings were raised by his mother. She was a nurse's aide, doing "all the crappy stuff, literally," he said.

His working days started in his teens, with jobs at a gas station, men's clothing stores and a movie theater. Scott still loves going to the movies, from a fiscally conservative perspective. "For seven bucks you get to watch a $400 million creation," he said. "It's hard to beat that."

Studying was not a priority until he met John Moniz, the owner of a local fast-food restaurant. Moniz became his mentor, preaching self-discipline. He died in 1985, and Scott formulated his mission statement while reflecting on Moniz's life.

Politics was one way to affect people's lives. In 1994, Scott worked as a gofer on the successful House campaign of Mark Sanford (who later became governor). The next year he was elected to the county council. Scott served as co-chairman of Republican Strom Thurmond's 1996 re-election campaign and calls the famous senator "a champion for the downtrodden."

Jack Kemp is another role model: Scott admired the former Housing and Urban Development secretary as someone who "espoused conservative virtues because of his open heart." He also was impressed by his football skills — Scott was a high school and college running back, and he cheers for the Dallas Cowboys.

In 2008, Scott won his race for the state House. He considered a run for lieutenant governor in 2010, but ultimately joined a crowded Republican field — including a son of Thurmond — trying to succeed GOP Rep. Henry E. Brown Jr., who was retiring. Supported during his campaign by prominent conservatives, including DeMint and 2008 GOP vice presidential nominee Sarah Palin, Scott finished first by a wide margin in the first round of voting. He easily dispatched Paul Thurmond in the runoff.

He then took almost two-thirds of the vote to win election in the solidly Republican district. He easily defeated Democrat Bobbie Rose, an educator and real estate business owner, in 2012.

Key Votes (while House member)

2012	
Extend a Social Security payroll tax cut and unemployment benefits	YES
Ease securities rules to expand small-business access to capital	YES
Extend for one year subsidized student loan interest rates financed by a cut in health care spending	YES
Cite Attorney General Eric H. Holder Jr. for contempt of Congress	YES
Create a visa program for foreign graduates in high-tech fields	YES
Extend most Bush-era income tax rates while allowing rates for top-bracket earners to rise (Jan. 1, 2013)	NO
2011	
Strike funding for F-35 alternative engine	YES
Prevent EPA from regulating greenhouse gas emissions to address climate change	YES
Extend certain provisions of Patriot Act for four years	YES
Declare opposition to use of ground troops in Libya	YES
Overhaul patent law	YES
Pass compromise debt limit increase plan and establish future spending limits	NO
Allow consideration of measures to implement three trade agreements	YES

CQ Vote Studies (while House member)

	PARTY UNITY		PRESIDENTIAL SUPPORT	
	SUPPORT	OPPOSE	SUPPORT	OPPOSE
2012	98%	2%	18%	82%
2011	97%	3%	20%	80%

Interest Groups (while House member)

	AFL-CIO	ADA	CCUS	ACU
2012	5%	5%	92%	100%
2011	0%	5%	94%	96%

Rep. Mark Sanford (R)

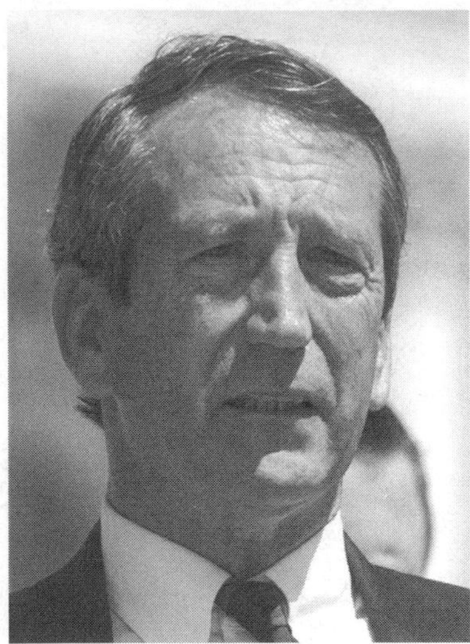

Capitol Office
225-3176
sanford.house.gov
332 Cannon Bldg. 20515; fax 225-3407

Committees
Has not been assigned committees

Residence
Charleston

Born
May 28, 1960; Fort Lauderdale, Fla.

Religion
Episcopalian

Family
Engaged to Maria Belen Chapur; four children

Education
Furman U., B.A. 1983 (business administration & economics); U. of Virginia, M.B.A. 1988

Military
Air Force Reserve, 2002-11

Career
Real estate investor; investment banker

Political Highlights
U.S. House, 1995-2001; governor, 2003-11

ELECTION RESULTS

2013 SPECIAL		
Mark Sanford (R)	77,600	54.0%
Elizabeth Colbert Busch (D)	64,961	45.2%

Previous Winning Percentages
1998 (91%); 1996 (96%); 1994 (66%)

Elected May 2013; 4th term

Also served 1995-2001

Twelve years after Sanford left Congress, a very strange political journey brought him back. In terms of his policy interests, he returned at a perfect time: He had been among the most fiscally conservative members of the House and a proponent of overhauling entitlement programs to keep them solvent. Since then, many more Republicans have come around to his way of thinking.

Of course, as he participates in those debates, he'll have to navigate the negative reactions to his famous personal indiscretions. After leaving the House, Sanford became the governor of South Carolina. In his second term, an extramarital affair led to his divorce, public humiliation, and a self-imposed exile from the public eye once he left office.

As Sanford mounted a political comeback in a 2013 special election, he did not dodge the issue — he was mostly introspective and contrite. Whatever qualms voters had about his behavior weren't enough to offset the strong Republican leanings of the 1st District, and he was sent back to Washington.

Sanford started out in Florida. His father, Marshall Sanford Sr., had been a cardiologist at Johns Hopkins Hospital in Baltimore, but he quit that job to start a medical practice in Fort Lauderdale. He also purchased Coosaw Plantation in the southeastern corner of South Carolina, and the family spent its vacations there. They moved there full-time when his father fell ill, as Sanford started his senior year of high school.

He worked for a real estate developer in Charleston after graduating from Furman University. He quit that job to pursue an MBA at the University of Virginia, and on earning that degree he worked real estate finance jobs in New York. While there, he met the future Jenny Sanford, who also worked in finance. They married in 1989 and eventually moved back to South Carolina, where Sanford started a real estate company.

Concerns about growing government debt spurred him to run for an open House seat in 1994, with his wife serving as his campaign manager. It was his first bid for public office, and he was proud of that fact. At one point, Sanford and his supporters donned hunting camouflage, declaring "open season" on career politicians who masquerade as citizen legislators. He pledged to serve no more than three terms, and he beat out experienced pols to win the seat.

Sanford sat on the precursors of the Oversight and Government Reform Committee and the Foreign Affairs Committee. He got some positive notices for his environmental voting record — he was sensitive to land conservation and possible damage to the coastal ecosystem of his district.

But he was mostly known as a staunch budget-cutter, often calling for reductions that even other Republicans wouldn't accept. (A notorious penny-pincher, he slept in his office for all six years of his first tenure, partly as a show of his frugality.) He often peppered his floor speeches with historical allusions and described American civilization as being at a crossroads: "Do we go back to what made us competitive and a world power in the first place, or do we stay on this happy but ultimately unsustainable cycle of upward government spending and upward government consumption?"

In his third term, he also promoted his plan to create private investment accounts in Social Security. One of his only regrets about his term limit pledge was that he did not get to see that proposal through, he told The Post and Courier of Charleston.

He honored his pledge, but within months he was plotting a campaign for governor. He defeated Democratic incumbent Jim Hodges and carried his policies to Columbia. Sanford clashed frequently with the Republican legislature — he vetoed scores of items in state budgets, and most of the vetoes were overturned. He pushed several tax cuts, and he tried to decline funds from the 2009 federal stimulus law, as he wasn't allowed to use them in the way he preferred. (The state supreme court overruled him.) He still wants local control of federal dollars — Sanford says transportation funding should be given to the states as a block grant with no strings attached.

The libertarian Cato Institute dubbed him the most fiscally conservative governor. His admirers said he created a pro-growth environment, while detractors said he did nothing to fight an economic recession.

Sanford seemed to be laying the groundwork for a possible presidential campaign when news of his affair broke in 2009. He had fallen in love with an Argentine woman he had first met in 2001. The affair started years later. It became a national story when Sanford disappeared for several days, with his whereabouts largely unknown; he told aides he would be hiking the Appalachian Trail, but he was in South America.

He admitted to the relationship and famously called the woman his "soul mate" — they are now engaged. Jenny Sanford filed for a divorce, which was finalized in 2010. Sanford also paid fines for ethics violations, as investigations of his travels revealed the use of taxpayer dollars for personal expenses. Attempts to impeach him fell short, and he completed his term and went back to Coosaw Plantation, dropping out of public life for a year.

Sanford eventually moved to Charleston and resumed a business career, but his return to politics surprised many people. Rep. Tim Scott — who served as gofer on Sanford's 1994 campaign — was appointed to the Senate at the start of 2013, leaving Sanford's old House seat vacant. Sanford has said that he asked his children for permission to run, and Jenny Sanford also grudgingly assented. He was the most familiar person in a 16-candidate primary field, and he won both the initial vote and a runoff several weeks later.

The race kept getting weirder. Democrats nominated Elizabeth Colbert Busch, a Clemson University official who is also the sister of political satirist Stephen Colbert. Sanford was the initial favorite, but the news broke that he had trespassed at his ex-wife's home, in violation of the terms of their divorce. (He said he was visiting his children.) The National Republican Congressional Committee pulled its financial support for his campaign, while Democratic groups redoubled their spending for Colbert Busch.

Sanford's political experience won out. He attended scores of events with voters, addressing their concerns in person. Colbert Busch, meanwhile, did little to define her political views. At one point, Sanford conducted a mock debate with a cardboard cutout of liberal Minority Leader Nancy Pelosi, using her as a stand-in for his opponent. The Republican base got the message — after many predictions of his demise, Sanford won by a comfortable margin.

South Carolina 1

Southern coast — part of Charleston; Hilton Head

History is on display in the 1st District: It is home to Fort Sumter, where the first battle of the Civil War took place; many of the colorful houses of downtown Charleston; and antebellum plantations dotting the countryside. The 1st is long and narrow, hugging the Atlantic coastline with the exception of an interior dive into Berkeley County to Lake Moultrie. Decennial remapping flip-flopped the geographic orientation of the 1st, trading South Carolina's northern beachfront in Horry County for territory all the way to Hilton Head Island near the Georgia border.

Tourism is the district's economic driver. Visitors flock to Charleston — part of which is in the 6th District — to take in its well-preserved historic downtown, top-flight restaurants and beaches. Resorts at Hilton Head and Kiawah Island lure affluent vacationers to their world-class golf courses. Hilton Head pulls in an estimated $1 billion annually in tourism dollars, and affiliated real estate jobs rely on the industry: Hundreds of real estate professionals are employed on the 42-square-mile island. Public beaches attract visitors to the barrier islands between Charleston and Hilton Head.

The defense industry is the second major employer in the district. Marine Corps Air Station Beaufort and the Marine Corps Recruit Depot at Parris Island are in the southern portion of the 1st. Parris Island is one of the Corps' recruit training installations. Although redistricting shifted the massive Joint Base Charleston (shared by the Air Force and Navy) into the 6th District to the west, its economic impact remains.

The 1st is largely white and is safe territory for the GOP, but it is more moderate than other portions of South Carolina. Republican Mitt Romney took the 1st by 16 percentage points in the 2012 presidential election.

Major Industry
Tourism, defense, service

Military Bases
Beaufort Marine Corps Air Station, 4,700 military, 667 civilian (2011); Marine Corps Recruit Depot Parris Island, 1,600 military, 430 civilian

Cities
Charleston (pt.), Mt. Pleasant, Hilton Head

Notable
The nation's first golf course, Harleston Green in what is now downtown Charleston, opened in 1786.

Rep. Joe Wilson (R)

Capitol Office
225-2452
joewilson.house.gov
2229 Rayburn Bldg. 20515-4002; fax 225-2455

Committees
Armed Services
(Military Personnel - Chairman)
Education & the Workforce
Foreign Affairs

Residence
Springdale

Born
July 31, 1947; Charleston, S.C.

Religion
Presbyterian

Family
Wife, Roxanne Wilson; four children

Education
Washington and Lee U., B.A. 1969 (political science); U. of South Carolina, J.D. 1972

Military
Army Reserve, 1972-75; S.C. National Guard, 1975-2003

Career
Lawyer; campaign aide; U.S. Energy Department official

Political Highlights
Pine Ridge town judge, 1974-76; Republican nominee for S.C. Senate, 1976; Springdale town judge, 1977-80; S.C. Senate, 1985-2001

ELECTION RESULTS

2012 GENERAL		
Joe Wilson (R)	196,116	96.3%
Write-In (WRI)	7,602	3.7%
2012 PRIMARY		
Joe Wilson (R)	23,062	80.6%
Phil Black (R)	5,557	19.4%

Previous Winning Percentages
2010 (54%); 2008 (54%); 2006 (63%); 2004 (65%); 2002 (84%); 2001 Special Election (73%)

Elected 2001; 6th full term

The dynamic Wilson backs as many conservative causes as his schedule will allow. Some people will always remember him for one outburst — blurting "You lie!" during a 2009 health care address by President Barack Obama. But his most substantial work has been on behalf of military servicemembers.

Democratic detractors have accused Wilson of self-promotion and valuing activity above legislative output. However, there's no denying that Wilson is ubiquitous on Capitol Hill. He sits on the Republican Policy Committee, belongs to the Republican Study Committee, and serves on the GOP whip team. C-SPAN junkies recognize him as one of the most frequent speakers on the House floor.

In the 112th Congress (2011-12), he also became "scoutmaster" to four enthusiastically conservative freshmen from his state. (All of them won re-election, and Tim Scott was appointed to the Senate.) Wilson preferred that title to dean, because it "has a level of respectability — that is, as scoutmaster, I know I cannot tell the scouts what to do. I can work hard to set an example, but they are their own person."

In 2011, the five men set the standard for hard-line fiscal conservatism in the House. Wanting more-dramatic constraints on non-defense spending, Wilson voted against the appropriations bills for fiscal 2011 and 2012 and an agreement to raise the federal debt limit. "The right questions are being asked," he said. "But the net result is simply not substantive."

The scoutmaster role is familiar, as Wilson's four sons are Eagle Scouts. They also have military experience. Three are in the South Carolina National Guard — where Wilson served for almost three decades — and one is in the Navy. That personal connection informs Wilson's work as chairman of the Armed Services Subcommittee on Military Personnel. He calls himself a "broken record" on supporting troops, military families and veterans. Regardless of the topics of his floor speeches, he often ends them the same way: "In conclusion, God bless our troops, and we will never forget September the 11th in the global war on terrorism."

Even as military budgets tighten, Wilson opposes increasing premiums for veterans' health benefits. When cost-cutters questioned the need for military-operated grocery and department stores, Wilson wrote in the Washington Times in 2011 that "few programs can match the power of the military resale systems to rally and solidify the strength of the military community."

He was particularly pleased with his provision in the fiscal 2012 defense policy law to facilitate the recruitment of homeschoolers and virtual-schoolers to military service. Wilson also supported that law's elevation of the head of the National Guard to a seat on the Joint Chiefs of Staff — a move that other service chiefs opposed as complicating command structures. He has pushed legislation to enable National Guard members and reservists to obtain retirement pay earlier.

Joining many Republicans, Wilson has lamented cuts to military spending and the Obama administration's plans to shrink the number of overall troops. He joined the Strategic Forces Subcommittee, which oversees the nuclear arsenal, in 2013. He immediately began stumping for a plutonium-processing center under construction at the Savannah River Site in his district — the Obama administration has proposed funding cuts for the over-budget facility, which is meant to turn weapons-grade plutonium into commercial nuclear-reactor fuel, per an arms reduction agreement with Russia in 2000.

On the Foreign Affairs Committee, Wilson advances his vision of America's role on the global stage: promoting democracy "everywhere in the world." As a state senator in 1990, Wilson was appointed by Republican National Committee Chairman Lee Atwater to observe the first democratic elections for the Bulgarian National Assembly; he has served in the House Democracy Partnership, a bipartisan group interacting with foreign legislative bodies. His wallet holds copies of his business cards printed in both Russian and Chinese.

Wilson has a particular affinity for the world's largest democracy. His father served in India during World War II as part of the famous Flying Tigers, and Wilson has professional ties to the Indian-American community. In working as a real estate lawyer, much of his practice involved representing Indian-Americans purchasing hotels and motels throughout South Carolina, the first state to elect an Indian-American female governor, Nikki R. Haley.

On the Education and the Workforce Committee, Wilson urges local control of education decisions; most federal involvement, he says, could be reduced to block grants to the states. In 2004, he won enactment of his bill to expand a loan forgiveness program for teachers in poverty-stricken public schools.

Wilson's full name is Addison Graves Wilson. He grew up in Charleston, the middle son of an Exxon sales manager — his family had been associated with Standard Oil as far back as 1895. The military presence in the city meant people in uniform were everywhere, and Wilson and his mother were great admirers of President Dwight D. Eisenhower. She worked as a Democratic poll manager, but only because "the word 'Republican' was not used in polite company" in the state until after the Barry Goldwater campaign in 1964, he said.

As a teenager, Wilson volunteered for Republican campaigns and attended a Goldwater rally in Washington. He met the woman who would later become his wife at a camp for GOP teenagers where she was a camper and he was a counselor. Wilson joined the staff of Rep. Floyd D. Spence, a South Carolina Republican, while in law school. He managed five of Spence's re-election campaigns and says he takes his philosophy of public service from his mentor: "Total dedication to the public by way of accessibility and accountability."

He lost a close race for state Senate in 1976, but unseated a GOP state senator eight years later. Spence died in 2001, and Wilson lapped the field in the race to succeed him. Re-elections were a breeze until 2008, when Democrat Rob Miller, a retired Marine and Iraq War veteran, held Wilson to just under 54 percent of the vote.

Incendiary remarks have sporadically put Wilson on the national radar; his 2009 outburst at Obama during a joint session drew an official reprimand from the House. Wilson also apologized to Obama. The incident juiced fundraising for both Wilson and Miller in their 2010 rematch, but the outcome was the same. After redistricting, Wilson had no Democratic opponent in 2012.

Wilson's oldest son, Alan, is currently South Carolina's attorney general.

Key Votes

2012	
Extend a Social Security payroll tax cut and unemployment benefits	NO
Ease securities rules to expand small-business access to capital	YES
Extend for one year subsidized student loan interest rates financed by a cut in health care spending	NO
Cite Attorney General Eric H. Holder Jr. for contempt of Congress	YES
Create a visa program for foreign graduates in high tech fields	YES
Extend most Bush-era income tax rates while allowing rates for top-bracket earners to rise (Jan. 1, 2013)	NO
2011	
Strike funding for F-35 alternative engine	NO
Prevent EPA from regulating greenhouse gas emissions to address climate change	YES
Extend certain provisions of Patriot Act for four years	YES
Declare opposition to use of ground troops in Libya	YES
Overhaul patent law	YES
Pass compromise debt limit increase plan and establish future spending limits	NO
Allow consideration of measures to implement three trade agreements	YES

CQ Vote Studies

	PARTY UNITY		PRESIDENTIAL SUPPORT	
	SUPPORT	OPPOSE	SUPPORT	OPPOSE
2012	99%	1%	16%	84%
2011	98%	2%	16%	84%
2010	97%	3%	24%	76%
2009	98%	2%	18%	82%
2008	98%	2%	82%	18%

Interest Groups

	AFL-CIO	ADA	CCUS	ACU
2012	10%	10%	92%	100%
2011	3%	10%	88%	96%
2010	7%	5%	75%	96%
2009	5%	0%	80%	96%
2008	7%	10%	100%	92%

South Carolina 2

Central — part of Columbia and suburbs, Aiken

The 2nd District runs from the central segment of the Georgia border to Lake Murray, then buttonhooks around Columbia to the north and east through Richland County in the state's Midlands. The district extends as far as the Shandon neighborhood within Columbia but stops short of the state Capitol and the University of South Carolina downtown. South Carolina received a new congressional district after reapportionment following the 2010 census. Remapping added all of Aiken County to the 2nd but moved all border counties south of Barnwell County as well as inland Bamberg County into the adjacent 6th.

The state government in Columbia and the Department of Energy's Savannah River Site outside of Aiken are the two economic centers. Devoted to nuclear energy cleanup and research, the Savannah River Site — shared with the 6th — has numerous facilities and a workforce of 12,000.

Thousands of residents work in Columbia's hospital complexes and government offices. The construction sector in the northern portion of the district remains strong as the suburbs around Lake Murray east of Columbia continue to grow. Lexington County has one of the lowest unemployment rates in the state: It relies on agribusiness, manufacturing, health care and nuclear energy jobs. Its economic outlook is in contrast to the swaths of the district south of Columbia and southeast of Aiken, which are rural and have among the highest unemployment rates in the state.

Lexington County is the population center and voters there overwhelmingly support Republican candidates. The highest proportion of black residents (44 percent) lives in rural Barnwell County, but not in sufficient numbers to challenge Republican dominance at the polls.

Major Industry
Energy, health care, defense, government, manufacturing

Military Bases
Fort Jackson (Army), 3,500 military, 3,500 civilian

Cities
Columbia (pt.), Aiken

Notable
In the late 19th century, Aiken served as a warm-weather colony for second homes of the Northeast's business magnates.

Rep. Jeff Duncan (R)

Capitol Office
225-5301
jeffduncan.house.gov
116 Cannon Bldg. 20515-4003; fax 225-3216

Committees
Foreign Affairs
Homeland Security
(Oversight and Management Efficiency - Chairman)
Natural Resources

Residence
Laurens

Born
Jan. 7, 1966; Greenville, S.C.

Religion
Baptist

Family
Wife, Melody Duncan; three children

Education
Clemson U., B.A. 1988 (political science)

Career
Real estate auction company owner; real estate broker; banker

Political Highlights
S.C. House, 2003-10

ELECTION RESULTS

2012 GENERAL		
Jeff Duncan (R)	169,512	66.5%
Brian Ryan Doyle (D)	84,735	33.3%
2012 PRIMARY		
Jeff Duncan (R)		unopposed
2010 GENERAL		
Jeff Duncan (R)	126,235	62.5%
Jane Dyer (D)	73,095	36.2%
John Dalen (CNSTP)	2,682	1.3%

Elected 2010; 2nd term

Duncan says that when he served in the state legislature, "folks didn't need to look at the voting board to know how I was going to vote." That has held true in the U.S. House. Duncan is an unflinching social and fiscal conservative who stays active in discussions of energy independence and foreign policy.

Along with the other self-assured South Carolinians of the Class of 2010, Duncan pulled no punches in attacking the Obama administration or the culture of Washington in the 112th Congress (2011-12). He showed allegiance to small-government principles over the priorities of the GOP House leadership.

Duncan opposed every major spending law of the 112th, protesting that they were irresponsible in the context of soaring budget deficits. When conservative opposition led to the defeat of a stopgap measure to fund the government through the start of fiscal 2012, GOP leaders arranged an embarrassing second vote; Duncan was among the 24 Republicans who still refused to support it. He initially expressed grudging support of a short-term measure for fiscal 2013 to keep spending decisions away from a lame-duck Congress — then voted against it.

He says a balanced-budget amendment to the Constitution is "absolutely" necessary and wants a version that includes spending caps and restrictions on Congress' ability to raise taxes. And he is not averse to eliminating federal institutions, such as the Education and Energy departments, that he feels are operating outside of constitutional authority.

About the only cuts he opposed in the 112th were reductions to defense accounts. Duncan, a member of the Foreign Affairs and Homeland Security committees, has indicated his preference for a "peace through strength" posture and tighter control of U.S. borders. He is the chairman of the Homeland Security subcommittee on oversight for the 113th Congress (2013-14).

Much as he resents perceived federal intrusions on state powers, he dislikes international intrusions on U.S. power. Duncan is the co-chairman, with Colorado Republican Doug Lamborn, of the Sovereignty Caucus, which seeks to combat the influence of international organizations and multilateral agreements on U.S. policy. In 2011, the Foreign Affairs Committee on a party-line vote adopted his amendment to a State Department authorization bill to block economic assistance to any government that opposes the United States in U.N. General Assembly and Security Council votes more than half the time.

"We're $14.3 trillion in debt," Duncan said in a written statement. "Why should we pay countries to hate us when they've shown they're willing to do it for free?"

Duncan's first major legislative success was enactment of his 2012 bill to address Iran's influence in the Western Hemisphere; the measure directs the secretary of State to send Congress an assessment of the threat posed by Iran's activities in the region, along with a strategy to respond to that country's growing influence. His effort on that measure began in earnest following a 2011 report that the Iranian government allegedly wanted members of Mexican drug cartels to carry out an assassination on U.S. soil.

Energy is a policy area where Duncan touts his expertise. While serving in the South Carolina House, he sat on a U.S. Interior Department planning committee for offshore oil and natural-gas leases. Now a member of the Natural Resources Committee, he supports expedited permitting of energy projects, more offshore drilling and expanded energy leasing on federal lands.

At a 2012 hearing he accused the Obama administration of trying "to handcuff or hold the reins back on American energy independence" by delaying fossil fuel projects. He is not keen on federal subsidies for alternative energy.

"I think the private market, if there is a market for that, has always stepped up to the plate and found innovative ways to make money through providing technology and other resources," he said.

With most of the Savannah River Site nuclear complex in the adjacent 2nd District, Duncan has a particular interest in promoting nuclear power. He supports the use of the Yucca Mountain facility in Nevada as a nuclear-waste depository and was cheered in 2012 by the issuing of a license for two new nuclear reactors in Fairfield County, in a neighboring district.

The Natural Resources Committee also handles bills that touch on some of Duncan's passions: He is an avid fisherman and hunter, and he sits on the subcommittee for fisheries and wildlife.

Duncan opposes abortion, supports gun rights and defines marriage as between a man and a woman. He also has significant concerns about government infringements on civil liberties. The conservative group Heritage Action for America gave him a 97 percent on its scorecard for the 112th Congress, which put him in a tie for first place. His only demerits were for votes against a free-trade agreement with South Korea — Duncan said the deal would hurt his state's textile sector — and for a package of disaster assistance for farmers.

Duncan was born in Greenville, but his father's job — turning around troubled textile plants — kept him on the move. The family relocated regularly, including stops in North Carolina and Virginia. His mother was a homemaker and later became a patient advocate at a local hospital when her two boys reached college.

He recalls Ronald Reagan as an early influence on his political views, finding resonance in both the president's small-government philosophy and his general attitude. "He inspired us to be proud to be Americans," Duncan said. Another guiding hand came from Republican Sen. Strom Thurmond. Duncan spent one summer interning for the South Carolina icon.

Both Duncan and his older brother attended Clemson University and made the football team at the school, which is located in the 3rd District. Duncan studied political science, then went into banking after graduation. In the mid-1990s he started his own real estate company, specializing in auctions. (He and Republican Billy Long of Missouri are the only professional auctioneers in Congress.) Duncan says he keeps his bid-calling skills sharp while driving, by counting telephone poles as he goes.

In 2010, he finished second in a six-candidate primary to succeed Republican J. Gresham Barrett, who ran unsuccessfully for governor. But he won the runoff, topping entrepreneur and anti-abortion activist Richard Cash by 3 points. He won almost 63 percent of the vote in the general election. In 2012, he was unopposed in the primary and again won easily.

Key Votes

2012	
Extend a Social Security payroll tax cut and unemployment benefits	NO
Ease securities rules to expand small-business access to capital	YES
Extend for one year subsidized student loan interest rates financed by a cut in health care spending	NO
Cite Attorney General Eric H. Holder Jr. for contempt of Congress	YES
Create a visa program for foreign graduates in high-tech fields	YES
Extend most Bush-era income tax rates while allowing rates for top-bracket earners to rise (Jan. 1, 2013)	NO
2011	
Strike funding for F-35 alternative engine	YES
Prevent EPA from regulating greenhouse gas emissions to address climate change	YES
Extend certain provisions of Patriot Act for four years	NO
Declare opposition to use of ground troops in Libya	YES
Overhaul patent law	NO
Pass compromise debt limit increase plan and establish future spending limits	NO
Allow consideration of measures to implement three trade agreements	YES

CQ Vote Studies

	Party Unity		Presidential Support	
	Support	Oppose	Support	Oppose
2012	98%	2%	13%	87%
2011	97%	3%	16%	84%

Interest Groups

	AFL-CIO	ADA	CCUS	ACU
2012	5%	10%	83%	100%
2011	3%	10%	81%	96%

South Carolina 3

Northwest — Anderson, Greenwood

The 3rd District takes in the hilly, forested northwestern portion of South Carolina. Mostly untouched by decennial redistricting, it runs from Edgefield and Saluda counties to the North Carolina border in Pickens County. Along its eastern edge, the 3rd includes portions of Newberry County, all of Laurens County, and the southern third of Greenville County.

Although rural, the 3rd boasts a diversified economy that keeps employment levels on par with the rest of the state. Edgefield and Saluda counties grow some of South Carolina's most bountiful peach crops — Saluda ranks among the top 10 counties in U.S. production. Anderson and Oconee counties produce cattle and eggs, respectively.

State-funded Clemson University in Pickens County is a major district employer, although it has shed thousands of jobs over the last decade. Nearby, Seneca has wealthier subdivisions but areas struggle with high poverty rates. Across Interstate 85 in Anderson, shuttered textile plants have been replaced by auto parts, refrigerator, high-tech fiber and tire plants. To the northwest in Oconee County, manufacturers range from aircraft and plastics companies to golf ball makers. The county is also home to a Duke Energy nuclear power plant.

With several large lakes, the 3rd is a popular water sports and fishing location. Lake Hartwell has hosted the Bassmaster Classic, the sport's largest tournament. Devils Fork State Park and Lake Jocassee in the district's north are popular for trout fishers and hikers.

The district votes solidly Republican in state and federal races. The less-populous counties in the 3rd's middle, including black-plurality McCormick County, are both more rural and more Democratic-leaning. Overall, the 3rd gave GOP nominee Mitt Romney a 31-point win over Barack Obama in the 2012 presidential race.

Major Industry
Manufacturing, agriculture, higher education

Cities
Anderson, Greenwood, Easley

Notable
The 70,000-acre Lake Thurmond, previously known as Clarks Hill Lake, was renamed for former GOP Sen. Strom Thurmond, the oldest person ever to serve in the Senate.

Rep. Trey Gowdy (R)

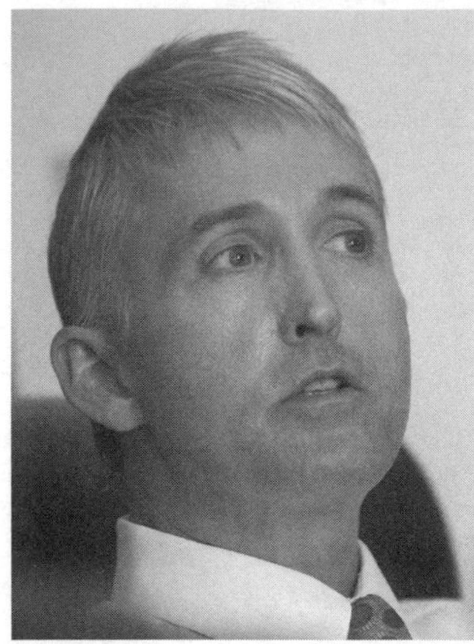

Capitol Office
225-6030
gowdy.house.gov
1404 Longworth Bldg. 20515-4004; fax 226-1177

Committees
Education & the Workforce
Ethics
Judiciary
(Immigration & Border Security - Chairman)
Oversight & Government Reform

Residence
Spartanburg

Born
Aug. 22, 1964; Greenville, S.C.

Religion
Baptist

Family
Wife, Terri Gowdy; two children

Education
Baylor U., B.A. 1986 (history); U. of South Carolina, J.D. 1989

Career
Lawyer

Political Highlights
Assistant U.S. attorney, 1994-2000; S.C. 7th Circuit solicitor, 2001-10

ELECTION RESULTS

2012 GENERAL		
Trey Gowdy (R)	173,201	64.9%
Deb Morrow (D)	89,964	33.7%
Jeff Sumerel (GREEN)	3,390	1.3%
2012 PRIMARY		
Trey Gowdy (R)		unopposed
2010 GENERAL		
Trey Gowdy (R)	137,586	63.4%
Paul Corden (D)	62,438	28.8%
Dave Edwards (CNSTP)	11,059	5.1%
Rick Mahler (LIBERT)	3,010	1.4%
C. Faye Walters (GREEN)	2,564	1.2%

Elected 2010; 2nd term

Gowdy's lawyerly and principled approach to legislative matters has won admirers in both parties, and when it comes to oversight, Republicans find him energizing. He describes his earlier work as a prosecutor as the best job he'll ever have, and he channels that enthusiasm into hard-nosed questioning of the executive branch.

Gowdy is one of the most conservative members of the House, although his work is defined less by politics and more by a high regard for personal and legal codes — perceived violations of either elicit passionate responses. He studied history at Baylor University and remains fascinated with the ancient Greeks and their concepts of honor. The Battle of Thermopylae is his favorite story, and he calls law enforcement officers "kind of modern-day Spartans to me."

He worked as a federal prosecutor for six years starting in 1994, then won election as the solicitor for South Carolina's 7th Circuit. Gowdy has three dogs: Judge, Jury and Bailiff. His wife "wouldn't go with Executioner," he said.

Both the Oversight and Government Reform and Judiciary committees made use of his talents as a freshman, and he joined the Ethics Committee for the 113th Congress (2013-14).

"I think if you were to ask my chairmen," he said, "they'd probably say, 'He's not that smart, but he does prepare, and he asks real good questions' — like you would expect a prosecutor to."

Republicans put Gowdy at the middle of a firestorm in his second term, awarding him the chairmanship of the Judiciary Subcommittee on Immigration and Border Security. The GOP's poor showing with Hispanic voters in 2012 led many to suggest that the party might accede to some overhaul of immigration law.

Gowdy is most likely to emphasize enforcement. In 2012, he blasted a policy directive by the Obama administration halting the deportation of some illegal immigrants brought into the country as children. If a secure border is a precursor to immigration changes, then it shouldn't be left to the Department of Homeland Security to define "secure," he said in 2013.

Gowdy rails against what he sees as politicized enforcement of the law. "If we don't have confidence in law enforcement and the criminal justice system, irrespective of political ideology, we're not going to make it as a republic," he said. But he also has been applauded for his legislative civility. On most issues he is not a firebrand, but a polite colleague with a wry sense of humor.

As a freshman, he chaired the Oversight subcommittee on the District of Columbia, which had been a hotbed of controversy in past Congresses. Republicans often tried to use the panel's jurisdiction to impose their preferences for gun control and abortion policy on the District.

Gowdy, however, called Democratic Del. Eleanor Holmes Norton "a very gracious hostess. ... Oversight does not necessarily have to be bitterly partisan, and I don't think anyone would tell you it has been." He voted "present" on a 2011 amendment in the Judiciary Committee that would have allowed non-District residents to bring concealed weapons into the city. "It was a combination of my preference to deal with D.C. gun laws in another vehicle and a general belief that the Second Amendment ... should not be subject to the vagaries of 50 different interpretations — 51 if you include the District," he said to The Washington Times. The amendment was defeated.

When Gowdy does get worked up, the subject is often law enforcement. He endeared himself to conservatives in the 112th Congress (2011-12) during the Oversight investigation of "Fast and Furious" — a gun-walking sting in which Justice Department officials allowed weapons to be sold into Mexico in order to build cases against drug cartels.

The Obama administration denied requests to release some documents related to the operation, and the House eventually voted to find Attorney General Eric H. Holder Jr. in contempt of Congress — many Democrats walked out in protest.

Throughout the investigation, Gowdy was one of the most aggressive questioners, often citing a duty to Border Patrol agent Brian Terry, who was killed in a shootout where guns from the operation were found on the scene. Before the contempt vote, Gowdy made an emotional, shouting plea to Democrats — akin to a closing argument — on behalf of Terry's family: "They want answers, they want justice, and they don't want part of it. They want all of it."

He lit up the blogosphere again at a hearing on the September 2012 attack on a U.S. consulate in Libya that left four American officials dead. He accused Obama administration officials of lying about the causes of the attack.

Gowdy is very conservative on fiscal matters, and he says a good way to cut spending is to limit the government to duties delineated in the Constitution. He sits on the Education and the Workforce Committee and favors a huge reduction of the Education Department. "I would probably leave one employee there," he said, "who could, if asked, share best practices among the 50 states." His wife is a public school teacher's aide, and he called education the single biggest issue in South Carolina — while maintaining that it should be a state and local concern.

Gowdy grew up in Spartanburg, the second of four children and the only son. His father was a pediatrician; his mother kept the house, helped out with the medical practice and worked as a victims' advocate in a district attorney's office.

He traces some of his interest in public service back to his family. "My father loves government and history and politics," he said, "and I would not have been elected without his popularity back home." Sen. Strom Thurmond was another influence: In 1980, Gowdy worked as an intern for the South Carolina icon. His duties included the occasional assignment to baby-sit Thurmond's daughter, Julie. "I loved him," Gowdy said of Thurmond. "The guy is and will remain legendary in South Carolina, the way he took care of people."

In 2010, Gowdy took on six-term Rep. Bob Inglis, who was something of a Republican maverick and had veered from his party on a few high-profile issues. Gowdy was able to paint Inglis as a Washington insider who became more moderate during his six terms in Congress.

Gowdy ran first in a five-candidate primary, then trounced Inglis in the runoff, winning more than 70 percent of the vote. He cruised to general-election victories in 2010 and 2012.

Key Votes

2012	
Extend a Social Security payroll tax cut and unemployment benefits	NO
Ease securities rules to expand small-business access to capital	YES
Extend for one year subsidized student loan interest rates financed by a cut in health care spending	NO
Cite Attorney General Eric H. Holder Jr. for contempt of Congress	YES
Create a visa program for foreign graduates in high-tech fields	YES
Extend most Bush-era income tax rates while allowing rates for top-bracket earners to rise (Jan. 1, 2013)	NO
2011	
Strike funding for F-35 alternative engine	NO
Prevent EPA from regulating greenhouse gas emissions to address climate change	YES
Extend certain provisions of Patriot Act for four years	YES
Declare opposition to use of ground troops in Libya	YES
Overhaul patent law	YES
Pass compromise debt limit increase plan and establish future spending limits	NO
Allow consideration of measures to implement three trade agreements	YES

CQ Vote Studies

	PARTY UNITY		PRESIDENTIAL SUPPORT	
	SUPPORT	OPPOSE	SUPPORT	OPPOSE
2012	99%	1%	16%	84%
2011	97%	3%	17%	83%

Interest Groups

	AFL-CIO	ADA	CCUS	ACU
2012	10%	10%	92%	100%
2011	3%	10%	88%	96%

South Carolina 4

North — Greenville, Spartanburg

Located in the northern part of the state, the 4th District is South Carolina's smallest by land area. It includes almost all of Spartanburg County and more than half of Greenville County, the latter of which is the most populous in the Palmetto State.

Manufacturing is vital to the economy, and the region is fast becoming an automotive haven. The 30 miles of Interstate 85 between Spartanburg and Greenville have collected an array of new facilities that drive the district's economy. French tiremaker Michelin has its North American headquarters in Greenville, which also hosts the world's largest gas turbine production plant, operated by General Electric. BMW builds its sports utility models in Spartanburg, and textile giant Milliken & Co. maintains its corporate headquarters there.

In conjunction with Clemson University (in the 3rd), Greenville has developed a public-private partnership to establish a 250-acre International Center for Automotive Research and has joined forces with technical colleges across the state. A satellite campus of the University of South Carolina is located in Spartanburg, and Clemson plans to move some of its graduate-level programs to Greenville.

Both counties grew substantially over the last decade, with Greenville posting a nearly 20 percent population boom. Greenville County, shared with the 3rd District, has one of the lowest unemployment rates in the state. Downtown Greenville's Falls Park on the Reedy draws tourists and locals with its 345-foot, curving Liberty Bridge.

While the majority of the district is white, there are areas where blacks are the majority, notably the city of Spartanburg, and much of the district has experienced an influx of Hispanic residents. The combination of business-oriented conservatives and values voters focused around Greenville's Bob Jones University keeps this district safely Republican.

Major Industry
Manufacturing, higher education

Cities
Greenville, Spartanburg

Notable
Spartanburg was named for the local "Spartan Rifles" Revolutionary War militia.

Rep. Mick Mulvaney (R)

Capitol Office
225-5501
mulvaney.house.gov
1207 Longworth Bldg. 20515-4005; fax 225-0464

Committees
Financial Services
Small Business

Residence
Indian Land

Born
July 21, 1967; Alexandria, Va.

Religion
Roman Catholic

Family
Wife, Pam Mulvaney; three children

Education
Georgetown U., B.S.F.S 1989 (international economics); U. of North Carolina, J.D. 1992

Career
Real estate developer; restaurateur; lawyer

Political Highlights
S.C. House, 2007-09; S.C. Senate, 2009-10

ELECTION RESULTS

2012 GENERAL		
Mick Mulvaney (R)	154,324	55.5%
Joyce Knott (D)	123,443	44.4%
2012 PRIMARY		
Mick Mulvaney (R)		unopposed
2010 GENERAL		
Mick Mulvaney (R)	125,834	55.1%
John M. Spratt Jr. (D)	102,296	44.8%

Elected 2010; 2nd term

Mulvaney calls himself a "dollars and cents guy," and he is comfortable when immersed in the technical details of government spending and manipulations of the economy. Opponents, however, cast him as a blunt instrument for spending reductions, and Mulvaney contributes to that perception with a sometimes abrasive way of doing business.

He shows little patience for continuing on the nation's current fiscal course. Mulvaney was one of the stalwarts demanding substantial spending cuts during deficit reduction negotiations at the end of the 112th Congress (2011-12). He was dismayed by passage of a package that mostly just extended lower income tax rates for earnings under $400,000. "Instead of turning the tide last night, we continued our lazy ride toward inevitable financial ruin," he said after the January 2013 vote.

Mulvaney blamed Republican leaders as much as Democrats. He was one of the organizers of an attempt to deny John A. Boehner a second term as speaker of the House in the 113th Congress (2013-14). Mulvaney canvassed support for the "coup" and, in the actual election of the speaker, abstained from voting. The episode fit the pattern of his relatively brief political career: He has deeply conservative views on fiscal matters and doesn't apologize for his urgency.

Born in suburban Washington, Mulvaney was a toddler when his family moved to Charlotte, N.C. His father was a homebuilder, and his mother was a teacher. Mulvaney went back to Washington to get a degree in international economics from Georgetown University, then returned to North Carolina to get a law degree. He eventually went to work for the family business and also owned and operated a Mexican restaurant.

Mulvaney moved over the state line to South Carolina in 2002, not far from the alleged birthplace of another occasionally prickly lawmaker who despised government debt — Andrew Jackson. According to Mulvaney, it was the profligate spending of Republicans that drew him into politics. He won a tough race in 2006 to secure a seat in the state House. The retirement of a state senator drew him into another hotly contested election in 2008, which he won with the backing of Republican Gov. Mark Sanford. Mulvaney had a strong anti-tax record and stepped on some toes in his own party. "He's a little bulldog," one Republican colleague told The Herald newspaper of Rock Hill. "If you were part of that Mark Sanford crowd, he had a great reputation. If not, we just tolerated him."

Mulvaney has had meaningful participation in spending debates. As the House pondered deficit reduction in the summer of 2011, Mulvaney, Jason Chaffetz of Utah and Reid Ribble of Wisconsin assembled the plan preferred by most conservative Republicans. Dubbed "Cut, Cap and Balance," it would have required $111 billion in spending reductions for fiscal 2012, established statutory caps to limit future spending and increased the debt ceiling — contingent on a balanced-budget amendment to the Constitution passing Congress and being sent to the states for ratification. It passed the House but died in the Senate.

During the January 2013 consideration of a relief bill for Superstorm Sandy victims, Mulvaney offered an amendment to offset $17 billion of that spending with a 1.63 percent across-the-board cut to all discretionary spending. It was defeated, but 157 Republicans voted for it.

He has been irked by the lack of support within his own party for freezing the Pentagon's budget. Mulvaney tried unsuccessfully to trim $17 billion from the fiscal 2012 Defense appropriations bill.

There's no denying that Mulvaney is willing to be showy to make a point. When the House was considering the fiscal 2013 budget, Mulvaney proposed President Barack Obama's highly criticized budget as a substitute amendment; Democrats decried the move as a meaningless stunt, but the tally was 0-414. Remembering an Obama promise not to raise taxes on those earning less than $250,000 a year, Mulvaney wrote a 2012 bill to eliminate a dozen taxes—many of them meant to pay for the 2010 health care law.

Mulvaney joined the Financial Services Committee for the 113th Congress. His background as a real estate developer gives him extra juice as Congress contemplates what to do with Fannie Mae and Freddie Mac. He seems inclined to end any government guarantee for mortgage-backed securities—the obligation that led to the federal bailout of those government-sponsored enterprises. At a 2011 Budget Committee hearing, he gave a sarcastic summary of a plan by California Republican John Campbell to continue the guarantee under a new system: "We know we screwed it up before; we know we've done a really, really lousy job in doing this in the past and it's cost literally trillions of dollars. But this time, we're going to be much smarter in doing this than everybody else who's been here before."

He buys into the idea that the 2010 financial regulatory overhaul is overburdening business and impeding the flow of capital in the marketplace. He also keeps an eye on monetary policy. Mulvaney was an original co-sponsor of a 2012 bill by Texas Republican Kevin Brady that would end the Federal Reserve's mandate to promote maximum employment, leaving it only the mission of maintaining stable prices.

Mulvaney's conservatism extends to social issues. He opposes abortion and restrictions to gun owners' rights. At times he will put South Carolina ahead of his fiscal philosophy. The only blemish on his pro-growth record as a freshman, according to conservative groups, was his vote against a 2011 free-trade pact with South Korea. Mulvaney worries that it will harm his state's textile industry.

At the onset of his state Senate career, Mulvaney said he was planning to be there awhile. He changed his mind in 2010, as Republicans were gaining grassroots strength. He challenged John M. Spratt Jr., the Democratic chairman of the Budget Committee, and scored a double-digit victory over the 14-term lawmaker. Redistricting for 2012 altered the 5th District a bit, and Mulvaney faced Democrat Joyce Knott, a small-business owner who had worked on Spratt's campaigns. He won by a similar margin.

As a freshman, Mulvaney joined the group of House members who sleep in their offices. He cited parenting costs as one reason for doing so—he is the father of young triplets.

Key Votes

2012	
Extend a Social Security payroll tax cut and unemployment benefits	NO
Ease securities rules to expand small-business access to capital	YES
Extend for one year subsidized student loan interest rates financed by a cut in health care spending	NO
Cite Attorney General Eric H. Holder Jr. for contempt of Congress	YES
Create a visa program for foreign graduates in high-tech fields	YES
Extend most Bush-era income tax rates while allowing rates for top-bracket earners to rise (Jan. 1, 2013)	NO
2011	
Strike funding for F-35 alternative engine	NO
Prevent EPA from regulating greenhouse gas emissions to address climate change	YES
Extend certain provisions of Patriot Act for four years	YES
Declare opposition to use of ground troops in Libya	YES
Overhaul patent law	YES
Pass compromise debt limit increase plan and establish future spending limits	NO
Allow consideration of measures to implement three trade agreements	YES

CQ Vote Studies

	Party Unity		Presidential Support	
	Support	Oppose	Support	Oppose
2012	94%	6%	28%	72%
2011	95%	5%	17%	83%

Interest Groups

	AFL-CIO	ADA	CCUS	ACU
2012	10%	25%	83%	96%
2011	3%	10%	88%	100%

South Carolina 5

North central — Rock Hill

The 5th District includes all or parts of 11 counties in the northern part of the state. It stretches from the North Carolina border to south of Sumter in the state's Midlands. Its population centers are in Rock Hill and Sumter, though it is mostly rural and dotted with small towns.

Rock Hill is a bedroom community of Charlotte, N.C., which is less than 30 miles away. Located in York County, Rock Hill includes white-collar workers with jobs in North Carolina and more traditional blue-collar workers who are employed in manufacturing. Winthrop University, originally a women's teaching college, is also in Rock Hill.

Sumter, in the district's southeast, is divided between the 5th and 6th districts and thrives on manufacturing. Caterpillar, the heavy machinery company, announced in 2012 it was expanding its operations in Sumter, a boon for an area that has above-average unemployment overall. Poultry producer Pilgrim's Pride also has a facility in the city. Shaw Air Force Base, to the west of Sumter, is home to the Air Force's largest combat F-16 wing.

York County has remained economically stable, but the more rural areas can struggle. Kershaw County ranks first in the state for the value of its agricultural products sold and leads in egg production. Lancaster County ranks second in turkeys. But of the eight counties wholly in the 5th, six have poverty levels of more than 19 percent.

The district has a significant proportion of black residents (28 percent), the third-highest statewide, behind only the majority-black 6th and the newly created 7th. Black residents make up most of the population in Fairfield and Lee counties. The district overall leans Republican, but Chester, Fairfield, Sumter and Lee counties are home to Democratic voters. GOP nominee Mitt Romney took 55 percent of the district's 2012 presidential vote.

Major Industry
Manufacturing, agriculture

Military Bases
Shaw Air Force Base, 7,700 military, 1,300 civilian

Cities
Rock Hill, Sumter

Notable
The annual Lee County Cotton Festival and Agricultural Fair celebrates the agricultural history of "King Cotton."

Rep. James E. Clyburn (D)

Capitol Office
225-3315
clyburn.house.gov
242 Cannon Bldg. 20515-4006; fax 225-2313

Committees
No committee assignments

Residence
Columbia

Born
July 21, 1940; Sumter, S.C.

Religion
African Methodist Episcopal

Family
Wife, Emily England Clyburn; three children

Education
South Carolina State College, B.A. 1962 (social studies)

Career
State agency official; teacher

Political Highlights
Candidate for S.C. House, 1970; S.C. human affairs commissioner, 1974-92; sought Democratic nomination for S.C. secretary of state, 1978, 1986

ELECTION RESULTS

2012 GENERAL		
James E. Clyburn (D)	218,717	93.6%
Nammu Y. Muhammad (GREEN)	12,920	5.5%
2012 PRIMARY		
James E. Clyburn (D)		unopposed
2010 GENERAL		
James E. Clyburn (D)	125,459	62.9%
Jim Pratt (R)	72,661	36.4%

Previous Winning Percentages
2008 (67%); 2006 (64%); 2004 (67%); 2002 (67%); 2000 (72%); 1998 (73%); 1996 (69%); 1994 (64%); 1992 (65%)

Elected 1992; 11th term

Clyburn is the assistant leader for House Democrats — a position that is versatile, in part because it is somewhat ill-defined. He serves as a bridge between urban liberals and red-state moderates, and he is also a confidant of President Barack Obama.

Clyburn began serving as the majority whip in 2007, under Speaker Nancy Pelosi. But when Democrats lost the House majority and the speakership in the 2010 elections, the leadership team shrank. Pelosi reclaimed her old job as minority leader, which set up a possible showdown between Clyburn and Steny H. Hoyer of Maryland for the minority whip job. Pelosi avoided that scuffle by creating the assistant leader job, which let Clyburn stay in the No. 3 slot on the leadership team.

But the job description is vague. One of Clyburn's best friends in the House, Democrat G.K. Butterfield of North Carolina, said in the fall of 2012 that "we still don't know how to really classify the Clyburn position." Other lawmakers and aides have reportedly been a bit confused about how the pieces of the new leadership team fit together.

Clyburn, meanwhile, has made clear his desire to climb the ladder, without committing to a future course of action. After the 2012 elections, he declined to challenge Hoyer for the whip post in the 113th Congress (2013-14). Still, he doesn't sit on his hands. He is a prolific fundraiser for his party, and he is the current chairman for national mobilization at the Democratic Congressional Campaign Committee.

A preacher's son, Clyburn has a sermon-like cadence on the stump and offers counsel to colleagues on the floor. At his annual fish fry in the Palmetto State, he serves catfish and advice to presidential aspirants and allies. He serves as Pelosi's emissary to church groups and the White House. "The president has given me permission to go to him directly, if I feel a need to," he said.

His connections yielded a spot on the Joint Select Committee on Deficit Reduction (aka the supercommittee), a bicameral, bipartisan panel created in 2011 and tasked with proposing ways to reduce the deficit by more than $1 trillion. Clyburn opposed cuts to entitlement programs unless there were GOP concessions on tax increases. "We're not going to sit there and agree to anything that puts an uneven and unfair burden on the least among us," he said.

He was one of 38 House members to support a fiscal 2013 budget based on the work of a 2010 special fiscal commission created by Obama, that became known as Simpson-Bowles; it proposed to cut deficits by $4 trillion over 10 years through a mix of spending reductions and revenue increases. Though not perfect, "it's a good default position," he said.

Most issues find Clyburn in the Democratic mainstream. In 2012, after the Supreme Court upheld the Democrats' 2010 health care overhaul, Clyburn urged implementation "with all deliberate speed," echoing the court's 1954 directive in Brown v. Board of Education. He opposes state-level mandates for voters to show photo ID at the polls, and in 2012 he promoted legislation to streamline voter registration. Much as there is a national voting age, "there ought to be one national qualification to vote," he said.

As a broker in South Carolina politics, Clyburn urged former President Bill Clinton to tone down criticism of Obama during the 2008 presidential primaries. When the primary season drew to a close, Clyburn was the first member of the House Democratic leadership team to endorse Obama.

But he sometimes shows glints of toughness when dealing with Obama's aides. In July 2010, he rebuked the administration for suddenly firing — then trying to rehire — Shirley Sherrod, the Agriculture Department's Georgia director of rural development. An edited video surfaced in which Sherrod told a story revealing her initial reluctance to help a white farmer 24 years ago. Clyburn told The New York Times that Obama "needs some black people around him" to prevent similar gaffes.

His ties to Obama grew closer during the 2010 campaign, when he joined the president for a round of golf on Martha's Vineyard and a private chat. "I feel much more warmth to him than I used to," Clyburn said. He also has a familial link to the administration. His daughter, Mignon, was appointed to a second term on the Federal Communications Commission in 2012.

Clyburn rose to become vice chairman of the House Democratic Caucus in 2003, then chairman in 2006. He was unopposed for the whip post at the start of the 110th Congress (2007-08) after a potential rival, Rahm Emanuel of Illinois, backed off. His second term as whip found him counting votes on the 2010 overhauls of health care and financial regulations.

A former appropriator, Clyburn called earmarks for projects back home "an important part of my job," allowing him to serve poor families and rural communities. He stepped down as board chairman of a planned International African American Museum in Charleston after critics questioned several related earmarks. Clyburn said his resignation would avoid a potential conflict involving a nephew who worked as a project architect. He often emphasizes rural initiatives, such as his push in the 111th Congress (2009-10) for rural energy-saving incentives and funding for counties with at least 20 percent of residents earning incomes below the poverty line.

Clyburn attended Mather Academy, an all-black boarding school. He read books about his hero, Harry S. Truman, but his family belonged to the GOP until the mid-1960s, a time when most elected Southern Democrats were still clinging to segregation. As a young man, Clyburn jumped into the civil rights movement, becoming an early member of the Student Nonviolent Coordinating Committee, affiliated with the Rev. Martin Luther King Jr.'s Southern Christian Leadership Conference. He was arrested several times.

After college, Clyburn became the state employment commission's lone black employee. In 1971, Democratic Gov. John West named him a special assistant for human resources, and in 1974 he became human affairs commissioner. In 1978 and 1986, he unsuccessfully sought the Democratic nomination for South Carolina secretary of state.

When 1992 redistricting created the black-majority 6th District, Clyburn saw his opening. He defeated four black Democrats in the primary, then became the first African-American elected to Congress from South Carolina since his great-uncle, George Washington Murray, served in the House during Reconstruction.

Key Votes

2012	
Extend a Social Security payroll tax cut and unemployment benefits	YES
Ease securities rules to expand small-business access to capital	YES
Extend for one year subsidized student loan interest rates financed by a cut in health care spending	NO
Cite Attorney General Eric H. Holder Jr. for contempt of Congress	?
Create a visa program for foreign graduates in high-tech fields	NO
Extend most Bush-era income tax rates while allowing rates for top-bracket earners to rise (Jan. 1, 2013)	YES
2011	
Strike funding for F-35 alternative engine	NO
Prevent EPA from regulating greenhouse gas emissions to address climate change	NO
Extend certain provisions of Patriot Act for four years	NO
Declare opposition to use of ground troops in Libya	NO
Overhaul patent law	YES
Pass compromise debt limit increase plan and establish future spending limits	YES
Allow consideration of measures to implement three trade agreements	NO

CQ Vote Studies

	PARTY UNITY		PRESIDENTIAL SUPPORT	
	SUPPORT	OPPOSE	SUPPORT	OPPOSE
2012	93%	7%	85%	15%
2011	92%	8%	86%	14%
2010	99%	1%	93%	8%
2009	99%	1%	97%	3%
2008	99%	1%	18%	82%

Interest Groups

	AFL-CIO	ADA	CCUS	ACU
2012	85%	70%	27%	4%
2011	93%	85%	31%	0%
2010	100%	95%	13%	0%
2009	100%	100%	29%	0%
2008	100%	95%	56%	0%

South Carolina 6

East central — parts of Columbia and Charleston

A black-majority, overwhelmingly Democratic district designed to combine African-American precincts around Columbia, Charleston and elsewhere in the state's southeast, the 6th includes all or parts of 16 counties. Decennial redistricting shifted it south to include three counties along the Georgia border, trading metropolitan Florence into the new 7th District.

Redistricting provided the 6th a maritime presence and several large economic plums formerly within the 1st. The new map placed massive Joint Base Charleston, operated by the Navy and Air Force, within the 6th, as well as the new Boeing 787 assembly plant. Altogether, the aviation-related assets in North Charleston account for more than 34,000 jobs. The 6th also shares one of the nation's largest cargo ports with the 1st.

Sharing Columbia with the 2nd, the 6th represents the central part of the city, including state government offices and the University of South Carolina. The 6th also extends north into black-majority suburbs along Interstates 77 and 20.

The 6th is home to Columbia's burgeoning health care industry centered on the Palmetto Health Alliance complex. A business-campus partnership between the University of South Carolina, the city and private enterprises south of the school, however, has yet to fully deliver its startup promise.

While the district is bookended by Charleston and Columbia, it is primarily rural. Employment opportunities in these other regions are challenging; many district residents have poor educational attainment and live below the poverty line. In Allendale County, along the Georgia border, the poverty rate is 42 percent.

Major Industry
Health care, defense, manufacturing

Military Bases
Joint Base Charleston, 10,500 military, 5,000 civilian (2012)

Cities
Columbia (pt.), Charleston (pt.), North Charleston, Sumter, Florence

Notable
Clarendon County (pop. 34,971) can claim five South Carolina governors, all related to each other.

Rep. Tom Rice (R)

Capitol Office
225-9895
rice.house.gov
325 Cannon Bldg. 20515-4209; fax 225-9690

Committees
Budget
Small Business
(Economic Growth, Tax & Capital Access - Chairman)
Transportation & Infrastructure

Residence
Myrtle Beach

Born
Aug. 4, 1957; Charleston, S.C.

Religion
Episcopalian

Family
Wife, Wrenzie Rice; three children

Education
U. of South Carolina, B.S. 1979 (accounting), J.D. 1982, M.Acc. 1982 (accounting)

Career
Lawyer; accountant

Political Highlights
Horry County Council chairman, 2010-12

ELECTION RESULTS

2012 GENERAL

Tom Rice (R)	153,068	55.5%
Gloria Bromell Tinubu (D)	122,389	44.4%

2012 PRIMARY RUNOFF

Tom Rice (R)	16,844	56.1%
Andre Bauer (R)	13,173	43.9%

Elected 2012; 1st term

Rice's quick ascension from county council to Congress has been propelled by his drive to create jobs in an economically challenged district.

Rice has spent most of his life in Horry County, and most of his career dealing with taxes and accounting. He settled in Myrtle Beach in the mid-1980s and worked as a tax attorney. In 1997 he started his own firm.

He was civically active, but his first real venture into politics was a 2010 race for chairman of the county council. Running on a platform of economic development, he scored an upset in the GOP primary en route to his election. Horry County, like the rest of the district, has struggled with an unemployment rate that surpasses the national average; Rice, a member of the conservative Republican Study Committee, says it's important to diversify the local economy so that it is less reliant on tourism and tobacco farming.

Rice chairs the Small Business Subcommittee on Economic Growth, Tax and Capital Access, and he has said that he wants Congress to focus on creating a "pro-startup environment."

He also sits on the Transportation and Infrastructure Committee, where he looks to extend the interstate highway system toward his hometown. "I'm not looking for earmarks," he said. "We have to ... allocate funding on the merit of the project, and having a place where 14 million people drive in and out of [to get to the beach] is certainly going to give it a lot of merit."

The 7th District had no incumbent, as it was created after South Carolina was awarded another House seat during decennial reapportionment. Andre Bauer, a former lieutenant governor and failed gubernatorial candidate, won the nine-person GOP primary, with Rice in second; Rice, who had the endorsement of Gov. Nikki R. Haley, won the runoff.

His Democratic opponent, Gloria Bromell Tinubu, had been serving in the Georgia House, but she resigned that post and moved back to her home state to seek the open seat. Rice won by 11 points.

South Carolina 7

Northeast — Florence, Myrtle Beach

The 7th District — created during decennial reapportionment — includes the northeastern portion of the state and is in the heart of the Pee Dee region. It stretches from the North Carolina border south to the Santee River, including all of the tourism-dependent counties of Horry and Georgetown, as well as the more rural counties of Chesterfield, Darlington, Dillon, Marion, Marlboro and almost all Florence.

Myrtle Beach is the heart of the district's coastline and commerce. The region around it, known as the Grand Strand, is highly dependent on tourism. The comfortable climate caters to outdoor enthusiasts; sandy beaches line the coast and golf courses abound.

Construction of Interstate 73 has been a long-planned, but yet-to-be-executed, project to connect eastern beachside communities with the heavily traveled Interstate 95, which bisects the 7th in Dillon and Florence counties. Congress made the infrastructure upgrade a priority several times in the 1990s, but funding problems and disagreements about the route have stalled construction. Many residents in and near Myrtle Beach support the project because of potential new jobs in the region, which has struggled to diversify beyond the oft vulnerable tourism industry.

Moving inland and away from the beaches, the district becomes much more rural, less populous, far more diverse and less affluent. Agriculture is important: Dillon, Darlington and Marlboro counties are leading cotton producers for the state. Florence, leading in soybeans, tobacco and corn, is on the western edges of the district. Health care is also a major industry here, and packaging products producer Sonoco has headquarters in Hartsville.

With a constituency that is nearly 30 percent black, the new 7th is generally in line with the demographic balance of South Carolina overall. It is considered a safe Republican district, but Marlboro, Dillon and Marion have Democratic bases. Mitt Romney won 54 percent of the district's 2012 presidential vote.

Major Industry
Tourism, agriculture

Cities
Florence, Myrtle Beach

Notable
On Pawleys Island, the legend of the "Gray Man" ghost says he appears to locals before major hurricanes, warning of nature's destructive power.

SOUTH DAKOTA

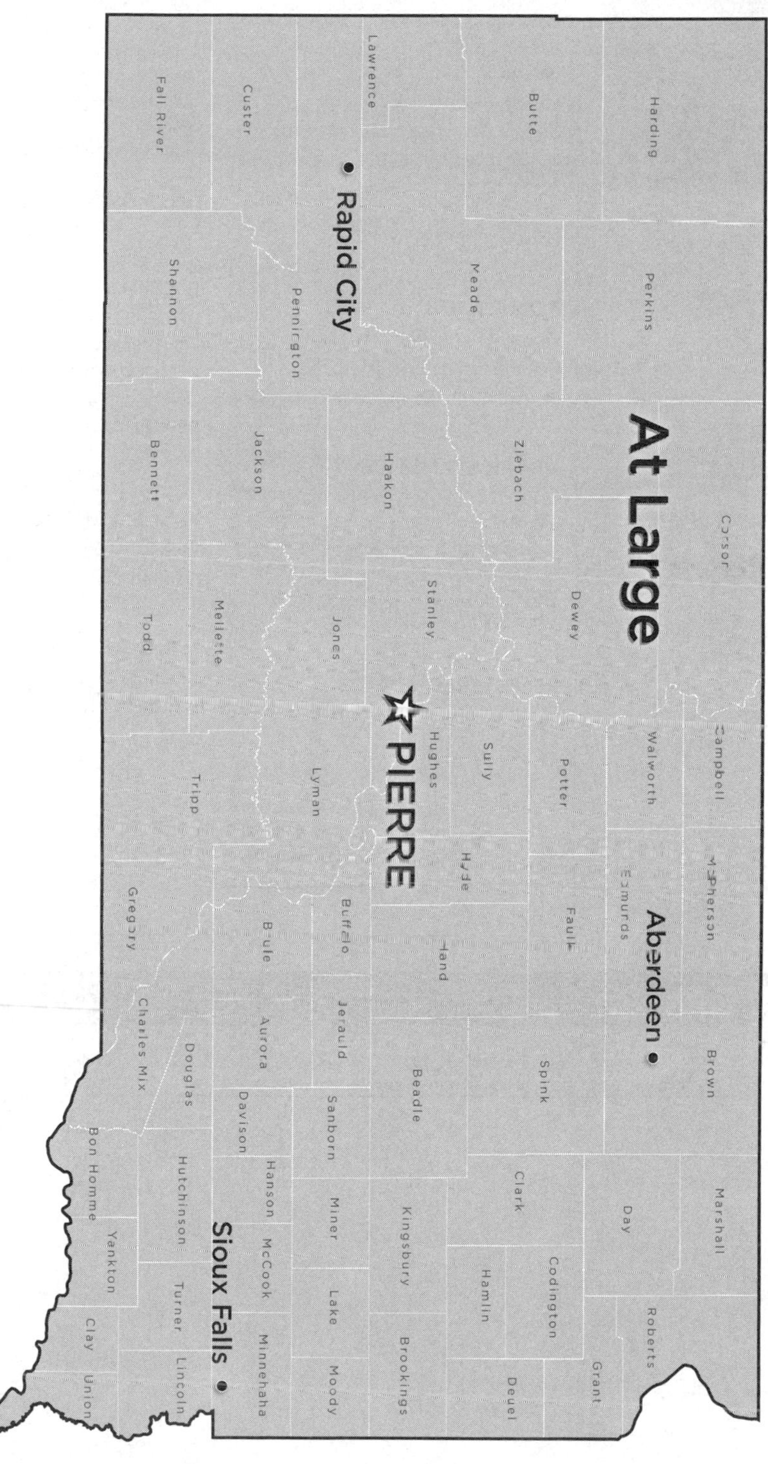

Gov. Dennis Daugaard (R)

First elected: 2010

Length of term: 4 years

Term expires: 1/15

Salary: $104,002

Phone: (605) 773-3212

Residence: Garretson

Born: June 11, 1953; Garretson, S.D.

Religion: Lutheran

Family: Wife, Linda Daugaard; three children

Education: U. of South Dakota, B.S. 1975 (government); Northwestern U., J.D. 1978

Career: Child welfare agency fundraiser and director; bank executive; lawyer

Political highlights: S.D. Senate, 1997-2003; lieutenant governor, 2003-11

ELECTION RESULTS

2010 GENERAL

Dennis Daugaard (R)	195,046	61.5%
Scott Heidepriem (D)	122,037	38.5%

Lt. Gov. Matt Michels (R)

First elected: 2010

Length of term: 4 years

Term expires: 1/15

Salary: $61,800

Phone: (605) 773-3661

LEGISLATURE

Legislature: January-March

Senate: 35 members, 2-year terms

2013 ratios: 28 R, 7 D; 29 men, 6 women

Salary: $6,000

Phone: (605) 773-3821

House: 70 members, 2-year terms

2013 ratios: 53 R, 17 D; 53 men, 17 women

Salary: $6,000

Phone: (605) 773-3851

TERM LIMITS

Governor: 2 consecutive terms

Senate: 2 consecutive terms

House: 4 consecutive terms

URBAN STATISTICS

CITY	POPULATION
Sioux Falls	153,888
Rapid City	67,956
Aberdeen	26,091
Brookings	22,056
Watertown	21,482

REGISTERED VOTERS

Republican	45%
Democrat	35%
Other	20%

POPULATION

2010 population	814,180
2000 population	754,844
1990 population	696,004
Percent change (2000-2010)	+7.9%
Rank among states (2010)	46
Median age	37.0
Born in state	66.1%
Foreign born	2.2%
Violent crime rate	186/100,000
Poverty level	14.2%
Federal workers	14,026
Military	3,910

ELECTIONS

STATE ELECTION OFFICIAL
(605) 773-3537

DEMOCRATIC PARTY
(605) 271-5405

REPUBLICAN PARTY
(605) 224-7347

MISCELLANEOUS

Web: www.sd.gov

Capital: Pierre

U.S. CONGRESS

Senate: 1 Democrat, 1 Republican

House: 1 Republican

STATISTICS BY DISTRICT

District	2012 Vote for President Obama	2012 Vote for President Romney	2008 Vote for President Obama	2008 Vote for President McCain	Black	Asian	Hispanic	Median Income	Over 64	Under 20	College Education	Rural	Sq. Miles
AL	40%	58%	45%	53%	1%	1%	3%	$48,321	15%	28%	26%	45%	75,811
STATE	40	58	45	53	1	1	3	48,321	15	28	26	45	75,811
U.S.	51	47	53	46	12	5	17	50,052	13	27	29	21	3,531,905

Sen. Tim Johnson (D)

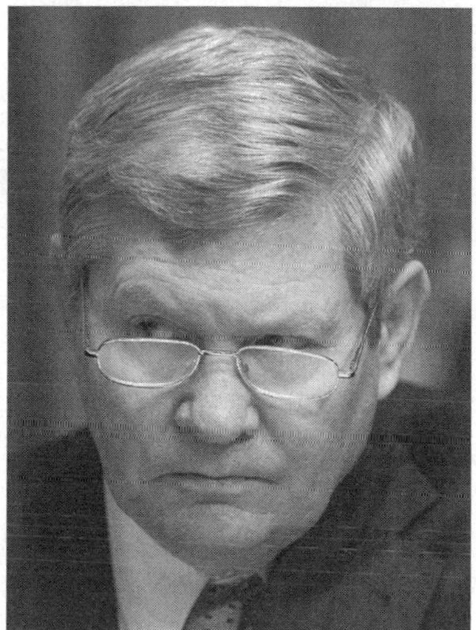

Capitol Office
224-5842
johnson.senate.gov
136 Hart Bldg. 20510; fax 228-5765

Committees
Appropriations
(Military Construction-VA - Chairman)
Banking, Housing & Urban Affairs - Chairman
Energy & Natural Resources
Indian Affairs

Residence
Sioux Falls

Born
Dec. 28, 1946; Canton, S.D.

Religion
Lutheran

Family
Wife, Barbara Johnson; three children

Education
U. of South Dakota, B.A. 1969 (government), M.A. 1970 (government), Michigan State U., attended 1970-71 (political science); U. of South Dakota, J.D. 1975

Career
Lawyer; county prosecutor; state legislative aide

Political Highlights
S.D. House, 1979-83; S.D. Senate, 1983-87; U.S. House, 1987-97

ELECTION RESULTS

2008 GENERAL

Tim Johnson (D)	237,889	62.5%
Joel Dykstra (R)	142,784	37.5%

2008 PRIMARY

Tim Johnson (D)	unopposed

Previous Winning Percentages
2002 (50%); 1996 (51%); 1994 House Election (60%); 1992 House Election (69%); 1990 House Election (68%); 1988 House Election (72%); 1986 House Election (59%)

Elected 1996; 3rd term

Johnson has stayed in Congress for more than 25 years by doting on the distinctive elements of South Dakota's economy — quiet prairie populism has helped him keep the public's support through a few close elections and some health crises. His success holding on to his Senate seat has yielded him the gavel of the Banking, Housing and Urban Affairs Committee, but he is giving it up at the end of the 113th Congress, when he will retire.

Johnson hasn't delved too deeply into his motivations for retiring, other than saying that he will be 68 at the end of his third term. But he is still feeling the effects of a 2006 brain hemorrhage, and his 2014 campaign had the potential to be grueling — President Barack Obama lost South Dakota by 18 points in 2012.

The Banking committee will keep him busy in the closing years of his career. Johnson's interest in financial services has its origins in his state's role as a location for credit card processing. He was serving in the state legislature in the 1980s when South Dakota adjusted its usury laws and landed the headquarters of Citibank's credit card operations. The industry has become a crucial part of the economy of Sioux Falls, the state's largest city.

He became Banking chairman in the 112th Congress (2011-12), about a year after the previous chairman, Democrat Christopher J. Dodd of Connecticut, engineered a major overhaul of financial services regulation. Johnson was atop the Subcommittee on Financial Institutions as that law, known as Dodd-Frank, was written. His seniority on the full committee allowed him to take over after Dodd retired.

Wary liberals weren't sure what to expect. Johnson was the lone Democratic vote against 2009 legislation that tightened credit card regulations, but he opposed a $700 billion rescue for the financial services industry in 2008.

So far, Johnson has been a moderating influence as the panel ponders the implementation and side effects of Dodd-Frank; a divided Congress hasn't done too much tinkering with the law. Johnson called a high-profile hearing in 2012 with JPMorgan Chase CEO Jamie Dimon following the bank's large trading losses, and he used the episode to press for faster implementation of regulations mandated by Dodd-Frank. "While risk cannot be eliminated from our economy, we can and must demand that banks take risk management seriously and maintain strong controls," Johnson said.

He entered the 112th Congress convinced that the status quo in housing markets was unsustainable, but the future of Fannie Mae, Freddie Mac and the mortgage industry are still up in the air in the 113th Congress (2013-14). Johnson has pressed for federal action on mortgage principal reductions to help struggling homeowners avoid foreclosure.

It's hard to peg Johnson as a partisan or a liberal, however. South Dakota has a conservative streak, but it has sustained several Democrats, such as Tom Daschle and George McGovern, through long Senate careers.

In both the Senate and the House (where he served for 10 years), Johnson has worked within that conservative tradition. He voted with Republicans on a welfare overhaul in 1996 and tax cuts in 2001. He was also one of two Democrats who voted in 2005 to cut off a filibuster against renewing the anti-terrorism law known as the Patriot Act. And his votes on gun measures earned him a 2008 endorsement from the National Rifle Association.

In addition to the Banking panel, Johnson's other committee assignments also address South Dakota interests. He sits on the Appropriations Committee and its subcommittees for agriculture, energy, federal lands and defense. He chairs its subcommittee on military construction and veterans programs.

Agriculture is the state's largest industry, and one of Johnson's signature achievements is the 2002 law requiring country-of-origin labeling for agricultural products.

Johnson spent his years in the House as a tenacious advocate for his state's farmers, seeking federal funds for local water projects, bridges and roads. In the 103rd Congress (1993-94), he chaired the House Agriculture Committee's Environment, Credit and Rural Development Subcommittee, where much of his work centered on overhauling federally backed crop insurance. He continued to back a robust crop insurance system in the Senate's 2012 version of a reauthorization of federal farm programs, which wasn't enacted. Johnson often must balance the interests of farmers in the eastern portion of the state with ranchers in the west.

South Dakota has a large population of American Indians, and Johnson has a seat on the Indian Affairs Committee.

He also serves on the Energy and Natural Resources Committee. He backs programs that encourage agriculture-based renewable fuels that can bolster his state's economy; Johnson was an early supporter of ethanol mixture requirements for motor vehicle fuels. He seeks to expand the development of wind energy, another resource South Dakota has in abundance.

The son of a college professor and a homemaker, Johnson is a fourth-generation South Dakotan. He met Barbara Brooks while at the University of South Dakota and married her shortly after getting his degree; he later got a master's degree and law degree from USD. Johnson worked as a budget analyst for the Michigan Senate while his wife got a master's in social work at Michigan State.

Their family has had its share of health problems. Johnson had successful surgery for prostate cancer in 2004, and his wife has twice fought breast cancer. He is deaf in his left ear as a result of surgery to remove a benign tumor discovered on his eardrum when he underwent a physical for the U.S. military during the Vietnam War. (He was denied admission.)

His biggest scare came in December 2006. A congenital arteriovenous malformation caused bleeding in his brain and produced stroke-like symptoms. Before Congress convened in January 2007, the Senate held its collective breath; Democrats had just won a majority by the narrowest of margins, gaining control of 51 seats to 49 for Republicans. Johnson was hospitalized for months and slowly regained strength, speech and mobility. He returned to work in September 2007.

After serving in the South Dakota legislature for eight years, Johnson ran for the state's lone House seat in 1986 as Democratic Rep. Tom Daschle ran for the Senate. Johnson easily beat a weak Republican opponent and was handily re-elected four times. He won his Senate seat by beating long-serving Republican Sen. Larry Pressler in a close 1996 contest.

Six years later, he nearly lost the seat. Republican Rep. John Thune, who followed Johnson into the state's House seat, was personally recruited by President George W. Bush to take on Johnson. Daschle, by then the Senate's Democratic leader, jumped in to defend Johnson, who prevailed by 524 votes. Thune unseated Daschle two years later, and he and Johnson have a comfortable working relationship.

Democratic colleagues raised funds for Johnson's 2008 campaign while he was still hospitalized. Republicans, uncertain whether they would face Johnson or another Democratic candidate, struggled to recruit a high-profile challenger. Johnson won easily.

When Johnson was elected to the House in 1986, his wife Barbara gave up her tenured position as a University of South Dakota social work professor to move to Washington, where she became a public school social worker. Their children went to school in Virginia but returned to South Dakota for college. Their son Brooks served in Iraq and Afghanistan with the Army.

Key Votes

2012	
Prohibit health insurance plans from denying coverage based on the sponsor's religious beliefs	YES
Require approval of the Keystone XL oil pipeline	NO
Ease securities rules to expand small-business access to capital	YES
Reauthorize farm and nutrition programs for five years	YES
Limit debate on a bill that would create private-sector cybersecurity standards	YES
Consent to ratification of a treaty setting global standard for the treatment of people with disabilities	YES
Provide $60.4 billion in disaster relief following Superstorm Sandy	YES
Extend most Bush-era income tax rates while allowing rates for top-bracket earners to rise (Jan. 1, 2013)	YES
2011	
Prevent EPA from regulating greenhouse gas emissions to address climate change	NO
Extend certain provisions of Patriot Act for four years	YES
Clear compromise debt limit increase plan and establish future spending limits	YES
Overhaul patent law	YES
Implement Colombia free trade agreement	YES
Limit debate on confirmation of Caitlin J. Halligan to D.C. Circuit Court of Appeals	YES
Extend payroll tax cut and unemployment benefits for two months	YES

CQ Vote Studies

	PARTY UNITY		PRESIDENTIAL SUPPORT	
	SUPPORT	OPPOSE	SUPPORT	OPPOSE
2012	95%	5%	99%	1%
2011	97%	3%	99%	1%
2010	98%	2%	100%	0%
2009	95%	5%	96%	4%
2008	80%	20%	44%	56%
2007	88%	12%	29%	71%
2006	83%	17%	57%	43%
2005	83%	17%	45%	55%
2004	90%	10%	60%	40%
2003	93%	7%	50%	50%

Interest Groups

	AFL-CIO	ADA	CCUS	ACU
2012	91%	90%	38%	0%
2011	84%	95%	64%	5%
2010	94%	85%	27%	0%
2009	89%	95%	57%	8%
2008	100%	80%	75%	12%
2007	89%	40%	80%	0%
2006	87%	85%	50%	12%
2005	86%	95%	60%	13%
2004	100%	85%	59%	11%
2003	100%	80%	39%	15%

Sen. John Thune (R)

Capitol Office
224-2321
thune.senate.gov
511 Dirksen Bldg. 20510-4103; fax 228-5429

Committees
Agriculture, Nutrition & Forestry
Commerce, Science & Transportation - Ranking Member
Finance

Residence
Sioux Falls

Born
Jan. 7, 1961; Pierre, S.D.

Religion
Protestant

Family
Wife, Kimberley Thune; two children

Education
Biola U., B.S. 1983 (business administration); U. of South Dakota, M.B.A. 1984

Career
Lobbyist; local governments association executive; U. S. Small Business Administration official; congressional aide

Political Highlights
S.D. Republican Party executive director, 1989-91; S.D. railroad director, 1991-93; U.S. House, 1997-2003; Republican nominee for U.S. Senate, 2002

ELECTION RESULTS

2010 GENERAL

John Thune (R)	unopposed

2010 PRIMARY

John Thune (R)	unopposed

Previous Winning Percentages
2004 (51%); 2000 House Election (73%); 1998 House Election (75%); 1996 House Election (58%)

Elected 2004; 2nd term

The consensus on Thune is that he "looks presidential," and his ease in communicating conservative values seems to suit a bigger stage. But lately, he has disavowed any plans to run for the White House, and spots on a national ticket are out of reach for a few years. The pressing question is how high he wants to rise in the Senate.

Waves of analysts have described his appeal: He is imposingly tall (6'4"), unfailingly polite, well-versed in conservative policy and unthreatening when he explains it on television. Added to that is his athleticism — he is a basketball player, and Runner's World called him "the fastest man in Congress" — and an ability to befriend, if not always agree with, Democrats. He is well-liked on Capitol Hill.

Thune pays close attention to South Dakota's concerns; one of his first moves as a senator was to oppose President George W. Bush's nominee for U.N. ambassador, as a way to cajole the administration out of closing an Air Force base in the state. But he was already a national figure when he joined the Senate, having defeated Minority Leader Tom Daschle to get there. He was named his party's chief deputy whip in 2007, then got elected to the No. 5 leadership post of conference vice chairman in late 2008. A surprise vacancy — John Ensign of Nevada resigned from the leadership team in the middle of a sex scandal — let him snag the No. 4 post of Republican Policy Committee chairman in mid-2009.

He removed himself from presidential contention in early 2011 (and was one of the first senators to endorse Mitt Romney), so when Tennessee's Lamar Alexander stepped down from the No. 3 post of conference chairman, Thune secured another promotion. After mulling runs for the No. 2 post of GOP whip or the chairmanship of the National Republican Senatorial Committee, Thune decided to stay put for the 113th Congress (2013-14).

As conference chairman, Thune helps set GOP strategy and messaging, and he identifies fiscal conservatism as a key: "That is the thing that unites all wings of the Republican Party," he said in 2010. Thune is socially conservative, but he personally tends to stay clear of the fray when issues such as abortion or gay marriage come up.

Thune also likes looking for solutions outside of Washington — he once ran a South Dakota association of local governments. "The big-government bureaucrats of the Obama administration have set their sights on our way of life," he said at the Republican National Convention in August 2012. "Instead of preserving family farms and ranches, President Obama's policies are effectively regulating them out of business."

He mentioned farms for good reason. South Dakota's biggest industry is agriculture, and one of Thune's most valued posts is his seat on the Agriculture, Nutrition and Forestry Committee. Thune was part of the bipartisan team that devised the Average Crop Revenue Election (ACRE) program included in a 2008 reauthorization of farming programs. That optional program allows farmers to give up countercyclical payments and some direct payments in exchange for payouts if statewide yields for their crops fall below 90 percent of recent annual averages.

Direct payments seem doomed for the next iteration of the farm bill, and in the 112th Congress (2011-12), Thune helped design a possible replacement of ACRE — a streamlined "shallow loss" program meant to supplement crop insurance, with payments tied to local yields instead of state yields. Some conservatives panned it as a government handout for farmers, but it was included in a Senate-passed version of the farm bill in 2012.

That measure wasn't enacted. A version approved by the committee in May 2013 still had the shallow-loss program, but Thune voted against it—he didn't like its inclusion of a "target price" program favored by Southerners.

Thune also keeps farmers in mind on the Finance Committee, which handles tax and trade policy. He wants a permanent end to the estate tax, which many farmers complain is devastating to the survival of family farming operations. As the top Republican on the international trade subcommittee in the 112th Congress, he urged the establishment of permanent normal trade relations with Russia, in part to help his state's agricultural exporters; that status was established in December 2012.

He lines up with most Republican stances on tax code simplification and rate reductions, but he will break with the GOP when South Dakota is involved. In the 112th, Thune was a major booster of extending the tax credit for wind energy producers, which went through in a January 2013 tax package. He and Minnesota Democrat Amy Klobuchar, a frequent legislative partner, tried to salvage some funding for the ethanol industry (another agricultural interest) as the Senate considered an end to tax benefits that help producers. They were not successful, however, and the benefits expired.

Thune added another feather to his cap at the start of 2013 when he became the ranking member of the Commerce, Science, and Transportation Committee. Surface transportation programs will expire in 2014, and in working on a reauthorization Thune will likely try to preserve funding levels for sparsely populated states such as his own. Like most Republicans, he hasn't been particularly enthusiastic about Amtrak, the passenger rail service that is up for reauthorization in 2013.

Thune was the top Republican on the aviation operations subcommittee in the 112th Congress, and the Senate passed his bill to prevent the European Union from hitting U.S. airlines with its emissions tax. Thune also backed a GOP proposal in early 2011 that would have barred the EPA from imposing a cap-and-trade system for greenhouse gas emissions by regulatory means.

Thune grew up in the small town of Murdo, about 40 miles south of Pierre. He comes from a family of New Deal Democrats but was won over by Ronald Reagan's policies and worldview.

He aspired to become a professional basketball player but said he was thwarted from realizing his NBA dreams by a "lack of leaping." However, his aptitude on the court helped him break into politics. Impressed with Thune's performance in a game during his freshman year of high school, GOP Rep. James Abdnor struck up a conversation with the young man — Abdnor had played high school basketball against Thune's father, a member of the South Dakota High School Basketball Hall of Fame.

Thune and Abdnor stayed in touch, and after Thune finished graduate school, he landed a job with then-Sen. Abdnor. When Abdnor was defeated for re-election in 1986 by Daschle, Thune followed him to the Small Business Administration. In 1989, Thune worked a few months as deputy staff director of the Senate Small Business Committee. He returned to South Dakota, where he served as executive director of the state Republican Party, then as the state's railroad director. In 1993, he was named executive director of the South Dakota Municipal League.

Three years later, Thune vied for the state's lone House seat, which was vacated by Democrat Tim Johnson, who ran successfully for the Senate. Thune bested Lt. Gov. Carole Hillard in the GOP primary and easily defeated longtime Daschle aide Rick Weiland in November.

In 2002, he challenged Johnson for his Senate seat, losing by 524 votes. He took a crack at Daschle in 2004. Thune successfully turned the election into a referendum on Daschle's role as leader of his party and his posh lifestyle as a Washingtonian. He beat Daschle by just more than 1 point. Democrats didn't field a candidate against Thune in 2010.

Key Votes

2012	
Prohibit health insurance plans from denying coverage based on the sponsor's religious beliefs	NO
Require approval of the Keystone XL oil pipeline	?
Ease securities rules to expand small-business access to capital	YES
Reauthorize farm and nutrition programs for five years	YES
Limit debate on a bill that would create private-sector cybersecurity standards	NO
Consent to ratification of a treaty setting global standard for the treatment of people with disabilities	NO
Provide $60.4 billion in disaster relief following Superstorm Sandy	NO
Extend most Bush-era income tax rates while allowing rates for top-bracket earners to rise (Jan. 1, 2013)	YES
2011	
Prevent EPA from regulating greenhouse gas emissions to address climate change	YES
Extend certain provisions of Patriot Act for four years	YES
Clear compromise debt limit increase plan and establish future spending limits	YES
Overhaul patent law	YES
Implement Colombia free trade agreement	YES
Limit debate on confirmation of Caitlin J. Halligan to D.C. Circuit Court of Appeals	NO
Extend payroll tax cut and unemployment benefits for two months	YES

CQ Vote Studies

	PARTY UNITY		PRESIDENTIAL SUPPORT	
	SUPPORT	OPPOSE	SUPPORT	OPPOSE
2012	88%	12%	50%	50%
2011	93%	7%	59%	41%
2010	99%	1%	33%	67%
2009	98%	2%	42%	58%
2008	95%	5%	76%	24%
2007	88%	12%	82%	18%
2006	95%	5%	87%	13%
2005	87%	13%	86%	14%

Interest Groups

	AFL-CIO	ADA	CCUS	ACU
2012	9%	15%	100%	77%
2011	16%	15%	91%	75%
2010	7%	0%	100%	100%
2009	6%	10%	86%	100%
2008	30%	10%	100%	84%
2007	16%	20%	55%	88%
2006	20%	0%	92%	100%
2005	21%	10%	93%	92%

Rep. Kristi Noem (R)

Capitol Office
225-2801
noem.house.gov
1323 Longworth Bldg. 20515-4101; fax 225-5823

Committees
Agriculture
Armed Services

Residence
Castlewood

Born
Nov. 30, 1971, Watertown, S.D.

Religion
Evangelical Christian

Family
Husband, Bryon Noem, three children

Education
Northern State U., attended 1990-92; South Dakota State U., B.S. 2011 (political science)

Career
Farmer; rancher; hunting lodge owner; restaurant manager

Political Highlights
S.D. House, 2007-11 (assistant majority leader, 2009-11)

ELECTION RESULTS

2012 GENERAL		
Kristi Noem (R)	207,640	57.4%
Matt Varilek (D)	153,789	42.6%
2012 PRIMARY		
Kristi Noem (R)		unopposed
2010 GENERAL		
Kristi Noem (R)	153,703	48.1%
Stephanie Herseth Sandlin (D)	146,589	45.9%
B. Thomas Marking (I)	19,134	6.0%

Elected 2010; 2nd term

The telegenic and youthful Noem has the potential for a bright future in the Republican Party. Her early tenure in the House has been spent mingling with the GOP leadership and establishing herself in farm policy debates.

Noem (NOHM) came to Congress with the budget-cutting, anti-regulation movement of 2010, and like many of those Republicans she said she wants "to change the way that Washington does business." So far, she has chosen to work within the GOP system.

As a freshman, she was named a regional chairwoman for the National Republican Congressional Committee, which deepened her involvement with party fundraising. She was also one of two liaisons between the Class of 2010 and the House leadership team. Noem was the more moderate of the two — the other, South Carolina's Tim Scott, was appointed to the Senate in early 2013.

Republicans are happy to have her in front of the cameras. Noem, a high school beauty queen, is a comfortable spokeswoman on a variety of topics; she made media appearances and spoke at news conferences to promote her party's plans on topics such as the economy and energy policy.

If she has a signature issue, it's agriculture, the dominant industry in her state. Born and raised in northeastern South Dakota, Noem, her sister and two brothers helped raise cattle, corn, wheat and soybeans on her family's farm and ranch. She went to college to study education, but in 1994 her father was killed in an accident while working on their farm.

Noem — then 22, attending college part-time, married and nearly eight months pregnant with her first child — left school to help take over the family operation. It was then that she found out they were going to be assessed estate taxes and would have to decide whether to sell land or take out a loan. In the end, the chose to get the loan. Noem said the experience is what kindled her interest in politics.

"It was tough for me to reconcile that because we had a tragedy in our family, now we had a financial situation, too. And that's what got me involved," she said. She later served in the state House for four years, two of those as assistant majority leader.

In the U.S. House, she sits on the Agriculture Committee. One of Noem's few public disputes with GOP leaders was over a five-year reauthorization of farm and nutrition programs that the committee approved in 2012. It never received a floor vote — leaders felt that conservative opposition to the bill would sink it — and programs lapsed for several months. Noem made a public campaign for a floor vote, insisting that safety net provisions were absolutely crucial, particularly in light of severe drought throughout her state.

During the panel's work on the bill, Noem focused on extensions of livestock disaster programs and "sodsaver" provisions, which cut back federal subsidies in order to remove unintended incentives that induced farmers to convert open prairies into cropland. She also tried to give South Dakota more flexibility to deal with pine beetle infestations. Noem endorsed billions in reductions to the Supplemental Nutrition Assistance Program but helped defeat deeper SNAP cuts favored by more-conservative panel members.

Noem re-introduced her sodsaver plan in the opening months of the 113th Congress (2013-14), working with Minnesota Democrat Tim Walz. She also produced a stand-alone bill to extend the livestock safety net programs.

She takes part in the GOP's anti-regulatory efforts. In 2011, the House passed her bill to preclude the EPA from increasing air quality standards regarding dust — there were reports that such action was under consideration, and farms kick up a lot of dust. The bill drew a veto threat, as the Obama administration said it was too ambiguous and could interfere with existing clean-air standards. The White House also insisted that it had no plans to further regulate farm dust. Noem wasn't swayed by such assurances: "The EPA hasn't always done the same thing that it said it was going to do," she said.

Noem joined the Armed Services Committee in the 113th Congress, giving up seats on the Natural Resources and Education and the Workforce panels to do so. Her chief concern there is Ellsworth Air Force Base, the only major military facility in South Dakota. Personnel issues are also pressing, as her state has an above-average number of veterans per capita.

Overall, Noem takes a fairly conservative tack, while not straying too far from the Republican line. She voted for an August 2011 deficit reduction package that some Republicans found too weak, and though she is a member of the conservative Republican Study Committee, she didn't support its more-austere fiscal 2013 budget.

Noem was one of the 85 House Republicans who voted for a January 2013 measure that extended lower income tax rates only for earnings under $400,000. She voiced reservations that it lacked spending cuts, but the deal had other elements she supported: an extension of the production tax credit for wind energy, a short-term extension of farm programs and a permanently higher exemption level for the estate tax.

Noem was the last person to enter the three-way GOP primary to run against popular Democratic Rep. Stephanie Herseth Sandlin in 2010. Emphasizing her experience as a farmer, rancher and small-business owner, she attracted an energetic following and won the primary with 42 percent of the vote. As the general election campaign picked up, polls showed a dead heat between the three-term incumbent and Noem, who was dubbed "Palin of the Plains" after former Alaska Gov. Sarah Palin.

Herseth Sandlin tried to emphasize her work across party lines and her moderate-to-conservative voting record — she voted against the 2010 health care law and 2009 cap-and-trade energy legislation. She also criticized Noem for a driving record that was reported to include 20 speeding tickets, six notices for failure to appear in court and two related arrest warrants.

Noem knocked her competitor for being part of a Democratic Congress plagued by reckless spending. With tea party backing and huge fundraising numbers, she captured the seat in November with 48 percent of the vote. She had no trouble holding it in 2012. She has been mentioned as a possible candidate for the Senate in 2014, as Democrat Tim Johnson is retiring, but as of spring 2013 she had not indicated plans to enter that race.

Noem resumed her college studies while in the state House, and she spent free time in 2011 completing a degree in political science at South Dakota State.

Key Votes

2012	
Extend a Social Security payroll tax cut and unemployment benefits	NO
Ease securities rules to expand small-business access to capital	YES
Extend for one year subsidized student loan interest rates financed by a cut in health care spending	YES
Cite Attorney General Eric H. Holder Jr. for contempt of Congress	YES
Create a visa program for foreign graduates in high-tech fields	YES
Extend most Bush-era income tax rates while allowing rates for top-bracket earners to rise (Jan. 1, 2013)	YES
2011	
Strike funding for F-35 alternative engine	YES
Prevent EPA from regulating greenhouse gas emissions to address climate change	YES
Extend certain provisions of Patriot Act for four years	YES
Declare opposition to use of ground troops in Libya	YES
Overhaul patent law	YES
Pass compromise debt limit increase plan and establish future spending limits	YES
Allow consideration of measures to implement three trade agreements	YES

CQ Vote Studies

	PARTY UNITY		PRESIDENTIAL SUPPORT	
	SUPPORT	OPPOSE	SUPPORT	OPPOSE
2012	93%	7%	12%	88%
2011	94%	6%	21%	79%

Interest Groups

	AFL-CIO	ADA	CCUS	ACU
2012	15%	0%	92%	84%
2011	0%	5%	100%	84%

South Dakota

At Large

Many residents of vast South Dakota hold generations-deep ties to an agrarian heritage, which is evident in the state's economy and also in its politics of small government and self-sufficiency. A fertile, agriculture-based economy keeps farmers and ranchers in business, but recently, the lure of the state's cities — and their finance, technology and health care jobs — has driven steady migration away from the grasslands and cornfields.

Nearly two-thirds of all counties in the state lost population between 2000 and 2010, but Sioux Falls in the east and Rapid City in the west gained residents during the same time period. Access to interstate highways and a concentration of jobs can account for the development; new residents have settled in state capital Pierre (pronounced PEER), as well.

The arid, hilly portion of the state around the Badlands, Mount Rushmore and other Black Hills attractions relies on ranching, mining and tourism. Officials hope to boost wind energy development through tax rebates.

South Dakota has one of the nation's highest percentages of American Indians, at almost 9 percent of the population. But gaming revenue from Indian casinos has failed to eliminate the poverty conditions on reservations. Several of the nation's poorest counties are entirely within reservations here, including Ziebach County, which has the state's highest poverty rate.

The Missouri River, which splits the state, used to be considered a political divide: east of the river, voters leaned more moderate and to the west more conservative. Now, western ranching conservatives and increasing numbers of Republicans in the east edge out urban and farming Democrats at the polls. The GOP enjoys a 10-percentage-point voter registration advantage overall. Republican presidential nominee Mitt Romney won the state by 18 percentage points in 2012 and lost in only nine counties.

Major Industry
Agriculture, finance, tourism

Military Bases
Ellsworth Air Force Base, 3,530 military, 777 civilian

Cities
Sioux Falls, Rapid City

Notable
About 200 Sioux were massacred in one day at Wounded Knee in 1890.

TENNESSEE

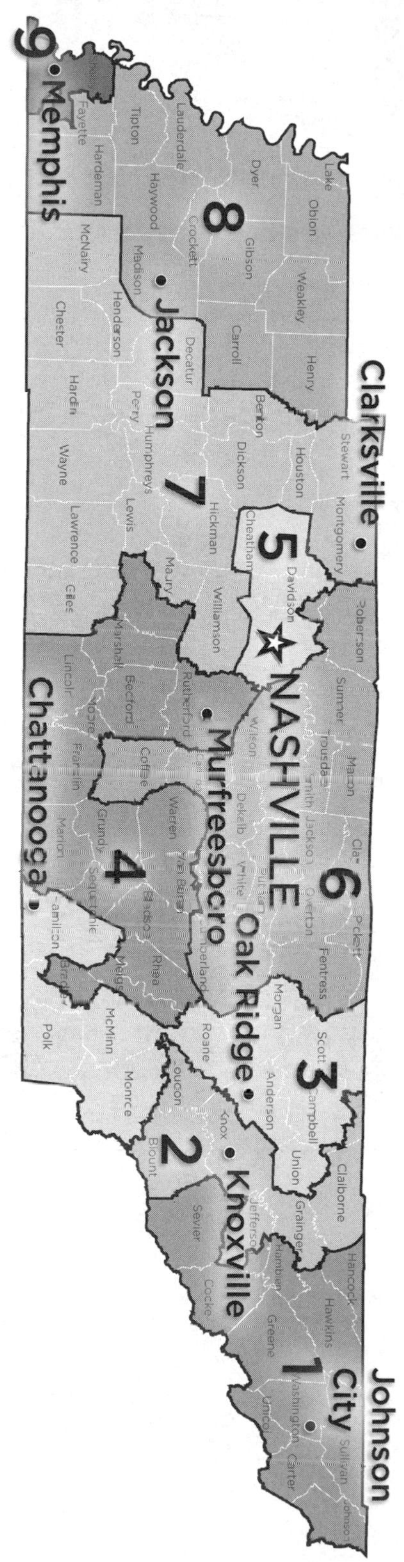

9
Memphis
8
Jackson
Clarksville
7
5
6
NASHVILLE
Murfreesboro
Chattanooga
4
Oak Ridge
3
2
Knoxville
1
Johnson City

Gov. Bill Haslam (R)

First elected: 2010
Length of term: 4 years
Term expires: 1/15
Salary: $178,356
Phone: (615) 741-2001
Residence: Knoxville
Born: Aug. 23, 1958; Knoxville, Tenn.
Religion: Presbyterian
Family: Wife, Chrissy Haslam; three children
Education: Emory U., B.A. 1980 (history)
Career: Gas station and travel center company president; online and catalog sales CEO
Political highlights: Mayor of Knoxville, 2003-11

ELECTION RESULTS

2010 GENERAL

Bill Haslam (R)	1,041,545	65.9%
Mike McWherter (D)	529,851	33.5%

Lt. Gov. Ronald L. Ramsey (R)

First elected: 2007*
Length of term: 2 years
Term expires: 1/13
Salary: $57,027
Phone: (615) 741-4824

*Elected by the Senate

LEGISLATURE

General Assembly: 90 days over 2 years starting in January
Senate: 33 members, 4-year terms
2013 ratios: 26 R, 7 D; 26 men, 7 women
Salary: $20,203
Phone: (615) 741-2730
House: 99 members, 2-year terms
2013 ratios: 70 R, 28 D, 1 I; 83 men, 16 women
Salary: $20,203
Phone: (615) 741-2901

TERM LIMITS

Governor: 2 terms
Senate: No
House: No

URBAN STATISTICS

CITY	POPULATION
Memphis	646,889
Nashville-Davidson	626,681
Knoxville	178,874
Chattanooga	167,674
Clarksville	132,929

REGISTERED VOTERS

Voters do not register by party.

POPULATION

2010 population	6,346,105
2000 population	5,689,283
1990 population	4,877,185
Percent change (2000-2010)	+11.5%
Rank among states (2010)	17
Median age	37.3
Born in state	62.1%
Foreign born	4.0%
Violent crime rate	668/100,000
Poverty level	17.1%
Federal workers	67,862
Military	3,511

ELECTIONS

STATE ELECTION OFFICIAL
(615) 741-7956
DEMOCRATIC PARTY
(615) 327-9779
REPUBLICAN PARTY
(615) 269-4260

MISCELLANEOUS

Web: www.tn.gov
Capital: Nashville

U.S. CONGRESS

Senate: 2 Republicans
House: 7 Republicans, 2 Democrats

STATISTICS BY DISTRICT

District	2012 Vote for President Obama	2012 Vote for President Romney	2008 Vote for President Obama	2008 Vote for President McCain	Black	Asian	Hispanic	Median Income	Over 64	Under 20	College Education	Rural	Sq. Miles
1	26%	73%	29%	70%	2%	1%	3%	$37,197	17%	23%	18%	45%	4,142
2	31	67	35	64	7	2	3	43,576	15	24	28	26	2,321
3	35	63	37	61	11	1	3	38,020	16	24	20	37	4,570
4	33	65	36	63	8	1	5	42,506	13	27	21	45	5,985
5	56	42	57	41	25	3	9	43,623	11	25	33	10	1,249
6	30	69	33	65	4	1	4	41,842	15	26	19	53	6,474
7	33	66	36	62	10	1	4	46,442	13	28	24	52	9,160
8	33	66	35	64	19	2	3	48,792	14	28	28	40	6,851
9	78	21	77	23	64	2	7	36,142	10	29	23	1	483
STATE	**39**	**60**	**42**	**57**	**17**	**1**	**5**	**41,693**	**14**	**26**	**23**	**34**	**41,235**
U.S.	**51**	**47**	**53**	**46**	**12**	**5**	**17**	**50,052**	**13**	**27**	**29**	**21**	**3,531,905**

Sen. Lamar Alexander (R)

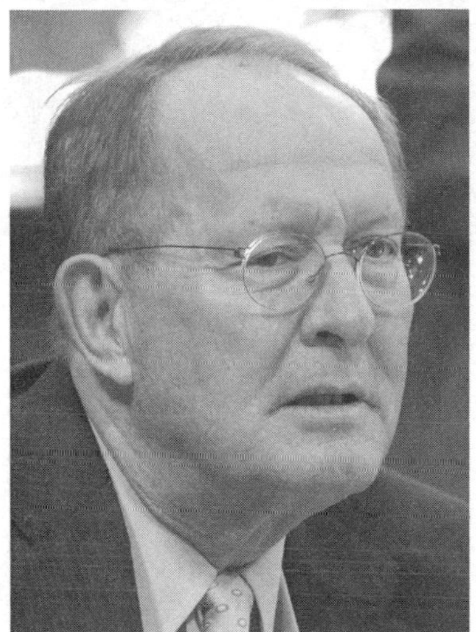

Capitol Office
224-4944
alexander.senate.gov
455 Dirksen Bldg. 20510-4204; fax 228-3398

Committees
Appropriations
Energy & Natural Resources
Health, Education, Labor & Pensions - Ranking Member
Rules & Administration

Residence
Walland

Born
July 3, 1940; Maryville, Tenn.

Religion
Presbyterian

Family
Wife, Honey Alexander, four children

Education
Vanderbilt U., B.A. 1962 (Latin American history); New York U., J.D. 1965

Career
Education consulting firm chairman; lobbyist; university president; White House and congressional aide; lawyer

Political Highlights
Republican nominee for governor, 1974; governor, 1979-87; Education secretary, 1991-93; sought Republican nomination for president, 1996, 2000

ELECTION RESULTS

2008 GENERAL		
Lamar Alexander (R)	1,579,477	65.1%
Robert D. Tuke (D)	767,236	31.6%
Edward L. Buck (I)	31,631	1.3%
2008 PRIMARY		
Lamar Alexander (R)	unopposed	

Previous Winning Percentages
2002 (54%)

Elected 2002; 2nd term

Alexander wants the Senate to be more aggressive in working on energy issues, education policy and the proper balance between federal and state power. He walked away from the GOP leadership team after 2011 to focus on those subjects. "I expect there to be politics," he said. "But the Senate has turned too much into a political playground, and we're not spending enough time on issues important to our country."

He was a two-term governor of Tennessee and secretary of Education for President George Bush. Like many lawmakers with a feel for executive power, Alexander puts a premium on output. He emphasizes that Republicans should cooperate with Democrats on areas of mutual agreement while offering substantive alternatives when the parties diverge.

Alexander tried to apply that philosophy through four years as chairman of the Senate Republican Conference, although partisan divisions in the chamber appeared to widen. He had expressed interest in moving up to become the Republican whip — which made his decision to leave the leadership team all the more surprising.

He still has plenty of opportunities to get things done as an independent operator. He is an ardent advocate for state and local governments, and nowhere is that more evident than in his efforts on elementary and secondary education. "We need to transfer to states and communities the decisions about whether teachers and schools are succeeding," he said.

Those standards will be revisited in the 113th Congress (2013-14) as the Senate again considers reauthorization of the education law known as No Child Left Behind. Alexander, who became the ranking member of the Health, Education, Labor and Pensions Committee in 2013, worked on a panel-approved reauthorization that stalled in the 112th Congress (2011-12).

The shift of responsibility to the states can be part of a "grand bargain," according to Alexander: States take responsibility for education, and the federal government takes full responsibility for Medicaid, the federal-state health insurance program for the poor. Outlays on Medicaid consume large portions of many states' budgets, and Alexander sees that situation getting substantially worse as the program is expanded under the 2010 health care law. That leaves less state support for things like higher education.

"Congress is just beginning to understand that we're the culprit and we're causing tuition to go up," Alexander said.

He is also a defender of his state's "right to work" laws and a critic of the National Labor Relations Board under the Obama administration. A January 2013 court ruling stated that several NLRB members were installed through recess appointments that were unconstitutional; Alexander said that funding to enforce decisions by those appointees should be blocked.

Alexander sits on the Appropriations Committee, where he is the top Republican on the Energy-Water Subcommittee. He also joined the Energy and Natural Resources Committee for the 113th Congress. For years, he has urged a new "Manhattan Project" to develop "clean" energy technology, including advanced batteries and methods for capturing the carbon emitted from using coal.

He would like to see a doubling of the number of electric vehicles (he drives a Nissan Leaf), increased use of nuclear power and a boost to spending on energy research and development. But he also has proposed ending the tax credit for wind energy production — he would use that revenue to offset the elimination of a tax on medical devices that was imposed by the 2010 health care law. Such devices are a major export for Tennessee.

He has worked with a bipartisan group of senators trying to deal with radioactive spent fuel piling up at power plants throughout the nation. The group, whose members represent the leadership of the relevant authorizing committees and appropriating subcommittees, supports language that would establish a limited interim-storage pilot project for nuclear waste.

Alexander has shown concern for both pollution and the potential burdens of environmental regulation. He introduced a measure with Thomas R. Carper, a Delaware Democrat, to sharply reduce nitrogen oxide, sulfur dioxide and mercury emissions from power plants. But he teamed with Arkansas Democrat Mark Pryor on a bill to give utilities six years to meet new emissions standards for mercury and other air toxins.

Alexander was the ranking member of the Rules and Administration Committee in the 112th Congress, and he uses his seat on that panel to try to accelerate the pace at which the Senate does its work — although he opposes dramatic changes to filibuster rules.

He worked with Chairman Charles E. Schumer of New York in 2011 to pass legislation that expedites confirmation of appointees to federal advisory boards and councils. The resolution was paired with a companion measure that eliminates the Senate confirmation requirement for roughly 200 lower-level executive branch appointees. President Barack Obama signed it into law in 2012. "It's a step toward helping the Senate work in a more effective way," Alexander said.

He has also sought to improve the work atmosphere of the Senate in more social ways. He and Virginia Democrat Mark Warner have hosted a series of bipartisan dinners meant to ease the tension that builds up during heated policy debates. "When the Senate runs off the track, when there's a fire, when there's a problem, somebody rings the bell and everybody who can shows up to try to fix it," Alexander told the Reuters news service.

A seventh-generation Tennessean, Alexander was born and raised in the state's mountainous east. He worked his way through Vanderbilt University, where, as a student newspaper editor, he led a campaign to desegregate the school. After graduating with a degree in Latin American history, he earned a law degree at New York University. An accomplished musician, he played trombone, tuba and washboard at a Bourbon Street nightclub while clerking for a federal judge in New Orleans.

His first run for office, at age 34, was an unsuccessful 1974 bid for governor against Democrat Ray Blanton. Four years later, with the help and advice of a mentor and friend, Senate GOP leader Howard H. Baker Jr. of Tennessee, Alexander ran again. This time, he gained national attention by traversing the state on foot — he is a lifelong hiker — in what would become his trademark red-and-black plaid shirt. Voters liked it, electing him with more than 55 percent of the vote.

During eight years as governor, Alexander developed a reputation as a pragmatist who brought businesses to Tennessee. He pushed a major education package through a Democratic General Assembly and then spent more than three years as the chief executive of Tennessee's state university system. He joined the Cabinet in 1991, serving as secretary of Education for two years.

Alexander geared up for the 1996 presidential election, but his campaign foundered and he dropped out after finishing third in the New Hampshire primary. He set his sights on the 2000 nomination but stopped campaigning in the summer of 1999, when George W. Bush became the front-runner.

Two years later, when Fred Thompson announced he was retiring after eight years in the Senate, Republicans looked to Alexander to take his place. In a bitter race against Rep. Bob Clement, Alexander won by 10 points. He had an easier time in 2008, prevailing over Robert D. Tuke, a former state Democratic Party chairman, with 65 percent of the vote.

Key Votes

2012	
Prohibit health insurance plans from denying coverage based on the sponsor's religious beliefs	NO
Require approval of the Keystone XL oil pipeline	YES
Ease securities rules to expand small-business access to capital	YES
Reauthorize farm and nutrition programs for five years	YES
Limit debate on a bill that would create private-sector cybersecurity standards	NO
Consent to ratification of a treaty setting global standard for the treatment of people with disabilities	NO
Provide $60.4 billion in disaster relief following Superstorm Sandy	NO
Extend most Bush-era income tax rates while allowing rates for top-bracket earners to rise (Jan. 1, 2013)	YES

2011	
Prevent EPA from regulating greenhouse gas emissions to address climate change	YES
Extend certain provisions of Patriot Act for four years	YES
Clear compromise debt limit increase plan and establish future spending limits	YES
Overhaul patent law	YES
Implement Colombia free trade agreement	YES
Limit debate on confirmation of Caitlin J. Halligan to D.C. Circuit Court of Appeals	NO
Extend payroll tax cut and unemployment benefits for two months	YES

CQ Vote Studies

	PARTY UNITY		PRESIDENTIAL SUPPORT	
	SUPPORT	OPPOSE	SUPPORT	OPPOSE
2012	83%	17%	62%	38%
2011	82%	18%	63%	37%
2010	87%	13%	52%	48%
2009	77%	23%	68%	32%
2008	92%	8%	77%	23%
2007	84%	16%	79%	21%
2006	94%	6%	93%	7%
2005	92%	8%	88%	12%
2004	95%	5%	98%	2%
2003	98%	2%	98%	2%

Interest Groups

	AFL-CIO	ADA	CCUS	ACU
2012	9%	20%	100%	68%
2011	16%	20%	91%	75%
2010	6%	10%	100%	80%
2009	39%	25%	86%	68%
2008	11%	25%	75%	72%
2007	21%	20%	82%	76%
2006	20%	5%	92%	72%
2005	21%	5%	100%	88%
2004	0%	15%	94%	92%
2003	0%	10%	100%	85%

Sen. Bob Corker (R)

Capitol Office
224-3344
corker.senate.gov
425 Dirksen Bldg. 20510-4205; fax 228-0566

Committees
Banking, Housing & Urban Affairs
Foreign Relations - Ranking Member
Special Aging

Residence
Chattanooga

Born
Aug. 24, 1952; Orangeburg, S.C.

Religion
Protestant

Family
Wife, Elizabeth Corker; two children

Education
U. of Tennessee, B.S. 1974 (industrial management)

Career
Commercial real estate developer; construction company owner

Political Highlights
Sought Republican nomination for U.S. Senate, 1994; Tenn. Finance and Administration Department commissioner, 1995-96; mayor of Chattanooga, 2001-05

ELECTION RESULTS

2012 GENERAL		
Bob Corker (R)	1,506,443	64.9%
Mark E. Clayton (D)	705,882	30.4%
Martin Pleasant (GREEN)	38,472	1.7%
2012 PRIMARY		
Bob Corker (R)	389,613	85.2%
Zach Poskevich (R)	28,311	6.2%
Fred R. Anderson (R)	15,951	3.5%
Mark Twain Clemens (R)	11,795	2.6%
Bronda S. Lenard (R)	11,384	2.5%

Previous Winning Percentages
2006 (51%)

Elected 2006; 2nd term

The habits Corker formed as an executive seem to shape his approach in the Senate. The moderate Republican is assertive, drawn to big ideas and willing to deal with Democrats to keep things moving. His actions sometimes clashed with the traditional expectations for a first-term senator, but at the start of his second term, the road has risen to meet him — Corker is poised to be a significant contributor on foreign policy, banking and fiscal issues.

Corker started a construction company at age 25, and his career building shopping centers around the country and investing in real estate has made him one of the richest members of Congress. His first elected post was as mayor of Chattanooga, and he launched a successful $120 million redevelopment of the city's waterfront. "Being mayor, you're able to create a vision and make it real," he said early in his Senate career. "It's like being CEO of a company. Being in the Senate is like being on the board of directors. You don't see that immediate impact."

Still, Corker has secured influence in the legislative environment. For the 113th Congress (2013-14), he is the top Republican on the Foreign Relations Committee.

Corker has criticized the Obama administration and the Foreign Relations Committee for what he calls a "hair on fire" approach — i.e., responding to crises rather than planning for the long term. He calls for a return to regular reauthorizations of State Department and foreign aid programs, saying such bills would provide the opportunity to define the national interest and take a more metrics-based approach to evaluating programs' effectiveness.

Corker calls himself "very market-oriented," and he considers supply-and-demand problems when thinking about U.S. interests. He suggests that Foreign Relations should take a deliberate look at how increased domestic energy production might change the nation's international posture.

He emphasizes the importance of business and economic relationships between nations. "The standard of living that we have in the U.S. is in large part because we are 25 percent of the world's GDP, which makes us very interconnected," he said. After a 2012 visit to Egypt to meet leaders of the Muslim Brotherhood government, Corker endorsed a $1 billion debt relief plan to help that country's struggling economy. "I know the quickest way for the democracy to fail is not improving the economic conditions," he said.

Corker is cautious about committing military forces. In 2012, he resisted calls for the United States to get involved in Syria's civil war, either by arming rebels fighting the forces of President Bashar al-Assad or by direct military intervention. In spring 2013, he continued to criticize the White House as being too reactive on Syria, but he still didn't want to deploy U.S. troops. "There's a clear humanitarian imperative to bring Assad's barbaric violence to an end," he said at a hearing. "But there are long-term challenges in Syria that we can't solve with a quick military fix." Corker, however, had warmed to the idea of arming Syrian rebels — namely, factions that are not affiliated with radical Islamist groups.

He has also stressed that as policy toward North Korea is reconsidered, it will still be necessary to enlist China as a partner in containing that regime.

Conservatives were frustrated by Corker's 2010 vote for a nuclear-arms-reduction treaty with Russia — he backed the Obama administration after securing a 10-year commitment for increased funding for the modernization of the nuclear stockpile. (Some of that work takes place at the Oak Ridge Laboratory in his state.) Two years later, though, Corker said there was no support or coordination on that spending from the White House, and he threatened to oppose other agreements — such as the Law of the Sea Treaty — if nothing changed.

Corker has made some deals on the Banking, Housing and Urban Affairs Committee, where he is the No. 3 Republican. In 2008, he helped write the $700 billion financial sector rescue package; he pressed for the funding to be doled out in installments, an idea that became part of the law.

In the 111th Congress (2009-10) he stepped on the toes of more-senior Republicans by leading negotiations with Democrats on an overhaul of financial regulations. Democrats cut talks short and issued their own bill, which Corker opposed; he felt it would burden smaller institutions and leave the government on the hook for bailouts when larger institutions collapsed. (Corker cited inadequate capitalization standards as his reason for opposing a 2012 reauthorization of the Export-Import Bank.)

Corker has proposed shifting to a fully privatized housing market over 10 years. He would first establish rules for a futures market where mortgage-backed securities could be traded, then gradually reduce the implied government guarantee behind such securities to zero — thereby allowing the private sector to wrest securitization business from Fannie Mae and Freddie Mac. He wants to get to a point where the private sector "provides that front-end buffer, so that it is absorbing all losses that take place."

In 2012, he devised a plan for overhauling the tax code and restructuring entitlement programs, which he shared with negotiators working on a major fiscal package at the end of the year. Earlier, he and Missouri Democrat Claire McCaskill introduced legislation to cap federal spending at 20 percent of GDP. Several times in 2012 he criticized the Federal Reserve's monetary policy: "Artificially lowering interest rates and printing more money will not solve our country's structural economic issues," he wrote.

Corker moved to Chattanooga at age 11 — his father, a DuPont engineer, was transferred there. He adjusted quickly and was president of his senior class in high school. He worked a variety of jobs as a teenager, earned a college degree in industrial management, then took a job as a construction superintendent. College friends with coat-and-tie jobs were shocked when they would visit him on a job site. "I might not have shaved. I was drinking day-old coffee," he said. "I had mud all over me."

He started his construction company with a pickup truck and $8,000 in savings. By the time he sold it in 1990, it was operating in 18 states. He also owned the Corker Group, a real estate development company, which he sold in 2006, retaining just two properties.

It was a church mission to Haiti in the 1980s that opened his eyes to poverty and stoked his interest in public service. He began working weekends back home to revitalize inner-city neighborhoods and started a nonprofit to help families secure affordable housing. He ran for the Senate in 1994, losing the primary to future Majority Leader Bill Frist, but GOP Rep. Don Sundquist won the governor's race and named Corker the state finance commissioner.

Corker was elected mayor in 2001. Three years into his term, he was invited to join Frist and the senator's two young sons on their annual hike. Frist convinced Corker that he should consider running for the Senate seat from which Frist was retiring. Corker poured his own money into the primary, and his branding as the only "non-career politician" in the field helped him win handily over two former House members. He defeated Democratic Rep. Harold E. Ford Jr., a five-term centrist from Memphis, in part by emphasizing his faith and his conservative values. Corker won by just less than 3 points.

He raised a hefty sum for his 2012 campaign, then had no reason to spend it. Democrat Mark E. Clayton won the primary and was abandoned by his party. He held no campaign events, raised no money and was accused of having anti-gay views. The Washington Post speculated that he might be "America's worst candidate."

Key Votes

2012	
Prohibit health insurance plans from denying coverage based on the sponsor's religious beliefs	NO
Require approval of the Keystone XL oil pipeline	YES
Ease securities rules to expand small-business access to capital	YES
Reauthorize farm and nutrition programs for five years	NO
Limit debate on a bill that would create private-sector cybersecurity standards	NO
Consent to ratification of a treaty setting global standard for the treatment of people with disabilities	NO
Provide $60.4 billion in disaster relief following Superstorm Sandy	NO
Extend most Bush-era income tax rates while allowing rates for top-bracket earners to rise (Jan. 1, 2013)	YES
2011	
Prevent EPA from regulating greenhouse gas emissions to address climate change	YES
Extend certain provisions of Patriot Act for four years	YES
Clear compromise debt limit increase plan and establish future spending limits	YES
Overhaul patent law	YES
Implement Colombia free trade agreement	YES
Limit debate on confirmation of Caitlin J. Halligan to D.C. Circuit Court of Appeals	NO
Extend payroll tax cut and unemployment benefits for two months	NO

CQ Vote Studies

	PARTY UNITY		PRESIDENTIAL SUPPORT	
	SUPPORT	OPPOSE	SUPPORT	OPPOSE
2012	86%	14%	56%	44%
2011	94%	6%	61%	39%
2010	91%	9%	47%	53%
2009	87%	13%	54%	46%
2008	90%	10%	72%	28%
2007	87%	13%	83%	17%

Interest Groups

	AFL-CIO	ADA	CCUS	ACU
2012	0%	15%	75%	92%
2011	11%	15%	100%	85%
2010	6%	5%	100%	92%
2009	28%	10%	71%	84%
2008	10%	20%	75%	83%
2007	26%	20%	82%	83%

Rep. Phil Roe (R)

Capitol Office
225-6356
roe.house.gov
407 Cannon Bldg. 20515-4201; fax 225-5714

Committees
Education & the Workforce
(Health, Employment, Labor & Pensions Chairman)
Veterans' Affairs

Residence
Johnson City

Born
July 21, 1945; Clarksville, Tenn.

Religion
Methodist

Family
Wife, Pam Roe; three children

Education
Austin Peay State U., B.S. 1967 (biology); U. of Tennessee, M.D. 1973

Military
Army Medical Corps, 1973-74

Career
Physician

Political Highlights
Johnson City Board of Commissioners, 2003-09 (mayor, 2007-09); sought Republican nomination for U.S. House, 2006

ELECTION RESULTS

2012 GENERAL		
Phil Roe (R)	182,252	76.0%
Alan Woodruff (D)	47,663	19.9%
Karen Sherry Brackett (I)	4,837	2.0%
Robert N. Smith (GREEN)	2,872	1.2%
2012 PRIMARY		
Phil Roe (R)		unopposed
2010 GENERAL		
Phil Roe (R)	123,006	80.8%
Michael Edward Clark (D)	26,045	17.1%
Kermit E. Steck (I)	3,110	2.0%

Previous Winning Percentages
2008 (72%)

Elected 2008; 3rd term

Roe bases his conservative convictions on his experiences as a doctor, a veteran, an employer and a mayor. Colorful and on-message, he regularly acts as a spokesman for Republican health care priorities.

He arrived in Congress in his mid-60s, but Roe is undeniably vigorous: He is an accomplished bluegrass guitarist, a college basketball fanatic, a history buff, a marathon runner and an outdoorsman. He climbed Mount Rainier for the fourth time on his 60th birthday in 2005.

His 31-year career as an OB-GYN shapes much of his congressional work. Roe was a frequent guest on news shows during the health care debate of the 111th Congress (2009-10). He opposed the Democratic overhaul and proposed finding ways to reduce administrative costs that free up money to cover more individuals. He also complained that Republican medical professionals in the House were never consulted in writing the overhaul.

Since 2011, Roe has been a key participant in the Republican effort to roll back the 2010 law. He chairs the Education and the Workforce Subcommittee on Health, Employment, Labor and Pensions.

His signature bill, passed as part of a legislative bundle in 2012, would repeal the Independent Payment Advisory Board created by the health care law. That panel is charged with generating cost-saving proposals for Medicare, and those proposals take effect unless Congress overrides them. Roe frequently rails against the introduction of bureaucracy into medical decisions — medicine is most cost-effective at the doctor-patient level, he says.

Roe predicts the IPAB will eventually restrict access to care, and he offers TennCare as a cautionary tale. In the 1990s, Tennessee expanded its Medicaid coverage through the use of managed care. As more people switched from private coverage to the state system, budget pressures led to cuts in provider reimbursements, which drove many doctors from the system and hurt many hospitals, Roe said. He thinks that pattern will repeat with the IPAB: "When you've got more demand for services at a fixed price than you got money to pay for it, you get in a line. That's how it works for everything."

The Senate didn't act on IPAB repeal in the 112th Congress (2011-12), and Roe reintroduced his bill in 2013 — with a handful of Democratic co-sponsors.

He has questioned whether employers can swing the health care law's coverage requirements — and in doing so he cites his years as an employer at his medical practice. Roe likes the premium support model, where people receive fixed amounts to help pay for the insurance plan of their choice. "What you're gonna have to do to make it work is to shift more of the responsibility to the consumer," he said. Roe also likes health savings accounts for that reason.

From the Veterans' Affairs Subcommittee on Health, Roe is interested in bringing efficiencies to the veterans health system. He supports community-based outpatient clinics and tele-health programs, which can extend services to rural regions (such as Roe's district) more easily than centralized VA health centers. Roe himself served in Korea in the Army Medical Corps from 1973 to 1974, and he says helping veterans is a "real passion" for him. He frequently mentions his service during hearings.

When labor issues come up, he's quick to note that he grew up in a union household. He lived on a farm in Stewart County in his early youth, but his father took a job at the B.F. Goodrich Rubber Co. plant in Clarksville. "I've had experience with seeing from a laborer's side," he said. "We would go on strike and he and I would go out and work. He would sand floors, and we would make a living any kind of way we could." The job went away when the plant was moved to Mexico in the 1970s.

But that sympathy hasn't translated to support of the National Labor Relations Board. Roe said the NLRB now clearly favors unions over employers, and in 2012 he opposed a new rule accelerating the timetable for union organizing elections by blocking employers' legal challenges until after the vote. He also strongly opposes any union-organizing method that is not a secret ballot.

In January 2013, a court ruled that several of President Barack Obama's recess appointments to the NLRB were unconstitutional. Roe introduced a bill to prevent the NLRB from taking actions requiring a quorum until the legal disputes were finally resolved. It passed the House on partisan lines.

Roe wears his mayor's hat when discussing education and regulation. He served on the Johnson City Board of Commissioners for six years, the last few as mayor. Like many Republicans, he believes in maximizing local control of education programs. "Set the standards, hold them to the standards, and let them decide how to work it out," he said. He calls the inner-city dropout rate a tragedy and touts increased support for charter schools as a way to increase educational alternatives.

According to Roe, federal regulations often make local projects a nightmare; rules on air pollution and stormwater runoff, for example, do not consider the economic drag on local governments. "If it is an unfunded mandate for local government, I am against it," Roe said. "I don't care if it cures cancer."

Roe belongs to the Republican Study Committee, the bloc of the most-conservative House members. He opposes abortion and same-sex marriage.

Roe graduated from high school in the final year in which the school system's black and white students were segregated. He decided to become a doctor because he enjoyed science; working on a tobacco patch on the family farm "convinced me chemistry wasn't that hard." On graduating medical school he was drafted into service in Vietnam, but received a one-year deferment to work at a local hospital. He ended up in Korea instead.

After establishing his practice in northeast Tennessee, he decided "it was time for me to give something back." Roe says he took no pay for his work as commissioner or mayor, donating his salary to scholarship funds.

Roe came in fourth in the 2006 GOP primary to fill an open House seat. David Davis won, guaranteeing election in a hugely Republican district. Roe came back in 2008, attacking Davis for his support of earmarks and ties to oil companies. Roe won by 482 votes, becoming the first Tennessee candidate in 42 years to defeat an incumbent congressman in a primary.

Though retired from medicine, Roe was pressed into service in 2011. On his way through the Charlotte, N.C., airport, he came to the aid of a man in cardiac arrest. Months later the man and his family toured the Capitol — with Roe as their guide.

Key Votes

2012	
Extend a Social Security payroll tax cut and unemployment benefits	NO
Ease securities rules to expand small-business access to capital	YES
Extend for one year subsidized student loan interest rates financed by a cut in health care spending	YES
Cite Attorney General Eric H. Holder Jr. for contempt of Congress	YES
Create a visa program for foreign graduates in high-tech fields	YES
Extend most Bush-era income tax rates while allowing rates for top-bracket earners to rise (Jan. 1, 2013)	NO
2011	
Strike funding for F-35 alternative engine	YES
Prevent EPA from regulating greenhouse gas emissions to address climate change	YES
Extend certain provisions of Patriot Act for four years	NO
Declare opposition to use of ground troops in Libya	YES
Overhaul patent law	YES
Pass compromise debt limit increase plan and establish future spending limits	YES
Allow consideration of measures to implement three trade agreements	YES

CQ Vote Studies

	PARTY UNITY		PRESIDENTIAL SUPPORT	
	SUPPORT	OPPOSE	SUPPORT	OPPOSE
2012	97%	3%	16%	84%
2011	96%	4%	16%	84%
2010	97%	3%	31%	69%
2009	96%	4%	26%	74%

Interest Groups

	AFL-CIO	ADA	CCUS	ACU
2012	19%	0%	100%	88%
2011	0%	10%	100%	88%
2010	7%	0%	88%	96%
2009	14%	5%	87%	92%

Tennessee 1

Northeast — 'tri-cities,' Morristown

Rolling hills and wooded Blue Ridge Mountain peaks cover the 1st District, which shares borders with Virginia and North Carolina. The eastern tip of the triangular district is industrial, while agriculture and tourism dominate the south and west. Many counties are plagued by high rates of unemployment. The district has been a Republican stronghold since the end of the Civil War — GOP nominee Mitt Romney took his statewide best percentage in the 1st with 73 percent of the district's 2012 presidential vote.

Collectively known as the tri-cities, the northeastern towns of Johnson City, Kingsport and Bristol drive much of the district's economic output. A diverse manufacturing sector produces chemicals, auto parts and plastics, but downturns in the economy make the workforce here vulnerable to layoffs. Johnson City serves as an education and health care hub for the surrounding area. Major employers include Eastern Tennessee State University, a large veterans' hospital and the Med Tech Business Park.

A portion of the Great Smoky Mountain National Forest, the nation's most-visited park, covers the district's southern tip and draws more than 9 million tourists annually. Gatlinburg and Pigeon Forge, home of Dolly Parton's Dollywood theme park, draw thousands of visitors.

Tobacco, forage crops and vegetables are harvested in Washington and Cocke counties. Greene County's cattle operations lead the state in beef and milk production. The areas of the district along the North Carolina border are some of most economically deprived areas in the state. More than one-fourth of Cocke County's residents have no high school diploma, and the median household income is under $29,000 — it is $43,000 statewide. Hancock County, on the northern border, is also severely impoverished and struggles with high rates of unemployment.

More than 17 percent of district residents are 65 or older. The first is overwhelmingly white, but the Hispanic population has grown significantly since 2000, especially in Sevier County.

Major Industry
Manufacturing, tourism, health care, agriculture

Cities
Johnson City, Kingsport, Morristown, Bristol

Notable
Jonesborough, the state's oldest settlement, is home to the National Storytelling Festival.

Rep. John J. Duncan Jr. (R)

Capitol Office
225-5435
duncan.house.gov
2207 Rayburn Bldg. 20515-4202; fax 225-6440

Committees
Oversight & Government Reform
Transportation & Infrastructure
(21st Century Freight Transportation - Chairman)

Residence
Knoxville

Born
July 21, 1947; Lebanon, Tenn.

Religion
Presbyterian

Family
Wife, Lynn Duncan; four children

Education
U. of Tennessee, B.S. 1969 (journalism); George Washington U., J.D. 1973

Military
Tenn. National Guard and Army Reserve, 1970-87

Career
Judge; lawyer; teacher

Political Highlights
Knox County Criminal Court judge, 1981-88

ELECTION RESULTS

2012 GENERAL

John J. Duncan Jr. (R)	196,894	74.4%
Troy Goodale (D)	54,522	20.6%
Norris Dryer (GREEN)	5,733	2.2%
Greg Samples (I)	4,382	1.7%
Brandon Stewart (I)	2,974	1.1%

2012 PRIMARY

John J. Duncan Jr. (R)	36,335	83.4%
Joseph R. Leinweber Jr. (R)	3,919	9.0%
Nick Ciparro (R)	3,317	7.6%

Previous Winning Percentages
2010 (82%); 2008 (78%); 2006 (78%); 2004 (79%); 2002 (79%); 2000 (89%); 1998 (89%); 1996 (71%); 1994 (90%); 1992 (72%); 1990 (81%); 1988 (56%); 1988 Special Election (56%)

Elected 1988; 13th full term

An unusual mix of old-school politicking and libertarian impulses makes Duncan very popular in his district, but it also keeps him out of the top tier of the Republican Party. He has burnished a reputation as a fiscal conservative while amassing expertise through decades of service on the Transportation and Infrastructure Committee.

Duncan's father represented the same Knoxville-based House district for 23 years, and in the 112th Congress (2011-12), Duncan surpassed that mark. He remembers his father as the "sweetest, kindest, toughest, hardest-working man I've ever known" and a model for how to conduct business. A backer advised him early on to take a high-tech approach to outreach. "One of the best decisions I ever made," Duncan said, "is that I just ignored everything that he said. I just kept doing a lot of the same things that my dad did, including giving away lucky pennies, and having the water booth at the fair, and having a barbecue each year before the election."

He is still set in his ways. Duncan has a curmudgeon's dislike for cellphones and email; he keeps constituents in the loop with a newsletter he writes himself, peppered with anecdotes and stats culled from whatever he consumes while indulging a voracious reading habit. He has stayed on the Transportation and Infrastructure Committee throughout his entire House career, and he is its vice chairman for the 113th Congress (2013-14).

Chairman Bill Shuster of Pennsylvania has plans for special panels to study transportation issues, and in April 2013 he tapped Duncan to lead the first one, examining intermodal freight transportation. Over the years, Duncan has led subcommittees touching on many facets of the national infrastructure system.

He chaired the Highways and Transit Subcommittee in the 112th Congress and was a key negotiator on the two-year authorization of surface transportation programs enacted in 2012. He considers provisions to expedite permitting and environmental reviews to be the most important parts of that law. He blames environmental groups for keeping development opportunities tied up in the courts.

Duncan backed the GOP's failed attempt to use federal oil and gas leases as a dedicated source of revenue for highway programs, and he thinks the idea will resurface; he also wouldn't mind taking transportation funding directly from the Treasury when needed. Rather than creating a national infrastructure bank, he'd just as soon see support for existing state infrastructure banks.

The 2012 transportation debate was complicated by the House ban on earmarks, which had been used in the past to secure members' support. Duncan considers the GOP-pushed ban "probably one of the dumbest things we've ever done, as far as the party goes. ... We didn't save any money, we just gave the money to the Obama administration and the bureaucrats."

For six years Duncan chaired the Aviation Subcommittee, where he had a reputation for even-handedness. He contributed to a significant increase in federal support for aviation programs, enacted in 2000, as well as tougher air security rules put in place after the Sept. 11 attacks. His current concern, however, is with bloat in security programs. Duncan calls for the abolition of the Federal Air Marshal Service and questions whether increases in airport security hiring have yielded improvements.

Despite his experience, Duncan has missed out on becoming the chairman of a full committee. Florida's John L. Mica jumped over Duncan and other senior Republicans in 2007 to take the top GOP slot on the transportation committee, as did Shuster in 2013. Party leaders bypassed Duncan for the chairmanship of the Natural Resources Committee in the 108th Congress

(2003-04) — and again in the 112th, when Washington Republican Doc Hastings took over. (The 113th is Duncan's first time away from Natural Resources; he instead is serving on the Oversight and Government Reform Committee.)

That's likely due to Duncan's voting record, which depicts him as independent with libertarian tints. In 2002, he was one of six Republicans to vote against the authorization of military action in Iraq. Duncan is critical of U.S. spending overseas and says "isolationist" is a label used to smear those who share his concerns: "I don't think I have an isolationist bone in my body. I think we should have trade and tourism and cultural and educational exchanges. I think we should help out to a limited extent during humanitarian crises."

A solid fiscal conservative, Duncan was one of 10 in his party to reject the GOP's fiscal 2013 budget — he liked its introduction of "free-enterprise-type principles" to entitlement programs but couldn't support its decades of budget deficits. Appropriations Chairman Harold Rogers of Kentucky "is probably my best friend in the Congress, yet I voted against almost all of his appropriations bills" in the 112th, Duncan said.

Still, Duncan isn't an across-the-board libertarian. He leans toward social conservatism, and over the years he has come to prefer "fair trade" to free trade, with more punitive measures against countries such as China should they attempt market manipulations.

The Duncan family wasn't exactly landed gentry. "My grandparents were good people, but they had 10 kids and an outhouse and not much more," Duncan remembers. "My dad hitchhiked into Knoxville with $5 in his pocket and worked his way through" the University of Tennessee. After World War II he became a lawyer, a career that Duncan thought he might follow.

But he also considered baseball. Duncan's father was part of a business group that brought minor league baseball to Knoxville in 1956. Young Duncan spent five and a half happy seasons as the Smokies' batboy and was the public address announcer during his first year in college. As a journalism major at UT, he also worked as a reporter for a local newspaper for a year. After graduating, he headed to D.C.; Duncan taught one year in Virginia at Alexandria's T.C. Williams High School while attending George Washington University's law school at night, then switched to full-time studies.

His legal career led to seven years as a criminal court judge in Knox County, a position he held when his father, in failing health, announced that the 100th Congress (1987-88) would be his last. His father died in 1988, shortly after that announcement. In his first House race, Duncan campaigned primarily as his father's successor, even appearing on the ballot as John J. Duncan, though he goes by Jimmy.

He won 56 percent of the vote and hasn't been seriously challenged since.

Key Votes

2012	
Extend a Social Security payroll tax cut and unemployment benefits	NO
Ease securities rules to expand small-business access to capital	YES
Extend for one year subsidized student loan interest rates financed by a cut in health care spending	YES
Cite Attorney General Eric H. Holder Jr. for contempt of Congress	YES
Create a visa program for foreign graduates in high-tech fields	YES
Extend most Bush-era income tax rates while allowing rates for top-bracket earners to rise (Jan. 1, 2013)	NO
2011	
Strike funding for F-35 alternative engine	YES
Prevent EPA from regulating greenhouse gas emissions to address climate change	YES
Extend certain provisions of Patriot Act for four years	NO
Declare opposition to use of ground troops in Libya	YES
Overhaul patent law	NO
Pass compromise debt limit increase plan and establish future spending limits	YES
Allow consideration of measures to implement three trade agreements	YES

CQ Vote Studies

	PARTY UNITY		PRESIDENTIAL SUPPORT	
	SUPPORT	OPPOSE	SUPPORT	OPPOSE
2012	89%	11%	30%	70%
2011	90%	10%	12%	88%
2010	96%	4%	22%	78%
2009	92%	8%	17%	83%
2008	94%	6%	67%	33%

Interest Groups

	AFL-CIO	ADA	CCUS	ACU
2012	30%	35%	92%	80%
2011	7%	20%	81%	96%
2010	14%	5%	88%	100%
2009	24%	10%	67%	92%
2008	0%	15%	72%	84%

Tennessee 2

East — Knoxville

From the Virginia and Kentucky borders in the north, the 2nd snakes down conservative eastern Tennessee through Knoxville into the Great Smoky Mountains National Park on the North Carolina border.

More than 60 percent of the district's population lives in Knoxville or surrounding Knox County. Government and higher education jobs at the University of Tennessee are key to the regional economy, making the workforce vulnerable to state and federal cutbacks. The Tennessee Valley Authority, which has its headquarters here, has expanded its nuclear power output. Scripps Networks Interactive, owner of HGTV and Food Network, is based downtown.

The University of Tennessee Volunteers' Neyland Stadium is the largest football stadium in the South, and its 104,079 seats become a sea of orange on home game Saturdays in the fall. College basketball and the Women's Basketball Hall of Fame also draw visitors to campus, and the city depends on their retail spending.

Loudon County's industrial parks are light manufacturing and distribution centers, serviced by rail and barge lines. Unemployment rates are among the lowest in the state and the county has experienced substantial population growth. Maryville College in Blount County began as a seminary school and was one of the first schools in the South to welcome blacks, women and American Indians.

Rural counties along the ridges of the Appalachians rely on agriculture and modest manufacturing operations, including furniture and auto parts, for employment. Grainger County produces tomatoes, cattle and tobacco.

The 2nd's Republican roots date back to the Civil War, and the district has not elected a Democrat to Congress since 1852. However, some Democrats are successful in Knoxville politics on the local and state level, especially in areas of the city with a substantial number of black voters.

Major Industry
Government, higher education, retail, manufacturing, agriculture

Cities
Knoxville, Farragut, Maryville

Notable
A statue in Knoxville's Haley Heritage Square honors "Roots" author Alex Haley.

Rep. Chuck Fleischmann (R)

Capitol Office
225-3271
fleischmann.house.gov
230 Cannon Bldg. 20515-4203; fax 225-3494

Committees
Appropriations

Residence
Ooltewah

Born
Oct. 11, 1962; Manhattan, N.Y.

Religion
Roman Catholic

Family
Wife, Brenda Fleischmann; three children

Education
U. of Illinois, B.A.L.A.S. 1983 (political science); U. of Tennessee, J.D. 1986

Career
Lawyer

Political Highlights
No previous office

ELECTION RESULTS

2012 GENERAL		
Chuck Fleischmann (R)	157,830	61.4%
Mary M. Headrick (D)	91,094	35.5%
Matthew Deniston (I)	7,905	3.1%
2012 PRIMARY		
Chuck Fleischmann (R)	29,947	39.1%
Scottie Mayfield (R)	23,779	31.0%
Weston Wamp (R)	21,997	28.7%
Ron Bhalla (R)	926	1.2%
2010 GENERAL		
Chuck Fleischmann (R)	92,032	56.8%
John Wolfe Jr. (D)	45,387	28.0%
Savas T. Kyriakidis (I)	17,077	10.5%
Mark DeVol (I)	5,773	3.6%

Elected 2010; 2nd term

Fleischmann cuts a peculiar figure on Capitol Hill. Although he is in his 50s, his diminutive frame, boyish face and sometimes unruly mop of hair can make him look like a prep school student breaking off from a tour group. There's no confusion about his politics, however. Fleischmann is a solid Republican vote from a solid Republican district.

A longtime lawyer, Fleischmann espouses small-government conservatism. He approved of the GOP's cost-cutting and anti-regulatory measures in the 112th Congress (2011-12), and he even formulated broad plans of his own. Less than a year into his House career, he issued his "Less Government, More Jobs" plan, a collection of "free-market-based solutions" that mirrored the GOP platform. It included a reduction in federal regulation, repeal of the 2010 health care and financial services overhauls, expansion of domestic energy production and support of free-trade agreements.

Fleischmann introduced a bill in 2011 to eliminate the capital gains tax for two years; in 2012, he sponsored a bill to freeze federal spending at $949 billion per year for the next 10 years. He didn't have the clout to advance such sweeping measures, but he promoted them when opportunities arose.

He gets to work directly on federal outlays as a member of the Appropriations Committee in the 113th Congress (2013-14) — an assignment that rewards his overall loyalty to his party. If his committee work as a freshman is any indication, he'll also use the panel to tend to district-based needs.

Fleischmann bounced around a bit in his first term. He was a member of the Natural Resources Committee, but he resigned to make space for Nevada Republican Mark Amodei, who had won a 2011 special election. He also served on the Small Business Committee, but he gave up that seat to move to the Transportation and Infrastructure Committee in June 2011.

His focus on that panel was replacement of the Chickamauga Lock on the Tennessee River. Fleischmann says maintenance on the original lock is the equivalent of "putting Band-Aids on stab wounds" and that a lock failure could shut down river traffic. Fleischmann wants changes to the Inland Waterways Trust Fund, which finances such projects, so that user fees are applied back to the lock where they were collected; the Olmsted Locks on the Ohio River are soaking up a disproportionate share of money, he said. He is a member of the Energy-Water Appropriations Subcommittee.

He calls infrastructure in the United States "woefully inadequate" and wants greater local control over federal transportation dollars. Fleischmann backed Republicans' original 2012 bill to reauthorize surface transportation programs, heaping extra praise on its lack of earmarks. He eventually voted for the two-year compromise worked out with the Senate.

As a member of the Science, Space and Technology Committee in his first term, he championed the Oak Ridge nuclear facility in his district. He supports the expansion of nuclear power as part of a long-term national energy strategy, and he joined most Republicans in voting for an amendment to the fiscal 2012 Energy-Water spending bill to increase funding for review of the Yucca Mountain nuclear-waste license application. He prefers private investment in research over direct government intervention. "That's where I think tax credits and other incentives are probably more appropriate," he said.

A member of the Republican Study Committee, Fleischmann extends his conservatism to social issues — he opposes abortion and supports gun rights.

Tennessee is a right-to-work state, and Fleischmann is supportive of efforts to curtail the powers of the National Labor Relations Board. He is critical of organized labor. "Unions may have served a role in a time and place when a balance needed to be struck between American business and the basic rights of American citizens, but that period in American labor history has long passed," he told the Chattanooga Area Chamber of Commerce in 2011. He sits on the Labor-HHS-Education Appropriations Subcommittee.

Fleischmann, an only child, was born in New York City. His father worked in food service, primarily on the purchasing side. When Fleischmann was 9, his mother was diagnosed with breast cancer; she died five years later. The family moved six times during his childhood as his father took various jobs around the Northeast and Midwest.

Fleischmann also held a number of jobs: scrubbing floors at McDonald's, babysitting, cutting lawns and packing and mailing posters for an art firm. He has sought out more odd jobs as a congressman. As part of his constituent outreach, Fleischmann spends some days in his district working for local employers; among other tasks, he has power-washed a bridge, pumped gas, cleaned hotel rooms and made milkshakes. Huge photos of those workdays adorn his office walls in Washington.

He was also a political junkie as a kid. His first campaign was going door to door in Yonkers, N.Y., as an eighth-grader for the House campaign of Republican Bruce F. Caputo. He remembers that the victory party was at a Carvel ice cream shop.

Fleischmann earned a political science degree from the University of Illinois and a law degree from the University of Tennessee. He and his wife, Brenda, ran their own law firm for more than two decades. Fleischmann worked in part as a personal injury lawyer. He applied to be attorney general of Tennessee in 1997, but his first bid for elective office was his 2010 race to succeed GOP Rep. Zach Wamp, who ran for governor.

In a rough-and-tumble 11-candidate primary, Fleischmann edged out former state GOP Chairwoman Robin Smith, who was endorsed by a number of senior Republicans, including soon-to-be House Majority Leader Eric Cantor of Virginia. The primary victory all but assured his election in the strongly Republican Chattanooga-based district. He defeated Democrat John Wolfe in November by nearly 30 points.

The GOP primary was again his highest hurdle in 2012. Weston Wamp, the 24-year-old son of Zach Wamp, entered the race in 2011. Scottie Mayfield, a popular businessman, dairy farmer and ice cream maven, also jumped into the fray. Wamp couldn't overcome charges of inexperience, and Mayfield was reluctant to engage in debates. Fleischmann ran a grass-roots campaign and won with 39 percent of the vote.

Physician Mary M. Headrick got the Democratic nomination but could do little to overcome the huge Republican advantage in the district.

Key Votes

2012	
Extend a Social Security payroll tax cut and unemployment benefits	YES
Ease securities rules to expand small-business access to capital	YES
Extend for one year subsidized student loan interest rates financed by a cut in health care spending	YES
Cite Attorney General Eric H. Holder Jr. for contempt of Congress	YES
Create a visa program for foreign graduates in high-tech fields	YES
Extend most Bush-era income tax rates while allowing rates for top-bracket earners to rise (Jan. 1, 2013)	NO
2011	
Strike funding for F-35 alternative engine	YES
Prevent EPA from regulating greenhouse gas emissions to address climate change	YES
Extend certain provisions of Patriot Act for four years	YES
Declare opposition to use of ground troops in Libya	YES
Overhaul patent law	YES
Pass compromise debt limit increase plan and establish future spending limits	NO
Allow consideration of measures to implement three trade agreements	YES

CQ Vote Studies

	PARTY UNITY		PRESIDENTIAL SUPPORT	
	SUPPORT	OPPOSE	SUPPORT	OPPOSE
2012	97%	3%	15%	85%
2011	97%	3%	24%	76%

Interest Groups

	AFL-CIO	ADA	CCUS	ACU
2012	15%	0%	92%	92%
2011	0%	5%	94%	88%

Tennessee 3

East — Chattanooga, Oak Ridge

The 3rd cuts south from the Kentucky border across Interstates 40 and 75 to North Carolina and Georgia. Across the lush Appalachian Plateau, flat-topped mountains separate sharp valleys. Part of Watts Bar Lake jogs through Roane County in the district's geographic center.

More than half of the district's population lives in Hamilton County, which includes Chattanooga. The Tennessee River snakes through the city and mountains provide a scenic backdrop. In the 1960s, a thick fog of air pollution drew national criticism, but revitalization efforts have turned it "green." Electric buses are manufactured here and provide free public transportation. Volkswagen chose it as the site for its only North American manufacturing plant, investing $1 billion into the economy and providing thousands of jobs. The city's public-owned electric company built a fiber-optic network that has become a model for advanced broadband.

To the east, McMinn, Monroe and Polk counties were once part of the Cherokee Nation, and their landscapes are dotted with historic sites. The rapids of the Ocoee River are a popular among white-water-rafting enthusiasts; deer, bears and wild boar bring hunters to Cherokee National Forest.

The 3rd's geographic center falls near Oak Ridge, where multidisciplinary high-tech national research facilities sprawl over parts of Anderson and Roane counties. The Y-12 National Security Complex is the nation's primary storehouse for weapons-grade uranium and was the site of the Manhattan Project. The U.S. Department of Energy is the area's largest employer.

Near Kentucky, industrial Scott County struggles with the highest unemployment rate in the state. Closure of the only hospital added to job losses; local leaders are working to reopen it.

Most voters back candidates who espouse low-tax fiscal policy and social conservatism. Republican Mitt Romney took 63 percent of the district's vote in the 2012 presidential contest overall.

Major Industry
Nuclear and high-tech research, manufacturing, technology

Cities
Chattanooga, East Ridge, Oak Ridge

Notable
Oak Ridge hosts an annual Secret City Festival commemorating the town's role in nuclear research.

Rep. Scott DesJarlais (R)

Capitol Office
225-6831
desjarlais.house.gov
413 Cannon Bldg. 20515-4204; fax 226-5172

Committees
Agriculture
Education & the Workforce
Oversight & Government Reform

Residence
South Pittsburg

Born
Feb. 21, 1964; Des Moines, Iowa

Religion
Episcopalian

Family
Wife, Amy DesJarlais; four children

Education
U. of South Dakota, B.S. 1987 (chemistry & psychology), M.D. 1991

Career
Physician

Political Highlights
No previous office

ELECTION RESULTS

2012 GENERAL		
Scott DesJarlais (R)	128,568	55.8%
Eric Stewart (D)	102,022	44.2%
2012 PRIMARY		
Scott DesJarlais (R)	36,088	76.8%
Shannon Kelley (R)	10,927	23.2%
2010 GENERAL		
Scott DesJarlais (R)	103,969	57.1%
Lincoln Davis (D)	70,254	38.6%
Paul H. Curtis (I)	3,178	1.7%
Gerald York (I)	2,159	1.2%

Elected 2010; 2nd term

DesJarlais was establishing himself as an inconspicuous conservative, but personal events dredged up from his past have imperiled his future in politics. As he tries to focus on legislative business, he takes a particular interest in health care and the nation's fiscal situation.

He held no political offices before joining the House in the 112th Congress (2011-12) — DesJarlais (DAY-zhur-lay) is a general-practice physician, though he has the physical frame of a linebacker. He was plain-spoken in hearings and fairly quiet everywhere else. DesJarlais rarely took to the House floor and made few media appearances outside of Tennessee.

But he openly touted his conservatism. On his campaign website, he wrote that he is "pro-gun, pro-life and pro-marriage and PROUD OF IT."

That posturing could be his undoing. During DesJarlais' 2010 campaign, Democrats publicized records from the divorce that ended his first marriage. They included allegations that DesJarlais had engaged in violent and threatening behavior.

It got worse in 2012. That October, the Huffington Post published a transcript from a 12-year-old phone conversation between DesJarlais and a patient with whom he had an affair — in it, DesJarlais encouraged the woman to get an abortion. As he wrestled with the media response, another former patient claimed to have had an affair with DesJarlais and to have smoked marijuana with him.

DesJarlais won a second term — his district is strongly Republican — but shortly after the election a transcript of his 2001 divorce trial was made public. It revealed that his first wife had two abortions and that DesJarlais had affairs with three co-workers and a drug representative while he was the chief of staff at Grandview Medical Center.

DesJarlais told the Knoxville News Sentinel that he didn't intentionally mislead voters, and he said his anti-abortion views had evolved since his first marriage. Republican colleagues didn't outwardly ostracize DesJarlais, saying it was a matter for voters to decide. Therein lies DesJarlais' problem: As one Tennessee GOP operative told Roll Call, "Religious faith is far more important to voters than party." Even before the start of the 113th Congress (2013-14), state Sen. Jim Tracy announced that he would run in the 2014 GOP primary, and his early fundraising totals were eye-popping.

As he sorts out his political future, DesJarlais continues to vote as a fiscal conservative. A member of the Republican Study Committee, DesJarlais in 2011 opposed three separate proposals to raise the federal debt limit, including one from Speaker John A. Boehner. "The debt limit debate provides us with a real opportunity to finally prioritize government spending," he wrote. "We need to sit down and open up the books to look at what government programs we can cut or eliminate."

In January 2013, he was one of 33 House Republicans to oppose another increase to the debt limit that was meant to last four months. He wrote that the increase needed to be bundled with spending cuts to win his support.

DesJarlais has a seat on the Agriculture Committee, and he voted to approve the panel's 2012 version of a long-term reauthorization of farm and nutrition programs. It included $16.1 billion in cuts to the Supplemental Nutrition Assistance Program (aka food stamps), and DesJarlais was one of the 13 panel Republicans supporting an unsuccessful amendment that would have doubled that amount. Late in 2011, he introduced a bill to stop bonus payments to states that have high enrollment levels for the food stamp program. "Why does the federal government need to incentivize states to spend taxpayer dollars with more taxpayer dollars?" he wrote.

The Agriculture Committee has jurisdiction over derivatives trading, and DesJarlais seeks assurances that the 2010 financial regulatory overhaul will not encumber entities, including agricultural cooperatives and farm credit system institutions, that use those financial instruments to mitigate risk.

He studies health care as a member of the Republican Doctors Caucus, the Education and the Workforce Committee and the Oversight and Government Reform Committee. As a freshman, DesJarlais paid particular attention to Medicare physician payments. DesJarlais wants a long-term change to the formula that sets payment rates, fearing that uncertainty will scare health care providers away from Medicare patients.

He opposed the 2010 health care overhaul, and especially the Independent Payment Advisory Board that it created. That 15-member panel is tasked with suggesting ways to reduce Medicare costs, and its recommendations are carried out unless Congress explicitly disapproves of them.

DesJarlais and California Republican Darrell Issa are spearheading a challenge to part of the overhaul's implementation. The law provides tax credits to assist those shopping for insurance in "exchanges" set up by states. But in 2011, the IRS issued a rule extending those credits to people shopping in a federally established exchange. Democrats said the rule was just correcting a drafting error in the law, but DesJarlais posited at a 2012 hearing that it was "a deliberate and premeditated action on the part of Democrats as a way to incentivize states to set up the exchanges." He maintains that the rule is illegal and introduced legislation to throw it out.

DesJarlais grew up in South Dakota, where his father was a barber and his mother was a nurse at a veterans hospital. He did all his higher education at the University of South Dakota, finishing with a medical degree. His practice took him to rural Tennessee.

Four-term Democratic incumbent Lincoln Davis, who carefully cultivated a centrist image, was not originally thought to be in electoral peril in 2010. DesJarlais won a five-way primary but didn't raise a lot of money. But Republicans tied Davis to the liberal Democratic leadership and criticized his support of President Barack Obama's $787 billion economic stimulus. DesJarlais won by almost 20 points.

Tennessee's new congressional map for 2012 included big changes to the 4th District — it lost counties to the north and west while adding the population center of Murfreesboro. More than half of its voters weren't previously represented by DesJarlais. But Democrat Eric Stewart, a former state senator, didn't have the time or campaign cash to capitalize on the scandals near the end of the campaign. DesJarlais won by 12 points.

Key Votes

2012	
Extend a Social Security payroll tax cut and unemployment benefits	NO
Ease securities rules to expand small-business access to capital	YES
Extend for one year subsidized student loan interest rates financed by a cut in health care spending	YES
Cite Attorney General Eric H. Holder Jr. for contempt of Congress	YES
Create a visa program for foreign graduates in high-tech fields	YES
Extend most Bush-era income tax rates while allowing rates for top-bracket earners to rise (Jan. 1, 2013)	NO
2011	
Strike funding for F-35 alternative engine	NO
Prevent EPA from regulating greenhouse gas emissions to address climate change	YES
Extend certain provisions of Patriot Act for four years	YES
Declare opposition to use of ground troops in Libya	YES
Overhaul patent law	YES
Pass compromise debt limit increase plan and establish future spending limits	NO
Allow consideration of measures to implement three trade agreements	YES

CQ Vote Studies

	PARTY UNITY		PRESIDENTIAL SUPPORT	
	SUPPORT	OPPOSE	SUPPORT	OPPOSE
2012	96%	4%	11%	89%
2011	97%	3%	21%	79%

Interest Groups

	AFL-CIO	ADA	CCUS	ACU
2012	19%	0%	100%	92%
2011	3%	5%	94%	88%

Tennessee 4

Southeastern Middle Tennessee — Murfreesboro

The 4th skips down from the outer reaches of the Nashville orbit to the state's southern border, wrapping around Chattanooga to Cleveland in the east and heading into McMinnville in the mountains of Middle Tennessee. The district includes all or part of 16 counties, but 38 percent of its residents live in Rutherford County, southeast of Nashville. Redistricting after the 2010 census made the 4th more compact and eliminated its reach to the northern edge of the state. Socially conservative voters here have strong GOP leanings despite the district's Democratic roots.

Rutherford is home to Murfreesboro, the largest city in the 4th, which has more than doubled its population since 1990. Middle Tennessee University has the most populous undergraduate student body in the state. Auto manufacturing is big here. Between Murfreesboro and Nashville, Smyrna has a long history with carmakers and builds Nissan's electric Leaf. Spring Hill (shared with the 7th) suffered job losses following a 2009 General Motors plant closure, and shops and homes emptied in nearby Columbia (also shared with the 7th). But unionized auto workers went back to work in 2012, when the plant reopened as a flexible manufacturing facility.

Near the Alabama border, Decherd hosts a Nissan luxury-car parts plant, and Daimler has announced plans to manufacture Mercedes-Benz engines nearby. The Episcopal Church-affiliated University of the South, commonly known as Sewanee for the town where it is based, churns out Rhodes scholars. Shelbyville is in the heart of Tennessee Walking Horse Country. Apples and Christmas trees are harvested in Bledsoe County, but its largest crop is pumpkins. Rhea County's Dayton still celebrates its heritage as a strawberry center. Marinas and campgrounds surround Watts Barr Lake (shared with the 3rd), one of the state's best sport fishing spots. The Cherokee Chieftain stands in downtown Cleveland commemorating Bradley County's Native American heritage.

Major Industry
Auto manufacturing, agriculture, higher education

Cities
Murfreesboro, Cleveland, Smyrna, Columbia (pt.), Spring Hill (pt.)

Notable
The Jack Daniel's sour mash whiskey distillery is in dry Moore County.

Rep. Jim Cooper (D)

Capitol Office
225-4311
cooper.house.gov
1536 Longworth Bldg. 20515-4205; fax 226-1035

Committees
Armed Services
Oversight & Government Reform

Residence
Nashville

Born
June 19, 1954; Nashville, Tenn.

Religion
Episcopalian

Family
Wife, Martha Hayes Cooper; three children

Education
U. of North Carolina, B.A. 1975 (history & economics); Oxford U., B.A., M.A. 1977 (Rhodes scholar); Harvard U., J.D. 1980

Career
Investment firm owner; lawyer; investment bank managing director

Political Highlights
U.S. House, 1983-95; Democratic nominee for U.S. Senate, 1994

ELECTION RESULTS

2012 GENERAL		
Jim Cooper (D)	171,621	65.2%
Brad Staats (R)	86,240	32.8%
John P. Miglietta (GREEN)	5,222	2.0%
2012 PRIMARY		
Jim Cooper (D)		unopposed
2010 GENERAL		
Jim Cooper (D)	99,162	56.2%
David Hall (R)	74,204	42.1%

Previous Winning Percentages
2008 (66%); 2006 (69%); 2004 (69%); 2002 (64%); 1992 (66%); 1990 (69%); 1988 (100%); 1986 (100%); 1984 (75%); 1982 (66%)

Elected 2002; 12th term

Also served 1983-95

Cooper can be bristly, thoughtful, funny and scolding, sometimes all in the same sentence. He has warned of a fiscal reckoning for years, and also of a Congress culturally incapable of responding. His efforts to change that culture have made him a field general for moderates of both parties.

Though technically a Democrat, Cooper places his allegiance with the notion of getting things done. He calls himself "a hard-core reformer," and New York Times columnist Joe Nocera has called him "the House's conscience." Speaking in a matter-of-fact monotone, he blames polarizing party leadership teams for creating an atmosphere where legislative breakthroughs are hard to come by and re-election is the top concern.

"Moderates are nearly extinct," Cooper said. "We had been the lifeblood of Congress, and now we're an endangered species."

Already a member of the fiscally conservative Blue Dog Coalition and the business-minded New Democrat Coalition, in the 112th Congress (2011-12) he helped organize No Labels, a nonpartisan grass-roots organization with no policy positions. Its recommendations are for changing Congress' work environment, including keeping members in Washington more weeks and requiring leaders from both parties to have regular joint meetings.

More than a few people scoffed at the group, but in January 2013, it had an undeniable victory. A law to suspend the limit on federal borrowing for four months included the "No Budget, No Pay" plan championed by Cooper — it would have suspended lawmaker salaries for a chamber that did not adopt a fiscal 2014 budget by April 15. When formulating a version of that proposal in 2012, he said it would "hire the most effective lobbyist on Earth to make sure Congress does the job" — a lawmaker's spouse. Whatever its motivation, for the first time in four years, the Senate adopted a budget.

Cooper, the Blue Dogs' co-chairman for policy and legislative strategy, has long seen the government's fiscal trajectory as perilous. In the 111th Congress (2009-10), he and Virginia Republican Frank R. Wolf were instrumental in goading President Barack Obama to create a fiscal commission, eventually known as Simpson-Bowles, to recommend long-term changes. Its work was the basis for a fiscal 2013 budget that Cooper introduced along with Ohio Republican Steven C. LaTourette.

Only 22 Democrats and 16 Republicans voted for it, which Cooper took as evidence of the challenges facing bipartisan legislation. He was one of 25 House Democrats to support a proposed balanced-budget amendment to the Constitution, despite worries about how to enforce it: "You can put that in the category of a bad idea whose time has come." He has introduced bills to ban all spending earmarks and root out duplicative federal programs.

The right spending level for the federal government, according to Cooper, is around 21 percent of gross domestic product. Getting and staying there will likely require changes to health care programs. Cooper supported Democrats' 2010 health care overhaul but does not see it as a "silver bullet." He has taught a class on health policy at Vanderbilt University for more than a decade, and he expects major adjustments from both parties in the years ahead. "There's an unlimited demand and there's a limited supply," he said. "So how do you curb the unlimited demand? It takes everything you've got."

Our federal fiscal woes would be even more pressing, Cooper believes, if we calculated them correctly. He scorns the cash-based accounting currently used to measure our deficits and urges a switch to accrual accounting, which puts all of the government's future financial obligations on a balance sheet.

Cooper brings his accounting concerns to the Armed Services Committee.

The Pentagon has been notoriously resistant to auditing over the years, which Cooper sees as a cultural problem. There are promises of improvement, but "they're just trying to wait out the current officeholders," he said.

Unsurprisingly, Cooper is not overly concerned with maintaining defense spending levels. Instead, he worries that the nation is not forward-thinking or nimble enough to process fast-changing military realities. At a 2011 hearing on the Navy's 30-year shipbuilding plan, he said it could be "a new type of pork preservative as people seek to lock in constituent facilities that may be popular back home, but may not strengthen America."

Discussions should be more about our shift toward "robot wars" or the nature of the United States' enemies; many Armed Services members simply do not understand the conflict in Afghanistan, Cooper said. The military is "not very good at nation building," and while the State Department might be better, "I think there are more military band members in Europe than there are State Department people worldwide." He is the ranking Democrat on the Strategic Forces Subcommittee, which oversees the nation's nuclear arsenal.

The studious Cooper — he happily dubs himself a "super nerd" — also has interests in energy policy, redistricting overhauls and intellectual-property rights (Nashville is home to many singer-songwriters). He indulges some of those as a member of the Oversight and Government Reform Committee, but generally he does not worry about jurisdictional constraints. "Newt Gingrich destroyed the committee system here, so it really doesn't matter what committee you're on," he said.

Cooper is the middle son of Prentice Cooper, Tennessee's governor during World War II, who died when Cooper was 14. He also fondly remembers his grandfather, who lived to be 91. Both men were born in the 1800s. "We did not have history in our house," he said. "It was current events." But he was not too exposed to politics as a child. He attended Groton, the prestigious Massachusetts prep school, zipped through the University of North Carolina in three years, went to Oxford as a Rhodes scholar and got a law degree from Harvard. In 1982 he defeated Senate Majority Leader Howard H. Baker Jr.'s daughter, Cissy, to become the youngest member of the House at age 28.

Cooper developed a reputation as a deal-maker and was a key player on health care and telecommunications policy. But when he ran for the Senate in 1994, he was trounced by actor and lawyer Fred Thompson. Cooper entered the investment banking world for eight years, and he called that time valuable experience for understanding how government regulation affects business.

An open House seat drew him back to politics in 2002. Cooper won easily.

His Washington roommate is Rep. Peter Welch, a fellow nerd and Democrat from Vermont. Welch is married to the cousin of Cooper's wife.

Key Votes

2012	
Extend a Social Security payroll tax cut and unemployment benefits	NO
Ease securities rules to expand small-business access to capital	YES
Extend for one year subsidized student loan interest rates financed by a cut in health care spending	NO
Cite Attorney General Eric H. Holder Jr. for contempt of Congress	NO
Create a visa program for foreign graduates in high-tech fields	YES
Extend most Bush-era income tax rates while allowing rates for top-bracket earners to rise (Jan. 1, 2013)	NO
2011	
Strike funding for F-35 alternative engine	YES
Prevent EPA from regulating greenhouse gas emissions to address climate change	NO
Extend certain provisions of Patriot Act for four years	YES
Declare opposition to use of ground troops in Libya	NO
Overhaul patent law	YES
Pass compromise debt limit increase plan and establish future spending limits	YES
Allow consideration of measures to implement three trade agreements	YES

CQ Vote Studies

	PARTY UNITY		PRESIDENTIAL SUPPORT	
	SUPPORT	OPPOSE	SUPPORT	OPPOSE
2012	81%	19%	70%	30%
2011	75%	25%	79%	21%
2010	81%	19%	66%	34%
2009	83%	17%	85%	15%
2008	92%	8%	28%	72%

Interest Groups

	AFL-CIO	ADA	CCUS	ACU
2012	81%	60%	58%	24%
2011	72%	70%	69%	16%
2010	43%	55%	63%	35%
2009	90%	90%	40%	16%
2008	79%	60%	72%	20%

Tennessee 5

Nashville

Home of the Grand Ole Opry and the Country Music Hall of Fame and Museum, the 5th's Nashville has long been known for its place in country music history. The state capital has left behind that one-dimensional image to become a cosmopolitan mecca for tourism, culture and education.

Honky-tonk music and cowboy boots still set the daily rhythm in Nashville. But state government jobs, a white-collar finance sector and hundreds of health care employers have helped the city emerge from years of declining album sales and recording-label restructuring plans at the dozens of studios that once filled the famous Music Row. Research facilities, including the Vanderbilt University Medical Center, and professional offices lure well-educated residents.

Despite the music industry's struggles, Gaylord Entertainment remains one of Nashville's top employers, and live music scenes still bounce in areas such as East Nashville and 12South. Destinations such as historic Printer's Alley and the Opry Mills Mall draw millions of tourists. Professional hockey (Predators) and football (Titans) add entertainment revenue, and newly renovated Nashville International Airport supports more than 39,000 jobs.

To the west, the district also captures most of Cheatham County and all of Dickson County, where rapid growth in the suburban population over the past decade has forced infrastructure upgrades.

The robust service economy has attracted a large immigrant population, and the 5th has a larger Hispanic community than any other district in the state. The nation's largest Kurdish population adds to the diversity, and more than 80 languages are spoken in Nashville public schools.

Andrew Jackson, founder of the Democratic Party, resided in The Hermitage, his plantation home outside Nashville, before and after his two terms in the White House. True to its roots, the 5th is a Democratic stronghold. Davidson County gave Barack Obama 58 percent in the 2012 presidential contest; he took 56 percent in the district overall.

Major Industry
Health care, higher education, music, government, tourism

Cities
Nashville-Davidson (pt.), Brentwood (pt.), Dickson

Notable
No Republican won Nashville's congressional seat during the 20th century.

Rep. Diane Black (R)

Capitol Office
225-4231
black.house.gov
1531 Longworth Bldg. 20515-4206; fax 225-6887

Committees
Budget
Ways & Means

Residence
Gallatin

Born
Jan. 16, 1951; Baltimore, Md.

Religion
Christian

Family
Husband, David Black; three children

Education
Anne Arundel Community College, A.S.N. 1971; Belmont U., B.S.N. 1992

Career
Nurse; nonprofit community and health organization fundraiser; college instructor

Political Highlights
Tenn. House, 1999-2005; Tenn. Senate, 2005-10

ELECTION RESULTS

2012 GENERAL		
Diane Black (R)	184,383	76.4%
Scott Beasley (I)	34,766	14.4%
Pat Riley (GREEN)	21,633	9.0%
2012 PRIMARY		
Diane Black (R)	44,949	69.4%
Lou Ann Zelenik (R)	19,836	30.6%
2010 GENERAL		
Diane Black (R)	128,517	67.3%
Brett Carter (D)	56,145	29.4%
Jim Boyd (I)	2,157	1.1%

Elected 2010; 2nd term

Black is a versatile lawmaker with ability as a communicator, legislator and campaigner. Well respected among House Republicans, she often is called upon to convey conservative priorities for health care, taxes and spending.

Black has two notable strengths as a messenger: she comes across as endearingly pleasant, and she knows how to make arguments accessible to a wide audience. She sits on the Ways and Means Committee, which is sometimes given to number- and policy-intensive debates.

But in hearings, she has pressed witnesses to explain what they mean by exemptions, subsidies, wealthy or poor, lamenting that the terms are used as rhetorical cudgels. Her own statements tend to have clear narrative structure and relatively plain language.

As a freshman, Black was chosen to lead the communications efforts for the National Republican Congressional Committee. She also was part of the agenda-setting Republican Policy Committee (where she still serves), and she took the microphone alongside party leaders at a number of media events.

Ways and Means handles health care, and in the 113th Congress (2013-14) Black addresses that subject as a vice chairwoman of the GOP Doctors Caucus. She worked for decades as an emergency room and long-term-care nurse, and she has said that the implementation of TennCare is what drew her into state government, where she served in both the House and Senate. That public insurance program greatly expanded coverage, nearly bankrupted the state and was significantly pared in 2005.

Black sees it as a cautionary tale for the implementation of the 2010 health care overhaul, which she describes as a drag on economic growth. She says "market-based" solutions are a better way to go.

As a state senator, Black unsuccessfully pushed a 2010 bill to allow Tennessee residents to opt out of the federal health care law. She supports some ends of the law, but not the means: She told the Daily News Journal of Murfreesboro that a pre-existing medical condition should not be grounds for denial of insurance coverage, but that she prefers the use of high-risk insurance pools to provide that coverage. It should be legal to sell health insurance across state lines, she says.

Black plucked some low-hanging fruit from the health care law, via her 2011 bill to change the formula that determines eligibility for Medicaid. Under the law, Social Security payments were not factored into a person's income level, allowing some people well above the federal poverty level to qualify for Medicaid. The measure had bipartisan support, and it was enacted as part of a package of tax changes.

A social conservative, Black inherited a major health initiative from Republican Mike Pence, who became Indiana's governor in 2013. She is now the lead sponsor of a bill to prevent abortion providers from getting federal grants for family planning and reproductive health services. Black has a harder edge when discussing the bill's main target, Planned Parenthood. Writing in Politico in early 2013, she said that organization's "sleight-of-hand accounting and dishonest PR campaign led much of the public to believe that women's health care is its primary function, which could not be further from reality."

In 2013, she also became the lead sponsor of a bill to protect "conscience rights" — it says no employers or religious institutions would have to provide coverage of abortion "or other item or service" if the employer or institution has a moral or religious objection. Nebraska Republican Jeff Fortenberry sponsored the bill in the 112th Congress (2011-12).

She also uses her Ways and Means post to stump for a simpler and fairer tax code. Her definition of "fairer" is that "everyone pays something as long as they're able. ... If you're an able person and you are working, I think that you should be paying something into the system. Because that gives us all ownership when we pay into the system."

She is supportive of the tax overhaul outlined by Chairman Dave Camp of Michigan over the course of the 112th.

On the Budget Committee, Black calls for mechanical adjustments to the spending machine. "I felt since I've been here that the budget process is broken," she said in 2011. She introduced a bill to switch budget measures from concurrent resolutions to joint resolutions with the force of law — meaning they would require passage in both chambers and the president's signature.

"All the different entities that are involved in making sure that a budget gets passed, it brings them together at the beginning of the process," she said.

Black has staked out conservative positions on other major issues, including immigration. The House adopted her amendment to the bill funding the Justice Department for fiscal 2013; it would prevent spending on lawsuits aimed at overturning or invalidating specific immigration laws in eight states. Black argues that states need to be able to enforce laws if the federal government won't. The same year, she amended the Homeland Security spending bill to block funds for a public advocate position that the Obama administration created to represent illegal immigrants. Neither spending bill was enacted.

Black was born in Baltimore, the third of four children. Her father was a World War II veteran and an electrician with Kaiser Aluminum. Her mother was a homemaker.

She moved to Tennessee in the 1980s, where she and her husband started Aegis Sciences Corp., a forensics and drug-testing company. Holdings in that company make Black one of the wealthiest members of Congress. She served six years in the Tennessee House, then six more in the state Senate, rising to become chairwoman of that chamber's GOP caucus.

The 6th District was represented by conservative Democrat Bart Gordon, whose popularity allowed him to hold his seat for 13 terms even as the state got more Republican. Black jumped into the race in late 2009 when Gordon announced his retirement. She won the GOP nomination by fewer than 300 votes in a seven-candidate primary, but the general election was a cakewalk.

As redrawn for the 2012 election, the 6th District lost its biggest population center — Murfreesboro was moved to the 4th District — but kept a very Republican lean. Black didn't mess around, raising more than $3.5 million for her campaign.

In the GOP primary she easily defeated Lou Ann Zelenik (the runner-up in the 2010 primary), and she didn't have a Democratic opponent in November.

Key Votes

2012	
Extend a Social Security payroll tax cut and unemployment benefits	NO
Ease securities rules to expand small-business access to capital	YES
Extend for one year subsidized student loan interest rates financed by a cut in health care spending	NO
Cite Attorney General Eric H. Holder Jr. for contempt of Congress	YES
Create a visa program for foreign graduates in high-tech fields	+
Extend most Bush-era income tax rates while allowing rates for top-bracket earners to rise (Jan. 1, 2013)	NO
2011	
Strike funding for F-35 alternative engine	NO
Prevent EPA from regulating greenhouse gas emissions to address climate change	YES
Extend certain provisions of Patriot Act for four years	YES
Declare opposition to use of ground troops in Libya	YES
Overhaul patent law	YES
Pass compromise debt limit increase plan and establish future spending limits	YES
Allow consideration of measures to implement three trade agreements	YES

CQ Vote Studies

	PARTY UNITY		PRESIDENTIAL SUPPORT	
	SUPPORT	OPPOSE	SUPPORT	OPPOSE
2012	99%	1%	13%	87%
2011	98%	2%	24%	76%

Interest Groups

	AFL-CIO	ADA	CCUS	ACU
2012	10%	5%	82%	100%
2011	0%	10%	100%	84%

Tennessee 6

Northeastern Middle Tennessee — Hendersonville

The vast Middle Tennessee 6th spans acres of fertile, rolling land cut by the curving Cumberland River and shares 130 miles of border with Kentucky. Population and economic growth fanning out from Nashville (in the 5th) has benefited much of the district. Nearly half of the district's population is clustered to the north and east of the capital city.

Hendersonville is the only city in the 6th with more than 50,000 people. On the scenic Old Hickory Lake, the town has attracted an affluent and well-educated population of Nashville commuters. Traffic congestion has increased and planners want denser urban development in Hendersonville and in neighboring Gallatin to increase use of mass transit. Four coal-fired generating units controlled by the Tennessee Valley Authority produce electricity in Gallatin. A medical center and community college Vol State also drive the economy. Cookeville is home to Tennessee Tech University.

Dell sold its Lebanon-based refurbishing facility to a logistics company in 2009 and slowly shed its employees, but officials recently landed a deal with Amazon, and the city is still home to headquarters for Cracker Barrel.

Tennessee's biggest tobacco farms dominate areas in the west, and Robertson County leads the state in production. In the east, the Cumberland Plateau supports the state's coal mining industry. Driven by environmental groups concerned about land depletion and endangered species, the state petitioned for a federal ban on surface mining in late 2010.

The overwhelmingly white district is socially conservative territory, where voters oppose gun control and abortion rights. Republicans easily captured the U.S. House seat when Democrat Bart Gordon retired in 2010 after 13 terms; Republican Mitt Romney took 69 percent of the district's vote in the 2012 presidential contest.

Major Industry
Higher education, health care, distribution, tobacco, coal mining

Military Bases
Arnold Air Force Base, 52 military, 389 civilian

Cities
Hendersonville, Gallatin, Cookeville, Lebanon

Notable
Manchester hosts the annual Bonnaroo Music and Arts Festival.

Rep. Marsha Blackburn (R)

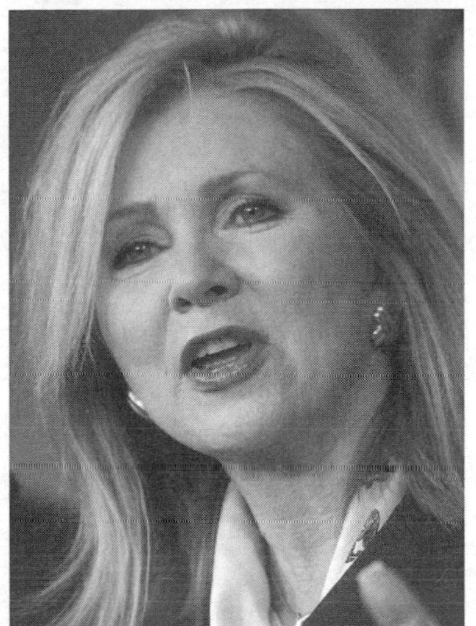

Capitol Office
225-2811
blackburn.house.gov
217 Cannon Bldg. 20515-4207; fax 225-3004

Committees
Budget
Energy & Commerce

Residence
Brentwood

Born
June 6, 1952; Laurel, Miss.

Religion
Presbyterian

Family
Husband, Chuck Blackburn; two children

Education
Mississippi State U., B.S. 1973 (home economics)

Career
Retail marketing company owner; state economic development official; sales manager

Political Highlights
Williamson County Republican Party chairwoman, 1989-91; Republican nominee for U.S. House, 1992; Tenn. Senate, 1999-2002

ELECTION RESULTS

2012 GENERAL		
Marsha Blackburn (R)	182,730	71.0%
Credo Amouzouvik (D)	61,679	24.0%
Howard M. Switzer (GREEN)	4,640	1.8%
Jack Arnold (I)	4,256	1.6%
William Ryan Akin (I)	2,740	1.1%
2012 PRIMARY		
Marsha Blackburn (R)		unopposed
2010 GENERAL		
Marsha Blackburn (R)	158,916	72.4%
Greg Rabidoux (D)	54,347	24.8%
J.W. "Bill" Stone (I)	6,320	2.9%

Previous Winning Percentages
2008 (69%); 2006 (66%); 2004 (100%); 2002 (71%)

Elected 2002; 6th term

The enterprising Blackburn has worked her way to the front lines as both a GOP spokeswoman and a policy bludgeon. Always active on fiscal issues, she has stepped up involvement with Internet policy and reshaping health care — and she wants her party to be more aggressive with its agenda.

She might be a born saleswoman. Blackburn's father sold oil field equipment, and she calls her mother a "professional volunteer" who headed up the Garden Clubs of Mississippi, PTA groups and the Homemakers Club.

Blackburn arrived in Tennessee for a summer job selling books door to door in the early 1970s. She worked her way up to sales manager and eventually went into marketing. She frequently invokes that enterprising spirit when outlining her goals on the Energy and Commerce Committee, where she now hold the informal title of vice chairwoman.

And Blackburn is not lacking in confidence: "I am great at team-building," she says. Blackburn serves on the GOP whip team, mentors freshmen and particularly keeps her door open to the women of Congress — though she chooses to be referred to as a congressman. In the 113th Congress (2013-14), she is overseeing the work of the five regional chairmen of the National Republican Congressional Committee, the campaign arm of the House GOP.

Blackburn was known in the Tennessee Senate for a relentless and ultimately successful crusade against a state income tax. She calls Tennessee's sales tax an "everybody-in system" with the broad base extolled by many Republicans; a national switch to a consumption-based tax code could happen if enough states make the change first, she said.

She also has an everybody-in sensibility on spending policy. Blackburn has started several Congresses by introducing bills to make across-the-board spending cuts to non-defense accounts — in 2013, she offered 1, 5, 10 and 15 percent options. The strategy has sometimes been criticized by both parties as too blunt, but Blackburn disagrees: "When you require everybody to participate ... you're going to get a more thoughtful result."

Her other economic plans usually involve keeping government out of the marketplace, particularly in regards to the Internet. "Conservatives need to wake up and understand that our core values are being challenged in debates over technology policy," she told the Conservative Political Action Conference in 2011. "The left has insidiously laid the groundwork for a massive expansion of federal authority."

That includes "network neutrality," the regulations put in place by the Federal Communications Commission in late 2011 to prevent Internet service providers from restricting or slowing access to various content. Blackburn views it as "nationalization of the Internet" and unprecedented federal intrusion on "our most innovative economic sector." She introduced a bill to block such regulation and considers it a top tech priority.

Regarding Internet privacy, she hopes to encourage the private sector to develop a series of best practices as it gathers and monetizes consumer information. "We don't need to pretend that government has all the answers," she said at a 2011 hearing.

Blackburn has been more proactive in fighting online piracy of intellectual property. Article 1, Section 8 of the Constitution outlines a federal "obligation to secure citizens' original works," Blackburn wrote in Roll Call in December 2011; she wants laws to ensure that copyright holders can pursue due process and to "choke off the money" to websites that facilitate piracy. "Online pirates are perpetuating the free entitlement culture that is plaguing the global economy," she wrote. "A culture of free dictates that every good idea America has ever produced holds no private value — that's not a sustainable model."

A co-founder of the Congressional Songwriters Caucus, Blackburn also has a local stake in the intellectual property battle: Memphis and Nashville are hotbeds for the industry, and she has musical roots. Blackburn played piano in her church growing up, minored in classical piano in college and knows her way around guitars and ukuleles.

Bach inventions are her favorite: "When you look at how your bass and your treble clef switch off with the melody in Bach ... it's like playing intellectual volleyball," she says. "I really like that a lot."

Blackburn also uses her seat on Energy and Commerce to jump in on health care discussions. She has repeatedly introduced her plan to allow seniors receiving Social Security to opt for vouchers to go toward health savings accounts or high-deductible insurance plans instead of standard Medicare benefits until age 70. She has produced legislation to allow health insurance to be sold across state lines, and in 2013 she and Republican Renee Ellmers of North Carolina released a series of principles for modifying Medicare.

And, like most House Republicans, she demands a decrease in federal regulation, particularly by the EPA. She wants the EPA and Energy Department merged into one agency.

Blackburn remembers her earliest political involvement growing up in Mississippi: handing out emery boards as a kid on behalf of her friend's father, who was running for district attorney. Her parents were active in the Jones County GOP and other groups such as 4-H; Blackburn herself won a 4-H college scholarship for food preservation. "I can beat anybody at canning tomatoes and making jam," she says. She also boasts of making the world's best chocolate chip cookies and having some mean barbecue skills.

She lost a 1992 race against Democratic Rep. Bart Gordon, then served a stint as executive director of Tennessee's Film, Entertainment and Music Commission before winning a state Senate seat in 1998. The state income tax issue boosted her in the 2002 Republican primary for an open seat, and she became the first woman from Tennessee to be elected to the House in her own right. She has easily won all of her re-election races.

One other distinction came her way in 2011. Israeli researchers were studying the relationship between lawmaker attractiveness and the frequency of TV appearances in the 110th Congress (2007-08), and they revealed that test groups rated Blackburn the most attractive lawmaker. She didn't complain. "Anything that gives me another opportunity to talk about preserving freedom, free markets, free people, I'm gonna take it," she said in 2012. "If they wanna think that a 59-year-old grandmother is at the top of the heap, God bless 'em and bring it on."

Key Votes

2012	
Extend a Social Security payroll tax cut and unemployment benefits	NO
Ease securities rules to expand small-business access to capital	YES
Extend for one year subsidized student loan interest rates financed by a cut in health care spending	YES
Cite Attorney General Eric H. Holder Jr. for contempt of Congress	YES
Create a visa program for foreign graduates in high-tech fields	YES
Extend most Bush-era income tax rates while allowing rates for top-bracket earners to rise (Jan. 1, 2013)	NO
2011	
Strike funding for F-35 alternative engine	YES
Prevent EPA from regulating greenhouse gas emissions to address climate change	YES
Extend certain provisions of Patriot Act for four years	YES
Declare opposition to use of ground troops in Libya	YES
Overhaul patent law	YES
Pass compromise debt limit increase plan and establish future spending limits	YES
Allow consideration of measures to implement three trade agreements	YES

CQ Vote Studies

	PARTY UNITY		PRESIDENTIAL SUPPORT	
	SUPPORT	OPPOSE	SUPPORT	OPPOSE
2012	99%	1%	11%	89%
2011	96%	4%	24%	76%
2010	98%	2%	32%	68%
2009	99%	1%	11%	89%
2008	99%	1%	78%	22%

Interest Groups

	AFL-CIO	ADA	CCUS	ACU
2012	10%	0%	92%	100%
2011	0%	5%	100%	87%
2010	0%	0%	88%	100%
2009	5%	0%	73%	100%
2008	0%	10%	83%	96%

Tennessee 7

Western Middle Tennessee — Clarksville, southern Nashville suburbs

The 7th is the state's geographically largest district. It borders Mississippi and Alabama to the south and Kentucky to the north. South of Nashville, the district takes in Williamson County, the state's fastest-growing county. Overall, the 7th spreads across 18 full counties and part of Maury County.

Williamson's suburban households bring in high incomes, and the area's economic growth is reflected in the development of once-open land. One retail hub is Cool Springs Galleria, the state's largest shopping center. Suburban Franklin, the county seat, hosts Nissan's corporate headquarters; its 2005 decision to move to the region has boosted auto manufacturing.

Montgomery County grew by more than 27 percent between 2000 and 2010. Activity in the county is focused on Fort Campbell, which straddles the Tennessee-Kentucky border, and its largest city, fast-growing Clarksville. In 2010, Clarksville landed a solar energy boon when Hemlock Semiconductor announced construction of a billion-dollar plant, but layoffs have raised questions. The state has invested in the industry, including a new engineering program at Austin Peay State University in Clarksville.

Forests and fields of hay, corn and soybeans cover the midsection of the district. Near Lexington, reservoirs of the Beech River Watershed provide recreation. In the southwest, Whiteville's two prisons provide jobs.

The district is majority-white, and its black population, the largest minority group in the 7th, is concentrated in Hardeman County. Barack Obama won Hardeman in the 2012 presidential election, but the 7th is overwhelmingly GOP territory and as a whole gave 66 percent of the vote that year to GOP nominee Mitt Romney.

Major Industry
Manufacturing, retail, agriculture

Military Bases
Fort Campbell, 30,438 military, 2,500 civilian (2011) (shared with Kentucky's 1st District)

Cities
Clarksville, Franklin, Brentwood (pt.), Spring Hill

Notable
Shiloh National Military Park memorializes the soldiers who died in one of the bloodiest battles of the Civil War.

Rep. Stephen Fincher (R)

Capitol Office
225-4714
fincher.house.gov
1118 Longworth Bldg. 20515-4208; fax 225-1765

Committees
Agriculture
Financial Services

Residence
Frog Jump

Born
Feb. 7, 1973; Memphis, Tenn.

Religion
United Methodist

Family
Wife, Lynn Fincher; three children

Education
Crockett County H.S., graduated 1990

Career
Farmer

Political Highlights
No previous office

ELECTION RESULTS

2012 GENERAL		
Stephen Fincher (R)	190,923	68.3%
Timothy D. Dixon (D)	79,490	28.4%
James L. Hart (I)	6,139	2.2%
Mark J. Rawles (I)	2,870	1.0%
2012 PRIMARY		
Stephen Fincher (R)	60,355	86.7%
Annette Justice (R)	9,288	13.3%
2010 GENERAL		
Stephen Fincher (R)	98,759	59.0%
Roy Herron (D)	64,960	38.8%
Donn Janes (I)	2,440	1.5%

Elected 2010; 2nd term

Fincher is a gospel-singing cotton farmer, which on paper makes him an outlier among colleagues on the Financial Services Committee. The seeming incongruity didn't keep him from scoring a major achievement as a freshman, and fellow Republicans have been impressed by his fundraising efforts.

The financial sector conjures up images of skyscrapers and MBAs wearing three-piece suits. Fincher comes from a town called Frog Jump, never went to college and held no political jobs prior to the 112th Congress (2011-12). He is the first Republican to represent the western Tennessee region since Reconstruction, and he joined Financial Services a few months into his first term.

He was a quick study of the GOP's agenda on the committee. Fincher fights the 2010 financial regulatory overhaul known as Dodd-Frank, which he says is "crippling the private sector."

Like many in his party, he states that rules designed for large banks are robbing smaller banks of the flexibility they need to help longtime, well-known customers. "Community banks are being punished for actions they are not responsible for and face excessive regulations preventing people from obtaining capital," he said in 2011.

Fincher has said that the law's requirements for high-cost mortgages are unintentionally damaging the manufactured housing industry (i.e., mobile homes), which has many producers and customers in his state. Because the loans are smaller and shorter than those for regular homes, the rates are often higher, which could subject them to Dodd-Frank regulations that result in more pass-through costs to borrowers, according to Fincher. He wants a workaround written into law.

But the biggest victory of his first term wasn't parochial in nature. Working with Delaware Democrat John Carney, he prepared a 2011 bill to ease filing and regulatory requirements for companies making public stock offerings. He said that reducing the costs of an IPO would "encourage more companies to go public" and "create more opportunity for companies to raise desperately needed capital to reinvest and grow business."

The measure drew the notice and support of the Wall Street Journal editorial page, and the House eventually passed it. Majority Leader Eric Cantor of Virginia made Fincher's bill the vehicle to carry several other measures meant to improve capital flows to smaller, growing businesses. The package was signed into law in 2012 by President Barack Obama and was one of the few overwhelmingly bipartisan laws produced by the 112th Congress.

Fincher's spot on Financial Services has helped his campaign fundraising efforts — political action committees associated with the finance sector accounted for almost one third of his PAC donations in the 2012 election cycle. But he didn't have problems before joining the committee. Fincher filed to run against John Tanner, a Democrat serving his 11th term, before Tanner announced his retirement in December 2009. Republicans were wowed by his fundraising efforts, which have continued apace. Facing no serious threat in 2012, he donated sizable amounts of cash to other Republican campaigns and organizations.

In general, Fincher has been a team player in the early stages of his House career, joining the party's push for greatly reduced spending. But there were signs at the start of the 113th Congress (2013-14) that his patience was wearing thin with GOP leaders. Republicans upset over Speaker John A. Boehner's handling of deficit reduction negotiations contemplated a coup to deny Boehner a second term as speaker. Fincher ultimately voted for Boehner, but only after a heated conversation with Majority Whip Kevin McCarthy of California on the House floor.

A seventh-generation cotton farmer, Fincher lives only two miles from the spot where the family farm originally started. He describes life in his hometown with the enthusiasm of a country song. A devout Christian, at age 9 he joined a singing ministry started by his grandmother known as "The Fincher Family." The group, which has its own recording studio, sings at more than 100 events throughout the year raising money for various charities. With his wife and three children, Fincher attends Archer's Chapel Methodist Church, which was built using lumber donated by one of Fincher's grandfathers on land donated by his other grandfather.

His family has not relocated to Washington. At his 2010 swearing-in, "I looked at my kids and said, 'Can you guys believe all this, isn't it amazing?' My son looks up at me and responds, 'Dad, do you know how many ducks we could have killed back home today?'"

Fincher had to leave the Agriculture Committee to join the "exclusive" Financial Services Committee in 2011, but in February 2013 he was granted a waiver and reclaimed a seat on the panel. His return lets him handle even more of the financial sector, as the Agriculture Committee oversees commodities markets. It also creates the potential for political headaches: He has been criticized for advocating small-government policies while accepting several million dollars in farm subsidies over the years.

Fincher joins the GOP chorus calling for a relaxed regulatory environment. He vocally supported the GOP attempt to block potential EPA regulation of farm dust, and he wants the agency to back off of possible rules regarding fuel storage containers that many farmers use.

He also casts some of his stances on the tax code as farmer-friendly. He opposes the estate tax and has suggested suspending the capital gains tax for 10 years. "Penalizing families for selling their homes, farms or investments has had an overall negative effect on our economy," he said.

Fincher fits the profile of a social conservative. He is anti-abortion, defends gun rights and opposes same-sex marriage. He introduced a bill in the 112th Congress to require all welfare applicants and recipients to submit to random drug testing for illegal substances.

Fincher had no political experience heading into the 2010 election; he said he ran at the urging of a friend. "Spending was out of control and needed to be stopped," he said. When Tanner cleared out of the race, Fincher won a five-way primary and went on to defeat Democratic state Sen. Roy Herron with 59 percent of the vote. Fincher credited conservative Democrats with adding to his margin of victory.

He easily won re-election in 2012.

Key Votes

2012	
Extend a Social Security payroll tax cut and unemployment benefits	YES
Ease securities rules to expand small-business access to capital	YES
Extend for one year subsidized student loan interest rates financed by a cut in health care spending	NO
Cite Attorney General Eric H. Holder Jr. for contempt of Congress	YES
Create a visa program for foreign graduates in high-tech fields	YES
Extend most Bush-era income tax rates while allowing rates for top-bracket earners to rise (Jan. 1, 2013)	NO
2011	
Strike funding for F-35 alternative engine	YES
Prevent EPA from regulating greenhouse gas emissions to address climate change	YES
Extend certain provisions of Patriot Act for four years	YES
Declare opposition to use of ground troops in Libya	YES
Overhaul patent law	YES
Pass compromise debt limit increase plan and establish future spending limits	YES
Allow consideration of measures to implement three trade agreements	YES

CQ Vote Studies

	PARTY UNITY		PRESIDENTIAL SUPPORT	
	SUPPORT	OPPOSE	SUPPORT	OPPOSE
2012	97%	3%	15%	85%
2011	97%	3%	20%	80%

Interest Groups

	AFL-CIO	ADA	CCUS	ACU
2012	5%	10%	92%	92%
2011	0%	5%	100%	88%

Tennessee 8

West — Jackson, eastern Memphis suburbs

The mighty Mississippi River separates the 8th from Missouri and Arkansas to the west, and the Tennessee River forms the northeastern corner of the district, with swamp land, rolling hills and farmland crisscrossed by streams in between. Taking in all or part of 15 counties, including a few neighborhoods in eastern Memphis, the 8th is the second-largest district in the state. In Shelby County (shared with the 9th), the 8th picks up many of the Republican voters there — those largely suburban voters have helped the GOP gain strength in this once-Democratic region.

Linked to Memphis by Interstate 40, Jackson sits 85 miles to the northeast and serves as a retail, health care and education hub. A faucet manufacturer and a Kellogg's Pringle plant are two of the largest employers.

In the northwestern corner of the district, residents hope completion of Interstate 69 from the Kentucky border to Memphis through Dyersburg will add jobs to a region struggling with high unemployment rates. Goodyear's announcement that it would shutter its Union City plant in late 2011 was a blow. In Memphis, west of Interstate 240, FedEx's headquarters is in the 8th and access to major roads enables next-day shipping to more major metro areas than from any other U.S. city. International Paper also has its global headquarters in the district. This stretch also includes the city's Jewish neighborhoods.

Rural stretches of the 8th are home to top-producing cotton, corn and soybean fields. Prisons also employ many regional residents.

Population growth in the suburbs surrounding Memphis began decades ago as "white flight," but now also includes middle-class blacks. The black population has risen in Fayette and Tipton counties, and accounts for half of the residents in Haywood. Barack Obama easily won Haywood County in the 2012 presidential election, but GOP nominee Mitt Romney dominated the other parts of the district, taking 66 percent in the 8th overall.

Major Industry
Distribution, manufacturing, agriculture

Cities
Memphis (pt.), Jackson, Collierville, Germantown (pt.)

Notable
Paris hosts the World's Biggest Fish Fry each spring.

Rep. Steve Cohen (D)

Capitol Office
225-3265
cohen.house.gov
2404 Rayburn Bldg. 20515-4209; fax 225-5663

Committees
Judiciary
Transportation & Infrastructure

Residence
Memphis

Born
May 24, 1949; Memphis, Tenn.

Religion
Jewish

Family
Single; one child

Education
Vanderbilt U., B.A. 1971 (history); Memphis State U., J.D. 1973

Career
Lawyer

Political Highlights
Democratic nominee for Tenn. House, 1970; Tenn. Constitutional Convention, 1977-78 (vice president, 1977-78); Shelby County Commission 1978-80; Shelby County General Sessions Court, 1980; defeated for election to Shelby County General Sessions Court, 1981; Tenn. Senate, 1983-2006; sought Democratic nomination for governor, 1994; sought Democratic nomination for U.S. House, 1996

ELECTION RESULTS

2012 GENERAL		
Steve Cohen (D)	188,422	75.1%
George S. Flinn Jr. (R)	59,742	23.8%
2012 PRIMARY		
Steve Cohen (D)	49,585	89.3%
Tomeka Hart (D)	5,944	10.7%
2010 GENERAL		
Steve Cohen (D)	99,827	74.0%
Charlotte Bergmann (R)	33,879	25.1%

Previous Winning Percentages
2008 (88%); 2006 (60%)

Elected 2006; 4th term

The macro picture for Cohen is "what I consider being progressive, looking for justice and equity and fairness in the system." The micro picture is taking care of Memphis: "For a Jewish guy, I bring home the bacon."

Whatever the subject — and there are lots — Cohen participates as a feisty liberal with self-assured flair. A sports nut, he got early training in competitive rhetoric as "Mr. Commodore," the Vanderbilt University mascot; his best friends "have all been linguists, wordsmiths and people kind of on the edge," including rocker Warren Zevon and journalist Christopher Hitchens.

Cohen speaks often on the House floor, and in the 112th Congress (2011-12) topics included the GOP campaign against the 2010 health care law. He compared that effort to the work of Nazi propagandist Joseph Goebbels. He also objected to a Republican plan to give Congress final approval on new major regulations, saying it would create a "big dark hole out there in the universe where all rules and regulations would go and die and never be seen again."

His style strikes a chord with Memphis. Cohen represented the city for 24 years in the state Senate, with a number of legislative successes to his name. The most famous was his two-decade campaign to create a state lottery that funds educational scholarships. He hopes for legislative victories in the House, but he sees his 2006 election as an accomplishment in itself: At the time, it made him the only white lawmaker elected from a black-majority district.

"If people hear about that enough, they'll realize that Memphis is a city that is more tolerant than other cities ... and that has more racial reconciliation," he said. "It's not Barack Obama getting to be president, but it's a microcosm." Cohen was denied in his attempt to join the Congressional Black Caucus after his election, but in 2008 the House adopted his resolution offering blacks a formal apology for slavery and the Jim Crow era.

Cohen, who earned a living as a criminal defense and personal injury lawyer, pursues justice issues on the Judiciary Committee. He has been a strong supporter of the Legal Services Corporation, a congressionally created nonprofit providing civil legal assistance to those who cannot afford it. The LSC has "never had an adequate amount of funding," he said.

He speaks up on any legal issue where he believes minority populations bear a disproportionate share of negative consequences. Cohen lobbied New York Mayor Michael Bloomberg on changing the city's "stop and frisk" law; and he has introduced a "second chance" bill to facilitate expunging nonviolent offenses from criminal records after sentences have been served.

Other issues fit under his quest for "fairness in the system," but with a grab-bag feel. He advocates a major rethinking of marijuana laws, and he wants to make it easier to discharge student loans through bankruptcy. In 2010, Obama signed his bill to prevent "libel tourism" by banning the recognition of foreign defamation judgments that do not meet the standards of U.S. courts.

He is the top Democrat on the Regulatory Reform, Commercial and Antitrust Law Subcommittee, and early in the 113th Congress (2013-14) he used that position to promote Memphis International Airport. He says that the merger of Northwest and Delta airlines resulted in a steep reduction in service to his city, and at a hearing on the proposed merger of US Airways and American, he gave executives a sales pitch for bringing more flights to Memphis.

He also promotes the city from the Transportation and Infrastructure Committee. A two-year surface transportation law enacted in 2012 contained his provision to include the development of "aerotropolis" systems — comprehensively planned infrastructure surrounding airports — as a goal of a national policy on freight transportation. Memphis is a major distribution center that includes the global hub for FedEx. Cohen embraces the notion of coordinated multi-nodal transportation systems contributing to "livability," as well as the common liberal belief that "there's no better way to stimulate the economy than through transportation."

Cohen has tried to stimulate Memphis' economy by steering home a number of grants, including funds for the airport, hospitals and the University of Tennessee's biocontainment lab. He helped persuade the Commerce Department to establish a Minority Development Business Center in Memphis; it opened in 2012.

But he also takes an interest in global affairs. Cohen says the United States has a "moral obligation" to provide economic development opportunities and humanitarian aid in struggling nations; he pens occasional opinion columns on African affairs and sits on the Commission on Security and Cooperation in Europe, known as the Helsinki Commission.

Cohen's father was a pediatrician and his mother was a housewife; he was the youngest of three children. He showed an early interest in politics. Cohen remembers listening to the 1958 debates for the governor's race on the radio, and he snapped a photo of his idol, John F. Kennedy, during a 1960 campaign stop in Memphis (the picture is on his House office wall).

Sports were also a passion, although Cohen contracted polio at age 5 and still walks with a noticeable limp. He frequently cites as a formative moment the time Cuban baseball star Minnie Minoso felt uncomfortable directly handing him an autographed baseball, because he was white. Cohen visited Minoso and other minority players at the Lorraine Motel — where Martin Luther King Jr. would later be assassinated.

Cohen's family moved to Florida for most of his teen years, then came back to Memphis; he attended Vanderbilt, then received a law degree from Memphis State University. He ran for office at 21, losing a bid for the state House.

Seven years later he was elected vice president of the Tennessee Constitutional Convention, and in 1983 he was elected to the state Senate. In 1996, he challenged Harold E. Ford Jr. in the Democratic primary for the House seat opened up by the retirement of Ford's father. Cohen was noticeably upset by his loss — he delivered a tirade on Memphis politics to reporters — but continued on in the Senate, eventually coming to praise Ford's work.

Ford gave up his seat 10 years later to run for the Senate. Cohen survived a 15-candidate primary in which his race was a major issue, winning 31 percent of the vote. He coasted to victory that November and has had overwhelming victories over subsequent primary challengers.

Cohen has never been married, but in recent years he learned that he has a college-age daughter from a past relationship. They are now close.

Key Votes

2012	
Extend a Social Security payroll tax cut and unemployment benefits	YES
Ease securities rules to expand small-business access to capital	NO
Extend for one year subsidized student loan interest rates financed by a cut in health care spending	NO
Cite Attorney General Eric H. Holder Jr. for contempt of Congress	NO
Create a visa program for foreign graduates in high-tech fields	YES
Extend most Bush-era income tax rates while allowing rates for top-bracket earners to rise (Jan. 1, 2013)	YES
2011	
Strike funding for F-35 alternative engine	YES
Prevent EPA from regulating greenhouse gas emissions to address climate change	NO
Extend certain provisions of Patriot Act for four years	NO
Declare opposition to use of ground troops in Libya	NO
Overhaul patent law	YES
Pass compromise debt limit increase plan and establish future spending limits	NO
Allow consideration of measures to implement three trade agreements	NO

CQ Vote Studies

	PARTY UNITY		PRESIDENTIAL SUPPORT	
	SUPPORT	OPPOSE	SUPPORT	OPPOSE
2012	97%	3%	88%	12%
2011	96%	4%	85%	15%
2010	98%	2%	89%	11%
2009	98%	2%	96%	4%
2008	99%	1%	14%	86%

Interest Groups

	AFL-CIO	ADA	CCUS	ACU
2012	95%	95%	33%	0%
2011	100%	90%	25%	4%
2010	100%	100%	14%	0%
2009	95%	100%	33%	0%
2008	100%	100%	61%	0%

Tennessee 9

Memphis

The 9th District takes in most of the state's largest city, Memphis, the birthplace of the blues. A compact district in western Shelby County, its 504 square miles cover less than half the land area of the next smallest district. Black residents account for 64 percent of the population, making the 9th the state's only minority-majority district.

Memphis is the largest city along the Mississippi River between St. Louis and New Orleans, and its port, five major rail lines and access to interstates make it a logistics hub. The Memphis International Airport ranks second in the world for air cargo traffic and serves as the home base for FedEx shipping, the city's largest private employer. Delta Airlines has cut flights, however, and officials hope the addition of Southwest Airlines will boost revenue. AutoZone also has its headquarters in the 9th. Major employer St. Jude Children's Research Hospital is expanding, and the University of Tennessee's medical campus adds health care jobs downtown.

Downtown Memphis has been the focus of revitalization efforts for decades, however the recent recession left many new retail storefronts vacant along the main commercial stretch. Beale Street, the heart of the city's vibrant music scene, includes the historic Orpheum Theatre. Mud Island and Harbor Town offer shopping and tourist destinations, and Overton Park hosts the Memphis Zoo and the Memphis Brooks Museum of Art. The Lorraine Hotel, site of Martin Luther King Jr.'s assassination in 1968, is now the National Civil Rights Museum.

Reflecting the racial composition and black political power in the district, the 9th sent African-American representatives to the U.S. House for decades until 2007. It is a Democratic stronghold that gave Barack Obama his highest percentage statewide in the 2008 and 2012 presidential contests.

Major Industry
Transportation, distribution, health care, government, tourism

Military Bases
Naval Support Activity Mid-South, 1,550 military, 1,880 civilian

Cities
Memphis (pt.), Millington

Notable
Graceland was the home of Elvis Presley.

TEXAS

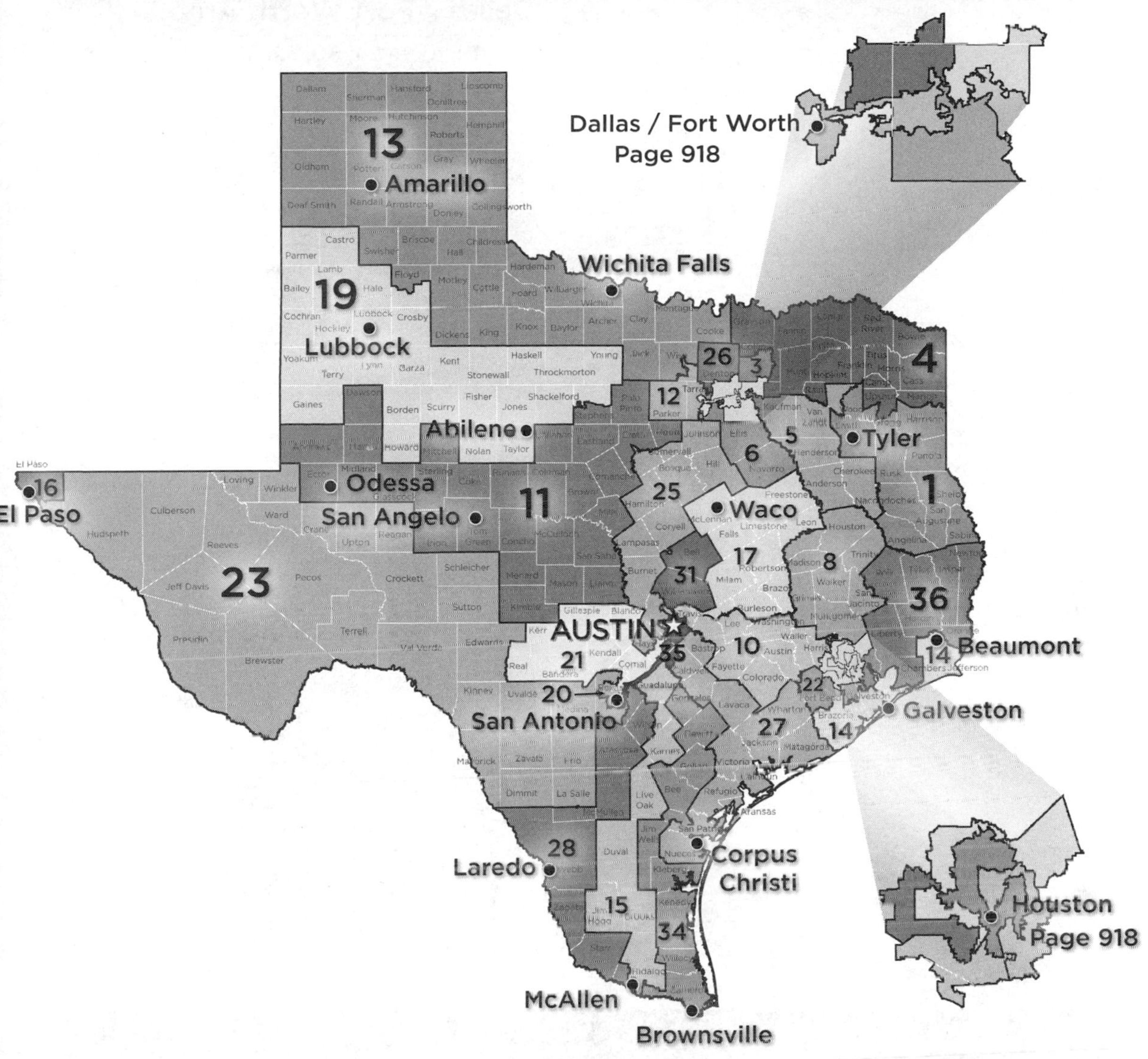

Statistics by District

District	2012 Vote for President: Obama	2012 Vote for President: Romney	2008 Vote for President: Obama	2008 Vote for President: McCain	Black	Asian	Hispanic	Median Income	Over 64	Under 20	College Education	Rural	Sq. Miles
1	27%	72%	30%	69%	18%	1%	16%	$41,834	14%	29%	20%	46%	7,859
2	36	63	37	62	13	6	30	69,181	9	29	38	2	309
3	34	64	38	62	8	13	15	83,724	8	30	51	3	481
4	25	74	29	70	11	1	13	46,846	15	28	20	53	10,123
5	34	65	37	62	14	2	26	42,887	12	30	18	34	5,044
6	41	58	42	57	19	5	23	55,788	9	31	27	12	2,148
7	39	60	41	59	12	10	31	63,282	9	28	46	0	162
8	22	77	26	73	8	2	20	56,919	12	29	26	35	6,054
9	78	21	76	23	39	9	37	41,354	8	30	23	0	166
10	39	59	43	56	10	5	26	58,080	11	29	35	25	5,071

Dallas / Fort Worth Area

Districts 24, 30, 32, 33

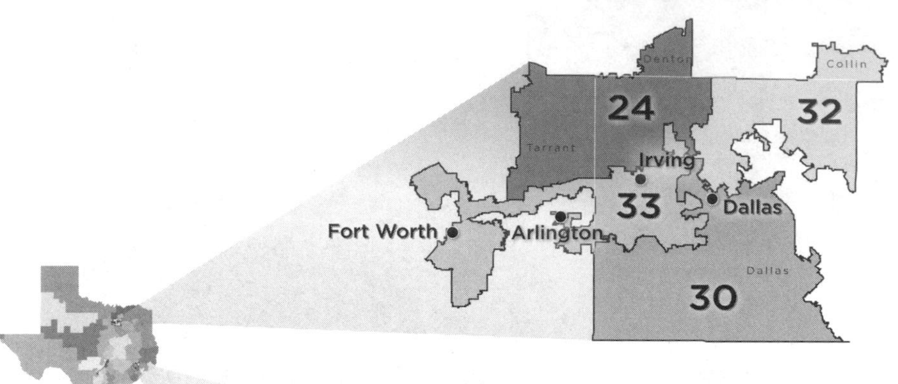

Houston Area

Districts 2, 7, 9, 18, 29

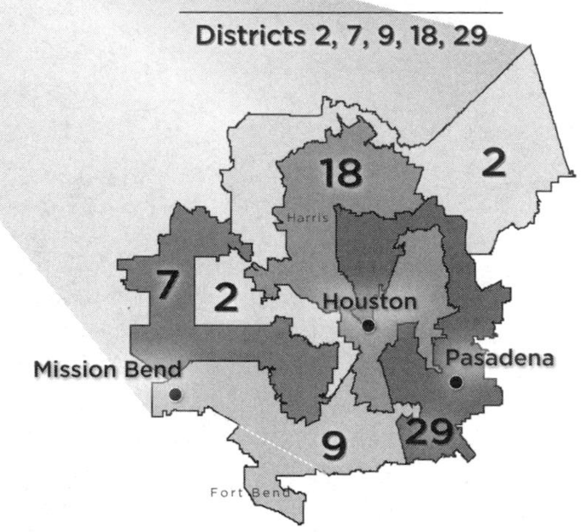

Statistics by District

District	2012 Vote for President Obama	2012 Vote for President Romney	2008 Vote for President Obama	2008 Vote for President McCain	Black	Asian	Hispanic	Median Income	Over 64	Under 20	College Education	Rural	Sq. Miles
11	20%	79%	23%	76%	4%	1%	34%	$44,607	15%	28%	19%	33%	27,832
12	32	67	36	64	8	3	21	56,155	11	28	28	13	1,441
13	19	80	22	77	6	2	25	45,739	14	29	20	33	38,349
14	39	59	42	57	21	3	23	50,178	12	28	22	15	2,441
15	57	42	57	42	2	1	80	37,000	10	35	19	16	7,804
16	64	35	65	35	4	1	79	41,434	11	32	23	2	710
17	38	60	41	58	13	4	23	41,989	11	28	27	27	7,651
18	76	23	77	23	39	4	41	37,079	8	31	19	<1	235
19	25	74	28	71	6	1	35	41,186	13	29	21	27	25,836
20	59	40	58	41	5	3	66	42,934	10	31	23	<1	200
21	38	60	42	57	3	3	28	57,219	13	24	44	22	5,921
22	37	62	39	61	12	17	25	81,392	8	31	39	7	1,033
23	48	51	50	49	2	1	71	46,232	11	33	21	26	58,059
24	38	60	41	59	11	10	24	59,229	9	26	43	<1	263

Gov. Rick Perry (R)

First elected: 2002; assumed office Dec. 21, 2000, following the resignation of George W. Bush, R, to become president

Length of term: 4 years

Term expires: 1/15

Salary: $150,000

Phone: (512) 463-2000

Residence: Austin

Born: March 4, 1950; Paint Creek, Texas

Religion: Methodist

Family: Wife, Anita Perry; two children

Education: Texas A&M U., B.S. 1972 (animal science)

Military service: Air Force, 1972-77

Career: Farmer; rancher

Political highlights: Texas House, 1984-90; Texas department of agriculture commissioner, 1990-98; lieutenant governor, 1999-2000

ELECTION RESULTS

2010 GENERAL

Rick Perry (R)	2,737,481	55.0%
Bill White (D)	2,106,395	42.3%
Kathie Glass (LIBERT)	109,211	2.2%

Lt. Gov. David Dewhurst (R)

First elected: 2002

Length of term: 4 years

Term expires: 1/15

Salary: $7,200

Phone: (512) 463-0001

LEGISLATURE

Legislature: January-May in odd-numbered years

Senate: 31 members, 4-year terms (to accommodate redistricting, 16 seats will have serve 2-year terms elegible for re-election in 2014.)

2013 ratios: 19 D, 12 R; 24 men, 7 women

Salary: $7,200

Phone: (512) 463-0100

House: 150 members, 2-year terms

2013 ratios: 95 R, 55 D; 119 men, 31 women

Salary: $7,200

Phone: (512) 463-0845

TERM LIMITS

Governor: No

Senate: No

House: No

URBAN STATISTICS

CITY	POPULATION
Houston	2,099,451
San Antonio	1,327,407
Dallas	1,197,816
Austin	790,390
Fort Worth	741,206

REGISTERED VOTERS

Voters do not register by party.

POPULATION

2010 population	25,145,561
2000 population	20,851,820
1990 population	16,986,510
Percent change (2000-2010)	+20.6%
Rank among states (2010)	2
Median age	33.0
Born in state	60.9%
Foreign born	15.0%
Violent crime rate	491/100,000
Poverty level	17.2%
Federal workers	244,856
Military	131,548

ELECTIONS

STATE ELECTION OFFICIAL
(512) 463-5650

DEMOCRATIC PARTY
(512) 478-9800

REPUBLICAN PARTY
(512) 477-9821

MISCELLANEOUS

Web: www.texas.gov

Capital: Austin

U.S. CONGRESS

Senate: 2 Republicans

House: 24 Republicans, 12 Democrats

STATISTICS BY DISTRICT

District	2012 Vote for President: Obama	2012 Vote for President: Romney	2008 Vote for President: Obama	2008 Vote for President: McCain	Black	Asian	Hispanic	Median Income	Over 64	Under 20	College Education	Rural	Sq. Miles
25	38%	60%	43%	56%	8%	3%	17%	$57,538	12%	29%	36%	36%	7,621
26	31	68	35	64	7	5	16	75,069	8	32	41	7	907
27	38	61	40	59	5	1	51	45,011	14	29	19	28	9,128
28	60	39	58	41	4	1	78	39,603	10	36	16	20	9,379
29	66	33	62	37	10	2	76	36,490	7	35	9	<1	187
30	80	20	79	21	45	2	36	40,107	9	31	20	1	356
31	38	60	43	56	11	4	23	58,960	9	30	33	14	2,154
32	41	57	44	55	11	7	28	61,356	10	29	40	<1	186
33	72	27	69	31	16	3	65	32,316	7	35	8	<1	212
34	61	38	60	39	1	1	83	32,333	12	34	13	18	8,190
35	63	35	63	36	10	2	64	36,792	8	31	15	4	594
36	26	73	30	70	10	2	23	50,790	12	29	18	35	7,126
STATE	**41**	**57**	**44**	**56**	**12**	**4**	**38**	**49,392**	**11**	**30**	**26**	**17**	**261,232**
U.S.	**51**	**47**	**53**	**46**	**12**	**5**	**17**	**50,052**	**13**	**27**	**29**	**21**	**3,531,905**

Sen. John Cornyn (R)

Capitol Office
224-2934
cornyn.senate.gov
517 Hart Bldg. 20510-4302; fax 228-2856

Committees
Finance
Judiciary

Residence
Austin

Born
Feb. 2, 1952; Houston, Texas

Religion
Christian non-denominational

Family
Wife, Sandy Cornyn; two children

Education
Trinity U., B.A. 1973 (journalism); St. Mary's U. (Texas), J.D. 1977; U. of Virginia, LL.M. 1995

Career
Lawyer; real estate agent

Political Highlights
Texas District Court judge, 1985-91; Texas Supreme Court, 1991-97; Texas attorney general, 1999-2002

ELECTION RESULTS

2008 GENERAL		
John Cornyn (R)	4,337,469	54.8%
Richard "Rick" Noriega (D)	3,389,365	42.8%
Yvonne Schick (LIBERT)	185,241	2.3%
2008 PRIMARY		
John Cornyn (R)	997,216	81.5%
Larry Kilgore (R)	226,649	18.5%

Previous Winning Percentages
2002 (55%)

Elected 2002; 2nd term

Cornyn is the No. 2 Republican in the Senate, though his ascent to the post of party whip was a little less triumphant than the party would have liked. A respected conservative, his long legal career positions him as an authority on law-and-order issues before Congress.

Cornyn secured his leadership job after a bittersweet year in 2012. He had served as chairman of the National Republican Senatorial Committee since 2009, making him the point man for efforts to regain the Senate majority. Republicans picked up seven seats in the 2010 elections, and Cornyn predicted they would get over the hump in 2012.

Instead, it was a painful cycle, with the GOP losing two seats. Democrats won most of the competitive races. In the months preceding the election, Cornyn faced criticism from colleagues such as Jim DeMint of South Carolina, who felt that Cornyn should have backed more-conservative candidates. (DeMint resigned to lead a conservative think tank.)

The results were sour enough that some people thought they might undo Cornyn's whip campaign — which had lasted almost two years, back to when the previous whip, Jon Kyl of Arizona, announced that he would retire at the end of the 112th Congress (2011-12). Cornyn noted that Republicans also lost the presidential race and that electoral woes weren't confined to any particular wing of the party. "We have a period of reflection and recalibration ahead," he said. No challenger materialized.

Cornyn studied the techniques of past whips, and as the 113th Congress (2013-14) began, he started road-testing his approach to the job. He is more media-friendly than Kyl or Minority Leader Mitch McConnell — his amiable personality and ability to turn a phrase, coupled with his NRSC job, made him a frequent guest on cable news shows throughout the 2012 election cycle. In the past, Cornyn was less harsh than many of his colleagues when denouncing Democratic plans — he frequently expresses a desire to work with Democrats on ideas for national security and the economy. But in early 2013, he made some tough criticisms of Democratic positions and strategies on gun control, the national debt and border security.

Cornyn does have a conservative voting record, and he was also a critic of President Barack Obama's plans during deficit reduction negotiations late in the 112th Congress. "Demanding higher taxes, more stimulus, no spending cuts, and no plan to preserve and protect Social Security and Medicare will not solve our fiscal crisis; it will make the crisis much worse," he said. He voted for a package that made the George W. Bush-era tax cuts permanent for income levels below $400,000 — but made sure to signal his displeasure with rate hikes on the wealthy.

In 2013, his proposal for a balanced-budget amendment to the Constitution was co-sponsored by all 44 other Senate Republicans. It would also require supermajorities to raise taxes or the debt limit and cap federal spending at 18 percent of gross domestic product. He told the Houston Chronicle in January that a government shutdown might be necessary to squeeze more spending cuts out of the Obama administration.

Cornyn addresses economic concerns as a member of the Finance Committee. He sits on its panels for taxation and health care, and he is the ranking member of the Energy, Natural Resources and Infrastructure Subcommittee.

He also sits on the Judiciary Committee and is the top Republican on its immigration policy panel. He strongly opposes the notion of an immigration overhaul that would provide a pathway to citizenship for illegal immigrants. In the 109th Congress (2005-06), he opposed Bush's attempt to engineer an immigration overhaul. (However, he is a good friend of Bush.) In 2010, he was instrumental in defeating a Democrat-backed measure to provide a path to legalization for young adults brought illegally to the United States as children, if they attended college or joined the U.S. military and met other requirements.

Nonetheless, Cornyn says he wants to move forward with comprehensively changing the immigration system. In the early months of the 113th Congress, he has continued to emphasize that any overhaul must start with border security and a crackdown on illegal immigrants.

He also highlights proposals to improve visa programs. In 2012, he sponsored legislation to issue 50,000 new green cards to skilled immigrants. Several other Republicans took up the cause, but House-Senate negotiations on a similar bill broke down. While Cornyn says immigration "can be a very complex topic, with strong feelings on all sides," he called the proposal "a sweet spot where Republicans and Democrats alike can agree that we should not suffer the brain drain that we currently have."

Cornyn is a former district court judge, state Supreme Court judge and Texas attorney general. He is a staunch critic of Fast and Furious, the Justice Department's botched gun-walking operation meant to build cases against drug cartels. He called on Attorney General Eric H. Holder Jr. to resign over his department's handling of the case. "We need an attorney general who will put justice before politics," he wrote in a 2012 editorial.

Cornyn is socially conservative. In the 108th Congress (2003-04), he chaired the Judiciary Subcommittee on the Constitution, and he pushed unsuccessfully for proposed constitutional amendments banning same-sex marriage and flag burning.

On becoming the whip, Cornyn relinquished seats on the Budget and Armed Services committees. He has called for a robust Pentagon budget, particularly regarding weapons spending. He opposed Senate approval of a strategic arms reduction treaty with Russia in December 2010. He also opposed Obama's original plan to relocate Guantánamo Bay detainees to U.S. prisons. In 2005, he was one of just nine senators — all Republicans — to vote against an amendment banning cruel, inhumane or degrading treatment of prisoners captured in the fight against terrorism.

Cornyn plays up his ties to Texas, often striding through the Senate in cowboy boots. He's also not afraid to poke fun at himself. In his 2008 re-election campaign, he recorded a video as cowboy-hatted, fringe-jacketed "Big Bad John," a take on the 1960s hit song of the same name. The video became popular on YouTube; it included the lyrics, "He rose to the top in just one term, kept Texas in power, made lesser states squirm."

Cornyn is the son of a World War II B-17 pilot. His family eventually settled in San Antonio, where his father became an Air Force pathologist. A wrestler in high school and college, Cornyn majored in journalism at Texas' Trinity University. He waited tables while earning his real estate license. When that career faltered in a sagging economy, he went to law school. He later practiced in San Antonio, specializing in defending doctors against medical malpractice suits.

In 1984, some Republican friends — looking to crack the Democrats' hold on Texas judicial elections — asked him to run for a state district court seat. He did, and he won. Six years later, he was elected to the state Supreme Court. In 1998, he won a bruising race to be attorney general against Democrat Jim Mattox.

When Republican Sen. Phil Gramm announced his retirement in 2002, Cornyn ran for the seat and won a primary against four little-known opponents. In the November race against former Dallas Mayor Ron Kirk, Cornyn ran on his loyalty to Bush and won with around 55 percent of the vote. Six years later he beat state Rep. Richard "Rick" Noriega, again with 55 percent.

Key Votes

2012	
Prohibit health insurance plans from denying coverage based on the sponsor's religious beliefs	NO
Require approval of the Keystone XL oil pipeline	YES
Ease securities rules to expand small-business access to capital	YES
Reauthorize farm and nutrition programs for five years	NO
Limit debate on a bill that would create private-sector cybersecurity standards	NO
Consent to ratification of a treaty setting global standard for the treatment of people with disabilities	NO
Provide $60.4 billion in disaster relief following Superstorm Sandy	NO
Extend most Bush-era income tax rates while allowing rates for top-bracket earners to rise (Jan. 1, 2013)	YES
2011	
Prevent EPA from regulating greenhouse gas emissions to address climate change	YES
Extend certain provisions of Patriot Act for four years	YES
Clear compromise debt limit increase plan and establish future spending limits	YES
Overhaul patent law	YES
Implement Colombia free trade agreement	YES
Limit debate on confirmation of Caitlin J. Halligan to D.C. Circuit Court of Appeals	NO
Extend payroll tax cut and unemployment benefits for two months	YES

CQ Vote Studies

	PARTY UNITY		PRESIDENTIAL SUPPORT	
	SUPPORT	OPPOSE	SUPPORT	OPPOSE
2012	98%	2%	41%	59%
2011	96%	4%	60%	40%
2010	99%	1%	38%	62%
2009	96%	4%	45%	55%
2008	97%	3%	73%	27%
2007	98%	2%	91%	9%
2006	97%	3%	91%	9%
2005	95%	5%	98%	2%
2004	97%	3%	96%	4%
2003	99%	1%	98%	2%

Interest Groups

	AFL-CIO	ADA	CCUS	ACU
2012	0%	0%	75%	88%
2011	16%	10%	100%	90%
2010	6%	0%	100%	100%
2009	17%	5%	71%	100%
2008	11%	20%	100%	79%
2007	0%	15%	80%	96%
2006	13%	0%	83%	96%
2005	14%	10%	89%	96%
2004	8%	5%	100%	100%
2003	0%	10%	100%	85%

Sen. Ted Cruz (R)

Capitol Office
224-5922
cruz.senate.gov
B40B Dirksen Bldg. 20510-4304; fax 228-0755

Committees
Armed Services
Commerce, Science & Transportation
Judiciary
Rules & Administration
Special Aging

Residence
Houston

Born
Dec. 22, 1970; Calgary, Canada

Religion
Baptist

Family
Wife, Heidi Cruz; two children

Education
Princeton U., A.B. 1992 (public and international affairs); Harvard U., J.D. 1995

Career
Lawyer; state solicitor general; U.S. Justice Department official; Federal Trade Commission policy director; presidential campaign aide

Political Highlights
No previous office

ELECTION RESULTS

2012 GENERAL		
Ted Cruz (R)	4,440,137	56.5%
Paul Sadler (D)	3,194,927	40.6%
John Jay Myers (LIBERT)	162,354	2.1%
2012 PRIMARY RUNOFF		
Ted Cruz (R)	631,812	56.8%
David Dewhurst (R)	480,126	43.2%

Elected 2012; 1st term

Cruz has already made his mark as an outspoken, stalwart constitutionalist — and irritated some colleagues in doing so. He has called fellow senators "squishes," filibustered alongside Kentucky Republican Rand Paul and stoked speculation about a possible presidential campaign. No other senator in recent memory has made such a strong first impression so quickly.

The son of a Cuban immigrant, Cruz won election with the support of the tea party movement. After finishing second in a nine-person GOP primary, he prevailed over Texas' lieutenant governor in a runoff.

Cruz had never been on a ballot before, but he was reputed among Republicans as having a sharp legal mind. He was Texas' first Hispanic solicitor general and the youngest person to hold that office in any state. He was also the first Hispanic clerk for the chief justice of the United States. Cruz was a pallbearer at the funeral of his former boss, William H. Rehnquist. He now holds a seat on the Judiciary Committee.

Cruz says there is a fundamental disconnect in America that he would like to bridge. "At the end of the day, there are sort of twin worlds," he said. "There is the world of Washington and the Beltway, and then there's the rest of the country. The spectrum in Washington — you've got career politicians in both parties that have been going along to get along a long, long time. And that's how we've gotten a national debt of $16 trillion."

Bridge-building goals aside, Cruz has become arguably the most outspoken freshman senator. As a member of the Armed Services Committee, he participated in the confirmation process for Defense Secretary Chuck Hagel in February 2013; he pressed Hagel to reveal the origins of various speaking fees, suggesting Hagel might have been paid by North Korea. Florida Democrat Bill Nelson — usually a reserved lawmaker — lectured Cruz on "comity and civility" in the committee, accusing the Texan of having "impugned the patriotism of the nominee."

Several weeks later on the Judiciary Committee, Cruz had a run-in with California Democrat Dianne Feinstein, the sponsor of a bill to ban "assault" weapons. Cruz, who strongly opposes proscriptions of gun rights, asked if she supported limiting First Amendment protections to a select list of books. "I'm not a sixth-grader," Feinstein snapped. " I've been on this committee for 20 years. I was a mayor for nine years. ... I've looked at bodies that have been shot with these weapons."

And Cruz was one of several GOP senators who contributed to Paul's "talking filibuster" in March 2013. They spoke for 13 hours against the nomination of John O. Brennan for CIA director, raising questions about the constitutionality of government use of drones to kill Americans on U.S. soil. Cruz addressed the legal issues surrounding their concerns and read supportive reaction from Twitter on the floor.

Cruz's criticism of his colleagues is pointed. He called some Republicans "squishes" at a FreedomWorks conference in Texas when discussing gun control. His colleagues have returned the name-calling: Arizona Republican John McCain referred to Cruz and Paul as "wacko birds" in an interview with the Huffington Post — although he later apologized.

Cruz has also won admirers with his passionate politics. Some conservatives have posited that criticism of Cruz is overblown — there are liberal news outlets that delight in disparaging politicians with tea party connections. Minority Leader Mitch McConnell named Cruz the vice chairman for grassroots outreach for the National Republican Senatorial Committee, to help the party recruit candidates who can avoid damaging battles in primary elections.

Early in his Senate career, Cruz hasn't wavered from conservative positions. The first bill he introduced was to repeal the 2010 health care overhaul. He voted against the confirmation of Hagel, and of Secretary of State John Kerry. He opposed a reauthorization of federal programs to combat domestic violence and assist its victims, on the grounds that "stopping and punishing violent criminals is primarily a state responsibility," his office said. He objected to a run-of-the-mill Senate resolution commemorating Multiple Sclerosis Awareness Week because, according to his office, he didn't have time to read it.

During an all-night voting session on a fiscal 2014 budget resolution, Cruz sponsored a point of order against any legislation that would provide taxpayer funds to the United Nations while any member nation forces citizens or residents of that nation to undergo involuntary abortions. The proposal led to a heated confrontation with Louisiana Democrat Mary L. Landrieu on the Senate floor.

Cruz's feelings about government stem in part from his family's history in Cuba. His father fought alongside Fidel Castro's rebels, but he was eventually imprisoned and beaten. He escaped thanks to a bribe. Cruz doesn't talk much about his father's experience, but gleaned some details from relatives. "He was a guerrilla, throwing Molotov cocktails and blowing up buildings," Cruz told the Austin American Statesman in 2006. In 1957, Cruz's father emigrated from Cuba to Austin with only $100 sewn into his underwear.

His father washed dishes to work his way through the University of Texas; his mother was the first in her family to attend college. "One of the most wonderful gifts a child can be given is to be the child of an immigrant," Cruz told the Statesman. "You have a profound appreciation for the miracle of opportunity in this country."

Cruz was born in Calgary and grew up in Houston. He expressed an early interest in law and politics, and he had a patron of sorts in Rolland Storey, a retired public relations executive who set up an education center to teach free-market economic theory. One of Storey's collaborators told the Dallas Morning News how Cruz memorized an outline of the Constitution and recited it for local civic clubs.

He was on the debate team at Princeton University, at one point winning an award for speaker of the year. He graduated Harvard Law School and edited the Harvard Law Review.

In 2000, he collected donations for Gov. George W. Bush's presidential campaign. He met a top Bush aide, Joshua B. Bolten, at a fundraiser in 1999. "He asked me what this campaign needed a lawyer for, and I started listing all of these policy concerns," Cruz told the Statesman. "The next thing I know, he asked me to join the campaign."

He ended up doing legal work to defend Bush's controversial win in Florida that year. It led to several jobs within the administration — and caught the attention of his eventual mentor, Texas Attorney General Greg Abbot. Cruz returned to Texas and served as solicitor general of Texas.

Cruz left that job in 2008 for a Houston law firm. He was considering a run for the Senate in 2012, and when Republican incumbent Kay Bailey Hutchison announced her retirement in January 2011, he entered the race within days. Initial polls put his support near 2 percent, but he climbed his way up and eventually defeated Lt. Gov. David Dewhurst. Numerous national conservative groups and icons endorsed him, including the Club for Growth and former Alaska Gov. Sarah Palin. He easily won the general election.

In the spring of 2013, National Review reported Cruz was thinking about a presidential bid — and Cruz responded by not denying the rumors on his Facebook page. "It is a continued source of amazement that the simple fact that I am working hard with like-minded Senators to keep my promise is seen as newsworthy and cause for wild speculation," he wrote.

Rep. Louie Gohmert (R)

Capitol Office
225-3035
gohmert.house.gov
2243 Rayburn Bldg. 20515-4301; fax 226-1230

Committees
Judiciary
Natural Resources

Residence
Tyler

Born
Aug. 18, 1953; Pittsburg, Texas

Religion
Baptist

Family
Wife, Kathy Gohmert; three children

Education
Texas A&M U., B.A. 1975 (history); Baylor U., J.D. 1977

Military
Army, 1978-82

Career
Lawyer; state prosecutor

Political Highlights
Smith County District Court judge, 1993-2002; Texas Court of Appeals chief justice, 2002-03

ELECTION RESULTS

2012 GENERAL		
Louie Gohmert (R)	178,322	71.4%
Shirley J. McKellar (D)	67,222	26.9%
Clark Patterson (LIBERT)	4,114	1.6%
2012 PRIMARY		
Louie Gohmert (R)		unopposed
2010 GENERAL		
Louie Gohmert (R)	129,398	89.7%
Charles Parkes (LIBERT)	14,811	10.3%

Previous Winning Percentages
2008 (88%); 2006 (68%); 2004 (61%)

Elected 2004; 5th term

Gohmert has a penchant for stirring controversy, presenting provocative proposals in a disarming drawl. He shows no fear of giving offense, employing a mix of conservative outrage and sarcasm to promote his beliefs.

Each year, Gohmert adds to his list of media kerfuffles. In 2010, he argued with CNN host Anderson Cooper over a theory that terrorist networks were sending women to the United States to give birth, so that their children could use their citizenship to later return to attack the country.

After the FBI briefed lawmakers on the January 2011 shooting that killed six and left Arizona Democratic Rep. Gabrielle Giffords seriously wounded, Gohmert complained that politics might have inhibited the bureau from providing him details on the alleged shooter. "It may be if the things he was reading, that he's a liberal, hates the flag, supports Marx, if those type of things turn out to be true, then it may be embarrassing to the current administration's constituents," he said.

And in October 2012, Gohmert was criticized for suggesting that policies that contradict Biblical teachings are worse than slavery. "Slavery was a blot on our existence, but the trouble is we have never as an entire nation overall been so far away from God's teaching," he said. A few weeks later, he was the only person to vote against a bill to remove the term "lunatic" from federal laws. "Not only should we not eliminate the word ... when the most pressing issue of the day is saving our country from bankruptcy, we should use the word to describe the people who want to continue with business as usual in Washington," he said. President Barack Obama signed the bill.

Gohmert has strained the patience of both Republicans and Democrats on occasion, but he makes no apologies for his candor, saying he is comfortable speaking his mind after serving 10 years as a trial judge. "As a judge, you have to look people in the eye and make decisions," he says. "Former judges don't seem to have a problem having the courage to stand up and say what we believe is right."

Gohmert admires bluntness among his colleagues. He joined Minnesota Republican Michele Bachmann in a widely criticized letter that sought to expose alleged allies of the Muslim Brotherhood within the Obama administration. "If she were more willing to compromise principles," Gohmert said of Bachmann, "she'd probably be a chairman of a subcommittee, but she's not a chairman of a subcommittee because she stands on principle."

In the 112th Congress (2011-12), votes on the deficit and spending were opportunities for Gohmert to stick to his principles. He was one of the most fiscally conservative Republicans, opposing every major enacted spending bill, usually because they weren't constraining enough. He was one of four House Republicans to vote against a 2011 resolution proposing a balanced-budget amendment to the Constitution, because he wanted a version that included spending caps. Gohmert is an advocate of "zero baseline" budgeting, in which every agency must justify its entire budget every year.

Gohmert went out on a conservative limb late in 2012. Republicans had a meeting to nominate their choice for speaker of the House for the 113th Congress (2013-14), and Gohmert was the only person to suggest someone other than John A. Boehner of Ohio. He proposed former Speaker Newt Gingrich. (The speaker does not have to be a member of the House.) No one seconded Gohmert's motion.

Gohmert sits on the Natural Resources Committee and pushes for more domestic energy production — oil and gas are among the major industries in his district. He has proposed that states should have regulatory control over hydraulic fracturing on federal lands within their borders. That practice, opposed by many environmentalists, involves the injection of high-pressure fluids into the ground to free up pockets of oil and natural gas.

He opposed a 2009 bill to create a cap-and-trade system for greenhouse gas emissions, and he supports blocking the EPA from regulating such gases in any effort to address climate change.

Gohmert uses his seat on the Judiciary Committee to advance a socially conservative agenda. He accused Obama of a "breach of his oath of office" over a policy to prioritize which illegal immigrants are subject to deportation. In 2009, he opposed an expansion of federal laws on hate crimes, saying in committee that "every human being in the world deserves to be equally protected, no matter who they are or who they go to bed with." Writing on the Human Events website, he called the bill a "great leap forward on the 'gay rights' agenda" and said that its vague definition of "sexual orientation" could one day force legal acceptance of orientation "toward children, or toward animals, or corpses, or shoes, or whatever."

Gohmert grew up in Mount Pleasant, an East Texas town where his father worked as an architect and his mother taught English. He hauled hay, pumped gas and worked at a construction site as a youth. He first won elective office as class president of his junior high school. He followed his father in attending Texas A&M University, where he was given an ROTC scholarship.

Gohmert earned a degree from Baylor University's law school, then worked as a state assistant district attorney while waiting for his call to active military duty. He served four years as an Army lawyer at Fort Benning, Ga.

Returning to Texas in 1982, he worked as a civil litigator. His mother's death in 1991 prompted him to consider her advice to become a judge. He ran in 1992 after he was unable to find anyone willing to challenge the Smith County District Court incumbent. He served for the next 10 years, then was appointed by GOP Gov. Rick Perry to the Texas Court of Appeals.

Gohmert has served as a deacon and still teaches Sunday school at a Baptist church in Texas. He credits snagging his wife to still having hair when they met. He misses Mexican food and barbecue when he's in Washington and hosts annual bipartisan barbecues on Capitol Hill; his closely guarded rib rub recipe is said to be a variation of one used by President Lyndon B. Johnson.

After House Majority Leader Tom DeLay orchestrated a GOP-dominated Texas redistricting plan, Gohmert unseated four-term Democratic Rep. Max Sandlin in 2004 by almost 24 points. Gohmert easily won again in 2006.

Democrats didn't field a candidate against him in 2008 or 2010. In 2012, Gohmert won with more than 70 percent of the vote over Democrat Shirley J. McKellar.

Key Votes

2012	
Extend a Social Security payroll tax cut and unemployment benefits	NO
Ease securities rules to expand small-business access to capital	YES
Extend for one year subsidized student loan interest rates financed by a cut in health care spending	YES
Cite Attorney General Eric H. Holder Jr. for contempt of Congress	YES
Create a visa program for foreign graduates in high-tech fields	YES
Extend most Bush-era income tax rates while allowing rates for top-bracket earners to rise (Jan. 1, 2013)	NO
2011	
Strike funding for F-35 alternative engine	YES
Prevent EPA from regulating greenhouse gas emissions to address climate change	YES
Extend certain provisions of Patriot Act for four years	YES
Declare opposition to use of ground troops in Libya	NO
Overhaul patent law	NO
Pass compromise debt limit increase plan and establish future spending limits	NO
Allow consideration of measures to implement three trade agreements	YES

CQ Vote Studies

	PARTY UNITY		PRESIDENTIAL SUPPORT	
	SUPPORT	OPPOSE	SUPPORT	OPPOSE
2012	94%	6%	22%	78%
2011	95%	5%	16%	84%
2010	95%	5%	29%	71%
2009	95%	5%	15%	85%
2008	92%	8%	63%	37%

Interest Groups

	AFL-CIO	ADA	CCUS	ACU
2012	11%	20%	72%	96%
2011	7%	10%	88%	92%
2010	0%	5%	75%	96%
2009	5%	0%	79%	100%
2008	7%	10%	75%	96%

Texas 1

Northeast — Tyler, Longview

The 1st District covers much of East Texas' Pineywoods region, an area with prodigious natural-gas and oil reserves under its forested swamplands. The resource-rich district borders Louisiana and includes 10 full counties and portions of two others.

Timber is the prominent industry in most counties of the 1st and has dominated the region's commerce since the late 1800s, coinciding with development of rail lines. Recently, increased demand for lumber from China, as well as a modest recovery of the U.S. housing market, has helped revive a declining industry. The Angeline and Sabine national forests along the district's southern border fared relatively well during the state's severe drought compared with its western stretches.

Natural-gas wells have proliferated in Harrison, Panola, Shelby and San Augustine counties as energy companies attempt to tap Haynesville and Bossier shale formations. With a population under 10,000, Carthage has named itself the Gas Capital of the United States.

Longview, in Gregg and western Harrison counties, was the starting point for the massive overland Big Inch oil pipeline during World War II before being converted to a natural-gas pipeline. Today the city is a hub for the Union Pacific railroad and an industrial center for chemicals and heavy equipment. It is also home to East Texas Regional Airport, a designated foreign-trade zone.

The district's largest city is Tyler, which has emerged as a health care center for the region, with multiple hospitals and health clinics, and is the headquarters for Brookshire grocery store chain.

Many communities here tout their elder services, to attract more of Texas' retiree population, and 14 percent of the district's population is older than 65. The population of this Republican district is about 60 percent white, with black and Hispanic populations at 18 and 16 percent, respectively.

Major Industry
Timber, oil and gas, manufacturing, agriculture

Cities
Tyler, Longview, Lufkin, Nacogdoches

Notable
Tyler boasts the nation's largest public rose garden, and each October visitors flock to the city's Texas Rose Festival.

Rep. Ted Poe (R)

Capitol Office
225-6565
poe.house.gov
2412 Rayburn Bldg. 20515-4302; fax 225-5547

Committees
Foreign Affairs
(Terrorism, Nonproliferation & Trade - Chairman)
Judiciary

Residence
Humble

Born
Sept. 10, 1948; Temple, Texas

Religion
Church of Christ

Family
Wife, Carol Poe; four children

Education
Abilene Christian College, B.A. 1970 (political science); U. of Houston, J.D. 1973

Military
Air Force Reserve, 1970-76

Career
County prosecutor; college instructor

Political Highlights
Harris County District Court judge, 1981-2003

ELECTION RESULTS

2012 GENERAL		
Ted Poe (R)	159,664	64.8%
Jim Dougherty (D)	80,512	32.7%
Kenneth Duncan (LIBERT)	4,140	1.7%
2012 PRIMARY		
Ted Poe (R)		unopposed
2010 GENERAL		
Ted Poe (R)	130,020	88.6%
David W. Smith (LIBERT)	16,711	11.4%

Previous Winning Percentages
2008 (89%); 2006 (66%); 2004 (56%)

Elected 2004; 5th term

Nearly every morning Congress is in session, Poe's face greets C-SPAN viewers when the House opens for debate. He likes to say he is a conservative first and a Republican second; he signs off his deliveries with Texas-sized confidence: "And that's just the way it is."

His seeming omnipresence at the microphone has earned a write-up in The New York Times. When C-SPAN tallied the number of days in the 110th, 111th and 112th Congresses (2007-12) that lawmakers appeared on the House floor, Poe, a former judge and prosecutor, came out on top. His only close rival has been a fellow Texan, Democrat Sheila Jackson Lee.

The conservative content of Poe's speeches is never in doubt. The issues vary, but they often relate to Texas; immigration and border control are frequent topics.

Poe is a member of the Judiciary Subcommittee on Immigration and Border Security, and in the 113th Congress (2013-14) he chairs the Foreign Affairs subcommittee on terrorism. He has referred to the U.S.-Mexico border as the "third front" in the war on terrorism, and he was among a bipartisan group of lawmakers who urged President Barack Obama to deploy National Guard troops to address criminal violence there related to Mexican cartels. He has suggested that military equipment no longer needed in Iraq or Afghanistan should be directed to the southern border.

Poe dislikes the idea of giving illegal immigrants already in the country a path to citizenship. But he supports attempts to overhaul immigration law. "We have de facto amnesty in this country," he told the U.S. Chamber of Commerce in April 2013. "So doing nothing is a vote for amnesty." He wants clear standards or non-federal input for determining "operational control" of the border, so that statistics aren't manipulated to give the impression of progress.

On the Foreign Affairs Committee, Poe is a big supporter of Israel, and he is very hawkish about combating terrorist networks linked to al-Qaida. He has questioned the oversight of some foreign-aid spending. After Osama bin Laden's death in May 2011, Poe introduced a bill to block all aid to Pakistan unless it could be shown that the Pakistani government had not helped harbor the terrorist leader.

He also studies the legal questions surrounding the prosecution of the war on terrorism. In February 2013, the Judiciary Committee debated whether a court should review drone strikes against U.S. citizens suspected of terrorism overseas — and whether reviews should come before or after the strike. Poe wasn't sure that the need for quick action justified post-strike reviews. "That doesn't do the dead guy much when we say, 'We made a mistake,'" he said.

His Foreign Affairs subcommittee also has jurisdiction over trade, which is a major interest for his suburban Houston district. Working with California Democrat Janice Hahn in 2011, Poe formed the Ports Caucus to better promote security and economic development of the nation's ports. Topping his list of priorities is a project to widen and deepen the Sabine-Neches Waterway, where a large amount of the nation's commercial jet fuel is produced and shipped.

He has also found Democratic partners in his efforts to improve privacy protections. Poe and California Democrat Zoe Lofgren maintain that there should be a better legal framework governing the use of drone aircraft for domestic surveillance. They have also teamed up on a bill to guarantee that Fourth Amendment protections extend to digital communications and geolocation data stored in mobile devices.

While Poe is known nationally for playing Cicero with his frequent House floor speeches, his constituents know him better from his previous career as a judge in Harris County. His unusual sentences made headlines and came to be labeled as "Poe-etic justice."

One punishment required an auto thief to serve jail time — and hand over the keys of his Trans Am to his victim, a 75-year-old grandmother who drove the car until her stolen vehicle was recovered. Poe once made a burglar stand on a sidewalk wearing a sign that read "I stole from this store," and he required convicted killers to keep pictures of their victims in their jail cells.

He now touts his get-tough stance as a founding member of the Victims' Rights Caucus. In 2012, Poe joined Judiciary Committee Democrats to vote against a reauthorization of federal programs to investigate and prosecute violent crimes against women. The GOP-authored version, Poe's office told the Houston Chronicle, might prevent illegal immigrants from reporting crimes committed against them. A Senate version that covered such immigrants was enacted in 2013 with Poe's support.

Born in Temple and raised in Houston, Poe has filled his Capitol Hill office with photographs that he snapped of the Texas countryside. He said a major turning point in his life occurred when he was in ninth grade. "I was shy so my daddy made me take speech class so that I would talk more. I've been talking ever since, I guess," he said.

Poe was influenced by his grandmother, a "Yellow Dog Democrat" who died at the age of 99. "She never forgave me for being a Republican," he said. "She told me once, 'I'm not sure you can go to Heaven being a Republican.' She might have meant it, too." A sixth-generation Texan, he also was moved by the story of William Barrett Travis, the Texas commander at the Battle of the Alamo. Posted at the door of Poe's office is a framed copy of Travis' Letter from the Alamo, which reads in part: "I am determined to sustain myself as long as possible and die like a soldier who never forgets what is due to his own honor and that of his country — Victory or Death."

Poe earned a political science degree from Abilene Christian College and a law degree from the University of Houston. Poe, who served in the Air Force Reserve, was an assistant district attorney and chief felony prosecutor for eight years and never lost a jury trial. He says he became a Republican when Gov. William Clements named him to the bench.

In 2004, Poe entered the race for the 2nd District, which had been redrawn to favor the GOP. The district included almost half the former 9th District represented by four-term Democrat Nick Lampson. Poe ousted Lampson with nearly 56 percent of the vote.

His re-elections have been fairly low-stress contests. Redistricting after the 2010 census did nothing to threaten his electoral prospects. He beat Democrat Jim Dougherty, a lawyer, by 32 points.

Key Votes

2012	
Extend a Social Security payroll tax cut and unemployment benefits	NO
Ease securities rules to expand small-business access to capital	YES
Extend for one year subsidized student loan interest rates financed by a cut in health care spending	YES
Cite Attorney General Eric H. Holder Jr. for contempt of Congress	YES
Create a visa program for foreign graduates in high-tech fields	YES
Extend most Bush-era income tax rates while allowing rates for top-bracket earners to rise (Jan. 1, 2013)	NO
2011	
Strike funding for F-35 alternative engine	YES
Prevent EPA from regulating greenhouse gas emissions to address climate change	YES
Extend certain provisions of Patriot Act for four years	YES
Declare opposition to use of ground troops in Libya	YES
Overhaul patent law	YES
Pass compromise debt limit increase plan and establish future spending limits	NO
Allow consideration of measures to implement three trade agreements	YES

CQ Vote Studies

	PARTY UNITY		PRESIDENTIAL SUPPORT	
	SUPPORT	OPPOSE	SUPPORT	OPPOSE
2012	96%	4%	16%	84%
2011	95%	5%	19%	81%
2010	99%	1%	24%	76%
2009	95%	5%	19%	81%
2008	94%	6%	68%	32%

Interest Groups

	AFL-CIO	ADA	CCUS	ACU
2012	19%	10%	92%	88%
2011	0%	5%	94%	96%
2010	0%	5%	75%	100%
2009	5%	5%	73%	92%
2008	7%	10%	56%	96%

Texas 2

Western and northwestern Houston; Humble

Confined to Harris County, the 2nd forms a narrow loop around Houston from the northeast to southwest. It edges the borders of Liberty and Montgomery counties through Northwest Houston communities, to subdivisions in the western part of the city, finally bending south into Rice University. Reflecting Houston's income segregation, the district encompasses mainly upper-income, master-planned neighborhoods, with a few exceptions between Beltway 8 and Loop 610 and in the inner city. Redistricting following the 2010 census pushed the 2nd inland.

The wooded community of Kingwood was plotted in the 1970s into 21 distinct villages. Nearby Atascocita is a popular retirement destination. Lake Houston is a source of recreation and a main water supply for the city, but droughts have rapidly depleted water, causing sustainability concerns.

The Champions, near George Bush Intercontinental Airport (in the 18th), is one of northwest Houston's oldest subdivisions. Neighboring Willowbrook has a major mall, a hospital and industrial parks. Fifteen minutes from downtown, the Sam Houston Race Park draws revenue. The 2nd captures Memorial Park, a former military camp converted into one of the nation's largest urban green spaces, and the Houston Arboretum.

Although Harris County will back Democratic presidential candidates, the 2nd's snake-like share — about one sixth of the county — supports the GOP. But the district's population is diverse: Asians account for 6 percent, black residents for 13 and Hispanics for 30, which carves away at the GOP base. Liberal votes can be found in Montrose, which has an eclectic reputation and is the heart of Houston's gay and lesbian community. Rice University sits at the district's southeastern terminus and brings in more Democratic support. Overall, though, the 2nd gave Republican Mitt Romney 63 percent of its presidential vote in 2012.

Major Industry

Technology, higher education, health care, retail, tourism

Cities

Houston (pt.), Atascocita (unincorp.), Spring (unincorp.) (pt.)

Notable

The Harris County War Memorial at Bear Creek Park honors county residents who died during military service; it continues to be updated with names from the Iraq and Afghanistan wars.

Rep. Sam Johnson (R)

Capitol Office
225-4201
samjohnson.house.gov
1211 Longworth Bldg. 20515-4303; fax 225-1485

Committees
Ways & Means
(Social Security - Chairman)
Joint Taxation

Residence
Plano

Born
Oct. 11, 1930; San Antonio, Texas

Religion
Methodist

Family
Wife, Shirley Johnson; three children (one deceased)

Education
Southern Methodist U., B.B.A. 1951; George Washington U., M.S.I.A. 1974 (international affairs)

Military
Air Force, 1951-79

Career
Home builder; Top Gun flight school director; Air Force pilot

Political Highlights
Texas House, 1985-91

ELECTION RESULTS

2012 GENERAL

Sam Johnson (R)		unopposed

2012 PRIMARY

Sam Johnson (R)	33,592	83.1%
Harry Pierce (R)	4,848	12.0%
Josh Caesar (R)	2,002	5.0%

2010 GENERAL

Sam Johnson (R)	101,180	66.3%
John Lingenfelder (D)	47,848	31.3%
Christopher J. Claytor (LIBERT)	3,602	2.4%

Previous Winning Percentages
2008 (60%); 2006 (63%); 2004 (86%); 2002 (74%); 2000 (72%); 1998 (91%); 1996 (73%); 1994 (91%); 1992 (86%); 1991 Special Runoff Election (53%)

Elected 1991; 11th full term

In his ninth decade, Johnson still flashes the vigor that established him as a leader among conservatives in the 1990s. Now a senior member of the Ways and Means Committee, he rallies Republicans around plans to reshape the tax code and entitlement programs.

Johnson was in his third full term when the Republican Study Committee, a group of House conservatives, dissolved following the 1994 Republican Revolution. Shortly after, he and three other lawmakers founded the Conservative Action Team, which was later rebranded into the current, far more influential version of the RSC — and grew to include most House Republicans.

With the departure of Indiana's Dan Burton at the end of the 112th Congress (2011-12), Johnson is the RSC's last remaining founder in Congress. National Journal deemed him the most conservative member of the House in 2010, a designation he termed a "badge of honor." He still hawks common conservative themes, such as shrinking the Education and Agriculture departments and eliminating executive branch "czars."

Younger lawmakers run the RSC these days, but Johnson is still an active member, making animated critiques of Democrats on the House floor. When President Barack Obama issued a 2012 policy directive to stop the deportation of some illegal immigrants, Johnson described Obama's "reprehensible steps that weaken our border security and undermine the rule of law in America." The presiding officer warned him not to engage in "personalities toward the president."

That incident aside, Johnson hasn't alienated himself from colleagues. He is quick to laugh and counts prominent members of both parties as friends — he has worked with Minority Whip Steny H. Hoyer of Maryland on immigration and Social Security issues and calls him "a good congressman." He has been part of a bipartisan House working group discussing immigration policy changes in the 113th Congress (2013-14). He also has earned unimpeachable respect as a former resident of the "Hanoi Hilton," the North Vietnamese prison that also held Arizona Republican Sen. John McCain.

In a nearly three-decade career in the Air Force, Johnson directed the Top Gun flight school. His military bearing still comes through at times. He declined a run at his party's top slot on Ways and Means in 2009 because he was the panel's No. 3 Republican. "I believe in seniority," he said.

Johnson, who is now the panel's No. 2 Republican, stands by the plans of Chairman Dave Camp of Michigan to attempt an overhaul of the tax code. In addition to lower corporate and individual tax rates, Johnson stresses simplification of the code by eliminating the carve-outs and deductions that have multiplied over the years.

"We need to start from scratch and eliminate them all," he said in 2012. "It's gonna be a fight regardless of what way we go ... [but] if we can just simplify the tax code, we'll be money ahead."

Johnson, who also sits on the Joint Taxation Committee, has not been timid in navigating the complexities of the current code. In the 112th Congress, he proposed granting recipients of the Korea Defense Service Medal preferential treatment for charitable donations; extending the reach of bonus depreciation savings for long-term contracts; delaying deadlines for the repayment of loans taken out against qualified retirement accounts; and making permanent a 2001 exclusion for employer-provided educational assistance.

Johnson wants to stop the refundable child tax credit — which provides cash payments to low-income parents who pay no federal income tax — from going to illegal immigrants. "I don't know how we can keep giving money away like that," he said. Keeping undocumented workers out of federal benefit programs has been one of his longtime goals.

Similarly, as the chairman of the Social Security Subcommittee, he tries to spotlight the flow of disability benefits to those who could be scamming the system. He says that people should not be allowed to simultaneously collect disability benefits and unemployment benefits.

Johnson is careful to emphasize that current retirees should not have their Social Security benefits reduced, but he also supported President George W. Bush's ill-fated proposal to allow personal accounts within the system. In 2005, he even suggested allowing workers to divert their entire Social Security payroll tax into a private account. He is open to using a "chained CPI" to calculate benefit increases, which would result in smaller annual bumps.

He is a member of the Health Subcommittee, and like most Republicans, he considers dismantling the 2010 health care law to be a top priority.

Johnson remains incredibly protective of military personnel and their benefits. In the 112th, he signed on to a number of bipartisan initiatives regaling "wounded warriors" with all types of honors. Parochially, he'd like to see a new Veterans Affairs Department health care facility in North Texas. Johnson has had surgeries for several joint problems over the years, which he traces in part to being held in leg chains for two years in Vietnam. His imprisonment lasted almost seven years and included solitary confinement.

He strongly supported the military effort in Iraq and has not been pleased with the Obama administration's focus on the withdrawal of troops from Afghanistan. Defense budget cuts put in place by a 2011 deficit reduction law "just stink," he said.

Johnson did not plan on a military career — participation in the ROTC was mandatory when he went to high school. He was aiming for a career in business and law when the Korean War intervened and his entire ROTC class at Southern Methodist University was called to duty. Accepted into flight training school, he fell in love with flying and was sold on an Air Force career. He flew combat missions over Korea and Vietnam and was a member of the Thunderbirds precision flying team for two years.

Johnson wrote a book about his POW experience, "Captive Warriors." He had three surgeries on his right hand after his 1973 release and resumed flying.

After retiring from the Air Force in 1979 as a colonel, Johnson went into the homebuilding business in Dallas. He got into local Republican Party affairs and won a seat in the Texas House in 1984. When GOP Rep. Steve Bartlett resigned in March 1991 to run for mayor of Dallas, Johnson won the special election to replace him. He has had no trouble since then in the solidly Republican district, and he ran unopposed in the 2012 general election.

Key Votes

2012	
Extend a Social Security payroll tax cut and unemployment benefits	YES
Ease securities rules to expand small-business access to capital	YES
Extend for one year subsidized student loan interest rates financed by a cut in health care spending	YES
Cite Attorney General Eric H. Holder Jr. for contempt of Congress	YES
Create a visa program for foreign graduates in high-tech fields	YES
Extend most Bush-era income tax rates while allowing rates for top-bracket earners to rise (Jan. 1, 2013)	NO
2011	
Strike funding for F-35 alternative engine	YES
Prevent EPA from regulating greenhouse gas emissions to address climate change	YES
Extend certain provisions of Patriot Act for four years	YES
Declare opposition to use of ground troops in Libya	YES
Overhaul patent law	YES
Pass compromise debt limit increase plan and establish future spending limits	YES
Allow consideration of measures to implement three trade agreements	YES

CQ Vote Studies

	PARTY UNITY		PRESIDENTIAL SUPPORT	
	SUPPORT	OPPOSE	SUPPORT	OPPOSE
2012	97%	3%	15%	85%
2011	97%	3%	25%	75%
2010	99%	1%	25%	75%
2009	98%	2%	10%	90%
2008	99%	1%	81%	10%

Interest Groups

	AFL-CIO	ADA	CCUS	ACU
2012	10%	0%	92%	96%
2011	0%	5%	100%	87%
2010	0%	0%	100%	100%
2009	5%	0%	79%	100%
2008	0%	0%	83%	96%

Texas 3

Most of Collin County — Plano, part of Frisco, McKinney

The 3rd, with the highest household median income in the state, takes the largest share of fast-growing Collin County, which is split between three districts. It stretches roughly from Frisco to Lavon Lake from east to west, and includes established Plano and McKinney. With a flood of Dallas County commuters, a massive $630-million transportation upgrade was completed in 2012 on Sam Rayburn Tollway, in the heart of the district.

Plano's office parks began attracting corporate headquarters, including J.C. Penney and Electronic Data Systems, in the 1980s. Both these firms have recently announced restructuring plans that include job cuts in the city. Other Fortune 500 firms based here include Dr Pepper Snapple Group, Rent-a-Center and Cinemark. Plano also has a large telecommunications and technology sector and major health care providers.

Frisco has developed into a recreation center for upper-middle income Metroplex suburbanites. Revenue generated from sales taxes on 8 million square feet of retail and dining space enabled the city to buy out a polluting battery plant. The city also hosts soccer's FC Dallas Stadium.

Despite rapid growth, McKinney has maintained enough ponds, parks, hiking trails and green spaces to earn national media attention as one of the best small cities to call home. Developers have experimented with environmentally friendly design in residential and commercial projects.

The University of Texas at Dallas campus in Richardson (shared with the 32nd) has been undergoing "green" construction and expansion. But the 3rd isn't immune to Texas' budget shortfalls, and public schools in the 3rd have had to cut programs and lay off staff and teachers.

Some communities have attracted an influx of Chinese-Americans, and combined with Hispanics, minorities account for about 30 percent of the population in the majority-white, solidly Republican district.

Major Industry
Telecommunications, professional services, health care, retail, tourism

Cities
Plano (pt.), Frisco (pt.), McKinney

Notable
Parker's Southfork Ranch, which was the home of the fictional Ewing family of television's "Dallas," now offers tours and a glimpse of the gun that shot J.R. Ewing.

Rep. Ralph M. Hall (R)

Capitol Office
225-6673
ralphhall.house.gov
2405 Rayburn Bldg. 20515-4304; fax 225-3332

Committees
Energy & Commerce
Science, Space & Technology

Residence
Rockwall

Born
May 3, 1923; Fate, Texas

Religion
Methodist

Family
Widowed; three children

Education
Texas Christian U., attended 1943 (pre-law); U. of Texas, attended 1946-47 (pre-law); Southern Methodist U., LL.B. 1951

Military
Navy, 1942-45

Career
Lawyer; aluminum company president

Political Highlights
Rockwall County judge, 1951-63; Texas Senate, 1963-73 (president pro tempore, 1968-69; served as a Democrat); sought Democratic nomination for lieutenant governor, 1972

ELECTION RESULTS

2012 GENERAL		
Ralph M. Hall (R)	182,679	73.0%
VaLinda Hathcox (D)	60,214	24.0%
Thomas Griffing (LIBERT)	7,262	2.9%
2012 PRIMARY		
Ralph M. Hall (R)	38,202	58.4%
Steve Clark (R)	13,719	21.0%
Lou Gigliotti (R)	13,532	20.7%

Previous Winning Percentages
2010 (73%); 2008 (69%); 2006 (64%); 2004 (68%); 2002 (58%); 2000 (60%); 1998 (58%); 1996 (64%); 1994 (59%); 1992 (58%); 1990 (100%); 1988 (66%); 1986 (72%); 1984 (58%); 1982 (74%); 1980 (52%)

Elected 1980; 17th term

Hall is the oldest person ever to cast a vote in the House and arguably one of the most entertaining members of the current Congress. Behind his larger-than-life personality are serious interests in energy, health care and science programs, and he is indulging them with his return to the Energy and Commerce Committee: "I want to spend my last years on it," he said.

Hall was born during the Harding administration, came to Washington as a conservative Democrat at the start of the Reagan administration, and switched to the Republican Party in the George W. Bush administration. No one questions his support of the GOP agenda — he opposes the 2010 health care law and pushes hard for domestic energy production — and he bristles when people question his age.

Of his colleagues, Hall says he "can outwork any of 'em." He runs two miles a day, rarely misses a vote and served as chairman of the Science, Space and Technology Committee in the 112th Congress (2011-12). He stepped down only to comply with GOP term limit rules for panel leaders.

To put voters at ease about his age in 2012, Hall went skydiving, because "you can't jump out of a damn airplane if you're too old," he said. "Nothing to it, I'd done it during the war." That would be World War II — Hall and Michigan Democrat John D. Dingell are the only two veterans of that conflict serving in the House.

Transcripts of congressional hearings are immeasurably improved by Hall's one-liners, and his humor and courtesy contribute to his good standing among colleagues. But he has mostly taken a non-showy approach in promoting the oil and gas industries. Hall took a leave of absence from Energy and Commerce when serving as Science chairman, but he reclaimed his seat in 2013. He sits on the Energy and Power Subcommittee, as well as the Environment and the Economy Subcommittee.

Hall takes the position that greater domestic energy production keeps the nation out of conflicts in resource-rich regions and aids economic development. He strongly supports oil drilling on federal land, off U.S. coastlines, and in Alaska's Arctic National Wildlife Refuge. "I'm almost one that would drill on cemetery lots if it'd keep my children from having to go to war," he said.

After the 2010 oil spill in the Gulf of Mexico, he criticized the Obama administration's moratorium on deep-water drilling and backed a measure that would overhaul an ultra-deep-water drilling research program to focus on safer drilling technologies. Hall helped create the existing program, which has been targeted for elimination by both the current and previous administration.

In early 2009, the House passed his bill promoting research on ways to purify and reuse brackish water produced when oil, gas and coal-bed methane are extracted from the ground.

Energy and Commerce oversees many health issues, and Hall said the results of the 2012 election were no reason to stop unified Republican opposition to the 2010 health care law. With Republicans controlling only the House, "we can't create, but we can kill," he said. He does favor some expansions of government health care, however. He has introduced bills to provide Medicaid coverage for optometry and Medicare coverage for CT colonography.

Hall still sits on the Science committee, now with the title of chairman emeritus. He has seats on the Space and Energy subcommittees.

He continues to assert his views on NASA, which has a large presence in Texas. While serving as chairman, Hall made several examinations of the agency's transition away from the space shuttle program. Hall worries that the United States is too reliant on Russia for access to the International Space Station, and he has criticized NASA's pace in developing its crew vehicle and heavy-lift rocket. He has been skeptical about the market viability of transportation for commercial crews and NASA's ability to oversee safety as companies develop these capacities.

He champions NASA's biomedical and basic science programs. "We're not going to find a cure for cancer here in this environment," he said. "We have to have the weightless environment up there if we're ever gonna find it."

As chairman, Hall criticized the energy policies of the Obama administration and said its proposed research budgets overemphasized alternative energy at the cost of basic research and energy sources such as oil and gas. He accused the administration of misusing science, saying at a hearing that "the president delivers a wink and a nod to EPA as it continues to regulate affordable energy out of existence, often on the basis of shaky and secretive and faulty science."

Hall helped pass legislation to boost math and science education, as well as funding for basic science research, during the 110th Congress (2007-08).

A social and fiscal conservative, Hall voted against the August 2011 debt limit law. He is a co-sponsor of a bill to eliminate the IRS and replace federal taxes with a single national sales tax.

Hall got an early start in politics, winning election as county judge (essentially, the chief executive) of Rockwall County in 1950 while still attending law school. Twelve years later, he moved to the state Senate and spent a decade there, rising to the post of president pro tempore.

After finishing fourth in the Democratic primary for lieutenant governor in 1972, he left public life for a while. But when Democrat Ray Roberts of the 4th District announced his retirement in 1980, Hall won the seat with 52 percent of the vote.

He always kept the liberal wing of the Democratic Party at arm's length. In 1995, Hall was a founder of the fiscally conservative Blue Dog Coalition, and he strayed from the party line more than any other House member in the early 2000s. His party switch in 2004 diminished his power when Democrats controlled the House from 2007 through 2010, but it also allowed him to survive in a district reconfigured to favor Republicans. He has won by comfortable margins. Former telecom executive Steve Clark challenged Hall in the GOP primary in both 2010 and 2012, but Hall won both races easily.

Colleagues of both parties took to the House floor to share stories about Hall in November 2012, on the day he became the oldest person to vote. Tales included Hall playing baseball with Ted Williams while in the Navy and once pumping gas for Bonnie and Clyde. "I've enjoyed the speeches I've listened to here," Hall said. "A lot of it was true."

Key Votes

2012	
Extend a Social Security payroll tax cut and unemployment benefits	NO
Ease securities rules to expand small-business access to capital	YES
Extend for one year subsidized student loan interest rates financed by a cut in health care spending	YES
Cite Attorney General Eric H. Holder Jr. for contempt of Congress	YES
Create a visa program for foreign graduates in high-tech fields	YES
Extend most Bush-era income tax rates while allowing rates for top-bracket earners to rise (Jan. 1, 2013)	NO
2011	
Strike funding for F-35 alternative engine	YES
Prevent EPA from regulating greenhouse gas emissions to address climate change	YES
Extend certain provisions of Patriot Act for four years	YES
Declare opposition to use of ground troops in Libya	YES
Overhaul patent law	YES
Pass compromise debt limit increase plan and establish future spending limits	NO
Allow consideration of measures to implement three trade agreements	YES

CQ Vote Studies

	PARTY UNITY		PRESIDENTIAL SUPPORT	
	SUPPORT	OPPOSE	SUPPORT	OPPOSE
2012	95%	5%	13%	87%
2011	97%	3%	19%	81%
2010	95%	5%	29%	71%
2009	92%	8%	31%	69%
2008	96%	4%	65%	35%

Interest Groups

	AFL-CIO	ADA	CCUS	ACU
2012	14%	5%	83%	84%
2011	4%	5%	94%	95%
2010	0%	0%	88%	96%
2009	14%	10%	93%	92%
2008	33%	30%	83%	84%

Texas 4

Northeast — Sherman, Paris, Texarkana

Situated in the northeastern corner of Texas, the 4th District grabs wealthy Dallas exurbs, much of the 12-million acre Pineywoods region and the Caddo National Grasslands. The Red River runs along its northern border, and it takes in the Texas half of Texarkana across the border from Arkansas.

The 4th is home to Rockwall County, the fastest-growing county in Texas and one of the most rapidly developing in the nation. With a total area of 144 square miles, Rockwall is geographically the smallest county in Texas but its population of more than 80,000 is predicted to almost triple by 2030. Major corporations have filled new office space, attracted by a highly educated workforce.

Transportation is a high priority, and planners take a regional approach. A future commuter rail link with Dallas' high-speed DART system could aid workers to the east. On the district's western flank, one of the busiest North American Free Trade Agreement corridors in the nation, Interstate 30, is crucial for Greenville's advanced manufacturing and Sulphur Spring's food processing sectors.

Texarkana's diverse blue-collar workforce survived recession-era setbacks, despite losing major manufacturer Alcoa. A tire plant, two paper mills supported by the region's timber industry, and a range of skilled manufacturers helped to keep unemployment low. With thousands of workers, Red River Army Depot's combat vehicle maintenance operation is the main employer near Texarkana. Between Texarkana and Rockwall County, away from the transportation corridors, the district is less populated. In Hopkins County, dairy and cattle are big industries.

The population of the 4th is the whitest among all Texas districts, at more than 80 percent. The constituency leans Republican and the upwardly mobile middle class in Rockwall harbors tea party tendencies.

Major Industry
Manufacturing, professional services, timber, military, distribution

Military Bases
Red River Army Depot, 2 military, 3,500 civilian

Cities
Rockwall, Texarkana, Greenville, Paris

Notable
Thousands of migratory birds fly south to spend winter in Hagerman National Wildlife Refuge each year.

Rep. Jeb Hensarling (R)

Capitol Office
225-3484
hensarling.house.gov
2228 Rayburn Bldg. 20515-4305; fax 226-4888

Committees
Financial Services - Chairman

Residence
Dallas

Born
May 29, 1957; Stephenville, Texas

Religion
Episcopalian

Family
Wife, Melissa Hensarling; two children

Education
Texas A&M U., B.A. 1979 (economics); U. of Texas, J.D. 1982

Career
Child support collection software firm owner; corporate communications executive; senatorial campaign committee executive director; congressional district and campaign aide; lawyer

Political Highlights
No previous office

ELECTION RESULTS

2012 GENERAL		
Jeb Hensarling (R)	134,091	64.4%
Linda S. Mrosko (D)	69,178	33.2%
Ken Ashby (LIBERT)	4,961	2.4%
2012 PRIMARY		
Jeb Hensarling (R)		unopposed
2010 GENERAL		
Jeb Hensarling (R)	106,742	70.5%
Tom Berry (D)	41,649	27.5%
Ken Ashby (LIBERT)	2,958	2.0%

Previous Winning Percentages
2008 (84%); 2006 (62%); 2004 (64%); 2002 (58%)

Elected 2002; 6th term

Hensarling often plays the heavy for the GOP, holding the conservative line in high-profile talks on government spending and the federal role in the finance sector. As the chairman of the Financial Services Committee, he has ambitious goals — and a challenging path to achieving them.

Hensarling (HENN-sur-ling) is a political and ideological heir to past Republican leaders from the Lone Star State, such as House Majority Leader Dick Armey and Sen. Phil Gramm, for whom he once worked as an aide. He is part strategist, part policy wonk.

In the 110th Congress (2007-08), he was the chairman of the Republican Study Committee, the large bloc of conservative House members. In the 111th Congress (2009-10), he served as finance chairman of the House Republicans' campaign organization. As his party returned to the majority in 2011, he became the chairman of the Republican Conference, the No. 4 leadership post.

Hensarling was also chosen to represent his party in major negotiations on the nation's fiscal future. In 2010, he was appointed to a special commission created by President Barack Obama to make recommendations on long-term deficit reduction measures. And in 2011, he was named co-chairman of the Joint Select Committee on Deficit Reduction (aka the supercommittee), a bipartisan, bicameral panel with a similar assignment.

The results — while certainly not solely attributable to Hensarling — were less than stellar. Both groups disbanded without striking any agreement, nor has their work been incorporated into new laws. Hensarling met Sen. Patty Murray, a Washington Democrat and the supercommittee's co-chairwoman, at that panel's first hearing. Their fast friendship had aides and lawmakers optimistic during the early days of the panel, but leaks and recriminations increased as its deadline for action approached.

Hensarling pinned the failure on Democrats' insistence on increasing taxes, as well as philosophical differences. "Ultimately, the committee did not succeed because we could not bridge the gap between two dramatically competing visions of the role government should play in a free society, the proper purpose and design of the social safety net, and the fundamentals of job creation and economic growth," he wrote in the Wall Street Journal.

There were also some rocky moments in his management of the Republican Conference during the 112th Congress (2011-12) — the 2010 elections brought a surge of new GOP House members, many with only intermittent loyalty to established party leaders. The office is typically a key part of the GOP's messaging apparatus, yet reporters and Republican aides complained of a meager and lethargic role for the Conference under Hensarling.

He gave up that job to become the Financial Services chairman in the 113th Congress (2013-14). Realistically, it will take intensive negotiations to advance changes to housing, regulatory and insurance policies that the Democratic Senate might accept. Compromise could be difficult — the ranking Democrat is Maxine Waters, a famously prickly Californian, and divisions among panel Republicans are big enough that Hensarling named Lynn Westmoreland of Georgia a committee whip. But some panel watchers are optimistic that Hensarling might be less hard-edged than he appears in hearings.

Hensarling boasts of a passion for intricate policy matters, and matters have been known to get fairly intricate on Financial Services. His devotion to free markets and small-government conservatism was on display during the debate over a financial industry regulatory overhaul in 2010. Hensarling denigrated the bill put forth by the panel's Democratic leadership. "It puts unparalleled discretionary powers to the federal government to pick winners and losers, ushering in a new era of crony capitalism," he said during the House and Senate conference on the legislation, which is known as Dodd-Frank. He is still skeptical that the law has solved the problem of financial institutions that are "too big to fail" and would require government bailouts — he wants to eliminate the liquidation authority given to federal agencies by the law.

In 2008, he opposed a bipartisan housing rescue plan allowing the government to extend credit to, and buy stock in, mortgage financiers Fannie Mae and Freddie Mac. "The bottom line: The taxpayer is about to be the big loser here," he said. "I came here to protect free enterprise, not big banks." Hensarling and Republican Scott Garrett of New Jersey have touted their goal of eliminating the federal guarantee behind home mortgages and shifting to a privatized housing finance system. He says federal attempts to promote home-ownership were partly responsible for the shaky loans that led to the market collapse.

Hensarling voted in 2008 against the $700 billion bailout for the financial services sector, calling it a "step down the slippery slope to socialism." He also would like to see the government get out of the flood insurance business.

Hensarling's fiscal outlook is paired with a dedicated social conservatism. He voted in both 2004 and 2006 for a constitutional amendment to ban same-sex marriage, and he opposes abortion, voting in 2006 to make it a felony to take a minor across state lines for the procedure. "I can come to no other conclusion than that life begins at conception," he wrote in 2012.

Born in Stephenville to a family of poultry farmers, Hensarling decided early that he wouldn't enter the family business. His first taste of politics came in 1964, when his Republican parents had him knocking on doors for presidential candidate Barry Goldwater. He started a Republican Club at his high school and acted as a GOP precinct captain at Texas A&M University, where he took a class on money and banking taught by Gramm.

After three years as a corporate lawyer, Hensarling was hired in 1985 to oversee Gramm's field offices in Texas. When Gramm became chairman of the National Republican Senatorial Committee in the 1992 campaign cycle, he made Hensarling its executive director.

Hensarling took a break from government to go home to Texas, where he started a computer software business: One product was used by government agencies to help single parents collect child support payments. His varied business career also included a stint as vice president of Austin-based Green Mountain Energy Co., a provider of electricity from wind and solar power.

Reapportionment after the 2000 census created an open House seat for 2002. Hensarling won a five-way primary, then beat Democrat Ron Chapman, a Dallas-area judge, by 18 points. He has coasted to re-election since.

Key Votes

2012	
Extend a Social Security payroll tax cut and unemployment benefits	YES
Ease securities rules to expand small-business access to capital	YES
Extend for one year subsidized student loan interest rates financed by a cut in health care spending	YES
Cite Attorney General Eric H. Holder Jr. for contempt of Congress	YES
Create a visa program for foreign graduates in high-tech fields	YES
Extend most Bush-era income tax rates while allowing rates for top-bracket earners to rise (Jan. 1, 2013)	NO
2011	
Strike funding for F-35 alternative engine	YES
Prevent EPA from regulating greenhouse gas emissions to address climate change	YES
Extend certain provisions of Patriot Act for four years	YES
Declare opposition to use of ground troops in Libya	YES
Overhaul patent law	YES
Pass compromise debt limit increase plan and establish future spending limits	YES
Allow consideration of measures to implement three trade agreements	YES

CQ Vote Studies

	PARTY UNITY		PRESIDENTIAL SUPPORT	
	SUPPORT	OPPOSE	SUPPORT	OPPOSE
2012	99%	1%	15%	85%
2011	97%	3%	22%	78%
2010	99%	1%	29%	71%
2009	99%	1%	11%	89%
2008	99%	1%	87%	13%

Interest Groups

	AFL-CIO	ADA	CCUS	ACU
2012	5%	0%	92%	96%
2011	0%	5%	100%	92%
2010	0%	0%	88%	100%
2009	5%	0%	73%	100%
2008	0%	5%	78%	100%

Texas 5

Part of Dallas and east suburbs — most of Mesquite and Garland; Palestine

Most of the 5th's land is a block of five counties and part of a sixth in eastern Texas, but nearly half of its population lives in Dallas County. Capturing Mesquite and northeastern Dallas neighborhoods miles from the glitzy downtown, even the most populous areas of the district have a down-home feel.

Tourists flock to the shores of White Rock Lake to visit the 66-acre Dallas Arboretum. The gardens draw more than 500,000 visitors each year, and residents in the historic homes surrounding the lake share an interest in environmental preservation. Nearby Casa Linda and its central shopping plaza were built on a family farm. Large lots, minimal traffic and tree-lined streets help the neighborhood maintain a country vibe.

Many middle-class Latino families have left the city for suburban Mesquite, where majority-Hispanic classrooms offer bilingual education. The city, home to a UPS distribution center, has become a logistics hub and supports manufacturing and retail jobs. Its popular arena is booking concerts and conventions in an attempt to diversify beyond its rodeo roots.

To the south, Seagoville has constructed new commercial space and experimented with tax increment financing zones for infrastructure improvements. Another high-growth area is Kaufman County's Forney.

The Trinity River flows along the eastern border of the district, through two wildlife management areas. Native prairie grasses, timbers and pastures cover Anderson, Van Zandt and Henderson counties. Salt and oil are still mined here and prisons are a major employer.

Whites are the majority in the district; the Dallas County population is 19 percent black and 37 percent Hispanic. Voters in Mesquite lean slightly Democratic, but the district as a whole votes Republican. GOP candidate Mitt Romney had a 31-point win here in the 2012 presidential contest.

Major Industry
Logistics, manufacturing, agriculture, oil

Cities
Dallas (pt.), Mesquite, Balch Springs

Notable
Grand Saline is home to the Salt Palace Museum, which commemorates its history as a center for salt mining.

Rep. Joe L. Barton (R)

Capitol Office
225-2002
joebarton.house.gov
2107 Rayburn Bldg. 20515-4306; fax 225-3052

Committees
Energy & Commerce

Residence
Ennis

Born
Sept. 15, 1949; Waco, Texas

Religion
Methodist

Family
Wife, Terri Barton; four children, two stepchildren

Education
Texas A&M U., B.S. 1972 (industrial engineering); Purdue U., M.S. 1973 (industrial administration)

Career
Engineering consultant; printing company plant manager

Political Highlights
Sought Republican nomination for U.S. Senate (special election), 1993

ELECTION RESULTS

2012 GENERAL		
Joe L. Barton (R)	145,019	58.0%
Kenneth Sanders (D)	98,053	39.2%
Hugh Chauvin (LIBERT)	4,847	1.9%
2012 PRIMARY		
Joe L. Barton (R)	26,192	63.2%
Joe Chow (R)	8,154	19.7%
Frank Kuchar (R)	4,725	11.4%
Itamar Gelbman (R)	2,356	5.7%
2010 GENERAL		
Joe L. Barton (R)	107,140	65.9%
David E. Cozad (D)	50,717	31.2%
Byron Severns (LIBERT)	4,700	2.9%

Previous Winning Percentages
2008 (62%); 2006 (60%); 2004 (66%); 2002 (70%); 2000 (88%); 1998 (73%); 1996 (77%); 1994 (76%); 1992 (72%); 1990 (66%); 1988 (68%); 1986 (56%); 1984 (57%)

Elected 1984; 15th term

Barton flourished during the George W. Bush administration as a Republican leader on energy policy. His power was sapped when he lost the party's top spot on the Energy and Commerce Committee, but he continues to fight for influence.

A former engineering consultant, Barton has been a go-to guy in the House for the oil and gas industries — as he noted at a 2013 hearing, "I represent a congressional district in Texas that at one time, had it been a nation, it would have been the fifth-largest oil-producing nation in the world." He became the Energy and Commerce chairman in February 2004 when Billy Tauzin of Louisiana stepped down due to his impending retirement.

Barton stayed on as the ranking member in the 110th and 111th Congresses (2007-10), and he hoped to reclaim the gavel when his party regained control in the 2010 elections. But he had reached the GOP's term limit for panel leaders, and colleagues didn't grant him a waiver. He took the title of chairman emeritus in the 112th Congress (2011-12), when at times he seemed out of step with elements of the new Republican majority.

That much was apparent during debate over legislation to dismantle an Energy Department program providing loan guarantees to companies in the renewable-energy sector. Barton is a prominent skeptic regarding man-made climate change, but he helped write the 2005 energy law that created the program, which supported innovative energy projects that reduce greenhouse gas emissions. It was expanded in the 2009 economic stimulus law to cover mature renewable-energy technologies, including wind and solar.

The 2011 bankruptcy of Solyndra Inc., a solar-panel manufacturer that received a $535 million loan guarantee under the expansion, brought on two oversight investigations and months of negative press from GOP critics. The stimulus law provisions expired at the end of 2011, but with the remaining program still well-subscribed, Barton bucked his party in 2012 by arguing that Congress didn't "have to throw the baby out with the bath water."

Less drastic changes backed by Barton were rebuffed, and the House passed a bill to block further loan guarantees in September 2012. It died in the Senate.

Some of Barton's setbacks have been of his own making. As the ranking member in 2010, he created a public relations nightmare by apologizing to the chief executive of BP during a hearing on the Gulf of Mexico oil spill caused by an explosion on one of the company's rigs. Barton said he was ashamed of President Barack Obama's effort — a "shakedown," he called it — to pressure BP to pay for the damages.

But he continues to stay involved in many policy discussions. As chairman emeritus, he sits on every Energy and Commerce subcommittee. He is also active in the Republican Study Committee, a bloc of House conservatives — he is leading its Energy Task Force in the 113th Congress (2013-14).

Several times in the 112th Congress, Barton appeared to be digging in his heels on behalf of conservative positions. He was one of 10 House Republicans to oppose the fiscal 2013 budget proposed by Budget Chairman Paul D. Ryan of Wisconsin — at a town hall meeting, he said it did not set spending levels low enough. He voted for Ryan's fiscal 2014 plan, pleased that it was designed to bring budgets into balance within 10 years.

Barton hasn't been celebrated as a bipartisan deal-maker, but he is more than familiar with the process. At the start of the 113th Congress, his 28 years in the House were evenly split between service in the majority and the minority. He crosses the aisle when he feels the need.

Privacy is one issue where he reaches out. He has worked with Democrats to ensure that the government and private sector respect the sanctity of users' personal information.

In 2012, he joined Massachusetts Democrat Edward J. Markey, his co-chairman on the Congressional Privacy Caucus, in opposing a bill to require the national intelligence director to promote voluntary information sharing between the federal intelligence community and the private sector. Barton said the lack of explicit privacy protections for individuals "is a greater threat to democracy and liberty" than cybersecurity threats. The bill's sponsors addressed privacy concerns for the 2013 edition of the bill, which passed the House with Barton's support.

In the 111th Congress, Barton did his best to fight Democrats as they pushed a health care overhaul through the Energy and Commerce Committee. In the 112th, he was critical of the Food and Drug Administration's medical device review process, calling for an end to the agency's user fees until it improves performance — he was satisfied by changes in a bipartisan reauthorization of those fees that was enacted in 2012.

On social issues, Barton supports amending the Constitution to ban same sex marriage and is a reliable anti-abortion vote. But he has backed federally supported stem cell research. He is hopeful that such work will help find cures to the ailments that felled his father, who died of complications from diabetes, and his brother, Texas District Judge Jon Barton, who succumbed to liver cancer in 2000 at age 44.

Born in Waco, Barton is the son of an agribusiness salesman and a teacher. His father later became a plant geneticist, breeding strains of cotton. Barton studied industrial engineering at Texas A&M University, then got a master's degree from Purdue University. He moved to Ennis and worked in several capacities for Ennis Business Forms.

In 1981, Barton was a White House fellow at the Energy Department. On his return to Texas, he worked as a natural gas consultant for Atlantic Richfield Co., and his first bid for elective office was a 1984 House race. He won the seat that had been held by Republican Phil Gramm, who moved to the Senate.

Barton has won re-elections easily. He made an unsuccessful bid for the Senate when Democrat Lloyd Bentsen left in 1993 to be President Bill Clinton's Treasury secretary. He considered a Senate run in 2002, when Gramm retired, but Bush endorsed John Cornyn and more or less cleared out the field. In 2006, he briefly campaigned for House minority leader before dropping out and endorsing the eventual winner, John A. Boehner.

Outside of politics, baseball is one of Barton's passions — although changes to the congressional map heading into the 2012 elections removed the stadium of the Texas Rangers from his district.

Key Votes

2012	
Extend a Social Security payroll tax cut and unemployment benefits	NO
Ease securities rules to expand small-business access to capital	YES
Extend for one year subsidized student loan interest rates financed by a cut in health care spending	YES
Cite Attorney General Eric H. Holder Jr. for contempt of Congress	YES
Create a visa program for foreign graduates in high-tech fields	YES
Extend most Bush-era income tax rates while allowing rates for top-bracket earners to rise (Jan. 1, 2013)	NO
2011	
Strike funding for F-35 alternative engine	YES
Prevent EPA from regulating greenhouse gas emissions to address climate change	YES
Extend certain provisions of Patriot Act for four years	YES
Declare opposition to use of ground troops in Libya	YES
Overhaul patent law	YES
Pass compromise debt limit increase plan and establish future spending limits	YES
Allow consideration of measures to implement three trade agreements	YES

CQ Vote Studies

	PARTY UNITY		PRESIDENTIAL SUPPORT	
	SUPPORT	OPPOSE	SUPPORT	OPPOSE
2012	94%	6%	18%	82%
2011	94%	6%	26%	74%
2010	97%	3%	29%	71%
2009	91%	9%	21%	79%
2008	98%	2%	82%	18%

Interest Groups

	AFL-CIO	ADA	CCUS	ACU
2012	24%	10%	92%	88%
2011	0%	10%	100%	86%
2010	0%	5%	86%	96%
2009	14%	5%	92%	96%
2008	14%	10%	94%	96%

Texas 6

Most of Arlington; Ellis and Navarro counties

Situated south of the Dallas-Fort Worth Metroplex, the 6th takes in all of Ellis and Navarro counties, but more than 70 percent of its population is concentrated in the southeastern corner of Tarrant County. This stretch includes the Central Meadowbrook and Handley neighborhoods in eastern Fort Worth, and most of Arlington (shared with the 33rd), blending suburban communities with rural, historically cotton-growing lands in the southern portion of the district. Redistricting after the 2010 census lopped off three counties and parts of two others to the south and southeast.

The 6th covers most of downtown Arlington and a portion of its manufacturing center, including a large GM plant undergoing a $200 million expansion. Southwest of downtown, enrollment has soared at the University of Texas at Arlington, thanks to aggressive recruitment and improvements to the campus, making it the second-largest school in the state system. The school is also one of the top employers in the region. Arlington has a relatively low unemployment rate in the state and median incomes on par with the state average.

No city south of Mansfield has more than 30,000 people, but proximity to interstate highways has helped Ennis, Waxahacie and Corsicana attract distribution centers for major retailers. Midlothian is a hub for the cement industry.

The district is majority white. Black residents make up more than half the population in the Hollow Hills area on the eastern side of Fort Worth, and Ennis has a large Hispanic community.

The GOP has done well here, especially in staunchly Republican Ellis County, where voters have not picked a Democratic presidential candidate since Jimmy Carter. Overall, the district gave GOP nominee Mitt Romney 58 percent of its 2012 presidential vote.

Major Industry
Manufacturing, higher education, transportation, agribusiness

Cities
Arlington (pt.), Mansfield (pt.), Waxahacie, Coriscana

Notable
The quarter-mile Texas Motorplex in Ennis hosts national hot rod races each fall, and was the first super-stadium built specifically for drag racing.

Rep. John Culberson (R)

Capitol Office
225-2571
culberson.house.gov
2352 Rayburn Bldg. 20515-2352; fax 225-4381

Committees
Appropriations
(Military Construction-VA - Chairman)

Residence
Houston

Born
Aug. 24, 1956; Houston, Texas

Religion
Methodist

Family
Wife, Belinda Culberson; one child

Education
Southern Methodist U., B.A. 1981 (history); South Texas College of Law, J.D. 1988

Career
Lawyer; political advertising agency employee; oil rig mud logger

Political Highlights
Texas House, 1987-2001

ELECTION RESULTS

2012 GENERAL		
John Culberson (R)	142,793	60.8%
James Cargas (D)	85,553	36.4%
Drew Parks (LIBERT)	4,669	2.0%
2012 PRIMARY		
John Culberson (R)	37,590	86.3%
Bill Tofte (R)	5,971	13.7%
2010 GENERAL		
John Culberson (R)	143,655	81.4%
Bob Townsend (LIBERT)	31,704	18.0%

Previous Winning Percentages
2008 (56%); 2006 (59%); 2004 (64%); 2002 (89%); 2000 (74%)

Elected 2000; 7th term

Culberson is an appropriator with a small-government philosophy. There are federal entities he defends, such as the space programs dear to his Houston district. But "the thing that I'm most interested in, and derive the greatest satisfaction from, is working to try to restore the 10th Amendment and individual liberty," he says.

That last item in the Bill of Rights reserves for the states all powers not delegated to the federal government — a central tenet of federalism, as defined by Thomas Jefferson. Culberson calls himself a "Jeffersonian Republican" and decorates his office with portraits of the third president.

In 2010, Culberson's desire to return more responsibilities to the state and local level led him to become a founding member of the 10th Amendment Task Force, an offshoot of the conservative Republican Study Committee. He also was a charter member of the House Tea Party Caucus.

He has offered solid support for Republican positions, but he isn't a disagreeable partisan. He counts Virginia Republican Frank R. Wolf and Texas Democrat Henry Cuellar, two of the most independent-minded House members, as his best friends in Congress.

At the start of the 112th Congress (2011-12) Culberson took the gavel of the Military Construction-VA Subcommittee, which handles spending on bases and veterans. Politically, neither account is easy to cut; Culberson pushed a fiscal 2013 measure that would increase discretionary spending for veterans by $2.3 billion over the previous year, while slicing $2.4 billion from the construction figure. The House overwhelmingly passed the measure.

Culberson wants to end the practice of requiring union-scale wages on building projects at military bases, which he says drives up costs. Early in the 113th Congress (2013-14), he also suggested at an oversight hearing that it might be worth privatizing the system for processing veterans benefits claims — lawmakers of both parties have agreed that government efforts to modernize and speed up the system have been uneven and vulnerable to waste.

There are traditional appropriations practices that Culberson does embrace. He often requested earmarks — funding set-asides for specific projects in a member's district — before House Republicans imposed a moratorium at the start of the 112th Congress.

He went along with the ban at first, but by spring 2012 he was expressing his frustration. He was planning to speed the expansion of a military facility in Ohio, "in light of new security threats to our country and our allies, " he told The Hill. "And because of the earmark ban, I can't move it. ... It's just nuts."

Still, he has not reflexively backed spending for his own district. In summer 2012, he sparked the ire of some Houston constituents when he worked to ban federal funds from going to a local light-rail project. He called it "unaffordable and unnecessary."

Beyond advocating for limited government, Culberson personally and professionally shares Jefferson's interest in science. He grew up in Houston and remembers the excitement surrounding every NASA mission — speaking at a 2013 hearing, he said that outside of the military, NASA is the one federal program that can "truly inspire a whole generation of young people to be their best and to achieve beyond what they ever thought possible." The Johnson Space Center is near his district, as are several research facilities.

Working with Wolf (the chairman of the Commerce-Justice-Science Subcommittee, to which Culberson belongs), Culberson has proposed restructuring NASA's management and funding. Under their plan, the president would appoint a director for a 10-year term, the NASA budget would be tied less to the annual budgeting process, and the agency could use multiyear procurement. Wolf and Culberson said the changes would facilitate the long-term planning needed for complex science programs.

Culberson has criticized presidents Barack Obama and George W. Bush as not sufficiently backing the Constellation program, which would have attempted more moon landings and manned spaceflight to Mars.

Immigration is one of Culberson's major terrestrial concerns. Like many conservatives, he was critical of Bush's immigration policies, telling the Los Angeles Times in 2006 that he would not support a guest-worker program until the borders are secured. He is no fan of the Obama administration's proposals either. In June 2012, Obama suspended deportation of many illegal immigrants who were brought to the country as children. In an email to constituents, Culberson called the move "unilateral and illegal."

"I genuinely love working on law enforcement, border security issues," he says, and he also sits on the Homeland Security Subcommittee.

Also like Jefferson, Culberson is a fossil collector. He initially led opposition to an omnibus lands bill in early 2009 because it included a provision that would set heavy penalties for taking any paleontological resource from federal lands without a permit. Ultimately the language was modified to forestall criminal prosecution of visitors who remove a few stones containing fossils.

The third of four children, Culberson was born in Houston. His father was a political consultant and graphic designer who worked on GOP Sen. John Tower's re-election in 1966, when Culberson was 10. He recalls going with his father on campaign trips and later was campus chairman at Southern Methodist University for George Bush's 1980 presidential campaign. (Culberson represents Bush's old House district.) After college, Culberson worked with his father while getting his law degree.

At 30, Culberson won a seat in the Texas House. He stayed there for 14 years while also practicing as a civil defense attorney. In that chamber, he waged an ultimately successful 11-year campaign to return control of the troubled Texas prison system to the state from the supervision of federal Judge William Wayne Justice. One of his goals is a constitutional amendment to give state legislatures the right to approve federal judges every 10 years.

When Rep. Bill Archer decided to retire in 2000, Culberson entered a crowded primary and won an expensive runoff, ensuring his election in the solidly Republican district. Even in the strong Democratic year of 2008, an opponent with a fundraising advantage finished only within 13 points of him. Democrats didn't field a candidate in his district in 2010.

In redistricting for 2012, his seat got even safer for a Republican. He beat Democrat James Cargas by 24 points.

Key Votes

2012	
Extend a Social Security payroll tax cut and unemployment benefits	YES
Ease securities rules to expand small-business access to capital	YES
Extend for one year subsidized student loan interest rates financed by a cut in health care spending	YES
Cite Attorney General Eric H. Holder Jr. for contempt of Congress	YES
Create a visa program for foreign graduates in high-tech fields	?
Extend most Bush-era income tax rates while allowing rates for top-bracket earners to rise (Jan. 1, 2013)	NO
2011	
Strike funding for F-35 alternative engine	YES
Prevent EPA from regulating greenhouse gas emissions to address climate change	YES
Extend certain provisions of Patriot Act for four years	YES
Declare opposition to use of ground troops in Libya	YES
Overhaul patent law	YES
Pass compromise debt limit increase plan and establish future spending limits	YES
Allow consideration of measures to implement three trade agreements	YES

CQ Vote Studies

	PARTY UNITY		PRESIDENTIAL SUPPORT	
	SUPPORT	OPPOSE	SUPPORT	OPPOSE
2012	95%	5%	14%	86%
2011	97%	3%	22%	78%
2010	97%	3%	26%	74%
2009	89%	11%	14%	86%
2008	97%	3%	77%	23%

Interest Groups

	AFL-CIO	ADA	CCUS	ACU
2012	16%	0%	90%	92%
2011	0%	10%	100%	86%
2010	0%	0%	100%	100%
2009	5%	0%	73%	100%
2008	7%	5%	88%	100%

Texas 7

Western Houston and suburbs — Bellaire, Jersey Village

The 7th contains some of Houston's wealthiest neighborhoods, home to highly educated professionals and business owners who make their fortunes in the city's oil and gas industry. Capturing the Uptown District and the city of Bellaire, the L-shaped 7th drops from Stone Gate to George Bush Park, swinging east through southwestern Houston.

Major white-collar employers in insurance and energy occupy the high-rise towers of Uptown, an economic center for the district. Its Galleria is one of the nation's largest retail spaces and a focal point for new residential development. Apartment complexes in Gulfton, south of the Southwest Freeway, are home to many Mexican and Latin American immigrants.

Western enclaves here have been overrun by the metropolitan area's growth and are often considered Houston neighborhoods, but they remain independent municipalities. In West University Place, or "West U," more than 85 percent of adult residents have a bachelor's degree, and streets are named after colleges, authors and poets. Bellaire is home to Chevron Pipe Line headquarters as well as a magnet school for foreign languages. Both cities harbor some Democratic votes.

Further west, Hunters Creek Village is the wealthiest community in the state, with nearby Bunker Hill and Piney Point not far behind. These areas provide the bulk of the district's dominant GOP vote.

Hispanic leaders mobilized for a new city council district covering the southwestern Houston part of the 7th that is expected to give Latinos a stronger voice in local politics. Growth trends have made the district more diverse — Hispanic residents alone account for more than 30 percent of the population — in an area that was once overwhelmingly white. Republican Mitt Romney won the new 7th District with 60 percent of the vote in the 2012 presidential race.

Major Industry
Energy, insurance, health care, retail

Cities
Houston (pt.), Bellaire, West University Place

Notable
America's biggest megachurch, Lakewood Church, draws about 44,000 worshipers for weekly services in the former home of the Houston Rockets.

Rep. Kevin Brady (R)

Capitol Office
225-4901
kevinbrady.house.gov
301 Cannon Bldg. 20515-4901; fax 225-5524

Committees
Ways & Means
(Health - Chairman)
Joint Economic - Chairman
Joint Taxation

Residence
The Woodlands

Born
April 11, 1955; Vermillion, S.D.

Religion
Roman Catholic

Family
Wife, Cathy Brady; two children

Education
U. of South Dakota, B.S. 1990 (mass communication)

Career
Chamber of commerce executive

Political Highlights
Texas House, 1991-96

ELECTION RESULTS

2012 GENERAL		
Kevin Brady (R)	194,043	77.3%
Neil Burns (D)	51,051	20.3%
Roy Hall (LIBERT)	5,958	2.4%
2012 PRIMARY		
Kevin Brady (R)	48,366	76.1%
Larry Youngblood (R)	15,181	23.9%
2010 GENERAL		
Kevin Brady (R)	161,417	80.3%
Kent Hargett (D)	34,694	17.2%
Bruce West (LIBERT)	4,988	2.5%

Previous Winning Percentages
2008 (73%); 2006 (67%); 2004 (69%); 2002 (93%); 2000 (92%); 1998 (93%); 1996 General Election Runoff (59%)

Elected 1996; 9th term

Brady is a Republican expert on trade, working diligently behind the scenes to promote "the freedom to buy, sell and compete with as little government interference as possible." As he urges conservatives to put trade higher on their list of priorities, he's also exploring new specialties as the chairman of the Ways and Means Subcommittee on Health.

Economic growth was a professional goal for Brady before it was a political one. For close to two decades before he came to the U.S. House, Brady worked as an official at local chambers of commerce. "I love trade," he says, describing it as one of Congress' best tools for promoting job creation.

It's a sticky issue, with conflicts forming along party and regional lines; many lawmakers see globalization as putting U.S. workers and companies at the mercy of foreign competitors and unscrupulous governments. Brady has therefore been flexible when trying to get trade agreements across the finish line. He is also noted as having a sunny disposition.

"He's conservative as hell. But the politics aside, he's a very nice guy," said liberal Democrat Jim McDermott of Washington. "And the politics doesn't get in the way of your being a friend with him. I have nothing but good things to say about Kevin." Brady often breaks the ice in intense negotiations with humor, sometimes in the form of a Vince Lombardi impression. "When others give up on something — it's kind of why he goes to that Vince Lombardi — he never gives up," said Majority Whip Kevin McCarthy of California. "He has the vision to figure out how to get to the end."

Brady and McDermott were the chairman and ranking member of the Ways and Means Trade Subcommittee in the 112th Congress (2011-12). Brady felt that President Barack Obama was uninterested in trade initially, but he applauded an uptick of activity in the 112th. He credited the administration with tweaking a South Korea deal to satisfy Democrats and automakers; that agreement, as well as pacts with Colombia and Panama, were approved in 2011. Democrats at the same time insisted on an expansion of the program assisting workers who lose their jobs because of international trade. Many conservatives voted against it, but Brady made a good-faith show of support.

The next year he helped ensure House passage of legislation to establish regular trade relations with Russia, which Obama signed. He also suggested granting the White House "fast-track" authority — which lets it submit trade deals to Congress for up-or-down votes with no amendments allowed — before negotiations conclude on the Trans-Pacific Partnership.

Brady hasn't been keen on attempts to punish China for manipulating the value of its currency, which gives it a trading advantage. He worries any duties imposed on China would result in retaliation that will drive up costs to U.S. consumers.

Brady has more political challenges on his plate as the Health chairman, a job that opened up when California Republican Wally Herger retired. (He still has the same ranking member — McDermott moved over with him.) Some parts of the 2010 health care law are "simply unworkable," he says, such as its Independent Payment Advisory Board and a tax on medical devices. He wants to examine ways to increase price transparency and competition in health care markets as a means to drive down costs.

Early in the 113th Congress (2013-14), Brady started shaping plans to eliminate the "sustainable growth rate" formula that sets Medicare payments to physicians. Both parties loathe the SGR, and Congress regularly overrides the steep cuts to reimbursements dictated by the formula.

He is also the chairman of the Joint Economic Committee, which provides analysis and recommendations on economic and fiscal policy. Brady dislikes the recent monetary policy pursued by the Federal Reserve. In 2012 and 2013, he introduced a bill to reshape the Fed dramatically, eliminating its mandate to maximize employment and weakening a lot of its monetary policy tools, which he says are interfering with market forces.

Transforming government is a Brady theme. He routinely sponsors legislation to set expiration dates for each federal agency, department and program unless they are affirmatively renewed. It's similar to a Texas law written by another current Ways and Means member, Democrat Lloyd Doggett.

Brady almost always votes with a majority of Republicans, but for a while he split with his party on the issue of gun rights. When he was 12, his father, a lawyer, was shot and killed in a South Dakota courtroom by the deranged spouse of a client, and the incident helped shape his outlook on gun control. As a state representative in Texas, Brady was one of two Republicans to oppose a bill allowing Texans to carry concealed weapons.

But more recently he said the law has not been abused and has protected many individuals and small businesses "in tough areas." In April 2009, he warned against "potential overreaction to the Mexican drug violence" that could lead to curbing gun owners' rights.

One of five children, Brady attended the University of South Dakota, where he was the center fielder on the baseball team. He left college without graduating because he had neglected to complete the paperwork for a work-study class. After an opponent in his first Texas House race in 1990 unearthed Brady's lack of a degree, he cleared up the incomplete grade.

Brady started working for the Rapid City Area Chamber of Commerce in 1979, then moved to Texas in 1982 to work for chambers in that state. He served six years in the Texas House. That tenure led straight to his run for the U.S. House when eight-term Republican Jack Fields announced he wasn't running for re-election in the 8th District in 1996.

Republican physician Gene Fontenot won the March primary for the GOP nomination but didn't capture a majority of the vote. Brady had stronger ties to the district and defeated Fontenot in the April runoff.

However, a three-judge federal panel redrew the 8th District and a dozen others in response to a Supreme Court ruling that found illegal racial gerrymandering at play in the Texas map. The court threw out the primary results. Fontenot was back on the ballot for the November election, along with two Democratic candidates; Brady won and Fontenot finished second. Brady then won a December runoff with 59 percent of the vote.

He has been safely ensconced since then. After redistricting for 2012, he took 77 percent of the vote.

Key Votes

2012	
Extend a Social Security payroll tax cut and unemployment benefits	YES
Ease securities rules to expand small-business access to capital	YES
Extend for one year subsidized student loan interest rates financed by a cut in health care spending	YES
Cite Attorney General Eric H. Holder Jr. for contempt of Congress	YES
Create a visa program for foreign graduates in high-tech fields	YES
Extend most Bush-era income tax rates while allowing rates for top-bracket earners to rise (Jan. 1, 2013)	YES
2011	
Strike funding for F-35 alternative engine	YES
Prevent EPA from regulating greenhouse gas emissions to address climate change	YES
Extend certain provisions of Patriot Act for four years	YES
Declare opposition to use of ground troops in Libya	YES
Overhaul patent law	YES
Pass compromise debt limit increase plan and establish future spending limits	YES
Allow consideration of measures to implement three trade agreements	YES

CQ Vote Studies

	Party Unity		Presidential Support	
	Support	Oppose	Support	Oppose
2012	98%	2%	18%	82%
2011	97%	3%	25%	75%
2010	97%	3%	26%	74%
2009	97%	3%	11%	89%
2008	94%	6%	77%	23%

Interest Groups

	AFL-CIO	ADA	CCUS	ACU
2012	14%	0%	100%	96%
2011	0%	5%	100%	92%
2010	0%	0%	88%	100%
2009	5%	0%	73%	100%
2008	7%	10%	88%	86%

Texas 8

East central — The Woodlands, Conroe

Capturing an outflow of Houston's highest educated, white-collar workers, Montgomery County serves as the core of the 8th and ranks among the fastest-growing counties in the nation. South of The Woodlands, the district grabs a tiny piece of Harris County, but most of its territory lies to the north in open prairies and rolling hills of pine and oak. More than 160,000 acres are blanketed by the Sam Houston National Forest, and it shares Lake Livingston, Houston's main water supply, with the 36th.

The 8th's old boundaries took it to the Louisiana border; decennial redistricting shifted it to the north and west, into former parts of the 6th and 17th districts.

Interstate 45, the link between Houston and Dallas, runs through the district. The professionals who have snapped up single-family homes, townhouses and golf-course estates in the planned communities of The Woodlands and Conroe clog the highway during rush hours. Flyovers are being added to Texas Highway 242, a frequently backed-up stretch in Montgomery County connected to the interstate. These densely populated suburban areas have become less dependent on Houston by expanding their retail and recreation offerings and new corporate development. Chevron Phillips Chemical, Huntsman and Lexicon Pharmaceuticals have offices in this part of the district.

Outside Montgomery County, the terrain becomes increasingly forested, making logging an important industry. Trinity and Houston counties in the district's northeastern corner are home to Davy Crockett National Forest.

The 8th is socially conservative territory, especially Montgomery County, and the voters in the district gave Republican Mitt Romney a secure 77 percent of their vote in the 2012 presidential election. Overall, the majority-white district is roughly 20 percent Hispanic.

Major Industry

Petrochemicals, timber, professional services, prisons

Cities

The Woodlands (unincorp.), Conroe, Huntsville

Notable

The Texas Prison Museum in Huntsville houses "Old Sparky," an electric chair that was the method of execution for 361 prisoners before being retired in 1964.

Rep. Al Green (D)

Capitol Office
225-7508
algreen.house.gov
2201 Rayburn Bldg. 20515-4309; fax 225-2947

Committees
Financial Services

Residence
Houston

Born
Sept. 1, 1947; New Orleans, La.

Religion
Baptist

Family
Divorced

Education
Florida A&M U., attended 1966-71; Tuskegee Institute of Technology, attended ; Texas Southern U., J.D. 1973

Career
Lawyer; NAACP chapter president

Political Highlights
Harris County Justice of the Peace Court judge, 1977-2004; candidate for mayor of Houston, 1981

ELECTION RESULTS

2012 GENERAL		
Al Green (D)	144,075	78.5%
Steve Mueller (R)	36,139	19.7%
2012 PRIMARY		
Al Green (D)		unopposed
2010 GENERAL		
Al Green (D)	80,107	75.7%
Steve Mueller (R)	24,201	22.9%
Michael W. Hope (LIBERT)	1,459	1.4%

Previous Winning Percentages
2008 (94%); 2006 (100%); 2004 (72%)

Elected 2004; 5th term

Green often works on behalf of people on the poorer end of the economic spectrum, wrapping his suggestions in appeals to human decency. His policy portfolio focuses on job security, higher wages, affordable housing and health care for all.

Born in New Orleans, Green has a background as diverse as the district he represents. He attended Florida A&M University and the Tuskegee Institute of Technology through work-study and grant programs. He never earned an undergraduate degree, but he went on to study at the Thurgood Marshall School of Law at Texas Southern University, where he earned his law degree. He co-founded a law practice and served as a criminal defense attorney. Among his adversaries was prosecutor Ted Poe, who now serves with Green in Congress, and whom he counts as a good friend.

Prior to his election to the House, Green also served as a justice of the peace and as president of his local NAACP chapter in the 1980s and early 1990s. Many of his sound bites have a ministerial feel, and he often wears a "God is Good" lapel pin.

He has said his calling is to speak for those who may not be able to speak for themselves. In his 2012 speech to the Democratic National Convention, Green urged fellow Democrats to make this mission their priority: "Our faith tells us we have a moral obligation to better our communities, to accept responsibility and care for each other."

Green sits on the Financial Services Committee, where many of his efforts involve housing. He supports the affordable-housing trust fund created by a 2008 law to provide money to build, rehabilitate and preserve rental housing. In July 2012, Financial Services Republicans advanced a bill to abolish the program — its major funding stream, contributions from Fannie Mae and Freddie Mac, dried up due to the precarious financial condition of those entities. Green offered an unsuccessful amendment to keep the trust fund in place even without contributions from Fannie and Freddie, arguing that more energy should be spent prosecuting those who abuse project funds. The underlying bill did not get a vote on the House floor.

In 2013, the House again passed Green's bill to establish a special assistant for veterans affairs in the Department of Housing and Urban Development, and to require agencies to report on efforts to help homeless veterans. He defended foreclosure assistance programs that Republicans sought to eliminate in 2011. "We can amend them; we need not end them," he said.

Green is protective of the 2010 financial regulatory overhaul known as Dodd-Frank, and he sees government backing of the housing finance market as necessary for the continued existence of the 30-year mortgage. In 2013, he was named the ranking member of the Oversight and Investigations Subcommittee, opposite Chairman Patrick T. McHenry of North Carolina. At the panel's first hearing, Green said lawmakers must balance "the rights of consumers and the needs of those in the financial services community."

Green proposes a substantial increase in the minimum wage. He has written legislation to require reassessments of the wage level every four years; he wants people working full-time minimum-wage jobs to earn annual pay 15 percent above the federal poverty level for a family of two.

His Houston-area district has a large number of poorer residents, and he will choose the direct economic interests of his constituents over standard Democratic positions. Green has been receptive to bills meant to bolster the oil industry, which is a major employer in the city. He joined 21 other Democrats in signing a 2011 letter urging President Barack Obama to approve the

Keystone XL pipeline from Canada's tar sands to Texas' refineries. He was one of 21 House Democrats voting for a 2012 bill to approve the pipeline, expand offshore drilling and open the Arctic National Wildlife Refuge to energy exploration.

He also keeps tabs on NASA. Green lamented the decision to end the space shuttle program, whose mission control headquarters was Johnson Space Center. Green and several other Texas lawmakers have positioned themselves as backers of the Orion Multi-Purpose Crew Vehicle project, which might produce the next generation of American manned space exploration vehicles — and an economic boon for the space center.

But Green's overall instincts are liberal. During debate on the 2010 health care overhaul, he called for a "robust public option," a government-run insurance program that did not make it into the final version of the legislation.

Green often recites the eight-verse poem "The Cold Within" by James Patrick Kenny, which tells the story of six people who died in the cold because greed and spite kept each from contributing to a fire that would have kept them all warm. "The point is this," he says. "If we don't learn to live together as brothers and sisters, we will perish as fools."

A broad interest in civil rights sometimes motivates Green to get involved in global affairs. In March 2012, he was arrested outside of the Sudanese Embassy while protesting violence against civilians and the humanitarian crisis in Sudan. Green, alongside actor George Clooney, several Democratic lawmakers, Martin Luther King III, NAACP President Ben Jealous and Enough Project co-founder John Prendergast, was released after posting bail.

"As Dr. King said, injustice anywhere is a threat to justice everywhere," Green said following his arrest. "We cannot allow the ongoing conflict in Sudan to continue, and we must stand together to protect those who are innocent victims of these senseless acts of violence."

Green represents a racially diverse district, and he is a member of both the Congressional Black Caucus and the Asian Pacific American Caucus. Green says he is comfortable moving in both circles, in part because he isn't entirely sure about his own ethnic background: "I don't know what I am."

When Texas congressional districts were remapped prior to the 2004 election, Green saw the demographics of the altered 9th District and decided to enter the Democratic primary. He handily defeated Rep. Chris Bell, which essentially guaranteed his election in November. In 2006 and 2008 he faced no major-party opposition, and in 2010 he won with 76 percent of the vote, despite being challenged by Republican Steve Mueller.

The 2012 cycle once again saw Green facing off with Mueller. He enjoyed another easy victory.

Key Votes

2012

Extend a Social Security payroll tax cut and unemployment benefits	YES
Ease securities rules to expand small-business access to capital	YES
Extend for one year subsidized student loan interest rates financed by a cut in health care spending	NO
Cite Attorney General Eric H. Holder Jr. for contempt of Congress	?
Create a visa program for foreign graduates in high-tech fields	NO
Extend most Bush-era income tax rates while allowing rates for top-bracket earners to rise (Jan. 1, 2013)	YES

2011

Strike funding for F-35 alternative engine	YES
Prevent EPA from regulating greenhouse gas emissions to address climate change	NO
Extend certain provisions of Patriot Act for four years	NO
Declare opposition to use of ground troops in Libya	NO
Overhaul patent law	YES
Pass compromise debt limit increase plan and establish future spending limits	NO
Allow consideration of measures to implement three trade agreements	NO

CQ Vote Studies

	Party Unity		Presidential Support	
	Support	Oppose	Support	Oppose
2012	88%	12%	83%	17%
2011	90%	10%	83%	17%
2010	98%	2%	95%	5%
2009	99%	1%	97%	3%
2008	99%	1%	14%	86%

Interest Groups

	AFL-CIO	ADA	CCUS	ACU
2012	95%	75%	33%	16%
2011	100%	90%	38%	8%
2010	93%	90%	25%	0%
2009	100%	100%	33%	0%
2008	100%	100%	67%	4%

Texas 9

Southern Houston and suburbs — Mission Bend, part of Missouri City

Curving around the southwestern quarter of Beltway 8, the 9th slices across stretches of metropolitan Houston and captures two wedges of northeastern Fort Bend County. Inside the South 610 Loop, the district takes in some of the city's major recreation sites and the famed Texas Medical Center. This 40-percent-black, 37-percent-Hispanic district has the smallest share of whites statewide. Democratic candidates perform well in elections here, and Barack Obama took 78 percent of the district's 2012 presidential vote.

The 9th reaches closest into Houston's urban center at Hermann Park, one of the most picturesque parts of the city and home to the Houston Zoo. Texas Medical Center sees about 160,000 visitors daily and employs nearly 100,000. Just to the south, Reliant Stadium hosts football's Texans across the street from the former home to baseball's Astros — the Astrodome faces an uncertain future.

Farther south, the 9th represents historically black Sunnyside and other low- and middle-income areas, where residents have banded together in "super neighborhoods" to better communicate their needs to city government. The Bellaire Boulevard corridor is home to many Asian-Americans, who account for 9 percent of the 9th's population overall, and the corridor is undergoing a multimillion-dollar infrastructure upgrade. Homes are newer and incomes are higher to the west, especially in Mission Bend.

Houston leads the nation in income segregation: More than $20,000 separates the median incomes of the 9th and its wealthier northern neighbor, the 7th. The southwestern corner of the district includes most of Missouri City, which helps boost the district's average income and diversity: its median household income is $80,000 and it is 40 percent black. More than 80 languages are spoken in classrooms of fast-growing Fort Bend County schools.

Major Industry

Health care, stadium events, tube and pipe manufacturing

Cities

Houston (pt.), Missouri City (pt.), Mission Bend (unincorp.)

Notable

Jade Buddha Temple is a place of worship that also serves as a Buddhist study and research center for many universities.

Rep. Michael McCaul (R)

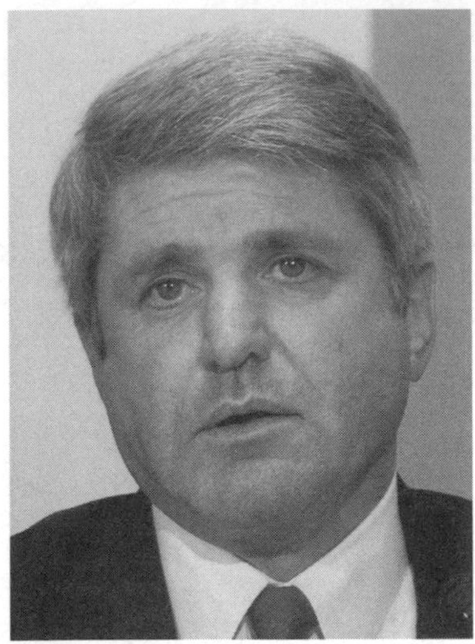

Capitol Office
255-2401
mccaul.house.gov
131 Cannon Bldg. 20515-4310; fax 225-5955

Committees
Foreign Affairs
Homeland Security - Chairman
Science, Space & Technology

Residence
Austin

Born
Jan. 14, 1962; Dallas, Texas

Religion
Roman Catholic

Family
Wife, Linda McCaul; five children

Education
Trinity U., B.A. 1984 (business & history); St. Mary's U. (Texas), J.D. 1987

Career
U.S. Justice Department official; state deputy attorney general; federal prosecutor; lawyer

Political Highlights
No previous office

ELECTION RESULTS

2012 GENERAL		
Michael McCaul (R)	159,783	60.5%
Tawana W. Cadien (D)	95,710	36.2%
Richard Priest (LIBERT)	8,526	3.2%
2012 PRIMARY		
Michael McCaul (R)	39,543	83.8%
Eddie Traylor (R)	7,664	16.2%
2010 GENERAL		
Michael McCaul (R)	144,980	64.7%
Ted Ankrum (D)	74,086	33.0%
Jeremiah Perkins (LIBERT)	5,105	2.3%

Previous Winning Percentages
2008 (54%); 2006 (55%); 2004 (79%)

Elected 2004; 5th term

Since arriving in the House in 2005, McCaul has worked on national security from as many angles as possible. His holistic approach and some smart politicking have yielded him the gavel of the Homeland Security Committee.

McCaul attributes his career in public service to the example set by his father — a B-17 pilot during World War II — and his education at the Jesuit College Preparatory School of Dallas. He was a prosecutor in the Justice Department's public integrity section before becoming a deputy to Texas Attorney General John Cornyn, who is now the Senate minority whip. He was later the chief of counterterrorism and national security in the U.S. attorney's office in Austin, and he led its Joint Terrorism Task Force.

He was assigned to the Homeland Security Committee as a freshman, but he has also been on the Foreign Affairs Committee and the Science, Space and Technology Committee throughout his House career — allowing him to round out his knowledge of the war on terrorism and the technology that factors into homeland defense. He is a founder of both the Congressional High Tech Caucus and the Congressional Cyber Security Caucus.

The former Homeland chairman, Peter T. King of New York, reached a GOP-imposed term limit at the end of the 112th Congress (2011-12), so McCaul threw his hat in the ring. In one of the closest chairman elections in the last 20 years, he edged out Candice S. Miller of Michigan and Mike D. Rogers of Alabama after several rounds of voting by the GOP Steering Committee.

McCaul sold his peers on his agenda across four areas: cybersecurity, terrorism, border controls, and management problems in the Department of Homeland Security. He has said that cybersecurity is paramount among those priorities in the 113th Congress (2013-14). He wants to codify the role of DHS in cybersecurity — some lawmakers would hand that role to the Pentagon — and offer liability protections to businesses to encourage coordination with the government.

In the 110th Congress (2007-08), he was the ranking member of the Subcommittee on Emerging Threats, alongside Democratic Chairman Jim Langevin of Rhode Island. That tandem co-chaired the Center for Strategic and International Studies Commission on Cybersecurity for the 44th Presidency, which issued a post-election report containing cybersecurity recommendations for President Barack Obama. McCaul has criticized Obama as dragging his feet on providing cybersecurity resources and appointing key personnel.

In both 2012 and 2013, the House overwhelmingly passed McCaul's bill to task federal science programs with developing a strategic research and development plan for cybersecurity. He has supported a more controversial measure, produced by the Intelligence Committee, to facilitate the sharing of classified information with private sector entities targeted by cyberattacks.

In the 112th Congress, McCaul chaired the Subcommittee on Oversight, Investigations and Management. DHS was created by glomming together 22 different agencies, and by almost any accounting it hasn't been a smooth process. Among other subjects, McCaul held hearings on fraud and ethical standards within the department. He wrote in Roll Call in late 2012 that the department has a "culture of corruption, waste, duplication and systemic management problems with little in the way of answers."

Like most Texas Republicans, McCaul describes illegal immigration as a major national security issue. He has led bipartisan efforts to increase the use of security technology on the U.S.-Mexico border. He applauded Obama's May 2010 decision to send National Guard troops to the border but said it wasn't enough. "I urge the Obama administration to show the same commitment to securing our borders as [Mexican] President [Felipe] Calderon has personally shown to tracking cartels, sharing intelligence and cooperating with the United States," he said. In April 2011, he proposed designating violent Mexican drug cartels as terrorist organizations.

For McCaul, border security and law enforcement trump any changes to immigration policies: "As a rule I oppose any effort to grant amnesty or create a path to citizenship for those who come here illegally and jumped the line ahead of people who have gone through the proper channels to enter lawfully," he wrote in June 2012.

His 2013 bill requiring DHS to develop a plan for achieving "operational control" of the U.S. border has bipartisan support. (It is based partly on work by Miller in 2012.) At his first hearing as chairman, he said that "the ability exists to gain effective control of our borders within three years."

Ethics is a common theme in McCaul's career, going back to his Justice Department days. From 2007 through 2012, he sat on the Ethics Committee. He was involved in investigations of Republican Rick Renzi of Arizona and California Democrat Maxine Waters; in 2010 he was the presiding Republican in the trial of New York Democrat Charles B. Rangel, who was censured.

McCaul was among the panel Republicans who criticized former Chairwoman Zoe Lofgren, a California Democrat, for delaying the trials of Rangel and Waters until after the 2010 elections. But internal committee documents later surfaced that indicated another possible reason for the delay: improper communications from staff members handling the case to McCaul and others.

His service on Ethics probably helped his bid for the Homeland gavel — it's a labor intensive job often taken as a favor to party leaders. McCaul has also been on the whip team and was his freshman class' liaison to GOP leaders.

McCaul's political debut was the 2004 GOP House primary, an eight-candidate free-for-all. He amassed support from Republican insiders and won the runoff with 63 percent of the vote. Democrats didn't field a candidate that November, and McCaul easily dispatched a libertarian opponent.

Despite good years for Democrats and actual opposition, he still won handily in 2006 and 2008. McCaul briefly contemplated a 2010 bid for state attorney general, but he told the Austin American-Statesman that he had decided to run for re-election "because the challenges we face in Washington have never been greater." He won with almost 65 percent of the vote. After redistricting for 2012, he won a fifth term with more than 60 percent.

Going by financial disclosure forms, McCaul is likely the richest member of Congress. Large transfers in wealth from his in-laws increased his minimum net worth to at around $306 million in 2011. McCaul's wife, Linda, is the daughter of Clear Channel Communications founder Lowry Mays.

Key Votes

2012

Extend a Social Security payroll tax cut and unemployment benefits	YES
Ease securities rules to expand small-business access to capital	YES
Extend for one year subsidized student loan interest rates financed by a cut in health care spending	YES
Cite Attorney General Eric H. Holder Jr. for contempt of Congress	YES
Create a visa program for foreign graduates in high-tech fields	YES
Extend most Bush-era income tax rates while allowing rates for top-bracket earners to rise (Jan. 1, 2013)	NO

2011

Strike funding for F-35 alternative engine	NO
Prevent EPA from regulating greenhouse gas emissions to address climate change	YES
Extend certain provisions of Patriot Act for four years	YES
Declare opposition to use of ground troops in Libya	YES
Overhaul patent law	YES
Pass compromise debt limit increase plan and establish future spending limits	YES
Allow consideration of measures to implement three trade agreements	YES

CQ Vote Studies

	PARTY UNITY		PRESIDENTIAL SUPPORT	
	SUPPORT	OPPOSE	SUPPORT	OPPOSE
2012	97%	3%	17%	83%
2011	96%	4%	23%	77%
2010	95%	5%	26%	74%
2009	94%	6%	26%	74%
2008	95%	5%	68%	32%

Interest Groups

	AFL-CIO	ADA	CCUS	ACU
2012	10%	0%	100%	95%
2011	0%	5%	100%	76%
2010	0%	0%	100%	96%
2009	16%	0%	87%	96%
2008	13%	25%	89%	96%

Texas 10

East central — northern Austin and suburbs, western Houston suburbs

The 10th spans approximately 150 miles of U.S. Highway 290, connecting the northern precincts of Austin to the Greater Houston region through a belt of rural counties. Nearly 70 percent of the district is anchored in Travis and Harris counties, while rolling hills and prairies stretch through the corridor between the cities. Overall, the 10th is a Republican and conservative district and gave Mitt Romney nearly 60 percent of its vote in the 2012 presidential race; the district's portion of Travis County is the only jurisdiction in the 10th to back Barack Obama in 2012.

Of the five districts sharing Travis County, the 10th has the largest share of Austin and includes some of its most historic upscale homes in North Austin. Formerly a top destination for technology jobs, the city has recently lost some of its clout as computer and semiconductor manufacturers have cut jobs. In response, the city council is working with developers to attract technology startups and more skilled workers. Grants helped it land a major new Apple operations center near the district. University of Texas' J.J. Pickle Research Campus is here, as is a National Guard facility. Northeast of Austin, the 10th grabs suburban Pflugerville, where the black population grew nearly threefold over the last decade.

To the east of the state capital, Bastrop County is expanding its hospitals to keep pace with rapid population growth. The broad mid-section of the district is covered by the oil-rich Austin Chalk formation, which brings drilling companies to Fayette, Lee and Washington counties. Hydrofracturing natural gas extraction operations are under way at the Eagle Ford Shale reserve.

As the 10th enters Harris County, it picks up wealthy suburban Houston neighborhoods. Outlet malls, shopping centers and megachurches typify the landscape in the western fringes of the district.

Major Industry
Technology, oil and gas, retail, health care

Cities
Houston (pt.), Austin (pt.), Pflugerville

Notable
The Attwater Prairie Chicken National Wildlife Refuge is home to one of the last populations of the endangered bird.

Rep. K. Michael Conaway (R)

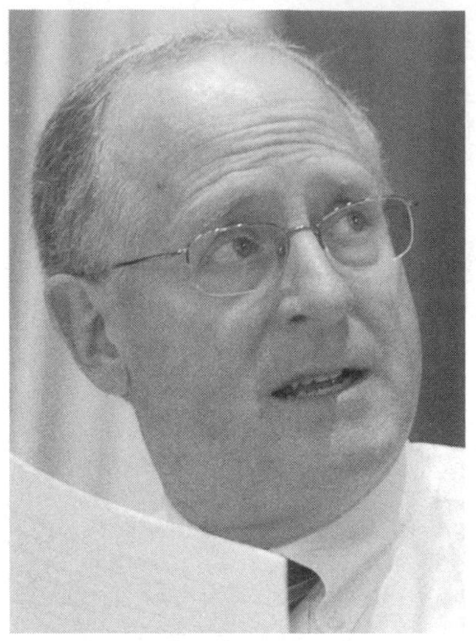

Capitol Office
225-3605
conaway.house.gov
2430 Rayburn Bldg. 20515-4311; fax 225-1783

Committees
Agriculture
(General Farm Commodities & Risk Management - Chairman)
Armed Services
Ethics - Chairman
Select Intelligence

Residence
Midland

Born
June 11, 1948; Borger, Texas

Religion
Baptist

Family
Wife, Suzanne Conaway; four children

Education
East Texas State U., B.B.A. 1970 (accounting)

Military
Army, 1970-72

Career
Accountant; bank chief financial officer; oil and gas exploration company chief financial officer

Political Highlights
Midland school board, 1985-88; Texas State Board of Public Accountancy, 1995-2002 (presiding officer, 1997-2002); candidate for U.S. House (special election), 2003

ELECTION RESULTS

2012 GENERAL		
K. Michael Conaway (R)	177,742	78.6%
Jim Riley (D)	41,970	18.6%
Scott J. Ballard (LIBERT)	6,311	2.8%
2012 PRIMARY		
K. Michael Conaway (R)	48,581	70.4%
Chris Younts (R)	12,917	18.7%
Wade Brown (R)	7,547	10.9%

Previous Winning Percentages
2010 (81%); 2008 (88%); 2006 (100%); 2004 (77%)

Elected 2004; 5th term

Conaway's ties to both financial management and the Republican Party are unusually strong. He was a friend and business partner to George W. Bush during the 1980s at their Midland-based energy company; Conaway, an accountant, served as the chief financial officer. When Bush became governor of Texas, he appointed Conaway to the state Board of Public Accountancy, where Conaway served seven years, including five as chairman.

He enjoys the minutiae of budgeting and champions fiscal restraint. "I am clearly in support of cutting spending," he said. "It's just how you cut that spending."

Conaway says his district buys in to the need to curb federal expenditures. But as the chairman of the Agriculture Subcommittee on General Farm Commodities and Risk Management, he found himself defending disaster aid for livestock producers affected by drought in the 112th Congress (2011-12).

He also challenged conservative criticisms of a five-year reauthorization of farm programs approved by the Agriculture Committee in 2012. That bill had substantial savings — more than $30 billion by some estimates — but maintained "target prices," with the government making up the difference when commodities sell below that price. "Farmers need price protection," he said.

The bill was not enacted, and Conaway is continuing his defense in the 113th Congress (2013-14). He is also concerned about the effect that a 2010 overhaul of the financial regulatory system is having on commodities markets. In 2013, he introduced a bill to require cost-benefit analyses of new regulations on derivatives.

Conaway is not shy about protecting farmers and agribusinesses. In 2010, he opposed a bipartisan effort to end federal subsidies for the production of mohair, which is made from the coats of Angora goats. The Mohair Council of America is located in his district. Immigrant labor is important to his district's farmers, and Conaway in the past has backed a limited immigration policy overhaul that would allow illegal immigrants to register as temporary workers, but without the possibility of becoming citizens.

As a member of the Armed Services Committee, he spent much of 2012 fighting potential "sequestration" cuts of $500 billion to defense budgets, put in place by an August 2011 deficit reduction law. Those cuts would go "beyond the pale," he said in 2012. "We will not be able to defend our country in the way most Americans presume she will be defended." The cuts began in 2013.

Republicans have tried to maximize the use of Conaway's professional talents. In the 111th Congress (2009-10), he was the ranking member of a special Armed Services panel studying the Pentagon's acquisitions process, and in the 112th Congress he chaired the short-term Defense Financial Management and Auditability Reform Panel — he has been a critic of the Pentagon's "outdated and cumbersome financial management systems." Robert E. Andrews of New Jersey was the top Democrat on both of those panels.

Conaway sees his positions on defense and agriculture as consistent with responsible fiscal spending — the federal government has a role to play in helping farmers and ranchers manage financial risks and in making sure national security is strong, he says. Like many Republicans, he sees the nation's fiscal health as dependent on an overhaul of mandatory entitlement programs that consume most of the budget. "Fixing the overall problems and limiting that fix to only a third of the budget is mathematically unsound," he said.

He has found enough members in the House and Senate who share his interest in numbers to form the bipartisan CPA and Accountants Caucus.

Conaway's close ties to the current crop of GOP leaders are demonstrated by his selection as chairman of the Ethics Committee for the 113th Congress. That labor-intensive job puts him in charge of reviewing thousands of financial disclosure forms and evaluating allegations of misconduct by House members. Conaway has been on the committee since 2009 — he sat on the special subcommittee that conducted a public trial of Charles B. Rangel, a New York Democrat. (In March 2013, the committee launched an investigation of Andrews over alleged misuses of campaign funds.)

Republican leaders have tapped him for special duties in the past. During the 110th Congress (2007-08), he led an internal audit team for the National Republican Congressional Committee, the House GOP's campaign arm. He found that the committee's treasurer, Christopher J. Ward, had been preparing false financial statements for years. The embezzlement was estimated at $725,000.

Conaway is also a member of the Intelligence Committee, where he has trained his accountant's eye on the spy community's financial practices. In July 2010, he wrote the Office of Management and Budget asking it to ensure that the intelligence community receives a clean financial audit because it "is currently unable to satisfactorily account for the tax dollars which it is given to protect the very individuals that provide that money."

Conaway played defensive end and offensive tackle on the Odessa Permian High School's first state championship football team. (The school's football program was the basis for the book "Friday Night Lights.") He won a football scholarship but had a limited college football career.

He was a pre-law major in college when a professor persuaded him to switch to accounting. He received his degree from East Texas State University (now Texas A&M University-Commerce) in 1970. Conaway worked as an oil rig worker, or "roughneck," while in college.

He was a military police officer at the Army's Fort Hood in Texas, then worked for Price Waterhouse & Co., settling in Midland. From 1981 to 1986, he served as chief financial officer of, and an investor in, Arbusto Energy Inc. (later Bush Exploration). Conaway backs expanded oil and gas production, and he says the Obama administration's push for the Defense Department to make big purchases of renewable fuels is economically unfeasible.

After working in the energy industry, he opened his own accounting firm in 1993. He also is an ordained Baptist deacon.

Republican Larry Combest resigned from the 19th District in 2003. In the race to replace him, Conaway lost a special-election runoff to fellow Republican Randy Neugebauer — by 587 votes. But GOP-led congressional redistricting heading into the 2004 election created an opportunity in the 11th District, and Conaway won that seat easily.

Key Votes

2012	
Extend a Social Security payroll tax cut and unemployment benefits	YES
Ease securities rules to expand small-business access to capital	YES
Extend for one year subsidized student loan interest rates financed by a cut in health care spending	YES
Cite Attorney General Eric H. Holder Jr. for contempt of Congress	YES
Create a visa program for foreign graduates in high-tech fields	YES
Extend most Bush-era income tax rates while allowing rates for top-bracket earners to rise (Jan. 1, 2013)	NO
2011	
Strike funding for F-35 alternative engine	NO
Prevent EPA from regulating greenhouse gas emissions to address climate change	YES
Extend certain provisions of Patriot Act for four years	YES
Declare opposition to use of ground troops in Libya	YES
Overhaul patent law	YES
Pass compromise debt limit increase plan and establish future spending limits	YES
Allow consideration of measures to implement three trade agreements	YES

CQ Vote Studies

	PARTY UNITY		PRESIDENTIAL SUPPORT	
	SUPPORT	OPPOSE	SUPPORT	OPPOSE
2012	99%	1%	15%	85%
2011	98%	2%	22%	78%
2010	99%	1%	26%	74%
2009	99%	1%	11%	89%
2008	97%	3%	76%	24%

Interest Groups

	AFL-CIO	ADA	CCUS	ACU
2012	10%	0%	83%	100%
2011	0%	5%	100%	88%
2010	0%	0%	88%	100%
2009	5%	0%	71%	100%
2008	0%	5%	89%	92%

Texas 11

West central — Midland, Odessa, San Angelo

The Republican-minded 11th stretches from the outskirts of Fort Worth in Hood County west to the New Mexico border, covering some of the high plains of central Texas and acres of chugging oil rigs. Traditional oil towns Midland and Odessa, along with San Angelo, have enjoyed petroleum-fueled boom times again. Decennial redistricting did not dramatically alter the boundaries of the 11th, however it did remove counties — its part of Nolan as well as Scurry and Gillespie — in the northwest and south, while extending it into the northeast through Palo Pinto and Hood counties.

The 1920s Texas oil boom started here in the Permian Basin. Odessa in particular still relies on oil and natural gas production, which has rebounded through hydraulic fracturing — or fracking — a method of natural gas extraction that has strained already scarce water resources. The area also has become a regional telecommunications and distribution hub.

Farms on the savannas and rolling hills of the Concho Valley to the southeast produce cotton, wheat and sorghum. Ranches here support the biggest goat and lamb market in the state as well as large herds of cattle. The region is also popular with hunters.

Agribusiness, including livestock processing, is a major industry for San Angelo, the valley's service and trade hub. Information technology also thrives here and is supported by Angelo State University.

Whites make up about 60 percent of the population in the district, while Hispanics are the fastest-growing group. The GOP has a strong sway in the district, which contains President George W. Bush's childhood home. Republican nominee Mitt Romney did not lose in any county in the district and won many by overwhelming margins in the 2012 presidential race.

Major Industry
Oil and gas, agriculture and livestock, technology

Military Bases
Goodfellow Air Force Base, 3,940 military, 1,019 civilian (2011)

Cities
Midland, Odessa, San Angelo

Notable
Brady hosts the World Championship BBQ Goat Cook-Off every Labor Day weekend.

Rep. Kay Granger (R)

Capitol Office
225-5071
kaygranger.house.gov
1026 Longworth Bldg. 20515-4312; fax 225-5683

Committees
Appropriations
(State-Foreign Operations - Chairwoman)

Residence
Fort Worth

Born
Jan. 18, 1943; Greenville, Texas

Religion
Methodist

Family
Divorced; three children

Education
Texas Wesleyan U., B.S. 1965

Career
Insurance agency owner; teacher

Political Highlights
Fort Worth Zoning Commission, 1981-89; Fort Worth City Council, 1989-91; mayor of Fort Worth, 1991-95

ELECTION RESULTS

2012 GENERAL		
Kay Granger (R)	175,649	70.9%
Dave Robinson (D)	66,080	26.7%
Matthew Solodow (LIBERT)	5,983	2.4%
2012 PRIMARY		
Kay Granger (R)	34,828	80.2%
Bill Lawrence (R)	8,611	19.8%
2010 GENERAL		
Kay Granger (R)	109,882	71.9%
Tracey Smith (D)	38,434	25.1%
Matthew Solodow (LIBERT)	4,601	3.0%

Previous Winning Percentages
2008 (68%); 2006 (67%); 2004 (72%); 2002 (92%); 2000 (63%); 1998 (62%); 1996 (58%)

Elected 1996; 9th term

Granger is a gatekeeper for foreign aid and State Department spending as an Appropriations subcommittee chairwoman. She supports well-defined aid programs but is sternly skeptical when their benefits are less than fully clear. Bono, the rock star and aid advocate, called her approach "tough love."

Foreign aid is never a highly popular spending account in Congress, and tighter fiscal times of late have made it even less so. Some advocates of foreign aid spending see more toughness than love in her approach. On Granger's watch in the 112th Congress (2011-12), the State-Foreign Operations Subcommittee proposed substantial cuts in foreign spending as compared to both Obama administration requests and recent funding levels.

Under her stewardship, the "frontline states" of strategic importance to the United States continued to receive relatively high levels of assistance, while other nations and regions fell behind. The favored nations were Iraq, Afghanistan, Pakistan, Israel and Texas's neighbor, Mexico, where drug violence has spread northward — even to Forth Worth, the city where Granger once served as mayor.

When Granger has backed funding for aid programs, she often has insisted on attaching tough preconditions for disbursing the money. That was the case with aid to Pakistan in the fiscal 2012 and 2013 bills.

In 2011 she wouldn't support relieving Egypt of $3.3 billion in debt without knowing who the country's next leader would be — and in 2012, she blocked a transfer of $450 million in financial assistance to the Egyptian government, when the government was mostly controlled by members of the Muslim Brotherhood. She argued in 2011 against aiding the Palestinian Authority after its president made a controversial bid for statehood in the United Nations. And in 2012 she backed cuts in aid to the U.N. Population Fund.

"In the past, we have been able to fund important projects and take the long view, knowing that someday what we plant would bear fruit," she said in 2011. "But today is a different time. We are facing a global recession unlike anything in recent memory."

She is dubious of the returns on spending for the International Monetary Fund and the World Bank. "If these institutions were being held to the same standards as our bilateral programs, the 'bang for the buck' argument might be credible, but they're not," she said at an April 2013 hearing.

Granger gets along very well with the top Democrat on her subcommittee, Nita M. Lowey of New York — who is also the ranking member of the full committee. At a hearing early in the 113th Congress (2013-14), Granger advised witnesses that "when we say this is bipartisan, it is. And when we say we're friends, we are. And we think that's important in the way we conduct our business, and we hope it spreads." Lowey dubbed them "the odd couple."

In addition to her job on the State-Foreign Operations panel, Granger sits on the Defense Subcommittee. From that position, she has looked out for defense contractors in and around her district, such as Lockheed Martin Corp. and Bell Helicopter Textron. When the Air Force proposed in its fiscal 2013 budget to move C-130 transport planes from her district to Montana, she helped make sure that language in the Defense spending bill barred any such moves; the plans to move the planes were eventually dropped.

Granger came out strongly against automatic cuts to defense accounts put in place by an August 2011 law. She wrote in a constituent newsletter that allowing the "sequestration" of more than $500 billion from defense spending will cause a "devastating blow to our nation's defense capabilities." Those cuts started in 2013.

Granger is a member of the conservative Republican Study Committee, but she does have some moderate tendencies. She calls herself a "pro-choice Republican," although she supports efforts to ban federal funding of abortion. She served as the vice chairwoman of the Republican Conference for the 110th Congress (2007-08), and she tried to help her party reach out to moderate voters by de-emphasizing hot-button issues such as abortion and same-sex marriage. She pushed to address family finances, advocating ideas such as full tax-deductibility for most medical expenses.

She expressed optimism in early 2009 regarding President Barack Obama's pledge of bipartisanship in addressing the economic crisis and tightening spending. But she raised a warning against potential tax hikes and cuts to the armed forces.

Granger also voted against Obama's $787 billion stimulus plan, saying she believed the bill should have focused on tax relief and provided more money for transportation and water infrastructure projects. (In 2013, she joined the Transportation-HUD Appropriations Subcommittee.)

As one of his first acts as president, Obama overturned the "Mexico City" policy that prohibited federal funding of groups that perform or promote abortion overseas, a perennial point of contention during consideration of the spending bill for which her subcommittee is responsible. Granger said his decision flouts a consensus that the United States should support family planning abroad, but nothing related to abortion.

Granger was born in Greenville to two public school teachers who divorced when she was 13. After working her way through college, she became a teacher in the same Birdville school district that named an elementary school after her mother. She taught literature and journalism for a decade, but grew restless. In the late 1970s, she went into the insurance business.

Shortly after her career change, she and her husband divorced, and she raised three children as a single mother. She later opened her own insurance agency. She is known in political circles for her superior preparation and organization skills.

In 1981, Granger was appointed to the Fort Worth Zoning Commission, where she served until she won a seat on the city council in 1989. Two years later, she won a nonpartisan election to become mayor.

Both parties courted her when Democratic Rep. Pete Geren decided not to seek re-election in 1996. Granger chose to run as a Republican and resigned as mayor. She won the nomination handily, then defeated another former Fort Worth mayor, Hugh Parmer, by nearly 17 points. She was the first Republican woman elected to the House from Texas.

Granger has not been in a close contest since then.

Key Votes

2012	
Extend a Social Security payroll tax cut and unemployment benefits	NO
Ease securities rules to expand small-business access to capital	YES
Extend for one year subsidized student loan interest rates financed by a cut in health care spending	YES
Cite Attorney General Eric H. Holder Jr. for contempt of Congress	YES
Create a visa program for foreign graduates in high-tech fields	YES
Extend most Bush-era income tax rates while allowing rates for top-bracket earners to rise (Jan. 1, 2013)	NO
2011	
Strike funding for F-35 alternative engine	YES
Prevent EPA from regulating greenhouse gas emissions to address climate change	YES
Extend certain provisions of Patriot Act for four years	YES
Declare opposition to use of ground troops in Libya	YES
Overhaul patent law	YES
Pass compromise debt limit increase plan and establish future spending limits	YES
Allow consideration of measures to implement three trade agreements	?

CQ Vote Studies

	PARTY UNITY		PRESIDENTIAL SUPPORT	
	SUPPORT	OPPOSE	SUPPORT	OPPOSE
2012	89%	11%	13%	87%
2011	95%	5%	28%	72%
2010	96%	4%	30%	70%
2009	88%	12%	21%	79%
2008	96%	4%	80%	20%

Interest Groups

	AFL-CIO	ADA	CCUS	ACU
2012	10%	5%	100%	83%
2011	0%	5%	100%	84%
2010	0%	0%	100%	100%
2009	6%	0%	77%	92%
2008	7%	5%	100%	92%

Texas 12

Western Fort Worth; Parker County

The 12th grabs the western side of Fort Worth, its northern Wise County suburbs and the rolling hills and plains of Parker County. The majority-white and Republican-leaning district captures some Northside neighborhoods in the city's outer reaches that are more than 90 percent Hispanic. Eagle Mountain Lake in the north and Lake Mineral Wells State Park and Trailway to the west provide fishing and recreation opportunities.

Fort Worth, where most of the district's population is concentrated, built its reputation as the "gateway to the West" with the arrival of the railroad. The 12th includes the headquarters for Burlington Northern Santa Fe Railroad and Union Pacific rail lines, and a downtown commuter and Amtrak train station. In the nearby cultural district, oil-rich philanthropists endowed Fort Worth with a wealth of museum attractions.

A thriving medical district now helps drive the economy of Forth Worth, which is home to several teaching hospitals, medical research centers and a public-private research consortium. Grants have attracted pharmaceutical and treatment research companies, as well as biosciences startups.

The area was settled as an Army fort along the West Fork and Clear Fork rivers that flow south of the city. A military presence is maintained at Naval Air Station Joint Reserve Base Fort Worth. The base recently underwent a round of energy upgrades to reduce its carbon footprint.

Republican voters in populous North Richland Hills and Haltom City outweigh the Democratic lean of more urban areas. Rural areas of the district trend heavily toward the GOP and helped Mitt Romney win 67 percent of the 12th's 2012 presidential vote.

Major Industry
Transportation, health care, pharmaceuticals, military

Military Bases
Naval Air Station Joint Reserve Base Fort Worth, 2,484 military, 1,306 civilian (2012)

Cities
Fort Worth (pt.), North Richland Hills, Haltom City (pt.), Weatherford

Notable
The Parker County Peach Festival in Weatherford attracts more than 30,000 visitors each summer; The National Cowgirl Museum and Hall of Fame is in Fort Worth.

Rep. Mac Thornberry (R)

Capitol Office
225-3706
thornberry.house.gov
2329 Rayburn Bldg. 20515-4313; fax 225-3486

Committees
Armed Services
(Intelligence, Emerging Threats & Capabilities - Chairman)
Select Intelligence

Residence
Clarendon

Born
July 15, 1958; Clarendon, Texas

Religion
Presbyterian

Family
Wife, Sally Thornberry; two children

Education
Texas Tech U., B.A. 1980 (history); U. of Texas, J.D. 1983

Career
Lawyer; cattleman; U.S. State Department official; congressional aide

Political Highlights
No previous office

ELECTION RESULTS

2012 GENERAL		
Mac Thornberry (R)	187,775	91.0%
John Robert Deek (LIBERT)	12,701	6.2%
Keith F. Houston (GREEN)	5,912	2.9%
2012 PRIMARY		
Mac Thornberry (R)	47,051	77.5%
Pam Barlow (R)	13,637	22.5%
2010 GENERAL		
Mac Thornberry (R)	113,201	87.0%
Keith Dyer (I)	11,192	8.6%
John T. Burwell (LIBERT)	5,650	4.3%

Previous Winning Percentages
2008 (78%); 2006 (74%); 2004 (92%); 2002 (79%); 2000 (68%); 1998 (68%); 1996 (67%); 1994 (55%)

Elected 1994; 10th term

Advancing national security is Thornberry's mission. Other priorities are a distant second. "If you can make a little bit of difference in national security, you can make a significant difference for the future of your country," he said.

In executing his mission, Thornberry has a clear goal: making sure laws evolve along with the technologies available to both the United States and its adversaries. That means ensuring that the government has the necessary legal authorities to protect cyberspace; to detain and prosecute alleged terrorists; to wage war against an enemy that does not play by any rules; to intercept electronic communications as necessary; and to avail itself of the most modern means of delivering strategic messages.

Thornberry is willing to give national security agencies expansive reach in exercising power, and his critics on the left and the far right sometimes see that approach as a threat to civil liberties. But almost to a person, they respect his seriousness and intelligence.

"The world is changing faster than the laws we produce change," he said. "If we can't stay updated for the way the world is changing, Congress will become increasingly irrelevant when things move so quickly."

Thornberry is now the No. 2 Republican on the Armed Services Committee, where he chairs the panel on Intelligence, Emerging Threats and Capabilities. He joined the Intelligence Committee in September 2004, and he received a waiver to stay there for the 113th Congress (2013-14) — in the House, service on that panel is usually limited to eight years. In 2011, he chaired a GOP task force that suggested changes to laws governing the public and private sectors in cyberspace.

During the 112th Congress (2011-12), Thornberry tried to broaden the 2001 authorization to use military force in response to the Sept. 11 attacks, so that it included not just the groups responsible for those attacks, but also affiliated groups. The provision was included in the House's fiscal 2012 defense policy bill but did not make it into the final law.

Working on the fiscal 2013 version, he fought attempts to ban indefinite detention of anyone held on terrorism charges in the United States — regardless of nationality — as well as to give such suspects access to U.S. criminal courts. No explicit ban was included in the final law.

Thornberry also won inclusion of his provision updating a 1948 law that was originally intended to prevent the State Department from using its foreign propaganda to influence Americans at home. In a modern context, it banned the government from using the Internet or satellite TV to communicate its messages, Thornberry argued. The ban on domestic broadcasting was lifted.

He also defeated an attempt to cut spending for the V-22 tiltrotor, made by Bell Helicopter in his district. He similarly watches out for the Pantex facility near Amarillo, where nuclear weapons are assembled and disassembled.

Despite his prominent role on security issues, Thornberry lost his bid to chair the Intelligence Committee in the 112th Congress, and in 2008 and 2009 he lost bids to become the top Republican on Armed Services. He still aspires to lead the Armed Services Committee in the future.

Thornberry's committee assignments have long provided him wide latitude to weigh in on national security.

Months before the Sept. 11 terrorist attacks, he drafted a bill to create a new department to oversee homeland security. It served as the foundation for 2002 legislation that created the Homeland Security Department. GOP leaders then granted him a seat on the new Homeland Security Committee, giving him oversight as the department was built. Another of his ideas became reality in

2005 with the creation of an assistant secretary for cybersecurity.

By then, Thornberry had moved to the Intelligence panel and was chairman of its new Oversight Subcommittee during the 109th Congress (2005-06). Established to monitor effectiveness of the law uniting U.S. intelligence functions under one director, the panel concluded in 2006 that implementation had been, in Thornberry's words, a "mixed bag." He found fault with the Office of the Director of National Intelligence's approach and concluded it should be focusing on high priorities such as information sharing.

For all his hawkishness, Thornberry looks beyond military power to combat America's enemies. He served on a bipartisan Smart Power Commission in 2007 that drew up recommendations for achieving U.S. national security goals with both lethal and non-lethal approaches.

Thornberry supported President George W. Bush's conduct of the Iraq War. When President Barack Obama released memos in April 2009 detailing the interrogation of detainees under the previous administration, Thornberry shied away from saying the detainees had been tortured. "I think people are too free with the use" of that word, he said on MSNBC. "Read these memos, because you will get a real feel for the carefully controlled, doctor-supervised circumstances under which these things were used."

Thornberry traces his conservatism to his upbringing on the cattle ranch that has been in his family for more than 70 years. "Someone in the federal government was telling us what to do on a farm seven miles down a dirt road outside a town of 2,000 people," he said. He still owns one-third of the Thornberry Brothers Cattle Partnership, and he is a big foe of the estate tax — a concern of many farmers and ranchers in his district.

Despite the dirt on his cowboy boots, most of Thornberry's formative professional experiences were in Washington. After graduating from the University of Texas law school in 1983, he worked for five years as a legislative aide and chief of staff to two Republican House members from Texas. In 1988, he was deputy assistant secretary of State for legislative affairs in the Reagan administration.

Thornberry took a break from politics in 1989 to work in an Amarillo law firm while helping to run his family's cattle ranch, but he was soon back in the game. In 1994, he sought the U.S. House seat held by Democrat Bill Sarpalius, who had become vulnerable after supporting tax increases as part of President Bill Clinton's 1993 budget plan.

Thornberry beat Sarpalius with 55 percent of the vote, and his re-elections have been by overwhelming margins. He fought off a rare primary challenge in 2012 with little difficulty, and Democrats did not field a candidate against him in the general election.

Key Votes

2012	
Extend a Social Security payroll tax cut and unemployment benefits	NO
Ease securities rules to expand small-business access to capital	YES
Extend for one year subsidized student loan interest rates financed by a cut in health care spending	YES
Cite Attorney General Eric H. Holder Jr. for contempt of Congress	YES
Create a visa program for foreign graduates in high-tech fields	YES
Extend most Bush-era income tax rates while allowing rates for top-bracket earners to rise (Jan. 1, 2013)	YES
2011	
Strike funding for F-35 alternative engine	NO
Prevent EPA from regulating greenhouse gas emissions to address climate change	YES
Extend certain provisions of Patriot Act for four years	YES
Declare opposition to use of ground troops in Libya	YES
Overhaul patent law	YES
Pass compromise debt limit increase plan and establish future spending limits	YES
Allow consideration of measures to implement three trade agreements	YES

CQ Vote Studies

	PARTY UNITY		PRESIDENTIAL SUPPORT	
	SUPPORT	OPPOSE	SUPPORT	OPPOSE
2012	97%	3%	16%	84%
2011	97%	3%	25%	75%
2010	99%	1%	26%	74%
2009	98%	2%	14%	86%
2008	98%	2%	82%	18%

Interest Groups

	AFL-CIO	ADA	CCUS	ACU
2012	10%	0%	92%	96%
2011	0%	5%	100%	88%
2010	0%	0%	88%	100%
2009	5%	0%	73%	100%
2008	0%	5%	89%	92%

Texas 13

Panhandle — Amarillo; Wichita Falls

Covering the Texas Panhandle and part of the Red River Valley along the border with Oklahoma, the 13th is the one of the nation's most conservative districts: In 2012, it gave GOP presidential nominee Mitt Romney his highest percentage statewide (80 percent).

The district sweeps up cattle country and croplands, taking in all or part of 41 counties, more than half of which are home to fewer than 10,000 people. Its population hubs, Amarillo and Wichita Falls, both developed as trading posts along rail lines. Part of the historic Western Trail for cattle drivers, Amarillo remains a major livestock processing center. More than 3 million animals move through its feedlots to livestock auctions and meat-processing plants, including Tyson foods. Hereford to the southwest stakes its claim as the beef production capital of the world.

The federal government also has a heavy economic impact outside Amarillo, operating the world's largest helium production operation. The nearby Pantex Plant assembles and disassembles part of the nation's nuclear-weapons stockpile. Boeing produces parts for the V-22 Osprey and other military helicopters in the city as well. To the east, Sheppard Air Force Base outside Wichita Falls was spared by 2005 base realignment. State hospitals and a prison employ many, but population growth remains stagnant. A new pipeline project will connect Permian Basin fields in West Texas through Wichita Falls to Gulf Coast markets.

Severe weather is a constant concern for Tornado Alley. The demanding environment is also hard on winter wheat farmers. A depleting supply of groundwater could force them into planting less-demanding, lower-yield sorghum. Overall, the 13th is aging — 14 percent of the population is 65 or older — and white. Roughly one-fourth of residents are Hispanic.

Major Industry

Agriculture, manufacturing, military

Military Bases

Sheppard Air Force Base, 2,440 military, 1,179 civilian (2012)

Cities

Amarillo, Wichita Falls

Notable

In the "Great Hanging" of 1862, 40 suspected Union sympathizers were hanged in Gainesville by Confederate Texans.

Rep. Randy Weber (R)

Capitol Office
225-2831
weber.house.gov
510 Cannon Bldg. 20515-1402; fax 225-0271

Committees
Foreign Affairs
Science, Space & Technology

Residence
Friendswood

Born
July 2, 1953; Houston, Texas

Religion
Baptist

Family
Wife, Brenda Weber; three children

Education
Alvin Community College, attended 1971-74; U. of Houston, Clear Lake, B.S. 1977 (public affairs)

Career
Air conditioning and heating company owner; recreational vehicle company clerk

Political Highlights
Pearland City Council, 1990-96; sought Republican nomination for Brazoria County Comissioners Court, 1996; candidate for Texas House (special election), 2007; Texas House, 2009-13

ELECTION RESULTS

2012 GENERAL		
Randy Weber (R)	131,460	53.5%
Nick Lampson (D)	109,697	44.6%
Zach Grady (LIBERT)	3,619	1.5%
2012 PRIMARY RUNOFF		
Randy Weber (R)	23,295	62.8%
Felicia Harris (R)	13,792	37.2%

Elected 2012; 1st term

An interest group once dubbed Weber the most conservative Republican in the Texas House. His record suggests that he'll get along fine with conservatives at the federal level, as he touts anti-tax, small-government positions.

Born in Houston, Weber has spent most of his life along the Gulf Coast. He started an air-conditioning company in 1981, and that business was the focus of his professional life until his election to the U.S. House. (The website for Weber's Air & Heat proudly proclaims: "Our customers are cool!")

Weber was civically active through his church, where he is a deacon, and other groups. He got involved in elective politics in the early 1990s, winning a seat on the Pearland City Council. After more than a decade out of office, he won a seat in the Texas House in 2008.

As a state legislator, Weber promoted the energy sector. He now sits on the Science, Space and Technology Committee and its panels on energy and the environment — the terminus of the proposed Keystone XL would be in the 14th District.

He also helped write a Texas law to help fight human trafficking; among other things it established a program to assist domestic victims. He continues his human rights work as a member of the Foreign Affairs Committee and its panel on global human rights.

Weber supports Israel. At a February 2013 hearing on anti-Semitism, he asked witnesses to promote domestic energy development — to slow down oil purchases from Saudi Arabia, which allegedly spreads anti-Semitic propaganda. "Can I get an amen?" he asked the panel. He got one.

The district had been represented by Ron Paul, a famous libertarian-leaning Republican. He eschewed re-election to focus on a 2012 presidential run. Weber and eight other Republicans fought for the nomination. He finished first in the primary, then easily won a runoff. In November, he beat Democrat Nick Lampson, a former five-term U.S. House member, by almost 9 points.

Texas 14

Northern Gulf Coast — Beaumont, League City, Galveston

The 14th District stretches along 120 miles of the Gulf Coast, from Port Arthur through Galveston to the San Bernard National Wildlife refuge, a winter hideaway for migrating geese. Ports, petrochemicals and coastal industries dominate the economy of the district, which encompasses all of Jefferson and Galveston counties and half of Brazoria County.

Petroleum has been crucial to eastern Jefferson County since the turn of the 20th century. The Beaumont-Port Arthur area, the district's population hub, is home to the nation's largest oil industry refining operations. Port Arthur is home to the the largest refinery in the nation. To the west in Texas City, a BP chemical plant is a top producer of petrochemicals used in solvents and dyes. Marathon maintains a refinery in the city as well.

Shipping is just as vital an industry across the district. Beaumont has the U.S. military's second-busiest port in the world and has shipped nearly half the cargo for operations in Afghanistan and Iraq. Port Arthur is a major exporter of timber products and metals, while the port of Galveston has attracted cruise ship traffic. The island-based city of Galveston — encompassing 32 miles of beaches, restaurants, Victorian houses and resorts — relies on tourism and fishing.

League City, between Houston and the Gulf Coast, grew rapidly over the last decade and is the largest city in Galveston County. The exurb, just over the district boundary from NASA's Johnson Space Center in the 36th District, boasts higher income and education levels than most of Houston.

The district is more than 50 percent white, with Hispanic and black communities each making up close to 20 percent of the population, and it will support unconventional, anti-establishment candidates, although it is still conservative and Republican-heavy. The 14th backed Mitt Romney in the 2012 presidential election with 59 percent of its vote.

Major Industry
Petrochemicals, transportation, tourism

Cities
Beaumont, League City (pt.), Port Arthur

Notable
Birdwatchers from around the world flock to the four bird sanctuaries on High Island, the tallest point in the Gulf of Mexico.

Rep. Rubén Hinojosa (D)

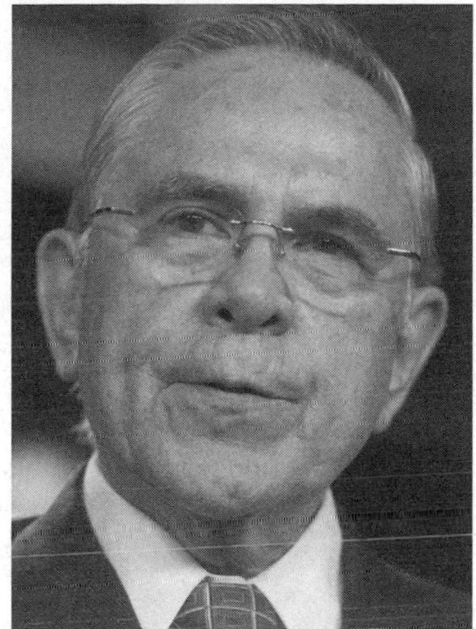

Capitol Office
225-2531
hinojosa.house.gov
2262 Rayburn Bldg. 20515-4315; fax 225-5688

Committees
Education & the Workforce
Financial Services

Residence
Mercedes

Born
Aug. 20, 1940; Edcouch, Texas

Religion
Roman Catholic

Family
Wife, Martha Hinojosa; five children

Education
U. of Texas, B.B.A. 1962; U. of Texas, Pan American, M.B.A. 1980

Career
Food processing executive

Political Highlights
Mercedes school board, 1972-74; Texas State Board of Education, 1974-84 (chairman of special populations)

ELECTION RESULTS

2012 GENERAL		
Rubén Hinojosa (D)	89,296	60.9%
Dale A. Brueggemann (R)	54,056	36.9%
Ronald Finch (LIBERT)	3,309	2.3%
2012 PRIMARY		
Rubén Hinojosa (D)	29,397	71.2%
David Cantu (D)	5,008	12.1%
Jane Cross (D)	4,208	10.2%
Ruben Ramon Ramirez (D)	2,012	4.9%
Johnny "JP" Partain (D)	687	1.7%
2010 GENERAL		
Rubén Hinojosa (D)	53,546	55.7%
Eddie Zamora (R)	39,964	41.6%
Aaron I. Cohn (LIBERT)	2,570	2.7%

Previous Winning Percentages
2008 (66%); 2006 (62%); 2004 (58%); 2002 (100%); 2000 (88%); 1998 (58%); 1996 (62%)

Elected 1996; 9th term

The Congressional Hispanic Caucus chose Hinojosa for its leader in the 113th Congress, giving the mild-mannered Democrat the most prominent role of his House career. Large parts of his agenda have not changed, however. He promotes the education programs and financial instruments most likely to help lower-income Hispanics.

The 113th Congress (2013-14) could be pivotal for the CHC. The caucus has grown in size, President Barack Obama has promised to put his weight behind a comprehensive overhaul of immigration law, and some GOP strategists are eager to improve their party's standing with the growing Hispanic segment of the electorate.

All those factors make Hinojosa an interesting choice for leader. He is not a masterful communicator, and his biggest legislative successes have been targeted efforts on education. "He's a little more quiet; he's a little more thoughtful," Texas Democratic political consultant Matt Angle said in 2011. "He's got a business background, so he thinks in terms of results."

Hinojosa's business instincts sometimes set him apart from a majority of Democrats. He supports free trade and expanded domestic oil production — he voted for pacts with Colombia and Panama in 2011, and he was one of 21 Democrats to back a 2012 bill to expand offshore drilling, allow exploration in the Arctic National Wildlife Refuge and approve the huge Keystone XL pipeline from Canada to Texas. He goes along with some GOP efforts to ease regulations that might stifle economic growth.

But Hinojosa digs in when his priorities are at stake. He and other South Texas lawmakers have opposed construction of a fence along the U.S.-Mexico border, arguing that it chokes off economic activity in their districts. He has dismissed "enforcement first" approaches to immigration law as "pointless political stunts and fear-mongering."

The first item on the CHC's list of principles for an immigration overhaul, issued shortly after the 2012 elections, was a path to citizenship for illegal immigrants already in the country. In particular, he promotes a Democratic measure to create a path for illegal immigrants who were brought to the country as children, should they enroll in college or the military.

Education has been Hinojosa's biggest issue, and he often cites his own educational journey. His parents spoke only Spanish when they fled Mexico during the 1910 revolution, but they "understood intuitively that education was the path to a better life," he said. Hinojosa attended a school where he and other Mexican-American children were segregated from white students. He then ended up at the University of Texas.

A member of the Education and the Workforce Committee, he emphasizes that Pell grants should not fall below their current amount and has said that federal loan programs should "offer all students an opportunity to register and attend college."

He is an advocate of the Education Department's TRIO programs, which provide outreach to, and support for, disadvantaged students. When the committee approved legislation in 2009 making the government the sole provider of federally guaranteed student loans, it included a Hinojosa proposal to significantly increase student aid and other funding for historically black colleges and Hispanic-serving institutions. He supported bills in 2007 and 2008 that authorized $200 million in grants over five years to help increase the number of Latino graduates in science, technology, engineering and mathematics.

Hinojosa is the top Democrat on the Subcommittee on Higher Education and Workforce Training. Republicans and Democrats agreed in 2012 that worker training programs need streamlining — the government operates 47 of them, and the Government Accountability Office reported in 2011 that 44 of those programs overlap in some way.

Republicans on the committee advanced their proposal to consolidate 27 of the programs into a single block grant to the states. Democrats led by Hinojosa, George Miller of California and John F. Tierney of Massachusetts argued that doing so would divert funds from the underserved populations, such as veterans or the homeless, that some programs were set up to help. Their alternative bill, rejected by the full committee, would enable local governments to contract with community colleges to train workers in sought-after skills, a priority for the Obama administration. When the subcommittee marked up another version of the GOP plan in March 2013, Hinojosa helped lead a walkout by panel Democrats, who said they had been cut out of negotiations.

Hinojosa is also a member of the Financial Services Committee, where he takes a particular interest in consumer protections and credit availability for poorer populations. He is an ardent defender of the Consumer Financial Protection Bureau created by the 2010 financial regulatory overhaul law.

He was a co-founder of the Rural Housing Caucus, which has the goal of increasing the availability and affordability of housing. He also co-founded the Financial and Economic Literacy Caucus, which ties in with his broader interest in education. His co-chairman for the 113th is Steve Stivers of Ohio.

After getting an undergraduate degree at the University of Texas, Hinojosa joined the family business, H&H Foods, serving 20 years as its president and chief financial officer. His ties to the businesses resulted in personal distress in late 2010. Hinojosa personally guaranteed a loan to the business, which was "forced into bankruptcy due to the recent economic downturn and financial market meltdown," he said in a written statement. He now ranks among the poorest members of Congress in terms of net worth.

Hinojosa was elected to the local school board in the early 1970s and later served a decade on the Texas State Board of Education. He made a successful bid for the U.S. House in 1996, winning a hotly contested five-way battle in the primary, then beating Republican minister Tom Haughey by 26 points. He won a rematch with Haughey in 1998 by 17 points and has won comfortably since.

His district was still recognizable after congressional maps were redrawn for the 2012 election, though it stretched a little further north to take in some areas east of San Antonio. It is still one of the least-educated and poorest districts in the country. Hinojosa appeared to be a little rusty in his re-election campaign. His fundraising was lackluster, and at an October debate with Republican Dale A. Brueggemann, he drew a blank trying to recall the Second Amendment. He still won easily, taking 61 percent of the vote.

Key Votes

2012	
Extend a Social Security payroll tax cut and unemployment benefits	YES
Ease securities rules to expand small-business access to capital	YES
Extend for one year subsidized student loan interest rates financed by a cut in health care spending	?
Cite Attorney General Eric H. Holder Jr. for contempt of Congress	?
Create a visa program for foreign graduates in high-tech fields	NO
Extend most Bush-era income tax rates while allowing rates for top-bracket earners to rise (Jan. 1, 2013)	YES
2011	
Strike funding for F-35 alternative engine	YES
Prevent EPA from regulating greenhouse gas emissions to address climate change	NO
Extend certain provisions of Patriot Act for four years	YES
Declare opposition to use of ground troops in Libya	NO
Overhaul patent law	YES
Pass compromise debt limit increase plan and establish future spending limits	YES
Allow consideration of measures to implement three trade agreements	?

CQ Vote Studies

	PARTY UNITY		PRESIDENTIAL SUPPORT	
	SUPPORT	OPPOSE	SUPPORT	OPPOSE
2012	92%	8%	86%	14%
2011	87%	13%	83%	17%
2010	97%	3%	90%	10%
2009	99%	1%	97%	3%
2008	97%	3%	22%	78%

Interest Groups

	AFL-CIO	ADA	CCUS	ACU
2012	95%	75%	33%	12%
2011	92%	80%	46%	0%
2010	100%	75%	38%	0%
2009	100%	90%	31%	0%
2008	100%	80%	59%	9%

Texas 15

South central — McAllen, part of Mission

The 15th slices a narrow, north-to-south strip of more than 250 miles from the eastern outskirts of San Antonio in Guadalupe County to the Rio Grande Valley.

The southern tip of the district, where three-fourths of the heavily Hispanic population lives, sits across the river from the large, drug-plagued Mexican city of Reynosa. McAllen is the 15th's largest city and a significant economic anchor for the southern Rio Grande Valley. The Pharr-Reynosa International Bridge is a key trade link and border access has attracted global manufacturing and warehousing companies. On the Mexican side of the border, maquiladoras — plants that use low-cost labor and import parts from the U.S. — have continued exporting at record levels, despite the drug violence. Federal budget cuts have made border policing more complicated, and Hidalgo County has struggled to attract federal grant funding to gate the gaps in its rust-red border fence.

The 15th covers the majority of Hidalgo County, where the state's top vegetable and sugar cane crops are produced. More cabbage, onions, cantaloupes, carrots and watermelons are harvested here than any other Texas county, often by farm workers who migrate seasonally. The poorest residents occupy unincorporated colonias along the border that may lack clean water, electricity or adequate sewage.

Populations between Guadalupe and Hidalgo counties are tiny, leaving open wide expanses of land for oil and gas exploration. Prospecting in Eagle Ford Shale has attracted energy companies and rigs in Duval County. A flurry of drilling in Karnes County's oil and gas reserves has caused property values to soar for land traditionally taken up by farms and ranches.

Guadalupe County is a Republican stronghold, but its votes cannot counter Democratic southern counties in the 80 percent Hispanic district.

Major Industry
Trade, agriculture, manufacturing

Cities
McAllen (pt.); Edinburg; Mission (pt.); Pharr (pt.); New Braunfels (pt.)

Notable
The world's largest pecan — a statue — is on display in Seguin, which also is home to a nutcracker museum.

Rep. Beto O'Rourke (D)

Capitol Office
225-4831
orourke.house.gov
1721 Longworth Bldg. 20515-4326; fax 225-2016

Committees
Homeland Security
Veterans' Affairs

Residence
El Paso

Born
Sept. 26, 1972; El Paso, Texas

Religion
Roman Catholic

Family
Wife, Amy Sanders O'Rourke; three children

Education
Columbia U., B.A. 1995 (English)

Career
Internet services company owner

Political Highlights
El Paso City Council, 2005-11

ELECTION RESULTS

2012 GENERAL		
Beto O'Rourke (D)	101,403	65.4%
Barbara Carrasco (R)	51,043	32.9%
Junart Sodoy (LIBERT)	2,559	1.6%
2012 PRIMARY		
Beto O'Rourke (D)	23,261	50.5%
Silvestre Reyes (D)	20,440	44.3%
Jerome Tilghman (D)	1,270	2.8%
Benjamin Eloy "Ben" Mendoza (D)	701	1.5%

Elected 2012; 1st term

El Paso sits on the U.S.-Mexico line, and as its representative, O'Rourke is a full-throated participant in discussions of border security. He notes that decisions on how to define a secure border will profoundly affect his district's economy, the national economy and the fate of any immigration law overhaul.

O'Rourke (first name: BET-oh) grew up in El Paso. During his childhood, his father, Pat, was an El Paso County commissioner and judge. Running as a Republican, Pat O'Rourke lost a bid for the U.S. House in 1992.

Beto O'Rourke went to college in New York City, and he stayed there after graduating to work at several Internet startups. For a time, he also toured the country as a guitarist in the band Foss. He returned to El Paso in 1998 and started an Internet services company. In 2005, at the age of 32, he won election to the city council; he says his goal was to improve the city's economy.

That is still a goal. He wants to spur investment in one of the country's largest land ports of entry, where long wait times create a chokepoint for shipping. He sits on the Homeland Security Subcommittee on Border and Maritime Security; as that panel considered a bill in early 2013 to help establish metrics of border security, he urged studies of how various security measures affect the flow of trade across the border. O'Rourke also has suggested that changes to U.S. drug policies could free up a lot of security bandwidth — he is an advocate for the legalization of marijuana.

His district includes Fort Bliss, one of the largest Army bases, and he sits on the Veterans' Affairs Committee. His first bill, to extend tuition assistance programs for servicemembers, was rolled into the fiscal 2013 spending law.

O'Rourke shocked a few people by beating eight-term Democrat Silvestre Reyes in an ugly primary that saw each man question the other's ethics. His cause was helped by an anti-incumbent super PAC that spent $240,000 trying to defeat Reyes. With that victory behind him, he did not have to campaign much to win the solidly Democratic 16th District.

Texas 16

West — El Paso and suburbs

The nation's busiest cross-border footpath connects the 16th District to its sister city in Mexico, Ciudad Juarez, forming the second largest bi-national community in the world. This rapidly growing bit of western Texas, encompassing El Paso and suburbs, is 80 percent Hispanic. Despite drug violence along the Rio Grande, the 16th continues to be a hub for international business.

Free-trade agreements in the 1990s attracted major U.S. manufacturers to Juarez. The resulting boom in import-export trade and increased traffic on ports, roads and trains, provided a boost to the district's economy and led to a major expansion of its international airport.

Many of the district's residents work in low-paying service jobs at technical and staffing support centers; El Paso's large pool of labor continues to attract businesses. Hispanic arts and Mexican cultural organizations also thrive, pulling in more than 325,000 visitors annually. The University of Texas, El Paso, founded as a mining college, has more than 20,000 students and is adding to its research profile.

The military brings billions of dollars to the economy of the 16th each year through the presence of the Army's Fort Bliss. Its influence is growing following the 2005 round of base realignments — an additional 20,000 troops and their families have arrived, and new hospital and residential construction is ongoing.

Despite rapid expansion, El Paso is a model for water conservation. The city ripped up grass from public places and replaced it with rock and cactus gardens, paying residents to do the same on their property. This conservation effort has become a model for desert cities.

Hispanic Democrats dominate state-level elections here, and Barack Obama won comfortably in 2008 and 2012. The strong Catholic tradition, however, tends to make voters more socially conservative.

Major Industry
Trade, military, manufacturing, office support

Military Bases
Fort Bliss (Army), 38,589 military, 13,079 civilian

Cities
El Paso

Notable
The National Border Patrol Museum boasts decades of historical memorabilia from the service.

Rep. Bill Flores (R)

Capitol Office
225-6105
flores.house.gov
1030 Longworth Bldg. 20515-4317; fax 225-0350

Committees
Budget
Natural Resources
Veterans' Affairs
(Economic Opportunity - Chairman)

Residence
Bryan

Born
Feb. 25, 1954; Warren Air Force Base, Wyo.

Religion
Baptist

Family
Wife, Gina Flores; two children

Education
Texas A&M U., B.B.A. 1976 (accounting); Houston Baptist U., M.B.A. 1985

Career
Energy company executive; oil drilling company financial manager; accountant

Political Highlights
No previous office

ELECTION RESULTS

2012 GENERAL		
Bill Flores (R)	143,284	79.9%
Ben Easton (LIBERT)	35,978	20.1%
2012 PRIMARY		
Bill Flores (R)	41,449	82.5%
George W. Hindman (R)	8,790	17.5%
2010 GENERAL		
Bill Flores (R)	106,696	61.8%
Chet Edwards (D)	63,138	36.6%
Richard B. Kelly (LIBERT)	2,808	1.6%

Elected 2010; 2nd term

Having spent years in the corner offices of energy companies, Flores calls himself a "big-picture guy" on economic issues. But he started out as an accountant, and he still leans heavily on numbers when making the case for his conservative positions.

Flores is very Republican, voting with a majority of his party almost every time it opposes a majority of Democrats. He is skeptical about political horse-trading. "There aren't many deals to be made here," he said. "You've got this huge ideological gulf between one view of America that's the '36 through '38 Roosevelt type of view, and the '81 through '84 Reagan type of view. I don't know how you deal in the middle."

He says his goal is to "get Washington fixed" and return to the private sector within eight years. While in office, "I want to be the go-to guy when somebody wants to know how the private sector, real-world economy works," he said.

On the Budget Committee, Flores asserts that private sector spending is far more efficient than government spending at fostering economic growth. He wants to restructure entitlement programs that drive huge portions of federal spending, even calling for a "more aggressive" approach than what was laid out in the fiscal 2012 and 2013 budgets of Chairman Paul D. Ryan of Wisconsin.

According to Flores, the methods the Congressional Budget Office uses to "score" the economic impact of legislation don't adequately account for the reactions businesses and individuals have to tax and spending changes. And he's no fan of "emergency" spending outside of the regular budget process. Flores voted early in the 113th Congress (2013-14) against $50 billion in disaster aid for Superstorm Sandy, but he said he could have supported a smaller bill offset by reductions in other areas of government. (His own district faced disaster in April 2013 when a fertilizer plant in West exploded.)

Flores also wants to be a "go-to guy on energy." He played that role for years as CEO of Phoenix Exploration Co., an oil and natural-gas firm; all told, he has spent more than 30 years managing the finances of various energy companies. On the Natural Resources Committee, Flores both defends his old industry and shows a willingness to render it obsolete.

Expansion of domestic-energy production is a priority for Flores, and in the 112th Congress (2011-12) he introduced bills to expedite the review of permits and extend certain leases for oil and gas development in the Gulf of Mexico. "The Obama administration is definitely opposed to continuing use of fossil fuels," he said, "and they're trying to have a very short-term phase-out" via the regulatory process.

While backing fossil fuels, he also is a huge fan of nuclear power, calling it the "ultimate energy source with a low carbon footprint." In July 2011, he told The Hill that nuclear plants could produce 80 percent of our power within 30 years, with "solar, biomass, natural gas, wind, you name it" picking up the slack. At a 2011 hearing, he boasted that he was the "largest residential producer of solar power in Brazos County."

Flores sees only two reasons for direct federal involvement in the energy sector: providing loan guarantees for nuclear power plant development, and funding basic research (he offers that the reprocessing of nuclear fuel rods would be a good place to start). All other loan guarantees and production tax credits, he could do without.

He calls the current regulatory environment "the worst I've ever seen." Flores is suspicious that the Obama administration is trying to implement a national oceans policy without congressional approval or industry input. A Flores amendment stripped $150 million from the Sandy relief measure for grants to help implement that policy.

His third panel is the Veterans' Affairs Committee, where he chairs the Economic Opportunity Subcommittee. Flores sees many problems of benefit programs as stemming from a poorly functioning bureaucracy. He said in 2011 that the Veterans Affairs Department is "really struggling to keep up" with benefit claims and delivery of services, and that Congress should examine new administrative models. He has floated the idea of outsourcing some functions, such as claims processing, to the private sector.

A member of the Republicans' Congressional Hispanic Conference, Flores opposes creating a path to citizenship for illegal immigrants. But he has no problems with a "multi-path visa program" for guest workers, including some expedited naturalization process for people who want to go that route.

Flores was born on the Wyoming Air Force base where his father was stationed — planes have continued to be a part of his life, as he got his pilot's license "the day I graduated from high school." The family ended up in his father's hometown of Stratford, Texas, when Flores was 3. His father started working as a day laborer, eventually establishing his own cattle ranch and selling insurance.

Flores got his first executive experience at home: As the oldest of six kids, "I guess I was sort of junior management," he says. Ranching and school filled much of his youth before he enrolled at Texas A&M, where he studied accounting. After graduation, he married a woman whom he had pursued in high school; he and Gina have two children and became grandparents early in 2011. Flores keeps a picture of his granddaughter on the card he uses to vote electronically on the House floor.

By 1980 he had started work in the energy industry. He went on to hold various executive positions at several companies. His political involvement flourished after 2000, mostly through large financial contributions to various candidates and causes. House passage of a 2009 bill to create a cap-and-trade system for regulating greenhouse gas emissions "sort of rung my bell," he said — he believes such a system would be economically devastating. He launched an exploratory effort to sound out local voters, then declared his candidacy toward the end of that year.

Flores finished first in a five-way GOP primary in 2010 and easily claimed the nomination in a runoff. He faced 10-term Democrat Chet Edwards, the chairman of an Appropriations subcommittee who also had the endorsement of the National Rifle Association. The district had become so Republican that Edwards couldn't hold on any longer. Flores won by 25 points.

Democrats fielded no candidate against Flores in 2012, and he took 80 percent of the vote against a libertarian opponent.

Key Votes

2012	
Extend a Social Security payroll tax cut and unemployment benefits	YES
Ease securities rules to expand small-business access to capital	?
Extend for one year subsidized student loan interest rates financed by a cut in health care spending	YES
Cite Attorney General Eric H. Holder Jr. for contempt of Congress	YES
Create a visa program for foreign graduates in high-tech fields	YES
Extend most Bush-era income tax rates while allowing rates for top-bracket earners to rise (Jan. 1, 2013)	NO
2011	
Strike funding for F-35 alternative engine	YES
Prevent EPA from regulating greenhouse gas emissions to address climate change	YES
Extend certain provisions of Patriot Act for four years	YES
Declare opposition to use of ground troops in Libya	YES
Overhaul patent law	YES
Pass compromise debt limit increase plan and establish future spending limits	YES
Allow consideration of measures to implement three trade agreements	YES

CQ Vote Studies

	PARTY UNITY		PRESIDENTIAL SUPPORT	
	SUPPORT	OPPOSE	SUPPORT	OPPOSE
2012	98%	2%	13%	87%
2011	99%	1%	20%	80%

Interest Groups

	AFL-CIO	ADA	CCUS	ACU
2012	6%	5%	100%	100%
2011	0%	5%	100%	92%

Texas 17

East central — Waco, College Station; part of northern Austin

The 17th takes in eight east-central counties and parts of four others. Waco in the northwest and College Station in the southeast serve as anchors of population amid sparsely populated woodland, hills and prairieland.

Decennial redistricting removed six counties between Waco and Dallas, which were replaced by a sliver of suburbs within Lee, Bastrop and Travis counties north of Austin. The Trinity River forms the 17th's eastern border.

One-third of the 17th's residents live in Waco or surrounding McLennan County. The city is the largest between Dallas and Austin and is home to Baylor University, a top employer and the state's oldest college. Aviation-related firms, two regional airports, defense contractors and health care networks provide additional jobs.

Texas A&M University in College Station drives the economy of Brazos County. The school's military and agricultural roots give it a conservative bent. A federal contract for bioterrorism preparedness research is expected to boost the fast-growing city's economy.

No county in the stretch between McLennan and Brazos contains more than 25,000 people. Wheat, hay, cotton and corn are grown on land that is not already occupied by cattle pastures.

The district is nearly one-fourth Hispanic, and that community continues to grow, especially in Bryan, near College Station. The 17th's new territory around Austin includes recently developed areas such as Scofield Farms, a wealthy community of white-collar, high-tech workers. Nearly 15 percent of the district's population lives near Austin, and the population is more diverse and slightly more liberal. But overall, the 17th backs GOP candidates — Republican Mitt Romney took 60 percent of the district's 2012 presidential vote.

Major Industry
Higher education, manufacturing, agriculture

Cities
Austin (pt.), Waco, College Station, Bryan, Pflugerville (pt.)

Notable
Crawford is home to George W. Bush's Prairie Chapel Ranch, dubbed the "Western White House" during his presidency.

Rep. Sheila Jackson Lee (D)

Capitol Office
225-3816
jacksonlee.house.gov
2160 Rayburn Bldg. 20515-4318; fax 225-3317

Committees
Homeland Security
Judiciary

Residence
Houston

Born
Jan. 12, 1950; Queens, N.Y.

Religion
Seventh-day Adventist

Family
Husband, Elwyn Lee; two children

Education
Yale U., B.A. 1972 (political science); U. of Virginia, J.D. 1975

Career
Lawyer; congressional aide

Political Highlights
Democratic nominee for Texas District Court judge, 1984; Democratic nominee for Harris County Probate Court judge, 1986; Houston municipal judge, 1987-89; Democratic nominee for Texas District Court judge, 1988; Houston City Council, 1990-95

ELECTION RESULTS

2012 GENERAL		
Sheila Jackson Lee (D)	146,223	75.0%
Sean Seibert (R)	44,015	22.6%
Christopher Barber (LIBERT)	4,694	2.4%
2012 PRIMARY		
Sheila Jackson Lee (D)		unopposed
2010 GENERAL		
Sheila Jackson Lee (D)	85,108	70.2%
John Faulk (R)	33,067	27.3%
Mike Taylor (LIBERT)	3,118	2.6%

Previous Winning Percentages
2008 (77%); 2006 (77%); 2004 (89%); 2002 (77%); 2000 (76%); 1998 (90%); 1996 (77%); 1994 (73%)

Elected 1994; 10th term

Jackson Lee has a reputation as a sharp-tongued Democrat, a difficult boss, and someone who never shies from expressing opinions to the media, presidents or anyone who will listen.

She added a new label in the 112th Congress (2011-12): cancer survivor. Diagnosed in 2011, Jackson Lee was quiet about her battle before announcing a year later that she had recovered after treatment that included "surgery, chemotherapy, radiation and other effects, including loss of hair."

The experience strengthened her commitment to supporting cancer research, and she introduced legislative proposals focusing on triple-negative breast cancer, which is often responsive to chemotherapy but not hormone treatments. Her disclosure had even her toughest critics wishing her well.

The diagnosis didn't change her way of doing business, however. Jackson Lee lambasted Republican leadership on a number of issues. She enraged GOP members in 2011 by saying on the House floor that attempts to repeal the 2010 health care law were unconstitutional and would mean "killing Americans." Jackson Lee speaks on the House floor more often than any other Democrat (since 2007, only Texas Republican Ted Poe has appeared more frequently), and in the 112th she filed more than 100 measures and amendments.

In a 2012 Washingtonian magazine survey of congressional aides, Jackson Lee was identified as the "meanest" House member, as well as the No. 1 "show horse." She has scored high in those categories for much of the past decade, taking the top spot on several occasions.

A 2011 study by the Houston Chronicle found that her office has a high staff turnover rate, with 11 chiefs of staff since 2000. Conservative writers have said the churn is evidence of problems and quoted former aides as saying Jackson Lee uses profane nicknames and berates workers over minor issues. She calls the "mean" label unfair and distracting, and she dismisses the reports about workplace issues, saying her staff "works hard and has fun."

Love her or hate her, many people will have to work with her in the 113th Congress (2013-14) — she is in the middle of the arena as the House contemplates border security and immigration changes. At the start of 2013, she became the top Democrat on the Homeland Security Subcommittee on Border and Maritime Security, and she returned as a member of the Judiciary Subcommittee on Immigration and Border Security.

As a Texan, Jackson Lee has been active on those issues in the past. She has introduced bills to foster cooperation with Mexican authorities and study whether racial profiling plays a role in traffic stops along the border. She has condemned efforts by states to enforce federal immigration law.

In spring 2013, she endorsed a bipartisan bill that would direct the Department of Homeland Security to formulate a plan for achieving "operational control" of the U.S. border, including metrics for measuring control. The bill "truly lays down the marker for moving ahead on comprehensive immigration reform," she said. However, she rejects the idea that operational control should be a precursor for changes to the immigration system.

She has retained her seat on the Homeland Security Subcommittee on Transportation Security, where she was the top Democrat from 2007 through 2012. That assignment put her at the center of a debate on whether the Transportation Security Agency should undergo a fundamental organizational shift. In the 112th Congress, she clashed with Republicans over their proposals to cut TSA staffing by at least 25 percent or to outsource most airport screening work to private contractors. Jackson Lee vehemently opposes the idea, saying it would revert security to a pre-Sept. 11 model and cripple TSA's ability to adapt to new mandates. "Privatization does not work, because any change in procedure is a change in a contract," she said in 2012. "We don't have full control. ... If you're a federalized workforce, it's much quicker."

Jackson Lee has mostly defended the TSA in a Congress where many have low regard for the agency. She approved of a 2011 decision to allow security workers collective bargaining powers — she had proposed legislation to do so in prior years — and TSA's moves to implement more "risk-based" security measures that rely on intelligence data to find potential terrorists.

But she is also a sharp critic of some agency policies, such as programs to train checkpoint workers to spot suspicious behavior. For years, she has urged more attention to surface transportation, instead of keeping the TSA focused on aviation.

On the Judiciary Committee, she has taken note of the perceived epidemic of bullying incidents. She introduced a 2012 bill to reauthorize the Juvenile Accountability Block Grants program to allow funding of anti-bullying initiatives. After an initial swell of support, the bill stalled.

Jackson Lee is a loyal Democrat, and she says her state is following suit. She predicts that Texas will be a "blue" state by 2014, when it holds its next gubernatorial election. A vice chairwoman of the liberal Congressional Progressive Caucus, she consistently supports President Barack Obama's budget requests. Some of her few departures from her party are on foreign affairs or security matters; she has backed several defense policy laws that many liberals scorned. She co-chairs the Congressional Pakistan Caucus.

Among Jackson Lee's role models was Democratic Rep. Barbara C. Jordan, the eloquent liberal from Houston who served from 1973 through 1978. Jackson Lee said she comes from a generation moved by the messages of Medgar Evers, Martin Luther King Jr. and Fannie Lou Hamer, and that she always "viewed my charge from their history and stories to be a change-maker."

She was born in Queens, N.Y., and educated at Yale and the University of Virginia School of Law, where she was one of three African-Americans in her class. She moved to Texas when her husband took a job with the University of Houston. After two unsuccessful bids for local judgeships, she was appointed a municipal judge in 1987.

Three years later, she won an at-large seat on the city council, where her initiatives included a law imposing penalties on gun owners who fail to keep weapons away from children. She also pushed for expanded summer hours at city parks and recreation centers as a way to reduce gang activity.

Jackson Lee came to Congress after beating incumbent Democrat Craig Washington in the 1994 primary. She has never taken less than 70 percent of the vote in a general election.

Key Votes

2012	
Extend a Social Security payroll tax cut and unemployment benefits	YES
Ease securities rules to expand small-business access to capital	YES
Extend for one year subsidized student loan interest rates financed by a cut in health care spending	NO
Cite Attorney General Eric H. Holder Jr. for contempt of Congress	?
Create a visa program for foreign graduates in high-tech fields	NO
Extend most Bush era income tax rates while allowing rates for top-bracket earners to rise (Jan. 1, 2013)	YES
2011	
Strike funding for F-35 alternative engine	NO
Prevent EPA from regulating greenhouse gas emissions to address climate change	NO
Extend certain provisions of Patriot Act for four years	NO
Declare opposition to use of ground troops in Libya	NO
Overhaul patent law	YES
Pass compromise debt limit increase plan and establish future spending limits	YES
Allow consideration of measures to implement three trade agreements	NO

CQ Vote Studies

	PARTY UNITY		PRESIDENTIAL SUPPORT	
	SUPPORT	OPPOSE	SUPPORT	OPPOSE
2012	94%	6%	85%	15%
2011	93%	7%	76%	24%
2010	99%	1%	84%	16%
2009	99%	1%	96%	4%
2008	98%	2%	14%	86%

Interest Groups

	AFL-CIO	ADA	CCUS	ACU
2012	94%	80%	20%	0%
2011	100%	95%	31%	4%
2010	93%	95%	25%	0%
2009	100%	95%	33%	0%
2008	100%	100%	59%	4%

Texas 18

Downtown Houston

The 18th District captures the glitz and glam of Houston as well as its considerable poverty. Heading past downtown through many of the cultural treasures of Museum Park, the district gathers up poor neighborhoods at its southern, eastern and northern spokes. This minority-majority district wraps nearly all the way around Houston.

Downtown's Skyline District is the city's largest employment center, with office towers connected by a network of underground tunnels that shield workers from the heat. Nearly half of the city's 23 Fortune 500 companies have their headquarters here. The city's convention center, performing arts venues and professional sports facilities — Minute Maid Park hosts baseball's Astros, basketball's Rockets play at the Toyota Center, and BBVA Compass Stadium is home to soccer's Dynamo — attract tourists to stay in a cluster of nearby hotels. Developers, spurred by the city's financial incentives, are adding residences to the downtown area.

Beyond downtown's commercial cathedrals, many stretches of the 18th include vacant and deteriorating low-income residential lots. The historically African-American Fifth Ward, east of the city, struggles with poverty, unemployment and lack of access to supermarkets.

The northern "C" of the district picks up George Bush Intercontinental Airport, the largest hub for United Airlines. It is slated for a $1 billion expansion and terminal renovation. The 18th also includes Texas Southern University, one of the nation's largest historically black colleges, and the 667-acre University of Houston.

Blacks account for roughly 40 percent of the population of the 2nd, with Hispanics comprising more than one-third. A combination of urban interests, minority voters and student populations has the 18th supporting Democrats — a contrast to the wealthier, strongly GOP outer Houston suburbs. Barack Obama won 76 percent of the district's 2012 presidential vote.

Major Industry
Energy, government, business services, entertainment, higher education

Cities
Houston (pt.)

Notable
The Third Ward's Emancipation Park, purchased by freed slaves in 1872, hosts an annual Juneteenth Festival.

Rep. Randy Neugebauer (R)

Capitol Office
225-4005
randy.house.gov
1424 Longworth Bldg. 20515-4319; fax 225-9615

Committees
Agriculture
Financial Services
(Housing and Insurance - Chairman)
Science, Space & Technology

Residence
Lubbock

Born
Dec. 24, 1949; St. Louis, Mo.

Religion
Baptist

Family
Wife, Dana Neugebauer; two children

Education
Texas Tech U., B.B.A. 1972 (accounting)

Career
Land developer; homebuilding company executive; bank executive

Political Highlights
Lubbock City Council, 1992-98

ELECTION RESULTS

2012 GENERAL		
Randy Neugebauer (R)	163,239	85.0%
Richard "Chip" Peterson (LIBERT)	28,824	15.0%
2012 PRIMARY		
Randy Neugebauer (R)	45,444	74.3%
Chris Winn (R)	15,707	25.7%
2010 GENERAL		
Randy Neugebauer (R)	106,059	77.8%
Andy Wilson (D)	25,984	19.1%
Richard "Chip" Peterson (LIBERT)	4,315	3.2%

Previous Winning Percentages
2008 (72%); 2006 (68%); 2004 (58%); 2003 Special Runoff Election (51%)

Elected 2003; 5th full term

Neugebauer says he got drafted into politics two decades ago for his "business guy" experience. It still defines him. He's a meticulous critic of expanded regulation of the financial sector and a contributor as Republicans try to shape the business side of agriculture and housing policies.

He was a homebuilder, real estate developer and bank executive before running for office. Neugebauer (NAW-geh-bow-er) said that as a leader of trade associations interacting with lawmakers, he saw "how little business experience a lot of those members have." Friends talked him into running for Lubbock City Council, where he served for most of the 1990s. He was one of the chief proponents for the Ports-to-Plains Corridor, a trucker-friendly highway route stretching from Mexico to Colorado.

Since coming to Congress, he has used his expertise on the Agriculture and Financial Services committees. He also votes as one of the more fiscally conservative members of the GOP Conference. Neugebauer is a member of the Republican Study Committee; he has worked on the GOP whip team and the National Republican Congressional Committee. "I don't go around rattling my conservative sword, but when it's time to speak, I speak up," he said.

If he knows the subject, he'll speak at length. A naturally friendly partisan, Neugebauer enjoys conversing about his committee work, and he has plenty to chat about as chairman of the Financial Services Subcommittee on Housing and Insurance.

Generally speaking, Neugebauer wants less government, and that goal holds true for his ideas for the housing sector. He would like to end or greatly reduce the federal guarantee behind many securitized home loans, in order to shift business back to the private sector. To eliminate the competitive advantages enjoyed by public entities, he wants a steady reduction to the size of loans that the Federal Housing Administration can guarantee, as well as increases to the fees Fannie Mae and Freddie Mac charge to "sanitize" mortgages.

He believes that the government does a poor job of "pricing risk," so he finds it troubling that the FHA has overstepped its original mission and now controls a huge share of the mortgage insurance market. "This is not your mother's or your father's FHA," he said at a 2013 hearing.

Neugebauer chaired the Subcommittee on Oversight and Investigations in the 112th Congress (2011-12), giving him the first crack at studying the 2010 financial services overhaul known as Dodd-Frank. He says the causes of the 2008 economic collapse could be addressed with "regulators doing their jobs" rather than more regulations. In hearings, he emphasized his belief that businesses can't flourish because the overhaul creates too much uncertainty. He calls Dodd-Frank "a 400-piece puzzle, but the puzzle pieces are turned upside down ... and we're not quite sure what it is that we're going to end up with."

Neugebauer hasn't approved of the picture thus far, contending that Dodd-Frank doesn't end the possibility of bailouts for "too big to fail" entities. He is put off by the law's new Consumer Financial Protection Bureau and the Office of Financial Research because their budgets are not set by Congress. And he says compliance costs of the new regulations spawned by Dodd-Frank will drive up prices of consumer goods.

Most Democrats disagree with those assertions, but Neugebauer did win bipartisan praise for investigations of the huge bankruptcy of MF Global, as well as claims that Barclays Bank manipulated the London interbank offered rate during the financial crisis. The LIBOR affects the costs of many global credit transactions, and U.S. authorities advised their British counterparts of possible wrongdoing at the time. Neugebauer cited the inaction as proof that regulators have enough tools to prevent a meltdown, but not enough focus.

Despite Neugebauer's worries about the government as an insurer, on the Agriculture Committee he has sought to manage risk for farmers and ranchers. Lawmakers didn't settle on a reauthorization of farm programs in the 112th, but there was at least consensus that federal crop insurance programs will be strengthened as direct payments to farmers are eliminated.

The farm bill approved by the panel in a May 2013 markup contains a version of Neugebauer's "supplemental coverage option." First proposed in the 110th Congress (2007-08), the program would let producers bolster their individual (and subsidized) insurance policies with another plan that pays out when their region experiences below-normal yields. Critics say the program could cost more than direct payments did, in years when the weather is bad. But Neugebauer argues that more insurance options are needed because many farming operations are now so large that capital outlays and potential losses are huge.

He also sits on the Science, Space and Technology Committee, where his work often involves agriculture. He questions whether EPA regulators use the best science available in setting rules for farmers and others.

Neugebauer is a social conservative and a deacon in his Baptist church. He doesn't usually step into the middle of social issues. However, in the last days of the 2010 health care debate in the House, he shouted out "baby killer" as Michigan Democrat Bart Stupak spoke about a deal he had struck on the overhaul legislation's abortion language. He later apologized and said he was referring to the policy, not to Stupak.

A St. Louis native, Neugebauer was raised in his mother's hometown of Lubbock. His father sold insurance; his mother was a real estate agent and interior designer. They divorced when Neugebauer was 9, and his father died soon after.

At Texas Tech University he became so skilled at back flips, twists and other moves that he joined a touring trampoline group called The Flying Matadors. He graduated with a degree in accounting and launched his business career. Neugebauer also married his high school sweetheart, Dana.

Republican Rep. Larry Combest resigned in 2003, and Neugebauer faced 13 Republicans and two Democrats in the special election to succeed him. In a runoff with accountant K. Michael Conaway, who had close ties to President George W. Bush, Neugebauer won by 587 votes. (Conaway was elected in 2004 in a neighboring district.)

After redistricting, his 2004 race pitted him against 26-year Democratic Rep. Charles W. Stenholm, the most conservative of congressional Democrats. Neugebauer defeated Stenholm by 18 points, and he has won by wide margins since then.

Key Votes

2012

Extend a Social Security payroll tax cut and unemployment benefits	NO
Ease securities rules to expand small-business access to capital	YES
Extend for one year subsidized student loan interest rates financed by a cut in health care spending	NO
Cite Attorney General Eric H. Holder Jr. for contempt of Congress	YES
Create a visa program for foreign graduates in high-tech fields	YES
Extend most Bush-era income tax rates while allowing rates for top-bracket earners to rise (Jan. 1, 2013)	NO

2011

Strike funding for F-35 alternative engine	YES
Prevent EPA from regulating greenhouse gas emissions to address climate change	YES
Extend certain provisions of Patriot Act for four years	YES
Declare opposition to use of ground troops in Libya	YES
Overhaul patent law	YES
Pass compromise debt limit increase plan and establish future spending limits	NO
Allow consideration of measures to implement three trade agreements	YES

CQ Vote Studies

	PARTY UNITY		PRESIDENTIAL SUPPORT	
	SUPPORT	OPPOSE	SUPPORT	OPPOSE
2012	98%	2%	12%	88%
2011	99%	1%	20%	80%
2010	99%	1%	30%	70%
2009	99%	1%	10%	90%
2008	98%	2%	80%	20%

Interest Groups

	AFL-CIO	ADA	CCUS	ACU
2012	10%	10%	83%	100%
2011	3%	5%	94%	96%
2010	0%	0%	88%	100%
2009	5%	0%	79%	100%
2008	0%	5%	82%	96%

Texas 19

West central — Lubbock, Abilene, Big Spring

The high, flat mesa of the 19th District produces one of the nation's top cotton crops. Beginning in Parmer and Castro counties in the Texas Panhandle, the district stretches across the South Plains and east through towns that sprouted along the path of the Texas and Pacific Railway. It captures both Lubbock and Abilene.

Lubbock serves as the cultural and retail hub for the high plains and the trade center for the cotton crop. Factories produce cotton gins as well as irrigation systems for the sandy soil; severe drought has depleted the Ogallala Aquifer and made conservation a key regional issue. Texas Tech University's 1,839-acre Spanish Renaissance-themed campus in Lubbock is the second-largest contiguous campus in the nation. Covenant Health Services and university medical centers make health care another important cog in the economy.

Visitors to Abilene, in the district's southeast, can learn about the town's railroad roots at the Frontier Texas! Museum. Local leaders are pushing for business growth, especially in health care, manufacturing and telecommunications sectors. Dyess Air Force Base has expanded its facilities but trimmed its civilian workforce because of budget cuts.

Sweeping winds have driven developers to the district's center: Nolan County's Roscoe Wind Complex is one of the world's largest wind farms.

In the late 1970s, the Lubbock region was Democratic enough that future Republican President George W. Bush lost a bid for Congress. Now, the one-third Hispanic 19th is Republican territory and gave Mitt Romney 74 percent of its vote in the 2012 presidential race.

Major Industry
Cotton, higher education, health care, energy, manufacturing

Military Bases
Dyess Air Force Base, , 4,325 military, 444 civilian (2011)

Cities
Lubbock, Abilene, Big Spring

Notable
Lubbock's Buddy Holly Center honors the local-native musician, who died in a February 1959 plane crash in Iowa.

Rep. Joaquin Castro (D)

Capitol Office
225-3236
castro.house.gov
212 Cannon Bldg. 20515-4320; fax 225-1915

Committees
Armed Services
Foreign Affairs

Residence
San Antonio

Born
Sept. 16, 1974; San Antonio, Texas

Religion
Roman Catholic

Family
Single

Education
Stanford U., A.B. 1996 (communications); Harvard U., J.D. 2000

Career
Lawyer; law instructor; city employee

Political Highlights
Texas House, 2003-13

ELECTION RESULTS

2012 GENERAL		
Joaquin Castro (D)	119,032	63.9%
David Rosa (R)	62,376	33.5%
A.E. "Tracy" Potts (LIBERT)	3,143	1.7%
2012 PRIMARY		
Joaquin Castro (D)		unopposed

Elected 2012; 1st term

Castro is one of the golden boys of the San Antonio political scene — the other one being his twin brother, Mayor Julián Castro. The two have been heralded as the identical new faces of Democratic politics, although Joaquin's service in the House is the first test of their governing skills on a larger stage.

The brothers grew up in San Antonio. Their mother, Rosie, was an activist and organizer of La Raza Unida, a radical group that focused on civil rights for Mexican-Americans. She kept her children involved in street-level politics throughout their childhood.

Both Castros went to Stanford, then Harvard Law School; when they returned to San Antonio they worked together as lawyers. Julián got involved with city politics, while Joaquin won election to the state House in 2002. His party was firmly in the minority for all five of his terms, so he has few signature legislative successes to point to — but several colleagues of both parties told the San Antonio Express-News that he was effective at forming relationships to nudge various policies to the benefit of his constituents.

He says his top priority in Texas was "getting more students to college and getting them to graduate," but he didn't snag a seat on the Education and the Workforce Committee. He does sit on the Armed Services Committee — which is relevant to the huge military population back home — and the Foreign Affairs Subcommittee on trade. He is a member of the business-friendly New Democrat Coalition.

The Castros also have some influence as media figures. Both brothers are regular guests on major news programs, and Julián gave the keynote address at the Democratic National Convention in 2012.

As Texas' congressional map took shape, Castro considered running in the 35th District against nine-term Democrat Lloyd Doggett. It was shaping up as a nasty primary, but the retirement of seven-term Democrat Charlie Gonzalez in the 20th District left Castro a clear path to the House.

Texas 20

Western San Antonio

The geographically small 20th District grabs San Antonio, the state's second-most-populous city, from the west. This metropolitan area was one of the nation's fastest-growing between 2000 and 2010, and although the city center of San Antonio experienced residential decline during that time, the 20th District takes in the western neighborhoods that experienced explosive population growth. The Democratic-leaning district includes both South Side rental units and sprawling estates with world-class golf courses in its northwestern reaches.

City leaders have attempted to revitalize subdivisions in northern and western areas of San Antonio, attracting native San Antonians from elsewhere as well as newcomers. Many of these new residents are Hispanic; the Latino community accounts for more than two-thirds of the district's population overall.

Expansion in the aerospace, energy and medical sectors, plus stable housing prices, have contributed to the area's population surge. Converting the former Kelly Air Force base to control by Port San Antonio has boosted shipping and logistics jobs, as well as lured military contractors and federal agencies. Boeing, the largest tenant, plans to move 400 more jobs in addition to the 2,800 already in San Antonio by transferring maintenance of Air Force One from Kansas. Tourism revenue rides the wave from Six Flags Fiesta Texas and a Sea World theme park.

To the north, the South Texas Medical Center (shared with the 21st) is a health care hub. Officials anticipate that six out of 10 high-growth professions in Bexar County (pronounced BEAR) will be in the medical sector. The University of Texas, San Antonio, pumps $1.2 billion into the local economy. Joint Base San Antonio, which includes the 20th's Lackland Air Force Base site, serves more Defense Department students than any other installation.

Major Industry
Military, aerospace, health care, tourism

Military Bases
Joint Base San Antonio, 24,205 military, 23,720 civilian (2011) (shared with the 21st, 23rd & 28th)

Cities
San Antonio (pt.)

Notable
Conjunto music, a South Texas genre featuring the button accordion, streams from Rosedale Park each summer during the Tejano Conjunto Festival.

Rep. Lamar Smith (R)

Capitol Office
225-4236
lamarsmith.house.gov
2409 Rayburn Bldg. 20515-4321, fax 225-8628

Committees
Homeland Security
Judiciary
Science, Space & Technology - Chairman

Residence
San Antonio

Born
Nov. 19, 1947; San Antonio, Texas

Religion
Christian Scientist

Family
Wife, Beth Schafer; two children

Education
Yale U., B.A. 1969 (American studies); Southern Methodist U., J.D. 1975

Career
Lawyer; rancher; reporter

Political Highlights
Texas House, 1981-82; Bexar County Commissioners Court, 1983-85

ELECTION RESULTS

2012 GENERAL		
Lamar Smith (R)	187,015	60.5%
Candace E. Duval (D)	109,326	35.4%
John-Henry Liberty (LIBERT)	12,524	4.0%
2012 PRIMARY		
Lamar Smith (R)	52,404	76.6%
Richard Mack (R)	10,111	14.8%
Richard Morgan (R)	5,868	8.6%
2010 GENERAL		
Lamar Smith (R)	162,924	68.9%
Lainey Melnick (D)	65,927	27.9%
James Arthur Strohm (LIBERT)	7,694	3.2%

Previous Winning Percentages
2008 (80%); 2006 (60%); 2004 (62%); 2002 (73%); 2000 (76%); 1998 (91%); 1996 (76%); 1994 (90%); 1992 (72%); 1990 (75%); 1988 (93%); 1986 (61%)

Elected 1986; 14th term

Smith has helped draw the Republican Party line on immigration and the war on terrorism, and his work on intellectual property law has put him in the national spotlight. He sits at or near the top of three committees, and he finds relatively genial ways to take oppositional stances against Democratic plans.

After serving six years as the top Republican on the Judiciary Committee, Smith bowed to GOP term limit rules and stepped down. He had a soft landing. For the 113th Congress (2013-14), he is the chairman of the Science, Space and Technology Committee. He is also the No. 2 Republican on the Homeland Security Committee.

Smith takes advantage of chances to advance his agenda across all of his committees. As he took the Science gavel, he indicated that promoting cybersecurity research would be high on his to-do list — it also factors into the work of the Homeland Security Committee and discussions of Internet law on the Judiciary Committee.

Citing a desire to keep America competitive, he embraces efforts to bolster education in science, technology, engineering and math, which are commonly referred to as the STEM fields. In 2012, he introduced a bill to grant 55,000 green cards to foreign students who graduate from American universities with advanced STEM degrees. His proposal would have offset the increase by shrinking an existing visa program — a provision that attracted Republican support but soured most Democrats on the bill.

The previous Science chairman, Ralph M. Hall, is also a Texan, and Smith is continuing the panel's rigorous looks at a few Texas interests: energy and the space program. He is a defender of hydraulic fracturing, a method of oil and gas extraction that environmentalists dislike. Smith sees NASA as drifting aimlessly under the Obama administration: "NASA needs decisive leadership from Congress," he wrote in February 2013.

Smith's run at the top of Judiciary was memorable, and it often focused on technology and innovation issues. In 2011, Smith achieved a goal he had pursued for years: the first major rewrite of U.S. patent law in decades. Smith and Senate Judiciary Chairman Patrick J. Leahy, a Vermont Democrat, led the charge in Congress, bringing U.S. standards closer to international norms.

Smith and Leahy also got together to extend expiring surveillance provisions in the 2001 anti-terrorism law known as the Patriot Act. Smith wanted six years, Leahy wanted two, and Congress signed off in 2011 when they settled on four. Smith led the fight during the 110th Congress (2007-08) to retain provisions in a foreign surveillance bill granting immunity protections for telecommunications companies that cooperate in such spying.

It wasn't all smooth sailing, however. Smith was caught in a blowup over his 2011 bill to fight Internet piracy. The measure would have given the Justice Department and intellectual property holders new tools to thwart foreign-based infringing websites, such as the ability to shut down a site by obtaining a court order.

Opponents said the measure would have a chilling effect on the Internet and allow action against almost any site reposting content it did not generate — therefore, most sites. Major websites "blacked out" their homepages in protest, and activists harangued Smith in a grass-roots campaign. He stopped pushing the bill, but, as with his early failed attempts at a patent overhaul, he quickly started searching for a more palatable approach.

Smith also stepped into election year politics as his panel and the House moved a 2012 reauthorization of federal programs to investigate and prosecute violent crimes against women. Unlike the Senate-passed version, the House bill did not require the extension of such programs to illegal immigrants and lesbian, gay, bisexual and transgender people. The reauthorization stalled, with Democrats using the delay as an example of what they called a GOP "war on women." A Senate-passed version became law in early 2013.

The Homeland Security and Judiciary panels give Smith opportunities to deal with border security and immigration. He has developed and defended the hard-line GOP stance: stopping illegal immigration through tighter border controls; tougher enforcement on those in the country illegally; and no path to legal status for those here illegally.

Smith has said that lax enforcement of immigration laws contributed to the 2001 terrorist attacks, and he opposed President George W. Bush's 2007 proposal to create a path to citizenship for illegal immigrants. He and other Republicans have accused the Obama administration of releasing dangerous criminals back into society when they should have been deported. When Obama decided to ease deportation practices against non-violent illegal immigrants, Smith called it "back-door amnesty" and introduced a measure to remove agencies' discretion on deportations.

Smith wants to require all employers to use E-Verify, an online system to check new employees' legal status — he says it would free up millions of jobs for unemployed Americans. "Right now it takes an unemployed American worker about nine months to find a job. But with E-Verify, we can open up a job in one to two minutes," he wrote. In 1996, Smith wrote a law that increased penalties for document fraud and the smuggling of illegal immigrants and made it easier for illegal immigrants to be detained at the border or deported.

Smith's family arrived in Texas around 1850, just five years after it became a state. The family's political involvement stretches back almost that long. His grandfather was district attorney in San Antonio and an unsuccessful House candidate. His great-grandfather was a San Antonio judge, and his great-great-great-grandfather was mayor of Galveston.

After graduating from Yale, Smith worked as a business reporter for The Christian Science Monitor in Boston. He then got a law degree and returned to San Antonio. He was elected to a seat in the state House, then served on the Bexar County Commissioners Court.

Republican Tom Loeffler gave up his House seat in 1986 to run for governor. After Bush, then a Midland oilman with one losing congressional race under his belt, decided not to seek the seat, Smith won a six-way primary. He then defeated former Democratic state Sen. Pete Snelson.

Smith has never dipped below 60 percent of the vote in a general election. Running in a reconfigured district in 2012, he beat Democrat Candace E. Duval by 25 points.

Key Votes

2012	
Extend a Social Security payroll tax cut and unemployment benefits	YES
Ease securities rules to expand small-business access to capital	YES
Extend for one year subsidized student loan interest rates financed by a cut in health care spending	YES
Cite Attorney General Eric H. Holder Jr. for contempt of Congress	YES
Create a visa program for foreign graduates in high-tech fields	?
Extend most Bush-era income tax rates while allowing rates for top-bracket earners to rise (Jan. 1, 2013)	YES
2011	
Strike funding for F-35 alternative engine	NO
Prevent EPA from regulating greenhouse gas emissions to address climate change	YES
Extend certain provisions of Patriot Act for four years	YES
Declare opposition to use of ground troops in Libya	YES
Overhaul patent law	YES
Pass compromise debt limit increase plan and establish future spending limits	YES
Allow consideration of measures to implement three trade agreements	YES

CQ Vote Studies

	PARTY UNITY		PRESIDENTIAL SUPPORT	
	SUPPORT	OPPOSE	SUPPORT	OPPOSE
2012	96%	4%	18%	82%
2011	95%	5%	29%	71%
2010	96%	4%	26%	74%
2009	86%	14%	22%	78%
2008	95%	5%	70%	30%

Interest Groups

	AFL-CIO	ADA	CCUS	ACU
2012	10%	0%	100%	88%
2011	0%	5%	100%	84%
2010	0%	0%	88%	100%
2009	10%	5%	87%	96%
2008	20%	15%	100%	88%

Texas 21

Central — northern San Antonio and suburbs, part of Austin and suburbs

The 21st District takes in the northeastern slope of the Balcones Escarpment, stretching from San Antonio to Austin. This heavily populated strip of the district connects through Comal County to a block of agricultural land on the Edwards Plateau to the west.

More than one-third of the district's residents live in San Antonio in ritzy neighborhoods such as Alamo Heights on its east side or in northern suburbs in Bexar (pronounced BEAR) County. The 21st encompasses Fort Sam Houston, part of Joint Base San Antonio, which includes the Brooke Army Medical Center. Civilian health care is a key component of the local economy as well, mostly centered on the booming South Texas Medical Center. The 21st also includes San Antonio International Airport.

Traveling to the district's north, Canyon Lake is a top spot for water skiers, boaters and fisherman. Approaching Austin from the south, the 21st takes in rapidly growing Buda and Lady Bird Lake. Within the capital city, the district brushes up against the University of Texas campus and takes in Zilker Park and the historic 6th Street entertainment district.

Bandera County is home to some of the nation's top-producing quail farms, while cattle and goats graze across Kerr, Kendall and Real counties. Gillespie County produces Texas' largest peach crop.

These rural counties, especially Gillespie, are Republican strongholds. Although Travis County and Austin lean Democratic, the 21st grabs southwestern and southern neighborhoods Oak Hill and Onion Creek that support GOP candidates. Overall, the 21st gave Republican Mitt Romney 60 percent of its vote in the 2010 presidential election.

Major Industry
Government, tourism, technology, higher education, agriculture

Military Bases
Joint Base San Antonio, 24,205 military, 23,720 civilian (shared with 20th, 23rd & 28th)

Cities
San Antonio (pt.), Austin (pt.), San Marcos, New Braunfels, Kerrville

Notable
Wonder World Park, centered on the Balcones Fault Line, offers visitors the chance to descend into an earthquake-formed cave.

Rep. Pete Olson (R)

Capitol Office
225-5951
olson.house.gov
312 Cannon Bldg. 20515-4322; fax 225-5241

Committees
Energy & Commerce

Residence
Sugar Land

Born
Dec. 9, 1962; Fort Lewis, Wash.

Religion
United Methodist

Family
Wife, Nancy Olson; two children

Education
Rice U., B.A. 1985 (computer science); U. of Texas, J.D. 1988

Military
Navy, 1988-98

Career
Congressional aide; Navy Senate liaison

Political Highlights
No previous office

ELECTION RESULTS

2012 GENERAL		
Pete Olson (R)	160,668	64.0%
Kesha Rogers (D)	80,203	32.0%
Steven Susman (LIBERT)	5,986	2.4%
Don Cook (GREEN)	4,054	1.6%
2012 PRIMARY		
Pete Olson (R)	35,838	76.5%
Barbara Carlson (R)	11,019	23.5%
2010 GENERAL		
Pete Olson (R)	140,537	67.5%
Kesha Rogers (D)	62,082	29.8%
Steven Susman (LIBERT)	5,538	2.7%

Previous Winning Percentages
2008 (52%)

Elected 2008; 3rd term

Olson shot for the moon — literally — but landed in Congress. Now in his third term, he has been a model conservative backbencher, reinforcing GOP positions across the board while locking in on subjects important to Houston.

His biography reads like a sampler of classic American dreams. Olson pursued careers as an athlete and an astronaut; he served as a naval aviator, then as a Navy liaison to the Senate. His work on Capitol Hill led to staff jobs with Texas Sens. Phil Gramm and John Cornyn before he became a lawmaker in his own right. He credits his former bosses with teaching him a guiding principle: "You have to be a man of your word."

When Olson speaks on the House floor or in committee, his words come quickly and sometimes on top of each other. What his delivery lacks in polish, he makes up in consistency. Joining the Energy and Commerce Committee in the 112th Congress (2011-12), he stood behind the GOP themes of increasing domestic energy production and ending what Republicans describe as over-regulation of various industries.

Olson was critical of the Obama administration's response to the 2010 Deepwater Horizon oil spill in the Gulf of Mexico. In 2011, he added to his plate the White House denial of a permit for Keystone XL, a proposed pipeline to take oil from Canada's tar sands as far as Texas refineries. The president "chose Hollywood elitists and radical environmentalists over American unions and the American people by putting the Keystone pipeline in limbo," Olson said on the House floor in 2012.

Believing that energy security is national security, Olson supports oil and gas development, particularly in Texas' Eagle Ford Shale and other fields opened by technological advances. In the 112th Congress, Democrats used tax credits for oil companies as examples of largesse for big industries, but Olson defended them as essential tools for smaller producers. Those companies are in the vanguard, he said, with bigger companies swooping in later to develop their discoveries. Tax credits are "encouraging these people to take chances," he said.

Olson calls federal regulation of hydraulic fracturing — the injection of high-pressure fluids into rock layers to allow access to new deposits of gas and oil — "double jeopardy." State regulation has been adequate, he says. In 2011, the House passed his provision requiring federal agencies to assess the impact a potential new rule could have on domestic employment. Another Olson bill was passed by the House with bipartisan support. It would shield electricity producers from EPA penalties for overproduction when other federal agencies order them to increase production to meet emergency needs.

"The Clean Air Act has become a weapon as opposed to a law to make sure that we have clean air," he said. His utilities bill stalled in the Senate, and he reintroduced it in 2013.

Olson once sat on the Science, Space and Technology Committee, and he still keeps tabs on NASA and the Johnson Space Center. Even in times of tight budgets, he supports spending on the space program — "the bang for the buck is amazing," he said. Olson has criticized President Barack Obama's proposed budgets for NASA and the move away from human space flight; while not opposed to the use of the private sector for such capabilities, he says companies are still too "unknown and untested" for the government to withdraw. He says NASA needs a clear mission and suggests a return to the moon, since it can be used as a training area or staging ground for missions farther afield.

Olson sees security needs in space as well. "Space is still the high ground," he said, and with our reliance on military and communications satellites, "I'm not saying we should militarize space, but we've got to stay up there and maintain our dominance."

Olson is part of a GOP team promoting a bill to restructure the management of NASA, so that it has a director with a 10-year term (similar to the FBI) and decisions on missions are less susceptible to shifts in political power.

Social conservatism colors some of Olson's work on health issues. Twice he has introduced a bill requiring states to report on any Medicaid payments to abortion providers. He was forceful in responding to a 2011 report that indicated federal funding for Planned Parenthood could be covering abortion services. "We can never tire," he said on the House floor. "We can never rest in our moral obligation to protect our nation's unborn children."

The oldest of three children, Olson was born at an Army medical center in Fort Lewis, Wash.; his father had enrolled in ROTC in college and spent two years on active duty. The family moved around as his dad, Richard, worked his way up in the paper manufacturing industry (he became CEO of Champion Paper). They eventually settled in Seabrook, a suburb of Houston.

Space and sports were all around, sometimes intertwining; Olson has mentioned that one of his youth football coaches was an astronaut. He played for legendary high school basketball coach Bill Krueger. Wanting to play Division I ball in college, he attended Rice University and walked on to the team — but after a year and half, "it became very clear that I did not have an NBA-caliber athletic ability." He got a degree in computer science, then found himself put off by a summer job in the field; he earned a law degree, then soured on that profession during summer clerkships.

He decided to pursue his dream of becoming an astronaut, and after passing the Texas bar exam in 1988, Olson joined the Navy, hoping the service would provide flight experience. He failed to win acceptance to test pilot school but did become a decorated aviator, flying missions over the Persian Gulf after Operation Desert Storm. He no longer flies, joking that it's "much more expensive when the government's not paying for your gasoline."

Assigned to Washington, he served with the Joint Chiefs of Staff, then got to know Gramm as a Senate liaison. When Gramm retired and Cornyn won his seat in 2002, Olson began a five-year stint as Cornyn's chief of staff.

The 22nd District was once the home turf of Majority Leader Tom DeLay. But Democrat Nick Lampson, a former four-term representative, captured the seat in 2006 after DeLay resigned following his indictment in a campaign finance case. Olson — with encouragement from his Texas connections — moved to the district to run for the seat in 2008. Despite carpetbagger charges, he had little trouble besting a primary challenger in a runoff. He ran 7 points ahead of Lampson in November. He won easily in 2010 and 2012.

Key Votes

2012	
Extend a Social Security payroll tax cut and unemployment benefits	NO
Ease securities rules to expand small-business access to capital	YES
Extend for one year subsidized student loan interest rates financed by a cut in health care spending	YES
Cite Attorney General Eric H. Holder Jr. for contempt of Congress	YES
Create a visa program for foreign graduates in high-tech fields	YES
Extend most Bush-era income tax rates while allowing rates for top-bracket earners to rise (Jan. 1, 2013)	NO
2011	
Strike funding for F-35 alternative engine	NO
Prevent EPA from regulating greenhouse gas emissions to address climate change	YES
Extend certain provisions of Patriot Act for four years	YES
Declare opposition to use of ground troops in Libya	YES
Overhaul patent law	YES
Pass compromise debt limit increase plan and establish future spending limits	YES
Allow consideration of measures to implement three trade agreements	YES

CQ Vote Studies

	PARTY UNITY		PRESIDENTIAL SUPPORT	
	SUPPORT	OPPOSE	SUPPORT	OPPOSE
2012	99%	1%	15%	85%
2011	97%	3%	27%	73%
2010	98%	2%	26%	74%
2009	97%	3%	13%	87%

Interest Groups

	AFL-CIO	ADA	CCUS	ACU
2012	10%	0%	92%	100%
2011	0%	5%	100%	84%
2010	0%	0%	88%	100%
2009	5%	0%	80%	100%

Texas 22

Southern Houston suburbs — Sugar Land, Pearland

The 22nd takes in three-fourths of Fort Bend County, one of the nation's fastest-growing areas, and half of Brazoria County south of Houston. It lost portions of Galveston County and the Johnson Space Center during decennial redistricting.

The planned communities sprouting up throughout the district are enclaves for upper-income professionals who work in Houston: The district's average median income tops $80,000. Most of the district's population is concentrated to the city's southwest, where residents live in unincorporated areas and subdivisions. A retail sector along Highway 6 through Sugar Land is part of a diverse economy in the district, which has been driven mainly by the energy industry.

Fort Bend's independent school district lures many families. Property tax rates have been rising parallel to the growth, but state budget shortfalls have officials worried about maintaining the quality of education. Transportation is another big concern, especially on U.S. Route 59, with highway-widening and tollway projects under way to improve access to the city.

To the east, Brazoria County's Pearland sits 20 minutes south of downtown Houston. A substantial bloc of its highly educated workforce is employed at Texas Medical Center (in the 9th). The city also has a healthy manufacturing and distribution sector.

Reflecting the diversity of Houston, the suburban fringe is a mix of races and cultures, where blacks and Hispanics account for roughly two-fifths of the population. It is home to the largest population of Asian residents among Texas districts (17 percent), including Pakistani, Vietnamese, Chinese and Indian immigrants. A Blue Dog Democrat briefly represented the district in the U.S. House, but voters here tend to favor the GOP and they gave Mitt Romney 62 percent of their vote in the 2012 presidential race.

Major Industry
Health care, transportation, retail, manufacturing

Cities
Houston (pt.), Pearland, Sugar Land, Friendswood (pt.), Rosenburg, Alvin

Notable
The Nolan Ryan Center in the Hall of Fame pitcher's hometown of Alvin has an interactive exhibit that gives visitors the chance to "catch" his famous fastball.

Rep. Pete Gallego (D)

Capitol Office
225-4511
gallego.house.gov
431 Cannon Bldg. 20515-4323; fax 225-2237

Committees
Agriculture
Armed Services

Residence
Alpine

Born
Dec. 2, 1961; Alpine, Texas

Religion
Roman Catholic

Family
Wife, Maria Elena Ramon; one child

Education
Sul Ross State U., B.A. 1982 (political science); U. of Texas, J.D. 1985

Career
Lawyer; county prosecutor; state assistant attorney general

Political Highlights
Texas House, 1991-2013

ELECTION RESULTS

2012 GENERAL		
Pete Gallego (D)	96,676	50.3%
Francisco "Quico" Canseco (R)	87,547	45.6%
Jeffrey C. Blunt (LIBERT)	5,841	3.0%
Ed Scharf (GREEN)	2,105	1.1%
2012 PRIMARY RUNOFF		
Pete Gallego (D)	15,815	54.8%
Ciro D. Rodriguez (D)	13,038	45.2%

Elected 2012; 1st term

Gallego was a respected state legislator, and he quickly distinguished himself in Washington by joining the Blue Dog Coalition — a group of fiscally conservative Democrats that has shrunk substantially in recent years.

He grew up in the small city of Alpine, near the middle of the vast district he now represents; his father, a World War II veteran, ran a family-owned restaurant and served on the local school board. Gallego (guy-AY-go) headed to Austin for law school at the University of Texas and worked as an assistant attorney general after passing the bar.

In 1990, he returned to Alpine and continued his legal career in private practice. That year, he was also elected to the first of 11 terms in the Texas House. As a freshman, he was chosen by his colleagues as the chairman of the Democratic Caucus, and on leaving that job after a decade, he had a long run as the chairman of the Mexican-American Legislative Caucus. He was known as a "member's member" and a subdued but effective facilitator of legislative action, even as Republicans cemented their hold on state government.

A lot of his personal interests back then involved criminal justice, but in the U.S. House he serves on the Armed Services and Agriculture committees, which are suited to his rural district. He keeps tabs on immigration and border discussions, as he represents more than one third of the U.S.-Mexico border. He also co-sponsored a balanced-budget amendment to the Constitution, put forth by the Blue Dogs, that has a firewall around Social Security spending.

To claim his seat, Gallego beat its two previous occupants. In the primary, he took on Ciro D. Rodriguez, who lost the seat by 5 points in 2010 after six terms. Environmental groups spent heavily against Rodriguez, helping to push Gallego to a runoff victory. In November, he faced freshman Rep. Francisco "Quico" Canseco, who had a big fundraising advantage — which was somewhat neutralized by huge spending against him by outside groups. Gallego won by less than 5 points.

Texas 23

Southwest — outer San Antonio, Socorro

Encompassing all or part of 29 counties, the 23rd is geographically the largest district in Texas and larger than most states east of the Mississippi. From the outskirts of El Paso, it heads toward San Antonio, forming pincers around the city from the west. Along the way it takes in the mountainous and arid Trans-Pecos region, Big Bend National Park and more than 700 miles of the Mexico border along the Rio Grande.

Most of the district's residents live in Bexar (pronounced BEAR) County in rapidly growing suburbs on three sides of San Antonio. The presence of Joint Base San Antonio, a combined Air Force and Army base that has the largest installation population of any U.S. military base, has lured business to suburban shopping centers, entertainment venues and hotels that accommodate base visitors. Military training facilities at Camp Bullis occupy 28,000 acres northwest of the city.

More than 20 million acres of the 23rd are devoted to farmland and ranches, and its pastures are among the top in the nation for goat and sheep production.

The wide open expanses of the Permian Basin have proved profitable for energy production. BP and other energy companies have funneled millions into wind farms in and around Pecos County, once a hotbed for oil production. Officials hope that unlike the constant fluctuation in commodity markets for petroleum, wind resources could be reliable development.

This district is the most politically competitive of the Rio Grande districts in Texas, particularly because of the 70 percent Hispanic vote and diverse concerns amongst constituents, varying from suburban development to border security and immigration to agriculture. While the 23rd sent a Democrat to the U.S. House in 2012, it supported Republican Mitt Romney in the presidential contest, though he only won by just more than 5,000 votes.

Major Industry
Agriculture, trade, mining, energy, tourism

Military Bases
Joint Base San Antonio, 24,205 military, 23,720 civilian (2011) (shared with 20th, 21st & 28th); Camp Bullis, 130 military, 585 civilian

Cities
San Antonio (pt.), Del Rio

Notable
Black-tailed jackrabbits are a common sighting along dirt roadsides in Big Bend National Park.

Rep. Kenny Marchant (R)

Capitol Office
225-6605
marchant.house.gov
1110 Longworth Bldg. 20515-4324; fax 225-0074

Committees
Education & the Workforce
Ways & Means

Residence
Coppell

Born
Feb. 23, 1951; Bonham, Texas

Religion
Nazarene

Family
Wife, Donna Marchant; four children

Education
Bethany Nazarene College, B.A. 1974 (religion); Nazarene Theological Seminary, attended 1975-76

Career
Real estate developer; homebuilding company owner

Political Highlights
Carrollton City Council, 1980-84 (mayor pro tempore, 1983-84); mayor of Carrollton, 1984-86; Texas House, 1987-2005

ELECTION RESULTS

2012 GENERAL		
Kenny Marchant (R)	148,586	61.0%
Tim Rusk (D)	87,645	36.0%
John Stathas (LIBERT)	7,258	3.0%
2012 PRIMARY		
Kenny Marchant (R)	27,926	67.9%
Grant Stinchfield (R)	13,184	32.1%
2010 GENERAL		
Kenny Marchant (R)	100,078	81.6%
David Sparks (LIBERT)	22,609	18.4%

Previous Winning Percentages
2008 (56%); 2006 (60%); 2004 (64%)

Elected 2004; 5th term

Colleagues respect Marchant for his expertise on financial matters and his judicious approach to his job. He's a fiscal conservative who loves committee work, never shows up a fellow lawmaker and has a prescient sense of what's politically possible — traits that have landed him a seat on the Ways and Means Committee.

A Democratic friend from the Texas House once told the Austin American-Statesman that Marchant was "a political poker player. ... He can see the future." Marchant (MARCH-unt) banked a lot of chips during 18 years in state government. He had a strong working relationship with Gov. George W. Bush, and he was the House Republican chairman in 2002 when Republicans took control of the Texas chamber.

And he did it modestly. "Being at the microphone and giving the speeches and all that never was part of my deal," he says. Marchant continues that approach in the U.S. House. He introduces relatively few bills, and as far as public speaking goes, his favorite format is the five minutes of question time he gets in hearings.

Many of those hearings are for the Ways and Means Committee, where Marchant has sat since 2011. He says that despite his leadership experience in Texas, his focus these days is committee work. "I have got the assignment I want," he said. (As a bonus, he was also given a seat on the Education and the Workforce Committee in 2013. He last served on that panel in his second term.)

In the 112th Congress (2011-12), Marchant and other Ways and Means Republicans used hearings in preparation for an attempted overhaul of the tax code in the 113th Congress (2013-14). Marchant likes the tenets outlined by Chairman Dave Camp of Michigan: fewer tax brackets with lower rates, elimination of many deductions or preferences, and a switch to "territorial" corporate taxation.

He sees three deductions surviving an overhaul: charitable contributions, mortgage interest on a primary residence and "the inside buildup of life insurance annuity income." Tax-deferred retirement plans such as 401(k)s and IRAs could continue as well, he said.

Marchant's district has lots of large corporate offices, as well as a major air cargo hub in the Dallas/Forth Worth International Airport. He often weighs in on the trade issues before Ways and Means. In 2012, he supported a bill to grant Russia permanent normal trade relations status, saying that "if it weren't for Russia being sympathetic to Syria and Iran, this'd be a no-brainer." The change went through late in the year.

He backs free-trade agreements and would like to see aggressive enforcement of pacts with China and Europe — both of which have been accused of manipulating markets to give their own exporters an advantage. Fears of a retaliatory "trade war" are overblown, Marchant says, because they won't risk losing access to U.S. markets.

The committee also handles some entitlement programs, such as Social Security. His emphasis for keeping those programs solvent is a careful vetting of program participants. "I don't think we're being nearly as aggressive as we can be on qualification," he says. Before cuts are made, Marchant wants lawmakers to reassess the eligibility standards for programs and make sure no benefits are going to ineligible recipients.

Marchant is a former member of the Financial Services Committee, and he chaired the Financial Institutions panel in the Texas House. His professional experiences as a homebuilder and developer versed him in housing issues and made him one of the wealthiest members of Congress.

Lawmakers are fleshing out plans for the government-sponsored housing giants, Fannie Mae and Freddie Mac, and Marchant plans to be involved. (He opposed the 2008 bailout that put those entities in conservatorship.) His own preference is to keep a federally insured housing entity, "but they don't ever hold the mortgages, they're just a pass-through entity that facilitates the marketing and the securitization." Once loans were securitized and sold off, the purchasers and reinsurers would be primarily responsible for covering losses, with the federal government having a minimal obligation.

Most of Marchant's heavy lifting is on fiscal matters. He belongs to the Republican Study Committee, and he joined the conservatives who voted against fiscal 2012 spending bills because they didn't cut enough. He pays extra attention to some parochial concerns — he is a staunch opponent of illegal immigration and any proposals to give such immigrants a path to citizenship. Several times, he has introduced a bill to prevent illegal immigrants from getting a loan insured by the Federal Housing Administration.

Marchant takes to the podium so infrequently that few might guess that he studied to be a minister. The oldest of five children, he grew up near Farmers Branch, where his father and two uncles owned a four-chair barbershop. Eulogizing his father on the House floor in 2012, he noted that his dad worked there for 46 years. Religion was a big part of their family life. "We went to church three or four times a week, and I went to church camps," Marchant recalls. "All of my activities basically revolved around the church."

He graduated from Bethany Nazarene college in Oklahoma and attended seminary in Missouri before having a change of heart. Instead of pursuing the ministry, he returned to Texas and became a roofing contractor, resuming work he had done to pay for college. That blossomed into his housing career. His faith remains an integral part of his life, however. One outlet is the Marchant Family Foundation, which provides scholarships for pastors' children; when Marchant was a part-time Texas legislator, the foundation was more active building and assisting churches and orphanages around the world.

Marchant chaired the local homebuilders association, which suspected city inspectors of soliciting bribes. Those concerns with local government helped spur him to run for Carrollton City Council in 1980. He won, and four years later, he was elected mayor. In 1987, he moved to the Texas House, where he served until he won his first congressional race in 2004. His re-elections have not been difficult.

Several Marchants have become involved with politics. Kenny's brother, Ron, is a Denton County commissioner. His son Matthew is the current mayor of Carrollton, and his son Luke is a Republican operative who has worked on the campaigns of Texas Rep. Pete Olson, Florida Sen. Marco Rubio and others.

Key Votes

2012	
Extend a Social Security payroll tax cut and unemployment benefits	YES
Ease securities rules to expand small-business access to capital	?
Extend for one year subsidized student loan interest rates financed by a cut in health care spending	YES
Cite Attorney General Eric H. Holder Jr. for contempt of Congress	YES
Create a visa program for foreign graduates in high-tech fields	YES
Extend most Bush-era income tax rates while allowing rates for top-bracket earners to rise (Jan. 1, 2013)	NO
2011	
Strike funding for F-35 alternative engine	YES
Prevent EPA from regulating greenhouse gas emissions to address climate change	YES
Extend certain provisions of Patriot Act for four years	YES
Declare opposition to use of ground troops in Libya	YES
Overhaul patent law	NO
Pass compromise debt limit increase plan and establish future spending limits	YES
Allow consideration of measures to implement three trade agreements	YES

CQ Vote Studies

	Party Unity		Presidential Support	
	Support	Oppose	Support	Oppose
2012	97%	3%	15%	85%
2011	96%	4%	21%	79%
2010	99%	1%	26%	74%
2009	98%	2%	15%	85%
2008	98%	2%	82%	18%

Interest Groups

	AFL-CIO	ADA	CCUS	ACU
2012	10%	10%	82%	92%
2011	0%	10%	94%	91%
2010	0%	5%	100%	95%
2009	11%	5%	73%	100%
2008	0%	0%	83%	100%

Texas 24

Northern 'mid-cities' region — Carrollton, Grapevine, Euless

Mainly within northern quadrants of Dallas and Tarrant counties, the 24th has an economy anchored by one of the nation's busiest airports. Dallas-Fort Worth International Airport annually pumps more than $16 billion into the region, and is the district's largest employer.

American Airlines corporate headquarters are here and are expected to remain following a merger between American and US Airways. To the east of the airport in Irving (shared with the 33rd), the Las Colinas mixed-development strip teems with corporate enterprises. ExxonMobil is among the Fortune 500 companies with headquarters here. Proximity to the international airport has also made the area a hub for foreign-owned companies. Irving's new convention center and hotels generate millions of dollars in taxes for the community, and a connecting light-rail line should draw city workers to the area.

Carrollton's designation as a foreign-trade zone has helped it attract manufacturing and major corporate firms — it already hosted Halliburton. Close to 40 percent of the city's adult population has at least a bachelor's degree. Pharmaceuticals and health care are important sectors here and in nearby Grapevine.

In the "mid-cities" region between Dallas and Fort Worth, suburban Bedford, Euless and Hurst work in a joint chamber of commerce to attract small businesses. The combined school district serving these middle-class communities frequently ranks among the best in the nation and offers its growing Hispanic student population a dual-language program beginning at the elementary level. Major employer Bell Helicopter, headquartered in Hurst, plans to expand and bring more workers to the region.

The 24th votes Republican in federal elections but remains politically competitive at the state level, with minorities becoming a growing influence. Hispanics, blacks and Asians make up nearly half the population.

Major Industry
Airports and transportation, hospitality, manufacturing, health care

Cities
Fort Worth (pt.), Irving (pt.), Carrollton (pt.), Euless (pt.)

Notable
Valley Ranch hosts the practice facilities of the Dallas Cowboys.

Rep. Roger Williams (R)

Capitol Office
225-9896
williams.house.gov
1122 Longworth Bldg. 20515-3209; fax 225-9692

Committees
Budget
Transportation & Infrastructure

Residence
Austin

Born
Sept. 13, 1949; Evanston, Ill.

Religion
Christian

Family
Wife, Patty Williams; two children

Education
Texas Christian U., B.S. 1972 (physical education)

Career
Car dealership owner; college baseball coach; professional baseball player

Political Highlights
Texas Department of Transportation Motor Vehicle Board, 2004-05; Texas secretary of state, 2005-07

ELECTION RESULTS

2012 GENERAL		
Roger Williams (R)	154,245	58.4%
Elaine M. Henderson (D)	98,827	37.4%
Betsy Dewey (LIBERT)	10,860	4.1%
2012 PRIMARY RUNOFF		
Roger Williams (R)	26,495	58.0%
Wes Riddle (R)	19,210	42.0%

Elected 2012; 1st term

Williams is not subtle in opposing the Democratic agenda, which he has described as the "path of socialism." On the campaign trail, he emphasized his career as a small-businessman and said he was trying "to stop the Obama economy."

Williams grew up in the Forth Worth area and played baseball at Texas Christian University. Drafted by the Atlanta Braves, he was an outfielder in the minor leagues for a few years, but an injury ended his dream of making it to the big leagues. Instead, he took over his father's auto dealership.

While attempting to buy the Texas Rangers with a group of other investors, he met and befriended George W. Bush (who did end up buying the team). Over the years, Williams was a prolific fundraiser for the Republican Party. In 2005, Gov. Rick Perry appointed him Texas secretary of state.

Williams says that regulations and taxes are killing small businesses. He sits on the Budget Committee and challenges Obama administration officials and House colleagues alike. "What the heck is wrong with being a millionaire?" he asked at a markup of the fiscal 2014 budget. "When you do that you become a job creator, you become a taxpayer. It's called the dream."

He also sits on the Transportation and Infrastructure Committee. At a March 2013 hearing, he suggested that one way to replenish funding for infrastructure would be eliminating fuel efficiency requirements for new cars, which would boost gas tax revenues.

Williams has pledged a conservative social agenda, opposing abortion, gay marriage and federal funding for stem cell research. He is a member of the conservative Republican Study Committee.

Williams was considering a Senate run in 2012, but he eventually opted for a campaign in the Republican-friendly 25th District. He took a quarter of the vote in a 12-person primary, then beat Wes Riddle, founder of the Central Texas Tea Party, in a runoff. He won by 21 points in November.

Texas 25

Part of Austin; southern Fort Worth suburbs

Grabbing a slice of Austin, the 25th takes in the state Capitol and the burnt orange pride at the University of Texas flagship campus. West of the city, the district stretches north through parts of 13 counties as far as a tiny speck of Tarrant County; it also heads south of Austin near Canyon Lake in central Texas. Formerly a Democratic bastion, the 25th was redrawn during decennial remapping to become a safe Republican seat — voters here gave Mitt Romney 60 percent of the vote in the 2012 presidential election.

More than one-third of the 25th's population is concentrated in Travis County, which includes a plurality of the black residents in this mostly white district. With more than 50,000 students, the University of Texas is among the nation's largest public colleges, providing more than $800 million to the local economy. It will soon add a medical campus.

Johnson County, in the northern portion of the district, has become a Fort Worth bedroom community. Cleburne and fast-growing Burleson, which straddles the border with Tarrant County, are two of the largest cities. Light manufacturing, railroads and natural gas are key to the economy. In neighboring Somervell County, Comanche Peak nuclear power plant outside Glen Rose provides energy and more than a thousand jobs.

Military jobs and prisons employ many residents in Coryell County. Five of Texas' 12 women's correctional facilities are located in or around Gatesville. Part of the county is taken up by Fort Hood, shared with the 31st and stretching into Bell County. The base boasts its role as the largest active-duty armored post in the nation. A substantial number of veterans reside in the district as well.

Hispanic residents account for 17 percent of the population in the 25th overall, but comprise more than one-fourth of the population in some areas.

Major Industry
Higher education, government, military

Military Bases
Fort Hood, 43,000 military, 5,249 civilian (shared with 31st)

Cities
Austin (pt.), Burleson, Copperas Cove

Notable
The Texas Memorial Museum on the UT campus began as the state's official natural sciences exhibit hall.

Rep. Michael C. Burgess (R)

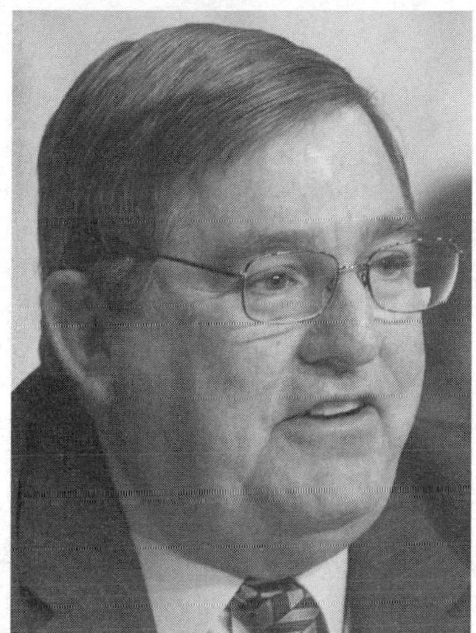

Capitol Office
225-7772
burgess.house.gov
2336 Rayburn Bldg. 20515-4326; fax 225-2919

Committees
Energy & Commerce
Rules

Residence
Lewisville

Born
Dec. 23, 1950; Rochester, Minn.

Religion
Episcopalian

Family
Wife, Laura Burgess; three children

Education
North Texas State U., B.S. 1972 (biology), M.S. 1976 (physiology); U. of Texas Health Science Center, Houston, M.D. 1977; U. of Texas Southwestern Medical Center, Dallas, M.S. 2000 (medical management)

Career
Physician

Political Highlights
No previous office

ELECTION RESULTS

2012 GENERAL		
Michael C. Burgess (R)	176,642	68.3%
David Sanchez (D)	74,237	28.7%
Mark Boler (LIBERT)	7,844	3.0%
2012 PRIMARY		
Michael C. Burgess (R)		unopposed
2010 GENERAL		
Michael C. Burgess (R)	120,984	67.0%
Neil L. Durrance (D)	55,385	30.7%
Mark Boler (LIBERT)	4,062	2.2%

Previous Winning Percentages
2008 (60%); 2006 (60%); 2004 (66%); 2002 (75%)

Elected 2002; 6th term

Burgess is a voluble conservative who never shies away from questioning Democrats. A former obstetrician-gynecologist, he takes pride in his reputation as one of the sharpest critics of the 2010 health care law.

The practice of medicine is a Burgess family tradition. His grandfather was an obstetrician who worked at the Royal Victoria Hospital in Montreal, his father was a general surgeon, his sister is a nurse and his brother is a pathologist. Distaste for government health care programs also runs in the family. Burgess says his father moved to the United States to get away from Canada's government-run health care system.

"I was just a little kid when Medicare came into being and heard from my dad what a mistake that was," Burgess said. "My dad's perception was that government getting a greater footprint in health care was not a good thing. Today, it's hard to imagine a world without Medicare."

Burgess founded the Republican-only Congressional Health Care Caucus in 2009 to disseminate information and ideas to fellow lawmakers. In the 112th Congress (2011-12) he became the No. 2 Republican on the Energy and Commerce Subcommittee on Health. He has kept that job for the 113th Congress (2013-14), while also becoming the No. 2 Republican on the Oversight and Investigations Committee — which is led by another health care professional, psychologist Tim Murphy of Pennsylvania.

In his office's summaries of activities for the 112th Congress, Burgess claimed to have attended 491 meetings or events related to health care. Around the one-year anniversary of the health care law, he released "Doctor in the House," a book detailing his perspective of the health care debate in the 111th Congress (2009-10) and his suggestions for replacing the law.

Burgess has a sense of urgency regarding repeal. Like Medicare, "this is going to be something that's impossible to unwind once it starts, and no one has a clear idea what the costs are," he said. He belongs to the conservative Republican Study Committee, and he has encouraged aggressive resistance to most of President Barack Obama's agenda; at an August 2011 tea party event in Texas, he said that impeachment of the president "needs to happen," if only as a way to tie up the administration for a while.

His own plans for health care tend to be market-based. Burgess has supported GOP budget proposals that suggest converting Medicare to a "premium support" model, with people receiving vouchers to shop for their own insurance. The cost of health benefits should be tax deductible, whether they are covered by an employer or paid directly by an individual, according to Burgess.

Another of his priorities is reining in medical malpractice suits, which to him is "an issue of fundamental fairness." Burgess, who estimates that he has delivered more than 3,000 babies, was sued in the late 1980s by a family whose baby died during a difficult cesarean section. He was not in charge of the delivery but was called in to assist another obstetrician; the incident helped convince him that the medical liability system needed to be overhauled, he said.

Some of his health care work is a little less contentious. Teaming up with Texas Democrat Gene Green, in 2012 he introduced a bill to require greater availability of pricing information for various hospital services: "Arming patients with cost information is an important step in improving our country's health care system with the focus on the patient," he wrote. Burgess and Wisconsin Democrat Ron Kind introduced a bill to extend Medicare immunosuppressant drug coverage for people who have received kidney transplants.

Burgess is also interested in changing the way some health care bills are "scored" by budget analysts. The Congressional Budget Office projects costs and savings of a bill over a 10-year window, but preventive health initiatives might shrink health care spending well beyond that period. Working with Democrat Donna M.C. Christensen — a fellow doctor and the delegate from the Virgin Islands — he has proposed a bill to require longer-term analysis, which would "bend the cost curve and provide long-term costs savings," he said in 2012. It did not have much Republican support.

Health care takes the lion's share of his attention, but Burgess is involved in other Energy and Commerce matters. He subscribes to the "all of the above" energy philosophy and has shown enthusiasm for energy efficiency programs. Overseeing Energy Department investments in 2012, Burgess and Democrat Edward J. Markey of Massachusetts asked for an investigation of the "floundering" United States Enrichment Corp., which processes uranium. They questioned the national security value of USEC's work, the company's technology and its activities' potential harm to the uranium mining industry.

Burgess unsuccessfully sought the Republican Policy Committee chairmanship in November 2008, following his party's weak showing at the polls. But in 2013, party leaders added him to the Rules Committee. He is also a member of the Commission on Security and Cooperation in Europe, which is also known as the Helsinki Commission; it studies human rights and other issues in that theater.

Burgess holds a pilot's license and is also a biker — something his aides didn't know until Burgess told them he wanted to do an event promoting motorcycle safety. He picked up the interest when his son went to serve in the military and made him promise to ride the motorcycle he left behind.

Burgess had no prior political experience when he entered the 2002 race to succeed Dick Armey — the Republican majority leader was retiring. Burgess was motivated in part by a desire to serve the country in some way after the Sept. 11 terrorist attacks.

"My country had been attacked, and what was I doing?" he said. "My son was in the service and I was writing birth control prescriptions." His campaign started off with an Internet query: "I Googled, 'How do you run for Congress?'"

To take Armey's place, Burgess had to defeat the nine-term lawmaker's son, Scott Armey. The 26th District had just been redrawn to favor the younger Armey — who finished first in the six-way Republican primary but did not win enough of the vote to avoid a runoff. Burgess finished in second, 93 votes ahead of the third-place finisher.

Burgess campaigned against Armey by handing out literature declaring, "My dad is not Dick Armey." He took almost 55 percent of the vote in the runoff, then won easily that November.

Key Votes

2012

Extend a Social Security payroll tax cut and unemployment benefits	NO
Ease securities rules to expand small-business access to capital	YES
Extend for one year subsidized student loan interest rates financed by a cut in health care spending	YES
Cite Attorney General Eric H. Holder Jr. for contempt of Congress	YES
Create a visa program for foreign graduates in high-tech fields	YES
Extend most Bush-era income tax rates while allowing rates for top-bracket earners to rise (Jan. 1, 2013)	NO

2011

Strike funding for F-35 alternative engine	YES
Prevent EPA from regulating greenhouse gas emissions to address climate change	?
Extend certain provisions of Patriot Act for four years	YES
Declare opposition to use of ground troops in Libya	YES
Overhaul patent law	NO
Pass compromise debt limit increase plan and establish future spending limits	YES
Allow consideration of measures to implement three trade agreements	YES

CQ Vote Studies

	PARTY UNITY		PRESIDENTIAL SUPPORT	
	SUPPORT	OPPOSE	SUPPORT	OPPOSE
2012	95%	5%	20%	80%
2011	94%	6%	20%	80%
2010	96%	4%	31%	69%
2009	96%	4%	17%	83%
2008	94%	6%	73%	27%

Interest Groups

	AFL-CIO	ADA	CCUS	ACU
2012	10%	10%	83%	96%
2011	0%	10%	93%	83%
2010	7%	5%	75%	96%
2009	0%	0%	71%	100%
2008	14%	10%	76%	96%

Texas 26

Denton County and northern Fort Worth suburbs

Denton County is the heart of the 26th District, which also includes a stretch of Tarrant County and slivers of Dallas County. Decennial remapping removed Cooke County from the district.

The communities of the 26th have grown rapidly since the 1970s, particularly along branches of Interstate 35. In the face of a national decline, home values here have been on the rise. Many residents who live in and around Denton face 40-mile commutes south to either Dallas or Fort Worth; the city recently invested in a commuter line to connect to Dallas' public transportation system and ease congestion.

Denton is home to two colleges, including the University of Northern Texas — its biggest employer and one of the state's largest public colleges. UNT boasts an engineering program that emphasizes nanotechnology research and applications. Manufacturing, retail and transportation are also growing sectors of the economy. The city's music scene is punctuated by the Denton Arts and Jazz Festival and the 35 Denton rock festival.

South Denton County developed quickly along with growth of Dallas-Fort Worth International Airport (in the 24th). Careful planning helped Flower Mound control the rate and character of development. Middle-class Lewisville capitalizes on retail and hotel activity from airport travelers. Rural parts of the county include Eastern Cross Timbers, prairies and large horse ranches — varying from dressage to barrel racing to therapy centers. In Tarrant County, Keller is also expanding rapidly, and the offices of Fidelity Investments and a new Deloitte training center are nearby.

The district is largely white, but Denton County's black and Hispanic population combined doubled between 2000 and 2010. Changing demographics and the college-attending population have given Democrats some hope in Denton, but the district tends to be GOP territory.

Major Industry
Transportation, higher education, manufacturing, horse farming

Cities
Frisco (pt.), Denton, Lewisville, Flower Mound, Keller

Notable
Established in 1946, the University of North Texas' jazz studies program was the first of its kind in the nation.

Rep. Blake Farenthold (R)

Capitol Office
225-7742
farenthold.house.gov
117 Cannon Bldg. 20515-4327; fax 226-1134

Committees
Judiciary
Oversight & Government Reform
(Federal Workforce, U.S. Postal Service and the Census - Chairman)
Transportation & Infrastructure

Residence
Corpus Christi

Born
Dec. 12, 1961; Corpus Christi, Texas

Religion
Episcopalian

Family
Wife, Debbie Farenthold; two children

Education
U. of Texas, B.S.R.T.F. 1985 (radio-television-film); St. Mary's U. (Texas), J.D. 1990

Career
Web services consulting company owner; lawyer

Political Highlights
No previous office

ELECTION RESULTS

2012 GENERAL		
Blake Farenthold (R)	120,684	56.8%
Rose Meza Harrison (D)	83,395	39.2%
Bret Baldwin (I)	5,354	2.5%
Corrie Byrd (LIBERT)	3,218	1.5%
2012 PRIMARY		
Blake Farenthold (R)	28,058	70.8%
Trey Roberts (R)	4,653	11.7%
Don Al Middlebrook (R)	3,676	9.3%
John Grunwald (R)	3,256	8.2%
2010 GENERAL		
Blake Farenthold (R)	51,001	47.8%
Solomon P. Ortiz (D)	50,226	47.1%
Edward C. Mishou (LIBERT)	5,372	5.0%

Elected 2010; 2nd term

The highly quotable Farenthold takes a media-centric approach to politics. As the self-described "advocate in chief" for South Texas, he zeroes in on conservative policies for the economic needs of the region. Republicans also have given him platforms to talk about technology and the federal workforce.

Farenthold (FAIR-enth-old) attributes his comfort with public messaging to his radio background — he promoted his computer consulting business by doing guest commentaries on technology issues. He's now an occasional guest on cable news shows, a media-minded questioner in hearings and the steward of @farenthold, one of the livelier Twitter feeds in Congress.

"I feel like I have more influence on policy by steering the discussion in the media than I do as one vote out of 535," he said in 2011. "I'm sure I'll eventually stick my foot in my mouth, go sulk in a corner for a month, but I haven't gotten there yet."

For the 113th Congress (2013-14), Farenthold is chairing the Oversight and Government Reform subcommittee overseeing the federal workforce and the ailing Postal Service. He is working closely with full-committee Chairman Darrell Issa of California, who in the 112th Congress (2011-12) had plans for both. Issa called federal salaries and pension plans "overly generous," and he proposed new entities to shutter many postal facilities and seize control if the Postal Service defaults on financial obligations for an extended period of time.

Farenthold is often on the same page with Issa. During the 112th, he was an energetic participant in Issa's probe of Fast and Furious, a Justice Department "gun walking" operation in which weapons initially tracked by the government were later found at the scene of a fatal shooting of a Border Patrol agent in Arizona. In a hearing, Farenthold said it was "one of the most shameful moments ... in our government's history." He called for the resignation of Attorney General Eric H. Holder Jr.

He no longer represents the Texas-Mexico border, but Farenthold says the economic vitality of the Rio Grande Valley has been sapped by real and perceived drug violence. He wants increased use of unmanned aircraft and remote sensing technology to secure the border, as well as more manpower both on the ground and in the air. He is "not a big fence fan," because "I've seen the fence."

As a new member of the Judiciary Committee in the 113th Congress, he will have a chance to work on immigration. In the past, he has opposed amnesty for illegal immigrants already in the country — but in 2013, he said it would be "a whole lot easier to support a path to citizenship" if the government did a better job tracking and removing people who overstayed their visas. He calls for a guest-worker program and expanded use of employee identification systems to reduce the number of "economic refugees" crossing the border.

Farenthold sits on the Judiciary subcommittee covering intellectual property and the Internet. One of the more tech-savvy lawmakers, he takes an interest in cybersecurity. "If you think your computers are not already compromised, you're an idiot," he says. He's also on the subcommittee covering commercial law and regulations. Farenthold, whose family has ties to the oil business, is a big proponent of relaxing federal regulations, particularly on the energy sector. The Eagle Ford Shale formation runs under part of his district.

On the Transportation and Infrastructure Committee, Farenthold is trying to accelerate the completion of Interstate 69 into the Rio Grande Valley. "The interstate highway network is just like a computer network. It increases value the more nodes that are on it," he said in 2011. The Rio Grande node would bring access to ports in Farenthold's district, which could benefit from increased trade generated by the Panama Canal expansion currently under way. Like most Republicans, Farenthold wants increased local control of federal transportation dollars.

A member of the conservative Republican Study Committee, he says a balanced-budget amendment to the Constitution is "our only hope" for spending discipline. He opposes tax increases and finds colorful ways to call for smaller government. The Corpus Christi Caller-Times reported on an August 2011 meeting with constituents: "I have to Google some of these agencies to find out what they do," Farenthold said. "If a congressman has to Google an agency, we probably don't need that agency."

He is also a defender of gun rights. In 2013, Connecticut gun manufacturers indicated that they might relocate, due to new state gun laws enacted in response to an elementary school shooting in Newtown. Farenthold circulated an open letter inviting the companies to move to Texas.

Farenthold was born into a well-to-do oil family. His father died when he was 11 — Randy Farenthold was murdered months before he was scheduled to testify in a criminal money laundering case. Farenthold was raised by his mother, a homemaker, and cites the influence of Hayden Head, his paternal grandmother's second husband, in shaping his conservatism. Another step-grandparent, Frances Tarlton "Sissy" Farenthold, was a liberal icon and gubernatorial candidate in Texas.

He landed his first radio job at 16, spinning on a local station under the name Blake Stevens; he also provided DJ services for dances and parties. His love of computers started early as well. In the early 1980s, he operated a kind of online chat room using Apple II computers. "I think the phone company thought I was a bookie, putting in 16 phone lines in my apartment," he said.

Farenthold worked as a lawyer, but an experience with computer consultants at his law office convinced him that he could do the job better. He opened his own company and eventually became a computer expert on a local radio show; that slot expanded over the years to a full-time volunteer co-hosting gig.

In 2010, he was upset with direction of the federal government and had just sold his computer business. "It was clear to me that it was time for a change in my life," he said, so he ran for Congress. He finished second in the four-way GOP primary, then won the runoff. His contest with 14-term Democrat Solomon P. Ortiz was very close — after a recount, he won by 775 votes.

Redistricting in Texas was ugly, and the map for 2012 was eventually drawn by a federal court. Farenthold couldn't complain. Democratic counties to the south were lopped off to form the new 34th District, and Republican-friendly territory to the north was added. Farenthold cruised to victory, while Democrat Filemon Vela — a longtime acquaintance — captured the 34th District.

Key Votes

2012	
Extend a Social Security payroll tax cut and unemployment benefits	NO
Ease securities rules to expand small-business access to capital	YES
Extend for one year subsidized student loan interest rates financed by a cut in health care spending	YES
Cite Attorney General Eric H. Holder Jr. for contempt of Congress	YES
Create a visa program for foreign graduates in high-tech fields	YES
Extend most Bush-era income tax rates while allowing rates for top-bracket earners to rise (Jan. 1, 2013)	NO
2011	
Strike funding for F-35 alternative engine	YES
Prevent EPA from regulating greenhouse gas emissions to address climate change	YES
Extend certain provisions of Patriot Act for four years	YES
Declare opposition to use of ground troops in Libya	YES
Overhaul patent law	YES
Pass compromise debt limit increase plan and establish future spending limits	YES
Allow consideration of measures to implement three trade agreements	YES

CQ Vote Studies

	PARTY UNITY		PRESIDENTIAL SUPPORT	
	SUPPORT	OPPOSE	SUPPORT	OPPOSE
2012	97%	3%	16%	84%
2011	97%	3%	21%	79%

Interest Groups

	AFL-CIO	ADA	CCUS	ACU
2012	14%	5%	83%	84%
2011	7%	15%	100%	80%

Texas 27

Central and Gulf Coast — Corpus Christi, Victoria

Decennial redistricting dramatically reshaped the 27th, which used to stretch south to the Mexico border with Corpus Christi at its northern edge. Now, the major port city is its southern terminus. The district covers seven Gulf Coast bays and runs through Matagorda and Wharton counties and the counties of the Golden Crescent. At Lavaca County it swings to the northwest through Caldwell and Bastrop counties outside Austin.

Nearly half of the district's population lives in Nueces County (Corpus Christi). Many members of the military earn their wings at the city's Naval Air Station. In addition to defense, top employers include oil rigs, refineries and industrial construction. Rail lines into the Port of Corpus Christi are expanding to keep pace with transport of wind turbines and drilling equipment integral to the exploration of Eagle Ford Shale in Gonzales and Lavaca counties. Oil and gas production is prevalent throughout the region, as are blue-collar fishing, shrimping and oystering jobs. Further inland, rivers wind through fields of rice, corn, cotton and sorghum.

Red, white and blue Interstate 69 signs have popped up along a stretch of U.S. Highway 77 near Robstown, the first federally funded interstate project in Texas since 1992; the upgraded roads will eventually join the high-volume route to Canada as well as capitalize on expansion of the Panama Canal. Victoria serves as the Golden Crescent's regional hub, home to hospitals and two universities. Plastics manufacturers provide many jobs in the county, and Caterpillar recently began producing excavators here.

Minorities are the majority in this district, with nearly half the population claiming Hispanic heritage — even though the 27th was redrawn to give Republicans an advantage in maintaining their tenuous hold on the seat.

Major Industry
Oil and gas, petrochemicals, fishing, agriculture, manufacturing

Military Bases
Naval Air Station Corpus Christi, 1,761 military, 8,174 civilian (2012); Corpus Christi Army Depot, 2,700 military, 7 civilian

Cities
Corpus Christi, Victoria, Bay City

Notable
Matagorda rings in the holidays with a Christmas Yuletide Sail-A-Bration and gumbo cookoff in its harbor.

Rep. Henry Cuellar (D)

Capitol Office
225-1640
cuellar.house.gov
2431 Rayburn Bldg. 20515-4328; fax 225-1641

Committees
Appropriations

Residence
Laredo

Born
Sept. 19, 1955; Laredo, Texas

Religion
Roman Catholic

Family
Wife, Imelda Cuellar; two children

Education
Laredo Community College, A.A. 1976 (political science); Georgetown U., B.S.F.S. 1978; U. of Texas, J.D. 1981; Laredo State U., M.B.A. 1982 (international trade); U. of Texas, Ph.D. 1998 (government)

Career
Lawyer; international trade firm owner

Political Highlights
Texas House, 1987-2001; Texas secretary of state, 2001; Democratic nominee for U.S. House, 2002

ELECTION RESULTS

2012 GENERAL		
Henry Cuellar (D)	112,456	67.9%
William R. Hayward (R)	49,309	29.8%
Patrick Hisel (LIBERT)	2,473	1.5%
2012 PRIMARY		
Henry Cuellar (D)		unopposed
2010 GENERAL		
Henry Cuellar (D)	62,773	56.3%
Bryan Underwood (R)	46,740	42.0%
Stephen Kaat (LIBERT)	1,889	1.7%

Previous Winning Percentages
2008 (69%); 2006 (68%); 2004 (59%)

Elected 2004; 5th term

Once considered an outsider within his own party, Cuellar has become a sounding board for the House Democratic leadership — while maintaining one of the most conservative voting records of any Democrat. "They know what they brought in," he said.

Cuellar endorsed George W. Bush for president in 2000, then served as Texas secretary of state under Bush's successor as governor, Republican Rick Perry. He entered Congress by taking out a popular incumbent Democrat, Ciro D. Rodriguez, in a primary.

Since 2011, however, he has served as a vice chairman of the Democratic Steering and Policy Committee. He tries to represent the fiscally conservative Blue Dog Coalition as the party shapes its messages. "I've sat down with the leadership and said, 'With this, please understand. ... Here's certain key votes that I'll stick with the leadership, but I've got to represent my district.'"

When Democrats were in the majority, Cuellar often made pragmatic choices on major bills, winning changes or promises before casting his vote in support. He was one of the last Democratic holdouts on the 2010 health care overhaul, citing his concern that it might allow federal funding of abortion. President Barack Obama's promise of an executive order banning such funding secured Cuellar's support — but he voted with Republicans in 2011 on a legislative version of that ban.

Fiscal concerns often separate him from a majority of Democrats. Cuellar has sponsored a proposed balanced-budget amendment to the Constitution, and he was one of the 25 House Democrats to vote for a Republican version of such an amendment in 2011.

That year, he also broke with most of his party in supporting free-trade pacts with Panama, Colombia and South Korea. Cuellar founded the Pro-Trade Caucus in 2009 and regularly works with Texas Republicans to facilitate trade with Mexico. He has a master's degree in international trade, briefly taught college classes on international commercial law and started a customs brokerage and international trade firm. His congressional website maintains that the North American Free Trade Agreement "has given rise to the greatest display of economic growth in the history of South Texas."

A fiscal 2013 spending law includes a provision, similar to a bill introduced by Cuellar and a bipartisan group of Texas lawmakers, to allow Customs and Border Protection to enter into public-private partnerships to fulfill some of its duties — which might be used to facilitate trade by alleviating congestion at border crossings. Laredo, Cuellar's hometown, is a major point of entry.

Cuellar is a proponent of government accountability and "performance-based" budgeting, the subject of his doctoral thesis. In 2010, he won the enactment of a provision to require agencies to develop performance measures for service and to conduct quarterly reviews. "If you talk to anyone who understands budgeting," he said, "it's the biggest change that we've had in 20 years."

At the start of the 113th Congress (2013-14), Cuellar began a more direct involvement with federal spending. He joined the Appropriations Committee and took seats on its Homeland Security and State-Foreign Operations panels.

Cuellar had been a member of the Homeland Security Committee. In the 112th Congress (2011-12), he was the ranking member on the Border and Maritime Security Subcommittee. Cuellar and panel Chairwoman Candice S. Miller of Michigan conducted a series of rigorous hearings on border security, cargo screening, ports and the visa system. "It's very rare that we disagree," Cuellar said.

Border fences to reduce illegal immigration are a "12th-century solution to a 21st-century problem," Cuellar has said. He supports the deployment of troops to the border with Mexico; he also has pushed, with Miller, for the repurposing of existing military technology — such as unmanned aerial vehicles — for use along the border. In 2012, President Barack Obama signed his bill to establish a permanent multi-agency task force designed to reduce security threats along the borders.

Mexico figures heavily in his work on the State-Foreign Operations panel. Cuellar argues that any assistance to our southern neighbor can be seen as an investment in fighting illegal immigration, since a more secure and economically stable Mexico gives its citizens less motivation to emigrate.

Cuellar used to sit on the Agriculture Committee, where he often heeded the concerns of Texas farm groups with regard to regulation. He was initially reluctant to vote for the Democrats' 2009 bill to create a cap-and-trade system for greenhouse gas emissions, but he voted for it after securing an amendment to bolster natural gas use. (The bill died in the Senate.) In the 112th, he voted for a number of GOP measures to limit the EPA's reach, including a bill to block the regulation of dust kicked up by farming operations.

Cuellar grew up speaking Spanish, in a home where he was the eldest of eight children. His parents were migrant workers who had only an elementary school education, but they insisted that their children go further. He earned law and business degrees in addition to a doctorate in government; he is currently the most degreed member of Congress.

He was elected to the Texas House in 1986 and served 14 years. Perry, whom Cuellar considers a friend, appointed him secretary of state in early 2001, but Cuellar resigned later that year to prepare for a 2002 campaign against Republican incumbent Henry Bonilla in the 23rd District. He lost by 4 points.

In 2004, a new congressional map moved part of Webb County, Cuellar's base, to the 28th District, a heavily Hispanic and primarily San Antonio-based district that had been represented since 1997 by Rodriguez. Cuellar challenged Rodriguez in the primary, even though Rodriguez had backed Cuellar's 2002 campaign against Bonilla. Cuellar eked out a 203-vote win.

Rodriguez was back to challenge Cuellar in 2006, but Cuellar touted his accessibility and his ability to bring federal funds to the district. He won the primary by almost 13 points. Court challenges to the district lines resulted in another redrawn map (and a new Democratic opponent) by the time the November elections rolled around, but Cuellar held the seat.

Cuellar rankled state Democrats during the 2012 redistricting process by siding with a compromise map that gave the GOP a projected 25-to-11 advantage in House seats. He noted, however, that the map gave the state two more Hispanic-majority districts. He won his race by 38 points.

Key Votes

2012	
Extend a Social Security payroll tax cut and unemployment benefits	YES
Ease securities rules to expand small-business access to capital	YES
Extend for one year subsidized student loan interest rates financed by a cut in health care spending	NO
Cite Attorney General Eric H. Holder Jr. for contempt of Congress	NO
Create a visa program for foreign graduates in high-tech fields	YES
Extend most Bush-era income tax rates while allowing rates for top-bracket earners to rise (Jan. 1, 2013)	YES
2011	
Strike funding for F-35 alternative engine	YES
Prevent EPA from regulating greenhouse gas emissions to address climate change	YES
Extend certain provisions of Patriot Act for four years	YES
Declare opposition to use of ground troops in Libya	YES
Overhaul patent law	YES
Pass compromise debt limit increase plan and establish future spending limits	YES
Allow consideration of measures to implement three trade agreements	YES

CQ Vote Studies

	PARTY UNITY		PRESIDENTIAL SUPPORT	
	SUPPORT	OPPOSE	SUPPORT	OPPOSE
2012	68%	32%	47%	53%
2011	66%	34%	68%	32%
2010	93%	7%	90%	10%
2009	91%	9%	92%	8%
2008	94%	6%	30%	70%

Interest Groups

	AFL-CIO	ADA	CCUS	ACU
2012	67%	40%	100%	36%
2011	69%	60%	88%	12%
2010	79%	75%	63%	13%
2009	90%	85%	60%	12%
2008	87%	80%	72%	12%

Texas 28

South central — Laredo, Mission

The overwhelmingly Hispanic and fast-growing 28th District abuts the Mexico border from Hidalgo County adjacent to the 15th District, to Webb County in the west. It stretches north into the suburbs of San Antonio, mainly west of Loop 410. Through decennial redistricting and changing demographics, the 28th has become safe Democratic territory.

Much of U.S.-Mexico trade passes through the 28th in rapidly growing Laredo, the population center of the district. The nation's "Gateway to Mexico" is its busiest inland port, while 12,000 commercial trucks cross its bridges over the Rio Grande each day. Commercial shippers also make heavy use of the city's air cargo terminal and rail lines.

An uptick in drug-related violence in the Mexican state of Tamaulipas has not slowed trade, but non-commercial traffic of vehicles and pedestrians has dropped off substantially. In rural border stretches, ranchers and sugar cane farmers have banded together to help state and federal agents crack down on smuggling operations. Zapata and Starr counties are among the most impoverished in the nation, with poverty rates topping 36 percent. Fewer than one in 10 residents of these counties have a college degree.

More than one-fifth of the population lives in south-central Texas' Bexar (pronounced BEAR) County along San Antonio's eastern flank. This part of the district includes Randolph Air Force Base in Universal City, a major flight training facility of the Joint Base San Antonio.

Heavy traffic from Eagle Ford Shale drilling operations has deteriorated roads in Atascosa County. Oil companies have paid billions for mineral rights in the region.

Major Industry
Trade, agriculture, oil and gas, defense

Military Bases
Joint Base San Antonio, 24,205 military, 23,720 civilian (shared with the 20th, 21st & 23rd) (2011)

Cities
Laredo, Mission (pt.)

Notable
The Texas Citrus Exchange in Mission is known for its signature Rio Red grapefruit juice.

Rep. Gene Green (D)

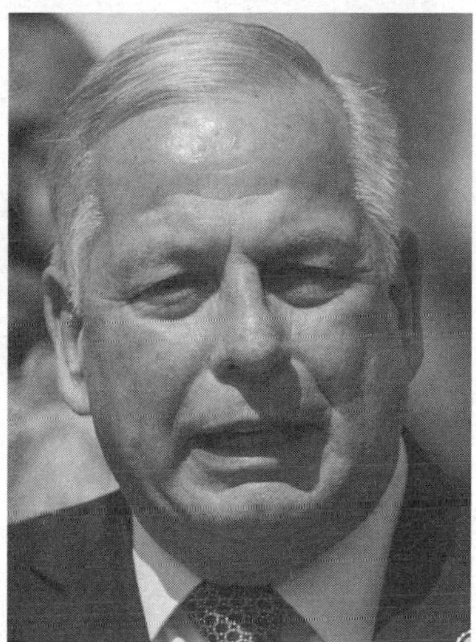

Capitol Office
225-1688
green.house.gov
2470 Rayburn Bldg. 20515-4329; fax 225-9903

Committees
Energy & Commerce

Residence
Houston

Born
Oct. 17, 1947; Houston, Texas

Religion
Methodist

Family
Wife, Helen Albers Green; two children

Education
U. of Houston, B.B.A. 1971; Bates College of Law, attended 1971-77

Career
Lawyer

Political Highlights
Texas House, 1973-85; Texas Senate, 1985-92

ELECTION RESULTS

2012 GENERAL		
Gene Green (D)	86,053	90.0%
James Stanczak (LIBERT)	4,996	5.2%
Maria Selva (GREEN)	4,562	4.8%
2012 PRIMARY		
Gene Green (D)		unopposed
2010 GENERAL		
Gene Green (D)	43,257	64.6%
Roy Morales (R)	22,825	34.1%
Brad Walters (LIBERT)	866	1.3%

Previous Winning Percentages
2008 (75%); 2006 (74%); 2004 (94%); 2002 (95%); 2000 (73%); 1998 (93%); 1996 (68%); 1994 (73%); 1992 (65%)

Elected 1992; 11th term

Green belongs to a dwindling group of Southern Democrats in the House. He's more willing than most to break from the party line, which is a necessity in a district reliant on chemical and oil companies.

Born, raised and educated in Houston, Green grew up in an area called "Redneck Alley," which is home to mostly working-class whites. During his early years, his father ran a hardware store, where he, his brother and his mother helped out. He attended the University of Houston, where he obtained a degree in business administration, and then began studying law.

Green parlayed that experience into a position with the Daily Court Review, a Houston legal newspaper. While still attending law school, at 25, he won a seat in the Texas Legislature. He served for nearly two decades, first as a representative and then as a state senator. He balanced his political work with a legal practice of civil cases and probate matters, and also his job as business manager at the paper. (Green never completed his law studies, but he did pass the Texas bar.)

Houston's economic interests are on his mind in the U.S. House. Green is skeptical of EPA regulation and eager to boost oil exploration, stances that are anathema to many in his party. But he won't always go along when Republicans try to use energy issues to hammer on Democrats. It's a fine line, but Green has managed to walk it during two decades in the House.

"Because I come from an industrial area, an oil and gas area, it's a natural conflict," he said in 2012. "Believe me, I want EPA to do their job, but I also want those jobs that my refiners and chemical plants generate."

Green is a member of the Energy and Commerce Committee. During the 112th Congress (2011-12), he was among Republicans' closest allies in urging President Barack Obama to approve an oil pipeline connecting the tar sands of Canada to refineries in Texas. Green argued that getting more oil from Canada would reduce U.S. dependence on nations in the Middle East. Environmentalists pushed Obama in the opposite direction, arguing that the Canadian oil was particularly dirty because of the laborious process involved in removing it from the ground. He has continued promoting the Keystone XL pipeline in the 113th Congress (2013-14).

But Green took issue with other attacks on Obama. He said that Republicans went too far as they criticized the administration for its investment in Solyndra Inc., a manufacturer of solar panels that went bankrupt in August 2011 after receiving $528 million in loan guarantees. Green says it's important to provide incentives for all kinds of energy development, from offshore drilling and natural gas exploration to solar and wind power. He is one of the four leaders of the Congressional Natural Gas Caucus for the 113th Congress.

And Green is willing to accept some EPA regulation. In 2009, he backed a House climate change bill pushed by his own party; it would have set a cap on emissions of greenhouse gases and required companies to buy allowances in order to pollute. Green helped broker a deal to protect refiners' bottom lines by providing them free emissions allowances. The measure died in the Senate.

Green had been the top Democrat on the Subcommittee on Environment and the Economy during the 112th Congress, but he yielded that job to New York Democrat Paul Tonko in 2013.

At the same time, Green returned to the Health Subcommittee. In 2010, he backed Democrats' health care overhaul — his district has a large number of uninsured working-age people. His vote on the health care bill was no surprise; he has long had an interest in the area. In 2007, his measure to upgrade states' trauma care systems was signed into law. It was a victory that Green had sought since hearing about a man who was seriously injured in a car accident and could not get treatment at a crowded Houston trauma center. The man had to be taken to Austin, where he died the next day.

In 2008, Green won enactment of legislation to expand community clinics and fight the spread of tuberculosis, which remains a problem in some border communities. In 2012, Green and Georgia Republican Phil Gingrey persuaded colleagues to include language in an overhaul of Food and Drug Administration user fee programs to provide incentives for pharmaceutical companies to develop more effective antibiotic drugs. It was enacted that July.

Working with Texas Republican Joe L. Barton, Green introduced a bill in 2013 to require all states to have continuous open enrollment for Medicaid and the Children's Health Insurance Program.

In addition to his differences with most Democrats on energy policy, Green sometimes parts from party colleagues on social issues. He has earned many "A" ratings from the National Rifle Association, and Green also has expressed reservations about legalizing same-sex marriage. He had an anti-abortion voting record in the Texas Legislature—however, he has voted many times in the U.S. House in defense of abortion rights.

As the two parties have become more polarized, Green has also been more willing to cross the aisle on matters of national security. He did so on two major foreign policy votes in 2011: He backed a resolution pushed by Republicans that June criticizing Obama's intervention in the Libyan civil war. Just a week earlier, he joined Republicans in adopting an amendment meant to ensure that alleged terrorists held at the U.S. military base at Guantánamo Bay in Cuba could not be brought to the United States to face trial in civilian courts.

Democrats have helped stymie some of his initiatives. Henry A. Waxman of California, the ranking member of Energy and Commerce, opposed Green's bill allowing the Homeland Security Department to continue writing rules governing the security of chemical facilities, arguing that Congress needs to take a firmer hand in ensuring that the rules are adequate.

In 1992, Green won a hard-fought five-way primary in a district that was drawn after the 1990 Census to enhance the political power of Houston's growing Hispanic population. Green bested Houston City Council member Ben Reyes in two runoffs; the first was voided after election officials found that some Republicans had illegally crossed over and cast ballots. Green won the general election with 65 percent of the vote, defeated Reyes in a rematch in the 1994 primary and has won easily since.

In 2012, Green ran in a redrawn 29th District that is still almost 75 percent Hispanic. His district has one of the highest percentages of adults without a high school diploma nationwide, and voter turnout is routinely low.

Key Votes

2012	
Extend a Social Security payroll tax cut and unemployment benefits	YES
Ease securities rules to expand small-business access to capital	NO
Extend for one year subsidized student loan interest rates financed by a cut in health care spending	NO
Cite Attorney General Eric H. Holder Jr. for contempt of Congress	NO
Create a visa program for foreign graduates in high-tech fields	NO
Extend most Bush-era income tax rates while allowing rates for top-bracket earners to rise (Jan. 1, 2013)	YES
2011	
Strike funding for F-35 alternative engine	YES
Prevent EPA from regulating greenhouse gas emissions to address climate change	NO
Extend certain provisions of Patriot Act for four years	-
Declare opposition to use of ground troops in Libya	YES
Overhaul patent law	NO
Pass compromise debt limit increase plan and establish future spending limits	YES
Allow consideration of measures to implement three trade agreements	-

CQ Vote Studies

	PARTY UNITY		PRESIDENTIAL SUPPORT	
	SUPPORT	OPPOSE	SUPPORT	OPPOSE
2012	78%	22%	75%	25%
2011	74%	26%	74%	26%
2010	97%	3%	88%	12%
2009	98%	2%	96%	4%
2008	94%	6%	26%	74%

Interest Groups

	AFL-CIO	ADA	CCUS	ACU
2012	89%	65%	18%	32%
2011	100%	90%	40%	20%
2010	100%	80%	25%	4%
2009	100%	100%	40%	0%
2008	100%	80%	59%	26%

Texas 29

Part of Houston and eastern suburbs — part of Pasadena

Taking in much of the industrial and petrochemical activity along the shores of the Houston Ship Channel, the 29th captures working-class Houston and most of Pasadena in eastern Harris County. The district's border flows along the eastern half of Beltway 8, darting outside the loop to include the North Belt Intercontinental Business Park and the Sterling Green neighborhood of suburban Channelview.

Economic activity is centered on East End Houston, a transportation hub bound by interstates 10 and 45. Railroads crisscross the area, and the Port of Houston leads the nation in imports, moving more than 200 million tons of cargo annually. Upgrades to the Panama Canal are expected to increase activity.

Petrochemicals and oil refining operations along the shores of the channel employ union workers, contributing to the district's Democratic lean and blue-collar feel. For residential communities such as Galena Park, near the industrial sites of the ship channel, air pollution and access to health care to treat problems related to chemical exposure have become a concern.

To the south, the city's oldest commercial airport, William P. Hobby, expects a boost in traffic and jobs thanks to a recently approved deal with Southwest Airlines. The planned $100 million expansion will open the airport to international flights in 2015.

More than three-fourths of the 29th's population is of Hispanic descent. The district includes historically Hispanic neighborhoods in Magnolia Park and parts of the Second Ward just east of downtown Houston.

Overall, the residents of the 29th have lower median incomes and rates of educational attainment than the rest of the state. The industrial district gave Barack Obama a 33-percentage-point win in the 2012 presidential election.

Major Industry
Transportation, shipping, petrochemicals, oil refining

Cities
Houston (pt.), Pasadena (pt.), Channelview (unincorp.) (pt.)

Notable
The University of Houston's Energy Research Park campus is in the district while the rest of the college is in the adjacent 18th.

Rep. Eddie Bernice Johnson (D)

Capitol Office
225-8885
ebjohnson.house.gov
2468 Rayburn Bldg. 20515-4330; fax 226-1477

Committees
Science, Space & Technology - Ranking Member
Transportation & Infrastructure

Residence
Dallas

Born
Dec. 3, 1935; Waco, Texas

Religion
Baptist

Family
Divorced; one child

Education
Texas Christian U., B.S. 1967 (nursing); Southern Methodist U., M.P.A. 1976

Career
Business relocation company owner; nurse; U.S. Health, Education & Welfare Department official

Political Highlights
Texas House, 1973-77; Texas Senate, 1987-93

ELECTION RESULTS

2012 GENERAL		
Eddie Bernice Johnson (D)	171,059	78.8%
Travis Washington Jr. (R)	41,222	19.0%
Ed Rankin (LIBERT)	4,733	2.2%
2012 PRIMARY		
Eddie Bernice Johnson (D)	23,346	70.1%
Barbara Mallory Caraway (D)	5,996	18.0%
Taj Clayton (D)	3,981	11.9%
2010 GENERAL		
Eddie Bernice Johnson (D)	86,322	75.7%
Stephen E. Broden (R)	24,668	21.6%
J.B. Oswalt (LIBERT)	2,988	2.6%

Previous Winning Percentages
2008 (82%); 2006 (80%); 2004 (93%); 2002 (74%); 2000 (92%); 1998 (72%); 1996 (55%); 1994 (73%); 1992 (72%)

Elected 1992; 11th term

Johnson started her political career as a trailblazer and nurtured it by taking care of constituents — factors that have made her politically bulletproof during the minor scandals dotting her dossier. Technology and transportation, two of Dallas's top industries, shape much of her Washington work.

In 1972, she became the first black woman from Dallas to win election to the state House. During the Carter administration, she served as a regional director of the Health, Education and Welfare Department — capitalizing on her background in nursing — and in the mid-1980s she won election to the state Senate. Johnson established local business ties in the 1980s via Eddie Bernice Johnson and Associates, which helped businesses expand or relocate in the Dallas-Fort Worth area.

Wielding her power in the state legislature, Johnson helped draw a U.S. House district preordained to elect her in 1992, and the firmly entrenched lawmaker has risen steadily to the top Democratic spot on the Science, Space and Technology Committee.

Johnson founded the Diversity and Innovation Caucus, and she has long tried to promote science education for minority populations. During the 111th Congress (2009-10) she added language to cybersecurity research and computer waste bills to encourage minority grant applicants.

The Science panel also lets her keep an eye on NASA, a major employer in Texas. In the 112th Congress (2011-12), Johnson made clear that she was "not real gung-ho" about the agency's plans to use commercial carriers to take people and cargo into space. At oversight hearings, she questioned whether the government takes too much of the risk in public-private partnerships with commercial carriers, and whether budgets for the commercial program might expand to crowd out planetary exploration accounts and other priorities. "I won't stand in the way of its development," she said. "I just don't want it to take the biggest chunk of the dollars available."

Johnson also sees a demand for research conducted at the International Space Station, particularly regarding viruses and climate change. She favors extending use of the space lab beyond its scheduled sunset date of 2020. "We have a very fertile, ready research lab ... if we would fund it," she said.

Johnson has advocated a permanent extension of the research and development tax credit and has been known to take some other business-friendly stances. She has indicated a desire to push the Congressional Black Caucus — which she chaired in the 107th Congress (2001-02) — into coalitions with business groups, rather than relying exclusively on its traditional allies in labor, the clergy and civil rights circles. In 2011, she was in the minority of House Democrats supporting free-trade pacts with South Korea and Panama.

But she is far more likely to defend the Democratic line. During the 112th Congress, Johnson enjoyed a cordial relationship with Science Chairman Ralph M. Hall, a fellow Texan, but as ranking member she accused the GOP of calling politicized hearings on oil research and nuclear power in the run-up to the 2012 elections. For the 113th Congress (2013-14), Hall handed the gavel to Lamar Smith, another Texan.

Water is the bridge between the Science panel and Johnson's other committee, Transportation and Infrastructure. In the 110th and 111th Congresses (2007-10) she chaired the Water Resources and Environment Subcommittee.

"Water availability and quality are essential for public health and a strong economy, but demands for, and threats to, these resources are growing," she said on the House floor in 2012, upon introducing two bills to coordinate federal research on water conservation and treatment.

From her Transportation subcommittee, Johnson in 2007 secured a $298 million authorization for the Dallas Floodway Extension in her district — although securing money for the project each year has proved challenging. In 2009, she pushed through the House a wastewater bill that included the first reauthorization of the Clean Water State Revolving Fund in 15 years, as well as legislation to boost security around wastewater plants.

Johnson has been adept at steering funds home — in the 110th Congress, she joined a Black Caucus committee that was established to help secure more earmarked funding for projects in black members' districts. (A report in CQ Weekly revealed that they were getting less than white-majority districts.) With earmarks banned in the 112th Congress, she sought Senate connections and other means to preserve transportation priorities, such as funding for mass transit systems.

She also has a passion for health care, dating to her childhood. Johnson was one of four children raised by her father, a preacher and store owner in segregated Waco. Her goal was to go to medical school and become a doctor, but her high school counselor encouraged her to become a nurse because "nurses were more feminine." Johnson earned an undergraduate degree in nursing and then a master's in public administration from Southern Methodist University. She rose to be chief psychiatric nurse at the veterans' hospital in Dallas.

She supported the 2010 health care overhaul but said its Medicare and Medicaid payment rates for some hospitals need to be adjusted. Hospitals that tend to a disproportionate number of Medicare and Medicaid patients — such as the Parkland Health and Hospital System in her district — need more cash, she said. Johnson has also championed a plan to steer more federal block grant funding toward local programs assisting the mentally ill.

Johnson would rather talk about policy than past scandals. The Dallas Morning News reported in 2010 that she had steered thousands of dollars in Congressional Black Caucus Foundation scholarships to her relatives, as well as children of a top aide, in violation of anti-nepotism rules. After initial hesitation, Johnson called her actions a mistake and repaid the foundation. Her constituents were forgiving. During the 108th Congress (2003-04), a former aide accused her of discrimination. Johnson insists she terminated a "nonfunctioning employee" and that her case was "airtight." A federal district court judge threw out the case for lack of evidence in October 2007.

Johnson's initial House victory in 1992 was a snap, but in 1996 the U.S. Supreme Court threw out some House districts in Texas as "racial gerrymanders." Johnson landed in a redrawn district that was 42 percent new to her. She captured 55 percent in an eight-person general-election contest. Since then, she has never taken less than 70 percent of the vote.

Key Votes

2012	
Extend a Social Security payroll tax cut and unemployment benefits	NO
Ease securities rules to expand small-business access to capital	NO
Extend for one year subsidized student loan interest rates financed by a cut in health care spending	NO
Cite Attorney General Eric H. Holder Jr. for contempt of Congress	?
Create a visa program for foreign graduates in high-tech fields	NO
Extend most Bush-era income tax rates while allowing rates for top-bracket earners to rise (Jan. 1, 2013)	YES
2011	
Strike funding for F-35 alternative engine	YES
Prevent EPA from regulating greenhouse gas emissions to address climate change	NO
Extend certain provisions of Patriot Act for four years	YES
Declare opposition to use of ground troops in Libya	NO
Overhaul patent law	YES
Pass compromise debt limit increase plan and establish future spending limits	YES
Allow consideration of measures to implement three trade agreements	YES

CQ Vote Studies

	PARTY UNITY		PRESIDENTIAL SUPPORT	
	SUPPORT	OPPOSE	SUPPORT	OPPOSE
2012	94%	6%	86%	14%
2011	94%	6%	83%	17%
2010	99%	1%	90%	10%
2009	99%	1%	97%	3%
2008	99%	1%	14%	86%

Interest Groups

	AFL-CIO	ADA	CCUS	ACU
2012	95%	90%	18%	4%
2011	93%	90%	38%	4%
2010	93%	85%	14%	0%
2009	100%	95%	29%	0%
2008	100%	100%	56%	0%

Texas 30

Southern Dallas County — Downtown Dallas, DeSoto

Confined to Dallas County, most of the 30th lies south of Interstate 30, taking in the southern half of the city and dipping into suburban DeSoto and Lancaster, where many of the city's black families have relocated. North of the interstate, it grabs Dallas Love Field Airport, parts of downtown and a sliver of modest residential neighborhoods below Forest Hills.

The 30th was designed two decades ago to cobble together African-American communities; black residents and a fast-growing Hispanic population now account for more than 80 percent of the population. This is a solidly Democratic district and it gave Barack Obama his highest statewide percentage in the 2012 election, with 80 percent of its vote.

Even before the recession, the 30th lagged behind the rest of North Texas in economic prosperity. Dallas' Main Street district was once the heart of its banking and insurance industries, but many of its skyscrapers have been converted into luxury condominiums as corporate tenants gradually shifted into the City Center district (in the 32nd). Downtown also lost the AT&T Cotton Bowl Classic when it was relocated from the stadium at the state fairgrounds to Arlington in 2010. Hockey's Stars and basketball's Mavericks remain downtown and share American Airlines Arena.

Transportation is a priority as roads here receive the brunt of commuter traffic into the state's third-largest city. The mass of ramps and lane mergers at the convergence of Interstates 35 and 30, known as the "mixmaster," got some relief in early 2012 when a new Trinity River bridge opened.

Accommodating 7 million travelers per year, Love Field is an economic bright spot. Traffic is expected to increase in 2014, when domestic flight restrictions imposed by the federal government are lifted. Southwest Airlines plans to expand its headquarters, which employs more than 7,000 people, and the airport is undergoing modernization through 2015.

Major Industry
Transportation, banking, technology, tourism

Cities
Dallas (pt.), DeSoto, Cedar Hill, Lancaster

Notable
Dealey Plaza and the Texas School Book Depository, where John F. Kennedy was assassinated in 1963, are in downtown Dallas.

Rep. John Carter (R)

Capitol Office
225-3864
carter.house.gov
409 Cannon Bldg. 20515-4331; fax 225-5886

Committees
Appropriations
(Homeland Security - Chairman)

Residence
Round Rock

Born
Nov. 6, 1941; Houston, Texas

Religion
Lutheran

Family
Wife, Erika Carter; four children

Education
Texas Technological College, B.A. 1964 (history); U. of Texas, J.D. 1969

Career
Lawyer; state legislative aide

Political Highlights
Candidate for Texas House, 1980; Texas District Court judge, 1981-2001

ELECTION RESULTS

2012 GENERAL		
John Carter (R)	145,348	61.3%
Stephen Wyman (D)	82,977	35.0%
Ethan Garofolo (LIBERT)	8,862	3.7%
2012 PRIMARY		
John Carter (R)	32,917	76.0%
Eric Klingemann (R)	10,400	24.0%
2010 GENERAL		
John Carter (R)	126,384	82.5%
Bill Oliver (LIBERT)	26,735	17.5%

Previous Winning Percentages
2008 (60%); 2006 (58%); 2004 (65%); 2002 (69%)

Elected 2002; 6th term

Carter is a modern Texas Republican straight out of Central Casting. He has personal ties to the oil industry, a hand in building GOP infrastructure, conservative beliefs and an interest in border and homeland security.

In the 113th Congress (2013-14), Carter wields influence as the new chairman of the Homeland Security Appropriations Subcommittee. And he emerged as a key negotiator in a bipartisan House working group trying to assemble a comprehensive overhaul of immigration law.

By Carter's account, the group of four conservatives and four liberals had been meeting "privately and without distractions" for almost four years when immigration suddenly returned to the national spotlight. Carter and Illinois Democrat Luis V. Gutierrez served as unofficial spokesmen for the group in the early months of 2013.

For his part, Carter outlined fairly clear precursors to immigration changes: a secure border that is confirmed by independent organizations; and making the E-Verify employment verification system mandatory. With those requirements in place, he wrote in March 2013, the nation can deal with the illegal immigrants already in the country "through common-sense court proceedings that preserve our rule of law with compassion."

Carter generally hasn't been thrilled with the Obama administration's approach to security. He accused the administration of being "more focused on groping grandma at the airport" — a reference to Transportation Security Administration guidelines — than on stopping drug smugglers and al-Qaida supporters from moving across the border with Mexico. He said the administration's fiscal 2014 budget request for homeland security had "shameful cuts to operations," and he has proposed shifting more spending to local law enforcement agencies along the border, as a "backup for our federal agents."

Carter had a comfortable upbringing as the son of John J. Carter, the general manager of Humble Oil and Refining Co. — the predecessor to Exxon. In high school, he worked summers on oil and gas pipelines.

As a law student at the University of Texas, he was one of a handful of conservatives on the Austin campus. "I think I had the only Goldwater button in law school. I got criticized by several professors," he remembered. During a summer in Holland, he worked on a pipeline project for Bechtel Corp. While there, he fell in love with the sister of the landlady for his rental flat. He and Erika were married in 1968.

His interest in politics was sparked when he worked as a counsel for the Texas Legislature. He moved his family to the small town of Round Rock, set up a law practice, and in 1980 ran unsuccessfully for a seat in the state House. Carter then briefly resumed his practice until he was appointed district court judge of Williamson County in 1981. The following year he won election to the position. Carter helped build up local GOP operations and has said that some people call him the "godfather" of the Republican Party in the county.

Carter says he left the bench after 20 years to run for Congress because of the Sept. 11 terrorist attacks. His focus never drifts far from national security. His district is home to Fort Hood, the largest Army post in the United States, and he is co-chairman of the House Army Caucus; he also sits on the Military Construction-VA Appropriations Subcommittee.

He has made a determined effort to get federal help for victims of the 2009 Fort Hood shooting, in which gunman Nidal Malik Hasan, an Army major of Palestinian descent, killed 13 people and wounded 32 others. In the 112th Congress (2011-12), Carter again introduced legislation to deem Fort Hood victims "combat casualties" and give survivors the according benefits; he criticized the Obama administration as having "political reasons" for denying "proper benefits." Carter wants whistle-blower protections for military and civilian personnel who report potential threats from radical Islamic sympathizers.

He takes the common GOP position that over-regulation is stifling the economy. He introduced legislation in the 112th Congress to block the U.S. Fish and Wildlife Service from listing Texas salamanders on the endangered species list — a designation that could make development of Texas oil fields more difficult. He similarly stumped against EPA regulations on mercury and fine-particle emissions from cement plants, which he said would be devastating to employment in the cement industry.

Carter sticks to the party line on most social and fiscal issues. Though he once sought earmarks for his district in spending bills, he said the process was "abused" and supports the GOP's recent ban on the practice.

He has served as a GOP point man on ethics problems confronting Democrats, although he has faced some ethical questions of his own over the years. He tried to focus public attention on Charles B. Rangel, a New York Democrat, who was censured by the House for a number of financial and fundraising violations. He was also one of a handful of Republican House members to sponsor a bill that would have required future presidential candidates to supply a copy of their birth certificate — a measure arising out of questions raised by some critics of President Barack Obama about where he was born.

Carter has been in the midst of ethics discussions since he came to the House in 2003 as an ally of House Majority Leader Tom DeLay, who, like him, is originally from the Houston area. When DeLay ran into trouble with a campaign fundraising investigation in 2005, Carter was one of 20 Republicans who voted to retain Republican-written rules allowing leaders to keep their jobs if indicted. The rules were later withdrawn.

Carter was among eight lawmakers, including DeLay (who resigned from the House in September 2005), who had accepted trips to South Korea from a registered foreign agent. The lawmakers said they were unaware that the organization paying for the trip was an agent of the South Korean government.

He also acknowledged that he failed to disclose nearly $300,000 in profits from the sale of Exxon stock in 2006 and 2007. He later amended his financial disclosure forms to include the amount of capital gains from past stock sales.

Carter served six years as conference secretary, the No. 6 post in the House, but he stepped down from that job at the end of 2012.

In his first U.S. House race in 2002, Carter won a primary runoff with 57 percent of the vote. He then received 69 percent of the vote in a defeat of Democrat David Bagley. He has been held under 60 percent only once, and he beat Democrat Stephen Wyman by 26 points in 2012.

Key Votes

2012	
Extend a Social Security payroll tax cut and unemployment benefits	NO
Ease securities rules to expand small-business access to capital	YES
Extend for one year subsidized student loan interest rates financed by a cut in health care spending	YES
Cite Attorney General Eric H. Holder Jr. for contempt of Congress	YES
Create a visa program for foreign graduates in high-tech fields	YES
Extend most Bush-era income tax rates while allowing rates for top-bracket earners to rise (Jan. 1, 2013)	NO
2011	
Strike funding for F-35 alternative engine	YES
Prevent EPA from regulating greenhouse gas emissions to address climate change	YES
Extend certain provisions of Patriot Act for four years	YES
Declare opposition to use of ground troops in Libya	YES
Overhaul patent law	YES
Pass compromise debt limit increase plan and establish future spending limits	YES
Allow consideration of measures to implement three trade agreements	YES

CQ Vote Studies

	PARTY UNITY		PRESIDENTIAL SUPPORT	
	SUPPORT	OPPOSE	SUPPORT	OPPOSE
2012	90%	10%	13%	87%
2011	96%	4%	29%	71%
2010	98%	2%	26%	74%
2009	89%	11%	16%	84%
2008	99%	1%	80%	20%

Interest Groups

	AFL-CIO	ADA	CCUS	ACU
2012	10%	5%	100%	84%
2011	0%	0%	100%	84%
2010	0%	0%	88%	100%
2009	10%	0%	79%	96%
2008	0%	5%	94%	96%

Texas 31

Central — parts of Round Rock and Killeen

Representing the rapidly growing area between Fort Hood and Austin, the 31st contracted geographically during redistricting; it shrank from seven counties to most of two — Bell and Williamson. These changes transformed the district into a largely suburban one, dominated by the presence of Fort Hood on its northern fringes and bisected by Interstate 35.

The Army is the dominant force in Killeen, the district's most populous city. One-fifth of its population is personnel serving at Fort Hood, and civilians rely heavily on the massive base (shared with the 25th) for employment. A large community college caters to the military population, and Texas A&M University in College Station is expanding its facilities here. Neighboring Temple is a health care hub and home to the headquarters of supply chain company McLane.

To the south, Williamson County has experienced explosive growth on the strength of its technology sector. Dell Computers employs 16,000 at its headquarters in Round Rock, and the city is home to high-tech firms that support heavy industry.

Although redistricting removed much of the 31st's agricultural base, cattle, cotton and grains remain an important part of Williamson County's economy east of Interstate 35.

Nearly 60 percent of the Republican-leaning population is white. The district is 23 percent Hispanic with many middle-class black families who have relocated from Austin to the suburbs. Republican Mitt Romeny won 60 percent of the district's 2012 presidential vote.

Major Industry
Defense, technology, manufacturing

Military Bases
Fort Hood, 43,000 military, 5,249 civilian (shared with the 25th)

Cities
Killeen, Round Rock, Temple, Cedar Park, Georgetown

Notable
In Georgetown at the Williamson County Courthouse in the 1920s, lawyer Dan Moody became the first lawyer to successfully prosecute members of the Ku Klux Klan.

Rep. Pete Sessions (R)

Capitol Office
225-2231
sessions.house.gov
2233 Rayburn Bldg. 20515-4332; fax 225-5878

Committees
Rules - Chairman

Residence
Dallas

Born
March 22, 1955; Waco, Texas

Religion
United Methodist

Family
Wife, Karen Sessions; two children, three stepchildren

Education
Southwest Texas State U., attended 1973-74; Southwestern U., B.S. 1978 (political science)

Career
Public policy analyst; telephone company executive

Political Highlights
Sought Republican nomination for U.S. House (special election), 1991; Republican nominee for U.S. House, 1994

ELECTION RESULTS

2012 GENERAL

Pete Sessions (R)	146,653	58.3%
Katherine Savers McGovern (D)	99,288	39.5%
Seth Hollist (LIBERT)	5,695	2.3%

2012 PRIMARY

Pete Sessions (R)	unopposed

2010 GENERAL

Pete Sessions (R)	79,433	62.6%
Grier Raggio (D)	44,258	34.9%
John Jay Myers (LIBERT)	3,178	2.5%

Previous Winning Percentages
2008 (57%); 2006 (56%); 2004 (54%); 2002 (68%); 2000 (54%); 1998 (56%); 1996 (53%)

Elected 1996; 9th term

Sessions ran House Republican campaign operations for the 2010 and 2012 elections. Hordes of analysts will never agree if he was brilliant, lackluster, savvy or overwhelmed as chairman of the National Republican Congressional Committee, but GOP leaders rendered a verdict of sorts — he is now setting the terms of legislative debates as the chairman of the Rules Committee.

Sessions was tapped by Speaker John A. Boehner, his friend and ally, to hold the Rules gavel in November 2012, ending speculation that the job might go to Doc Hastings of Washington.

The announcement came a week after Republicans lost a handful of House seats in the general election. The losses weren't taken lightly, but in the grand scheme of things they weren't that bad — the party easily kept the House majority, even as Mitt Romney lost his presidential bid and the GOP had poor results in Senate races.

It was a fittingly ambiguous end to Sessions' tenure. In 2009, he started an ambitious reorganization of the NRCC. He restructured its programs to make them more metrics-driven, so that candidates would bear more responsibility to reach fundraising and organizational benchmarks.

Republicans picked up 63 seats and the House majority in 2010. Doubters said the results were attributable to national political trends and the strength of the tea party movement, rather than anything Sessions did. His backers said his decision to return as NRCC chairman for the 112th Congress (2011-12) — rather than move to a high-ranking leadership post — showed his desire to emphasize teamwork over individual accomplishment. Boehner called him the "architect" of the Republican takeover.

Engaging in professionally required optimism, Sessions pledged that the GOP would expand its majority by a dozen seats or more in 2012. He focused on recruiting embattled incumbents into the Patriot Program, which gives participants fundraising and logistical assistance. Far fewer incumbents signed up than Sessions hoped.

Approval ratings of Congress stayed low, in part because Boehner had trouble persuading hard-line conservatives to go along with his plans. Sessions bears some responsibility: He took on the role of mentor to the 80 new Republicans in the House. Many freshmen were unreceptive to his overtures. Conservatives played a big role in shooting down an expansive debt reduction deal that Boehner struck with President Barack Obama in 2011.

Fundraising also lagged, as the NRCC competed with outside conservative groups (such as Karl Rove's American Crossroads) for donations. Sessions' efforts to keep pace with the Democratic fundraising machine were criticized in March 2012, when CBS News ran a segment on a fundraiser at a Florida resort where lobbyists paid thousands of dollars to interact with lawmakers. Sessions was featured prominently in hidden-camera video of the festivities.

Despite those ill omens, the elections were not a catastrophe — but it's hard to pinpoint why. To some extent, redistricting after the 2010 census cushioned the GOP. Analysts could only guess at the effect of big-spending political action committees allowed by a 2010 Supreme Court decision. Or Sessions might have engineered results far better than the GOP should have expected with Obama at the top of the Democratic ticket.

Whatever the analysis, Sessions is now devising strategies for the House floor as the Rules chairman. He was the No. 2 Republican on the panel in the 112th Congress, and he succeeded California's David Dreier, who retired. His NRCC deputy, Greg Walden of Oregon, took his place on the campaign team — another implied endorsement of Sessions' work.

A member of the conservative Republican Study Committee, Sessions opposed the Democrats' signature legislative victories of 2010. He panned the health care overhaul, even though census figures indicated that his district had the highest rate of uninsured people of any Republican-controlled district in the country.

There is one issue on which Sessions regularly reaches across the aisle. The father of a son with Down syndrome, Sessions worked with Democrat Henry A. Waxman of California on a 2006 law to help families with incomes above the poverty line buy into Medicaid coverage for children with special needs. He co-chairs the bipartisan Congressional Down Syndrome Caucus.

Sessions is the son of William S. Sessions, a former federal judge who served as director of the FBI from 1987 to 1993. He was born in Waco and got his degree from Southwestern University in Georgetown, Texas. After college, he went to work at Southwestern Bell Telephone Co. and Bell Communications Research.

He ran for Congress in 1991, finishing sixth in a special election to determine the successor to 3rd District GOP Rep. Steve Bartlett, who resigned to run for mayor of Dallas. In 1994, Sessions quit his job and made an unsuccessful bid against incumbent Democrat John Bryant of the 5th District. After that, he worked as vice president for public policy at the National Center for Policy Analysis, a conservative think tank in Dallas.

When Bryant gave up his seat in 1996 to run for the Senate, Sessions took 53 percent of the vote in the race to replace him. Following redistricting after the 2000 census, Sessions ran in the newly created 32nd District, which had more Republican voters. His house was still in the 5th, but a mere two blocks from the boundary. Sessions cruised to victory in 2002 with 68 percent of the vote. In 2003, state Republicans redrew the map again. The race for the new 32nd District pitted Sessions against 13-term Democrat Martin Frost. Sessions prevailed with 54 percent in the costliest House election of 2004.

Demographic shifts made his district minority-majority by 2010, but many of the Hispanic residents were not voting citizens. Sessions is an immigration hard-liner and favors ending automatic citizenship for children born in the United States if their parents are in the country illegally.

But he says he is "very aware of Hispanic needs and ... in tune with their needs as parents on the issues of jobs, health care and education." Sessions was married to a Mexican woman for 27 years, but they divorced in August 2011. (In 2012, he married Karen Diebel, who ran in a 2010 House primary in Florida.)

New district lines in for the 2012 election included more white Republican neighborhoods to the north of Dallas. Sessions won 58 percent of the vote.

Key Votes

2012	
Extend a Social Security payroll tax cut and unemployment benefits	NO
Ease securities rules to expand small-business access to capital	YES
Extend for one year subsidized student loan interest rates financed by a cut in health care spending	YES
Cite Attorney General Eric H. Holder Jr. for contempt of Congress	YES
Create a visa program for foreign graduates in high-tech fields	YES
Extend most Bush-era income tax rates while allowing rates for top-bracket earners to rise (Jan. 1, 2013)	YES
2011	
Strike funding for F-35 alternative engine	NO
Prevent EPA from regulating greenhouse gas emissions to address climate change	YES
Extend certain provisions of Patriot Act for four years	YES
Declare opposition to use of ground troops in Libya	YES
Overhaul patent law	YES
Pass compromise debt limit increase plan and establish future spending limits	YES
Allow consideration of measures to implement three trade agreements	YES

CQ Vote Studies

	PARTY UNITY		PRESIDENTIAL SUPPORT	
	SUPPORT	OPPOSE	SUPPORT	OPPOSE
2012	98%	2%	17%	83%
2011	98%	2%	19%	81%
2010	99%	1%	26%	74%
2009	99%	1%	12%	88%
2008	99%	1%	85%	15%

Interest Groups

	AFL-CIO	ADA	CCUS	ACU
2012	14%	0%	100%	96%
2011	0%	5%	100%	92%
2010	0%	0%	88%	100%
2009	0%	0%	75%	100%
2008	0%	5%	100%	92%

Texas 32

Northern Dallas; most of Richardson and Garland

Situated in the northeastern quarter of Dallas County, the compact 32nd District takes in a northern chunk of the city, affluent suburban enclaves and most of business-friendly Richardson. It also grabs the majority of Garland and the western side of Lake Ray Hubbard before reaching north to Wylie in Collin County.

The district's stretch of North Dallas is eclectic and wealthy. It includes part of the Oak Lawn neighborhood, with a lively entertainment scene that serves as the hub for Dallas' gay and lesbian community. A haven for artists, lawyers and creative types, Junius Heights is the city's largest historic district. University Park — home to Southern Methodist University — and Highland Park are known as the "Park Cities." They host the estates of sports stars and wealthy Dallas CEOs, and are almost entirely white.

The metro area's vibrant telecom corridor, based in Richardson, includes AT&T, Cisco and Verizon in an office park the 32nd shares with the 3rd. More corporate customers are lined up to move into a data center, being partially financed by redevelopment funds from the city. Texas Instruments also has its headquarters nearby, but the company has struggled.

Garland has varied manufacturing interests. Raytheon's intelligence and information systems headquarters (just over the border in the 5th) employ more than 8,000. Development in the past decade includes the mixed-use 5th Street Crossing, which sits adjacent to the Dallas Area Rapid Transit line to accommodate the city's many commuters, and the vast Firewheel Town Center Mall.

Whites are the majority here, but a fast-growing Hispanic population makes up one-fourth of the population and black residents account for 13 percent. The district shifted east after decennial redistricting, and the GOP still tends to dominate elections here.

Major Industry
Telecommunications, defense, health care, retail

Cities
Dallas (pt), Garland (pt.), Richardson (pt.), Rowlett (pt.), Wylie (pt.)

Notable
The George W. Bush Presidential Library and Museum was dedicated on SMU's campus in April 2013.

Rep. Marc Veasey (D)

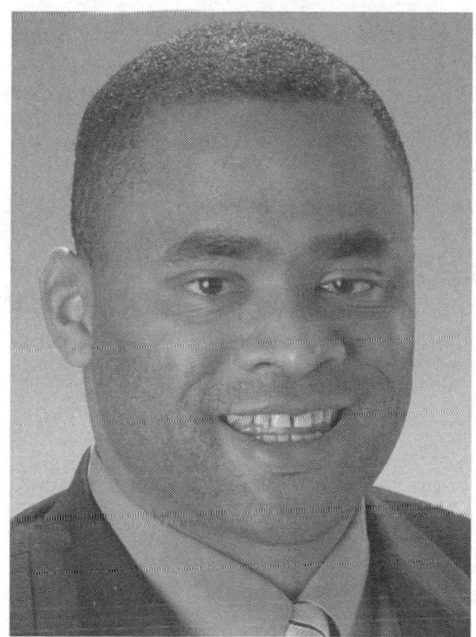

Capitol Office
225-9897
veasey.house.gov
414 Cannon Bldg. 20515-1801; fax 225-9702

Committees
Armed Services
Science, Space & Technology

Residence
Fort Worth

Born
Jan. 3, 1971; Fort Worth, Texas

Religion
Baptist

Family
Wife, Tonya Veasey; one child

Education
Texas Wesleyan U., B.S. 1995 (mass communications)

Career
Real estate broker; congressional district aide; news assistant; teacher

Political Highlights
Texas House, 2005-13

ELECTION RESULTS

2012 GENERAL		
Marc Veasey (D)	85,114	72.5%
Chuck Bradley (R)	30,252	25.8%
Ed Lindsay (GREEN)	2,009	1.7%
2012 PRIMARY RUNOFF		
Marc Veasey (D)	10,766	52.7%
Domingo Garcia (D)	9,653	47.3%

Elected 2012; 1st term

As Veasey tries to make connections in Washington, he is working just as hard to reach out to Democratic constituents at home; Hispanics make up most of his district's population, and their interests have jumped to the top of Veasey's list of priorities.

Veasey spent his early years in the Fort Worth area, but he moved with his mother and brother to the small town of Como, east of Dallas, after his parents divorced. He came back to Fort Worth for high school, then college at Texas Wesleyan University. He had a few different jobs after graduating, including a stint on the sports desk of the Fort Worth Star-Telegram. But he was always intrigued by politics, and after volunteering for the 1998 campaign of Democratic Rep. Martin Frost, he was hired as a district aide for the congressman.

Going door to door and working on constituent service prepared him for his first run for office. In 2004, he beat a Democratic incumbent and claimed a seat in the Texas House. He served there until his election to the U.S. House.

Veasey sits on the Armed Services Committee and on the Science, Space and Technology Committee. On the latter, he serves on the Energy panel, which is relevant to the Dallas-Forth Worth economy — even his mostly urban district has hundreds of active oil and gas wells.

He has also made conspicuous displays of support for a comprehensive overhaul of immigration law and for improved access to education, which happens to make good political sense, given his constituency.

Many people expected the new 33rd District to elect a Hispanic representative. Eleven Democrats entered the primary, with Veasey and former state Rep. Domingo Garcia finishing first and second. The runoff was fairly intense; Garcia accused Veasey of being too complacent, while critics of Garcia called him too combative. Veasey's mobilization of the district's black voters proved decisive in a low-turnout contest. He won easily in November.

Garcia is reportedly considering another run for the seat in 2014.

Texas 33

Parts of Fort Worth, Irving and Grand Prairie

The 33rd District was drawn during decennial remapping to group together North Texas Latino communities. The district's population is 65 percent Hispanic and and nearly 20 percent black. It stretches from Fort Worth's stockyards, across part of Arlington and into Dallas' Oak Cliff section. The Trinity River winds through the region, supporting the 1,300-acre River Legacy Park, and planners are working to enhance access to the urban waterfront. Many of the communities in this district experienced significant population growth between 2000 and 2010, mainly among minority groups.

Cowboys still drive Longhorn steers down the brick streets of Fort Worth's historic stockyards district twice daily. While embracing its former "cowtown" past, the city boasts strong health care, life sciences and aviation sectors. Alcon, the world's largest specialized eye care company, has its headquarters in the 33rd.

To the south, the Forest Hill and Everman neighborhoods of Fort Worth have relatively large black populations and growing Hispanic communities.

Each summer, Arlington — which is known for its warehousing sector — draws thousands of visitors to the Six Flags Over Texas amusement park. Others head to the Rangers' ballpark for baseball, and the fall brings enormous crowds to Cowboys Stadium to watch football. In addition to tourism dollars, manufacturing helps support the district's economy. Lockheed Martin assembles its F-35 aircraft in Grand Prairie.

Home values and incomes decline moving east from suburban Grand Prairie and the residential Irving into western Dallas. Wynnewood was designed around a village shopping center, which has fallen into decline; redevelopment is under way, including for senior citizen residences. Oak Cliff neighborhoods have worked to combat high rates of crime.

Democratic votes are heavily concentrated in a district designed to serve the interest of Metroplex minorities; Barack Obama received 72 percent of the district's vote in the 2012 presidential election.

Major Industry
Tourism, manufacturing, health care

Cities
Dallas (pt.), Fort Worth (pt.), Arlington (pt.)

Notable
Billy Bob's Texas, in Fort Worth, is the world's largest honky-tonk; Grand Prairie is home to the National Championship Indian Pow Wow.

Rep. Filemon Vela (D)

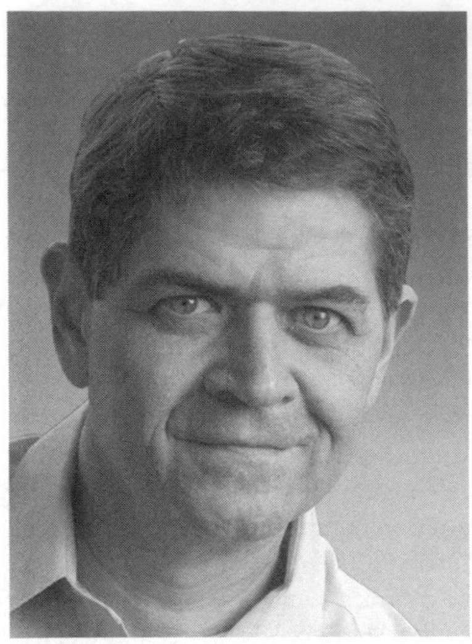

Capitol Office
225-9901
vela.house.gov
437 Cannon Bldg. 20515-1902; fax 226-0475

Committees
Agriculture
Homeland Security

Residence
Brownsville

Born
Feb. 13, 1963; Harlingen, Texas

Religion
Roman Catholic

Family
Wife, Rose Vela

Education
Loyola U. New Orleans, attended 1981-82; Georgetown U., B.A. 1985 (government); U. of Texas, J.D. 1987

Career
Lawyer

Political Highlights
Candidate for Corpus Christi City Council, 1993

ELECTION RESULTS

2012 GENERAL		
Filemon Vela (D)	89,606	61.9%
Jessica Puente-Bradshaw (R)	52,448	36.2%
Steven "Ziggy" Shanklin (LIBERT)	2,724	1.9%
2012 PRIMARY RUNOFF		
Filemon Vela (D)	15,628	66.6%
Denise Saenz Blanchard (D)	7,824	33.4%

Elected 2012; 1st term

In South Texas, Vela's name is his calling card — he comes from a family tradition of public service. His personal record as an officeholder, however, began when he was sworn into the U.S. House.

His mother, Blanca Sanchez Vela, was mayor of Brownsville. His father, Filemon Vela Sr., served on the Brownsville City Commission. The elder Vela was nominated as a U.S. District judge by President Jimmy Carter in 1980 and held that post until his death in 2004. Vela's wife, Rose, was a justice on Texas' 13th Court of Appeals, an elected position. She was formerly a Democrat but served as a Republican. After winning his primary in late July, Vela (full name: FEE-lay-mon VAY-la) told the Dallas Morning News, "I've lived with her for 22 years. If I can get along with her, I can get along with them."

Vela, who worked as a lawyer, had been described as a grass-roots activist. But aside from a failed bid for the Corpus Christi city council in 1993, he passed up opportunities to seek elective office before 2012. He has now joined the New Democrat Coalition, a group often seen as business-minded and centrist.

Farming is one of the biggest segments of his district's economy, and he holds a seat on the Agriculture Committee. He also touts his assignment to the Homeland Security Committee. Vela has banded with other border-district representatives to seek ways to expedite the flow of trade with Mexico. He insists that an overhaul of immigration law should not require an "arbitrary declaration of border security" before changes take hold. Demands for such a trigger are an "overt attempt to thwart reform efforts," he said.

In the race for the new and solidly Democratic 34th District, Vela had both his famous name and superior financial resources — the amount he loaned his own campaign surpassed the fundraising totals of his seven opponents in the primary. One of his chief rivals was indicted for racketeering weeks before the election. After winning the primary, he easily beat Denise Saenz Blanchard, a former chief of staff to former Rep. Solomon P. Ortiz, in the runoff.

Texas 34

South central — Brownsville, southern Gulf Coast, Kingsville

Anchored by Cameron County in the southernmost tip of Texas, the 34th sweeps as far north as Gonzales County nearly 300 miles away. This new district runs along the Gulf Coast, taking in tourist-friendly South Padre Island, through Kleberg County.

Of the three south Texas districts slicing through most of the Rio Grande Valley, this strip has the highest proportion of Hispanic residents — more than 80 percent. It is reliably Democratic and gave Barack Obama 61 percent of its vote in the 2012 election.

Brownsville, the district's largest city, has one of the nation's highest poverty rates. This border town has implemented federal initiatives to help fight chronic poverty, targeting colonias — unincorporated border communities — that lack access to basic utilities and infrastructure. Fortunately the cost of living, especially in Harlingen, is one of the nation's lowest. International trade at Brownsville's port provides transportation jobs.

The decline of the shrimping industry, caused by high fuel prices and an influx of frozen catches, has hurt Port Isabel. Rio Grande Valley schools strain to provide meals and support to students. A new medical school from the University of Texas system could provide needed assistance.

Offshore wind energy projects proposed for Gulf Coast waters have been stalled to allow for environmental impact studies, but wind turbines are springing up on Willacy County's land. Nearby fields of cotton and sorghum, agricultural mainstays here, were socked by exceptional drought in recent years.

Historic 825,000-acre King Ranch, home to 60,000 cattle and 300 quarterhorses, sprawls across much of Kleberg and Kenedy counties in the central stretch of the district. Uranium mining operations near Kingsburg caused concerns about the safety of wells here, the source of water for drinking, irrigation and livestock for generations of ranchers.

Major Industry
Transportation, agriculture, fishing, tourism

Cities
Brownsville, Harlingen, Kingsville

Notable
The annual Charro Days Fiesta celebrated in Brownsville and its Mexican sister city, Matamoros, pays homage to bi-national heritage.

Rep. Lloyd Doggett (D)

Capitol Office
225-4865
doggett.house.gov
201 Cannon Bldg. 20515-4325; fax 225-3073

Committees
Ways & Means

Residence
Austin

Born
Oct. 6, 1946; Austin, Texas

Religion
Methodist

Family
Wife, Libby Belk Doggett; two children

Education
U. of Texas, B.B.A. 1967, J.D. 1970

Career
Lawyer

Political Highlights
Democratic nominee for U.S. Senate, 1984; Texas Senate, 1973-85; Texas Supreme Court, 1989-94

ELECTION RESULTS

2012 GENERAL		
Lloyd Doggett (D)	105,626	63.9%
Susan Narvaiz (R)	52,894	32.0%
Ross Lynn Leone (LIBERT)	4,082	2.5%
Meghan Owen (GREEN)	2,540	1.5%
2012 PRIMARY		
Lloyd Doggett (D)	14,559	73.2%
Sylvia Romo (D)	4,212	21.2%
Maria Luisa Alvarado (D)	1,105	5.6%
2010 GENERAL		
Lloyd Doggett (D)	99,967	52.8%
Donna Campbell (R)	84,849	44.8%
Jim Stutsman (LIBERT)	4,431	2.3%

Previous Winning Percentages
2008 (66%); 2006 (67%); 2004 (68%); 2002 (84%); 2000 (85%); 1998 (85%); 1996 (56%); 1994 (56%)

Elected 1994; 10th term

Doggett still has something of the trial lawyer in him, embracing theatrics when he makes his liberal case in his native Texas twang. He sharply promotes Democratic priorities on a host of subjects, with particular attention to taxes, fiscal policy and the social safety net.

Before his House tenure, Doggett was anchored in Austin. Born and raised there, he stayed in town to attend the University of Texas; he was a student body president during the turbulent 1960s. A few years out of UT's law school, he was elected to the Texas Senate, which meets downtown. The defiantly liberal city had a senator to match. In 1994, the Austin American-Statesman said Doggett "was once the golden boy of Austin politics and sometime bad boy of the Texas Senate."

As a senator, Doggett took an aggressive approach to consumer and environmental protection. He filibustered bills he disliked — the comfortable shoes he used for those efforts hang in his D.C. office — and made headlines in 1979 by hiding out with a group of colleagues to prevent Senate action on a proposal to alter the state's primary elections. Doggett worked as a plaintiff's attorney and burnished his reputation as a consumer-protection advocate during a six-year run on the Texas Supreme Court.

Doggett transferred his lively style to Washington in 1995, at the start of the Republican Revolution. He quickly became known for a flood of partisan and bristly speeches. Near the end of his first year, he was reprimanded for calling Speaker Newt Gingrich a "crybaby" from the House floor.

The frequency of those speeches has diminished over the years, although their spirit lives on in Doggett's work on the Ways and Means Committee. Since 2011, he has been the ranking member on the Human Resources Subcommittee, which has jurisdiction over welfare programs.

Debating a short-term extension of the Temporary Assistance for Needy Families program in late 2011, Doggett said, "This bill today does so little to address that tattered safety net, which is increasingly more hole than net." He lamented that TANF supplemental grants to states such as Texas were not included in a short-term extension enacted in 2012.

Republicans have tried to walk back the recession-spurred expansion of federal unemployment insurance to the usual 26-week benefit. Doggett has slammed them as disregarding the plight of the working person. "While our belts should be tightened, it should not be done around the necks of the unemployed," he wrote in Roll Call in 2011.

That year, Doggett worked on a bill with subcommittee Chairman Geoff Davis of Kentucky to reauthorize two child-welfare programs. It also allowed states to use federal foster-care funds to test new programs for child welfare. Doggett touted its enactment — and also made sure to note that it did not do enough for children. In early 2013, President Barack Obama signed a Doggett bill to create a commission to study child fatalities from abuse and neglect and to evaluate current federal programs addressing those problems.

Ways and Means handles taxes, and for more than a decade Doggett's pet cause has been to block the "international shenanigans" that allow some multinational corporations to avoid U.S. taxes. When Obama unveiled his plan in May 2009 to significantly change how U.S.-based multinationals are taxed, it included aspects of Doggett's proposals. Doggett supported a free-trade deal with Panama in 2011 because Panama had changed its banking-secrecy laws to combat the use of the country as a tax haven.

With a possible tax code overhaul in the works, Doggett has harped on "the distorted Republican theology that, when the question is taxes, less always means more. It's political alchemy. It's like turning hay into gold." He calls for all tax expenditures — the exemptions, credits and deductions meant to encourage various activities by companies or individuals — to be regularly evaluated to determine whether they are achieving their desired result.

In fact, he has proposed "sunset" legislation calling for periodic congressional review of all federal programs. Under his plan, Congress would have to reauthorize most programs at least once a decade to keep them running. Doggett based his bill on a Texas law he wrote when he was a state senator.

Still, Doggett's overall vision of fiscal prudence does not mesh with that of Republicans. In the 112th Congress (2011-12), he opposed the budgets of Wisconsin Republican Paul D. Ryan as well as the GOP's insistence on deficit reduction before the federal debt limit was increased. "They demand that we jeopardize the security for the very young with educational opportunities, and for the old with Social Security and Medicare," he said in July 2011. "Their ransom demands do not share the sacrifice, but they sure do spread the pain — to the young, to the old, to those who are trying to climb up the economic ladder or just not slide backwards."

Doggett is a strong environmentalist and thinks the government should support a broad shift to renewable sources of energy. In the 110th Congress (2007-08), he wrote climate change legislation that would have gone further to reduce greenhouse gases than bills supported by his party's leaders.

In 1984 he ran for the U.S. Senate, winning the Democratic primary but getting crushed by GOP Rep. Phil Gramm. Doggett spent several years as a trial lawyer, then won election to the Texas Supreme Court. He was on the bench when 16-term Democrat J.J. Pickle (a Ways and Means member) announced his retirement. Doggett got the jump on Democratic rivals, had an easy primary and won by 16 points that November.

Doggett's antagonism toward Republicans has made him a target when redistricting comes around. When his 10th District was dismantled by a 2003 Republican redraw of the electoral map, he jumped to the new 25th District, which had been drawn to elect a Hispanic candidate and which stretched to the Mexico border. The Supreme Court struck down that map in 2006, making Doggett's district more compact and less Hispanic.

The redraw for 2012 seemed like it would pit Doggett against Democratic state Rep. Joaquin Castro in a Hispanic-majority district stretching from San Antonio to Austin. A bitter primary was shaping up, with some liberal groups saying Doggett was not active enough on issues such as gay rights and immigration. But when the map was settled, Castro ran in the open 20th District. Doggett beat Sylvia Romo, the tax assessor-collector for Bexar County (which includes San Antonio), in the primary. He cruised to a 10th term in November.

Key Votes

2012	
Extend a Social Security payroll tax cut and unemployment benefits	YES
Ease securities rules to expand small-business access to capital	YES
Extend for one year subsidized student loan interest rates financed by a cut in health care spending	NO
Cite Attorney General Eric H. Holder Jr. for contempt of Congress	NO
Create a visa program for foreign graduates in high-tech fields	NO
Extend most Bush-era income tax rates while allowing rates for top-bracket earners to rise (Jan. 1, 2013)	YES
2011	
Strike funding for F-35 alternative engine	YES
Prevent EPA from regulating greenhouse gas emissions to address climate change	NO
Extend certain provisions of Patriot Act for four years	NO
Declare opposition to use of ground troops in Libya	YES
Overhaul patent law	YES
Pass compromise debt limit increase plan and establish future spending limits	YES
Allow consideration of measures to implement three trade agreements	NO

CQ Vote Studies

	PARTY UNITY		PRESIDENTIAL SUPPORT	
	SUPPORT	OPPOSE	SUPPORT	OPPOSE
2012	95%	5%	87%	13%
2011	96%	4%	87%	13%
2010	95%	5%	86%	14%
2009	95%	5%	89%	11%
2008	97%	3%	11%	89%

Interest Groups

	AFL-CIO	ADA	CCUS	ACU
2012	95%	85%	25%	8%
2011	97%	85%	25%	0%
2010	86%	95%	13%	4%
2009	95%	95%	33%	12%
2008	100%	90%	50%	8%

Texas 35

Downtown San Antonio and parts of Austin

The new 35th District includes both downtown San Antonio and parts of Austin. It runs in a narrow oxtail-shaped stretch between the cities down Interstate 35, nicking five counties along the way.

Just less than half of the district's population resides in Bexar (pronounced BEAR) County. The 35th boasts most of San Antonio's leading tourist attractions, including the Alamo and River Walk, helping the city lure 20 million visitors annually. The 750-foot Tower of the Americas offers impressive vistas from its observation deck. The AT&T Center hosts basketball's Spurs, while the city's annual Stock Show and Rodeo draws more than a million people. The 35th also takes in the 1,200-acre Brooks City-Base planned retail and residential park, previously an Air Force base and where Charles A. Lindbergh learned to fly while in the military.

Tourism is also important up Interstate 35 to the northeast in middle-class New Braunfels (shared with the 21st). Schlitterbahn, a 65-acre water park themed on the community's German heritage, gives visitors the opportunity to float the Guadalupe and Comal rivers.

North of downtown Austin, the district grabs some technology and travel sector employers and the city's international airport, which is expected to receive a $50 million expansion. The North Lamar corridor has become a primary destination for Latino immigrants. East of the city, the Walter E. Long Lake doubles as a power plant cooling reservoir and a popular bass fishing location.

Overall, the district lags in educational attainment: Only 15 percent of its residents have at least a bachelor's degree. Hispanic and black residents account for more than 70 percent of the 35th's population, and the district is strongly Democratic. Barack Obama won here by a 28-percentage-point margin in the 2012 presidential election.

Major Industry
Tourism, retail, technology, transportation

Cities
San Antonio (pt.), Austin (pt.), New Braunfels (pt.), San Marcos (pt.)

Notable
First celebrated in 1891 to commemorate victory at the Battle of San Jacinto and the fallen at the Alamo, the Battle of Flowers parade takes place during San Antonio's annual fiesta.

Rep. Steve Stockman (R)

Capitol Office
225-1555
stockman.house.gov
326 Cannon Bldg. 20515-6601; fax 226-0396

Committees
Foreign Affairs
Science, Space & Technology

Residence
Friendswood

Born
Nov. 14, 1956; Bloomfield Hills, Mich.

Religion
Christian

Family
Wife, Patti Ferguson

Education
San Jacinto College, attended 1985-86; U. of Houston, Clear Lake, B.S. 1990 (accounting)

Career
Youth political activism organization director; computer salesman

Political Highlights
Sought Republican nomination for U.S. House, 1990; Republican nominee for U.S. House, 1992; U.S. House, 1995-97; defeated for re-election to U.S. House, 1996; sought Republican nomination for Texas Railroad Commission, 1998; candidate for U.S. House (special election), 2006

ELECTION RESULTS

2012 GENERAL		
Steve Stockman (R)	165,405	70.7%
Max Martin (D)	62,143	26.6%
Michael K. Cole (LIBERT)	6,284	2.7%
2012 PRIMARY RUNOFF		
Steve Stockman (R)	21,472	55.3%
Stephen Takach (R)	17,378	44.7%

Previous Winning Percentages
1994 (52%)

Elected 2012; 2nd term

Also served 1995-97

Stockman was a freshman lawmaker in 1995, and he became a sophomore in 2013. A lot changed in Washington during his 16-year absence, but he seems to be the same. He is still a staunch fiscal and social conservative who energizes admirers and detractors alike with incendiary rhetoric.

The details of Stockman's past can be hard to come by — he shuns many mainstream media requests, preferring social media — but he is a native of Michigan and the son of two teachers. He moved to Texas in search of employment and eventually studied at San Jacinto College in the mid-1980s. For a time he was jobless and living out of his car in Fort Worth. He eventually became a born-again Christian, and he received a bachelor's degree in accounting from the University of Houston Clear Lake in 1990, at age 34.

That same year, he made his first run for the House, hoping to challenge Democratic Rep. Jack Brooks. He lost in the Republican primary. Two years later, he clinched the nomination, but lost to Brooks by 10 points.

In 1994, Republicans were surging nationwide. Brooks, as the chairman of the Judiciary Committee, put his support behind a 1994 crime measure that included a controversial ban on "assault" weapons — even though he had defended gun rights in the past. His constituents were not pleased. In his third attempt, Stockman beat Brooks by 6 points, ending the incumbent's House career at 42 years. He credited the dustup over the crime law as a major factor in his victory.

But in 1996, the Supreme Court threw out Texas' congressional map, forcing Stockman into a considerably more Democratic district. He was beaten by Jefferson County tax assessor Nick Lampson. While redistricting may have been pivotal, Stockman made many political foes with his brusque and often controversial style. His outspokenness included writing an article for Guns & Ammo magazine, published shortly after the Oklahoma City bombing, suggesting that the Clinton administration raided the Branch Davidian compound in Waco in 1993 to gain support for the assault weapons ban.

Stockman added to his notoriety in the opening months of the 113th Congress (2013-14). One of his first votes was against the re-election of John A. Boehner as speaker of the House. He said that the "fiscal cliff" deal from the end of the 112th Congress (2011-12), which raised income taxes on earnings over $400,000 and had no spending reductions, was a "betrayal of conservative principle and economic reality." Stockman voted "present" in the selection of the speaker.

The hallway outside Stockman's Washington office was briefly the site of the "Obama Failometer," a 10-foot-long billboard of unemployment metrics meant to illustrate President Barack Obama's failure to create jobs. After House officials ordered its removal, Stockman was defiant. "The Obama Failometer may not be allowed in Congress, but it will be back somewhere, and bigger," he wrote. "Tearing it down created more labor than Obama has."

In protest of Obama's push for gun control legislation, Stockman invited the Motor City Madman — rock star Ted Nugent — as his guest to the 2013 State of the Union address. Nugent is a noted gun rights advocate. It was a stark contrast with members who had invited victims of gun violence. Stockman has sponsored several bills meant to remove or prevent gun restrictions, including one to repeal prohibitions on firearms in school zones.

He also proposed the "Stockman smartquester," a series of spending cuts targeting renewable-energy programs, nutrition assistance programs and alleged overpayments in subsidies for health insurance exchanges established by the 2010 health care law. They would replace across-the-board spending cuts put in place by an August 2011 deficit reduction law.

Stockman sits on the Science, Space and Technology Committee, after serving on its predecessor in his first term. He sits on the Space Subcommittee and is the vice chairman of the Research Subcommittee. Stockman, whose district is home to the Johnson Space Center, has already used his seat to support NASA and push for an increased American space presence.

While advocating small budgets for most areas of the federal government, he has argued that spending on NASA has educational and security value. "Not only can you increase NASA funding while balancing the budget, cutting spending, cutting taxes and reducing the debt, it's the fiscally responsible thing to do," he said. "Every dollar spent on NASA produces real value for our economy and our defense." He co-sponsored a bill to direct NASA to develop a plan for returning to the moon and establishing a human presence there.

Stockman is also on the Foreign Affairs Committee. He sits on the Subcommittee for Europe, Eurasia and Emerging Threats, which is chaired by Dana Rohrabacher of California — one of his good friends in Congress. Speaking to the Houston Chronicle about Stockman, Rohrabacher said that "there's nothing pretentious about him. He could be the guy fixing the plumbing in your house or making sure the dead tree in the lawn is removed."

Along with other Republicans on Foreign Affairs, Stockman called for the Obama administration to release information regarding the September 2012 attack on a U.S. consulate in Libya, which killed four Americans. He also expressed hope for new leadership in Venezuela upon the death of President Hugo Chavez. "Chavez's agenda, hailed by many Democrats, produced nothing but poverty, violence and oppression," he wrote. Stockman also sits on the subcommittee covering global human rights.

Stockman told National Review that he eased off of politics after his 1996 defeat to take care of his father, who suffered from Alzheimer's disease. He eventually placed his father in a veterans' home and was forced to file for bankruptcy due to the cost of his care. He lost a bid for the Texas Railroad Commission in 1998 and finished a very distant third in the 2006 special election to replace former House Majority Leader Tom DeLay.

Texas was awarded four new House seats for the 2012 elections, and one of them was an open seat covering much of the eastern suburbs of Houston. Twelve people entered the Republican primary. Stockman raised relatively little money and did not engage other candidates much, but he finished second to Stephen Takach, a financial planner who spent heavily from his own personal wealth during the crowded contest.

Stockman won the runoff by more than 10 points. He had no problems in the general election, as the district is very conservative.

Texas 36

Eastern Houston suburbs — Baytown, Highlands; Orange

The new 36th — made up of parts of three former districts — runs from the Louisiana border through eight East Texas counties, but suburbs and refinery towns in a small part of Harris County east of Houston sop up a large portion of the district's residents and include three-fourths of its Hispanic population. Overall, Hispanics make up more than 20 percent of the 36th, with whites accounting for much of the rest of the population.

Channelview is named for its proximity to the Houston Ship Channel that curves through its part of Harris County. This part of the district relies on the refining and transport of petrochemicals and oil. Both ExxonMobil and Chevron Phillips operate large petrochemical complexes in Baytown at the mouth of Trinity Bay.

Shipping also is important to the southeastern corner of the district — the former shipbuilding hub of Orange falls into the orbit of Port Arthur (in the 14th). Rail traffic within the district helps transport its oil, natural gas and timber reserves to far-flung markets.

During decennial redistricting, the 36th wrested the Johnson Space Center from the 22nd along with the suburb of Clear Lake, which many NASA employees call home.

Away from the coast, much of the 36th is forested. Bottomland hardwood forest in the Trinity River National Wildlife Refuge north of Liberty offers prime birding. The Big Thicket National Preserve blankets the northern stretches of the district with towering pines and cypress bogs. The district also contains swatches of the Angelina and Sabine national forests along its northernmost edge.

The 36th promises to be a Republican stronghold and gave Mitt Romney 73 percent of its vote in the 2012 presidential election.

Major Industry
Oil refining, petrochemicals, aerospace, timber, shipping

Cities
Pasadena, League City, Baytown

Notable
The Battleship Texas, docked at the San Jacinto Battleground state park, became the nation's first battleship memorial museum in 1948.

UTAH

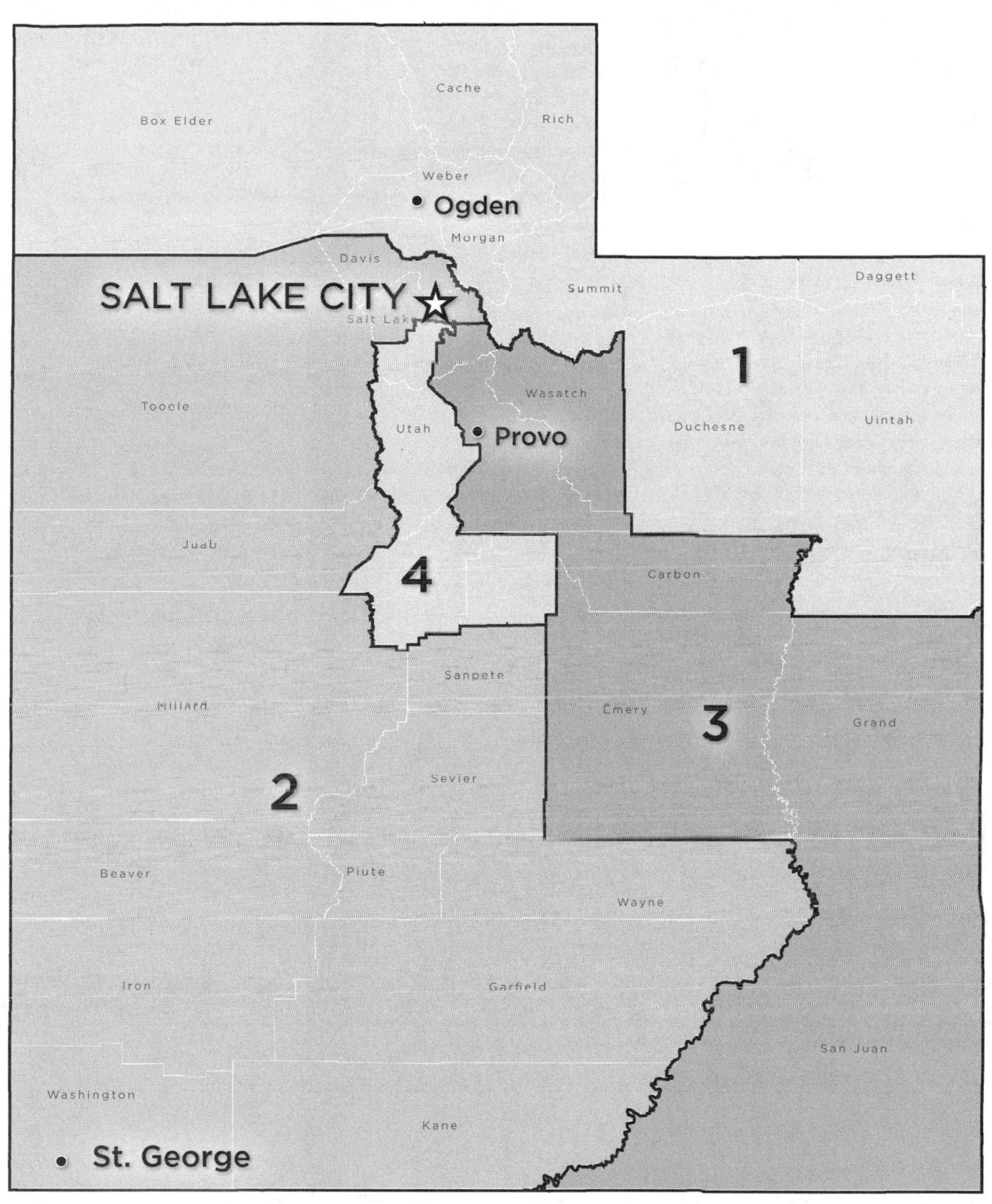

Cache
Box Elder
Rich
Weber
Ogden
Morgan
Davis
SALT LAKE CITY
Salt Lake
Summit
Daggett
1
Wasatch
Tooele
Utah
Provo
Duchesne
Uintah
Juab
4
Carbon
Sanpete
Millard
Emery
3
Grand
Sevier
2
Beaver
Piute
Wayne
Iron
Garfield
San Juan
Washington
Kane
St. George

Gov. Gary R. Herbert (R)

First elected: 2010; assumed office Aug. 11, 2009, following the resignation of Jon Huntsman Jr., R, to become ambassador to China.

Length of term: 4 years

Term expires: 1/13

Salary: $109,900

Phone: (801) 538-1000

Residence: Orem

Born: May 7, 1947; American Fork, Utah

Religion: Mormon

Family: Wife, Jeanette Herbert; six children

Education: Brigham Young U., attended 1965-70

Military Service: Utah National Guard 1970-76

Career: Realtor; child care center owner

Political highlights: Utah County Commission, 1990-2004; lieutenant governor, 2005-09

ELECTION RESULTS

2010 GENERAL

Gary R. Herbert (R)	412,151	64.1%
Peter Corroon (D)	205,246	31.9%
Farley Anderson (I)	13,038	2.0%
Andrew McCullough (LIBERT)	12,871	2.0%

Lt. Gov. Gregory S. Bell (R)

First elected: 2010; assumed office Sept. 1, 2009, following the elevation of Herbert to governor.

Length of term: 4 years

Term expires: 1/13

Salary: $104,405

Phone: (801) 538-1041

LEGISLATURE

Legislature: 45 days yearly January-March

Senate: 29 members, 4-year terms

2013 ratios: 24 R, 5 D; 24 men, 5 women

Salary: $273/day

Phone: (801) 538-1035

House: 75 members, 2-year terms

2013 ratios: 61 R, 14 D; 63 men, 12 women

Salary: $273/day

Phone: (801) 538-1029

TERM LIMITS

Governor: 3 terms

Senate: No

House: No

URBAN STATISTICS

CITY	POPULATION
Salt Lake City	186,440
West Valley City	129,480
Provo	112,488
West Jordan	103,712
Orem	88,328

REGISTERED VOTERS

Registration by party began in May 1999, however, not all voters have declared an affiliation and the numbers are kept on a county basis.

POPULATION

2010 population	2,763,885
2000 population	2,233,169
1990 population	1,722,850
Percent change (2000-2010)	+23.8%
Rank among states (2010)	34
Median age	28.5
Born in state	62.5%
Foreign born	7.6%
Violent crime rate	213/100,000
Poverty level	11.5%
Federal workers	41,880
Military	6,237

ELECTIONS

STATE ELECTION OFFICIAL
(801) 538-1041

DEMOCRATIC PARTY
(801) 328-1212

REPUBLICAN PARTY
(801) 533-9777

MISCELLANEOUS

Web: www.utah.gov

Capital: Salt Lake City

U.S. CONGRESS

Senate: 2 Republicans

House: 3 Republicans, 1 Democrat

STATISTICS BY DISTRICT

District	2012 Vote for President: Obama	2012 Vote for President: Romney	2008 Vote for President: Obama	2008 Vote for President: McCain	Black	Asian	Hispanic	Median Income	Over 64	Under 20	College Education	Rural	Sq. Miles
1	20%	77%	29%	68%	1%	1%	12%	$56,973	9%	35%	28%	20%	19,561
2	29	68	38	59	1	2	15	49,178	11	33	29	17	39,988
3	19	78	30	68	1	2	11	59,687	9	36	35	10	20,071
4	30	67	41	56	1	3	16	57,124	8	34	27	4	2,550
STATE	**25**	**73**	**34**	**63**	**1**	**2**	**13**	**55,869**	**9**	**35**	**29**	**13**	**82,170**
U.S.	**51**	**47**	**53**	**46**	**12**	**5**	**17**	**50,052**	**13**	**27**	**29**	**21**	**3,531,905**

Sen. Orrin G. Hatch (R)

Capitol Office
224-5251
hatch.senate.gov
104 Hart Bldg. 20510 4402, fax 224-6331

Committees
Finance - Ranking Member
Health, Education, Labor & Pensions
Judiciary
Special Aging
Joint Taxation

Residence
Salt Lake City

Born
March 22, 1934; Pittsburgh, Pa.

Religion
Mormon

Family
Wife, Elaine Hatch; six children

Education
Brigham Young U., B.S. 1959 (history); U. of Pittsburgh, J.D. 1962

Career
Lawyer; songwriter

Political Highlights
Sought Republican nomination for president, 2000

ELECTION RESULTS

2012 GENERAL		
Orrin G. Hatch (R)	657,608	65.3%
Scott N. Howell (D)	301,873	30.0%
Shaun McCausland (CNSTP)	31,905	3.2%
2012 PRIMARY		
Orrin G. Hatch (R)	157,101	66.5%
Dan Liljenquist (R)	79,261	33.5%

Previous Winning Percentages
2006 (62%); 2000 (66%); 1994 (69%); 1988 (67%); 1982 (58%); 1976 (54%)

Elected 1976; 7th term

Hatch is the most senior Senate Republican. He plans on his seventh term being his last, and he has a major goal for the closing chapter of his career: an overhaul of the nation's much-despised tax code. "It's going to take a real effort by both parties, and both parties know that we have to do it," Hatch said in 2012, adding that "good will" between Democrats and Republicans would be crucial.

Work has begun in the pivotal panels. Republican leaders of the House Ways and Means Committee hope to move an overhaul by the end of 2013, and Democratic Chairman Max Baucus of Montana set the Finance Committee in motion in the early months of the 113th Congress (2013-14) — his last before his retirement.

Hatch has been the top Republican on the Finance Committee since 2011, and his track record suggests he could be integral in the tax effort. During stints as the top Republican on the Judiciary Committee and the Health, Education, Labor and Pensions Committee, he worked out bipartisan compromises and cleared landmark laws related to national security and health care.

Also, electoral pressure is no longer a factor. A common perception of Hatch in recent years is that he tried to court the most conservative Republicans. Many people were stunned in 2010 when three-term Utah Sen. Robert F. Bennett was denied the GOP Senate nomination, as conservatives at the party's nominating convention lined up behind two challengers. Hatch had two years to prepare for a similar battle. He established ties to the tea party movement and engaged in aggressive fundraising. He publicly apologized to conservative groups for some past stances, such as support for a $700 billion rescue package for the financial sector in 2008.

The Salt Lake Tribune reported that Hatch spent "a record $10 million" to defend his seat in the 2012 primary, and he was aided by an endorsement from GOP presidential contender Mitt Romney. He won nearly two-thirds of the vote to defeat state Sen. Dan Liljenquist — but as that victory seemed more certain, he showed hints of his usual pragmatism. "In order to pass legislation, you're going to have to have a few Democrats with you," Hatch said to Utah's KSL news station amid the primary fight. "So you can't just say no to everything. If you do that, you are not representing the state."

Over the years, Hatch has been both the foe and the surprising ally of Democrats. He earned the enmity of many through his ardent defense of Clarence Thomas during his 1991 Supreme Court confirmation. More recently, Hatch voted against President Barack Obama's nominees to the highest court, Sonia Sotomayor and Elena Kagan, saying he feared that they would legislate from the bench.

But he has worked well with even the most liberal Democrats when their interests have aligned. Hatch and Edward M. Kennedy of Massachusetts worked to create the federal-state health insurance program for children living in or near poverty. Tom Harkin of Iowa was his ally in preparing a 1994 law that has limited the Food and Drug Administration's ability to withdraw dietary supplements from stores (supplements are a huge industry in Utah). A law credited with making generic medicines more widely available is named for Hatch and Democratic California Rep. Henry A. Waxman.

The GOP's right wing sometimes finds fault with his tendency to join with Democrats. After the Sept. 11 attacks, the Judiciary Committee came under heavy pressure to rapidly approve a major expansion of law enforcement's investigative powers, raising concerns about possible encroachments on civil liberties. The George W. Bush administration negotiated with Chairman

Patrick J. Leahy, a liberal Democrat from Vermont. Hatch, worried that the talks would break down, quietly conducted parallel discussions with Leahy. He courted support from Democrats Joseph R. Biden Jr. of Delaware, Dianne Feinstein of California and Charles E. Schumer of New York.

"This way, if the negotiations with Leahy broke down, we would still have a compromise acceptable to a majority on the committee," Hatch said in his autobiography, titled "Square Peg." The bill, known as the Patriot Act, passed the Senate overwhelmingly; it became law in 2001.

Hatch has worked with his fellow Republicans in the effort to dismantle the 2010 health care overhaul. He is one of the leading opponents of the excise tax on medical devices created by that law, and in 2013, Hatch and Republican Lamar Alexander of Tennessee introduced a bill to repeal the "individual mandate" to have insurance. Hatch has also outlined a package of changes for Medicare and Medicaid, should Congress try to restructure those programs in a bigger deal to address long-term deficits. He proposes allowing private health plans to compete with traditional fee-for-service Medicare, in the hope that competition can drive down costs.

As lawmakers consider immigration policy, Hatch takes a particular interest in expanding the number of visas available to high-skilled workers. He is the chairman of the Senate Republican High-Tech Task Force.

Hatch is now known now for a degree of political savvy, but he started in 1977 as a combative freshman with no prior legislative experience. "In that first year, he fought everybody on everything," longtime Hatch aide Frank Madsen told the Tribune. "I think the difference over the years has been that he has discovered if all you are going to do is fight, you are going to get nowhere because you are not a player."

Born in Pittsburgh, Hatch grew up in poverty. His family lost their home during the Great Depression, so Hatch's father, a lathe operator, borrowed $100 to buy an acre of land in the hills above Pittsburgh, where he built a home of blackened lumber salvaged from a fire. The family grew their own food; Hatch tended the chickens and sold their eggs.

During World War II, when Hatch was 11, his beloved older brother, Jesse, a B-24 nose gunner, died in a bombing raid over Italy. Just weeks afterward, a lock of hair over Hatch's forehead turned white. When it came time for Hatch to serve his mission as a young Mormon, he chose to serve two, one for himself and one for Jesse.

He worked his way through Brigham Young University in Utah and law school at the University of Pittsburgh as a janitor, an all-night desk clerk in a girls' dormitory and a lathe operator. To house a growing family — three of his six children were born by the time he finished law school — he plastered the inside of his family's old chicken coop.

He returned to Utah in 1969 and became an attorney with a thriving private practice. He decided in 1976 to run for the Senate seat then held by Democrat Frank Moss. He won the GOP nomination over Jack W. Carlson, a former assistant secretary of Interior, then defeated Moss with 54 percent of the vote.

A frugal workaholic, Hatch is also an urbane clotheshorse, art lover and successful songwriter whose work has been performed by the Osmonds and Gladys Knight. Hatch is friendly with U2 lead singer Bono. Hooked on music since he started taking piano lessons at age 6, Hatch started writing poetry in college. In 1996, singer-songwriter Janice Kapp Perry asked him to write some hymns with her. He wrote 10 songs in a weekend, the core of the "My God Is Love" album. Since then, he has produced several discs of religious, romantic and patriotic songs.

Hatch's only electoral defeat came in 2000, during a quixotic bid for the GOP presidential nomination. He finished last in Iowa's GOP caucuses and dropped out the next week, endorsing George W. Bush.

Key Votes

2012	
Prohibit health insurance plans from denying coverage based on the sponsor's religious beliefs	NO
Require approval of the Keystone XL oil pipeline	YES
Ease securities rules to expand small-business access to capital	YES
Reauthorize farm and nutrition programs for five years	NO
Limit debate on a bill that would create private-sector cybersecurity standards	NO
Consent to ratification of a treaty setting global standard for the treatment of people with disabilities	NO
Provide $60.4 billion in disaster relief following Superstorm Sandy	NO
Extend most Bush-era income tax rates while allowing rates for top-bracket earners to rise (Jan. 1, 2013)	YES
2011	
Prevent EPA from regulating greenhouse gas emissions to address climate change	YES
Extend certain provisions of Patriot Act for four years	YES
Clear compromise debt limit increase plan and establish future spending limits	NO
Overhaul patent law	YES
Implement Colombia free trade agreement	YES
Limit debate on confirmation of Caitlin J. Halligan to D.C. Circuit Court of Appeals	P
Extend payroll tax cut and unemployment benefits for two months	YES

CQ Vote Studies

	PARTY UNITY		PRESIDENTIAL SUPPORT	
	SUPPORT	OPPOSE	SUPPORT	OPPOSE
2012	92%	8%	41%	59%
2011	96%	4%	57%	43%
2010	97%	3%	46%	54%
2009	85%	15%	58%	42%
2008	93%	7%	80%	20%
2007	82%	18%	76%	24%
2006	93%	7%	88%	12%
2005	96%	4%	93%	7%
2004	98%	2%	94%	6%
2003	98%	2%	99%	1%

Interest Groups

	AFL-CIO	ADA	CCUS	ACU
2012	0%	0%	71%	92%
2011	17%	10%	90%	100%
2010	8%	0%	100%	100%
2009	22%	20%	86%	88%
2008	20%	10%	100%	80%
2007	29%	30%	91%	76%
2006	20%	5%	92%	84%
2005	14%	5%	100%	92%
2004	8%	10%	100%	96%
2003	0%	10%	100%	80%

Sen. Mike Lee (R)

Capitol Office
224-5444
lee.senate.gov
316 Hart Bldg. 20510-4403; fax 228-1168

Committees
Armed Services
Energy & Natural Resources
Judiciary
Joint Economic

Residence
Alpine

Born
June 4, 1971; Mesa, Ariz.

Religion
Mormon

Family
Wife, Sharon Lee; three children

Education
Brigham Young U., B.A. 1994 (political science), J.D. 1997

Career
Lawyer; gubernatorial aide

Political Highlights
Assistant U.S. attorney, 2002-05

ELECTION RESULTS

2010 GENERAL		
Mike Lee (R)	390,179	61.6%
Sam F. Granato (D)	207,685	32.8%
Scott N. Bradley (CNSTP)	35,937	5.7%
2010 PRIMARY		
Mike Lee (R)	98,512	51.2%
Tim Bridgewater (R)	93,905	48.8%

Elected 2010; 1st term

Some lawmakers and attorneys would consider it an insult if they were described as "lawyerly." For Lee, a conservative dedicated to a limited role for government, it's a compliment.

Like most national politicians, Lee can deliver practiced talking points. But just as often, he pauses before answering a question and delivers a well-thought-out response — an argument, really, as if he were making a case before a judge or jury.

It's a skill that comes naturally. Lee sat in on most of the arguments his father, Rex Lee, made before the Supreme Court as solicitor general in the 1980s. The younger Lee went on to clerk for Justice Samuel A. Alito Jr. and was an assistant U.S. attorney under President George W. Bush.

Lee, a member of the Judiciary Committee, says the federal government should return to constitutional principles. He argues that the clearest legislative path to that goal is a constitutional amendment to require a balanced budget. Just one month into his Senate career, he introduced a version that would require not just balance between income and outgo, but would limit outlays to 18 percent of gross domestic product and require a two-thirds vote in each chamber to raise taxes.

It went nowhere, but Lee is willing to be creative. Colorado Democrat Mark Udall also favors an amendment — although a less stringent version. In 2013 they suggested packaging two competing proposals into a single measure that might make it out of Congress. States could then decide which one they like better. "There is no single formula that could carry the magic bullet, but we do know ... if we don't try anything, we're never going to get there," Lee said during his 2010 campaign.

Lee has earned a reputation as someone unafraid to speak up, even as a junior member of the clubby Senate. "My role is not to adhere to convention for the sake of convention," he said. A senior Republican Senate aide told Roll Call in 2011 that Lee "tends to talk very loudly and very authoritatively, not in a conversational way that invites discussion." A GOP lobbyist labeled him brash — but also described him as "a very effective, conservative-thought leader."

The conservative advocacy group Heritage Action for America put Lee in a first-place tie for the title of most conservative senator in the 112th Congress (2011-12). The man he tied with, Jim DeMint of South Carolina, resigned at the start of 2013 to become the president of the Heritage Foundation — the think tank associated with Heritage Action. At the start of the 113th Congress (2013-14), Lee also had a perfect career rating from the Club for Growth, an influential free-market, anti-tax organization. He is a member of the Joint Economic Committee, which has no legislative power but initiates many policy discussions on fiscal matters.

Despite his reputation, Lee was not particularly brazen as discussions of an immigration overhaul began in 2013. Instead, he objected to the idea of a comprehensive approach: "Good policy rarely flows from massive bills that seek to fix every problem in a single sweeping piece of legislation," he said at a Judiciary hearing. Lee's bills on the subject have mostly dealt with legal immigration, trying to extend the stays of certain agricultural guest workers and eliminate the per-country percentage caps on visas available to high-skilled workers.

Lee is a defender of the protections outlined in the Fourth Amendment. He and Judiciary Chairman Patrick J. Leahy of Vermont are pursuing an update of the law governing electronic communications. Their bill would require law enforcement officials to get a warrant before accessing the emails and other electronic data of U.S. citizens, regardless of how old the data is.

He also defends the Second Amendment. Lee was wary of gun control proposals that came before the Senate in April 2013 — all of which were defeated. "We all wanted to find answers that would reduce crime and prevent the next senseless act of violence," Lee wrote. But "the primary effect of most of the bills we voted on today ... was to limit the rights of law-abiding citizens."

On the Energy and Natural Resources Committee, Lee supports opening up the nation's natural energy resources. He has backed proposals to drill for oil and gas in the Arctic National Wildlife Refuge in Alaska, and to extract shale oil from rock in Utah, Colorado and Wyoming. He also scrutinizes proposals to designate wilderness areas or protected habitats in his state. Most of Utah is federally owned, and those designations often come with regulatory restrictions that can limit economic activity on the land.

Lee also sits on the Armed Services Committee, having moved there in 2013 after serving on the Foreign Relations Committee for two years. After President Barack Obama committed U.S. forces to help rebels fighting the government of Muammar el-Qaddafi in Libya in 2011, Lee co-sponsored a measure that called for Obama to delineate policy objectives and limitations on military involvement. He supports the removal of most U.S. forces from Afghanistan, as "our original goals have largely been achieved."

He was critical of a Senate-passed measure to impose tariffs on China if that country was shown to be manipulating the value of its currency for a trade advantage. "There are better, more productive ways to create jobs than to threaten a trade war with our largest trading partner," he said.

Lee grew up in Utah and Washington, D.C., and earned his undergraduate and law degrees at Brigham Young University in Utah.

After graduating from law school, he served as a law clerk for a district court judge in Utah, then for Alito, who at the time was on the U.S. Court of Appeals for the 3rd Circuit. He practiced appellate and Supreme Court litigation in D.C. before moving back to Utah to serve as an assistant U.S. attorney.

He was general counsel to Republican Gov. Jon Huntsman before returning to Washington for a one-year clerkship with Alito, who had joined the Supreme Court. It was then back to Utah to work in private practice.

Conservative activists were looking for a candidate to take on incumbent Republican Robert F. Bennett, who had supported the $700 billion financial industry rescue in 2008 and had chafed those to his right in the party with his stances on health care and immigration. The early front-runner was state Attorney General Mark Shurtleff. But citing family concerns, he withdrew a year before the election. That left Bennett to contend with Lee and businessman Tim Bridgewater.

Utah Republicans pick their candidates at a convention, using a primary as a runoff if one person does not have overwhelming support. Lee was steamed by a mailer sent to convention delegates. On the surface, it seemed to support his candidacy; it put a picture of Lee in front of the Mormon temple in Salt Lake City, and a picture of Bennett in front of the U.S. Capitol, with a line asking which candidate had Utah's values.

Many voters found the use of the religious image in a political attack offensive — but Lee hadn't sent the mailer. Tim Stewart, a longtime Bennett aide, had engineered the campaign. (He is also the brother of Chris Stewart, the new representative from the 2nd District.) Lee ended up finishing second at the convention, but still ahead of Bennett. He squeaked past Bridgewater in the primary a month later.

That was tantamount to election in heavily Republican Utah, and Lee cruised past Democrat Sam F. Granato, a Salt Lake City restaurateur, with nearly 62 percent of the vote.

Key Votes

2012	
Prohibit health insurance plans from denying coverage based on the sponsor's religious beliefs	NO
Require approval of the Keystone XL oil pipeline	YES
Ease securities rules to expand small-business access to capital	YES
Reauthorize farm and nutrition programs for five years	NO
Limit debate on a bill that would create private-sector cybersecurity standards	NO
Consent to ratification of a treaty setting global standard for the treatment of people with disabilities	NO
Provide $60.4 billion in disaster relief following Superstorm Sandy	NO
Extend most Bush-era income tax rates while allowing rates for top-bracket earners to rise (Jan. 1, 2013)	NO
2011	
Prevent EPA from regulating greenhouse gas emissions to address climate change	YES
Extend certain provisions of Patriot Act for four years	NO
Clear compromise debt limit increase plan and establish future spending limits	NO
Overhaul patent law	NO
Implement Colombia free trade agreement	YES
Limit debate on confirmation of Caitlin J. Halligan to D.C. Circuit Court of Appeals	NO
Extend payroll tax cut and unemployment benefits for two months	YES

CQ Vote Studies

	PARTY UNITY		PRESIDENTIAL SUPPORT	
	SUPPORT	OPPOSE	SUPPORT	OPPOSE
2012	91%	9%	17%	83%
2011	93%	7%	51%	49%

Interest Groups

	AFL-CIO	ADA	CCUS	ACU
2012	0%	10%	75%	100%
2011	22%	10%	73%	100%

Rep. Rob Bishop (R)

Capitol Office
225-0453
robbishop.house.gov
123 Cannon Bldg. 20515-4401; fax 225-5857

Committees
Armed Services
Natural Resources
(Public Lands and Environmental Regulations - Chairman)
Rules

Residence
Brigham City

Born
July 13, 1951; Salt Lake City, Utah

Religion
Mormon

Family
Wife, Jeralynn Bishop; five children

Education
U. of Utah, B.A. 1974 (political science)

Career
Teacher; lobbyist

Political Highlights
Utah House, 1979-95 (speaker, 1993-95); Utah Republican Party chairman, 1997-2001

ELECTION RESULTS

2012 GENERAL		
Rob Bishop (R)	175,487	71.5%
Donna M. McAleer (D)	60,611	24.7%
Sherry Phipps (CNSTP)	9,430	3.8%
2012 PRIMARY		
Rob Bishop (R)	unopposed	
2010 GENERAL		
Rob Bishop (R)	135,247	69.2%
Morgan E. Bowen (D)	46,765	23.9%
Kirk D. Pearson (CNSTP)	9,143	4.7%
Jared Paul Stratton (LIBERT)	4,307	2.2%

Previous Winning Percentages
2008 (65%); 2006 (63%); 2004 (68%); 2002 (61%)

Elected 2002; 6th term

The federal government owns huge tracts of land in Utah and neighboring states. Bishop is the House member in charge of framing Republican plans for that property, and most of his ideas are rooted in his belief that government should be as hands-off as constitutionally possible.

"The only advantage you have from the federal level is in uniformity," he said at a 2012 news conference. "If everyone has to have the exact same thing at the exact same time, Washington is the perfect place to mandate that. If you want something like helping people, then you need to involve the states in that type of approach."

Bishop has a good sense of humor, which was surely an asset when he was teaching history and government to public high school students. But he takes small-government principles seriously. In the 111th Congress (2009-10) he founded the 10th Amendment Task Force, a unit within the conservative Republican Study Committee dedicated to "federalism," which translates to dispersing federal control back to the states.

Applied to the management of public lands, federalism can result in striking policy suggestions. A former speaker of the Utah House, Bishop attended a 2012 ceremony as Gov. Gary R. Herbert signed a bill demanding that the federal government cede most public lands to the state by the end of 2014. His presence had extra meaning because he is the chairman of the Natural Resources subcommittee with jurisdiction over public lands. He has said that giving land to states would help the economy (states allow more development) and eliminate federal management costs.

Bishop has smaller designs, if those plans don't pan out. He watches the Interior Department for possible implementation of a "wild lands" policy — Bishop and his allies worry that it's an administrative way of putting public lands off-limits to economic and recreational activity without congressional approval. He was similarly put off when President Barack Obama used the century-old Antiquities Act to declare five new national monuments in 2013.

Obama signed his 2011 bill, worked on with Colorado Democratic Sen. Mark Udall, to allow the Agriculture Department to permit a wider range of sporting activities, such as skiing, in national forests.

For the 113th Congress (2013-14), Bishop's subcommittee has jurisdiction over the National Environmental Policy Act, which requires environmental impact studies for many federal agency actions. That gives Bishop more license to promote energy development on public lands and criticize the government as blocking such activity. In 2013, he and GOP Sen. David Vitter of Louisiana introduced companion bills to raise the cap on revenue that states receive from offshore energy leases.

More than once, Bishop has used a favorite metaphor to contrast GOP plans with Obama's. Speaking on the House floor in 2012, he again said White House policies would result in a future like the altered reality in "Back to the Future II," in which "Biff actually does have the sports sheets and he is able to win all those bets and get control of everything."

(Bishop likes pop culture references. Upset with Senate inaction on a fiscal 2012 budget, he wrote that "I am frustrated. 'Dancing with the Stars' would not be exciting if each participant didn't have a partner. It does indeed take two to tango.")

National security is one of the few areas where Bishop feels comfortable with the federal government staying out front; providing for the common defense is "one of the few things to which we are constitutionally bound," he says. In the 112th Congress (2011-12), that principle intermingled with his public-lands agenda, as he reintroduced a bill to exempt the Border Patrol from complying with a number of environmental restrictions when operating on public lands. The House passed a version of his measure as part of another bill, and Democrats warned of environmental disaster should it become law. Bishop maintained that the agency is hamstrung when trying to put security infrastructure along the southern border.

"I hate to say this, but the drug cartel who was coming over doesn't care about wilderness designation," he said on the House floor in 2012. "They don't care about endangered species habitat. They don't care about the endangered species — unless it can be eaten. What they do is simply leave behind all of the trash as they are coming through."

Bishop is back on the Armed Services Committee for the 113th Congress — he took a leave of absence to serve a second stint on the Rules Committee in the 112th, but GOP leaders have allowed him to serve on both committees this time around. He has lots of parochial defense concerns, with a number of military installations in the Salt Lake City area, as well as defense and NASA contractor ATK Aerospace. Bishop is a fiscal conservative, but he says he is wary of recent cuts to defense budgets.

On occasion, Bishop will put civil liberties above defense needs. In 2006, he was one of 13 Republicans to vote against a reauthorization of the anti-terrorism law known as the Patriot Act, and he opposed an extension of some of its surveillance provisions in 2011.

Bishop's father was an accountant, but he also served as mayor of Kaysville, as a GOP delegate and as a campaign volunteer. "I remember him vividly, sitting at the telephone at the kitchen table, calling delegates. I thought that everybody did that," Bishop said.

After college, Bishop taught high school English, debate and history, later adding German and Advanced Placement government courses. (He spent two years in Germany as part of his Mormon mission experience.) He believes strongly in local control of education and has introduced a plan to allow states to treat their share of federal education funding as a block grant.

Bishop was also active in community theater and coached baseball.

He continued teaching after he won election to the Utah House (a part-time legislative body). He served 16 years, the last two as speaker. He kept teaching after leaving the House, and he also worked as a part-time lobbyist and the state Republican Party chairman.

Bishop jumped into the 2002 race to succeed retiring Republican James V. Hansen in the U.S. House. He defeated state House Majority Leader Kevin S. Garn for the GOP nomination, then won the general election with 61 percent of the vote. He has had no trouble getting re-elected.

Key Votes

2012	
Extend a Social Security payroll tax cut and unemployment benefits	NO
Ease securities rules to expand small-business access to capital	YES
Extend for one year subsidized student loan interest rates financed by a cut in health care spending	YES
Cite Attorney General Eric H. Holder Jr. for contempt of Congress	YES
Create a visa program for foreign graduates in high-tech fields	YES
Extend most Bush-era income tax rates while allowing rates for top-bracket earners to rise (Jan. 1, 2013)	NO
2011	
Strike funding for F-35 alternative engine	NO
Prevent EPA from regulating greenhouse gas emissions to address climate change	YES
Extend certain provisions of Patriot Act for four years	NO
Declare opposition to use of ground troops in Libya	YES
Overhaul patent law	NO
Pass compromise debt limit increase plan and establish future spending limits	NO
Allow consideration of measures to implement three trade agreements	YES

CQ Vote Studies

	PARTY UNITY		PRESIDENTIAL SUPPORT	
	SUPPORT	OPPOSE	SUPPORT	OPPOSE
2012	96%	4%	17%	83%
2011	95%	5%	10%	90%
2010	97%	3%	26%	74%
2009	96%	4%	11%	89%
2008	96%	4%	78%	22%

Interest Groups

	AFL-CIO	ADA	CCUS	ACU
2012	17%	5%	92%	88%
2011	14%	20%	75%	95%
2010	8%	0%	88%	100%
2009	5%	0%	79%	100%
2008	8%	0%	81%	100%

Utah 1

North

In the late 1840s, Mormon pioneers led by Brigham Young journeyed into the mountainous terrain of northern Utah. Today, the 1st — covering the northernmost part of the state — retains a strongly Mormon bent. Although Salt Lake City was drawn into the 2nd and 4th districts following redistricting after the 2010 census, the 1st has held on to the steadily growing Wasatch Front cities of Logan, in Cache County, and Ogden, in Weber County. It also takes in a large portion of the Great Salt Lake and expanses of forests in the east and desert in the west.

Ogden was once a lively railroad town but today includes facilities for car safety systems manufacturer Autoliv and the IRS, which operates a call center downtown. Defense jobs are important to the 1st's economy: Hill Air Force Base, just south of Ogden in Davis County, is one of the state's largest employers; the 1st, not surprisingly, hosts the most civilian veterans among the state's four districts. To the northwest, Proctor & Gamble operates a plant in Box Elder County.

The 1st contains much of the north-central Utah ski country, including Park City, a wealthy and liberal resort town southeast of Salt Lake City. Farming is key in eastern Box Elder County, and the main campus of Utah State University, which has agricultural centers throughout the region, is in Logan.

The wealthy suburbs in Davis County combine with strongly Republican rural areas to put the district firmly in GOP hands. Republican Mike Lee cruised to the U.S. Senate in 2010, earning particularly wide margins in Uintah and Duchesne counties — he was held to a narrower win in Park City's Summit County. Republican Mitt Romney — whose mother was a native of Logan — earned 77 percent of the district's vote in the 2012 presidential election.

Major Industry
Manufacturing, defense, agriculture, tourism

Military Bases
Hill Air Force Base, 4,341 military, 12,534 civilian (2012)

Cities
Ogden, Layton, Logan

Notable
The Sundance Film Festival is held annually in Park City; Bear Lake, shared with Idaho, is called the "Caribbean of the Rockies" for its turquoise color.

Rep. Chris Stewart (R)

Capitol Office
225-9730
stewart.house.gov
323 Cannon Bldg. 20515-0924; fax 225-5629

Committees
Homeland Security
Natural Resources
Science, Space & Technology
(Environment - Chairman)

Residence
Farmington

Born
July 15, 1960; Logan, Utah

Religion
Mormon

Family
Wife, Evie Stewart; six children

Education
Utah State U., B.S. 1984 (economics)

Military
Air Force, 1984-98

Career
Management and leadership consulting company executive; author

Political Highlights
No previous office

ELECTION RESULTS

2012 GENERAL		
Chris Stewart (R)	154,523	62.2%
Jay Seegmiller (D)	83,176	33.5%
Jonathan D. Garrard (CNSTP)	5,051	2.0%
Joseph Andrade (NPA)	2,971	1.2%
Charles E. Kimball (NPA)	2,824	1.1%
2012 PRIMARY		
Chris Stewart (R)		unopposed

Elected 2012; 1st term

In the spirit of his best-sellers, here are seven points about Stewart:

1) He's one of 10 children of an Air Force pilot. On leaving the service, his father settled on a dairy farm — where Stewart was raised — and also worked as a teacher. The family is Mormon, and Stewart has six kids of his own.

2) After college, he joined the Air Force himself. In a 14-year career, he flew helicopters and bombers, and he helped set the record for the fastest nonstop flight around the world. He now sits on the Homeland Security Committee.

3) He became an accomplished author upon leaving the service. Media host Glenn Beck helped catapult "The Miracle of Freedom: Seven Tipping Points that Saved the World," to the New York Times best-seller list. Stewart also wrote "Seven Miracles that Saved America" and several techno-thrillers.

4) He is new to politics. Stewart said he couldn't "stand on the sidelines" any longer because the United States is facing a "financial tipping point." He beat out numerous candidates at the state GOP nominating convention and easily won the heavily Republican district. But his brother Tim was once an aide to GOP Sen. Robert F. Bennett, and in the 2010 campaign, Tim reportedly was involved in a campaign to make it seem as though Mike Lee was questioning Bennett's Mormon faith. Lee defeated Bennett.

5) He is the chairman of the Science, Space and Technology Subcommittee on Environment. Energy policy "has the potential of changing the world in a very positive way," he says. He also was the CEO of a consulting company where environmental compliance was a big part of the business. He contends that many Obama administration rules are based on "controversial scientific assertions and conclusions."

6) He also sits on the Natural Resources Committee, which ties in to energy and economic development on public lands (which make up most of Utah).

7) On joining the 113th Congress (2013-14), he became a member of the conservative Republican Study Committee.

Utah 2

Most of Salt Lake City; southwest

Taking in the southern reaches of the Great Salt Lake, the 2nd District grabs all but a tiny slice of Salt Lake City and covers federally owned and rural land to the state's southwestern corner. Remapping following the 2010 census combined the urban state capital and some of its western suburbs with deserts and national parks into the state's geographically largest district.

Salt Lake City is the district's population center. The focal point of the Mormon faith, the city's Temple Square includes the Tabernacle and the headquarters of the Church of Jesus Christ of Latter-day Saints. Salt Lake City International Airport also is in the 1st, as is the EnergySolutions Arena, home to basketball's Jazz. Private firms are pushing for "smart growth" initiatives for the city, including the expansion of commuter rail to outlying suburbs and development of convention and tourism districts. Salt Lake City boasts an unemployment rate below 5 percent.

In the southwestern corner of the state, Washington was Utah's second fastest-growing county from 2000 to 2010, and St. George has attracted retirees for decades. Land-use issues are also important in the 2nd. Despite employment growth in the health care and education sectors, parts of the 2nd, including Washington as a whole, have struggled more than the rest of the state, and unemployment rates have hovered near the double digits.

Many areas of Salt Lake City lean Democratic at the state and federal levels, but wealthy suburbs in heavily populated Salt Lake and Davis counties give the district its solid Republican lean. Most of the rural areas strongly favor Republicans, and GOP nominee Mitt Romney took large margins in the 2nd (68 percent overall) as he won every county in the state in the 2012 presidential election.

Major Industry
Government, technology, ranching, mining, distribution, manufacturing

Military Bases
Dugway Proving Ground, 401 military, 717 civilian (2012); Tooele Army Depot, 2 military, 524 civilian (2012)

Cities
Salt Lake City (pt.), West Valley City (pt.), St. George

Notable
Antelope Island in the Great Salt Lake, the largest saltwater lake in the Western Hemisphere, hosts reintroduced populations of the namesake wildlife.

Rep. Jason Chaffetz (R)

Capitol Office
225-7751
chaffetz.house.gov
2464 Rayburn Bldg. 20515-4403; fax 225-5629

Committees
Homeland Security
Judiciary
Oversight & Government Reform
(National Security - Chairman)

Residence
Alpine

Born
March 26, 1967; Los Gatos, Calif.

Religion
Mormon

Family
Wife, Julie Chaffetz; three children

Education
Brigham Young U., B.A. 1989 (communications)

Career
Public relations firm owner; gubernatorial and campaign aide; pharmaceutical company marketing executive; alternative fuel company marketing executive; personal care products company executive

Political Highlights
Utah Valley University Board of Trustees, 2007-08

ELECTION RESULTS

2012 GENERAL		
Jason Chaffetz (R)	198,828	76.6%
Soren Simonsen (D)	60,719	23.4%
2012 PRIMARY		
Jason Chaffetz (R)		unopposed
2010 GENERAL		
Jason Chaffetz (R)	139,721	72.3%
Karen Hyer (D)	44,320	22.9%
Douglas Sligting (CNSTP)	4,596	2.4%
Jake Shannon (LIBERT)	2,945	1.5%

Previous Winning Percentages
2008 (66%)

Elected 2008; 3rd term

One of the more visible and younger conservatives, Chaffetz has designs on amassing power, whether in the House, Utah or elsewhere. He enjoys his overseer's role, and he's also an enthusiastic participant when Congress considers technology and security.

In 2011, Chaffetz (CHAY-fits) became the chairman of the Oversight and Government Reform subcommittee on homeland and national security. He admits to being "very vocal" with GOP leaders about wanting to lead the full committee someday. "Inevitably there's always somebody doing something stupid, and Congress has a constitutional duty to hold the administration accountable," he told the Deseret Morning News. "I love that 'good government, good use of taxpayer resources,' the whole gambit. I love all of it."

He has also reportedly been interested in chairing the Budget Committee, running for the Senate and running for governor. He was a big supporter of Mitt Romney's 2012 presidential campaign, and he didn't rule out serving in the executive branch if Romney won. He is, in short, an ambitious guy.

From his subcommittee, he has pushed for a less-intrusive government — the Transportation Security Administration is a frequent target. Chaffetz criticized the TSA for security breaches, pat-downs and its plan to use imaging machines instead of explosive-sniffing dogs. In 2011, after a TSA screener frisked a 6-year-old, he introduced legislation requiring the agency to seek parental consent before searching a child.

Chaffetz was added to the Homeland Security Committee at the start of the 113th Congress (2013-14), and he sits on its panels for cybersecurity and counterterrorism. He also continues to serve on the Judiciary Committee and its panels on the Internet, terrorism and homeland security.

From those vantage points, he can look into technology issues — whether it means promoting high-tech solutions to security problems, or addressing some of the intellectual property and privacy conundrums of the digital age. For the 2014 campaign cycle, he is also studying the political uses of technology as the "vice chairman for digital" at the National Republican Congressional Committee, the campaign arm of the House GOP.

The expanded use of GPS tracking has set off alarms among civil liberties advocates, Chaffetz included. He has introduced a bill to require law enforcement to show probable cause and obtain a search warrant to track suspects using geolocation information involving cellphones and GPS devices.

Chaffetz also is concerned that intellectual property policies haven't kept up with the times. He and Colorado Democrat Jared Polis have proposed a bill to equalize the royalty rates paid by Internet-based radio services with those paid by other digital providers — rates for the Internet were statutorily set much higher, at a time when Internet radio hardly existed. A coalition of recording artists and record companies vehemently opposes the change.

He and Oregon Democrat Peter A. DeFazio have worked on legislation to discourage "patent trolls," companies that obtain patent rights only to sue other businesses for licensing fees. Their plan is to make the losers of many patent suits pay all the litigation costs, to discourage frivolous filings.

His seats on the Judiciary and Homeland Security committees also put him in the middle of immigration discussions. Chaffetz opposes offering a path toward citizenship for illegal immigrants, a position that resonates with Utah voters — that was a key stance that propelled Chaffetz to victory in a 2008 primary against Republican Rep. Chris Cannon.

Still, the House passed his 2011 bill to eliminate country-based caps on the annual number of employment visas and boost similar limits for immigrants sponsored by a spouse or relative in the United States. He introduced a similar measure in 2013.

Chaffetz has tried to highlight perceived areas of waste, fraud and abuse. In 2012, the House passed his bill to create a pilot program for the disposal of unused federal properties; he introduced another version in 2013. He has proposed several measures to deny federal employment or contracts to people or businesses late paying their taxes.

He also is involved in big-picture spending debates. In the 112th Congress (2011-12) he was a member of the Budget Committee, and the lead sponsor of a conservative-favored measure known as "Cut, Cap and Balance." It would have cut fiscal 2012 spending by $111 billion, limited future spending to a percentage of the gross domestic product and required that a balanced-budget constitutional amendment be submitted to the states before limits on federal borrowing were raised.

The House passed the bill, which many Republicans cited as their preferred fiscal plan. Chaffetz and 65 other Republicans in the House opposed the less-stringent compromise plan enacted in August. He said its potential $2.4 trillion in cuts were "not deep enough."

Chaffetz is willing to extend budget-cutting to defense accounts, which he feels are just as susceptible to waste and abuse. "Everything has to be on the table," he said. "We're in fiscal peril. We've got to come to that realization." He offered an amendment with Vermont Democrat Peter Welch to the fiscal 2012 defense policy bill that would require U.S. ground troops to withdraw from Afghanistan, leaving in place just those who are involved in small, targeted counterterrorism operations.

His family moved around when he was a boy, and Chaffetz eventually went to play football as a placekicker at Brigham Young University. His father's first wife was Kitty Dickson, who later married Massachusetts Gov. Michael S. Dukakis. While in college, Chaffetz — then a Democrat — was a Utah co-chairman of Dukakis' 1988 presidential campaign.

Inspired by President Ronald Reagan, Chaffetz became a Republican after college and continued to dabble in politics. He worked 11 years for Nu Skin Enterprises, mostly as a spokesman; a few years later, he and his brother formed a corporate communications and marketing firm, Maxtera Inc., before Chaffetz went into politics full time.

He worked on Jon Huntsman Jr.'s gubernatorial campaign in 2003—first as communications director then as campaign manager. When Huntsman won in 2004, he named Chaffetz his chief of staff. He resigned less than a year later and went back into corporate communications until his 2007 decision to run against Cannon. Since that primary, his elections have been easy wins.

Key Votes

2012	
Extend a Social Security payroll tax cut and unemployment benefits	NO
Ease securities rules to expand small-business access to capital	YES
Extend for one year subsidized student loan interest rates financed by a cut in health care spending	YES
Cite Attorney General Eric H. Holder Jr. for contempt of Congress	YES
Create a visa program for foreign graduates in high-tech fields	YES
Extend most Bush-era income tax rates while allowing rates for top-bracket earners to rise (Jan. 1, 2013)	NO
2011	
Strike funding for F-35 alternative engine	NO
Prevent EPA from regulating greenhouse gas emissions to address climate change	YES
Extend certain provisions of Patriot Act for four years	NO
Declare opposition to use of ground troops in Libya	YES
Overhaul patent law	NO
Pass compromise debt limit increase plan and establish future spending limits	NO
Allow consideration of measures to implement three trade agreements	YES

CQ Vote Studies

	PARTY UNITY		PRESIDENTIAL SUPPORT	
	SUPPORT	OPPOSE	SUPPORT	OPPOSE
2012	96%	4%	17%	83%
2011	95%	5%	15%	85%
2010	93%	7%	21%	79%
2009	96%	4%	11%	89%

Interest Groups

	AFL-CIO	ADA	CCUS	ACU
2012	10%	5%	92%	88%
2011	0%	15%	87%	100%
2010	0%	10%	75%	100%
2009	5%	0%	80%	100%

Utah 3

Southern Wasatch Front and rural southeast

Taking in plateaus, towering cliffs, forests and mountain trails, the 3rd cuts diagonally from east of Salt Lake City southeast to Four Corners. Although decennial remapping cut most of the Salt Lake City area out of this district — formerly numbered the 2nd — the current 3rd District still sweeps in some of its bedroom communities and slides down much of the Wasatch Front, taking in Sandy, Draper, Orem and Provo.

Populous Provo's predominately Mormon Brigham Young University is one of the state's largest employers and is home to more than 30,000 students. BYU and nearby colleges continue to lure businesses to Utah County's thriving Provo-Orem area. Some big-name software firms maintain key facilities here, and companies in the dietary supplement and health care industries have headquarters in the 3rd. Utah's National Guard headquarters are in the Salt Lake County portion of Draper. In less-populated Grand County, on the eastern edge of the state, artists and residents who rely on seasonal tourism-based jobs populate Moab, a haven for outdoor enthusiasts.

In contrast to Utah County's prosperity, large swathes of the 3rd struggle economically. Nearly 30 percent of residents in San Juan County, home to part of the Navajo Nation, live in poverty, by far the highest percentage in the state. The 3rd also takes in counties with Utah's highest unemployment rates.

The 3rd is GOP territory. Grand County can provide some Democratic votes. In the 2012 presidential election, Grand gave Democrat Barack Obama his second-highest percentage in the state (44 percent), as he lost statewide by large margins to GOP nominee Mitt Romney; Romney, however, took his highest percentage statewide in the 3rd overall (78 percent). Republican Rep. Jason Chaffetz only won Grand by a few dozen votes while surpassing 75 percent in the district overall.

Major Industry
Higher education, technology, tourism

Cities
Provo, Orem, Sandy (pt.)

Notable
Philo T. Farnsworth, credited with inventing television, lived in Provo; San Juan County includes Utah's portion of Monument Valley.

Rep. Jim Matheson (D)

Capitol Office
225-3011
matheson.house.gov
2211 Rayburn Bldg. 20515-4402; fax 225-5638

Committees
Energy & Commerce

Residence
Salt Lake City

Born
March 21, 1960; Salt Lake City, Utah

Religion
Mormon

Family
Wife, Amy Matheson; two children

Education
Harvard U., A.B. 1982 (government); U. of California, Los Angeles, M.B.A. 1987

Career
Energy consulting firm owner; energy company project manager; environmental policy think tank advocate

Political Highlights
No previous office

ELECTION RESULTS

2012 GENERAL		
Jim Matheson (D)	119,803	48.8%
Mia Love (R)	119,035	48.5%
Jim L. Vein (LIBERT)	6,439	2.6%
2012 PRIMARY		
Jim Matheson (D)		unopposed
2010 GENERAL		
Jim Matheson (D)	127,151	50.5%
Morgan Philpot (R)	116,001	46.1%
Randall Hinton (CNSTP)	4,578	1.8%

Previous Winning Percentages
2008 (63%); 2006 (59%); 2004 (55%); 2002 (49%); 2000 (56%)

Elected 2000; 7th term

Matheson marshaled all of his political talents in 2012 to remain the only Democrat in the congressional delegation of what could be America's reddest state. His business-focused, fiscally conservative views often put him in agreement with Republicans — who will nonetheless keep gunning for his seat.

Matheson considers his father, the late Utah Gov. Scott Matheson, to be his political hero. "He set the example for how you behave in politics," he said. "You try to get people together and solve problems. It's not really a complicated equation. ... Dad would tell me he knew that when he was being beat up by both the left and the right he was doing the right thing."

If there's truth to that wisdom, then Matheson was doing the right thing in the 112th Congress (2011-12). He started out by voting against Democratic leader Nancy Pelosi in the election of the speaker of the House. Even so, Matheson was named a chief deputy whip for House Democrats — then spent 2011 and 2012 splitting with a majority of his party on considerably more than half of the votes where they opposed most Republicans.

Republicans still came after him in 2012. Running in Utah's new 4th District, he faced Saratoga Springs Mayor Mia Love, an African-American convert to Mormonism and one of the GOP's most touted emerging stars. Matheson was endorsed by the U.S. Chamber of Commerce and John Huntsman Sr., father of the former governor and Republican presidential candidate. He eked out a 768-vote victory to secure both a seventh term and his reputation as one of the more astute political number-crunchers in Congress. Matheson started the 113th Congress (2013-14) by voting against Pelosi again.

The genial Matheson is budget-conscious in life — he reportedly calls around to find the cheapest dry cleaner — and especially in politics. He is a member of the Blue Dog Coalition of fiscally conservative Democrats. He was in the minority of his party in voting for a balanced-budget amendment to the Constitution in 2011, and he was one of only four House Democrats to vote for a disapproval resolution when President Barack Obama raised the federal debt limit in September 2011.

At the close of the 112th Congress, he was one of 16 House Democrats to vote against the "fiscal cliff" deal that extended lower income tax rates on earnings under $400,000. Matheson was one of the Democrats who voted for those lower tax rates in 2001 and 2003, but he said the January 2013 bill should have included "a strong framework for real deficit reduction."

Matheson sits on the Energy and Commerce Committee, and in the 112th he agreed with some GOP measures to rein in federal regulations and expand domestic energy production. He voted for a 2011 bill to bar the EPA from regulating greenhouse gases in an effort to address climate change. In 2012, he voiced support for construction of the Keystone XL pipeline from Canada to Texas, more offshore drilling, and a package of measures meant to stop rules and regulations that could impede the coal industry.

But Matheson also pursues Democratic and nonpartisan goals. He sponsored bipartisan legislation in the 112th to accelerate the production and use of natural-gas-fueled cars and trucks, and a bill to track the supply chain of pharmaceuticals from manufacturing to sale.

"The majority needs to be inclusive and the minority needs to be constructive for bipartisanship things to work," Matheson said in 2012. "That's something not always remembered around here ... on both sides."

The federal government is the biggest landlord in Utah, and Matheson has worked well with Republicans to petition the landlord. He and former Utah GOP Sen. Robert F. Bennett worked for years on a bill to set development guidelines for Washington County, the southwestern corner of the state that includes most of Zion National Park. It was enacted as part of a 2009 omnibus lands law. Matheson has criticized the Bureau of Land Management for creating national monuments in the West without local input.

Matheson approves of the Obama administration's efforts to shut down the planned nuclear waste dump at Nevada's Yucca Mountain. He has also joined with Utah Republicans in an effort to win resumption of federal compensation to people who became ill as a result of exposure to radiation from atomic bomb testing in Nevada. Compensation for those "downwinders" ended in 2000. The issue resonates with Matheson, whose father died in 1990 of bone marrow cancer, a disease linked to radiation exposure. He had lived in an area of southern Utah affected by the nuclear tests.

On education and labor issues, Matheson usually goes along with Democrats. He also signed off on some of his party's major legislative accomplishments of recent years. He supported the $787 billion economic stimulus law in 2009, believing it would boost job creation, and a 2010 overhaul of financial regulations. But he opposed the 2010 health care law, saying it did not do enough to control costs. He declined to vote for its repeal in 2011, but when Republicans called another repeal vote in 2012, Matheson was one of five House Democrats to vote "yes."

Matheson's ancestors converted to Mormonism in Dundee, Scotland, and settled in southern Utah in the 1850s. His grandfather was the first member of the family to graduate from high school; he was appointed U.S. attorney by President Harry S. Truman. Matheson's older brother Scott is a federal judge on the U.S. Court of Appeals for the 10th Circuit.

Matheson considers his mother, who still lives four houses away and has been involved in countless civic projects, to be his conscience. "We speak almost every day. She's my political sounding board," he says.

While majoring in government at Harvard, Matheson served a summer internship in the office of House Speaker Thomas P. O'Neill Jr. After college, he worked at an environmental policy think tank in Washington for three years, got an MBA and returned to Utah. He eventually started an energy consulting business.

In 2000, Matheson ran for Congress against executive Derek Smith, who, after some bad press over his past business practices, lost by 15 points. Republican state Rep. John Swallow came within 1,641 votes of Matheson in 2002, but the next four elections were relatively easy wins.

In 2010, he was forced into a primary by Democrats dissatisfied with his centrism. He prevailed by a 2-1 margin, however, and in November he beat former GOP state Rep. Morgan Philpot by 4 points.

Key Votes

2012	
Extend a Social Security payroll tax cut and unemployment benefits	YES
Ease securities rules to expand small-business access to capital	YES
Extend for one year subsidized student loan interest rates financed by a cut in health care spending	YES
Cite Attorney General Eric H. Holder Jr. for contempt of Congress	YES
Create a visa program for foreign graduates in high-tech fields	YES
Extend most Bush-era income tax rates while allowing rates for top-bracket earners to rise (Jan. 1, 2013)	NO
2011	
Strike funding for F-35 alternative engine	YES
Prevent EPA from regulating greenhouse gas emissions to address climate change	YES
Extend certain provisions of Patriot Act for four years	YES
Declare opposition to use of ground troops in Libya	YES
Overhaul patent law	YES
Pass compromise debt limit increase plan and establish future spending limits	YES
Allow consideration of measures to implement three trade agreements	YES

CQ Vote Studies

	PARTY UNITY		PRESIDENTIAL SUPPORT	
	SUPPORT	OPPOSE	SUPPORT	OPPOSE
2012	32%	68%	31%	69%
2011	47%	53%	58%	42%
2010	82%	18%	74%	26%
2009	84%	16%	75%	25%
2008	86%	14%	32%	68%

Interest Groups

	AFL-CIO	ADA	CCUS	ACU
2012	57%	20%	100%	56%
2011	66%	60%	88%	41%
2010	71%	60%	75%	17%
2009	67%	55%	80%	24%
2008	67%	55%	78%	36%

Utah 4

Central

The 4th is the geographically smallest district, mostly carved out of populous Salt Lake and Utah counties during redistricting after Utah gained a U.S. House seat following the 2010 census. From South Salt Lake, the L-shaped district follows Interstate 15 south through growing exurbs, swallows up almost all of the mountain-lined Utah Lake, and stretches to the rural areas near Mount Pleasant.

Salt Lake County's Latino population has boomed since 2000, and the 4th has the state's highest proportion of Hispanic residents (16 percent). Overall the district remains majority white and heavily Mormon — Brigham Young University is nearby in the 3rd. Filling in Salt Lake City's bedroom communities with families, the district's residents are also relatively young.

West Jordan, 13 miles south of Salt Lake City, is the fourth largest city in the state and its population growth is supported by the construction sector and health care and education jobs. Dannon also expanded a yogurt plant in the city. Mining is important in the 4th — to the west, the Bingham Canyon copper mine is among the deepest open-pit mines in the world.

Parts of the district near Bluffdale, in the southern stretch of Salt Lake exurbs, experienced 50 percent population growth between 2000 and 2010. The National Security Agency is also building a data center near the town.

Agriculture is a mainstay of the district's economy. Despite losing some influence to the north, the traditional economic foundation remains important in the district's more rural, less populated south.

Expected to support GOP candidates at the federal level, the new 4th was drawn by a Republican-controlled legislature in 2011 to reduce the impact of Democratic voters in Salt Lake County. Democratic Rep. Jim Matheson held on to his U.S. House seat with a slim plurality against GOP nominee Mia Love by taking a majority in the district's portion of Salt Lake County while losing in the 4th's portions of Juab, Sanpete and Utah counties. Mitt Romney took 67 percent of the 4th's vote in the 2012 presidential election.

Major Industry
Government, agriculture, mining, construction, manufacturing

Cities
Salt Lake City (pt.), West Valley City (pt.), West Jordan, Sandy (pt.)

Notable
Rio Tinto Stadium in Sandy hosts soccer's Real Salt Lake.

VERMONT

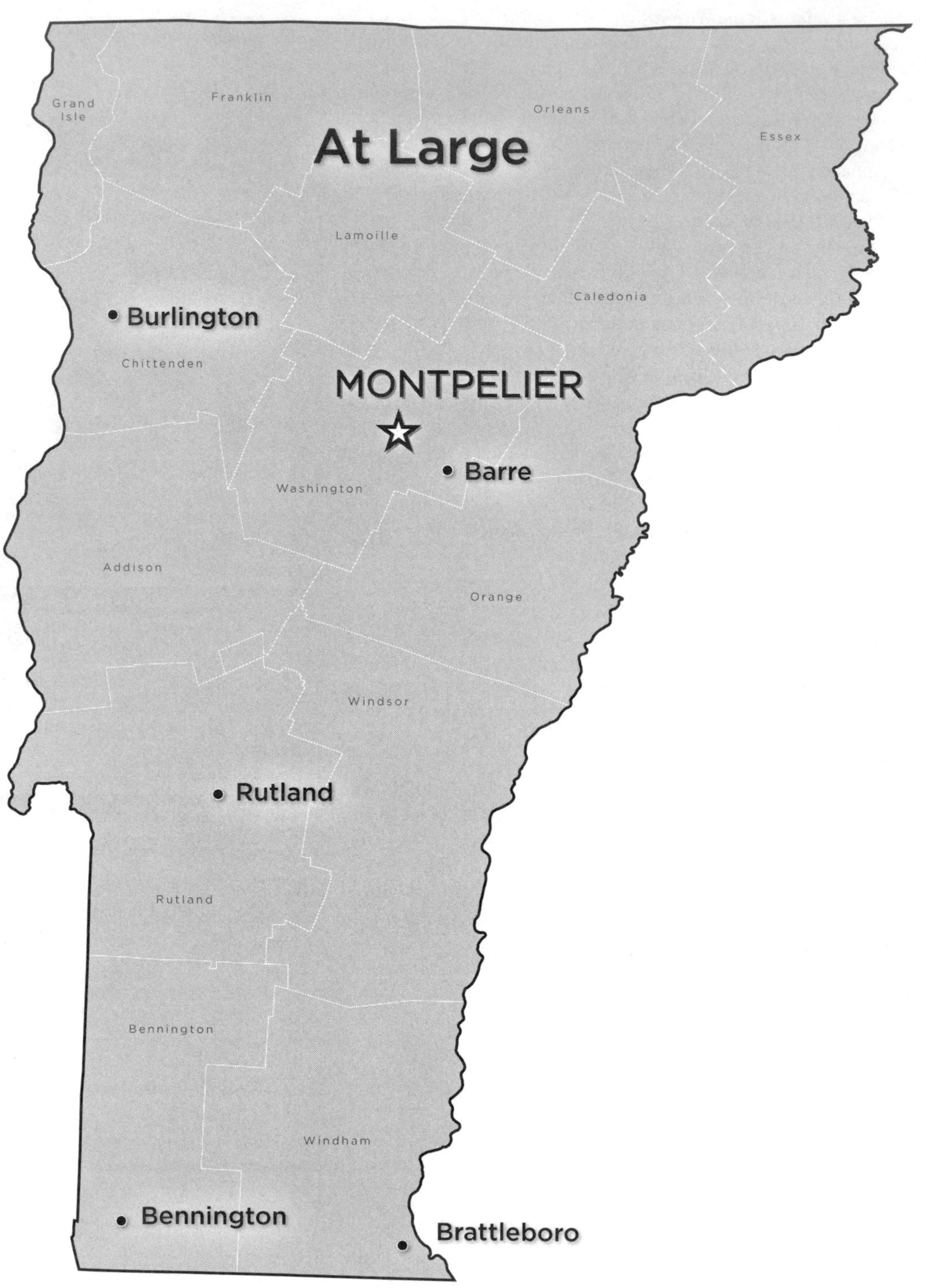

Grand Isle
Franklin
Orleans
Essex
At Large
Lamoille
Caledonia
Burlington
Chittenden
MONTPELIER
Barre
Washington
Addison
Orange
Windsor
Rutland
Rutland
Bennington
Windham
Bennington
Brattleboro

Gov. Peter Shumlin (D)

First elected: 2010

Length of term: 2 years

Term expires: 1/13

Salary: $142,542

Phone: (802) 828-3333

Residence: Putney

Born: March 24, 1956; Brattleboro, Vt.

Religion: Unspecified

Family: Divorced; two children

Education: Wesleyan U., B.A. 1979 (government)

Career: Travel organization director; dairy farm owner

Political highlights: Putney Board of Selectmen, 1983-90 (chairman, 1983-90); Vt. House, 1989-93; Vt. Senate, 1993-2003 (minority leader, 1995-96; president pro tempore, 1997-2003); Democratic nominee for lieutenant governor, 2002; Vt. Senate, 2007-11 (president pro tempore, 2007-11)

ELECTION RESULTS

2012 GENERAL

Peter Shumlin (D)	170749	57.8%
Randy Brock (R)	110940	37.6%
Others	13,723	4.6%

Lt. Gov. Phil Scott (R)

First elected: 2010

Length of term: 2 years

Term expires: 1/13

Salary: $60,507

Phone: (802) 828-2226

LEGISLATURE

General Assembly: January-April

Senate: 30 members, 2-year terms

2013 ratios: 20 D, 7 R, 1 PRO, 2 other; 21 men, 9 women

Salary: $647/week

Phone: (802) 828-2241

House: 150 members, 2-year terms

2013 ratios: 93 D, 33 R, 23 other, 1 PRO; 86 men, 64 women

Salary: $647/week

Phone: (802) 828-2247

TERM LIMITS

Governor: No

Senate: No

House: No

URBAN STATISTICS

CITY	POPULATION
Burlington	42,417
Essex	19,587
South Burlington	17,904
Colchester	17,067
Rutland	16,495

REGISTERED VOTERS

Voters do not register by party.

POPULATION

2010 population	625,741
2000 population	608,827
1990 population	562,758
Percent change (2000-2010)	+2.8%
Rank among states (2010)	49
Median age	40.6
Born in state	52.2%
Foreign born	3.7%
Violent crime rate	131/100,000
Poverty level	11.4%
Federal workers	6,917
Military	565

ELECTIONS

STATE ELECTION OFFICIAL
(802) 828-2464

DEMOCRATIC PARTY
(802) 229-1783

REPUBLICAN PARTY
(802) 223-3411

MISCELLANEOUS

Web: www.vermont.gov

Capital: Montpelier

U.S. CONGRESS

Senate: 1 Democrat, 1 Independent

House: 1 Democrat

STATISTICS BY DISTRICT

District	2012 Vote for President		2008 Vote for President										
	Obama	Romney	Obama	McCain	Black	Asian	Hispanic	Median Income	Over 64	Under 20	College Education	Rural	Sq. Miles
AL	67%	31%	67%	30%	1%	1%	1%	$52,776	15%	23%	35%	67%	9,217
STATE	67	31	67	30	1	1	1	52,776	15	23	35	67	9,217
U.S.	51	47	53	46	12	5	17	50,052	13	27	29	21	3,531,905

Sen. Patrick J. Leahy (D)

Capitol Office
224-4242
leahy.senate.gov
437 Russell Bldg. 20510-4502; fax 224-3479

Committees
Agriculture, Nutrition & Forestry
Appropriations
(State-Foreign Operations - Chairman)
Judiciary - Chairman
Rules & Administration
Joint Library

Residence
Middlesex

Born
March 31, 1940; Montpelier, Vt.

Religion
Roman Catholic

Family
Wife, Marcelle Leahy; three children

Education
St. Michael's College, B.A. 1961 (political science); Georgetown U., J.D. 1964

Career
Lawyer

Political Highlights
Chittenden County state's attorney, 1966-75

ELECTION RESULTS

2010 GENERAL		
Patrick J. Leahy (D)	151,281	64.3%
Len Britton (R)	72,699	30.9%
Daniel Freilich (I)	3,544	1.5%
Cris Ericson (USM)	2,731	1.2%
Stephen J. Cain (I)	2,356	1.0%
2010 PRIMARY		
Patrick J. Leahy (D)	64,515	89.1%
Daniel Freilich (D)	7,892	10.9%

Previous Winning Percentages
2004 (71%); 1998 (72%); 1992 (54%); 1986 (63%); 1980 (50%); 1974 (50%)

Elected 1974; 7th term

Leahy, the most senior senator, has mastered the art of being partisan, pragmatic or patient, as circumstances require. His wry humor and jovial demeanor have helped him withstand the rigors of chairing the Judiciary Committee, one of the busiest and most divisive panels in Congress.

His patience came into play in the 112th Congress (2011-12), as a years-long effort finally bore fruit: In 2011, President Barack Obama signed the first major rewrite of U.S. patent law in decades. Leahy and Texas Republican Rep. Lamar Smith led the charge, bringing U.S. standards closer to international norms — most notably by changing a "first to invent" system to a "first to file" system, in which the first party to file paperwork receives the patent.

Opponents say that the law now favors large companies over small inventors with fewer bureaucratic resources; Leahy maintains that it will foster innovation, speed the processing of applications and bolster the economy.

Leahy is a liberal, and in the 112th he willingly took up partisan causes that were likely to fail in the Republican House. He led a push for a reauthorization of federal programs to prosecute domestic and sexual violence crimes. House conservatives balked, as the usually noncontroversial measure included expansions of some protections to illegal immigrants and gay victims. Leahy rode out the uproar and won another battle — after a tepid showing in the 2012 elections and facing the increasing perception that their party is hostile to women, House Republican leaders were ready to pass the bill over the objections of conservatives. It was enacted in the early months of the 113th Congress (2013-14).

And judicial nominations, particularly for the Supreme Court, have shown Leahy's pragmatic side. He has been on the Judiciary Committee since 1979, and he has participated in confirmation hearings for every sitting Supreme Court justice. Democrats sometimes call him too accommodating on GOP choices, and Republicans sometimes roll their eyes at his opposition.

He backed John G. Roberts Jr., President George W. Bush's nominee for chief justice, but opposed conservative nominee Samuel A. Alito Jr. In 2009, he praised Sonia Sotomayor — Obama's first Supreme Court nominee — as a "restrained, experienced and thoughtful judge." A year later he went to bat for former Harvard Law School dean Elena Kagan, who had never served as a judge of any kind. Leahy has been a longtime proponent of looking beyond federal appellate courts for Supreme Court nominees.

Leahy uses the Judiciary Committee to defend open government and his version of the correct balance between security and civil liberties. He was Judiciary chairman during the Sept. 11 terrorist attacks, and he had a hand in the first major law enacted in response: the 2001 anti-terrorism law known as the Patriot Act. "As draconian as it was, the terrorism bill was far more constitutional than it would have been had I not been chairman," he said.

He opposed the U.S. invasion of Iraq, and he was a frequent critic of Bush's conduct of the war and of related policies in the war on terrorism, such as detainee and interrogation policies. He fell short in his effort to add stronger oversight provisions to an update of the Foreign Intelligence Surveillance Act in late 2012. And in 2013, he and Utah Republican Mike Lee rolled out a bill to set a uniform standard requiring a warrant to access individuals' email and other electronic data.

One marquee issue found Leahy and Bush working together: immigration. "I'd love to see a comprehensive immigration bill," including a path to citizenship for those in the country illegally, Leahy said in 2012.

By April 2013, such a bill had been referred to his committee. He has a few personal preferences for any overhaul: allowing visas for same-sex couples, and making sure that temporary work visa programs are suited to Vermont's dairy industry.

He also looks out for his state's farmers on the Agriculture, Nutrition and Forestry Committee, which he chaired for eight years starting in the late 1980s. He defends Northeastern dairy farmers during conflicts with other dairy-producing regions. In 2008, he engineered the renewal of the Milk Income Loss Contract Program, a price-support subsidy for dairy farmers.

Leahy is a member of the Appropriations Committee, and he had the option of being its top Democrat after the December 2012 death of Chairman Daniel K. Inouye of Hawaii. He opted to remain the Judiciary chairman.

But he still holds the gavel of the State-Foreign Operations Appropriations Subcommittee. He has sought to increase spending for humanitarian efforts overseas, and he has been critical of proposals to trim foreign assistance. He has long campaigned against the use of land mines. The Leahy War Victims Fund, established as part of the foreign aid budget in 1989, provides millions of dollars in aid each year to civilian victims of armed conflict.

He broke with the Obama administration when it waived conditions on aid to Egypt that were put in place after that nation's Arab Spring uprising. Leahy had co-written language in a fiscal 2012 spending law withholding military aid until the administration certified that the government in Cairo is upholding democracy and protecting human rights and civil liberties.

Leahy has an intriguing assortment of cultural interests. He is a devotee of the band the Grateful Dead, and he delivered a eulogy at the 1981 funeral of folk-rock musician Harry Chapin, a good friend. Despite limited vision in one eye, he is an avid photographer who has taken his camera all over the world — his work has been published in newspapers and magazines. In his office, photos abound, with subjects ranging from a Bill Clinton bill-signing to kids flying a kite from a clifftop in Turkey to the view from Leahy's front porch in Vermont.

He is also a die-hard Batman fan, with cameos in Batman movies released in 2008 and 2012. He jokes that his "good looks and thick head of hair" got him the parts; actually, his roles stem from his collaboration on Batman and Superman comic books used to educate children of the dangers of land mines. "The Batman one was on the desk of every single senator who came to the vote on banning the export of land mines," he said.

Leahy and his wife live on a tree farm in Middlesex. Their 19th-century farmhouse boasts "one of the prettiest views in all of central Vermont," he says. His oldest son and his daughter-in-law live nearby, and "grandchildren come skipping down the road to visit."

His father was an Irish-American who ran a printing business in Montpelier out of the same building that housed the family. When he went to school, Leahy walked by, and sometimes through, the state Capitol. His mother rented rooms to lawmakers when the legislature was in session. Members of his mother's family — Italian immigrants — worked in Vermont's granite quarries.

Leahy's first exposure to the Senate was in the early 1960s when he was a student at Georgetown University's law school. Aiming to be a prosecutor or a U.S. senator, he ended up doing both, serving as a local prosecutor for eight years before being elected to the Senate in 1974. A Watergate-fueled voter backlash helped him beat a favored Republican. At 34, he was the youngest elected senator in state history.

He withstood the GOP landslide of 1980 to win his first re-election by just 2,755 votes. Subsequent victories have been easy, thanks in part to the retail politics of the small rural state. "If I'm in the grocery store, or putting gas in my car, or coming out of church, or whatever, everybody calls me by my first name," he says.

Key Votes

2012	
Prohibit health insurance plans from denying coverage based on the sponsor's religious beliefs	YES
Require approval of the Keystone XL oil pipeline	NO
Ease securities rules to expand small-business access to capital	NO
Reauthorize farm and nutrition programs for five years	YES
Limit debate on a bill that would create private-sector cybersecurity standards	YES
Consent to ratification of a treaty setting global standard for the treatment of people with disabilities	YES
Provide $60.4 billion in disaster relief following Superstorm Sandy	YES
Extend most Bush-era income tax rates while allowing rates for top bracket earners to rise (Jan. 1, 2013)	YES
2011	
Prevent EPA from regulating greenhouse gas emissions to address climate change	NO
Extend certain provisions of Patriot Act for four years	NO
Clear compromise debt limit increase plan and establish future spending limits	YES
Overhaul patent law	YES
Implement Colombia free trade agreement	YES
Limit debate on confirmation of Caitlin J. Halligan to D.C. Circuit Court of Appeals	YES
Extend payroll tax cut and unemployment benefits for two months	NO

CQ Vote Studies

	PARTY UNITY		PRESIDENTIAL SUPPORT	
	SUPPORT	OPPOSE	SUPPORT	OPPOSE
2012	97%	3%	96%	4%
2011	99%	1%	95%	5%
2010	100%	0%	98%	2%
2009	98%	2%	96%	4%
2008	98%	2%	30%	70%
2007	95%	5%	35%	65%
2006	97%	3%	46%	54%
2005	97%	3%	36%	64%
2004	94%	6%	58%	42%
2003	97%	3%	51%	49%

Interest Groups

	AFL-CIO	ADA	CCUS	ACU
2012	100%	100%	38%	4%
2011	83%	95%	45%	5%
2010	100%	100%	0%	0%
2009	100%	95%	43%	8%
2008	100%	100%	50%	4%
2007	100%	95%	36%	0%
2006	93%	95%	33%	0%
2005	86%	100%	28%	0%
2004	100%	100%	50%	8%
2003	85%	85%	35%	16%

Sen. Bernard Sanders (I)

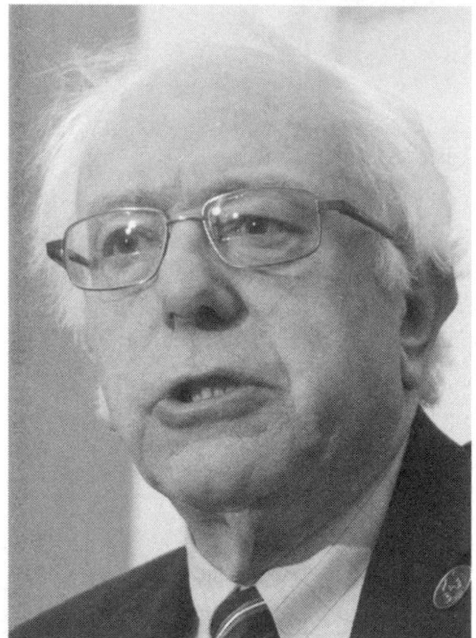

Capitol Office
224-5141
sanders.senate.gov
332 Dirksen Bldg. 20510-4503; fax 228-0776

Committees
Budget
Energy & Natural Resources
Environment & Public Works
Health, Education, Labor & Pensions
(Primary Health & Aging - Chairman)
Veterans' Affairs - Chairman
Joint Economic

Residence
Burlington

Born
Sept. 8, 1941; Brooklyn, N.Y.

Religion
Jewish

Family
Wife, Jane O'Meara Sanders; four children

Education
Brooklyn College, attended 1959-60; U. of Chicago, A.B. 1964 (political science)

Career
College instructor; freelance writer; documentary filmmaker; carpenter

Political Highlights
Liberty Union candidate for U.S. Senate, 1972; Liberty Union candidate for governor, 1972; Liberty Union candidate for U.S. Senate, 1974; Liberty Union candidate for governor, 1976; mayor of Burlington, 1981-89; independent candidate for governor, 1986; independent candidate for U.S. House, 1988; U.S. House, 1991-2007

ELECTION RESULTS

2012 GENERAL

Bernard Sanders (I)	207,848	71.0%
John MacGovern (R)	72,898	24.9%
Cris Ericson (UMJ)	5,924	2.0%

Previous Winning Percentages
2006 (65%); 2004 House Election (67%); 2002 House Election (64%); 2000 House Election (69%); 1998 House Election (63%); 1996 House Election (55%); 1994 House Election (50%); 1992 House Election (58%); 1990 House Election (56%)

Elected 2006; 2nd term

Sanders identifies himself as a socialist, lists himself as an independent and caucuses with the Democratic Party. When he was a House member, his lone-wolf style of politics seemed to marginalize him in national policy debates. But as a senator, he must be reckoned with, and on his signature issues he has tried to pull his colleagues to the left.

Most of Sanders' thoughts on government and the economy could be described as populist, and he has a devoted following among liberal activists. No one doubts his passion — and his perpetually mussed hair adds to his mystique. He stridently protects Social Security benefits, urges congressional action to address climate change and criticizes corporate America.

His defense of tax increases on the wealthy and his rebukes of the tea party movement led to publication in 2011 of his electronic book, "The Speech: A Historic Filibuster on Corporate Greed and the Decline of Our Middle Class." The book is a transcript of a December 2010 floor speech that lasted more than eight hours and generated widespread attention among social media followers.

Sanders says the public reaction to his speech demonstrated "a perception on the part of many people that there is something fundamentally wrong. ... Poverty is increasing and the gap is growing between the rich and everyone else." The only self-identified socialist ever elected to the Senate, he keeps a plaque on his office wall honoring Eugene V. Debs, founder of the Socialist Party of America.

After the 2009 death of Massachusetts Democrat Edward M. Kennedy, Sanders became perhaps the most vocal liberal regarding health care. He is the chairman of the Health, Education, Labor and Pensions Subcommittee on Primary Health and Aging.

One of his priorities for the 113th Congress (2013-14) is a reauthorization of the Older Americans Act, which governs social services for seniors; to lay the groundwork, in 2012 he introduced a bill that would boost funding by about 50 percent over fiscal 2011 levels for nutrition services (such as Meals on Wheels), the Senior Community Service Employment Program, and disease prevention and health promotion programs.

Sanders says the government is not doing enough to encourage doctors to become primary care physicians, and he has also called for increased Medicaid reimbursements for oral care. "We're not just talking about a pretty smile," he said. "What we're talking about is people going through their lives with severe pain."

As the Senate worked on a health care overhaul in the 111th Congress (2009-10), Sanders promoted the use of community health centers. The law dramatically increased access to health care in rural and underserved urban areas, a development that meshed well with Vermont's progress toward a "single payer" health care system. Local health centers serve more than 100,000 of the state's residents.

Republicans turned his zeal against him during the debate. Sanders offered an amendment running more than 700 pages to establish a "single-payer, Medicare-for-all health care system," something he has advocated for years. Tom Coburn of Oklahoma demanded a full reading, forcing Sanders to pull the amendment before a vote — a reading would have consumed hours of valuable floor time. But Sanders still touted the discussion of such a plan as a historic milestone.

In the 113th Congress, Sanders has a new, specialized role in promoting and defending federal benefits — he is now the chairman of the Veterans'

Affairs Committee. On winning the job he touted his work to provide robust health care for disabled veterans, as well as education benefits.

At an April 2013 hearing, Sanders said his main criticism of the Veterans Affairs Department is that "they forget to tell the world what they're doing." Success stories from the VA health system go unnoticed, and many veterans are unaware of the benefits they are eligible to receive.

Environmental issues have always piqued his interest, and Sanders sits on both the Energy and Natural Resources Committee and the Environment and Public Works Committee. He has proposed establishing a "carbon tax" to discourage the continued use of fossil fuels.

The 2010 oil spill in the Gulf of Mexico spurred Sanders to slam offshore drilling and call for more "sustainable energy," but he doesn't count nuclear power as an option. In 2011, he delayed action on the renomination of Nuclear Regulatory Commission member William Ostendorff—until he received assurance that the federal government would not intervene on behalf of Entergy, the operator of the Vermont Yankee nuclear plant, in a lawsuit filed against Vermont. The state government has considered shutting down the plant once its current license expires.

Sanders also sits on the Budget Committee. He supports increased taxes on those with high incomes and opposes reducing Social Security benefits or raising the retirement age. An August 2011 deal to cut spending and raise the federal debt limit was "grotesquely unfair, and it is also bad economic policy," he said. He has co-sponsored a bill to establish a tax on trades of financial securities; in addition to raising revenue, he has argued that it would discourage speculators.

Sanders has been noted as one of the most effective senators in using social media—an offshoot of his grass-roots approach to Vermont politics. He has been ranked by the Edelman firm as No. 1 in influence and engagement among all lawmakers in "TweetLevel rankings."

Sanders was born and raised in the New York borough of Brooklyn. His mother died at 46, when he was 19. His father, a Jewish immigrant from Poland whose family was killed in the Holocaust, was a paint salesman.

After college, Sanders lived on a kibbutz in Israel. He returned briefly to New York, then in 1968 joined the wave of liberals abandoning urban life for pastoral Vermont. Sanders held a variety of jobs, from freelance writer to carpenter, and built a foundation in left-wing politics.

While other transplants flocked to the Democratic Party, Sanders helped found the Liberty Union Party. He ran unsuccessfully for statewide office four times in the 1970s. He then focused on local office and in 1981 unseated the Democratic mayor of Burlington by 10 votes. He became the city's first socialist mayor and won three more two-year terms. He pursued populist goals while presiding over the revitalization of the city's downtown.

In 1988 he ran for Vermont's lone House seat, which was vacated when Republican James M. Jeffords ran for the Senate. He lost to Republican Peter Smith by only 4 points, and in a rematch two years later, he won with 56 percent of the vote. Sanders barely held on during the national Republican wave of 1994. In 2000, he captured the highest margin of victory in his House career with 69 percent of the vote.

When Jeffords announced plans to retire from the Senate, Sanders jumped in to the 2006 race. Campaigning as a Democrat, he had no trouble beating four political unknowns in the primary. He then ran as an independent in the general election. His Republican rival, software magnate Rich Tarrant, spent $7 million of his own money and tried to paint Sanders as a radical. Sanders won with 65 percent of the vote, with some financial support from the Democratic Senatorial Campaign Committee. Its chairman, New York Sen. Charles E. Schumer, had attended the same schools as Sanders in Brooklyn.

His campaign for a second term in 2012 was a blowout.

Key Votes

2012	
Prohibit health insurance plans from denying coverage based on the sponsor's religious beliefs	YES
Require approval of the Keystone XL oil pipeline	NO
Ease securities rules to expand small-business access to capital	NO
Reauthorize farm and nutrition programs for five years	YES
Limit debate on a bill that would create private-sector cybersecurity standards	YES
Consent to ratification of a treaty setting global standard for the treatment of people with disabilities	YES
Provide $60.4 billion in disaster relief following Superstorm Sandy	YES
Extend most Bush-era income tax rates while allowing rates for top-bracket earners to rise (Jan. 1, 2013)	YES
2011	
Prevent EPA from regulating greenhouse gas emissions to address climate change	NO
Extend certain provisions of Patriot Act for four years	NO
Clear compromise debt limit increase plan and establish future spending limits	NO
Overhaul patent law	YES
Implement Colombia free trade agreement	NO
Limit debate on confirmation of Caitlin J. Halligan to D.C. Circuit Court of Appeals	YES
Extend payroll tax cut and unemployment benefits for two months	NO

CQ Vote Studies

	PARTY UNITY		PRESIDENTIAL SUPPORT	
	SUPPORT	OPPOSE	SUPPORT	OPPOSE
2012	97%	3%	88%	12%
2011	96%	4%	88%	12%
2010	99%	1%	95%	5%
2009	97%	3%	86%	14%
2008	98%	2%	30%	70%
2007	97%	3%	33%	67%
2006	98%	2%	15%	85%
2005	97%	3%	15%	85%
2004	98%	2%	29%	71%
2003	95%	5%	15%	85%

Interest Groups

	AFL-CIO	ADA	CCUS	ACU
2012	100%	100%	13%	8%
2011	89%	80%	30%	5%
2010	100%	95%	0%	4%
2009	100%	100%	29%	12%
2008	100%	100%	38%	8%
2007	100%	95%	27%	4%
2006	100%	100%	27%	8%
2005	93%	100%	33%	8%
2004	100%	95%	30%	4%
2003	100%	100%	14%	20%

Rep. Peter Welch (D)

Capitol Office
225-4115
welch.house.gov
2303 Rayburn Bldg. 20515-4501; fax 225-6790

Committees
Energy & Commerce
Oversight & Government Reform

Residence
Norwich

Born
May 2, 1947; Springfield, Mass.

Religion
Roman Catholic

Family
Wife, Margaret Cheney; eight children

Education
College of the Holy Cross, A.B. 1969 (history); U. of California, Berkeley, J.D. 1973

Career
Lawyer; county public defender

Political Highlights
Vt. Senate, 1981-89 (minority leader, 1983-85; president pro tempore, 1985-89); sought Democratic nomination for U.S. House, 1988; Democratic nominee for governor, 1990; Vt. Senate, 2002-06 (president pro tempore, 2003-06)

ELECTION RESULTS

2012 GENERAL		
Peter Welch (D)	208,600	71.9%
Mark Donka (R)	67,543	23.3%
James "Sam" Desrochers (I)	8,302	2.9%
Jane Newton (LU)	4,065	1.4%
2012 PRIMARY		
Peter Welch (D)	36,863	99.0%
2010 GENERAL		
Peter Welch (D)	154,006	64.6%
Paul D. Beaudry (R)	76,403	32.0%
Gus Jaccaci (I)	4,704	2.0%
Jane Newton (S)	3,222	1.4%

Previous Winning Percentages
2008 (83%); 2006 (53%)

Elected 2006; 4th term

Welch's stature in the House has grown, not so much for his liberal beliefs as for his way of articulating them. "If you want to influence policy," he says, "I think you've got to be clear and early."

Welch began public life as a community activist. He sees a powerful role for government in effecting economic and social change. He speaks frequently on the House floor and cable news shows, putting a pleasantly nerdy face on progressive priorities. Illinois Republican Peter Roskam told The Hill that Welch is "a happy warrior"; Michigan Democrat Sander M. Levin once called him "the very active gentleman from Vermont." He serves as a chief deputy whip for House Democrats.

He is skilled at framing debates. In recent battles over the federal debt limit, Welch was well out front, laying out Democratic rhetoric and strategies months in advance — and his predictions of GOP tactics were prescient. Near the end of the 111th Congress (2009-10), he got 53 Democrats to sign a concise letter protesting a deal extending the George W. Bush-era tax cuts for the top two income brackets. "The very same people who support this addition to our debt will oppose raising the debt ceiling to pay for it," he wrote.

As conflict over the debt limit materialized in the 112th Congress (2011-12), Welch publicly outlined what he called a "sensible" fiscal position for his party: "When it came to be crunch time, the debate would be about whether you pay your bills or you default," he said. Writing in Roll Call in March 2011, he urged colleagues not to trade budget cuts for a hike in the debt limit, as it would allow Republicans to "take hostage our nation's full faith and credit."

Welch demanded a vote on a no-strings-attached increase of the debt limit, and in May 2011, Republicans accommodated him — hoping to put Democrats on the record. A slight majority of the caucus voted for Welch's position. Democratic leaders were irked with GOP leaders, not Welch; he was praised in caucus meetings. Observers have noted that Welch also makes himself useful to potential next-generation leaders in the Democratic Party.

But Welch has also been able to reach across the aisle. Late in 2011, he joined the bipartisan "Go Big" coalition, which urged development of a plan to cut the deficit by $4 trillion over 10 years through spending cuts and revenue increases. He has hosted bipartisan "Costco lasagna parties" for colleagues and seeks GOP collaborators on his favorite issues, such as energy efficiency.

His favorite person to work with is "whoever I can get to say yes." Welch and Colorado Republican Cory Gardner formed the Energy Savings Performance Caucus in late 2012; it promotes the government's use of contracts with private companies that specialize in lowering energy use at public buildings. Companies pay for the upgrades and are paid a portion of the energy savings.

President Barack Obama has lauded a 2010 House-passed Welch measure to provide rebates to consumers who improve the energy efficiency of their homes. Welch introduced a modified version with West Virginia Republican David B. McKinley in 2012, and they are continuing to work on the issue in the 113th Congress (2013-14). He sees promotion of energy efficiency as some of his most non-ideological work: "Whatever fuel source your prefer, less is more. Coal, solar, oil. You use less, you save more." He also thinks it is appropriate for the federal government to encourage a transition to renewable energy.

In 2013, Welch returned to the Energy and Commerce Committee after a two-year hiatus — he was forced off the panel in 2011 due to his party's losses in the 2010 election. He is a new member of the Commerce, Manufacturing and Trade Subcommittee, which handles some consumer protections. Welch has proposed new limits on the swipe fees that credit card companies charge businesses, contending that they are exorbitant and hurt small businesses.

Welch also sits on the Oversight and Government Reform Subcommittee on National Security. He opposes U.S. involvement in Afghanistan as fruitless nation building and got Utah Republican Jason Chaffetz, the panel chairman, to partner with him on a 2011 proposal requiring a military withdrawal.

Welch sat on the Agriculture Committee in the 112th Congress (2011-12) and is a founder of the Dairy Farmers Caucus. For Vermont's dairy industry, he favors implementation of a "growth management" system, whereby the government aims at price stability by using tax penalties to discourage large increases in production by farmers.

Like most people in his state, Welch has environmentalist tendencies. But he is sympathetic to complaints of overregulation of farms and other businesses. Environmentalists, he said, "have the greatest responsibility to make sure those environmental regulations are doing what they're supposed to, but not more. ... I'm all in on regulatory review."

He grew up in Springfield, Mass., the third of six children. His father was a dentist, and his mother was a homemaker. He attended Cathedral Catholic High School, where he helped his team win the 1964 and 1965 city championships in basketball — a big deal in the city where the game was invented.

Welch enrolled at the nearby College of the Holy Cross, which his father attended, but he left in his junior year for a community organizing project in Chicago. He eventually returned to wrap up a history degree, then went back to Illinois to fight discriminatory housing policies.

After earning a law degree at the University of California at Berkeley in 1973, Welch spent six months backpacking the Pan-American Highway down to Santiago, Chile. Back in the states, he went to work as a public defender in White River Junction, Vt. His future wife, Joan Smith, was a professor at Dartmouth College across the Connecticut River. They married in 1976.

He was elected to the state Senate in the early 1980s and soon became minority leader. His party took over the chamber a few years later. After running unsuccessfully for governor in 1990, Welch went behind the scenes in politics while working in a law firm and caring for his wife, who was diagnosed with cancer in the mid-1990s. She died in 2004. (Welch remarried in 2009 to Margaret Cheney, a state representative and cousin of the wife of Jim Cooper — the Tennessee Democrat whom Welch lives with in Washington.)

He supported Democrat Howard Dean's gubernatorial re-election in 2000 and got an appointment to return to the state Senate in 2002. Welch served as an adviser to Dean's presidential campaign in 2004.

He won 53 percent of the vote in the 2006 race for an open seat and has been re-elected by wide margins three times.

Key Votes

2012	
Extend a Social Security payroll tax cut and unemployment benefits	NO
Ease securities rules to expand small-business access to capital	YES
Extend for one year subsidized student loan interest rates financed by a cut in health care spending	NO
Cite Attorney General Eric H. Holder Jr. for contempt of Congress	NO
Create a visa program for foreign graduates in high-tech fields	NO
Extend most Bush-era income tax rates while allowing rates for top-bracket earners to rise (Jan. 1, 2013)	YES
2011	
Strike funding for F-35 alternative engine	NO
Prevent EPA from regulating greenhouse gas emissions to address climate change	NO
Extend certain provisions of Patriot Act for four years	NO
Declare opposition to use of ground troops in Libya	NO
Overhaul patent law	YES
Pass compromise debt limit increase plan and establish future spending limits	NO
Allow consideration of measures to implement three trade agreements	NO

CQ Vote Studies

	Party Unity		Presidential Support	
	Support	Oppose	Support	Oppose
2012	95%	5%	92%	8%
2011	94%	6%	82%	18%
2010	96%	4%	83%	17%
2009	98%	2%	92%	8%
2008	98%	2%	15%	85%

Interest Groups

	AFL-CIO	ADA	CCUS	ACU
2012	95%	100%	25%	4%
2011	97%	95%	25%	8%
2010	93%	95%	13%	4%
2009	100%	90%	33%	0%
2008	100%	90%	56%	8%

Vermont

At Large

Resting on the shores of Lake Champlain and rolling through the rustic Green Mountains, the nation's second-least-populous state feels like a good, small-town neighbor.

Small businesses and family farms make up the majority of Vermont's workforce. The once-prosperous dairy industry, which still comprises a significant portion of the state's agricultural output, has been hit hard by increased production in the West and volatile demand and pricing trends. The manufacturing sector depends on a few key employers, such as IBM, as well as the arrival of new manufacturers drawn by state incentives. Municipal and statewide budget shortfalls have cast doubt on the stability of government jobs.

Officials also hope to lure tourists, so prevalent on the ski slopes in the winter, to the state year-round. In addition, they continue to attempt to persuade urban dwellers from other states — flatlanders, as they are called here — to buy summer homes, especially in the northeast. Local leaders in the northeast are also hoping to lure overseas investors.

Once a remote rural bastion of Yankee Republicanism, Vermont moved solidly to the left decades ago as young liberal urbanites joined the remnants of the late-1960s counterculture settlers. In state and federal races, the strongly progressive voters in Burlington and surrounding Chittenden County — the state's most populous — outvote libertarian conservatives. In some years, the state's liberal Progressive Party and other left-leaning independents have split Democratic voters, occasionally aiding GOP victories.

The state's rural areas, including the Northeast Kingdom, still hold small pockets of GOP votes, but Democrats dominate central Vermont and the southeastern corner. Many small urban centers, such as Montpelier and Rutland, support Democratic candidates. Republican Gov. Jim Douglas held office for eight years, but Democrat Peter Shumlin narrowly defeated Republican Brian Dubie in the 2010 gubernatorial race and took 58 percent two years later.

Major Industry
Manufacturing, dairy farming, tourism

Cities
Burlington, South Burlington, Rutland

Notable
Ben & Jerry's ice cream began in a renovated Burlington gas station.

VIRGINIA

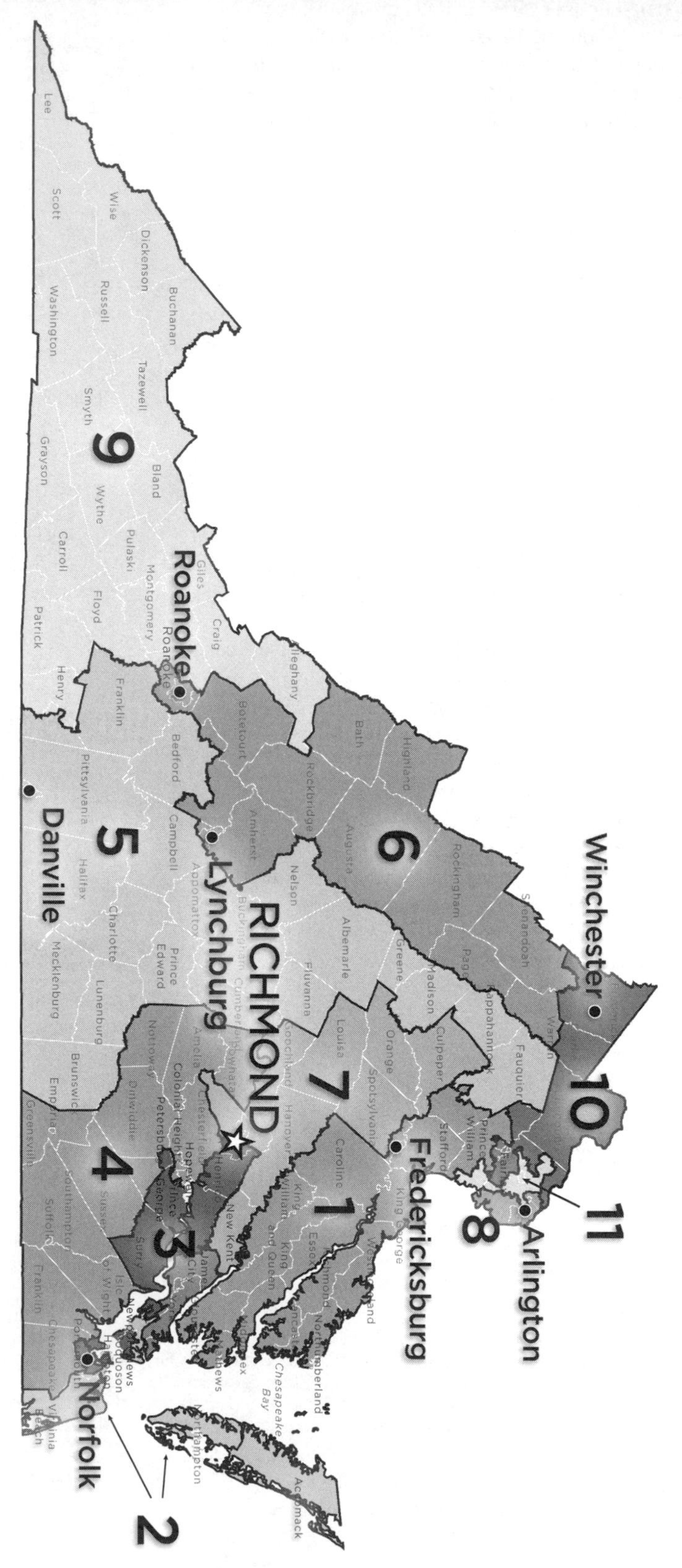
RICHMOND
Roanoke
Lynchburg
Danville
Winchester
Fredericksburg
Arlington
Norfolk
1
2
3
4
5
6
7
8
9
10
11
Lee
Scott
Wise
Dickenson
Buchanan
Russell
Washington
Tazewell
Smyth
Grayson
Bland
Wythe
Carroll
Pulaski
Giles
Montgomery
Floyd
Patrick
Craig
Roanoke
Henry
Franklin
Alleghany
Botetourt
Bath
Highland
Bedford
Pittsylvania
Rockbridge
Amherst
Campbell
Augusta
Rockingham
Halifax
Nelson
Appomattox
Charlotte
Albemarle
Greene
Madison
Prince Edward
Mecklenburg
Lunenburg
Fluvanna
Louisa
Orange
Culpeper
Fauquier
Nottoway
Amelia
Brunswick
Dinwiddie
Caroline
Stafford
Greensville
Southampton
Suffolk
Sussex
Surry
Franklin
New Kent
Chesapeake
Northumberland
Chesapeake Bay
Northampton
Accomack

Gov. Bob McDonnell (R)

First elected: 2009

Length of term: 4 years

Term expires: 1/14

Salary: $175,000

Phone: (804) 786-2211

Residence: Glen Allen

Born: June 15, 1954; Philadelphia, Pa.

Religion: Roman Catholic

Family: Wife, Maureen McDonnell; five children

Education: U. of Notre Dame, B.B.A. 1976 (management); Boston U., M.S. 1980 (business administration and management); CBN U., M.A. 1989 (public policy), J.D. 1989

Career: Lawyer; city prosecutor; newspaper sales manager; hospital supply company manager

Political highlights: Va. House, 1991-2005; Va. attorney general, 2006-09

ELECTION RESULTS

2009 GENERAL

Bob McDonnell (R)	1,163,651	58.6%
Creigh Deeds (D)	818,950	41.3%

Lt. Gov. Bill Bolling (R)

First elected: 2005

Length of term: 4 years

Term expires: 1/14

Salary: $36,321

Phone: (804) 786-2078

LEGISLATURE

General Assembly: 60 days January-March in even-numbered years; 45 days January-February in odd-numbered years

Senate: 40 members, 4-year terms

2013 ratios: 20 R, 20 D; 34 men, 6 women

Salary: $18,000

Phone: (804) 698-7410

House: 100 members, 2-year terms

2013 ratios: 67 R, 32 D, 1 I; 81 men, 19 women

Salary: $17,640

Phone: (804) 698-1500

TERM LIMITS

Governor: No consecutive terms

Senate: No

House: No

URBAN STATISTICS

CITY	POPULATION
Virginia Beach	437,994
Norfolk	242,803
Chesapeake	222,209
Richmond	204,214
Newport News	180,719

REGISTERED VOTERS

Voters do not register by party.

POPULATION

2010 population	8,001,024
2000 population	7,078,515
1990 population	6,187,358
Percent change (2000-2010)	+13.0%
Rank among states (2010)	12
Median age	36.7
Born in state	50.5%
Foreign born	9.8%
Violent crime rate	227/100,000
Poverty level	10.5%
Federal workers	289,166
Military	63,160

ELECTIONS

STATE ELECTION OFFICIAL
(804) 864-8901

DEMOCRATIC PARTY
(804) 644-1966

REPUBLICAN PARTY
(804) 780-0111

MISCELLANEOUS

Web: www.virginia.gov

Capital: Richmond

U.S. CONGRESS

Senate: 2 Democrats

House: 8 Republicans, 3 Democrats

Statistics by District

	2012 Vote for President		2008 Vote for President										
District	Obama	Romney	Obama	McCain	Black	Asian	Hispanic	Median Income	Over 64	Under 20	College Education	Rural	Sq. Miles
1	46%	53%	47%	52%	17%	3%	10%	$74,283	13%	28%	34%	36%	3,684
2	50	49	51	48	22	5	7	60,101	12	26	31	10	992
3	79	20	78	22	57	2	5	40,304	11	26	21	5	947
4	49	50	49	50	31	2	5	59,061	12	27	24	26	4,310
5	46	53	48	51	21	1	3	48,187	17	24	26	67	10,030
6	39	59	42	57	11	2	4	46,350	16	25	24	37	5,930
7	42	57	44	55	14	4	5	68,596	13	26	39	27	2,776
8	68	31	68	31	14	11	18	91,027	10	23	60	<1	149
9	35	63	40	58	6	1	2	36,634	17	23	19	60	9,114
10	49	50	52	48	7	12	12	109,505	9	31	52	16	1,372
11	62	36	62	37	12	18	17	100,146	10	26	54	<1	185
STATE	**51**	**47**	**53**	**46**	**19**	**5**	**8**	**61,882**	**13**	**26**	**34**	**27**	**39,490**
U.S.	**51**	**47**	**53**	**46**	**12**	**5**	**17**	**50,052**	**13**	**27**	**29**	**21**	**3,531,905**

Sen. Mark Warner (D)

Capitol Office
224-2023
warner.senate.gov
475 Russell Bldg. 20510; fax 224-6295

Committees
Banking, Housing & Urban Affairs
(National Security & International Trade and Finance - Chairman)
Budget
Commerce, Science & Transportation
(Competitiveness, Innovation & Export Promotion - Chairman)
Rules & Administration
Select Intelligence
Joint Economic
Joint Printing

Residence
Alexandria

Born
Dec. 15, 1954; Indianapolis, Ind.

Religion
Presbyterian

Family
Wife, Lisa Collis; three children

Education
George Washington U., B.A. 1977 (political science); Harvard U., J.D. 1980

Career
Technology venture capitalist; campaign aide and party fundraiser

Political Highlights
Commonwealth Transportation Board, 1990-94; Va. Democratic Party chairman, 1993-95; Democratic nominee for U.S. Senate, 1996; governor, 2002-06

ELECTION RESULTS

2008 GENERAL

Mark Warner (D)	2,369,327	65.0%
James S. Gilmore III (R)	1,228,830	33.7%

2008 PRIMARY

Mark Warner (D)	unopposed

Elected 2008; 1st term

Warner calls himself a "radical centrist" and fondly remembers the sense of urgency during his tenure as Virginia's governor. As he nears the end of his first term in the Senate, he has adjusted to the chamber's unhurried pace — but that's not to say he enjoys it.

Virginia is the only state that doesn't allow governors to serve consecutive terms. Warner was famously impatient to get things done as the state's top executive from 2002 to 2006. "My mind-set when I was governor was: Every day that you're not putting points on the board is a day you're not going to get back," he said.

Upon leaving the governor's mansion, he considered running for president in the 2008 election, but within a year he decided to skip that contest. He ran for the Senate instead. Some political observers thought that he might seek another term as governor in 2013, then use that job as a springboard for a 2016 presidential campaign — but he announced in November 2012 that he had no plans of reclaiming his old job.

Presidential politics became a source of frustration for Warner in the 112th Congress (2011-12), as the campaign atmosphere was inhospitable to his top priority: moving on a comprehensive budget agreement. "I didn't get the memo that you're supposed to take presidential years off," he said.

Warner has attempted to serve as a consensus-builder on economic issues. In 2011, he was part of the "gang of six," a bipartisan group of senators that unsuccessfully tried to produce a budget proposal — widely seen as middle ground — including $4 trillion in deficit reduction, increases in federal revenue and changes to entitlement programs. Late that year, almost half the Senate signed on to a bicameral, bipartisan "Go Big" coalition urging action along those lines; Warner and Georgia Republican Saxby Chambliss led the effort in their chamber.

In 2012, Warner tried to build connections with business leaders and other groups that might help the campaign for broad fiscal changes. "While people talk about bipartisan compromise, there is in fact no institutional support for it," he said. "All of the organized groups are organized around the status quo."

Warner has also sought to improve bipartisan relationships in the Senate. He and Tennessee Republican Lamar Alexander are the co-hosts of a series of dinners meant to ease the tension that builds up during heated policy debates.

Warner had considerable success in the business world. After finishing law school and working for a time as a Democratic National Committee fundraiser, he started ventures in energy and real estate, then hit it big as an early investor in cellular company Nextel.

His business-minded proposals often involve Republican partners. In May 2012 Warner sponsored legislation with Democrat Chris Coons of Delaware and Republicans Jerry Moran of Kansas and Marco Rubio of Florida to overhaul the visa entry process for entrepreneurs and incentivize investment in startup companies. An updated version — with Missouri Republican Roy Blunt replacing Rubio — was introduced in February 2013.

Warner also worked on a bipartisan manufacturing jobs initiative in 2012, to encourage repatriation of jobs that have been moved overseas back to rural areas. With Republican Olympia J. Snowe of Maine, he wrote a bill to make more broadcast spectrum available for wireless broadband Internet access, a concern dear to constituents in rural Virginia communities. In April 2013, he was named the chairman of the Commerce, Science and Transportation Subcommittee on Competitiveness, Innovation and Export Promotion.

Warner pays considerable attention to government operations. He was selected during his first year in the Senate to lead a bipartisan task force on government performance, operating out of the Budget Committee. He resumed that role in 2013. He seeks new approaches to federal regulation — such as offsetting the economic impact of new rules by removing old ones.

With Republicans Rob Portman of Ohio and Susan Collins of Maine, he introduced 2012 legislation to require independent agencies to analyze the costs and benefits of new regulations. Warner also champions the standardization of the reporting and disclosure of federal spending, to allow easier tracking of how various programs are using taxpayer dollars.

Whatever his efforts at collaboration, Warner still supports Democrats on key legislative votes. In 2010 he voted for overhauls of the health care system and financial regulations. In 2011, he voted to clear a compromise debt limit increase plan.

Warner spent long hours preparing the financial regulatory overhaul as a member of the Banking, Housing and Urban Affairs Committee. "I don't think ever when you pass major legislation you get it 100 percent right," he said. "The challenge at this point on Dodd-Frank and health care is that, particularly in the House, there's a group of people [where] there's not an interest in fixing it. It's either repeal or nothing."

Warner was raised in Indiana and Connecticut by Republican parents. His father, Robert, is a World War II Marine veteran, while his mother, Marjorie, died in 2010 after a long struggle with Alzheimer's disease. Warner became interested in politics at an early age; an eighth-grade social studies teacher inspired him to work on social change during the tumultuous year of 1968. By the time he was a high school senior — during the 1972 re-election bid of Richard Nixon — it was evident his politics would differ from those of his parents.

He was the valedictorian for his 1977 George Washington University class and the first in his family to graduate from college. During school, he worked for former Sen. Abraham Ribicoff, a Connecticut Democrat.

Warner briefly worked for Sen. Christopher J. Dodd of Connecticut and the DNC after attending Harvard Law School, where he graduated in 1980. He never launched a legal career, instead making his name as a venture capitalist. As he made money, he stayed active in the Democratic political scene, managing L. Douglas Wilder's successful 1989 campaign in Virginia to become the nation's first elected black governor. He also served as state party chairman from 1993 to 1995.

Warner first ran for the Senate in 1996, spending $10 million of his fortune in an unsuccessful campaign against Republican incumbent John W. Warner (no relation). His close loss enhanced his standing in Democratic circles and helped lay the groundwork for his successful statehouse run in 2001.

As governor, he did away with a budget deficit in part by raising taxes. He also collaborated with GOP leaders in Richmond to produce a fiscal package that included spending cuts. He implemented businesslike changes to state government, especially at Virginia's transportation department. As chairman of the National Governors Association in 2004 and 2005, he led a national education initiative. His efforts propelled his approval ratings to the mid-70s.

John W. Warner's retirement announcement in 2007 led him to try for the Senate again. He faced Republican James S. Gilmore III, his predecessor as governor. Warner coasted to victory with 65 percent of the vote.

Warner has a number of pursuits outside the Senate; he has been noted for his philanthropy. In 1992, he helped create the Virginia Health Care Foundation, a public-private partnership that helps uninsured Virginians receive medical care.

Virginia's junior senator, former Gov. Tim Kaine, is a longtime friend and political partner of Warner — he served as Warner's lieutenant governor.

Key Votes

2012	
Prohibit health insurance plans from denying coverage based on the sponsor's religious beliefs	YES
Require approval of the Keystone XL oil pipeline	NO
Ease securities rules to expand small-business access to capital	YES
Reauthorize farm and nutrition programs for five years	YES
Limit debate on a bill that would create private-sector cybersecurity standards	YES
Consent to ratification of a treaty setting global standard for the treatment of people with disabilities	YES
Provide $60.4 billion in disaster relief following Superstorm Sandy	?
Extend most Bush-era income tax rates while allowing rates for top-bracket earners to rise (Jan. 1, 2013)	YES
2011	
Prevent EPA from regulating greenhouse gas emissions to address climate change	NO
Extend certain provisions of Patriot Act for four years	YES
Clear compromise debt limit increase plan and establish future spending limits	YES
Overhaul patent law	YES
Implement Colombia free trade agreement	YES
Limit debate on confirmation of Caitlin J. Halligan to D.C. Circuit Court of Appeals	YES
Extend payroll tax cut and unemployment benefits for two months	YES

CQ Vote Studies

	PARTY UNITY		PRESIDENTIAL SUPPORT	
	SUPPORT	OPPOSE	SUPPORT	OPPOSE
2012	86%	14%	96%	4%
2011	91%	9%	99%	1%
2010	90%	10%	97%	3%
2009	92%	8%	96%	4%

Interest Groups

	AFL-CIO	ADA	CCUS	ACU
2012	89%	85%	38%	13%
2011	83%	90%	70%	5%
2010	81%	80%	36%	8%
2009	89%	95%	43%	24%

Sen. Tim Kaine (D)

Capitol Office
224-4024
kaine.senate.gov
B40C Dirksen Bldg. 20510-4604; fax 228-6363

Committees
Armed Services
Budget
Foreign Relations
(International Development - Chairman)

Residence
Richmond

Born
Feb. 26, 1958; St. Paul, Minn.

Religion
Roman Catholic

Family
Wife, Anne Holton; three children

Education
U. of Missouri, A.B. 1979 (economics); Harvard U., J.D. 1983

Career
Lawyer

Political Highlights
Richmond City Council, 1994-2001 (mayor, 1998-2001); lieutenant governor, 2002-06; governor, 2006-10; Democratic National Committee chairman, 2009-11

ELECTION RESULTS

2012 GENERAL		
Tim Kaine (D)	2,010,067	52.9%
George Allen (R)	1,785,542	47.0%
2012 PRIMARY		
Tim Kaine (D)		unopposed

Elected 2012; 1st term

Kaine called the shots in his previous political jobs, first as the governor of Virginia, then as the titular leader of the Democratic Party. Even so, he isn't viewing his new job as junior senator as a step backward. It affords him the opportunity to work in tandem with a close friend and longtime political ally — senior senator Mark Warner — on behalf of their state.

According to Kaine, "the junior senator / senior senator relationship in Virginia is the closest in the 50 states." Kaine and Warner met in 1980, when they were at Harvard Law School. They reconnected in 1989, while working together on the successful gubernatorial campaign of L. Douglas Wilder.

Warner helped Kaine's launch into local politics, a successful 1994 campaign for Richmond city council. Kaine returned the favor by supporting Warner in his unsuccessful bid for a U.S. Senate seat in 1996. When Warner won a gubernatorial race in 2001, Kaine was elected as his lieutenant governor, and four years later Kaine succeeded Warner.

Both men also worked for the Democratic National Committee. Warner was a DNC fundraiser early in his career, and Kaine served as DNC chairman during the 111th Congress (2009-10), acting as a media salesman for the Obama administration's priorities. And both men portray themselves as political moderates.

"Our careers have kind of braided back and forth together," Kaine said. "It's nice to be working in partnership." In the 113th Congress (2013-14), Virginia and West Virginia are the only states where both senators are former governors.

Kaine and Warner serve together on the Budget Committee. As governor, Kaine had the difficult task of balancing Virginia's budget as the national economy tanked. He and the General Assembly made up more than $7 billion in shortfalls using a number of techniques, including elimination of a pay raise for state employees, tapping a "rainy day" fund and cutting spending for a number of programs. The assembly rejected a tax increase that Kaine proposed in the closing weeks of his tenure.

In regard to government spending, "there's no pain-free cut," Kaine said, "but you can make them a lot better." He warns that government should "never do across-the-board cuts. That's always the wrong strategy, because everything isn't worth everything else."

Kaine advocates a return to "regular order" as the best means to improving the nation's fiscal situation: "The right way to make decisions about spending and taxes and deficit reduction is not as part of some one-off gimmick. It's annual budgets." His maiden speech on the Senate floor was to protest the automatic "sequestration" cuts that were created by a 2011 deficit reduction law and began taking hold in 2013.

Outside of the Budget Committee, Kaine and Warner have a decent division of labor for committee work, with Kaine handling foreign affairs and looking after the state's military establishment.

Kaine sits on the Armed Services Committee and its panels with jurisdiction over personnel issues and military readiness. He urges the Pentagon to adopt policies that would help servicemembers market the skills they acquired in the military when they transition to the civilian workforce. "We have to figure out ways to help our active-duty before they become veterans," he said. Kaine would like to see easily transferable, universally understood "credentials" bestowed on active servicemembers.

"We're failing them, and we're not getting the value of all the leadership and technical talent they have," he said. "If your hiring officer doesn't have military experience ... they don't understand what the people bring to the table." Although he did not secure a seat on the Health, Education, Labor and Pensions Committee, Kaine has contacted Chairman Tom Harkin of Iowa about fostering additional workforce development initiatives.

On the Foreign Relations Committee, Kaine chairs the Subcommittee on International Development. He also sits on the panel overseeing the Western Hemisphere. As a young man, Kaine flirted with missionary work — he left law school after his first year and spent nine months teaching at a Jesuit school in El Progreso, Honduras.

By Kaine's reckoning, there is a strong need to expand international relationships, starting with the countries right in America's backyard. "So often, foreign policy is kind of east-west," he said. "I think we need to have a foreign policy on a north-south axis too."

He points to Brazil, Chile and Colombia as burgeoning economies, and he describes Mexico as a manufacturing powerhouse we'd be wise to work with. Trying to single-handedly win economic battles with rising population centers such as China and India is a fool's errand, Kaine said: "If we do more economic cooperation throughout the Americas, now we're not 300 million. We're a billion — or more, if we do it throughout the entire hemisphere."

He's convinced that building stronger relationships doesn't require the United States to cut a lot of checks. "Relationship-building in the Americas is less about aid, it's more about economic exchanges and finding ways to do more trade," he said. Kaine lists trade agreements and information exchange programs as critical growth strategies. An overhaul of immigration law also plays a part. "We want to be the talent nation ... the most attractive place for people who are talented in intellect, or talented in work ethic, or talented in creativity," he said. "I do think that there is a moment for the institution to get this right after a lot of talking about it."

Kaine, the oldest of three sons, was born in Minnesota. His family moved to Kansas when he was 2, settling in the Kansas City suburbs. His father ran an iron-working shop, and his mother was a home economics teacher.

Kaine attended an all-boys Jesuit high school. He was the president of the student council. As a junior, he delivered money to the Honduran mission where he would later teach. Kaine has tried to balance his social conservatism with some parts of the Democratic platform. He opposes abortion, but does not actively try to legislate against it.

While studying law at Harvard, Kaine met fellow student Anne Holton, whom he later married. She is the daughter of former Virginia Republican Gov. Linwood Holton Jr., who was elected in 1969 and made high-profile stances against racial segregation. He lost a Senate bid in 1978. Kaine calls his father-in-law his political role model and thanked him during his victory speech on Election Night in 2012. Holton "played an amazingly important role in the life of this commonwealth and in the life of this country," Kaine said. "And he did it in a courageous way, at a political cost to himself."

Kaine and his wife settled in Richmond. He worked as a civil rights attorney, and his wife eventually became a juvenile court judge.

He entered public life by serving as an independent city councilman in Richmond. At that time, the city council chose the city's mayor, and Kaine served in that capacity for three years starting in the middle of 1998.

The retirement of Democratic Sen. Jim Webb created an open seat in 2012 that Republicans were hoping to pick up. They had an experienced but vulnerable candidate in George Allen, a former senator and governor. Kaine announced his candidacy in April 2011. Republicans tried to paint him as a Democratic shill because of his DNC work, but Kaine said he always worked to be civil in that post: "I tried not to be a name-caller or a super-negative guy with respect to Republicans." Kaine took 53 percent of the vote, running several points ahead of President Barack Obama in the state.

Rep. Rob Wittman (R)

Capitol Office
225-4261
wittman.house.gov
2454 Rayburn Bldg. 20515-4601; fax 225-4382

Committees
Armed Services
(Readiness - Chairman)
Natural Resources

Residence
Montross

Born
Feb. 3, 1959; Washington, D.C.

Religion
Episcopalian

Family
Wife, Kathryn Wittman; two children

Education
Virginia Polytechnic Institute and State U., B.S. 1981 (biology); U. of North Carolina, M.P.H. 1990 (health policy and administration); Virginia Commonwealth U., Ph.D. 2002 (public policy and administration)

Career
State health agency official; environmental health inspector; fisherman

Political Highlights
Montross Town Council, 1986-96 (mayor 1992-96); Westmoreland County Board of Supervisors, 1996-2005 (chairman 2004-05); Va. House, 2006-07

ELECTION RESULTS

2012 GENERAL		
Rob Wittman (R)	200,845	56.3%
Adam M. Cook (D)	147,036	41.2%
G. Gail "for Rail" Parker (IGREEN)	8,308	2.3%
2012 PRIMARY		
Rob Wittman (R)		unopposed
2010 GENERAL		
Rob Wittman (R)	135,564	63.9%
Krystal M. Ball (D)	73,824	34.8%
G. Gail "for Rail" Parker (IGREEN)	2,544	1.2%

Previous Winning Percentages
2008 (57%); 2007 Special Election (61%)

Elected 2007; 3rd full term

Wittman has prospered in politics for more than two decades, in part by harmonizing two priorities of his coastal constituents: preserving the Chesapeake Bay and protecting military installations and shipbuilding.

Eager and down-to-earth, he grew up hunting and fishing along the bay. After college, he worked as a fisherman in the Northern Neck — a peninsula between the Potomac and the Rappahannock rivers that includes the birthplaces of George Washington and James Monroe. He went on to became an environmental specialist for Virginia's health department and worked his way up to field director of the shellfish sanitation division.

Wittman continues to push for restoration and protection of the bay. In the 112th Congress (2011-12), when Republicans were often critical of spending and environmental regulations, Wittman was willing to break ranks when water quality or conservation programs were at issue.

His higher-profile work, however, is on the Armed Services Committee. In 2013, he became the chairman of the Readiness Subcommittee.

Wittman was handed that gavel by fellow Virginia Republican J. Randy Forbes, who now chairs the Seapower and Projection Forces Subcommittee — where Wittman also serves. As the Readiness chairman, he is charged with studying the Pentagon's ability to handle current and potential military engagements.

He says his goal is to "make sure strategy drives the budget" for defense spending — a sentiment shared by Forbes. At a 2011 hearing, he lamented that "we're constantly reacting to events rather than planning for them."

While serving as chairman of the Oversight and Investigations Subcommittee in the 112th Congress (2011-12), Wittman conducted a year-long evaluation of the Navy's 30-year shipbuilding plan; he has expressed the concern that the service simply does not have enough ships to fulfill future missions. "Quantity is a quality all its own," he quipped in 2012. He would like to see faster production of Virginia-class attack submarines and the replacement for the Ohio-class submarine — he views them as crucial as the nation's military focus shifts to the Pacific.

Attempts to reduce military spending have often met his disapproval. In February 2011, he voted against an attempt to reduce funding for an alternative engine to the F-35 Joint Strike Fighter. He also opposes further base closings until America restructures its global military strategy — Wittman says a 2005 round of closures and realignments has not achieved projected savings, and at a 2013 hearing he said that eliminating bases because of the overall decrease in active-duty personnel is "shortsighted."

He was pleased when the Obama administration dropped its request to move a Norfolk-based aircraft carrier to a new home base in Florida. Military leaders had suggested that spreading out carriers would hedge risk to the fleet; Wittman and other Virginians questioned the expense and strategic value of such a move, which would have cost the region numerous jobs.

As the Oversight chairman, he attempted to spotlight the return of several former Guantánamo Bay detainees to the battlefield, urging agencies to keep better tabs on prisoners after they are released to other countries. But a 2012 committee report on the topic was harshly criticized by Wittman's ranking member, Democrat Jim Cooper of Tennessee, as a dumbed-down study meant to scare voters and gain partisan advantage.

Wittman's advocacy for the Chesapeake Bay takes place on the Natural Resources Committee. In late 2008, he cheered as blue crab populations were designated a "resource disaster," which resulted in $20 million in funding to help address the situation. Six months later, he announced reports indicating signs of a recovery. In 2011, the committee approved his bill to require a multi-agency budget for bay restoration activities.

The committee held a 2011 hearing on his bill to require consideration of certain scientific information before the government sets annual catch limits for fisheries. Wittman is an avid sport fisherman; he has a fiberglass replica of a 308-pound tuna that he caught off the coast of Mexico hanging in his D.C. office. He's also a duck hunter, and his bill to authorize states to issue electronic duck stamps passed the House in early 2012. He re-introduced it in 2013. President Barack Obama signed his 2010 bill to allow funds from Canadian sources to match federal contributions to conservation programs protecting waterfowl habitats in Canada.

Joining many Republicans, he supports offshore drilling — even off the coasts of Virginia, as long as environmental considerations are made. And another offshore energy source has piqued his interest: "I think wind energy off of Virginia has tremendous, tremendous potential," he said.

Wittman served on the Montross Town Council for a decade, the last four years as mayor. In 1995 he was elected to the Westmoreland County Board of Supervisors and then won an election to the Virginia Legislature in 2005. Though he applauds spending to help local projects, he believes Washington needs to "get back to the conservative principles of controlling spending, particularly when it comes to federal earmarks." Even before House Republicans voluntarily banned the practice in 2010, Wittman requested earmarks only for military construction and certain other defense-related projects.

Like many of his constituents, he commutes to Washington each day, and Wittman introduced legislation in 2009 and 2011 that would allow an income tax credit for expenses incurred in teleworking. He supported a measure that would require the creation of federal telework policies in each agency.

He was born in the District of Columbia in 1959. Eight months later he was adopted and moved to Richmond. His mother was a homemaker before earning a teaching degree. His father, an auditor, often worked in the Northern Neck. Wittman spent summers there working on fishing boats and tomato farms. He attended Benedictine Military Institute, an all-boys military school in Richmond, and was active in student government and the school newspaper. He earned a bachelor's degree in biology in 1981 from Virginia Tech.

Wittman won a special election in December 2007 to replace Republican Rep. Jo Ann Davis, who had died of breast cancer. At the nominating convention he was one of 11 Republicans — and the only sitting elected official vying for the seat. Wittman won in the fifth round of balloting, then had little trouble capturing the seat. His re-elections have been fairly routine.

Key Votes

2012	
Extend a Social Security payroll tax cut and unemployment benefits	YES
Ease securities rules to expand small-business access to capital	YES
Extend for one year subsidized student loan interest rates financed by a cut in health care spending	YES
Cite Attorney General Eric H. Holder Jr. for contempt of Congress	YES
Create a visa program for foreign graduates in high-tech fields	YES
Extend most Bush-era income tax rates while allowing rates for top-bracket earners to rise (Jan. 1, 2013)	NO
2011	
Strike funding for F-35 alternative engine	NO
Prevent EPA from regulating greenhouse gas emissions to address climate change	YES
Extend certain provisions of Patriot Act for four years	YES
Declare opposition to use of ground troops in Libya	YES
Overhaul patent law	YES
Pass compromise debt limit increase plan and establish future spending limits	YES
Allow consideration of measures to implement three trade agreements	YES

CQ Vote Studies

	PARTY UNITY		PRESIDENTIAL SUPPORT	
	SUPPORT	OPPOSE	SUPPORT	OPPOSE
2012	94%	6%	20%	80%
2011	92%	8%	23%	77%
2010	90%	10%	31%	69%
2009	88%	12%	31%	69%
2008	93%	7%	63%	37%

Interest Groups

	AFL-CIO	ADA	CCUS	ACU
2012	19%	0%	92%	84%
2011	0%	10%	100%	72%
2010	7%	5%	88%	92%
2009	19%	5%	87%	92%
2008	20%	35%	83%	92%

Virginia 1

East — Fredericksburg, Williamsburg

The 1st hugs the western bank of the Potomac River to the Chesapeake Bay, stretching from the southernmost exurban outskirts of Washington, D.C., through the sparsely populated Northern Neck and Middle Peninsula to portions of Hampton Roads. Military bases are scattered throughout the conservative-leaning district, and the southern region is home to historical tourist destinations such as Jamestown, Williamsburg and Yorktown.

Military and government jobs keep the economy of the 1st relatively stable. Northern counties such as Prince William and Stafford continue to grow as white-collar Washington professionals move further from the capital city. The region is also home to research and technology firms and government contractors within commuting distance of both Washington and Richmond. The Williamsburg area is a popular retirement destination.

The 1st is home to two major military training facilities: Marine Corps Base Quantico in the district's north and the Army's Fort A.P. Hill. Quantico also serves as a research and development center for military communication technology. The main campus of the Marine Corps University is south of Quantico. At its southern edge, the 1st takes in part of the Hampton Roads region, including a major naval weapons facility. Joint Base Langley-Eustis and Newport News' shipyards lay just south of the district.

The population centers of the 1st have grown rapidly in the past decade. Decennial redistricting increased the 1st's footprint in Prince William County near Manassas, where Hispanic population growth is steady. Redistricting kept this district solidly Republican and removed the city of Newport News, which has a large black population.

Major Industry

Defense, technology, tourism, shipbuilding

Military Bases

Marine Corps Base Quantico, 6,609 military, 11,380 civilian (2012); Fort A.P. Hill (Army), 57 military, 430 civilian; Naval Surface Warfare Center, Dahlgren Division, 10 military, 3,415 civilian (2012); Naval Weapons Station Yorktown, 1,393 military, 689 civilian

Cities

Newport News (pt.), Fredericksburg, Williamsburg

Notable

Jamestown (1607) was the first permanent English settlement in North America.

Rep. Scott Rigell (R)

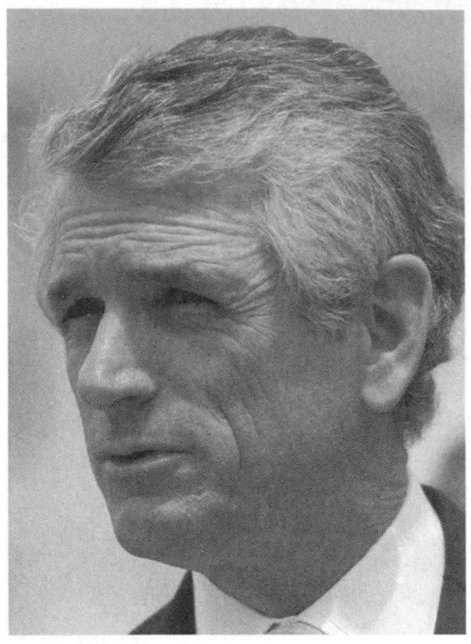

Capitol Office
225-4215
rigell.house.gov
418 Cannon Bldg. 20515-4602; fax 225-4218

Committees
Armed Services
Budget

Residence
Virginia Beach

Born
May 28, 1960; Titusville, Fla.

Religion
Protestant

Family
Wife, Teri Rigell; four children

Education
Brevard Community College, A.A. 1981; Mercer U., B.B.A 1983 (management); Regent U., M.B.A. 1990

Military
Marine Corps Reserve, 1978-84

Career
Car dealership owner

Political Highlights
Va. Motor Vehicle Dealer Board, 1995-99

ELECTION RESULTS

2012 GENERAL		
Scott Rigell (R)	166,231	53.8%
Paul Hirschbiel (D)	142,548	46.1%
2012 PRIMARY		
Scott Rigell (R)		unopposed
2010 GENERAL		
Scott Rigell (R)	88,340	53.1%
Glenn Nye (D)	70,591	42.4%
Kenny E. Golden (I)	7,194	4.3%

Elected 2010; 2nd term

Rigell casts himself as a pragmatic conservative interested in changing the work environment in Washington, as well as government spending practices. It's an approach suited to the 2nd District, which contains a huge Republican-leaning military presence and large Democratic-leaning population centers.

Before coming to Congress in 2011, Rigell (RIDGE-uhl) worked as an auto dealer, and he often cites his small-business experiences when commenting on fiscal issues. He regularly appeared in television advertisements for his dealership—giving out his home phone number to potential customers—and now stars in video vignettes produced by his congressional office.

As a lawmaker, however, he doesn't meet the stereotype of a fast-talking salesman. Rigell is deliberate and careful in his political speech, and he got national attention in the 112th Congress (2011-12) for laying out his reasoning when he broke ranks with the Republican Party.

Rigell calls for more federal revenue, and he was one of the first public defectors from the Americans for Tax Reform pledge, a highly publicized promise to never raise taxes. In 2011, he started advancing his view that not even House Republicans were willing to support spending cuts large enough to balance the federal budget under current revenue levels.

During deficit reduction talks in December 2012, he sent an open letter to GOP colleagues. "We need to examine what it means to be a fiscal conservative," he wrote. "Surely, in addition to fighting for smaller government, it means paying for the size and scope of government for which we have voted." He voted against legislation to increase tax rates on earnings over $400,000, however. He said spending cuts should have been packaged with the rate increase, which later became law.

A few months earlier, Rigell was one of two House Republicans to vote against holding Attorney General Eric H. Holder Jr. in criminal contempt of Congress over the withholding of documents on a botched gun-trafficking sting. He supported a civil contempt citation and wrote to his constituents that the harsher measure was needless.

Along with several moderate Democrats and Wisconsin Republican Reid Ribble, Rigell created the Fix Congress Now Caucus in 2012. He is affiliated with No Labels, a nonpartisan organization that focuses on ways to increase the legislative output of Congress, and he belongs to both the conservative Republican Study Committee and the moderate Main Street Partnership.

Rigell is making his economic pitches from the Budget Committee in the 113th Congress (2013-14). "I've borrowed money; I've paid it back," he says. "I have firsthand knowledge of the kind of lending environment we need for business to grow."

He also sits on the Armed Services Committee. Rigell says defense accounts are being slashed too aggressively. He called the $500 billion "sequestration" cuts that were put in place by an August 2011 deficit reduction law "a violent, unwise, unconscionable, sharp-direction turn for the Department of Defense." In preparing its fiscal 2013 defense policy bill, the House adopted Rigell's amendment to eliminate those cuts for fiscal 2013 if an offsetting amount was cut from other parts of the federal budget. It was not included in the final law.

The Navy fleet could stand to be larger, Rigell says, in part to protect U.S. trade interests in the Pacific from Chinese interference. Along with the rest of the Virginia delegation, he has worked to block the move of one aircraft carrier from its Norfolk base to Florida. He applauded when the Obama administration left funding for the relocation out of its fiscal 2013 budget request.

Rigell voices some constitutional concerns from his Armed Services seat.

The fiscal 2013 defense policy law contains his amendment to affirm habeas corpus rights of military detainees captured in the United States. And he was a prominent opponent of the U.S. involvement in Libya in 2011, which came without congressional approval. He called the mission "an egregious, ongoing breach of the Separation of Powers." The House rejected his attempt to block funding for Libya operations.

He has military experience, having served as a Marine Corps reservist. He is also the father and son of a Marine. He balks at attempts to increase the fees veterans pay for health benefits, calling it a "breach of trust."

Rigell no longer sits on the Science, Space and Technology Committee, but he has a personal interest in the space program. The youngest of four children, he grew up in Florida; his father was a NASA engineer who served as deputy launch director of the Apollo 11 mission.

The Wallops Flight Facility — one of the oldest launch sites in the world — is located in his district. Rigell has tried to open up a parcel of land near Wallops to development as a technology park; the federal government gave the land to Accomack County in 1976 on the condition that it would be used for recreation. The House passed his 2011 bill to lift the deed restriction, but it didn't move in the Senate.

Rigell's first business out of college was a cleaning service, which initially consisted of him and his wife, Teri. By 1990 he had earned an MBA. He opened an auto dealership in the Virginia Beach area. Around that time, he began contributing to, and volunteering for, Republican candidates. He was also active in numerous business and charitable organizations.

Music is another facet of his public life. Along with current state Sen. Jeff McWaters, Rigell belongs to the band Guava Jam — he plays the drums, and often sits in with other bands at public functions when asked.

Rigell won a six-way GOP primary with about 40 percent of the vote in 2010, then faced first-term Democrat Glenn Nye. In a solidly Republican year, Rigell won by nearly 11 points.

The redrawn congressional map for 2012 added Republican areas of Newport News to the 2nd District, but Rigell's re-election was no sure thing — Democrats poured millions of dollars into the Virginia Beach media market as part of the presidential campaign.

The Democratic nominee was Paul Hirschbiel, a venture capitalist and friend of Democratic Sen. Mark Warner. Though the candidates were personally acquainted through philanthropic work, Hirschbiel said Rigell's dissents from his party were mostly calculated to win favor with voters.

Rigell, one of the richest members of Congress, dipped into his personal fortune to supplement his fundraising. He won by less than 8 points.

Key Votes

2012	
Extend a Social Security payroll tax cut and unemployment benefits	YES
Ease securities rules to expand small-business access to capital	YES
Extend for one year subsidized student loan interest rates financed by a cut in health care spending	YES
Cite Attorney General Eric H. Holder Jr. for contempt of Congress	NO
Create a visa program for foreign graduates in high-tech fields	YES
Extend most Bush-era income tax rates while allowing rates for top-bracket earners to rise (Jan. 1, 2013)	NO
2011	
Strike funding for F-35 alternative engine	NO
Prevent EPA from regulating greenhouse gas emissions to address climate change	YES
Extend certain provisions of Patriot Act for four years	YES
Declare opposition to use of ground troops in Libya	YES
Overhaul patent law	YES
Pass compromise debt limit increase plan and establish future spending limits	YES
Allow consideration of measures to implement three trade agreements	YES

CQ Vote Studies

	PARTY UNITY		PRESIDENTIAL SUPPORT	
	SUPPORT	OPPOSE	SUPPORT	OPPOSE
2012	93%	7%	20%	80%
2011	93%	7%	19%	81%

Interest Groups

	AFL-CIO	ADA	CCUS	ACU
2012	14%	5%	83%	84%
2011	0%	15%	100%	80%

Virginia 2

Southeast — Virginia Beach, part of Newport News, Eastern Shore

Naval warships are a common sight in the waterways of the 2nd, situated on Virginia's southeastern edge at the mouth of the Chesapeake Bay. The district takes in much of the Hampton Roads region, including Virginia Beach and parts of Norfolk and Newport News, and a high concentration of military bases. It also includes less-populated Accomack and Northampton counties, Virginia's portion of the eastern shore of the Chesapeake.

Defense spending, tourism and commercial shipping support a stable economy around Hampton Roads. Norfolk Naval Base (shared with the 3rd) is the world's largest naval station. The region's ports serve a number of international shipping businesses, and shipbuilding has long been a major industry at the mouth of the James River, where aircraft carriers and submarines are constructed. Huntington Ingalls is developing an industry training center in Newport News.

Virginia Beach also relies on the tourists drawn to the Atlantic. While unemployment rates have remained low, the financial crisis led to an uptick in foreclosures. With the BRAC closure of Fort Monroe in 2011, the land became a national monument and development plans are ongoing.

The population is nearly one-fourth black and has a conservatism rooted in military and economic issues that may be boosted after redistricting extended the district to the Army's Fort Eustis. Buoyed by strong African-American turnout, Barack Obama narrowly won a 50 percent victory in the 2012 presidential election.

Major Industry
Defense, tourism, shipbuilding, tourism

Cities
Virginia Beach, Norfolk (pt.), Newport News (pt.), Hampton (pt.)

Military
Naval Station Norfolk (shared with the 3rd), 49,328 military, 19,323 civilian (2011); Joint Base Langley-Eustis (shared with the 3rd), 13,566 military, 6,331 civilian; Joint Expeditionary Base Little creek-Fort Story, 10,676 military, 3,378 civilian (2011); Naval Air Station Oceana, 10,473 civilian, 2,042 military; Naval Air Station Oceana Dam Neck Annex, 2,437 military, 1,592 civilian

Notable
The Norfolk Botanical Garden has more than 40 themed gardens.

Rep. Robert C. Scott (D)

Capitol Office
225-8351
bobbyscott.house.gov
1201 Longworth Bldg. 20515-4603; fax 225-8354

Committees
Education & the Workforce
Judiciary

Residence
Newport News

Born
April 30, 1947; Washington, D.C.

Religion
Episcopalian

Family
Divorced

Education
Harvard U., A.B. 1969; Boston College, J.D. 1973

Military
Mass. National Guard, 1970-74; Army Reserve, 1974-76

Career
Lawyer

Political Highlights
Va. House, 1978-83; Va. Senate, 1983-93; Democratic nominee for U.S. House, 1986

ELECTION RESULTS

2012 GENERAL		
Robert C. Scott (D)	259,199	81.3%
Dean L. Longo (R)	58,931	18.5%
2012 PRIMARY		
Robert C. Scott (D)		unopposed
2010 GENERAL		
Robert C. Scott (D)	114,754	70.0%
C.L. "Chuck" Smith Jr. (R)	44,553	27.2%
James J. Quigley (LIBERT)	2,383	1.4%
John D. Kelly (I)	2,039	1.2%

Previous Winning Percentages
2008 (97%); 2006 (96%); 2004 (69%); 2002 (96%); 2000 (98%); 1998 (76%); 1996 (82%); 1994 (79%); 1992 (79%)

Elected 1992; 11th term

Scott calls his approach to governing "evidence-based," and his number-crunching efforts are most often in the name of reshaping the criminal justice system and equalizing educational opportunities. He is a steady liberal who also holds some civil libertarian views.

A lawyer by trade, Scott is the top Democrat on the Judiciary Subcommittee on Crime, Terrorism, Homeland Security and Investigations. He chaired the panel when Democrats were in the majority. His mantra: "Evidence-based crime policy reduces crime and saves money. All the studies show it. You can't debate it."

Much of his signature work has been to improve the lot of those on the wrong side of the law. He challenges the perception that mandatory minimum sentences reduce criminal recidivism. "Sound bites and slogans have resulted in a massive increase in overincarceration, particularly with minorities," he said. He wants judges to "ascertain objectively" in sentencing. Scott boasts that he has greatly reduced the number of bills that leave the committee with mandatory-minimum-sentence provisions. In 2013, Scott and subcommittee Chairman Jim Sensenbrenner of Wisconsin are leading a task force studying what they call the "over-criminalization" of the justice system.

Scott's fingerprints were on an August 2010 law on cocaine sentencing. Previously, offenses involving a small amount of crack cocaine drew a minimum five years of jail time; powder cocaine offenses required 100 times the quantity to trigger a similar punishment. Since crack is more prevalent in cities, Scott said the law disproportionately affected poor blacks. The law did not achieve his goal of parity — the ratio is now 18-1 — but Scott, a member of the Congressional Black Caucus, called it "good progress."

Scott sees "second chance" programs, which assist ex-offenders in returning to society, as a means to cut government overhead. By reducing recidivism, he said, they create savings that materialize within a year or two.

In 2011, the House passed his bill to require states receiving federal grants for law enforcement to report prisoner deaths to the attorney general. The Senate did not act on it.

The Judiciary Committee has given Scott a place in civil liberties battles. He opposed the 2001 anti-terrorism law known as the Patriot Act and called its surveillance provisions a trampling of individual liberties. He voted in 2011 against a four-year extension of expiring provisions in the law, which was later enacted. He also frowned on the fiscal 2012 defense policy law, citing a provision that he felt would "allow the indefinite military detention without charge or trial of anyone, including U.S. citizens, accused or suspected of involvement with terrorism."

Scott supports plans to update electronic privacy laws, so that warrants are needed to track people through the geolocation data on their mobile devices.

Republican efforts involving faith-based organizations have given him pause. In 2007, Scott helped remove a provision from a Head Start reauthorization bill that would have let faith-based providers consider applicants' adherence to the groups' beliefs when hiring. "If you allow discrimination in federally funded programs, you essentially lose your moral authority to enforce civil rights laws," he said. When the House passed a 2011 resolution affirming "In God We Trust" as the official motto of the United States, Scott called it an unconstitutional endorsement of one religious view over another.

On the Education and the Workforce Committee, Scott focuses on federal means to equalize school experiences across economic strata.

His own education took him to Massachusetts. Scott is the son of a surgeon and a teacher. When local white officials resisted court-ordered integration of the public school system, the Scotts used a voucher to send their son to Groton, the prestigious Massachusetts preparatory school. He went on to Harvard, then the Boston College law school.

Today, he has shown a passion for assisting troubled youths. He would like to modify federal education law to address drop-out rates and the achievement gap between students — one of his suggestions is improving the distribution of highly qualified teachers, so that good instructors end up at schools facing the biggest challenges. He said that despite its flaws, the 2001 education law known as No Child Left Behind rightly "quantified school failure" with its testing regimen. He introduced his own measure in 2011 to improve the calculation and reporting of secondary-school graduation rates.

Scott also has military credentials. He is a former member of the Army Reserve and National Guard.

He has joined with Republicans in the state delegation to protect military installations in Virginia, but they were unsuccessful in halting the 2011 closure of the Norfolk-based Joint Forces Command, which coordinated cooperation among the services and employed about 6,000 military and civilian personnel. Some of the JFC functions (and jobs) remained in the region, but Scott saw no justification for the move beside cost-cutting. (He has not joined his state colleagues, however, in calling for offshore oil and gas exploration in Virginia, citing environmental concerns. He's OK with offshore wind farms.)

Scott was an early proponent of letting tax cuts from 2001 and 2003 expire: "I believe when people start putting numbers on a page, instead of just giving speeches, that they will notice that although it's unpopular, it's a lot less unpopular than major cuts in Social Security, Medicare and defense." He was one of just 16 House Democrats to vote against the January 2013 "fiscal cliff" deal that permanently extended those tax rates for earnings under $400,000. He said the agreement made it far more likely that entitlement programs would be cut in future deficit reduction negotiations.

After law school, Scott returned to Newport News and became active in local civic groups, which eventually led him into politics. He won a seat in the state House in 1977 and in five years moved to the state Senate. He was unsuccessful in his first run for Congress in 1986, but made another run six years later — redistricting resulted in a 3rd District that was 64 percent black. With no incumbent running, he won the primary and breezed to victory that November. He became the first black House member from Virginia since 1891.

A federal panel struck down the 3rd District's boundaries in 1997, and new lines drawn by the General Assembly set the black population at 54 percent. Scott still won handily and has easily won re-election since then.

Key Votes

2012

Extend a Social Security payroll tax cut and unemployment benefits	NO
Ease securities rules to expand small-business access to capital	NO
Extend for one year subsidized student loan interest rates financed by a cut in health care spending	NO
Cite Attorney General Eric H. Holder Jr. for contempt of Congress	?
Create a visa program for foreign graduates in high-tech fields	NO
Extend most Bush-era income tax rates while allowing rates for top-bracket earners to rise (Jan. 1, 2013)	NO

2011

Strike funding for F-35 alternative engine	NO
Prevent EPA from regulating greenhouse gas emissions to address climate change	NO
Extend certain provisions of Patriot Act for four years	NO
Declare opposition to use of ground troops in Libya	NO
Overhaul patent law	YES
Pass compromise debt limit increase plan and establish future spending limits	NO
Allow consideration of measures to implement three trade agreements	NO

CQ Vote Studies

	PARTY UNITY		PRESIDENTIAL SUPPORT	
	SUPPORT	OPPOSE	SUPPORT	OPPOSE
2012	95%	5%	81%	19%
2011	94%	6%	79%	21%
2010	97%	3%	86%	14%
2009	98%	2%	96%	4%
2008	99%	1%	11%	89%

Interest Groups

	AFL-CIO	ADA	CCUS	ACU
2012	95%	90%	25%	0%
2011	97%	75%	25%	4%
2010	100%	100%	13%	0%
2009	100%	95%	33%	4%
2008	100%	100%	53%	8%

Virginia 3

Southeast — most of Richmond, Hampton and Norfolk

The 3rd District combines two of the state's most populous regions with an emphasis on government and military: The district collects most of the capital city of Richmond, small-town Petersburg and parts of the maritime Hampton Roads region. It is the only district statewide where black residents account for a majority of the population (60 percent).

Urban Richmond is a commercial and cultural hub along the James River. The city's unemployment rate has not spiked, due to a diverse economy, government jobs and the Port of Virginia. Capital One financial services and banks are top employers, along with one of the nation's largest cigarette factories and the Virginia Commonwealth University medical center.

The coastal plain region known as Hampton Roads is dominated by the naval base in Norfolk (shared with the 2nd) and associated facilities and contractors. Shipbuilding has long been lucrative here. The Port of Virginia also makes this a commercial shipping, distribution and passenger cruise center. Norfolk is expected to experience more growth with an Amtrak line connecting it to Washington, D.C., via Richmond.

During decennial redistricting, the 3rd gained Petersburg and an expanded footprint in Richmond while losing a portion of Norfolk and New Kent County. Richmond and Portsmouth are black-majority, and Hampton Roads is home to numerous military veterans. Redistricting further concentrated Democratic support in the safe seat for the party. The 3rd gave Barack Obama his best showing in the state at nearly 80 percent in 2012.

Major Industry

Defense, shipbuilding, shipping and distribution, health care, government

Military Bases

Naval Station Norfolk, 10,676 military, 3,378 civilian (2011) (shared with the 2nd); Joint Base Langley-Eustis, 13,566 military, 6,331 civilian (shared with the 2nd); Fort Lee (Army), 4,694 military, 3,401 civilian (2012) (shared with the 4th); Naval Medical Center Portsmouth, 3,155 military, 1,848 civilian (2012); Norfolk Naval Shipyard at Portsmouth, 500 military, 4,200 civilian

Cities

Norfolk (pt.), Richmond (pt.), Newport News (pt.), Hampton (pt.)

Notable

Norfolk is home to the North American headquarters of NATO.

Rep. J. Randy Forbes (R)

Capitol Office
225-6365
forbes.house.gov
2135 Rayburn Bldg. 20515-4604; fax 226-1170

Committees
Armed Services
(Seapower & Projection Forces - Chairman)
Judiciary

Residence
Chesapeake

Born
Feb. 17, 1952; Chesapeake, Va.

Religion
Baptist

Family
Wife, Shirley Forbes; four children

Education
Randolph-Macon College, B.A. 1974 (political science); U. of Virginia, J.D. 1977

Career
Lawyer; state legislative aide

Political Highlights
Va. House, 1990-97 (Republican floor leader, 1994-97); Va. Republican Party chairman, 1996-2000; Va. Senate, 1997-2001 (Republican floor leader, 1998-2000)

ELECTION RESULTS

2012 GENERAL		
J. Randy Forbes (R)	199,292	56.9%
Ella P. Ward (D)	150,190	42.9%
2012 PRIMARY		
J. Randy Forbes (R)	26,294	89.7%
R.M. "Bonnie" Girard (R)	3,017	10.3%
2010 GENERAL		
J. Randy Forbes (R)	123,659	62.3%
Wynne V.E. LeGrow (D)	74,298	37.4%

Previous Winning Percentages
2008 (60%); 2006 (76%); 2004 (64%); 2002 (98%); 2001 Special Election (52%)

Elected 2001; 6th full term

Forbes is direct and polished, reflecting the Pentagon brass he deals with when overseeing military matters. The longtime GOP operative is assertive in just about all of his work — including his leadership of the Congressional Prayer Caucus.

For the 113th Congress (2013-14), Forbes has taken the gavel of the Armed Services Subcommittee on Seapower and Projection Forces. His efforts there build on the principles he laid out while chairing the Readiness Subcommittee in the 112th Congress (2011-12).

In that job, Forbes had two goals: first, making sure the U.S. military is never in a fair fight; and second, "when a Chinese admiral or an Iranian general looks across the field ... and he sees American soldiers, I want him to say, 'Not today.' " He sees the military as a tool for the common defense, but "with technology the way it is, with the world situation the way it is, we've gotta be all over the globe."

He supports a shift of military emphasis to the Pacific theater, but he says that the Navy and Air Force will need improved capabilities in the region — especially forward-based assets that allow rapid military mobilizations. "We have developed a force replete with aging equipment and dwindling numbers," he wrote in Roll Call in 2011.

Forbes feels Americans have not been clearly told the risks of diminished defense spending, and China is a frequent foil when he outlines those risks. Forbes observed Chinese shipbuilding and military modernization during an official visit in 2005 and has warned that we know too little about the aspiring superpower. China has more ships than the U.S. Navy, infrastructure for cyberwar and a growing nuclear stockpile, and "we've already ceded space over to them, pretty much," he said. Forbes founded the Congressional China Caucus and co-chairs it with Madeleine Z. Bordallo, a Democrat from Guam.

Speaking to the American Enterprise Institute in 2013, he said that military spending in regards to China should have a strategic goal: "To deter China from aggression until the inherent unsustainability of China's economic model causes the country's leaders to focus internally on domestic concerns."

Some Atlantic-based assets have also gotten his attention, particularly those in his district. Forbes was born in Chesapeake and lives 180 feet from the house he grew up in — "I haven't gone too far in the world," he jokes. Forbes was instrumental in protecting Fort Lee in the 2005 round of base closures. And he joined other Virginians in successfully opposing the Navy's plan to move a Norfolk-based aircraft carrier, and many jobs, to Florida. (They were not able to preserve Joint Forces Command in Norfolk, however.)

Forbes has been wary of altering military benefits and wants extensive polling to determine the effects on morale before any changes are made. Such studies were undertaken before repealing the "don't ask, don't tell" policy on gay servicemembers, he notes.

He voted against the final fiscal 2012 defense policy law, to protest its lower spending levels for the military. And he was one of just 10 Republicans to oppose the party's fiscal 2014 budget proposal, because it did not plan to undo defense cuts from a 2011 deficit reduction law. Forbes has been hawkish on most other fiscal issues, however. He opposes tax increases.

Forbes, an attorney who mostly practiced corporate business law, also sits on the Judiciary Committee. He takes a tough-on-crime approach. In 2006, he won House passage of a bill targeting illegal immigrants who belong to criminal gangs, and he has excoriated Obama administration officials for what he sees as selective enforcement of immigration law.

The Judiciary panel launched some of Forbes' most high-profile work in 2011: a resolution reaffirming "In God We Trust" as the national motto. Democrats said GOP leaders were wasting time by scheduling a vote on the resolution — it was adopted 396-9 — in the middle of raging fiscal disputes. Forbes defended it as an appropriate measure for challenging times, often citing the faith of the nation's founders. (One wall of his office features a copy of the Declaration of Independence and portraits of all 56 signers.)

Forbes, a Sunday school teacher for more than 20 years, co-founded the Congressional Prayer Caucus in 2005. It has more than 100 members, and its goals include working "to preserve the presence of religion, faith and morality in the marketplace of ideas." He calls for displaying the national motto in public places. The caucus provides guidance to state-level groups in that effort.

Forbes has an interest in research. Introduced in several Congresses, his "New Manhattan Project" bill would incentivize private sector research by offering big prize money for renewable-energy innovations; it has gotten rave reviews from publications such as The Wall Street Journal but little legislative support. He wants targeted federal spending for medical research, believing that attacking Alzheimer's, Parkinson's and diabetes can dramatically cut health care expenses in the future. Forbes is also a fan of computer modeling and simulation, and in 2008 he helped win enactment of grants to enhance universities' programs in those areas.

Forbes is the middle of three children. His father sold life insurance and was a friend and adviser to the community: "He always had this kind of love and belief that you had to pay back whatever you had." Forbes worked as a shoe salesman through high school, then clerked and did research for law firms when he headed off to college.

After a few years of private practice, he won a seat in the House of Delegates with little Republican support; instead, he relied on goodwill built up by his father. Forbes remembers people repaying favors his father had done 20 years before as they supported his first campaign. He rose to become Republican floor leader and later served in the state Senate.

When a former law school classmate, George Allen, became governor, he made Forbes chairman of the state Republican Party. Under Forbes' watch from 1996 to 2000, the party became the dominant power in Virginia politics. In 2001, he geared up to run for lieutenant governor, but when conservative Democrat Norman Sisisky died that March, Forbes ran for the House.

Many voters broke along racial lines in his contest with state Sen. Louise Lucas, a black Democrat and former shipyard worker. Forbes won 52 percent of the vote. Redistricting changed the composition of the district somewhat, but Forbes hasn't faced serious opposition since.

Key Votes

2012	
Extend a Social Security payroll tax cut and unemployment benefits	NO
Ease securities rules to expand small-business access to capital	YES
Extend for one year subsidized student loan interest rates financed by a cut in health care spending	YES
Cite Attorney General Eric H. Holder Jr. for contempt of Congress	YES
Create a visa program for foreign graduates in high-tech fields	YES
Extend most Bush-era income tax rates while allowing rates for top-bracket earners to rise (Jan. 1, 2013)	NO
2011	
Strike funding for F-35 alternative engine	NO
Prevent EPA from regulating greenhouse gas emissions to address climate change	YES
Extend certain provisions of Patriot Act for four years	YES
Declare opposition to use of ground troops in Libya	YES
Overhaul patent law	YES
Pass compromise debt limit increase plan and establish future spending limits	NO
Allow consideration of measures to implement three trade agreements	YES

CQ Vote Studies

	PARTY UNITY		PRESIDENTIAL SUPPORT	
	SUPPORT	OPPOSE	SUPPORT	OPPOSE
2012	95%	5%	10%	90%
2011	93%	7%	25%	75%
2010	94%	6%	26%	74%
2009	90%	10%	25%	75%
2008	95%	5%	60%	40%

Interest Groups

	AFL-CIO	ADA	CCUS	ACU
2012	14%	0%	91%	88%
2011	0%	10%	94%	84%
2010	7%	5%	75%	100%
2009	10%	0%	86%	96%
2008	25%	25%	78%	91%

Virginia 4

Southeast — Chesapeake, Suffolk, Chester

The sprawling 4th District tiptoes around Richmond and Norfolk and includes rambling stretches of rural Virginia. Swinging around the farming counties west and southwest of the capital, it heads down to the North Carolina border from Greensville County east through Chesapeake. Most residents live south of the James River near Norfolk or in communities between Petersburg and the Richmond orbit along Interstate 95.

The military has a major presence here. Naval Station Norfolk is just over the border in the 3rd, and support facilities and defense contractors are scattered through Chesapeake and fast-growing Suffolk; but the 2011 closure of the Joint Forces Command eliminated thousands of jobs. To the north, the Army's Fort Lee (shared with the 3rd) employs thousands near Petersburg, and the southern outskirts of Richmond host a Defense Supply Center. To the west is the National Guard's Fort Pickett in rural Blackstone.

Chesapeake and Suffolk depend on military and support sites, as well as the nearby Port of Virginia. Beyond the cities, tobacco and peanut farming are key, and Smithfield hosts a meat processing plant.

After decennial redistricting, the 4th lost the black-majority and liberal Petersburg. Still, nearly one-third of the district's population is black — the second-largest proportion statewide — and its Southside counties are nearly 60 percent black. The district trends Republican but Democrats can do well at the local level. The more populated and black-majority areas favored Barack Obama, but Republican presidential candidates won slim majorities from residents within these boundaries in 2008 and 2012.

Major Industry
Military, agriculture, tobacco, health care, manufacturing

Military Bases
Fort Lee (Army), 4,694 military, 3,401 civilian (2012) (shared with the 3rd); Naval Support Activity Norfolk, Northwest Annex, 841 military, 549 civilian; Defense Supply Center Richmond, 2,814 civilian, 104 military

Cities
Chesapeake, Suffolk, Hopewell, Chester (unincorp.)

Notable
Suffolk, which calls itself the peanut capital of the world, is the birthplace of Planters' Mr. Peanut and hosts an annual Suffolk Peanut Festival.

Rep. Robert Hurt (R)

Capitol Office
225-4711
hurt.house.gov
125 Cannon Bldg. 20515-4605; fax 225-5681

Committees
Financial Services

Residence
Chatham

Born
June 16, 1969; Manhattan, N.Y.

Religion
Presbyterian

Family
Wife, Kathy Hurt; three children

Education
Hampden-Sydney College, B.A. 1991 (English); Mississippi College, J.D. 1995

Career
Lawyer; county prosecutor

Political Highlights
Chatham Town Council, 2000-01; Va. House, 2002-08; Va. Senate, 2008-11

ELECTION RESULTS

2012 GENERAL		
Robert Hurt (R)	193,009	55.4%
John Wade Douglass (D)	149,214	42.9%
Kenneth J. Hildebrandt (IGREEN)	5,500	1.6%
2012 PRIMARY		
Robert Hurt (R)		unopposed
2010 GENERAL		
Robert Hurt (R)	119,560	50.8%
Tom Perriello (D)	110,562	47.0%
Jeffrey A. Clark (I)	4,992	2.1%

Elected 2010; 2nd term

Hurt comes from the district that holds Thomas Jefferson's Monticello, and parts of his home turf were represented by James Madison in the 1st Congress. Appropriately, his conservative agenda jibes with the platform of Republicans from the early 1800s: He wants to shrink the national debt and scale down the reach of the federal government.

Also like those Virginians, Hurt has a background in the law. He worked as a county prosecutor before starting a general practice based in Chatham. He first served in political office as a member of the town council, eventually moving on to six years in the House of Delegates and three years in the state Senate.

In D.C., he lines up with social and fiscal conservatives as a member of the Republican Study Committee. Much of his legislative work takes place on the Financial Services Committee, but he also keeps up on the issues of interest to the farms that make up a huge chunk of his district.

On fiscal matters, Hurt broadly supports GOP efforts to reduce spending, and in his first year in the House he argued that Congress didn't cut enough — he opposed the final version of a catchall spending bill for fiscal 2011 that would have trimmed spending by $40 billion, saying that the reduction was inadequate.

He likes the idea of a balanced-budget amendment to the Constitution and has approved of the budgets put forth by Wisconsin Republican Paul D. Ryan. The fiscal 2012 budget "reforms Medicare in a way that I think will save it for current beneficiaries and for future generations, in a way that I think is very intelligent," Hurt said in 2011. "It really does infuse competition into the system, and we will see the benefits of it."

Hurt sometimes puts his district before his party, however. He voted against a free-trade pact with South Korea in 2011, agreeing with several lawmakers from Virginia and the Carolinas that it could hurt textile producers in the area.

From the Financial Services Committee, Hurt makes a common critique of the 2010 financial regulatory overhaul known as Dodd-Frank — that the law "is offensive because of all the regulations that are going to get passed down to the small banks, the community banks."

In June 2011, the committee approved his bill to reduce Securities and Exchange Commission reporting requirements for many private equity companies. Hurt said such investors are crucial to the health of businesses in his district. He reintroduced it in March 2013.

For the 113th Congress (2013-14), Hurt was named the vice chairman of the Subcommittee on Capital Markets and Government Sponsored Enterprises. He favors the gradual withdrawal of the federal government from the housing finance market, citing the "moral hazard that's associated with having lending policy tied up with the finances that underpin" the economy. "I think it's just bad, bad, bad," he said.

In 2011, Hurt wrote a bill to require the director of the Federal Housing Finance Agency — which controls Fannie Mae and Freddie Mac — to review the GSEs' substantial portfolios of patents and determine which ones are "non-mission critical" and could be sold. The measure also would have required Fannie and Freddie to sell off some of their mortgage data, to both raise revenue and give private lenders more access to such information. The Financial Services Committee never approved the bill, but it appeared on the House's calendar in September 2012.

Democrats complained, and the bill was pulled. "It's a terrible idea to announce to the buyers that you're going to have a fire sale," said Barney Frank of Massachusetts, the top Democrat on Financial Services at the time.

Much of Hurt's anti-regulatory work has to do with agriculture. He pushed hard for House passage of a 2011 bill by South Dakota Republican Kristi Noem to bar the EPA from regulating dust kicked up by farm activities. EPA officials said they had no intention of regulating such dust, but Hurt blanched at the notion of the agency asking Congress to back off.

"We'll tell you what the policy is, and then you execute it," Hurt said in 2011. "That's so fundamental. Any fifth-grader knows that that's the reason there's separation of powers in our Constitution."

The Transportation and Infrastructure Committee approved Hurt's 2012 bill to modify the Clean Water Act so that EPA permits wouldn't be required for many instances of farmers or ranchers discharging dredged or fill material into navigable waters, including wetlands. Hurt said that regulators were overstepping their statutory authority and hurting agricultural activity.

Hurt's family came from Virginia, but he was born in New York, where his father was working as an editor for Reader's Digest in Pleasantville. Hurt's brother, Charles, is also a journalist; he has worked as the Washington bureau chief for the New York Post, written columns for the Washington Times and chipped in for the news aggregation site The Drudge Report.

Hurt does have some professional backup in the family. His sister works as an attorney, but "on the other side" — whereas he was a prosecutor, she has worked in a public defender's office in Pennsylvania.

The family came back south before Hurt's teen years, and "we've got four generations sitting on the back row in Chatham Presbyterian Church," he said in 2011. That includes his grandmother, who drove the first bookmobile for Pittsylvania County and took the kids to see historic sites around the state.

One-term Democrat Tom Perriello was viewed as vulnerable in 2010 because of his support of key items in his party's agenda, including the 2009 economic stimulus law, a cap-and-trade energy bill and the 2010 health care overhaul. At first, some tea party activists were skeptical of Hurt because of his support for a 2004 state tax increase. But he won a seven-way primary by a wide margin. He got plenty of help from the National Republican Congressional Committee and beat Perriello by about 4 points.

Neither the tea party nor Perriello challenged Hurt in 2012, and retired Air Force Gen. John Wade Douglass got the Democratic nomination — he had planned to challenge Republican Frank R. Wolf in the 10th District, but changed his mind.

Douglass played up his military experience and took some spirited digs at Hurt, but Hurt enjoyed a significant fundraising advantage and was largely unflappable. He won by more than 12 points.

Key Votes

2012

Extend a Social Security payroll tax cut and unemployment benefits	YES
Ease securities rules to expand small-business access to capital	YES
Extend for one year subsidized student loan interest rates financed by a cut in health care spending	YES
Cite Attorney General Eric H. Holder Jr. for contempt of Congress	YES
Create a visa program for foreign graduates in high-tech fields	YES
Extend most Bush-era income tax rates while allowing rates for top-bracket earners to rise (Jan. 1, 2013)	NO

2011

Strike funding for F-35 alternative engine	NO
Prevent EPA from regulating greenhouse gas emissions to address climate change	YES
Extend certain provisions of Patriot Act for four years	YES
Declare opposition to use of ground troops in Libya	YES
Overhaul patent law	YES
Pass compromise debt limit increase plan and establish future spending limits	YES
Allow consideration of measures to implement three trade agreements	YES

CQ Vote Studies

	PARTY UNITY		PRESIDENTIAL SUPPORT	
	SUPPORT	OPPOSE	SUPPORT	OPPOSE
2012	97%	3%	16%	84%
2011	97%	3%	22%	78%

Interest Groups

	AFL-CIO	ADA	CCUS	ACU
2012	16%	0%	92%	88%
2011	4%	10%	94%	[illegible]

Virginia 5

Central — most of Fauquier County, Charlottesville, Danville

The 5th District sweeps from the North Carolina border north to Warrenton-area horse country, taking up Shenandoah foothills, forests and Civil War sites. Its main population centers are Danville, a blue-collar industrial city on the North Carolina border, and Charlottesville, a historic college town in the heart of central Virginia.

Although Virginia's unemployment rates have been lower than national averages, Southside counties such as Halifax, Mecklenburg and Brunswick have yet to replace lost manufacturing jobs. Danville, a historical tobacco and textile center, has struggled with industrial decline for decades. Downtown tobacco warehouses are being redone for commercial use, and the city hopes to expand its technology and advanced manufacturing sectors.

Charlottesville is known for its historic ties to Thomas Jefferson and James Monroe, especially Jefferson's self-designed neoclassical home, Monticello. The city is also home to the University of Virginia, founded by Jefferson and home to more than 21,000 students. Charlottesville's diverse economy is driven by health care, service and education. A defense-related sector is growing thanks to the 2010 relocation of the Defense Intelligence Agency to the city. The university and its medical center account for the most jobs in the city, and there are plans for steady expansion over the next decade. Charlottesville's downtown has seen significant commercial and residential growth, and beyond campus, rolling hills host wineries.

The 5th added several rural counties north of Albemarle County during remapping following the 2010 census and now stretches north of Interstate 66. These changes did little to alter its Republican-leaning tilt, which washes out Democratic majorities in Charlottesville and Danville. Barack Obama took Charlottesville's Albemarle County by double digits and the city of Danville by more than 20 points in the 2012 presidential election, but the 5th overall gave Republican Mitt Romney 53 percent of its vote.

Major Industry

Agriculture, higher education, manufacturing, textiles, service

Cities

Charlottesville, Danville

Notable

The annual four-day Virginia Film Festival is hosted at the University of Virginia in Charlottesville.

Rep. Robert W. Goodlatte (R)

Capitol Office
225-5431
goodlatte.house.gov
2309 Rayburn Bldg. 20515-4606; fax 225-9681

Committees
Agriculture
Judiciary - Chairman

Residence
Roanoke

Born
Sept. 22, 1952; Holyoke, Mass.

Religion
Christian Scientist

Family
Wife, Maryellen Goodlatte; two children

Education
Bates College, B.A. 1974 (government); Washington and Lee U., J.D. 1977

Career
Lawyer; congressional aide

Political Highlights
Roanoke City Republican Committee chairman, 1980-83; 6th Congressional District Republican Party chairman, 1983-88

ELECTION RESULTS

2012 GENERAL		
Robert W. Goodlatte (R)	211,278	65.2%
Andrew B. Schmookler (D)	111,949	34.6%
2012 PRIMARY		
Robert W. Goodlatte (R)	21,808	66.5%
Karen U. Kwiatkowski (R)	10,991	33.5%
2010 GENERAL		
Robert W. Goodlatte (R)	127,487	76.3%
Jeffrey W. Vanke (I)	21,649	13.0%
Stuart M. Bain (LIBERT)	15,309	9.2%
write-ins (WRI)	2,709	1.6%

Previous Winning Percentages
2008 (62%); 2006 (75%); 2004 (97%); 2002 (97%); 2000 (99%); 1998 (69%); 1996 (67%); 1994 (100%); 1992 (60%)

Elected 1992; 11th term

As the chairman of the Judiciary Committee, Goodlatte has ownership of some of the most divisive issues before the 113th Congress — immigration and gun control among them. He has signaled his preference to take deliberate approaches to those issues, to the delight of House Republicans.

Goodlatte (GOOD-lat) promotes classic GOP themes: more competition, more free enterprise, and less government intervention. He often says his top priority is "dealing with out-of-control government spending." In 2011, he finally saw action on his proposal for a balanced-budget amendment to the Constitution. It fell 23 votes short of the two-thirds majority required for adoption. In 2013, Republican leaders again reserved the symbolic designation of "House Joint Resolution 1" for his proposal.

His secondary priorities are nothing to sneeze at. He took the Judiciary gavel in 2013, as Republicans were mulling whether to budge on an overhaul of the immigration system. Before coming to Congress, Goodlatte was a lawyer specializing in immigration law.

"I will continue working closely with my colleagues in Congress to pass much-needed reforms to grant local and state agencies authority to enforce the law and crack down on illegal immigration," he wrote in late 2012. He does not support the idea of granting illegal immigrants already in the country a means to achieving citizenship. "People have a pathway to citizenship right now," he told NPR in 2013. "It's to abide by the immigration laws."

In spring 2013, as the Democratic Senate worked on a comprehensive overhaul, Goodlatte said changes should go through the committee process. He started work on smaller measures: one to expand an employment verification system, and his bill to revamp agricultural guest worker programs. Some Democrats would describe his positions as hard-line, but Goodlatte is mostly mild-mannered.

In the 112th Congress (2011-12) he chaired the Subcommittee on Intellectual Property, Competition and the Internet, placing him among the House members with the most influence on technology policy. "The Internet should not be regulated," he said. "But it also should not become the wild, wild West of the 21st century." Goodlatte seeks solutions that "throw the book at the bad guys but don't overregulate the good guys."

He opposed "network neutrality" rules finalized by the Federal Communications Commission in 2011. The rules are designed to prevent broadband providers from blocking or slowing the delivery of certain Internet content to users, but critics have worried that regulators could use them to promote a political agenda. Goodlatte prefers antitrust law as a mechanism to combat any private sector wrongdoing.

But he backed an anti-piracy measure, known as SOPA (the Stop Online Piracy Act), which drew substantial media attention and stalled after opposition from Internet companies. The bill would have allowed law enforcement agencies to shut down offending websites by obtaining a court order, which Goodlatte said would strengthen the ability of innovators to enforce property rights abroad and thus encourage innovation and job creation.

In 2006, he steered into law a bill to curb online gambling by prohibiting Internet-based businesses from accepting credit cards and electronic transfers for betting. "The Internet is a challenge to the sovereignty of civilized communities, states and nations to decide what is appropriate and decent behavior," he said on the House floor in 1999.

Over the years, Goodlatte has worked on legislation to protect computer users' privacy, shield children from indecent material and allow export of encryption technology. In 2007, he backed a bill sponsored by Democrat Anna G. Eshoo of California to ban Internet access taxes permanently, but the two wound up reluctantly endorsing a compromise seven-year extension of the existing moratorium.

Goodlatte has an interest in spreading technology to rural areas, and he once used information technology to build up his Roanoke law practice. He sees communications technology today as comparable to the railroad in the 19th century. "If the railroad came through your town and connected you with the rest of the country, you'd boom. If it didn't, you'd go bust," he said.

Goodlatte handled a wealth of rural concerns as chairman of the Agriculture Committee in the 108th and 109th Congresses (2003-06). He helped pass President George W. Bush's forest initiative, which expedited the cutting of timber in areas prone to wildfires, and a buyout program for tobacco farmers.

He is now the No. 2 Republican on the panel. Goodlatte says that farm bills have historically been "major federal government interference in the ... agricultural marketplace."

"You want to design a farm program that promotes free enterprise and also helps farmers deal" with crop failure and overproduction. He prefers futures trading and forward contracting to prevent overproduction. His solution for addressing crop failure: expanding crop insurance to cover nearly all agricultural products and using upgraded technology to assess insurance prices according to risks in a region. Price supports, disaster payments and direct payments to farmers all give him pause.

He particularly wants to end the federal requirement for renewable-fuel production, as the diversion of corn to ethanol production has created supply problems for farms and other businesses that rely on corn.

Goodlatte grew up in western Massachusetts, where his father managed a Friendly's ice cream store and his mother worked part time in a department store. His parents liked to visit places of historical significance, which nurtured his interest in presidential history. As of 2012, he had visited at least one home of every deceased president. Goodlatte gives talks in his district to historical societies and other groups about history and presidential homes. He is also a baseball fan, and has about 50 or 60 signed baseballs.

Goodlatte was president of the College Republicans at Bates College in Maine. After getting a law degree at Washington and Lee University in Lexington, Va., he entered private practice and also worked for the area's Republican congressman, M. Caldwell Butler. He considered running for Congress in 1986, but the birth of his second child at the start of the campaign season kept him out of the race. In 1992, Democrat Jim Olin opted to retire, and Goodlatte decided the time was right. He won easily and has done so ever since.

Key Votes

2012	
Extend a Social Security payroll tax cut and unemployment benefits	NO
Ease securities rules to expand small-business access to capital	YES
Extend for one year subsidized student loan interest rates financed by a cut in health care spending	YES
Cite Attorney General Eric H. Holder Jr. for contempt of Congress	YES
Create a visa program for foreign graduates in high-tech fields	YES
Extend most Bush-era income tax rates while allowing rates for top-bracket earners to rise (Jan. 1, 2013)	NO
2011	
Strike funding for F-35 alternative engine	NO
Prevent EPA from regulating greenhouse gas emissions to address climate change	YES
Extend certain provisions of Patriot Act for four years	YES
Declare opposition to use of ground troops in Libya	YES
Overhaul patent law	YES
Pass compromise debt limit increase plan and establish future spending limits	YES
Allow consideration of measures to implement three trade agreements	YES

CQ Vote Studies

	PARTY UNITY		PRESIDENTIAL SUPPORT	
	SUPPORT	OPPOSE	SUPPORT	OPPOSE
2012	95%	5%	18%	82%
2011	95%	5%	22%	78%
2010	95%	5%	26%	74%
2009	96%	4%	14%	86%
2008	94%	6%	64%	36%

Interest Groups

	AFL-CIO	ADA	CCUS	ACU
2012	14%	0%	92%	88%
2011	0%	5%	100%	90%
2010	7%	0%	88%	100%
2009	5%	0%	73%	100%
2008	14%	15%	83%	96%

Virginia 6

West — Roanoke, Lynchburg, Front Royal

The 6th hugs part of the West Virginia border, covering the Blue Ridge Mountains and towns to the east. At its southern edge is Roanoke, the district's main population center, and at its northern edge it dips into the Shenandoah County. In between are farms, national forests and the cities of Lynchburg and Harrisonburg.

Roanoke is the largest city in Virginia west of Richmond, with a diverse and relatively stable economy. Roanoke's unemployment was low before the financial crisis and remained lower than state and national averages afterward. The city's historic downtown buildings, including the City Market, have undergone renovations and are luring new vendors. The city is also promoting a medical research cluster.

Lynchburg's traditional manufacturing base is retooling toward health care, education and nuclear technology sectors. The city is home to the world's largest nuclear plant designer and manufacturer, Areva NP. Harrisonburg, home to James Madison University, has attracted a significant Hispanic population and has grown by more than 20 percent since 2000.

The region's lands are top producers of poultry, beef and dairy. The 6th hews closely to Virginia's section of the Appalachian Trail, which draws outdoors tourism, and the 100 miles of scenic Skyline Drive forms part of the district's eastern border. During decennial redistricting, the 6th lost the town of Salem and gained a swath of rural small towns from Shenandoah to Front Royal along its northeastern edge, where national park management preserves lushly forested hills.

A reliably Republican district, its brand of conservatism is moderate. Democrats and independents can win some local elections here. In 2012, Republican Mitt Romney took 59 percent of the district's vote, his second-highest percentage statewide.

Major Industry
Manufacturing, agriculture, livestock, higher education, tourism

Cities
Roanoke, Lynchburg, Harrisonburg

Notable
Luray Caverns, in Page County, features a pipe organ made of stalactites; The historic Homestead resort in Hot Springs, which opened in 1766, has hosted 22 U.S. presidents.

Rep. Eric Cantor (R)

Capitol Office
225-2815
cantor.house.gov
303 Cannon Bldg. 20515-4607; fax 225-0011

Committees
No committee assignments

Residence
Glen Allen

Born
June 6, 1963; Richmond, Va.

Religion
Jewish

Family
Wife, Diana Fine Cantor; three children

Education
George Washington U., B.A. 1985 (political science); College of William & Mary, J.D. 1988; Columbia U., M.S. 1989 (real estate development)

Career
Lawyer; real estate developer; campaign aide

Political Highlights
Va. House, 1992-2001

ELECTION RESULTS

2012 GENERAL		
Eric Cantor (R)	222,983	58.4%
E. Wayne Powell (D)	158,012	41.4%
2012 PRIMARY		
Eric Cantor (R)	37,369	79.4%
Floyd C. Bayne (R)	9,668	20.6%
2010 GENERAL		
Eric Cantor (R)	138,209	59.2%
Rick E. Waugh Jr. (D)	79,616	34.1%
Floyd C. Bayne (IGREEN)	15,164	6.5%

Previous Winning Percentages
2008 (63%); 2006 (64%); 2004 (76%); 2002 (69%); 2000 (67%)

Elected 2000; 7th term

Officially, Cantor is the House majority leader. Unofficially, he serves as the GOP leadership team's bridge to the younger and more conservative segments of the Republican Party. He is a powerful ally (and reputed occasional rival) of Speaker John A. Boehner.

Cantor wears stylish suits and speaks in a Southern drawl. Widely viewed as a speaker-in-waiting, he made clear after tough elections in 2012 that he would not challenge Boehner, calling him a mentor in a "real partnership" that is "focused on trying to deliver results."

"I stand with Speaker Boehner when he says, 'Let's rise above the dysfunction, and do the right thing together for our country,'" he said in November 2012. "Economic growth, entitlement reform and solving our spending crisis are our top priorities."

Those were also their priorities for the 112th Congress (2011-12), when Cantor ascended to his current post. The new GOP majority in 2011 included a huge freshman class and a number of small-government conservatives energized by the tea party movement.

Boehner and Cantor took a laissez-faire approach to managing their caucus, letting various factions get votes on their preferred bills and often declining to mete out punishment when those factions refused to support the leadership's plans. At times the results were politically damaging. The law governing federal farm programs lapsed for the last three months of 2012, as internal disputes in the party prompted Cantor to delay floor action on a reauthorization. To salvage a two-year surface transportation bill, Cantor stressed to conservatives "why we've got to do what we have to do," he said. "What gets results around here ... is education."

For the 113th Congress (2013-14), Cantor has the option to be more forceful. Tweaks to GOP Conference rules allow him to bring more bills to the House floor under suspension of the rules, a process that limits debate and requires a two-thirds majority for passage; there will be fewer opportunities for obstruction. The Class of 2010 had two representatives on the leadership team; now it's down to one.

What's unchanged is Cantor's efficiency in setting the House calendar. A move to align schedules with the Senate in the 113th Congress — while allowing week-long district work periods — earned bipartisan praise.

There has been tension between Cantor and Boehner when Cantor seems to push the interests of the conservative wing of the party. Unlike Boehner and GOP Whip Kevin McCarthy of California, Cantor retains membership in the conservative Republican Study Committee. In early 2011, he resisted a plan devised by Boehner and President Barack Obama for pairing spending cuts with increases in revenue. In January 2013, he voted against the "fiscal cliff" deal that allowed higher tax rates on income over $400,000, while permanently extending lower rates under that threshold. Boehner voted for it.

But he has also hit a few snags when trying to favor leadership plans over the desires of conservatives. He scheduled an April 2013 vote on a bill to modify Democrats' 2010 health care law; it would have shifted money from the Prevention and Public Health Fund to high-risk insurance pools that had been closed to new enrollment. Several prominent conservative groups criticized the measure as an acceptance of the overhaul law and said Republicans should focus only on repeal. As outside pressure increased and the outcome of the vote became less certain, Cantor pulled the bill from the floor.

Cantor, a former member of the Ways and Means Committee, hones GOP strategy on business-related themes. He is a lawyer with a master's degree in real estate development from Columbia University. He helped secure enactment of a 2012 law to ease regulations on startup businesses.

In 2003, Cantor became chief deputy to GOP Whip Roy Blunt of Missouri. Blunt lost a race against Boehner for the position of minority leader in early 2006, but Cantor passed on that opportunity to challenge Blunt for the whip job. Two years later, Blunt stepped aside, and Cantor won election to succeed him. In his lone term as whip, Cantor displayed a smooth style as the chief GOP vote counter. He was elected majority leader in November 2010 without opposition.

Cantor wrote a 2010 book with McCarthy and Wisconsin Republican Paul D. Ryan — the Budget Committee chairman and 2012 GOP vice presidential nominee — outlining their vision for the party. A leader of the "Young Guns" candidate recruitment program, he raised more than $5 million for his leadership political action committee in the 2012 cycle. He helped raise a comparable amount for the YG Action Network PAC.

He has a penchant for bold moves to help his allies. When redistricting prompted freshman Rep. Adam Kinzinger and 10-term Rep. Donald Manzullo to oppose each other in a 2012 Illinois primary, Cantor angered some in the party by openly supporting Kinzinger, who won. Boehner stayed neutral.

Cantor grew up in a well-to-do, politically active Richmond family. His father, Eddie, was on the board of the Virginia Housing Development Authority, and his mother, Mary Lee, was a board member of the Family and Children's Trust Fund and the Science Museum of Virginia. He is the only Jewish Republican in Congress, and he leads colleagues on visits to Israel.

While in college, Cantor interned for Rep. Thomas J. Bliley Jr. of Virginia, driving the Republican's campaign car around the district. He also worked as an aide to Walter A. Stosch, a member of the Virginia House of Delegates.

Cantor worked in the family real estate business before he was elected to Congress. His wife, Diana, serves as board chairwoman of the Virginia Retirement System, a public employee pension fund, and is a director of Media General Inc. and Domino's Pizza.

When Stosch ran for the state Senate in 1991, the 28-year-old Cantor won election to become the youngest member of the House of Delegates. Bliley's campaign machinery helped Cantor, and he frequently served as Bliley's campaign chairman. Bliley announced his retirement in 2000, and Cantor won election to replace him — after eking out a 263-vote win over state Sen. Stephen H. Martin in the Republican primary.

His re-elections have been easy contests. Running in a redrawn district in 2012, Cantor had his most competitive race in a decade — but he still defeated retired U.S. Army Colonel E. Wayne Powell by 17 points.

Key Votes

2012

Extend a Social Security payroll tax cut and unemployment benefits	YES
Ease securities rules to expand small-business access to capital	YES
Extend for one year subsidized student loan interest rates financed by a cut in health care spending	YES
Cite Attorney General Eric H. Holder Jr. for contempt of Congress	YES
Create a visa program for foreign graduates in high-tech fields	YES
Extend most Bush-era income tax rates while allowing rates for top-bracket earners to rise (Jan. 1, 2013)	NO

2011

Strike funding for F-35 alternative engine	NO
Prevent EPA from regulating greenhouse gas emissions to address climate change	YES
Extend certain provisions of Patriot Act for four years	YES
Declare opposition to use of ground troops in Libya	YES
Overhaul patent law	YES
Pass compromise debt limit increase plan and establish future spending limits	YES
Allow consideration of measures to implement three trade agreements	YES

CQ Vote Studies

	PARTY UNITY		PRESIDENTIAL SUPPORT	
	SUPPORT	OPPOSE	SUPPORT	OPPOSE
2012	98%	2%	17%	83%
2011	97%	3%	26%	74%
2010	98%	2%	27%	73%
2009	97%	3%	21%	79%
2008	98%	2%	79%	21%

Interest Groups

	AFL-CIO	ADA	CCUS	ACU
2012	14%	0%	100%	95%
2011	0%	5%	100%	80%
2010	0%	0%	88%	100%
2009	5%	0%	71%	100%
2008	7%	5%	94%	92%

Virginia 7

Central — Richmond and suburbs, Culpeper County

The conservative 7th District takes in Richmond's heavily populated West End and South Side suburbs, stretching northeast through the small towns and farmland of central Virginia until it reaches the Washington, D.C., exurbs in Spotsylvania and Culpeper counties.

As the center of state government and a major tobacco industry headquarters, Richmond has white-collar professionals who live in the wealthy suburbs of Henrico County to the north and east and Chesterfield County to the southwest. Historic mansions and old-money estates are part of the West End. The city, which is a financial hub, has long had a manufacturing base, and Altria's Philip Morris tobacco company continues to be one of the largest employers. In growing Midlothian and surrounding Chesterfield County, extensive commercial growth is a concern for residents who want to maintain a small-town, community vibe. Agriculture is important to counties in the 7th: Culpeper produces sod and Orange is a top grower of wine grapes.

At the district's northeast, Culpeper and Spotsylvania have grown steadily as Washington's professional class moves farther from the city — battling clogged commuting routes — and parts of the region have increasingly begun to identify themselves with Northern Virginia. Spotsylvania is home to Richmond commuters and has recently attracted new technology firms.

Richmond is a black-majority city, but the total population of the 7th is less than 15 percent black. Redistricting bolstered the 7th's Republican slant, cutting out Madison and Rappahannock counties as well as parts of northern Richmond. The district gained a larger share of Spotsylvania County in the north and all of rural New Kent County east of Richmond down Interstate 64. The new map makes the 7th even safer for the GOP. Republican Bob McDonnell won nearly 70 percent in the 2009 gubernatorial race within the new borders, his best showing statewide. Mitt Romney took 57 percent of the vote in the 2012 presidential election.

Major Industry

Agriculture, government, manufacturing, retail

Cities

Richmond (pt.); Tuckahoe (unincorp.); Mechanicsville (unincorp.)

Notable

James Madison's Montpelier estate is in Orange County.

Rep. James P. Moran (D)

Capitol Office
225-4376
moran.house.gov
2252 Rayburn Bldg. 20515-4608; fax 225-0017

Committees
Appropriations

Residence
Arlington

Born
May 16, 1945; Buffalo, N.Y.

Religion
Roman Catholic

Family
Divorced; four children

Education
College of the Holy Cross, B.A. 1967 (economics); City U. of New York, Bernard M. Baruch School of Finance, attended 1967-68; U. of Pittsburgh, M.P.A. 1970

Career
Investment broker; congressional aide; U.S. Health, Education and Welfare Department analyst

Political Highlights
Alexandria City Council, 1979-84 (vice mayor, 1982-84); mayor of Alexandria, 1985-90 (served as an independent 1985-88)

ELECTION RESULTS

2012 GENERAL		
James P. Moran (D)	226,847	64.6%
J. Patrick Murray (R)	107,370	30.6%
Jason J. Howell (I)	10,180	2.9%
Janet Murphy (IGREEN)	5,985	1.7%
2012 PRIMARY		
James P. Moran (D)	23,018	74.2%
Bruce B. Shuttleworth (D)	8,006	25.8%
2010 GENERAL		
James P. Moran (D)	116,404	61.0%
J. Patrick Murray (R)	71,145	37.3%
J. Ron Fisher (IGREEN)	2,707	1.4%

Previous Winning Percentages
2008 (68%); 2006 (66%); 2004 (60%); 2002 (60%); 2000 (63%); 1998 (67%); 1996 (66%); 1994 (59%); 1992 (56%); 1990 (52%)

Elected 1990; 12th term

Moran is often his own worst enemy, as his turbulent personal life and bouts of ill temper overshadow his talents as a negotiator. But Democrats are still happy to have him defending their priorities as an effective senior member of the Appropriations Committee.

Over the course of his House career, Moran has started a shoving match with colleagues while leaving the House floor; publicly expressed a desire to break the noses of numerous politicians; endured some testy elections; and impolitically suggested that the Jewish community pushed for the 2003 invasion of Iraq. His third marriage ended in 2012. It dissolved more amicably than the second one — that union ended after a call to the police during a domestic argument and allegations that Moran squandered a small fortune on the stock market. Later financial disclosures and reports have confirmed his sizable stock losses.

Moran's son Patrick resigned as field director of his father's campaign in 2012, after conservative filmmakers captured him on camera offering advice on how to commit voter fraud. That December, Patrick pleaded guilty to assaulting his girlfriend, with police reports indicating he slammed her head into a metal garbage container. (Not all Moran family news for 2012 was bad; Moran's youngest brother, Brian, wrapped up a successful run as chairman of the Virginia Democratic Party.)

Moran's ability to attract negative publicity has cost him. He was kicked off the Democratic whip team for his remarks on Iraq, and fellow Democrats sometimes feel the need to distance themselves from him. Even so, his long run on the Appropriations Committee — he has served there for all but two terms of his House career — has allowed him to take the top Democratic spot on the Interior-Environment Subcommittee.

Moran gets favorable notices from environmental groups, and in the 112th Congress (2011-12) he said it was "incumbent on me to lead the effort to reject the anti-environmental riders that have been attached to the Interior appropriations bill." Republicans made several attempts to curtail the EPA's powers and budget, all of which Moran resisted. He says that addressing climate change is a "moral and ethical obligation," and he got several religious groups to endorse his 2012 resolution calling for congressional action on that front.

He also has seats on the Defense and Legislative Branch panels. Moran has opposed the Iraq and Afghanistan wars, even calling the Afghanistan conflict unwinnable in a 2010 MSNBC appearance. During deficit reduction negotiations at the end of 2012, Moran was the most prominent Democrat signing a letter requesting defense cuts as part of that effort — though the letter said the cuts should be carefully selected, and not across-the-board reductions.

A lot of Moran's longevity is attributable to old-school, parochial appropriating via earmarks — provisions in bills that direct federal spending toward specific projects in a lawmaker's district. He told a group of supporters in 2006 that if he became a subcommittee chairman the next year, he would "earmark the shit out of it."

The Republican majority started an earmark ban in 2011, and Moran has unsuccessfully pressed for its end. Before the ban, he had managed to secure scads of dollars for mass transit and infrastructure in his traffic-clogged Northern Virginia district, as well as a wide variety of social services programs. "Much of our economic development is around locating people in areas where they can live and work and shop and play without having to get into their car," he said. "That kind of lifestyle appeals to many people, appeals certainly to the type of workforce we are trying to attract." He often pushes for better pay and retirement benefits for federal workers.

Moran touts his work with the Tahirih Justice Center (which helps victims of sex trafficking) as well as the money he secured for a children's hospital and clinic in Washington after his own daughter developed a malignant brain tumor. "I know that I've made a difference in a number of areas," he said.

Some of Moran's rhetoric seems to come straight from the liberal playbook, as he routinely supports federal programs assisting lower-income Americans. But he is not easy to pigeonhole. His district is one of the wealthiest and most educated in the nation, and he is a founding member of the New Democrat Coalition. That business-friendly group of House Democrats sits somewhere between the liberal Congressional Progressive Caucus (to which he also belongs) and the fiscally conservative Blue Dog Coalition.

He strongly supports free trade and voted for pacts with South Korea, Panama and Colombia in 2011. Moran similarly backs federal actions to bolster research and employment at the many high-tech companies he represents. "Much of this district is involved in research and development and innovation, and it requires a certain investment from the federal government to keep it productive," he says.

And despite his pugilism, Moran is known as a results-oriented deal-maker, particularly when it comes to helping Northern Virginia. In 2012, the group No Labels welcomed him as a member of the "problem-solvers bloc," a group of lawmakers "dedicated to working across the aisle to find effective, principled and pragmatic solutions."

Moran grew up in the suburbs of Boston as the oldest of seven siblings. His father, James P. Moran Sr., was a Roosevelt Democrat, a probation officer and a former football player for the Boston Redskins. Moran played football for the College of the Holy Cross and fought as an amateur boxer, but he eventually ended up in Washington crunching numbers for the Health, Education and Welfare Department. He later became a staffer for the Senate Appropriations Committee.

First elected to the Alexandria City Council in 1979, Moran saw his career derail briefly five years later — he resigned as vice mayor after pleading no contest to a misdemeanor conflict-of-interest charge. He had used money from a political action committee to rent a tuxedo and buy Christmas cards. He ran as an independent the next year and unseated the incumbent mayor.

He was serving as mayor in 1990 when he ran for Congress. He took 52 percent of the vote to upset six-term Republican Stan Parris. Even with his unusually high number of public embarrassments, Moran has not had any particularly close re-elections, as his district has a strong Democratic lean. He won by 34 points in 2012.

Key Votes

2012	
Extend a Social Security payroll tax cut and unemployment benefits	NO
Ease securities rules to expand small-business access to capital	YES
Extend for one year subsidized student loan interest rates financed by a cut in health care spending	NO
Cite Attorney General Eric H. Holder Jr. for contempt of Congress	NO
Create a visa program for foreign graduates in high-tech fields	YES
Extend most Bush-era income tax rates while allowing rates for top-bracket earners to rise (Jan. 1, 2013)	NO
2011	
Strike funding for F-35 alternative engine	NO
Prevent EPA from regulating greenhouse gas emissions to address climate change	NO
Extend certain provisions of Patriot Act for four years	NO
Declare opposition to use of ground troops in Libya	NO
Overhaul patent law	YES
Pass compromise debt limit increase plan and establish future spending limits	NO
Allow consideration of measures to implement three trade agreements	YES

CQ Vote Studies

	PARTY UNITY		PRESIDENTIAL SUPPORT	
	SUPPORT	OPPOSE	SUPPORT	OPPOSE
2012	94%	6%	82%	18%
2011	95%	5%	85%	15%
2010	97%	3%	85%	15%
2009	98%	2%	97%	3%
2008	98%	2%	15%	85%

Interest Groups

	AFL-CIO	ADA	CCUS	ACU
2012	95%	85%	42%	0%
2011	00%	05%	31%	4%
2010	93%	100%	13%	8%
2009	100%	85%	50%	0%
2008	100%	95%	61%	0%

Virginia 8

Washington suburbs — Arlington, Alexandria, part of Fairfax County

The diverse and Democratic 8th contains the heavily populated close-in Washington, D.C., suburbs of Arlington and Alexandria, as well as part of McLean. It rides along the Potomac River, across from the nation's capital, south to Occoquan Bay. This bustling, affluent region is home to highly paid government workers and myriad technology and service firms.

The Northern Virginia suburbs have a stable economy that outperforms national averages. Home to the Pentagon and Ronald Reagan Washington National Airport in Arlington County and the U.S. Patent and Trademark Office in Alexandria, the 8th is replete with contractors as well as major law, public policy and consulting firms. This combination lures an educated workforce with high-income professional jobs that are recession-resistant.

The 8th is also emblematic of Northern Virginia's changing demographic. Exchanging parts of Springfield and Annandale for Tyson's Corner and Reston during decennial redistricting, it now has the state's highest proportion of Hispanic residents (19 percent) and substantial black and Asian populations. Overall the district is about 40 percent minority.

Politically, redistricting may have added more conservative voters to the 8th from its portions of McLean, but it remains Virginia's most solidly Democratic district outside of the black-majority 3rd District. The 8th's suburban young professionals tend to be socially liberal and support a proactive role for government. In 2008 and 2012, 2-to-1 advantages in the 8th were instrumental to Barack Obama carrying the state.

Major Industry
Government, defense, technology, service, tourism

Cities
Arlington (unincorp.), Alexandria, Falls Church

Military Bases
Pentagon; Fort Belvoir, 8,000 military, 24,000 civilian; Joint Base Myer-Henderson Hall, 9,800 military, 1,000 civilian (shared with District of Columbia) (2012)

Notable
George Washington's estate, Mount Vernon, lies on the banks of the Potomac River in Fairfax County; Arlington National Cemetery is located near the Pentagon in Arlington.

Rep. Morgan Griffith (R)

Capitol Office
225-3861
morgangriffith.house.gov
1108 Longworth Bldg. 20515; fax 225-0076

Committees
Energy & Commerce

Residence
Salem

Born
March 15, 1958; Philadelphia, Pa.

Religion
Protestant

Family
Wife, Hilary Griffith; three children

Education
Emory & Henry College, B.A. 1980 (history); Washington and Lee U., J.D. 1983

Career
Lawyer

Political Highlights
Salem Republican Committee chairman, 1986-88, 1991-94; Va. House, 1994-2011 (majority leader, 2000-11)

ELECTION RESULTS

2012 GENERAL		
Morgan Griffith (R)	184,882	61.3%
Anthony J. Flaccavento (D)	116,400	38.6%
2012 PRIMARY		
Morgan Griffith (R)		unopposed
2010 GENERAL		
Morgan Griffith (R)	95,726	51.2%
Rick Boucher (D)	86,743	46.4%
Jeremiah D. Heaton (I)	4,282	2.3%

Elected 2010; 2nd term

Griffith is quirky, conservative and energized by parliamentary pugilism. He had more chances to plot legislative battles when he was the Republican majority leader in the Virginia House, but as a congressional backbencher he zestfully scraps over energy policies that are crucial to the 9th District.

"Nerdy" is a description Griffith doesn't shy from — he has a geeky enthusiasm for history and biology, and food allergies to fit the nerd stereotype. In 2000, he became the first GOP majority leader in the long history of the House of Delegates, and he used his bookishness to master floor procedures. He employed that expertise aggressively in the fast-paced state legislature. Virginia Sen. Mark Warner, a Democratic governor during Griffith's tenure, said Griffith "loved the back and forth, but it was never personal."

Griffith has a host of ideas for speeding up House action; he maintains that inefficient floor procedures take time away from "doing the other business of the people." Most of his work, however, takes place on the Energy and Commerce Committee.

Coal is a linchpin of the 9th District's economy. Griffith unseated 14-term Democrat Rick Boucher in 2010 partly by criticizing Boucher's vote for a 2009 bill to establish a cap-and-trade system to limit greenhouse gas emissions. He has expressed skepticism that climate change is a man-made phenomenon.

When energy companies in the region announced closures or layoffs during the 112th Congress (2011-12), Griffith affixed the blame to the regulatory environment created by the Obama administration. He has accused the EPA of trying to "kill" the coal industry "to appease far-left environmentalists."

His signature effort in the 112th was a bill to require the delay of certain EPA standards for emissions from industrial boilers. Griffith said the upgrades required for compliance would be too costly for many facilities, and that "you've got to give people more time" to comply with standards. The House passed the measure in October 2011 and unsuccessfully tried to include its language in a tax law at the end of that year.

Revised final standards issued in December 2012 were narrower and had a longer compliance window. Griffith wrote that he preferred his bill, but "I appreciate that the EPA is showing a willingness to work with businesses making genuine efforts to comply."

Griffith, a member of the Energy and Power Subcommittee, supports expansion of oil and natural gas development, and he said the Obama administration was "fighting us tooth and nail" to prevent the development of energy resources off Virginia's coast. He began pushing for such development in 2004 from the state House. "I'm a big believer that if the state thinks it's right for them ... then we probably ought to give them some authority," he said.

He also weighs in on national energy issues. In 2012, after President Barack Obama denied a permit for the Keystone XL pipeline from Canada's tar sands to U.S. refineries, Griffith said the president had ignored reports in favor of the pipeline. He took to the House floor to compare the president to his sixth-grade daughter. "Abby doesn't like to do her homework. She would much rather be talking to her friends or watching TV," he said. "President Obama apparently doesn't like to do his homework, either. He would much rather be speaking to friends that tell him how great he is."

On the Oversight and Investigations Subcommittee, Griffith exercises skills developed as a lawyer. He took a particular interest in the probe of a $535 million Energy Department loan guarantee to Solyndra Inc., a manufacturer of solar panels that went bankrupt in 2011. His ire was stoked by an Energy Department decision to give investors other than the government priority in recovering the first $75 million in the event of a bankruptcy. "I don't think there's any question they broke the law," he said.

Griffith said that "philosophically, I can see some value" in tax credits and loan guarantees to spur energy development, particularly for things like clean-coal technology. His current objection is fiscal: "We don't have money."

Generally, Griffith is a fiscal conservative. He opposed the fiscal 2011 and 2012 spending laws, as well as the August 2011 agreement to cut spending and raise the federal debt limit. All of those were insufficiently austere for his tastes. He has been more open than most Republicans to reductions in defense accounts. He was the only person to vote for a 2011 House proposal to split the bill funding military construction and veterans programs into two pieces—he said that severing the construction accounts from popular veterans' issues would make them easier to trim.

In the 113th Congress (2013-14), he has an entry point to study a big driver of government spending—he now sits on the Health Subcommittee.

Griffith grew up in Salem and has spent most of his life along the Interstate 81 corridor. He went south to get a history degree at Emory & Henry College, then north to get a law degree at Washington and Lee. His legal practice specialized in criminal traffic law, constitutional law and civil litigation.

His love of history goes back a ways: As a student council president, he tried to get a new high school named after Revolutionary War Gen. Andrew Lewis, a personal idol whom Griffith believes spurred westward expansion in the late 18th century. Lewis is buried in Salem, and Griffith's wedding was near the grave site.

History sometimes shapes his policy stands. In 2011, Griffith was one of 31 Republicans to reject four-year reauthorizations of certain surveillance provisions in the anti-terrorism law known as the Patriot Act. In explaining his vote, he pointed to the abuse of warrants by King George III. "The Founding Fathers would never have wanted us to go so far," he said. Griffith read a letter from Thomas Jefferson to James Madison to explain his opposition to a defense policy bill that might allow indefinite detention of U.S. citizens.

In 2010, Griffith was the consensus party choice to take on Boucher, a senior member of Energy and Commerce who had not been seriously challenged since 1984. In his defense, Boucher argued that he helped include protections for the coal industry in the cap-and-trade measure. But Griffith took 51 percent of the vote in a very strong year for Republicans.

Farmer and agricultural activist Anthony J. Flaccavento was the Democrat facing Griffith in 2012, but the first time political candidate had a lackluster fundraising effort and gained little traction. Griffith won by more than 22 points.

Key Votes

2012	
Extend a Social Security payroll tax cut and unemployment benefits	NO
Ease securities rules to expand small-business access to capital	YES
Extend for one year subsidized student loan interest rates financed by a cut in health care spending	YES
Cite Attorney General Eric H. Holder Jr. for contempt of Congress	YES
Create a visa program for foreign graduates in high-tech fields	YES
Extend most Bush-era income tax rates while allowing rates for top-bracket earners to rise (Jan. 1, 2013)	NO
2011	
Strike funding for F-35 alternative engine	NO
Prevent EPA from regulating greenhouse gas emissions to address climate change	YES
Extend certain provisions of Patriot Act for four years	NO
Declare opposition to use of ground troops in Libya	YES
Overhaul patent law	YES
Pass compromise debt limit increase plan and establish future spending limits	NO
Allow consideration of measures to implement three trade agreements	YES

CQ Vote Studies

	PARTY UNITY		PRESIDENTIAL SUPPORT	
	SUPPORT	OPPOSE	SUPPORT	OPPOSE
2012	92%	8%	20%	80%
2011	92%	8%	25%	75%

Interest Groups

	AFL-CIO	ADA	CCUS	ACU
2012	19%	5%	100%	76%
2011	10%	25%	87%	84%

Virginia 9

Southwest — Blacksburg, Salem, Bristol

Bordering four states in Virginia's southwestern corner, the mountainous 9th collects blue-collar mining towns and college campuses. An area of rolling green hills and Appalachian ridges, the region prides itself on its political independence from Richmond and the rest of the state.

Blacksburg is home to the commonwealth's only land-grant university, Virginia Tech, whose 30,000 students drive Montgomery County's economics and culture. The campus has become an anchor for a cluster of technology and research firms. The city also has a manufacturing base in auto parts and Virginia Tech has programs in automotive and transportation research. Among the district's other population centers, Christiansburg is a retail hub and Radford is home to Radford University, with nearly 10,000 students.

The mining towns along the West Virginia and Kentucky borders are part of Appalachian coal country. These areas have some of the state's highest poverty and lowest education rates: The 9th has the lowest rate of college-educated residents and the lowest median household income among districts statewide. Towns along the southern border are more dependent on manufacturing. Much of Virginia's portion of the Appalachian Trail lies within the 9th's Jefferson National Forest. Decennial redistricting moved Martinsville Speedway, home to several NASCAR races, into the 9th.

The district's population is more than 90 percent white, making it Virginia's least racially diverse district. Moderate Democrats can win if they court coal union voters, but Republicans have won several recent high-profile races. The 9th gave 66 percent of its gubernatorial vote to Bob McDonnell in 2009. In 2008, John McCain won 59 percent of the current district's presidential vote — his strongest showing in the state — while Mitt Romney's backing of the coal industry in 2012 helped him crush Barack Obama in the 9th and get his highest statewide percentage with 63 percent.

Major Industry
Manufacturing, coal mining, agriculture, higher education

Cities
Blacksburg, Salem, Christiansburg, Bristol

Notable
Abingdon's still-thriving Barter Theatre allowed local residents to exchange excess produce and livestock for admission during the Depression.

Rep. Frank R. Wolf (R)

Capitol Office
225-5136
wolf.house.gov
233 Cannon Bldg. 20515-4610; fax 225-0437

Committees
Appropriations
(Commerce-Justice-Science - Chairman)

Residence
Vienna

Born
Jan. 30, 1939; Philadelphia, Pa.

Religion
Presbyterian

Family
Wife, Carolyn Wolf; five children

Education
Pennsylvania State U., B.A. 1961 (political science); Georgetown U., LL.B. 1965

Military
Army Reserve, 1962-63

Career
Lawyer; U.S. Interior Department official; congressional aide; lobbyist

Political Highlights
Sought Republican nomination for U.S. House, 1976; Republican nominee for U.S. House, 1978

ELECTION RESULTS

2012 GENERAL		
Frank R. Wolf (R)	214,038	58.4%
Kristin A. Cabral (D)	142,024	38.8%
J. Kevin Chisholm (I)	9,855	2.7%
2012 PRIMARY		
Frank R. Wolf (R)		unopposed
2010 GENERAL		
Frank R. Wolf (R)	131,116	62.9%
Jeffrey R. Barnett (D)	72,604	34.8%
William B. Redpath (LIBERT)	4,607	2.2%

Previous Winning Percentages
2008 (59%); 2006 (57%); 2004 (64%); 2002 (72%); 2000 (84%); 1998 (72%); 1996 (72%); 1994 (87%); 1992 (64%); 1990 (61%); 1988 (68%); 1986 (60%); 1984 (63%); 1982 (53%); 1980 (51%)

Elected 1980; 17th term

Wolf has been in the House for more than three decades, and his intensity regarding his chosen issues hasn't ebbed. What's more, he chooses issues of all sizes — he is relentless when pursuing his goals for human rights, the space program or eradicating stink bugs in Virginia. The fast-moving legislator prides himself on being a thorn in the side of high-ranking officials, whether they are Republicans, Democrats or from a foreign government.

Wolf counts William Wilberforce, the 18th-century British abolitionist, as a political hero. A devoted Christian who has long met with other lawmakers for a weekly Bible study, he sees himself as a loudspeaker for addressing worldwide human rights abuses.

In his 2011 book, "Prisoner of Conscience: One Man's Crusade for Global Human and Religious Rights," he evinces anger at the U.S. government for its inaction on human rights abuses. "We can't say that we didn't know," Wolf writes. "We must stand up and speak out for those who suffer around the globe — no matter how hard the battle, nor how long it takes."

His simple strategy: "Keep speaking out." Wolf controls one forum as chairman of the Appropriations subcommittee with jurisdiction over the Justice Department; he also sits on the State-Foreign Operations Subcommittee. And he is a co-chairman of the Tom Lantos Human Rights Commission.

One of his proudest accomplishments is a 1998 law that established a government body to monitor religious freedom abroad. He said the International Religious Freedom Commission has given victims of persecution "a forum to speak truth" and to put pressure on U.S. policymakers to act on their behalf. The law was reauthorized in the 112th Congress (2011-12), with a new report required on the best uses of foreign assistance to promote religious freedom. It also requires religious-freedom training for Foreign Service officers.

He also advocates the creation of a religious-freedom special envoy for the Near East and South Central Asia regions.

Wolf criticized President George W. Bush for attending the 2008 Olympics in China, citing its government's human rights record and its support for the regime in Sudan — which is widely believed to be responsible for genocide in the Darfur region. The first member of the House to travel to Darfur, Wolf has said the Obama administration is "setting us back on human rights" and should be doing more to address the situation there. He also has scolded the White House for what he perceives as silence on the deportations of Christians from Morocco.

He opts to travel without the formality of a congressional delegation — he went to Tibet in 1997, under the radar of the Chinese government, and believes he is the only member of Congress to do so.

Wolf was one of the lawmakers behind the creation of the Iraq Study Group, a panel composed of policy experts that recommended a new course in Iraq in late 2006 — though not the one eventually taken. Now he is pushing for an Afghanistan-Pakistan Study Group.

Special panels and commissions clearly appeal to Wolf. In the 111th Congress (2009-10), he joined with Democrat Jim Cooper of Tennessee to push legislation creating a commission to study ways to cut the federal budget deficit. That effort was superseded by President Barack Obama's creation of a deficit commission by executive order. Wolf has supported budgets based on the work of that commission (which is known as Simpson-Bowles).

He has also called for a special committee to investigate a September 2012 attack on a U.S. consulate in Libya, and the Obama administration's response to that attack. Wolf maintains the White House has been less than forthcoming about the terrorist ties of the people involved in the attack.

The subcommittee Wolf chairs also handles funding for the Commerce Department and federal science programs. Even as budgets for many agencies shrink, he has been supportive of strong funding for the National Weather Service. "No one should be able to say that there have been damages, loss of life or anything because the weather bureau says, 'We don't have the money,'" he said at a 2013 hearing. In 2012, he reached an agreement with NASA officials that the agency's commercial crew program should focus on shuttling U.S. astronauts to the space station, not developing a commercial crew industry.

Wolf's district is home to thousands of federal employees, and in 2009 he was one of three original GOP co-sponsors of legislation to grant them up to four weeks of paid parental leave; he is also a leading proponent of telecommuting and its potential to relieve the region's clogged roads. He wants to increase research on Lyme disease and stink bugs, an invasive pest infesting many apple and grape crops.

A history buff, Wolf is involved in efforts to preserve historic sites in his district. In 2008, he won enactment of a law designating a 175-mile corridor from Gettysburg, Pa., to Charlottesville, Va., as a National Heritage Area, over the objections of people who said it could impede local development.

Wolf was born and raised in Philadelphia. He is the son of a police officer and a cafeteria worker. His interest in politics grew out of a boyhood fascination with history and a desire to find a way to overcome a stutter. In college, Wolf majored in political science, then earned his law degree from Georgetown University in Washington. He says his first job on Capitol Hill was in the 1960s — he did some construction work and helped build the Rayburn House Office Building.

He became an aide to Pennsylvania GOP Rep. Edward G. Biester, then a deputy assistant in the Interior Department during the Nixon and Ford administrations. Later, he worked as a lobbyist for baby food and farm implement manufacturers.

Most members of his family were Democrats. Wolf says he joined the Republican Party because of his beliefs in lower taxes, strong national defense and a tough approach to fighting communism during the Cold War.

He credits President Ronald Reagan with getting him into office. He fell short when seeking a House seat in 1976 and 1978, but he rode the Reagan surge to a narrow victory in 1980.

He had a tough re-election race in 1982, but since then his elections haven't been remotely close — when Democrats were surging in 2006, Wolf won by more than 16 points. There is frequent speculation about his retirement, but Wolf has filed to run for re-election in 2014.

Key Votes

2012	
Extend a Social Security payroll tax cut and unemployment benefits	NO
Ease securities rules to expand small-business access to capital	YES
Extend for one year subsidized student loan interest rates financed by a cut in health care spending	YES
Cite Attorney General Eric H. Holder Jr. for contempt of Congress	YES
Create a visa program for foreign graduates in high-tech fields	YES
Extend most Bush-era income tax rates while allowing rates for top-bracket earners to rise (Jan. 1, 2013)	NO
2011	
Strike funding for F-35 alternative engine	NO
Prevent EPA from regulating greenhouse gas emissions to address climate change	YES
Extend certain provisions of Patriot Act for four years	YES
Declare opposition to use of ground troops in Libya	YES
Overhaul patent law	NO
Pass compromise debt limit increase plan and establish future spending limits	YES
Allow consideration of measures to implement three trade agreements	YES

CQ Vote Studies

	PARTY UNITY		PRESIDENTIAL SUPPORT	
	SUPPORT	OPPOSE	SUPPORT	OPPOSE
2012	86%	14%	22%	78%
2011	87%	13%	27%	73%
2010	89%	11%	29%	71%
2009	79%	21%	43%	57%
2008	87%	13%	66%	34%

Interest Groups

	AFL-CIO	ADA	CCUS	ACU
2012	30%	10%	91%	64%
2011	10%	10%	94%	64%
2010	7%	10%	88%	92%
2009	29%	10%	93%	80%
2008	21%	30%	94%	79%

Virginia 10

North — outer Washington suburbs, Loudoun County

The 10th District sits along Virginia's northernmost border, stretching from the rural tranquility of Frederick County bordering the West Virginia panhandle to the heavily populated and rapidly developing suburbs of Washington, D.C. It includes all of Loudoun County, the palatial estates of northern Fairfax County and commuter enclaves Manassas and Chantilly.

The 10th's economy is dominated by its proximity to the nation's capital. It supports technology firms, manufacturers and defense contractors, particularly near Dulles International Airport in eastern Loudoun. Residents are largely young, white-collar professionals with families, and commuter rail and road expansions are priorities. Northern Virginia has maintained some of the lowest unemployment rates in the state and median incomes here top $100,000.

Following decennial redistricting, the 10th takes in Haymarket and Manassas portions of Prince William County. Prince William and Loudoun have been two of the state's fastest-growing counties since 2000. The region's Hispanic population in particular has boomed, but remapping carved several large Latino communities out of the 10th near Bull Run and Herndon.

As the district rambles northwest of the Capital Beltway, leafy countryside and farmland quickly takes over. Solidly conservative Frederick County, at the state's northern tip, is more sparsely populated and known for its plentiful apple orchards.

The changing demographics of Northern Virginia augurs future competitiveness, but the 10th leans decidedly Republican. In decennial remapping, the 10th lost southern McLean and a wide swath of northern Warren and Fauquier counties, shoring up its conservative bent. While Barack Obama won 53 percent of the former 10th in 2008, he won only 49 percent within the district's current, redrawn borders.

Major Industry
Technology, government, manufacturing, agriculture

Cities
McLean (unincorp.) (pt.), Leesburg, Ashburn (unincorp.), Manassas

Notable
CIA headquarters is in Langley; Winchester hosts the annual Shenandoah Apple Blossom Festival.

Rep. Gerald E. Connolly (D)

Capitol Office
225-1492
connolly.house.gov
424 Cannon Bldg. 20515-4611; fax 225-3071

Committees
Foreign Affairs
Oversight & Government Reform

Residence
Fairfax

Born
March 30, 1950; Boston, Mass.

Religion
Roman Catholic

Family
Wife, Catherine Connolly; one child

Education
Maryknoll College, B.A. 1971 (literature); Harvard U., M.P.A. 1979

Career
Government relations executive; congressional aide; nonprofit international aid organization director

Political Highlights
Fairfax County Board of Supervisors, 1995-2003; Fairfax County Board of Supervisors chairman, 2004-09

ELECTION RESULTS

2012 GENERAL		
Gerald E. Connolly (D)	202,606	61.0%
Chris S. Perkins (R)	117,902	35.5%
Mark T. Gibson (I)	3,806	1.1%
2012 PRIMARY		
Gerald E. Connolly (D)		unopposed
2010 GENERAL		
Gerald E. Connolly (D)	111,720	49.2%
Keith Fimian (R)	110,739	48.8%

Previous Winning Percentages
2008 (55%)

Elected 2008; 3rd term

Connolly has bottom-up knowledge of Northern Virginia governments and their symbiotic relationships with their federal neighbor. He is most effective — and collaborative — when working on the infrastructure, workplace and security issues at the top of the region's to-do list.

But he'll still take partisan digs. "I think the 112th Congress has been the most anti-federal-employee, anti-environmental, socially Darwinian Congress in history," he said in 2012. "I do not appreciate the Republican war on federal employees."

Much of Connolly's congressional agenda has its roots in his 14 years on the Fairfax County Board of Supervisors, which included five years as chairman. Now on the Oversight and Government Reform Committee, he focuses on protections for government workers, bolstering transportation and infrastructure, promoting "green" jobs and augmenting telecommuting opportunities.

In the 113th Congress (2013-14), he is the top Democrat on the Government Operations Subcommittee, which was created in 2013 — its chairman is John L. Mica of Florida, the former head of the Transportation and Infrastructure Committee. It has similar jurisdiction to the old Subcommittee on Technology, Information Policy, Intergovernmental Relations and Procurement, where Connolly was the top Democrat in the 112th Congress (2011-12).

In 2010, President Barack Obama signed a federal telework bill written by Connolly, Republican Frank R. Wolf of the neighboring 10th District and Baltimore-area Democrat John Sarbanes. It increased eligibility for telework and requires the Office of Personnel Management to track the results. "The biggest problem we have is cultural — a mentality among some managers that if I can't see you, you're not working," he said. Connolly touts telework as a means to reduce traffic congestion and a way to keep the government operating in the event of a terrorist attack on the capital.

He will support some defense and cybersecurity measures — in April 2013, the House passed a bill by Mica, Connolly and the leaders of the full committee that would require federal agencies to create information security programs approved by the Office of Management and Budget.

Connolly is a vice chairman of the business-minded New Democrat Coalition and one of the architects of its "innovation agenda," which includes cybersecurity, "cloud" computing, research and development tax credits, education and infrastructure.

Connolly spent most of the 1980s as a staff member on the Senate Foreign Relations Committee, and he now sits on its House counterpart. He highlights free trade as a priority. He was in the minority of House Democrats who supported 2011 pacts with South Korea, Colombia and Panama.

Human rights issues also have grabbed his attention in recent years. "If there's anything the United States stands for ... it is to champion personal autonomy, personal freedom," he said. "We can never countenance something that negates that."

Connolly and several colleagues raised a red flag about purported forced-labor camps in Vietnam, writing a 2012 letter asking the U.S. ambassador there to call publicly for their closure.

He also has addressed reports of human trafficking by U.S. contractors operating in Iraq and Afghanistan. The fiscal 2013 defense authorization law includes a bipartisan amendment, backed by Connolly and other Oversight members, that requires improved monitoring and reporting to prevent any trafficking abuses by contractors.

Connolly became the steward of a new cause in 2013: restructuring foreign aid programs. California Democrat Howard L. Berman, a former chairman of the Foreign Affairs Committee, had been developing an overhaul for years with Connolly's assistance. But Berman was defeated for re-election in 2012, and Connolly took the cause as his own. The plan would centralize foreign aid, humanitarian response and arms sales under the umbrella of the U.S. Agency for International Development and give its administrator a permanent seat on the National Security Council.

Connolly grew up in Boston, where his grandmother settled after leaving Northern Ireland at age 17. His father helped spark his passion for politics, bringing 8-year-old Gerald along to set up placards for Sen. John F. Kennedy's re-election campaign in Boston. Connolly's mother was a nurse, and his father worked in life insurance and served as a ward committee member, which pretty much tied the family to Democrat Thomas P. O'Neill Jr., speaker of the House from 1977 to 1987. Connolly used O'Neill's gavel, a gift from a constituent, when he first presided over the House in 2009.

In the mid-1960s, he was a student at Maryknoll Fathers Junior Seminary in Pennsylvania. But doubts about a life of celibacy, as well as disillusionment over the church's silence on the Vietnam War, led him away from the priesthood. Still, he calls politics a "logical extension" of his earlier study of religion.

After graduating from Maryknoll College with a degree in literature in 1971, he worked for nonprofit organizations, including the American Freedom from Hunger Foundation. That's where he met his future wife, Catherine Smith, a former nun. Connolly earned a master's degree in public administration from Harvard, then went to work for the Senate. Ten years later he returned to the private sector, serving as vice president for the Washington office of SRI International, formerly the Stanford Research Institute.

Connolly was elected to the Fairfax County Board of Supervisors in 1995 and became chairman in 2004. During his tenure, he oversaw implementation of military base realignments. He also helped pave the way for the largest expansion of Metro rail service in a generation — the first phase of which should welcome new riders in 2013, with the final stretch into neighboring Loudoun County scheduled for completion by 2016.

Connolly won a heated 2008 House primary, then handily defeated Republican challenger Keith Fimian in the contest to succeed retiring Republican Thomas M. Davis III. Their 2010 rematch proved to be a nail-biter, with Connolly edging out Fimian by fewer than 1,000 votes in a race that wasn't certified until a week after Election Day.

He briefly considered a 2012 run for the Senate, but dropped those plans when former Gov. Tim Kaine entered the race. Running in a redrawn 11th District, Connolly took 61 percent of the vote for his easiest win to date.

Key Votes

2012	
Extend a Social Security payroll tax cut and unemployment benefits	NO
Ease securities rules to expand small-business access to capital	YES
Extend for one year subsidized student loan interest rates financed by a cut in health care spending	NO
Cite Attorney General Eric H. Holder Jr. for contempt of Congress	NO
Create a visa program for foreign graduates in high-tech fields	NO
Extend most Bush-era income tax rates while allowing rates for top-bracket earners to rise (Jan. 1, 2013)	YES
2011	
Strike funding for F-35 alternative engine	NO
Prevent EPA from regulating greenhouse gas emissions to address climate change	NO
Extend certain provisions of Patriot Act for four years	NO
Declare opposition to use of ground troops in Libya	YES
Overhaul patent law	YES
Pass compromise debt limit increase plan and establish future spending limits	YES
Allow consideration of measures to implement three trade agreements	YES

CQ Vote Studies

	PARTY UNITY		PRESIDENTIAL SUPPORT	
	SUPPORT	OPPOSE	SUPPORT	OPPOSE
2012	91%	9%	83%	17%
2011	90%	10%	88%	12%
2010	90%	10%	93%	7%
2009	97%	3%	96%	4%

Interest Groups

	AFL-CIO	ADA	CCUS	ACU
2012	85%	65%	42%	17%
2011	86%	80%	44%	4%
2010	86%	85%	25%	4%
2009	95%	95%	47%	0%

Virginia 11

Washington suburbs — parts of Fairfax and Prince William counties

The 11th District takes up some Northern Virginia suburbs outside Washington, D.C.; it is centered on Fairfax County and the independent city of Fairfax and grabs a slice of eastern Prince William County. The area is home to highly paid, white-collar professionals who work for the federal government or the many technology, media and consulting businesses linked to it. Changing demographics in the area will make this seat increasingly politically competitive and attractive to moderates running for office.

While not completely immune to the recession, the region has weathered the economic downturn better than many other parts of the state. Workers in Fairfax and Vienna are directly linked to Washington by the Metrorail system, although traffic remains a major district-wide concern. Tysons Corner is a booming retail and corporate office hub. Redistricting drew racially diverse and generally affluent communities such as Reston, Herndon, Fair Lakes and Centreville into the 11th, giving it the commonwealth's highest proportion of Asian residents (18 percent) and the second-highest proportion of Hispanic residents (17 percent).

Infrastructure is a concern, especially given the high number of commuters and rapid development. Reston was one of Virginia's first planned communities and continues to try to manage its growth. Further south, the 11th's new portion of Prince William County includes communities along the Potomac River, north of Marine Corps Base Quantico.

The 11th was one of Virginia's most geographically altered districts in the decennial remapping process, losing portions of southern Fairfax County, including Fort Belvoir, and parts of Prince William County. The new borders shore up the district's current Democratic lean — the parts of Prince William here gave Barack Obama 70 percent of the presidential vote in 2012; overall he took 62 percent in the district.

Major Industry
Government, technology, service, retail

Cities
Reston (unincorp.), Centreville (unincorp.) (pt.), Dale City (unincorp.) (pt.)

Notable
The Fairfax city-owned Blenheim Estate once housed Union soldiers during the Civil War, and graffiti written by soldiers is still visible in the house's attic — the house is preserved as a Civil War museum and hosts Fairfax's annual Civil War Weekend.

WASHINGTON

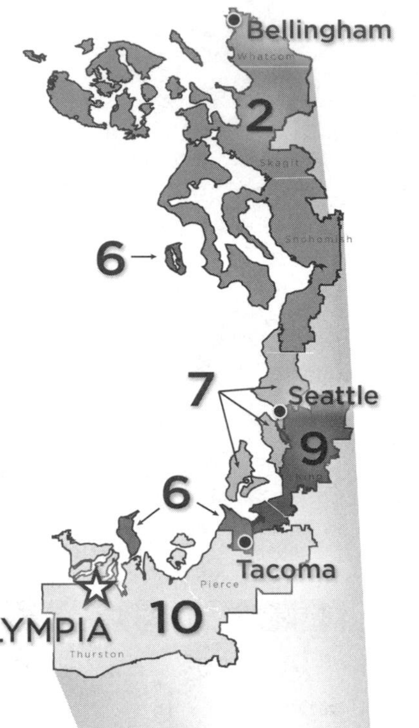

Seattle Area

Districts 2, 7, 9, 10
- Part of 6

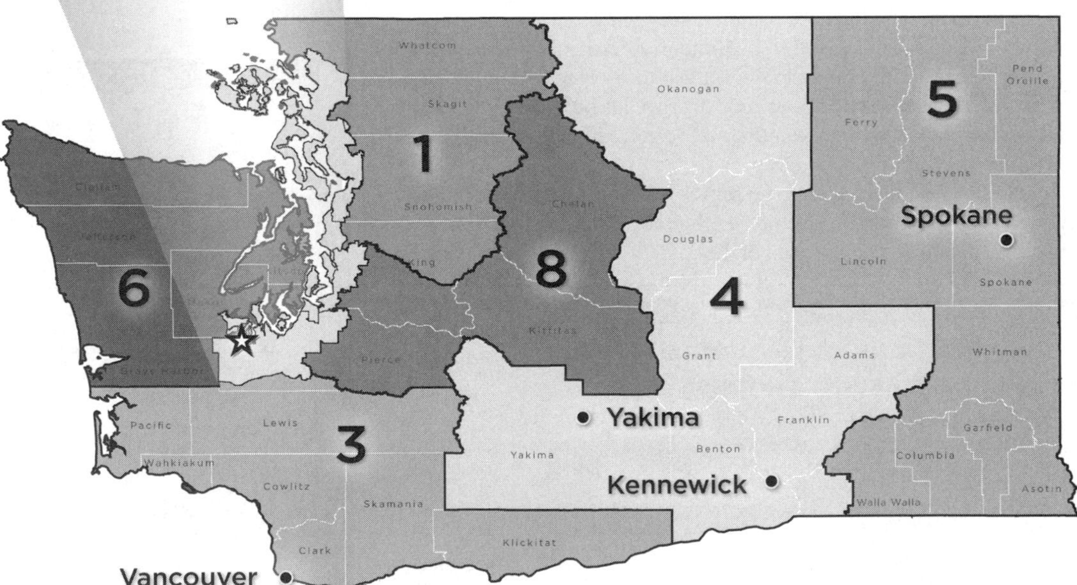

Gov. Jay Inslee (D)

First elected: 2012

Length of term: 4 years

Term expires: 1/17

Salary: $166,891

Phone: (360) 902-4111

Residence: Bainbridge Island

Born: Feb. 9, 1951; Seattle, Wash.

Religion: Protestant

Family: Wife, Trudi Inslee; three children

Education: Stanford U., attended 1969-70; U. of Washington, B.A. 1973 (economics); Willamette U., J.D. 1976

Career: Lawyer

Political highlights: Wash. House, 1989-93; U.S. House, 1993-95; defeated for re-election to U.S. House, 1994; sought Democratic nomination for governor, 1996; U.S. House, 1999-2012

ELECTION RESULTS

2010 GENERAL

Jay Insell (D)	1,582,802	51.5%
Rob McKenna (R)	1,488,245	48.5%

Lt. Gov. Brad Owen (D)

First elected: 1996

Length of term: 4 years

Term expires: 1/17

Salary: $93,948

Phone: (360) 786-7700

LEGISLATURE

Legislature: 105 days January-May in odd-numbered years; 60 days in January-March in even-numbered years

Senate: 49 members, 4-year terms

2013 ratios: 26 D, 23 R; 32 men, 17 women

Salary: $42,106

Phone: (360) 786-7550

House: 98 members, 2-year terms

2013 ratios: 55 D, 43 R; 70 men, 28 women

Salary: $42,106

Phone: (360) 786-7750

TERM LIMITS

Governor: No

Senate: No

House: No

URBAN STATISTICS

CITY	POPULATION
Seattle	608,660
Spokane	208,916
Tacoma	198,397
Vancouver	161,791
Bellevue	122,363

REGISTERED VOTERS

Voters do not register by party.

POPULATION

2010 population	6,724,540
2000 population	5,894,121
1990 population	4,866,692
Percent change (2000-2010)	+14.1%
Rank among states (2010)	13
Median age	36.8
Born in state	47.2%
Foreign born	11.7%
Violent crime rate	331/100,000
Poverty level	12.3%
Federal workers	92,594
Military	46,161

ELECTIONS

STATE ELECTION OFFICIAL
(360) 902-4180

DEMOCRATIC PARTY
(206) 583-0664

REPUBLICAN PARTY
(425) 460-0570

MISCELLANEOUS

Web: www.access.wa.gov

Capital: Olympia

U.S. CONGRESS

Senate: 2 Democrats

House: 6 Democrats, 4 Republicans

STATISTICS BY DISTRICT

District	2012 Vote for President: Obama	2012 Vote for President: Romney	2008 Vote for President: Obama	2008 Vote for President: McCain	Black	Asian	Hispanic	Median Income	Over 64	Under 20	College Education	Rural	Sq. Miles
1	54%	43%	56%	42%	1%	9%	8%	$77,382	11%	27%	39%	21%	6,186
2	59	38	60	38	2	8	10	54,964	13	24	29	19	1,015
3	48	50	51	47	1	3	8	51,366	14	27	23	29	9,114
4	38	60	39	59	1	2	37	47,594	12	32	21	29	19,250
5	44	53	46	51	2	2	6	45,714	14	26	28	25	15,473
6	56	41	57	41	4	5	7	51,982	16	23	27	26	6,903
7	79	18	80	18	5	10	7	61,747	12	19	55	2	144
8	50	48	51	47	2	7	9	67,046	11	29	30	20	7,360
9	68	30	69	30	11	21	12	62,381	11	25	37	<1	183
10	56	41	57	41	5	6	10	54,917	12	27	26	8	827
STATE	**56**	**41**	**58**	**41**	**4**	**7**	**11**	**56,835**	**13**	**26**	**31**	**18**	**66,456**
U.S.	**51**	**47**	**53**	**46**	**12**	**5**	**17**	**50,052**	**13**	**27**	**29**	**21**	**3,531,905**

Sen. Patty Murray (D)

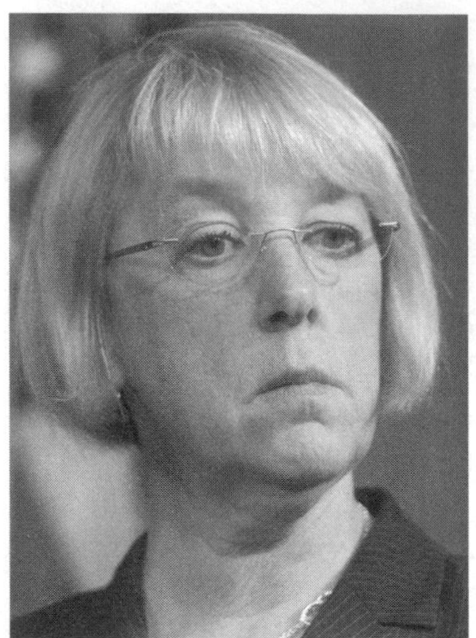

Capitol Office
224-2621
murray.senate.gov
154 Russell Bldg. 20510-4704; fax 224-0238

Committees
Appropriations
(Transportation-HUD - Chairwoman)
Budget - Chairwoman
Health, Education, Labor & Pensions
Rules & Administration
Veterans' Affairs

Residence
Seattle

Born
Oct. 11, 1950; Bothell, Wash.

Religion
Roman Catholic

Family
Husband, Rob Murray; two children

Education
Washington State U., B.A. 1972

Career
Parenting class instructor; homemaker; secretary

Political Highlights
Candidate for Shoreline School Board, 1983; Shoreline School Board, 1983-89; Wash. Senate, 1989-93

ELECTION RESULTS

2010 GENERAL		
Patty Murray (D)	1,314,930	52.4%
Dino Rossi (R)	1,196,164	47.6%
2010 PRIMARY (Open)		
Patty Murray (D)	670,284	46.2%

Previous Winning Percentages
2004 (55%); 1998 (58%); 1992 (54%)

Elected 1992; 4th term

Unassuming but tough, Murray has worked her way into the inner circle of the Democratic leadership team. She has frequently been enlisted as a leader of bipartisan negotiations, and in those talks she acts as a liberal who defends government intervention in the economy.

Murray serves as the Democratic Conference secretary, the No. 4 position in the party's leadership structure. She helped Democrats expand their majority as the chairwoman of the Democratic Senatorial Campaign Committee in the 2012 cycle — the second time she held that job. And she has also become the voice of Senate Democrats on matters of economic policy.

The August 2011 law raising the debt limit also created a bipartisan, bicameral panel charged with making recommendations to reduce the deficit by more than $1 trillion over a decade. Murray and Texas Republican Rep. Jeb Hensarling co-chaired the "supercommittee," which ultimately disbanded without achieving its goal — Republicans balked at proposed tax increases, while Democrats weren't interested in further spending reductions.

But it did place Murray out front in a major political debate, which was something of a change. She had generally kept a lower profile than other members of the Democratic leadership, such as media-savvy Majority Whip Richard J. Durbin of Illinois and voluble Conference Vice Chairman Charles E. Schumer of New York. Her reputation for smoothing over disputes within the party helped her land the supercommittee assignment.

And her ability to stay on message didn't hurt, either. As some lawmakers looked to avert spending cuts put in place by the 2011 debt limit law, Murray held fast. "If we can't get a good deal, a balanced deal that calls on the wealthy to pay their fair share, then I will absolutely continue this debate into 2013 rather than lock in a long-term deal this year that throws middle-class families under the bus," she said in a July 2012 speech.

She has continued the debate in the 113th Congress (2013-14), as the new chairwoman of the Budget Committee. Under Murray's leadership, the panel produced a fiscal 2014 budget that the Senate adopted by the narrowest of margins — 50-49, with four Democrats joining all Republicans in opposition.

It was the first budget that the chamber had adopted in four years, and it reflected priorities Murray laid out the year before. It calls for close to a trillion dollars in revenue increases over 10 years, and its deficit reduction targets were much smaller than those in the budget of the Republican House. Murray carefully managed the rhetoric surrounding the blueprint, describing it as a "balanced" approach and a "pro-growth, pro-middle-class agenda."

"I feel very strongly that it doesn't make sense to replace our budget deficits with deficits in education and infrastructure and research and development," she said at a February 2013 hearing.

There was a time when Murray had difficulty being taken seriously. Her first Senate election in 1992 was often dismissed as a fluke, and congressional staffers rated her in 2002 and 2004 as one of the least intelligent senators in Washingtonian Magazine's "Best and Worst of Congress" list. Now, she has a hand in a number of domestic policy issues — everything from Amtrak funding to early-childhood education — and other things that she says affect everyday Americans.

Murray is a senior member of the Appropriations Committee and the chairwoman of its Transportation-HUD panel. After the 2008 economic meltdown, she was a prominent proponent of stimulating the economy via transportation and infrastructure projects, and she proposed an additional $25 billion for such activities during the debate on President Barack Obama's economic stimulus package in early 2009.

She will try to steer that funding home, as well. Murray has been compared favorably to Washington's legendary Democratic Sen. Warren Magnuson, who secured billions of federal dollars for the state.

Murray promotes two of her state's biggest employers, Microsoft Corp. and Boeing Co. She repeatedly denounced the federal antitrust case against Microsoft. When competitors of Boeing were awarded a $35 billion contract to build Air Force refueling tankers in 2008, Murray protested the decision. She threatened to withhold funds for the tankers or impose penalties on the Air Force, arguing that U.S. tax dollars should not boost the foreign company, EADS, that won. The deal was scrapped once the Government Accountability Office found that the Air Force had violated its own contracting rules. Bidding was re-opened, and Boeing won the contract in 2011.

Murray chaired the Veterans' Affairs Committee in the 112th Congress (2011-12), and in that role she claimed several bipartisan achievements. She and her House counterpart, Florida Republican Jeff Miller, combined parts of their bills to promote the hiring of veterans, producing a measure signed by Obama in late 2011. The next year, she tried to woo Republican support for a bill that would establish a federal jobs corps for veterans. She included several GOP provisions in the measure, but Republicans ultimately blocked the bill via a procedural vote — they said the spending in the bill would exceed the spending cap enacted in the 2011 debt limit law.

Murry is also a member of the Health, Education, Labor and Pensions Committee. She is a frequent critic of what she calls GOP attacks on women's health rights, and she supports requiring employers to provide insurance that includes contraception among the preventive services available without a co-pay. In 2011, Murray also challenged the Department of Health and Human Services to explain the decision to prevent women younger than 17 from obtaining emergency contraception without a prescription. Murray once threatened to hold up the nomination of the Food and Drug Administration commissioner until the agency ruled on making such morning-after contraception available.

Murray's work ethic and support for government social programs stem from her childhood. She and her six siblings put in long hours at their father's dime store. They often made their own clothes and went without health care. When Murray was a teenager, her father was diagnosed with multiple sclerosis and stopped working. The family briefly went on welfare until her mother completed a government-funded program that enabled her to work as a bookkeeper. When Murray went to college, she worked to help pay for her education. Her jobs included working in a glass shop, as a secretary and, one summer, cleaning bathrooms in a state park.

In the early 1980s, Murray was angered when the state legislature planned to eliminate a parenting education program that she was teaching. She packed the kids into the car and drove to the capital to complain. She says she was dismissed by a legislator who told her, "You can't make a difference. You're just a mom in tennis shoes."

"I drove home as angry as I could be, saying he has no right to tell me I can't make a difference," Murray said. She organized a successful campaign to revive the program. That led Murray to serve six years on a school board and four years in the state Senate.

In her 1992 quest for a seat in the U.S. Senate, she bested better-known moderates with years of congressional experience in both the primary and general elections. She was re-elected in 1998 with 58 percent of the vote. In 2004, she faced George Nethercutt, a Republican House member who had beaten Democratic Speaker Thomas S. Foley in 1994. Murray won by 12 points. Her 2010 race against Republican Dino Rossi, a two-time candidate for governor, was her closest contest. She bested Rossi by less than 5 points.

Key Votes

2012

Prohibit health insurance plans from denying coverage based on the sponsor's religious beliefs	YES
Require approval of the Keystone XL oil pipeline	NO
Ease securities rules to expand small-business access to capital	NO
Reauthorize farm and nutrition programs for five years	YES
Limit debate on a bill that would create private-sector cybersecurity standards	YES
Consent to ratification of a treaty setting global standard for the treatment of people with disabilities	YES
Provide $60.4 billion in disaster relief following Superstorm Sandy	YES
Extend most Bush-era income tax rates while allowing rates for top-bracket earners to rise (Jan. 1, 2013)	YES

2011

Prevent EPA from regulating greenhouse gas emissions to address climate change	NO
Extend certain provisions of Patriot Act for four years	NO
Clear compromise debt limit increase plan and establish future spending limits	YES
Overhaul patent law	YES
Implement Colombia free trade agreement	YES
Limit debate on confirmation of Caitlin J. Halligan to D.C. Circuit Court of Appeals	YES
Extend payroll tax cut and unemployment benefits for two months	YES

CQ Vote Studies

	PARTY UNITY		PRESIDENTIAL SUPPORT	
	SUPPORT	OPPOSE	SUPPORT	OPPOSE
2012	98%	2%	96%	4%
2011	96%	4%	97%	3%
2010	97%	3%	98%	2%
2009	97%	3%	95%	5%
2008	99%	1%	28%	72%
2007	97%	3%	38%	62%
2006	92%	8%	59%	41%
2005	95%	5%	33%	67%
2004	91%	9%	63%	37%
2003	97%	3%	49%	51%

Interest Groups

	AFL-CIO	ADA	CCUS	ACU
2012	100%	100%	38%	0%
2011	84%	95%	55%	5%
2010	100%	95%	27%	0%
2009	94%	95%	43%	0%
2008	100%	95%	63%	0%
2007	100%	90%	64%	0%
2006	93%	95%	50%	4%
2005	79%	95%	44%	0%
2004	92%	90%	75%	8%
2003	85%	90%	43%	10%

Sen. Maria Cantwell (D)

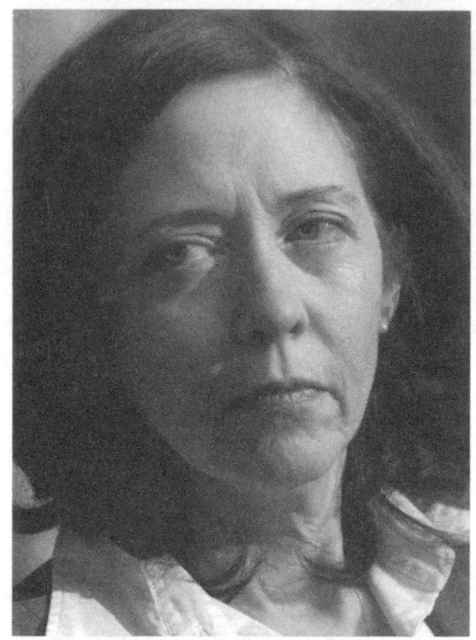

Capitol Office
224-3441
cantwell.senate.gov
311 Hart Bldg. 20510-4705; fax 228-0514

Committees
Commerce, Science & Transportation
(Aviation Operations, Safety & Security - Chairwoman)
Energy & Natural Resources
Finance
Indian Affairs - Chairwoman
Small Business & Entrepreneurship

Residence
Edmonds

Born
Oct. 13, 1958; Indianapolis, Ind.

Religion
Roman Catholic

Family
Single

Education
Miami U. (Ohio), B.A. 1980 (public policy)

Career
Internet audio company executive; public relations consultant

Political Highlights
Wash. House, 1987-92; U.S. House, 1993-95; defeated for re-election to U.S. House, 1994

ELECTION RESULTS

2012 GENERAL		
Maria Cantwell (D)	1,855,493	60.4%
Michael Baumgartner (R)	1,213,924	39.5%
2012 PRIMARY (Open)		
Maria Cantwell (D)	772,058	55.7%
Timmy "Doc" Wilson (D)	31,817	2.3%

Previous Winning Percentages
2006 (57%); 2000 (49%);
1992 House Election (55%)

Elected 2000; 3rd term

Cantwell has become increasingly assertive in the Senate, expending her considerable energy on efforts that matter most to her state's economy. She speaks of the importance of free markets, with a liberal's instincts to use a vigorous government to protect her notions of fairness in those markets.

Many people go on to private sector success upon leaving politics, while others come to Congress after succeeding in the business world. Cantwell fits both descriptions. Her father, Paul, was a congressional aide and later an Indiana politician; Cantwell followed the same path and became a campaign operative, a state legislator and a one-term member of the U.S. House.

After her failed re-election bid in 1994, she landed a job at RealNetworks, a Seattle-based Internet startup. Cantwell rose to the position of senior vice president of consumer products — the company grew rapidly, as did the value of her stock holdings. She used her new personal fortune to bankroll her 2000 Senate campaign (though the stock price plummeted late that year). She returned to Congress, professing respect for the power of technology and innovation to spur economic growth.

As a lawmaker, Cantwell is still businesslike — in 2012, the Seattle Times described her as "intense and demanding." Her committee work has national significance, but her home state's companies and economic interests are often what draw her into any particular fight. The Chamber of Commerce endorsed Cantwell in her 2012 campaign for a third term.

Cantwell sits on the Finance Committee, which has jurisdiction over taxes and trade; she was a leading Senate proponent of a 2012 reauthorization of the Export-Import Bank, which helps U.S. companies sell products abroad. Its biggest beneficiary is Boeing Co., a major Seattle-area employer. Cantwell introduces targeted measures to promote Washington's shipping industry and reduce duties that affect its technology companies. In the 112th Congress (2011-12), she was the only Democrat on the Finance Committee to vote for "fast-tracking" of votes on the Trans-Pacific Partnership.

She adheres to some common Democratic positions on free trade — Cantwell said in 2012 that her support for normalizing trade relations with Russia was contingent on provisions to address human rights and election violations there. A normalization bill was enacted late that year.

Cantwell also looks out for Boeing as the chairwoman of the Commerce, Science and Transportation subcommittee on aviation, a position she has held since 2011. As Congress wrapped up a 2012 reauthorization of federal aviation programs, Commerce Chairman Jay Rockefeller of West Virginia touted Cantwell's contributions on provisions regarding NextGen, a new GPS-based air traffic control system. "She's brilliant on technology and all those things, and she's very organized," he said.

Working with fellow Washington Democrat Patty Murray, in the 112th she secured a $20 million Labor Department grant to train community college students for aerospace jobs, an important gain for a state projecting 20,000 new jobs over the next 10 years to fill orders at Boeing and its contractors.

Cantwell sides with her state's technology sector in a fight with Hollywood over intellectual-property protections. In 2011, Congress debated whether copyright laws should be strengthened to allow law enforcement officials to go after foreign websites offering pirated materials — in some cases, shutting the sites down via a court order. Cantwell and several partners introduced a bill to route infringement disputes to the International Trade Commission, which she said would preserve due process rights.

She supports "network neutrality" rules that the Federal Communications

Commission put in place in 2011, which are written to prevent broadband providers from restricting access to certain Internet content. However, she introduced a 2011 bill that would have extended such rules to wireless platforms, which the FCC rules did not.

On the Energy and Natural Resources Committee, Cantwell supports tax credits for energy production from "clean" sources. She has also called for a permanent ban on offshore drilling along the West Coast.

She backs the regulation of greenhouse gas emissions, but the cap-and-trade system Democrats tried to advance in the 111th Congress (2009-10) gave her pause. She worried that such a system, which would allow polluters to trade emissions credits, would create a secondary financial market in energy that would be vulnerable to speculation and risk. Cantwell and Maine Republican Susan Collins proposed a "cap and dividend" system that would limit trading only to polluting entities.

Her worries about market abuses have tempered her business agenda several times. Cantwell voted against a 2010 financial regulatory overhaul because the Senate bill lacked provisions she sought to "further clamp down on Wall Street." She and Arizona Republican John McCain in 2009 and 2010 tried to revive some Depression-era restrictions on the trading activities of commercial banks.

Cantwell has been a fixture on the Indian Affairs Committee, and she became its chairwoman at the start of the 113th Congress (2013-14). She told a tribal group in 2013 that she supports a "Carcieri fix" — legislation to overturn a 2009 Supreme Court decision that prevents tribes recognized after 1934 from placing land into a federal trust that exempts it from state and local laws and taxes. Such arrangements have been used to facilitate American Indian gaming facilities.

Cantwell is socially liberal. She defends abortion rights and same-sex marriage. But she opposed a successful 2012 state ballot initiative to legalize marijuana for recreational use.

Born in Indianapolis, Cantwell spent part of her childhood in Washington, D.C., while her father worked for Rep. Andrew Jacobs Jr., an Indiana Democrat. When the family moved back to Indiana, her father held a seat as a county commissioner.

Cantwell earned a degree in public policy at Miami University in Ohio. She worked on the unsuccessful gubernatorial campaign of Jerry Springer, who went on to talk-show fame. In 1983, she moved to the Seattle area to be a political organizer for Democratic presidential candidate Alan Cranston, a U.S. senator from California. She worked in public relations, then was elected to the state legislature, serving from 1987 to 1992. She was elected to the U.S. House in 1992, the same year her father was elected to the Indiana House. She couldn't survive the Republican tide of 1994.

Her interlude at RealNetworks gave her a huge money advantage in her 2000 Senate campaign. Cantwell blew past a favored Democrat in the "open" primary, then spent $11.6 million — much of that her own — to unseat incumbent Republican Slade Gorton by around 2,000 votes. Her net worth plummeted when RealNetworks' stock price fell, but her campaign still has not repaid her for all of those loans.

She scored a 17-point victory over Republican Mike McGavick in 2006, and Cantwell was heavily favored heading into the 2012 election. Her fund-raising effort dissuaded most challengers. The Seattle Times reported that she "collected hundreds of thousands of dollars from executives at corporations with stakes in alternative energy, biotech, aviation and other issues."

Her opponent, state Sen. Michael Baumgartner, raised only $1 million. Cantwell's lead in the polls was enough that she spent much of the campaign helping other Democrats in statewide races. She took more than 60 percent of the vote.

Key Votes

2012	
Prohibit health insurance plans from denying coverage based on the sponsor's religious beliefs	YES
Require approval of the Keystone XL oil pipeline	NO
Ease securities rules to expand small-business access to capital	YES
Reauthorize farm and nutrition programs for five years	YES
Limit debate on a bill that would create private-sector cybersecurity standards	YES
Consent to ratification of a treaty setting global standard for the treatment of people with disabilities	YES
Provide $60.4 billion in disaster relief following Superstorm Sandy	YES
Extend most Bush-era income tax rates while allowing rates for top-bracket earners to rise (Jan. 1, 2013)	YES
2011	
Prevent EPA from regulating greenhouse gas emissions to address climate change	NO
Extend certain provisions of Patriot Act for four years	NO
Clear compromise debt limit increase plan and establish future spending limits	YES
Overhaul patent law	NO
Implement Colombia free trade agreement	YES
Limit debate on confirmation of Caitlin J. Halligan to D.C. Circuit Court of Appeals	YES
Extend payroll tax cut and unemployment benefits for two months	YES

CQ Vote Studies

	PARTY UNITY		PRESIDENTIAL SUPPORT	
	SUPPORT	OPPOSE	SUPPORT	OPPOSE
2012	97%	3%	97%	3%
2011	92%	8%	97%	3%
2010	92%	8%	95%	5%
2009	94%	6%	95%	5%
2008	97%	3%	28%	72%
2007	94%	6%	39%	61%
2006	92%	8%	54%	46%
2005	92%	8%	36%	64%
2004	90%	10%	66%	34%
2003	96%	4%	52%	48%

Interest Groups

	AFL-CIO	ADA	CCUS	ACU
2012	91%	100%	38%	4%
2011	84%	95%	55%	10%
2010	94%	90%	45%	12%
2009	94%	95%	43%	8%
2008	100%	100%	50%	12%
2007	95%	95%	64%	4%
2006	87%	95%	58%	12%
2005	86%	95%	56%	8%
2004	83%	95%	65%	8%
2003	85%	90%	39%	15%

Rep. Suzan DelBene (D)

Capitol Office
225-6311
delbene.house.gov
318 Cannon Bldg. 20515-4701; fax 226-1606

Committees
Agriculture
Judiciary

Residence
Medina

Born
Feb. 17, 1962; Selma, Ala.

Religion
Episcopalian

Family
Husband, Kurt DelBene; two children

Education
Reed College, B.A. 1983 (biology); U. of Washington, M.B.A. 1990

Career
Micro-financing nonprofit management consultant; Microsoft executive; data software company executive; health sciences researcher; online convenience store executive

Political Highlights
Democratic nominee for U.S. House, 2010; Wash. Department of Revenue director, 2011-12

ELECTION RESULTS

2012 SPECIAL		
Suzan DelBene (D)	216,144	60.4%
John Koster (R)	141,591	39.6%
2012 GENERAL		
Suzan DelBene (D)	177,025	53.9%
John Koster (R)	151,187	46.1%
2012 PRIMARY (Open)		
Suzan DelBene (D)	33,670	22.5%
Darcy Burner (D)	20,844	13.9%
Laura Ruderman (D)	10,582	7.1%
Steve Hobbs (D)	10,279	6.9%
Darshan Rauniyar (D)	4,134	2.8%

Elected 2012; 1st full term

DelBene started out in biotechnology and worked as a Microsoft executive; her deliberative style was suited to industries where research takes time and new products require incubation. But as a businesswoman, she also speaks of the need for timely action: "In the end, you have to decide to get stuff done."

At first glance, DelBene (full name: like "Susan" dell-BEN-ay) seems to be a mild-mannered version of Maria Cantwell, the junior senator from her state. Both women accrued personal fortunes from their ties to tech companies, both women emphasize their insight into the business community, and both women are Democrats. But Cantwell comes from a family tradition of politics, whereas DelBene is relatively new to the game.

DelBene was not born a millionaire. Her parents divorced when she was a toddler, and she went with her mother after the split. Her stepfather lost his job as a pilot, and the family moved around the country as he sought stable work. Eventually, her stepfather got a job in Iran, and DelBene got a scholarship at a boarding school in Connecticut — Choate Rosemary Hall, which counts John F. Kennedy as an alumnus.

She says her politics were shaped in part by watching her parents struggle to pay the bills. "My dad lost his job when I was young, and he never got back on track financially," DelBene says. "I had the opportunity to go to college through financial aid, student loans and work study, and everyone should have access to similar opportunities."

At Reed College in Portland, Ore., DelBene got a degree in biology. A few years after graduating, she ended up in Seattle at a biotech startup company. As she got interested in the business side of operations, she worked toward an MBA at the University of Washington. An internship at Microsoft led to her first job there; she also met Kurt DelBene, whom she married in 1997. He is currently the president of the Microsoft Office Division.

DelBene left the company and served as an executive for two Internet start-up companies. When she returned to Microsoft in 2004, she served as a vice president of marketing for the mobile communications division. After a few years, she left again to work at a microfinance nonprofit.

In 2010, she mounted a challenge to Republican Rep. Dave Reichert of the 8th District. DelBene put more than $2 million of her own money into the race, but Reichert is an experienced politician, and Republicans were having a great year. She lost by 4 points.

A few weeks after the election, Gov. Christine Gregoire appointed her as director of the state Department of Revenue, saying there was a need for her "business savvy." DelBene says the job gave her an appreciation for how policies need to hold up in the real world: "We have a lot of policy that is incredibly complicated, and the people it impacts don't understand it, and sometimes we don't get the result we want, even though the intent might be good."

The job also might have provided a lesson in politics. DelBene's proposal to streamline the state's business tax system — mostly by having the state take over tax collection — was scuttled as city governments resisted the possible reduction in their revenue and control.

She quit that job to pursue a second, successful run for the House. DelBene represents a swing district and a plethora of interests from Washington state: specialty crop agriculture, tech companies and middle-class families.

She has seats on the Agriculture and Judiciary committees. DelBene has gravitated toward issues where differences are more regional than partisan.

On the Judiciary Committee, DelBene hopes to represent the interests of northern border states in immigration policy debates — her district borders

Canada. She aligns with the usual Democratic Party preferences for an immigration overhaul; she would like to see an "earned path" to citizenship for illegal immigrants who are working in the United States.

She does not want enhanced border security to impede the flow of commerce and workers who commute through border crossings each day. "Reforms must support the workforce needs of our local employers, including long-term and seasonal agricultural workers, as well as highly trained technical workers," she wrote in a January 2013 opinion piece.

DelBene sits on the Courts, Intellectual Property and Internet panel. As Congress works to modernize intellectual property protections, adaptability is key, she says. Whatever is put in place, we shouldn't "think it's going to sit there for years. ... Our economy moves quickly, our business environment and innovation change really quickly, and we need to get policy up to date with what's happening out there."

She wants to update privacy rules for the digital age. In one of her first actions of the 113th Congress (2013-14), DelBene co-sponsored a bill by California Democrat Zoe Lofgren to require the government to obtain warrants for both digital communications and geolocation data.

DelBene, a member of the New Democrat Coalition, is also in favor of requiring online retailers to collect state sales tax.

On the Agriculture Committee, DelBene will look out for the interests of specialty crop farmers and try to maintain funding for agriculture research.

The congressional map drawn after the 2010 census included a 1st District that seemed to be the most politically competitive turf in the state. It soon became an open seat — Democratic Rep. Jay Inslee resigned to focus on his campaign for governor. (He won.)

Washington has a "top two" primary system, where all candidates are on the same ballot and the top two, regardless of party affiliation, advance to the general election. John Koster of the Snohomish County Council was the only Republican on the ballot, and he finished in first place. DelBene competed with several Democrats in an expensive and at times bitter race. She finished in second with less than 23 percent of the vote.

Democrats rallied around her in the general election, and she defeated Koster by almost 8 points. She simultaneously won a special election to complete Inslee's term in the 112th Congress (2011-12), which gave her a boost in seniority over other members who were first elected in November 2012. She spent close to $3 million of her own money on the campaign.

When DelBene arrived on Capitol Hill, she took an office not far from that of New York Republican Richard Hanna — another graduate of her alma mater. "We have the bipartisan Reed College Caucus here in the corner," she said.

Key Votes

2012	
Create a visa program for foreign graduates in high-tech fields	**NO**
Extend most Bush-era income tax rates while allowing rates for top-bracket earners to rise (Jan. 1, 2013)	**YES**

Interest Groups

	AFL-CIO	ADA	CCUS	ACU
2012			50%	

Washington 1

Northeastern Seattle suburbs and Cascade Mountains

Extending from the Cascade Mountains to the Puget Sound north of Bellingham and also to the northeastern Seattle suburbs, the 1st covers a mostly rural, inland area representative of the state as a whole. The 1st has coastal fishing, orchards and dairy farms, as well as high-tech jobs and congested interstates. Most of the district's population is in the Seattle-area King and Snohomish counties. The 1st takes up much of Whatcom and Skagit, but only about 50 percent of each county's population.

The northern tier of King County offers a rich vein of computer and software jobs. Redmond is home to the massive Microsoft corporate headquarters and research campus, and most of the city's workforce is affiliated with the industry giant. On the other side of Interstate 405, Google's Pacific Northwest facilities are in Kirkland. Nearby Medina hosts some of the wealthiest residents in the state. North of Seattle, white-collar commuters live in outer suburbs in Snohomish; other residents work at Boeing.

Agriculture is vital to the rest of the district. Whatcom County's raspberries and dairy farms contribute $1 billion annually to the local economy. Some of the space on the agricultural plain between the mountains and the populous corridor near the Sound could be useful to the wind-energy sector. Jobs at Cherry Point's smelting facilities, oil refinery and international shipping port provide steady employment, although environmental concerns have caused officials to reconsider expansion at the sites.

Decennial remapping created a competitive district as inland portions of Whatcom, Skagit and Snohomish were separated from much of the Puget Sound north of Seattle and added to close-in Seattle-area suburbs. Whatcom is Democratic overall, but the portion within the 1st backed Republicans in 2012. Competitive Snohomish and Skagit both back Democrats, but less strongly than the liberal King County portions of the district. In the 2012 presidential race, Barack Obama took 54 percent of the vote here overall.

Major Industry
Software, internet technology, agriculture, manufacturing

Cities
Redmond, Kirkland, Mount Vernon

Notable
The Junior Softball World Series is played each summer in Kirkland.

Rep. Rick Larsen (D)

Capitol Office
225-2605
larsen.house.gov
2113 Rayburn Bldg. 20515-4702; fax 225-4420

Committees
Armed Services
Transportation & Infrastructure

Residence
Everett

Born
June 15, 1965; Arlington, Wash.

Religion
Methodist

Family
Wife, Tiia Karlen; two children

Education
Pacific Lutheran U., B.A. 1987 (political science); U. of Minnesota, M.P.A. 1990

Career
Dental association lobbyist; port economic development official

Political Highlights
Snohomish County Council, 1998-2000 (chairman, 1999)

ELECTION RESULTS

2012 GENERAL		
Rick Larsen (D)	184,826	61.1%
Dan Matthews (R)	117,465	38.9%
2012 PRIMARY (Open)		
Rick Larsen (D)	79,632	57.2%
2010 GENERAL		
Rick Larsen (D)	155,241	51.1%
John Koster (R)	148,722	48.9%

Previous Winning Percentages
2008 (62%); 2006 (64%); 2004 (64%); 2002 (50%); 2000 (50%)

Elected 2000; 7th term

Larsen calls himself the deputy mayor of the small cities and towns dotting Puget Sound, but the region's needs are a gateway to global affairs. He is a moderate Democrat with nuts-and-bolts involvement on aviation, defense, trade and China.

In the working environment of the Capitol, Larsen plays well with others. He describes his world view as communitarian: "I grew up believing that one's obligation to the community is equal to one's obligation to oneself." He pairs that philosophy with a self-effacing sense of humor — in the past, Larsen has finished well in a charity stand-up comedy competition for D.C. notables, cracking jokes about politics and his hairline.

In the 112th Congress (2011-12), he put his good will to use during the fact-finding tour conducted by the Armed Services Committee's Panel on Business Challenges Within the Defense Industry. Larsen, a member (and now vice chairman) of the business-friendly New Democrat Coalition, served as the ranking member to Pennsylvania Republican Bill Shuster. Several panel recommendations for improving the contracting process for small businesses were included in the fiscal 2013 defense policy law.

Larsen says that smaller businesses, such as the many tech companies and subcontractors along the Interstate 5 corridor in his district, offer some of the best opportunities for growth. He sees strategic benefits in using the "nimbleness" of small companies to make things "that a warfighter can use and needs to use more immediately" than the products of decadelong procurement deals. Export controls and Pentagon auditing standards could be adjusted for small companies, which sometimes lack the resources to comply.

But Larsen also cheers for the big guy. For several years, he fought for the Boeing Co.'s bid to build a new Air Force refueling tanker. A year after Boeing landed the contract in 2011, the company announced that it was stopping tanker work at its Kansas facilities and moving it to Washington. Boeing has major operations in Larsen's district. In the 113th Congress (2013-14), Larsen is serving as the ranking member of the Transportation and Infrastructure Aviation Subcommittee.

He voted in 2002 against authorizing the use of force in Iraq, and he has also called for accelerated removal of U.S. forces from Afghanistan. Larsen is a key figure in the inclusion of "global security contingency fund" provisions in defense policy bills. The language allows the Defense and State departments to pool financial resources when trying to help qualifying nations build their own security forces. He inherited the cause from former Armed Services Chairman Ike Skelton of Missouri.

Geography figures to keep Larsen in the loop as the country shifts military and diplomatic resources to the Pacific. "Some people call Asia the Far East," he said. "I call it my Near West."

Larsen co-founded the U.S.-China Working Group, and with Republican co-chairman Charles Boustany Jr. of Louisiana, he visited China in 2011 to meet with political and military leaders. China should not be feared as an adversary, he said, but understood as a growing nation with clear economic needs. Larsen has supported retaliatory tariffs on countries that may be using non-market systems to gain trade advantages. However, in 2012 Larsen predicted that "in the next five to seven years, you're going to see the leadership [of China] turn more inward" as economic inequality forces the Communist Party to build a social safety net and switch from an export-based economy to a consumption economy.

That would present an opportunity for U.S. businesses and the shipping interests in the Northwest. Larsen will break with his party on trade. He was one of 25 Democrats to vote in 2002 to give the president fast-track authority to negotiate trade agreements that Congress cannot amend. He supported free-trade pacts with Colombia, Panama and South Korea in 2011.

That year, President Barack Obama signed a bill allowing special credentials that expedite the travel of American businessmen who frequently visit certain Asian nations. Larsen had been stumping for such cards since the 111th Congress (2009-10).

On the Transportation and Infrastructure Committee, Larsen gets to be more overt in his "deputy mayor" duties. He frequently introduces bills to improve security on ferries (a common sight on Puget Sound), and he says federal funding for ferry programs should be formula-based rather than discretionary. He also got behind Shuster's 2011 bill to enhance pipeline safety, which became law. In his freshman term, Larsen helped enact a safety law after a 1999 pipeline accident in Bellingham killed three people.

In the 112th, he was the top Democrat on the Coast Guard and Maritime Transportation Subcommittee; he and Chairman Frank A. LoBiondo of New Jersey helped produce a Coast Guard reauthorization enacted in late 2012. (LoBiondo now chairs the Aviation panel.) He shines a spotlight on the need for more icebreaking vessels, as he says the failure to invest in ships now will give other countries an advantage in the scramble for the Arctic's resources.

Tourism is an economic draw in Larsen's district. In the 110th Congress (2007-08), he succeeded in designating 106,000 acres of land 60 miles northeast of Seattle as a protected wilderness area. He was pleased when Obama created a national monument in the San Juan Islands in 2013.

Larsen, whose lineage traces to Norway, was born and raised in Snohomish County. He is one of eight children of a utility company power-line worker. Both his parents were civically active, and his father was a city councilman.

After earning a master's in public affairs, he worked for the Port of Everett, helping businesses comply with clean-water requirements. He then became the director of public affairs for the Washington Dental Association. He waged a successful door-to-door campaign for the Snohomish County Council in 1997, then became its chairman in 1999.

Larsen ran to succeed retiring Republican Rep. Jack Metcalf in 2000, and he prevailed by 12,000 votes against GOP state Rep. John Koster. The district stayed competitive after redistricting following the 2000 census, but Larsen built up enough support over a decade to survive a close race in the very Republican year of 2010 — once again, he beat Koster.

His district shrank dramatically in size in the latest round of redistricting; it now hugs the coast. He easily defeated Republican Dan Matthews in 2012.

Key Votes

2012	
Extend a Social Security payroll tax cut and unemployment benefits	YES
Ease securities rules to expand small-business access to capital	YES
Extend for one year subsidized student loan interest rates financed by a cut in health care spending	NO
Cite Attorney General Eric H. Holder Jr. for contempt of Congress	NO
Create a visa program for foreign graduates in high-tech fields	NO
Extend most Bush-era income tax rates while allowing rates for top-bracket earners to rise (Jan. 1, 2013)	YES
2011	
Strike funding for F-35 alternative engine	NO
Prevent EPA from regulating greenhouse gas emissions to address climate change	NO
Extend certain provisions of Patriot Act for four years	NO
Declare opposition to use of ground troops in Libya	NO
Overhaul patent law	YES
Pass compromise debt limit increase plan and establish future spending limits	YES
Allow consideration of measures to implement three trade agreements	YES

CQ Vote Studies

	Party Unity		Presidential Support	
	Support	Oppose	Support	Oppose
2012	90%	10%	85%	15%
2011	90%	10%	91%	9%
2010	98%	2%	95%	5%
2009	98%	2%	97%	3%
2008	98%	2%	16%	84%

Interest Groups

	AFL-CIO	ADA	CCUS	ACU
2012	86%	75%	42%	4%
2011	90%	80%	44%	0%
2010	93%	90%	25%	0%
2009	100%	100%	43%	0%
2008	100%	90%	56%	0%

Washington 2

Northern Puget Sound — Everett, islands; Bellingham

Sliding north along Interstate 5 from the northern Seattle suburbs to Bellingham, and taking in some of the state's northwestern islands, the 2nd District is defined by aerospace engineering, maritime industries and Democratic voters. As a result of decennial redistricting, the 2nd lost its portion of the Cascade Range and the farmland west of it to the newly drawn and renumbered 1st District.

The densely populated corridor on Interstate 5 near Seattle hosts technology companies and white-collar residents. Everett is the most populous city in Snohomish County and is home to Boeing's largest aerospace facility. The Future of Flight Aviation Center and Boeing Tour in nearby Mukilteo draws tourists. Firms linked to Seattle's technology industries are located in the district, and many Snohomish residents here have jobs in the city.

Some of the district's blue-collar employment is based at the ports in Everett and Bellingham. The district's last remaining agricultural production comes from the islands in Puget Sound and in areas outside Mt. Vernon (in the 1st) west of Interstate 5 between the 2nd's population hubs. The district's two military bases — Naval Air Station Whidbey Island and Naval Station Everett — provide thousands of jobs to district residents.

White-majority overall, Snohomish provides the bulk of the district's minority population. Some areas, particularly around Bellingham and in San Juan County, provide more than 2-to-1 margins of victory for statewide and federal Democratic candidates. Also Democratic, slow-paced San Juan County — a collection of islands southwest of Bellingham that are closer to Vancouver, British Columbia, than Seattle — lures tourists and has attracted retirees — it has the highest median age in the state (52 years).

Major Industry
Aerospace, technology

Military Bases
Naval Air Station Whidbey Island, 6,900 military, 2,420 civilian; Naval Station Everett, 5,000 military, 1,000 civilian

Cities
Everett, Bellingham, Marysville

Notable
There are no stoplights on the San Juan Islands.

Rep. Jaime Herrera Beutler (R)

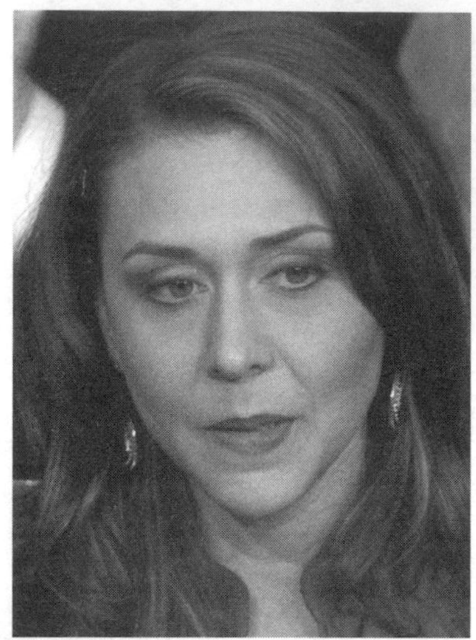

Capitol Office
225-3536
herrerabeutler.house.gov
1130 Longworth Bldg. 20515; fax 225-3478

Committees
Appropriations
Small Business

Residence
Camas

Born
Nov. 3, 1978; Glendale, Calif.

Religion
Christian

Family
Husband, Daniel Beutler

Education
Seattle Pacific U., attended 1996-98; Bellevue Community College, A.A. 2003; U. of Washington, B.A. 2004 (communications)

Career
Congressional aide

Political Highlights
Wash. House, 2007-11

ELECTION RESULTS

2012 GENERAL		
Jaime Herrera Beutler (R)	177,446	60.4%
Jon T. Haugen (D)	116,438	39.6%
2012 PRIMARY (Open)		
Jaime Herrera Beutler (R)	68,603	56.5%
2010 GENERAL		
Jaime Herrera Beutler (R)	152,799	53.0%
Denny Heck (D)	135,654	47.0%

Elected 2010; 2nd term

Herrera Beutler is young, female, Hispanic and fairly moderate — a virtual composite of demographic segments that GOP strategists would like to win over. She participates in that outreach effort while also paying meticulous attention to infrastructure development and business needs in her district.

Herrera Beutler (full name: JAY-me HER-air-ah BUT-ler) is the second-youngest woman in Congress — only Hawaii Democrat Tulsi Gabbard is younger — but she isn't without political experience. She interned in the George W. Bush White House, worked for fellow Washington Republican Cathy McMorris Rodgers in D.C. and served three years in the state House.

As a freshman, she took a number of centrist positions. On the most heated votes of the 112th Congress (2011-12) — those regarding spending and deficit reduction — Herrera Beutler supported the measures endorsed by House Republican leaders rather than join the conservatives who demanded larger cuts and tighter spending restrictions.

Party leaders awarded her a seat on the Appropriations Committee for the 113th Congress (2013-14). Herrera Beutler has also been recruited to help the party target Hispanic voters; she serves as a vice chairwoman for coalitions at the National Republican Congressional Committee for the 2014 election cycle. Plus, she has an in with the Republican leadership team — her former boss, McMorris Rodgers, is the GOP Conference chairwoman.

Herrera Beutler is positioned to continue work she started as a freshman. A former member of the Transportation and Infrastructure Committee, she now sits on the Transportation-HUD Appropriations Subcommittee.

Many Northwest politicians have called for construction of a $3.5 billion bridge across the Columbia River on Interstate 5, connecting Oregon and Washington. Despite criticism in the local media, Herrera Beutler declined to push for federal funding, insisting that Clark County residents needed to vote on the taxes and tolls that may be required to cover local funding.

A proposed sales tax hike to pay for a light-rail extension on the bridge was defeated in a November 2012 referendum. She continued to call for local input into the planning process in 2013, protesting that one bridge design under review might not allow for passage of ships used by local manufacturers.

Herrera Beutler similarly opposes the construction of a flood mitigation system along Interstate 5. She said in 2012 that plans for that project protected only federal property and not local homeowners or businesses.

Her seat on the Interior-Environment Appropriations Subcommittee gives her opportunities to weigh in on regulations and land use issues that affect forestry. In voting for a 2011 bill to nullify new EPA rules on industrial boiler emissions, she said biomass plants in her timber-rich district couldn't afford compliance upgrades without shedding hundreds of jobs.

Working with Oregon Democrat Kurt Schrader in the 112th, she tried to codify the classification of forest roads as a "non-point" pollution source under the Clean Water Act, as has been the case for several decades. A decision by the 9th U.S. Circuit Court of Appeals reclassified them, subjecting landowners to new permitting requirements and environmental reviews. The lawmakers added a one-year moratorium on the change to a bill enacted in late 2011. The Supreme Court overturned the 9th Circuit decision in March 2013.

Herrera Beutler also has a seat on the Small Business Committee. Southwest Washington has struggled with higher unemployment than most regions of the state, and she points to regulatory burdens on small businesses and financial institutions as a reason why. She frequently uses her question time in hearings to detail the challenges of businesses in her district.

She wants faster reviews of applications to the Small Business Lending Fund, which was created in 2010 to channel $30 billion to banks and open capital flows. She spoke up on behalf of banks in her district that had waited six months for a response.

The fiscal 2013 defense authorization law included a provision by Herrera Beutler and Schrader to expand the use of Small Business Administration advocates, who help small businesses compete for federal contracts. Involving those workers in the planning stages of acquisition programs, instead of bringing them in around the time bidding starts, would result in more opportunities for small businesses, they said.

Herrera Beutler wants an overall smaller federal government, but she has sought some nuance when voting on spending reductions. "The challenge is learning what is your preference and what is your conscience," she told The Seattle Times in 2011. "I would never vote against my conscience."

She was one of two Republicans to vote against a 2011 bill to end a federal program that provides emergency loans to unemployed homeowners facing foreclosure. She voted that year to strip funding for Planned Parenthood — as a social conservative, she opposes abortion — but she told the Times that she did so after determining that women in her district would still have some access to contraceptive counseling and related health services.

Herrera Beutler has credited her parents with fostering her conservatism. Her father, a printer, is Mexican-American (her great-grandparents were the immigrants), and her mother is white. She grew up with two siblings and three cousins in southwest Washington and was home-schooled through 9th grade. Her parents encouraged civic participation. Linda Smith, a Republican representative in the 1990s, told The Columbian newspaper that Herrera Beutler "door-belled for me."

She studied nursing for several years, then took a break from school. She eventually earned a degree in communications from the University of Washington in 2004. While working for McMorris Rodgers, she was appointed to the state House in 2007 and was elected in her own right the following year.

The 3rd District seat opened when six-term Democrat Brian Baird announced he was retiring. Herrera Beutler and Democrat Denny Heck, a communications entrepreneur, emerged from the "top two" primary. She won 53 percent of the vote in November despite Heck's fundraising advantage.

The redistricting process for 2012 removed Olympia from her district, which made it more favorable to Republican candidates. Herrera Beutler raised more than $1.6 million while her Democratic opponent raised less than $14,000, and she won by almost 21 points. At the same time, Heck was elected in the newly created 10th District.

Key Votes

2012	
Extend a Social Security payroll tax cut and unemployment benefits	YES
Ease securities rules to expand small-business access to capital	YES
Extend for one year subsidized student loan interest rates financed by a cut in health care spending	YES
Cite Attorney General Eric H. Holder Jr. for contempt of Congress	YES
Create a visa program for foreign graduates in high-tech fields	YES
Extend most Bush-era income tax rates while allowing rates for top-bracket earners to rise (Jan. 1, 2013)	YES
2011	
Strike funding for F-35 alternative engine	NO
Prevent EPA from regulating greenhouse gas emissions to address climate change	YES
Extend certain provisions of Patriot Act for four years	NO
Declare opposition to use of ground troops in Libya	YES
Overhaul patent law	YES
Pass compromise debt limit increase plan and establish future spending limits	YES
Allow consideration of measures to implement three trade agreements	YES

CQ Vote Studies

	PARTY UNITY		PRESIDENTIAL SUPPORT	
	SUPPORT	OPPOSE	SUPPORT	OPPOSE
2012	89%	11%	23%	77%
2011	91%	9%	25%	75%

Interest Groups

	AFL-CIO	ADA	CCUS	ACU
2012	29%	5%	100%	76%
2011	4%	15%	100%	66%

Washington 3

Southwest — Vancouver

Located in Washington's southwestern corner, the 3rd District runs along the Columbia River border with Oregon from the Pacific Ocean east through Skamania County and north into southern Thurston County. On both sides of Interstate 5 — which bisects the district from Vancouver toward Olympia — open rural territory hosts farms, forests and state parks.

The district's population center is Clark County (Vancouver), where nearly two-thirds of the 3rd's residents live. Tens of thousands of residents cross the Columbia River each day to jobs in Oregon. Population growth and economic expansion over the last two decades slowed during nationwide downturns and had a significant impact on Clark's homebuilding sector and housing market.

Economic struggles also affected the 3rd's extensive timber industry — the vast stretches of woodlands to the east in the Cascade Mountains and to the west in Wahkiakum and Pacific counties supply the lumber for homes and commercial construction. Paper mill giant Weyerhaeuser has several locations in the district. Fishing and oyster harvesting are prominent on Pacific County's coast, and Lewis County grows Christmas trees.

Unemployment is a concern in rural areas, and aging infrastructure — particularly the bridges into Oregon — is a key issue in the city of Vancouver near Portland, Ore. The 3rd lost state capital Olympia to the new 10th District during decennial redistricting, taking in GOP-friendly Klickitat County and leaving only one enclave of strongly liberal Democratic voters: Vancouver.

Although two-term GOP Rep. Jaime Herrera Beutler expanded her margin of victory in 2012 and won every county in the district, several counties backed Democrats for president, U.S. senator and governor. Overall, the 3rd supported Mitt Romney for president in the 2012 contest, although he only won by a 2-percentage-point margin

Major Industry
Timber, agriculture, manufacturing, fishing

Cities
Vancouver, Longview

Notable
Mount St. Helens erupted May 18, 1980, killing 57 people and destroying enough timber for 300,000 two-bedroom homes; The World Kite Museum and Hall of Fame is on the Long Beach peninsula and hosts an annual kite festival.

Rep. Doc Hastings (R)

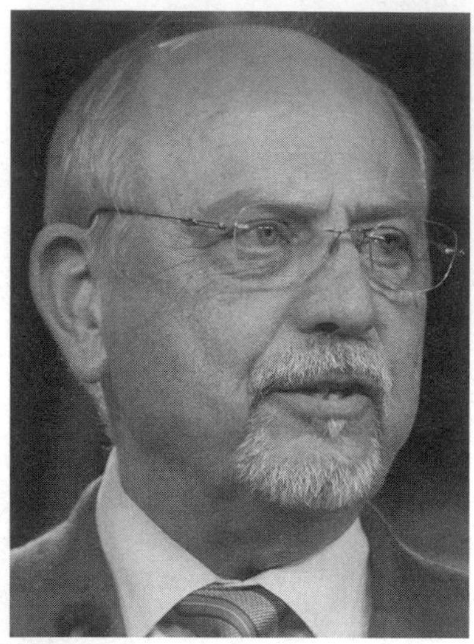

Capitol Office
225-5816
hastings.house.gov
1203 Longworth Bldg. 20515-4704; fax 225-3251

Committees
Natural Resources - Chairman
Oversight & Government Reform

Residence
Pasco

Born
Feb. 7, 1941; Spokane, Wash.

Religion
Protestant

Family
Wife, Claire Hastings; three children

Education
Columbia Basin College, attended 1959-61;
Central Washington U., attended 1964

Military
Army Reserve, 1964-69

Career
Paper supply business owner

Political Highlights
Wash. House, 1979-87; Republican nominee for U.S. House, 1992

ELECTION RESULTS

2012 GENERAL		
Doc Hastings (R)	154,749	66.2%
Mary Baechler (D)	78,940	33.8%
2012 PRIMARY (Open)		
Doc Hastings (R)	60,774	59.3%
Jamie Wheeler (R)	11,581	11.3%
2010 GENERAL		
Doc Hastings (R)	156,726	67.6%
Jay Clough (D)	74,973	32.4%

Previous Winning Percentages
2008 (63%); 2006 (60%); 2004 (63%); 2002 (67%); 2000 (61%); 1998 (69%); 1996 (53%); 1994 (53%)

Elected 1994; 10th term

Hastings is a trusted party man, although he hasn't achieved national fame for his service to House Republicans. As chairman of the Natural Resources Committee, he advances the GOP's "all of the above" energy agenda, and he is also reputed as an expert tactician in legislative battles.

Born Richard Norman Hastings, he has been known as "Doc" since childhood. Before coming to Congress, he ran his family's paper supply business in Pasco and was active in local GOP politics. He was elected to the state House in 1978 and served eight years, including stints as assistant majority leader and chairman of the GOP caucus.

Hastings is often described as having a subdued personality, but he worked his way into the good graces of congressional Republicans in the 1990s. He served several election cycles on the National Republican Congressional Committee, the campaign arm of the House GOP. In his second term, leaders put him on the Rules Committee, which sets the terms of floor debate.

He's remembered by some politics junkies as the lawmaker presiding over the House during the historic vote on President George W. Bush's Medicare prescription drug bill in November 2003 — Hastings held the vote open for an extraordinary three hours while the speaker and the GOP whip team worked the floor and the phones to furiously round up the final votes they needed to win passage.

In 2001, he accepted an appointment to the Ethics Committee, a labor-intensive panel that parses hundreds of reports from congressional offices, investigates allegations of misconduct and offers no opportunities to please constituents. Hastings stayed there for eight years. When Joel Hefley of Colorado was term-limited out of the chairmanship in 2005, Hastings was chosen by leaders as the panel's new chairman. Many observers called the transition a "purge" by party leaders upset over investigations of Majority Leader Tom DeLay of Texas — several staffers and two other GOP lawmakers were also removed from the committee. But Hefley in 2012 described Hastings as "a level-headed guy and thoughtful. Not bombastic."

All of his legwork for the party positioned Hastings to return to the Natural Resources Committee in the 111th Congress (2009-10) as the ranking member — although he hadn't served on the panel since 1996. He became the chairman in the 112th Congress (2011-12) as Republicans retook the majority. It was his first front-line legislative assignment in years. Under party rules, he can hold the gavel through the end of the 113th Congress (2013-14).

Hastings unsuccessfully tried to expand his panel's power for the 112th by urging party leaders to give it primary jurisdiction over energy issues. But even after that defeat, he willingly executed the GOP's energy agenda. Hastings used the panel to advance measures to expand oil and gas production, clamp down on regulations that he described as harmful to the coal industry, and increase economic activity on federal land. Just about all of those efforts hit a wall in the Democratic Senate.

He kept pushing. In September 2012, many coal-related bills backed by Republicans were repackaged into a new measure and passed by the House just before lawmakers headed back to their districts for their last flurry of campaigning. "The Obama administration has waged a war on coal — coal jobs and the small businesses in the mining supply chain and the low-cost energy that millions of Americans rely on," he said on the House floor.

Hastings supports the expansion of offshore drilling and introduced legislation to open additional areas in California, South Carolina, the mid-Atlantic and Alaska for oil and gas development. He also prepared a bill containing the

Obama administration's proposed offshore leasing plan, then steered both measures to a vote to get lawmakers' preferences on record. Massachusetts Democrat Edward J. Markey accused Hastings of trying to "embarrass" President Barack Obama. The first bill passed; the second was defeated.

His district's needs motivate some of Hastings' work on Natural Resources. Agriculture and timber are major industries in central Washington, and he has tried to limit funding for the enforcement of the Endangered Species Act. He has called for a major overhaul of that law, which he says is ineffective at helping species recover while still tying up economic activity. "Congress can no longer kick the can down the road while millions of dollars are wasted on frivolous lawsuits, resources are diverted away from true species recovery, and jobs are lost due to regulatory red tape that does little, if anything, to protect species," Hastings wrote in a 2012 Washington Times opinion piece.

As founder and chairman of the House Nuclear Cleanup Caucus, he seeks to expedite environmental restoration of radioactive-waste sites. His district is home to the Hanford Nuclear Reservation, once a major employer as the leading producer of nuclear material for weapons. It now stands idle as the nation's most toxic relic of the Cold War, and Hastings has secured hundreds of millions of dollars over the years to clean it up. Hanford's B Reactor was designated a National Historic Landmark in 2008. In the fall of 2012, Hastings introduced legislation to establish historical national parks at the Manhattan Project sites in Oak Ridge, Tenn.; Los Alamos, N.M.; and Hanford. The measure was defeated on the House floor when those opposing the bill said the United States shouldn't celebrate the deaths of innocent civilians.

He was not pleased, however, when Obama used a 1906 law to designate five new national monuments, including one in Washington state. Several designated areas include private land, and Hastings said the White House was trying to "spend money it doesn't have on property it doesn't even own."

Hastings was out of state government for several years when GOP Rep. Sid Morrison eschewed re-election to run (unsuccessfully, as it turned out) for governor in 1992. Hastings had the support of religious activists and was considered the most conservative of the four Republicans in the open primary. He finished first with 24 percent of the vote. Democrat Jay Inslee was second, but in the general election Inslee scored a narrow victory.

Republicans had a great year in 1994, and Hastings came back for a rematch. He cast the campaign as a referendum on Inslee's support for President Bill Clinton, took more than 53 percent of the vote in November and has won handily since then. Hastings was mentioned as a possible Rules chairman for the 113th Congress, but that job went to Pete Sessions of Texas, who had finished his run as the chairman of the NRCC.

Key Votes

2012	
Extend a Social Security payroll tax cut and unemployment benefits	YES
Ease securities rules to expand small-business access to capital	YES
Extend for one year subsidized student loan interest rates financed by a cut in health care spending	YES
Cite Attorney General Eric H. Holder Jr. for contempt of Congress	YES
Create a visa program for foreign graduates in high-tech fields	NO
Extend most Bush-era income tax rates while allowing rates for top-bracket earners to rise (Jan. 1, 2013)	YES
2011	
Strike funding for F-35 alternative engine	NO
Prevent EPA from regulating greenhouse gas emissions to address climate change	YES
Extend certain provisions of Patriot Act for four years	?
Declare opposition to use of ground troops in Libya	YES
Overhaul patent law	YES
Pass compromise debt limit increase plan and establish future spending limits	YES
Allow consideration of measures to implement three trade agreements	YES

CQ Vote Studies

	PARTY UNITY		PRESIDENTIAL SUPPORT	
	SUPPORT	OPPOSE	SUPPORT	OPPOSE
2012	90%	10%	20%	80%
2011	96%	4%	25%	75%
2010	98%	2%	27%	73%
2009	89%	11%	19%	81%
2008	98%	2%	70%	30%

Interest Groups

	AFL-CIO	ADA	CCUS	ACU
2012	10%	5%	92%	84%
2011	0%	5%	100%	77%
2010	0%	0%	88%	100%
2009	5%	0%	80%	96%
2008	13%	15%	88%	96%

Washington 4

Central — Yakima and 'tri-cities'

Mainly east of the Cascade Range in central Washington, the 4th — the state's geographically largest — includes some of the region's most fertile land, a piece of the Canada border, and stretches of the Columbia River (shared with the 3rd and forming part of its border with the 8th).

The southwestern leg of the district is the Yakima Valley, known as the fruit bowl of the Northwest. Heavily irrigated agriculture drives its economy, with apple and pear orchards and fields of hops. The valley accounts for 75 percent of the total U.S. hops acreage and hosts the Hop Growers of America. The Yakima Valley also has productive vineyards, and other wine grape and potato farms are hydrated by the Columbia Basin Project — the Grand Coulee Dam is the nation's largest hydropower producer. Okanogan County, which borders Canada, is known for ranches and orchards.

The tri-cities population hub in the district's south includes Kennewick, Pasco and Richland along the first northward bend in the Columbia River. The Pacific Northwest National Laboratory is located in Richland, and the research facility is the leading employer in the county. The Energy Department also operates the Hanford Nuclear Energy site, the nation's most contaminated nuclear site and a target for accelerated cleanup efforts, in Richland. Part of the military's 327,000-acre Yakima Training Center is here; it is shared with the 8th.

The Yakima Valley takes in the Yakama Indian Reservation, and the Colville Indian Reservation occupies parts of Okanogan and Ferry counties (in the 5th). Many agrarian areas have attracted Hispanic-majority populations — the 4th has the largest proportion of Hispanic residents of any district statewide, and every county here has a sizable Latino population.

Predominately conservative, the 4th backs Republicans at all levels. Most counties in the district provide at least 2-to-1 margins for the GOP in federal and statewide races, although Yakima gave incumbent Democrat Maria Cantwell a slim victory during her 2012 U.S. Senate re-election bid.

Major Industry
Agriculture, energy

Cities
Yakima, Kennewick, Pasco, Richland

Notable
There is enough concrete in the Grand Coulee Dam to build a highway from Seattle to Miami.

Rep. Cathy McMorris Rodgers (R)

Capitol Office
225-2006
mcmorrisrodgers.house.gov
203 Cannon Bldg. 20515-4705; fax 225-3392

Committees
Energy & Commerce

Residence
Spokane

Born
May 22, 1969; Salem, Ore.

Religion
Christian non-denominational

Family
Husband, Brian Rodgers; two children

Education
Pensacola Christian College, B.A. 1990 (pre-law); U. of Washington, M.B.A. 2002

Career
Fruit orchard worker; state legislative aide

Political Highlights
Wash. House, 1994-2004 (minority leader, 2002-03)

ELECTION RESULTS

2012 GENERAL		
Cathy McMorris Rodgers (R)	191,066	61.9%
Rich Cowan (D)	117,512	38.1%
2012 PRIMARY (Open)		
Cathy McMorris Rodgers (R)	83,186	55.8%
Randall Yearout (R)	11,894	8.0%
2010 GENERAL		
Cathy McMorris Rodgers (R)	177,235	63.7%
Daryl Romeyn (D)	101,146	36.3%

Previous Winning Percentages
2008 (65%); 2006 (56%); 2004 (60%)

Elected 2004; 5th term

McMorris Rodgers is the highest-ranking Republican woman in Congress. In relatively short order, she has become a valued member of the GOP House leadership team and a spokeswoman for her party. Given her youth and her ability to appeal to a broad segment of the electorate, many people have great expectations for the next stages of her political career.

She jumped from political aide to politician at the age of 24, with her appointment to the state House. Over the course of a decade, she rose to the post of minority leader. The U.S. House has been no less kind. In 2008, at the end of her fourth year, she was elected GOP Conference vice chairwoman, with the backing of Minority Leader John A. Boehner.

After four more years, she was elected Conference chairwoman, this time with the blessing of Speaker Boehner. She defeated Tom Price of Georgia, a more conservative lawmaker, to become the No. 4 House Republican — and a key figure as the party tries to reach out to demographics that shunned the GOP message in the 2012 elections.

In the opening months of the 113th Congress (2013-14), McMorris Rodgers revamped and expanded the Conference's communications team, with new hires meant to target Hispanics, women and younger voters. Her team has emphasized rapid responses to media requests, and she has tried to provide more coaching services to lawmakers making media appearances.

McMorris Rodgers herself has appeal as a media messenger — she presents a family-friendly image that contrasts with negative stereotypes about Republicans. She was highly visible in 2012 as the fight for female voters spilled into congressional debates and the race for the White House. The parties clashed over pay equity, insurance coverage of contraception and a reauthorization of programs to combat domestic violence. Some Democrats described a GOP "war on women," a characterization McMorris Rodgers disputed.

"It is a myth," she said on MSNBC in May 2012. "They're creating distractions. They're trying to divide America and really trying to distract women from the real issues that face this country right now. Women are concerned about the economy. They're concerned about the debt."

As a leader, McMorris Rodgers has to balance the demands of centrists and the GOP's right wing — she belongs to both the conservative Republican Study Committee and the moderate Main Street Partnership. She has spoken in favor of fiscal restraint. "We need to simplify the tax code, stop burdensome government regulation, reduce government spending and balance the budget," she told The Spokesman-Review of Spokane when asked her top priority for 2013. "That will give families, small-business owners and farmers the confidence they need to invest, innovate and expand."

But in January 2013, she sided with Boehner to vote for the "fiscal cliff" deal, which allowed tax rates to increase on earnings over $400,000 while preserving lower rates under that threshold. Most Republicans voted against it.

McMorris Rodgers joined the Energy and Commerce Committee in 2011. She is a leading supporter of hydropower — which is plentiful in her district and overlooked elsewhere, she says. She launched the Congressional Hydropower Caucus in 2008 to advocate its expansion to boost domestic energy supplies. Her bill to streamline the permitting for smaller hydropower projects, written in collaboration with Colorado Democrat Diana DeGette, passed the House easily in 2012. The Senate didn't act, so they reintroduced it in 2013; it was quickly passed, 422-0.

She sits on the Health Subcommittee, where some of her advocacy has a deeply personal origin. As the mother of a child with Down syndrome, she helped launched the Congressional Down Syndrome Caucus to promote research and raise educational expectations and outcomes for children with the syndrome, and to help provide family and community support. "I feel like in many ways, I've had my eyes opened," she said of her son, Cole. "He's given me a whole new purpose for being in Congress."

In the 110th Congress (2007-08), she co-chaired the Congressional Caucus for Women's Issues. She supported a 2008 law that bans discrimination by insurers or employers based on the results of genetic testing. She is also a leader of the Congressional Neuroscience Caucus.

Locally, she looks out for Fairchild Air Force Base, home to much of the Air Force's West Coast tanker fleet. She co-chairs the Congressional Military Families Caucus, which she helped found to address the needs of military spouses and children — her husband is a retired Navy officer. Throughout her career, she has promoted policies to encourage family-friendly workplaces. She is the first congresswoman to give birth to two children while in office.

McMorris Rodgers is a descendant of pioneers who traveled the Oregon Trail to the Pacific Northwest in the 1850s. Born in Salem, she lived in British Columbia as a small child. Her family moved to Kettle Falls on the Columbia River, 30 miles south of the Canadian border, as she and her brother were preparing to enter high school. Her father bought an orchard and opened a fruit stand, where she pruned, thinned, picked and sold produce.

Her father also chaired the Stevens County Republican Party and was the president of the local Chamber of Commerce. She was the first in her family to attend college. She worked her way through school in several jobs, including stints at McDonald's and as a housekeeper.

When she graduated, family friend Bob Morton asked her to manage his campaign for the state House. He won, and she became a legislative assistant in his office. When Morton was appointed to the state Senate in 1993, she was appointed to replace him in the state House. She won the seat in her own right the next year and was elected minority leader in 2002.

Two years later, while Republican George Nethercutt was unsuccessfully attempting to unseat Democratic Sen. Patty Murray, McMorris Rodgers won a three-way primary in the quest for his House seat. She then trounced the Democratic candidate, Spokane businessman Don Barbieri, by 19 points.

In 2005, while she was home over the August recess, a campaign volunteer brought her brother to the congresswoman's "pink flamingo" fundraiser. The two talked only briefly, but Brian Rodgers followed up with a letter. They married a year later, in the midst of her first re-election campaign. She won that race with 56 percent of the vote, even in a climate that had turned hostile to the GOP. She hasn't dipped below 60 percent of the vote since then.

Key Votes

2012	
Extend a Social Security payroll tax cut and unemployment benefits	YES
Ease securities rules to expand small-business access to capital	YES
Extend for one year subsidized student loan interest rates financed by a cut in health care spending	YES
Cite Attorney General Eric H. Holder Jr. for contempt of Congress	YES
Create a visa program for foreign graduates in high-tech fields	YES
Extend most Bush-era income tax rates while allowing rates for top-bracket earners to rise (Jan. 1, 2013)	YES
2011	
Strike funding for F-35 alternative engine	NO
Prevent EPA from regulating greenhouse gas emissions to address climate change	YES
Extend certain provisions of Patriot Act for four years	YES
Declare opposition to use of ground troops in Libya	YES
Overhaul patent law	YES
Pass compromise debt limit increase plan and establish future spending limits	YES
Allow consideration of measures to implement three trade agreements	YES

CQ Vote Studies

	Party Unity		Presidential Support	
	Support	Oppose	Support	Oppose
2012	97%	3%	18%	82%
2011	97%	3%	21%	79%
2010	97%	3%	28%	72%
2009	95%	5%	23%	77%
2008	95%	5%	64%	36%

Interest Groups

	AFL-CIO	ADA	CCUS	ACU
2012	19%	0%	100%	84%
2011	0%	5%	100%	80%
2010	0%	0%	100%	96%
2009	5%	0%	80%	96%
2008	20%	20%	89%	92%

Washington 5

East — Spokane

With beautiful forests and lush fields, the 5th is anchored by the greater Spokane region, which accounts for more than two-thirds of the district's population and is an economic hub for the Inland Northwest. Stretching from Canada to Oregon and along the state's entire border with Idaho, most of the district is remote, dotted with rural communities.

The largest city between Seattle and Minneapolis, Spokane also serves as a nexus for retail, trade and telecommunications companies. Fairchild Air Force Base, 10 miles west of downtown, is one of the area's key employers. Land use plans around the base are a concern for local officials, who have to balance the continued growth of the Spokane region with protecting the airspace and access to the base.

North of Spokane, among national and state forests, no city surpasses the 5,000-resident mark. Declining logging and mining sectors have stalled economic growth in many areas. The southern 5th's fertile soil produces some of the world's most sought-after wheat, wine grapes and the Walla Walla sweet onion. At the foot of the Blue Mountains near Oregon, Walla Walla hosts a thriving dining and arts community and two colleges. Higher education plays a role elsewhere in the district, as well: Gonzaga University in Spokane, Eastern Washington University in Cheney and Washington State University in Pullman.

Outside of Spokane and Walla Walla, the district is sparsely populated and not racially diverse; rural counties struggle with high poverty rates. The 5th is a Republican stronghold — Democratic Sen. Maria Cantwell lost all the counties here during her successful re-election in 2012, despite winning 60 percent of the state's vote; Mitt Romney easily won the 5th in the 2012 presidential race while losing the state by 15 percentage points.

Major Industry
Agriculture and wine production, health care, higher education, military

Military Bases
Fairchild Air Force Base, 2,844 military, 77 civilian

Cities
Spokane, Spokane Valley, Walla Walla, Pullman

Notable
The Fort Walla Walla Museum's "Living History" performances celebrate the city's heritage and the lives of 19th-century residents.

Rep. Derek Kilmer (D)

Capitol Office
225-5916
kilmer.house.gov
1429 Longworth Bldg. 20515-6601; fax 226-3575

Committees
Armed Services
Science, Space & Technology

Residence
Gig Harbor

Born
Jan. 1, 1974; Port Angeles, Wash.

Religion
Methodist

Family
Wife, Jennifer Kilmer; two children

Education
Princeton U., A.B. 1996 (public and international affairs); Oxford U., D.Phil. 2003 (Marshall scholar)

Career
County economic development executive; management consultant

Political Highlights
Wash. House, 2005-07; Wash. Senate, 2007-12

ELECTION RESULTS

2012 GENERAL		
Derek Kilmer (D)	186,661	59.0%
Bill Driscoll (R)	129,725	41.0%
2012 PRIMARY (Open)		
Derek Kilmer (D)	86,436	53.4%

Elected 2012; 1st term

Kilmer has big shoes to fill as the successor to Norm Dicks, an 18-term Democrat who was the party's top appropriator. Although 33 years younger than Dicks, he has a fairly impressive record as a politician and policy expert.

Kilmer, the son of two teachers, grew up on the Olympic Peninsula. He crossed the country to attend college at Princeton, then crossed the Atlantic to get a doctorate at Oxford as part of the prestigious Marshall Scholarship program. (His wife, the current director of the Washington State Historical Society, was also in the program.) He studied social policy with a focus on economic development.

When he returned home, he worked as a management consultant for a few years, then took a job with the Economic Development Board for Tacoma-Pierce County, trying to spur job creation in an area that once relied on the timber industry. He was part of several local business groups, and he is now a member of the New Democrat Coalition.

Kilmer won a seat in the state House in 2004, and two years later he moved to the state Senate. He was known as a budget expert, and he helped enact a $1 billion stimulus law in 2012 that used debt financing to speed up public works projects that had already been approved.

He sits on the Armed Services Committee and its seapower panel — the Puget Sound shipyard is in his district. He also sits on the Science, Space and Technology Committee. He has shown particular interest in the development of a workforce that can tackle cybersecurity demands. He is pursuing federal recognition of worker-owned, employer-matched savings plans — similar to a 401(k) — that are geared toward worker education and training.

When Kilmer entered the 2012 race to succeed Dicks, who was retiring, other Democrats cleared out. Of the seven people in the "open" primary, he was the only one from his party. He took more than half the vote to easily win the primary, then won the seat by 18 points.

Washington 6

West — Bremerton, Tacoma, Olympic Peninsula

Olympic National Park and Olympic National Forest constitute roughly one-third of the 6th's land and make the Olympic Mountains region a popular destination for hikers and backpackers. Surrounding the mountains, communities are striving to move beyond traditional — and often diminishing — timber, paper mill and fishing industries.

To the southwest, the Port of Grays Harbor is a shipping center, and Port Angeles and Port Townsend along the Olympic Peninsula's northern shores rely on the ferries, airports and bridges that deliver tourists and connect residents to the central Puget Sound area. More than two-thirds of the 6th's residents live in Kitsap and Pierce counties in the south Puget Sound region, including downtown Tacoma and the city's suburbs.

Revitalization efforts downtown have not been able to stem a decade of population loss from Tacoma. The 6th hosts the University of Washington at Tacoma and the University of Puget Sound; the more diverse South Tacoma neighborhood; and manufacturing and shipping jobs in the onetime hub of railroad activity.

A military posture on the west side of Puget Sound — there are several naval facilities on the Kitsap Peninsula and Bainbridge Island — stabilizes the district's economy. The 6th also has a significant Coast Guard presence. Bainbridge Island is an outlying destination for Seattle-based tourists who can take a 35-minute ferry from the city.

In the 2012 presidential race, Barack Obama won the parts of every county wholly or partially in the Democratic-leaning district — his slim margins in Clallam and Mason counties were more than offset by solid support in populous King and Pierce.

Major Industry
Shipping, military, timber, health care, tourism

Military Bases
Naval Base Kitsap, 13,000 military, 13,000 civilian (2011); Puget Sound Naval Shipyard and Intermediate Maintenance Facility, 10,600 civilian, 680 military; Naval Underwater Warfare Center Keyport, 28 military, 1,500 civilian

Cities
Tacoma (pt.), Bremerton, Bainbridge Island

Notable
Poulsbo is home to the annual Scandinavian celebration Viking Fest.

Rep. Jim McDermott (D)

Capitol Office
225-3106
mcdermott.house.gov
1035 Longworth Bldg. 20515-4707; fax 225-6197

Committees
Budget
Ways & Means

Residence
Seattle

Born
Dec. 28, 1936, Chicago, Ill.

Religion
Episcopalian

Family
Divorced; two children

Education
Wheaton College (Ill.), B.S. 1958; U. of Illinois, M.D. 1963

Military
Navy Medical Service Corps, 1968-70

Career
Psychiatrist; Foreign Service officer

Political Highlights
Wash. House, 1971-73; sought Democratic nomination for governor, 1972; Wash. Senate, 1975-87; Democratic nominee for governor, 1980; sought Democratic nomination for governor, 1984

ELECTION RESULTS

2012 GENERAL		
Jim McDermott (D)	298,368	79.6%
Ron Bemis (R)	76,212	20.3%
2012 PRIMARY (Open)		
Jim McDermott (D)	124,692	70.9%
Andrew Hughes (D)	10,340	5.9%
Charles Allen (D)	4,367	2.5%
Donovan Rivers (D)	2,688	1.5%
2010 GENERAL		
Jim McDermott (D)	232,649	83.0%
Bob Jeffers-Schroder (I)	47,741	17.0%

Previous Winning Percentages
2008 (84%); 2006 (79%); 2004 (81%); 2002 (74%); 2000 (73%); 1998 (88%); 1996 (81%); 1994 (75%); 1992 (78%); 1990 (72%); 1988 (76%)

Elected 1988; 13th term

The fiery McDermott has big ambitions for expanding the role of the public sector, but with Republicans in control of the House, he has focused just as much on protecting past Democratic gains.

The most prevalent theme of his work is making government more responsive to the needs of the poor. In January 2013, he was one of just 16 House Democrats to vote against the "fiscal cliff" deal, which raised income tax rates on earnings above $400,000—while locking in lower rates on earnings below that threshold. The deal "does not generate the revenue necessary to invest in people and help the poor," he said.

He serves on the Ways and Means Committee, and for the 113th Congress (2013-14) he is the top Democrat on the Health Subcommittee, alongside Chairman Kevin Brady of Texas—they worked together in the 112th Congress (2011-12) as the leaders of the Trade Subcommittee. The chairman is "more conservative than I am, but he's not unreasonable," McDermott said. "Do I want to control costs? Yes. Does Kevin Brady want to control costs? Yes."

He says changes to the Medicare physician reimbursement system could offer the best current opportunity for doing so: "If you want to deal with the question of cost, then you have to start saying you have to pay for value, not volume."

McDermott, a former psychiatrist, has dreamed of government-run health care in the United States—he has introduced a bill that would require every state to set up its own "single payer" system. But he has no qualms about supporting the 2010 health care overhaul law written by Democrats. He scoffs at efforts to repeal the law and vows that in 2013, "we'll implement the last of the major pieces of safety net social insurance in this country."

By his standards, that's a fairly mild vow. McDermott's public statements are often dripping with derision for Republican policy plans and the logic behind them. He says it's not that big of a deal, and that media posturing is less important than behind-the-scenes relationships built in quiet discussions. "I talk to everybody," he said. "I learned a long time ago that what we say on the floor doesn't mean anything."

McDermott was able to work with Republicans on some trade issues—he has called his home of Seattle the most trade-dependent city in America. He found a few GOP allies to support his position that China is providing illegal subsidies to its state-owned companies. After a court threw out one of the tariffs the United States has traditionally imposed on Chinese goods, he helped push legislation through the House in 2012 that made it clear Congress approved of the trade penalties.

Most liberals have opposed free-trade agreements in recent years, but McDermott voted for pacts with South Korea and Panama in 2011.

When Democrats controlled the House from 2007 through 2010, McDermott was the chairman of the Subcommittee on Income Security and Family Support. He shepherded several bills and amendments aimed at helping people down on their luck. That included a major overhaul of the country's child welfare system, aimed at encouraging adoption of foster children and preparing them for life after leaving foster homes. It was enacted in 2008.

After the financial crisis struck that year, he pushed hard to expand the length of time that unemployed workers can receive insurance payments from the government. The 2009 economic stimulus law included a $5 billion emergency fund championed by McDermott to help states train jobless residents.

Whatever his legislative output, McDermott will forever be associated with some of the partisan attacks he has leveled against Republicans. In the most notorious incident, he was ordered in 2008 to pay John A. Boehner of Ohio — who is now speaker of the House — nearly $1.1 million. McDermott had received a recording of an intercepted 1996 cell phone call between Boehner and then-Speaker Newt Gingrich of Georgia, and he released it to the media. In May 2007, a federal appeals court determined that he violated House rules by leaking the call. He maintains it was worth the fight, and the settlement, to protect free speech.

McDermott says that he will call Republicans out whenever he thinks they go too far on the issues he cares most about, such as free speech, human rights and poverty: "Bullies will make you back up your whole life. I don't back up."

McDermott protested U.S. involvement in Vietnam in the 1960s, and he voted against the 2002 resolution authorizing the use of military force in Iraq. He was featured as a critic of the war in Michael Moore's 2004 documentary "Fahrenheit 9/11," and he opposed the "surge" of more troops to Afghanistan early in the Obama administration. He joined 55 lawmakers in sending a letter to President Barack Obama in September 2009, warning of a "military quagmire" in a time of economic turmoil.

Still, he refused to join Republicans in June 2011 when they pushed through the House a resolution criticizing Obama's use of air power to aid Libyan rebel forces seeking to overthrow Muammar el-Qaddafi. McDermott endorsed Obama's approach, saying that "the violence in Libya is unconscionable" and that the "international community must unite in opposition."

Born and raised in Illinois, McDermott came from a poor, conservative and deeply religious family. His father, a bond underwriter, and his mother, a telephone operator and homemaker, started a church in the garage of their two-bedroom home. His three siblings slept in one bedroom; his parents in the other. McDermott, the oldest child, had the couch.

He attended the conservative evangelical Wheaton College. His bend toward liberalism began during medical school at the University of Illinois, when he voted for John F. Kennedy in the 1960 presidential election.

McDermott's residency training took him to Seattle. After a two-year stint in the Navy Medical Service Corps, he launched a career in Seattle. He won a seat in the state House in 1970 running on an anti-war platform. Two years later, he ran for governor and lost, but he won a seat in the state Senate in 1974. He made two more failed gubernatorial bids, in 1980 and 1984.

McDermott left office in 1987 and went to Africa as a Foreign Service medical officer. Less than a year later, Democratic Rep. Mike Lowry announced his plans to run for the Senate, and McDermott announced — from Kinshasa, Zaire — his intention to run for Lowry's seat. He won the 1988 primary with 38 percent of the vote and easily won the general election.

Key Votes

2012	
Extend a Social Security payroll tax cut and unemployment benefits	NO
Ease securities rules to expand small-business access to capital	NO
Extend for one year subsidized student loan interest rates financed by a cut in health care spending	NO
Cite Attorney General Eric H. Holder Jr. for contempt of Congress	NO
Create a visa program for foreign graduates in high-tech fields	NO
Extend most Bush-era income tax rates while allowing rates for top-bracket earners to rise (Jan. 1, 2013)	NO
2011	
Strike funding for F-35 alternative engine	YES
Prevent EPA from regulating greenhouse gas emissions to address climate change	NO
Extend certain provisions of Patriot Act for four years	NO
Declare opposition to use of ground troops in Libya	NO
Overhaul patent law	YES
Pass compromise debt limit increase plan and establish future spending limits	NO
Allow consideration of measures to implement three trade agreements	YES

CQ Vote Studies

	PARTY UNITY		PRESIDENTIAL SUPPORT	
	SUPPORT	OPPOSE	SUPPORT	OPPOSE
2012	99%	1%	84%	16%
2011	97%	3%	89%	11%
2010	99%	1%	88%	12%
2009	99%	1%	93%	7%
2008	98%	2%	17%	83%

Interest Groups

	AFL-CIO	ADA	CCUS	ACU
2012	100%	95%	25%	0%
2011	93%	90%	25%	4%
2010	100%	100%	13%	0%
2009	100%	95%	36%	4%
2008	100%	95%	50%	8%

Washington 7

Most of Seattle and inner suburbs

The most populous city in the Pacific Northwest, Seattle is nicknamed the "Emerald City," and it remains the gem of the Evergreen State. The city anchors the 7th, which is diverse, liberal and well-educated. From the top of the iconic Space Needle on a clear day, tourists can see the Seattle skyline and the Cascade and Olympic Mountain ranges.

Seattle's high-tech sector includes leaders such as Amazon.com, as well as biotechnology and software companies. Amazon's headquarters in the South Lake Union neighborhood are just east of the new campus of the Bill and Melinda Gates Foundation. The University of Washington is east of Interstate 5 along the Portage and Union bays, and several other Seattle-based colleges are here. The district's maritime industry — centered on the bustling Port of Seattle — remains a key employer. Other downtown destinations include Safeco Field, home of baseball's Mariners, and CenturyLink Field, home of football's Seahawks and soccer's Sounders. The famous Pike Place Market and other fish markets lure shoppers and tourists.

Vashon Island, once a remote agricultural haven, now is filled with commuters who ride the ferry into Seattle for work, although local farms still produce strawberries. North of Seattle, the 7th takes in some of Snohomish County, including Edmonds, where a recent redevelopment of downtown encouraged foot traffic to retail and dining locations.

Transportation is a perennial issue in Seattle. Multi-use development plans for downtown and light-rail expansion have targeted alleviating the notorious traffic congestion, and ferry service transports residents and visitors across Puget Sound.

Asians make up 10 percent of the district's population, and Hispanics another 7 percent — only the other Seattle-based district (the 9th) has more Asian residents. The politics here are solidly liberal, and Democrats regularly dominate the district in all races — Barack Obama won 79 percent of the district's 2012 presidential vote, his highest percentage statewide.

Major Industry
Internet technology, software, trade, health care, tourism

Cities
Seattle (pt.), Shoreline, Edmonds

Notable
The Fraternal Order of Eagles was founded in 1898 at a Seattle shipyard.

Rep. Dave Reichert (R)

Capitol Office
225-7761
reichert.house.gov
1127 Longworth Bldg. 20515-4708; fax 225-4282

Committees
Ways & Means
(Human Resources - Chairman)

Residence
Auburn

Born
Aug. 29, 1950; Detroit Lakes, Minn.

Religion
Lutheran - Missouri Synod

Family
Wife, Julie Reichert; three children

Education
Concordia College (Ore.), A.A. 1970

Military
Air Force Reserve, 1971-76

Career
Police officer; grocery warehouse worker

Political Highlights
King County sheriff, 1997-2005

ELECTION RESULTS

2012 GENERAL		
Dave Reichert (R)	180,204	59.6%
Karen Porterfield (D)	121,886	40.3%
2012 PRIMARY (Open)		
Dave Reichert (R)	66,220	50.6%
Keith Swank (R)	10,942	8.4%
Ernest Huber (R)	4,165	3.2%
2010 GENERAL		
Dave Reichert (R)	161,296	52.0%
Suzan DelBene (D)	148,581	48.0%

Previous Winning Percentages
2008 (53%); 2006 (51%); 2004 (52%)

Elected 2004; 5th term

Reichert helped capture a serial killer, and for a period during high school he lived out of his car. In relative terms, the political challenges he faces are small potatoes, and he approaches them confidently. He blends fiscal conservatism with moderate views on social policy and the environment.

The oldest of seven children of an abusive father, Reichert (RIKE-ert) grew up in a two-bedroom duplex in a rough neighborhood. The boys slept in the garage. "There were times I attended high school out of my car in order to escape difficult family circumstances," he wrote in 2013. But he also took on the role of protector to his siblings.

It stuck, and he began thinking about a career in police work. A tuition waiver at a two-year college in Oregon got him on track; serving as the quarterback on the football team brought out his leadership skills, he said.

Reichert started as a patrol officer in King County in 1972; he later became an undercover agent and made sergeant in 1990. Seven years later, he was elected sheriff — four years before the 2001 capture of Gary Ridgway, the Green River Killer. Ridgway confessed to killing at least 49 women in the early 1980s in the Seattle area.

Reichert had supervised the case earlier in his career, and the story made him a media star. But he decided to see the case to its conclusion rather than run for governor. He waited for another opportunity to run for office and jumped in when Republican Rep. Jennifer Dunn decided to retire in 2004. The national party campaign committees spent more on that contest than on any other House race that year, and Reichert prevailed by 5 points over well-known radio commentator Dave Ross.

His district was not safe GOP territory, however, and he was targeted by Democrats in the next three elections. He held on by building partnerships with Democrats and Republicans alike (and by facing a few inexperienced opponents). He says law enforcement developed his approach to legislating: "I was a hostage negotiator when I was with the sheriff's office. It's come in handy back here."

Since 2009, Reichert has been a member of the Ways and Means Committee, and in the 113th Congress (2013-14) he chairs the Human Resources Subcommittee, which handles social welfare programs — the assignment is an extension of his desire to help those in need, he said.

He also sits on the Trade Subcommittee, an assignment he wanted since his first day in the House. "The importance of trade to our little part of the world is very high," he said. Reichert is a member of the President's Export Council, and he boasts a relationship with former Commerce Secretary Gary Locke, who is now ambassador to China. Locke was in the King County prosecutor's office while Reichert was a detective there.

Free-trade agreements with South Korea, Colombia and Panama in 2011 met his approval, and he was pleased when permanent normal trade relations were extended to Russia in 2012. He plans to be involved as the Trans-Pacific Partnership, a multilateral agreement for the Asia-Pacific region, is shaped in 2013 and beyond. Reichert has concerns about China's currency policies and intellectual property theft, but he wants to keep trade doors open.

The Ways and Means Committee is tackling an overhaul of the tax code in the 113th Congress, and Reichert has already contributed to the discussion. He and Wisconsin Democrat Ron Kind produced a 2013 bill to revamp tax code incentives for investments in "S corporations" — a common configuration for small, privately held businesses. Several of their ideas were incorporated in a draft tax overhaul proposal by committee leaders.

A former member of the Health Subcommittee, Reichert has focused in particular on children's health care. He was one of 40 House Republicans voting for a 2009 law expanding the Children's Health Insurance Program, which covers children from low-income families that make too much money to qualify for Medicaid. Reichert's daughter adopted two drug-addicted children, and the proceeds from Reichert's book on the Green River case go to a clinic that cares for drug-addicted babies.

He did not support the 2010 health care overhaul, however, believing it failed to address crucial issues, including cost containment. Despite White House lobbying, he also opposed the 2009 economic stimulus law.

Reichert, a member of the moderate Main Street Partnership, sometimes aligns with Democrats on environmental, labor and social issues. In early 2011, he did not support proposed cuts to Justice Department drug and policing programs, many EPA programs and the Forest Service. He voted in support of collective bargaining rights for Federal Aviation Administration and Transportation Security Administration employees.

Most notably, he voted for a 2009 bill to create a cap-and-trade system for regulating greenhouse gas emissions — he said he liked parts of the bill that increased federal support for nuclear, wind and solar technologies. He teamed up with Oregon Democrat Earl Blumenauer on a 2011 bill to extend a tax credit for renewable-energy production. He said the key to winning acceptance from conservatives is requiring actual energy production before the credit can be received. Reichert and Maryland Democrat Chris Van Hollen are the co-chairmen of the Renewable Energy and Energy Efficiency Caucus.

Reichert was King County sheriff for eight years and is a strong advocate for increased federal support of DNA research for law enforcement. In the early stages of the Green River case, "we were still checking fingerprints with a magnifying glass and counting the loops and whorls by hand," he said. DNA technology was crucial in catching the killer years later.

Even with his law enforcement days behind him, Reichert stays in shape: He works out religiously, often to the music of James Brown.

In the 2006 and 2008 elections, Reichert beat Microsoft executive Darcy Burner in close contests. In 2010, he underwent brain surgery for an injury sustained when a tree branch hit his head while he was chopping wood. He recovered, and went on to beat another Microsoft executive, Democrat Suzan DelBene, with 52 percent of the vote. (She won in the 1st District in 2012.)

His district was made a little safer for a Republican in the congressional map drawn after the 2010 census (although President Barack Obama still won its presidential vote in 2012). Reichert took almost 60 percent of the vote for his easiest victory to date.

Key Votes

2012	
Extend a Social Security payroll tax cut and unemployment benefits	YES
Ease securities rules to expand small-business access to capital	YES
Extend for one year subsidized student loan interest rates financed by a cut in health care spending	YES
Cite Attorney General Eric H. Holder Jr. for contempt of Congress	YES
Create a visa program for foreign graduates in high-tech fields	YES
Extend most Bush-era income tax rates while allowing rates for top-bracket earners to rise (Jan. 1, 2013)	YES
2011	
Strike funding for F-35 alternative engine	NO
Prevent EPA from regulating greenhouse gas emissions to address climate change	YES
Extend certain provisions of Patriot Act for four years	YES
Declare opposition to use of ground troops in Libya	YES
Overhaul patent law	YES
Pass compromise debt limit increase plan and establish future spending limits	YES
Allow consideration of measures to implement three trade agreements	YES

CQ Vote Studies

	PARTY UNITY		PRESIDENTIAL SUPPORT	
	SUPPORT	OPPOSE	SUPPORT	OPPOSE
2012	84%	16%	22%	78%
2011	78%	22%	35%	65%
2010	80%	20%	38%	62%
2009	68%	32%	56%	44%
2008	75%	25%	53%	47%

Interest Groups

	AFL-CIO	ADA	CCUS	ACU
2012	38%	5%	83%	62%
2011	46%	30%	100%	41%
2010	7%	20%	100%	67%
2009	62%	45%	80%	60%
2008	60%	60%	78%	56%

Washington 8

Southeastern Seattle suburbs and central Cascade Mountains

The 8th takes in most of King and Pierce counties outside Seattle and Tacoma, including some wealthier suburban communities. These less populous portions of King and Pierce are home to wide-ranging farm production — including berries, vegetables, livestock and nursery plants — and their eastern halves rise into vast forests and the Cascade Range, which extend through Kittitas and Chelan counties. Most of Mount Rainier National Park — including the peak itself, which is the highest point in Washington and in the Cascades — is in the 8th in the southeastern corner of Pierce County.

Much of the district is rural, and the stretch of suburbs from Sammamish and Issaquah to Auburn serves as its population hub. Growth in these cities gives a more metropolitan feel to the western edge of the district, although the urban areas — and Democratic voters — in the region were excised from the 8th during decennial remapping. Auburn straddles the King-Pierce line, and is home to a major Boeing airplane assembly plant and related parts manufacturers that employ thousands of local residents.

Agriculture dominates the economy in the plains west of the Cascades, and in remote Chelan and Kittitas. The Army's Yakima Training Center (shared with the 4th) and fertile farmland, including vineyards, in Kittitas County take up the southeastern corner of the district. The Wenatchee National Forest still provides some timber jobs in Chelan. Central Washington University in Ellensburg is a top employer in Kittitas County.

Redistricting solidified incumbent Republican Rep. Dave Reichert's hold on the 8th, but moderate voters here are willing to back Democrats for U.S. Senate and president. In 2012, the district's portion of King — which accounts for nearly 60 percent of the population — backed Sen. Maria Cantwell and Barack Obama for re-election but opted for former Rep. Jay Inslee's GOP opponent in the gubernatorial contest.

Major Industry
Agriculture, aviation, tourism, military

Cities
Auburn, Wenatchee, Ellensburg

Notable
Mount Rainier, an active volcano, is the most heavily glaciated peak in the lower 48 states.

Rep. Adam Smith (D)

Capitol Office
225-8901
adamsmith.house.gov
2264 Rayburn Bldg. 20515-4709; fax 225-5893

Committees
Armed Services - Ranking Member

Residence
Bellevue

Born
June 15, 1965; Washington, D.C.

Religion
Episcopalian

Family
Wife, Sara Smith; two children

Education
Fordham U., B.A. 1987 (political science); U. of Washington, J.D. 1990

Career
City prosecutor; lawyer

Political Highlights
Wash. Senate, 1991-97

ELECTION RESULTS

2012 GENERAL		
Adam Smith (D)	192,034	71.6%
James Postma (R)	76,105	28.4%
2012 PRIMARY (Open)		
Adam Smith (D)	72,868	61.2%
Tom Cramer (D)	8,376	7.0%
2010 GENERAL		
Adam Smith (D)	123,743	54.8%
Richard "Dick" Muri (R)	101,851	45.1%

Previous Winning Percentages
2008 (65%); 2006 (66%); 2004 (63%); 2002 (59%); 2000 (62%); 1998 (65%); 1996 (50%)

Elected 1996; 9th term

Smart and businesslike, Smith takes pride in solving problems. "I've been doing this for a while," he said. "I think I'm good at it." He has plenty of problems to work on as the top Democrat on the Armed Services Committee.

Smith considers the federal debt to be a national security threat. Reducing it, he says, requires that Congress and the administration address every factor by increasing revenue and decreasing spending on entitlements, some domestic discretionary programs and, yes, the Pentagon. "If we don't start looking at the big picture, we are going to be in a world of hurt," he said in a 2012 speech.

He therefore takes pride in being an Armed Services leader who wants to shrink defense budgets without gutting them. When Smith chaired the Air and Land Forces Subcommittee, it was arguably the toughest oversight panel in Congress in limiting spending on programs plagued by ballooning costs, schedule delays and technical snafus. He took penetrating looks at the Army's now-defunct Future Combat Systems and the F-35 fighter jet.

More recently, he has come out as a strong advocate of another round of base closures. "It needs to be done in order to get our force in the right structure and save money that needs to be saved," he said in 2013.

Smith has acted as a moderate on the Armed Services Committee. On some issues he leans left, defending the rights of openly gay people to serve in the military and of people accused of terrorism to defend themselves in court. On others, he leans right, advocating defense spending levels higher than liberal colleagues would like.

But it was party loyalty that helped him nab the ranking member position starting in 2011. Smith occasionally breaks with Democratic leaders on trade (not uncommon for Democrats in the Seattle area) and certain national security issues. However, over the course of his career he has become more inclined to stand with a majority of his party when it opposes a majority of Republicans.

Once a strong supporter of President George W. Bush's policy in Iraq — he sided with Republicans in 2006 against setting a troop withdrawal deadline — Smith became one of Bush's toughest critics after Democrats took the majority in 2007. That year, he opposed the surge of troops to that theater.

After President Barack Obama took office, Smith praised his announcement in December 2009 that he would boost forces in Afghanistan and Pakistan. He then backed the president's June 2011 proposal to withdraw most forces by the end of 2014. As is the case on many defense issues, Smith stands squarely in the middle on Afghanistan: urging a withdrawal as soon as possible but hastening to add that it should be done "responsibly."

He split the difference again after Obama committed U.S. forces to help stem the violence in Libya in early 2011. He was somewhat supportive of the policy while suggesting that the president should have included Congress before the decision to involve Americans was made.

And while Smith has backed the administration's use of targeted killings and surveillance authorities when fighting terrorism overseas, civil libertarians of both parties were pleased with his attempt to secure a provision in the fiscal 2013 defense authorization law that would bar indefinite detention without trial for terrorism suspects. It fell short.

He was more successful persuading the House to agree to an amendment relaxing exports of satellites and related equipment. That provision figures to be a boon to Boeing Co., which has a major facility near Smith's district and has thrown its financial support behind many of his campaigns. Smith was a major Boeing ally in protesting the Air Force's 2008 decision to award a new multibillion-dollar air tanker contract to a consortium of Northrop Grumman Corp. and the North American division of the European Aeronautic Defence & Space Co., the parent company of Airbus. Boeing won the contract in a reopened competition in 2011.

Smith also looks out for Joint Base Lewis-McChord. He no longer represents the base, after the most recent round of redistricting took effect at the start of the 113th Congress (2013-14). But its proximity still makes the base and its personnel hugely important to his agenda.

Even before becoming the ranking member of Armed Services, Smith had extensive defense and foreign policy credentials. He chaired two Armed Services subcommittees: Terrorism and Unconventional Threats and Capabilities, which oversees special operations units; and Air and Land Forces, which has responsibility for most Air Force and Army equipment.

He also served on the House Foreign Affairs and Intelligence panels and is a seasoned world traveler. He views national and global security not just as a matter of military strength, but also a product of diplomacy, economic vitality, education, good governance and other factors.

A member of the business-friendly New Democrat Coalition, he is an advocate of intellectual property protections and generally backs free trade. In 2002, he split with his party's leaders and backed legislation giving the president fast-track authority to negotiate trade agreements that Congress cannot amend. He voted against the 2005 Central America Free Trade Agreement, pleasing unions that had criticized his earlier pro-trade votes but antagonizing many businesses in his trade-friendly district.

By 2007, he returned to the pro-trade side, and in 2011 he voted for pacts with South Korea, Panama and Colombia.

Smith's father, who worked as a baggage handler at Seattle-Tacoma International Airport, died of a heart attack when Smith was 19. The family went on welfare, and Smith worked his way through college loading trucks for UPS. He was a Teamsters union member and still supports organized labor on most issues other than trade.

The fall after he earned his law degree in 1990, he won a state Senate seat in an upset and, at 25, became the youngest state senator in the country. The victory was bittersweet, however. Just days before his election, his mother suffered a stroke and died.

In 1996, Smith challenged incumbent Rep. Randy Tate — a favorite of social conservatives, who had ridden into office on the GOP wave of 1994. Smith won by 3 points and has been re-elected fairly comfortably since then. Even in the strong Republican year of 2010, he won by almost 10 points. Running in a reconfigured district in 2012, he took more than 71 percent of the vote.

Key Votes

2012	
Extend a Social Security payroll tax cut and unemployment benefits	NO
Ease securities rules to expand small-business access to capital	YES
Extend for one year subsidized student loan interest rates financed by a cut in health care spending	NO
Cite Attorney General Eric H. Holder Jr. for contempt of Congress	NO
Create a visa program for foreign graduates in high-tech fields	-
Extend most Bush-era income tax rates while allowing rates for top-bracket earners to rise (Jan. 1, 2013)	NO
2011	
Strike funding for F-35 alternative engine	NO
Prevent EPA from regulating greenhouse gas emissions to address climate change	NO
Extend certain provisions of Patriot Act for four years	YES
Declare opposition to use of ground troops in Libya	NO
Overhaul patent law	YES
Pass compromise debt limit increase plan and establish future spending limits	NO
Allow consideration of measures to implement three trade agreements	YES

CQ Vote Studies

	PARTY UNITY		PRESIDENTIAL SUPPORT	
	SUPPORT	OPPOSE	SUPPORT	OPPOSE
2012	93%	7%	87%	13%
2011	88%	12%	93%	7%
2010	96%	4%	90%	10%
2009	93%	7%	94%	6%
2008	97%	3%	20%	80%

Interest Groups

	AFL-CIO	ADA	CCUS	ACU
2012	95%	70%	36%	8%
2011	90%	75%	38%	12%
2010	86%	90%	0%	8%
2009	95%	95%	47%	0%
2008	100%	85%	67%	4%

Washington 9

Eastside Seattle suburbs — Bellevue, Renton, Kent

Decennial reapportionment gave Washington one new district, and the resulting map made the 9th more compact — the district, which is crisscrossed by interstates, runs from Seattle and Bellevue in the north to the Port of Tacoma in the south. The 9th grabbed Bellevue, which is east of Seattle, from the 8th, but lost portions of Pierce County, including a major military base and densely populated suburbs. The redistricting process also drew the 9th as Washington's first minority-majority district.

Suburbs outside of Seattle, including Eastside communities and Mercer Island, boast high-salaried residents and low rates of unemployment; much of the workforce there works in white-collar technology industries. Residents in some urban areas, such as Tukwila, still struggle with poverty.

Aviation is big business in the 9th. Despite years of layoffs and uncertainty over the company's expansion in other regions, Boeing remains a key fixture in the district's economy — major assembly and corporate facilities in Renton, Bellevue and Tukwila provide thousands of jobs. Seattle-Tacoma International Airport and the surrounding hotels and restaurants are important to economic stability. The 9th is also home to technology and Internet industries: the Expedia headquarters are in Bellevue, and many residents in the district work for Microsoft in the neighboring 1st. Truck manufacturer PACCAR has its corporate headquarters in Bellevue, and timber giant Weyerhaeuser's corporate headquarters and main campus are in Federal Way.

In the district's portion of Seattle, the Chinatown-International District has a large concentration of Chinese, Filipino, Japanese, Vietnamese and other Southeast Asian residents. Bellevue is one of the state's most diverse cities: Roughly one-fourth of its population is Asian and more than 30 percent is foreign-born. Blacks and Hispanics each make up more than 10 percent of the population in the 9th. The strongly Democratic district gave Barack Obama 68 percent of its presidential vote in 2012.

Major Industry
Aviation, technology, trade

Cities
Seattle (pt.), Tacoma (pt.), Bellevue, Kent, Renton

Notable
The Jimi Hendrix Memorial in Renton celebrates the musical contribution of the Seattle native.

Rep. Denny Heck (D)

Capitol Office
225-9740
dennyheck.house.gov
425 Cannon Bldg. 20515-6601; fax 225-0129

Committees
Financial Services

Residence
Olympia

Born
July 29, 1952; Vancouver, Wash.

Religion
Lutheran

Family
Wife, Paula Heck; two children

Education
Evergreen State College, B.A. 1973; Portland State U., attended 1974-75

Career
Public affairs television broadcaster; gubernatorial aide; political consulting company owner; credit union marketing director; school district administrative assistant; congressional district aide; union representative; state legislative aide

Political Highlights
Wash. House, 1977-85 (majority leader, 1983-85); Wash. House chief clerk, 1985-87; candidate for Wash. Superintendent of Public Instruction, 1988; Democratic nominee for U.S. House, 2010

ELECTION RESULTS

2012 GENERAL		
Denny Heck (D)	163,036	58.6%
Richard "Dick" Muri (R)	115,381	41.4%
2012 PRIMARY (Open)		
Denny Heck (D)	51,047	39.7%
Jennifer Ferguson (D)	14,026	10.9%

Elected 2012; 1st term

Heck once led the Democratic majority in the Washington House. He took a 28-year hiatus from legislating, but he wasn't spinning his wheels. Occupations in the public sector and in the private sector now shape his work on the Financial Services Committee.

Born in Vancouver, Heck is the son of a truck driver and a phone operator. When he was 20, his former high school social studies teacher — who was also a state representative — helped him get a job as an education analyst in the state legislature. That was followed by jobs with a school district and a union representing school workers. He was elected to the state House in his mid-20s, and by his fourth (and final) term, he was the majority leader. Heck helped write a law that overhauled the state's education funding system.

Heck went on to serve as chief of staff to Gov. Booth Gardner. He then founded, ran and appeared as a host on TVW, the state's public affairs TV network. He later created a company offering business-oriented education and training and was an early investor in RealNetworks.

On several occasions, Heck has said that his business experiences shifted his views on policy from his state House days, when he was seen as a more partisan lawmaker. He is a member of the business-minded New Democrat Coalition, and his seat on Financial Services lets him address the concerns of the private sector in any number of ways. He also links economic growth to enhanced education and training, and he supports an increase in funding for federal education programs.

Heck ran for the open 3rd District seat in 2010, losing by 6 points to Republican Jaime Herrera Beutler. Washington was awarded a new House seat for 2012, and as drawn it favored a Democratic candidate. Heck ran again, and he easily defeated Republican Richard Muri, a retired Air Force officer.

Heck has a creative streak. He has self-published a mystery novel and wrote and performed the one-man play "Our Times."

Washington 10

Southern Puget Sound region — Olympia, Puyallup

The newly created 10th District was carved out of the former 3rd and 9th after decennial reapportionment assigned the state an additional U.S. House seat. The Capital District takes in northern Thurston County and Olympia, northwestern Pierce County and a small corner of southeastern Mason County.

Pierce County includes populous suburbs south of Tacoma (most of the downtown is in the 6th and 9th), including Lakewood and Parkland. Residing in the heart of the district, Joint Base Lewis-McChord — a merged "mega base" created after the most recent BRAC round — employs tens of thousands of military and civilian personnel in this area. Nearby Dupont along Interstate 5 is home to an Intel facility.

Government is the cornerstone of the 10th's portion of Thurston County. Olympia hosts state and county government offices, as well as regional American Indian tribal government operations. Evergreen State College is known for a liberal student body, adding diversity and youth to the population. Local officials have worked to lure private sector employers to the city in order to diversify the economy, and retail sector and health care jobs are already important to residents in the area's suburban communities.

Half of the Capitol State Forest, shared with the 6th, occupies most of the district's southwestern corner. Other less-populous areas of the 10th include farmland along the district's southern tier.

Most of the district's voters live in Pierce County, which gave Democrats Barack Obama, Maria Cantwell and Denny Heck comfortable margins of victory in the presidential, U.S. Senate and U.S. House elections in 2012. The liberal lean of Olympia provides even more votes for Democrats in Thurston County.

Major Industry
Government, service, military

Military Bases
Joint Base Lewis-McChord, 36,500 military, 15,100 civilian

Cities
Lakewood, Olympia, Puyallup

Notable
The 17-day Western Washington Fair in Puyallup is the largest annual event in the state.

WEST VIRGINIA

Gov. Earl Ray Tomblin (D)

First elected: 2012; Took office Nov. 15, 2010, due to the resignation of Joe Manchin III, D, who was elected to the U.S. Senate.

Length of term: 4 years

Term expires: 1/17

Salary: $150,000

Phone: (304) 558-2000

Residence: Chapmanville

Born: March 15, 1952; Logan County, W.Va.

Religion: Presbyterian

Family: Wife, Joanne Jaeger Tomblin; one child

Education: West Virginia U., B.S. 1974; Marshall U., 1975 M.B.A

Career: Property manager; teacher

Political highlights: W.Va. House, 1975-81; W.Va. Senate, 1981-present (president, 1995-present)

ELECTION RESULTS

2012 GENERAL

Earl Ray Tomblin (D)	335,468	50.5%
Bill Maloney (R)	303,291	45.6%
Jesse Johnson (MOUNT)	16,787	2.5%
David Moran (LIBERT)	8,909	1.3%

Senate President Jeffrey V. Kessler (D)

(no lieutenant governor)

Phone: (304) 845-2580

LEGISLATURE

Legislature: January or February-March, limit of 60 days

Senate: 34 members, 4-year terms

2013 ratios: 25 D, 9 R; 33 men, 1 woman

Salary: $20,000

Phone: (304) 357-7800

House: 100 members, 2-year terms

2013 ratios: 54 D, 46 R; 79 men, 21 women

Salary: $20,000

Phone: (304) 340-3200

TERM LIMITS

Governor: 2 consecutive terms

Senate: No

House: No

URBAN STATISTICS

CITY	POPULATION
Charleston	51,400
Huntington	49,138
Parkersburg	31,492
Morgantown	29,660
Wheeling	28,486

REGISTERED VOTERS

Democrat	51%
Republican	29%
Other	20%

POPULATION

2010 population	1,852,994
2000 population	1,808,344
1990 population	1,793,477
Percent change (2000-2010)	+2.5%
Rank among states (2010)	37
Median age	40.4
Born in state	71.5%
Foreign born	1.3%
Violent crime rate	267/100,000
Poverty level	17.7
Federal workers	26,740
Military	1,199

ELECTIONS

STATE ELECTION OFFICIAL
(304) 558-6000

DEMOCRATIC PARTY
(304) 342-8121

REPUBLICAN PARTY
(304) 768-0493

MISCELLANEOUS

Web: www.wv.gov

Capital: Charleston

U.S. CONGRESS

Senate: 2 Democrats

House: 2 Republicans, 1 Democrat

STATISTICS BY DISTRICT

District	2012 Vote for President Obama	2012 Vote for President Romney	2008 Vote for President Obama	2008 Vote for President McCain	Black	Asian	Hispanic	Median Income	Over 64	Under 20	College Education	Rural	Sq. Miles
1	36%	62%	42%	57%	2%	1%	1%	$39,170	16%	23%	20%	45%	6,276
2	38	60	44	55	3	1	2	41,260	16	24	20	50	8,017
3	33	65	42	56	4	<1	1	34,826	17	23	15	60	9,745
STATE	**36**	**62**	**43**	**56**	**3**	**1**	**1**	**38,482**	**16**	**24**	**18**	**52**	**24,038**
U.S.	**51**	**47**	**53**	**46**	**12**	**5**	**17**	**50,052**	**13**	**27**	**29**	**21**	**3,531,905**

Sen. Jay Rockefeller (D)

Capitol Office
224-6472
rockefeller.senate.gov
531 Hart Bldg. 20510-4802; fax 224-7665

Committees
Commerce, Science & Transportation - Chairman
Finance
(Health Care - Chairman)
Veterans' Affairs
Select Intelligence
Joint Taxation

Residence
Charleston

Born
June 18, 1937; Manhattan, N.Y.

Religion
Presbyterian

Family
Wife, Sharon Percy; four children

Education
International Christian U. (Tokyo), attended 1957-60; Harvard U., A.B. 1961 (Asian languages & history)

Career
College president; VISTA volunteer

Political Highlights
W.Va. House, 1967-69; W.Va. secretary of state, 1969-73; Democratic nominee for governor, 1972; governor, 1977-85

ELECTION RESULTS

2008 GENERAL		
Jay Rockefeller (D)	447,560	63.7%
Jay Wolfe (R)	254,629	36.3%
2008 PRIMARY		
Jay Rockefeller (D)	271,425	77.1%
Sheirl L. Fletcher (D)	51,073	14.5%
Billy Hendricks Jr. (D)	29,707	8.4%

Previous Winning Percentages
2002 (63%); 1996 (77%); 1990 (68%); 1984 (52%)

Elected 1984; 5th term

Rockefeller has been a towering presence in the Senate, but he plans to depart the chamber at the end of the 113th Congress. He still has a window to move major legislation — and help his adopted home state — as chairman of the Commerce, Science and Transportation Committee.

He already has several historic achievements to his name. In the 111th Congress (2009-10), he successfully concluded a two-decade quest with enactment of the 2010 health care overhaul — he is also the chairman of the Finance Subcommittee on Health Care.

The 112th Congress (2011-12) didn't offer the same degree of opportunity, as Republicans took control of the House. But Rockefeller kept an active pace as Commerce chairman, conducting oversight of consumer safety, online privacy and space exploration. Working closely with ranking Republican Kay Bailey Hutchison of Texas, he helped move a two-year reauthorization of surface transportation programs and a four-year reauthorization of federal aviation programs.

There are some loose ends for the 113th Congress (2013-14), most notably regarding cybersecurity. Rockefeller and other Democrats have pushed for greater federal oversight of critical infrastructure (such as water and power utilities) that experts say is vulnerable to online attacks by terrorists and other nefarious interests. Hutchison sided with businesses that opposed handing the government greater policing powers over infrastructure largely owned by the private sector. A Senate bill to set new cybersecurity standards couldn't clear procedural hurdles in 2012.

Rockefeller also butts heads with the GOP by defending regulations for "network neutrality," which are meant to stop broadband providers from blocking certain Internet traffic or establishing tiered pathways for Internet content. They were put in place by the Federal Communications Commission in 2011. Democrats call those rules a consumer protection, while Republicans see them as unprecedented regulation of the Internet. Rockefeller is a big proponent of federal programs to spread broadband service to schools and underserved regions.

He also has transportation issues to deal with. Debates on infrastructure spending will re-open, as the surface transportation law expires in 2014. And Amtrak is due for reauthorization in 2013. Rockefeller has been wary of any attempts to privatize the financially beleaguered passenger rail service.

For all these issues, Rockefeller has a new negotiating partner. Hutchison retired at the end of the 112th, and John Thune has taken her place. By all accounts, the South Dakotan is personable, but he's also the GOP Conference chairman — meaning he has a vested interest in reinforcing the Republican platform of small-government fiscal conservatism.

Rockefeller is less bothered by many government-centered solutions. As Congress debated the health care overhaul, he was unsuccessful in trying to include a government-run "public option" insurance plan as part of the final legislation. He voted for the bill anyway — he had been the chief congressional surrogate for President Bill Clinton's proposed health care overhaul.

The Finance Committee is looking at reworking the tax code in the 113th, and Rockefeller, who also sits on the Joint Taxation Committee, has endorsed a number of standard Democratic tax proposals. He wants higher-earning Americans to pay taxes at higher rates (on both income and capital gains) and wants tax credits for oil and ethanol producers eliminated.

Rockefeller's recent focus on domestic matters is a reversal from his priorities during the presidency of George W. Bush. He chaired the Intelligence

Committee then, and he clashed frequently with Republicans over the war in Iraq, the treatment of detainees and other intelligence-related issues.

He remains a committed liberal on social issues and a reliable vote for the Obama administration and his party's leadership. But there was speculation well ahead of his January 2013 retirement announcement that he has been vexed by the increasingly conservative politics of his state. Coal is a huge part of West Virginia's economy and culture, and he made blistering remarks about the industry in 2012.

Speaking in June against a resolution to void limits on mercury emissions from coal-fired power plants, Rockefeller accused coal operators of spreading misinformation instead of tackling health and environmental issues associated with coal-fueled energy. "The reality is that many who run the coal industry today would rather attack false enemies and deny real problems than find solutions," he said on the Senate floor. "Scare tactics are a cynical waste of time, money and, worst of all, coal miners' hopes. But sadly, these coal operators have closed themselves off from any other opposing voices and few dared to speak out for change — even though it's been staring them in the face for years."

Those remarks directly challenged a story line the industry was pushing in his state and elsewhere — that the Obama administration had initiated a "war on coal." Rockefeller was echoing comments made by revered West Virginia Democratic Sen. Robert C. Byrd, the son of a coal miner, before his death in 2010. But Rockefeller's remarks were widely criticized at home.

Rockefeller then attended the 2012 Democratic National Convention, where President Barack Obama — deeply unpopular in West Virginia — was nominated for a second term. Other prominent Democrats in the state steered clear of the event. Shortly after the November elections, Republican Rep. Shelley Moore Capito announced that she would run for the Senate in 2014. Rockefeller told The Associated Press that he's retiring to spend more time with his family — but it wasn't going to be an easy re-election campaign.

Even so, it's impossible to question Rockefeller's devotion to his adopted home. He sank deep roots in the state, arriving in 1964 as a 27-year-old VISTA volunteer in possession of youthful idealism and one of the most famous names in American history.

The path to the Mountain State was perhaps an unlikely one for Rockefeller, the great-grandson of Standard Oil Co. founder John D. Rockefeller, who at one point was considered the world's richest man. Jay grew up on the Upper East Side of Manhattan — far from the coal mines and poverty of West Virginia. He studied at Phillips Exeter Academy and Harvard University, and he spent three years studying in Japan.

The time he spent as a volunteer in Emmons, a small town on the Big Coal River in West Virginia, would forever change his life. He can still get misty when recalling his VISTA days. During a late-night markup of the health care overhaul in 2009, Rockefeller described the experience as being "reborn," becoming emotional as he described the poverty he encountered in the hardscrabble town. "I could not leave. And it was because I [had] become so devoted to those people and the unfairness," he said.

Although he had planned to stay only one year, he became active in local politics, later winning a seat in the state legislature and serving as secretary of state. Rockefeller lost a bid for governor in 1972, but he became the president of West Virginia Wesleyan College and used that opportunity to broaden his connections to the state.

He won in his second attempt at the governor's office in 1976, serving two terms before taking the seat of retiring Democratic Sen. Jennings Randolph in 1984. In that contest, he barely squeaked out a win, securing just 52 percent of the vote despite spending $12 million of his vast personal fortune. He was re-elected four times by more comfortable margins.

Key Votes

2012	
Prohibit health insurance plans from denying coverage based on the sponsor's religious beliefs	**YES**
Require approval of the Keystone XL oil pipeline	**NO**
Ease securities rules to expand small-business access to capital	**NO**
Reauthorize farm and nutrition programs for five years	**YES**
Limit debate on a bill that would create private-sector cybersecurity standards	**YES**
Consent to ratification of a treaty setting global standard for the treatment of people with disabilities	**YES**
Provide $60.4 billion in disaster relief following Superstorm Sandy	**YES**
Extend most Bush-era income tax rates while allowing rates for top-bracket earners to rise (Jan. 1, 2013)	**YES**
2011	
Prevent EPA from regulating greenhouse gas emissions to address climate change	**NO**
Extend certain provisions of Patriot Act for four years	**YES**
Clear compromise debt limit increase plan and establish future spending limits	**YES**
Overhaul patent law	**?**
Implement Colombia free trade agreement	**NO**
Limit debate on confirmation of Caitlin J. Halligan to D.C. Circuit Court of Appeals	**YES**
Extend payroll tax cut and unemployment benefits for two months	**YES**

CQ Vote Studies

	PARTY UNITY		PRESIDENTIAL SUPPORT	
	SUPPORT	OPPOSE	SUPPORT	OPPOSE
2012	96%	4%	99%	1%
2011	99%	1%	96%	4%
2010	97%	3%	97%	3%
2009	98%	2%	100%	0%
2008	84%	16%	45%	55%
2007	91%	9%	35%	65%
2006	84%	16%	55%	45%
2005	93%	7%	40%	60%
2004	88%	12%	64%	36%
2003	96%	4%	50%	50%

Interest Groups

	AFL-CIO	ADA	CCUS	ACU
2012	100%	90%	17%	4%
2011	100%	100%	40%	0%
2010	100%	85%	27%	8%
2009	93%	85%	40%	0%
2008	100%	85%	63%	0%
2007	100%	85%	45%	8%
2006	100%	60%	83%	10%
2005	86%	100%	50%	4%
2004	100%	90%	41%	12%
2003	92%	100%	30%	15%

Sen. Joe Manchin III (D)

Capitol Office
224-3954
manchin.senate.gov
306 Hart Bldg. 20510-4801; fax 228-0002

Committees
Armed Services
(Airland - Chairman)
Banking, Housing & Urban Affairs
Energy & Natural Resources
(Public Lands, Forests and Mining - Chairman)
Special Aging

Residence
Fairmont

Born
Aug. 24, 1947; Fairmont, W.Va.

Religion
Roman Catholic

Family
Wife, Gayle Manchin; three children

Education
West Virginia U., B.A. 1970 (business administration)

Career
Coal brokerage company owner; carpet store owner

Political Highlights
W.Va. House, 1983-85; sought Democratic nomination for governor, 1996; W.Va. Senate, 1987-97; W.Va. secretary of state, 2001-05; governor, 2005-10

ELECTION RESULTS

2012 GENERAL		
Joe Manchin III (D)	399,898	60.6%
John Raese (R)	240,787	36.5%
Bob Henry Baber (MOUNT)	19,517	3.0%
2012 PRIMARY		
Joe Manchin III (D)	163,891	79.9%
Sheirl L. Fletcher (D)	41,118	20.1%
2010 SPECIAL		
Joe Manchin III (D)	283,358	53.5%
John Raese (R)	230,013	43.4%
Jesse Johnson (MOUNT)	10,152	1.9%
Jeff Becker (CNSTP)	6,425	1.2%

Elected 2010; 1st full term

Manchin, a former governor, is willing to deploy the full resources of the federal government to his state's benefit — a practice perfected by Democrat Robert C. Byrd, his legendary predecessor. But on a host of other issues, he walks a fine line between the national party and his state's more moderate political inclinations.

Byrd did most of his state-friendly work on the Appropriations Committee. Thus far, Manchin has had to work elsewhere. He sits on the Energy and Natural Resources Committee, and in the 113th Congress (2013-14) he holds a gavel of great importance to his state: He is now the chairman of the Public Lands, Forests and Mining Subcommittee. He also retained his seats on the Energy Subcommittee and the Water and Power Subcommittee. Packaged together, those panels make him a central player when the Senate considers the coal industry that carries West Virginia's economy.

Manchin participates when Democrats (and some Republicans) push for improvements to energy efficiency and development of renewable energy sources. But he doesn't want coal, or the mining industry, left behind. As some Democrats dusted off proposals for a tax on greenhouse gas emissions at the start of the 113th — which would likely drive down demand for fossil fuels — Manchin was indignant. "Why the hell would I want a carbon tax?" he said. "I don't know how it would be good for the economy, unless you are trying to just shift money from one group to another group."

He supports approval of the Keystone XL pipeline from Canada's tar sands to U.S. refineries, over the objection of environmentalists. He has sponsored a bill to block the EPA from revoking water permits for mining projects that other agencies have granted — a direct response to a mining dispute in West Virginia. And he has worked on a mine safety overhaul with fellow West Virginia Democrat Jay Rockefeller.

The EPA is one of his most frequent targets — he sued the agency when he was governor. He co-authored a bill with Indiana Republican Dan Coats in November 2011 to extend the time for utilities to comply with EPA rules on cross-border air pollution and coal- and gas-fueled electricity generators. And Manchin was one of four Democrats to vote in April 2011 to block the EPA from regulating stationary sources of carbon dioxide and other greenhouse gases to address climate change.

In addition to his advocacy for coal, Manchin has reflected his state's growing fiscal conservatism. "I have never put together a budget, be it my family's or as governor, that was based on how much we wanted to spend, but on what we had," Manchin said in 2011. That year, he voted for a proposed balanced-budget amendment to the Constitution that would allow deficit spending only with the approval of a congressional supermajority.

He's also sensitive to socially conservative elements in the state. Manchin is a foe of abortion and has not endorsed same-sex marriage. He opposed the 2010 law to repeal the statutory "don't ask, don't tell" policy barring openly gay people from serving in the military. (But he then sent out a statement saying that the policy "probably should be repealed in the near future.")

Many West Virginians also favor robust gun rights. Having just won a full six-year term in 2012, Manchin wasn't taking too much of a risk in early 2013 when he and Pennsylvania Republican Patrick J. Toomey proposed a system of expanded background checks for gun purchases. Their plan was actually a compromise — a plan favored by New York Democrat Charles E. Schumer was far more rigorous. But when it was put on the Senate floor in April 2013, it fell six votes short. An avid hunter, Manchin still opposes most gun control measures—an iconic moment from the 2010 campaign came when he fired a rifle shot through a copy of the Democrats' bill to create a cap-and-trade system regulating greenhouse gas emissions.

A member of the Armed Services Committee, Manchin was named the chairman of the Airland Subcommittee in 2013. (His state has no Defense Department bases, but it does have National Guard facilities.)

Manchin has been critical of U.S. strategy in the Middle East. On several occasions, he has accused the Pentagon of prioritizing nation-building over countering terrorism. "Enough is enough. It's time to rebuild America, not Afghanistan," he said in an October 2011 hearing. Manchin similarly supported the end of U.S. military involvement in Iraq and called for an end to civilian and contracting projects in that country.

Representing a state that has one of the highest per-capita populations of seniors, Manchin also serves on the Special Aging Committee. At the end of 2010, Congress voted to reduce the payroll taxes funding Social Security for one year; late in 2011, Manchin opposed extension of the lower rate. "We'll never have the political will to go back" to the original tax level, he said on MSNBC. Manchin and Patrick J. Leahy of Vermont were the only Senate Democrats to vote against the bill. (The lower rates did expire at the end of 2012, however.)

His newest assignment is a seat on the Banking, Housing and Urban Affairs Committee that he took in 2013. Some of his first inquiries on the panel regarded community banks—he worries they are being swamped by new regulations and capitalization rules that were designed for larger financial institutions, which were the culprits in the 2008 economic collapse.

He has also become the honorary co-chairman of No Labels, a nonpartisan group dedicated to improving the functionality of Congress.

Manchin hails from the small coal-mining town of Farmington. He went to West Virginia University on a football scholarship, then went into business, owning a carpet store and a coal brokerage company.

He got his start in politics in the state House, winning election in 1982 and serving one term, then moving to the state Senate two years later, where he served until 1997. He ran for the Democratic nomination for governor in 1996, losing to Charlotte Pritt, but came back to win election as secretary of state four years later. He was elected governor in 2004 and was re-elected in 2008. As governor, Manchin enjoyed approval ratings consistently around 70 percent.

After Byrd died in June 2010, Manchin appointed Democrat Carte P. Goodwin, his former general counsel, to fill the spot. The state legislature then cleared a bill clarifying that the seat would be filled by a special election in November. Manchin signed it.

Manchin quickly entered the race and took 73 percent of the vote in an August primary. The GOP's potentially strongest option, Rep. Shelley Moore Capito, opted not to enter the race. Instead, businessman John Raese won the nomination.

Considered a moderate, Manchin campaigned at a distance from the White House, promising not to "rubber stamp" President Barack Obama's policies. Early on, he had kind words for the Democrats' health care overhaul enacted in March 2010. He later tried to back away from the law, although he stopped short of calling for its repeal.

Polls showed a close contest for most of the campaign, with the popular Manchin being dragged down by Obama's unpopularity in the state. In the end, Manchin topped Raese by 10 points.

Byrd's original term expired at the end of the 112th Congress (2011-12), so Manchin had to run for re-election. He again ran apart from the national Democratic Party, skipping its September 2012 convention. Raese secured the GOP nomination for a rematch, but this time Manchin won by 24 points.

Key Votes

2012	
Prohibit health insurance plans from denying coverage based on the sponsor's religious beliefs	NO
Require approval of the Keystone XL oil pipeline	YES
Ease securities rules to expand small-business access to capital	YES
Reauthorize farm and nutrition programs for five years	YES
Limit debate on a bill that would create private-sector cybersecurity standards	YES
Consent to ratification of a treaty setting global standard for the treatment of people with disabilities	YES
Provide $60.4 billion in disaster relief following Superstorm Sandy	YES
Extend most Bush-era income tax rates while allowing rates for top-bracket earners to rise (Jan. 1, 2013)	YES
2011	
Prevent EPA from regulating greenhouse gas emissions to address climate change	YES
Extend certain provisions of Patriot Act for four years	YES
Clear compromise debt limit increase plan and establish future spending limits	YES
Overhaul patent law	YES
Implement Colombia free trade agreement	NO
Limit debate on confirmation of Caitlin J. Halligan to D.C. Circuit Court of Appeals	YES
Extend payroll tax cut and unemployment benefits for two months	NO

CQ Vote Studies

	PARTY UNITY		PRESIDENTIAL SUPPORT	
	SUPPORT	OPPOSE	SUPPORT	OPPOSE
2012	76%	24%	85%	15%
2011	75%	25%	84%	16%
2010	88%	12%	90%	10%

Interest Groups

	AFL-CIO	ADA	CCUS	ACU
2012	91%	70%	63%	28%
2011	74%	80%	45%	15%
2010	100%		75%	33%

Rep. David B. McKinley (R)

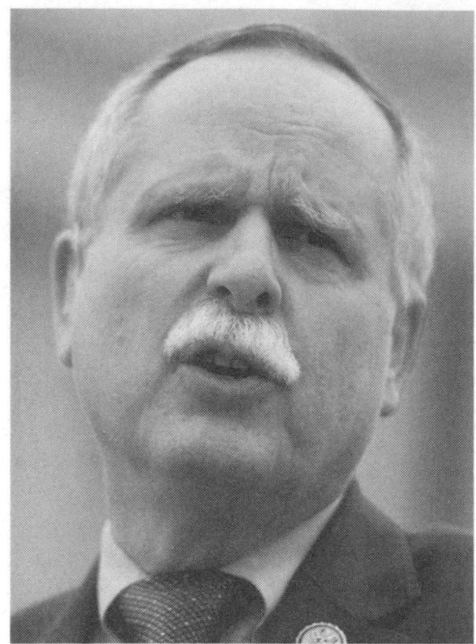

Capitol Office
225-4172
mckinley.house.gov
412 Cannon Bldg. 20515-4801; fax 225-7564

Committees
Energy & Commerce

Residence
Wheeling

Born
March 28, 1947; Wheeling, W.Va.

Religion
Episcopalian

Family
Wife, Mary McKinley; four children

Education
Purdue U., B.S.C.E. 1969

Career
Architectural engineering company owner; civil engineer

Political Highlights
W.Va. Republican Party chairman, 1990-94; W.Va. House, 1980-95; sought Republican nomination for governor, 1996

ELECTION RESULTS

2012 GENERAL		
David B. McKinley (R)	133,809	62.5%
Sue Thorn (D)	80,342	37.5%
2012 PRIMARY		
David B. McKinley (R)		unopposed
2010 GENERAL		
David B. McKinley (R)	90,660	50.4%
Mike Oliverio (D)	89,220	49.6%

Elected 2010; 2nd term

McKinley, a mustachioed civil engineer with a businesslike manner, looks after his district with the loyalty of a seventh-generation resident — John McKinley settled in the Wheeling area in the 1760s. "This is my history," he said. "This is my heritage." For the fiscal conservative, that heritage means bucking his party when local interests are at stake and maintaining a spirited defense of coal.

McKinley was one of just four House Republicans to vote against the fiscal 2012 budget prepared by Wisconsin's Paul D. Ryan. He criticized its proposed changes to Medicare as too rapid to allow for long-term financial planning. "I wish it had been an option, not the option," he said. West Virginia has one of the oldest populations in the United States, and McKinley is "going to protect my senior citizens," he said. He opposed Ryan's 2013 and 2014 budgets, too.

A one-year extension of lower payroll taxes was enacted in 2012 with bipartisan support, but McKinley panned it as attacking the funding stream for Social Security. "I'm not convinced that everyone even understands what the payroll tax is, unless they've been in business," he said. He advocates a "firewall" to keep the Social Security trust fund exclusively for beneficiaries, and he opposes raising the retirement age.

In July 2011, McKinley was one of six Republicans to oppose a short-term reauthorization of aviation programs that limited subsidies for airports such as Morgantown's. A few months later, he was one of seven Republicans who rejected a bill to curtail the powers of the National Labor Relations Board, saying it could overturn protections for construction workers and miners. And he voted against free-trade pacts with Colombia, Panama and South Korea — while voting for an expanded program to benefit workers whose jobs are displaced by international trade.

With more than four decades of experience as a small-businessman, he hews closer to the Republican line in attacking federal regulations. McKinley started his first company at the age of 24; he notes that he operated a business longer than some House colleagues have been alive. Legislators without a business background often "don't understand the effects a regulatory body has," he said. In terms of the business environment, "I'm trying to remove uncertainty."

His focus in that effort is the coal industry. McKinley often refers to a "war on coal" by the Obama administration, and he has launched counterattacks from the Energy and Commerce Committee. "I'm not trying to do away with the EPA," he said of a favorite target. "I'm just trying to ask them to be more responsible in the economic conditions that we're dealing with right now."

With Republicans hammering the Obama administration on regulations in the 112th Congress (2011-12), McKinley took the lead in fighting rules on coal ash, a byproduct from the burning of coal that is used in construction and agriculture and for other purposes. In 2011, the House passed his bill to establish a system of state-level regulation for coal ash and prevent the EPA from designating coal ash as hazardous waste; McKinley said doing so would remove a "stigma" on coal use, reduce waste-disposal costs, keep energy costs for manufacturers low and allow coal-burning projects to continue.

McKinley worked to include a coal ash provision in the 2012 surface transportation law, only to see it dropped in the negotiations that produced the final version. That exclusion led to a spat with West Virginia Democratic Sen. Jay Rockefeller, who declined to back McKinley's language in the negotiations.

The House passed an updated version of the coal ash bill in September 2012 as part of a coal-themed package, which also included a McKinley amendment to prevent the EPA from disapproving mountaintop mining permits issued by the Army Corps of Engineers — a bill designed to reverse a decision on West Virginia's Spruce No. 1 Mine. He has continued to pursue certainty for coal ash and mining permits in the 113th Congress (2013-14).

Fiscally, McKinley says cutting spending is a top priority. He supports a balanced-budget constitutional amendment. But he is not as ardent about spending reductions as some conservative groups would like. McKinley has gotten low marks from the Club for Growth, among others.

McKinley has some interest in health issues. When he was a member of the West Virginia Legislature, he wrote a law to stop insurers from canceling the coverage of people with HIV. He introduced a 2012 measure to limit cost-sharing requirements for patients with serious chronic diseases who need specialty medications — it was reintroduced in 2013. McKinley himself suffers from significant hearing loss.

The second of five brothers, McKinley was born in Wheeling. His father was an engineer, working on sewer and water line design, and his mother was a homemaker. He studied engineering at Purdue University while working a series of jobs. "One of my more pleasant jobs, quite frankly, was working in a sorority as a waiter," he fondly recalls. "The environment was lovely."

After several years in construction and teaching night classes, McKinley started his first venture. The architectural and engineering business of McKinley and Associates grew, with acquisitions, to more than 40 employees; he is one of the wealthier members of Congress.

Business sometimes makes way for football, however. West Virginia University is in his district — a WVU banner and football helmet decorate his office, along with a life-sized photo of a coal miner — and on fall weekends, he finds himself in Morgantown. "Thirty years I've had the same seat," he said. "Mountaineer Field on Saturday, 60,000 people, with everyone yelling. It's very therapeutic for me. My wife has caught me more than one time yelling when there's no reason to be yelling."

From 1980 to 1995, McKinley served in the West Virginia House of Delegates — he called it "a good learning exercise." He was the state Republican Party chairman from 1990 to 1994. He lost in the GOP gubernatorial primary in 1996, then turned his focus to business before trying politics again in 2010.

State Sen. Mike Oliverio defeated scandal-plagued, 14-term incumbent Alan B. Mollohan in the Democratic primary, making McKinley's task more difficult than it might have been. Oliverio ran as a conservative Democrat, but McKinley prevailed by 1,440 votes in the seventh-closest House race of 2010. Oliverio thought about a rematch in 2012 but ultimately declined. McKinley beat Democrat Sue Thorn by 25 points.

Key Votes

2012	
Extend a Social Security payroll tax cut and unemployment benefits	NO
Ease securities rules to expand small-business access to capital	YES
Extend for one year subsidized student loan interest rates financed by a cut in health care spending	YES
Cite Attorney General Eric H. Holder Jr. for contempt of Congress	YES
Create a visa program for foreign graduates in high-tech fields	YES
Extend most Bush-era income tax rates while allowing rates for top-bracket earners to rise (Jan. 1, 2013)	NO
2011	
Strike funding for F-35 alternative engine	YES
Prevent EPA from regulating greenhouse gas emissions to address climate change	YES
Extend certain provisions of Patriot Act for four years	YES
Declare opposition to use of ground troops in Libya	YES
Overhaul patent law	YES
Pass compromise debt limit increase plan and establish future spending limits	YES
Allow consideration of measures to implement three trade agreements	YES

CQ Vote Studies

	PARTY UNITY		PRESIDENTIAL SUPPORT	
	SUPPORT	OPPOSE	SUPPORT	OPPOSE
2012	88%	12%	13%	87%
2011	90%	10%	23%	77%

Interest Groups

	AFL-CIO	ADA	CCUS	ACU
2012	18%	5%	100%	68%
2011	59%	30%	88%	64%

West Virginia 1

North — Parkersburg, Wheeling, Morgantown

The 1st District includes most of West Virginia's northern border, a collection of small cities and rural communities wedged between Ohio, Pennsylvania and Maryland. As in the rest of the state, the district relies on energy, mining and extraction industries, especially in coal. Plastics and polymers are staples of the region's manufacturing industry, while the steel sector remains important — particularly in northern cities such as Wheeling, a short commute from Pittsburgh — and hopes to get a boost from new energy initiatives in the state.

West Virginia is the nation's second-largest coal-producing state: Every county in the 1st District produces the energy resource, and Marion, Marshall and Monongalia are among the top statewide. Environmental regulations affecting the industry are hot-button issues here.

Rail yards and shipping docks on the Ohio River make the northern panhandle a trade hub. Parkersburg, in the southwestern corner of the district and its largest city, has worked with Ohio following a natural gas boom near the Mid-Ohio Valley. Recent development in shale extraction has drawn energy conglomerates back to the state's northwest, with the promise of expanded gas fields and plants offering a boost to local industries, including steel, even as statewide poverty rates remain high.

Morgantown is one of several cities to ban gas drilling, despite criticism from pro-business groups. The hilly city hosts West Virginia University, which contracts with the FBI for biometric identification programs. The FBI' Criminal Justice Information Services Division is a top employer in Clarksburg. NASA and Lockheed Martin also maintain labs in the area, as do smaller firms of the state's technology corridor along Interstate 79.

The district favors conservative candidates and will split party tickets. Monongalia and adjacent Marion were the district's only two counties to favor Barack Obama in 2008 — neither backed him in 2012.

Major Industry
Technology, coal and steel, manufacturing, energy, government

Cities
Parkersburg, Morgantown, Wheeling, Weirton

Notable
Confederate Gen. Thomas "Stonewall" Jackson was born in Clarksburg.

Rep. Shelley Moore Capito (R)

Capitol Office
225-2711
capito.house.gov
2366 Rayburn Bldg. 20515-4802; fax 225-7856

Committees
Financial Services
(Financial Institutions & Consumer Credit - Chairwoman)
Transportation & Infrastructure

Residence
Charleston

Born
Nov. 26, 1953; Glen Dale, W.Va.

Religion
Presbyterian

Family
Husband, Charles L. Capito Jr.; three children

Education
Duke U., B.S. 1975 (zoology); U. of Virginia, M.Ed. 1976 (counselor education)

Career
University system information center director; college career counselor

Political Highlights
W.Va. House, 1997-2001

ELECTION RESULTS

2012 GENERAL		
Shelley Moore Capito (R)	158,206	69.8%
Howard Swint (D)	68,560	30.2%
2012 PRIMARY		
Shelley Moore Capito (R)	35,088	83.0%
Jonathan Miller (R)	4,711	11.1%
Michael Davis (R)	2,495	5.9%
2010 GENERAL		
Shelley Moore Capito (R)	126,814	68.5%
Virginia Lynch Graf (D)	55,001	29.7%
Phil Hudok (CNSTP)	3,431	1.8%

Previous Winning Percentages
2008 (57%); 2006 (57%); 2004 (57%); 2002 (60%); 2000 (48%)

Elected 2000; 7th term

Capito has finally jumped into a statewide campaign: She hopes to become her state's next senator. In building to her decision, she has been a model of West Virginia Republicanism — moderation with a focus on coal and transportation — while scrutinizing the implementation of the 2010 financial regulatory overhaul.

Political observers have anticipated her campaign for years, given her popularity and family history. Capito (CAP-ih-toe) was 3 when her father, Arch A. Moore Jr., began a 12-year run in the House; he later served three non-consecutive terms as governor. Political functions and speeches were part of her childhood (she attended John F. Kennedy's funeral with her dad), and she credits Moore with teaching her a great lesson about the job: "To be able to compartmentalize. Leave it at the end of the day."

She's less vitriolic than many pols. When Missouri Democrat Emanuel Cleaver II founded the Civility Caucus in 2006, Capito became the second member. She has criticized colleagues who take intraparty disputes public. "I'd rather have us air our dirty laundry behind closed doors," she said. As a member of the moderate Main Street Partnership, she sometimes sides with Democrats on labor, trade and health care issues.

When Capito was a member of the state House of Delegates, she sat on its banking committee. In the U.S. House, she has been on the Financial Services Committee since its creation in 2001. Formerly the top Republican on the housing panel, she now chairs the Subcommittee on Financial Institutions and Consumer Credit. Her stated approach: "Always an eye towards getting the economy moving and getting government out of the way."

During the 112th Congress (2011-12), she avoided talk of repealing the 2010 overhaul, which is known as Dodd-Frank. Instead, she studied provisions of the law that might gum up markets or unintentionally restrict capital flow.

Capito wants enhanced oversight of the new Consumer Financial Protection Bureau, which she has called a "layered-on bureaucracy" duplicating the work of other agencies. Her panel produced a package of changes: making it easier to overturn CFPB regulations; transferring governing power to a five-person board instead of a director; and (based on a Capito bill) requiring a Senate-confirmed director before the bureau could start work.

"Nothing in this package weakens or changes the ability of the CFPB to make rules and regulations for consumer protection," she said when the House passed the bill in July 2011.

Working with Democrat Carolyn B. Maloney of New York, her ranking member at the time, she produced a bill to codify a process for banks to appeal federal regulators' examination reports — a concern of community banks fretting over Dodd-Frank compliance. The bill was reintroduced in 2013. Capito used hearings to suggest that Dodd-Frank and capitalization requirements are crushing smaller banking institutions.

Federal bailouts are also on her mind. Capito voted against a $700 billion rescue package for the ailing financial services sector in 2008, saying it lacked adequate protection for taxpayers. She has been in the vanguard of lawmakers warning of dwindling reserves at the Federal Housing Administration, which took a larger role in the mortgage market after the federal takeover of housing giants Fannie Mae and Freddie Mac. She'd like to see the federal role in the housing sector restored to what she views as its original intent: "to get money toward the moderate- and low-income folks."

Capito's stances on energy and transportation are integral to her statewide appeal. She co-founded the Coal Caucus, and she has a sharper edge when accusing the Obama administration of trying to "destroy coal" through regulation. "For decades, the EPA has successfully cleaned up our air and streams without slowing down the economy," she wrote in 2011. "Now, at the worst possible time, the EPA is advancing an extreme agenda that threatens millions of jobs across America."

Capito opposes EPA regulation of greenhouse gases, and she calls for more economic analysis before EPA regulations kick in. Three coal-fired power plants in her district announced closures in 2011, citing the cost of complying with new EPA rules; businesses need more time to adapt than EPA allows, Capito said. "Everybody knows you work better with a deadline, but I'm wondering, do they ever consult with industry when they make these timelines."

Her seat on the Transportation and Infrastructure Committee gives her some oversight of EPA's enforcement of the Clean Water Act, which affects mountaintop removal mining. She also used it in 2012 to promote a GOP plan to tie transportation funding to energy. Capito introduced a bill to dedicate money from oil and gas leases toward infrastructure development, and she backed a 2012 version of a highway bill with a similar plan. It was not included in the two-year highway bill enacted later that year.

But Capito was on the conference committee that finalized that two-year reauthorization, and she voted for it. She was particularly pleased with its provisions to speed up environmental reviews of proposed infrastructure projects. She supports local discretion in spending federal transportation dollars.

Her family comes from Glen Dale, a small town that was home to the Marx toy company. Her parents still live there. Her father's career ended in 1990 when he pleaded guilty to federal charges that included taking illegal contributions for his gubernatorial campaign. He served three years in prison and eventually paid a $750,000 settlement to the state.

Capito went to Duke University planning to become a doctor. (All three of her children are Blue Devils.) She found hospital work not to her liking; instead she wound up as a college counselor and administrator. Capito was a governor's daughter when she met her husband on a blind date — he now works as a financial services executive. She waited until her youngest child was 11 to enter politics, winning a seat in the House of Delegates in 1996.

She won an open U.S. House seat in 2000, narrowly beating wealthy class-action attorney Jim Humphreys. The 2002 rematch was the most expensive House campaign that year, but she won by 20 points.

Capito won a seventh term and almost immediately put her name in for the 2014 Senate race. Soon after, incumbent Democrat Jay Rockefeller announced that he was retiring. Some conservative groups panned Capito's legislative record and vowed to search for a challenger to back in the GOP primary.

Key Votes

2012	
Extend a Social Security payroll tax cut and unemployment benefits	YES
Ease securities rules to expand small-business access to capital	YES
Extend for one year subsidized student loan interest rates financed by a cut in health care spending	YES
Cite Attorney General Eric H. Holder Jr. for contempt of Congress	YES
Create a visa program for foreign graduates in high-tech fields	YES
Extend most Bush-era income tax rates while allowing rates for top-bracket earners to rise (Jan. 1, 2013)	NO
2011	
Strike funding for F-35 alternative engine	YES
Prevent EPA from regulating greenhouse gas emissions to address climate change	YES
Extend certain provisions of Patriot Act for four years	YES
Declare opposition to use of ground troops in Libya	YES
Overhaul patent law	YES
Pass compromise debt limit increase plan and establish future spending limits	YES
Allow consideration of measures to implement three trade agreements	YES

CQ Vote Studies

	PARTY UNITY		PRESIDENTIAL SUPPORT	
	SUPPORT	OPPOSE	SUPPORT	OPPOSE
2012	88%	12%	15%	85%
2011	91%	9%	24%	76%
2010	86%	14%	36%	64%
2009	76%	24%	44%	56%
2008	82%	18%	46%	54%

Interest Groups

	AFL-CIO	ADA	CCUS	ACU
2012	38%	0%	100%	68%
2011	31%	20%	100%	60%
2010	8%	10%	100%	82%
2009	40%	30%	93%	75%
2008	73%	60%	78%	48%

West Virginia 2

Central — Charleston, Eastern Panhandle

Taking in a strip of central West Virginia reaching from the western Ohio River border to the eastern panhandle, the 2nd is the fastest-growing and most economically resilient district in the state. It includes the capital city of Charleston, rural mining communities surrounding it and booming panhandle towns benefiting from proximity to Washington, D.C., Baltimore and other major markets.

Coal mining is especially big in the extraction-dependent counties northwest of Charleston and the Kanawha Valley, but Kanawha County itself — the state's most populous county and home to more than 30 percent of the district's residents — has been insulated from the vagaries of the coal industry due to its location as a transportation and distribution hub served by well-connected interstates and waterways. Chemical companies have been a major driver in the region, with firms such as Union Carbide, DuPont and Monsanto making up half of Kanawha's manufacturing employment — although the industry has suffered layoffs through the economic crisis.

About an hour's drive from Washington, D.C., the tip of the eastern panhandle — Martinsburg and surrounding Berkeley and Jefferson counties — is the fastest-growing region in the state, thanks in part to government employers. Large data centers for the U.S. Coast Guard and other federal agencies provide thousands of jobs in Berkeley County, which is also home to numerous distribution centers, construction materials plants and printing centers. As a result, Berkeley also has some of the lowest poverty rates in this high-poverty state.

Redistricting following the 2010 census moved Mason County out of the 2nd — the only change statewide. The 2nd gave Republican Mitt Romney a comfortable 60 percent in the 2012 presidential election, but it was his lowest among all three of the districts.

Major Industry

Chemicals, manufacturing, coal, government, distribution

Cities

Charleston, Martinsburg

Notable

The Martinsburg branch of the Bureau of Alcohol, Tobacco and Firearms includes the federal licensing center for explosives and firearms, as well as the National Tracing Center.

Rep. Nick J. Rahall II (D)

Capitol Office
225-3452
rahall.house.gov
2307 Rayburn Bldg. 20515-4803; fax 225-9061

Committees
Transportation & Infrastructure - Ranking Member

Residence
Beckley

Born
May 20, 1949; Beckley, W.Va.

Religion
Presbyterian

Family
Wife, Melinda Rahall; three children

Education
Duke U., B.A. 1971 (political science); George Washington U., attended 1972 (graduate studies)

Career
Broadcasting executive; travel agent; congressional aide

Political Highlights
No previous office

ELECTION RESULTS

2012 GENERAL		
Nick J. Rahall II (D)	108,199	54.0%
Rick Snuffer (R)	92,238	46.0%
2012 PRIMARY		
Nick J. Rahall II (D)		unopposed
2010 GENERAL		
Nick J. Rahall II (D)	83,636	56.0%
Elliott E. "Spike" Maynard (R)	65,611	44.0%

Previous Winning Percentages
2008 (67%); 2006 (69%); 2004 (65%); 2002 (70%); 2000 (91%); 1998 (87%); 1996 (100%); 1994 (64%); 1992 (66%); 1990 (52%); 1988 (61%); 1986 (71%); 1984 (67%); 1982 (81%); 1980 (77%); 1978 (100%); 1976 (46%)

Elected 1976; 19th term

Rahall is known at home as "Nicky Joe," and he has a sanguine, good-old-boy style. His perennial goals are protecting the coal industry and steering federal resources to West Virginia. He has been resilient over the years, and his challenges have multiplied as of late — the Obama administration is not popular in his state, and he has some association with its agenda as the top Democrat on the Transportation and Infrastructure Committee.

Rahall (RAY-haul) learned his trade from the late Democratic Sen. Robert C. Byrd. He was an aide to Byrd in the 1970s before joining him in Congress, and he has said that he was closer to Byrd than any man other than his own father. His office is filled with coal paraphernalia (he and Byrd hail from the state's biggest coal-producing region) and pictures of the two men together.

Byrd's skill at sending federal largesse to his state was legendary, and Rahall does his best to emulate his mentor. However, the 112th Congress (2011-12) found him deprived of the best tools for that job. The Republican majority in the House instituted a ban on earmarks, the provisions in bills that direct funding to specific projects in a lawmaker's district.

Earmarks were particularly common on bills from the Transportation and Infrastructure Committee, where Rahall became the ranking member in 2011. The 2005 reauthorization of surface transportation programs was famously greased through Congress with more than 6,000 such provisions.

Senior members of both parties complained that the lack of earmarks had turned normally bipartisan bills into tough policy slogs. Rahall was among the first to speak up, saying lawmakers "have a legitimate insight, deciding local projects that are best for our people, rather than leaving them to bureaucracies of presidents of the United States, regardless of who occupies that office."

Rahall has worked to cajole the bureaucracy of the Obama administration into pointing grants the way of his constituents, but the strain on the Transportation Committee has been noticeable.

Republican Chairman John L. Mica of Florida declined Rahall's request to petition GOP leaders for lifting the earmark ban for a 2012 reauthorization of surface transportation programs. Rahall said that House Democrats were largely shut out of the process of writing the five-year bill the GOP introduced, and that it "would lead America's transportation programs down a reckless path toward bankruptcy" — he opposed the Republican plan to feed the Highway Trust Fund with revenue from expanded oil and gas leases.

Rahall supported a two-year compromise version, including provisions to speed up permitting and reviews of infrastructure projects; he also acceded to the addition of a provision, later removed before enactment, to block the EPA from regulating coal ash, a byproduct of coal combustion, as hazardous waste. The law expires in 2014, so work will resume in the 113th Congress (2013-14). Mica, however, has been replaced by Pennsylvania Republican Bill Shuster.

In 2011, Rahall led Democrats through a bruising battle with the GOP over a reauthorization of the Federal Aviation Administration — one that included a politically damaging shutdown of the FAA during the summer travel season. Democrats objected to a provision that would reverse a National Mediation Board rule change that airlines complained would give unions an upper hand in organizing efforts. As with the highway bill, Rahall held out for a compromise version worked out in early 2012 by House and Senate leaders; he was one of just 24 House Democrats to vote in favor.

Rahall chaired the Natural Resources Committee in the 110th and 111th Congresses (2007-10). He used his seat on that committee to defend the coal industry, but he also curried favor with environmentalists by pushing for conservation measures and trying to reduce tax advantages for oil producers.

He opposed a 2007 energy bill that increased fuel economy standards for new automobiles — only three other House Democrats joined him — partly because the bill didn't include provisions to curtail oil company subsidies or to promote experimental clean-coal technology. He opposes comprehensive climate change legislation, and specifically cap-and-trade systems to regulate greenhouse gas emissions. In 2011, Rahall voted for GOP-authored legislation to prohibit the EPA from regulating greenhouse gases.

One area where he will allow an increased regulatory burden is mine safety. Rahall supported legislation in 2010 and 2011 to toughen safety laws, after a 2010 explosion in the Upper Big Branch mine killed 29 people. He and Sen. Jay Rockefeller, a fellow West Virginia Democrat, continue to push for its passage.

Rahall's ties to Byrd and adherence to the mores of his district have helped him survive as a Democrat in an increasingly conservative part of the country. He deviates sharply from his fellow Democrats on many social issues. Following earlier anti-abortion votes in his career, he joined with House Republicans in 2011 to pass a bill blocking federal funding of abortion services. He says he is against "amnesty" for illegal immigrants already in the country.

The grandson of Lebanese immigrants, Rahall is among the few outspoken House critics of U.S. policy toward Israel. He encourages closer ties with Arab countries and was one of eight lawmakers who opposed a resolution expressing unconditional support for Israel in its 2006 conflict with the Lebanese terrorist group Hezbollah.

Unlike Byrd, Rahall grew up affluent. His paternal grandfather peddled goods in coal camps. Rahall's father ran a five-and-dime store and later a clothing shop, which enabled him to invest in radio and TV stations.

Rahall graduated from Duke University. After working for Byrd, he returned to his family's broadcasting business. He ran for the House in 1976, taking advantage of Democratic Rep. Ken Hechler's decision to run for governor. Rahall spent family money on a media campaign his foes couldn't match and won the nomination with 37 percent of the vote. Hechler, who lost his primary, mounted a write-in drive to keep his seat, but Rahall prevailed.

Rahall has had some fits and starts: gambling debts in the mid-1980s; a guilty plea to an alcohol-related reckless driving charge in 1988; bad publicity surrounding trips taken at lobbyists' expense in the 1990s; and questions about his professional relationship with his sister, who is a registered lobbyist.

Republicans have been enthusiastic about toppling him in recent years, capitalizing on Obama's unpopularity. After winning by 12 points in 2010, he saw that margin shrink to 8 points against Rick Snuffer in 2012. Rahall has opted against a Senate bid for 2014, and Republicans are targeting him again.

Key Votes

2012	
Extend a Social Security payroll tax cut and unemployment benefits	YES
Ease securities rules to expand small-business access to capital	YES
Extend for one year subsidized student loan interest rates financed by a cut in health care spending	NO
Cite Attorney General Eric H. Holder Jr. for contempt of Congress	YES
Create a visa program for foreign graduates in high-tech fields	NO
Extend most Bush-era income tax rates while allowing rates for top-bracket earners to rise (Jan. 1, 2013)	YES
2011	
Strike funding for F-35 alternative engine	NO
Prevent EPA from regulating greenhouse gas emissions to address climate change	YES
Extend certain provisions of Patriot Act for four years	YES
Declare opposition to use of ground troops in Libya	NO
Overhaul patent law	YES
Pass compromise debt limit increase plan and establish future spending limits	YES
Allow consideration of measures to implement three trade agreements	NO

CQ Vote Studies

	PARTY UNITY		PRESIDENTIAL SUPPORT	
	SUPPORT	OPPOSE	SUPPORT	OPPOSE
2012	81%	19%	64%	36%
2011	71%	29%	65%	35%
2010	94%	6%	88%	12%
2009	97%	3%	94%	6%
2008	97%	3%	18%	82%

Interest Groups

	AFL-CIO	ADA	CCUS	ACU
2012	86%	70%	33%	24%
2011	07%	75%	00%	24%
2010	93%	60%	25%	8%
2009	95%	85%	53%	12%
2008	93%	85%	67%	8%

West Virginia 3

South — Huntington, Beckley

Coal has long been king in the largely rural 3rd District, which grabs the state's southern counties and borders Ohio, Kentucky and Virginia. It remains the top coal-producing region in the state, where miners' union matters and safety regulations are important issues. But the decline of the coal industry and the manufacturing plants it once powered, and decades of high unemployment and persistent poverty, have taken their toll. The 3rd was the only district in the state to have a decrease in population between 2000 and 2010, as residents abandoned the area. The district overall is also aging, with 17 percent of its population over the age of 65.

Huntington, on the district's western edge, is the second-largest city in the state. With a strong manufacturing tradition, the city — along with nearby communities in Ohio and Kentucky — has been hurt by steel industry dips. Metal works, shipping and distribution centers as well as health care facilities round out the economy. Huntington also hosts Marshall University.

At the district's eastern edge are lush forest parklands and the Appalachian Mountains, which attract outdoor tourism such as skiing and white-water rafting. The Greenbrier, in White Sulphur Springs, is a luxury resort that hosts golf tournaments, conferences and congressional retreats, and stands in stark contrast to much of the poverty surrounding its grounds. All of the district's counties have poverty rates of nearly 20 percent or more; none has been harder hit than McDowell, the southernmost county in the state, where more than one third of all residents live in poverty and the population declined by nearly 20 percent since 2000.

The 3rd has long favored conservative Democrats for Congress but has increasingly supported Republican presidential candidates. The district gave Republican John McCain 56 percent of its vote in the 2008 presidential race but four years later gave Mitt Romney 65 percent; in 2012, all of the district's counties supported Democrat Joe Manchin III for the U.S. Senate.

Major Industry
Coal, timber, manufacturing, distribution, tourism

Cities
Huntington, Beckley

Notable
The Port of Huntington Tri-State is the nation's largest inland shipping port; the annual Webster County Woodchopping Festival brings lumberjacks from around the world.

WISCONSIN

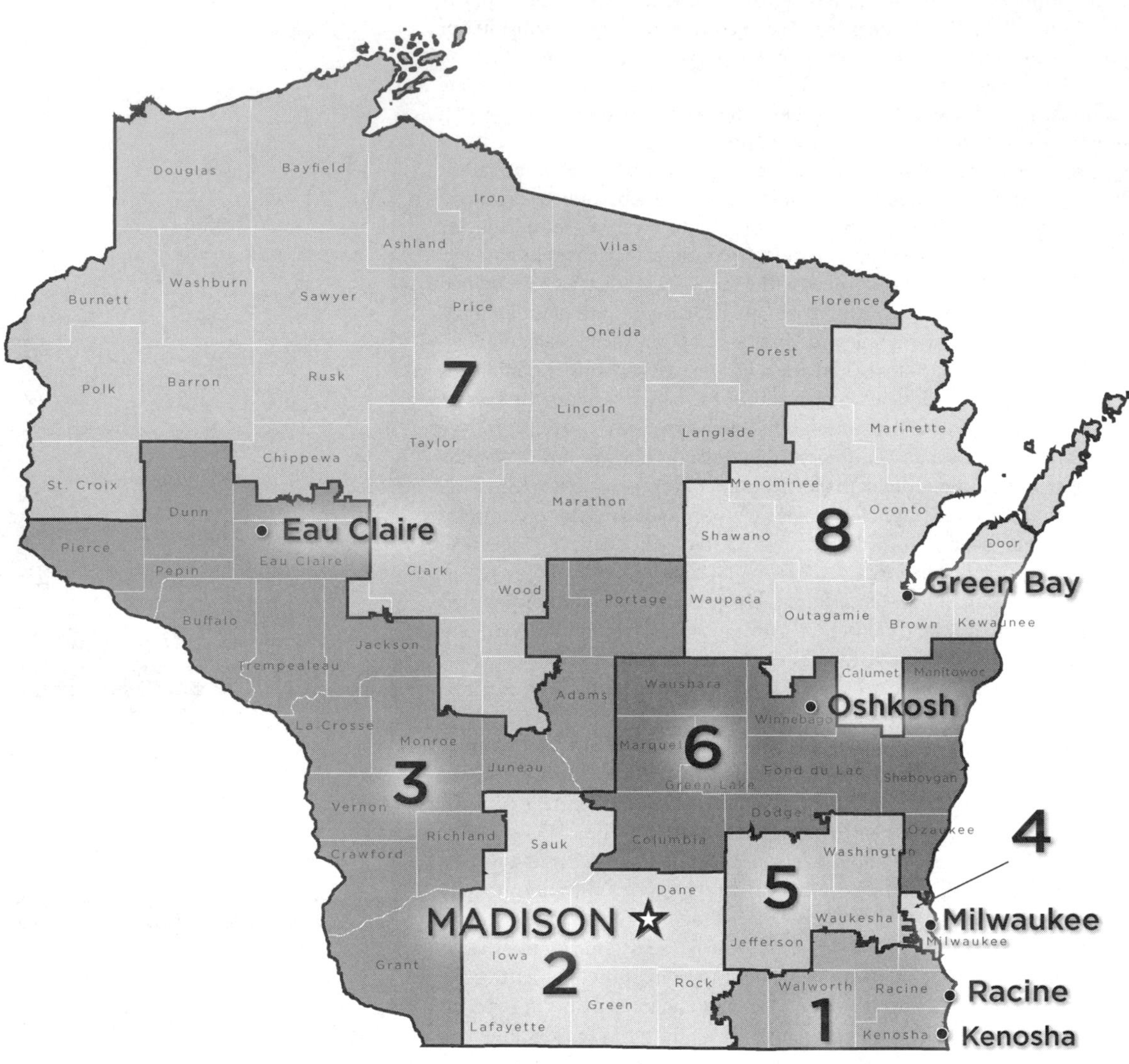

Douglas
Bayfield
Iron
Ashland
Vilas
Burnett
Washburn
Sawyer
Price
Florence
Oneida
Forest
Polk
Barron
Rusk
7
Lincoln
Marinette
Langlade
Taylor
Chippewa
St. Croix
Menominee
Marathon
Oconto
Dunn
Eau Claire
8
Shawano
Door
Pierce
Eau Claire
Pepin
Clark
Green Bay
Wood
Portage
Waupaca
Outagamie
Brown
Kewaunee
Buffalo
Jackson
Trempealeau
Calumet
Manitowoc
Adams
Waushara
Oshkosh
Winnebago
La Crosse
Monroe
Marquette
6
Juneau
Fond du Lac
Sheboygan
3
Green Lake
Vernon
Dodge
Ozaukee
4
Richland
Sauk
Columbia
Washington
Crawford
Dane
5
MADISON
Waukesha
Milwaukee
Milwaukee
Jefferson
Iowa
Grant
2
Rock
Walworth
Racine
Racine
Green
1
Lafayette
Kenosha
Kenosha

Gov. Scott Walker (R)

First elected: 2010
Length of term: 4 years
Term expires: 1/15
Salary: $144,425
Phone: (608) 266-1212
Residence: Wauwatosa
Born: Nov. 2, 1967; Colorado Springs, Colo.
Religion: Non-denominational Christian
Family: Wife, Tonette Walker; two children
Education: Marquette U., attended 1986-90
Career: Humanitarian relief nonprofit fundraiser
Political highlights: Wis. House, 1993-2002; Milwaukee County executive, 2002-10

ELECTION RESULTS

2010 GENERAL

Scott Walker (R)	1,128,941	52.3%
Tom Barrett (D)	1,004,303	46.5%

Lt. Gov. Rebecca Kleefisch (R)

First elected: 2010
Length of term: 4 years
Term expires: 1/15
Salary: $76,262
Phone: (608) 266-3516

LEGISLATURE

Legislature: 10 floor periods of varying lengths over a 2-year session
Senate: 33 members, 4-year terms
2013 ratios: 18 R, 15 D; 24 men, 9 women
Salary: $49,943
Phone: (608) 266-2517
Assembly: 99 members, 2-year terms
2013 ratios: 60 R, 39 D; 75 men, 24 women
Salary: $49,943
Phone: (608) 266-1501

TERM LIMITS

Governor: No
Senate: No
House: No

URBAN STATISTICS

CITY	POPULATION
Milwaukee	594,833
Madison	233,209
Green Bay	104,057
Kenosha	99,218
Racine	78,860

REGISTERED VOTERS

Voters do not register by party.

POPULATION

2010 population	5,686,986
2000 population	5,363,675
1990 population	4,891,769
Percent change (2000-2010)	+6.0%
Rank among states (2010)	20
Median age	37.8
Born in state	71.9%
Foreign born	4.3
Violent crime rate	257/100,000
Poverty level	12.4%
Federal workers	37,022
Military	2,046

ELECTIONS

STATE ELECTION OFFICIAL
(608) 266-8005
DEMOCRATIC PARTY
(608) 255-5172
REPUBLICAN PARTY
(608) 257-4765

MISCELLANEOUS

Web: www.wisconsin.gov
Capital: Madison

U.S. CONGRESS

Senate: 1 Democrat, 1 Republican
House: 5 Republicans, 3 Democrats

STATISTICS BY DISTRICT

District	2012 Vote for President		2008 Vote for President										
	Obama	Romney	Obama	McCain	Black	Asian	Hispanic	Median Income	Over 64	Under 20	College Education	Rural	Sq. Miles
1	47%	52%	51%	48%	6%	2%	9%	$56,022	13%	27%	26%	16%	1,728
2	68	30	70	29	4	4	6	56,089	12	26	38	23	4,537
3	55	44	59	39	1	2	2	46,448	15	26	23	50	11,112
4	75	24	74	25	34	3	16	35,729	10	29	26	0	128
5	38	61	42	57	2	2	5	61,272	15	26	33	15	1,891
6	46	53	49.4	49.2	2	2	4	51,995	15	25	24	35	4,918
7	48	51	53	45	1	1	2	45,868	17	25	20	72	23,037
8	48	51	54	45	1	2	4	51,914	14	26	23	42	6,807
STATE	**53**	**46**	**56**	**42**	**6**	**2**	**6**	**50,395**	**14**	**26**	**26**	**34**	**54,158**
U.S.	**51**	**47**	**53**	**46**	**12**	**5**	**17**	**50,052**	**13**	**27**	**29**	**21**	**3,531,905**

Sen. Ron Johnson (R)

Capitol Office
224-5323
ronjohnson.senate.gov
328 Hart Bldg. 20510-4904; fax 228-6965

Committees
Budget
Commerce, Science & Transportation
Foreign Relations
Homeland Security & Governmental Affairs
Small Business & Entrepreneurship

Residence
Oshkosh

Born
April 8, 1955; Mankato, Minn.

Religion
Lutheran

Family
Wife, Jane Johnson; three children

Education
U. of Minnesota, B.S. 1977 (accounting), attended 1977-79 (business administration)

Career
Plastics manufacturing company owner; shipping supply company machine operator; accountant

Political Highlights
No previous office

ELECTION RESULTS

2010 GENERAL		
Ron Johnson (R)	1,125,999	51.9%
Russ Feingold (D)	1,020,958	47.0%
Rob Taylor (CNSTP)	23,473	1.1%
2010 PRIMARY		
Ron Johnson (R)	504,644	84.8%
Dave Bond Westlake IV (R)	61,633	10.4%
Stephen M. Finn (R)	28,929	4.9%

Elected 2010; 1st term

Johnson believes that the federal government, at its current size, is a drag on economic growth. His attempts to do something about it have thus far been frustrated by the working environment of the Senate, and he has sought non-legislative ways to spread his message of fiscal conservatism.

Born and raised in Minnesota, Johnson earned money as a kid by mowing lawns, shoveling snow from driveways, delivering newspapers, baling hay and working as a golf caddie. In his teen years, he was a dishwasher and night manager at a Walgreen's Grill. To earn extra money, his family worked in its basement to produce soap balls to sell to a local bath factory, according to a profile in the Milwaukee Journal Sentinel.

Johnson lived at home and worked full time while attending the University of Minnesota. He says he was able to graduate from college debt free, with $7,000 in the bank. "The greatest compliment my parents would ever give somebody is, 'That person is a really hard worker.' It's a part of who you are," he told the Journal Sentinel.

He worked as an accountant for Josten's, which sells school rings and yearbooks, then moved to Oshkosh in 1979 to help launch a plastics manufacturing firm with his brother-in-law. The company, Pacur, produces a specialty plastic used in medical-device packaging and high-tech printing applications. That business made him very wealthy, and he used part of his wealth to fund his successful 2010 Senate campaign — his first bid for public office. In that campaign, Johnson vowed to reduce federal spending and spur economic growth. He was criticized by his opponent, Democratic Sen. Russ Feingold, for offering few specific plans to do so. "I don't think this election is about details," Johnson once responded, according to the St. Paul Pioneer Press.

His first two years in the Senate weren't entirely about details, either; he offered little in the way of bills or amendments. But his voting record placed him among the most fiscally conservative senators. The American Conservative Union gave Johnson a perfect rating on its voting scorecard, and he was close to perfect on the scorecard of the Club for Growth, an influential anti-tax organization. (In contrast, Wisconsin chose one of the most liberal House members, Democrat Tammy Baldwin, to be the state's junior senator in the 2012 elections.)

During the 112th Congress (2011-12), Johnson was also a conservative island on the Appropriations Committee, often casting the only vote in opposition to spending bills as they were marked up. He didn't return to the panel in the 113th Congress (2013-14), and he told the Journal Sentinel that it was a voluntary departure, as he was fed up with the "dysfunction" on the committee. He instead took seats on the Commerce, Science and Transportation Committee, the Foreign Relations Committee and the Small Business and Entrepreneurship Committee.

Some Republican Senate aides have complained that Johnson is not particularly invested in building up working relationships with all his colleagues. But he clearly has the ear of fiscal conservatives. Late in 2011, he narrowly lost a bid for the No. 5 slot on the Senate GOP leadership team. Running against Roy Blunt of Missouri for vice chairman of the GOP Conference, Johnson got 22 votes in the secret ballot, to Blunt's 25. "I don't think anybody thought I would be able to get 22 votes, so that's a pretty encouraging sign," Johnson told Oshkosh's WOSH-AM. A few months after that election, Johnson openly turned the focus of his Senate office toward political messaging and communicating the GOP agenda heading into the 2012 elections. He is a frequent guest on TV news programs.

Despite departing Appropriations, Johnson still serves on committees that let him address federal spending. He has returned to the Budget Committee. And he is the top Republican on the Homeland Security and Governmental Affairs Subcommittee on Financial and Contracting Oversight.

Johnson often questions the government's accounting and business practices. In 2011, he challenged officials about whether the federal government has been too quick to put itself on the hook for recovery costs from damaging events that are not truly disasters.

He also has questioned how well the government can negotiate with unions. "If unions go too far, they bargain for too-high wages, too-high benefits. They put their business at risk, and if the business goes out of business, they lose their jobs. So you have that market discipline," Johnson said at an October 2011 hearing. "That same discipline does not operate within the public sector unions." He introduced a bill to shrink the federal workforce by 10 percent through attrition by 2015.

And he wants to bring entitlement programs — the bulk of federal spending — into the discretionary budget. Deficits would shrink, he said at a 2011 hearing, "if we were appropriating all the entitlements ... and actually tweaking the programs like businesses have to do with their health care. Every year you have to maybe increase your deductibles to make it affordable."

Johnson also signed on as a co-sponsor of legislation by Tennessee Republican Bob Corker and Missouri Democrat Claire McCaskill that would limit all discretionary and mandatory spending to a percentage of the gross domestic product.

The conservative Weekly Standard magazine dubbed Johnson an "Ayn Rand-loving, pro-life Lutheran," and he sticks with the conservative GOP agenda. He opposes abortion and regulations on gun ownership. He wants to undo the 2010 health care overhaul and cut federal regulations; he introduced a 2011 bill that would block major federal regulatory action unless the national unemployment rate is at or below 7.7 percent.

He banded with Democrats, however, on at least one regional issue. Joining Minnesota Democrats Amy Klobuchar and Al Franken, Johnson in 2011 pushed for Congress to support a new St. Croix River bridge by supporting an exemption from federal law protecting wild and scenic rivers. Johnson argued that the new bridge would improve traffic flows and encourage economic development. He also noted how delays in the project have swelled its projected cost. "When this was proposed back in 1992, the original construction cost would have been $80 million," Johnson said at a hearing. "Today it is close to $700 million." President Barack Obama signed a bill granting the exemption in March 2012.

He also is willing to consider creating a path to citizenship or legal status for illegal immigrants already in the country. Johnson opposes "amnesty," but "if you're asking people to pay a fine, it's not amnesty," he told Patch Media in 2013.

In the autumn of 2009, Johnson was invited to speak to a group of tea party activists in Oshkosh. His scathing dissertation on the health care overhaul inspired some of the participants to urge him to get into the Senate race. He later swept to the GOP nomination, winning both the state party endorsement at a May convention and the support of tea party activists. He easily captured the nomination in the September primary, winning 85 percent of the vote over small-business owner Dave Bond Westlake, and became the challenger to Feingold, a three-term senator.

Despite Johnson's "rich guy" reputation and lack of experience and Feingold's career-long advocacy for stricter campaign regulations, the incumbent outraised and outspent Johnson about 3-to-2, according to the Center for Responsive Politics. About two-thirds of Johnson's money was his own. On election night, Johnson topped Feingold by more than 100,000 votes.

Key Votes

2012	
Prohibit health insurance plans from denying coverage based on the sponsor's religious beliefs	NO
Require approval of the Keystone XL oil pipeline	YES
Ease securities rules to expand small-business access to capital	YES
Reauthorize farm and nutrition programs for five years	NO
Limit debate on a bill that would create private-sector cybersecurity standards	NO
Consent to ratification of a treaty setting global standard for the treatment of people with disabilities	NO
Provide $60.4 billion in disaster relief following Superstorm Sandy	NO
Extend most Bush-era income tax rates while allowing rates for top-bracket earners to rise (Jan. 1, 2013)	YES
2011	
Prevent EPA from regulating greenhouse gas emissions to address climate change	YES
Extend certain provisions of Patriot Act for four years	YES
Clear compromise debt limit increase plan and establish future spending limits	NO
Overhaul patent law	NO
Implement Colombia free trade agreement	YES
Limit debate on confirmation of Caitlin J. Halligan to D.C. Circuit Court of Appeals	NO
Extend payroll tax cut and unemployment benefits for two months	NO

CQ Vote Studies

	PARTY UNITY		PRESIDENTIAL SUPPORT	
	SUPPORT	OPPOSE	SUPPORT	OPPOSE
2012	95%	5%	47%	53%
2011	99%	1%	51%	49%

Interest Groups

	AFL-CIO	ADA	CCUS	ACU
2012	0%	0%	75%	100%
2011	11%	5%	73%	100%

Sen. Tammy Baldwin (D)

Capitol Office
224-5653
baldwin.senate.gov
717 Hart Bldg. 20510; fax 224-9787

Committees
Budget
Health, Education, Labor & Pensions
Homeland Security & Governmental Affairs
Special Aging

Residence
Madison

Born
Feb. 11, 1962; Madison, Wis.

Religion
Unspecified

Family
Dissolved partnership

Education
Smith College, A.B. 1984 (math & government); U. of Wisconsin, J.D. 1989

Career
Lawyer

Political Highlights
Madison City Council, 1986; Dane County Board of Supervisors, 1986-94; Wis. Assembly, 1993-99; U.S. House, 1999-2013

ELECTION RESULTS

2012 GENERAL		
Tammy Baldwin (D)	1,547,104	51.4%
Tommy G. Thompson (R)	1,380,126	45.9%
Joseph Kexel (LIBERT)	62,240	2.1%
2012 PRIMARY		
Tammy Baldwin (D)		unopposed
2010 GENERAL		
Tammy Baldwin (D)	191,164	61.8%
Chad Lee (R)	118,099	38.2%
2010 PRIMARY		
Tammy Baldwin (D)		unopposed

Previous Winning Percentages
2008 House Election (69%); 2006 House Election (63%); 2004 House Election (63%); 2002 House Election (66%); 2000 House Election (51%); 1998 House Election (52%)

Elected 2012; 1st term

The moment she was sworn in, Baldwin made history as the first openly gay senator. While she embraces the role of champion for gay rights, many of her priorities involve the difficult economy — especially as it pertains to Wisconsinites — and her established interests in health care policy and progressive ideals.

Baldwin was born in Madison, home to the University of Wisconsin and a hotbed of liberalism. She was raised by her maternal grandparents while her mother attended the university and participated in civil rights and anti-war demonstrations. Her grandfather was a biochemist, and her grandmother worked at the costume lab at the university theater.

Baldwin got into politics while she was in law school. In 1986, at age 24, she won election as a Dane County supervisor. She says she was inspired in part by the Democrats' nomination two years earlier of Geraldine A. Ferraro for vice president. After four terms as a county supervisor, in 1992 she was elected to the Wisconsin Assembly, where she served six years. That was followed by seven terms in the U.S. House, then her election to the Senate.

She sits on the Health, Education, Labor and Pensions Committee, which puts her front and center for the implementation of the health care overhaul enacted in 2010.

As a member of the House, Baldwin served on the Energy and Commerce Committee during the 111th Congress (2009-10), when that law was being written. Like other liberals, she supported inclusion of a "public option" — a government-run health insurance program that would compete with private insurers. (Her longtime goal is universal health coverage.) Congress and the White House ultimately scrapped that idea, but Baldwin helped press for provisions that survived, including one to allow children to stay on their parents' insurance until age 26.

In addition to overseeing implementation of the overhaul, Baldwin hopes to examine the increasing costs of health care, saying she wants to "push reforms in our health care delivery system in ways that we can make health care more affordable and higher-quality without cutting people's benefits." She has called Medicare not just a program, but "a promise."

The HELP Committee also handles workforce issues, and Baldwin has worked in the past to extend various employment protections to gay, lesbian, bisexual and transgender workers. She is a strong backer of Democratic efforts to codify more guarantees of equal wages between the genders.

She also sees a strong federal role in worker retraining programs — "our investments in education are the key to a strong economic future," she said — and she emphasizes her support of legislation to impose fines on China in response to the country's presumed currency manipulation. "Part of my focus will be on making sure that globally and internationally, there's a level playing field for U.S. manufacturing and Wisconsin manufacturing specifically," Baldwin said. "Wages have been stagnant in recent years, and people want to get back to the times when if you worked hard enough and played by the rules, you could get ahead."

She has a seat on the Budget Committee, and the fiscal 2014 blueprint adopted by the Senate included her amendment to propose a "deficit-neutral reserve fund to create regional manufacturing hubs that develop and deploy new manufacturing technologies," as she put it.

Baldwin also sits on the Homeland Security and Governmental Affairs Committee, and her subcommittees there focus on the governmental affairs side of the panel. Baldwin supports the extension of benefits to same-sex partners of federal employees.

Even though her sexual orientation was mostly a non-issue during the 2012 campaign, the gay-themed magazine Advocate named her its Person of the Year in January 2013. "One of the phrases I used on the campaign trail about what difference I might make was, 'When you're not in the room, the conversation is about you. When you're in the room, the conversation is with you,'" she said. "When you're in the Senate, the conversation is with you, not about you."

In March 2013, Baldwin attended oral arguments as the Supreme Court considered a challenge to the law defining marriage, for the purposes of the federal government, as being between a man and a woman. She was a lead sponsor of the measure that helped repeal "don't ask, don't tell," the military policy banning openly gay military personnel.

For the most part, Baldwin is very liberal and supportive of the positions favored by Democratic leaders. Each of her 14 years in the House, she voted with a majority of her party at least 96 percent of the time when it opposed a majority of Republicans. She was a vice chairwoman of the Congressional Progressive Caucus in the 112th Congress (2011-12).

During the 112th, Baldwin was the House sponsor of the "Buffett Rule" — named for billionaire Warren Buffett — a bill which would impose a surtax on Americans making more than $1 million per year. At a Budget hearing in February 2013, she continued to frame government spending in rich-against-poor terms.

"In my home state, do we kick 900 Wisconsin children out of Head Start, or do we close oil and gas tax loopholes for one of the world's most profitable set of companies?" she asked. "Do we ensure that 23,000 Wisconsinites continue to get job search assistance to get them back on their feet or do we continue with tax breaks for companies who ship American jobs overseas?"

Baldwin says that "powerful lobbyists have too much impact in writing the rules. ... There are loopholes that ordinary citizens don't get to enjoy but hedge fund managers do."

Baldwin won her House seat in 1998 with her own impressive fundraising and help from EMILY's List, a political action committee that supports Democratic female candidates who back abortion rights. She edged out two well-known opponents in the primary, then beat former state Insurance Commissioner Josephine Musser by 6 points in the general election. In 2000, she scored a 3-point victory over Republican John Sharpless, a history professor. The rest of her House races were easy.

The retirement of four-term Democrat Herb Kohl created an open Senate seat for 2012. Baldwin was unopposed in the primary but faced a formidable GOP opponent in Tommy G. Thompson, a former four-term governor who had also served as the secretary of Health and Human Services during the George W. Bush administration. Early on, pundits wondered if Baldwin was too liberal too win a statewide campaign.

Thompson campaigned on repealing the 2010 health care law, and he highlighted Baldwin's plans to expand the federal role in health care. Baldwin emphasized her defense of social safety net programs.

The so-called Tommy-Tammy race attracted lots of money from outside groups — unions and women's organizations ponied up for Baldwin, and super PACs such as Crossroads GPS spent on behalf of Thompson.

Baldwin won by more than 5 points, as President Barack Obama carried the state by a slightly wider margin. In 2013, she said the transition from the House wasn't too difficult, as the smaller number of colleagues made it easier to get acquainted with her fellow senators.

For the 2014 election cycle, Baldwin is leading the Democratic Senatorial Campaign Committee's program to recruit new female candidates and protect female incumbents.

Key Votes (while House member)

2012	
Extend a Social Security payroll tax cut and unemployment benefits	YES
Ease securities rules to expand small-business access to capital	YES
Extend for one year subsidized student loan interest rates financed by a cut in health care spending	NO
Cite Attorney General Eric H. Holder Jr. for contempt of Congress	NO
Create a visa program for foreign graduates in high-tech fields	?
Extend most Bush-era income tax rates while allowing rates for top-bracket earners to rise (Jan. 1, 2013)	YES
2011	
Strike funding for F-35 alternative engine	YES
Prevent EPA from regulating greenhouse gas emissions to address climate change	NO
Extend certain provisions of Patriot Act for four years	NO
Declare opposition to use of ground troops in Libya	NO
Overhaul patent law	NO
Pass compromise debt limit increase plan and establish future spending limits	NO
Allow consideration of measures to implement three trade agreements	NO

CQ Vote Studies (while House member)

	PARTY UNITY		PRESIDENTIAL SUPPORT	
	SUPPORT	OPPOSE	SUPPORT	OPPOSE
2012	97%	3%	88%	12%
2011	98%	2%	76%	24%
2010	99%	1%	85%	15%
2009	99%	1%	96%	4%
2008	99%	1%	14%	86%
2007	99%	1%	3%	97%
2006	99%	1%	13%	87%
2005	99%	1%	13%	87%
2004	98%	2%	32%	68%
2003	99%	1%	18%	82%

Interest Groups (while House member)

	AFL-CIO	ADA	CCUS	ACU
2012	95%	85%	30%	0%
2011	100%	90%	13%	4%
2010	100%	100%	13%	0%
2009	100%	95%	45%	0%
2008	100%	100%	56%	0%
2007	96%	100%	45%	0%
2006	100%	95%	20%	0%
2005	93%	100%	30%	0%
2004	100%	100%	29%	4%
2003	100%	100%	23%	12%

Rep. Paul D. Ryan (R)

Capitol Office
225-3031
paulryan.house.gov
1233 Longworth Bldg. 20515-4901; fax 225-3393

Committees
Budget - Chairman
Ways & Means

Residence
Janesville

Born
Jan. 29, 1970; Janesville, Wis.

Religion
Roman Catholic

Family
Wife, Janna Ryan; three children

Education
Miami U. (Ohio), B.A. 1992 (political science & economics)

Career
Congressional aide; economic policy analyst

Political Highlights
Republican nominee for vice president, 2012

ELECTION RESULTS

2012 GENERAL		
Paul D. Ryan (R)	200,423	54.9%
Rob Zerban (D)	158,414	43.4%
Keith Deschler (LIBERT)	6,054	1.7%
2012 PRIMARY		
Paul D. Ryan (R)		unopposed
2010 GENERAL		
Paul D. Ryan (R)	179,819	68.2%
John Heckenlively (D)	79,363	30.1%
Joseph Kexel (LIBERT)	4,311	1.6%

Previous Winning Percentages
2008 (64%); 2006 (63%); 2004 (65%); 2002 (67%); 2000 (67%); 1998 (57%)

Elected 1998; 8th term

As the GOP vice presidential nominee in 2012, Ryan hoped one of his jobs in the 113th Congress would be presiding over the Senate. Instead, he is back in the House, and his political brand is largely untarnished. He is still the face of the Republican fiscal agenda, with the potential to once again become a national candidate.

For most people, the federal budget is numbers in a ledger. For Ryan, the Budget Committee chairman, it's a cause. "It's not an accounting exercise," he said in 2013. "It's not root canal economics. It's pro-growth economics that gets people the kind of opportunity that they've always known about in America growing up."

His plans would amend the social contract between the government and the governed, and he says that change is not a choice, but a necessity. He argues that the nation is headed for a debt crisis unless spending is cut and federal health care programs such as Medicare and Medicaid are restructured. He believes that his ideas are gaining currency among Americans.

"They know we're on the wrong track," he said in July 2012. "They just sort of know instinctively that government, politicians from both political parties — Republicans are equally to blame on this — have made a whole bunch of empty promises to people that there's no way the government can keep."

Ryan had reached the Republican-imposed term limit for panel leaders, but his party gave him a waiver so he could return as Budget chairman in 2013. He is also a high-ranking member of the Ways and Means Committee, which directly shapes the taxes and benefit programs that factor so heavily into his fiscal blueprints.

After taking his gavel in 2011, the energetic Ryan sold Republicans on his plans, which contained some politically risky elements — chiefly, a proposal to control the growing cost of Medicare by converting it into a voucher-based "premium support" program for those under 55. That idea became the most controversial part of the budget resolution the House adopted in 2011.

Democrats attacked the plan, which they said would shift costs to seniors; an independent group cut an ad in which a Ryan look-alike dumps an elderly woman in a wheelchair off a cliff. For a while, it seemed Ryan was retreating into a less prominent role. He was not among the lawmakers appointed to a special joint congressional committee created by an August 2011 law and charged with producing a $1.2 trillion deficit reduction plan.

But in the spring of 2012, Ryan persuaded the GOP Conference to back a second budget resolution that was much like the first. The fiscal 2013 version, however, added a traditional fee-for-service Medicare option to the premium support proposal, based on a plan Ryan had created with Oregon Democratic Sen. Ron Wyden. The framework also called for cutting $4 trillion in spending over a decade and simplifying the tax code.

When Mitt Romney named Ryan as his running mate in August 2012, the decision stunned many — especially those who believed he would make the ticket vulnerable to Democratic charges that the GOP wants to dismantle the nation's social welfare system.

But even after his defeat on the presidential ticket, Ryan has continued to update his plans. His fiscal 2014 resolution made concessions to conservative Republicans, by calling for the elimination of federal deficits in 10 years — faster than his earlier budgets. He also joined a five-person working group to plot out political strategy regarding federal spending; all the other members have chaired the conservative Republican Study Committee.

Ryan has been working on his ideas since he first came to Congress, but

GOP support for his work has swelled in recent years. In January 2010, he gained considerable attention when he unveiled his second "Roadmap for America's Future," a proposal to eliminate projected future federal deficits by overhauling the tax code, Social Security and the health care system.

Ryan was highly visible during debate on health care overhaul legislation in the 111th Congress (2009-10). He and California Republican Devin Nunes joined a pair of Republican senators, Tom Coburn of Oklahoma and Richard M. Burr of North Carolina, in introducing an alternative that would have authorized state health insurance exchanges and provided tax credits to families for insurance purchases while repealing the tax deduction for employer-provided health insurance. Ryan strongly opposed the law enacted in 2010, calling it "paternalistic" and "arrogant."

He says his philosophy of individualism and entrepreneurial capitalism was influenced most deeply by novelist Ayn Rand. He lists the late New York Rep. Jack F. Kemp, his former boss and the 1996 GOP vice presidential nominee, as his political role model. "Jack had a huge influence on me, his brand of inclusive conservatism, his pro-growth, happy-warrior style. That was infectious to me," Ryan told the Milwaukee Journal Sentinel in 2009.

Even though he is a member of the RSC, Ryan sometimes splits with conservatives. In 2008, he voted in favor of the $700 billion financial sector rescue package, saying it was needed to avoid economic collapse. He also supported aid to the domestic auto industry, which historically has had a major presence in Ryan's hometown of Janesville. He voted for the "fiscal cliff" agreement in January 2013, which allowed higher tax rates on earnings above $400,000.

The youngest of four children, Ryan was 16 when his father died. His mother used Social Security survivor's benefits to help pay for his college education. He said that helped shape his personal and political beliefs. "It made me more of a self-starter and scrapper," he said.

After college, he took a job as an aide to Wisconsin GOP Sen. Bob Kasten. His direct speaking style mirrors that of his two mentors, Kemp and William J. Bennett, former Republican Cabinet secretaries and co-founders of the now-defunct Empower America, a conservative think tank where Ryan worked.

After five years in Washington, Ryan returned to Wisconsin, briefly joining his family's earth-moving and construction business. When GOP Rep. Mark W. Neumann ran for the Senate in 1998, Ryan sought the open seat. His opponent was Democrat Lydia Spottswood, a former Kenosha City Council president who nearly beat Neumann in 1996. Ryan was the superior campaigner and won easily. At 28, he was the youngest member of the freshman class.

With his attention on the presidential race in 2012, Ryan took his lowest share of the vote in any of his House campaigns, at around 55 percent.

Key Votes

2012	
Extend a Social Security payroll tax cut and unemployment benefits	NO
Ease securities rules to expand small-business access to capital	YES
Extend for one year subsidized student loan interest rates financed by a cut in health care spending	YES
Cite Attorney General Eric H. Holder Jr. for contempt of Congress	YES
Create a visa program for foreign graduates in high-tech fields	YES
Extend most Bush-era income tax rates while allowing rates for top-bracket earners to rise (Jan. 1, 2013)	YES
2011	
Strike funding for F-35 alternative engine	YES
Prevent EPA from regulating greenhouse gas emissions to address climate change	YES
Extend certain provisions of Patriot Act for four years	YES
Declare opposition to use of ground troops in Libya	YES
Overhaul patent law	YES
Pass compromise debt limit increase plan and establish future spending limits	YES
Allow consideration of measures to implement three trade agreements	YES

CQ Vote Studies

	PARTY UNITY		PRESIDENTIAL SUPPORT	
	SUPPORT	OPPOSE	SUPPORT	OPPOSE
2012	97%	3%	13%	87%
2011	95%	5%	26%	74%
2010	98%	2%	24%	76%
2009	97%	3%	17%	83%
2008	97%	3%	86%	14%

Interest Groups

	AFL-CIO	ADA	CCUS	ACU
2012	24%	5%	91%	84%
2011	28%	20%	100%	80%
2010	0%	0%	88%	96%
2009	10%	0%	73%	96%
2008	20%	15%	83%	84%

Wisconsin 1

Southeast — Kenosha, Racine

The 1st is a snapshot of the Midwest and is made up of: some Lake Michigan shoreline; two interstates; rural areas; bedroom communities outside Milwaukee to the north and Chicago to the south; and numerous lakes. The largest cities are Racine and Kenosha in the east and Janesville to the west. Unlike other districts in the state, the 1st's lines did not change much during decennial remapping, although now it includes a greater portion of Waukesha County than it had in the past and is slightly more conservative.

Rural areas that depend on tourism — such as Lake Geneva and Lake Delavan — cater to wealthy Chicagoans in Walworth County, with wine festivals, large resorts and downtowns with small shops. But more blue-collar Kenosha also has a growing resort-like feel and has been revitalized with the development of Harborpark, an old industrial region renovated to include a marina and museums, as well as commercial and residential properties.

Historically, however, there is a heavy reliance on manufacturing and agriculture in the 1st. SC Johnson, the household products manufacturer, has its headquarters in Racine. Janesville was hurt by the closure of its GM plant in 2009; many residents and officials had hoped it would reopen, but it remains idle. But other businesses, such as Woodman's Markets' new headquarters, have boosted Janesville, and expanding Blackhawk Technical College is a vocational school. Kenosha also lost jobs when its Chrysler plant closed as assembly line jobs moved to Mexico and Michigan.

The district has been represented by Rep. Paul D. Ryan, a conservative Republican, since 1998, but is less consistent when it comes to other races. In 2012, both Kenosha and Racine counties supported Democrat Tammy Baldwin for U.S. Senate and Barack Obama in the presidential race; Racine backed Ryan, and Kenosha went for his Democratic opponent. In 2008, Obama won the 1st with 51 percent of the vote, but having Ryan on the GOP ticket in 2012 swung the district 4 percentage points and out of the president's column.

Major Industry
Manufacturing, agriculture, tourism

Cities
Kenosha, Racine, Janesville

Notable
C. Latham Sholes invented the typewriter in Kenosha.

Rep. Mark Pocan (D)

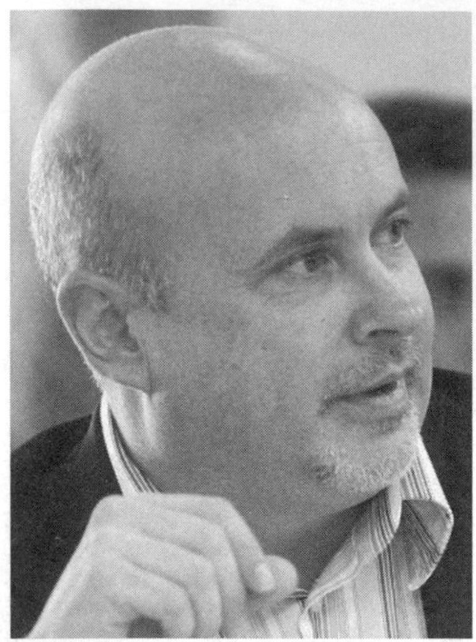

Capitol Office
225-2906
pocan.house.gov
313 Cannon Bldg. 20515-0925; fax 225-6942

Committees
Budget
Oversight & Government Reform

Residence
Madison

Born
Aug. 14, 1964; Kenosha, Wis.

Religion
Unspecified

Family
Husband, Philip Frank

Education
U. of Wisconsin, B.A. 1986 (journalism)

Career
Sign manufacturing company owner; Realtor association public relations director

Political Highlights
Dane County Board of Supervisors, 1991-96; Wis. Assembly, 1999-2013

ELECTION RESULTS

2012 GENERAL		
Mark Pocan (D)	265,422	67.9%
Chad Lee (R)	124,683	31.9%
2012 PRIMARY		
Mark Pocan (D)	43,171	72.2%
Kelda Helen Roys (D)	13,081	21.9%
Matt Silverman (D)	2,365	4.0%
Dennis Hall (D)	1,163	1.9%

Elected 2012; 1st term

Voters of the 2nd District liked what they had with Rep. Tammy Baldwin, who is now a senator. They found a great replacement in Pocan. Like his friend and predecessor, he has experience in county and state government, he is very liberal, and he is openly gay.

Pocan (poe-CAN) grew up in Kenosha, where his father was a city councilman and the proprietor of a sign shop. He eventually followed his father in both pursuits. After getting a journalism degree at the University of Wisconsin in Madison, he opened his own sign and printing business in the capital city.

He has said that his civic activism was spurred in part by a gay-bashing incident — he was attacked by two men upon leaving a gay bar. He was elected in 1991 to the Dane County Board of Supervisors, representing downtown Madison and serving with Baldwin. In 1998, Baldwin gave up a state House seat to run for the U.S. House, and Pocan ran to succeed her — he joked to The Capital Times that his shop made the yard signs for his opponents.

Initially known for sneering criticisms of Republicans, Pocan toned it down after a few years and became a respected legislator. He ended up organizing the 2008 campaign that gave his party the majority, and afterward he co-chaired the budget-writing committee.

He now sits on the Budget Committee in the U.S. House. He is also on the Oversight and Government Reform subcommittee on economic growth and job creation. A member of the Congressional Progressive Caucus, Pocan is a big supporter of union labor, and he was a strident foe of Republican Gov. Scott Walker's 2011 initiative to end collective bargaining for state workers. He is also a proponent of public financing of elections.

Pocan had little trouble in his campaign to succeed Baldwin a second time. He had a well-funded and spirited primary opponent in state Rep. Kelda Helen Roys, but he beat her by 50 points en route to a general election landslide.

Among his non-political talents, Pocan is an accomplished magician.

Wisconsin 2

South — Madison

Winter temperatures in Madison routinely drop into the single digits, but the capital city is at the geographic and economic center of the 2nd District and politics always raise the mercury.

The capital city is home to the flagship campus of the University of Wisconsin; founded in 1848, it hosts 40,000 students. The areas in Madison and surrounding Dane County are populated by white-collar workers focused on academics and politics. Health care and health services companies add diversity to the economy, and American Family Insurance has its headquarters to the northeast of the city. Dane County, which has median household incomes above the statewide average, experienced large population growth (nearly 15 percent) between 2000 and 2010 and has the lowest unemployment rate in the state, at under 6 percent.

Outside of Madison, the district bears a stronger resemblance to the rest of the state: It takes in rural landscapes with manufacturing and agriculture-based economies. Dane and Green counties are some of state's largest producers of milk and grow corn and soybeans. Areas to the east, including Iowa and Lafayette counties, which were both moved into the 2nd District following decennial redistricting, produce nearly as much as Dane and Green.

Tourism also plays a vital role in the economy, with residents employed at the facilities of the tourist-driven Wisconsin Dells in the north (in the neighboring 6th District), and the Swiss-themed town of New Glarus in the south. There are also several water parks, rivers and lakes throughout the area, which welcome vacationers from across the region.

The reliably Democratic district has many strongly liberal residents in and near Madison, where issues regarding public employee unions can spur discord. Barack Obama took 70 percent of the district's vote in his 2008 election for president and then 68 percent in the 2012 contest. Iowa, Dane and Rock counties supported Democrat Tom Barrett in Republican Gov. Scott Walker's 2012 recall election.

Major Industry
Higher education, government, agriculture, tourism

Cities
Madison, Beloit

Notable
The first capital of Wisconsin was Belmont in Lafayette County — today tourists visit buildings depicting early 19th-century life and see where the legislature first met in 1836.

Rep. Ron Kind (D)

Capitol Office
225-5506
kind.house.gov
1502 Longworth Bldg. 20515-4903; fax 225-5739

Committees
Ways & Means

Residence
La Crosse

Born
March 16, 1963; La Crosse, Wis.

Religion
Lutheran

Family
Wife, Tawni Kind; two children

Education
Harvard U., A.B. 1985; London School of Economics, M.A. 1986; U. of Minnesota, J.D. 1990

Career
County prosecutor; lawyer

Political Highlights
No previous office

ELECTION RESULTS

2012 GENERAL

Ron Kind (D)	217,712	64.1%
Ray Boland (R)	121,713	35.8%

2012 PRIMARY

Ron Kind (D)	unopposed

2010 GENERAL

Ron Kind (D)	126,380	50.3%
Dan Kapanke (R)	116,838	46.5%
Michael Krsiean (I)	8,001	3.2%

Previous Winning Percentages
2008 (63%); 2006 (65%); 2004 (56%); 2002 (63%); 2000 (64%); 1998 (71%); 1996 (52%)

Elected 1996; 9th term

A proud moderate, Kind supports federal investments in the economy if they meet his standards for efficiency and affordability. He's the chairman of the business-friendly New Democrat Coalition, and as a member of the Ways and Means Committee he has a hand in shaping programs and tax provisions central to the national deficit and economic growth.

Kind comes from a blue-collar background; his father was a telephone repairman and union leader. Kind was a standout high school football and basketball player who won an academic scholarship to Harvard University. He played quarterback there before suffering a career-ending shoulder injury. As a summer intern for frugal Wisconsin Democrat William Proxmire in 1984, he did research for the senator's annual "Golden Fleece" awards, which showcased what Proxmire considered to be wasteful federal spending.

Kind shares Proxmire's brand of fiscal conservatism, and it sometimes separates him from his caucus. He was one of 25 House Democrats who voted for a balanced-budget amendment to the Constitution in 2011. The next year, he was one of 22 supporting a budget based on the work of the 2010 fiscal commission known as Simpson-Bowles; it proposed $4 trillion in deficit reduction over 10 years through a mix of spending cuts and revenue increases. Kind swore off earmarks well before Republicans banned them in 2011.

In the 112th Congress (2011-12), most Democrats voted for the liberal Nancy Pelosi of California when the House selected its speaker, but Kind chose one of the most fiscally conservative Democrats, his colleague and collaborator Jim Cooper of Tennessee.

Late in 2012, Kind was chosen to chair the New Democrats for the 113th Congress (2013-14). Deficit reduction is part of the group's mission, but Kind places equal emphasis on government investments in education, job training, infrastructure and technology. "I see the great economic challenge of our time as increased global competition," he said. "So we need to be approaching policy from that perspective, not just as it relates to businesses, but what can we do to ensure all of our citizens are full participants in the 21st-century global economy."

Kind has pressed his ideas on economic growth and health care from the Ways and Means Committee. In the 113th, he sits on the Health and Trade subcommittees. He supports a targeted repeal of the estate tax for family-owned small businesses and family farms; in 2012, he proposed a reduction on the effective tax rate paid by domestic manufacturers.

He angered large parts of his district by supporting the Democrats' 2010 health care overhaul. Kind, who is now the chairman of the Rural Health Care Coalition, justified the law as a first step toward containing medical costs and noted that official budget scores indicated its costs were offset by projected savings. The law includes health insurance "exchanges" designed to allow for competition and price comparison, a concept similar to a plan sponsored by Kind in both 2008 and 2009.

It wasn't the first time Kind ruffled feathers at home. Agriculture is a big part of his district's economy, and he criticizes many federal farm programs as creating unhealthy dynamics in the marketplace. As Congress considered a reauthorization of farm programs in the 110th Congress (2007-08), Kind joined forces with Republicans Paul D. Ryan of Wisconsin and Jeff Flake of Arizona to try to cut direct farm subsidies and apply the savings to conservation, rural development and deficit reduction. He has proposed consolidating federal conservation programs, as well.

Direct payments are likely to end in the next enacted farm bill, but Kind is not enthusiastic about a possible shift in emphasis to subsidized crop insurance. "They're trying to take all risk out of farming," he said in 2012. "When you do that, it leads to huge market distortions that are tough to justify and result in bad decisions being made."

Still, Kind looks out for the dairy industry; his district leads the state in dairy production. He has supported extensions of the Milk Income Loss Contract program, a decade-old price support.

Raised in La Crosse on the banks of the Mississippi River, Kind grew up hunting, fishing and camping. He has passed his love of the outdoors on to his family. His sons' high school football commitments in 2012 ended an eight-year tradition: Kind took time every August to visit a different national park with his family. "It is a neat concept when you think about it," Kind says, "that it doesn't matter who you are, that because of your birthright as an American you are co-owner of some of the most beautiful and some of the most expensive lands in the entire world."

He supports tax incentives for states that promote outdoor recreation to combat childhood obesity, which he believes will improve children's health and lower health care costs.

One of Kind's most distinctive achievements is the Veterans History Project at the Library of Congress, which collects video and audio tapes, letters, cards, photographs, drawings and other mementos from soldiers in the wars of the 20th and 21st centuries. Kind introduced the bill creating the project in September 2000, and it sped through Congress in less than a month. He got the idea after taping his father and uncle — veterans of the Korean conflict and of World War II, respectively — telling war stories at a family gathering.

Kind is also a Civil War enthusiast. The political arguments of that era are similar to arguments today, he says: "It's the tension between the role of federal government in our lives versus state rights versus individual rights."

After graduate school and law school, Kind worked two years at a Milwaukee law firm, then returned to La Crosse to become a county prosecutor. When GOP Rep. Steve Gunderson announced his retirement, Kind entered the 1996 race. With little money, he waged a grass-roots campaign and beat Jim Harsdorf with 52 percent of the vote. He had little trouble with re-election until 2010, when he came under fire for his health care vote. He prevailed by less than 4 points over GOP state Sen. Dan Kapanke.

Republican Ray Boland, a retired Army colonel and former secretary of the Wisconsin Department of Veterans, challenged Kind in a mostly unchanged 3rd District in 2012. The race was described by many news outlets as remarkably civil. Boland's small-government message wasn't persuasive enough to knock off the incumbent. Kind won by 28 points.

Key Votes

2012	
Extend a Social Security payroll tax cut and unemployment benefits	NO
Ease securities rules to expand small-business access to capital	YES
Extend for one year subsidized student loan interest rates financed by a cut in health care spending	NO
Cite Attorney General Eric H. Holder Jr. for contempt of Congress	YES
Create a visa program for foreign graduates in high-tech fields	YES
Extend most Bush-era income tax rates while allowing rates for top-bracket earners to rise (Jan. 1, 2013)	YES
2011	
Strike funding for F-35 alternative engine	YES
Prevent EPA from regulating greenhouse gas emissions to address climate change	NO
Extend certain provisions of Patriot Act for four years	YES
Declare opposition to use of ground troops in Libya	NO
Overhaul patent law	NO
Pass compromise debt limit increase plan and establish future spending limits	YES
Allow consideration of measures to implement three trade agreements	?

CQ Vote Studies

	PARTY UNITY		PRESIDENTIAL SUPPORT	
	SUPPORT	OPPOSE	SUPPORT	OPPOSE
2012	88%	12%	80%	20%
2011	87%	13%	88%	12%
2010	95%	5%	87%	13%
2009	86%	14%	83%	17%
2008	95%	5%	28%	72%

Interest Groups

	AFL-CIO	ADA	CCUS	ACU
2012	86%	85%	50%	8%
2011	86%	75%	31%	8%
2010	100%	95%	13%	4%
2009	86%	90%	47%	8%
2008	100%	80%	72%	8%

Wisconsin 3

West and central — Eau Claire, La Crosse, Stevens Point

The Y-shaped 3rd sits along the state's southwestern border. Its eastern fork roughly traces the area between the Wisconsin River and Interstate 39, while its western fork fills in between the Mississippi River and Interstate 94 to Dunn County. The 3rd includes La Crosse, Eau Claire and rural areas. The 3rd changed markedly during decennial redistricting, with the new district grabbing about one-fourth of its land from the old 7th to the north.

The cities to the east of Castle Rock Lake and its northern tributaries add a more conservative bent to this left-leaning district. The 3rd, with blue-collar roots, supports moderate Democrats, although most of the counties here supported Republican Gov. Scott Walker in the unsuccessful election to remove him from office in 2012.

The 3rd appeals to those who work in large cities, either in Wisconsin or in neighboring states, but prefer the less expensive living that towns such as Eau Claire can offer. Regional planning commissioners, however, rejected a proposed rail link between Minneapolis-Saint Paul and Eau Claire in early 2012, citing buses or other transportation initiatives as more beneficial.

The economic engine of the 3rd is the state's famous dairy farmers. The district still leads the state in dairy production, and although uncertainty remains regarding federal dairy policy, milk prices are expected to rise. Farmers here are becoming dependent on immigrant workers, leading to an influx of Hispanic residents in an overwhelmingly white district. Following declines in manufacturing, many residents here have had to look to other sectors for jobs. Higher education is an established industry here: Six of the state's 13 four-year public colleges are in the 3rd. The district is also home to an Army training base at Fort McCoy.

Major Industry
Agriculture, health care, higher education

Military Bases
Fort McCoy, 454 military, 1,549 civilian (2012)

Cities
Eau Claire, La Crosse, Stevens Point

Notable
Laura Ingalls Wilder's birthplace in Pepin has a recreation of her home and a museum in her name.

Rep. Gwen Moore (D)

Capitol Office
225-4572
gwenmoore.house.gov
2245 Rayburn Bldg. 20515-4904; fax 225-8135

Committees
Budget
Financial Services

Residence
Milwaukee

Born
April 18, 1951; Racine, Wis.

Religion
Baptist

Family
Single; three children

Education
Marquette U., B.A. 1978 (political science)

Career
State agency legislative analyst; city development specialist; VISTA volunteer

Political Highlights
Wis. Assembly, 1989-92; Wis. Senate, 1993-2004 (president pro tempore, 1997-98)

ELECTION RESULTS

2012 GENERAL		
Gwen Moore (D)	235,257	72.2%
Dan Sebring (R)	80,787	24.8%
Robert R. Raymond (I)	9,277	2.8%
2012 PRIMARY		
Gwen Moore (D)		unopposed
2010 GENERAL		
Gwen Moore (D)	143,559	69.0%
Dan Sebring (R)	61,543	29.6%
Eddie Ahmad Ayyash (I)	2,802	1.3%

Previous Winning Percentages
2008 (88%); 2006 (71%); 2004 (70%)

Elected 2004; 5th term

Moore's personal encounters with domestic violence and social welfare programs have made her a committed spokeswoman for federal activism in addressing societal ills. She also engages in counterattacks, "challenging the rhetoric" of the Republican majority when opportunities arise.

She became interested in politics as a student in Milwaukee's public schools in the late 1960s, inspired by the Rev. Martin Luther King Jr. and the civil rights movement. At 18, during her freshman year at Marquette University, Moore became pregnant and began receiving welfare benefits. Still, she continued her studies in political science, earning her bachelor's degree after eight years — an outcome she credits to federal programs for low-income students.

Moore sits on the Budget Committee, and in the 112th Congress (2011-12) she harshly criticized Republican blueprints for spending reductions and entitlement program changes. "We can't cut ourselves into prosperity and not take one dime from millionaires and billionaires and corporations," she said. "To the extent that we cut benefits for middle-class people, we are preventing our economy from thriving."

Budget Chairman Paul D. Ryan, a Wisconsin Republican, set off a liberal fusillade in 2011 when he fretted that the social safety net was sometimes used as a "hammock." Moore was among the incensed: "You're going to block-grant Medicaid? Most funding is for 85-year-old women in nursing homes. How dare you say they're in a hammock."

In 2012, the Obama administration tried to offer states some wiggle room to modify the work requirements in welfare programs, which were put in place by a 1996 law. Some Republicans were outraged, and Moore was outraged right back. She said it was untrue that the 1996 law "was a raging success that took people out of poverty, gave them dignity and put them in good jobs. What it really did was kick poor people off the rolls."

A good deal of Moore's focus is on the downtrodden or abused. In May 2009, she shepherded into law a reauthorization of assistance programs for the homeless. The law expanded the definition of "homeless" — and thus eligibility for aid — to include those fleeing from domestic violence with no place to go, as well as individuals and families who are within 14 days of losing their housing. One of her proudest achievements is language to protect the identity of domestic violence victims who receive homeless assistance. Moore's fear was that abusers could track their victims through federal databases. That measure was enacted as part of a 2006 reauthorization of federal programs to prevent and prosecute violent crimes against women.

Moore herself is a victim, and she took her story to the House floor in March 2012 when another reauthorization was under discussion. "Domestic violence has been a thread throughout my personal life, up to and including being a child repeatedly sexually assaulted, up to and including being an adult who has been raped," she said. "This is not a partisan issue, and it would be very, very devastating to women of all colors, creeds and sexual orientations for us not to address this." After some partisan disputes over extensions of the programs to illegal immigrants and same-sex couples, a reauthorization was enacted early in the 113th Congress (2013-14).

Moore also sits on the Financial Services Committee. After college, she worked as a VISTA volunteer and organized a community credit union in her North Milwaukee neighborhood. During the 2010 debate over the financial regulatory overhaul known as Dodd-Frank, she sought to strengthen the hand of regulators and pushed for a $1 billion loan program to assist unemployed individuals at risk of home foreclosure. It was included in the law.

She voted for a $700 billion Wall Street rescue package in 2008, but she is wary of further taxpayer-funded bailouts; her hope is that Dodd-Frank will end the notion of companies that are "too big to fail." She's also wary that some regulations inspired by the financial crisis might go too far. In 2012 she opposed a Securities and Exchange Commission plan to alter rules for money market mutual funds, writing in The Hill that it would "needlessly disrupt markets."

She has tried to make flood insurance more affordable. The House passed her 2012 bill calling for study of voluntary "group coverage" plans, where local governments would buy a policy for a community, funded by property taxes or a utility-style bill. She reintroduced it in 2013.

Moore has supported President Barack Obama's agenda, backing his economic stimulus and job creation proposals as well as the 2010 health care overhaul. She belongs to Congressional Black Caucus and the Congressional Progressive Caucus, a group of the most-liberal House members.

Moore was born in Racine, the eighth of nine children. Her father was factory worker and her mother was a teacher. She said her father taught her self-reliance, a trait that propelled her through school and her career.

She served as student council president of North Division High School, where she pushed city officials to replace an aging building that lacked science labs and showers for athletes. Moore also organized a school walkout over a lack of textbooks describing the post-slavery history of African-Americans.

She held a variety of government jobs, including a post as a neighborhood development specialist for Milwaukee's city government. In 1988, she was elected to the Wisconsin Assembly, and in her first re-election bid she beat Republican Scott Walker, the state's current governor. Moore was heavily involved in the failed 2012 campaign to recall Walker, which was spurred by his efforts to modify collective bargaining rights for public employees.

Democrat Gerald D. Kleczka decided to retire from the House in 2004, and Moore easily won a three-way primary for her party's nomination. That November, she took almost 70 percent of the vote to become the first African-American member of Congress from Wisconsin.

Moore's victory was somewhat marred by the January 2005 arrest of her 25-year-old son, Sowande Omokunde, one of five workers for the Kerry-Edwards presidential campaign charged with slashing the tires of GOP get-out-the-vote vehicles on Election Day. The judge sentenced Omokunde and three co-defendants to several months in jail.

Moore received more unwanted press later that year when a newspaper reported that her sister had been paid $44,000 for work on Moore's campaign, although she lives in Georgia. Regardless, Moore has won re-election with ease. She took more than 72 percent of the vote in 2012.

Key Votes

2012	
Extend a Social Security payroll tax cut and unemployment benefits	YES
Ease securities rules to expand small-business access to capital	YES
Extend for one year subsidized student loan interest rates financed by a cut in health care spending	NO
Cite Attorney General Eric H. Holder Jr. for contempt of Congress	?
Create a visa program for foreign graduates in high-tech fields	NO
Extend most Bush-era income tax rates while allowing rates for top-bracket earners to rise (Jan. 1, 2013)	YES
2011	
Strike funding for F-35 alternative engine	YES
Prevent EPA from regulating greenhouse gas emissions to address climate change	NO
Extend certain provisions of Patriot Act for four years	NO
Declare opposition to use of ground troops in Libya	?
Overhaul patent law	NO
Pass compromise debt limit increase plan and establish future spending limits	+
Allow consideration of measures to implement three trade agreements	NO

CQ Vote Studies

	PARTY UNITY		PRESIDENTIAL SUPPORT	
	SUPPORT	OPPOSE	SUPPORT	OPPOSE
2012	98%	2%	91%	9%
2011	96%	4%	81%	19%
2010	96%	4%	87%	13%
2009	99%	1%	99%	1%
2008	99%	1%	19%	81%

Interest Groups

	AFL-CIO	ADA	CCUS	ACU
2012	95%	100%	25%	0%
2011	100%	90%	13%	0%
2010	93%	100%	13%	0%
2009	100%	100%	33%	0%
2008	100%	95%	50%	4%

Wisconsin 4

Milwaukee

There were few changes to the 4th's borders during decennial remapping, but those that did take place benefit Republicans elsewhere in Wisconsin. The district, situated on the shores of Lake Michigan, included all of the city of Milwaukee — a longtime Democratic stronghold — and a few southern suburbs. It gained several left-leaning northern suburbs in order to maintain Republican footing in the more conservative adjacent 5th District.

Once a major manufacturing city, Milwaukee suffered large losses in the latter half of the 20th century as manufacturing jobs went abroad. Several major firms with historic roots in the city still operate. The Miller Brewing Co., which became MillerCoors in 2007, has been in the city since 1850. A number of smaller breweries and microbreweries also operate the city. Harley-Davidson's founders sold their first motorcycle there in 1903 and its headquarters are on Juneau Avenue. Today's largest employers for the area are primarily in the health care sector and include Aurora Health Care and Wheaton Franciscan Healthcare. Kohl's Corp. department stores are based just outside of the district in Waukesha County.

Milwaukee has experienced a surge in redevelopment. The city's historic and formerly industrial Third Ward is now a bustling arts, shopping and nightlife area. Brady Street is known for its eclectic establishments. The Menomonee Valley, with its productive machine shops, has come back from decline as well; it boasts nature trails, the Harley-Davidson Museum, Miller Park baseball stadium and a casino run by the Potawatomi tribe.

While Milwaukee County experienced minimal change in overall population since 2000, it did see a jump in minority populations. In particular, the number of Hispanic residents increased by 53 percent; the number of Asian residents, by 34 percent. In the city, much of the population increase centered on the Third Ward and its surrounding area. Overall nearly 20 percent of Milwaukee city claims a German heritage.

Major Industry
Manufacturing, health care, retail, tourism, beer manufacturing

Cities
Milwaukee

Notable
The original manuscripts for J.R.R. Tolkien's "The Hobbit" and "The Lord of the Rings" reside in Marquette University's Raynor Library collections.

Rep. Jim Sensenbrenner (R)

Capitol Office
225-5101
sensenbrenner.house.gov
2449 Rayburn Bldg. 20515-4905; fax 225-3190

Committees
Judiciary
(Crime, Terrorism, Homeland Security & Investigations - Chairman)
(Over-Criminalization Task Force - Chairman)
Science, Space & Technology

Residence
Menomonee Falls

Born
June 14, 1943; Chicago, Ill.

Religion
Anglican Catholic

Family
Wife, Cheryl Sensenbrenner; two children

Education
Stanford U., A.B. 1965 (political science); U. of Wisconsin, J.D. 1968

Career
Lawyer

Political Highlights
Wis. Assembly, 1969-75; Wis. Senate, 1975-79

ELECTION RESULTS

2012 GENERAL		
Jim Sensenbrenner (R)	250,335	67.7%
Dave Heaster (D)	118,478	32.0%
2012 PRIMARY		
Jim Sensenbrenner (R)		unopposed
2010 GENERAL		
Jim Sensenbrenner (R)	229,642	69.3%
Todd P. Kolosso (D)	90,634	27.4%
Robert R. Raymond (I)	10,813	3.3%

Previous Winning Percentages
2008 (80%); 2006 (62%); 2004 (67%); 2002 (86%); 2000 (74%); 1998 (91%); 1996 (74%); 1994 (100%); 1992 (70%); 1990 (100%); 1988 (75%); 1986 (78%); 1984 (73%); 1982 (100%); 1980 (78%); 1978 (61%)

Elected 1978; 18th term

Sensenbrenner is a renowned curmudgeon — even his wife calls his attitude "crabby." He is also a forceful conservative voice on criminal justice issues and a skilled legislator. Although he fell short in his bid to lead the Science, Space and Technology Committee for the 113th Congress, he still holds the gavel of the Judiciary subcommittee on crime and terrorism.

Sensenbrenner has been hawkish about giving law enforcement agencies tools to aggressively fight terrorism. He was the chairman of the full Judiciary Committee at the time of the Sept. 11 attacks, and he sponsored the landmark anti-terrorism law known as the Patriot Act. For the 112th Congress (2011-12), "my top priority was getting the Patriot Act reauthorized," he said. "That's done." In 2011, President Barack Obama signed an extension of three surveillance provisions in the law.

Critics say that the spying powers infringe on civil liberties, but Sensenbrenner has called them "integral to defending America against enemy nations, terrorist groups and individual terrorists." Early in the 113th Congress (2013-14), his panel considered an update of electronic privacy laws. Whereas some lawmakers blanch at Internet providers storing any information on users, Sensenbrenner favors "data preservation," where some records are stored for people suspected of wrongdoing. "Neither law enforcement nor the service [provider] community are going to get everything that they want," he said — in a display of his usual bluntness.

The Science committee has been his staging ground for battles with the EPA. Under the Obama administration, Sensenbrenner says, the agency is using regulatory power to implement a cap-and-trade system for greenhouse gas emissions — a Democrat-favored approach that died in the Senate in the 111th Congress (2009-10). "The people's representatives voted no, and an appointed bureaucrat wants to reverse that," he said.

Sensenbrenner has sparred with Democrats over the science of climate change and its economic implications — from 2007 through 2010, he was the ranking member on the Select Committee on Energy Independence and Global Warming. Writing in Roll Call in late 2010, he urged the incoming GOP majority not to eliminate the panel, but to "rebrand" it as a watchdog "to ensure the administration doesn't bend to unrealistic international demands — and that the EPA doesn't attempt to do what Congress wouldn't." His remarks foreshadowed the role that he would take on himself.

He is on a mission to reverse the EPA's June 2012 decision to allow the sale of E15, a gasoline-ethanol fuel blend. "I started out on that by writing letters to all 14 automobile manufacturers, and every one of them said the engines would be wrecked by E15," he said. Before the EPA decision, he introduced a bill to prohibit the EPA from granting a waiver on prohibitions on new fuels that would cause or contribute to damage to vehicle engines. In 2013, he wrote a bill to block the use of E15 until further studies of its effects are done.

Sensenbrenner's clashes with the administration have gone beyond climate change and alternative-fuel issues. In late 2011, he was overheard criticizing first lady Michelle Obama's healthy-eating campaign; he included the dig that "she has a large posterior herself." His office tried to clarify, saying that his criticism was that government shouldn't tell Americans what to eat. But as fodder for gossip blogs and big newspapers alike, the story compelled the delivery of a written apology to the first lady.

He was just as prickly during the George W. Bush administration, however. In 2005, he ended a hearing on the Patriot Act by deriding the questioning by lawmakers as off-topic. Democrats were still talking when the meeting was closed by Sensenbrenner's walking out of the room, gavel in hand. A GOP colleague told The New York Times in 2006 that Sensenbrenner treats everyone equally — "like dogs." A day later, Sensenbrenner circulated a basket of dog biscuits at a committee meeting.

But his gruff, no-nonsense persona doesn't get in the way of his relationship with constituents. Dubbed the 2010 Town Hall King by CQ Roll Call, he typically holds about 100 public meetings a year in his district.

And when he isn't taking on the Obama administration, he sometimes teams with Democrats. He joined with Maxine Waters of California on a bill to keep state and local governments from using their power of eminent domain to seize private property for economic development purposes. It passed the House easily in 2012.

In 2008, he worked with Democrat Steny H. Hoyer of Maryland to push through Congress a bill to expand the category of people classified as disabled, and to ensure that protections under the Americans with Disabilities Act aren't withheld from anyone meeting those standards. Lawmakers said that Supreme Court rulings had imposed unwarranted limits on the law's reach. Sensenbrenner's wife, Cheryl, disabled since age 22 by a spinal cord injury, is a past board chairwoman for the American Association of People with Disabilities.

Sensenbrenner has parted with key Republicans at times. In 2006, during his final months as Judiciary chairman, he defied Bush on immigration policy by emphasizing border security over the creation of a path to citizenship for illegal immigrants. Some of Sensenbrenner's ideas made it into law, including a plan to build a 700-mile-long fence on the U.S.-Mexico border. That year he also won an extension of the 1965 Voting Rights Act, and he was riled that Republicans threw up roadblocks by trying to eliminate requirements for bilingual assistance at polling places.

Sensenbrenner has spent his entire career in politics and government since graduating from law school in 1968 — as the heir to the Kimberly-Clark paper and cellulose manufacturing fortune, he is one of the wealthiest members of Congress. As a teenager, he helped his math teacher win a race for county surveyor. He studied political science at Stanford University, earned a law degree from the University of Wisconsin, then was elected to the state Assembly. He spent a decade in the legislature.

When Rep. Bob Kasten, a Republican, ran unsuccessfully for governor in 1978, Sensenbrenner, with a solid political base in Milwaukee's affluent suburbs bordering Lake Michigan, was the obvious successor. He dipped into family wealth to overcome primary opponent Susan Engeleiter, a fellow state legislator, by fewer than 1,000 votes. He then won the general election with 61 percent of the vote and has not faced a significant challenge since.

Key Votes

2012	
Extend a Social Security payroll tax cut and unemployment benefits	NO
Ease securities rules to expand small-business access to capital	YES
Extend for one year subsidized student loan interest rates financed by a cut in health care spending	YES
Cite Attorney General Eric H. Holder Jr. for contempt of Congress	YES
Create a visa program for foreign graduates in high-tech fields	YES
Extend most Bush-era income tax rates while allowing rates for top-bracket earners to rise (Jan. 1, 2013)	NO
2011	
Strike funding for F-35 alternative engine	YES
Prevent EPA from regulating greenhouse gas emissions to address climate change	YES
Extend certain provisions of Patriot Act for four years	YES
Declare opposition to use of ground troops in Libya	YES
Overhaul patent law	NO
Pass compromise debt limit increase plan and establish future spending limits	YES
Allow consideration of measures to implement three trade agreements	YES

CQ Vote Studies

	PARTY UNITY		PRESIDENTIAL SUPPORT	
	SUPPORT	OPPOSE	SUPPORT	OPPOSE
2012	93%	7%	24%	76%
2011	93%	7%	20%	80%
2010	98%	2%	24%	76%
2009	98%	2%	15%	85%
2008	98%	2%	82%	18%

Interest Groups

	AFL-CIO	ADA	CCUS	ACU
2012	10%	15%	75%	96%
2011	3%	10%	94%	92%
2010	7%	0%	88%	100%
2009	5%	0%	73%	100%
2008	0%	10%	67%	96%

Wisconsin 5

Southeast — Milwaukee suburbs

The 5th covers the suburbs of Madison to the west and Milwaukee to the east, taking in the Interstate 94 corridor that connects Wisconsin's most populous cities. Redistricting after the 2010 census removed its lakefront presence north of Milwaukee and larger chunks of Waukesha County but added Dodge County to the northeast.

Closer to Milwaukee, areas in the district are fast growing and are some of the wealthiest in the state. At more than $60,000, the 5th has the highest median household income among districts statewide. Population gains within its lines were particularly notable south of Interstate 94, near Lake Mills and Waukesha, and in areas southeast of Watertown. The city of Waukesha, about 25 minutes from downtown Milwaukee, has developed a new riverwalk along the Fox River, recently restored its downtown to attract urbanites out to the suburbs, and has plans to build a hotel and convention center.

Despite the nationwide decline in the manufacturing sector, industry is still represented in the 5th. Small-engine manufacturer Briggs and Stratton has its headquarters in Wauwatosa, where insulation manufacturer Gaco Western is building a new facility to move its various components under one roof and allow for increased employment. Kohl's Department Store has its headquarters in Menomonee Falls and plans to build a new corporate facility; and GE Healthcare is located in Waukesha. The 5th is not as reliant on agriculture as other parts of the state, although a number of farms cover the more agricultural land to the district's west.

The district is a conservative stronghold, with most areas supporting Republicans in statewide and federal contests. The 5th gave Republican Mitt Romney 61 percent of its vote in the 2012 presidential election. Barack Obama won only in the district's portions of Milwaukee and Walworth counties; Romney took 70 percent in Washington County.

Major Industry
Construction, health care, manufacturing

Cities
Waukesha, West Allis

Notable
Mary Todd Lincoln spent time in the health-spa city of Waukesha, seeking solace after the president's death.

Rep. Tom Petri (R)

Capitol Office
225-2476
petri.house.gov
2462 Rayburn Bldg. 20515-4906; fax 225-2356

Committees
Education & the Workforce
Transportation & Infrastructure
(Highways & Transit - Chairman)

Residence
Fond du Lac

Born
May 28, 1940; Marinette, Wis.

Religion
Lutheran

Family
Wife, Anne Neal Petri; one child

Education
Harvard U., A.B. 1962 (government), J.D. 1965

Career
Lawyer; White House aide; Peace Corps volunteer

Political Highlights
Wis. Senate, 1973-79; Republican nominee for U.S. Senate, 1974

ELECTION RESULTS

2012 GENERAL		
Tom Petri (R)	223,460	62.1%
Joseph C. Kallas (D)	135,921	37.8%
2012 PRIMARY		
Tom Petri (R)	73,376	82.3%
Lauren Stephens (R)	15,821	17.7%
2010 GENERAL		
Tom Petri (R)	183,271	70.7%
Joseph C. Kallas (D)	75,926	29.3%

Previous Winning Percentages
2008 (64%); 2006 (99%); 2004 (67%); 2002 (99%); 2000 (65%); 1998 (93%); 1996 (73%); 1994 (99%); 1992 (53%); 1990 (100%); 1988 (74%); 1986 (97%); 1984 (76%); 1982 (65%); 1980 (59%); 1979 Special Election (50%)

Elected 1979; 17th full term

Petri exudes dignified gentility, and his brand of Republicanism has remained popular with voters even as Wisconsin's electorate has fractured. After three decades of House service, he often plays the role of experienced backbencher — a throwback to when members remained in Washington on weekends and socialized with the opposition.

In the 1960s, Petri (PEA-try) helped found the Ripon Society, a redoubt of moderate Republicanism. Its founding statement says that "the future of our party lies not in extremism, but in moderation." He takes to heart the examples of his political heroes, George Washington and Dwight D. Eisenhower, who succeeded in part by being less faction-focused than their contemporaries.

"Hamilton and Jefferson didn't trust each other, but they trusted Washington," he said. "Eisenhower would always say that the strength of a country is the moral fiber of its people and the capacity of the economy."

Petri's pragmatic bent may have hindered his personal rise to power in an increasingly conservative party, however. He is the fourth-most senior House Republican, but since 2001 he has been passed over four times when the top GOP slot on one of his committees has opened up. Today, he is the No. 2 Republican on the Education and the Workforce Committee and No. 3 on Transportation and Infrastructure.

He has managed to head up some powerful subcommittees, however. In the 113th Congress (2013-14), he is the chairman of the Highways and Transit panel, which will be working on a reauthorization of surface transportation programs as their 2014 expiration approaches.

From 2007 through 2012, Petri was the top Republican on the Aviation Subcommittee. That was a boon for his district, which is home to manufacturers that have a stake in the aviation industry. Petri and other panel leaders in the 112th Congress (2011-12) moved a bill to shield U.S. companies from paying European Union taxes and fees on aircraft emissions; they said such taxes would kill U.S. jobs. President Barack Obama signed it in November 2012.

Petri couldn't muster much bipartisanship for other measures. The Federal Aviation Administration shut down temporarily in the summer of 2011 as the parties battled over a long-term reauthorization of aviation programs; Democrats objected to a provision in the House bill to undo a rule making it easier for airline workers to organize. Petri has been more accommodating to labor causes than many GOP colleagues, often voting to preserve "prevailing wage" requirements for federal contracts. A compromise measure — negotiated by party leadership teams, with Petri largely sidelined — was enacted in 2012.

Petri has been a proponent of robust infrastructure spending; in 2009 he opposed Obama's $787 billion stimulus package because not enough of its funding went to infrastructure. When the House considered a long-term bill to authorize surface transportation programs in 2012, he was the only committee Republican to vote against it — he said Wisconsin was being short-changed by the bill's new spending formula. Petri also tried to restore authorizations for "transportation enhancements," such as bike paths. Leaders eventually pulled the long-term bill, and a two-year version was enacted.

The Education and the Workforce Committee had less work product in the 112th, but Petri has already made waves in the 113th with a proposed overhaul of federal student loans. His bill would streamline the program to offer only one kind of loan, with interest rates tied to the 10-year Treasury rate. It would leave only one method of loan payment: paycheck withholdings equivalent to 15 percent of discretionary income. Petri has said that his plan would eliminate confusion and lower the rate of defaults.

Petri has also proposed the creation of new teacher and principal training academies, as well as allowing new kinds of computerized testing to assess student achievement. He is an advocate for increased charter school funding.

Born Thomas Rudolph Everett Jr., Petri spent his early childhood in Puerto Rico, where his Navy pilot father was stationed. After his father was killed in action over Germany during World War II, his mother remarried. Although Petri eventually took the surname of his stepfather, he continued to be known to family and friends as "Tim," a nickname his grandmother gave him at age 2 to distinguish him from his biological father.

As a teenager, Petri got his first job as a disc jockey at the local radio station. He soon became the host of "Teen Time," a weekly show that made him the Badger State's youngest on-air personality. He earned both an undergraduate and a law degree, working his way through Harvard as a bank teller. During his days in Boston, he was a member of the NAACP and picketed Woolworth's over its segregation policies in the South — an act he calls "not overly heroic," as it took place in Massachusetts. He clerked for Judge James E. Doyle Sr. — whose son would become a Democratic governor of Wisconsin — before joining the Peace Corps for a stint in Somalia. Once home, he started a law practice in Fond du Lac. In 1972, at age 32, he won a state Senate seat.

Petri was the GOP Senate nominee against Democrat Gaylord Nelson in 1974, but lost in the aftermath of the Watergate scandal. A longtime environmentalist, Petri was joined on the campaign trail for a canoe trip down the Milwaukee River by former Attorney General Elliott Richardson, a hero to moderate Republicans. Richardson later invited Petri to become a fellow at the Wilson Center, a D.C. research institute, where Petri shared a room with Richard Darman, future head of the Office of Management and Budget. While there, he shared lunches with diplomat George Kennan and Andrew Goodpaster, a former aide to Dwight D. Eisenhower.

Exposure from the 1974 race helped Petri win a 1979 special election to replace Republican Rep. William A. Steiger, who had died one month after winning his seventh term. Petri triumphed over six candidates in the primary, including Tommy G. Thompson — it was the only electoral defeat in the career of the future governor, at least until the 2012 Wisconsin Senate race. Petri won a full term in 1980. He coasted until his 1992 campaign, when he was hit by negative publicity about 77 overdrafts at the private bank for House members. He took less than 53 percent of the vote, his worst re-election result ever.

One of the wealthiest members of Congress, Petri recently has been criticized for not paying any state taxes from 2002 to 2005, mainly due to heavy losses at Lloyd's of London, the insurer where Petri is an investor. It has not significantly affected his standing at the polls.

Key Votes

2012	
Extend a Social Security payroll tax cut and unemployment benefits	NO
Ease securities rules to expand small-business access to capital	YES
Extend for one year subsidized student loan interest rates financed by a cut in health care spending	YES
Cite Attorney General Eric H. Holder Jr. for contempt of Congress	YES
Create a visa program for foreign graduates in high-tech fields	YES
Extend most Bush-era income tax rates while allowing rates for top-bracket earners to rise (Jan. 1, 2013)	NO
2011	
Strike funding for F-35 alternative engine	YES
Prevent EPA from regulating greenhouse gas emissions to address climate change	YES
Extend certain provisions of Patriot Act for four years	YES
Declare opposition to use of ground troops in Libya	YES
Overhaul patent law	NO
Pass compromise debt limit increase plan and establish future spending limits	YES
Allow consideration of measures to implement three trade agreements	YES

CQ Vote Studies

	PARTY UNITY		PRESIDENTIAL SUPPORT	
	SUPPORT	OPPOSE	SUPPORT	OPPOSE
2012	93%	7%	15%	85%
2011	90%	10%	20%	80%
2010	94%	6%	38%	62%
2009	89%	11%	26%	74%
2008	91%	9%	62%	38%

Interest Groups

	AFL-CIO	ADA	CCUS	ACU
2012	33%	5%	92%	76%
2011	34%	20%	94%	72%
2010	14%	10%	88%	88%
2009	24%	10%	80%	92%
2008	33%	40%	72%	80%

Wisconsin 6

East central — Oshkosh, Sheboygan, Fond du Lac

The 6th starts in the center of the state and extends east to Lake Michigan, sweeping in the northern outer suburbs of Madison and Milwaukee.
It reaches as far north as Oshkosh and takes in the western side of 130,000-acre Lake Winnebago.

Overwhelmingly white, the district is made up of counties with proportions of minority residents in the single digits. However, farmers are becoming reliant upon immigrant workers, driving small but sudden growth of the Hispanic population of the district. The area is home to a vibrant agricultural industry, including corn and Wisconsin's famous dairy production. The northwestern part of the 6th is known for a profitable Christmas tree industry: The state is among the top producers of evergreens.

The district has long been home to an array of manufacturers, most noteworthy being the shipbuilding industry centered around Manitowoc County. The county now leans on jobs in health care, as well as industrial and technical manufacturing. Further south, Sheboygan is known for food processors, notably cheese maker Sargento Foods, owing to its location near areas heavy in produce and dairy production. In the district's western tip, the tourism-driven Wisconsin Dells provides jobs.

Traditional manufacturing has been hit hard since the recent housing slump. Faucet maker Kohler, from the city that shares its name, has shed jobs in recent years, including closing plants and consolidating its operations.

The 6th has transitioned from a relatively moderate district to one designed to back Republicans. Gone are the more left-leaning parts from the northern portion of the old 6th, such as a chunk of Winnebago County.

Major Industry
Manufacturing, agriculture, tourism

Cities
Oshkosh, Sheboygan, Fond du Lac

Notable
Fond du Lac's Silver Wheel Manor Doll Museum features more than 3,000 dolls from six generations; Known as the Bratwurst Capital of the World, Sheboygan holds a festival in its honor every summer.

Rep. Sean P. Duffy (R)

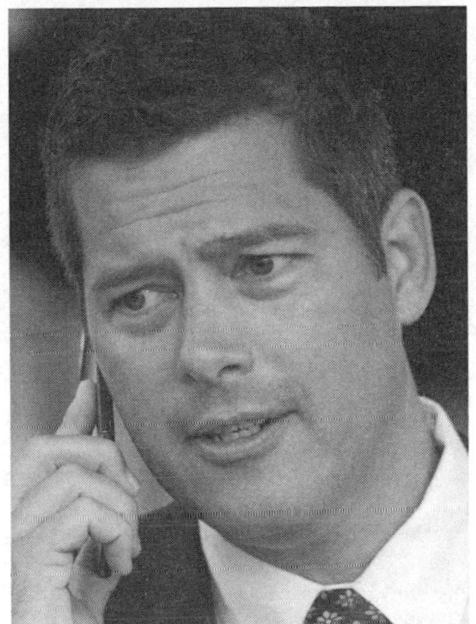

Capitol Office
225-3365
duffy.house.gov
1208 Longworth Bldg. 20515-4907; fax 225-3240

Committees
Budget
Financial Services
Joint Economic

Residence
Weston

Born
Oct. 3, 1971; Hayward, Wis.

Religion
Roman Catholic

Family
Wife, Rachel Campos-Duffy; six children

Education
St. Mary's College (Minn.), B.A. 1994 (marketing), William Mitchell College of Law, J.D. 1999

Career
County prosecutor; lawyer; bus driver, professional timber sports competitor; reality show personality

Political Highlights
Ashland County district attorney, 2002-10

ELECTION RESULTS

2012 GENERAL		
Sean P. Duffy (R)	201,720	56.1%
Pat Kreitlow (D)	157,524	43.8%
2012 PRIMARY		
Sean P. Duffy (R)		unopposed
2010 GENERAL		
Sean P. Duffy (R)	132,551	52.1%
Julie Lassa (D)	113,018	44.4%
Gary Kauther (I)	8,397	3.3%

Elected 2010; 2nd term

Duffy is a handsome former television star, and some of his biggest battles in Congress have been with preconceptions. Early on, he was dismissed by foes as an empty suit, while a few Republicans eyed him as a new leader for the party's youth movement. In practice, he's a conventional member of the GOP Conference, making modest contributions on the Financial Services Committee and working to broaden his appeal in a district that Democrats held for 40 straight years.

He came to the 112th Congress (2011-12) after eight years as a district attorney, but most people focus on the other parts of his résumé. Duffy was born and raised in heavily wooded northern Wisconsin, the 10th of 11 children. Lumber is a big part of his family's history, going all the way back to his great-great-grandfather, who worked for the Northwestern Lumber Company.

Duffy followed in that tradition by competing in, and winning, numerous lumberjack competitions. The money he earned from such events helped pay his way through college and law school. His oldest children — Duffy is a father of six — are involved in logrolling contests, and he keeps a 6-pound Australian ax in his Washington office.

Duffy was in law school when he was selected as a cast member for "The Real World," the pioneering reality show on MTV. Several years later, he returned to the network on "Road Rules." It was on that show where he met Rachel Campos, his future wife. When he finally settled into a legal career, Duffy served as a county prosecutor; he was appointed to the district attorney post, then won re-election several times.

He says he ran for Congress in response to the huge amounts of spending in the 2009 economic stimulus package. That bill was shepherded in part by his representative: Democrat David R. Obey was chairman of the Appropriations Committee at the time. Duffy was initially seen as facing a very tough campaign, but Obey announced in May 2010 that he would retire after 40 years in the House. That left Duffy to face a state senator, whom he defeated by about 8 points.

Duffy hasn't panned out as the made-for-TV politician that some people expected. He's an enthusiastic speaker but by no means a polished one; at present, he's not particularly skilled at snapping off tidy policy arguments. He has proved to be immensely likable among GOP colleagues, who volunteer their personal warmth toward Duffy. He maintains that civility is important. "I like to get input from a lot of people — even those, and especially those, who don't agree with me," he said in 2011.

Parts of the liberal blogosphere openly sneered at Duffy during his freshman term, but his charisma and district work clearly paid off. He sponsored several measures with bipartisan appeal in the 112th Congress. The House passed his 2012 bill to freeze federal salaries, including those of congressmen, for a year. Another Duffy bill encouraged the use of blind trusts by lawmakers and their senior staff members in order to eliminate the appearance of using "insider" information to make stock trades. Elements of his proposal were incorporated into a 2012 law on that subject.

Duffy sits on the Financial Services Committee, where his overriding concern is the health of community banks and other smaller financial institutions. His contention, shared by many Republicans, is that an overhaul of financial regulations enacted in 2010 is creating standards that small banks can't hope to meet — which ultimately hinders their ability to make loans or forces them into mergers. He told a 2012 conference of credit union officials that the number of consolidations in the financial sector might be moving the U.S. toward a "Canadian-style banking system."

The Consumer Financial Protection Bureau created by the 2010 law is criticized by Republicans as concentrating too much power over the financial sector in a federal bureaucracy. The CFPB "only gives a voice to big Wall Street banks and leaves small banks out of the conversation," Duffy said. He similarly suggests that small banks were not adequately represented in the "Basel III" talks setting international banking conventions.

Duffy introduced a bill in 2011 to ease the review process for overturning CFPB regulations. It became the vehicle for several other Republican-backed measures to modify the CFPB, including one to replace the agency's director with a bipartisan five-person commission. The package passed the House with Duffy's support.

He has regulatory concerns outside of the financial services law. He lauded a 2011 EPA decision to revise standards on hazardous waste caused by industrial boilers and incinerators, which would affect the forest products industry in his district. "Mandating unattainable EPA standards on our businesses will cost millions of dollars at a time when our businesses are struggling to stay alive," he said.

Duffy is a fiscal conservative, though not necessarily a hard-liner. He voted for a compromise fiscal 2011 appropriations package that still cut overall spending, as well as an August 2011 deficit reduction deal. Duffy is a member of the conservative Republican Study Committee, but he voted against the fiscal 2013 and 2014 budgets produced by the RSC.

He instead supported the less austere blueprints of fellow Wisconsin Republican Paul D. Ryan, the Budget Committee chairman. "Paul has done a very good job of advocating for policies that will truly move the country forward, and doing it in a way that is not vitriolic," he said. Duffy was given a seat on the Budget Committee in 2013, and he also returned as a member of the Joint Economic Committee.

Like many of his constituents, Duffy is a social conservative. He opposes federal funding of abortion and restrictions to gun owners' rights. He also opposes same-sex marriage and civil unions that resemble marriages.

A redrawn congressional map for 2012 moved several Democratic-leaning areas out of Duffy's district, but Democrats still hoped to recapture the seat — Obey's long career there convinced them that it was a viable pickup. Pat Kreitlow, a former state senator and newscaster, got their nomination.

Both candidates had outside groups spending heavily to influence the race on their behalf. But Duffy beat Kreitlow 2-to-1 in head-to-head fundraising, aided in part by his seat on Financial Services and the campaign donations that it attracts. He won by more than 12 points.

Key Votes

2012	
Extend a Social Security payroll tax cut and unemployment benefits	YES
Ease securities rules to expand small-business access to capital	YES
Extend for one year subsidized student loan interest rates financed by a cut in health care spending	YES
Cite Attorney General Eric H. Holder Jr. for contempt of Congress	YES
Create a visa program for foreign graduates in high-tech fields	YES
Extend most Bush-era income tax rates while allowing rates for top-bracket earners to rise (Jan. 1, 2013)	NO
2011	
Strike funding for F-35 alternative engine	YES
Prevent EPA from regulating greenhouse gas emissions to address climate change	YES
Extend certain provisions of Patriot Act for four years	YES
Declare opposition to use of ground troops in Libya	YES
Overhaul patent law	YES
Pass compromise debt limit increase plan and establish future spending limits	YES
Allow consideration of measures to implement three trade agreements	YES

CQ Vote Studies

	PARTY UNITY		PRESIDENTIAL SUPPORT	
	SUPPORT	OPPOSE	SUPPORT	OPPOSE
2012	96%	4%	17%	83%
2011	94%	6%	21%	79%

Interest Groups

	AFL-CIO	ADA	CCUS	ACU
2012	33%	0%	100%	84%
2011	10%	10%	100%	88%

Wisconsin 7

Northwest — Wausau, Superior

The state's largest district, the 7th stretches north and west from central counties, travels across farmland, forests and lakes, and reaches the Apostle Islands in the waters of Lake Superior.

Farming sustains the economy, although cold weather in the north shaves a month off the growing season. Dairy farms are the agricultural heart of the 7th. Centrally located Clark and Marathon counties lead Wisconsin in dairy production. Paper and woodworking plants are scattered throughout the 7th, but the historic, influential paper industry has suffered, and plants have closed across the state. Numerous Native American-run casinos are located in the 7th and are key employers in the northern counties. Areas in the central part of the district also host companies in the insurance industry.

The tranquil lifestyle in small towns appeals to senior citizens and the 7th's lakes in the north are a draw for tourists. A large number of Hmong immigrants have settled in Marathon County. One fast-growing area of the district is St. Croix County, which capitalizes on its proximity to the Minneapolis-St. Paul metropolitan area.

Blue-collar regions along Lake Superior consistently vote Democratic, however many of the rural voters of north-central Wisconsin voted for Barack Obama in 2008 while supporting Republican Gov. Scott Walker in his 2012 recall election. Evangelical Christians and socially conservative Catholics in the district's southern counties tend to favor the GOP.

After decennial redistricting, the redrawn 7th now includes the conservative exurbs of St. Croix County and rural Vilas and Florence counties. Obama carried the old 7th with 56 percent of its vote in the 2008 presidential election, but the newly drawn district gave Republican Mitt Romney 51 percent of its presidential vote in 2012, and the race was tight in most counties.

Major Industry
Agriculture, paper, manufacturing, insurance

Cities
Wausau, Superior, Marshfield

Notable
The American Birkebeiner, from Cable to Hayward, is North America's largest cross-country ski marathon.

Rep. Reid Ribble (R)

Capitol Office
225-5665
ribble.house.gov
1513 Longworth Bldg. 20515-4908; fax 225-5729

Committees
Agriculture
Budget
Transportation & Infrastructure

Residence
Sherwood

Born
April 5, 1956; Neenah, Wis.

Religion
Baptist

Family
Wife, DeaNa Ribble; two children

Education
Appleton East H.S., graduated 1974

Career
Roofing construction company president

Political Highlights
No previous office

ELECTION RESULTS

2012 GENERAL		
Reid Ribble (R)	198,874	55.9%
Jamie Wall (D)	156,287	44.0%
2012 PRIMARY		
Reid Ribble (R)		unopposed
2010 GENERAL		
Reid Ribble (R)	143,998	54.8%
Steve Kagen (D)	118,646	45.1%

Elected 2010; 2nd term

Ribble's opinions of Congress are informed by his experience as president — of a roofing company. "The constant political bickering, posturing, partial truths, all those things drive me insane," he said. "Coming out of the business climate, you have the tendency to be more pragmatic. ... Efficiency drives the day because inefficiency costs profitability, right?"

The energetic and likable Ribble held no political offices before joining the House in 2011, and he has leveraged his outsider status to become a leader in the movement to "fix" the functionality of the nation's legislative body. In 2012, he created the Fix Congress Now Caucus with Republican Scott Rigell of Virginia and Democrats Jim Cooper of Tennessee and Kurt Schrader of Oregon.

The co-founders are also affiliated with No Labels, a nonpartisan group that has no policy positions outside of plans to cajole Congress toward legislative output. Ribble has proposed constitutional amendments to lengthen the terms of House members and impose term limits on both chambers.

He and Cooper also helped prepare and promote the "Go Big" letter in 2011, a bipartisan note from 100 House members urging enactment of a package to reduce deficits by at least $4 trillion over 10 years. As fiscal negotiations were struggling along late that year, Ribble renounced the Americans for Tax Reform "pledge," which demands that signatories oppose revenue increases. (Almost the entire GOP Conference has signed it at one point.)

Ribble's overtures to productivity have co-existed with his fiscally conservative voting record. He sits on the Budget Committee and emphasizes that business owners need confidence in the government in order to flourish. He says that streamlining the tax system in a way to create that confidence, and he keeps a hefty copy of the U.S. tax code on a table in his D.C. office. "That's a reminder to me, that every day when I walk in here, that's my agenda — to fix that," he said.

A member of the conservative Republican Study Committee, he co-wrote a 2011 bill with Republicans Jason Chaffetz of Utah and Mick Mulvaney of South Carolina that became conservatives' rallying point in deficit reduction negotiations that summer.

The bill, titled the Cut, Cap and Balance Act, would have cut spending by $111 billion for fiscal 2012, established statutory caps to limit spending in future years and increased the debt ceiling — the last part being contingent on a balanced-budget amendment to the Constitution passing Congress and being sent to the states for ratification. Praised by conservatives, the bill passed in the Republican House in July 2011 — but was soon tabled in the Democratic Senate.

Ribble has a seat on the Agriculture Committee. His district has extensive forests, as well as apple and cherry orchards and vineyards. Regarding a long-term reauthorization of farm programs, Ribble says his constituents are OK with shrinking subsidies and mainly want government "out of the way."

But when lawmakers were assembling a "fiscal cliff" measure to extend certain tax rates due to expire at the start of 2013, Ribble fought to include a provision extending a subsidy for dairy farmers in times of market volatility. He said it was necessary to maintain the program until it could be replaced by a long-term farm bill. Ribble wasn't pleased that the final package extended lower tax rates only for earnings under $400,000 — he wanted spending cuts included as well — but the dairy extension helped win his support.

Overall, he supports a move in farm policy away from direct payments and toward risk-management-based safety nets. He wants to bolster job growth in the organic sector, and to make sure that farm bills include competitive research grants and formula funding for land grant institutions.

Ribble also sits on the Transportation and Infrastructure Committee. He was part of the conference committee that assembled a two-year extension of surface transportation programs in 2012, and he was among those who worked to include provisions that streamline environmental permitting requirements for infrastructure projects.

As a freshman, Ribble called for a moratorium on federal rule-making to create a "cooling off period" for small businesses. But his concerns go back years. In 1995, he was a witness at a Small Business Committee hearing on regulations regarding workplace falls. Ribble called the standards unnecessary and said they even "insulted" his employees, "who for years have taken pride not only in their workmanship, but in their ability to complete their work in a safe fashion."

He started the Job Creators Caucus in 2011, and Rigell was another founder. Its members consider business acumen a part of their professional skill set.

Ribble was born in Wisconsin, the youngest of eight children. His father, Ralph, was a World War II veteran. He started a roofing company when Ribble was a toddler. Ralph was also a Baptist minister.

While attending Appleton East High School, Ribble played on the volleyball team, and as an adult he ended up coaching it for 20 years. He's also a football fan — representing Green Bay, Ribble has stadium seats from Lambeau Field displayed prominently in his Washington office.

He considered becoming a full-time minister but instead joined his father's company. He became its president in 1981. Ribble got involved with the National Roofing Contractors Association in the mid-1980s and served a term as its president in 2005 and 2006.

Ribble has two sons, both of whom are musicians. He operated a production company called Reel Loud Records for a number of years.

Two-term Democrat Steve Kagen was something of an anomaly in the 8th District, a blue-collar region that had mostly elected Republicans. Kagen won 51 percent and 54 percent of the vote in strong Democratic years. In 2010, Ribble hopped on to the national wave of Republican support, and the district's voters returned to form, giving him a nearly 10-point win.

In the 2012 cycle, he was unopposed in his primary race. He faced Democrat Jamie Wall, a management consultant and Rhodes Scholar, in the general election. Ribble took nearly 56 percent of the vote.

At the start of the 113th Congress (2013-14), he was named one of the leaders of the Patriot Program — the National Republican Congressional Committee's operation for helping incumbent members.

Key Votes

2012	
Extend a Social Security payroll tax cut and unemployment benefits	YES
Ease securities rules to expand small-business access to capital	YES
Extend for one year subsidized student loan interest rates financed by a cut in health care spending	YES
Cite Attorney General Eric H. Holder Jr. for contempt of Congress	YES
Create a visa program for foreign graduates in high-tech fields	YES
Extend most Bush-era income tax rates while allowing rates for top-bracket earners to rise (Jan. 1, 2013)	YES
2011	
Strike funding for F-35 alternative engine	YES
Prevent EPA from regulating greenhouse gas emissions to address climate change	YES
Extend certain provisions of Patriot Act for four years	YES
Declare opposition to use of ground troops in Libya	YES
Overhaul patent law	YES
Pass compromise debt limit increase plan and establish future spending limits	YES
Allow consideration of measures to implement three trade agreements	YES

CQ Vote Studies

	PARTY UNITY		PRESIDENTIAL SUPPORT	
	SUPPORT	OPPOSE	SUPPORT	OPPOSE
2012	95%	5%	21%	79%
2011	97%	3%	18%	82%

Interest Groups

	AFL-CIO	ADA	CCUS	ACU
2012	19%	5%	100%	88%
2011	0%	5%	100%	91%

Wisconsin 8

Northeast — Green Bay, Appleton

On autumn Sundays, all eyes in Wisconsin turn to the 8th to watch football's Green Bay Packers. Regardless of the team's fortunes, the Packers represent the emotional heart of the state and they pull in millions of dollars. But the 8th's traditional blue-collar economy depends on its natural resources. Taking up the northeastern portion of the state, the 8th encompasses the Door Peninsula, the areas northeast of Lake Winnebago and the state's third largest city, Green Bay.

While urban areas in the district between Green Bay and Appleton experienced modest population gains between 2000 and 2010, rural counties, notably Marinette County, have shed residents. Once a dominant industry, paper mills still churn, although many have closed or cut jobs following the recent recession. A Kimberly-Clark plant closed in 2008 — it had operated since 1889. Along with meat-packing and shipping, these blue-collar mill jobs are disappearing and a new service sector economy is forming in the region, albeit slowly. In Green Bay, health care facilities also employ many residents, although the city has a median household income rate lower than the statewide average.

Door County, with its tree-lined shoreline, lighthouses, resorts and small cabins, is a popular vacation spot as downstate residents and out-of-state tourists seek the "Cape Cod of the Midwest." The district overall is home to a number of American Indian tribes and casinos. Brown County, at the mouth of the Door Peninsula, is home to numerous Indian gaming sites.

The district is blue-collar and Catholic, and its voting patterns do not fall along traditional left-right lines. Voters here will back the more conservative candidate, and gave GOP presidential candidate Mitt Romney 51 percent of their vote in the 2012 election. That same year, voters across the 8th, except for Menominee County, supported Republican Gov. Scott Walker in a recall election.

Major Industry
Agriculture, casinos, paper, tourism

Cities
Green Bay, Appleton

Notable
Owing to the town's tradition of magic, Appleton, home of Harry Houdini, hosts hands-on exhibits at its history museum dedicated to the escapist.

WYOMING

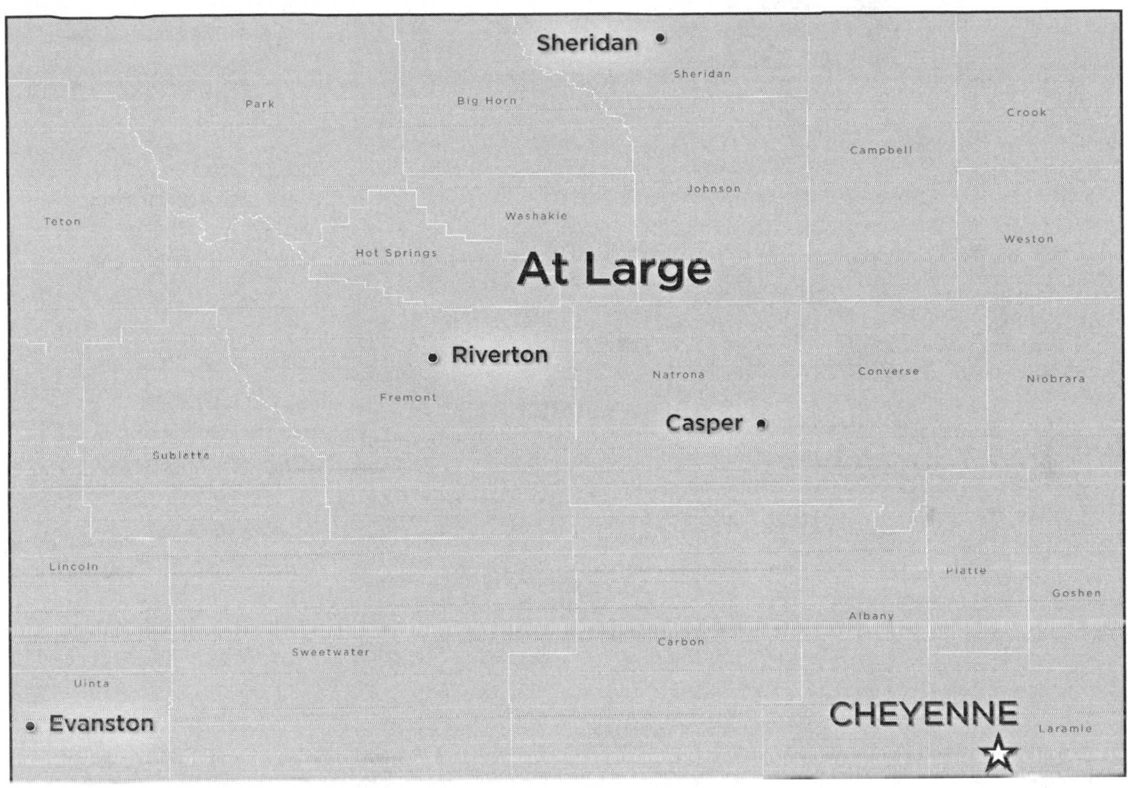

Sheridan
Sheridan
Park
Big Horn
Crook
Campbell
Johnson
Teton
Washakie
Weston
Hot Springs
At Large
Riverton
Natrona
Converse
Niobrara
Fremont
Casper
Sublette
Lincoln
Platte
Goshen
Albany
Carbon
Sweetwater
Uinta
Evanston
CHEYENNE
Laramie

Gov. Matt Mead (R)

First elected: 2010
Length of term: 4 years
Term expires: 1/15
Salary: $105,000
Phone: (307) 777-17434
Residence: Cheyenne
Born: March 11, 1962; Jackson, Wyo.
Religion: Episcopalian
Family: Wife, Carol Mead; two children
Education: U. of Texas, B.A. 1984 (communications); U. of Wyoming, J.D. 1987
Career: Rancher; lawyer; deputy county attorney; federal prosecutor; special assistant state attorney general
Political highlights: U.S. attorney, 2001-07

ELECTION RESULTS

2010 GENERAL

Matt Mead (R)	123,780	71.8%
Leslie Petersen (D)	43,240	25.1%
Mike Wheeler (LIBERT)	5,362	3.1%

Secretary of State Max Maxfield (R)

(no lieutenant governor)
First elected: 2006
Length of term: 4 years
Term expires: 1/15
Salary: $92,000
Phone: (307) 777-5333

LEGISLATURE

Legislature: 40 days January-March in odd-numbered years; 20 days February-March in even-numbered years
Senate: 30 members, 4-year terms
2013 ratios: 26 R, 4 D; 28 men, 2 women
Salary: $150/day in session
Phone: (307) 777-7881
House: 60 members, 2-year terms
2013 ratios: 52 R, 8 D; 47 men, 13 women
Salary: $150/day in session
Phone: (307) 777-7881

TERM LIMITS

Governor: 2 terms
Senate: No
House: No

URBAN STATISTICS

CITY	POPULATION
Cheyenne	59,466
Casper	55,316
Laramie	30,816
Gillette	29,087

REGISTERED VOTERS

Republican	65%
Democrat	21%
Other	14%

POPULATION

2010 population	563,626
2000 population	493,782
1990 population	453,588
Percent change (2000-2010)	+14.1%
Rank among states (2010)	50
Median age	36.7
Born in state	42.0%
Foreign born	2.6%
Violent crime rate	228/100,000
Poverty level	9.8%
Federal workers	8,121
Military	3,407

ELECTIONS

STATE ELECTION OFFICIAL
(307) 777-7186
DEMOCRATIC PARTY
(307) 473-1457
REPUBLICAN PARTY
(307) 234-9166

MISCELLANEOUS

Web: www.wyoming.gov
Capital: Cheyenne

U.S. CONGRESS

Senate: 2 Republicans
House: 1 Republican

STATISTICS BY DISTRICT

District	2012 Vote for President: Obama	2012 Vote for President: Romney	2008 Vote for President: Obama	2008 Vote for President: McCain	Black	Asian	Hispanic	Median Income	Over 64	Under 20	College Education	Rural	Sq. Miles
AL	28%	69%	33%	65%	1%	1%	9%	$56,322	13%	27%	25%	38%	97,093
STATE	28	69	33	65	1	1	9	56,322	13	27	25	38	97,093
U.S.	51	47	53	46	12	5	17	50,052	13	27	29	21	3,531,905

Sen. Michael B. Enzi (R)

Capitol Office
224-3424
enzi.senate.gov
379A Russell Bldg. 20510-5004; fax 228-0359

Committees
Budget
Finance
Health, Education, Labor & Pensions
Homeland Security & Governmental Affairs
Small Business & Entrepreneurship

Residence
Gillette

Born
Feb. 1, 1944; Bremerton, Wash.

Religion
Presbyterian

Family
Wife, Diana Enzi; three children

Education
George Washington U., B.A. 1966 (accounting); U. of Denver, M.S. 1968 (retail marketing)

Military Service
Wyoming Air National Guard, 1967-73

Career
Accountant; computer programmer; shoe store owner

Political Highlights
Mayor of Gillette, 1975-83; Wyo. House, 1987-91; Wyo. Senate, 1991-96

ELECTION RESULTS

2008 GENERAL		
Michael B. Enzi (R)	189,046	75.6%
Chris Rothfuss (D)	60,631	24.3%
2008 PRIMARY		
Michael B. Enzi (R)		unopposed

Previous Winning Percentages
2002 (73%); 1996 (54%)

Elected 1996; 3rd term

One of Enzi's favorite stories to tell is that of negotiating with the Senate's liberal lion, the late Edward M. Kennedy. The two worked alongside each other as chairman and ranking member of the Health, Education, Labor and Pensions Committee, negotiating and passing legislation by what they coined the "80/20 rule."

If you can agree on 80 percent of the issues in a bill, and can't come to agreement on the other 20 percent, you write a bill with just the 80 percent you agree on. That bill will still do great things, Enzi says.

That outlook still guides him. It was evident in the 112th Congress (2011-12) as he worked on an overhaul of the K-12 federal education law with HELP Chairman Tom Harkin, an Iowa Democrat. They sprinkled the bill with sweeteners for both sides. For Democrats, it would write into law the Obama administration's signature competitive grants, such as the Race to the Top program. For Republicans, it would expand charter schools. "This is not a perfect bill, nor does it solve every education issue," Enzi wrote at its release. "But it will make a huge, positive difference to our nation's young people."

The Senate never voted on the bill, nor did the House vote on a version of its own; the reauthorization is on the to-do list for the 113th Congress (2013-14). However, Enzi now has a diminished role. Republican term limit rules forced him from the top GOP spot on the HELP panel, and Lamar Alexander of Tennessee took his place. Enzi is now the ranking member of the Children and Families Subcommittee.

But his ability to find common ground should keep him relevant. Despite a conservative voting record, he still has the attitude of a deal-maker, rather than an ideologue. For example, Enzi and Harkin shepherded a five-year reauthorization of Food and Drug Administration user fee programs to the president's desk in 2012. It reauthorized the fees that fund the agency's approval process for prescription drugs and medical devices. It created new fees for generic drugs and generic biological medicines. "We've had a great teamwork effort," Enzi said. He had several successes working with Kennedy, such as laws to expand insurance coverage of mental-health treatment.

He showed zero tolerance for the partisan politics leading up to the 2012 presidential election. He was visibly perturbed after a bill he assembled with Democrat Patty Murray of Washington and Republican Johnny Isakson of Georgia — to set up a national workforce training system — stalled. And he took particular offense to the partisan mudslinging over proposals to prevent the interest rates on federal student loans from doubling. (They are set by statute, and a lower rate was expiring.) He wanted the measures to come through the HELP Committee.

"Bills that don't go to committee are designed to fail," he said, imploring Majority Leader Harry Reid to pull legislation from the Senate floor and start over. "The ones that come through, most of them pass."

That is a common Enzi refrain, so there was a twinge of irony in spring 2013 as one of Enzi's signature efforts skipped the committee process. For years, he has wanted to enact a bill to overturn a 1992 Supreme Court decision and allow states to collect sales taxes from online retailers outside their borders. He has a powerful partner in his effort — Majority Whip Richard J. Durbin of Illinois. The latest version of their bill includes an exemption for retailers with less than $1 million in gross sales. Enzi maintains that the change would be a huge boon for state revenue and eliminate an unfair advantage enjoyed by online retailers.

Reid brought the bill straight to the floor, likely to avoid Finance Chairman

Max Baucus of Montana — his state has no sales tax, and he says the change would be burdensome to its retailers. It passed with 69 votes.

Enzi is an accountant by trade, and he sits on the Finance Committee as well — he is the top Republican on its taxation subcommittee. He is eager for the tax code overhaul the panel might attempt in the 113th. He has proposed an international taxation bill meant to help U.S. companies compete with foreign counterparts.

He will also continue to push his "Penny Plan," which he says would balance the budget in five years by cutting a single penny off of every dollar the government spends for each of five years. In 2013, he joined the Homeland Security and Governmental Affairs Committee, which gives him a new venue for studying federal outlays and management practices.

And he will work outside of committees if he sees the need. In the 112th Congress he was part of the bipartisan "gang of six" (later eight) senators trying to generate legislative proposals incorporating both increased revenue and spending cuts to improve the nation's fiscal outlook. He has touted budget ideas outlined by a 2010 special fiscal commission, widely known as Simpson-Bowles; by most accounts, they would trim deficits by $4 trillion over 10 years through revenue increases, spending cuts and modifications to entitlement programs.

Enzi generally favors liberalized foreign trade, including agricultural trade with Cuba and expanded ties with China, something that could help his state's farmers and ranchers. In 2007 he cast the only dissenting vote on extending a ban on U.S. imports from Myanmar; he said unilateral sanctions often hurt U.S. businesses. But he voted against the 2005 Central America Free Trade Agreement, which was opposed by the Wyoming Stock Growers Association because it did not include a requirement for country-of-origin labeling for beef.

For the most part, Enzi displays the prototypical Western conservative's skepticism about an overweening federal government. He is also a solid social conservative, opposing abortion rights and gay marriage.

Enzi was born in Bremerton, Wash., where his father had worked in the naval shipyards during World War II. The family moved to Wyoming soon after his birth. After graduating from high school in Sheridan, he headed east to George Washington University in Washington, D.C., where he earned an accounting degree. He returned west to the University of Denver, where he collected a master's in retail marketing in 1968.

The following year, he married and moved to Wyoming with his wife, Diana. They settled in Gillette, where they started their own small business, NZ Shoes. (He is also a member of the Small Business and Entrepreneurship Committee.) They later added stores in Sheridan and Miles City, Mont.

Enzi began his political career by winning the 1974 mayoral election in Gillette when he was 30. In 1986, he won a seat in the state House and by 1991 was serving in the state Senate. When Republican Sen. Alan K. Simpson decided to retire after 18 years, Enzi sought the seat. He narrowly won the 1996 primary over John Barrasso — who is now his Senate colleague — by building a network of supporters drawn in part from the Wyoming Christian Coalition. He took the general election by 12 points over Democrat Kathy Karpan, a former two-term Wyoming secretary of state. (Simpson went on to become a co-chairman of the 2010 fiscal commission.)

In 2002, he won re-election with 73 percent of the vote over Democrat Joyce Jansa Corcoran, the former mayor of Lander. Six years later, he took almost 76 percent against University of Wyoming professor Chris Rothfuss. Enzi's re-election was never in doubt, but he refused to have his campaign take any polls.

"I don't do polls because, on a weekend, I talk to more people than a pollster does," he told The Associated Press.

Key Votes

2012	
Prohibit health insurance plans from denying coverage based on the sponsor's religious beliefs	NO
Require approval of the Keystone XL oil pipeline	YES
Ease securities rules to expand small-business access to capital	YES
Reauthorize farm and nutrition programs for five years	YES
Limit debate on a bill that would create private-sector cybersecurity standards	NO
Consent to ratification of a treaty setting global standard for the treatment of people with disabilities	NO
Provide $60.4 billion in disaster relief following Superstorm Sandy	NO
Extend most Bush-era income tax rates while allowing rates for top-bracket earners to rise (Jan. 1, 2013)	YES
2011	
Prevent EPA from regulating greenhouse gas emissions to address climate change	YES
Extend certain provisions of Patriot Act for four years	YES
Clear compromise debt limit increase plan and establish future spending limits	YES
Overhaul patent law	YES
Implement Colombia free trade agreement	YES
Limit debate on confirmation of Caitlin J. Halligan to D.C. Circuit Court of Appeals	NO
Extend payroll tax cut and unemployment benefits for two months	YES

CQ Vote Studies

	PARTY UNITY		PRESIDENTIAL SUPPORT	
	SUPPORT	OPPOSE	SUPPORT	OPPOSE
2012	91%	9%	47%	53%
2011	99%	1%	53%	47%
2010	97%	3%	42%	58%
2009	98%	2%	43%	57%
2008	99%	1%	78%	22%
2007	96%	4%	89%	11%
2006	98%	2%	91%	9%
2005	94%	6%	84%	16%
2004	97%	3%	98%	2%
2003	99%	1%	97%	3%

Interest Groups

	AFL-CIO	ADA	CCUS	ACU
2012	0%	5%	75%	92%
2011	11%	10%	100%	89%
2010	7%	5%	100%	96%
2009	11%	10%	86%	100%
2008	10%	5%	75%	96%
2007	5%	10%	55%	96%
2006	8%	5%	91%	96%
2005	21%	10%	78%	96%
2004	9%	5%	100%	96%
2003	0%	5%	100%	80%

Sen. John Barrasso (R)

Capitol Office
224-6441
barrasso.senate.gov
307 Dirksen Bldg. 20510-5003; fax 224-1724

Committees
Energy & Natural Resources
Environment & Public Works
Foreign Relations
Indian Affairs - Vice Chairman

Residence
Casper

Born
July 21, 1952; Reading, Pa.

Religion
Presbyterian

Family
Wife Bobbi Barrasso; three children

Education
Georgetown U., B.S. 1974 (biology), M.D. 1978

Career
Surgeon

Political Highlights
Sought Republican nomination for U.S. Senate, 1996; Wyo. Senate, 2003-07

ELECTION RESULTS

2012 GENERAL		
John Barrasso (R)	185,250	75.6%
Tim Chesnut (D)	53,019	21.6%
Joel Otto (WCP)	6,176	2.5%
2012 PRIMARY		
John Barrasso (R)	73,516	89.9%
Thomas Bleming (R)	5,080	6.2%
Emmett A. Mavy (R)	2,873	3.5%
2008 GENERAL		
John Barrasso (R)	183,063	73.4%
Nick Carter (D)	66,202	26.5%
2008 PRIMARY		
John Barrasso (R)		unopposed

Elected 2008; 1st full term

Appointed 2007

Barrasso, the chairman of the Republican Policy Committee, puts a clinical sheen on the GOP agenda in the Senate. The party's anti-regulatory stances play very well in his adopted home state, and as an orthopedic surgeon, he is prepared to offer alternatives to Democratic health care plans.

He has been known to set politics aside when colleagues of either party need a little unofficial medical advice. "I'm happy to visit with folks and do it with great frequency," he said, noting that the collection of lawmakers with aches and pains is "a very bipartisan group." He keeps a small lending library of reassuring brochures and pamphlets on common ailments.

Bedside manner is less of a priority when he develops and delivers the Republican message. His television appearances are more starchy than fiery — he seldom smiles or raises his voice — but he is very good at drawing the conservative line. Even before joining the Senate, he had ample experience at communicating through the media. He wrote a newspaper column called "Keeping Wyoming Healthy" and gave health and fitness commentaries on television. For two decades, he hosted state broadcasts of the annual Jerry Lewis Telethon.

His rise to the party's No. 4 leadership position began in late 2010, when he became vice chairman of the Republican Conference (the No. 5 post). Alaska's Lisa Murkowski had resigned from that job to focus on her write-in campaign for a second term. A year later, Tennessee's Lamar Alexander stepped down from the conference chairmanship, and Barrasso moved one rung up the ladder in the reshuffling.

In the 112th Congress (2011-12), he contended that Majority Leader Harry Reid had severed bipartisan relations with Republicans — but he did not hesitate to pick at the wound.

Tasked with curating and disseminating talking points to colleagues and constituents alike, Barrasso frequently focuses on the Democrats' 2010 health care overhaul. Even before heading the Policy Committee, he began commissioning colorfully named studies on the subject, including "Bad Medicine," "Grim Diagnosis" and "Warning: Side Effects."

Barrasso makes regular visits to the well of the Senate to deliver a "doctor's second opinions" on the law, and he frequently discusses it on cable news programs. "The president continued to confuse the word 'coverage' with 'care,'" Barrasso said on Fox Business Network in June 2012. "He focused so much on coverage by putting 17 million more Americans on Medicaid, but not ... on getting care to people — and affordable care. That's where the health care law has failed miserably."

The principles he outlines for an overhaul are common GOP refrains: increasing free-market practices in the health sector and making changes to medical malpractice law.

Barrasso also chairs the GOP's Western Caucus, and his committee assignments are tailored to the job. He sits on the Energy and Natural Resources Committee, the Environment and Public Works Committee, and the Indian Affairs Committee.

"I worry that the rules and regulations coming out of Washington can hurt our use of public lands in Wyoming," Barrasso said. He will on occasion put those lands off limits — Barrasso's first bill, eventually enacted as part of a 2009 omnibus lands measure, was to protect 1.2 million acres in Bridger-Teton National Forest from oil and gas development.

But he has fought attempts to set up a cap-and-trade system to curb greenhouse gas emissions, as well as regulations that he feels are threatening to

Wyoming's coal industry. Arguing on the Senate floor for a 2012 amendment to limit EPA regulation of coal-fired power plants, he accused the agency of "cooking the books" by exaggerating the health benefits of tougher standards. In 2010, he made similar accusations of data manipulation against a United Nations report on the effects of climate change.

Early in the 113th Congress (2013-14), Barrasso has led a charge for an expansion of hydropower. He is the Senate sponsor of a bill to allow small hydro projects on existing federal canals throughout the West; the proposal has bipartisan support in both chambers.

Pro-energy and anti-regulatory themes extend to his work on the Indian Affairs Committee, where he is the top Republican. Barrasso and Daniel K. Akaka, a Hawaii Democrat, introduced a 2011 bill to grant tribes more autonomy and financial resources to enter development leases without federal approval. That same year, Barrasso unveiled legislation to ease restrictions on tribes hoping to lease or develop lands held in trust.

Barrasso also sits on the Foreign Relations Committee, where he avows a "Wyoming first" agenda that includes support of free-trade agreements to boost the state's agricultural exports. In 2012, he was one of several Republicans opposing approval of the Law of the Sea Treaty, believing it would subject U.S. corporations to new regulation.

Over his political career, Barrasso has become more socially conservative. In a 1996 GOP primary race for the Senate — won by Michael B. Enzi — he opposed federal funding for abortions through Medicaid but said a decision on the procedure should be between a woman and her doctor. During four years in the state Senate, he took increasingly conservative positions and sponsored a bill to increase the penalty for killing a pregnant woman. He said most forms of abortion should be banned, and he opposes expanded federal funding of embryonic stem cell research.

He is a regular at the Senate's Prayer Breakfast and describes "a lot of bipartisan camaraderie" at the events.

Barrasso grew up in Reading, Pa., in a blue-collar Republican family. His paternal grandfather worked as a cement finisher after emigrating from Italy in the early 1900s. His father, also named John, quit school in ninth grade and joined the industry to supplement the family's income during the Great Depression. He eventually enlisted in the Army during World War II.

After the war, his father returned to cement finishing, and his mother stayed home with their three children. At age 8, Barrasso made his first trip to Washington, for the 1961 inauguration of John F. Kennedy as president — even though, as he recalls, his father had voted for Richard Nixon. He later returned to Washington to study at Georgetown University, where he majored in biology and went on to earn a medical degree.

He spent summers in Reading, laying cement during the week and working at a racetrack on weekends. As a college student, he visited Wyoming and fell in love with the Western landscape. After finishing his medical residency in New Haven, Conn., he and his now-ex-wife moved to Casper, where they raised two children. Barrasso remarried on New Year's Day in 2008.

His first campaign for public office was his 1996 bid to replace retiring Republican Sen. Alan K. Simpson; after losing to Enzi by less than 3 points in the primary, he signed on as Enzi's finance chairman.

Barrasso was elected to the Wyoming Senate in 2002 and re-elected in 2006. He was appointed to the U.S. Senate in 2007, after Republican Craig Thomas succumbed to leukemia. Wyoming had a Democratic governor, but state law required that he select a replacement from a slate of candidates chosen by the incumbent senator's party.

Barrasso easily won a special election in 2008 to fill out the remainder of the term, taking 73 percent of the vote. He did even better running for a full term in 2012, taking more than three-quarters of the vote.

Key Votes

2012	
Prohibit health insurance plans from denying coverage based on the sponsor's religious beliefs	NO
Require approval of the Keystone XL oil pipeline	YES
Ease securities rules to expand small-business access to capital	YES
Reauthorize farm and nutrition programs for five years	YES
Limit debate on a bill that would create private-sector cybersecurity standards	NO
Consent to ratification of a treaty setting global standard for the treatment of people with disabilities	YES
Provide $60.4 billion in disaster relief following Superstorm Sandy	NO
Extend most Bush-era income tax rates while allowing rates for top-bracket earners to rise (Jan. 1, 2013)	YES
2011	
Prevent EPA from regulating greenhouse gas emissions to address climate change	YES
Extend certain provisions of Patriot Act for four years	YES
Clear compromise debt limit increase plan and establish future spending limits	YES
Overhaul patent law	YES
Implement Colombia free trade agreement	YES
Limit debate on confirmation of Caitlin J. Halligan to D.C. Circuit Court of Appeals	NO
Extend payroll tax cut and unemployment benefits for two months	YES

CQ Vote Studies

	PARTY UNITY		PRESIDENTIAL SUPPORT	
	SUPPORT	OPPOSE	SUPPORT	OPPOSE
2012	89%	11%	48%	52%
2011	99%	1%	54%	46%
2010	98%	2%	37%	63%
2009	98%	2%	44%	56%
2008	99%	1%	76%	24%
2007	96%	4%	84%	16%

Interest Groups

	AFL-CIO	ADA	CCUS	ACU
2012	0%	10%	75%	88%
2011	11%	10%	100%	89%
2010	6%	0%	100%	100%
2009	11%	5%	86%	100%
2008	10%	5%	75%	96%
2007	0%	10%	75%	100%

Rep. Cynthia M. Lummis (R)

Capitol Office
225-2311
lummis.house.gov
113 Cannon Bldg. 20515-5001; fax 225-3057

Committees
Natural Resources
Oversight & Government Reform
Science, Space & Technology
(Energy - Chairwoman)

Residence
Cheyenne

Born
Sept. 10, 1954; Cheyenne, Wyo.

Religion
Lutheran - Missouri Synod

Family
Husband, Al Wiederspahn; one child

Education
U. of Wyoming, B.S. 1976 (animal science), B.S. 1978 (biology), J.D. 1985

Career
Rancher; lawyer; gubernatorial aide

Political Highlights
Wyo. House, 1979-83, 1985-93; Wyo. Senate, 1993-95; Wyo. State Lands and Investment acting director, 1997-98; Wyo. treasurer, 1999-2007

ELECTION RESULTS

2012 GENERAL		
Cynthia M. Lummis (R)	166,452	68.9%
Chris Henrichsen (D)	57,573	23.8%
Richard Brubaker (LIBERT)	8,442	3.5%
Daniel Cummings (CONSTI)	4,963	2.0%
Don Wills (WCP)	3,775	1.6%
2012 PRIMARY		
Cynthia M. Lummis (R)	73,153	98.1%
write-ins (R)	1,393	1.9%
2010 GENERAL		
Cynthia M. Lummis (R)	131,661	70.4%
David Wendt (D)	45,768	24.5%
John V. Love (LIBERT)	9,253	4.9%

Previous Winning Percentages
2008 (53%)

Elected 2008; 3rd term

Lummis considers Wyoming the best-run state in the union, bolstering her belief that most decisions should be pushed away from the federal level. If anything, she wants Washington to take more cues from her home in sorting out the nation's finances — a problem she considers a "moral imperative."

She has worked as a state legislator, gubernatorial aide and state treasurer, but three decades in politics haven't dulled her identity as a rancher. Lummis (LUH-miss) grew up in the business and owns huge chunks of property; while passionate about fiscal issues, she lights up when talking about cows. "They're my favorite non-human friends," she said. "They have lovely personalities."

By her accounting, she has ridden, trained, branded, castrated, vaccinated, shot, butchered, judged, driven, and been kicked by cattle; Lummis has pulled calves, "shoveled more poop than you can shake a stick at" and once jumped into a swollen creek to rescue a drowning calf.

That workload was excellent preparation for budget debates in the 112th Congress (2011-12), but they did not turn out to Lummis' liking. She was a member of the Appropriations Committee, but she voted against most of the bills it produced, exasperated that they didn't do more to tame deficits. "We know how to fix these problems, and we don't have the political gumption to do it," she said. Lummis took the somewhat unconventional step of leaving the committee after one term.

She was one of 16 Republicans to vote for a fiscal 2013 budget based on the work of President Barack Obama's 2010 fiscal commission (which is widely known as Simpson Bowles). The baseline plan called for $4 trillion in deficit reduction over 10 years through a combination of spending cuts, revenue increases and entitlement program changes. Lummis introduced a 2011 bill to raise the eligibility age for Social Security benefits to improve that program's solvency; she reintroduced it in 2013. When Congress extended reduced rates for the payroll tax funding Social Security at the end of 2011, she was appalled: "When do we get to the point where we stand up in front of the American people and say we can't afford this?" she asked on Fox Business Network.

Wyoming could teach the federal government something about financial planning, she said: "We balance our budgets, and we frequently do it in the face of a boom-and-bust economy" heavily tied to mineral prices. Lummis suggests that the federal government can enlist states in cost-control efforts simply by converting many programs to block grants with minimal restrictions; states can then use their knowledge of local realities to achieve results superior to federal "one-size-fits-all policies." In 2010, she helped launch the 10th Amendment Task Force, aimed at promoting the dispersal of decision-making and funding away from Washington and back to states, local governments and individuals.

On her departure from the Appropriations Committee, Lummis negotiated a return to the Natural Resources Committee, where she served as a freshman; she also joined the Science, Space and Technology Committee, which oversees many EPA activities. She chairs its Energy Subcommittee.

Joining many Western conservatives (she co-chairs the Western Caucus), Lummis wants to shrink government involvement in land and environmental management. She has focused on a 1980 law that reimburses attorney's fees for those who successfully sue the government — environmental groups with litigation shops have abused the law to defray the costs of repeated attempts to slow the development or use of public lands, she says. Her bill to narrow eligibility for the program was approved by the Judiciary Committee in late 2011; she also added sterner reporting requirements for reimbursements to a regulatory bill passed by the House in 2012.

Lummis asserts that states can manage public lands in an economically beneficial and environmentally sound manner, and she has resisted attempts to extend federal wilderness designations (and restrictions that come with them) to new tracts. "Saddling Americans with 20 more years of inactivity, slow-walking development of domestic uranium, oil, natural gas and clean coal, and making back-room deals with litigation-happy environmentalists is the legacy" of the Obama administration, she wrote in 2011.

Lummis takes the same tack on the management of endangered species. She consistently pushes for Wyoming to have greater control over its wolf population; those defending themselves or their property should not worry about lawsuits, she maintains. She was happy with the removal of gray wolves from the endangered species list in 2012. (Her family has encountered wolves on its property.) In May 2013, she and Natural Resources Chairman Doc Hastings of Washington formed a working group to study a possible overhaul of the Endangered Species Act.

A member of the conservative Republican Study Committee, Lummis is a social conservative who strongly defends gun owners' rights and opposes abortion and gay marriage.

Her family arrived in Cheyenne one year after the railroad in the 1860s. Her great-grandfather opened a hardware store, then acquired ranch land when he bought out his partner. The property stayed in the family, with Lummis and her siblings buying out many of their cousins and expanding.

The third of four children, she went to a "little bitty four-room Lutheran school. ... It was school, church and 4-H all wrapped into one. Very, very simple, wonderful life," she remembers. Ranching was always in her career plans, but she "fell head over heels for the Wyoming Legislature" during an internship with the state Senate to wrap up her college requirements. Her husband, Al Wiederspahn, is a former Democratic colleague in the state House. He is now a Cheyenne attorney.

At 24, she became the youngest woman elected to the state legislature, where an early assignment to the Judiciary Committee convinced her to attend law school. She later returned to serve 12 years in the state House and two years in the state Senate before twice being elected state treasurer.

After failing to win appointment to the Senate following the 2007 death of GOP Sen. Craig Thomas, Lummis announced her candidacy for the seat being vacated by Republican Barbara Cubin. She won a four-way GOP primary, then faced Democrat Gary Trauner, a businessman who had lost to Cubin in 2006 by less than 1 point. Lummis won that November with 53 percent of the vote, then improved to 70 percent in 2010. She had a similar result in 2012.

Key Votes

2012	
Extend a Social Security payroll tax cut and unemployment benefits	NO
Ease securities rules to expand small-business access to capital	YES
Extend for one year subsidized student loan interest rates financed by a cut in health care spending	YES
Cite Attorney General Eric H. Holder Jr. for contempt of Congress	YES
Create a visa program for foreign graduates in high-tech fields	YES
Extend most Bush-era income tax rates while allowing rates for top-bracket earners to rise (Jan. 1, 2013)	NO
2011	
Strike funding for F-35 alternative engine	YES
Prevent EPA from regulating greenhouse gas emissions to address climate change	YES
Extend certain provisions of Patriot Act for four years	YES
Declare opposition to use of ground troops in Libya	YES
Overhaul patent law	NO
Pass compromise debt limit increase plan and establish future spending limits	YES
Allow consideration of measures to implement three trade agreements	YES

CQ Vote Studies

	PARTY UNITY		PRESIDENTIAL SUPPORT	
	SUPPORT	OPPOSE	SUPPORT	OPPOSE
2012	96%	4%	24%	76%
2011	95%	5%	19%	81%
2010	95%	5%	26%	74%
2009	98%	2%	10%	90%

Interest Groups

	AFL-CIO	ADA	CCUS	ACU
2012	14%	20%	92%	92%
2011	3%	5%	94%	92%
2010	0%	0%	88%	100%
2009	5%	0%	80%	100%

Wyoming

At Large

Wyoming, the least populated state in the nation, basks in its wide-open spaces, which define its libertarian politics and natural-resources-based economy. The Grand Tetons' jagged peaks rise from the floor of the Jackson Hole Valley to their nearly 14,000-foot apex, less than 10 miles from the nation's steepest ski slopes at Jackson Hole Mountain.

Tourist attractions such as Yellowstone National Park, the first national park, are economic staples. The state relies on ranching and mining, but wind turbines have been popping up along the landscape. Although the state lacks a highly diversified economy, stability in retail and government jobs attracted some out-of-state workers from areas hit hard by the nationwide recession. Consistent population growth in the state has added roughly 80,000 residents since 2000, and only two of the state's counties — Hot Springs and Platte — shed residents between 2000 and 2010. Most residents are happy with relative seclusion, a tranquil lifestyle and moderate population growth.

Residents savor their land and resources and reject government intrusion, especially regarding land use. State lawmakers are loath to raise taxes. Wyoming, with a statewide 4 percent sales tax, has no corporate or personal income taxes.

Voters here favor the GOP but sometimes allow personality to triumph over party if a Democrat is moderate and unaffiliated with the national party. Mitt Romney won 69 percent of Wyoming's 2012 presidential vote, his second-best statewide showing in the nation. Wyoming, which has not elected a Democrat to the U.S. House since 1976, chose a Democratic governor in seven of the last 10 elections. But Republican Matt Mead easily won the 2010 gubernatorial race, taking every county in the state.

Major Industry
Mining, tourism, agriculture

Military Bases
Francis E. Warren Air Force Base, 2,585 military, 995 civilian (2011)

Cities
Cheyenne, Casper, Laramie, Gillette

Notable
In 1920, Jackson became the first U.S. town ever to elect an all-female slate — mayor, council and marshal.

Delegates

Del. Eni F.H. Faleomavaega (D)

Capitol Office
225-8577
house.gov/faleomavaega
2422 Rayburn Bldg. 20515-5201; fax 225-8757

Committees
Foreign Affairs
Natural Resources

Residence
Pago Pago

Born
Aug. 15, 1943; Vailoatai, A.S.

Religion
Mormon

Family
Wife, Hinanui Bambridge Hunkin; five children

Education
Brigham Young U., A.A. 1964, B.A. 1966 (political science); Texas Southern U., attended 1969 (law); U. of Houston, J.D. 1972; U. of California, Berkeley, LL.M. 1973

Military
Army, 1966-69; Army Reserve, 1983-2001

Career
Lawyer; territorial prosecutor; congressional aide

Political Highlights
Democratic candidate for U.S. House, 1984; lieutenant governor, 1985-89

ELECTION RESULTS

2012 GENERAL		
Eni F.H. Faleomavaega (D)	7,221	55.2%
Aumua Amata (C)	4,420	33.8%
Rosie F. Tago Lancaster (I)	697	5.3%
Kereti Mata'utia Jr. (D)	438	3.4%
Fatumalala Leulua'ial'i Al-Sheri (NPA)	300	2.3%
2010 GENERAL		
Eni F.H. Faleomavaega (D)	6,176	56.3%
Aumua Amata (R)	4,438	40.4%
Tuika Tuika (NPA)	357	3.2%

Previous Winning Percentages
2008 (60%); 2006 (47%); 2004 (65%); 2002 (41%); 2000 (46%); 1998 (86%); 1994 (64%); 1992 (65%); 1990 (55%); 1988 (51%)

Elected 1988; 13th term

Faleomavaega looks out for the little guy. He applies that ethic not only to his tiny homeland, but to his work on the Foreign Affairs Committee, where he is the top Democrat on the increasingly important Subcommittee on Asia and the Pacific.

He traces his long career in public service to his society's elders. Samoa "is kind of like an Indian reservation," he says. "Chief tells the son, go get a white man's education, learn how to speak English. Then you come back to the reservation, supposedly with all this new knowledge." He is now a chief himself — Faleomavaega is actually his title, and his family name is Hunkin.

Faleomavaega (full name: EN-ee FOL-ee-oh-mav-ah-ENG-uh) enlisted in the Army and fought in the Vietnam War; after finishing law school, he worked as an aide to American Samoa's unofficial representative in Washington. He then switched for six years to the office of Rep. Phillip Burton, the scorchingly progressive San Francisco Democrat who chaired the subcommittee overseeing the U.S. territories.

Though outwardly less fiery than his former boss, he credits Burton with teaching him a lesson: "Don't worry about these big corporations. They have batteries of lawyers that can help them. You keep an eye after the guy out there who's trying to make ends meet."

Dealing with Samoa's economic realities therefore requires a balancing act. Many of his constituents qualify as "trying to make ends meet," but Faleomavaega estimates that 80 percent of the local economy relies on two companies in the tuna industry. A 2007 law was designed to bring Samoa's dramatically lower minimum wage into alignment with rates on the U.S. mainland by 2016, but Faleomavaega has fought regular increases — Chicken of the Sea cited increased labor costs when it closed a cannery in 2009.

That facility was eventually purchased by Tri-Marine, which has made some positive investments, opening a cold storage facility in 2013 and announcing plans to base its fishing fleet in American Samoa. Starkist operates the other cannery in the territory.

There is potential for economic growth, Faleomavaega says. He sits on the Natural Resources Committee and would like to see new investment in aquaculture in the ocean surrounding the territory. He has opposed expansion of marine sanctuaries in the region unless arrangements are made for continued economic activity by locals. The tourism sector is promising, he said.

Faleomavaega has also tried to stir interest in mining minerals found in the seabed. We study what's in the seabed, "but then other countries are taking it," he said. With China dominating the global supply of rare-earth minerals — often used in technology manufacturing — extracting such resources from the oceans could have national security benefits. "You have to have the federal government involved as a facilitator" to get production going, he said.

He tries to keep his Samoa-related legislation bipartisan and noncontroversial, acknowledging that "our needs are certainly not as big" as those of the states. On the Foreign Affairs Committee, where he has sat for two decades, he is less inhibited. Faleomavaega scorns unilateralism and sympathizes with more-vulnerable nations or populaces.

As the chairman of the Asia and the Pacific Subcommittee in the 110th and 111th Congresses (2007-10), Faleomavaega called attention to the effect of the defoliant Agent Orange on the health of the Vietnamese people. Despite the protests of the Japanese government, he encouraged House passage of a 2007 resolution calling for Japan to atone for the use of sex slaves by its military in World War II. And he pushed for assistance to the countries he believes are most vulnerable to dangers posed by global climate change.

In 2011, he became the ranking member. He urged the Obama administration to lift economic sanctions on the military-controlled government of Fiji; the 2006 coup in that nation was understandable considering the longtime cultural and ethnic strains on that island, he said. In 2013, he accused the United States of unfairly criticizing Sri Lanka for alleged human rights abuses, as its government was emerging from a long battle with terrorist groups.

Faleomavaega says he understands the political status of many Asian nations — their leaders end up as socialists or Marxists "because the worst examples of democracy and freedom were these European countries that came to colonize them." He sees inherent hypocrisy straining U.S. dealings on issues such as nuclear nonproliferation, believing nations are motivated by self-defense in their efforts to obtain weapons.

Our problems, he says, stem from the unilateralist approach of the George W. Bush era: "We just come charging in there, like we are the big mighty America, and we're gonna kick ass and we're gonna set the terms." Faleomavaega is highly dubious that the Iraq War will have long-term benefits and believes the decision to break off engagement with North Korea was disastrous.

He agrees with the Obama administration's preference to address international issues on "the community basis." Adversarial relations with China are not necessary, he said: "I don't think the U.S. can do anything without China's participation or consultation. And China also realizes its economy is just as much dependent on the U.S. So there's a mutual need." But he worries about apparent attempts by China to control shipping lanes in the South China Sea.

Faleomavaega was born on Samoa, the second of eight children. His father was a communications operator for the Navy and brought the family to Hawaii when he was transferred there. During his time in Hawaii, Faleomavaega played high school football and performed in Polynesian dancing shows, once meeting Elvis Presley during a film shoot. He also worked as a canoe paddler — and in 1987, he was the Samoan representative on a Tahiti-to-Hawaii trip of the famous Hokule'a voyaging canoe. The four-week journey "was one of the most spiritual experiences in my life," he said.

He was "just a grunt" in Vietnam, and he resented the treatment of U.S. troops, "where we were being accused of being baby-killers and monsters." He finished law school and spent eight years in Washington before returning to Pago Pago. Faleomavaega served as a prosecutor and lieutenant governor before his election as delegate in 1988.

Faleomavaega hopes for an eventual change in his homeland's relationship to the United States. "Being an unincorporated and unorganized territory is not positive," he said.

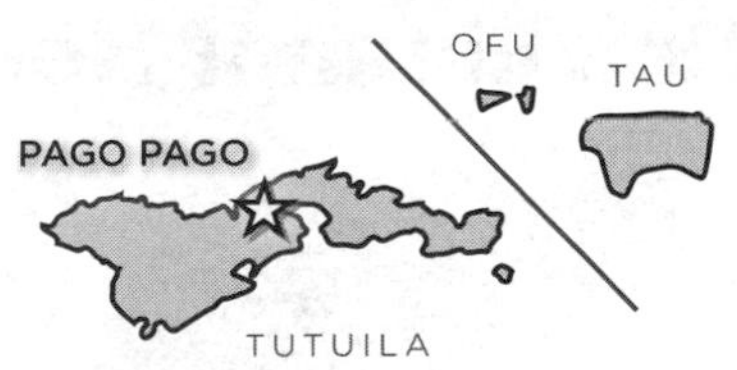

American Samoa

Capital: Pago Pago

Governor: Lolo Matalasi Moliga (I), elected 2012, 4-year term

Lieutenant governor: Lemanu Peleti Mauga (I), elected 2012, 4-year term

Legislative branch: Nonpartisan, bicameral assembly

House: 20 members, 1 non-voting delegate, 2-year terms

Senate: 18 members elected by and from local chiefs, 4-year terms

Web: americansamoa.gov

2010 population: 55,519

2000 population: 57,291

American Samoa

At Large

In the heart of Polynesia, American Samoa is the nation's southernmost territory. Located about 2,500 miles southwest of Hawaii, it is composed of five volcanic islands and two outlying coral atolls. Its total land area is 77 square miles, slightly more than the District of Columbia. Tourists venture here for snorkeling, fishing, hiking and the islands' secluded beaches.

An 1899 treaty gave the United States control over the islands in the eastern portion of the Samoan archipelago. During World War II, the U.S. Marine Corps, attracted by the deep-water harbor at Pago Pago, made the island an advanced training and staging center. Today it is an unincorporated territory of the United States, administered by the Interior Department. Residents are U.S. nationals, not citizens, and the territory has had a non-voting delegate since 1981.

The largest and main island of Tutuila, called "The Rock," is where most of the population lives. Most land on the islands is communally owned. Per capita income is very low ($8,000), and federal aid, including welfare and the Supplemental Nutrition Assistance Program, is vital. Economic growth, even in the promising tourism sector, is hindered by American Samoa's isolation, limited transportation and susceptibility to hurricanes and tsunamis.

In recent years, there has been a concerted government effort to cope with the islands' limited resources of fresh water, and in 2010 the island made it illegal for stores to hand out plastic bags, hoping to protect the islands' habitats.

Tuna fishing and processing is key to the private sector economy. Widespread unemployment — estimated to be close to 25 percent — across the territory concerns officials and residents.

Nearly all residents here claim native Pacific Islander heritage, with a small percentage of Asian descent. Almost half of Samoans are Christian Congregationalist and another 20 percent or so are Roman Catholic, and the residents are devout, with many stores closed on Sundays.

Major Industry

Government, fishing, handicrafts, tourism

Villages

Tafuna, Nu'uuli, Pago Pago

Notable

Anthropologist Margaret Mead studied on Ta'u and wrote "Coming of Age in Samoa."

Del. Eleanor Holmes Norton (D)

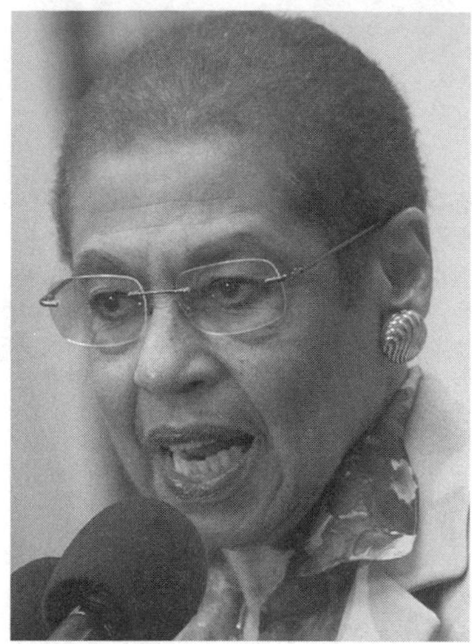

Capitol Office
225-8050
norton.house.gov
2136 Rayburn Bldg. 20515-5100; fax 225-3002

Committees
Oversight & Government Reform
Transportation & Infrastructure

Residence
Washington

Born
June 13, 1937; Washington, D.C.

Religion
Episcopalian

Family
Divorced; two children

Education
Antioch College, B.A. 1960 (history); Yale U., M.A. 1963 (American studies), LL.B. 1964

Career
Professor; lawyer

Political Highlights
New York City Commission on Human Rights, 1970-77; Equal Employment Opportunity Commission chairwoman, 1977-81

ELECTION RESULTS

2012 GENERAL		
Eleanor Holmes Norton (D)	246,664	88.5%
Bruce Majors (LIBERT)	16,524	5.9%
Natale "Lino" Stracuzzi (SGREEN)	13,243	4.8%
2012 PRIMARY		
Eleanor Holmes Norton (D)	52,881	97.3%
write-ins (D)	1,474	2.7%
2010 GENERAL		
Eleanor Holmes Norton (D)	117,990	88.9%
Missy Reilly Smith (R)	8,109	6.1%
Rick Tingling-Clemmons (GREEN)	4,413	3.3%
write-ins (WRI)	1,359	1.0%

Previous Winning Percentages
2008 (92%); 2006 (97%); 2004 (91%); 2002 (93%); 2000 (90%); 1998 (90%); 1996 (90%); 1994 (89%); 1992 (85%); 1990 (62%)

Elected 1990; 12th term

Norton manages an impressive dichotomy in her congressional work. Sometimes described as "the Warrior on the Hill," she can be scathing to those who oppose D.C. voting rights and autonomy. But she also garners respect from all quarters as an effective promoter of the capital's economy.

Her rhetoric on the city's political status is borrowed from the Revolutionary era — she has been a key figure in reviving the "no taxation without representation" slogan. She describes as "self-evident" the city's rights to a voting representative and a local government free from congressional interference. The purpose of home rule, granted in 1973, was "to restore, not to create, rights," she has said.

Her conviction recalls the civil rights era. Norton is a third-generation Washingtonian. Her mother taught elementary school, and her lawyer father worked on housing issues for the city government; they were Roosevelt Democrats. Norton attended the segregated and prestigious Dunbar High School, within view of the Capitol — it was a de facto magnet school for blacks hoping to attend college. She was there May 17, 1955, when the Supreme Court handed down its desegregation decision in Brown v. Board of Education.

A strong education was essential "to get around the segregation, to get around the strictures in the District," she said. At the famously liberal Antioch College in Ohio, she became involved in protests through the NAACP, and she continued her activism while studying law at Yale.

Living in New York, Norton worked as an assistant legal director for the American Civil Liberties Union and later chaired the New York City Commission on Human Rights from 1970 to 1977. That led to her appointment as head of the Equal Employment Opportunity Commission during the Jimmy Carter administration. She is still energetic — Norton often race-walks around the city — as she approaches her late 70s.

Norton's first bill in 1991, often reintroduced since, was to admit D.C. to the union as a state. She has also pursued a slew of proposals to protect or expand local autonomy and representation. In 2007 and 2009 she almost secured voting representation in the House, but those efforts collapsed over Democrat-opposed amendments to nullify the city's gun control laws.

She sits on the Oversight and Government Reform Committee. In the 112th Congress (2011-12), she boasted an excellent working relationship with two influential Republicans: Darrell Issa of California, the full-panel chairman, and Trey Gowdy of South Carolina, the chairman of the subcommittee with jurisdiction over D.C. "Everybody's grown-up on this committee," she said in 2012. At the start of 2013, a reorganization made D.C. affairs the purview of the full committee, to Norton's approval.

Issa has pleasantly surprised her with his efforts to eliminate the need for congressional approval of the city's budget. Delays caused by the approval process make life difficult for city government and hurt the District on the municipal bond market, Norton says. She called Issa's proposal "very close to my own." There was a sticking point in 2012, however: possible Republican amendments restricting city funding of abortion providers. "We don't bargain away our rights," Norton said. The bill did not move, and Issa and Norton are continuing their efforts in the 113th Congress (2013-14).

Although she fights to become a full-voting House member, Norton says that her current status has not hindered her work. Her record on economic development seems to support that claim. Washington's high-cost housing drives many taxpayers into Virginia and Maryland, and Norton won 1997 enactment (and continual renewal) of a $5,000 tax credit for homebuyers in the District. Similarly, some people leave the city to take advantage of in-state tuition rates for state college systems. In 1999, she secured annual grants of up to $10,000 for D.C. students to go to any state-supported institution in the country.

And then there's property development. Norton worked her way onto the Transportation and Infrastructure Subcommittee on Economic Development, Public Buildings and Emergency Management — she says it "may be the best decision I have ever made in the Congress." She chaired the panel from 2007 through 2010 and is now its ranking member. Among other things, it decides on leases and construction projects in the federal city.

Norton steered the new headquarters for the Department of Homeland Security to the city's economically stagnant Ward 8, where it is under construction. She also has helped free up federal land along the Anacostia River for economic development by the private sector. She wants the National Park Service to enter into more public-private partnerships to provide services to consumers — she envisions more bike rental stations and economic activity along the National Mall.

Plus, she would like to keep the famous Smithsonian museums free for all visitors, and urges more transparency for the Smithsonian bureaucracy.

Her subcommittee's emergency response portfolio gave her a chance to scold federal officials for their response to the 2011 earthquake that shook the city. The chaotic mobilization of resources and instructions to commuters showed that the city is unprepared to respond to terrorist attacks, she said.

Norton looks beyond the District, usually with a liberal gaze, on a number of issues. She has constantly pushed for an expansion of pre-kindergarten programs offered by school districts, and she has suggested using grants as incentives for such expansion. Doing so would maximize the use of existing educational infrastructure and lower child-raising costs, she says.

With a nod to her EEOC days, she often introduces a measure to "prohibit discrimination in the payment of wages on account of sex, race, or national origin." In 2011, she made headlines by walking out of an Oversight hearing when Republicans refused to accept a Georgetown University Law Center student as a witness on contraception in health care plans provided by religion-affiliated institutions. (Georgetown is a Jesuit school.)

Norton herself was teaching law at Georgetown in 1990 when Democratic Del. Walter E. Fauntroy stepped down to run for mayor. She won that year with almost 62 percent of the vote, and she has never won less than 84 percent since.

She still teaches a class at Georgetown: "I need that part of my brain," she said, "so I go to fetch it every other week." She is also a fan of the theater, attending plays in the city when she can.

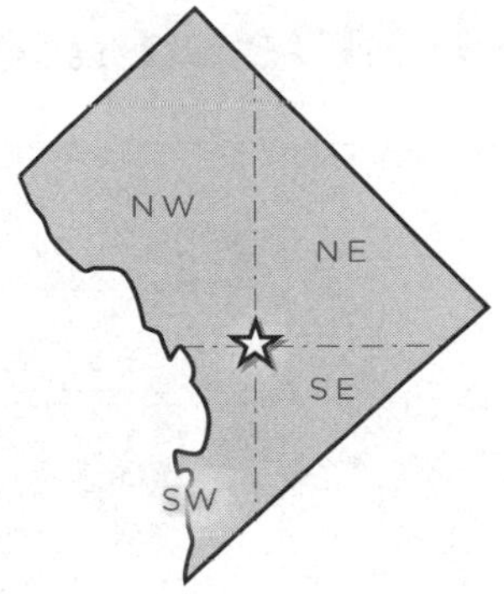

District of Columbia

Capital: Washington

Mayor: Vincent C. Gray (D), elected 2010, 4-year term

Legislature: City council with 13 members, 4-year terms. Actions of the council can be overturned by the U.S. Congress.

2013 council ratios: 11 D, 2 I

Web: dccouncil.us/council

2010 population: 601,723

2000 population: 572,059

Median age: 34.1

District of Columbia

At Large

"Taxation Without Representation." That slogan on the District's license plates sums up residents' displeasure at not being able to participate fully in a democracy they host. The city's budget and laws are subject to review and veto by Congress, a body in which residents have no vote.

Although residents do vote for president, a non-voting delegate in the House (continuously since 1971) and an elected mayor (since 1974), efforts to gain full participation in the U.S. government — including bids for statehood — have not yet succeeded. Local politics are dominated by Democrats, but elections are plagued by low turnout despite the politics-driven atmosphere of the city.

It is no surprise that the main business of the nation's capital is government. Hundreds of thousands of District residents work for the federal or local governments or in related private sector work, such as lobbying, law and journalism. It also is no surprise that the District draws hordes of tourists — from high school students to foreign travelers — who come to see the Smithsonian museums and national monuments. Clogged roads and local transportation improvements remain top concerns for residents.

The city's wealth is mainly concentrated in its Northwest quadrant, but some revitalized areas, such as those east of the U.S. Capitol, attract bars, restaurants and young professionals. Development efforts along the Anacostia River and in the Northeast quadrant are ongoing and may spur economic growth. The District's population has grown since 2000, but its longtime black majority has dwindled to just 51 percent.

Major Industry

Government, professional services, tourism, retail

Military Bases

Joint Base Anacostia-Bolling, 13,405 military, 2,977 civilian (2011); Joint Base Myer-Henderson Hall, 9,800 military, 1,000 civilian (shared with Virginia's 8th) (2012); Naval Support Activity Washington, 3,658 military, 14,622 civilian

City

Washington, D.C.

Notable

Since residents began casting votes for president in 1964, the Republican candidate's share has ranged from a high of 22 percent in 1972 to a low of less than 7 percent in 2008.

Del. Madeleine Z. Bordallo (D)

Capitol Office
225-1188
bordallo.house.gov
2441 Rayburn Bldg. 20515-5301; fax 226-0341

Committees
Armed Services
Natural Resources

Residence
Tamuning

Born
May 31, 1933; Graceville, Minn.

Religion
Roman Catholic

Family
Widowed; one child

Education
Saint Mary's College (Ind.), attended 1952-53; The College of St. Catherine, attended 1953

Career
Guam first lady; shoe company founder; radio show host

Political Highlights
Guam Senate, 1981-83, 1987-95; Democratic nominee for governor, 1990; lieutenant governor, 1995-2003

ELECTION RESULTS

2012 GENERAL		
Madeleine Z. Bordallo (D)	19,765	59.9%
Frank Flores Blas Jr. (R)	12,995	39.4%
2012 PRIMARY		
Madeleine Z. Bordallo (D)	7,866	73.1%
Karlo Dizon (D)	2,829	26.3%
2010 GENERAL		
Madeleine Z. Bordallo (D)		unopposed

Previous Winning Percentages
2008 (95%); 2006 (96%); 2004 (97%); 2002 (65%)

Elected 2002; 6th term

Bordallo has been near the center of Guam politics for four decades, first as a governor's wife and then as an elected official in her own right. Her latest and most momentous mission is orchestrating a military buildup on Guam as part of America's "strategic pivot" to the Pacific theater.

She has a reputation for being both gracious and tenacious, even if she has slowed somewhat at 80 years of age. Bordallo (bore-DAA-yo) describes much of her work as being a "lobbyist" for Guam and her biggest challenge as keeping the distant island on the minds of fellow lawmakers: "Just to show them, you know, that we exist." To that end, she has employed tactics from hosting congressional delegations on the island to arranging Guam theme days in the members dining room.

Her job has gotten a little easier in recent years, with the Obama administration's stated intention of shifting many military and diplomatic resources to the Pacific. Bordallo fully supports that notion — and just about any initiative to sustain the military — as the top Democrat on the Armed Services Subcommittee on Readiness. She has held that post since 2011.

America should "never cut funding from the military forces," she said. Though an active participant on military debates spanning the globe, she is particularly hawkish when it comes to the multibillion-dollar buildup of the military presence on Guam initiated in the mid-2000s.

Part of her interest is strategic. Guam and the Northern Marianas are the westernmost territories, putting them closer to China and North Korea than any other U.S. soil. "It's important for the United States to have a forward military presence that is capable of responding to nuclear threats, and in a timely manner," she said, citing 2012 missile tests by North Korea. That regime "continues to demonstrate the need for the U.S. to remain a visible power in the Asia-Pacific area. The distribution of U.S. Marine Corps forces in Guam and throughout the Pacific will definitely play a significant role in promoting regional stability." In April 2013, the Pentagon announced that a land-based missile defense system was on its way to Guam.

The military buildup also has huge implications for Guam's economy, which is supported in large part by defense spending. As lawmakers discussed buildup plans, Bordallo worked to codify various contracting preferences for island businesses; in 2005, President George W. Bush signed a bill with her provision to designate Guam as a "HUB Zone," giving small businesses there advantages when competing for federal contracts.

In the 112th Congress (2011-12), Bordallo found herself fighting a possible downgrade to buildup plans. The Obama administration announced new talks with Japan to reconsider reallocations of U.S. military resources from that nation. Bordallo warned constituents in a radio address that original estimates of more than 8,000 Marines shifted to Guam might be cut in half, and she called on local officials to present a united front in presenting concerns to the Pentagon. She has been worried that recent defense policy laws have not included specific authorizations for spending on civilian infrastructure in Guam to accommodate an influx of military population.

Bordallo has eggs in other economic baskets, however. She has kept an eye on China, co-chairing the Congressional China Caucus with J. Randy Forbes of Virginia, the Seapower and Projection Forces Subcommittee chairman. The biggest problem with China, she says, is its secrecy: "At least we know where we are with North Korea." But she has courted Chinese (and Russian) visitors, attempting since 2008 to allow visa waivers for those headed to Guam or the Northern Marianas — tourism is another driver of local development.

Bordallo went against most House Democrats in calling for approval of a South Korea free-trade agreement in 2011. She introduced a bill to make Guam and other territories eligible to compete for various federal grant programs bolstering infrastructure projects, with a particular eye on a possible ferry system linking Guam and the Northern Marianas.

She has also looked to address high energy costs, a common problem in the territories. Bordallo sits on the Natural Resources Committee, and from 2007 through 2010 she chaired the Subcommittee on Fisheries, Oceans, Wildlife and Insular Affairs. "I think Guam is behind" in the development of alternative energy sources, she said, and she hopes for more study of energy generated from ocean waves. She laments that too many bills on ocean policy from her time as chairwoman died in the Senate.

One Bordallo effort from that era was revived and enacted in the fiscal 2012 defense policy law: an update of the law (known as the Sikes Act) governing natural resources management on land under the Pentagon's jurisdiction. Bordallo's provision expanded it to National Guard facilities, many of which cover large coastal areas around Guam, in the hope of allowing further recreational and economic uses. She still pursues changes to make administration of the Sikes Act more nimble.

For all her ties to the territory, Bordallo was born in Minnesota, where her father was a school superintendent. In her teen years, he landed a job as a principal in Guam and moved the family nearly 7,000 miles. Bordallo came back to the mainland to study music — she told McClatchy News in 2006 that she dreamed of being an opera star — but a romance brought her back to her adopted home. She married Ricardo J. Bordallo, the scion of a wealthy and connected island family. His election as governor in the mid-1970s made her Guam's first lady. She later won election to the Guam Senate.

In 1990, caught up in a corruption case, Ricardo Bordallo wrapped himself in the Guam flag, chained himself to a statue on the island's main thoroughfare and shot himself in the head. "It was probably the most difficult time of my life," Bordallo said, but she credits the Guam custom of mourning with helping her recover. "You are never left alone; you are always surrounded by family and friends."

That year, she lost the gubernatorial race to Republican Joseph F. Ada. She remained in the legislature and later served eight years as lieutenant governor. In 2002, when five-term Democratic Del. Robert A. Underwood ran unsuccessfully for governor, Bordallo defeated Ada in the U.S. House race with 65 percent of the vote. She was the first woman to seek the island's delegate post.

Bordallo beat 20-something Karlo Dizon in the 2012 primary, then defeated Guam Sen. Frank Flores Blas Jr. — her first Republican challenger since 2002.

Guam

Capital: Hagatna

Governor: Eddie Calvo (R), elected 2010, 4-year term

Lieutenant governor: Ray Tenorio (R), elected 2010, 4-year term

Legislative branch: Senate with 15 members, 2-year terms

2013 Senate ratios: 9 D, 6 R

Web: www.guamlegislature.com

2010 Population: 159,358

2000 Population: 154,805

Median age: 27.4

Guam

At Large

"Where America's day begins," Guam is the largest and most southerly island in the Marianas archipelago. At 212 square miles, it is about three times the size of the District of Columbia and is made up of 19 municipalities, or villages. More than 3,800 miles west of Hawaii and across the International Date Line from the U.S. mainland, Guam is closer to Tokyo than to Honolulu.

The indigenous people, the Chamorros (38 percent of the island's population claims heritage), first had contact with Europeans in 1521 with the visit of Ferdinand Magellan. Spain ceded Guam to the United States in 1898, and the U.S. Navy administered Guam until 1950, when residents were granted U.S. citizenship and elected a local government. Guam has had a non-voting delegate in the House since 1973. Although residents are citizens, they may not vote in presidential elections.

Guam's economy is heavily dependent on a U.S. military presence, which is expected to increase here by 2014, when thousands of U.S. Marines will begin relocation to Guam from bases in Japan. Officials hope Guam increases in importance as a strategic hub in the Asia-Pacific region. A tropical climate, pristine beaches with coral reefs and a picturesque countryside make the island an ideal vacation spot; tourism — including a significant number of visitors from Japan — is vital to the local economy. Per capita income in 2012 was $12,864.

Most food and other consumer goods are imported. In recent years, Guam has had to cope with large influxes of illegal immigrants, who pay smugglers to sneak them onto the island to seek asylum in the United States. The island is also vulnerable to large storms.

Major Industry

Military, tourism, construction, shipping

Military Bases

Naval Base Guam, 4,000 military, 2,000 civilian; Andersen Air Force Base, 2,334 military, 400 civilian

Districts

Dededo, Yigo, Tamuning

Notable

At the bottom of Apra Harbor, scuba divers can see the remains of the German ship SMS Cormoran, scuttled in WWI, and the Japanese cargo ship Tokai Maru, which sank during WWII, side by side.

Del. Gregorio Kilili Camacho Sablan (D)

Capitol Office
225-2646
sablan.house.gov
423 Cannon Bldg. 20515-5201; fax 226-4249

Committees
Education & the Workforce
Natural Resources

Residence
Saipan

Born
Jan. 19, 1955; Saipan, N. Marianas

Religion
Roman Catholic

Family
Wife, Andrea C. Sablan; six children

Education
U. of Hawaii, Manoa, attended 1989-90

Military
Army Reserve, 1981-86

Career
Election commission director; gubernatorial aide

Political Highlights
N. Marianas Democratic Party chairman, 1982-83; N. Marianas House, 1982-86

ELECTION RESULTS

2012 GENERAL		
Gregorio Kilili Camacho Sablan (D)	9,829	79.7%
Ignacia Tudela Demapan (R)	2,503	20.3%
2010 GENERAL		
Gregorio Kilili Camacho Sablan (D)	4,896	43.2%
Joseph Camacho (COV)	2,744	24.2%
Juan N. Babauta (R)	1,978	17.5%
Jesus Borja (D)	1,707	15.1%

Previous Winning Percentages
2008 (24%)

Elected 2008; 3rd term

Sablan has the fewest constituents of any member of Congress, but no shortage of problems to tackle. While his political sensibilities place him squarely in the Democratic Caucus, he emphasizes gratitude as he tries to shape perceptions of the Northern Marianas. "When I go home," he said, "I tell people that when they see an American taxpayer, say 'thank you.'"

He set his sights on the delegate position while working in the office of Democratic Sen. Daniel K. Inouye of Hawaii as part of a fellowship. That was in 1986, two decades before the post even existed. When the seat was created, "I didn't have a decision to make," he said. "I'd already made it 22 years ago."

His wait was not rewarded with enviable circumstances. Notorious lobbyist Jack Abramoff counted the government of the Commonwealth of the Northern Mariana Islands, or CNMI, as a client, and his 2006 conviction for corruption and fraud made the territory politically radioactive to many. The garment industry that had propped up much of the local economy completely collapsed in the middle of the decade, and the islands' population and gross domestic product have dropped at an alarming pace.

What's more, Sablan has often been at cross purposes with local leaders. "I know that some of the problems are in the leadership of our government — self-inflicted," he said. "When we had the garment industry and we had the boom years, we didn't invest in the future, and those are decisions that have come back to haunt us now." Sablan had numerous disputes with Republican Gov. Benigno Fitial — who resigned in February 2013, shortly after he was impeached on allegations of corruption and financial mismanagement.

In Washington, Sablan has made an effort at rebuilding political bridges destroyed by the Abramoff scandal, while also seeking any means to get the local economy on its feet again. The CNMI has varying degrees of participation in a number of federal programs. Sablan's ultimate goal is parity with the states, but for now, he's "just trying to catch up with the other territories."

For the 113th Congress (2013-14), he regained a seat on the Education and the Workforce Committee, where he sat as a freshman. He calls education his No. 1 priority: "I truly believe that training and educating our people would bring us the prosperity we need to get to, whether it's going to be physicians or teachers or people that flip burgers — whatever it is, it's in the training and education."

He was very pleased with the more than $40 million the commonwealth received in "stabilization" funds from the 2009 stimulus law, as much of it went toward schools. Sablan emphasizes the importance of formula grants for his district and supports an increased focus on vocational training programs.

Many workforce issues for the CNMI are tied to immigration. A 2008 law extended federal immigration law to the territory, via a phase-in period that is scheduled to conclude in 2014. The transition has created economic and demographic turmoil. The CNMI has a large number of foreign "contingent workers," many of whom came in with the garment industry. (Increases in the territory's minimum wage — which Sablan supports — and reports of labor abuses led to the collapse of that industry.)

Sablan worries that U.S. citizens are losing jobs to foreigners, and he criticized the Department of Homeland Security in 2011 for allowing more than 22,000 foreign workers to remain during the transition.

At the same time, he is wary of decimating the workforce — it is still not clear how many contingent workers will be allowed after 2014, or if longtime residents would be asked to leave. Sablan shared his concerns with a group of senators negotiating an immigration overhaul at the start of 2013, and a section on the Marianas was included in the bill they produced.

From the Natural Resources Committee, Sablan has tried to win the CNMI control of submerged lands off its coasts. He is the ranking member of the Fisheries, Wildlife, Oceans and Insular Affairs panel, and the House has overwhelmingly endorsed his bill to let the local government manage the waters up to three miles offshore — a privilege enjoyed by every other coastal state and territory. The federal government "does nothing with the potential of these lands," Sablan said on the House floor in 2011, and he believes aquaculture could help spur economic growth. The bill has stalled in the Senate, but he was optimistic that the 2013 version might see action.

The House has also passed his bill to order a feasibility study for a National Park site on the lightly developed island of Rota, which he paints as an ecotourism destination for travelers looking to escape the huge cities of Asia. Sablan has pushed for visa waivers for countries such as Russia and China, whose citizens treat the islands as a vacation spot.

Known as Kilili at home, Sablan is the first Chamorro (the indigenous people of the Mariana Islands) to serve in Congress. He is solidly built, smokes cigarettes, has a prominent tattoo on his hand and hints at a wild youth. Sablan "wasn't exactly your good kid," he said. "I hung around with people much older than me."

Any rebelliousness might have been stoked by the fact that he has six sisters and no brothers; Sablan himself has one son and five daughters. His life took a turn for the better, he said, when he was sent to a Jesuit boarding school on the Micronesian island of Chuuk at age 11. He was the only Chamorro there, so "I know how it feels to be a minority of one." Several summers were spent exploring the islands of the South Pacific.

Sablan's father worked for Bank of America and was also involved in the commonwealth government. Several family members have political ties — Sablan's uncle was the mayor of Saipan.

Sablan finished high school in Saipan and attended college in Guam and California, returning home when his father lost his job with the bank. He lost a 1980 bid to join the CNMI's relatively young government (commonwealth status was granted in 1976), but he served as a gubernatorial aide and won in his second attempt. He served two terms, then went to work for Inouye in D.C.

During the 1990s, he served as an aide to two more governors, then was named executive director of the Commonwealth Election Commission in 1999. He held that position until resigning to run for the newly created delegate position in 2008. Sablan won a nine-way race for the U.S. House seat that year — thanks to the small population of the island, he garnered fewer than 2,500 votes in his victory — and was easily re-elected in 2010 and 2012.

Northern Mariana Islands

Capital: Saipan

Governor: Eloy S. Inos, promoted from lieutenant governor in February 2013, 5-year term expires January 2015

Lieutenant governor: Jude U. Hofschneider, promoted from Senate president in February 2013, 5-year term expires January 2015

Legislative branch: Bicameral assembly

House: 20 members, 2-year terms

2013 House ratios: 12 I, 4 R, 4 C*

Senate: 9 members, staggered 4-year terms

2013 Senate ratios: 5 R, 4 I

Web: www.cnmileg.gov.mp

2010 population: 53,883

2000 population: 69,221

Median age: 33.4

*Note: Covenant Party

Northern Mariana Islands

At Large

A string of more than a dozen mostly volcanic islands forming the eastern boundary of the Philippine Sea in the tropical Pacific Ocean, the Northern Mariana Islands rely on the federal government and tourism. Saipan, the commonwealth's largest island and capital, supports more than 90 percent of the population and most of the local economy. Tinian and Rota are the commonwealth's other inhabited islands. Pagan consists of two stratovolcanoes, one of which had a major eruption most recently in 1981.

After three centuries of colonization by Spain, decades of control by Germany and then Japan, and participation in a territorial structure with other Micronesian islands, the Northern Marianas in 1976 became a commonwealth of the United States. Residents are U.S. citizens but cannot vote in presidential elections. Formerly represented in Washington by a resident representative, the Northern Marianas gained a delegate to the U.S. House with a two-year term in 2009.

Tourists and prospective members of the workforce arrive in large numbers from Asia, and Asians make up a significant portion of the population. Filipinos and Chamorros, a native island population, make up the largest individual ethnic groups, and many residents here identify multiple ethnic backgrounds. More than 85 percent of the population speaks a language other than English at home.

The federal government is a stable source of jobs, as well as a source of economic subsidies. Hotels are among the largest employers on the islands, but employment rates, family incomes and the islands' population have decreased over the past decade. The garment industry used to be a major, and controversial, employer, but the last factory closed in 2009. Household incomes in the Northern Marianas tend hover in the $20,000s. The islands have a small agricultural sector, mainly producing vegetables, cattle, melons and coconuts.

Major Industry
Government, tourism

Islands
Saipan, Tinian, Rota

Notable
The islands' national anthem is "Gi Talo Gi Halom Tasi," which translates to "In the Middle of the Sea."

Res. Cmmsr. Pedro R. Pierluisi (D)

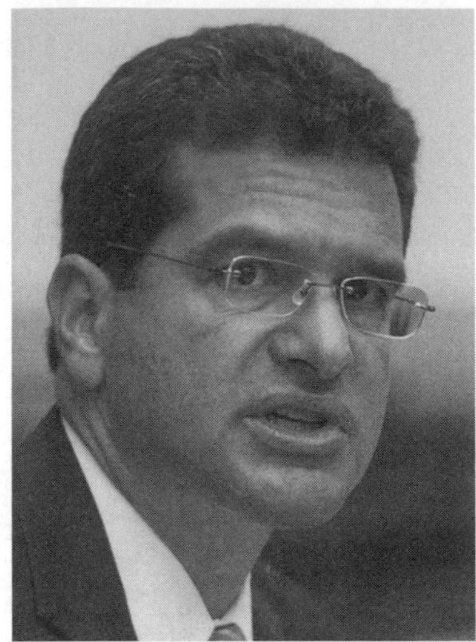

Capitol Office
225-2615
pierluisi.house.gov
1213 Longworth Bldg. 20515-5401; fax 225-2154

Committees
Ethics
Judiciary
Natural Resources

Residence
San Juan

Born
April 26, 1959; San Juan, P.R.

Religion
Roman Catholic

Family
Wife, Maria Elena Carrion; four children

Education
Tulane U., B.A. 1981 (American history); George Washington U., J.D. 1984

Career
Lawyer

Political Highlights
P.R. secretary of Justice, 1993-96

ELECTION RESULTS

2012 GENERAL

Pedro R. Pierluisi (D)	895,003	48.7%
Rafael Cox Alomar (POPDEM)	873,113	47.6%
Juan Manuel Mercado Nieves (PRI)	37,844	2.1%

Previous Winning Percentages
2008 (53%)

Elected 2008; 2nd term

Pierluisi represents close to 3.7 million Puerto Ricans, a job that would be shared among seven congressmen should his hopes for statehood be realized. For now, he attempts to expand the federal presence in the commonwealth and cultivates alliances within the Democratic Party. "Representing a place like ours that is pretty much disenfranchised, you better be well liked," he says. "Otherwise, you're gonna get fried."

His youthful appearance is complemented by general animation. Pierluisi is a lawyer who once served as Puerto Rico's attorney general; law-and-order issues are a big part of his workload.

He belongs to the business-friendly New Democrat Coalition and is very much a party loyalist. In the 112th Congress (2011-12), he oversaw community mobilization plans for the Democratic Congressional Campaign Committee, he aided the Democratic National Committee, and he served on the Ethics Committee — an often unwanted assignment that is sometimes taken as a favor to party leaders. He still serves there in the 113th Congress (2013-14).

Although Pierluisi cannot vote on the House floor in the Committee of the Whole — delegates were stripped of that power in 2011 — he has served as a regional whip. He finds it "offensive and even embarrassing to ... not be able to vote on behalf of my people."

Statehood would erase that condition. Pierluisi says the only real question is when that will happen. A relationship of more than a century has resulted in strong economic, governmental and cultural ties to the United States. "The world has been getting smaller," he said. "The idea of having a Hispanic state ... located in the Caribbean is going to be more and more acceptable." He paints it as a logical way forward for those who believe in participatory democracy.

In a two-part plebiscite in November 2012, 54 percent of voters indicated that they do not want Puerto Rico's current status to continue. Given a list of three alternative statuses, 61 percent chose statehood.

There were some mixed signals: many people left the second question blank; the pro-statehood governor, Luis Fortuño, lost a very close election; and the pro-statehood party lost control of the legislature. Pierluisi, who also appears on Puerto Rican ballots as a member of the pro-statehood party, won a second term by scarcely more than 1 point. (To add to the confusion, on the federal level, Fortuño identifies as a Republican.)

But Pierluisi saw the results as a call to action, and the White House has indicated support for a federally sponsored status vote. Pierluisi would like to start plotting out how a possible transition to statehood might work. Like other territories, Puerto Rico has patchwork eligibility for federal programs and funding. Equal treatment can be phased in, Pierluisi says, along with federal income taxes — the commonwealth currently does not pay them.

Among other things, Pierluisi sees statehood as a boon for a territory where the unemployment rate is consistently much higher than the national average. "I believe that Puerto Rico's economy will never unleash its tremendous potential under its current political status," he said in 2011.

In the meantime, he attempts to boost the economy in other ways. With thoughts of attracting investment, he introduced a 2011 bill to allow some companies incorporated in Puerto Rico to operate as domestic U.S. companies, mitigating the tax impact when profits are "repatriated" into the United States. He applauded the territory's reduction of its corporate and individual tax rates as "pro-growth." And at his request, the federal government agreed in 2011 to study how the Jones Act affects the territorial economy. That law prevents foreign-registered vessels from cruising between U.S. ports, possibly stifling employment in Puerto Rico's yachting industry.

Pierluisi helped expand the territory's Medicaid funding under the 2010 health care law and wants better Medicare reimbursement rates for Puerto Rican hospitals. He believes Puerto Rico's disabled citizens should be eligible for Supplemental Security Income. Critics have noted that Puerto Ricans don't pay income taxes to the Treasury, from where that program is funded; Pierluisi points out that "pretty much half" of U.S. households don't pay income taxes, yet have eligibility thanks to geographic circumstance.

As a member of the Judiciary Committee, he has tried to steer attention to drug violence in Puerto Rico. Homicides spiked early in Pierluisi's tenure as attorney general in the 1990s, and his 28-year-old brother was killed in a carjacking in 1994. At that time, Pierluisi helped obtain designation of Puerto Rico as a high-intensity drug-trafficking area.

Today, he sees increased drug-fighting efforts on the Southwest border as steering traffickers back to the Caribbean, with another spike in violence (the homicide rate in Puerto Rico is significantly higher than in any state). The Caribbean is especially appealing to criminals, Pierluisi notes, because drugs that slip into Puerto Rico or the U.S. Virgin Islands can be moved to the mainland without going through customs. He has called for a Caribbean border initiative to better coordinate the agencies combatting drug traffic.

On the immigration subcommittee, he deflects the criticism that the Obama administration selectively enforces immigration law. With limited enforcement resources, it is appropriate to focus on the removal of "dangerous criminal aliens," he said at a July 2011 hearing.

He also sits on the Natural Resources Committee, which oversees territorial affairs; he has used that committee to promote El Yunque National Forest.

Pierluisi was born in San Juan. His father, Jorge, was the president of the Puerto Rico chapter of the Associated General Contractors. Jorge served as the secretary of housing for eight years starting in the late 1970s, has been active in the pro-statehood party and still works as an arbitrator on construction issues. Pierluisi's mother was a homemaker who raised five children.

Pierluisi studied law at George Washington University. He worked as a part-time aide to Baltasar Corrada, a former resident commissioner, during the 1980s. After serving as attorney general, he returned to private law practice.

He still lives in San Juan and looks to his family when trying to relax. Whenever possible, he reserves Sundays for leisurely luncheons with relatives. And Pierluisi likes to get outdoors: He enjoys kayaking, paddleboarding and downhill skiing, though "I stick to the blues."

In 2008, he defeated Alfredo Salazar to succeed Fortuño, who was running for governor. Pierluisi is the only House member who serves a four-year term.

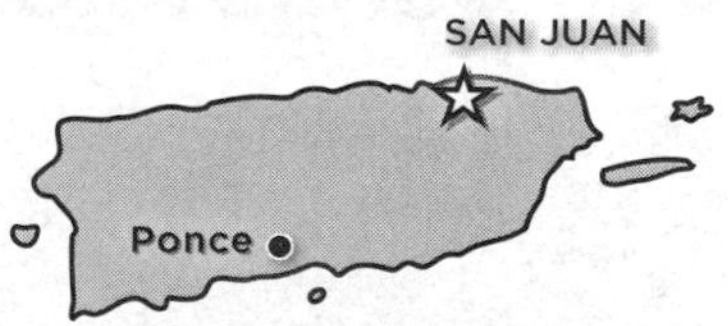

Puerto Rico

Capital: San Juan

Governor: Alejandro Javier García Padilla (POPDEM), elected 2012, 4-year term

Secretary of State: David Bernier (POPDEM), appointed 2013, 4-year term

Legislature: Bicameral assembly. Parties are aligned largely around the issue of statehood. Popular Democrats (POPDEM) favor "enhanced commonwealth" status. New Progressives (PNP) favor statehood. The Independence Party (PRI) favors independence.

House: 51 members, 4-year terms

2013 House ratios: 28 POPDEM, 23 PNP

Senate: 27 members, 4-year terms

2013 Senate ratios: 18 POPDEM, 8 PNP, 1 PRI

Web: www.camaraderepresentantes.org; www.senadopr.us

2010 Population: 3,725,789

2000 Population: 3,808,610

Median age: 36.8

Puerto Rico

At Large

Puerto Rico, the largest and most populated (3.7 million) of the territories, has been a self-governing commonwealth of the United States since 1952. Median household income here in 2009 was about $18,000 — high by Caribbean standards, but still less than half that of the poorest state — and the island has lost population since 2000.

Christopher Columbus arrived in Puerto Rico in 1493, and the Spanish arrived 15 years later along with slaves to work in the sugar cane fields; slavery was not abolished on the island until 1873. Spain ceded the territory to the United States in 1898 following the Spanish-American War. Its residents became U.S. citizens in 1917, but they cannot vote for president.

Since 1901, Puerto Ricans have been represented in the House by a resident commissioner. The island's political status has been a long-standing issue, with various factions favoring continued commonwealth status, statehood or independence. A 2012 referendum showed solid support for statehood, but a pro-statehood governor — former Res. Cmmsr. Luis Fortuño — lost his re-election bid, while a party colleague, Pedro R. Pierluisi, kept his spot in the U.S. House.

Puerto Rico's economy, one of the most stable in the Caribbean, relies on its tourism industry and industrial sector. Millions of tourists visit Puerto Rico each year, although some arrive via cruise ship and only stop for a day. Popular destinations include: El Yunque tropical forest; Old San Juan and its Castillo San Cristobal and Castillo San Felipe del Morro; and local beaches. Additional direct flights from the U.S. and new or renovated luxury hotels may drive more tourism to the island. Mainland U.S. firms also invest heavily here, encouraged by tax incentives and by duty-free access to the United States. High crime rates still plague the island, driving numerous residents to immigrate to the U.S.

Major Industry

Manufacturing, service, tourism

Military Bases

Fort Buchanan

Cities

San Juan (unincorp.), Bayamón (unincorp.)

Notable

Coliseo Roberto Clemente was named after the baseball star and Puerto Rico native.

Del. Donna M.C. Christensen (D)

Capitol Office
225-1790
donnachristensen.house.gov
1510 Longworth Bldg. 20515-5501; fax 225-5517

Committees
Energy & Commerce

Residence
St. Croix

Born
Sept. 19, 1945; Teaneck, N.J.

Religion
Moravian

Family
Divorced; two children

Education
Saint Mary's College (Ind.), B.S. 1966 (biology); George Washington U., M.D. 1970

Career
Physician; health official

Political Highlights
Virgin Is. Democratic Territorial Committee, 1980-97 (chairwoman, 1980-82); Virgin Is. Board of Education, 1984-86; Virgin Is. acting commissioner of health, 1993-94; sought Democratic nomination for U.S. House, 1994

ELECTION RESULTS

2012 GENERAL		
Donna M.C. Christensen (D)	13,273	56.6%
Warren B. Mosler (I)	3,968	16.9%
Norma Pickard-Samuel (I)	3,386	14.4%
Holland Redfield (R)	2,409	10.3%
Guillaume Mimoun (I)	375	1.6%
2010 GENERAL		
Donna M.C. Christensen (D)	19,844	71.7%
Jeffrey Moorhead (None)	5,063	18.3%
Vincent Emile Danet (R)	2,329	8.4%
Guillaume Mimoun (None)	419	1.5%

Previous Winning Percentages
2008 (100%); 2006 (63%); 2004 (66%); 2002 (68%); 2000 (78%); 1998 (80%); 1996 General Runoff Election (52%)

Elected 1996; 9th term

Christensen is an authority on the health issues facing minority groups and a steadfast supporter of President Barack Obama. But the most pressing task for the even-keeled doctor might be drumming up attention and relief for the economic calamity in the Virgin Islands.

Many woes of the territory are tied to distressingly high energy costs, which Christensen can address as the only delegate on the Energy and Commerce Committee. She became a member of the Energy and Power Subcommittee at the start of the 113th Congress (2013-14).

The islands are "100 percent dependent" on deteriorating diesel-powered generators, Christensen said in 2012. She helped win funding in 2011 to study whether the Virgin Islands power grid could be connected to nearby Puerto Rico's system, allowing for the purchase of surplus electricity.

Christensen is intrigued by ocean thermal energy conversion plants; she also would love construction of plants burning natural gas, though she acknowledges that the territory, with a population under 110,000, doesn't benefit from economies of scale that might attract such development.

But those are long-term plans. In February 2013, she organized a meeting of officials from various federal agencies to discuss which assistance programs might be able to quickly bring down costs to ratepayers; the islands "are in dire need of unusual and uncommon remedies," she said. Even amid the crisis, Christensen has resisted when Republicans assail EPA regulation of fossil-fuel-burning power plants. The EPA has been "very cooperative" in understanding local needs, she said.

The energy and economic crises in the Virgin Islands were intensified in early 2012, when the HOVENSA oil refinery on St. Croix, a major provider of gasoline and diesel for the islands, ceased operations — with a loss of more than 2,000 jobs. That closure came shortly after the territorial government announced layoffs of at least 500 government workers because of budget shortfalls. Christensen described the job losses as an "economic earthquake" sure to shake ancillary employment.

Several times, the House has passed her measure to create a chief financial officer for the Virgin Islands; citizens, unions and territorial legislators have "no trust" in the numbers produced by the governor's office, she said. Another of her plans would allow territorial taxpayers to transfer retirement accounts into a special fund, where taxes on distributions — she has estimated $250 million annually — would go to infrastructure development in the territory.

Christensen would like to boost tourism, the biggest driver of the local economy, by establishing a National Heritage Area for St. Croix. And she has worked to defend and increase the rebate that the territorial government receives on excise taxes on rum sold to the 50 states.

Her national concerns are rooted in her background as a family practice physician. Christensen planned to be a medical technologist working in a lab. As a college sophomore, she picked up a United Negro College Fund booklet urging African-Americans to go into medicine, to give to a friend. She read it herself, and "the next morning decided I was going to be a doctor. Whoever wrote that brochure did a really good job." Over her 20-year career, she worked in clinics and hospitals on St. Croix and later became acting commissioner of health. She was the first female doctor elected to Congress.

"I don't miss the business side of medicine at all," she says. But she dove into it while working on the 2010 health care overhaul as a member of the Health Subcommittee. Christensen believes the key to controlling health care costs is on the prevention side — in part by improving the use of information technology and encouraging comparative effectiveness research. As chairwoman of the Congressional Black Caucus Health Braintrust, she especially pushed for a community-based approach to reducing health disparities for minority populations and women. She and her staff were "in the trenches" to secure such provisions in the overhaul, she said.

As implementation of the law proceeds, Christensen has kept a close eye on funding for community health centers, community health workers and programs to diversify the health workforce. When comparative effectiveness research is conducted, she wants it to study health trends in minority groups and other subpopulations. In touting the CBC's fiscal 2012 budget plan, she said it addressed "the social, the environmental and the economic determinants of our health." When Republicans pitched a deficit reduction plan dubbed "Cut, Cap and Balance," she called it "their latest slash, burn and kill Medicare and Medicaid bill."

She has not succeeded in removing the federal cap on Medicaid funding for the territories, but Christensen has tried to ensure that the Virgin Islands are eligible for various grants under the health care law.

Christensen's father was from St. Croix, and her mother was from New York. After serving in the Army in World War II, her father finished his studies at Columbia Law. Almeric L. Christian was "one of the first native attorneys to come home," she said, and President Dwight D. Eisenhower appointed him to a panel determining the federal laws that apply to the territory. He eventually served as a U.S. attorney and District Court judge — though Christensen says he hated politics.

He also owned some race horses, and Christensen remembers going to the track with him. She still relaxes at home by heading to the Randall "Doc" James Racetrack with friends.

Christensen "lived in the library" as a girl and eventually went to boarding schools in Puerto Rico and New York. She attended medical school at George Washington University in the late 1960s, and she credits some of her interest in public life to working on Martin Luther King Jr.'s Poor People's Campaign when it came to Washington. She returned to the Virgin Islands after her postgraduate training.

She lost her first race for delegate in 1994. But in 1996, she edged out the incumbent, Victor O. Frazer. She has won easily since then. In a five-person race in 2012, she beat the second-place finisher by almost 40 points.

The Virgin Islands, like several territories, has some questions about its future status — the territory has never even adopted a constitution. Should the political relationship with the United States change, Christensen said she tends toward favoring free association.

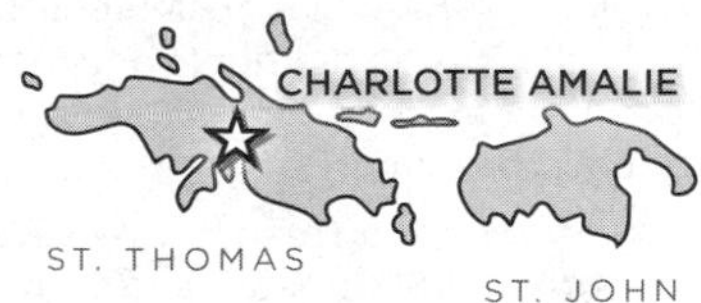

Virgin Islands

Capital: Charlotte Amalie

Governor: John Percy de Jongh Jr. (D), first elected 2006, 4-year term

Lieutenant governor: Gregory R. Francis (D), first elected 2006, 4-year term

Legislative branch: Senate with 15 members, 2-year terms

2013 Senate ratios: 10 D, 4 I, 1 ICM*

Web: www.legvi.org

2010 population: 106,405

2000 population: 108,612

Median age: 38.5

*Note: Independent Citizens Movement

Virgin Islands

At Large

The Virgin Islands, just east of Puerto Rico, are known for their subtropical climate, beautiful beaches, duty-free shopping and — far too often — being in the path of tropical storms. The first three characteristics have helped build a tourism industry, while the storms and, more recently, budget shortfalls have made economic development an uneven and difficult process.

Spain asserted its authority over the islands after Christopher Columbus arrived in 1493, and over the next century Spanish settlers killed or drove out the native Indians. But Spain showed no real interest in setting up a colony on the Virgin Islands. Denmark established a colony on St. Thomas in the mid-17th century, and sugar plantations drove the islands' economy until slavery was abolished in 1848. The U.S. government bought the islands from Denmark for $25 million in 1917.

The Virgin Islands form an unincorporated territory under the jurisdiction of the Interior Department. The territory is composed of 68 islands and cays, but only four are inhabited. Its population is roughly 110,000. Residents are U.S. citizens but may not vote for president. The Virgin Islands have had a non-voting House delegate since 1973.

Cruise ships make regular stops at the islands, principally at the capital of Charlotte Amalie on St. Thomas but also in neighboring St. Croix, which is the largest of the islands. Passengers stream ashore to take advantage of duty-free shopping, and most tourists leave without spending a night. A majority of St. John is a national park, with swamps, sub-tropical forests and semi-arid scrublands: Some 800 plant species inhabit the park. Ecotourism is becoming increasingly popular as the islands seek to balance development with the natural habitats.

A rum distillery on St. Croix, as well as light industry on other islands, are the primary sources of private sector jobs. In 2012, a large petroleum refinery on St. Croix announced it would close, although the government hopes to negotiate a reprieve.

Major Industry

Tourism, petroleum refining, rum distilling

Cities

Charlotte Amalie, Christiansted

Notable

The Virgin Islands is the only U.S. territory where traffic travels on the left.

Member Statistics

Following several cycles of electoral turnover, more than one-third of House members and more than one-fourth of Senate members of the 113th Congress are new to their chamber since 2010.

Despite some young members — seven representatives were born in 1980 or later, and 35 members (including one senator) were under 40 at the start of the 113th — the average age is 63.

Women increased their representation in both chambers after the 2012 election, with the Senate seating a record 20 — both California and New Hampshire are represented by a pair of female senators.

The 113th Congress has 15 Mormons, three Buddhists, two Muslims and the first Hindu to serve in the House. Catholics continue to be the single largest denomination, with 162 members.

113th Congress by the Numbers

710,767 The average population of a congressional district based on reapportionment following the 2010 census.

1,933 The approximate number of miles between the hometowns of House Speaker John A. Boehner. (West Chester Township, Ohio) and Senate Majority Leader Harry Reid (Searchlight, Nev.).

209 The number of congressional districts that President Barack Obama won in the 2012 election, versus 242 in the 2008 presidential contest. Districts had been redrawn following the 2010 census.

177 The number of political science/government degrees held by members of Congress.

60 The difference in age between the oldest member of Congress, Rep. Ralph M. Hall, R-Texas, and the youngest, Rep. Patrick Murphy, D-Fla.

20 The number of terms Rep. Pete Stark, D-Calif., had served before being defeated by Eric Swalwell, D-Calif., in 2012. Stark was the longest-serving member to lose a re-election bid in November.

11 Number of states with a single-party congressional delegation. Five states (Connecticut, Delaware, Hawaii, Massachusetts and Rhode Island) are represented by Democrats, and five (Idaho, Kansas, Nebraska, Oklahoma and Wyoming) are represented by Republicans. There are no Republicans in Vermont's delegation (Sen. Patrick J. Leahy and Rep. Peter Welch are Democrats and Sen. Bernard Sanders is an independent who caucuses with the Democrats).

10 The number of members of the 113th Congress who served in the 111th Congress or earlier, but not in the 112th (Reps. Bill Foster, D-Ill.; Alan Grayson, D-Fla.; Ann Kirkpatrick, D-Ariz.; Dan Maffei, D-N.Y.; Rick Nolan, D-Minn.; Carol Shea-Porter, D-N.H.; Matt Salmon, R-Ariz.; Mark Sanford, R-S.C.; Steve Stockman, R-Texas; Dina Titus, D-Nev.). Nolan spent 32 years out of congressional service; he previously served from 1975-81, a tenure he ended before three of his current House colleagues were born.

-18 The change in the number of seats New York has held in the U.S. House since 1940; it is the largest decrease of any state.

Get to know the 113th Congress by perusing these fact files, charts and statistics. They provide a handy reference guide to the demographic characteristics of members, as well as details on who belongs to which committees and caucuses. And you can test your congressional IQ with "Did You Know?"

Pronunciation Guide for Congress

Some members of Congress whose names are frequently mispronounced:

Rep. Robert B. Aderholt, R-Ala. — ADD-er-holt
Rep. Justin Amash, R-Mich. — ah-MAHSH
Rep. Mark Amodei, R-Nev. — AM-uh-day
Sen. Kelly Ayotte, R-N.H. — EYH-ott
Rep. Spencer Bachus, R-Ala. — BACK-us
Rep. Ami Bera, D-Calif. — AH-mi BEAR-uh
Rep. Gus Bilirakis, R-Fla. — bil-uh-RACK-iss
Rep. John A. Boehner, R-Ohio — BAY-ner
Rep. Suzanne Bonamici, D-Ore. — bon-a-ME-chee
Sen. John Boozman, R-Ark. — BOZE-man
Del. Madeleine Z. Bordallo, D-Guam — bore-DAA-yo
Rep. Charles Boustany Jr., R-La. — boo-STAN-knee
Rep. Paul Broun, R-Ga. — BROWN
Rep. Larry Bucshon, R-Ind. — boo-SHON
Rep. Shelley Moore Capito, R-W.Va. — CAP-ih-toe
Rep. Michael E. Capuano, D-Mass. — KAP-you-AH-no
Rep. Steve Chabot, R-Ohio — SHAB-it
Rep. Jason Chaffetz, R-Utah — CHAY-fits
Rep. David Cicilline, D-R.I. — sis-uh-LEE-nee
Sen. Michael D. Crapo, R-Idaho — CRAY-poe
Rep. Diana DeGette, D-Colo. — de-GET
Rep. Suzan DelBene, D-Wash. — Like "Susan" dell-BEN-ay
Rep. Scott DesJarlais, R-Tenn. — DAY-zhur-lay
Rep. Ted Deutch, D-Fla. — DOYTCH
Del. Eni F.H. Faleomavaega, D-Am. Samoa — EN-ee FOL-ee-oh-mav-ah-ENG-uh
Rep. Blake Farenthold, R-Texas — FAIR-enth-old
Rep. Chaka Fattah, D-Pa. — SHOCK-ah fa-TAH
Sen. Dianne Feinstein, D-Calif. — FINE-stine
Rep. Rodney Frelinghuysen, R-N.J. — FREE-ling high-zen
Rep. Pete Gallego, D-Texas — guy-AY-go
Rep. Jim Gerlach, R-Pa. — GUR-lock
Sen. Kirsten Gillibrand, D-N.Y. — KEER-sten JILL-uh-brand
Rep. Robert W. Goodlatte, R-Va. — GOOD-lat
Rep. Paul Gosar, R-Ariz. — go-SAR
Rep. Raúl M. Grijalva, D-Arz. — gree-HAHL-va
Sen. Martin Heinrich, D-N.M. — HINE-rick
Rep. Jeb Hensarling, R-Texas — HENN-sur-ling
Rep. Jaime Herrera Beutler, R-Wash. — JAY-me HER-air-ah BUT-ler
Sen. John Hoeven, R-N.D. — HO-ven
Rep. Tim Huelskamp, R-N.D. — HYOOLS-camp
Rep. Bill Huizenga, R-Mich. — HI-zing-uh
Sen. James M. Inhofe, R-Okla. IN-hoff
Rep. Darrell Issa, R-Calif. — EYE-sah
Rep. Hakeem Jeffries, D-N.Y. — HA-keem
Sen. Mike Johanns, R-Neb. — JOE-hans
Sen. Amy Klobuchar, D-Minn. — KLO-buh-shar
Rep. Jim Langevin, D-R.I. — LAN-juh-vin
Rep. Zoe Lofgren, D-Calif. — ZO LOFF-gren
Rep. Blaine Luetkemeyer, R-Mo. — LUTE-ka-myer
Rep. Cynthia M. Lummis, R-Wyo. — LUH-miss
Rep. Dan Maffei, D-N.Y. — muh-FAY
Rep. Kenny Marchant, R-Texas — MARCH-unt
Rep. Michael H. Michaud, D-Maine — ME-shoo
Rep. Jerrold Nadler, D-N.Y. — NAD-ler
Rep. Randy Neugebauer, R-Texas — NAW-geh-bow-er
Rep. Kristi Noem, R-S.D. — NOHM
Rep. Devin Nunes, R-Calif. — NEW-ness
Rep. Beto O'Rourke, D-Texas — BET-oh
Rep. Ed Pastor, D-Ariz. — pas-TORE
Rep. Tom Petri, R-Wis. — PEA-try
Rep. Chellie Pingree, D-Maine — Like "Shelley"
Rep. Mark Pocan, D-Wis. — poe-CAN
Rep. Mike Pompeo, R-Kan. — pom-PAY-oh
Rep. Nick J. Rahall II, D-W.Va. — RAY-haul
Rep. Dave Reichert, R-Wash. — RIKE-ert
Rep. James B. Renacci, R-Ohio — reh-NAY-see
Rep. Scott Rigell, R-Va. — RIDGE-uhl
Rep. Dana Rohrabacher, R-Calif. — ROAR-ah-BAH-ker
Rep. Todd Rokita, R-Ind. — ro-KEE-ta
Rep. Ileana Ros-Lehtinen, R-Fla. — il-ee-AH-na ross-LAY-tin-nen
Del. Gregorio Kilili Camacho Sablan, D-N. Marianas — greg OREO key-LEE-lee ka-MAH-cho sab-LAHN
Rep. Steve Scalise, R-La. — skuh-LEASE
Rep. Jan Schakowsky, D-Ill. — shuh-KOW-ski
Rep. Terri A. Sewell, D-Ala. — SUE-ell
Rep. Kyrsten Sinema, D-Ariz. — KEER-sten SIN-eh-ma (like "cinema")
Rep. Albio Sires, D-N.J. — SEAR-eez (like "series")
Rep. Jackie Speier, D-Calif. — SPEAR
Rep. Pat Tiberi, R-Ohio — TEA-berry
Rep. Niki Tsongas, D-Mass. — SONG-gus
Rep. David Valadao, R-Calif. — val-a-DAY-oh
Rep. Filemon Vela, D-Texas — FEE-lay-mon VAY-la
Rep. Tim Walz, D-Minn. — WALLS

Republicans

House Republicans determine seniority by length of service. Members who previously served in the House are usually given credit for most of that service. For members who joined at the beginning of a Congress, service is credited from the first day of the session. Seniority for members who won special elections is credited from the date of the election. No credit is given for other service, such as a senator or governor.

1	C.W. Bill Young, Fla.	Jan. 21, 1971
2	Don Young, Alaska	March 6, 1973
3	Jim Sensenbrenner, Wis.	Jan. 15, 1979
4	Tom Petri, Wis.	April 3, 1979
5	Ralph M. Hall, Texas	Jan. 5, 1981
6	Harold Rogers, Ky.	Jan. 5, 1981
7	Christopher H. Smith, N.J.	Jan. 5, 1981
8	Frank R. Wolf, Va.	Jan. 5, 1981
9	Joe L. Barton, Texas	Jan. 3, 1985
10	Howard Coble, N.C.	Jan. 3, 1985
11	Lamar Smith, Texas	Jan. 6, 1987
12	Fred Upton, Mich.	Jan. 6, 1987
13	John J. Duncan Jr., Tenn.	Nov. 8, 1988
14	Dana Rohrabacher, Calif.	Jan. 3, 1989
15	Ileana Ros-Lehtinen, Fla.	Aug. 29, 1989
16	John A. Boehner, Ohio	Jan. 3, 1991
17	Dave Camp, Mich.	Jan. 3, 1991
18	Sam Johnson, Texas	May 18, 1991
19	Spencer Bachus, Ala.	Jan. 5, 1993
20	Ken Calvert, Calif.	Jan. 5, 1993
21	Robert W. Goodlatte, Va.	Jan. 5, 1993
22	Peter T. King, N.Y.	Jan. 5, 1993
23	Jack Kingston, Ga.	Jan. 5, 1993
24	Howard "Buck" McKeon, Calif.	Jan. 5, 1993
25	John L. Mica, Fla.	Jan. 5, 1993
26	Ed Royce, Calif.	Jan. 5, 1993
27	Frank D. Lucas, Okla.	May 10, 1994
28	Rodney Frelinghuysen, N.J.	Jan. 4, 1995
29	Doc Hastings, Wash.	Jan. 4, 1995
30	Walter B. Jones, N.C.	Jan. 4, 1995
31	Tom Latham, Iowa	Jan. 4, 1995
32	Frank A. LoBiondo, N.J.	Jan. 4, 1995
33	Mac Thornberry, Texas	Jan. 4, 1995
34	Edward Whitfield, Ky.	Jan. 4, 1995
35	Robert B. Aderholt, Ala.	Jan. 7, 1997
36	Kevin Brady, Texas	Jan. 7, 1997
37	Kay Granger, Texas	Jan. 7, 1997
38	Joe Pitts, Pa.	Jan. 7, 1997
39	Pete Sessions, Texas	Jan. 7, 1997
40	John Shimkus, Ill.	Jan. 7, 1997
41	Steve Chabot, Ohio	Jan. 5, 2011
		Also served 1995-2009
42	Gary G. Miller, Calif.	Jan. 6, 1999
43	Paul D. Ryan, Wis.	Jan. 6, 1999
44	Mike Simpson, Idaho	Jan. 6, 1999
45	Lee Terry, Neb.	Jan. 6, 1999
46	Greg Walden, Ore.	Jan. 6, 1999
47	Eric Cantor, Va.	Jan. 3, 2001
48	Shelley Moore Capito, W.Va.	Jan. 3, 2001
49	Ander Crenshaw, Fla.	Jan. 3, 2001
50	John Culberson, Texas	Jan. 3, 2001
51	Sam Graves, Mo.	Jan. 3, 2001
52	Darrell Issa, Calif.	Jan. 3, 2001
53	Mike Rogers, Mich.	Jan. 3, 2001
54	Pat Tiberi, Ohio	Jan. 3, 2001
55	Bill Shuster, Pa.	May 15, 2001
56	J. Randy Forbes, Va.	June 19, 2001
57	Jeff Miller, Fla.	Oct. 16, 2001
58	Joe Wilson, S.C.	Dec. 18, 2001
59	Rodney Alexander, La.	Jan. 7, 2003
60	Rob Bishop, Utah	Jan. 7, 2003
61	Marsha Blackburn, Tenn.	Jan. 7, 2003
62	Jo Bonner, Ala.	Jan. 7, 2003
63	Michael C. Burgess, Texas	Jan. 7, 2003
64	John Carter, Texas	Jan. 7, 2003
65	Tom Cole, Okla.	Jan. 7, 2003
66	Mario Diaz-Balart, Fla.	Jan. 7, 2003
67	Trent Franks, Ariz.	Jan. 7, 2003
68	Scott Garrett, N.J.	Jan. 7, 2003
69	Jim Gerlach, Pa.	Jan. 7, 2003
70	Phil Gingrey, Ga.	Jan. 7, 2003
71	Jeb Hensarling, Texas	Jan. 7, 2003
72	Steve King, Iowa	Jan. 7, 2003
73	John Kline, Minn.	Jan. 7, 2003
74	Candice S. Miller, Mich.	Jan. 7, 2003
75	Tim Murphy, Pa.	Jan. 7, 2003
76	Devin Nunes, Calif.	Jan. 7, 2003
77	Mike D. Rogers, Ala.	Jan. 7, 2003
78	Michael R. Turner, Ohio	Jan. 7, 2003
79	Randy Neugebauer, Texas	June 3, 2003
80	Charles Boustany Jr., La.	Jan. 4, 2005
81	K. Michael Conaway, Texas	Jan. 4, 2005
82	Charlie Dent, Pa.	Jan. 4, 2005
83	Jeff Fortenberry, Neb.	Jan. 4, 2005
84	Virginia Foxx, N.C.	Jan. 4, 2005
85	Louie Gohmert, Texas	Jan. 4, 2005
86	Kenny Marchant, Texas	Jan. 4, 2005
87	Michael McCaul, Texas	Jan. 4, 2005
88	Patrick T. McHenry, N.C.	Jan. 4, 2005
89	Cathy McMorris Rodgers, Wash.	Jan. 4, 2005
90	Ted Poe, Texas	Jan. 4, 2005
91	Tom Price, Ga.	Jan. 4, 2005
92	Dave Reichert, Wash.	Jan. 4, 2005
93	Lynn Westmoreland, Ga.	Jan. 4, 2005
94	John Campbell, Calif.	Dec. 7, 2005
95	Steve Pearce, N.M.	Jan. 5, 2011
		Also served 2003-09
96	Michele Bachmann, Minn.	Jan. 4, 2007
97	Gus Bilirakis, Fla.	Jan. 4, 2007
98	Vern Buchanan, Fla.	Jan. 4, 2007
99	Jim Jordan, Ohio	Jan. 4, 2007
100	Doug Lamborn, Colo.	Jan. 4, 2007
101	Kevin McCarthy, Calif.	Jan. 4, 2007
102	Peter Roskam, Ill.	Jan. 4, 2007
103	Adrian Smith, Neb.	Jan. 4, 2007
104	Matt Salmon, Ariz.	Jan. 3, 2013
		Also served 1995-2001
105	Paul Broun, Ga.	July 17, 2007
106	Bob Latta, Ohio	Dec. 11, 2007
107	Rob Wittman, Va.	Dec. 11, 2007
108	Steve Scalise, La.	May 3, 2008
109	Mark Sanford, S.C.	May 15, 2013
		Also served 1995-2001

110 Bill Cassidy, La. Jan. 6, 2009
111 Jason Chaffetz, Utah Jan. 6, 2009
112 Mike Coffman, Colo. Jan. 6, 2009
113 John Fleming, La. Jan. 6, 2009
114 Brett Guthrie, Ky. Jan. 6, 2009
115 Gregg Harper, Miss. Jan. 6, 2009
116 Duncan Hunter, Calif. Jan. 6, 2009
117 Lynn Jenkins, Kan. Jan. 6, 2009
118 Leonard Lance, N.J. Jan. 6, 2009
119 Blaine Luetkemeyer, Mo. Jan. 6, 2009
120 Cynthia M. Lummis, Wyo. Jan. 6, 2009
121 Tom McClintock, Calif. Jan. 6, 2009
122 Pete Olson, Texas Jan. 6, 2009
123 Erik Paulsen, Minn. Jan. 6, 2009
124 Bill Posey, Fla. Jan. 6, 2009
125 Phil Roe, Tenn. Jan. 6, 2009
126 Tom Rooney, Fla. Jan. 6, 2009
127 Aaron Schock, Ill. Jan. 6, 2009
128 Glenn Thompson, Pa. Jan. 6, 2009
129 Tom Graves, Ga. June 8, 2010
130 Tom Reed, N.Y. Nov. 2, 2010
131 Marlin Stutzman, Ind. Nov. 2, 2010
132 Michael G. Fitzpatrick, Pa. Jan. 5, 2011
Also served 2005-07
133 Tim Walberg, Mich. Jan. 5, 2011
Also served 2007-09
134 Justin Amash, Mich. Jan. 5, 2011
135 Lou Barletta, Pa. Jan. 5, 2011
136 Dan Benishek, Mich. Jan. 5, 2011
137 Diane Black, Tenn. Jan. 5, 2011
138 Mo Brooks, Ala. Jan. 5, 2011
139 Larry Bucshon, Ind. Jan. 5, 2011
140 Rick Crawford, Ark. Jan. 5, 2011
141 Jeff Denham, Calif. Jan. 5, 2011
142 Scott DesJarlais, Tenn. Jan. 5, 2011
143 Sean P. Duffy, Wis. Jan. 5, 2011
144 Jeff Duncan, S.C. Jan. 5, 2011
145 Renee Ellmers, N.C. Jan. 5, 2011
146 Blake Farenthold, Texas Jan. 5, 2011
147 Stephen Fincher, Tenn. Jan. 5, 2011
148 Chuck Fleischmann, Tenn. Jan. 5, 2011
149 Bill Flores, Texas Jan. 5, 2011
150 Cory Gardner, Colo. Jan. 5, 2011
151 Bob Gibbs, Ohio Jan. 5, 2011
152 Chris Gibson, N.Y. Jan. 5, 2011
153 Paul Gosar, Ariz. Jan. 5, 2011
154 Trey Gowdy, S.C. Jan. 5, 2011
155 Tim Griffin, Ark. Jan. 5, 2011
156 Morgan Griffith, Va. Jan. 5, 2011
157 Michael G. Grimm, N.Y. Jan. 5, 2011
158 Richard Hanna, N.Y. Jan. 5, 2011
159 Andy Harris, Md. Jan. 5, 2011
160 Vicky Hartzler, Mo. Jan. 5, 2011
161 Joe Heck, Nev. Jan. 5, 2011
162 Jaime Herrera Beutler, Wash. Jan. 5, 2011
163 Tim Huelskamp, Kan. Jan. 5, 2011
164 Bill Huizenga, Mich. Jan. 5, 2011
165 Randy Hultgren, Ill. Jan. 5, 2011
166 Robert Hurt, Va. Jan. 5, 2011
167 Bill Johnson, Ohio Jan. 5, 2011
168 Mike Kelly, Pa. Jan. 5, 2011
169 Adam Kinzinger, Ill. Jan. 5, 2011
170 Raúl R. Labrador, Idaho Jan. 5, 2011
171 James Lankford, Okla. Jan. 5, 2011
172 Billy Long, Mo. Jan. 5, 2011
173 Tom Marino, Pa. Jan. 5, 2011
174 David B. McKinley, W.Va. Jan. 5, 2011
175 Patrick Meehan, Pa. Jan. 5, 2011
176 Mick Mulvaney, S.C. Jan. 5, 2011
177 Kristi Noem, S.D. Jan. 5, 2011
178 Rich Nugent, Fla. Jan. 5, 2011
179 Alan Nunnelee, Miss. Jan. 5, 2011
180 Steven M. Palazzo, Miss. Jan. 5, 2011
181 Mike Pompeo, Kan. Jan. 5, 2011
182 James B. Renacci, Ohio Jan. 5, 2011
183 Reid Ribble, Wis. Jan. 5, 2011
184 Scott Rigell, Va. Jan. 5, 2011
185 Martha Roby, Ala. Jan. 5, 2011
186 Todd Rokita, Ind. Jan. 5, 2011
187 Dennis A. Ross, Fla. Jan. 5, 2011
188 Jon Runyan, N.J. Jan. 5, 2011
189 David Schweikert, Ariz. Jan. 5, 2011
190 Austin Scott, Ga. Jan. 5, 2011
191 Steve Southerland II, Fla. Jan. 5, 2011
192 Steve Stivers, Ohio Jan. 5, 2011
193 Scott Tipton, Colo. Jan. 5, 2011
194 Daniel Webster, Fla. Jan. 5, 2011
195 Steve Womack, Ark. Jan. 5, 2011
196 Rob Woodall, Ga. Jan. 5, 2011
197 Kevin Yoder, Kan. Jan. 5, 2011
198 Todd Young, Ind. Jan. 5, 2011
199 Steve Stockman, Texas Jan. 3, 2013
Also served 1995-97
200 Mark Amodei, Nev. Sept. 13, 2011
201 Thomas Massie, Ky. Nov. 13, 2012
202 Andy Barr, Ky. Jan. 3, 2013
203 Kerry Bentivolio, Mich. Jan. 3, 2013
204 Jim Bridenstine, Okla. Jan. 3, 2013
205 Susan W. Brooks, Ind. Jan. 3, 2013
206 Chris Collins, N.Y. Jan. 3, 2013
207 Doug Collins, Ga. Jan. 3, 2013
208 Paul Cook, Calif. Jan. 3, 2013
209 Tom Cotton, Ark. Jan. 3, 2013
210 Kevin Cramer, N.D. Jan. 3, 2013
211 Steve Daines, Mont. Jan. 3, 2013
212 Rodney Davis, Ill. Jan. 3, 2013
213 Ron DeSantis, Fla. Jan. 3, 2013
214 George Holding, N.C. Jan. 3, 2013
215 Richard Hudson, N.C. Jan. 3, 2013
216 David Joyce, Ohio Jan. 3, 2013
217 Doug LaMalfa, Calif. Jan. 3, 2013
218 Mark Meadows, N.C. Jan. 3, 2013
219 Luke Messer, Ind. Jan. 3, 2013
220 Markwayne Mullin, Okla. Jan. 3, 2013
221 Scott Perry, Pa. Jan. 3, 2013
222 Robert Pittenger, N.C. Jan. 3, 2013
223 Trey Radel, Fla. Jan. 3, 2013
224 Tom Rice, S.C. Jan. 3, 2013
225 Keith Rothfus, Pa. Jan. 3, 2013
226 Chris Stewart, Utah Jan. 3, 2013
227 David Valadao, Calif. Jan. 3, 2013
228 Ann Wagner, Mo. Jan. 3, 2013
229 Jackie Walorski, Ind. Jan. 3, 2013
230 Randy Weber, Texas Jan. 3, 2013
231 Brad Wenstrup, Ohio Jan. 3, 2013
232 Roger Williams, Texas Jan. 3, 2013
233 Ted Yoho, Fla. Jan. 3, 2013
234 Jason Smith, Mo. June 4, 2013

Democrats

House Democrats determine seniority by length of service. Members who previously served in the House are given some credit for that service — when they return, they are ranked above other members of that entering class. For members who joined at the beginning of a Congress, service is credited from the first day of the session. Seniority for members who won special elections is credited from the date of the election. No credit is given for other previous service, such as a senator or governor.

1	John D. Dingell, Mich.	Dec. 13, 1955
2	John Conyers Jr., Mich.	Jan. 4, 1965
3	Charles B. Rangel, N.Y.	Jan. 21, 1971
4	George Miller, Calif.	Jan. 14, 1975
5	Henry A. Waxman, Calif.	Jan. 14, 1975
6	Edward J. Markey, Mass.	Nov. 2, 1976
7	Nick J. Rahall II, W.Va.	Jan. 4, 1977
8	Steny H. Hoyer, Md.	May 19, 1981
9	Marcy Kaptur, Ohio	Jan. 3, 1983
10	Sander M. Levin, Mich.	Jan. 3, 1983
11	Peter J. Visclosky, Ind.	Jan. 3, 1985
12	Peter A. DeFazio, Ore.	Jan. 6, 1987
13	John Lewis, Ga.	Jan. 6, 1987
14	Louise M. Slaughter, N.Y.	Jan. 6, 1987
15	Nancy Pelosi, Calif.	June 2, 1987
16	Frank Pallone Jr., N.J.	Nov. 8, 1988
17	Eliot L. Engel, N.Y.	Jan. 3, 1989
18	Nita M. Lowey, N.Y.	Jan. 3, 1989
19	Jim McDermott, Wash.	Jan. 3, 1989
20	Richard E. Neal, Mass.	Jan. 3, 1989
21	José E. Serrano, N.Y.	March 20, 1990
22	Robert E. Andrews, N.J.	Nov. 6, 1990
23	David E. Price, N.C.	Jan. 7, 1997 *Also served 1987-95*
24	Rosa DeLauro, Conn.	Jan. 3, 1991
25	James P. Moran, Va.	Jan. 3, 1991
26	Collin C. Peterson, Minn.	Jan. 3, 1991
27	Maxine Waters, Calif.	Jan. 3, 1991
28	Ed Pastor, Ariz.	Sept. 24, 1991
29	Jerrold Nadler, N.Y.	Nov. 3, 1992
30	Jim Cooper, Tenn.	Jan. 7, 2003 *Also served 1983-95*
31	Xavier Becerra, Calif.	Jan. 5, 1993
32	Sanford D. Bishop Jr., Ga.	Jan. 5, 1993
33	Corrine Brown, Fla.	Jan. 5, 1993
34	James E. Clyburn, S.C.	Jan. 5, 1993
35	Anna G. Eshoo, Calif.	Jan. 5, 1993
36	Gene Green, Texas	Jan. 5, 1993
37	Luis V. Gutierrez, Ill.	Jan. 5, 1993
38	Alcee L. Hastings, Fla.	Jan. 5, 1993
39	Eddie Bernice Johnson, Texas	Jan. 5, 1993
40	Carolyn B. Maloney, N.Y.	Jan. 5, 1993
41	Lucille Roybal-Allard, Calif.	Jan. 5, 1993
42	Bobby L. Rush, Ill.	Jan. 5, 1993
43	Robert C. Scott, Va.	Jan. 5, 1993
44	Nydia M. Velázquez, N.Y.	Jan. 5, 1993
45	Melvin Watt, N.C.	Jan. 5, 1993
46	Bennie Thompson, Miss.	April 13, 1993
47	Sam Farr, Calif.	June 8, 1993
48	Lloyd Doggett, Texas	Jan. 4, 1995
49	Mike Doyle, Pa.	Jan. 4, 1995
50	Chaka Fattah, Pa.	Jan. 4, 1995
51	Sheila Jackson Lee, Texas	Jan. 4, 1995
52	Zoe Lofgren, Calif.	Jan. 4, 1995
53	Elijah E. Cummings, Md.	April 16, 1996
54	Earl Blumenauer, Ore.	May 21, 1996
55	Danny K. Davis, Ill.	Jan. 7, 1997
56	Diana DeGette, Colo.	Jan. 7, 1997
57	Rubén Hinojosa, Texas	Jan. 7, 1997
58	Ron Kind, Wis.	Jan. 7, 1997
59	Carolyn McCarthy, N.Y.	Jan. 7, 1997
60	Jim McGovern, Mass.	Jan. 7, 1997
61	Mike McIntyre, N.C.	Jan. 7, 1997
62	Bill Pascrell Jr., N.J.	Jan. 7, 1997
63	Loretta Sanchez, Calif.	Jan. 7, 1997
64	Brad Sherman, Calif.	Jan. 7, 1997
65	Adam Smith, Wash.	Jan. 7, 1997
66	John F. Tierney, Mass.	Jan. 7, 1997
67	Gregory W. Meeks, N.Y.	Feb. 3, 1998
68	Lois Capps, Calif.	March 10, 1998
69	Barbara Lee, Calif.	April 7, 1998
70	Robert A. Brady, Pa.	May 19, 1998
71	Michael E. Capuano, Mass.	Jan. 6, 1999
72	Joseph Crowley, N.Y.	Jan. 6, 1999
73	Rush D. Holt, N.J.	Jan. 6, 1999
74	John B. Larson, Conn.	Jan. 6, 1999
75	Grace F. Napolitano, Calif.	Jan. 6, 1999
76	Jan Schakowsky, Ill.	Jan. 6, 1999
77	Mike Thompson, Calif.	Jan. 6, 1999
78	William Lacy Clay, Mo.	Jan. 3, 2001
79	Susan A. Davis, Calif.	Jan. 3, 2001
80	Michael M. Honda, Calif.	Jan. 3, 2001
81	Steve Israel, N.Y.	Jan. 3, 2001
82	Jim Langevin, R.I.	Jan. 3, 2001
83	Rick Larsen, Wash.	Jan. 3, 2001
84	Jim Matheson, Utah	Jan. 3, 2001
85	Betty McCollum, Minn.	Jan. 3, 2001
86	Adam B. Schiff, Calif.	Jan. 3, 2001
87	Stephen F. Lynch, Mass.	Oct. 16, 2001
88	Timothy H. Bishop, N.Y.	Jan. 7, 2003
89	Raúl M. Grijalva, Ariz.	Jan. 7, 2003
90	Michael H. Michaud, Maine	Jan. 7, 2003
91	C.A. Dutch Ruppersberger, Md.	Jan. 7, 2003
92	Tim Ryan, Ohio	Jan. 7, 2003
93	Linda T. Sánchez, Calif.	Jan. 7, 2003
94	David Scott, Ga.	Jan. 7, 2003
95	Chris Van Hollen, Md.	Jan. 7, 2003
96	G.K. Butterfield, N.C.	July 20, 2004
97	John Barrow, Ga.	Jan. 4, 2005
98	Emanuel Cleaver II, Mo.	Jan. 4, 2005
99	Jim Costa, Calif.	Jan. 4, 2005
100	Henry Cuellar, Texas	Jan. 4, 2005
101	Al Green, Texas	Jan. 4, 2005
102	Brian Higgins, N.Y.	Jan. 4, 2005
103	Daniel Lipinski, Ill.	Jan. 4, 2005
104	Gwen Moore, Wis.	Jan. 4, 2005
105	Allyson Y. Schwartz, Pa.	Jan. 4, 2005
106	Debbie Wasserman Schultz, Fla.	Jan. 4, 2005
107	Doris Matsui, Calif.	March 8, 2005
108	Albio Sires, N.J.	Nov. 13, 2006
109	Bruce Braley, Iowa	Jan. 4, 2007
110	Kathy Castor, Fla.	Jan. 4, 2007

111	Yvette D. Clarke, N.Y.	Jan. 4, 2007
112	Steve Cohen, Tenn.	Jan. 4, 2007
113	Joe Courtney, Conn.	Jan. 4, 2007
114	Keith Ellison, Minn.	Jan. 4, 2007
115	Hank Johnson, Fla.	Jan. 4, 2007
116	Dave Loebsack, Iowa	Jan. 4, 2007
117	Jerry McNerney, Calif.	Jan. 4, 2007
118	Ed Perlmutter, Colo.	Jan. 4, 2007
119	John Sarbanes, Md.	Jan. 4, 2007
120	Tim Walz, Minn.	Jan. 4, 2007
121	Peter Welch, Vt.	Jan. 4, 2007
122	John Yarmuth, Ky.	Jan. 4, 2007
123	Rick Nolan, Minn.	Jan. 3, 2013
		Also served 1975-81
124	Niki Tsongas, Mass.	Oct. 16, 2007
125	André Carson, Ind.	March 11, 2008
126	Jackie Speier, Calif.	April 8, 2008
127	Donna Edwards, Md.	June 17, 2008
128	Marcia L. Fudge, Ohio	Nov. 18, 2008
129	Gerald E. Connolly, Va.	Jan. 6, 2009
130	Jim Himes, Conn.	Jan. 6, 2009
131	Ben Ray Luján, N.M.	Jan. 6, 2009
132	Gary Peters, Mich.	Jan. 6, 2009
133	Chellie Pingree, Maine	Jan. 6, 2009
134	Jared Polis, Colo.	Jan. 6, 2009
135	Kurt Schrader, Ore.	Jan. 6, 2009
136	Paul Tonko, N.Y.	Jan. 6, 2009
137	Carol Shea-Porter, N.H.	Jan. 3, 2013
		Also served 2007-11
138	Mike Quigley, Ill.	April 7, 2009
139	Judy Chu, Calif.	July 14, 2009
140	John Garamendi, Calif.	Nov. 3, 2009
141	Bill Owens, N.Y.	Nov. 3, 2009
142	Bill Foster, Ill.	Jan. 3, 2013
		Also served 2008-11
143	Ted Deutch, Fla.	April 13, 2010
144	Karen Bass, Calif.	Jan. 5, 2011
145	John Carney, Del.	Jan. 5, 2011
146	David Cicilline, R.I.	Jan. 5, 2011
147	Colleen Hanabusa, Hawaii	Jan. 5, 2011
148	William Keating, Mass.	Jan. 5, 2011
149	Cedric L. Richmond, La.	Jan. 5, 2011
150	Terri A. Sewell, Ala.	Jan. 5, 2011
151	Frederica S. Wilson, Fla.	Jan. 5, 2011
152	Alan Grayson, Fla.	Jan. 3, 2013
		Also served 2009-11
153	Ann Kirkpatrick, Ariz.	Jan. 3, 2013
		Also served 2009-11
154	Dan Maffei, N.Y.	Jan. 3, 2013
		Also served 2009-11
155	Dina Titus, Nev.	Jan. 3, 2013
		Also served 2009-11
156	Janice Hahn, Calif.	July 12, 2011
157	Suzanne Bonamici, Ore.	Jan. 31, 2012
158	Ron Barber, Ariz.	June 12, 2012
159	Suzan DelBene, Wash.	Nov. 13, 2012
160	Donald M. Payne Jr., N.J.	Nov. 15, 2012
161	Joyce Beatty, Ohio	Jan. 3, 2013
162	Ami Bera, Calif.	Jan. 3, 2013
163	Julia Brownley, Calif.	Jan. 3, 2013
164	Cheri Bustos, Ill.	Jan. 3, 2013
165	Tony Cárdenas, Calif.	Jan. 3, 2013
166	Matt Cartwright, Pa.	Jan. 3, 2013
167	Joaquin Castro, Texas	Jan. 3, 2013
168	John Delaney, Md.	Jan. 3, 2013
169	Tammy Duckworth, Ill.	Jan. 3, 2013
170	Bill Enyart, Ill.	Jan. 3, 2013
171	Elizabeth Esty, Conn.	Jan. 3, 2013
172	Lois Frankel, Fla.	Jan. 3, 2013
173	Tulsi Gabbard, Hawaii	Jan. 3, 2013
174	Pete Gallego, Texas	Jan. 3, 2013
175	Joe Garcia, Fla.	Jan. 3, 2013
176	Denny Heck, Wash.	Jan. 3, 2013
177	Steven Horsford, Nev.	Jan. 3, 2013
178	Jared Huffman, Calif.	Jan. 3, 2013
179	Hakeem Jeffries, N.Y.	Jan. 3, 2013
180	Joseph P. Kennedy III, Mass.	Jan. 3, 2013
181	Dan Kildee, Mich.	Jan. 3, 2013
182	Derek Kilmer, Wash.	Jan. 3, 2013
183	Ann McLane Kuster, N.H.	Jan. 3, 2013
184	Alan Lowenthal, Calif.	Jan. 3, 2013
185	Michelle Lujan Grisham, N.M.	Jan. 3, 2013
186	Sean Patrick Maloney, N.Y.	Jan. 3, 2013
187	Grace Meng, N.Y.	Jan. 3, 2013
188	Patrick Murphy, Fla.	Jan. 3, 2013
189	Gloria Negrete McLeod, Calif.	Jan. 3, 2013
190	Beto O'Rourke, Texas	Jan. 3, 2013
191	Scott Peters, Calif.	Jan. 3, 2013
192	Mark Pocan, Wis.	Jan. 3, 2013
193	Raul Ruiz, Calif.	Jan. 3, 2013
194	Brad Schneider, Ill.	Jan. 3, 2013
195	Kyrsten Sinema, Ariz.	Jan. 3, 2013
196	Eric Swalwell, Calif.	Jan. 3, 2013
197	Mark Takano, Calif.	Jan. 3, 2013
198	Juan C. Vargas, Calif.	Jan. 3, 2013
199	Mark Veasey, Texas	Jan. 3, 2013
200	Filemon Vela, Texas	Jan. 3, 2013
201	Robin Kelly, Ill	April 11, 2013

Party Switchers

Three current members changed their party affiliation after they were elected to Congress. Several other members switched before coming to Congress; they are not listed below.

House

Rodney Alexander, La.
Democrat to Republican on Sept. 7, 2004

Ralph M. Hall, Texas
Democrat to Republican on Jan. 5, 2004

Senate

Richard C. Shelby, Ala.
Democrat to Republican on Nov. 9, 1994

Senate Seniority

Seniority is determined by the length of consecutive Senate service from the date of swearing-in.

Tie-breakers for those who join the Senate on the same day, in order of precedence, are: previous Senate service, service as the vice president, previous House service, service in the Cabinet, service as a state governor. If a tie still exists, they are ranked according to their state's population at the time of swearing in. Independents Bernard Sanders and Angus King caucus with the Democrats. Richard C. Shelby was a Democrat, and the GOP Conference credited that service toward his seniority ranking.

DEMOCRATS

1	Patrick J. Leahy, Vt.	Jan. 14, 1975
2	Max Baucus, Mont.	Dec. 15, 1978
3	Carl Levin, Mich.	Jan. 15, 1979
4	Tom Harkin, Iowa	Jan. 3, 1985
5	Jay Rockefeller, W.Va.	Jan. 15, 1985
6	Barbara A. Mikulski, Md.	Jan. 6, 1987
7	Harry Reid, Nev.	Jan. 6, 1987
8	Dianne Feinstein, Calif.	Nov. 4, 1992
9	Barbara Boxer, Calif.	Jan. 5, 1993
10	Patty Murray, Wash.	Jan. 5, 1993
11	Ron Wyden, Ore.	Feb. 6, 1996
12	Richard J. Durbin, Ill.	Jan. 7, 1997
13	Tim Johnson, S.D.	Jan. 7, 1997
14	Jack Reed, R.I.	Jan. 7, 1997
15	Mary L. Landrieu, La.	Jan. 7, 1997
16	Charles E. Schumer, N.Y.	Jan. 6, 1999
17	Bill Nelson, Fla.	Jan. 3, 2001
18	Thomas R. Carper, Del.	Jan. 3, 2001
19	Debbie Stabenow, Mich.	Jan. 3, 2001
20	Maria Cantwell, Wash.	Jan. 3, 2001
21	Mark Pryor, Ark.	Jan. 7, 2003
22	Robert Menendez, N.J.	Jan. 18, 2006
23	Benjamin L. Cardin, Md.	Jan. 4, 2007
24	Sherrod Brown, Ohio	Jan. 4, 2007
25	Bob Casey, Pa.	Jan. 4, 2007
26	Claire McCaskill, Mo.	Jan. 4, 2007
27	Amy Klobuchar, Minn.	Jan. 4, 2007
28	Sheldon Whitehouse, R.I.	Jan. 4, 2007
29	Jon Tester, Mont.	Jan. 4, 2007
30	Mark Udall, Colo.	Jan. 6, 2009
31	Tom Udall, N.M.	Jan. 6, 2009
32	Jeanne Shaheen, N.H.	Jan. 6, 2009
33	Mark Warner, Va.	Jan. 6, 2009
34	Kay Hagan, N.C.	Jan. 6, 2009
35	Jeff Merkley, Ore.	Jan. 6, 2009
36	Mark Begich, Alaska	Jan. 6, 2009
37	Michael Bennet, Colo.	Jan. 22, 2009
38	Kirsten Gillibrand, N.Y.	Jan. 27, 2009
39	Al Franken, Minn.	July 7, 2009
40	Joe Manchin III, W.Va.	Nov. 15, 2010
41	Chris Coons, Del.	Nov. 15, 2010
42	Richard Blumenthal, Conn.	Jan. 5, 2011
43	Brian Schatz, Hawaii	Dec. 27, 2012
44	Tammy Baldwin, Wis.	Jan. 3, 2013
45	Joe Donnelly, Ind.	Jan. 3, 2013
46	Christopher S. Murphy, Conn.	Jan. 3, 2013
47	Mazie K. Hirono, Hawaii	Jan. 3, 2013
48	Martin Heinrich, N.M.	Jan. 3, 2013
49	Tim Kaine, Va.	Jan. 3, 2013
50	Elizabeth Warren, Mass.	Jan. 3, 2013
51	Heidi Heitkamp, N.D.	Jan. 3, 2013
52	William "Mo" Cowan, Mass.	Feb. 7, 2013

REPUBLICANS

1	Orrin G. Hatch, Utah	Jan. 4, 1977
2	Thad Cochran, Miss.	Dec. 27, 1978
3	Charles E. Grassley, Iowa	Jan. 5, 1981
4	Mitch McConnell, Ky.	Jan. 3, 1985
5	Richard C. Shelby, Ala.	Jan. 6, 1987
6	John McCain, Ariz.	Jan. 6, 1987
7	James M. Inhofe, Okla.	Nov. 30, 1994
8	Pat Roberts, Kan.	Jan. 7, 1997
9	Jeff Sessions, Ala.	Jan. 7, 1997
10	Susan Collins, Maine	Jan. 7, 1997
11	Michael B. Enzi, Wyo.	Jan. 7, 1997
12	Michael D. Crapo, Idaho	Jan. 6, 1999
13	Lisa Murkowski, Alaska	Dec. 20, 2002
14	Saxby Chambliss, Ga.	Jan. 7, 2003
15	Lindsey Graham, S.C.	Jan. 7, 2003
16	Lamar Alexander, Tenn.	Jan. 7, 2003
17	John Cornyn, Texas	Jan. 7, 2003
18	Richard M. Burr, N.C.	Jan. 4, 2005
19	Tom Coburn, Okla.	Jan. 4, 2005
20	John Thune, S.D.	Jan. 4, 2005
21	Johnny Isakson, Ga.	Jan. 4, 2005
22	David Vitter, La.	Jan. 4, 2005
23	Bob Corker, Tenn.	Jan. 4, 2007
24	John Barrasso, Wyo.	June 25, 2007
25	Roger Wicker, Miss.	Dec. 31, 2007
26	Mike Johanns, Neb.	Jan. 6, 2009
27	Jim Risch, Idaho	Jan. 6, 2009
28	Mark S. Kirk, Ill.	Nov. 29, 2010
29	Dan Coats, Ind.	Jan. 5, 2011
30	Roy Blunt, Mo.	Jan. 5, 2011
31	Jerry Moran, Kan.	Jan. 5, 2011
32	Rob Portman, Ohio.	Jan. 5, 2011
33	John Boozman, Ark.	Jan. 5, 2011
34	John Hoeven, N.D.	Jan. 5, 2011
35	Marco Rubio, Fla.	Jan. 5, 2011
36	Patrick J. Toomey, Pa.	Jan. 5, 2011
37	Ron Johnson, Wis.	Jan. 5, 2011
38	Rand Paul, Ky.	Jan. 5, 2011
39	Mike Lee, Utah	Jan. 5, 2011
40	Kelly Ayotte, N.H.	Jan. 5, 2011
41	Dean Heller, Nev.	May 9, 2011
42	Jeff Flake, Ariz.	Jan. 3, 2013
43	Tim Scott, S.C.	Jan. 3, 2013
44	Ted Cruz, Texas	Jan. 3, 2013
45	Deb Fischer, Neb.	Jan. 3, 2013

INDEPENDENTS

1	Bernard Sanders, Vt.	Jan. 4, 2007
2	Angus King, Maine	Jan. 3, 2013

Former Governors

Eleven senators and one House member have served as governor.

Member	Years	Member	Years
Sen. Lamar Alexander, R-Tenn.	1979-87	Sen. Joe Manchin III, D-W.Va.	2005-10
Sen. Thomas R. Carper, D-Del.	1993-2001	Sen. Jim Risch, R-Idaho	2006
Sen. John Hoeven, R-N.D.	2000-10	Sen. Jay Rockefeller, D-W.Va.	1977-85
Sen. Mike Johanns, R-Neb.	1999-2005	Rep. Mark Sanford, R-S.C.	2003-11
Sen. Tim Kaine, D-Va.*	2006-10	Sen. Jeanne Shaheen, D-N.H.	1997-2003
Sen. Angus King, I-Maine*	1995-2003	Sen. Mark Warner, D-Va.	2002-06

Former Lieutenant Governors

Four senators, three House members and two delegates have served as lieutenant governor.

Member	Years	Member	Years
Del. Madeleine Z. Bordallo, D-Guam	1995-2003	Sen. Tim Kaine, D-Va.*	2002-06
Rep. John Carney, D-Del.	2001-09	Sen. Harry Reid, D-Nev.	1971-75
Del. Eni F.H. Faleomavaega, D-Am. Samoa	1985-89	Sen. Jim Risch, R-Idaho	2003-06, 2007-09
Rep. John Garamendi, D-Calif.	2007-09	Sen. Brian Schatz, D-Hawaii	2010-12
Sen. Mazie K. Hirono, D-Hawaii	1994 2002		

Former Representatives in the Senate

25 Democrats, 23 Republicans, 1 independent

Member	House Service	Member	House Service
Tammy Baldwin, D-Wis. †	1999-2013	Tim Johnson, D-S.D.	1987-97
Max Baucus, D-Mont.	1975-78	Mark S. Kirk, R-Ill.	2001-10
Roy Blunt, R-Mo.	1997-2011	John McCain, R-Ariz.	1983 87
John Boozman, R-Ark.	2001-11	Robert Menendez, D-N.J.	1993-2006
Barbara Boxer, D-Calif.	1983-93	Barbara A. Mikulski, D-Md.	1977-87
Sherrod Brown, D Ohio	1993-2007	Jerry Moran, R-Kan.	1997-2011
Richard M. Burr, R-N.C.	1995-2005	Christopher S. Murphy, D-Conn. †	2007-13
Maria Cantwell, D-Wash.	1993-95	Bill Nelson, D-Fla.	1979-91
Benjamin L. Cardin, D-Md.	1987-2007	Rob Portman, R Ohio	1993-2005
Thomas R. Carper, D-Del.	1983-93	Jack Reed, D-R.I.	1991-97
Saxby Chambliss, R-Ga.	1995-2003	Harry Reid, D-Nev.	1983-87
Dan Coats, R-Ind.	1981 89	Pat Roberts, R-Kan.	1981-97
Tom Coburn, R-Okla.	1995-2001	Bernard Sanders, I-Vt.	1991-2007
Thad Cochran, R-Miss.	1973-78	Charles E. Schumer, D-N.Y.	1981-99
Michael D. Crapo, R-Idaho	1993-99	Richard C. Shelby, R-Ala.	1979-87
Joe Donnelly, D-Ind. †	2007-13	Debbie Stabenow, D-Mich.	1997-2001
Richard J. Durbin, D-Ill.	1983-97	John Thune, R-S.D.	1997-2003
Jeff Flake, R-Ariz. †	2001-13	Patrick J. Toomey, R-Pa.	1999-2005
Kirsten Gillibrand, D-N.Y.	2007-09	Mark Udall, D-Colo.	1999-2009
Lindsey Graham, R-S.C.	1995-2003	Tom Udall, D-N.M.	1999-2009
Charles E. Grassley, R-Iowa	1975-81	David Vitter, R-La.	1999-2005
Tom Harkin, D-Iowa	1975-85	Roger Wicker, R-Miss.	1995-2007
Martin Heinrich, D-N.M.	2009-13	Ron Wyden, D-Ore.	1981-96
Mazie K. Hirono, D-Hawaii †	2007-13		
James M. Inhofe, R-Okla.	1987-94		
Johnny Isakson, R-Ga.	1999-2005		

*New to Congress
† New to the Senate

Women in Congress

Senate (16 D, 4 R)
Kelly Ayotte, R-N.H.
Tammy Baldwin, D-Wis.
Barbara Boxer, D-Calif.
Maria Cantwell, D-Wash.
Susan Collins, R-Maine
Dianne Feinstein, D-Calif.
Deb Fischer, R-Neb.*
Kirsten Gillibrand, D-N.Y.
Kay Hagan, D-N.C.
Heidi Heitkamp, D-N.D.*
Mazie K. Hirono, D-Hawaii
Amy Klobuchar, D-Minn.
Mary L. Landrieu, D-La.
Claire McCaskill, D-Mo.
Barbara A. Mikulski, D-Md.
Lisa Murkowski, R-Alaska
Patty Murray, D-Wash.
Jeanne Shaheen, D-N.H.
Debbie Stabenow, D-Mich.
Elizabeth Warren, D-Mass.*

House (62 D, 19 R)
Michele Bachmann, R-Minn.
Karen Bass, D-Calif.
Joyce Beatty, D-Ohio*
Diane Black, R-Tenn.
Marsha Blackburn, R-Tenn.
Suzanne Bonamici, D-Ore.
Madeleine Z. Bordallo, D-Guam
Susan W. Brooks, R-Ind.*
Corrine Brown, D-Fla.
Julia Brownley, D-Calif.*
Cheri Bustos, D-Ill.*
Shelley Moore Capito, R-W.Va.
Lois Capps, D-Calif.
Kathy Castor, D-Fla.
Donna M.C. Christensen, D-V.I.
Judy Chu, D-Calif.
Yvette D. Clarke, D-N.Y.
Susan A. Davis, D-Calif.
Diana DeGette, D-Colo.
Rosa DeLauro, D-Conn.
Suzan DelBene, D-Wash.
Tammy Duckworth, D-Ill.*
Donna Edwards, D-Md.
Renee Ellmers, R-N.C.
Anna G. Eshoo, D-Calif.
Elizabeth Esty, D-Conn.*
Virginia Foxx, R-N.C.
Lois Frankel, D-Fla.*
Marcia L. Fudge, D-Ohio
Tulsi Gabbard, D-Hawaii*
Kay Granger, R-Texas
Janice Hahn, D-Calif.
Colleen Hanabusa, D-Hawaii
Vicky Hartzler, R-Mo.
Jaime Herrera Beutler, R-Wash.
Sheila Jackson Lee, D-Texas
Lynn Jenkins, R-Kan.
Eddie Bernice Johnson, D-Texas
Marcy Kaptur, D-Ohio
Robin Kelly, D-Ill.*
Ann Kirkpatrick, D-Ariz.
Ann McLane Kuster, D-N.H.*
Barbara Lee, D-Calif.
Zoe Lofgren, D-Calif.
Nita M. Lowey, D-N.Y.
Michelle Lujan Grisham, D-N.M.*
Cynthia M. Lummis, R-Wyo.
Carolyn B. Maloney, D-N.Y.
Doris Matsui, D-Calif.
Carolyn McCarthy, D-N.Y.
Betty McCollum, D-Minn.
Cathy McMorris Rodgers, R-Wash.
Grace Meng, D-N.Y.*
Candice S. Miller, R-Mich.
Gwen Moore, D-Wis.
Grace F. Napolitano, D-Calif.
Gloria Negrete McLeod, D-Calif.*
Kristi Noem, R-S.D.
Eleanor Holmes Norton, D-D.C.
Nancy Pelosi, D-Calif.
Chellie Pingree, D-Maine
Martha Roby, R-Ala.
Ileana Ros-Lehtinen, R-Fla.
Lucille Roybal-Allard, D-Calif.
Linda T. Sánchez, D-Calif.
Loretta Sanchez, D-Calif.
Jan Schakowsky, D-Ill.
Allyson Y. Schwartz, D-Pa.
Terri A. Sewell, D-Ala.
Carol Shea-Porter, D-N.H.
Kyrsten Sinema, D-Ariz.*
Louise M. Slaughter, D-N.Y.
Jackie Speier, D-Calif.
Dina Titus, D-Nev.
Niki Tsongas, D-Mass.
Nydia M. Velázquez, D-N.Y.
Ann Wagner, R-Mo.*
Jackie Walorski, R-Ind.*
Debbie Wasserman Schultz, D-Fla.
Maxine Waters, D-Calif.
Frederica S. Wilson, D-Fla.

* New to Congress

Minorities in Congress

AMERICAN INDIAN

House (2 R)
Tom Cole, R-Okla.
Markwayne Mullin, R-Okla.*

ASIAN

Senate (1 D)
Mazie K. Hirono, D-Hawaii

House (10 D)
Ami Bera, D-Calif.*
Judy Chu, D-Calif.
Tammy Duckworth, D-Ill.*
Eni F.H. Faleomavaega, D-Am.Samoa
Colleen Hanabusa, D-Hawaii
Michael M. Honda, D-Calif.
Doris Matsui, D-Calif.
Grace Meng, D-N.Y.*
Gregorio Kilili Camacho Sablan, D-N. Marianas
Mark Takano, D-Calif.*

HISPANIC

Senate (2 R, 1 D)
Ted Cruz, R-Texas*
Robert Menendez, D-N.J.
Marco Rubio, R-Fla.

House (24 D, 5 R)
Xavier Becerra, D-Calif.
Tony Cárdenas, D-Calif.*
Joaquin Castro, D-Texas*
Henry Cuellar, D-Texas
Mario Diaz-Balart, R-Fla.
Bill Flores, R-Texas
Pete Gallego, D-Texas*
Joe Garcia, D-Fla.*
Raúl M. Grijalva, D-Ariz.
Luis V. Gutierrez, D-Ill.
Jaime Herrera Beutler, R-Wash.
Rubén Hinojosa, D-Texas
Raúl R. Labrador, R-Idaho
Ben Ray Luján, D-N.M.
Michelle Lujan Grisham, D-N.M.*
Grace F. Napolitano, D-Calif.
Gloria Negrete McLeod, D-Calif.*
Ed Pastor, D-Ariz.
Pedro R. Pierluisi, D-P.R.
Ileana Ros-Lehtinen, R-Fla.
Lucille Roybal-Allard, D-Calif.
Raul Ruiz, D-Calif.*
Linda T. Sánchez, D-Calif.
Loretta Sanchez, D-Calif.
José E. Serrano, D-N.Y.
Albio Sires, D-N.J.
Juan C. Vargas, D-Calif.*
Filemon Vela, D-Texas*
Nydia M. Velázquez, D-N.Y.

BLACK

Senate (1 D, 1 R)
William "Mo" Cowan, D-Mass.*
Tim Scott, R-S.C.

House (43 D)
Karen Bass, D-Calif.
Joyce Beatty, D-Ohio*
Sanford D. Bishop Jr., D-Ga.
Corrine Brown, D-Fla.
G.K. Butterfield, D-N.C.
André Carson, D-Ind.
Donna M.C. Christensen, D-V.I.
Yvette D. Clarke, D-N.Y.
William Lacy Clay, D-Mo.
Emanuel Cleaver II, D-Mo.
James E. Clyburn, D-S.C.
John Conyers Jr., D-Mich.
Elijah E. Cummings, D-Md.
Danny K. Davis, D-Ill.
Donna Edwards, D-Md.
Keith Ellison, D-Minn.
Chaka Fattah, D-Pa.
Marcia L. Fudge, D-Ohio
Al Green, D-Texas
Alcee L. Hastings, D-Fla.
Steven Horsford, D-Nev.*
Sheila Jackson Lee, D-Texas
Hakeem Jeffries, D-N.Y.*
Eddie Bernice Johnson, D-Texas
Hank Johnson, D-Ga.
Robin Kelly, D-Ill.*
Barbara Lee, D-Calif.
John Lewis, D-Ga.
Gregory W. Meeks, D-N.Y.
Gwen Moore, D-Wis.
Eleanor Holmes Norton, D-D.C.
Donald M. Payne Jr., D-N.J.
Charles B. Rangel, D-N.Y.
Cedric L. Richmond, D-La.
Bobby L. Rush, D-Ill.
David Scott, D-Ga.
Robert C. Scott, D-Va.
Terri A. Sewell, D-Ala.
Bennie Thompson, D-Miss.
Marc Veasey, D-Texas*
Maxine Waters, D-Calif.
Melvin Watt, D-N.C.
Frederica S. Wilson, D-Fla.

PACIFIC ISLANDER

House (1 D)
Tulsi Gabbard, D-Hawaii*

* New to Congress

Former Congressional Staffers

Below are the 76 members who previously worked as paid, full-time congressional aides. Internships, fellowships and campaign work are not included.

Member	Congressional Office	Years
Sen. Lamar Alexander, R-Tenn.	Sen. Howard H. Baker Jr., R-Tenn.	1967-68
Rep. Ron Barber, D-Ariz.	Rep. Gabrielle Giffords, D-Ariz.	2007-11
Rep. Andy Barr, R-Ky.*	Rep. Jim Talent, R-Mo.	1996-98
Sen. Richard Blumenthal, D-Conn.	Sen. Abraham Ribicoff, D-Conn.	1975-76
Rep. Jo Bonner, R-Ala.	Rep. Sonny Calahan, R-Ala.	1985-2002
Sen. Barbara Boxer, D-Calif.	Rep. John L. Burton, D-Calif.	1974-76
Rep. Dave Camp, R-Mich.	Rep. Bill Schuette, R-Mich.	1984-87
Rep. John Carney, D-Del.	Sen. Joseph R. Biden Jr., D-Del.	1987-89
Rep. William Lacy Clay, D-Mo.	House Clerk	1977-83
Sen. Dan Coats, R-Ind.	Rep. Dan Quayle, R-Ind.	1976-80
Rep. Tom Cole, R-Okla.	Rep. Mickey Edwards, R-Okla.	1982-84
Sen. Susan Collins, R-Maine	Rep./Sen. William S. Cohen, R-Maine	1975-87
Rep. Gerald E. Connolly, D-Va.	Senate Foreign Relations Committee	1979-89
Rep. John Conyers Jr., D-Mich.	Rep. John D. Dingell, D-Mich.	1958-61
Rep. Jim Costa, D-Calif.	Rep. John Krebs, D-Calif.	1975-76
Rep. Rodney Davis, R-Ill.*	Rep. John Shimkus, R-Ill.	1997-2012
Rep. Peter A. DeFazio, D-Ore.	Rep. James Weaver, D-Ore.	1977-82
Rep. Rosa DeLauro, D-Conn.	Sen. Christopher J. Dodd, D-Conn.	1981-87
Rep. Charlie Dent, R-Pa.	Rep. Don Ritter, R-Pa.	1982
Del. Eni F.H. Faleomavaega, D-Am. Samoa	Del. A.U. Fuimaono, D-Am. Samoa	1973-75
Rep. Jeff Fortenberry, R-Neb.	Senate Governmental Affairs subcommittee	1985-86
Rep. Marcia L. Fudge, D-Ohio	Rep. Stephanie Tubbs Jones, D-Ohio	1999
Rep. Tulsi Gabbard, D-Hawaii*	Sen. Daniel K. Akaka, D-Hawaii	2006-09
Rep. Cory Gardner, R-Colo.	Sen. Wayne Allard, R-Colo.	2002-05
Rep. Robert W. Goodlatte, R-Va.	Rep. M. Caldwell Butler, R-Va.	1977-79
Rep. Tim Griffin, R-Ark.	House Government Reform Committee	1997-99
Sen. Tom Harkin, D-Iowa	Rep. Neal Smith, D-Iowa	1969-70
Rep. Denny Heck, D-Wash.*	Rep. Mike McCormack, D-Wash.	1974-75
Rep. Jeb Hensarling, R-Texas	Sen. Phil Gramm, R-Texas	1985-89
Rep. Jaime Herrera Beutler, R-Wash.	Rep. Cathy McMorris Rodgers, R-Wash.	2005-07
Rep. George Holding, R-N.C.*	Sen. Jesse Helms, R-N.C.	1998-2001
Rep. Richard Hudson, R-N.C.*	Rep. Robin Hayes, R-N.C.	1999-2005
	Rep. Virginia Foxx, R-N.C.	2005-06
	Rep. John Carter, R-Texas	2006-08
	Rep. K. Michael Conaway, R-Texas	2008-2011
Rep. Bill Huizenga, R-Mich.	Rep. Peter Hoekstra, R-Mich.	1997-2003
Rep. Randy Hultgren, R-Ill.	Rep. J. Dennis Hastert, R-Ill.	1988-90
Rep. Steve Israel, D-N.Y.	Rep. Richard L. Ottinger, D-N.Y.	1980-83
Rep. Sheila Jackson Lee, D-Texas	House Select Committee on Assassinations	1977-78
Sen. Angus King, I-Maine*	Senate Labor and Public Welfare subcommittee	1972-75
Sen. Mark S. Kirk, R-Ill.	Rep. John Edward Porter, R-Ill.	1984-89
	House International Relations Committee	1995-2000
Rep. Ann McLane Kuster, D-N.H.*	Rep. Paul Norton "Pete" McCloskey Jr., R-Calif.	1978-81
Rep. Barbara Lee, D-Calif.	Rep. Ronald V. Dellums, D-Calif.	1975-86
Rep. Daniel Lipinski, D-Ill.	Rep. Rod R. Blagojevich, D-Ill.	1999-2000
Rep. Zoe Lofgren, D-Calif.	Rep. Don Edwards, D-Calif.	1970-79
Rep. Dan Maffei, D-N.Y.	Sen. Bill Bradley, D-N.J.	1995-96
	Sen. Daniel Patrick Moynihan	1997-98
	House Ways and Means Committee	1999-2005
Rep. Kevin McCarthy, R-Calif.	Rep. Bill Thomas, R-Calif.	1987-2002
Sen. Mitch McConnell, R-Ky.	Sen. Marlow W. Cook, R-Ky.	1969-70
Rep. Jim McGovern, D-Mass.	Rep. Joe Moakley, D-Mass.	1981-1993
Rep. Patrick Meehan, R-Pa.	Sen. Arlen Specter, R-Pa.	1990, 1992-94
Sen. Jeff Merkley, D-Ore.	Congressional Budget Office	1985-89
Rep. Luke Messer, R-Ind.*	House Government Reform subcommittee	1996-97
	Rep. Ed Bryant, R-Tenn.	1997-98
	Rep. John J. Duncan Jr., R-Tenn.	1998-99

Rep. John L. Mica, R-Fla.	Sen. Paula Hawkins, R-Fla.	1981-85
Rep. James P. Moran, D-Va.	Senate Appropriations Committee	1976-79
Rep. Rick Nolan, D-Minn.	Sen. Walter F. Mondale, D-Minn.	1966-68
Rep. Pete Olson, R-Texas	Sen. Phil Gramm, R-Texas	1998-2002
	Sen. John Cornyn, R-Texas	2002-07
Rep. Erik Paulsen, R-Minn.	Rep. Jim Ramstad, R-Minn.	1990-94
Rep. Nick J. Rahall II, D-W.Va.	Sen. Robert C. Byrd, D-W.Va.	1971-74
Sen. Pat Roberts, R-Kan.	Sen. Frank Carlson, R-Kan.	1967-68
Rep. Tom Rooney, R-Fla.	Sen. Connie Mack, R-Fla.	1993
Rep. Peter Roskam, R-Ill.	Rep. Tom DeLay, R-Texas	1985-86
	Rep. Henry J. Hyde, R-Ill.	1986-87
Rep. Paul D. Ryan, R-Wis.	Sen. Bob Kasten, R-Wis.	1992
	Rep./Sen. Sam Brownback, R-Kan.	1995-97
Rep. Tim Ryan, D-Ohio	Rep. James A. Traficant Jr., D-Ohio	1995-97
Rep. Jackie Speier, D-Calif.	Rep. Leo Ryan, D-Calif.	1976-78
Rep. Mac Thornberry, R-Texas	Rep. Tom Loeffler, R-Texas	1983-85
	Rep. Larry Combest, R-Texas	1985-88
Sen. John Thune, R-S.D.	Rep. James Abdnor, R-S.D.	1985-86
	Senate Small Business Committee	1989
Rep. Pat Tiberi, R-Ohio	Rep. John R. Kasich, R-Ohio	1983-91
Sen. Tom Udall, D-N.M.	Sen. Joseph R. Biden Jr., D-Del.	1973
Rep. Fred Upton, R-Mich.	Rep. David A. Stockman, R-Mich.	1977-81
Rep. Chris Van Hollen, D-Md.	Sen. Charles McC. Mathias Jr., R-Md.	1985-87
	Senate Foreign Relations Committee	1987-89
Rep. Marc Veasey, D-Texas*	Rep. Martin Frost, D-Texas	1998-2004
Rep. Nydia M. Velázquez, D-N.Y.	Rep. Edolphus Towns, D-N.Y.	1983-84
Rep. Peter J. Visclosky, D-Ind.	Rep. Adam Benjamin Jr., D-Ind.	1977-82
Rep. Greg Walden, R-Ore.	Rep. Denny Smith, R-Ore.	1981-86
Sen. Roger Wicker, R-Miss.	Rep. Trent Lott, R-Miss.	1980-82
Rep. Frank R. Wolf, R-Va.	Rep. Edward G. Biester, R-Pa.	1968-71
Rep. Rob Woodall, R-Ga.	Rep. John Linder, R-Ga.	1994-2010
Rep. John Yarmuth, D-Ky.	Sen. Marlow W. Cook, R-Ky.	1971-74
Rep. Todd Young, R-Ind.	Sen. Richard G. Lugar, R-Ind.	2001-03

* New to Congress

Born in D.C.

Rep. Hank Johnson, D-Ga.
Del. Eleanor Holmes Norton, D-D.C.
Rep. Bill Posey, R-Fla.
Rep. Robert C. Scott, D-Va.
Rep. Adam Smith, D-Wash.
Rep. Rob Wittman, R-Va.

Former Pages

There are seven members of Congress who once served as congressional pages:

	Years
Sen. Michael Bennet, D-Colo.	—
Rep. Jim Cooper, D-Tenn.	1970
Rep. John D. Dingell, D-Mich.	1938-42
Rep. Rush D. Holt, D-N.J.	1963-64
Sen. Mike Lee, R-Utah	1987
Sen. Mark Pryor, D-Ark.	1982
Sen. Roger Wicker, R-Miss.	1967

Members Who Served in the Military

There are 104 members with military service, including in the National Guard and reserves. The years of service include both active and inactive duty. An asterisk denotes a combat veteran, and a dagger denotes a member who served after Sept. 11, 2001, in Iraq, Afghanistan or both.

Senate (11 R, 5 D)	Years
Richard Blumenthal, D-Conn.	1970-76
Thomas R. Carper, D-Del.*	1968-91
Dan Coats, R-Ind.	1966-68
Thad Cochran, R-Miss.	1959-61
Michael B. Enzi, R-Wyo.	1967-73
Lindsey Graham, R-S.C.	1982-96, 2003-present
Tom Harkin, D-Iowa	1962-67, 1968-74
James M. Inhofe, R-Okla.	1957-58
Johnny Isakson, R-Ga.	1966-72
Mark S. Kirk, R-Ill.	1989-present
John McCain, R-Ariz.*	1958-81
Bill Nelson, D-Fla.	1965-71
Jack Reed, D-R.I.	1971-91
Pat Roberts, R-Kan.	1958-62
Jeff Sessions, R-Ala.	1973-86
Roger Wicker, R-Miss.	1976-2004

House (66 R, 22 D)	Years
Rodney Alexander, R-La.	1965-71
Mark Amodei, R-Nev.	1983-87
Spencer Bachus, R-Ala.	1969-71
Kerry Bentivolio, R-Mich.*	1970-71, 1974, 1990-2009
Sanford D. Bishop Jr., D-Ga.	1971
John A. Boehner, R-Ohio	1968
Jim Bridenstine, R-Okla.*†	1998-2007, 2010-present
Paul Broun, R-Ga.	1964-73, 2010-present
Vern Buchanan, R-Fla.	1970-76
Larry Bucshon, R-Ind.	1989-98
G.K. Butterfield, D-N.C.	1968-70
Howard Coble, R-N.C.*	1952-56, 1960-82, 1977-78
Mike Coffman, R-Colo.*†	1972-74, 1975-94, 2005-06
Doug Collins, R-Ga.*†	2002-present
K. Michael Conaway, R-Texas	1970-72
John Conyers Jr., D-Mich.*	1948-57
Paul Cook, R-Calif.*	1966-92
Tom Cotton, R-Ark.*†	2004-09
Rick Crawford, R-Ark.*	1985-89
Peter A. DeFazio, D-Ore.	1967-71
Jeff Denham, R-Calif.	1984-2000
Ron DeSantis, R-Fla.*†	2004-present
John D. Dingell, D-Mich.*	1944-46
Tammy Duckworth, D-Ill.*†	1991-present
John J. Duncan Jr., R-Tenn.	1970-87
Bill Enyart, D-Ill.	1969-75, 1982-2012
Eni F.H. Faleomavaega, D-Am. Samoa	1966-69, 1983-2001
John Fleming, R-La.	1976-82
Rodney Frelinghuysen, R-N.J.*	1969-71
Tulsi Gabbard, D-Hawaii*†	2003-present
Chris Gibson, R-N.Y.*†	1986-2010
Louie Gohmert, R-Texas	1978-82
Tim Griffin, R-Ark.*†	1996-present
Michael G. Grimm, R-N.Y.*	1989-97
Brett Guthrie, R-Ky.	1987-2002
Ralph M. Hall, R-Texas*	1942-45
Andy Harris, R-Md.	1988-2005
Doc Hastings, R-Wash.	1964-69
Joe Heck, R-Nev.*†	1991-present
Duncan Hunter, R-Calif.*†	2002-08
Darrell Issa, R-Calif.	1970-72, 1976-88
Bill Johnson, R-Ohio	1973-78, 1979-99
Sam Johnson, R-Texas*	1951-79
Walter B. Jones, R-N.C.	1967-71
Peter T. King, R-N.Y.	1968-73
Adam Kinzinger, R-Ill.*†	2001-present
John Kline, R-Minn.*	1969-94
Edward J. Markey, D-Mass.	1968-73
Jim McDermott, D-Wash.	1968-70
Gary G. Miller, R-Calif.	1967
Tim Murphy, R-Pa.	2009-present
Rich Nugent, R-Fla.	1969-75
Pete Olson, R-Texas	1988-98
Bill Owens, D-N.Y.	1971-82
Steven M. Palazzo, R-Miss.*	1988-96, 1997-present
Bill Pascrell Jr., D-N.J.	1961, 1962-67
Steve Pearce, R-N.M.*	1970-76
Scott Perry, R-Pa.*†	1980-present
Gary Peters, D-Mich.	1993-2000, 2001-05
Collin C. Peterson, D-Minn.	1963-69
Joe Pitts, R-Pa.*	1963-69
Ted Poe, R-Texas	1970-76
Mike Pompeo, R-Kan.	1986-91
Charles B. Rangel, D-N.Y.*	1948-52
Dave Reichert, R-Wash.	1971-76
Scott Rigell, R-Va.	1978-84
Phil Roe, R-Tenn.	1973-74
Harold Rogers, R-Ky.	1956-63
Mike Rogers, R-Mich.	1985-88
Tom Rooney, R-Fla.	2000-04
Bobby L. Rush, D-Ill.	1963-68
Gregorio Kilili Camacho Sablan, D-N. Marianas	1981-86
Mark Sanford, R-S.C.	2002-11
Robert C. Scott, D-Va.	1970-76
José E. Serrano, D-N.Y.	1964-66
John Shimkus, R-Ill.	1980-2008
Chris Stewart, R-Utah	1984-98
Steve Stivers, R-Ohio*†	1988-present
Mike Thompson, D-Calif.*	1969-73
Tim Walz, D-Minn.	1981-2005
Brad Wenstrup, R-Ohio*†	1998-present
Edward Whitfield, R-Ky.	1967-73

Members Who Served in the Military, cont.

Joe Wilson, R-S.C.	1972-2003	C.W. Bill Young, R-Fla.	1948-57
Frank R. Wolf, R-Va.	1962-63	Don Young, R-Alaska	1955-57
Steve Womack, R-Ark.	1979-2009	Todd Young, R-Ind.	1995-2000

Peace Corps Volunteers

Member	Country	Years
Rep. Sam Farr, D-Calif.	Colombia	1964-66
Rep. John Garamendi, D-Calif.	Ethiopia	1966-68
Rep. Michael M. Honda, D-Calif.	El Salvador	1965-67
Rep. Joseph P. Kennedy III, D-Mass.	Dominican Republic	2004-06
Rep. Tom Petri, R-Wis.	Somalia	1966-67

Eagle Scouts

Sen. Lamar Alexander, R-Tenn.
Rep. Lou Barletta, R-Pa.
Rep. Sanford D. Bishop Jr., D-Ga.
Rep. Jim Bridenstine, R-Okla.
Sen. Sherrod Brown, D-Ohio
Sen. Thad Cochran, R-Miss.
Rep. Chris Collins, R-N.Y.
Rep. Jim Cooper, D-Tenn.
Sen. Michael D. Crapo, R-Idaho
Sen. Michael B. Enzi, R-Wyo.
Rep. Michael G. Fitzpatrick, R-Pa.
Rep. John Garamendi, D-Calif.
Rep. Louie Gohmert, R-Texas
Rep. Sam Graves, R-Mo.
Rep. Jeb Hensarling, R-Texas
Sen. Mike Lee, R-Utah
Rep. David B. McKinley, R-W.Va.
Sen. Jeff Merkley, D-Ore.
Rep. Phil Roe, R-Tenn.
Rep. Dana Rohrabacher, R-Calif.
Sen. Jeff Sessions, R-Ala.
Rep. Pete Sessions, R-Texas
Rep. Christopher H. Smith, R-N.J.
Rep. Steve Stivers, R-Ohio
Rep. Glenn Thompson, R-Pa.
Sen. Patrick J. Toomey, R-Pa.
Rep. Greg Walden, R-Ore.

Fastest Members of Congress

Some members participate in an annual 3-mile footrace in Washington, D.C. Here are the times posted by those who ran in the May 2013 race. Sen. John Thune, who has run the race in less than 20 minutes, could not participate in 2013 due to injury.

Member	Time	Member	Time
Rep. Tom Cotton, R-Ark.	17:55	Rep. Earl Blumenauer, D-Ore.	28:28
Rep. Eric Swalwell, D-Calif.	19:45	Sen. Jack Reed, D-R.I.	29:18
Rep. Daniel Lipinski, D-Ill.	19:56	Rep. Bill Huizenga, R-Mich.	29:37
Rep. Tom Graves, R-Ga.	22:27	Rep. José E. Serrano, D-N.Y.	29:49
Rep. Rodney Davis, R-Ill.	23:59	Rep. David Schweikert, R-Ariz.	30:14
Rep. Tim Walz, D-Minn.	24:23	Rep. Cheri Bustos, D-Ill.	31:21
Sen. Rob Portman, R-Ohio	24:47	Sen. Charles E. Grassley, R-Iowa	32:52
Rep. Kyrsten Sinema, D-Ariz.	25:13	Sen. Kay Hagan, D-N.C.	36:34
Rep. Matt Cartwright, D-Pa.	25:18	Rep. Michael R. Turner, R-Ohio	36:53
Sen. Kelly Ayotte, R-N.H.	26:44	Rep. Mark Meadows, R-N.C.	38:18
Rep. Shelley Moore Capito, R-W.Va.	26:49	Rep. Marc Veasey, D-Texas	40:34
Rep. Rob Wittman, R-Va.	27:17	Sen. Heidi Heitkamp, D-N.D.	46:48
Rep. Chris Gibson, R-N.Y.	27:59	Rep. Cynthia M. Lummis, R-Wyo.	52:31
Rep. Scott Rigell, R-Va.	28:09		

Congressional Half-Life

Members who have served more than half of their life in Congress. Length of service and percentage figures are as of the start of the 113th Congress.

Member	Age at Swearing-In	Length of Service	Percent of Life in Congress
Rep. John D. Dingell, D-Mich.	29 years, 158 days	57 years, 21 days	66
Rep. John Conyers Jr., D-Mich.	35 years, 233 days	46 years	57
Rep. Nick J. Rahall II, D-W.Va.	27 years, 229 days	34 years	57
Rep. George Miller, D-Calif.	29 years, 242 days	36 years	56
Rep. Edward J. Markey, D-Mass.	30 years, 114 days	36 years, 62 days	54
Sen. Max Baucus, D-Mont.	33 years, 34 days	38 years	53
Rep. Christopher H. Smith, R-N.J.	27 years, 307 days	32 years	53
Sen. Thad Cochran, R-Miss.	35 years, 27 days	40 years	53
Sen. Patrick J. Leahy, D-Vt.	34 years, 289 days	38 years	52
Sen. Tom Harkin, D-Iowa	35 years, 56 days	38 years	52
Rep. Henry A. Waxman, D-Calif.	35 years, 124 days	38 years	52
Sen. Charles E. Schumer, D-N.Y.	30 years, 43 days	32 years	52
Rep. C.W. Bill Young, R-Fla.	40 years, 36 days	42 years	51
Rep. Charles B. Rangel, D-N.Y.	40 years, 224 days	42 years	51
Sen. Ron Wyden, D-Ore.	31 years, 247 days	32 years	50
Rep. Don Young, R-Alaska	39 years, 270 days	39 years, 303 days	50

Note: Lawmakers who will join the list during the 113th Congress are Rep. Jim Sensenbrenner, R-Wis. (Oct. 26, 2013), and Sen. Charles E. Grassley, R-Iowa (Sept. 8, 2014).

Members Whose Parent Served in Congress

There are 22 members with a parent who served in Congress. Walter B. Jones is the only one listed who belongs to a different political party than his parent.

Member	Parent	Years Parent Served
Sen. Mark Begich, D-Alaska	Rep. Nick Begich, D-Alaska	1971-72
Rep. Gus Bilirakis, R-Fla.*	Rep. Michael Bilirakis, R-Fla	1983-2007
Rep. Shelley Moore Capito, R-W.Va.	Rep. Arch A. Moore Jr., R-W.Va.	1957-69
Rep. William Lacy Clay, D-Mo.*	Rep. William L. Clay, D-Mo.	1969-2001
Rep. John D. Dingell, D-Mich.*	Rep. John D. Dingell Sr., D-Mich.	1933-55
Rep. John J. Duncan Jr., R-Tenn.*	Rep. John J. Duncan, R-Tenn.	1965-88
Rep. Rodney Frelinghuysen, R-N.J.	Rep. Peter H. Frelinghuysen, R-N.J.	1953-75
Rep. Rush D. Holt, D-N.J.	Sen. Rush Dew Holt, D-W.Va.	1935-41
Rep. Duncan Hunter, R-Calif.*	Rep. Duncan Hunter, R-Calif.	1981-2009
Rep. Walter B. Jones, R-N.C.	Rep. Walter B. Jones Sr., D-N.C.	1966-92
Rep. Joseph P. Kennedy III, D-Mass.	Rep. Joseph P. Kennedy II, D-Mass.	1987-98
Rep. Bob Latta, R-Ohio	Rep. Delbert L. Latta, R-Ohio	1959-89
Rep. Daniel Lipinski, D-Ill.*	Rep. William O. Lipinski, D-Ill.	1983-2005
Sen. Lisa Murkowski, R-Alaska*	Sen. Frank H. Murkowski, R-Alaska	1981-2002
Rep. Donald M. Payne Jr., D-N.J.*	Rep. Donald M. Payne, D-N.J.	1989-2012
Rep. Nancy Pelosi, D-Calif.	Rep. Thomas D'Alesandro Jr., D-Md.	1939-47
Sen. Mark Pryor, D-Ark.	Rep./Sen. David Pryor, D-Ark.	1966-73, 1979-97
Rep. Lucille Roybal-Allard, D-Calif.	Rep. Edward R. Roybal, D-Calif.	1963-93
Rep. John Sarbanes, D-Md.	Rep./Sen. Paul S. Sarbanes, D-Md.	1971-2007
Rep. Bill Shuster, R-Pa.*	Rep. Bud Shuster, R-Pa.	1973-2001
Sen. Mark Udall, D-Colo.	Rep. Morris K. Udall, D-Ariz.	1961-91
Sen. Tom Udall, D-N.M.	Rep. Stewart L. Udall, D-Ariz.	1955-61

* Directly succeeded his or her parent in the same seat

Dean of the Delegation

These are the longest-serving members of Congress from each state.

State	Member	First Elected
Alabama	Sen. Richard C. Shelby, R	*1978
Alaska	Rep. Don Young, R	1973
Arizona	Sen. John McCain, R	*1982
Arkansas	Sen. John Boozman, R	*2000
California	Rep. George Miller, D	† † 1974
	Rep. Henry A. Waxman, D	† † 1974
Colorado	Rep. Diana DeGette, D	1996
Connecticut	Rep. Rosa DeLauro, D	1990
Delaware	Sen. Thomas R. Carper, D	*1982
Florida	Rep. C. W. Bill Young, R	1970
Georgia	Rep. John Lewis, D	1986
Hawaii	Sen. Mazie K. Hirono, D	*2006
Idaho	Sen. Michael D. Crapo, R	*1992
Illinois	Sen. Richard J. Durbin, D	*1982
Indiana	Rep. Peter J. Visclosky, D	1984
Iowa	Sen. Charles E. Grassley, R	†*1974
Kansas	Sen. Pat Roberts, R	*1980
Kentucky	Rep. Harold Rogers, R	1980
Louisiana	Sen. Mary L. Landrieu, D	1996
Maine	Sen. Susan Collins, R	1996
Maryland	Sen. Barbara A. Mikulski, D	*1976
Massachusetts	Rep. Edward J. Markey, D	1976
Michigan	Rep. John D. Dingell, D	1955
Minnesota	Rep. Collin C. Peterson, D	1990
Mississippi	Sen. Thad Cochran, R	*1972
Missouri	Sen. Roy Blunt, R	*1996
Montana	Sen. Max Baucus, D	*1974
Nebraska	Rep. Lee Terry, R	1998
Nevada	Sen. Harry Reid, D	*1982
New Hampshire	Sen. Jeanne Shaheen, D	# 2008
New Jersey	Rep. Christopher H. Smith, R	1980
New Mexico	Sen. Tom Udall, D	*1998
New York	Rep. Charles B. Rangel, D	1970
North Carolina	Rep. Howard Coble, R	1984
North Dakota	Sen. John Hoeven, R	2010
Ohio	Rep. Marcy Kaptur, D	1982
Oklahoma	Sen. James M. Inhofe, R	*1986
Oregon	Sen. Ron Wyden, D	*1980
Pennsylvania	Rep. Mike Doyle, D	† † 1994
	Rep. Chaka Fattah, D	† † 1994
Rhode Island	Sen. Jack Reed, D	*1990
South Carolina	Rep. James E. Clyburn, D	1992
South Dakota	Sen. Tim Johnson, D	*1986
Tennessee	Rep. John J. Duncan Jr., R	1988
Texas	Rep. Ralph M. Hall, R	1980
Utah	Sen. Orrin G. Hatch, R	1976
Vermont	Sen. Patrick J. Leahy, D	1974
Virginia	Rep. Frank R. Wolf, R	1980
Washington	Rep. Jim McDermott, D	1988
West Virginia	Rep. Nick J. Rahall II, D	1976
Wisconsin	Rep. Jim Sensenbrenner, R	1978
Wyoming	Sen. Michael B. Enzi, R	1996

*First elected to the House

† Sen. Tom Harkin, D, also was elected to the House in 1974, but Grassley reached the Senate four years before Harkin.

† † Reps. George Miller, D, and Henry A. Waxman, D, both were elected in 1974.
Reps. Mike Doyle, D, and Chaka Fattah, D, both were elected in 1994.

Rep. Carol Shea-Porter, D, also served the same number of years as Shaheen; however, it was split service.

Members Whose Spouse Served in Congress

Member	Spouse	Spouse's Service
Rep. Lois Capps, D-Calif.	Rep. Walter Capps, D-Calif.	1997
Rep. Doris Matsui, D-Calif.	Rep. Robert T. Matsui, D-Calif.	1979-2005
Rep. Niki Tsongas, D-Mass.	Rep./Sen. Paul E. Tsongas, D-Mass.	1975-85

Relatives Serving Together in Congress

Siblings	Years Serving
Sen. Carl Levin, D-Mich.	1979-present
Rep. Sander M. Levin, D-Mich.	1983-present

Siblings	Years Serving
Rep. Linda T. Sánchez, D-Calif.	2003-present
Rep. Loretta Sanchez, D-Calif.	1997-present

Cousins	
Sen. Mark Udall, D-Colo.*	1999-present
Sen. Tom Udall, D-N.M.*	1999-present

* First elected to the House

Most and Least Legislation

These members served in the entire 112th Congress (2011-12) and introduced the most and least legislation. Members whose names are in italics are no longer in Congress.

Most — Senate	
Bob Casey, D-Pa.*	232
Robert Menendez, D-N.J.*	209
Charles E. Schumer, D-N.Y.*	148
Sherrod Brown, D-Ohio*	118
*John Kerry, D-Mass.**	118
Kay Hagan, D-N.C.	116
Dianne Feinstein, D-Calif.*	99
Amy Klobuchar, D-Minn.	96
Kirsten Gillibrand, D-N.Y.	82
Ron Wyden, D-Ore.	82

Most — House	
Steve Israel, D-N.Y.	65
Carolyn B. Maloney, D-N.Y.*	65
Don Young, R-Alaska	65
Jim Gerlach, R-Pa.	58
Melvin Watt, D-N.C.	57
Edward J. Markey, D-Mass.	56
*Bob Filner, D-Calif.**	54
Eleanor Holmes Norton, D-D.C.	54
Laura Richardson, D-Calif.	54
*Ron Paul, R-Texas**	53

Least — Senate	
Jim Risch, R-Idaho †	3
Saxby Chambliss, R-Ga.	4
Dan Coats, R-Ind.	6
Bob Corker, R-Tenn. †	7
Ron Johnson, R-Wis.	7
Richard C. Shelby, R-Ala. †	8
John Boozman, R-Ark.	9
Thad Cochran, R-Miss. †	9
Jon Kyl, R-Ariz. †	9
Lamar Alexander, R-Tenn.	10

Least — House	
Luis V. Gutierrez, D-Ill.	1
Ed Pastor, D-Ariz.	1
David Scott, D-Ga. †	1
Mario Diaz-Balart, R-Fla.	2
Bob Gibbs, R-Ohio	2
Tim Holden, R-Pa.	2
John Olver, D-Mass. †	2
Nancy Pelosi, D-Calif.	2
Henry A. Waxman, D-Calif.	2
Martha Roby, R-Ala.	3
Todd Rokita, R-Ind.	3
Peter J. Visclosky, D-Ind.	3

* Also in the top 10 in the 111th Congress

† Also in the bottom 10 in the 111th Congress

Roll Call's Clout Index

The clout index tracks the political influence of each state on national affairs. States are scored from 1 to 100 using a formula that accounts for a wide variety of criteria, including size of the delegation, seniority, number of full-committee chairmen and ranking members, and per capita federal spending received.

Overall Rank

State	Clout Index
California	100
Florida	88.7
Texas	80
Louisiana	68
New York	64.4
Virginia	51.7
Michigan	51.6
New Jersey	44.4
Maryland	43.2
Pennsylvania	38.6

Rank Per Member

State	Clout Index
Alaska	100
Delaware	90.4
North Dakota	89
Hawaii	84.4
Louisiana	83.3
South Dakota	78.9
Montana	75.5
Vermont	74
Maine	62.6
Rhode Island	60.4

Member Occupations

	HOUSE			SENATE			113th
	Democrat	Republican	Total	Democrat	Republican	Total	Congress
Public Service/Politics	156	110	266	34*	26	60	326
Business	91	152	243	14*	19	33	276
Law	100	84	184	37*	29	66	250
Education	53	32	85	14*	7	21	106
Real Estate	5	32	37	2	5	7	44
Agriculture	5	22	27	1	4	5	32
Medicine/Doctor	4	17	21	0	4	4	25
Labor/Blue Collar	9	8	17	2*	2	4	21
Journalism	6	9	15	4*	1	5	20
Homemaker/Domestic	12	4	16	5	0	5	21
Health Care	9	5	14	0	0	0	14
Military	1	8	9	0	1	1	10
Secretarial/Clerical	11	4	15	1	0	1	16
Law Enforcement	0	5	5	0	0	0	5
Engineering	5	3	8	0	0	0	8
Entertainment/Actor	0	1	1	1	1	2	3
Professional Sports	1	4	5	0	0	0	5
Science	4	1	5	0	0	0	5
Technical	2	4	6	1	0	1	7
Artistic/Creative	0	1	1	2*	0	2	3
Clergy	2	4	6	0	0	0	6
Aeronautics	0	1	1	0	0	0	1
Miscellaneous/None	3	0	3	1	0	1	4

Notes: Some members have had more than one occupation, and some members have had more than one separate occupation within a category. Delegates are not included.* Total includes independents Angus King, Maine, and Bernard Sanders, Vt.

Oldest in Congress

Member	Birth date
Rep. Ralph M. Hall, R-Texas	5/3/1923
Rep. John D. Dingell, D-Mich.	7/8/1926
Rep. John Conyers Jr., D-Mich.	5/16/1929
Rep. Louise M. Slaughter, D-N.Y.	8/14/1929
Rep. Charles B. Rangel, D-N.Y.	6/11/1930
Rep. Sam Johnson, R-Texas	10/11/1930
Rep. C.W. Bill Young, R-Fla.	12/16/1930
Rep. Howard Coble, R-N.C.	3/18/1931
Rep. Sander M. Levin, D-Mich.	9/6/1931
Del. Madeleine Z. Bordallo, D-Guam	5/31/1933
Rep. Don Young, R-Alaska	6/9/1933
Sen. Dianne Feinstein, D-Calif.	6/22/1933
Sen. Charles E. Grassley, R-Iowa	9/17/1933
Sen. Orrin G. Hatch, R-Utah	3/22/1934

Youngest in Congress

Member	Birth date
Rep. Patrick Murphy, D-Fla.	3/30/1983
Rep. Aaron Schock, R-Ill.	5/28/1981
Rep. Tulsi Gabbard, D-Hawaii	4/12/1981
Rep. Eric Swalwell, D-Calif.	11/16/1980
Rep. Joseph P. Kennedy III, D-Mass.	10/4/1980
Rep. Jason Smith, R-Mo.	6/16/1980
Rep. Justin Amash, R-Mich.	4/18/1980
Rep. Jaime Herrera Beutler, R-Wash.	11/3/1978
Rep. Ron DeSantis, R-Fla.	9/14/1978
Rep. Adam Kinzinger, R-Ill.	2/27/1978
Rep. Markwayne Mullin, R-Okla.	7/26/1977
Rep. Tom Cotton, R-Ark.	5/13/1977
Rep. David Valadao, R-Calif.	4/14/1977
Rep. Duncan Hunter, R-Calif.	12/7/1976

Car Dealers

Rep. Vern Buchanan, R-Fla.
Rep. John Campbell, R-Calif.
Rep. Mike Kelly, R-Pa.
Rep. Scott Rigell, R-Va.
Rep. Bill Shuster, R-Pa.
Rep. Roger Williams, R-Texas

M.D.s

Member	Field
Sen. John Barrasso, R-Wyo.	orthopedic surgeon
Rep. Dan Benishek, R-Mich.	surgeon
Rep. Ami Bera, D-Calif.	physician
Rep. Charles Boustany Jr., R-La.	heart surgeon
Rep. Paul Broun, R-Ga.	physician
Rep. Larry Bucshon, R-Ind.	heart surgeon
Rep. Michael C. Burgess, R-Texas	obstetrician
Rep. Bill Cassidy, R-La.	gastroenterologist
Del. Donna M.C. Christensen, D-V.I.	physician
Sen. Tom Coburn, R-Okla.	obstetrician
Rep. Scott DesJarlais, R-Tenn.	physician
Rep. John Fleming, R-La.	physician
Rep. Phil Gingrey, R-Ga.	obstetrician
Rep. Andy Harris, R-Md.	physician
Rep. Joe Heck, R-Nev.	physician
Rep. Jim McDermott, D-Wash.	psychiatrist
Sen. Rand Paul, R-Ky.	ophthalmologist
Rep. Tom Price, R-Ga.	orthopedic surgeon
Rep. Phil Roe, R-Tenn.	physician
Rep. Raul Ruiz, D-Calif.	physician
Rep. Brad Wenstrup, R-Ohio	surgeon

Professors

Rep. Robert E. Andrews, D-N.J.
Rep. Joyce Beatty, D-Ohio
Rep. Ami Bera, D-Calif.
Rep. Judy Chu, D-Calif.
Rep. Tom Cole, R-Okla.
Rep. Virginia Foxx, R-N.C.
Rep. Rush D. Holt, D-N.J.
Rep. Daniel Lipinski, D-Ill.
Rep. Dave Loebsack, D-Iowa
Rep. Zoe Lofgren, D-Calif.
Rep. Alan Lowenthal, D-Calif.
Rep. Tim Murphy, R-Pa.
Del. Eleanor Holmes Norton, D-D.C.
Rep. David E. Price, D-N.C.
Rep. Dina Titus, D-Nev.
Rep. Nydia M. Velázquez, D-N.Y.
Sen. David Vitter, R-La.
Sen. Elizabeth Warren, D-Mass.
Sen. Ron Wyden, D-Ore.

Professional Athletes

Member	Sport
Rep. Sean P. Duffy, R-Wis.	timber sports competitor
Rep. Jared Huffman, D-Calif.	national team volleyball player
Rep. Jon Runyan, R-N.J.	football player
Rep. Roger Williams, R-Texas	baseball player

Note: Rep. Patrick Meehan, R-Pa., was a professional hockey referee

Nurses

Member

Rep. Karen Bass, D-Calif.
Rep. Diane Black, R-Tenn.
Rep. Lois Capps, D-Calif.
Rep. Renee Ellmers, R-N.C.
Rep. Eddie Bernice Johnson, D-Texas
Rep. Carolyn McCarthy, D-N.Y.

Law Enforcement Officers

Member	Job
Rep. Michael G. Grimm, R-N.Y.	FBI agent
Rep. Jeff Miller, R-Fla.	deputy county sheriff
Rep. Rich Nugent, R-Fla.	county sheriff
Rep. Dave Reichert, R-Wash.	county sheriff, police officer
Rep. Mike Rogers, R-Mich.	FBI agent

Engineers and Physicists

Member	Job
Rep. Joe L. Barton, R-Texas	engineering consultant
Rep. Bill Foster, D-Ill.	physicist
Sen. Martin Heinrich, D-N.M.	mechanical draftsman
Rep. Rush D. Holt, D-N.J.	physicist
Rep. David B. McKinley, R-W.Va.	civil engineer
Rep. Jerry McNerney, D-Calif.	wind engineer
Rep. Bill Posey, R-Fla.	space program engineering inspector
Rep. Steve Scalise, R-La.	software engineer
Rep. Brad Schneider, D-Ill.	industrial engineer
Rep. Paul Tonko, D-N.Y.	state public works engineer

Member Religious Affiliations

	HOUSE			SENATE			113th
	Democrat	Republican	Total	Democrat	Republican	Total	CONGRESS
Roman Catholic	75	61	136	17	9	26	162
Baptist	25	41	66	0	9	9	75
Protestant - Unspecified	13	43	56	7	6	13	69
Methodist	10	24	34	2	5	7	41
Presbyterian	8	19	27	6	8	14	41
Jewish	21	1	22	10*	0	10	32
Episcopalian	14	18	32	2*	2	4	36
Lutheran	8	10	18	0	1	1	23
Mormon	1	7	8	2	5	7	15
Unspecified	9	0	9	2	0	2	11
Eastern Orthodox	2	3	5	0	0	0	5
United Church of Christ/ Congregationalist	2	2	4	1	0	1	5
African Methodist Episcopal	4	0	4	0	0	0	4
Buddhist	2	0	2	1	0	1	3
Christian Scientist	0	2	2	0	0	0	2
Muslim	2	0	2	0	0	0	2
Seventh-day Adventist	2	0	2	0	0	0	2
Atheist	0	0	0	0	0	0	0
Community of Christ	0	0	0	0	0	0	0
Christian Reformed Church	0	1	1	0	0	0	1
Quaker	1	0	1	0	0	0	1
Unitarian	1	0	1	0	0	0	1
Hindu	1	0	1	0	0	0	1
Pentecostal	0	2	2	0	0	0	2

Delegates are not included

* Includes independents Angus King, Maine, and/or Bernard Sanders, Vt.

Born Abroad

There are 18 lawmakers and three delegates who were born outside the 50 states and Washington, D.C.

Member	Birthplace	Member	Birthplace
Del. Eni F.H. Faleomavaega, D-Am. Samoa	Am. Samoa	Del. Kilili Sablan, D-N. Marianas	N. Marianas
Rep. Tulsi Gabbard, D-Hawaii	Am. Samoa	Rep. Chris Van Hollen, D-Md.	Pakistan
Sen. Ted Cruz, R-Texas	Canada	Sen. John McCain, R-Ariz	Panama Canal Zone
Rep. Sean Patrick Maloney, D-N.Y.	Canada	Rep. Jim Himes, D-Conn.	Peru
Rep. Ileana Ros-Lehtinen, R-Fla.	Cuba	Res. Cmmsr. Pedro R. Pierluisi, D-P.R.	Puerto Rico
Rep. Albio Sires, D-N.J.	Cuba	Rep. Raúl R. Labrador, R-Idaho	Puerto Rico
Rep. Mark Meadows, R-N.C.	France	Rep. José E. Serrano, D-N.Y.	Puerto Rico
Sen. Michael Bennet, D-Colo.	India	Rep. Nydia M. Velázquez, D-N.Y.	Puerto Rico
Rep. Diana DeGette, D-Colo.	Japan	Rep. Tammy Duckworth, D-Ill.	Thailand
Sen. Mazie K. Hirono, D-Hawaii	Japan	Rep. Ron Barber, D-Ariz.	United Kingdom
Rep. Raul Ruiz, D-Calif.	Mexico		

New to Congress

Senate (4 D, 2 R, 1 I)
William "Mo" Cowan, D-Mass.
Ted Cruz, R-Texas
Deb Fischer, R-Neb.
Heidi Heitkamp, D-N.D.
Tim Kaine, D-Va.
Angus King, I-Maine
Elizabeth Warren, D-Mass.

House (41 D, 33 R)
Andy Barr, R-Ky.
Joyce Beatty, D-Ohio
Kerry Bentivolio, R-Mich.
Ami Bera, D-Calif.
Jim Bridenstine, R-Okla.
Susan W. Brooks, R-Ind.
Julia Brownley, D-Calif.
Cheri Bustos, D-Ill.
Tony Cárdenas, D-Calif.
Matt Cartwright, D-Pa.
Joaquin Castro, D-Texas
Chris Collins, R-N.Y.
Doug Collins, R-Ga.
Paul Cook, R-Calif.
Tom Cotton, R-Ark.
Kevin Cramer, R-N.D.
Steve Daines, R-Mont.
Rodney Davis, R-Ill.
John Delaney, D-Md.
Ron DeSantis, R-Fla.
Tammy Duckworth, D-Ill.
Bill Enyart, D-Ill.
Elizabeth Esty, D-Conn.
Lois Frankel, D-Fla.
Tulsi Gabbard, D-Hawaii
Pete Gallego, D-Texas
Joe Garcia, D-Fla.
Denny Heck, D-Wash.
George Holding, R-N.C.
Steven Horsford, D-Nev.
Richard Hudson, R-N.C.
Jared Huffman, D-Calif.
Hakeem Jeffries, D-N.Y.
David Joyce, R-Ohio
Robin Kelly, D-Ill.
Joseph P. Kennedy III, D-Mass.
Dan Kildee, D-Mich.
Derek Kilmer, D-Wash.
Ann McLane Kuster, D-N.H.
Doug LaMalfa, R-Calif.
Alan Lowenthal, D-Calif.
Michelle Lujan Grisham, D-N.M.
Sean Patrick Maloney, D-N.Y.
Mark Meadows, R-N.C.
Grace Meng, D-N.Y.
Luke Messer, R-Ind.
Markwayne Mullin, R-Okla.
Patrick Murphy, D-Fla.
Gloria Negrete McLeod, D-Calif.
Beto O'Rourke, D-Texas
Scott Perry, R-Pa.
Scott Peters, D-Calif.
Robert Pittenger, R-N.C.
Mark Pocan, D-Wis.
Trey Radel, R-Fla.
Tom Rice, R-S.C.
Keith Rothfus, R-Pa.
Raul Ruiz, D-Calif.
Brad Schneider, D-Ill.
Kyrsten Sinema, D-Ariz.
Jason Smith, R-Mo.
Chris Stewart, R-Utah
Eric Swalwell, D-Calif.
Mark Takano, D-Calif.
David Valadao, R-Calif.
Juan C. Vargas, D-Calif.
Marc Veasey, D-Texas
Filemon Vela, D-Texas
Ann Wagner, R-Mo.
Jackie Walorski, R-Ind.
Randy Weber, R-Texas
Brad Wenstrup, R-Ohio
Roger Williams, R-Texas
Ted Yoho, R-Fla.

Senators Up for Election in 2014

20 Democrats, 14 Republicans
Lamar Alexander, R-Tenn.
Max Baucus, D-Mont.*
Mark Begich, D-Alaska
Saxby Chambliss, R-Ga.*
Thad Cochran, R-Miss.
Susan Collins, R-Maine
Chris Coons, D-Del.
John Cornyn, R-Texas
William "Mo" Cowan, D-Mass.***
Richard J. Durbin, D-Ill.
Michael B. Enzi, R-Wyo.
Al Franken, D-Minn.
Lindsey Graham, R-S.C.
Kay Hagan, D-N.C.
Tom Harkin, D-Iowa *
James M. Inhofe, R-Okla.
Mike Johanns, R-Neb.*
Tim Johnson, D-S.D.*
Mary L. Landrieu, D-La.
Carl Levin, D-Mich.*
Mitch McConnell, R-Ky.
Jeff Merkley, D-Ore.
Mark Pryor, D-Ark.
Jack Reed, D-R.I.
Jim Risch, R-Idaho
Pat Roberts, R-Kan.
Jay Rockefeller, D-W.Va.*
Brian Schatz, D-Hawaii**
Tim Scott, R-S.C.**
Jeff Sessions, R-Ala.
Jeanne Shaheen, D-N.H.
Mark Udall, D-Colo.
Tom Udall, D-N.M.
Mark Warner, D-Va.

* Not running for re-election
** Appointed and will stand for election in 2014
***Appointed and will not stand for election in 2014

Republican Wins in Obama Districts

In 2012, 17 Republicans won in districts whose voters preferred Democrat Barack Obama for president. The second column of numbers shows the percentage with which Obama won in the district, and the last column shows how far the House Republican ran ahead or behind Obama in the district.

	Member's win	Obama	+/-
Dave Reichert, Wash. (8)	60	50	10
Erik Paulsen, Minn. (3)	58	50	8
C.W. Bill Young, Fla. (13)	58	50	8
Ileana Ros-Lehtinen, Fla. (27)	60	53	7
Peter T. King, N.Y. (2)	59	52	7
John Kline, Minn. (2)	54	49	5
Scott Rigell, Va. (2)	54	50	4
Frank A. LoBiondo, N.J. (2)	58	54	4
David Valadao, Calif. (21)	58	55	3
Jon Runyan, N.J. (3)	54	52	2
Jeff Denham, Calif. (10)	53	51	2
Tom Latham, Iowa (3)	52	51	1
Chris Gibson, N.Y. (19)	53	52	1
Joe Heck, Nev. (3)	50	50	0
Michael G. Grimm, N.Y. (11)	52	52	0
Gary G. Miller, Calif. (31)	55	57	-2
Mike Coffman, Colo. (6)	48	52	-4

Democratic Wins in Romney Districts

In 2012, nine Democrats won in districts whose voters preferred Republican Mitt Romney for president. The second column of numbers shows the percentage with which Romney won in the district, and the last column shows how far the House Democrat ran ahead or behind Romney in the district.

	Member's win	Romney	+/-
Collin C. Peterson, Minn. (7)	60	54	6
Ron Barber, Ariz. (2)	50	50	0
Pete Gallego, Texas (23)	50	51	-1
Ann Kirkpatrick, Ariz. (1)	49	50	-1
John Barrow, Ga. (12)	54	55	-1
Patrick Murphy, Fla. (18)	50	52	-2
Mike McIntyre, N.C. (7)	50	59	-9
Nick J. Rahall II, W.Va. (3)	54	65	-11
Jim Matheson, Utah (4)	49	67	-18

Richest Districts

Congressional districts with the highest median household income in 2011:

District	Income	Member
Virginia 10	$109,505	Wolf, R
Virginia 11	100,146	Connolly, D
California 18	97,001	Eshoo, D
New York 3	95,699	Israel, D
New Jersey 7	95,189	Lance, R
New Jersey 11	93,655	Frelinghuysen, R
California 17	92,030	Honda, D
Virginia 8	91,027	Moran, D
Maryland 8	90,959	Van Hollen, D
California 45	89,383	Campbell, R

Poorest Districts

Congressional districts with the lowest median household income in 2011:

District	Income	Member
New York 15	$23,894	Serrano, D
Kentucky 5	29,627	Rogers, R
Michigan 13	29,863	Conyers, D
Alabama 7	30,327	Sewell, D
Mississippi 2	31,084	Thompson, D
South Carolina 6	31,313	Clyburn, D
Arizona 7	31,611	Pastor, D
North Carolina 1	32,009	Butterfield, D
Ohio 11	32,014	Fudge, D
Georgia 2	32,049	Bishop, D

Least Educated Districts

Congressional districts with the largest percentage of people 25 and older without a high school diploma:

District	Percent	Member
California 40	49.1	Roybal-Allard, D
California 21	43.0	Valadao, R
Texas 33	42.6	Veasey, D
Texas 29	41.5	Gene Green, D
New York 15	39.6	Serrano, D
California 44	39.4	Hahn, D
California 34	38.7	Becerra, D
California 16	36.1	Costa, D
Texas 34	35.4	Vela, D
California 46	35.4	Sanchez, D

Most Educated Districts

Congressional districts with the largest percentage of people 25 and older with at least a bachelor's degree:

District	Percent	Member
New York 12	68.6	Maloney, D
California 33	62.4	Waxman, D
Virginia 8	59.8	Moran, D
California 18	57.3	Eshoo, D
New York 10	57.2	Nadler, D
Georgia 6	56.3	Price, R
Washington 7	54.8	McDermott, D
California 52	54.6	Peters, D
California 12	54.4	Pelosi, D
Virginia 11	53.7	Connolly, D

Oldest Districts

Congressional districts with the highest median age:

District	Median Age	Member
Florida 11	50.7	Nugent, R
Florida 16	49.6	Buchanan, R
Florida 19	47.7	Radel, R
Florida 13	46.8	Young, R
Florida 8	46	Posey, R
Florida 17	45.7	Rooney, R
Florida 6	45.6	DeSantis, R
Florida 18	45.4	Murphy, D
Florida 22	44.7	Frankel, D
Michigan 1	44.7	Benishek, R

Youngest Districts

Congressional districts with the lowest median age:

District	Median Age	Member
Utah 3	27.2	Chaffetz, R
Arizona 7	27.9	Pastor, D
California 21	28.3	Valadao, R
Texas 29	28.7	Gene Green, D
Texas 33	28.7	Veasey, D
California 16	28.8	Costa, D
Calfornia 40	28.8	Roybal-Allard, D
Utah 1	29.2	Bishop, R
California 41	29.3	Takano, D
California 35	29.6	Negrete McLeod, D

Statistics in the boxes appearing on pp. 1126-1127 are from the U.S. Census Bureau

Hispanic Districts

Congressional districts with the largest percentage of Hispanics (Hispanics may be of any race):

District	Percent	Member
California 40	86.6	Roybal-Allard, D
Texas 34	82.6	Vela, D
Texas 15	80.2	Hinojosa, D
Texas 16	79.3	O'Rourke, D
Texas 28	78.4	Cuellar, D
Texas 29	76.4	Gene Green, D
Florida 27	72.7	Ros-Lehtinen, R
California 21	72.1	Valadao, D
Illinois 4	71.8	Gutierrez, D
Texas 23	70.8	Gallego, D

Black Districts

Congressional districts with the largest percentage of black residents:

District	Percent	Member
Mississippi 2	65.2	Thompson, D
Alabama 7	64.1	Sewell, D
Tennessee 9	63.8	Cohen, D
Louisiana 2	62.9	Richmond, D
Pennsylvania 2	58.6	Fattah, D
Georgia 5	58.3	Lewis, D
Michigan 14	57.2	Peters, D
Virginia 3	57.2	Scott, D
Georgia 4	56.9	Johnson, D
South Carolina 6	56.9	Clyburn, D

Asian Districts

Congressional districts with the largest percentage of Asians:

District	Percent	Member
Hawaii 1	51.0	Hanabusa, D
California 17	48.9	Honda, D
New York 6	36.4	Meng, D
California 27	36.4	Chu, D
California 14	31.4	Speier, D
California 12	31.0	Pelosi, D
California 39	28.3	Royce, R
California 15	28.1	Swalwell, D
California 19	25.8	Lofgren, D
Hawaii 2	25.1	Gabbard, D

American Indian Districts

Congressional districts with the largest percentage of American Indians:

District	Percent	Member
Arizona 1	23.2	Kirkpatrick, D
New Mexico 3	17.2	Luján, D
Alaska AL	14.2	Young, R
Oklahoma 2	13.2	Mullin, R
South Dakota AL	8.7	Noem, R
North Carolina 8	7.1	Hudson, R
Montana AL	6.7	Daines, R
New Mexico 2	6.0	Pearce, R
Oklahoma 1	5.9	Bridenstine, R
North Dakota AL	5.6	Cramer, R

Senate Presidential Support and Opposition

Support scores represent how often a senator sided with President Obama on roll call votes on which the president took a clear position beforehand. Opposition scores represent how often a senator voted against the president's position. During the 112th Congress (2011-12), there were 168 Senate votes on which the president took a position. Only members who voted on more than half of those are listed.

112TH CONGRESS: TOP SCORERS

Support — Democrats

Tim Johnson, S.D.	98.8
John Kerry, Mass.*	98.7
Dianne Feinstein, Calif.	98.2
Charles E. Schumer, N.Y.	98.1
Jeanne Shaheen, N.H.	98.1
Thomas R. Carper, Del.	97.6
Mark Warner, Va.	97.5
Bill Nelson, Fla.	97.5
Jay Rockefeller, W.Va.	97.3
Daniel K. Inouye, Hawaii*	97.2
Maria Cantwell, Wash.	97
Chris Coons, Del.	97
Jeff Bingaman, N.M.*	96.9
Kent Conrad, N.D.*	96.9
Amy Klobuchar, Minn.	96.9
Ron Wyden, Ore.	96.9
Michael Bennet, Colo.	96.4
Benjamin L. Cardin, Md.	96.4
Richard J. Durbin, Ill.	96.3
Patty Murray, Wash.	96.3
Mark Udall, Colo.	96.3

Opposition — Democrats

Joe Manchin III, W.Va.	15.8
Ben Nelson, Neb.*	14
Bernard Sanders, Vt. †	12
Jon Tester, Mont.	7.9
Tom Harkin, Iowa	7.7
Mary L. Landrieu, La.	7.5
Kay Hagan, N.C.	6.9
Mark Begich, Alaska	6.8
Jeff Merkley, Ore.	6.8
Jim Webb, Va.*	6.8
Mark Pryor, Ark.	6.7
Claire McCaskill, Mo.	6.3
Bob Casey, Pa.	6.2
Max Baucus, Mont.	6.1
Sherrod Brown, Ohio	6
Harry Reid, Nev.	6
Sheldon Whitehouse, R.I.	5.5
Jack Reed, R.I.	5.4
Frank R. Lautenberg, N.J.*	5.3
Tom Udall, N.M.	5
Debbie Stabenow, Mich.	4.9
Al Franken, Minn.	4.8
Barbara Boxer, Calif.	4.6

Support — Republicans

Susan Collins, Maine	75
Scott P. Brown, Mass.*	73.8
Olympia J. Snowe, Maine*	73
Lisa Murkowski, Alaska	66.6
Richard G. Lugar, Ind.*	63.8
Lamar Alexander, Tenn.	62.7
Lindsey Graham, S.C.	59.8
Bob Corker, Tenn.	59
John McCain, Ariz.	58.2
John Hoeven, N.D.	57.5
Mike Johanns, Neb.	56.8
Jon Kyl, Ariz.*	56.8
Kelly Ayotte, N.H.	56.7
Dan Coats, Ind.	55.7
Thad Cochran, Miss.	55.7
Kay Bailey Hutchison, Texas*	55.6
Jerry Moran, Kan.	54.8
Rob Portman, Ohio	54.6
John Thune, S.D.	54.6
John Barrasso, Wyo.	51.2
Jeff Sessions, Ala.	51.2

Opposition — Republicans

Jim DeMint, S.C.*	69.5
Mike Lee, Utah	65.3
Rand Paul, Ky.	62.5
David Vitter, La.	58.2
Jim Risch, Idaho	56.3
Marco Rubio, Fla.	55
James Inhofe, Okla.	54.2
Tom Coburn, Okla.	53.3
Michael D. Crapo, Idaho	52.5
Richard M. Burr, N.C.	51.7
Ron Johnson, Wis.	50.9
Mitch McConnell, Ky.	50.6
Richard C. Shelby, Ala.	50.3
Orrin G. Hatch, Utah	50
Dean Heller, Nev.	50
Roy Blunt, Mo.	49.7
John Boozman, Ark.	49.4
Saxby Chambliss, Ga.	49.4
Michael B. Enzi, Wyo.	49.4
Johnny Isakson, Ga.	49.4
Pat Roberts, Kan.	49.4
Patrick J. Toomey, Pa.	49.4
Roger Wicker, Miss.	49.4

* No longer in Congress

† Independents in the 112th Congress, Lieberman and Sanders, caucused with the Democrats

Senate Party Unity and Opposition

Support scores represent how often a senator voted with his or her party's majority against a majority of the other party. Opposition scores represent how often a senator voted against his or her party's majority. In the 112th Congress (2011-12), there were 270 such "party unity" votes in the Senate. Only members who voted on more than half of those are listed.

112TH CONGRESS: TOP SCORERS

Support — Democrats

Tom Udall, N.M.	100
Benjamin L. Cardin, Md.	99.2
Al Franken, Minn.	98.1
Kirsten Gillibrand, N.Y.	97.7
Patrick J. Leahy, Vt.	97.7
Barbara Boxer, Calif.	97.5
Frank R. Lautenberg, N.J.*	97.5
Sherrod Brown, Ohio	97.3
Richard J. Durbin, Ill.	97.3
Tom Harkin, Iowa	97.3
Charles E. Schumer, N.Y.	97.3
Jay Rockefeller, W.Va.	97.2
Jeff Bingaman, N.M.*	97
Jack Reed, R.I.	97
Daniel K. Akaka, Hawaii*	96.9
Patty Murray, Wash.	96.9
Richard Blumenthal, Conn.	96.6
Ron Wyden, Ore.	96.5
Robert Menendez, N.J.	96.2
Jeff Merkley, Ore.	96.2
Bernard Sanders, Vt.†	96.2
Sheldon Whitehouse, R.I.	96.2

Support — Republicans

John Cornyn, Texas	97
Ron Johnson, Wis.	97
Jim Risch, Idaho	95.8
Michael D. Crapo, Idaho	95.5
Tom Coburn, Okla.	94.8
Mitch McConnell, Ky.	94.8
James Inhofe, Okla.	94.5
Jim DeMint, S.C.*	94.2
Michael B. Enzi, Wyo.	94.2
Orrin G Hatch, Utah	94.2
Patrick J. Toomey, Pa.	93.9
Richard M. Burr, N.C.	93.7
Jeff Sessions, Ala.	93.6
John Barrasso, Wyo.	93.4
Saxby Chambliss, Ga.	93.1
Jon Kyl, Ariz.*	92.9
Marco Rubio, Fla.	92.2
Mike Lee, Utah	92.1
Johnny Isakson, Ga.	91
David Vitter, La.	90.9
Rand Paul, Ky.	90.8
Kelly Ayotte, N.H.	90.6

Opposition — Democrats

Joe Manchin III, W.Va.	24.3
Ben Nelson, Neb.*	22
Claire McCaskill, Mo.	21.4
Joseph I. Lieberman, Conn.* †	14.8
Mark Pryor, Ark.	14.7
Jim Webb, Va.*	14.4
Kay Hagan, N.C.	11.6
Mark Warner, Va.	11.5
Mary L. Landrieu, La.	11
Thomas R. Carper, Del.	10
Jon Tester, Mont.	10
Bill Nelson, Fla.	9.3
Max Baucus, Mont.	9
Michael Bennet, Colo.	8.6
Mark Udall, Colo.	8.6
Herb Kohl, Wis.*	8.1
Mark Begich, Alaska	7.9
Amy Klobuchar, Minn.	7.8
Bob Casey, Pa.	7.5
Debbie Stabenow, Mich.	7.5

Opposition — Republicans

Susan Collins, Maine	57.1
Scott P. Brown, Mass.*	54.7
Olympia J. Snowe, Maine*	50.2
Lisa Murkowski, Alaska	40.3
Dean Heller, Nev.	27.1
John Hoeven, N.D.	26.6
Thad Cochran, Miss.	26.3
Richard G. Lugar, Ind.*	23.3
Roy Blunt, Mo.	20.2
Lamar Alexander, Tenn.	17.5
Lindsey Graham, S.C.	16.9
Mike Johanns, Neb.	16.8
Jerry Moran, Kan.	16.4
Kay Bailey Hutchison, Texas*	15.2
Charles E. Grassley, Iowa	13.8
Roger Wicker, Miss.	13.8
Pat Roberts, Kan.	12.3
Rob Portman, Ohio	11.2
John Boozman, Ark.	10.7
Bob Corker, Tenn.	10.7

* No longer in Congress

† Independents in the 112th Congress, Lieberman and Sanders, caucused with the Democrats

House Presidential Support and Opposition

Support scores represent how often a House member sided with President Obama on roll call votes on which the president took a clear position beforehand. Opposition scores represent how often a member voted against the president's position. During the 112th Congress (2011-12), there were 156 House votes on which the president took a position. Only members who voted on more than half of those are listed.

112TH CONGRESS: TOP SCORERS

Support — Democrats

Chris Van Hollen, Md.	94.2
Steny H. Hoyer, Md.	93.5
Allyson Y. Schwartz, Pa.	93.4
Sander M. Levin, Mich.	92.9
Ted Deutch, Fla.	92.6
Nita M. Lowey, N.Y.	92.6
Debbie Wasserman Schultz, Fla.	92.4
Jim Langevin, R.I.	92.2
Kathy Castor, Fla.	91.9
Nancy Pelosi, Calif.	91.8
Adam B. Schiff, Calif.	91.6
Howard L. Berman, Calif.*	91.3
Susan A. Davis, Calif.	91.0
David E. Price, N.C.	91.0
Adam Smith, Wash.	90.8
Steven R. Rothman, N.J.	90.7
Gary L. Ackerman, N.Y.	90.5
Bill Pascrell Jr., N.J.	90.5
Lois Capps, Calif.	90.3
Steve Israel, N.Y.	90.1
Gary Peters, Mich.	90.1
Russ Carnahan, Mo.*	90.0
John Yarmuth, Ky.	90.0

Opposition — Democrats

Mike McIntyre, N.C.	62.0
Dan Boren, Okla.*	61.2
Collin C. Peterson, Minn.	55.8
Mike Ross, Ark.*	54.6
John Barrow, Ga.	52.3
Jim Matheson, Utah	52.3
Jason Altmire, Pa.*	45.8
Joe Donnelly, Ind.**	43.4
Heath Shuler, N.C.*	41.5
Ben Chandler, Ky.*	41.2
Larry Kissell, N.C.*	40.4
Henry Cuellar, Texas	39.7
Jerry F. Costello, Ill.*	38.4
Tim Holden, Pa.*	37.2
Bill Owens, N.Y.	36.8
Kathy Hochul, N.Y.*	35.8
Leonard Boswell, Iowa*	35.7
Nick J. Rahall II, W.Va.	35.5
Jim Costa, Calif.	35.4
Mark Critz, Pa.*	35.3
Sanford D. Bishop Jr., Ga.	34.9
Dennis Cardoza, Calif.*	30.7
Peter A. DeFazio, Ore.	29
Kurt Schrader, Ore.	27.5

Support — Republicans

Robert Dold, Ill.*	34.4
Justin Amash, Mich.	33.1
Walter B. Jones, N.C.	32.3
Chris Gibson, N.Y.	32.1
Nan Hayworth, N.Y.*	31.4
Steven C. LaTourette, Ohio*	30.3
Timothy V. Johnson, Ill.*	30.1
Dave Reichert, Wash.	29.8
Charles Bass, N.H.*	29.2
Ileana Ros-Lehtinen, Fla.	29.0
Judy Biggert, Ill.	28.4
Mario Diaz-Balart, Fla.	27.9
Patrick Meehan, Pa.	27.6
Todd R. Platts, Pa.*	27.1
Charlie Dent, Pa.	26.9
Rodney Frelinghuysen, N.J.	26.9
Leonard Lance, N.J.	26.9
Brian P. Bilbray, Calif.*	26.8
Jon Runyan, N.J.	26.6
Christopher H. Smith, N.J.	26.6
Aaron Schock, Ill.	26.5
Ron Paul, Texas*	26.4
David Dreier, Calif.*	26.3

Opposition — Republicans

Jim Jordan, Ohio	16.3
Jeff Miller, Fla.	16.3
Don Young, Alaska	16.3
Connie Mack, Fla.*	16.2
Todd Rokita, Ind.	16.2
Joe Wilson, S.C.	16.2
Randy Hultgren, Ill.	16.1
Jeff Landry, La.*	16.1
Phil Roe, Tenn.	16.0
Marlin Stutzman, Ind.	15.9
Bobby Schilling, Ill.*	15.8
Jason Chaffetz, Utah	15.5
John Fleming, La.	15.5
Dana Rohrabacher, Calif.	15.4
Jack Kingston, Ga.	14.8
Dennis A. Ross, Fla.	14.8
Austin Scott, Ga.	14.8
Jeff Duncan, S.C.	14.7
Tom Graves, Ga.	14.7
Todd Akin, Mo.*	14.5
Jean Schmidt, Ohio*	14.0
Dan Burton, Ind.*	13.5
Virginia Foxx, N.C.	13.5
Rob Bishop, Utah	12.8

* No longer in Congress ** Elected to the Senate in 2012

House Party Unity and Opposition

Support scores represent how often a House member voted with his or her party's majority against a majority of the other party. Opposition scores represent how often a member voted against his or her party's majority. In the 112th Congress (2011-12) there were 1194 such "party unity" votes in the House. Only members who voted on more than half of those are listed.

112TH CONGRESS: TOP SCORERS

Support — Democrats		Support — Republicans	
Bob Filner, Calif.*	99.1	K. Michael Conaway, Texas	98.4
Keith Ellison, Minn.	98.7	Randy Neugebauer, Texas	98.4
Edward J. Markey, Mass.	98.6	Mike Pompeo, Kan.	98.4
John W. Olver, Mass.*	98.6	Bill Flores, Texas	98.3
Frank Pallone Jr., N.J.	98.4	Doug Lamborn, Colo.	98.3
Richard E. Neal, Mass.	98.2	Mike Pence, Ind.*	98.3
Donald M. Payne, N.J.*	98.2	Pete Sessions, Texas	98.2
Jan Schakowsky, Ill.	98.2	Diane Black, Tenn.	98.1
Judy Chu, Calif.	98.1	Joe Wilson, S.C.	98.1
Grace F. Napolitano, Calif.	98.1	Todd Akin, Mo.*	98
Lucille Roybal-Allard, Calif.	98.1	John Kline, Minn.	98
Karen Bass, Calif.	98	Trey Gowdy, S.C.	97.9
Mazie K. Hirono, Hawaii**	98	Jeb Hensarling, Texas	97.9
Linda T. Sánchez, Calif.	98	Wally Herger, Calif.*	97.9
Janice Hahn, Calif.	97.9	Lynn Jenkins, Kan.	97.9
Michael M. Honda, Calif.	97.9	Bob Latta, Ohio	97.9
Jim McGovern, Mass.	97.9	John Fleming, La.	97.8
Nancy Pelosi, Calif.	97.8	Darrell Issa, Calif.	97.8
Yvette D. Clarke, N.Y.	97.7	Austin Scott, Ga.	97.8
Diana DeGette, Colo.	97.7	Ann Marie Buerkle, N.Y.*	97.7
Barbara Lee, Calif.	97.7	Francisco "Quico" Canseco, Texas*	97.7
John Lewis, Ga.	97.7	Ben Quayle, Ariz.*	97.7
Pete Stark, Calif.*	97.7	Dennis A. Ross, Fla.	97.7
Paul Tonko, N.Y.	97.7	Steve Scalise, La.	97.7
		Tim Scott, S.C.***	97.7
		Lynn Westmoreland, Ga.	97.7

Opposition — Democrats		Opposition — Republicans	
Dan Boren, Okla.*	63.5	Walter B. Jones, N.C.	34.9
Jim Matheson, Utah	59	Chris Gibson, N.Y.	28.1
Mike Ross, Ark.	54.9	Timothy V. Johnson, Ill.*	22
Collin C. Peterson, Minn.	53.5	Michael G. Fitzpatrick, Pa.	21.6
Jason Altmire, Pa.*	44.7	Robert Dold, Ill.*	21.1
Heath Shuler, N.C.*	43.6	Charles Bass, N.H.*	20.2
John Barrow, Ga.	42.5	Frank A. LoBiondo, N.J.	19.6
Jim Costa, Calif.	41.1	Ron Paul, Texas*	19.4
Mike McIntyre, N.C.	41.1	Christopher H. Smith, N.J.	19.3
Joe Donnelly, Ind.**	40.4	Dave Reichert, Wash.	19.2
Larry Kissell, N.C.*	34.9	Steven C. LaTourette, Ohio*	17.6
Bill Owens, N.Y.	33.6	Jim Gerlach, Pa.	16.7
Henry Cuellar, Texas	33	Richard Hanna, N.Y.	16.3
Ben Chandler, Ky.*	31.9	Charlie Dent, Pa.	16
Dennis Cardoza, Calif.*	31.8	Patrick Meehan, Pa.	15.9
Tim Holden, Pa.*	29	Todd R. Platts, Pa.*	15.5
Mark Critz, Pa.*	28.7	Nan Hayworth, N.Y.*	13.5
Nick J. Rahall II, W.Va.	25	Frank R. Wolf, Va.	13.4
Gene Green, Texas	24.5	Judy Biggert, Ill.	13.3
Sanford D. Bishop Jr., Ga.	24.1	Peter T. King, N.Y.	12.7
Jim Cooper, Tenn.	22.9	Justin Amash, Mich.	12.6
Jerry F. Costello, Ill.*	22.6	Michael G. Grimm, N.Y.	12.5
Kathy Hochul, N.Y.*	22.3	Jeff Fortenberry, Neb.	12.4
Kurt Schrader, Ore.	21.5	Ileana Ros-Lehtinen, Fla.	12.3

* No longer in Congress ** Elected to the Senate in 2012 *** Appointed to the Senate in 2013

House Members Who Voted Against Boehner or Pelosi

On Jan. 3, 2013, members of the 113th Congress voted for speaker of the House. John A. Boehner, speaker in the 112th Congress, was elected by a vote of 229-197, though a handful of House Republicans opposed his nomination. A majority of Democrats voted for Minority Leader Nancy Pelosi in support of their party. These members voted for someone other than Boehner or Pelosi:

Voted for Rep. Eric Cantor, R-Va.
Jim Bridenstine, R-Okla.*
Steve Pearce, R-N.M.
Ted Yoho, R-Fla.*

Voted for former Rep. Allen B. West, R-Fla.
Paul Broun, R-Ga.
Louie Gohmert, R-Texas

Voted for Rep. Raúl R. Labrador, R-Idaho
Justin Amash, R-Mich.

Voted for Rep. Justin Amash, R-Mich.
Thomas Massie, R-Ky.*

Voted for former comptroller general David Walker
Walter B. Jones, R-N.C.

Voted for Rep. Jim Cooper, D-Tenn.
Daniel Lipinski, D-Ill.
Mike McIntyre, D-N.C.

Voted for Rep. John Lewis, D-Ga.
John Barrow, D-Ga.

Voted for Rep. Jim Jordan, D-Ohio
Tim Huelskamp, R-Kan.

Voted for former Secretary of State Colin Powell
Jim Cooper, D-Tenn.

Voted for Rep. John D. Dingell, D-Mich.
Jim Matheson, D-Utah

Voted Present
Steve Stockman, R-Texas

Did not vote
John A. Boehner, R-Ohio

New Democrat Coalition

The New Democrats are a group of pro-business Democratic House moderates.

Chairman: Ron Kind, Wis..

Ron Barber, Ariz.
John Barrow, Ga.
Ami Bera, Calif.*
Lois Capps, Calif.
John Carney, Del.
André Carson, Ind.
Joaquin Castro, Texas*
Gerald E. Connolly, Va.
Jim Cooper, Tenn.
Joe Courtney, Conn.
Susan A. Davis, Calif.
John Delaney, Md.*
Suzan DelBene, Wash.
Eliot L. Engel, N.Y.
Elizabeth Esty, Conn.*
Bill Foster, Ill.
Joe Garcia, Fla.*
Colleen Hanabusa, Hawaii
Denny Heck, Wash.*
Jim Himes, Conn.
Rush D. Holt, N.J.
Derek Kilmer, Wash.
Rick Larsen, Wash.
Dan Maffei, N.Y.
Sean Patrick Maloney, N.Y.*
Carolyn McCarthy, N.Y.
Mike McIntyre, N.C.
Gregory W. Meeks, N.Y.
James P. Moran, Va.
Patrick Murphy, Fla.*
Bill Owens, N.Y.
Ed Perlmutter, Colo.
Gary Peters, Mich.
Scott Peters, Calif.*
Pedro R. Pierluisi, P.R.
Jared Polis, Colo.
Mike Quigley, Ill.
Cedric L. Richmond, La.
Loretta Sanchez, Calif.
Adam B. Schiff, Calif.
Brad Schneider, Ill.*
Kurt Schrader, Ore.
Allyson Y. Schwartz, Pa.
David Scott, Ga.
Terri A. Sewell, Ala.
Adam Smith, Wash.
Juan C. Vargas, Calif.*
Filemon Vela, Texas*

* New to Congress

Blue Dog Coalition

The Blue Dogs are a group of the House's most fiscally conservative Democrats.

Co-Chairmen: John Barrow, Ga.; Kurt Schrader, Ore.; Jim Cooper, Tenn.

Sanford D. Bishop Jr., Ga.
Jim Costa, Calif.
Henry Cuellar, Texas
Pete Gallego, Texas*
Daniel Lipinski, Ill.
Jim Matheson, Utah
Mike McIntyre, N.C.
Michael H. Michaud, Maine
Collin C. Peterson, Minn.
Loretta Sanchez, Calif.
David Scott, Ga.
Mike Thompson, Calif.

Congressional Progressive Caucus

The Progressive Caucus is a group of liberal lawmakers. All members are House Democrats, except independent Sen. Bernard Sanders.

Co-Chairmen: Keith Ellison, Minn., and Raúl M. Grijalva, Ariz.

André Carson, Ind.
Donna M.C. Christensen, V.I.
Judy Chu, Calif.
David Cicilline, R.I.
Yvette D. Clarke, N.Y.
William Lacy Clay, Mo.
Emanuel Cleaver II, Mo.
Steve Cohen, Tenn.
John Conyers Jr., Mich.
Elijah E. Cummings, Md.
Danny K. Davis, Ill.
Peter A. DeFazio, Ore.
Rosa DeLauro, Conn.
Donna Edwards, Md.
Sam Farr, Calif.
Chaka Fattah, Pa.
Lois Frankel, Fla.*
Marcia L. Fudge, Ohio
Alan Grayson, Fla.
Luis V. Guiterrez, Ill.
Janice Hahn, Calif.
Michael M. Honda, Calif.
Jared Huffman, Calif.*
Shelia Jackson Lee, Texas
Hakeem Jeffries, N.Y.*
Eddie Bernice Johnson, Texas
Hank Johnson, Ga.
Marcy Kaptur, Ohio
Joseph P. Kennedy III., Mass.
Ann McLane Kuster, N.H.*
Barabara Lee, Calif.
John Lewis, D-Ga.
Dave Loebsack, Iowa
Ben Ray Luján, N.M.
Michelle Lujan Grisham, N.M.*
Carolyn B. Maloney, N.Y.
Edward J. Markey, Mass.
Jim McDermott, Wash.
Jim McGovern, Mass.
George Miller, Calif.
Gwen Moore, Wis.
James P. Moran, Va.
Jerrold Nadler, N.Y.
Rick Nolan, Minn.
Eleanor Holmes Norton, D.C.
Frank Pallone Jr., N.J.
Ed Pastor, Ariz.
Chellie Pingree, Maine
Mark Pocan, Wis.*
Jared Polis, Colo.
Charles B. Rangel, N.Y.
Lucille Roybal-Allard, Calif.
Linda T. Sánchez, Calif.
Bernard Sanders, Vt.
Jan Schakowsky, Ill.
José E. Serrano, N.Y.
Louise M. Slaughter, N.Y.
Mark Takano, Calif.*
Bennie Thompson, Miss.
John F. Tierney, Mass.
Nydia M. Velázquez, N.Y.
Maxine Waters, Calif.
Melvin Watt, N.C.
Peter Welch, Vt.

* New to Congress

Republican Study Committee

The RSC is the most conservative bloc and dominant force within the House Republican caucus. The list below is not comprehensive, as the caucus permits individual members to decide whether to publicize their membership.

Chairman: Steve Scalise, La.

Robert B. Aderholt, Ala.
Justin Amash, Mich.
Michele Bachmann, Minn.
Spencer Bachus, Ala.
Andy Barr, Ky.*
Joe L. Barton, Texas
Dan Benishek, Mich.
Kerry Bentivolio, Mich.*
Gus Bilikrakis, Fla.
Rob Bishop, Utah
Diane Black, Tenn.
Marsha Blackburn, Tenn.
Kevin Brady, Texas
Jim Bridenstine, Okla.*
Mo Brooks, Ala.
Susan W. Brooks, Ind.*
Paul Broun, Ga.
Vern Buchanan, Fla.
Larry Bucshon, Ind.
Michael C. Burgess, Texas
John Campbell, Calif.
Eric Cantor, Va.
John Carter, Texas
Bill Cassidy, La.
Steve Chabot, Ohio
Jason Chaffetz, Utah
Tom Cole, Okla.
Chris Collins, N.Y.*
Doug Collins, Ga.*
K. Michael Conaway, Texas
Tom Cotton, Ark.*
Kevin Cramer, N.D.*
Rick Crawford, Ark.
John Culberson, Texas
Steve Daines, Mont.*
Jeff Denham, Calif.
Ron DeSantis, Fla.*
Scott DesJarlais, Tenn.
Sean P. Duffy, Wis.
Jeff Duncan, S.C.
Renee Ellmers, N.C.
Blake Farenthold, Texas
Stephen Fincher, Tenn.
Chuck Fleischmann, Tenn.
John Fleming, La.
Bill Flores, Texas
J. Randy Forbes, Va.
Jeff Fortenberry, Neb.
Virginia Foxx, N.C.
Trent Franks, Ariz.
Cory Gardner, Colo.
Scott Garrett, N.J.
Bob Gibbs, Ohio
Phil Gingrey, Ga.
Louie Gohmert, Texas
Robert W. Goodlatte, Va.
Paul Gosar, Ariz.
Trey Gowdy, S.C.
Kay Granger, Texas
Sam Graves, Mo.
Tom Graves, Ga.
Tim Griffin, Ark.
Michael G. Grimm, N.Y.
Ralph Hall, Texas
Richard Hanna, N.Y.
Gregg Harper, Miss.
Andy Harris, Md.
Vicky Hartzler, Mo.
Jeb Hensarling, Texas
Jaime Herrera Beutler, Wash.
George Holding, N.C.*
Richard Hudson, N.C.*
Tim Huelskamp, K.S.
Bill Huizenga, Mich.
Randy Hultgren, Ill.
Duncan Hunter, Calif.
Robert Hurt, Va.
Darrell Issa, Calif.
Lynn Jenkins, Kan.
Bill Johnson, Ohio
Sam Johnson, Texas
Jim Jordan, Ohio
David Joyce, Ohio*
Mike Kelly, Pa.
Steve King, Iowa
Jack Kingston, Ga.
John Kline, Minn.
Raúl R. Labrador, Idaho
Doug LaMalfa, Calif.*
Doug Lamborn, Colo.
James Lankford, Okla.
Bob Latta, Ohio
Billy Long, Mo.
Frank D. Lucas, Okla.
Blaine Luetkemeyer, Mo.
Cynthia M. Lummis, Wy.
Kenny Marchant, Texas
Thomas Massie, Ky.
Michael McCaul, Texas
Tom McClintock, Calif.
Patrick T. McHenry, N.C.
Howard "Buck" McKeon, Calif.
David B. McKinley, W.Va.
Cathy McMorris Rodgers, Wash.
Mark Meadows, N.C.*
Luke Messer, Ind.*
Jeff Miller, Fla.
Markwayne Mullin, Okla.*
Mick Mulvaney, S.C.
Randy Neugebauer, Texas
Kristi Noem, S.D.
Rich Nugent, Fla.
Alan Nunnelee, Miss.
Pete Olson, Texas
Steven M. Palazzo, Miss.
Steve Pearce, N.M.
Scott Perry, Pa.*
Robert Pittenger, N.C.*
Joe Pitts, Pa.
Ted Poe, Texas
Mike Pompeo, Kan.
Bill Posey, Fla.
Tom Price, Ga.
Trey Radel, Fla.*
Tom Reed, N.Y.
James B. Renacci, Ohio
Reid Ribble, Wis.
Tom Rice, S.C.*
Scott Rigell, Va.
Phil Roe, Tenn.
Mike D. Rogers, Ala.
Todd Rokita, Ind.
Peter Roskam, Ill.
Dennis A. Ross, Fla.
Keith Rothfus, Pa.*
Ed Royce, Calif.
Paul D. Ryan, Wis.
Matt Salmon, Ariz.
David Schweikert, Ariz.
Austin Scott, Ga.
Pete Sessions, Texas
John Shimkus, Ill.
Adrian Smith, Neb.
Lamar Smith, Texas
Steve Southerland II, Fla.
Chris Stewart, Utah*
Steve Stivers, Ohio
Steve Stockman, Texas
Marlin Stutzman, Ind.
Mac Thornberry, Texas
Scott Tipton, Colo.
Michael R. Turner, Ohio
Ann Wagner, Mo.*
Tim Walberg, Minn.
Jackie Walorski, Ind.*
Randy Weber, Texas
Daniel Webster, Fla.
Brad Wenstrup, Ohio*
Lynn Westmoreland, Ga.
Roger Williams, Texas*
Joe Wilson, S.C.
Rob Wittman, Va.
Steve Womack, Ark.
Rob Woodall, Ga.
Kevin Yoder, Kan.
Ted Yoho, Fla.*
Todd Young, Ind.

* New to Congress

Main Street Partnership

The Main Street Partnership is considered a moderate or centrist bloc in the Republican Party. In the House, a good number of its members also belong to the Tuesday Group, a less-formal organization of GOP moderates.

Chairman: Former Rep. Steven C. LaTourette, R-Ohio

Susan W. Brooks, Ind.*
Larry Buschon, Ind.
Ken Calvert, Calif.
Dave Camp, Mich.
Shelley Moore Capito, W.Va.
Chris Collins, N.Y.*
Susan Collins, Maine.
Paul Cook, Calif.*
Rodney Davis, Ill.*
Jeff Denham, Calif.
Charlie Dent, Pa.
Mario Diaz-Balart, Fla.
Sean P. Duffy, Wis.
Michael G. Fitzpatrick, Pa.
Jeff Fortenberry, Neb.
Rodney Frelinghuysen, N.J.
Jim Gerlach, Pa.
Chris Gibson, N.Y.
Michael G. Grimm, N.Y.
Richard Hanna, N.Y.
Jaime Herrera Beutler, Wash.
Lynn Jenkins, Kan.
Bill Johnson, Ohio
David Joyce, Ohio*
Mike Kelly, Pa.
Peter T. King, N.Y.
Adam Kinzinger, Ill.
Mark S. Kirk, Ill.
Leonard Lance, N.J.
Tom Latham, Iowa
Frank A. LoBiondo, N.J.
John McCain, Ariz.
David B. McKinley, W.Va.
Cathy McMorris Rodgers, Wash.
Patrick Meehan, Pa.
Tim Murphy, Pa.
Erik Paulsen, Minn.
Tom Petri, Wis.
Tom Reed, N.Y.
Dave Reichert, Wash.
James B. Renacci, Ohio
Scott Rigell, Va.
Jon Runyan, N.J.
Aaron Schock, Ill.
Mike Simpson, Idaho
Steve Stivers, Ohio
Lee Terry, Neb.
Pat Tiberi, Ohio
Michael R. Turner, Ohio
Fred Upton, Mich.
David Valadao, Calif.*
Greg Walden, Ore.
Edward Whitfield, Ky.
Frank R. Wolf, Va.
Todd Young, Ind.

Other Caucus Leadership

Congressional Asian Pacific American Caucus
Rep. Judy Chu, D-Calif., chairwoman

Congressional Black Caucus
Rep. Marcia L. Fudge, D-Ohio, chairwoman

Congressional Caucus for Women's Issues
Rep. Jaime Herrera Beutler, R-Wash., co-chairwoman
Rep. Donna Edwards, D-Md., co-chairwoman

Congressional Hispanic Caucus
Rep. Rubén Hinojosa, D-Texas, chairman

Tea Party Caucus
Rep. Michele Bachmann, R-Minn., chairwoman

* New to Congress

Winners Outspent by Opponents

General-election winners in 2012 who spent less than their opponents. Totals cover the period of Jan. 1, 2011, through Dec. 31, 2012. Losing incumbents are in *italics*.

(in order of spending margin)

Senate

Senator	Expenditures	Opponent	Expenditures
Christopher S. Murphy, D-Conn.	$10,436,219	Linda E. McMahon, R	$50,196,249
Bob Casey, D-Pa.	12,363,026	Tom Smith, R	37,681,326
Joe Donnelly, D-Ind.	5,588,317	Richard E. Mourdock, R	9,009,500
Dean Heller, R-Nev.	9,192,588	Rep. Shelley Berkley, D	11,625,854
Heidi Heitkamp, D-N.D.	5,498,044	Rep. Rick Berg, R	6,344,251
Deb Fischer, R-Neb.	5,176,461	Bob Kerrey, D	5,662,682
Martin Heinrich, D-N.M.	6,720,126	Heather A. Wilson, R	7,108,688
Mazie K. Hirono, D-Hawaii	5,644,499	Linda Lingle, R	5,839,282

House

Member	Expenditures	Opponent	Expenditures
Patrick Murphy, D-Fla. (18)	$4,480,428	*Allen B. West, R*	$18,471,216
Chris Collins, R-N.Y. (27)	1,420,830	*Kathy Hochul, D*	4,858,496
Ed Perlmutter, D-Colo. (7)	2,988,391	Joe Coors, R	4,832,075
Brad Schneider, D-Ill. (10)	3,029,605	*Robert Dold, R*	4,543,849
Rick Nolan, D-Minn. (8)	1,230,233	*Chip Cravaack, R*	2,377,366
Sean Patrick Maloney, D-N.Y. (18)	2,246,008	*Nan Hayworth, R*	3,317,572
Gloria Negrete McLeod, D-Calif. (35)	344,428	*Joe Baca, D*	1,162,457
Justin Amash, R-Mich. (3)	1,293,711	Steve Pestka, D	2,096,680
Pete Gallego, D-Texas (23)	1,767,938	*Francisco "Quico" Canseco, R*	2,534,135
Steve Cohen, D-Tenn. (9)	820,327	George S. Flinn Jr., R	1,568,657
Keith Rothfus, R-Pa. (12)	2,015,330	*Mark Critz, D*	2,709,384
Eric Swalwell, D-Calif. (15)	799,576	*Pete Stark, D*	1,397,139
Raul Ruiz, D-Calif. (36)	1,925,464	*Mary Bono Mack, R*	2,423,516
Daniel Webster, R-Fla. (10)	1,498,872	Val B. Demings, D	1,955,180
Bill Owens, D-N.Y. (21)	1,998,276	Matt Doheny, R	2,445,626
Cheri Bustos, D-Ill. (17)	2,187,283	*Bobby Schilling, R*	2,571,550
Andy Barr, R-Ky. (6)	2,211,676	*Ben Chandler, D*	2,533,044
Julia Brownley, D-Calif. (26)	2,106,886	Tony Strickland, R	2,377,030
Alan Lowenthal, D-Calif. (47)	1,171,131	Gary DeLong, R	1,418,740
Jerry McNerney, D-Calif. (9)	2,744,514	Ricky Gill, R	2,947,420
Bill Enyart, D-Ill. (12)	1,167,686	Jason Plummer, R	1,346,211
Carol Shea-Porter, D-N.H. (1)	1,696,703	*Frank Guinta, R*	1,869,673
Derek Kilmer, D-Wash. (6)	1,706,202	Bill Driscoll, R	1,827,361
Kerry Bentivolio, R-Mich. (11)	585,302	Syed Taj, D	698,355
John F. Tierney, D-Mass. (6)	2,299,261	Richard Tisei, R	2,352,537
Dan Maffei, D-N.Y. (24)	2,047,007	*Ann Marie Buerkle, R*	2,059,235

Closest Elections of 2012

Race	Winner	Votes	Loser	Votes	Margin
North Carolina 7	Rep. Mike McIntyre, D	168,695	David Rouzer, R	168,041	654
Utah 4	Rep. Jim Matheson, D	119,803	Mia P. Love, R	119,035	768
Illinois 13	Rodney Davis, R	137,034	David Gill, D	136,032	1,002
Michigan 1	Rep. Dan Benishek, R	167,060	Gary McDowell, D	165,179	1,881
Florida 18	Patrick Murphy, D	166,257	Rep. Allen B. West, R	164,353	1,904
Arizona 2	Rep. Ron Barber, D	147,338	Martha McSally, R	144,884	2,454
N.D. Senate	Heidi Heitkamp, D	161,163	Rep. Rick Berg, R	158,282	2,881
Illinois 10	Brad Schneider, D	133,890	Rep. Robert Dold, R	130,564	3,326
Indiana 2	Jackie Walorski, R	134,033	Brendan Mullen, D	130,113	3,920
Nebraska 2	Rep. Lee Terry, R	133,964	John W. Ewing, D	129,767	4,197

Fewest Votes Received

Winning House candidates in contested elections who received the fewest votes in 2012:

Member	Votes Received
Charles Boustany Jr., R-La. (3) †	58,820
David Valadao, R Calif. (21)	67,164
Lucille Roybal-Allard, D-Calif. (40)	73,940
Gloria Negrete McLeod, D-Calif. (35)	79,698
Jim Costa, D-Calif. (16)*	84,649
Marc Veasey, D-Texas (33)	85,114
Gene Green, D-Texas (29)*	86,053
Gary G. Miller, R-Calif. (31)	88,964
Rubén Hinojosa, D-Texas (15)*	89,296
Filemon Vela, D-Texas (34)	89,606

*Also finished in the top 10 in the 2010 election

†December runoff election

Most Votes Received

Winning House candidates who received the most votes in 2012:

Member	Votes Received
Chaka Fattah, D-Pa. (2)	318,176
Jim McDermott, D-Wash. (7)*	298,368
Gary Peters, D-Mich. (14)	270,450
William Lacy Clay, D-Mo. (1)	267,927
Mark Pocan, D-Wis. (2)	265,442
Earl Blumenauer, D-Ore. (3)*	264,979
Stephen F. Lynch, D-Mass. (8)	263,999
Keith Ellison, D-Minn. (5)	262,102
Richard E. Neal, D-Mass. (1)	261,936
David E. Price, D-N.C. (4)	259,534

*Also finished in the top 10 in the 2010 election

Top 10 Winning Senate Spenders in 2012

Based on FEC reports of expenditures from Jan. 1, 2011, through Dec. 31, 2012, the first column lists the top spenders who were elected or re-elected in the 2012 election. Campaign spending includes contributions made to other candidates or party organizations.

Member	Expenditures	Opponent	Expenditures
Elizabeth Warren, D-Mass.	$42,211,677	Sen. Scott P. Brown, R	$35,058,354
Sherrod Brown, D-Ohio	21,914,316	Josh Mandel, R	18,868,809
Claire McCaskill, D-Mo.	19,720,542	Rep. Todd Akin, R	6,165,888
Tim Kaine, D-Va.	17,918,247	George Allen, R	14,221,931
Kirsten Gillibrand, D-N.Y.	14,257,872	Wendy Long, R	759,747
Ted Cruz, R-Texas	14,618,864	Paul Sadler, D*	515,439
Tammy Baldwin, D-Wis.	15,650,797	Tommy G. Thompson, R	9,832,888
Bill Nelson, D-Fla.	15,494,167	Rep. Connie Mack, R	7,526,151
Dianne Feinstein, D-Calif.	15,661,462	Elizabeth Emken, R	1,110,209
Robert Menendez, D-N.J.	13,290,088	Joseph M. Kyrillos, R	4,564,876

*Republican David Dewhurst spent $33,935,911

Top 10 Winning House Spenders in 2012

Based on FEC reports of expenditures from Jan. 1, 2011, through Dec. 31, 2012, the first column lists the top spenders who were elected or re-elected in the 2012 election. Campaign spending includes contributions made to other candidates or party organizations.

Member	Expenditures	Opponent	Expenditures
Michele Bachmann, R-Minn. (6)	$25,580,916	Jim Graves, D	$2,551,801
John A. Boehner, R-Ohio (8)	21,197,801	None	n/a
Eric Cantor, R-Va. (7)	7,485,667	E. Wayne Powell, D	956,747
Paul D. Ryan, R-Wis. (1)	6,651,221	Rob Zerban, D	2,364,426
Brad Sherman, D-Calif. (30)	6,372,614	Rep. Howard L. Berman, D	5,772,180
Alan Grayson, D-Fla. (9)	5,352,174	Todd Long, R	148,812
Tammy Duckworth, D-Ill. (8)	5,208,691	Rep. Joe Walsh, R	2,008,415
Charles Boustany Jr., R-La. (3)*	4,867,555	Rep. Jeff Landry, R	2,244,000
Fred Upton, R-Mich. (6)	4,724,798	Mike O'Brien, D	292,383
John Delaney, D-Md. (6)	4,601,988	Rep. Roscoe G. Bartlett, R	1,371,544

* Includes runoff election expenditures

10 Least Expensive Winning Campaigns in 2012

Based on FEC reports of expenditures from Jan. 1, 2011, through Dec. 31, 2012. Campaign spending includes contributions made to other candidates or party organizations.

Member	Expenditures	Member	Expenditures
José E. Serrano, D-N.Y. (15)	$209,532	Jeff Fortenberry, R-Neb. (1)	$381,322
Gloria Negrete McCleod, D-Calif. (35)	344,428	Luis V. Gutierrez, D-Ill. (4)	383,849
Al Green, D-Texas (9)	365,844	Trent Franks, R-Ariz. (8)	399,105
Steve Stockman, R-Texas (36)	368,712	Rob Bishop, R-Utah (1)	403,467
Tim Huelskamp, R-Kan. (1)	370,530	Rob Woodall, R-Ga. (7)	426,844

House Committees

House standing and select committees are listed by their full names. Membership is in order of seniority on the panel. Leadership committees are listed on page 1163.

Republicans are in roman type and Democrats are in italics. A vacancy indicates that a committee or subcommittee seat had not been filled as of press time, June 2013. Subcommittee vacancies do not necessarily indicate vacancies on full committees and vice versa.

Agriculture

Phone: (202) 225-2171 **Office: 1301 Longworth**

REPUBLICANS (25)

Frank D. Lucas, Okla., Chairman
Robert W. Goodlatte, Va.
Steve King, Iowa
Randy Neugebauer, Texas
Mike D. Rogers, Ala.
K. Michael Conaway, Texas
Glenn Thompson, Pa.
Bob Gibbs, Ohio
Austin Scott, Ga.
Scott Tipton, Colo.
Rick Crawford, Ark.
Martha Roby, Ala.
Scott DesJarlais, Tenn.
Chris Gibson, N.Y.
Vicky Hartzler, Mo.
Reid Ribble, Wis.
Kristi Noem, S.D.
Dan Benishek, Mich.
Jeff Denham, Calif.
Stephen Fincher, Tenn.
Doug LaMalfa, Calif.
Richard Hudson, N.C.
Rodney Davis, Ill.
Chris Collins, N.Y.
Ted Yoho, Fla.

DEMOCRATS (21)

Collin C. Peterson, Minn., Ranking Member
Mike McIntyre, N.C.
David Scott, Ga.
Jim Costa, Calif.
Tim Walz, Minn.
Kurt Schrader, Ore.
Marcia L. Fudge, Ohio
Jim McGovern, Mass.
Suzan DelBene, Wash.
Gloria Negrete McLeod, Calif.
Filemon Vela, Texas
Michelle Lujan Grisham, N.M.
Ann McLane Kuster, N.H.
Rick Nolan, Minn.
Pete Gallego, Texas
Bill Enyart, Ill.
Juan C. Vargas, Calif.
Cheri Bustos, Ill.
Sean Patrick Maloney, N.Y.
Joe Courtney, Conn.
John Garamendi, Calif.

Conservation, Energy & Forestry
Thompson (chairman), Rogers, Gibbs, Tipton, Crawford, Roby, Ribble, Noem, Benishek
Walz, Negrete McLeod, Kuster, Nolan, McIntyre, Schrader, DelBene

Department Operations, Oversight & Nutrition
King (chairman), Goodlatte, Gibbs, Scott, Roby, Fincher
Fudge, McGovern, Lujan Grisham, Negrete McLeod, Vacancy

General Farm Commodities & Risk Management
Conaway (chairman), Neugebauer, Rogers, Gibbs, Scott, Crawford, Roby, Gibson, Hartzler, Noem, Benishek, LaMalfa, Hudson, Davis, Collins
Scott, Vela, Gallego, Enyart, Vargas, Bustos, Maloney, Walz, Negrete McLeod, Costa, Garamendi, Vacancy

Horticulture, Research, Biotechnology & Foreign Agriculture
Scott (chairman), Hartzler, Denham, LaMalfa, Davis, Collins, Yoho, Fincher
Schrader, DelBene, Costa, Fudge, Kuster, Vargas, Maloney

Livestock, Rural Development & Credit
Crawford (chairman), Goodlatte, King, Neugebauer, Rogers, Conaway, Thompson, DesJarlais, Gibson, Ribble, Denham, Hudson, Yoho
Costa, McIntyre, Scott, Vela, Lujan Grisham, Gallego, Enyart, Bustos, Schrader, Nolan, Courtney

Appropriations

Phone: (202) 225-2771 **Office: H-307 Capitol**

REPUBLICANS (29)

Harold Rogers, Ky., Chairman
C.W. Bill Young, Fla.
Frank R. Wolf, Va.
Jack Kingston, Ga.
Rodney Frelinghuysen, N.J.
Tom Latham, Iowa
Robert B. Aderholt, Ala.
Kay Granger, Texas
Mike Simpson, Idaho
John Culberson, Texas
Ander Crenshaw, Fla.
John Carter, Texas
Rodney Alexander, La.
Ken Calvert, Calif.
Jo Bonner, Ala.
Tom Cole, Okla.
Mario Diaz-Balart, Fla.
Charlie Dent, Pa.
Tom Graves, Ga.
Kevin Yoder, Kan.
Steve Womack, Ark.
Alan Nunnelee, Miss.
Jeff Fortenberry, Neb.
Tom Rooney, Fla.
Chuck Fleischmann, Tenn.
Jaime Herrera Beutler, Wash.
David Joyce, Ohio
David Valadao, Calif.
Andy Harris, Md.

DEMOCRATS (22)

Nita M. Lowey, N.Y., Ranking Member
Marcy Kaptur, Ohio
Peter J. Visclosky, Ind.
José E. Serrano, N.Y.
Rosa DeLauro, Conn.
James P. Moran, Va.
Ed Pastor, Ariz.
David E. Price, N.C.
Lucille Roybal-Allard, Calif.
Sam Farr, Calif.
Chaka Fattah, Pa.
Sanford D. Bishop Jr., Ga.
Barbara Lee, Calif.
Adam B. Schiff, Calif.
Michael M. Honda, Calif.
Betty McCollum, Minn.
Tim Ryan, Ohio
Debbie Wasserman Schultz, Fla.
Henry Cuellar, Texas
Chellie Pingree, Maine
Mike Quigley, Ill.
Bill Owens, N.Y.

Agriculture
Aderholt (chairman), Latham, Nunnelee, Yoder, Fortenberry, Rooney, Valadao
Farr, DeLauro, Bishop, Pingree

Commerce-Justice-Science
Wolf (chairman), Culberson, Aderholt, Bonner, Graves, Rooney, Harris
Fattah, Schiff, Honda, Serrano

Defense
Young (chairman), Frelinghuysen, Kingston, Granger, Crenshaw, Calvert, Bonner, Cole, Womack
Visclosky, Moran, McCollum, Ryan, Owens, Kaptur,

Energy-Water
Frelinghuysen (chairman), Simpson, Alexander, Nunnelee, Calvert, Carter, Fleischmann
Kaptur, Visclosky, Pastor, Fattah

Financial Services
Crenshaw (chairman), Bonner, Diaz-Balart, Graves, Yoder, Womack, Herrera Beutler
Serrano, Quigley, Kaptur, Pastor

Homeland Security
Carter (chairman), Aderholt, Culberson, Frelinghuysen, Latham, Dent, Fleischmann
Price, Roybal-Allard, Cuellar, Owens

Interior-Environment
Simpson (chairman), Calvert, Cole, Graves, Herrera Beutler, Joyce, Valadao
Moran, McCollum, Pingree, Serrano

Labor-HHS-Education
Kingston (chairman), Alexander, Simpson, Womack, Fleischmann, Joyce, Harris
DeLauro, Roybal-Allard, Lee, Honda

Legislative Branch
Alexander (chairman), Young, Fortenberry, Valadao, Harris
Wasserman Schultz, Moran, Bishop

Military Construction-VA
Culberson (chairman), Young, Carter, Nunnelee, Diaz-Balart, Fortenberry, Rooney
Bishop, Farr, Price, Fattah

State-Foreign Operations
Granger (chairwoman), Wolf, Diaz-Balart, Dent, Crenshaw, Kingston, Yoder
Lowey, Schiff, Lee, Wasserman Schultz, Cuellar

Transportation-HUD
Latham (chairman), Wolf, Dent, Granger, Cole, Herrera Beutler, Joyce
Pastor, Price, Quigley, Ryan

Armed Services

Phone: (202) 225-4151 **Office: 2120 Rayburn**

REPUBLICANS (34)
Howard "Buck" McKeon, Calif., Chairman
Mac Thornberry, Texas
Walter B. Jones, N.C.
J. Randy Forbes, Va.
Jeff Miller, Fla.
Joe Wilson, S.C.
Frank A. LoBiondo, N.J.
Rob Bishop, Utah
Michael R. Turner, Ohio
John Kline, Minn.
Mike D. Rogers, Ala.
Trent Franks, Ariz.
Bill Shuster, Pa.
K. Michael Conaway, Texas
Doug Lamborn, Colo.
Rob Wittman, Va.
Duncan Hunter, Calif.
John Fleming, La.
Mike Coffman, Colo.
Scott Rigell, Va.
Chris Gibson, N.Y.
Vicky Hartzler, Mo.
Joe Heck, Nev.
Jon Runyan, N.J.
Austin Scott, Ga.
Steven M. Palazzo, Miss.
Martha Roby, Ala.
Mo Brooks, Ala.
Rich Nugent, Fla.
Kristi Noem, S.D.
Paul Cook, Calif.
Jim Bridenstine, Okla.
Brad Wenstrup, Ohio
Jackie Walorski, Ind.

DEMOCRATS (28)
Adam Smith, Wash., Ranking Member
Loretta Sanchez, Calif.
Mike McIntyre, N.C.
Robert A. Brady, Pa.
Robert E. Andrews, N.J.
Susan A. Davis, Calif.
Jim Langevin, R.I.
Rick Larsen, Wash.
Jim Cooper, Tenn.
Madeleine Z. Bordallo, Guam
Joe Courtney, Conn.
Dave Loebsack, Iowa
Niki Tsongas, Mass.
John Garamendi, Calif.
Hank Johnson, Ga.
Colleen Hanabusa, Hawaii
Jackie Speier, Calif.
Ron Barber, Ariz.
André Carson, Ind.
Carol Shea-Porter, N.H.
Dan Maffei, N.Y.
Derek Kilmer, Wash.
Joaquin Castro, Texas
Tammy Duckworth, Ill.
Scott Peters, Calif.
Bill Enyart, Ill.
Pete Gallego, Texas
Marc Veasey, Texas

Intelligence, Emerging Threats & Capabilities
Thornberry (chairman), Miller, Kline, Shuster, Nugent, Franks, Hunter, Gibson, Hartzler, Heck
Langevin, Davis, Johnson, Carson, Maffei, Kilmer, Castro, Peters

Military Personnel
Wilson (chairman), Jones, Heck, Scott, Wenstrup, Walorski, Gibson, Noem
Davis, Brady, Bordallo, Loebsack, Tsongas, Shea-Porter

Oversight & Investigations
Roby (chairwoman), Conaway, Brooks, Jones, Scott, Bridenstine
Tsongas, Andrews, Speier, Duckworth

Readiness
Wittman (chairman), Bishop, Hartzler, Scott, Noem, Forbes, LoBiondo, Rogers, Lamborn, Rigell, Palazzo
Bordallo, Courtney, Loebsack, Hanabusa, Speier, Barber, Shea-Porter, Enyart, Gallego

Seapower & Projection Forces
Conaway, Hunter, Rigell, Palazzo, Wittman, Coffman, Runyan, Noem, Cook
McIntyre, Courtney, Langevin, Larsen, Johnson, Hanabusa, Kilmer, Peters

Strategic Forces
Rogers (chairman), Franks, Lamborn, Coffman, Brooks, Wilson, Turner, Fleming, Nugent, Bridenstine
Cooper, Sanchez, Langevin, Larsen, Garamendi, Johnson, Carson, Veasey

Tactical Air & Land Forces
Turner (chairman), LoBiondo, Fleming, Gibson, Runyan, Roby, Cook, Bridenstine, Wenstrup, Walorski, Thornberry, Jones, Bishop
Sanchez, McIntyre, Cooper, Garamendi, Barber, Maffei, Castro, Duckworth, Enyart, Gallego, Veasey

Budget

Phone: (202) 226-7270 **Office: 207 Cannon**

REPUBLICANS (22)
Paul D. Ryan, Wis., Chairman
Scott Garrett, N.J.
John Campbell, Calif.
Ken Calvert, Calif.
Tom Cole, Okla.
Tom Price, Ga.
Tom McClintock, Calif.
James Lankford, Okla.
Diane Black, Tenn.
Reid Ribble, Wis.
Bill Flores, Texas
Todd Rokita, Ind.
Rob Woodall, Ga.
Marsha Blackburn, Tenn.
Alan Nunnelee, Miss.
Scott Rigell, Va.
Vicky Hartzler, Mo.
Jackie Walorski, Ind.
Luke Messer, Ind.
Tom Rice, S.C.
Roger Williams, Texas
Sean P. Duffy, Wis.

DEMOCRATS (17)
Chris Van Hollen, Md., Ranking Member
Allyson Y. Schwartz, Pa.
John Yarmuth, Ky.
Bill Pascrell Jr., N.J.
Tim Ryan, Ohio
Gwen Moore, Wis.
Kathy Castor, Fla.
Jim McDermott, Wash.
Barbara Lee, Calif.
David Cicilline, R.I.
Hakeem Jeffries, N.Y.
Mark Pocan, Wis.
Michelle Lujan Grisham, N.M.
Jared Huffman, Calif.
Tony Cárdenas, Calif.
Earl Blumenauer, Ore.
Kurt Schrader, Ore.

Education & the Workforce

Phone: (202) 225-4527 **Office: 2181 Rayburn**

REPUBLICANS (23)

John Kline, Minn., Chairman
Tom Petri, Wis.
Howard "Buck" McKeon, Calif.
Joe Wilson, S.C.
Virginia Foxx, N.C.
Tom Price, Ga.
Kenny Marchant, Texas
Duncan Hunter, Calif.
Phil Roe, Tenn.
Glenn Thompson, Pa.
Tim Walberg, Mich.
Matt Salmon, Ariz.
Brett Guthrie, Ky.
Scott DesJarlais, Tenn.
Todd Rokita, Ind.
Larry Bucshon, Ind.
Trey Gowdy, S.C.
Lou Barletta, Pa.
Martha Roby, Ala.
Joe Heck, Nev.
Susan W. Brooks, Ind.
Richard Hudson, N.C.
Luke Messer, Ind.

DEMOCRATS (18)

George Miller, Calif., Ranking Member
Robert E. Andrews, N.J.
Robert C. Scott, Va.
Rubén Hinojosa, Texas
Carolyn McCarthy, N.Y.
John F. Tierney, Mass.
Rush D. Holt, N.J.
Susan A. Davis, Calif.
Raúl M. Grijalva, Ariz.
Timothy H. Bishop, N.Y.
Dave Loebsack, Iowa
Joe Courtney, Conn.
Marcia L. Fudge, Ohio
Jared Polis, Colo.
Gregorio Kilili Camacho Sablan, N. Marianas
John Yarmuth, Ky.
Frederica S. Wilson, Fla.
Suzanne Bonamici, Ore.

Early Childhood, Elementary & Secondary Education
Rokita (chairman), Kline, Petri, Foxx, Marchant, Hunter, Roe, Thompson, Roby, Brooks
McCarthy, Scott, Davis, Grijalva, Fudge, Polis, Sablan, Wilson

Health, Employment, Labor & Pensions
Roe (chairman), Wilson, Price, Marchant, Salmon, Guthrie, DesJarlais, Bucshon, Gowdy, Barletta, Roby, Heck, Brooks, Messer
Andrews, Holt, Loebsack, Scott, Hinojosa, Tierney, Grijalva, Courtney, Polis, Yarmuth, Wilson

Higher Education & Workforce Training
Foxx (chairwoman), Petri, McKeon, Thompson, Walberg, Salmon, Guthrie, Barletta, Heck, Brooks, Hudson, Messer
Hinojosa, Tierney, Bishop, Yarmuth, Bonamici, McCarthy, Holt, Davis, Loebsack

Workforce Protections
Walberg (chairman), Kline, Price, Hunter, DesJarlais, Rokita, Bucshon, Hudson
Courtney, Andrews, Bishop, Fudge, Sablan, Bonamici

Energy & Commerce

Phone: (202) 225-2927 **Office: 2125 Rayburn**

REPUBLICANS (30)

Fred Upton, Mich., Chairman
Ralph M. Hall, Texas
Joe L. Barton, Texas
Edward Whitfield, Ky.
John Shimkus, Ill.
Joe Pitts, Pa.
Greg Walden, Ore.
Lee Terry, Neb.
Mike Rogers, Mich.
Tim Murphy, Pa.
Michael C. Burgess, Texas
Marsha Blackburn, Tenn.
Phil Gingrey, Ga.
Steve Scalise, La.
Bob Latta, Ohio
Cathy McMorris Rodgers, Wash.
Gregg Harper, Miss.
Leonard Lance, N.J.
Bill Cassidy, La.
Brett Guthrie, Ky.
Pete Olson, Texas
David B. McKinley, W.Va.
Cory Gardner, Colo.
Mike Pompeo, Kan.
Adam Kinzinger, Ill.
Morgan Griffith, Va.
Gus Bilirakis, Fla.
Bill Johnson, Ohio
Billy Long, Mo.
Renee Ellmers, N.C.

DEMOCRATS (24)

Henry A. Waxman, Calif., Ranking Member
John D. Dingell, Mich.
Edward J. Markey, Mass.
Frank Pallone Jr., N.J.
Bobby L. Rush, Ill.
Anna G. Eshoo, Calif.
Eliot L. Engel, N.Y.
Gene Green, Texas
Diana DeGette, Colo.
Lois Capps, Calif.
Mike Doyle, Pa.
Jan Schakowsky, Ill.
Jim Matheson, Utah
G.K. Butterfield, N.C.
John Barrow, Ga.
Doris Matsui, Calif.
Donna M.C. Christensen, V.I.
Kathy Castor, Fla.
John Sarbanes, Md.
Jerry McNerney, Calif.
Bruce Braley, Iowa
Peter Welch, Vt.
Ben Ray Luján, N.M.
Paul Tonko, N.Y.

Commerce, Manufacturing & Trade
Terry (chairman), Lance, Blackburn, Harper, Guthrie, Olson, McKinley, Pompeo, Kinzinger, Bilirakis, Johnson, Long, Barton, Upton
Schakowsky, Butterfield, Sarbanes, McNerney, Welch, Dingell, Rush, Matheson, Barrow, Christensen, Waxman

Communications & Technology
Walden (chairman), Latta, Shimkus, Terry, Rogers, Blackburn, Scalise, Lance, Guthrie, Gardner, Pompeo, Kinzinger, Long, Ellmers, Barton, Upton
Eshoo, Markey, Doyle, Matsui, Braley, Welch, Luján, Dingell, Pallone, Rush, DeGette, Matheson, Waxman

Energy & Power
Whitfield (chairman), Scalise, Hall, Shimkus, Pitts, Terry, Burgess, Latta, Cassidy, Olson, McKinley, Gardner, Pompeo, Kinzinger, Griffith, Barton, Upton
Rush, McNerney, Tonko, Markey, Engel, Green, Capps, Doyle, Barrow, Matsui, Christensen, Castor, Waxman

Environment & the Economy
Shimkus (chairman), Gingrey, Hall, Whitfield, Pitts, Murphy, Latta, Harper, Cassidy, McKinley, Bilirakis, Johnson, Barton, Upton
Tonko, Pallone, Green, DeGette, Capps, McNerney, Dingell, Schakowsky, Barrow, Matsui, Waxman

Health
Pitts (chairman), Burgess, Whitfield, Shimkus, Rogers, Murphy, Blackburn, Gingrey, McMorris Rodgers, Lance, Cassidy, Guthrie, Griffith, Bilirakis, Ellmers, Barton, Upton
Pallone, Dingell, Engel, Capps, Schakowsky, Matheson, Green, Butterfield, Barrow, Christensen, Castor, Sarbanes, Waxman

Oversight & Investigations
Murphy (chairman), Burgess, Blackburn, Gingrey, Scalise, Harper, Olson, Gardner, Griffith, Johnson, Long, Ellmers, Barton, Upton
DeGette, Braley, Luján, Markey, Schakowsky, Butterfield, Castor, Welch, Tonko, Green, Waxman

Financial Services

Phone: (202) 225-7502 **Office: 2129 Rayburn**

REPUBLICANS (33)	**DEMOCRATS (28)**
Jeb Hensarling, Texas, Chairman	*Maxine Waters, Calif., Ranking Member*
Spencer Bachus, Ala.	*Carolyn B. Maloney, N.Y.*
Peter T. King, N.Y.	*Nydia M. Velázquez, N.Y.*
Ed Royce, Calif.	*Melvin Watt, N.C.*
Frank D. Lucas, Okla.	*Brad Sherman, Calif.*
Gary G. Miller, Calif.	*Gregory W. Meeks, N.Y.*
Shelley Moore Capito, W.Va.	*Michael E. Capuano, Mass.*
Scott Garrett, N.J.	*Rubén Hinojosa, Texas*
Randy Neugebauer, Texas	*William Lacy Clay, Mo.*
Patrick T. McHenry, N.C.	*Carolyn McCarthy, N.Y.*
John Campbell, Calif.	*Stephen F. Lynch, Mass.*
Michele Bachmann, Minn.	*David Scott, Ga.*
Kevin McCarthy, Calif.	*Al Green, Texas*
Steve Pearce, N.M.	*Emanuel Cleaver II, Mo.*
Bill Posey, Fla.	*Gwen Moore, Wis.*
Michael G. Fitzpatrick, Pa.	*Keith Ellison, Minn.*
Lynn Westmoreland, Ga.	*Ed Perlmutter, Colo.*
Blaine Luetkemeyer, Mo.	*Jim Himes, Conn.*
Bill Huizenga, Mich.	*Gary Peters, Mich.*
Sean P. Duffy, Wis.	*John Carney, Del.*
Robert Hurt, Va.	*Terri A. Sewell, Ala.*
Michael G. Grimm, N.Y.	*Bill Foster, Ill.*
Steve Stivers, Ohio	*Dan Kildee, Mich.*
Stephen Fincher, Tenn.	*Patrick Murphy, Fla.*
Marlin Stutzman, Ind.	*John Delaney, Md.*
Mick Mulvaney, S.C.	*Kyrsten Sinema, Ariz.*
Randy Hultgren, Ill.	*Joyce Beatty, Ohio*
Dennis A. Ross, Fla.	*Denny Heck, Wash.*
Robert Pittenger, N.C.	
Ann Wagner, Mo.	
Andy Barr, Ky.	
Tom Cotton, Ark.	
Keith Rothfus, Pa.	

Capital Markets & Government Sponsored Enterprises
Garrett (chairman), Bachus, King, Royce, Lucas, Neugebauer, Bachmann, McCarthy, Westmoreland, Huizenga, Hurt, Grimm, Stivers, Fincher, Mulvaney, Hultgren, Ross, Wagner
Maloney, Sherman, Hinojosa, Lynch, Moore, Perlmutter, Scott, Himes, Peters, Ellison, Watt, Foster, Carney, Sewell, Kildee

Financial Institutions & Consumer Credit
Capito (chairwoman), Bachus, Miller, McHenry, Campbell, McCarthy, Pearce, Posey, Fitzpatrick, Westmoreland, Luetkemeyer, Duffy, Stutzman, Pittenger, Barr, Cotton, Rothfus
Meeks, Maloney, Watt, Hinojosa, McCarthy, Scott, Green, Ellison, Velázquez, Lynch, Capuano, Murphy, Delaney, Heck

Housing and Insurance
Neugebauer (chairman), Royce, Miller, Capito, Garrett, Westmoreland, Luetkemeyer, Duffy, Hurt, Stivers, Ross
Capuano, Velázquez, Cleaver, Clay, Sherman, Himes, McCarthy, Sinema, Beatty

Monetary Policy & Trade
Campbell (chairman), Lucas, Pearce, Posey, Huizenga, Grimm, Fincher, Stutzman, Mulvaney, Pittenger, Cotton
Clay, Moore, Peters, Perlmutter, Foster, Carney, Sewell, Kildee, Murphy

Oversight & Investigations
McHenry (chairman), King, Bachmann, Fitzpatrick, Duffy, Grimm, Fincher, Hultgren, Wagner, Barr, Rothfus
Green, Cleaver, Ellison, Perlmutter, Maloney, Delaney, Sinema, Beatty, Heck

Ethics

Phone: (202) 225-7103 **Office: 1015 Longworth**

REPUBLICANS (5)	**DEMOCRATS (5)**
K. Michael Conaway, Texas, Chairman	*Linda T. Sánchez, Calif., Ranking Member*
Charlie Dent, Pa.	*Pedro R. Pierluisi, P.R.*
Patrick Meehan, Pa.	*Michael E. Capuano, Mass.*
Trey Gowdy, S.C.	*Yvette D. Clarke, N.Y.*
Susan W. Brooks, Ind.	*Ted Deutch, Fla.*

Foreign Affairs

Phone: (202) 225-5021 **Office: 2170 Rayburn**

REPUBLICANS (25)

Ed Royce, Calif., Chairman
Christopher H. Smith, N.J.
Ileana Ros-Lehtinen, Fla.
Dana Rohrabacher, Ca-
lif. Steve Chabot, Ohio
Joe Wilson, S.C.
Michael McCaul, Texas
Ted Poe, Texas
Matt Salmon, Ariz.
Tom Marino, Pa.
Jeff Duncan, S.C.
Adam Kinzinger, Ill.
Mo Brooks, Ala.
Tom Cotton, Ark.
Paul Cook, Calif.
George Holding, N.C.
Randy Weber, Texas
Scott Perry, Pa.
Steve Stockman, Texas
Ron DeSantis, Fla.
Trey Radel, Fla.
Doug Collins, Ga.
Mark Meadows, N.C.
Ted Yoho, Fla.
Luke Messer, Ind.

DEMOCRATS (21)

Eliot L. Engel, N.Y., Ranking Member
Eni F.H. Faleomavaega, A.S.
Brad Sherman, Calif.
Gregory W. Meeks, N.Y.
Albio Sires, N.J.
Gerald E. Connolly, Va.
Ted Deutch, Fla.
Brian Higgins, N.Y.
Karen Bass, Calif.
William Keating, Mass.
David Cicilline, R.I.
Alan Grayson, Fla.
Juan C. Vargas, Calif.
Brad Schneider, Ill.
Joseph P. Kennedy III, Mass.
Ami Bera, Calif.
Alan Lowenthal, Calif.
Grace Meng, N.Y.
Lois Frankel, Fla.
Tulsi Gabbard, Hawaii
Joaquin Castro, Texas

Africa, Global Health, Global Human Rights & International Organizations
Smith (chairman), Marino, Weber, Stockman, Meadows
Bass, Cicilline, Bera

Asia & the Pacific
Chabot (chairman), Rohrabacher, Salmon, Brooks, Holding, Perry, Collins, Messer
Faleomavaega, Bera, Gabbard, Sherman, Connolly, Keating

Europe, Eurasia & Emerging Threats
Rohrabacher (chairman), Poe, Marino, Duncan, Cook, Holding, Stockman
Keating, Meeks, Sires, Higgins, Lowenthal

Middle East & North Africa
Ros-Lehtinen (chairwoman), Chabot, Wilson, Kinzinger, Cotton, Weber, DeSantis, Radel, Collins, Meadows, Yoho, Messer
Deutch, Connolly, Higgins, Cicilline, Grayson, Vargas, Schneider, Kennedy, Meng, Frankel

Terrorism, Nonproliferation & Trade
Poe (chairman), Wilson, Kinzinger, Brooks, Cotton, Cook, Perry, Yoho
Sherman, Lowenthal, Castro, Vargas, Schneider, Kennedy

Western Hemisphere
Salmon (chairman), Smith, Ros-Lehtinen, McCaul, Duncan, DeSantis, Radel
Sires, Meeks, Faleomavaega, Deutch, Grayson

Homeland Security

Phone: (202) 226-8417 **Office: H2-176 Ford**

REPUBLICANS (18)

Michael McCaul, Texas, Chairman
Lamar Smith, Texas
Peter T. King, N.Y.
Mike D. Rogers, Ala.
Paul Broun, Ga.
Candice S. Miller, Mich.
Patrick Meehan, Pa.
Jeff Duncan, S.C.
Tom Marino, Pa.
Jason Chaffetz, Utah
Steven M. Palazzo, Miss.
Lou Barletta, Pa.
Chris Stewart, Utah
Richard Hudson, N.C.
Steve Daines, Mont.
Susan W. Brooks, Ind.
Scott Perry, Pa.
Vacancy

DEMOCRATS (14)

Bennie Thompson, Miss., Ranking Member
Loretta Sanchez, Calif.
Sheila Jackson Lee, Texas
Yvette D. Clarke, N.Y.
Brian Higgins, N.Y.
Cedric L. Richmond, La.
William Keating, Mass.
Ron Barber, Ariz.
Donald M. Payne Jr., N.J.
Beto O'Rourke, Texas
Tulsi Gabbard, Hawaii
Filemon Vela, Texas
Steven Horsford, Nev.
Eric Swalwell, Calif.

Border & Maritime Security
Miller (chairwoman), Duncan, Marino, Palazzo, Barletta, Stewart
Jackson Lee, Sanchez, O'Rourke, Gabbard

Counterterrorism & Intelligence
King (chairman), Broun, Meehan, Chaffetz, Stewart
Higgins, Sanchez, Keating

Cybersecurity, Infrastructure Protection & Security Technologies
Meehan (chairman), Rogers, Chaffetz, Daines, Perry, Vacancy
Clarke, Keating, Vela, Horsford

Emergency Preparedness, Response & Communications
Brooks (chairwoman), King, Marino, Palazzo, Perry
Payne, Clarke, Higgins

Oversight and Management Efficiency
Duncan (chairman), Broun, Hudson, Daines, Vacancy
Barber, Payne, O'Rourke

Transportation Security
Hudson (chairman), Rogers, Miller, Barletta, Brooks
Richmond, Jackson Lee, Swalwell

House Administration

Phone: (202) 225-8281 **Office: 1309 Longworth**

REPUBLICANS (6)	DEMOCRATS (3)
Candice S. Miller, Mich., Chairwoman	*Robert A. Brady, Pa., Ranking Member*
Gregg Harper, Miss.	*Zoe Lofgren, Calif.*
Phil Gingrey, Ga.	*Juan C. Vargas, Calif.*
Aaron Schock, Ill.	
Todd Rokita, Ind.	
Rich Nugent, Fla.	

Judiciary

Phone: (202) 225-3951 **Office: 2138 Rayburn**

REPUBLICANS (23)	DEMOCRATS (17)
Robert W. Goodlatte, Va., Chairman	*John Conyers Jr., Mich., Ranking Member*
Jim Sensenbrenner, Wis.	*Jerrold Nadler, N.Y.*
Howard Coble, N.C.	*Robert C. Scott, Va.*
Lamar Smith, Texas	*Melvin Watt, N.C.*
Steve Chabot, Ohio	*Zoe Lofgren, Calif.*
Spencer Bachus, Ala.	*Sheila Jackson Lee, Texas*
Darrell Issa, Calif.	*Steve Cohen, Tenn.*
J. Randy Forbes, Va.	*Hank Johnson, Ga.*
Steve King, Iowa	*Pedro R. Pierluisi, P.R.*
Trent Franks, Ariz.	*Judy Chu, Calif.*
Louie Gohmert, Texas	*Ted Deutch, Fla.*
Jim Jordan, Ohio	*Luis V. Gutierrez, Ill.*
Ted Poe, Texas	*Karen Bass, Calif.*
Jason Chaffetz, Utah	*Cedric L. Richmond, La.*
Tom Marino, Pa.	*Suzan DelBene, Wash.*
Trey Gowdy, S.C.	*Joe Garcia, Fla.*
Mark Amodei, Nev.	*Hakeem Jeffries, N.Y.*
Raúl R. Labrador, Idaho	
Blake Farenthold, Texas	
George Holding, N.C.	
Doug Collins, Ga.	
Ron DeSantis, Fla.	
Vacancy	

Constitution & Civil Justice
Franks (chairman), Jordan, Chabot, Forbes, King, Gohmert, DeSantis, Vacancy
Nadler, Conyers, Scott, Cohen, Deutch

Courts, Intellectual Property & the Internet
Coble (chairman), Marino, Sensenbrenner, Smith, Chabot, Issa,Poe, Chaffetz, Amodei, Farenthold, Holding, Collins, DeSantis, Vacancy
Watt, Conyers, Johnson, Chu, Deutch, Bass, Richmond, DelBene, Jeffries, Nadler, Lofgren, Jackson Lee

Crime, Terrorism, Homeland Security & Investigations
Sensenbrenner (chairman), Gohmert, Coble, Bachus, Forbes, Franks, Chaffetz, Gowdy, Labrador
Scott, Pierluisi, Chu, Gutierrez, Bass, Richmond

Immigration & Border Security
Gowdy (chairman), Poe, Smith, King, Jordan, Amodei, Labrador, Holding
Lofgren, Jackson Lee, Gutierrez, Garcia, Pierluisi

Regulatory Reform, Commercial & Antitrust Law
Bachus (chairman), Farenthold, Issa, Marino, Holding, Collins, Vacancy
Cohen, Johnson, DelBene, Garcia, Jeffries

Over-Criminalization Task Force
Sensenbrenner (chairman), Bachus, Gohmert, Labrador, Holding
Scott, Nadler, Cohen, Bass Jeffries

Natural Resources

Phone: (202) 225-2761 **Office: 1324 Longworth**

REPUBLICANS (26)	DEMOCRATS (21)
Doc Hastings, Wash., Chairman	*Edward J. Markey, Mass., Ranking Member*
Don Young, Alaska	*Peter A. DeFazio, Ore.*
Louie Gohmert, Texas	*Eni F.H. Faleomavaega, A.S.*
Rob Bishop, Utah	*Frank Pallone Jr., N.J.*
Doug Lamborn, Colo.	*Grace F. Napolitano, Calif.*
Rob Wittman, Va.	*Rush D. Holt, N.J.*
Paul Broun, Ga.	*Raúl M. Grijalva, Ariz.*
John Fleming, La.	*Madeleine Z. Bordallo, Guam*
Tom McClintock, Calif.	*Jim Costa, Calif.*
Glenn Thompson, Pa.	*Gregorio Kilili Camacho Sablan, N. Marianas*
Cynthia M. Lummis, Wyo.	*Niki Tsongas, Mass.*
Dan Benishek, Mich.	*Pedro R. Pierluisi, P.R.*
Jeff Duncan, S.C.	*Colleen Hanabusa, Hawaii*
Scott Tipton, Colo.	*Tony Cárdenas, Calif.*
Paul Gosar, Ariz.	*Steven Horsford, Nev.*
Raúl R. Labrador, Idaho	*Jared Huffman, Calif.*
Steve Southerland II, Fla.	*Raul Ruiz, Calif.*
Bill Flores, Texas	*Carol Shea-Porter, N.H.*
Jon Runyan, N.J.	*Alan Lowenthal, Calif.*
Mark Amodei, Nev.	*Joe Garcia, Fla.*
Markwayne Mullin, Okla.	*Matt Cartwright, Pa.*
Chris Stewart, Utah	
Steve Daines, Mont.	
Kevin Cramer, N.D.	
Doug LaMalfa, Calif.	
Vacancy	

Energy & Mineral Resources
Lamborn (chairman), Gohmert, Bishop, Wittman, Broun, Fleming, Thompson, Lummis, Benishek, Duncan, Gosar, Flores, Amodei, Daines, Cramer, Vacancy
Holt, Horsford, Cartwright, Costa, Tsongas, Huffman, Lowenthal, DeFazio, Cárdenas, Grijalva, Hanabusa, Ruiz, Garcia, Vacancy, Vacancy

Fisheries, Wildlife, Oceans & Insular Affairs
Fleming (chairman), Young, Wittman, Thompson, Duncan, Southerland, Flores, Runyan, Vacancy, Vacancy
Sablan, Faleomavaega, Pallone, Bordallo, Pierluisi, Shea-Porter, Lowenthal, Garcia

Indian & Alaska Native Affairs
Young (chairman), Benishek, Gosar, Mullin, Daines, Cramer, LaMalfa
Hanabusa, Cárdenas, Ruiz, Faleomavaega, Grijalva

Public Lands and Environmental Regulations
Bishop (chairman), Young, Gohmert, Lamborn, Broun, McClintock, Lummis, Tipton, Labrador, Amodei, Stewart, Daines, Cramer, LaMalfa
Grijalva, DeFazio, Tsongas, Holt, Bordallo, Sablan, Pierluisi, Hanabusa, Horsford, Shea-Porter, Garcia, Cartwright

Water & Power
McClintock (chairman), Lummis, Tipton, Gosar, Labrador, Mullin, Stewart, LaMalfa
Napolitano, Costa, Huffman, DeFazio, Cárdenas, Ruiz

Oversight & Government Reform

Phone: (202) 225-5074 **Office: 2157 Rayburn**

REPUBLICANS (23)	DEMOCRATS (18)
Darrell Issa, Calif., Chairman	*Elijah E. Cummings, Md., Ranking Member*
John L. Mica, Fla.	*Carolyn B. Maloney, N.Y.*
Michael R. Turner, Ohio	*Eleanor Holmes Norton, D.C.*
John J. Duncan Jr., Tenn.	*John F. Tierney, Mass.*
Patrick T. McHenry, N.C.	*William Lacy Clay, Mo.*
Jim Jordan, Ohio	*Stephen F. Lynch, Mass.*
Jason Chaffetz, Utah	*Jim Cooper, Tenn.*
Tim Walberg, Mich.	*Gerald E. Connolly, Va.*
James Lankford, Okla.	*Jackie Speier, Calif.*
Justin Amash, Mich.	*Matt Cartwright, Pa.*
Paul Gosar, Ariz.	*Mark Pocan, Wis.*
Patrick Meehan, Pa.	*Tammy Duckworth, Ill.*
Scott DesJarlais, Tenn.	*Robin Kelly, Ill.*
Trey Gowdy, S.C.	*Danny K. Davis, Ill.*
Blake Farenthold, Texas	*Peter Welch, Vt.*
Doc Hastings, Wash.	*Tony Cárdenas, Calif.*
Cynthia M. Lummis, Wyo.	*Steven Horsford, Nev.*
Rob Woodall, Ga.	*Michelle Lujan Grisham, N.M.*
Thomas Massie, Ky.	
Doug Collins, Ga.	
Mark Meadows, N.C.	
Kerry Bentivolio, Mich.	
Ron DeSantis, Fla.	

Economic Growth, Job Creation and Regulatory Affairs
Jordan (chairman), Duncan, McHenry, Gosar, Meehan, DesJarlais, Hastings, Lummis, Collins, Meadows, Bentivolio, DeSantis
Cartwright, Duckworth, Connolly, Pocan, Kelly, Davis, Horsford, Lujan Grisham, Vacancy, Vacancy

Energy Policy, Health Care and Entitlements
Lankford (chairman), McHenry, Jordan, Chaffetz, Walberg, Meehan, DesJarlais, Farenthold, Hastings, Woodall, Massie
Speier, Norton, Cooper, Cartwright, Duckworth, Cárdenas, Lujan Grisham, Davis, Horsford

Federal Workforce, U.S. Postal Service and the Census
Farenthold (chairman), Walberg, Gowdy, Collins, DeSantis
Lynch, Norton, Clay

Government Operations
Mica (chairman), Turner, Amash, Massie, Meadows
Connolly, Cooper, Pocan

National Security
Chaffetz (chairman), Mica, Duncan, Amash, Gosar, Gowdy, Lummis, Woodall, Bentivolio
Tierney, Maloney, Lynch, Speier, Kelly, Welch, Lujan Grisham

Rules

Phone: (202) 225-9191 **Office: H-312 Capitol**

REPUBLICANS (9)	DEMOCRATS (4)
Pete Sessions, Texas, Chairman	*Louise M. Slaughter, N.Y., Ranking Member*
Virginia Foxx, N.C.	*Jim McGovern, Mass.*
Rob Bishop, Utah	*Alcee L. Hastings, Fla.*
Tom Cole, Okla.	*Jared Polis, Colo.*
Rob Woodall, Ga.	
Rich Nugent, Fla.	
Daniel Webster, Fla.	
Ileana Ros-Lehtinen, Fla.	
Michael C. Burgess, Texas	

Legislative & Budget Process
Woodall (chairman), Foxx, Nugent, Webster, Burgess
Hastings, Polis

Rules & the Organization of the House
Nugent (chairman), Bishop, Webster, Ros-Lehtinen, Sessions
McGovern, Slaughter

Science, Space & Technology

Phone: (202) 225-6371 **Office: 2321 Rayburn**

REPUBLICANS (22)

Lamar Smith, Texas, Chairman
Jim Sensenbrenner, Wis.
Ralph M. Hall, Texas
Dana Rohrabacher, Calif.
Frank D. Lucas, Okla.
Randy Neugebauer, Texas
Michael McCaul, Texas
Paul Broun, Ga.
Steven M. Palazzo, Miss.
Mo Brooks, Ala.
Randy Hultgren, Ill.
Larry Bucshon, Ind.
Steve Stockman, Texas
Bill Posey, Fla.
Cynthia M. Lummis, Wyo.
David Schweikert, Ariz.
Thomas Massie, Ky.
Kevin Cramer, N.D.
Jim Bridenstine, Okla.
Randy Weber, Texas
Chris Stewart, Utah
Vacancy

DEMOCRATS (18)

Eddie Bernice Johnson, Texas, Ranking Member
Zoe Lofgren, Calif.
Daniel Lipinski, Ill.
Donna Edwards, Md.
Frederica S. Wilson, Fla.
Suzanne Bonamici, Ore.
Eric Swalwell, Calif.
Dan Maffei, N.Y.
Alan Grayson, Fla.
Joseph P. Kennedy III, Mass.
Scott Peters, Calif.
Derek Kilmer, Wash.
Ami Bera, Calif.
Elizabeth Esty, Conn.
Marc Veasey, Texas
Julia Brownley, Calif.
Mark Takano, Calif.
Robin Kelly, Ill.

Energy
Lummis (chairwoman), Hall, Lucas, Neugebauer, McCaul, Hultgren, Massie, Cramer, Weber
Swalwell, Lofgren, Lipinski, Grayson, Kennedy, Veasey, Takano

Environment
Stewart (chairman), Sensenbrenner, Rohrabacher, Neugebauer, Broun, Weber, Vacancy
Bonamici, Edwards, Grayson, Brownley, Takano

Oversight
Broun (chairman), Sensenbrenner, Posey, Schweikert, Cramer
Maffei, Swalwell, Peters

Research
Bucshon (chairman), Palazzo, Brooks, Stockman, Lummis, Bridenstine
Lipinski, Lofgren, Bera, Esty

Space
Palazzo (chairman), Rohrabacher, Lucas, Hall, McCaul, Brooks, Bucshon, Stockman, Posey, Schweikert, Bridenstine, Stewart
Edwards, Wilson, Bonamici, Maffei, Kennedy, Kilmer, Bera, Veasey, Brownley

Technology
Massie (chairman), Hultgren, Schweikert, Bridenstine, Vacancy
Wilson, Peters, Kilmer

Select Intelligence

Phone: (202) 225-4121
Office: HVC-304 Capitol Visitor Center

REPUBLICANS (12)
Mike Rogers, Mich., Chairman
Mac Thornberry, Texas
Jeff Miller, Fla.
K. Michael Conaway, Texas
Peter T. King, N.Y.
Frank A. LoBiondo, N.J.
Devin Nunes, Calif.
Lynn Westmoreland, Ga.
Michele Bachmann, Minn.
Tom Rooney, Fla.
Joe Heck, Nev.
Mike Pompeo, Kan.

DEMOCRATS (9)
C.A. Dutch Ruppersberger, Md., Ranking Member
Mike Thompson, Calif.
Jan Schakowsky, Ill.
Jim Langevin, R.I.
Adam B. Schiff, Calif.
Luis V. Gutierrez, Ill.
Ed Pastor, Ariz.
Jim Himes, Conn.
Terri A. Sewell, Ala.

Small Business

Phone: (202) 225-5821 **Office: 2361 Rayburn**

REPUBLICANS (14)
Sam Graves, Mo., Chairman
Steve Chabot, Ohio
Steve King, Iowa
Mike Coffman, Colo.
Blaine Luetkemeyer, Mo.
Mick Mulvaney, S.C.
Scott Tipton, Colo.
Jaime Herrera Beutler, Wash.
Richard Hanna, N.Y.
Tim Huelskamp, Kan.
David Schweikert, Ariz.
Kerry Bentivolio, Mich.
Chris Collins, N.Y.
Tom Rice, S.C.

DEMOCRATS (11)
Nydia M. Velázquez, N.Y., Ranking Member
Kurt Schrader, Ore.
Yvette D. Clarke, N.Y.
Judy Chu, Calif.
Janice Hahn, Calif.
Donald M. Payne Jr., N.J.
Grace Meng, N.Y.
Brad Schneider, Ill.
Ron Barber, Ariz.
Ann McLane Kuster, N.H.
Patrick Murphy, Fla.

Agriculture, Energy & Trade
Tipton (chairman), King, Luetkemeyer, Mulvaney, Hanna, Huelskamp
Murphy, Schrader, Meng, Barber

Contracting & Workforce
Hanna (chairman), King, Mulvaney, Tipton, Huelskamp, Bentivolio
Meng, Clarke, Chu, Vacancy

Economic Growth, Tax & Capital Access
Rice (chairman), Chabot, King, Coffman, Mulvaney, Schweikert
Chu, Payne, Schneider, Barber

Health and Technology
Collins (chairman), King, Coffman, Luetkemeyer, Herrera Beutler, Huelskamp
Hahn, Schrader, Schneider, Vacancy

Investigations, Oversight & Regulations
Schweikert (chairman), Chabot, Herrera Beutler, Bentivolio, Collins, Rice
Clarke, Chu, Kuster, Vacancy

Transportation & Infrastructure

Phone: (202) 225-9446 **Office: 2165 Rayburn**

REPUBLICANS (33)

Bill Shuster, Pa., Chairman
Don Young, Alaska
Tom Petri, Wis.
Howard Coble, N.C.
John J. Duncan Jr., Tenn.
John L. Mica, Fla.
Frank A. LoBiondo, N.J.
Gary G. Miller, Calif.
Sam Graves, Mo.
Shelley Moore Capito, W.Va.
Candice S. Miller, Mich.
Duncan Hunter, Calif.
Rick Crawford, Ark.
Lou Barletta, Pa.
Blake Farenthold, Texas
Larry Bucshon, Ind.
Bob Gibbs, Ohio
Patrick Meehan, Pa.
Richard Hanna, N.Y.
Daniel Webster, Fla.
Steve Southerland II, Fla.
Jeff Denham, Calif.
Reid Ribble, Wis.
Thomas Massie, Ky.
Steve Daines, Mont.
Tom Rice, S.C.
Markwayne Mullin, Okla.
Roger Williams, Texas
Trey Radel, Fla.
Mark Meadows, N.C.
Scott Perry, Pa.
Rodney Davis, Ill.
Vacancy

DEMOCRATS (27)

Nick J. Rahall II, W.Va., Ranking Member
Peter A. DeFazio, Ore.
Eleanor Holmes Norton, D.C.
Jerrold Nadler, N.Y.
Corrine Brown, Fla.
Eddie Bernice Johnson, Texas
Elijah E. Cummings, Md.
Rick Larsen, Wash.
Michael E. Capuano, Mass.
Timothy H. Bishop, N.Y.
Michael H. Michaud, Maine
Grace F. Napolitano, Calif.
Daniel Lipinski, Ill.
Tim Walz, Minn.
Steve Cohen, Tenn.
Albio Sires, N.J.
Donna Edwards, Md.
John Garamendi, Calif.
André Carson, Ind.
Janice Hahn, Calif.
Rick Nolan, Minn.
Ann Kirkpatrick, Ariz.
Dina Titus, Nev.
Sean Patrick Maloney, N.Y.
Elizabeth Esty, Conn.
Lois Frankel, Fla.
Cheri Bustos, Ill.

Aviation

LoBiondo (chairman), Petri, Coble, Duncan, Graves, Farenthold, Bucshon, Meehan, Webster, Denham, Ribble, Massie, Daines, Williams, Radel, Meadows, Davis, Shuster

Larsen, DeFazio, Norton, Johnson, Capuano, Lipinski, Cohen, Carson, Nolan, Titus, Maloney, Bustos, Brown, Rahall

Coast Guard & Maritime Transportation

Hunter (chairman), Young, Coble, LoBiondo, Meehan, Southerland, Rice, Radel, Shuster, Vacancy

Garamendi, Cummings, Brown, Larsen, Bishop, Hahn, Frankel, Rahall

Economic Development, Public Buildings & Emergency Management

Barletta (chairman), Petri, Mica, Crawford, Farenthold, Mullin, Meadows, Perry, Shuster, Vacancy

Norton, Michaud, Edwards, Nolan, Kirkpatrick, Titus, Walz, Rahall

Highways & Transit

Petri (chairman), Young, Coble, Duncan, Mica, LoBiondo, Miller (Calif.), Graves, Capito, Hunter, Crawford, Barletta, Farenthold, Bucshon, Gibbs, Hanna, Southerland, Ribble, Daines, Rice, Mullin, Williams, Perry, Davis, Shuster

DeFazio, Nadler, Johnson, Capuano, Michaud, Napolitano, Walz, Cohen, Sires, Edwards, Carson, Hahn, Nolan, Kirkpatrick, Titus, Maloney, Esty, Frankel, Bustos, Rahall

Railroads, Pipelines & Hazardous Materials

Denham (chairman), Duncan, Mica, Miller (Calif.), Graves, Capito, Miller (Mich.), Barletta, Bucshon, Gibbs, Meehan, Hanna, Webster, Massie, Williams, Radel, Perry, Shuster

Brown, Lipinski, Nadler, Cummings, Michaud, Napolitano, Walz, Sires, Esty, DeFazio, Capuano, Cohen, Titus, Rahall

Water Resources & Environment

Gibbs (chairman), Young, Miller (Calif.), Capito, Miller (Mich.), Crawford, Hanna, Webster, Denham, Ribble, Massie, Daines, Rice, Mullin, Meadows, Davis, Shuster, Vacancy

Bishop, Edwards, Garamendi, Kirkpatrick, Frankel, Norton, Johnson, Napolitano, Esty, Michaud, Nolan, Hahn, Maloney, Rahall

21st Century Freight Transportation

Duncan (chairman), Miller (Calif.), Crawford, Hanna, Webster, Mullin

Nadler, Brown, Lipinski, Sires, Hahn

Veterans' Affairs

Phone: (202) 225-3527 **Office: 335 Cannon**

REPUBLICANS (14)

Jeff Miller, Fla., Chairman
Doug Lamborn, Colo.
Gus Bilirakis, Fla.
Phil Roe, Tenn.
Bill Flores, Texas
Jeff Denham, Calif.
Jon Runyan, N.J.
Dan Benishek, Mich.
Tim Huelskamp, Kan.
Mark Amodei, Nev.
Mike Coffman, Colo.
Brad Wenstrup, Ohio
Paul Cook, Calif.
Jackie Walorski, Ind.

DEMOCRATS (11)

Michael H. Michaud, Maine, Ranking Member
Corrine Brown, Fla.
Mark Takano, Calif.
Julia Brownley, Calif.
Dina Titus, Nev.
Ann Kirkpatrick, Ariz.
Raul Ruiz, Calif.
Gloria Negrete McLeod, Calif.
Ann McLane Kuster, N.H.
Beto O'Rourke, Texas
Tim Walz, Minn.

Disability Assistance & Memorial Affairs
Runyan (chairman), Lamborn, Bilirakis, Amodei, Cook
Titus, O'Rourke, Ruiz, Negrete McLeod

Economic Opportunity
Flores (chairman), Runyan, Coffman, Cook, Wenstrup
Takano, Brownley, Titus, Kirkpatrick

Health
Benishek (chairman), Roe, Denham, Huelskamp, Walorski, Wenstrup, Vacancy
Brownley, Brown, Ruiz, Negrete McLeod, Kuster

Oversight & Investigations
Coffman (chairman), Lamborn, Roe, Huelskamp, Benishek, Walorski
Kirkpatrick, Takano, Kuster, O'Rourke, Walz

Ways & Means

Phone: (202) 225-3625 **Office: 1102 Longworth**

REPUBLICANS (23)

Dave Camp, Mich., Chairman
Sam Johnson, Texas
Kevin Brady, Texas
Paul D. Ryan, Wis.
Devin Nunes, Calif.
Pat Tiberi, Ohio
Dave Reichert, Wash.
Charles Boustany Jr., La.
Peter Roskam, Ill.
Jim Gerlach, Pa.
Tom Price, Ga.
Vern Buchanan, Fla.
Adrian Smith, Neb.
Aaron Schock, Ill.
Lynn Jenkins, Kan.
Erik Paulsen, Minn.
Kenny Marchant, Texas
Diane Black, Tenn.
Tom Reed, N.Y.
Todd Young, Ind.
Mike Kelly, Pa.
Tim Griffin, Ark.
James B. Renacci, Ohio

DEMOCRATS (16)

Sander M. Levin, Mich., Ranking Member
Charles B. Rangel, N.Y.
Jim McDermott, Wash.
John Lewis, Ga.
Richard E. Neal, Mass.
Xavier Becerra, Calif.
Lloyd Doggett, Texas
Mike Thompson, Calif.
John B. Larson, Conn.
Earl Blumenauer, Ore.
Ron Kind, Wis.
Bill Pascrell Jr., N.J.
Joseph Crowley, N.Y.
Allyson Y. Schwartz, Pa.
Danny K. Davis, Ill.
Linda T. Sánchez, Calif.

Health
Brady (chairman), Johnson, Ryan, Nunes, Roskam, Gerlach, Price, Buchanan, Smith
McDermott, Thompson, Blumenauer, Kind, Pascrell

Human Resources
Reichert (chairman), Young, Kelly, Griffin, Renacci, Reed, Boustany
Doggett, Lewis, Crowley, Davis

Oversight
Boustany (chairman), Black, Jenkins, Marchant, Reed, Paulsen, Kelly
Lewis, Crowley, Davis, Sánchez

Select Revenue Measures
Tiberi (chairman), Paulsen, Marchant, Gerlach, Schock, Reed, Young
Neal, Larson, Schwartz, Sánchez

Social Security
Johnson (chairman), Tiberi, Griffin, Renacci, Schock, Kelly, Brady
Becerra, Doggett, Thompson, Schwartz

Trade
Nunes (chairman), Brady, Reichert, Buchanan, Smith, Schock, Jenkins, Boustany, Roskam
Rangel, Neal, Larson, Blumenauer, Kind

House Leadership

DEMOCRATIC LEADERS

Minority Leader........Nancy Pelosi
Minority Whip........Steny H. Hoyer
Assistant Leader........James E. Clyburn
Caucus Chairman........Xavier Becerra
Caucus Vice Chairman........Joseph Crowley
Organization, Study and Review Chairwoman........Karen Bass

Chief Deputy Whips: John Lewis (senior), G.K. Butterfield, Diana DeGette, Keith Ellison, Ben Ray Luján, Jim Matheson, Jan Schakowsky, Terri A. Sewell, Debbie Wasserman Schultz, Peter Welch, Jared Polis (parliamentarian)

DEMOCRATIC CONGRESSIONAL CAMPAIGN COMMITTEE

863-1500 **430 S. Capitol St. SE 20003**

Chairman........Steve Israel
National Finance Chairman........Jim Himes
DC Finance Chairman........Joseph Crowley
National Candidate Services Chairman........Jared Polis
National Mobilization Chairman........James E. Clyburn
Frontline Program Chairman........Tim Walz
Recruitment Committee Chairwoman....Donna Edwards

Business Council Co-Chairmen: Richard E. Neal, Terri A. Sewell

Latino Council Co-Chairmen: Henry Cuellar, Ben Ray Luján

Women LEAD Co-Chairwomen: Lois Frankel, Chellie Pingree

DEMOCRATIC STEERING & POLICY COMMITTEE

225-0100 **235 Cannon**

Chairwoman........Nancy Pelosi
Steering Co-Chairwoman........Rosa DeLauro
Policy Co-Chairman........Robert E. Andrews
Vice Chairwoman........Allyson Y. Schwartz
Vice Chairman........Henry Cuellar
Freshman Class Representative........Dan Kildee

Members: John Barrow, Karen Bass, Xavier Becerra, Bruce Braley, G.K. Butterfield, John Carney, Yvette D. Clarke, James E. Clyburn, Joseph Crowley, Susan A. Davis, Peter A. DeFazio, Diana DeGette, Mike Doyle, Tammy Duckworth, Keith Ellison, Rubén Hinojosa, Steny H. Hoyer, John B. Larson, Barbara Lee, Sander M. Levin, John Lewis, Nita M. Lowey, Ben Ray Luján, Carolyn B. Maloney, Jim Matheson, Betty McCollum, George Miller, Gwen Moore, Frank Pallone Jr., Nancy Pelosi, Jared Polis, Cedric L. Richmond, Bobby L. Rush, Tim Ryan, Jan Schakowsky, Terri A. Sewell Louise M. Slaughter, Jackie Speier, Niki Tsongas, Chris Van Hollen, Nydia M. Velázquez, Tim Walz, Debbie Wasserman Schultz, Maxine Waters, Henry A. Waxman, Peter Welch, John Yarmuth

REPUBLICAN LEADERS

Speaker........John A. Boehner
Majority Leader........Eric Cantor
Majority Whip........Kevin McCarthy
Conference Chairwoman........Cathy McMorris Rodgers
Conference Vice Chairwoman........Lynn Jenkins
Conference Secretary........Virginia Foxx
Class of 2010 Representative........Steve Southerland II
Freshman Class Representative........Ann Wagner

NATIONAL REPUBLICAN CONGRESSIONAL COMMITTEE

479-7000 **320 First St. SE 20003**

Chairman........Greg Walden
Deputy Chairman........Lynn Westmoreland
Finance Vice Chairman........Steve Stivers
Recruitment Vice Chairman........Patrick T. McHenry
Policy Vice Chairman........Tom Price
Digital Vice Chairman........Jason Chaffetz
Coalitions Vice Chairmen........Tom Graves, Jaime Herrera Beutler
Patriot Program Vice Chairmen........Cory Gardner, Reid Ribble
Regional Vice Chairwoman........Marsha Blackburn

Regional Chairmen: Martha Roby (southern), Steve Daines (central west), Adam Kinzinger (midwest), Devin Nunes (western), Tom Reed (northeast)

REPUBLICAN POLICY COMMITTEE

225-2132 **228 Cannon**

Chairman........James Lankford

Members: Gus Bilirakis, Rob Bishop, Diane Black, Paul Broun, Larry Bucshon, Michael C. Burgess, Steve Daines, Jeff Denham, Renee Ellmers, Michael G. Fitzpatrick, John Fleming, Cory Gardner, Chris Gibson, Phil Gingrey, Tom Graves, Morgan Griffith, Michael G. Grimm, Andy Harris, Bill Huizenga, Robert Hurt, Bill Johnson, Steve King, Cynthia M. Lummis, Markwayne Mullin, Mick Mulvaney, Randy Neugebauer, Mike Pompeo, James B. Renacci, Reid Ribble, Scott Rigell, Mike D. Rogers, Keith Rothfus, Austin Scott, Lee Terry, Glenn Thompson, Brad Wenstrup, Joe Wilson, Steve Womack, Rob Woodall, Kevin Yoder, Don Young

REPUBLICAN STEERING COMMITTEE

225-0600 **H-232 Capitol**

Chairman........John A. Boehner

Senate Committees

The standing and select committees of the Senate are listed by their full names. Membership is given in order of seniority on the panel. Leadership committees are on page 1171.

Democrats are shown in roman type and Republicans in italics. A vacancy indicates that a committee or subcommittee seat had not been filled as of press time, June 2013. Subcommittee vacancies do not necessarily indicate vacancies on full committees and vice versa.

Agriculture, Nutrition & Forestry

Phone: (202) 224-2035 **Office: 328A Russell**

DEMOCRATS (11)

Debbie Stabenow, Mich., Chairwoman
Patrick J. Leahy, Vt.
Tom Harkin, Iowa
Max Baucus, Mont.
Sherrod Brown, Ohio
Amy Klobuchar, Minn.
Michael Bennet, Colo.
Kirsten Gillibrand, N.Y.
Joe Donnelly, Ind.
Heidi Heitkamp, N.D.
William "Mo" Cowan, Mass.

REPUBLICANS (9)

Thad Cochran, Miss., Ranking Member
Mitch McConnell, Ky.
Pat Roberts, Kan.
Saxby Chambliss, Ga.
John Boozman, Ark.
John Hoeven, N.D.
Mike Johanns, Neb.
Charles E. Grassley, Iowa
John Thune, S.D.

Commodities & Markets

Donnelly (chairman), Baucus, Heitkamp, Harkin, Brown, Gillibrand
Chambliss, Roberts, Boozman, Hoeven, Johanns

Conservation, Forestry & Natural Resources

Bennet (chairman), Harkin, Klobuchar, Leahy, Baucus, Heitkamp
Boozman, McConnell, Chambliss, Thune, Roberts

Jobs, Rural Economic Growth & Energy Innovation

Heitkamp (chairwoman), Brown, Klobuchar, Bennet, Donnelly, Cowan
Johanns, Hoeven, Grassley, Thune, Boozman

Livestock and Dairy

Gillibrand (chairwoman), Leahy, Baucus, Klobuchar, Donnelly, Cowan
Roberts, McConnell, Boozman, Johanns, Grassley

Nutrition, Specialty Crops, Food & Agricultural Research

Cowan (chairman), Leahy, Harkin, Brown, Gillibrand, Bennet
Hoeven, McConnell, Chambliss, Grassley, Thune

Appropriations

Phone: (202) 224-7363 **Office: S-128 Capitol**

DEMOCRATS (16)

Barbara A. Mikulski, Md., Chairwoman
Patrick J. Leahy, Vt.
Tom Harkin, Iowa
Patty Murray, Wash.
Dianne Feinstein, Calif.
Richard J. Durbin, Ill.
Tim Johnson, S.D.
Mary L. Landrieu, La.
Jack Reed, R.I.
Mark Pryor, Ark.
Jon Tester, Mont.
Tom Udall, N.M.
Jeanne Shaheen, N.H.
Jeff Merkley, Ore.
Mark Begich, Alaska
Vacancy

REPUBLICANS (14)

Richard C. Shelby, Ala., Ranking Member
Thad Cochran, Miss.
Mitch McConnell, Ky.
Lamar Alexander, Tenn.
Susan Collins, Maine
Lisa Murkowski, Alaska
Lindsey Graham, S.C.
Mark S. Kirk, Ill.
Dan Coats, Ind.
Roy Blunt, Mo.
Jerry Moran, Kan.
John Hoeven, N.D.
Mike Johanns, Neb.
John Boozman, Ark.

Agriculture

Pryor (chairman), Harkin, Feinstein, Johnson, Tester, Udall, Merkley
Blunt, Cochran, McConnell, Collins, Moran, Hoeven

Commerce-Justice-Science

Mikulski (chairwoman), Leahy, Feinstein, Reed, Pryor, Landrieu, Shaheen, Merkley, Vacancy
Shelby, McConnell, Alexander, Collins, Murkowski, Graham, Kirk, Boozman

Defense

Durbin (chairman), Leahy, Harkin, Feinstein, Mikulski, Murray, Johnson, Reed, Landrieu, Pryor
Cochran, McConnell, Shelby, Alexander, Collins, Murkowski, Graham, Coats, Blunt

Energy-Water

Feinstein (chairwoman), Murray, Johnson, Landrieu, Harkin, Tester, Durbin, Udall, Vacancy
Alexander, Cochran, McConnell, Shelby, Collins, Murkowski, Graham, Hoeven

Financial Services
Vacancy (chairman), Durbin, Udall
Johanns, Moran

Homeland Security
Landrieu (chairwoman), Leahy, Murray, Tester, Begich, Vacancy
Coats, Cochran, Shelby, Murkowski, Moran

Interior-Environment
Reed (chairman), Feinstein, Leahy, Johnson, Tester, Udall, Merkley, Begich
Murkowski, Cochran, Alexander, Blunt, Hoeven, Johanns

Labor-HHS-Education
Harkin (chairman), Murray, Landrieu, Durbin, Reed, Pryor, Mikulski, Tester, Shaheen, Merkley
Moran, Cochran, Shelby, Alexander, Graham, Kirk, Johanns, Boozman

Legislative Branch
Shaheen (chairwoman), Merkley, Begich
Hoeven, Boozman

Military Construction-VA
Johnson (chairman), Murray, Reed, Pryor, Tester, Udall, Shaheen, Begich
Kirk, McConnell, Collins, Murkowski, Coats, Hoeven, Johanns

State-Foreign Operations
Leahy (chairman), Harkin, Mikulski, Durbin, Landrieu, Shaheen, Begich, Vacancy
Graham, McConnell, Kirk, Coats, Blunt, Johanns, Boozman

Transportation-HUD
Murray (chairwoman), Mikulski, Durbin, Leahy, Harkin, Feinstein, Johnson, Pryor, Reed, Vacancy
Collins, Shelby, Alexander, Graham, Kirk, Coats, Blunt, Moran, Boozman

Armed Services

Phone: (202) 224-3871 **Office: 228 Russell**

DEMOCRATS (14)	**REPUBLICANS (12)**
Carl Levin, Mich., Chairman	*James M. Inhofe, Okla., Ranking Member*
Jack Reed, R.I.	*John McCain, Ariz.*
Bill Nelson, Fla.	*Jeff Sessions, Ala.*
Claire McCaskill, Mo.	*Saxby Chambliss, Ga.*
Mark Udall, Colo.	*Roger Wicker, Miss.*
Kay Hagan, N.C.	*Kelly Ayotte, N.H.*
Joe Manchin III, W.Va.	*Deb Fischer, Neb.*
Jeanne Shaheen, N.H.	*Lindsey Graham, S.C.*
Kirsten Gillibrand, N.Y.	*David Vitter, La.*
Richard Blumenthal, Conn.	*Roy Blunt, Mo.*
Joe Donnelly, Ind.	*Mike Lee, Utah*
Mazie K. Hirono, Hawaii	*Ted Cruz, Texas*
Tim Kaine, Va.	
Angus King, Maine (I)	

Airland
Manchin (chairman), Nelson, McCaskill, Gillibrand, Blumenthal, Donnelly
Wicker, McCain, Sessions, Chambliss, Blunt

Emerging Threats & Capabilities
Hagan (chairwoman), Reed, Nelson, Udall, Manchin, Shaheen, Gillibrand
Fischer, McCain, Wicker, Graham, Vitter, Cruz

Personnel
Gillibrand (chairwoman), Hagan, Blumenthal, Hirono, Kaine, King (I)
Graham, Chambliss, Ayotte, Blunt, Lee

Readiness & Management Support
Shaheen (chairwoman), McCaskill, Udall, Manchin, Donnelly, Hirono, Kaine
Ayotte, Chambliss, Fischer, Blunt, Lee, Cruz

Seapower
Reed (chairman), Nelson, Hagan, Shaheen, Blumenthal, Hirono, Kaine, King (I)
McCain, Sessions, Wicker, Ayotte, Graham, Vitter, Cruz

Strategic Forces
Udall (chairman), Reed, McCaskill, Donnelly, King (I)
Sessions, Fischer, Vitter, Lee

Banking, Housing & Urban Affairs

Phone: (202) 224-7391 **Office: 534 Dirksen**

DEMOCRATS (12)
Tim Johnson, S.D., Chairman
Jack Reed, R.I.
Charles E. Schumer, N.Y.
Robert Menendez, N.J.
Sherrod Brown, Ohio
Jon Tester, Mont.
Mark Warner, Va.
Jeff Merkley, Ore.
Kay Hagan, N.C.
Joe Manchin III, W.Va.
Elizabeth Warren, Mass.
Heidi Heitkamp, N.D.

REPUBLICANS (10)
Michael D. Crapo, Idaho, Ranking Member
Richard C. Shelby, Ala.
Bob Corker, Tenn.
David Vitter, La.
Mike Johanns, Neb.
Patrick J. Toomey, Pa.
Mark S. Kirk, Ill.
Jerry Moran, Kan.
Tom Coburn, Okla.
Dean Heller, Nev.

Economic Policy
Merkley (chairman), Tester, Warner, Hagan, Manchin, Heitkamp
Heller, Coburn, Vitter, Johanns, Crapo

Financial Institutions & Consumer Protection
Brown (chairman), Reed, Schumer, Menendez, Tester, Merkley, Hagan, Warren
Toomey, Shelby, Vitter, Johanns, Moran, Heller, Corker

Housing, Transportation & Community Development
Menendez (chairman), Reed, Schumer, Brown, Merkley, Manchin, Warren, Heitkamp
Moran, Corker, Toomey, Kirk, Coburn, Heller, Shelby

National Security & International Trade & Finance
Warner (chairman), Brown, Manchin
Kirk, Moran

Securities, Insurance & Investment
Tester (chairman), Reed, Schumer, Menendez, Warner, Hagan, Warren, Heitkamp
Johanns, Corker, Shelby, Vitter, Toomey, Kirk, Coburn

Budget

Phone: (202) 224-0642 **Office: 624 Dirksen**

DEMOCRATS (12)
Patty Murray, Wash., Chairwoman
Ron Wyden, Ore.
Bill Nelson, Fla.
Debbie Stabenow, Mich.
Bernard Sanders, Vt. (I)
Sheldon Whitehouse, R.I.
Mark Warner, Va.
Jeff Merkley, Ore.
Chris Coons, Del.
Tammy Baldwin, Wis.
Tim Kaine, Va.
Angus King, Maine (I)

REPUBLICANS (10)
Jeff Sessions, Ala., Ranking Member
Charles E. Grassley, Iowa
Michael B. Enzi, Wyo.
Michael D. Crapo, Idaho
Lindsey Graham, S.C.
Rob Portman, Ohio
Patrick J. Toomey, Pa.
Ron Johnson, Wis.
Kelly Ayotte, N.H.
Roger Wicker, Miss.

Commerce, Science & Transportation

Phone: (202) 224-0411 **Office: 254 Russell**

DEMOCRATS (13)
Jay Rockefeller, W.Va., Chairman
Barbara Boxer, Calif.
Bill Nelson, Fla.
Maria Cantwell, Wash.
Mark Pryor, Ark.
Claire McCaskill, Mo.
Amy Klobuchar, Minn.
Mark Warner, Va.
Mark Begich, Alaska
Richard Blumenthal, Conn.
Brian Schatz, Hawaii
William "Mo" Cowan, Mass.
Vacancy

REPUBLICANS (11)
John Thune, S.D., Ranking Member
Roger Wicker, Miss.
Roy Blunt, Mo.
Marco Rubio, Fla.
Kelly Ayotte, N.H.
Dean Heller, Nev.
Dan Coats, Ind.
Tim Scott, S.C.
Ted Cruz, Texas
Deb Fischer, Neb.
Ron Johnson, Wis.

Aviation Operations, Safety & Security
Cantwell (chairwoman), Boxer, Nelson, Pryor, Klobuchar, Warner, Begich, Schatz, Cowan, Vacancy
Ayotte, Wicker, Blunt, Rubio, Heller, Scott, Cruz, Fischer, Johnson

Communications, Technology & the Internet
Pryor (chairman), Boxer, Nelson, Cantwell, McCaskill, Klobuchar, Warner, Begich, Blumenthal, Schatz, Cowan, Vacancy
Wicker, Blunt, Rubio, Ayotte, Heller, Coats, Scott, Cruz, Fischer, Johnson

Competitiveness, Innovation & Export Promotion
Warner (chairman), Klobuchar, Pryor, Begich, Blumenthal, Cowan
Scott, Blunt, Coats, Fischer, Johnson

Consumer Protection, Product Safety & Insurance
McCaskill (chairwoman), Boxer, Pryor, Klobuchar, Blumenthal, Schatz, Cowan
Heller, Blunt, Ayotte, Coats, Cruz, Fischer

Oceans, Atmosphere, Fisheries & Coast Guard
Begich (chairman), Nelson, Cantwell, Blumenthal, Schatz, Cowan, Vacancy
Rubio, Wicker, Ayotte, Coats, Scott, Cruz

Science & Space
Nelson (chairman), Boxer, Pryor, Klobuchar, Warner, Blumenthal, Cowan
Cruz, Wicker, Rubio, Heller, Coats, Johnson

Surface Transportation and Merchant Marine
Vacancy (chairman), Boxer, Cantwell, Pryor, McCaskill, Klobuchar, Warner, Begich, Blumenthal, Schatz, Cowan
Blunt, Wicker, Rubio, Ayotte, Heller, Coats, Scott, Cruz, Fischer, Johnson

Energy & Natural Resources

Phone: (202) 224-4971 **Office: 304 Dirksen**

DEMOCRATS (12)	REPUBLICANS (10)
Ron Wyden, Ore., Chairman	*Lisa Murkowski, Alaska, Ranking Member*
Tim Johnson, S.D.	*John Barrasso, Wyo.*
Mary L. Landrieu, La.	*Jim Risch, Idaho*
Maria Cantwell, Wash.	*Mike Lee, Utah*
Bernard Sanders, Vt. (I)	*Dean Heller, Nev.*
Debbie Stabenow, Mich.	*Jeff Flake, Ariz.*
Mark Udall, Colo.	*Tim Scott, S.C.*
Al Franken, Minn.	*Lamar Alexander, Tenn.*
Joe Manchin III, W.Va.	*Rob Portman, Ohio*
Chris Coons, Del.	*John Hoeven, N.D.*
Brian Schatz, Hawaii	
Martin Heinrich, N.M.	

Energy
Franken (chairman), Johnson, Landrieu, Cantwell, Sanders (I), Stabenow, Udall, Manchin, Coons, Heinrich
Risch, Heller, Flake, Alexander, Portman, Hoeven

National Parks
Udall (chairman), Landrieu, Sanders (I), Stabenow, Coons, Schatz, Heinrich
Portman, Barrasso, Lee, Alexander, Hoeven

Public Lands, Forests and Mining
Manchin (chairman), Johnson, Landrieu, Cantwell, Udall, Franken, Coons, Schatz, Heinrich
Barrasso, Risch, Lee, Heller, Flake, Scott, Alexander, Hoeven

Water & Power
Schatz (chairman), Johnson, Cantwell, Sanders (I), Stabenow, Manchin, Franken
Lee, Barrasso, Risch, Heller, Flake, Scott

Environment & Public Works

Phone: (202) 224-8832 **Office: 410 Dirksen**

DEMOCRATS (10)	REPUBLICANS (8)
Barbara Boxer, Calif., Chairwoman	*David Vitter, La., Ranking Member*
Max Baucus, Mont.	*James M. Inhofe, Okla.*
Thomas R. Carper, Del.	*John Barrasso, Wyo.*
Benjamin L. Cardin, Md.	*Jeff Sessions, Ala.*
Bernard Sanders, Vt. (I)	*Michael D. Crapo, Idaho*
Sheldon Whitehouse, R.I.	*Roger Wicker, Miss.*
Tom Udall, N.M.	*John Boozman, Ark.*
Jeff Merkley, Ore.	*Deb Fischer, Neb.*
Kirsten Gillibrand, N.Y.	
Vacancy	

Clean Air & Nuclear Safety
Carper (chairman), Baucus, Cardin, Sanders (I), Whitehouse, Udall
Sessions, Barrasso, Crapo, Wicker, Boozman

Green Jobs & the New Economy
Merkley (chairman), Carper, Sanders (I)
Wicker, Sessions

Oversight
Whitehouse (chairman), Baucus, Vacancy
Inhofe, Boozman

Superfund, Toxics & Environmental Health
Udall (chairman), Baucus, Merkley, Gillibrand, Vacancy
Crapo, Inhofe, Wicker, Fischer

Transportation & Infrastructure
Baucus (chairman), Carper, Cardin, Sanders (I), Udall, Gillibrand, Vacancy
Barrasso, Inhofe, Sessions, Crapo, Wicker, Fischer

Water & Wildlife
Cardin (chairman), Carper, Whitehouse, Merkley, Gillibrand, Vacancy
Boozman, Inhofe, Barrasso, Sessions, Fischer

Finance

Phone: (202) 224-4515 **Office: 219 Dirksen**

DEMOCRATS (13)

Max Baucus, Mont., Chairman
Jay Rockefeller, W.Va.
Ron Wyden, Ore.
Charles E. Schumer, N.Y.
Debbie Stabenow, Mich.
Maria Cantwell, Wash.
Bill Nelson, Fla.
Robert Menendez, N.J.
Thomas R. Carper, Del.
Benjamin L. Cardin, Md.
Sherrod Brown, Ohio
Michael Bennet, Colo.
Bob Casey, Pa.

REPUBLICANS (11)

Orrin G. Hatch, Utah, Ranking Member
Charles E. Grassley, Iowa
Michael D. Crapo, Idaho
Pat Roberts, Kan.
Michael B. Enzi, Wyo.
John Cornyn, Texas
John Thune, S.D.
Richard M. Burr, N.C.
Johnny Isakson, Ga.
Rob Portman, Ohio
Patrick J. Toomey, Pa.

Energy, Natural Resources & Infrastructure
Stabenow (chairwoman), Baucus, Rockefeller, Wyden, Cantwell, Nelson, Carper, Bennet
Cornyn, Grassley, Crapo, Enzi, Thune, Burr, Isakson

Fiscal Responsibility & Economic Growth
Casey (chairman), Baucus, Brown
Portman, Burr

Health Care
Rockefeller (chairman), Stabenow, Cantwell, Nelson, Menendez, Carper, Cardin, Casey
Roberts, Hatch, Grassley, Enzi, Cornyn, Burr, Toomey

International Trade, Customs & Global Competitiveness
Wyden (chairman), Rockefeller, Schumer, Stabenow, Cantwell, Menendez, Brown, Bennet
Isakson, Hatch, Grassley, Roberts, Thune, Portman

Social Security, Pensions & Family Policy
Brown (chairman), Rockefeller, Schumer, Nelson, Cardin
Toomey, Crapo, Isakson, Portman

Taxation & IRS Oversight
Bennet (chairman), Baucus, Wyden, Schumer, Menendez, Carper, Cardin, Casey
Enzi, Hatch, Crapo, Roberts, Cornyn, Thune, Toomey

Foreign Relations

Phone: (202) 224-4651 **Office: 444 Dirksen**

DEMOCRATS (10)

Robert Menendez, N.J., Chairman
Barbara Boxer, Calif.
Benjamin L. Cardin, Md.
Bob Casey, Pa.
Jeanne Shaheen, N.H.
Chris Coons, Del.
Richard J. Durbin, Ill.
Tom Udall, N.M.
Christopher S. Murphy, Conn.
Tim Kaine, Va.

REPUBLICANS (8)

Bob Corker, Tenn., Ranking Member
Jim Risch, Idaho
Marco Rubio, Fla.
Ron Johnson, Wis.
Jeff Flake, Ariz.
John McCain, Ariz.
John Barrasso, Wyo.
Rand Paul, Ky.

African Affairs
Coons (chairman), Cardin, Shaheen, Durbin, Udall
Flake, McCain, Barrasso, Paul

East Asian & Pacific Affairs
Cardin (chairman), Boxer, Casey, Udall, Murphy
Rubio, Johnson, Flake, McCain

European Affairs
Murphy (chairman), Casey, Shaheen, Coons, Durbin
Johnson, Risch, Flake, Barrasso

International Development
Kaine (chairman), Coons, Durbin, Udall, Murphy
Barrasso, Risch, Flake, Paul

International Operations & Organizations
Boxer (chairwoman), Casey, Shaheen, Durbin, Kaine
Paul, Risch, Rubio, Johnson

Near Eastern & South & Central Asian Affairs
Casey (chairman), Boxer, Cardin, Shaheen, Coons
Risch, Rubio, Johnson, McCain

Western Hemisphere & Global Narcotics Affairs
Udall (chairman), Boxer, Murphy, Kaine
McCain, Rubio, Barrasso, Paul

Health, Education, Labor & Pensions

Phone: (202) 224-5375 **Office: 428 Dirksen**

DEMOCRATS (12)

Tom Harkin, Iowa, Chairman
Barbara A. Mikulski, Md.
Patty Murray, Wash.
Bernard Sanders, Vt. (I)
Bob Casey, Pa.
Kay Hagan, N.C.
Al Franken, Minn.
Michael Bennet, Colo.
Sheldon Whitehouse, R.I.
Tammy Baldwin, Wis.
Christopher S. Murphy, Conn.
Elizabeth Warren, Mass.

REPUBLICANS (10)

Lamar Alexander, Tenn., Ranking Member
Michael B. Enzi, Wyo.
Richard M. Burr, N.C.
Johnny Isakson, Ga.
Rand Paul, Ky.
Orrin G. Hatch, Utah
Pat Roberts, Kan.
Lisa Murkowski, Alaska
Mark S. Kirk, Ill.
Tim Scott, S.C.

Children & Families

Hagan (chairwoman), Mikulski, Murray, Sanders (I), Casey, Franken, Bennet, Murphy, Warren
Enzi, Kirk, Burr, Isakson, Paul, Hatch, Roberts

Employment & Workplace Safety

Casey (chairman), Murray, Franken, Bennet, Whitehouse, Baldwin
Isakson, Paul, Hatch, Scott

Primary Health & Aging

Sanders (I) (chairman), Mikulski, Hagan, Whitehouse, Baldwin, Murphy, Warren
Burr, Roberts, Murkowski, Enzi, Kirk

Homeland Security & Governmental Affairs

Phone: (202) 224-2627 **Office: 340 Dirksen**

DEMOCRATS (9)

Thomas R. Carper, Del., Chairman
Carl Levin, Mich.
Mark Pryor, Ark.
Mary L. Landrieu, La.
Claire McCaskill, Mo.
Jon Tester, Mont.
Mark Begich, Alaska
Tammy Baldwin, Wis.
Heidi Heitkamp, N.D.

REPUBLICANS (7)

Tom Coburn, Okla., Ranking Member
John McCain, Ariz.
Ron Johnson, Wis.
Rob Portman, Ohio
Rand Paul, Ky.
Michael B. Enzi, Wyo.
Kelly Ayotte, N.H.

Efficiency of Federal Programs

Tester (chairman), Pryor, McCaskill, Begich, Baldwin, Heitkamp
Portman, Johnson, Paul, Enzi

Emergency Management & District of Columbia

Begich (chairman), Levin, Pryor, Landrieu, Tester, Heitkamp
Paul, McCain, Portman, Enzi

Financial & Contracting Oversight

McCaskill (chairwoman), Levin, Pryor, Landrieu, Begich, Baldwin
Johnson, McCain, Enzi, Ayotte

Permanent Investigations

Levin (chairman), Pryor, Landrieu, McCaskill, Tester, Baldwin, Heitkamp
McCain, Johnson, Portman, Paul, Ayotte

Indian Affairs

Phone: (202) 224-2251 **Office: 838 Hart**

DEMOCRATS (8)

Maria Cantwell, Wash., Chairwoman
Tim Johnson, S.D.
Jon Tester, Mont.
Tom Udall, N.M.
Al Franken, Minn.
Mark Begich, Alaska
Brian Schatz, Hawaii
Heidi Heitkamp, N.D.

REPUBLICANS (6)

John Barrasso, Wyo., Vice Chairman
John McCain, Ariz.
Lisa Murkowski, Alaska
John Hoeven, N.D.
Michael D. Crapo, Idaho
Deb Fischer, Neb.

Judiciary

Phone: (202) 224-7703 **Office: 224 Dirksen**

DEMOCRATS (10)
Patrick J. Leahy, Vt., Chairman
Dianne Feinstein, Calif.
Charles E. Schumer, N.Y.
Richard J. Durbin, Ill.
Sheldon Whitehouse, R.I.
Amy Klobuchar, Minn.
Al Franken, Minn.
Chris Coons, Del.
Richard Blumenthal, Conn.
Mazie K. Hirono, Hawaii

REPUBLICANS (8)
Charles E. Grassley, Iowa, Ranking Member
Orrin G. Hatch, Utah
Jeff Sessions, Ala.
Lindsey Graham, S.C.
John Cornyn, Texas
Mike Lee, Utah
Ted Cruz, Texas
Jeff Flake, Ariz.

Antitrust, Competition Policy & Consumer Rights
Klobuchar (chairwoman), Schumer, Franken, Coons, Blumenthal
Lee, Graham, Grassley, Flake

Bankruptcy & Courts
Coons (chairman), Durbin, Whitehouse, Klobuchar, Franken
Sessions, Grassley, Flake, Cruz

Constitution, Civil Rights & Human Rights
Durbin (chairman), Franken, Coons, Blumenthal, Hirono
Cruz, Graham, Cornyn, Hatch

Crime & Terrorism
Whitehouse (chairman), Feinstein, Schumer, Durbin, Klobuchar
Graham, Cruz, Sessions, Lee

Immigration, Refugees & Border Security
Schumer (chairman), Leahy, Feinstein, Durbin, Klobuchar, Blumenthal, Hirono
Cornyn, Grassley, Hatch, Sessions, Flake, Cruz

Oversight, Federal Rights & Agency Actions
Blumenthal (chairman), Leahy, Klobuchar
Hatch, Flake

Privacy, Technology & the Law
Franken (chairman), Feinstein, Schumer, Whitehouse, Coons, Hirono
Flake, Hatch, Lee, Cornyn, Graham

Rules & Administration

Phone: (202) 224-6352 **Office: 305 Russell**

DEMOCRATS (10)
Charles E. Schumer, N.Y., Chairman
Dianne Feinstein, Calif.
Richard J. Durbin, Ill.
Patty Murray, Wash.
Mark Pryor, Ark.
Tom Udall, N.M.
Mark Warner, Va.
Patrick J. Leahy, Vt.
Amy Klobuchar, Minn.
Angus King, Maine (I)

REPUBLICANS (8)
Pat Roberts, Kan., Ranking Member
Mitch McConnell, Ky.
Thad Cochran, Miss.
Saxby Chambliss, Ga.
Lamar Alexander, Tenn.
Richard C. Shelby, Ala.
Roy Blunt, Mo.
Ted Cruz, Texas

Select Ethics

Phone: (202) 224-2981 **Office: 220 Hart**

DEMOCRATS (3)
Barbara Boxer, Calif., Chairwoman
Mark Pryor, Ark.
Sherrod Brown, Ohio

REPUBLICANS (3)
Johnny Isakson, Ga., Vice Chairman
Pat Roberts, Kan.
Jim Risch, Idaho

Select Intelligence

Phone: (202) 224-1700 **Office: 211 Hart**

DEMOCRATS (8)
Dianne Feinstein, Calif., Chairwoman
Jay Rockefeller, W.Va.
Ron Wyden, Ore.
Barbara A. Mikulski, Md.
Mark Udall, Colo.
Mark Warner, Va.
Martin Heinrich, N.M.
Angus King, Maine (I)

REPUBLICANS (7)
Saxby Chambliss, Ga., Ranking Member
Richard M. Burr, N.C.
Jim Risch, Idaho
Dan Coats, Ind.
Marco Rubio, Fla.
Susan Collins, Maine
Tom Coburn, Okla.

Small Business & Entrepreneurship

Phone: (202) 224-5175 **Office: 428A Russell**

DEMOCRATS (10)
Mary L. Landrieu, La., Chairwoman
Carl Levin, Mich.
Tom Harkin, Iowa
Maria Cantwell, Wash.
Mark Pryor, Ark.
Benjamin L. Cardin, Md.
Jeanne Shaheen, N.H.
Kay Hagan, N.C.
Heidi Heitkamp, N.D.
William "Mo" Cowan, Mass.

REPUBLICANS (8)
Jim Risch, Idaho, Ranking Member
David Vitter, La.
Marco Rubio, Fla.
Rand Paul, Ky.
Tim Scott, S.C.
Deb Fischer, Neb.
Michael B. Enzi, Wyo.
Ron Johnson, Wis.

Special Aging

Phone: (202) 224-5364 **Office: G31 Dirksen**

DEMOCRATS (11)

Bill Nelson, Fla., Chairman
Ron Wyden, Ore.
Bob Casey, Pa.
Claire McCaskill, Mo.
Sheldon Whitehouse, R.I.
Kirsten Gillibrand, N.Y.
Joe Manchin III, W.Va.
Richard Blumenthal, Conn.
Tammy Baldwin, Wis.
Joe Donnelly, Ind.
Elizabeth Warren, Mass.

REPUBLICANS (9)

Susan Collins, Maine, Ranking Member
Bob Corker, Tenn.
Orrin G. Hatch, Utah
Mark S. Kirk, Ill.
Dean Heller, Nev.
Jeff Flake, Ariz.
Kelly Ayotte, N.H.
Tim Scott, S.C.
Ted Cruz, Texas

Veterans' Affairs

Phone: (202) 224-9126 **Office: 412 Russell**

DEMOCRATS (8)

Bernard Sanders, Vt. (I), Chairman
Jay Rockefeller, W.Va.
Patty Murray, Wash.
Sherrod Brown, Ohio
Jon Tester, Mont.
Mark Begich, Alaska
Richard Blumenthal, Conn.
Mazie K. Hirono, Hawaii

REPUBLICANS (6)

Richard M. Burr, N.C., Ranking Member
Johnny Isakson, Ga.
Mike Johanns, Neb.
Jerry Moran, Kan.
John Boozman, Ark.
Dean Heller, Nev.

Senate Leadership

DEMOCRATIC LEADERS

President .... Vice President Joseph R Biden Jr.
President Pro Tempore .... Patrick J. Leahy
Majority Leader .... Harry Reid
Majority Whip .... Richard J. Durbin
Conference Vice Chairman .... Charles E. Schumer
Conference Secretary .... Patty Murray
Chief Deputy Whip .... Barbara Boxer

Deputy Whips: Thomas R. Carper, Mark Pryor

DEMOCRATIC SENATORIAL CAMPAIGN COMMITTEE

224-2447 **120 Maryland Ave. NE 20002**

Chairman .... Michael Bennet

POLICY AND COMMUNICATIONS COMMITTEE

224-3232 **419 Hart**

Chairman .... Charles E. Schumer
Vice Chairwoman .... Debbie Stabenow

STEERING AND OUTREACH COMMITTEE

224-9048 **712 Hart**

Chairman .... Mark Begich
Vice Chairwoman .... Jeanne Shaheen

Members: Max Baucus, Barbara Boxer, Kent Conrad, Chris Coons, Richard J. Durbin, Kirsten Gillibrand, Tom Harkin, Carl Levin, Patrick J. Leahy, Robert Menendez, Mark Pryor, Harry Reid, Jay Rockefeller

REPUBLICAN LEADERS

Minority Leader .... Mitch McConnell
Minority Whip .... John Cornyn
Conference Chairman .... John Thune
Conference Vice Chairman .... Roy Blunt
Chief Deputy Whip .... Michael D. Crapo

Deputy Whips. Kelly Ayotte, Roy Blunt, Saxby Chambliss, Susan Collins, Michael D. Crapo, Rob Portman, David Vitter, Roger Wicker

NATIONAL REPUBLICAN SENATORIAL COMMITTEE

675-6000 **425 Second St. NE 20002**

Chairman .... Jerry Moran
Vice Chairman of Finance .... Rob Portman
Vice Chairman .... Ted Cruz

POLICY COMMITTEE

224-2946 **347 Russell**

Chairman .... John Barrasso

COMMITTEE ON COMMITTEES

224-6142 **239 Dirksen**

Chairman .... Michael D. Crapo

Joint Committees

JOINT ECONOMIC

(202) 224-5171 G-01 Dirksen

SENATE MEMBERS

DEMOCRATS (6)

Amy Klobuchar, Minn., Vice Chairwoman
Bob Casey, Pa.
Mark Warner, Va.
Bernard Sanders, Vt. (I)
Christopher S. Murphy, Conn.
Martin Heinrich, N.M.

REPUBLICANS (4)

Dan Coats, Ind.
Mike Lee, Utah
Roger Wicker, Miss.
Patrick J. Toomey, Pa.

HOUSE MEMBERS

REPUBLICANS (6)

Kevin Brady, Texas, Chairman
John Campbell, Calif.
Sean P. Duffy, Wis.
Justin Amash, Mich.
Erik Paulsen, Minn.
Richard Hanna, N.Y.

DEMOCRATS (4)

Carolyn B. Maloney, N.Y.
Loretta Sanchez, Calif.
Elijah E. Cummings, Md.
John Delaney, Md.

JOINT PRINTING

(202) 225-8281 1309 Longworth

SENATE MEMBERS

DEMOCRATS (3)

Charles E. Schumer, N.Y., Chairman
Tom Udall, N.M.
Mark Warner, Va.

REPUBLICANS (2)

Pat Roberts, Kan.
Saxby Chambliss, Ga.

HOUSE MEMBERS

REPUBLICANS (3)

Gregg Harper, Miss., Vice Chairman
Candice S. Miller, Mich.
Rich Nugent, Fla.

DEMOCRATS (2)

Robert A. Brady, Pa.
Juan C. Vargas, Calif.

JOINT LIBRARY

(202) 224-6352 305 Russell

SENATE MEMBERS

DEMOCRATS (3)

Charles E. Schumer, N.Y., Vice Chairman
Richard J. Durbin, Ill.
Patrick J. Leahy, Vt.

REPUBLICANS (2)

Pat Roberts, Kan.
Roy Blunt, Mo.

HOUSE MEMBERS

REPUBLICANS (3)

Gregg Harper, Miss., Chairman
Candice S. Miller, Mich.
Rodney Alexander, La.

DEMOCRATS (2)

Robert A. Brady, Pa.
Zoe Lofgren, Calif.

JOINT TAXATION

(202) 225-3621 1625 Longworth

SENATE MEMBERS

DEMOCRATS (3)

Max Baucus, Mont., Vice Chairman
Jay Rockefeller, W.Va.
Ron Wyden, Ore.

REPUBLICANS (2)

Orrin G. Hatch, Utah
Charles E. Grassley, Iowa

HOUSE MEMBERS

REPUBLICANS (3)

Dave Camp, Mich., Chairman
Sam Johnson, Texas
Kevin Brady, Texas

DEMOCRATS (2)

Sander M. Levin, Mich.
Charles B. Rangel, N.Y.

Did You Know?

The 113th Congress has its share of firsts. For example, Democrat Tammy Baldwin of Wisconsin is the first openly gay senator, and Mazie K. Hirono of Hawaii is the first Asian-American woman to serve in that chamber.

But the lawmakers on Capitol Hill also have lots of personal and professional distinctions to their names.

Republican Rep. Jon Runyan of New Jersey played in two Super Bowls. Democratic Sen. Tim Kaine is both a former governor of Virginia and the son-in-law of a former Republican governor of Virginia. Long before Republican Sean P. Duffy represented Wisconsin, he was a reality show star on MTV.

Others have equally interesting tales. Did you know:

Michigan Republican Rep. **Justin Amash**'s father lived in a Palestinian refugee camp as a child before his family immigrated to the United States in the 1950s.

Rep. **Robert E. Andrews**, D-N.J., used Rahm Emanuel — later his House colleague, then White House chief of staff and now mayor of Chicago — as an opposition researcher in his first campaign in 1990.

New Hampshire Republican Sen. **Kelly Ayotte** is attached to a famous Supreme Court case: *Ayotte v. Planned Parenthood of Northern New England*, which involved a challenge to the state's parental notification abortion law.

The first jobs that Rep. **Lou Barletta**, R-Pa., ever had were at Angela Park, an amusement park owned by his family.

Rep. **Karen Bass**, D-Calif., has brown belts in tae kwon do and hapkido martial arts.

As a young man, Sen. **Max Baucus**, D-Mont., hitchhiked around Europe with the Roma and says he had an epiphany to enter public service while traveling in the Belgian Congo.

Michigan Republican Rep. **Kerry Bentivolio** is the proprietor of Old Fashion Santa and Co.; he owns reindeer that are featured in local Christmas events, where he impersonates Santa.

Sen. **Richard Blumenthal**, D-Conn., was once a tennis partner of Donald H. Rumsfeld, when the George W. Bush-era Defense secretary was head of the Office of Economic Opportunity in the Nixon administration.

Sen. **Barbara Boxer**, D-Calif., is the author of two political thrillers featuring a heroic liberal Democratic senator from California.

In the 1990s, Rep. **Mo Brooks**, R-Ala., served under **Jeff Sessions** as a special assistant attorney general while the senator was Alabama's attorney general.

The son of a longtime Georgia state senator, Georgia Republican Rep. **Paul Broun** used to give up his bedroom when his father's colleague from Plains, Jimmy Carter, would visit Athens.

North Carolina Republican Sen. **Richard M. Burr** is a descendant of Aaron Burr, the New York senator and vice president who killed Alexander Hamilton in a famous duel.

A fourth-generation Californian, Republican Rep. **John Campbell** is a member of the Sons of Union Veterans and has occasionally participated in Civil War re-enactments. His great-grandfather on his father's side, Alexander, was elected to the California Assembly in 1860 on the same GOP ticket as Abraham Lincoln.

Rep. **Shelley Moore Capito**, R-W.Va., was the first Cherry Blossom Princess elected to Congress; Republican Sen. **Lisa Murkowski** of Alaska was the second.

Delaware is the only state represented by lawmakers whose last names begin with the same letter: Sens. **Thomas R. Carper** and **Chris Coons** and Rep. **John Carney**, all Democrats.

Rep. **André Carson**, D-Ind., was an aspiring rapper during high school, performing at local variety shows under the stage name "Juggernaut."

Georgia Republican Sens. **Saxby Chambliss** and **Johnny Isakson** met in college. When their stay-at-home wives (who were in the same sorority) are in Washington, the couples frequently dine together. When they're not, Chambliss and Isakson are part of a group of Republican men who eat out together and gather at one another's homes. The pack has included Sens. **Lindsey Graham** of South Carolina, **Tom Coburn** of Oklahoma, **John Thune** of South Dakota and **Richard M. Burr** of North Carolina, and occasionally House Speaker **John A. Boehner** of Ohio.

To pay for his education at the University of Maryland, Rep. **William Lacy Clay**, D-Mo., was a U.S. House of Representatives doorman for seven years.

To prove his environmental bona fides, Democratic Missouri Rep. **Emanuel Cleaver II** uses a 1998 Ford Econoline van converted to run on vegetable oil as an office on wheels in his district.

Rep. **James E. Clyburn**, D-S.C., is the first African-American elected to Congress from South Carolina since 1896, when his great-uncle, George Washington Murray, was in the House.

Rep. **Steve Cohen**, D-Tenn., was diagnosed with polio as a child, but he was too young to take the vaccine that his father, a doctor, was helping Jonas Salk test.

Rep. **Chris Collins**, R-N.Y., is a big fan of Lean Six Sigma, a management system he used to turn around several businesses he owned. Rep. **Tom Latham**, R-Iowa, is another promoter of that system.

Rep. **Bill Enyart**, D-Ill., is currently the highest-ranking military officer serving in Congress. He was the leader of the Illinois National Guard.

When Rep. **Anna G. Eshoo**, D-Calif., was in high school in Connecticut, President Harry S. Truman once gave her a ride home from school.

Del. **Eni F.H. Faleomavaega**, D-Am. Samoa, is a "matai," or chief. Faleomavaega is actually his title; his family name is Hunkin.

Rep. **Blake Farenthold**, a conservative Texas Republican, is the step-grandson of longtime liberal Democratic activist Frances Tarleton "Sissy" Farenthold.

Rep. **Chaka Fattah**, D-Pa., was born Arthur Davenport. Fattah's mother changed his name when she married activist David Fattah. She called him "Chaka" in honor of a Zulu warrior.

Rep. **John Fleming**, R-La., owns 30 Subway restaurant franchises.

Democratic Rep. **Lois Frankel** was the first woman to be elected minority leader of the Florida House. In her spare time, she is an amateur modernist painter.

Rep. **Rodney Frelinghuysen**, R-N.J., is the sixth member of his family to serve in Congress.

Sen. **Charles E. Grassley**, R-Iowa, works on the family farm on weekends and tucks a cell phone inside his cap while driving the tractor so he will feel the vibrations of an incoming call.

Rep. **Morgan Griffith**, R-Va., is an admirer of Revolutionary War Gen. Andrew Lewis, and he has dressed up as Lewis at several events. Sen. **Angus King**, I-Maine, has studied Civil War Gen. Joshua Chamberlain — he lives in Brunswick, the same town where Chamberlain lived.

In December 2012, Texas Republican **Ralph M. Hall** became the oldest person to ever serve in the House.

As a young Hill aide on a 1969 trip to Vietnam, Sen. **Tom Harkin,** D-Iowa, discovered the "tiger cages," squalid underground cells where the South Vietnamese government secretly kept prisoners of war.

Sen. **Orrin G. Hatch**, R-Utah, has written songs and movie soundtracks performed by the Osmonds and Gladys Knight. He often scribbles lyrics between votes and has produced several discs of religious, romantic and patriotic songs.

Rep. **Rush D. Holt**, D-N.J., a physicist, is a former champion on the TV quiz show "Jeopardy." Sen. **Charles E. Schumer**, D-N.Y., appeared on the high school quiz program "It's Academic" in 1967 and was captain of his team.

Rep. **Steven Horsford,** D-Nev., was the first African-American majority leader in the Nevada Senate, the youngest person to hold that post.

Rep. **Jared Huffman**, D-Calif., was a member of the 1987 world champion U.S. volleyball team.

There are more Buddhists in Congress (**Hank Johnson** of Georgia and Hawaii's **Mazie K. Hirono** and **Colleen Hanabusa**) than Muslims (**Keith Ellison** of Minnesota and **André Carson** of Indiana). All are Democrats.

Rep. **Sam Johnson**, R-Texas, spent almost seven years in a North Vietnamese prison camp. For a brief stretch, he shared a cell with fellow prisoner of war Sen. **John McCain**, R-Ariz.

Democratic Rep. **Dan Kildee** of Michigan was the president of a land use think tank, where he worked on "shrinking" cities such as his hometown of Flint.

Rep. **Adam Kinzinger**, R-Ill., served in both Illinois and Wisconsin Air National Guard units, and he conducted five tours in Iraq and Afghanistan as a pilot.

During his service in the Marine Corps, Minnesota Republican Rep. **John Kline** carried the "football" — the briefcase with nuclear war codes — for Jimmy Carter and Ronald Reagan and flew the presidential helicopter, Marine One.

Rep. **James Lankford**, R-Okla., has a master's of divinity degree with a focus on biblical languages.

Utah Republican Sen. **Mike Lee** clerked for Supreme Court Justice Samuel A. Alito Jr.; his father, Rex Lee, argued cases before the high court when he served as solicitor general under President Ronald Reagan.

At Duke University, the judge of Illinois Democrat **Daniel Lipinski**'s doctoral thesis was Democratic Rep. **David E. Price** of North Carolina, who was between congressional stints.

Rep. **Billy Long**, R-Mo., was voted best auctioneer in the Ozarks seven years in a row.

While serving as New Mexico's state aging agency director, Democratic Rep. **Michelle Lujan Grisham** went undercover and checked herself into a local nursing home as a stroke victim to test the care facilities.

Rep. **Cynthia M. Lummis**, R-Wyo., owns a huge ranch in her home state and has wide experience wrangling and caring for her cows: She once jumped into a swollen creek to rescue a drowning calf. Sen. **Deb Fischer**, R-Neb., married into a ranching family and also has extensive experience working with cattle.

Rep. **Stephen F. Lynch**, D-Mass., donated more than half his liver to his brother-in-law.

The husband of Rep. **Sean Patrick Maloney**, D-N.Y., is the star of "My Flipp'n Brother," a reality television show on A&E that debuted in late 2012.

Rep. **Thomas Massie**, R-Ky., built his own "off the grid" house that gets its electricity from solar panels, geothermal sources and other means.

Rep. **Patrick Meehan**, R-Pa., is a former National Hockey League referee.

Rep. **Candice S. Miller**, R-Mich., earned the honorary title "Old Goat" in 2001 when she competed in her 25th Port Huron to Mackinac Island sailboat race.

Rep. **George Miller**, D-Calif., and Sens. **Charles E. Schumer,** D-N.Y., and **Richard J. Durbin**, D-Ill., have shared a Capitol Hill rowhouse of such notorious disarray that it merited a New York Times write-up and a visit from an ABC News television crew in early 2007.

Republican Sen. **Lisa Murkowski** is the first woman to represent Alaska, the first person ever appointed to the Senate by her father and the first person to win election as a write-in candidate since Strom Thurmond in 1954.

Pennsylvania GOP **Rep. Tim Murphy** taught himself to play guitar and once opened for banjo legend Earl Scruggs. Murphy also dug graves to earn money for college.

Rep. **Randy Neugebauer**, R-Texas, was so skilled at back flips, twists and other moves that while at Texas Tech he joined the Flying Matadors trampoline troupe.

Republican Rep. **Kristi Noem** won the South Dakota Snow Queen contest and traveled the state giving speeches.

Texas Democratic Rep. **Beto O'Rourke** once toured with the punk-rock band Foss.

As a girl, Minority Leader **Nancy Pelosi**, D-Calif., slept above stacks of the Congressional Record. Her father, Thomas D'Alesandro Jr., was a Maryland congressman and stored them under her bed in their Baltimore rowhouse.

Wisconsin Republican Rep. **Tom Petri**'s first job was hosting a radio show called "Teen Time."

Democrat **Pedro R. Pierluisi**, the resident commissioner from Puerto Rico, is the only member of Congress with a four-year term.

During a 1997 trip to Colombia, Rep. **Mark Pocan,** D-Wis., was taken hostage for five days by rebels. He entertained his fellow captives with magic shows — he is an accomplished magician.

Rep. **Bill Posey**, R-Fla., is an experienced stock-car racer and won an award for short-track driver achievement.

Rep. **Dave Reichert**, R-Wash., was the original lead detective in the Green River serial killer task force. Almost 20 years later, as the King County sheriff, he announced the arrest of Gary Ridgway in 2001.

Sen. **Harry Reid**, D-Nev., took on organized crime as chairman of the Nevada Gaming Commission. A bomb was once found under the hood of his car.

Rep. **James B. Renacci**, R-Ohio, has been an owner of an Arena Football League team, the Columbus Destroyers, and a minor league baseball team, the Lancaster JetHawks of the California League.

Kansas Republican **Pat Roberts** is the first person ever to have served as chairman and ranking member of the House Agriculture Committee and ranking member of the Senate Agriculture panel.

Rep. **Dana Rohrabacher**, R-Calif., says John Wayne taught him how to drink tequila.

Idaho Republican Sen. **Jim Risch** thrived in the courtroom as the prosecutor for Ada County, but his efforts to crack down on narcotics almost cost him his life when leaders of a drug ring made a failed attempt to plant a bomb in his car. Risch became Idaho's shortest-tenured governor when he filled out the last seven months of the term of Gov. Dirk Kempthorne, who had left the state in 2006 to be President George W. Bush's Interior secretary.

Florida Republican Rep. **Tom Rooney** is the grandson of Pittsburgh Steelers founder Art Rooney. As a youth, he spent summers working as a ball boy. He went on to play football at Washington and Jefferson College and Syracuse University.

Illinois Democratic Rep. **Bobby L. Rush** is a former Black Panther who served six months in prison on a weapons charge. Rush also is the only politician to ever defeat Barack Obama in an election — a 2000 Democratic primary for the House.

House Budget Chairman **Paul D. Ryan**, R-Wis., says his philosophy of individualism and entrepreneurial capitalism was influenced most deeply by novelist and objectivist philosopher Ayn Rand.

Rep. **Brad Schneider**, D-Ill., is an industrial engineer by trade, and he worked in Israel in a kibbutz wire factory.

Republican Sen. **Tim Scott** of South Carolina worked on the 1994 campaign that brought **Mark Sanford** to the House. In 2012, Sanford won a special election to fill the House seat left empty when Scott was appointed to the Senate.

Reps. **Jim Sensenbrenner**, R-Wis., and **Kevin McCarthy**, R-Calif., are both lottery winners. Sensenbrenner put his $250,000 toward charities and investments; McCarthy invested the $5,000 from his scratch-off ticket to open "Kevin O's Deli."

Rep. **José E. Serrano**, D-N.Y., learned to speak English by listening to Frank Sinatra records.

Democratic Rep. **Terri A. Sewell** is the first African-American woman from Alabama to serve in Congress.

Rep. **Kyrsten Sinema**, D-Ariz., does not state a religious affiliation and has been described as agnostic. She is also the first openly bisexual member of Congress.

Rep. **Chris Stewart**, R-Utah, was a senior project officer for the team that set the world record for the fastest non-stop flight around the world.

Rep. **Mike Thompson**, D-Calif., a wine enthusiast, grows organic sauvignon grapes. House Minority Leader **Nancy Pelosi** owns a vineyard in Thompson's hometown and California Republican Rep. **Devin Nunes** is part owner of the Alpha Omega winery.

Colorado Democrats **Mark Udall** and **Michael Bennet** were the first pair to represent their state in the Senate as freshmen since 1995, when Republicans Bill Frist and Fred Thompson represented Tennessee.

In 1983, while working as a White House aide, Rep. **Fred Upton**, R-Mich., proposed to his wife during a Baltimore Orioles baseball game, hiring an airplane to fly overhead with a banner reading, "Amey this is the inning to say yes."

Rep. **Juan C. Vargas**, D-Calif., trained as a Jesuit novice and Sen. **Tim Kaine**, D-Va., traveled with Jesuit missionaries. Both Reps. **Gerald E. Connolly**, D-Va., and **Peter J. Visclosky**, D-Ind., pursued seminary studies in their teens.

Michigan Republican **Tim Walberg** holds a House seat that changed hands four times in four elections — Democrat Joe Schwarz won the seat in 2004 after Republican Nick Smith retired; Walberg won in 2006; Democrat Mark Schauer unseated Walberg in 2008; and Walberg recaptured the seat in 2010.

Rep. **Tim Walz**, D-Minn., earned the rank of command sergeant major in the Army National Guard, making him the highest-ranking enlisted soldier ever to serve in Congress.

Sen. **Elizabeth Warren**, D-Mass., graduated high school at 16 and then went to George Washington University on a debate scholarship.

Ohio Republican Rep. **Brad Wenstrup** was the chief of surgery at the Abu Ghraib complex in Iraq. The prisoner abuse scandal had already passed, and he was responsible for providing medical care for both U.S. soldiers and military prisoners.

Rep. **Roger Williams**, R-Texas, was drafted by the Atlanta Braves and spent a few years as an outfielder in the minor leagues before an injury ended his playing career.

Glossary of Congressional Terms

Congress has a language all its own. Below are some terms often heard during legislative debate on the floor and in committee, and sprinkled throughout the profiles of lawmakers found in the 2012 edition of CQ Roll Call's Politics in America.

Act: Legislation that has passed both houses of Congress and been signed into law by the president.

Adjourn: To close a legislative day.

Amendment: A change in a bill or document by adding, substituting or deleting portions.

Appropriations Bill: Legislation that provides funding for government agencies and programs.

Authorization Bill: Legislation establishing or extending a program and setting funding limits and policy.

Bill: Legislation introduced in either the House or Senate that, if enacted, has the force of law.

Budget Resolution: Concurrent resolution that establishes spending and revenue targets for the upcoming fiscal year. It does not become law but provides a framework for Congress as it considers other measures.

By Request: Phrase used when a member introduces a bill at the request of an executive agency or private organization but does not necessarily endorse the legislation.

Calendar: List and schedule of bills to be considered by a committee or chamber.

Caucus: Collection of members of Congress, usually organized by party or shared interest. In the House, the party caucuses are known as the Republican Conference and Democratic Caucus. In the Senate, both are formally known as conferences.

Chairman/Chairwoman: Presiding officer of a committee or the Committee of the Whole.

Chamber: Place where the entire House or Senate meets to conduct business; also can refer to the House of Representatives or the Senate itself.

Clean Bill: A new bill, reflecting revisions made by a committee to an earlier version of the legislation.

Cloakrooms: Small rooms off the House and Senate floor where members can rest and hold informal conferences.

Closed Hearings: Hearings closed to all but members, staff and witnesses testifying; also called executive hearings.

Closed Rule: In the House, a rule that prohibits floor amendments.

Cloture: Method of limiting debate or ending a filibuster in the Senate. At least 60 senators must vote in favor before cloture can be invoked. Once cloture is invoked, there can be 30 more hours of debate.

Cosponsor: Member who joins in sponsoring legislation but who is not the principal sponsor or the one who introduced the legislation.

Committee: A group of members assigned to give special consideration to certain bills that fall into subject areas within the committee's jurisdiction.

Committee of the Whole: A mechanism to expedite business in the House whereby the House itself meets as a committee, allowing for less rigid rules and a quorum of 100 instead of 218.

Companion Bills: Identical, or nearly identical, bills introduced separately in both the Senate and the House.

Concurrent Resolution: Legislation used to express the position of the House and Senate. Does not have the force of law, if enacted.

Conference Committee: Meeting between representatives and senators to resolve differences when two versions of a bill have been passed by the House and Senate. It can produce a conference report that is sent to both chambers for approval.

Congressional Record: Official transcript of the proceedings in Congress.

Continuing Resolution: A joint resolution to appropriate funds, usually for a short period of time and often in the absence of a regular appropriations bill. It is frequently used at the beginning of a fiscal year if work on appropriations measures has not been completed.

Discharge Petition: In the House, a petition for the purpose of removing a bill from the control of a committee. A discharge petition must be signed by a majority of members.

Discretionary Spending: Funding for programs or agencies determined by Congress through the appropriations process.

Earmark: There is considerable debate about what qualifies as an earmark, but generally it is congressionally directed funding, issued through an appropriations or authorization bill, for a project in a member's district or state.

Engrossed Bill: Final copy of a bill passed by either the House or Senate with amendments. The bill is then delivered to the other chamber.

Enrolled Bill: Final copy of a bill that has passed both the House and Senate in identical form.

Extension of Remarks: When a member of Congress inserts material in the Congressional Record that is not directly related to the debate under way.

Filibuster: Tactic used in the Senate whereby a minority intentionally delays a vote by extending proceedings such as using unlimited debate. The cloture process can overcome a filibuster.

Final Passage: Approval of a bill after all amendments have been voted on.

Fiscal Year: Accounting year. For the federal government, the fiscal year begins Oct. 1.

Five-Minute Rule: Rule that allows any House member to propose an amendment and debate it for five minutes. Opponents and supporters of the amendment have five minutes to debate it.

Floor Manager: A member who attempts to direct a bill through the debate and amendment process to a final vote.

Germane: Amendments that are relevant to the underlying bill. All amendments in the House must be germane. A non-germane amendment would add new and different subject matter, or its subject matter may be irrelevant to the bill or other measure it seeks to amend. Senate rules permit non-germane amendments in all but a few specific circumstances — most often, after cloture is invoked.

Hearing: Committee sessions for receiving testimony from witnesses.

Holds: A courtesy afforded senators that allows them to delay legislation. The senator placing the hold must do so in writing, and the notice is published in the Congressional Record.

Hopper: Box on the desk of the clerk of the House where sponsors submit their bills.

Hour Rule: When the House is sitting as the full House, each member has one hour to debate amendments. In the Committee of the Whole, the five-minute rule is in effect.

Jefferson's Manual: Basic rules of parliamentary procedure drafted by Thomas Jefferson that guide both chambers.

Joint Committee: Committee composed of members of both the House and Senate.

Joint Resolution: Legislation similar to a bill that has the force of law if passed by both houses and signed by the president, generally used for special circumstances and to propose constitutional amendments.

Lame Duck: Member of Congress (or the president) who was defeated for, or did not seek, re-election but whose term has not yet expired.

Leader Time: In the Senate, 10 minutes given to the majority and minority leaders at the beginning of each day Congress is in session.

Legislative Day: In the Senate, the period of time between convening until the Senate adjourns, not necessarily a calendar day.

Lobbying: The process of attempting to influence the passage, defeat or content of legislation by individuals or a group other than members of Congress.

Logrolling: Quid pro quo process whereby members help each other get particular measures passed. One member will help another on one piece of legislation in return for similar help.

Mandatory Spending: Funding for programs or agencies provided directly through authorization bills, such as entitlement programs.

Majority Leader: Chief spokesman and strategist for the majority party, elected by members of the majority party. In the House, the majority leader is the second-ranking lawmaker, behind the Speaker.

Marking Up a Bill: Process, usually in committee, of analyzing a piece of legislation section by section and making changes.

Member: A U.S. senator or U.S. representative.

Minority Leader: Chief spokesman and strategist for the minority party, elected by members of the minority party.

Modified Open Rule: In the House, permission to offer amendments to a particular bill during floor debate under certain restrictions set by the Rules Committee, such as a time limit or a requirement that the amendments be printed ahead of time in the Congressional Record.

Motion: Proposal presented to a legislative body for consideration.

Motion to Concur: Proposal to agree to the other chamber's altered version of a measure passed by both the House and the Senate. The chamber can also vote on a motion to concur with further amendments to the measure.

Motion to Recommit: Proposal to send a bill or resolution back to a committee. The motion to recommit can contain instructions for the committee, such as amending the legislation. The minority party in the House may use the motion to recommit to propose changes immediately prior to a vote on final passage.

Motion to Table: Proposal to kill a bill or amendment by cutting off consideration of it. Such motions are not debatable.

Omnibus Bill: Legislation that combines different bills regarding a single broader subject into one measure, such as appropriations bills.

One-Day Rule. In the Senate, a requirement that measures reported from committee be held for at least one legislative day before being brought to the floor.

Open Rule: In the House, permission to offer any amendments to a particular bill during floor debate.

Override a Veto: When both the House and Senate vote by a two-thirds majority to enact a bill over a presidential veto of the legislation.

Pairing: System whereby two members jointly agree not to vote on a particular matter.

Party Unity Score: CQ's measure of the percentage of votes in which a member sides with his or her party when a majority of one party votes against a majority of the other party.

Petition: Plea by an individual or organization for a chamber to consider particular legislation.

Pocket Veto: When the president kills a bill by withholding his signature when Congress has recessed or adjourned, preventing him from returning the measure. A true pocket veto denies Congress the opportunity to override the veto, but presidents and Congresses have disagreed about when pocket vetoes may occur.

Point of Order: An objection that language, an amendment or bill is in violation of a rule.

President of the Senate: The vice president of the United States is designated by the Constitution as the president of the Senate. That individual casts a vote only in cases of a tie.

Previous Question: In the House, a request to end all debate and force a vote on the motion, bill or other measure under consideration.

Private Bill: Bill designed to benefit a certain individual or business.

President Pro Tempore: Senator who presides over the Senate in the absence of the vice president of the United States. The president pro tem is usually the longest-serving member of the majority party.

Public Law: Designation used for legislation that has been passed by both chambers and signed by the president or enacted over a presidential veto. Private bills become private laws.

Quorum: The number of senators or representatives who must be present

before a legislative body can conduct official business.

Quorum Call: In the Senate, a method of determining whether there is a quorum. Often used to suspend debate without adjourning.

Ranking Member: The leading member of the minority party on a committee. The ranking member may be referred to as the ranking Democrat or ranking Republican, depending on which party is in the minority of the relevant chamber.

Recess: Temporary halt to proceedings, with a time set for proceedings to resume. It also describes periods when the House or Senate is not in session.

Reconciliation: Process in which the budget resolution includes instructions to committees to report legislation that changes laws dealing with mandatory spending or taxes. The resulting measures are not subject to filibusters in the Senate.

Recorded Vote: Vote in which members of Congress indicate their vote for listing in the Congressional Record.

Rescission Bill: Legislation that revokes spending authority previously granted by Congress.

Resolution: A measure adopted only in one house to express the sentiment of that chamber. A simple resolution does not have the force of law.

Rider: A measure added to another, often unrelated, bill with the purpose of one piece of legislation passing on the strength of another.

Roll Call Vote: A vote in which a record is kept. The House uses electronic vote recording; the Senate uses oral voting.

Seniority: A member's rank in a chamber based on length of congressional service and other factors, including tenure in certain other elected offices. Often used to determine rank on committees.

Seriatim Consideration: Consideration of a motion line by line.

Sine Die: Final adjournment at the end of a session, of which there are two in each Congress. Bills under consideration but not enacted by the end of the Congress must be reintroduced in the next session.

Speaker: The presiding officer of the House, elected by members of that chamber.

Sponsor: The representative or senator who introduces a measure.

Suspend the Rules: Procedural action to expedite debate in the House. A motion to suspend the rules requires the votes of two-thirds of those present and is debatable for 40 minutes. Members cannot offer amendments.

Teller Vote: A vote in the House in which members file past tellers who count the votes. The total vote is recorded, but no record is kept on how each member voted. A teller vote is rarely used.

Three-Day Rule: In the House, a requirement that legislation be held for at least three calendar days (not counting weekends and holidays) before being brought to the floor. Similar to the One-Day Rule in the Senate.

Unanimous Consent: A procedure whereby a matter is considered agreed to if no member on the floor objects. It can be used to pass legislation or set the terms for floor debate. Unanimous consent motions save time by eliminating the need for a vote.

Unlimited Debate: In the Senate, the right of any senator to talk as long as desired during floor debates on a bill.

Whip: Assistant leader for each party in each chamber who keeps other members of the party informed of the legislative agenda of the leader. Also tracks sentiment among party members for certain legislation and tries to persuade members to be present and vote for measures important to the leadership.

Yield: Permission granted by the member who has the floor to another member who wishes to make a comment or ask a question.

Index

A

B

C

D

H

I

J

K

L

M

N

O

P

Q

S

T

U

V

W

Y